# Formation of Government Contracts

## Fourth Edition

Wolters Kluwer
Law & Business

# Formation of Government Contracts

## Fourth Edition

John Cibinic, Jr.
Ralph C. Nash, Jr.
Christopher R. Yukins

The
George
Washington
University
WASHINGTON DC

# PREFACE

The first edition of *Formation of Government Contracts* was published in 1983, followed by editions in 1986 and 1998. The second and third editions were necessary to update the material based on the enactment of the Competition in Contracting Act in 1984 and the Federal Acquisition Streamlining Act in 1994. The third edition also encompassed the major rewrite of Part 15 of the Federal Acquisition in 1997. This fourth edition provides the opportunity to see how all of these changes have impacted the process of entering into government contracts by reviewing all of the statutory and regulatory changes since that time as well as the decisions of the Government Accountability Office and the Court of Federal Claims. The book is focused entirely on the *formation* of a contract – from the earliest planning until contract award. For our purposes, the award of a contract begins the process of contract administration and that is covered by Cibinic, Nash & Nagle, *Administration of Government Contracts*, 4th ed. 2006.

One of the major changes that has occurred since the third edition of *Formation of Government Contracts* is the widespread use of interagency contracting. For that reason, we have added a new Chapter 8 covering this complex field. As agencies began to make use of interagency contracts in large measure at the beginning of the 21st Century, many difficulties were encountered – providing fertile ground for investigations by Inspectors General and the Government Accountability Office. However, rather than documenting in detail the difficulties that were encountered along the way, we focus on the current rules governing the use of these contracts and the litigation that has ensued. They are clearly contracting devices that serve a useful purpose when adroitly used, making this chapter a vital resource for both government and contractor personnel. My good friend, Vernon Edwards, has authored this new chapter with his usual skill and comprehension of a difficult area of government procurement.

As with our earlier editions, our goal has been to make the reader aware of the statutes, regulations and decisions that establish the complex rule structure that is followed in the process of entering into government contracts. As all seasoned practitioners recognize, only when these elements of the process are synthesized can one truly know the rules of the game. This synthesis is carried out in each chapter of the book and we recommend that, to most effectively use the book, our readers become well versed in the detailed organization that is depicted in numerous topical subheads. We have also provided an index to assist in this process.

Having noted that the rule structure governing contract formation is complex, we hasten to add that federal contracting agencies are primarily responsible for the undue complexity of this field. Since the passage of the Competition in Contracting Act in 1984, making competitive negotiation the major contracting process, the agencies have adopted practices that make contract formation far too expensive and time consuming. We address these practices in detail in Chapter 6 and have published a companion book, Nash, Cibinic & O'Brien-DeBakey, *Competitive Negotiation: The Source Selection Process*, 3d ed. 2011. While we are critical of these practices and have made numerous attempts to persuade agencies to streamline them, we confess that we have been less than successful. Contractors participating in the competitive negotiation process must reconcile themselves to the fact that they will be required to expend excessive amounts of time and money, frequently requiring the use of their most talented personnel, if they are to win a significant number of contracts.

The other major change that has occurred since the publication of the third edition is in the selection of the proper type of contract – addressed in Chapter 9. As this book is published, we are in one of those periods when cost-reimbursement contracts are in disrepute and the emphasis is on more fixed-price type contracts. Further, new statutes and regulations have made the cost-plus-award-fee contract an undesirable arrangement. We trace these periodic swings of the pendulum in Cibinic & Nash, *Cost Reimbursement Contracting*, 3d ed. 2004 – including some discussion of the consequences of the over-use of fixed-price type contracts. For many years we have observed a tradition for new people coming into the top positions in the Executive Branch to latch on to the theory that cost-reimbursement contracts are intrinsically bad and to attempt to move away from them. They neither know nor learn from past experience – which demonstrates conclusively that fixed-price contracts are only beneficial when, as FAR Part 16 clearly states, risks have been narrowed and rational prices can be arrived at.

Finally, I want to acknowledge the work of Chris Yukins as he takes the place of John Cibinic as a coauthor. I am grateful for his work. We have kept John's name on the book as an author because he is truly the author of much of the underlying logic of the book and was instrumental in working with me to lay out the fundamental principles of government contract formation. We worked together as a team for over 40 years and were both aware that we could not have written these books without our close collaboration.

Ralph C. Nash, Jr.
Washington, D.C.

August, 2011

# ABOUT THE AUTHORS

## JOHN CIBINIC, JR.

John Cibinic, Jr. was Professor Emeritus at The George Washington University Law School where he taught from 1963 to 1993. From 1966 to 1974, he was Director of the Government Contracts Program. A respected spokesman in the field of government contracts, Professor Cibinic conducted seminars and conferences on government contracts for professionals in government and corporations, and for lawyers. He also served as a consultant to government agencies, private corporations, and law firms. He was vice-chairman of the Cost and Pricing Committee of the Public Contract Section of the American Bar Association. Professor Cibinic coauthored several books, including *Formation of Government Contracts*, *Administration of Government Contracts*, *Competitive Negotiation: The Source Selection Process*, and *Construction Contracting*. He received an A.B. from the University of Pittsburgh and a J.D. from George Washington University. Together, with Professor Ralph Nash he coauthored the *Nash & Cibinic Report*, a monthly newsletter.

## RALPH C. NASH, JR.

Ralph C. Nash, Jr., is Professor Emeritus of Law of The George Washington University, Washington, D.C., from which he retired in 1993. He founded the Government Contracts Program of the university's National Law Center in 1960, was Director of the Program from 1960 to 1966 and from 1979 to 1984, and continues to be actively involved in the Program. He was Associate Dean for Graduate Studies, Research and Projects, of the Law Center from 1966 to 1972. Professor Nash has specialized in the area of Government Procurement Law. He worked for the Navy Department as a contract negotiator from 1953 to 1959, and for the American Machine and Foundry Company as Assistant Manager of Contracts and Counsel during 1959 and 1960. He graduated *magna cum laude* with an A.B. degree from Princeton University in 1953, and earned his Juris Doctor degree from The George Washington University Law School in 1957. He is a member of Phi Beta Kappa, Phi Alpha Delta, and the Order of the Coif.

Professor Nash is active as a consultant for government agencies, private corporations, and law firms on government contract matters. In recent years, he has served widely as neutral advisor or mediator/arbitrator in alternate dispute resolution proceedings. He is active in the Public Contracts Section of the American Bar Association, is a member of the Procurement Round Table, and is a Fellow and serves on the Board of Advisors of the National Contract Management Association.

During the 1990s, Professor Nash was active in the field of acquisition reform. He served on the "Section 800 Panel" that recommended revisions to all laws affecting Department of Defense procurement, the Defense Science Board Task Force on Defense Acquisition Reform, and the Blue Ribbon Panel of the Federal Aviation Administration.

He is the coauthor with John Cibinic, Jr. of a casebook, *Federal Procurement Law* (3d ed., Volume I, 1977, and Volume II, 1980). He and Professor Cibinic also coauthored five textbooks: *Formation of Government Contracts* (3d ed. 1998), *Administration of Government Contracts* (4th ed. 2006), *Cost Reimbursement Contracting* (3d ed. 2004), *Government Contract Claims* (1981) and *Competitive Negotiation: The Source Selection Process* (2d ed. 1999). He is coauthor with Leonard Rawicz of the textbook *Intellectual Property in Government Contracts* (6th ed. 2008), coauthor with seven other authors of the textbook *Construction Contracting* (1991), coauthor with Vernon Edwards, Steven L. Schooner and Karen O'Brien-DeBakey of *The Government Contracts Reference Book* (3d ed. 2007) and coauthor with Steven Feldman of *Government Contract Changes* (3d ed. 2007). He has written several monographs for The George Washington University Government Contracts Program monograph series, and has published articles in various law reviews and journals. Since 1987 he has been coauthor of a monthly analytical report on government contract issues, *The Nash & Cibinic Report*.

# CHRISTOPHER R. YUKINS

Professor Christopher Yukins teaches on government contract formations and performance issues, anti-corruption measures, bid challenges, government contracts litigation, and comparative issues in public procurement law at The George Washington University Law School. He is an active member of the Public Contract Law Section of the American Bar Association, and is a member of the Procurement Roundtable, an organization of senior members of the U.S. procurement community. He is a faculty advisor to the *Public Contract Law Journal*, and has published on procurement reform in numerous journals, nationally and internationally. He regularly addresses audiences around the world on issues of procurement law and policy, anti-corruption, and international trade. Together with Professor Steven Schooner, he runs a colloquium series on procurement reform at The George Washington University Law School. In private practice, Professor Yukins has been an associate, partner and counsel at leading national firms; he is currently of counsel to the firm of Arnold & Porter LLP. He is an advisor to the U.S. delegation to the working group on reform of the UNCITRAL Model Procurement Law.

# SUMMARY TABLE OF CONTENTS

# CONTENTS

# CHAPTER 1

# BASIC PRINCIPLES OF FEDERAL PROCUREMENT

This book covers contracts of *Executive Branch agencies* for the *procurement* of goods and services where the government is acting in the role of a buyer. While procurement is a major form of contracting activity of the federal government, it is only one of several types of contracting in which the government engages. Other types of contractual arrangements include sales of personal property, purchases and sales of real property, grants, cooperative agreements, and employment contracts. Many of the legal principles and general rules applicable to these nonprocurement transactions are the same as those applied to procurement. Thus, many statutes, regulations, and decisions involving these principles and general rules will apply to both procurement and nonprocurement transactions. However, this book does not cover the detailed rules that apply to these nonprocurement transactions

Procurement of goods and services by the United States Government is a unique form of activity dominated by numerous specialized rules. These rules arise out of the nature of the government as a contracting party and the distinctive forms and procedures used in the procurement process. The rules governing this process are contained in statutes, regulations, and decisions, many of which are designed to protect the public's interest while assuring fair treatment to those who deal with the government. Most of these rules are of general application but some apply only to specific agencies. In addition, procurement is conducted under the general rules governing all contracts entered into by the federal government. This general rule structure is exemplified by the basic principles of contract law discussed in Chapter 2.

This chapter covers issues that are fundamental to the federal procurement process. The first section illustrates the role of procurement in the operation of the government by examining the variety of government organizations that procure goods and services and the statutes and regulations that cover this area. It also describes the different types of contractual transactions in which the government engages in order to show the relationship of procurement to other transactions. The next three sections consider how the special nature of the government as a contracting party is recognized by legal principles aimed at protecting the public from unauthorized or improper activity. This consideration starts with an examination of the statutes and regulations that control the procurement activities of government agencies and the methods of oversight used to assure compliance with these authorities. The next two sections analyze the special rules that apply to the authority of individual government personnel as well as the binding nature of the activities of contractor personnel. The chapter concludes with a survey of the standards of conduct required of those representing or dealing with the government.

# I.  TRANSACTIONS AND AGENCIES

Procurement is an essential element of the operation of almost every organization within the executive branch. To achieve a full understanding of the procurement process, it is necessary to see the relationship of procurement to the other types of contractual transactions carried out by these agencies. To understand the full scope of the procurement process, one must be aware of the variety of agencies within the executive branch of the government and the statutes and regulations that govern the procurement activities of these agencies.

## A.  Transactions

As noted earlier, procurement is only one of a number of contractual transactions in which the government regularly engages. Thus, procurement has a large number of special rules, and it also shares, in general, rules applicable to all contractual transactions of the federal government. These general rules of contract law are most frequently found in judicial decisions where fundamental contract law issues are raised. Similarly, statutes and regulations dealing with litigation against the federal government or with socioeconomic policies are often broadly applicable to contracts regardless of the nature of the transaction. In contrast, statutes and regulations dealing with contracting *procedures* are usually more specific in their application and may affect only particular types of transactions. However, here too there is a large degree of commonality in the rule structure. Many of the procedural rules developed for one type of activity have been adopted for others. Since procurement contracts have attracted the greatest degree of statutory and regulatory attention, the procurement rules are often used as models for rules in other types of contracting. Thus, while the discussion in this book is directed specifically to procurement contracts, some of the cases cited as precedent have involved other types of government contracts, and some of the procurement rules have application to other types of contracts.

The major categories of government transactions utilizing contractual agreements are:

- Procurement of goods and services

- Purchase of real property

- Sale of real or personal property

- Grants, cooperative agreements, cooperative research and development agreements, and "other transactions"

- Employment of personnel

Ordinarily, each of these transactions can be readily distinguished from the others. However, there can be a significant overlap between procurement transactions and other types of contractual arrangements. This section first discusses the types of transactions that are considered to be procurement of goods and services and the statutes and regulations applying to those contracts. It then considers the other types of government contracts and analyzes their relationship to procurement contracts.

## 1. Procurement (Acquisition)

Government procurement, or "acquisition" as it is called in the Federal Acquisition Regulation (FAR), involves contracting for goods and services. The following guidance on the use of procurement contracts is provided at 31 U.S.C. § 6303:

> An executive agency shall use a procurement contract as the legal instrument reflecting a relationship between the United States Government and a State, a local government, or other recipient when —
>
> > (1) the principal purpose of the instrument is to acquire (by purchase, lease, or barter) property or services for the direct benefit or use of the United States Government; or
> >
> > (2) the agency decides in a specific instance that the use of a procurement contract is appropriate.

Compare the definition of "acquisition" in FAR 2.101:

> Acquisition means the acquiring by contract with appropriated funds of supplies or services (including construction) by and for the use of the Federal Government through purchase or lease, whether the supplies or services are already in existence or must be created, developed, demonstrated and evaluated. . . .

In noting that this definition omitted the word "barter," the court ruled that a barter transaction where no appropriated funds were used was not a procurement contract, *Marketing & Mgmt. Information, Inc. v. United States*, 57 Fed. Cl. 665 (2003). The court reasoned that 31 U.S.C. § 6303 "does not purport to be a definition of a procurement contract."

The provision in 31 U.S.C. § 6303 requiring that a procurement contract be for the direct benefit and use of the United States Government has not been applied literally. For example, in *Civic Action Inst.*, 61 Comp. Gen. 637 (B-206372), 82-2 CPD ¶ 270, the Government Accountability Office (GAO) held that if the instrument required performance, procurement was appropriate even though the performance was being acquired for others. There is also no requirement that the government pay for services in order to have a procurement contract. See Comp. Gen. Dec. B-257430, 1994 U.S. Comp. Gen. LEXIS 887, where a "memorandum of understanding" with an organization to assist it, at no cost, in conducting a study was found to be a procurement contract because the primary purpose of the agreement was to "obtain services in direct support of" the agency's statutory functions. However, a contract can only be a procurement contract if the agency obtains goods or services. Thus, in *Coastal Corp. v. United States*, 713 F.2d 728 (Fed. Cir. 1983), the implied contract to treat a bid honestly and fairly was held not to be a procurement contract because it calls for no goods and services. Neither will a contract be a procurement contract unless it is issued by "an executive agency." See, for example, *Nutritional Support, Inc.*, AGBCA 2002-141-1, 03-1 BCA ¶ 32,115 (service contract issued by a state using federal grant-in-aid funds was not a procurement contract); *CDK Contracting Co.*, ASBCA 44997, 93-3 BCA ¶ 26,068 (construction contract issued by the state National Guard using federal funds not a procurement contract).

While this statute mentions only property and services, other statutes may be more specific. In addition, the regulations contain a detailed description of the types of services included. The major categories of procurement are:

- supplies

- construction

- services

- research and development

- rental of real property

Within each of these major categories are numerous specialized types of procurement. The classification of these types of procurement is extremely important for purposes of funding, types of contracts to be used, applicability of contract clauses, and coverage of socioeconomic provisions. See FAR 52.300 providing a matrix of solicitation provisions and contract clauses for specific types of procurement.

### a. *Personal Property (Supplies)*

FAR 2.101 defines "supplies" as follows:

Supplies means all property except land or interest in land. It includes (but is not limited to) public works, buildings, and facilities; ships, floating equipment, and vessels of every character, type, and description, together with parts and accessories; aircraft and aircraft parts, accessories, and equipment; machine tools; and the alteration or installation of any of the foregoing.

This definition of "supplies" is much more expansive than the meaning otherwise used in the FAR and is somewhat confusing. For example, contracts for the construction or repair of buildings and other permanent improvements to land are considered to be construction contracts, not supply contracts, FAR Part 36. However, contracts for the "construction" of ships are considered to be supply contracts, FAR 36.102. Nevertheless, some construction rules may be applied to contracts for work on ships. See, for example, *Southwest Marine, Inc.*, 64 Comp. Gen. 714 (B-218875.2), 85-2 CPD ¶ 104 (Miller Act performance and payment bonds applicable to ship conversion contract).

There are special rules and procedures governing the acquisition of certain types of supplies. For example, "major systems" are governed by OMB Circular A-109 and FAR Part 34. Detailed guidance on such procurements is contained in DoD Directive 5000.01, "The Defense Acquisition System," Nov. 20, 2007, and DoD Instruction 5000.02, "Operation of the Defense Acquisition System," Dec. 8, 2008. NASA Guidance is contained in NASA Management Instruction 7100.14, "Major Systems Acquisitions."

For many years there were special rules governing the acquisition of automatic data processing equipment in the Brooks Act, 40 U.S.C. § 759. However, this Act was repealed by § 5101 of the Clinger-Cohen Act of 1996, and a new Information Technology Management Reform Act of 1996, Pub. L. No. 104-106, 40 U.S.C. § 11101 et seq. was substituted. This Act was implemented by Executive Order 13011, 61 Fed. Reg. 37657, July 16, 1996. The special rules in this Act are implemented in FAR Part 39.

### b.  Construction

FAR 2.101 contains the following definition of "construction:"

Construction means construction, alteration, or repair (including dredging, excavating, and painting) of buildings, structures, or other real property. For purposes of this definition, the terms " buildings, structures, or other real property" include but are not limited to, improvements of all types, such as bridges, dams, plants, highways, parkways, streets, subways, tunnels, sewers, mains, power lines, cemeteries, pumping stations, railways, airport facilities, terminals, docks, piers, wharves, ways, lighthouses, buoys, jetties, breakwaters, levees, canals, and channels. Construction does not include the manufacture, production, furnishing, construction, alteration, repair, processing, or assembling of vessels, aircraft, or other kinds of personal property.

Construction contracts are unique because they generally involve improvements to government-owned property. Special rules governing these contracts are contained in FAR Part 36 and the matrix of contract clauses and solicitation provisions in FAR 52.301 covers construction as a separate category of procurement.

General authority for construction of buildings for the federal government is vested in the General Services Administration (GSA), 40 U.S.C. § 583. Regulations on the design and construction of buildings are in 41 C.F.R. Part 102-76. In addition to this general authority, many agencies have independent authority to construct various facilities for their own use.

The Clinger-Cohen Act of 1996 added 10 U.S.C. § 2305a and 41 U.S.C. § 253m (now 41 U.S.C. § 3309), permitting the acquisition of construction using a special two-phase design-build selection procedure. This procedure may be used when there will be significant costs in competing for the award. See FAR Subpart 36.3.

In order to provide protection for subcontractors, suppliers, and laborers, the Miller Act, 40 U.S.C. § 270a, requires that performance and payment bonds be obtained for all construction contracts for fixed prices over $100,000, 40 U.S.C. § 3131 et seq. The Act also requires that the FAR contain payment protection on contracts from $25,000 to $100,000. See FAR 28.102. Bid guarantees are normally used when performance and payment bonds are required, FAR 28.101.

### c.  Services

FAR 37.101 defines a "service contract" as follows:

"Service contract" means a contract that directly engages the time and effort of a contractor whose primary purpose is to perform an identifiable task rather than to furnish an end item of supply. A service contract may be either a nonpersonal or personal contract. It can also cover services performed by either professional or nonprofessional personnel whether on an individual or organizational basis. Some of the areas in which service contracts are found include the following:

(1) Maintenance, overhaul, repair, servicing, rehabilitation, salvage, modernization, or modification of supplies, systems, or equipment.

(2) Routine recurring maintenance of real property.

(3) Housekeeping and base services.

(4) Advisory and assistance services.

(5) Operation of Government-owned equipment, facilities, and systems.

(6) Communications services.

(7) Architect-Engineering (see Subpart 36.6).

(8) Transportation and related services (see Part 47).

(9) Research and development (see Part 35).

Several types of services contracts are the subject of special statutory authorizations or procedures that supplement the general procurement statutes and regulations. One special type of services contract is architect-engineer (A-E) services. A-E services contracts are generally subject to the procurement statutes and regulations but are to be acquired under special negotiation procedures prescribed by the Brooks Architect-Engineering Act, 40 U.S.C. § 1101 et seq. See Chapter 7 for a discussion of these procedures. Other types of services contracts are discussed below.

## (1) TRANSPORTATION AND TRAVEL SERVICES

Transportation and travel services may be acquired under procurement contracts subject to the procurement statutes and FAR Part 47, or under government bills of lading, travel requests, and other such documents under the provisions of the Transportation Act of 1940, 49 U.S.C. § 10721and § 13712. Services procured under the Transportation Act are not subject to procurement statutes and regulations, FAR 47.000(a)(2). See *Petchem Inc.*, 65 Comp. Gen. 328 (B-220902), 86-1 CPD ¶ 179. 40 U.S.C. § 602 makes the GSA responsible for prescribing policies and methods of procurement and supply for transportation and travel services and authorizes the Administrator of GSA to enter into contracts on behalf of executive agencies. These statutes are implemented in the Federal Property Management Regulations (FPMR). 41 C.F.R § 102-117 of this regulation deals with Transportation Management covering freight and household goods of government employees. 41 C.F.R. § 102-117.20 indicates that the Department of Defense (DoD) and uniformed members of civilian agencies are exempt from this regulation. For other agencies, 41 C.F.R. § 102-117.30 provides the following choices in procuring these services:

When you acquire transportation or related services you may:

(a) Use the GSA tender of service;

(b) Use another agency's contract or rate tender with a TSP only if allowed by the terms of that agreement or if the Administrator of General Services delegates authority to another agency to enter an agreement available to other Executive agencies;

(c) Contract directly with a TSP using the acquisition procedures under the Federal Acquisition Regulation (FAR) (48 CFR chapter 1); or

(d) Negotiate a rate tender under a Federal transportation procurement statute, 49 U.S.C. 10721 or 13712.

DFARS Subparts 247.1 and 247.2 contain procedures applicable to DoD procurement of these transportation services. See *CW Gov't Travel, Inc.*, Comp. Gen. Dec. B-295530, 2005 CPD ¶ 59, where GAO denied a protest that the minimum was too low on an IDIQ travel agent contract, and *ABF Freight Sys., Inc.*, Comp. Gen. Dec. B-291185, 2002 CPD ¶ 201, where GAO denied protests of the terms of multiple award IDIQ contracts for transportation of "freight of all kinds."

Travel services are covered by separate regulations. 41 C.F.R. §§ 300-304 contain the Federal Travel Regulation which provides detailed rules on the permissible expenses for travel by employees of civilian agencies. GSA also enters into travel management services contracts for use by executive agencies. In 2003 GSA awarded three 10-year E-Travel contracts that agencies can use to obtain these services. In addition, other agencies — primarily in DoD — issue travel service contracts. Many of these contracts are no-cost-no-fee contracts which have been held to be permissible under the procurement statutes and regulations, *T.V. Travel, Inc.*, 65 Comp. Gen. 109 (B-218198.6), 85-2 CPD ¶ 640; *N&N Travel & Tours, Inc.*, Comp. Gen. Dec. B-283731.2, 99-2 CPD ¶ 113. Payment under these contracts is frequently made by using travel cards issued to government employees under the authority of FAR 13.301.

## (2) PUBLIC UTILITY SERVICES

The GSA Administrator is authorized under 40 U.S.C. § 501(a) to acquire "public utility services" for the use of executive agencies. However, DoD and the Department of Energy (DOE) have independent authority to procure utility services, and other agencies may obtain such authority by delegation from the GSA, FAR 41.103(b). Contracts for utility services are subject to FAR Part 41 and may be made for periods not exceeding 10 years.

"Utility service" is not defined at 40 U.S.C. § 501(a), but FAR 41.101 contains the following definition:

> Utility service means a service such as furnishing electricity, natural or manufactured gas, water, sewage, thermal energy, chilled water, steam, hot water, or high temperature hot water. The application of part 41 to other services (e.g., rubbish removal, snow removal) may be appropriate when the acquisition is not subject to the Service Contract of 1965 (see 37.107).

Additionally, in *GSA Procurement of Equip. under 40 U.S.C. § 481(a)(3)*, 62 Comp. Gen. 569 (B-208422) (1983), GAO found that a procurement of telephone equipment and related installation and maintenance services from a nontariffed supplier was a procurement of public utility services. The supplier of such services need not be a "regulated, monopolistic public utility" in order for the services to be classified as a public utility service subject to 40 U.S.C. § 501(a), 45 Comp. Gen. 59 (B-155725) (1965). Even though a service may fit the definition of a "public utility," FAR Part 41 procedures may not apply. See FAR 41.102(b) for utilities that are exempted from these procedures. See also DFARS Subpart 239.74.

Utility services above the simplified acquisition threshold must be acquired by a bilateral written contract regardless of whether rates or terms or conditions of service are fixed or adjusted by a regulatory body, FAR 41.201(b). If a utility supplier refuses to execute a contract, the agency is required to obtain a written refusal signed by an official of the supplier. This document, along with statements of the reasons for the refusal and the record of negotiations, are to be sent to the GSA, FAR 41.202(c). The government generally procures utility services competitively, FAR 41.201(a), except for electricity when such competition is inconsistent with state law, FAR 41.201(e). GSA also has issued areawide contracts for use by federal agencies, FAR 41.204. When public utility services are being acquired by procurement contract, they are subject to the competition requirements of the procurement statutes, *R.C.A. Alaska Commc'ns, Inc.*, Comp. Gen. Dec. B-178442, 74-1 CPD ¶ 336.

Energy contracts have frequently been awarded on the basis of a share of savings where the contractor is compensated by a percentage of the savings achieved by introducing energy-saving measures. The Energy Policy Act of 1992, Pub. L. No. 102-486, 42 U.S.C. § 8287, permits agencies to enter into "energy savings performance contracts" (ESPCs) for up to 25 years. The Federal Energy Management Program of DOE "Super ESPCs," which are indefinite-delivery/indefinite-quantity contracts that can be used by any agency to enter into delivery orders for a share-in-savings contract at a specific site. See *http://www.eren.doe.gov/femp*. DoD also had statutory authority in 10 USC § 2865(c) to develop "a simplified method of contracting for shared energy savings contract services," but this statute was repealed in 2006 and replaced by 10 USC § 2911, calling for DoD to implement a comprehensive plan to save energy.

Telecommunications services have been procured for the entire federal government by GSA under FTS 2000, FTS 2001 and Networx contracts (*www.gsa.gov/Portal/gsa/ep/contentView.do?contentType=gsa_OVERVIEW&contentId=16100*). These are dual source contracts obtained on a competitive basis for multiple years. These contracts are not mandatory but are used by many agencies.

### (3) ADVISORY AND ASSISTANCE SERVICES

Contracts for advisory and assistance services have been subject to special scrutiny and oversight because these services are closely related to inherently governmental functions. See Chapter 3 for a discussion of inherently governmental functions. These contracts are subject to FAR Subpart 37.2. FAR 2.101 contains the following definition of advisory and assistance services:

> Advisory and assistance services means those services provided under contract by nongovernmental sources to support or improve: organizational policy development; decision-making; management and administration; program and/or project management and administration; or R&D activities. It can also mean the furnishing of professional advice or assistance rendered to improve the effectiveness of Federal management processes or procedures (including those of an engineering and technical nature). In rendering the foregoing services, outputs may take the form of information, advice, opinions, alternatives, analyses, evaluations, recommendations, training and the day-to-day aid of support personnel needed for the successful performance of ongoing Federal operations All advisory and assistance services are classified in one of the following definitional subdivisions:

(1) Management and professional support services, i.e., contractual services that provide assistance, advice or training for the efficient and effective management and operation of organizations, activities (including management and support services for R&D activities), or systems. These services are normally closely related to the basic responsibilities and mission of the agency originating the requirement for the acquisition of services by contract. Included are efforts that support or contribute to improved organization of program management, logistics management, project monitoring and reporting, data collection, budgeting, accounting, performance auditing, and administrative technical support for conferences and training programs.

(2) Studies, analyses and evaluations, i.e., contracted services that provide organized, analytical assessments/evaluations in support of policy development, decision-making, management, or administration. Included are studies in support of R&D activities. Also included are acquisitions of models, methodologies, and related software supporting studies, analyses or evaluations.

(3) Engineering and technical services, i.e., contractual services used to support the program office during the acquisition cycle by providing such services as systems engineering and technical direction (see 9.505-1(b)) to ensure the effective operation and maintenance of a weapon system or major system as defined in OMB Circular No. A-109 or to provide direct support of a weapon system that is essential to research, development, production, operation or maintenance of the system.

FAR 37.203(a) permits the use of advisory and assistance services "to help managers achieve maximum effectiveness or economy in their operations." However, FAR 37.203(c) prohibits contracting for advisory and assistance services:

(1) Used in performing work of a policy, decision-making, or managerial nature which is the direct responsibility of agency officials;

(2) Used to bypass or undermine personnel ceilings, pay limitations, or competitive employment procedures;

(3) Contracted for on a preferential basis to former Government employees;

(4) Used under any circumstances specifically to aid in influencing or enacting legislation;

(5) Used to obtain professional or technical advice which is readily available within the agency or another Federal agency.

Concern over the possible improper use of advisory and assistance services has resulted in the imposition of numerous management controls. 10 U.S.C. § 2304b and 41 U.S.C. § 4105 contain limitations on task order contracts for advisory and assistance services, including a five-year maximum length of such contracts. These statutes are implemented in FAR 16.504(c)(2). In addition, OFPP Policy Letter 93-1, May 18,

1994 (*http://www.acqnet.gov/Library/OFPP/PolicyLetters*) deals with management oversight of service contracting and incorporates many provisions of rescinded OMB Circular A-120 which dealt specifically with advisory and assistance services.

## (4) CONCESSION CONTRACTS

The government often obtains services under concession contracts. Under these arrangements, fees are charged to the public and the government obtains the services or provides the services to recipients at no cost to the government. See, for example, Systems Planning Corp., Comp. Gen. Dec. B-244697.4, 92-1 CPD ¶ 516 (operation of Securities Exchange Commission Lost and Stolen Securities Program), and *Ann Riley & Assocs.*, Comp. Gen. Dec. B-241309.2, 91-1 CPD ¶ 142 (stenographic services at public hearing). Although no public funds are expended under these contracts, they are considered procurement and the procurement statutes are applicable if the government receives a benefit from the transaction. The benefit may be one received by the government or it may be the discharge of an obligation of the government. See *Total Med. Mgmt., Inc. v. United States*, 104 F.3d 1314 (Fed. Cir.), *cert. denied*, 522 U.S. 857 (1997), which involved a Memorandum of Understanding (MOU) between the government and a health care provider. The court stated at 1320:

> Finally, the government argues that, if contracts, the MOUs are not subject to the Contract Disputes Act, 41 U.S.C. § 602(a), because they are not procurement contracts for the benefit of the government. The government argues that the MOUs are solely for the benefit of the military dependents who receive the medical care. We reject this argument since it is clear that the government has legal obligations to military dependents and benefits by obtaining said dependents' care at a reduced cost.

The determination of whether a sufficient benefit is received by the government is done on a case-by-case basis. See *Bararossa Reiseservice GmbH*, 66 Comp. Gen. 474 (B-225641), 87-1 CPD ¶ 529 (agreement providing for official travel services subject to procurement rules and agreement only for unofficial travel not subject to procurement rules). In *Maritime Global Bank Group*, Comp. Gen. Dec. B-272552, 96-2 CPD ¶ 62, GAO dismissed a protest against the Navy's execution of an agreement with a bank for the provision of on-base services, reasoning:

> Where a concession or similar type of transaction results in a benefit to the government, the transaction is one for the procurement of property or services, and is thus subject to our bid protest jurisdiction; whether the performance of the business opportunity in question relates to the advancement of the agency's mission depends, in turn, upon whether the agency's workload will be reduced or whether the effort is somehow rendered, either directly or indirectly, in support of the agency's mission requirements. Thus, for example, our Office has assumed jurisdiction over a protest against the award of a photocopy concession to provide copying services paid for by the public, where the services in question are a part

of the agency's mission requirement of furnishing copies of documents to the public. *West Coast Copy, Inc.*; *Pacific Photocopy and Research Servs.*, B-254044; B-254044.2, Nov. 16, 1993, 93-2 CPD ¶ 283. Similarly, we have found jurisdiction where the agency was granting a concession for providing initial haircuts to new recruits at an Air Force base because the record reasonably established that receiving an initial haircut was an important aspect of the training experience, the provision of which was integral to the agency's mission. *Gino Morena Enters.*, 66 Comp. Gen. 231 (1987), 87-1 CPD ¶ 121, *aff'd on recons.*, B-224235.2, May 13, 1987, 87-1 CPD ¶ 501. We also have found jurisdiction where the government receives a benefit in connection with the transaction, even where the benefit is not, strictly speaking, related to fulfilling the agency's mission. *See Americable Int'l, Inc.*, B-225570.2, July 20, 1987, 87-2 CPD ¶ 64 (agreement requiring cable television service provider to furnish free cable television services to all Navy ships and duty rooms on base confers benefit on government).

On the other hand, where any benefit to the government is speculative or contingent, we have found jurisdiction lacking, and have declined to consider the merits of the protest, even though earmarks of a procurement were present. *See North Florida Shipyards, Inc.*, B-243575, May 3, 1991, 91-1 CPD ¶ 434 (although solicitation for the lease of a drydock facility by the Navy to a private concern required offerors to submit a capital maintenance plan with their offers, the agency was not obligated to obtain the services under the terms of the contract, and thus any procurement aspect of the transaction was merely speculative).

Here, GAO found no benefit to the agency sufficient to establish jurisdiction, pointing out that the services were for the direct benefit of Navy personnel, not the Navy. Moreover, Navy personnel were not required to use the services and the bank was not required to provide such services.

The fact that the agency receives compensation from a concessionaire does not convert a concession contract into a procurement contract. See, e.g., *Good Food Serv., Inc.*, Comp. Gen. Dec. B-253161, 93-2 CPD ¶ 107 (cafeteria and vending service concession at federal office building); *YRT Servs. Corp. v. United States*, 28 Fed. Cl. 366 (1993) (concession awarded by the National Park Service executed under The National Park Systems Concessions Policy Act of 1965, 16 U.S.C. § 20 et seq.); and *Amfac Resorts, L.L.C. v. Department of Interior*, 282 F.3d 818 (D.C. Cir. 2002). In *Amfac* the court agreed with the regulations of the National Park Service stating that a concession contract was not a procurement contract, stating at 834-35:

Section 51.3 of the regulations states that concession contracts are not "contracts" within the meaning of the Contract Disputes Act. 36 C.F.R. § 51.3 (2000). With this we agree. The Act applies to any "express or implied contract" for the "procurement" of "property," "services" or "construction." 41 U.S.C. § 602(a)(2). A procurement contract, the Park Service reasoned, "is a contract for which the government bargains for, and pays for, and receives goods and services." 65 Fed. Reg. at 20,635. Concession contracts are not of that sort. Their function is not to procure services or goods for the government. Instead, as the Park Service put it, concession contracts "authorize third parties to provide services to park area visitors." *Id.*

This decision was vacated and remanded in *National Park Hospitality Ass'n v. Department of Interior*, 538 U.S. 803 (2003), on the ground that the case was not ripe for decision because the regulation created no "adverse effects of a strictly legal kind." The Court did not comment on the substantive holding of the circuit court. Even though a concession contract is not subject to procurement rules, modifications of the contract could be subject to the procurement statutes if they provide for the expenditure of public funds. See *Great South Bay Marina, Inc.*, Comp. Gen. Dec. B-296335, 2005 CPD ¶ 135, agreeing that a "pure" concession contract to provide services to park visitors is not a procurement contract but holding that a concession contract requiring the investment of significant funds to rehabilitate and improve the buildings in the park is a procurement contract. See also *Yosemite Park & Curry Co. v. United States*, 217 Ct. Cl. 360, 582 F.2d 582 (1978).

## d. *Research and Development*

Research and development is a specialized form of service contracting dealt with in FAR Part 35. The matrix of contract clauses and solicitation provisions in FAR 52.301 covers research and development as a separate category of procurement. Most agencies also have a separate appropriation for research and development contracts — requiring that this work be segregated from other types of work. FAR 35.001 contains definitions of applied research and development. FAR 35.002 contains the following statement of general principles applicable to contracting for research and development:

> The primary purpose of contracted R&D programs is to advance scientific and technical knowledge and apply that knowledge to the extent necessary to achieve agency and national goals. Unlike contracts for supplies and services, most R&D contracts are directed toward objectives for which the work or methods cannot be precisely described in advance. It is difficult to judge the probabilities of success or required effort for technical approaches, some of which offer little or no early assurance of full success. The contracting process shall be used to encourage the best sources from the scientific and industrial community to become involved in the program and must provide an environment in which the work can be pursued with reasonable flexibility and minimum administrative burden.

There are a number of techniques used to acquire research and development in addition to the standard negotiation technique. Basic research may be procured through broad agency announcements, 10 U.S.C. § 2302(2)(B) and 41 U.S.C. § 152. Contracts for research and development may also be awarded on the basis of unsolicited proposals. In addition, all major agencies must use a designated percentage of their research and development funds in awards of research contracts to small businesses, 15 U.S.C. § 638. See Chapter 7 for a discussion of procedures followed when broad agency announcements are used to obtain research contracts.

In a very questionable decision, the Court of Federal Claims ruled that it did not have jurisdiction of a protest concerning a research and development contract because it was not a "procurement" contract, *R&D Dynamics Corp. v. United States*, 80 Fed. Cl. 715 (2007), *aff'd*, 309 Fed. Appx. 388 (Fed. Cir. 2009). The court apparently believed that the Small Business Innovative Research contract being protested was more in the nature of a grant and seems to have been influenced by the fact that R&D appropriations are separate from "procurement" appropriations. GAO has regularly taken jurisdiction of SBIR protests, understanding that they are procurements. See, for example, *Quimba Software*, Comp. Gen. Dec. B-299000, 2007 CPD ¶ 14; and *R&D Dynamics Corp.*, Comp. Gen. Dec. B-298766, 2006 CPD ¶ 195.

### e.  *Rental of Real Property*

The rental of real property is also subject to procurement rules. See *Forman v. United States*, 767 F.2d 875 (Fed. Cir. 1985), holding that the exclusion in the Office of Federal Procurement Policy Act (OFPP Act), 41 U.S.C. § 401 et seq. (now 41 U.S.C. § 1101 et seq.), of contracts for the acquisition of "real property in being" only applies to the acquisition of leases already in existence. Thus, the court held that acquiring a "new" lease (i.e., renting real property) was a procurement subject to the OFPP Act and the Contract Disputes Act. General authority for leasing real property for the federal government is vested in the GSA, 40 U.S.C. § 585. The GSA has, in turn, delegated authority for leasing of certain types of property and locations to other agencies, 41 C.F.R. § 102-72.30. Regulations on leasing real property are set forth in 41 C.F.R. Part 102-73. In addition, some agencies have independent authority to lease real property without regard to these regulations, 41 C.F.R. § 102-73.50. In *Aerolease Long Beach & Satsuma Inv. Co. v. United States*, 31 Fed. Cl. 342, *aff'd*, 39 F.3d 1198 (Fed. Cir. 1994), the court dealt with a provision of the GSA regulations that conflicted with a FAR provision. The court held that, in the absence of an authorized deviation (none was present in this case), the GSA provision was invalid.

## 2.  *Other Contractual Arrangements*

There are numerous other types of contractual relationships in which the federal government engages. The major nonprocurement transactions and their relationship to procurement are discussed in this section.

### a.  *Purchase of Real Property*

The purchase of real property is not covered by the procurement statutes. See 10 U.S.C. § 2303(a), stating that the Armed Services Procurement Act (ASPA) applies to the procurement of "all property (other than land)," and 40 U.S.C. § 501(b) (1)(A), stating that GSA will procure and supply "personal property." In addition, the FAR system applies to the procurement of "property other than real property in being," 41 U.S.C. § 1121(c)(1)(A). 41 U.S.C. § 14 (pre-2011 codification) provides that "[n]o land shall be purchased on account of the United States, except under a law authorizing such purchase."

## b. Sale of Property

Article IV, Section 3, Clause 2 of the Constitution gives Congress the exclusive authority to dispose of federal government property. See, e.g., *Royal Indemn. Co. v. United States*, 313 U.S. 289 (1941). 40 U.S.C. § 541 et seq., grants the authority to "supervise and direct the disposition of surplus property" to the GSA Administrator, who may delegate this authority to other agencies. The statute is implemented by the Federal Management Regulations, 41 C.F.R. Part 102-38, and by subsidiary agency regulations such as the Defense Material Disposition Manual, DoD Manual 4160.21-M, August 1997 (*http://www.dla.mil/dlaps/DoD/416021m/guide.asp*). In addition to this general authority, specific statutory authority to dispose of property is granted to some agencies. See, for example, 16 U.S.C. § 472a granting the Secretary of Agriculture authority to sell timber from the national forests. The FAR does not apply to sales of property, *Sandia Die & Cartridge Co.*, Comp. Gen. Dec. B-218011, 85-1 CPD ¶ 308. See also *Monchamp Corp. v. United States*, 19 Cl. Ct. 797 (1990), holding that neither the procurement statutes nor the FAR apply to timber sales.

There can be considerable overlap between a property disposal contract and a procurement contract. In some cases, work that would ordinarily be accomplished under a procurement contract may be made a part of the property disposal contract. For example, 16 U.S.C. § 535 gives the Secretary of Agriculture authority to provide for the acquisition, construction, and maintenance of roads within and near national forests by placing requirements on purchasers of national forest timber. The Miller Act, 40 U.S.C. § 3131 et seq., has been held not to apply to road construction under such contracts, *Keller v. United States*, No. 2356 (D. Mont. 1975). On the other hand, contracts for the "dismantling, demolition, or removal of improvements" are considered service contracts as provided under FAR Subpart 37.3. Under FAR 37.303(a)(2), such contracts may require the contractor to pay the government for the right to salvage and remove materials resulting from the dismantling or demolition of operations. In a similar vein, the Secretary of Labor, in regulations promulgated under the Service Contract Act, found that while timber sale contracts generally do not constitute service contracts, contracts for the removal of diseased or dead timber would be service contracts under the Act, 29 C.F.R. § 4.111 and § 4.131. See also *Alamo Aircraft Supply, Inc.*, Comp. Gen. Dec. B-278215, 98-1 CPD ¶ 5, holding that a contract to sell surplus property and give the government 80% of the proceeds of the sale was a contract to sell property subject to the Federal Property and Administrative Services Act not a procurement contract.

## c.   Grants and Cooperative Agreements

Grants and cooperative agreements are used when the federal government intends to provide assistance or support to private organizations or to state and local governments. A grant without any contractual obligations on the part of the recipient may be characterized as a gift. See *Alabama v. Schmidt*, 232 U.S. 168 (1914) (Alabama had no contractual obligation to use land granted by Congress for public schools); *King County, Wash. v. Seattle School Dist. No. 1*, 263 U.S. 361 (1923) (congressional intent that grant money be used for public schools is not a requirement that grant money be used for public schools); and *Madison County Bd. of Educ. v. Illinois Cent. R.R. Co.*, 939 F.2d 292 (1991) (grant of land for public schools was a gift and not an honorary trust arrangement). However, most grants now require the recipient to use the funds or property only for specified purposes, 42 Comp. Gen. 289 (B-149441) (1962). Such grants are contractual agreements but are not procurement contracts, *Thermalon Indus., Ltd. v. United States*, 34 Fed. Cl. 411 (1995). See also *Westmoreland Human Opportunities, Inc. v. Walsh*, 246 F.3d 233 (3d Cir. 2001), treating a grant as a contract at a preliminary stage of the litigation, and *San Juan City College v. United States*, 391 F.3d 1357 (Fed. Cir. 2004), treating a grant in the form of a "program participation agreement" as a contract. Compare *D.R. Smalley & Sons, Inc. v. United States*, 178 Ct. Cl. 593, 372 F.2d 505, *cert. denied*, 389 U.S. 835 (1967), holding that a highway contractor with a state using federal highway grant funds could not sue the federal government because the state was not an agent of the federal government and such grants are "in reality gifts or gratuities." In *Bennett v. Kentucky Dep't of Education*, 470 U.S. 656 (1985), the Court held that a grant to a state should be treated like a normal contract for breach analysis rather than applying a standard of bad faith. The court also held that the grant provisions, which were specified by Congress, should not be subject to the normal interpretation rule that ambiguous provisions are interpreted against the drafter. See also *Bell v. New Jersey*, 461 U.S. 773 (1983).

Cooperative agreements have also been held to be contracts even though they are not procurement contracts, United States v. Harvard College, 323 F. Supp. 2d 151 (D. Mass. 2004); Quiman, S.A. de C.V. v. United States, 39 Fed. Cl. 171 (1997). Compare Trauma Serv. Group, Ltd. v. United States, 33 Fed. Cl. 426 (1995), *aff'd*, 104 F.3d 1321 (Fed. Cir. 1997), holding that a cooperative agreement for shared health services under 10 U.S.C. § 1096, in which the government made no promise to compensate the recipient, was not a contract. The Federal Circuit affirmed the decision in Trauma based on the fact that the cooperative agreement did not call for the payment claimed by the plaintiff not on the basis that the agreement was not a contract. The court stated at 1326:

> [A]ny agreement can be a contract within the meaning of the Tucker Act, provided that it meets the requirements for a contract with the Government, specifically: mutual intent to contract including an offer and acceptance, consideration, and a Government representative who had actual authority to bind the Government.

See *City of El Centro [v. United States]*, 922 F.2d [816 (Fed. Cir. 1990)] at 820; Thermalon, 34 Fed. Cl. at 414. As such, contrary to the opinion of the trial court, a MOA can also be a contract - whether this one is, we do not decide.

Unlike procurement contracts, which agencies have the inherent authority to use in carrying out authorized activities, assistance agreements require that an agency have specific statutory authority for their use, *Federal Facility Contributions to Capital Costs of Sewage Treatment Projects*, 59 Comp. Gen. 1 (B-194912) (1979). Many agencies have such statutory authority. See, for example, 6 U.S.C. § 112(b)(2) (DHS may "make contracts, grants, and cooperative agreements, and to enter into agreements with other executive agencies"); 10 U.S.C. § 2358(b) (DoD may perform research and development by "contract, cooperative agreement, or grant"); 15 U.S.C. § 638(g) (agencies may award "funding agreements" — contracts, grants or cooperative agreements — to small businesses to carry out the SBIR program); 42 U.S.C. § 2473(c)(5) (NASA may enter into and perform such contracts, leases, cooperative agreements, or other transactions as may be necessary); 42 U.S.C. § 7256 (DOE may enter into and perform such contracts, leases, cooperative agreements, or other similar transactions). Although there is no overall grant procedural statute, individual statutes authorizing assistance programs often contain procedural and other requirements. See, for example, 7 U.S.C. § 450i(b) establishing the Department of Agriculture Research Grant Program (implemented in 7 C.F.R. Part 3400), and the National Science Foundation Act of 1950, 42 U.S.C. § 1862. See also 42 U.S.C. § 2731 (DOE may award grants for training); and 42 U.S.C. § 2486d (NASA may award grants to assist any space grant and fellowship program).

Neither grants nor cooperative agreements are governed by the procurement statutes or the FAR, *Trauma Serv. Group, Ltd. v. United States*, 33 Fed. Cl. 426 (1995), *aff'd*, 104 F.3d 1321 (Fed. Cir. 1997). However, there are a few statutes and a number of regulations that govern these assistance agreements. Broad guidance for assistance agreements is promulgated by the Office of Management and Budget (OMB). This guidance is in 2 C.F.R. Parts 180 (nonprocurement debarment and suspension) and 182 (drug-free workplace requirements) (formerly in the "Grants Management Common Rule"); 2 C.F.R. Part 215, Uniform Administrative Requirements for Grants and Agreements with Institutions of Higher Education, Hospitals and Other Nonprofit Organizations (formerly OMB Circular A-110); 2 C.F.R. Part 220, Cost Principles for Educational Institutions (formerly OMB Circular A-21); 2 C.F.R. Part 225, Cost Principles for State, Local, and Indian Tribal Governments (formerly OMB Circular A-87); 2 C.F.R. Part 230, Cost Principles for Non-Profit Organizations (formerly OMB Circular A-122); and OMB Circular A-102, Grants and Cooperative Agreements with State and Local Governments, 59 Fed. Reg. 52224 (1994), amended, 62 Fed. Reg. 45934 (1997). Provisions concerning the disposition of patent rights in "funding agreements" (grants, cooperative agreements, and procurement contracts) with small businesses and nonprofit organizations are specified in 35 U.S.C. § 200 et seq. These provisions are implemented by the Department of Commerce in 37 C.F.R. Part 401. A few agencies have issued guidance on grants and cooperative agreements. See, for example, the DoD Grant and Agreement Regulations (DoDGARs), 68 Fed. Reg. 47150, August 7, 2003. These regulations are published at 32 C.F.R. Part 21 through Part 37. See also the NASA Grant and Cooperative Agreement Handbook, 14 C.F.R. Part 1260.

Whether an assistance agreement takes the form of a grant or a cooperative agreement depends upon the government's degree of involvement in the activity being supported, *Xcavators, Inc.*, 59 Comp. Gen. 758 (B-198297), 80-2 CPD ¶ 229. The following guidance on the use of grants is provided at 31 U.S.C. § 6304:

> An executive agency shall use a grant agreement as the legal instrument reflecting a relationship between the United States Government and a State, a local government, or other recipient when —
>
> > (1) the principal purpose of the relationship is to transfer a thing of value to the State or local government or other recipient to carry out a public purpose of support or stimulation authorized by a law of the United States instead of acquiring (by purchase, lease, or barter) property or services for the direct benefit or use of the United States Government; and
> >
> > (2) substantial involvement *is not expected* between the executive agency and the State, local government, or other recipient when carrying out the activity contemplated in the agreement (emphasis added).

The conditions for use of cooperative agreements are specified in 31 U.S.C. § 6305 as follows:

> An executive agency shall use a cooperative agreement as the legal instrument reflecting a relationship between the United States Government and a State, a local government, or other recipient when —
>
> > (1) the principal purpose of the relationship is to transfer a thing of value to the State, local government, or other recipient to carry out a public purpose of support or stimulation authorized by a law of the United States instead of acquiring (by purchase, lease, or barter) property or services for the direct benefit or use of the United States Government; and
> >
> > (2) substantial involvement *is expected* between the executive agency and the State, local government, or other recipient when carrying out the activity contemplated in the agreement (emphasis added).

FAR 35.003(a) implements this statute by stating that "[g]rants or cooperative agreements should be used when the principal purpose of the transaction is to stimulate or support research and development for [a] public purpose [other than acquisition of supplies or services for the direct benefit or use of the federal government]." An agency may not avoid compliance with the procurement rules by using a cooperative agreement when a procurement contract is the proper vehicle, 67 Comp. Gen. 13 (B-

227084.5) (1987), *recons. denied*, Comp. Gen. Dec. B-227084.6, 1988 U.S. Comp. Gen. LEXIS 1586 (procurement contract rather than cooperative agreement should be used to turn over operation of a facility to private company when agency was main user of facility); *R&R Enters.*, IBCA 2417, 89-2 BCA ¶ 21,708 (agreement to run a concession is a procurement contract, not a cooperative agreement); Comp. Gen. Dec. B-257430, Sept. 12, 1994, *Unpub.* (arrangement to conduct a survey was a procurement contract, not an "assistance relationship"); *Environmental Protection Agency-Inspector General — Cooperative Agreement — Procurement*, Comp. Gen. Dec. B-262110, 97-1 CPD ¶ 131 (support services to run a conference should be obtained under a procurement contract not a cooperative agreement). The distinction in these cases is between procuring services and providing assistance, with the cases holding that an arrangement to obtain services, even when other parties pay for them, will require the use of a procurement contract, *West Coast Copy, Inc.*, Comp. Gen. Dec. B-254044 , 93-2 CPD ¶ 283. Compare *Montana Human Rights Comm'n*, HUDBCA 90-5305-C8, 91-2 BCA ¶ 23,993 (cooperative agreement properly used in an arrangement where the federal agency assisted a state in developing a complaint resolution process), *Capital Health Servs., Inc.*, Comp. Gen. Dec. B-281439.3, 99-1 CPD ¶ 63 (cooperative agreement correct instrument for sharing health services for military personnel and their dependents); and *Strong Envtl., Inc.*, Comp. Gen. Dec. B-311005, 2008 CPD ¶ 57 (cooperative agreement properly used for disposal and recycling of equipment).

A recipient of a grant or cooperative agreement is not in a position to dictate an agency's choice of the instrument and is not liable to the government if the agency makes the wrong choice, Comp. Gen. Dec. B-198846, Feb. 24, 1981, *Unpub.* (grant); Environmental *Protection Agency*, Comp. Gen. Dec. B-262110, 97-1 CPD ¶ 131 (cooperative agreement).

The distinction between procuring services and providing assistance is most obscure when an agency provides funds to support basic or applied research. In that situation, some agencies use grants while other agencies use procurement contracts. NASA provides guidance on the appropriate choice of award instruments for various types of grants at 14 C.F.R. § 1260.12. See *Energy Conversion Devices, Inc.*, Comp. Gen. Dec. B-260514, 95-2 CPD ¶ 121, holding that a cooperative agreement could properly be used when the primary purpose of the research was to "advance the state-of-the-art by supporting and stimulating research and development."

One of the purposes of the Federal Grant and Agreement Act was to "encourage competition in making grants and cooperative agreements," 31 U.S.C. § 6301. However, there is no overall statutory requirement for competition in such awards, *Burgos & Assocs.*, 58 Comp. Gen. 785 (B-194140), 79-2 CPD ¶ 194, and GAO will not consider protests that improper procedures have been used to award grants or cooperative agreements, *Sprint Commc'ns Co.*, Comp. Gen. Dec. B-256586, 94-1 CPD ¶ 300 (protest will only consider whether procurement contract should have been used and whether there was a conflict of interest). In some cases, individual statutes require competition. See, for example, 7 U.S.C. § 450i(b).

### d.  Other Transactions

Several major agencies have the authority to enter into "other transactions" that are neither procurement contracts, grants, nor cooperative agreements. See 10 U.S.C. § 2371(a), stating:

> Additional Forms of Transactions Authorized — The Secretary of Defense and the Secretary of each military department may enter into transactions (other than contracts, cooperative agreements, and grants) under the authority of this subsection in carrying out basic, applied, and advanced research projects. The authority of this subsection is in addition to the authority provided in section 2358 of this title to use contracts, cooperative agreements, and grants in carrying out such projects.

Section 845 of the National Defense Authorization Act for Fiscal Year 1994, Pub. L. No. 103-160, granted this authority on a temporary basis for "prototype projects that are directly relevant to weapons or weapon systems to be acquired or developed by the Department of Defense." This authority has been periodically extended with the current extension granting the authority until September 30, 2013, § 823 of the National Defense Authorization Act for FY 2008, Pub. L. No. 110-181.

NASA has similar authority. See 42 U.S.C. § 2473, stating that the Administrator is authorized:

> to enter into and perform such contracts, leases, cooperative agreements, or other transactions as may be necessary in the conduct of its work and on such terms as it may deem appropriate, with any agency or instrumentality of the United States, or with any State, Territory, or possession, or with any political subdivision thereof, or with any person, firm, association, corporation, or educational institution.

Under this authority, NASA uses "Space Act Agreements" which are not procurement contracts. See *Rocketplane Kistler*, Comp. Gen. Dec. B-310741, 2008 CPD ¶ 22, and *Exploration Partners, LLC*, Comp. Gen. Dec. B-298804, 2006 CPD ¶ 201 holding that such an agreement to provide funding to encourage the development of a private space transportation system was not a procurement contract.

The DOE also has this type of authority with regard to its nonnuclear research, development, demonstration, and commercial application program, 42 U.S.C. § 7256(g), while DHS has the same authority as DoD to use the authority for both research and prototype contracts, 6 U.S.C. § 391(a).

These agencies can use this "other transactions" authority for any type of work within the scope of the statutory delegation. See, however, *Energy Conversion Devices, Inc.*, Comp. Gen. Dec. B-260514, 95-2 CPD ¶ 121, where GAO denied a protest that a procurement contract should have been used in lieu of a DoD other transaction on the grounds that the principal purpose of the agreement was to stimulate and support the development of new manufacturing technology not to acquire services. The discussion in this decision indicates that GAO might rule that the other transactions authority could not be properly used if the agency was merely procuring services. Such a ruling would appear to be in conflict with the express statutory provisions.

When an agency uses its other transactions authority, it need not comply with the procurement statutes, the FAR, or the statutes and regulations applying to grants and cooperative agreements. However, it will be required to comply with any other statute that applies to contractual transactions in general. To make this determination, the terms of each statute must be analyzed closely. There is no uniform guidance as to which statutes apply to these other transactions. However, the DoDGARs contains substantial guidance in 32 C.F.R. Part 21 through Part 37.

See Chapter 7 of Nash & Rawicz, *Intellectual Property in Government Contracts*, 6th ed. 2008, for a more complete discussion of other transactions.

### e. *Cooperative Research and Development Agreements*

Another form of contract is the cooperative research and development agreement (CRADA). The Federal Technology Transfer Act (FTTA), 15 U.S.C. § 3710a(d), defines a CRADA as follows:

> (1) [T]he term "cooperative research and development agreement" means any agreement between one or more Federal laboratories and one or more non-Federal parties under which the Government, through its laboratories, provides personnel, services, facilities, equipment, intellectual property, or other resources with or without reimbursement (but not funds to non-Federal parties) and the non-Federal parties provide funds, personnel, services, facilities, equipment, intellectual property, or other resources toward the conduct of specified research or development efforts which are consistent with the missions of the laboratory; except that such term does not include a procurement contract or cooperative agreement as those terms are used in sections 6303, 6304, and 6305 of title 31, United States Code;

15 U.S.C. § 3710a authorizes the directors of federal laboratories to enter into CRADAs. The purpose of these CRADAs is to "transfer federally owned or originated technology to State and local governments and to the private sector," 15 U.S.C. § 3710a(1). To accomplish this purpose, the Act permits federal laboratories to provide any resources *except federal funds* to the parties entering into CRADAs. The other parties can, and generally do, provide funding to support the work of the laboratory. Agencies with the authority to enter into other transactions could enter into an agreement similar to a CRADA and provide federal funds as part of the arrangement.

A CRADA cannot be awarded when a procurement contract is the proper instrument, *Chem Serv., Inc. v. Environmental Monitoring Sys. Lab.*, 12 F.3d 1256 (3d Cir. 1993). GAO will only consider protests to the award of CRADAs if there is an allegation that a procurement contract should have been used or that there is a conflict of interest, *Management Dev. Group*, 64 Comp. Gen. 669 (B-219245), 85-2 CPD ¶ 34. In *Spire Corp.*, Comp. Gen. Dec. B-258267, 94-2 CPD ¶ 257, GAO gave the following guidance as to how this issue would be decided:

> The FTTA sets forth specific requirements for using a CRADA which are different from the more general requirements for using a cooperative agreement specified in the FGCA. As a general matter, CRADAs under the FTTA may only be used where the purpose of the agreement is to transfer technology from a federal laboratory to a nonfederal entity for the purpose of conducting specified scientific research or development work in collaboration with the nonfederal entity. 15 U.S.C. §§ 3702, 3710a(c)(2) (1988). Given the more specific requirements under the FTTA, the terms of that statute would be the basis for determining whether a CRADA was appropriate here. It follows that the agency's actions would have to be shown to be impermissible under the terms of the FTTA in order for our Office to object to the agency's use of a CRADA.

CRADAs are not subject to the procurement statutes, the FAR, the statutes and regulations governing grants and cooperative agreements, or the statutes governing "other transactions." Furthermore, there is no governmentwide regulatory guidance and very little agencywide guidance on the use of CRADAs. Thus, each agency is free to follow its own procedures. As with the case of "other transactions," other statutes pertaining to contracting by the federal government must be carefully analyzed to determine if they apply to CRADAs.

See Chapter 7 of Nash & Rawicz, *Intellectual Property in Government Contracts*, 6th ed. 2008, for a more complete discussion of CRADAs.

## f.  *Employment Contracts*

The employment of individuals by the federal government is accomplished pursuant to civil service laws. See generally 5 U.S.C. § 2101 et seq. However, services may be acquired under a procurement contract, *either from an individual or an organization,* as long as an employer-employee relationship is not established between the government and the persons performing the services, *Sunbelt Props., Inc.*, Comp. Gen. Dec. B-249469, 92-2 CPD ¶ 353. As discussed above, the federal government enters into numerous contracts with different types of organizations for the performance of a wide variety services. In addition, 5 U.S.C. § 3109 permits agencies to "procure by contract the temporary (not in excess of one year) or intermittent services of experts or consultants" when authorized by an appropriation or other statute.

In order to prevent agencies from circumventing the personnel laws, there are strict limitations on obtaining additional employees by contract. These limitations are implemented in the FAR 37.104(b) provision stating that "personal services contracts" are prohibited unless specifically authorized by statute. However, FAR 2.101 defines the term "personal services contract" as:

a contract that, by its express terms or as administered, makes the contractor personnel appear to be, in effect, Government employees (see 37.104).

This definition does not appear to encompass contracts with individuals but only addresses contracts with organizations. However, the limitations on obtaining additional employees by contract applies to both types of contract. The only FAR guidance on contracts with individuals is the confusing statement in FAR 37.104(f) that the contracting officer must coordinate with the appropriate personnel office prior to entering into "personal services contracts" with individual experts or consultants.

Contracts with a particular individual can avoid the prohibition on establishing an employer-employee relationship by treating the individual as an independent contractor. See, for example, *Payment by Nat'l Mediation Bd. to A. Robert Lowry, Inc.*, Comp. Gen. Dec. B-217468, June 25, 1985, *Unpub.*, which involved a contract for the services of a specific individual to act as an independent-contractor neutral arbitrator. In other cases, a contract for the personal services of an individual might be subject to government supervision. See *Lynn Francis Jones*, 63 Comp. Gen. 507 (B-214432) (1984), where GAO stated at 509:

> In view of the purely personal nature of the services provided to the Army by Mr. Jones as an individual and of the contract provision for Government supervision over the services rendered by Mr. Jones, we regard the contract as establishing an employer-employee relationship between him and the Government rather than an independent contractor relationship. See 26 Comp. Gen. 188 (1946), 27 Comp. Gen. 46 (1947) and 53 Comp. Gen. 542 (1974).

There is no prohibition in the FAR of awarding contracts with individuals when they are treated as independent contractors. However, such contracts may not establish an employer-employee relationship.

There is considerably more guidance on contracts with service contractors. There, it is clear that it is improper for the federal government to, in effect, hire employees through the creation of an employer-employee relationship between the government and a contractor's employees in a procurement contract, *United States Advisory Comm'n on Pub. Diplomacy*, 61 Comp. Gen. 69 (B-202159), 81-2 CPD ¶ 404. FAR 37.104(c) contains the following guidance for determining when an employer-employee relationship is created under a service contract:

> (1) An employer-employee relationship under a service contract occurs when, as a result of (i) the contract's terms or (ii) the manner of its administration during performance, contractor personnel are subject to the relatively continuous supervision and control of a Government officer or employee. However, giving an order for a specific article or service, with the right to reject the finished product or result, is not the type of supervision or control that converts an individual who is an independent contractor (such as a contractor employee) into a Government employee.

(2) Each contract arrangement must be judged in the light of its own facts and circumstances, the key question always being: Will the Government exercise relatively continuous supervision and control over the contractor personnel performing the contract? The sporadic, unauthorized supervision of only one of a large number of contractor employees might reasonably be considered not relevant, while relatively continuous Government supervision of a substantial number of contractor employees would have to be taken strongly into account (see (d) below).

FAR 37.104 (d) contains additional guidance on this issue:

The following descriptive elements should be used as a guide in assessing whether or not a proposed contract is personal in nature:

(1) Performance on site.

(2) Principal tools and equipment furnished by the Government.

(3) Services are applied directly to the integral effort of agencies or an organizational subpart in furtherance of assigned function or mission.

(4) Comparable services, meeting comparable needs, are performed in the same or similar agencies using civil service personnel.

(5) The need for the type of service provided can reasonably be expected to last beyond 1 year.

(6) The inherent nature of the service, or the manner in which it is provided, reasonably requires directly or indirectly, Government direction or supervision of contractor employees in order to —

(i) Adequately protect the Government's interest;

(ii) Retain control of the function involved; or

(iii) Retain full personal responsibility for the function supported in a duly authorized Federal officer or employee.

In *Lodge 1858, AFGE v. Webb*, 580 F.2d 496 (D.C. Cir.), *cert. denied*, 439 U.S. 927 (1978), the court held that *supervision* is the all-important factor in determining whether services are being performed under an employment arrangement or under an independent contractor relationship. The court recognized that either actual supervision or the contractual right to supervise could create an employer-employee relationship. Supervision was defined as "control of the individual workman's physical conduct." In this case, the service contracts were held not to violate the proscription because the government did not directly control the contractor's employees since all government orders were issued through the contractor's management. The court discussed all the FAR factors and held that it was not necessary for all the factors to be present; the critical item is supervision. See also *Hines v. United States*, 60 F.3d 1442 (9th Cir. 1995) (contractual right of Postal Service to screen driving records of independent contractor's employees is not supervision); *Information Ventures, Inc.*, Comp. Gen. Dec. B-290785, 2002 CPD ¶ 152 (requirement that government project officer monitor all work of contractor not the type of continuous supervision that creates a personal services contract); *Carr's Wild Horse Center*, Comp. Gen. Dec. B-285833, 2000 CPD ¶ 210 (performing work that is also to be done by government employees not an indication of a personal services contract); *Danoff & Donnelly*, Comp. Gen. Dec. B-243368, 91-2 CPD ¶ 95 (key personnel clause and required approval of personnel does not create personal services contract); *Minority Commc'ns, Inc.*, Comp. Gen. Dec. B-228230.2, 88-1 CPD ¶ 88 (fact that government approval is required for contractor to substitute employees for those identified in proposal does not constitute supervision even though contractor's traditional management prerogatives are infringed); *Work Sys. Design, Inc.*, Comp. Gen. Dec. B-213451, 84-2 CPD ¶ 226 (failure of contract to specify details of work direction does not create employer-employee relationship if written technical instructions are given to contractor's management); *Computer Sciences Corp.*, Comp. Gen. Dec. B-210800, 84-1 CPD ¶ 422 (criticizing excessive lower level management not an indication that agency will supervise contractor's employees); and *Cerberonics, Inc.*, Comp. Gen. Dec. B-192161, 78-2 CPD ¶ 354 (clause limiting contractor's replacement of key personnel not an indication that a personal services contract was created). See *Encore Mgmt., Inc.*, Comp. Gen. Dec. 278903.2, 99-1 CPD ¶ 33, holding that the agency properly canceled a contract for clerical and administrative support services because the agency Inspector General had ruled that it was a personal services contract. Compare *Costner v. United States*, 229 Ct. Cl. 87, 665 F.2d 1016 (1981), holding that supervision is only one of three elements that must be met to create an employment contract with the government — the other two being appointment as an employee and performance of a federal function. This decision would indicate that the FAR guidance is incorrect.

## B. Agencies Covered by Procurement Statutes

The terms "government" and "federal government" are used extensively in statutes, regulations, and in this book to refer to the United States in its contractual dealings. However, contracts are not made by the United States generally but are entered into by individual organizations in all three branches of the government. These numerous organizations are varied in nature, ranging from old-line departments to recently formed corporations. Some have very large procurement budgets and procurement organizations with thousands of employees while others perform a modest amount of contracting with a small number of personnel engaged in such activity. **Figure 1-1** contains the Organization Chart of the United States Government depicting the major governmental units.

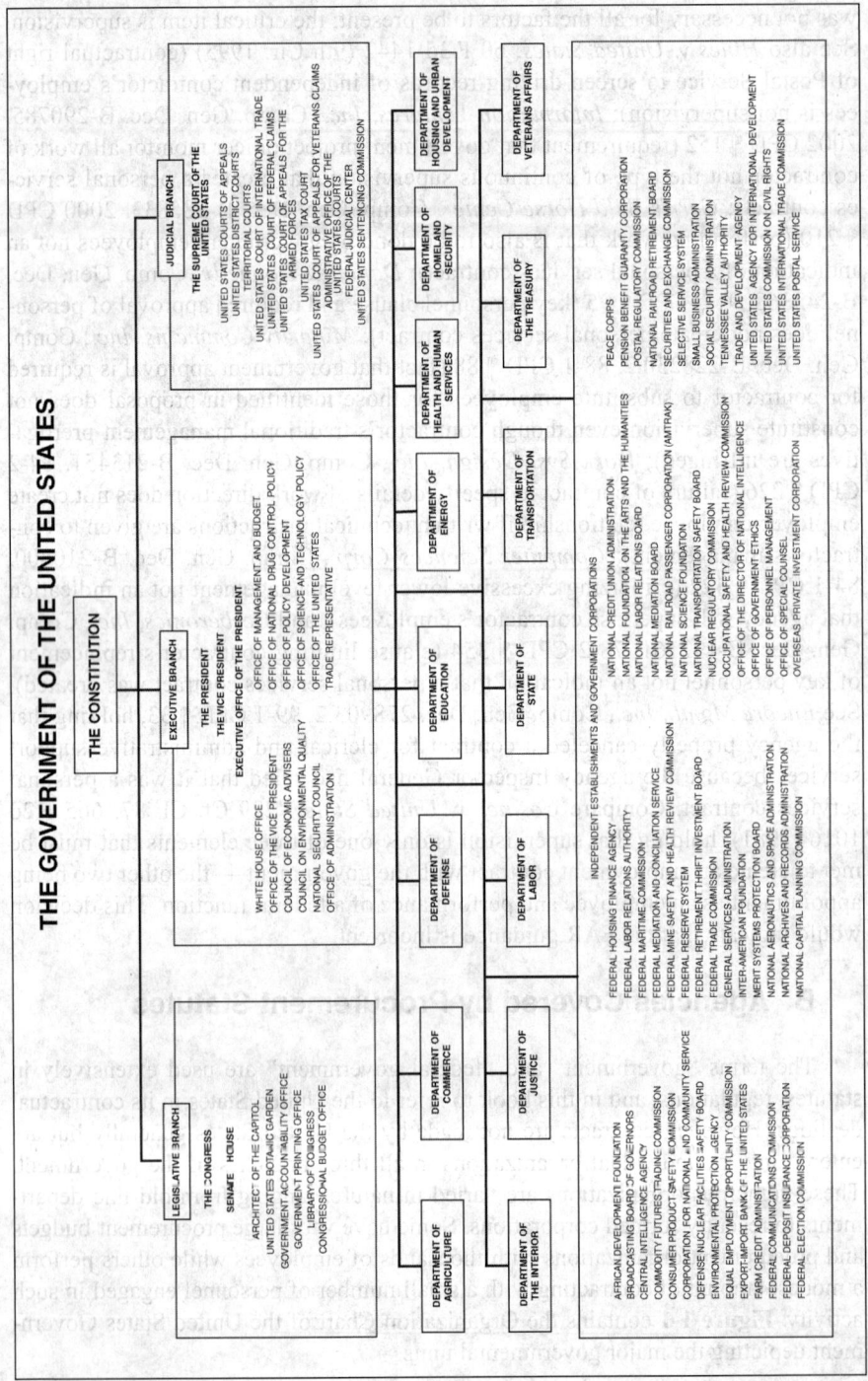

## THE GOVERNMENT OF THE UNITED STATES

THE CONSTITUTION

**LEGISLATIVE BRANCH**

THE CONGRESS

SENATE    HOUSE

ARCHITECT OF THE CAPITOL
UNITED STATES BOTANIC GARDEN
GOVERNMENT ACCOUNTABILITY OFFICE
GOVERNMENT PRINTING OFFICE
LIBRARY OF CONGRESS
CONGRESSIONAL BUDGET OFFICE

**EXECUTIVE BRANCH**

THE PRESIDENT

THE VICE PRESIDENT

EXECUTIVE OFFICE OF THE PRESIDENT

WHITE HOUSE OFFICE
OFFICE OF THE VICE PRESIDENT
COUNCIL OF ECONOMIC ADVISERS
COUNCIL ON ENVIRONMENTAL QUALITY
NATIONAL SECURITY COUNCIL
OFFICE OF ADMINISTRATION

OFFICE OF MANAGEMENT AND BUDGET
OFFICE OF NATIONAL DRUG CONTROL POLICY
OFFICE OF POLICY DEVELOPMENT
OFFICE OF SCIENCE AND TECHNOLOGY POLICY
OFFICE OF THE UNITED STATES
TRADE REPRESENTATIVE

**JUDICIAL BRANCH**

THE SUPREME COURT OF THE UNITED STATES

UNITED STATES COURTS OF APPEALS
UNITED STATES DISTRICT COURTS
TERRITORIAL COURTS
UNITED STATES COURT OF INTERNATIONAL TRADE
UNITED STATES COURT OF FEDERAL CLAIMS
UNITED STATES COURT OF APPEALS FOR THE
ARMED FORCES
UNITED STATES TAX COURT
UNITED STATES COURT OF APPEALS FOR VETERANS CLAIMS
ADMINISTRATIVE OFFICE OF THE
UNITED STATES COURTS
FEDERAL JUDICIAL CENTER
UNITED STATES SENTENCING COMMISSION

DEPARTMENT OF AGRICULTURE
DEPARTMENT OF COMMERCE
DEPARTMENT OF DEFENSE
DEPARTMENT OF EDUCATION
DEPARTMENT OF ENERGY
DEPARTMENT OF HEALTH AND HUMAN SERVICES
DEPARTMENT OF HOMELAND SECURITY

DEPARTMENT OF THE INTERIOR
DEPARTMENT OF JUSTICE
DEPARTMENT OF LABOR
DEPARTMENT OF STATE
DEPARTMENT OF TRANSPORTATION
DEPARTMENT OF THE TREASURY
DEPARTMENT OF VETERANS AFFAIRS
DEPARTMENT OF HOUSING AND URBAN DEVELOPMENT

INDEPENDENT ESTABLISHMENTS AND GOVERNMENT CORPORATIONS

AFRICAN DEVELOPMENT FOUNDATION
BROADCASTING BOARD OF GOVERNORS
CENTRAL INTELLIGENCE AGENCY
COMMODITY FUTURES TRADING COMMISSION
CONSUMER PRODUCT SAFETY COMMISSION
CORPORATION FOR NATIONAL AND COMMUNITY SERVICE
DEFENSE NUCLEAR FACILITIES SAFETY BOARD
ENVIRONMENTAL PROTECTION AGENCY
EQUAL EMPLOYMENT OPPORTUNITY COMMISSION
EXPORT-IMPORT BANK OF THE UNITED STATES
FARM CREDIT ADMINISTRATION
FEDERAL COMMUNICATIONS COMMISSION
FEDERAL DEPOSIT INSURANCE CORPORATION
FEDERAL ELECTION COMMISSION

FEDERAL HOUSING FINANCE AGENCY
FEDERAL LABOR RELATIONS AUTHORITY
FEDERAL MARITIME COMMISSION
FEDERAL MEDIATION AND CONCILIATION SERVICE
FEDERAL MINE SAFETY AND HEALTH REVIEW COMMISSION
FEDERAL RESERVE SYSTEM
FEDERAL RETIREMENT THRIFT INVESTMENT BOARD
FEDERAL TRADE COMMISSION
GENERAL SERVICES ADMINISTRATION
INTER-AMERICAN FOUNDATION
MERIT SYSTEMS PROTECTION BOARD
NATIONAL AERONAUTICS AND SPACE ADMINISTRATION
NATIONAL ARCHIVES AND RECORDS ADMINISTRATION
NATIONAL CAPITAL PLANNING COMMISSION

NATIONAL CREDIT UNION ADMINISTRATION
NATIONAL FOUNDATION ON THE ARTS AND THE HUMANITIES
NATIONAL LABOR RELATIONS BOARD
NATIONAL MEDIATION BOARD
NATIONAL RAILROAD PASSENGER CORPORATION (AMTRAK)
NATIONAL SCIENCE FOUNDATION
NATIONAL TRANSPORTATION SAFETY BOARD
NUCLEAR REGULATORY COMMISSION
OCCUPATIONAL SAFETY AND HEALTH REVIEW COMMISSION
OFFICE OF THE DIRECTOR OF NATIONAL INTELLIGENCE
OFFICE OF GOVERNMENT ETHICS
OFFICE OF PERSONNEL MANAGEMENT
OFFICE OF SPECIAL COUNSEL
OVERSEAS PRIVATE INVESTMENT CORPORATION

PEACE CORPS
PENSION BENEFIT GUARANTY CORPORATION
POSTAL REGULATORY COMMISSION
NATIONAL RAILROAD RETIREMENT BOARD
SECURITIES AND EXCHANGE COMMISSION
SELECTIVE SERVICE SYSTEM
SMALL BUSINESS ADMINISTRATION
SOCIAL SECURITY ADMINISTRATION
TENNESSEE VALLEY AUTHORITY
TRADE AND DEVELOPMENT AGENCY
UNITED STATES AGENCY FOR INTERNATIONAL DEVELOPMENT
UNITED STATES COMMISSION ON CIVIL RIGHTS
UNITED STATES INTERNATIONAL TRADE COMMISSION
UNITED STATES POSTAL SERVICE

**Figure 1-1**

While there is a small amount of procurement carried out by the legislative branch and the judicial branch, the vast majority of all procurement is done by the executive branch of the government.

## *1. Statutes Governing Procurement*

Congress has not adopted a single procurement statute for the entire government. Instead, there are two major statutes covering most government procurement — the Armed Services Procurement Act (ASPA), 10 U.S.C. § 2302 et seq., and the Federal Property and Administrative Services Act (FPASA), 41 U.S.C. § 251 et seq. The ASPA was passed in 1948, and the FPASA, which was modeled after the ASPA, was enacted in 1949. Through the years, the ASPA has been modified extensively, but the FPASA tends to be modified infrequently. In 1984, through the Competition in Contracting Act (CICA), Pub. L. No. 98-369, Congress made these two statutes almost identical. However, changes were subsequently made to both Acts with the result that over the next decade, the two statutes again diverged. The Federal Acquisition Streamlining Act of 1994 (FASA), Pub. L. No. 103-355, again brought the two statutes into closer conformity. The Clinger-Cohen Act of 1996, Pub. L. No. 104-106, retains this conformity by amending both statutes in most cases. Since that time, the ASPA has continued to be modified on a regular basis while the FPASA has not.

There are a few minor agencies not covered by either of these two statutes, most of which conduct their procurement under Revised Statutes 3709 and 3710, 41 U.S.C. § 5 and 41 U.S.C. § 8, respectively (pre-2011 codification). There are also several agencies, most notably the Postal Service and the Federal Aviation Administration, which have been specifically authorized to conduct their procurement without following the major procurement statutes. Finally, there is an overriding statute, the Office of Federal Procurement Policy Act (OFPPA), 41 U.S.C. § 1101 et seq., that contains a number of procurement rules covering almost all government agencies. The problems inherent in this unnecessarily complex and burdensome statutory scheme were recognized in the President's Blue Ribbon Commission on Defense Management, *A Quest for Excellence — Final Report to the President* (June 1986), which stated at 55, "[W]e recommend that Congress work with the Administration to recodify federal laws governing procurement in a single, consistent, and greatly simplified procurement statute." However, there has been no significant effort to enact a single procurement statute for the entire federal government.

There are also numerous statutes that have an impact on the procurement process because they govern the internal workings of the government. A number of these statutes are listed in **Figure 1-2**.

| ORGANIZATIONAL TERMINOLOGY OF THE FEDERAL GOVERNMENT | | |
| --- | --- | --- |
| **Statute or Regulation** | **Organizational Element** | **Definition** |
| 5 U.S.C. § 101 Government Organization and Employees | Executive Departments | Departments of State, Treasury, Defense, Justice, Interior, Agriculture, Commerce, Labor, HHS, HUD, Transportation, Energy, Education, Veterans Affairs, and Homeland Security |
| 5 U.S.C. § 102 Government Organization and Employees | Military Departments | Departments of the Army, Navy, and Air Force |
| 5 U.S.C. § 102 Government Organization and Employees | Government Corporations | A corporation owned or controlled by the Government of the United States (Government-controlled corporation does not include a corporation owned by the Government of the United States) |
| 5 U.S.C. § 104 | Independent Establishment | An establishment in the executive branch (other than the United States Postal Service or the Postal Regulatory Commission) that is not an executive department, military department, Government corporation, or part thereof, or part of an independent establishment and the Government Accountability Office |
| 31 U.S.C. § 101 Money and Finance | Agency | A department, agency or instrumentality of the United States Government |
| 40 U.S.C. § 102 Public Buildings, Property, and Works* | Executive Agency | Any executive department of independent establishment in the executive branch of the Government including any wholly owned Government corporations |
| 40 U.S.C. § 102 Public Buildings, Property, and Works* | Federal Agency | Any executive agency or any establishment in the legislative or judicial branch of the Government (except the Senate, the House of Representatives, and the Architect of the Capitol and any activities under its direction) |
| 41 U.S.C. § 133 | Executive Agency | An executive department, a military department, an independent establishment, and a wholly owned Government corporation |
| *FAR 2. 101 contains substantially the same definitions. | | |

Figure 1-2

It can be seen that these statutes use different terms to describe the agencies that they cover — with the result that there is no uniform terminology describing agencies of the executive branch.

In addition, procurement rules may be found in statutes creating an agency or in funding statutes. As a result, the specific rules that apply to procurements must be determined agency by agency. This section examines the coverage of the four major procurement statutes.

## a. Armed Services Procurement Act

The applicability of the ASPA is specified at 10 U.S.C. § 2303 as follows:

(a) This chapter applies to the procurement by any of the following agencies, for its use or otherwise, of all property (other than land) and all services for which payment is to be made from appropriated funds:

(1) The Department of Defense.

(2) The Department of the Army.

(3) The Department of the Navy.

(4) The Department of the Air Force.

(5) The Coast Guard.

(6) The National Aeronautics and Space Administration.

When a provision in the ASPA states that it is to be implemented by "the head of an agency," all of the agencies listed above are covered. However, some sections and paragraphs call for implementation by "the Secretary of Defense." In those cases, the provisions apply only to defense agencies, including the military services, but not to the Coast Guard and NASA.

## b. Federal Property and Administrative Services Act

41 U.S.C. § 3101(c) makes the FPASA applicable to procurements of "executive agencies" except that it does not apply:

(A) to the Department of Defense, the Coast Guard, and the National Aeronautics and Space Administration; or

(B) except as provided in paragraph (2), when this division [41 U.S.C. § 3101 et seq.] is made inapplicable pursuant to law.

In order to ascertain the coverage of the FPASA, it is necessary to determine whether the contracting organization is an executive agency and whether it is exempted by some other law. 40 U.S.C. § 113 contains a list of exemptions and there are other exemptions in other laws applicable to specific agencies. The following material considers the meaning of the term "executive agency" and the breadth of the exemptions.

## (1) EXECUTIVE AGENCY

The term "executive agency" is defined in 40 U.S.C. § 102 as follows:

(4) The term "executive agency" means — (A) an executive department or independent establishment in the executive branch of the Government; and (B) a wholly owned Government corporation.

Organizations other than the departments, establishments, and corporations listed in **Figure 1-1** can also be considered to be executive agencies if they perform procurement functions for the executive agencies. However, the mere fact that the government provides funding for the operation of an organization will not make that agency a federal instrumentality, *United States v. Orleans*, 425 U.S. 807 (1976). The total factual circumstances surrounding the creation of the organization must be considered in determining whether it constitutes an executive agency under a particular statute, *Motor Coach Indus., Inc. v. Dole*, 725 F.2d 958 (4th Cir. 1984). In that case, the Federal Aviation Agency required a trust to be formed by airlines for purposes of receiving airport landing fees due to the United States and using those fees for the purchase of buses for passenger transportation to the airport. All the employees of the trust were airline personnel. However, the court held that the trust was an executive agency and that the FPASA applied to its purchases, stating at 964-65:

Whether a trust becomes a public instrumentality must be determined by analyzing the total factual circumstances surrounding its creation. See, e.g., *United States v. Orleans*, 425 U.S. 807, 815, 96 S. Ct. 1971, 1976, 48 L.Ed.2d 390 (1976) (whether an agency acts as an instrumentality of the government depends on the day-to-day supervision over its operations by the government); *Lewis v. United States*, 680 F.2d 1239, 1240 (9th Cir. 1982) (degree of control, source of finances, and public character of the agency's mission are important criteria for determining whether the entity is governmental in nature); *Federal Reserve Bank of St. Louis v. Metrocentre Improvement District No. 1*, 657 F.2d 183, 185 (8th Cir. 1981) (the governmental or private character of the agency's function is important in determining whether it is a governmental instrumentality). We must consider, at a minimum, the purposes for which the trust was established; the public or private character of the entity spearheading the trust's creation; the identity of the trust's beneficiary and administrators; the degree of control exercised by the public agency over disbursements and other details of administration; and the method by which the trust is funded.

The Trust was established at the urging of the FAA to accomplish an objective it had long sought — improved public access to Dulles Airport. The documents governing the Trust not only made the FAA the sole beneficiary, but gave the agency a prominent, if not exclusive, role in the Trust's administration. The FAA established the airlines' contribution formula, monitored collections with its own staff, exercised final approval power over disbursements, and participated in every phase of the decision to award Eagle the bus contract.

An organization may be considered to be an executive agency for purposes of the procurement statutes but not a federal agency under other statutes. See *Flight Int'l Group, Inc. v. Federal Reserve Bank of Chicago*, 583 F. Supp. 674, *vacated because of parties' settlement*, 597 F. Supp. 462 (N.D. Ga. 1984), where procurement by a Federal Reserve Bank was found to be governed by the FPASA. The court noted that 40 U.S.C. § 102 (previously § 472) does not explicitly define an independent establishment, and it therefore applied the definition of that term contained in 5 U.S.C. § 104 and deemed the Federal Reserve Bank an executive agency subject to the FPASA. The court observed that the Board of Governors of the Federal Reserve System, the members of which are appointed by the President, is listed among the "Independent Establishments and Government Corporations" under the executive branch in *The United States Government Organization Manual*. See also *Dorsey v. Federal Reserve Bank of St. Louis*, 451 F. Supp. 683 (N.D. Mo. 1978), where a bank was held to be an executive agency for purposes of application of Title VII of the Civil Rights Act. Compare *Lewis v. United States*, 680 F.2d 1239 (9th Cir. 1982) (Federal Reserve Board does not exercise sufficient control over member banks to have bank be considered a federal agency for purposes of the Federal Tort Claims Act); *Mendrala v. Crown Mortgage Co.*, 955 F.2d 1132 (7th Cir. 1992) (Federal Home Loan Mortgage Corporation can be a federal agency for other purposes — estoppel); and *Lee Constr. Co. v. Federal Reserve Bank of Richmond*, 558 F. Supp. 165 (D. Md. 1982) (court held, without analysis, that a Federal Reserve Bank was neither a federal agency nor an executive agency under 40 U.S.C. § 472(a) or (b) (now § 102) and that the 40 U.S.C. § 484 (now § 541 et seq.) restrictions on disposal of surplus government property did not apply).

Even an Article I court may be considered an executive agency under the FPASA, despite its being listed within the judicial branch in **Figure 1-1.** Article I courts include the United States Court of Federal Claims, the United States Court of Military Appeals, the United States Court of Veterans Appeals, and the United States Tax Court.

## (2) 40 U.S.C. § 113 EXEMPTIONS

40 U.S.C. § 113 does not explicitly grant exemptions to the FPASA but provides that nothing "in this subtitle impairs or affects the authority" of 20 listed organizations whose transactions are totally or partially subject to its coverage. It is not clear whether this provision is intended to grant exemptions to the organizations listed or is merely supportive of exemption authority independently granted by some other statute. In addition, some of the exemptions have limited application.

## (3) OTHER LAWS

The phrase "other law" used in 41 U.S.C. § 3101(c) has been interpreted to require that the statute relied upon for exemption contain "express terms" exempting the procurements from 41 U.S.C. § 3101 et seq. before the agency will be exempted. See *Andrus v. Glover Constr. Co.*, 446 U.S. 608 (1980), where the Court held that the Buy Indian Act, which authorizes the Secretary of the Interior to purchase "the products of Indian industry . . . in open market," does not authorize an exemption from the FPASA. The "express terms" exemption is apparently satisfied by 39 U.S.C. § 410(a), which states that "no Federal law dealing with public or Federal contracts . . . shall apply to the exercise of the powers of the Postal Service." The intent of Congress to exempt the Postal Service from the FPASA seems evident, even though the FPASA is not specifically mentioned. A clear exemption is contained in Pub. L. No. 104-50, stating that after April 1, 1996, the Federal Aviation Administration will not be subject to a list of statutes including the FPASA, the OFPPA, 41 U.S.C. § 3101 et seq., and the Small Business Act, 15 U.S.C. § 631 et seq. See also the statutory language applicable to the Tennessee Valley Authority (TVA), 16 U.S.C. § 831h(b), and the Bonneville Power Administration (BPA), 16 U.S.C. § 832a(f). These statutes permit these organizations to enter into contracts "upon such terms and conditions and in such manner as [they] may deem necessary." In *Inryco, Inc. v. Tennessee Valley Auth.*, 471 F. Supp. 59 (D. Tenn. 1978), the court held that the FPASA did not apply to TVA projects and cited the predecessor TVA statute, 16 U.S.C. § 831h(b), and 40 U.S.C. § 474(12) in support of its decision. Similarly, the BPA is not subject to either the FPASA or the FAR, *International Line Builders*, 67 Comp. Gen. 8 (B-227811), 87-2 CPD ¶ 345.

When a statute does contain the proper express terms exemption from the FPASA, the court will scrutinize the action taken under the statute to ensure that the statute is not being invoked in order to circumvent the FPASA provisions. See *Chem Serv., Inc. v. Environmental Monitoring Sys. Lab.*, 12 F.3d 1256 (3d Cir. 1993), where the court found that although the Federal Technology Transfer Act (FTTA) explicitly allowed research and development agreements without following the FPASA provisions, an agreement made under the FTTA that manifested the features of a traditional procurement contract had improperly bypassed the FPASA provisions.

### c.  Revised Statutes 3709 and 3710

These basic procurement statutes originally applied to all government agencies. They were codified in 41 U.S.C. § 5 and § 8 prior to the 2011 codification of Title 41, and applied to procurement by "federal agencies" when the ASPA and the FPASA did not apply, 41 U.S.C. § 252(a) (pre-2011 codification). Thus, unless otherwise excepted, they applied to procurement by all government organizations not within the executive branch. Exemptions from 41 U.S.C. § 5 did not necessarily exempt an agency from other procurement statutes. For example, the Buy American

Act, 41 U.S.C. § 8302, provides that "[o]nly unmanufactured articles, materials, and supplies that have been mined or produced in the United States, and only manufactured articles, materials, and supplies that have been manufactured in the United States . . . shall be acquired for public use." (Prior to the 2011 codification, the Act included the phrase "notwithstanding any other provision of law")

## d. Office of Federal Procurement Policy Act

The OFPPA, 41 U.S.C. § 1101 et seq., also applies to "executive agencies," which were defined in 41 U.S.C. § 403(1) (pre-2011 codification), as follows:

[T]he term "executive agency" means —

    (A) an executive department specified in section 101 of title 5, United States Code;

    (B) a military department specified in section 102 of such title;

    (C) an independent establishment as defined in section 104(1) of such title; and

    (D) a wholly owned Government corporation fully subject to the provisions of chapter 91 of title 31, United States Code.

This definition was removed in the 2011 codification. The Act creates the Office of Federal Procurement Policy (OFPP) in the Office of Management and Budget (OMB) and gives its Administrator broad powers to "provide overall direction of Governmentwide procurement policies, regulations, procedures, and forms for executive agencies," 41 U.S.C. § 1101(b)(1). It also contains a number of sections applicable to all "executive agencies," 41 U.S.C. § 1127 (limitations on compensation of contractor executives), § 1702 (requirement for "chief acquisition officers" in all but DoD), § 1704 (requirement to plan for and train the acquisition workforce), § 1705 (requirement for competition advocates), § 1708 (requirement for procurement notices), § 1709 (rules governing contracting out of agency work), § 1711 (value engineering requirement), § 1712 (requirement for record of procurements), § 1501-06 (establishment of cost accounting standards), §§ 1901-05 (simplified acquisition rules), § 1906 (laws inapplicable to commercial item procurements), § 1907 (laws inapplicable to commercial off-the-shelf item procurements), §§ 2101-07 (procurement integrity requirements), § 2301 (electronic commerce requirement), § 2308 (information technology procurement requirements),§ 2309 (protection of constitutional rights of contractors), § 2310 (encouragement of performance-based service contracts), and § 2312 (establishing a Contingency Contracting Corps). These sections have been added to the statute periodically when Congress enacts a provision applicable to the entire executive branch without amending both the ASPA and the FPASA.

## 2. *Federal Acquisition Regulation System*

Although Congress has not enacted a single statute covering all agencies, it has provided that a *single regulation* be promulgated in this area, 41 U.S.C. § 1121(b). This regulation is known as the Federal Acquisition Regulation (FAR). It is written by the Defense Acquisition Regulations Council and the Civilian Agency Acquisition Council, FAR 1.201-1, and published under the auspices of the Secretary of Defense, the Administrator of National Aeronautics and Space, and the Administrator of General Services, 41 U.S.C. § 1303(a).

All of the major agencies with procurement functions issue supplementary regulations to implement the FAR. However, these FAR Supplements are required to be limited in scope in accordance with 41 U.S.C. § 1303(a)(2), as follows:

> Other regulations relating to procurement issued by an executive agency shall be limited to (A) regulations essential to implement Government-wide policies within the agency; and (B) additional policies and procedures required to satisfy the specific and unique needs of the agency.

The Administrator of the OFPP has the authority to rescind, revise, or deny promulgation of any regulation that does not meet these standards, 41 U.S.C. § 1303(a)(5). The Administrator also has the authority to issue regulations if the three designated agencies do not issue necessary regulations in a timely manner, 41 U.S.C. § 1121(d). However, these reserve powers have not been used, as the promulgation of the FAR has been achieved in a collegial manner.

The FAR and its many supplements are known as the "FAR system." **Figure 1-3** depicts this system, and **Figure 1-4** contains a listing of the agency supplemental regulations. The FAR became effective April 1, 1984.

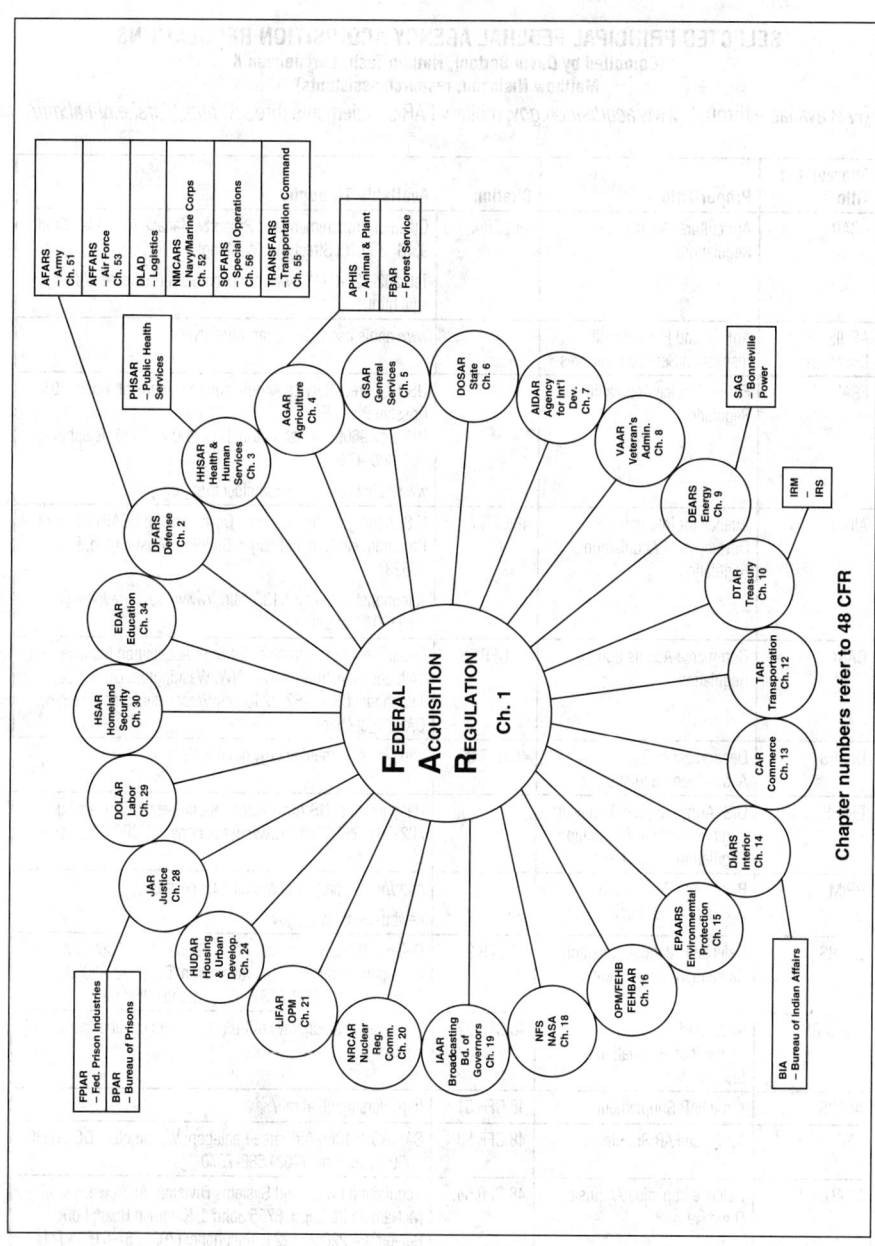

**Figure 1-3**

**SELECTED PRINCIPAL FEDERAL AGENCY ACQUISITION REGULATIONS**
(Compiled by David Bertoni, Nathan Tash, Lori Jensen &
Matthew Nisinson, research assistants)
(FAR available through *www.acquisition.gov*, military FAR supplements through *http://farsite.hill.af.mil/*)

| Abbreviated Title | Proper Title | Citation | Available Through |
|---|---|---|---|
| AGAR | Agricultural Acquisition Regulations | 48 CFR 4 | Office of Procurement and Property Management; Mail Stop 9301; 300 7th Street SW; Washington, DC 20024<br><br>Tel. 202-720-9448; www.dm.usda.gov/procurement/policy/agar.html |
| APHIS Directives | Animal and Plant Health Inspection Service Directives | | www.aphis.usda.gov/library/directives/ |
| FSAR | Forest Service Acquisition Regulation | | USDA, Forest Service Acquisition Management: Room 706, Rosslyn Plaza-E P.O. Box 96090; Washington, D.C. 20090-6090; Telephone: 703-605-4744<br><br>www.fs.fed.us/business/incident/ref_reg.php |
| AIDAR | Agency for International Development Acquisition Regulation | 48 CFR 7 | U.S. Agency for International Development; USAID Office of Procurement; Ronald Reagan Building; Washington, D.C. 20523<br><br>Telephone: 202-712-5130; http://www.usaid.gov/policy/ads/300/aidar.pdf |
| CAR | Commerce Acquisition Regulation | 48 CFR 13 | Department of Commerce, Office of Acquisition Management; 14th and Constitution Ave., NW; Washington, DC 20230; Telephone: (202) 482-4248; http://oam.eas.commerce.gov/CAPPS_car.html |
| DEARS | Department of Energy Acquisition Regulation | 48 CFR 9 | http://management.energy.gov/DEAR.htm |
| EFARS | U.S. Army Corps of Engineers: Engineer Federal Acquisition Regulation Supplement | | Headquarters, US Army Corps of Engineers: Contracting 202-761-0567; http://www.usace.army.mil/CECT/Pages/EFARS.aspx |
| BPIM | Bonneville Purchasing Instructions Manual | | http://www.bpa.gov/corporate/business/bpi/<br><br>newbusiness@bpa.gov |
| DFARS | Defense Federal Acquisition Regulation Supplement | 48 CFR 2 | Defense Procurement and Acquisition Policy; 3060 Defense Pentagon; Room 3B855; Washington, DC 20301-3060; Telephone: 703-602-0131; http://farsite.hill.af.mil |
| NMCARS | Navy Marine Corps Acquisition Regulation Supplement | 48 CFR 52 | https://acquisition.navy.mil/rda/home/policy_and_guidance/nmcars |
| AFARS | Army FAR Supplement | 48 CFR 51 | http://farsite.hill.af.mil/ |
| AFFARS | Air Force FAR Supplement | 48 CFR 53 | SAF/AQC; 1060 Air Force Pentagon; Washington, DC 20330-1060; Telephone: (703) 588-7070 |
| DLAD | Defense Logistics Acquisition Directive | 48 CFR 54 | Acquisition Policy and Systems Division; Andrew T. McNamara Building; 8725 John J. Kingman Road; Fort Belvoir, VA 22060-6221; Telephone: (703) 767-6155 xJ71; http://www.dla.mil/j-3/j-3311/dlad/rev5.htm |
| DIARS | Department of the Interior Acquisition Regulation | 48 CFR 14 | Office of Acquisition and Property Management; Department of the Interior;<br><br>http://www.doi.gov/pam/pamareg.html |

**Figure 1-4 (cont'd on next page)**

| Abbreviated Title | Proper Title | Citation | Available Through |
|---|---|---|---|
| DOLAR | Department of Labor Acquisition Regulation | 48 CFR 29 | Office of the Assistant Secretary for Administration and Management; 200 Constitution Avenue, NW, Room S1524; Washington, D.C. 20210; Telephone: 202-693-4028 |
| EDAR | Education Department Acquisition Regulation | 48 CFR 34 | Contracts and Acquisition Management; Office of the Chief Financial Officer; Department of Education; Telephone: 202-245-8059 |
| EPAAR | Environmental Protection Agency Acquisition Regulation | 48 CFR 15 | Office of Acquisition Management; Environmental Protection Agency; http://www.epa.gov/oam/ |
| HSAR | Homeland Security Acquisition Regulation | 48 CFR 30 | http://www.dhs.gov/xopnbiz/regulations/ |
| GSAM | General Services Administration Acquisition Manual | 48 CFR 5 | Office of Acquisition Policy; General Services Administration; Telephone: (202) 501-1224 http://www.gsa.gov/portal/category/21220 |
| HHSAR | Health and Human Services Acquisition Regulation | 48 CFR 3 | Division of Acquisition; Office of Grants and Acquisition Policy and Accountability; Department of Health and Human Services; http://www.hhs.gov/asfr/ogapa/acquisition/index.html |
| HUDAR | Housing and Urban Development Acquisition Regulation | 48 CFR 24 | http://portal.hud.gov/hudportal/HUD?src=/program_offices/cpo |
| JAR | Justice Acquisition Regulation | 48 CFR 28 | Department of Justice Chief Acquisition Officer http://www.justice.gov/jmd/pe/ |
| BPAP | Bureau of Prisons Acquisition Policy | | http://www.bop.gov/business/acquisition.jsp |
| NFS | National Aeronautics and Space Administration FAR Supplement | 48 CFR 18 | http://www.hq.nasa.gov/office/procurement/ |
| NSFAR | National Science Foundation FAR Supplement | 48 CFR 25 | https://www.acquisition.gov/agency_supp_regs.asp |
| DTAR | Department of the Treasury Acquisition Regulation | 48 CFR 10 | Office of the Procurement Executive https://treas.gov/offices/management/dcfo/procurement/ |
| DOSAR | Department of State Acquisition Regulation | 48 CFR 6 | Office of the Procurement Executive http://www.statebuy.state.gov/ |
| IRSAP | IRS Acquisition Procedure | | http://www.irs.gov/pub/irs-procure/guide_irsap_interim.pdf |
| TAR | Department of Transportation Acquisition Regulation | 48 CFR 12 | Acquisition and Financial Assistance Management; Department of Transportation; http://www.dot.gov/ost/m60/tamtar/tar.htm |
| VAAR | Veterans Administration Acquisition Regulation | 48 CFR 8 | Office of Acquisition and Logistics http://www1.va.gov/oamm/ |
| | Office of Personnel Management Federal Acquisition Regulation Supplement | 48 CFR 17 | http://www.opm.gov/doingbusiness/contract/policies.aspx |
| SSAR | Social Security Acquisition Regulation | 48 C.F.R. 23 | SSA Office of Acquisition and Grants 1st Floor, Rear Entrance; 7111 Security Blvd.; Baltimore, MD 21244 Agency Specific Acquisition Polices & Procedures: (410) 965-9519 |

**Figure 1-4 (cont'd from previous page)**

## II.  CONTRACTING POWERS

Although the Constitution does not expressly refer to contracts, the United States Government has the inherent power to use procurement contracts in carrying out its duties and exercising its powers, *United States v. Maurice*, 26 F. Cas. 1211 (No. 15747) (C.C.D. Va. 1823). This contracting power is shared by the legislative and executive branches of the government. The executive branch, which has the constitutional power to execute the laws, enters into contracts. Congress, which is granted the power to make the laws and appropriate money, enacts statutes which authorize programs or activities and provide funds for their accomplishment.

Statutes delegate power to the government agencies. In addition, they often contain requirements to be followed when contracts are used. Thus, statutes serve two purposes in the government contracting process. First, they are the principal means of authorizing and funding programs that are implemented, in whole or in part, by contracting with private parties. Second, they are used to place *limitations* on the way in which those contracting powers are exercised.

Statutes are supplemented by regulations that specify rules that must be followed in awarding contracts and that require the use of specified terms and conditions. When promulgated pursuant to statutory authority, regulations take on the status of law. Together, statutes and regulations are of supreme importance because the government can be contractually bound only through the proper exercise of validly conferred powers.

However, statutes and regulations are not self-enforcing. Control over the day-to-day activities of a government agency is usually vested in the head of the agency, who normally has great discretion in making contracts to carry out government programs. In most cases, these delegated powers are performed properly. However, differences of opinion often arise in interpreting statutes and regulations that may result in an improper use of power. In addition, whether by inadvertence or design, there are instances where an agency's contracting activity violates statutory or regulatory authority. Congress uses a number of oversight techniques to give reasonable assurance that the contracting powers are properly exercised.

This section discusses the statutory mechanisms that Congress uses to delegate powers and to provide funding to the government agencies; the degree of control that various statutes and regulations have over the contracting process; and the techniques used to oversee government agencies in the contracting process.

### A.  Congressional Delegation of Power

The primary means that Congress uses to delegate power to the executive branch is the enactment of laws establishing new programs and the appropriation of funds to pay for these programs. This activity occurs each year in the "budget and appropriations" process of the federal government. This process is controlled by the Congressional Budget and Impoundment Control Act of 1974, 2 U.S.C. § 621 et seq., and various sections of Title 31. See also the Government Accountability Office, Principles of Federal Appropriations Law. (*http://www.gao.gov/legal/redbook.html*) There is now a third edition of Volume I, January 2004, Volume II, February 2006, and Volume III, September 2008, with annual updates of these volumes.

This subsection first considers the legal requirements for congressional appropriations before contracts can be awarded. It then reviews the budget and appropriations process which is the primary means of conferring contracting power. Finally, it summarizes the manner that appropriations law impacts the contracting process.

## 1. Need for Congressional Appropriation

Congress exerts authority over the contracting process through the use of its constitutional powers. Article 1, Section 9, Clause 7, of the Constitution provides that "[n]o money shall be drawn from the Treasury, but in Consequence of Appropriations made by Law." This provision of the Constitution prohibits any *payments* by agencies unless funds have been approved by Congress. Congress has extended this control mechanism by restricting government agencies from *obligating funds* unless there is existing congressional authority. This proposition is embodied in the Anti-Deficiency Act, 31 U.S.C. § 1341(a), which states:

(1) An officer or employee of the United States Government or of the District of Columbia government may not —

(A) make or authorize an expenditure or obligation exceeding an amount available in an appropriation or fund for the expenditure or obligation; or

(B) involve either government in a contract or obligation for the payment of money before an appropriation is made unless authorized by law.

In the contracting process the signing of a contract legally obligates the funds necessary to carry out the contract. Thus, government agencies cannot make *payments* under a contract or *enter into* a contract unless Congress has given them proper authority.

In order to obligate the government by contract, the agency must have received sufficient funds in an existing appropriations statute to cover the obligation, or there must be some other statute by which Congress specifically empowers an agency to make contracts without regard to the need for appropriations. The authority inherent in both types of statutes is called "budget authority." See 2 U.S.C. § 622(2), which states:

The term "budget authority" means the authority provided by Federal law to incur financial obligations, as follows:

(i) provisions of law that make funds available for obligation and expenditure (other than borrowing authority), including the authority to obligate and expend the proceeds of offsetting receipts and collections;

(ii) borrowing authority, which means authority granted to a Federal entity to borrow and obligate and expend the borrowed funds, including through the issuance of promissory notes or other monetary credits;

(iii) contract authority, which means the making of funds available for obligation but not for expenditure; and

(iv) offsetting receipts and collections as negative budget authority, and the reduction thereof as positive budget authority.

The first, and most common, form of budget authority is an appropriation. Congress allows agencies to incur obligations and make payments for obligations through appropriations. They give agencies the power to enter into and pay for work under contracts. This type of budget authority will be discussed in more detail in subsequent sections.

"Borrowing authority," referred to at 2 U.S.C. § 622(2)(ii), can also apply to contracts. Borrowing authority allows government agencies to incur obligations and liquidate these obligations out of borrowed funds. Agencies with borrowing authority can enter into contracts and make payments with borrowed monies. See, for example, Comp. Gen. Dec. B-223857, Feb. 27, 1987, *Unpub.* (Commodity Credit Corporation violated the Anti-Deficiency Act because it had used all funds available from its borrowing authority but still had contractual obligations). Borrowing authority may consist of the authority to borrow from the Treasury, authority to borrow directly from the public, authority to borrow from the Federal Financing Bank, or a combination, *Principles of Federal Appropriations Law* 2-7 (3d ed. 2004). However, since direct appropriations provides more congressional control than borrowing authority, the Congressional Budget Act requires new borrowing authority to be limited to the extent or amounts provided in appropriations acts, 2 U.S.C. § 651(a).

"Contract authority," referred to at 2 U.S.C. § 622(2)(iii), is found in statutes authorizing contracts without regard to appropriations. See, for example, *People's Bank & Trust Co. v. United States*, 11 Cl. Ct. 554 (1987) (court found "contract authority" in applicable statutes and regulations governing FmHA); *New York Airways, Inc. v. United States*, 177 Ct. Cl. 800, 369 F.2d 743 (1966) (although Congress did not grant appropriations, government was not relieved of contractual obligation because appropriations restrictions did not apply to 49 U.S.C. § 1376(c) giving contract authority). 31 U.S.C. § 1301(d) provides that for a law to be construed to authorize a contract for payment of money in excess of an appropriation, it must specifically state that such a contract may be made. Contract authority can be given in appropriations acts but is more frequently conferred in other legislation, *Principles of Federal Appropriations Law* 2-6 (3d ed. 2004). Like borrowing authority,

2 U.S.C. § 651(a) also restricts the use of new "contract authority" in future statutes by providing that it will be out of order for either house to consider any bill, resolution, conference report, or amendment that provides "new spending authority" beyond the amount of the appropriations for that fiscal year.

Another form of budget authority, which is characterized as "offsetting receipts and collections" in 2 U.S.C. § 622(2)(iv), is a revolving fund. Revolving funds allow government corporations and offices to generate income as well as expend money. Agencies are allowed to conduct public or intragovernmental transactions which generate income. Specific statutory authority allows these agencies to deposit the income in an appropriation or fund account. The agency is then permitted to make use of such income to finance continued operations. See *Principles of Federal Appropriations Law* 2-9 (3d ed. 2004). For an example of a revolving fund, see 31 U.S.C. § 5142, which establishes such a fund for the Bureau of Engraving and Printing.

## 2. Budget and Appropriations Process

The budget and appropriations process is the involved means that the federal government uses to arrive at the annual budget that supports its varied programs. The "budget and appropriations" process has three phases: the budget formulation phase, the authorization phase, and the appropriations phase.

### a. Budget Formulation Phase

The budgetary phase of the process begins with the administrative process of budget preparation and review. Agencies gather information through reviews of current operations, program objectives, and future plans. This, along with information from other federal departments, is used to prepare the President's budget, which must be submitted on or before the first Monday in February for the fiscal year starting the following October 1. See 2 U.S.C. § 631.

Upon receipt of the President's budget, the Budget Committees of the House of Representatives and the Senate begin work on a budget resolution which packages the entire federal budget for the following year. By February 15, the Congressional Budget Office must submit a budget report to the Budget Committees, and within 10 days of that date all other congressional committees with oversight over agency programs are required to submit their views and estimates to the Budget Committees. Then the Senate Budget Committee reports a concurrent resolution on the budget, and by April 15, Congress is required to complete action on the concurrent resolution. After the concurrent resolution is passed, annual authorization and appropriation bills can be considered, 2 U.S.C. § 631. The concurrent resolution establishes "target ceilings" for expenditures which are used to evaluate individual appropriations legislation, *Principles of Federal Appropriations Law* 1-17 (3d ed. 2004).

## b. *Authorization of Appropriations*

The next phase in the process is the authorization of appropriations. Before an appropriations statute is passed, there usually must be some separate statute authorizing the program or activity that is the subject of the appropriation. Although there is no general statutory provision to this effect, House of Representatives Rule XXI(2) prohibits the reporting out of general appropriations unless the proposed expenditures were "previously authorized by law." The Senate has similar rules, *Principles of Federal Appropriations Law* 1-29 (3d ed. 2004). In addition, Congress has required annual authorizations for some agencies. See, for example 42 U.S.C. § 7270 (DOE); 10 U.S.C. § 114 (DoD); and 42 U.S.C. § 2460 (NASA). GAO has described authorizations in *Principles of Federal Appropriations Law* (3d ed. 2004), stating at 2-41:

> Authorizations take many different forms, depending in part on whether they are contained in the organic legislation [of an agency] or are separate. Authorizations contained in organic legislation may be "definite" (setting dollar limitations either in the aggregate or for specific fiscal years) or "indefinite" (authorizing "such sums as may be necessary to carry out the provisions of this act"). An indefinite authorization serves little purpose other than to comply with House Rule XXI. Appropriation authorizations enacted as separate legislation resemble appropriations acts in structure, for example, the annual Department of Defense Authorization Acts.

Under this description, the authorization for an appropriation may be the organic act that established the agency, a separate statute establishing a particular program, or the annual authorization statutes required for some agencies. The purpose of these authorizations is to ensure that the legislative committees with oversight of specific agencies retain control over the programs that these agencies undertake.

Even if authorization statutes specify definite amounts that may not be exceeded, they are not binding on Congress in passing an appropriations act. Congress can appropriate a greater amount, 36 Comp. Gen. 240 (B-128902) (1956), or a lesser amount, 53 Comp. Gen. 695 (B-180517) (1974). When the amount appropriated is greater than that authorized, the intent to fund the program at the higher level must be clear, 64 Comp. Gen. 282 (B-214172) (1985) (table in appropriations conference report showing higher amounts than authorization not clear evidence that lump sum appropriation exceeded authorization levels).

Although the Anti-Deficiency Act prohibits obligation of funds in excess of the amount *"available in an appropriation,"* GAO has ruled that it is also a violation of the Act to obligate funds in excess of an authorization which has not clearly been increased by an appropriation, 64 Comp. Gen. 282 (B-214172) (1985) (relying on 60 Comp. Gen. 440 (B-201260) (1980)). This holding was based on the reasoning that funds exceeding the authorization were not "available" for obligation.

Annual authorization statutes usually contain a number of provisions governing the procurement process. See, for example, the National Defense Authorization Act for Fiscal Year 2010, Pub. L. No. 111-84, Title VIII.

### c. Appropriations Statutes

The final stage of the process is the passage of the annual appropriations statutes. In order to ensure that funds are available to operate the government in the fiscal year beginning on October 1, all appropriations acts should be enacted by September 30. There are 12 appropriations statutes, as follows:

- Departments of Agriculture, Rural Development, Foods and Drug Administration, and related agencies

- Departments of Commerce, Justice, Science, and related agencies

- Department of Defense

- Department of State, Foreign Operations, and related programs

- Department of the Interior, Environment, and related agencies

- Departments of Labor, Health and Human Services, and Education, and related agencies

- Department of Homeland Security

- Departments of Transportation, Housing and Urban Development, and related agencies

- Energy and Water Development, and related agencies

- Financial Services and General Government

- Legislative Branch

- Military Construction, Veterans Affairs, and related agencies

In most years, Congress has been unable to meet the statutory requirements for carrying out the appropriations process by the beginning of the fiscal year. In that case, appropriations called "continuing resolutions" are passed to permit agencies to continue their operations. See, for example, Joint Resolution, Pub. L. No. 110-92, appropriating funds to most agencies of the government through November 16, 2007 "for continuing projects or activities . . . that were conducted in fiscal year 2007," with several provisions restricting higher expenditure rates. This was followed by three subsequent continuing resolutions, Pub. L. No. 110-116, Pub. L. No. 110-137, and Pub. L. No. 110-149, extending through December 31, 2007. In ad dition, Congress has frequently combined several appropriations bills into a single "Consolidated Appropriations Act." See, for example, the Consolidated Appropriations Act, 2010, Pub. L. No. 111-117, containing six appropriations acts.

Appropriations being considered by either house of Congress in the absence of an authorization statute are subject to being ruled out of order. However, if the point of order is not raised and the appropriation is passed, it would appear that the impropriety was waived by Congress. See 65 Comp. Gen. 524 (B-222323) (1986); 57 Comp. Gen. 34 (B-145136) (1977). See, however, *Atchison, Topeka & Santa Fe Ry. Co. v. Callaway*, 382 F. Supp. 610 (D.D.C. 1974), holding that the failure to raise a point of order would not cure the invalidity of an appropriation passed in the absence of an authorizing statute.

Most agencies have separate appropriations for functions such as operation and maintenance, procurement, construction, and research and development. A typical functional breakdown for the DoD is set forth in the DoD Appropriations Act, Fiscal Year 2010, Pub . L. No. 111-118, as follows:

Title I Military Personnel

Title II Operation and Maintenance

Title III Procurement

Title IV Research, Development, Test and Evaluation

Title V Revolving and Management Funds

Title VI Other Department of Defense Programs

Title VII Related Agencies

Such appropriations can be, and sometimes are, further divided so that specific amounts are allocated to particular programs, such as the construction of individual buildings, or to separate subcomponents of an agency, such as a bureau, command, or administration within a department.

Each of these statutes may contain numerous special sections, called "riders," directing certain contractual actions or limiting the use of the appropriation for specified purposes. See, for example, the DoD Appropriations Act, 2010, Pub. L. No. 111-118, § 8001 ("No part of any appropriation contained in this Act shall be used for publicity or propaganda purposes not authorized by the Congress") and § 8011 ("None of the funds provided in this Act shall be available to initiate: (1) a multiyear contract that employs economic order quantity procurement in excess of $20,000,000 in any 1 year of the contract or that includes an unfunded contingent liability in excess of $20,000,000, or (2) a contract for advance procurement leading to a multiyear contract that employs economic order quantity procurement in excess of $20,000,000 in any 1 year, unless the congressional defense committees have been notified at least 30 days in advance of the proposed contract award"); the Consolidated Appropriations Act, 2010, Pub. L. No. 111-117, § 404 ("The expenditure of any appropriation under this Act for any consulting service through procurement contract pursuant to section 3109 of title 5, United States Code, shall be limited to those contracts where such expenditures are a matter of public record and available for public inspection, except where otherwise provided under existing law, or under existing Executive order issued pursuant to existing law.")

## 3.  Appropriations Law As It Affects the Contracting Process

The same means by which Congress delegates power to the executive branch — appropriations and authorizations — also enables Congress to limit that power. Thus, appropriations law is an important part of the contracting process.

This subsection first reviews the rules determining the scope of each appropriation. It then considers the requirements that contracts be made only for purposes covered by an appropriation. Finally it addresses the rule that contracts may be entered into only during the time that the appropriation is available for obligation.

### a.  Scope of Appropriations

Appropriations are made for *designated purposes* during *specified fiscal years.* Thus, in entering into a contract, an agency must determine if an appropriation covers the activity being procured and if the appropriated funds may be used at the time the contract is formed. This determination is based on an analysis of the statute making funds available to the agency. For a law to be construed as an appropriation, 31 U.S.C. § 1301(d) requires that "the law specifically states that an appropriation is made." See *Principles of Federal Appropriations Law* (3d ed. 2004) stating at 2-16:

> An appropriation is a form of budget authority that makes funds available to an agency to incur obligations and make expenditures. 2 U.S.C. § 622(2)(A)(i). See also 31 U.S.C. § 701(2)(C) ("authority making amounts available for obligation or expenditure"). Consequently, while the authority must be expressly stated, it is not necessary that the statute actually use the word "appropriation." If the statute contains a specific direction to pay and a designation of the funds to be used, such as a direction to make a specified payment or class of payments  "out of any money in the Treasury not otherwise appropriated," then this amounts to an appropriation. 63 Comp. Gen. 331 (1984); 13 Comp. Gen. 77 (1933). See also 34 Comp. Gen. 590 (1955).

Appropriations acts are not substantive law. Thus, the mere appropriation of money for a program does not mean that other laws applicable to the program may be ignored. In *Tennessee Valley Auth. v. Hill*, 437 U.S. 153 (1978), the Court ruled that the unspecified inclusion of funds to construct a dam did not constitute a repeal by implication of the Endangered Species Act, which had previously been held by the Supreme Court to prohibit construction of the dam.

### b.  Purpose of Appropriations

31 U.S.C. § 1301(a) states that "[a]ppropriations shall be applied only to the objects for which the appropriations were made except as otherwise provided by law." In other words, appropriations may be used only for the purpose for which they were appropriated. Thus, Congress has limited the government agencies' expenditure of appropriated funds by denying the agencies the power to use funds for a purpose beyond that which the appropriations act allows. Agencies have considerable discretion in incurring all expenses reasonably necessary to carry out the purpose of the appropriation, Comp. Gen. Dec. B-252467, June 3, 1994, *Unpub.*, but they are not authorized to use appropriated funds (1) for purposes that do not bear a logical relationship to the appropriation, (2) for purposes that are prohibited by law, or (3) from a general appropriation for an item that is specifically covered in another appropriation, Comp. Gen. Dec. B-230304, Mar. 18, 1988, *Unpub.* See also 73 Comp. Gen.44 (B-254666) (1993); 67 Comp. Gen. 276 (B-226132) (1988). If two or more appropriations are available for the same purpose, the agency may choose between appropriations; once the choice is made, however, the agency must continue to use that appropriation, 59 Comp. Gen. 518 (B-195732) (1980); 67 Comp. Gen. 276 (B-226132) (1988).

The determination of the purposes covered by an appropriation is largely a question of determining the intent of Congress in making the appropriation. In interpreting the meaning of an appropriation, GAO relies primarily on the statutory language itself. The fact that a program has been specifically presented to the congressional committee during budget hearings will be considered by GAO, 35 Comp. Gen. 220 (B-124672) (1955), but the mere inclusion of an item in a budget justification does not enlarge the purpose of the appropriation where such an expenditure is otherwise expressly prohibited by law, 26 Comp. Gen. 545 (B-62700) (1947). Similarly, a limitation expressed in the legislative history will not restrict the use of the funds in a broadly worded appropriation, Comp. Gen. Dec. B-258000, Aug. 31, 1994, *Unpub.* In *LTV Aerospace Corp.*, 55 Comp. Gen. 307 (B-183851), 75-2 CPD ¶ 203, GAO considered whether statements from the Congressional Conference Report on an appropriations act indicating that certain funds could only be used for a specified purpose imposed a legal restriction on the use of such funds. In determining that the Navy was not required to spend the funds in accordance with the Conference Report restriction, GAO noted at 325-26:

To be binding as a matter of law, an intention to so restrict the legal availability of the funds provided would have to be expressed in the statute. However, if the issue is whether a particular aircraft is in fact a " military aircraft," as that term is used in the statute, resort to legislative history is required.

\* \* \*

As observed above, this does not mean agencies are free to ignore clearly expressed legislative history applicable to the use of appropriated funds. They ignore such expressions of intent at the peril of strained relations with the Congress. The executive branch — as the Navy has recognized — has a practical duty to abide by such expressions. This duty, however, must be understood to fall short of a statutory requirement giving rise to a legal infraction where there is a failure to carry out that duty.

See also *Forest Serv.*, Comp. Gen. Dec. B-231711, Mar. 28, 1989, *Unpub.* (congressional committee's recommendation that a specific dollar amount be used for liquidating the debt of prior fiscal year was not binding because Congress did not impose the requirement in the appropriations act); *Newport News Shipbuilding & Dry Dock Co.*, 55 Comp. Gen. 812 (B-184830), 76-1 CPD ¶ 136 (specific dollar amount for one ship in an appropriations committee report did not limit the amount the procuring agency could obligate for that ship out of an appropriation covering two ships).

Executive agencies have a measure of flexibility so that they can make adjustments for unforeseen developments or changed circumstances. Congress grants this flexibility by appropriating funds in lump sum amounts. Such an appropriation is a *general purpose appropriation* — one appropriation made for a group of objects necessary for the performance of a broad function. The great majority of appropriations presently used for the procurement of supplies, services, research and development, ships, aircraft, and missiles are general purpose appropriations. Appropriations are also made for the accomplishment of a single object. Such appropriations are *specific purpose appropriations.*

Congress may stipulate, by statute, that certain types of appropriations only be authorized via specific purpose appropriations. For example, 41 U.S.C. § 6303, states:

A contract to erect, repair, or furnish a public building, or to make any public improvement, shall not be made on terms requiring the Federal Government to pay more than the amount specifically appropriated for the activity covered by the contract.

This statute has been interpreted as imposing a special rule prohibiting the construction of public buildings or improvements unless appropriations specifically provide for the item, 38 Comp. Gen. 758 (B-138598) (1959) (appropriation for "necessary expenses" not broad enough to include the cost of construction for building alterations nor definite enough to comply with 41 U.S.C. § 6303 (previously § 12) requiring specific authorization for such work). In referring to this statute, GAO has stated that expenditures for such projects must "be authorized by specific appropriations," 42 Comp. Gen. 212 (B-146728) (1962). The use of the words "specific appropriations" is misleading, however, since the statute appears to require no more than a reference in an appropriations act or its legislative history that indicates that congressional authority for a project has, in fact, been granted. For example, in 38 Comp. Gen. 392 (B-137094) (1958) GAO denied a request to construct a special building for hydrostatic testing, painting, and maintaining helium tank cars under an appropriation designated for "acquiring and developing helium properties." In the absence of any legislative history establishing a congressional intent to attribute a broadened meaning to those general terms, GAO concluded that the necessary express statutory authority was lacking. With respect to the definitions of the terms "public building" and "public improvement," GAO has uniformly held that any structure in the form of a building not clearly of a temporary character qualifies as a public building or public improvement, 42 Comp. Gen. 212 (B-146728) (1962).

"Riders" on appropriations acts, whether for general or specific purpose, frequently impose explicit statutory restrictions that are binding on the agency. See Comp. Gen. Dec. B-254086, May 2, 1994, *Unpub.* (§ 9047 of 1993 DoD Appropriations Act prohibited the DoD from using funds to implement consolidation plans for data processing centers without submitting a report to appropriation committees); Comp. Gen. Dec. B-251481.4, Sept. 30, 1994, *Unpub.* (§ 207 of the Legislative Branch Appropriation Act prohibited executive agencies from using appropriated funds to procure duplicating services from any source except the Government Printing Office); and Comp. Gen. Dec. B-300192, Nov. 13, 2002, *Unpub.* (§ 117 of 2003 Continuing Resolution prohibits implementing the Office of Management and Budget Memorandum M-02-07calling for private sector printing, and no funds are available to pay for the printing of the President's Budget other than through the Government Printing Office). However, since annual appropriations acts are, by their nature, nonpermanent legislation, there is a presumption that legislative riders in annual appropriations are effective only for that fiscal year, *Building & Constr. Trades Dep't , AFL-CIO v. Martin,* 961 F.2d 269 (D.C. Cir.), *cert. denied,* 506 U.S. 915 (1992); 70 Comp. Gen. 351 (B-242142) (1991). A provision in an appropriations act may not be construed as permanent legislation unless the language or nature of the provision expresses a clear intent of Congress to make the provision permanent, *Atlantic Fish Spotters Ass'n v. Evans,* 321 F.3d 220 (1st Cir. 2003); Comp. Gen. Dec. B-230110, Apr. 11, 1988, *Unpub.* The principal means of establishing permanence is to include "words of futurity" in the provision of the appropriations act, Comp. Gen. Dec. B-230110, Apr. 11, 1988, *Unpub.* Other indications of permanence are if the provision is general in nature and bears no relation to the objects of the appropriations acts or if the provision would be meaningless if it were not interpreted to be a permanent legislation, 65 Comp. Gen. 588 (B-222097) (1986). See *Principles of Federal Appropriations Law* (3d ed. 2004) 2-33 through 2-39 for extensive analysis of this issue.

31 U.S.C. § 1532 also ensures that appropriations are only used for the purposes covered by the appropriations act. This statute specifically prohibits transfer

between appropriations unless specifically authorized by statute. See also 70 Comp. Gen. 592 (B-238024) (1991); 33 Comp. Gen. 216 (B-117393) (1953). However, the shifting of funds between objects in a lump sum appropriation is not a transfer but a *reprogramming*. Reprogramming is a nonstatutory accommodation between government agencies and legislative committees. See *Principles of Federal Appropriations Law* 2-31 (3d ed. 2004). However, reprogramming agreements with Congress do not have the force and effect of law, *Blackhawk Heating & Plumbing Co. v. United States*, 224 Ct. Cl. 111, 622 F.2d 539 (1980); *A.R.F. Prod., Inc.*, 56 Comp. Gen. 201 (B-186248), 76-2 CPD ¶ 541, and failure to follow reprogramming procedures will not justify cancellation of a contract entered into as a result of the shifting of funds, *LTV Aerospace Corp.*, 55 Comp. Gen. 307 (B-183851), 75-2 CPD ¶ 203. Furthermore, the denial of approval for reprogramming from one program element to another does not prohibit the agency from using other funds within the same program element, 65 Comp. Gen. 360 (B-220113) (1986).

## c. Obligation of Appropriations

Congress controls the expenditure of public funds by restricting the time in which appropriations may be used to incur *obligations*. For procurement transactions, 31 U.S.C. § 1501(a) provides that "[a]n amount shall be recorded as an obligation of the United States Government only when supported by documentary evidence." This would normally require a properly executed, written contractual document. However, the obligation arises when the government incurs a liability even though the documentary evidence is not yet available to support its recordation, 38 Comp. Gen. 81 (B-114876) (1958). Thus, if the government acts in a way that legally binds it under contract law concepts, an obligation will have occurred.

In addition to the Anti-Deficiency Act preclusion of obligations not supported by appropriations or contract authority, 31 U.S.C. § 1517 requires an *apportionment* before an appropriation may be obligated. An apportionment is a distribution of appropriated funds made by the President through the OMB to executive agencies. Apportionments are made by time periods, usually quarters, and by activities to maintain control over the rate of obligation and expenditure of funds.

### (1) TIME FOR OBLIGATION

The time when obligations may be made depends upon the type of appropriation. Basically, three types of appropriations are used. These are *annual appropriations*, *multiple-year appropriations*, and *no-year appropriations*. If an obligation is properly incurred during the period of availability of the appropriated funds, the appropriation will be available for *expenditure* to pay for the incurred obligation during the five subsequent fiscal years, 31 U.S.C. § 1552. Thereafter, the appropriation is canceled and the money is no longer available for expenditure — even if it was properly obligated before such cancellation, *United States Capitol Police — Advances to Volpe*

*Center Working Capital Fund*, Comp. Gen. Dec. B-319349, 2010 U.S. Comp. Gen. LEXIS 109. The result of this rule is that a contractor may not be paid from funds properly obligated to its contract after the five-year period has expired.

Annual appropriations may be obligated only in the specified fiscal year. Under an annual appropriation, if no obligation is made during the year for which the money was appropriated, the appropriation is said to "expire" and is no longer available for obligation. However, as discussed below, it will still be available to fund some additional contractual activities under contracts that were entered into during the fiscal year. Multiple-year appropriations are governed by the same principles except that they are available for obligation for a specified number of years rather than a single year. No-year appropriations are available for obligation until completely obligated and are not limited by time.

## (2) BONA FIDE NEEDS RULE

Another limitation on obligation of annual appropriations is the "bona fide needs" rule, based on 31 U.S.C. § 1502(a), which states:

> The balance of an appropriation or fund limited for obligation to a definite period is available only for payment of expenses properly incurred during the period of availability or to complete contracts properly made within that period of availability and obligated consistent with section 1501 of this title. However, the appropriation or fund is not available for expenditure for a period beyond the period otherwise authorized by law.

Thus, annual funds, as well as multiple-year funds, may be used only to fulfill the *bona fide needs* of the fiscal year(s) for which the funds were appropriated. Agencies cannot obligate an annual appropriation for the needs of prior or subsequent years, Comp. Gen. Dec. B-229873, Nov. 29, 1988, *Unpub.;* Comp. Gen. Dec. B-226801, Mar. 2, 1988, *Unpub.* Neither can they obligate multiple-year funds for the needs of subsequent fiscal years, Comp. Gen. Dec. B-235678, July 30, 1990, *Unpub.*; 68 Comp. Gen. 170 (B-232024) (1989); 55 Comp. Gen. 768 (B-132900) (1976).

A need may arise and be contracted for in one fiscal year but deliveries may not occur until the following or subsequent fiscal years because of necessary lead time. Thus, articles procured with annual funds do not have to be delivered or used in that fiscal year, so long as the need for the articles arose during the fiscal year, *U.S. Geological Survey*, Comp. Gen. Dec. B-226198, July 21, 1987, *Unpub.* In addition, annual funds may be used to replenish stock for future use, Comp. Gen. Dec. B-251706, Aug. 17, 1994, *Unpub.*; 21 Comp. Gen. 1159 (A-44006) (1941). However, if too long a period exists between contract award and delivery, especially for items that will be available on the open market at the time needed for use, the contract will not be considered as having fulfilled the needs of the fiscal year for which the funds were appropriated, 38 Comp. Gen. 628 (B-138574) (1959) (excessively long period to satisfy need where the units were ordered in April 1958 but would not be delivered until the later part of fiscal year 1960). But see 70 Comp. Gen. 296 (B-238940) (1991), where the agency was permitted to charge fiscal year 1989 appropriations for the cost of a training course scheduled to begin the first day of fiscal year 1990 because the two-week period between procurement and performance was not excessive.

It is also a violation of the bona fide needs rule to transfer funds (called "parking") to another agency for use in a subsequent fiscal year without a clear definition of the work to be obtained by the other agency, *Expired Funds and Interagency Agreements between GovWorks and the Dep't of Defense*, Comp. Gen. Dec. B-308944, 2007 CPD ¶ 157. See Chapter 8 for detailed coverage of the rules governing parking of funds.

Services that extend beyond the fiscal year may only be procured with annual funds to the extent they are nonseverable. GAO defined severable and nonseverable services in Comp. Gen. Dec. B-240264, Feb. 7, 1994, *Unpub.*, stating that services are severable if they can be divided into components that independently meet a separate need of the government. If the services constitute a specific, entire job with a defined end result that cannot be feasibly subdivided for separate performance, then they are nonseverable. See Comp. Gen. Dec. B-235678, July 30, 1990, *Unpub.*, holding that cost-reimbursement level of effort (term) contracts can be nonseverable depending on the circumstances (modifying the statement in 65 Comp. Gen. 154 (B-214597) (1985) that such contracts are, by their nature, severable). This reasoning is explained in *Funding for Air Force Cost Plus Fixed Fee Level of Effort Contract*, Comp. Gen. Dec. B-277165, 2000 CPD ¶ 54, as follows:

> [W]e recognized that even though a contract is denoted a CPFF term contract, the value of the required performance could in some theoretical instance be an end product. In such a case, the contract should be treated for obligational purposes as a nonseverable service contract. Thus, fairly read, B-235678 stands for the proposition that a CPFF term contract is presumptively a severable service contract, unless the actual nature of the work warrants a different conclusion (i.e., clearly calls for an end product). Further, one might reasonably conclude that the initial agency determination whether the contract is for funding purposes severable or nonseverable takes place roughly contemporaneously with agency selection of contract type (term or completion).

After a thorough analysis of the facts, GAO concluded that the contract in question was severable with the result that annual funds could not be used for work in the subsequent fiscal year. See also *Chemical Safety and Hazard Investigation Board — Interagency Agreement with the General Servs. Admin.*, Comp. Gen. Dec. B-318425, 2009 Comp. Gen. LEXIS 257, holding that maintenance of Personal Identity Verification cards was a severable service, precluding the use of annual funds to perform this service during future years. See *Principles of Federal Appropriations Law* (3d ed. 2004) 5-23 through 5-28 for extensive analysis of the difference between severable and nonseverable services.

Services that are nonseverable should be charged to the year when the need for the services was identified and the contract awarded, even though performance may extend beyond the fiscal year, 71 Comp. Gen. 428 (B-241415) (1992) (expert and consulting services contract may not be incrementally funded but must be funded from appropriation in year of contract award); 73 Comp. Gen. 77 (B-240264) (1994) (research work orders may not be incrementally funded but must be charged to appropriation for year of issuance of order). See also 60 Comp. Gen. 452 (B-174226) (1981); 50 Comp. Gen. 589 (B-171457) (1971). However, if the services are severable and continuous in nature, they must be charged to the appropriation current when the services are rendered, *Acumenics Research & Tech., Inc.*, Comp. Gen. Dec. B-224702, 87-2 CPD ¶ 128; 60 Comp. Gen. 219 (B-198574) (1981). When the agency has a multiple year appropriation, severable services can be procured for the years covered by that appropriation, *Severable Service Contracts*, Comp. Gen. Dec. B-317636, 2009 CPD ¶ 89.

If a bona fide need is identified in one year but the agency chooses not to satisfy the need in that year, it will be treated as a bona fide need of the year when the obligation was incurred. GAO has called this the "continuing need rule," Comp. Gen. Dec. B-207433, Sept. 16, 1983, *Unpub.* See *Principles of Federal Appropriations Law* (3d ed. 2004) stating at 5-20:

> The essential requirements of the "continuing need" corollary are that (1) the need, unmet in the year in which it arose, must continue to exist in the subsequent obligational period; (2) the incurring of an obligation must have been discretionary with the agency to begin with; and (3) no obligations was in fact incurred during the prior year.

In order to facilitate the procurement of severable services, Congress has created statutory exceptions to the bona fide needs rule that authorize contracts covering periods that do not correspond to the fiscal year. The DoD has authority to contract for certain types of services for 12-month periods beginning at any time during the fiscal year and to charge the appropriation current when the contract is made for the full 12 months of services, 10 U.S.C. § 2410a. See *Funding of Maintenance Contract Extending Beyond Fiscal Year*, Comp. Gen. Dec. B-259274, 96-1 CPD ¶ 247. NASA has similar authority, 42 U.S.C. § 2459a.

The bona fide needs rule applies to all types of procurement in which Congress has limited the period of availability of funds. See 64 Comp. Gen. 163 (B-215825) (1984), where GAO applied it to prohibit procurement of sixth and seventh year needs on a multiyear program Congress had authorized for five years. However, it has been held not to apply to no-year appropriations, 43 Comp. Gen. 657 (B-152766) (1964). See 67 Comp. Gen. 553 (B-208637.2) (1988); Comp. Gen. Dec. B-226922, May 21, 1987, *Unpub.*

## (3) Contract Modifications

When performance of contracts continues beyond the fiscal year of an annual or multiple-year appropriation, the question arises as to which fiscal year's appropriation is chargeable for changes and modifications. Generally, contract modifications that are found to be within the scope of the original contract are considered bona fide needs of the fiscal year when the original contract was made. Thus, the funds used on the original contract have been properly used to fund changes issued under the Changes clause, 23 Comp. Gen. 943 (B-41903) (1944), overruns on cost-reimbursement contracts resulting from the Negotiated Overhead Rates clause, 59 Comp. Gen. 518 (B-195732) (1980), and price adjustments under an Economic Price Adjustment, Price Redetermination or Incentive Price Revision clause, 34 Comp. Gen. 418 (B-121982) (1955). This rule is premised on the theory that these clauses do not create new liabilities but simply make existing ones certain.

Modifications that are not within the scope of such clauses must use appropriations current at the time of the modification, Comp. Gen. Dec. B-257617, Apr. 18, 1995, *Unpub.* (funds available from downward price adjustment could not be used in subsequent fiscal year to buy additional quantities on indefinite-quantity contract); Comp. Gen. Dec. B-207433, Sept. 16, 1979, Unpub. (funds available from downward price reduction could not be used in subsequent fiscal year to buy additional quantities even though their need had been identified in year contract was issued); 44 Comp. Gen. 399 (B-155876) (1965) (appropriation for year of contract award could not be used to fund change order to use better data to improve the quality of a completed study); 25 Comp. Gen. 332 (B-50425) (1945) (appropriation for year of contract award could not be used to fund change order issued after contract was completed because contractor was not required to perform such work).

In some cases, modifications arguably within the scope of the contract are not considered bona fide needs of the year in which the original agreement was made, and any price adjustments arising out of these modifications must be charged to a later year's appropriation, 59 Comp. Gen. 518 (B-195732) (1980). Letter contracts and contracts containing "limitation of cost" clauses are examples in which price adjustments must be charged to the later-year appropriations. In *Financial Crimes Enforcement Network — Obligations Under a Cost-Reimbursement, Nonseverable Services Contract*, Comp. Gen. Dec. B-317139, 2009 CPD ¶ 158, GAO held that discretionary cost increases in cost-reimbursement contracts that exceed contractually stipulated ceilings set forth in a Limitation of Cost clause must be treated as a bona fide need of the year when the overrun is funded. This decision was based on *Environmental Protection Agency*, 61 Comp. Gen. 609 (B-195732), 82-2 CPD ¶ 491, where GAO stated at 612:

> [I]t would not be reasonable to require that amounts for cost increases beyond the contract's ceiling . . . be reserved. There is no way to estimate the anticipated amount of such increases or the need for them in any future years and it would therefore be difficult to consider them as bona fide needs of an earlier year.

The same result was reached in 65 Comp. Gen. 741 (B-219829) (1986).

The same reasoning was used for letter contract conversions. In *Obligating Letter Contracts*, Comp. Gen. Dec. B-197274, 84-1 CPD ¶ 90, GAO held that the maximum liability that may be incurred under the letter contract is chargeable to the year's appropriation current when the letter contract was made, and the amount of the definitized contract is chargeable to the year's appropriation current when the contract was definitized. GAO equated letter contracts to cases in which there is a cost increase that exceeds contractually stipulated ceilings and that is not based on antecedent liability enforceable by the contractor. In both cases, the government is not legally liable beyond the amount set forth in the original contract until the government and contractor agree on the modifications. Settlement of claims not related to contracts must be funded out of current year funds, *National Endowment of the Arts — Dep't of Justice — Appropriations Availability — Payment of Settlement*, Comp. Gen. Dec. B-255772, *Unpub.* Similarly, settlement of contract claims at a board or court must be funded out of current year funds, *Bureau of Land Management — Reimbursement of Contract Disputes Act Payments*, 63 Comp. Gen. 308 (B-211229) (1984). GAO concluded that such claims gave rise to a "new liability." In contrast, this decision indicated that settlement of contract claims by a contracting officer could be funded out of funds used on the original contract. Compare *National Science Found. — Potential Antideficiency Act Violation by the National Science Board Office*, Comp. Gen. Dec. B-317413, 2009 CPD ¶ 94, holding that agreement by a contracting officer to give an equitable adjustment to cover an unauthorized commitment of an agency official was a new liability that had to be funded from current year funds. GAO stated in this decision that if the contracting officer had ratified the unauthorized commitment, it could have been funded out of prior year funds.

It is also improper to use current-year funds to finance a contract that has been awarded using prior year funds in violation of the Anti-Deficiency Act. See 55 Comp. Gen. 768 (B-132900) (1976), stating at 773-74:

> The purpose of [31 U.S.C. § 1502(a)] is to restrict the use of annual appropriations to expenditures required for the service of the particular fiscal year for which they were made. *See* 42 Comp. Gen. 272, 275 (1962). We have long held, consistent with the above statute, as well as 31 U.S.C. [§ 1341(a)] and 41 U.S.C. § 1, that a claim against a fixed year appropriation, when otherwise proper, is chargeable to the appropriation for the fiscal year in which the liability was incurred. *See, e.g.,* 18 Comp. Gen. 363, 365 (1938); 50 Comp. Gen. 589 (1971). The same rule requires, of course, that all liabilities and expenditures attributable to contracts made under the instant 3-year procurement appropriations remain chargeable to those appropriations.
>
> As we understand the proposal, the prior year contracts under which the funds were originally obligated, would not be canceled. Rather, only the source of funding those obligations would be changed, so that current year funds would be used

to pay for performance already contracted for in previous years. Under these circumstances, 31 U.S.C. [§ 1502(a)] would preclude the use of current appropriations to fund these prior year contracts since such transactions would constitute neither "the payment of expenses properly incurred" nor "the fulfillment of contracts properly made" in fiscal year 1976.

See also 71 Comp. Gen. 502 (B-245856.7) (1992) stating that the only courses of action when an agency has violated the Anti-Deficiency Act by entering into contracts in excess of appropriations is to obtain a deficiency appropriation to pay the overobligations or obtain statutory authorization to pay the overobligations out of current appropriations.

## (4) REPLACEMENT CONTRACTS

If a contract is terminated for default, the amount of a reprocurement contract that is timely issued should be charged to the appropriation that was used for the original contract, 2 Comp. Gen. 130 (1922); 34 Comp. Gen. 239 (B-121248) (1954). *Principles of Federal Appropriations Law* 5-28-32 (3d ed. 2004) calls such contracts "replacement contracts." This replacement contract rule will not apply if the default termination is not issued in a timely manner, 32 Comp. Gen. 565 (B-114334) (1965) (contract not terminated until three and one-half years after award), or if the reprocurement is not conducted in a timely fashion, 60 Comp. Gen. 591 (B-198074) (1981). In Comp. Gen. Dec. B-160834, Apr. 7, 1967, *Unpub.*, GAO stated that this rule would not apply if the work on the reprocurement contract differed from the work on the original contract, but permitted use of the appropriations current at the time of the original contract where the reprocurement contract was for different vehicles but they served the same purpose and were the vehicles currently available in the open market.

The replacement contract rule has also been applied to contracts issued after a termination for convenience. See, for example, 34 Comp. Gen. 239 (B-121248) (1954) permitting use of the appropriation used for the original contract when that contract was terminated for default and subsequently converted to a termination for convenience by the agency. After ruling in 60 Comp. Gen. 591 (B-198074) (1981) that the replacement contract rule did not apply to convenience terminations, GAO reversed that position in *Funding of Replacement Contracts*, 68 Comp. Gen.158 (B-232616), 88-2 CPD ¶ 602, and held that the rule did apply to contracts that were awarded after the original contract was terminated for convenience as the result of a successful bid protest. In *Navy, Replacement Contract*, 70 Comp. Gen. 230 (B-238548), 91-1 CPD ¶ 117, GAO extended the rule to terminations for convenience when the agency determined, on its own accord, that the original award had been improperly made. See *Herman Miller, Inc.*, 70 Comp. Gen. 287 (B-241582), 91-1 CPD ¶ 184, holding that this rule would only apply if the agency had made the original award "in good faith." See also 55 Comp. Gen. 1351 (B-185405) (1976) where the replacement contract rule was applied when an agency awarded a contract on the condition that the contractor was a small business and subsequently canceled the contract because the condition had not been fulfilled.

## (5) Contingent or Indefinite Liabilities

Where the government's liability is not definite in amount, there is a question as to the proper amount to be obligated. GAO has stated that when an agency signs a contract, it must obligate its "maximum potential liability" at that time, Comp. Gen. Dec. B-300480.2, June 6, 2003, *Unpub*. See, however, 34 Comp. Gen. 418 (B-121982) (1955) permitting a substantial amount of flexibility in determining the amount to be recorded as obligations for contracts involving liabilities that are indefinite in amount. In that decision, GAO agreed with a proposed DoD directive establishing the following policy with respect to obligations for various types of contracts that were subject to price redetermination or revision:

| Type of Contract | Obligation Amount |
|---|---|
| Fixed-price contracts with economic price adjustment | Original fixed price |
| Price redeterminable contract | Original fixed price |
| Incentive contract | Target or billing price |
| Variations in quantity contracts | Price of quantity specified |
| Letter contracts | Specified maximum liability |

GAO stipulated, however, that to safeguard against the possibility of violating the Anti-Deficiency Act, the agency should administratively reserve sufficient funds to cover at least the excess of estimated increases over decreases of all such contracts. Thereafter, the amount recorded as the original obligation was required to be increased or decreased to reflect price revisions at the time such revisions were made. See also 55 Comp. Gen. 812 (B-184830) (1976). In such cases, an administrative reserve, called a "commitment," may be made of the estimated amount of liability. See DoD 7000.14-R, *Dep't of Defense Financial Mgmt. Regulations*, Vol. 3, Chap. 8 (Nov. 2000). There are no uniform procedures governing the use of commitments. The decision to commit funds is made on a contract-by-contract basis depending on the likelihood of an under-obligation of funds, the amount of money available in the appropriation, and the need for flexibility in administering the appropriation.

When the government's liability under a contract is contingent on some future event that is not certain to occur, there is considerable controversy as to the proper treatment. In 37 Comp. Gen. 691 (B-114876) (1958) GAO ruled that claims made under the Changed Conditions clauses of several excavation contracts that were denied by the contracting officer did not require obligation of funds because they were contingent liabilities. At the same time GAO agreed with the agency involved that amounts to cover these contingent liabilities should be administratively reserved. However, GAO has stated that, absent specific statutory authority, indemnity provisions that subject the United States to contingent and undetermined liabilities and contain no limitations contravene the Anti-Deficiency Act, 62 Comp. Gen. 361 (B-201072), 83-1 CPD ¶ 501. In response to this decision the standard Insurance — Liability to Third Persons clause in FAR 52.228-7, which makes the government liable for claims of third parties not compensated by the contractor's insurance, was amended to include the following paragraph:

> (d) The Government's liability under paragraph (c) of this clause is subject to the availability of appropriated funds at the time a contingency occurs. Nothing in this contract shall be construed as implying that the Congress will, at a later date, appropriate funds sufficient to meet deficiencies.

The last sentence of this provision was included to overcome criticisms that indemnity provisions may create "coercive deficiencies." See *Project Stormfury*, 59 Comp. Gen. 369 (B-198206) (1980), where GAO stated that an agreement that is solely contingent on Congress passing an appropriation for its fulfillment may not violate the letter of the Act but violates its spirit; it could be considered a coercive deficiency in that Congress has little choice in such a situation.

GAO has continued to object to "open-ended indemnification agreements," Comp. Gen. Dec. B-260063, 96-1 CPD ¶ 122; Comp. Gen. Dec. B-242146, Aug. 16, 1991, *Unpub.* See also *E.I. DuPont de Nemours & Co. v. United States*, 54 Fed. Cl. 361 (2002); and *Union Pacific Railroad Corp. v. United States*, 52 Fed. Cl. 730 (2002), refusing to enforce a indemnification clauses because they violated the Anti-Deficiency Act. The decision in *DuPont* was reversed on the grounds that the Contract Settlement Act of 1944, 41 U.S.C. § 101 et seq., gave contract authority under the Anti-Deficiency Act to make agreements in excess of appropriations and the government had used that authority when it entered into a termination settlement at the end of the Second World War, 365 F.3d 1367 (Fed. Cir. 2004). The court did not disagree with the basic proposition that indemnification clauses were subject to the Act. See also *Hercules, Inc. v. United States*, 516 U.S. 417 (1996), recognizing GAO's view on indemnification clauses.

Even if the amount is determinable, a clause subjecting the government to a contingent liability could violate the statute. See *Federal Data Corp.*, 60 Comp. Gen. 584 (B-194709), 81-2 CPD ¶ 28, where the agency was found to have violated the Anti-Deficiency Act by obligating only the rental payments but agreeing to be liable for the full price of the item in case of loss. GAO stated at 590:

> Agreements to assume the risk of loss for contractor-owned equipment have often been disapproved by our Office on the basis of 31 U.S.C. § [1341] and 41 U.S.C. § 11 (1976), for the reason that such agreements could subject the United States to a contingent liability in an indeterminate amount which could exceed the available appropriation. See 54 Comp. Gen. 824, *supra.* Here, the agency only obligates a sum sufficient to meet the monthly payments required by the [lease-purchase] for the current fiscal year. Any loss which might occur during the first 2 years of the [lease-purchase] would exceed that amount and therefore unobligated

funds must be available in the appropriation to cover such a contingency. While in this case the agency's maximum liability is determinable, the amount of a loss could be such as to exceed the unobligated portion of the appropriation.

The government may possess statutory authority, which is the equivalent of contract authority, to include indemnification agreements in certain instances. For example, 10 U.S.C. § 2354 permits indemnification for research and development activity, and the Price-Anderson Act, 42 U.S.C. § 2210, covers indemnification for nuclear risks. In addition, Exec. Order 11610, 36 Fed. Reg. 13755 (1971), uses Pub. L. No. 85-804 to permit heads of specified agencies to indemnify contractors from risks arising from unusually hazardous or nuclear activity. See FAR 50.403.

## B. Control and Oversight of Procurement

There are a number of techniques that Congress and the executive agencies use to control and oversee the conduct of procurement. The primary techniques for control are the limitations on the exercise of contracting power contained in statutes and regulations. One of the major methods of overseeing compliance with these requirements is the contract award protest process discussed in Chapter 12. In addition, organizations in both legislative and executive branches review whether procurement of authorized programs has been carried out in accordance with laws and regulations. The following material discusses the proper roles of the executive and legislative branches with respect to procurement and considers the major techniques used to control and oversee the process.

### 1. Executive Branch

The primary method of control of procurement in the executive branch is through the promulgation of regulations. The major executive branch oversight of procurement is conducted by Inspectors General.

#### a. Regulations

Rules affecting contracting are promulgated in a number of different types of regulations. Executive Orders, issued by the President, OMB Circulars, and OFPP Policy Letters deal with matters having broad application throughout the executive branch. These regulations may be published to implement statutes or may be based upon executive branch policies. Another type of regulation affecting procurement is issued by an agency with oversight of a specific government program or policy. For example, the Department of Labor has issued regulations in Volume 29 of the Code of Federal Regulations under the Davis-Bacon Act, 40 U.S.C. § 276(a) (29 C.F.R. Part 5), and the Service Contract Act, 41 U.S.C. §§ 6701-07 (29 C.F.R. Part 4).

The most important regulations governing procurement are the regulations in the FAR system, discussed earlier. When these regulations use the term "must" or "shall," they are binding on contracting agencies, FAR 2.101. However, if the regulations are less specific regarding an issue, an agency has the discretion to take action. FAR 1.102 contains a "statement of guiding principles" for the FAR system, and FAR 1.102(d) states:

> The role of each member of the Acquisition Team is to exercise personal initiative and sound business judgment in providing the best value product or service to meet the customer's needs. In exercising initiative, Government members of the Acquisition Team may assume if a specific strategy, practice, policy or procedure is in the best interests of the Government and is not addressed in the FAR nor prohibited by law (statute or case law), Executive order or other regulation, that the strategy, practice, policy or procedure is a permissible exercise of authority.

Many regulations regarding procurement are required to be posted for notice and an opportunity for comment before taking effect. 41 U.S.C. § 1707 requires notice and an opportunity for public comment prior to publication of procurement policies, regulations, procedures, or forms having a "significant effect beyond the internal operating procedures of the agency" or a "significant cost or administrative impact on contractors or offerors." Thus, final regulations in the FAR system may not take effect until 60 days after publication in the *Federal Register.* However, procurement policies, regulations, procedures, or forms may take effect earlier than 60 days after the publication date when there are compelling circumstances for the earlier effective date, but in no circumstances can the effective date be less than 30 days after the publication date. If the prepromulgation notice is impracticable, the agency head may issue a temporary regulation with public comment invited before final promulgation.

Several agencies are moving significant parts of their procurement regulations to guidance documents which are not issued following the rules governing the issuance of formal regulations. See Procedures, Guidance and Information (PGI) of DoD (*www.acq.osd.mil/dpap/dars/dfarspgi/current/index.html),* the Acquisition Guide of DOE *(management.energy.gov/policy_guidance/Acquisition_Guide.html*), the Department of Homeland Security Acquisition Manual (*www.dhs.gov/xlibrary/ assets/opnbiz/HSAM_WITH_Notice_06-02.pdf*), the Transportation Acquisition Guide (*fasteditapp.faa.gov/dot/do_action?do_action=ListTOC&contentUID=1& contentVersionUID=912*), and the GSA Acquisition Manual (GSAM) (*www.acqui- sition.gov/gsam/gsam.html*). Such documents are unlikely to be given the legal status of formal regulations.

The legal status of a specific provision in a regulation is a subject of great uncertainty. The provision may be found to be an "interpretative" or "housekeeping" rule, which is intended as instructions to government personnel or to indicate the agency's interpretation of a statute. Other provisions may be found to be "substantive" or "legislative" rules that implement a statute. Either type of regulation may serve as notice of limitations on the authority of government employees or as an aid in determining the intention of the contracting parties. However, regulations will have the "force and effect of law" only if authorized by Congress, *Chrysler Corp. v. Brown*, 441 U.S. 281 (1979). There is not complete agreement as to the nature and extent of the required congressional authorization. *G.L. Christian & Assocs. v. United States*, 160 Ct. Cl. 1, 312 F.2d 418, *reh'g denied*, 160 Ct. Cl. 58, 320 F.2d 345, *cert. denied*, 375 U.S. 954 (1963), is the leading case for the proposition that provisions in procurement regulations that do not implement specific statutes may have the force and effect of law. In finding that an Armed Services Procurement Regulation (ASPR) provision mandating inclusion of a Termination for Convenience of the Government clause in defense contracts had the force and effect of law even though there was no specific statutory authority for such provision, the court looked to the general authority of the agency to issue procurement regulations and then considered the importance of the government policy. More recently, the focus has been on finding a nexus between the regulatory provision and specific statutory authority rather than on the importance of the policy. In *Liberty Mut. Ins. Co. v. Friedman*, 639 F.2d 164 (4th Cir. 1981), the court considered the congressional authority required to support Exec. Order 11246 and its implementing regulations, stating at 169:

> A congressional grant of legislative authority need not be specific in order to sustain the validity of regulations promulgated pursuant to the grant, but a court must " reasonably be able to conclude that the grant of authority contemplates the regulations issued." [*Chrysler Corp. v. Brown*, 441 U.S. 281] at 308, 99 S. Ct. at 721. Our examination of the possible statutory sources of congressional authorization for Executive Order 11,246 convinces us that none of the statutes reasonably contemplates that Liberty, as a provider of workers' compensation insurance to government contractors, may be required to comply with Executive Order 11,246. We conclude therefore that none of the cited statutes authorize the action taken by defendants.

The court went on to hold that the delegation of general procurement power by Congress to the executive branch by the FPASA, 40 U.S.C. § 471 et seq. (pre-2011 codification), would support regulations not specifically authorized only to the extent that they were adopted to further the congressional purpose of achieving an "economical and efficient system" of procurement. The court rejected the "proposition that equal employment goals themselves, reflecting important national policies, validate the use of procurement power" to impose affirmative action requirements on an insurer. In doing so, it disagreed with *United States v. New Orleans Pub. Serv., Inc.*, 553 F.2d 459 (5th Cir. 1977), *vacated & remanded on other grounds*, 436 U.S. 942 (1978), to the extent that the case held that no nexus between the purpose of the congressional act and the provision of a regulation was required. In *Muller of Gary Aircraft Corp.*, 698 F.2d 775 (5th Cir.), *cert. denied*, 464 U.S. 820 (1983), the court held that the Disputes clause mandated by the ASPR did not have the force and effect of law because the clause was not specifically authorized by the Armed Services Procurement Act. Though the Contract Disputes Act of 1978 statutorily mandates the inclusion of a Disputes clause, it did not apply to this case because it was not in effect at the time of the contracts. The court did not discuss either the general authority of the Secretary of Defense to draft regulations contained in 10 U.S.C. § 2202 or the efficiency and economy nexus found necessary in the *Liberty Mutual* case. Arguably, the Disputes clause with its remedial provisions would satisfy this requirement. In *AFL-CIO v. Kahn*, 618 F.2d 784 (D.C. Cir.), *cert. denied*, 443 U.S. 915 (1979), the court upheld the requirement for government contractors to certify compliance with "voluntary" wage and price guidelines under Exec. Order 12092. It found that the Executive Order's predominant objective of containing procurement costs furnished the required nexus to the Procurement Act's criteria of efficiency and economy. However, in *Chamber of Commerce v. Reich*, 74 F.3d 1322 (D.C. Cir. 1996), the court held that the President did not have authority under the FPASA to issue an executive order authorizing the Secretary of Labor to disqualify employers with federal contracts exceeding $100,000 that hire permanent replacement workers during a lawful economic strike. In distinguishing *Kahn*, the court stated at 1322:

> [T]he President, even under the Procurement Act, does not have unlimited authority to make decisions he believes will likely result in savings to the government. We cautioned that our decisions did not "write a blank check for the President to fill in at his will. The procurement power must be exercised consistently with the structure and purposes of the statute that delegates that power." Despite our expansive reasoning [in *Kahn*] upholding President Carter's Executive Order, we stressed the importance of the "nexus between the wage and price standards and likely savings to the government."

The court found that the executive order was not rationally related to the statutory objective of providing an economical and efficient system of federal procurement but, rather, was premised on labor relations policy. Thus, the court held that the executive order was preempted by the National Labor Relations Act. See also *UAW-Labor Employment & Training Corp. v. Chao*, 325 F.3d 360 (D.C. Cir. 2003), finding sufficient nexus to the Procurement Act in the provision of Executive Order 13201 requiring contractors to post notices of the rights of their employees.

In order for a regulation to affect legal relations, the contractor must have actual or constructive notice of the regulation. Constructive notice occurs when regulations have been published in the *Federal Register*, *Federal Crop Ins. Corp. v. Merrill*, 332 U.S. 380 (1947). The Freedom of Information Act, 5 U.S.C. § 552(a)(1), precludes constructive notice for matters "required to be published in the *Federal Register* and not so published," stating:

> Except to the extent that a person has actual and timely notice of the terms thereof, a person may not in any manner . . . be adversely affected by a matter required to be published in the *Federal Register* and not so published.

It also provides that "substantive rules" must be published in the *Federal Register*. Thus, for a regulation to have the force and effect of law either it must be published in the *Federal Register* or the affected person must have actual notice. As provided at 5 U.S.C. § 552(a)(2)(C), "administrative staff manuals and instructions to staff that affect a member of the public" need only be made available for public inspection or copies offered for sale.

Contractors have been held to have notice of regulations not published in the *Federal Register* even though there was no actual notice. In *Planning Research Corp.*, 55 Comp. Gen. 911 (B-184926), 76-1 CPD ¶ 202, the contractor was held to have constructive notice of the contents of an agency manual that was incorporated in the contract by reference. The agency manual, though not published, was available for public inspection, as required by § 552(a)(2)(C). See also *Timber Access Indus. Co. v. United States*, 213 Ct. Cl. 648, 553 F.2d 1250 (1977), where the plaintiff was held to have had actual and timely notice of regulations contained in an unpublished Forest Service Manual and was therefore bound by the terms of the manual.

### b.  Inspectors General

Under the Inspector General Act of 1978, 5 U.S.C. App. § 2, Inspectors General have been established in the following departments and agencies listed in 5 U.S.C. App. § 11:

> Agency for International Development, Agriculture, Commerce, Community Development Financial Institutions Fund, Corporation for National & Community Service, Defense, Education, Energy, Environmental Protection Agency, Export-Import Bank, Federal Deposit Insurance Corporation, Federal Emergency Management Agency, General Services Administration, Health & Human Services, Homeland Security, Housing & Urban Development, Interior, Justice, Labor, NASA, Nuclear Regulatory Commission, Office of Personnel Management, Railroad Retirement Board, Resolution Trust Corporation, Small Business Administration, Social Security Administration, State, Tennessee Valley Authority, Transportation, Treasury, Veterans Affairs

The Inspectors General have broad investigative powers, and their investigations are required to be free of agency influence, 5 U.S.C. App. § 3(a). They may make such investigations as they consider to be necessary or desirable. They have access to all records relating to any agency's programs and operations, 5 U.S.C. App. § 6(a)(1), and may issue subpoenas for "all information, documents, reports, answers, records, accounts, papers, and other data and documentary evidence necessary in the performance" of their duties, 5 U.S.C. App. § 6(a)(4). In *United States v. Iannone*, 610 F.2d 943 (D.C. Cir. 1979), the court held that this subpoena power relates to documents only and cannot be used to compel oral testimony.

Inspectors General have the following broad duties and responsibilities, as set forth at 5 U.S.C. App. § 4(a):

> It shall be the duty and responsibility of each Inspector General, with respect to the establishment within which his Office is established —

(1) to provide policy direction for and to conduct, supervise, and coordinate audits and investigations relating to the programs and operations of such establishment;

(2) to review existing and proposed legislation and regulations relating to programs and operations of such establishment and to make recommendations in the semiannual reports required by section 5(a) concerning the impact of such legislation or regulations on the economy and efficiency in the administration of programs and operations administered or financed by such establishment or the prevention and detection of fraud and abuse in such programs and operations;

(3) to recommend policies for, and to conduct, supervise, or coordinate other activities carried out or financed by such establishment for the purpose of promoting economy and efficiency in the administration of, or preventing and detecting fraud and abuse in, its programs and operations;

(4) to recommend policies for, and to conduct, supervise, or coordinate relationships between such establishment and other Federal agencies, State and local governmental agencies, and nongovernmental entities with respect to (A) all matters relating to the promotion of economy and efficiency in the administration of, or the prevention and detection of fraud and abuse in, programs and operations administered or financed by such establishment, or (B) the identification and prosecution of participants in such fraud or abuse; and

(5) to keep the head of such establishment and the Congress fully and currently informed, by means of the reports required by section 5 and otherwise, concerning fraud and other serious problems, abuses, and deficiencies relating to the administration of programs and operations administered or financed by such establishment, to recommend corrective action concerning such problems, abuses, and deficiencies, and to report on the progress made in implementing such corrective action.

In addition, 5 U.S.C. App. § 5(a) requires the submission of semiannual reports to the head of the agency who, in turn, is required to submit the report to the appropriate congressional committees. The reports are required to contain the following information:

(1) a description of significant problems, abuses, and deficiencies relating to the administration of programs and operations of such establishment disclosed by such activities during the reporting period;

(2) a description of the recommendations for corrective action made by the Office during the reporting period with respect to significant problems, abuses, or deficiencies identified pursuant to paragraph (1);

(3) an identification of each significant recommendation described in previous semiannual reports on which corrective action has not been completed;

(4) a summary of matters referred to prosecutive authorities and the prosecutions and convictions which have resulted;

(5) a summary of each report made to the head of the establishment under section 6(b)(2) during the reporting period; and

(6) a listing of each audit report completed by the Office during the reporting period.

Limitations on the scope of the DoD Inspector General's investigative and reporting roles for classified and other sensitive matters are contained in 5 U.S.C. App. § 8.

Inspector Generals have played a significant role in auditing and investigating the effectiveness of procurement by agencies in the executive branch.   See, for example, GSA IG Rep't, *Procurement Reform and the Multiple Award Schedule Program* (*http://oig.gsa.gov/reform1.htm*); DoD IG Rep't D-2004-015, *Contracts for Professional, Administrative, and Management Support Services* (*http://www. DoDig.osd.mil/audit/reports/fy04/04015.htm*); NASA IG Rep't IG-04-007, *Review of Sole-Source and Limited Competition Contract Actions Citing "Urgent and Compelling Urgency"* (*http://www.hq.nasa.gov/office/oig/hq/ig-04-007.pdf*); VAIG Rep't, *Audit of VA Acquisitions for Other Government Agencies* (*http://www.va.gov/ oig/52/reports/2006/VAOIG-04-03178-139.pdf*).

## 2.  Legislative Branch

Congressional control over the procurement function is manifested in require-ments and limitations included in procurement statutes, authorization acts, appro-priations acts, and other statutes. Oversight of the procurement function by the leg-islative branch is conducted by Congress itself and by its agent, the Comptroller General of the United States, the head of the Government Accountability Office.

### a.  Congressional Oversight

Among the principal means of congressional oversight are the investigations and hearings of its committees. Oversight of general procurement matters is largely carried out by the Homeland Security and Governmental Affairs Committee in the Senate, by the Government Reform Committee in the House of Representatives, and by the Small Business Committees of both houses of Congress. However, each legislative committee of Congress with authority over the programs of a procuring agency, such as the Armed Services Committees of the Senate and House, monitors the procurement practices of that agency, and the Appropriations Committees are quite active in reviewing selective procurement policies. Even when these congres-sional committees do not formally adopt statutory language establishing binding procurement rules, their views are normally given great respect by agencies in for-mulating contracting policies. Failure of the agencies to follow the "recommenda-tions" of committees often leads to additional statutory requirements or limitations.

Historically, there have been a number of cases where Congress authorized a program and appropriated funds but the executive agency failed or refused to carry out the program or delayed or reduced the scope of the program. Such actions have been called *impoundments*. In litigation over impoundments, it was held that the executive branch had no inherent authority to refuse to allot funds where Congress had mandated their use. See, e.g., *Train v. City of N.Y.*, 420 U.S. 35 (1975), and *Train v. Campaign Clean Water, Inc.*, 420 U.S. 136 (1975), holding that there was a clear statutory interest and direction for the funds to be obligated in those cases. In response to increased litigation and political controversy over such impoundments, Congress passed the Congressional Budget and Impoundment Control Act of 1974, 2 U.S.C. § 681 et seq. The Act divides impoundments into *rescissions*, which cancel previously granted budget authority still unused and available for obligation, and *deferrals*, which delay the obligation or expenditure of budget authority. For a rescission to take place, the President must send a message to Congress requesting rescission of budget authority and must obtain a rescinding bill. If both houses of Congress do not pass a rescinding bill within 45 days of continuous session after the message is received, the funds must be made available for obligation. The President can defer funds by sending a special deferral message to Congress; if either house passes a simple resolution disapproving the deferral, funds must be made available for obligation. If there is no disapproval the deferral remains in effect for the remainder of the fiscal year, at which time funds must be released or a new message sent. Although a number of separation of powers issues were raised by the Act, it stipulates that it shall not be construed as "asserting or conceding the constitutional powers or limitations of either Congress or the President," 2 U.S.C. § 681(1). The executive branch has, for the most part, complied with the Act. However, in *City of New Haven v. United States*, 634 F. Supp. 1449 (D.D.C. 1986), the court held that the one-House veto provision on deferrals violated the Constitution's separation of powers under the holding of *Immigration & Naturalization Serv. v. Chadha*, 462 U.S. 919 (1983). As a result, the court held that the deferral authority under the Act could not be used by the executive branch to defer the expenditure and issued an injunction ordering that the funds be made available. The court refused to decide the question of the President's authority to impound independently of the Act because the Act had been relied upon to defer the spending. After Congress passed legislation rejecting the deferrals, the D.C. Circuit dismissed an appeal of the decision as moot but agreed with the reasoning of the District Court, *City of New Haven v. United States*, 809 F.2d 900 (D.C. Cir. 1987). It has been held that the Act does not require the application of some part of the funds in a lump sum appropriation to all of the objects for which it is appropriated so long as all of the funds in the appropriation are obligated, *International Union, United Automobile, Aerospace & Agricultural Implement Workers v. Donovan*, 746 F.2d 855 (D.C. Cir. 1984), *cert. denied*, 474 U.S. 825 (1985). The court reasoned that the only clear statutory intent and directive in a lump sum appropriation is to obligate all of the funds.

Another example of congressional retention of power over implementation of statutes after they have been enacted into law was present in the statute creating the

Cost Accounting Standards Board (CASB), 50 U.S.C. App. § 2168. The board was granted authority to promulgate regulations and cost accounting standards but was established as an agent of the Congress, independent of the executive branch, 50 U.S.C. § 2168(a). In addition, the Comptroller General was designated as the Chairman of the Board with the authority to appoint all of its members. The constitutionality of the CASB's rulemaking power was open to question in view of *Buckley v. Valeo*, 424 U.S. 1 (1976). In that case, dealing with the Federal Election Commission, the Court stated that rule-making is an administrative function and can be carried out only by persons appointed in compliance with Article II, Section 2, Clause 2 of the Constitution. The CASB did not meet this appointment criteria. See *Bowsher v. Synar*, 478 U.S. 714 (1986), holding that the Comptroller General was an agent of Congress. These constitutional issues were resolved when the CASB was reestablished by 41 U.S.C. § 422 (now §§ 1501-06) with membership composed entirely of members of the executive branch and members of the public.

In 1997 Congress attempted to decrease its Constitutional power by giving the President the power to veto parts of a bill in the Line Item Veto Act, 2 U.S.C. § 691 et seq. This Act was declared unconstitutional in *Byrd v. Raines*, 956 F. Supp. 25 (D.D.C. 1997), but that decision was vacated and reversed in *Raines v. Byrd*, 521 U.S. 811 (1997), on the grounds that the plaintiff Senators and Congressmen had no standing to bring the action. Subsequently, in *Clinton v. City of New York*, 524 U.S. 417 (1998), the Court held that the Act was unconstitutional because it violated the Presentment Clause of the Constitution, Art. I, § 7, cl. 2.

### b.  Comptroller General

The Comptroller General of the United States and the Government Accountability Office (GAO), headed by the Comptroller General, have been given a prominent role in the oversight of government procurement and procurement-related functions. The office and the organization (called the General Accounting Office until 2004) were created by the Budget and Accounting Act of 1921, 42 Stat. 20, to provide Congress with a continuing review of the government's financial affairs. When originally established, GAO was given a number of responsibilities previously performed in the Treasury Department. The Act gave the office additional auditing functions, and from time to time, Congress has given new responsibilities to the Comptroller General. Currently, GAO audits government agencies and their contractors, decides contract award controversies and other procurement related disputes, finally settles government financial accounts, and prescribes executive agency accounting principles.

In *Bowsher v. Synar*, 478 U.S. 714 (1986), the Court, in an opinion of five justices, held that since the Comptroller General is under the control of Congress, it violates the separation of powers doctrine of the Constitution for the Comptroller General to perform the executive functions of establishing a final estimate of expenditures and revenues. Thus, the Gramm-Rudman-Hollings Act, 2 U.S.C. § 901 et seq., was held unconstitutional. A concurring opinion agreed that the Comptroller General and GAO were part of the legislative branch but disagreed with the conclusion that the functions being performed by the Comptroller under the Act were executive functions. However, it held the Act to be unconstitutional under *Immigration & Naturalization Serv. v. Chadha*, 462 U.S. 919 (1983), because Congress could not delegate such a fundamental power to formulate national policy to an individual agent of Congress.

GAO procurement-related functions that are clearly legislative would be constitutional to the extent that they do not delegate to GAO powers that must be exercised by Congress itself. Clearly within this category of powers would be the broad investigative and audit powers of the Comptroller. These powers include the investigation of all matters relating to the receipt, disbursement, and use of public money, 31 U.S.C. § 712; the auditing of the financial transactions of each government agency, 31 U.S.C. § 3523; and the evaluation of programs and activities of government agencies, 31 U.S.C. § 717. In the performance of this audit function, GAO has access to all government records, and each agency is required to supply information GAO requires concerning audit of the agency, 31 U.S.C. § 716. This statute also grants GAO subpoena power to compel the production of documents. In addition, GAO has the right to audit directly the pertinent books and records of contractors that are awarded negotiated contracts, 10 U.S.C. § 2313(b) and 41 U.S.C. § 4706(d). Thus, these substantial oversight powers are preserved. In carrying out these powers, GAO regularly issues audit reports evaluating various agency's implementation of the procurement process and recommending improvements. See, for example, *Defense Acquisitions: Key Decisions To Be Made on Future Combat System*, GAO-07-376, March 15, 2007; *Interagency Contracting: Franchise Funds Provide Convenience, But Value to DoD Is Not Demonstrated*, GAO-05-456, July 29, 2005; *Contract Management: Guidance Needed to Promote Competition for Defense Task Orders*, GAO-04-874, July 30, 2004; *Defense Acquisitions: Assessments of Major Weapon Programs*, GAO-04-248, March 31, 2004; *Contract Management: Restructuring GSA's Federal Supply Service and Federal Technology Service*, GAO-04-132T, October 2, 2003.

For many years, GAO had several functions that were executive in nature and thus of questionable validity under *Bowsher*. Such functions included the power to settle all claims of or against the United States, 31 U.S.C. § 3702, the authority to collect or compromise claims due to the United States, 31 U.S.C. § 3711. These functions were transferred to agencies in the executive branch by The General Accounting Office Act of 1996, Pub. L. No. 104-316, § 202 and § 115. See also Pub. L. No. 105-85, § 1012.

GAO has been granted numerous powers dealing with the financial accounts to be maintained by executive agencies and the liability of government certifying and disbursing officers for losses or improper disbursement of funds. See, for example, 31 U.S.C. § 3511 (prescription of agency accounting principles); 31 U.S.C. § 3512(f) (review and approval of agency accounting systems); 31 U.S.C. § 3526(a) (settlement of financial accounts conclusive on executive agencies); and 31 U.S.C. § 3527 (relief of accountable officers for losses). These would appear to be executive powers.

One of the most effective control and oversight techniques used by GAO is the power to give advance decisions to certifying or disbursing officers involving payments or vouchers, 31 U.S.C. § 3529. Such decisions are almost always respected by agencies because they indicate how GAO will rule when reviewing financial accounts if payment is made. However, as a matter of law, these decisions are advisory only and are binding only upon GAO, 31 U.S.C. § 3526(b). See *Greene County Planning Bd. v. Federal Power Comm'n*, 559 F.2d 1227 (2d Cir. 1976), *cert. denied*, 434 U.S. 1086 (1978). Thus, this provision would not appear to be constitutionally offensive. However, it might lose its effectiveness if GAO's power to disallow accounts under 31 U.S.C. § 3526(a) were held to be an unconstitutional delegation of executive powers.

The most significant use of the 31 U.S.C. § 3529 advance-decision power in the past was in the area of contract award controversies. Although the statute mentions only decisions requested by certifying or disbursing officers, GAO agreed to give such advance decisions at the request of disappointed bidders and other parties who had an interest in a procurement. GAO's power in the contract award controversy area was formally authorized by the Competition in Contracting Act, Pub. L. No. 98-369, 31 U.S.C. § 3551 et seq., giving GAO the power to make recommendations on award controversies and requiring agencies to stay their procurements until a protest has been decided (with limited power for the agency to override the stay). In *Ameron, Inc. v. United States Army Corps of Eng'rs*, 809 F.2d 979 (3d Cir. 1986), this statute was held not to violate the Constitution because the protest procedure neither gives GAO executive power nor "interferes impermissibly with the executive's performance of its procurement duties." The Supreme Court granted certiorari, 485 U.S. 958 (1988), but subsequently dismissed the writ, 488 U.S. 915 (1988), without hearing argument. Accord, *Lear Siegler, Inc. v. Lehman*, 842 F.2d 1102, 1105 (9th Cir. 1988), *mod. on other grounds*, 893 F.2d 205 (9th Cir. 1989). The entire subject of contract award controversies is discussed in detail in Chapter 12.

GAO also has significant powers under the Congressional Budget and Impoundment Control Act of 1974, 2 U.S.C. § 681 et seq. The Act gives GAO a key role in impoundment. GAO:

- receives and reviews all deferral or rescission messages and informs Congress of the findings,

- reports any executive withholding of funds where the executive has not sent a message to Congress,

- reports to Congress if it is determined that a presidential deferral should be classed as a rescission, and

- has authority to bring suit to require that budget authority be made available

It would appear that these responsibilities are not executive branch functions.

## C. Contracts Varying from Statutory or Regulatory Requirements

Government agencies quite frequently use procedures or enter into contracts that, either intentionally or inadvertently, vary from the requirements of statutes or regulations. Some variations from the controls imposed by the applicable statutes and regulations are authorized since the need for flexibility is frequently recognized by provisions permitting *waiver* or *deviation*. However, without a waiver or deviation, the failure to follow precisely the prescribed procedures may result in an unauthorized transaction. Where no waiver or deviation is permitted, the failure to comply with the statute or regulation will also result in an unauthorized transaction. The following section discusses waiver and deviation procedures and the effect of noncompliance.

### 1.  Deviations and Waivers

The commonly used terminology describes departures from regulations as "deviations" and from statutes as "waivers." The procedures for deviating from regulations and waiving statutory requirements are generally strictly enforced.

### a.  Deviations from Regulations

Authority and procedures for obtaining deviations from the regulations in the interest of providing some flexibility in the system are contained in FAR Subpart 1.4. FAR 1.402 states:

Unless precluded by law, executive order, or regulation, deviations from the FAR may be granted as specified in this subpart when necessary to meet the specific needs and requirements of each agency. The development and testing of new techniques and methods of acquisition should not be stifled simply because such action would require a FAR deviation. The fact that deviation authority is required should not, of itself, deter agencies in their development and testing of new techniques and acquisition methods. Refer to 31.101 for instructions concerning deviations pertaining to the subject matter of Part 31, Contract Cost Principles and Procedures. Deviations are not authorized with respect to 30.201-3 and 30.201-4, or the requirements of the Cost Accounting Standards Board (CASB) rules and regulations (48 CFR Chapter 99 (FAR Appendix). Refer to 30.201-5 for instructions concerning waivers pertaining to Cost Accounting Standards.

Individual deviations, affecting only one "contract action," may be granted by agency heads, FAR 1.403. Class deviations, affecting more than one contract action, may be granted by agency heads, with the power delegated in some agencies, FAR 1.404. In addition, when a agency knows that it will require a class deviation on a permanent basis, it should propose a FAR revision. An individual deviation may not be granted for a procurement aimed at awarding a number of contracts for various geographic regions because such a procurement is not a single "contract action," *La Gloria Oil & Gas Co. v. United States*, 56 Fed. Cl. 211 (2003); *Tesoro Hawaii Corp. v. United States*, 58 Fed. Cl. 65 (2003), *rev'd on other grounds*, 405 F.3d 1339 (Fed. Cir. 2005). There is no similar deviation procedure for other executive branch regulations such as Executive Orders, OMB circulars, and OFPP policy letters.

When deviation authority is delegated, it is invariably given to a subordinate official in charge of the acquisition process. See, for example, DFARS Subpart 201.4. Thus, deviations by other officials will be ineffective. In *G.L. Christian & Assocs. v. United States*, 160 Ct. Cl. 1, 312 F.2d 418, *reh'g denied*, 160 Ct. Cl. 58, 320 F.2d 345, *cert. denied*, 375 U.S. 954 (1963), the court refused to find that a proper deviation had been obtained when an Assistant Secretary of Defense in charge of housing policy approved the omission of a required clause from a housing contract. The court held that the deviation was only authorized if it was granted by the Assistant Secretary with authority to grant a deviation, stating at 70:

> The Armed Services Procurement Regulations contemplated a specific mechanism for receiving permission to deviate from required forms or articles. . . . There is no proof, or offer to prove, that this mechanism was used. It is said, however, that the general agreement of the Assistant Secretary of Defense (Properties and Installations) with the Federal Housing Commissioner upon a number of forms, including a form of housing contract, constituted sufficient permission to eliminate the termination-for-convenience clause. Here, too, there is lacking any proof that this particular Assistant Secretary was empowered to approve alterations in articles mandatorily required by the ASPR. More importantly, we are not persuaded that a conscious decision was made, at the appropriate level in the Defense Department, to eliminate the required termination article and thus to subject the Government to the full common-law measures of damages (including unearned profits).

See also *Johnson Mgmt. Group CFC, Inc. v. Martinez*, 308 F.3d 1245 (Fed. Cir. 2002), and *McDonnell Douglas Corp. v. United States*, 229 Ct. Cl. 323, 670 F.2d 156 (1982), holding that deviation from the precise wording of a prescribed clause without obtaining approval pursuant to the regulations was beyond the authority of the contracting officer. In *Whittaker Corp.*, ASBCA 18422, 81-1 BCA ¶ 15,055, the board refused to find that a deviation was required when, after award of the contract, the contracting officer entered into a modification giving a board of contract appeals jurisdiction over a claim specifically excluded from jurisdiction by a mandatory contract clause. The board noted that the government received consideration for the modification and that the "granting of such a waiver was well within the ambit of the contracting officer's authority to administer the contract." The impact of the board's decision is that while the contracting officer had no authority to modify or exclude the clause without a deviation when the contract was formed, such authority existed during contract administration.

## b.  Waiver of Statutory Requirements

In the absence of a specific statutory provision granting such authority, government officials do not have the authority to waive statutory requirements, *Centech Group, Inc. v. United States*, 554 F.3d 1029 (Fed. Cir. 2009) (agency policy memorandum cannot waive the statutory requirement in 15 U.S.C. § 644(o)(1)(A) that a small business must perform 50% of the work with its own employees); *M-R-S Mfg. Co. v. United States*, 203 Ct. Cl. 551, 492 F.2d 835 (1974) (requirements of the Truth in Negotiations Act not waivable by the contracting officer); *Harry L. Lowe & Assocs.*, 53 Comp. Gen. 620 (B-178307), 74-1 CPD ¶ 96 (requirement for a valid ICC operating authority for interstate motor transportation services cannot be waived by a government agency). However, Congress has provided such authority in a significant number of statutes. For example, see 41 U.S.C. § 8301(a)(1) (heads of agencies may waive the requirements of the Buy American Act upon determination that the cost of compliance is unreasonable or application is inconsistent with the public interest); 40 U.S.C. § 3131(d) (contracting officers may waive Miller Act bond requirements with respect to as much of the work as is to be performed in a foreign country if it is impracticable for the contractor to furnish such bonds); 40 U.S.C. § 3134(a) (department secretaries may waive the Miller Act bond requirements with respect to cost type contracts for construction of public buildings and procurement of certain material and supplies for the Army, Navy, Air Force, and Coast Guard); 40 U.S.C. § 501(a)(2) (Secretary of Defense may exempt the DoD from certain procurement methods and policies prescribed by the GSA unless the President directs otherwise); 41 U.S.C. § 40 (Secretary of Labor may provide exemptions from wage and hour requirements of the Walsh-Healey Act and the President may suspend certain sections of the Act upon judgment that such action would be in the public interest); 40 U.S.C. § 3706 (Secretary of Labor may provide "limitations, variations, tolerances, or exemptions" from the Contract Work Hours and Safety Standards Act); 41 U.S.C. § 6508 (Secretary of Labor may provide "limitations, variations, tolerances, or exemptions" from the Service Contract Act of 1965); 40 U.S.C. § 3147 (the President may suspend the provisions of the Davis-Bacon Act in the event of a national emergency); 46 U.S.C. § App. 1241(b) (the President or the Secretary of Defense may temporarily waive requirements of the Cargo Preference Act upon declaration that an emergency exists justifying such action); 10 U.S.C. § 2306a(b) (1)(B) and 41 U.S.C. § 3503(a)(3) (head of procuring activity may waive requirement for cost or pricing data in exceptional cases).

A judicially forged exception to the requirement for specific statutory authority for a government official to waive a statute has been applied to the Assignment of

Claims Act, 41 U.S.C. § 6305(b). This statute states that any prohibited assignment "shall cause the annulment of the contract." In *Tuftco Corp. v. United States*, 222 Ct. Cl. 277, 614 F.2d 740 (1980), the court held that a contracting officer possessed the necessary authority to waive the statute. This seemingly controverts not only conventional concepts of sources of authority, but also the specific policies inherent in the Act.

## 2. Unauthorized Variations

When unauthorized procedures or terms and conditions are used, a variety of consequences may follow. In some cases, the government may be permitted to avoid the contract. In other instances, the contract may be rewritten to add a mandatory clause or exclude a prohibited clause. Finally, the contractor may be able to require the government to abide by mandatory procedures.

### a. Contract Avoidance

The most drastic consequence of a contract made in violation of a statute or a regulation with the force and effect of law is that the government has the right to avoid the contract. Such contracts have been variously described as "void ab initio," *Trilon Educ. Corp. v. United States*, 217 Ct. Cl. 266, 578 F.2d 1356, *aff'd*, 217 Ct. Cl. 284 (1978); "invalid," *Prestex Inc. v. United States*, 162 Ct. Cl. 620, 320 F.2d 367 (1963); or "illegal," *Alabama Rural Fire Ins. Co. v. United States*, 215 Ct. Cl. 442, 572 F.2d 727 (1978). Government avoidance is limited to clear-cut violations of statutes or regulations, *John Reiner & Co. v. United States*, 163 Ct. Cl. 381, 325 F.2d 438 (1963), *cert. denied*, 377 U.S. 931 (1964). In *Reiner*, the court held that an improper "cancellation" should be treated as a termination for the convenience of the government, stating that the "binding stamp of nullity" should only be imposed when the illegality is "plain." In *United States v. Amdahl Corp.*, 786 F.2d 387 (Fed. Cir. 1986), the court stated that in determining whether an award is "plainly or palpably illegal," consideration should be given to whether a statute or regulation was violated because of some action or statement by the contractor or if the contractor was on direct notice that the procedures followed violated such rules. See *Total Med. Mgmt., Inc. v. United States*, 104 F.3d 1314 (Fed. Cir. 1997), where the court held the contract to be void because it was in direct conflict with governing regulations and the contractor knew that those regulations were controlling. Following avoidance, the contractor may not recover under the contract. Further, the contractor may be denied any compensation if fraud or other criminal conduct of the contractor was involved, *K & R Eng'g Co. v. United States*, 222 Ct. Cl. 340, 616 F.2d 469 (1980) (contractor not entitled to payments due for completed work on contracts involving a violation of the conflict of interest statute, 18 U.S.C. § 208, and government entitled to recover amounts already paid), or if the government received no benefit from the contractor's efforts, *Prestex Inc. v. United States*, 162 Ct. Cl. 620, 320 F.2d 367 (1963) (government permitted to reject a shipment of supplies that conformed to the contract but not to the IFB). However, where there has been no criminal conduct and the government has received a benefit from the contractor's performance, the contractor has been permitted to recover the value of the benefit conferred. See *United States v. Amdahl Corp.*, 786 F.2d 387 (Fed. Cir. 1986), where the court stated at 393:

> [I]n many circumstances it would violate good conscience to impose upon the contractor all economic loss from having entered an illegal contract. Where a benefit has been conferred by the contractor on the government in the form of goods or services, which it accepted, a contractor may recover at least on a quantum valebant or quantum meruit basis for the value of the conforming goods or services received by the government prior to the rescission of the contract for invalidity. The contractor is not compensated under the contract, but rather under an implied-in-fact contract.

* * *

> Even though a contract be unenforceable against the Government, because not properly advertised, not authorized, or for some other reason, it is only fair and just that the Government pay for goods delivered or services rendered and accepted under it. In certain limited fact situations, therefore, the courts will grant relief of a quasi-contractual nature when the Government elects to rescind an invalid contract. No one would deny that ordinary principles of equity and justice preclude the United States from retaining the services, materials, and benefits and at the same time refusing to pay for them on the ground that the contracting officer's promise was unauthorized, or unenforceable for some other reason. However, the basic fact of legal significance charging the Government with liability in these situations is its retention of benefits in the form of goods or services.

See also *New York Mail & Newspaper Transp. Co. v. United States*, 139 Ct. Cl. 751, 154 F. Supp. 271, *cert. denied*, 355 U.S. 904 (1957) (contract "null and void" for violating the advertising statute, but contractor entitled to recover for the value of services rendered to the date of avoidance not limited to quantum meruit); *Urban Data Sys., Inc. v. United States*, 699 F.2d 1147 (Fed. Cir. 1983) (contract invalid for violation of cost-plus-a-percentage-of-cost prohibition, but recovery permitted on quantum valebant basis); *Interagency Agreements*, Comp. Gen. Dec. B-309181, 2007 CPD ¶ 163 (leases violating the leasing statutes, 40 U.S.C. § 585 and 10 U.S.C. § 2661, were void ab initio but recovery might be possible on quantum meruit basis); and *Veridyne Corp. v. United States*, 83 Fed. Cl. 575 (2008) (interpreting *Amdahl* to require recovery of money paid for work performed only if the contractor has a conflict of interest or has bribed a government official).

Contractors have had great difficulty in proving that a contract that violated a statute was void. In a number of cases, the court has ruled that the intent of Congress was not to void a contract if it was violated. See *American Tel. & Tel. Co. v. United States*, 177 F.3d 1368 (Fed. Cir. 1999) (en banc), *reversing*, 124 F.3d 1471 (Fed. Cir.

1997), holding that a contract was not invalid because it did not comply with the requirements of § 8118 of the 1988 Fiscal Year Department of Defense Appropriations Act, Pub. L. No. 100-202 limiting the use of fixed-price type contracts. The court refused to find the contract void, stating at 1374:

> Invalidation of the contract is not a necessary consequence when a statute or regulation has been contravened, but must be considered in light of the statutory or regulatory purpose, with recognition of the strong policy of supporting the integrity of contracts made by and with the United States. In *United States v. Mississippi Valley Generating Co.*, 364 U.S. 520, 81 S. Ct. 294, 5 L. Ed. 2d 268 (1961) the Court explained that when a statute "does not specifically provide for the invalidation of contracts which are made in violation of [its provisions]" the court shall inquire "whether the sanction of nonenforcement is consistent with and essential to effectuating the public policy embodied in [the statute]." Id. at 563, 81 S. Ct. 294. Thus the policy underlying the enactment must be considered in determining the remedy for its violation, when the statute itself does not announce the sanction of contract invalidity.

The opinion then noted congressional responses to past noncompliances with the statute and stated at 1375:

> These congressional responses, made with knowledge of the agency's imperfect compliance with § 8118, negate any reasonable inference that Congress intended simply to render void ab initio, even after full performance, any fixed price contract for which the Under Secretary's review of risk allocation and the report to the Committees were omitted. Congress can not have intended to charge the contracting partner with adverse consequences depending on whether the Defense Department carried out the internal responsibilities and filed the reports that Congress required.

In a later opinion, the Federal Circuit also denied the contractor's appeal that the contract should be reformed from a fixed-price type contract to a cost-reimbursement contract, *American Tel. & Tel. Co. v. United States*, 307 F.3d 1374 (Fed. Cir. 2002), *cert. denied*, 540 U.S. 937 (2003). The court stated at 1380-81:

> The reformation that AT&T seeks is not minor, but strikes to the core of the contract bargain. In the fixed-price contract, for example, AT&T agreed, in essence, to assume the risk associated with its lower technical rating. Had the contract required cost reimbursement, however, the Navy would have assumed the risk that AT&T's inferior technical capability would result in more costly performance. Under a cost-reimbursement scheme, this court perceives that the Navy may have refused to assume the risk of AT&T's technical competency. Instead, the Navy might have avoided that risk by awarding the RDA contract to one of AT&T's technically superior competitors — a contingency of which AT&T surely was aware. In sum, competition on a cost-reimbursement basis may have taken AT&T out of the game. In any event, this court is not inclined to change the rules and the scoring after the game has been played.

The same result was reached in *Northrop Grumman Corp. v. United States*, 47 Fed. Cl. 20 (2000), where the court found that § 8118 of the 1988 Fiscal Year Department of Defense Appropriations Act had been violated but denied relief on either a theory of implied contract or contract reformation. The court granted some relief for the constructive changes that had occurred on the fixed-price type contract. See also *Northrop Grumman Corp. v. United States*, 63 Fed. Cl. 38 (2004), denying relief on another contract violating § 8118, and *United Pac. Ins. Co. v. United States*, 464 F.3d 1325 (Fed. Cir. 2006), rejecting the argument that a contract was illegal because it violated statutory expenditure limitations on a military construction project.

## b. Nonenforcement of Clause

Violation of a statute or a regulation with the force and effect of law can also lead to nonenforcement of a contract clause. If the clause benefits the contractor, this will result the contractor's inability to recover money in accordance with the provisions of that clause. For example, in *Johnson Mgmt. Group CFC, Inc. v. Martinez*, 308 F.3d 1245 (Fed. Cir. 2002), the court held that a special clause allowing subcontractor payments to constitute liquidation of advance payments should not be enforced because it conflicted with the statutory advance payments provisions. Similarly, in *E.I. DuPont de Nemours & Co. v. United States*, 54 Fed. Cl. 361 (2002), the court ruled that an Indemnification clause was "void and unenforceable" because it violated the Anti-Deficiency Act, 31 U.S.C. § 1341 — with the result that the contractor was denied recovery under the clause. In 365 F.3d 1367 (Fed. Cir. 2004), the Federal Circuit agreed that the Act barred enforcement of an open-ended Indemnification clause but found that the Contract Settlement Act of 1944, 41 U.S.C. § 101 et seq.(pre-2011 codification), had granted contract authority to agree to the indemnification. Open-ended indemnification provisions have also been declared void by GAO, 7 Comp. Gen. 507 (A-21633) (1928); 35 Comp. Gen. 85 (B-117057) (1955); *Assumption by Government of Contractor Liability to Third Persons,* Comp. Gen. Dec. B-201072, 82-1 CPD ¶ 406, *recons. denied*, 62 Comp. Gen. 361, 83-1 CPD ¶ 501.

Nonenforcement of a clause can also result in the government's inability to enforce a clause against the contractor. For example, in *Mapco Alaska Petroleum, Inc. v. United States*, 27 Fed. Cl. 405 (1992), the court refused to enforce an Economic Price Adjustment clause that was not permitted by the FAR. The same result was reached in *Gold Line Refining, Ltd. v. United States*, 54 Fed. Cl. 285 (2002), and *La Gloria Oil & Gas Co. v. United States*, 56 Fed. Cl. 211 (2003). The opposite result was reached in *Williams Alaska Petroleum, Inc. v. United States*, 57 Fed. Cl. 789 (2003). In *Tesoro Haw. Corp. v. United States*, 405 F.3d 1339 (Fed. Cir. 2005), the court adopted the *Williams* view that the clause was in conformance with the FAR even though the great majority of the judges in the Court of Federal Claims had followed the *Mapco* reasoning. When an Economic Price Adjustment clause has been found unenforceable because it does not conform to the FAR, the court has fashioned different remedies. See *Barrett Refining Corp. v. United States*, 242 F.3d 1055 (Fed. Cir. 2001), granting relief for an implied-in-fact contract promising to pay fair market value, and *Beta Sys., Inc. v. United States*, 838 F.2d 1179 (Fed. Cir. 1988), granting reformation to bring the clause into conformance.

## c.  Inclusion or Exclusion of Mandatory Clause

A statute or a regulation with the force and effect of law may also impact the contract language to which the parties agreed. Thus, if a mandatory clause is required to be included in the contract, the contract will be read to include it even though it is not physically incorporated in the document, *G.L. Christian & Assocs. v. United States*, 160 Ct. Cl. 1, 312 F.2d 418, *reh'g denied*, 160 Ct. Cl. 58, 320 F.2d 345, *cert. denied*, 375 U.S. 954 (1963) (Termination for the Convenience of the Government clause); *Santa Fe — Andover Oil Co.*, ASBCA 35256, 88-2 BCA ¶ 20,607 (Disputes clause); *Bromley Contracting Co.*, DOTCAB 1284, 84-2 BCA ¶ 17,233 (Payment of Interest on Contractors' Claims clause); *Dayron Corp.*, ASBCA 24919, 84-1 BCA ¶ 17,213 (Government Property clause); *Benjamin P. Garcia*, ASBCA 18035, 73-2 BCA ¶ 10,196 (Equal Opportunity clause). Similarly, if a certain clause is prohibited, it will be read out of the contract even though it is physically present, *Johnson Mgmt. Group CFC, Inc. v. Martinez*, 308 F.3d 1245 (Fed. Cir. 2002) (special Liquidation of Advanced Payments clause); *Charles Beseler Co.*, ASBCA 22669, 78-2 BCA ¶ 13,483 (Value Engineering clause).

In the early application of this rule, it was held to apply only to clauses that contained significant procurement policies, *Chamberlain Mfg. Co.*, ASBCA 18103, 74-1 BCA ¶ 10,368 (Government Property clause). Subsequently, cases appeared to apply the rule to all mandatory clauses without analyzing whether they contained significant policies. See, for example, *Balimoy Mfg. Co.*, ASBCA 43768, 93-1 BCA ¶ 25,437 (First Article Approval clause); *Rodgers Constr., Inc.*, IBCA 2777, 92-1 BCA ¶ 24,503 (Assignment of Claims clause); *M.E. McGeary Co.*, ASBCA 36788, 90-1 BCA ¶ 22,512 (Disputes Concerning Labor Standards clause); and *Fireman's Fund Ins. Co.*, ASBCA 38284, 91-1 BCA ¶ 23,439 (Dispute clause). Some later cases did, however, analyze whether the mandatory clause contained significant policies. See, for example, *Miller's Moving Co.*, ASBCA 42114, 92-1 BCA ¶ 24,707 (Services Contract Act provisions incorporated in contract because the Act was an "obligatory congressional enactment"); and *H&R Machinists Co.*, ASBCA 38440, 91-1 BCA ¶ 23,373 (Default clause incorporated in the contract because it implemented "fundamental procurement policy").

Other cases incorporated a mandatory clause without discussion, but these clauses did deal with more significant issues. See, for example, *Technical & Mgmt. Servs. Corp.*, ASBCA 39999, 93-2 BCA ¶ 25,681 (Limitation of Price and Contractor Obligation clause); *Telesec Library Servs.*, ASBCA 42968, 92-1 BCA ¶ 24,650

(Fair Standards Act and Service Contract Act — Price Adjustment clause); and *OFEGRO*, HUDBCA 88-3410-C7, 91-3 BCA ¶ 24,206 (Default clause).

In 1993, the Federal Circuit announced that the rule applied when the clause contained a significant procurement policy *or* when it was written to "benefit or protect the party seeking incorporation," *General Eng'g & Mach. Works v. O'Keefe*, 991 F.2d 775 (Fed. Cir. 1993) (correct Payments clause carries out significant procurement policy). Most decisions thereafter articulated one of these grounds when they incorporated a clause. See *Dawkins General Contractors & Supply, Inc.*, AS-BCA 48535, 03-2 BCA ¶ 32,305 (Time-and-Materials Payments clause "expresses a purpose sufficiently ingrained in public procurement policy" to require incorporation); *Labat-Anderson, Inc. v. United States*, 42 Fed. Cl. 806 (1999) (Protest After Award clause incorporated in contract "on either ground"); and *Amoroso Constr. Co. v. United States*, 12 F.3d 1072 (Fed. Cir. 1993) (Buy American Act clause incorporated because it carried out a significant procurement policy). Compare *Lambrecht & Sons, Inc.*, ASBCA 49515, 97-2 BCA ¶ 29,105, *recons. denied*, 98-1 BCA ¶ 29,389, refusing to incorporate a Variation in Estimated Quantities clause because it reflected "no significant or deeply ingrained public procurement policy."

In *Rehabilitation Servs.*, ASBCA 47085, 96-2 BCA ¶ 28,324, the board incorporated a Government Furnished Property clause in the contract because it was a "mandatory contract clause that expresses a significant and deeply ingrained strand of public procurement policy," but in *American Bank Note Co.*, AGBCA 2004-146-1, 05-1 BCA ¶ 32,867, the board reached the opposite conclusion and refused to incorporate the Government Furnished Property clause in the contract. See also *Computing Application Software Tech., Inc.*, ASBCA 47554, 96-1 BCA ¶ 28,204, where the board refused to incorporate a mandatory NASA Government Furnished Property clause placing the risk of loss on the contractor. The board stated that this clause had the opposite effect of the standard FAR clause and that it was to be used in the special circumstance of contracts for the repair or modification of government property. The board found that this was such a narrow category of contracts that it was not covered by the FAR provisions on government property and therefore it was not "fundamental policy."

There are cases subsequent to the *General Engineering* decision incorporating clauses into a contract without a discussion of whether they expressed significant policy. See, for example, *Gerald Cunningham*, AGBCA 98-155-2, 98-2 BCA ¶ 29,908 (Disputes clause 90-day appeal provision); *C&J Assocs. v. VA Med. Ctr.*, VABCA 3892, 95-2 BCA ¶ 27,834 (Termination for Convenience clause incorporated in a purchase order but Default clause not incorporated because it was not mandatory); *GAI Consultants, Inc.*, ENGBCA 6030, 95-2 BCA ¶ 27,620 (correct Changes clause incorporated in a contract for archeological investigation); *Alta Constr. Co.*, PSBCA 1463, 94-3 BCA ¶ 27,961 (regulatory language read into Termination for Convenience clause that was placed in the contract); and *Unit Data Servs. Corp. v. Department of Veterans Affairs*, GSBCA 10775-P-R, 93-3 BCA ¶ 25,964 (clause requiring small business set-aside contractor to perform at least 50% of the work with its own employees incorporated in contract). See *Boeing Defense & Space Group*, ASBCA 50048, 98-2 BCA ¶ 28,927, where the government filed a motion for reconsideration contesting the board's use of the Christian doctrine to add loss adjustment language to the Termination for Convenience clause without making a finding citing one of the *General Engineering* factors. The board denied the motion stating at 148,097:

> Respondent's argument that our decision improperly extended the *Christian* doctrine is based on the misinterpretation that our decision held that FAR 49.203(b) (3) was incorporated in contract 12 by operation of law. We did not so hold. There is more to the *Christian* case than what is commonly referred to as the *Christian Doctrine*. Our decision held, unremarkably, that in interpreting what the terms of the FAR 52.249-2 convenience termination clause in contract 12 required, namely —
>
>> if it appears that the Contractor would have sustained a loss on the entire contract had it been completed, the Contracting Officer shall reduce the settlement to reflect the indicated rate of loss
>
> a tribunal properly may consider for guidance any pertinent authority which has the force and effect of law pursuant to *Christian,* including FAR 49.203(b). Clearly the contracting officer was obliged to adhere to FAR 49.203(b). Moreover, even ignoring FAR 49.203(b), the most obvious application of the FAR 52.249-2 (f)(2)(iii) convenience termination clause's loss provision is to reduce the settlement payment proportionate to the indicated rate of loss "on the entire contract."

Compare *Lockheed Martin Librascope Corp.*, ASBCA 50508, 99-1 BCA ¶ 30,635, where the board did not incorporate the Incentive Price Revision (Firm Target) clause in the contract and did not follow the clause in calculating the final price because the parties had included another clause on that issue in the contract and the standard clause was not "of such importance as to reflect a deeply ingrained strand of, or a legislative intent for, public procurement policy, or a major government principle."

If the statute or regulation is not mandatory with respect to the use of a clause, this rule will not apply. See *Professional Servs. Unified, Inc.*, ASBCA 48883, 96-1 BCA ¶ 28,073, where the board held that a contracting officer had correctly interpreted the FAR in using a Federal, State and Local Taxes clause which did not provide for price adjustments for subsequent tax increases. The board found that the clause giving price adjustments was to be used only in noncompetitive procurements and the procurement at issue was competitive. See also *Parcel 49C Ltd. Partnership v. General Servs. Admin.*, GSBCA 16377, 05-2 BCA ¶ 33,098 (GSA Equitable Adjustment clause in lease); *Mktg. & Mgmt. Info., Inc. v. United States*, 57 Fed. Cl. 665 (2003) (Termination for Convenience clause in commissary barter contract); *Ace-Federal Reporters, Inc.*, GSBCA 13298-REM, 02-2 BCA ¶ 31,913 (regulation providing an exception to mandatory use of the Federal Supply Schedule for lower-priced items); *Empresa de Viacao Terceirense*, ASBCA 49827, 00-2 BCA ¶ 31,120 (DFARS 252.237-7020 Restriction on Severance Payments to Foreign Nationals clause); *Shawn K. Chistensen*, AGBCA 95-188-R, 95-2 BCA ¶ 27,724 (Differing Site Conditions clause); *Jamsar, Inc.*, GSBCA 4396, 76-2 BCA ¶ 12,053 (Changes clause in building services contract); *Jacqueline Howell, Ltd.*, ASBCA 27026, 82-2 BCA ¶ 16,086 (Liquidated Damages clause); *Palmer & Sicard, Inc.*, ASBCA 23485, 81-1 BCA ¶ 15,029 (Government Delay of Work clause); *Muncie Gear Works, Inc.*, ASBCA 16153, 72-1 BCA ¶ 9429 (Duty-Free Entry clause).

## 3. Contractor Benefit

These rules involving statutes and regulations have been used primarily for the benefit of the government. Thus, courts have been prone to rule that, absent clear evidence of Congressional intent, statutes and regulations do not evidence such intent. See *Cessna Aircraft Co. v. Dalton*, 126 F.3d 1442 (Fed. Cir. 1997), *cert. denied*, 525 U.S. 818 (1998), stating at 1451-52:

> We must still determine whether the provision is a binding regulation, whose breach a contractor may assert against the government. The primary benefit of a statute or regulation must be to protect or benefit a class of persons in order for that class to be able to bring suit against the government for violating the statute or regulation.

> \* \* \*

> If the primary intended beneficiary of a statute or regulation is the government, then a private party cannot complain about the government's failure to comply with that statute or regulation, even if that party derives some incidental benefit from compliance with it.

See also *American Tel. & Tel. Co. v. United States*, 307 F.3d 1374 (Fed. Cir. 2002), *cert. denied*, 540 U.S. 937 (2003), stating at 1379:

> [T]he language of section 8118 provides for legislative oversight and enforcement. The section does not create a cause of action inviting private parties to enforce the provision in courts. In that context, AT&T's suit for reformation presumes to undertake a challenge as a private party to the propriety of the otherwise valid . . . contract. AT&T's earlier attack on that contract's validity similarly presumed to undertake Congress's role as the enforcement mechanism for section 8118. Section 8118, however, does not permit this form of enforcement. As this court en banc refused to void the otherwise valid and performed . . . contract, so this court again acknowledges as correct the trial court's refusal to entertain AT&T's request for contract reformation. Section 8118 simply does not provide implicitly or explicitly for any enforcement of its supervisory and congressional oversight provisions in a judicial forum.

* * *

AT&T also alleges that the Navy violated a variety of procurement regulations and directives that guide a contracting officer's selection of contract type. See, e.g., 48 C.F.R. §§ 16.104, 35.006, 216.101, 216.104 (1987); DoD Directive 5000.1 (Sept. 1, 1987). Those regulations and directives grant the contracting officer the discretion to select the type of contract.

* * *

Even if the contracting officer abused his discretion by negotiating the RDA contract on a fixed-price basis — a finding which the trial court properly declined to make on this record — that finding still would not provide AT&T a remedy. These cautionary and informative regulations and directives provide only internal governmental direction. Like section 8118, these provisions supply no remedy for private parties in a judicial forum. Cf. *Thompson v. Thompson*, 484 U.S. 174, 188-92, 98 L. Ed. 2d 512, 108 S. Ct. 513 (1988) (Scalia, J., concurring) ("This Court has long since abandoned its hospitable attitude towards implied rights of action. . . . The recent history of our holdings is one of repeated rejection of claims of an implied right."). As this court's predecessor stated: "The fact that a procurement practice is prohibited does not necessarily mean that it is therefore actionable. The discipline to be administered in such cases is a responsibility of the cognizant procurement officials within the agency . . . [and not] by this court." *E. Walters & Co. v. United States*, 217 Ct. Cl. 254, 576 F.2d 362, 367 (Ct. Cl. 1978).

See also *Gould, Inc. v. United States*, 66 Fed. Cl. 253 (2005), where the court held that the contractor was not entitled to relief because of violation of the multi-year contract statute, 10 U.S.C. § 2306(h)(1)(D), reasoning that the statute was a means that Congress had adopted to oversee the Department of Defense rather than the granting of a remedy to contractors if the statute was violated.

In contrast, there are some recent cases holding that regulations were for the benefit of a contractor or an offeror. See *Todd Constr. L.P. v. United States*, 94 Fed. Cl. 100 (2010), holding that the performance evaluation scheme in FAR 36.201 was for the benefit of contractors, with the result that evaluations could be challenged in a suit before the court, and *BLR Group of America, Inc. v. United States*, 94 Fed. Cl. 354 (2010), holding that the performance rating scheme in FAR Subpart 42.15 was intended to benefit both the contractor and the government, with the result that the court had jurisdiction to hear a challenge of the rating. See also *Magnum Opus Techs., Inc. v. United States*, 94 Fed. Cl. 512 (2010), holding that the requirement in FAR 17.207(f) that unevaluated options be competed was for the benefit of potential competitors — allowing a protest on this issue. *Magnum Opus* is illustrative of numerous protests that are based on a claimed violation of statute or regulation.

There are some earlier cases where contractors have obtained relief when statutes and regulations have been violated. In *Fletcher v. United States*, 183 Ct. Cl. 1, 392 F.2d 266 (1968), the court held that regulations that are intended to define or state the rights of a class of persons are presumably intended for the benefit of those persons. Such regulations can be asserted for a contractor's benefit, *Moran Bros., Inc. v. United States*, 171 Ct. Cl. 245, 346 F.2d 590 (1965) (Atomic Energy Commission procurement regulation that permitted appeals within 60 days had the effect of law, and appeal was timely even though it exceeded the 30-day limit included in the contract); 47 Comp. Gen. 457 (B-162272) (1968) (mandatory government liability for insurance premiums read into the contract); *Bethlehem Steel Corp. v. United States*, 191 Ct. Cl. 141, 423 F.2d 300 (1970) (regulation prescribing technique for determining the profit for defense contractors used for the benefit of contractors); *Chris Berg, Inc. v. United States*, 192 Ct. Cl. 176, 426 F.2d 314 (1970) (ASPR provision giving contractors the right to correct clerical mistakes in bids binding on the government).

## III. AUTHORITY OF GOVERNMENT AND CONTRACTOR PERSONNEL

The formation or modification of a government contract may involve many government and contractor personnel with varying degrees of authority. Specialists representing both parties engage in activities such as cost and price analysis, technical review, preaward surveys, negotiation, and preparation of contract documents. Accountants, attorneys, auditors, engineers, and other specialists may represent both parties. The ultimate aim of their activity is the creation of a legally enforceable agreement. In the vast majority of the cases, this goal is achieved. However, legal problems concerning the authority of these personnel are frequently encountered — most often when the government refuses to recognize an alleged contractual agreement on the grounds that the contractor has dealt with an unauthorized person. Contractors occasionally raise the same defenses, but with much less success. This section first considers the legal principles relevant to determining the authority of government personnel, the consequences of dealing with unauthorized personnel, and the effect of notice of limitations on authority. It then examines a number of the same principles as applied to contractor personnel.

### A.  Government Personnel

The fundamental rule regarding government personnel is that the government is not bound by unauthorized acts of its officers or agents, *Wilber Nat'l Bank v. United States*, 294 U.S. 120 (1935). The government has taken advantage of this rule by allocating the major grant of contractual authority to *a special and limited class of employees* called *contracting officers*. Contracting officers have the sole authority to legally bind the government to contracts and contract modifications, FAR 1.601(a). However, they are frequently not involved in the day-to-day activities that occur in the contract formation process. In some agencies, the designated contracting officer may be an active participant in the steps leading to signature of a contract, while in others, the contracting officer's role may be only to sign the document. Thus, during the formation process, a contractor may deal primarily with government personnel bearing titles such as contract specialist, contract negotiator, cost analyst, project manager, engineer, contracting officer's representative, auditor, and attorney. In many cases, those personnel who are not contracting officers may be delegated authority to perform specific functions even though the general grant of contractual authority is made only to contracting officers. Additionally, the authority of contracting officers may range from full authority, regardless of the nature and size of the transaction (plenary authority), to authority to perform only a limited class of contractual activities described by type and dollar amount. This fragmentation of authority in the contracting process has created difficult legal problems.

## 1. Actual Authority Required

In private agency law, an employer will be bound by an employee under the legal theory of *apparent authority* if the employer has permitted the employee to assume authority or has held out the employee as possessing authority. See *Restatement, Second, Agency* § 8. Recognizing the importance of effective government control over the conduct of its agents, the courts and boards have rejected the apparent-authority rule, holding that *actual authority* is required to bind the government. See *Federal Crop Ins. Corp. v. Merrill*, 332 U.S. 380 (1947), where the Court stated at 383:

> Whatever the form in which the Government functions, anyone entering into an arrangement with the Government takes the risk of having accurately ascertained that he who purports to act for the Government stays within the bounds of his authority. The scope of this authority may be explicitly defined by Congress or be limited by delegated legislation, properly exercised through the rule-making power. And this is so even though, as here, the agent himself may have been unaware of the limitations upon his authority. See, e.g., *Utah Power & Light Co. v. United States*, 243 U.S. 389, 409 (1917); *United States v. Stewart*, 311 U.S. 60 (1940).

For cases where government employees with apparent authority were found to have no actual authority, see *P.R. Burke Corp. v. United States*, 277 F.3d 1346 (Fed. Cir. 2002) (Assistant Plant Manager had no authority to permit deviation from specifications); *Starflight Boats v. United States*, 48 Fed. Cl. 592 (2001) (Deputy Chief of Procurement had no authority to order contractor to assist in investigation); *Total Procurement Serv., Inc.*, ASBCA 53258, 01-2 BCA ¶ 31,436 (Executive Director of Business Office had no authority to bind government to an electronic commerce agreement); *Healthcare Practice Enhancement Network, Inc.*, VABCA 5864, 01-1 BCA ¶ 31,383 (Chief Financial Officer of Veterans Administration medical center had no contracting officer authority); *Melrose Assocs., L.P. v. United States*, 43 Fed. Cl. 124 (1999) (Director of HUD State Field Office had no authority to waive regulations); *Jascourt v. United States*, 207 Ct. Cl. 955, *cert. denied*, 423 U.S. 1032 (1975) (government not bound by the actions of the Deputy Assistant Secretary of Labor for Labor Relations, or the Director of the Division of Public Employees, since neither official had the authority to enter into a contract); *Housing Corp. v. United States*, 199 Ct. Cl.

705, 468 F.2d 922 (1972) (HUD Secretary's unauthorized signature would not bind government as a third party responsible for costly changes); *Byrne Org., Inc. v. United States*, 152 Ct. Cl. 578, 287 F.2d 582 (1961) ("letters of intent" issued by director and chief administrative officer of the National Capital Sesquicentennial Commission not binding on the government); and *Gordon Woodroffe Corp. v. United States*, 122 Ct. Cl. 723, 104 F. Supp. 984 (1952) (special assistant to State Department coordinator for aid to Greece and Turkey had no authority to purchase equipment).

The fact that an official appears to be a superior of a contracting officer does not establish the authority of that official. See *Inter-Tribal Council of Nev., Inc.*, IBCA 1234-12-78, 83-1 BCA ¶ 16,433, stating at 81,745-46:

> The facts that the Assistant Area Director for Education was the " boss" for Area education matters, . . . that the CO sought his approval for a contract budget modification, . . . and that he was named as the "contact person" for negotiations for an upcoming contract . . . are irrelevant in this context. The best that can be said about them is that they are probative of the fact and conclusion that the Assistant Area Director had *apparent* authority here, which we have already noted is insufficient authority for [the contractor's] reliance under the *Federal Crop Insurance* rule. The reason for excepting the Government from the rule of apparent authority generally applicable to private contracts has been oft-stated as grounded in the difference between protecting the public treasury, a public right or a public interest on the one hand, and protecting private concerns on the other. *Federal Crop Insurance Corp. v. Merrill, supra* at 385, and *Utah Power & Light Co. v. United States*, 243 U.S. 389, 37 S. Ct. 387, 391 (1917). Also, the Government practice of specifically designating only one person, the CO, as having exclusive actual authority for dealing with the administration of a contract avoids the chaos and lack of protection for those Government interests which would result if a contractor were allowed to rely on the authority of any one of dozens or potentially hundreds of Government "agents" who might have some relationship with the contract. See *Dresser Industries, Inc. v. United States*, [596 F.2d 1231, 1237 (5th Cir. 1979)].

See also *Henry Burge & Alvin White*, PSBCA 2431, 89-3 BCA ¶ 21,910, where a project manager was held to have no authority to relax the specifications. Compare *Zoubi v. United States*, 25 Cl. Ct. 581 (1992), where an "acting program director" was held to have authority to contract for services because he was responsible for obtaining such services and had obtained them in the past.

Within contracting offices, personnel with official-sounding titles such as contract specialist, contract negotiator, and contract administrator work for contracting officers and handle the day-to-day contracting activity of the government, but such personnel generally do not have authority to order additional work or to commit the government by virtue of their position. Contractors are expected to recognize this lack of authority. In *General Elec. Co.*, ASBCA 11990, 67-1 BCA ¶ 6377, *rev'd on other grounds*, 188 Ct. Cl. 620, 412 F.2d 1215 (1969), the board stated at 29,525-26:

> [The contract specialist's] only function was to serve as contact point between the Government and [the contractor]. He can be considered little more than a messenger. There is no evidence that he was delegated any power to bind the Government; on the contrary the testimony establishes that he was delegated no authority to bind the Government. No authority to bind the Government for additional funds by demanding the report notwithstanding the funding situation can be implied from [his] position.

Thus, when a contractor negotiates a contract or a contract modification with a contract specialist, it must recognize that there will be no binding agreement until an actual contracting officer signs the contract or modification. See *Mil-Spec Contractors, Inc. v. United States*, 835 F.2d 865 (Fed. Cir. 1987) (government not bound by alleged oral agreement by contract negotiator); *Anchor/Darling Valve Co.*, ASBCA 46109, 95-1 BCA ¶ 27,595 (procurement assistant had no authority to waive delivery schedule); *Precision Standards, Inc.*, ASBCA 41375, 96-2 BCA ¶ 28,461 (contract administrator working for ACO had no authority to waive delivery schedule); and *Total Procurement Serv., Inc.*, ASBCA 53258, 01-2 BCA ¶ 31,436 (Executive Director of program office had no authority to enter into contract). In *Kahaluu Constr. Co.*, ASBCA 33248, 90-2 BCA ¶ 22,663, the government argued that a binding agreement had been reached on a "Board on Changes Report" signed by a contractor's representative and government members of the board. However, the board found that neither the government members nor the contractor's representatives had authority to bind their respective parties.

## 2. Delegation of Authority

The contracting authority in each agency flows from the head of the agency to contracting officers. See FAR 1.601, stating:

> [A]uthority and responsibility to contract for authorized supplies and services are vested in the agency head. The agency head may establish contracting activities and delegate broad authority to manage the agency's contracting functions to heads of such contracting activities. Contracts may be entered into and signed on behalf of the Government only by contracting officers. In some agencies, a relatively small number of high level officials are designated contracting officers solely by virtue of their positions. Contracting officers below the level of a head of a contracting activity shall be selected and appointed under 1.603.

This regulation recognizes two types of officials with contracting officer authority. At the upper level of the agency, in secretarial positions or as head of a contracting activity, officials have contracting authority "by virtue of their positions." These officials are not required to meet the qualification requirements for appointment and generally do not act as contracting officers except on special matters. Yet they have full authority to act as contracting officers. Below these officials are the *designated contracting officers*, appointed in accordance with the regulations discussed below.

Each agency is authorized to delegate contracting officer authority in accordance with its own procedures. See FAR 1.603-1, stating that the agency shall

> establish and maintain a procurement career management program and a system for the selection, appointment, and termination of appointment of contracting officers. Agency heads or their designees may select and appoint contracting officers and terminate their appointments.

Thus, agency heads may appoint contracting officers or may delegate this authority. In some agencies authority has been delegated to appoint subsidiary contracting officers or other representatives. FAR 1.602-1(a) requires clear instructions in the appointment document, as follows:

> Contracting officers may bind the Government only to the extent of the authority delegated to them. Contracting officers shall receive from the appointing authority (see 1.603-1) clear instructions in writing regarding the limits of their authority. Information on the limits of contracting officers' authority shall be readily available to the public and agency personnel.

The term "contracting officer" is used to describe those individuals with the authority to execute contractual documents that bind the government and to sign determinations and findings and other internal documents. FAR 2.101 contains the following definition:

> Contracting Officer means a person with the authority to enter into, administer, and/or terminate contracts and make related determinations and findings. The term includes certain authorized representatives of the contracting officer acting within the limits of their authority as delegated by the contracting officer. "Administrative contracting officer (ACO)" refers to a contracting officer who is administering contracts. "Termination contracting officer (TCO)" refers to a contracting officer who is settling terminated contracts. A single contracting officer may be responsible for duties in any or all of these areas. Reference in this regulation to administrative contracting officer or termination contracting officer does not (a) require that a duty be performed at a particular office or activity or (b) restrict in any way a contracting officer in the performance of any duty properly assigned.

The first sentence of this FAR definition refers to the official who has been designated as a contracting officer. However, the second sentence creates confusion by stating that *the term includes* any "authorized representative" of the contracting officer. This broad definition of contracting officer is also included in the Definitions clause in FAR 52.202-1.

The inclusion of "authorized representatives" within the definition of contracting officer is very misleading, because formally designated contracting officers will normally have a much broader grant of authority than authorized representatives. In addition, not all representatives are appointed in the same manner or with the same degree of authority. The following discussion explores the method of appointment and stated scope of authority of three categories of government employees — designated contracting officers, contracting officer representatives, and other employees with contractual duties.

## a. Designated Contracting Officers

FAR 1.603-3 calls for the appointment of designated contracting officers *by name* using the Certificate of Appointment, Standard Form 1402. See **Figure 1-5**. In addition, each agency is required to establish a system that ensures that each designated contracting officer is fully qualified by experience and training. The following guidance for selection criteria is given in FAR 1.603-2:

> In selecting contracting officers, the appointing official shall consider the complexity and dollar value of the acquisitions to be assigned and the candidate's experience, training, education, business acumen, judgment, character, and reputation. Examples of selection criteria include —
>
> (a) Experience in Government contracting and administration, commercial purchasing, or related fields;
>
> (b) Education or special training in business administration, law, accounting, engineering, or related fields;
>
> (c) Knowledge of acquisition policies and procedures, including this and other applicable regulations;
>
> (d) Specialized knowledge in the particular assigned field of contracting; and
>
> (e) Satisfactory completion of acquisition training courses.

More precise and demanding requirements have been called for in recent years. See, for example, Executive Order 12931, 59 Fed. Reg. 52387 (1994), requiring heads of agencies to:

> (h) Establish career education programs for procurement professionals, including requirements for successful completion of educational requirements or mandatory training for entry level positions and for promotion to higher level positions, in order to ensure a highly qualified procurement work force.

See also the Office of Personnel Management Standard for GS-1102 (the series for contracting professionals), which contains educational or experience requirements. A number of agencies have adopted higher standards for their contracting officers. See, for example, DFARS 201.603-2, imposing the following requirements on contracting officers in DoD:

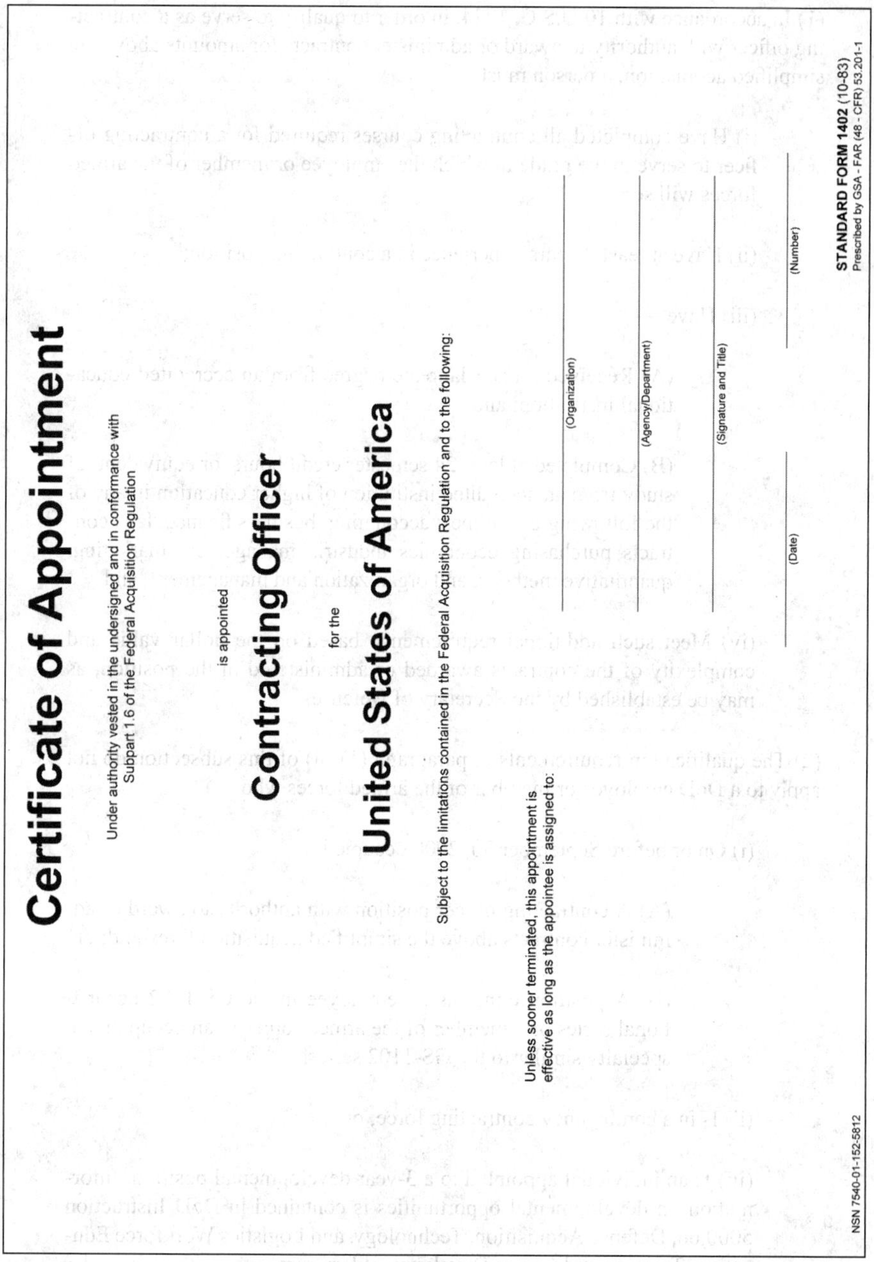

# Certificate of Appointment

Under authority vested in the undersigned and in conformance with
Subpart 1.6 of the Federal Acquisition Regulation

is appointed

## Contracting Officer

for the

## United States of America

Subject to the limitations contained in the Federal Acquisition Regulation and to the following:

Unless sooner terminated, this appointment is
effective as long as the appointee is assigned to:

_____ (Organization)

_____ (Agency/Department)

_____ (Signature and Title)

_____ (Date)

_____ (Number)

STANDARD FORM 1402 (10-83)
Prescribed by GSA - FAR (48 - CFR) 53.201-1

NSN 7540-01-152-5812

Figure 1-5

(1) In accordance with 10 U.S.C. 1724, in order to qualify to serve as a contracting officer with authority to award or administer contracts for amounts above the simplified acquisition, a person must

(i) Have completed all contracting courses required for a contracting officer to serve in the grade in which the employee or member of the armed forces will serve;

(ii) Have at least 2 years experience in a contracting position;

(iii) Have —

(A) Received a baccalaureate degree from an accredited educational institution; and

(B) Completed at least 24 semester credit hours, or equivalent, of study from an accredited institution of higher education in any of the following disciplines: accounting, business finance, law, contracts, purchasing, economics, industrial management, marketing, quantitative methods, and organization and management; and

(iv) Meet such additional requirements, based on the dollar value and complexity of the contracts awarded or administered in the position, as may be established by the Secretary of Defense.

(2) The qualification requirements in paragraph (1)(iii) of this subsection do not apply to a DoD employee or member of the armed forces who

(i) On or before September 30, 2000 occupied

(A) A contracting officer position with authority to award or administer contracts above the simplified acquisition threshold; or

(B) A position either as an employee in the GS-1102 occupational series or a member of the armed forces in an occupational specialty similar to the GS-1102 series;

(ii) Is in a contingency contracting force; or

(iii) Is an individual appointed to a 3-year developmental position. Information on developmental opportunities is contained in DoD Instruction 5000.66, Defense Acquisition, Technology, and Logistics Workforce Education, Training and Career Development Program.

(3) Waivers to the requirements in paragraph (1) of this subsection may be authorized. Information on waivers is contained in DoD Instruction 5000.66.

## (1) INTERNAL LIMITATIONS ON AUTHORITY

In each agency there are one or more contracting officers with plenary authority. Even these contracting officers, however, may be subject to internal regulations governing how that authority is exercised, and the contractor is responsible for being aware of any regulations made known to it through publication or otherwise, *Federal Crop Ins. Corp. v. Merrill*, 332 U.S. 380 (1947). In *Porter v. United States*, 204 Ct. Cl. 355, 496 F.2d 583 (1974), *cert. denied*, 420 U.S. 1004 (1975), published regulations delegated authority to the high commissioner and the director of the Office of Territories to contract for shipping services "on behalf of the Trust Territory of the Pacific Islands." The contractor was deemed to have notice that these officials were acting for the Trust Territory government and had no authority to bind the United States. See also *Johnson Mgmt. Group, CFC, Inc. v. Martinez*, 308 F.3d 1245 (Fed. Cir. 2002) (contracting officer lacked authority to insert a clause in a contract that deviated from the FAR); *Harbert/Lummus Agrifuels Projects v. United States*, 142 F.3d 1429 (Fed. Cir. 1998), *cert. denied*, 525 U.S. 1177 (1999) (contracting officer lacked authority to enter into an oral, unilateral contract to continue guaranteeing future borrowing requests until completion of a construction project because the delegation of authority required the preparation of a "separate prior written approval"); *Total Medical Mgmt. v. United States*, 104 F.3d 1314 (Fed. Cir. 1997) (person with contracting authority did not have authority to agree to provisions violating agency regulations); and *OAO Corp. v. United States*, 17 Cl. Ct. 91 (1989) (government not bound by handshake of contracting officer when approval of higher authority required; however, court did find an implied-in-fact contract). See also *Johnson Mgmt. Group, CFC, Inc.*, HUDBCA 96-C-132-C, 00-2 BCA ¶ 31,116, holding that under the "relevant regulations" a contracting officer did not have the authority to enter into an oral contract, citing *Mil-Spec Contractors, Inc. v. United States*, 835 F.2d 865 (Fed. Cir. 1987), and *SCM Corp. v. United States*, 291 Ct. Cl. 459, 595 F.2d 595 (1979).

Contractors are not bound by limitations in unpublished regulations, *Texas Instruments, Inc. v. United States*, 922 F.2d 810 (Fed. Cir. 1990) (government bound by ACO signature on agreement even though internal regulations required internal approvals). See also *Western Aviation Servs., Inc. v. General Servs. Admin.*, GSBCA 14165, 00-2 BCA ¶ 31,123 (contractor not bound by internal government manual); *NI Indus., Inc. v. United States*, 841 F.2d 1104 (Fed. Cir. 1988) (contractor not bound by limitations set forth in unpublished value engineering change proposal rule); *A-1 Garbage Disposal & Trash Serv.*, ASBCA 30623, 89-1 BCA ¶ 21,323 (contractor not bound by unpublished regulation of Small Business Administration); and *New England Tank Indus. of N.H., Inc.*, ASBCA 26474, 88-1 BCA ¶ 20,395, *vacated & remanded on other grounds*, 861 F.2d 685 (Fed. Cir. 1988) (government bound to modification signed by contracting officer even though unpublished regulation prohibited agreement). See also *Devil's Lake Sioux Tribe*, IBCA 1953, 88-1 BCA ¶ 20,320, where the board held that the contractor was not bound by a published regulation that was so vague and ambiguous that it could not be understood by a typical contractor. Compare *Trauma Serv. Group v. United States*, 104 F.3d 1321 (Fed. Cir. 1997), holding that a memorandum of agreement was not binding on the government even though it was signed by an official with proper authority because a DoD Instruction required approval of higher authority. The court did not discuss whether the instruction was available to the public.

If the contractor is aware of the unpublished regulation, it will be bound by the limitations contained therein. See *D.M. Summers, Inc.*, VABCA 2750, 89-3 BCA ¶ 22,123 (contractor could not recover for lost work because it had actual knowledge of changes in internal agency regulations that reduced the requirements of the contract). In *LDG Timber Enters., Inc. v. Glickman*, 114 F.3d 1140 (Fed. Cir. 1997), the court held that the government had the burden of proving that an internal regulation barred a contracting officer from taking normal action within his or her authority.

## (2) FUNCTIONAL CONTRACTING OFFICERS

In the DoD, different types of contracting officers perform different functions. Contracting officers that award contracts are known as procuring contracting officers (PCOs); contracting officers that administer contracts are known as administrative contracting officers (ACOs); and contracting officers that handle contract terminations are known as terminating contracting officers (TCOs). In most other agencies, there is no such fragmentation of authority, with the result that the contracting officers who award contracts usually retain authority to administer or terminate them. There may be additional specialized contracting officers with limited scopes of authority, such as corporate administrative contracting officers (CACOs).

FAR 1.603-3 requires that limitations on authority be included in the certificate of appointment of each contracting officer and that contractors be responsible for ascertaining the limits of authority of contracting officers. See, for example, *Strick Corp.*, ASBCA 15921, 73-2 BCA ¶ 10,077 (modification not binding because ACO had no authority to sign it); and *Atlantic, Gulf & Pac. Co.*, ASBCA 13533, 72-1 BCA ¶ 9415 (termination settlement not binding because TCO acted beyond authority). However, such limitations on authority will not control if they are neither published nor communicated to the contractor. See *Texas Instruments, Inc. v. United States*, 922 F.2d 810 (Fed. Cir. 1990) (government bound by ACO signature on agreement even though internal regulations required internal approvals).

FAR 42.302 contains a long list of functions that are normally delegated to contract administration offices (CAOs). When an agency has a separate ACO that person will generally be the head of a CAO and will generally have the functions listed in FAR 42.302(a) — some of which entail legally obligating the government. Note, however, that FAR 42.302(b) warns that the following functions are permitted only when specifically delegated:

(1) Negotiate or negotiate and execute supplemental agreements incorporating contractor proposals resulting from change orders issued under the Changes clause. Before completing negotiations, coordinate any delivery schedule change with the contracting office.

(2) Negotiate prices and execute priced exhibits for unpriced orders issued by the contracting officer under basic ordering agreements.

(3) Negotiate or negotiate and execute supplemental agreements changing contract delivery schedules.

\* \* \*

(7) Negotiate and definitize adjustments to contract prices resulting from exercise of an economic price adjustment clause (see subpart 16.2).

(8) Issue change orders and negotiate and execute resulting supplemental agreements under contracts for ship construction, conversion, and repair.

## (3) SPECIFIC DESIGNATION BY CONTRACT

There is also a difference in the way contracting officer authority is distributed relative to supply versus construction contracts. In construction contracts, the contractor can generally expect to be informed of a single named individual who has authority to bind the government. There is usually no designation of ACOs; the field functions relating to the day-to-day administration of the contract are performed through contracting officer representatives (CORs). In supply contracts, there is usually no designation of a single person to serve as contracting officer. Thus, any employee of the agency who has been properly designated a contracting officer may act on any contract of the agency, provided that he or she is acting within the limits of this authority. This procedure gives the agency much greater internal operating flexibility, but it creates difficulties for contractors in ascertaining the authority of the person with whom they are dealing.

## (4) DOLLAR LIMITATIONS ON AUTHORITY

There are frequently various tiers of contracting officers with decreasing amounts of authority given to each succeeding lower tier. This practice is particularly prevalent in supply and service contracting. At the top may be the contracting officer who signed the contract and has full ("plenary") authority within the agency. Below may be a contracting officer with authority to sign contracts, task or delivery orders and changes up to $500,000 in value, and another step down may be a contracting officer with authority to sign changes and task or delivery orders up to $25,000. The contractor must know this internal structure and be aware of the personnel and organizational changes that occur within the agency in order to determine whether a particular employee has authority at any given time. Since, as a general rule, no notice is given to contractors of such personnel or organizational changes, this task is a difficult one for the contractor that does not deal with the agency regularly.

Contractors must ascertain the monetary limitations on the authority of subsidiary contracting officers. See *Biofunction, LLC v. United States*, 92 Fed. Cl. 167 (2010) (pilot program costing $360,000 could not be procured by contracting officer with $10,000 limitation on authority); *Comspace Corp.*, DOTBCA 3095, 98-2 BCA ¶ 30,037 (delivery order not binding because it was in excess of $25,000 authority of contracting officer that signed it); *Edwards v. United States*, 22 Cl. Ct. 411 (1991) (government not bound when contracting officer agreed to modification above dollar limitation for agreements without approval of higher authority); and *Danac, Inc.*, ASBCA 30227, 90-3 BCA ¶ 23,246 (government would not have been bound by a settlement agreement above dollar limitation in contract, without approval of higher authority as provided for in contracting officer's warrant).

## b.  Authorized Representatives

A considerable degree of confusion surrounds the term "authorized representative." One source of the confusion is the regulatory definition of contracting officer, discussed above, which defines the term to include "the authorized representatives of the contracting officer acting within the limits of their authority," FAR 2.101. However, authorized representatives traditionally have *a much narrower scope of authority* than those specifically appointed as contracting officers, and it should be clear that generally authorized representatives *do not have the authority to sign contracts or contract modifications*. See *Essen Mall Properties v. United States*, 21 Cl. Ct. 430 (1990), rejecting the argument that an authorized representative had the full authority of a contracting officer because of the regulatory definition.

Further confusion results from the varying methods used by contracting officers to appoint representatives — with some representatives being formally designated as contracting officer representatives and other representatives merely being assigned functions to be performed in the procurement process without specific use of the term "authorized representative" in their selection or appointment. For this reason, these two types of representatives are discussed separately.

### (1) FORMALLY DESIGNATED REPRESENTATIVES

There are a number of formally designated representatives who act on behalf of the government — primarily during contract administration. Depending upon the agency involved, these representatives may bear the title of contracting officer representative (COR), contracting officer technical representative (COTR), government technical representative (GTR), or government technical evaluator (GTE). See Cibinic, Nagle & Nash, *Administration of Government Contracts* (4th ed. 2006) for a detailed discussion of the appointment of such representatives and their major responsibilities.

These formally designated representatives frequently participate in modifications to contracts. However, limitations on authority of CORs or COTRs with regard to such modifications that have been communicated to the contractor are binding on the contractor. See *Winter v. Cath-dr/Balti Joint Venture*, 497 F.3d 1339 (Fed. Cir. 2007), holding pursuant to specific contract clauses that a COR had no authority to agree to contract modifications even though the contracting officer had informed the contractor that the COR had broad authority in administering the contract. The court stated that DFARS 201.602-2 *prohibited* the delegation of contracting officer authority to CORs. See also *Elter S.A.*, ASBCA 52349, 01-2 BCA ¶ 31,547 & ASBCA 52791, 02-1 BCA ¶ 31,672 (government's construction representatives clearly had no authority to order changes); *California Consulting Eng'rs,* ASBCA 50355, 98-2 BCA ¶ 29,995 (COR had no authority to order extra work); *Niko Contracting Co. v. United States*, 39 Fed. Cl. 795 (1997) (COTR had no authority to promise that modification could be reopened); *Toloff Constr.*, AG-BCA 95-227-3, 96-1 BCA ¶ 28,156 (COR had no authority to order extra work); *David W.E. Cabell*, VABCA 3402, 93-2 BCA ¶ 25,598 (COR has no authority to interpret an unambiguous contract in a manner that leads to additional compensation); *HTC Indus., Inc.*, ASBCA 40562, 93-1 BCA ¶ 25,560, *recons. denied*, 93-2 BCA ¶ 25,701, *aff'd*, 22 F.3d 1103 (Fed. Cir. 1994) (COTR had no authority to order contractor to continue performance while he sought additional funding in view of the specific language in the contract); *David W.E. Cabell*, VABCA 3402, 93-2 BCA ¶ 25,598 (COR had no authority to interpret an unambiguous contract in a manner that leads to additional compensation); *Construction Equip. Lease Co. v. United States*, 26 Cl. Ct. 341 (1992) (COR technical project officer had no authority to change contract in face of explicit language in appointment letter); *Essen Mall Properties v. United States*, 21 Cl. Ct. 430 (1990) (project manager acting as authorized representative had no authority to bind government agency to contract); and *Carothers & Carothers Co.*, ENGBCA 4015, 88-3 BCA ¶ 21,162 (COR had no authority to issue major change). The proper course of action when receiving an order for extra or changed work from such an employee is to demand that the order be issued by the contracting officer, *Adventure Group, Inc.*, ASBCA 50188, 97-2 BCA ¶ 29,081 (contractor compensated for delay due to government refusal to resolve the need for extra work ordered by contract administrator).

Prior to *Winter v. Cath-dr/Balti*, there were numerous decisions holding the government bound by the actions of a COR or COTR acting within the scope of his or her authority, even if additional work was called for. See *Oliver Eng'g Servs.*, DOTBCA 2549, 94-3 BCA ¶ 27,203 (providing faulty technical information within scope of COTR's duties); *Hudson Contracting, Inc.*, ASBCA 41023, 94-1 BCA ¶ 26,466 (making government property available to contractor within authority of COR); *Diversified Marine Tech, Inc.*, DOTBCA 2455, 93-2 BCA ¶ 25,720 (granting permission to perform work within scope of COR's delegation when, as the government representative at the site, he was the most logical person to act); *MJW Enters., Inc.*, ENGBCA 5813, 93-1 BCA ¶ 25,405 (interpretation of vague specification within scope of COR's authority); and *Farr Bros., Inc.*, ASBCA 42658, 92-2 BCA ¶ 24,991 (COR had authority to order work suspension). In view of *Winter v. Cath-dr/Balti,* there is a significant question whether the boards or courts will be able to reach such a conclusion in the future. See *Sinil Co.*, ASBCA 55819, 09-2 BCA ¶ 34,213 (no authority for COR to order additional or substituted work); *States Roofing Corp.*, ASBCA 55500, 09-1 BCA ¶ 34,036 (COR had no authority to direct contractor to employ a full-time safety official).

## (2) OTHER REPRESENTATIVES

The vast majority of personnel involved in the contract formation process are designated neither as contracting officers nor authorized representatives. Some of these personnel, such as program managers, engineers and scientists, generate and fund the agency requirement which initiates the contracting process. Others are organizationally separate specialists, such as attorneys and auditors, from whom the contracting officer is required to request advice, FAR 1.602-2(c). All such personnel may receive information from contractors and may, in the course of their duties, participate in discussions or negotiations. Thus, their role may be seen as independent government representatives or as informally recognized representatives of the contracting officer. The regulations in this area do not clearly delineate the authority of these personnel and rarely require specific written designation as CORs.

In the past, the absence of formal delegation as a "representative" did not prevent the courts and boards of contract appeals from finding that these personnel were authorized representatives of the contracting officer. See, for example, *Cessna Aircraft Co.*, ASBCA 37726, 95-1 BCA ¶ 27,373 (government "evaluators" had authority to issue technical directions that changed contract because their direction was reportedly followed by COTR and contracting officer); *Zoubi v. United States*, 25 Cl. Ct. 581 (1992) (program director had authority to enter into a contract for interpreter services because his job carried with it an implied authorization to obtain all necessary personnel); *H. Landau & Co. v. United States*, 886 F.2d 322 (Fed. Cir. 1989) (employees with contract administration authority bound the government when they stated that the government would guarantee payment for materials); *Walter Straga*, ASBCA 26134, 83-2 BCA ¶ 16,611 (project manager proper official to respond to technical inquiries and "was a representative of the contracting officer"); and *Contractors Equip. Rental Co.*, ASBCA 13052, 70-1 BCA ¶ 8183 (statement by contracting officer that official was "the man to satisfy" and deferral to him for equipment needs held "tantamount to a delegation de facto" as contracting officer's authorized representative). However, after the decision of the Federal Circuit in *Winter v. Cath-dr/Balti Joint Venture*, 497 F.3d 1339 (Fed. Cir. 2007), decisions have tended to refuse to find such delegation of authority. See, for example, *Dubar v. Dep't of Agriculture*, CBCA 1895, 10-2 BCA ¶ 34,497 (agency "contact person" had no authority to contract for more work); *Hambone Constr., Inc. v. Department of Agriculture*, CBCA 1088, 09-2 BCA ¶ 34,258 (agency engineer had no authority to agree to pay for extra work); *Corners & Edges, Inc.*, ASBCA 55767, 09-1 BCA 34,019 (project officers had no authority to increase the work); *Corners & Edges, Inc. v. Department of Health & Human Servs.*, CBCA 648, 07-2 BCA ¶ 33,706 ("certified project officer" had no authority to extend performance period); and *California Business Tels. v. Department of Agriculture*, CBCA 135, 07-1 BCA ¶ 33,553 ("program analyst" that was the "point of contact" on the contract had no authority to order extra work).

When a contractor is expressly informed of limitations on the authority of these representatives, the contractor is generally unable to recover for unauthorized acts. Such notifications are often contained in letters to contractors or in contract clauses. One standard clause containing such an express statement is ¶ (d) of the Inspection of Construction clause in FAR 52.246-12. For cases denying relief based on this provision, see *DeKonty Corp.*, ASBCA 32140, 89-2 BCA ¶ 21,586; *Commercial Contractors, Inc.*, ASBCA 30675, 88-3 BCA ¶ 20,877; and *Allen's of Fla., Inc.*, ASBCA 14656, 71-1 BCA ¶ 8646. For a rare case where the government was held liable in the face of this clause, see *Townsco Contracting Co.*, ASBCA 13742, 71-2 BCA ¶ 8962, where a government inspector gave the contractor faulty direction.

Similar contract language has been used to deny relief to contractors. See, for example, *Winter v. Cath-dr/Balti Joint Venture*, 497 F.3d 1339 (Fed. Cir. 2007), where the contract contained a clause stating that "In no event shall any understanding or agreement between the Contractor and any Government employee other than the Contracting Officer on any contract, modification, change order, letter or verbal direction to the Contractor be effective or binding upon the Government."; and *Woodcraft Corp. v. United States*, 146 Ct. Cl. 101, 173 F. Supp. 613 (1959), where the contract contained a clause advising the contractor that "[t]he Inspector has no authority to advise or direct a contractor to use a particular method of production." See also *S & M Mgmt., Inc. v. United States*, 82 Fed. Cl. 2 (2008) (contract clause stated limits of authority); *Jerry DoDds*, ASBCA 51682, 02-1 BCA ¶ 31,844 (two agency clauses warned the contractor that only the contracting officer had authority to change the contract); *Gavosto Assocs., Inc.*, PS-BCA 4058, 01-1 BCA ¶ 31,389 (agency clause and a warning at the pre-construction meeting informed the contractor of limitations on authority); *King Fisher Co. v. United States*, 51 Fed. Cl. 94 (2001) (agency clause required contracting officer approval of changes); *Twigg Corp. v. General Servs. Admin.*, GSBCA 14064, 98-1 BCA ¶ 29,452 (clause warned contractor that only contracting officer could order extra work); *Crow & Sutton Assocs.*, ASBCA 44392, 93-1 BCA ¶ 25,503 (two agency clauses warned that inspectors had no authority to order changes); and *Inez Kaiser & Assocs.*, ASBCA 22212, 88-2 BCA ¶ 20,732 (contract stated that only the contracting officer could order changes).

Letters limiting the authority of representatives generally have the same result. See *Franchi Realty Trust v. General Servs. Admin.*, GSBCA 11149, 92-3 BCA ¶ 25,180; and *F.H. Antrim Constr. Co.*, IBCA 882-12-70, 71-2 BCA ¶ 8983. Notice on the minutes of project meetings of technical personnel stating that only "no-cost" changes could be approved by such personnel precluded recovery, *Metric Constructors, Inc.*, ASBCA 49374, 96-2 BCA ¶ 28,418, and the contractor's acknowledgment that it had been told that an inspector had no authority also precluded recovery, *AAA Eng'g & Drafting, Inc.*, ASBCA 44605, 96-1 BCA ¶ 28,182.

## 3. Dealing with Personnel Lacking Full Contractual Authority

As previously indicated, the vast majority of government personnel with whom a contractor deals do not possess full contractual authority; this does not mean, however, that dealings with such unauthorized personnel are without legal significance. This section considers several of the theories used to bind the government when the contractor has dealt with personnel possessing less than full authority to bind the government. The first of these theories is implied authority, where no authority has been specifically granted; the second is contracting officer ratification of the unauthorized act or statement; and the third is imputation of knowledge of unauthorized representatives to contracting officers.

### a.  Implied Authority

While "apparent authority" will not be sufficient to bind the government, the courts and boards have frequently granted contractors relief on the basis of "implied authority." The implied authority cases primarily involve determining what delegations would mean under a "reasonable person" standard. Thus, precise written delegations leave little room for implication of authority, while broad general delegations provide a greater opportunity for finding implied authority, *DOT Sys., Inc.*, DOT-CAB 1208, 82-2 BCA ¶ 15,817. Most of the cases finding implied authority have involved delegations by contracting officers to project managers, engineers, inspectors, and other personnel involved in contract administration. Although the principle of implied authority is not necessarily inapplicable to designated contracting officers, the nature of the Certificate of Appointment and pertinent regulations leave relatively little room for its application, *Strick Corp.*, ASBCA 15921, 73-2 BCA ¶ 10,077.

The Court of Federal Claims explained the concept of implied authority in *Aero-Abre, Inc. v. United States*, 39 Fed. Cl. 654 (1997), as follows at 657:

> In order to find implied actual authority, a court must conclude that the government intended to grant such authority but failed to do so explicitly due to some oversight or that such authority inheres in a particular position. See, e.g., *Cruz-Pagan v. United States*, 35 Fed. Cl. 59, 62-63 (1996) ("the doctrine of implied actual authority ... serves to fill in the gap when an agency reasonably must have intended cer-

tain representatives to possess contracting authority but failed expressly to grant that authority"). Actual authority to bind the government has not been implied when a regulation, a contract, or a letter to the contractor expressly states that the employee does not have actual authority. See *Cruz-Pagan*, 35 Fed. Cl. at 62-63; *Construction Equip. Lease Co. v. United States*, 26 Cl. Ct. 341, 346-47 (1992); *Essen Mall Properties v. United States*, 21 Cl. Ct. 430, 444-45 (1990).

To find implied authority, there must have been some authority delegated. See *California Sand & Gravel, Inc. v. United States*, 22 Cl. Ct. 19 (1990), *aff'd*, 937 F.2d 624 (Fed. Cir. 1991), where the Claims Court stated at 27:

[A] person with some limited actual authority impliedly may have broader authority. However, a person with no actual authority may not gain actual authority through the court-made rule of implied actual authority. Specifically, the court may not substitute itself unconditionally for the executive in granting authority to an unauthorized person. The most the court can do is interpret the limited authority of an authorized person in a broader manner than ordinarily would be the case.

## (1) EMERGENCY SITUATIONS

The courts and boards have found that government employees with no authority to act in the contracting process have authority to bind the government in an emergency situation, *Philadelphia Suburban Corp. v. United States*, 217 Ct. Cl. 705 (1978) (firefighting foam to put out ship fire); *Halvorson v. United States*, 126 F. Supp. 898 (E.D. Wash. 1954) (equipment to deal with blizzard); *Sigma Constr. Co.*, ASBCA 37040, 91-2 BCA ¶ 23,926 (small alterations to ensure that concrete cured properly). However, this means of overcoming the lack of authority has been construed narrowly. See *City of El Centro v. United States*, 922 F.2d 816 (Fed. Cir. 1990), *cert. denied*, 501 U.S. 1230 (1991), where the court found no emergency when border patrol agents had agreed to pay for hospital services for illegal aliens injured in a high-speed chase, and *Gardiner v. Virgin Islands Water & Power Authority*, 145 F.3d 635 (3d Cir. 1998), where the court refused to find an emergency where the contractor had provided services for ten weeks following the occurrence of a hurricane.

## (2) INTEGRAL PART OF DUTY THEORY

Authority to bind the government is generally implied when such authority is considered to be an integral part of the duties assigned to a government employee, *H. Landau & Co. v. United States*, 886 F.2d 322 (Fed. Cir. 1989). See *Stevens Van Lines, Inc. v. United States*, 80 Fed. Cl. 276 (2008), finding that upper level officials in the agency had the authority to guarantee that the government would reimburse the contractor for fees that were not included in the contract price. See also *First Fed. Lincoln Bank v. United States*, 54 Fed. Cl. 446 (2002), and *Commercial Fed. Corp. v. United States*, 55 Fed. Cl. 595 (2003), holding that making contractual agreements was an integral part of promoting the acquisition of failing thrift organizations. In *Cruz-Pagan v. United States*, 35 Fed. Cl. 59 (1996), the court framed the test as whether there was a "reasonably efficient alternative" to achieve the agency's objective. In holding that field agents of the Drug Enforcement Administration (DEA) had no implied authority to contract with informants, the court stated at 61:

> DEA could efficiently create . . . an expectation of compensation [by informants] without granting contracting authority to its field agents. For example, DEA could adopt internal procedures that grant contracting authority to supervisors of the field agents and oblige the field agents to secure approval from their supervisors before agreeing to provide compensation for assistance. Alternatively, DEA could establish procedures by which DEA would evaluate the value of the information or service provided, and based on that evaluation grant compensation to informants on a fair and reasonable basis.

See also *Strickland v. United States*, 382 F. Supp. 2d 1334 (M.D. Fla. 2005), finding that agreeing that extra work was necessary on a ship repainting contract was not an integral part of the duties of port engineers; *Cornejo-Ortega v. United States*, 61 Fed. Cl. 371 (2004), finding that promising rewards to informants was not an integral part of the duties of field agents of the FBI; and *MTD Transcribing Serv.*, ASBCA 53104, 01-1 BCA ¶ 31,304, finding that arranging for transcription of a hearing was not an integral part of the job of an equal employment opportunity specialist. Compare *Leonardo v. United States*, 63 Fed. Cl. 552 (2005), *aff'd*, 163 Fed. Appx. 180 (Fed. Cir. 2006), where the court found that a Cultural Affairs Officer whose job was to "plan, coordinate and carry out cultural programs in support of public diplomacy objectives identified in the Country Plan" had implied authority (but that she did not ratify the arrangement of a lower-level employee). The court stated at 560:

> In contrast to the DEA field agents in Cruz-Pagan, who reported to field supervisors . . . Ms. Ignatius oversaw all programs and activities at the ACC and "reported directly to the Country Public Affairs Officer." The court sees no "reasonably efficient alternative," *Cruz-Pagan*, 35 Fed. Cl. at 61, to vesting Ms. Ignatius with authority to enter into contracts with artists that enables her effectively and efficiently to discharge her duties and fulfill the ACC's cultural mission. Nor has defendant presented any such alternatives. The court agrees with plaintiff that Ms. Ignatius' ability to enter into contracts was integral to the successful "planning, coordinating and carrying out [the United States Information Agency's] cultural programs," and to "managing the activities of the Cultural Center" efficiently.

### (3) IMPLIED DELEGATION

The most recent decision of the Federal Circuit, *Winter v. Cath-dr/Balti Joint Venture*, 497 F.3d 1339 (Fed. Cir. 2007), holds that there can be no implied delegation of authority within the Department of Defense because it is prohibited by DFARS 201.602-2. However, there have been a number of cases finding that there has been an implied delegation of authority. See, for example, *Jordan & Nobles Constr. Co.*, GSBCA 8349, 91-1 BCA ¶ 23,659 (on-site representative had authority to determine whether supplies met contract requirements and to direct the work under the contract). Similarly, inspectors with authority to accept or reject the work have been held to bind the government when they: misinterpreted the specifications, *Dan Rice Constr. Co.*, ASBCA 52160, 04-1 BCA ¶ 32,595; insisted on performance beyond the specification requirements, *A & D Fire Protection, Inc.*, ASBCA 53103, 02-2 BCA ¶ 32,053; improperly rejected the work, *Donohoe Constr. Co.*, ASBCA 47310, 98-2 BCA ¶ 30,076 and *Gonzales Custom Painting, Inc.*, ASBCA 39527, 90-3 BCA ¶ 22,950; ordered minor adjustment to the work, *Construction Foresite, Inc.*, ASBCA 42350, 93-1 BCA ¶ 25,515; ordered extra work in the course of contract administration, *Gricoski Detective Agency*, GSBCA 8901, 90-3 BCA ¶ 23,131; or prescribed additional testing procedures, *Switlik Parachute Co.*, ASBCA 17920, 74-2 BCA ¶ 10,970. See also *CEMS, Inc. v. United States*, 59 Fed. Cl. 168 (2003) (project engineer/on-site representative has implied authority because he was given broad discretion by contracting officer); *Kumin Assocs., Inc.*, LBCA 94-BCA-3, 98-2 BCA ¶ 30,007 (authorized representative and project manager had implied authority to change work because contracting officer relied on them); *Urban Pathfinders, Inc.*, ASBCA 23134, 79-1 BCA ¶ 13,709 (project officer with authority to certify vouchers, receive progress reports, perform inspections, and accept work, held to have the implied authority to issue a change order where immediate action was required); *Tasker Indus., Inc.*, DOTCAB 71-22, 75-2 BCA ¶ 11,372 (authority to issue engineering interpretations or to reject end product, erroneously exercised, amounted to constructive change even though contractor was on notice that representative was not authorized to "order" any changes); *WRB Corp. v. United States*, 183 Ct. Cl. 409 (1968) (authority to inspect, reject, and require replacement implied authority to "order" constructive change); and *Cameo Curtains, Inc.*, ASBCA 3574, 58-2 BCA ¶ 2051 (inspector authorized to reject work had implied authority to change work through improper rejection). There is a question as to whether this line of reasoning will be followed in the future in view of the decision in *Winter v. Cath-dr/Balti*.

It has been held that a contractor is not obligated to appeal to the contracting officer if a representative with such implied authority erroneously construes the contract, *WRB Corp. v. United States*, 183 Ct. Cl. 409 (1968). However, prudent contract administration demands that contractors bring to the attention of the contracting officer any interpretation or instruction issued by an official who lacks formal contracting authority, rather than rely on the implied authority doctrine, and there are numerous decisions finding no implied authority where the contractor knew authority was lacking. See *Singer Co. v. United States*, 215 Ct. Cl. 281, 568 F.2d 695 (1977), denying a constructive-change claim based upon interpretations issued by a technical coordinating group where the contractor was aware that the group lacked formal contracting officer authority but failed to bring the interpretations to the attention of the contracting officer. See also *Thai Hai*, ASBCA 53375, 02-2 BCA ¶ 31,971, *aff'd*, 82 Fed. Appx. 226 (Fed. Cir. 2003) (real estate officer told contractor he had no contracting officer authority); *Eurovan Movers, S.A.*, ASBCA 53302, 02-1 BCA ¶ 31,843 (no proof that any government personnel with whom contractor dealt had contracting officer authority); *Northrop Grumman Corp. v. United States*, 47 Fed. Cl. 20 (2000) ("field marines" had no authority to constructively change contract); *John C. Grimberg Co.*, ASBCA 51693, 99-2 BCA ¶ 30,572 (trial counsel had no authority to settle claim); *Safeco Credit & Fraley Assocs., Inc. v. United States*, 44 Fed. Cl. 96 (1999) (Assistant Resident Officer in Charge of Construction had no authority to bind the government); *Contel of California, Inc. v. United States*, 37 Fed. Cl. 68 (1996) (technical personnel had no authority to approve extra work); *AAA Eng'g & Drafting, Inc.*, ASBCA 44605, 96-1 BCA ¶ 28,182 (inspector had no authority to order change); *P.J. Dick Inc. v. General Servs. Admin.*, GSBCA 12033, 95-2 BCA ¶ 27,739 (resident engineer had no authority to approve overtime work); *J.S. Alberici Constr. Co.*, GSBCA 10977, 91-3 BCA ¶ 24,204 (architect had no authority to order corrections of defective work); *RMTC Sys.*, AGBCA 88-198-1, 91-2 BCA ¶ 23,873 (shipment before purchase order in response to an unauthorized request did not form a contract); *United Food Servs., Inc. v. United States*, 19 Cl. Ct. 539 (1990), *aff'd*, 928 F.2d 411 (Fed. Cir. 1991) (mess sergeant had no authority to order extra work); *J.S. Alberici Constr. Co.*, GSBCA 10977, 91-3 BCA ¶ 24,204 (architect had no authority to order corrections of defective work); *RMTC Sys.*, AGBCA 88-198-1, 91-2 BCA ¶ 23,873 (shipment before purchase order in response to an unauthorized request did not form a contract). Such action is particularly necessary when the contract contains a clause informing the contractor of the limited authority of government personnel, *Brand S Roofing*, ASBCA 24688, 82-1 BCA ¶ 15,513 (Designation of Technical Representative clause); *W.W. Wilkinson, Inc.*, ASBCA 23031, 80-2 BCA ¶ 14,749 (Government Inspectors clause).

### b. Ratification

Ratification is the adoption of an unauthorized act resulting in the act being given effect as if originally authorized, *Restatement, Second, Agency* § 82. In government contracting, representatives' unauthorized actions may subsequently be ratified by those with authority to bind the government. If the ratifying government official has actual or constructive knowledge of a representative's unauthorized act and expressly or impliedly adopts the act, ratification will be found, *Williams v. United States*, 130 Ct. Cl. 435, 127 F. Supp. 617, *cert. denied*, 349 U.S. 938 (1955). See also *Moran Bros. Co. v. United States*, 39 Ct. Cl. 486 (1904) ("[I]f upon a full knowledge of the facts, the superior officer ratifies and confirms the action of his subordinate, is not that in law equivalent to an express authority in the subordinate at the time he ordered the performance of the labor?").

### (1) AUTHORITY TO RATIFY

In general, the authority to ratify has been considered to be an integral part of an agent's authority without the need for specific statutory or regulatory coverage. For many years, the procurement regulations contained no specific ratification provisions. However, the government was held bound on the basis of ratifications without reference to regulatory authorities, *Michael Guth*, ASBCA 22663, 80-2 BCA ¶ 14,572; *Norwood Precision Prods.*, ASBCA 24083, 80-1 BCA ¶ 14,405.

In the 1970s and 1980s, agency regulations began to provide for ratification of unauthorized acts and to specify how such ratifications should be handled. Finally, in 1988, the following governmentwide guidance was added to FAR 1.602-3:

(b) *Policy.* (1) Agencies should take positive action to preclude, to the maximum extent possible, the need for ratification actions. Although procedures are provided in this section for use in those cases where the ratification of an unauthorized commitment is necessary, these procedures may not be used in a manner that encourages such commitments being made by Government personnel.

(2) Subject to the limitations in paragraph (c) of this subsection, the head of the contracting activity, unless a higher level official is designated by the agency, may ratify an unauthorized commitment.

(3) The ratification authority in subparagraph (b)(2) of this subsection may be delegated in accordance with agency procedures, but in no case shall the authority be delegated below the level of chief of the contracting office.

(4) Agencies should process unauthorized commitments using the ratification authority of this subsection instead of referring such actions to the General Accounting Office for resolution. (See 1.602-3(d).)

(5) Unauthorized commitments that would involve claims subject to resolution under the Contract Disputes Act of 1978 should be processed in accordance with Subpart 33.2, Disputes and Appeals.

(c) *Limitations.* The authority in subparagraph (b)(2) of this subsection may be exercised only when —

(1) Supplies or services have been provided to and accepted by the Government, or the Government otherwise has obtained or will obtain a benefit resulting from performance of the unauthorized commitment;

(2) The ratifying official has the authority to enter into a contractual commitment;

(3) The resulting contract would otherwise have been proper if made by an appropriate contracting officer;

(4) The contracting officer reviewing the unauthorized commitment determines the price to be fair and reasonable;

(5) The contracting officer recommends payment and legal counsel concurs in the recommendation, unless agency procedures expressly do not require such concurrence;

(6) Funds are available and were available at the time the unauthorized commitment was made; and

(7) The ratification is in accordance with any other limitations prescribed under agency procedures.

While these procedures are quite explicit, they have not prevented a finding of express ratification, *Tri-West Contractors, Inc.*, AGBCA 95-200-1, 97-1 BCA ¶ 28,662, or implied ratification, *Reliable Disposal Co.*, ASBCA 40100, 91-2 BCA ¶ 23,895. In the latter case, three contracting officers supported a request to pay the contractor for extra work but did not follow the FAR procedures. The board found that the failure to follow the FAR was not a bar to a finding of implied ratification. See also *Kumin Assocs., Inc.*, LBCA 94-BCA-3, 98-2 BCA ¶ 30,007, where the contracting officer's review of changed drawings was found to show implied ratification, and *Tripod, Inc.*, ASBCA 21305, 89-1 BCA ¶ 21,305, where the contracting officer's knowledge of the contractor's complaints and review of inspection reports evidenced implied ratification. For a similar ruling under prior regulations, see *Driftwood of Ala.*, GSBCA 5429, 81-2 BCA ¶ 15,169. Compare *Kearfott Guidance & Navigation Corp.*, ASBCA 49271, 04-2 BCA ¶ 32,757, where the ratification regulation was invoked to deny ratification because the act was not performed by the head of the contracting activity, and *Fish & Wildlife Serv.*, Comp. Gen. Dec. B-208730, 83-1 CPD ¶ 75, where ratification regulations were specifically invoked to support a finding of ratification.

Courts and boards do not possess the authority to ratify; they may only determine whether a ratification has occurred. They have recommended, however, that ratification authority be liberally exercised in cases where an injustice would result if the government did not become bound. See *Globe Indem. Co. v. United States*, 102 Ct. Cl. 21 (1944), *cert. denied*, 324 U.S. 852 (1945), where the court stated at 38:

> The head of the department, or his duly authorized agent, of course, could have ratified these unauthorized acts, and in our opinion should have done so, since the work was necessary and for [the Government's] benefit, but he did not do so, and we are powerless to do it for him.

> From this case two lessons are to be drawn: (1) contracting officers and heads of departments should exercise the great powers conferred on them by these contracts to do equity; they should not feel under obligation to take advantage of technicalities, where to do so would defeat justice; (2) contractors must study their contracts and insist on compliance with their terms; before relying on any promise they should ascertain that it is made by a person having authority to make it.

## (2) AUTHORITY TO PERFORM OR AUTHORIZE ACTS BEING RATIFIED

The ratifying official must have the power to perform or authorize the unauthorized act, 22 Comp Gen. 1083 (B-33769) (1943). Thus, an official lacking the authority to enter into contracts cannot ratify an agreement, *Consortium Venture Corp. v. United States*, 5 Cl. Ct. 47 (1984); *Western Contract Furnishers*, PSBCA 317, 76-2 BCA ¶ 12,216. Similarly, illegal actions cannot be ratified because officials lack the authority to enter into illegal agreements. In *Trio Mach. Works, Inc.*, NASABCA 480-6, 82-1 BCA ¶ 15,465, *recons. denied*, 82-2 BCA ¶ 15,968, an alleged agreement between the contractor and a representative — whereby the contractor, for keeping a modification under a certain dollar amount, was to receive preferred treatment in future contract awards — was illegal and beyond the contracting officer's ratification authority. Similarly, where an agency purchased spark plugs on a sole source basis in violation of statutes requiring formal advertising, the Assistant Secretary of War could not subsequently ratify the transaction by classifying the spark plugs as an experimental item subject to negotiated procurement, 15 Comp. Gen. 618 (A-66806) (1936).

Proper authority to ratify was found in *Telenor Satellite Servs. v. United States*, 71 Fed. Cl. 114 (2006) (Deputy Assistant Secretary of State could ratify bailment contract); *Romac, Inc.*, ASBCA 41150, 91-2 BCA ¶ 23,918 (officer in charge of construction could order additional work); *Fish & Wildlife Serv.*, Comp. Gen. Dec. B-208730, 83-1 CPD ¶ 75 (acting director of Fish and Wildlife Service had authority to issue a split procurement); *Mil-Pak Co.*, GSBCA 5849, 83-1 BCA ¶ 16,482 (contracting officer had authority to issue a change order); and *W. Southard Jones, Inc.*, ASBCA 6321, 61-2 BCA ¶ 3182 (contracting officer had authority to alter contract). Compare *Kearfott Guidance & Navigation Corp.*, ASBCA 49271, 04-2 BCA ¶ 32,757, holding that an ACO had no authority to ratify because he was not the head of the contracting activity as required by the FAR. In contrast, in *B.V. Constr., Inc.*, ASBCA 47766, 04-1 BCA ¶ 32,604, the board found that a contracting officer had ratified actions allowing the contractor to perform work to correct defective specifications because a contract specialist who was required to report to the contracting officer had know of the action and accepted the benefits. The decision does not discuss the FAR requirement that ratification be given by the head of the contracting activity.

Under these rules, ratification normally requires action or inaction by a specific individual having the requisite authority to ratify the previously unauthorized act. However, some cases have found ratification without identifying such a specific individual (known as "institutional ratification"). In *Silverman v. United States*, 230 Ct. Cl. 701, 679 F.2d 865 (1982), the court found that the agency ratified the agreement by accepting the benefits flowing from the unauthorized official's promise. See also *Rapp v. United States*, 2 Cl. Ct. 694 (1983), where the court found ratification where a government auctioneer's authority to extend the winning bidder's period of payment was in dispute: "[I]f any question remains as to the auctioneer's authority, it is rendered moot by the Customs Service's ratification of the announcement." Compare *City of El Centro v. United States*, 922 F.2d 816 (Fed. Cir. 1990), *cert. denied*, 501 U.S. 1230 (1991), where the Federal Circuit reversed a finding of institutional ratification by the Claims Court (16 Cl. Ct. 500 (1989)). See also *Choe-*

*Kelly, Inc.*, ASBCA 43481, 94-1 BCA ¶ 26,431, refusing to apply the institutional ratification logic. See, however, *Janowsky v. United States*, 133 F.3d 888 (Fed. Cir. 1998), remanding a case to the Court of Federal Claims to determine if institutional ratification occurred. See also *Hawkins & Powers Aviation, Inc. v. United States*, 46 Fed. Cl. 238 (2000) (denying institutional ratification claim because government received no benefit); *Dolmatch Group, Ltd. v. United States*, 40 Fed. Cl. 431 (1998) (denying motion for summary judgment because plaintiff might be able to prove institutional ratification).

In *Catel, Inc.*, ASBCA 54627, 05-1 BCA ¶ 32,966, the board found at 163,299 that *Janowsky* stood for the proposition that —

> Institutional ratification may occur giving rise to a contract where a government agency accepts benefits followed by a promise of payment by the agency or approval of payment by a senior agency official with authority to obtain reimbursement for the one providing those benefits.

See also *Digicon Corp. v. United States*, 56 Fed. Cl. 425 (2003), stating that "it is well established that an agency can 'institutionally' ratify the contract, even in the absence of specific ratification by an authorized official" and finding such ratification when the agency accepted the benefits of the contested contract for 16 months. Similarly, in *Healthcare Practice Enhancement Network, Inc.*, VABCA 5864, 01-1 BCA ¶ 31,383, institutional ratification was found in where a committee including the contracting officer knew of an agreement made by the Chief Fiscal Officer of the agency and accepted the benefits of the agreement. Compare *Gary v. United States*, 67 Fed. Cl. 202 (2005), concluding that institutional ratification cannot be found from the acts of "low-ranking Government employees" because that would subject the government to "wholly uncontrollable" expenditures. See also *Doe v. United States*, 58 Fed. Cl. 479 (2003), rejecting institutional ratification because there was no "active acceptance" of the plaintiff's performance.

### (3) KNOWLEDGE OF UNAUTHORIZED ACTS

A prerequisite to ratification is the ratifying official's knowledge, either actual or constructive, of the facts affecting the unauthorized action. In *United States v. Beebe*, 180 U.S. 343 (1901), the Court stated at 354:

> Where an agent has acted without authority and it is claimed that the principal has thereafter ratified his act, such ratification can only be based upon a full knowledge of all the facts upon which the unauthorized action was taken. This is as true in the case of the Government as in that of an individual. Knowledge is necessary in any event. Story on Agency, 9th ed. sec. 239, notes 1 and 2. If there be want of it, though such want arises from the neglect of the principal, no ratification can be based upon any act of his. Knowledge of the facts is the essential element of ratification, and must be shown or such facts proved that its existence is a necessary inference from them.

See *Dureiko v. United States*, 62 Fed. Cl. 340 (2004), finding no ratification when the contracting officer testified that he had no knowledge of the alleged agreement; *California Sand & Gravel, Inc. v. United States*, 22 Cl. Ct. 19 (1990), *aff'd*, 937 F.2d 624 (Fed. Cir. 1991), holding that there could be no ratification without "full knowledge of all facts" pertinent to the unauthorized commitment; *Durocher Dock & Dredge, Inc.*, ENGBCA 5768, 91-3 BCA ¶ 24,145, where ratification was denied because the contracting officer, as the only official with authority to ratify, had no knowledge of the events; and *Tymshare*, PSBCA 206, 76-2 BCA ¶ 12,218, where there was no ratification of an unauthorized representative's agreement because the authorized official neither knew nor should have known of the unauthorized agreement.

The ratifying official may obtain actual knowledge from various sources, *Mick DeWall Constr.*, PSBCA 2580, 91-1 BCA ¶ 23,510 (contracting officer received notice within 10 days that COR had agreed to modification); *Brown Constr. Co.*, ASBCA 22648, 79-1 BCA ¶ 13,745 (contracting officer participated in a preconstruction conference where a representative stated that construction policy required a contract change); *Globe Constr. Co.*, GSBCA 2197, 67-2 BCA ¶ 6478 (contracting officer received notice of prior actions from his representative and through the contractor's formal claim for additional compensation).

A ratifying official may also gain knowledge constructively. Constructive notice was found in *Williams v. United States*, 130 Ct. Cl. 435, 127 F. Supp. 617, *cert. denied*, 349 U.S. 938 (1955), where an unauthorized Air Force officer and the contractor agreed that the contractor could use the Air Force's asphalt plant in return for seal coating the base's roads. The base contracting officer was held to have constructive knowledge of the agreement because the roads were wholly within the base where he was located.

Imputed knowledge from representatives may also serve as constructive knowledge of a ratifying official. See, for example, *W. Southard Jones, Inc.*, ASBCA 6321, 61-2 BCA ¶ 3182, where base technical personnel knew that the contractor's performance did not conform to contract drawings. This knowledge was imputed to the contracting officer, who frequently met with the base engineer and discussed projects at the base. When the relationship between two persons creates a presumption that one would have informed the other of certain events, the boards may impute the knowledge of one to the other, *Leiden Corp.*, ASBCA 26136, 83-2 BCA ¶ 16,612. In *Southwestern Sheet Metal Works, Inc.*, ASBCA 22748, 79-1 BCA ¶ 13,744, *recons. denied*, 79-2 BCA ¶ 13,949, inspectors functioned as the contracting officer's " eyes and ears"; hence, the contracting officer had actual or constructive knowledge of the inspector's directive changing contract terms, where the inspector lacked authority to issue such a change. In *B.V. Constr., Inc.*, ASBCA 47766, 04-1 BCA ¶ 32,604, the knowledge of a contract specialist was imputed to the contracting officer.

## (4) ADOPTION OF UNAUTHORIZED ACTS

The contractor must show that an authorized official has adopted the unauthorized action, either expressly, by conduct, or by silence. In *DBA Sys., Inc.*, NASABCA 481-5, 82-1 BCA ¶ 15,468, ratification did not occur because the contracting officer "consistently and expressly disavowed the purported funding agreement and likewise did nothing which, by implication, could be reasonably interpreted as his concurrence with [his representative's] belief that the overrun should be funded." See also *Prestex Inc. v. United States*, 162 Ct. Cl. 620, 320 F.2d 367 (1963) (upon learning of deviations from specifications, the government repudiated the contract, never having accepted or used the product, so that no ratification of deviations existed).

An express adoption of an unauthorized act clearly establishes ratification, *Fish & Wildlife Serv.*, Comp. Gen. Dec. B-208730, 83-1 CPD ¶ 75 (authorized official signed a document expressing his intent to ratify the unauthorized act); *Globe Constr. Co.*, GSBCA 2197, 67-2 BCA ¶ 6478 (contracting officer stated that his subordinate's prior action had been done "within his authority").

An authorized official's adoption of an unauthorized act may result from conduct, *B.V. Constr., Inc.*, ASBCA 47766, 04-1 BCA ¶ 32,604 (sending a revised statement of work and an unpriced contract modification containing revised drawings); *Boeing Computer Servs.*, ASBCA 42674, 94-3 BCA ¶ 27,114 (acceptance of user manual containing procedure modifying the contract specifications); *T.W. Cole*, PSBCA 3076, 92-3 BCA ¶ 25,091 (acceptance of work with knowledge of order to modify it); *Henry Burge & Alvin White*, PSBCA 2431, 89-3 BCA ¶ 21,910 (acceptance of work with knowledge of modification); *Norwood Precision Prods.*, ASBCA 24083, 80-1 BCA ¶ 14,405 (payment for products accepted after a default termination indicated the official's adoption of the inspector's unauthorized acceptance); *Mil-Pak Co.*, GSBCA 5849, 83-1 BCA ¶ 16,482 (contracting officer ratified a "change order by unilaterally fixing the amount of the equitable adjustment"). But see *Leonardo v. United States*, 63 Fed. Cl. 552 (2005), finding inadequate proof of ratification when the plaintiff testified about relatively vague discussions with a government official with implied authority and the government did not call the official as a witness, and *Metcalf & Assocs.*, GSBCA 3190, 72-2 BCA ¶ 9516, where the board held that a contracting officer's award of compensation to a contractor for certain changes directed by unauthorized representatives did not constitute a ratification but was an attempt at settlement not binding upon the government.

Silence or inaction may also constitute adoption by an authorized official. See *KRW, Inc.*, DOTBCA 2572, 94-1 BCA ¶ 26,435 (contracting officer acquiesced in alteration of work product); *HFS, Inc.*, ASBCA 43748, 92-3 BCA ¶ 25,198 (contracting officer took no action on letter describing the order for extra work); *Gri-*

*coski Detective Agency*, GSBCA 8901, 90-3 BCA ¶ 23,131 (total inaction after letter was sent to contracting officer describing an order to change the method of performance); *Lox Equip. Co.*, ASBCA 8985, 1964 BCA ¶ 4463 (failure of contracting officer "to take effective action to correct the situation" adopted his inspector's directives); *Michael Guth*, ASBCA 22663, 80-2 BCA ¶ 14,572 (contracting officer affirmed by not questioning a manager's interpretation of liability provisions); *Brown Constr. Co.*, ASBCA 22648, 79-1 BCA ¶ 13,745 (contracting officer silent when unauthorized official prohibited the use of contract-designated plywood); and *Triangle Elec. Mfg. Co.*, ASBCA 15995, 74-2 BCA ¶ 10,783 (contracting officer's silence regarding representatives' interpretation "was conduct amounting to consent to the performance of such duties"). Compare *SAE Americon*, PSBCA 3866, 00-1 BCA ¶ 30,867, where no ratification by silence was found where the COR promptly notified the contractor that a construction technique was not required after finding out about the purported direction to use the technique. See also *Harbert/Lummus Agrifuels Projects v. United States*, 142 F.3d 1429 (Fed. Cir. 1998), *cert. denied*, 525 U.S. 1177 (1999), finding no ratification when a contracting officer heard an unauthorized official make an oral promise to the contractor but did not object or warn the contractor. The court reasoned at 1433-34:

> In our case, the trial court merely found that the CO was present when the Deputy Director made the offer and was silent after the offer was made. There was no finding that the CO even heard the statement. This is not sufficient evidence to support a finding of actual knowledge by the CO of the offer. In addition, the facts as found by the trial court do not support imputing to the CO constructive knowledge of the unilateral contract. The mere fact that Harbert/Lummus continued performing its construction activities would not have put the CO on notice of the existence of a new, unilateral contract because Harbert/Lummus had been performing its construction activities before the offer by the Deputy Director in accordance with its construction contract with Agrifuels. In the absence of either actual or constructive knowledge of the unilateral contract, the CO's silence cannot be a ratification of the unilateral contract.

Acquiescence has been premised on the ratifying official's constructive notice coupled with silence. See *Williams v. United States*, 130 Ct. Cl. 435, 127 F. Supp. 617, *cert. denied*, 349 U.S. 938 (1955); *Southwestern Sheet Metal Works, Inc.*, ASBCA 22748, 79-1 BCA ¶ 13,744, *recons. denied*, 79-2 BCA ¶ 13,949; and *W. Southard Jones, Inc.*, ASBCA 6321, 61-2 BCA ¶ 3182.

## (5) Ratification and Quantum Meruit

GAO has often held that ratification by authorized officials is required before it will approve payment to persons conferring a benefit on the government. In discussing recovery under quantum meruit or quantum valebant theories, GAO in *Acme, Inc.*, Comp. Gen. Dec. B-182584, 74-2 CPD ¶ 310, stated:

Before a right to payment under such basis may be recognized it must be shown that the Government has received a benefit, and that the unauthorized goods or services were expressly or impliedly ratified by authorized contracting officials.

See *Checker Van Lines*, Comp. Gen. Dec. B-206542, 82-2 CPD ¶ 219 (obligation of funds beyond a 180-day period was statutorily prohibited; therefore, ratification could not support the requisite implied-in-fact contract for recovery); and Comp. Gen. Dec. B-164087, July 1, 1968, *Unpub.* (no basis for quantum meruit recovery where the authorized contracting officials were not aware of the project director's action and immediate action was taken to curtail such activity when it became known). See also *Equal Employment Opportunity Comm'n*, Comp. Gen. Dec. B-207492, 82-2 CPD ¶ 112 (failure of authorized representatives to curtail contractor's activities constituted adoption); *Mathews Furniture Co.*, Comp. Gen. Dec. B-195123, 79-2 CPD ¶ 131 (acquiescence by an authorized official determined from his negotiations seeking a settlement); *Defense Mapping Agency*, Comp. Gen. Dec. B-183915, 75-2 CPD ¶ 15 (recommendation for payment); and *INTASA, Inc.*, Comp. Gen. Dec. B-180876, 74-1 CPD ¶ 148 (unauthorized notice to proceed affirmed by intention to formalize a contract and recommendation for payment).

Ratification has been found even after the authorized contracting officer refused to adopt the unauthorized act. In *Acme, Inc.*, Comp. Gen. Dec. B-182584, 74-2 CPD ¶ 310, an officer exceeded his authority by soliciting informal quotations. The authorized contracting officer found that the work was necessary, the government benefited, and the contractor performed in good faith at a reasonable price, but the contracting officer refused to ratify the procurement. However, payment was recommended by the director of fiscal management. GAO inferred an implied ratification from the contracting officer's determination that the work performed was in the best interest of the government and from the director's recommendation for payment. Similarly, although authorized contracting officers refused to ratify an unauthorized order for a contractor to conduct training sessions in *Singer Co.*, Comp. Gen. Dec. B-183878, 75-1 CPD ¶ 406, "primarily because the officials had no basis to determine if the price was reasonable," implied ratification was inferred "from the issuance of a contract for a subsequent identical training session" to be conducted by the contractor. See also *Maintenance Serv. & Sales Corp.*, 70 Comp. Gen. 664 (B-242019) (1991), where the contracting officer refused to ratify and took no action, but GAO granted relief under quantum meruit; and *Interagency Agreements*, Comp. Gen. Dec. B-309181, 2007 CPD ¶ 163, where the General Services Administration refused to ratify a lease but GAO stated that relief might be granted under quantum meruit.

## c. Knowledge Imputed to Authorized Personnel

In many cases it is important to determine whether the contracting officer or other authorized representative has knowledge of certain facts. Such knowledge may be important because the contract requires that information be furnished to the authorized person or that notice be given of events such as delays or constructive changes. In other situations, the legal significance of statements or acts of an authorized person depends upon whether the person was in possession of specific knowledge. Almost all instances of imputed knowledge arise in the contract administration process, but the legal principles are equally applicable to contract formation.

The authorized person is held to have knowledge under the common-law concept that a principal is charged with knowledge that an agent has a duty to deliver to the principal, *Restatement, Second, Agency* § 272. In applying this rule to government contracts, the courts and boards have imputed knowledge to contracting officers and other authorized persons when the nature of the relationship between the authorized person and the representative establishes a presumption that the authorized person would be informed. Thus, in *Sociometrics, Inc.*, ASBCA 51620, 00-1 BCA ¶ 30,620, the board imputed knowledge that the contractor was performing work even though an option had not been exercised because the COR was the "eyes and ears" of the contracting officer.

In most cases involving imputed knowledge, the unauthorized representative possesses actual knowledge obtained within the scope of his or her duties. However, two cases have held a contracting officer to have imputed knowledge although only constructive knowledge on the part of the representatives was demonstrated, *Inet Power*, NASABCA 566-23, 68-1 BCA ¶ 7020, and *W. Southard Jones, Inc.*, ASBCA 6321, 61-2 BCA ¶ 3182. Constructive notice to a representative has been expressly rejected in cases involving cost or pricing data. Because of the contractor's affirmative duty to submit such data, knowledge would not be imputed to the government if auditors lack actual knowledge. See *Libby Welding Co.*, ASBCA 15084, 73-1 BCA ¶ 9859 (contractor listed costs twice on bill that auditors overlooked and imputation held improper); and *Sylvania Elec. Prods., Inc.*, ASBCA 13622, 70-2 BCA ¶ 8387, *aff'd*, 202 Ct. Cl. 16, 479 F.2d 1342 (1973) (auditors did not cross-check data and therefore failed to uncover a material cost error, but absent auditors' actual knowledge, the contracting officer was not charged with knowledge).

Knowledge of a wide variety of government officials has been imputed to the contracting officer. Thus, knowledge of technical personnel is frequently imputed, *Glenda R. Whitaker*, PSBCA 3443, 94-2 BCA ¶ 26,643 (knowledge of contractor's protests, having been communicated to those authorized by the contracting officer to administer the contract, may be imputed to the contracting officer); *Walter Straga*, ASBCA 26134, 83-2 BCA ¶ 16,611 (project manager's knowledge that the contractor's interpretation of the drawings differed from his own imputed to contracting officer); *Carl J. Bonidie, Inc.*, ASBCA 25769, 82-2 BCA ¶ 15,818 (Changes clause notice requirement was satisfied by knowledge of base civil engineer, whose recommendations apparently determined the contracting officer's contractual decisions). However, information possessed by a technical representative will not be imputed if the information is not the type that technical representatives would be presumed to convey to a contracting officer. See *Donat Gerg Haustechnik*, ASBCA 41197, 97-2 BCA ¶ 29,272, refusing to impute knowledge of technical person of nonconforming work, and *Franchi Realty Trust v. General Servs. Admin.*, GSBCA 11149, 92-3 BCA ¶ 25,180, not imputing a directive by a Drug Enforcement Administration representative concerning construction work.

Information obtained by inspectors that is pertinent to their duties has also been imputed to the contracting officer. See *Hudson Contracting, Inc.*, ASBCA 41023, 94-1 BCA ¶ 26,466, where the board upheld a government inspector's oral agreement for the furnishing of government property in return for the contractor providing equipment and an operator for unrelated government work. The board found that the government project manager, with authority to provide the government property involved, had imputed knowledge of the agreement "by virtue of [his] supervision of the inspector . . . [and his] extensive day-to-day involvement in the progress of the contract." However, not all relationships between contracting officers and inspectors are sufficiently close to raise the presumption that the contracting officer would be informed of relevant facts. See, for example, *Canadian Commercial Corp.*, ASBCA 17187, 76-2 BCA ¶ 12,145, *recons. denied*, 77-2 BCA ¶ 12,758, where an inspector's knowledge of design defects was not imputed to the contracting officer because "close contact between the resident Canadian inspector and the [government's] contract administration or technical personnel" was not established.

Knowledge of administrative and clerical personnel is far less likely to be imputed to the contracting officer. Compare *KRW, Inc.*, DOTBCA 2572, 94-1 BCA ¶ 26,435, where a contract administrator's knowledge was imputed to the contracting officer because the contractor had been directed to send reports to the contract administrator, with *JGB Enters. v. United States*, 63 Fed. Cl. 319 (2004), where a small business specialist's knowledge of a subcontractor's difficulties in obtaining payment was not imputed to the contracting officer, and *M.J. Newsom*, ASBCA 9799, 1964 BCA ¶ 4444, where an airman's knowledge of the contractor's causes of delay was not imputed because his relationship with the contracting officer was not sufficient to establish a presumption that the information would be reported.

Since auditors are expected to convey information to the contracting officer, information related to the audit function will be imputed. In *Chrysler Corp.*, ASBCA 17259, 75-1 BCA ¶ 11,236, *recons. denied*, 76-1 BCA ¶ 11,665, Army Audit Agency knowledge of the contractor's accrual account and the manner in which it operated was imputed to the contracting officer. Similarly, in *E-Sys., Inc.*, ASBCA 18877, 76-1 BCA ¶ 11,797, where the Defense Contract Audit Agency was aware of the contractor's pooling and allocation of material costs, this information was imputed to the contracting officer. See also *United States v. Hanna Nickel Smelting Co.*, 253 F. Supp. 784 (D. Ore. 1966), *aff'd on other grounds*, 400 F.2d 944 (9th Cir. 1968) (contractor's accounting practices regarding allocation of capital items known by auditors); and *Western Elec. Co.*, ASBCA 21294, 79-1 BCA ¶ 13,550.

See Cibinic, Nagle & Nash, *Administration of Government Contracts*, 4th ed. 2005, for a more complete discussion of imputed knowledge.

## B. Contractor Personnel

In contrast to the special rules pertaining to government representatives, general principles of agency law apply to contractor's representatives. There is considerably less litigation in this area.

### 1. Delegation

Authority may be expressly or impliedly delegated to contractor's representatives. When a corporation is involved, the plenary authority to transact all the ordinary business of the corporation within its charter powers is vested in the board of directors. Express delegation of authority to others is normally contained in resolutions of the board of directors, which are often furnished to the government agencies with whom the corporate contractor does business.

The guidance in the FAR concerning the authority of corporate officials is the provision in FAR 4.102 stating:

(a) Individuals. A contract with an individual shall be signed by that individual. A contract with an individual doing business as a firm shall be signed by that individual, and the signature shall be followed by the individual's typed, stamped, or printed name and the words, "an individual doing business as _____" [insert name of firm].

(b) Partnerships. A contract with a partnership shall be signed in the partnership name. Before signing for the Government, the contracting officer shall obtain a list of all partners and ensure that the individual(s) signing for the partnership have authority to bind the partnership.

(c) Corporations. A contract with a corporation shall be signed in the corporate name, followed by the word "by" and the signature and title of the person authorized to sign. The contracting officer shall ensure that the person signing for the corporation has authority to bind the corporation.

(d) Joint venturers. A contract with joint venturers may involve any combination of individuals, partnerships, or corporations. The contract shall be signed by each participant in the joint venture in the manner prescribed in paragraphs (a) through (c) above for each type of participant. When a corporation is participating, the contracting officer shall verify that the corporation is authorized to participate in the joint venture.

(e) Agents. When an agent is to sign the contract, other than as stated in paragraphs (a) through (d) above, the agent's authorization to bind the principal must be established by evidence satisfactory to the contracting officer.

## 2. *Apparent Authority*

The major difference between the legal rules applicable to government and contractor representatives is that a contractor may be bound by a representative possessing apparent authority. See *American Anchor & Chain Corp. v. United States*, 166 Ct. Cl. 1, 331 F.2d 860 (1964), where the court stated at 4:

> Although the Federal Government still stands on the stricter requirements of actual authority for its own agents (see, e.g., *Federal Crop Ins. Corp. v. Merrill*, 332 U.S. 380 (1947)), the agents of Government contractors are governed by the usual rules.

See also *Kaco Contracting Co.*, ASBCA 44937, 01-2 BCA ¶ 31,584, and *Western Box-O-Matic Corp.*, GSBCA 3562, 73-1 BCA ¶ 9968, where it was held that the government was entitled to rely on the apparent authority of the contractor's plant manager to interpret contract language. Similarly, in *Deep Joint Venture v. General Servs. Admin.*, GSBCA 14511, 02-2 BCA ¶ 31,914, the person that negotiated and signed a lease for a joint venture was held to have apparent authority. In *Menches Tool & Die, Inc.*, ASBCA 21469, 78-1 BCA ¶ 13,167, the board rejected the contractor's arguments that it had never authorized its attorney to make certain statements, stating "[t]he Government has the right to assume an agent has actual or apparent authority to bind its principal."

However, if government employees know or should know that a contractor representative does not have contracting authority, that representative will not be found to have apparent authority. See, for example, *Tectonics Asia Architects & Eng'rs, Inc.*, ASBCA 17067, 75-2 BCA ¶ 11,456, where the board stated at 54,567:

> It is also clear from the record that Mr. a'Becket was not an officer of the corporation and this fact should have been known to AID contracting personnel since he always signed correspondence and invoices as contract administrator, acted in that capacity and did not represent himself as a corporate officer. There is nothing in the record to indicate that AID was ever notified that Mr. a'Becket had contracting authority. His participation in negotiations for Amendment No. 1, together with [the contractors's] vice-president Mr. Anderson, did not clothe him with apparent or implied authority on which AID personnel could have been [relying.] The authorities cited in [the Government's] brief (*American Anchor & Chain Corporation v. United States*, 166 Ct. Cl. 1 (1964) and *Video Engineering Company, Inc.*, DOT CAB No. 72-5, 72-1 BCA ¶ 9432) involve distinctly different factual situations and thus do not support the proposition that Mr. a'Becket had apparent authority to act for the corporation and bind it contractually.

See also *Peter Bauwens Bauunternehmung GmbH & Co. KG*, ASBCA 44679, 98-1 BCA ¶ 29,551 (contractor not bound be agreements of its project manager because government "knew or had reason to know" that he had no contracting authority); *Piracci Corp.*, GSBCA 6007, 82-2 BCA ¶ 16,047 (contractor not bound by a settlement negotiated by attorney when government negotiator had no reason to believe that attorney had authority to settle a claim); *Ray Wilson Co.*, ASBCA 17084, 74-1 BCA ¶ 11,066 (government was not justified in inferring that a second-tier subcontractor's employees had authority to bind the contractor); Comp. Gen. Dec. B-171802, March 2, 1971, *Unpub.* (contractor not bound by the actions of its employees who had no real, implied, or apparent authority); *Colorado Security Agency, Inc.*, GSBCA 5650, 84-1 BCA ¶ 16,940 (contractor not bound because contracting officer knew contractor's employee had no authority); and *Kahaluu Constr. Co.*, ASBCA 33248, 90-2 BCA ¶ 22,663 (proposed settlement agreement approved by an agent of a contractor and an agent of the government, both without authority, was not an offer to settle).

## 3. *Ratification and Estoppel*

Even though the government deals with an unauthorized representative, the contractor will be bound if the action is ratified by an authorized official. In *Tectonics Asia Architects & Eng'rs, Inc.*, ASBCA 17067, 75-2 BCA ¶ 11,456, the contractor was held bound by an unauthorized amendment when it had continued performance for 2½ months with full knowledge of the terms of the amendment.

The principles of estoppel are also similarly applicable to the contractor. In *Ampex Corp.*, GSBCA 5913, 82-1 BCA ¶ 15,738, *recons. denied*, 82-2 BCA ¶ 15,858, the board held that the contractor was estopped to deny an agreement where a contractor's representative had informed the government that the contractor had agreed to accept the agreement. The board found that the representative did not have authority to make the agreement but did have the authority to convey information to the government, stating at 77,861:

> Granted, [the contractor's representative] was not an agent of the company authorized to bind it contractually. We have already indicated that we do not consider that to be the point in dispute. Rather, the issue is whether [the representative] had the authority to tell the Government that [the contractor] had agreed to be bound. If she had that authority, then [the contractor] is bound by her representation:
>
> > Except as to statements with relation to the agent's authority, in actions brought upon a contract or to rescind a contract, a disclosed or partially disclosed principal is responsible for unauthorized representations made incidental to it, if the contract is otherwise authorized and if true representations as to the same subject matter are within the authority or the apparent authority of the agent, unless the other party thereto has notice that the representations are untrue or unauthorized.

Restatement (Second), Agency (1958), § 162.

See also *E. Walters & Co. v. United States*, 217 Ct. Cl. 254, 576 F.2d 362 (1978), where the contractor was estopped from seeking additional compensation for the performance of an allegedly improperly exercised option because it had performed the work without objection, and *Detroit Diesel Allison Div., Gen. Motors Corp.,* ASBCA 20199, 77-1 BCA ¶ 12,414, where the contractor was estopped to deny applicability of longstanding accounting practice. Contractors have also been held to be estopped from denying that they are subject to the standard disputes process after they have participated in that process to a significant extent, *H.R. Henderson & Co. v. United States,* 169 Ct. Cl. 228 (1965); *Norair Eng'g. Corp.,* ENGBCA 5244, 97-1 BCA ¶ 28,917. Compare *CRF v. United States,* 224 Ct. Cl. 312, 624 F.2d 1054 (1980), stating that the contractor was not estopped to deny the validity of a contract awarded in a manner contrary to the regulations. In *E.L. Hamm & Assocs. v. England,* 26 Fed. Appx. 936 (Fed. Cir. 2002), the court held that a contractor was not estopped to assert a claim by a letter offering to perform at no cost because the government had not proved the authority of the person that sent the letter or that the government relied on the letter. Similarly, in *Piracci Corp.,* GSBCA 6007, 82-2 BCA ¶ 16,047, the board that held the contractor was not estopped on the basis, among others, that there was no justifiable reliance by the government.

## IV. GOVERNMENT BOUND BY CONDUCT OF ITS AUTHORIZED AGENTS

Since the government can act only through its agents and employees, it is clear that it will be bound when authorized agents carry out their duties properly. However, government personnel cannot be expected to act only in ways favorable to the United States. Whether resulting from mistakes, negligence, or poor judgment, their statements, acts, or omissions are sometimes contrary to the government's best interests. This may become evident from later reflection or subsequent events, or it may be determined by the agents' advisers, superiors, or successors. In such cases, attempts may be made to avoid the consequences by repudiating or countermanding the agents' acts. There are two major concepts that are invoked to prevent the government from disowning authorized agents' acts or agreements, thereby making them binding on the government. The first concept is finality, the second is estoppel.

### A. Finality

The actions of a government employee acting within the scope of his or her employment are the actions of the government itself, and as with any contracting party, once the government has taken the final step toward committing a contractual act, it is bound by it. Once an authorized representative enters into a contract, not even Congress has the authority to abrogate it, *United States v. Winstar Corp.,* 518 U.S. 839 (1996).

#### 1. Sources of Finality

Finality of contractual acts may attach as a result of either the application of a legal rule or a provision of the contract that is interpreted as providing that finality attaches to a decision or action of a government agent. The clearest example of a legal rule creating finality occurs in the contract formation process where the normal binding effect of the acceptance of an offer is applied to the government. This rule of contract law states that at the time an offer is accepted, a binding contract is formed. See *United States v. Purcell Envelope Co.*, 249 U.S. 313 (1919), where the Court held that the government was bound when the Postmaster General accepted the offer of a company in a formally advertised procurement. Similarly, the government will be bound if an authorized official enters into a contract modification adjusting the price after a change has been ordered, *Liberty Coat Co.*, ASBCA 4119, 57-2 BCA ¶ 1576. See also *Airmotive Eng'g. Corp.*, ASBCA 15235, 71-2 BCA ¶ 8988, where the board held that the government was bound when a contracting officer entered into a contract amendment modifying the price to reflect the adoption of a value engineering proposal.

The most direct example of a contract clause providing for finality is the Disputes clause, which allows contracting officers to make final decisions when a dispute cannot be settled. The government was held bound by such decisions in *Bell Helicopter Co.*, ASBCA 17776, 74-1 BCA ¶ 10,411. Another such clause is the Inspection clause, which states that government acceptance of work will be final, with certain exceptions. In *C.H. McQuagge v. United States*, 197 F. Supp. 460 (W.D. La. 1961), the contracting officer had issued a certificate of final acceptance despite the knowledge of the government that the concrete used in airport taxiways did not measure up to the specifications. The court found the acceptance final and conclusive, stating at 468:

> In a case such as this, the government can only act through those to whom it has delegated authority to make decisions. It was within the discretion of the Contracting Officers to determine whether the work was acceptable to the government, and final acceptance by such officers was subject to being opened or questioned only upon evidence of collusion, fraud, or obvious error.

See also *Shea-Ball (JV)*, ENGBCA 5608, 99-1 BCA ¶ 30,277; *Mil-Spec Contractors, Inc. v. United States*, 835 F.2d 865 (Fed. Cir. 1987); *S.E.R., Jobs for Progress, Inc. v. United States*, 759 F.2d 1 (Fed. Cir. 1985); *Walsky Constr. Co.*, ASBCA 19875, 77-1 BCA ¶ 12,388; *Conrad Weihnacht Constr., Inc.*, ASBCA 20767, 76-2 BCA ¶ 11,963; and *Genuine Motor Parts of Pa., Inc.*, See also SBCA 19063, 76-1 BCA ¶ 11,860.

Finality has also been found when the government acts under contract clauses that do not expressly state that the action is "final." One such clause that has been interpreted as creating finality is the Allowable Cost and Payment clause, FAR 52.216-7. See *Chrysler Corp.*, ASBCA 17259, 75-1 BCA ¶ 11,236, *recons. denied*, 76-1 BCA ¶ 11,665, holding that the predecessor Allowable Cost, Fixed Fee and Payment clause should be interpreted to bar the government from contesting the allowability of costs after final payment on the contract has been made. See also *MPR Assocs., Inc.*, ASBCA 54689, 05-2 BCA ¶ 33,115, holding the government bound to the agreements made in a final overhead rate negotiation even though the parties had not yet signed an "indirect cost rate agreement." In *Bell Aircraft Corp. v. United States*, 120 Ct. Cl. 398, 100 F. Supp. 661 (1951), the court held that approval and payment of invoices under a cost-reimbursement contract was binding on the government at the time the payment was made. The same result was reached in *United States v. Mason & Hanger Co.*, 260 U.S. 323 (1922), and *Leeds & Northrup Co. v. United States*, 101 F. Supp. 999 (E.D. Pa. 1951). Finality was also found when a contracting officer made a decision to fund an overrun under the Limitation of Cost clause, *General Elec. Co. v. United States*, 188 Ct. Cl. 620, 412 F.2d 1215, *mot. for reh'g denied*, 189 Ct. Cl. 116, 416 F.2d 1320 (1969), and where an award fee official determined the award fee under an Award Fee clause, *URS Consultants, Inc.*, IBCA 4285-2000, 02-1 BCA ¶ 31,812. Neither the Allowable Cost, Fixed Fee and Payment clause, the Limitation of Cost clause nor the Award Fee clause contains explicit language stating that decisions or actions of the contracting officer or award fee official will be final, yet the courts and boards have interpreted the clauses to have this effect. Compare *Litton Sys., Inc., Guidance & Control Sys. Div.*, ASBCA 45400, 94-2 BCA ¶ 26,895, holding that an administrative contracting officer's determination that the contractor was not in compliance with Cost Accounting Standards 405 and 410 was not entitled to finality because no contract clause provided that such decisions would be final. See also *JC&N Maint., Inc.*, ASBCA 51283, 02-1 BCA ¶ 31,799, finding no finality in pre-dispute representations of contracting officers which were not labeled final decisions and were part of an evolving course of negotiations between the contractor and the agency.

Finality has been found in a few instances where the act of the government was not communicated to the contractor at the time the act was taken. In *General Elec. Co. v. United States*, 188 Ct. Cl. 620, 412 F.2d 1215, *mot. for reh'g denied*, 189 Ct. Cl. 116, 416 F.2d 1320 (1969), the court found a final decision because the contracting officer had signed an internal memorandum stating that an overrun would be funded, even though this contracting officer's decision was not communicated to the contractor. The same result was reached in *Texas Instruments, Inc. v. United States*, 922 F.2d 810 (Fed. Cir. 1990), where an ACO had signed a price negotiation memorandum (PNM) agreeing to a negotiated settlement of a claim. The court found that this was a final decision, stating at 813-14:

> Under *General Electric*, the law presumes that when an ACO acquainted with the underlying facts signs an internal document, such as the PNM, that she has decided to express a definite opinion on the merits of the claim in the absence of contrary testimony or evidence. Such contrary evidence or testimony is lacking here.

These cases indicate that the government will be bound during contract administration by the doctrine of finality whenever an authorized employee signs a document or takes an action that is properly construed as resolving the issue at hand. See also *Boeing Co. v. United States*, 75 Fed. Cl. 34 (2007), holding that the award fee determination of the contractually designated Award Fee Determination Official was binding on the government even though internal agency procedures called for review of the decision at the Secretarial level (where it was disapproved).

A variety of other actions and determinations by government officials may also be final and binding on the government. For example, a determination by a contracting officer that the contractor's labor cost estimating technique was not defective was final and binding on the government and could not be revoked or overruled by his successor, *Bell Helicopter Co.*, ASBCA 17776, 74-1 BCA ¶ 10,411. In *Southern Waldrip & Harvick Co. v. United States*, 167 Ct. Cl. 488, 334 F.2d 245 (1964), the court held that the chief of engineers could not overrule a finding of the contracting officer that a telegraphic bid modification had been timely received. The instructions to bidders had stated that a determination of timeliness of modifications would rest with the contracting officer. These instructions constituted an agreement between the government and the contractor and left the chief of engineers without authority to determine timeliness independently.

## 2. Authority Required

For the action to be binding and final, the government employee must be acting within his or her authority. See *Trevco Eng'g & Sales*, VACAB 1021, 73-2 BCA ¶ 10,096, where the board found that an inspector had not been delegated the authority to make final acceptance. See also Comp. Gen. Dec. B-170360, Apr. 6, 1971, *Unpub.*, stating that an award by a contracting officer to the second low bidder could be overruled by his superiors, because the contracting officer had no authority to make a valid award to anyone but the low responsible bidder; and 35 Comp. Gen. 63 (B-120714) (1955), stating that no finality attaches to payment contrary to the cost-plus-a-percentage-of-cost prohibition. Acts of unauthorized representatives that are ratified by an authorized official are also accorded finality, *Tucker & Assocs. Contracting, Inc.*, IBCA 1468-6-81, 83-1 BCA ¶ 16,140.

Since no government employee has the authority to violate the law, finality will not attach to a decision that violates public policy. See, for example, *ENCORP Int'l, Inc.*, ASBCA 49474, 99-1 BCA ¶ 30,254, finding an agreement of a contracting officer to release Miller Act payment bonds not entitled to finality because it was in violation of an important public policy. The board stated at 149,608:

> The Miller Act manifests a public policy to protect suppliers of labor and material on Federal construction projects through payment bonds. "Recognizing that sovereign immunity left subcontractors and suppliers without a remedy against the Government when the general contractor became insolvent, Congress enacted the Miller Act (and its predecessor the Heard Act) to protect these workers." *Department of the Army v. Blue Fox, Inc.*, [525 U.S. 255] (1999). See also *Clifford F. MacEvoy Co. v. United States*, 322 U.S. 102, 107 (1944) (Miller Act entitled to a liberal construction and application). The Miller Act requires prime contractors to furnish payment bonds for the protection of suppliers and provides a one year period of limitation for suits to be brought on the bonds. This period can be expected to run past acceptance of the work. Enforcing the Government's promise

in Modification No. P00012 would enable appellant to avoid full compliance with the Miller Act, leaving its suppliers without the protection intended by Congress. We conclude, therefore, that enforcement of the promise would harm the public policy represented by the Miller Act.

## 3.  *Government Bound by Prejudicial Decisions*

The government is bound by the acts of its authorized representatives, even if their decisions are the result of poor judgment that is injurious to the government. In *Liberty Coat Co.*, ASBCA 4119, 57-2 BCA ¶ 1576, the contracting officer issued findings and determinations that certain changes reduced the contractor's costs and adjusted the contract price accordingly. A successor contracting officer issued new determinations and findings on the same changes and greatly increased the reductions in price. In ruling for the contractor that the original contracting officer's decision was binding, the board stated at 5671-72:

> The Government makes no allegation of mutual mistake and, while admitting that it has no other evidence of fraud or collusion, argues that we are required to draw such an inference from the gross disparity between the equitable adjustments agreed to by the original contracting officer and the " correct and equitable adjustment for the deviation[s]" as found by the successor contracting officer. Assuming for the purposes of decision on [the contractor's] motion, the validity of the successor contracting officer's determination of " correct and equitable" price adjustments, in the absence of even a scintilla of other evidence of fraud and collusion, we think the proper inference is that, relying on erroneous advice of his price analysts, the original contracting officer made a bad bargain. We are not aware of any authorities, nor has counsel invited our attention to any, holding that an agreement is vitiated by this fact alone.

> The Government seeks to distinguish these cases from our prior holdings on the ground that in their determination the Board did not consider its present argument that the original contracting officer acted " outside the bounds of his authority" in agreeing to allegedly grossly inadequate price adjustments. Under the terms of the standard " Changes" article of these contracts, and procurement regulations, the contracting officer had clear authority to make changes in the specifications of the contracts. Upon doing so he was specifically charged with the responsibility of determining whether the change caused " an increase or decrease in the cost of . . . this contract . . . ," and, upon such a determination, the clause continues, " an equitable adjustment shall be made in the contract price . . . and the contract shall be modified in writing accordingly." The Government's argument, reduced to its lowest common denominator, is that while the contracting officer had authority to make a good bargain, he had no authority to make a bad one. We are unable to accept such an argument. It confuses the contracting officer's authority to act with the judgment displayed by him in performing the act. It seeks to measure authority by the results obtained upon its exercise. Counsel has not cited, and we have been unable to find, any cases supporting this method of measuring authority.

While it cannot be said that the government "authorizes" its agents to make negligent decisions or to commit torts, it is liable for the agent's action if it is within the scope of his or her authority. See *Cooke v. United States*, 91 U.S. (1 Otto) 389 (1875), where the Court stated at 398:

> Laches is not imputable to the government, in its character as sovereign, by those subject to its dominion. Still a government may suffer loss through the negligence of its officers. If it comes down from its position of sovereignty, and enters the domain of commerce, it submits itself to the same laws that govern individuals there. Thus, if it becomes the holder of a bill of exchange, it must use the same diligence to charge the drawers and indorsers that is required of individuals; and, if it fails in this, its claim upon the parties is lost. Generally, in respect to all the commercial business of the government, if an officer specially charged with the performance of any duty, and authorized to represent the government in that behalf, neglects that duty, and loss ensues, the government must bear the consequences of his neglect. But this cannot happen until the officer specially charged with the duty, if there be one, has acted, or ought to have acted. As the government can only act through its officers, it may select for its work whomsoever it will; but it must have some representative authorized to act in all the emergencies of its commercial transactions. If it fails in this, it fails in the performance of its own duties, and must be charged with the consequences that follow such omissions in the commercial world.

See also *Rockwell Int'l Corp.*, EBCA C-9509187, 97-1 BCA ¶ 28,814 (government bound by provisions of settlement agreement entered into by Department of Justice and accepted by court); *Steward/Tampke, JV*, ASBCA 48929, 96-2 BCA ¶ 28,320 (government bound by settlement agreement to pay Contract Disputes Act interest); *Honeywell Fed. Sys., Inc.*, ASBCA 39974, 92-2 BCA ¶ 24,966 (government bound by contracting officer's determination that cost or pricing data not required because contractor met commercial item exemption); *Sterling Millwrights, Inc. v. United States*, 26 Cl. Ct. 49 (1992) (government bound where contracting officer made progress payments with full knowledge of costs included therein); and *Summit Contractors*, AGBCA 81-252-1, 86-1 BCA ¶ 18,632 (government bound by contract modification favorable to contractor).

It appears that the doctrine of finality will prevent recovery by the government when the government agent makes a unilateral mistake but not when the mistake is mutual. See *Chrysler Corp.*, ASBCA 17259, 75-1 BCA ¶ 11,236, *recons. denied*, 76-1 BCA ¶ 11,665, holding the government bound by incorrect determinations of an allowable cost but commenting that finality would not bar recovery on the theory of mutual mistake. See also *United States v. Hadden*, 192 F.2d 327 (6th Cir. 1951), holding that the government could not recover mistaken payments made to contractor's creditors because there was no "mistake of fact" and the "bankrupt had no knowledge of the mistake." Similarly, in *URS Consultants, Inc.*, IBCA 4285-2000, 02-1 BCA 31,812, *recons. denied*, 02-2 BCA ¶ 31,917, the government was held bound to allegedly mistaken award fee computations made by the award official and contracting officer in a CPAF contract. The board rejected the argument that the mistaken calculations were simple mathematical errors that might have been correctable. Compare *Institutional & Environmental Mgmt., Inc.*, ASBCA 32924, 90-3 BCA ¶ 23,118, holding that the government was not bound when the contracting officer mistakenly agreed to increase the contract price when state unemployment insurance taxes were increased. The board reasoned that this was a pure mistake because the contract placed the risk of higher state taxes on the contractor, stating at 116,073:

> Finality does not apply to this situation where the contracting officer was not exercising discretion or powers granted to her by virtue of the contract and her position. The contracting officer simply misinterpreted the contract to provide reimbursement to appellant of amounts which appellant was obligated by contract to include within its bid.

Of course, the government will not be bound by a bad decision of an employee who lacks authority, *Winn-Senter Constr. Co. v. United States*, 110 Ct. Cl. 34, 75 F. Supp. 255 (1948) (absent special circumstances, government agent has no authority to order contractor to increase wages and agree to government reimbursement).

## B. Equitable Estoppel

Equitable estoppel is a concept that prohibits a party from escaping liability for statements, actions, or inactions if they have been relied on by the other party. It has traditionally been thought that two prerequisites exist for estopping the government: (1) the government's representative must have been acting within the scope of his or her authority, and (2) the government must be acting in its proprietary capacity rather than its sovereign capacity, *United States v. Georgia-Pacific Co.*, 421 F.2d 92 (9th Cir. 1970). The Supreme Court has altered the focus of the first prerequisite to the requirement that the act of the government must be one that is not barred by statute or published regulation, *OPM v. Richmond*, 496 U.S. 414, *reh'g denied*, 497 U.S. 1046 (1990). Once these threshold requirements are met, the normal common-law rules of estoppel apply. Thus, the government can be estopped based on its actions in the contracting process. See *Burnside-Ott Aviation Training Ctr., Inc. v. United States*, 985 F.2d 1574 (Fed. Cir. 1993), stating at 1581:

> The Claims Court improperly relied on *Richmond* to conclude that Burnside-Ott's equitable estoppel claim is barred as a matter of law. In particular, the Claims Court erred in concluding that *Richmond* stands for the proposition that equitable estoppel will not lie against the government for any monetary claim. The *Richmond* holding is not so broad. *Richmond* is limited to "claim(s) for the payment of money from the Public Treasury *contrary to a statutory appropriation*." 496 U.S. at 424 (emphasis added). Indeed, because the Supreme Court's analysis in *Richmond* is based entirely on the Appropriations Clause of the Constitution, Article 1, Section 9, Clause 7, which provides that "No Money shall be drawn from the

Treasury, but in Consequence of Appropriations made by Law," its holding must be limited to claims of entitlement contrary to statutory appropriations.

*Burnside-Ott's* assertion of a right to payment of money from the Public Treasury, however, is not based upon a statutory entitlement. Burnside-Ott's assertion is instead based upon its contract with the Navy. Nor does Burnside-Ott claim entitlement contrary to statutory eligibility criteria, as did Richmond. Thus, neither the holding nor analysis in *Richmond* is applicable in this case, and Burnside-Ott's equitable estoppel claim is not barred as a matter of law because of *Richmond.* Equitable estoppel may or may not apply in this case depending on facts yet to be established.

In *Emeco Indus. v. United States*, 202 Ct. Cl. 1006, 485 F.2d 652 (1973), the court specified that four elements were required before estoppel could be invoked, listing them at 1015:

(1) The party to be estopped must know the facts; (2) he must intend that his conduct shall be acted on or must so act that the party asserting the estoppel has a right to believe it is so intended; (3) the latter must be ignorant of the true facts; and (4) he must rely on the former's conduct to his injury.

Additionally, the contractor must show affirmative misconduct by the government. See *Zacharin v. United States*, 213 F.3d 1366 (Fed. Cir. 2000), stating at 1371:

Although the Supreme Court has not adopted a per se rule prohibiting the application of equitable estoppel against the government under any circumstances, it has made it clear that "the government may not be estopped on the same terms as any other litigant." *Heckler v. Community Health Servs.*, 467 U.S. 51, 60, 81 L. Ed. 2d 42, 104 S. Ct. 2218 (1984). In particular, the Court has suggested that if equitable estoppel is available at all against the government some form of affirmative misconduct must be shown in addition to the traditional requirements of estoppel. See *Richmond*, 496 U.S. at 421; *INS v. Miranda*, 459 U.S. 14, 19, 74 L. Ed. 2d 12, 103 S. Ct. 281 (1982); *Schweiker v. Hansen*, 450 U.S. 785, 788, 67 L. Ed. 2d 685, 101 S. Ct. 1468 (1981). While the Supreme Court has not squarely held that affirmative misconduct is a prerequisite for invoking equitable estoppel against the government, this court has done so, see *Henry v. United States*, 870 F.2d 634, 637 (Fed. Cir. 1989); *Hanson v. Office of Personnel Management*, 833 F.2d 1568, 1569 (Fed. Cir. 1987), as has every other court of appeals, see *Tefel v. Reno*, 180 F.3d 1286, 1303 (11th Cir. 1999) (citing cases).

For other cases stating that affirmative misconduct must be proved to estop the government, see *Bernard Cap Co.*, ASBCA 56679, 10-1 BCA ¶ 34,387 (claim of equitable tolling of statute of limitations rejected for lack of proof of affirmative misconduct); *Data Computer Corp. of American v. United States*, 80 Fed. Cl. 606 (2008); *Alliant Techsystems, Inc. v. United States*, 74 Fed. Cl. 577 (2007) (no affirmative misconduct when contracting officers led contractor to believe that they were agreeing to final overhead rates); (no affirmative misconduct estopping government from asserting that settlement agreement included claimed costs); *Kaeper Mach.*,

*Inc. v. United States*, 74 Fed. Cl. 1 (2006) (no affirmative misconduct when government allowed purchase order to lapse when contractor failed to deliver units); *Ervin
& Assocs. v. United States*, 59 Fed. Cl. 267 (2004), *aff'd*, 120 Fed. Appx. 353 (Fed.
Cir. 2005) (no affirmative misconduct found when agency gave contractor's data to
competitors); *United Pacific Ins. Co.*, ASBCA 52419, 04-1 BCA ¶ 32,494, *aff'd*,
401 F.3d 1362 (Fed. Cir. 2005) (no affirmative misconduct when parties miscalculated contract balance at time of entering into takeover agreement and contracting
officer did not inform surety when mistake was found); *Demarco Durzo Dev. Co. v.
United States*, 60 Fed. Cl. 632 (2004) (no affirmative misconduct when contracting
officer misstated date when lease would be terminated); and *Melrose Assocs., L.P.
v. United States*, 45 Fed. Cl. 56 (1999) (no affirmative misconduct when government employee that executed two amendments failed to confirm her authority in
advance, was ignorant as to the limitations on her authority and did not notify the
contractor when she was made aware of the possible limitations on her authority).
See also *Westinghouse Elec. Corp. v. United States*, 41 Fed. Cl. 229 (1998), discussing the need for affirmative misconduct but rejecting an estoppel argument on other
grounds. In *Rumsfeld v. United Techs. Corp.*, 315 F.3d 1361 (Fed. Cir.), *cert. denied*,
540 U.S. 1012 (2003), the court remanded the case for trial on the estoppel issue, but
the board denied the claim for lack of affirmative misconduct, *United Techs. Corp.*,
ASBCA 47416, 06-1 BCA ¶ 33,289. The board decision contains a thorough discussion of the application of the affirmative misconduct requirement.

Prior to the Federal Circuit's ruling that affirmative misconduct was an essential
element of an estoppel claim, when the official was acting within the scope of delegated authority and the actions were not prohibited by statute or regulation, estoppel
would be found even though the action was based upon *a mistaken interpretation* of
the government's obligations, *USA Petroleum Corp. v. United States*, 821 F.2d 622
(Fed. Cir. 1987); *Portmann v. United States*, 674 F.2d 1155 (7th Cir. 1982); *Broad
Ave. Laundry & Tailoring v. United States*, 231 Ct. Cl. 1, 681 F.2d 746 (1982). Note,
however, that *Broad Avenue Laundry* was questionable precedent since the contracting
officer's statement was contrary to a published regulation. In *Kozak Micro Sys., Inc.*,
GSBCA 10519, 91-1 BCA ¶ 23,342, *recons. denied*, 91-1 BCA ¶ 23,593, the board
stated that where government representatives acting within their scope of authority
make statements to contractors that result in factual interpretations not consistent with
the contract or its provisions, and the recipients of these statements can prove the elements of estoppel, the government cannot act contrary to its representations.

The courts and boards were reluctant to estop the government from recovering overpayments even before the affirmative misconduct element was added.
See *JANA, Inc. v. United States*, 936 F.2d 1265 (Fed. Cir. 1991), *cert. denied*, 502
U.S. 1030 (1992), finding no estoppel because the contract contained a right to
audit the payments that had been erroneously made. Similarly, in *General Eng'g
& Mach. Works v. O'Keefe*, 991 F.2d 775 (Fed. Cir. 1993), the court held that
the government was not estopped to recover overpaid material handling charges
because the government personnel did not understand the contractor's account-

ing system, and in *Dawkins General Contractors & Supply, Inc.*, ASBCA 48535, 03-2 BCA ¶ 32,305, the board found no estoppel because the there was no evidence that government personnel knowingly overpaid the contractor on a time and materials contract. Compare *Bank of America Nat'l Trust & Sav. Ass'n v. United States*, 23 F.3d 380 (Fed. Cir. 1994), holding that the government could not recover an "overpayment" when it freely entered into a settlement agreement knowing all of the facts.

Because estoppel accomplishes the same result as finality, the two concepts are often confused. However, there are two important differences between finality and estoppel. Estoppel requires *detrimental reliance* by the party who seeks to invoke it, while reliance is not an element of finality. The other difference is that the statement or action leading to finality is by its very nature contractually binding upon the government through the operation of legal principles such as offer and acceptance, acceptance of goods, etc. The government is held bound by estoppel, however, because it would be *unfair* not to do so even though the statement, action, or inaction would not be contractually binding. Thus, the government has been estopped through its course of conduct as well as through its verbal representations. See *Dynamic Concepts, Inc.*, ASBCA 44738, 93-2 BCA ¶ 25,689 (government estopped when the contracting officer paid invoices exceeding the contract ceiling and the contractor continued performance in reliance on such conduct); *Peninsular ChemResearch, Inc.*, ASBCA 14384, 71-2 BCA ¶ 9066 (government required to accept results of accounting method it previously approved by implication); and *Litton Sys., Inc. v. United States*, 196 Ct. Cl. 133, 449 F.2d 392 (1971) (government's knowledge of, acquiescence to, and approval of contractor's accounting system precluded retroactive disallowance of cost).

## 1. Government Not Estopped by Unauthorized Actions

The government will not be estopped by the unauthorized actions of its representatives, *United States v. Georgia-Pacific Co.*, 421 F.2d 92 (9th Cir. 1970). Frequently, the lack of authority results from the action being contrary to statutory requirements. In such cases, courts will construe authority narrowly, *Schweiker v. Hansen*, 450 U.S. 785 (1981) (all courts have a duty to observe conditions defined by Congress for charging the public treasury); *OPM v. Richmond*, 496 U.S. 414, *reh'g denied*, 497 U.S. 1046 (1990) (government cannot be bound by payment contravening explicit statutory limitation). Similarly, in *Singer Co.*, ASBCA 17604, 75-2 BCA ¶ 11,401, *aff'd*, 217 Ct. Cl. 225, 576 F.2d 905 (1978), the contractor submitted cost or pricing data that the government representative knew were not current. Since the government official had no authority to waive the requirements of the Truth in Negotiations Act, 10 U.S.C. § 2306a, the government could not be estopped from obtaining a price reduction. The board stated at 54,288:

In the appeal before us, no Government representative had authority to waive the statutory requirement of disclosure of accurate, complete and current data. We need not further discuss the application of estoppel since it fails at a threshold question. We note parenthetically that a far different case would exist had [the contractor] fully disclosed its data in relation to its proposal and the Government then, for whatever reason, failed to make use of the data in the negotiation process. *Muncie Gear Works, Inc.*, ASBCA No. 18184, [75-2 BCA ¶ 11,380]; *Levinson Steel Co.*, ASBCA No. 16520, 73-2 BCA ¶ 10,116.

The same rule applies when the employee is acting contrary to delegated authority, *Atlantic Gulf & Pac. Co. of Manila v. United States*, 207 Ct. Cl. 995 (1975) (no estoppel to disavow settlement agreement negotiated without required advance approval).

GAO has consistently ruled that the government can not be estopped from rejecting bids that are nonresponsive or offers that do not meet the government's needs in a negotiated procurement. See *International Waste Indus.*, Comp. Gen. Dec. B-210500.2, 83-1 CPD ¶ 652, stating that "erroneous advice given by agency officials cannot estop the agency from rejecting a nonresponsive bid, since the agency is required to do so by law." The same result was reached in *Jensen Corp.*, 60 Comp. Gen. 543 (B-200277.2), 81-1 CPD ¶ 524; and *Trident Indus. Prod., Inc.*, 59 Comp. Gen. 742 (B-199138), 80-2 CPD ¶ 222. See also *International Med. Indus., Inc.*, 62 Comp. Gen. 31 (B-208235), 82-2 CPD ¶ 386, where no estoppel was found when a bidder was found nonresponsive in step two of a two-step sealed bidding procurement even though the nonconformity was present in the step one proposal which was accepted by the government. In *Eastern Marine, Inc.*, Comp. Gen. Dec. B-213945, 84-1 CPD ¶ 343, the same rule was applied to negotiated procurements by holding that the government cannot be estopped from rejecting a nonconforming proposal from the competitive range. In that case, GAO formulated the rule as a matter of legal authority by stating that "there exists no basis under the legal doctrine of estoppel for requiring the government to consider for award a proposal which does not meet the government's minimum needs." See also *Toyo Menka Kaisha, Ltd. v. United States*, 220 Ct. Cl. 210, 597 F.2d 1371 (1979), where the court held that the government was not estopped to deny the validity of a contract since the contracting officer was not authorized to make an award on a nonresponsive bid.

Other cases finding no estoppel because of lack of authority include: *California Bus. Tels. v. Department of Agriculture*, CBCA 135, 07-1 BCA ¶ 33,553 (program analyst had no authority to expand scope of contract); *Conner Bros. Constr. Co. v. United States*, 65 Fed. Cl. 657 (2005) (contracting officer had limited authority); *Healthcare Practice Enhancement Network, Inc.*, VABCA 5864, 01-1 BCA ¶ 31,383 (Chief Financial Officer of agency health center had no authority to enter into contract); *Seaboard Lumber Co. v. United States*, 45 Fed. Cl. 404 (1999) (Forest Service supervisor lacked authority to agree to cancel contract); *Grigor E. Atonian v. General Services Admin.*, GSBCA 12765, 95-1 BCA ¶ 27,444 (non-contracting officer had no authority to state that claim would be paid); *Essen*

*Mall Properties v. United States*, 21 Cl. Ct. 430 (1990) (Postal Service negotiator lacked implied authority to bind Postal Service); *Lance Dickinson & Co.*, AS-BCA 36408, 89-3 BCA ¶ 22,198, *recons. denied*, 90-1 BCA ¶ 22,511 (no implied contract where contractor knew that government employee lacked authority to contract); *Eastern Marine, Inc. v. United States*, 5 Cl. Ct. 34 (1984) (no estoppel when Source Evaluation Board Chairman without contracting officer authority induced offeror to compete by making numerous erroneous statements about the specification requirements); *Aetna Casualty & Surety Co. v. United States*, 208 Ct. Cl. 515, 526 F.2d 1127 (1975), *cert. denied*, 425 U.S. 973 (1976) (government not estopped from recovering illegal payment); *Carroll Beaver*, Comp. Gen. Dec. B-184130, 75-2 CPD ¶ 14 (government not bound to rental exceeding maximum authorized amount); *California-Pacific Utilities Co. v. United States*, 194 Ct. Cl. 703 (1971) (no authority to include indemnity provision in contract); and *Fansteel Metallurgical Corp. v. United States*, 145 Ct. Cl. 496, 172 F. Supp. 268 (1959) (unauthorized overpayment does not bind government).

In *Urban Data Sys., Inc. v. United States*, 699 F.2d 1147 (Fed. Cir. 1983), a small business contract contained a cost-plus-percentage-of-cost pricing clause at the government's insistence. Because agents lack the authority to compensate contractors under such a clause, the government was not estopped to deny its validity. Urban was entitled to compensation, however, under quantum valebant.

## 2. Sovereign Capacity Exception

It has been stated that the government will not be estopped from performing sovereign acts, *United States v. Georgia-Pacific Co.*, 421 F.2d 92 (9th Cir. 1970). In *United States v. Lazy FC Ranch*, 481 F.2d 985 (9th Cir. 1973), the court considered both the questions of lack of authority and actions within the government's sovereign capacity. Citing *Georgia-Pacific, Moser v. United States*, 341 U.S. 41 (1951), *Brandt v. Hickel*, 427 F.2d 53 (9th Cir. 1970), and *Schuster v. C.I.R.*, 312 F.2d 311 (9th Cir. 1962), the court stated at 989:

> The *Moser-Brandt-Schuster* line of cases establish the proposition that estoppel is available as a defense against the government if the government's wrongful conduct threatens to work a serious injustice and if the public's interest would not be unduly damaged by the imposition of estoppel. *Gestuvo v. District Dir. of I.N.S.*, 337 F. Supp. 1093 (C.D. Cal. 1971). This proposition is true even if the government is acting in a capacity that has traditionally been described as sovereign (as distinguished from proprietary) although we may be more reluctant to estop the government when it is acting in this capacity. See *Georgia-Pacific, supra.*

This case rejects the sovereign-capacity exception and also appears to reject the rule that the government is not estopped by unauthorized acts. However, the court found that "the agency's published regulations arguably permitted" the action taken by the government's representatives. The Supreme Court has not ruled on whether estoppel lies against the government when the government acted in its sovereign capacity. In *Schweiker v. Hansen*, 450 U.S. 785 (1981), the Court referred to *Lazy FC Ranch* in a footnote, stating, "We do not need to consider the correctness of these cases."

## 3. Reliance

Reasonable reliance by the contractor is an essential element of estoppel, *California-Pacific Utilities Co. v. United States*, 194 Ct. Cl. 703 (1971). In this case, the court held that the contractor could not claim reliance on an alleged agreement to include an indemnification clause in a permit when it had notice that the government official who allegedly agreed to include the clause did not have authority to do so. There are numerous decisions finding the contractor's alleged reliance to be unreasonable. See, for example, *Melrose Assocs., L.P. v. United States*, 45 Fed. Cl. 56 (1999) (unreasonable to rely on government employees' signing contract amendments without checking to determine if they had authority); *C Constr. Co.*, ASBCA 41706, 94-1 BCA ¶ 26,263 (unreasonable to rely on inadvertent specification deviation approved by architect/engineer); *Turner Constr. Co. v. General Servs. Admin.*, GSBCA 11361, 93-2 BCA ¶ 25,115 (unreasonable to rely on contracting officer's interpretation of standard contract clause); *Diamond v. Federal Emergency Mgmt. Agency*, 689 F. Supp. 163 (E.D.N.Y. 1988) (reliance in contradiction of policy provision was unreasonable).

Reliance on opinions or statements of future intention are frequently found to be unreasonable. See *Brenda R. Ronhaar*, AGBCA 98-147-1, 99-1 BCA ¶ 30,591 (reliance on opinion that options would be exercised unreasonable); *Robert Shaw Control Sys. Div. v. Department of the Army*, GSBCA 12714-P, 94-2 BCA ¶ 26,713 (reliance on government lawyer's opinion on legal rule unreasonable); *State Street Mgmt. Corp. v. General Servs. Admin.*, GSBCA 12374, 94-1 BCA ¶ 26,500 (unreasonable to rely on statement of future intention).

Reliance cannot occur when the contractor's action took place *before* the government act that is alleged to have created the estoppel. Thus, in *George G. Sharp, Inc.*, ASBCA 55385, 09-1 BCA ¶ 34,117, no reliance was found because a recommendation to fund overruns occurred after costs had been incurred. See *Rockwell Int'l Corp.*, ASBCA 20304, 76-2 BCA ¶ 12,131 (contractor changed its accounting system before the government acted), and *Codex Corp.*, ASBCA 17983, 75-2 BCA ¶ 11,554, *remanded on other grounds*, 226 Ct. Cl. 693 (1981) (costs were incurred before action by contracting officer). Estoppel was also denied in *Blount, Inc.*, VABCA 3719, 95-2 BCA ¶ 27,874, where the board found that although the subcontractor probably relied on the VA review finding that its system appeared to meet the specification requirements, there was no detrimental reliance by the prime contractor. The board outlined three factors leading to this conclusion at 139,059:

> The first factor is that Blount [the prime contractor] included the SBS [the subcontractor] quote as a part of its (MHS) bid to the VA *before* the VA's notification

to SBS that, in effect, the Bavis product was a functionally equivalent system. The second factor against detrimental reliance is that Blount also signed the subcontract which it proffered to SBS *before* the VA's favorable evaluation of the Bavis system. Finally, the VA awarded the contract to Blount *before* the agency had even communicated its evaluation of the Bavis system to SBS. Thus, Blount, the only party to this contract with the Government, had already committed itself to furnish and install an MHS system which met the VA's specifications by the time of the VA's Bavis evaluation. Blount could not possibly have relied on the later actions by the VA in this respect.

The contractor must prove that it actually relied on the government statement or act. In *Mountain Plains Educ. & Economic Dev. Program, Inc.*, ASBCA 21714, 78-1 BCA ¶ 13,083, the government was not estopped to deny the reasonableness of payments under employment contracts where the contractor could not show that it relied upon the contracting officer's concurrence in the validity of the proposed payments. See also *General Elec. Co. v. United States*, 60 Fed. Cl. 782 (2004) (no proof that contractor relied on government position on costs in sale of division); *General Sec. Servs. Corp. v. General Servs. Admin.*, GSBCA 11381, 92-2 BCA ¶ 24,897 (no reliance on an alleged government waiver of the specification was found because the contractor did not indicate in negotiations that it was relying on the waiver); *Snowbird Indus., Inc.*, ASBCA 33027, 89-3 BCA ¶ 22,065 (no reliance where contractor did not know of government act alleged to create estoppel); *Meridian Inc.*, PSBCA 2203, 89-2 BCA ¶ 21,648 (no evidence that contractor action occurred because of government act); and *Baifield Indus., Div. of A-T-O, Inc.*, ASBCA 19025, 75-1 BCA ¶ 11,245 (no indication that contractor would have altered actions if government had made demand earlier).

The Supreme Court's ruling in *Heckler v. Community Servs. of Crawford County, Inc.*, 467 U.S. 51 (1984), casts doubt as to the validity of reliance on oral advice as the basis for asserting estoppel against the government. The Court stated at 65:

> The appropriateness of respondent's reliance is further undermined because the advice it received from Travelers was oral. It is not merely the possibility of fraud that undermines our confidence in the reliability of official action that is not confirmed or evidenced by a written instrument. Written advice, like a written judicial opinion, requires its author to reflect about the nature of the advice that is given to the citizen, and subjects that advice to the possibility of review, criticism, and reexamination. The necessity for ensuring that governmental agents stay within the lawful scope of their authority, and that those who seek public funds act with scrupulous exactitude, argues strongly for the conclusion that an estoppel cannot be erected on the basis of the oral advice that underlay respondent's cost reports.

GAO has consistently held that, even with contractor's detrimental reliance in formulating its bid, a bidder relies "on any oral explanation at its own risk," *International Waste Indus.*, Comp. Gen. Dec. B-210500.2, 83-1 CPD ¶ 652. See also *Eastern Marine, Inc.*, Comp. Gen. Dec. B-213945, 84-1 CPD ¶ 343, rejecting a claim of estoppel against the government because it was based upon oral advice, allegedly received during telephone conversations, that was in direct conflict with the provisions in the RFP.

## 4. Knowledge of Facts

When a claim of estoppel is based on the government not revealing facts, the contractor must prove that it did not know those facts. See *Henry H. Norman v. General Servs. Admin.*, GSBCA 15070, 02-2 BCA ¶ 32,042, denying recovery because, while the contractor did not know all of the detailed facts in the possession of the government with regard to the possibility of injury because of an insecure government building, it was aware of many of these facts. See also *H. Bendzulla Contracting*, ASBCA 51869, 01-2 BCA ¶ 31,655 (contractor knew of specification problems at time of bidding); *Western Aviation Maint., Inc. v. General Servs. Admin.*, GSBCA 14165, 00-2 BCA ¶ 31,123 (parties had equal but incomplete knowledge of the facts); *Davis Group, Inc.*, ASBCA 48431, 95-2 BCA ¶ 27,702 (contractor knew the contents of a contract clause).

## 5. Injury

Injury is essential to estoppel. The contractor must establish that its reliance has placed it in a worse position than it would have been in otherwise, *Chula Vista City School Dist. v. Bennett*, 824 F.2d 1573 (Fed. Cir. 1987), *cert. denied*, 484 U.S. 1042 (1988). See also *Grigor E. Atoian v. General Servs. Admin.*, GSBCA 12765, 95-1 BCA ¶ 27,444 (contractor's delay in filing claim in reliance on advice from government employee caused no loss or harm to contractor); *Okaw Indus., Inc.*, ASBCA 17863, 75-1 BCA ¶ 11,321, *recons. denied*, 75-2 BCA ¶ 11,571 (no injury to contractor from disallowance of settlement); *Simmonds Precision Prods., Inc.*, ASBCA 18110, 74-1 BCA ¶ 10,472 (government not estopped from assessing liquidated damages after two years absent proof of prejudice from delay); and *General Dynamics Corp.*, ASBCA 13868, 69-2 BCA ¶ 8044 (contractor not deprived of recovery of allocable costs by retroactive change of accounting system).

## 6. Waiver

Closely related to and sometimes used interchangeably with estoppel is the concept of waiver — the relinquishment of a legal right. See *American Nat'l Bank & Trust Co. v. United States*, 23 Cl. Ct. 542 (1991); *Branch Bunking & Trust Co. v. United States*, 120 Ct. Cl. 72, 98 F. Supp. 757, *cert. denied*, 342 U.S. 893 (1951); and Comp. Gen. Dec. B-174410, June 30, 1972, *Unpub*. As with estoppel, the government will be bound by a waiver if the contractor relies upon it to its detriment, *De Vito v. United States*, 188 Ct. Cl. 979, 413 F.2d 1147 (1969). However, a waiver may be retracted if it is not supported by consideration or if the contractor has not relied upon the waiver to its detriment, *Mark Dunning Indus.*, ASBCA 29599, 86-1 BCA ¶ 18,521.

The term "waiver" is frequently used in connection with the government's failure to promptly terminate a delinquent contractor when that contractor has relied on the government's failure to terminate by continuing performance or preparation for performance with the government's knowledge and express or implied consent. In such cases, the government will have waived its right to terminate the contractor for default. In *Freeway Ford Truck Sales, Inc. v. General Servs. Admin.*, GSBCA 10662, 93-3 BCA ¶ 26,019, a default termination was held to be improper despite the contractor's late delivery. The board found that the government had waived its right to terminate by allowing the contractor to continue with production. In *Marci Enters., Inc. v. General Servs. Admin.*, GSBCA 12197, 94-1 BCA ¶ 26,563, the board held that the government improperly terminated the contract, stating that the government had waived the delivery date by telling the contractor to delay the shipment for inspection and by continuing to encourage the contractor to correct the deficiencies. See also *Applied Cos.*, ASBCA 43210, 94-2 BCA ¶ 26,837 (government waived delivery date by rescheduling a date for witnessing the first article test and approving engineering change proposals after the contract delivery date); *Vista Scientific Corp.*, ASBCA 25974, 87-1 BCA ¶ 19,603 (government waived completion date by encouraging and participating in contractor's efforts to fulfill contract after due date); and *S.T. Research Corp.*, ASBCA 39600, 92-2 BCA ¶ 24,838 (government waived right to terminate where the contracting officer told the contractor to continue and proposed a new delivery schedule). For a thorough discussion of this doctrine, see Chapter 10, Cibinic, Nash & Nagle, *Administration of Government Contracts*, 4th ed. 2006.

The government's acceptance of nonspecification performance under a prior or current contract may give rise to a constructive waiver of specifications. The Court of Federal Claims explained the concept of constructive waiver of specifications in *Miller Elevator Co. v. United States*, 30 Fed. Cl. 662 (1994), at 687:

> While the constructive waiver of specifications incorporates estoppel theories into the legal doctrine of waiver, the theory finds basis in any certain interpretation given to a contract specification by the contracting parties. Once the parties continue performance under the interpretation, one party may not later seek to enforce a contrary interpretation, even if the former interpretation results in the constructive waiver of specifications.

The Court of Federal Claims has adopted a four-part test for constructive waiver. In *Hannon Elec. Co. v. United States*, 31 Fed. Cl. 135 (1994), the court stated at 147 that to establish a constructive waiver of specifications, the contractor must show that:

> (1) The [contracting officer] had notice that the work differed from the contract requirements. (2) Action or inaction of the [contracting officer] indicated that the non-specification performance was acceptable. (3) The contractor relied on the [contracting officer's] action or inaction. (4) It would be unfair to permit the Government to retract the waiver.

In *Gresham & Co. v. United States*, 200 Ct. Cl. 97, 470 F.2d 542 (1972), the contract called for dishwashers with automatic detergent dispensers. The government had accepted dishwashers without automatic dispensers in the previous 21 contracts. The Court of Claims held that the government's knowing acceptance of nonspecification dishwashers effectively removed the specification requirement in question. In *Hannon Elec.*, however, the contractor disregarded the contract's size requirements for load banks (electrical testing devices) and built larger, nonspecification load banks. Unbeknownst to the contractor, the government discovered that the load banks were too large before they were completed. Because the contractor was unaware of the government's knowledge of the deviation, no waiver was found because it could not have relied on the government's alleged acquiescence.

Acceptance of a small number of deviating performances will not constitute waiver, *Western States Constr. Co.*, ASBCA 37611, 92-1 BCA ¶ 24,418 (waiver on only two prior contracts — one with another contractor); *Kvaas Constr. Co.*, ASBCA 45965, 94-1 BCA ¶ 26,513 (waiver on four prior contracts). Waiver can, however, occur on a single contract. See *General Motors Corp.*, ASBCA 15807, 72-1 BCA ¶ 9405, where the government was held to have waived the reliability requirement by knowingly authorizing the contractor to proceed with production despite nonconformity with reliability criteria; and *Walsky Constr. Co.*, ASBCA 36940, 90-2 BCA ¶ 22,934, where waiver was found when the contracting officer permitted seal coating of a road at temperatures below the specified minimum.

Waiver of a required contract provision may require a higher standard of proof. See *Kearfott Guidance & Navigation Corp.*, ASBCA 49271, 04-2 BCA ¶ 32,757, *recons. denied*, 05-1 BCA ¶ 32,845, finding inadequate proof that the government had waived a paragraph of the Incentive Price Revision — Firm Target clause in FAR 52.216-16.

## 7. Estoppel Improperly Used

In numerous cases involving finality of action, the boards and courts have unnecessarily used the term estoppel in holding that the government is bound. This, of course, has led to confusion because it has been the operation of the legal principle involved (acceptance of offer or goods, interpretation of contract, etc.) rather than the doctrine of equitable estoppel that has bound the government. See, for example, *LDG Timber Enters., Inc.*, AGBCA 91 213-1, 95-2 BCA ¶ 27,906, where the board held the government was not estopped by a letter from the contracting officer granting a time extension. The board reasoned the contractor had not proved that it relied on the letter. In reversing this decision, the Federal Circuit held that the estoppel analysis was misused because the government was bound by the *promise* in the letter in accordance with "ordinary contract principles," *LDG Timber Enters., Inc. v. Glickman*, 114 F.3d 1140 (Fed. Cir. 1997). Similarly, in *McTeague Constr. Co. v. General Servs. Admin.*, GSBCA 14765, 01-1 BCA ¶ 31,203, the board rejected an estoppel claim and went on to analyze whether the government had entered into a contract to settle specified claims. See also *H & M Moving, Inc. v. United States*, 204 Ct. Cl. 696, 499 F.2d 660 (1974) (ambiguous term construed in contractor's favor); *Emeco Indus. v. United States*, 202 Ct. Cl. 1006, 485 F.2d 652 (1973) (implied-in-fact contract existed based upon government's actions); *Dana Corp. v. United States*, 200 Ct. Cl. 200, 470 F.2d 1032 (1972) (contractor's offer accepted); *Gresham & Co. v. United States*, 200 Ct. Cl. 97, 470 F.2d 542 (1972) (ambiguous term construed in contractor's favor based upon similar interpretation by government representative); *Manloading & Mgmt. Assocs. v. United States*, 198 Ct. Cl. 628, 461 F.2d 1299 (1972) (oral agreement at bidder's conference not precluded by parol evidence rule); *Mercury Mach. & Mfg. Co.*, ASBCA 20068, 76-1 BCA ¶ 11,809; *Fink Sanitary Serv., Inc.*, 53 Comp. Gen. 502 (B-179040), 74-1 CPD ¶ 36; and *Unidynamics/ St. Louis, Inc.*, ASBCA 17592, 73-2 BCA ¶ 10,360.

A good example of the confusion that exists in the use of the term "estoppel" is *Lockheed Shipbuilding & Constr. Co.*, ASBCA 18460, 75-1 BCA ¶ 11,246, *recons. denied*, 75-2 BCA ¶ 11,566. This controversial case involved broad multicontract, multiservice negotiations between Deputy Secretary of Defense Packard and the contractor whereby an overall settlement plan was negotiated. Pursuant to these negotiations, the contractor agreed to assume a fixed loss of $200 million under its C-5A contracts with the Air Force and to accept a $62 million settlement on its Navy contracts. The board held that Deputy Secretary Packard had impliedly assured the contractor that the $62 million settlement would be approved by "higher authorities" in the Navy, as required by regulations. Although the overall agreement between Deputy Secretary Packard and the contractor appeared to have all the elements of an enforceable contract, the board used the doctrine of estoppel to hold that the Navy higher authorities could not refuse to approve the $62 million settlement.

# V. SUITS AGAINST GOVERNMENT EMPLOYEES

Suits against government officers, employees, or agents are either of two types. First is the suit, almost always for monetary damages, that seeks to obtain relief directly from the officer, employee, or agent. The second seeks *relief from the government* by a suit against the employee, officer, or agent in his or her official capacity. Such suits were the normal means of seeking injunctive relief against the government prior to 1976.

Both types of litigation are generally subject to some form of "immunity" defense. Suits against the individual personally will invariably be challenged on the ground that the employee is entitled to the *personal immunity* that attaches to public employees. In suits against the officer or employee in his or her official capacity, the government may move for dismissal if it has not waived its *sovereign immunity* from such suits. Such suits are no longer necessary because 5 U.S.C. § 702, as amended in 1976, Pub. L. No. 94-574, 90 Stat. 2721, permits such suits to be filed directly against the "United States" in order to obtain injunctive relief against adverse agency action. Thus, the only necessity of naming the employee in such suits is to specify who should be enjoined in the event the plaintiff prevails. This section considers the first type of suit against government employees — those attempting to obtain monetary relief against the employees personally.

Traditionally, government employees were *immune from personal suit* when acting within the scope of their authority. The courts have recognized the necessity of protecting the freedom of federal officers and employees to exercise the discretion that is required for the proper execution of their duties by prohibiting suits against such employees in their personal capacity. In *Ove Gustavsson Contracting Co. v. Floete*, 299 F.2d 655 (2d Cir. 1962), *cert. denied*, 374 U.S. 827 (1963), a contractor brought suit against federal employees in their private capacities, seeking damages for alleged intentional and malicious falsification of progress reports filed with the government. Affirming the district court's grant of summary judgment for the government employees, the court stated at 658:

> [O]fficials of the federal Government are not personally liable for alleged torts based upon acts, done within the scope of their duties, which necessarily involved the exercise of a judgment or discretion which public policy requires be made without fear of personal liability.

This type of immunity has been referred to as *absolute immunity.*

When the government officer or employee is charged with violating a person's *constitutional rights*, a *qualified immunity* rather than an absolute immunity will be invoked. In *Scheuer v. Rhodes*, 416 U.S. 232 (1974), involving a suit under 42 U.S.C. § 1983 against the governor of Ohio and other high state officials for killing four demonstrators, the Court ruled that state officials could claim only a "qualified immunity." Thus, they would be immune only to the extent that the acts were within the scope of their duties, that they were done with a good faith belief that they were correct, and that such belief was reasonable in light of the facts as they existed at the time of the acts. The Supreme Court extended this rule to federal government employees in *Butz v. Economou*, 438 U.S. 478 (1978), when violations of constitutional rights were alleged. Absolute immunity for constitutional violations was held to apply only to "those exceptional situations where it is demonstrated that absolute immunity is essential for the conduct of the public business." Subsequently, the Court has indicated that absolute immunity for constitutional violations is to be accorded to legislators and judges in their legislative and judicial capacities, respectively, to prosecutors and similar officials of executive agencies, and to executive officers engaged in adjudicative functions. Other federal officials who seek absolute exemption from personal liability for unconstitutional conduct must bear the burden of showing that public policy requires an exemption of that scope based on their functions, not merely their positions. See *Harlow v. Fitzgerald*, 457 U.S. 800 (1982).

In *Harlow*, senior presidential aides and advisers were charged with violating Fitzgerald's constitutional and statutory rights. The Court held that absolute immunity is not "an incident of the office of every presidential subordinate based in the White House." However, an official would be entitled to absolute immunity for constitutional violations by showing (1) "that the responsibilities of his office embraced a function so sensitive as to require a total shield from liability," and (2) "that he was discharging the protected function when performing the act for which liability is asserted." With respect to qualified immunity, the Court stated that it would not apply if the official "knew or reasonably should have known that the action he took within his sphere of official responsibility would violate the constitutional rights of the [plaintiff], or if he took the action with malicious intention to cause a deprivation of constitutional rights or other injury," further stating that "government officials performing discretionary functions generally are shielded from liability for civil damages insofar as their conduct does not violate clearly established statutory or constitutional rights of which a reasonable person would have known." The judge is to determine the threshold question of whether a clearly established law existed at the time of the action of which the government employee "knew or should have known."

The Supreme Court placed another limitation on absolute immunity in *Westfall v. Erwin*, 484 U.S. 292 (1988), ruling that absolute immunity would be granted only if the act was discretionary in nature. Thus, not all acts of high-level officials would necessarily be subject to absolute immunity. The Court also described at 295-96 the following policy reasons as supporting such immunity:

> The purpose of such official immunity is not to protect an erring official, but to insulate the decision making process from the harassment of prospective litigation. The provision of immunity rests on the view that the threat of liability will make federal officials unduly timid in carrying out their official duties, and that effective government will be promoted if officials are freed of the costs of vexatious and often frivolous damages suits. . . . This Court always has recognized, however, that official immunity comes at a great cost. An injured party with an otherwise meritorious tort claim is denied compensation simply because he had the misfortune to be injured by a federal official. Moreover, absolute immunity contravenes the basic tenet that individuals be held accountable for their wrongful conduct. We therefore have held that absolute immunity for federal officials is justified only when "the contributions of immunity to effective government in particular contexts outweighs the perhaps recurring harm to individual citizens." *Doe v. McMillan*, [412 U.S. 306, 320 (1973)].

In response to the Court's decision in *Westfall*, Congress enacted the Federal Employees Liability Reform and Tort Compensation Act of 1988, Pub. L. No. 100-694, which contained the following statement:

> It is the purpose of this Act to protect Federal employees from personal liability for common law torts committed within the scope of their employment, while

providing persons injured by the common law torts with an appropriate remedy against the United States.

To achieve this purpose, the Act amended the Federal Torts Claims Act (FTCA), 28 U.S.C. § 1346(b) and § 2671 et seq., to restore the immunity that the Supreme Court had taken away in *Westfall*. The Act restored absolute immunity for suits for money damages when common-law torts are alleged and did not make the immunity dependent upon the discretionary nature of the employee's duties. In such cases, only the government may be sued. See 28 U.S.C. § 2679(b). This absolute immunity is broadly construed, *Hui v. Castaneda*, 130 S. Ct. 1845 (2010).

As a result, government employees have absolute immunity from suits for monetary compensation unless such suit is based on (1) an act totally outside of the scope of their employment, or (2) an act that deprives a person of his or her constitutional rights and the employee is not a member of the class of employees that has absolute immunity. The Supreme Court has held that this immunity applies even "when an FTCA exception precludes recovery against the government," *United States v. Smith*, 499 U.S. 160 (1991).

Under 28 U.S.C. § 2679(d), the Attorney General is to make a determination as to whether the act was accomplished within the scope of employment and may defend the employee and the United States if it is so determined. A certification that the employee was acting within the scope of employment has two effects: (1) the government is substituted as the defendant, and (2) the case is removed to federal district court if it has been filed in a state court. The certification or lack of certification is reviewable by the district court with regard to the substitution of the government as the proper party but a certification is conclusive as to removal from a state court, *Gutierrez de Martinez v. Lamagno*, 515 U.S. 417 (1995). This can lead to the anomalous result that, if a court finds the certification incorrect, the government employee becomes the defendant but the case remains in federal district court, *Garcia v. United States*, 88 F.3d 318 (5th Cir. 1996); *Ross v. Bryan*, 309 F.3d 830 (4th Cir. 2002). In *Osborn v. Haley*, 549 U.S. 225 (2007), the Court ruled that this review of the correctness of the certification applied in the situation where the defense was that the conduct never occurred as well as where the issue was whether the conduct was within the scope of employment. The Court also ruled that a district court rejection of the certification that the conduct was within the scope of employment could not be based on the pleadings but had to be based on the facts accepted by the judge in a trial. The Court recognized that this deprived the plaintiff of a jury trial but concluded that was the intent of 28 U.S.C. § 2679(d).

There is a further anomaly in this procedure. If the Attorney General refuses to certify, the defendant can appeal the lack of certification to a federal court. If that court finds that the conduct is not within the scope of employment, it will remand the case to state court under 28 U.S.C. § 2679(d)(3), and such remand is not appealable under 28 U.S.C. § 1447(d). The scope of this statute is discussed in

*Powerex Corp. v. Reliant Energy Servs., Inc,* 551 U.S. 224 (2007). If the state court then concludes that the conduct was within the scope of employment, it will have to send the case back to the federal court. The unfairness of this procedure to the government employee accused of tortious conduct is discussed in *Foster v. Hill,* 497 F.3d 695 (7th Cir. 2007).

In *Aversa v. United States,* 99 F.3d 1200 (1st Cir. 1996), the court held that while federal law "does determine whether a person is a federal employee and the nature and contours of his or her federal responsibilities . . . state law governs whether the person was acting within the scope of that employment and those responsibilities." A good summary of the standards that are applied to determine whether actions are within the scope of employment is contained in *Davric Maine Corp. v. U.S. Postal Service,* 238 F.3d 58 (1st Cir. 2001), at 66:

> Under Maine law an employee's actions are within the scope of employment if they are of the kind that he is employed to perform, they occur within authorized time and space limits, and they are actuated by a purpose to serve the employee's master. See Restatement (Second) of Agency § 228, at 504 (1958), cited in *Bergeron [v. Henderson*], 47 F. Supp. 2d [61 (D.Maine 1999)] at 65. Under the Restatement (Second), an action may be within the scope of employment although "forbidden, or done in a forbidden manner," see Restatement (Second) § 230, or even "consciously criminal or tortious," see *id.* § 231. Actions "relating to work" and "done in the workplace during working hours" are typically within the scope. See id. §§ 229, 233, 234. Whether the motivation of the employee is to serve the master's interest or his or her own private purposes is often an important element in this determination. See id. §§ 228, 235-236; see also *Lyons [v. Brown*], 158 F.3d [650 (1st Cir. 1998)] at 609. Where seemingly work-related acts taken by the federal employee are done with a private purpose on the employee's part to retaliate or discriminate against the plaintiff, they may fall outside the scope of employment under Maine law; where the acts were done in good faith to serve the employer's interest, even if the federal employee's judgment was mistaken, then the conduct is likely within the scope of employment. See Lyons, 158 F.3d at 610.

Several situations have been held to be outside of the scope of employment, making the employee personally liable for his or her conduct. See *Johnson v. United States,* 534 F.3d 958 (8th Cir. 2008) (arrest by Bureau of Indian Affairs correctional officer); *Sullivan v. Shimp,* 324 F.3d 397 (6th Cir. 2003) (automobile accident returning from work site to home — Ohio law); *Ross v. Bryan* (an automobile accident while commuting to work — Virginia law); *Borneman v. United States,* 213 F.3d 819 (4th Cir. 2000) (intentional tort such as assault and battery during work frequently, but not always, outside of scope of employment — North Carolina law); *Mackey v. Milam,* 154 F.3d 64 (6th Cir. 1998) (sexual harassment outside scope of employment if done by employee with no control over plaintiff but within scope of employment if done by supervisor or other person with control over plaintiff — Ohio law). However, tortious conduct between employees in the workplace has been held to be within the scope of employment, *United States v. Tomscha,* 150 Fed. Appx. 18

(2d Cir. 2005) (circulating email allegedly libeling union leader); *Taboas v. Mlync-zak*, 149 F.3d 576 (7th Cir. 1998) (allegedly malicious and vindictive complaints lodged against a fellow employee within the scope of employment — Illinois law); *McLachlan v. Bell*, 261 F3d 908 (9th Cir. 2001) (alleged circulation of false rumors and malicious gossip within scope of employment — California law). In addition, tortious conduct by a superior is held to be within the scope of employment, *Hendrix v. Snow*, 170 Fed. Appx. 68 (11th Cir. 2006), *cert. denied*, 549 U.S. 1208 (2007) (alleged discrimination and retaliation after filing complaints); *Singleton v. United States*, 277 F3d 864 (6th Cir. 2002) (alleged efforts of superior to have employee removed from his job, filing of false and degrading reports, punished him for pursuing his legal rights, and leaking confidential information about him within scope of employment — Ohio law); *Heuton v. Anderson*, 75 F3d 357 (8th Cir. 1996) (posting pictures characterizing employees as pigs within scope of supervisor's employment — Iowa law). See also *Kashin v. Kent*, 457 F.3d 1033 (9th Cir. 2006), finding, under District of Columbia law, that a foreign service officer was acting within the scope of his employment when he had an automobile accident driving home from work in Russia. It is also held that individuals performing work for the government are not employees for these purposes if they qualify as independent contractors, *Creel v. United States*, 598 F.3d 210 (5th Cir. 2010); *Rodriguez v. Sarabyn*, 129 F.3d 760 (5th Cir. 1997).

## VI. STANDARDS OF CONDUCT

In order to maintain public confidence in the federal procurement process, government and contractor employees must follow exemplary standards of conduct. There are numerous statutory and regulatory provisions outlining the standards to be followed and the stringent penalties for noncompliance. This section discusses these standards in three broad categories — those dealing with improper influence on government decisions, those requiring honesty and disclosure of relevant facts in dealing with the government, and those barring improperly disclosing or obtaining information. The focus of the material is on proscribed conduct.

### A. Sanctions

Each statute prohibiting a certain type of conduct contains its own sanction or penalty. Since most of these sanctions involve straightforward criminal or civil fines or imprisonment, this section does not discuss the precise way that these penalties have been interpreted and enforced. In this regard, a government contractor or a government employee is treated the same as any other person guilty of a "white collar" crime. However, government contractors are also subject to additional sanctions that are considerably broader than the normal criminal and civil sanctions. In many if not most cases, these broader sanctions are a more serious threat to government contractors than the criminal or civil sanctions contained in the specific statutes covering the prohibited conduct. There are also additional sanctions applicable to government employees. This section considers those additional sanctions that provide drastic penalties for those engaged in improper conduct in the contracting process.

## 1. Forfeiture and Cancellation

The first of these general sanctions against government contractors is *forfeiture* of all rights under the contract. The Supreme Court has held that the government can cancel a contract and need not pay for work done or benefit conferred if it is tainted with illegal conduct, *United States v. Mississippi Valley Generating Co.*, 364 U.S. 520 (1961) (conflict of interest); *Pan Am. Petroleum & Transp. Co. v. United States*, 273 U.S. 456 (1927). The Court of Claims went even further and held that the government can recover the full amount paid on a *completed contract* that is subsequently found to have been tainted with illegal conduct, *K & R Eng'g Co. v. United States*, 222 Ct. Cl. 340, 616 F.2d 469 (1980) (bribery and conflict of interest). See also *Bureau of Land Mgmt.: Payment of Pocatello Field Office Photocopying Costs*, Comp. Gen. Dec. B-290901, 2003 CPD ¶ 2, holding that contract was void and unenforceable because it violated 44 U.S.C. § 501 requiring agencies to obtain all printing services through the Government Printing Office, and *Schuepferling GmbH & Co., KG*, ASBCA 45567, 98-2 BCA ¶ 29,828, holding that it was proper to refuse to pay for work on 22 fully performed delivery orders because the contractor had bribed the contracting specialist at the inception of the contract. While it has been held that a contract containing a contingent fee arrangement is also void and unenforceable, *Quinn v. Gulf & Western Corp.*, 644 F.2d 89 (2d Cir. 1981); *LeJohn Mfg. Co. v. Webb*, 222 F.2d 48 (D.C. Cir. 1955), the government may not cancel a contract for breach of the covenant where it knew of the arrangement during prolonged negotiations and the arrangement had many indicia of a bona fide covenant, *Companhia Atlantica De Desenvolvimento E Exploracao De Minas v. United States*, 148 Ct. Cl. 71, 180 F. Supp. 342, *cert. denied*, 364 U.S. 862 (1960). See also *Paradyne Corp. v. United States*, 647 F. Supp. 1228 (D.D.C. 1986), prohibiting the government from exercising a contract option at the same time it was charging the contractor with fraud pertaining to the option.

The fact that Congress may have specifically provided for other statutory or criminal sanctions does not deprive the United States of the right to cancel contracts "tainted with illegal conduct," *United States v. Acme Process Equip. Co.*, 385 U.S. 138 (1966) (statutory sanction for violation of Anti-Kickback Act, 41 U.S.C. § 51); *Horton J. Brown v. United States*, 207 Ct. Cl. 768, 524 F.2d 693 (1975) (criminal sanction for violation of False Statement Act, 18 U.S.C. § 1001). However, the question has been raised concerning which officials in the government are authorized to cancel contracts and the nature of the activity that would entitle the government to cancel. In *Medico Indus., Inc.*, ASBCA 22141, 80-2 BCA ¶ 14,498, *recons. denied*, 80-2 BCA ¶ 14,665, *mot. to suspend hearings granted*, 81-1 BCA ¶ 14,983, it was held that the contracting officer was not authorized to cancel a contract because of improper conduct by a former government employee. The board distinguished *Mississippi Valley Generating Co.* on the grounds that it involved the more serious violation of action by a public official having simultaneous conflicting interests. The board also questioned whether improper conduct of a former government employee was a sufficiently serious violation to allow the government to cancel. Following the board's suspension of the hearing, the government sued in U.S. District Court for a declaratory judgment that the contract cancellation was authorized. The district court granted the contractor's motion to dismiss for lack of jurisdiction but in *United States v. Medico Indus., Inc.*, 685 F.2d 230 (7th Cir. 1982), the circuit court reversed, holding that the board of contract appeals did not have jurisdiction under the Disputes clause to determine whether 18 U.S.C. § 207(a) was violated and remanded the matter to the district court for disposition. Contrast *Four-Phase Sys., Inc.*, ASBCA 27487, 84-1 BCA ¶ 17,122, suggesting that the Contract Disputes Act gives jurisdiction to the appeals boards over a government affirmative defense of cancellation for a violation of 18 U.S.C. § 208. 18 U.S.C. § 218 provides for cancellation by the President or, under regulations prescribed by him, the head of any department or agency if there has been a final conviction for offenses involving bribery, gratuities, and conflicts of interest during and after government employment. Executive Order 12448, 48 Fed. Reg. 51281 (1983), delegates the authority to exercise this power to heads of executive agencies and provides that implementing regulations should contain specified procedural protections. FAR 3.705 sets forth the procedures for exercising this authority.

Pursuant to 28 U.S.C. § 2514 fraudulent claims are also subject to forfeiture. This statute calls for forfeiture of any claim presented to the Court of Federal Claims if there is fraud in the presentation of the claim or in the performance of the contract to which the claim is related. See *Daewoo Eng'g & Constr. Co. v. United States*, 73 Fed. Cl. 547 (2006), *aff'd*, 557 F.3d 1332 (Fed. Cir.), *cert. denied*, 130 Sup. Ct. 490 (2009) (forfeiture of potentially valid part of claim when major part was fraudulent); *Long Island Savings Bank, FSB v. United* States, 476 F.3d 917 (Fed. Cir. 2007) (entire claim forfeited because of fraud in the inducement); *First Fed'l Savings Bank of Hegewisch v. United States*, 52 Fed. Cl. 774 (2002); *UMC Elecs. Co. v. United States*, 43 Fed. Cl. 776, 790 (1999), *aff'd*, 249 F.3d 1337 (Fed. Cir. 2001). To obtain forfeiture under this statute, the government must prove its fraud claim by clear and convincing evidence, *Glendale Fed'l Bank, FSB v. United States*, 239 F.3d 1374, 1379 (Fed. Cir. 2001); *Commercial Contractors, Inc. v. United States*, 154 F.3d 1357, 1362 (Fed. Cir. 1998). See also *O'Brien Gear & Mach. Co. v. United States*, 219 Ct. Cl. 187, 591 F.2d 666 (1979) (forfeiting a renegotiation claim because it was tainted with fraud); and *Supermex, Inc. v. United States*, 35 Fed. Cl. 29 (1996) (forfeiting a contract claim because the contractor had bribed a government official during contract performance).

The boards of contract appeals cannot use 28 U.S.C. § 2514 to forfeit claims, *DEL Mfg. Co.*, ASBCA 43801, 94-3 BCA ¶ 27239, and are precluded by 41

U.S.C. § 605(a) from litigating the issue of fraud, *Simko Constr., Inc. v. United States*, 852 F.2d 540 (Fed. Cir. 1988). However, if a court has found that the contractor has committed fraud during the performance of the contract, the board will follow this determination and dismiss the case, *Beech Gap, Inc.*, ENGBCA 5585, 95-2 BCA ¶ 27879, *aff'd* 86 F.3d 1177 (Fed. Cir. 1996), or award the government any amount that has been paid to the contractor as a result of the fraud, *Medica, S.A.*, ENGBCA PCC 142, 00-2 BCA ¶ 30,966. Furthermore, a board's granting of an appeal finding a claim valid is not binding if the government later obtains a court ruling of fraud, *J.E.T.S., Inc. v. United States*, 838 F.2d 1196 (Fed. Cir. 1988), *cert. denied*, 486 U.S. 1057 (1988). In *Morse Diesel Int'l, Inc. v. United States*, 74 Fed. Cl. 601 (2007), claims for $53,534,679.16 were forfeited because the contractor had submitted false invoices and had paid illegal kickbacks. The claims were originally submitted to the GSBCA which had no jurisdiction under 28 U.S.C. § 2514 but were removed to the Court of Federal Claims under 41 U.S.C. § 609(d) (now § 7107(d)), permitting consolidation of claims on a contract, when the contractor filed claims on other contracts in that court, *Morse Diesel Int'l, Inc. v. United States*, 69 Fed. Cl. 558 (2006). This permitted the government to assert the fraud counterclaim. When the contractor asked for mandamus returning the original claims to the GSBCA because the claims were on different contracts, the Federal Circuit refused, *In re Morse Diesel Int'l, Inc.*, 163 Fed. Appx. 878 (Fed. Cir. 2006).

41 U.S.C. § 604 (now § 7103(c)(2)) provides that if a contractor is unable to support any part of its claim because of misrepresentation of fact or fraud, the contractor will be liable to the government for the amount of such fraudulent claim. In *Daewoo Engineering* this led to a judgment for the government on a counterclaim under this statute for $50,629,855.88, the amount of the claim that was found to be fraudulent because it had been added "to get the attention of the contracting officer."

## *2. Debarment*

The second broad sanction is debarment of the contractor or its employees, that is, precluding participation in the government contracts process for a stated period of time. FAR 9.406-2 contains a long list of causes for debarment which are discussed in detail in Chapter 4.

Debarment precludes contracts with any agency of the federal government for a period of up to three years, FAR 9.406-4. However, some debarments last considerably longer. See, for example, *Roderick Nielson*, HUDBCA 99-C-107-D6, 99-2 BCA ¶ 30,569, where, over the opposition of the government, the board terminated a debarment that had been in effect for ten years. Debarment of a company has been sustained for submitting false claims, *Dowling Group v. Williams*, Civ. Action No. 82-1775 (D.D.C. 1982), for bribery and collusive bidding, *Robinson v. Cheney*, 876 F.2d 152 (D.C. Cir. 1989); and for bribery, *Atlantic Chem. Co.*,

GSBCA 5822-D, 80-2 BCA ¶ 14,801. Debarment of an officer of a company was also sustained when the company bribed government officials, *Taylor v. Marsh*, Civ. Action No. 81-2643 (D.D.C. 1982). For a rare case where the agency refused to debar a company and the court ordered the prior temporary action of suspension to be voided ab initio, see *Leon Sloan, Sr. & Jimmy Lee Furby v. Department of Housing & Urban Development*, 231 F.3d 10 (D.C. Cir. 2000). See also *Lion Raisins, Inc. v. United States*, 51 Fed. Cl. 238 (2001), where the court found a debarment to be an abuse of discretion because the agency had awarded five contracts between the time it found about the acts that allegedly indicated a lack of integrity and it issued the suspension order, and *Dantran, Inc., v. Department of Labor*, 171 F.3d 58 (1st Cir. 1999), where the court overturned a debarment for improper wage payments because there was substantial evidence that the contractor had complied with agency procedures. See Chapter 4 for a more complete discussion of debarment and suspension of contractors.

Debarment is a particularly harsh sanction because when an agency *proposes* to debar a contractor, it is immediately placed in the Excluded Parties List System, FAR 9.404(b)(1), and may not receive contract awards or solicitations thereafter, FAR 9.405(a), or subcontract awards, FAR 9.405-2. See *IMCO, Inc. v. United States*, 97 F.3d 1422 (Fed. Cir. 1996), sustaining the dismissal of a protest where the agency deprived the Small Business Administration of the opportunity to issue a certificate of competency by proposing to debar the offeror. See also *FAS Support Servs., LLC*, Comp. Gen. Dec B-402464, 2010 CPD ¶ 105 (denying protest that agency failed to reinstate contractor after suspension was lifted); *Aardvark Keith Moving, Inc.*, Comp. Gen. Dec. B-290565, 2002 CPD ¶ 134 (denying protest that the agency declared the protester ineligible because it was affiliated with a company that had been proposed for debarment five years earlier).

Even after a contractor is removed from the List, its name remains on the GSA website containing the List as a firm that has been previously debarred. In *Hickey v. Chadick*, 649 F. Supp. 2d 770 (S.D. Ohio 2009), the court ruled that it had jurisdiction to hear a claim that this had injured the contractor because this aspect of the List could be used in making a future responsibility determination.

Debarment can be imposed simultaneously with civil or criminal penalties for the improper conduct. See *United States v. Glymph*, 96 F.3d 722 (4th Cir. 1996), holding that conviction for criminal fraud was proper because the prior debarment was not punitive but remedial — thus precluding any defense of double jeopardy. Accord, *United States v. Hatfield*, 108 F.3d 67 (4th Cir. 1997). See also *Hudson v. United States*, 522 U.S. 93 (1997), finding no double jeopardy in a criminal prosecution following a settlement that included a civil fine and an agreement to refrain from participation in government programs without written authorization from the agency.

## 3.  Suspension or Dismissal of Government Employees

A third broad sanction is suspension or dismissal of a government employee who has violated the standards of conduct. Such actions must be taken in accordance with 5 U.S.C. § 7513, which permits appeal by the employee to the Merit System Protection Board. See 5 C.F.R. Part 1200. Dismissal of employees was upheld in *Lachance v. Erickson*, 522 U.S. 262 (1998), where they gave false statements during investigations of misconduct. See also *Pollock v. Department of the Navy*, 369 Fed. Appx. 133 (Fed. Cir. 2010) (medical technician dismissed for failure to provide urine sample for random drug test); *Stevenson v. Department of Justice*, 189 Fed. Appx. 973 (Fed. Cir. 2006) (employee dismissed for failure to report arrest as required by agency standards of conduct); *Womer v. Hampton*, 496 F.2d 99 (5th Cir. 1974) (government inspector dismissed for taking payments from a contractor and not giving a satisfactory explanation for the payments); and *Polcover v. Secretary of Treasury*, 477 F.2d 1223 (D.C. Cir. 1973) (dismissal upheld when employee accepted a bribe even though he was later acquitted in a criminal prosecution — reasoning that the evidence was sufficient to meet a "preponderance of the evidence" test in the dismissal proceeding despite failing to meet the "beyond a reasonable doubt" test of the criminal action). The Court of Claims repeatedly held that agencies have broad discretion in selecting administrative sanctions for acceptances of bribes and gratuities. In *Jones v. United States*, 223 Ct. Cl. 138, 617 F.2d 233 (1980), the court upheld a decision of the Civil Service Commission Appeals Review Board sustaining the dismissal of a Department of Agriculture meat inspector who had accepted a single bottle of whiskey from a meat packer. In *Parker v. United States*, 224 Ct. Cl. 618, 650 F.2d 287 (1980), the court rejected the contention that dismissal of an employee who had accepted meals and entertainment valued at more than $3,000 from a contractor constituted an abuse of agency discretion. In *Lane v. United States*, 225 Ct. Cl. 209, 633 F.2d 1384 (1980), the court upheld the dismissal of IRS auditors who had accepted a "whole series" of free meals from a firm being audited. See also *Baker v. Department of Health & Human Services*, 912 F.2d 1448 (Fed. Cir. 1990), sustaining dismissal of an employee that accepted a lunch during which he disclosed internal agency information; *Monahan v. United States*, 173 Ct. Cl. 734, 354 F.2d 306 (1965), sustaining the dismissal of a procuring agency employee for permitting a contractor to pay for hotel rooms and accepting loans from three contractors; and *Miller v. United States Postal Serv.*, 712 F.2d 1006 (6th Cir. 1983), sustaining the dismissal of an employee for using inside information to benefit a company in which he had an interest.

Dismissal of an employee was also upheld for falsification of records which was a violation of 18 U.S.C. § 1001, *Santornino v. Department of Veterans Affairs*, 45 F.3d 442 (Fed. Cir. 1994) (affirming ruling of administrative law judge in unpublished opinion). See also *Pararas-Carayannis v. Department of Commerce*, 9 F.3d 955 (Fed. Cir. 1993) (upholding indefinite suspension without pay for laundering money for escort/prostitution operations, in violation of 18 U.S.C. § 1956(a)(3)); *Brook v. Corrado*, 999 F.2d 523 (Fed. Cir. 1993) (dismissal for possession of cocaine with intent to distribute it); *Stanek v. Department of Transportation*, 805 F.2d 1572 (Fed. Cir. 1986) (dismissal for solicitation of loan from company that might have benefited from employee's research); *Kumferman v. Department of Navy*, 785 F.2d 286 (Fed. Cir. 1986) (dismissal for theft of government property). *Brewer v. United States Postal Serv.*, 227 Ct. Cl. 276, 647 F.2d 1093 (1981), *cert. denied*, 454 U.S. 1144 (1982) (dismissal of an employee with 27 years of service for falsifying time cards). Compare *Miguel v. Department of Army*, 727 F.2d 1081 (Fed. Cir. 1984), reversing an agency decision to dismiss an employee with 24 years of service for stealing two bars of soap.

## B. Codes of Conduct

For many years government employees have been subject to strict codes of conduct, Executive Order 11222, May 8, 1965. General rules governing such conduct are contained in the regulations of the Office of Personnel Management, 5 C.F.R. § 735. In addition, the Office of Government Ethics has promulgated detailed standards of conduct in 5 C.F.R. Part 2635. Agencies can supplement these regulations with the concurrence of the Officer of Government Ethics, 5 C.F.R. ¶ 2635.105. The following material elaborates on most of these ethical standards.

Government contractors are also expected to have codes of conduct governing their employees, 41 U.S.C. § 2303. See FAR 3.1002 stating:

> (b) Contractors should have a written code of business ethics and conduct. To promote compliance with such code of business ethics and conduct, contractors should have an employee business ethics and compliance training program and an internal control system that —

> > (1) Are suitable to the size of the company and extent of its involvement in Government contracting;

> > (2) Facilitate timely discovery and disclosure of improper conduct in connection with Government contracts; and

> > (3) Ensure corrective measures are promptly instituted and carried out.

Mandatory codes of conduct are required for contracts of over $5 million that have a period of performance of over 120 days, FAR 3.1004(a). Such contracts must contain the Contractor Code of Business Ethics and Conduct clause at FAR 52.203-13:

CONTRACTOR CODE OF BUSINESS ETHICS AND CONDUCT (APR 2010)

> (a) *Definitions.* As used in this clause —

Agent means any individual, including a director, an officer, an employee, or an independent Contractor, authorized to act on behalf of the organization.

*Full cooperation* — (1) Means disclosure to the Government of the information sufficient for law enforcement to identify the nature and extent of the offense and the individuals responsible for the conduct. It includes providing timely and complete response to Government auditors' and investigators' request for documents and access to employees with information;

(2) Does not foreclose any Contractor rights arising in law, the FAR, or the terms of the contract. It does not require —

(i) A Contractor to waive its attorney-client privilege or the protections afforded by the attorney work product doctrine; or

(ii) Any officer, director, owner, or employee of the Contractor, including a sole proprietor, to waive his or her attorney client privilege or Fifth Amendment rights; and

(3) Does not restrict a Contractor from —

(i) Conducting an internal investigation; or

(ii) Defending a proceeding or dispute arising under the contract or related to a potential or disclosed violation.

*Principal* means an officer, director, owner, partner, or a person having primary management or supervisory responsibilities within a business entity (e.g., general manager; plant manager; head of a division or business segment; and similar positions).

*Subcontract* means any contract entered into by a subcontractor to furnish supplies or services for performance of a prime contract or a subcontract.

*Subcontractor* means any supplier, distributor, vendor, or firm that furnished supplies or services to or for a prime contractor or another subcontractor.

*United States* means the 50 States, the District of Columbia, and outlying areas.

(b) *Code of business ethics and conduct.* (1) Within 30 days after contract award, unless the Contracting Officer establishes a longer time period, the Contractor shall —

(i) Have a written code of business ethics and conduct;

(ii) Make a copy of the code available to each employee engaged in performance of the contract.

(2) The Contractor shall —

(i) Exercise due diligence to prevent and detect criminal conduct; and

(ii) Otherwise promote an organizational culture that encourages ethical conduct and a commitment to compliance with the law.

(3)(i) The Contractor shall timely disclose, in writing, to the agency Office of the Inspector General (OIG), with a copy to the Contracting Officer, whenever, in connection with the award, performance, or closeout of this contract or any subcontract thereunder, the Contractor has credible evidence that a principal, employee, agent, or subcontractor of the Contractor has committed —

(A) A violation of Federal criminal law involving fraud, conflict of interest, bribery, or gratuity violations found in Title 18 of the United States Code; or

(B) A violation of the civil False Claims Act (31 U.S.C. 3729-3733).

(ii) The Government, to the extent permitted by law and regulation, will safeguard and treat information obtained pursuant to the Contractor's disclosure as confidential where the information has been marked "confidential" or "proprietary" by the company. To the extent permitted by law and regulation, such information will not be released by the Government to the public pursuant to a Freedom of Information Act request, 5 U.S.C. Section 552, without prior notification to the Contractor. The Government may transfer documents provided by the Contractor to any department or agency within the Executive Branch if the information relates to matters within the organization's jurisdiction.

(iii) If the violation relates to an order against a Governmentwide acquisition contract, a multi-agency contract, a multiple-award schedule contract such as the Federal Supply Schedule, or any other procurement instrument intended for use by multiple agencies, the Contractor shall notify the OIG of the ordering agency and the IG of the agency responsible for the basic contract.

(c) *Business ethics awareness and compliance program and internal control system.* This paragraph (c) does not apply if the Contractor has represented itself as a small business concern pursuant to the award of this contract or if this contract is for the acquisition of a commercial item as defined at FAR 2.101. The Contractor shall establish the following within 90 days after contract award, unless the Contracting Officer establishes a longer time period:

(1) An ongoing business ethics awareness and compliance program.

(i) This program shall include reasonable steps to communicate periodically and in a practical manner the Contractor's standards and procedures and other aspects of the Contractor's business ethics awareness and compliance program and internal control system, by conducting effective training programs and otherwise disseminating information appropriate to an individual's respective roles and responsibilities.

(ii) The training conducted under this program shall be provided to the Contractor's principals and employees, and as appropriate, the Contractor's agents and subcontractors.

(2) An internal control system.

(i) The Contractor's internal control system shall —

(A) Establish standards and procedures to facilitate timely discovery of improper conduct in connection with Government contracts; and

(B) Ensure corrective measures are promptly instituted and carried out.

(ii) At a minimum, the Contractor's internal control system shall provide for the following:

(A) Assignment of responsibility at a sufficiently high level and adequate resources to ensure effectiveness of the business ethics awareness and compliance program and internal control system.

(B) Reasonable efforts not to include an individual as a principal, whom due diligence would have exposed as having engaged in conduct that is in conflict with the Contractor's code of business ethics and conduct.

(C) Periodic reviews of company business practices, procedures, policies, and internal controls for compliance with the Contractor's code of business ethics and conduct and the special requirements of Government contracting, including —

(1) Monitoring and auditing to detect criminal conduct;

(2) Periodic evaluation of the effectiveness of the business ethics awareness and compliance program and internal control system, especially if criminal conduct has been detected; and

(3) Periodic assessment of the risk of criminal conduct, with appropriate steps to design, implement, or modify the business ethics awareness and compliance program and the internal control system as necessary to reduce the risk of criminal conduct identified through this process.

(D) An internal reporting mechanism, such as a hotline, which allows for anonymity or confidentiality, by which employees may report suspected instances of improper conduct, and instructions that encourage employees to make such reports.

(E) Disciplinary action for improper conduct or for failing to take reasonable steps to prevent or detect improper conduct.

(F) Timely disclosure, in writing, to the agency OIG, with a copy to the Contracting Officer, whenever, in connection with the award, performance, or closeout of any Government contract performed by the Contractor or a subcontractor thereunder, the Contractor has credible evidence that a principal, employee, agent, or subcontractor of the Contractor has committed a violation of Federal criminal law involving fraud, conflict of interest, bribery, or gratuity violations found in Title 18 U.S.C. or a violation of the civil False Claims Act (31 U.S.C. 3729-3733).

(1) If a violation relates to more than one Government contract, the Contractor may make the disclosure to the agency OIG and Contracting Officer responsible for the largest dollar value contract impacted by the violation.

(2) If the violation relates to an order against a Governmentwide acquisition contract, a multi-agency contract, a multiple-award schedule contract such as the Federal Supply Schedule, or any other procurement instrument intended for use by multiple agencies, the contractor shall notify the OIG of the ordering agency and the IG of the agency responsible for the basic contract, and the respective agencies' contracting officers.

(3) The disclosure requirement for an individual contract continues until at least 3 years after final payment on the contract.

(4) The Government will safeguard such disclosures in accordance with paragraph (b)(3)(ii)
of this clause.

(G) Full cooperation with any Government agencies
responsible for audits, investigations, or corrective
actions.

(d) *Subcontracts.* (1) The Contractor shall include the substance of this clause,
including this paragraph (d), in subcontracts that have a value in excess of
$5,000,000 and a performance period of more than 120 days.

(2) In altering this clause to identify the appropriate parties, all disclosures
of violation of the civil False Claims Act or of Federal criminal law shall
be directed to the agency Office of the Inspector General, with a copy to
the Contracting Officer.

In addition to the requirement for a code of conduct meeting the requirements
of this clause, contractors subject to the clause must *disclose* unethical conduct to
the government in a timely manner. This mandatory disclosure requirement was
subject to considerable debate when the regulation was issued. See 73 Fed. Reg.
67064-090, Nov. 12, 2008, for a full discussion of the intent of this requirement.

Contractors with contracts under the thresholds for application of the clause
are still subject to suspension or debarment for failure to meet these standards of
conduct. See FAR 3.1003(a) stating:

(2) Whether or not the clause at 52.203-13 is applicable, a contractor may be
suspended and/or debarred for knowing failure by a principal to timely disclose
to the Government, in connection with the award, performance, or closeout of a
Government contract performed by the contractor or a subcontract awarded thereunder, credible evidence of a violation of Federal criminal law involving fraud,
conflict of interest, bribery, or gratuity violations found in Title 18 of the United
States Code or a violation of the civil False Claims Act. Knowing failure to timely
disclose credible evidence of any of the above violations remains a cause for
suspension and/or debarment until 3 years after final payment on a contract (see
9.406-2(b)(1)(vi) and 9.407-2(a)(8)).

Contractors are also subject to sanctions for failure to promptly remit an overpayment to the government. See FAR 3.1003(a) stating:

(3) The Payment clauses at FAR 52.212-4(i)(5), 52.232-25(d), 52.232-26(c), and
52.232-27(l) require that, if the contractor becomes aware that the Government has
overpaid on a contract financing or invoice payment, the contractor shall remit the
overpayment amount to the Government. A contractor may be suspended and/or
debarred for knowing failure by a principal to timely disclose credible evidence of a
significant overpayment, other than overpayments resulting from contract financing
payments as defined in 32.001 (see 9.406-2(b)(1)(vi) and 9.407-2(a)(8)).

## C. Improper Influence of Government Decisions

One of the most serious threats to the integrity of the procurement process is the possibility of conduct by contractors that will improperly influence the decisions of contracting officers and other government employees. To protect against this threat, there are a number of very strict criminal statutes.

### 1. Bribery

18 U.S.C. § 201(b) makes it a criminal offense to *offer* or *give* a bribe to a government official or for a government official to *solicit* or *receive* a bribe. The crimes are defined as follows:

(b) Whoever —

> (1) directly or indirectly, corruptly gives, offers or promises anything of value to any public official or person who has been selected to be a public official, or offers or promises any public official or any person who has been selected to be a public official to give anything of value to any other person or entity, with intent —

>> (A) to influence any official act; or

>> (B) to influence such public official or person who has been selected to be a public official to commit or aid in committing, or collude in, or allow, any fraud, or make opportunity for the commission of any fraud, on the United States; or

>> (C) to induce such public official or such person who has been selected to be a public official to do or omit to do any act in violation of the lawful duty of such official or person;

> (2) being a public official or person selected to be a public official, directly or indirectly, corruptly demands, seeks, receives, accepts, or agrees to receive or accept anything of value personally or for any other person or entity, in return for:

>> (A) being influenced in the performance of any official act;

>> (B) being influenced to commit or aid in committing, or to collude in, or allow, any fraud, or make opportunity for the commission of any fraud, on the United States; or

>> (C) being induced to do or omit to do any act in violation of the official duty of such official or person.

## a. Thing of Value

To constitute bribery, the statute requires that something "of value" be given, offered, promised, solicited, or received. Courts have adopted an expansive reading of the value requirement for both bribery and gratuities. Most cases involving bribery under the statute understandably concern cash payments, *United States v. Huff*, 609 F.3d 1240 (11th Cir. 2010) (cash and merchandise to steer contracts to company); *United States v. Lianidis*, 599 F.3d 273 (3d Cir. 2010) (cash to steer contracts to company); *United States v. Peleti*, 576 F.3d 377 (7th Cir. 2009) (cash payment for assistance in obtaining contract); *United States v. Kinter*, 235 F.3d 192 (8th Cir. 2000), *cert. denied*, 532 U.S. 937 (2001) (cash payment to technical employee advising contracting officer during source selection); *United States v. Hollingshead*, 672 F.2d 751 (9th Cir. 1982) (cash payment to employee of Federal Reserve Bank); *United States v. Myers*, 635 F.2d 932 (2d Cir.), *cert. denied*, 449 U.S. 956 (1980) (cash paid by undercover agents to members of Congress); *United States v. Johnson*, 621 F.2d 1073 (10th Cir. 1980) (cash payment offered to FAA procurement official); *United States v. Strand*, 574 F.2d 993 (9th Cir. 1978) (cash payment by undercover agent to summer border guard); *United States v. Arroyo*, 581 F.2d 649 (7th Cir. 1978), *cert. denied*, 439 U.S. 1069 (1979) (cash payments to Small Business Administration loan officers from loan applicant); *United States v. Brasco*, 516 F.2d 816 (2d Cir. 1975), *cert. denied*, 423 U.S. 860 (1975) (cash payments to Post Office officials to obtain contracts); *United States v. Deutsch*, 475 F.2d 55 (5th Cir. 1973) (cash payments to Post Office employees to obtain stolen credit cards); *United States v. Rosner*, 485 F.2d 1213 (2d Cir. 1973), *cert. denied*, 417 U.S. 950 (1974) (cash payments by lawyer to undercover agent to obtain secret grand jury minutes); and *United States v. Jacobs*, 431 F.2d 754 (2d Cir. 1970), *cert. denied*, 402 U.S. 950 (1971) (cash payment to IRS auditor). However, a variety of other benefits have also been considered as " value" by courts in relation to bribery charges, *United States v McDade*, 28 F.3d 283 (3d Cir. 1994), *cert. denied*, 514 U.S. 1003 (1995) (travel expenses); *United States v. Harary*, 457 F.2d 471 (2d Cir. 1972) (prostitutes and cameras); *United States v. Ellenbogen*, 365 F.2d 982 (2d Cir. 1966), *cert. denied*, 386 U.S. 923 (1967) (an automobile). It is not necessary for the government to establish the exact value of a bribe, since the express language of 18 U.S.C. § 201(b)(1) defines the offense as giving "anything of value" to a public official, *United States v. Rasco*, 853 F.2d 501 (7th Cir.), *post-conviction proceedings*, 697 F. Supp. 343 (N.D. Ill.), *cert. denied*, 488 U.S. 959 (1988).

## b. Corrupt Intent

To establish a violation of the provision, a specific "corrupt" intent on the part of the giver or receiver of the bribe must be proved. The requisite intent is proved by showing a quid pro quo — an expectation of a favorable official act in return for the bribe. In *United States v. Strand*, 574 F.2d 993 (9th Cir. 1978), where a U.S. Customs Service official was found to have violated this provision by soliciting and accepting an $800 payment in return for allowing drugs to be smuggled through a border checkpoint, the court discussed the intent required under 18 U.S.C. § 201(c) (now § 201(b)(2)(c)) at 995:

> To be guilty under § 201(c)(3), Strand must have " corruptly" accepted the $800 from the Customs agent for himself or some other person in return for knowingly violating his official duty. The requisite " corrupt" intent has been defined as " incorporating a concept of the bribe being the prime mover or producer of the official act." *United States v. Brewster*, 165 U.S. App. D.C. 1, 21, 506 F.2d 62, 82 (D.C. Cir. 1974). It is this element of quid pro quo that distinguishes the heightened criminal intent requisite under the bribery sections of the statute from the simple mens rea required for violation of the gratuity sections.

In proving the exchange or quid pro quo element, the accompanying intent to influence some identifiable public act must be shown. See *United States v. Abbey*, 560 F.3d 513 (6th Cir. 2009), holding that there need not be an explicit promise to perform of a specific, identifiable act as long as the is an expectation of future acts to benefit the giver of the bribe. In *United States v. Heffler*, 402 F.2d 924 (3d Cir. 1968), a government technical employee was convicted for having solicited a bribe in return for an offer to influence an award, even though he was not the awarding officer. The nexus between solicitation and intent was found in the employee's purported ability to indirectly affect award, his offer to do so, and the specificity of the act to be performed. Similarly, in *United States v. Arroyo*, 581 F.2d 649 (7th Cir. 1978), *cert. denied*, 439 U.S. 1069 (1979), an SBA loan officer was convicted of accepting a bribe even though the loan had already been consummated, because the loan officer had told the borrower that the loan had not yet been finalized. In *United States v. Pommerening*, 500 F.2d 92 (10th Cir.), *cert. denied*, 419 U.S. 1088 (1974), loan applicants were convicted of bribery for giving an SBA official a $5,000 automobile in exchange for expediting a $200,000 loan application to finance their car dealership. The number of reported cases involving government procurement officials and contractors is relatively small. The typical case involves payments made in the hope of influencing contract awards. In *United States v. Johnson*, 621 F.2d 1073 (10th Cir. 1980), the court found the requisite indicia of an expected quid pro quo where the contractor, who had given a $10,000 check to a government procurement agent, credited it on its books to government contracts it expected to win. *United States v. Iaconetti*, 540 F.2d 574 (2d Cir.), *cert. denied*, 429 U.S. 1041 (1976), involved a GSA inspector who was assigned to conduct a preaward survey of a contractor and was convicted of soliciting a bribe for offering to ensure the favorable treatment of the contractor by the " upper echelon" of GSA in exchange for 1% of the contract price.

Corrupt intent can be found even though some of the payments are for services rendered. For example, in *United States v. Biaggi*, 909 F.2d 662 (2d Cir. 1990), the court found corrupt intent in payments made by a contractor to a law firm that had rendered services because part of the payment was for "services" demanded by a Congressman who was "of counsel" to the firm.

### c. Public Official

The statute prohibits payments to a "public official," defined at 18 U.S.C. § 201(a), as follows:

Member of Congress, Delegate, or Resident Commissioner, either before or after such official has qualified, or an officer or employee or person acting for or on behalf of the United States, or any department, agency or branch of Government thereof, including the District of Columbia, in any official function under or by authority of any such department, agency, or branch of Government, or a juror.

The class of "public officials" is an expansive one, consisting of federal prison administrators, *United States v. Alessio*, 528 F.2d 1079 (9th Cir.), *cert. denied*, 426 U.S. 948 (1976); IRS agents, *United States v. Johnson*, 647 F.2d 815 (8th Cir. 1981); congressional aides, *United States v. Carson*, 464 F.2d 424 (2d Cir. 1972), *cert. denied*, 409 U.S. 949 (1972); *United States v. Dixon*, 658 F.2d 181 (3d Cir. 1981); a privately employed grain inspector licensed by the Department of Agriculture, *United States v. Kirby*, 587 F.2d 876 (7th Cir. 1978); and a contracting officer's representative, *K & R Eng'g Co. v. United States*, 222 Ct. Cl. 340, 616 F.2d 469 (1980).

Generally, persons that are in a position of public trust with regard to government funds are classified as public officials even though they are not directly employed by the federal government. See *United States v Kenney*, 185 F.3d 1217 (11th Cir. 1999) (government contractor); *United States v Hang*, 75 F.3d 1275 (8th Cir. 1996) (employee of local housing authority); *United States v Strissel*, 920 F.2d 1162 (4th Cir. 1990) (director of local housing authority); *United States v. Velazquez*, 847 F.2d 140 (4th Cir. 1988) (county jailer where jail housed federal as well as state prisoners, county jailers supervised federal inmates, and jail was subject to inspections by federal prison authorities); *United States v. Kirby*, 587 F.2d 876 (7th Cir. 1978) (privately employed grain inspector licensed by the Department of Agriculture); *United States v. Griffin*, 401 F. Supp. 1222 (S.D. Ind. 1975), *aff'd without op.* 541 F.2d 284 (7th Cir. 1976) (privately employed broker under a HUD contract). Compare *United States v. Loschiavo*, 531 F.2d 659 (2d Cir. 1976) (Model Cities program administrator was not acting on behalf of federal government by suggesting leasing arrangement with one who bribed administrator).

## 2. Gratuities

18 U.S.C. § 201(c) makes it a crime to offer or give a gratuity to a Government official or for a Government official to solicit or receive a gratuity. The crimes are defined as follows:

(c) Whoever —

(1) otherwise than as provided by law for the proper discharge of official duty —

>> (A) directly or indirectly gives, offers, or promises anything of value to any public official, former public official, or person selected to be a public official, for or because of any official act performed or to be performed by such public official, former public official, or person selected to be a public official; or

>> (B) being a public official, former public official, or person selected to be a public official, otherwise than as provided by law for the proper discharge of official duty, directly or indirectly demands, seeks, receives, accepts, or agrees to receive or accept anything of value personally for or because of any official act performed or to be performed by such official or person.

This statute is implemented by Exec. Order No. 12674, 54 Fed. Reg. 15159 (1989), as modified by Exec. Order No. 12731, 55 Fed. Reg. 42547 (1990), and by the regulations at 5 C.F.R. § 2635 Subpart B, which provide a uniform set of rules for all executive branch employees.

### a.  *Thing of Value*

A variety of benefits have been deemed to constitute "value" in relation to gratuities, including cash, meat, liquor, and clothing, *United States v. Romano*, 583 F.2d 1 (1st Cir. 1978); paid vacations, *United States v. Hartley*, 678 F.2d 961 (11th Cir. 1982); loans and promise of future employment, *United States v. Gorman*, 807 F.2d 1299 (6th Cir. 1986), *cert. denied*, 484 U.S. 815 (1987); and golf clubs, *United States v. Hoffmann*, 556 F.3d 871 (8th Cir. 2009). In *Gorman*, the court noted that the term "anything of value" should be broadly construed and not limited to gratuities as that word is commonly understood. In determining what constitutes a "thing of value," the court placed the focus on the subjective value the receiver of the gratuity attached to the items received. See *United States v. McDade*, 827 F. Supp. 1153 (E.D. Pa. 1993), *aff'd*, 28 F.3d 283 (3d Cir. 1994), where a United States congressman charged with accepting illegal gratuities argued that many of the gifts allegedly received, such as a golf jacket, a golf bag, and a golf umbrella, had only nominal value and were thus not "things of value" under the gratuities statute. The congressman cited *Gorman* to support the proposition that the term "anything of value" should be construed as meaning "substantial value." The court could find nothing in *Gorman* to support this argument and denied the congressman's motion to dismiss the indictment. The court noted that even the smallest of the items allegedly received was objectively valuable enough under the gratuities statute, and that the items may have also had additional subjective value to the congressman. As an example, the court noted that the golf jacket was a green jacket similar to the one awarded each year to the winner of the Masters Golf Tournament and, thus, presumably covetable by a golf lover.

The federal standards of conduct in 5 C.F.R. § 2635 contain extensive guidance on "gifts" to federal employees. 5 C.F.R. § 2635.203(b) provides the following definition of the term "gift:"

> *Gift* includes any gratuity, favor, discount, entertainment, hospitality, loan, forbearance, or other item having monetary value. It includes services as well as gifts of training, transportation, local travel, lodgings, and meals, whether provided in-kind, by purchase of a ticket, payment in advance, or reimbursement after the expense has been incurred.

This regulation contains nine exceptions to this definition as follows:

> (1) Modest items of food and refreshments, such as soft drinks, coffee and donuts, offered other than as part of a meal;
>
> (2) Greeting cards and items with little intrinsic value, such as plaques, certificates, and trophies, which are intended solely for presentation;
>
> (3) Loans from banks and other financial institutions on terms generally available to the public;
>
> (4) Opportunities and benefits, including favorable rates and commercial discounts, available to the public or to a class consisting of all Government employees or all uniformed military personnel, whether or not restricted on the basis of geographic considerations;
>
> (5) Rewards and prizes given to competitors in contests or events, including random drawings, open to the public unless the employee's entry into the contest or event is required as part of his official duties;
>
> (6) Pension and other benefits resulting from continued participation in an employee welfare and benefits plan maintained by a former employer;
>
> (7) Anything which is paid for by the Government or secured by the Government under Government contract;

NOTE: Some airlines encourage those purchasing tickets to join programs that award free flights and other benefits to frequent fliers. Any such benefit earned on the basis of Government-financed travel belongs to the agency rather than to the employee and may be accepted only insofar as provided under 41 CFR part 301-53.

> (8) Any gift accepted by the Government under specific statutory authority, including:
>
>> (i) Travel, subsistence, and related expenses accepted by an agency under the authority of 31 U.S.C. 1353 in connection with an employee's attendance at a meeting or similar function relating to his official duties which takes place away from his duty station.

The agency's acceptance must be in accordance with the implementing regulations at 41 CFR part 304-1; and

(ii) Other gifts provided in-kind which have been accepted by an agency under its agency gift acceptance statute; or

(9) Anything for which market value is paid by the employee.

(c) Market value means the retail cost the employee would incur to purchase the gift. An employee who cannot ascertain the market value of a gift may estimate its market value by reference to the retail cost of similar items of like quality. The market value of a gift of a ticket entitling the holder to food, refreshments, entertainment, or any other benefit shall be the face value of the ticket,

5 C.F.R. § 2635.204 contains detailed guidance on a number of additional exceptions that pertain to special situations. See, for example, the small value exception in 5 C.F.R. § 2635.204(a), which permits employees to accept unsolicited gifts with a value of $20 or less and an aggregate annual value of $50 per giver; 5 C.F.R. § 2635.204(b), which permits acceptance of gifts based on a personal relationship; 5 C.F.R. § 2635.204(d), which permits the acceptance of awards and honorary degrees with a value of no more than $200; 5 C.F.R. § 2635.204(e), which permits acceptance of gifts based on outside employment or business relationships; 5 C.F.R. § 2635.204(f), which permits acceptance of gifts in connection with political activities; 5 C.F.R. § 2635.204(g), which permits acceptance of free attendance for speakers and panelists in public meetings; and 5 C.F.R. § 2635.204(h), which permits acceptance of food and refreshments at social events where the invitation has been issued by other than a prohibited source. This regulation contains detailed guidance on these exceptions including numerous specific examples of their application.

Even though acceptance of a gift may be permitted by one of the described exceptions, the regulations note at 5 C.F.R. § 2635.204 that "it is never inappropriate and frequently prudent for an employee to decline a gift offered by a prohibited source or because of his official position." Additionally, 5 C.F.R. § 2635.202(c) contains the following broad restrictive guidance:

Notwithstanding any exception provided in this subpart . . . an employee shall not:

(1) Accept a gift in return for being influenced in the performance of an official act:

(2) Solicit or coerce the offering of a gift;

(3) Accept gifts from the same or different sources on a basis so frequent that a reasonable person would be led to believe that the employee is using his public office for private gain;

(4) Accept a gift in violation of any statute . . . ;

(5) Accept vendor promotional training contrary to applicable regulations, policies or guidance relating to the procurement of supplies and services for the Government, except pursuant to § 2635.204(l).

This would appear to make it inappropriate for a government employee to accept any gift from a contractor if the employee has official duties with regard to the contract. See 5 C.F.R. § 3601.103 for supplemental guidance provided for DoD employees.

## b. Purpose of Gratuity

The gratuity must be linked to a *specific* act that the official has performed or is expected to perform, *United States v. Sun-Diamond Growers of California*, 526 U.S. 398 (1999). In reaching this conclusion, the Court held the statute did not intend to make it a crime to give gifts to employees merely because they held high positions in the government. See also *United States v. Arthur*, 544 F.2d 730 (4th Cir. 1976), stating that a gift given to create goodwill was not a gratuity. In earlier cases, some circuits had construed the statute more broadly. See, for example, *United States v. Campbell*, 684 F.2d 141 (D.C. Cir. 1982), concluding that a gift offered or solicited merely to "generally influence" an official was sufficient to satisfy the "for or because of" element of the statute. See also *United States v Evans*, 572 F.2d 455 (5th Cir.), *cert. denied*, 439 U.S. 870 (1978), stating at 480:

> The purpose of these statutes is to reach any situation in which the judgment of a government agent might be clouded because of payments or gifts made to him by reason of his position "otherwise than as provided by law for the proper discharge of official duty." Even if corruption is not intended by either the donor or the donee, there is still a tendency in such a situation to provide conscious or unconscious preferential treatment of the donor by the donee, or the inefficient management of public affairs. These statutes, like the predecessor legislation, are a congressional effort to eliminate the temptation inherent in such a situation.

In *United States v. Niederberger*, 580 F.2d 63 (3d Cir. 1978), where an IRS employee violated this statute by accepting five golfing trips, the court discussed the different degrees of intent required for establishing violations of the bribery and gratuity sections, at 68:

> It is clear, then, that § 201(c)(1) [now § 201(b)(1)] requires as one of its elements a quid pro quo. In fact, we find this to be the primary distinction between subsections (c)(1) and (g) [now § 201(c)]. Support for this view is found in *United States v. Brewster*, 165 U.S. App. D.C. 1, 506 F.2d 62 (1974), where the court, analyzing the differences between subsections (c)(1) and (g), held that " [t]he bribery section [(c)(1)] makes necessary an explicit quid pro quo which need not exist if only an illegal gratuity is involved." *Id.*, at 11, 506 F.2d at 72.

Thus, we find it unnecessary for the Government to allege in an indictment charging a § 201(g) offense that a gratuity received by a public official was, in any way, generated by some specific, identifiable act performed or to be performed by the official. A quid pro quo is simply foreign to the elements of a subsection (g) offense.

In *United States v. Bishton*, 463 F.2d 887 (D.C. Cir. 1972), a supervisor was convicted under this section for soliciting a $400 gift from an employee for whom the supervisor had previously obtained a promotion. In *United States v. Evans*, 572 F.2d 455 (5th Cir. 1978), acceptance of a $500 gratuity by an official who had previously accepted an offer of government employment but had not commenced work was sufficient to establish a violation of this section.

Since a gratuity need only be paid "for or because of any official act" (18 U.S.C. § 201(c)) and no quid pro quo need be proved, it may be difficult to discern whether the alleged payment was made out of friendship or other disinterested motive. While it is clear that *corrupt* intent need not be shown, the government must at least demonstrate *some* nexus between the giving or receiving of the thing of value and the employee's official position. In *United States v. Standefer*, 610 F.2d 1076 (3d Cir. 1979), *aff'd*, 447 U.S. 10 (1980), sufficient evidence of intent was found despite a corporate officer's assertion that certain vacation trips to Florida given to an IRS employee were motivated by disinterested friendship, because no evidence was offered that similar gifts were given either prior or subsequent to the recipient's employment in the government, and a subordinate of the corporate officer characterized the relationship as a "business friendship." However, many of the reported cases actually involve facts reflecting an expectation of a quid pro quo, perhaps reflecting a prosecutorial reluctance to impose bribery sanctions in cases involving small payments. For example, in *United States v. Mosley*, 659 F.2d 812 (7th Cir. 1981), an Illinois state official, whose salary was entirely paid by the federal government under the CETA program, was convicted of violating 18 U.S.C. § 201(g) (now § 201(c)(1)(B)) for soliciting $50 payments from applicants for CETA jobs in exchange for favorable referral to CETA hiring agencies. In *United States v. Kirby*, 587 F.2d 876 (7th Cir. 1978), the defendants were convicted of conspiring to violate 18 U.S.C. § 201(f) (now § 201(c)(1)(A)) by making payments to grain inspectors in exchange for false certifications that inspected grain was of a higher quality than it actually was.

## c.  Contract Termination

10 U.S.C. § 2207 requires that all Department of Defense contracts over the simplified acquisition threshold contain a clause giving the government the right to terminate the contract if gratuities have been offered or paid. The standard clause used for this purpose the Gratuities clause in FAR 52.203-3. FAR 3.202 requires this clause to be used by all agencies. However, it is not applicable to contracts for personal services and contracts between the military departments or defense agencies and foreign governments that do not obligate Department of Defense funds, FAR 3.202. In addition to the right to terminate the contract, the clause gives agencies the right to damages for breach of contract and gives the Department of Defense

the right to exemplary damages from three to ten times the "cost incurred by the contractor in giving [the] gratuities."

There are several cases indicating that contractors can be subjected to severe penalties for bribery or gratuities under this clause. See, for example, *Erwin Pfister General-Bauunternehmen*, ASBCA 43980, 02-1 BCA ¶ 31,431, where the government terminated the contracts, refused to pay for work performed, refused to pay for claimed extra work and assessed substantial exemplary damages. The board denied the contractor's appeal to recover the payments owed on the contract on the basis of the contractor's conviction of bribing a contract specialist. The same result was reached in *Andreas Boehm Malergrossbetrieb*, ASBCA 44017, 01-1 BCA ¶ 31,354; *Schneider Haustechnik GmbH*, ASBCA 43969, 01-1 BCA ¶ 31,264; and *Schuepferling GmbH & Co., KG*, ASBCA 45567, 98-2 BCA ¶ 29,828. In these cases, the board rejected the argument that the government had ratified the contracts by allowing performance to continue after it learned of the bribes. Similarly, in *Howema Bau-GmbH*, Comp. Gen. Dec. B-245356, 91-2 CPD ¶ 214, a competitor was properly excluded from competition for a suspected bribe, and in *Litton Sys., Inc.*, 68 Comp. Gen. 422 (B-234060), 89-1 CPD ¶ 450, *recons. denied*, 68 Comp. Gen. 677 (B-234060.2), 89-2 CPD ¶ 228, GAO directed an agency to terminate a major contract because a high-ranking official was bribed.

See also *Heinrich Wilhem Koehler v. United States*, 37 Cont. Cas. Fed. (CCH) ¶ 76,241 (D.D.C. 1991), where the court found proper an agency's decision to suspend a foreign contractor on the ground that the contractor offered gratuities to government personnel in violation of regulations. The court stated that given the fact that all government contracts involving defense appropriations are to contain a clause indicating the government's right to terminate a contractor's right under a contract if the contractor offered a gratuity in order to obtain a contract, it was presumed that the contract in question contained the clause and the contractor was thus on notice of the illegality of the gifts.

## 3. Conduct of Former Employees

The government has sought to prevent former government employees and military officers from making unfair use of their prior positions and affiliations. At the same time, the government recognizes the legitimate interest and rights of former employees to seek employment and to enter into business ventures. Thus, activity that seeks to influence government action or that would undermine confidence in the fairness of government activities is prohibited, but former government employees and military officers retain a great amount of freedom to pursue legally permissible activity.

### a. General Restrictions

18 U.S.C. § 207 restricts "officers and employees" in the following circumstances:

1. A former employee is prohibited for life from representing anyone else before the government on a particular matter the employee handled personally and substantially while a government official.

2. A former employee is prohibited for two years from representing a party on a particular matter that had been under the employee's official responsibility during the final year of the employee's government service.

3. A former employee is prohibited for one year from assisting others in trade or treaty negotiations in which the employee had been personally and substantially engaged during the employee's final year of government service.

4. A former senior level employee is prohibited for one year from making any communication or appearance before the employee's former agency regardless of prior involvement in the matter.

5. A former "very senior level" employee is prohibited for two years from contacting employees of the executive branch of the government.

6. A former senior level employee is prohibited for one year from representing any foreign entity before the government.

Criminal prosecutions under this statute are rare and a violation will not make invoices on a contract false claims, *United States ex rel. Siewick v. Jamieson Science & Eng'g, Inc.*, 214 F.3d 1372 (D.C. Cir. 2000). However, alleged violations of this statute are frequently raised in contesting the validity of contracts. The most egregious conduct falling within this provision is hiring government employees before the award of a contract when they have worked on the procurement. A contracting officer's disqualification of an offeror for such conduct was sustained in *NKF Eng'g, Inc. v. United States*, 805 F.2d 372 (Fed. Cir. 1986). In that case, a former Navy civilian employee, who had participated substantially in the procurement process on a particular RFP, left federal employment to take a job with one of the offerors before the contract was awarded. That offeror subsequently submitted a price revision that was 33% lower than its earlier offer. The court upheld the disqualification of the offeror on the basis of an appearance of impropriety, even though the offeror claimed that it had carefully isolated the former government employee from its preparation of the final offer. The court agreed that the potential for an unfair competitive advantage so tainted the procurement process that the integrity of the process had been damaged.

### (1) PARTICULAR MATTER

Violations of the first two restrictions require participation in a "particular matter" that was in the agency during the official's employment. See 5 C.F.R. § 2641.201(h) stating:

(1) Basic concept. The prohibition applies only to communications or appearances made in connection with a "particular matter involving a specific party or parties." Although the statute defines "particular matter" broadly to include "any investigation, application, request for a ruling or determination, rulemaking, contract, controversy, claim, charge, accusation, arrest, or judicial or other proceeding," 18 U.S.C. 207(i)(3), only those particular matters that involve a specific party or parties fall within the prohibition of section 207(a)(1). Such a matter typically involves a specific proceeding affecting the legal rights of the parties or an isolatable transaction or related set of transactions between identified parties, such as a specific contract, grant, license, product approval application, enforcement action, administrative adjudication, or court case.

Excluded are formulation of general policy, rulemaking, and legislation, 5 C.F.R. § 2641.201(h)(2). For a violation to occur, the subsequent representation must concern the same matter in which the employee participated during employment, 5 C.F.R. § 2641.201(h)(3). These regulations contain numerous examples to illustrate the application of these rules.

There is little judicial interpretation of this term. See, however, *CACI, Inc.-Fed. v. United States*, 1 Cl. Ct. 352, *rev'd*, 719 F.2d 1567 (Fed. Cir. 1983), where the Justice Department issued an RFP for ADPE services for the Information Systems Support Group (ISSG) of the department. Before award was made, an offeror who had provided these services for some time alleged that a conflict existed in that a vice president of a competitor had previously served as chief of the ISSG. In issuing an injunction barring award, the Claims Court found that the employee was involved in the "same particular matter" while working for the government, a criterion that satisfies either § 207(a) or § 207(b). The Federal Circuit reversed, holding that a follow-on service contract did not cover the "same particular matter" as the prior contract because the nature of the services had evolved and were broader than those on the earlier contract. The court appears to have read the statute narrowly in arriving at this conclusion. Contrast the *CACI* decision with *United States v. Medico Indus., Inc.*, 784 F.2d 840 (7th Cir. 1986), holding that a contract amendment adding a large quantity of units to an existing contract was sufficiently related to the original contract to be the same particular matter. See also *United States v. Walters*, 2009 U.S. Dist. LEXIS 58370 (S.D. Miss. 2009), finding that advice on how to obtain loans was a particular matter regarding the employee that then went to work for the company that he had advised.

## (2) PERSONAL AND SUBSTANTIAL PARTICIPATION

Violation of the first restriction occurs only when there has been a personal and substantial participation in the matter during employment, as stated at 5 C.F.R. § 2641.201(i) stating:

(1) Participate. To "participate" means to take an action as an employee through decision, approval, disapproval, recommendation, the rendering of advice, inves-

tigation, or other such action, or to purposefully forbear in order to affect the outcome of a matter. An employee can participate in particular matters that are pending other than in his own agency. An employee does not participate in a matter merely because he had knowledge of its existence or because it was pending under his official responsibility. An employee does not participate in a matter within the meaning of this section unless he does so in his official capacity.

(2) Personally. To participate "personally" means to participate:

(i) Directly, either individually or in combination with other persons; or

(ii) Through direct and active supervision of the participation of any person he supervises, including a subordinate.

(3) Substantially. To participate "substantially" means that the employee's involvement is of significance to the matter. Participation may be substantial even though it is not determinative of the outcome of a particular matter. However, it requires more than official responsibility, knowledge, perfunctory involvement, or involvement on an administrative or peripheral issue. A finding of substantiality should be based not only on the effort devoted to a matter, but also on the importance of the effort. While a series of peripheral involvements may be insubstantial, the single act of approving or participating in a critical step may be substantial. Provided that an employee participates in the substantive merits of a matter, his participation may be substantial even though his role in the matter, or the aspect of the matter in which he is participating, may be minor in relation to the matter as a whole. Participation in peripheral aspects of a matter or in aspects not directly involving the substantive merits of a matter (such as reviewing budgetary procedures or scheduling meetings) is not substantial.

These regulations contain numerous examples to illustrate the application of these terms. Review of a proposed notice of income tax deficiency and recommendation for its issuance constituted personal and substantial participation, *United States v. Nasser*, 476 F.2d 1111 (7th Cir. 1973). Preparing a memorandum and answering a legal question were also held to be such participation. Review of a patent application was held to be sufficient involvement in *Kearney & Trecker Corp. v. Giddings & Lewis, Inc.*, 452 F.2d 579 (7th Cir. 1971), *cert. denied*, 405 U.S. 1066 (1972).

## (3) REPRESENTATION

The basic prohibition in 18 U.S.C. § 207(a)(1) is on representational activities carried out "with the intent to influence." "Representation" may occur in the course of communications or appearances. 5 C.F.R. § 2641.201(c) states:

(d) Communication or appearance — (1) Communication. A former employee makes a communication when he imparts or transmits information of any kind, including facts, opinions, ideas, questions or direction, to an employee of the United States, whether orally, in written correspondence, by electronic media, or by any other means. This includes only those communications with respect to which the former employee intends that the information conveyed will be attributed to himself, although it is not necessary that any employee of the United States actually recognize the former employee as the source of the information.

> (2) Appearance. A former employee makes an appearance when he is physically present before an employee of the United States, in either a formal or informal setting. Although an appearance also may be accompanied by certain communications, an appearance need not involve any communication by the former employee.

> (3) Behind-the-scenes assistance. Nothing in this section prohibits a former employee from providing assistance to another person, provided that the assistance does not involve a communication to or an appearance before an employee of the United States.

5 C.F.R. § 2641.201(e) provides the following guidance on the "intent to influence" element of this rule:

> (e) With the intent to influence — (1) Basic concept. The prohibition applies only to communications or appearances made by a former Government employee with the intent to influence the United States. A communication or appearance is made with the intent to influence when made for the purpose of:

>> (i) Seeking a Government ruling, benefit, approval, or other discretionary Government action; or

>> (ii) Affecting Government action in connection with an issue or aspect of a matter which involves an appreciable element of actual or potential dispute or controversy.

5 C.F.R. § 2641.201(e)(2)(vi) makes it clear that there is no violation when a former employee makes a communication, at the initiation of the government, concerning work performed or to be performed under a government contract, during a routine government site visit to a contractor, "in the ordinary course of evaluation, administration, or performance of an actual or proposed contract." The regulation contains the following example:

> An agency official visits the premises of a prospective contractor to evaluate the testing procedure being proposed by the contractor for a research contract on which it has bid. A former employee of the agency, now employed by the contractor, is the person most familiar with the technical aspects of the proposed testing procedure. The agency official asks the former employee about certain technical features of the equipment used in connection with the testing procedure. The former employee may provide factual information that is responsive to the questions posed by the agency official, as such information is requested by the Government under circumstances for its convenience in reviewing the bid. However, the former employee may not argue for the appropriateness of

the proposed testing procedure or otherwise advocate any position on behalf of the contractor.

See *Robert E. Derecktor of R.I., Inc. v. United States*, 762 F. Supp. 1019 (D.R.I. 1991), where the court, interpreting the predecessor to § 207(a), held that a former employee's delivery of a bid package to his former agency did not constitute an appearance within the meaning of this restriction and that the employee did not deliver the bid with the intent to influence. See, however, *United States v. Coleman*, 805 F.2d 474 (3d Cir. 1986), where a former employee's presence at a meeting related to tax cases, which had been within the employee's supervisory responsibility before retiring, was found to constitute representation within the meaning of this restriction.

18 U.S.C. § 207(j)(5) permits "communications solely for the purpose of furnishing scientific or technological information" to the agency. See *J. L. Assocs.*, Comp. Gen. Dec. B-201331.2, 82-1 CPD ¶ 99, where this exception was applied by the Air Force to a " briefing" by a retired military officer concerning the same activity that he had commanded. The briefing concerned the contractor's experience on similar work with other agencies and occurred before issuance of an RFP.

Under a predecessor statute, participation in the preparation of a claim for reimbursement was held not to violate the statute since it did not amount to "prosecution" of a claim, *Acme Process Equip. Co. v. United States*, 171 Ct. Cl. 324, 347 F.2d 509 (1965), *rev'd on other grounds*, 385 U.S. 138 (1966).

### (4) TYPES OF EMPLOYMENT OR CONTRACTING PERMITTED

Absent a violation of the specific provisions of 18 U.S.C. § 207, there is no general prohibition in this statute against *employment* of a former government employee by a contractor. 5 C.F.R. § 2641.101 provides:

18 U.S.C. § 207 prohibits certain acts by former employees (including current employees who formerly served in "senior" or "very senior" employee positions) which involve, or may appear to involve, the unfair use of prior Government employment. None of the restrictions of section 207 prohibits any former employee, regardless of Government rank or position, from accepting employment with any particular private or public employer. Rather, section 207 prohibits a former employee from providing certain services to or on behalf of non-Federal employers or other persons, whether or not done for compensation. These restrictions are personal to the employee and are not imputed to other.

For cases not applying this statute to mere employment, see *Perini/Jones, Joint Venture*, Comp. Gen. Dec. B-285906, 2002 CPD ¶ 68 (former employee that will serve as company's project manager who was in the procuring agency at time proposals were submitted and evaluated); *Medical Dev. Int'l*, Comp. Gen. Dec. B-281484.2, 99-1 CPD ¶ 68 (former employee that will serve as Associate Director of company and had policy position in agency); *Culp/Wesner/Culp*, Comp. Gen. Dec. B-212318, 84-1 CPD ¶ 17 (former agency employee in charge of preparing solicitation subsequently awarded subcontract); and *Bray Studios, Inc.*, Comp. Gen. Dec. B-207723, 82-2 CPD ¶ 373 (former agency employee now president of contractor and working in same area).

Neither is there any general prohibition against entering into contracts with former government employees, *Sterling Med. Assocs.*, 62 Comp. Gen. 230 (B-209493), 83-1 CPD ¶ 215 (former employee of Veterans Administration awarded contract by the Department of the Navy); *Edward R. Jereb*, 60 Comp. Gen. 298 (B-200092), 81-1 CPD ¶ 178 (restriction prohibiting award of services contract to former agency employees held invalid); *Western Eng'g & Sales Co.*, Comp. Gen. Dec. B-205464, 82-2 CPD ¶ 277 (former employee awarded contract by agency based on proposal submitted after employment terminated). See, however, *KAR Contracting, LLC*, Comp. Gen. Dec. B-310454, 2007 CPD ¶ 226, where the agency properly refused to contract with company whose founder had prepared the contract drawings; and *Aviation Enters., Inc. v. Orr*, 29 Cont. Cas. Fed. (CCF) ¶ 82,053 (D.D.C. 1981), *vacated*, 716 F.2d 1403 (D.C. Cir. 1983), where a contract award to a company owned by a former military officer was enjoined because of a "conflict of interest," without reference to the statute. In *KAR Contracting* GAO stated:

> In our view, the restrictions of 18 U.S.C. § 207 do not set the outer boundaries for a CO's reasonable exercise of discretion about whether the award of a contract will create the appearance of impropriety. Specifically, even if KAR can argue that the facts here would not support a criminal conviction for violation of the post-employment restrictions, that would not mean there was no reasonable basis for concluding that KAR was ineligible for award.

### b.  Additional Statutory Restrictions

A broader post-employment restriction applicable to specific "former officials" is set forth in the Procurement Integrity Act at 41 U.S.C. § 2104, stating:

> (a) Prohibition. A former official of a Federal agency may not accept compensation from a contractor as an employee, officer, director, or consultant of the contractor within a period of one year after such former official —
>
> > (1) served, when the contractor was selected or awarded a contract, as the procuring contracting officer, the source selection authority, a member of the source selection evaluation board, or the chief of a financial or technical evaluation team in a procurement in which that contractor was selected for award of a contract in excess of $10,000,000;
> >
> > (2) served as the program manager, deputy program manager, or administrative contracting officer for a contract in excess of $10,000,000 awarded to that contractor; or

(3) personally made for the Federal agency a decision to —

(A) award a contract, subcontract, modification of a contract or subcontract, or a task order or delivery order in excess of $10,000,000 to that contractor;

(B) establish overhead or other rates applicable to one or more contracts for that contractor that are valued in excess of $10,000,000;

(C) approve issuance of one or more contract payments in excess of $10,000,000 to that contractor; or

(D) pay or settle a claim in excess of $10,000,000 with that contractor.

(b) When compensation may be accepted. Subsection (a) does not prohibit a former official of a Federal agency from accepting compensation from a division or affiliate of a contractor that does not produce the same or similar products or services as the entity of the contractor that is responsible for the contract referred to in paragraph (1), (2), or (3) of subsection (a).

FAR 3.104-3(d)(2) provides detailed guidance on the calculation of the one-year period. FAR 3.104-3(d)(3) states that the statute does not prohibit employment by a division or affiliate of a contractor that does not produce the same or similar products or services as the division with which the official had previous contact. FAR 3.104-6 contains guidance on obtaining advice from agency ethics officials on the application of these rules. 41 U.S.C. § 2106 also provides that protests may no longer be filed based on an allegation that this statute has been violated unless the violation has been reported to the contracting agency within 14 days of learning of the violation. See *Honeywell Tech. Solutions, Inc.*, Comp. Gen. Dec. B-400771, 2009 CPD ¶ 49 (protest denied because protester did not file within 14 days of learning that winning offeror had hired an agency official as a consultant). However GAO has ruled on protests alleging that a contractor had obtained an unfair competitive advantage through revolving door violations, *Day & Zimmermann Pantex Corp.*, Comp. Gen. Dec. B-286016, 2001 CPD ¶ 96 (no indication that hired official impacted award decision); *PRC, Inc.*, Comp. Gen. Dec. B-274698.2, 97-1 CPD ¶ 115, *recons. denied*, 97-2 CPD ¶ 10 (no impropriety in the employment of the former Commanding Officer of the procuring agency who had obtained an opinion that he was not a procurement official under the statute although he had concurred in the acquisition plan and appointed the source selection official).

This restriction replaces prior restrictions in 41 U.S.C. § 423(f) (pre-2011 codification) that became applicable when an employee's participation occurred during the conduct of a procurement. In that event, the former procurement official was prohibited for two years from participating with a competing contractor in subsequent negotiations on that contract or from participating in the performance of that contract. Those restrictions also applied to first- and second-tier subcontractors with contracts in excess of $100,000, subcontractors who significantly assisted the contractor in negotiations of the contract, subcontractors specifically directed to the contractor by the procurement official, and subcontractors reviewed or approved by the procurement official. GAO held that the interpretation and enforcement of the postemployment restrictions found in 41 U.S.C. § 423 were primarily matters for the procuring agency and the Department of Justice — with the result that protests would determine only "whether any action of the former government employee may have resulted in prejudice for, or on behalf of, the awardee," *Central Texas College*, 71 Comp. Gen. 164 (B-245233.4), 92-1 CPD ¶ 121. In *FHC Options, Inc.*, Comp. Gen. Dec. B-246793.3, 92-1 CPD ¶ 366, GAO denied a protest based on the employment of a former government employee by the awardee's subcontractor because, although the former employee had assisted in the initial development of the performance work statement and the source selection plan for the solicitation, he had left the government before the RFP was issued, was not involved in the preparation of the awardee's proposal, and would not be involved in performing the contract.

There were also special purpose post-employment restrictions applicable only to defense or procurement personnel, 10 U.S.C. § 2397c. These provisions were repealed by § 4304(b)(1) of the Clinger-Cohen Act of 1996.

Formerly, a retired military officer was subject to two additional restrictions under 37 U.S.C. § 801 and 18 U.S.C. § 281. The Federal Acquisition Streamlining Act of 1994, Pub. L. No. 103-355, repealed 37 U.S.C. § 801. Under the provisions of that statute, a retired regular officer could not be paid from any appropriation for three years after retirement if the former officer was selling for himself or herself or for others or was contracting or negotiating to sell supplies or war materials to the DoD, the Coast Guard, NASA, or the Public Health Service. Section 4304(b)(3) of the Clinger-Cohen Act of 1996 repealed 18 U.S.C. § 281. This statute made it unlawful for a period of two years after retirement for a former military officer to be compensated for representing any person in the sale of goods or services to the military service from which the officer retired.

Section 4304(b)(6) of the Clinger-Cohen Act of 1996 also repealed 42 U.S.C. § 7216, prohibiting the Department of Energy from using employees of "energy concerns" in departmental matters involving that concern for a period of one year after employment. In *TRW Envtl. Safety Sys., Inc. v. United States*, 18 Cl. Ct. 33 (1989), award to an offeror was permanently enjoined when the court found a violation of that statute. In that case, an ex-employee of a competitor had participated in drafting the statement of work and was appointed chairman of the source evaluation board within the one-year period.

## 4. *Conduct of Current Employees*

There are numerous statutes and regulations circumscribing the activities of government employees. See, for example, 18 U.S.C. § 203 (limitation on receiving payment from others for official activity); 18 U.S.C. § 205 (prohibition against prosecuting claims); and 18 U.S.C. § 209 (prohibition against receiving compensation from other than United States for official duties). This section discusses the two major statutes applicable to government contracting. It also discusses administrative restrictions on contracting with organizations owned or controlled by government employees.

### a. *General Restrictions*

Officers and employees of the government with a financial interest in an organization are prohibited from participating personally and substantially in any matter concerning that organization and the government, 18 U.S.C. § 208. This provision was intended to expand the proscriptions against employee participation with the private sector beyond the prior § 434, which merely prohibited certain "transactions of business."

#### (1) EXTENT OF FINANCIAL INTEREST

The Standards of Ethical Conduct contained in 5 C.F.R. § 2635 Subpart D provide detailed guidance implementing this statutory proscription. The following definition of "financial interest" is found at 5 C.F.R. § 2635.403(c):

> (1) Except as provided in paragraph (c)(2) of this section, the term financial interest is limited to financial interests that are owned by the employee or by the employee's spouse or minor children. However, the term is not limited to only those financial interests that would be disqualifying under 18 U.S.C. § 208(a) and § 2635.402. The term includes any current or contingent ownership, equity, or security interest in real or personal property or a business and may include an indebtedness or compensated employment relationship. It thus includes, for example, interests in the nature of stocks, bonds, partnership interests, fee and leasehold interests, mineral and other property rights, deeds of trust, and liens, and extends to any right to purchase or acquire any such interest, such as a stock option or commodity future. It does not include a future interest created by someone other than the employee, his spouse or dependent child or any right as a beneficiary of an estate that has not been settled.

> (2) The term financial interest includes service, with or without compensation, as an officer, director, trustee, general partner or employee of any person, including a nonprofit entity, whose financial interests are imputed to the employee under § 2635.402(b)(2)(iii) or (iv).

The Ethics in Government Act of 1978, 5 U.S.C. App. § 201 et seq., further requires the public disclosure of financial information by all political appointees and all civil service employees of GS-16 and above.

A financial interest is present if it is more than insubstantial, remote, or inconsequential. The Office of Government Ethics ruled in 83 OGE 1 (1983), that vested rights in a private corporation's pension plan constituted a financial interest. In another ruling dated August 17, 1979, the Office ruled that leaves of absence or reemployment rights with a former employer were financial interests in that company.

Case law indicates that a statutory violation occurs when the employee has both a financial stake in the outcome of the transaction and a sufficient contact with the transaction. It seems clear that the threshold is quite low for both elements. In *United States v. Mississippi Valley Generating Co.*, 364 U.S. 520 (1961), the Court gave an expansive reading to the term "transacting business" in prior § 434 and found a violation of the statute where the employee's financial stake consisted of the potential business he had generated for another employer and where his contact with the transaction involved him in preliminary contract negotiations on behalf of both parties. In that case, a temporary employee of the Bureau of the Budget who served at the request of the bureau chief without pay also served as an officer of a bank. An offeror on an RFP for construction of a power plant negotiated the early stages of the contract with the temporary employee and also asked him to inquire into financing with bank officials. The temporary employee was not involved in the final contract negotiations but confidentially suggested revisions to the offeror's second proposal. Regarding the employee's financial stake, the Court held that positive corruption is not a prerequisite for violation of the conflicts statute and stated at 550, "[T]he statute is more concerned with what might have happened than with what actually happened." See also *Smith v. United States*, 305 F.2d 197 (9th Cir. 1962), where the court found a violation of § 434 even though the "transaction" consisted merely of an employee's failure to circumscribe the activities of subordinates who were involved in a conflict.

Although § 208 is much broader in scope than was § 434, the cases decided under this section do not appear to have given it as strict an interpretation as was given to the prior statute. See *United States v. Ponnapula*, 246 F.3d 576 (6th Cir. 2001), finding no conflict where a person acting for the Small Business Administration in the sale of foreclosed property took a $5,000 retainer for future employment from the buyer but had no substantial participation in the transaction because her actions with regard to the sale were only ministerial; *Cexec, Inc. v. Department of Energy*, GSB-CA 12909-P, 95-1 BCA ¶ 27,380, finding no conflict when an employee, whose wife had a financial interest in the winning contractor, had only peripheral contact with the procurement; and *United States v. Tierney*, 947 F.2d 854 (8th Cir. 1991), finding no conflict because the fact that prosecutor's husband was representing defendant's insurance company was too remote a connection. See also *Grassetti v. Weinberger*, 408 F. Supp. 142 (N.D. Cal. 1976), where a grant applicant had been denied a grant by the National Cancer Institute, a division of the National Institutes of Health, whose evaluation team consisted of members also competing for research grants. Though the team had sufficient contact with the transaction, the court stated that although a conflict would arise where team members contributed to a decision as to whether to award themselves a grant, the allegation that a denial of a grant to another applicant would leave more money for the team was too remote to create a conflict.

The cases that have enforced § 208 have dealt with considerably greater financial interests and contact than that in *Mississippi Valley* or *Smith*. See, for example, *United States v. Selby*, 557 F.3d 968 (9th Cir. 2009) (employee promoted the agency's use of software sold by husband's company); *United States v Bouchey*, 860 F. Supp. 890 (D.D.C. 1994) (alleged participation by government employee in conspiracy to pay inflated consulting fees); *K & R Eng'g Co. v. United States*, 222 Ct. Cl. 340, 616 F.2d 469 (1980) (chief of a branch of the Corps of Engineers took kickbacks and profits from contracts awarded by his office to a particular contractor after giving contractor advance notice of the IFB and of the maximum amount the Corps would pay); *United States v. Conlon*, 628 F.2d 150 (D.C. Cir. 1980) (indictment under § 208 reinstated where it was shown that the director of the Bureau of Engraving, who was also president of the American Bank Note Development Corp. (ABNC), participated in decisionmaking regarding replacement of a Bureau signature system with one developed by ABNC); *United States v. Irons*, 640 F.2d 872 (7th Cir. 1981) (program officer for HEW recommended to a contracting officer that an IFB be sent to a company he established for the purpose of receiving the IFB); and *United Tel. Co.*, GSBCA 10031-P, 89-3 BCA ¶ 22,108 (offeror disqualified because its subcontractor had used a government employee participating in the procurement as a consultant during the competition).

## (2) EMPLOYMENT DISCUSSIONS

Conducting employment negotiations has also been held to be a conflict of interest under 18 U.S.C. § 208. Employment discussions are considered a financial interest by the Standards of Ethical Conduct, 5 C.F.R. § 2635.603. The following definition of "seeking employment" is found at 5 C.F.R. § 2635.603(b):

> An employee is seeking employment once he has begun seeking employment within the meaning of paragraph (b)(1) of this section and until he is no longer seeking employment within the meaning of paragraph (b)(2) of this section.
>
> (1) An employee has begun seeking employment if he has directly or indirectly:
>
> > (i) Engaged in negotiations for employment with any person. For these purposes, as for 18 U.S.C. § 208(a), the term negotiations means discussion or communication with another person, or such person's agent or intermediary, mutually conducted with a view toward reaching an agreement regarding possible employment with that person. The term is not limited to discussions of specific terms and conditions of employment in a specific position;
>
> > (ii) Made an unsolicited communication to any person, or such person's agent or intermediary, regarding possible employment

with that person. However, the employee has not begun seeking employment if that communication was:

(A) For the sole purpose of requesting a job application; or

(B) For the purpose of submitting a resume or other employment proposal to a person affected by the performance or nonperformance of the employee's duties only as part of an industry or other discrete class. The employee will be considered to have begun seeking employment upon receipt of any response indicating an interest in employment discussions; or

(iii) Made a response other than rejection to an unsolicited communication from any person, or such person's agent or intermediary, regarding possible employment with that person.

(2) An employee is no longer seeking employment when:

(i) The employee or the prospective employer rejects the possibility of employment and all discussions of possible employment have terminated; or

(ii) Two months have transpired after the employee's dispatch of an unsolicited resume or employment proposal, provided the employee has received no indication of interest in employment discussions from the prospective employer.

(3) For purposes of this definition, a response that defers discussions until the foreseeable future does not constitute rejection of an unsolicited employment overture, proposal, or resume nor rejection of a prospective employment possibility.

Negotiations for employment were found in *United States v. Schaltenbrand*, 930 F.2d 1554 (11th Cir. 1991), *cert. denied*, 502 U.S. 1005 (1991), where an Air Force reserve officer approached a prospective employer, filled out an application, came for an interview, discussed his qualifications and indicated a willingness to meet company officials, even though neither side made any formal offer until after he was finished with the project; *United States v. Lord*, 710 F. Supp. 615 (E.D. Va. 1989), *aff'd*, 902 F.2d 1567 (4th Cir.1990), where a government program manager discussed employment with a contractor; *United States v. Gorman*, 807 F.2d 1299 (6th Cir. 1986), *cert. denied*, 484 U.S. 815 (1987), where the government employee had an initial conversation with a company and gave them a list of conditions for employment. The Principal Deputy Assistant Secretary of the Air Force for Acquisition also pled guilty to a violation of § 208 when she met with an officer of a company to discuss future employment at the same time she was negotiating a major contract with that company. See *Lockheed Martin Aeronautics Co.*, Comp. Gen. Dec. B-295401, 2005 CPD ¶ 41, for a description of this plea agreement. Compare *Air Line Pilots Assn., Int'l v. Department of Transportation*, 899 F.2d 1230 (D.C. Cir. 1990), where no conflict was found when the Secretary of Transportation made a regulatory ruling at the time he was negotiating for employment with a law firm. The court based its conclusion of the fact that the law firm was not representing any of the parties to the regulatory ruling.

Once an employment discussion has commenced, it may be terminated by "rejection" of any possibility of employment. However, it is clear that terminating an immediate employment discussion will not result in "rejection" of an offer of employment if the discussion is only deferred. See *Express One Int'l, Inc. v. United States Postal Serv.*, 814 F. Supp. 93 (D.D.C. 1992), where the court enjoined award of a contract because the employee of a consultant of the procuring agency had told the winning offeror "he would not be available for a personal meeting or to discuss a position until after [award of the contract]."

Violations of § 208 are valid grounds for rejecting an offer. In *AT&T Communications, Inc.*, GSBCA 9252-P, 88-2 BCA ¶ 20,805 , an offeror was disqualified after receiving information from a government employee with whom it had discussed employment. Less stringent enforcement of this rule occurred in *Chemonics Int'l Consulting Div.*, 63 Comp. Gen. 14 (B-210426), 83-2 CPD ¶ 426, where GAO held that it was improper to withhold award from a firm that had offered employment to a government employee who had attended subsequent negotiations, and *CACI, Inc.-Fed. v. United States*, 1 Cl. Ct. 352, *rev'd*, 719 F.2d 1567 (Fed. Cir. 1983), where the court found no violation of § 208 when contract negotiations with a government employee occurred 16 months after an employment discussion had occurred. In *Four-Phase Sys., Inc.*, ASBCA 26794, 86-2 BCA ¶ 18,924, a violation of § 208 was found where employment negotiations occurred during the negotiation of a change order. As a result, the board held that the violation of § 208 was a valid defense to a breach of contract claim based on the change order.

## b.  Procurement Integrity Restrictions

Additional restrictions on employment contacts or discussions are contained in 41 U.S.C. § 2103, stating:

> (a) Actions required. An agency official participating personally and substantially in a Federal agency procurement for a contract in excess of the simplified acquisition threshold who contacts or is contacted by a person that is a bidder or offeror in that Federal agency procurement regarding possible non-Federal employment for that official shall —

>> (1) promptly report the contact in writing to the official's supervisor and to the designated agency ethics official (or designee) of the agency in which the official is employed; and

>> (2) (A) reject the possibility of non-Federal employment; or

(B) disqualify himself or herself from further personal and substantial participation in that Federal agency procurement until the agency authorizes the official to resume participation in the procurement, in accordance with the requirements of section 208 of title 18 and applicable agency regulations on the grounds that —

(i) the person is no longer a bidder or offeror in that Federal agency procurement; or

(ii) all discussions with the bidder or offeror regarding possible non-Federal employment have terminated without an agreement or arrangement for employment.

The Act is implemented in FAR 3.104-3(c)(2) which defines a "contact" as "any of the actions included as 'seeking employment' in 5 C.F.R. § 2635.603(b)" as well as "unsolicited communications from offerors regarding possible employment." FAR 3.104-5(a) also warns that contacts by "agents or other intermediaries" of an offeror may fall within these procedures. The first step in this procedure is an immediate reporting requirement when an agency official receives an employment contract, FAR 3.104-3(c)(1). This report must be submitted to the official's supervisor and the agency ethics official. The second step is for the official to either "reject the possibility of non-Federal employment" or disqualify himself or herself from further participation in the procurement. This disqualification decision appears to be in the sole discretion of the official. However, FAR 3.104-8(c) states that an official who "refuses to terminate employment discussions may be subject to agency administrative actions under 5 C.F.R. § 2635.604(d) if the official's disqualification from participation in a particular procurement interferes substantially with the individual's ability to perform assigned duties." Thus, an agency retains considerable control over this decision under the regulations.

FAR 3.104-5(b) contains the following additional reporting requirements:

(b) *Disqualification notice.* In addition to submitting the contact report required by 3.104-3(c)(1), an agency official who must disqualify himself or herself pursuant to 3.104-3(c)(1)(ii) must promptly submit written notice of disqualification from further participation in the procurement to the contracting officer, the source selection authority if other than the contracting officer, and the agency official's immediate supervisor. As a minimum, the notice must —

(1) Identify the procurement;

(2) Describe the nature of the agency official's participation in the procurement and specify the approximate dates or time period of participation; and

(3) Identify the offeror and describe its interest in the procurement.

After disqualification, FAR 3.104-5(c) places the decision on reinstatement of the official in the sole discretion of the agency as follows:

(c) *Resumption of participation in a procurement.* (1) The official must remain disqualified until such time as the agency, at its sole and exclusive discretion, authorizes the official to resume participation in the procurement in accordance with 3.104-3(c)(1)(ii).

(2) After the conditions of 3.104-3(c)(1)(ii)(A) or (B) have been met, the head of the contracting activity (HCA), after consultation with the agency ethics official, may authorize the disqualified official to resume participation in the procurement, or may determine that an additional disqualification period is necessary to protect the integrity of the procurement process. In determining the disqualification period, the HCA must consider any factors that create an appearance that the disqualified official acted without complete impartiality in the procurement. The HCA's reinstatement decision should be in writing.

(3) Government officer or employee must also comply with the provisions of 18 U.S.C. 208 and 5 CFR part 2635 regarding any resumed participation in a procurement matter. Government officer or employee may not be reinstated to participate in a procurement matter affecting the financial interest of someone with whom the individual is seeking employment, unless the individual receives —

(i) A waiver pursuant to 18 U.S.C. 208(b)(1) or (b)(3); or

(ii) An authorization in accordance with the requirements of subpart F of 5 CFR part 2635.

The Act also narrows the scope of these restrictions. First, the rule only applies to contracts over the simplified acquisition threshold of $150,000. Second, the rule applies only to "Federal agency procurement" — which excludes sole source contracts and contract modifications. Note, however, that entertaining employment discussions or negotiations during such transactions would be a violation of 18 U.S.C. § 208 and 5 C.F.R. § 2635.603(b). A third narrowing is that the Act restricts only bidders and offerors making contacts to officials regarding future employment. However, FAR 3.104-5(a) warns that the disqualification may be required even where contacts are through an agent or intermediary of the bidder or offeror because that contact would be a violation of 18 U.S.C. § 208. See also 5 C.F.R. § 2635.603(c).

## 5.  *Contracting with Government Employees*

Government employees who do not fall within the proscriptions of 18 U.S.C. § 208 because they are not involved in the procurement process are, nevertheless, restricted from entering into contracts with any agency of the government. FAR 3.601(a) states:

Except as specified in 3.602, a contracting officer shall not knowingly award a contract to a Government employee or to a business concern or other organization owned or substantially owned or controlled by one or more Government employees. This policy is intended to avoid any conflict of interest that might arise between the employees' interests and their Government duties, and to avoid the appearance of favoritism or preferential treatment by the Government toward its employees.

*Valiant Sec. Agency*, Comp. Gen. Dec. B-205087, 81-2 CPD ¶ 367, *recons. denied*, 81-2 CPD ¶ 501, explains this policy as follows:

Contracts between the Government and its employees are not expressly prohibited by statute except where the employee acts for both the Government and the contractor in a particular transaction or where the service to be rendered is such as could be required of the contractor in his capacity as a Government employee. 18 U.S.C. § 208 (1976); *Hugh Maher*, B-187841, March 31, 1977, 77-1 CPD ¶ 204. However, it has long been recognized that such contracts are undesirable because among other reasons they invite criticism as to alleged favoritism and possible fraud and that they should be authorized only in exceptional cases where the Government cannot reasonably be otherwise supplied. 27 Comp. Gen. 735 (1948); *Capital Aero, Inc.*, B-183833, September 30, 1975, 75-2 CPD ¶ 201; *Burgos & Associates, Inc.*, 59 Comp. Gen. 273 (1980), 80-1 CPD ¶ 155. The fact that a service would be more expensive if not obtained from an employee of the Government does not by itself provide support for a determination that the service cannot reasonably be obtained from other sources. 55 Comp. Gen. 681 (1976).

The sole exception to this prohibition is in FAR 3.602 which requires a determination by a high-level official that there is a "most compelling reason" to enter into a contract with a former government employee, such as when the government's needs cannot reasonably be otherwise met. The contracting officer has discretion in determining whether this exemption applies. Compare the *Valiant* case with *International Alliance of Sports Officials*, Comp. Gen. Dec. B-210172, 83-2 CPD ¶ 328, sustaining a contracting officer's decision to award a contract at approximately $223,000 in contrast to the next low offer of $275,000.

Substantial ownership or control is determined by the facts of each individual case. Mere employment by a government contractor is not prohibited by this restriction. See *National Serv. Corp.*, Comp. Gen. Dec. B-205629, 82-2 CPD ¶ 76 (no substantial ownership or control when government employee gave up partnership and became part-time bookkeeper); and *H H & K Bldrs., Inc.*, Comp. Gen. Dec. B-238095, 90-1 CPD ¶ 219 (sole owner's husband was government employee, but sufficient separation of ownership). Compare *Elecs. West, Inc.*, Comp. Gen. Dec. B-209720, 83-2 CPD ¶ 127 (change in title from President to Treasurer did not prevent disqualification). An agency does not have to establish with certainty that an employee has a substantially controlling interest but rather needs only to have a reason to believe that the government employee has such control, *Gurley's Inc.*, Comp. Gen. Dec. B-253852, 93-2 CPD ¶ 123. See *Eugene Thurman*, Comp. Gen. Dec. B-206325, 82-1 CPD ¶ 487 (award to wife of government employee improper when husband in fact ran the business); *American Truss & Mfg. Corp.*, Comp. Gen. Dec. B-205962, 82-1 CPD ¶ 477 (award improper where government employee owned 50% of stock and wife owned balance); *Marc Indus.*, Comp. Gen. Dec. B-246528, 92-1 CPD ¶ 273 (substantial control found where government employee represented the firm in prework conferences under prior contracts with the agency, served as the contact for any complaints about contract performance, and, based on his involvement with the firm, was disciplined for violating his agency's conflict of interest regulations); *KSR, Inc.*, Comp. Gen. Dec. B-250160, 93-1 CPD ¶ 37 (substantial control found where government employee was president and was one of five owners); and *Asia Resource Partners K.K.*, Comp. Gen. Dec. B-400552, 2008 CPD ¶ 201 (exclusion of company when husband of contracting officer was its president and majority owner). The restriction does not apply when a contractor employee has a similar conflict with a subcontractor, *Science Pump Corp.*, Comp. Gen. Dec. B-255737, 94-1 CPD ¶ 246.

Some agencies have further restrictions on contracting with members of a former government employee's family. See, for example, *Joann Flora*, Comp. Gen. Dec. B-212776, 83-2 CPD ¶ 520 (regulations prohibiting contract with immediate member of the household of agency employee barred contract with unmarried party living as spouse); and *Heidi Holley*, Comp. Gen. Dec. B-211746, 83-2 CPD ¶ 241 (regulations stating that contracts should generally not be awarded to members of an agency employee's family and requiring close scrutiny barred award to spouse of agency employee required to supervise contract).

If the contracting officer inadvertently makes an award to a company owned or controlled by a government employee, GAO will not disturb the award absent an indication of favoritism or other impropriety, *Sterling Medical Assocs.*, 62 Comp. Gen. 230 (B-209493), 83-1 CPD ¶ 215; *Biosystems Analysis, Inc.*, Comp. Gen. Dec. B-198846, 80-2 CPD ¶ 149. In both cases, the employee worked for an agency other than the one awarding the contract.

## 6. Anti-Kickback Act

Contractors and subcontractors are prohibited from soliciting, accepting, or attempting to accept any kickbacks from their subcontractors by the Anti-Kickback Act of 1986, 41 U.S.C. §§ 8701-07. The Act contains a broad definition of the term "kickback," as follows:

> The term "kickback" means any money, fee, commission, credit, gift, gratuity, thing of value, or compensation of any kind that is provided to a prime contractor, prime contractor employee, subcontractor, or subcontractor employee to improperly obtain or reward favorable treatment in connection with a prime contract or a subcontract relating to a prime contract.

The purpose of this statute is to prevent payments that impede the competitive process. The typical kickback is paid to a purchasing agent of a contractor or subcontractor to obtain the award of a subcontract without having to participate in a fair competition. The purchasing agent, in turn, takes some action that distorts the competition. The presumption is that the government eventually pays the amount of the kickback in higher prices, and the Act permits the procuring agency to reduce the price by the amount of the kickback, 41 U.S.C. § 8705(b). The Act also contains criminal and civil sanctions, 41 U.S.C. §§ 8706 and 8707.

The Act is implemented in FAR 3.502 and the Anti-Kickback Procedures clause at FAR 52.203-7. This clause requires the contractor to have internal procedures to detect and prevent kickbacks. It also requires the prompt reporting of kickbacks and cooperation with government agencies in the investigation of kickbacks. The clause is not required for contracts under $150,000 or contracts for the acquisition of commercial items, § 4104 (civilian agency acquisitions) and § 8301 (armed services acquisitions) of the Federal Acquisition Streamlining Act of 1994, Pub. L. No. 103-355. However, such procurements are still subject to the Act.

There has been very little significant litigation under this Act. However, see *Morse Diesel Int'l, Inc. v. United States*, 66 Fed. Cl. 788 (2005), 74 Fed. Cl. 601 (2007), finding a violation of the Act when the contractor's surety bond broker paid 50% of its commissions to the contractor in exchange for the right to be its exclusive broker. See also *Aalco Forwarding, Inc.*, Comp. Gen. Dec. B-277241.8, 97-2 CPD ¶ 110, holding that payment of commissions or rebates from tariff rates from carriers to brokers under government contract were not per se violations of the Act, and *United States v Guthrie*, 64 F.3d 1510 (10th Cir. 1995), holding that contractors can be required to pay restitution for violations of the Act.

There was considerable litigation under a prior Act that was narrower in scope. There the courts required proof of specific intent and construed the value and intent elements of the kickback prohibition, following the cases on bribery, *Howard v. United States*, 345 F.2d 126 (1st Cir.), *cert. denied*, 382 U.S. 838 (1965). In addition, it was held that the government was not precluded from suing under both this Act and the False Claims Act, *United States v. General Dynamics Corp.*, 19 F.3d 770 (2d Cir. 1994).

## 7. Covenant Against Contingent Fees

The government has a longstanding policy against the payment of contingent fees. This policy developed because of the government's concern that contingent fee arrangements expose government agencies to corrupting influences. It also reflects the government's recognition that such agreements could allow for the payment of exorbitant fees by contractors, leading to higher costs for the government, thereby resulting in an unnecessary waste of public funds. See *Quinn v. Gulf & Western Corp.*, 644 F.2d 89 (2d Cir. 1981). Thus, a clause is required in negotiated contracts by statute, 10 U.S.C. § 2306(b) and 41 U.S.C. § 254(a) (pre-2011 codification), and in sealed bid procurements by regulation, FAR 3.404. The FASA removes the requirement for such a clause in contracts at or below the simplified acquisition threshold of $150,000 (§ 4103(c) and § 4102(b), civilian agencies and armed services, respectively) or in contracts for the acquisition of commercial items (§ 8204(b) and § 1105(a), civilian agency and armed services, respectively). The clause to be used is contained in FAR 52.203-5:

### COVENANT AGAINST CONTINGENT FEES (APR 1984)

(a) The Contractor warrants that no person or agency has been employed or retained to solicit or obtain this contract upon an agreement or understanding for a contingent fee, except a bona fide employee or agency. For breach or violation of this warranty, the Government shall have the right to annul this contract without liability or, in its discretion, to deduct from the contract price or consideration, or otherwise recover, the full amount of the contingent fee.

(b) "Bona fide agency," as used in this clause, means an established commercial or selling agency, maintained by a contractor for the purpose of securing business, that neither exerts nor proposes to exert improper influence to solicit or obtain Government contracts nor holds itself out as being able to obtain any Government contract or contracts through improper influence.

"Bona fide employee," as used in this clause, means a person, employed by a contractor and subject to the contractor's supervision and control as to time, place, and manner of performance, who neither exerts nor proposes to exert improper influence to solicit or obtain Government contracts nor holds out as being able to obtain any Government contract or contracts though improper influence.

"Contingent fee," as used in this clause, means any commission, percentage, brokerage, or other fee that is contingent upon the success that a person or concern has in securing a Government contract.

"Improper influence," as used in this clause, means any influence that induces or tends to induce a Government employee or officer to give consideration or to act regarding a Government contract on any basis other than the merits of the matter.

The covenant does not prohibit the payment of all contingent fees — only those made for the purpose of obtaining a contract. In *Browne v. R & R Eng'g Co.*, 264 F.2d 219 (3d Cir. 1959), the court held that contingent fee services in connection with a proposed contract that did not involve any dealings with officials responsible for the award of contracts were not prohibited. GAO has followed this ruling. See *Holmes & Narver Servs., Inc.*, 70 Comp. Gen. 424 (B-242240 ), 91-1 CPD ¶ 373, where an incumbent contractor offered to sell access to its employees and competitively useful contract information to potential offerors who agreed to purchase inventory and equipment at set prices if they won the contract. GAO held that this was not a prohibited contingent fee arrangement because the payment would not be made for the purpose of soliciting or obtaining the contract at issue and the arrangement did not involve any dealings with government officials. See also *Kasler Elec. Co.*, DOTCAB 1425, 84-2

BCA ¶ 17,374, where a payment to a nonemployee estimator was contingent on award of the contract. The board held that the arrangement did not violate the covenant, since the estimator's function was to price out a bid and not to solicit a government contract. Compare *Howard Johnson Lodge*, Comp. Gen. Dec. B-244302.2, 92-1 CPD ¶ 305, finding a violation of the covenant because the sales agent was directly contacting government agencies about potential contracts.

In addition, the covenant does not apply to a "bona fide employee" or a "bona fide agency." See *Acme Process Equip. Co. v. United States*, 171 Ct. Cl. 251, 347 F.2d 538 (1965), setting forth factors to be considered in determining whether the recipient of a contingent fee falls within this "bona fide" rule. The FAR contains no guidance on this issue. However, an earlier version of the FAR contained the following factors at FAR 3.408-2(c):

(1) The fee should not be inequitable or exorbitant when compared to the services performed or to customary fees for similar services related to commercial business.

(2) The agency should have adequate knowledge of the contractor's products and business, as well as other qualifications necessary to sell the products or services on their merits.

(3) The contractor and the agency should have a continuing relationship or, in newly established relationships, should contemplate future continuity.

(4) The agency should be an established concern that has existed for a considerable period, or be a newly established going concern likely to continue in the future. The business of the agency should be conducted in the agency name and characterized by the customary indicia of the conduct of regular business.

(5) While an agency that confines its selling activities to Government contracts is not disqualified, the fact that an agency represents the contractor in Government and commercial sales should receive favorable consideration.

Established sales arrangements that are not confined to sales to the government do not violate the covenant, *Puma Indus. Consulting, Inc. v. Daal Assocs., Inc.*, 808 F.2d 982 (2d Cir. 1987). In *General Sales Agency*, Comp. Gen. Dec. B-247133.2, 92-1 CPD ¶ 544, a newly established arrangement with a sales organization for a 7½% contingent fee was held proper because the parties anticipated that the arrangement would be longstanding and no improper influence had been exerted to obtain the contract. See also *Howard Johnson Lodge*, Comp. Gen. Dec. B-244302.2, 92-1 CPD ¶ 305, where a 10% contingent fee was held proper because there was "no hint" of improper influence in the arrangement, Similarly, in *Convention Mktg. Servs.*, Comp. Gen. Dec. B-245660.3, 92-1 CPD ¶ 144, no violation was found where contractors had entered into contingent fee arrangements with sales agents to assist in the acquisition and preparation of contracts, but they had exerted no improper influence to solicit or obtain the contracts. GAO stated:

The fact that an agent's fee is contingent upon the contractor receiving the contract award is insufficient to bring a fee arrangement under the contingent fee prohibition; rather, the regulation contemplates a specific demonstration that an agent is retained for the express purpose of contacting Government officials.

See *Wickes Indus., Inc.*, ASBCA 17376, 75-1 BCA ¶ 11,180, for a decision in which the government was not allowed to cancel a contract where a contingency arrangement was "bona fide" considering the factors set forth in the DAR. See also Comp. Gen. Dec. B-157815, Jan. 21, 1966, *Unpub.*

The bona fide employee exemption focuses on the nature of the arrangement between the agent and the contractor, FAR 3.408-2(b). In *Quinn v. Gulf & Western Corp.*, 644 F.2d 89 (2d Cir. 1981), a contract was held to be unenforceable because the contingent fee arrangement between the turbine blade manufacturer and the owner of the consulting firm, who was also a special government employee, failed to satisfy the "bona fide employee" criterion.

## D. Honesty in Dealing

One of the most important requirements of the public contracting process is that contractors and subcontractors be honest in their dealings with governmental agencies and contractors. This section reviews this requirement by first discussing the applicable statutes and then considering the major types of conduct that have been found to violate this requirement.

### 1. Statutory Requirements

In federal contracting, the requirement for honesty in dealing with the government is supported by a number of criminal and civil statutes imposing a variety of penalties on contractors and others who do not comply with the minimum standards of honesty.

#### a. False Claims

The fundamental federal statute with the goal of promoting honesty in dealing is the False Claims Act. This Act was originally enacted in 1863 to prevent fraud in Civil War defense contracts and is now divided into a civil provision in 31 U.S.C. § 3729 and a criminal provision in 18 U.S.C. § 287.

##### (1) CIVIL FRAUD

For many years this provision was set forth in 31 U.S.C. § 231. In 1982, it was codified in 31 U.S.C. § 3729, and then it was amended by the False Claims Amendments Act of 1986, Pub. L. No. 99-562, the Fraud Enforcement & Recovery Act of

2009, Pub. L. No. 111-21, and the Patient Protection & Affordable Care Act, Pub. L. No. 111-148, to read as follows:

(a) Liability for certain acts.

(1) In general. Subject to paragraph (2), any person who —

(A) knowingly presents, or causes to be presented, a false or fraudulent claim for payment or approval;

(B) knowingly makes, uses, or causes to be made or used, a false record or statement material to a false or fraudulent claim;

(C) conspires to commit a violation of subparagraph (A), (B), (D), (E), (F), or (G);

(D) has possession, custody, or control of property or money used, or to be used, by the Government and knowingly delivers, or causes to be delivered, less than all of that money or property;

(E) is authorized to make or deliver a document certifying receipt of property used, or to be used, by the Government and, intending to defraud the Government, makes or delivers the receipt without completely knowing that the information on the receipt is true;

(F) knowingly buys, or receives as a pledge of an obligation or debt, public property from an officer or employee of the Government, or a member of the Armed Forces, who lawfully may not sell or pledge property; or

(G) knowingly makes, uses, or causes to be made or used, a false record or statement material to an obligation to pay or transmit money or property to the Government, or knowingly conceals or knowingly and improperly avoids or decreases an obligation to pay or transmit money or property to the Government, is liable to the United States Government for a civil penalty of not less than $5,000 and not more than $10,000, as adjusted by the Federal Civil Penalties Inflation Adjustment Act of 1990 (28 U.S.C. 2461 note; Public Law 104-410), plus 3 times the amount of damages which the Government sustains because of the act of that person.

In *Hughes Aircraft Co. v. Schumer*, 520 U.S. 939 (1997), the Court held that the 1986 amendment does not apply to actions that took place prior to its enactment.

A claim is not "false" when the law is unclear or when there is a legitimate good faith disagreement about the applicable law. See *United States ex rel. K & R Ltd. Partnership v. Massachusetts Housing Finance Agency*, 530 F.3d 980 (D.C. Cir. 2008) (terms for calculating housing subsidy with HUD ambiguous); *United States ex rel. Ramadoss v. Caremark, Inc.*, 586 F. Supp.2d 668 (W.D. Tex. 2008) (Medicaid reimbursement rules subject to "good-faith disagreement").

## (A) SPECIFIC INTENT

Under the False Claims Act, as amended in 1986, the government can establish liability without showing that the contractor had a specific intent to defraud as long as the act is committed "knowingly." Not defined in the original Act, "knowingly" is now defined in 31 U.S.C. § 3729(b) as (1) actual knowledge of the information, (2) acting in deliberate ignorance of the truth or falsity of the information, or (3) acting in reckless disregard of the truth or falsity of the information. Further, the Act specifically states that "no proof of specific intent to defraud is required." See *United States v. TDC Mgmt. Corp.*, 24 F.3d 292 (D.C. Cir. 1994), stating at 298:

> To prevail under the False Claims Act, the government must prove either that TDC actually knew it had omitted material information from its monthly progress reports or that it recklessly disregarded or deliberately ignored that possibility. The government need not prove that TDC intended to deceive the government by omitting such information.

Reckless disregard has been called the "loosest" of the three standards, *United States ex rel. Siewick v. Jamieson Science & Eng'g., Inc.*, 214 F.3d 1372 (D.C. Cir. 2000). Thus, failure to review Medicare claims prepared by others has been held to be reckless disregard, *United States v. Krizek*, 111 F.3d 934 (D.C. Cir. 1997). Similarly, filing an equitable adjustment claim for "actual costs" when estimates are used is reckless disregard, *UMC Elecs. Co. v. United States*, 43 Fed. Cl. 776 (1999). However, failing to consult a lawyer prior to submitting a claim for payment is not reckless disregard, *United States ex rel. Quirk v. Madonna Towers, Inc.*, 278 F.3d 765 (8th Cir. 2002). Reckless disregard does not extend to simple negligence or mistakes, *United States v. United Tech. Corp.*, 51 F. Supp. 2d 167 (D. Conn. 1999) (no liability for honest mistake); *Wang ex rel. United States v. FMC Corp.*, 975 F.2d 1412 (9th Cir. 1992) (engineering miscalculations and lack of engineering insight no more than innocent mistake); *First Interstate Bank v. United States*, 27 Fed. Cl. 348 (1992) (mere negligence by bank would not satisfy requirement of "knowing").

Since what constitutes the offense is not an intent to deceive but a knowing presentation of a claim that is either "fraudulent" or simply "false," the fact that the germane government officials knew of a claim's falsity is not a defense, *Hagood v. Sonoma Cty. Water Agency*, 92 F.2d 1416 (9th Cir. 1991) (government officials condoned contractor's inaccurate cost allocation violating federal water supply law). However, the government's knowledge may be relevant in proving that the defendant did not submit a claim with "deliberate ignorance" or "reckless disregard" of the "truth or falsity of the information." For example, in *Chemray Coatings Corp. v. United States*, 29 Fed. Cl. 278 (1993), the court held that the government's knowledge of the condition of paint pigment contaminated by fire debris for which the contractor received payment under a termination for convenience settlement was relevant to the determination of liability under the Act, stating at 284:

> GSA's knowledge of the contents of the drums is relevant for purposes of section 3729(a). Intent to deceive need not be proved under the Act. . . . What must be proved is that the contractor knowingly presented a false or fraudulent claim. . . . If GSA officials knew that the drums referred to in the termination for convenience settlement contained debris and [the contractor] did not know that its representation of the contents was false, [the contractor] is not guilty of "knowingly" making a false or fraudulent statement to the Government.

Similarly, in *United States ex rel. Durcholz v. FKW, Inc.*, 189 F.3d 542 (7th Cir. 1999), the court held that the government's approval of the particulars of a claim demonstrated that the claim was not "knowingly" false, and in *United States ex rel. Lamers v. City of Green Bay*, 168 F.3d 1013 (7th Cir. 1999), the court held that discussions of a method of using grant funds with city officials showed lack of knowing falsehood. See also *United States ex rel. Becker v. Westinghouse Savannah River Co.*, 305 F.3d 284 (4th Cir. 2002), finding no false claim where the company changed its accounts to reflect a pending change in congressional appropriations at the request of the government agency. The court found that the company may have "negligently disregarded" whether Congress had approved the change, this did not meet the scienter requirement of the Act.

Generally, proof that a statement or action was in accord with a reasonable interpretation of the contract or regulation will be sufficient to demonstrate a lack of intent. See *United States ex rel. Lamers v. City of Green Bay*, 168 F.3d 1013 (7th Cir. 1998) (even though the city's interpretation of regulations was questionable, a review of all of the facts indicated that it did not intend to defraud the government); *United States ex rel. Hochman v. Nackman*, 145 F.3d 1069 (9th Cir. 1998) (good faith interpretation of contract indicates lack of intent); *United States ex rel. Lindenthal v. General Dynamics Corp.*, 61 F.3d 1402 (9th Cir. 1995) (parties' interpretation of ambiguous specification indicated lack of intent). Contrast *United States ex rel. Oliver v. Parsons Co.*, 195 F.3d 457 (9th Cir. 1999), where the court held that the question of reasonableness of the interpretation of a regulation was not dispositive but that the district court should address the question of intent directly. The result of this reasoning could be that a false claim could be found because the contractor's interpretation was not made in good faith but with the intent to defraud the government. Accord, *United States ex rel. Minnesota Assoc. of Nurse Anesthetists v. Allina Health Sys. Corp.*, 276 F.3d 1032 (8th Cir. 2002) (submitting a bill based on a reasonable interpretation of an ambiguous regulation is a false claim if the submitter knows that the government interprets the regulation differently). See also *United States v. Rule Indus., Inc.*, 878 F.2d 535 (1st Cir. 1989), where the court affirmed a jury determination that the contractor had defrauded the government by following its interpretation of the ambiguous Buy American Act.

## (B) DEFINITION OF CLAIM

A "claim" for purposes of the False Claims Act is any demand upon the government for the payment of money or the transfer of property, *United States v. Tieger*, 234 F.2d 589 (3d Cir.), *cert. denied*, 352 U.S. 941 (1956). For example, in *Tieger* the court found no claim, although the defendant had fraudulently induced the government to guarantee loans, because no demand for satisfaction of the guarantee had been made against the government. Similarly, no claim was found in *United States ex rel. Butler v. Hughes Helicopters, Inc.*, 71 F.3d 321 (9th Cir. 1995), when the contractor submitted a DD 250 "Material Inspection and Receiving Report." See also *United States v. Farina*, 153 F. Supp. 819 (D.N.J. 1957), where a bidder had conspired with a government employee to submit a lower bid after the bids had been opened. While the court recognized that such conduct subverted the competitive bidding process, it found no claim because no contract had been awarded and, hence, no request for payment was made. But any request for payment will constitute a claim. See *United States ex rel. Marcus v. Hess*, 317 U.S. 537 (1943), where the Court found a claim because the contractor submitted a payment voucher on a contract obtained through collusive bidding. The Court held that the Act covered all claims "grounded in fraud." See also *Bly-Magee v. California*, 236 F.3d 1014 (9th Cir. 2001), finding a claim when the defendant allegedly defrauded the state on a federal program where overpayments to a state would not revert to the United States Treasury but would be distributed to other states; and *United States ex rel. Luther v. Consolidated Indus.*, 720 F. Supp. 919 (N.D. Ala. 1989), finding a claim where the defendant submitted false invoices even though government discovered fraud and withheld payments.

The definition of claim was broadened in the 2009 amendments by stating that a claim occurs if the money claimed is to be "spent or used on the Government's behalf or to advance a Government program or interest." This is in accord with the decision in *United States ex rel. DRC, Inc. v. Custer Battles LLC*, 562 F.3d 295 (4th Cir. 2009), holding the contractor liable for submitting a false claim to the Coalition Provisional Authority in Iraq because part of the funding for the authority came from the government.

The demand for payment need not be one based on an existing contractual relationship since the Act encompasses all fraudulent attempts to cause the government to pay out a sum of money, *United States v. Neifert-White Co.*, 390 U.S. 228 (1968) (false application to Federal Commodity Credit Corp. for loan held to be claim). The Act has been held to apply to a subcontractor's failure to comply with specifications, *United States ex rel. Varljen v. Cleveland Gear Co.*, 250 F.3d 426 (6th Cir. 2001); a knowing misrepresentation about the need for and cost of using a subcontractor, *Harrison v. Westinghouse Savannah River Co.*, 176 F.3d 776 (4th Cir. 1999); endorsement and deposit of government checks known to have been issued by mistake, *United States v. McLeod*, 721 F.2d 282 (9th Cir. 1983); repeated inclusion of rejected items in shipments, *United States v. Milton Marks Corp.*, 240 F.2d 838 (3d Cir. 1957); fraudulently submitted Medicare health insurance claim forms by health care providers, *United States v. Lorenzo*, 768 F. Supp. 1127 (E.D. Pa. 1991); cashing fraudulently obtained social security checks, *United States v. Fowler*, 282 F. Supp. 1 (E.D.N.Y. 1968); and submission of false payroll reports, *United States v. Greenberg*, 237 F. Supp. 439 (S.D.N.Y. 1965).

Some courts have held that a demand for payment can be false if the contractor submitting the invoice is not in compliance with contract requirements at the time of submission. Thus, some courts have held that there is an "implied certification of compliance in such situations." See *United States ex rel. Augustine v. Century Health Servs., Inc.*, 289 F.3d 409 (6th Cir. 2002) (implied certification that contractor would continue to be in compliance with regulations after submission of cost report); *Shaw v. AAA Eng'g & Drafting, Inc.*, 213 F.3d 519 (10th Cir. 2000) (implied certification that contractor was in compliance with environmental requirements of contract); *BMY-Combat Sys. Div. of Harsco Corp. v. United States*, 38 Fed. Cl. 109 (1997) (invoices of contractor impliedly but falsely represented contractual compliance which was "critical to defendant's decision to pay"); *United States ex rel. Pogue v. American Healthcorp, Inc.*, 914 F. Supp. 1507 (M.D. Tenn. 1996) (by submitting Medicare claims defendants implicitly certified compliance with the statutes, rules, and regulations governing the Medicare program); *Ab-Tech Constr., Inc. v. United States*, 31 Fed. Cl. 429 (1994), *aff'd*, 57 F.3d 1084 (Fed. Cir. 1995) ("payment vouchers represented an implied certification by Ab-Tech of its continuing adherence to the requirements for participation in the [minority-owned business] program"). Not all courts have agreed with this theory, holding that there can be a false claim of this nature only when a certification is an express condition of payment of the claim. See *Mikes v. Straus*, 274 F.3d 687 (2d Cir. 2001); *United States ex rel. Siewick v. Jamieson Science & Eng'g., Inc.*, 214 F.3d 1372 (D.C. Cir. 2000);   *Harrison v. Westinghouse Savannah River Co.*, 176 F.3d 776 (4th Cir. 1999); *United States ex rel. Thompson v. Columbia/HCA Healthcare Corp.*, 125 F.3d 899 (5th Cir. 1997); *United States ex rel. Hopper v. Anton,* 91 F.3d 1261 (9th Cir.1996); and *United States ex rel. Joslin v. Community Home Health of Md., Inc.*, 984 F. Supp. 374 (D. Md. 1997).

"Reverse false claims" also fall under the Act, 31 U.S.C. § 3729(a)(7). These are actions taken to prevent the government from making a claim against the contractor or obtaining the full amount owed by a contractor. For example, in *United States v. Pemco Aeroplex, Inc.*, 195 F.3d 1234 (11th Cir. 1999), a false claim was found where the contractor identified valuable and usable inventory as scrap and bought it at a very low price. See also  *United States v. Eilberg*, 507 F. Supp. 267 (E.D. Pa. 1980) (false claim when Congressman submitted false certification that toll telephone calls pertained to government business in order to prevent the government from demanding reimbursement of funds previously paid); and *United States v. Raymond & Whitcomb Co.*, 53 F. Supp. 2d 436 (S.D.N.Y. 1999) (claims include false statement intended to conceal obligation to government). Compare *American Textile Mfrs. Inst., Inc. v. The Limited, Inc.*, 190 F.3d 729 (6th Cir. 1999), holding that false statements made to avoid payment of fines were not reverse false claims because the obligation to the government must exist before the false statement is made, and *United States v. Q Int'l Courier, Inc.*, 131 F.3d 770 (8th Cir. 1997), finding no reverse false claim because there was no "existing, specific legal duty in the nature of a debt" was owed to the government.

## (C) PRESENTMENT

Prior to the 2009 amendments to the Act, a claim had to be "presented" to the government in order to constitute a false claim. Thus, a claim submitted to Amtrak, an organization receiving government funding, did not fall under the Act because Amtrak was not a government entity, *United States ex rel. Totten v. Bombardier Corp.*, 380 F.3d 488 (D.C. Cir. 2004). See also *Allison Engine Co. v. United States ex rel. Sanders*, 553 U.S. 662 (2008), holding that if the false claim was based on the submission of a false statement to a non-government entity, it only met the presentment requirement if it could be proved that the submitter of the statement intended that the government rely on it as a condition of payment. These holdings tended to relieve subcontractors and contractors with non-government entities from liability.

The 2009 amendments to the Act were intended to bring these type situation under the Act. Thus, § 3729(a)(1)(B) now states that it will be a false claim to knowingly make, use, or cause to be made a false record or statement if it is *material* to a false or fraudulent claim. Furthermore, the definition of "claim" in § 3729(b)(2) was revised to include demands "presented" not only to "an officer, employee, or agent of the United States" but also demands made to "a contractor, grantee, or other recipient" of government funds. This will likely increase the liability of subcontractors and third parties dealing with government contractors.

## (D) MATERIALITY

Although the original Act was silent on the issue, some courts held that liability only attached if the false claim was material. False claims have been held to be material only if they are "an essential, important, or pertinent part of the claim," *Tyger Constr. Co. v. United States*, 28 Fed. Cl. 35 (1993). In that case, the court held the contractor's legal arguments in a Contract Disputes Act claim were not false claims because they were opinions not facts — hence did not have a tendency to influence a decision-maker in the government. See *United States ex rel. Berge v. Bd. of Trs.*, 104 F.3d 1453 (4th Cir. 1997), holding that minor misstatements on a grant application did not influence the decision to award the grant. See also *United States v. Intervest Corp.*, 67 F. Supp. 2d 637 (S.D. Miss. 1999), holding that false statements about the condition of property did not influence the decision to pay invoices for the property (based on testimony of a government employee that she would know the true condition when she authorized payment). Compare *United States ex rel. Longhi v. Lithium Power Techs., Inc.*, 530 F. Supp.2d 888 (S.D. Tex. 2008), *aff'd*, 575 F.3d 458 (5th Cir.

2009), holding that a number of relatively minor misstatements about an offeror's past work amounted to a material misrepresentation of the type covered by the Act. See also *United States v. United Techs. Corp.*, No. 3:99-cv-093 (S.D. Ohio 2008), *rev'd on other grounds*, 626 F.3d 313 (6th Cir. 2010), holding that three false statements in BAFO regarding how contractor calculated certain costs were material to major pricing of jet engines.

### (E) Qui Tam

Any person may bring a civil action (termed "qui tam") under the Act "for the person and the United States," and the action is "brought in the name of the United States," 31 U.S.C. § 3730(b). The qui tam plaintiff (termed "the relator") files a civil complaint. The complaint is sealed while the government decides whether to take over the case. If the government intervenes, it bears primary responsibility for prosecuting the action, 31 U.S.C. § 3730(c)(1). If the government elects not to proceed with the action, the person who initiated the action has the right to conduct the action, 31 U.S.C. § 3730(c)(3).

Qui tam action are barred if they are based upon a "public disclosure" in a federal hearing, audit or investigation or in the press of the fraudulent activity unless the relator is an "original source" of the information on which the fraud allegations are based, 31 U.S.C. § 3730(e)(4). This limitation on qui tam suits has generated a substantial amount of litigation which is peripheral to the actual proof of the fraud. Public disclosure occurs when the allegations upon which the qui tam suit is based are affirmatively disclosed to the public, *United States ex rel. Ramseyer v. Century Healthcare Corp.*, 90 F.3d 1514 (10th Cir. 1996). In this case, the court held that a relator whose allegations were similar to findings made in a routine state audit report did not base her suit upon publicly disclosed information because the report remained in government files and was never released to the public. Compare *United States ex rel. v. MK-Ferguson Co.*, 99 F.3d 1538 (10th Cir. 1996), holding that a qui tam suit filed by a former government auditor was barred under § 3730(e). The court found that the complaint was substantially identical to a government audit report that had been sent to a state without any restriction on dissemination. See also *United States ex rel. Fine v. Advanced Sciences, Inc.*, 99 F.3d 1000 (10th Cir. 1996), affirming a district court's holding that a qui tam suit filed by a former government auditor was barred under § 3730(e). The court found that the action was substantially identical to a memorandum, which contained allegations and transactions set out in a government audit, that the relator had given to his representative in an unrelated age discrimination case. The court found that the memorandum was made public when it was disclosed to an American Association of Retired Persons representative. In *United States ex rel. Doe v. John Doe Corp.*, 960 F.2d 318 (2d Cir. 1992), a public disclosure occurred when federal investigators executing a search warrant informed employees of their investigation into fraudulent overcharging.

Providing material in response to a FOIA request constitutes a public disclosure, *United States ex rel Kirk v. Schindler Elevator Corp.*, 131 S. Ct. 1885 (2011).

If public disclosure is found, the suit will not be barred unless it is based on the disclosed information. Most courts hold that this is determined by comparing the allegations to the disclosed information. Using this test, a suit can be found to be based on disclosed information even if the relator did not learn of the allegations from the disclosure. Thus, in *United States ex rel. v. MK-Ferguson Co.*, 99 F.3d 1538 (10th Cir. 1996), the court examined whether a qui tam complaint was based upon a publicly disclosed audit report. The court held that "based upon" means "supported by" and the inquiry is "whether the relator's complaint is 'substantially identical' to the allegations contained in the public disclosure." The court compared the audit report with the complaint and found substantial identity and, thus, barred the action. See also *United States ex rel. Mistick PBT v. Housing Auth. of Pittsburgh*, 186 F.3d 376 (3d Cir. 1999) (public disclosure contained essential elements of complaint); *United States ex rel. Biddle v. Bd. of Trs.*, 161 F.3d 533 (9th Cir. 1998), *cert. denied*, 526 U.S. 1066 (1999) (irrelevant if source of knowledge is different from public disclosure if allegations are the same); *United States ex rel. McKenzie v. BellSouth Tel., Inc.*, 123 F.3d 935 (6th Cir. 1997), *cert. denied*, 522 U.S. 1077 (1998) (suit partially based upon the allegations brought in other suits). The Second Circuit has held that "based upon" should be defined as "the same as," *United States ex rel. Doe v. John Doe Corp.*, 960 F.2d 318 (2d Cir. 1992). Other circuits interpret the phrase "based upon" to mean "derived from." See *United States ex rel. Siller v. Becton Dickinson & Co.*, 21 F.3d 1339 (4th Cir.), *cert. denied*, 513 U.S. 928 (1994), stating that the "derived from" definition would grant jurisdiction when the relator's suit would not be "based upon" public disclosures of which the relator had no knowledge. In this case, the relator learned of the overcharging through an independent source and thus the court held that the information was not based upon public disclosures. When the facts show that the relator used the disclosed information, it will be barred under either test. See, for example, *United States ex rel. Fine v. Advanced Sciences, Inc.*, 99 F.3d 1000 (10th Cir. 1996), finding that the plaintiff's qui tam complaint was "based upon" a memorandum that had been publicly disclosed. The court noted that the plaintiff admitted that the costs specified in the memorandum provided the basis for the allegations in his complaint. The plaintiff also stated that his knowledge about the practices of Advanced Sciences came in part from the work papers of the report.

If the relator is the original source of the information, public disclosure will not be a bar to the suit. The determination as whether the relator is an original source is made by comparing the original disclosure with the amended complaint, *Rockwell Int'l Corp. v. United States*, 549 U.S. 457 (2007). Prior to 2010, to be considered an original source a plaintiff had to have direct and independent knowledge of the allegations in the qui tam suit and voluntarily provide the information to the government before filing the suit, 31 U.S.C. § 3730(e)(4). In *United States ex rel. Barth v. Ridgedale Elec., Inc.*, 44 F.3d 699 (8th Cir. 1995), the court stated at 703:

"Independent knowledge" has been consistently defined as knowledge that is not dependent on public disclosure. See, e.g., *United States ex rel. Stinson, Lyons, Gerlin & Bustamante, P.A. v. Prudential Ins. Co.*, 944 F.2d 1149, 1160 (3d Cir. 1991) . . .

\* \* \*

"Direct" knowledge under the Act has been defined as knowledge "marked by absence of an intervening agency," *United States ex rel. Springfield Terminal Ry. v. Quinn*, 304 U.S. App. D.C. 347, 14 F.3d 645, 656 (D.C. Cir. 1994) (citing *Prudential*, 944 F.2d at 1160), or "unmediated by anything but [the plaintiff's] own labor." *Wang [v. FMC Corp.*, 975 F.2d 1412 (9th Cir. 1992)], at 1417. A relator is said to have direct knowledge of fraud when he "saw [it] with his own eyes." *Id.* The direct knowledge requirement was intended to avoid parasitic lawsuits by "disinterested outsiders" who "simply stumble across an interesting court file." *United States ex rel. Stinson, Lyons, Gerlin & Bustamante v. Provident Life & Accident Ins. Co.*, 721 F. Supp. 1247, 1258 (S.D. Fla. 1989) . . .

As the Act was amended in 2010, there is a less stringent standard for determining who is an original source. The Act now defines "original source" as "an individual who either —

(1) prior to a public disclosure . . . has voluntarily disclosed to the Government the information on which allegations or transactions in a claim are based, or

(2) who has knowledge that is independent of and materially adds to the publicly disclosed allegations or transactions, and who has voluntarily provided the information to the Government before filing an action under this section.

In *United States ex rel. Devlin, Sidicane, & Kodman v. State of California*, 84 F.3d 358 (9th Cir. 1996), the court held that the relators could not meet the original source test because, while they were a source for a news article, they had learned of the fraud from an employee of the defendant and did not have sufficient first-hand information to satisfy the direct knowledge prong of the original source test. In *United States ex rel. Fine v. MK-Ferguson Co.*, 99 F.3d 1538 (10th Cir. 1996), the court held that the plaintiff did not have direct and independent knowledge because the plaintiff did not discover the alleged fraud but, rather, was the supervisor to whom the auditors reported the fraud. See also *Seal 1 v. Seal A*, 255 F.3d 1154 (9th Cir. 2001), holding that the relator of information against one contractor was not an original source for the information as it was used against another contractor because he did not play a sufficient role with regard to the second contractor. Government contracts attorneys who learned of the information during a bid protest are not original sources, *United States ex rel. Grayson & Hodges v. Advanced Mgmt. Tech., Inc.*, 221 F.3d 580 (4th Cir. 2000). Compare *United States ex rel. Minnesota Assn. of Nurse Anesthetists v. Allina Health Sys. Corp.*, 276 F.3d 1032 (8th Cir. 2002), holding that an association can be an original source because its members had direct knowledge of the alleged fraud. A person who is obligated as part of his or her job to investigate and report fraud will not be considered an original source, *United States ex rel. LeBlanc v. Raytheon Co.*, 913 F.2d 17 (1st Cir. 1990) (quality assurance specialist); *United States ex rel. Fine v. Chevron U.S.A., Inc.*, 72 F.3d 740 (9th Cir. 1995), *cert. denied*, 517 U.S. 1233 (1996) (Inspector General auditor); *United States ex rel. Biddle v. Bd. of Trs.*, 161 F.3d 533 (9th Cir. 1998), *cert. denied*, 526 U.S. 1066 (1999) (administrative contracting officer). But see *Hagood v. Sonoma County Water Agency*, 81 F.3d 1465 (9th Cir. 1996), where a government attorney was held to be an original source because his job did not entail exposing fraud.

An "original source" must also have voluntarily provided the information to the government if it is the basis of the claim or if it adds to the publicly disclosed information. Under the prior Act, there was a conflict among the courts over the result if there has been a public disclosure of that information before the relator provided it to the government. Some courts looked to the "plain meaning" of the statute, holding the relator must only provide the information to the government before it filed its suit, regardless of whether there has been a public disclosure of the information at that point, *United States ex rel. Duxbury v. Ortho Biotech Prods., L.P.*, 579 F.3d 13 (1st Cir. 2009), *cert. denied*, 130 S. Ct. 3454 (2010); and *Siller v. Becton Dickinson & Co.*, 21 F. 3d 1339 (4th Cir. 1994). Other courts held that the relator must provide the information *prior* to its public disclosure, but that it is not necessary that the information be provided to the specific agency or organization that was responsible for the subsequent disclosure of that information, *United States ex rel D.J. Findley v. FPC-Boron Employees' Club*, 105 F.3d 675 (D.C. Cir. 1997); and *United States ex rel McKenzie v. BellSouth Telecommunications, Inc.* 123 F.3d 95 (6th Cir. 1997). Still other courts held that not only must the relator provide the information prior to its public disclosure, but also that it be provided to the party who was responsible for its disclosure, in effect requiring that the relator's information be the source for that public disclosure, *United States ex rel. W. Gordon Dick v. Long Island Lighting Co.*, 912 F.2d 13 (2d Cir. 1990); and *Chen-Cheng Wang ex rel. United States v. FMC Corp.*, 975 F.2d 1412 (9th Cir. 1992). The 2010 amendment to the Act may resolve some of these issues.

Prior to the 2010 amendments to the Act, once a qui tam suit had been filed, no other person could file a "parasitic" suit based on the same facts. See 31 U.S.C, § 3730(b)(5) providing that "when a person brings a [qui tam action], no person other than the government may intervene or bring a related action based on the facts underlying the pending action." See *United States ex rel. Prawer & Co. v. Fleet Bank*, 24 F.3d 320 (1st Cir. 1994), holding that a suit against a different defendant was not parasitic because the defendant could not have been brought into the prior suit. Compare *United States ex rel. Lujan v. Hughes Aircraft Co.*, 243 F.3d 1181 (9th Cir. 2001), holding that this provision barred a claim even though the plaintiff had added a few facts to the previously filed suit. Under the new definition of "original source," a person apparently file a parasitic suit if the information provided "materially adds to the publicly disclosed allegations or transactions."

Relators are given a share of the government's monetary recovery and are granted whistleblower protection. The amount depends on whether the government elects to proceed with the action. 31 U.S.C. § 3730(d) provides that if the government proceeds with an action, the relator will receive at least 15% but not more than 25% of the proceeds, "depending upon the extent to which the person substantially contributed to the prosecution of the action." However, the relator is permitted to receive no more than 10% of the recovery if the action is based primarily on disclosures of specific information, allegations, or transactions in a criminal, civil, or administrative hearing; in a congressional, administrative, or GAO report, hearing, audit, or investigation; or from the news media. If the government does not take over the case, the relator receives not less than 25% nor more than 30% of the proceeds. In either case, the relator receives an amount for reasonable expenses plus reasonable attorneys' fees and costs.

There is a disagreement over whether the government has the right to challenge a settlement in a case in which it chose not to intervene. In *United States ex rel. Killingsworth v. Northrop Corp.*, 25 F.3d 715 (9th Cir. 1994), the court held that the government had no right to challenge the settlement agreed to between the relator and the defendant. In *Searcy, Trustee for Bankruptcy Estate of C&P Bus. World Inc. v. Philips Elecs. N. Am. Corp.*, 117 F.3d 154 (5th Cir. 1997), the court took the opposite position, allowing the government to enter the case to contest the settlement. See also *United States v. Health Possibilities, P.S.C.*, 207 F.3d 335 (6th Cir. 2000), barring a settlement without the written consent of the Attorney General. See *Riley v. St. Luke's Episcopal Hosp.*, 252 F.3d 749 (5th Cir. 2001), for a full discussion of the powers of the federal government after it chooses not to intervene in a qui tam suit.

## (2) CRIMINAL FRAUD

As amended by the False Claims Amendments Act of 1986, 18 U.S.C. § 287 provides:

> Whoever makes or presents to any person or officer in the civil, military, or naval service of the United States, or to any department or agency thereof, any claim upon or against the United States, or any department or agency thereof, knowing such claim to be false, fictitious, or fraudulent, shall be imprisoned not more than five years and shall be subject to a fine in the amount provided in this title.

The same issues have arisen under this provision as those discussed with regard to civil fraud.

### (A) SPECIFIC INTENT

The courts have held that proof of specific intent to defraud the government is not necessary to prove criminal intent. Acting with "knowledge that the claim is false or fictitious is sufficient," *United States v. Maher*, 582 F.2d 842 (4th Cir.), *cert. denied*, 439 U.S. 1115 (1978); *United States v. Precision Medical Labs., Inc.*, 593 F.2d 434 (2d Cir. 1978); *United States v. Milton*, 602 F.2d 231 (9th Cir. 1979). See also *United States v. Catton*, 89 F.3d 387 (7th Cir.1996) (willfulness need not be charged); *Giuliano v. Everything Yogurt, Inc.*, 819 F. Supp. 240 (E.D.N.Y. 1993) (dishonesty, recklessness, deceptiveness, and deliberate disregard satisfied the intent requirement for fraud); and *United States v. Irwin*, 654 F.2d 671 (10th Cir. 1981) (comparing the language of the False Statements Act — which includes the term "willfully" — and concluding that the False Claims Act intentionally excludes the question of the state of mind of the claimant). Deliberate ignorance has been found sufficient to prove intent, *United States v. Wallace*, 40 F. Supp. 2d 131 (E.D.N.Y. 1999). However, no intent to defraud the government was found when a claim was submitted to the government of the Virgin Islands without knowledge that federal funds were involved, *United States v. Gumbs*, 283 F.3d 128 (3d Cir. 2002). In contrast, an intent to defraud has been found when the defendant presented a claim to a state knowing that a federal program was involved, *United States v. Beasley*, 550 F.2d 261 (5th Cir.), *cert. denied*, 434 U.S. 863 (1977). See also *United States v. Prigmore*, 243 F.3d 1 (1st Cir. 2001), holding that a defendant charged with violating regulation is entitled to an interpretation of that regulation that is "most congenial to their case theory and yet also objectively reasonable."

### *(B) Definition of Claim*

The courts have followed the rule used in the Civil False Claims Act that a criminal false claim can occur only if there is a request for the payment of money or the transfer of property. However, a valid request for payment will be a false claim if it is made under a contract obtained by fraudulent means, *United States v. Winchester*, 407 F. Supp. 261 (D. Del. 1975). Presenting a voucher for payment knowing that the goods had not been properly inspected and accepted was also held to be a false claim, *United States v. U.S. Cartridge Co.*, 198 F.2d 456 (8th Cir. 1952), *cert. denied*, 345 U.S. 910 (1953).

The Act encompasses claims submitted indirectly to the government. For example, a claim submitted to a contractor processing Medicare claims for the government was held to be a false claim, *United States v. Precision Medical Labs., Inc.*, 593 F.2d 434 (2d Cir. 1978). Similarly, in *United States v. Beasley*, 550 F.2d 261 (5th Cir.), *cert. denied*, 434 U.S. 938 (1977), the court held that a claim submitted to the state of Louisiana for housing units never constructed was a claim against the federal government since federal funds were to be used for the payments.

### *(C) Materiality*

The courts disagree on whether proof of materiality of the claim is an element of this criminal offense. The majority of the circuits have held that a conviction is proper without proof of materiality of the claim, *United States v. Saybolt*, 577 F.3d

195 (3d Cir. 2009); *United States v. Lawrence*, 405 F.3d 888 (10th Cir. 2005), *cert. denied*, 546 U.S. 955 (2006); *United States v. Logan*, 250 F.3d 350 (6th Cir.), *cert. denied*, 534 U.S. 895 (2001); *United States v. Upton*, 91 F.3d 677 (5th Cir. 1996); *United States v. Taylor*, 66 F.3d 254 (9th Cir. 1995); *United States v. Parsons*, 967 F.2d 452 (10th Cir. 1992); *United States v. Elkin*, 731 F.2d 1005 (2d Cir. 1984), *overruled on other grounds by United States v. Ali*, 68 F.3d 1468 (2d Cir. 1995). However, two circuits and the Court of Federal Claims have held that materiality is a necessary element of the offense, *United States v. Wells*, 63 F.3d 745 (8th Cir. 1995), *vacated on other grounds*, 519 U.S. 482 (1997); *United States ex rel. Berge v. Bd. of Trustees*, 104 F.3d 1453 (4th Cir. 1997); *Tyger Constr. Co. v. United States*, 28 Fed. Cl. 35 (1993). See also *United States v. Foster*, 229 F.3d 1196 (5th Cir. 2000), where the court stated that its view of *Neder v. United States*, 527 U.S. 1 (1999), was that the Supreme Court is now requiring a jury instruction that it must find materiality.

## b.  False Statements

The False Statements Act, 18 U.S.C. § 1001 provides:

(a) Except as otherwise provided in this section, whoever, in any matter within the jurisdiction of the executive, legislative, or judicial branch of the Government of the United States knowingly and willfully —

(1) falsifies, conceals or covers up by any trick, scheme, or device a material fact;

(2) makes any materially false, fictitious or fraudulent statements or representation; or

(3) makes or uses any false writing or document knowing the same to contain any materially false, fictitious or fraudulent statement or entry;

shall be fined under this title, imprisoned not more than 5 years or, if the offense involves international or domestic terrorism (as defined in [18 USCS § 2331]), imprisoned not more than 8 years, or both.

The key elements of the conduct prohibited by this statute are "knowingly and willfully" making a false "statement." Courts added the requirement that the statement be material prior to its inclusion in the statute, *United States v. Gafyczk*, 847 F.2d 685 (11th Cir. 1988); *United States v. Godwin*, 566 F.2d 975 (5th Cir. 1978); *United States v. Rose*, 570 F.2d 1358 (9th Cir. 1978).

### (1) DEFINITION OF STATEMENT

The scope of the False Statements Act is considerably broader than that of the False Claims Act. It has been held that the Act covers all false statements which might support fraudulent claims or which might pervert or corrupt the authorized functions of a government agency to which the statement was made, *United States v. Bedore*, 455 F.2d 1109 (9th Cir. 1972). The statement need not be on a government form if it affects the government, *United States v. Heuer*, 4 F.3d 723 (9th Cir.1993), *cert. denied*, 510 U.S. 1164 (1994) (bill of lading). The Act covers oral as well as written statements and unsworn as well as sworn statements, *United States v. Massey*, 550 F.2d 300 (5th Cir. 1977), as well as "private discussions" between members of the executive and legislative branches of the government, *United States v. Poindexter*, 951 F.2d 369 (D.C. Cir. 1991). It also covers the omission of information on a certified statement when the information should have been included, *United States v. Irwin*, 654 F.2d 671 (10th Cir. 1981). In *United States v. Johnson*, 937 F.2d 392 (8th Cir. 1991), the court stated at 395:

> It is generally recognized that section 1001 creates two distinct offenses with different elements: (1) concealing material facts from a federal agency by trick, scheme, or device; (2) making false or fraudulent statements of material facts to a federal agency. See *United States v. Mayberry*, 913 F.2d 719, 722 n.7 (9th Cir. 1990); *United States v. St. Michael's Credit Union*, 880 F.2d 579, 590 (1st Cir. 1989).

The transferring of acceptance stamps from goods that had been accepted to goods that had not been inspected was held to be a false statement, *United States v. Steiner Plastics Mfg. Co.*, 231 F.2d 149 (2d Cir. 1956). Statements made during settlement negotiations were also found to be false statements, *New York v. Sokol*, 113 F.3d 303 (2d Cir.1997). Similarly, a padded estimate in a request for equitable adjustment was held to be a false statement, *United States v. White*, 765 F.2d 1469 (11th Cir. 1985). False statements were also found to be made by an employee of a contractor who included false information on a security questionnaire, *United States v. Dale*, 991 F.2d 819 (D.C. Cir. 1993); *Pitts v. United States*, 263 F.2d 353 (9th Cir.), *cert. denied*, 360 U.S. 935 (1959); and by an applicant for employment with a defense contractor who included false statements on the employment application, *United States v. Giarraputo*, 140 F. Supp. 831 (E.D.N.Y. 1956). False statements have also been found to have been made by government employees when they included false entries on documents during the transaction of government business, *United States v. Leviton*, 193 F.2d 848 (2d Cir. 1951), *cert. denied*, 343 U.S. 946 (1952); *United States v. Eisenmann*, 396 F.2d 565 (2d Cir. 1968). The question of the authority of the agency to seek or obtain the statement is not relevant if the false statement influences the agency, *United States v. Arcadipane*, 41 F.3d 1 (1st Cir. 1994).

The Act applies to matters that involve a government agency's activity even though the false statement is not made to the government, *Ebeling v. United States*, 248 F.2d 429 (8th Cir.), *cert. denied sub nom. Emerling v. United States*, 355 U.S. 907 (1957) (false invoices submitted by subcontractor to contractor under price redeterminable contract); *United States v. Huber*, 603 F.2d 387 (2d Cir. 1979), *cert. denied*, 445 U.S. 927 (1980) (false statements made to hospitals receiving money under federal programs). See also *United States v. Popow*, 821

F.2d 483 (8th Cir. 1987) (false identification presented to custom inspector is a matter concerning INS); and *United States v. Herring*, 916 F.2d 1543 (11th Cir. 1990) (Georgia Department of Labor involves activity of United States Department of Labor).

## (2) KNOWINGLY AND WILLFULLY

To fall within the scope of the Act, the statement must have been made with the intent to deceive, but the government need not prove an intent to defraud, *United States v. Lichenstein*, 610 F.2d 1272 (5th Cir. 1980); *United States v. Leo*, 941 F.2d 181 (3d Cir. 1991). In *United States v. Starnes*, 583 F.3d 196 (3d Cir. 2009), the court held that "specific intent" need not be proved and provided a thorough analysis of the term "knowingly and willfully." One court stated that the knowing and willful intent requirement was met when the government proved that the defendant knew that the false statement was necessary for the fraudulent scheme to succeed, *United States v. Beck*, 615 F.2d 441 (7th Cir. 1980). See also *United States v. Cutaia*, 511 F. Supp. 619 (E.D.N.Y. 1981), where criminal intent was found when the defendant was advised of the government's requirements and deliberately gave answers to avoid compliance. However, there can be no intent to deceive unless the statement is false at the time it is made, *United States v. McCarrick*, 294 F.3d 1286 (11th Cir. 2002) (alleged wrongdoing occurred after document was signed).

An honest misinterpretation on government forms precludes conviction under the Act, *United States v. Weatherspoon*, 581 F.2d 595 (7th Cir. 1978), but reckless disregard of the truthfulness of the statement and a conscious effort to avoid learning the truth will be deemed to be a knowing and willful false statement, *United States v. Evans*, 559 F.2d 244 (5th Cir. 1977), *cert. denied*, 434 U.S. 1015 (1978). See also *United States v. Puente*, 982 F.2d 156 (5th Cir.), *cert. denied*, 508 U.S. 962 (1993), holding that it was reckless disregard to sign a government form certifying that the offeror had never been convicted of a felony without reading it.

Generally proof that the contractor followed a reasonable interpretation of an ambiguous regulation or contract is sufficient to demonstrate that there was no intent to make a false statement. See *United States v. Whiteside*, 285 F.3d 1345 (11th Cir. 2002), holding that an ambiguous regulation prevented a finding of the requisite intent. The court stated at 1351-52:

> In a case where the truth or falsity of a statement centers on an interpretive question of law, the government bears the burden of proving beyond a reasonable doubt that the defendant's statement is not true under a reasonable interpretation of the law. *United States v. Migliaccio*, 34 F.3d 1517, 1525 (10th Cir. 1994) (holding that the government bears the burden to negate any reasonable interpretations that would make the defendant's statement correct); *United States v. Johnson*, 937 F.2d 392, 399 (8th Cir. 1991) (holding that one cannot be guilty of a false state-

ment beyond a reasonable doubt when his statement is a reasonable construction); *United States v. Race*, 632 F.2d 1114, 1120 (4th Cir. 1980) (same); *United States v. Anderson*, 579 F.2d 455, 460 (8th Cir. 1978) (same); see also *United States v. Calhoon*, 97 F.3d 518, 526 (11th Cir. 1996) (noting that even though the Medicare regulations were clear regarding the royalty fees paid to a related party, the government failed to establish as a matter of *fact* that the fees claimed were actually in excess of what was clearly allowed under the regulations, and thus, had "failed to sustain its burden to prove the claim false by virtue of the nonreimbursable nature of the interest").

However, if the court finds the contractor's interpretation unreasonable, intent to defraud the government will be found, *United States v. White*, 765 F.2d 1469 (11th Cir. 1985) (rule not applicable because contractor's interpretation unreasonable); *United States v. Dale*, 991 F.2d 819 (D.C. Cir. 1993) (rule not applicable because defendant's interpretation "far too restrictive"). In addition, one circuit has held that the argument of ambiguity will not prevail if there is sufficient evidence that the contractor knew that the government had a contrary interpretation, *United States v. Carrier*, 654 F.2d 559 (9th Cir. 1981).

It has been held that the maker of the false statement can be convicted even if he does not know that the federal government is involved in the transaction, *United States v. Baker*, 626 F.2d 512 (5th Cir. 1980); *United States v. Wright*, 988 F.2d 1036 (10th Cir. 1993).

### (3) MATERIALITY

Although the Act did not originally mention materiality, the courts were in general agreement that a statement must be material to fall within the scope of the Act, *United States v. Ali*, 68 F.3d 1468, *amended on denial of reh'g*, 86 F.3d 275 (2d Cir. 1996); *Gonzales v. United States*, 286 F.2d 118 (10th Cir. 1960), *cert. denied*, 365 U.S. 878 (1961). The test of materiality is whether a statement has a natural tendency to influence, or is capable of influencing, the actions of a federal agency, *Kungys v. United States*, 485 U.S. 759 (1988); *United States v. Gaudin*, 515 U.S. 506 (1995); *United States v. McBane*, 433 F.3d 344 (3d Cir. 2005). There is no need to prove either reliance by the government, *United States v. Hicks*, 619 F.2d 752 (8th Cir. 1980), or actual pecuniary loss by the government, *United States v. Lichenstein*, 610 F.2d 1272 (5th Cir. 1980). Thus, a criminal false statement can occur even if the government employee hearing the statement knows that it is false at the time, *United States v. Goldfine*, 538 F.2d 815 (9th Cir. 1976) (statements made during administrative "compliance investigation"); *United States v. LeMaster*, 54 F.3d 1224 (6th Cir. 1995) (statements to FBI agents during investigation); *United States v. Turner*, 551 F.3d 657 (7th Cir. 2008) (statements to FBI agents during investigation). In *United States v. Safavian*, 644 F. Supp.2d 1 (D.D.C. 2009), *aff'd*, 2011 U.S. App. Lexis 9740 (D.C. Cir. 2011), the court refused to overturn a jury verdict that held the defendant liable for making false statements to an agency ethics officer in the course of obtaining an advisory opinion. In *United States v. Coastal Contracting & Eng'g Co.*, 174 F. Supp. 474 (D. Md. 1959), a contractor knowingly submitted fictitious statements in connection with a change order proposal. They were not relied upon by the government negotiator because he thought the prices were entirely out of line. Nevertheless, the contractor violated the Act because the misstatements were material and were calculated to induce reliance and action.

Materiality in a false statement is a question of fact to be decided by the jury, *United States v. Gaudin*, 515 U.S. 506 (1995). Prior to *Gaudin* there were numerous decisions holding that materiality was a question of law.

### c.  Truth in Negotiations

The Truth in Negotiations Act (TINA) was added to the Armed Services Procurement Act in 1962 to improve the government's ability to negotiate contracts and contract modifications by ensuring that the government has the same factual data as the contractor at the time of price negotiations. The Act does this by requiring that offerors and contractors submit and certify "cost or pricing data" in circumstances where the government has no way, other than cost analysis, to determine that a price is reasonable. The requirement was added to the Federal Property and Administrative Services Act in 1985. The Federal Acquisition Streamlining Act of 1994, Pub. L. No. 103-355, amended these statutes to contain the same requirements in 10 U.S.C. § 2306a and 41 U.S.C. §§ 3501-09. These statutes now require the submission of cost or pricing data on all negotiated contracts over $700,000 but prohibit obtaining such data when one of four exceptions applies. FAR Subpart 15.4 gives guidance on the procedures when obtaining data is mandatory. The application of these requirements is discussed in Chapter 10.

These statutes contain elaborate guidance on the contractual remedies available to the government if a contractor fails to comply with their requirements. See 10 U.S.C. § 2306a(e) stating:

> Price Reductions for Defective Cost or Pricing Data. (1)(A) A prime contract (or change or modification to a prime contract) under which a certificate under subsection (a)(2) is required shall contain a provision that the price of the contract to the United States, including profit or fee, shall be adjusted to exclude any significant amount by which it may be determined by the head of the agency that such price was increased because the contractor (or any subcontractor required to make available such a certificate) submitted defective cost or pricing data.
>
> (B) For the purposes of this section, defective cost or pricing data are cost or pricing data which, as of the date of agreement on the price of the contract (or another date agreed upon between the parties), were inaccurate, incomplete, or noncurrent. If for the purposes of the preceding sentence the parties agree upon a date other than the date of

agreement on the price of the contract, the date agreed upon by the parties shall be as close to the date of agreement on the price of the contract as is practicable.

(2) In determining for purposes of a contract price adjustment under the contract provision required by paragraph (1) whether, and to what extent, a contract price was increased because the contractor (or a subcontractor) submitted defective cost or pricing data, it shall be a defense that the United States did not rely on the defective data submitted by the contractor or subcontractor.

(3) It is not a defense to an adjustment of the price of a contract under a contract provision required by paragraph (1) that —

(A) the price of the contract would not have been modified even if accurate, complete, and current cost or pricing data had been submitted by the contractor or subcontractor because the contractor or subcontractor —

(i) was the sole source of the property or services procured; or

(ii) otherwise was in a superior bargaining position with respect to the property or services procured;

(B) the contracting officer should have known that the cost or pricing data in issue were defective even though the contractor or subcontractor took no affirmative action to bring the character of the data to the attention of the contracting officer;

(C) the contract was based on an agreement between the contractor and the United States about the total cost of the contract and there was no agreement about the cost of each item procured under such contract; or

(D) the prime contractor or subcontractor did not submit a certification of cost or pricing data relating to the contract as required under subsection (a)(2).

41 U.S.C. § 3506(a) contains substantially the same requirement. The statutory provisions are implemented, with almost no additional guidance, in FAR 15.407-1 and two mandatory contract clauses: Price Reduction for Defective Cost or Pricing Data in FAR 52.215-10 and Price Reduction for Defective Cost or Pricing Data — Modifications in FAR 52.215-11.

## (1) WHEN THE GOVERNMENT IS ENTITLED TO A REDUCTION

Although the statutes provide for price reduction only when the effect of the defective data is to increase the contract price by a "significant amount," the government has been permitted to recover any amount that the price has been increased by a defect. See, for example, *Conrac Corp. v. United States*, 214 Ct. Cl. 561, 558 F.2d 994 (1977), where the court interpreted the statutory language as relieving agencies from having to pursue trivial claims but permitted claims in any amount that an agency considered to be meaningful. In that case, the claim was for an over-pricing of $8,050 on a $548,100 contract. In *American Bosch Arma Corp.*, ASBCA 10305, 65-2 BCA ¶ 5280, the board held that a claim for $20,746 on a contract over $15 million was significant. In *Kaiser Aerospace & Elecs. Corp.*, ASBCA 32098, 90-1 BCA ¶ 22,489, *recons. denied*, 90-2 BCA ¶ 22,695, the board awarded a price reduction of $5,527.82 on orders under a basic ordering agreement of $2,754,581, holding that even if this might "appear to be insignificant," it was bound to award that amount by *Conrac*.

## (2) GOVERNMENT RELIANCE ON DEFECTIVE DATA

In order to obtain a price reduction, the government must demonstrate that the contract price negotiated by the parties was increased because of government reli-ance on defective data. The government is aided in this task by the "natural and prob-able consequence" rule developed by the Armed Services Board in *Lambert Eng'g Co.*, ASBCA 13338, 69-1 BCA ¶ 7663; *McDonnell Douglas Corp.*, ASBCA 12786, 69-2 BCA ¶ 7897. This rule holds that the natural and probable consequence of the furnishing of defective data is a dollar-for-dollar increase in the negotiated price. This rule has been termed a "rebuttable presumption," *American Mach. & Foundry Co.*, ASBCA 15037, 74-1 BCA ¶ 10,409. However, it has the effect of requiring the contractor, in order to avoid a price reduction, to demonstrate that the price was not impacted by the defective data, *Sylvania Elec. Prods., Inc. v. United States*, 202 Ct. Cl. 16, 479 F.2d 1342 (1973). See *EDO Corp.*, ASBCA 41448, 93-3 BCA ¶ 26,135, where the price was reduced by the full amount of a reduced price that a supplier gave a subcontractor, because the contractor could not furnish evidence to overcome the presumption that the contract price had been impacted by this amount.

The natural and probable consequence rule has led to a number of rulings that the contractor was responsible for a dollar-for-dollar price increase. See *Hughes Aircraft Co.*, ASBCA 46321, 97-1 BCA ¶ 28,972; *Limpiezas Corona S.A.*, ASBCA 45504, 96-1 BCA ¶ 28,137; *P.A.L. Sys. Co.*, GSBCA 10858, 91-3 BCA ¶ 24,259; *Millipore Corp.*, GSBCA 9453, 91-1 BCA ¶ 23,345; *Kaiser Aerospace & Elecs. Corp.*, ASBCA 32098, 90-1 BCA ¶ 22,489, *recons. denied*, 90-2 BCA ¶ 22,695; *Etowah Mfg. Co.*, ASBCA 27267, 88-3 BCA ¶ 21,054; *Boeing Military Airplane Co.*, ASBCA 33168, 87-2 BCA ¶ 19,714; *Sylvania Elec. Prods., Inc.*, ASBCA 13622, 70-2 BCA ¶ 8387, *aff'd*, 202 Ct. Cl. 16, 479 F.2d 1342 (1973); and *Aerojet-General Corp.*, ASBCA 12264, 69-1 BCA ¶ 7664, *modified*, 70 BCA ¶ 8140.

Contractors have been successful in demonstrating lack of reliance in several cases. See, for example, *United Techs. Corp.*, ASBCA 51410, 05-1 BCA ¶ 32,860, *aff'd*, 463 F.3d 1261 (Fed. Cir. 2006), where the board held that the presumption of reliance was rebutted by proof that no government employees actually reviewed the defective data in preparing for the price negotiation. Similarly, in *Texas Instruments, Inc.*, ASBCA 30836, 89-1 BCA ¶ 21,489; and *Hughes Aircraft Co.*, ASBCA 30144, 90-2 BCA ¶ 22,847, the board found that the government would not have used current prices of materials because the contract price had been negotiated using average prices of materials based on accumulated costs after the materials went through the manufacturing process. Thus, the board concluded that no price reduction was called for because the government would not have used the data had it been disclosed. See also *Levinson Steel Co.*, ASBCA 16520, 73-2 BCA ¶ 10,116 (contracting officer testified he would not have used data); *Muncie Gear Works, Inc.*, ASBCA 18184, 75-2 BCA ¶ 11,380 (auditor would not have used data because he rejected similar data as inaccurate); and *Rose, Beaton & Rose*, PSBCA 459, 80-1 BCA ¶ 14,242 (government would not have reduced its offer because it contained far less overhead than indicated by undisclosed data).

Several defenses demonstrating that the government did not rely on defective data have been barred by the language in 10 U.S.C. § 2306a(3) and 41 U.S.C. § 3506(c):

- the price of the contract would not have been modified even if accurate, complete, and current cost or pricing data had been submitted because the contractor or subcontractor was a sole source or was in a superior bargaining position

- The contracting officer should have known that the cost and pricing data in issue were defective even though the contractor or subcontractor took no affirmative action to bring the character of the data to the attention of the contracting officer

- the contract was based on agreement on the total cost of the contract and there was no agreement about the cost of each item procured under such contract

- the contractor or subcontractor did not submit a certification of cost and pricing data

Thus, it may no longer be possible to argue that there was no reliance because the contractor would not have accepted a lower price. This argument had been used successfully in *Universal Restoration, Inc. v. United States*, 798 F.2d 1400 (Fed. Cir. 1986). See also *Luzon Stevedoring Corp.*, ASBCA 14851, 71-1 BCA ¶ 8745 (contractor made take-it-or-leave-it offer); and *American Mach. & Foundry Co.*, ASBCA 15037, 74-1 BCA ¶ 10,409 (contractor in strong bargaining position). Similarly, in *J.S. Latsis Group of Cos.*, ENGBCA 4276, 86-2 BCA ¶ 18,853, the board denied any price reduction for nondisclosure of detailed information on overhead because the contracting officer had negotiated overhead rates on a gross basis without regard to the contents of the overhead pool.

## (3) Computing the Price Reduction

In computing the amount of a price reduction, the court or board must determine (1) the dollar amount that would have been included in the price had the data been disclosed and (2) the dollar amount that was included in the contract price because of the nondisclosure. The determination of the latter amount has led to significant controversy. In *Sperry Corp. Computer Sys.*, ASBCA 29525, 88-3 BCA ¶ 20,975, *aff'd sub nom., Unisys Corp. v. United States*, 888 F.2d 841 (Fed. Cir. 1989), the board used the labor dollars that the government's documents indicated had been included in the contract price. The board rejected the contractor's argument that a lower amount should be used because the parties had arrived at the price through a "bottom line" settlement. In *Grumman Aerospace Corp.*, ASBCA 35188, 90-2 BCA ¶ 22,842, the board used the labor rates agreed to by the parties in the negotiation of the contract price rather than the labor rate originally proposed by the contractor because "a contractor is not liable for overstated costs that were eliminated during the price negotiation process." In that case, the board rejected the government's argument that the labor hours in the contract price would have been derived from labor hours on a prior contract projected down a learning curve. The board found that the parties had concluded during the price negotiation that difficulties in performing the work would prevent learning and had therefore used the same number of hours for the new contract as had been incurred on the previous contract. In *McDonnell Douglas Helicopter Sys.*, ASBCA 50341, 99-2 BCA ¶ 30,546, the board stated that the correct amount was the amount the government should cost team used to establish the government's negotiating position. In *Etowah Mfg. Co.*, ASBCA 27267, 88-3 BCA ¶ 21,054, the board used the government estimate prior to the negotiation rather than the considerably higher amount included in the contract price. The board apparently concluded that the contractor's nondisclosure of relevant data was not the cause of the government's willingness to include a higher amount in the price and, therefore, that the contractor was not responsible for any amount greater than the difference between the government estimate and the amount derived from the undisclosed data.

The dollar amount that would have been included in the contract price had the data been disclosed has also created controversy. In *Sperry Corporation Computer System*, the board used the undisclosed labor dollars incurred in manufacturing the product 18 months before the negotiations even though there was evidence that the parties had agreed in the negotiations that a higher figure would be required for the instant contract because of decreases in volume. The precise amount in the undisclosed data was also used in *Etowah Manufacturing*. In earlier cases, the boards had been more willing to base the computation of this figure on the record of the actual negotiations. For example, in *Aerojet-General Corp.*, ASBCA 12873, 69-1 BCA ¶ 7585, the board noted that the parties had arrived at the contract price by splitting the difference in their final negotiation positions. The board therefore assumed that the defective data would have decreased the government's negotiation position by the amount of the defect and that the parties would have split the difference — resulting in a price reduction of one-half of the amount of the defective data. Similarly, in *Bell & Howell Co.*, ASBCA 11999, 68-1 BCA ¶ 6993, the board concluded that had the data been disclosed, the parties would not have been able to negotiate a firm-fixed-price contract. It therefore assumed that they would have negotiated an incentive contract with a 60/40 share and awarded a price reduction in the amount of 60 percent of the defect. For a later case using the negotiation history, see *Aerojet Ordnance Tenn.*, ASBCA 36089, 95-2 BCA ¶ 27,922, where the board concluded that the parties would not have arrived at a price reduced by the entire amount of the defects in submitting the data. The board reached a compromise reduction based on the figures generated by each party in a precontract technical analysis.

In order to make a full computation of the impact of the price reduction on the contract price, the price must be reconstructed using the pricing structure that the parties used in the original negotiation. Thus, the computation must also include all elements of the contractor's costs that would normally be added to the cost item that is adjusted because of the defective data. See, for example, *Grumman Aerospace Corp.*, ASBCA 35188, 90-2 BCA ¶ 22,842, where the board computed the price reduction for defective data on labor dollars by adding all categories of work that were estimated as percentages of labor dollars (manufacturing engineering, sustaining engineering, program management, and foreign sales) plus all applicable overheads, general and administrative expense, and profit. Similarly, in *Kaiser Aerospace & Elecs. Corp.*, ASBCA 32098, 90-1 BCA ¶ 22,489, *recons. denied*, 90-2 BCA ¶ 22,695, the price reduction for defective data on labor rates was computed by adding overhead, general and administrative expense, warranty, and profit.

## (4) OFFSET

Early in the litigation of price reductions for defective cost or pricing data, it was determined that a contractor was entitled, up to the amount of any price reduction, to offset any amount due to underpricing that had occurred because of defective data in the same pricing action, *Cutler-Hammer, Inc. v. United States*, 189 Ct. Cl. 76, 416 F.2d 1306 (1969); *Lockheed Aircraft Corp. v. United States*, 193 Ct. Cl. 86, 432 F.2d 801 (1970). This rule was incorporated in the statutes in 10 U.S.C. § 2306a(e) and 41 U.S.C. § 3506(d), as follows:

(4)(A) A contractor shall be allowed to offset an amount against the amount of a contract price adjustment under a contract provision required by paragraph (1) if —

(i) the contractor certifies to the contracting officer (or to a designated representative of the contracting officer) that, to the best of the contractor's knowledge and belief, the contractor is entitled to the offset; and

(ii) the contractor proves that the cost or pricing data were available before the date of agreement on the price of the contract (or price of the modification) and that the data were not submitted as specified in subsection (a)(3) before such date.

(B) A contractor shall not be allowed to offset an amount otherwise authorized to be offset under subparagraph (A) if —

(i) the certification under subsection (a)(2) with respect to the cost or pricing data involved was known to be false when signed; or

(ii) the United States proves that, had the cost or pricing data referred to in subparagraph (A)(ii) been submitted to the United States before the date of agreement on the price of the contract (or price of the modification), the submission of such cost or pricing data would not have resulted in an increase in that price in the amount to be offset.

Offsets are permitted only when the contractor proves that there was an understatement of "factual pricing data," *J.S. Latsis Group of Cos.*, ENGBCA 4276, 86-2 BCA ¶ 18,853. In that case, the board found that the evidence was very unclear, but if there were any errors to which a low price could be attributed, they were errors of judgment, not errors in cost or pricing data. Compare *Hughes Aircraft Co.*, ASBCA 46321, 97-1 BCA ¶ 28,972, where offsetting mistakes in the same packages of data as the nondisclosed reduced cost were permitted as offsets.

Offsets may not be made between different contracts, *Norris Indus., Inc.*, AS-BCA 15442, 74-1 BCA ¶ 10,482; *Minnesota Mining & Mfg. Co.*, ASBCA 20266, 77-2 BCA ¶ 12,823, or between unrelated contract modifications, *Muncie Gear Works, Inc.*, ASBCA 18184, 75-2 BCA ¶ 11,380. Neither can offsets lead to a price increase by the contractor, *Baldwin Elecs., Inc.*, ASBCA 19683, 76-2 BCA ¶ 12,199 (offsets exceeding the claimed price reduction led to sustaining of contractor's appeal), or be used when the omitted costs have been recovered from the government through inclusion in an overhead account, *Aerojet Ordnance Tenn.*, ASBCA 36089, 95-2 BCA ¶ 27,922. However, offsets are proper even when the contractor has intentionally understated the dollar amounts in the data, *Rogerson Aircraft Controls*, AS-BCA 27954, 85-1 BCA ¶ 17,725, *aff'd*, 785 F.2d 296 (Fed. Cir. 1986) (government knew of understatements and was not "hindered or deceived" by them). Offsets are also proper when a contractor is informed of an error and does not correct it when submitting its BAFO, *United Techs. Corp.*, ASBCA 51410, 04-1 BCA ¶ 32,556. A contractor has also been permitted to offset its omitted in-house costs of completing work from an overstated subcontract price for the same work, *TGS Int'l, Inc.*, AS-BCA 31120, 87-2 BCA ¶ 19,683, *recons. denied*, 87-3 BCA ¶ 19,989.

## (5) DEFECTIVE SUBCONTRACTOR DATA

If subcontractor cost or pricing data have been submitted to the government before the negotiation of the contract price of a firm-fixed-price contract, the contractor is liable for defects in that data, *Lockheed Aircraft Corp. v. United States*, 193 Ct. Cl. 86, 432 F.2d 801 (1970). In that case, the court held the contractor liable even though the subcontractor data had been submitted directly to the government, not to the contractor. The court reasoned that the contractor's liability was dictated by the contract clause requiring price reductions. See also *McDonnell Aircraft Co.*, ASBCA 44504, 97-1 BCA ¶ 28,977 (contractor liable for not furnishing updated subcontractor information when it had furnished original subcontractor data with its proposal). If subcontractor cost or pricing data are not submitted to the contractor until after the negotiation of the price of a firm-fixed-price contract, there is no contractor liability for a price reduction because there could be no government reliance on that data.

The contractor is expected to include price reduction clauses in all subcontracts under cost-reimbursement or fixed-price-incentive or redeterminable contracts, and price reductions obtained through such clauses are expected to be credited to the costs billed to the government, FAR 15.407-1(f)(2). This applies even though the subcontractor's cost or pricing data were never submitted to the government or used as the basis for the original contract price.

## (6) INTEREST AND PENALTIES

The statutes require the addition of interest and penalties in certain cases where the government has overpaid the contractor as a result of defective cost or pricing data, as stated at 10 U.S.C. § 2306a and 41 U.S.C. § 3507:

(f) Interest and penalties for certain overpayments. (1) If the United States makes an overpayment to a contractor under a contract with an executive agency subject to this section and the overpayment was due to the submission by the contractor of defective cost or pricing data, the contractor shall be liable to the United States —

(A) for interest on the amount of such overpayment, to be computed —

(i) for the period beginning on the date the overpayment was made to the contractor and ending on the date the contractor repays the amount of such overpayment to the United States; and

(ii) at the current rate prescribed by the Secretary of the Treasury under section 6621 of the Internal Revenue Code of 1986; and

(B) if the submission of such defective data was a knowing submission, for an additional amount equal to the amount of the overpayment.

(2) Any liability under this subsection of a contractor that submits cost or pricing data but refuses to submit the certification required by subsection (a)(2) with respect to the cost or pricing data shall not be affected by the refusal to submit such certification.

## d.  Contract Disputes Act of 1978

The Contract Disputes Act of 1978, 41 U.S.C. § 7103(b), provides that each claim over $100,000 must be certified with regard to four specific elements:

> For claims of more than $100,000 made by a contractor, the contractor shall certify that (A) the claim is made in good faith, (B) the supporting data are accurate and complete to the best of the contractor's knowledge and belief, (C) the amount requested accurately reflects the contract adjustment for which the contractor believes the Federal Government is liable, and (D) the certifier is authorized to certify the claim on behalf of the contractor.

Neither the statutes nor regulations specifically require the submission of supporting data. All that is expressly required is that the contractor certify that "supporting data" are accurate and complete. Although a certification that the data are "complete" could be interpreted as a requirement for submission, there has been disagreement over whether the contractor is affirmatively required to submit data. See *Joseph P. Mentor*, GSBCA 6757, 85-1 BCA ¶ 17,887, where the board held that the certification was not intended to force contractors to submit evidence in support of their claims, but was merely an "honesty" requirement designed to discourage inflated claims. However, the scope of the certification of data is broad. See *LaBarge Elecs.*, ASBCA 44401, 93-2 BCA ¶ 25,617, holding that supporting data for a claim cannot be limited to data concerning the amount but must also include data in support of entitlement. See also *Triasco Corp.*, ASBCA 42465, 91-2 BCA ¶ 23,969, stating that this certification covers "all supporting data." See Chapter 13 of Cibinic, Nash & Nagle, *Administration of Government Contracts*, 4th ed. 2006, for an in-depth discussion of the certification requirements under the Contract Disputes Act.

The Contract Disputes Act contains drastic sanctions for the misrepresentation of facts when submitting a claim. 41 U.S.C. § 7103(c)(2) provides:

> If a contractor is unable to support any part of the contractor's claim and it is determined that such inability is attributable to misrepresentation of fact or fraud by the contractor, then the contractor is liable to the Federal Government for an amount equal to the unsupported part of the claim plus all of the Federal Government's costs attributable to the cost of reviewing the unsupported part of the claim. Liability under this paragraph shall be determined within 6 years of the commission of the misrepresentation of fact or fraud.

The Act contains no definition of fraud. However, 41 U.S.C. § 7101(9) defines "misrepresentation of fact" as follows:

> The term "misrepresentation of fact" means a false statement of substantive fact, or conduct that leads to a belief of a substantive fact material to proper understanding of the matter in hand, made with intent to deceive or mislead.

The boards of contract appeals have refused to rule on a counterclaim for the penalty prescribed in § 7103(c)(2) based on the following language in the original 41 U.S.C. § 605(a):

> Each claim by a contractor against the government relating to a contract and each claim by the government against a contractor relating to a contract shall be submitted within 6 years after the accrual of the claim. The preceding sentence does not apply to a claim by the government against a contractor that is based on a claim by the contractor involving fraud. . . . The authority of this subsection shall not extend to a claim or dispute for penalties or forfeitures prescribed by statute or regulation which another Federal agency is specifically authorized to administer, settle or determine.

See *Comada Corp.*, ASBCA 26613, 83-2 BCA ¶ 16,681 ("actions to enforce the Government's rights under [Section 604] would be solely the responsibility of the Department of Justice and would be instituted by the United States in a court of competent jurisdiction"); or on a defense that the claim was fraudulent, *Schmalz Constr., Ltd.*, AGBCA 86-207-1, 91-3 BCA ¶ 24,183 ("[I]t is sufficient for the Board to determine whether statements in a claim are correct or incorrect. The Board does not need to determine whether incorrect statements were made knowingly or with an intent to deceive . . ."). Thus, the remedy in the boards of contract appeals for claims that have been found in another proceeding to be "tainted by fraud" is dismissal of the claim, *Beech Gap, Inc.*, ENGBCA 5585, 95-2 BCA ¶ 27,879, *aff'd*, 86 F.3d 1177 (Fed. Cir. 1997); *P.H. Mech. Corp. v. General Servs. Admin.*, GSBCA 10567, 94-2 BCA ¶ 26,785. Following this view that the appeals boards have no jurisdiction over claims involving § 604, a board has also refused to hear a contractor's claim that the contracting officer improperly assessed the penalty prescribed in that section, *Warren Beaves*, DOTCAB 1324, 83-1 BCA ¶ 16,232. The codification of this provision in 41 U.S.C. § 7103 contains slightly different wording but it is likely that the boards will continue to rule that they have no jurisdiction in this area.

The result is that the statutory penalty has only been imposed by the Court of Federal Claims when the government asserts a counterclaim in a contractor suit. Such counterclaims can be asserted in the same manner that all fraud counterclaims are asserted in that court without a prior decision of the contracting officer, *Simko Constr., Inc. v. United States*, 852 F.2d 540 (Fed. Cir. 1988). This provision making the contractor liable to the government for the amount of the fraudulent claim is probably the most drastic sanction for submitting a false claim. See *Daewoo Eng'g & Constr. Co. v. United States*, 73 Fed. Cl. 547 (2006), *aff'd*, 557 F.3d 1332 (Fed. Cir. 2009), *cert. denied*, 130 S. Ct. 490 (2009), holding that the contractor was liable for $50,629,855.88, the amount it had added to a claim to get the government's attention.

Such counterclaims are generally asserted along with counterclaims under the False Claims Act and the False Statements Act, *UMC Elecs. Co. v. United States*, 43 Fed. Cl. 776 (1999); *Crane Helicopter Servs., Inc. v. United States*, 45 Fed. Cl. 410

(1999); *Commercial Contractors, Inc. v. United States*, 154 F.3d 1357 (Fed. Cir. 1998); *Chemray Coatings Corp. v. United States*, 29 Fed. Cl. 278 (1993); *Tyger Constr. Co. v. United States*, 28 Fed. Cl. 35 (1993). See *JANA, Inc. v. United States*, 34 Fed. Cl. 447 (1995), where the court held that the government's counterclaim alleging fraud under the CDA was timely because the Act's six-year statute of limitations for fraud could begin to run no earlier than the submission of the contractor's certified claim, regardless of when the conduct rendering the contractor's false claim allegedly occurred.

### e.  10 U.S.C. § 2410 Certification

Another statute dealing with certifying supporting data for requests for equitable adjustment and requests for relief under Pub. L. No. 85-804 on DoD contracts is 10 U.S.C. § 2410. This statute was amended by the Federal Acquisition Streamlining Act of 1994, Pub. L. No. 103-355, to make it clear that the provision applies only to requests for equitable adjustment or for relief under Pub. L. No. 85-804. As amended, 10 U.S.C. § 2410 establishes the following certification requirement:

> (a) Certification Requirement. — A request for equitable adjustment to contract terms or request for relief under Public Law 85-804 (50 U.S.C. 1431 et seq.) that exceeds the simplified acquisition threshold may not be paid unless a person authorized to certify the request on behalf of the contractor certifies, at the time the request is submitted, that —
>
> > (1) the request is made in good faith, and
>
> > (2) the supporting data are accurate and complete to the best of that person's knowledge and belief.

This statute also does not contain a clear requirement for the submission of data. The Federal Acquisition Streamlining Act of 1994 also repealed the DoD-unique claim certification requirement contained in 10 U.S.C. § 2410e, thus leaving the Contract Disputes Act claim certification as the single governmentwide standard.

## 2.  Types of Illegal Conduct

Since the 1980s government contractors have been heavily investigated and sued for failure to deal openly and honestly with the federal government. The major types of conduct that are subject to lawsuits are discussed below.

### a.  Product Substitution

Product substitution generally refers to attempts by the contractor to deliver to the government a product that does not conform to the contract requirements. Such substitution can occur by mismarking products, deviating from specifications, and other types of conduct that may indicate an intention to deceive the government in the performance of the contract. Such conduct may subject contractors to criminal or civil sanctions under the False Claims Act. See, for example, *BMY-Combat Sys. Div. of Harsco Corp. v. United States*, 38 Fed. Cl. 109 (1997), finding false claims when the contractor knowingly failed to fully inspect military equipment. The court also voided final acceptance of the equipment and held the contractor liable for breach of contract. See also *Varljen v. Cleveland Gear Co.*, 250 F.3d 426 (6th Cir. 2001) (false claim when subcontractor changed manufacturing process without approval after qualifying item); *United States ex rel. Roby v. Boeing Co.*, 100 F. Supp. 2d 619 (S.D. Ohio 2000) (false claim to knowingly furnish helicopter transmission gears known to be defective); *United States v. Hangar One, Inc.*, 563 F.2d 1155 (5th Cir. 1977) (false claim to rig inspection system to omit required inspections and deliver rejected items); *Imperial Meat Co. v. United States*, 316 F.2d 435 (10th Cir.), *cert. denied*, 375 U.S. 820 (1963) (false claim when contractor substituted an inferior grade of meat on a DoD contract). In *United States v. National Wholesalers*, 236 F.2d 944 (9th Cir. 1956), *cert. denied*, 353 U.S. 930 (1957), the contractor indicated to the government that it would supply brand name regulators, but instead manufactured the regulators itself and attached false brand name labels before delivery. The court found the contractor liable for a false claim even though the regulators were in fact equal. See also *United States v. Aerodex, Inc.*, 469 F.2d 1003 (5th Cir. 1972), where the court found a false claim when the contractor knowingly substituted aircraft bearings which differed from the contract specifications, even though there was no proof that they were inferior. Other statutes used to prosecute product substitution include the False Statements Act, 18 U.S.C. § 1001, the conspiracy statutes, 18 U.S.C. § 286 and § 371, the mail and wire fraud statutes, 18 U.S.C. § 1341 and § 1343, and the Racketeer Influenced and Corrupt Organizations Act, 18 U.S.C. §§ 1961-1968.

Product substitution with an intent to defraud has also led to the loss of disputes cases in the boards of contract appeals. For example, in *D & H Constr. Co.*, ASBCA 37482, 89-3 BCA ¶ 22,070, the contractor's substitution of refrigerators with counterfeited certification labels rose to the level of fraud and voided final acceptance. Similarly, a default termination will be sustained if the contractor has fraudulently performed defective work, *Beech Gap, Inc.*, ENGBCA 5585, 95-2 BCA ¶ 27,879, *aff'd*, 86 F.3d 1177 (Fed. Cir. 1997).

When a contractor does not deliver goods that conform precisely to contract requirements there may not be an intent to defraud but the government still has contract remedies. Thus, it may obtain a price reduction equivalent to the amount of costs saved plus overhead and profit, *Santa Fe Eng'rs., Inc.*, ASBCA 44906, 93-1 BCA ¶ 25,298 (substitution of less expensive door); *Arnold M. Diamond, Inc.*, ASBCA 38974, 92-2 BCA ¶ 24,869 (use of fewer expansion joints than called for by specifications); *J.S. Alberici Constr. Co.*, GSBCA 10630, 92-1 BCA ¶ 24,392 (substitution of less expensive doors); *Bruce Andersen Co.*, ASBCA 29412, 89-2 BCA ¶ 21,872 (omission of work called for by contract). Even if the substitute is equal to that specified in the contract, acceptance may harm the procurement system, which is based on all competitors offering to furnish only the product called for in the contract. Allowing offerors to substitute products according to their own judgment would defeat the concept of bidding on an equal basis. See *Ideal Restaurant Supply Co.*, VACAB 570, 67-1 BCA ¶ 6237, where the board found that the government was justified in rejecting equivalent supplies that did not meet contract specifications and noted that allowing the contractor to substitute aluminum for nickel alloy and stainless steel in steam kettle parts could have a negative effect on the competitive bidding process. Similarly, in *J.L. Malone & Assocs.*, VABCA 2335, 88-3 BCA ¶ 20,894, *aff'd*, 879 F.2d 841 (Fed. Cir. 1989), the government rejected a contractor's substitution of a technically equivalent computer in the installation of a fire alarm system. The board stated that the preservation of the integrity of the competitive procurement system was more important than any benefits that could derive from replacing the specified computer with even a more advanced one at no extra cost to the government. See also *C.H. Hyperbarics, Inc.*, ASBCA 49375, 04-1 BCA ¶ 32,568, holding that the government properly rejected valves that were not of the same manufacture as other parts of the system, as required by the specifications.

### b. Mischarging/Accounting Fraud

Mischarging is the term used to describe a particular type of fraud involving the accounting treatment of costs by contractors. Mischarging is the false description and the improper charging of costs to a government contract. The contractual remedy for mischarging is the disallowance of the costs including all costs incurred because of the mischarging. See FAR 31.205-15 providing:

> (b) Costs incurred in connection with, or related to, the mischarging of costs on Government contracts are unallowable when the costs are caused by, or result from, alteration or destruction of records, or other false or improper charging or recording of costs. Such costs include those incurred to measure or otherwise determine the magnitude of the improper charging, and costs incurred to remedy or correct the mischarging, such as costs to rescreen and reconstruct records.

Mischarging can arise in several instances, including improper allocation of costs and charging of expressly unallowable costs to a contract. If a contractor includes an "expressly unallowable" cost in a proposal to settle indirect costs, the agency must assess a penalty against the contractor, in addition to disallowance of the cost, in the amount of the cost claimed plus interest on those costs, 10 U.S.C. § 2324(b); 41 U.S.C. § 4303(b). These sections also provide that the penalty will be double the amount of the claimed cost if it had been "determined to be unallowable in the case of such contractor before the submission of such proposal."

Mischarging is also subject to criminal and civil sanctions under the False Claims Act as well as other criminal sanctions. For example, in *United States v. McGunnigal*, 151 F.2d 162 (1st Cir.), *cert. denied*, 326 U.S. 776 (1945), a criminal conspiracy was found between welders and counters who manufactured and constructed ships under a cost-reimbursement contract resulted in inflated payroll costs. See *United States v.*

*Maher*, 582 F.2d 842 (4th Cir. 1978), *cert. denied*, 439 U.S. 1115 (1979), where false claims requesting payments under a time-and-materials contract were submitted. The accountant involved was instructed to inflate labor hours on monthly billings, prepare new time sheets that conformed to the changes, trace over employees' signatures on the new time sheets, and destroy the originals. See also *Morse Diesel Int'l, Inc. v. United States*, 74 Fed. Cl. 601 (2007) (invoicing bond premiums before payment to surety); *United States v. Newport News Shipbuilding, Inc.*, 276 F. Supp. 2d 539 (E.D. Va. 2003) (charging costs of designing commercial ships to IR&D); *United States ex rel. Newsham v. Lockheed Missile & Space Co.*, 190 F.3d 963 (9th Cir. 1999) (allegedly billing costs of unproductive labor and time workers spent on personal projects); *Jana, Inc. v. United States*, 41 Fed. Cl. 735 (1998) (altering time cards); *United States ex rel. Mayman v. Martin Marietta Corp.*, 894 F. Supp. 218 (D.C. Md. 1995) (proposing low costs for work with intention of charging costs of performance to IR&D); *Young-Montenay, Inc. v. United States*, 15 F.3d 1040 (Fed. Cir. 1994) (altering subcontractor invoice in order to inflate progress payment); *United States v. TDC Mgmt. Corp.*, 24 F.3d 292 (D.C. Cir. 1994) (omission of information from cost reports);*United States v. Sperry Corp.*, Civ. 89-2472 (E.D.N.Y. 1991) (contractor employees falsely filled out time cards indicating work on one contract when the work was properly chargeable to other jobs); *United States v. Lagerbusch*, 361 F.2d 449 (3d Cir. 1966) (false representations in invoices submitted to cost-type contractor). See also *United States v. Richmond*, 700 F.2d 1183 (8th Cir. 1983). For an in-depth analysis of other mischarging cases, see Graham, *Mischarging: A Contract Dispute or a Criminal Fraud?*, 15 Pub. Cont. L.J. 208 (1985).

### c.  Fraudulent Pricing

As discussed previously, the Truth in Negotiations Act requires that before price negotiations for negotiated contracts, government contractors must disclose the facts relevant to those negotiations and certify that the facts are accurate, complete, and current. However, the failure to submit complete, current, and accurate cost or pricing data has been treated as fraud in only a few cases. There are two types of defective pricing situations that are often treated as instances of fraud — the falsification of cost or pricing data, and the submission of inaccurate estimates.

### (1) FRAUDULENT DATA

For many years, *United States v. Foster Wheeler Corp.*, 447 F.2d 100 (2d Cir. 1971), which affirmed a district court decision that the contractor had committed civil fraud by submitting defective cost or pricing data, was the only reported decision in this area. More recently, in *UMC Elecs. Co. v. United States*, 43 Fed. Cl. 776 (1999), fraud was found when the contractor submitted full cost or pricing data to support its claim but listed its "actual costs" by summarizing its purchase order prices even though there were several instances where subcontractors and suppliers had not invoiced for work at those prices. The court found that the contractor knew full well the difference between actual costs and estimates because it had made the difference clear in prior submissions of cost or pricing data. The court therefore found that the inclusion by the contractor of uninvoiced costs in its statement of "actual costs" was a fraudulent statement. Similarly, in *United States v. Leo*, 941 F.2d 181 (3d Cir.1991), fraud was found when a contractor's negotiator affirmatively stated that its estimate of subcontract prices would be difficult to attain when it had knowingly failed to provide the government with subcontract prices that had been substantially reduced, and in *United States v. Pimental & Duroyd Mfg. Co.*, 810 F.2d 366 (2d Cir. 1987), fraud was found when the contractor obtained quotations from eight vendors but submitted only the highest quote to the contracting officer while buying at the low price. See also *United States v. Poarch*, 878 F.2d 1355 (11th Cir. 1989), where the circuit court affirmed the conviction of a defense firm's contracts administrator for conspiracy to defraud the United States and for criminal false statements. Fraud was found when an administrator (1) told an employee to charge time to a wrong account in order to build up labor hours, and (2) omitted current labor-hour data from the submission of cost or pricing data that had been required by the contracting officer. A number of fraud cases in this area involve the creation and submission of false data by the contractor. See *United States v. Barnette*, 800 F.2d 1558 (11th Cir. 1986), *cert. denied*, 480 U.S. 935 (1987), where the contractor created false payroll records and false invoices from bogus vendors to inflate its proposed contract prices; and *United States v. Busher*, 817 F.2d 1409 (9th Cir. 1987), where the contractor falsified data relating to performance of work by subcontractors.

Cases litigating the issue of whether the government should obtain a price reduction for defective pricing appear to be easily distinguishable from those involving prosecution for civil or criminal fraud. Price reduction cases largely deal with technical interpretations of the submission requirement. In most instances, the contractor has made major submissions but has omitted some discrete data. The fraud cases generally involve either falsification of data or a scheme to obtain a higher price. Thus, if a contractor makes a serious effort to disclose the cost or pricing data used in preparing its proposal, it is probably not in jeopardy of being charged with fraud. However, a contractor that adopts practices that permit regular nondisclosure of such data is taking an unreasonable business risk. If the government concludes that higher prices are being obtained through the use of such practices, a charge of fraud is likely.

## (2) INACCURATE ESTIMATES

In a few cases, contractors have been held liable for submitting egregiously inaccurate estimates. In the original case of this type, *United States ex rel. Taxpayers Against Fraud v. Singer Co.*, 889 F.2d 1327 (4th Cir. 1989), the fraud was found in not submitting the contractor's "best estimates" as certified on the Standard Form 1411 as follows:

> This proposal is submitted in response to the RFP, contract, modification, etc. in Item 1 and reflects our best estimates and/or actual costs as of this date and conforms with the instructions in FAR 15.804-6(b)(1). . . .

Similarly, in *United States v. Sperry Corp.*, Civ. 89-2472 (E.D.N.Y. 1991), the government alleged that the contractor submitted a low estimate on the original contract and after buying in submitted high estimates on the follow-on contracts where the contractor was the sole source. Subsequently, in *United States v. Bicoastal Corp.*, Cr. No. 92-CR-261 (N.D.N.Y. 1992), a contractor pleaded guilty to charges arising from the submission of inflated, fraudulent labor estimates on negotiated sole source contracts for flight simulators. The contractor had submitted cost estimates that included amounts allocated for fictitious jobs and personnel that purported to be necessary costs. The contractor certified that each cost estimate was its best estimate, while it routinely concealed a lower estimate. The Standard Form 1411 has been removed from the FAR but Table 15-2 — Instructions for Submitting Cost/Price Proposals When Cost or Pricing Data Are Required, FAR 15.408, contains the following required statement (removing the word "best") on such proposals:

> This proposal reflects our estimates and/or actual costs as of this data and conforms with the instructions in FAR 15.403-5(b)(1) and Table 15-2. . . .

This removes the issue of whether the estimate submitted was the "best" estimate but does not affect the question of whether the estimate was fraudulently compiled.

Other fraud cases also involve the submission of estimates of a contract's cost of performance when the contractor is aware that the estimate does not reflect its anticipated allowable costs. See *United States v. White*, 765 F.2d 1469 (11th Cir. 1985), where the contractor submitted an estimate of the cost of fully performed work under change orders that was far higher than the actual costs that had been incurred and recorded in its accounting data. The court held that the contractor had represented to the government that its estimate reflected actual costs. See also *Daewoo Eng'g & Constr. Co. v. United States*, 73 Fed. Cl. 547 (2006), *aff'd*, 557 F.3d 1332 (Fed. Cir. 2009), *cert. denied*, 130 S. Ct. 490 (2009) (false claim to add over $50 million to claim to get the attention of the contracting officer); *United States v. United Techs. Corp.*, No. 3:99-cv-093 (S.D. Ohio 2008), *rev'd on other grounds*, 626 F.3d 313 (6th Cir. 2010) (false claim to misstate the way that a complex estimate was calculated); *Harrison v. Westinghouse Savannah River Co.*, 176 F.3d 776 (4th Cir. 1999) (false claim to misstate the scope and length of work to be subcontracted in order to obtain government approval to subcontract); *United States v. General Dynamics Corp.*, 19 F.3d 770 (2d Cir. 1994) (false claim to include kickbacks paid to subcontractor in cost estimates submitted to the government).

## (3) BUYING-IN

Submitting a low price in order to obtain additional compensation during contract performance or through obtaining follow-on contracts is not per se fraudulent, *United States ex rel. Bettis v. Odebrecht Contractors of California, Inc.*, 297 F. Supp. 2d 272 (D.D.C. 2004), *aff'd*, 393 F.3d 1321 (D.C. Cir. 2005).

After concluding that contracting at a low price could not be equated with false-ly claiming money to which the contractor was not entitled, the district court reasoned at 281:

> The fact that a deflated bid alone cannot suffice to impose liability under the FCA is not, however, cured by merely adding a claim that defendant sought monies above and beyond the bid price. Such a proposition completely ignores the reality of government contracting where it is common for a contract that was bid at one price to ultimately cost far more. For instance, as previously noted, in a unit-price contract, such as [this] contract, the final price will neces-sarily be different if the actual quantities of materials turn out to be greater than the government's original quantity estimates. Further, as plaintiff concedes..., it is perfectly acceptable for the government to modify the scope of work or to change the design specifications. Alternatively, the final price can be increased if the government's representations about the nature of the project turn out to be inaccurate. Since there are a myriad of legitimate adjustments that can in-crease a contract price beyond the bid price, it necessarily follows that plaintiff cannot rest only on proof of a fraudulently induced contract by means of a low bid and an attempt by the bidder to obtain monies in excess of the bid price. Rather, there must be a claim "for money to which...[the contractor] is not legitimately entitled."

### d. Equitable Adjustment Claims

Making false statements or allegations in equitable adjustment claims has also been found to be fraudulent. For example, in *United States ex rel. Wilkins v. North Am. Constr. Corp.*, 101 F. Supp.2d 500 (S.D. Tex. 2000), the court found a proper allegation of fraud when the contractor based a differing site conditions claim on allegedly defective information that had been provided by the govern-ment when it had considerable information that the government information was accurate. In *Commercial Contractors, Inc. v. United States*, 154 F.3d 1357 (Fed. Cir. 1998), the court also found fraud in the substantive allegations in a differing site condition claim. Similarly, in *P.H. Mech. Corp. v. General Servs. Admin.*, GSBCA 10567, 94-2 BCA ¶ 26,785, fraud was found where a contractor falsified receipts, invoices and records supporting an equitable adjustment claim. See also *Shaw v. AAA Eng'g & Drafting, Inc.*, 213 F.3d 519 (10th Cir. 2000), where the contractor falsely inflated numbers on official work orders used to support an eq-uitable adjustment claim. In *AAA Engrg. & Drafting, Inc.*, ASBCA 47940, 01-1 BCA ¶ 31,256, the board denied a subsequent equitable adjustment claim based on this court decision.

## E.  Obtaining Information Improperly

There are several sanctions for improperly disclosing or obtaining informa-tion related to the procurement process. 18 U.S.C. § 1905 imposes criminal sanctions on any government employee that discloses trade secrets and other propri-etary data obtained from any person or organization. The procurement integrity provisions in the Office of Procurement Policy Act, prohibit any person from disclosing "contractor bid or proposal information" or "source selection informa-tion" before contract award, 41 U.S.C. § 2102(a) or obtaining such information, 41 U.S.C. § 2102(b). There may also be improper conduct involved in obtaining information about a competitor. These various aspects of improperly obtaining information are discussed below. Improper access to information is also consid-ered to be an organizational conflict of interest which is discussed in Chapter 4.

## 1. Disclosure of Confidential Information by Government Employees

18 U.S.C. § 1905 provides:

Whoever, being an officer or employee of the United States or of any depart-ment or agency thereof, any person acting on behalf of the Office of Federal Housing Enterprise Oversight, or agent of the Department of Justice as de-fined in the Antitrust Civil Process Act (15 U.S.C. 1311 — 1314), or being an employee of a private sector organization who is or was assigned to an agency under Chapter 37 of title 5, publishes, divulges, discloses, or makes known in any manner or to any extent not authorized by law any information coming to him in the course of his employment or official duties or by reason of any ex-amination or investigation made by, or return, report or record made to or filed with, such department or agency or officer or employee thereof, which infor-mation concerns or relates to the trade secrets, processes, operations, style of work, or apparatus, or to the identity, confidential statistical data, amount or source of any income, profits, losses, or expenditures of any person, firm, partnership, corporation, or association; or permits any income return or copy thereof or any book containing any abstract or particulars thereof to be seen or examined by any person except as provided by law; shall be fined under this title, or imprisoned not more than one year, or both; and shall be removed from office or employment.

The conviction of a government employee under 18 U.S.C. § 1905 for improper disclosure of information was affirmed in *United States v. Wallington*, 889 F.2d 573 (5th Cir. 1989). The court held that the Act was not overly broad to constitute a valid criminal statute.

## 2. Disclosure of and Obtaining Bid or Proposal Information or Source Selection Information

The Clinger-Cohen Act of 1996 amended the Procurement Integrity Act, 41 U.S.C. § 2102, to streamline the provisions on disclosure of and obtaining information. The amended Act contains two provisions relating to such transmission of information. 41 U.S.C. § 2102(a), prohibits a "person" from knowingly disclosing "contractor bid or proposal information" or "source selection information" before award of a contract. The "persons" covered were defined in 41 U.S.C. § 423(a)(2) as any person who

(A) is a present or former official of the United States, or a person who is acting or has acted for or on behalf of, or who is advising or has advised the United States with respect to, a Federal agency procurement; and

(B) by virtue of that office, employment, or relationship has or had access to contractor bid or proposal information or source selection information.

This definition was omitted from the 2011 codification of these provisions. However, the term "official" is defined in 41 U.S.C. § 2101(5) as (1) an officer as defined in 5 U.S.C. § 2104, (2) an employee as defined in 5 U.S.C. § 2105, and (3) a member of the uniformed forces as defined in 5 U.S.C. § 2101(3). FAR 3.104-3 adds to this the category of "special Government employees" as defined in 18 U.S.C. § 202. This statute gives a new test as to what persons are covered by this paragraph of the Act. They are persons who have either "acted" or "advised" regarding a federal agency procurement and have obtained information through that contact with the procurement. Neither the statute nor the implementation of this part of the Act in FAR 3.104-4 contain any guidance on the meaning of the terms "acted" or "advised," with the apparent effect that this rule applies to persons who have acted or advised no matter how small their contact with the procurement. This would seem to apply this part of the Act to virtually anyone who obtained information in the course of participating in the procurement, unless he or she was a total bystander that obtained information in the course of observing the procurement.

The second prohibition is in 41 U.S.C. § 2102(b), prohibiting a "person" from knowingly obtaining "contractor bid or proposal information" or "source selection information" before award of a contract to which the information pertains. The Act contains no definition of the "persons" covered by this paragraph with the result that it appears to apply to any contractor, other business entity, or individual that obtains information even if that person is not participating in the procurement. It also seems to apply the prohibition without regard to the source of the information, with the result that it could arguably be a violation to obtain the information from a newspaper reporter or some other person not connected with the procurement. The only narrowing of the rule is that it is no longer a violation of the Act to solicit information if the information is not obtained.

The Act applies only to a "federal agency procurement," and this term is defined in 41 U.S.C. § 2101(f)(4) to mean only acquisitions using competitive procedures. This is an important reduction from the coverage of the prior Act because officials who have participated in sole source procurements or contract modifications are not covered by the current Act. However, the implementation of this provision of the Act in FAR 3.104-4 applies these rules without regard to this statutory limitation as follows:

(a) Except as specifically provided for in this subsection, no person or other entity may disclose contractor bid or proposal information or source selection information to any person other than a person authorized, in accordance with applicable agency regulations or procedures, by the head of the agency or the contracting officer to receive such information.

(b) Contractor bid or proposal information and source selection information must be protected from unauthorized disclosure in accordance with 14.401, 15.207, applicable law, and agency regulations.

This broadening of the prohibition beyond the scope of the Procurement Integrity Act reflects the fact that 18 U.S.C. § 1905 is a blanket prohibition of disclosure of proprietary information.

The two types of information protected from disclosure are defined in 41 U.S.C. § 2101 as follows:

(2) The term "contractor bid or proposal information" means any of the following information submitted to a Federal agency as part of or in connection with a bid or proposal to enter into a Federal agency procurement contract, if that information has not been previously made available to the public or disclosed publicly:

(A) Cost or pricing data (as defined by section 2306a(h) of title 10 with respect to procurements subject to that section, and section 3501(a) of this title, with respect to procurements subject to that section).

(B) Indirect costs and direct labor rates.

(C) Proprietary information about manufacturing processes, operations, or techniques marked by the contractor in accordance with applicable law or regulation.

(D) Information marked by the contractor as "contractor bid or proposal information", in accordance with applicable law or regulation.

(7) The term "source selection information" means any of the following information prepared for use by a Federal agency to evaluate a bid or proposal to enter into a Federal agency procurement contract, if that information has not been previously made available to the public or disclosed publicly:

(A) Bid prices submitted in response to a Federal agency solicitation for sealed bids, or lists of those bid prices before public bid opening.

(B) Proposed costs or prices submitted in response to a Federal agency solicitation, or lists of those proposed costs or prices.

(C) Source selection plans.

(D) Technical evaluation plans.

(E) Technical evaluations of proposals.

(F) Cost or price evaluations of proposals.

(G) Competitive range determinations that identify proposals that have a reasonable chance of being selected for award of a contract.

(H) Rankings of bids, proposals, or competitors.

(I) The reports and evaluations of source selection panels, boards, or advisory councils.

(J) Other information marked as "source selection information" based on a case-by-case determination by the head of the agency, his designee, or the contracting officer that its disclosure would jeopardize the integrity or successful completion of the Federal agency procurement to which the information relates.

41 U.S.C. § 2107 contains a number of "savings provisions," as follows:

(h) *Savings Provisions.* This chapter does not —

(1) restrict the disclosure of information to, or its receipt by, any person or class of persons authorized, in accordance with applicable agency regulations or procedures, to receive that information;

(2) restrict a contractor from disclosing its own bid or proposal information or the recipient from receiving that information;

(3) restrict the disclosure or receipt of information relating to a Federal agency procurement after it has been canceled by the Federal agency before contract award unless the Federal agency plans to resume the procurement;

(4) prohibit individual meetings between a Federal agency official and an offeror or potential offeror for, or a recipient of, a contract or subcontract under a Federal agency procurement, provided that unauthorized disclosure or receipt of contractor bid or proposal information or source selection information does not occur;

(5) authorize the withholding of information from, nor restrict its receipt by, Congress, a committee or subcommittee of Congress, the Comptroller General, a Federal agency, or an inspector general of a Federal agency;

(6) authorize the withholding of information from, nor restrict its receipt by, the Comptroller General of the United States in the course of a protest against the award or proposed award of a Federal agency procurement contract; or

(7) limit the applicability of any requirements, sanctions, contract penalties, and remedies established under another law or regulation.

These provisions are implemented at FAR 3.104-4(e) and (f). It seems clear that these rules should not prevent open communication between contracting agencies and potential offerors regarding the work to be procured and the procurement strategy before solicitations are issued as long as specific finalized source selection plans and technical evaluation plans are not revealed. It also places no limitations on obtaining information during litigation. See *Pikes Peak Family Housing, LLC v United States*, 40 Fed. Cl. 673 (1998), permitting normal discovery in an award protest citing ¶ (7) above providing for discovery in a court proceeding as a "remedy" covered by the saving provisions of the Act. However, they will permit disqualification of an offeror that has improperly obtained access to such information. See *Guardian Techs. Int'l*, Comp. Gen. Dec. B-270213, 96-1 CPD ¶ 104, where GAO agreed that it was proper to disqualify an offeror that had hired a government employee that had access to source selection information.

There are severe penalties for violation these provisions. See 41 U.S.C. § 2105 stating:

(a) Criminal penalties. A person that violates section 2102 of this title to exchange information covered by section 2102 of this title for anything of value or to obtain or give a person a competitive advantage in the award of a Federal agency procurement contract shall be fined under title 18, imprisoned for not more than 5 years, or both.

(b) Civil penalties. The Attorney General may bring a civil action in an appropriate district court of the United States against a person that engages in conduct that violates section 2102, 2103, or 2104 of this title. On proof of that conduct by a preponderance of the evidence —

(1) an individual is liable to the Federal Government for a civil penalty of not more than $50,000 for each violation plus twice the amount of compensation that the individual received or offered for the prohibited conduct; and

(2) an organization is liable to the Federal Government for a civil penalty of not more than $500,000 for each violation plus twice the amount of compensation that the organization received or offered for the prohibited conduct.

## 3. Information about Competitors

The techniques for gaining information about competitors are diverse and may or may not be proper. These techniques range from the benign, such as reading a competitor's sales brochure, to the potentially criminal, such as business espionage. In *Compliance Corp. v. United States*, 22 Cl. Ct. 193 (1990), *aff'd*, 960 F.2d 157 (Fed. Cir. 1992), the offeror approached employees of the incumbent contractor, who was competing for a follow-on services contract, to obtain detailed information on how the incumbent contractor was performing the work and to discover the contents of the incumbent's proposal for the follow-on work. Upon learning of this conduct, the contracting officer disqualified the offeror, and GAO sustained this action, *Compliance Corp.*, Comp. Gen. Dec. B-239252, 90-2 CPD ¶ 126, *recons. denied*, B-239252.3, 90-2 CPD ¶ 435. The Claims Court agreed with this decision, stating at 204:

> The court finds actual or attempted "industrial espionage" to be outside the realm of normal business practices, and the contracting officer is entitled to disqualify those who engage in such conduct, not only to protect the integrity of the contracting process, but also to deter others from similar conduct.

Similarly, in *Kellogg Brown & Root Servs., Inc.*, Comp. Gen. Dec. B-400787.2, 2009 CPD ¶ 54, GAO agreed that it was proper to disqualify a contractor from competing for task orders where it had been inadvertently sent information as to its competitors pricing strategy and had refused to isolate recipients of the information from performance of the task orders, and in *Computer Tech. Assocs., Inc.*, Comp. Gen. Dec. B-288622, 2001 CPD ¶ 187, GAO agreed that a competitor should be disqualified when it obtained and read e-mail transcripts of its competitors' oral presentations. The latter decision cites the Procurement Integrity Act provisions barring such conduct. See also *Huynh Serv. Co.*, Comp. Gen. Dec. 242297.2, 91-1 CPD ¶ 562, where GAO concurred with an agency decision to terminate a contract for the convenience of the government after it learned that the low bidder might have obtained a competitor's pricing information before it submitted its bid, and *Litton Sys., Inc.*, 68 Comp. Gen. 422 (B-234060), 89-1 CPD ¶ 450, *recons. denied*, 68 Comp. Gen. 677 (B-234060.2), 89-2 CPD ¶ 228, where GAO disqualified an offeror that had obtained source selection information through a marketing consultant. Generally, however, GAO will not rule on protests that one competitor acted improperly with regard to another competitor — stating that this is a private dispute to be resolved in the courts, *Advanced Communications Sys., Inc.*, Comp. Gen. Dec. B-271040, 96-1 CPD ¶ 274 (allegation that competitor improperly obtained protester's proposal strategy and pricing information by hiring its employee); *Bildon, Inc.*, Comp. Gen. Dec. B-241375, 90-2 CPD ¶ 332 (allegation that company improperly obtained competitor's information by hiring employee who prepared proposal); *Garrett Corp.*, Comp. Gen. Dec. B-182991, 76-1 CPD ¶ 20 (allegation that competitor had obtained proprietary drawings by improper means); *York Indus., Inc.*, Comp. Gen. Dec. B-186958, 76-2 CPD ¶ 453 (allegation that competitor had used proprietary drawings in violation of license agreement).

## 4. Exchanging Information with Competitors

Offerors in fixed-price contracts are required by FAR 3.103-1 to certify that prices were arrived at independently without collusion between prospective contractors. This provision is implemented by the Certificate of Independent Price Determination solicitation provision in FAR 52.203-2. The contracting officer is directed to reject an offer if the certificate is altered, FAR 3.103-2(b).

Sanctions have been imposed on firms that entered into agreements on prices to be bid, *United States v. Portsmouth Paving Corp.*, 694 F.2d 312 (4th Cir. 1982) (criminal sanctions for bid rigging), as well as an agreement not to bid on a procurement, *Leitman v. McAusland*, 934 F.2d 46 (4th Cir. 1991) (debarment for collusive bidding). Collusive bidding will not be found unless there is proof of concerted action between two or more parties. In *Federal Trade Comm'n v. Lukens Steel Co.*, 454 F. Supp. 1182 (D.D.C. 1978), the court found no concerted action between Lukens and United States Steel Company in the pricing of steel plates for Navy ships when the two companies followed each other's published prices or prices obtained from the shipbuilder. The court stated at 1193 that: "The actions of each defendant appear to be based upon independent judgment, a consideration of the defendant's own business interest, and an assessment of the competition."

GAO usually will not rule on protests requesting that competing offerors be disqualified because of collusive bidding, *Shel-Ken Props., Inc.*, Comp. Gen. Dec. B-261443, 95-2 CPD ¶ 139; *Seyforth Roofing Co.*, Comp. Gen. Dec. B-241719.2, 91-1 CPD ¶ 268; *Automated Datatron, Inc.*, Comp. Gen. Dec. B-184022, 75-2 CPD ¶ 153. However, in denying such protests GAO has frequently stated that the alleged conduct was not improper. Thus, it has stated that it is not a violation of the independent pricing certificate for competitors to propose to use the same subcontractor, *McCombs Fleet Servs.*, Comp. Gen. Dec. B-278330, 98-1 CPD ¶ 24; for competitors to use a common subcontractor, *Ross Aviation, Inc.*, Comp. Gen. Dec. B-236952, 90-1 CPD ¶ 83; for affiliated firms to submit separate bids prepared by the same person, 51 Comp. Gen. 403 (B-174449) (1972); for a firm to bid as a joint venturer and also submit bids to competitors to perform work as a subcontractor, *Southern Maryland Gen. Contractors, Inc.*, 57 Comp. Gen. 277 (B-190270), 78-1 CPD ¶ 121; for partners sharing the same business address to submit separate bids, *Ace Reforestation, Inc.*, 65 Comp. Gen. 151 (B-220276), 85-2 CPD ¶ 704; or for a firm to mail letters to several potential competitors warning of possible legal action if they infringed patents, Comp. Gen. Dec. B-167152, Aug. 14, 1969, *Unpub.*

An agreement to fix prices in a government contract may also be illegal under the Sherman Act, 15 U.S.C. §§ 1–7. Agencies are required to report bids and proposals to the Attorney General if there is substantial evidence of a violation of antitrust laws, 10 U.S.C. § 2305(b)(5) and 41 U.S.C. § 3707. See FAR 3.303.

In many circumstances, however, information may legally be exchanged with competitors. Generally, if the prospective offeror legally obtains information directly from a competitor without any restriction on the ability to use that information, it is appropriate and legal to use that information in preparing proposals.

## F. Conspiracy

It is a crime for two or more persons to agree to (1) commit any offense against the United States, 18 U.S.C. § 371, or (2) defraud the United States, 18 U.S.C. § 286, if any of the persons perform an act to effect the conspiracy. The unlawful object of a conspiracy could be the violation of any civil or criminal statute, *United States v. Feola*, 420 U.S. 671 (1975). A conspiracy to commit bribery is clearly included, and conspiracies involving gratuities or conflicts of interest also fall within 18 U.S.C. § 371, *United States v. Razete*, 199 F.2d 44 (6th Cir.), *cert. denied*, 344 U.S. 904 (1952). However, it is not necessary for the agreed-upon action to be a violation of statute. An agreement to defraud the United States in any manner would qualify. It is not necessary that the government lose money or property as a result of the fraud. All that is required is that "[the government's] legitimate official action and purpose shall be defeated by misrepresentation, chicane or . . . overreaching," *Hammerschmidt v. United States*, 265 U.S. 182 (1924).

An agreement to give preferential treatment to an offeror for a government contract is prohibited, Executive Order 12674, § 101(h) as modified by Executive Order 12731; 5 C.F.R. § 2635.101(b)(8). In proving the existence of such an agreement, the government is not required to establish a formal express agreement but can show a tacit understanding between the parties, *United States v. Paramount Pictures, Inc.*, 334 U.S. 131 (1948). This understanding can be proved by circumstantial evidence, *Hamling v. United States*, 418 U.S. 87 (1974); *Glasser v. United States*, 315 U.S. 60 (1942).

# CHAPTER 2

# CONTRACT FORMATION PRINCIPLES

Although the federal government's purchasing procedures are governed extensively by statutes and regulations, the creation or modification of a contractual relationship between the government and the contractor is, for the most part, determined by common-law legal rules. See *Winstar v. United States,* 518 U.S. 839, 895 (1996) ("When the United States enters into contract relations, its rights and duties therein are governed generally by the law applicable to contracts between private individuals." (quoting *Lynch v. United States,* 292 U.S. 571 (1934))); *Priebe & Sons, Inc. v. United States,* 332 U.S. 407 (1947). As these rules have been applied to government contract cases, a body of federal law has developed as the primary source of law in this area. This federal law is generally consistent with the legal rules summarized in the *Restatement, Second, Contracts.* See, for, example, *Long Island Sav. Bank, FSB v. United States,* 503 F.3d 1234, 1245 (Fed. Cir. 2007). The *Uniform Commercial Code* (U.C.C.), although not binding upon the federal government, is also used to determine the rights and liabilities of the contracting parties when not inconsistent with federal law.

Enforceable promises are the essential requirements for a contract. See *Restatement, Second, Contracts* § 1, which defines "contract" as —

> a promise or a set of promises for the breach of which the law gives a remedy, or the performance of which the law in some way recognizes as a duty.

This chapter focuses on the legal principles used by the courts (primarily the U.S. Court of Appeals for the Federal Circuit and the U.S. Court of Federal Claims), the Government Accountability Office (GAO), and the boards of contract appeals to determine whether the government has entered into a relationship involving one or more enforceable promises. It first considers whether the parties have entered into a contractual relationship — whether they have manifested mutual assent. It then deals with whether their agreement is binding. Where applicable, the chapter includes a discussion of contract formation issues involving electronic transactions.

## I. MANIFESTATION OF MUTUAL ASSENT

In order to create a contractual relationship, the parties must each assent to the same terms and conditions, *Anderson v. United States,* 344 F.3d 1343, 1353 (Fed. Cir. 2003) ("To form an agreement binding upon the government, four basic requirements must be met: (1) mutuality of intent to contract; (2) lack of ambiguity in offer and acceptance; (3) consideration; and (4) a government representative having actual authority to bind the United States in contract."). This mutual assent occurs when one party manifests an intent to be bound to a set of terms and conditions and the other party timely agrees to that relationship. Most often this process can be analyzed in terms of an offer and an acceptance. The party making the offer, referred to as the "offeror," communicates to the other party an intention to form a contract. To accept the offer forming a contract, the other party must assent in the manner invited or authorized. The manifestation of mutual assent may also occur absent an identifiable offer or acceptance. These concepts are stated in *Restatement, Second, Contracts* § 22, which provides:

> (1) The manifestation of mutual assent to an exchange ordinarily takes the form of an offer or proposal by one party followed by an acceptance by the other party or parties.

> (2) A manifestation of mutual assent may be made even though neither offer nor acceptance can be identified and even though the moment of formation cannot be determined.

See also U.C.C. § 2-204; *Northeast Sav. v. United States,* 63 Fed. Cl. 507 (2005) (looking to ambiguous offer and acceptance).

This section first covers basic requirements, specifically capacity to contract and contractual intent and definiteness. It then analyzes the rules of offer and acceptance as they have been applied to the various types of contractual relationships entered into by the federal government. The section concludes with a discussion of the circumstances where the actions of the parties create an implied-in-fact contract.

## A. Basic Requirements

There are a number of basic requirements which must be satisfied in order for parties' communications to result in contractual obligations. Both parties must possess the legal capacity to contract, they must have contractual intent, and their agreement must be sufficiently definite to permit enforcement by a court or board of contract appeals.

### 1. Capacity to Contract

Capacity to contract refers to the common law principle which provides that a person cannot be bound unless that person "has capacity to incur at least avoidable contractual duties," *Restatement, Second, Contracts* § 12. This rule is applicable to government contracts although its application is not common. There are also a number of special government contracts rules which deal with the same or analogous issues. For example, questions concerning the legal capacity of government agencies to contract are dealt with in Chapter 1, Section II under the topic "contracting powers." Similarly, those seeking to deal with the government are subject to rules concerning eligibility, suspension and debarment. See Chapter 4, Section II.

In some cases, the term "capacity to contract" has been used, mistakenly, to refer to the question of whether a specific officer, employee or agent has the authority to bind an offeror. *See Video Eng'g Co.*, DOTCAB 72-5, 72-1 BCA ¶ 9432. Questions concerning such authority are dealt with in Chapter 1, Section III.

## a.  Nature of Capacity to Contract

Determination of a party's capacity to contract depends on whether the party is a natural person, a partnership, a joint venture, or a corporation. For natural persons, *Restatement, Second, Contracts* § 12 states:

> A natural person who manifests assent to a transaction has the full legal capacity to incur contractual duties thereby unless he or she is:
>
> (a) under guardianship, or
>
> (b) an infant, or
>
> (c) mentally ill or defective, or
>
> (d) intoxicated.

However, this does not mean that such parties cannot enter into contracts. If a contracting party has no knowledge, or reason to know, that the other party is mentally ill or intoxicated, the lack of capacity will not prevent the formation of a contract. Further, a contract will be found if the party fails to disaffirm the transaction within a reasonable time after recovering from the mental illness or intoxication. With respect to infancy, the other party's notice or reason to know of the infancy is not required in order to permit the infant from rescinding the agreement. However, the failure to do so within a reasonable time after reaching the age of majority will permit the other party to enforce the contract, *Lonchyna v. Brown*, 491 F. Supp. 1352 (N.D. Ill. 1980) (armed services enlistment contract). These types of agreements are commonly referred to as "voidable."

Corporations are artificial persons and their contracting capacity is determined by their charters or articles of incorporation. Agreements which are not within the authority of such documents are called "ultra vires" and are considered to be *void ab initio*, meaning that a contract never came into being, *Rose Island Co. v. United States*, 105 Ct. Cl. 192 (1945). There, the court permitted the government to cancel an agreement for the purchase of stone on the grounds that the corporation it dealt with had no legal capacity to contract. The court found that the corporation's charter authorized it to conduct a public entertainment and amusement park but not to sell stone from a quarry which it owned. The laws of the state of incorporation will determine whether a corporation has the capacity to contract, *BLH, Inc. v. United States*, 2 Cl. Ct. 463 (1983); *Mather Constr. Co. v. United States*, 201 Ct. Cl. 219,

475 F.2d 1152 (1973). Thus, if questions arise concerning capacity to contract, a certificate from the proper agency of the state of incorporation will be used to determine capacity, *Valley Constr. Co.*, Comp. Gen. Dec. B-184391, 75-2 CPD ¶ 393.

Most of the cases challenging corporate capacity involve situations where a corporation's charter has been suspended for failure to pay taxes or failure to file reports. State corporation laws contain elaborate provisions governing the conduct of a corporation whose charter has been suspended for such reasons. See *Easterbrook/ Ramco*, ASBCA 42176, 94-2 BCA ¶ 26,658, where the board dismissed an appeal without prejudice because the company had entered into the contract during a period when its charter had been suspended but the applicable California law appeared to permit the company to sue for restitution of any benefits it had conferred on the party to the contract. Compare *Micro Tool Eng'g, Inc.*, ASBCA 31136, 86-1 BCA ¶ 18,680, where the board dismissed an appeal with prejudice because the company had entered into a contract at a time when it had been "involuntarily dissolved" for failure to file annual reports and the time for reinstatement under Florida law had expired. The same result was reached in *West Point Research, Inc.*, ASBCA 27185, 83-2 BCA ¶ 16,845 (applying Connecticut law); and *Services, Inc.*, ASBCA 42929, 93-1 BCA ¶ 25,514 (applying South Carolina law).

Loss of corporate capacity may also preclude a contractor from bringing a suit or appeal concerning a contract that was entered into when the company had capacity. See *Computer Prods., Int'l, Inc. v. United States*, 26 Cl. Ct. 518 (1992), where a suit was dismissed because it was filed during a period when the company's charter had been suspended by the state of California and the Contract Disputes Act statute of limitations had run during the period of suspension. Compare *TPS, Inc.*, ASBCA 52421, 01-1 BCA ¶ 31,375 (board rejected motion to dismiss because according to Florida law, the facts giving rise to the claim occurred before dissolution and therefore was part of winding up the affairs of the corporation); *Ricmar Eng'g, Inc.*, ASBCA 44260, 97-2 BCA ¶ 29,084 (board rejected motion to dismiss because the company had been reinstated by the state of California and the board construed state law to require no prejudicial action to companies that had filed suits during suspension); *Teller Envtl. Sys., Inc.*, ASBCA 42092, 93-1 BCA ¶ 25,330 (board rejected motion to dismiss because the appeal had been filed within three years of dissolution, as permitted by Massachusetts law); *Allied Production Mgmt., Inc.*, DOTCAB 2466, 92-1 BCA ¶ 24,585 (board rejected motion to dismiss because California law permitted suits during suspension if company subsequently reinstated).

Questions concerning the contracting capacity of a partnership or a joint venture would be determined by reference to the partnership or joint venture agreement. See GSAR 552.270-3(b) providing that for leases of real property, "a copy of either the partnership agreement or current Certificate of Limited Partnership" shall be furnished if required by the government. FAR 4.102(d) provides as follows with respect to joint ventures:

A contract with joint venturers may involve any combination of individuals, partnerships, or corporations. The contract shall be signed by each participant in the joint venture in the manner prescribed in paragraphs (a) through (c) above for each type of participant. When a corporation is participating, the contracting officer shall verify that the corporation is authorized to participate in the joint venture.

As long as an organization possesses the capacity to contract, it is not necessary to spell out that capacity in the contract, *Pacific Far East Line, Inc.*, ASBCA 7629, 1963 BCA ¶ 3835.

## b.  Time for Determining Capacity to Contract

A number of cases have involved the question of whether a corporation's capacity to contract is to be determined at time of bidding or time of award. In *West Point Research, Inc.*, ASBCA 27185, 83-2 BCA ¶ 16,845, no valid contract was found where the company had capacity at the time of bid opening but had lost capacity, through revocation of its corporate charter, at the time of award. See also *P.I.O. GmbH Bau und Ingenieurplanung*, GSBCA 15934-IBB, 04-1 BCA ¶ 32,592 (board, in general, will follow laws under which a legal entity was organized to determine what powers may have survived its dissolution); *Rosinka Joint Venture*, ASBCA 48143, 97-1 BCA ¶ 28,653 (same). Conversely, in *Casper Constr. Co.*, Comp. Gen. Dec. B-253887, 93-2 CPD ¶ 247, a corporation had been dissolved at the time of bid opening. It later became reinstated and under the laws of the state of incorporation, the reinstatement was made retroactive to the time of dissolution. Nevertheless, GAO held that the bid could not be accepted, reasoning:

> As a general rule, a sealed bid award may not be made to any entity different from that which submitted the bid, and where a bid represents that it was submitted by a corporation, it should be disregarded if no such corporation exists. *General Chem. Servs. Inc.*, B-241595, Jan. 30, 1991, 91-1 CPD ¶ 94. Otherwise, irresponsible parties could undermine sound competitive bidding procedures by submitting bids that could be avoided or backed up by real principals as their interests might dictate. *Id.* We believe Casper's bid was properly rejected. At the time of bid opening, on June 7, the corporation had been dissolved under the laws of Oregon since January 20, and was not reinstated until after award on June 15. Consequently, at the time of bid opening Casper was not a legally sufficient corporation for bidding purposes.

GAO reached the opposite result in a line of cases holding that bids may be accepted even though submitted in a corporate name prior to the date of incorporation. See *PHE/Master, Inc.*, 70 Comp. Gen. 689 (B-238367.5), 91-2 CPD ¶ 210, stating at 695:

> As PHE/Master pointed out to the Air Force in its letter dated May 22, 1990, there is ample legal authority permitting an entity, formed for the purpose of perform-

ing a particular government contract, to submit a proposal in the name of the corporation prior to formally incorporating. *See Telex Commc'ns, Inc., Mil-Tech Sys., Inc.*, B-212385; B-212385.2, [84-1 CPD ¶ 127, *recons. denied*, 84-1 CPD ¶ 440]; *see also Protectors, Inc.*, B-194446, Aug. 17, 1979, 79-2 CPD ¶ 128; *Oscar Holmes & Son, Inc.*; *Blue Ribbon Refuse Removal Inc.*, B-184099, Oct. 24, 1975, 75-2 CPD ¶ 251. At a minimum, these cases provided PHE/Master with a good faith basis for submitting its initial proposal under the corporate name. Accordingly, we find no reasonable basis for the Air Force to conclude that PHE/Master engaged in misrepresentation by submitting its proposal in the name of the corporation that was formally incorporated after proposal submission.

It is difficult to understand this distinction. It would seem that the offeror, by not going forward with the incorporation, would have the same ability to avoid any obligation as would the bidder in Casper. The bridge between the two lines of cases may lie in *Telex Commc'ns, Inc.,* Comp. Gen. Dec. B-212385, 84-1 CPD ¶ 127, *recons. denied*, 84-1 CPD ¶ 440, which held that, because the previously unincorporated bidder was bound under state law to fulfill its contractual obligations if the bid was accepted, protecting the government from the risk of nonperformance, the bid was properly considered by the government (citing *Protectors, Inc.*, Comp. Gen. Dec. B-194446, 79-2 CPD ¶ 128).

In *Tours, Lodging & Conferences, Inc.*, Comp. Gen. Dec. B-270478, 96-1 CPD ¶ 144, GAO held that an award to a joint venture was proper even though one of the venturers was a corporation which had been dissolved at time of submission of the offer but had been reinstated prior to award. The fact that the other joint venturer possessed the capacity to contract would appear to justify this result; because, again, the government was protected from the risk of nonperformance.

GAO has also dealt with the situation where an award was made to an offeror, which at the time of proposal submission and the time of award, had its corporate status automatically terminated for "an apparently inadvertent failure to pay an annual registration fee." *Triad Research, Inc.*, Comp. Gen. Dec. B-225793, 87-2 CPD ¶ 16. GAO held that the award was proper since the award was made to the "same entity" which submitted the offer. See also *Forbes Aviation, Inc.*, Comp. Gen. Dec. B-248056, 92-2 CPD ¶ 58. In these cases, GAO relied on state statutes which provided "that the corporation is responsible for any liabilities incurred during the period of termination, including 'contracts, acts, matters and things made, done or performed in its name and on its behalf by its officers and agents prior to its reinstatement, as if its articles of incorporation had remained at all times in full force and effect.'"

## 2. *Contractual Intent and Definiteness*

In order for a contract to be formed, the parties must possess contractual intent and their agreement must be sufficiently definite to be enforced, *Modern Sys. Tech.*

*Corp. v. United States*, 24 Cl. Ct. 360 (1991), *aff'd*, 979 F.2d 200 (Fed. Cir. 1992). While the absence of definite terms may be evidence that the parties do not intend to enter into a contractual relationship, their existence does not necessarily require a finding that the parties had contractual intent.

### a. Contractual Intent

Whether the parties have indicated an intent to enter into a contractual relationship will be determined on a case-by-case basis, taking into consideration all the facts and circumstances surrounding the transaction. See *Mayfair Constr. Co.*, NASABCA 478-6, 80-2 BCA ¶ 14,772 ("entire context" of government granting of contractor's request for deviation was contractual).

### (1) PRELIMINARY NEGOTIATIONS

One of the problems in determining contractual intent is whether the communications between the parties are merely preliminary negotiations contemplating future contractual agreements or whether they indicate an intent to presently enter into a contract.

Occasionally, the government announces publicly its desire to receive proposals for specified programs, services, or commodities. They may be included in statutes, regulations, circulars, or other media. Normally, these announcements are treated as preliminary inquiries or requests for offers, *Primary Metal & Mineral Corp. v. United States*, 214 Ct. Cl. 90, 556 F.2d 507 (1977) (Department of Treasury regulation stating that all "requests" for silver bullion in exchange for silver certificates be directed to the fiscal assistant secretary held not to be an offer). If the statement merely reflects a future intent or a desire to begin negotiations, it will not be considered an offer. Such statements are invitations to begin negotiations or to submit offers and cannot be accepted to form a contract for goods and services. See *Elkhorn-Hazard Coal Co. v. Kentucky River Corp.*, 20 F.2d 67 (6th Cir. 1927).

However, they may constitute offers if they are sufficiently definite. In *Radium Mines, Inc. v. United States*, 139 Ct. Cl. 144, 153 F. Supp. 403 (1957), the Atomic Energy Commission issued a circular expressing the Commission's desire to stimulate domestic production of uranium ore. The circular contained information as to the minimum price to be paid for ore, the time period in which the commission would purchase ore, grade specifications, and application instructions. The court held that the circular constituted an offer since it was sufficient to induce performance. Similarly, in *Griffin v. United States*, 215 Ct. Cl. 710 (1978), the service secretary published procedures and guidelines requesting meritorious suggestions relating to Minuteman Missile silos. Since the service secretary adopted suggestions that benefited the service, the court held that a valid contract was created. But see *Hayes v. United States*, 20 Cl. Ct. 150 (1990), which held that although a suggestion of a former Postal Service employee was implemented as part of the Employee Suggestion Program, a contractual relationship was not formed between the former employee and the government. The court found that the statutory and procedural requirements necessary to elevate such an agreement to the level of a contract had not been met. Similarly, in *Baker v. United States,* 50 Fed. Cl. 483, 495 (2001), the court noted that "[s]o long as it is reasonably apparent that some further act of the offeror is necessary, the offeree has no power to create contractual relations by an act of his own, and there is as yet no operative offer." Compare *Cutler-Hammer, Inc. v. United States*, 194 Ct. Cl. 788, 441 F.2d 1179 (1971), where a Treasury Department regulation regarding the sale of silver at a specific price was held not to be an offer because it was interpreted not to contain a promise by the government.

## (2) Non-Contractual Agreements

The government enters into several different types of agreements which it specifically indicates are not contracts. FAR 16.702 describes "basic agreements," which are instruments of "understanding" between agencies and contractors on contract clauses that will be used in future contracts between the parties. FAR 16.702(a) states that "[a] basic agreement is not a contract." "Basic ordering agreements," described in FAR 16.703, contain not only contract clauses, but a description of supplies or services to be provided and methods for "pricing, issuing, and delivering future orders" under the agreement. However, FAR 16.703(a) states that "[a] basic ordering agreement is not a contract." In addition, FAR 16.703(c) states:

> *Limitations.* A basic ordering agreement shall not state or imply any agreement by the Government to place future contracts or orders with the contractor or be used in any manner to restrict competition.

"Blanket purchase agreements," described in FAR 13.303, are agreements that agencies establish with contractors for placing repetitive orders in the future within the simplified acquisition threshold. FAR 13.303-3(a)(2) requires that such agreements contain a statement that the government "is obligated only to the extent of authorized purchases actually made." See *Production Packaging*, ASBCA 53662, 03-2 BCA ¶ 32,338, holding that the holder of the BPA had "no legal expectation to receive exclusive orders."

FAR 8.405-3 allows the use of blanket purchase agreements with General Services Administration (GSA) Federal Supply Schedules contracts, and purchases under BPAs entered into in conjunction with these GSA multiple award schedule contracts are not subject to the same dollar limitations that curb purchases under simplified acquisition BPAs in accordance with FAR 13.303-5(b)(1). While the FAR is silent on the contractual nature of these BPAs, it seems clear that they are not contracts but merely vehicles to allow agencies to place future orders. For a critique of these agreements see *Agencies Are Not Maximizing Opportunities for Competi-*

*tion or Savings Under Blanket Purchase Agreements Despite Significant Increase in Usage*, GAO-09-792, Sept. 9, 2009.

The line between "basic" agreements and enforceable contracts continues to shift, as the federal acquisition system evolves. *Modern Sys. Tech. Corp. v. United States*, 24 Cl. Ct. 360 (1991), *aff'd*, 979 F.2d 200 (Fed. Cir. 1992), dealt with a basic pricing agreement used by the Postal Service. The court concluded that the "plain language" of the agreement "appears to be contemplative of future contracts." It found "no language indicating any present intent that either party be bound," and concluded that the agreement was more like a basic ordering agreement.

Another type of agreement envisioning future transactions is a "trading partner agreement." To engage in electronic commerce (Electronic Data Interchange (EDI) or Electronic Funds Transfer (EFT)), a contractor must become a trading partner, which means, in this context, that it has agreed to exchange business information electronically. In order to become a trading partner, a contractor must first register with the government's Central Contractor Registration, *www.ccr.gov*. It then must execute a trading partner agreement which prescribes the general procedures and policies when using EDI. The General Services Administration uses EDI when its contractors have entered into a trading partner agreement. See GSAR 516.506(a) requiring the use of the Placement of Orders clause at GSAR 552.216-72, requiring contractors to enter into such an agreement in order to receive EDI delivery orders. In addition to a trading partner agreement, some agencies require a trading partner to sign another agreement setting forth the standard contract clauses for electronic solicitations; the goal is, if possible, to allocate risks before electronic transactions begin, as the "gap-filler" rules for failures in electronic commerce are not fully mature. See Uniform Electronic Transactions Act (UETA) (1999) (uniform state law, broadly adopted, for allocating electronic commerce risks governed by state law) (*www.law.upenn.edu/bll/ulc/uecicta/eta1299.htm*); Electronic Signatures in Global and National Commerce (ESIGN) Act, Pub. L. No. 106-229 (2000) (allocating electronic commerce risks in interstate commerce); Yukins & Vacura, *Emerging Issues in DoD's Shift to E-Business*, 43 Gov't Contractor ¶ 32 (Jan. 24, 2001).

## b. Definiteness

The parties' agreement must be sufficiently complete and certain in its terms so that the promises and performances to be rendered can be reasonably determined. However, this does not mean that there be complete agreement on all terms. See *Penn-Ohio Steel Corp. v. United States*, 173 Ct. Cl. 1064, 354 F.2d 254 (1965), where the court found a contract because there had been agreement on "major matters in issue." Similarly, in *Town of North Bonneville, Wash. v. United States*, 5 Cl. Ct. 312 (1984), the court found a binding agreement in spite of the need for future agreements because the parties had indicated a present intent to be bound.

*Restatement, Second, Contracts* § 33 recognizes that:

(1) Even though a manifestation of intention is intended to be understood as an offer, it cannot be accepted so as to form a contract unless the terms of the contract are reasonably certain.

(2) The terms of a contract are reasonably certain if they provide a basis for determining the existence of a breach and for giving an appropriate remedy.

(3) The fact that one or more terms of a proposed bargain are left open or uncertain may show that a manifestation of intention is not intended to be understood as an offer or as an acceptance.

See *Western States Constr. Co.*, ASBCA 16003, 72-2 BCA ¶ 9508 (contract found to exist even though price of contract was never agreed upon).

## (1) AGREEMENTS TO AGREE

When the parties have agreed to negotiate some of the terms of the contract in the future, the lack of definiteness may not preclude the existence of a binding contract. Such arrangements are called "agreements to agree" and have been found binding if they are sufficiently definite to permit their enforcement. See *Folk Constr. Co.*, ENGBCA 5839, 93-3 BCA ¶ 26,094, finding that the parties mutually agreed to rescind the contract. The government argued that the condition that the unit prices would be determined through future negotiations made the bargain unenforceable. The board rejected this defense, stating at 129,726:

Agreements in which certain terms are reserved for future negotiation ("agreements to agree"), while not favored traditionally, have been gaining approval where the criteria for resolution of the terms to be negotiated are sufficiently definite. The reservation of some terms for future agreement does not necessarily preclude a finding that a binding agreement has been made. However, this arrangement impliedly places an obligation on the parties to negotiate in good faith in an effort to resolve the outstanding issues. Courts then will evaluate the *bona fides* of the parties toward negotiation in order to ascertain when a breach has occurred if the remaining issues are not resolved.

The degree of definiteness necessary to form a binding contract has been decided on a case-by-case basis. In *Modern Sys. Tech. Corp. v. United States*, 24 Cl. Ct. 360 (1991), *aff'd*, 979 F.2d 200 (Fed. Cir. 1992), the court stated that, to be binding, a contract generally must be "sufficiently definite to permit determination of breach and remedies." In *Trauma Serv. Group, Ltd. v. United States*, 33 Fed. Cl. 426 (1995), *aff'd*, 104 F.3d 1321 (Fed. Cir. 1997), the court held that the CHAMPUS Memoranda of Understanding (MOU) at issue was unenforceable because it did not contain any indication of how to compute the salary of a person that was required to be furnished by the contractor. In contrast, in *Total Med. Mgmt., Inc. v. United*

*States*, 104 F.3d 1314 (Fed. Cir. 1997), the court held that, in general, CHAMPUS MOUs were enforceable agreements because they called for the contractor to provide discounted medical services while the hospital was to provide free space and support staff and encourage military dependents to use the services, including payment details for most services. The court held that the determination of damages or specific performance would flow naturally from a breach of these duties. See also *Gardiner, Kamya & Assocs. v. United States*, 369 F.3d 1318 (Fed. Cir. 2004), holding that an agreement to negotiate the terms of a contract extension was sufficiently definite to form a binding contract.

Once an agreement to agree is found sufficiently definite, the question arises as to the extent of the duty concerning the undefined terms. As stated in *Folk Construction* the duty is to negotiate in good faith. In *North Star Steel Co. v. United States*, 477 F.3d 1324 (Fed. Cir. 2007), the court held that failure to reveal information necessary to proceed with the contemplated negotiations would be a lack of good faith. See also *City of Tacoma v. United States*, 31 F.3d 1130 (Fed. Cir. 1994) (city had to agree to "reasonable" rates when they were subject to negotiation); *Aviation Contractor Employees, Inc. v. United States*, 945 F.2d 1568 (Fed. Cir. 1991) (refusal to negotiate would be lack of good faith); and *Tennessee Valley Auth. v. United States*, 60 Fed. Cl. 665 (2004) (refusing to negotiate breached duty of good faith and fair dealing).

## (2) LETTER CONTRACTS

Federal procurement law recognizes a distinct class of agreements known as "letter contracts." A letter contract is a "written preliminary contractual instrument that authorizes the contractor to begin immediately manufacturing supplies or performing services," FAR 16.603-1. 10 U.S.C. § 2326 calls such contracts "undefinitized contractual actions" and requires that they be used only in urgent situations. See also FAR 16.603-2 permitting their use only when "(1) the Government's interests demand that the contractor be given a binding commitment so that work can start immediately and (2) negotiating a definitive contract is not possible in sufficient time to meet the requirement." See DFARS Subpart 217.74 for detailed guidance on the use of such contracts. A letter contract is typically followed by a more detailed agreement "definitizing" the parties' earlier agreement. See FAR 16.603-4 (required clauses).

The terms of a letter contract have been found sufficiently definite to bind the parties even though the parties failed to definitize the contract. In *Saul Bass & Assocs. v. United States*, 205 Ct. Cl. 214, 505 F.2d 1386 (1974), the government issued a letter of intent incorporating a contractor's design agreement, stating a monetary limitation and proposing the execution of a formal contract. The contractor performed, but no formal contract was agreed upon. The court found contractual agreement on the basis of the letters exchanged between the parties. For another case providing a remedy when the contractor completed performance but the parties failed to definitize the letter contract, see *Sanders Assocs. v. United States*, 191 Ct. Cl. 157, 423 F.2d 291 (1970). See also *Wilco Floor Serv., Inc. v. United States*, 197 Ct. Cl. 902 (1972) (plaintiff entitled to costs from beginning of letter-contract term as opposed to date of definitized contract); *Kavourvas, Inc.*, Comp. Gen. Dec. B-226782, Oct. 20, 1987, *Unpub.* (even though expected definitized contract never came into existence, GAO ordered claimant be paid according to terms of letter contract).

## B. Offer and Acceptance

*Restatement, Second, Contracts* § 24 defines "offer" as follows:

An offer is the manifestation of willingness to enter into a bargain, so made as to justify another person in understanding that his assent to that bargain is invited and will conclude it.

*Restatement, Second, Contracts* § 50(1) defines "acceptance" as follows:

Acceptance of an offer is a manifestation of assent to the terms thereof made by the offeree in a manner invited or required by the offer.

The time, manner, form, and any other conditions associated with the method of acceptance are generally within the control of the offeror and may be specified in the offer. When the offeror requests that the acceptance be in the form of a return promise the acceptance creates what is termed a "bilateral contract." The offeror may also request that the acceptance be in the performance of an act or forbearance; this being referred to as a "unilateral contract."

Except for simplified acquisitions, the government prefers to have the contractor make the offer, thereby obtaining the favored position of offeree. The government then has full control of when the contract is formed because it will not be bound to that contract until it manifests its acceptance. This is extremely important as it enables the contracting officer to determine which offer is most advantageous to the government and whether funds are available before deciding to accept. The government controls the terms of the offer by requiring that offerors agree to submit their offers in accordance with the terms provided in the solicitation.

### 1. Solicitation and Submission of Offers or Quotations

#### a. Sealed Bidding

In sealed bidding, the government solicits offers by issuing an Invitation for Bids (IFB) on Standard Form 33 (FAR 53.301-33). See Chapter 5, Figure 5-1. The

IFB is not an offer by the government to purchase goods or services. The prospective contractor's bid is intended to be the offer and the government's award is the acceptance. See 42 Comp. Gen. 490 (B-150798) (1963), which noted that a bid submitted in response to a solicitation is an offer that may be accepted if sufficiently responsive. While the IFB is not an offer, it contains virtually all of the essential terms of the offer (standard and special clauses and the description of the work) except the price. This permits the government to ensure that all of the bidders compete on an equal basis, as discussed in Chapter 5.

## b.  Negotiated Procurement

The process of negotiated procurement is more complex than that of sealed bidding. The opportunity to hold oral or written discussions in the procurement process raises the possibility that offerors may be requested to submit sequential offers. See *United States v. John McShain, Inc.*, 258 F.2d 422 (D.C. Cir. 1958), *cert. denied*, 358 U.S. 832 (1958), where the court stated at 424:

> Negotiation is a process of submission and consideration of offers until an acceptable offer is made, and accepted, or until it becomes apparent that no acceptable offer will be made.

The negotiation process is sufficiently flexible so that the government can also make an offer during the course of negotiations. The various forms of negotiated procurement are discussed below.

### (1) REQUEST FOR PROPOSALS OR OFFERS

The major form of solicitation in negotiated procurement is the Request for Proposals (RFP). This type of solicitation is generally accomplished using Optional Form 307 (FAR 53.302-307) or Standard Form 33. The RFP is not an offer but, like the IFB, requests the proposer to submit an offer, *Space Research Corp. v. United States*, 225 Ct. Cl. 721 (1980). See FAR 15.203(a). However, also like IFBs, when competition is solicited, the RFP will contain virtually all of the essential terms of the offer (standard and special clauses and the description of the work) except price and any enhancements that are being solicited. See Chapter 6 for a complete discussion of this process.

In competitive negotiation, if acceptance without discussions is not possible or desirable, the government conducts oral or written negotiations with all offerors within the competitive range. These offerors are then given the opportunity to submit another offer, which is called a "final proposal revision," FAR 15.307(b). Before FAR Part 15 was rewritten in 1997, see FAC 97-02, 62 Fed. Reg. 51,225, Sept. 30, 1997, these offers were called "best and final offers" (BAFOs), FAR 15.611(a) (pre-1997 FAR). If the government is not satisfied with any such offer the process may be repeated and, in rare cases, the government may be the party making the ultimate offer.

## (2) REQUEST FOR QUOTATIONS

When the government does not intend that offers be submitted in response to the initial solicitation in a negotiated procurement, it uses a Request for Quotations (RFQ) rather than an RFP. This procedure traditionally was used most commonly with sole source procurements, though the use of RFQs is now very common with multiple-award indefinite-delivery/indefinite-quantity contracts, including the Gen-

| REQUEST FOR QUOTATION (THIS IS NOT AN ORDER) | | THIS RFQ ☐ IS ☐ IS NOT A SMALL BUSINESS SET-ASIDE | | | PAGE OF PAGES |
|---|---|---|---|---|---|
| 1. REQUEST NO. | 2. DATE ISSUED | 3. REQUISITION/PURCHASE REQUEST NO. | | 4. CERT. FOR NAT. DEF. UNDER BDSA REG. 2 AND/OR DMS REG. 1 ▶ | RATING |
| 5a. ISSUED BY | | | | 6. DELIVER BY (Date) | |
| 5b. FOR INFORMATION CALL (NO COLLECT CALLS) | | | | 7. DELIVERY | |
| NAME | | TELEPHONE NUMBER | | ☐ FOB DESTINATION | ☐ OTHER (See Schedule) |
| | | AREA CODE | NUMBER | 9. DESTINATION | |
| 8. TO: | | | | a. NAME OF CONSIGNEE | |
| a. NAME | b. COMPANY | | | b. STREET ADDRESS | |
| c. STREET ADDRESS | | | | c. CITY | |
| d. CITY | e. STATE | f. ZIP CODE | | d. STATE | e. ZIP CODE |
| 10. PLEASE FURNISH QUOTATIONS TO THE ISSUING OFFICE IN BLOCK 5a ON OR BEFORE CLOSE OF BUSINESS (Date) | IMPORTANT: This is a request for information and quotations furnished are not offers. If you are unable to quote, please so indicate on this form and return it to the address in Block 5a. This request does not commit the Government to pay any costs incurred in the preparation of the submission of this quotation or to contract for supplies or service. Supplies are of domestic origin unless otherwise indicated by quoter. Any representations and/or certifications attached to this Request for Quotation must be completed by the quoter. | | | | |

### 11. SCHEDULE (Include applicable Federal, State and local taxes)

| ITEM NO. (a) | SUPPLIES/ SERVICES (b) | QUANTITY (c) | UNIT (d) | UNIT PRICE (e) | AMOUNT (f) |
|---|---|---|---|---|---|
| | | | | | |
| | | | | | |
| | | | | | |
| | | | | | |

| 12. DISCOUNT FOR PROMPT PAYMENT ▶ | a. 10 CALENDAR DAYS (%) | b. 20 CALENDAR DAYS (%) | c. 30 CALENDAR DAYS (%) | d. CALENDAR DAYS | |
|---|---|---|---|---|---|
| | | | | NUMBER | PERCENTAGE |

NOTE: Additional provisions and representations ☐ are ☐ are not attached.

| 13. NAME AND ADDRESS OF QUOTER | | | 14. SIGNATURE OF PERSON AUTHORIZED TO SIGN QUOTATION | | 15. DATE OF QUOTATION |
|---|---|---|---|---|---|
| a. NAME OF QUOTER | | | | | |
| b. STREET ADDRESS | | | 16. SIGNER | | |
| | | | a. NAME (Type or print) | | b. TELEPHONE |
| c. COUNTY | | | | | AREA CODE |
| d. CITY | e. STATE | f. ZIP CODE | c. TITLE (Type or print) | | NUMBER |

| AUTHORIZED FOR LOCAL REPRODUCTION Previous edition not usable | STANDARD FORM 18 (REV. 6-95) Prescribed by GSA-FAR (48 CFR) 53.215-1(a) |
|---|---|

**Figure 2-1**

eral Services Administration's schedule contracts. RFQs are sometimes prepared on Standard Form 18 (FAR 53.301-18). See **Figure 2-1.** Unlike bids or proposals following an IFB or RFP, quotations submitted in response to an RFQ are not considered to be offers that can be accepted, FAR 13.004(a). Thus, as discussed further below, the government's order in response to the quotation does not form a contract; the agreement (offer and acceptance) arises only when the supplier accedes to the government's order (offer). Prior to FAC 97-02, the FAR permitted the use of RFQs in negotiated procurement. The FAR is now silent on this issue.

A variety of procedures may be used following the receipt of a quotation. In some cases, a quotation serves as the basis for beginning negotiations. Following the conclusion of these negotiations in major procurements, the government usually requests the prospective contractor to submit an offer that can be accepted by the government. This is often accomplished by the government sending a formal contract document to be signed by the contractor and presented to the government for acceptance. However, various other procedures may be followed, and in some instances the government becomes the offeror.

### c. Simplified Acquisition

FAR Part 13 sets forth procedures for simplified acquisitions. The standard procedure for simplified acquisitions is for the government to request quotations and to make offers through the issuance of purchase orders. The quoter is then free to reject or accept the offer. See *Computer Assocs. Int'l, Inc.,* Comp. Gen. Dec. B-292077.6, 2004 CPD ¶ 110 (in an RFQ situation, "it is the government that makes the offer . . . and no binding agreement is created until the vendor accepts the offer. . . . A vendor submitting a price quotation therefore could, the next moment, reject an offer from the government at its quoted price"). FAR 13.004(a) provides in part:

> Therefore, issuance by the Government of an order in response to a supplier's quotation does not establish a contract. The order is an offer by the Government to the supplier to buy certain supplies or services upon specified terms and conditions. A contract is established when the supplier accepts the offer.

See *Harney County Gypsum Co.,* AGBCA 93-190-1, 94-1 BCA ¶ 26,455, in which the firm's response to a request for price quotes and discussion of the firm's availability did not manifest an offer by the firm that could be accepted by the government. Once the purchase order has been issued, the supplier may then manifest acceptance through promise or performance, FAR 13.004(b). See *Sunshine Cordage Corp.,* ASBCA 38904, 90-1 BCA ¶ 22,382 (initial request for quotation on price of rope was not an offer, but purchase order by government in response to quotation by supplier was an offer). See Chapter 7 for a discussion of simplified acquisition procedures.

The purchase order, in simplified acquisitions, may be made on Optional Form 347 (FAR 53.302-347) or, for purchases not exceeding $3,000, the micro-purchase threshold, Standard Form 44 (FAR 53.301-44). See FAR 53.213; FAR 13.306. Agencies may use their own forms and the military agencies must use DD Form 1155 (DFARS 253.303-1155). See DFARS 213.505-2.

## d. Obligation to Consider Responses

Although the issuance of a solicitation may not be an offer by the government to contract for goods or services, the government may be obligated to fairly and honestly consider responses conforming to the solicitation. In determining whether such an obligation exists, the courts have used offer-and-acceptance analysis to find that the government entered into an implied-in-fact contract when the offer was submitted. This analysis served as the basis for giving the Court of Federal Claims jurisdiction to grant relief over award protests under the then-current version of 28 U.S.C. § 1491, *United States v. John C. Grimberg Co.*, 702 F.2d 1362 (Fed. Cir. 1983). See also *Aerolease Long Beach & Satsuma Inv. Co. v. United States*, 31 Fed. Cl. 342, *aff'd*, 39 F.3d 1198 (Fed. Cir. 1994), and *CACI, Inc.-Fed. v. United States*, 1 Cl. Ct. 352, *rev'd*, 719 F.2d 1567 (Fed. Cir. 1983), holding that issuance of a solicitation implied an offer to fairly and honestly consider all bids or proposals. When the Court of Federal Claims was given independent protest jurisdiction under 28 U.S.C. § 1491(b), there was a question as to whether the implied-in-fact jurisdiction under 28 U.S.C. § 1491(a) remained in effect. This issue was partially addressed in *Resource Conservation Group, LLC v. United States*, 597 F.3d 1238 (Fed. Cir. 2010), holding that the implied-in-fact contract jurisdiction under 28 U.S.C. § 1491(a)(1) remains in effect for nonprocurement contracts. See also *Terry v. United States*, 96 Fed. Cl. 131 (2010), holding that the implied-in-fact contract jurisdiction under 28 U.S.C. § 1491(a)(1) remains in effect for nonappropriated fund activity contracts. Two judges of the Court of Federal Claims have ruled that dicta in *Resource Conservation* deprives the court of implied-in-fact jurisdiction over procurement contracts under § 1491(a)(1), *Metropolitan Van & Storage, Inc. v. United States*, 92 Fed. Cl. 232 (2010); *Linc Gov't Servs., LLC v. United States*, 96 Fed. Cl. 672 (2010). Three other judges have ruled that the dicta should not be construed as depriving the court of such jurisdiction, *FAS Support Servs., LLC v. United States*, 93 Fed. Cl. 687 (2010); *L-3 Commc'ns Integrated Sys., L.P. v. United States*, 94 Fed. Cl. 394 (2010); *Bilfinger Berger AG Sede Secondaria Italiana v. United States*, 97 Fed. Cl. 96 (2010).

The government has also been held to have made an offer to give fair and impartial consideration to responses to a procurement notice published by the government, *Standard Mfg. Co. v. United States*, 7 Cl. Ct. 54 (1984); *Magnavox Elec. Sys. Co. v. United States*, 26 Cl. Ct. 1373 (1992). But see *Motorola, Inc. v. United States*, 988 F.2d 113 (Fed. Cir. 1993), which criticized the rationale of *Standard Manufacturing* and *Magnavox*, stating at 116:

Government requests for information and responses from prospective bidders are not the equivalents of offer and acceptance. Such exchanges are not carried on with an expectation to presently affect legal relations. Rather, the parties are dealing . . . with an eye to the future, each being free, . . . to withdraw from the dialogue.

The court then differentiated this situation from the situation that arises when a bid actually has been submitted, finding at 116:

> In that circumstance there is a promise — the contractor's bid — which empowers the Government, upon acceptance, to bind the contractor to the terms of the solicitation. The essence of the contractor's engagement — the manifestation of an intention to be bound — warrants reading into the situation a reciprocal commitment from the Government, i.e., a promise to fairly and honestly consider the contractor's bid.

Similarly, in *El Dorado Springs v. United States*, 28 Fed. Cl. 132 (1993), the court held that a Department of Housing and Urban Development invitation to submit an application for mortgage insurance did not imply a request for offers by the government. The court was therefore unwilling to find that an implied contract to fairly and honestly consider all offers existed. See also *Garchik v. United States*, 37 Fed. Cl. 52 (1996), where the court held that a *CBD* notice of procurement opportunity stating explicitly that it was not a request for offers did not create an implied contract to fairly and honestly consider the response. The court stated that the *Motorola* decision "implicitly" overruled *Standard Manufacturing* and *Magnovox*. Subsequently, in *Emery Worldwide Airlines, Inc. v. United States*, 264 F.3d 1071 (Fed. Cir. 2001), the Federal Circuit declined to decide whether the Court of Federal Claims had implied-in-fact jurisdiction in a case where the plaintiff had not submitted an offer but was contesting a sole source award, citing the fact that the *Motorola* court had "harshly criticized" *Standard Manufacturing*. See also *Pure Power!, Inc. v. United States*, 70 Fed. Cl. 739 (2006), holding that no implied-in-fact contract was created when a company submitted its products for testing to determine if they met the government's needs.

## 2. Requests for Information

When the government needs information on prices, delivery or other terms, it may use a Request for Information (RFI). Responses to RFIs are not offers that can be accepted, FAR 15.201(e).

## 3. Withdrawal or Modification of Offers

According to general contract-law principles, unless an offeror has made an enforceable agreement not to revoke an offer, the offer is freely revocable. See *Restatement, Second, Contracts* § 42:

> An offeree's power of acceptance is terminated when the offeree receives from the offeror a manifestation of an intention not to enter into the proposed contract

Despite this general rule, there are a number of limitations on revocability. See *Restatement, Second, Contracts* § 87, which provides:

(1) An offer is binding as an option contract if it

(a) is in writing and signed by the offeror, recites a purported consideration for the making of the offer, and proposes an exchange on fair terms within a reasonable time; or

(b) is made irrevocable by statute.

(2) An offer which the offeror should reasonably expect to induce action or forbearance of a substantial character on the part of the offeree before acceptance and which does induce such action or forbearance is binding as an option contract to the extent necessary to avoid injustice.

These general limitations on revocability have been subsumed, to a degree, in the rules developed for government contracts. However, the term "option contract" has not been used in government contracts to describe all irrevocable offers.

In the procurement of goods and services, the revocability of an offer is dependent upon the type of procurement involved and the stage of the procurement. Revocation may occur through either modification or withdrawal of the offer. In sealed bidding, offers may be modified or withdrawn prior to the time set for bid opening, FAR 14.303. Another longstanding rule, however, is that bids may not be modified or withdrawn after the exact time for bid opening unless they are based on a mistake, *Refining Assocs. v. United States*, 124 Ct. Cl. 115, 109 F. Supp. 259 (1953). However, the Late Submissions, Modifications, and Withdrawal solicitation provision in FAR 52.214-7(b)(2) states that a late modification of an otherwise successful bid that makes it terms more favorable to the government "will be considered and may be accepted."

In negotiated procurement, proposals (offers) may be withdrawn at any time prior to award, FAR 15.208(e). See ¶ (c)(8) of the Instructions to Offerors — Competitive Acquisition solicitation provision in FAR 52.215-1, which states:

Proposals may be withdrawn at any time before award. Withdrawals are effective upon receipt of notice by the Contracting Officer.

See *United Elec. Motor Co.*, Comp. Gen. Dec. B-191996, 78-2 CPD ¶ 206.

"Modifications" and "revisions" of proposals are dealt with differently in FAR Part 15. With regard to modifications, ¶ (c)(6) of the Instructions to Offerors — Competitive Acquisition solicitation provision in FAR 52.215-1, states:

> Offerors may submit modifications to their proposals at any time before the so-
> licitation closing date and time, and may submit modifications in response to an
> amendment, or to correct a mistake at any time before award.

This confusing provision presumably means that a modification to a proposal submitted after the closing date and time would be "late" and therefore not considered.
However, FAR 15.208(b)(2) provides that a late modification of an otherwise successful proposal that would make its terms more favorable to the government "will
be considered at any time it is received and may be accepted." In addition, the above
provision appears to allow a modification submitted in response to an amendment
to be considered if it is submitted by the time specified in the amendment. It also
appears to permit an offeror to submit a modification to correct a mistake at any time
prior to award, but GAO has not interpreted it in this manner. See Chapter 6 for a
discussion of the late proposal and correction of mistake decisions.

The rule on proposal revisions is stated in ¶ (c)(7) of the Instructions to Offerors
— Competitive Acquisition solicitation provision in FAR 52.215-1:

> Offerors may submit revised proposals only if requested or allowed by the Con-
> tracting Officer.

This provision is apparently a reference to FAR 15.307(b) which states that a contracting officer may request or allow proposal revisions "to clarify and document understandings reached during negotiations." That paragraph also discusses "final proposal
revisions" that can be submitted by offerors after negotiations are concluded. All such
revisions are, in effect, new offers which must also meet the strict timeliness rules.
See, however, *NCR Gov't Sys. LLC*, Comp. Gen. Dec. B-297959, 2006 CPD ¶ 82,
permitting acceptance of such a late proposal revision because it modified a proposal
that was acceptable to the government. In contrast, in *Sunrise Med. HHG, Inc.*, Comp.
Gen. Dec. B-310230, 2007 CPD ¶ 7, the agency properly refused to accept a late proposed price reduction because the offeror was not the "otherwise successful offeror."
See Chapter 6 for a complete discussion of the rules regarding proposal revisions.

These rules would appear to indicate that offerors are not bound in any way
when they submit a proposal. However, the standard form used as a cover sheet for
solicitations, Standard Form 33, FAR 53.301-33, creates confusion here because it
contemplates much less flexibility in the proposal process. The specific provision in
Item 12 of this form requires the offeror to agree to be bound if its "offer is accepted
within" a specified number of days "from the date of receipt of offers." This could be
interpreted to be an adoption of the firm bid rule described in the above *Restatement*.
However, it is likely that the issue will be governed by the more specific solicitation
provisions discussed above.

The government also uses option clauses, giving it the right to order additional
goods or services. Such options are offers by the contractor that are irrevocable for

the stipulated period, *Contel Page Servs., Inc.*, ASBCA 32100, 87-1 BCA ¶ 19,540 (government timely exercised its option to extend contract when it sent the contractor written notice as well as an unsigned bilateral modification). See Chapter 9 for a complete discussion of the legal rules governing options.

The legal theories supporting the irrevocability of government contract offers have never been fully articulated. There is no government contract statute similar to U.C.C. § 2-205, which makes "firm" offers irrevocable. In dealing with sealed bids, the court in *Refining Assocs. v. United States*, 124 Ct. Cl. 115, 109 F. Supp. 259 (1953), enforced the solicitation provision precluding withdrawal on the grounds that otherwise "innumerable frauds could be perpetrated against the United States." Irrevocability might also be supported on the theory that the offeror responding to solicitations receives consideration for agreeing not to revoke the offer in the form of the government's obligation to fairly and honestly consider all bids and proposals. As FAR 2.101 defines "option" as a "unilateral right" in an already existing contract, the consideration supporting the irrevocability of offers in option clauses is provided by the consideration present in the contract that contains the option clause, *Holly Corp.*, ASBCA 24975, 83-1 BCA ¶ 16,327.

While the theory of detrimental reliance in ¶ (2) of *Restatement, Second, Contracts* § 87 is potentially available to support the irrevocability of offers to contract with the government, it would appear to be applicable only to sealed bid contracting and to offers for amendments to existing contracts. In these situations, the government's expenditure of time and effort in evaluating the offers and preparing for acceptance could well be sufficient to bind offerors that agreed not to revoke. Although significantly more effort is expended by the government in negotiated procurements, the offeror's broad right of withdrawal makes this theory inapplicable.

Government offers in the form of purchase orders for simplified acquisitions may also be revoked at any time prior to acceptance, FAR 13.004(c). See *Harney County Gypsum Co.*, AGBCA 93-190-1, 94-1 BCA ¶ 26,455 (government's withdrawal of a purchase order for the rental of an excavator and operator did not constitute a breach of contract when the contractor had not yet accepted the offer in writing nor furnished an excavator and operator). The contracting officer may also modify purchase orders, without the contractor's written acceptance of the modification, FAR 13.302-3. See *University Sys., Inc. v. Department of Commerce*, GSBCA 10896-COM, 92-3 BCA ¶ 25,182 (insertion of a Termination for Default clause by unilateral modification to an already existing contract did not have to be accepted in writing by the contractor).

The procedures for withdrawing offers contain safeguards. Withdrawal is to be accomplished by written or telegraphic notice, facsimile, or in person if the identity of the person withdrawing the bid is established and such person signs a receipt, FAR 14.303. Guidance also may be found in the solicitation provision, FAR 52.214-7. Less detailed guidance for negotiated procurements is found in FAR 15.208(e). See also *John A. Maney*, GSBCA 6550, 83-2 BCA ¶ 16,744 (withdrawal of offers in government contracts regulated by provisions specific to the field and not necessarily by common law).

## 4. Acceptance of Bids, Proposals, and Purchase Orders

To be binding, an acceptance must contain a manifestation of present intention to be bound. See *D&S Universal Mining, Inc.*, Comp. Gen. Dec. B-200815, 81-2 CPD ¶ 186, where GAO stated:

> In order for a binding contract to result, the contracting officer must unequivocally express an intent to accept an offer. Also, the acceptance of a contractor's offer by the Government must be clear and unconditional; it must appear that both parties intended to make a binding agreement at the time of the acceptance of the contractor's offer.

In *DeMatteo Constr. Co. v. United States*, 220 Ct. Cl. 579, 600 F.2d 1384 (1979), mere notification to an offeror that its offer was "selected as the lowest responsive bid" did not constitute an acceptance. Similarly, in *Greenwood Co.*, AS-BCA 12232, 67-2 BCA ¶ 6650, the contracting officer asked the bidder to come in and sign contract documents and to bring payment and performance bonds. The bidder complied. Subsequently, the contracting officer determined that it would be to the government's advantage to split the award as permitted by the IFB. The bidder contended that the entire contract had been awarded, but the board disagreed, finding that there had been no contract made for full performance because the contracting officer's request was not a "clear-cut expression of intention" to accept, stating at 30,829:

> Here, no clear-cut expression of intention to accept the bid and award a contract exists. [The bidder] was asked to bring in the payment and performance bonds undated, indicating that a contract date had not been established and the contract not yet awarded. In fact, the bonds were provisional, subject to annulment if a contract was not entered into. Nor did the contracting officer even sign the proposed contract on behalf of the Government, after [the bidder] had signed on its own behalf. In this light, that which transpired on 20 and 21 June 1966 must be considered as preparatory to the homologation of the contract. When the contracting officer failed to sign the proposed instrument signed by [the bidder], he did not, acting on behalf of [the Government], breach a contract, but preserved the STATUS QUO ANTE that no contract had yet come into existence.

See also *City of Klawock v. United States*, 2 Cl. Ct. 580 (1983), *aff'd*, 732 F.2d 168 (Fed. Cir. 1984), and *Edwards v. United States*, 22 Cl. Ct. 411 (1991), which appear to find no present intent to be bound because there were details remaining to be resolved. In both cases, the communications between the parties were susceptible to being read as conditional acceptances. In *Goldberger Foods, Inc. v. United States*,

23 Cl. Ct. 295 (1991), neither telephonic notice to a bidder that it was the lowest bidder nor public release of award information constituted a binding acceptance.

New modes of electronic commerce add interesting elements to these well-established rules regarding acceptance. FAR Subpart 4.5 allows government agencies to use electronic commerce in lieu of traditional paper-based contracting. The rules governing electronic commerce in government procurement continue to evolve. See Office of Management & Budget Memorandum MM-00-15, *Guidance on Implementing the Electronic Signatures in Global and National Commerce Act* (Sept. 25, 2000), *www.omb.gov*. What is clear is that the generally accepted standard for an enforceable electronic signature — an electronic symbol that manifests an intention to sign under the Uniform Electronic Transactions Act § 2, or, pursuant to FAR 2.101, a "present intention to authenticate the writing" — should mean that the government and contractors may, under appropriate circumstances, be bound by "signatures" created and conveyed electronically.

### a. Time for Acceptance

Acceptance must occur within the time stated in the offer or a reasonable time if no time is stated. See *Restatement, Second, Contracts* § 41, which provides:

> (1) An offeree's power of acceptance is terminated at the time specified in the offer, or, if no time is specified, at the end of a reasonable time.

> (2) What is a reasonable time is a question of fact, depending on all the circumstances existing when the offer and attempted acceptance are made.

In IFBs and RFPs using Standard Form 33, the standard acceptance period is 60 days from opening of bids (in the case of IFBs) or from the date set for receipt of proposals (in the case of RFPs). Note that Item 12 of this form uses the term "date for receipt of offers" to imprecisely describe both situations. This clause also permits offerors to insert a longer or shorter acceptance period. But see *Imperial Maint., Inc.*, 71 Comp. Gen. 407 (B-247371), 92-1 CPD ¶ 464 (a 56-day bid guarantee period, made in the form of letters of credit, established the bid acceptance period even though the bidder did not insert that period in the bid form); *Dep't of the Army — Reconsideration*, B-251527.3, 93-2 CPD ¶ 178 (absent proof that contractor intended to hold earlier proposal open for possible acceptance, subsequent offers superseded earlier proposal).

The regulations also provide for the use of minimum acceptance periods. In construction IFBs and RFPs using Standard Form 1442 (FAR 53.301-1442), the contracting officer is required to insert a minimum acceptance period in Item 13D, and the offeror is permitted to offer a longer period in Item 17. FAR 52.214-16, applicable to contracts for other than construction, contains a solicitation provision for IFBs that is to be used when the contracting officer determines that a minimum acceptance period is necessary, FAR 14.201-6(j).

If acceptance does not occur during the specified period, no contract is formed. See 46 Comp. Gen. 371 (B-159639) (1966), stating at 372:

[I]t is clear that expiration of the acceptance period operated to deprive the Government of any right to create a contract by acceptance action and to confer upon the bidder a right to refuse to perform any contract awarded to him thereafter.

This rule is applied strictly in the case of an attempted exercise of an option, *International Tel. & Tel. v. United States*, 197 Ct. Cl. 11, 453 F.2d 1283 (1972).

Where no time for acceptance is specified by the offer, the government must accept within a reasonable time, *International Graphics, Div. of Moore Business Forms, Inc. v. United States*, 4 Cl. Ct. 515 (1984) (reasonable period held to be "obviously in excess of 14 days"). See *National Movers Co. v. United States*, 181 Ct. Cl. 419, 386 F.2d 999 (1967), where acceptance at 3:00 p.m. on Friday, two days after bid opening, was held to be within a reasonable time even though work was required to begin on the following Monday morning. See also *Eagle Aviation, Inc. v. United States*, 9 Cl. Ct. 128 (1985), holding that a notice of award 32 days after submission of the proposal was a valid acceptance of the contractor's offer, and *One Way Constr., Inc.*, AGBCA 84-301-1, 85-1 BCA ¶ 17,839, holding that 23 days is not "an unduly long period of time from bid opening to award of contract."

The acceptance period may be extended in a number of different ways. The contracting officer may request offerors to extend the period if administrative difficulties prevent award before expiration of the bids, FAR 14.404-1(d), or if a protest prevents awarding the contract before expiration of the offers, FAR 33.103(f)(2) (agency-level protests); FAR 33.104(b)(3) (GAO protests). The acceptance period may also be extended on negotiated procurements without reopening discussions with offerors, *Science Info. Servs., Inc.*, Comp. Gen. Dec. B-207149.2, 82-2 CPD ¶ 477. While offerors are not required to extend their offers, such extensions are commonly granted because the offeror wishes to continue to be considered for award. However, it may be disadvantageous for a low bidder to extend in view of FAR 33.103(f)(2) and FAR 33.104(b)(3), which suggest that the contracting officer should consider award prior to resolution of a protest and expiration of a bid if the bidder refuses to extend the offer.

The acceptance period may also be extended through the submission of a bid protest. GAO has held that such an extension of the protester's acceptance period is automatic until the date of the decision and may be extended for a reasonable time thereafter, 52 Comp. Gen. 863 (B-177165) (1973). In *International Graphics v. United States*, 4 Cl. Ct. 515 (1984), the court ruled that an acceptance period may be extended through and beyond protest litigation if the "parties, through litigation or otherwise, have actually or constructively expressed their intent to accept the award." See also *Ulstein Maritime, Ltd. v. United States*, 833 F.2d 1052 (1st Cir. 1987), explaining that the "expiration period on public contract solicitations is for the benefit of the bidders, who have the option of waiving this protection." In *Uffnor Textile Corp.*, Comp. Gen. Dec. B-205050, 81-2 CPD ¶ 443, GAO found another type of automatic extension when the bidder withdrew from the protest but agreed to accept the contracting officer's decision, reasoning that such expression of interest had the effect of extending the acceptance period.

Offerors submitting offers with acceptance periods equal to or greater than those requested by the solicitation have been permitted to revive their offers after the period has expired if doing so will not compromise the integrity of the competitive bidding system, *Consultants, Inc.*, Comp. Gen. Dec. B-286688.2, 2001 CPD ¶ 92; *Strom Contracting Co.*, Comp. Gen. Dec. B-216115, 84-2 CPD ¶ 705; *Rubbermaid, Inc.*, Comp. Gen. Dec. B-238631, 90-1 CPD ¶ 444; *Strom Contracting Co.*, Comp. Gen. Dec. B-216115, 84-2 CPD ¶ 705. See also *Rentfrow, Inc.*, Comp. Gen. Dec. B-243215, 91-2 CPD ¶ 25, holding that where a firm proposed an adequate acceptance period in its original proposal, it could revive the offer once the original acceptance period had passed because doing so would not prejudice other offerors. Accord *Shel-Ken Props., Inc.*, Comp. Gen. Dec. B-261443.3, 96-1 CPD ¶ 243. However, a bidder that offers a bid acceptance period shorter than that requested in an IFB may not extend that period or revive the bid in order to qualify for award because such an extension would be prejudicial to other bidders that offered the requested acceptance period. However, where the contract is awarded to another firm within the shorter acceptance period and the bidder that offered the shorter period protests the award, that bid may be accepted if the protest is sustained even though the acceptance period otherwise would have expired, *Phillips Cartner & Co., Inc.*, 69 Comp. Gen. 105 (B-236416), 89-2 CPD ¶ 492; *Professional Materials Handling Co.*, Comp. Gen. Dec. B-205969, 82-1 CPD ¶ 297, *recons. denied*, 82-1 CPD ¶ 501.

### b.  *Time When Acceptance Occurs*

The time when acceptance occurs depends upon the type of acceptance requested by the offer and the mode of communication used. When the parties are face-to-face or communicating by telephone or teletype, the acceptance occurs as soon as the offeree has given assent to the transaction by statement or signature, *Restatement, Second, Contracts* § 64. There is little opportunity for controversy in such cases. Where the communication is by mail or telegraph, there are two views as to when acceptance occurs. The private common-law view holds that acceptance is effective when dispatched, *Adams v. Lindsell*, 106 Eng. Rep. 250 (K.B. 1818). This is commonly referred to as the "mailbox rule" and requires only that the offeree properly dispatch the notice of acceptance, *Restatement, Second, Contracts* § 63. In government contracts, a contrary view was adopted by the Court of Claims, which ruled that an acceptance must be received by the offeror before a contract is created, *Rhode Island Tool Co. v. United States*, 130 Ct. Cl. 698, 128 F. Supp. 417 (1955). That decision was premised on postal regulations that permitted reclaiming letters after deposit in the mail and on solicitation language that stated that a binding contract would be formed upon "receipt" of the notice of award.

Subsequently, the solicitation language was changed by the government to provide that a binding contract is formed when a notice of award is "mailed or otherwise furnished" to the offeror, FAR 52.214-10(d) and FAR 52.215-1(f)(10). Litigation involving solicitations containing this revised language has demonstrated that a potential conflict still remains. A concurring opinion in *G.C. Casebolt Co. v. United States*, 190 Ct. Cl. 783, 421 F.2d 710 (1970), stated that "a valid contract is not formed until the acceptance is received by the offeror." The majority of the court disposed of the case on other grounds. In *Best Foam Fabricators, Inc. v. United States*, 38 Fed. Cl. 627 (1997), the court found that acceptance was communicated when the agency received the contractor's duly executed contracts. Similarly, in *Emeco Indus. v. United States*, 202 Ct. Cl. 1006, 485 F.2d 652 (1973), the court endorsed the requirement for an actual "communication" of the acceptance. See also *Romala Corp. v. United States*, 20 Cl. Ct. 435 (1990) (provisions included in letter sent by government after acceptance of original offer had been communicated were not part of contract). In contrast, the appeals boards have followed the reasoning of GAO in finding that the acceptance need only be mailed for a valid contract to come into being when specific language to that effect is used in the solicitation. See *Singleton Contracting Corp.*, IBCA 1770-1-84, 86-2 BCA ¶ 18,800 (relief from bid error was denied because board found mailed notice of award had already completed the contract as designated in solicitation); *Cisco Supply Co.*, GSBCA 5678, 81-1 BCA ¶ 15,103 (IFB required removal of purchased property within 15 days after award, and board found that time period began to run when notice of award was mailed as per solicitation language); and *Computer Wholesale Corp.*, GSBCA 4217, 76-1 BCA ¶ 11,859, *recons. denied*, 76-2 BCA ¶ 12,163 (board's reasoning was not necessarily inconsistent with the Court of Claims when solicitation specifically provided that once a written acceptance of award was mailed, contract was formed). In cases involving an acceptance not governed by this solicitation language, it has been held that the Court of Claims rule should be followed, *Titan Atlantic Constr. Corp.*, ASBCA 26007, 83-2 BCA ¶ 16,791.

The mailbox rule requires that the notice of award be placed in the United States mail, not delivered by a private overnight service, *G.E. Sales & Rentals*, GSBCA 13304, 1995 GSBCA LEXIS 409, nor placed in the agency mail system, *Albert H. Voight, Inc.*, GSBCA 4433, 76-1 BCA ¶ 11,789. The government, as offeree, carries the burden of proving timely and proper mailing of the award notice. See *C & L Petroleum Co.*, ASBCA 39844, 91-1 BCA ¶ 23,490, where the government failed to mail the notice of award by either registered or certified mail and thus could only submit evidence of usual practices to prove timely acceptance. The board found that type of evidence insufficient to carry the burden.

There is unanimity regarding the rule for exercise of options under existing contracts. Unless a contrary agreement is shown, all authorities hold that the acceptance is not effective until *received* by the offeror, *Dynamics Corp. of Am. v. United States*, 182 Ct. Cl. 62, 389 F.2d 424 (1968); and *Restatement, Second, Contracts* § 63(b). FAR 17.207(a) requires that written notice of the exercise of the option be "provided" to the contractor within the time specified in the contract. While the *Restatement* uses the term "option contract" broadly to apply to all irrevocable offers — those in new contracts as well as those in existing contracts — the special acceptance rule for options has generally not been applied to firm offers for new government contracts. As discussed above, the *Rhode Island Tool* case reached the same conclusion. In *Cessna Aircraft Co.*, ASBCA 43196, 96-1 BCA ¶ 27,966, the board held that an option exercised by facsimile at 6:00 p.m. on a Saturday and received on the contractor's fax machine was effective even though the contractor did not become aware of the fax until the following Monday. The government had warned the contractor that it intended to exercise the option, which was due to expire at 12:00 midnight on Saturday, as soon as funds became available. It alerted the contractor to "stand by their fax machine."

When acceptance is to be accomplished by performance rather than promise, such as in simplified acquisitions, *Restatement, Second, Contracts* § 45 provides that *the beginning of performance* binds the offeror (the government) but not the offeree (the contractor). FAR 13.004(b) attempts nevertheless to permit later government withdrawal of its unilateral offer by defining acceptance as occurring when the supplier either furnishes the supplies or services or substantially performs the work. The FAR definition does not address, and should not alter, the *Restatement* rule that the contractor is not bound. The appeals boards have followed the FAR, to some degree, in determining when performance binds the government. See *Comtech Corp.*, ASBCA 55526, 08-2 BCA ¶ 33,982, finding that manufacturing noncompliant products was "substantial enough" to prevent the government from withdrawing its purchase order offer. See also *Harney County Gypsum Co.*, AGBCA 93-190-1, 94-1 BCA ¶ 26,455 (board found no acceptance, citing the substantial performance requirement in the FAR, but finding no significant performance); *Eastman Kodak Co.*, Comp. Gen. Dec. B-271009, 96-1 CPD ¶ 215 (an order for supplies or services in response to a seller's quotation does not establish a contract); *Federal Acquisition Mgmt. Training Serv.*, Comp. Gen. Dec. B-248871, 92-2 CPD ¶ 214 (agency may cancel purchase order prior to beginning of performance); *Sunshine Cordage Corp.*, ASBCA 38904, 90-1 BCA ¶ 22,382 (finding that the supplier/offeror is not bound to perform under a government offer for a unilateral contract).

When the government is bound to hold its purchase order offer open because the contractor has accepted by performance, the offer remains open only until the delivery date specified in the purchase order. Thus, if the contractor delivers no goods or defective goods on that date, there is no longer a contract, *Commwise, Inc.*, ASBCA 56580, 09-2 BCA ¶ 34,240 (defective goods). See *Comtech Corp.*, ASBCA 55526, 08-2 BCA ¶ 33,982, containing a complete explanation of the rules governing "unilateral" contracts and treating the rule governing the expiration of the offer at 168,082:

The "offer" presented by the POs is to buy certain supplies on specified terms and conditions if the offer is accepted by the act of delivering those goods on or before the date that the offer specifies. *Sunshine Cordage, supra,* 90-1 BCA ¶ 22,382 at 112,471; *Amplitronics, Inc.,* ASBCA No. 33732, 87-2 BCA ¶ 19,906 at 100,703; *Ordnance Parts & Engineering Co.,* ASBCA No. 31166, 86-1 BCA ¶ 18,545 at 93,154; FAR 13.004(a). If complete performance in accordance with the offer's terms and conditions is not tendered, the "offer" lapses by its own terms. *E.g., Master Research & Manufacturing, Inc.,* ASBCA No. 46341, 94-2 BCA ¶ 26,747 at 133,071; *Ordnance Parts & Engineering Co.,* ASBCA No. 37985, 89-2 BCA ¶ 21,805 at 109,704; *Amplitronics, supra,* 87-2 BCA ¶ 19,906 at 100,704. When an offer lapses by its own terms, the offeree (supplier) bears the costs of nonperformance. *Alsace Industrial, Inc.,* ASBCA No. 51709, 99-1 BCA ¶ 30,227 at 149,542, *recons. denied,* 1999 ASBCA LEXIS 47; *Western Mfg. Co.,* ASBCA No. 25089, 81-1 BCA ¶ 15,024 at 74,346.

## c. Conditional Acceptance

Under certain circumstances, the contracting officer wants to accept the offer but is unable or unwilling to obligate the government at that time. The most common situations occur when the contracting officer's acceptance is contingent upon either the availability of funding for the contract or the approval of higher authority. FAR 32.703-2 permits the contracting officer to initiate a contracting action properly chargeable to funds of the new fiscal year before these funds are available, provided that the solicitation and contract document include the following clause at FAR 52.232-18:

AVAILABILITY OF FUNDS (APR 1984)

Funds are not presently available for this contract. The Government's obligation under this contract is contingent upon the availability of appropriated funds from which payment for contract purposes can be made. No legal liability on the part of the Government for any payment may arise until funds are made available to the Contracting Officer for this contract and until the Contractor receives notice of such availability, to be confirmed in writing by the Contracting Officer.

The contracting officer may use this procedure for procurements involving operation and maintenance and continuing services necessary for normal operations, and for which Congress previously has consistently appropriated funds, unless statutory authority exists for use in other areas, FAR 32.703-2.

Another type of conditional acceptance is one subject to approval of higher authority. FAR 4.103 requires that the contracting officer use the following clause at FAR 52.204-1 in solicitations and contract documents if required by agency procedures:

APPROVAL OF CONTRACT (DEC 1989)

This contract is subject to the written approval of [*identify title of designated agency official here*] and shall not be binding until so approved.

If the condition occurs within a stated or reasonable time without attempted withdrawal by either party, both parties will be bound, *Thomson v. United States*, 174 Ct. Cl. 780, 357 F.2d 683 (1966) (once condition of approval of contract by Attorney General's office was attained, parties to contract were bound); *Delco Elecs. Corp. v. United States*, 12 Cl. Ct. 367 (1987) (failure to issue required formal modification of contract prevented formation of a binding contract). Further, if the condition never occurs, neither party is bound unless one party has undertaken an obligation regarding the occurrence of the condition, *Monroe v. United States*, 184 U.S. 524 (1902) (lack of approval by chief of engineers as specified in contract prevented contract from being enforceable); *Municipal Leasing Corp. v. United States*, 1 Cl. Ct. 771 (1983) (government's motion for summary judgment denied due to its failure to use "best efforts" to secure the necessary funding that was condition of contract). See also *United States v. Newport News Shipbuilding & Dry Dock Co.*, 571 F.2d 1283 (4th Cir.), *cert. denied*, 439 U.S. 875 (1978) (negotiated settlement not binding on the government because condition of ultimate approval by Attorney General never received); and *Blackhawk Heating & Plumbing Co.*, VACAB 823, 81-2 BCA ¶ 15,400 (government not obligated to pay contractor full amount due under a settlement agreement because the agreement made the government's payment obligation contingent upon the availability of funds and Congress withdrew the appropriation of funds for the agreement before the final payment was due). But compare *Cherokee Nation v. Leavitt*, 543 U.S. 631 (2005) (Court rejected government's argument that government not bound to pay tribes because of "insufficient appropriations," notwithstanding qualifying statements in appropriations' legislative history).

There is less certainty as to the degree to which either party is bound during the period prior to the occurrence of the condition or the passage of a reasonable or stated time for its occurrence. Since the offeror has usually invested considerable effort in the procurement, there is normally no desire to withdraw. Thus, most of the cases in this area have involved the government's refusal to proceed with the contractual action. One view of this legal issue is that either party is free to withdraw during this period. See *2 Williston on Contracts*, § 6:14 (4th ed. 1992), stating, in part, that an acceptance to take effect in the future is one that:

> adopts unequivocally the terms of the offer but states that it will not be effective until a certain contingency happens or fails to happen. . . . [T]here is, in effect, so to speak, an acceptance in escrow, which is not to take effect until the future. In the meanwhile, of course, neither party is bound and either may withdraw. Moreover, if the time at which the acceptance is to become effectual is unreasonably remote, the offer may lapse before the acceptance becomes effective. If neither party withdraws and the delay is not unreasonable, however, a contract will arise when the contingency happens or the stipulated event occurs.

The applicability of this reasoning should depend upon which party has control of the condition. If the condition is under the control of a third party, there would appear to be no sound reason for permitting either party to withdraw from such a conditional acceptance envisioned in the terms of the solicitation. In such an agreement, it could be argued that since neither party has control of the condition, both have agreed to be bound while awaiting its outcome. See, however, *City of Klawock v. United States*, 2 Cl. Ct. 580 (1983), *aff'd*, 732 F.2d 168 (Fed. Cir. 1984), and *American Gen. Leasing, Inc. v. United States*, 218 Ct. Cl. 367, 587 F.2d 54 (1978), both supporting the proposition that if a contract is conditioned upon the action of a third party, no contract comes into existence until such action is completed. A better rule would be that a contract for the goods or services does not come into being but that the parties are contractually bound to await the occurrence of the condition for a reasonable period of time.

The more common conditions included in government contract solicitations are those within the control of the government. In such cases, typically some official above the contracting officer or outside the contracting agency must approve the transaction or provide funding. In *American Gen. Leasing, Inc. v. United States*, 218 Ct. Cl. 367, 587 F.2d 54 (1978), it was held that the approving or funding official is under no obligation to the offeror. Similarly, in *Congress Constr. Corp. v. United States*, 161 Ct. Cl. 50, 314 F.2d 527 (1963), *cert. denied*, 375 U.S. 817 (1963), the court assumed, *arguendo*, that the government was legally bound to use its "best efforts" to obtain the higher approval needed to complete negotiations, but that such efforts did not include "unreasonable and improper conduct," such as ignoring the orders of a superior officer. This would indicate that the government had a good faith obligation to attempt to obtain the required approval. See *Essen Mall Props. v. United States*, 21 Cl. Ct. 430 (1990), finding no "bad faith" in not approving contract because negotiations continued for four months after agency had decided not to go forward with deal. See also *Peninsula Group Capital Corp. v. United States*, 93 Fed. Cl. 720 (2010), where the court found no contract when the approval of the Secretary of the Army was blocked by legislation requiring competitive procedures to be used. Compare *Municipal Leasing Corp. v. United States*, 1 Cl. Ct. 771 (1983), where the contract provided that the Air Force would "use its best efforts to obtain appropriations." The court found that the Conditional Funding clause was modified by this provision. If the ultimate decision-maker within the government has no obligation, the government also is free of obligation as a practical matter.

If the government can freely avoid obligation in this manner, basic contract principles would give the offeror the same right unless there is an independent promise to be bound. For example, a conditional acceptance should not override a bidder's agreement not to withdraw a sealed bid. Once the period has expired, the bidder should be free to withdraw unless the government has assumed some obligation such as to use good faith in the decisional process. However, in one case, GAO held that a bidder could not withdraw following a conditional acceptance, 31 Comp. Gen. 477 (B-103842) (1952). There was no discussion of government obligation and no indication that the required approval was obtained within the bid acceptance period. The decision was supported by the questionable reasoning that a bid bond provided an independent basis for liability.

An offeror should not be bound to conditions not included in solicitations but unilaterally inserted by the offeree at the time of attempted acceptance. Since such an "acceptance" would not conform to the terms of the offer, no contract would be formed, *United States v. Braunstein*, 75 F. Supp. 137 (S.D.N.Y. 1947). This rule has been applied to the attempted exercise of an option where the board held that the contractor was not bound by an acceptance conditioned on the availability of funds; this clause was not present in the original contract which the contractor had satisfactorily performed, *Lear Siegler Inc.*, ASBCA 30224, 86-3 BCA ¶ 19,155. See also *CTA Inc.*, ASBCA 47062, 00-2 BCA ¶ 30,946, holding that the contractor had the right to accept or reject the contracting officer's overture to "renegotiate" the contract's production option.

### d. Nonacceptance Responses to Offers

In some cases, offerees' communications are not intended to be acceptances; in others, attempted acceptances do not properly manifest an intent to accept. In such situations, the communication may be held to be a rejection of the offer, a counteroffer, or a request that the offeror alter the terms of the offer. Under traditional contract law, an acceptance must unequivocally conform to the terms of the offer in order to create a binding contractual agreement. See *United States v. Braunstein*, 75 F. Supp. 137 (S.D.N.Y. 1947). *Restatement, Second, Contracts* § 58 provides:

> An acceptance must comply with the requirements of the offer as to the promise to be made or the performance to be rendered.

However, an acceptance is not invalid if it merely requests a change or addition to terms and is not made to depend on assent to the changed or added terms, *Restatement, Second, Contracts* § 61. See *Best Foam Fabricators, Inc. v. United States*, 38 Fed. Cl. 627 (1997), where the government argued that the contractor never accepted the offer because its letter accompanying the signed contract took exception to the inclusion of MIL-I-45208 and, therefore, constituted a counteroffer. The court disagreed, stating that the contractor's letter unequivocally requested that the contract be modified to remove MIL-I-45208. The court stated that neither this request nor any other portion of the letter even remotely suggested that the contractor's acceptance was dependent on the government's assent to the deletion. Thus, the court held that the request was not a counteroffer and did not invalidate the contractor's acceptance. See also *Walsh Constr. Co.*, ASBCA 52952, 02-2 BCA ¶ 32,024, holding that the government's correction of mathematical errors in the extension of unit prices at the time it accepted a bid was not a counteroffer but merely a proper interpretation of the bid.

Rejections and counteroffers terminate the offer unless a different intention is manifested. See *Restatement, Second, Contracts* § 38 and § 39:

§ 38. Rejection

(1) An offeree's power of acceptance is terminated by his rejection of the offer, unless the offeror has manifested a contrary intention.

(2) A manifestation of intention not to accept an offer is a rejection unless the offeree manifests an intention to take it under further advisement.

§ 39. Counter-offers

(1) A counter-offer is an offer made by an offeree to his offeror relating to the same matter as the original offer and proposing a substituted bargain differing from that proposed by the original offer.

(2) An offeree's power of acceptance is terminated by his making of a counter-offer, unless the offeror has manifested a contrary intention or unless the counter-offer manifests a contrary intention of the offeree.

The *Restatement* further provides that a rejection or counteroffer does not necessarily terminate an offer where there is a binding promise by the offeror not to revoke the offer, *Restatement, Second, Contracts* § 37. In government contracts, this latter rule would prevent termination of offers in option clauses and in irrevocable offers in sealed bid procurements. In contrast, offers in negotiated contracts would be terminated by a rejection or counteroffer in view of the offeror's broad right to revoke the offer.

The most common type of counteroffer in government contracts occurs where the offeree attempts to conclude the transaction with different terms. Thus, an acceptance by the government that materially varies from the contractor's offer will be treated as a counteroffer, 26 Comp. Gen. 567 (B-63244) (1947) (government's insertion of level of permitted price increase in its acceptance made such acceptance a counteroffer); *Aero Corp.*, ASBCA 8178, 1963 BCA ¶ 3665 (purchase order by government containing terms "not previously set out, referred to or incorporated" turned purchase order into counteroffer); *Northpoint Investors*, Comp. Gen. Dec. B-209816, 83-1 CPD ¶ 523 (government's acceptance conditioned upon future actions by government was neither clear nor unconditional and thus constituted a counteroffer); *Ford Aerospace & Commc'ns Corp.*, ASBCA 34994, 91-3 BCA ¶ 24,108 (government's acceptance of offer only at lower sales rate found to be a counteroffer and not an acceptance); *Fedcar Co., Ltd.*, Comp. Gen. Dec. B-310980, 2008 CPD ¶ 70 (government acceptance of lease containing "material changes" to offer a counteroffer). The *Aero Corporation* case holds further that such a counteroffer may then be accepted by the original offeror. See also *First Commerce Corp. v. United States*, 60 Fed. Cl. 570 (2004), where a bank accepted the government's counteroffer by performing in accordance with its terms; and *Bloch Lumber Co.*, ASBCA 23512, 79-2 BCA ¶ 14,167, where the government accepted a counteroffer by accepting delivered items without objecting to the new terms. Compare, however, *Ford Aerospace & Commc'ns Corp.*, where before and during performance, the contractor maintained that a discrepancy had to be corrected by the government. The board refused to find acceptance by the contractor through performance because the government was unclear and ambiguous as to what course of action it would take. In *Dunrite Tool & Die Corp.*, ASBCA 16708, 73-1 BCA ¶ 9940, the board found that there were two counteroffers. The government was found to have made one counteroffer when it included different terms in its purported acceptance. The second counteroffer was found when the offeror's response incorporated different terms. Since the government subsequently rejected the offeror's counteroffer, the board concluded that no contract was ever formed. A government notice of award citing the RFP was held to be a counteroffer to an offer containing specifications different from those in the RFP, *Data Gen. Corp.*, ASBCA 21865, 79-2 BCA ¶ 14,185.

Generally, late acceptances have also been treated as counteroffers. See *Restatement, Second, Contracts* § 70, which states in part:

> A late or otherwise defective acceptance may be effective as an offer to the original offeror.

In order to prevent these types of acceptance communications from terminating the offer, the offeree must manifest an intention to keep the offer open. If such an intention is manifested, the offeree can make inquiries, suggest different terms, or propose a counteroffer while retaining the right to accept the original offer. See *Dudek & Bock Spring Mfg. Co.*, ASBCA 9753, 65-2 BCA ¶ 4931, where a government telegram requesting that a bidder confirm the unit price, provide an extended price, and confirm that it had received certain data was held not to terminate the government's power to accept the offer.

## C. Implied-in-Fact Contracts

An implied-in-fact contract occurs when the conduct of the parties indicates that they have actually manifested their mutual assent but an express offer or acceptance is absent. See *Restatement, Second, Contracts* § 4 and § 19, stating that promises may be inferred and that mutual assent may be determined from words or acts. Implied-in-fact contracts are also recognized in government contracts, *Baltimore & Ohio R.R. v. United States*, 261 U.S. 592 (1923). In *Barrett Refining Corp. v. United States*, 242 F.3d 1055, 1060 (Fed. Cir. 2001), the Federal Circuit cited "four requirements of an implied-in-fact contract: (1) mutuality of intent to contract, (2) consideration; (3) lack of ambiguity in offer and acceptance; and (4) actual authority in the government representative to bind the government." As was noted above, and as was pointed out by the Federal Circuit in *Anderson v. United States*, 344 F.3d 1343, 1353 n.3 (Fed. Cir. 2003), these are the same elements that generally must be met to form a binding government contract, both express and implied-in-fact.

However, as in the case of express contracts, implied-in-fact contracts must be consistent with statutory and regulatory requirements, *Prestex Inc. v. United States*,

162 Ct. Cl. 620, 320 F.2d 367 (1963), and based on the conduct of authorized employees, *Peninsula Group Capital Corp. v. United States*, 93 Fed. Cl. 720 (2010); *D & F Marketing, Inc.*, ASBCA 56043, 09-1 BCA ¶ 34,108; *Humlen v. United States*, 49 Fed. Cl. 497 (2001); *Essen Mall Properties v. United States,* 21 Cl. Ct. 430 (1990); *Pacific Gas & Elec. Co. v. United States,* 3 Cl. Ct. 329 (1983), *aff'd*, 738 F.2d 452 (Fed. Cir. 1984); *Woodcraft Corp. v. United States*, 146 Ct. Cl. 101, 173 F. Supp. 613 (1959). It has been very difficult for contractors to prove that they have met all of the elements of an implied-in-fact contract.

In recent years there have been a number of decisions involving "implied-in-fact" contracts as a result of litigation in the wake of the "savings and loan crisis" of the 1980s. See, e.g., *Home Sav. of Am. v. United States*, 399 F.3d 1341 (Fed. Cir. 2005) (discussing background to crisis). This line of cases is known generally as the *Winstar* cases, named after the Supreme Court's decision in *United States v. Winstar Corp.,* 518 U.S. 839 (1996). The Court's decision in *Winstar* confirmed that the owners of solvent savings and loan banks, that had originally negotiated favorable accounting agreements with the government when they purchased ailing savings and loan banks and then were damaged by a congressional change in banking reserve rules, could, under certain circumstances, recover damages from the government. These *Winstar* decisions, which have come primarily from the Court of Federal Claims (where over 100 *Winstar* cases were filed), and the Federal Circuit, obviously stem from nonprocurement contracts. Nevertheless, these decisions have helped clarify many areas of government contract law doctrine, including rules regarding implied-in-fact contracts.

## 1. *Course of Conduct*

The implied-in-fact agreement may be established from a course of conduct followed by the parties. See *Forest Glen Props., LLC v. United States,* 79 Fed. Cl. 669 (2007), where a series of retroactive instruments confirmed implied-in-fact contracts, and *La Van v. United States*, 53 Fed. Cl. 290 (2002), *aff'd*, 382 F.3d 1340 (Fed. Cir. 2004), where extensive negotiations between the bank and officials of the FDIC indicated that they intended to enter into a binding contract. In the latter decision, the court cited *California Fed. Bank, FSB v. United States*, 245 F.3d 1342 (Fed. Cir. 2001), *cert. denied*, 534 U.S. 1113 (2002), where a binding contract was found based on the documents that were exchanged during extensive negotiations. The Federal Circuit did not identify whether it was finding an express contract or an implied-in-fact contract. In *Algonac Mfg. Co. v. United States*, 192 Ct. Cl. 649, 428 F.2d 1241 (1970), a contract was awarded for the production of armor-plated gun carriage parts. By a contract modification, the government was to furnish the necessary armor plate and the contractor was to maintain, repair, protect, and preserve it so long as it was in its possession. Following completion of performance, the contractor asked the government to remove the surplus armor plate from its plant. It was not removed. The contractor stored it for 11 years and later informed the government that it would assess a storage charge for that time. The court held that the government was liable for a reasonable charge on the basis of an implied-in-fact contract, stating at 676:

> In view of the duties, responsibilities, and obligations imposed on the [contractor] by the foregoing provisions to maintain, repair, protect, and preserve the armor plate as long as it was in its possession, it was reasonable for the [contractor] to conclude, after the contract was finished and it had requested the government several times in writing, as outlined above, to take possession of the property and the government failed to do so, that the government wished it to continue to care for, preserve, and store such property and that the government would pay it for doing so.

Similarly, in *Bruce-Andersen Co.*, ASBCA 28125, 83-2 BCA ¶ 16,892, a contractor made an agreement with the government to substitute five-eighth-inch plywood furring for the three-quarter-inch solid furring called for in the contract in order to correct a one-eighth-inch gap resulting from the government's contract drawings. At the time this agreement was reached, it was clear to both parties that each would benefit from the change. The contractor was silent as to the matter of potential net increased cost of the change. In addition, the contractor knew, or should have known, that the government agent with whom it dealt did not have the authority to approve changes involving additional costs to the government. Nevertheless, a year later, the contractor attempted to claim increased costs from the government for the change. The board held that, under the circumstances, there was an implied-in-fact agreement that the change was to be made on a no-cost basis, stating at 84,060:

> [The contractor] is in error in conceiving that express words that the change would be on a no-cost basis was [sic] the only mode for making an agreement to that effect. It is well settled that an agreement may be effected not only through the exchange of express verbal undertakings by the parties but also through conduct between them that, evaluated in the light of surrounding circumstances, manifests a mutual, albeit tacit, intent to be contractually bound. Such an agreement, implied in fact from such conduct is as actual as one reached verbally.

See also *OAO Corp. v. United States,* 17 Cl. Ct. 91 (1989), where the government encouraged the contractor to begin performance before the contract was awarded but later canceled the acquisition. The court granted relief for the contractor's costs based on an implied-in-fact contract. Compare *Northrop Grumman Corp. v. United States*, 63 Fed. Cl. 38 (2004), where the court could find no implied-in-fact contract based upon the parties' actions.

## 2. Acceptance of Benefits

Implied-in-fact contracts may also be created through the acceptance of benefits with the knowledge that the contractor expects to be compensated, *Pacific Maritime Ass'n v. United States*, 123 Ct. Cl. 667, 108 F. Supp. 603 (1952) (labor referral services by the contractor accepted with knowledge that compensation was expected); *Buffalo & Fort Erie Pub. Bridge Auth. v. United States*, 106 Ct. Cl. 731, 65 F. Supp. 476 (1946) (premises used with knowledge that contractor expected compensation); *Equitable Life Assurance Soc'y*, GSBCA 8909, 90-3 BCA ¶ 23,130 (directive to contractor/lessor to replace carpet in leased office space made with knowledge that contractor expected compensation); *Robert J. DiDomenico*, GSBCA 5539, 82-2 BCA ¶ 16,093 (building alterations not called for in the contract ordered with knowledge that contractor expected compensation).

Since implied-in-fact contracts require conduct of the parties manifesting assent, the mere conferring of a benefit on the government does not create a contractual relationship, *Mega Constr. Co. v. United States*, 29 Fed. Cl. 396 (1993). In private transactions, conferring a benefit may permit recovery under a restitutionary theory. In government contracts, however, sovereign immunity from suit has not been waived for restitutionary actions. Such claims have been called "quasi-contract" or "implied-in-law" contract claims, which are not actionable under the Tucker Act, 28 U.S.C. § 1491, or the Contract Disputes Act of 1978, 41 U.S.C. § 7101 et seq. These statutes waiving sovereign immunity for suits on express or implied contracts have been held to exclude suits on contracts implied in law. See *Trauma Serv. Group v. United States,* 104 F.3d 1321 (Fed. Cir. 1997); *Dureiko v. United States*, 62 Fed. Cl. 340 (2004). See *Merritt v. United States*, 267 U.S. 338 (1925), stating at 341:

> The Tucker Act does not give a right of action against the United States in those cases where, if the transaction were between private parties, recovery could be had upon a contract implied in law.

In *Russell Corp. v. United States*, 210 Ct. Cl. 596, 537 F.2d 474 (1976), the court recognized this distinction and its inability to grant remedies on quasi-or implied-in-law contracts, stating at 609:

> Implied-in-fact contracts differ from contracts implied in law (quasi-contracts), where a duty is imposed by operation of law without regard to the intent of the parties. Such arrangements are treated as contracts for the purposes of remedy only. This court, of course, has no jurisdiction to render judgment against the United States based upon a contract implied in law.

See also *United States v. Mitchell,* 463 U.S. 206 (1983), confirming that the Tucker Act does not waive sovereign immunity for claims based on contracts implied in law. Therefore, the Court of Federal Claims and the boards of contract appeals lack jurisdiction in such cases.

### 3. Incomplete Contract Formation

Implied-in-fact contracts have also been found to exist where the government and the contractor have unsuccessfully attempted to form an express contract,

*Hughes Transp., Inc. v. United States*, 128 Ct. Cl. 221, 121 F. Supp. 212 (1954). Similarly, such contracts have sometimes been found to exist where the government and a contractor enter into an incomplete agreement. If the parties have nonetheless exhibited contractual intent, a contract will be found to exist. See *Western States Constr. Co.*, ASBCA 16003, 72-2 BCA ¶ 9508, where the board commented on the failure of the parties to agree to a contract price at 44,302:

> In this case there was no manifestation of mutual assent or "meeting of the minds" as to the contract price. [The contractor] took the firm position that the legal contract price was $1,208,300, and the Government knew it. The Government took the equally firm position that the correct legal contract price was $1,098,300, and [the contractor] knew it. Each party clearly manifested to the other party its position as to the correct contract price, and each party manifested to the other party its disagreement with the other party's position as to the contract price. It does not follow, however, that the failure of the parties to arrive at a meeting of the minds on the contract price resulted in there being no contract. An agreed on contract price is not essential to the existence of a contract when there is agreement on all the other terms of contract and a manifestation of intent to make a contract, such as we have here.

See also *Howard Nettleton*, PSBCA 3454, 94-3 BCA ¶ 27,038, where the absence of an express agreement on price was insufficient to prevent recovery on a contract implied-in-fact.

An implied-in-fact contract may be found to exist on the basis of an implied acceptance of an express offer. In *Thomson v. United States*, 174 Ct. Cl. 780, 357 F.2d 683 (1966), acceptance of a contractor's offer to perform surveying services was contingent upon approval of higher authority. The contracting office received notice of such approval but did not inform the contractor of that fact, and did not therefore expressly accept the offer. However, the court held that there was an implied acceptance by the actions and communications of the contracting officer that encouraged the contractor to perform. As a result, an implied-in-fact contract was held to have come into existence. In discussing the relationship between an implied acceptance and an implied-in-fact contract, the court stated at 791:

> It is fundamental, however, that acceptance of an offer may be manifested either expressly (as by words) or impliedly by conduct indicating assent to the proposed bargain. *Restatement 2d, Contracts* §§ 5, 21, 21A, 52 (Comment c) (Tent. ed. 1, 1964); I *Williston, Contracts* §§ 90, 91A (3d ed. 1957). The notion that assent to the terms of an agreement (i.e., acceptance) may be evinced by action or conduct underlies the rule, repeatedly recognized by the courts, that contracts may be "implied in fact."

See also *Padbloc Co. v. United States*, 161 Ct. Cl. 369 (1963), where because the contractor stipulated that the government could use its data only if the data were kept confidential, the government's use of the data constituted an implied promise of confidentiality.

## II.  BINDING THE PARTIES

The manifestation of mutual assent is not in itself sufficient to bind a party to perform as promised. The law requires either that something be exchanged for the promise or that the promise be reasonably relied upon. The term given by the law to the former is "consideration," while the latter is called "promissory estoppel."

### A.  Requirement for Signed Document

In private contract law, state Statutes of Frauds permit a party being charged in a contract suit who has not signed a document evidencing a contract to plead that failure — the lack of a signed document — as a defense. See generally *Restatement, Second, Contracts* § 110 and § 138; and U.C.C. § 2-201. There is no similar statute concerning government contracts, and it has been held that the absence of a signed written document does not preclude the enforceability of a government contract, *Escote Mfg. Co. v. United States*, 144 Ct. Cl. 452, 169 F. Supp. 483 (1959) (valid contract existed despite the absence of the contracting officer's signature on the government's acceptance form because the form was sent with a letter indicating acceptance that was signed by the contracting officer).

### 1.  *Written or Electronic Notice*

Although there is no federal Statute of Frauds, there are a number of statutory and regulatory references indicating that contracts should be awarded in writing or by electronic means. See 10 U.S.C. § 2305(b)(3) and (b)(4); 41 U.S.C. § 3702(c) and § 3703(d), as well as FAR 14.408-1. Thus, the guidance which traditionally requires written notices of award for sealed bid and competitive negotiated procurement now contemplates electronic transmissions as well. See FAR Subpart 4.5 requiring the use of electronic commerce "whenever practicable or cost-effective." See also Department of Justice, *Legal Considerations in Designing and Implementing Electronic Processes: A Guide for Federal Agencies* (Nov. 2000), *www.cyber-crime.gov/eprocess.htm* (noting statutory and evidentiary requirements for traditional, hard-copy documents).

The FAR 2.101 definition of "contracts" states that the term "includes all types of commitments that obligate the Government . . . and that, except as otherwise authorized, are in writing." "In writing," in turn, is defined by FAR 2.101 to include "any worded or numbered expression that can be read, reproduced, and later communicated, and includes electronically transmitted and stored information." The term "writing" is defined in 1 U.S.C. § 1 to include "printing and typewriting and reproductions of visual symbols by photographing, multigraphing, mimeographing, manifolding, or otherwise." The fiscal statutes also contain a provision relating to this issue. 31 U.S.C. § 1501(a)(1) states that one of the bases for recording an obligation of the United States is a "binding agreement . . . in writing . . . and executed." GAO has held that for purposes of the statute, electronic data interchanges constitute writings, *National Inst. of Standards & Tech.*, 71 Comp. Gen. 109 (B-245714), 96-2 CPD ¶ 225.

In *United States v. American Renaissance Lines, Inc.*, 494 F.2d 1059 (D.C. Cir.), *cert. denied*, 419 U.S. 1020 (1974), the court construed the appropriations recording statute to be a Statute of Frauds in refusing to hold a contractor to an oral agreement. The court rejected the government's argument that the statute was merely for purposes of recording obligations to facilitate auditing and that it was not applicable to government contracts. *Escote Mfg. Co. v. United States*, 144 Ct. Cl. 452, 169 F. Supp. 483 (1959), and *Penn-Ohio Steel Corp. v. United States*, 173 Ct. Cl. 1064, 354 F.2d 254 (1965), earlier Court of Claims cases holding that government contracts need not be in writing to be binding, were dismissed in a statement that in neither case did a citation to the statute appear. The court's interpretation of the statute has not been followed by other courts. See *Narva Harris Constr. Corp. v. United States*, 216 Ct. Cl. 238, 574 F.2d 508 (1978), where the Court of Claims recognized that an implied contract could exist even though some of the indicia of the agreement were oral statements concerning the transaction. In rejecting the government's claim that 31 U.S.C. § 1501 barred the contractor's recovery, the court stated at 244:

> In almost all such cases, there is some sort of oral representation on the part of some Government agent. Although the party seeking to recover from the Government may not rely on the oral representation, and may rely totally on other, independent facts to establish the presence of an implied in fact contract or to recover in quantum meruit, the Government now seeks to make the mere existence of the oral representation, characterized as an oral express contract not reduced to writing, sufficient to compel this court to close its eyes to all other surrounding facts. Clearly such an expansive interpretation of § 200 [1501] is unacceptable.

See also *Arakaki v. United States*, 62 Fed. Cl. 244 (2004) (refusing to dismiss, on bare jurisdictional grounds, claim based on alleged oral contract). In *Lublin Corp. v. United States*, 84 Fed. Cl. 678 (2008), the Court of Federal Claims rejected the government's argument that 31 U.S.C. § 1501 barred holding that an oral contract was binding, explaining at 688-89:

> [N]early a dozen decisions have chosen to follow [*Narva Harris*] in concluding that section 1501(a)(1) neither prohibits express oral nor implied-in-fact contracts.[18] A number of other cases, among them several in the Court of Claims, conclude that unwritten contracts are enforceable under the Tucker Act.[19]

[18] See, e.g., *Pacord Inc. v. United States*, 139 F.3d 1320, 1322 (9th Cir. 1998); *Kenney v. United States*, 41 Fed. Cl. 353, 357 (1998) ("Implied-in-fact contracts with the government have been enforced despite statutory or regulatory requirements that contracts be in writing."); *Al-Kurdi v. United States*, 25 Cl. Ct. 599, 602 n.4 (1992) (noting that Federal law does not have a requirement that contracts "must be in writing," and citing the holding in *Narva Harris*); *Johns-Manville Corp. v. United States*, 12 Cl. Ct. 1, 19 (1987) ("Even when a party contracts with the Federal Government, it is not essential that the contract be in written form."); *People's Bank & Trust Co. v. United States*, 11 Cl. Ct. 554, 566 (1987) (same); *South La. Grain Servs., Inc. v. United States*, 1 Cl. Ct.

281, 290 n.7 (1982) ("Defendant does not argue 31 U.S.C. § 200 (1976) . . . as a basis for denial of plaintiff's oral agreement claim, presumably because a like argument was rejected by the Court of Claims in *Narva Harris*."); *Integral Systems, Inc. v. Dep't of Commerce*, [GSBCA 16321-COM, 05-2 BCA ¶ 32,984] ("Section [1501] is intended for internal and bookkeeping and fiscal control purposes. It does not govern the relationships between the government and any outside parties with which it deals."); see also *Willard L. Boyd III*, "Implied-in-Fact Contract: Contractual Recovery Against the Government Without an Express Agreement," 21 Pub. Con. L.J. 84, 85-87 & n.12 (1991) ("There is no express statute of frauds applicable to government contracts requiring that contracts be in writing, and the clear majority of cases have held that a signed document need no exist in order for a binding contract to exist.").

[19] See, e.g., *Penn-Ohio Steel Corp. v. United States*, 354 F.2d 254, 267, 173 Ct. Cl. 1064 (Ct. Cl. 1965); *Escote Mfg. Co. v. United States*, 169 F. Supp. 483, 488, 144 Ct. Cl. 452 (Ct. Cl. 1959); *Ship Constr. & Trading Co. v. United States*, 91 Ct. Cl. 419, 456 (1940), cert. denied, 312 U.S. 699, 61 S. Ct. 737, 85 L. Ed. 1133, 92 Ct. Cl. 629 (1941); *People's Bank & Trust Co.*, 11 Ct. Cl. at 566; *ATL, Inc. v. United States*, 4 Cl. Ct. 672, 675 (1984), aff'd, 735 F.2d 1343 (Fed. Cir. 1984); *Pacific Gas & Elec. Co. v. United States*, 3 Cl. Ct. 329, 338-39 (1983), aff'd, 738 F.2d 452 (Fed. Cir. 1984); *Harbridge House, Inc.*, 77-2 BCA P 12,653, at 61,341 (1977); see also *United States v. Purcell Envelope Co*, 249 U.S. 313, 319, 39 S. Ct. 300, 63 L. Ed. 620, 54 Ct. Cl. 190 (1919) ("It makes no difference that the contract was not formally signed [because] . . . formal execution . . . was not essential to the consummation of the contract.").

The *American Renaissance Lines* holding is also inapplicable where the contracts involve the obligation of nonappropriated funds. See *Sam Won Dev. Co.*, ASBCA 16541, 74-2 BCA ¶ 10,730, recognizing a binding oral contract and distinguishing *American Renaissance Lines* on the ground that the statute has no application to agreements where nonappropriated funds are involved. See also *Robert P. Maier, Inc.*, GSBCA 4382, 76-1 BCA ¶ 11,873, and *Robert P. Maier, Inc.*, Comp. Gen. Dec. B-185177, 76-1 CPD ¶ 137, *recons. denied*, 76-2 CPD ¶ 163, holding that *American Renaissance Lines* is not applicable to sales of government property.

*American Renaissance Lines* was also distinguished where the government's bidding documents specify that acceptance will be oral, *Ross Indus.*, ASBCA 19563, 75-1 BCA ¶ 11,212, and where the parties acted with the mutual understanding that a contract had been formed, *Superior Asphalt & Concrete Co.*, AGBCA 75-142, 76-2 BCA ¶ 12,022, *recons. denied*, 77-2 BCA ¶ 12,851. In the latter case, the board stated at 62,559:

We are persuaded that the weight of authority to the effect that there is no Federal Statute of Frauds applies in the case before us. Where the terms and conditions are fixed by the writing in the bid package which becomes the offer, oral acceptance with execution of the document intended by both parties in a routine manner results in an enforceable contract even though the parties fail to actually execute the document. The oral acceptance must, of course, be by a duly authorized contracting officer acting within the scope of his authority.

For a similar discussion, see the concurring opinion in *Eastern Salvage Assocs.*, ENGBCA 4046, 80-1 BCA ¶ 14,216. However, the Claims Court opinion in *Prestex Inc. v. United States*, 3 Cl. Ct. 373 (1983), contains *dicta* in note 5 stating that express oral contracts fail on the ground that they violate the recording statute.

The Claims Court has also noted that while 31 U.S.C. § 1501 "is rarely, if ever, the sole basis for invalidating an otherwise valid express oral agreement[,] . . . the provision manifests the general view that generally oral agreements provide a very shaky basis for granting relief by way of money judgments," *Edwards v. United States*, 22 Cl. Ct. 411 (1991).

## 2. *Signature*

A handwritten signature is probably the most universally accepted evidence of an agreement to be bound by a contract's terms. As early as 1951, however, GAO held that a signature does not have to be handwritten and that "any symbol adopted as one's signature when affixed with his knowledge and consent is a binding and legal signature," Comp. Gen. Dec. B-104590, Sept. 12, 1951, *Unpub.* 1 U.S.C. § 1 provides that "'signature' or 'subscription' includes a mark when the person making the same intended it as such." Under common law, it has been determined that audio tape recordings can be considered to constitute a "signed writing" and are sufficient to create a contract. See *Ellis Canning Co. v. Berstein*, 348 F. Supp. 1212 (D. Colo. 1972).

In the commercial sphere, the scope of recognizable "signatures" has expanded greatly with electronic commerce and with the federal and state laws to guide that commerce, the Electronic Signatures in Global and National Commerce (ESIGN) Act, 15 U.S.C. § 7001 et seq., and the Uniform Electronic Transactions Act (UETA). The ESIGN Act, for example, lends electronic signatures equal status with traditional signatures, and defines "electronic signatures" broadly to include any "electronic sound, symbol, or process, attached to or logically associated with a contract or other record and executed or adopted by a person with the intent to sign the record," 15 U.S.C. § 7006. UETA, for its part, contemplates an enormous range of signs and symbols of acquiescence as permissible electronic "signatures." The commentary to § 2 of UETA (*http://www.law.upenn.edu/bll/ulc/fnact99/1990s/ueta99.htm*) notes, for example:

> One's voice on an answering machine may suffice [as an electronic signature] if the requisite intention is present. Similarly, including one's name as part of an electronic mail communication also may suffice, as may the firm name on a facsimile. It also may be shown that the requisite intent was not present and accordingly the symbol, sound or process did not amount to a signature. . . . In any case the critical element is the intention to execute or adopt the sound or symbol or process for the purpose of signing the related record

Although UETA is a uniform state statute, broadly adopted across the United States, it is not binding on federal procurement. Nor, in fact, is the ESIGN Act binding on federal agencies' procurement. See 15 U.S.C. § 7004. At the same time, however, the liberal approach taken by the two acts suggests that the boards and the courts are likely to take a similarly broad view of what qualifies as a permissible "signature" in electronic records used for federal contracting. See FAR 4.502 stating:

(d) Agencies may accept electronic signatures and records in connection with Government contracts.

See also FAR 2.101 stating:

*Signature* or *signed* means the discrete, verifiable symbol of an individual that, when affixed to a writing with the knowledge and consent of the individual, indicates a present intention to authenticate the writing. This includes electronic symbols.

The earlier cases laid the groundwork for the current broad understanding of "signatures" in an age of electronic contracting. In 1996, for example, GAO concluded that Electronic Data Interchange (EDI) technology, one of the earliest forms of electronic commerce, offered evidence of an intent to be bound that had the same attributes as a handwritten signature, *National Inst. of Standards & Tech.*, 71 Comp. Gen. 109 (B-245714), 96-2 CPD ¶ 225. In that case, GAO held that EDI systems using message authentication codes that follow the National Institute of Standards and Technology's (NIST) Computer Data Authentication Standard or digital signatures following NIST's Digital Standard, can produce a form of evidence of a signature.

Sending a signed document electronically may not be accepted as an electronic signature. *See General Dynamics C4 Sys.*, ASBCA 54988, 09-2 BCA ¶ 34,150, *rev'd on other grounds*, 633 F.3d 1356 (Fed. Cir. 2010), rejecting the argument that "electronic images" of delivery orders were signed documents because they did not contain a "digital signature" of the contracting officer. Similarly, GAO has rejected the acceptance of electronically submitted bid bonds on sealed bid procurements because there is no guarantee that such documents have not been altered from the actual original written bond, *TJ's Marine Constr. LLC*, Comp. Gen. Dec. B-402227, 2010 CPD ¶ 19; *Excel Bldg. & Dev. Corp.*, Comp. Gen. Dec. B-401955, 2009 CPD ¶ 262. See also *Teknocraft, Inc.*, ASBCA 55438, 08-1 BCA ¶ 33,846 (CDA claim sent by email with "// signed //" not valid because it contained no authenticated signature).

The requirement for authenticated signatures, transmitted using highly secure technologies, may prove out of step with evolving procurement law, which has traditionally accepted signatures in many forms, from faxes to photocopies. Where facsimile transmission is authorized, for example, GAO has held that a facsimile signature will be sufficient. In *American Eagle Indus., Inc.*, Comp. Gen. Dec. B-256907, 94-2 CPD ¶ 156, GAO held that a bidder's faxed modification did not render its bid nonresponsive merely because it instructed the agency to replace the original first page of its bid with a faxed page, thereby replacing the authorized agent's original signature with a faxed copy of the same agent's signature. Similarly, in *International Shelter Sys., Inc.*, 71 Comp. Gen. 142 (B-245466), 92-1 CPD ¶ 34, the protester argued that the facsimile and photocopy signatures did not equal an original signature and thus the bid was nonresponsive. GAO denied the protest and held that a photocopy of a signed bid document is binding as a duplicate of the original signed document because the signature still prevents the bidder from disavowing its obligations under the signed document.

An appeals board has followed GAO's reasoning that evidence of an intent to be bound has the same attributes as a handwritten signature. In *Regional Trucking, Inc.*, PSBCA 3918, 97-1 BCA ¶ 28,733, the board held that the hand-printed name and title of the contractor's president constituted acceptable evidence of the contractor's intent to be bound by the bid on which it was placed. The president had also hand-signed three other documents that were submitted as part of the bid and referred to the specific solicitation involved and the contractor subsequently completed, signed, and returned the preaward surveys. In reaching its decision, the board stated at 143,404:

> Courts, as well as the General Accounting Office, have long indicated a willingness to accept other than a handwritten signature on executory documents such as bid proposals. *See Ohl & Co. v. Smith Iron Works*, 288 U.S. 170, 176 (1932) (initials); *Benedict v. Lebowitz*, 346 F.2d 120 (2d Cir. 1965) (typed name); *Tabas v. Emergency Fleet Corporation*, 9 F.2d 648, 649 (E.D. Penn., 1926) (typed, printed or stamped signatures); *See also National Institute of Standards and Technology*, 71 Comp. Gen. 109 (1991) (use of electronic data interchange technology to create valid obligations). What is necessary is evidence of an intent to be bound. *Benedict v. Lebowitz, supra; see also, Peter J. O'Brien*, 96-2 CPD ¶ 91 (Aug. 29, 1996). In this case, Appellant hand printed the title of the corporation on the signature line, and hand printed "M.C. Johnson President" on the line calling for the name and title of the bidder. Mr. Johnson also hand signed three other documents which were submitted as a part of its bid, all of which either referred to the solicitation or highway route number. These actions constitute sufficient evidence of an intent to be bound by the bid documents. Furthermore, the fact that Appellant subsequently completed, signed and returned to Respondent the pre-award surveys, resolve any doubt of Appellant's intent to be bound by the bid it submitted.

## 3. Superseding Requirement for Writing

Even though, as a general rule, oral agreements will bind the parties, a written document may be required by statutory or regulatory provisions or by limitations in a delegation of authority to a contracting officer. See, for example, *Harbert/Lummus Agrifuels Projects v. United States*, 142 F.3d 1429 (Fed. Cir. 1998), *cert. denied*, 525 U.S. 1177 (1999), holding that the government was not bound by an oral agreement of the contracting officer when his delegation of authority specifically required agreements to be in writing. See also *American Gen. Leasing, Inc. v. United States*, 218 Ct. Cl. 367, 587 F.2d 54 (1978), finding the government not bound by an oral agreement because both Standard Form 33 and the definition of "contract" in the Federal Procurement Regulation required contracts to be in writing.

Most cases of this type deal with contract modifications where the regulations have been interpreted as requiring a writing. See FAR 43.301(a)(1) requiring supplemental agreements (contract modifications) to be issued on Standard Form (SF) 30. In *SCM Corp. v. United States*, 219 Ct. Cl. 459, 595 F.2d 595 (1979), the court held that the contractor and the contracting officer did not intend to be bound by their oral agreement settling a claim because of this requirement, stating at 464:

> Oral understandings which contemplate the finalization of the legal obligations in a written form are not contracts in themselves. When legal obligations between the parties *will be deferred* until the time when a written document is executed, there will not be a contract until that time. *See Restatement of Contracts* § 26 (1932). *See also Corbin on Contracts* § 30 (1963). Under the regulations, Government funds were not obligated until the execution of standard form 30. The parties were well aware of the fact that only the written contract modification could finalize their agreement. No commitments in the oral understanding to act in any way by either party were to be consummated until execution of the supplemental agreement. Whether the parties had reached a clear understanding of the terms of the settlement makes no difference and we specifically intimate no decision on that issue. We thus conclude that neither party was bound by its negotiations until standard form 30 was executed. This interpretation of the understanding and intent of the parties is supported by the actions of plaintiff in later seeking inclusion in the contract of an additional term for interest. Thus, we conclude that the representations made by telephone on January 6, 1976, did not constitute a contract.

> We note that this case does not squarely present the question of the enforceability of oral contracts with the Government. Instead, the case deals with the problem of what effect the parties' clear understanding of the procedures and regulations governing settlements had on their intent to consummate a binding contract. It should be kept in mind that oral understandings must first be contracts before they are enforceable. In this case, we simply hold that the understanding between the parties was not a contract and cannot sustain a breach of contract action in this court.

While the *SCM Corporation* decision was clearly based upon the conclusion that both parties did not intend to have a binding agreement until a SF 30 was signed, later decisions have focused on the need for a signed writing to modify an integrated contract. In *Mil-Spec Contractors, Inc. v. United States*, 835 F.2d 865 (Fed. Cir. 1987), the court cited the regulatory requirement for the use of a signed SF 30 in holding that an oral agreement was not a binding contract amendment. Board decisions have held that FAR 43.301 requires modifications to be in writing, *Kato Corp.*, ASBCA 51462, 06-2 BCA ¶ 33,293; *Johnson Mgmt. Group CFC, Inc.*, HUDBCA 96-C-132-C15, 00-2 BCA ¶ 31,116; *Marshall Associated Contractors, Inc., & Columbia Excavating, Inc. (J.V.)*, IBCA 1901, 98-1 BCA ¶ 29,965. See also *National Surety Corp. v. United States*, 118 F.3d 1542 (Fed. Cir.1997) (contract clause required modifications to be in writing); *Cooper Realty Co. v. United States*, 36 Fed. Cl. 284 (1996) ("Having failed to comply with the USPS rules and regulations, the oral agreement is not a valid contractual modification."). See also *Daly Constr., Inc. v. Garrett*, 5 F.3d 520 (Fed. Cir. 1993), stating at 521:

To recover on an express agreement with a government agency, the agreement must be in writing and signed by an authorized person. *Mil-Spec Contractors, Inc. v. United States*, 835 F.2d 865 (Fed. Cir. 1987). We need not here discuss whether any circumstances might warrant departure from that standard, for as to this particular contract modification Daly, although poorly used by the pattern of lengthy negotiation, apparent agreement, unwarranted delay, and broken promises, was not deceived. Daly knew the government was not bound in contract until a formal written modification was executed.

In contrast, the use of SF 30 was held to be a "mere formality" as long as the parties' agreement was in a signed writing, *Robinson Contracting Co. v. United States*, 16 Cl. Ct. 676 (1989), *aff'd*, 895 F.2d 1420 (Fed. Cir. 1989). See also *Adams Constr. Co.*, VABCA 4669, 97-1 BCA ¶ 28,801. While these decisions affect modifications to contracts, they do not deal with the initial formation of a contract.

## B. Consideration

Consideration can be described as the price bargained and paid for a promise. It may consist of an act, a forbearance, or a return promise. *Restatement, Second, Contracts* § 71 defines "consideration" as follows:

(1) To constitute consideration, a performance or a return promise must be bargained for.

(2) A performance or return promise is bargained for if it is sought by the promisor in exchange for his promise and is given by the promisee in exchange for that promise.

(3) The performance may consist of

(a) an act other than a promise, or

(b) a forbearance, or

(c) the creation, modification, or destruction of a legal relation.

(4) The performance or return promise may be given to the promisor or to some other person. It may be given by the promisee or by some other person.

The requirement for consideration flowing to the government is supported not only by the common-law rules but also by the rule that government officials generally do not have the authority to give up vested rights of the government without receiving consideration, *Simpson v. United States*, 172 U.S. 372 (1899). See also *Aviation Contractor Employees, Inc. v. United States*, 945 F.2d 1568 (Fed. Cir. 1991); *Metzger, Shadyac & Schwarz v. United States*, 12 Cl. Ct. 602 (1987); and *Joseph Pickard's Sons Co.*, ASBCA 13585, 73-1 BCA ¶ 10,026. The major exception to this rule is Pub. L. No. 85-804, 50 U.S.C. §§ 1431-35, which authorizes executive agencies to make or amend contracts without consideration when to do so would facilitate national defense. See FAR Part 50.

## 1. Form of Consideration

Generally, consideration in the typical sealed bid or negotiated government contract is found in the exchange of promises to perform positive duties. A bid or proposal is a promise to furnish supplies or services offered in exchange for the government's promise to pay for the work. The promise of compensation induces the offeror's promise of performance, and the offeror's promise to perform induces the award of the contract containing the government's promise to pay upon completion. Each party's promise serves as consideration for the other's. In unilateral contracts, as in some simplified acquisitions, consideration takes the form of an act, i.e., performance, induced by the government's promise to pay.

Consideration in contract modifications normally takes the form of promises by the contractor to perform work that is different from that originally required in exchange for the government's promise to pay a different price. See, for example, *Gardiner, Kamya & Assocs., P.C. v. Jackson*, 369 F.3d 1318 (Fed. Cir. 2004) (court, reversing board, found adequate consideration in agency's agreement to reprice earlier work in return for contractor's agreement in modification to perform certain work). In some cases, the consideration may be the agreement to forbear from exercising a right such as asserting a claim.

### a. Promises to Perform Duties

Cases in which consideration is not present may arise under different fact situations. In one type of case, the alleged promise or performance confers no benefit on the other party. In government contracts, this most often occurs when the government modifies a contract to benefit the contractor but receives no additional or different promise or performance in return. Under *Restatement, Second, Contracts* § 73, such modifications are without consideration because they involve performance of a preexisting duty that is neither doubtful nor the subject of honest dispute. See *Alpine Computers, Inc.*, ASBCA 54659, 05-2 BCA ¶ 32,997 (subcontractor delivery of equipment to agency when it was not paid by defaulted contractor); *National Micrographics Sys., Inc. v. United States*, 38 Fed. Cl. 46 (1997) (subcontractor delivery of computers to National Security Agency not valid consideration because insolvent contractor was already contractually obligated to deliver them); *AAA Eng'g & Drafting, Inc.*, ASBCA 36176, 91-2 BCA ¶ 23,812 (contract clause that provided for additional compensation as workload increased unenforceable where the government did not order the minimum amount of work specified in the contract); *Montefiore Hosp. v. United States*, 5 Cl. Ct. 471 (1984) (alleged agreement to modify contractual interest rate unenforceable because government received no benefit); *States Roof ing & Metal Co.*, ASBCA 22091, 78-2 BCA ¶ 13,287 (change order that directed contractor to do work required under original contract for increased compensation not binding); and *A.O. Smith Corp.*, ASBCA 16788, 72-2 BCA ¶ 9688 (modification covering repair costs unenforceable since contractor was already obligated to make repairs). Furthermore, GAO has stated that a defaulted firm's bid on a reprocurement contract must be rejected if it is higher than the original contract price, on the grounds that acceptance of a higher bid would be tantamount to a contract modification increasing the price without any consideration for the government, *A.R.E. Mfg. Co.*, Comp. Gen. Dec. B-246161, 92-1 CPD ¶ 210; *Air, Inc.,* Comp. Gen. Dec. B-233501 , 88-2 CPD ¶ 505. See, however, *Salsbury Indus. v. United States*, 17 Cl. Ct. 47 (1989), *aff'd*, 905 F.2d 1518 (Fed. Cir. 1990), indicating that the requirement to give notice would be sufficient to enforce the contract.

Another situation where no consideration exists is where one party has a right to avoid any contractual duties. See *Restatement, Second, Contracts* § 77. See also *3 Williston, Contracts* § 7:13 (4th ed., 1992), which states at 271, "An agreement wherein one party reserves the right to cancel at his pleasure cannot create a contract." This issue has been raised concerning the present Termination for the Convenience of the Government clause. An early government contracts case dealing with the question of lack of consideration and termination clause is *Sylvan Crest Sand & Gravel Co. v. United States*, 150 F.2d 642 (2d Cir. 1945), where the clause stated, "Cancellation by the Procurement Division may be effected at any time." The appellate court held that the contract was not illusory because it contained an implied promise by the government to give notice of cancellation within a reasonable time if it did not want to accept the goods. In *Torncello v. United States*, 231 Ct. Cl. 20, 681 F.2d 756 (1982), the court extensively discussed the consideration issue and concluded that the scope of termination rights had to be limited to prevent the absence of consideration. The court also indicated that it disagreed with the reasoning in *Sylvan Crest* that the bare requirement to give notice constituted consideration. See also *Salsbury Indus. v. United States*, 17 Cl. Ct. 47 (1989), *aff'd*, 905 F.2d 1518 (Fed. Cir. 1990), where the court in a footnote reiterated that notice of impending termination might not constitute sufficient consideration in a contract with a Termination clause. In *Krygoski Constr. Co. v. United States*, 94 F.3d 1537 (Fed. Cir. 1996), the court interpreted *Torncello* to impose only the limitation of bad faith on such terminations without discussing whether this constituted consideration. See *Judiciary Plaza Limited Partnership v. Securities & Exchange Comm'n*, GSBCA 12920-SEC, 96-2 BCA ¶ 28,596, holding that a lease that granted the landlord broad termination rights was not invalid for lack of consideration. The board stated that upon signing the lease, the parties became subject to the obligations thereunder. The lease expressly described the parties' obligations in the event of a termination. See generally McConnell, *Note: Bad Faith as a Limitation on Terminations for Convenience: As Bad As They Say, Or Not So Bad?,* 32 Pub. Cont. L.J. 411 (2003).

In *Green Mgmt. Corp. v. United States*, 42 Fed. Cl. 411 (1998), the court held that the government's decision *not* to exercise its right to terminate for convenience was consideration for the contractor's agreement to a modification imposing restrictions on its method of performance. Since the government has very broad powers to terminate a contract for its convenience, this argument could be used to support modifications whenever a termination for convenience was in the interest of the government.

## b. Forbearance

Forbearance is a kind of consideration that does not involve the performance of any additional or modified duties. Perhaps the most common type of forbearance is involved in the settlement of claims. See *Restatement, Second, Contracts* § 74(1), which states:

> Forbearance to assert or the surrender of a claim or defense which proves to be invalid is not consideration unless
>
>> (a) the claim or defense is in fact doubtful because of uncertainty as to the facts or the law, or
>>
>> (b) the forbearing or surrendering party believes that the claim or defense may be fairly determined to be valid.

See *Penn-Ohio Steel Corp. v. United States*, 173 Ct. Cl. 1064, 354 F.2d 254 (1965), where the government argued that a contractor's agreement to vacate a building was not consideration because a contract clause entitled the government to revoke the lease in case of a national emergency. The court found consideration because the contractor could have instituted a suit to enjoin the contractor's eviction from the plant under this legally questionable provision. Thus, the forbearance need not be on a claim that is legally correct. In *American Air Filter Co.*, ASBCA 14794, 72-1 BCA ¶ 9219, the government believed that a high-pressure cutout switch was a required item in a contract to furnish air conditioners. The contractor contended that the item was not required. The board held that the position of the contractor was incorrect, but because the claim was not completely unreasonable or in bad faith, the settlement of the claim by the government through contract modification was supported by consideration (the agreement by contractor to withdraw the claim). Compare *Institutional & Envtl. Mgmt.*, ASBCA 32924, 90-3 BCA ¶ 23,118, where a modification lacked consideration because the contractor's relinquished claim had "no color or claim of right." The board's reasoning is consistent with the general principle that consideration exists if one party is relinquishing a legal right or forbearing to exercise it in exchange for something from the other party, *Busby School Bd. of the N. Cheyenne Tribe*, IBCA 3007, 94-1 BCA ¶ 26,327; *ITT Gilfillan, Inc. v. United States*, 200 Ct. Cl. 367, 471 F.2d 1382 (1973). Several savings and loan cases have held that the government's forbearance in exercising its right to enforce regulatory requirements qualified as consideration for its contracts, *Hughes v. United States*, 498 F.3d 1334 (Fed. Cir. 2007), *cert. denied*, 552 U.S. 1309 (2008); *Franklin Fed. Sav. Bank v.*

*United States*, 431 F.3d 1360 (Fed. Cir. 2005); *Admiral Financial Corp. v. United States*, 378 F.3d 1336 (Fed. Cir. 2004); *First Commerce Corp. v. United States*, 63 Fed. Cl. 627 (2005).

Another type of consideration through forbearance exists where the parties agree to release each other from a contract that has not been completely performed on either side. In *Savage Arms Corp. v. United States*, 266 U.S. 217 (1924), the Court stated at 220-21:

> A good deal is said by [the contractor] to the effect that this agreement was without consideration; but we need not stop to review the contention. It is enough to say that the parties to a contract may release themselves, in whole or in part, from its obligations so far as they remain executory, by mutual agreement without fresh consideration. The release of one is sufficient consideration for the release of the other. If authority for a rule so elementary be required, see, for example: *Hanson & Parker v. Wittenberg*, 205 Mass. 319, 326; *Collyer & Co. v. Moulton*, 9 R.I. 90, 92; *McCreery v. Day*, 119 N.Y. 1, 7; *Dreifus, Block & Co. v. Salvage Co.*, 194 Pa. St. 475, 486.

One example of such an agreement would be the no-cost termination authorized in FAR 49.402-4(c) (and set forth in FAR 49.603-6 and 49.603-7), through which a contractor, typically to avoid the threat of default termination, will agree to waive all claims in a "no cost" termination. In *Folk Constr. Co.*, ENGBCA 5839, 93-3 BCA ¶ 26,094, although not following the reasoning of *Savage Arms*, the board found that the release of claims for additional compensation was valid consideration, stating at 129,728:

> [We] conclude that the release of claims element of the agreement satisfies the requirement for consideration. The claims were neither meritless on their face nor manufactured. Even if a tribunal subsequently determines that released or settled claims would have been resolved on their merits against the party advancing them, it will not *nunc pro tunc* divest the settlement of its consideration value. . . . Furthermore, withdrawal of even specious claims has been recognized as supplying consideration, where the defendant realizes the "nuisance value" of not defending against the allegations. See *Restatement, Second, Contracts* § 74(1).

Similarly, in *Aviation Contractor Employees, Inc. v. United States*, 945 F.2d 1568 (Fed. Cir. 1991), the claims were determined by the court to be meritless but were held to be the subject of an "honest dispute," with the result that their withdrawal was found to constitute consideration for a modification. See *Buesing v. United States*, 47 Fed. Cl. 621 (2000) ("A settlement agreement is a contract; mutual forbearance supplies the consideration.").

## 2. *Adequacy of Consideration*

It is a well-established rule that the boards and courts will inquire only into whether there has been a bargained-for exchange and not into the adequacy of the consideration, *Silverman v. United States*, 230 Ct. Cl. 701, 679 F.2d. 865 (1982); *Mills v. United States*, 187 Ct. Cl. 696, 410 F.2d 1255 (1969). There is no requirement that the parties' obligations be relatively equal, *United States v. American Trading Co.*, 138 F. Supp. 536 (N.D. Cal. 1956); *Aywon Wire & Metal Corp.*, ASBCA 4966, 1963 BCA ¶ 3912. The Claims Court has stated that a contract does not lack mutuality merely because a particular promise is not offset by a similar promise or obligation. Rather, "the pertinent question is whether the agreement as a whole is supported by mutual consideration," *Florida Keys Aqueduct Auth. v. United States*, 7 Cl. Ct. 297 (1985), *aff'd*, 790 F.2d 95 (Fed. Cir. 1986). See also *Bailer v. United States*, 54 Fed. Cl. 459 (2002), *aff'd*, 94 Fed. Appx. 828 (Fed. Cir. 2004), where the court responded to the argument that the bank's bargain was so "bad" that it should not be enforced, stating at 499:

> The court, however, does not evaluate the adequacy of consideration, only the ex-
> istence of consideration. Whether the arrangements were a "good deal" for one or
> the other or both parties is not a matter for the court. An implied-in-fact contract
> is a mutual endeavor, requiring a meeting of minds of both parties on all of the
> elements of a contract, including consideration. It is a long established rule that
> the court will inquire only into whether there has been a bargained for exchange,
> and not into the adequacy of consideration. The United States Court of Claims
> has stated: "As there is no indication of fraud or misrepresentation on the part of
> the plaintiff, the court is not concerned with the adequacy of the consideration
> furnished by the plaintiff." *Silverman v. United States*, 230 Ct. Cl. 701, 711, 679
> F.2d 865, 871 (1982).

However, if the consideration furnished by a party is so inadequate as to cause the tribunal to determine that the agreement would be unconscionable, it will not be enforced. See *Hume v. United States*, 132 U.S. 406 (1889), stating at 410:

> That an agreement to pay $1200 a ton for shucks, actual worth not more than $35
> a ton, is a grossly unconscionable bargain, defined in Bouvier's Law Dictionary to
> be "a contract which no man in his senses, not under delusion, would make, on the
> one hand, and which no fair and honest man would accept on the other," nobody
> can doubt. Such a contract, whether founded on fraud, accident, mistake, folly, or
> ignorance, is void at common law. It is not necessary to invoke the aid of a court
> of equity to reform it. Courts of law will always refuse to enforce such a bargain,
> as against the public policy of honesty, fair dealing, and good morals.

Similarly, GAO has indicated that it will not inquire into adequacy of the bargain when determining whether consideration exists. See, for example, 47 Comp. Gen. 170 (B-160886) (1967), stating at 173:

> However, it is well settled that the legal sufficiency of a promise or benefit is
> not dependent upon the adequacy of the bargain. In other words, an extravagant
> promise for an inadequate consideration will still be held to constitute legally
> sufficient consideration. See *Contracts*, 17 Am. Jur. 2d, sections 85, 92 and 102.
> Accordingly, we conclude that the portion of the amendment dealing with the
> culler-stacker is supported by consideration.

GAO has indicated that the reasoning behind the refusal to address the adequacy of the consideration lies in the belief that it is an issue of contract administration, better left to the individual agencies. See *Stancil-Hoffman Corp.*, Comp. Gen. Dec. B-193001.2, 80-2 CPD ¶ 226, stating:

> The issue as to adequacy of the consideration received by the Air Force for relaxing the delivery schedule of VRC's contract pertains to a matter of contract administration since the reinstatement of the contract has been found to be proper. As such, it is not for resolution within our bid protest function. See *Acadian Airmotive Inc.*, B-196414, 80-1 CPD ¶ 270.

## 3. Severability of Consideration

Government contracts involve a number of obligations of or benefits to each party. In general, such contracts are not divided into individual exchanges. Thus, the total benefit or detriment of one party is normally thought to be consideration for the total obligations of the other. Further, a single obligation or benefit can support a number of promises. See *Home Sav. of Am., F.S.B. v. United States*, 70 Fed. Cl. 303 (2006), finding that a single promise was adequate to constitute consideration for numerous promises by the other party, quoting 2 *Corbin on Contracts* § 5.12: "A single and undivided consideration may be bargained for and given as the agreed equivalent of one promise or of two promises or of many promises." However, these rules do not apply when the agreements are severable, for example, when a benefit or promise runs to only one portion of the contract. See *Telex Commc'ns, Inc. v. United States,* 40 Fed. Cl. 703 (1998), rejecting the contractor's argument that purchase orders based on a master contract were separate contracts, each subject to consideration requirement.

A few cases have found severable promises. In *Pennsylvania Exch. Bank v. United States*, 145 Ct. Cl. 216, 170 F. Supp. 629 (1959), the contract called for work in four steps. Steps I, II, and III required the contractor to tool up and get ready to manufacture exchange tees. Step IV required the contractor to stand by and be prepared to manufacture the tees. The contractor claimed it was not bound since the government was not obligated to order any tees under Step IV. The court first found that the contract was not severable. It then held that consideration existed even though the contractor was reimbursed only for its costs in Steps I, II, and III. The contractor was benefited by obtaining, at government expense, the capacity to produce the tees. Similarly, in *Shipco Gen., Inc.*, ASBCA 29206, 86-2 BCA ¶ 18,973, the government granted an extension of the contract completion date in consideration of the contractor's release of a valid claim. The contract modification contained a separate provision applying liquidated damages to a more demanding delivery requirement. The board held that the parties did not intend that the time extension relate to the altered provisions regarding the delivery schedule. Therefore, the agreements were severable and the revised delivery schedule failed for lack of consideration by the government. See also 47

Comp. Gen. 170 (B-160886) (1967), where GAO divided a contract amendment into three separate agreements for the purpose of consideration and found one to lack sufficient consideration, and *Hemet Valley Flying Serv. Co. v. United States*, 7 Cl. Ct. 512 (1985), where the Forest Service paid the contractor to be available to fly. This payment was an indivisible part of the contract which furnished consideration for the contractor's obligation to satisfy all the Forest Service's flight order needs. Similarly, in *Enron Fed. Sys., Inc. v. United States*, 80 Fed. Cl. 382 (2008), the court rejected the contractor's argument that the amortization of capital improvements was divisible from balance of the contract, and in *Parcel 49C Limited Partnership v. General Servs. Admin.*, GSBCA 15222, 00-2 BCA ¶ 31,073, the board rejected the government's argument that a lease and its supplemental agreements were separate agreements.

Because a release of a claim must be supported by consideration, severability of consideration has been used to avoid general releases included in change orders. For example, compensation for the increased costs of change orders was held to be inadequate to support a general release of the contractor's subsequent claims arising from the defective government property that precipitated the change orders, *Dero Indus., Inc.*, ASBCA 16473, 72-1 BCA ¶ 9462. See also *Sam Won Dev. Co.*, ASBCA 16541, 74-2 BCA ¶ 10,730, where the board stated that such a release by the contractor would be gratuitous. Furthermore, when the parties do not intend a time extension to be the sole consideration for a change order, claims for additional compensation arising from the change order are not precluded, *Discon Corp.*, ASBCA 15981, 71-2 BCA ¶ 9069. Where, however, the amount agreed upon by the negotiating parties is not clearly related solely to the change order involved, or there is a good faith dispute concerning either the entitlement to the adjustment or its amount, the inclusion of a broader release or waiver will be supported by the compromise agreement, *Boston Shipyard Corp. v. United States Military Sealift Command*, 886 F.2d 451 (1st Cir. 1989); *Spellman Eng'g Inc.*, NASABCA 367-11, 69-2 BCA ¶ 7891. Of course, a release already called for by the contract upon completion of performance is not lacking consideration even though the contractor receives only amounts otherwise due, *IMS Engineers-Architects, P.C. v. United States*, 92 Fed. Cl. 52 (2010); *Optimum Designs, Inc.*, ASBCA 16986, 74-1 BCA ¶ 10,622; *Inland Empire Builders, Inc. v. United States*, 191 Ct. Cl. 742, 424 F.2d 1370 (1970) (citing authorities). Such releases are based on the consideration contained in the government's promises in the original contract.

### 4.  Consideration in Variable Quantity Contracts

When the government wishes to obtain firm contractual commitments from contractors but is unable to forecast its precise needs, an indefinite-quantity contract is often used. There are three basic types of indefinite-quantity contracts. One of the most commonly used is the requirements contract, where the government agrees to purchase its "needs" or "requirements" from one contractor for a specified period of time. See FAR 16.503(a). There is no issue of consideration in this type of agreement because the contractor is bound to furnish items and the government's agrees to purchase its requirements solely from the contractor, *United States v. Purcell Envelope Co.*, 249 U.S. 313 (1919); *Ceredo Mortuary Chapel, Inc. v. United States*, 29 Fed. Cl. 346 (1993); *Vehicle Maint. Servs. v. General Servs. Admin.*, GSBCA 11663, 94-2 BCA ¶ 26,893. In *Machlett Labs., Inc.*, ASBCA 16194, 73-1 BCA ¶ 9929, the board found an enforceable contract even though the government never placed a single order. Similarly, in 52 Comp. Gen. 732 (B-176901) (1973), it was held that the use of a clause providing that "no guarantee is given that any quantities will be purchased" did not render a requirements contract unenforceable for lack of consideration.

An unusual case where the court enforced a requirements contract is *Torncello v. United States*, 231 Ct. Cl. 20, 681 F.2d 756 (1982). In this case, the contractor was awarded a requirements contract by the Navy for grounds maintenance and refuse removal. The contractor's bid itemization, accepted by the government, specified a per-call charge of $500 for any call under the pest control item. It turned out, however, that the Navy only needed gopher-control work which was customarily cheaper than $500 per call. Therefore, the Navy did not call the contractor for this work but instead requested such work from a competing bidder on the original solicitation. The contractor claimed that the Navy had breached its contract when it diverted work to a competing bidder. The court agreed and rejected the government's argument that the Termination for Convenience clause creates in the government an implicit right to refrain from giving a contractor work if it is not in the best interests of the government. The court stated at 42:

> It must be concluded, then, that the government's promise to turn to Soledad for all of its pest control work, if it was also implicit in the termination for convenience clause that the Government could give Soledad none, was no promise at all. The contract would thus fail [for lack of consideration].

A second type of indefinite-quantity contract requires the contractor to furnish all supplies or services ordered by the government but obligates the government to order only a stated minimum quantity. These are commonly referred to as "Indefinite-Delivery/Indefinite-Quantity" ("IDIQ") contracts. See FAR 16.504 and FAR 52.216-22. After the government has ordered the minimum quantity, it is free to order the remainder of its "needs" or "requirements" from either the same contractor or from any other source. However, the contractor continues to be bound to supply all that is ordered from it even after the minimum amount. Consideration to support this obligation of the contractor is found in the government's agreement to order the minimum quantity. See *J. Cooper & Assocs., Inc. v. United States,* 53 Fed. Cl. 8 (2002), *aff'd*, 65 Fed. Appx. 731 (Fed. Cir. 2003), stating at 17:

> Because the buyer is not obligated to purchase all requirements from the seller, unless the buyer contracts to purchase a minimum quantity, an IDIQ contract

is "illusory and the contract unenforceable against the seller." *Mason v. United States*, 222 Ct. Cl. at 443 n.5, 615 F.2d at 1346, n. 5, (citing *Willard, Sutherland & Co. v. United States*, 262 U.S. at 493, 43 S. Ct. 592; Corbin, *Contracts* § 157; *see also Coyle's Pest Control, Inc. v. Cuomo*, 154 F.3d 1302, 1304 (Fed. Cir.1998)).

The minimum order, however, must be for more than just a nominal amount in order for consideration to exist. See FAR 16.504(a)(2) stating:

> To ensure that the contract is binding, the minimum quantity must be more than a nominal quantity, but it should not exceed the amount that the Government is fairly certain to order.

See *Tennessee Soap Co. v. United States*, 130 Ct. Cl. 154, 126 F. Supp. 439 (1954), holding that a $10 minimum amount was nominal. However, IDIQ contracts with very small minimums have been held to have sufficient consideration. See *Travel Centre v. Barram*, 236 F.3d 1316 (Fed. Cir. 2001) ($100 minimum revenue); *CW Gov't Travel, Inc.*, Comp. Gen. Dec. B-295530, 2005 CPD ¶ 59, *recons. denied*, 2005 CPD ¶ 205 ($2,500 minimum amount on a contract with the $15,000,000 maximum order amount); *ABF Freight Sys., Inc.*, Comp. Gen. Dec. B-291185, 2002 CPD ¶ 201 (minimum of a "few hundred dollars"); *TRS Research*, Comp. Gen. Dec. B-290644, 2002 CPD ¶ 159 ($10,000 minimum on contract with estimated value of $45 million). In *C.W. Over & Sons, Inc.*, Comp. Gen. Dec. B-274365, 96-2 CPD ¶ 223, GAO held that the requirement that the value of an IDIQ contract be more than nominal does not apply to individual task orders under a contract. In this case, GAO found it sufficient that there was a guarantee minimum value of $800,000 for the base contract period.

Another type of indefinite-quantity contract is one that does not bind the government either to purchase its requirements or to place a minimum order. Such contracts are often referred to as "wish, want or will" contracts and are unenforceable for lack of consideration where no order is placed, *Modern Sys. Tech. Corp.*, 24 Cl. Ct. 360 (1991); *Updike v. United States*, 69 Ct. Cl. 394 (1930). However, if the government places an order with the contractor, it will be treated as an offer that the contractor may accept to form a binding agreement as to that particular order. See, for example, *Bel Pre Health Care Ctr. v. United States*, 24 Cl. Ct. 495 (1991); *Ann Riley & Assocs.*, DOTBCA 2418, 93-3 BCA ¶ 25,963. In *Ralph Constr., Inc. v. United States*, 4 Cl. Ct. 727 (1984), the court found lack of consideration in an indefinite-quantity contract that contained no promised minimum quantity and no firm requirements promise because the government had reserved the right to assign work to its own workforce. However, rather than finding that the entire contract was unenforceable for lack of consideration, the court found that it was valid only to the extent it was performed. On this basis, the court held that the contractor was entitled to the reasonable value of the work completed but was not entitled to additional costs. See also *Satellite Servs., Inc.*, Comp. Gen. Dec. B-280945, 98-2 CPD ¶ 125, finding lack of consideration when the contract contained a government promise to allow awardees to enter into limited competition for future task orders, but the contracting officer could deny contractors the right to compete if it was "in the best interest of the government."

If a contract is susceptible to interpretation as either an indefinite-quantity contract without a specified minimum order or a requirements contract, the general rule is that the court should uphold it as a requirements type, *A-Transport Northwest Co. v. United States,* 27 Fed. Cl. 206 (1992).

## 5.  *Consideration to Contractor*

Although it is clear that the government must receive consideration for the execution of a contract modification, there is a split of authority on the need for the contractor to receive consideration. GAO has held that a contractor need not receive consideration to be bound by a contract modification, Comp. Gen. Dec. B-151383, Nov. 3, 1966, *Unpub.* See also *Mid-State Prods. Co. v. Commodity Credit Corp.*, 196 F.2d 416 (7th Cir. 1952); and *Equipment Corp. v. United States*, 98 Ct. Cl. 159 (1942).

It is doubtful if this rule will be followed at the current time. Several boards of contract appeals have held that a contractor must receive consideration. In one case, a $700 credit to the government for substitution of a conforming brand was held to be without consideration since the government was obligated to accept a conforming brand under the original contract, *Hunt Bldg. Marts*, DOTCAB 69-6, 69-2 BCA ¶ 8042. A second case involved the government's reduction of the contract price for a nonconforming item. Having determined that the item was acceptable, the board held that the agreement reducing the price was without consideration and, thus, not binding, *Airco Eng'rs*, AGBCA 245, 72-1 BCA ¶ 9215. In a third case, the government issued a unilateral contract modification adding a Liquidated Damages clause to the contract. The board held that because the amount of liquidated damages to be assessed in the event of delay is a vital condition affecting the price of a contract, the government's unilateral modification was not supported by consideration and, therefore, was not binding upon the contractor, *Jacqueline Howell, Ltd.*, ASBCA 27026, 82-2 BCA ¶ 16,086. See also *Yardney Tech. Prods., Inc.*, ASBCA 53866, 09-2 BCA ¶ 34,277, finding no consideration when the contractor agreed to correct a specification error for no increase in price.

In addition, at least one board of contract appeals has adopted the view in *Restatement, Second, Contracts* § 89 that allows modification of an executory agreement without consideration to the contractor —

> (a) if the modification is fair and equitable in view of circumstances not anticipated by the parties when the contract was made; or (b) to the extent provided by statute; or (c) to the extent that justice requires enforcement in view of a material change of position in reliance on the promise.

See *Florida East Coast Props., Inc.*, GSBCA 7538, 86-3 BCA ¶ 19,070; *Universal Bldg. Servs. Inc.*, GSBCA 7396, 85-1 BCA ¶ 17,732; *Zebra Corp.*, GSBCA 4723, 80-2 BCA ¶ 14,484.

## C. Promissory Estoppel

Promissory estoppel is a concept developed by the courts to enforce agreements on the basis of fairness and justice when consideration is not present but a person has reasonably relied on a promise. Whereas equitable estoppel is used to bar a party from raising a defense or objection, promissory estoppel is used to create a cause of action, *Knaub v. United States*, 22 Cl. Ct. 268 (1991). The necessary requirements for application of promissory estoppel are stated in *Restatement, Second, Contracts* § 90:

> (1) A promise which the promisor should reasonably expect to induce action or forbearance on the part of the promisee or a third person and which does induce such action or forbearance is binding if injustice can be avoided only by enforcement of the promise. The remedy granted for breach may be limited as justice requires.

Promissory estoppel has been infrequently used in government contracts, and it would appear that in some of the cases where is has been applied, it has been used unnecessarily. See, for example, *George H. Whike Constr. Co. v. United States*, 135 Ct. Cl. 126, 140 F. Supp. 560 (1956), where the bidder entered into a written contract and performed it upon the assurance that the provision for reimbursement included in its bid would protect it from increased costs resulting from changes in labor regulations. It seems apparent that either the contractor's agreement or its subsequent performance should have been sufficient consideration. There was no need to resort to promissory estoppel since the "acts in reliance" were the very things bargained for by the government. See also *Lockheed Shipbuilding & Constr. Co.*, ASBCA 18460, 75-1 BCA ¶ 11,246, *recons. denied*, 75-2 BCA ¶ 11,566, and *Mercury Mach. & Mfg. Co.*, ASBCA 20068, 76-1 BCA ¶ 11,809, where all of the elements of consideration were present but the board held for the contractor based on "equitable or promissory estoppel." In *Louisiana Lamps & Shades*, ASBCA 45294, 95-1 BCA ¶ 27,577, the board held that the government did not establish promissory estoppel because the government did not prove that the terminating contracting officer relied on the contractor's promise to deliver the work by a certain date when deciding not to terminate the contractor for default.

There is a long line of decisions holding that the Court of Federal Claims has no jurisdiction over claims against the government on the theory of promissory estoppel because it is, in effect, a contract implied-in-law, over which the court has no jurisdiction. See *Steinberg v. United States*, 90 Fed. Cl. 435, 443 (2009) ("Promissory estoppel . . . requires the court find an implied-in-law contract, [and therefore the court has no jurisdiction, because such] a claim [is one] for which the United States has not waived its sovereign immunity."); *LaMirage, Inc. v. United States*,

44 Fed. Cl. 192 (1999) ("It is well settled that this court is without jurisdiction to entertain claims arising from a contract, based on the theory of promissory estoppel, or based on contracts implied-in-law."); *Hubbs v. United States*, 20 Cl. Ct. 423, 427 (1990) ("[p]romissory estoppel is another name for an implied-in-law contract claim."). See *Craig-Buff Ltd. P'ship v. United States*, 69 Fed. Cl. 382 (2006), and *Sinclair v. United States*, 56 Fed. Cl. 270 (2003), reasoning that promissory estoppel is a theory used to "create" a contract "that would not otherwise exist" and such a contract must be an implied-in-law contract over which the court has no jurisdiction. The Federal Circuit has not ruled on this issue. See, however, *Pacific Gas & Elec. Co. v. United States*, 3 Cl. Ct. 329 (1983), *aff'd*, 738 F.2d 452 (Fed. Cir. 1984), affirmed a decision denying a claim of promissory estoppel without a discussion of promissory estoppel.

This rationale does not recognize the distinction between promissory estoppel and implied-in-law contracts. Although both concepts are based upon considerations of justice and fairness, promissory estoppel requires that the person being charged make an actual promise, express or implied in fact. On the other hand, the "promises" referred to in contracts implied in law (alternatively referred to as "quasi contracts") are legal fictions. They are "implied" by courts to recognize that a person of good faith would want to pay compensation for a benefit that they received from another. They are based upon the legal and equitable rules of restitution, which, according to the Supreme Court, are not covered by the Tucker Act, *Merritt v. United States*, 267 U.S. 338 (1925).

The boards of contract appeals have also ruled that they have no jurisdiction over claims based on promissory estoppel. See *P.J. Dick, Inc. v. General Servs. Admin.*, CBCA 461, 07-1 BCA ¶ 33,534; *RGW Commc'ns, Inc.*, ASBCA 54495, 05-2 BCA ¶ 32,972; *Embarcadero Center, Ltd.*, GSBCA 8526, 89-1 BCA ¶ 21,362. In *RGW Commc'ns* the board rejected the applicability of a prior case, *United Pacific Ins. Co.*, ASBCA 52419, 04-1 BCA ¶ 32,494, *aff'd*, 401 F.3d 1362 (Fed. Cir. 2005), which had discussed whether the elements of promissory estoppel existed because that discussion was in "a 'straw man' or 'even if' fashion." For other cases discussing whether the elements of promissory estoppel are present, see *Systems Mgmt. Am. Corp.*, ASBCA 45704, 97-1 BCA ¶ 28,820 (claim reinstated to determine whether contractor's reliance was based on assurances that option would be exercised); *State Street Mgmt. Corp. v. General Servs. Admin.*, GSBCA 12374, 94-1 BCA ¶ 26,500 (government statements not specific enough for reliance); and *Louisiana Lamps & Shades, ASBCA* 45294, 95-1 BCA ¶ 27,577 (government did not prove reliance in its claim based on promissory estoppel).

In *Law Mathematics & Tech., Inc. v. United States*, 779 F.2d 675 (Fed. Cir. 1985), on appeal from a board of contract appeals, the contractor argued that it took certain actions in reliance on the government's assurances that it would provide additional funds on the contract. The court held that even if the government had made such assurances and the contractor had relied upon them, the contractor still could not recover. The court held that the contractor's reliance would not have been reasonable, stating at 679:

> Finally, even if LMT had relied to its detriment on any promises or assertions, such reliance could not have been reasonable in this case. Dr. Sponsler is an attorney, with the ability to understand the specific limitations of the contract language. Moreover, Sponsler is also a former Navy employee, and should have been, if he was not, familiar with the uncertainty of relying on additional allocations to Navy research contracts.

In another appeal from a board of contract appeals, the government argued that promissory estoppel was not available against the government. In a decision not for precedent, the court did not address this argument, disposing of the appeal on the grounds that the contractor did not offer "any concrete evidence that it relied on a promise to change its position for the worse," *Delfour, Inc. v. Runyon*, 95 F.3d 1163 (Fed. Cir. 1996).

# CHAPTER 3

# ACQUISITION PLANNING

"Acquisition planning" is an expansive term that includes actions aimed at stating the government's needs, identifying potential sources, and determining the techniques to be used to satisfy those needs. It is the first step in the procurement process. FAR 2.101 contains the following broad definition:

> "Acquisition planning" means the process by which the efforts of all personnel responsible for an acquisition are coordinated and integrated through a comprehensive plan for fulfilling the agency need in a timely manner and at a reasonable cost. It includes developing the overall strategy for managing the acquisition.

A well-planned procurement will be structured to comply with the numerous acquisition laws and regulations as well as to obtain, most effectively, the goods or services needed by the agency. A procurement that is not well planned can lead to numerous problems that waste the time and funds of both the procuring agency and the offerors.

This chapter reviews all elements of acquisition planning conducted by a procuring agency. The first section explains the planning process as mandated by law and implemented by regulation. The next two sections cover the requirement for competition and the selection of the contracting technique. The fourth section addresses identifying sources for obtaining goods or services. The fifth section deals with the preparation of the statement of work. The sixth section deals with the consideration of overall cost to the government in the acquisition planning process. The final section covers public announcements and solicitations.

## I.  PLANNING PROCESS

The planning process brings all members of the acquisition team together to formulate the strategy that will be used to conduct a procurement.

### A.  Requirement for Planning

As a result of deficiencies in the planning process, a number of agencies began to focus on the need for more formalized acquisition planning in the 1970s. Congress also identified this need during discussions on the Competition in Contracting Act of 1984 (CICA). As a result, the Armed Services Procurement Act and the Federal Property and Administrative Services Act now require that an executive agency "use advance procurement planning and market research" in preparing for the procurement of property or services, 10 U.S.C. § 2305(a)(1)(A)(ii); 41 U.S.C. § 3306(a)(1)(B). FAR Part 7 implements this requirement.

FAR 7.102 (b) states that "[t]he purpose of this planning is to ensure that the government meets its needs in the most effective, economical, and timely manner." The acquisition planning requirement in FAR 7.102 is pervasive:

> Agencies shall perform acquisition planning and conduct market research (see part 10) for all acquisitions in order to promote and provide for —
>
> (1) Acquisition of commercial items or, to the extent that commercial items suitable to meet the agency's needs are not available, nondevelopmental items, to the maximum extent practicable (10 U.S.C. 2377 and 41 U.S.C. 251, *et seq.*); and
>
> (2) Full and open competition (see part 6), or, when full and open competition is not required in accordance with part 6, to obtain competition to the maximum extent practicable, with due regard to the nature of the supplies or services to be acquired (10 U.S.C. 2301(a)(5) and 41 U.S.C. 253a(a)(1)).

In some cases, the lack of adequate acquisition planning will place the agency in a position where it will attempt to acquire supplies and services without obtaining full and open competition. See *Freund Precision, Inc.*, 66 Comp. Gen. 90 (B-223613), 86-2 CPD ¶ 543 (failure to plan ahead precluded agency from evaluating protester's alternate product and resulted in sole source procurement); and *TeQcom, Inc.*, Comp. Gen. Dec. B-224664, 86-2 CPD ¶ 700 (failure to plan ahead effectively deprived offerors of any opportunity to qualify their products so that they could compete with the brand name manufacturer). In this regard, lack of advance planning does not justify noncompetitive procurement, as stated in 10 U.S.C. § 2304(f)(4) and 41 U.S.C. § 3304(e)(5)(a)(i):

> In no case may the head of an agency —
>
> (A) enter into a contract for property or services using procedures other than competitive procedures on the basis of the lack of advance planning.

See also FAR 6.301(c) prohibiting justification of contracting without full and open competition based on a lack of advance planning.

Cases finding a lack of advance planning include *eFedBudget Corp.*, Comp. Gen. Dec. B-298627, 2006 CPD ¶ 159 (no record of steps taken by agency to overcome proprietary software); *VSE Corp.*, Comp. Gen. Dec. B-290452.3, 2005 CPD ¶ 103 (no effort to plan for a competitive bridge contract when agency knew it would cancel solicitation for follow on contract); *Signals & Sys., Inc.*, Comp. Gen. Dec. B-288107, 2001 CPD ¶ 168 (agency took two years to draft performance specification permitting competition); *TLC Servs., Inc.*, Comp. Gen. Dec. B-252614, 93-1 CPD ¶ 481 (agency could not prepare work statement because of inadequate and inexperienced staff); *K-Whit Tools, Inc.*, Comp. Gen. Dec. B-247081, 92-1 CPD

¶ 382 (agency took 10 months to determine requirements when it knew that the items were required by a fixed deadline); *Service Contractors*, Comp. Gen. Dec. B-243236, 91-2 CPD ¶ 49 (procurement process for ongoing services commenced six months after expiration of prior contract); and *Pacific Sky Supply, Inc.*, 66 Comp. Gen. 370 (B-225513), 87-1 CPD ¶ 358 (nine-week delay in processing paperwork on qualification requirement).

Advance planning need not be entirely error-free or actually successful, *Sprint Commc'ns Co.*, Comp. Gen. Dec. B-262003.2, 96-1 CPD ¶ 24. See also *Filtration Dev. Co., LLC v. United States*, 60 Fed. Cl. 371 (2004) (agency made several un-successful attempts to address the problem before issuing the urgent procurement); *Bannum, Inc.*, Comp. Gen. B-289707, 2002 CPD ¶ 61 (while the agency's planning ultimately was unsuccessful, this was due to unanticipated events, not a lack of planning). However, the planning actions must be reasonable. In *New Breed Leasing Corp.*, Comp. Gen. Dec. B-274201, 96-2 CPD ¶ 202, GAO sustained a protest, find-ing that had the agency engaged in reasonable advance planning, it would not have taken more than a year after the solicitations were issued to realize that the solicita-tions were fundamentally flawed in failing to contain basic information. Similarly, in *Commercial Drapery Contractors, Inc.*, Comp. Gen. Dec. B-271222, 96-1 CPD ¶ 290, an agency sought to justify its issuance of purchase orders to a Multiple Award Federal Supply Schedule contractor at higher prices than offered by other Federal Supply Schedule contractors by arguing that it urgently needed the supplies and only the selected contractor could meet the delivery time. GAO sustained the protest, finding that the urgency resulted from delays caused by the agency's prior improper issuance of purchase orders to the same contractor for the same require-ment and the subsequent cancellation of those orders in response to clearly meritori-ous protests. See, however, *Datacom, Inc.*, Comp. Gen. Dec. B-274175, 96-2 CPD ¶ 199, rejecting the protester's claim that the urgency necessitating a noncompetitive sole source award and contract modification resulted from the lack of advance plan-ning. GAO found that the Air Force had failed to compete its procurement because a congressional report directing the agency to go no further in its effort to hold a competition of any kind. See also *Argon ST, Inc.*, Comp. Gen. Dec. B-402908, 2011 CPD ¶ 4 (planning adequate when agency took over a year to formulate plan for competition); *Diversified Tech. & Servs. of Virginia., Inc.*, Comp. Gen. Dec. B-282497, 99-2 CPD ¶ 16 (refusing to fault agency where the procurement was delayed by the agency's efforts to implement a long-term acquisition plan).

Potential bidders' ability to assess and challenge agencies' acquisition plan-ning is complicated by the mechanics of the bid protest process. Offerors gen-erally have little real access to the agencies' internal planning documents, as those materials are generally not made public. See *Holmes & Narver Servs., Inc./ Morrison-Knudsen Servs., Inc.*, Comp. Gen. Dec. B-235906, 89-2 CPD ¶ 379 (acquisition plan to be released to erase competitive imbalance). Moreover, even if a protest is brought GAO has shown deference to agency planning process-es, even if only minimal, *Warden Assocs., Inc.*, Comp. Gen. Dec. B-291440,

2002 CPD ¶ 223 (agency conducted sufficient planning under FAR Subpart 8.4 by simply contacting vendors); *Sales Res. Consultants, Inc.*, Comp. Gen. Dec. B-284943, 2000 CPD ¶ 102 (surveying schedule vendors adequate, so long as appropriately documented); *Wescam, Inc.*, Comp. Gen. Dec. B-285792, 2000 CPD ¶ 168 (agency produced written plan and emails reflecting internal planning); *N&N Travel & Tours, Inc.*, Comp. Gen. Dec. B-285164.2, 2000 CPD ¶ 146 (challenges to inadequate planning for IDIQ task order were outside GAO's limited jurisdiction). Furthermore, GAO has held that, if an agency does have a plan and deviates from that plan, that deviation is not a ground for protest, *Hubbell Elec. Heater Co.*, Comp. Gen. Dec. B-289098, 2000 CPD ¶ 15 ("Acquisition plans are internal agency instructions and as such do not give outside parties any rights."). Protesters at GAO must also show that they were prejudiced by a failure in the planning process, as GAO explained in *Frasca Int'l, Inc.*, Comp. Gen. Dec. B-293299, 2004 CPD ¶ 38:

> We need not reach the issue of whether the Navy has sufficiently justified its consolidation of the requirements because the record does not show that the protester has suffered any prejudice, even if the requirements were improperly consolidated. Competitive prejudice is an essential element of every viable protest; where the record does not demonstrate that, but for the agency's actions, the protester would have had a reasonable chance of receiving the award, our Office will not sustain a protest, even if a deficiency in the procurement is found.

As a practical matter, therefore, sound acquisition planning is more likely to result from internal agency pressures than from external challenges by bidders. See FAR 7.104(d)(1) requiring that acquisition planning be coordinated with the agency small business specialist.

The fact that a procurement is noncompetitive does not necessarily establish that there was a lack of acquisition planning. See *Starwin Indus.*, Comp. Gen. Dec. B-401576, 2009 CPD ¶ 199, where the agency made a reasonable decision to waive first article testing requirements; and *Honeycomb Co. of Am.*, Comp. Gen. Dec. B-225685, 87-1 CPD ¶ 579, where the agency made a reasonable but unsuccessful effort to obtain competition. GAO distinguished such a case from those where there was an absence of advance planning. See also *Sprint Commc'ns Co., L.P.*, Comp. Gen. Dec. B-262003.2, 96-1 CPD ¶ 24, stating that there was no requirement that planning be successful. In *Rex Sys., Inc.*, Comp. Gen. Dec. B-239524, 90-2 CPD ¶ 185, the agency's continued negotiations with a failing contractor placed it in a position of urgency requiring a sole source award. Although GAO in "hindsight" indicated that it might disagree with how long the negotiations were allowed to continue, it was unable to say that such actions were unreasonable. GAO found that the efforts sought to establish the failing contractor as an alternate source and were therefore related to procurement planning and fostering competition. The fact that the efforts were unsuccessful did not constitute a lack of planning.

## B.  Statement of Need

The acquisition plan should begin with a brief statement of need. The need for the acquisition is identified and documented by the program or technical personnel in the agency who prepare the budget justification. Generally, the need will have been fully justified during the budget process and can merely be restated in the acquisition plan. See OMB Circular A-11: *Preparation, Submission and Execution of the Budget* (2004), available at *www.omb.gov* (outlining steps to budget review process). If the acquisition planning is being done prior to preparing the budget, the agency will have to analyze its needs in a thorough manner as part of the acquisition plan.

The plan should "[s]pecify the required capabilities or performance characteristics of the supplies or the performance standards of the services being acquired and state how they are related to the need," FAR 7.105(a)(4). This requirement should assist the agency in identifying restrictive provisions in the statement of work that may preclude potential contractors from participating in the procurement. When such provisions are identified, an agency can address possible ways to eliminate them. The guidance on restrictive specifications is reviewed below in the discussion of specifications.

## C.  Contents of Plan

The acquisition plan must identify all actions essential to the conduct of a successful procurement and establish milestones for their performance. See FAR 7.105, which provides the following general guidance regarding the elements of the acquisition plan:

> In order to facilitate attainment of the acquisition objectives, the plan must identify those milestones at which decisions should be made (see subparagraph (b)(18) below). The plan must address all the technical, business, management, and other significant considerations that will control the acquisition. The specific content of plans will vary, depending on the nature, circumstances, and stage of the acquisition.

FAR 7.105(a) contains a brief description of the elements of the acquisition plan under the category "Acquisition Background and Objectives," while FAR 7.105(b) describes additional elements under the category "Plan of Action." The Background and Objectives section considers what the government is buying, how it will evaluate price and other cost factors, where the work is to be performed, and the risks involved. The Plan of Action section describes the steps necessary to procure the identified articles or services. Although the elements are discussed separately, they are interrelated. For a model acquisition plan published by one civilian agency, see U.S. Department of Justice, Justice Management Division, "The Department of Justice Systems Development Life Cycle Guidance Document," App. C-6 (Jan. 2003), available at *http://www.usdoj.gov/jmd/irm/lifecycle/appendixc6.htm.*

The contents of the acquisition plan also should include a summary of any contractual history, FAR 7.105(a). This summary, normally done by the contracting officer, should identify each previous procurement that impacts the current planning. This is a key element in the planning process because it identifies how the current procurement fits in the overall conduct of the agency's business. The contractual history also identifies those cases where the procurement is part of an ongoing program, such as the development of a new product. In such cases, the agency normally will have adopted an acquisition plan for the entire program, and the planning for each step in the program will merely verify that the overall plan is still valid. On the other hand, the contractual history may identify previous procurements that have been unsuccessful — indicating that a new approach is needed. Thus, the contractual history is a key starting point for the preparation of the plan.

The plan should contain a concise statement of the acquisition strategy to be followed. See, for example, DoD Instruction 5000.02, "Operation of the Defense Acquisition System" (Dec. 8, 2008), *http://www.dtic.mil/whs/directives/corres/pdf/5000002p.pdf,* which contains general guidance on arriving at a sound acquisition strategy within the Department of Defense (DoD). This regulation describes the planning of an acquisition strategy for a new system as an iterative process that becomes increasingly more definitive as the system progresses from the initial stages of advanced research to production. Curiously, the FAR does not require agencies to include a summary of the acquisition strategy in the plan. Nonetheless, planners should strive to draft a clear and explicit statement of the agency's strategy to ensure that all agency personnel understand how the procurement goal is to be achieved.

In formulating the acquisition strategy, the entire planning team should review all acquisition alternatives that could be used to conduct the procurement. Any acquisition strategy that will enhance the procurement should be considered as an alternative, and all members of the team should be encouraged to propose ideas. This element of the plan calls for innovative thinking, especially if the acquisition techniques used in the past have not been fully successful.

The Plan of Action called for by FAR 7.105(b) also should include such considerations as the method for obtaining and using priorities, allocations, and allotments; consideration of make-or-buy programs; description of the test and evaluation program of the contractor and government; description of logistical support; applicable environmental issues associated with the acquisition; how security will be established, maintained, and monitored; what government property or information will be furnished to the contractor; what management system will be used by the government to monitor the contractor's effort; as well as any other consideration that might impact the procurement. For a discussion of these elements of the acquisition plan, see Chapter 1 of Nash, Cibinic & O'Brien-DeBakey, *Competitive Negotiation: The Source Selection Process* (3d ed. 2011).

## 1. Acquisition Milestones

Each acquisition plan should contain a specific set of milestones for the procurement. The basic milestones are set forth in FAR 7.105(b)(20):

Acquisition plan approval.

Statement of work.

Specifications.

Data requirements.

Completion of acquisition-package preparation.

Purchase request.

Justification and approval for other than full and open competition where applicable and/or any required D&F approval.

Issuance of synopsis.

Issuance of solicitation.

Evaluation of proposals, audits, and field reports.

Beginning and completion of negotiations.

Contract preparation, review, and clearance.

Contract award.

Any additional steps that are required to implement the acquisition plan should also be included in the milestone chart.

## 2. Applicable Conditions

This part of the plan identifies the constraints that must be imposed on the end product of the procurement, as set forth in FAR 7.105(a)(2):

*Applicable conditions.* State all significant conditions affecting the acquisition, such as

(i) requirements for compatibility with existing or future systems or programs and

(ii) any known cost, schedule, and capability or performance constraints.

Precise identification of significant conditions early in the procurement process enables the agency to explore steps that can be taken to reduce or eliminate constraints that could have a detrimental impact on the procurement being planned. For example, if a product to be procured must be fully compatible with items in the agency's inventory, the agency may have to provide detailed drawings in the procurement package or induce the original manufacturer to license other sources in order to obtain sufficient competition to ensure a reasonable price. In this case, identification of this constraint would lead to the adoption of a strategy that would make detailed drawings available to a number of competitors.

Of course, identification of a constraint does not guarantee that there is a strategy that will completely overcome it. Many constraints must be accepted as an inherent element of the procurement. However, early identification of such constraints is beneficial because it assists all members of the planning team in recognizing the limitations that must be accepted in the conduct of the procurement being planned.

### 3. Justifications and Approvals

When the acquisition plan proposes a strategy that entails using a procurement procedure that is "other than competitive," 41 U.S.C. § 253(f)(2) and 10 U.S.C. § 3304(e)(2) require the contracting officer to provide written justification for the use of such procedures, containing the following six elements:

(A) a description of the agency's needs;

(B) an identification of the statutory exception from the requirement to use competitive procedures and a demonstration, based on the proposed contractor's qualifications or the nature of the procurement, of the reasons for using that exception;

(C) a determination that the anticipated cost will be fair and reasonable;

(D) a description of the market survey conducted or a statement of the reasons a market survey was not conducted;

(E) a listing of the sources, if any, that expressed in writing an interest in the procurement; and

(F) a statement of the actions, if any, the agency may take to remove or overcome any barrier to competition before a subsequent procurement for such needs.

See FAR 6.303-2 for additional guidance on the contents of this justification.

This justification must be certified as accurate and complete by the contracting officer responsible for awarding the contract, 41 U.S.C. § 3304(e)(1)(A), 10 U.S.C. § 2304(f)(1)(A). It must then be reviewed and approved pursuant to 41 U.S.C. § 3304(e)(1)(B) and 10 U.S.C. § 2304(f)(1)(B), as follows:

| Contract Amount | | Approval Authority |
|---|---|---|
| Over | Not in Excess of | |
| $500,000 | $10,000,000 | Competition advocate without delegation |
| $10,000,000 | $50,000,000 | Head of Procuring Activity or delegate (Flag Officer or GS-16 rank or above) |
| $50,000,000 | — — — — — — | Senior Procurement Executive of Agency without delegation |

In addition such Justifications and Approvals (J&As) must be published, 41 U.S.C. § 3304(f) and 10 U.S.C. § 2304(f)(4). See FAR 6.305 calling for such publication on *www.fedbizopps.gov* and providing guidance on the time and contents of this publication.

J&As should be prepared and approved during the acquisition planning process. However, they may be written subsequently and even after award if circumstances warrant, such as when preparation and approval prior to award would unreasonably delay the acquisition, FAR 6.303-1(e). While late preparation of a J&A may not represent good planning, the lateness will not affect the validity of an otherwise proper J&A, *Systems Integration & Mgmt., Inc.*, Comp. Gen. Dec. B-402785.2, 2010 CPD ¶ 207 (J&A written one week after protest was filed); *AUTOFLEX, Inc.*, Comp. Gen. Dec. B-240012, 90-2 CPD ¶ 294, *recons. denied*, 90-2 CPD ¶ 370 (J&A executed after the closing date for receipt of proposals but prior to award); and *Magnavox Elec. Sys. Co.*, Comp. Gen. Dec. B-258076.2, 94-2 CPD ¶ 266 (J&A not invalidated even though modified and signed by the approving authority after the lower-level officials had signed it and after a protest was filed). Similarly, if additional facts are learned after a J&A has been prepared, an amended J&A will satisfy the detailed requirements for information that must be included, *Minowitz Mfg. Co.*, Comp. Gen. Dec. B-228502, 88-1 CPD ¶ 1.

A procurement may be overturned if the J&A does not contain a reasonable explanation for the avoidance of full and open competition, *Racal Corp.*, Comp. Gen. Dec. B-233240, 89-1 CPD ¶ 169 (agency couldn't demonstrate its need to use a specific make and model specification); *Sturm, Ruger & Co.*, Comp. Gen. Dec. B-235938, 89-2 CPD ¶ 375 (documentation not meeting the specific requirements applicable to J&As was insufficient to justify the avoidance of full and open competition); *NI Indus., Inc., Vernon Div.*, Comp. Gen. Dec. B-223941, 86-2 CPD ¶ 674 (elimination of one of two mobilization base contractors was not adequately justified where the J&A contained no statement of the particular facts and circumstances that would justify a sole source award); or if the J&A does not bear a reasonable relationship to the agency's actual requirements, *Sabreliner Corp.*, Comp. Gen. Dec. B-288030, 2001 CPD ¶ 170. See also *Google, Inc. v. United States*, 95 Fed. Cl. 661 (2011), where the court enjoined a sole source procurement because the justification was signed by an unauthorized official well after the procurement commenced and did not analyze the costs the agency would incur by dealing with only one contractor.

Class J&As are permitted if approved in writing in accordance with agency procedures, FAR 6.303-1(c). When class J&As are used, the approval level should be determined by the estimated total value of the class, FAR 6.304(c). Class J&As will not be sufficient if they do not relate to the particular facts and circumstances of the specific procurement being questioned, *NI Indus., Inc., Vernon Div.*, Comp. Gen. Dec. B-223941, 86-2 CPD ¶ 674.

## D. Preparation of Plan

An effective plan must be timely prepared and have the participation of all agency personnel whose input can affect its viability. In addition, attention should be given to program requirements as well as individual contracts.

### 1. Time of Preparation

It is essential that acquisition planning be done early in the process to ensure that all actions necessary to carry out an effective procurement can be performed within the procurement cycle. FAR 7.104(a) provides that "[a]cquisition planning should begin as soon as the agency need is identified, preferably well in advance of the fiscal year in which contract award or order placement is necessary." This recognizes that a complex procurement may require up to several years from the time the requirement is identified until a contract is awarded. In such cases, acquisition planning must start at essentially the same time as the budget process and must be executed simultaneously. This, of course, means that if the requirement is ultimately not funded, some planning effort will be wasted. However, to ensure that the ultimate procurement is carried out effectively, such a risk may be unavoidable.

DoD Directive 5000.1, Mar. 15, 1996, identified that, in the acquisition of a new system, the acquisition process is concurrent with both the budgeting process and the requirements generation process. See **Figure 3-1**. These three key management processes, then, are completely interactive, and acquisition planning must be done very early in the life of a new system. While this directive has been replaced with later instructions that do not include this guidance, this is still good guidance on the time that acquisition planning should commence.

Feb 23, 91
5000.1 (Part 2)

PART 2

## INTEGRATED MANAGEMENT FRAMEWORK

A. OVERVIEW

The policies established in Part 1 forge a closer, more effective interface among the Department's three major decisionmaking support systems affecting acquisition. These are the:

- Requirements Generation System.
- Acquisition Management System.
- Planning, Programming, and Budgeting System.

This part describes the major characteristics of each system and highlights the complex relationships that must be maintained for effective decisionmaking. These characteristics and relationships define the integrated management framework for defense acquisition. This part describes the disciplined integration of the three systems and is not intended to establish policy. Elements of the decisionmaking systems described below are adjusted as necessary to assist the Secretary of Defense in decisionmaking as circumstances change.

## THE THREE SYSTEMS

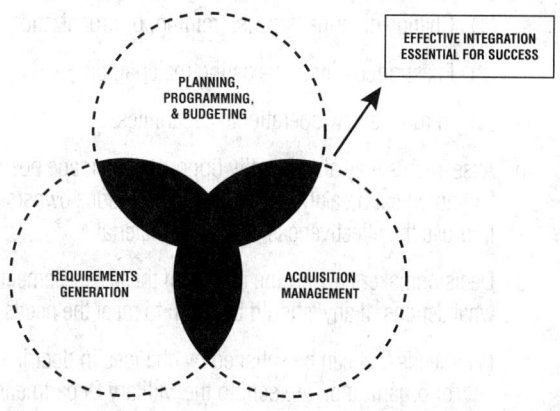

Figure 3-1 (cont'd on next page)

B.    REQUIREMENTS GENERATION SYSTEM

   1.   Overview. The requirements generation system produces information for decisionmakers on projected mission needs.

     a.   The needs identified are expressed initially in broad operational terms. They are progressively translated into system-specific performance requirements.

     b.   This evolutionary approach enables decisionmakers to make informed cost-performance-schedule trade-offs at critical points in a program's implementation.

### REQUIREMENTS EVOLUTION

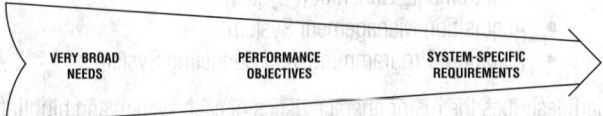

   2.   Identifying and Processing Mission Needs. Mission needs are identified as a direct result of continuing assessments of current and projected capabilites in the context of changing military threats and national defense policy.

     a.   The assesments are conducted by the Unified and Specified Commands, the Military Departments, the Office of the Secretary of Defense, and the Chairman of the Joint Chiefs of Staff. Their purpose is to identify deficiencies that may result in a need to:

       (1)   Change doctrine, tactics, training, or organization;

       (2)   Fix shortcomings in existing material; or

       (3)   Introduce new operational capabilites.

     b.   Assesments may also identify opportunities made possible by technological breakthroughs that could reduce ownership costs or improve the effectiveness of current material.

     c.   Decisionmakers review the results of these assessments to determine what actions, if any, should be taken to meet the needs identified.

       (1)   Needs that can be satisfied by changes in doctrine, tactics, training, or organization are sent to the Military Departments for consideration and action.

**Figure 3-1 (cont'd from previous page)**

Other agencies have also sought to ensure that acquisition planning is conducted on a timely basis. For example, NFS 1807.7102-1 requires NASA field centers to prepare "Master Buy Plans" for major procurements and obtain NASA Headquarters approval on a timely basis.

The acquisition plan should be revised and changed whenever necessary. FAR 7.104(a) provides:

> At key dates specified in the plan or whenever significant changes occur, and no less often than annually, the planner shall review the plan and, if appropriate, revise it.

## 2. Form of Plan

The FAR does not deal with the question of when written acquisition plans should be prepared but, rather, places this responsibility on agency heads, FAR 7.103(d). Some agencies, such as the DoD, require written plans only for large-dollar acquisitions (acquisitions for development when costs are $10 million or more and for production or services when costs are $50 million or more for all years) but permit the use of written plans for smaller procurements, DFARS 207.103(d)(i)(C).

Civilian agencies tend to require written acquisition plans at lower-dollar thresholds. For example, the General Services Administration requires plans almost all acquisitions, allowing "oral plans in "unusual and compelling situations," GSA Acquisition Manual, ¶ 507.105(b). NASA requires written plans for procurement over $10 million and leaves it to the procuring activity to establish thresholds for written plans for smaller procurements, NFS 1807.103.

## 3. Responsibility for Preparing Plan

Although FAR 7.102 requires agencies to conduct acquisition planning, it does not require the contracting officer to manage the planning process — it merely permits each procuring agency to designate the person or office responsible for acquisition planning. The DoD provides that the program manager, or other official responsible for the program, has overall responsibility for acquisition planning, DFARS 207.103(g). The Navy states that the acquisition program manager has overall responsibility for acquisition planning and implementing the acquisition plan, Department of the Navy Acquisition Planning Guide (Apr. 1992). The Air Force requires that an acquisition strategy panel be held for many acquisitions, although that requirement is waivable, AFFARS 5307.104-90. NASA similarly requires a "Procurement Strategy Meeting" for larger contracts, NFS 1807.170.

FAR 7.104(a) contemplates that acquisition planning be performed by a team:

In developing the plan, the planner shall form a team consisting of all those who will be responsible for significant aspects of the acquisition, such as contracting, fiscal, legal, and technical personnel. The planner should review previous plans for similar acquisitions and discuss them with the key personnel involved in those acquisitions.

FAR 1.102(c) also states that the "Acquisition Team" should include the users of the supplies or services being procured. See also FAR 1.102-2(a)(7) stating:

> All members of the Team are required to employ planning as an integral part of the overall process of acquiring products or services. Although advance planning is required, each member of the Team must be flexible in order to accommodate changing or unforeseen mission needs. Planning is a tool for the accomplishment of tasks, and application of its discipline should be commensurate with the size and nature of a given task.

The members of the team should be identified in the acquisition plan, FAR 7.105(b)(10).

One of the most comprehensive listing of team members was found in the Department of the Navy Acquisition Planning Guide (April 1992), since superseded, but which provided useful guideline for shaping the planning team, stating at paragraph 2.1:

> The APM [Acquisition Program Manager] is responsible for convening acquisition planning meetings with representatives from logistics, technical, fiscal, security, contracting, legal counsel, small business, and other areas, as appropriate, to prepare initial [acquisition plans] or revise [acquisition plans].
>
> All personnel engaged in the management of the acquisition process; including program, contracts, logistics, technical and financial personnel; are essential to the comprehensive acquisition planning and preparations necessary to achieve the acquisition objectives. These personnel must be made cognizant of their responsibilities and actively participate in the development and preparation of the [acquisition plan], if acquisition planning is to be successful. Planning meetings are strongly encouraged in order to coordinate planning efforts, which should significantly reduce [acquisition plan] development time.

Although the FAR does not discuss the role of competition advocates in the planning process, their participation is essential in each executive agency and in each procuring activity within the agency. Appointed pursuant to 41 U.S.C. § 1705 and 10 U.S.C. § 2318, competition advocates are responsible for challenging barriers to competition and promoting full and open competition. The competition advocate for the Defense Logistics Agency (DLA) described his role as follows, on the DLA website (*http://www.dscr.dla.mil/sbo/competition_advocate.htm*):

> The Competition in Contracting Act established the Competition Advocate (COMPAD) position for the purpose of removing all barriers to a competitive acquisition process. In theory, competition in the market place should result in better prices from all potential sources, and avoid the "horror stories" of the early

1980's. The Competition Advocate is NOT an avenue for protest. However, if you believe competition is being hampered in any way contact the Competition Advocate's office for clarification or action.

Agency-level advocates are given the additional duty of providing an annual report to the senior procurement executive on the agency's use of competition in contracting. They have been actively involved in acquisition planning in many procuring agencies. They generally work at a high level in the procuring agency with commensurate influence in determining the strategy that will be used by the agency in the prospective procurement. They also approve or review virtually all justifications for the use of other than competitive procedures. Thus, their agreement with the acquisition plan is essential to ensuring the success of the procurement.

### 4. Scope of Plan

Acquisition planning has been performed by some agencies in a sporadic and fragmented manner. Requirements have often been identified and justified on a contract-by-contract basis without regard for long-term acquisition needs. There are, after all, relatively few regulations requiring plans to be made on a program-wide basis. DoD provides that written acquisition plans for large-dollar acquisitions should be prepared on a program basis, while other acquisition plans may be written on either a program or individual-contract basis, DFARS 207.103(e).

## II. COMPETITION REQUIREMENT

A major goal of acquisition planning is to use competition whenever feasible. In *HEROS, Inc.,* Comp. Gen. Dec. B-292043, 2003 CPD ¶ 111, GAO explained the link between acquisition planning and effective competition, and noted that, though there may be exceptions to competition, a lack of planning is no excuse for inadequate competition:

> [U]nder no circumstances may noncompetitive procedures be used due to a lack of advance planning by contracting officials. 10 U.S.C. § 2304(f)(5) . . . . Our Office has recognized that, while the requirement for advance planning does not mean that such planning must be completely error-free, . . . as with all procurement actions taken by an agency, the advance planning required under 10 U.S.C. § 2304 must be reasonable.

> In enacting CICA, Congress explained: "Effective competition is predicated on advance procurement planning and an understanding of the marketplace." S. Rep. No. 50, 98th Cong., 2d Sess. 18 (1984), *reprinted in* 1984 U.S.C.C.A.N. 2191. The Senate Report also quoted with approval the following testimony regarding the need for advance planning:

>> Opportunities for obtaining or improving competition have often been lost because of untimely, faulty, or the total lack of advance procurement plan-

ning. Noncompetitive procurement or inadequate competition also has resulted many times from the failure to develop specifications . . . . By requiring effective competition, Congress will serve notice on the agencies that they will need to do more than the minimum to comply with the statute. . . .

Finally, in interpreting this statutory requirement, our Office has noted that contracting officials have a duty to promote and provide for competition and to obtain the most advantageous contract for the government. . . . In other words, contracting officials must act affirmatively to obtain and safeguard competition; they cannot take a passive approach and remain in a sole source situation when they could reasonably take steps to enhance competition.

See also *Barnes Aerospace Group*, Comp. Gen. Dec. B-298864, 2006 CPD ¶ 204 (the requirement for advance planning does not mean that the planning must be error-free, "but, as with all actions taken by an agency, the advance planning required under 10 U.S.C. § 2304 must be reasonable").

The Competition in Contract Act of 1984 (CICA) specifically requires "full and open competition" to be attained by executive agencies in the conduct of sealed bid or competitive negotiation except as specifically permitted by statute. CICA also lists five other "competitive procedures." Full and open competition and other than full and open competition are discussed in this section.

## A. Full and Open Competition

The extent of competition required by the procurement statutes has been the subject of extensive debate and a number of statutory changes. Prior to passage of the CICA, the statutes provided that specifications and invitations for bids (IFBs) for formal advertising (now sealed bidding) "permit such free and full competition as is consistent with the procurement of property and services needed by the agency concerned," 10 U.S.C. § 2305(a) (pre-CICA version). See also the prior version of 41 U.S.C. § 253. For negotiated procurement, the Armed Services Procurement Act required that proposals be solicited from "the maximum number of qualified sources consistent with the nature and requirements of the supplies or services to be procured," 10 U.S.C. § 2304(g) (pre-CICA version). In 1984, the CICA required that "full and open competition" be used in sealed bid and competitive proposal procurements except when specifically exempted, 10 U.S.C. § 2304(a)(1)(A) and 41 U.S.C. § 253(a)(1)(A) (now 41 U.S.C. § 3301(a)(1)). The CICA defined the term "full and open competition" to mean that "all responsible sources are permitted to submit sealed bids or competitive proposals on the procurement," 41 U.S.C. § 403(6) (now 41 U.S.C. § 107).

Based upon claims that receipt in some cases of inordinately large numbers of proposals placed an undue and unnecessary burden on procurements, attempts were made to narrow the statutory definition. One draft of the Clinger-Cohen Act of 1996 provided for "efficient competition." However, the definition was not changed. Instead, § 4101 of the Act added a new provision to 10 U.S.C. § 2304(j) and 41 U.S.C. § 3301(c), as follows:

> The Federal Acquisition Regulation shall ensure that the requirement to obtain full and open competition is implemented in a manner that is consistent with the need to efficiently fulfill the Government's requirements.

Efficiency in competition was addressed in § 4103 of the Act, which provides that the contracting officer may limit the number of proposals in the competitive range "to the greatest number that will permit an efficient competition among the offerors rated most highly," 10 U.S.C. § 2305(b)(4)(B) and 41 U.S.C. § 3703(b). This was a radical change from the earlier approach, which, under the prior regulation FAR 15.609, was that the contracting officer was to include in the competitive range any "proposals that [had] 'a reasonable chance' of being selected for award, that is, those proposals which [were] technically acceptable as submitted or which [were] reasonably susceptible of being made acceptable through discussions." See *DBA Sys., Inc.,* Comp. Gen. Dec. B-241048, 91-1 CPD ¶ 36. This narrower approach to "competitive range" meant, in effect, that normal competitive procedures could, in practice, be narrowed to accommodate agencies' efficiency concerns. Congress also left in place, however, other "competitive procedures," discussed below, under which all potential responsible offerors are not necessarily permitted to submit bids or proposals. Nevertheless, Congress has by statute provided that these procurements, when properly conducted, are included in the definition of full and open competition. 10 U.S.C. § 2302(2) and 41 U.S.C. § 152 specify five special procedures that are "competitive procedures" meeting the statutory requirement for full and open competition. See Section III for a listing of these special procedures.

Under the previous statutory provisions, GAO upheld awards if the government obtained "adequate competition" and stated that the adequacy of competition did not depend upon whether every prospective bidder was afforded an opportunity to bid. See *Culligan, Inc.,* 56 Comp. Gen. 1011 (B-189307), 77-2 CPD ¶ 242, which involved advertised procurement, and *John Bransby Prods., Ltd.,* Comp. Gen. Dec. B-198360, 80-2 CPD ¶ 419, which dealt with a negotiated procurement. These decisions were based upon the government's reasonable efforts to inform offerors generally of the proposed procurements and upon the absence of probative evidence that the government had a conscious or deliberate intent to impede the participation of the prospective bidders.

GAO has continued this line of cases and will not require cancellation of a solicitation or an award merely because a prospective offeror was not furnished a copy of the solicitation, absent probative evidence of a conscious or deliberate effort to exclude the offeror. See *International Ass'n of Fire Fighters,* Comp. Gen. Dec. B-220757, 86-1 CPD ¶ 31, stating:

Generally, the risk of nonreceipt of a solicitation amendment rests with the offeror. *Maryland Computer Services, Inc.*, B-216990, Feb. 12, 1985, 85-1 CPD ¶ 187. The propriety of a particular procurement is determined on the basis of whether full and open competition was achieved and reasonable prices were obtained, *Metro Medical Downtown*, B-220399, Dec. 5, 1985, 85-2 CPD ¶ 631, and whether the agency made a conscious and deliberate effort to exclude an offeror from competing for the contract. *Reliable Service Technology*, B-217152, Feb. 25, 1985, 85-1 CPD ¶ 234.

See also *Shemya Constructors*, Comp. Gen. Dec. B-232928.2, 89-1 CPD ¶ 108 (24 firms were solicited and there was no attempt by the agency to exclude the offeror from the competition); *Metro Med. Downtown*, Comp. Gen. Dec. B-220399, 85-2 CPD ¶ 631 (full and open competition was present despite failure to solicit firm through apparent oversight since *Commerce Business Daily* (CBD) notice resulted in solicitation of 24 firms, of which four submitted offers); and *Denver X-Ray Instruments, Inc.*, Comp. Gen. Dec. B-220963, 85-2 CPD ¶ 562 (no evidence that prospective offeror was deliberately excluded from competition).

In *Kendall Healthcare Prods. Co.,* Comp. Gen. Dec. B-289381, 2002 CPD ¶ 42, GAO spelled out the reasoning in this line of cases, and noted the allocation of risks and responsibilities under the broader policy goals of CICA:

> The Competition in Contracting Act of 1984 (CICA) generally requires contracting agencies to obtain full and open competition through the use of competitive procedures, the dual purpose of which is to ensure that a procurement is open to all responsible sources and to provide the government with the opportunity to receive fair and reasonable prices. 41 U.S.C. § 253(a)(1)(A) (1994) . . . . In pursuit of these goals, a contracting agency has the affirmative obligation to use reasonable methods to publicize its procurement needs and to timely disseminate solicitation documents to those entitled to receive them. Concurrent with the agency's obligations in this regard, prospective contractors also must avail themselves of every reasonable opportunity to obtain the solicitation documents. . . . Consequently, where a prospective contractor fails to do so, we will not sustain the protest even if the agency failed in its solicitation dissemination obligations, and in considering such situations, we consider whether the agency or the protester had the last clear opportunity to avoid the protester's being precluded from competing.

The agencies have not, however, always prevailed in these cases. In *Trans World Maint., Inc.*, 65 Comp. Gen. 401 (B-220947), 86-1 CPD ¶ 239, GAO found that the agency failed to obtain full and open competition when it failed to solicit bids from the incumbent contractor, which had requested a copy of the solicitation at least four times before its issuance. In addition, the agency's published CBD notice did not indicate the date of the solicitation or of the bid opening. See also *Bonneville Blue Print Supply*, 67 Comp. Gen. 96 (B-228183), 87-2 CPD ¶ 492; and *Dan's Moving & Storage, Inc.*, Comp. Gen. Dec. B-222431, 86-1 CPD ¶ 496. In *Abel Converting, Inc. v. United States*, 679 F. Supp. 1133 (D.D.C. 1988), the court held that an agency's failure to solicit an incumbent contractor on a 33-item procurement would not be adequately remedied by GAO's recommendation that the agency resolicit the 14 items on which it had received only one bid, because the agency had not received full and open competition. The court reasoned at 1141:

> While the GAO concluded that two bids constituted adequate competition on nineteen of the line items, the Court disagrees. When so few bidders participate in a solicitation, the absence of even one responsible bidder significantly diminishes the level of competition. This is particularly so when the absent bidder is the incumbent contractor since that contractor previously submitted the lowest bids. Because GSA's actions "prevented a responsible source from competing[,] . . . the CICA mandate for full and open competition was not met."

In *Republic Floors, Inc.*, Comp. Gen. Dec. B-242962, 91-1 CPD ¶ 579, the agency failed to send the protester two material solicitation amendments, in violation of applicable regulatory requirements governing the dissemination of solicitation materials. GAO found that as a result of the agency's actions, of the four bids received, only two were responsive and where so few firms participate in a competition, the absence of even one responsive firm due to the agency's regulatory violation so diminished the level of competition and undermined the CICA mandate for full and open competition that it constituted a compelling reason to resolicit the requirement. See also *Custom Envtl. Serv., Inc.*, 70 Comp. Gen. 563 (B-242900), 91-1 CPD ¶ 578, where competition was found to be inadequate where only one responsive bid was received and at least three other prospective bidders were eliminated from the bidding as a result of using an obsolete mailing list.

These issues of publication and notice have shifted dramatically in recent years, as electronic means of publicizing the government's business opportunities have transformed the federal marketplace. As is discussed further below, opportunities are now published not in a newspaper — the old *Commerce Business Daily* — but rather on a central website, *www.fedbizopps.gov*. See FAR Part 5. At the same time, sophisticated data intermediaries have emerged, private firms which gather and sell information on pending federal opportunities. With this evolution in the marketplace, it has become far easier for vendors to identify and track potential opportunities, so long as those opportunities are publicized through the standard, centralized government channels.

Despite the statutory changes in 1996, there continues to be disagreement over when agencies must obtain full and open competition. For example, in 2002 a dispute arose between Congress and DoD involving the lease of Boeing 737 aircraft. In § 8147 of the Department of Defense Appropriations Act for Fiscal Year 2003, Pub. L. No. 107-248, 116 Stat. 1519, 1572 (2002), Congress specifically provided that none of the funds appropriated by the Act could be used for leasing of transport/VIP aircraft "under any contract entered into *under any procurement procedures other than pursuant to the Competition [in] Contracting Act*," (emphasis added.)

DoD concluded that it could use an *exception* within CICA — one of the exceptions discussed below — to lease such aircraft without using normal competitive procedures. Senator John McCain requested GAO to review this action. GAO reported that § 8147 only required DoD to procure pursuant to CICA, and that the Defense Department could, therefore, properly use any noncompetitive procedure countenanced by CICA, *Use of Fiscal Year 2003 Funds for Boeing 737 Aircraft Lease Payments*, Comp. Gen. Dec. B-300222, 2003 U.S. Comp. Gen. LEXIS 227. See also *EADS North Am., Inc.*, Comp. Gen. Dec. B-291805, 2003 CPD ¶ 51.

## B. Other Than Full and Open Competition

"Other than competitive procedures" are not statutorily defined; the statutes merely list seven specific procurement situations where full and open competition is not required. Depending upon the circumstances, such procurements may be made on either a sole source basis or with limited competition. These exceptions, set forth in 41 U.S.C. § 3304(a) and 10 U.S.C. § 2304(c), state that other than competitive procedures may be used *only* in the following situations:

(1) the property or services needed by the executive agency are available from only one responsible source (or, for the Defense Department, or only from a limited number of responsible sources), and no other type of property or services will satisfy the needs of the executive agency;

(2) the agency's need for the property or services is of such an unusual and compelling urgency that the United States would be seriously injured unless the agency is permitted to limit the number of sources from which it solicits bids or proposals;

(3) it is necessary to award the contract to a particular source or sources in order (A) to maintain a facility, producer, manufacturer, or other supplier available for furnishing property or services in case of a national emergency or to achieve industrial mobilization, (B) to establish or maintain an essential engineering, research, or development capability to be provided by an educational or other nonprofit institution or a federally funded research and development center, or (C) to procure the services of an expert for use, in any litigation or dispute (including any reasonably foreseeable litigation or dispute) involving the Federal Government, in any trial, hearing, or proceeding before any court, administrative tribunal, or agency, or to procure the services of an expert or neutral for use in any part of an alternative dispute resolution process, whether or not the expert is expected to testify;

(4) the terms of an international agreement or a treaty between the United States and a foreign government or international organization, or the written directions of a foreign government reimbursing the agency for the cost of the procurement of the property or services for such government, have the effect of requiring the use of procedures other than competitive procedures;

(5) subject to subsection (h), a statute expressly authorizes or requires that the procurement be made through another executive agency or from a specified source, or the agency's need is for a brand-name commercial item for authorized resale;

(6) the disclosure of the agency's needs would compromise the national security unless the agency is permitted to limit the number of sources from which it solicits bids or proposals; or

(7) the head of the agency —

    (A) determines that it is necessary in the public interest to use procedures other than competitive procedures in the particular procurement concerned, and

    (B) notifies the Congress in writing of such determination not less than 30 days before the award of the contract.

Where an agency had incorrectly relied upon one exception (the "expert" exception under ¶ (3)(C)), but the record supported the use of the ¶ (1) exception, GAO allowed the sole source procurement to stand, *SEMCOR, Inc.,* Comp. Gen. Dec. B-279794, 98-2 CPD ¶ 43.

Justification for the use of other than competitive procedures on the basis of any exception other than ¶ (1) does not necessarily permit the use of sole source contracting. Competition is required from as many potential sources as is practicable. See 41 U.S.C. § 3304(d) and 10 U.S.C. § 2304(e), which state:

The head of an agency . . . using procedures other than competitive procedures to procure property or services by reason of the application of [¶ (2) or ¶ (6)] shall request offers from as many potential sources as is practicable under the circumstances.

The FAR requirement to solicit offers from as many sources as is practicable is not limited to ¶ (2) and ¶ (6) only. FAR 6.301(d), set forth below, is applicable to the statutory exceptions under ¶ (3), ¶ (4), ¶ (5), and ¶ (7) as well:

When not providing for full and open competition, the contracting officer shall solicit offers from as many potential sources as is practicable under the circumstances.

Thus, procurements under all paragraphs except ¶ (1) (which generally applies when there is "only one responsible source") should be conducted with some degree of competition when circumstances permit.

Protests in this area have primarily been under ¶ (2) ("unusual and compelling urgency"), which is discussed further below. In *Total Indus. Packaging Corp.,* Comp. Gen. Dec. B- 295434, 2005 CPD ¶ 38, GAO outlined its standard for deciding cases under ¶ (2):

Although CICA requires that the agency request offers from as many potential sources as is practicable under the circumstances, 10 U.S.C. 2304(e); see Federal Acquisition Regulation (FAR 6.302(c)(2)), an agency may still limit the procurement to the only firm it reasonably believes can properly perform the work in the available time. *McGregor Mfg. Corp.*, B-285341, Aug. 18, 2000, 2000 CPD ¶ 151 at 6; *Hercules Aerospace Co.*, B-254677, Jan. 10, 1994, 94-1 CPD ¶ 7 at 3. We will object to the agency's determination only where the decision lacks a reasonable basis. *Signals & Sys., Inc.*, B-288107, Sept. 21, 2001, 2001 CPD ¶ 168 at 12.

Through this line of decisions, for instance, GAO has held that even though urgency permitted a procurement without full and open competition, the agency violated the statute by awarding a sole source contract, *Data Based Decisions, Inc.*, Comp. Gen. Dec. B-232663, 89-1 CPD ¶ 87; *TMS Bldg. Maint.*, 65 Comp. Gen. 222 (B-220588), 86-1 CPD ¶ 68. GAO has also held that an agency violated the statute where it had conducted the procurement so inefficiently that a competitor did not have time to compete for the entire quantity, *Arrow Gear Co.*, 68 Comp. Gen. 612 (B-235081), 89-2 CPD ¶ 135. Other such protests have been sustained in *WorldWide Language Res., Inc.*, Comp. Gen. Dec. B-296993, 2005 CPD ¶ 206 (agency's lack of advance planning was unreasonable where the justification was premised on the conclusion that awardee was the only responsible source); *Kahn Indus., Inc.*, Comp. Gen. Dec. B-251777, 93-1 CPD ¶ 356 (agency failed to contact one of the potential sources because the firm's phone number was missing from the file and the agency opined that three quotes would be "good enough" in a situation of urgency); *Ferranti Int'l Def. Sys., Inc.*, Comp. Gen. Dec. B-237760, 90-1 CPD ¶ 317 (agency could have negotiated with a third source that had expressed interest and had prior experience, without significantly delaying the ongoing procurement); *Charles Snyder*, 68 Comp. Gen. 659 (B-235409), 89-2 CPD ¶ 208 (agency could have solicited nonlocal company that had previously expressed interest in procurement); and *AT&T Info. Servs., Inc.*, 66 Comp. Gen. 58 (B-223914), 86-2 CPD ¶ 447 (agency could have conducted fast negotiations with another known source of the work). In *Earth Prop. Servs., Inc.*, Comp. Gen. Dec. B-237742, 90-1 CPD ¶ 273, the agency was prohibited from soliciting only one source in an urgent procurement where a second offeror, which had previously done similar work for the agency, was available to perform on short notice. Similarly, in *Olympic Marine Servs., Inc.*, Comp. Gen. Dec. B-246143 , 92-1 CPD ¶ 205, GAO sustained a protest where an agency failed to solicit a firm that had previously done similar work and had specifically requested to be solicited by the agency in the future. See also *Bay Cities Servs., Inc.*, Comp. Gen. Dec. B-239880, 90-2 CPD ¶ 271, holding that the incumbent contractor's refusal to provide cost data did not justify failing to solicit a proposal for an urgent procurement of additional effort for four months (two other proposals had been solicited).

## 1. Only One Source Available

The first exception is the broadest and possibly most utilized exception to the requirement for full and open competition, FAR 6.302-1. It is intended to permit a sole source procurement "only when truly warranted," *Competition in Contracting Act: Report of Government Affairs Committee to Accompany S. 338*, S. Rep. No. 8-50, 98th Cong., 1st Sess. 21 (1983). GAO's standards for evaluating challenges under this exception were set forth in *Kearfott Guidance & Navigation Corp.*, Comp. Gen. Dec. B- 292895.2, 2004 CPD ¶ 123:

> When an agency uses noncompetitive procedures under 10 U.S.C. § 2304(c)(1), it is required to execute a written J & A [Justification & Approval] with sufficient facts and rationale to support the use of the cited authority, and publish a notice to permit potential competitors an opportunity to challenge the agency's decision to procure without full and open competition. See 10 U.S.C. § 2304(f)(1)(A), (B); Federal Acquisition Regulation §§ 6.302-1(d)(1), 6.303, 6.304; *Marconi Dynamics, Inc.*, B-252318, June 21, 1993, 93-1 CPD ¶ 475 at 5. Our review of the agency's decision to conduct a sole source procurement focuses on the adequacy of the rationale and conclusions set forth in the J & A. When the J & A sets forth a reasonable justification for the agency's actions, we will not object to the award.

This section discusses the decisions contesting sole source procurements under both the prior statutes and the current statute to determine the meaning of this exception.

### a. Agency Discretion

An agency determination that a proposed contractor is the only source capable of meeting the technical needs of the agency is subject to close scrutiny but will not be overturned if the agency has properly justified its needs and there is a reasonable basis for its determination, *Mine Safety Appliances Co.*, Comp. Gen. Dec. B-233052, 89-1 CPD ¶ 127; *WSI Corp.*, Comp. Gen. Dec. B-220025, 85-2 CPD ¶ 626. The fact that the protester disagrees with the agency's technical evaluation does not in itself render the evaluation unreasonable, *International Sys. Mktg., Inc.*, Comp. Gen. Dec. B-215174, 85-2 CPD ¶ 166. However, when a responsible source has expressed interest in the procurement, the agency must make reasonable efforts to permit the source to compete, *Neil R. Gross & Co.*, 69 Comp. Gen. 292 (B-237434), 90-1 CPD ¶ 212. If such efforts fail, however, GAO is reluctant to question agency decisions. See, for example, *Automated Prod. Equip. Corp.*, Comp. Gen. Dec. B-210476, 84-1 CPD ¶ 269, where, despite observing that the agency's technical personnel were impressed with the protester's equipment demonstration, GAO did not disturb the agency's determination that the protester did not supply sufficient data from which the agency could evaluate the functional equivalence of the protester's equipment. Similarly, in *Technology for Commc'ns Int'l*, Comp. Gen. Dec. B-236922, 89-2 CPD ¶ 603, GAO did not question an agency's determination that the protester, in response to a CBD notice seeking sources, did not submit sufficient technical data to justify permitting the protester to compete on the basis of developing a new product if it won the competition. See also *Lyntronics, Inc.*, Comp. Gen. B-292204, 2003 CPD ¶ 140 (based on protester's limited evidence of potential schedule for delivery of materials from alternative new source,

GAO concluded "we have no basis for questioning the agency's position that deliveries by a new source would be materially delayed").

GAO has, though, held that the availability of only one source has to be demonstrated "convincingly," *Daniel H. Wagner Assocs.*, 65 Comp. Gen. 305 (B-220633), 86-1 CPD ¶ 166. In most protests of sole source awards, agencies have been able to meet this test. For example, in *Amray, Inc.*, Comp. Gen. Dec. B-209186, 83-2 CPD ¶ 45, the protester complained of a sole source procurement for a scanning microscope on the grounds that it, too, could meet the agency's needs. In rejecting the protest, GAO noted that the agency's technical personnel reviewed the literature published by various manufacturers, spoke to their representatives, including Amray's, and reasonably determined the microscope to be unique. See also *Raytheon Co. Integrated Def. Sys.*, Comp. Gen. Dec. B-400610, 2009 CPD ¶ 8 (sole source awards of follow-on contract are "unobjectionable" where agency determined that award to any other source would cause unacceptable delays); *EADS N. Am., Inc.*, Comp. Gen. Dec. B-291805, 2003 CPD ¶ 51 (sole source to Boeing proper when statute specifically authorized the lease of "Boeing 737 aircraft in commercial configuration"); *McKesson Automation Sys., Inc.*, Comp. Gen. Dec. B-290969, 2003 CPD ¶ 24 (agency computer security requirement not an unreasonable barrier, even though it left only one competitor); *Mnemonics, Inc.*, Comp. Gen. Dec. B-261476.3, 96-1 CPD ¶ 7 (agency reasonably determined that only one source could supply critically required items under an expedited delivery schedule); *Navistar Marine Instrument Corp.*, Comp. Gen. Dec. B-262221, 95-2 CPD ¶ 232 (sole source procurement proper where no other barometer had the ability to fit into a preexisting opening on the instrument control panel of the engine); *Nomura Enter., Inc.*, Comp. Gen. Dec. B-260977.2, 95-2 CPD ¶ 206 (sole source contract for engineering support services related to howitzer proper because agency reasonably concluded that unacceptable delays would occur if award was made to another source); *Pilkington Aerospace, Inc.*, Comp. Gen. Dec. B-259173, 95-1 CPD ¶ 180 (agency reasonably awarded sole source contract for advanced design windshields for the F-15 aircraft); *Midwest Dynamometer & Eng'g Co.*, Comp. Gen. Dec. B-257323, 94-2 CPD ¶ 91 (agency reasonably determined that only one source could furnish a dynamometer system meeting its requirement for a system capable of running on existing software); *Litton Computer Servs.*, Comp. Gen. Dec. B-256225, 94-2 CPD ¶ 36 (agency reasonably determined that only the developer of the original system had the necessary extensive system knowledge and experience to accomplish task); *Essex Electro Eng'rs, Inc.*, Comp. Gen. Dec. B-250437, 93-1 CPD ¶ 74 (procurement from only immediately available source justified to obtain backup electric power plants, which were in short supply because of Operation Desert Storm — even though units would be placed on standby status); *AGEMA Infrared Sys.*, Comp. Gen. Dec. B-240961, 91-1 CPD ¶ 4 (protester's equipment did not contain essential technical features needed by agency); *EG&G Astrophysics Research Corp.*, Comp. Gen. Dec. B-241171, 90-2 CPD ¶ 525 (agency had thoroughly reviewed protester's equipment and had reasonably determined it did not meet agency's needs); *Elbit Computers, Ltd.*, Comp. Gen. Dec. B-239038, 90-2 CPD ¶ 26 (agency's determination that no other contractor could supply the equipment reasonable); and *C & S Antennas, Inc.*, Comp. Gen. Dec. B-224549, 87-1 CPD ¶ 161 (agency determination that only one product was compatible with its needs reasonable even though protester was meeting similar needs of another agency).

Protests of sole source determinations have, however, been sustained if the facts indicate that other sources could satisfactorily meet the government's needs. In *Sidereal Corp.*, Comp. Gen. Dec. B-210969, 83-2 CPD ¶ 92, GAO sustained a protest to a sole source award for automatic data processing equipment. The protester had recently won contracts for equipment similar to that which was procured, thus demonstrating that meaningful competition was possible. See also *Design Pak, Inc.*, Comp. Gen. Dec. B-212579, 83-2 CPD ¶ 336, sustaining a protest to a noncompetitive award because the agency confused its requirements with the characteristics of the sole source contractor's product, and *Data Based Decisions, Inc.*, Comp. Gen. Dec. B-232663, 89-1 CPD ¶ 87, where a protest was sustained because the incumbent contractor was not solicited although able to compete for the work. See also *eFedBudget Corp.*, Comp. Gen. Dec. B-298627, 2006 CPD ¶ 159 (protest sustained where the agency never considered whether the costs associated with a purchase of additional license rights outweighed the benefits of competition); *Lockheed Martin Sys. Integration — Owego*, Comp. Gen. Dec. B-287190.2, 2001 CPD ¶ 110 (protest sustained because agency gave potential competitor incorrect information on requirements, and thus competitor could not fairly demonstrate its ability to meet agency's requirements); *National Aerospace Group, Inc.*, Comp. Gen. Dec. B-282,843, 99-2 CPD ¶ 43 (agency's sole source justification was inadequate because documentation did not reasonably show that only named produce would satisfy agency's needs, and did not show that agency's allegedly urgent need was not created by a lack of advance planning).

In making a determination that only one contractor is capable of meeting an agency's needs, it is improper for an agency to rely on the putative sole source contractor for technical advice and expertise. The agency should independently evaluate technical data and draw its own conclusions, *Aero Corp. v. Dep't of the Navy*, 558 F. Supp. 404 (D.D.C. 1983). See also *National Aerospace Group, Inc.*, Comp. Gen. Dec. B-282843, 99-2 CPD ¶ 43 (agency criticized for "unquestioning acceptance . . . of the [original equipment manufacturer's] apparent insistence that its product is unique in ways that are essential to its function but cannot be revealed").

## b. Privately Developed Items

The determination to procure on a sole source basis may be justified under certain circumstances if the items being procured were developed at private expense. The following material discusses the circumstances that preclude or permit sole source procurement of privately developed items. For a complete discussion of the policies in this area see Chapter 8 of Nash & Rawicz, *Intellectual Property in Government Contracts* (6th ed. 2008).

## (1) Patented Items

The fact that an item is patented will *not* justify a sole source procurement. See FAR 27.1021(b) ("Generally, the Government will not refuse to award a contract on the grounds that the prospective contractor may infringe a patent."). The statutory basis for this rule is 28 U.S.C. § 1498(a), which gives patent owners the right to reasonable compensation if an invention is used "by or for the United States without license," but does not permit patent owners to enjoin the use of patents in such cases. In 38 Comp. Gen. 276 (B-136916) (1958), GAO ruled that this statute requires the use of competitive procurement techniques when purchasing patented items, reasoning at 278:

> It is our view, however, that section 1498 appears clearly to constitute a modification of the patent law by limiting the rights of patentees insofar as procurement of supplies by the Government may be concerned, and by vesting in the Government a right to the use of any patents granted by it upon payment of reasonable compensation for such use. We believe that the statute is not consistent with any duty on the part of a contracting agency of the Government to protect the interests of patentees or licensees with respect to articles which it proposes to purchase, since the statute itself defines and provides an exclusive remedy for enforcement of the patentee's rights as to the Government. Any other interpretation would appear to us to impose an impossible burden upon Government procurement officials to determine the applicability and validity of any patents affecting any articles desired.

See also 53 Comp. Gen. 270 (B-177835) (1973), indicating that competitive negotiation could be used to obtain patented items if the circumstances for negotiation are present. It is proper to use a Patent Indemnity clause (transferring the risk of patent infringement to the contractor) in such cases, *Barrier-Wear*, Comp. Gen. Dec. B-240563, 90-2 CPD ¶ 421. Prior regulations explicitly permitted this technique but the current FAR is silent on this use of a Patent Indemnity clause to attempt to overcome the competitive advantage that this policy gives to the infringer.

## (2) Copyrighted Items

Although 28 U.S.C. § 1498(b) contains substantially the same language relating to copyrights as 28 U.S.C. § 1498(a), the presence of a copyright has been held to be a valid reason for sole source procurement. See *ALK Assocs.*, Comp. Gen. Dec. B-237019, 90-1 CPD ¶ 113, upholding a sole source procurement of copyrighted software because the agency needed the identical software to meet its needs. GAO apparently reasoned that competitors could not re-create such software and/or that the agency or its contractors could not take the software through eminent domain procedures (as can occur with patents). See also *MFVega & Assocs., LLC,* Comp. Gen. Dec. B-291605.3, 2003 CPD ¶ 65 (agency properly sole-sourced to incumbent software provider, because agency "may properly take into account the existence of software data rights and licenses when determining whether only one responsible source exists"). The same logic probably explains the copyright provisions in ¶ (c)(2) of the Rights in Data — General clause in FAR 52.227-14 and ¶ (d) of the Rights in Technical Data — Noncommercial Items clause in DFARS 252.227-7013, stating that a contractor may not use copyrighted material in the performance of the contract without the consent of the contracting officer unless it obtains a license from the owner of the copyright.

### (3) ITEMS DESCRIBED BY PROPRIETARY DATA

Since there is no statute comparable to 28 U.S.C. § 1498 covering proprietary data, it is the policy of the government to honor proprietary rights in technical data, FAR 27.402(b). This policy, now incorporated in 41 U.S.C. § 2302(a)(1) and 10 U.S.C. § 2320(a)(1), states that procurement regulations may not impair "any other right in technical data otherwise established by law." However, 10 U.S.C. § 2320(c)(1) does permit the use of contract clauses calling for expiration of a contractor's proprietary rights to the technical data after no more than seven years, a policy that is implemented at DFARS 227.7103-5(b)(2) (calling for a "nominal" five year expiration of government-purpose rights). The government's policy of honoring proprietary rights in technical data does not prevent the government from meeting its needs with an independent development project.

In some cases, GAO has held that agencies should prepare data packages or use performance specifications to facilitate competitive procurement. The fact that the agency would incur substantial cost in drafting a specification that could be used for competitive procurement was not adequate justification for sole source procurement in *Techniarts*, Comp. Gen. Dec. B-193263, 79-1 CPD ¶ 246. But see *Compressor Eng'g Corp.*, Comp. Gen. Dec. B-213032, 84-1 CPD ¶ 180, where GAO stated that it would be unreasonable for the agency to bear the cost of testing parts that would facilitate a competitive procurement. In *Command, Control & Commc'ns Corp.*, Comp. Gen. Dec. B-210100, 83-2 CPD ¶ 448, GAO rejected the agency's arguments that the urgency of its needs and the lack of proprietary data precluded a competitive award. While GAO recognized that the agency might have to satisfy its immediate needs on a sole source basis, urgency could not justify acquisition of computer systems over a five-year period where the systems were not complex technologically and the agency acknowledged that other vendors could duplicate the system " if given enough time."

Agencies occasionally create nonproprietary technical data packages by reverse engineering proprietary products. Reverse engineering is the process of developing design specifications by inspection and analysis of a product. Although DFARS 217.7503 provides that reverse engineering by the government is the least desirable means of obtaining competition in the face of proprietary data, this practice has been found to be legal, *Westech Gear Corp. v. Department of the Navy*, 907 F.2d 1225 (D.C. Cir. 1990); *American Hoist & Derrick, Inc. v. United States*, 3 Cl.

Ct. 198 (1983). Sometimes nonproprietary technical data packages are created by awarding a contract to perform the reverse engineering, *EG&G Sealol*, Comp. Gen. Dec. B-232265, 88-2 CPD ¶ 558. When reverse engineering is too expensive to justify the effort to obtain competition, an agency can reasonably decide to continue the sole source procurement, *Gel Sys., Inc.*, Comp. Gen. Dec. B-231680, 88-2 CPD ¶ 316. See also *Kearfott Guidance & Navigation Corp.*, Comp. Gen. Dec. 292895.2, 2004 CPD ¶ 123, agreeing that the product was too complicated to permit success- ful reverse engineering, and *AAI ACL Techs., Inc.*, Comp. Gen. Dec. 258679.4, 95-2 CPD ¶ 243, finding a sole source award proper given the risk and cost associated with reverse engineering.

The most prevalent form of reverse engineering is for the government to sug- gest that companies reverse engineer a product in order to compete for a quantity of items to be procured. The major way that an agency initiates this type of reverse engineering is by providing proprietary items to competitors. With regard to spare parts, this procedure is encouraged by 10 U.S.C. § 2320(d), which states:

> The Secretary of Defense shall by regulation establish programs which provide domestic business concerns an opportunity to purchase or borrow replenishment parts from the United States for the purpose of design replication or modification, to be used by such concerns in the submission of subsequent offers to sell the same or like parts to the United States.

This technique is sometimes called "competitive copying."

Agencies also attempt to obtain competition in the face of proprietary data by having the contractor with the proprietary data license other contractors. In *Leigh Instruments, Ltd.*, Comp. Gen. Dec. B-233642, 89-1 CPD ¶ 149, the licensee com- plained that the contractor had failed to honor the license with the result that the licensee could not successfully compete on a procurement. GAO did not entertain the protest, characterizing such situations as disputes between two private parties.

GAO has sustained sole source procurements where the product being procured could only be described by proprietary data, *Aerospace Eng'g & Support, Inc.*, Comp. Gen. Dec. B-258546, 95-1 CPD ¶ 18; *TSI Microelectronics Corp.*, Comp. Gen. Dec. B-243889, 91-2 CPD ¶ 172; *Hydra Rig Cryogenics, Inc.*, Comp. Gen. Dec. B-234029, 89-1 CPD ¶ 442; *Turbo Mech., Inc.*, Comp. Gen. Dec. B-231807, 88-2 CPD ¶ 299; *Quality Diesel Engines, Inc.*, Comp. Gen. Dec. B-210215, 83 2 CPD ¶ 1. In such cases, GAO generally will not question an agency's legal deter- mination that the sole source contractor has proprietary rights, *Fil-Coil Co.*, Comp. Gen. Dec. B-198105, 80-2 CPD ¶ 304. See *KSD, Inc. v. United States*, 72 Fed. Cl. 236 (2006), where the court upheld a sole source procurement because the contrac- tor had created an entirely proprietary data package using IR&D funds in response to the agency's request for companies to devise solutions to a current problem.

Sole source procurements have also been justified where, "as a practical matter," it was not feasible to create a nonproprietary data package. See *Kessler Int'l Corp.*, Comp. Gen. Dec. B-230662, 88-2 CPD ¶ 27, where it was held that the agency reasonably determined that only one source could timely supply the needed part because it was a critical application part necessary for performing safety, mission, and readiness requirements. The government had no technical data package because the item had been developed at private expense under a nondevelopmental item. In *Rack Eng'g Co.*, Comp. Gen. Dec. B-194470, 79-2 CPD ¶ 385, GAO upheld the Navy's sole source procurement for interchangeable spare parts cabinets because the supplier had already supplied 87% of the Atlantic Fleet Carrier Force's needs, reasoning that the cost of redesigning and retooling to meet the interchangeability requirement would necessarily preclude any other offerors from competing. Thus, the most economically sound alternative to ensure interchangeability was to procure sole source from the existing supplier. In *Worldwide Marine, Inc.*, Comp. Gen. Dec. B-212640, 84-1 CPD ¶ 152, GAO acknowledged there may have been some degree of agency negligence in failing to draft specifications, but nevertheless held that, faced with an urgent need for the purchase in question, the agency was justified in making a sole source award to the only company that possessed adequate data to produce the item. See also *Piezo Crystal Co.*, 69 Comp. Gen. 97 (B-236160), 89-2 CPD ¶ 477, and *Rotek, Inc.*, Comp. Gen. Dec. B-240252, 90-2 CPD ¶ 341, where GAO upheld sole source procurements justified by the agency's lack of a data package and an urgent need for initial deliveries of the product. In *Masbe Corp.*, Comp. Gen. Dec. B-260253.2 , 95-1 CPD ¶ 253, GAO upheld a sole source procurement for a critical military aircraft engine part because the agency did not have adequate data to establish qualification requirements for the part because this data was possessed by the original designer of the engine.

The Small Business and Federal Procurement Competition Enhancement Act of 1984, Pub. L. No. 98-577, and the Defense Reform Act of 1984, Pub. L. No. 98-525, both contained provisions requiring agencies to consider requiring offerors for development and production contracts for major systems to propose methods for obtaining competition. See 10 U.S.C. § 2305(d) (the parallel provision for civilian agencies is at 41 U.S.C. § 3308(b)), which describes this requirement as follows:

(1) (A) The Secretary of Defense shall ensure that, in preparing a solicitation for the award of a development contract for a major system, the head of an agency consider requiring in the solicitation that an offeror include in its offer proposals described in subparagraph (B). In determining whether to require such proposals, the head of the agency shall give due consideration to the purposes for which the system is being procured and the technology necessary to meet the system's required capabilities. If such proposals are required, the head of the agency shall consider them in evaluating the offeror's price.

(B) Proposals referred to in the first sentence of subparagraph (A) are the following:

(i) Proposals to incorporate in the design of the major system items which are currently available within the supply system of the Federal agency responsible for the major system, available elsewhere in the national system, or commercially available from more than one source.

(ii) With respect to items that are likely to be required in substantial quantities during the system's service life, proposals to incorporate in the design of the major system items which the United States will be able to acquire competitively in the future.

(2) (A) The Secretary of Defense shall ensure that, in preparing, in preparing a solicitation for the award of a production contract for a major system, the head of an agency consider requiring in the solicitation that an offeror include in its offer proposals described in subparagraph (B). In determining whether to require such proposals, the head of the agency shall give due consideration to the purposes for which the system is being procured and the technology necessary to meet the system's required capabilities. If such proposals are required, the head of the agency shall consider them in evaluating the offeror's price.

(B) Proposals referred to in the first sentence of subparagraph (A) are proposals identifying opportunities to ensure that the United States will be able to obtain on a competitive basis items procured in connection with the system that are likely to be reprocured in substantial quantities during the service life of the system. Proposals submitted in response to such requirement may include the following:

(i) Proposals to provide to the United States the right to use technical data to be provided under the contract for competitive reprocurement of the item, together with the cost to the United States, if any, of acquiring such technical data and the right to use such data.

(ii) Proposals for the qualification or development of multiple sources of supply for the item.

10 U.S.C. § 2320(e) was added to the statute to impose a requirement on program managers to structure procurements to obtain competition, stating:

(e) The Secretary of Defense shall require program managers for major weapon systems and subsystems of major weapon systems to assess the long-term technical data needs of such systems and subsystems and establish corresponding acquisition strategies that provide for technical data rights needed to sustain such systems and subsystems over their life cycle. Such strategies may include the development of maintenance capabilities within the Department of Defense or competition for contracts for sustainment of such systems or subsystems. Assessments and corresponding acquisition strategies developed under this section with respect to a weapon system or subsystem shall —

(1) be developed before issuance of a contract solicitation for the weapon system or subsystem;

(2) address the merits of including a priced contract option for the future delivery of technical data that were not acquired upon initial contract award;

(3) address the potential for changes in the sustainment plan over the life cycle of the weapon system or subsystem; and

(4) apply to weapon systems and subsystems that are to be supported by performance-based logistics arrangements as well as to weapons systems and subsystems that are to be supported by other sustainment approaches.

## c. Unsolicited Proposals

Unsolicited proposals can provide the basis for a determination that the property or services are available from only one source. See 41 U.S.C. § 3304(b)(1), which states:

> [in the case of] a contract for property or services to be awarded on the basis of acceptance of an unsolicited research proposal, the property or services shall be considered to be available from only one source if the source has submitted an unsolicited research proposal that demonstrates a unique and innovative concept the substance of which is not otherwise available to the United States and does not resemble the substance of a pending competitive procurement.

10 U.S.C. § 2304(d)(1)(A) is substantively the same.

FAR Subpart 15.6 goes beyond these statutes and provides guidance on the handling of all unsolicited proposals for research work and other types of work. FAR 15.606-2(a) requires that each proposal be comprehensively evaluated, considering, at a minimum, the following factors:

(1) Unique, innovative and meritorious methods, approaches, or concepts demonstrated by the proposal;

(2) Overall scientific, technical, or socioeconomic merits of the proposal;

(3) Potential contribution of the effort to the agency's specific mission;

(4) The offeror's capabilities, related experience, facilities, techniques, or unique combinations of these that are integral factors for achieving the proposal objectives;

(5) The qualifications, capabilities, and experience of the proposed principal investigator, team leader, or key personnel who are critical to achieving the proposal objectives; and

(6) The realism of the proposed cost.

FAR 15.607 contains limitations on award of contracts based on unsolicited proposals:

(a) A favorable comprehensive evaluation of an unsolicited proposal does not, in itself, justify awarding a contract without providing for full and open competition. The agency point of contact shall return an unsolicited proposal to the offeror, citing reasons, when its substance —

(1) Is available to the Government without restriction from another source;

(2) Closely resembles a pending competitive acquisition requirement;

(3) Does not relate to the activity's missions; or

(4) Does not demonstrate an innovative and unique method, approach, or concept, or is otherwise not deemed a meritorious proposal.

FAR 15.607(b) goes on to state that if the unsolicited proposal has received a favorable comprehensive evaluation and is not subject to the above impediments, the agency can procure the work covered by the proposal. If it is for research work, such procurement can be on a sole source basis in accordance with FAR 6.302-1(a)(2)(i):

Supplies or services may be considered to be available from only one source if the source has submitted an unsolicited research proposal that [meets the statutory requirements].

If the proposal is for other than research work, FAR 15.607(b) requires full and open competition unless one of the statutory exceptions is justified.

GAO has held that these provisions *do not* require award of a contract to a submitter of an unsolicited proposal — they merely *permit* award if the proposal is unique and innovative. Even when the proposal is unique and innovative, agencies have the discretion not to award a sole source contract. See *Digital Healthcare, Inc.*, Comp. Gen. Dec. B-296489, 2005 CPD ¶ 166, where the agency concluded that the information in the proposal was not unique and properly conducted a competitive procurement containing a general statement of its needs. See also *S. T. Research Corp.*, Comp. Gen. Dec. B-231752, 88-2 CPD ¶ 152; *University of Dayton Research Inst.*, Comp. Gen. Dec. B-220589, 86-1 CPD ¶ 108. Further, GAO "does not consider it appropriate to review a protest that an agency should procure from a particular firm on a sole source basis," *Arctic Energies Ltd.*, Comp. Gen. Dec. B-224672, 86-2 CPD ¶ 571. Thus, it is very difficult to challenge an agency decision to reject an unsolicited proposal.

It is appropriate for an agency not to issue a sole source contract based on an unsolicited proposal where the data necessary for a competitive procurement are otherwise available to the government, *Saratoga Indus.*, Comp. Gen. Dec. B-219341, 85-2 CPD ¶ 247 (information in the unsolicited proposal was available from previous specifications or from publicly available information); *Georgetown Air & Hydro Sys.*, Comp. Gen. Dec. B-210806, 84-1 CPD ¶ 186 (unsolicited proposal incorporated information related to a forthcoming solicitation). In *LW Planning Group*, Comp. Gen. Dec. B-215539, 84-2 CPD ¶ 531, the government was found to have properly decided that the work in the unsolicited proposal required the work of an architect-engineer contractor and thus the work could not be done by the submitter.

It appears that a proposal could be "unique and innovative" even if it did not include proprietary information. FAR 15.609 permits unsolicited proposals to contain a legend prohibiting the disclosure, outside the government, of all information in the proposal or the use of such information for any purpose other than evaluation of the proposal. This regulation also establishes a procedure for government protection of the information even if the legends are not placed on the proposal. It has been held that the government does not violate a protectable trade secret by competitively soliciting for the item using data that were independently developed by the government, *Zodiac of N. Am., Inc.*, Comp. Gen. Dec. B-220012, 85-2 CPD ¶ 595; *Sellers, Connor & Cuneo*, 53 Comp. Gen. 161 (B-177436), *recons. denied*, 74-1 CPD ¶ 126. When the government makes such a claim, the protester must show with clear and convincing evidence that the specifications were derived from protester's proprietary data, *November Group, Inc.*, Comp. Gen. Dec. B-292483, 2003 CPD ¶ 165; *Ingersoll-Rand Co.*, Comp. Gen. Dec. B-236495, 89-2 CPD ¶ 542.

Many agencies now screen unsolicited research proposals to determine if they can be reviewed and considered under the broad agency announcement in effect at the time of receipt of the proposal. In most cases, the proposal will fall within one of the categories of research covered by this announcement and can be treated as a research proposal.

### d. Follow-On Contracts

Follow-on contracts are awards made to the contractor that has previously been awarded a design or manufacturing contract for the same item or that has previously performed the services being procured. CICA enacted two different provisions on this issue. Sole source contracting for follow-on contracts is permitted by 41 U.S.C. § 3304(b)(2) in the following circumstances:

[in the case of] a follow-on contract for the continued development or production of a major system or highly specialized equipment, the property may be deemed to be available only from the original source and may be procured through procedures other than competitive procedures when it is likely that award to a source other than the original source would result in (i) substantial duplication of cost to the Government which is not expected to be recovered through competition, or (ii) unacceptable delay in fulfilling the executive agency's needs.

The same provision is contained in 10 U.S.C. § 2304(d)(1)(B) with additional language making it applicable to follow-on contracts for "highly specialized services." The Act requires the agency to determine and document that the cost of the initial capital investment made by the developer of new items cannot be offset by savings that would result from openly competing the item.

There have been very few decisions on the scope of these statutes. See *Magnavox Elec. Sys. Co. v. United States*, 26 Cl. Ct. 1373 (1992) (enjoined sole source procurement because defense agency, relying on statutory exception for follow-on contracts, had not adequately explored alternative sources); and *Nomura Enters., Inc.*, Comp. Gen. Dec. B-260977, 95-2 CPD ¶ 206 (Army reasonably cited statutory justification for sole source award for interim period pending competitive procurement of these services). However, GAO has considered the issue of follow-on contracts in a variety of cases. In *Pegasus Global Strategic Solutions, LLC*, Comp. Gen. Dec. B-400422.3, 2009 CPD ¶ 73, GAO denied a protest where the agency reasonably determined from market research and testing that only the contract holder could meet its urgent requirements. Similarly, in *Raytheon Co.*, Comp. Gen. Dec. B-400610, 2009 CPD ¶ 8, GAO held that sole source procurements were unobjectionable where the agency reasonably found that award to any other source would likely cause unacceptable delays. In *International Harvester Co.*, 61 Comp. Gen. 388 (B-205073), 82-1 CPD ¶ 459, involving a sole source award to the company that developed and hand-built four prototypes, GAO urged the Army to limit its first production run to the minimum number needed to validate a data package and to consider whether competing the remainder of its requirements would result in savings despite the initial tooling cost incurred by the incumbent contractor. In *Sprint Commc'ns Co.*, Comp. Gen. Dec. B-262003.2, 96-1 CPD ¶ 24, the agency justified a 15-month "bridge" contract on a sole source basis to the original contractor to permit the award of several contracts designated to achieve significant economies of scale. See also *Univox Cal., Inc.*, Comp. Gen. Dec. B-225449.2, 87-2 CPD ¶ 569, permitting the limitation of competition to the two contractors that had developed competitive prototypes, but recommended that the agency quickly obtain technical data packages so that quantities in future years could be fully competed. Compare *Berkey Mktg. Cos.*, Comp. Gen. Dec. B-224481, 86-2 CPD ¶ 596, where the agency was permitted to continue buying "the only commercially available item within an acceptable price range that would meet the [agency's] minimum requirements," and *SEAVAC Int'l, Inc.*, Comp. Gen. Dec. B-231016, 88-2 CPD ¶ 134, where urgency justified the agency's continuing to buy services from the incumbent contractor. See also *Magnavox Elec. Sys. Co.*, Comp. Gen. Dec. B-258076.2, 94-2 CPD ¶ 266, finding that a sole source award on a follow-on contract was permissible because award to any other source would cause unacceptable delays. GAO noted that another basis for awarding sole source to a follow-on contractor would be if the award to any other source would result in substantial duplication of cost that would not be expected to be recovered through competition. Since the decision was based on unreasonable delay, GAO did not address the question of duplication of costs.

Mere prior experience of a contractor has been found to be insufficient grounds to support a sole source procurement. In *Electronic Sys., U.S.A., Inc.*, Comp. Gen. Dec. B-200947, 81-1 CPD ¶ 309, GAO stated:

A company's prior experience with the procuring agency which may facilitate the company's performance of the required services and enable it to better anticipate problems in the implementation of the system is not a legally adequate justification to support a sole-source procurement. Furthermore, the fact that a particular contractor may be able to perform the services with greater ease than any other contractor does not justify a noncompetitive procurement to the exclusion of others.

In another decision, a sole source procurement of repairs to an oil distribution system was improper when justified on the basis that the selected contractor had installed the original system and had previously made repairs to it, *Titan Atl. Constr. Corp.*, Comp. Gen. Dec. B-200986, 81-2 CPD ¶ 12. See also *Metropolitan Radiology Assocs.*, Comp. Gen. Dec. B-195559, 80-1 CPD ¶ 265, where GAO ruled that a sole source procurement was not justified on the basis of a past long-standing relationship with a single contractor.

Justifications for award of sole source procurements to the prior contractor have been most successfully challenged by the submission of proof that the competitor is equally capable of performing the work. For example, in *Techniarts*, Comp. Gen. Dec. B-193263, 79-1 CPD ¶ 246, GAO determined that the protester was capable of producing the desired product, and the sole source procurement was therefore improper. Similarly, sole source procurements were found improper in *Berkshire Computer Prods.*, Comp. Gen. Dec. B-240327, 91-1 CPD ¶ 464 (protester sold compatible equipment and software for a computer system); *Aerospace Research Assocs.*, Comp. Gen. Dec. B-201953, 81-2 CPD ¶ 36 (agency was aware of two other contractors that could possibly "satisfy the Government's minimum needs without undue technical risk . . . within the required time," yet failed to contact them about the solicitation); *Federal Data Corp.*, Comp. Gen. Dec. B-196221, 80-1 CPD ¶ 167 (after the agency's publication of intent to procure on a sole source basis, the agency received alternative responses indicating the likelihood that other concerns could meet the government's needs); and *Consolidated Elevator Co.*, 56 Comp. Gen. 434 (B-187624), 77-1 CPD ¶ 210 (companies other than the manufacturers of elevators could meet the government's maintenance needs).

## 2.  *Unusual and Compelling Urgency*

The second exception in the statute permits a procurement without full and open competition based on "unusual and compelling" urgency. This exception is narrowly construed because the acquisition planning process is intended to overcome all but the most compelling urgency situations. In *Filtration Dev. Co. v. United States*, 59 Fed. Cl. 658 (2004), the court outlined some of the substantive and temporal limitations on this CICA exception at 633:

In keeping with its preference for "full and open competition," the statute indicates that "the head of an agency using procedures other than competitive procedures . . . by reason of the application of subsection (c)(2) . . . shall request offers from as many potential sources as practicable under the circumstances." 10 U.S.C. § 2304(e). The agency head's discretion to invoke the exception is also not unfettered; a justification is required and "[e]ach justification shall contain sufficient facts and rationale to justify the use of the specific authority cited." 48 C.F.R. § 6.303- 2(a). In addition, the exception has been interpreted as containing an implicit limitation that "the agency take reasonable steps to accurately determine its needs and describe them." *Matter of Signals & Sys., Inc.,* B-288107, 2001 CPD ¶ 168, at 12, . . . . (Sept. 21, 2001). The agency head's discretion is subject to this limitation because "the urgency justification cannot support the procurement of more than a minimum quantity needed to satisfy the immediate urgent requirement." *Id.*

Urgency has generally been found in circumstances where the agency has made reasonable efforts to obtain competition but has been unable to accomplish this goal because of insufficient time to fulfill critical agency requirements. For example, the need to continue weapon tests vital to the national security has met the urgency requirement, *Support Sys. Assocs.*, Comp. Gen. Dec. B-232473, 89-1 CPD ¶ 11. Urgency was also found to exist in *T-L-C Sys.*, Comp. Gen. Dec. B-44369, 2008 CPD ¶ 195 (agency showed that immediate replacement of 51 failed fire alarms was necessary to prevent serious injury to property or loss of life); *McGregor Mfg. Corp.*, Comp. Gen Dec. B-285341, 2000 CPD ¶ 151 (exclusion of competitor was reasonable because the competitor's inability to provide usable parts caused the agency's urgency for procurement); *BlueStar Battery Sys. Corp.*, Comp. Gen. Dec. B-270111.2, 96-1 CPD ¶ 67 (procurement restricted to two manufacturers that had supplied batteries to the Army under previous contracts); *Alektronics, Inc.*, Comp. Gen. Dec. B-261431, 95-2 CPD ¶ 146 (sole source award of a critical military item reasonable where there was an inventory shortage and awardee was the only approved source); *All Points Int'l, Inc.*, Comp. Gen. Dec. B-260134, 95-1 CPD ¶ 252 (only one contractor was capable of meeting requirement relating to the growing Cuban and Haitian refugee population at the U.S. Naval Facility); *Purdy Corp.*, Comp. Gen. Dec. B-257432, 94-2 CPD ¶ 127 (no other source possessed or could reasonably access test stand that was needed quickly for examining discovered gearbox problem); *Logics, Inc.*, Comp. Gen. Dec. B-256171, 94-1 CPD ¶ 314 (agency solicited only known sources that had successfully manufactured filter assemblies because the agency encountered a critical supply shortage); *Sargent & Greenleaf, Inc.*, Comp. Gen. Dec. B-255604.3, 94-1 CPD ¶ 208 (sole source award to only qualified firm for limited quantities of security containers because existing mechanical locks placed classified information at risk); *E. Huttenbauer & Son, Inc.*, Comp. Gen. Dec. B-252320.2, 93-1 CPD ¶ 499 (agency reasonably determined that only one known firm was capable of meeting urgent supply requirement caused by Operation Restore Hope in Somalia); *Greenbrier Indus., Inc.*, Comp. Gen. Dec. B-241304, 91-1 CPD ¶ 92 (Marine Corps reasonably determined that only one company was capable of immediately supplying chemical protective suits for use in Operation Desert Shield); *Rotair Indus.*, Comp. Gen. Dec. B-239503, 90-2 CPD ¶ 154 (competition limited to two sources with qualified products when the protester had not completed the qualification of its product and the agency could wait no longer);

and *Racal Corp.*, Comp. Gen. Dec. B-235441, 89-2 CPD ¶ 213 (contract awarded to the only contractor that could proceed without first article testing and the agency had concluded that the risk of failure by another contractor was too great). Similarly, in *Gentex Corp.*, Comp. Gen. Dec. B-233119, 89-1 CPD ¶ 144, the agency was justified in refusing to consider an untested competitive product in a weapons program, and in *Forster Enters., Inc.*, Comp. Gen. Dec. B-237910, 90-1 CPD ¶ 363, a sole source contract was permitted to the only company with a qualified product for an unforeseen quantity of essential military items needed during the period the protester was qualifying its product under a new contract. Compare *Al Ghanim Combined Group Co. Gen. Trad. & Cont. W.L.L. v. United States*, 56 Fed. Cl. 502 (2003) (defendant agency suggested basis for urgency exception may have eroded once President declared end of major hostilities in Iraq in May 2003).

Unusual and compelling circumstances have also been found when there was insufficient time to test a nondevelopmental item, *Astron*, Comp. Gen. Dec. B-236922.2, 90-1 CPD ¶ 441. A finding of urgency has also been justified where the contractor currently performing the work provided an additional quantity while competition was being conducted for future requirements, *Elbit Computers, Ltd.*, Comp. Gen. Dec. B-239038, 90-2 CPD ¶ 26; *Abbott Prods., Inc.*, Comp. Gen. Dec. B-231131, 88-2 CPD ¶ 119, and while an award protest was being decided, *Unified Indus., Inc.*, 70 Comp. Gen. 142 (B-241010), 91-1 CPD ¶ 11. However, unusual and compelling circumstances will not be found if the agency is slow in conducting the procurement. For example, in *Honeycomb Co. of Am.*, Comp. Gen. Dec. B-227070, 87-2 CPD ¶ 209, GAO held that no urgency could be justified when the agency took eight months to award a contract for products to be delivered from 16 months to four years after award.

Unusual and compelling circumstances also will not be found when there is a lack of advance planning, *RBC Bearings Inc.*, Comp. Gen Dec. B-401661, 2009 CPD ¶ 207; *New Breed Leasing Corp.*, Comp. Gen. Dec. B-274201, 96-2 CPD ¶ 202; *TLC Servs., Inc.*, Comp. Gen. Dec. B-252614, 93-1 CPD ¶ 481. Agencies may not justify contracting without providing for full and open competition simply because of a lack of planning, 10 U.S.C. § 2304(f)(4)(A); FAR 6.301(c)(1); *Signals & Sys., Inc.*, Comp. Gen. Dec. B-288107, 2001 CPD ¶ 168. Compare *Bannum, Inc.*, Comp. Gen. Dec. B-289707, 2002 CPD ¶ 61 (while the agency's planning ultimately was unsuccessful, this was due to unanticipated events, not a lack of planning); and *Diversified Tech. & Servs. of Virginia, Inc.*, Comp. Gen. Dec. B-282497, 99-2 CPD ¶ 16 (refusing to fault the agency where procurement was delayed by the agency's efforts to implement a long-term acquisition plan).

Although urgency does not necessarily justify sole source procurement, an agency conducting a procurement under the urgency exception may limit competition to the only firm it reasonably believes can perform the work promptly and properly, *Arthur Young & Co.*, Comp. Gen. Dec. B-221879, 86-1 CPD ¶ 536; *Gentex Corp.*, Comp. Gen. Dec. B-221340, 86-1 CPD ¶ 195. See also *IMR Sys.*

*Corp.*, Comp. Gen. Dec. B-222465, 86-2 CPD ¶ 36, where urgency justified a sole source procurement even though the protester had notified the agency that it could take over the work on three to five days' notice. Compare *Earth Prop. Serv., Inc.*, Comp. Gen. Dec. B-237742, 90-1 CPD ¶ 273, sustaining a protest of a sole source procurement based on urgency because the protester showed that it could begin performance "on short notice."

Although the statute does not indicate what type of "serious injury" must result to justify limiting competition, GAO has included possible financial injury within the scope of the term, *Arthur Young Co.*, Comp. Gen. Dec. B-221879, 86-1 CPD ¶ 536. In that case, the Navy was permitted to make a sole source award because it claimed that the incumbent was the only firm that could perform a management study in time and that the study was necessary to achieve an estimated $1.5 billion savings. Serious injury was also found in a potential failure of the agency's telephone system, *AT&T Info. Servs., Inc.*, 66 Comp. Gen. 58 (B-223914), 86-2 CPD ¶ 447, and potential poor operation of the agency's computer facility, *Data Transformation Corp.*, Comp. Gen. Dec. B-220581, 86-1 CPD ¶ 55. In addition, changed conditions, such as policy decisions to reduce budgets or reorder procurement priorities, do not generally indicate a lack of advance planning by an agency. See *Magnavox Elec. Corp.*, Comp. Gen. Dec. B-258076, 94-2 CPD ¶ 266, where problems in a data program created an unforeseen need for substantial additional quantities of its alternative.

Potential expiration of funds is not a justification under the urgency exception, FAR 6.301(c)(2); *AAI ACL Tech., Inc.*, Comp. Gen. Dec. B-258679.4, 95-2 CPD ¶ 243 (distinguishing the expiration of funds from the unavailability of funds). See *Computer Lines*, GSBCA 8206-P, 86-1 BCA ¶ 18,653, where the board stated at 93,805:

> We can first quickly dispel the notion that [the agency's] actions in this acquisition are somehow made legitimate by its concern that the period of availability for obligation of its funds was shortly to expire. *See* 31 U.S.C. § 1552(a)(2) (1982) (the unobligated balance of funds available for obligation for a definite period is withdrawn at the end of the period of availability for obligation, and it reverts to the Treasury). The procurement provisions of the CICA have put an end to the idea that the statutory duty to obtain maximum practicable competition is somehow suspended at the end of each fiscal year. The legislative history of the CICA clearly depicts Congressional disgust with unconscionable year-end spending abuses. *See,* H.R. Rep. No 98-861, 98th Cong., 2d Sess. 1428 (1984), *reprinted in* 1984 U.S. Code Cong. & Ad. News 2116. We do not suggest that this acquisition was the sort of abusive spending that Congress had in mind when it prohibited agencies from entering into noncompetitive contracts "on the basis of the lack of advance planning or concerns related to the amount of funds available to the agency for procurement functions." [10 U.S.C. § 2304(f)(5)(A)] Nonetheless, we have previously held that concerns as to expiring funds have no place in protest proceedings before this Board, *Wordplex Corp.*, GSBCA No.

8193-P, 86-1 BCA ¶ 18,655 (Dec. 3, 1985), and we see no reason to depart from that holding here.

Frequently, the threat of appropriations expiring occurs because of a protest against the award. See, for example, *Federal Tech. Corp.*, GSBCA 10188-P, 89-3 BCA ¶ 22,134, where the board refused to permit award pending the outcome of a protest that could have resulted in a decision on the last day of the fiscal year. This problem has been ameliorated with regard to protests before the agency, GAO, or the courts by the provisions of 31 U.S.C. § 1558(a), which keep appropriations from expiring for 100 calendar days after the date of the final ruling on the protest.

When agencies use the urgency exception, they must limit the quantity of the supplies or services being procured to only the amount necessary to meet their needs prior to the time when competition can be obtained. See *SSI Tech., Inc.*, Comp. Gen. Dec. B-298212, 2006 CPD ¶ 183, where GAO analyzed the agency's computation of the number of units being procured under the urgency exception and found that it was greater than needed before a competitive procurement was completed. See also *Filtration Dev. Co., LLC v. United States*, 60 Fed. Cl. 371 (2004) (agency limited quantity to its minimum needs); *Signals & Sys., Inc.*, Comp. Gen. Dec. B-288107, 2001 CPD ¶ 168 (unreasonable to procure large quantity based on inadequate data on actual needs of agency). In *EOD Tech., Inc. v. United States*, 82 Fed. Cl. 12 (2008), the court denied a motion to enjoin the override of a stay that awarded a six month bridge contract but enjoined the agency from proceeding on a sole source basis "absent exigent circumstances."

### 3. Industrial Mobilization and Maintaining Critical Capability

The third exception permits a procurement under less than competitive procedures in order to achieve industrial mobilization or to establish or maintain critical engineering, research, or development capability provided by an educational or other nonprofit organization or federally funded research and development center, FAR 6.302-3(a)(2)(i) & (ii). An agency's decision under this exception will not be questioned as long as it can demonstrate that its determinations are related to its industrial mobilization needs, *Minowitz Mfg. Co.*, Comp. Gen. Dec. B-228502, 88-1 CPD ¶ 1. See also *Ridgeline Indus. Inc.*, Comp. Gen. Dec. B-402105, 2010 CPD ¶ 22 (sole source contract to preserve the industrial base was reasonable where protester only had experience in producing tent components, not complete tents); *Right Away Foods/Shelf Stable Foods*, Comp. Gen. Dec. B-259859.3, 95-2 CPD ¶ 34 (award to third mobilization base producer proper where agency reasonably determined that the failure of either of the current producers would be catastrophic in the event of a military emergency); *Kilgore Corp.*, Comp. Gen. Dec. B-253672, 93-2 CPD ¶ 220 (sole source award to operate and maintain an ammunition plant based on mobilization need); *Lance Ordnance Co.*, Comp. Gen. Dec. B-246849, 92-2 CPD ¶ 29 (sole source award made to one of two mobilization base producers for smoke and illumination signals); *Greenbrier Indus., Inc.*, Comp. Gen. Dec. B-248177, 92-2 CPD ¶ 74 (agency divided its requirements for chemical suits among four active mobilization base producers to provide a continuation of each firm's minimum sustaining rate of production); and *Propper Int'l, Inc.*, Comp. Gen. Dec. B-229888, 88-1 CPD ¶ 296 (Navy hat considered an essential part of the enlisted person's uniform and designated industrial mobilization item).

The exception under FAR 6.302-3(a)(2)(iii) extends as well to a sole source procurement to "acquire the services of an expert or neutral person for any current or anticipated litigation or dispute." In *SEMCOR, Inc.*, Comp. Gen. Dec. B-279794, 98-2 CPD ¶ 43, the Air Force had attempted to use this exception in acquiring, on a sole source basis, the services of a group of litigation support personnel who had long experience with certain Air Force litigation. GAO rejected that justification, finding that the litigation support personnel at issue hardly possessed true expertise, "special skill or knowledge of a particular subject, that may be combined with experience, which enables them to provide opinions, information, advice, or recommendations to those who call upon them."

## 4. Terms of International Agreement or Treaty

This exception may be used when the terms of an international agreement or treaty have the effect of requiring the use of other than competitive procedures, FAR 6.302-4. See *Goddard Indus., Inc.*, Comp. Gen. Dec. B-275643, 97-1 CPD ¶ 104 (agency's sole source purchase as part of foreign military sale at foreign government's request was permissible); *Pilkington Aerospace, Inc.*, Comp. Gen. B-260397, 95-2 CPD ¶ 122 (Israeli order for parts on sole source basis through U.S. agency). There is no requirement that the foreign government initiate a sole source designation. Thus, in the absence of bad faith or an intention to circumvent competition, it is immaterial whether a United States agency recommends specific items or advises a foreign government as to what items might satisfy its needs. See *Electro Design Mfg., Inc.*, Comp. Gen. Dec. B-280953, 98-2 CPD ¶ 142 (upholding agency's decision to combine system requirements into single procurement at foreign customer's request); *Julie Research Labs. Inc.*, GSBCA 8070-P, 85-3 BCA ¶ 18,375; and *Kahn Indus., Inc.*, Comp. Gen. Dec. B-225491, 87-1 CPD ¶ 343.

## 5. Authorized by Another Statute

The use of other than competitive procedures is permitted when a statute expressly authorizes or requires that a procurement be made through another agency or from a specified source. See, for example, *Diversified Mgt. Group, A Joint Venture*, Comp. Gen. Dec. B-288443.2, 2001 CPD ¶ 175 (appropriate to sole-source per Javits-Wagner-O'Day statute). Although FAR 6.302-5 lists a number of statutory set-aside authorities that *may* make sole source procurement appropriate, in *HAP Constr., Inc.*,

Comp. Gen. Dec. B-280044, 98-2 CPD ¶ 76, GAO emphasized that FAR 6.302-5 does not mean that the procuring agency *must* use those statutory authorities.

Sole source awards under the Small Business Act's § 8(a) set-aside program are usually justified under this exception. See *Bosco Contracting Inc.*, Comp. Gen. Dec. B-236989, 89-2 CPD ¶ 346, holding that CICA's mandate for full and open competition does not apply to a procurement being conducted as a § 8(a) set-aside under 15 U.S.C. § 637(a). 10 U.S.C. § 2304(c)(5) also authorizes the use of other than competitive procedures when "the agency's need is for a brand-name commercial item for authorized resale." See *Defense Commissary — Request for Advance Decision*, Comp. Gen. Dec. B-262047, 96-1 CPD ¶ 115, holding that under CICA, the Defense Commissary Agency could noncompetitively procure items bearing the USO Always Home brand name for resale in military stores.

## 6. National Security

This exception permits an agency to limit the number of sources from which it solicits offers if the disclosure of the agency's needs would compromise the national security. There are no reported protests on the use of this exception. See generally Clark, *Overcoming the Critical Challenges of Contingency Contracting: Understanding the Flexibility Permitted by CICA, Simplified Acquisition Procedures, and Small Purchases*, 28 Pub. Cont. L.J. 503, 512-13 (1999) (discussing CICA exceptions).

## 7. Public Interest

This exception enables the head of the agency to make a determination that it is necessary in the public interest to use other than competitive procedures in a particular procurement. See *Sikorsky Aircraft Corp.*, Comp. Gen. Dec. B-403471, 2010 CPD ¶ 271, denying a protest that the Navy had improperly used this exception to buy Russian helicopters for the Afghanistan Air Force. GAO found that the Secretary of the Navy had properly determined that providing a helicopter with which the Afghans were familiar would assist the war effort. See also *Zublin Del., Inc.*, Comp. Gen. Dec. B-227003.2, 87-2 CPD ¶ 149, denying a protest that the Navy, after submission of initial offers, unreasonably restricted competition to United States firms for construction of Navy housing in the Philippines. GAO held that the Secretary of the Navy, under 10 U.S.C. § 2304(c)(7), made the required determination that such a restriction was in the public interest because hiring foreign firms could jeopardize United States bases in the Philippines.

In late 2003, DoD cited this exception under FAR 6.302-7, to bar other nations which had joined the United States' coalition in Iraq from competing for certain Iraqi reconstruction contracts. See Deputy Secretary of Defense Paul Wolfowitz December 5, 2003 Memorandum: Contracting in Iraq, available at *http:// japan.usembassy.gov/e/p/tp-20031211-04.html*. The decision triggered an international uproar, and raised concerns as to whether that exercise of sole source authority violated the United States' obligations to allow equal access to U.S. procurement under the World Trade Organization's Government Procurement Agreement. See Pitchas, *World Trade Organisation/United States: Award of Prime Contracts for Infrastructure Reconstruction in Iraq — An Assessment Under the WTO Agreement,* 2004 Pub. Proc. L. Rev. NA85.

## 8.  Competition Excluding Particular Sources

41 U.S.C. § 3303(a)(1) provides that executive agencies are permitted to exclude particular sources in order to establish or maintain alternate sources if the agency head determines that to do so would —

(A) increase or maintain competition and likely result in reduced overall costs for such procurement, or an anticipated procurement, of property or services;

(B) be in the interest of national defense in having a facility (or a producer, manufacturer, or other supplier) available for furnishing the property or service in case of a national emergency or industrial mobilization;

(C) be in the interest of national defense in establishing or maintaining an essential engineering, research, or development capability to be provided by an educational or other nonprofit institution or a Federally funded research and development center;

(D) ensure the continuous availability of a reliable source of supply of the property or service;

(E) satisfy projected needs for the property or service determined on the basis of a history of high demand for the property or service; or

(F) satisfy a critical need for medical, safety, or emergency supplies.

Substantially the same provision is contained in 10 U.S.C. § 2304(b)(1).

The second and third of these reasons are similar to the former 10 U.S.C. § 2304(a)(16), which permitted the use of negotiated procurement for mobilization purposes. The first reason gives statutory authority for developing a competitive second source by precluding an existing sole source contractor from participating in the second source competition or maintaining an alternate source by precluding the primary source from being awarded all of an agency's requirements. FAR 6.202(a) states the following justifications that may be used for the action:

Agencies may exclude a particular source from a contract action in order to establish or maintain an alternate source or sources for the supplies or services being acquired if the agency head determines that to do so would —

(1) Increase or maintain competition and likely result in reduced overall costs for the acquisition, or for any anticipated acquisition;

(2) Be in the interest of national defense in having a facility (or a producer, manufacturer, or other supplier) available for furnishing the supplies or services in case of a national emergency or industrial mobilization;

(3) Be in the interest of national defense in establishing or maintaining an essential engineering, research, or development capability to be provided by an educational or other nonprofit institution or a federally funded research and development center;

(4) Ensure the continuous availability of a reliable source of supplies or services;

(5) Satisfy projected needs based on a history of high demand; or

(6) Satisfy a critical need for medical, safety, or emergency supplies.

See *Hawker Eternacell, Inc.*, Comp. Gen. Dec. B-283586, 99-2 CPD ¶ 96 (agency decision to exclude incumbent encompassed most reasons for exclusion under FAR).

FAR 6.202(b) provides that a determination and findings (D&F) by an agency head or designee must support the decision to exclude particular sources. Class D&Fs are not permitted; thus, a D&F must be made for each individual procurement action. After exclusion of particular sources, an agency is required to establish full and open competition using one of the competitive procedures, FAR 6.201.

## 9. Reprocurement after Default Termination

FAR 49.402-6(b) provides that after a default termination, reprocurements of no more than the amount of work remaining to be performed are not subject to the statutory competition requirements, while reprocurements over the remaining quantity of work are to be treated as "new acquisitions." The FAR requires in the former case that the agency obtain competition "to the maximum extent practicable." GAO has held that in the case of a reprocurement after default, the statutes and regulations governing regular federal procurements are not strictly applicable, *Aerosonic Corp.*, 68 Comp. Gen. 179 (B-232730), 89-1 CPD ¶ 45. See *AT&T Corp.*, Comp. Gen. Dec. B-270344, 96-1 CPD ¶ 117, denying a protest against the sole source award of a contract for a telecommunications circuit following the protester's default termination; *Marvin Land Sys., Inc.*, Comp. Gen. Dec. B-276434, 97-2 CPD ¶ 4, denying a protest by the defaulted contractor that the agency had issued a sole source contract, and *Bluff Springs Paper Co., Ltd./R.D. Thompson Paper Products Co. Joint Venture*, Comp. Gen. Dec. B-286797.3, 2001 CPD ¶ 160, denying a protest that the agency did not award to the second low bidder on the prior procurement. But see *Master Sec., Inc.*, Comp. Gen. Dec. B-235711, 89-2 CPD ¶ 303, ruling that the inclusion of two one-year options in a sole source reprocurement of a defaulted service contract was unreasonable. In reaching this conclusion, GAO used the same reasoning applied under the statutory requirements — because there was adequate time to obtain competition for this optional work, not obtaining such competition was improper. Contracting officers are invested with wide latitude to determine how needed supplies or services are to be reprocured after a default, *Vereinigte Gebaudereinigungsgesellschaft*, Comp. Gen. Dec. B-280805, 98-2 CPD ¶ 117, and may automatically exclude a defaulted contractor from the competition for the reprocurement, *Montage Inc.*, Comp. Gen. Dec. B-277923.2, 97-2 CPD ¶ 176.

## C. Ordering Work Under Existing Contracts

Merely because work is added to an existing contract by modification or change order does not justify the use of "other than competitive" procedures if the work is in reality a new procurement action. Thus, it is necessary to determine whether the work can properly be ordered on a noncompetitive basis under existing contracts.

### 1. Change Orders

Change orders issued under the various Changes clauses may be made on a sole source basis if they are within the general scope of the contract. Although GAO does not review contract administration matters, it will review an allegation that the government action should have been the subject of a new procurement, *LDDS WorldCom*, Comp. Gen. Dec. B-266257, 96-1 CPD ¶ 50; *Arjay Elecs. Corp.*, Comp. Gen. Dec. B-243080, 91-2 CPD ¶ 3; *Memorex Corp.*, 61 Comp. Gen. 42 (B-200722), 81-2 CPD ¶ 334; *Webcraft Packaging*, Comp. Gen. Dec. B-194087, 79-2 CPD ¶ 120.

Changes outside of the scope of the work have been called "cardinal changes." A "scope of the competition" test is employed to determine whether work has been improperly added to a contract. See *American Air Filter Co.*, 57 Comp. Gen. 567 (B-188408), 78-1 CPD ¶ 443, stating at 573:

> The impact of any modification is in our view to be determined by examining whether the alteration is within the scope of the competition which was initially conducted. Ordinarily, a modification falls within the scope of the procurement provided that it is of a nature which potential offerors would have reasonably anticipated under the changes clause.

> To determine what potential offerors would have reasonably expected, consideration should be given, in our view, to the procurement format used, the history of the present and related past procurements, and the nature of the supplies or services sought. A variety of factors may be pertinent, including: whether the requirement was appropriate initially for an advertised or negotiated procurement; whether a standard off-the-shelf or similar item is sought; or whether,

*e.g.*, the contract is one for research and development, suggesting that broad changes might be expected because the Government's requirements are at best only indefinite.

GAO held that a change substituting diesel for gasoline engines in heating units was beyond the scope of an advertised manufacturing contract because it required significant development work, doubled the performance time, and increased the price by 29%. In *W.H. Mullins*, Comp. Gen. Dec. B-207200, 83-1 CPD ¶ 158, a modification of an existing requirements contract was also found to be beyond the scope of competition for the original contract because the parties could not have reasonably anticipated such a major change. See also *DynCorp Int'l LLC,* Comp. Gen. Dec. B-402349, 2010 CPD ¶ 59, where the task order requests for proposal were not reasonably contemplated under the original contract quantities; *Poly-Pacific Techs., Inc.*, Comp. Gen. Dec. B-296029, 2005 CPD ¶ 105, where a modification to solid waste disposal was outside the scope of work anticipated by the underlying solicitation; *MCI Telecomms. Corp.*, Comp. Gen. Dec. B-276659.2, 97-2 CPD ¶ 90, where a modification of the FTS 2000 contract under which AT&T Commc'ns, Inc. supplied 60% of the federal government's intercity telecommunications services exceeded the scope of the original contract and therefore had to be purchased on a competitive basis. In the latter decision, GAO distinguished the network design and management services at issue purchased under the modification from the services purchased under earlier modifications, thereby distinguishing the case from *AT&T Commc'ns, Inc. v. Wiltel, Inc.*, 1 F.3d 1201 (Fed. Cir. 1993). See, however, *LDDS WorldCom*, Comp. Gen. Dec. B-266257, 96-1 CPD ¶ 50, finding the modification at issue there to be within the scope of the original contract because the added services could have been anticipated from the face of the contract and the added services were not materially different from the services currently produced under the contract.

A slightly different test was used in *Cray Research v. Department of the Navy*, 556 F. Supp. 201 (D.D.C. 1982), where the court stated at 203:

> The "cardinal change" doctrine prevents government agencies from circumventing the competitive process by adopting drastic modifications beyond the original scope of a contract. The basic standard is whether the modified contract calls for essentially the same performance as that required by the contract when originally awarded so that the modification does not materially change the field of competition.

Utilizing this analysis, the court examined the claim that installation by an incumbent contractor of more advanced computer equipment following a performance test failure of the specified equipment was a "cardinal change." The court held that where new equipment is provided at no additional cost and the original contract specifications remain unchanged, the field of competition is not changed sufficiently to constitute a cardinal change.

The Court of Federal Claims, in the case of *Cardinal Maint. Serv., Inc. v. United States,* 63 Fed. Cl. 98 (2004), drew together the precedents of GAO and the Court of Federal Claims on this issue of "cardinal change," stating at 106-07:

> Both this court and the GAO, in the exercise of its bid protest jurisdiction, have looked to a variety of factors to determine whether a contract, as modified, calls for "essentially the same performance." Several cases have endorsed the factors identified by the Comptroller General in *Matter of: Neil R. Gross & Co., Inc.,* Comp. Gen. B-237434, . . . : "In determining the materiality of a modification, we consider factors such as the extent of any changes in the type of work, performance period and costs between the contract as awarded and modified." . . . . Most recently, in *CW Government Travel, Inc. v. United States,* 61 Fed. Cl. 559 (2004), the court found that the addition, by contract modification, of traditional travel services to a contract to provide military travel services using a paperless automated travel management system was a material change; thus the contracting agency's failure to issue a competitive solicitation for traditional travel services violated CICA. As the *CW Government Travel* court explained, a "modification generally falls within the scope of the original procurement if potential bidders would have expected it to fall within the contract's changes clause." . . .

Compare *Chapman Law Firm v. United States,* 63 Fed. Cl. 519 (2005) (declining to apply *Cardinal Maintenance* factors).

The General Services Board of Contract Appeals followed essentially the same analysis as that used by GAO. See *MCI Telecomms. Corp. v. General Servs. Admin.,* GSBCA 11963-P, 93-1 BCA ¶ 25,541 . In *Wiltel, Inc. v. General Servs. Admin.,* 93-1 BCA ¶ 25,314, *rev'd,* 1 F.3d 1201 (Fed. Cir. 1993), the board held that a modification to a telecommunications contract to add a new service that had become available commercially after contract award was outside the scope of the services for which the contract had been awarded. However, the Federal Circuit reversed, stating that the services added by the modification would have been anticipated by the original competitors because the solicitation called for services that were commercially available and the contract contained a "Service Improvements" clause, *AT&T Commc'ns, Inc. v. Wiltel, Inc.,* 1 F.3d 1201 (Fed. Cir. 1993). The court noted that "a broad original competition may validate a broader range of later modifications."

Contract actions held to be outside the scope of the procurement include a change order issued almost immediately after contract award substituting a mail delivery system of electric cars on fixed tracks in lieu of the specialized system of stationary trays on moving belts, *Lumson Dtv. of Diebold, Inc.,* Comp. Gen. Dec. B-196029.2, 80-1 CPD ¶ 447; a modification substituting a newer model disk drive and changing an "option to purchase" or a "lease-to-ownership" plan envisioning a five-year lease period, *Memorex Corp.,* 61 Comp. Gen. 42 (B-200722), 81-2 CPD ¶ 334; an extension of a requirements contract for word processing equipment, *CPT Corp.,* Comp. Gen. Dec. B-211464, 84-1 CPD ¶ 606; and a modification to the performance specifications in the purchase description for aircraft generator test stands, *Avtron Mfg., Inc.*, 67 Comp. Gen. 404 (B-229972), 88-1 CPD ¶ 458.

## 2. *Extensions and Options*

Contract extensions, exercise of contract options, and lease renewals can also constitute de facto sole source procurements. Extensions adding only time to permit the contractor to complete performance of the original work are almost always within the scope of the procurement. However, if the original contract is seen as a procurement of services for a specified period of time, extensions calling for additional time will frequently be held to be de facto sole source procurements. GAO has stated that "competition should be sought whenever it appears likely that the Government's position can be improved whether in terms of cost or performance," 51 Comp. Gen. 57 (B-165218) (1971). In *Washington Nat'l Arena Ltd P'ship*, 65 Comp. Gen. 25 (B-219136), 85-2 CPD ¶ 435, the government issued an amendment retroactively extending a contract that had expired four months earlier. GAO held that this action constituted a cardinal change and an improper de facto sole source award. See also *Intermem Corp.*, Comp. Gen. Dec. B-187607, 77-1 CPD ¶ 263, where a mandatory requirements contract was modified twice to extend its expiration date. The agency issued a D&F (a written approval by an authorized official, clearly justifying the specific determination made), concluding that the extensions were in the best interests of the government because a lapse would disrupt a government-wide mandatory source of equipment and services, and user agencies would lose accumulated purchase credits. GAO found that the extensions became necessary only because the agency failed to timely solicit a follow-on contract, and the extensions were therefore not justified. In *Varian Assocs.*, Comp. Gen. Dec. B-208281, 83-1 CPD ¶ 160, the exercise of a contract option by the contracting agency constituted an unjustifiable sole source procurement even though the contracting officer sought and obtained a reduction in the price called for in the original contract. In *Federal Data Corp.*, Comp. Gen. Dec. B-196221, 80-1 CPD ¶ 167, a short renewal of an ADPE lease pending replacement with government-owned equipment constituted an unjustified sole source procurement where responses to a CBD notice evidenced competitive interests in a solicitation. See also *Major Contracting Servs., Inc.*, Comp. Gen. Dec. B-401472, 2009 CPD ¶ 170, *recons. denied*, 2009 CPD ¶ 250; and *Techno-Sciences, Inc.*, Comp. Gen. Dec. B-257686, 94-2 CPD ¶ 164, finding that the agencies had improperly extended contracts on a sole source basis, stating that other responsible sources could have competed for the requirement had the agency engaged in adequate advance procurement planning.

Before an agency may exercise an option, in order to satisfy the requirement for full and open competition, "the option must have been evaluated as part of the initial competition," FAR 17.207(f). See also FAR 6.001, which contains the following statement of applicability of the competition requirements:

This part applies to all acquisitions except —

\* \* \*

(c) Contract modifications, including the exercise of priced options that were evaluated as part of the initial competition (see 17.207(f)), that are within the scope and under the terms of an existing contract.

If an option is not evaluated under the initial competition, FAR 17.207(f) prevents its exercise absent an appropriate justification and authorization that full and open competition is not required, *Kollsman Instrument Co.*, Comp. Gen. Dec. B-233759, 89-1 CPD ¶ 243. See *Stoehner Sec. Servs., Inc.*, Comp. Gen. Dec. B-248077.3, 92-2 CPD ¶ 285. Furthermore, an option may only be exercised at an amount that is "reasonably determinable from the terms of the basic contract," FAR 17.207(f). See *Magnum Opus Techs., Inc. v. United States*, 94 Fed. Cl. 512 (2010), rejecting exercise of options where the agency had agreed that the prices in the contract were unenforceable.

Even if it has been determined that government action in modifying a contract has gone beyond the scope of the procurement, and therefore constitutes a de facto sole source procurement, GAO will deny the protest if a new sole source procurement could have been justified. See *Pegasus Global Strategic Solutions, LLC*, Comp. Gen. Dec. B-400422.3, 2009 CPD ¶ 73, finding that the Army's sole source modification of a contract was reasonable based on market research and testing that only the contract holder could meet its urgent requirements. In *Tilden-Coil Constructors, Inc.*, Comp. Gen. Dec. B-211189.3, 83-2 CPD ¶ 236, the Army modified an ongoing contract, for the construction of eight buildings and a central energy plant, to authorize the incumbent to construct two additional buildings. GAO accepted the Army's explanation that additional costs and delayed completion dates would result from the overcrowding of the congested work site occasioned by the presence of another contractor. Similarly, in *Die Mesh Corp.*, Comp. Gen. Dec. B-190421, 78-2 CPD ¶ 36, modifications incorporating Phase II research into Phase I contracts, although outside of the scope of the procurement, were allowed. The procuring agency had claimed that Phase II was treated as a new (noncompetitive) procurement and that the contracts were modified "purely for administrative convenience." GAO found sufficient sole source justification to support the amendment because award to a new source would have precluded meeting statutory deadlines for the program. See also *Mediax Assocs.*, Comp. Gen. Dec. B-211350, 84-1 CPD ¶ 71, declining to determine whether a modification exceeded the scope of a procurement after first concluding that a sole source award was justified. Similarly, in *Hercules Aerospace Co.*, Comp. Gen. Dec. B-254677, 94-1 CPD ¶ 7, the protester asserted that a contract modification for additional rocket motors and engineering services amounted to a de facto sole source procurement. Without deciding this issue, GAO held that the agency's decision to modify the contract of the only qualified contractor due to unusual and compelling circumstances was reasonable. Compare *Kent Watkins & Assocs.*, Comp. Gen. Dec. B-191078, 78-1 CPD ¶ 377, where the government apparently added another year's work by modification and later wrote a sole source justification for a new procurement after the protest had been lodged. The supporting reasons cited included that the incumbent contractor submitted the only response to the solicitation, the incumbent had gained special experience, and additional costs would be incurred in changing contractors. However, because the agency was aware of other companies interested in the solicitation, GAO found the sole source award improper. In 41 Comp. Gen. 484 (B-145598) (1962), a Navy decision to renovate a portion of Bancroft Hall at the Naval Academy by giving a change order to a contractor that was performing other work at the Academy was held to be improper. GAO found invalid the Navy's effort to ensure that the incumbent contractor performed the work.

## 3.  Task and Delivery Orders

Task (services) and delivery (supplies) order contracts are contracts that do not specify a "firm quantity," 10 U.S.C. § 2304d(1) and (2) and 41 U.S.C. § 4101(1) and (2). FAR 16.5 provides that task or delivery order contracts may take the form of requirements contracts or indefinite-quantity (IDIQ) contracts. See Chapter 9 for a complete discussion of this type of contracting.

Procurement notices and competition are generally not required for the issuance of task or delivery orders under either single-award or multiple-award contracts, 10 U.S.C. § 2304c(a) and 41 U.S.C. § 1708(b)(1)(D). However, 10 U.S.C. § 2304c(b) and 41 U.S.C. § 4104(b)(2)(B) require that each contractor receiving a multiple-award contract be "provided a fair opportunity to be considered" for each order unless:

(1) the [executive] agency's need for the services or property ordered is of such unusual urgency that providing such opportunity to all such contractors would result in unacceptable delays in fulfilling that need;

(2) only one such contractor is capable of providing the services or property required at the level of quality required because the services or property ordered are unique or highly specialized;

(3) the task or delivery order should be issued on a sole source basis in the interest of economy and efficiency because it is a logical follow-on to a task or delivery order already issued on a competitive basis; or

(4) it is necessary to place the order with a particular contractor in order to satisfy a minimum guarantee.

The statutory exemption of task and delivery orders from competition is implemented in FAR 6.001(d)-(f). Limited competition requirements for certain orders, such as those issued for work paid funded by the American Recovery and Reinvestment Act, are set forth in FAR Subparts 8.4 and 16.5.

A task or delivery order may not "increase the scope, period or maximum value" of the contract. Such increases may only be accomplished "by modification of the contract," 10 U.S.C. § 2304a(e) and 41 U.S.C. § 4103(e). Although not specifically stated in these sections, procurement notices and competition would be required for such actions unless a noncompetitive award could be justified since the exemption from competition is only applicable to task orders. In contrast, contract modifications of task orders for advisory and assistance services are explicitly stated to be subject to competition requirements, 10 U.S.C. § 2304b(f)(2) and 41 U.S.C. § 4105(g)(2). Under limited circumstances, a one-time extension not exceeding six months may be made on a "sole source basis," 10 U.S.C. § 2304b(g) and 41 U.S.C. § 4105(h).

FASA permits the award of task and delivery order contracts using "[a] statement of work, specifications, or other description that reasonably describes the general scope, nature, complexity, and purposes of the services or property to be procured under the contract," 10 U.S.C. § 2304a(b)(3) and 41 U.S.C. § 4103(b)(3). Thus, task orders can potentially cover a broad spectrum, depending upon the nature of the work statement. Although no cases on this issue have been decided under the new FASA rules, a number of cases decided under the prior rules have dealt with the question of what could be ordered noncompetitively under indefinite-quantity and requirements contracts.

In *Bulova Techs., Inc.*, Comp. Gen. Dec. B-252660, 93-2 CPD ¶ 23, GAO suggested that the criterion for determining whether an order or modification is outside the scope is whether potential offerors would have considered that such a modification might be made:

> Preservation of the integrity of the competitive procurement system requires that contracting parties not make changes to contracts which have the effect of circumventing the competitive procurement statutes; this principle is violated when a modification so substantially changes the purpose or nature of a contract that the contract for which the competition was held and the contract which is to be performed are essentially different. Ordinarily, a modification falls within the scope of the contract originally competed where potential offerors could reasonably have anticipated that such a modification might be made under the changes or other contract clauses.

See also *AT&T Commc'ns, Inc. v. Wiltel, Inc.*, 1 F.3d 1201 (Fed. Cir. 1993), where the court noted that the length of the contract and the need to meet changing government needs placed the competitors on notice that "a broad range of modifications would fall within the scope," stating at 1205:

> In determining whether a modification falls within CICA's competition requirement, this court examines whether the contract as modified materially departs from the scope of the original procurement. [citations omitted] The analysis thus focuses on the scope of the entire original procurement in comparison to the scope

of the contract as modified. Thus a broad original competition may validate a broader range of later modifications without further bid procedures.

Similarly, in *Astronautics Corp. of Am.*, 70 Comp. Gen. 554 (B-242782), 91-1 CPD ¶ 531, GAO stated that the protesters there were precluded from contesting the issuance of a delivery order on the ground that the statement of work in the contract was too broad, reasoning at 557:

> Since the delivery order falls within the scope of the existing engineering services contract, there is no basis to require a separately-competed procurement as urged by the protester. *See Stanford Telecommunications. Inc.*, B-241449, Dec. 10, 1990, 90-2 CPD ¶ 475.

> Here, the basic contract appears to encompass an extremely broad spectrum of items and services, which prompted the protester to hypothesize that DoD could use the contract routinely to obtain a wide range of electronic items without meaningful competition. While on the limited record presented in this case we could not resolve the question, we recognize that where an agency conducts a procurement for a total package or for broadly aggregated needs without a legitimate basis for bundling its requirements rather than breaking them out, competition is inhibited in derogation of the mandate for " full and open competition" under the Competition in Contracting Act of 1984, 10 U.S.C. § 304(a)(1)(A) (1988). *See LaBarge Prods., Inc.*, B-232201, Nov. 23, 1988, 88-2 CPD ¶ 510; *Pacific Sky Supply, Inc.*, B-228049, Nov. 23, 1987, 87-2 CPD ¶ 504; *Systems, Terminals & Communications Corp.*, B-218170, May 21, 1985, 85-1 CPD ¶ 578. However, as the protester also acknowledges, the [*Commerce Business Daily*] synopsis indicated the broad range of services which could be acquired. [The protester] did not timely protest the scope of the procurement in 1988. To the extent that [the protester] is now protesting the scope of the requirements under the basic contract, the protest is untimely.

Task orders were also found to be within the scope of the contract in *Information Ventures, Inc.*, Comp. Gen. Dec. B-240458, 90-2 CPD ¶ 414 (tasks "logically related to the overall purpose" of the agreement); *Liebert Corp.*, Comp. Gen. Dec. B-232234.5, 91-1 CPD ¶ 413 (work within the general scope but quantity beyond maximum stated in contract outside scope); and *Lockheed Martin Fairchild Sys.*, Comp. Gen. Dec. B-275034, 97-1 CPD ¶ 28 (modernization of computer-based training within scope of contract for automatic data processing systems integration and support services).

The background and circumstances surrounding the award of a contract may indicate that an order under an otherwise broad work statement is not within the scope of the contract. In *DynCorp Int'l LLC*, Comp. Gen. Dec. B-402349, 2010 CPD ¶ 59, GAO found that task orders for the mentoring and training of Afghani troops were outside the scope of IDIQ contracts for the DoD Counter Narcoterrorism Technology Program Office. Similarly, in *Anteon Corp.*, Comp. Gen. Dec. B-293523, 2004 CPD ¶ 51, a task order request for cloth cover sheets for electronic passport covers was found to be outside the scope of a contract for credit card-sized plastic cards. See also *Dynamac Corp.*, Comp. Gen. Dec. B-252800, 93-2 CPD ¶ 37, determining that an order for support of a computerized information system was outside the scope of a contract that was intended to provide engineering support for an agency's information resources management systems because the original solicitation for the contract did not adequately advise offerors of the potential for this type of order. Similar reasoning was used in *Data Transformation Corp.*, Comp. Gen. Dec. B-274629, 97-1 CPD ¶ 10, where operation of a nationwide debt collection system was held to be outside of the scope of a litigation support contract. GAO stated that one factor supporting the decision was that the agency had "historically procured [the work] under a separate contract." In *Comdisco, Inc.*, Comp. Gen. Dec. B-277340, 97-2 CPD ¶ 105, GAO sustained a protest where an agency exceeded the scope of its task orders for computer equipment and related services by permitting computer hardware/software to constitute more than its allotted share of a contract. See also *Marvin J. Perry & Assocs.*, Comp. Gen. Dec. B-277684, 97-2 CPD ¶ 128, finding that the Navy's modification of Federal Supply Schedule delivery orders to permit substitution of lower-grade, less expensive furniture materially altered the nature of the orders from those originally issued and thereby prejudiced the protester.

The issue of "out-of-scope" task orders exploded in importance in the summer of 2004, when it emerged that the Army had purchased interrogation services for Baghdad's Abu Ghraib prison through an information technology services contract. See Fay, *AR 15-6 Investigation of the Abu Ghraib Detention Facility and 205th Military Intelligence Brigade,* 47-52, 116-17, available at *http://news.findlaw.com/nytimes/docs/dod/fay82504rpt.pdf.* The Interior Department's Inspector General (it was an Interior unit that coordinated the interrogator task orders) also articulated, step by step, how the customer agencies abused the flexible task-order contracts to obtain these services. See Devaney, Inspector General, U.S. Department of the Interior, *Review of 12 Procurements Placed Under General Services Administration Federal Supply Schedules 70 and 871 by the National Business Center (Assignment No. W-EV-OSS-0075-2004)* (July 16, 2004), *www.oig.doi.gov/upload/CACI%20LETTER3.pdf.* See generally McCullough & Edmonds, *Contractors on the Battlefield Revisited: The War in Iraq and Its Aftermath,* 04-06 Briefing Papers 1, 11-12 (May 2004). A high point in the controversy came in mid-December 2004, when the GSA Inspector General released a compendium of audits, collectively over 400 pages long, on procurement practices at various GSA regional centers. GSA IG, Compendium of Audits of the Federal Technology Service Regional Client Support Centers (Dec. 14, 2004), *www.gsa.gov/gsa/cm_attachments/GSA_DOCUMENT/COMPENDIUM_R2-sM2T_0Z5RDZ-i34K-pR.pdf.* See Hardy, FTS Pledges Improvement, Fed. Computer Week, *www.fcw.com/fcw/articles/2004/1213/web-fts-12-17-04.asp.* These audits presented a sweeping critique of task-order contracting practices across many GSA regional centers, and identified failures in competition and contracting practices in literally hundreds of GSA task orders.

In the wake of these various controversies, generally involving orders under IDIQ contracts sponsored by centralized purchasing agencies, more competition and notice requirements were introduced into the ordering process. See FAR 8.405 and FAR 16.505. Further, Congress permitted protests to GAO of IDIQ orders over $10 million, 10 U.S.C. § 2304c(e) and 41 U.S.C. § 253j(e). The protest authority was extended to September 30, 2016 by § 825 of the Ike Skelton National Defense Authorization Act for Fiscal Year 2011. At the same time, IDIQ contracting (known more commonly as "framework" contracting abroad) gained broader acceptance in other nations, and became an accepted method of procurement internationally. See Yukins, *Are IDIQs Inefficient? Sharing Lessons with European Framework Contracting,* 37 Pub. Cont. L.J. 545 (2008).

## III. SELECTION OF CONTRACTING TECHNIQUE

One of the major changes to procurement policy in CICA was the elimination of the absolute preference for formal advertising (renamed "sealed bidding") over negotiation. Instead, CICA substituted the following rule in 10 U.S.C. § 2304(a)(2) and 41 U.S.C. § 3301(b)(1):

In determining the competitive procedures appropriate under the circumstance, [an agency shall] —

(A) solicit sealed bids if —

(i) time permits the solicitation, submission, and evaluation of sealed bids;

(ii) the award will be made on the basis of price and other price-related factors;

(iii) it is not necessary to conduct discussions with the responding sources about their bids; and

(iv) there is a reasonable expectation of receiving more than one sealed bid . . . .

10 U.S.C. § 2304(a)(1)(B) and 41 U.S.C. § 3301(a)(2) provide that in conducting a procurement, an agency shall —

use the competitive procedure or combination of competitive procedures that is best suited under the circumstances of the procurement.

These provisions are implemented by FAR 6.401, which states:

Sealed bidding and competitive proposals, as described in Parts 14 and 15 are both acceptable procedures for use under Subparts 6.1, 6.2 and, when appropriate, under Subpart 6.3. Contracting Officers shall exercise good judgment in selecting the method of contracting that best meets the needs of the Government. If the choice is to use competitive proposals rather than sealed bidding, the contracting officer shall briefly explain, in writing, which of the four conditions [in the above mentioned statute] has not been met. No additional documentation or justification is required.

FAR 6.401(b) provides, in turn, that when the four conditions for sealed bids listed above "are not appropriate," contracting officers may request competitive proposals. Moreover, FAR 6.401(b)(2) specifically provides that because of differences in laws, regulations and business practices abroad, competitive proposals — which allow for discussions between agencies and offerors — are generally to be used for proposed contracts to be made and performed outside the United States.

## A. Sealed Bidding

Contracting officers must use sealed bidding if none of the four exceptions set forth in 10 U.S.C. § 2304(a)(2) and 41 U.S.C. § 3301(a)(1) can be demonstrated. GAO enunciated this rule in *Defense Logistics Agency*, 67 Comp. Gen. 16 (B-227055.2), 87-2 CPD ¶ 365 at 17:

> It is true . . . that CICA eliminates the specific preference for formally advertised procurements ("sealed bids") and directs an agency to use the competitive procedures, or combination of procedures, that is best suited under the circumstances of the procurement. However, CICA . . . does provide, in determining which competitive procedure is appropriate under the circumstances, that an agency "shall solicit sealed bids if": (1) time permits, (2) award will be based on price, (3) discussions are not necessary, and (4) more than one bid is expected to be submitted. As is evident, the plain language of the CICA provision is mandatory in nature. When the enumerated statutory conditions are present, the solicitation of sealed bids is, therefore, required, leaving no room for the exercise of discretion by the contracting officer in determining which competitive procedure to use.

In reaching this conclusion, GAO relied on the legislative history of CICA, stating:

> The legislative history of CICA also indicates the mandatory nature of the requirement to use sealed bidding when the statutory conditions are present. Senate Report No. 98-50, 98th Cong., 2d Sess., *reprinted in* 1984 U.S. Code Cong. & Admin. News 2191, states, in pertinent part:
>
>> While competitive negotiation is recognized in S.338 as a bona fide competitive procedure, the Committee emphasizes that traditional formal advertising procedures are by no means cast aside. In fact, agencies are *required* . . . to solicit sealed bids [when the enumerated conditions are present]. . . .
>
> House Conference Report No. 98-861, 98th Cong., 2d Sess., *reprinted in* 1984 U.S. Code Cong. & Admin. News 2110, states:

> In effect, the substitute, like the Senate amendment, removes the restriction from — and written justification required for — competitive proposal procedures and places them on a par with sealed bid procedures. *The substitute maintains minimum criteria for sealed bid procedures to ensure their use when appropriate.*

Thus, where all the elements enumerated in CICA for the use of sealed bidding procedures are present, agencies are required to use these procedures and do not have the discretion to use negotiated procedures, *Knoll N. Am., Inc.*, Comp. Gen. Dec. B-250234, 93-1 CPD ¶ 26. In *Racal Corp.*, 70 Comp. Gen. 127 (B-240579), 90-2 CPD ¶ 453, GAO ruled that negotiation could not be used in a price-only procurement to ensure that offerors had a complete understanding of the specifications and to permit changes to the agency's requirements after submission of offerors. See also *Northeast Constr. Co.*, 68 Comp. Gen. 406 (B-234323), 89-1 CPD ¶ 402, holding that negotiation was not appropriate because the procurement was based on price alone and the RFP did not call for technical proposals.

An agency's decision to use sealed bidding procedures instead of competitive negotiation will be upheld unless it is clearly unreasonable. In *Eagle Fire Inc.*, Comp. Gen. Dec. B-257951, 94-2 CPD ¶ 214, the protester argued that technical proposals were needed and discussions required; thus, the procurement should have been conducted using competitive procedures rather than sealed bidding procedures. GAO found no basis to object to the Navy's choice of using sealed bidding because there was no ambiguity in the specification requirements and the Navy could conduct a preaward survey to determine whether the low bidder was qualified and capable of performing the contract. See also *Tennessee Apparel Corp.*, Comp. Gen. Dec. B-253178.3, 94-1 CPD ¶ 104, where the protester contended that negotiation procedures were required. GAO found that the specifications identified in the IFB made price and price-related factors the only relevant evaluation criteria and made discussions unnecessary. Further, GAO stated that the matters identified by the protester as necessary for discussions concerned a bidder's capacity to perform, which could be resolved through the conduct of a preaward survey. In *Machinewerks, Inc.*, Comp. Gen. Dec. B-258123, 94-2 CPD ¶ 238, GAO found sealed bidding with bid samples an appropriate technique to ensure that the proposed product met the agency's needs. The protester had argued that a negotiated procurement requiring first articles was less burdensome on the competitors. Similarly, in *Virginia Blood Servs.*, B-259717, 95-1 CPD ¶ 185, GAO upheld the agency's decision to use sealing bidding procedures, stating that the agency reasonably concluded that there was no reason to conduct discussions or to consider factors other than price in selecting the contractor. Likewise, in *Pfizer, Inc.*, Comp. Gen. Dec. B-276362, 97-1 CPD ¶ 205, GAO found unobjectionable an agency decision to only use price factors when it reasonably determined that competing drugs were technically equal.

## B. Competitive Negotiation

It is frequently determined in the planning process that one of the statutory conditions for the use of sealed bidding is absent. In such cases, competitive negotiation is the proper procurement technique. See *Weeks Marine, Inc. v. United States*, 575 F.3d 1352 (Fed. Cir. 2009), reversing the Court of Federal Claims (79 Fed. Cl. 22 (2007)) because it had substituted its judgment as to the need for negotiation for that of the agency. The court stated at 1370-71:

> [W]e hold that the Corps's decision to issue the MATOC solicitation "evince[es] rational reasoning and consideration of relevant factors." Were we to conclude otherwise, we would be second-guessing the Corps's action. That is something we are not permitted to do. "'If the court finds a reasonable basis for the agency's action, the court should stay its hand even though it might, as an original proposition, have reached a different conclusion as to the proper administration and application of the procurement regulations.'" *Honeywell, Inc. v. United States*, 870 F.2d 644, 648 (Fed. Cir. 1989) (quoting *M. Steinthal & Co. v. Seamans*, 455 F.2d 1289, 1301, 147 U.S. App. D.C. 221 (D.C. Cir. 1971)) . . .

See also *Ceres Envtl. Servs., Inc.*, Comp. Gen. Dec. B-310902, 2008 CPD ¶ 48 ("The determination as to whether circumstances support the use of negotiated procedures is largely a discretionary matter within the purview of the contracting officer. . . . However, an agency must reasonably conclude that the conditions requiring use of sealed bidding are not present.").

## 1. No Time Nor Expectation of Receiving More Than One Bid

Conditions (i) and (iv) of 10 U.S.C. § 2304(a)(2) and 41 U.S.C. § 3301(a)(1) do not frequently arise in protests of the use of competitive negotiation. When these conditions are called into question, GAO gives contracting officers a large amount of discretion. In *Milbar Corp.*, Comp. Gen. Dec. B-232158, 88-2 CPD ¶ 509, the contracting officer used competitive negotiation because only one offer was anticipated on a number of the items being procured. GAO denied the protest even though the contracting officer's logic was questionable. Although five firms participated in the previous procurement, only two firms were expected to bid on the current procurement. The contracting officer expected to receive only one offer on nine of the 32 items and expected the other firm to be financially capable of supplying only three of the items. The contracting officer therefore determined that the agency could not reasonably expect more than one bid on the vast majority of items.

## 2. Non-Price-Related Factors

The most common reason for using competitive proposals (negotiation) will probably be the need to make award on the basis of non-price-related factors. There appears to be little controversy as to the discretion of agencies to use negotiation procedures in these circumstances. See *Ceres Envtl. Servs., Inc.*, Comp. Gen. Dec. B-310902, 2008 CPD ¶ 48, where an agency reasonably concluded that an accelerated construction schedule required consideration of non-price related factors in selecting a proposal. See also *Integrity Mgmt. Int'l, Inc.*, Comp. Gen. Dec. B-219998.2, Feb. 18, 1986, *Unpub.*, where GAO dismissed the protest against the use of competitive proposals without requesting a separate report from the agency because the solicitation indicated award would not be based solely on price and price-related factors. In both *A.J. Fowler Corp.*, Comp. Gen. Dec. B-233326, 89-1 CPD ¶ 166, and *KIME Plus, Inc.*, Comp. Gen. Dec. B-231906, 88-2 CPD ¶ 237, GAO sustained the decision to use competitive negotiation in order to award on the basis of technical/management factors as well as price, although the work was relatively routine and had been previously obtained through sealed bidding. In *Premiere Vending*, Comp. Gen. Dec. B-256437, 94-1 CPD ¶ 380, the solicitation was initially issued as an IFB, but the contracting officer subsequently decided that the procurement should be conducted using competitive proposals. GAO upheld the agency's decision to use negotiated procedures, stating that award would be based on non-price-related factors and that discussions might be required. Similarly, in *Specialized Contract Servs., Inc.*, Comp. Gen. Dec. B-257321, 94-2 CPD ¶ 90, GAO upheld an agency's decision to use negotiated procedures because the agency reasonably determined that, based on its experience, it was desirable to evaluate technical factors in addition to price. In *Vantex Serv. Corp.*, Comp. Gen. Dec. B-266199, 96-1 CPD ¶ 29, GAO found that the agency properly determined to use competitive negotiation. The RFP listed three technical evaluation factors that the agency stated would be evaluated on a go/no-go basis. Thus, GAO stated that award would be based on technical acceptability and price — not just price, as the protester contended. In addition, based on prior performance problems, GAO found that the agency reasonably determined that discussions would be necessary to ensure that offerors understood the requirements. See also *Comfort Inn South*, Comp. Gen. Dec. B-270819.2, 96-1 CPD ¶ 225, finding that the use of negotiated procedures was justified because the agency reasonably determined that it was necessary to evaluate offeror past performance.

This trade-off between price and non-price (or quality) factors is the crux of negotiated procurement. Negotiated procurements allow agencies the flexibility to make a "best-value" trade-off of price for quality, and thus to balance the agency's needs against available resources. To succeed, negotiated procurement requires a sophisticated acquisition team, which can accurately gauge the agency's available resources, the agency's true spending priorities, and the marginal value to the agency of higher quality goods and services. Because negotiated procurement vests such discretion in purchasing officials, it runs the risk of expending excessive amounts to obtain minimal differences in quality of performance. At the same time, though, because negotiated procurement allows vendors to offer their own technical solutions (rather than bidding against the government's predetermined solution in sealed bidding), it can afford the government to opportunity to introduce new technology and innovation into its operations.

## 3. Need to Conduct Discussions

When the agency intended to make award on the basis of only price and price-related factors, traditionally the use of negotiation procedures was subject to much greater scrutiny. See *ARO Corp.*, Comp. Gen. Dec. B-227055, 87-2 CPD ¶ 165, *recons. denied*, 67 Comp. Gen. 16 (B-227055.2), 87-2 CPD ¶ 365, finding that the use of negotiation procedures in order to conduct price negotiations violated the statute because discussions were not necessary and all of the other conditions for sealed bidding had been met. One case found that in order to justify negotiation on the basis of discussions, the agency was required to solicit technical proposals, *Saxon Corp.*, Comp. Gen. Dec. B-221054, 86-1 CPD ¶ 225. However, there have been subsequent cases where negotiation has been permitted without obtaining technical proposals. See *Enviroclean Sys., Inc.*, Comp. Gen. Dec. B-278261, 97-2 CPD ¶ 172, where GAO found that the Army reasonably decided that, because discussions might be necessary, it was appropriate to use negotiation procedures. See also *Carter Chevrolet Agency, Inc.*, Comp. Gen. Dec. B-228151, 87-2 CPD ¶ 584, where negotiation was permitted because prior sealed bid procurements had demonstrated that offerors had many exceptions to the solicitation and that only one bid had been submitted on a number of bid items. Similarly, in *Claude E. Atkins Enters., Inc.*, Comp. Gen. Dec. B-241047, 91-1 CPD ¶ 42, GAO permitted negotiation of a construction contract where the specifications were complex and prior sealed bid procurements had indicated that the agency could expect numerous queries as to the proper interpretation of the specifications. The distinguishing feature in many of these cases was the prior experience of the agency on similar procurements, indicating that discussions might be needed to effect a successful procurement. In *Saxon Corp.*, Comp. Gen. Dec. B-216148, 85-1 CPD ¶ 87, negotiation was held appropriate for a base vehicle operations and maintenance services contract requiring a high level of technical and managerial competence that could not be defined adequately in the specifications. GAO reasoned that prebid conferences and preaward surveys would not be adequate substitutes for discussions. See also *Vantex Serv. Corp.*, Comp. Gen. Dec. B-2166199, 96-1 CPD ¶ 29 (agency properly determined that discussions were necessary to ensure that offerors understood the requirements of the solicitation before award); *JT Constr. Co.*, Comp. Gen. Dec. B-244404.2, 92-1 CPD ¶ 1 (use of competitive negotiation procedures was appropriate where contracting officer determined that discussions were necessary to gauge offeror understanding of complex specifications); and *Essex Electro Eng'rs, Inc.*, 65 Comp. Gen. 242 (B-221114), 86-1 CPD ¶ 92 (refusing to question the judgment of the agency that technical data regarding a new engine were sufficiently important to warrant discussions).

## 4. Fixed-Price Contract Not Appropriate

Another reason for not using sealed bidding is that the agency determines that a firm-fixed-price or fixed-price with economic price adjustment type contract cannot be used for the procurement. If this choice is correctly made, it will rule out sealed bidding and require the use of one of the other competitive procedures — in most cases the solicitation of competitive proposals. For example, in *United Food Servs., Inc.*, Comp. Gen. Dec. B-220367, 86-1 CPD ¶ 177, GAO found that the Army's decision to use a cost-plus-award-fee contract for food service was justified by a number of factors, including the uncertainty in the quantities of meals to be served. GAO had found in an earlier decision, *United Food Servs., Inc.*, 64 Comp. Gen. 880 (B-217211), 85-2 CPD ¶ 326, that variation in quantity alone was not a sufficient justification for the use of a cost-type contract requiring negotiation. In *United Food Servs., Inc. — Recons.*, 65 Comp. Gen. 643 (B-218165.2), 86-1 CPD ¶ 538, GAO modified the 64 Comp. Gen. 880 decision to recommend that the Army assess the overall risks and uncertainties to determine whether use of a cost-type contract would be warranted. See also *Surface Trans. Corp.*, Comp. Gen. Dec. B-288317, 2001 CPD ¶ 147, where a cost-plus-incentive-fee contract for the performance of shipboard preservation services was reasonable given the unpredictable nature of the work.

## C. Other Competitive Procedures

41 U.S.C. § 152 specifies five special procedures that are "competitive procedures" meeting the statutory requirement for full and open competition:

(1) procurement of architectural or engineering services conducted in accordance with chapter 11 of title 40 (40 U.S.C. § 1101 et seq.);

(2) the competitive selection of basic research proposals resulting from a general solicitation and the peer review or scientific review (as appropriate) of those proposals;

(3) the procedures established by the Administrator of General Services for the multiple award schedule program of the General Services Administration if —

(A) participation in the program has been open to all responsible sources; and

(B) orders and contracts under those procedures result in the lowest overall cost alternative to meet the needs of the Federal Government;

(4) procurements conducted in furtherance of section 15 of the Small Business Act (15 U.S.C. 644) as long as all responsible business concerns that are entitled to submit offers for such procurements are permitted to compete; and

(5) a competitive selection of research proposals resulting from a general solicitation and peer review or scientific review (as appropriate) solicited pursuant to section 9 of the Small Business Act (15 U.S.C. 638).

The same procedures are specified in 10 U.S.C. § 2302(2). These procedures are generally used in preference to sealed bidding or competitive negotiation when the special circumstances set forth in the statutes apply. See Chapters 7 and 8 for a detailed discussion of these procedures.

## D. Commercial Supplies and Services

FASA added 10 U.S.C. § 2377 and 41 U.S.C. § 3307, stating a preference for the acquisition of commercial items. Agencies are required to "define requirements in terms that enable and encourage offerors to supply commercial items," FAR 11.002(a)(2)(ii). In addition, offerors of commercial items are to be provided an opportunity to compete in any procurement, FAR 11.002(a)(2)(iii). When commercial items are procured, certain statutes and clauses applicable to other procurements do not apply and special price analysis does apply. FAR 12.203 provides that contracting officers are required to use the policies unique to the acquisition of commercial items in conjunction with the policies and procedures for solicitation, evaluation and award prescribed in FAR Part 13, FAR Part 14, or FAR Part 15, as appropriate for the particular acquisition. The contracting officer may use the streamlined procedure for soliciting offers for commercial items prescribed in FAR 12.603. For acquisitions exceeding the simplified acquisition threshold but not exceeding $6.5 million contracting activities must use the simplified procedures authorized by Subpart 13.5 to the maximum extent practicable. A detailed discussion of commercial item procedures in contained in Chapter 7.

## E. Simplified Acquisition

In order to promote efficiency and economy in contracting, Congress enacted a provision under FASA for special simplified procedures for contracts for acquisition of property and services at amounts not greater than the simplified acquisition threshold. FAR 2.101 provides the following definition:

"Simplified acquisition procedures" means the methods prescribed in part 13 for making purchases of supplies or services.

FAR 13.003(g) provides broad guidance on the procedures that may be used for acquisitions not expected to exceed:

(1) The simplified acquisition threshold for other than commercial items, use any appropriate combination of the procedures in Parts 13, 14, 15, 35, or 36, including the use of Standard Form 1442, Solicitation, Offer, and Award (Construction, Alteration, or Repair), for construction contracts (see 36.701(a)); or

(2) $6.5 million ($20 million for acquisitions as described in 13.500(c)) [for contingency contracting or certain anti-terrorism purchases] for commercial items, use any appropriate combination of the procedures in Parts 12, 13, 14, and 15 (see paragraph (d) of this section).

In choosing among these techniques, contracting officers are required to use the "simplified manner that is most suitable, efficient, and economical in the circumstances of each acquisition," FAR 13.003(g).

The simplified acquisition threshold of $100,000 in 41 U.S.C. § 134 has been increased to purchases not exceeding $150,000, FAR 2.101. FAR 13.003 provides, in part:

(a) Agencies shall use simplified acquisition procedures to the maximum extent practicable for all purchases of supplies or services not exceeding the simplified acquisition threshold (including purchases at or below the micro-purchase threshold).

* * *

(c)(1) The contracting officer shall not use simplified acquisition procedures to acquire supplies and services if the anticipated award will exceed-

(i) The simplified acquisition threshold; or

(ii) $6.5 million ($20 million for acquisitions as described in 13.500(e)), including options, for acquisitions of commercial items using Subpart 13.5.

(2) Do not break down requirements aggregating more than the simplified acquisition threshold (or for commercial items, the threshold in Subpart 13.5) or the micro-purchase threshold into several purchases that are less than the applicable threshold merely to-

(i) Permit use of simplified acquisition procedures; or

(ii) Avoid any requirement that applies to purchases exceeding the micro-purchase threshold

(d) The contracting officer shall not use simplified acquisition procedures to acquire supplies and services if the anticipated award will exceed the simplified acquisition threshold (or $6,500,000), including options, for acquisitions of commercial items using Subpart 13.5). Do not break down requirements aggregating more than the simplified acquisition threshold (or for commercial items, the threshold in Subpart 13.5) or the micro-purchase threshold into several purchases that are less than the applicable threshold merely to —

(1) Permit use of simplified acquisition procedures; or

(2) Avoid any requirement that applies to purchases exceeding the micro-purchase threshold.

The use of simplified acquisition procedures requires that the procurement be within the threshold at two stages in the procurement action — the solicitation stage and the award stage. First, the government's estimate of the dollar value of the procurement determines whether the procurement can be solicited using simplified acquisition procedures. Next, the quoted or offered prices determine whether a simplified acquisition award can be made. For example, if the government's estimate of the procurement is $148,500, a simplified acquisition solicitation can be issued. However, if the lowest price received exceeds $150,000, a simplified acquisition award cannot be made unless a price reduction is obtained that brings the amount within the threshold. Thus, in this example, if the lowest quotation received is $152,500, the contracting officer can seek to obtain price reductions to come within the $150,000 threshold. If that fails, the procurement must be resolicited using sealed bid or competitive proposal procedures. A detailed discussion of simplified acquisition procedures is contained in Chapter 7.

## IV. IDENTIFYING SOURCES

In planning a procurement, it is necessary to determine what sources, if any, exist to meet the government's needs. The number and nature of the sources will, in large part, determine the technique that can be used in the procurement. Other determinations that must be made in the planning stages deal with whether to satisfy the agency's needs from private or government sources. It is also essential to determine whether there are any mandatory sources.

The prospective sources of supplies and/or services that can meet the need must be stated in the acquisition plan, FAR 7.105(b)(1). In determining what sources can be used to fulfill their needs, the agencies may not be free to make a choice. Statutes, regulations, and existing contractual obligations often dictate what sources may or may not be used. One example is when purchases are required to be set aside for performance solely by small business concerns, 15 U.S.C. § 644(j). Indeed, one of the primary uses of market research is to determine whether there are small businesses available to fulfill particular requirements, on a set-aside basis. See *Information Ventures, Inc.*, Comp. Gen. Dec. B-294267, 2004 CPD ¶ 205 (market research inadequate because agency did not review known sources of information on small business sources); *SWR, Inc.*, Comp. Gen. Dec. B-294266, 2004 CPD ¶ 219; *Rochester Optical Mfg. Co.*, Comp. Gen. Dec. B-292247, 2003 CPD ¶ 138. Another example of a socioeconomic issue that must be addressed during market research is when products or services fall under the Buy American Act, 41 U.S.C. §§ 10a-d. See Chapter 11 for an in-depth discussion of collateral policies, including important socioeconomic policies, that play a role in determining what sources are available to meet the government's procurement needs.

In most cases, the agency technical and program personnel and the contracting officer will know of potential sources that should be solicited. In addition, the contracting officer may find it necessary to publicize the requirement with a solicitation of sources. The contracting officer will also determine whether the procurement must be directed to a mandatory source or set aside for small or disadvantaged businesses.

## A. Market Research

Market research is defined in FAR 2.101:

"Market research" means collecting and analyzing information about capabilities within the market to satisfy agency needs.

In *Coulter Corp.*, Comp. Gen. Dec. B-258713, 95-1 CPD ¶ 70, GAO stated the purpose of market research:

CICA requires that agencies use market research during the planning stage for the procurement of property or services. 41 U.S.C. § 253a(a)(1)(B). A market survey is an attempt to ascertain whether other qualified sources capable of satisfying the government's requirements exist and may be informal, i.e., phone calls to federal or non-federal experts, or formal, i.e., sources-sought announcements in the CBD or solicitations for information or planning purposes. Federal Acquisition Regulation § 7.101.

An increased emphasis on market research began in the early 1980s. In hearings before the Senate Armed Services Committee, GAO stated that the failure to perform market research was a "major processing deficiency." Many witnesses testified that the failure to perform market research was one of the key factors responsible for the absence of competition in government procurement, *Competition in Contracting Act of 1983: Hearings on S. 338 Before the Committee on Armed Services, United States Senate*, 98th Cong., 1st Sess. (1983). The Senate Report on the CICA stated that "[c]ompetition in contracting depends on the procuring agency's understanding of the marketplace . . . [M]arket research is essential to developing this understanding," S. Rep. No. 50, 98th Cong., 2d Sess. (1984).

As a result, CICA included a general requirement for market research in 10 U.S.C. § 2305(a)(1)(A)(ii) and 41 U.S.C. § 253a(a)(1)(B) (now 41 U.S.C. § 3306(a)(1)(B)). The Federal Acquisition Streamlining Act of 1994 (FASA) added new, more specific provisions at 10 U.S.C. § 2377(c) which (as amended) require that market research be conducted "appropriate to the circumstances:"

(A) before developing new specifications for a procurement by that agency;

(B) before soliciting bids or proposals for a contract in excess of the simplified acquisition threshold; and

(C) before awarding a task order or delivery order in excess of the simplified acquisition threshold.

The civilian agency statute, 41 U.S.C. § 264b(c), contained only (A) and (B) and was omitted in the 2011 codification of Title 41. These statutes imposed a unique requirement that market research be conducted *before* new specifications are prepared. This is to ensure, in part, that such specifications are drafted to maximize the use of commercial items.

These statutes are implemented in new FAR Part 10. FAR 10.002(a) provides that the government's need should be stated in sufficient terms to allow market research to be conducted. Once the acquisition need is sufficiently stated, market research is conducted to determine if commercial items or nondevelopmental items are available to meet the government's needs or could be modified to meet the government's needs, FAR 10.002(b). Market research can also be used to determine the availability of additional or more competent sources to perform government work. The extent of market research conducted varies depending on the circumstances and complexity of the procurement, FAR 10.002(b)(1).

When other than full and open competition procedures are used, FAR 6.303-2(a)(8) requires that justifications describe the market research conducted or the reasons why it was not conducted. GAO has held that an agency's reason for not conducting a market survey was adequate where it had supported the fact that a directed source was designated pursuant to an international agreement, *PacOrd*, Comp. Gen. Dec. B-238366, 90-1 CPD ¶ 466. GAO also upheld an agency's decision not to conduct a market survey where the agency stated that it had recently determined that there was only one domestic source for a product, *Lister Bolt & Chain, Ltd.*, Comp. Gen. Dec. B-224473, 86-2 CPD ¶ 305. The technique used for the market survey is in the discretion of the contracting officer, *AAA Eng'g & Drafting, Inc.*, Comp. Gen. Dec. B-236034.3, 93-1 CPD ¶ 295.

## 1. Inadequate Market Research

Inadequate market research can be a fatal defect in the procurement process if there are sources available to meet the agency's needs that were not discovered. In *K-Whit Tools, Inc.*, Comp. Gen. Dec. B-247081, 92-1 CPD ¶ 382, GAO held that the failure to conduct a market survey indicated that the need to contract sole source was due to a lack of advance planning and was unauthorized. See also *TMS Bldg. Maint.*, 65 Comp. Gen. 222 (B-220588), 86-1 CPD ¶ 68 (failure to contact other potential sources or to conduct a market survey evidenced a lack of advance planning and rendered the sole source award improper); *BFI Medical Waste Sys. of Arizona, Inc.*, Comp. Gen. Dec. B-270881, 96-1 CPD ¶ 239 (failure to conduct market survey led to improper small business set aside); *Jervis B. Webb Co.*, Comp. Gen. Dec. B-211724, 85-1 CPD ¶ 35 (lack of even a limited market survey led, in part, to a finding that the Defense Logistics Agency's sole source justification was inadequate). In contrast, the results of a market survey may justify a sole source award, *Interscience Sys., Inc.*, Comp. Gen. Dec B-201943, 82-2 CPD ¶ 187 (upholding determination to award contract on a sole source basis as a result of two market surveys). The results of a market survey have also been used to support the reasonableness of a bid price, *Eclipse Sys., Inc.*, Comp. Gen. Dec. B-216002, 85-1 CPD ¶ 267.

## 2.  Solicitations for Planning Purposes

One technique for conducting market research is the use of solicitations for information or planning purposes. FAR 15.201(e) permits requests for information (RFIs) to be used in this manner as follows:

RFIs may be used when the Government does not presently intend to award a contract, but wants to obtain price, delivery, other market information, or capabilities for planning purposes. Responses to these notices are not offers and cannot be accepted by the Government to form a binding contract. There is no required format for RFIs.

FAR 14.105-1 refers to this provision permitting its use on sealed bid procurements.

## 3.  Sources-Sought Synopsis

Another technique for identifying potential sources is the issuance of a sources-sought synopsis. Those synopses were traditionally published in paper form, in the Commerce Business Daily (CBD); now they are published on a website, *www. fedbizopps.gov*, the "Governmentwide Point of Entry" (GPE), the single point where government contracting opportunities greater than $25,000 can be accessed electronically by the public. FAR 5.204 requires that "presolicitation notices" be disseminated using the GPE. FAR 5.205(a) states that contracting officers may publish in the GPE advance notices of their interest in potential research and development programs when market research does not produce a sufficient number of concerns to obtain adequate competition. These notices are called "Research and Development Sources Sought." Although the FAR appears to limit this technique for identifying potential sources to research and development contracts, it has been used for all types of procurement. See FAR 5.205(c) permitting use of the GPE to transmit "special notices:"

Contracting officers may transmit to the GPE special notices of procurement matters such as business fairs, long-range procurement estimates, prebid or preproposal conferences, meetings, and the availability of draft solicitations or draft specifications for review.

If an agency uses a sources-sought synopsis, it must make its essential requirements clear to potential offerors and allow them an opportunity to demonstrate their ability to comply before rejecting them as potential sources. In *Masstor Sys. Corp.*, 64 Comp. Gen. 118 (B-215046), 84-2 CPD ¶ 598, GAO sustained a protest where the agency rejected a potential source for failing to demonstrate compliance with a requirement that was neither set forth in the sources-sought synopsis nor otherwise made known to the vendor. The government should not, however, include proprietary information in the sources-sought synopsis. In *Research, Analysis & Dev., Inc. v. United States*, 8 Cl. Ct. 54 (1985), the plaintiff submitted an unsolicited proposal pertaining to a novel concept in state-of-the-art aircraft-sensor technology. The proposal included the proper restrictive proprietary legend. After having agreed to maintain the confidentiality of the information, the agency issued a sources-sought synopsis requesting responses regarding the feasibility of a sensor system concept identical to that proposed by the plaintiff. The court held that the disclosure in the CBD of the proprietary information associated with the unsolicited proposal violated the government's implied-in-fact contractual obligation to protect the data and entitled the company to damages.

The results of a sources-sought synopsis may bear on GAO's review of an agency's reasonableness in choosing specifications. In *Motorola, Inc.*, Comp. Gen. Dec. B-247913.2, 92-2 CPD ¶ 240, the protester challenged the agency's choice of procuring on a nondevelopmental item (NDI) basis. In concluding that the agency had a reasonable basis for its selection of NDI-only specifications, GAO stated that through a sources-sought synopsis, the agency learned that there were offerors who would have an NDI available either by making minor modifications to existing items or by developing an item that would meet the agency's specifications and that such items would be available by the time the agency would award the contract. Thus, GAO found that the agency had a sufficient basis to conclude that an NDI procurement was feasible.

Similarly, the results of a sources-sought synopsis may support GAO's finding that an agency reasonably awarded on a sole source basis. In *Standard Bent Glass Corp.*, Comp. Gen. Dec. B-401212, 2009 CPD ¶ 143, the agency had sought competitors for a sole source product by issuing several sources-sought synopses but had not been able to delay the procurement for a sufficient time for the protester to qualify its product. GAO denied the protest concluding that the protester was partly responsible for the delay. See also *Polaris, Inc.*, Comp. Gen. Dec. B-218008, 85-1 CPD ¶ 401, rejecting a protest alleging that the agency improperly awarded a sole source contract. GAO stated that the agency had made a significant effort to determine whether other firms could meet the agency's needs by issuing a sources-sought synopsis and received responses from six potential offerors. The agency, however, determined that none of the six potential offerors could meet all of its requirements. In denying the protest, GAO stated that it was incumbent upon the protester in responding to the CBD announcement to do more than restate the agency's needs.

Sources-sought synopses are a frequent means of determining whether there are two or more qualified small businesses allowing the agency to set aside the procurement for small businesses. See *Assessment & Training Solutions Consulting Corp. v. United States,* 92 Fed. Cl. 722 (2010), where the agency correctly concluded that a procurement should be placed under the 8(a) program (either as a set-aside or sole source) based on the responses to its sources-sought synopsis. In contrast, in *Metasoft, LLC*, Comp. Gen. Dec. B-402800, 2010 CPD ¶ 170, and *RhinoCorps Ltd. Co. v. United States*, 87 Fed. Cl. 261 (2009), the agency properly concluded from the responses to the synopsis that there were not two small businesses that could perform

50% of the work with their own forces. See also *Totolo/King v. United States*, 87 Fed. Cl. 680 (2009), where the agency was able to determine from the responses to the synopsis that there were not two small businesses with sufficient bonding capacity to perform the contract; *EMMES Corp.*, Comp. Gen. Dec. B-402245, 2009 CPD ¶ 53, where the agency was able to conclude, as a result of the responses to a sources-sought synopsis that there were not two qualified small business firms; and *Information Ventures, Inc.*, Comp. Gen. Dec. B-400604, 2008 CPD ¶ 232, where none of the 26 small businesses that responded to the synopsis were found to be qualified.

GAO will not consider a protest against a procuring agency issuing a potential sources-sought announcement in the GPE. *See Lockheed Martin Sys. Integration — Owego*, Comp. Gen. Dec. B-287190.2, 2001 CPD ¶ 110. GAO considers only protests against solicitations already issued by agencies and awards made or proposed to be made under those solicitations, *Pancor Corp.*, Comp. Gen. Dec. B-234168, 89-1 CPD ¶ 328.

## B. Contractor versus Government Performance

Once a need has been identified by a government agency, there are usually a number of sources available to satisfy those needs. These sources may either be private commercial sources or government agencies, including the procuring agency itself.

This section first examines the executive branch policy of reliance on private sources, which was reshaped in the 2003 rewrite of Office of Management and Budget (OMB) Circular No. A-76, *Performance of Commercial Activities* (May 2003) (Circular A-76), *www.whitehouse.gov/OMB/circulars/index.htm*. It then considers mandatory sources and procurements through other government agencies.

### 1. Reliance on Private Sources

As a result of concerns that government competition with the private sector is detrimental to the free enterprise system, the executive branch policy has been that, to the extent practicable, the government should rely on the private sector for commercially available goods and services. This policy was first enunciated in Bureau of the Budget Bulletin No. 55-4, Jan. 15, 1955. Subsequently it has been embodied in Circular A-76. By the 1990s this Circular called for a two-step acquisition process when an agency identified commercial work that was being performed by government personnel. The first step was a competition among contractors to determine which contractor was best able to compete for the work. The second step was a competition with the government organization performing the work. This proved to be a cumbersome, time-consuming process that was judged to be ineffective. As a result, a blue-ribbon panel, the Commercial Activities Panel, was established per § 832 of the Floyd D. Spence National Defense Authorization Act for 2001, Pub. L. No. 106-398, to undertake a study of government sourcing methods. The independent panel, which was chaired by Comptroller General David Walker and included representatives from government, industry, and government employee unions, published its report in April 2002. The Commercial Activities Panel's report (*www.gao.gov/a76panel/dcap0201.pdf*) set forth the following consensus principles for sourcing decisions by the government:

1. Support agency missions, goals, and objectives.

2. Be consistent with human capital practices designed to attract, motivate, retain, and reward a highperforming federal workforce.

3. Recognize that inherently governmental and certain other functions should be performed by federal workers.

4. Create incentives and processes to foster high-performing, efficient, and effective organizations throughout the federal government.

5. Be based on a clear, transparent, and consistently applied process.

6. Avoid arbitrary full-time equivalent (FTE) or other arbitrary numerical goals.

7. Establish a process that, for activities that may be performed by either the public or the private sector, would permit public and private sources to participate in competitions for work currently performed in-house, work currently contracted to the private sector, and new work, consistent with these guiding principles.

8. Ensure that, when competitions are held, they are conducted as fairly, effectively, and efficiently as possible.

9. Ensure that competitions involve a process that considers both quality and cost factors.

10. Provide for accountability in connection with all sourcing decisions.

See generally Walker, *The Future of Competitive Sourcing*, 33 Pub. Cont. L.J. 299 (2004) (discussing principles).

Based on these principles, OMB's Circular A-76 was completely rewritten in 2003, reflecting the goal of the Bush administration to maximize "competitive sourcing." See Office of Management & Budget, *The President's Management Agenda* 17 (2002). In the private sector, meanwhile, outsourcing (including "offshoring" abroad) was rapidly evolving into very sophisticated methods for "strategic sourcing." See Gottfredson, Puryear & Phillips, *Strategic Sourcing: From Peripher to the Core*, Harv. Bus. Rev., Feb. 1, 2005, *www.hbr.org*. The current policy of the federal government places less emphasis on moving more work to the private sector but is addressed, rather, at establishing firmer guidelines on what work should not be performed by the private sector because it is an "inherently governmental function." See proposed OFPP policy letter, *Work Reserved for Performance by Federal Government Employees*, March 31, 2010, 75 Fed. Reg. 16188. Legislative agencies are not subject to Circular A-76's requirements, *International Graphics v. United States*, 4 Cl. Ct. 186 (1983).

This policy was implemented by FAR Subpart 7.3 until the revised Circular was published. Then the detailed guidance was removed from the FAR, with the result that contracting agencies must use the detailed rules in attachments to the Circular for guidance on the procedures to be followed. FAR 7.302 merely contains the following summary of A-76's policy:

(a) The Circular provides that it is the policy of the Government to —

(1) Perform inherently governmental activities with Government personnel; and

(2) Subject commercial activities to the forces of competition.

(b) As provided in the Circular, agencies shall —

(1) Not use contractors to perform inherently governmental activities;

(2) Conduct public-private competitions in accordance with the provision of the Circular and, as applicable, these regulations;

(3) Give appropriate consideration relative to cost when making performance decisions between agency and contractor performance in public-private competitions;

(4) Consider the Agency Tender Official an interested party in accordance with 31 U.S.C. 3551 to 3553 for purposes of filing a protest at the Government Accountability Office; and

(5) Hear contests in accordance with OMB Circular A-76, Attachment B, Paragraph F.

(c) When using sealed bidding in public-private competitions under OMB Circular A-76, contracting officers shall not hold discussions to correct deficiencies.

The Circular provides that it is the policy of the government to (a) rely generally on private commercial sources for supplies and services, if certain criteria are met, while recognizing that some functions are inherently governmental and must be performed by government personnel, and (b) give appropriate consideration to relative cost in deciding between government performance and performance under contract. In comparing the costs of government and contractor performance, the Circular provides that agencies shall base the contractor's cost of performance on firm offers.

As amended, Circular A-76 requires that each agency designate an official at the assistant secretary or equivalent level, the "Competitive Sourcing Official" (CSO), to be responsible for implementing its policies. Under the revised Circular A-76, agencies must prepare annual inventories, as required by the Federal Activities Inventory Reform Act of 1998 (FAIR Act), Pub. L. No. 105-270, 31 U.S.C. § 501 note, of all their activities that are performed by federal employees but are not inherently governmental (i.e., are commercial). OMB is to review each agency's Commercial Activities Inventory and consult with the agency regarding its content. Upon the completion of this review and consultation, the agency must transmit a copy of the inventory to Congress and make it available to the public. The FAIR Act establishes an administrative appeals process under which an interested party may challenge the omission or the inclusion of a particular activity on the inventory. See Circular A-76, Attachment A, § D.

To compile these inventories each agency must evaluate its activities and functions and determine which are inherently governmental and which are commercial. All the commercial activities are listed on an inventory that includes known expansions and new requirements. Activities involving 10 full-time equivalent (FTE) personnel or fewer are listed separately from those with more than 10 FTEs. The inventory must, at a minimum, describe the number of FTEs involved, the nature and location of the activity, and the dates of last and next reviews. "Commercial" activities being performed by government personnel may be subject to competitive sourcing (the competitive outsourcing process described below); "inherently governmental" functions are not. The revised Circular A-76 includes the following guidance on what constitute "inherently governmental" activities at Attachment A, § B.1.:

> a. An inherently governmental activity is an activity that is so intimately related to the public interest as to mandate performance by government personnel. These activities require the exercise of substantial discretion in applying government authority and/or in making decisions for the government. Inherently governmental activities normally fall into two categories: the exercise of sovereign government authority or the establishment of procedures and processes related to the oversight of monetary transactions or entitlements. An inherently governmental activity involves:
>
> > (1) Binding the United States to take or not to take some action by contract, policy, regulation, authorization, order, or otherwise;
> >
> > (2) Determining, protecting, and advancing economic, political, territorial, property, or other interests by military or diplomatic action, civil or criminal judicial proceedings, contract management, or otherwise;
> >
> > (3) Significantly affecting the life, liberty, or property of private persons; or

(4) Exerting ultimate control over the acquisition, use, or disposition of United States property (real or personal, tangible or intangible), including establishing policies or procedures for the collection, control, or disbursement of appropriated and other federal funds.

The definition of "inherently govermental" in the revised Circular A-76 was written against the backdrop of decades of decisions — and debate — on that topic.. In *Nuclear Regulatory Comm'n Licensing Examiners*, 70 Comp. Gen. 682 (B-242942), Aug. 29, 1991, GAO found that the Nuclear Regulatory Commission's (NRC) use of contract employees to perform testing procedures involved in licensing operators for nuclear facilities did not involve the performance of inherently governmental functions. Although the contract examiners prepared, administered, and graded examinations, the NRC's internal guidelines provided such extensive detail and guidance that the contract examiners could not exercise discretion and make value judgments to decide who would passed the examination and be licensed. However, in *Socolar*, Comp. Gen. Dec. B-237356, Dec. 29, 1989, *Unpub.*, GAO found that determining eligibility for a DOE security clearance was an inherently governmental function. In this case, the hearing officers had to consider and rule on disputed matters, make specific findings as to the truth of the information provided, and preliminarily determine whether the access should be granted, denied, or invoked.

"Commercial" activities, which are not reserved to government employees, are defined as follows at Attachment A, § B.2 of the revised Circular A-76:

Commercial Activities. A commercial activity is a recurring service that could be performed by the private sector and is resourced, performed, and controlled by the agency through performance by government personnel, a contract, or a fee-for-service agreement. A commercial activity is not so intimately related to the public interest as to mandate performance by government personnel. Commercial activities may be found within, or throughout, organizations that perform inherently governmental activities or classified work.

Activities that are deemed "commercial" are subject to special competitive processes, called "A-76 competitions," which are outlined in Attachment B to the revised Circular A-76. These competitions are to be between a "Most Efficient Organization" (MEO) made up, generally, of current government employees performing the function, which presents the "agency tender," versus offerors from the private sector.

As originally written, the revised Circular A-76 contemplated two types of "A-76" processes: "streamlined" processes, which could be used for activities involving 65 or fewer people, and "standard" competitions for larger activities. The "streamlined" process would not require a formal competition before the activity could be converted to commercial performance. See Circular A-76, Attachment B, § A.5. In 2004, however, Congress enacted § 8014 of the Department of Defense Appropriations Act, 2005, Pub. L. No. 108-287, which severely limited the use of streamlined competitions, at least in the Department of Defense. Other legislation limited streamlined competitions in other agencies, as well. See McCullough, Melander & Alerding, *Feature Comment: Year 2003 OMB Circular A-76 Decisions and Developments,* 46 Gov. Contractor ¶ 27 (Jan. 21, 2004).

The first step in the standard competition process under the revised Circular A-76 is the naming of a Performance Work Statement team, to develop the statement of work against which the MEO and private offerors can compete. This team and the contracting officer and the source selection official are a separate team that runs the competition. Additionally, the agency must appoint an Agency Tender Official (ATO) to represent the MEO. This agency team that is competing for the work is required to be totally separated from the source selection team. The competition can be run as a sealed bid or as a negotiated procurement, and if negotiated procurement is selected the agency can use a "lowest price technically acceptable, phased evaluation, [or] tradeoff" process, Circular A-76, Attachment B, ¶ D.3.a.(3). Once the statement of work is completed, bids or proposals are solicited. Concurrently, an in-house estimate is prepared for submission to the contracting officer not later than the time established for receipt of proposals or bid opening, Circular A-76, Attachment B, ¶ D.3.a.(5). The evaluation procedure to be followed in the standard A-76 competition after the contracting officer receives the cost estimate from the ATO and the responses to the solicitation differs from conventional contracting procedures. Under what is termed the "conversion differential" — a price advantage given the MEO on the assumption that shifting the work from existing government employees will entail additional costs — 10% or $10 million is added to the price or cost of the "incumbent source" (generally the best offer from a contractor). See Circular A-76, Attachment B, ¶ D.5.c.(4)(c), stating:

> The conversion differential is a cost that is the lesser of 10 percent of the MEO's personnel-related costs . . . or $10 million over all the performance periods stated in the solicitation. This conversion differential is added to the cost of performance by a non-incumbent source. If the incumbent provider is a private sector or public reimbursable source, the conversion differential is added to the cost of agency performance. If the agency is the incumbent provider, the conversion differential is added to the cost of private sector or public reimbursable performance. The conversion differential precludes conversions based on marginal estimated savings, and captures non-quantifiable costs related to a conversion, such as disruption and decreased productivity.

Attachment B of Circular A-76 contains very detailed instructions on each step of this standard competition procedure, including use of the tradeoff process when the offers are evaluated on both price and non-price factors. However, the complexity of this process and the difficulty of applying such factors to MEOs has led most agencies to use a process where the selection is based on price alone. This policy decision is heavily influenced by the fact that the Circular requires that standard procedures be completed within one year of the time of the public announcement of the competition, Circular A-76, Attachment B, ¶ D.1.

The revised Circular A-76 explicitly contemplates "contests," or bid protests, brought through the agency-level bid protest process outlined in FAR 33.103, Circular A-76, Attachment B, ¶ F.1. These contests, to be brought only by "directly interested parties," may review any of the following actions taken in connection with a standard competition:

(1) a solicitation;

(2) the cancellation of a solicitation;

(3) a determination to exclude a tender or offer from a standard competition;

(4) a performance decision, including, but not limited to, compliance with the costing provisions of this circular and other elements in an agency's evaluation of offers and tenders; or

(5) a termination or cancellation of a contract or letter of obligation if the challenge contains an allegation that the termination or cancellation is based in whole or in part on improprieties concerning the performance decision.

While the Circular does not specifically provide for protests before GAO, GAO traditionally reviewed whether an offeror was unfairly treated because the agency failed to conduct an A-76 cost comparison in accordance with applicable procedures, *Dyneteria, Inc.*, Comp. Gen. Dec. B-222581.3, 87-1 CPD ¶ 30. See, for example, *Tecom, Inc.*, Comp. Gen. Dec. B-253740.3, July 7, 1994, *Unpub.*, finding that the agency had followed applicable procedures and that the protester failed to show that the methodology used in its cost comparison was unreasonable or inconsistent with A-76. Compare *DynCorp*, Comp. Gen. Dec. B-233727.2, 89-1 CPD ¶ 543, sustaining a protest, stating that the agency failed to include all costs required for in-house performance and otherwise miscalculated costs in conducting a cost comparison. GAO looked to see not only if the agency failed to follow established procedures, but that the failure could have materially affected the outcome of the cost comparison, *Trajen, Inc.*, Comp. Gen. Dec. B-284310, 2000 CPD ¶ 61. However, GAO would not review the validity of an agency cost comparison until the protester had exhausted the administrative appeals procedure provided by the agency, *RAI, Inc.*, Comp. Gen. Dec. B-244725, 91-2 CPD ¶ 48.

After the revised Circular A-76 was in place, debate continued on what role GAO should have in reviewing competitive sourcing decisions. One immediate issue was whether government employees whose jobs are at stake should have standing to challenge A-76 awards at GAO. GAO originally published a notice soliciting comments on that question, and ultimately addressed the in-house competitor standing issue in *Dan Duefrene,* Comp. Gen. Dec. B-293590.2, 2004 CPD ¶ 82. In that decision, GAO concluded that, notwithstanding the revisions to Circular A-76, the in-house competitor in a public-private competition conducted under the Circular was not an offeror and, therefore, under the current language of CICA, no representative of an in-house competitor was an interested party eligible to maintain a protest before GAO. At the same time, however, GAO suggested to Congress that it might want to consider amending CICA to allow GAO to decide such protests. Congress then included a provision in the Ronald W. Reagan National Defense Authorization Act for Fiscal Year 2005, Pub. L. No. 108-375, specifically authorizing protests on behalf of federal employees by the ATO. The Act also provided that an ATO's decision on whether to file a protest would not be subject to review. Subsequently, the National Defense Authorization Act for Fiscal Year 2008, Pub. L. No. 110-181, authorized protests by "Designated Employee Agents" (DEAs) as well as ATOs and expanded the scope of such protests. GAO amended its protest regulations to permit such protests in 4 C.F.R. § 21.0(a), defining an "interested party" as follows:

> (2) In a public-private competition conducted under Office of Management and Budget Circular A-76 regarding performance of an activity or function of a Federal agency, or a decision to convert a function performed by Federal employees to private sector performance without a competition under OMB Circular A-76, interested party also means
>
> > (A) The official responsible for submitting the Federal agency tender, and
> >
> > (B) Any one individual, designated as an agent by a majority of the employees performing that activity or function, who represents the affected employees.

In contrast, employees do not have standing to challenge these competitions in court, *National Federation of Federal Employees v. Cheney*, 883 F2d 1038 (D.C. Cir. 1989), *cert. denied*, 496 U.S. 936 (1990).

ATOs and DEAs have the authority to challenge any issue related to a competition that was started on or after January 28, 2008. With regard to competitions that were started prior to that date, they can only challenge the source selection decision. See *Gary Johnson — Designated Employee Agent*, Comp. Gen. Dec. B-310910.3, 2009 CPD ¶ 22; *Bruce Bancroft — Agency Tender Official*, Comp. Gen. Dec. B-400404.2, 2008 CPD ¶ 200. The strict timeliness rules apply to these officials, *Rhonda Podojil — Agency Tender Official*, Comp. Gen. Dec. B-311310, 2008 CPD ¶ 94. Protests of award to contractors were sustained in *Frank A. Bloomer — Agency Tender Official*, Comp. Gen. Dec. B-401482.2, 2009 CPD ¶ 203 (agency unreasonably accepted offeror's revised fringe benefit ratios in its cost realism analysis, its unsupported assumption that it could perform a significant portion of the workload 10% more efficiently, and (3) its omission of labor cost associated with the material supply function from its cost proposal); and *Rosemary Livingston — Agency Tender Official*, Comp. Gen. Dec. B-401102.2, 2009 CPD ¶ 135 (record contains inconsistent statements by the agency in its contemporaneous evaluation and inadequate documentation of it's findings regarding the tender's shortcomings). A protest of an award to an MEO was sustained in *New Dynamics Corp.*, Comp. Gen. Dec. B-401272, 2009 CPD ¶ 150 (agency failed to reasonably consider whether agency tender's material and supply costs were realistic).

GAO will not review the decision of whether to contract out because this is a matter of executive branch policy, *Schonstedt Instrument Co.*, Comp. Gen. Dec. B-215531, 84-2 CPD ¶ 141; *Research, Analysis & Mgmt. Corp.*, Comp. Gen. Dec. B-215712.2, 85-1 CPD ¶ 54. Thus, GAO will not review an agency decision to cancel the solicitation for an A-76 competition, *Aleut Facilities Support Servs., LLC*, Comp. Gen. Dec. B-401925, 2009 CPD ¶ 202. Likewise, the courts have held that agency decisions under A-76 are internal managerial decisions that are not subject to judicial review, *International Graphics v. United States*, 4 Cl. Ct. 186 (1983).

## 2. Exceptions

Paragraph 5. of Circular A-76 contains the following limitations on the contracting-out policy:

b. As provided by Attachment A, the CSO may exempt a commercial activity performed by government personnel from performance by the private sector.

c. The CSO (without delegation) shall receive prior written OMB approval to deviate from this circular (e.g., time limit extensions, procedural deviations, or costing variations for a specific streamlined or standard competition, or inventory process deviations). Agencies shall include any OMB approved deviations in the public announcement and solicitation for a streamlined or standard competition. Agencies are encouraged to use this deviation procedure to explore innovative alternatives to standard or streamlined competitions, including public-private partnerships, public-public partnerships, and high performing organizations.

d. A streamlined or standard competition is not required for private sector performance of a new requirement, private sector performance of a segregable expansion to an existing commercial activity performed by government personnel, or continued private sector performance of a commercial activity. Before government personnel may perform a new requirement, an expansion to an existing commercial activity, or an activity performed by the private sector, a streamlined or standard competition shall be used to determine whether government personnel should perform the commercial activity. [*See OMB Memorandum M-08-11 (February 20, 2008), number 4, when applying this provision*]

## 3. Statutory Limitations on Contracting Out

Congress has placed a number of statutory limitations on the procurement of services by contract.

### a. Department of Defense

Chapter 146 of Title 10 of the U.S. Code regulates the DoD's contracting-out process. 10 U.S.C. § 2461 prohibits direct conversion of work performed by civilian employees without first conducting a competition following the procedures of Circular A-76. 10 U.S.C. § 2463 requires the agency to issue guidelines and procedures "to ensure that consideration is given to using, on a regular basis . . . civilian employees to perform new functions and functions that are performed by contractors and could be performed by [such] civilian employees." These guidelines must give special consideration to using civilian employees to perform any function that

(1) is performed by a contractor and —

> (A) has been performed by Department of Defense civilian employees at any time during the previous 10 years;
>
> (B) is a function closely associated with the performance of an inherently governmental function;
>
> (C) has been performed pursuant to a contract awarded on a non-competitive basis; or
>
> (D) has been performed poorly, as determined by a contracting officer during the 5-year period preceding the date of such determination, because of excessive costs or inferior quality; or

(2) is a new requirement, with particular emphasis given to a new requirement that is similar to a function previously performed by Department of Defense civilian employees or is a function closely associated with the performance of an inherently governmental function.

This statutory provision also contains restrictions on using the A-76 procedures with such civilian functions.

10 U.S.C. § 2464 requires the agency to identify "core logistics capabilities" and the workload necessary to maintain these capabilities. This workload must be "sufficient . . . . to ensure cost efficiency and technical competence in peacetime while preserving the surge capacity and reconstitution capabilities necessary to support fully the [agency's] strategic and contingency plans." This workload may not be contracted out pursuant to Circular A-76 unless the Secretary of Defense waives this requirement. These provisions do not apply to commercial items but the Act requires that Congress be notified when the agency determines that a military product is a commercial item.

Another restriction is in 10 U.S.C. § 2466, whereby defense agencies and military departments are prevented from contracting out more than 50% of their respective depot maintenance workloads. Any funds that are not used for such a contract must be used for the performance of depot-level maintenance and repair workload by employees of the DoD.

10 U.S.C. § 2465 prohibits contracting out of firefighting or security-guard functions at any military installation or facility. This restriction does not apply to

contracts outside of the United States and contracts for such work at contractor operated, government owned facilities.

## b.  National Park Service

The Volunteers in the Parks Act of 1969, amended by Pub. L. No. 98-540, 98 Stat. 2718 (1984), 43 U.S.C. § 1457a note, stated that Circular A-76 was not to apply to activities conducted by the National Park Service, United States Fish and Wildlife Service, and the Bureau of Land Management if those activities involve 10 FTEs or fewer. This was applicable for fiscal years 1985 through and including 1988. Three cases challenging to the cost comparisons conducted by the National Park Service were dismissed as moot because this statute deprived the contracting officer of authority to contract out the work. See *Applicators, Inc.*, IBCA 1797(A-76), 85-1 BCA ¶ 17,797; *Crimson Enters., Inc.*, IBCA 1876(A-76), 85-1 BCA ¶ 17,798; and *B&W Serv. Indus., Inc.*, IBCA 1859(A-76), 85-1 BCA ¶ 17,799. In another case, the same board affirmed a prior dismissal for lack of jurisdiction over an appeal of a decision not to renew a contract. The board did not rely on Pub. L. No. 98-540 as it did in the above cases, but chose rather to rely on A-76. The board stated that A-76 did not provide for an appeal "for a decision to terminate a contracted service resulting from a cost comparison study," despite an Office of Federal Procurement Policy letter to the appellant that an appeal should be heard, *Ontario Flight Serv., Inc.*, IBCA 1812(A-76), 84-3 BCA ¶ 17,630, *recons. denied*, 85-1 BCA ¶ 17,775.

## c.  Department of Veterans Affairs

In enacting the Veterans' Compensation, Education and Employment Act of 1982, Pub. L. No. 97-306, Congress decided that cost savings alone would not justify a conversion of patient-care-related services from in-house performance to contractor performance. See S. Rep. No. 97-550, 97th Cong., 2d Sess. 100 (1982). 38 U.S.C. § 8110(a)(5), now provides:

> Notwithstanding any other provision of this title or of any other law, funds appropriated for the Department under the appropriation accounts for medical care, medical and prosthetic research, and medical administration and miscellaneous operating expenses may not be used for, and no employee compensated from such funds may carry out any activity in connection with, the conduct of any study comparing the cost of the provision by private contractors with the cost of the provision by the Department of commercial or industrial products and services for the Veterans Health Administration unless such funds have been specifically appropriated for that purpose.

See also 38 U.S.C. § 8110(c) requiring annual reports to Congress on contracting out activities. These two provisions establish clear congressional intent that activities relating to veterans' patient care should be performed by federal employees. In its Fiscal Year 2005 budget report on the Department of Veterans Affairs, the White

House noted that the "Administration will work with the Congress to remove legislative impediments to advance this effort which has been demonstrated to generate savings and could free up additional resources to be used to provide direct medical services to veterans," *www.whitehouse.gov/omb/budget/fy2005/va.html*. However, no statutory changes resulted from this effort.

### d. General Services Administration

General Services Administration guards, elevator operators, messengers, and custodians were protected by Pub L. No. 97-377, 96 Stat. 1830, 1913 (1983), which prohibited the use of funds available under the Act from being expended for these services. As a result, GAO dismissed a protest to the cancellation of a solicitation for custodial services as "academic" because the GSA was prohibited by the Act from awarding such a contract, *Consolidated Maint. Co.*, Comp. Gen. Dec. B-209766, 83-1 CPD ¶ 225.

## 4. Mandatory Sources

Various statutes and regulations require agencies to attempt to satisfy their needs for goods and services from specific sources prior to contracting with commercial sources. FAR Part 8 contains detailed guidance on mandatory sources. See also DFARS Part 208 for guidance on mandatory sources for defense procurement.

FAR 8.002 ranks mandatory sources in order of priority. Existing agency inventory is the first source considered. If the needed supply is not available from existing inventory, FAR 8.002 directs the agency to consider other sources in the following order: other agencies (excess supplies), Federal Prison Industries, the Committee for Purchase from People Who Are Blind or Severely Disabled, government wholesale supply sources, mandatory federal supply schedules, optional use federal supply schedules, and commercial sources. If the agency's requirement is for services, sources are considered in the following sequence: the Committee for Purchase from People Who Are Blind or Severely Disabled, mandatory federal supply schedules, optional use federal supply schedules, Federal Prison Industries, and commercial sources. The following discussion examines these other sources of supply.

### a. Excess Personal Property

The administrator of the GSA is authorized to prescribe policies and methods to promote utilization of excess personal property by the federal agencies pursuant to 40 U.S.C. § 521 et seq. This statute requires agencies to utilize excess personal property of other agencies to the fullest extent possible. The statute also charges agencies with the duty of monitoring excess property and either transferring or disposing of it as promptly as possible, 40 U.S.C. § 529. The GSA maintains catalogs of available excess property, issues bulletins, and provides other assistance to facilitate acquisition of excess personal property. FAR 8.102 requires procurement personnel to make "positive efforts" to utilize excess personal property before taking other procurement action.

## b. Government Printing Office

Virtually all printing, binding, and blank-book work for Congress, the Executive Office of the President, the judiciary (except the Supreme Court), and every executive department, independent office, and establishment of the government must be done by or through the Government Printing Office (GPO). Exceptions include those classes of work the Congressional Joint Committee on Printing considers sufficiently urgent or necessary to be done elsewhere, as well as work printed in field printing plants operated by an executive department, 44 U.S.C. § 501. FAR 8.802 mandates compliance with the regulations of the Congressional Joint Committee on Printing and vests responsibility for obtaining waivers and dealing with the Joint Committee in certain officials.

Section 207 of the Legislative Branch Appropriations Act of 1993, Pub. L. No. 102-392, prohibits, with limited exceptions, the use of appropriated funds by the executive branch agencies for the procurement of printing other than by or through the GPO. Section 207 was amended by the Legislative Branch Appropriations Act of 1995, Pub. L. No. 103-283, and added "duplicating" to the definition of "printing." Congress specifically deleted language from the proposed amendment that would have added to the definition of "printing" those processes involving "production of an image on paper or other substrate." The conference report accompanying the amendment stated that the deletion was made so that the revised definition would not encompass "ADP output, CD-ROMs, video discs, and other material that fall within the Brooks Act or other statutes," H.R. Conf. Rep. 567, 103 Cong. 2d Sess. 13 (1994). See *Bureau of Land Mgmt.: Payment of Pocatello Field Office Photocopying Costs*, Comp. Gen. Dec. B-290901, 2003 CPD ¶ 2, holding that printing includes photocopying, and Comp. Gen. Dec. B-251481.4, Sept. 30, 1994, *Unpub.*, holding that printing includes duplicating processes using high-speed duplicating equipment. But see Comp. Gen. Dec. B-251481.3, Feb. 15, 1994, *Unpub.*, stating that a contract modification requiring a design system to have the capability of developing "reproducible masters" from the technical manual source data did not fall within the definition of printing. See also *Bureau of Land Mgmt.: Payment of Printing Costs by the Milwaukee Field Office*, Comp. Gen. Dec. B-290900, 2003 U.S. Comp. Gen. LEXIS 241, holding that sharing in the cost of printing a brochure under a cooperative agreement did not fall under this prohibition because the brochure was not "for the government" under 44 U.S.C. § 501.

Individual printing orders costing not more than $1,000 are, under certain conditions, not required to be printed by the GPO, Pub. L. No.102-392, Title II § 207(a), codified at 44 U.S.C. § 501 note.

In 2002, the Office of Management and Budget issued OMB Memorandum M-02-07, *www.whitehouse.gov/omb/memoranda/m02-07.pdf,* stating that executive agencies should purchase duplicating and printing services at best value, whether from GPO or private vendors. This guidance was based on an opinion of the Office of Legal Counsel of the Department of Justice that GPO was under the control of the legislative branch and hence could not control executive branch activities. Congress responded by enacting Pub. L. No. 107-240, 116 Stat. 1492 (October 11, 2002), which amended § 117 of Pub. L. No. 107-229, 116 Stat. 1465 (September 30, 2002), finding that the laws requiring the use of GPO were binding and prohibiting the use of any appropriated funds to comply with the OMB memorandum. In *The Effect of Section 117 of P.L. 107-229, 116 Stat. 1465,* Comp. Gen. Dec. B-300192, 2002 U.S. Comp. Gen. LEXIS 272, Nov. 13, 2002, GAO ruled that this statute was binding because it was based on the power of Congress to designate the proper use of appropriations.

In June 2003, OMB and GPO announced a new "compact," or agreement between the agencies. See Government Printing Office, Press Release: GPO and OMB Announce a New Compact for Government Printing (June 6, 2003), *www.gpo.gov/images/pdfs/compact.pdf.* Under the compact, GPO is to sponsor a new contracting vehicle, modeled on the General Services Administration's Multiple Award Schedule contracts, which will allow printers across the country to be eligible, under a standing contract, to provide services to any federal agency. The new contract vehicle is to include a fee to cover GPO's costs and, like the GSA schedule contracts, will include a most favored customer pricing commitment from participating printers. All stakeholders in the debate — GPO, OMB, the printing industry, and the librarians (who were concerned that government materials printed outside GPO will not make their way into library depositories) — supported the agreement. See FAR Subpart 8.8 for guidance on procuring printing.

### c.  General Services Administration Stores Stock

The administrator of the GSA is authorized to operate supply centers and procure and supply personal property for executive agencies, 40 U.S.C. § 501. Pursuant to this authority, the GSA operates supply distribution facilities and maintains an inventory of stock items that constitute a mandatory source for executive agencies located within the United States. See 41 C.F.R. § 101-26.301. The GSA publishes a supply catalog that lists all items available from GSA stock. The GSA also has an electronic catalog, "GSAXcess," which tracks excess property and which is available through the GSA home page, GSA Advantage!," which is an on-line ordering system that allows agencies to search through all GSA sources of supply and select the item that best meets their requirements.

### d.  General Services Administration Motorpools

The Federal Property and Administrative Services Act of 1949 authorizes GSA to provide motor vehicles to agencies of the federal government. See 40 U.S.C. § 602 directing GSA to —

(1) take over from executive agencies and consolidate, or otherwise acquire, motor vehicles and related equipment and supplies;

(2) provide for the establishment, maintenance, and operation (including servicing and storage) of motor vehicle pools or systems; and

(3) furnish motor vehicles and related services to executive agencies for the transportation of property and passengers.

40 U.S.C. § 603 provides guidance on the implementation of this requirement and calls for the issuance of regulations on motor vehicles. See 41 C.F.R. Part 101-39. The Act authorizes the GSA to enter into rental or other arrangements and to utilize government-owned vehicles. The Act provides that requisitioning agencies should be charged for services rendered at prices calculated to recover all elements of cost. See FAR Subpart 8.11 for guidance on leasing motor vehicles.

## e.  Federal Prison Industries

Federal Prison Industries, Inc. (FPI), also known as "UNICOR," is a wholly owned government corporation created by Congress in 1934 to administer industrial operations in federal penal and correctional institutions. FPI is authorized to produce commodities for consumption in penal institutions or for sale to the government, but is prohibited from selling to the public, 18 U.S.C. § 4122. For many years, all government agencies were required to purchase available quantities that met their needs from FPI.

The FPI's preference was modified by § 637 of the Consolidated Appropriations Act for 2005, Pub. L. No. 108-447, and the amendment of 10 U.S.C. § 2410n. FAR 8.602(a) implements these statutes by requiring agencies to —

(1) Before purchasing an item of supply listed in the FPI Schedule, conduct market research to determine whether the FPI item is comparable to supplies available from the private sector that best meet the Government's needs in terms of price, quality, and time of delivery. This is a unilateral determination made at the discretion of the contracting officer. The arbitration provisions of 18 U.S.C. 4124(b) do not apply;

(2) Prepare a written determination that includes supporting rationale explaining the assessment of price, quality, and time of delivery, based on the results of market research comparing the FPI item to supplies available from the private sector;

(3) If the FPI item is comparable, purchase the item from FPI following the ordering procedures at *http://www.unicor.gov,* unless a waiver is obtained in accordance with 8.604; and

(4) If the FPI item is not comparable in one or more of the areas of price, quality, and time of delivery. —

(i) Acquire the item using —

(A) Competitive procedures (e.g., the procedures in 6.102, the set-aside procedures in subpart 19.5, or competition conducted in accordance with part 13); or

(B) The fair opportunity procedures in 16.505, if placing an order under a multiple award delivery-order contract;

(ii) Include FPI in the solicitation process and consider a timely offer from FPI for award in accordance with the item description or specifications, and evaluation factors in the solicitation —

(A) If the solicitation is available through the Governmentwide point of entry (FedBizOpps), it is not necessary to provide a separate copy of the solicitation to FPI;

(B) If the solicitation is not available through FedBizOpps, provide a copy of the solicitation to FPI;

(iii) When using a multiple award schedule issued under the procedures in Subpart 8.4 or when using the fair opportunity procedures in 16.505–

(A) Establish and communicate to FPI the item description or specifications, and evaluation factors that will be used as the basis for selecting a source, so that an offer from FPI can be evaluated on the same basis as the contract or schedule holder; and

(B) Consider a timely offer from FPI;

(iv) Award to the source offering the item determined by the agency to provide the best value to the Government; and

(v) When the FPI item is determined to provide the best value to the Government as a result of FPI's response to a competitive solicitation, follow the ordering procedures at *http://www.unicor.gov*.

## f.  *Surplus Strategic and Critical Materials*

FAR 8.003 requires agencies to procure strategic and critical materials as follows:

(d) Strategic and critical materials (e.g., metals and ores) from inventories exceeding Defense National Stockpile requirements (detailed information is available from the Defense National Stockpile Center, 8725 John J. Kingman Rd., Suite 3229, Fort Belvoir, VA 22060-6223.

### g.  The Committee for Purchase from People Who Are Blind or Severely Disabled

Pursuant to the Javits-Wagner-O'Day Act (the JWOD Act), and the rules implementing the AbilityOne program, federal agencies are required to procure goods and services from a nonprofit agency serving people who are blind or a nonprofit agency serving people with other severe disabilities if those agencies can provide the needed commodities or services, 41 U.S.C. § 8501 et seq. This committee, appointed by the President, compiles a list of supplies and services that qualified agencies may provide (known as the Procurement List). Agencies must purchase these supplies or services if they are available within the period required, FAR 8.704. FAR 8.703 notes that many items on the Procurement List are identified in the GSA Supply Catalogs or in catalogs issued by the Defense Supply Agency and the Department of Veterans Affairs. The procedures for ordering these supplies and services are set forth in FAR 8.705 and procedures for administering these orders are provided in FAR 8.706-716.

### h.  Jewel Bearings and Related Items

Pub. L. No. 90-469 provided for the operation, by contract or otherwise, of the William Langer Jewel Bearing Plant to produce jewel bearings and related items for government use or for sale at prices to be determined by the GSA to be sufficient to cover the estimated or actual costs of production, including depreciation, without fiscal year limitation. In 1995, § 2852 of Pub. L. No. 104-201 conveyed the land that the plant is on (including the improvements and all associated personal property) to the Job Development Authority of the city of Rolla, North Dakota, subject to the condition that the land and property be used "for economic development relating to the jewel bearing plant." Section 4301 of the Clinger-Cohen Act of 1996 provided for the elimination of certain regulatory certification requirements for contractors and offerors that are not specifically imposed by statute. As a result of this Act, FAR Subpart 8.2, requiring the acquisition of jewel bearings from the William Langer Plant, was removed by FAC 90-45, Jan. 2, 1997.

## 5.  Procurement through Another Government Agency

In some cases, the most efficient procurement can be achieved by obtaining the goods and services through another agency. This permits agencies to pool their requirements to achieve higher volume procurements or to reduce the administrative expenses of multiple procurement actions. The numerous types of interagency contracts are discussed in Chapter 8.

# V.  DESCRIBING THE WORK

The selection of the specification is a key element of the acquisition planning process because it is inherently related to the extent of competition and the procurement technique that can be used. Another critical decision is the amount of work that will be included in each solicitation. As discussed earlier, "new specifications" may not be prepared until market research has been conducted, 10 U.S.C. § 2377(c) and 41 U.S.C. § 264b(c) (pre-2011 codification).

## A.  Specifications

The term "specifications" is used in this material to refer to work descriptions generally, including statements of work, drawings, and documents bearing the title "specifications."

With respect to specifications to be used in the procurement process, 10 U.S.C. § 2305(a)(1)(B) provides:

> Each solicitation under this subchapter shall include specifications which —
>
>> (A) consistent with the provisions of this subchapter, permit full and open competition;
>
>> (B) include restrictive provisions or conditions only to the extent necessary to satisfy the needs of the executive agency or as authorized by law.

41 U.S.C. § 3306(a)(2) contains substantially the same requirements.

To meet the requirement for seeking "full and open competition," agencies should draft specifications "in terms that enable and encourage offerors to supply commercial items" to the maximum extent possible. This requires that specifications be drafted only after there is full knowledge of what goods and services are commercially available. See FAR 11.002(a)(2)(ii).

### 1.  Generic Nature of Specifications

Once the market situation is known, agencies can choose among a number of types of specifications or combine types of specifications to explain their needs. 41 U.S.C. § 3306(a)(3) and 10 U.S.C. § 2305(a)(1)(C) provide:

> [T]he type of specification included in a solicitation shall depend on the nature of the needs of the executive agency and the market available to satisfy such needs. Subject to such needs, specifications may be stated in terms of —

(A) function, so that a variety of products or services may qualify;

(B) performance, including specifications of the range of acceptable characteristics or of the minimum acceptable standards; or

(C) design requirements.

FAR 11.002(a)(2)(i) sets forth the same concepts, albeit in slightly different language:

State requirements with respect to an acquisition of supplies or services in terms of —

(A) Functions to be performed;

(B) Performance required; or

(C) Essential physical characteristics;.

These provisions state no preference regarding the type of specification to be used, giving the agency full discretion to prepare the type of specification best suited to satisfy its needs. See, however, FAR 11.101(a), which states a preference for "performance-oriented" specifications over "design-oriented" specifications. See also FAR 11.002(a)(2)ii) requiring agencies to define their requirements in terms that allow offerors to provide commercial or nondevelopmental items. Regardless of the type of specification used, it must contain only those provisions necessary to meet the agency's needs.

Note that few specifications are composed solely of one type. The government must often combine specification types in order to describe its needs adequately and ensure full and open competition. See *Blake Constr. Co. v. United States*, 987 F.2d 743 (Fed. Cir. 1993), stating at 746:

[T]he distinction between design and performance specifications is not absolute, and does not dictate the resolution of this case. Contracts may have both design and performance characteristics. *See, e.g., Utility Contractors, Inc. v. United States*, 8 Cl. Ct. 42, 50 n.7 (1985) ("Certainly one can find numerous government contracts exhibiting both performance and design specifications."), *aff'd mem.*, 790 F.2d 90 (Fed. Cir. 1986); *Aleutain Constructors v. United States*, 24 Cl. Ct. 372, 379 (1991) ("Government contracts not uncommonly contain both design and performance specifications." It is not only possible, but likely that a contractor will be granted at least limited discretion to find the best way to achieve goals within the design parameters set by a contract. *See, e.g., Penguin Indus., Inc. v. United States*, 209 Ct. Cl. 121, 530 F.2d 934, 937 (Ct. Cl. 1976). "On occasion the labels 'design specification' and 'performance specification' have been used to connote the degree to which the government has prescribed certain details of performance on which the contractor could rely. However, those labels do not independently create, limit, or remove a contractor's obligations." *Zinger Constr. Co. v. United States*, 807 F.2d 979, 981 (Fed. Cir. 1986) (citations omitted). These labels merely help the court discuss the discretionary elements of a contract. It is the obligations imposed by the specification which determine the extent to which it is "performance" or "design," not the other way around.

See also *Purification Envtl.*, Comp. Gen. Dec. B-270762, 96-1 CPD ¶ 203, where the performance specification included a requirement that only a specified type of water treatment system be used. In such a case, GAO noted that —

> where the government does specify a certain design, it has long been established that the risk that the design is unsuited for the intended purpose is allocated to the government, based on a theory of implied warranty.

## a. Design Specifications

In *Blake Constr. Co. v. United States*, 987 F.2d 743 (Fed. Cir. 1993), the court described design specifications at 744:

> Design specifications . . . describe in precise detail the materials to be employed and the manner in which the work is to be performed. The contractor has no discretion to deviate from the specifications, but is "required to follow them as one would a road map." "Detailed design specifications contain an implied warranty that if they are followed, an acceptable result will be produced." *Stuyvesant Dredging Co. v. United States*, 834 F.2d 1576, 1582 (Fed. Cir. 1987) (*citing United States v. Spearin*, 248 U.S. 132 (1918)).

When the government uses a design specification, it impliedly warrants that the specifications are suitable for their intended purposes. See *White v. Edsall Constr. Co., Inc.,* 296 F.3d 1081 (Fed. Cir. 2002), stating at 1084-85:

> When the Government provides a contractor with design specifications, such that the contractor is bound by contract to build according to the specifications, the contract carries an implied warranty that the specifications are free from design defects. *United States v. Spearin*, 248 U.S. 132, 136, 54 Ct. Cl. 187, 39 S. Ct. 59, 63 L. Ed. 166 (1918); *see also Essex Electro Eng'rs, Inc. v. Danzig,* 224 F.3d 1283, 1289 (Fed. Cir.2000); *USA Petroleum Corp. v. United States*, 821 F.2d 622, 624 (Fed. Cir.1987). This implied warranty attaches only to design specifications detailing the actual method of performance. It does not accompany performance specifications that merely set forth an objective without specifying the method of obtaining the objective. Because the implied warranty protects contractors who fully comply with the design specifications, the contractors are not responsible for the consequences of defects in the specified design. *Spearin*, 248 U.S. at 136.

See also *CEMS, Inc. v. United States*, 59 Fed. Cl. 168 (2003) ("It is established in government contract law that the government warrants the 'performability' of the design specifications it issues"). For complete coverage of the implied warranty of design specifications see Chapter 3 of Cibinic, Nash & Nagle, *Administration of Government Contracts* (4th ed. 2006).

## b. Performance Specifications

In *Blake Constr. Co. v. United States*, 987 F.2d 743 (Fed. Cir. 1993), the court discussed performance specifications at 744:

> Performance specifications "set forth an objective or standard to be achieved, and the successful bidder is expected to exercise his ingenuity in achieving that objective or standard of performance, selecting the means and assuming a corresponding responsibility for that selection." *J.L. Simmons Co. v. United States*, 188 Cl. Ct. 684, 412 F.2d 1360, 1362 (Ct. Cl. 1969).

In general, performance type specifications describe the government's requirements in terms of the end result that the agency desires rather than in terms of a precise description of the work to be done. In many cases, they promote more competition by giving contractors more flexibility. GAO denied a protest that the use of such specifications placed too much risk on the contractor by requiring substantial design effort, *McDermott Shipyards*, Comp. Gen. Dec. B-237049, 90-1 CPD ¶ 121. It cited *Pitney Bowes*, 68 Comp. Gen. 249 (B-233100), 89-1 CPD ¶ 157, for the view that such specifications are favored under CICA. See also *Flight Safety Int'l*, Comp. Gen. Dec. B-290595, 2002 CPD ¶ 138, where a separate contract line item number was not necessary when the agency provided enough information for offerors to use its business judgment to amortize pilot training costs; and *SouthEastern Techs., Inc.*, Comp. Gen. Dec. B-275636, 97-1 CPD ¶ 96, where the solicitation described the information with enough detail to enable all interested parties to prepare expressions of interest.

Performance specifications are much less likely than design specifications to be found to be unduly restrictive unless they contain a restrictive design feature. See, for example, *Sun Refining & Mktg. Co.*, Comp. Gen. Dec. B-239973, 90-2 CPD ¶ 305 (requirement for delivery of oil products by pipeline rather than by truck). Performance requirements, however, can be unduly restrictive in some instances, *Prime-Mover Co.*, Comp. Gen. Dec. B-201970, 81-2 CPD ¶ 325 (unnecessary speed and mechanical requirements for forklift vehicles); *Globe Air, Inc.*, Comp. Gen. Dec. B-180969.2, 75-1 CPD ¶ 57 (requirement that rotor blades on helicopter be no more than 37 feet in diameter). Compare *Glock, Inc.*, Comp. Gen. Dec. B-236614, 89-2 CPD ¶ 593 (requirement that handguns be double-action first shot, single-action subsequent shots reasonable for safety purposes); *Fluid Eng'g Assocs.*, 68 Comp. Gen. 447 (B-234540), 89-1 CPD ¶ 520 (requirement for independent roughing/backing pump system reasonable based on analysis of agency needs); and *Hallmark Packaging Prods., Inc.*, Comp. Gen. Dec. B-232218, 88-2 CPD ¶ 390 (requirement that trash bags pass tear-resistance test reasonable because it is a standard commercial test).

A DoD manual, Defense Standardization Program, DoD 4120.24-M, DSP Policies & Procedures (March 2000), at App. 1, ¶ AP1.66, defined a performance specification as one that "states requirements in terms of the required results with criteria for verifying compliance, but without stating the methods for achieving the required results. A performance specification defines the functional requirements for the item, the environment in which it must operate, and interface and interchange-ability characteristics."

There are four types of performance-based specifications: commercial item descriptions (CIDs), guide specifications, standard performance specifications, and program-peculiar performance specifications. CIDs are only to describe require-ments in terms of function, performance, and essential form and fit requirements. The guidance for CIDs is in the General Services Administration's *Federal Stan-dardization Manual-2000*, and in DoD Manual 4120.24-M. Numerous military specifications are CID candidates.

Guide specifications standardize the function or performance requirements of common procurements like systems, subsystems, equipments, and assemblies. The guidance for guide specifications is also in the DoD Manual 4120.24-M.

## c.  Functional Specifications

A functional specification describes the work to be performed in terms of end purpose or the government's ultimate objective, rather than how the work is to be performed. Functional specifications may be regarded as a particular type of perfor-mance specification — ones that describe the government's ultimate need or objec-tive without specifying any particular approach or type of product that should be used to achieve the objectives. This should be contrasted with a so-called "product-oriented" performance type specification, which indicates the ultimate performance objectives of the government but also specifies a particular type of product or ap-proach that must be used and the performance standards that must be met. Function-al specifications have the advantage of permitting the widest possible competition. However, before functional specifications are introduced, the commercial market should be examined to guarantee that the needs of the government can and will be met through use of such specifications.

It has been very difficult to distinguish functional specifications from perfor-mance specifications when drafting a specification for procurement of equipment. See, for example, Federal Property Management Regulation Temporary Regulation E-69, 45 Fed. Reg. 9269, Feb. 12, 1980, which implemented a policy favoring purchase of commercially available products through so-called commercial item descriptions (CIDs) by providing the following definition of "functional specifications" at § 7(i):

Functional specification. A description of a product in terms of its performance characteristics and intended use. It may include a statement of the qualitative nature of the product and, when necessary, will contain those minimum essential characteristics to which the product must conform.

Section 11(b) emphasized the use of functional specifications in both CIDs and any new or revised federal specifications:

> Stressing functional or performance requirements. Functional or performance requirements will be specified instead of design requirements. Design will be specified only to the extent that controls are necessary to achieve commonality and interchangeability or when it is clearly more efficient and effective to do so and is reflective of general industry practice. Design requirements such as dimensions, materials, composition, and formulation may be included only to the extent that these requirements are essential to the end use . . . and when the requirements are common practice.

Thus, functional specifications used on contracts for equipment are only slightly broader than performance specifications.

Functional specifications must be carefully prepared to ensure that competitors are not misled by overly general statements of the agency's requirements. In *CompuServe*, Comp. Gen. Dec. B-188990, 77-2 CPD ¶ 182, GAO discussed the benefits and disadvantages of functional specifications:

> To use the approach advocated by the protester — functional specifications — in a procurement such as the present one can increase competition, which is desirable. However, using functional specifications is not free from complex, and potentially costly, difficulties. Initially, the Government must expend considerable effort in drafting the specifications. Offerors must then translate the specifications into their own individual equipment and software approaches. This can involve a considerable amount of detail, may result in a variety of solutions to the Government's requirements and may be quite costly. A substantial effort on the part of the Government is then required to evaluate the proposals. Whether an agency conducting a procurement like the present one should be required to take a functional approach, as opposed to specifying a DBMS package, is a question which cannot be answered in the abstract.

In *Project Software & Dev., Inc.*, GSBCA 8471-P, 86-3 BCA ¶ 19,082, the board held that the agency's failure to use a completely functional specification was not improper since major portions of the specification were stated in functional terms.

## 2. Sources of Specifications

For many years, government specifications were required to be used when available. However, the FAR was revised in 1995 to drop this requirement and substitute the following broad guidance in FAR 11.101(a):

Agencies may select from existing requirements documents, modify or combine existing requirements documents, or create new requirements documents to meet agency needs, consistent with the following order of precedence:

(1) Documents mandated for use by law.

(2) Performance-oriented documents.

(3) Detailed design-oriented documents.

(4) Standards, specifications and related publications issued by the Government outside the Defense or Federal series for the non-repetitive acquisition of items.

## a. Government Specifications

Federal and military specifications are generally detailed and include specific requirements on the characteristics of a product and the standards that it must meet. They provide for a clearly stated, mandatory level of quality that any contractor subject to them will be required to meet.

### (1) MILITARY SPECIFICATIONS

Traditionally, DoD had used thousands of military specifications and standards in its procurements. However, it became increasingly difficult to keep these specifications and standards attuned to normal commercial practices. In 1994, Defense Secretary William Perry issued a DoD policy mandating greater use of performance and commercial specifications in lieu of military specifications. The Memorandum for Secretaries of the Military Departments (June 29, 1994), *http://www.dsp.dla.mil/policy/perry.html*, stated in relevant part:

Military Specifications and Standards: Performance specifications shall be used when purchasing new systems, major modifications, upgrades to current systems, and nondevelopmental and commercial items, for programs in any acquisition category. If it is not practicable to use a performance specification, a non-government standard shall be used. Since there will be cases when military specifications are needed to define an exact design solution because there is no acceptable non-government standard or because the use of a performance specification or non-government standard is not cost effective, the use of military specifications and standards is authorized as a last resort, with an appropriate waiver.

The intent of the policy was not to eliminate military specifications altogether, but to curtail the automatic development and imposition of unique military specifications as the cultural norm at DoD. When DoD was the leader in advanced technology, military specifications served a logical purpose. In recent years, however, industry has taken the lead in technological developments, and military specifications in lieu of industry standards are no longer optimal or cost-effective for either the government or the contractor. Thus, a modern DoD solicitation must describe the agency's needs with performance specifications or non-government standards. According to the policy of the Secretary Perry memorandum, military specifications are to be used only as a "last resort," and only after obtaining the proper waiver.

Although industry was generally pleased with the cancellation of overly burdensome "how to" military specifications, there was concern from some in industry, including, for example, the Aerospace Industry Association (AIA), regarding the effect of canceling specifications that define parts and materials used in aircraft manufacture worldwide. As DoD canceled specifications that constituted state of the art in actual commercial practices, the burden fell on industry to prepare new documents to replace those that were canceled. The AIA argued that where a military specification had in fact become a de facto commercial specification or international standard, its cancellation might well not result in cost savings to the government or its contractors.

In addition, the shift from military specifications to commercial specifications in principle required successful offerors to assume substantially greater levels of performance risk when the commercial specification was performance-oriented. In such cases, contractors encountering performance problems could no longer routinely assert that the contract requirements were met by showing that military specifications were precisely followed. The use of performance specifications also threatened the availability of the traditional government contractor defense to tort liability.

Approved specifications are listed in the DoD Index of Specifications and Standards (DODISS), online at the Defense Automated Printing Service (DAPS), eAccess database, *http://stinet.dtic.mil/str/dodiss4_fields.html*. A special section lists standard performance specifications that are used in multiple applications. The guidance for program-peculiar performance specifications is still being developed.

## (2) FEDERAL SPECIFICATIONS

There are four basic categories of federal standardization documents that control the content of solicitations from the various federal agencies. First, federal specifications describe essential and technical requirements for items, materials, or services bought by the federal government. Federal specifications are coordinated with interested government agencies and industry during their development and are mandatory for use in procurement by government agencies.

Second, federal standards provide standard data for reference in federal specifications. There are two major categories of standards: federal test method standards, which are developed by the federal government when appropriate industry standards are not available; and packaging, marking, and material identification standards.

Third, Commercial Item Descriptions are simplified specifications intended to be used in the acquisition of products available in the commercial marketplace. Finally, Qualified Products Lists are lists of products, by plant, that have been tested for conformance with the appropriate specification requirements. A complete list of all federal standardization documents can be found in the *Index of Federal Specifications, Standards and Commercial Item Descriptions* (FPMR 101-29.1), *http://apps.fss.gsa.gov/pub/fedspecs/*.

## b.  Nongovernment Standards

Nongovernment standards are authored and published privately, usually with the help of and in conjunction with professional and technical societies or associations, such as the National Defense Industrial Association. Two common sources of nongovernment standards are the American Society for Testing and Materials and the American National Standards Institute.

## 3.  Improper Specifications

Specifications must promote full and open competition. Thus, specifications are improper if they unnecessarily require certain features or preclude certain products or services from being offered, or are unclear or ambiguous.

## a.  Unduly Restrictive Specifications

The use of unduly restrictive specifications is prohibited by 41 U.S.C. § 3306(a)(2)(B) and 10 U.S.C. § 2305(a)(1)(B). An unduly restrictive specification is one that limits competition by including a requirement that exceeds the needs of the government, *Kohler Co.*, Comp. Gen. Dec. B-257162, 94-2 CPD ¶ 88. See *NCS Techs., Inc.*, Comp. Gen. Dec. B-403435, 2010 CPD ¶ 281 (requiring all computer monitors to be made by same manufacturer); *SMARTnet, Inc.*, Comp. Gen. Dec. B-406512, 2009 CPD ¶ 34 (requirement that equipment be certified by agency at time of quotation); *Apex Support Servs., Inc.*, Comp. Gen. Dec. B-288936, 2001 CPD ¶ 202 (unnecessary bonding requirements); *Hoechst Marion Roussel, Inc.*, Comp. Gen. Dec. B-279073, 98-1 CPD ¶ 127 (restricting solicitation for Diltiazem to lower dosage strengths lacked any basis in the agency's needs); *Chadwick-Helmuth Co.*, Comp. Gen. Dec. B-279621.2, 98-2 CPD ¶ 44 (requirement for a test instrument capable of operating existing program-specific software unduly restrictive, where the requirement did not accurately reflect the agency's actual needs); *Falcon Indus.*, Comp. Gen. Dec. B-256419, 94-1 CPD ¶ 337 (exclusion of alternative technology based solely on cost considerations unduly restrictive). Compare *Vaden Indus., Inc.*, Comp. Gen. Dec. B-299338, 2007 CPD ¶ 48 (performance bond equal to 100% of the contract value and a payment bond equal to 10% of the contract value not unreasonable); *Instrument Specialists, Inc.*, Comp. Gen. Dec. B-279714, 98-2 CPD ¶ 1 (requirements for monthly service calls and a 15-working- day turn-around time for off-site repairs of surgical instruments not unduly restrictive); *Caswell Int'l Corp.,* Comp. Gen. Dec. B-278103, 98-1 CPD ¶ 6 (requirement to obtain interoperable equipment to ensure operational safety and military readiness reasonably related to agency's needs); *Laidlaw Envtl,* Comp. Gen. Dec. B-272139, 96-2 CPD ¶ 109 (prohibition against using open burn/open detonation technologies to demilitarize conventional munitions unobjectionable where it reflected Congress' legitimate environmental concerns).

The procuring agency has considerable discretion in determining its needs, and GAO will not disturb the agency's determination unless a protester shows that the restrictive provision is unreasonable. See *AT&T Corp.,* Comp. Gen. Dec. B-270841, 96-1 CPD ¶ 237, stating:

> The governing statutes and regulations allow contracting agencies broad discretion in determining their minimum needs and the appropriate method for accommodating them. See 10 U.S.C. § 2305(a)(1)(A) (1994); Federal Acquisition Regulation §§ 6.101(b) and 7.103(c). Government procurement officials who are familiar with the conditions under which supplies, equipment, or services have been used in the past, and how they are to be used in the future, are generally in the best position to know the government's actual needs, and therefore, are best able to draft appropriate specifications. *Gel Sys., Inc.,* B-234283, May 8, 1989, 89-1 CPD ¶ 433. Although an agency is required to specify its needs in a manner designed to achieve full and open competition, and is required to include restrictive provisions or conditions only to the extent necessary to satisfy its needs, without a showing that competition is restricted, agencies are permitted to determine how best to accommodate their needs, *Mine Safety Appliances Co.,* B-242379.2 ; B-242379.3, Nov. 27, 1991, 91-2 CPD ¶ 506, and we will not substitute our judgment for that of the agency. *Simula, Inc.,* B-251749, Feb. 1, 1993, 93-1 CPD ¶ 86; *Purification Envtl.,* B-259280, Mar. 14, 1995, 95-1 CPD ¶ 142.

In spite of this discretion, GAO has noted that, "[w]here a protester challenges a specification as unduly restrictive, the procuring agency has the responsibility of establishing that the specification is reasonably necessary to meet its needs," *Dynamic Access Sys.,* Comp. Gen. Dec. B-295356, 2005 CPD ¶ 34; *Boehringer Ingelheim Pharmaceuticals, Inc.,* Comp. Gen. Dec. B-294944.3, 2005 CPD ¶ 32; *Military Waste Mgmt., Inc.,* Comp. Gen. Dec. B-294645.2, 2005 CPD ¶ 13; *Ocean Servs., LLC,* Comp. Gen. Dec. B-292511.2, 2003 CPD ¶ 206. GAO has also held that an agency's basis for using a restrictive specification will be held to be reasonable if it can "withstand logical scrutiny," *Glock, Inc.,* Comp. Gen. Dec. B-236614, 89-2 CPD ¶ 593. However, a stricter rule is applicable when the provision limits the competition to a single source. In that instance the agency must show convincingly that its needs cannot be met by firms possessing other than the exact experience stated, *Daniel H. Wagner, Assocs.,* 65 Comp. Gen. 305 (B-220633), 86-1 CPD ¶ 166.

GAO will not rule on protests that the specification was less restrictive than proper to meet the needs of an agency, *Aptus Co.,* Comp. Gen. Dec. B-281289, 99-1

CPD ¶ 40; *Purification Envtl.*, Comp. Gen. Dec. B-259280, 95-1 CPD ¶ 142; *Technology Scientific Servs., Inc.*, Comp. Gen. Dec. B-245039, 91-2 CPD ¶ 233; *Terex Corp.*, 64 Comp. Gen. 691 (B-217053), 85-2 CPD ¶ 76.

Of the various kinds of specifications, design specifications are the most likely to be unduly restrictive. They are likely to contain specific requirements that are not necessary to meet the agency's needs but that preclude some contractors from competing. See, for example, *Laidlaw Envtl. Servs.*, Comp. Gen. Dec. B-272139, 96-2 CPD ¶ 109 (prohibition of open burn/open detonation techniques); *Kohler Co.*, Comp. Gen. Dec. B-257162 , 94-2 CPD ¶ 88 (requirement that diesel engines in power generators be four-cycle); *Bardex Corp.*, Comp. Gen. Dec. B-252208, 93-1 CPD ¶ 461 (requirement for electromechanical shiplift rather than hydraulic lifting devices); *Data-Team, Inc.*, 68 Comp. Gen. 368 (B-233676), 89-1 CPD ¶ 355 (requirement that copying machines use dry toner); *North Am. Reporting, Inc.*, 60 Comp. Gen. 64 (B-198448), 80-2 CPD ¶ 364 (exclusion of electronic stenographic equipment); *Lanier Business Prods., Inc.*, Comp. Gen. Dec. B-193693, 79-1 CPD ¶ 232 (overly intricate features on text editing equipment); and *Constantine N. Polites & Co.*, Comp. Gen. Dec. B-189214, 78-2 CPD ¶ 437 (exclusion of metric threaded parts).

Specifications written around a certain product are particularly susceptible to being found unduly restrictive. See, for example, *Racal Corp.*, Comp. Gen. Dec. B-233240, 89-1 CPD ¶ 169 (make and model specification); *Southern Techs., Inc.*, 66 Comp. Gen. 208 (B-224328), 87-1 CPD ¶ 42 (specific product required); *Jarrell-Ash Div. of the Fisher Scientific Co.*, Comp. Gen. Dec. B-185582, 77-1 CPD ¶ 19 (specified feature found in only one product); and 48 Comp. Gen. 345 (B-164993) (1968) ("commercial" specification describing, in great part, the desk of one manufacturer). See, however, *Stavely Instruments, Inc.*, Comp. Gen. Dec. B-259548.3, 95-1 CPD ¶ 256, where GAO held that the specifications for X-ray units were not unduly restrictive even though only one company manufactured the product and the specifications were written around that product; Stavely did not challenge the technical specifications or otherwise assert that the specifications overstated or otherwise exceeded the Air Force's actual needs. Similarly, in *Messier-Bugatti Safran Group*, Comp. Gen. Dec. B-401064, 2009 CPD ¶ 109, a requirement that a product meet a specified design was held not unduly restrictive based on the agency's demonstration that the protester's design had a higher life-cycle cost.

A specification will not be held to be unduly restrictive if the agency can show that it has a legitimate need for the specified restrictive feature. See, for example, *JGB/Naylor Station I, LLC*, Comp. Gen. Dec. B-402807.2, 2010 CPD ¶ 194 (requirement that contractor have all necessary permits other than building permit at time of submission of proposal); *JLT Group, Inc.*, Comp. Gen. Dec. B-402603.2, 2010 CPD ¶ 181 (requirement that leased buildings have nine foot headroom in parking area); *CHE Consulting, Inc.*, Comp. Gen. Dec. B-297534.4, 2006 CPD ¶ 84 (requirement that contractor for maintenance of critical computer equipment have agreement with original manufacturer to support work); *LBM, Inc.*, Comp. Gen. Dec.

B-286271, 2000 CPD ¶ 194 (requirement that contracting be ISO-9000 registered); *CHE Consulting, Inc.*, Comp. Gen. Dec. B-284110, 2000 CPD ¶ 51 (requirement that contractor for maintenance of critical computer equipment have agreement with original manufacturer covering at least 65% of the equipment); *Purification Envtl.*, Comp. Gen. Dec. B-270762, 96-1 CPD ¶ 203 (requirement to use one particular design approach (oxidation process rather than new accelerated chemical treatment process) not unduly restrictive because agency reasonably determined that it was the only way to remove the contaminant without creating a hazardous waste); *Building Sys. Contractors, Inc.*, Comp. Gen. Dec. B-266180, 96-1 CPD ¶ 18 (specifications for a brand name computerized energy management control system not unduly restrictive because the system had to be compatible with the other 23 facilities at the base); *T&S Products, Inc.*, Comp. Gen. Dec. B-261852, 95-2 CPD ¶ 161 (requirement for pressure-sensitive adhesive shipping tape with a specified length not unduly restrictive where agency reasonably demonstrated that tape quality was necessary to secure fiberboard shipping boxes); *Fisons Instruments, Inc.*, Comp. Gen. Dec. B-261371, 95-2 CPD ¶ 31 (specifications for a mass spectrometry system not unduly restrictive); *Electronic Office Env'ts*, Comp. Gen. Dec. B-254571, 93-2 CPD ¶ 342 (detailed design specifications for file cabinets not unduly restrictive because necessary to maintain aesthetic appearance); *Lenderking Metal Prods.*, Comp. Gen. Dec. B-252035, 93-1 CPD ¶ 393 (suspension system incorporating features of brand name product not unduly restrictive because agency experience indicated that features necessary to meet agency's needs); *Absecon Mills, Inc.*, Comp. Gen. Dec. B-251685, 93-1 CPD ¶ 332 (upholstery fabrics to be used by Federal Prison Industries not unduly restrictive because necessary for aesthetics); *Trilectron Indus., Inc.*, Comp. Gen. Dec. B-248475, 92-2 CPD ¶ 130 (requiring air conditioners to use new coolant that reduces ozone release not unduly restrictive even though EPA regulations do not require its use); *Electro-Methods, Inc.*, 70 Comp. Gen. 53 (B-239141.2), 90-2 CPD ¶ 363 (buying entire modification kits rather than individual parts not unduly restrictive); *Pulse Elecs., Inc.*, Comp. Gen. Dec. B-240105, 90-2 CPD ¶ 309 (MIL-Q-9858A quality assurance requirement not unduly restrictive for complex item); *Allen Organ Co.*, Comp. Gen. Dec. B-231473.2, 88-2 CPD ¶ 196 (requirement for wind-blown pipe organ to harmonize with historic building not unduly restrictive even though it excluded electronic organs); *Milcare, Inc.*, Comp. Gen. Dec. B-230876, 88-2 CPD ¶ 29 (inward-opening doors on storage cabinets not unduly restrictive when agency had space shortage); and *Honeywell Inc.*, Comp. Gen. Dec. B-230224, 88-1 CPD ¶ 568 (detailed salient characteristics describing features of brand name product not unduly restrictive when agency demonstrated its need for specified features).

## b.  Unclear or Ambiguous Specifications

If specifications are vague or ambiguous, they will not communicate the exact needs of the agency to the offerors. This will generally result in proposals that do not fully meet the agency's needs or do not give rise to the most satisfactory product or service that the offeror can provide. It may even result in some potential offerors deciding not to submit proposals because they assume the agency is not seeking their product or service. The outcome of such specifications is, thus, either reduced competition or the need for considerably greater clarification or discussion after the proposals have been submitted.

Specifications must provide a common basis for competition by allowing the competitors to price the same requirement. See *Deknatel Div., Pfizer Hosp. Prod. Group, Inc.,* Comp. Gen. Dec. B-243408, 91-2 CPD ¶ 97 (finding that the agency violated the FAR by failing to provide the same specification to all offerors); and *Valenzuela Eng'g, Inc.,* Comp. Gen. Dec. B-277979, 98-1 CPD ¶ 51 (chastising the Army because its "impermissibly broad" statement of work failed to give potential offerors reasonable notice of the scope of the proposed contract).

Most protests of ambiguous or vague specifications have occurred in sealed bid procurements where specification problems cannot be cleared up easily after bid opening. While there is more flexibility in negotiated procurements, agencies are still required to provide clear and unambiguous specifications. GAO stated the following rule in *Alpha Q, Inc.,* Comp. Gen. Dec. B-248706, 92-2 CPD ¶ 189:

> The government has a general obligation when seeking bids or proposals to draft solicitations in a way that identifies the agency's needs with sufficient detail and clarity so that all vendors have a common understanding of what is required under the contract in order that they can compete on an equal basis. *Dynalectron Corp.,* B-198679, Aug. 11, 1981, 81-2 CPD ¶ 115; *Worldwide Marine, Inc.,* B-212640, Feb. 7, 1984, 84-1 CPD ¶ 152. This means that a contracting agency normally must provide or at least reference the applicable specifications and drawings which are to govern the contractor's performance. Federal Acquisition Regulation (FAR) 10.008(d). Solicitations are not required to be so detailed as to eliminate all uncertainties, *AAA Eng'g & Drafting, Inc.,* B-236034, Oct. 31, 1989, 89-2 CPD ¶ 404, and in some cases the government cannot provide drawings or other data because they are either not available or not releasable. See *Oktel,* B-244956, B-244956.2, Dec. 4, 1991, 91-2 CPD 512; *American Diesel Engineering Co., Inc.,* B-245534, Jan. 16, 1992, 92-1 CPD ¶ 79. However, where relevant information is available for inclusion in a solicitation and would give offerors seeking to meet government requirements a clearer understanding of those requirements than they would otherwise have, the information should be provided.

The following discussion includes decisions on both sealed bid and competitively negotiated procurements where guidance is provided to ensure fair competition and obtain the best product or service to meet the agency's needs.

## (1) REQUIREMENT FOR CLARITY

Specifications and solicitations that are susceptible to more than one reasonable interpretation of what kind of performance is contemplated are ambiguous, requiring the amendment or cancellation of the solicitation, *Ashe Facility Servs. Inc.*, Comp. Gen. Dec. B-292218.3, 2004 CPD ¶ 80; *Arora Group, Inc.*, Comp. Gen. Dec. B-288127, 2001 CPD ¶ 154; *Flow Tech., Inc.*, Comp. Gen. Dec. B-228281, 87-2 CPD ¶ 633. As a general rule, the contracting agency must give offerors sufficient detail in a solicitation to enable them to compete intelligently and on a relatively equal basis. There is no requirement, though, that a competition be based on specifications drafted in such detail as to eliminate completely any risk or remove every uncertainty from the mind of every prospective offeror, *Aramark Servs., Inc.*, Comp. Gen. Dec. B-282232.2, 99-1 CPD ¶ 110; *RMS Indus.*, Comp. Gen. Dec. B-248678, 92-2 CPD ¶ 109.

Such specifications are objectionable because they impede full and open competition by failing to ensure that offerors are competing on a "common" or "equal" basis. This rule is strictly enforced in sealed bid procurements and would appear to be equally applicable to competitively negotiated procurements using design specifications. See *North Am. Reporting, Inc.*, 60 Comp. Gen. 64 (B-198448), 80-2 CPD ¶ 364, stating at 69:

> We agree with the protester that the term "other service" as used in the amended IFB is ambiguous. . . . [T]he term "other service" may be *any* other delivery service each bidder cares to offer as long as the FERC is so advised. Thus, the bidders are, in effect, defining the term and, as they do so differently, their bids are not comparable because they are not bidding on the same delivery bases. *See* 39 Comp. Gen. 570, 572 (1960). Therefore, we believe that this portion of the IFB accelerated delivery specification is not sufficiently definite to permit the preparation and evaluation of bids on a common basis.

In *M.J. Rudolph Corp.*, Comp. Gen. Dec. B-196159, 80-1 CPD ¶ 84, GAO recommended resolicitation of a contract to lease cranes for loading ships where the specifications were susceptible to more than one reasonable interpretation as to the necessary performance characteristics of the cranes. See also *Allied Signal, Inc.*, Comp. Gen. Dec. B-275032, 97-1 CPD ¶ 136 (solicitation ambiguous where two parties had reasonable interpretations as to backwards compatibility to two existing intelligence terminals); *MLC Fed., Inc.*, Comp. Gen. Dec. B-254696, 94-1 CPD ¶ 8 (RFP's system architecture requirement that equipment proposed be of the latest line could have referred only to the conceptual structure and functional behavior of the machine as distinct from the physical design); *Consolidated Devices, Inc. — Recons.*, Comp. Gen. Dec. B-225602.2, 87-1 CPD ¶ 437 (RFP did not adequately define the torque/force tension ranges within which the calibrators were to operate); *University Research Corp.*, 64 Comp. Gen. 273 (B-216461), 85-1 CPD ¶ 210 (RFP contained vague description of training courses with result that incumbent contractor had unfair advantage); *Maron Constr. Co.*, Comp. Gen. Dec. B-193106, 79-1 CPD ¶ 169 (specifications ambiguous as to the quantity of doors and frames required); *Kemp Indus., Inc.*, Comp. Gen. Dec. B-192301, 78-2 CPD ¶ 248 (specifications ambiguous regarding a requirement that a specific motor assembly be used in the power pack supplying howitzers); *Orthopedic Equip. Co.*, Comp. Gen. Dec. B-189971, 78-1 CPD ¶ 391 (specifications unclear as to whether or not leaded steel could be used in the production of mountain pilon snap links); *Flo Tek, Inc.*, 56 Comp. Gen. 378 (B-187571), 77-1 CPD ¶ 129 (specifications ambiguous as to the type of stainless steel required under the contract); *Allied Contractors, Inc.*, Comp. Gen. Dec. B-186114, 76-2 CPD ¶ 55 (specification ambiguous as to whether prefabricated metal building was needed in sewage treatment plant); *Learning Res. Mfg. Co.*, Comp. Gen. Dec. B-180642, 74-1 CPD ¶ 308 (specifications did not indicate whether modular counter units were to be constructed of particle board or plywood and particle board); *Air Plastics, Inc.*, 53 Comp. Gen. 622 (B-179836), 74-1 CPD ¶ 100 (specifications did not detail descriptive data required); *Jacobs Transfer, Inc.*, 53 Comp. Gen. 797 (B-180195), 74-1 CPD ¶ 213 (specifications failed to estimate the number of work units required); and 51 Comp. Gen. 635 (B-174813) (1972) (specifications did not indicate whether photocomposition, Linotron 1010 system, or master typography program was to be furnished).

Specifications are not ambiguous when they contain clear performance requirements. Thus, an agency can properly elect to state its needs in terms of performance or functional requirements in order to encourage greater competition. See *University Research Corp.*, Comp. Gen. Dec. B-228895, 87-2 CPD ¶ 636, finding that a solicitation provided sufficient detail when most information had been given or was unnecessary for preparation of bid; and *Memorex Corp.*, Comp. Gen. Dec. B-212660, 84-1 CPD ¶ 153, finding that it was proper to define the requirement in terms of the "required capability and characteristics of the requested equipment" in order to invite innovative and independent approaches to meeting the agency's needs. In the latter case GAO relied to some extent on the fact that five proposals had been submitted in response to the RFP. See also *Jackson Jordan, Inc.*, Comp. Gen. Dec. B-198072, 80-2 CPD ¶ 104, where, on a sealed bid procurement, GAO held that a specification requiring "tamping 100% of the switch" was not ambiguous, although performance was impossible, because it provided the "best method presently available" to describe the performance characteristic. It is also proper to define the work in terms of sample tasks, *International Sec. Tech., Inc.*, Comp. Gen. Dec. B-215029, 85-1 CPD ¶ 6.

An agency may also impose risks on competitors when it does not have necessary information. See *Jones, Russotto & Walker*, Comp. Gen. Dec. B-283288, 99-2 CPD ¶ 111 (statement of work was detailed enough to permit prospective parties to apply their own cost data regarding tasks and responsibilities); *ANV Enters., Inc.*, Comp. Gen. Dec. B-270013, 96-1 CPD ¶ 40 (specification to test soil for the proper fertilizer requirements and to furnish and apply fertilizer did not impose undue risk where agency provided information on the types and quantities of fertilizer used historically); *Cobra Techs., Inc.*, Comp. Gen. Dec. B-254890, 94-1 CPD ¶ 35 (failure to include an estimate of the hours required to assist tenant moves not undue risk because there was no historical data to use and the IFB described what was to be required); *Newport News Shipbuilding & Dry Dock Co.*, Comp. Gen. Dec.

B-221888, 86-2 CPD ¶ 23 (statement that offerors should assume the work was similar to prior overhauls and that, if not, price would be adjusted provided sufficient clarity); *Korean Maint. Co.*, 66 Comp. Gen. 12 (B-223780), 86-2 CPD ¶ 379 (requirement that offeror bear risk of utility costs for three-year performance period not undue risk where past usage data were included in RFP); *Dynalectron Corp.*, 65 Comp. Gen. 290 (B-220518), 86-1 CPD ¶ 151 (requirement that offeror bear risk of amount of materials needed to perform work not undue risk where neither agency nor offerors could make a good estimate because the past usage data were not segregated); *Analytics Inc.*, Comp. Gen. Dec. B-215092, 85-1 CPD ¶ 3 (requirement that equipment function with other unspecified equipment to be procured in the future not overly vague); and *Klein-Sieb Advertising & Pub. Relations, Inc.*, Comp. Gen. Dec. B-200399, 81-2 CPD ¶ 251, *recons. denied*, 82-1 CPD ¶ 101 (statement that agency could not compute amount of services required not overly vague where seven proposals received).

The apparent confusion of bidders evidenced by their varied responses to the solicitation can be indicative of ambiguity in the specification. One solicitation was canceled because six of nine bidders took exception to the specifications, Comp. Gen. Dec. B-177660, Apr. 24, 1973, *Unpub.* See also *Dynamic Corp.*, Comp. Gen. Dec. B-296366, 2005 CPD ¶ 125 (agency canceled solicitation when bidders submitted widely varying unit prices); *Brickwood Contractors, Inc.*, Comp. Gen. Dec. B-292171, 2003 CPD ¶ 120 (agency canceled solicitation when it found that a reasonable interpretation of specification would not meet its needs); *Neals Janitorial Serv.*, Comp. Gen. Dec. B-276625, 97-2 CPD ¶ 6 (agency canceled solicitation where specifications were so inadequate that bidders did not have a common basis on which to prepare bids); *Ferguson-Williams, Inc.*, Comp. Gen. Dec. B-258460, 95-1 CPD ¶ 39 (agency canceled solicitation where refuse collection and disposal requirements did not identify the agency's actual requirements and the three low bidders were misled). However, in *Bentley, Inc.*, Comp. Gen. Dec. B-200561, 81-1 CPD ¶ 156, GAO overturned the agency's decision to cancel a solicitation for alleged ambiguity, relying in part upon the fact that none of the several bidders had complained that the solicitation was ambiguous. The mere fact that there is a great variation in bid prices is not sufficient evidence of inadequate specifications to require cancellation, *Broken Lance Enters., Inc.*, Comp. Gen. Dec. B-193066, 78-2 CPD ¶ 328 (submission of low bids does not indicate ambiguity and is not a basis to challenge an award); *Arvol D. Hays Constr. Co.*, Comp. Gen. Dec. B-187526, 76-2 CPD ¶ 378 (wide disparity in bid prices does not automatically indicate defective IFB); *J.C.L. Servs., Inc.*, Comp. Gen. Dec. B-181009, 74-1 CPD ¶ 198 (wide range of bids does not necessarily indicate defect in the specifications).

## (2) Errors or Omissions in Specifications

Specifications may be improper due to errors or omissions even though they are definite and unambiguous, *Day & Zimmerman, Inc.*, Comp. Gen. Dec. B-212017,

84-1 CPD ¶ 377 (current operating data needed for competition for services); 50 Comp. Gen. 50 (B-169977) (1970) (erroneous provision expressed fixed level of man hours required as opposed to estimated level); 51 Comp Gen. 426 (B-174010) (1972) (solicitation omitted data requirements); Comp. Gen. Dec. B-173740.1, Nov. 17, 1971, *Unpub.* (specifications omitted test capability and one specific item); Comp. Gen. Dec. B-178482, July 10, 1973, *Unpub.* (explosive was erroneously classified in specifications as class " C" rather than class " B" ); *Kleen-Rite Janitorial Servs., Inc.*, Comp. Gen. Dec. B-180345, 74-1 CPD ¶ 210 (bid sheet omitted blank space for an itemized price). Failure of a solicitation to list an item's salient characteristics may improperly restrict competition by precluding potential offerors of equal products from determining what characteristics are considered essential for their items to be accepted, and cancellation of the solicitation may required, *T-L-C Sys*, Comp. Gen. Dec. B-227470, 87-2 CPD ¶ 283; *Bluco Corp.*, Comp. Gen. Dec. B-260368, 95-2 CPD ¶ 125.

Government construction contracts often attempt to overcome this problem of missing information by including an Omissions and Misdescriptions clause which requires the contractor to perform any omitted or misdescribed details of the work that are necessary to carry out the intent of the drawings or specifications. See ¶ (d) of the *Contract Drawings, Maps & Specifications* clause in DFARS 252.236-7001. However, this clause applies only to details, not to new sections of unspecified work. For example, in *Strauss Constr. Co.*, ASBCA 22791, 79-1 BCA ¶ 13,578, a contractor was not required to provide a particular fire extinguishing system whose description was omitted from the specifications because the particular system was not a "detail" under the clause. See *M.A. Mortenson Co.*, ASBCA 50716, 99-1 BCA ¶ 30,270, stating that the clause only covers the omission of work that is "manifestly" necessary to carry out the work.

Furthermore, the government may include contract clauses that require the contractor to assume the risk of specification or drawing errors or omissions. In 48 Comp. Gen. 750 (B-165953) (1968), GAO approved the use of such a clause, stating at 754:

> [W]e are not aware of any situations where [the] doctrine of implied warranty or representation as to the adequacy of Government specifications has been extended to cases where the Government discloses the inadequacies of such specifications and permits or requires the contractor to make necessary corrections.

See also *Rixon Elecs., Inc. v. United States*, 210 Ct. Cl. 309, 536 F.2d 1345 (1976); *Varo, Inc.*, Comp. Gen. Dec. B-193789, 80-2 CPD ¶ 44.

### (3) OPEN OR INDEFINITE SPECIFICATIONS

Provisions permitting offerors to select the applicable specification, like ambiguous specifications, may preclude competition on a common basis. In *Alpha Q*,

*Inc.*, Comp. Gen. Dec. B-248706, 92-2 CPD ¶ 189, GAO ruled that a specification was improper because it required offerors to deliver parts for General Electric engines meeting "the latest revision of the General Electric drawing." GAO reasoned that FAR 10.008(b) required that the government furnish such information. That provision, now in FAR 11.201(a), states:

> Do not use general identification references, such as "the issue in effect on the date of the solicitation."

See also *Pulse Elecs., Inc.*, Comp. Gen. Dec. B-244764, 91-2 CPD ¶ 468, finding a specification improper because it required offerors to comply with military specifications and standards "in effect as of the date set for receipt of proposals."

## B. Bundling

One of the major decisions that must be made in the acquisition planning process is how much work to bundle or package in a single procurement. The bundling (also known as " packaging") decision is usually a tradeoff between the type of competition that is obtained and the achievement of efficiencies in procuring the work. When different types of work are bundled into a single procurement, there will inevitably be some companies that cannot compete because they are only capable of performing a segment of the work. On the other hand, other companies with broader capabilities will be attracted to the job and may be more vigorous competitors than if the work were fragmented into a number of procurements. Thus, the type of competition shifts when bundling occurs. In addition, efficiencies are achieved through bundling. One efficiency is a reduction of the administrative costs of awarding contracts by reducing the number of procurements that must be processed. Another efficiency is frequently achieved by having only one contractor responsible for coordinating the work. This ensures that the work is performed in a more coherent manner than if it were performed by multiple contractors. An additional efficiency is the reduction in the amount of contract administration that the procuring agency must perform. These efficiencies make bundling an attractive alternative when planning procurements.

At the same time, however, bundling raises serious policy concerns because it may, in practical effect, preclude at least some small businesses from competing. Indeed, the Small Business Act defines "bundling" as a threat to small businesses' procurement opportunities. 15 U.S.C. § 632(o) contains the following definition:

> The term "bundling of contract requirements" means consolidating 2 or more procurement requirements for goods or services previously provided or performed under separate smaller contracts into a solicitation of offers for a single contract that is likely to be unsuitable for award to a small-business concern due to —
>
> (A) the diversity, size, or specialized nature of the elements of the performance specified;

(B) the aggregate dollar value of the anticipated award;

(C) the geographical dispersion of the contract performance sites; or

(D) any combination of the factors described in subparagraphs (A), (B), and (C).

The Small Business Reauthorization Act of 1997, Pub. L. No. 105-135, initiated the effort to limit bundling by adding the following provision to 15 U.S.C. § 631:

(j) Contract bundling. In complying with the statement of congressional policy expressed in subsection (a), relating to fostering the participation of small business concerns in the contracting opportunities of the Government, each Federal agency, to the maximum extent practicable, shall —

(1) comply with congressional intent to foster the participation of small business concerns as prime contractors, subcontractors, and suppliers;

(2) structure its contracting requirements to facilitate competition by and among small business concerns, taking all reasonable steps to eliminate obstacles to their participation; and

(3) avoid unnecessary and unjustified bundling of contract requirements that precludes small business participation in procurements as prime contractors.

The Small Business Administration issued a final rule on October 20, 2003, 68 Fed. Reg. 60006, implementing its statute. See 13 C.F.R. § 125.2 setting forth procedures that are to be followed to deal with unnecessary and unjustified bundling.

10 U.S.C. § 2382, enacted through § 801 of the National Defense Authorization Act for Fiscal Year 2004, Pub. L. No. 108-136, requires each military department and contracting activity to ensure that "decisions . . . regarding contract consolidation . . . are made with a view to providing small business concerns with appropriate opportunities to participate in Department of Defense procurements as prime contractors and appropriate opportunities to participate in such procurements as subcontractors." This statute also requires that before activities consolidate requirements worth cumulatively over $5 million, the senior procurement executive involved must analyze the situation (with market research) and must conclude that no other acquisition strategy, more friendly to small business, would be workable, and that consolidation is "necessary and justified." See also DFARS 207.170, implementing 10 U.S.C. § 2382 and raising the threshold to $6 million, and the Small Business Jobs & Credit Act of 2010, Pub. L. No. 111-240, requiring the Office of Federal Procurement Policy to establish a government-wide policy for contract bundling, and requiring market research and senior approval before opportunities are bundled on contracts over $2 million.

FAR 7.107 sets forth the steps that must be taken during acquisition planning to address bundling:

(a) Bundling may provide substantial benefits to the Government. However, because of the potential impact on small business participation, the head of the agency must conduct market research to determine whether bundling is necessary and justified (15 U.S.C. 644(e)(2)). Market research may indicate that bundling is necessary and justified if an agency or the Government would derive measurably substantial benefits (see 10.001(a)(2)(iv) and (a)(3)(vi)).

(b) Measurably substantial benefits may include, individually or in any combination or aggregate, cost savings or price reduction, quality improvements that will save time or improve or enhance performance or efficiency, reduction in acquisition cycle times, better terms and conditions, and any other benefits. The agency must quantify the identified benefits and explain how their impact would be measurably substantial. Except as provided in paragraph (d) of this section, the agency may determine bundling to be necessary and justified if, as compared to the benefits that it would derive from contracting to meet those requirements if not bundled, it would derive measurably substantial benefits equivalent to —

(1) Ten percent of the estimated contract or order value (including options) if the value is $94 million or less; or

(2) Five percent of the estimated contract or order value (including options) or $9.4 million, whichever is greater, if the value exceeds $94 million.

(c) Without power of delegation, the service acquisition executive for the military departments, the Under Secretary of Defense for Acquisition, Technology and Logistics for the defense agencies, or the Deputy Secretary or equivalent for the civilian agencies may determine that bundling is necessary and justified when

(1) The expected benefits do not meet the thresholds in paragraphs (b)(1) and (b)(2) of this section but are critical to the agency's mission success; and

(2) The acquisition strategy provides for maximum practicable participation by small business concerns.

(d) Reduction of administrative or personnel costs alone is not sufficient justification for bundling unless the cost savings are expected to be at least 10 percent of the estimated contract or order value (including options) of the bundled requirements.

(e) Substantial bundling is any bundling that results in a contract or order that meets the dollar amounts specified in 7.104(d)(2). When the proposed acquisition strategy involves substantial bundling, the acquisition strategy must additionally —

(1) Identify the specific benefits anticipated to be derived from bundling;

(2) Include an assessment of the specific impediments to participation by small business concerns as contractors that result from bundling;

(3) Specify actions designed to maximize small business participation as contractors, including provisions that encourage small business teaming;

(4) Specify actions designed to maximize small business participation as subcontractors (including suppliers) at any tier under the contract, or order, that may be awarded to meet the requirements;

(5) Include a specific determination that the anticipated benefits of the proposed bundled contract or order justify its use; and

(6) Identify alternative strategies that would reduce or minimize the scope of the bundling, and the rationale for not choosing those alternatives.

(f) The contracting officer must justify bundling in acquisition strategy documentation.

(g) In assessing whether cost savings would be achieved through bundling, the contracting officer must consider the cost that has been charged or, where data is available, could be charged by small business concerns for the same or similar work.

Traditionally, agencies had considerable discretion in determining what work will be consolidated into a single procurement. These cases were decided based on the extent that they restricted competition. See *LaBarge Prods., Inc.*, Comp. Gen. Dec. B-232201, 88-2 CPD ¶ 510, stating that the decision to consolidate contract requirements was highly discretionary. Thus, it was permissible to include design and manufacture of a product in a single contract and limit competition to firms capable of performing both types of work, *Argus Research Corp.*, Comp. Gen. Dec. B-249055, 92-2 CPD ¶ 260. See also *Express Signs Int'l.*, Comp. Gen. Dec. B-227144, 87-2 CPD ¶ 243, denying a protest of packaging design and installation services in a single procurement.

GAO also denied protests against packaging of work in numerous situations where the agency was able to describe a satisfactory benefit to be derived from the packaging. See, for example, *Reedsport Mach. & Fabrication*, Comp. Gen. Dec. B-293556, 2004 CPD ¶ 91 (agency reasonably demonstrated that its combination of two groups of motor lifeboats was necessary to satisfy its minimum dollar amount for an IDIQ contract); *S&K Elecs.*, Comp. Gen. Dec. B-282167, 99-1 CPD ¶ 111 (combining desktop computing requirements will provide substantial technical benefits); *Aalco Forwarding, Inc.*, Comp. Gen. Dec. B-277241.12, 97-2 CPD ¶ 175 (pilot program to reengineer the personal property of military service members and civilian employees did not constitute improper bundling); *Phoenix Tech. Servs.*, Comp. Gen. Dec. B-274694.2, 97-2 CPD ¶ 142 (Air Force's decision to consolidate engineering support services for C-130 and C-141 aircraft systems for purposes of systems integration upheld); *Advanced Elevator Servs., Inc.*, Comp. Gen. Dec. B-272340, 96-2 CPD ¶ 125 (use of five regional task order contracts instead of 103 local contracts for elevator maintenance necessary because of agency downsizing and budget reductions); *Building Sys. Contractors, Inc.*, Comp. Gen. Dec. B-266180, 96-1 CPD ¶ 18 (requirement for heating ventilation and air conditioning installation bundled with the acquisition of a computerized energy management control system); *Border Maint. Serv., Inc.*, Comp. Gen. Dec. B-260954, 95-1 CPD ¶ 287 (putting building maintenance services at separate facilities in four cities into a total-package commercial facilities management procurement); *Iowa-Illinois Cleaning Co.*, Comp. Gen. Dec. B-260463, 95-1 CPD ¶ 272 (custodial and mechanical maintenance services for single building in one procurement); *Magnavox Elec. Sys. Co.*, Comp. Gen. Dec. B-258037.2, 94-2 CPD ¶ 227 (bundling of guidance system and the missile it serves into one procurement); *Tucson Mobilephone, Inc.*, Comp. Gen. Dec. B-256802, 94-2 CPD ¶ 45 (single contract to provide, install, and warrant equipment for emergency communications system); *Titan Dynamics Simulations, Inc.*, Comp. Gen. Dec. B-257559, 94-2 CPD ¶ 139 (bundling requirements for weapon simulators); and *Resource Consultants, Inc.*, Comp. Gen. Dec. B-255053, 94-1 CPD ¶ 59 (combining several tasks to support a modification to a weapon training system).

In contrast, GAO sometimes found that consolidating large amounts of work in a single procurement restricted competition without providing a commensurate benefit to the government. See, for example, *Pemco Aeroplex, Inc.*, Comp. Gen. Dec. B-280397, 98-2 CPD ¶ 79, sustaining a protest when the Air Force was unable to show that consolidated programmed depot maintenance for the KC-135 aircraft, inspections and painting of the A-10 aircraft, and overhaul and repair requirements for hydraulic components, electrical accessories, and flight instruments, was reasonably required to satisfy its needs. Other decisions finding restrictive consolidations of requirements include *Vantex Serv. Corp.*, Comp. Gen. Dec. B-290415, 2002 CPD ¶ 131 (no reasonable basis to consolidate portable latrine rental services with waste removal services); *Better Serv.*, Comp. Gen. Dec. B-265751.2, 96-1 CPD ¶ 90 (consolidating copier machine service for government-owned machines with sales of copiers under a federal supply schedule unduly restricted competition); *Allfast Fastening Sys., Inc.*, Comp. Gen. Dec. B-251315, 93-1 CPD ¶ 266 (agency had packaged a three-year indefinite-quantity procurement of 97 types of rivets into four lots, precluding one of three competitors from participating in the procurement); *National Customer Eng'g*, Comp. Gen. Dec. B-251135, 93-1 CPD ¶ 225 (consolidating computer hardware and software maintenance restricted competition because it clearly excluded companies that performed only one of these types of maintenance); *Southern Techs., Inc.*, Comp. Gen. Dec. B-239431, 90-2 CPD ¶ 191 (requirement that the product be designed, manufactured, and delivered by a contractor); *Airport Markings of Am., Inc.*, 69 Comp. Gen. 511 (B-238490), 90-1 CPD ¶ 543 (procuring work on 84 airfields in four regional procurements unduly restricted competition); *Pacific Sky Supply, Inc.*, Comp. Gen. Dec. B-228049, 87-2 CPD ¶ 504 (package all replacement parts for an aircraft engine in a five-year requirements contract).

After the statutory and regulatory changes limiting the use of bundling, GAO has addressed this issue as a matter of restrictiveness as well as statutory compliance. See *USA Information Sys., Inc.*, Comp. Gen. Dec. B-291417, 2002 CPD ¶ 224, discussing the differences in the two approaches. There have been a number of decisions granting protests because of improper bundling. See *2B Brokers*, Comp. Gen. Dec. B-298651, 2006 CPD ¶ 178 (consolidation of transportation coordination and freight transportation services); *EDP Enterprises, Inc.*, Comp. Gen. Dec. B-284533.6, 2003 CPD ¶ 93 (bundling would impair competition from small businesses and administrative convenience not a legal basis to justify bundling); *TRS Research*, Comp. Gen. Dec. B-290644, 2002 CPD ¶ 159 (consolidation of previously separate contracts for intermodal containers inappropriate because it would likely preclude participation by small businesses).

There have also been a significant number of cases finding that the benefits of bundling outweighed the impact on small business. See *U.S. Electrodynamics, Inc.*, Comp. Gen. Dec. B-403516, 2010 CPD ¶ 275 (consolidation of requirements for global satellite services would result in improved performance, efficiency, and services, less redundancy, and significant cost savings); See *Nautical Eng'g, Inc.*, Comp. Gen. Dec. B-309955, 2007 CPD ¶ 204 (consolidation of all maintenance and repair work for Coast Guard cutters, including drydock and dockside services, would result in similar savings as 5.29% saved by Navy when it followed this practice with destroyers); *B.H. Aircraft Co.*, Comp. Gen. Dec. B-295399.2, 2005 CPD ¶ 13 (bundling of requirements for spare parts for aircraft engine would allow contractor to draw down inventory saving significant sums); *Teximara, Inc.*, Comp. Gen. Dec. B-293221.2, 2004 CPD ¶ 151 (consolidation of all base operation support functions would reduce overlapping functions saving significant sums); *AirTrak Travel*, Comp. Gen. Dec. B-292101, 2003 CPD ¶ 117 (consolidating travel services into fewer regions provided significant efficiency and did not significantly small businesses' ability to compete). See also *Future Solutions, Inc.*, Comp. Gen. Dec. B-293194, 2004 CPD ¶ 39, rejecting a bundling protest because the protester had told the agency it was fully capable of performing the bundled contract.

If an agency bundles requirements but sets the procurement aside for small business, GAO will not consider a protest claiming that the agency violated the anti-bundling statute, *Health & Human Servs. Group*, Comp. Gen. Dec. B-294703, 2005 CPD ¶ 6. Thus, the only challenge available to a potential protester in such cases will be a claim that this is restrictive of competition. See *Frasca Int'l, Inc.*, Comp. Gen. Dec. B-293299, 2004 CPD ¶ 38 (consolidating requirements for pilot training with flight training devices not restrictive because protester did not show it could not compete).

## C. Draft Solicitations and Specifications

As noted above, FAR 15.201 explicitly recommends that agencies work aggressively to exchange information with industry, to improve the agencies' ultimate procurement decisionmaking. Some agencies have for many years used use draft solicitations or draft specifications (which FAR 15.201 now specifically endorses) as a means of improving their clarity when the procurement is complex or of a high dollar amount. See NFS 1815.201 making draft RFPs mandatory for all competitive negotiated procurements over $10 million. See *Formal Source Selection for Major Acquisitions*, AFFARS Appendix AA, stating at paragraph AA-104:

> (e) Early industry involvement including the use of draft RFPs is recommended to obtain industry comments. The contracting officer may request industry feedback on contract type, performance, schedule, Contract Data Requirements Lists (CDRLs), specifications, statements of work, and other requirements that impact costs or restrict technical solutions. Equal access for all potential offerors must be afforded and a cutoff date will be established for receipt of comments to permit government evaluation and incorporation of accepted changes into the formal solicitation. The Program Office shall evaluate recommendations, make appropriate changes and provide industry feedback on disposition of the recommendations.

See also *NAVSEA Source Selection Guide* § 5.1 (Mar. 1989), which encouraged the use of draft RFPs to obtain feedback from prospective offerors and states:

> A draft RFP is a solicitation which includes all the requirements (statement of work, specifications, data requirements, and general and specific provisions), but which is sent to prospective offerors to request information. An offeror's response to a draft RFP is not an offer and cannot be accepted by the Government to create a binding contract.

When draft solicitations or specifications are circulated for comment, they should be sent to all prospective offerors, and a *fedbizopps.gov* announcement of their availability should be published. See FAR 5.205(c) permitting publication of federal business opportunities. Sufficient time should be given to potential bidders or offerors to submit meaningful comments, and the agency should take steps to assure all submitters that their comments have been given full consideration. The use of a draft RFP led GAO to reject a protest that a procuring agency had given insufficient performance time in a subsequent procurement, *International Tech. Corp.*, Comp. Gen. Dec. B-233742.2, 89-1 CPD ¶ 497.

## VI. OVERALL COST TO THE GOVERNMENT

One of the major considerations in acquisition planning is the overall cost to the government. Acquisition techniques should be chosen to induce contractors to provide products and services at the lowest possible cost commensurate with high quality and timely performance. The costs considered should be both the initial acquisition cost of the product or service and the operating or usage costs because the amount to be paid to a contractor may not be the only, or even the major, expenditure by the government in using the work obtained. Thus, it is important for the govern ment to consider more than the contract price in determining what award is most advantageous to the government. FAR 7.105(a)(3) states:

> *Cost.* Set forth the established cost goals for the acquisition and the rationale supporting them, and discuss related cost concepts to be employed, including, as appropriate,
>
>> (i) *Life-cycle cost.* Discuss how life-cycle cost will be considered. If it is not used, explain why. If appropriate, discuss the cost model used to develop life-cycle-cost estimates.
>>
>> (ii) *Design-to-cost.* Describe the design-to-cost objective(s) and underlying assumptions, including the rationale for quantity, learning-curve, and economic adjustment factors. Describe how objectives are to be applied, tracked, and enforced. Indicate specific related solicitation and contractual requirements to be imposed.
>>
>> (iii) *Application of should-cost.* Describe the application of should-cost analysis to the acquisition (see 15.407-4).

This part of the plan contains the agency's best analysis of the expected cost of the procurement and some of the techniques that will be used to ensure that this cost is reasonable and attainable.

## A.  Acquisition Cost

The plan must contain the agency's estimate of the amount of funds that will be needed to support the contract effort. Prior to FAC 97-02, Sept. 30, 1997, FAR 15.803(b) contained the following requirement:

> Before issuing a solicitation, the contracting officer shall (when it is feasible to do so) develop an estimate of the proper price level or value of the supplies or services to be purchased. Estimates can range from simple budgetary estimates to complex estimates based on inspection of the product itself and review of such items as drawings, specifications, and prior data.

Although this requirement was deleted from the FAR, it is still good practice to develop an estimate of the cost of the procurement. Ideally, this estimate of the acquisition cost will be made in conjunction with the budget process so that sufficient funds can be obtained to carry out the procurement. The cost estimate can be made using parametric data on the class of products or services being procured, data from past procurements of the same or similar products or services, or any other data that are relevant to arriving at the estimate. The higher the degree of accuracy of this cost estimate, the more smoothly the procurement will proceed because funds will be available as necessary to execute it. Thus, good acquisition planning demands that the agency devote sufficient effort to arriving at a valid cost estimate to ensure a satisfactory degree of accuracy.

The plan should also address measures that will be taken to ensure reasonable acquisition costs. When price competition is anticipated, it is generally assumed that the government will be able to contract at a reasonable price. Where price competition is not anticipated, the acquisition plan must address the efforts that will be made to ensure that reasonable prices can be negotiated. See Chapter 10 for a full discussion of this issue. In this situation, the acquisition plan should also address the type of contract that will be used to share the risks and motivate the contractor to control the costs of performance. Chapter 9 sets forth the guidance on selecting the contract type.

## B.  Life-Cycle Cost

The plan must contain a discussion of how life-cycle cost logic will be used in the procurement. FAR 7.101 defines life-cycle cost to mean "the total cost to the Government of acquiring, operating, supporting, and (if applicable) disposing of the items being acquired," but contains no guidance on the application of this technique. See also DFARS 207.106(S-70), which requires, in planning for a major weapon system or subsystem, that a strategy be adopted to obtain sufficient proprietary rights and licenses to sustain the systems over their life cycle.

Essentially, assessing life-cycle costs attempts to identify products that are likely to impose the lowest costs on the agency over the total period that the product will be used and to plan for competition in procuring spare parts, as well as upgrade and overhaul of the product. To use the technique, acquisition officials must factor the prospective costs of using a product into the original source selection decision (which is frequently otherwise generally based made only on the basis of the initial acquisition costs). The best guidance available on the use of this technique is found in the DoD Contract Pricing Reference Guides, at § 5.6, *www.acq.osd.mil/dpap/contractpricing/index.htm,* discussing life-cycle costing as part of an effective contract pricing strategy.

In instances where the cost of operating and maintaining the acquired product will be much greater than the initial acquisition cost, conducting a procurement without factoring in life-cycle costs can greatly increase the ultimate costs to the government. For example, it may be more expensive to purchase equipment with a low initial price that requires significantly more personnel or energy to operate than higher priced equipment. Similarly, low-priced equipment that will be expensive to maintain may not be the best buy for the agency. Generally, these life-cycle costs are included in a procurement in one of two ways: (1) by including specific contract provisions establishing design goals or stating mandatory contract requirements for such factors as operating costs, maintainability, and reliability; or (2) by making life-cycle costs a part of the evaluation process in competitive source selections when the agency has a methodology to evaluate such costs during source selection.

Factoring life-cycle costs into a procurement by using clauses containing mandatory contract requirements forces the contractor to consider the cost in computing the contract price. Thus, a warranty clause calling for the equipment to function over a specified period of time would induce the contractor to include in its price either the cost of repair of equipment that did not meet the warranty or the cost of designing and manufacturing equipment that had the required life. Similarly, a clause requiring the contractor to reimburse the government for all energy costs over a certain required amount would motivate the contractor to include such costs in the price if its equipment did not meet the requirement. Such clauses are the most direct way of factoring life-cycle costs into the procurement process because they ensure that the offered prices include each offeror's evaluation of the cost impact of the requirement. It is difficult, however, for agencies to formulate a complete set of contract clauses covering all life-cycle costs anticipated in the use of a product. Agencies must also consider that, while such warranties or other provisions as to excess costs will in effect shift risks to the contractor, such techniques may deter some companies from participating in the competition.

Another way to deal with life-cycle costs is to include contract clauses establishing goals, such as maintenance man-hours per aircraft flight hour or fuel consumption of vehicles. In order to ensure that such goals are effective, agencies frequently specify contractual penalties for missing the goal or incentives for making the goal. Alternatively, these goals can be taken into account in subjective award-fee determinations. Such clauses generally have a less direct impact on the contractor than a clause requiring full reimbursement of the government for failure to meet the life-cycle cost requirement.

The use of evaluation factors in the source selection process is the another way of addressing life-cycle costs. If sufficient information is available, the agency can, for example, make a reasonable estimate of the life-cycle costs of each competitor and add that estimate to the offered prices to determine whose which competitor's price is, in fact, lowest overall, *Columbia Inv. Group*, Comp. Gen. Dec. B-214324, 84-2 CPD ¶ 632, or the life-cycle cost estimate can be used indirectly to assist the source selection official in making a best value determination, *Storage Tech. Corp.*, Comp. Gen. Dec. B-215336, 84-2 CPD ¶ 190. See *Sikorsky Aircraft Co.*, Comp. Gen. Dec. B-299145, 2007 CPD ¶ 45, where the Air Force used a normalized calculation of "Most Probable Life-Cycle Cost" when it had obtained actual data from the offerors on prior usage of their helicopters. GAO granted the protest, reasoning that asking for the data obligated the agency to use the data. Subsequently, the Air Force amended the RFP to provide for a subjective evaluation of life-cycle costs without allowing the competitors to submit revised prices. GAO granted a protest of this procedure in *Sikorsky Aircraft Co.*, Comp. Gen. Dec. B-299145.5, 2007 CPD ¶ 155. See also *Lockheed Missile & Space Co. v. Department of the Treasury*, GS-BCA 11776-P, 93-1 BCA ¶ 25,401, where the board found proper the agency's cost/technical tradeoff that resulted in an award to the highest technical, highest price offeror. The agency compared the differences in the value of technical features with the difference in overall cost to the government. Overall cost to the government included the offeror's prices for equipment, software, maintenance, support and any other solicited items, while the differences in value included the "productivity" of the proposed computer systems. Even though the agency paid hundreds of millions more in acquisition costs in order to obtain higher productivity, the Federal Circuit affirmed the decision of the board, *Lockheed Missiles & Space Co. v. Bentsen*, 4 F.3d 955 (Fed. Cir. 1993).

Another possible technique is to make a subjective evaluation of life-cycle costs in the evaluation of the technical competence of the offeror. Such evaluation techniques will be far more accurate if the agency has valid information on the prospective life-cycle costs of the offered equipment — such as its energy usage or maintenance costs.

## C. Design-to-Cost

When the acquisition is for the development of a new product, the plan must also contain a discussion of the use of design-to-cost techniques. FAR 2.101 defines "design-to-cost" as

> a concept that establishes cost elements as management goals to achieve the best balance between life-cycle cost, acceptable performance, and schedule. Under this concept, cost is a design constraint during the design and development phases and a management discipline throughout the acquisition and operation of the system or equipment.

The purpose of this technique is to focus the contractor on the need to design an item that can be manufactured at an affordable cost. FAR 7.105a)(3)(ii) describes the elements of this technique as follows:

> Describe the design-to-cost objective(s) and underlying assumptions, including the rationale for quantity, learning-curve, and economic adjustment factors. Describe how objectives are to be applied, tracked, and enforced. Indicate specific related solicitation and contractual requirements to be imposed.

In the 1990s DoD addressed this issue in different terminology — adopting the practice of treating "cost as an independent variable." Paragraph 3.3.3.1 of DoD 5000.2-R, Mandatory Procedures for Major Defense Acquisition Programs and Major Automated Information System Acquisition Programs, March 15, 1996, called for continual cost/performance tradeoffs during system design and contemplated lowering performance requirements in order to achieve life-cycle goals. The Defense Acquisition Guidebook, *http://at.dod.mil/docs/DefenseAcquisitionGuidebook.pdf*, describes this concept as follows at ¶ 3.2.4:

> As stated in DoD Directive 5000.1, all participants in the acquisition system are expected to recognize the reality of fiscal constraints, and to view cost as

an independent variable. Cost in this context refers to Lifecycle cost, which should be treated as equally important to performance and schedule in program decisions. To institutionalize this principle, program managers should consider developing a formal Cost As an Independent Variable (CAIV) plan as part of the acquisition strategy.

The current DoD guidance for weapon system procurement, DoD Instruction 5000.02, *Operation of the Defense Acquisition System*, Dec. 8, 2008, does not discuss either design-to-cost or cost as an independent variable but merely states that development contracts should be written to encourage "design for producibility."

# VII. PROCUREMENT NOTICES

Procurement notices are aimed at soliciting proposals or increasing meaningful competition by explaining the government's requirements. They are basic elements of a transparent public procurement system. There are several ways to disseminate information concerning the government's needs; in practical terms, the primary method today is *www.fedbizopps.gov*, the website that is the government's "Governmentwide Point of Entry" (GPE) to federal business opportunities. There are also different techniques used to publicize solicitations, such as mailing lists and public posting of solicitations. This section covers the various notice requirements and concludes with a discussion on the use of publicizing procurements electronically through the use of the Internet, and e-mail.

## A. Presolicitation Notices and Conferences

Some procurement notices are designed primarily to give notice of present and planned procurements. The primary vehicle used is a synopsis of the proposed procurement posted at fedbizopps.gov. Agencies may also use presolicitation notices and conferences or other techniques to develop competition well in advance of the prospective procurement.

### 1. GPE Notice Requirements

The Small Business Act, 15 U.S.C. § 637(e), and the Office of Procurement Policy Act, 41 U.S.C. § 1708, establish *minimum standards* for the development of competition by requiring that contracting officers transmit a notice (synopsis) to the GPE (*fedbizopps.gov*) for each covered contract action proposed procurement in excess of $25,000 and for proposed orders under basic agreements, basic ordering agreements, or similar agreements exceeding $25,000. FAR 5.101(b) suggests other methods of publicizing solicitations:

(1) Preparing periodic handouts listing proposed contracts, and displaying them as in 5.101(a)(2).

(2) Assisting local trade associations in disseminating information to their members.

(3) Making brief announcements of proposed contracts to newspapers, trade journals, magazines, or other mass communication media for publication without cost to the Government.

(4) Placing paid advertisements in newspapers or other communications media, subject to [restrictions].

The purposes served by this policy of publicizing proposed contract actions is stated as follows in FAR 5.002:

Contracting officers must publicize contract actions in order to —

(a) Increase competition;

(b) Broaden industry participation in meeting Government requirements; and

(c) Assist small business concerns, veteran-owned small business concerns, service-disabled veteran-owned small business concerns, HUB-Zone small business concerns, small disadvantaged business concerns, and women-owned small business concerns in obtaining contracts and subcontracts.

This publicizing policy gives potential competitors a short period to determine if they are capable of performing the proposed work. It provides that solicitations may not be issued earlier than 15 days after publication of the notice, and the closing date for the receipt of proposals may not be earlier than 30 days after issuance of the solicitation, FAR 5.203. FAR 5.203(d) calls for a "response time" of not less than 30 days from issuance of the notice for architect-engineer services and orders under basic ordering agreements. For research and development procurements, the required waiting period for the closing date for receipt of proposals is 45 days, FAR 5.203(e). For commercial items, FAR 12.603 permits the use of a combined synopsis/solicitation with a response time of not less than 15 days. These requirements set forth minimum periods only; many procuring agencies have found that extending the periods increases competition.

FAR 5.203(g) provides that contracting officers may, unless they have evidence to the contrary, presume that the notices are published one day after transmittal to the GPE, but this presumption does not negate the statutory waiting periods. See *AUL Instruments, Inc.*, 64 Comp. Gen. 871 (B-216543), 85-2 CPD ¶ 324, reaching this same conclusion under earlier rules. Thus, FAR 5.203(g) requires contracting officers, upon learning that the notice was not published within the presumed one day period, to determine whether the date for receipt of proposals should be extended or the notice requirement waived under FAR 5.202(a)(2). In *Shiloh Forestry, Inc.*, Comp. Gen. Dec. B-235449, 89-2 CPD ¶ 229, GAO upheld a decision to waive the requirement based on the urgency of the procurement even though the notice was never published. See also *Hercules Aerospace Co.*, Comp. Gen. Dec. B-254677, 94-1 CPD ¶ 7, where the contractor abandoned its argument that the Navy did not synopsize the solicitation after the Navy responded that there was an unusual and compelling urgency; *Electro-Methods, Inc.*, Comp. Gen. Dec. B-250931, 93-1 CPD ¶ 181, where the Air Force reasonably decided it had an "urgent need" for airplane engine duct supports and was therefore not required to synopsize the proposed acquisition. Similarly, in *JRW Mgmt. Co.*, Comp. Gen. Dec. B-260396.2, 95-1 CPD ¶ 276, GAO held that the agency's need for shuttle bus services had been classified as urgent, and the procurement was consequently exempt from the FAR's general synopsis and time period requirements.

According to 15 U.S.C. § 637(f) and 41 U.S.C. § 1708(c), the following information must be contained in GPE notices:

(1) [An] accurate description of the property or services to be contracted for, which description (A) shall not be unnecessarily restrictive of competition, and (B) shall include, as appropriate, the agency nomenclature, National Stock Number or other part number, and a brief description of the item's form, fit, or function, physical dimensions, predominant material of manufacture, or similar information that will assist a prospective contractor to make an informed business judgment as to whether a copy of the solicitation should be requested;

(2) provisions that —

(A) state whether the technical data required to respond to the solicitation will not be furnished as part of such solicitation, and identify the source in the Government, if any, from which the technical data may be obtained; and

(B) state whether an offeror, its product, or service must meet a qualification requirement in order to be eligible for award, and, if so, identify the office from which the qualification requirement may be obtained;

(3) the name, business address, and telephone number of the contracting officer;

(4) a statement that all responsible sources may submit a bid, proposal, or quotation (as appropriate) which shall be considered by the agency;

(5) in the case of a procurement using procedures other than competitive procedures, a statement of the reason justifying the use of such procedures and the identity of the intended source; and

(6) in the case of a contract in an amount estimated to be greater than $25,000 but not greater than the simplified acquisition threshold [or, where appropriate, a contract for the procurement of commercial items using simplified procedures], or a contract for the procurement of commercial items using simplified procedures —

(A) a description of the procedures to be used in awarding the contract; and

(B) a statement specifying the periods for prospective offerors and the contracting officer to take the necessary preaward and award actions.

A number of exemptions from the requirement for GPE notices are contained in 15 U.S.C. § 637(g) and 41 U.S.C. § 1708(b). These are summarized as follows in FAR 5.202:

The contracting officer need not submit the notice required by 5.201 when —

(a) The contracting officer determines that —

(1) The synopsis cannot be worded to preclude disclosure of an agency's needs and such disclosure would compromise the national security (*e.g.*, would result in disclosure of classified information). The fact that a proposed solicitation or contract action contains classified information, or that access to classified matter may be necessary to submit a proposal or perform the contract does not, in itself, justify use of this exception to synopsis;

(2) The proposed contract action is made under the conditions described in 6.302-2 (or, for purchases conducted using simplified acquisition procedures, if unusual and compelling urgency precludes competition to the maximum extent practicable) and the Government would be seriously injured if the agency complies with the time periods specified in 5.203;

(3) The proposed contract action is one for which either the written direction of a foreign government reimbursing the agency for the cost of the acquisition of the supplies or services for such government, or the terms of an international agreement or treaty between the United States and a foreign government, or international organizations, has the effect of requiring that the acquisition shall be from specified sources;

(4) The proposed contract action is expressly authorized or required by a statute to be made through another Government agency, including acquisitions from the Small Business Administration (SBA) using the authority of section 8(a) of the Small Business Act (but see 5.205(f)), or from a specific source such as a workshop for the blind under the rules of the Committee for the Purchase from the Blind and Other Severely Handicapped;

(5) The proposed contract action is for utility services other than telecommunications services and only one source is available;

(6) The proposed contract action is an order placed under Subpart 16.5;

(7) The proposed contract action results from acceptance of a proposal under the Small Business Innovation Development Act of 1982 (Pub. L. 97-219);

(8) The proposed contract action results from the acceptance of an unsolicited research proposal that demonstrates a unique and innovative concept (see 2.101) and publication of any notice complying with 5.207 would improperly disclose the originality of thought or innovativeness of the proposed research, or would disclose proprietary information associated with the proposal. This exception does not apply if the proposed contract action results from an unsolicited research proposal and acceptance is based solely upon the unique capability of the source to perform the particular research services proposed (see 6.302-1(a)(2)(i));

(9) The proposed contract action is made for perishable subsistence supplies, and advance notice is not appropriate or reasonable;

(10) The proposed contract action is made under conditions described in 6.302-3, or 6.302-5 with regard to brand name commercial items for authorized resale, or 6.302-7, and advance notice is not appropriate or reasonable;

(11) The proposed contract action is made under the terms of an existing contract that was previously synopsized in sufficient detail to comply with the requirements of 5.207 with respect to the current proposed contract action;

(12) The proposed contract action is by a Defense agency and the proposed contract action will be made and performed outside the United States and its outlying areas, and only local sources will be solicited. This exception does not apply to proposed contract actions covered by the World Trade Organization Government Procurement Agreement or a Free Trade Agreement (see Subpart 25.4);

(13) The proposed contract action —

(i) Is for an amount not expected to exceed the simplified acquisition threshold;

(ii) Will be made through a means that provides access to the notice of proposed contract action through the GPE; and

(iii) Permits the public to respond to the solicitation electronically; or

(14) The proposed contract action is made under conditions described in 6.302-3 with respect to the services of an expert to support the Federal Government in any current or anticipated litigation or dispute.

(b) The head of the agency determines in writing, after consultation with the Administrator for Federal Procurement Policy and the Administrator of the Small Business Administration, that advance notice is not appropriate or reasonable.

It has also been held that the synopsis requirement is not directly applicable to reprocurements against defaulted contracts, *United States Pollution Control, Inc.*, Comp. Gen. Dec. B-225372, 87-1 CPD ¶ 96.

The government's failure to properly publish the required notice may invalidate a procurement. See *TMI Mgmt. Sys., Inc.*, Comp. Gen. Dec. B-401530, 2009 CPD ¶ 191, where GAO held that FEMA's misclassification for facilities support services on the GPE site under a "miscellaneous" product classification code improperly deprived vendors of an appropriate opportunity to respond to the solicitation. Similarly, in *Gourmet Distribs.*, Comp. Gen. Dec. B-259083, 95-1 CPD ¶ 130, GAO held that an agency did not use reasonable methods to obtain full and open competition when it improperly classified the announcement of a beverage vending services procurement under the classification category for leasing or renting equipment. See also *Information Ventures, Inc.*, Comp. Gen. Dec. B-293518, 2004 CPD ¶ 76 (synopsis lacked necessary information because it did not accurately describe the agency's requirements); *RII*, Comp. Gen. Dec. B-251436 , 93-1 CPD ¶ 223 (cancellation and resolicitation proper where agency had misclassified a listing in the CBD as "research and development" instead of "professional, administrative, and management support services"); *Frank Thatcher Assocs.*, 67 Comp. Gen. 77 (B-228744), 87-2 CPD ¶ 480 (misclassification of notice held to be a statutory violation requiring the award of protest costs (the contract had been performed)); *Pacific Sky Supply, Inc.*, Comp. Gen. Dec. B-225420, 87-1 CPD ¶ 206 (notice not listing all of the items to be procured from a single source was defective); and *United States Marshals Serv.*, Comp. Gen. Dec. B-224277.3, 87-1 CPD ¶ 430 (improper synopsis of procurement based on national security when it failed to include a full explanation of its use of this exception). Compare *Morris Guralnick Assocs.*, Comp. Gen. Dec. B-214751.2, 84-2 CPD ¶ 597, where the CBD notice appeared in the section for communications equipment rather than in the section on services where it properly belonged. GAO refused to recommend cancellation of the contract because the statute contains no expression of congressional intent to require agencies to cancel otherwise proper awards where the exact letter of the statute was not followed. GAO noted that the Navy complied with the spirit of the statute because notice was actually published and two firms were aware of the procurement. In *Pilkington Aerospace, Inc.*, Comp. Gen. Dec. B-259173, 95-1 CPD ¶ 180, where the Air Force failed to publish an amended CBD synopsis increasing the quantity of goods from 35 to 325, GAO agreed with the protester that the Air Force erred but denied the protest because the protester was not capable of meeting the increased needs. See also *Gott Corp.*, Comp. Gen. Dec. B-222586, 86-2 CPD ¶ 154, refusing to cancel the award for improper notice because the protester actually knew of the procurement in time to compete. Similarly, in *Space Vector Corp.*, Comp. Gen. Dec. B-253295.2, 93-2 CPD ¶ 273, GAO held that although the "GPS receiver integration" was a critical factor in the agency's sole source determination that should have been disclosed in the CBD synopsis, the protester was informed of this requirement during qualification discussions and was given the opportunity to demonstrate its capability.

One of the major functions of GPE notices is to alert potential competitors that an agency intends to conduct a procurement using other than competitive procedures. Thus, notices of procurements involving other than competitive procedures must contain a statement of the reason justifying such procedures and must identify the intended source, 41 U.S.C. § 1708(c)(5); FAR 5.207 (c)(2)(xiv). The failure to comply with this publication requirement was held not to require termination of the resulting sole source award in *AUL Instruments, Inc.*, 64 Comp. Gen. 871 (B-216543), 85-2 CPD ¶ 324, because there was no prejudice to the protester who did not appear able to meet the urgent requirements.

However, the publication of this notice is mandatory and when a potential contractor responds to such a notice, the agency must consider the response, 10 U.S.C. § 2304(f)(1)(C); 41 U.S.C. § 253(f)(1)(C) (pre-2011 codification). See *Masstor Sys. Corp.*, 64 Comp. Gen. 118 (B-215046), 84-2 CPD ¶ 598, holding that a sole source award was unreasonable because the agency rejected the responding offer for reasons not stated in the notice or otherwise made known to the offeror. See also *Standard Mfg. Co. v. United States*, 7 Cl. Ct. 54 (1984), where the court held that the protester's reply to a CBD notice stating that it was capable of performing the proposed work bound the government to an implied promise to fairly and honestly consider the response. Similarly, in *Magnavox Elec. Sys. Co. v. United States*, 26 Cl. Ct. 1373 (1992), the court held that the government's CBD market survey notice and prospective bidder's response resulted in an implied contract to give fair and impartial consideration to a bid. But see *Motorola, Inc. v. United States*, 988 F.2d 113 (Fed. Cir. 1993), where the court stated that it is only the contractor's submission of a formal bid manifesting its intent to be bound by the solicitation's provision that justifies implying a reciprocal government commitment to fairly and honestly consider the bid. *Motorola* impliedly overrules *Standard* and *Magnavox* to the extent that those cases held that anything less than a formal, responsive bid can create an implied contract of fair and honest dealing. See *Garchik v. United States*, 37 Fed. Cl. 52 (1996), holding that the court had no jurisdiction because the protester had responded to a request for information, which response was not a formal, responsive bid.

Mere inclusion in the notice of the identity of the intended source and the reason justifying the lack of competition may be insufficient. In *Berkshire Computer Prods.*, Comp. Gen. Dec. B-240327, 91-1 CPD ¶ 464, GAO indicated that the notice should contain sufficient information to permit prospective offerors to respond in a meaningful way with alternative approaches. In *Racal-Milgo*, 66 Comp. Gen. 430 (B-225681), 87-1 CPD ¶ 472, GAO held that this did not require the inclusion of the agency's evaluation factors in the notice.

If a potential competitor fails to submit a timely expression of interest in response to a notice that other than competitive procedures will be used, it will be precluded from contesting the agency decision before GAO. Thus, when the agency specified in the a CBD notice that there was a 45-day period for the submission of expressions of interest in competing on a procurement, GAO refused to rule on a protest from a firm that had not responded within that time, *Fraser-Volpe Corp.*, Comp. Gen. Dec. B-240499, 90-2 CPD ¶ 397. See also *Allerion, Inc.*, Comp. Gen. Dec. B-256986, 94-1 CPD ¶ 281 (protester must respond to CBD notices with a timely expression of interest in fulfilling the potential sole source requirement and must receive a negative agency response as a prerequisite to filing a protest challenging the agency's sole source decision); *Norden Sys., Inc.,* Comp. Gen. Dec. B-254684, 92-1 CPD ¶ 32 (same); *DCC Computers, Inc.*, 70 Comp. Gen. Dec. 534 (B-244149, 91-1 CPD ¶ 514 (same). When a potential competitor submits a timely expression of interest that is subsequently rejected, a protest will be untimely if it is not filed within 10 days of the rejection, *Keco Indus., Inc.*, Comp. Gen. Dec. B-238301, 90-1 CPD ¶ 490.

## 2.  *Presolicitation Exchanges with Industry*

As noted above, FAR 15.201 encourages early exchanges with industry when competitive negotiations are employed. It states:

(a) Exchanges of information among all interested parties, from the earliest identification of a requirement through receipt of proposals, are encouraged. Any exchange of information must be consistent with procurement integrity requirements (see 3.104). Interested parties include potential offerors, end users, Government acquisition and supporting personnel, and others involved in the conduct or outcome of the acquisition.

(b) The purpose of exchanging information is to improve the understanding of Government requirements and industry capabilities, thereby allowing potential offerors to judge whether or how they can satisfy the Government's requirements, and enhancing the Government's ability to obtain quality supplies and services, including construction, at reasonable prices, and increase efficiency in proposal preparation, proposal evaluation, negotiation, and contract award.

(c) Agencies are encouraged to promote early exchanges of information about future acquisitions. An early exchange of information among industry and the program manager, contracting officer, and other participants in the acquisition process can identify and resolve concerns regarding the acquisition strategy, including proposed contract type, terms and conditions, and acquisition planning schedules; the feasibility of the requirement, including performance requirements, statements of work, and data requirements; the suitability of the proposal instructions and evaluation criteria, including the approach for assessing past performance information; the availability of reference documents; and any other industry concerns or questions.

The techniques used to promote early exchanges of information are set forth in FAR 15.201(c), as follows:

(1) Industry or small business conferences;

(2) Public hearings;

(3) Market research, as described in part 10;

(4) One-on-one meetings with potential offerors (any that are substantially involved with potential contract terms and conditions should include the contracting officer; also see paragraph (f) of this section regarding restrictions on disclosure of information);

(5) Presolicitation notices;

(6) Draft RFPs;

(7) RFIs;

(8) Presolicitation or preproposal conferences; and

(9) Site visits.

As stated in ¶ (a) it is important that any information exchanged with potential offerors be consistent with the Procurement Integrity Act. FAR 15.201 also provides guidance on the type of information that can be exchanged and the precautions that must be taken once a solicitation has been released, stating:

(f) General information about agency mission needs and future requirements may be disclosed at any time. After release of the solicitation, the contracting officer shall be the focal point of any exchange with potential offerors. When specific information about a proposed acquisition that would be necessary for the preparation of proposals is disclosed to one or more potential offerors, that information shall be made available to the public as soon as practicable, but no later than the next general release of information, in order to avoid creating an unfair competitive advantage. Information provided to a particular offeror in response to that offeror's request shall not be disclosed if doing so would reveal the potential offeror's confidential business strategy. When a presolicitation or preproposal conference is conducted, materials distributed at the conference should be made available to all potential offerors, upon request.

Note that one-on-one exchanges with potential offerors meets the procurement integrity requirements, FAR 15.201(c)(4), but agency officials must exercise great care in treating potential offerors evenhandedly when one-on-one meetings are conducted. Thus, if such a meeting is held with one potential offeror, all other known companies that can meet the requirement should be offered a one-on-one meeting.

Alternatively, the agency can post a notice of its willingness to hold one-on-one meetings on the GPE.

After a presolicitation conference has been held, attendees must be diligent in following up with the agency to ensure that they receive an RFP. See *Ketch Corp.*, Comp. Gen. Dec. B-240578, 90-2 CPD ¶ 447, where a protest was denied when the protester inadvertently did not receive a copy of the RFP. GAO held that no recourse was available because the protester made only one inquiry to the agency in the two months between the presolicitation conference and the mailing of the RFP. See also *O.J. Best Servs., Inc.*, Comp. Gen. Dec. B-276954, 97-1 CPD ¶ 23, holding that the protester bore the risk of nonreceipt where the record established that the RFP and the two subsequent amendments were mailed to the protester.

## B. Solicitation of Bids or Proposals

Traditionally each agency of the government maintained mailing lists of potential offerors and publicly posted solicitations. However, mailing lists were abolished in 2003, 68 Fed. Reg. 43855, July 24, 2003. During the same period electronic commerce became the primary means of distributing solicitations. See FAR 4.502 stating:

> (a) The Federal Government shall use electronic commerce whenever practicable or cost-effective. The use of terms commonly associated with paper transactions (e.g., "copy," "document," "page," "printed," "sealed envelope," and "stamped") shall not be interpreted to restrict the use of electronic commerce. Contracting officers may supplement electronic transactions by using other media to meet the requirements of any contract action governed by the FAR (e.g., transmit hard copy of drawings).

> (b) Agencies may exercise broad discretion in selecting the hardware and software that will be used in conducting electronic commerce. However, as required by Section 30 of the OFPP Act (41 U.S.C. 426), the head of each agency, after consulting with the Administrator of OFPP, shall ensure that systems, technologies, procedures, and processes used by the agency to conduct electronic commerce —

>> (1) Are implemented uniformly throughout the agency, to the maximum extent practicable;

>> (2) Are implemented only after considering the full or partial use of existing infrastructures;

>> (3) Facilitate access to Government acquisition opportunities by small business concerns, small disadvantaged business concerns, women-owned, veteran-owned, HUBZone, and service-disabled veteran-owned small business concerns;

>> (4) Include a single means of providing widespread public notice of acquisition opportunities through the Governmentwide point of entry and a means of responding to notices or solicitations electronically; and

(5) Comply with nationally and internationally recognized standards that broaden interoperability and ease the electronic interchange of information, such as standards established by the National Institute of Standards and Technology.

(c) Before using electronic commerce, the agency head shall ensure that the agency systems are capable of ensuring authentication and confidentiality commensurate with the risk and magnitude of the harm from loss, misuse, or unauthorized access to or modification of the information.

(d) Agencies may accept electronic signatures and records in connection with Government contracts.

The electronic commerce technique that is used to disseminate solicitations is the GPE. See FAR 5.102 stating:

(a)(1) Except as provided in paragraph (a)(5) of this section, the contracting officer must make available through the GPE solicitations synopsized through the GPE, including specifications, technical data, and other pertinent information determined necessary by the contracting officer. Transmissions to the GPE must be in accordance with the interface description available via the Internet at *http:// www.fedbizopps.gov*.

(2) The contracting officer is encouraged, when practicable and cost-effective, to make accessible through the GPE additional information related to a solicitation.

(3) The contracting officer must ensure that solicitations transmitted using electronic commerce are forwarded to the GPE to satisfy the requirements of paragraph (a)(1) of this section.

(4) When an agency determines that a solicitation contains information that requires additional controls to monitor access and distribution (e.g., technical data, specifications, maps, building designs, schedules, etc.), the information shall be made available through the enhanced controls of the GPE, unless an exception in paragraph (a)(5) of this section applies. The GPE meets the synopsis and advertising requirements of this part.

(5) The contracting officer need not make a solicitation available through the GPE as required in paragraph (a)(4) of this section, when

(i) Disclosure would compromise the national security (e.g., would result in disclosure of classified information, or information subject to export controls) or create other security risks. The fact that access to classified matter may be necessary to submit a proposal or perform the contract does not, in itself, justify use of this exception;

(ii) The nature of the file (e.g., size, format) does not make it cost-effective or practicable for contracting officers to provide access to the solicitation through the GPE; or

(iii) The agency's senior procurement executive makes a written determination that access through the GPE is not in the Government's interest.

In *NuWestern USA Constructors, Inc.*, Comp. Gen. Dec. B-275514, 97-1 CPD ¶ 90, GAO held that an agency's issuance of a solicitation only in electronic format (CD-ROM) was not unduly restrictive of competition or otherwise inconsistent with applicable law and regulation, stating:

> Federal agencies have traditionally issued their solicitations on paper and furnished paper copies to interested vendors, who then responded with paper proposals. With advances in the information technology field, however, agencies have found that the use of an electronic format, in place of a paper format, can be more efficient and economical. For example, submission of quotation prices on a floppy disk was required in *Latins American, Inc.*, 71 Comp. Gen. 436 (1992), 92-1 CPD ¶ 519, cost spreadsheets were required on disk in *D.O.N. Protective Servs., Inc.*, B-249066, Oct. 23, 1992, 92-2 CPD ¶ 277, and complete cost proposals on a disk were required in *W.B. Jolley*, 68 Comp. Gen. 443 (1989), 89-1 CPD ¶ 512. Further, in both *Continental Airlines, Inc.*, B-258271, B-258271.4, July 31, 1995, 95-1 CPD [¶ 5], and *Spectronics Corp.*, B-260924, July 27, 1995, 95-2 CPD ¶ 47, the agency furnished offerors with certain solicitation-related information on a computer disk, while in *Arcy Mfg. Co., Inc.*, et al., B-261538 et al., Aug. 14, 1995, 95-2 CPD ¶ 283, the agency conducted entire procurements electronically, posting solicitations on its electronic bulletin board and requiring electronic responses only. Moreover, with the enactment of the Federal Acquisition Streamlining Act of 1994, which called for the development and utilization of a federal acquisition computer network, 41 U.S.C. § 426 (1994), Congress clearly signaled its desire that agencies use electronic acquisition methods.

The solicitation was sent to 63 firms. GAO found nothing in the procurement statutes or the Small Business Act that requires agencies to provide paper copies of solicitation documents upon request. Requiring firms to have access to computerized CD-ROM printing equipment or incur a charge to have another company do the printing was not considered unduly burdensome to prospective contractors. See also *Commonwealth Indus. Specialties, Inc.*, Comp. Gen. Dec. B-277833, 97-2 CPD ¶ 151, finding that requiring responses to a request for quotations be submitted though the agency's electronic bulletin board would promote efficiency and economy, and not be overly burdensome to prospective vendors.

## 1. Alternate Means of Issuing Solicitations

In some cases, an agency may choose a means other than the GPE as the means of disseminating a solicitation.

### a. Paper or CD-ROM

FAR 5.102 contains the following guidance:

(b) When the contracting officer does not make a solicitation available through the GPE pursuant to paragraph (a)(5) of this section, the contracting officer —

(1) Should employ other electronic means (e.g., CD-ROM or electronic mail) whenever practicable and cost-effective. When solicitations are provided electronically on physical media (e.g., disks) or in paper form, the contracting officer must —

(i) Maintain a reasonable number of copies of solicitations, including specifications and other pertinent information determined necessary by the contracting officer (upon request, potential sources not initially solicited should be mailed or provided copies of solicitations, if available);

(ii) Provide copies on a "first-come-first-served" basis, for pickup at the contracting office, to publishers, trade associations, information services, and other members of the public having a legitimate interest (for construction, see 36.211); and

(iii) Retain a copy of the solicitation and other documents for review by and duplication for those requesting copies after the initial number of copies is exhausted; and

(2) May require payment of a fee, not exceeding the actual cost of duplication, for a copy of the solicitation document.

## b. *Facsimile*

FAR 15.203(d) permits the solicitation and receipt of proposals by facsimile, as follows:

Contracting officers may issue RFPs and/or authorize receipt of proposals modifications, or revisions by facsimile.

(1) In deciding whether or not to use facsimiles, the contracting officer should consider factors such as —

(i) Anticipated proposal size and volume;

(ii) Urgency of the requirement;

(iii) Availability and suitability of electronic commerce methods; and

(iv) Adequacy of administrative procedures and controls for receiving, identifying, recording, and safeguarding facsimile proposals, and ensuring their timely delivery to the designated proposal delivery location.

(2) If facsimile proposals are authorized, contracting officers may request offeror(s) to provide the complete, original signed proposal at a later date.

Although the FAR is silent as to the use of facsimile for sealed bid procurements, this would appear to be permissible.

### c. Oral Solicitations

Oral solicitations may be used for any procurement falling within the simplified acquisition threshold, FAR 13.106-1(c). In addition, FAR 15.203(f) permits the use of oral solicitations for negotiated procurements, as follows:

> Oral RFPs are authorized when processing a written solicitation would delay the acquisition of supplies or services to the detriment of the Government and a notice is not required under 5.202 (*e.g.*, perishable items and support of contingency operations or other emergency situations). Use of an oral RFP does not relieve the contracting officer from complying with other FAR requirements.

(1) The contract files supporting oral solicitations should include —

(i) A description of the requirement;

(ii) Rationale for use of an oral solicitation;

(iii) Sources solicited, including the date, time, name of individuals contacted, and prices offered: and

(iv) The solicitation number provided to the prospective offerors.

(2) The information furnished to potential offerors under oral solicitations should include appropriate items from paragraph (e) of this section.

## C. Omission of Firms

There have been numerous instances where firms did not receive notice of a procurement or were not sent solicitations, either through mistake or because the agency heads determined that they were not qualified to meet the agency's needs. With the advent of electronic commerce, these occurrences are less likely to occur through fault of the procuring agency because offerors are expected to monitor websites to determine when opportunities exist or solicitations are being made available.

### 1. Inadvertent Omission

Before the passage of CICA, GAO upheld awards if the government obtained "adequate competition" and held that the adequacy of competition did not depend upon whether every prospective offeror was afforded an opportunity to submit a proposal, *John Bransby Prods., Ltd.*, 60 Comp. Gen. 104 (B-198360), 80-2 CPD ¶ 419. This decision was based upon the government's reasonable efforts to inform offerors generally of the proposed procurement and upon the absence of probative evidence that the government had a conscious or deliberate intent to impede the participation of the prospective bidders.

In spite of the language of the CICA that all responsible sources be "permitted" to submit bids or proposals, GAO has continued to follow this line of cases and not require cancellation of a solicitation or an award merely because a prospective offeror was not furnished a copy of the solicitation, absent clear evidence of government fault. See *Price Waterhouse*, Comp. Gen. Dec. B-239525, 90-2 CPD ¶ 192, stating:

> A firm bears the risk of not receiving solicitation materials unless it is shown that the contracting agency made a deliberate effort to prevent the firm from competing, or that, even if not deliberate, the agency failed to provide the solicitation materials after the firm availed itself of every reasonable opportunity to obtain it. *Crown Management Servs., Inc.*, B-232431.4 , Apr. 20, 1989, 89-1 CPD ¶ 393; *Uniform Rental Serv.*, B-228293 , Dec. 9, 1987, 87-2 CPD ¶ 571.

See also *Kendall Healthcare Prods. Co.*, Comp. Gen. Dec. B-289381, 2002 CPD ¶ 42 (protest that the solicitation was misclassified in the CBD denied where agency mailed solicitation to protester and a company protester recently acquired); *Sentinel Security & Patrol Servs.*, Comp. Gen. Dec. B-261018, 95-2 CPD ¶ 67 (inadvertent failure to provide solicitation amendment that set the revised bid opening date); *Lewis Jamison Inc. & Assocs.*, Comp. Gen. Dec. B-252198, 93-1 CPD ¶ 433 (inadvertent mailing of solicitation to wrong address); *International Ass'n of Fire Fighters*, Comp. Gen. Dec. B-220757, 86-1 CPD ¶ 31 (inadvertent failure to mail solicitation amendment); *Viktoria F.I.T., GmbH*, Comp. Gen. Dec. B-233125, 89-1 CPD ¶ 70 (inadvertent mailing of solicitation amendments to wrong address). In *Eagle Creek Archaeological Servs., Inc.*, Comp. Gen. Dec. B-258480, 95-1 CPD ¶ 43, GAO found a series of errors by the agency to be inadvertent. Here, the protester had informed the agency of a change of address and had subsequently received a solicitation amendment at its new address. However, the contracting officer failed to update the mailing list with the result that a second amendment was mailed to the protester's former address and subsequently returned by mail to the agency rather than forwarded to the new address. Further, a personnel shortage resulted in the agency's failure to promptly forward the amendment to the protester. The protest was denied because these inadvertent errors did not show any deliberate attempt by the agency to exclude the protester. Compare *EMSA Ltd. P'ship*, Comp. Gen. Dec. B-237846, 90-1 CPD ¶ 326, finding agency fault when the offeror had requested that the RFP and its amendments be sent by Federal Express and the agency did not send them until the day before the proposal was due. GAO found sufficient diligence by the offeror, which apparently believed that the procurement had been delayed.

More recently, GAO again confirmed that, absent inappropriate action by the agency, the contractor will bear the risk if, once on notice, the contractor fails to take reasonable steps to retrieve a copy of the solicitation. See *Allied Materials & Equipment Co.,* Comp. Gen. Dec. B-293231, 2004 CPD ¶ 27, stating:

> The Competition in Contracting Act of 1984 generally requires contracting agencies to obtain full and open competition through the use of competitive procedures, the dual purpose of which is to ensure that a procurement is open to all responsible sources and to provide the government with the opportunity to receive fair and reasonable prices. . . . In pursuit of these goals, a contracting agency has the affirmative obligation to use reasonable methods to publicize its procurement needs and to timely disseminate solicitation documents to those entitled to receive them. To that end, FAR § 5.102(a)(1) generally requires that solicitations that are synopsized on the GPE also be available on the GPE. However, concurrent with the agency's obligations in this regard, prospective contractors also must avail themselves of every reasonable opportunity to obtain the solicitation documents. *Laboratory Sys. Servs., Inc.,* B-258883, Feb. 15, 1995, 95-1 CPD ¶ 90 at 2. Where a prospective contractor fails in this duty, we will not sustain its protest challenging the agency's failure to meet its solicitation dissemination obligations. *Wind Gap Knitwear, Inc.,* B-276669, July 10, 1997, 97-2 CPD ¶ 14 at 3. In considering such situations, we look to see whether the agency or the protester had the last clear opportunity to avoid the protester's being precluded from competing.

See also *Jess Bruner Fire Suppression,* Comp. Gen. Dec. B-296533, 2005 CPD ¶ 163 (protest denied when presolicitation notice and solicitation were on *fedbizopps* by geographic area which protester could have found with diligent search); *Linguistic Sys., Inc.,* Comp. Gen. Dec. B-296221, 2005 CPD ¶ 104 (protest denied when quotation was late because protester did not carefully read electronic "Q & A" amendment to determine that due time was noon); *USA Info. Sys., Inc.,* Comp. Gen. Dec. B-291488, 2002 CPD ¶ 205 (protest denied because protester failed to avail itself of every reasonable opportunity to obtain an amendment by either registering for e-mail notification or checking the Internet site).

## 2. Incumbent Contractors

Although it might be expected that agencies would be required to exercise special care to ensure that incumbent contractors are solicited in order to ensure full and open competition, there does not appear to be any special rule with regard to such offerors. See *Rut's Moving & Delivery Serv., Inc.,* 67 Comp. Gen. 240 (B-228406), 88-1 CPD ¶ 139, where GAO found that the requirement for full and open competition had been met even though the agency inadvertently failed to solicit the incumbent contractor. The agency had publicized the procurement in the CBD and had received three proposals. See also *Cutter Lumber Prods.,* Comp. Gen. Dec. B-262223.2, 96-1 CPD ¶ 57, finding that the agency's inadvertent failure to solicit the incumbent contractor did not warrant sustaining the protest where the RFP had been issued to 62 prospective small business contractors and the agency received 12 offers.

When the agency is at fault in omitting the incumbent, a lack of full and open competition has been found. See *Qualimetrics, Inc.*, Comp. Gen. Dec. B-262057, 95-2 CPD ¶ 228 (agency mailed solicitation to wrong address after having been advised that the contractor had executed a novation agreement approved by another agency and of the correct address of the successor contractor); *Professional Ambu lance Inc.*, Comp. Gen. Dec. B-248474, 92-2 CPD ¶ 145 (agency failed to mail a solicitation to the incumbent contractor and received only three offers); *Kimber Guard & Patrol, Inc.*, Comp. Gen. Dec. B-248920, 92-2 CPD ¶ 220 (agency failed to mail a solicitation to the incumbent contractor and received only one bid); and *Pratt & Lambert, Inc.*, Comp. Gen. Dec. B-245537, 92-1 CPD ¶ 48 (agency failed to mail a solicitation to the incumbent contractor and received only one offer).

## D. Central Contractor Registration

The Central Contractor Registration (CCR) system is envisioned as a method for the government to have one list of all entities wishing to contract with any agency of the government. Although it was initiated by DoD, the system serves the entire government, and it facilitates many aspects of the procurement process, including publicity, responsibility determinations, and payments. See FAR 2.101 stating that the CCR database is "the primary Government repository for contractor information required for the conduct of business with the Government." Essentially, it displaced solicitation mailing lists maintained by individual agencies. The Federal Electronic Commerce Acquisition Registration Instructions (FECAI) state that "[w]e are creating a single, master registration database of all contractors that want to do business with any Federal government agency," the "primary purpose" of which is to "avoid registrations with each procurement office." FAR 4.1102(a) requires all prospective contractors to be registered in the CCR database except for:

(1) Purchases that use a Governmentwide commercial purchase card as both the purchasing and payment mechanism, as opposed to using the purchase card only as a payment method;

(2) Classified contracts (see 2.101) when registration in the CCR database, or use of CCR data, could compromise the safeguarding of classified information or national security;

(3) Contracts awarded by —

(i) Deployed contracting officers in the course of military operations, including, but not limited to, contingency operations as defined in 10 U.S.C. 101(a)(13) or humanitarian or peacekeeping operations as defined in 10 U.S.C. 2302(7); or

(ii) Contracting officers in the conduct of emergency operations, such as responses to natural or environmental disasters or national or civil emergencies, e.g., Robert T. Stafford Disaster Relief and Emergency Assistance Act (42 U.S.C. 5121);

(4) Contracts to support unusual or compelling needs (see 6.302-2);

(5) Awards made to foreign vendors for work performed outside the United States, if it is impractical to obtain CCR registration; and

(6) Micro-purchases that do not use the electronic funds transfer (EFT) method for payment and are not required to be reported (see subpart 4.6).

Registration in the CCR system, done through *www.ccr.gov.*, is now a prerequisite for federal contracting. The Central Contractor Registration clause at FAR 52.204-7 spells out the procedures for registration, and warns those that fail to register in a timely manner that they may, in effect, disqualify themselves from award even if they otherwise qualify as a successful offeror. DFARS 204.1104 requires DoD activities to use Alternate A of this clause at DFARS 252.204-7004. However, see *TEC/WEST-TEC JV*, Comp. Gen. Dec. B-402573.3, 2010 CPD ¶ 174 (protest that awardee was not registered prior to submission of proposal denied because no such requirement); *Computer Cite*, Comp. Gen. Dec. B-400830, 2009 CPD ¶ 40 (protest that awardee's parent company not registered denied because no such requirement); *Command Mgmt. Servs., Inc., ,* Comp. Gen. Dec. B-310261, 2008 CPD ¶ 29 (protest that awardee's name was not registered denied because other indicia (DUNS and TIN numbers) indicated name discrepancy was "mere clerical error"); *Kloppenburg Enters., Inc.,* Comp. Gen. Dec. B-294709, 2004 CPD ¶ 246 (protest denied where, though awardee's office that would perform work was not yet registered in CCR, awardee had otherwise registered in CCR and was coordinating with contracting officer).

FAR 4.1103 contains the following instructions to contracting officers on how to deal with offerors that are not registered on the CCR:

(b) If the contracting officer, when awarding a contract or agreement, determines that a prospective contractor is not registered in the CCR database and an exception to the registration requirements for the award does not apply (see 4.1102), the contracting officer shall —

(1) If the needs of the requiring activity allow for a delay, make award after the apparently successful offeror has registered in the CCR database. The contracting officer shall advise the offeror of the number of days it will be allowed to become registered. If the offeror does not become registered by the required date, the contracting officer shall award to the next otherwise successful registered offeror following the same procedures (i.e., if the next apparently successful offeror is not registered, the contracting officer shall advise the offeror of the number of days it will be allowed to become registered, etc.); or

(2) If the needs of the requiring activity do not allow for a delay, proceed to award to the next otherwise successful registered offeror, provided that written approval is obtained at one level above the contracting officer.

The CCR system is also being used to perform market research and GAO has affirmed that information in the system as to small business status is valid information to make socio-economic determinations, *MCS Portable Restroom Serv.*, Comp. Gen. Dec. B-299291, 2007 CPD ¶ 55.

# CHAPTER 4

# CONTRACTOR QUALIFICATION

An essential step in every procurement involves a determination that the potential contractor is qualified to serve as a government contractor. This is based on the well-established policy that awards will be made only to "responsible" contractors. (While other procurement systems typically refer to contractors that are "qualified," the federal government system refers more specifically to "responsible" contractors in describing those eligible to contract.) It has long been recognized that the government has broad discretion in determining those firms with which it will enter into contractual agreements. The basic rule was stated in *Perkins v. Lukens Steel Co.*, 310 U.S. 113 (1940), at 127:

> Like private individuals and businesses, the Government enjoys the unrestricted power to produce its own supplies, to determine those with whom it will deal, and fix the terms and conditions upon which it will make needed purchases.

While this rule has been modified in recent years, it still retains its basic vitality.

Determination of contractor qualification requires consideration of whether the firm: (1) can be expected to complete the contract work on time and in a satisfactory manner; (2) is organized in such a way that doing business with it will promote various social and economic goals; and (3) satisfies other special standards of eligibility imposed by statutes and regulations.

The government uses three separate techniques to avoid awarding contracts to unqualified firms: (1) nonresponsibility determinations, (2) disqualification because of an organizational conflict of interest (OCI), and (3) debarment and suspension actions. The most critical difference between these types of disqualification techniques is that a nonresponsibility determination or an OCI disqualification is made by a contracting officer and results in disqualification from a specific contract, while a debarment or suspension action is taken by an agency official or agency board and results in disqualification on an extended (or even permanent) basis. This chapter analyzes the important substantive and procedural aspects of each of these disqualification techniques.

## I. RESPONSIBILITY

While government agencies had long followed the practice of refraining from awarding contracts to firms lacking qualifications to perform the specified work, 7 Comp. Gen. 547 (A-21012) (1928); *O'Brien v. Carney*, 6 F. Supp. 761 (D.C. Mass. 1934), the concept of responsibility was not formalized as part of the procurement process until 1948. At that time, the Armed Services Procurement Act (ASPA) adopted the following language relevant to advertised procurement at 10 U.S.C. § 2305(c):

> Awards shall be made with reasonable promptness by giving written notice to the responsible bidder whose bid conforms to the invitation and will be the most advantageous to the United States, price and other factors considered.

Similar language was included in the Federal Property and Administrative Services Act of 1949, 41 U.S.C. § 253(b). In 1962, when 10 U.S.C. § 2304(g) was added to the ASPA to provide negotiation procedures, the concept of responsibility was specifically recognized as applying to negotiation as well as to contracting by formal advertising (now sealed bidding). The Competition in Contracting Act of 1984 (CICA), Pub. L. No. 98-369, which amended 10 U.S.C. § 2305 and 41 U.S.C. § 253, provided fresh emphasis on the imperative of contractor responsibility. That Act reiterated earlier policy on providing for award in negotiated procurements only to a "responsible source," 10 U.S.C. § 2305(b)(4)(C); 41 U.S.C. § 253b(d)(2) (now 41 U.S.C. § 3702(b)), and for award in sealed bid procurements only to a "responsible bidder," 10 U.S.C. § 2305(b)(3); 41 U.S.C. § 253b(4) (now 41 U.S.C. § 3703(c)).

The regulations promulgated pursuant to these statutes have expressly required an *affirmative responsibility determination* as a prerequisite to award of a government contract. This requirement, as well as an expression of the policy on which it is based, is contained in FAR 9.103:

> (a) Purchases shall be made from, and contracts shall be awarded to, responsible prospective contractors only.

> (b) No purchase or award shall be made unless the contracting officer makes an affirmative determination of responsibility. In the absence of information clearly indicating that the prospective contractor is responsible, the contracting officer shall make a determination of nonresponsibility. If the prospective contractor is a small business concern, the contracting officer shall comply with subpart 19.6, Certificates of Competency and Determinations of Responsibility. (If Section 8(a) of the Small Business Act (15 U.S.C. 637) applies, see Subpart 19.8.)

> (c) The award of a contract to a supplier based on lowest evaluated price alone can be false economy if there is subsequent default, late deliveries, or other unsatisfactory performance resulting in additional contractual or administrative costs. While it is important that Government purchases be made at the lowest price, this does not require an award to a supplier solely because that supplier submits the lowest offer. A prospective contractor must affirmatively demonstrate its responsibility, including, when necessary, the responsibility of its proposed subcontractors,

As noted in ¶ (b) of this regulation, when the offeror is a small business, the Small Business Administration (SBA) may override a contracting officer's determination of nonresponsibility by issuing a Certificate of Competency (COC). Under the Small Business Act and the procedures set forth at FAR 19.6, an agency is not to find a small business nonresponsible without referring the matter to the SBA, which has the ultimate authority to determine the responsibility of small businesses under its COC procedures. See *Capitol CREAG LLC*, Comp. Gen. Dec. B-294958.4, 2005 CPD ¶ 31. See Chapter 11 for a complete discussion of this procedure.

Unlike the issue of "responsiveness" (discussed in Chapter 5), the responsibility of a prospective contractor is judged as of the time of award and not as of the time of submission of the offer, *CardioMetrix*, Comp. Gen. Dec. B-255748.2, 94-1 CPD ¶ 364; *Vulcan Eng'g Co.*, Comp. Gen. Dec. B-214595, 84-2 CPD ¶ 403; *Heli-Jet Corp. v. United States*, 2 Cl. Ct. 613 (1983). Thus, a firm that appears unqualified at the time of bid opening may nevertheless gain eligibility for award of the contract so long as it takes the steps necessary to become responsible by the time of award. In addition, information pertaining to how performance requirements will be met (rather than to the requirements themselves) relates to bidder responsibility and not to bid responsiveness; such information may be provided at any time prior to award, *LORS Med. Corp.*, Comp. Gen. Dec. B-259829.2, 95-1 CPD ¶ 222. The distinction between matters of responsiveness and responsibility is reviewed in detail in Chapter 5.

In most situations, this timing issue does not become a source of controversy because the prospective contractor's status will not be expected to vary significantly between the time of evaluation and the time of award. However, when there is a marked change of status, the rule can affect the outcome. For example, when a low bidder obtained adequate financing by forming a joint venture after bid opening, GAO held that the responsibility determination should be based on the resources of the joint venture, *International Bus. Invs.*, Comp. Gen. Dec. B-206474, 82-1 CPD ¶ 500; *Masoneilan Regulator Co.*, Comp. Gen. Dec. B-189908, 77-2 CPD ¶ 343. Similarly, it has been held that a bidder is responsible if it obtains required licenses and permits after bid opening but before award, even though the invitation required the inclusion of the permits with the bids, *International Bus. Invs.*, Comp. Gen. Dec. B-206474, 82-1 CPD ¶ 500; 47 Comp. Gen. 539 (B-163156) (1968). See *United Seguranca, Ltda.*, Comp. Gen. Dec. B-294388, 2004 CPD ¶ 207, for a discussion of the impact of permits on responsibility. This principle is also reflected in the timing of the submission of the FAR 52.222-25 certification of affirmative action program requirements that need not be submitted until immediately prior to award, *McCarthy Mfg. Co.*, 56 Comp. Gen. 369 (B-186550), 77-1 CPD ¶ 116; *Royal Indus.*, Comp. Gen. Dec. B-185571, 76-1 CPD ¶ 139. Administrative convenience does not justify making a responsibility determination at the time of negotiations rather than at the time of award, *Mercury Consol., Inc.*, Comp. Gen. Dec. B-212077.2, 84-2 CPD ¶ 186, *recons. denied, CFE Servs., Inc.*, Comp. Gen. Dec. B-212077.3, 84-2 CPD ¶ 459.

GAO's rules, revised as of 2003, make it clear that it will not review affirmative determinations of responsibility. See 4 C.F.R. § 21.5(c):

(c) *Affirmative determination of responsibility by the contracting officer*. Because the determination that a bidder or offeror is capable of performing a contract is largely committed to the contracting officer's discretion, GAO will generally not consider a protest challenging such a determination. The exceptions are protests that allege that definitive responsibility criteria in the solicitation were not met and those that identify evidence raising serious concerns that, in reaching a particular responsibility determination, the contracting officer unreasonably failed to consider available relevant information or otherwise violated statute or regulation.

See *FN Mfg., Inc.*, Comp. Gen. Dec. B-297172, 2005 CPD ¶ 212 (discussing history and purposes of revised GAO bid protest rule).

## A. Standards of Responsibility

There are two basic issues addressed in making responsibility determinations. The first is whether the prospective contractor will perform the contract. The second is whether the prospective contractor meets the eligibility requirements imposed by statute or regulation for the type of procurement. In the following material, the term "responsibility" is broadly used to encompass all matters relating to determination of contractor eligibility made on a contract-by-contract basis. However, statutes and regulations setting forth collateral social and economic standards of eligibility frequently do not use the term "responsibility."

### 1. Performance-Related Standards of Responsibility

Performance-related standards are of two basic types: (1) general standards, which are mandated by the procurement regulations for application to all prospective contractors regardless of whether there is any mention of responsibility in the solicitation; and (2) special standards, or "definitive criteria," which are imposed in the solicitation at the discretion of the contracting officer. Special standards may be desirable when it is evident that unusual expertise or special facilities are needed for adequate contract performance, FAR 9.104-2.

#### a. General Standards

General standards of responsibility address two distinct issues relating to whether the prospective contractor will perform in accordance with the contract terms. First, they deal with the question of whether the contractor possesses *the ability to render satisfactory performance*, that is, whether it can perform the work. Second, they relate to whether the contractor has *the determination to use this ability* to complete the contract work in a satisfactory manner and whether the contractor has sufficient *integrity* to justify reliance on its agreement to perform.

## (1) ABILITY TO PERFORM

In determining whether a firm possesses the capability to satisfactorily perform the work, the contracting officer is required to consider several distinct aspects of the prospective contractor's business structure.

### (A) FINANCIAL RESOURCES

A prospective contractor must, according to FAR 9.104-1(a):

[h]ave adequate financial resources to perform the contract, or the ability to obtain them (see 9.104-3(a)).

Although the FAR does not contain specific guidance on techniques for determining financial responsibility, the criteria in practice are those traditionally used to gauge the financial health of any business organization. They include the ratio of assets to liabilities, working capital, cash flow projections, and credit ratings. Other factors, such as the firm's profitability and the liquidity of assets, are also frequently considered.

The contracting officer has broad discretion to use any current facts indicating financial weakness in making responsibility determinations. Thus, GAO has deferred to agency findings of nonresponsibility based on inadequate financial information, *Melbourne Commerce, LLC*, Comp. Gen. B-400049.2, 2009 CPD ¶ 14 (approved bank loan not proof of availability of funds); *Acquest Dev. LLC*, Comp. Gen. B-287439, 2001 CPD ¶ 101 (contradictory information). In 39 Comp. Gen. 895 (B-143208) (1960), GAO upheld a determination of nonresponsibility of a bidder on a $4.7 million contract to charter aircraft to the Military Transportation Service. The procuring agency based its determinations on the facts that the bidder's net worth amounted to only $66,000 and that it had incurred an operating loss of $22,000 thus far that year. Even with the bidder's promised bank loan of $300,000, the cash flow position was still deemed unsatisfactory because it appeared that the contractor would suffer a loss on the contract. Although not necessarily endorsing such action, GAO found that the procuring agency did not abuse its discretion by not informing the bidder of the amount of working capital that it believed sufficient to permit a finding of financial responsibility. In *Costec Assocs.*, Comp. Gen. Dec. B-215827, 84-2 CPD ¶ 626, GAO concluded that a new business with unproven profitability was properly held nonresponsible based upon a financial responsibility report finding that the protester's working capital of $32,500 was insufficient to maintain a $230,000 contract. Similarly, in *Tomko, Inc.*, 63 Comp. Gen. 218 (B-210023.2), 84-1 CPD ¶ 202, an offeror was found nonresponsible because it acquired only merchants' lines of credit rather than a bank line of credit. GAO ruled that the contracting officer and the SBA properly determined that a bank line of credit was necessary to assure performance. See also *West State, Inc.*, Comp. Gen. Dec. B-255693, 94-1

CPD ¶ 211, where the contracting officer reasonably determined that the receipt of a judgment and the obtaining of a loan did not cure the negative net worth and negative working capital situation that had led to the prior SBA denial of a COC. Conversely, in *Schwendener/Riteway (J.V.)*, Comp. Gen. Dec. B-250865.2, 93-1 CPD ¶ 203, GAO reversed a finding of nonresponsibility when it concluded that the contracting officer had misinterpreted information concerning the protester's bonding capacity and schedule of values, and had also failed to seek relevant information regarding the true status of its current performance, thereby deciding unreasonably that the protester was financially and otherwise nonresponsible. Similarly, in *ESCO Marine, Inc.* Comp. Gen. Dec. B-401438, 2009 CPD ¶ 234, GAO reversed a finding of responsibility when it found that the contracting officer had miscalculated the amount of funds necessary to perform the contract. See also *CapRock Gov't Solutions, Inc.*, Comp. Gen. Dec. B-402490, 2010 CPD ¶ 124, denying a protest that the contracting officer should not have looked to the parent company's financial situation in finding that the offeror was responsible.

An offeror whose financial resources are questionable may obtain necessary assistance through association with another firm. The form of association may vary. However, if the entity submitting the bid or proposal ceases to exist as a legal entity, award may not be made to the firm that has succeeded to the interests of the offeror. Another limitation is that the transaction may not appear to be the mere transfer of a bid to a nonbidding entity. Arrangements that have been found to be appropriate include the establishment of a joint venture after bid opening, *Harper Enters.*, 53 Comp. Gen. 496 (B-179026), 74-1 CPD ¶ 131; the sale of all the offeror's stock to an organization with the necessary financial resources, *Telex Communications, Inc.*, Comp. Gen. Dec. B-212385, 84-1 CPD ¶ 127; and the sale of all the offeror's assets to an organization that has agreed to "assume" all open contracts and has guaranteed the performance of the transaction in question, *Gull Airborne Instruments, Inc.*, 57 Comp. Gen. 67 (B-188743), 77-2 CPD ¶ 344. In *Gull Airborne*, the transaction was approved on the grounds that the offeror did not cease to exist as a legal entity. GAO appears to have ignored the prohibition against transferring a bid to a nonbidding party. This prohibition will preclude any arrangement involving the acquisition of an offeror with insubstantial assets, *Mil-Tech Sys., Inc. v. United States*, 6 Cl. Ct. 26 (1984).

A bidder may demonstrate financial capability by offering a performance bond, 33 Comp. Gen. 549 (B-119030) (1954). See also *G & C Enters., Inc.*, Comp. Gen. Dec. B-186748, 77-1 CPD ¶ 155, stating that additional resources may be obtained through a subcontractual or guaranteeship arrangement.

The fact that a contractor has filed a petition of bankruptcy does not, per se, require a finding of nonresponsibility, *Hunter Outdoor Prods., Inc.*, 54 Comp. Gen. 276 (B-179922), 74-2 CPD ¶ 207; *Domar Indus. Co.*, Comp. Gen. Dec. B-202735, 81-2 CPD ¶ 199, but may be considered as a factor in such determination, *Harvard Interiors Mfg. Co.*, Comp. Gen. Dec. B-247400, 92-1 CPD ¶ 413;

*Wallace & Wallace, Inc.*, Comp. Gen. Dec. B-209859.2, 83-2 CPD ¶ 142. The appropriate question is whether the contractor has the necessary financial capability in spite of the bankruptcy.

## (B) ABILITY TO COMPLY WITH DELIVERY SCHEDULE

According to FAR 9.104-1(b), a prospective contractor must:

[b]e able to comply with the required or proposed delivery or performance schedule, taking into consideration all existing commercial and governmental business commitments.

A variety of factors may indicate inability to meet the schedule. See *Gray Graphics Corp.*, Comp. Gen. Dec. B-295421, 2005 CPD ¶ 37 (GAO deferred to agency's nonresponsibility determination based upon protester's late deliveries under recent contracts); *50 State Security Serv., Inc.*, Comp. Gen. Dec. B-272114, 96-2 CPD ¶ 123 (GAO upheld a contracting officer's determination that the protester did not have the ability to have a sufficient number of guards in place when performance of the contract was to begin because there were only 18 days remaining prior to commencement of contract performance and the protester had not provided a list of names of prospective employees). In *X-Tyal Int'l Corp.*, Comp. Gen. Dec. B-190101, 78-1 CPD ¶ 748, GAO upheld a contracting officer's determination that X-Tyal would not be able to comply with the required delivery schedule where it had recently moved to a new facility, had undergone a labor strike, and had delivery problems with a majority of its other government contracts. In *System Dev. Corp.*, Comp. Gen. Dec. B-212624, 83-2 CPD ¶ 644, SDC's failure to present written confirmation of suppliers' and subcontractors' commitments to deliver items and equipment with long lead times led to a negative responsibility determination. In *Sermor, Inc.*, Comp. Gen. Dec. B-210872, 83-2 CPD ¶ 87, the procuring agency found the protester nonresponsible because eight of its ten current contracts were delinquent under original performance schedules and six continued to be delinquent under revised schedules. In *Johnson Graphic Indus. Inc.*, Comp. Gen. Dec. B-205070, 82-1 CPD ¶ 409, a nonresponsibility determination was reasonably based on the firm's record of late deliveries under two of six contracts during the preceding four-month period. See *Victor Graphics, Inc.*, Comp. Gen. Dec. B-249297, 92-2 CPD ¶ 252, where the protester's late deliveries under a number of recent contracts were found to provide a reasonable basis for a nonresponsibility determination in view of the solicitation's short (27-workday) delivery schedule. See also *Computer Support Sys., Inc.*, Comp. Gen. Dec. B-261166, 95-2 CPD ¶ 30, where a protester was properly found nonresponsible when the contracting officer observed and obtained information during a preaward survey that it lacked the resources and ability to comply with the IFB's short delivery schedule.

## (C) FACILITIES AND EQUIPMENT

A prospective contractor must, according to FAR 9.104-1(f):

[h]ave the necessary production, construction, and technical equipment and facilities, or the ability to obtain them (see 9.104-3(a)).

See *S.A.F.E. Export Corp.*, Comp. Gen. Dec. B-208744, 83-1 CPD ¶ 437, *recons.
denied*, 83-2 CPD ¶ 90, where GAO upheld the contracting officer's determination
of nonresponsibility based in part on the fact that S.A.F.E. apparently had no plant in
either the United States or Europe, although the prospective contract required work
in both places.

Contractors that do not have the necessary equipment and facilities at the time
of evaluation for award can demonstrate responsibility by submitting "acceptable
evidence" of ability to obtain the required resources, as stated at FAR 9.104-3(a):

Acceptable evidence normally consists of a commitment or explicit arrangement,
that will be in existence at the time of contract award, to rent, purchase, or otherwise acquire the needed facilities, equipment, other resources, or personnel.

See also *McLaughlin Research Corp.*, Comp. Gen. Dec. B-247118, 92-1 CPD ¶ 422,
where the agency reasonably relied upon an "intent to leave" agreement as demonstrating the awardee's ability to use certain warehouse facilities during its performance; and *Norfolk Shipbuilding & Drydock Corp.*, Comp. Gen. Dec. B-248549.2,
92-2 CPD ¶ 127, where a certification of drydocking availability was deemed to
relate to a contractor's ability to perform and therefore was a matter of responsibility (not responsiveness) that need only be met prior to award. GAO stated that the
solicitation cannot convert a matter of responsibility into one of responsiveness.

GAO upheld a contracting officer's nonresponsibility determination based on
the offeror's lack of a "written commitment" for the purchase of essential equipment, but did comment that the offeror should have been given the chance to prove
that it could have acquired the equipment by the time needed for performance, 52
Comp. Gen. 240 (B-176227) (1972).

Plant and equipment are evaluated for safety as well as capacity to meet contract
requirements, and the failure to correct prior safety deficiencies may be a basis for a
finding of nonresponsibility, Comp. Gen. Dec. B-175545, Aug. 17, 1972, *Unpub.*

## (D) MANAGEMENT AND TECHNICAL CAPABILITY

According to FAR 9.104-1(e), a prospective contractor must:

[h]ave the necessary organization, experience, accounting and operational controls, and technical skills, or the ability to obtain them (including, as appropriate, such elements as production control procedures, property control systems, quality assurance measures, and safety programs applicable to materials to be produced or services to be performed by the prospective contractor and subcontractors) (see 9.104-3(a)).

The best means of ascertaining whether the offeror has these capabilities is to appraise the offeror's present organization. See, for example, *Certified Testing Corp.*, Comp. Gen. Dec. B-212242, 83-2 CPD ¶ 542, where GAO affirmed the finding that the low bidder was not responsible in part because its quality control manager was unfamiliar with the quality assurance provisions of the solicitation. The preaward survey report showed that the company's quality control manager lacked knowledge of quality control procedures and test equipment. See also *Omneco, Inc.*, Comp. Gen. Dec. B-218343, 85-1 CPD ¶ 660 (protester's inability to implement an adequate quality assurance program plan in time to meet the performance schedule constituted a reasonable basis for a determination of nonresponsibility); and *Products Research & Chem. Corp.*, Comp. Gen. Dec. B-214293, 84-2 CPD ¶ 122 (poor quality control system, production capacity, and purchasing ability).

When the offeror is a joint venture, the capability of the new entity should be investigated. See *McKissack+Delcan JV II*, Comp. Gen. Dec. B-401973.2, 2010 CPD ¶ 28, holding that it was improper to find the joint venture nonresponsible based on its proposed accounting system when there was no apparent reason why the accounting system was inadequate for the cost-reimbursement contract that was to be awarded.

The determination of capability is often approached by investigating the prior experience of the prospective contractor. Determinations as to types and degree of experience and the method of proving experience are solely within the discretion of the procuring agency, but any such requirements must be necessary to meet the agency's needs, 39 Comp. Gen. 173 (B-140481) (1959). Nonresponsibility can be based on either experience demonstrating unsatisfactory performance, *Daisung Co.*, Comp. Gen. Dec. B-294142, 2004 CPD ¶ 196 (contracting officer's nonresponsibility determination reasonably based upon collateral investigations of vendor's poor performance on prior contracts); *Columbus Jack Corp.*, Comp. Gen. Dec. B-211829, 83-2 CPD ¶ 348 (poor quality assurance history), or lack of experience, Comp. Gen. Dec. B-169160, May 4, 1970, *Unpub.* (firm had no experience in type of work being procured). A responsibility finding was properly based on the individual experience of a firm's principal officers in *D.H. Kim Enters., Inc.*, Comp. Gen. Dec. B-255124, 94-1 CPD ¶ 86.

The past performance of a contractor can be used to determine that it does not have the capability to perform the current contract. For example, in *Pittman Mech. Contractors, Inc.*, Comp. Gen. Dec. B-242499, 91-1 CPD ¶ 439, GAO affirmed determinations of nonresponsibility based on a thorough evaluation of the performance records from eight prior contracts. The contracting officers had concluded that this performance record indicated that the contractor had problems with the quality of the work, the timeliness of performance, the effectiveness of management, and compliance with labor and safety standards. See also *North Am. Constr. Corp.*, Comp. Gen. Dec. B-270085, 96-1 CPD ¶ 44. Similarly, in *Shepard Printing*, Comp. Gen. Dec. B-260362, 95-2 CPD ¶ 119, GAO agreed with a determination of nonresponsibility based on the contractor's performance record on several recent contracts for the same type of work.

The performance of a predecessor firm may be considered in determining the bidder's technical and management capability. For example, in *Sun Elec. Corp.*, Comp. Gen. Dec. B-202325, 81-2 CPD ¶ 112, although the prospective contractor was not established until 1980, it was the successor in interest to a prior corporation that had manufactured a similar product. The contracting officer properly considered this information in concluding that the prospective awardee had the requisite experience. Similarly, in *Oklahoma County Newspapers, Inc.*, Comp. Gen. Dec. B-270849, 96-1 CPD ¶ 213, the experience of the predecessor firm was relevant because the new firm had retained all of the key employees of the predecessor firm. GAO stated that the "key consideration is whether the experience evaluated reasonably can be considered predictive of the offeror's performance under the contract." It is also proper to evaluate the experience of key employees who have worked for another firm, *J.D. Miles & Sons, Inc.*, Comp. Gen. Dec. B-251533, 93-1 CPD ¶ 300; *Hawco Mfg. Co.*, Comp. Gen. Dec. B-265795, 95-2 CPD ¶ 191.

A contracting agency may also consider the experience of an offeror's parent firm in evaluating a proposal where the offeror has represented that all of the parent's resources would be committed to the project, *Tri-Star Indus., Inc.*, Comp. Gen. Dec. B-254767.2, 94-1 CPD ¶ 20; *Hardie-Tynes Mfg. Co.*, 69 Comp. Gen. 359 (B-237938), 90-1 CPD ¶ 347. Compare *Pope, Evans & Robbins, Inc.*, Comp. Gen. Dec. B-200265, 81-2 CPD ¶ 29, which affirmed a contracting officer's determination that a bidder was nonresponsible even though the parent corporation stated it would "stand behind" its subsidiary. See *Medical Servs. Consultants, Inc.*, Comp. Gen. Dec. B-203998, 82-1 CPD ¶ 93, where GAO stated that in evaluating the experience of a newly formed subsidiary, an agency could use, but was not obligated to consider, the experience of a parent company.

In evaluating the management and technical capability of a corporation, it is proper to consider the experience of one or more of its principal officers, 36 Comp. Gen. 673 (B-130910) (1957). In *Hydromatics Int'l Corp.*, Comp. Gen. Dec. B-180669, 74-2 CPD ¶ 66, a newly formed company was declared nonresponsible for reasons of inadequate management because the firm's president and general manager had been instrumental in managing contracts awarded to other firms on which there was an unsatisfactory record of performance. Similarly, in *Data Flow Corp.*, 62 Comp. Gen. 506 (B-209499), 83-2 CPD ¶ 57, GAO specifically held that in evaluating a new business, an agency could consider the experience of supervisory personnel.

GAO has made it clear that, with regard to this element of responsibility as with others, it will generally defer to a contracting officer's determination. As GAO observed in *American Indian Ctr., Inc.*, Comp. Gen. B-278678, 98-1 CPD ¶ 66, whether "an offeror has the organization and financial controls necessary for successful performance is a matter bearing on its responsibility." Thus, "where a protester argues that an awardee lacks these elements, it is in essence challenging the contracting officer's affirmative determination of the awardee's responsibility." GAO cautioned that because "the determination that an offeror is capable of performing a contract is based in large measure on subjective judgments which generally are not readily susceptible of reasoned review," GAO would not consider such challenges "absent a showing of possible bad faith on the part of government officials or that definitive responsibility criteria in the solicitation were not met." See 4 C.F.R. § 21.5 (GAO rule stating that it generally will not hear protests of affirmative findings of responsibility).

Contracting officers frequently include provisions in the solicitation specifying precise minimum-experience requirements. These so called "definitive criteria" of responsibility are discussed in the section on special standards of responsibility.

## (E) LICENSES AND PERMITS

FAR 9.104-1(g) provides generally that a prospective contractor must be "otherwise qualified" to receive an award under applicable laws and regulations. The major application of this provision is with regard to licenses and permits. The decisions, which have been somewhat confusing, have focused on whether the licenses and permits are federal, state, or local and whether they are specifically required by the solicitation. However, two rules appear to have clearly emerged regardless of these considerations.

First, an affirmative determination of responsibility may be made if the offeror can obtain the license or permit prior to the time of performance even though it has not been obtained prior to award, 46 Comp. Gen. 326 (B-160085) (1966) (Atomic Energy Commission license and California license); *New Haven Ambulance Serv., Inc.*, 57 Comp. Gen. 361 (B-190223), 78-1 CPD ¶ 225 (license from the state office of Emergency Medical Services); *Carolina Waste Sys., Inc.*, Comp. Gen. Dec. B-215689.3, 85-1 CPD ¶ 22 (state certification of waste disposal sites); *Impact Instrumentation, Inc.*, Comp. Gen. Dec. B-250968.2, 93-1 CPD ¶ 241 (premarketing approval by Food & Drug Administration); *Olson & Assocs. Eng'g, Inc.*, Comp. Gen. Dec. B-215742, 84-2 CPD ¶ 129 (state surveyor's license); *United Seguranca, Ltda.*, Comp. Gen. Dec. B-294388, 2004 CPD ¶ 207 (security guard licenses); *Solar Plexus, LLC*, Comp. Gen. Dec. B-402061, 2009 CPD ¶ 256 (state registration as construction contractor).

Second, a determination of nonresponsibility will be upheld if the contracting officer reasonably concludes that a required or necessary license or permit will, if not obtained, impair performance, *What-Mac Contractors, Inc.*, 58 Comp. Gen. 767 (B-192188), 79-2 CPD ¶ 179 (state license, not required by solicitation, which state intended to enforce); *U.S. Jet Aviation*, Comp. Gen. Dec. B-214093, 84-1 CPD ¶ 575 (FAA certificate required by solicitation). Thus, if the contracting officer determines that the work can be performed without the license, it is proper to hold the offeror responsible, *Transcontinental Enters., Inc.*, Comp. Gen. Dec. B-294765, 2004 CPD ¶ 240 (GAO would not disturb responsibility finding because most of work could be performed without missing permits).

There is a great deal of discussion in the cases concerning the degree of specificity of the solicitation requirement for licenses or permits. This discussion is primarily related to the question of whether the contracting officer must consider the lack of a license or permit in making a responsibility determination. Where the solicitation merely includes a statement requiring offerors to "obtain any necessary licenses," as in the Permits and Responsibilities clause for construction contracts in FAR 52.236-7, the contracting officer is not required to consider state or local licenses or permits. The contracting officer can leave the matter of such licenses or permits to be resolved between the contractor and the state or local authorities, *P&R Water Taxi, Ltd.*, Comp. Gen. Dec. B-279014, 98-1 CPD ¶ 119; *Mercury Bus. Servs., Inc.*, Comp. Gen. Dec. B-237220, 89-2 CPD ¶ 443; *James C. Bateman Petroleum Servs., Inc.*, 67 Comp. Gen. 591 (B-232325), 88-2 CPD ¶ 170; *North Park Vill. Homes, Inc.*, Comp. Gen. Dec. B-216862, 85-1 CPD ¶ 129; *John Baker Janitorial, Inc.*, Comp. Gen. Dec. B-206292, 82-1 CPD ¶ 157; *E.I.L. Instruments, Inc.*, 54 Comp. Gen. 480 (B-182004), 74-2 CPD ¶ 339. However, where the contracting officer reasonably determines that enforcement attempts by state or local officials are likely and that there is a reasonable possibility that such enforcement attempts could interrupt and delay performance if award is made to the unlicensed contractor, the contracting officer may consider lack of such license as bearing on responsibility, *Recyc Sys., Inc.*, Comp. Gen. Dec. B-216772, 85-2 CPD ¶ 216; *What-Mac Contractors, Inc.*, 58 Comp. Gen. 767 (B-192188), 79-2 CPD ¶ 179. If the contracting officer does not have reasonable grounds for determining that enforcement attempts by the state will impair performance, the absence of a license or permit cannot properly be considered, *Career Consultants, Inc.*, Comp. Gen. Dec. B-195913, 80-1 CPD ¶ 215. These same rules have been held to be applicable to federal licenses and permits, *Chipman Van & Storage, Inc.*, Comp. Gen. Dec. B-188917, 77-2 CPD ¶ 299. See, however, *What-Mac Contractors, Inc.*, 58 Comp. Gen. 767 (B-192188), 79-2 CPD ¶ 179, which indicates that the contracting officer must make a determination regarding federal licenses or permits in this situation. See also *Israel Aircraft Indus. Ltd.*, Comp. Gen. Dec. B-242552, 91-1 CPD ¶ 454, where denial of an Israeli import license was deemed sufficient to render an offeror nonresponsible.

License and permit requirement have also been interpreted to be a matter of contract administration rather than a matter of eligibility for award of a contract. See

*Nilson Van & Storage, Inc.*, Comp. Gen. Dec. B-403009, 2010 CPD ¶ 198, holding that the IFB statement that "prospective contractors shall be approved and hold" federal and state licenses should be interpreted to allow award to a contractor before the licenses had been obtained. The same result was reached in *United Seguranca, Ltda.*, Comp. Gen. Dec. B-294388, 2004 CPD ¶ 207.

A contracting officer may include a specific requirement for a state or local license or permit in the solicitation if it is reasonably determined that it is necessary to have a licensed contractor, 53 Comp. Gen. 51 (B-174634) (1973). Federal licensing requirements are not subject to such limitations but may be freely incorporated in solicitations. When such mandatory requirements for licenses or permits are placed in solicitations, the contracting officer must consider whether the offeror has, or will be able to obtain, the license or permit in making the responsibility determination. Thus, GAO has treated such requirements as definitive responsibility criteria, *Coastal Elecs., Inc.*, Comp. Gen. Dec. B-250718, 93-1 CPD ¶ 144; *Aero Sys., Inc.*, Comp. Gen. Dec. B-215892, 84-2 CPD ¶ 374; *Fry Commc'ns, Inc.*, 62 Comp. Gen. 164 (B-207605), 83-1 CPD ¶ 109; *Sillco, Inc.*, Comp. Gen. Dec. B-188026, 77-1 CPD ¶ 296. The language of the solicitation relative to licenses and permits will be read very closely to determine whether the requirement is general or specific. See, for example, *AJT & Assocs., Inc.*, Comp. Gen. Dec. B-284305, 2000 CPD ¶ 60 (general license requirements did not establish specific responsibility requirement that had to be met prior to award); *Mark Danning Indus., Inc.*, Comp. Gen. Dec. B-258373, 94-2 CPD ¶ 226 (contract line item requiring a bid price for a refuse disposal fee not a specific requirement for a dumping franchise agreement with a local government); *Honolulu Marine, Inc.*, Comp. Gen. Dec. B-248380, 92-2 CPD ¶ 87 (solicitation statement "directing" offerors to state hazardous waste materials requirement not a specific requirement); and *Washington Patrol Serv., Inc.*, Comp. Gen. Dec. B-195900, 80-2 CPD ¶ 132 (requirement to meet state laws regarding security services not specific requirement to obtain state handgun permits).

## (2) WILL TO PERFORM

Offerors having the requisite ability to perform may, nevertheless, be declared nonresponsible if there is evidence indicating that they lack the will to complete the work in a satisfactory way. Determining whether an offeror possesses the necessary will to perform generally involves the evaluation of two factors: (1) tenacity and perseverance and (2) integrity.

The information to be consulted by the contracting officer in making these determinations has expanded substantially in recent years. The Federal Awardee Performance and Integrity Information System (FAPIIS), FAR 9.104-6, launched in 2010, has integrated much of the information that a contracting officer is to review in making a responsibility determination. FAPIIS was established under § 872 of the Duncan Hunter National Defense Authorization Act of 2009, Pub. L. No. 110-

417. In addition to providing contracting officers with ready access to contractor suspension and debarment information, and to contractor past performance information, FAPIIS also includes nonresponsibility determinations, default terminations, defective pricing determinations, administrative agreements entered into to resolve suspension or debarment proceedings, and information (self-reported by contractors) on criminal convictions, civil judgments, and adverse administrative actions related to past federal contracts or grants. The legislation, and the implementing regulations, ensured that there are procedural mechanisms in place for contractors to challenge adverse information in FAPIIS. See 75 Fed. Reg. 14059, Mar. 23, 2010 (final rule); 75 Fed. Reg. 60258, Sept. 29, 2010 (additional information to be added to FAPIIS). See also *Todd Constr., L.P. v. United States,* 94 Fed. Cl. 100 (2010) (Court of Federal Claims had jurisdiction to hear challenges to adverse past performance evaluations, under Contract Disputes Act). Contracting officers must use care in assessing this information because some of it will be based on preliminary determinations of contracting agencies (such as default terminations) that have not yet been finally resolved. However, contracting officers have considerable discretion in this regard. See, for example, *Commissioning Solutions Global, LLC*, Comp. Gen. Dec. B-403542, 2010 CPD ¶ 272, denying a protest that a contracting officer had considered a default termination in evaluating past performance even though it had been converted to a termination for convenience.

Further legislation, § 3010 of Pub. L. No. 111-212, required the posting of FAPIIS information, excluding past performance information, on a publicly available website; that information became publicly available as of April 15, 2011, 76 Fed. Reg. 4188, Jan. 24, 2011. While previously much (if not all) of this information had, at least in principle, been available to contracting officials on inquiry, FAPIIS marked a significant step forward in consolidating this adverse information on contractor responsibility, and in making much of it publicly available on the Internet. It marked a high-water mark in a longstanding debate over how much transparency to bring to federal contracting; notably, at roughly the same time, regulators abandoned a parallel initiative to make all federal contracts publicly available on the Internet, in part because of concerns over the costs and risks of posting sensitive contractor information in a public forum, 76 Fed. Reg. 7522, Feb. 10, 2011.

Before awarding a contract in excess of the simplified acquisition threshold, contracting officers must review the information available in FAPIIS (*www.ppirs.gov*) and other past performance information, and must document how the FAPIIS information was considered, FAR 9.104-6. The past performance information relevant to the responsibility determination is broadly defined in FAR Subpart 42.15 to include relevant information, for future source selection purposes, regarding a contractor's actions under previously awarded contracts. This past performance information can include a contractor's record of conforming to contract requirements and standards of good workmanship, the contractor's record of cost control, of meeting contract schedules, the contractor's history of "reasonable and cooperative behavior and commitment to customer satisfaction," certain large contractor's diligence in reporting executive compensation (per FAR Subpart 4.14), the contractor's record of integrity and business ethics, and "the contractor's business-like concern for the interest of the customer."

## (A) TENACITY AND PERSEVERANCE

A prospective contractor's performance record must be satisfactory to demonstrate responsibility, FAR 9.104-1(c). This qualification standard is essentially related to the issue of whether a prospective contractor has the will to perform, and is treated as an independent basis of responsibility by FAR 9.104-3(b), which states:

> *Satisfactory performance record.* A prospective contractor that is or recently has been seriously deficient in contract performance shall be presumed to be nonresponsible, unless the contracting officer determines that the circumstances were properly beyond the contractor's control, or that the contractor has taken appropriate corrective action. Past failure to apply sufficient tenacity and perseverance to perform acceptably is strong evidence of nonresponsibility. Failure to meet the quality requirements of the contract is a significant factor to consider in determining satisfactory performance. The contracting officer shall consider the number of contracts involved and the extent of deficient performance in each contract when making this determination. If the pending contract requires a subcontracting plan pursuant to Subpart 19.7, The Small Business Subcontracting Program, the contracting officer shall also consider the prospective contractor's compliance with subcontracting plans under recent contracts.

This provision creates a strong presumption that a poor performance record indicates a lack of tenacity and perseverance. *See Information Res. Inc.*, Comp. Gen. Dec. B-271767, 96-2 CPD ¶ 38, where GAO upheld the agency's finding that the protester was nonresponsible based on poor past performance while contracts were awarded to other firms with poor records that recently had experienced serious performance deficiencies on similar contracts with the same agency, where the performance records of the other firms were substantially better than the protester's. See also *Mine Safety Appliances Co.*, Comp. Gen. Dec. B-266025, 96-1 CPD ¶ 86, where GAO upheld the contracting officer's determination of nonresponsibility based on a history of serious deficient contract performance; and, *Blocacor, LDA*, Comp. Gen. Dec. B-282122.3, 99-2 CPD ¶ 25, where GAO found that the contracting officer reasonably concluded that the protester would have been found nonresponsible based upon dumped materials allegedly traceable to the protester. This presumption that poor performance reflects a lack of tenacity may be applied to the poor performance history of a subcontractor that is proposed for a major portion of the work, *L & M Mercadeo Int'l, S.A.*, Comp. Gen. Dec. B-250637, 93-1 CPD ¶ 124.

The issue in judging tenacity and perseverance is whether a firm that possesses adequate capability will apply it in sufficient measure to ensure satisfactory completion of the contract, *United Power & Control Sys., Inc.*, Comp. Gen. Dec. B-184662,

78-2 CPD ¶ 436; *Eastern Tank, Inc.*, Comp. Gen. Dec. B-188559, 77-2 CPD ¶ 76; *Boiler Servs.*, Comp. Gen. Dec. B-187080, 77-1 CPD ¶ 372.

Tenacity and perseverance, by their nature, must be determined from past performance, *Ford Motor Co.*, Comp. Gen. Dec. B-207179, 83-1 CPD ¶ 72; *Particle Data, Inc.*, Comp. Gen. Dec. B-179144, 74-2 CPD ¶ 30. This may include performance on both private and government contracts, and such determination must be based on substantial evidence, 51 Comp. Gen. 288 (B-171729) (1971). The fact of poor performance or of a default on one or several prior contracts is not per se a sufficient reason for a determination that the contractor lacks the requisite tenacity and perseverance — inquiry must be made into the nature and causes of the poor performance, *Marine Eng'rs Beneficial Ass'n*, Comp. Gen. Dec. B-181265, 74-2 CPD ¶ 298; 39 Comp. Gen. 705 (B-142055) (1960). If the offeror was delinquent in performance of numerous contracts while possessing the necessary equipment and production personnel, a finding of lack of tenacity and perseverance is justified, 49 Comp. Gen. 139 (B-166969) (1969); *Pittman Mech. Contractors, Inc.*, Comp. Gen. Dec. B-242499, 91-1 CPD ¶ 439. In *United Power & Control Sys., Inc.*, Comp. Gen. Dec. B-184662, 78-2 CPD ¶ 436, GAO affirmed the Navy's nonresponsibility determination where the bidder delivered nonconforming items under current government contracts that were similar to those called for in the procurement at hand even though it had the ability to perform. Similarly, in Comp. Gen. Dec. B-170224, Oct. 8, 1970, *Unpub.*, performance deficiencies were properly attributed to lack of tenacity and perseverance where previous contract administrators had tried to work with the contractor to improve its performance but the contractor was unresponsive to their suggestions. See, however, 49 Comp. Gen. 600 (B-168917) (1970) and 39 Comp. Gen. 868 (B-142939) (1960) for cases in which GAO stated that it will not affirm a nonresponsibility determination based on a bidder's lack of tenacity and perseverance where the evidence fails to (1) relate to those nonresponsibility factors or (2) adequately establish a reasonable basis for the determination.

A contractor may be found nonresponsible for lack of tenacity and perseverance based on prior failures to adhere to contract specifications, *Kennedy Van & Storage Co.*, Comp. Gen. Dec. B-180973, 74-1 CPD ¶ 334, even where the alleged deficiencies are still the subject of dispute between the contractor and the agency, *Halo Optical Prods., Inc.*, Comp. Gen. Dec. B-178573, 74-1 CPD ¶ 263; *Howard Elec. Co.*, 58 Comp. Gen. 303 (B-193899), 79-1 CPD ¶ 137; *Ford Motor Co.*, Comp. Gen. Dec. B-207179, 83-1 CPD ¶ 72. A lack of tenacity or perseverance has been found based on late deliveries caused by factors within the contractor's control, such as poor business practices, *Transport Tire Co.*, Comp. Gen. Dec. B-179098, 74-1 CPD ¶ 27; poor management and technical judgment, *Campbell Indus.*, Comp. Gen. Dec. B-238871, 90-2 CPD ¶ 5; a failure to diligently or aggressively take action to correct production problems, *Marine Eng'rs Beneficial Ass'n*, Comp. Gen. Dec. B-181265, 74-2 CPD ¶ 298; a failure to perform safely on a prior contract, *Air Unlimited*, Comp. Gen. Dec. B-189428, 77-2 CPD ¶ 294; and inadequate surveillance and supervision of subcontractors, *Bill Ward Painting & Decorating*, Comp. Gen. Dec. B-184612,

76-1 CPD ¶ 57. Even though a contractor has substantially performed its prior contracts on time, meeting minimum contract requirements, it may still be found to lack
tenacity and perseverance based on the cumulative effect of a number of relatively
minor deficiencies that, individually, would not warrant termination for default or
finding unsatisfactory performance, 43 Comp. Gen. 257 (B-151121) (1963) (numerous minor deficiencies in performance of 11 of last 12 contracts); 49 Comp. Gen.
139 (B-166969) (1969) (almost 60% of recent contracts not completed on schedule);
*Leslie & Elliott Co.*, Comp. Gen. Dec. B-237190, 90-1 CPD ¶ 100 (numerous deficiencies in five previous contracts). But see *Pulse Cos.*, Comp. Gen. Dec. B-184463,
76-1 CPD ¶ 376, where GAO objected to a nonresponsibility determination after the
contractor had taken steps necessary to prevent recurrence of deficiencies.

The contracting officer has considerable discretion in determining what information will be used in appraising past performance. See *Standard Register Co.*,
Comp. Gen. B-289579, 2002 CPD ¶ 54, where GAO deferred to the agency's decision to use performance at different contract facilities as a measure of nonresponsibility. In *Flameco Div. of Barnes Group, Inc.*, Comp. Gen. Dec. B-243872, 91-2
CPD ¶ 123, a finding of nonresponsibility was properly reached after consultation
with the administrative contracting officer and consideration of inadequate performance under prior contracts for manufacture of the same part. See also *S.A.F.E.
Export Corp.*, Comp. Gen. Dec. B-208744, 83-1 CPD ¶ 437, where a determination of nonresponsibility was found proper because it was based on default terminations of four previous contracts plus performance difficulties on two others.
Even if there have been no default terminations, nonresponsibility can be properly
determined based on delinquencies in performance, *Gray Graphics Corp.*, Comp.
Gen. Dec. B-295421, 2005 CPD ¶ 37 (agency's nonresponsibility determination
was reasonable based on information showing that protester had made late deliveries under recent contracts); *NJCT Corp.*, 64 Comp. Gen. 883 (B-219434), 85-2
CPD ¶ 342 (delinquencies on numerous contracts); *C.W. Girard, C.M.*, 64 Comp.
Gen. 175 (B-216004), 84-2 CPD ¶ 704 (a number of delinquencies on one contract);
*Pittman Mech. Contractors, Inc.*, Comp. Gen. Dec. B-242243.2, 91-1 CPD ¶ 525
(recent contract performance on similar work inadequate); *Marathon Watch Co.,
Ltd.*, Comp. Gen. Dec. B-247043, 92-1 CPD ¶ 384 (serious performance problems
on four recent contracts). Conversely, the contracting officer may make an affirmative determination of responsibility despite unfavorable information concerning
past performance, *REDM Corp.*, Comp. Gen. Dec. B-211197, 83-1 CPD ¶ 428. Both
the FAR and GAO decisions in this area indicate that circumstances surrounding
nonperformance must be weighed to ascertain the seriousness of the delinquency in
performance. See *Girard*, stating at 178:

> [T]he mere fact of unsatisfactory performance under one prior contract does not
> necessarily establish a lack of responsibility. Nevertheless, the circumstances of
> the contractor's failure to perform properly and in a timely manner under the
> contract are for consideration, and may provide a reasonable basis for a nonre-
> sponsibility determination. 39 Comp. Gen. 705 (1960).

Thus, GAO will not normally review protests of favorable determinations of responsibility even if the successful offeror had a previous contract terminated for default, *Pacific Fabrication*, Comp. Gen. Dec. B-219837.2, 85-2 CPD ¶ 263, or failed to meet obligations on prior contracts, *Norfolk Shipbuilding & Drydock Corp.*, Comp. Gen. Dec. B-218618, 85-1 CPD ¶ 604.

Information necessary to determine responsibility is generally obtained after bid opening or receipt of offer, FAR 9.105-1(b). However, FAR 9.104-6(a) requires the contracting officer to review the FAPIIS for adverse information "before award." A determination of nonresponsibility based on unsatisfactory performance is generally based on serious deficiencies in current or recent contracts, FAR 9.104-3(b). In *United Office Machs.*, 56 Comp. Gen. 411 (B-187193), 77-1 CPD ¶ 195, GAO held that the contracting officer's determination of nonresponsibility for lack of tenacity and perseverance may not be based on events that occurred more than three years prior to the determination when there is an adequate record of more recent experience. See *Universal Am. Enters., Inc.*, Comp. Gen. Dec. B-185430, 76-2 CPD ¶ 373, and *Consolidated Airborne Sys., Inc.*, 55 Comp. Gen. 571 (B-183293), 75-2 CPD ¶ 395, indicating that contracts completed within one year of the responsibility determination are "recent" contracts. Compare *Maywood Cab Co.*, Comp. Gen. Dec. B-187550, 77-1 CPD ¶ 288, finding improper a determination of nonresponsibility based on termination for default of similar contracts nine months earlier, where no preaward survey had been conducted in the interim and the deficiencies were readily correctable.

## *(B) INTEGRITY*

FAR 9.104-1(d) states that a prospective contractor must have "a satisfactory record of integrity and business ethics," but it does not define the term "integrity." However, the term has been given its generally accepted connotation of probity, honesty, and uprightness, 48 Comp. Gen. 769 (B-165915) (1969). As in most cases involving nonresponsibility determinations based on lack of integrity, the finding in that case was based on criminal violations — the indictment of an officer and the conviction of an employee of the company for criminal offenses, income tax evasion, and fraud. See also *Traffic Moving Sys., Inc.*, Comp. Gen. Dec. B-248572, 92-2 CPD ¶ 152, affirming a nonresponsibility determination based upon a prior criminal conviction of the protester's president; and *Myers Investigative & Sec. Servs., Inc.*, Comp. Gen. Dec. B-288468, 2001 CPD ¶ 189, broadly deferring to agency's reasonable determination that awardee was responsible, despite conflicting submissions asserting that awardee may have attempted to mislead agency regarding necessary permits.

Assessments of a vendor's integrity will gain new complexity as more information becomes available to contracting officials. Under FAR 9.406-2 and the standard clause at FAR 52.203-13, a contractor must make a mandatory report, to the contracting officer and the cognizant inspector general, if the contractor has substantial evidence that the contractor has engaged in certain crimes (such as bribes or gratuities), has received significant overpayments, or has committed a civil fraud in violation of the False Claims Act. See American Bar Association, *Guide to the Mandatory Disclosure Rule* (Huffman & Levy, eds., 2010). The FAR contemplates that the bad acts that trigger a mandatory disclosure may be identified through a contractor's own internal compliance system, which is also generally required by FAR 52.203-13. Those mandatory self-disclosures may, as a matter of course, lead to suspension or debarment proceedings, and if the vendor settles such a proceeding through an administrative agreement with the government, that agreement must, as described above, appear in the FAPIIS system.

GAO has held that the causes for suspension, now enumerated in FAR 9.407-2, may be used to determine a bidder's integrity, *Drexel Indus., Inc.*, Comp. Gen. Dec. B-189344, 77-2 CPD ¶ 433. These causes also primarily deal with the violation of criminal statutes. Findings of lack of integrity have been upheld based on an allegedly false certification submitted under requirements of prior government contracts, *Mayfair Constr. Co.*, Comp. Gen. Dec. B-192023, 78-2 CPD ¶ 187; repeated violations of state environmental laws, *Standard Tank Cleaning Corp.*, Comp. Gen. Dec. B-245364, 92-1 CPD ¶ 3; an indictment that had been dismissed because of procedural deficiencies, *P.T. & L. Constr. Co.*, 55 Comp. Gen. 343 (B-183966), 75-2 CPD ¶ 208; a pending debarment for violations of the Service Contract Act, *Greenwoods's Transfer & Storage Co.*, Comp. Gen. Dec. B-186438, 76-2 CPD ¶ 167; and a plea of nolo contendere in an antitrust case, *Colonial Baking Co.*, Comp. Gen. Dec. B-185305, 76-2 CPD ¶ 59. See, however, *Pulse Cos.*, Comp. Gen. Dec. B-184463, 76-1 CPD ¶ 376, where GAO found insufficient proof to sustain a finding of lack of integrity where the offeror had corrected isolated violations of the Service Contract Act on prior contracts; *Universal Techs. Inc.*, Comp. Gen. Dec. B-248808.2, 92-2 CPD ¶ 212, where failure to identify criminal convictions did not influence an affirmative responsibility determination because it was not made in bad faith; and *Tutor-Saliba Corp.*, Comp. Gen. Dec. B-255756, 94-1 CPD ¶ 223, where allegations of involvement in Brazilian government scandals were found to be insubstantial.

See also *Garten-und Landschaftsbau GmbH Frank Mohr*, Comp. Gen. Dec. B-237276, 90-1 CPD ¶186, and *Frank Cain & Sons, Inc.*, Comp. Gen. Dec. B-236893, 90-1 CPD ¶ 44, where the agency reasonably determined that the protester was nonresponsible based upon a criminal investigation report that called into question the protester's integrity under recent procurements; *Becker & Schwindenhammer, GmbH*, Comp. Gen. Dec. B-225396, 87-1 CPD ¶ 235, where the contracting officer properly relied on an Army CID report of improper substitution of materials to support a nonresponsibility determination; *Americana de Comestibles S.A.*, Comp. Gen. Dec. B-210390, 84-1 CPD ¶ 289, where GAO upheld a nonresponsibility determination based on confidential information contained in a discontinued Army CID investigative file; and *Drexel Indus., Inc.*, Comp. Gen. Dec. B-189344, 77-2 CPD ¶ 433, where GAO overturned a nonresponsibility determination for lack of integrity because the evidence in the contract file indicated that the contractor's prior performance problems were apparently due to financial circumstances and not lack of integrity.

Determinations of nonresponsibility may be based on the lack of integrity of those having close relationships with the offeror. In *Bilfinger Berger AG Sede Secondaria Italiana*, Comp. Gen. Dec. B-402496, 2010 CPD ¶ 125, GAO upheld a nonresponsibility determination based on the fact that a related company had been debarred and the two companies had shared resources. See also *Speco Corp.*, Comp. Gen. Dec. B-211353, 83-1 CPD ¶ 458 (lack of integrity of a bidder's key employee properly constituted grounds for finding bidder nonresponsible when it appeared that significant influence might be exercised by the key employee in performance of the contract); *Americana de Comestibles S.A.*, Comp. Gen. Dec. B-210390, 84-1 CPD ¶ 289 (unsatisfactory record of integrity of company's president deemed sufficient in itself to justify the contracting officer's finding that the firm was not responsible). Compare *Najlaa Int'l Catering Servs.*, Comp. Gen. Dec. B-402434, 2010 CPD ¶ 107, holding that the contracting officer had properly found a company responsible even though a former director had bribed an agency to obtain a contract because the director had acted independently and the company had dismissed him when it learned of this conduct.

Similarly, the integrity of a predecessor firm may be considered in determining the responsibility of a bidder. In *R.H. Ritchey*, Comp. Gen. Dec. B-205602, 82-2 CPD ¶ 28, GAO based its nonresponsibility determination on the fact that the managing partner of the predecessor firm had been convicted of false pretenses in connection with a previous contract. A low bidder's relationship with another contractor that, it was conceded, lacked integrity, may also support a finding of nonresponsibility, *John Carlo, Inc.*, Comp. Gen. Dec. B-204928, 82-1 CPD ¶ 184. In that case, although the protester argued there was no substantial relationship between it and the disreputable contractor, GAO found that there were both past and present dealings between the two contractors in which the protester allowed the other to both bid and perform work in the protester's name.

Determinations of nonresponsibility based upon lack of integrity involve special considerations because of the rule requiring "due process" if such a determination "stigmatizes" the offeror, *Old Dominion Dairy Prods., Inc. v. Secretary of Def.*, 631 F.2d 953 (D.C. Cir. 1980); *Related Indus., Inc. v. United States*, 2 Cl. Ct. 517 (1983). See *Omneco, Inc.*, Comp. Gen. Dec. B-218343, 85-1 CPD ¶ 660, stating that this rule does not apply to an initial determination of nonresponsibility. The elements of such "due process" are discussed below.

### b.  *Special Standards*

Contracting officers are permitted to define the responsibility criteria more specifically by including special standards of responsibility, sometimes called "definitive performance criteria," in the solicitation. Such definitive responsibility criteria "concern the capability of the offeror, not a specific product, and they are objective standards established by the agency as a precondition to award," *Vador Ventures, Inc.*, Comp. Gen. Dec. B-296394, 2005 CPD ¶ 155. In discussing such definitive responsibility criteria, FAR 9.104-2(a) states:

> When it is necessary for a particular acquisition or class of acquisitions, the contracting officer shall develop, with the assistance of appropriate specialists, special standards of responsibility. Special standards may be particularly desirable when experience has demonstrated that unusual expertise or specialized facilities are needed for adequate contract performance. The special standards shall be set forth in the solicitation (and so identified) and shall apply to all offerors.

As was noted above, although GAO has changed its rules generally to bar protests involving affirmative responsibility determinations, it left the door open to protests "that allege that definitive responsibility criteria in the solicitation were not met," 4 C.F.R. § 21.5(c). Thus, despite GAO's general reluctance to review agencies' determinations that contractors *are* responsible, GAO will still allow protests that challenge an agency's failure to enforce such definitive responsibility criteria. See *Public Facility Consortium I, LLC*, Comp. Gen. B-295911, 2005 CPD ¶ 170 (discussing exception).

As GAO noted in *Charter Envtl., Inc.*, Comp. Gen. Dec. B-297219, 2005 CPD ¶ 213, definitive responsibility criteria, "which must be met as a precondition to award, limit the class of contractors to those meeting specified qualitative and quantitative qualifications necessary for adequate performance, e.g., unusual expertise or specialized facilities." Since imposition of special standards has the effect of limiting competition, they must be thoughtfully drawn. However, when they are based on essential government needs, they effectively narrow the field of eligible firms by warning unqualified firms not to expend needless effort in preparing offers.

Contracting officers may not waive special standards of responsibility, *Mary Kathleen Collins Trust*, Comp. Gen. Dec. B-261019.2, 96-1 CPD ¶ 164. Thus, an affirmative determination of responsibility will be overruled if the contracting officer does not have a reasonable basis to conclude that the low responsible bidder satisfies a special responsibility standard, *George Hyman Constr. Co.*, Comp. Gen. Dec. B-265798, 95-2 CPD ¶ 173 (there was a "reasonable possibility of prejudice" in the waiver of a "very restrictive" key personnel experience requirement).

The contracting officer is, however, granted some discretion in determining whether the offeror has the equivalent experience to meet such special standards of responsibility, and the contracting officer may look beyond the offeror itself in concluding that the specific responsibility criteria are met. See *Firma Hermann Leis*, Comp. Gen. Dec. B- 295956, 2005 CPD ¶ 102 ("In determining compliance with a definitive responsibility criterion, in the absence of RFP language to the contrary, an agency may consider the experience of the corporation's principal officers, the experience of the firm's employees, and the experience of a predecessor company acquired by the 'bidding entity.'"); *Haughton Elevator Div., Reliance Elec. Co.*, 55 Comp. Gen. 1051 (B-184865), 76-1 CPD ¶ 294 (employee's experience used to satisfy corporate experience requirement); *Evans, Inc.*, Comp. Gen. Dec. B-216260.2, 85-1 CPD ¶ 535 (regular dealer permitted to certify as manufacturer). See also *Aero Sys., Inc.*, Comp. Gen. Dec. B-215892, 84-2 CPD ¶ 374, where GAO determined that despite the offeror's failure to meet the precise definitive criteria, it could still be found responsible because it had clearly demonstrated that it had equivalent capability (possession of Canadian license instead of FAR 13.5 certificate), and *Stocker & Yale, Inc.*, Comp. Gen. Dec. B-238251, 90-1 CPD ¶ 475, where the agency's right to determine if an awardee's licenses were the equivalent of the IFB requirements was acknowledged. This discretion is not granted, however, if the definitive criteria are stated with specificity, *Power Sys.*, Comp. Gen. Dec. B-210032, 83-2 CPD ¶ 232. In that case, the solicitation required experience on the same product offered in the bid, and GAO ruled that experience on no other product would suffice.

The definitive criteria must be necessary to assure satisfaction of the government's needs. See *Software City*, Comp. Gen. Dec. B-217542, 85-1 CPD ¶ 475, concurring with an agency requirement that offerors present a letter from the source of the goods guaranteeing the supply of the product because the agency needed a continuous supply. Compare *Keeson, Inc.*, Comp. Gen. Dec. B-245625, 92-1 CPD ¶ 108, where GAO found the following requirement unduly restrictive:

> The [contractor] has an established asbestos abatement business for 5 years; has conducted within the last 3 years 5 asbestos abatement projects 3 of which are of comparable complexity and dollar value with this project; has not defaulted on any project within the last five years; has not been cited or has not been a defending party of any legal action for violation of asbestos regulations during the last five years; [and] . . . has an adequate number of qualified personnel available for this project.

GAO found the provisions on regulatory violations and prior defaults unreasonably broad and the provision requiring that the organization have five years' experience unduly restrictive in that it did not recognize experience of the personnel working for the organization. See also *Haughton Elevator Div., Reliance Elec. Co.*, 55 Comp. Gen. 1051 (B-184865), 76-1 CPD ¶ 294, where GAO found that an experience requirement was unduly restrictive because the awardee, while not meeting the requirement, was successfully performing the contract. In *International Computaprint Corp.*, 55 Comp. Gen. 1043 (B-185403), 76-1 CPD ¶ 289, and *Topley Realty Co.*, 65 Comp. Gen. 510 (B-221459), 86-1 CPD ¶ 398, GAO found definitive responsibility criteria unduly restrictive because the agency had ignored the requirement in making the award. To the extent that a special standard requires the offeror to complete a "testing or other quality assurance demonstration" before award, it must be justified in writing pursuant to 10 U.S.C. § 2319 or 41 U.S.C. § 253c. See

FAR Subpart 9.2. In *Altex Enters., Inc.*, 67 Comp. Gen. 184 (B-228200), 88-1 CPD ¶ 7, a blanket requirement that all individual sureties provide a first deed of trust on the unencumbered value of real estate was found not reasonably related to the needs of the agency because there were no unusual circumstances justifying its presence.

To qualify as definitive responsibility criteria, solicitation provisions must be specific, objective, and mandatory, *John C. Grimberg Co. v. United States*, 185 F.3d 1297 (Fed. Cir. 1999). See *Eggs & Bacon, Inc.*, Comp. Gen. Dec. B-402591.2, 2010 CPD ¶ 193 ("in order to be a definitive responsibility criterion, the solicitation provision must reasonably inform offerors that they must demonstrate compliance with the standard as a precondition to receiving the award"). In *Weldtest, Inc.*, Comp. Gen. Dec. B-216747.2, 84-2 CPD ¶ 612, a requirement that "offerors may be required to prove that they have experience in comparable work" was held to be neither "specific and objective" nor "mandatory." In *AT&T Corp.*, Comp. Gen. Dec. B-260447.4, 96-1 CPD ¶ 200, GAO found a lack of specificity when the solicitation stated that the "facilities and services under the contract shall be in accordance with all applicable tariffs, rates, charges, rules, regulations or requirements of the FCC." Similarly, a provision "reserving the right" to consider performance in the last two years was held not to meet these requirements, *Old Dominion Sec.*, Comp. Gen. Dec. B-216534, 85-1 CPD ¶ 78, and a requirement for "corporate experience" was held not to be sufficiently specific or objective, *Alliance Props. Inc.*, Comp. Gen. Dec. B-214769, 84-2 CPD ¶ 14. Compare *J. Baranello & Sons*, 58 Comp. Gen. 509 (B-192221), 79-1 CPD ¶ 322, where the standards were met by a solicitation requiring three years' experience and installation of comparable equipment on two prior projects.

Definitive responsibility criteria must also be distinguished from specification requirements. See *Power Testing Inc.*, Comp. Gen. Dec. B-197190, 80-2 CPD ¶ 72, where a statement in the solicitation requiring the contractor to use a foreperson with at least five years' experience was treated as a statement of how the work was to be performed rather than an aspect of responsibility that had to be satisfied at the time of award. See also *Thames Towboat Co.*, Comp. Gen. Dec. B-282982, 99-2 CPD ¶ 100 ("Specifications of minimum technical requirements do not establish standards relating to an offeror's ability to perform the contract," and thus do not reflect responsibility; "rather, they describe the item offerors are to furnish if they are awarded the contract."). Compare *J2A² JV, LLC*, Comp. Gen. Dec. B-401663.4, 2010 CPD ¶ 102 ("requirements that a prospective contractor have a specified number of years of experience in a particular area and a designated number of projects completed within a specified time period are definitive responsibility criteria; that is, they are specific and objective standards designed to measure a prospective contractor's ability to perform the contract"). Specification statements rather than definitive responsibility criteria were also found in *Markhurd Aerial Surveys, Inc.*, Comp. Gen. Dec. B-210108, 83-1 CPD ¶ 51, where a solicitation requirement stated that the contractor was required to use personnel with minimum crew experience; *Data Gen. Corp.*, Comp. Gen. Dec. B-252239, 93-1 CPD ¶ 457, where the solicitation stated that "all personnel performing under the resulting contract must have a minimum of one year experience" in similar work; and *Satellite Servs., Inc.*, Comp. Gen. Dec. B-219679, 85-2 CPD ¶ 224, where the solicitation stated that all personnel must be fully qualified to perform.

In order to properly find that an awardee meets the criteria, an agency must base its determination upon adequate and objective evidence, *T. Warehouse Corp.*, Comp. Gen. Dec. B-248951, 92-2 CPD ¶ 235. In that case, GAO reviewed the facts and determined that they did not support the agency's determination that the criteria had been met. Similarly, in *Prime Mortgage Corp.*, 69 Comp. Gen. 618 (B-238680.2), 90-2 CPD ¶ 48, GAO reversed a finding of responsibility when the contracting officer had no objective evidence that the offeror had $100,000 working capital as required by the solicitation. Compare *Coastal Elecs., Inc.*, Comp. Gen. Dec. B-250718, 93-1 CPD ¶ 144, where GAO reviewed certificates of training and determined that they met the criteria.

A contract requirement that a commercial product be furnished is not a definitive responsibility criterion, *PTR-Precision Techs., Inc.*, Comp. Gen. Dec. B-243439, 91-2 CPD ¶ 110; *Blue Tee Corp.*, Comp. Gen. Dec B-246623, 92-1 CPD ¶ 289. See also *Symtron Sys., Inc.*, Comp. Gen. Dec. B-242244, 91-1 CPD ¶ 282, holding that a commercial product requirement involves an affirmative determination of responsibility and generally is not reviewable. At one time, GAO ruled that requirements that commercial products be furnished were definitive responsibility criteria, *Data Test, Inc.*, 54 Comp. Gen. 499 (B-181199), 74-2 CPD ¶ 365, *recons. denied*, 54 Comp. Gen. 715, 75-1 CPD ¶ 138. In *Clausing Mach. Tools*, Comp. Gen. Dec. B-216113, 85-1 CPD ¶ 533, GAO stated that this rule had been changed. See, however, *Presto Lock, Inc.*, Comp. Gen. Dec. B-218766, 85-2 CPD ¶ 183, following the *Data Test* rule and not citing *Clausing*. See also *Evans, Inc.*, Comp. Gen. Dec. B-216260.2, 85-1 CPD ¶ 535, holding that a required manufacturer's certification that spare parts be available for 10 years was a definitive criterion.

One of the most common types of special standards deals with experience requirements. GAO has recognized the propriety of limiting contract awards to those bidders that have had a minimum amount of experience doing work comparable to that required by the contract, 35 Comp. Gen. 161 (B-124614) (1955) (service contract); *American Sterilizer Co.*, Comp. Gen. Dec. B-207518, 82-2 CPD ¶ 453 (supply contract for biohazardous use); *Karl Doll GmbH*, Comp. Gen. Dec. B-213556, 84-1 CPD ¶ 604 (boiler firing services); *Urban Masonry Corp.*, Comp. Gen. Dec. D-213196, 84-1 CPD ¶ 48 (erection of precast concrete); *R.R. Mongeau Eng'rs, Inc.*, Comp. Gen. Dec. B-213330, 84-1 CPD ¶ 333 (installation of cathodic protection equipment). GAO has accepted the use of such provisions where the interests of the government would thereby be served, provided that the special standards are included in the invitation, 37 Comp. Gen. 196 (B-133707) (1957); 45 Comp. Gen. 4 (B-156520) (1965).

Requirements for special facilities have also been expressed as definitive responsibility criteria, *Aero Corp.*, Comp. Gen. Dec. B-201581, 81-1 CPD ¶ 338. See *Auto*

*Discount Rent-N-Drive Sys., Inc.*, Comp. Gen. Dec. B-197236, 80-2 CPD ¶ 73, finding that a requirement that the awardee demonstrate that its dispatching facility was located in a certain geographical area was a definitive criterion. Business reference requirements have been treated as definitive responsibility criteria, *Ampex Corp.*, Comp. Gen. Dec. B-212356, 83-2 CPD ¶ 565. Accreditation requirements have also been treated as definitive responsibility criteria, *United States Crane Certification Bureau, Inc.*, Comp. Gen. Dec. B-197433, 80-1 CPD ¶ 247; *School for Educ. Enrichment*, Comp. Gen. Dec. B-199003, 80-2 CPD ¶ 286. See *E.J. Nachtwey*, Comp. Gen. Dec. B-209562, 83-1 CPD ¶ 104, where a music degree from a special music school was held to be a definitive responsibility criterion, and *Townsco Contracting Co.*, Comp. Gen. Dec. B-240289, 90-2 CPD ¶ 313, where a requirement for bidders that have been regularly engaged "in airfield paving for the three years immediately preceding" was found to be a definitive responsibility criteria.

Definitive responsibility criteria can be demonstrated by showing that affiliates or subcontractors meet the criteria, *Tutor-Saliba Corp.*, Comp. Gen. Dec. B-255756, 94-1 CPD ¶ 223. In that case, GAO stated:

> As a general rule, the experience of a technically qualified subcontractor or third party — such as an affiliate or consultant — may be used to satisfy definitive responsibility criteria relating to experience for a prospective prime contractor. *Gelco Servs., Inc.*, B-253376, Sept. 14, 1993, 93-2 CPD ¶ 163, *recon. denied*, B-253376.2, Oct. 27, 1993, 93-2 CPD ¶ 261; *Tama Kensetsu Co., Ltd, and Nippon Hodo*, B-233118, Feb. 8, 1989, 89-1 CPD ¶ 128. However, where a solicitation contains a criterion which by its express language prohibits satisfying a particular experience requirement through the experience of a prospective subcontractor, such a provision limits the prime contractor from relying on a subcontractor to comply with the experience criterion. See *Allen-Sherman-Hoff Co.*, B-231552, Aug. 4, 1988, 88-2 CPD ¶ 116.

GAO has also held that a joint venture meets a definitive criteria requirement if only one of the venturers satisfies the requirement, *Hellenic Technodomiki, S.A.*, Comp. Gen. Dec. B-265931, 96-1 CPD ¶ 91. Experience of employees working for other companies can also be used to demonstrate that the offeror meets an experience requirement, *Tucson Mobilephone, Inc.*, Comp. Gen. Dec. B-258408.3, 95-1 CPD ¶ 267.

For a number of years, GAO held that these special standards or "definitive criteria" of responsibility could be waived if the agency determined that the contractor was responsible even though it did not meet the standards, 39 Comp. Gen. 881 (B-143073) (1960). In one case, GAO held that the contracting officer could not declare an offeror nonresponsible for failure to meet the "literal requirements" of such provisions, 45 Comp. Gen. 4 (B-156520) (1965). This line of decisions was expressly reversed in *Haughton Elevator Div., Reliance Elec. Co.*, 55 Comp. Gen. 1051 (B-184865), 76-1 CPD ¶ 294, because of the potential prejudicial effect of waiving definitive responsibility criteria, and further clarified in *Lesko Assocs.*, Comp. Gen.

Dec. B-209703, 83-1 CPD ¶ 443, where GAO stated that a waiver is misleading and prejudicial both to offerors that met the requirement and to any prospective offerors that did not participate in the competition because of the stated requirement.

If the matter involves a small business and an issue of potential nonresponsibility is therefore shifted to the Small Business Administration, under FAR Subpart 9.6, in assessing the possible issuance of a Certificate of Competency, the SBA must consider, but is not bound by, the definitive responsibility criteria in the solicitation, *Baxter & Sons Elevator Co.*, 60 Comp. Gen. 97 (B-197595), 80-2 CPD ¶ 414; *E-Systems, Inc.*, 60 Comp. Gen. 283 (B-199550.5), 81-1 CPD ¶ 137. Thus, GAO will not review the proper application of a definitive responsibility criterion unless the SBA has not been informed of its application to the procurement under protest, *Eastern Marine, Inc.*, 63 Comp. Gen. 551 (B-212444.2), 84-2 CPD ¶ 232.

## 2.  Collateral Requirements

Offerors that do not meet specific requirements imposed by statute or regulation may be excluded from contracting even though they appear otherwise fully able and willing to perform the work specified in the solicitation. These requirements are termed "collateral" because they are not involved with the performance of the work called for by the contract. In some cases, they are closely related to the responsibility issue, while in others they are separate eligibility considerations. See, however, FAR 9.104-1(g) (to be determined responsible, prospective contractor must be "otherwise qualified and eligible to receive an award under applicable laws and regulations"), which apparently makes all such issues matters of responsibility.

### a.  Equal Employment Opportunity

The equal employment opportunity policies of the federal government are covered in Chapter 11. A major element of these policies is the development of affirmative action plans and programs. FAR 22.802(b) prohibits award of a contract to a person "who has been found ineligible" by the Office of Federal Contract Compliance Programs (OFCCP) of the Department of Labor. In addition, 41 C.F.R. § 60-2.2(b) requires a nonresponsibility determination if a contracting officer finds that a contractor does not have an affirmative action program that complies with the government's standards. See 51 Comp. Gen. 551 (B-174816) (1972), where GAO, citing 41 C.F.R. § 60-2.2, stated that the contracting officer was correct in finding the prospective contractor nonresponsible because the contractor was not in compliance with the equal employment opportunity requirements at one of its establishments.

For awards of contracts of $10 million or more, excluding construction, the contracting officer must request a determination from the OFCCP that the contract is "awardable," FAR 22.805(a).

## b.  Small Business Subcontracting

In 1978, Pub. L. No. 95-507 amended 15 U.S.C. § 637 to require that solicitations for certain contracts that offer subcontracting possibilities contain a clause requiring any bidder who is selected for award to submit a detailed small business subcontracting plan to the procuring agency. 15 U.S.C. § 637(d)(5)(B) indicates that failure to comply with these requirements will result in a nonresponsibility determination:

> If, within the time limit prescribed in regulations of the Federal agency concerned, the bidder selected to be awarded the contract fails to submit the subcontracting plan required by this paragraph, such bidder shall become ineligible to be awarded the contract. Prior compliance of the bidder with other subcontracting plans shall be considered by the Federal agency in determining the responsibility of such bidder for the award of the contract. The subcontracting plan of the bidder awarded the contract shall be included in and made a material part of the contract.

See *Devcon Sys. Corp.*, Comp. Gen. Dec. B-197935, 80-2 CPD ¶ 46, affirming the contracting officer's holding that submission of a small business subcontracting plan is a matter of responsibility rather than responsiveness, and permitting the firm, until the time of award, to submit an acceptable plan. Accord *A.B. Dick Co.*, Comp. Gen. Dec. B-233142, 89-1 CPD ¶ 106. Thus, because the negotiation and ultimate approval of a subcontracting plan involved a question of the successful offeror's responsibility, those negotiations do not involve evaluation and discussion of the successful offeror's proposal, and do not trigger the obligation to open discussions with all offerors, *General Dynamics — Ordnance & Tactical Sys.*, Comp. Gen. Dec. B-295987, B-295987.2, 2005 CPD ¶ 114; *AmClyde Engineered Prods. Co.*, Comp. Gen. Dec. B-282,271, 99-2 CPD ¶ 5; *Kahn Instruments, Inc.*, Comp. Gen. Dec. B-277973, 98-1 CPD ¶ 11. See also *Columbia Research Corp.*, 61 Comp. Gen. 194 (B-202762), 82-1 CPD ¶ 8, finding a 16-page plan adequate although the offeror proposed no small business subcontracts for the procurement under consideration.

## c.  Government Employees

An agency's decision to contract with a firm directly or indirectly controlled by a government employee raises unique, and potentially serious, issues of responsibility because of potential conflicts of interest. See generally Luci, Jr., *Contracting with Government Employees: An Overly Restrictive Rule, A Comparison, and a Compromise,* 27 Pub. Cont. L.J. 37 (1997). FAR 3.601(a) provides explicit policy guidance on contracting with employees of the federal government:

> Except as specified in 3.602, a contracting officer shall not knowingly award a contract to a Government employee or to a business concern or other organization owned or substantially owned or controlled by one or more Government employees. This policy is intended to avoid any conflict of interest that might arise between the employees' interests and their Government duties, and to avoid

the appearance of favoritism or preferential treatment by the Government toward its employees.

GAO's decision in *Valiant Sec. Agency*, Comp. Gen. Dec. B-205087, 81-2 CPD ¶ 367, *recons. denied*, 81-2 CPD ¶ 501, explained:

> Contracts between the Government and its employees are not expressly prohibited by statute except where the employee acts for both the Government and the contractor in a particular transaction or where the service to be rendered is such as could be required of the contractor in his capacity as a Government employee. 18 U.S.C. § 208 (1976); *Hugh Maher*, B-187841, March 31, 1977, 77-1 CPD ¶ 204. However, it has long been recognized that such contracts are undesirable because among other reasons they invite criticism as to alleged favoritism and possible fraud and that they should be authorized only in exceptional cases where the Government cannot reasonably be otherwise supplied. 27 Comp. Gen. 735 (1948); *Capital Aero, Inc.*, B-183833, September 30, 1975, 75-2 CPD ¶ 201; *Burgos & Associates, Inc.*, 59 Comp. Gen. 273 (1980), 80-1 CPD ¶55. The fact that a service would be more expensive if not obtained from an employee of the Government does not by itself provide support for a determination that the service cannot reasonably be obtained from other sources. 55 Comp. Gen. 681 [B-184716] (1976).

The sole exception to the prohibition in FAR 3.601 is in FAR 3.602, which requires a determination by a high-level official that there is a "most compelling reason to [enter into a contract], such as when the Government's needs cannot reasonably be otherwise met." The contracting officer has discretion in determining whether this exemption applies. Compare the *Valiant* case with *International Alliance of Sports Officials*, Comp. Gen. Dec. B-210172, 83-2 CPD ¶ 328, sustaining a contracting officer's decision to award a contract to an employee-owned company at approximately $223,000 in contrast to the next low offer of $275,000.

Substantial ownership or control is determined by the facts of each individual case. Mere employment by a government contractor is not prohibited by this restriction. See *National Serv. Corp.*, Comp. Gen. Dec. B-205629, 82-2 CPD ¶ 76 (no substantial ownership or control when government employee gave up partnership and became part-time bookkeeper); *HH & K Builders, Inc.*, Comp. Gen. Dec. B-238095, 90-1 CPD ¶ 219 (sole owner's husband was government employee, but sufficient separation of ownership). Compare *Electronics W., Inc.*, Comp. Gen. Dec. B-209720, 83-2 CPD ¶ 127 (change in title from president to treasurer did not prevent disqualification). An agency does not have to establish with certainty that an employee has a substantially controlling interest but rather need only have "a reason to believe" that the government employee has such control, *Gurley's, Inc.*, Comp. Gen. Dec. B-253852, 93-2 CPD ¶ 123. See *Elogene Thurman*, Comp. Gen. Dec. B-206325, 82-1 CPD ¶ 487 (award to wife of government employee improper when husband in fact ran the business); *Applied Res. Corp.*, Comp. Gen. Dec. B-249258, 92-2 CPD ¶ 272 (disqualification proper where spouse of firm's president was the contracting officer's supervisor and relationship was not disclosed on financial disclosure form); *American Truss & Mfg. Corp.*, Comp. Gen. Dec. B-205962, 82-1 CPD ¶ 477 (award improper where government employee owned 50% of stock and wife owned balance); *Marc Indus.*, Comp. Gen. Dec. B-246528, 92-1 CPD ¶ 273 (substantial control found where government employee represented the firm in prework conferences under prior contracts with the agency, served as the contact for any complaints about contract performance, and, based on his involvement with the firm, was disciplined for violating his agency's conflict of interest regulations); and *KSR, Inc.*, Comp. Gen. Dec. B-250160, 93-1 CPD ¶ 37 (substantial control found where government employee was president and was one of five owners).

Some agencies have restrictions on dealing with close relatives of employees. See *Joann Flora*, Comp. Gen. Dec. B-212776, 83-2 CPD ¶ 520 (regulation prohibiting contract with "immediate member of the household" of agency employee barred contract with unmarried party living as spouse); and *Heidi Holley*, Comp. Gen. Dec. B-211746, 83-2 CPD ¶ 241 (regulations stating that contracts should generally not be awarded to members of an agency employee's family and requiring close scrutiny barred award to spouse of agency employee required to supervise contract). However, see *J. Allen Grafton*, Comp. Gen. Dec. B-212986, 84-1 CPD ¶ 263, in which GAO found that an agency unreasonably rejected a quotation from the son of an agency employee, when there was no showing that the employee had responsibility for the resulting contract and no indication that the father had disclosed any confidential agency information or otherwise influenced the procurement.

If the contracting officer inadvertently makes an award to a company owned or controlled by a government employee, GAO will not disturb the award absent an indication of favoritism or other impropriety, *Sterling Med. Assocs.*, Comp. Gen. Dec. B-209493, 83-1 CPD ¶ 215; *Biosystems Analysis, Inc.*, Comp. Gen. Dec. B-198846, 80-2 CPD ¶ 149. In both cases, the employee worked for an agency other than the one awarding the contract.

### d.  Guard and Security Service

The Anti-Pinkerton Act of 1893, a very dated statutory bar against contracting for armed guards, is set forth at 5 U.S.C. § 3108, and states:

> An individual employed by the Pinkerton Detective Agency, or similar organization, may not be employed by the Government of the United States or the government of the District of Columbia.

This Act has been narrowly construed by FAR 37.109, to bar only the hiring of "quasi-military armed forces," by stating:

Contracts with "Pinkerton Detective Agencies or similar organizations" are prohibited by 5 U.S.C. § 3108. This prohibition applies only to contracts with organizations that offer quasi-military armed forces for hire, or with their employees, regardless of the contract's character. An organization providing guard or protective services does not thereby become a "quasi-military armed force," even though the guards are armed or the organization provides general investigative or detective services.

This guidance limiting the application of the Act to "quasi-military" forces is derived from *United States ex rel. Weinberger v. Equifax, Inc.*, 557 F.2d 456 (5th Cir. 1977), *cert. denied*, 434 U.S. 1035 (1978). It was adopted by GAO in 57 Comp. Gen. 524 (B-139965) (1978). In *Old Dominion Security*, Comp. Gen. Dec. B-216534, 85-1 CPD ¶ 78, it was held that the low bidder was not precluded by the Anti-Pinkerton Act from receiving a contract for security guard services since all personnel assigned to the project were licensed and employed solely as uniformed security guards. Whether a prospective contractor must be precluded from government contracting due to the Anti-Pinkerton Act is a matter for contracting officer determination subject to GAO review, *Inter-Con Sec. Sys., Inc.*, Comp. Gen. Dec. B-192188, 79-1 CPD ¶ 86. Notably, GAO in 1978 itself questioned the continuing relevance of the Anti-Pinkerton Act, 57 Comp. Gen. 524 (B-139965), and others have noted that the Act may not be viable, given the vast increase in the use of private armed guards by the government, including the use of private guards to defend highly sensitive missions abroad. See Davidson, *Ruck Up: An Introduction to the Legal Issues Associated with Civilian Contractors on the Battlefield,* 29 Pub. Cont. L.J. 233, 253-54 (2000).

## II. ORGANIZATIONAL CONFLICTS OF INTEREST

It is the policy of the government to avoid awarding contracts where the contractor would have either an actual or potential bias in making judgments required by contract performance or have an unfair competitive advantage in competing for future contracts, FAR 9.505. In implementing this policy, the contracting officer must decide whether to disqualify an offeror or to include a contract provision imposing restraints designed to "avoid, neutralize, or mitigate" the bias or competitive advantage, FAR 9.504(a)(2). The particular action the contracting officer should take depends on the nature of the potential organizational conflict of interest (OCI), and the point in the procurement process at which it is identified. Agency heads or their designees are permitted to waive the rules restricting award of contracts to contractors with OCIs, FAR 9.503, and GAO will "not make an independent determination of the matter" in such cases, *MCR Fed., LLC*, Comp. Gen. Dec. B-401954.2, 2010 CPD ¶ 196; *CIGNA Gov't Servs., LLC*, Comp. Gen. Dec. B-401068.4, 2010 CPD ¶ 230.

### A. Types of OCIs

FAR Subpart 9.5 contains a description of four scenarios where OCIs exist plus nine specific examples of applying the rules in this area. However, it leaves the determination of whether such a conflict exists and the preparation of appropriate contract language to each contracting officer. More detailed guidance must be obtained from GAO decisions in this area. In that regard, GAO concluded in *Aetna Gov. Health Plans, Inc.*, Comp. Gen. Dec. B-254397.15, 95-2 CPD ¶ 129, that there are three basic types of OCI — unequal access to information, setting biased ground rules, and impaired objectivity. See also Gordon, *Organizational Conflicts of Interest: A Growing Integrity Challenge*, 35 Pub. Cont. L.J. 25 (Fall 2005); Guttman, *Governance by Contract: Constitutional Visions: Time for Reflection and Choice*, 33 Pub. Cont. L.J. 321 (2004).

The rules governing OCIs continue to evolve, in part because of an acute policy concern with contractors' involvement in the workings of government. In December 2010, in accordance with § 207 of the Weapons System Acquisition Reform Act of 2009, Pub. L. No. 111-23, the DFARS was amended to address potential conflicts in those producing major weapons system, 75 Fed. Reg. 81908, Dec. 29, 2010. Those changes to the DFARS urged contracting officers, rather than disqualifying offerors, to mitigate OCIs, where possible, through mitigation plans negotiated with contractors, and the final rule included a model clause, DFARS 252.209-7009, to be used where the Defense Department and the contractor can reach agreement on a mitigation plan.

A total rewrite of the FAR OCI rules is also in progress with new rules anticipated in 2011 or 2012. It is likely that these rules will adopt GAO logic on the types of OCIs.

## 1.  Unequal Access To Information

FAR 9.505 contains the following general guidance on this type of OCI:

(b) *Preventing unfair competitive advantage.* In addition to the other situations described in this subpart, an unfair competitive advantage exists where a contractor competing for award for any Federal contract possesses —

> (1) Proprietary information that was obtained from a Government official without proper authorization; or

> (2) Source selection information (as defined in [FAR] 2.101) that is relevant to the contract but is not available to all competitors, and such information would assist that contractor in obtaining the contract.

FAR 9.505-4 contains more explicit guidance as follows:

(a) When a contractor requires proprietary information from others to perform a Government contract and can use the leverage of the contract to obtain it, the contractor may gain an unfair competitive advantage unless restrictions are imposed. These restrictions protect the information and encourage companies to provide it when necessary for contract performance. They are not intended to protect information (1) furnished voluntarily without limitations on its use or (2) available to the Government or contractor from other sources without restriction.

(b) A contractor that gains access to proprietary information of other companies in performing advisory and assistance services for the Government must agree with the other companies to protect their information from unauthorized use or disclosure for as long as it remains proprietary and refrain from using the information for any purpose other than that for which it was furnished. The contracting officer shall obtain copies of these agreements and ensure that they are properly executed.

(c) Contractors also obtain proprietary and source selection information by acquiring the services of marketing consultants which, if used in connection with an acquisition, may give the contractor an unfair competitive advantage. Contractors should make inquiries of marketing consultants to ensure that the marketing consultant has provided no unfair competitive advantage.

This guidance describes the types of information covered by this rule as "proprietary information" and "source selection information" In *Aetna*, GAO described the information covered as "nonpublic information." To fall in this category, the information must be *specific information* that gives a potential competitor a competitive advantage. However, it need not be proprietary information or source selection information. For example, in *Johnson Controls World Servs., Inc.*, Comp. Gen. Dec. B-286714.2, 2001 CPD ¶ 20, GAO found this type of OCI when the awardee's proposed subcontractor for a maintenance contract was, under another contract, maintaining the agency's Executive Management Information System (EMIS) database, which provided detailed information on the agency's maintenance activities, reasoning:

FAR 9.505(b) cites two kinds of information that can provide an offeror an unfair competitive advantage: proprietary information obtained from the government without proper authorization, and source selection information. However, the regulation recognizes that "conflicts may arise in situations not expressly covered in this section 9.505. . . . Each individual contracting situation should be examined on the basis of its particular facts and the nature of the proposed contract." FAR 9.505. The information principally in question here, EMIS data, does not fall within either category specified in the regulation, since it was presumably obtained with proper authorization and not in the course of the source selection process. However, if the information is as [the protester] alleges, it clearly could have provided the [awardee/subcontractor] team with an advantage in the competition. That advantage would be an unfair competitive advantage to the extent that the [awardee/subcontractor] team, and no other offeror, had relevant nonpublic information — beyond that which would be available to a typical incumbent installation logistics support contractor — that would assist it in obtaining the contract.

Potential OCIs of this type were found in *B.L. Harbert-Brasfield & Gorrie, JV*, Comp. Gen. Dec. B-402229, 2010 CPD ¶ 69, and *McCarthy/Hunt, JV*, Comp. Gen. Dec. B-402229.2, 2010 CPD ¶ 68 (parent company of consultant that had participated in planning procurement was negotiating to purchase subcontractor of selected contractor); *VRC, Inc.*, Comp. Gen. Dec. B-310100, 2007 CPD ¶ 202 (employee of a company that was a major stockholder in a proposed subcontractor worked directly for the contracting officer, had access to all source selection information, and was expected to assist the evaluators); *United States ex rel. Harrison v. Westinghouse Savannah River Co.*, 352 F.3d 908 (4th Cir. 2003) (employee of potential subcontractor had prepared internal documents justifying subcontracting training work); and *Ktech Corp.*, Comp. Gen. Dec. B-285330, 2002 CPD ¶ 77 (subcontractor had access to protester's technical information through its work in assisting the agency in monitoring the protester's performance on prior contract). However, most protests have been denied because the protester could not prove that the winning offeror had specific information that gave it a competitive advantage. See *ITT Corp. — Elec. Sys.*, Comp. Gen. Dec. B-202808, 2010 CPD ¶ 178 (agency had contractual right to provide information); *Alabama Aircraft Indus., Inc. v. United States*, 83 Fed. Cl. 666 (2008), *aff'd*, 586 F.3d 1372 (Fed. Cir. 2009) (work on prior engineering services contract provided no specific information giving competitive advantage on aircraft maintenance contract); *Masai Techs. Corp. v. United States*, 79 Fed. Cl. 433 (2007) (contracting officer found that subcontractors to winning offeror did not have access to detailed information on program for which contract was awarded); *ARINC Eng'g Servs., LLC v. United States*, 77 Fed. Cl. 196 (2007) (work on prior contract was different and unrelated to work on new contract); *Chenega Fed. Sys., LLC*, Comp. Gen. Dec. B-299310.2, 2007 CPD ¶ 196 (winning offeror hired government technical representative on prior contract but he had performed only "low-level administrative functions"); *Mechanical Equip. Co.*, Comp. Gen. Dec. B-292789.2, 2004 CPD ¶ 192 (prospective subcontractor working in the agency did not have access to critical information); *Perini/Jones, Joint Venture*, Comp. Gen. Dec. B-285906, 2002 CPD ¶ 68 (no proof that prospective project manager gained access to proprietary information when working for the agency at the time proposals were submitted); and *TRW, Inc.*, Comp. Gen. Dec. B-282162, 99-2 CPD ¶ 12 (no proof that subcontractor had gained access to proprietary information when serving as support service contractor). In *ARINC* the court stated at 203-04 that to prove this type of OCI, a protester would have to show that —

> (i) the awardee was so embedded in the agency as to provide it with insight into the agency's operations beyond that which would be expected of a typical government contractor; (ii) the awardee had obtained materials related to the specifications or statement of work for the instant procurement; or (iii) some other "preferred treatment or . . . agency action" has occurred.

It is clear that to prove this type of OCI, a protester must show evidence beyond the fact that the winning offeror has gained information because it has been the incumbent contractor. See *Systems Plus, Inc. v. United States*, 69 Fed. Cl. 757 (2006), where the court found no OCI when the winning offeror had worked with the agency in designing its information technology infrastructure and planning the process. Although the protester claimed that this gave the contractor a "superior understanding of [the agency's] network architecture, objectives, and requirements," the court found that the contractor did not have "the kind of specific, sensitive information that would create an OCI." The court noted that merely being an incumbent contractor did not generally create an OCI, stating at 771:

> Incumbent status, without more, typically does not constitute "unequal access to information" for purposes of showing an OCI. See *Gulf Group, Inc. v. United States*, 56 Fed. Cl. 391, 398 & n.13 (2003) ("While an agency may not unduly tip the scales in favor of an incumbent, it certainly may weigh the competitive advantages offered by that incumbent via its relevant experience and performance with the contract subject matter."); *Winstar Commc'ns, Inc. v. United States*, 41 Fed. Cl. 748, 763 (1998) (citing *Matter of Versar, Inc.*, B-254464.3, 94-1 CPD ¶ 230, 1994 WL 120013, at *7 (GAO Feb. 16, 1994)) ("An offeror's competitive advantage gained through incumbency is generally not an unfair advantage that must be eliminated.").

See also *PAI Corp. v. United States*, 614 F.3d 1347 (Fed. Cir. 2010); *Integrated Concepts & Research Corp.*, Comp. Gen. Dec. B-309803, 2008 CPD ¶ 117, and *Council for Adult & Experiential Learning*, Comp. Gen. Dec. B-299798.2, 2007 CPD ¶ 151.

This type of OCI does not exist with regard to information that has been furnished to an agency without proprietary legends. See *Snell Enters., Inc.*, Comp. Gen. Dec. B-290113, 2002 CPD ¶ 115, finding no OCI because the information had been furnished to the agency voluntarily with no proprietary markings. Neither does it exist when a company employs a person that worked for a competitor and had access to proprietary information, *Elwood Nat'l Forge Co.*, Comp. Gen. Dec. B-402089.3, 2010 CPD ¶ 250.

This type of OCI can be overcome by disclosing the information in the RFP. See *KPMG Peat Marwick*, 73 Comp. Gen. 15 ( B-251902.3), 93-2 CPD ¶ 272 (information obtained by Freedom of Information Act request during competition). Of course, this would be improper if the information was proprietary.

## 2. Setting Biased Ground Rules

*Aetna* describes this as a situation —

> in which a firm, as part of its performance of a government contract, has in some sense set the ground rules for another government contract by, for example, writing the statement of work or the specifications. In these "biased ground rules" cases, the primary concern is that the firm could skew the competition, whether intentionally or not, in favor of itself. FAR 9.505-1, 9.505-2. These situations

may also involve a concern that the firm, by virtue of its special knowledge of the agency's future requirements, would have an unfair advantage in the competition for those requirements.

FAR 9.505 describes two types of situations in which an OCI of this type is most likely to arise. The first situation is procurement of systems engineering and technical direction. FAR 9.505-1 contains the following bar when a contractor performs such work:

> (a) A contractor that provides systems engineering and technical direction for a system but does not have overall contractual responsibility for its development, its integration, assembly, and checkout, or its production shall not (1) be awarded a contract to supply the system or any of its major components or (2) be a subcontractor or consultant to a supplier of the system or any of its major components.

> (b) Systems engineering includes a combination of substantially all of the following activities: determining specifications, identifying and resolving interface problems, developing test requirements, evaluating test data, and supervising design. Technical direction includes a combination of substantially all of the following activities: developing work statements, determining parameters, directing other contractors' operations, and resolving technical controversies.

DFARS 209.571-1 contains a much broader definition of "systems engineering and technical assistance," including "performing technology assessments," "developing acquisition strategies," "conducting risk assessments," and "developing cost estimates." Further, this rule excludes the FAR requirement that "substantially all" of the activities be performed by the contractor — allowing a contracting officer to find that a contractor has an OCI if it performs any one of the listed tasks. DFARS 209.571-7 also carries out the statutory requirement that when a company has this type of OCI, no *affiliate* can participate in the development or production of the weapon system for which the contractor has provided systems engineering and technical assistance.

It has been held that "sustaining engineering" by a contractor on an aircraft program did not bar that contractor from performance of overhaul and maintenance contracts on the same aircraft because sustaining engineering was not the same as technical direction or systems engineering, *Hayes Int'l Corp. v. McLucas*, 509 F.2d 247 (5th Cir.), *cert. denied*, 423 U.S. 864 (1975). See also *Masai Techs. Corp. v. United States*, 79 Fed. Cl. 433 (2007), finding that work on prior contracts did not constitute systems engineering, and *Central Texas Coll.*, 71 Comp. Gen. 164 (B-245233.4) (1992), finding that mere employment of a former government employee, who was familiar with the type of work required but not privy to the contents of proposals or any other "inside" information, did not confer any unfair competitive advantage. Compare *MAR, Inc.*, Comp. Gen. Dec. B-215798, 85-1 CPD ¶ 121, where a contract for "scientific, engineering, analytical, technical and prototype-fabrication services" was held to involve a potential conflict of interest.

The second situation where there is an OCI is the preparation of complete specifications for nondevelopmental items. See FAR 9.505-2 stating:

(a)(1) If a contractor prepares and furnishes complete specifications covering
nondevelopmental items, to be used in a competitive acquisition, that contractor
shall not be allowed to furnish these items, either as a prime contractor or as a
subcontractor, for a reasonable period of time including, at least, the duration of
the initial production contract. This rule shall not apply to —

(i) Contractors that furnish at Government request specifications
or data regarding a product they provide, even though the specifications or data may have been paid for separately or in the price
of the product; or

(ii) Situations in which contractors, acting as industry representatives, help Government agencies prepare, refine, or coordinate
specifications, regardless of source, provided this assistance is
supervised and controlled by Government representatives.

(2) If a single contractor drafts complete specifications for nondevelopmental equipment, it should be eliminated for a reasonable time from competition for production based on the specifications. This should be done in
order to avoid a situation in which the contractor could draft specifications
favoring its own products or capabilities. In this way the Government can be
assured of getting unbiased advice as to the content of the specifications and
can avoid allegations of favoritism in the award of production contracts.

\* \* \*

(b)(1) If a contractor prepares, or assists in preparing, a work statement to be used
in competitively acquiring a system or services-or provides material leading directly, predictably, and without delay to such a work statement that contractor may
not supply the system, major components of the system, or the services unless—

(i) It is the sole source;

(ii) It has participated in the development and design work; or

(iii) More than one contractor has been involved in preparing the
work statement.

This situation may occur where the specifications contain substantial detail,
*Nelson Erection Co.*, Comp. Gen. Dec. B-217556, 85-1 CPD ¶ 482 (specifications
for repair of hangar door outlining specific repairs needed), as well as where the
specifications are very general, *LW Planning Group*, Comp. Gen. Dec. B-215539,
84-2 CPD ¶ 531 (broad work statement for contract to revise a facility's master plan).
This type of OCI has been found in a number of cases where the contractor played
a major but not sole role in drafting a work statement. See *B.L. Harbert-Brasfield*

& *Gorrie, JV*, Comp. Gen. Dec. B-402229, 2010 CPD ¶ 69, and *McCarthy/Hunt, JV*, Comp. Gen. Dec. B-402229.2, 2010 CPD ¶ 68 (parent company of consultant that had participate in preparation of design concept for hospital was negotiating to purchase subcontractor of selected contractor); *L-3 Servs., Inc.*, Comp. Gen. Dec. B-400134.11, 2009 CPD ¶ 171 (OCI because contractor assisted in planning the procurement and writing the business case); *Lucent Techs. World Servs., Inc.*, Comp. Gen. Dec. B-295462, 2005 CPD ¶ 55, 47 GC ¶ 190 (OCI even though agency technical personnel participated in the preparation of the specifications by commenting on them as the contractor submitted drafts); *Basile, Baumann, Prost & Assocs., Inc.*, Comp. Gen. Dec. B-274870, 97-1 CPD ¶ 15 (OCI where offeror prepared statement of work and agency cost estimate); *Ressler Assocs., Inc.*, Comp. Gen. Dec. B-244110, 91-2 CPD ¶ 230 (OCI where protester had earlier prepared portions of the statement of work without contracting officer's knowledge); and *Network Solutions, Inc. v. Department of the Air Force*, GSBCA 11498-P, 92-3 BCA ¶ 25,083 (OCI where offeror, under an RFP for engineering of LANs, had previously installed the network on which a sample task set out in the RFP was based). Because most services, including construction, will be construed to involve non-development work, contractors drafting specifications for such work will generally be excluded under this rule. See *Danish Arctic Contractors*, Comp. Gen. Dec. B-212957, 84-1 CPD ¶ 131; and *Ressler Assocs.*, Comp. Gen. Dec. B-244110, 91-2 CPD ¶ 230. Compare *Detica*, Comp. Gen. Dec. B-400523, 2008 CPD ¶ 217, where no OCI was found because an agency official hired by the winning offeror had not participated in preparing the final work statement; *Operational Res. Consultants, Inc.*, Comp. Gen. Dec. B-299131.1, 2007 CPD ¶ 38, where no OCI was found because the winning offeror had no role in drafting specifications; and *Analytic Scis. Corp.*, Comp. Gen. Dec. B-218074, 85-1 CPD ¶ 464, where GAO questioned the exclusion of a company that had prepared a broad work statement because it was not clear whether the work statement involved existing software or software to be newly developed.

This type of OCI can exist even if the company assisting in the preparation of the specification believes that there will be no competition, *Energy Sys. Group*, Comp. Gen. Dec. B-402324, 2010 CPD ¶ 73, where the company participated as a subcontractor in preparing a feasibility study for an energy-saving contract believing that the utility contractor would be awarded the contract on a sole source basis. When the agency later decided to use a competitive procurement, GAO ruled that the subcontractor had an OCI and could not participate in the competition.

No OCI will be found in this situation unless the offeror has a significant interest in the outcome of the competition. See *American Mgmt. Sys., Inc.*, Comp. Gen. Dec. B-285645, 2000 CPD ¶ 163, holding that there was no OCI where a firm performing work for the agency, KPMG Peat Marwick, only had a "marketing alliance" with several of the competitors but had no relationship with regard to the procurement in question. The decision contains the following summary:

We find the potential benefit to KPMG here is speculative and too remote from the present procurement to establish a significant organizational conflict of interest that the contracting agency must avoid, neutralize or mitigate pursuant to FAR Subpart 9.5. Compare *Professional Gunsmithing Inc.*, B-279048.2, Aug. 24, 1998, 98-2 CPD ¶ 49 at 3-4 (entitlement of consultant employed by the agency to help evaluate proposals to trademark royalties from awardee on products other than those to be provided under the contract is an interest that is speculative and too remote to create a significant conflict of interest) and *International Management and Communications Corp.*, B-272456, Oct. 23, 1996, 96-2 CPD ¶ 156 at 4 (awardee's interest in receiving repayment of debt owed to its affiliate organization by a potential recipient of advice and assistance under the awarded support services contract is not a significant conflict of interest because the relationship between the awardee/contract and the repayment of the debt is indirect) with *Aetna Gov't Health Plans, Inc.; Foundation Health Fed'l Servs., Inc.*, [Comp. Gen. Dec. B-254397.15, 95-2 CPD ¶ 129] at 13-17 (significant organizational conflict of interest exists where a corporate affiliate of a major subcontractor under one proposal evaluates proposals for the procuring agency).

The major exception to this type of OCI is for contractors that have designed a product under contract with the government. FAR 9.505-2 provides:

(a)(3) In development work, it is normal to select firms that have done the most advanced work in the field. These firms can be expected to design and develop around their own prior knowledge. Development contractors can frequently start production earlier and more knowledgeably than firms that did not participate in the development, and this can affect the time and quality of production, both of which are important to the Government. In many instances the Government may have financed the development. Thus, while the development contractor has a competitive advantage, it is an unavoidable one that is not considered unfair; hence no prohibition should be imposed.

This exception was not applied in *SSR Engineers, Inc.*, Comp. Gen. Dec. B-282244, 99-2 CPD ¶ 27, sustaining the agency's decision that an OCI blocked an architect-engineer from competing for a design-build project because it had prepared the master plan and the budget estimate for the project. The decision does not discuss why this prior effort was not permissible "design" effort. Other cases have refused to apply this exception because the work was not "developmental." See *LW Planning Group*, Comp. Gen. Dec. B-215539, 84-2 CPD ¶ 531, where an OCI was found when a contractor had prepared a work statement for a subsequent contract to revise a master plan, and *Basile, Baumann, Prost & Assocs., Inc.*, Comp. Gen. Dec. B-274870, 97-1 CPD ¶ 15, where an OCI was found when the contractor prepared a work statement for follow-on work during performance of a contract calling for the evaluation of government land for its suitability for recreational uses. In one unusual case, a development contractor was found to have an OCI barring it from competing for a follow-on contract for more design and development work because it has surreptitiously prepared a work statement for that contract, *Ressler Assocs., Inc.*, Comp. Gen. Dec. B-244110, 91-2 CPD ¶ 230. GAO reasoned that the development

2004 CPD ¶ 177, finding an OCI in a contract for analytical and technical support services for an agency in evaluating the performance of weapons manufactured by the contractor when the services being procured involved "analysis, evaluation and judgment." Compare *Serco, Inc.*, Comp. Gen. Dec. B-404033, 2011 CPD ¶ 302 (no OCI because the contractor was not required to make recommendations); *Software Eng'g Servs., Inc.*, Comp. Gen. Dec. B-401645, 2010 CPD ¶ 150 (no OCI in award-ing contract to operate and maintain system to contractor that prepared requirements for system when another contractor developed the system); *Overlook Sys. Techs., Inc.*, Comp. Gen. Dec. B-298099.4, 2006 CPD ¶ 185 (OCI could be mitigated be-cause only a small part of the work required the exercise of judgment); *Computers Universal, Inc.*, Comp. Gen. Dec. B-292794, 2003 CPD ¶ 201 (no OCI because the contract task of preparing a quality assurance program did not involve subjective judgment when the actual inspection of the company's work was to be done by others); and *Tymshare, Inc.*, Comp. Gen. Dec. B-198020, 80-2 CPD ¶ 267 (no OCI under a solicitation that called for the contractor to provide "technical assistance" to the government in evaluating the reliability of the data system being procured). Similarly, in *TDS, Inc.*, Comp. Gen. Dec. B-292674, 2003 CPD ¶ 204, no OCI was found when a subcontractor with an existing contract with the agency for "monitor-ing" work on new contracts did not have the task of "evaluating" the performance of the prospective contractor on the new contract. GAO reasoned:

> [M]onitoring, standing alone, does not necessarily create the potential for im-paired objectivity. Rather, as noted above, an impaired objectivity conflict typi-cally arises where a firm is evaluating its own activities because the objectivity necessary to impartially evaluate performance may be impaired by the firm's in-terest in the entity being evaluated. . . . While we do not exclude the possibility in a different context of monitoring activities resulting in an impaired objectivity OCI, here there is no evidence that [deleted] will be evaluating the performance of the help desk contractor, and there is nothing otherwise objectionable in the in-terrelationship of activities performed by [deleted] on the two contracts. Instead, the record shows that the help desk contractor's performance must at least meet the minimum standards outlined in the [Request for Quotations] and that the con-tracting officer's technical representative will be responsible for evaluating the adequacy of the firm's performance for purposes of assessing the firm's overall performance, deciding whether or not to award option year requirements, and determining the firm's compensation under the [service level agreement].

See also *Wyle Labs., Inc.*, Comp. Gen. Dec. B-288892, 2002 CPD ¶ 12, finding no OCI where a contractor operated a top-level laboratory and several lower-level laboratories. GAO accepted the agency's argument that government personnel would do the actual monitoring of performance of all of the laboratories. Similarly, in *Bat-telle Mem'l Inst.*, Comp. Gen. Dec. B-218538, 85-1 CPD ¶ 726, a contract to prepare general methodologies to solve a technical program, including the summarization of technical data from past contract performance, was properly awarded to a contractor that was performing one of the prior contracts. GAO reasoned that the contract did not require the assessment of the adequacy of its performance under the prior contract.

Neither will there be an OCI if the contractor has no financial interest in the application of its judgment on the new contract. See, for example, *Marinette Marine Corp.*, Comp. Gen. Dec. B-400697, 2009 CPD ¶ 16, finding no OCI when a consultant advised both the agency and the winning offeror because the consultant had no financial interest in the outcome of the competition. Similarly, in *Karrar Sys. Corp.*, Comp. Gen. Dec. B-310661, 2008 CPD ¶ 55, an OCI was avoided by severing the relationship between the winning offeror for administrative services and one of the competitors. See also *Teledyne-Commodore, LLC*, Comp. Gen. Dec. B-278408.5, 99-1 CPD ¶ 60, finding no OCI where an agency used a company to assist in evaluating proposals but the company had no financial interest in the outcome of the competition. GAO rejected the contention that the company had an OCI because it would favor the technology that it had previously recommended. See also *CH2M Hill, Ltd.*, Comp. Gen. Dec. B-259511, 95-1 CPD ¶ 203, finding no conflict of interest when the president of a subcontractor chaired a community commission that was the focal point for relocation efforts caused by government downsizing. GAO concluded that the commission had no control over the agency's efforts that would be facilitated by the contract. Compare *Greenleaf Constr. Co.*, Comp. Gen. Dec. B-293105.18, 2006 CPD ¶ 19, where a firm that had won a contract for home marketing and management services divested its interest in a firm that was the closing agent of the homes being managed. GAO ruled that an OCI still existed because, while the firm had sold its interest in the closing firm, it had accepted compensation over a period covered by the contract — with the potential that it might make biased recommendations to keep that firm viable until it had been paid.

GAO has also used this provision in determining whether there was impropriety in proposing the use of a government agency to assist in evaluating work when that agency had employees on the source selection team, *Battelle Mem'l Inst.*, Comp. Gen. Dec. B-278673, 98-1 CPD ¶ 107. GAO found that the agency had properly considered the matter and determined the conflict was not sufficient to require barring the offeror from the competition.

## B. Disqualification

When the contracting officer identifies a potential OCI, the offeror must be disqualified unless a restraint can be included in the contract to neutralize or mitigate the conflict. Contracting officers must exercise great care in disqualifying contractors because the result can be loss of competition on the instant contract or future contracts. On the other hand, allowing contractors with OCIs can pose a considerable risk that the contractor will have an unfair advantage or provide biased opinions. Disqualification can occur in two ways — (1) by not allowing a contractor with an OCI to compete on a current requirement or (2) by including a clause in a contract precluding the contractor from competing for future work.

GAO has recognized the judgmental nature of decisions in this area and has stated that the responsibility for determining whether award to a particular firm would result in an OCI lies with the procuring agency. Such determinations are subject to objection only if they are directly contrary to statute or regulation or are shown to be clearly unreasonable, *Abt Assocs.*, Comp. Gen. Dec. B-253220.2, 93-2 CPD ¶ 269; *NAHB Research Found., Inc.*, Comp. Gen. Dec. B-219344, 85-2 CPD ¶ 248; *John J. McMullen Assocs.*, Comp. Gen. Dec. B-188703, 77-2 CPD ¶ 270.

## 1. Disqualification on Current Procurement

If the conflict results from past actions of the contractor, disqualification may be the only logical course of action. Frequently this occurs when a prior contract has included a clause restraining participation in the present procurement. However, the absence of a clause does not preclude disqualification, *LW Planning Group*, Comp. Gen. Dec. B-215539, 84-2 CPD ¶ 531 (contractor that had participated in the drafting of specifications or work statements); *Acumenics Research & Tech., Inc.*, Comp. Gen. Dec. B-211575, 83-2 CPD ¶ 94 (contract that required the firm to evaluate the usefulness of its own work under an earlier contract); *Cardiocare*, 59 Comp. Gen. 355 (B-195827), 80-1 CPD ¶ 237 (potential bias where the offeror was determined ineligible to do the follow-up service work on pacemakers because approximately 50% of them were produced by the offeror's parent company).

Disqualification is mandatory with regard to contracts for products where the offeror has performed systems engineering or technical direction, FAR 9.505-1(a); DFARS 209.571-7. See *Filtration Dev. Co. v. United States*, 60 Fed. Cl. 371 (2004) (disqualifying systems engineering contractor from providing components of system). It is also mandatory for a period of time it the offeror has drafted the specification for a nondevelopmental item, FAR 9.505-2(a). See *Lucent Techs. World Servs., Inc.*, Comp. Gen. Dec. B-295462, 2005 CPD ¶ 55 (contractor had prepared technical specification for procurement); *SSR Engineers, Inc.*, Comp. Gen. Dec. B-282244, 99-2 CPD ¶ 27 (architect-engineer barred from competing for a design-build project because it had prepared the master plan and the budget estimate for the project); *Basile, Baumann, Prost & Assocs., Inc.*, Comp. Gen. Dec. B-274870, 97-1 CPD ¶ 1 (contractor that had prepared a work statement for follow-on work during performance of a contract calling for the evaluation of government land for its suitability for recreational uses barred from competing for follow-on contract); *Ressler Assocs., Inc.*, Comp. Gen. Dec. B-244110, 91-2 CPD ¶ 230 (development contractor barred from competing for a follow-on contract for more design and development work when it has surreptitiously prepared a work statement for that contract); *LW Planning Group*, Comp. Gen. Dec. B-215539, 84-2 CPD ¶ 531 (protester disqualified from competing on work for which it had drafted the statement of work in performing a prior task order issued by the agency). Agencies have also included a clause in the original contract to prepare specifications barring the contractor from competing for production of the item, *Analytic Scis. Corp.*, Comp. Gen. Dec. B-218074, 85-1 CPD ¶ 464.

Disqualification under a current procurement may also be required in the other types of OCIs. In some unequal access to information cases, no other remedy is feasible because the risk of transmission of the information has already occurred. For example, in *VRC, Inc.*, Comp. Gen. Dec. B-310100, 2007 CPD ¶ 202, disqualification was found to be the only feasible course of action when a contracting officer did not learn until after receipt of proposals that a subcontractor had access to all of the agency's internal information about the procurement. See also *L-3 Servs., Inc.*, Comp. Gen. Dec. B-400134.11, 2009 CPD ¶ 171, where disqualification was required when the contractor had assisted in planning the procurement and a proposed mitigation plan was not submitted until after the work had been done, and *NKF Eng'g, Inc. v. United States*, 805 F.2d 372 (Fed. Cir. 1986), where a company was properly disqualified from a procurement when it hired a member of the agency's source selection board prior to the submission of best and final offers. Disqualification was also required in *Axion Res. Mgmt., Inc. v. United States*, 78 Fed. Cl. 576 (2007), *rev'd*, 564 F.3d 1374 (Fed. Cir. 2009), where the court found that information gained on one phase of a project would provide an undue competitive advantage in competing for the next phase. GAO had concluded that disqualification was not required in *Axion Res. Mgmt., Inc.*, Comp. Gen. Dec. B-298870.3, 2007 CPD ¶ 117, and the Federal Circuit agreed because the Court of Federal Claims decision calling for disqualification was based on inadmissible new evidence outside of the administrative record before the agency and was made by reviewing the decision of the agency de novo rather than on an arbitrary and capricious standard.

The same result frequently occurs in the impaired objectivity situations where the new contract requires the evaluation of work that a contractor has performed on a prior contract. For example, in *Leboeuf v. Abraham*, 347 F.3d 315 (D.C. Cir. 2003), a law firm was barred from competing when the contract required it to analyze legal opinions it had rendered on a prior contract. See also *PURVIS Sys., Inc.*, Comp. Gen. Dec. B-293807.3, 2004 CPD ¶ 177 (agency's review of OCI mitigation plans insufficient because it failed to consider potential conflicts of interest that would be created by awardee's involvement in evaluating the performance of undersea warfare systems that have been manufactured by the awardee or by the awardee's competitors), *Acumenics Research & Tech., Inc.*, Comp. Gen. Dec. B-211575, 83-2 CPD ¶ 94 (protester barred from competing for a contract that required it to evaluate the adequacy and applicability of specification that it had prepared under an earlier contract); *Cardiocare*, 59 Comp. Gen. 355 (B-195827), 80-1 CPD ¶ 237 (producer of medical equipment disqualified from competing for a contract to monitor the performance of that type equipment).

## 2. Adopting a Contract Clause Calling for Future Disqualification

When the contracting officer knows that the work on a contract will lead to an OCI on future work, both the solicitation and the contract should contain a clause which provides for disqualification for the future work or some other restraint, FAR 9.507(a). However, the FAR contains no clauses for this purpose. A broad clause, used by NASA, is contained in NFS 1852.209-71:

LIMITATION OF FUTURE CONTRACTING (DEC 1988)

(a) The Contracting Officer has determined that this acquisition may give rise to a potential organizational conflict of interest. Accordingly, the attention of prospective offerors is invited to FAR Subpart 9.5 — Organizational Conflicts of Interest.

(b) The nature of this conflict is [describe the conflict].

(c) The restrictions upon future contracting are as follows:

(1) If the Contractor, under the terms of this contract, or through the performance of tasks pursuant to this contract, is required to develop specifications or statements of work that are to be incorporated into a solicitation, the Contractor shall be ineligible to perform the work described in that solicitation as a prime or first-tier subcontractor under an ensuing NASA contract. This restriction shall remain in effect for a reasonable time, as agreed to by the Contracting Officer and the Contractor, sufficient to avoid unfair competitive advantage or potential bias (this time shall in no case be less than the duration of the initial production contract). NASA shall not unilaterally require the Contractor to prepare such specifications or statements of work under this contract.

(2) To the extent that the work under this contract requires access to proprietary, business confidential, or financial data of other companies, and as long as these data remain proprietary or confidential, the Contractor shall protect these data from unauthorized use and disclosure and agrees not to use them to compete with those other companies.

DFARS 252.209-7008 and -7009 call for use of the following clauses for systems engineering and technical assistance contracts on major systems:

NOTICE OF PROHIBITION RELATING TO ORGANIZATIONAL CONFLICT OF INTEREST — MAJOR DEFENSE ACQUISITION PROGRAM (DEC 2010)

(a) *Definitions.* "Major subcontractor" is defined in the clause at 252.209-7009, Organizational Conflict of Interest — Major Defense Acquisition Program.

(b) This solicitation is for the performance of systems engineering and technical assistance for a major defense acquisition program or a pre-major defense acquisition program.

(c) *Prohibition.* As required by paragraph (b)(3) of section 207 of the Weapons System Acquisition Reform Act of 2009 (Pub. L. 111-23), if awarded the contract, the contractor or any affiliate of the contractor is prohibited from participating as a prime contractor or a major subcontractor in the development or production of a weapon system under the major defense acquisition program or pre-major defense acquisition program, unless the offeror submits, and the Government approves, an Organizational Conflict of Interest Mitigation Plan.

(d) *Request for an exception.* If the offeror requests an exception to the prohibition of paragraph (c) of this provision, then the offeror shall submit an Organizational Conflict of Interest Mitigation Plan with its offer for evaluation.

(e) *Incorporation of Organizational Conflict of Interest Mitigation Plan in contract.* If the apparently successful offeror submitted an acceptable Organizational Conflict of Interest Mitigation Plan, and the head of the contracting activity determines that DoD needs the domain experience and expertise of the highly qualified, apparently successful offeror in accordance with FAR 209.571-7(c), then the Contracting Officer will incorporate the Organizational Conflict of Interest Mitigation Plan into the resultant contract, and paragraph (d) of the clause at 252.209-7009 will become applicable.

### ORGANIZATIONAL CONFLICT OF INTEREST — MAJOR DEFENSE ACQUISITION PROGRAM (DEC 2010)

(a) *Definition.* "Major subcontractor," as used in this clause, means a subcontractor that isawarded a subcontract that equals or exceeds —

> (1) Both the cost or pricing data threshold and 10% of the value of the contract under which the subcontracts are awarded; or

> (2) $50 million.

(b) This contract is for the performance of systems engineering and technical assistance for a major defense acquisition program or a pre-major defense acquisition program.

(c) *Prohibition.* Except as provided in paragraph (d) of this clause, as required by paragraph (b)(3) of section 207 of the Weapons System Acquisition Reform Act of 2009 (Pub. L. 111-23), the Contractor or any affiliate of the Contractor is prohibited from participating as a prime contractor or major subcontractor in the development or production of a weapon system under the major defense acquisition program or pre-major defense acquisition program.

(d) *Organizational Conflict of Interest Mitigation Plan.* If the Contractor submitted an acceptable Organizational Conflict of Interest Mitigation Plan that has been incorporated into this contract, then the prohibition in paragraph (c) of this clause does not apply. The Contractor shall comply with the Organizational Conflict of Interest Mitigation Plan. Compliance with the Organizational Conflict of Interest Mitigation Plan is a material requirement of the contract. Failure to comply may result in the Contractor or any affiliate of the Contractor being prohibited from participating as a contractor or major subcontractor in the development or production of a weapon system under the program, in addition to any other remedies available to the Government for noncompliance with a material requirement of a contract.

See also DEAR 952.209-72 and 48 C.F.R. § 2052.209-72 (Nuclear Regulatory Commission) for other agency clauses.

Clauses barring participation in future procurements have been used to eliminate bias in drafting specifications, *Analytic Scis. Corp.*, Comp. Gen. Dec. B-218074, 85-1 CPD ¶ 464. Similarly, a clause may only warn a contractor that disqualification in future contracts could result from biased drafting of specifications, *Iris Int'l, Inc.*, Comp. Gen. Dec. B-216084.2, 85-1 CPD ¶ 524. Other types of restraints have been used to eliminate bias. For example, in *Columbia Research Corp.*, 61 Comp. Gen. 194 (B-202762), 82-1 CPD ¶ 8, the agency included a clause requiring the contractor to give notice of any organizational conflicts during a study and providing for default termination if the notice was not given.

## 3. Avoiding Disqualification

When it is possible to formulate an effective plan to mitigate an OCI, adoption of such a plan is generally more desirable than disqualifying a contractor. It can be argued that the contracting officer is required to attempt to negotiate restraints, when appropriate, before disqualifying an offeror because of an OCI, FAR 9.505. See *Orkand Corp.*, Comp. Gen. Dec. B-209662.2, 83-1 CPD ¶ 349, where GAO agreed with an agency determination that a contracting officer should have attempted to negotiate an appropriate contract clause. With respect to unfair advantage resulting from obtaining proprietary data of competitors, FAR 9.505-4 appears to indicate that a restraint is the proper course of action.

In some instances it has been determined that no mitigation is feasible. For example, in *Aetna Gov. Health Plans, Inc.*, Comp. Gen. Dec. B-254397.15, 95-2 CPD ¶ 129, where a major subcontractor of an offeror was affiliated with a company giving advice to the agency on the selection of the source, GAO ruled that no mitigation was possible where the subcontract was projected to be in the amount of $183 million and the company giving the advice was an integral part of the evaluation of proposals and the source selection process. GAO concluded that a firewall between elements of a single company was not an effective mitigation technique. See also *Cahaba Safeguard Administrators, LLC*, Comp. Gen. Dec. B-401842.2, 2010 CPD ¶ 39, and *C2C Solutions, Inc.*, Comp. Gen. Dec. B-401106.5, 2010 CPD ¶ 38, where

GAO concluded that there was considerable doubt as to whether using a firewalled subcontractor for conflicted work was an effective remedy, and *First Coast Serv. Options, Inc.*, Comp. Gen. Dec. B-401429, 2010 CPD ¶ 6, where GAO held that the agency had properly rejected a mitigation plan calling for a firewalled subcontractor. A similar result was reached in *Nortel Gov't Solutions, Inc.*, Comp. Gen. Dec. B-299522.5, 2009 CPD ¶ 10, where GAO reasoned:

> SRA's proposal to separate its . . . personnel through use of a firewall appears to be of little, if any, help in resolving the OCI here. In this regard, the proposed firewall provides for SRA to manage the two contracts using "separate organizations with separate interests" and "distinct business objectives." It also prohibits SRA and subcontractor personnel working on one contract from providing support under the other contract, without written approval from the contracting officer. However, while a firewall arrangement may resolve and "unfair access to information" OCI, it is virtually irrelevant to an OCI involving potentially impaired objectivity. See *Aetna Gov't Health Plans* . . . This is because the conflict at issue pertains to the organization, and not the individual employees. Thus, while the firewall proposed by SRA may created the appearance of separation to mitigate the OCI, The fact remains that personnel under both contracts will be working for the same organization with an incentive ti benefit SRA overall.

On the other hand, a firewall between a contractor and its subcontractor has been accepted as an effective mitigation technique because it prevents the organization with the OCI from performing work for which it has previously performed services to the agency. See *Business Consulting Assocs., LLC*, Comp. Gen. Dec. B-299758.2, 2007 CPD ¶ 134 (contractor with OCI agreed to transfer work impacted by the OCI to firewalled subcontractor); *Alion Sci. & Tech. Corp.*, Comp. Gen. Dec. B-297022.4, 2006 CPD ¶ 146 (contractor with OCI agreed to transfer the one-third of work impacted by the OCI to a firewalled subcontractor); *Deutche Bank*, Comp. Gen. Dec. B-289111, 2001 CPD ¶ 210 (contractor with OCI agreed to transfer work impacted by the OCI to firewalled subcontractor that would report directly to agency); *Epoch Eng'g, Inc.*, Comp. Gen. Dec. B-276634, 97-2 CPD ¶ 72 (contractor agreed not to assign work impacted by a subcontractor's OCI to that firewalled subcontractor); *SC&A, Inc.*, Comp. Gen. Dec. B-270160.2, 96-1 CPD ¶ 197 (contractor agreed not to assign work impacted by a subcontractor's OCI to that firewalled subcontractor). In *Overlook Sys. Techs., Inc.*, Comp. Gen. Dec. B-298099.4, 2006 CPD ¶ 185, GAO accepted a mitigation plan that included a number of elements — firewalling the subcontractor with an OCI, precluding assigning that subcontractor work impacted by the OCI, conducting regular OCI training, and requiring enhanced government oversight of the subcontractor with the OCI. See also *PRI, Inc.*, Comp. Gen. Dec. B-210714, 84-1 CPD ¶ 345, denying a protest of bias concerning the overlapping roles of the awardee in separate contracts with the agency. It was held that potential bias could be avoided by having the agency monitor the placing of task orders to avoid such conflict.

Clauses establishing firewalls have also been accepted to mitigate unequal access to information situation OCIs where they prohibited the dissemination of that information to any person that has not worked on the contract and precluded any of those personnel from participating in a procurement of follow-on work. See *LEADS Corp.*, Comp. Gen. Dec. B-292465, 2003 CPD ¶ 197, accepting a mitigation plan of this type on a task order contract where it was providing procurement services to the agency. The plan also included a provision where the contractor would notify the contracting officer of any task order for which it desired to compete so that the agency could avoid using the contractor's personnel on that task order. Similar plans have been accepted in *Research Analysis & Maint., Inc.* Comp. Gen. Dec. B-272261, 96-2 CPD ¶ 131 (delivery orders for which subcontractor had OCI would be given by agency to another delivery order contractor); and *Deloitte & Touche*, 69 Comp. Gen. 463 (B-238371), 90-1 CPD ¶ 486 (task orders where subcontractor had OCI would be performed by contractor). It is questionable whether an agency would accept even this type of broad restraint because of the fear that it was unenforceable. See, for example, § (b)(2)(i)(B) of the DEAR 952.209-72 clause precluding competing for such work for a designated period. For partial implementation of such a restraint, see FAR 9.505-4(b) requiring contractors performing advisory and assistance services to "agree with other companies to protect their information from unauthorized use and disclosure." See *MAR, Inc.*, Comp. Gen. Dec. B-215798, 85-1 CPD ¶ 121, where GAO agreed with the use of such a clause even though a protester contended that no competitors would disclose the data under such conditions.

## III. DEBARMENT AND SUSPENSION

Debarment and suspension are drastic sanctions, precluding a company or individual from contracting with executive agencies. Debarments are defined as actions which "exclude a contractor from Government contracting and Government-approved subcontracting for a reasonable, specified period," FAR 2.101. Suspensions are temporary exclusions "pending the completion of investigation or legal proceedings, when it has been determined that immediate action is necessary to protect the Government's interest," FAR 9.407-1(b)(1). Contractors "proposed for debarment" are also excluded temporarily, FAR 9.404 (b)(1). While this exclusion appears to relate only to contractors proposed for debarment for procurement violations, it has also been permitted in the case of a contractor proposed for debarment under the Davis-Bacon Act, *Salazar Constr. Co.*, 67 Comp. Gen. 115 (B-228071), 87-2 CPD ¶ 542.

There are two types of debarments: *procurement* and *inducement.* Procurement debarments and suspensions are carried out following the procedures in FAR Subpart 9.4, with the purpose of avoiding certain business risks associated with engaging in a contractual relationship with a firm. These risks relate directly to the procurement involved and include delivery of unacceptable products or services, waste of public funds, and contractor fraud. Thus, procurement debarment and suspension are the "appropriate means to effectuate" an express regulatory policy of ensuring "the Government's protection" by allowing contracting " with responsible contractors only," FAR 9.402(a)-(b). This basis for debarment and suspension involves behavior "of so serious or compelling a nature that it affects the present responsibility" of the contractor, FAR 9.406-2(c) and FAR 9.407-2(c). This type of sanction, referred to as "procurement," "nonresponsibility," or "administrative" debarment or suspension, is used by procuring agency officials as an integral part of the procurement process.

Inducement debarments have a different purpose— to induce contractors to perform government contracts in ways that will further fundamental social and economic goals, such as equal employment opportunity, the payment of prescribed minimum wages, and environmental protection. Debarments based upon a contractor's failure to participate effectively in furtherance of these goals have been referred to as "inducement" or "statutory" debarments because they are generally based upon statutory provisions. The grounds and procedures for these debarments are set forth in a variety of regulations issued by agencies outside of the procurement process such as the Department of Labor (DOL) and the Environmental Protection Agency (EPA). While the statutes, executive orders, and regulations creating and implementing these debarments are often imprecise in their terminology (using either "listing" or "ineligible," for example, apparently to mean the same thing) all sanctions that preclude contract awards for a specific period of time are encompassed in the discussion of debarment in this section (suspension is not used to induce contractors to carry out these goals). FAR 9.400(b) describes inducement debarments as declarations of "ineligibility" and states that it does not prescribe the policies or procedures applicable to them. However, they have the same effect as debarments issued by the procuring agencies.

All contractors that are "debarred, suspended, proposed for debarment or declared ineligible" are included in the Excluded Parties List System (EPLS), FAR 9.404(a). The EPLS also includes all entities excluded from nonprocurement transactions, formerly found in Executive Order 12549, 51 Fed. Reg. 6370 (1986), FAR 9.404(b). This includes recipients of grants and other agreements, 2 C.F.R. § 215.13, making debarments of such entities applicable to procurement contracts. This list is compiled by the General Services Administration (GSA) and is posted on the Internet at *http://epls.gov*, FAR 9.404(d). This list is used by contracting officers in carrying out the policies regarding debarred and suspended contractors.

Procurement debarment or suspension decisions are made by agency heads or designees rather than contracting officers. FAR 9.403 defines these designees as the "debarring official" and the "suspending official"; typically, authority over the suspension and debarment functions is lodged in one official. Debarment or suspension actions preclude contracting officers awarding contracts to debarred or suspended contractors, FAR 9.405(a). Thus, debarment and suspension override the responsibility determination process including the SBA COC procedure.

Procurement and inducement debarments are treated differently when contracts are awarded to debarred firms through government inadvertence. Contracts awarded to firms debarred under statutes are void ab initio, *Paisner v. United States*, 138 Ct. Cl. 420, 150 F. Supp. 835 (1957), *cert. denied*, 355 U.S. 941 (1958), while contracts awarded to firms debarred pursuant to agency regulation are voidable at the option of the government, *P.E.C. Corp.*, ASBCA 14241, 69-2 BCA ¶ 8056.

This section discusses the bases for debarment and suspension, the impact of these actions, and the procedures used to impose these sanctions.

## A. Exercise of Discretion

Even though the purposes of procurement and inducement debarments are different, both require the exercise of discretion in making the debarment or suspension decision. Thus, even though a cause for debarment has been clearly demonstrated, the debarring official must consider such factors as the seriousness of the improper conduct, mitigating circumstances, and remedial actions that have been taken.

## 1. *Procurement Debarments or Suspensions*

Procurement debarments or suspensions are generally considered actions to be taken to protect the government from future misconduct, as FAR 9.402(b) states:

> The serious nature of debarment and suspension requires that these sanctions be imposed only in the public interest for the Government's protection and not for purposes of punishment. Agencies shall impose debarment or suspension to protect the Government's interest and only for the causes and in accordance with the procedures set forth in this subpart.

Under this policy, the primary consideration in imposing these sanctions should be the offeror's "present and likely future responsibility" rather than the mere fact that a past offense has been committed, *Roemer v. Hoffman*, 419 F. Supp. 130 (D.D.C. 1976). While most circuit courts have rejected the contention that debarment is punitive, *Bae v. Shalala*, 44 F.3d 489 (7th. Cir. 1995); *United States v. Bizzell*, 921 F.2d 263 (10th Cir. 1990), or that debarment is a form of criminal punishment, *United States v. Hatfield*, 108 F.3d 67 (4th Cir. 1997), one circuit court has stated that every debarment "is a form of punishment," *Fischer v. RTC*, 59 F.3d 1344 (D.C. Cir. 1995).

Conduct constituting grounds for debarment is sufficient to raise doubts concerning present responsibility. However, debarment officials must consider the seriousness of the contractor's conduct and any mitigating circumstances in deciding whether to impose debarment. FAR 9.406-1(a) provides:

> The existence of a cause for debarment, however, does not necessarily require that the contractor be debarred; the seriousness of the contractor's acts or omis-

sions and any remedial measures or mitigating factors should be considered in making any debarment decision.

This regulatory policy establishes two key points. First, debarment is not to be an automatic consequence of a cause for debarment; rather, the debarment official is to exercise discretion. Second, it is appropriate not to debar in circumstances where the contractor's acts or omissions are not serious or where mitigating factors are strong. For example, the Housing and Urban Development (HUD) Board of Contract Appeals did not impose debarment where the contractor had rectified the misdeeds (making false statements to HUD) and produced letters indicating its present responsibility, *Lawrence C. Shank*, HUDBCA 82-724-D43, 83-1 BCA ¶ 16,439. In *Roemer*, the court remanded the debarment of a contractor based upon a conviction for accepting monies from a manufacturer's representative because the agency had not given a "hard look" to factors affecting the question of the firm's "present responsibility." The court discussed the kind of mitigating factors it considered relevant at 132:

> [T]he plaintiff has suggested a number of factors which appear to diminish the force of that conviction as an indication of Roemer's present responsibility. These factors touch on Roemer's character before the offense occurred, the circumstances surrounding the offense, the deterrent effect of the prior 29-month suspension, of the conviction, and of the payment to the government of $3,600 in restitution, the length of time which has passed since the offense and since the conviction, and Roemer's character since the offense and conviction.

In *Silverman v. Defense Logistics Agency*, 817 F. Supp. 846 (S.D. Cal. 1993), the court terminated a debarment based on a plea of guilty to a misdemeanor (with a fine of $250), because the debarring official had failed to consider the mitigating circumstance that the plea had been made to avoid an indictment for an offense of which the plaintiff did not believe he was guilty. The court also doubted if the agency was correct in finding the plaintiff not presently responsible when it had continued to contract with his company for six years after the alleged offense. In *C. & J. Harmon*, AGBCA 77-198, 79-1 BCA ¶ 13,705, the Agriculture board overturned a debarment based upon a firm's failure to satisfy contract requirements where the agency "mechanically" applied the debarment sanction without giving consideration to "surrounding" circumstances. Compare *Puma Co.*, GSBCA 6934-D, 83-1 BCA ¶ 16,349, and *Atlantic Chem. Co.*, GSBCA 5822 D, 80 2 BCA ¶14,801, where the board agreed that mitigating factors should be considered but deferred to the discretionary decision of the debarring official. See *David K. Alberta*, AGBCA 93-189-7, 94-2 BCA ¶ 26,923, where the board reduced the length of a contractor's debarment because its conviction for previous illegal activities did not demonstrate that it lacked present responsibility justifying continuation of the debarment. In *United States Testing Co.*, EPADEBAR 89-0021-00, Apr. 23, 1991, *Unpub.*, the board analogized the standard of "adequate evidence" in support of suspension to that of "probable cause" in support of a warrant. It noted that an adequate evidence showing need not rise to the level of that necessary for a successful criminal prosecution or a formal debarment. Similarly, in *Kirkpatrick v. White,* 351 F. Supp. 2d 1261, 1282 (N.D. Ala. 2004), the district court described the "adequate evidence" standard as "an extremely low standard of proof."

DFARS 209.406-1(a) has placed certain limitations on the debarring official's discretion to forgo debarment, stating:

> (ii) Before the debarring official decides not to suspend or debar in the case of an indictment or conviction for a felony, the debarring official must determine that the contractor has addressed adequately the circumstances that gave rise to the misconduct, and that appropriate standards of ethics and integrity are in place and are working.

This reflects a broader reliance upon compliance systems by enforcement officials to ensure the integrity of the contracting process. DFARS 209.406-1 provides:

> (a)(i) When the debarring official decides that debarment is not necessary, the official may require the contractor to enter into a written agreement which includes —

>> (A) A requirement for the contractor to establish, if not already established, and to maintain the standards of conduct and internal control systems prescribed by Subpart 203.70; and

>> (B) Other requirements the debarring official considers appropriate.

See Zucker & Fratarcangeli, *Administrative Compliance Agreements: An Effective Tool In The Suspension And Debarment Process,* 15 Clause 4 (Board of Contract Appeals Bar Ass'n Winter 2004 (*http://www.bcabar.org/the_clause.htm*)); Seymour, Note, *Refining the Source of the Risk: Suspension and Debarment in the Post-Andersen Era,* 34 Pub. Cont. L.J. 357 (2005). Ultimately, however, suspension or debarment is a matter for the reviewing official's discretion, and it is the contractor's burden to show that suspension or debarment is not warranted, for example because adequate controls have been put in place, FAR 9.406-1(a). See Thomas, Annotation, *Judicial Review of Administrative Order Debarring Defense Contractor from Contracting with Federal Government,* 91 A.L.R. Fed. 868.

## 2. Inducement Debarments

Statutes and other regulations providing for inducement debarments do not contain the clear statement of purpose included in FAR 9.402(b), but similar principles have been applied. These debarments are now subject to the governmentwide Nonprocurement Common Rule (NCR) which sets forth the common policies and procedures that federal agencies must use in taking suspension or debarment actions. See 2 C.F.R. Part 180.

Nonetheless, these agencies have broad discretion in determining to debar a firm or person. Thus, under the Service Contract Act of 1965, 41 U.S.C. § 6706, the Secretary of Labor is given discretion to refrain from debarring violators upon a finding of "unusual circumstances." See *White Glove Bldg. Maint., Inc. v. Hodgson*, 459 F.2d 175 (9th Cir. 1972), affirming the discretion of the Secretary not to debar violators under the pre-1972 version of the Act, which simply stated that contracts should not be awarded to violators "unless the Secretary otherwise recommends." In *Washington Moving & Storage Co.*, SCA-168, Mar. 12, 1974, the Secretary of Labor identified the factors to be considered in deciding whether "unusual circumstances" are present:

> Whether "unusual circumstances" are present in a case within the meaning of the Act must be determined on the basis of the facts and circumstances of the particular case. Some of the principal factors which must be considered in making this determination are whether there is a history of repeated violations of the Act; the nature, extent, and seriousness of past or present violations; whether the violations were willful, or the circumstances show there was culpable neglect to ascertain whether certain practices were in compliance, or culpable disregard of whether they were or not, or other culpable conduct (such as deliberate falsification of records); whether the respondent's liability turned on bona fide legal issues of doubtful certainty; whether the respondent has demonstrated good faith, cooperation in the resolution of issues, and a desire and intention to comply with the requirements of the Act; and the promptness with which employees were paid the sums determined to be due them. It is clear that the mere payment of sums found due employees after an administrative proceeding, coupled with an assurance of future compliance, is not in itself sufficient to constitute "unusual circumstances" warranting relief from the ineligible list sanction. It is also clear that a history of recurrent violations of identical nature, such as repeated violations of identical minimum wage or recordkeeping provisions, does not permit a finding of "unusual circumstances."

See also *Federal Food Serv., Inc. v. Donovan*, 658 F.2d 830 (D.C. Cir. 1981), where the court reversed a decision of the Secretary of Labor debarring a contractor for "de minimis" underpayments under the Service Contract Act, concluding that the Secretary's failure to consider whether the facts warranted a finding of "unusual circumstances" constituted an "arbitrary" act. The court held that "use of debarment against innocent and petty violations was not intended." But see the Department of Labor Administrative Review Board's decision in *Coast Indus., Inc.*, DOL ARB No. 04-004, ALJ No. 2002-SCA-003 (Feb. 28, 2005), which pointed out that the SCA's debarment provision "is a particularly unforgiving provision of a demanding statute," and that a "contractor seeking an 'unusual circumstances' exemption from debarment must, therefore, run a narrow gauntlet." The board there noted, per *Vigilantes v. Administrator of Wage and Hour Div.*, 968 F.2d 1412, 1418 (1st Cir. 1992), that the "legislative history of the SCA makes clear that debarment of a contractor who violated the SCA should be the norm, not the exception, and only the most compelling of justifications should relieve a violating contractor from that sanction." See also *Dantran, Inc. v. Department of Labor*, 246 F.3d 36, 41 (1st Cir. 2001) (discussing violator's burden in establishing "unusual circumstances").

The Davis-Bacon Act, 40 U.S.C. § 276a, authorizes GAO to debar firms that have "disregarded their obligations" under the Act. GAO acts on recommendations of the Secretary of Labor, and has held that it will exercise limited discretion— debarring firms for "substantial violations" but not for "technical violations," *Bryant Paint Contracting, Inc.*, 64 Comp. Gen. 549 (B-217337) (1985). Thus, in *Rams-Head Constr., Inc.*, Comp. Gen. Dec. B-222063, Aug. 13, 1986, *Unpub.*, GAO refused to follow the debarment recommendation of the Secretary of Labor because there was insufficient evidence of "willful" violation of the Act; the contractor's not paying workers was based on either inadvertence or a justified concern that they had improperly reported hours worked. Compare *Phoenix Paint Co.*, Comp. Gen. Dec. B-242728, Jan. 2, 1992, *Unpub.*, debarring a contractor that had falsified payroll records even though it claimed that the violation was inadvertent (based on bad advice), had cooperated in the investigation, and had made restitution to the workers. See also *Mashburn Elec. Co.*, Comp. Gen. Dec. B-189471, 78-1 CPD ¶ 277, holding that such mitigating circumstances will not preclude debarment when there have been substantial violations of the Act. The Secretary of Labor also exercises discretion in determining whether to recommend debarment of a firm to GAO per the standards set forth at 29 C.F.R. § 5.12. See also *Thomas & Sons Bldg. Contractors, Inc.*, ARB No. 98-164, ALJ No. 96-DBA-33, at n.3 (June 8, 2001) (comparing Davis-Bacon and SCA debarment procedures).

Executive Order 11246, as amended, gives the Secretary of Labor the power to refrain from debarring firms not in compliance with contractual equal employment obligations, because § 209 of the executive order states that the Secretary "may" provide for debarment of noncomplying firms. See also the implementing regulations, at 41 C.F.R. § 60-1.24(c)(2), indicating that the director of the DOL's Office of Federal Contract Compliance Programs (OFCCP) should seek to resolve instances of violations through "informal means," such as conciliation agreements, before invoking sanctions. See Hordell, McWilliams III, Hoffman & Persico, *Employment Law for Contractors: A Primer,* 39 Proc. Lawyer 3 (ABA Winter 2004).

Clean Air Act and Federal Water Pollution Control Act regulations provide for the debarment of companies that violate the Acts, 40 C.F.R. § 32.110(d). See *Burke v. Environmental Protection Agency*, 127 F. Supp. 2d 235 (D.D.C. 2001) (five year debarment not arbitrary because debarring official had considered potential mitigating factors); *Brent Stromberg*, EPA No. 07-0226-03, 2008 EPADEBAR LEXIS 4 (one year debarment based on conviction of perjury, with a thorough review of mitigating circumstances). However, an agency or the EPA debarring official may grant an exception to the regulations and permit a contractor to be eligible for a contract, 40 C.F.R. § 32.120.

The Buy American Act also provides for debarment, 41 U.S.C. § 10b (now § 8303(c)). See *Glazer Constr. Co. v. United States*, 50 F. Supp. 2d 85 (D. Mass. 1999), holding that debarment was mandatory under the Act but, if not, there was no abuse of discretion.

# B. Causes for Debarment

Statutes and regulations list a number of causes that, in the absence of mitigating or other circumstances, will support debarment.

## 1. Procurement Debarments

FAR 9.406-2 contains a list of acts that are sufficiently serious to warrant debarment proceedings— *conviction* of or *civil judgment* for offenses showing lack of business integrity, *serious* violation of contract terms, and other causes showing a lack of present responsibility.

### a. Lack of Business Integrity

FAR 9.406-2(a) lists types of conduct that indicate a lack of business integrity:

(1) Commission of fraud or a criminal offense in connection with (i) obtaining, (ii) attempting to obtain, or (iii) performing a public contract or subcontract;

(2) Violation of Federal or State antitrust statutes relating to the submission of offers;

(3) Commission of embezzlement, theft, forgery, bribery, falsification or destruction of records, making false statements, tax evasion, violating Federal criminal tax laws, or receiving stolen property;

(4) Intentionally affixing a label bearing a "Made in America" inscription (or any inscription having the same meaning) to a product sold in or shipped to the United States or its outlying areas, when the product was not made in the United States or its outlying areas (see Section 202 of the Defense Production Act (Pub. L. 102-558)); or

(5) Commission of any other offense indicating a lack of business integrity or business honesty that seriously and directly affects the present responsibility of a Government contractor or subcontractor.

Most business integrity debarments have been based upon conviction of criminal offenses in dealing with the federal government. Included are such acts as bid rigging and mail fraud in violation of 18 U.S.C. § 1341, *John F. Azzarelli*, HUDBCA 82-671-D12, 82-1 BCA ¶ 15,677; bribing public officials in violation of 18 U.S.C. § 201, *Thomas P. Prickett*, GSBCA 6311-D, 82-1 BCA ¶ 15,736; perjury before a grand jury in connection with investigation of another government contractor, *William A. Fuhrman*, HUDBCA 79-431-D46, Oct. 14, 1980, *Unpub.*; presenting fraudulent claims in violation of 18 U.S.C. § 287, *Ira F. Gassman*, GSBCA D-3, 79-1 BCA ¶ 13,771; submitting false income tax information in violation of 18 U.S.C. § 1001, *Clarence L. White*, HUDBCA 79-382-D32, July 12, 1979, *Unpub.*

(later reinstated); failing to file a federal income tax return in violation of 26 U.S.C. § 7203, *Nathan A. Hicks*, HUDBCA 79-438-D51, Jan. 7, 1980, *Unpub.*; taking kickbacks in violation of 18 U.S.C. § 874, *Thomas M. Zakucia*, HUDBCA 79-348-D7, Dec. 3, 1979, *Unpub.*; failing to immediately notify the appropriate agency of an unlawful release of a hazardous substance as required by 42 U.S.C. § 9603(b), *John R. Fields*, EPADEBAR 93-0289-00, Nov. 13, 1995, *Unpub.*; and knowingly failing to dispose of asbestos contaminated material in accordance with the Clean Air Act, 42 U.S.C. § 7412, *Ellis "Ray" Kiser*, EPADEBAR 93-0253-01, Nov. 2, 1995, *Unpub.*

Occasionally, a debarment will be based upon convictions of criminal acts in connection with other governmental dealings. See, for example, *Lundin Constr. Co.*, DOT Fin. Asst. Pgm. Dkt. No. 2, Mar. 11, 1985, 43 Fed. Cont. Rep. 657 (bid rigging conviction in state court). The FAR gives no guidance as to what other offenses might indicate a lack of business integrity or honesty. See generally Seymour, Note, *Refining the Source of the Risk: Suspension and Debarment in the Post-Andersen Era,* 34 Pub. Cont. L.J. 357 (2005) (discussing cases where debarments arose based on bad acts outside federal contracting, and arguing that there should be a nexus between bad act and government contracting). It is not clear, for example, whether conviction for commission of a crime of violence might fall within this category.

FAR 2.101 contains the following broad definition of "conviction":

"Conviction" means a judgment or conviction of a criminal offense by any court of competent jurisdiction, whether entered upon a verdict or a plea, and includes a conviction entered upon a plea of nolo contendere.

Generally, convictions establish the facts necessary to support a debarment without the submission of additional evidence to the debarring official. However, there is some disagreement on this rule in the case of a conviction based on a plea of nolo contendere. Despite the clearly stated intention of the government in the above definition, the HUD Board of Contract Appeals held that independent evidence must be introduced in a debarment proceeding to prove the alleged criminal acts when a conviction is based upon a plea of nolo contendere, *Milton H. Girard*, HUDBCA 82-730-D47, 83-1 BCA ¶ 16,544; *Willie J. Hope*, HUDBCA 80-521-D52, 81-1 BCA ¶ 15,045. See also *Sam Ligon*, HUDBCA 83-798-D29, Jan. 4, 1984, *Unpub.*, where independent evidence of the facts was used to prove the commission of the criminal act in lieu of the plea of nolo contendere. The EPA board has reached a similar conclusion. In *Mark P. Young*, EPADEBAR 93-00-25-03, Jan. 6, 1994, *Unpub.*, the board stated that "fundamental fairness requires that the respondents be provided an opportunity to complete their submission of information and arguments."

## b. *Serious Violation of Contract Terms*

FAR 9.406-2 contains the following description of this category of debarment, for failure to comply with a contract's terms:

The debarring official may debar —

\* \* \*

(b)(1) A contractor, based upon a preponderance of the evidence, for any of the following —

> (i) Violation of the terms of a Government contract or subcontract so serious as to justify debarment, such as—

>> (A) Willful failure to perform in accordance with the terms of one or more contracts; or

>> (B) A history of failure to perform, or of unsatisfactory performance of, one or more contracts.

This provision appears to give considerable discretion to debarring officials — both as to the conduct that will justify debarment and the amount of evidence necessary to prove the conduct. Thus, failure to perform repairs within the time specified in the contract and failure to obtain a timely extension of the period of performance provided grounds for debarment in *Wilbert T. Alexander & Alexander Realty Co.*, HUDBCA 81-648-D47, 82-1 BCA ¶ 15,649. See also *WEDJ/Three C's, Inc. v. Department of Def.*, 2006 U.S. Dist. LEXIS 50363 (M.D. Pa. 2006) (alteration of test reports to hide product deficiencies); *Andrew Calhoun*, HUDBCA 82-676-D14, 82-2 BCA ¶ 15,921 (unexcused failure to perform 17 contracts for purchase and repair of rental property); *Mayer Co.*, HUDBCA 81-544-D1, 82-1 BCA ¶ 15,473 (serious inadequacies in supervision and control by corporate managers of a property management firm, including the failure to make mortgage payments and obtain liability insurance); *Donald Schutte*, AGBCA 77-189, 79-2 BCA ¶ 13,902 (three-year debarment for installing a well within a building foundation in violation of state requirements the contractor knew or should have known); *Howard Bigelow*, HUDBCA 80-467-D15, 82-2 BCA ¶ 15,798 (three-year debarment for persistent failure to supervise employees and poor business practices leading to noncompliance with HUD regulations). However, in *Rudy Barnes & Rudy Barnes Co.*, HUDBCA 81-588-D15, 82-2 BCA ¶ 16,001, the contractor's failure to complete two HUD contracts was held insufficient where the contractor's difficulties arose in part from an excessive agency delay in awarding one of the contracts, and a history of failure on a large number of contracts was not involved.

FAR 9.406-2(b)(1) also permits debarment, based on a preponderance of the evidence, for violations of the Drug-Free Workplace Act, intentionally mislabeling a product "Made in America," or commission of an unfair practice relating to foreign trade, and federal tax delinquency. In a major shift in federal procurement law, in late 2008 the rule was broadened, to call for "mandatory disclosure" of certain wrongful acts, so that a contractor may be subject to debarment under FAR 9.406-2(b)(1) upon:

(vi) Knowing failure by a principal, until 3 years after final payment on any Government contract awarded to the contractor, to timely disclose to the Government, in connection with the award, performance, or closeout of the contract or a subcontract thereunder, credible evidence of—

(A) Violation of Federal criminal law involving fraud, conflict of interest, bribery, or gratuity violations found in Title 18 of the United States Code;

(B) Violation of the civil False Claims Act (31 U.S.C. 3729-3733); or

(C) Significant overpayment(s) on the contract, other than overpayments resulting from contract financing payments as defined in 32.001.

The implementing clause, Contractor Code of Business Ethics and Conduct in FAR 52.203-13, also calls for comprehensive contractor compliance systems, to support those disclosure obligations by identifying and addressing violations of law. See generally American Bar Association, Public Contract Law Section, *Guide to the Mandatory Disclosure Rule: Issues, Guidelines, and Best Practices* (2010).

## c.  Other Causes Showing Lack of Present Responsibility

FAR 9.406-2(c) contains the following omnibus category of causes for debarment:

Any other cause of so serious or compelling a nature that it affects the present responsibility of a Government contractor or subcontractor.

This provision, which gives extremely broad discretion to the debarring official, can relate either to performance or integrity issues. See, for example, *Robert Walker, Mark Walker, Alto Leasing Corp.*, GSBCA 7585-D, Mar. 11, 1985, *Unpub.*, where the board found that the contractor's misrepresentation to third parties of its contractual relationship with the GSA demonstrated absence of integrity and lack of present responsibility, and *Kiesel Co.*, EPADEBAR 94-0091-00, Aug. 28, 1995, *Unpub.*, where the charge was improper storage of one drum of hazardous waste (PCB) without required markings. In *Robinson v. Cheney*, 876 F.2d 152 (D.C. Cir. 1989), the court affirmed the debarment of a military clothing supplier that had been indicted for bribing a government official and collusive bidding. The court found no abuse of discretion in finding that the contractor did not have present responsibility based on uncontroverted evidence supplied by one witness that had been granted immunity from criminal prosecution.

## 2.  Inducement Debarments

Causes for inducement debarments are specifically enunciated in each statute or regulation covering the public policy at issue.

## a. Equal Employment Opportunity

Section 209(a)(6) of Executive. Order No. 11246 empowers the Secretary of Labor to debar any firm that fails to comply with the terms of the Equal Employment clause in FAR 52.222-26. Paragraph (c)(9) of this clause incorporates this policy, specifically stating that "the Contractor may be declared ineligible for further Government contracts" as a possible sanction for violation of these requirements. See *BFI Waste Servs.*, 68 Fed. Reg. 7394 (2003) (consent decree because of inadequate compliance); *Goya de Puerto Rico, Inc.*, 67 Fed. Reg. 53028 (2002) (same).

This debarment sanction has been invoked against firms failing to submit acceptable affirmative action plans, *Ingersoll Milling Mfg. Co.*, 42 Fed. Reg. 41330 (1977); *Loffland Bros. Co.*, 44 Fed. Reg. 22835 (1979). In the latter debarment action, the director of OFCCP rejected the contractor's contention that its failure to submit an acceptable affirmative action plan should not be grounds for debarment since it had successfully completed performance of the specified contract work. Failure to meet the minority utilization goals in an affirmative action plan has also been used as the basis for debarment, *Anastasia Bros. Corp.*, 42 Fed. Reg. 42932 (1977). See also *Painting Corp. of Detroit, Inc.*, 43 Fed. Reg. 30919 (1978), where a debarment action was based in part upon a contractor's failure to make a good faith effort to meet minority utilization goals.

The debarment authority under Executive. Order No. 11246 has also been invoked for certain procedural violations. In *Uniroyal, Inc. v. Marshall*, 482 F. Supp. 364 (D.D.C. 1979), the court upheld an OFCCP debarment order based upon the contractor's failure to comply with regulations giving the government access to employment records needed to conduct a discrimination investigation. In *First Alabama Bank of Montgomery v. Donovan*, 692 F.2d 714 (11th Cir. 1982), the court upheld a debarment based upon a refusal to cooperate in a compliance review under Executive. Order No. 11246. See also *OFCCP v. Prudential Ins. Co.*, 23 F.E.P. Cases 492 (DOL 1980), where debarment resulted from a contractor's failure to give OFCCP computer tapes containing detailed personnel, salary, and organizational material, and *Painting Corp. of Detroit, Inc.*, 43 Fed. Reg. 22836 (1978), where a debarment order was based in part upon a firm's refusal to supply workforce data.

## b. Labor Statutes

While only the Davis-Bacon Act, 40 U.S.C. § 276a-2(a), the Walsh-Healey Act, 41 U.S.C. § 6504, and the Service Contract Act, 41 U.S.C. § 6706, specifically provide for debarment, the Secretary of Labor has adopted a rule authorizing debarment for violations of labor-related statutes that do not, in themselves, specifically authorize debarment, 29 C.F.R. § 5.1. The Contract Work Hours and Safety Standards Act, 40 U.S.C. § 3701 *et seq.*, is perhaps the most important among these. See *Copper Plumbing & Heating Co. v. Campbell*, 290 F.2d 368 (D.C. Cir. 1961), and *Janik Paving & Constr., Inc. v. Brock*, 828 F.2d 84 (2d Cir. 1987), sustaining the right of the Secretary of Labor to debar in the absence of statutory provisions. See also *Foundation for Fair Contracting, Ltd. v. G & M Eastern Contracting & Double E, LLC*, 259 F. Supp. 2d 329 (D.N.J. 2003) (reviewing regulatory scheme for enforcement, and holding administrative proceedings for potential debarment foreclosed False Claims Act action by qui tam relator). The standard for debarment under the Davis-Bacon Act is a showing of disregard of obligations to employees and subcontractors. The standard in the other labor statutes is aggravated or willful violation of the statutory requirements, 29 C.F.R. § 5.12(a)(1).

The DOL has also adopted the debarment sanction for violations of the Vietnam-Era Veterans Readjustment Assistance Act of 1974, 41 C.F.R. § 60-250.28(e), and the Rehabilitation Act of 1973, 41 C.F.R. § 60-741.28(e). See *Commonwealth Aluminum Corp.*, 59 Fed. Reg. 22178 (1994); *Blaine Constr. Co.*, 59 Fed. Reg. 17120 (1994); and *Layton Constr. Co.*, 58 Fed. Reg. 61922 (1993).

### c.  Buy American

41 U.S.C. § 8303(c) authorizes the head of a contracting agency to debar a contractor from receiving future construction contracts for violations of the Buy American Act in performing construction contracts. See FAR 25.206(c)(4) implementing this statute.

Although Buy American Act requirements also apply to supply contracts, neither the statute nor the FAR explicitly provides for debarment for violations. However, it would appear that debarment in this area could be accomplished as a serious violation of contract terms under FAR 9.406-2(b).

### d.  Environmental Statutes

The EPA is authorized to declare facilities (not contractors) ineligible to receive contracts if they are convicted of violations of the Clean Water Act, 33 U.S.C. § 1368, and the Clean Air Act, 42 U.S.C. § 7606. These statutes are implemented by Executive Order 11738, 38 Fed. Reg. 25161 (1973), which was initially addressed in the governmentwide nonprocurement common rule (NCR), 68 Fed. Reg. 66534 (2003); the statutory requirements are now addressed in the EPA provisions under OMB's governmentwide nonprocurement debarment guidance, at 2 C.F.R. Part 1532. Part 1532 adopts the OMB governmentwide guidance, 2 C.F.R. Part 180, as the EPA policies and procedures for nonprocurement debarments and suspensions under the governing environmental statutes. The EPA rules, which supplement the general OMB guidance, explain how persons and firms will be debarred or suspended for certain criminal violations of the Clean Water Act and the Clean Air Act. EPA specifically reserves the right to suspend or debar other facilities of firms that might not fall under the mandatory suspension and debarment provisions, 2 C.F.R. § 1532.1115.

The EPA regulations 2 C.F.R. § 1532.1130 - .1135 warn contractors that they are immediately placed on the EPLS when they are convicted of a violation of the Clean Water Act and the Clean Air Act and that they will stay on the list until they have demonstrated to the debarring official "certifies that the condition giving rise to your conviction has been corrected." The prior EPA rule contained broader grounds for debarment which were upheld in *United States v. Del Monte de Puerto Rico, Inc.*, 9 E.R.C. 1495 (D.P.R. 1976); *United States v. Interlake, Inc.*, 432 F. Supp. 987 (N.D. Ill. 1977); and *United States v. United States Steel*, 10 E.R.C. 1751 (N.D. Ill. 1977). In *ITT Rayonier Inc. v. United States*, 651 F.2d 343 (5th Cir. 1981), the plaintiff contended that these opinions did not examine the legislative history of the Federal Water Pollution Control Act, which would show that EPA was denied this authority. The court deemed the issue moot and did not rule on it.

## C. Causes for Suspension

The causes for suspension are somewhat narrower than those for debarment. There are no inducement-type causes, and the procurement causes are limited to integrity issues and "serious and compelling" causes that affect the present responsibility of the contractor. However, there is considerable discretion because the test is "*suspected, upon adequate evidence*" rather than conviction or civil judgment.

FAR 9.407-2 specifies the following causes for suspension:

(a) The suspending official may suspend a contractor suspected, upon adequate evidence, of —

(1) Commission of fraud or a criminal offense in connection with (i) obtaining, (ii) attempting to obtain, or (iii) performing a public contract or subcontract;

(2) Violation of Federal or State antitrust statutes relating to the submission of offers;

(3) Commission of embezzlement, theft, forgery, bribery, falsification or destruction of records, making false statements, tax evasion, violating Federal criminal tax laws, or receiving stolen property; or

(4) Violations of the Drug-Free Workplace Act of 1988 (Public Law 100-690), as indicated by —

(i) Failure to comply with the requirements of the clause at 52.223-6, Drug-Free Workplace; or

(ii) Such a number of contractor employees convicted of violations of criminal drug statutes occurring in the workplace as to indicate that the contractor has failed to make a good faith effort to provide a drug-free workplace (see 23.504);

(5) Intentionally affixing a label bearing a "Made in America" inscription (or any inscription having the same meaning) to a product sold in or shipped to the United States or its outlying areas, when the product was not made in the United States or its outlying areas (see section 202 of the Defense Production Act (Public Law 102-558));

(6) Commission of an unfair trade practice as defined in 9.403 (see section 201 of the Defense Production Act (Pub. L. 102-558)); or

(7) Delinquent Federal taxes in an amount that exceeds $3,000. See the criteria at 9.406-2(b)(1)(v) for determination of when taxes are delinquent; or

(8) Knowing failure by a principal until 3 years after final payment on any Government contract awarded to the contractor, to timely disclose to the Government, in connection with the award, performance, or closeout of the contract or a subcontract thereunder, credible evidence of—

(i) Violation of Federal criminal law involving fraud, conflict of interest, bribery, or gratuity violations found in Title 18 of the United States Code;

(ii) Violation of the civil False Claims Act (31 U.S.C. 3729-3733); or

(iii) Significant overpayment(s) on the contract, other than overpayments resulting from contract financing payments as defined in 32.001; or

(9) Commission of any other offense indicating a lack of business integrity or business honesty that seriously and directly affects the present responsibility of a Government contractor or subcontractor.

(b) Indictment for any of the causes in paragraph (a) above constitutes adequate evidence for suspension.

(c) The suspending official may upon adequate evidence also suspend a contractor for any other cause of so serious or compelling a nature that it affects the present responsibility of a Government contractor or subcontractor.

Because suspensions may be ordered before conviction or judgment, the FAR requires that a suspension action be based upon "adequate evidence." *See Lion Raisins, Inc. v. United States,* 51 Fed. Cl. 238 (2001) (applying test to find suspension arbitrary and capricious when agency continued to award contracts to contractor *after* learning of alleged bad acts but *before* suspension). FAR 9.407-1(b)(1) provides:

Suspension is a serious action to be imposed on the basis of adequate evidence, pending the completion of investigation or legal proceedings, when it has been determined that immediate action is necessary to protect the Government's interest. In assessing the adequacy of the evidence, agencies should consider how much information is available, how credible it is given the circumstances, whether or not important allegations are corroborated, and what inferences can reasonably be drawn as a result. This assessment should include an examination of basic documents such as contracts, inspection reports, and correspondence.

FAR 9.407-2(b) indicates that an outstanding indictment for criminal conduct of the type identified in the regulations as grounds for debarment by itself constitutes "adequate evidence" of criminal conduct upon which a suspension may be based. See *James A. Merritt & Sons v. Marsh*, 791 F.2d 328 (4th Cir. 1986), and *Alexander & Alexander, Ltd.*, HUDBCA 82-727-D46, 83-1 BCA ¶ 16,229. However, the Department of Transportation has held an indictment to be a rebuttable presumption of adequate evidence, thereby shifting the burden of rebutting the adequacy of the evidence to the contractor, *Mainelli, DOT Fin. Asst. Prog.*, Dkt. No. 12, July 22, 1985. Adequate evidence has been likened to the probable cause necessary for an arrest, a search warrant, or a preliminary hearing, *Horne Bros., Inc. v. Laird*, 463 F.2d 1268 (D.C. Cir. 1972); *Kirkpatrick v. White*, 351 F. Supp. 2d 1261 (N.D. Ala. 2004); *McCoy's Super Tread, Inc.*, GSBCA 7039-S, 83-2 BCA ¶ 16,751. In *Bio-Tech Research Labs., Inc.*, HUDBCA 94-C-154-D21, Sept. 28, 1995, *Unpub.*, the HUD board defined the "adequate evidence" needed to support a suspension as a "minimal standard of proof" and as " information sufficient to support the reasonable belief that a particular act or omission has occurred." See also *United States Testing Co.*, EPADEBAR 89-0021-00, Apr. 23, 1991, *Unpub.*

Historically, GAO reviewed suspensions for arbitrary or capricious action. In *TS Generalbau GmbH*, Comp. Gen. Dec. B-246034, 92-1 CPD ¶ 189, GAO approved a suspension that was based upon "an ongoing investigation of the alleged bribery of Government employees." In *SDA Inc.*, Comp. Gen. Dec. B-253355, 93-2 CPD ¶ 132, approval was given to a suspension based upon "unrebutted, detailed allegations" of misconduct involving fraudulent real estate transactions and substantial sums of money that were contained in a civil complaint filed by the Resolution Trust Corporation (a government entity). See also *BASIX, Inc.*, Comp. Gen. Dec. B-255613, 94-1 CPD ¶ 194, where GAO approved exclusion of a company from a competition because of its suspension based upon an indictment alleging conspiracy to commit securities fraud, bank fraud, and mail fraud. In *Shinwha Elecs.*, Comp. Gen. Dec. B-290603, 2002 CPD ¶ 154, however, GAO announced that it would no longer hear challenges to agency suspension and debarment decisions:

[O]ur Office will no longer review, even under a limited standard, protests that an agency improperly suspended or debarred a contractor from receiving government contracts. Because the FAR sets forth specific procedures for both imposing and challenging a suspension or debarment action, see FAR §§ 9.406-3(b), 9.407-3(b), we conclude that the appropriate forum for resolving such disputes is with the contracting agency.

## D. Scope and Duration

Because debarments and suspensions are for the protection of the government, debarring officials have considerable discretion in tailoring their scope and duration. In certain areas, however, the regulations limit this discretion but provide for waivers or exemptions. This section discusses the government agencies that must respect debarment or suspension orders, the entities to which such orders apply, the duration of such orders, their effect during the procurement process, and the permissible activities of debarred or suspended entities.

### 1. Agencies Affected

FAR 9.406-1(c) and FAR 9.407-1(d) provide that debarments and suspensions are "effective throughout the executive branch" unless waived by the procuring agency. It is clear that these provisions make debarments and suspensions by any executive branch agency binding on all other executive branch agencies. FAR 9.404 requires the GSA to administer the internet-based Excluded Parties List System, which contains the names of all contractors that are debarred, suspended, proposed for debarment, or ineligible for contracts, as well as all entities excluded from participation in nonprocurement transactions under the "Nonprocurement Common Rule" (NCR), 2 C.F.R. Part 180. FAR 9.403 defines the NCR, giving examples of these nonprocurement transactions as "grants, cooperative agreements, scholarships, fellowships, contracts of assistance, loans, loan guarantees, subsidies, insurance, payments for specified use and donation agreements." Since FAR 9.405 precludes contracting officers from awarding contracts to any entity on this list, this "common rule" bars contracting with a broad spectrum of entities that have been excluded from participation in federal programs.

It is clear from the statutes that most inducement-type debarments are binding throughout the federal government. Debarments ordered by the Secretary of Labor under the Walsh-Healey Act, 41 U.S.C. § 6504, the Service Contract Act, 41 U.S.C. § 6706, and debarments ordered by GAO for violations of the Davis-Bacon Act, 40 U.S.C. § 276a-2(a), are mandatory for all government agencies. Listing of a facility by the EPA for violations of the Clean Air Act and the Clean Water Act generally precludes all government agencies from making award of any contract to be performed at the listed facility. The construction provisions of the Buy American Act, 41 U.S.C. § 8303(c), also apply to all agencies of the government. In contrast, equal employment debarments under Executive Order 11246 apply only to executive branch agencies. All of these inducement debarments are included on the GSA consolidated list.

Procuring agencies generally are permitted to contract with debarred or suspended firms or individuals. FAR 9.406-1(c) and FAR 9.407-1(d) provide that such waivers may be made by the agency head or the agency head's designee and must be based on "compelling reasons." The NCR similarly contemplates exceptions allowed, for example, by the head of the agency involved. See 2 C.F.R. § 180.135.

While these provisions appear to permit contracting in the face of all debarments, the only statutory provisions that explicitly grant such discretion to procuring activities are the Clean Air Act and the Clean Water Act. DFARS 209.405 contains the following guidance on the "compelling reasons" that may warrant granting an exception:

Examples of compelling reasons are —

(i) Only a debarred or suspended contractor can provide the supplies or services;

(ii) Urgency requires contracting with a debarred or suspended contractor;

(iii) The contractor and a department or agency have an agreement covering the same events that resulted in the debarment or suspension and the agreement includes the department or agency decision not to debar or suspend the contractor; or

(iv) The national defense requires continued business dealings with the debarred or suspended contractor.

## 2. Entities Covered

Debarment and suspension orders may apply to those entities sufficiently connected with the misconduct to make dealing with them detrimental to the interest of the government. Under FAR 9.406-1(a) and FAR 9.407-1(a), "contractors" are debarred or suspended. FAR 9.403 contains the following definition:

*Contractor* means any individual or other legal entity that —

(1) Directly or indirectly (e.g., through an affiliate), submits offers for or is awarded, or reasonably may be expected to submit offers for or be awarded, a Government contract, including a contract for carriage under Government or commercial bills of lading, or a subcontract under a Government contract; or

(2) Conducts business, or reasonably may be expected to conduct business, with the Government as an agent or representative of another contractor.

This definition includes affiliates of a company as well as its officers and employees. It also reaches companies for which tainted officers or employees perform work. The following discussion treats business entities separately from officers and employees.

### a. Business Entities

The government deals with a variety of types of business entities. An entity may be debarred or suspended based on the acts of its own employees or based upon its association with entities or individuals that have committed improper acts. An entity may also escape debarment or suspension if it purges itself by severing its relationship with offending individuals or entities.

FAR 9.406-1(b) deals with the breadth of the debarment with respect to business entities and permits the debarring official to include "affiliates" within the scope of the debarment:

> Debarment constitutes debarment of all divisions or other organizational elements of the contractor, unless the debarment decision is limited by its terms to specific divisions, organizational elements, or commodities. The debarring official may extend the debarment decision to include any affiliates of the contractor if they are —
>
> > (1) Specifically named; and
> >
> > (2) Given written notice of the proposed debarment and an opportunity to respond (see 9.406-3(c)).

FAR 9.403 contains the following definition of "affiliates":

> Business concerns, organizations, or individuals are affiliates of each other if, directly or indirectly, (1) either one controls or has the power to control the other, or (2) a third party controls or has the power to control both. Indicia of control include, but are not limited to, interlocking management or ownership, identity of interests among family members, shared facilities and equipment, common use of employees, or a business entity organized following the debarment, suspension, or proposed debarment of a contractor which has the same or similar management, ownership, or principal employees as the contractor that was debarred, suspended, or proposed for debarment.

One of the issues raised by these provisions is whether an entire entity should be debarred or suspended. Although FAR 9.406-1 gives broad discretion, it has been very rare for a debarment or suspension to cover less than the entire business entity. See GSA Press Release, *GSA Suspends Enron and Arthur Andersen and Former Officials*, Press Release No. 9930 (Mar. 15, 2002) (available at *www.gsa.gov*) (entire corporations suspended). Compare Air Force Press Release, *Air Force Lifts Boeing Suspension*, Press Release No. 020305 (Mar. 4, 2005) (suspension of only three business units related to bad acts) (*http://www.af.mil/pressreleases/release.asp?storyID=123009959*).

For a case narrowing the scope of a procurement debarment, see *Peter Kiewit & Sons' Co. v. U.S. Army Corps of Eng'rs*, 534 F. Supp. 1139 (D.D.C. 1982), *rev'd on other grounds*, 714 F.2d 163 (D.C. Cir. 1983), where the district court held that the contractor "should not be prevented from doing business with the United States." The court reasoned that criminal acts that had been committed by two small subsidiaries and one small division were not sufficient to exclude the balance of the organization from being awarded contracts for different types of work, given that the contractor had discharged the employees responsible for the illegal acts. The circuit did not rule on this issue but reversed on the grounds that the district court should not have taken the case until the administrative process had been completed. Compare *Dowling Group v. Williams*, Civ. Action No. 82-1775 (D.D.C. 1982), permitting debarment of all entities of a small company and agreeing with the debarring official's distinction of the *Kiewit* case on the ground that *Kiewit* was "a large corporation with over 11,000 employees."

FAR 9.406-1(b) also gives broad discretion to include affiliates in a debarment order if notice is given. Debarment of affiliates is proper to prevent circumvention of the sanctions by operating through separate entities. Normally, however, an affiliate generally would not be debarred if it was not connected in any way to the entity that committed the improper act. See 51 Comp. Gen. 65 (B-173016) (1971), affirming an agency decision not to debar an affiliate because there could have been valid reasons for the creation of the affiliate other than avoidance of the debarment. See also *Roy C. Markey*, HUDBCA 82-712-D33, 83-2 BCA ¶ 16,688, affirming the decision to debar two companies as long as they were controlled by an individual who had committed improper acts in his capacity as a sole proprietor. Even though there was no proof that they had participated in the improper acts, it was clear that these affiliates could be used to circumvent the debarment were they not included within the scope of it. See also Zucker, *The Boeing Suspension: Has Increased Consolidation Tied the United States Department of Defense's Hands*, 2004 Pub. Proc. L. Rev. 260, 271 (discussing Air Force strategy in suspending only three Boeing units); Madsen, *The Government's Debarment Process: Out-of-Step with Current Ethical Standards*, 2004 Pub. Proc. L. Rev. 252 (arguing that a "debarment system that is overly focused on individuals or narrowly drawn operational segments within a company and which too freely permits waivers for contractors with questionable business ethics contrasts sharply, and is out-of-step, with other government efforts to reform and reemphasize responsibility and accountability in corporate governance").

Affiliation depends on control, and control is a question of fact to be determined by the debarment official. For example, in *Alexandria Printing & Photo Servs.*, EBCA 285-3-83(D), 83-2 BCA ¶ 16,570, the appellant company argued that it was not an affiliate because it was a sole proprietorship under the control of Mary P., who was legally separated from Earl P. and who had filed for divorce. However, in looking at all the facts, including the facts that the wife was employed as a full-time cashier at another store, was not an experienced printer, and was subsidized in her business operations by the husband, the board found a factual basis for debarment of the appellant company on the ground of affiliation. See also *Robinson v. Cheney*, 876 F.2d 152 (D.C. Cir. 1989) (founder and owner of equitable interest was "affiliate" for purposes of debarment); *Michael C. Kantrow*, HUDBCA 95-A-109-D7, Aug. 2, 1995, *Unpub.* (affiliation where an individual who pleaded guilty to causing submission of a false change order was part owner of and exercised management authority over the affiliated company); *Detek, Inc.*, Comp. Gen. Dec. B-261678,

95-2 CPD ¶ 177 (affiliation where one entity was purchased by a key employer of the other, both shared several key management employees, and they planned to engage in a prime/subcontractor relationship); and *ABL Indus., Inc.*, Comp. Gen. Dec. B-207335, 82-2 CPD ¶ 119 (affiliation when the owner of a suspended firm transferred ownership of another firm to his wife, and that second firm used the key employees and facilities of the suspended firm). Compare *Provident Maint. Servs., Inc.*, GSBCA 7640-D, Apr. 23, 1985, *Unpub.*, where no affiliation was found even though there was friendship, joint use of office space, and previous business relationships. GAO has also upheld an agency determination that a debarred company's wholly owned subsidiary was ineligible for award where the debarred company created the affiliate after the agency debarred the parent company, *Solid Waste Servs., Inc.*, Comp. Gen. Dec. B-218445, 85-1 CPD ¶ 703.

FAR 9.406-5(c) provides that entities participating in a joint venture may be debarred for acts of the venture:

> The fraudulent, criminal, or other seriously improper conduct of one contractor participating in a joint venture or similar arrangement may be imputed to other participating contractors if the conduct occurred for or on behalf of the joint venture or similar arrangement, or with the knowledge, approval, or acquiescence of these contractors. Acceptance of the benefits derived from the conduct shall be evidence of such knowledge, approval, or acquiescence.

Generally, misconduct of an officer or employee of a business entity may result in the debarment or suspension of the entity. FAR 9.406-5(a) recognizes this fact but implicitly recognizes that there may be circumstances when such acts should not be imputed to the business entity:

> The fraudulent, criminal, or other seriously improper conduct of any officer, director, shareholder, partner, employee or other individual associated with a contractor may be imputed to the contractor when the conduct occurred in connection with the individual's performance of duties for or on behalf of the contractor, or with the contractor's knowledge, approval, or acquiescence. The contractor's acceptance of the benefits derived from the conduct shall be evidence of such knowledge, approval, or acquiescence.

Thus, a debarment probably would be improper if an employee's misconduct was totally outside the knowledge or control of the business entity.

Where the employee is an officer of the entity or exercises significant control over the entity, the acts are generally imputed to the entity. See, for example, *Robinson v. Cheney*, 876 F.2d 152 (D.C. Cir. 1989), where a company was debarred for acts of its president even though the other employees knew nothing of the acts. See also *Mikulec v. Department of the Air Force*, Civ. Action No. 84-2248 (D.D.C. 1985) (president at time of misconduct and "corporate official" at time of suspension); *Park Poly Bag Corp.*, GSBCA 5744-S, 80-2 BCA ¶ 14,600 (president, vice president, and sole shareholders); *Arun Gaind, & Gaind Assocs., Inc.*, EPADEBAR 92-0007-01, Mar. 3, 1995, *Unpub.* (president at all times); and *Hy-Tex Mktg., Inc.*, EPADEBAR 93-0217-04, Nov. 22, 1994, *Unpub.* (president, principal stockholder, and sole managerial employee). In *Joseph E. Berrigan & Berrigan, Daniel, Litchfield & Olsen*, HUDBCA 84-894-D46, July 12, 1985, *Unpub.*, a lawyer was debarred but his law firm was not because there was no evidence that the law firm was aware of the lawyer's culpable conduct or that the lawyer controlled the firm. Business entities have also been debarred because they have associated with persons who were debarred or guilty of prior misconduct. In such cases, the entity is described as an affiliate and control is required. See, for example, *Thomas P. Prickett*, GSBCA 6311-D, 82-1 BCA ¶ 15,736, where a company was debarred based on the previous debarment of its sole shareholder. Compare *Canales v. Paulson*, 2006 U.S. Dist. LEXIS 61915 (D.D.C. 2006), temporarily barring a debarment of a company based on a misdemeanor of the person forming the company. The court was persuaded that the debarment might have been improper because the conduct occurred prior to the formation of the company when its founder was a government employee. After the agency withdrew the debarment of the company, the individual's debarment was held improper because of failure of the debarring official to consider mitigating factors, *Canales v. Paulson*, 2007 U.S. Dist. LEXIS 50924 (D.D.C. 2007).

The issue of control may be mitigated by a compliance agreement between the agency and the contractor corporation facing potential suspension or debarment, if the contractor can show that the employee(s) engaged in bad acts have been removed from any control of the corporation. In *Jerry A. Costacos*, GSBCA 7547-D, Apr. 9, 1985, *Unpub.*, a company escaped debarment by showing that its debarred vice president for operations did not "control" the company because he was "walled off" from involvement in government contracts. Compare *Robinson*, where the court sustained debarment of a company where the president and sole stockholder placed the company in trust after being indicted for alleged criminal conduct. The court agreed that, in such a situation, there was not a sufficient divesting of interest.

## b. Individuals

The FAR does not directly discuss the debarment of individuals, but FAR 9.403 includes within the definition of "contractor" "any individual" who "[c]onducts business, or reasonably may be expected to conduct business, with the Government as an agent or representative of another contractor." In addition, FAR 9.406-5(b) permits imputation of acts of a contractor to any employee or other person connected to the misconduct:

> The fraudulent, criminal, or other seriously improper conduct of a contractor may be imputed to any officer, director, shareholder, partner, employee, or other individual associated with the contractor who participated in, knew of, or had reason to know of the contractor's conduct.

It can be seen that the scope of this provision is very broad. Thus, not being a contractor employee does not shield an individual from being debarred from future government contracts.

The debarment of an individual operating as a sole proprietorship was accomplished under the Federal Procurement Regulation (predecessor to the FAR) pursuant to regulations that permitted debarment of individuals. See *Dimitrious A. Mavrophilipos*, GSBCA D-5, 80-1 BCA ¶ 14,446. Under HUD regulations, individuals operating as a sole proprietorship were debarred as contractors, *Robert C. Gennaro*, HUDBCA 81-632-D37, 83-1 BCA ¶ 16,141. This result also could be proper under the current FAR. The confusion of terminology in this area is illustrated in *Charles Kirkland*, HUDBCA 80-541-D60, 82-1 BCA ¶ 15,743, where an individual was debarred for improper conduct, and a sole proprietorship and a company through which he dealt were also debarred as affiliates. See also *Edward M. Alba*, HUDBCA 83-820-D39, 84-2 BCA ¶ 17,242. In *Harold Estes*, HUDBCA 83-793-D24, 84-2 BCA ¶ 17,241, an individual was debarred for illegal acts as a subcontractor and his sole proprietorship was debarred as an affiliate.

When an individual has not been operating as a sole proprietorship but is an employee of a business entity, debarment has been based on several different theories. Under the prior HUD regulations, at former 24 C.F.R. § 24.105, employees were debarred under a broad definition of "contractor." See *Marvin B. Awaya*, HUDBCA 84-834-D6, 84-2 BCA ¶17,3200, where a housing program analyst came within the definition of contractor because he administered funds; *Nathaniel H. Armstrong, John A. Breland & Bo-rite Co.*, HUDBCA 82-687-D20, 84-3 BCA ¶ 17,634, where officers, directors, and part owners of a subcontractor came within the definition of contractor because they were indirect recipients of HUD funds; and *John F. Azzarelli*, HUDBCA 82-671-D12, 82-1 BCA ¶ 15,677, where a vice president of a company was debarred for illegal acts because he was a "contractor." See also *Facchiano Constr. Co. v. Department of Labor*, 987 F.2d 206 (3d Cir. 1993), where the court concluded that the DOL had the authority to debar "responsible officers" of a contractor but not officers who did not know of the conduct; *Janik Paving & Constr., Inc. v. Brock*, 828 F.2d 84 (2d Cir. 1987), where the court affirmed the debarment of a company's president without discussing his connection to the misconduct; and *TS Generalbau GmbH*, Comp. Gen. Dec. B-246034, 92-1 CPD ¶ 189, where GAO approved a DOD suspension of "an individual authorized to sign contracts" by imputing the contractor's misconduct (bribery) to the individual. Compare *John R. Morris*, HUDBCA 84-836-D8, 84-2 BCA ¶ 17,245, where the government did not prove that a maintenance man was a contractor. Under the predecessor regulation, the FPR, which provided for debarment of individuals, the corporation's president and vice president who participated in the illegal conduct were suspended, *Park Poly Bag Corp.*, GSBCA 5744-S, 80-2 BCA ¶ 14,600.

Under the FAR standard, individuals can be debarred if they "participated in, knew of or had reason to know" of the contractor's misconduct, FAR 9.406-5(b).

See *American Floor Consultants & Installations, Inc. v. United States,* 70 Fed. Cl. 235 (2006) (controlling individuals and affiliates reached by debarment order); *WEDJ/Three C's, Inc. v. Department of Def.*, 2006 U.S. Dist. LEXIS 50363 (M.D. Pa. 2006) (violation of contractor imputed to president and owner, contract administrator and project engineer); *Glazer Constr. Co. v. United States,* 52 Fed. Cl. 513 (2002) (violations of contractor imputed to senior employee with knowledge); *Kisser v. Cisneros*, 14 F.3d 615 (D.C. Cir. 1994) (debarment of executive vice president who had participated in the alleged misconduct sustained, rejecting the argument that the debarring agency was required to explain why all officers and employees who participated in the conduct were not similarly debarred). Compare *Alf v. Donley*, 666 F. Supp. 2d 60 (D.D.C. 2009) (debarment of CEO of company enjoined because debarring official did not consider all evidence in the record and imputing knowledge of offenses merely because official was CEO was improper (relying on *Novicki*)); *Impresa Construzioni Geom. Domenico Garufi v. United States*, 238 F.3d 1324 (Fed. Cir. 2001) ("past criminal activities by a corporate officer do not automatically establish that the bidder fails the responsibility requirement"); *Novicki v. Cook*, 946 F.2d 938 (D.C. Cir. 1991) (debarment of the president and CEO of a contractor vacated because there was inadequate proof of "reason to know" of the misconduct, and the agency may have erroneously applied a strict liability or "should have known" standard to the individual's conduct); *Caiola v. Carroll*, 851 F.2d 395 (D.C. Cir. 1988) (debarment of two company officers that was based on the "reason to know" standard overturned when the agency could not explain why it had terminated debarment proceedings against a third officer, seemingly in similar circumstances). See also *Taylor v. Marsh*, Civ. Action No. 81-2643 (D.D.C. 1982), where an officer and 50% shareholder was debarred under the DAR based upon her own negligence, and *Mikulec v. Department of the Air Force*, Civ. Action No. 84-2248 (D.D.C. 1985), where the president of a company was suspended following an indictment.

### 3.  *Duration of Orders*

Debarment orders are normally for a specified fixed period of time, while suspension orders are for an indefinite but limited period.

### a.  *Debarment Orders*

FAR 9.406-4 contains the following provision concerning the duration of procurement debarment:

(a)(1) Debarment shall be for a period commensurate with the seriousness of the cause(s). Generally, debarment should not exceed 3 years, except that —

(i) Debarment for violation of the provisions of the Drug-Free Workplace Act of 1988 (see 23.506) may be for a period not to exceed 5 years; and

(ii) Debarments under 9.406-2(b)(2) shall be for one year unless extended pursuant to paragraph (b) of this subsection.

(2) If suspension precedes a debarment, the suspension period shall be considered in determining the debarment period.

(b) The debarring official may extend the debarment for an additional period, if that official determines that an extension is necessary to protect the Government's interest. However, a debarment may not be extended solely on the basis of the facts and circumstances upon which the initial debarment action was based. Debarments under 9.406-2(b)(2) may be extended for additional periods of one year if the Secretary of Homeland Security or the Attorney General determines that the contractor continues to be in violation of the employment provisions of the Immigration and Nationality Act. If debarment for an additional period is determined to be necessary, the procedures of 9.406-3 shall be followed to extend the debarment.

(c) The debarring official may reduce the period or extent of debarment, upon the contractor's request, supported by documentation, for reasons such as —

(1) Newly discovered material evidence;

(2) Reversal of the conviction or civil judgment upon which the debarment was based;

(3) Bona fide change in ownership or management;

(4) Elimination of other causes for which the debarment was imposed; or

(5) Other reasons the debarring official deems appropriate.

FAR 9.406-1(a) requires the debarring official to consider "the seriousness of the contractor's acts or omissions and any remedial measures or mitigating factors" in making the debarment decision. See *Glazer Constr. Co. v. United States,* 50 F. Supp. 2d 85 (D. Mass. 1999), questioning the finding that a contractor had "willfully" violated the Buy American Act but sustaining the debarment based on the fact of the violation. Compare *Watts-Healy Tibbitts A JV v. United States,* 84 Fed. Cl. 253 (2008), agreeing that a contracting officer properly considered corrective measures and mitigating factors in declaring responsible a contractor that had been guilty of bid-rigging.

These issues are also considered in determining the period of a debarment. See *Thomas M. Zakucia,* HUDBCA 79-348-D7, Dec. 3, 1979, *Unpub.*, where a proposed debarment of five years for taking illegal kickbacks was reduced to 30 months where there was no evidence that the individual had acted improperly in the intervening six years since the conviction, and he was remorseful for his criminal activities. Similarly, in *Normal D. Wilhelm,* HUDBCA 82-679-D15, 82-2 BCA ¶ 16,002, the board reduced a debarment period based on a corporate president's conviction for bid rigging because it was convinced he had partially reformed. A "nominal period of debarment" was still necessary, however, because the president did not seem to understand why collusive bidding was illegal, because he did not sufficiently alter the operations of the firm, and because he retained individuals formerly involved in the crime. In *Bruce E. Betterton*, EPADEBAR 93-0217-02, Apr. 25, 1995, *Unpub.*, mitigating circumstances, including lesser culpability for the offenses and cooperation with investigating officials, persuaded the board to reduce the debarment to a two-year period including the suspension period. In *Ellis "Ray" Kiser*, EPADEBAR 93-0253-01, Nov. 2, 1995, *Unpub.*, a three-year debarment of the CEO and owner of a contractor that had improperly disposed of asbestos was reduced to two years after considering the owner's one-year preliminary exclusion under the FAR, the seriousness of the misconduct, the fact that the present facility contained no asbestos, and information presented as mitigating factors and remedial measures. See also *James J. Wannamacher*, HUDBCA 81-585-D14, 82-1 BCA ¶ 15,474, where the board stated that the contractor's conviction for submission of a false certification, based on a plea of nolo contendere, along with extensive evidence showing the violation to be of a continuing pattern and practice, would normally warrant the imposition of a substantial period of debarment. However, only a one-year debarment was imposed because the term was all the agency had sought. In *Shane Meat Co. v. Department of Def.*, 800 F.2d 334 (3d Cir. 1986), the court affirmed a three-year debarment based on the failure of the contractor to ensure that delivery of defective products would not be repeated by changing its senior officers. The court held that the debarring official was reasonable in reaching this conclusion even though the contractor had a record of satisfactory performance for the five years subsequent to the illegal conduct. In *Sidney Spiegal*, HUDBCA 91-5908, 93-1 BCA ¶ 25,294, the board held that the fact that bid rigging was a regular practice in public real estate auctions in the District of Columbia did not excuse or mitigate the practice and should not be used to reduce an individual's three-year debarment.

Debarments for periods longer than three years have been affirmed when the causes for the actions have been egregious. See *Coccia v. Defense Logistics Agency*, Civ. Action No. 89-6544 (E.D. Pa. 1992), where the court affirmed the DLA's debarment of an individual for 15 years because, acting as a procurement official, he had seriously corrupted the procurement system by taking bribes in exchange for procurement information. The court agreed with the judgment of the debarring official that the evidence did not demonstrate that the individual could deal honestly with the government within the 15-year period. See also *Martin Dale Jeffus*, 2003 EPADEBAR 4, Aug. 14, 2003, debarring an official of a company for 10 years. It appears, however, that long debarments will be carefully scrutinized. See, for example, *Lake Doctors, Inc.*, EPADEBAR 93-0133-00, Aug. 8, 1995, *Unpub.*, where a five-year debarment for using pesticides in a manner inconsistent with their labeling was reduced to a four-year period with full credit for the period of suspension, due to the presence of mitigating and remedial measures. See also *William R. Absalom*, HUDBCA 82-746-D45, 83-1 BCA ¶ 16,390, where, even though the appellant's mitigating factors were unpersuasive, the board reduced the period of debarment from five to three years because the government's evidence did not support the longer period for the contractor's false statements made to HUD.

The FAR does not specifically address the permissibility of debarments for indefinite periods. However, under the prior HUD regulations, a few such debarments were ordered in exceptional cases. In *Don L. Blankenship*, HUDBCA 81-547-D3, Mar. 27, 1981, *Unpub.*, the board imposed debarment for an indefinite period of time because the firm willfully violated the terms of a prior debarment settlement agreement; in 1993, the board declined to reinstate Blankenship because his conduct "remains unexplained, uncorrected and unrepented," *Don Louis Blankenship*, HUDBCA 93-C-D15, June 29, 1993, *Unpub.* In *Charles Kirkland*, HUDBCA 80-541-D60, 82-1 BCA ¶ 15,743, an individual who procured two false certifications, breached his fiduciary obligations as a broker to the parties in a HUD-assisted transaction, and willfully violated HUD regulations and procedures displayed a course of conduct "so fraught with improprieties" that debarment "for an indefinite period of not less than five years" was imposed. Some years later, in *Charles Kirkland*, HUDBCA 90-5285-D57, Jan. 14, 1991, *Unpub.*, the HUD board, after comparing Kirkland's sanctions to those imposed for similar violations, granted his request for reinstatement and ordered the debarment terminated immediately. See also *Charles Howell*, HUDBCA 85-933-D17, Sept. 13, 1985, *Unpub.*, where the board reversed an indefinite debarment imposed five-and-one-half years earlier, on the basis of newly discovered material evidence that the conduct that gave rise to the debarment was neither egregious nor willful. In *Joseph A. Strauss, The Phoenix Assocs., Ltd.*, HUDBCA 95-G-113-D11, May 19, 1995, *Unpub.*, the board considered an imposing list of mitigating factors and changed an indefinite debarment to a five-year debarment with credit given for the period of suspension; in *Philip D. Winn*, HUDBCA 95-G-108-D6, June 9, 1995, *Unpub.*, an indefinite debarment was changed to a four-year debarment.

FAR 9.406-4(b) and (c) provide guidance on extending the period of debarment. See *Lasmer Indus., Inc. v. Defense Supply Ctr. Columbus*, 2008 U.S.Dist. LEXIS 51460 (S.D. Ohio 2008), where the court took limited jurisdiction of a request to enjoin such an extension. The agency had given notice of an extended debarment because the contractor continued to accept contracts during the period it was debarred. In *S.A.F.E. Export Corp.*, 65 Comp. Gen. 530 (B-222308), 86-1 CPD ¶ 413, GAO permitted the extension of an earlier debarment based on continued lack of integrity by the company in subsequent business dealings.

FAR 9.406-4(a)(2) provides that debarring officials shall give consideration to a preceding period of suspension in determining the period of debarment. Under prior regulations, the board, in *Park Poly Bag Corp.*, GSBCA 5826-D, Mar. 9, 1981, *Unpub.*, held that setting a debarment period without considering a preceding period of suspension was arbitrary and capricious. See *Thomas P. Prickett*, GSBCA 6311-D, 82-1 BCA ¶ 15,736, remanding a case to the debarring official to consider adjusting the debarment period. Although the HUD regulations did not contain such a provision, the HUD Board of Contract Appeals followed this practice, *Curtis Jerome Kennedy*, HUDBCA 78-319-D49, 79-2 BCA ¶ 13,896; *Thomas M. Zakucia*, HUDBCA 79-348-D7, Dec. 3, 1979, *Unpub.* See also *Bradley Shane Hartman*, HUDBCA 93-0133-10, Oct. 11, 1995, *Unpub.*, where the board, after considering the record, agreed to a two-and-one-half-year debarment "with full credit for the period of suspension." Compare, however, *Andrew Nuccitelli*, HUDBCA 78-321-D51, July 17, 1979, *Unpub.*, where the board refused to reduce the debarment period by the period of suspension because of the particularly egregious nature of the contractor's activities and the absence of mitigating factors. In *Arun Gaind, & Gaind Assocs., Inc.*, EPADEBAR 92-0007-01, Mar. 3, 1995, *Unpub.*, the board, after considering limited mitigating factors and finding that the original violations were egregious, sustained the refusal to "give credit" for Gaind's 33-month suspension in imposing a three-year debarment.

The duration of inducement debarments is controlled primarily by the statute or regulations establishing the debarment. For example, the Davis-Bacon Act specifies a three-year period of debarment for firms found to be in violation of the statute, 40 U.S.C. § 276a-2(a). While the Walsh-Healey Act, 41 U.S.C. § 6504, and the Service Contract Act of 1965, 41 U.S.C. § 6706, also specify a three-year debarment period, the Secretary of Labor has discretion to impose a shorter-term or no debarment. The Buy American Act, 41 U.S.C. § 8303(c), also specifies a three-year period. In *J.B. Kies Constr. Co.*, Comp. Gen. Dec. B-250797, 93-1 CPD ¶ 127, the company was debarred for five and one-half years because the debarment was effective for three years after date of publication of the list of ineligible firms, and the company's name was not included on the list until two and one-half years after it was debarred.

In contrast, facilities listed for noncompliance with the Clean Water Act and the Clear Air Act will remain on the list until compliance is demonstrated. EPA regulations at 2 C.F.R. § 1532.1205 state that a written petition to reinstate the eligibility of a facility may be submitted to the EPA debarring official. The petitioner bears the burden of providing sufficient information and documentation to establish, by a preponderance of the evidence, that the condition giving rise to the ineligibility finding has been corrected.

Section 209(a)(6) of Executive Order 11246 also provides that the Secretary of Labor may debar a firm " until such contractor has satisfied the Secretary of Labor that such contractor has established and will carry out personnel and employment policies in compliance with the provisions of this order." Thus, 41 C.F.R. § 60-1.27 permits debarments for an indefinite period. Firms declared ineligible may be entitled to reinstatement upon submitting proof that "they have established and will carry out employment policies and practices in compliance with the Order and implementing regulations (the equal opportunity clause)," 41 C.F.R. § 60-1.31.

Debarring officials may not have as much discretion to reduce the duration of all inducement debarments. See *Mashburn Elec. Co.*, Comp. Gen. Dec. B-189471,

78-1 CPD ¶ 277, where GAO stated that while the duration of debarments under the Walsh-Healey Act and Service Contract Act could be reduced, there was no similar authority to reduce the duration of a debarment under the Davis-Bacon Act. See 29 C.F.R. § 5.12(c), stating that firms shall be removed from the ineligible bidders list upon demonstrating current responsibility to comply with the labor standards of the applicable statutes.

### b.  Suspension Orders

FAR 9.407-4 gives specific guidance on the duration of suspension orders:

(a) Suspension shall be for a temporary period pending the completion of investigation and any ensuing legal proceedings, unless sooner terminated by the suspending official or as provided in this subsection.

(b) If legal proceedings are not initiated within 12 months after the date of the suspension notice, the suspension shall be terminated unless an Assistant Attorney General requests its extension, in which case it may be extended for an additional 6 months. In no event may a suspension extend beyond 18 months, unless legal proceedings have been initiated within that period.

(c) The suspending official shall notify the Department of Justice of the proposed termination of the suspension, at least 30 days before the 12-month period expires, to give that Department an opportunity to request an extension.

The regulation was promulgated in response to *Horne Bros., Inc. v. Laird*, 463 F.2d 1268 (D.C. Cir. 1972), where the court criticized an indefinite suspension. The regulation, however, provides for suspension as long as a criminal proceeding is actively being conducted without regard to the total length of the suspension. For instance, in *BASIX, Inc.*, Comp. Gen. Dec. B-255613, 94-1 CPD ¶ 194, the suspension remained in effect "pending resolution of the indictment" of the contractor's CEO. Similarly, in *MetaTRACE, Inc.*, EPADEBAR 90-0001-00, Aug 30, 1990, *Unpub.*, the suspension remained in effect "pending completion of investigation or ensuing proceedings, including debarment action." There is some question as to whether this complies with the spirit of the *Horne Brothers* decision. In *U.S. Testing Co.*, EPADEBAR 89-0021-00, Apr. 23, 1991, *Unpub.*, the board, after concluding that additional information evidenced "an altered corporate culture as well as organizational and procedural changes," ordered the company's suspension terminated.

## 4.  Effect of Listing

FAR 9.405(a) precludes the award of contracts or the solicitation of offers from contractors that are debarred, suspended, or proposed for debarment. FAR 9.405(b) refers contracting officers to the EPLS, issued by the GSA, to determine which contractors are subject to this requirement. However, contractors on the list might submit bids or proposals, even if listed. Thus, FAR 9.405(d) contains the following procedures to ensure that the government does not deal with listed contractors:

(1) After the opening of bids or receipt of proposals, the contracting officer shall review the EPLS.

(2) Bids received from any listed contractor in response to an invitation for bids shall be entered on the abstract of bids, and rejected unless the agency head determines in writing that there is a compelling reason to consider the bid.

(3) Proposals, quotations, or offers received from any listed contractor shall not be evaluated for award or included in the competitive range, nor shall discussions be conducted with a listed offeror during a period of ineligibility, unless the agency head determines, in writing, that there is a compelling reason to do so. If the period of ineligibility expires or is terminated prior to award, the contracting officer may, but is not required to, consider such proposals, quotations, or offers.

(4) Immediately prior to award, the contracting officer shall again review the EPLS to ensure that no award is made to a listed contractor.

Contracting officers have been permitted to refuse to deal with companies that are closely related to companies on the EPLS. For example, in *Bilfinger Berger AG Sede Secondaria Italiana*, Comp. Gen. Dec. B-402496, 2010 CPD ¶ 125, the protester was properly declared nonresponsible because the contracting officer believed that a debarred firm to which it was closely related would perform part of the work. GAO concluded that the contracting officer had properly rejected the firm's representation that it would not use the debarred firm. The Court of Federal Claims reached the opposite conclusion in *Bilfinger Berger AG Sede Secondaria Italiana v. United States*, 389 Fed. Cl. 94 (2010). See also *Aardvark Keith Moving, Inc.*, Comp. Gen. Dec. B-290565, 2002 CPD ¶ 134, where a contracting officer properly rejected the proposal of a firm because it was affiliated with a firm that was proposed for debarment. The contracting officer had reached this conclusion from information submitted with the proposal and a Dun & Bradstreet report— which GAO found sound evidence even though the protester submitted evidence in the protest that there was no affiliation.

This regulation gives the contracting officer considerable discretion in deciding whether to reinstate an offeror if a debarment or suspension is lifted during the competition. See *FAS Support Servs., LLC*, 93 Fed. Cl. 687 (2010), and *FAS Support Servs., LLC*, Comp. Gen. Dec. B-402464, 2010 CPD ¶ 105, finding no abuse of discretion when a contracting officer did not reinstate such an offeror because he determined that there was little likelihood that it could win the competition and reinstatement would have delayed the procurement. Under prior similar regulations, it was held that a contracting officer could properly refuse to award a contract to a bidder that had been proposed for debarment at the time of bid opening but had settled the issues (ending the debarment proceedings) at the time of award, *Instruments by*

*Precision Ltd.*, Comp. Gen. Dec. B-235339, 89-2 CPD ¶ 138. Compare *Tracor Applied Sci., Inc.*, Comp. Gen. Dec. B-221230.2, 86-1 CPD ¶ 189, holding that a contracting officer had discretion to award to a firm that was suspended or debarred at the time the offer was submitted, so long as it was not ineligible at the time of award, or to deny award even if the suspension or debarment was being reconsidered at the time of evaluation.

The FAR gives the contracting officer discretion to award to an offeror on the EPLS when there is a "compelling reason," but it appears that agencies may be reluctant to find such compelling reasons. See *J.B. Kies Constr. Co.*, Comp. Gen. Dec. B-250797, 93-1 CPD ¶ 127, affirming a finding of no compelling reason where the bids were opened two days before the debarment ended and the debarment had been delayed for over two years because of "administrative oversight." In *TS Generalbau GmbH*, Comp. Gen. Dec. B-246034, 92-1 CPD ¶ 189, GAO rejected the argument that the contractor had been arbitrarily suspended "just days before the bid opening and contract award," and in *Baxter Healthcare Corp.*, Comp. Gen. Dec. B-253455.3, 94-1 CPD ¶ 301, the protester was found ineligible for award where its suspension was not lifted until the afternoon after award and the contracting officer did not know that the suspension was about to end.

Contracting officers must be diligent in determining the status of offerors. See *R.J. Crowley, Inc.*, Comp. Gen. Dec. B-253783, 93-2 CPD ¶ 257, where GAO sustained a protest when the contracting officer had checked the latest monthly list but had not reviewed the electronic update, and the "monthly" list was several months out of date.

One contractor was found to have standing to bring a suit to have its name removed for the EPLS archive, *Hickey v. Chadick*, 649 F. Supp. 2d 770 (S.D. Ohio 2009). The court concluded that contracting officers might use the archive to determine that the contractor was nonresponsible. For a description of the multiple efforts of this contractor to overcome the impact of a debarment, see *Lasmer Indus., Inc v. AM Gen., LLC*, 741 F. Supp. 2d 829 (S.D. Ohio 2010) (statute of limitations barred suit against competitor that allegedly gave agency false information leading to the debarment).

## 5. Permissible Activities

While debarment and suspension are government-wide, they do not bar entities from all activities related to government contracting. Some inducement debarments are limited to a certain type of activity. Further, debarments and suspensions do not necessarily affect existing contracts or subcontracting activities.

### a. Limited Debarments

Some inducement debarments are limited in nature. For example, a Buy American Act debarment under 41 U.S.C. § 8303(c) extends to contracts for construction, alterations, or repairs of public buildings or public works. The statute is silent as to other types of work. In debarments under the Clean Air Act and the Clean Water Act, debarments apply only to a "facility."

## b. Existing Contracts

FAR 9.405-1 provides guidance on whether current contracts are to be continued:

(a) Notwithstanding the debarment, suspension, or proposed debarment of a contractor, agencies may continue contracts or subcontracts in existence at the time the contractor was debarred, suspended, or proposed for debarment unless the agency head directs otherwise. A decision as to the type of termination action, if any, to be taken should be made only after review by agency contracting and technical personnel and by counsel to ensure the propriety of the proposed action.

(b) For contractors debarred, suspended, or proposed for debarment, unless the agency head makes a written determination of the compelling reasons for doing so, ordering activities shall not —

(1) Place orders exceeding the guaranteed minimum under indefinite quantity contracts;

(2) Place orders under optional use Federal Supply Schedule contracts, blanket purchase agreements, or basic ordering agreements; or

(3) Add new work, exercise options, or otherwise extend the duration of current contracts or orders.

General Services Administration regulations provide that termination for default is appropriate if the circumstances giving rise to the debarment or suspension also constitute a default in performance under the contract. If the debarment is based on reasons unrelated to performance, default termination is inappropriate. However, termination for convenience or cancellation is authorized if "the contractor presents a significant risk to the Government in completing a current contract," GSAR 509.405-1(a). See *Integrated Sys. Group, Inc. v. Department of the Army*, GSBCA 12613-P, 94-2 BCA ¶ 26,618, where the board approved the convenience termination of a contractor that had been proposed for debarment. There is no special DoD regulatory provision on the effect of debarment on termination of current contracts, although DFARS 209.405-1, as with FAR 9.405-1, warns against placing orders in excess of the minimum amount on an indefinite quantity contract, or against Federal Supply Schedule contracts. This regulation also states that "[t]his includes the exercise of options."

## c. Subcontracts

FAR 9.405-2(a) provides that contracting officers may not consent to subcontracts "subject to consent" under FAR Subpart 44.2. FAR 9.409 requires the inclusion of the Protecting the Government's Interests When Subcontracting with Contractors Debarred, Suspended or Proposed for Debarment clause at FAR 52.209-6 in all contracts with a value exceeding $30,000. Paragraph (b) of this clause provides:

> Other than a subcontract for a commercially available off-the-shelf item, the Contractor shall not enter into any subcontract, in excess of $ 30,000 with a Contractor that is debarred, suspended, or proposed for debarment by any executive agency unless there is a compelling reason to do so.

Paragraph (d) of this clause requires notification of the contracting officer prior to the award of any subcontract to a listed subcontractor.

The pre-2010 FAR was silent as to the eligibility of debarred firms for subcontracts where the contract did not require approval of the subcontractor selected by the contractor. See 51 Comp. Gen. 65 (B-173016) (1971), where GAO stated that debarment did not preclude the sale of products to the government through a distributor. See also Comp. Gen. Dec. B-149781, Oct. 29, 1962, *Unpub.*, where GAO precluded the nonresponsibility determination of a contractor planning to use a debarred subcontractor. Even under the prior regulations on this issue, however, a contractor ran the risk of being declared nonresponsible if significant purchases were made from debarred or suspended subcontractors. Thus, the proposed use of a debarred subcontractor was considered partially relevant to the determination of responsibility of a contractor in *Medical Devices of Fall River, Inc.*, Comp. Gen. Dec. B-232336, 88-2 CPD ¶ 247, and *Nuclear Supply & Serv. Co.*, Comp. Gen. Dec. B-151543, Jan. 17, 1964, *Unpub.*

Some inducement debarments have always covered subcontractors. It seems clear under EPA regulations that agencies may not award contracts where part of the performance would take place in a subcontractor facility that has been listed for violation of the Clean Air Act or the Clean Water Act. See 2 C.F.R. § 1532.220.

## E. Debarment and Suspension Procedures

This section considers the debarment and suspension procedures employed by the various contracting agencies and discusses the procedural due process requirements in debarment and suspension actions. Because suspension and debarment of a firm is quite serious and may even be fatal, the courts have recognized that certain due process protections must be afforded before these measures are invoked. See FAR 9.406-3(b) and FAR 9.407-3(b), stating that agencies shall establish procedures governing the debarment and suspension decision-making process that are "as informal as is practicable, consistent with principles of fundamental fairness." Executive Order 12549 created a set of procedural "Common Rules" that retained the due process structure outlined in FAR 9.406-3(b) and FAR 9.407-3(b). The final guidelines were accepted, with certain modifications, by 28 administrative agencies, including the EPA, HUD, and the DOE, 53 Fed. Reg. 19161 (1988).

The governmentwide Nonprocurement Common Rule (NCR), was updated by the member agencies in 2003, 68 Fed. Reg. 66534. On May 11, 2004, 69 Fed. Reg. 26,276, OMB established a new title 2 of the Code of Federal Regulations, which is comprised of two subtitles. Subtitle A, entitled "Government-wide Grants and Agreements," contains OMB policy guidance to Federal agencies on grants and agreements. Part 180 of that Subtitle sets forth the OMB Guidelines to agencies (the NCR) on governmentwide debarment and suspension, regarding nonprocurement actions. Subtitle B, entitled "Federal Agency Regulations for Grants and Agreements," contains the regulations of Federal agencies implementing the OMB guidance, as those regulations apply to grants and other financial assistance agreements and nonprocurement transactions. The FAR procedures and the NCR procedures are, by design, closely parallel.

## 1.  Notice

An agency is not required to provide notice that it is contemplating the suspension of a contractor. Many small contractors receive the notice that they have been proposed for debarment or are suspended after they have been included on the EPLS. Large contractors generally overcome the lack of a notice requirement by tracking investigative actions so that they can present their arguments before they are place on the EPLS.

### a.  Referral and Investigation

FAR 9.406-3(a) requires agencies to establish "procedures for the prompt reporting, investigation, and referral to the debarring official of matters appropriate for that official's consideration." Usually, suspension and debarment actions are initiated upon receipt by the agency of information of an indictment or conviction. Suspension and debarring officials receive indictment and conviction notice from U.S. Attorneys' offices, Inspector General offices, and other government investigative organizations, as well as such sources as newspaper articles, competitors, and qui tam relators. However, any employee of an agency can refer a matter to the debarring official.

### b.  No Presuspension Notice

No notice of contemplated proceedings is required. Although there have been initiatives to require such notice, agencies have resisted. While there may be valid arguments that lack of advance notice of suspension or proposed debarment violates due process, the courts have not yet reached this conclusion. In *Shermco Indus., Inc. v. Secretary of the Air Force*, 584 F. Supp. 76 (N.D. Tex. 1984), the court observed at 88:

> Whether notice given a suspended contractor is sufficient depends on several considerations. The first is whether timing of the notice allowed meaningful opportunity to rebut the charges. Two recent Court of Appeals decisions seem to impose

different due process requirements for the timing of notice of a suspension. In *Transco [Security, Inc. v. Freeman*, 639 F.2d 318, 323 (6th Cir.), *cert. denied*, 454 U.S. 820 (1981)], the contractor received no notice until after the suspension. Although the Sixth Circuit discussed whether the notice there involved was constitutionally infirm due to vagueness and the inconsistent explanations given by the agency for its decision to suspend, the court gave no indication that notice, to be constitutionally sufficient, had to be given before suspension.

On the other hand, in *Old Dominion Dairy Products, Inc. v. Secretary of Defense*, 631 F.2d 953 (D.C. Cir. 1980), the D.C. Circuit held that a contractor was denied due process when it was not told, before two non-responsibility determinations, that it was under investigation and, after the determinations, was told only that they were based on the lack of a " satisfactory record of integrity."

\* \* \*

Under the circumstances of this case, the constructive notice provided to Shermco, by way of a draft of the proposed indictment against it, was constitutionally sufficient. This draft indictment was delivered to Shermco several months before suspension proceedings were instituted; it sufficiently informed Shermco of the existence of an investigation and the substance of the charges against it.

This same issue arises with the listing of contractors that are proposed for debarment—the notice is received after they are included on the list.

Some agencies have adopted the practice of sending an informal notice, commonly known as a "shock and alarm" letter. This letter informs the recipient that suspension is contemplated but that the respondent is being afforded a presuspension opportunity to submit information in opposition to the proposed suspension.

While agencies reject any notion that presuspension notice is required, they generally will allow a contractor the opportunity to present matters of present responsibility prior to suspension if the contractor so requests and if a timely meeting can be scheduled. Thus, a contractor that knows an indictment or suspension is imminent is well advised to request an opportunity to present information and argument before any action by the agency is taken. From the agency's perspective, early notice and negotiations increase the chances that the matter will be resolved through compliance efforts, rather than sanctions and potential litigation.

The procedures for such preventive communication vary with each agency. For example, the DoD has incorporated a particular avenue of communication into its acquisition regulations, stating at DFARS 209.402, App. H-103:

A contractor who becomes aware of a pending indictment or allegations of wrongdoing that the contractor believes may lead to a suspension or debarment action may contact that debarring and suspending official or designee to provide information as to the contractor's present responsibility.

This communication may take the form of appealing to the agency's pragmatism. For instance, the contractor may argue to the agency that it would be against its interest to begin debarment procedures because debarment or listing will disrupt the flow of a product that is indispensable to the government or will affect future procurements that have few competitors.

If the contractor is successful in proving its responsibility to the agency's satisfaction, the result is usually described in a settlement or compliance agreement. This document sets forth the findings of the informal communications between the parties and the terms upon which the finding of responsibility has been conditioned. Such administrative agreements are made public by posting on the online Federal Awardee Performance and Integrity Information System (FAPIIS), FAR 9.406-3(f) (1) (debarment); FAR 9.407-3(e)(1) (suspension). In the event that this exchange does not prevent a debarment, early recognition of the problem will accelerate the fact-finding and hearing process and result in the removal of the contractor's name from the proposed debarment list with as little damage as possible (assuming, of course, that the proposed debarment is unsuccessful).

## c.  Notice of Suspension or Notice of Proposed Debarment

Contractors must be given notice of the grounds upon which suspension and debarment actions are based, FAR 9.406-3(c) (proposed debarment); FAR 9.407-3(c) (suspension); NCR § 180.615. However, as stated above, once a contractor receives notice that it has been proposed for debarment or suspension, it is already included on the EPLS, FAR 9.404. In *Horne Bros., Inc. v. Laird*, 463 F.2d 1268 (D.C. Cir. 1972), the court concluded that a contractor could not be subjected to a "protracted suspension" without being given "some specific notice" of the charges upon which the suspension was based. In *Transco Sec., Inc. v. Freeman*, 639 F.2d 318 (6th Cir. 1981), the court overturned the suspension of a contractor suspected of fraud in obtaining a government contract since the agency had failed to give adequate notice of the charges, stating at 323:

> The general notice which appellants received did not permit adequate preparation for participation in a meaningful way in any forthcoming hearing or equivalent proceeding. Appellants were suspended for, among other things, "billing irregularities." At the time this information was received, appellants had performed a number of contracts for the GSA over several years at various locations. Appellants were not told to which of these contracts the "billing irregularities" referred. Without further identifying information of at least the contract involved, and approximate date of misbillings, it would be at best onerous and at worst virtually impossible to effectively gather and present relevant information refuting this general charge.

See also *ATL, Inc. v. United States*, 736 F.2d 677 (Fed. Cir. 1984), requiring notice "sufficiently specific to permit the suspended contractor to collect and present relevant evidence refuting the charges," and *Electro-Methods, Inc. v. United States*, 728 F.2d 1471 (Fed. Cir. 1984), finding adequate notice where the contractor had been provided and in fact rebutted all the evidence considered by the suspension authority. In *SDA Inc.*, Comp. Gen. Dec. B-253355, 93-2 CPD ¶ 132, GAO found sufficient notice where a contractor had been suspended on the basis of detailed, unrebutted allegations of misconduct contained in a civil complaint filed by the federal government. See also *Reeve Aleutian Airways, Inc. v. United States*, 982 F.2d 594 (D.C. Cir. 1993), where the court found sufficient notice in a letter referring to an adverse report on the contractor's performance.

FAR 9.406-3(c) requires that contractors and "specifically named affiliates" be given advance notification of proposed debarment actions as well as at least a general statement of the reasons for the proposed debarment. See *S.A.F.E. Export Corp.*, Comp. Gen. Dec. B-222308.2, 86-2 CPD ¶ 44, where GAO found adequate notice to an unnamed affiliate because the principal officer of the affiliate and the principal company received actual notice. With respect to suspension actions, the regulations provide for notice *immediately after* the suspension has been invoked, FAR 9.407-3(c).

### d.  Designation of Lead Agency

Because contractors often do business with various government agencies, more than one agency may have an interest in suspension or debarment of an entity. FAR 9.402(d) provides for the designation of a lead agency as follows:

> When more than one agency has an interest in the debarment or suspension of a contractor, the Interagency Committee on Debarment and Suspension, established under Executive Order 12549, and authorized by Section 873 of the National Defense Authorization Act for Fiscal year 2009 (Pub. L. 110-417), shall resolve the lead agency issue and coordinate such resolution among all interested agencies prior to the initiation of any suspension, debarment, or related administrative action by any agency.

See also NCR § 180.620 The procedures for designating the lead agency are informal. Where a contractor is known to have involvement with more than one agency, the agencies consult with one another to determine which agency will handle the matter. Often, the agency with which the contractor does the most business (based on dollar value of contracts and subcontracts) is designated the lead agency. However, there may be extenuating circumstances where there is an overriding interest in another agency being the lead agency. For example, the EPA may take the lead for cases involving violations of the environmental laws.

### 2.  Presentation of Matters in Opposition

Basic fairness in debarment proceedings requires that a party be given an "opportunity to present evidence," *Gonzales v. Freeman*, 118 U.S. App. D.C. 180, 334 F.2d 570

(D.C. Cir. 1964). Moreover, after a reasonable period of time following imposition of a suspension, the firm may be entitled to a "hearing" involving at least an opportunity to refute the basis for the suspension, unless a hearing would be inappropriate for reasons of national security or would prejudice a pending or imminent criminal prosecution of the firm, *Horne Bros., Inc. v. Laird*, 463 F.2d 1268 (D.C. Cir. 1972).

## a.  Opportunity to Be Heard in Opposition

FAR 9.406-3(b)(1) and FAR 9.407-3(b)(1) contain the minimal guidance that debarment and suspension proceedings "shall afford the contractor (and any specifically named affiliates) an opportunity to submit, in person, in writing, or through a representative, information and argument in opposition to the proposed" action. FAR 9.406-3(b)(2) and FAR 9.407-3(b)(2) then state that in debarment actions not based on conviction or civil judgment and in suspension actions not based on an indictment, if it is found that the contractor's submission *raises a genuine dispute over facts material to the proposed action*, the agency must:

(i) Afford the contractor an opportunity to appear with counsel, submit documentary evidence, present witnesses, and confront any person the agency presents; and

(ii) Make a transcribed record of the proceedings and make it available at cost to the contractor upon request, unless the contractor and the agency, by mutual agreement, waive the requirement for a transcript.

Agencies have been granted considerable discretion in following this two-step procedure in deciding whether there is a genuine dispute of fact to justify such an actual hearing. See *Robinson v. Cheney*, 876 F.2d 152 (D.C. Cir. 1989), affirming the agency's denial of a hearing on the grounds that the alleged factual disputes were minor in nature and did not go to the central issues in the case. See also *IMCO, Inc. v. United States*, 33 Fed. Cl. 312 (1995), affirming the debarring official's denial of a hearing on the basis that there were no seriously contested facts. This limited-hearing approach was also upheld in *Transco Sec., Inc. v. Freeman*, 639 F.2d 318 (6th Cir. 1981), where the court stated at 322-23:

Under the present regulations, promulgated following *Horne Brothers*, suspended contractors denied a hearing are provided the opportunity to present information or argument, in person, in writing, or through representation in opposition to the suspension. Thus under the current regulations, suspended contractors will not "dangle in suspension for a period of one year or more" before being given an opportunity to rebut charges. 463 F.2d at 1271. Under most circumstances, this opportunity coupled with proper notice will timely cure such errors as suspending the wrong contractor or suspending a contractor based on mere suspicion, unfounded allegation, or error.

Thus, when an agency follows this two-step procedure, a contractor that is proposed for debarment or is suspended must, in order to obtain a hearing, demonstrate in its initial written submission that there are significant factual disputes. On the other hand, there is nothing in the FAR precluding an agency from granting hearings in less restrictive circumstances.

FAR 9.406-3(d) and FAR 9.407-3(d)(2) call for written findings of fact when an actual hearing is conducted. They also permit the debarring official to delegate the conduct of such a hearing by stating that "matters involving disputed material facts" may be referred to another official. Some agencies have established a separate hearing officer as a matter of course. For example, GSA provides that if there is a genuine dispute of material fact, the suspending official must refer the matter to the fact-finding official, GSAR 509.406-3(d)(3). See also DFARS Appendix H-104 stating:

> (a) . . . If the debarring and suspending official has determined a genuine dispute of material fact(s) exists, a designated fact-finder will conduct the fact-finding proceeding. The proceeding before the fact-finder will be limited to a finding of the facts in dispute as determined by the debarring and suspending official.

> (b) The designated fact-finder will establish the date for a fact-finding proceeding, normally to be held within 45 working days of the contractor's presentation of matters in opposition. An official record will be made of the fact-finding proceeding.

> (c) The Government's representative and the contractor will have an opportunity to present evidence relevant to the facts at issues. The contractor may appear in person or through a representative in the fact-finding proceeding.

> (d) Neither the Federal Rules of Evidence nor the Federal Rules of Civil Procedure govern fact-finding. Hearsay evidence may be presented and will be given appropriate weight by the fact-finder.

> (e) Witnesses may testify in person. Witnesses will be reminded of the official nature of the proceeding and that any false testimony given is subject to criminal prosecution. Witnesses are subject to cross-examination.

Obtaining a hearing does not necessarily give the contractor the same due process rights it would have in civil litigation. For example, in *Electro-Methods, Inc. v. United States*, 728 F.2d 1471 (Fed. Cir. 1984), the court, commenting on a suspension, held that the "concept of due process cannot be extended so far, in the circumstances of this case, as to mandate that a 'meaningful' hearing include permitting the contractor to subpoena and examine FBI agents involved in an on-going criminal investigation, as well as other government and industry officials, to prove its case." However, some minimal evidentiary standards may apply. See *James J. Burnett*, HUDBCA 80-501-D42, 82-1 BCA ¶ 15,716, where the board held that hearsay evidence alone would not normally be sufficient to support a debarment.

During fact finding the contractor is not be permitted to challenge facts that were the basis of a conviction or civil judgment, NCR § 180.830.

## b.  Right of Confrontation

Although the court in *Horne Bros., Inc. v. Laird*, 463 F.2d 1268 (D.C. Cir. 1972), suggested that there may be a right to confront adverse witnesses if a suspension is protracted, FAR 9.406-3(b)(2)(i) and FAR 9.407-3(b)(2)(i) provide for an opportunity to confront agency witnesses *only* when there is a dispute as to material facts. *Robinson v. Cheney*, 876 F.2d 152 (D.C. Cir. 1989), significantly limits this right by analogizing the situation to that of courts deciding motions for summary judgment without a hearing. See also *Reeve Aleutian Airways, Inc. v. United States*, 982 F.2d 594 (D.C. Cir. 1993), commenting that a hearing where no government witnesses were present was sufficient because the contractor could have called them.

Cross-examination of adverse witnesses is generally permitted during fact finding. See the DFARS above, GSAR 509.406-3(d)(3)(viii), and NCR § 180.840. However, confrontation and cross-examination of adverse witnesses have not been required where material facts are not in dispute, *Titan Constr. Co. v. Weinberger*, Civ. Action No. 85-5533 (D.N.J. 1986); *Taylor v. Marsh*, Civ. Action No. 81-2643 (D.D.C. 1982); *Commonwealth Labs., Inc.*, AGBCA 94-0059-01, Apr. 17, 1995, *Unpub.*

## 3.  Timing Requirements

FAR 9.406-3(c) and NCR § 180.820, provide that within 30 days of receipt of notice of proposed debarment or suspension, the respondent may present information or argument in opposition. In actions based upon "a conviction or judgment, or in which there is no genuine dispute over material facts," the debarring official will make a decision based upon the administrative record. No time is specified for this decision. If no suspension is in effect, the decision must be made within 30 working days after receipt of "any information and argument submitted by the contractor, unless the debarring official extends this period for good cause," FAR 9.406-3(d).

## F.  De Facto Debarment and Suspension

There have been a number of decisions finding actions of the government that exclude contractors from the opportunity to receive award to be de facto debarments. The reasoning in such cases is that since the effect of the action was the same as a suspension or debarment, it was improper, because the agency did not observe due process requirements. The FAR contains no guidance on the type of actions that constitute de facto debarments. The decisions giving such guidance are covered in this section.

## 1.  Multiple Nonresponsibility Determinations

Multiple determinations of nonresponsibility may be tantamount to a debarment. See 43 Comp. Gen. 140 (B-151269) (1963), holding it improper to make successive nonresponsibility determinations for the same criminal offense without initiating debarment proceedings. See also Comp. Gen. Dec. B-175845, Mar. 9, 1973, *Unpub.*, where GAO upheld a nonresponsibility determination for alleged labor violations without the agency having undertaken formal debarment proceedings, but stated that "continued refusal to award contracts . . . as a result of a nonresponsibility determination based upon the same alleged labor violations as involved here without invoking and following the applicable debarment procedures would be of doubtful validity." In *Myers & Myers, Inc. v. United States Postal Serv.*, 527 F.2d 1252 (2d Cir. 1975), the court found de facto debarment where the Postal Service refused to renew six delivery contracts because of suspected criminal conduct. See *Dynamic Aviation v. Department of the Interior*, 898 F. Supp. 11 (D.D.C. 1995), where the court recognized a possibility of a de facto debarment in the government's one-year revocation of a contractor's pilot's credentials coupled with a refusal to test and inspect until a federal bureau specifically requested the contractor's services, which would not occur until a card has been issued; and *Leslie & Elliott Co. v. Garrett*, 732 F. Supp. 191 (D.D.C. 1990), where a de facto debarment was found because the Navy attacked the contractor's integrity and developed a policy to declare the contractor nonresponsible on all contracts. In *Shermco Indus. v. Secretary of the Air Force*, 584 F. Supp. 76 (N.D. Tex. 1984), involving integrity issues, the court stated "a procuring agency cannot make successive determinations of nonresponsibility on the same basis; rather it must initiate suspension or debarment procedures at the earliest practicable date following the first determination of nonresponsibility."

GAO has refused to find de facto debarments when the finding of nonresponsibility can be referred to the SBA for the granting of a Certificate of Competency, *Sermor, Inc.*, Comp. Gen. Dec. B-219132.2, 85-2 CPD ¶ 444 (five consecutive nonresponsibility determinations based on financial capability); *Pittman Mech. Contractors, Inc.*, Comp. Gen. Dec. B-242499, 91-1 CPD ¶ 439 (four contemporaneous nonresponsibility determinations). GAO has also refused to find de facto debarments when a number of nonresponsibility determinations have been made contemporaneously, *Mexican Intermodal Equip., S.A. de C.V.*, Comp. Gen. Dec. B-270144, 96-1 CPD ¶ 31 (two nonresponsibility determinations did "not demonstrate that they were part of a long-term disqualification attempt . . . [but were] . . . merely a reflection of the fact that the determinations were based on the same current information"); *Shepard Printing*, Comp. Gen. Dec. B-260362, 95-2 CPD ¶ 119 (seven nonresponsibility determinations within three-month period based on same information as to deficient quality); *Government Contract Advisory Servs., Inc.*, Comp. Gen. Dec. B-255918, 94-1 CPD ¶ 181 (three concurrent nonresponsibility determinations by different contracting officers based on same information); *Garten-und Landschaftsbau GmbH Frank Mohr*, Comp. Gen. Dec. B-237276, 90-1 CPD ¶ 186 (two nonresponsibility determinations based on integrity issues). It seems clear that a single nonresponsibility determination will not be considered to be a de facto debarment, *Redondo-Borges v. United States HUD*, 421 F.3d 1 (1st Cir. 2005).

GAO has cautioned that in order for an agency's nonresponsibility determinations to qualify as a de facto suspension or debarment, the agency must have had an intent to exclude. In *Quality Trust, Inc.*, Comp. Gen. Dec. B-289445, 2002 CPD ¶ 41, for example, GAO noted that "de facto debarment occurs when the government uses nonresponibility determinations as a means of excluding a firm from government contracting or subcontracting, rather than following the debarment regulations and procedures set forth at FAR Subpart 9.4." A necessary element of a de facto debarment, GAO noted, "is that an agency intends not to do business with the firm in the future."

## 2. Blacklists, Holdups, and Passovers

Actions or communications indicating a refusal to deal with a contractor in the future have been held to be de facto debarments or suspension. In *Airco, Inc. v. Cecil D. Andrus*, 26 Cont. Cas. Fed. (CCF) ¶ 83,636 (D.D.C. 1979), the contractor was threatened with placement of an "informal blacklist" by the Department of the Interior (DOI). Specifically, the agency threatened to notify its customers and contractors that Airco was in violation of an agency regulation that would prevent such customers from doing business with Airco. The court found that while the DOI had not canceled or terminated any contract with Airco and had not put Airco on an "ineligible" list, the effect on Airco was the same as a formal debarment but without the protective procedures to which Airco would have been entitled by a formal debarment action. Similarly, in *Peter Kiewit & Sons' Co. v. U.S. Army Corps of Eng'rs*, 534 F. Supp. 1139 (D.D.C. 1982), *rev'd on other grounds*, 714 F.2d 163 (D.C. Cir. 1983), the court found a de facto debarment by the Army when it held Kiewit in abeyance under a "temporary declaration of ineligibility" and denied it a contract award without providing notice and an opportunity to be heard. See also *Highview Eng'g, Inc. v. Corps of Engineers*, 2010 U.S. Dist. LEXIS 75102 (W.D. Ky. 2010) (agency employees statements that they did not want a subcontractor included in proposals demonstrated de facto debarment); *Art-Metal USA, Inc. v. Solomon*, 473 F. Supp. 1 (D.D.C. 1978) (de facto debarment where the GSA terminated contract for convenience and then held in abeyance four other contract awards pending the completion of a GSA investigation into possible contract abuses).

Informal statements of the contracting officer may be sufficient to indicate an intention not to award future contracts. For example, in *Related Indus., Inc. v. United States*, 2 Cl. Ct. 517 (1983), the court found de facto debarment where the contracting officer proposed to find Related nonresponsible on one award but also declared that he would not award any future contract to plaintiff or to any company with which plaintiff was associated. Compare *Community Econ. Dev. Corp. v. United States*, 577 F. Supp. 425 (D.D.C. 1983), where there was a justifiable basis for a single nonresponsibility determination. Although the contractor contended that the contracting officer told him he was debarred, the subsequent deposition of the contracting officer stating that the contractor was welcome to bid on future procurements and regularly would be sent future solicitations led the court to conclude that the alleged statement, if true, was made in the heat of the moment. In *Bannum, Inc.*, Comp. Gen. Dec. B-249758, 92-2 CPD ¶ 373, while an agency official's remark that she and her supervisors "were tired of Bannum's rhetoric," a remark made over two years earlier, may have reflected a lack of judgment, the facts did not support the contractor's contention that it had been de facto debarred.

It has also been held that the "passover" procedure under Executive Order 11246, where contractors are found not in compliance with equal employment obligations, constitutes a de facto debarment, *Pan Am. World Airways, Inc. v. Marshall*, 439 F. Supp. 487 (S.D.N.Y. 1977); *Sundstrand Corp. v. Marshall*, 17 FEP Cases 432 (N.D. Ill. 1978).

Although not decided under the de facto debarment rubric, two cases have found that stigmatizing communications that inhibit the award of future contracts constitute a deprivation of a contractor's "liberty interest," *Old Dominion Dairy Prods., Inc. v. Secretary of Defense*, 631 F.2d 953 (D.C. Cir. 1980); *Conset Corp. v. Community Servs. Admin.*, 655 F.2d 1291 (D.C. Cir. 1981). In both cases, the stigmatizing communications related to the integrity of the contractor, and there is some question as to whether this logic would apply to other grounds of nonresponsibility. See *John Carlo, Inc. v. Corps of Eng'rs of the U.S. Army*, 539 F. Supp. 1075 (N.D. Tex. 1982), listing four factors to consider when deciding if a finding of nonresponsibility amounts to a de facto debarment:

(1) were other persons or government agencies apprised of the contracting officer's finding of nonresponsibility; (2) was the information circulated for the purpose of preventing [contractor] from securing future contracts with the government; (3) did circulation of the information in fact stigmatize [contractor]; and (4) has [contractor] suffered any losses in government business attributable to the contracting officer's determination of nonresponsibility.

In *Frank Cain & Sons, Inc.*, Comp. Gen. Dec. B-236893, 90-1 CPD ¶ 44, GAO found proper the contracting agency's determination that the bidder was nonresponsible based on information in a criminal investigation report that called into question the bidder's integrity.

# CHAPTER 5

# SEALED BIDDING

Sealed bidding, previously known as formal advertising and often called "tendering" internationally, has long been used by the federal government to select contractors on the basis of price competition with publicly opened bids. Congress passed the first statute dealing with advertising in 1809, requiring that "all purchases and contracts for supplies or services . . . shall be made either by open purchase, or by previously advertising for proposals," 2 Stat. 536. The Attorney General stated that the purpose of this statute was to prevent favoritism, 2 Ops. Att'y Gen. 257 (1829), and to prevent the notorious mischief of making contracts privately, 6 Ops. Att'y Gen. 99 (1853). From time to time, additional formalities were adopted. See, e.g., 5 Stat. 522, 526 (1842), 5 Stat. 614, 617 (1843), 5 Stat. 790, 795 (1845). In 1861, the statutory requirements for advertising were reaffirmed, 12 Stat. 220. This statute was subsequently incorporated into Revised Statute 3709, the forerunner of 41 U.S.C. § 5 (pre-2011 codification). In the years that followed, numerous Comptroller of the Treasury, Comptroller General, and court decisions implemented the statute by further defining the procedures to be followed in formal advertising. Following World War II, these procedures were adopted by Congress in the Armed Services Procurement Act of 1947, 10 U.S.C. § 2301 et seq., and the Federal Property and Administrative Services Act, 41 U.S.C. § 252 et seq. (pre-2011 codification). These statutes were further modified by the Competition in Contracting Act of 1984 (CICA), Pub. L. No. 98-369, and the Federal. Acquisition Streamlining Act of 1994 (FASA), Pub. L. No. 103-355.

Sealed bidding was the predominant technique used in government contracting until World War II. During the war its use was suspended in order to efficiently award contracts to obtain necessary war materials. After the war the statutes reinstated it as the preferred technique, but negotiation was permitted under specified statutory exceptions. Thereafter, sealed bidding was used for the majority of federal procurement actions, but the more significant dollar expenditures were made using negotiation procedures. As discussed in Chapter 3, the CICA ended the practice of "favoring" the use of sealed bidding when it made sealed bidding and competitive negotiation parallel procedures for meeting the statutory competition requirements. At the present time, less than 10% of federal procurement dollars are spent in sealed bid procurements.

The statutory procedures for sealed bidding are now contained in 10 U.S.C. § 2305 and 41 U.S.C. § 3702. The key provisions describing the unique features of sealed bidding are in 10 U.S.C. § 2305(b)(3):

Sealed bids shall be opened publicly at the time and place stated in the solicitation. The head of the agency shall evaluate the bids in accordance with paragraph (1) without discussions with the bidders and, except as provided in paragraph (2), shall award a contract with reasonable promptness to the responsible bidder whose bid conforms to the solicitation and is most advantageous to the United States, considering only price and the other price-related factors included in the solicitation. The award of a contract shall be made by transmitting, in writing or by electronic means, notice of the award to the successful bidder. Within three days after the date of contract award, the head of the agency shall notify, in writing or by electronic means, each bidder not awarded the contract that the contract has been awarded.

Substantially the same language is in 41 U.S.C. § 3702. The statutory requirements for sealed bidding are implemented in FAR Part 14.

This chapter first considers the procedures applicable to the submission and public opening of sealed bids. It then deals with the concept of responsiveness — whether the bid conforms in all material respects to the invitation. The evaluation of bids and the award of the contract is next discussed. The last two sections cover mistakes in bids and two-step sealed bidding. The other key aspect of sealed bidding — determining whether the prospective contractor is responsible — is covered in Chapter 4.

## I. BIDDING AND OPENING PROCEDURE

The fundamental concept of sealed bidding is that the public interest is best served when the government describes its needs with precision, conducts an open competition to obtain the best price, opens the bids publicly, and awards to the responsible bidder that submits the lowest price and agrees without qualification to meet all the material contract requirements. In this system, discretion of government employees is reduced to a minimum, and public opening ensures that the award decision is subject to public scrutiny. Thus, it has been stated that sealed bidding is aimed at securing the most advantageous contract for the government by maximizing free and open competition; preventing favoritism, collusion, or fraud; and giving all interested parties an opportunity to compete, *United States v. Brookridge Farm, Inc.*, 111 F.2d 461 (10th Cir. 1940). Bidders must prepare their bids independently without the knowledge of whether other bidders are competing for award or of the contents of other bids. Public opening ensures all parties that the award is being made in conformance with the solicitation. Bids are "firm" for a specified period of time — with the result that withdrawal or modification of a bid after opening is permitted only in the limited circumstances of mistake.

Sealed bidding does not afford the government the option of evaluating the merits of technical proposals and paying somewhat more to obtain a higher quality product or service. It *requires* that if award is made, it must be made to the responsive bidder with the lowest price even if the product or service offered is only minimally acceptable. Thus, its successful use is almost completely dependent on the government's ability to describe its needs in a way that ensures that the winning contractor will be *contractually bound* to perform satisfactory work.

## A. Solicitation of Bids

The solicitation of sealed bids is accomplished through a written document called an Invitation for Bids (IFB). The government makes copies of IFBs available to prospective bidders, typically electronically using the federal central posting site, *www.fedbizopps.gov*, and may give further notice of the solicitation through advertising or posting notices of the solicitation in public places. See Chapter 3, Section IV for a discussion of public announcements and solicitations.

### 1. Invitations for Bids

In order to ensure that all bidders compete on an equal basis, IFBs must contain all of the essential terms of the contract so that bidders may submit offers by merely filling in the price and schedule, if required, completing the necessary certifications, and signing the offer, FAR 14.101(a). Solicitations are issued on multipurpose standard forms used for both sealed bid and negotiated procurements. The contracting officer may use Standard Form 33 (Solicitation, Offer and Award) (see Figure 5-1) or Standard Form 1447 (Solicitation/Contract) or may issue the solicitation on a special form, FAR 14.201-2(a); FAR 53.214. Standard Form 1442 (Solicitation, Offer, and Award) is prescribed for use on construction contracts, FAR 36.701(b); FAR 53.236-1(e). One of these standard forms is used in most cases because they contain blanks with the essential information that must be filled in by both the contracting officer and the bidder. This entire package is designed so that all bidders can make legally sufficient and comparable offers under the same terms and conditions by furnishing the required information and inserting their price and delivery schedule.

FAR 14.201-1 requires, with certain exceptions such as construction contracts, that solicitations and resulting contracts be prepared using the Uniform Contract Format "to the maximum practicable extent." Standard Form 33 is the most commonly used standard form because it is structured to use this format. However, the contracting officer is permitted to use a "simplified contract format," FAR 14.201-9, and should use Standard Form 1447 when this format is used, FAR 53.214(d).

The Uniform Contract Format consists of the following Parts and Subparts:

| Section | Title |
|---|---|
| **Part I — The Schedule** | |
| A | Solicitation/contract form |
| B | Supplies or services and prices |
| C | Description/specifications |
| D | Packaging and marking |
| E | Inspection and acceptance |
| F | Deliveries or performance |
| G | Contract administration data |
| H | Special contract requirements |
| **Part II — Contract Clauses** | |
| I | Contract clauses |
| **Part III — List of Documents, Exhibits, and Other Attachments** | |
| J | List of documents, exhibits, and other attachments |
| **Part IV — Representations and Instructions** | |
| K | Representations, certifications, and other statements of bidders |
| L | Instructions, conditions, and notices to bidders |
| M | Evaluation factors for award |

This format is structured so that Parts I, II, and III become the contract, when awarded, while Part IV is retained in the contract file, FAR 14.201-1(c). Part I of the format contains the unique provisions pertaining to the procurement, including, as Section A, Standard Form 33, FAR 14.201-2. Part II, Section I, contains the clauses for the proposed contract, FAR 14.201-3, including standard contract clauses contained in FAR Part 52 and special clauses used by the agency and not included in Part I. FAR 52.3 contains a matrix giving guidance on the required and optional clauses to be incorporated into the various types of contracts. FAR 52.102-1 encourages incorporation of clauses by reference, "to the maximum extent practicable," if permitted by FAR 52.3 or if they are contained in agency-wide procurement regulations such as the Department of Defense Federal Acquisition Regulation Supplement (DFARS).

Part III, Section J, contains a list of all attachments to the contract, providing the title, date, and number of pages for each document, FAR 14.201-4. Part IV, Section K, contains all representations and certifications as well as any other provision that must be filled in by the bidders, FAR 14.201-5(a). This section, by clustering all of these requirements in a single section, reduces the possibility of bidders failing to fill out a necessary form. Many of those certifications may be provided online, through the Online Representations and Certifications Application (ORCA) website at *https://orca.bpn.gov*, see 69 Fed. Reg. 76,340, Dec. 20, 2004. Section L contains all of the instructions to bidders on procedures that will be followed in evaluating bids and selecting the bidders — commonly known as "solicitation provisions." See FAR 52.101, which defines a solicitation provision as "a term or condition used only in solicitations and applying only before contract award." FAR 14.201-6 contains a long list of the standard solicitation provisions used in sealed bid procurements. Section M contains all of the "price-related factors" other than bid price that will be evaluated in selecting the low bidder, FAR 14.201-5(c).

Once a solicitation is issued, communication between the procuring agency and prospective bidders is discouraged except through the procurement official named in the solicitation for that purpose. Routine questions that do not require an amendment to the solicitation or do not involve the clarification of ambiguous provisions may be answered orally or by letter. If the procurement is complex or numerous questions have been raised, the procuring agency may convene a prebid conference for all interested parties. See FAR 14.208, 14.211. A prebid conference, however, is "never [to] be used as a substitute for amending a defective or ambiguous invitation," FAR 14.207.

The solicitation therefore serves a number of functions in the procurement process. It must: (1) lay out the ground rules of the competition, including the information to be supplied by bidders and the bid opening time; (2) contain the specifications or incorporate them by reference when permitted; and (3) contain all the terms and conditions of the proposed contract. Both the substantive requirements of the solicitation and the procedures by which it is publicized can influence the degree of competition that is obtained.

## 2. Amendment of IFBs

A contracting officer may — because of revised needs, or errors or deficiencies in the solicitation — find it necessary to change the solicitation by issuing an amendment. FAR 14.208 outlines the procedures for the issuance of amendments to IFBs:

(a) If it becomes necessary to make changes in quantity, specifications, delivery schedules, opening dates, etc., or to correct a defective or ambiguous invitation, such changes shall be accomplished by amendment of the invitation for bids using Standard Form 30, Amendment of Solicitation/Modification of Contract. The fact that a change was mentioned at a pre-bid conference does not relieve the necessity for issuing an amendment. Amendments shall be sent, before the time for bid opening, to everyone to whom invitations have been furnished and shall be displayed in the bid room.

(b) Before amending an invitation for bids, the period of time remaining until bid opening and the need to extend this period shall be considered. When only a short time remains before the time set for bid opening, consideration should be given to notifying bidders of an extension of time by telegrams or telephone. Such extension must be confirmed in the amendment.

(c) Any information given to a prospective bidder concerning an invitation for bids shall be furnished promptly to all other prospective bidders as an amendment to the invitation —

(1) if such information is necessary for bidders to submit bids or

(2) if the lack of such information would be prejudicial to uninformed bidders. The information shall be furnished even though a pre-bid conference is held. No award shall be made on the invitation unless such amendment has been issued in sufficient time to permit all prospective bidders to consider such information in submitting or modifying their bids.

Only information that would cause prejudice to uninformed bidders needs to be distributed per FAR 14.208, *Hunt Constr. Group, Inc. v. United States*, 281 F.3d 1369 (Fed. Cir. 2002).

Even though the regulations provide that an amendment shall be sent to each concern to whom the IFB has been furnished, GAO has consistently held that a bidder bears the risk of not receiving an amendment, assuming that such failure is not the result of a failure to follow the regulations governing distribution of solicitation materials, *Navistar Marine Instrument Corp.*, Comp. Gen. Dec. B-277143, 98-1 CPD ¶ 53, or the product of a conscious and deliberate effort by the agency to exclude the bidder from participating in the competition, *Monterey Advanced Imaging Ctr.*, Comp. Gen. Dec. B-253152, 93-2 CPD ¶ 118; *Southwestern Enters., Inc.*, Comp. Gen. Dec. B-245491.2, 92-1 CPD ¶ 88; *GSX Gov't Servs., Inc.*, Comp. Gen. Dec. B-239549.2, 91-1 CPD ¶ 12; *Crown Mgmt. Servs., Inc.*, Comp. Gen. Dec. B-232431.4, 89-1 CPD ¶ 393; *C-Way Constr. Co.*, Comp. Gen. Dec. B-198885, 80-2 CPD ¶ 41.

The underlying theory is that the agency discharges its legal responsibility when it issues and dispatches an amendment in sufficient time to permit all bidders to consider the amendment in formulating their bids, *Southern Techs., Inc.*, 67 Comp. Gen. 204 (B-228516), 88-1 CPD ¶ 57; *Maintenance Pace Setters, Inc.*, Comp. Gen. Dec. B-212757, 84-1 CPD ¶ 98; *Eugene Ricciardelli, Inc.*, Comp. Gen. Dec. B-212871, 83-2 CPD ¶ 640. Hence, in *Electro-Mechanical Indus., Inc.*, 52 Comp. Gen. 281 (B-176839) (1972), an amendment issued to the bidder, but addressed incorrectly, provided no basis for cancellation. GAO stated that "the propriety of a particular procurement must be determined from the Government's point of view upon the basis of whether adequate competition and reasonable prices were obtained, not upon whether every possible prospective bidder was afforded an opportunity to bid." Thus, late receipt of an amendment will require cancellation and resolicitation if adequate competition is not received as a result of the transmission defect. For example, in *Andero Constr., Inc.*, 61 Comp. Gen. 253 (B-203898), 82-1 CPD ¶ 133, GAO ignored the general rule that the bidder bears the risk of nondelivery of an amendment to the solicitation, because the agency failed to affirmatively establish that it complied with DAR 2-208 (similar to FAR 14.208), and three of four bidders appeared not to have received the amendment in the mail. The agency never affirmatively stated that the amendments were mailed, and thus GAO recommended that the agency cancel the IFB and resolicit its requirements. See also *Gadsden Moving & Storage Co.*, Comp. Gen. Dec. B-250658, 93-1 CPD ¶ 134, where GAO found that the agency had deprived the protester of the opportunity to compete by not providing the protester with a copy of the amendment in a timely manner. GAO stated that the agency conceded that it used an incorrect mailing address, the protester took reasonable steps to obtain the amendment, and the agency had received only one bid. In *Phillip Sitz Constr.*, Comp. Gen. Dec. B-245941, 92-1 CPD ¶ 101, GAO found that because the agency had sent the IFB to the protester, it was required to place the protester on the mailing list and to send it any solicitation amendments. The agency conceded that the protester was not included on the mailing list and that it did not send the amendment. Further, GAO stated that as a result of the agency's actions, only one responsive bid was received, thereby undermining the CICA mandate for full and open competition.

### 3.  Time for Submission of Bids

Bidders must be given sufficient time to submit bids. See FAR 14.202-1, which states:

> (a) *Policy.* A reasonable time for prospective bidders to prepare and submit bids shall be allowed in all invitations, consistent with the needs of the Government. (For construction contracts, see 36.303(a).) A bidding time (i.e., the time between issuance of the solicitation and opening of bids) of at least 30 calendar days shall be provided when synopsis is required by Subpart 5.2.
>
> (b) *Factors to be considered.* Because of unduly limited bidding time, some potential sources may be precluded from bidding and others may be forced to include amounts for contingencies that, with additional time, could be eliminated. To avoid unduly restricting competition or paying higher-than-necessary prices, consideration shall be given to such factors as the following in establishing a reasonable bidding time: (1) degree of urgency; (2) complexity of requirement; (3) anticipated extent of subcontracting; (4) whether use was made of preinvitation notices; (5) geographic distribution of bidders; and (6) normal transmittal time for both initiations and bids.

Contracting officers may extend (or postpone) the bidding time in order to increase competition, *Ling Dynamic Sys., Inc.*, Comp. Gen. Dec. B-252091, 93-1 CPD ¶ 407; *Combustion Equip. Co.*, Comp. Gen. Dec. B-228291, 87-2 CPD ¶ 627.

FAR 14.208(b) provides that no award should be made on an invitation unless an amendment has been issued in sufficient time to permit all prospective bidders to consider such information in submitting or modifying their bids. However, the amount of time necessary will be determined by the complexity of the amendment.

In *Pacific Contractors, Inc.*, Comp. Gen. Dec. B-190568, 78-2 CPD ¶ 97, GAO found that the contracting officer acted reasonably in affording four of five bidders less than one day and a fifth bidder less than one hour to consider the effect of an amendment, where the amendment was simple in nature and none of the bidders (including the protester) objected prior to bid opening. In *Tom Walsh & Assocs.*, Comp. Gen. Dec. B-212750, 84-1 CPD ¶ 78, GAO again determined that the protester had been given sufficient time (six days) to consider the amendment. Conversely, 45 Comp. Gen. 651 (B-158766) (1966) held that no award should be made where amendments to the IFB were furnished to prospective bidders only two days before bid opening. GAO rejected the government's argument that since six bidders were able to respond, sufficient time was available; the six bidders were all located nearer to the bidding site than the protester.

It is within the contracting officer's discretion to extend the bidding time when it appears that there was insufficient time to consider an amendment to a solicitation. See *Tolina Constr. Co.*, Comp. Gen. Dec. B-213028, 84-1 CPD ¶ 244, where it was determined that the contracting officer had not abused his discretion when he extended bid opening by one week in order to allow potential bidders additional time to consider a material amendment to the IFB. The contracting officer made this decision on the day prior to bid opening because no bids had been received and he feared that competition had been restricted by the issuance of the amendment. Compare *T & A Painting, Inc.*, Comp. Gen. Dec. B- 229655, 88-1 CPD ¶ 435 (contracting officer appropriately refused to extend time for response).

## B. Submission of Bids

Bids that are submitted in accordance with the IFB bind the bidder once they are opened. However, the regulations permit their withdrawal before bid opening.

### 1. Method of Submission

As discussed in Chapter 2, bids are *offers* submitted in the precise form specified by the government in the IFB. The method of submission of sealed bids is covered by a standard solicitation provision set forth in FAR 52.214-5:

SUBMISSION OF BIDS (MAR 1997)

(a) Bids and bid modifications shall be submitted in sealed envelopes or packages (unless submitted by electronic means) —

(1) Addressed to the office specified in the solicitation, and

(2) Showing the time and date specified for receipt, the solicitation number, and the name and address of the bidder.

(b) Bidders using commercial carrier services shall ensure that the bid is addressed and marked on the outermost envelope or wrapper as prescribed in subparagraphs (a)(1) and (2) of this provision when delivered to the office specified in the solicitation.

(c) Telegraphic bids will not be considered unless authorized by the solicitation; however, bids may be modified or withdrawn by written or telegraphic notice.

(d) Facsimile bids, modifications, or withdrawals, will not be considered unless authorized by the solicitation.

(e) Bids submitted by electronic commerce shall be considered only if the electronic commerce method was specifically stipulated or permitted by the solicitation.

Bids may be submitted through the United States Postal Service, any other delivery service, or may be hand delivered. Bids should be submitted in a sealed envelope or package on the forms provided in the IFB. However, such submission is not required if the bidder is careful to comply fully with the IFB. Failure to seal a bid envelope is a minor informality that will not prevent the consideration of the bid, Comp. Gen. Dec. B-153288, Mar. 19, 1964, *Unpub.*; *Rhoads Constr. Co.,* Comp. Gen. Dec. B-242992, 91-1 CPD ¶ 561. Upon receipt of an unsealed bid the government should place the bid in a sealed envelope. Last-minute changes on the packaging may well prove ineffective: unsigned or uninitialed bid modifications noted on the outside of the bid envelopes may not be accepted by the receiving agency unless the bid or modification is otherwise accompanied by evidence of the bidder's intent to be bound by the modification, *R.F. Lusa & Sons Sheetmetal, Inc.*, Comp. Gen. Dec. B-281180.2, 98-2 CPD ¶ 157.

Bids must be submitted prior to bid opening. Paragraph (c) of the Late Submissions, Modifications, and Withdrawals of Bids solicitation provision in FAR 52.214-7 states:

> Acceptable evidence to establish the time of receipt at the Government installation includes the time/date stamp of that installation on the bid wrapper, other documentary evidence of receipt maintained by the installation, or oral testimony or statements of Government personnel.

This provision has been strictly enforced, *General Power Eng'g Assocs., Inc.*, Comp. Gen. Dec. B-292170, 2003 CPD ¶ 109; *Pershield, Inc.*, Comp. Gen. Dec. B-256827, 94-2 CPD ¶ 46; *Isometrics, Inc.*, Comp. Gen. Dec. B-245095, 91-2 CPD ¶ 477; *Monitor Northwest Co.*, Comp. Gen. Dec. B-193357, 79-1 CPD ¶ 437.

## a. *Bids Submitted By Other Means*

The Submission of Bid solicitation provision allows submission of bids electronically, by facsimile or telegraphically *only* if there is another solicitation provi-

sion permitting submission using that method. The FAR contains standard solicitation provisions for the submission of telegraphic bids (Telegraphic Bids, FAR
52.214-13) and facsimile bids (Facsimile Bids, FAR 52.214-31). However, there
is no standard provision for the submission of electronic bids. If there is no separate solicitation provision allowing submission using one of these methods, such
a bid must be rejected, *Heath Constr., Inc.*, Comp. Gen. Dec. B-403417, 2010
CPD ¶ 202 (facsimile bid); *H. Bendzulla Contracting*, Comp. Gen. Dec. B-246112,
91-2 CPD ¶ 441 (facsimile bid); *Marbex, Inc.*, Comp. Gen. Dec. B-221995, 86-1
CPD ¶ 212 (telegraphic bid); *Electro-Mechanical Indus., Inc.*, 52 Comp. Gen.
281 (B-176839) (1972) (telegraphic bid). See also *Recreonics Corp.*, Comp. Gen.
Dec. B-246339, 92-1 CPD ¶ 249 (bid nonresponsive where bidder acknowledged
a material amendment by facsimile transmission, which was not permitted by the
solicitation); and *Michelin Aircraft Tire Corp.*, Comp. Gen. Dec. B-248498, 92-2
CPD ¶ 142 (agency properly rejected a bid modification sent by facsimile when the
bidder had been orally advised by an agency contract specialist that the modification should be sent in that manner because the agency's telegraphic equipment had
become inoperative).

If the IFB contains either the Telegraphic Bids solicitation provision or the
Facsimile Bids solicitation provision, the bidder may submit the bid in the form
permitted, but care must be exercised to ensure that the bid precisely complies with
the technical requirements of the applicable provision. For example, both clauses
require that all required representations and information be submitted just as if the
bid had been mailed, *Triple D Orchards, Inc.*, Comp. Gen. Dec. B-219648, 85-2
CPD ¶ 525. The Telegraphic Bids provision also requires the submission of a signed
confirming copy of the bid. The Facsimile Bids provision requires that a proper
signature be included and makes the offeror responsible for all defects in the bid due
to faulty transmission or reception. This provision has been strictly enforced against
the offeror even in cases where the offeror had proof of transmission of the facsimile, *Southern CAD/CAM*, 71 Comp. Gen. 78 (B-244745), 91-2 CPD ¶ 453; *S.W.
Elecs. & Mfg. Corp.*, Comp. Gen. Dec. B-249308, 92-2 CPD ¶ 320; *Microscope
Co.*, Comp. Gen. Dec. B-257015, 94-2 CPD ¶ 157. Bids transmitted by facsimile
must be received in the office designated for the receipt of bids before the time set
for bid opening, *Butt Constr. Co.*, Comp. Gen. Dec. B-258507, 95-1 CPD ¶ 45. The
controlling time is the time the *last page* of the bid is received by the agency (not
when the transmission begins), *Radar Devices, Inc.*, Comp. Gen. Dec. B 249118,
92-2 CPD ¶ 287. However, if the bid is late due to mishandling on the part of the
government, the bid will be considered timely. Bidders must be certain to correctly
and carefully instruct telegraph company employees on such matters as the exact
date, time, and place of delivery. In *Western Alaska Contractors, J.V.*, Comp. Gen.
Dec. B-241839, 91-1 CPD ¶ 248, the telegraph company attempted to send telephone notice of a bid modification to the agency, but stated to the agency employee
that it had a "bid wire." The agency employee reasonably assumed that this was an
attempted telephone bid, which was not permitted by the IFB. The agency employee
so informed the telegraph company and hung up the telephone. GAO sustained the

agency's decision to reject the protester's subsequent written modification, which was received after bid opening.

The Submission of Bids solicitation provision permits submission of bid modifications telegraphically. However, if the IFB does not contain a current telex number, the bidder assumes the risk in using a prior number in sending a modification to the agency's telex machine, *Kings Point Indus., Inc.*, Comp. Gen. Dec. B-244398, 91-2 CPD ¶ 331. In that case, GAO ruled that the contracting officer had properly rejected proof that a modification had been received by the agency's telex machine when the agency had discontinued its direct receipt of such communications. On the other hand, if the solicitation contains telex numbers, it is improper to disconnect the machine without informing bidders, *Kings Point Mfg. Co.*, Comp. Gen. Dec. B-199992, 81-1 CPD ¶ 293; *Singleton Contracting Co.*, Comp. Gen. Dec. B-215186, 84-2 CPD ¶ 471; to allow the telex machine to run out of paper, *Hydro Fitting Corp.*, 54 Comp. Gen. 999 (B-183438), 75-1 CPD ¶ 331; or to lose the service because of failure to pay the service fee, *Standard Prods. Co.*, Comp. Gen. Dec. B-215832, 85-1 CPD ¶ 86.

Although there is no standard clause for the submission of electronic bids, as discussed in Chapter 3, electronic commerce is the preferred method. This is recognized by FAR 14.202-8 authorizing contracting officers to call for the submission of electronic bids and stating that "if electronic bids are authorized, the solicitation shall specify the electronic commerce method(s) that bidders may use." While the normal method of submitting an electronic bid would be through *www.fedbizopps. gov*, agencies have used different strategies for using electronic commerce, only some of which have proven successful. *See, e.g., USA Info. Sys., Inc.*, Comp. Gen. Dec. B- 291488, 2002 CPD ¶ 205 (vendor bore burden of triggering electronic updates); *Jack Faucett Assocs., Inc.*, Comp. Gen. Dec. B-279347, 98-1 CPD ¶ 155 (procurement under the Federal Acquisition Computer Network (FACNET), a failed experiment in federal electronic commerce); *Comspace Corp.*, Comp. Gen. Dec. B-274037, 96-2 CPD ¶ 186 (electronic quotations forwarded by private intermediary); *Total Procurement Servs., Inc.*, Comp. Gen. Dec. B-272891, 96-2 CPD ¶ 92 (description of FACNET system); Godes, Note, *Government Contracting on the Internet: Abandoning FACNET as the Government's Network for Electronic Commerce,* 26 Pub. Cont. L.J. 663 (1997).

### b.  Notice of Nonsubmission of Bid

Traditionally, as part of the formal, paper-based exchange between vendor and agency, the vendor was to advise the agency if the vendor, although declining to bid, wanted to receive future solicitation materials. That clause (FAR 52.214-9) was dropped from the FAR as agencies moved to electronic systems for distributing notices of bidding opportunities. See 68 Fed. Reg. 43854, July 24, 2003.

## 2. Firm Bid Rule

As discussed in Chapter 2, sealed bids are subject to the "firm bid rule," which prohibits modification or withdrawal of bids after bid opening. The rationale for this rule is that it would be detrimental to the competitive bidding system if bidders were allowed to change their bids after they have had an opportunity to discover what other bidders have offered. The only major exceptions to the firm bid rule are for mistakes in bid, discussed below, and for reverse auctions, which though not specifically addressed in the FAR, are increasingly common in federal procurement. See 72 Fed. Reg. 46,614, Aug. 21, 2007 (notice seeking industry input on use of reverse auctions); 65 Fed. Reg. 65,232, Oct. 21, 2000 (outreach seeking input on whether regulations on reverse auctions are necessary); *Wyse Tech., Inc.,* Comp. Gen. Dec. B-297454, 2006 CPD ¶ 23 (challenge regarding use of reverse auction mechanism); Volk, Note, *A Principles-Oriented Approach to Regulating Reverse Auctions,* 37 Pub. Cont. L.J. 127 (2007); Yukins, *A Case Study in Comparative Procurement Law: Assessing UNICTRAL's Lessons for U.S. Procurement,* 35 Pub. Cont. L.J. 457 (2006). In a reverse auction, unlike a traditional sealed bid procurement, bidders are allowed to lower their bids in response to their competitors' bids, in an extended competition to win the award.

Under traditional sealed bidding, in contrast, bidders are expected to submit and remain committed to a firm bid. The firm bid rule is incorporated in both Standard Form 33 and Standard Form 1447. Block 12 of Standard Form 33 provides:

> [T]he undersigned agrees, if this offer is accepted within calendar days (60 calendar days unless a different period is inserted by the offeror) from the date for receipt of offers specified above, to furnish any or all items upon which prices are offered at the price set opposite each item, delivered at the designated point(s), within the time specified in the schedule.

Block 11 of Standard Form 1447 provides:

> If offer is accepted by the government within calendar days (60 calendar days unless offeror inserts a different period) from the date set forth in blk 9 above, the contractor agrees to hold its offered prices firm for the items solicited herein and to accept any resulting contract subject to the terms and conditions stated herein.

In *W.A. Scott v. United States,* 44 Ct. Cl. 524 (1909), the Court of Claims recognized the distinction between private and government contracts and would not allow the withdrawal of a bid deposit, and explained why concerns about corruption played such an important part in the government's relatively inflexible rules for bidding. The court stated at 527:

> The agents of the Government stand upon a different footing from private individuals in the matter of advertising for the letting of contracts in behalf of the United States. They have no discretion. They must accept the lowest or the highest re-

sponsible bid, or reject all and readvertise. Private individuals are not required thus to act. Hence it is apparent that Government agents should be allowed a reasonable time after the opening of bids before they are allowed to be withdrawn so they can be afforded opportunities to ascertain whether collusion or fraud had been perpetrated against the United States by the parties engaged in the bidding. It is also apparent that if the rule of allowing immediate withdrawals after the results of the bidding are made known, frauds innumerable could be perpetrated against the United States and thus public justice would be greatly hampered.

In *Refining Assocs. v. United States*, 124 Ct. Cl. 115, 109 F. Supp. 259 (1953), the court reiterated that bids were irrevocable for the time stated in the invitation. In that case, the invitation for bids stipulated that after the opening of bids no bid could be withdrawn. In holding the bid to be irrevocable, the court stated at 122:

> [The bidder] submitted its bid subject to these provisions, and agreed that [the Government] should have 15 days from the date of opening to consider the bids. In so doing, [the bidder] was accorded the right of having its bid considered on the merits, and this right was conditioned on the premise that the bid would remain open during the time specified.

See *Nation-Wide Reporting & Convention Coverage*, GSBCA 8309, 88-2 BCA ¶ 20,521, where the IFB specifically required that the bidder keep its offer open for 90 days from the opening of bids. The board held that the bidder could not revoke its bid during this period and that, once the bids were opened, the government's "acceptance after an attempted withdrawal . . . create[d] a valid contract" and failure to perform after this acceptance justified default termination. See also *Western Adhesives*, GSBCA 7449, 85-2 BCA ¶ 17,961 (acceptance of bid during an extended acceptance period created a valid contract even though bidder attempted to withdraw bid); and 19 Comp. Gen. 761 (B-8531) (1940) (agreement to perform contract if awarded within 20 days of bid opening is held the same as an agreement not to revoke offer in that period). Compare *Granco Indus., Inc.*, GSBCA 14900, 01-1 BCA ¶ 31,173 (contractor not bound by firm bid rule as to line items that were withdrawn when contractor agreed to extend bid pending government review).

## 3. Modification or Withdrawal of Bids Prior to Bid Opening

Bids may be freely modified or withdrawn as long as this is accomplished no later than *the exact time set for bid opening*. Such modification or withdrawal is effective if it is in accordance with the procedures set forth in the Late Submissions, Modifications, and Withdrawal of Bids solicitation provision in FAR 52.214-7. These procedures are summarized in FAR 14.303 as follows:

> (a) Bids may be modified or withdrawn by any method authorized by the solicitation, if notice is received in the office designated in the solicitation not later than the exact time set for opening of bids. Unless proscribed by agency regula-

tions, a telegraphic modification or withdrawal of a bid received in such office by telephone from the receiving telegraph office shall be considered. However, the message shall be confirmed by the telegraph company by sending a copy of the written telegram that formed the basis for the telephone call. If the solicitation authorizes facsimile bids, bids may be modified or withdrawn via facsimile received at any time before the exact time set for receipt of bids, subject to the conditions specified in the provision prescribed in 14.201-6(v). Modifications received by telegram (including a record of those telephoned by the telegraph company) or facsimile shall be sealed in an envelope by a proper official. The official shall write on the envelope (1) the date and time of receipt and by whom, and (2) the number of the invitation for bids, and shall sign the envelope. No information contained in the envelope shall be disclosed before the time set for bid opening.

(b) A bid may be withdrawn in person by a bidder or its authorized representative if, before the exact time set for opening of bids, the identity of the persons requesting withdrawal is established and that person signs a receipt for the bid.

(c) Upon withdrawal of an electronically transmitted bid, the data received shall not be viewed and shall be purged from primary and backup data storage systems.

Paragraph (c) of FAR 14.303 was added in 1995 as part of a broader initiative to address the use of electronic commerce in federal government contracting. The provision reflects the concern with protecting the confidentiality of withdrawn bids, in an era when a paper-based bid can no longer be simply withdrawn and destroyed. Under the new ¶ (c), the electronically submitted bid is not to be viewed and electronic records of the withdrawn bid are to be purged, as well.

These procedures have been held to preclude a bidder from withdrawing a bid by telephone, *Ruggiero v. United States*, 190 Ct. Cl. 327, 420 F.2d 709 (1970); *John A. Maney*, GSBCA 6550, 83-2 BCA ¶ 16,744. See *Satellite Servs.*, Comp. Gen. Dec. B-207631.2, 83-1 CPD ¶ 357, where a bidder telephonically requested that the agency return its bid. When the agency failed in its attempt to comply with the request, the bidder continued to participate in the procurement and was eventually awarded the contract. GAO denied a protest of a competitor, holding that a telephone request for withdrawal from other than a telegraph company will not be honored. It appears that a valid withdrawal would have occurred if the agency had returned the bid. Withdrawal in person is permitted, but failure to return the bid has been considered sufficient evidence that such withdrawal did not occur, *Tomahawk Constr. Co.*, Comp. Gen. Dec. B-243582, 91-2 CPD ¶ 137.

Bid modifications must be submitted in sufficient time so that they will be delivered to the bid opening room prior to opening. When they are sent telegraphically, time must be allowed for the receiving employee to take the telegram (or telephone message from the telegraph company) to the bid opening. See *Roy McGinnis & Co.*, Comp. Gen. Dec. B-275988, 97-1 CPD ¶ 156 (bid modification received five seconds before deadline was insufficient); and *Sanchez Painting & Constr. Co.*, Comp.

Gen. Dec. B-232287, 88-2 CPD ¶ 554, (bid received one minute before deadline was insufficient). See also *Monitor Nw. Co.*, Comp. Gen. Dec. B-193357, 79-1 CPD ¶ 437, where GAO stated that it is unrealistic to assume that a document not marked as a bid or bid modification received five minutes before bid opening would reach the designated office on time. When, under traditional procedures, the telegraph company attempted to notify the agency by telephone that a modification had been sent, the bidder bore bears the risk that the agency would reject the call, *Western Alaska Contractors, J.V.*, Comp. Gen. Dec. B-241839, 91-1 CPD ¶ 248. In case of an IFB for multiple items, a telegraphic modification could include prices on items that were not in the original bid, 39 Comp. Gen. 163 (B-140552) (1959).

## C. Cancellation of Procurement Before Opening

Agencies have considerable discretion in cancelling a procurement before the time of bid opening. FAR 14.209 states:

(a) The cancellation of an invitation for bids usually involves a loss of time, effort, and money spent by the Government and bidders. Invitations should not be cancelled unless cancellation is clearly in the public interest; e.g., (1) where there is no longer a requirement for the supplies or services or (2) where amendments to the invitation would be of such magnitude that a new invitation is desirable.

Determining whether cancellation is "in the public interest" is a highly discretionary decision. See *Diversified Mgmt. Group, A Joint Venture*, Comp. Gen. Dec. B-288443.2, 2001 CPD ¶ 175 (cancellation appropriate where failed to determine whether procurement should be set aside); *Lynch Machinery Co.*, Comp. Gen. Dec. B-256279.2, 94-2 CPD ¶ 15 (cancellation appropriate to amend restrictive specification).

## D. Public Opening

Public opening of bids is one of the key elements of sealed bidding, and public bid opening is recognized internationally as an important protection against corruption. The importance of public opening was recognized by GAO in *Computer Network Corp.*, 55 Comp. Gen. 445 (B-183639), 75-2 CPD ¶ 297, stating at 451:

The public advertising statute, 41 U.S. Code §253(b) (1970), requires that: "All bids shall be publicly opened at the time and place stated in the advertisement." We have interpreted this requirement for a public opening to mean that the bid must publicly disclose the essential nature and type of the products offered and those elements of the bid which relate to price, quantity and delivery terms. 53 Comp. Gen. 24 (1973). The purpose of public opening of bids for public contracts is to protect both the public interest and bidders against any form of fraud, favoritism or partiality and such openings should be conducted to leave no room for any suspicion of irregularity, *Page Airways, Inc., et al.*, 54 Comp. Gen. 120 (1974), 74-2 CPD ¶ 99; 48 Comp. Gen. 413 (1968).

Bids must be closely guarded prior to opening to ensure that no bidder has access to the bids of competitors. FAR 14.401 provides the following guidance on the safeguarding of bids received prior to the time for bid opening:

> (a) All bids (including modifications) received before the time set for the opening of bids shall be kept secure. Except as provided in paragraph (b) of this section, the bids shall not be opened or viewed, and shall remain in a locked bid box, a safe, or in a secured, restricted-access electronic bid box. If an invitation for bids is cancelled, bids shall be returned to the bidders. Necessary precautions shall be taken to ensure the security of the bid box or safe. Before bid opening, information concerning the identity and number of bids received shall be made available only to Government employees. Such disclosure shall be only on a "need to know" basis. When bid samples are submitted, they shall be handled with sufficient care to prevent disclosure of characteristics before bid opening.

> (b) Envelopes marked as bids but not identifying the bidder or the solicitation may be opened solely for the purpose of identification, and then only by an official designated for this purpose. If a sealed bid is opened by mistake (e.g., because it is not marked as being a bid), the envelope shall be signed by the opener, whose position shall also be written thereon, and delivered to the designated official. This official shall immediately write on the envelope (1) an explanation of the opening, (2) the date and time opened, and (3) the invitation for bids number, and shall sign the envelope. The official shall then immediately reseal the envelope.

If a bid is returned unopened to the bidder, it may not be considered even if the basis for return was improper, *Leggett & Platt, Inc.*, Comp. Gen. Dec. B-246733, 92-1 CPD ¶ 314 (Federal Express envelope contained two bids, and agency returned envelope to bidder unopened because of action taken with respect to the other procurement); *Dima Contracting Corp.*, Comp. Gen. Dec. B-186487, 76-2 CPD ¶ 208 (bid was returned unopened because of reference on envelope to another IFB).

The procedures for public opening of unclassified bids are contained in FAR 14.402-1:

> (a) The bid opening officer shall decide when the time set for opening bids has arrived and shall inform those present of that decision. The officer shall then (1) personally and publicly open all bids received before that time, (2) if practical, read the bids aloud to the persons present, and (3) have the bids recorded. The original of each bid shall be carefully safeguarded, particularly until the abstract of bids required by 14.403 has been made and its accuracy verified.

> (b) Performance of the procedure in paragraph (a) above may be delegated to an assistant, but the bid opening officer remains fully responsible for the actions of the assistant.

> (c) Examination of bids by interested persons shall be permitted if it does not interfere unduly with the conduct of Government business. Original bids shall not be allowed to pass out of the hands of a Government official unless a duplicate

bid is not available for public inspection. The original bid may be examined by the public only under the immediate supervision of a Government official and under conditions that preclude possibility of a substitution, addition, deletion, or alteration in the bid.

Under these procedures requiring public bid opening, bids "are publicly opened . . . and the bid prices are generally announced and available for examination by interested persons," *Neals Janitorial Serv.*, Comp. Gen. Dec. B-279633, 98-1 CPD ¶ 156. Although FAR 14.402-1 does not specifically address the opening of electronically submitted bids, the World Bank's procurement guidelines, in addressing the same question, state that bids shall be opened in public, and that "bidders or their representatives shall be allowed to be present (in person or online, when electronic bidding is used)." World Bank, *Guidelines — Procurement Under IBRD Loans and IDA Credits* § 2.45 (2006), *http://go.worldbank.org/1KKD1KNT40.*

For national security reasons, a different bid opening procedure must be used for classified bids. See FAR 14.402-2 stating:

> The opening of classified bids shall not be accessible to the general public. Openings may be witnessed and the results recorded by those bidder representatives (a) who have been previously cleared from a security standpoint and (b) who represent bidders who were invited to bid. Bids shall be made available to those persons authorized to attend the opening of bids. No public record shall be made of bids or bid prices received in response to classified invitations for bids.

Public opening is required even if only one bid is received and the contracting officer knows before reading the bid that it will be rejected, *Wessel Co.*, Comp. Gen. Dec. B-189629, 77-2 CPD ¶ 152.

Inherent in the public opening procedure is the availability of the bid and its accompanying documents for public inspection. Typically the bid prices are recorded on an Abstract of Offers form (Standard Form 1409), which is also made available for public inspection per FAR 14.403(b). See *Neals Janitorial Serv.*, Comp. Gen. Dec. B-279633, 98-1 CPD ¶ 156. Thus, it is improper to fail to read an unclassified bid publicly and to make it available for public inspection, Comp. Gen. Dec. B-170049, Aug. 2, 1970, *Unpub.* However, the failure to publicly read a bid is a deviation of form, not substance, which does not affect the validity of an otherwise proper award. If the bidders have an opportunity to examine the awardee's bid, there is no prejudice in failing to publicly read it, *A. A. Beiro Constr. Co.*, Comp. Gen. Dec. B-192664, 78-2 CPD ¶ 425. See also *George C. Martin, Inc.*, 55 Comp. Gen. 110 (B-182175), 75-2 CPD ¶ 55; and *Moir Ranch & Constr. Co.*, Comp. Gen. Dec. B-191616, 78-1 CPD ¶ 423. However, bids that may not be publicly read because they contain information that the bidder considers "proprietary" must be rejected as nonresponsive, *Spotless Janitorial Servs., Inc.*, Comp. Gen. Dec. B-295620, 2005 CPD ¶ 36, even if the bidder authorizes disclosure after bids are opened, *Sperry-Univac*, Comp. Gen. Dec. B-200378, 81-1 CPD ¶ 38; *Computer Network Corp.*, 55

Comp. Gen. 445 (B-183639), 75-2 CPD ¶ 297. See also *Industrial Acoustics Co.*, Comp. Gen. Dec. B-255123.2, 94-1 CPD ¶ 220 (prohibition against disclosing required test data); *Prestex, Inc.*, Comp. Gen. Dec. B-195251.2, 79-2 CPD ¶ 411 (prohibition against revealing place of performance in a small business set-aside); *Warner Labs., Inc.*, Comp. Gen. Dec. B-189502, 77-2 CPD ¶ 314 (prohibition against disclosure of unit prices); and 53 Comp. Gen. 24 (B-178140) (1973) (prohibition against disclosure of descriptive data relating to responsiveness of bid). However, a prohibition on disclosure of information that deals only with a bidder's responsibility will not require rejection, *Ace-Federal Reporters, Inc.*, 54 Comp. Gen. 340 (B-181451), 74-2 CPD ¶ 239.

The premature opening of bids raises a serious question regarding the propriety of the procurement. Ordinarily such a circumstance requires that all bids be rejected and the matter resolicited unless later bidders did not obtain an unfair advantage, 34 Comp. Gen. 395 (B-122707) (1955). In *Chemical Compounding Corp.*, Comp. Gen. Dec. B-210317, 83-1 CPD ¶ 499, GAO held that it was not unreasonable to cancel a solicitation where the premature opening coincided with inadequate and ambiguous specifications. In determining whether the solicitation should be canceled when bids are prematurely opened through error or inadvertence, GAO considers the impact on both the bidders who submitted the prematurely opened bids and the other bidders. An alternate remedy is to give the bidder whose bid has been prematurely opened sufficient time to revise its bid, even if that requires extending the period for bidding, *Bartomeli Co.*, 71 Comp. Gen. 237 (B-246060), 92-1 CPD ¶ 170. See *Leach Corp.*, Comp. Gen. Dec. B-212534, 83-2 CPD ¶ 623, and *Boyd Lumber Co.*, Comp. Gen. Dec. B-189641, 77-2 CPD ¶ 315, holding that giving the bidders of the prematurely opened bids the opportunity to confirm, modify, or withdraw the bids was sufficient protection. It is not clear how the opportunity to modify a bid assists the bidder whose bid has been prematurely opened when there is evidence that other bidders have learned of the amount of the bid. However, there is no adequate means of correcting this error once it has been made, and to restrict the procurement to the bidders whose bids have been opened prematurely would be prejudicial to other bidders, *Air, Inc.*, 69 Comp. Gen. 504 (B-238468), 90-1 CPD ¶ 533.

## E.  Bid Opening Time

To be considered for award, bids must be "submitted so that they will be received in the office designated in the Invitation for Bids . . . not later than the exact time set for opening of bids," FAR 14.302(a). The regulations provide that the contracting officer should announce to those present when the time for bid opening has arrived, FAR 14.402-1(a). A bid may be submitted up to, or simultaneously with, the time the bid opening officer announces that the time for bid opening has arrived, *Carothers Constr., Inc. v. United States*, 18 Cl. Ct. 745 (1989); *Amfel Constr., Inc.*, Comp. Gen. Dec. B-233493.2, 89-1 CPD ¶ 477.

The determination of the bid opening officer of when the opening time has arrived is binding unless it is clearly unreasonable. See *W.W. Asphalt*, Comp. Gen. Dec. B-235560, 89-2 CPD ¶ 106, upholding a determination that a bid was untimely when late by the opening officer's clock even though it was one minute early by the Federal Express courier's hand-held computer. See also *Swinerton & Walberg Co.*, Comp. Gen. Dec. B-242077.3, 91-1 CPD ¶ 318, and *Chattanooga Office Supply Co.*, Comp. Gen. Dec. B-228062, 87-2 CPD ¶ 221 (bid untimely when late by bid opening office clock even though timely by telephonic report); *Lambert Constr. Co.*, Comp. Gen. Dec. B-181794, 74-2 CPD ¶ 131 (bid modification found to be late based on agency time stamp even though modification was timely according to Western Union); and 51 Comp. Gen. 173 (B-173392) (1971) (bid found to be late based on the time shown on the clock in the bid opening room even though bid was timely according to the clock in the hall). See also *General Eng'g Corp.*, Comp. Gen. Dec. B-245476, 92-1 CPD ¶ 45, upholding a determination that a bid was late based on the bid opening room clock even though the watch of an Army civil engineering technician, who was in the bid room when the protester first appeared with its bid, stated that the time was 10:59 and 45 seconds a.m., and the bid opening room clock was shown, after bid opening, to be about three minutes fast.

Occasionally, a bid opening officer's declaration of bid opening time has been shown to be unreasonable. See *William F. Wilke, Inc. v. Department of the Army*, 485 F.2d 180 (4th Cir. 1973), where a bid that was hand delivered four minutes after the scheduled bid opening could not be considered even though no other bids had been opened, and the bid opening officer announced after receipt of the late bid: "It is now 3:00 p.m." Similarly, contracting officers cannot arbitrarily use the time on their own watch as evidence of the bid opening time when the clock in the bid opening room shows another time, 41 Comp. Gen. 807 (B-148972) (1962). However, opening officers may reasonably rely on the time shown by their watch if the bid opening room is not equipped with a clock, and only "persuasive independent evidence" will rebut the reasonableness of this reliance, *Tate Architectural Prods., Inc.*, Comp. Gen. Dec. B-191361, 78-1 CPD ¶ 389. This rule is based on GAO's view that the bid opening officer's declaration is prima facie evidence of the time for bid opening. Unless there is a clear record to contradict this evidence, the authorized declaration serves as the criterion of lateness, *MACETO, Inc.*, Comp. Gen. Dec. B-207878, 82-2 CPD ¶ 300; *Peter Kiewit & Sons' Co.*, Comp. Gen. Dec. B-189022, 77-2 CPD ¶ 41; *Hyster Co.*, 55 Comp. Gen. 267 (B-182995), 75-2 CPD ¶ 176. See *Nueva Constr. Co.*, Comp. Gen. B-270009, 96-1 CPD ¶ 84, where the agency properly rejected bid as late when the protester submitted its bid seconds after the bid opening officer reasonably declared that the set time for bid opening had arrived even though the bid opening clock continued to display the same minute in time.

If the government admits that its time determination was incorrect, it may accept a bid that was determined to be late but was actually submitted on time. In *Washington Mech. Contractors, Inc. v. United States*, 612 F. Supp. 1243 (N.D. Cal. 1984), bids were due by 2:30 p.m., and the bidder's agent had been standing at a wall phone until 2:29 p.m. waiting for a final figure. The agent had previously synchronized his watch with the phone company's time service. The agent received the final figure and inserted it into the bid forms, walked to the bid opening room (which took less than 30 seconds), and tried to submit its bid. The bid opening officer said the bid was late and would not stamp it. An assistant who was present in the room said that the bid opening officer should at least stamp the envelope as received. By this time 30 seconds had passed, and the stamp read 2:31 p.m. Subsequent testing by the government indicated that the clock was one to three minutes fast and the bid was held to have been properly accepted.

The relevant time for determining whether a bid is timely received by the government is that time when the bidder relinquishes possession of its bid. If a bidder does not relinquish control of a bid prior to the bid opening officer's announcement of bid opening, it will be considered late even if the bid is time/date stamped before bid opening. In *J. C. Kimberly Co.*, Comp. Gen. Dec. B-255018.2, 94-1 CPD ¶ 79, although the bid was time/date stamped 2:29 p.m., the bid was late because it was not tendered to the bid opening officer until after the 2:30 p.m. announcement that the time for receipt of bids has passed. Similarly, in *Reliable Bldrs., Inc.*, Comp. Gen. Dec. B-249908.2, 93-1 CPD ¶ 116, a bid that was time/date stamped at 2:01 p.m. was not considered late because the record showed that the bidder relinquished control of the bid by 2:00 p.m., the exact time called for in the solicitation, and prior to the bid opening officer's declaration of the time for bid opening. A bid handed to and returned by the agency receptionist outside the designated bid opening room does not constitute submission of the bid, *J.C.N. Constr. Co.*, Comp. Gen. Dec. B-250815, 93-1 CPD ¶ 166. Even if the bidder is in the bid opening room, a bid received an instant late must be rejected. In *Lucero*, Comp. Gen. Dec. B-228425, 87-2 CPD ¶ 566, GAO rejected a bid as late under the following circumstances:

> Bids were due by 2:00 p.m. September 25, 1987 in the conference room of the District Ranger's Office. At approximately 1:50 or 1:55 p.m. of that day, Lucero entered the conference room after returning from an unsuccessful attempt to locate and inspect the timber sale area. When Lucero arrived, the bid receiving agent introduced himself, inquired as to whether Lucero had an updated form, advised him to complete the appropriate forms " right away," and answered Lucero's questions. Another Forest Service agent then assisted Lucero in completing the forms and at 1:59 p.m. advised him that he had one minute remaining in which to submit the bid. At 1:59 p m. and 55 seconds, Lucero placed the unsealed envelope in front of him, but did not submit it. At 2:00 the bid receiving agent announced that the time for receiving sealed bids had expired. Lucero attempted then to submit his bid but was advised that it could not be accepted since it was after 2:00 p.m.

A bid that is relinquished simultaneously with the announcement of closing will be considered timely. In *Carothers Constr., Inc. v. United States*, 18 Cl. Ct. 745 (1989), the court upheld GAO decision that the bid was submitted on time. In holding that the decision had a rational basis, the court stated at 750:

GAO's finding that Townsend relinquished control of Barron's bid (including all bid documents) simultaneously with Quinton's announcement that the time for receipt of bids had passed had ample support in the record. GAO based its finding on the unsworn declarations of Quinton, Brignole and Thoele. The Comptroller General focused on the following: Quinton declared that she was watching the clock, and "when the second hand reached the 12 she began to announce that the time for receipt of bids had passed. At that time . . . [Townsend] threw the other copies of the bid (and other bid documents) on the table in front of her." Supporting this was the statement of Brignole that Townsend placed the other bid documents simultaneously with Quinton's announcement. Finally, the Comptroller General noted Thoele's declaration that he picked up the documents on the table. Based on these unsworn declarations, the court finds that a rational basis existed for GAO's decision.

The timeliness requirement is not satisfied merely because the bid is in the government's possession. The bid must be delivered to the exact location specified in the solicitation or it will be considered late, unless the failure to arrive on time is a result of government mishandling, *Alpha Tech. Servs., Inc.*, Comp. Gen. Dec. B-243715, 91-2 CPD ¶ 56 (bid delivered to government installation approximately two hours before bid opening but not received in bid opening room until next day was late); *Larry J. Robinson & Co.*, Comp. Gen. Dec. B-234991, 89-1 CPD ¶ 559 (delivery to central switchboard area insufficient); *Four Thirteen, Inc.*, ASBCA 28638, 84-1 BCA ¶ 17,155 (telegram delivered to guard in lobby approximately three hours before opening insufficient).

FAR 14.402-3 permits bid opening officers to postpone the time scheduled for bid opening. Generally this occurs when the contracting officer has reason to believe that an "important segment" of bidders have been delayed for causes beyond their control and without their fault or negligence (i.e., flood, fire, weather conditions), or when an emergency or unanticipated event interrupts the normal government process, making the scheduled bid opening impractical. See *B.L.I. Constr. Co.*, Comp. Gen. Dec. B-239246.2, 90-2 CPD ¶ 85, in which an extension was permitted so that bidders could get to the designated room on time. Note, however, that postponing the date set for bid opening is strictly within the contracting officer's discretion, *Educational Planning & Advice, Inc.*, Comp. Gen. Dec. B-274513, 96-2 CPD ¶ 173 (determination to proceed with bid opening despite hurricane not an abuse of discretion). When a postponement occurs due to an interruption in the normal government process and urgent government requirements prevent amendment of the solicitation under FAR 14.208, bid opening is extended to "the first work day on which normal government processes resume," at the same time of day as originally specified in the solicitation.

## F.  Late Bids

The government has adopted very strict requirements precluding the consideration of late bids unless precisely defined exceptions are met. See FAR 14.304, which was revised in 1999 as part of an effort to provide a single standard for late offers under commercial, sealed bid, and negotiated acquisitions. The FAR provision states:

> (b)(1) Any bid, modification, or withdrawal of a bid received at the Government office designated in the IFB after the exact time specified for receipt of bids is "late" and will not be considered unless it is received before award is made, the contracting officer determines that accepting the late bid would not unduly delay the acquisition; and —
>
>> (i) If it was transmitted through an electronic commerce method authorized by the IFB, it was received at the initial point of entry to the Government infrastructure not later than 5:00 p.m. one working day prior to the date specified for receipt of bids; or
>>
>> (ii) There is acceptable evidence to establish that it was received at the Government installation designated for receipt of bids and was under the Government's control prior to the time set for receipt of bids.
>
> (2) However, a late modification of an otherwise successful bid, that makes its terms more favorable to the Government, will be considered at any time it is received and may be accepted.

\* \* \*

> (f) The contracting officer must promptly notify any bidder if its bid, modification, or withdrawal was received late, and must inform the bidder whether its bid will be considered, unless contract award is imminent and the notices prescribed in 14.409 would suffice.

Bids that cannot meet the exceptions in the regulations are considered late even though received immediately after the bid opening time. See *James L. Ferry & Sons, Inc.*, Comp. Gen. Dec. B-181612, 74-2 CPD ¶ 245 (hand-delivered bid not considered even though only three minutes late); *National Blower & Sheet Metal Co.*, Comp. Gen. Dec. B-194895, 79-2 CPD ¶ 240 (bid not accepted though only two minutes late and no bids had yet been opened); and *Parmatic Filter Corp.*, Comp. Gen. Dec. B-209296, 83-1 CPD ¶ 234 (telegraphic bid recorded as being received two minutes late was rejected where protester was unable to prove record was inaccurate).

## 1. Bids In Paper Form

A bid in paper form that is under the control of the government at the specified time is not late. However, the bidder must have proof that it had relinquished control to an official at the government office when the bid is not delivered to the specified office on time. See *Stephen Lucas Constr., LLC*, Comp. Gen. Dec. B-402654, 2010 CPD ¶ 138 (Federal Express tracking sheet showing that agency employee signed for bid before specified time adequate evidence that bid was under contract of agency). If there is any fault on the part of the bidder, the bid will be considered late, *Aquaterra Contracting, Inc.*, Comp. Gen. Dec. B-400065, 2008 CPD ¶ 138 (protest denied because protester failed to take reasonable steps to ensure proper delivery, and failure to take available steps to ensure timely delivery was paramount cause of bid's late receipt); *InfoGroup, Inc.*, Comp. Gen. Dec. B-294610, 2004 CPD ¶ 190 (lateness due to contractor fault in not providing correct room number to Federal Express). On the other hand, if the lateness is due to government fault, the bid can be accepted. See *Weeks Marine, Inc.*, Comp. Gen. Dec. B-292586, 2003 CPD ¶ 183, holding that the contracting officer properly accepted a bid delivered to the opening room one minute late because the IFB specified the wrong room.

Under the late bid rule in effect prior to 1999, bids were not late if the failure to receive them at the specified office was due to government mishandling. The decisions on this old rule may be instructive in deciding whether a bid is in the control of the agency (under the new rule). Under the mishandling rule, GAO assessed the reasonableness of agency determinations that late receipt of a hand-carried bid was due primarily to government mishandling, *Department of Housing & Urban Dev.— Reconsideration*, Comp. Gen. Dec. B-279575.2, 98-2 CPD ¶ 105.

In *Watson Agency, Inc.*, Comp. Gen. Dec. B-241072, 90-2 CPD ¶ 506, GAO found government mishandling where a guard placed the bid in the wrong safe, and the agency subsequently failed to remove the bid from the guardhouse and deliver it to the Center's Classified Mails and Files Branch for distribution, in accordance with agency procedures. Government mishandling was found in *John J. Kirlin, Inc.*, Comp. Gen. Dec. B-250244, 92-2 CPD ¶ 419, where a contractor representative delivered a hand-carried bid to the wrong bid opening officer, relying upon a sign on the entrance door to the building that the bid opening room for an IFB for "Compilation of 13 Construction Jobs" had been changed. The representative interpreted the sign to mean that the IFB for his construction project had been combined with other solicitations and that the room had been changed. Compounding the confusion, the bid opening officer for the combined construction jobs accepted the bid and clocked it at 1:46 p.m. without noticing that the envelope listed a different solicitation number. Mishandling was also found in *AABLE Tank Servs., Inc.*, Comp. Gen. Dec. B-273010, 96-2 CPD ¶ 180 (contract specialist identified in the solicitation as contact person for further information misdirected bid); *Gair's Med. Transcription Servs.*, Comp. Gen. Dec. B-257426, 94-2 CPD ¶ 115 (contracting officer failed to remove bid from safe prior to bid opening); *Victoria Inn Ltd.*, Comp. Gen. Dec. B-256724, 94-2 CPD ¶ 37 (bid package misfiled in bid cabinet); and *Data Gen. Corp.*, Comp. Gen. Dec. B-252239, 93-1 CPD ¶ 457 (installation postal authorities received bid two days prior to bid opening but did not deliver bid to contracting office due to the absence of a driver with a security clearance). No mishandling was found in *PDP Analytical Servs.*, Comp. Gen. Dec. B-251776.2, 93-1 CPD ¶ 294 (due to accumulation of mail over the Christmas holidays, the mail took longer to sort and was not distributed until after bid opening); *Environmental Control Techs.*, Comp. Gen. Dec. B-250859, 93-1 CPD ¶ 172 (bid received at the installation post office 40 minutes prior to bid opening but, as a result of the installation's normal mail delivery, did not arrive at the place for receipt of bids until after bid opening).

If the bidder significantly contributed to late receipt of a bid, any subsequent government mishandling was not the paramount reason for the bid's late receipt. See *Adirondack Constr. Corp.*, Comp. Gen. Dec. B-280015, 98-2 CPD ¶ 55 (while the agency changed the bid opening room less than one hour before bid opening, the bidder's actions significantly contributed to the late receipt of the bid); *Boines Constr. & Equip. Co.*, Comp. Gen. Dec. B-279575, 98-1 CPD ¶ 175 (bidder's erroneous labeling was paramount cause of delayed delivery); *Bill Strong Enters., Inc.*, Comp. Gen. Dec. B-260721, 95-2 CPD ¶ 10 (Federal Express, contributed significantly to the late receipt of the bid by not including the correct label on the bid).

Although the prior rule referred to government mishandling only at the government installation after receipt, GAO avoided strict application of the rule where government mishandling in the process of receipt caused the lateness. See, for example, *Kings Point Mfg. Co.*, Comp. Gen. Dec. B-199992, 81-1 CPD ¶ 293 (government cancellation of authorized Western Union terminal without notice constituted government mishandling); *I & E Constr. Co.*, 55 Comp. Gen. 1340 (B-186766), 76-2 CPD ¶ 139 (locking the building designated for receipt of bids constituted government mishandling under the "intent and the spirit" of the late bid regulations); *Sun Int'l*, Comp. Gen. Dec. B-208146, 83-1 CPD ¶ 78 (government failure to follow established procedures for receiving express mail on the weekends was the paramount cause of the bid's late receipt; the bid was therefore acceptable despite never being in the government's possession); *Howard Mgmt. Group*, Comp. Gen. Dec. B-221889, 86-2 CPD ¶ 28 (mishandling found when agency misinformed bidder that it had a telex machine); and *Standard Prods. Co.*, Comp. Gen. Dec. B-215832, 85-1 CPD ¶ 86 (mishandling found when agency failed to pay for telex service). In *Microflect*, 66 Comp. Gen. 269 (B-225118), 87-1 CPD ¶ 173 (bid mailed by express mail was delivered to the post office four and one-half hours before bid opening but was not picked up by the agency in time for bid opening).

As required by the current rule, government mishandling could not be found until the bidder established, with documented evidence, that the bid was actually received at the government facility prior to bid opening, *Power Connector, Inc.*, Comp. Gen. Dec. B-256362, 94-1 CPD ¶ 369. See *Pacific Tank Cleaning Servs., Inc.*, Comp. Gen. Dec. B-279111, 98-2 CPD ¶ 2 (evidence did not establish that bid was timely received and remained under the government's control until it was first discovered six days after bid opening); *J.C.N. Constr. Co.*, Comp. Gen. Dec. B-270068, 96-1 CPD ¶ 42 (record of a commercial carrier insufficient evidence to support the contention that the bid was timely delivered). However, commercial carrier records could be considered if the record contained corroborating relevant evidence, including statements by government personnel, *Santa Cruz Constr., Inc.*, Comp. Gen. Dec. B-226773 , 87-2 CPD ¶ 7. In *Eliscu & Co.*, Comp. Gen. Dec. B-211617, 84-1 CPD ¶ 75, GAO refused to consider the issue of government mishandling because the only proof available for bid receipt was the government stamp that recorded the delivery as being late.

## 2. Electronically Submitted Bids

FAR 14.304(b)(1)(i) contains separate language covering bid that are submitted electronically requiring that, if they are not received on time at the designated office, they will be accepted if they were received in the agency one day ahead of the bid opening date. In *Sea Box, Inc.*, Comp. Gen. Dec. B-291056, 2002 CPD ¶ 181, GAO ruled that the parallel provision pertaining to the submission of competitive proposals established an exclusive rule that barred the assertion that the proposal was late due to government mishandling. In that case the electronic proposal was received on time at the agency server but not transmitted to the designated agency office on time. See also *PMTech, Inc.*, Comp. Gen. Dec. B-291082, 2002 CPD ¶ 172, strictly interpreting this electronic submission rule. Compare *Watterson Constr. Co. v. United States*, 98 Fed. Cl. 84 (2011), reaching the opposite conclusion from *Sea Box*.

Prior to the 1999 revision of the rule, the government mishandling rule was applied to bids submitted by facsimile or electronically. Thus, in *Hydro Fitting Mfg. Corp.*, 54 Comp. Gen. 999 (B-183438), 75-1 CPD ¶ 331, a telegraphic bid received late due to the malfunction of a government telex machine was considered government mishandling. See also *Brazos Roofing, Inc.*, Comp. Gen. Dec. B-275113, 97-1 CPD ¶ 43 (where the agency amended a solicitation so close to the deadline for submitting bids that submission by facsimile was the only practicable alternative to bidders, a bid received late due to an inoperable facsimile machine considered government mishandling); *Butt Constr. Co.*, Comp. Gen. Dec. B-258507, 95-1 CPD ¶ 45 (government mishandling the paramount cause of late receipt of a facsimile bid modification received at least seven minutes prior to bid opening time where the facsimile machine was only a short distance from the opening room). However, the rule was strictly applied. See *Roy McGinnis & Co.*, Comp. Gen. Dec. B-275988, 97-1 CPD ¶ 156 (bidder did not allow sufficient time for facsimile bid to be brought to bid room); *Stack-On Prods. Co.*, Comp. Gen. Dec. B-181862, 74-2 CPD ¶ 220 (late bid modification could not be considered even though it was received on the telex machine on time but was not transcribed for 50 minutes because the operator was busy). In an unusual case, *Scherr Constr. Co. v. United States*, 5 Cl. Ct. 249 (1984), the failure of the government to inform a bidder of the flex-time schedule during which the government officer operated was found to be the primary cause of the nonreceipt of the contractor's telegraphic modification on the day before bid opening. The late bid rule, however, remained intact since the court ultimately determined that Western Union's lack of diligence in delivering the modification the following day when the government office was open was the primary cause for nonreceipt.

## 3. Hand-Carried Bids

The regulations have never provided exceptions for late bids that are hand carried. See *Nueva Constr. Co.*, Comp. Gen. Dec. B-270009, 96-1 CPD ¶ 84 (hand-carried bid delivered seconds after bid opening officer declared that the time for bid opening stated in the solicitation had arrived was late); *J. C. Kimberly Co.*, Comp. Gen. Dec. B-255018.2, 94-1 CPD ¶ 79 (hand-carried bid received after bid opening officer declared that the time for bid opening had arrived was late); and *GS Edwards*, Comp. Gen. Dec. B-255202, 94-1 CPD ¶ 54 (hand-carried bid delivered three minutes late could not be considered); *George W. Kane, Inc.*, Comp. Gen. Dec. B-245382.2, 92-1 CPD ¶ 143 (bid late although hand carried to bid opening room because it was not delivered to the bid depository location on time). See also *Boulder Constr., Inc.*, Comp. Gen. Dec. B-250671, 93-1 CPD ¶ 122; *Wyoming Sawmills, Inc.*, Comp. Gen. Dec. B-248331, 92-2 CPD ¶ 45; and *General Eng'g Corp.*, Comp. Gen. Dec. B-245476, 92-1 CPD ¶ 45.

A bid that is delivered by commercial carrier is considered to be "hand carried" and is considered late if it does not arrive timely at the location designated in the solicitation, *Barnes Elec. Co.*, Comp. Gen. Dec. B-241391.2, 91-1 CPD ¶ 10; *Hans Olsen Egg Co.*, Comp. Gen. Dec. B-235085, 89-2 CPD ¶ 75.

Late hand-carried bids have been properly accepted where the government was responsible for the lateness. See *Palomar Grading & Paving, Inc.*, Comp. Gen. Dec. B-274885, 97-1 CPD ¶16 (incorrect address specified in the solicitation for the delivery of bids); *Ed Kocharian & Co.*, Comp. Gen. Dec. B-271186, 96-1 CPD ¶ 170 (office designated for bid opening was locked); *Kelton Contracting, Inc.*, Comp. Gen. Dec. B-262255, 95-2 CPD ¶ 254 (agency properly accepted a late hand-carried bid where agency clerk placed the bid package in the wrong mail slot); *Power Connector, Inc.*, Comp. Gen. Dec. B-256362 , 94-1 CPD ¶369 (agency personnel misdirected delivery of bid package to the wrong floor); *Pearl Props.*, Comp. Gen. Dec. B-249519, 92-2 CPD ¶ 333 (bid received three-and-one-half hours prior to bid opening but placed in the bottom of a mail tote); *Ranco Constr., Inc.*, Comp. Gen. Dec. B-246345, 92-1 CPD ¶ 234 (employee failed to expedite delivery of package as instructed and instead placed bid in normal delivery); *Richards Painting Co.*, Comp. Gen. Dec. B-232678, 89-1 CPD ¶76 (hand-carried bid delivered three minutes after bid opening because the front door of the government building was locked, and the bid opening room was different from the unstaffed room designated for the receipt of hand-carried bids); *Baeten Constr., Co.*, Comp. Gen. Dec. B-210681, 83-2 CPD ¶ 203 (government official misdirected the delivery person); *Dale Woods*, Comp. Gen. Dec. B-209459, 83-1 CPD ¶ 396 (government changed the room for bid delivery without informing all bidders); *Empire Mech. Contractors, Inc.*, Comp. Gen. Dec. B-202141, 81-1 CPD ¶ 471 (commercial carrier delivered the bid before opening, but the bid was delivered late to the opening official due to mishandling); *Scot, Inc.*, Comp. Gen. Dec. B-189345, 77-2 CPD ¶ 425 (commercial carrier delivered the bid late due to government misdirection); *LeChase Constr. Corp.*, Comp. Gen. Dec. B-183609, 75-2 CPD ¶ 5 (delay was caused by a change in the room designated for bid opening); and *Fredericks Rubber Co.*, 51 Comp. Gen. 69 (B-172974) (1971) (bid was placed in the wrong box due to the government's failure to mark the correct bid box clearly).

If the government is not the cause of the lateness of the hand-carried bid, generally no other excuse will assist the bidder in having its bid considered. See *Great Plains Asbestos Control, Inc.*, Comp. Gen. Dec. B-271841, 96-2 CPD ¶ 19 (commercial carrier leaving bid at military installation's freight terminal no excuse); *Ironhorse, Ltd.*, Comp. Gen. Dec. B-256582, 94-1 CPD ¶ 176, and *B.E.C. Med. Prods.*, Comp. Gen. Dec. B-256483, 94-1 CPD ¶ 159 (severe weather no excuse); *Braceland Bros., Inc.*, Comp. Gen. Dec. B-248234, 92-2 CPD ¶ 69 (messenger delivering bids to wrong address no excuse); *John Holtman & Sons, Inc.*, Comp. Gen. Dec. B-246062, 92-1 CPD ¶ 187 (bid delivered to warehouse rather than the office specified in the solicitation was late); *High Vacuum Equip. Corp.*, Comp. Gen. Dec. B-224511, 86-2 CPD ¶ 189 (flight delays no excuse); *National Minority Research Dev. Corp.*, Comp. Gen. Dec. B-220057, 85-2 CPD ¶ 303 (automobile accident no excuse); *Key Airlines*, Comp. Gen. Dec. B-214122, 84-1 CPD ¶ 242 (late bid properly rejected despite bidder never receiving an official copy of the IFB); *Northwest Instrument*, Comp. Gen. Dec. B-200873, 80-2 CPD ¶ 373 (traffic delays and business necessity do not excuse late bid); and *Unitron Eng'g Co.*, 58 Comp. Gen. 748 (B-194707), 79-2 CPD ¶ 155 (closing of a common carrier's offices due to the Three Mile Island nuclear emergency did not serve as an excuse for late delivery of hand-carried bid).

Similarly, a bidder's failure to follow solicitation procedures will generally be considered the primary reason for the late delivery rather than improper government action, *Sencland CDC Enters.*, Comp. Gen. Dec. B-252796, 93-2 CPD ¶ 36 (bid rejected as late where commercial carrier delivered bids to the mail room rather than to the bid depository for hand-carried bids in accordance with the solicitation instructions); *Gould Metal Specialists Inc.*, Comp. Gen. Dec. B-246686, 92-1 CPD ¶ 311 (bid was delivered to the mailing address rather than the address for hand-carried bids).

## II. RESPONSIVENESS

A key element of the sealed bidding system is that nonresponsive bids may not be considered by contracting officers and must be rejected. This *responsiveness* requirement is derived from the statutory provision providing that award be made to the bidder "whose bid conforms to the solicitation," 10 U.S.C. § 2305(b)(3); 41 U.S.C. § 3702(b). The purpose of this requirement is to promote fairness and objectivity, and to encourage wide competition by requiring all bidders to bid on exactly the same work and to the same terms and conditions — permitting the selection of the winning bidder solely on the basis of price. Thus, the responsiveness requirement ensures that a bidder will not receive an award by offering to perform the work perhaps less expensively but in a manner that represents a material deviation from the terms of the IFB. This promotes the integrity of the procurement process by protecting other bidders that might also have proposed such a method had they known that the government was willing to accept it. At the same time, however, the strict responsiveness requirement may result in the government's loss of the benefit of diverse and innovative solutions — explaining, in part, why over time federal agencies have shifted away from the use of sealed bidding for more complex requirements.

The mandatory rejection rule also prevents bidders with ambiguous bids from having "two bites at the apple" by contending, after seeing the competing bids, that their bids conformed to the solicitation (or did not conform), depending on the interpretation that is most beneficial to them.

The requirement for mandatory rejection has made responsiveness a focal point for award controversies. If the low bidder can be disqualified as nonresponsive, the next bidder in line becomes eligible to receive the award at a higher price. Thus, both the government and the bidder could be "losers" if a bid is found to be nonresponsive. This section first examines the criteria used in determining whether a nonconformity is sufficient to require the bid being classified as nonresponsive. It next considers the disposition of nonconforming bids and the limited circumstances under which an award may be made on the basis of a nonresponsive bid. The section concludes with an analysis of the types of nonconforming bids and the factors that determine whether such bids are nonresponsive.

## A.  Criteria for Determining Responsiveness

A bid is nonconforming if it fails to comply exactly with the literal requirements of the IFB. However, not all nonconforming bids are nonresponsive. In determining whether a nonconforming bid is nonresponsive, the focus may be either on the nature of the nonconformity or on the effect of the nonconformity on the competition. This section first considers whether the nonconformity is *sufficiently material* to warrant rejection of the bid or is merely an *immaterial deviation* that may be waived. It then examines the extent to which *prejudice to other bidders* resulting from a nonconformity determines responsiveness. The section concludes with a discussion of the distinction between responsiveness of bids and responsibility of bidders.

### 1.  Materiality of Nonconformity

The FAR defines responsiveness in terms of materiality of the nonconformity See FAR 14.301(a), stating:

> To be considered for award, a bid must comply in all material respects with the invitation for bids. Such compliance enables bidders to stand on an equal footing and maintain the integrity of the sealed bidding system.

Thus, a bid that contains an immaterial nonconformity is not considered to be a nonresponsive bid. Such nonconformities are called *minor informalities*. FAR 14.405 defines a "minor informality":

an acceptable bid. In *AABCO, Inc. v. United States*, 3 Cl. Ct. 109 (1983), the failure of a bidder to code each of the prices on a magnetic tape exactly as required by the solicitation was properly waived as a minor informality. The Claims Court held that there was no doubt whatsoever as to the intended bids, stating at 119:

> A mere glance at the printout that accompanied the submitted tape would confirm the exact dollars and cents that the [contractor] intended to bid.

See also *Sere Constr. Corp.*, Comp. Gen. Dec. B-205098, 82-1 CPD ¶ 453 (failure to provide unit prices waivable because single unit price provided sufficient bidding pattern to allow accurate pricing of any contract modification); *MKB Constructors (J.V.)*, Comp. Gen. Dec. B-250413, 93-1 CPD ¶ 50 (failure to submit a price for 1 of 60 line items was a minor informality where the intended price of the missing line item could be determined from the bid itself); *Mike Johnson, Inc.*, Comp. Gen. Dec. B-271943, 96-2 CPD ¶ 66 (failure to break the contract work into three line items of work per revised bid schedule was a minor informality because the revised schedule did not add any additional work beyond that encompassed in the original bid schedule). However, when the bid fails to provide sufficient information to allow the contracting officer to determine the details of the intended bid, it must be rejected. See *Childrey Contract Servs., Inc.*, Comp. Gen. Dec. B-258653, 95-1 CPD ¶ 60 (insufficient information in bid to determine what prices bidder intended to bid for option years without prices); and *Norris Paint & Varnish Co.*, Comp. Gen. Dec. B-206079, 82-1 CPD ¶ 425 (no information in bid to determine whether bidder had a valid Qualified Products List test number as required by IFB).

Statements in invitations as to the automatic effect of noncompliance with certain provisions on responsiveness are not controlling where noncompliance involves a minor deviation, *Mid-South Metals, Inc.*, Comp. Gen. Dec. B-257056, 94-2 CPD ¶ 78 (submission of multiple credit card accounts as bid guarantee was responsive, even though solicitation prohibited the use of multiple credit card accounts); *Isometrics, Inc.*, Comp. Gen. Dec. B-212434, 83-2 CPD ¶ 618 (failure to supply shipping information as required by the IFB does not render bid nonresponsive when agency was able to derive the information from other bids). In *D.N. Owens Co.*, 57 Comp. Gen. 231 (B-190749), 78-1 CPD ¶ 66, even though the solicitation required rejection of bids for nonresponsiveness if bidders failed to submit bid samples, GAO held that the failure to submit the sample was a minor irregularity since the extent of detail in the specifications made the sample unnecessary.

The decision as to whether a particular nonconformity constitutes a minor deviation has sometimes been characterized as a discretionary one for the contracting officer, Comp. Gen. Dec. B-172227, May 13, 1971, *Unpub*. Cases where proper waiver was found include *Consolidated Contracting Eng'g*, Comp. Gen. Dec. B-274319, 96-2 CPD ¶ 174 (failure to acknowledge amendment properly waived where the amendment results in less stringent obligations on the bidder); *Elliott Co.*, Comp. Gen. Dec. B-212897, 84-1 CPD ¶ 130 (failure to include Qualified Price

List information was properly waived when the information could be obtained from other facts within the bid); *Massee Bldrs., Inc.*, 61 Comp. Gen. 227 (B-204450), 82-1 CPD ¶ 72 (failure to utilize additive method in bid construction as stated in IFB properly waived); *Gillette Indus., Inc.*, Comp. Gen. Dec. B-194552, 79-2 CPD ¶ 59 (failure to acknowledge "trivial amendment" properly waived).

GAO has required waiver in several cases and has suggested award to the protester, even though the contracting officer "in his discretion" had previously refused to waive the nonconformity, *Fort Mojave/Hummel, J.V.,* Comp. Gen. Dec. B-296961, 2005 CPD ¶ 181 (low bidder's failure to acknowledge amendment that merely clarified requirements already contained in the solicitation and otherwise had a negligible effect on the quality and price of the project); *Jackson Enters.,* Comp. Gen. Dec. B-286688, 2001 CPD ¶ 25 (failure to acknowledge amendment setting forth agency answers to bidders' questions that did not contain material information and did not alter bidders' legal obligations); *Schuster Eng'g, Inc.*, Comp. Gen. Dec. B-275044, 97-1 CPD ¶ 29 (failure to acknowledge amendment because the amendment only relaxed performance requirements); *Legare Constr. Co.*, Comp. Gen. Dec. B-257735, 94-2 CPD ¶ 173 (failure to meet price limitation); *Shipco Gen., Inc.*, Comp. Gen. Dec. B-204259, 81-2 CPD ¶ 161 (failure to complete size status certifications); *National Radio Co.*, Comp. Gen. Dec. B-198240, 80-2 CPD ¶ 67, *recons. denied*, 80-2 CPD ¶ 165 (failure to list separate price for first article testing, regardless of IFB warnings, because the bid indicated that such cost was included in the price of the basic item); *MB Assocs.*, Comp. Gen. Dec. B-197566, 80-1 CPD ¶ 383 (failure to acknowledge amendment that decreased performance costs). In an unusual case, *Champion Road Mach. Int'l Corp.*, Comp. Gen. Dec. B-200678, 81-2 CPD ¶ 27, GAO reversed the contracting officer by ruling that a two horsepower difference between the item offered and the performance required constituted a minor deviation. Another example of a liberal interpretation of the minor deviation rule is *Albano Cleaners, Inc. v. United States*, 197 Ct. Cl. 450, 455 F.2d 556 (1972), where the contractor had qualified the bid by refusing delivery services for orders of less than $50. The court held that the contracting officer should have waived the deviation because the qualification was not a substantial deviation from the solicitation.

## 2. Prejudice to Other Bidders

A number of cases have focused on the prejudice to other bidders rather than on the degree of nonconformity in determining whether a bid is nonresponsive. Thus, a material nonconformity that gives the bidder no advantage or that operates only to the disadvantage of the bidder will not require rejection. See *Gibraltar Indus., Inc.*, Comp. Gen. Dec. B-218537.3, 85-2 CPD ¶ 24 (failure to acknowledge amendment that reduced quantity of items required under the contract properly waived); and *Action Mfg. Co.*, Comp. Gen. Dec. B-208205.2, 82-2 CPD ¶ 526 (failure to indicate which of two equally acceptable designs would be used, as required by the IFB, waived and bid properly accepted). In *Davidson-Kelson, Inc.*, Comp. Gen. Dec.

B-212551, 83-2 CPD ¶ 589, where an amendment reduced the cost of performance, and no competitive advantage accrued to the bidder as a result of its failure to acknowledge, the error was waived. GAO stated:

> [T]he bidder's failure to acknowledge an amendment containing a lessened requirement could only be prejudicial to the bidder's own competitive position and even possibly beneficial to the position of the other bidders.

See also *Conrad Indus., Inc.*, Comp. Gen. Dec. B-213974.2, 84-2 CPD ¶ 156 (failure to acknowledge amendment changing delivery terms from "f.o.b. destination" to "f.o.b. origin" properly waived); and *Patterson Enters. Ltd.*, Comp. Gen. Dec. B-207105, 82-2 CPD ¶ 133 (failure to acknowledge amendment extending completion deadline for construction project properly waived). However, a different result is obtained when, in addition to reducing performance cost, the amendment imposes additional work, *Hutto Appliance & Refrigeration Serv.*, Comp. Gen. Dec. B-201585, 81-1 CPD ¶ 495. See also *Childrey Contract Servs., Inc.*, Comp. Gen. Dec. B-258653, 95-1 CPD ¶ 60 (failure to clearly demonstrate that bid price includes work added by amendment renders bid nonresponsive).

For other cases involving application of the "no prejudice" rule, see *Keco Indus., Inc.*, 64 Comp. Gen. 48 (B-216396.2), 84-2 CPD ¶ 491 (second low bidder could not conceivably become low even if permitted the same nonconformity); *Leslie & Elliott Co.*, 64 Comp. Gen. 279 (B-216676), 85-1 CPD ¶ 212 (failure to provide a price for a bid item waived); and *Energy Maint. Corp.*, 64 Comp. Gen. 425 (B-215281.3), 85-1 CPD ¶ 341 (ambiguity as to low bidder's price waived where bid would be low by a significant margin under least favorable interpretation). Thus, GAO has, under limited circumstances, required waiver of an otherwise significant deviation where no competitive advantage would result.

## 3. Responsiveness versus Responsibility

It is critical to determine whether a nonconformity deals with the responsiveness of a bid or the responsibility of the bidder. Responsiveness, an area in which the contracting officer has limited discretion, deals with the question of whether the contractor *has promised to do exactly what the government has requested.* Responsibility, on the other hand, involves the question of whether the contractor *can or will perform as it has promised*, and the contracting officer is accorded a great deal of discretion in reaching this conclusion. Questions of responsiveness are determined only on the basis of information submitted with the bid and on the facts available at the time of bid opening. Conversely, responsibility determinations are made on the basis of all information that may be submitted or available up to the time of award. These concepts are often confused, particularly when the IFB contains specific requirements concerning bidders' responsibility characteristics — such as the requirement for submission of information relating to responsibility. As a general rule, matters that deal with bidder responsibility cannot be converted into matters of responsiveness merely by inserting a provision into the IFB requiring rejection of bids that do not comply, *SourceLink Ohio, LLC*, Comp. Gen. Dec. B-299258, 2007 CPD ¶ 50 (requirement that bidders submit data source agreement describing how health data would be protected related to responsibility, not responsiveness); *Joint Venture Conscoop-Meyerinck,* Comp. Gen. Dec. B-278243, 98-1 CPD ¶ 83 (agency properly took corrective action in treating information required with bid regarding systems integrator to perform work as a matter of responsibility, not responsiveness); *LORS Med. Corp.*, Comp. Gen. Dec. B-259829, 95-1 CPD ¶ 222 (requirement for submission of information regarding company's policies and procedures relates to responsibility even though IFB required information to be submitted with bid); *Employers Sec. Co.*, GSBCA 6917, 85-1 BCA ¶ 17,885 (requirement that bidder possess an operating license properly relates to responsibility, notwithstanding solicitation language stating that it affects responsiveness); *Lithographic Pubs. Inc.*, Comp. Gen. Dec. B-217263, 85-1 CPD ¶ 357 (solicitation provision stating that bids would be considered nonresponsive if the bidder had defaulted on prior government contract could not convert a matter of responsibility into one of responsiveness); *Marine Power & Equip. Co.*, Comp. Gen. Dec. B-208393, 82-2 CPD ¶ 514 (specific solicitation provisions could not convert the issue of an agent's authority into a matter of bid responsiveness). However, some matters, such as those discussed below, although dealing with the likelihood of obtaining promised performance, have been permitted to be treated as matters of responsiveness.

### a.  Quantity in Use Provisions

The requirement that a product have a "quantity in use" for a stated period of time may be considered to deal with responsiveness, even though the requirement deals more with a bidder's ability to satisfy the government's needs than with the bidder's agreement to do so. See Comp. Gen. Dec. B-175493.1, Apr. 20, 1972, *Unpub.*, where GAO discussed quantity in use requirements in a responsiveness context. In *Sunsav, Inc.*, Comp. Gen. Dec. B-205004.2, 82-2 CPD ¶ 476, GAO held that if the requirement relates to the performance history and reliability of the contract *product* and the solicitation requires that the information be furnished, the requirement relates to bid responsiveness and evidence of compliance must be submitted prior to bid opening. The same result was reached by the General Services Administration Board of Contract Appeals in *Micro Star Co.*, GSBCA 8717-P, 87-1 BCA ¶ 19,474.

The key is whether the solicitation clearly establishes that the agency is seeking to assure itself of the reliability of the equipment rather than the capability of the offeror, *National Energy Res., Inc.*, Comp. Gen. Dec. B-206275, 83-1 CPD ¶ 108 (requirement of coal analysis reports related to the suitability of the product and not to the producer's qualifications). However, the distinction between quantity in use requirements and "experience" requirements is often obscure. For example, in *Cubic Western Data, Inc.*, 57 Comp. Gen. 17 (B-189578), 77-2 CPD ¶ 279, GAO found the statement that "each bidder, in order to demonstrate his qualifications . . . shall . . . show that he has successfully executed a contract for the design . . . of equipment of the complexity of this contract within . . . two years" related to the bidder's responsibility. Thus, if a quantity in use requirement does not pertain exclusively to the item procured, but includes generally similar equipment previously produced by the offeror, the quantity in use requirement is a matter of responsibility, *Carco Elecs.*, Comp. Gen. Dec. B-186747, 77-1 CPD ¶ 172; *United Power & Control Sys., Inc.*, Comp. Gen. Dec. B-184662, 76-1 CPD ¶ 340; 52 Comp. Gen. 647 (B-175254.2) (1973). Similarly, if information regarding use of the product is requested, but the agency has established no standards for measuring the level of successful use, it will be a matter of responsibility and not responsiveness, *W.M. Schlosser Co.*, Comp. Gen. Dec. B-258284, 94-2 CPD ¶ 234.

## b. Bid Guarantees

Another area where the concepts of responsiveness and responsibility are confused is that of bid guarantees. Such bid guarantees, commonly in the form of bid bonds, are necessary when a performance bond is required from the winning bidder, FAR 28.101-1(a). Despite the fact that the bid guarantee relates to whether the contractor will perform (responsibility), it is considered such a material requirement that it has been made a matter of bid responsiveness. Thus, ¶ (a) of the Bid Guarantee solicitation provision in FAR 52.228-1 states that failure to furnish a required bid guarantee by the time of bid opening "may be cause for rejection of the bid." FAR 28.101-4(a) *requires* rejection of bids not including required bid guarantees, but FAR 28.101-4(c) gives the contracting officer discretion to waive noncompliance as follows:

Noncompliance with a solicitation requirement for a bid guarantee shall be waived in the following circumstances unless the contracting officer determines in writing that acceptance of the bid would be detrimental to the Government's interest when —

(1) Only one offer is received. In this case, the contracting officer may require the furnishing of the bid guarantee before award;

(2) The amount of the bid guarantee submitted is less than required, but is equal to or greater than the difference between the offer price and the next higher acceptable offer;

(3) The amount of the bid guarantee submitted, although less than that required by the solicitation for the maximum quantity offered, is sufficient for a quantity for which the offeror is otherwise eligible for award. Any award to the offeror shall not exceed the quantity covered by the bid guarantee;

(4) The bid guarantee is received late, and late receipt is waived under 14.304;

(5) A bid guarantee becomes inadequate as a result of the correction of a mistake under 14.407 (but only if the bidder will increase the bid guarantee to the level required for the corrected bid);

(6) A telegraphic offer modification is received without corresponding modification of the bid guarantee, if the modification expressly refers to the previous offer and the offeror corrects any deficiency in bid guarantee;

(7) An otherwise acceptable bid bond was submitted with a signed offer, but the bid bond was not signed by the offeror;

(8) An otherwise acceptable bid bond is erroneously dated or bears no date at all; or

(9) A bid bond does not list the United States as obligee, but correctly identifies the offeror, the solicitation number, and the name and location of the project involved, so long as it is acceptable in all other respects.

GAO acceded to this policy in 38 Comp. Gen. 532 (B-137319) (1958) on the grounds that permitting bidders to submit bid bonds after bids had been opened gave them "two bites at the apple." This damaged the integrity of the procurement process by providing the low bidder that had not furnished a bond with the option of winning the competition by furnishing the bond or dropping out by not furnishing it. Since that time, rejection of bids as nonresponsive because of the lack of a proper bid guarantee has been sustained, *Morrison Constr. Servs.*, Comp. Gen. Dec. B-266233, 96-1 CPD ¶ 26; *Johnston Eng'g, Inc.*, Comp. Gen. Dec. B-258180, 94-2 CPD ¶ 246; *Secur-Data Sys., Inc.*, Comp. Gen. Dec. B-255090, 94-1 CPD ¶ 68; *Hugo Key & Son, Inc.*, Comp. Gen. Dec. B-251053.4, 93-2 CPD ¶ 21; *Minority Enters., Inc.*, Comp. Gen. Dec. B-216667, 85-1 CPD ¶ 57. For a circuit court case agreeing with this reasoning, see *Professional Bldg. Concepts, Inc. v. City of Central Falls*, 974 F.2d 1 (1st Cir. 1992). This issue must be determined based on the documents submitted with the bid. Thus, it is improper to reject a bid with a facially proper bid guarantee because of knowledge that the surety will not provide the performance bond if the bidder is awarded the contract, *Aeroplate Corp. v. United States*, 67 Fed. Cl. 4 (2005).

Contracting officers' decisions to waive the requirement that bid security be submitted with the bid have been sustained when one of the FAR situations applies or where there is another valid reason for waiver, *R.P. Richards Constr. Co.*, Comp. Gen. Dec. B-260965, 95-2 CPD ¶ 128 (bid bond with incorrect solicitation number but with other indicia tying it to the IFB); *Centex-Great Southwest Corp.*, Comp. Gen. Dec. B-258578, 95-1 CPD ¶ 19 (bid bond less than 20% of bid price but greater than difference between low and next low bid); *S.J. Amoroso Constr. Co.*, Comp. Gen. Dec. B-240687, 90-2 CPD ¶ 432 (bid bond not listing United States as obligee but containing other indicia that it was for the bid). In a few cases, GAO has also sustained protests that the contracting officer failed to waive this requirement,

*Hostetter, Keach & Cassada Constr., LLC*, Comp. Gen. Dec. B-403329, 2010 CPD ¶ 246 (discrepancy between name of bidder and name of bid bond principal but record showed they were the same entity);*Castle Floor Covering*, 70 Comp. Gen. 530 (B-242718), 91-1 CPD ¶ 510 (cashier's check made out to "Farmers Home Bureau, U.S. Government" in lieu of "Farmers Home Administration" is minor error); *Haag Elec. & Constr., Inc.*, 70 Comp. Gen. 180 (B-240974), 91-1 CPD ¶ 29 (bid bond for less than amount required but more than difference between bid and next low bid). See also *Tip Top Constr., Inc. v. United States*, 563 F.3d 1338 (Fed. Cir. 2009), holding that a contracting officer properly rejected a bid guarantee that pledged mined coal which was not an acceptable form of security.

### c. Ability to Perform

The argument that a bidder's inability to perform should be taken to mean that it does not intend to perform and that the bid is therefore nonresponsive is usually rejected, *Tessa Structures, LLC*, Comp. Gen. Dec. B-298835, 2006 CPD ¶ 199 (agency determination that inability to meet contract schedule was matter of responsiveness); *Peterson Accounting*, Comp. Gen. Dec. B-257411 , Sept. 24, 1994, *Unpub.* (agency allegation that bidder failed to submit information to demonstrate ability to perform work); *Luhr Bros., Inc.*, Comp. Gen. Dec. B-248423, 92-2 CPD ¶ 88 (allegation that "bidder-generated production rate" used to determine low bidder on IFB calling for payment based on bid unit prices "is so much a part of the price structure that it has been elevated to a matter of responsiveness"); *American KAL Enters., Inc.*, Comp. Gen. Dec. B-211938, 84-1 CPD ¶ 66 (protest that bidder was unable to meet domestic products requirement); *Grace Indus., Inc.*, Comp. Gen. Dec. B-212263.3, 84-1 CPD ¶ 212 (allegation that bidder was unable to comply with IFB requirement); *Gillette Indus., Inc.*, Comp. Gen. Dec. B-203157, 81-1 CPD ¶ 389 (allegation that low bidders could not perform contract at their bid prices); *Data Test Corp.*, 54 Comp. Gen. 499 (B-181199), 74-2 CPD ¶ 365 (allegation that the bidder did not have an "off the shelf" item as required by the IFB, however, protest sustained on the basis of nonresponsibility).

For a unique case where a bid valid on its face was held nonresponsive, see 46 Comp. Gen. 275 (B-159560), Oct. 7, 1966, where it was found that the bidder did not intend to comply with the IFB although the bid conformed to the IFB. GAO found that contacts between the bidder and government personnel prior to bidding indicated that the bidder was unable and did not intend to perform in accordance with the IFB. Compare *Radio TV Reports, Inc.*, Comp. Gen. Dec. B-192958, 79-2 CPD ¶ 27, where GAO, holding that an allegation that the bidder did not intend to perform was a matter of responsibility, distinguished 46 Comp. Gen. 275, stating:

> In its bid, Birmingham promised to perform all the work required and further indicated that it intended to use its owned and operated facilities in the four metropolitan areas for contract performance. However, prior to award, the Army learned that Birmingham did not own monitoring, recording, and transcribing facilities in

Chicago and New York. When questioned about this, Birmingham provided the Army's preaward survey team addresses in the two cities, and explained it had representatives at those locations who could easily obtain the requisite tapes and transcripts from the broadcasting stations.

* * *

Radio TV contends, however, that the contract should be terminated because the Army awarded the contract knowing that Birmingham had no facilities in either Chicago or New York. In support of its position, the protester submits that the facts in this case are sufficiently similar to those in B-159560, October 7, 1966, where we recommended a contract be canceled, to warrant a similar result. In that case, the Navy awarded a contract following advertisement for trash removal services to a company knowing that the contractor planned to use a trash collection method which deviated from the specifications. We determined that although the contractor's bid appeared valid on its face, contracting officials, by making the award, in effect improperly agreed to waive the specifications requirements for the benefit of one bidder.

We do not believe the present case is sufficiently analogous to B-159560, *supra*, to warrant a similar result, because in our view, there was no Government waiver of a substantive contract provision for the benefit of Birmingham. For example, the IFB provision quoted above which the protester relies upon for the most part as his basis for protest does not *require* the contractor to perform the desired services either through the use of its own personnel *or* by subcontract. If, as Birmingham alleges, the materials can be obtained directly from the broadcasters who presumably make the recordings for their own purposes, we believe no subcontracts are involved and the clause requiring evidence of a "commitment or specific arrangement" is not called into play.

## d.  Certification Requirements

Bidders are frequently required to submit certifications and representations with their bids. This practice often led to confusion on the part of the bidders when these requirements were scattered throughout the IFB, Comp. Gen. Dec. B-176148, Aug. 14, 1973, *Unpub*. However, under the Uniform Contract Format required by FAR 14.201-1, all certifications and representations must be included in Section K of the IFB. Nonetheless, certifications and representations are often omitted or are furnished with signatures or other information missing. This raises a question of whether a bid submitted with an incomplete, missing, or defective certification or representation must be rejected, as being nonresponsive. As a general rule, if the information in the certification deals with the bidder's responsibility, the bid should not be rejected and the missing information may properly be submitted after bid opening, *J. Morris & Assocs.*, Comp. Gen. Dec. B-259767, 95-1 CPD ¶ 213 (certification that bidder is or is not a small, disadvantaged business is not a matter of responsiveness); *Norfolk Shipbuilding & Drydock Corp.*, Comp. Gen. Dec. B-248549, 92-2 CPD ¶ 127 (although a solicitation required certification of drydocking availability to be submitted with bid, certification concerns bidder's capability to perform and is a matter of responsibility); *PacifiCorp Capital, Inc.*, GSBCA 10884-P, 91-1 BCA ¶ 23,598 (requirement that reconditioned equipment be "certified as new" not a matter of responsiveness); *Grifco*, Comp. Gen. Dec. B-240549, 90-2 CPD ¶ 143 (certificate disclosing whether any facilities are on the EPA list of facilities violating the Clean Air Act or the Clean Water Act is a matter of bidder responsibility); *Intermountain Elec., Inc.*, Comp. Gen. Dec. B-236953.2 , 90-1 CPD ¶ 143 (certificate regarding status as debarred or suspended bidder a matter of responsibility); *Jersey Maid Distribs., Inc.*, Comp. Gen. Dec. B-217307, 85-1 CPD ¶ 307 (bid certifications were not necessary to determine whether the bid meets specifications requirements since they relate to responsibility); *Deterline Corp.*, Comp. Gen. Dec. B-208986, 83-1 CPD ¶ 427 (certification that bidder is a regular dealer or manufacturer of product may be submitted up to time of award); *C.R. Hipp, Inc.*, Comp. Gen. Dec. B-212093, 83-2 CPD ¶ 418 (failure to complete Standard Form 19-B, "Representations and Certifications," relates to bidder's responsibility); *Fisher Berkeley Corp.*, Comp. Gen. Dec. B-196432, 80-1 CPD ¶ 26 (failure to include testing certification may be waived if bid indicates equipment has been tested and meets the specifications); *Jets, Inc.*, Comp. Gen. Dec. B-194017, 79-1 CPD ¶ 269 (failure to accurately complete affidavit regarding surety net worth is a matter of responsibility).

Bidders are now required to submit their certifications and representations annually by submitting the Online Representations and Certifications Application, FAR Subpart 4.12. This policy is implemented by the inclusion of the Annual Representations and Certifications clause in FAR 52.204-8 in IFBs. The expiration of this registration does not make a bid nonresponsive because it can be updated prior to award, *Veterans Constr. of South Carolina, LLC*, Comp. Gen. Dec. B-401723.2, 2010 CPD ¶ 36.

However, if a missing or defective certificate raises doubt over whether the bidder has agreed to perform in accordance with the IFB or whether the product offered meets the contract requirements, the bid must be rejected, *New Zealand Fence Sys.*, Comp. Gen. Dec. B-257460, 94-2 CPD ¶ 101 (failure to certify that bidder under a total small business set-aside for supply items would provide end items manufactured or produced by small business concerns); *Camar Corp.*, Comp. Gen. Dec. B-248485, 92-2 CPD ¶ 140 (failure to submit certified test report that product had been tested under specified conditions); *Koch Corp.*, Comp. Gen. Dec. B-212304.4, 84-2 CPD ¶ 132 (failure to certify product's performance history relates to product quality); *Phaostron Instrument & Elec. Co.*, Comp. Gen. Dec. B-214169, 84-1 CPD ¶ 474 (failure to certify that bidder would supply previously approved, identified components); *B.K. Instrument Inc.*, Comp. Gen. Dec. B-212162.2, 84-1 CPD ¶ 189 (failure to meet source control certification requirements); *Fraser-Volpe Corp.*, Comp. Gen. Dec. B-213910, 84-1 CPD ¶ 35 (failure to certify that component parts would be purchased from a designated group).

On occasion, the government has treated certifications that serve an important public policy as matters of responsiveness even though they relate more directly to issues of responsibility. See *Northeast Constr. Co. v. Romney*, 485 F.2d 752 (D.C.

Cir. 1973); *Rossetti Contracting Co. v. Brennan*, 508 F.2d 1039 (7th Cir. 1974); and *Astro Pak Corp.*, Comp. Gen. Dec. B-183556, 75-2 CPD ¶ 97, which deal with affirmative action plans for equal employment opportunity that were required to be submitted along with the bids. In *Northeast Construction*, the bidder failed to fill in its affirmative action goals in the space provided but did sign the document agreeing to comply with the plan included in the IFB, which specified the minimum acceptable goals. Nevertheless, the bid was considered nonresponsive because the omissions created doubts regarding enforceability of the bidder's commitment because its bid was inconsistent with the instructions of the plan. These decisions have been mooted with respect to EEO certificates because of changes in the procedures making the certificate a matter of responsibility, FAR 14.405(f).

The government had identified proper completion of the Certificate of Procurement Integrity as a matter of responsiveness for procurements that exceeded $100,000. This requirement was upheld even though the Procurement Integrity Act, 41 U.S.C. § 423(e), merely called for obtaining the certificate before award, *S.J. Amoroso Constr. Co. v. United States*, 981 F.2d 1073 (9th Cir. 1992); *McMaster Constr., Inc. v. United States*, 23 Cl. Ct. 679 (1991); *P & R Roofing & Sheet Metal, Inc.*, Comp. Gen. Dec. B-258388, 94-2 CPD ¶ 254; *Stamatis Lykos*, Comp. Gen. Dec. B-257843, 94-2 CPD ¶ 186. Submission of an unsigned certificate was also held to make the bid nonresponsive, *Holly's, Inc.*, Comp. Gen. Dec. B-246444, 92-1 CPD ¶ 261. However, submission of a photocopy of a properly executed certificate met the responsiveness requirement, *C.B.S. Enters., Inc.*, Comp. Gen. Dec. B-252484, 93-1 CPD ¶ 495. Similarly, an undated certificate met the requirement, *General Elec. Ocean & Radar Sys. Div.*, Comp. Gen. Dec. B-250418, 93-1 CPD ¶ 30. This certification requirement was been repealed by § 4301 of the Clinger-Cohen Act of 1996, Pub. L. No. 104-106.

In *Worcester Elec. Assocs.*, Comp. Gen. Dec. B-193064, 79-1 CPD ¶ 236, a specification requirement that bidders submit Underwriter Laboratories (UL) listing cards was held to be a matter of responsiveness, because the purpose of the cards was to provide evidence that the equipment being offered conformed to certain standards of safety and performance. But see *Fisher Berkeley Corp.*, Comp. Gen. Dec. B-196432, 80-1 CPD ¶ 26, where the UL certification itself was considered a matter of responsibility as long as the bidder promised that its product would be and was UL certified.

### e. Information or Data to Be Submitted

When data or information is required to be submitted with the bid, the purpose for which the data or information is to be used will determine whether it is a matter of responsiveness or responsibility. Thus, if descriptive data are to be used to determine a bidder's *ability or capacity to perform*, the matter will be one of *responsibility*, and failure to submit the information with the bid will not cause its rejection, *Savin Business Machs. Corp.*, Comp. Gen. Dec. B-191163, 78-1 CPD ¶ 447 (failure to furnish preventive maintenance plan, key operator instruction plan, and samples of paper to be used with photocopying equipment did not render bid nonresponsive); *Science Applications, Inc.*, Comp. Gen. Dec. B-193479, 79-1 CPD ¶ 167 (failure to submit personnel resumes did not render bid nonresponsive); *Career Consultants, Inc.*, Comp. Gen. Dec. B-198727, 80-2 CPD ¶ 285 (IFB requirement for statement of licensing status was not a matter of responsiveness); *Seacoast Trucking & Moving Co.*, Comp. Gen. Dec. B-200315, 80-2 CPD ¶ 235 (failure to submit description of equipment to be used in performing refuse services did not render bid nonresponsive because equipment was matter of capability to perform); *Career Consultants, Inc.*, Comp. Gen. Dec. B-200506.2, 81-1 CPD ¶ 414 (requirement for security clearances is a matter of responsibility); *Skyline Credit Corp.*, Comp. Gen. Dec. B-209193, 83-1 CPD ¶ 257 (failure to include written performance procedures did not render bid nonresponsive); *Commercial Window & Door Co.*, Comp. Gen. Dec. B-211280, 83-2 CPD ¶ 582 (bid that failed to include test results concerning product performance held responsive because IFB failed to warn bidders that submission requirement involved responsiveness and the information was not necessary to determine conformance with specifications); *Siska Constr. Co.*, 64 Comp. Gen. 384 (B-218208.2), 85-1 CPD ¶ 331 (affiliation and parent company data as well as certificate of independent pricing concern bidder responsibility and may be submitted after bid opening); *Master Power, Inc.*, Comp. Gen. Dec. B-238468.2, 90-2 CPD ¶ 434 (furnishing incorrect qualification test number for qualified product a matter of responsibility); *RKR, Inc.*, Comp. Gen. Dec. B-247619.2, 92-2 CPD ¶ 289 (failure to submit adequate evidence of compliance with zoning laws a matter of responsibility); *CardioMetrix*, Comp. Gen. Dec. B-255748.2, 94-1 CPD ¶ 364 (failure to designate place of performance is matter of responsibility).

On the other hand, information or data may be required to be submitted with the bid for purposes of more precisely determining *the nature of the work that the bidder is agreeing to accomplish.* Such data can be considered to go to the *responsiveness* of the bid. Requiring the submission of such data can protect the government from bids that are responsive on their face, because they take no exception to the IFB but are based on performing in a manner that does not conform to the solicitation. The two major techniques used by the government for this purpose are requirements for *descriptive literature* and *bid samples.*

Neither of these techniques should be used indiscriminately because they may unduly increase the cost of bidding. FAR 14.202-4(b) gives the following guidance regarding the use of bid samples:

> The use of bid samples would be appropriate for products that must be suitable from the standpoint of balance, facility of use, general "feel," color, pattern, or other characteristics that cannot be described adequately in the specification. However, when more than a minor portion of the characteristics of the product cannot be adequately described in the specification, products should be acquired by two-step sealed bidding or negotiation, as appropriate.

FAR 14.202-5(a) provides the following guidance with respect to descriptive literature:

> Contracting officers must not require bidders to furnish descriptive literature unless it is needed before award to determine whether the products offered meet the specification and to establish exactly what the bidder proposes to furnish.

Where the purpose of the data is to enable the procuring agency to determine precisely what the bidder intends to supply, the matter will be considered to deal with responsiveness. This is the only purpose for which bid samples may be submitted, FAR 14.202-4(a)(2). For example, in *Western Waterproofing Co.*, Comp. Gen. Dec. B-183155, 75-1 CPD ¶ 306, the bidder was required to furnish data demonstrating that the stone proposed for use met the IFB criteria. GAO reasoned that this provision did not deal with the bidder's ability to perform but was aimed at describing the articles to be supplied. See also *American Material Handling, Inc.*, Comp. Gen. Dec. B-278107, 97-2 CPD ¶ 177 (reservation of right in descriptive literature to make specification changes without notice made bid nonresponsive); *FFR-Bauelemente + Bausanierung GmbH*, Comp. Gen. Dec. B-274828, 97-1 CPD ¶ 7 (failure to include descriptive literature to ascertain whether item met salient characteristics of brand name product made bid nonresponsive); *RMTC Sys., Inc. v. Department of the Army*, GSBCA 12637-P, 94-2 BCA ¶ 26,614 (failure to submit descriptive literature to demonstrate that product was "equal" to the specified brand name makes bid nonresponsive); *B.E.C. Med. Prods.*, Comp. Gen. Dec. B-256483, 94-1 CPD ¶ 159 (late submission of bid sample makes bid nonresponsive); *National Energy Res., Inc.*, Comp. Gen. Dec. B-206275, 83-1 CPD ¶ 108 (failure to include data regarding the suitability of the coal to be provided was a matter of responsiveness); and *Thermal Reduction Co.*, Comp. Gen. Dec. B-211405, 83-2 CPD ¶ 180 (failure to include descriptive literature assuring conformance with specifications makes bid nonresponsive).

## B. Consequences of Nonconforming Bids

The consequences of submitting a nonconforming bid depend on the nature of the nonconformity and the time it is discovered.

### 1. Minor Informalities

Once a defect is found to be minor, award must be made if at all, to the low bidder who is otherwise responsible. The contracting officer has the choice of either giving the bidder an opportunity to cure the deficiency or waiving it, whichever is in the best interest of the government, FAR 14.405; *Champion Road Mach. Int'l Corp.*, Comp. Gen. Dec. B-200678, 81-2 CPD ¶ 27; *Astrophysics Research Corp.*, 66 Comp. Gen. 211 (B-224532), 87-1 CPD ¶ 65. If the bidder refuses to cure the deficiency, then award may be made on the basis of the bid as submitted.

If a sealed bid procurement is canceled because the agency determines that the only bid at a reasonable price is nonresponsive, and the agency subsequently determines that the defect in the bid was a minor informality, the agency may reinstate the IFB and award to that bidder, *Bilt-Rite Contractors, Inc.*, Comp. Gen. Dec. B-259106.2, 95-1 CPD ¶ 220.

## 2. Material Nonconformities

This section discusses the requirement for rejection of nonresponsive bids, the legal effect of an award on the basis of a nonresponsive bid, and the limited cases in which such awards are sanctioned by GAO.

### a. Rejection Required

FAR 14.404-2(a) states that "any bid that fails to conform to the essential requirements of the solicitation shall be rejected." In commenting on the rationale for this rule, the court, in *Toyo Menka Kaisha, Ltd. v. United States*, 220 Ct. Cl. 210, 597 F.2d 1371 (1979), stated at 219-20:

These principles rest upon and effectuate important public policies. "Rejection of irresponsive bids is necessary if the purposes of formal advertising are to be attained, that is, to give everyone an equal right to compete for Government business, to secure fair prices, and to prevent fraud." *Prestex Inc. v. United States*, *supra*, 162 Ct. Cl. at 626, 320 F.2d at 372 (footnote omitted). The requirement that a bid be responsive is designed to avoid unfairness to other contractors who submitted a sealed bid on the understanding that they must comply with all of the specifications and conditions in the invitation for bids, and who could have made a better proposal if they imposed conditions upon or variances from the contractual terms the government had specified. The rule also avoids placing the contracting officer in the difficult position of having to balance the more favorable offer of the deviating bidder against the disadvantages to the government from the qualifications and conditions the bidder has added. In short, the requirement of responsiveness is designed to avoid a method of awarding government contracts that would be similar to negotiating agreements but which would lack the safeguards present in either that system or in true competitive bidding. See R. Nash & J. Cibinic, *Federal Procurement Law*, 260 (3d ed. 1977).

Responsiveness is determined by reference to the bids when they are opened and not by reference to subsequent changes in a bid. *Id.* at 261. Allowing a bidder to modify a nonresponsive bid when, upon opening the bids, it appears that the variations will preclude an award, would permit the very kind of bid manipulation and negotiation that the rule is designed to prevent. Otherwise bidders would be encouraged to submit nonresponsive bids on terms favorable to the government but subject to certain conditions, in the hope that if their bids were the top ones, they could then negotiate about and retain some of their proposed changes. In this way they could obtain a contract that they could not have received had they complied with the specification in the invitation for bids.

It is immaterial whether the nonconformity is deliberate or occurs by mistake, or whether the bidder is willing to correct or modify the bid to conform to the terms of the invitation, *Legeay, Inc.*, Comp. Gen. Dec. B-218307, 85-1 CPD ¶ 338 (fact that bidder alleged mistake and offered to correct an insufficient acceptance period held irrelevant); *AVS Inc.*, Comp. Gen. Dec. B-218205, 85-1 CPD ¶ 328 (irrelevant that bid guarantee deficiency may have resulted from innocent error on the part of the surety); *Public Entity Underwriters, Ltd.*, Comp. Gen. Dec. B-213745, 84-2 CPD ¶ 326 (clerical error may not be corrected after opening to make bid responsive). In *Amendola Constr. Co.*, Comp. Gen. Dec. B-214258, 84-1 CPD ¶ 255, GAO stated:

> The fact that [the protester] has subsequently explained that the 15-day period it offered was a mistake and that it is willing to waive its restriction is irrelevant. A bid which is nonresponsive on its face may not be changed, corrected or explained by the bidder after bid opening since to permit this would give the firm the option of accepting or rejecting a contract after bids are exposed.

See also *Parco, A Div. of Blue Mountain Prods., Inc.*, Comp. Gen. Dec. B-211016, 83-1 CPD ¶ 318, refusing to allow a nonresponsive bid to be considered for correction after bid opening because to permit a change after bid opening would be tantamount to permitting the submission of a new bid after the competitors' bids have been revealed.

### b.  Validity of Award

Award to a bidder whose bid contains a material nonconformity has been held to be void ab initio, *Prestex Inc. v. United States*, 162 Ct. Cl. 620, 320 F.2d 367 (1963). See also *Albano Cleaners, Inc. v. United States*, 197 Ct. Cl. 450, 455 F.2d 556 (1972), where the court stated at 455:

> [The Government] may disclaim a contract on the ground of voidness *ab initio* because of the nonresponsiveness of the bid. Where a public contract is to be let pursuant to formal advertising, the strictures upon [the Government's] contracting agent are such " that the contract awarded must be the contract advertised and *** if it is not, the Government is not bound, since [the Government's] contracting agent could not bind the Government beyond his actual authority." *Prestex Inc. v. United States*, 162 Ct. Cl. 620, 625, 320 F.2d 367, 371 (1963).

Thus, a bidder who receives such an award runs a great risk if the government decides to cancel the award. If the contract is declared void ab initio, the contractor will generally be entitled to payment only for benefits conferred on the government, *United States v. Amdahl Corp.*, 786 F.2d 387 (Fed. Cir. 1986). However, to the extent that any expenditures made in performance do not confer a benefit upon the government, they may not be recovered, *Toyo Menka Kaisha, Ltd. v. United States*, 220 Ct. Cl. 210, 597 F.2d 1371 (1979).

GAO has recommended termination for convenience rather than cancellation when there has been an award to a nonresponsive bidder, *Fischer-White-Rankin Contractors, Inc.*, Comp. Gen. Dec. B-213401, 84-1 CPD ¶ 471, *withdrawn because much work done*, 84-1 CPD ¶640; *Harris Constr. Co.*, 64 Comp. Gen. 628 (B-218387), 85-1 CPD ¶ 710. This result follows the reasoning that cancellation is only proper when the illegality of the contract is "plain," *John Reiner & Co. v. United States*, 163 Ct. Cl. 381, 325 F.2d 438 (1963), *cert. denied*, 377 U.S. 931 (1964), or "palpable," *Warren Bros. Roads Co. v. United States*, 173 Ct. Cl. 714, 355 F.2d 612 (1965). This reasoning was also followed by the General Services Board of Contract Appeals, *International Bus. Machs. Corp.*, GSBCA 9703-P, 89-1 BCA ¶ 21,389, *rev'd on other grounds*, 892 F.2d 1006 (Fed. Cir. 1989).

## c. Award

On a number of occasions GAO has sanctioned awards on the basis of nonresponsive bids. This is generally done only if all the bids submitted are nonresponsive, the bid in question satisfies the government's requirements, and no competing bidder would be prejudiced as a result of the award. In *K. B. Constr.*, Comp. Gen. Dec. B-214192, 84-1 CPD ¶ 223, the failure of all bidders to submit required test manufacturer's data permitted award to the low bidder.

A crucial element in the decisions sanctioning award to a nonresponsive bidder is GAO's finding that, under the circumstances, acceptance of the nonresponsive bid would not prejudice other bidders, *Singleton Contracting Corp.*, Comp. Gen. Dec. B-211259, 83-2 CPD ¶ 270 (award proper where both bids were nonresponsive for same material nonconformity, and acceptance resulted in a contract that satisfied government needs). In *E.F. Matelich Constr. Co.*, Comp. Gen. Dec. B-207600, 82-2 CPD ¶ 291, GAO stated that "[t]he test of prejudice . . . is whether it is reasonably clear that another bidder, given the benefit of a similarly relaxed requirement . . . would have bid in such a manner that it would have been in line for award." See *Esko & Young, Inc.*, 61 Comp. Gen. 192 (B-204053), 82-1 CPD ¶ 5, where the failure of the sole bidder to include a conforming bid acceptance period did not require rejection since "no bidding advantage accrues to the single bidder . . . because there were no competitors who . . . subjected themselves to the risks of maintaining their bid process for the longer period." See also *Fluid Sys, Inc.*, Comp. Gen. Dec. B-225880, 87-1 CPD ¶ 20, where an award was upheld where the IFB required a two-inch-diameter drain for feed pump lube oil modification kits, but the low bidder could supply only a one-and-three-quarter-inch-diameter model because it was the only model available. GAO reasoned that the substituted product met the government's needs and no other bidders were prejudiced.

In a number of these cases, award is sanctioned because cancellation of the procurement after bids have been exposed is seen as a greater evil. In *Big State Enters.*, 64 Comp. Gen. 482 (B-218055), 85 1 CPD ¶ 459, GAO stated at 484:

> [W]e believe that in spite of the specification deficiency, the determination to make an award was reasonable and less of a compromise to the competitive bidding system than resolicitation after exposure of all prices would have been. *See GAF Corp. et al.*, 53 Comp. Gen. 586 (1974), 74-1 CPD ¶68.

These GAO decisions sanctioning award on the basis of the most advantageous nonresponsive bid are based on pragmatism. The standard alternatives would be for the contracting officer to reject all bids and resolicit sealed bids, *Gulf & Western Healthcare, Inc.*, Comp. Gen. Dec. B-209684, 83-2 CPD ¶ 248, competitive proposals, or two-step sealed bids, 34 Comp. Gen. 364 (B-121831) (1965). In case of urgency, it might also be possible to negotiate with all bidders if less than full and open competition could be justified. See *Bus Indus. of Am., Inc.*, Comp. Gen. Dec. B-208366, 83-1 CPD ¶ 222, approving this technique in a case that arose prior to the Competition in Contracting Act. Since these alternatives would all involve the expenditure of additional time and effort, it is clearly more expedient to make the award to the bidder submitting the most advantageous, albeit nonresponsive, bid.

This pragmatism, however, may be shortsighted. It ignores the possibility that the requirement that was not met may have deterred other potential bidders from entering the competition at all. These decisions also ignore decisions such as *Prestex Inc. v. United States*, 162 Ct. Cl. 620, 320 F.2d 367 (1963), holding that award to a nonresponsive bidder constitutes a prohibited waiver of responsiveness criteria and does not obligate the government. The courts focus more on the prejudice to potential bidders, while GAO addresses the issue of prejudice only in terms of actual bidders.

For a questionable case in which GAO held that the government could accept a nonresponsive bid even though the second low bid was responsive, see *Dunlin Corp.*, Comp. Gen. Dec. B-207964, 83-1 CPD ¶ 7. The protester, who believed that it was the only bidder with a supply of the window sealant required by the IFB, submitted a bid price of $24.80 per unit. The awardee, offering an alternative sealant that rendered its bid nonresponsive, submitted a bid price of $18.10 per unit. Claiming that the alternative sealant would meet its needs and that the specifications had overstated the needs, the government made the award to the low bidder. Even though GAO held that this action was proper, more effective competition could have been promoted by a cancellation and resolicitation in which both those submitting bids and those refraining from bidding could compete to the revised specifications.

## C. Types of Nonconforming Bids

The determination of whether a nonconformity is material depends upon the facts of the case and the nature of the nonconformity. This section examines some of the common types of nonconforming bids.

## 1. Differing Products or Services

Any bid that fails to conform to the essential requirements or applicable specifications of an invitation must be rejected. FAR 14.404-2(b) states that bids offering materially differing products or services from those solicited must be rejected as nonresponsive. See, for example, *Kincaid Equip. Mfg.*, Comp. Gen. Dec. B-246079, 92-1 CPD ¶ 140 (bid offering a belt-driven threshing cylinder rejected as nonresponsive where IFB required a hydrostatically driven threshing cylinder); *Mobile Drilling Co.*, Comp. Gen. Dec. B-216989, 85-1 CPD ¶ 199 (an offer to furnish a drill with a torque capacity of 6,000 ft.-lbs. at 27 R.P.M. instead of the required capacity of 5,800 ft.-lbs. at 50 R.P.M. was properly rejected); *Jensen Corp.*, Comp. Gen. Dec. B-213677, 84-1 CPD ¶ 544 (a bid offering a two-roll flatwork commercial ironer when the IFB called for a four-roll ironer held nonresponsive); and *Sheffield Bldg. Co.*, Comp. Gen. Dec. B-181242, 74-2 CPD ¶ 108 (bidder's failure to include spud engines when the specifications called for derrickboats equipped with spud engines resulted in bid rejection).

When the government solicits products on a "brand name or equal" basis, a bidder offering an "equal" product must establish that it conforms to all the salient characteristics of the brand name product listed in the IFB. A failure to do so will result in bid rejection, *RCP Shelters, Inc.*, Comp. Gen. Dec. B-256258, 94-1 CPD ¶ 336 (descriptive literature submitted with bid failed to show compliance with the salient characteristics listed in the IFB); *Alternate Power & Energy Corp.*, Comp. Gen. Dec. B-228746, 87-2 CPD ¶ 440 (although offered product possessed required features, bid rejected where literature submitted with bid did not clearly show conformance with IFB requirements). Any information used to show conformance to the salient characteristics must have been commercially available prior to bid opening and must not have been developed afterward, *Elastomeric Roofing Assocs.*, 68 Comp. Gen. 426, (B-234125), 89-1 CPD ¶ 451. To allow bidders to submit other than preexisting, commercially available material would give the bidder control over the responsiveness of its bid, *Monitronics*, Comp. Gen. Dec. B-228219, 87-2 CPD ¶ 527. However, bidders have been permitted to submit such information after bid opening. See *Lappen Auto Supply Co.*, Comp. Gen. Dec. B-261475, 95-2 CPD ¶ 68.

Bids that fail to meet salient characteristics of the solicitation must be rejected as nonresponsive even if the offered items function as well as the brand name units and satisfy the intent of the specifications, *SDV Furniture & Servs., LLC*, Comp. Gen. Dec. B-401221, 2009 CPD ¶ 108 (bid offering acoustic panels with "better" internal sound baffling" rejected because dimensions did not match salient characteristics); *Advanced Med. Sys., Inc.*, Comp. Gen. Dec. B-258945, 95-1 CPD ¶ 67 (bid rejected as nonresponsive where proposed "equal" product could digitally display one fetal heart rate, but IFB for fetal heart monitor required digital display of two fetal heart rates); *T & T Prods., Inc.*, Comp. Gen. Dec. B-243898, 91-2 CPD ¶ 139 (bid stating "equal" product had cable diameter of "0.75 inches nominal" rejected as nonresponsive where IFB required a cable diameter between 0.8 and 0.875 inches); *United Mach.*, Comp. Gen. Dec. B-227923, 87-2 CPD ¶ 54 (bid rejected as nonresponsive where, although the offered "equal" washer extractor may have functioned as well as the brand name, the protester conceded that the offered product did not meet all the specifications of the IFB); *Paul F. Pugh & Associated Prof'l Eng'rs*, Comp. Gen. Dec. B-199920, 80-2 CPD ¶ 358 (although aluminum conductors offered may function as well as brand-name units, bid was properly rejected as nonresponsive because IFB for power cables listed copper as a salient characteristic). Even a brand-name product listed in the IFB may not be accepted as responsive if it fails to meet listed salient characteristics and, in effect, constitutes a "differing" product, *Vista Scientific Corp.*, Comp. Gen. Dec. B-185170, 76-1 CPD ¶ 212. But see *Central Power Eng'g Corp.*, Comp. Gen. Dec. B-215658.2, 85-1 CPD ¶ 85, where the bid listed a brand-name model number that represented an upgraded version of the brand-name model solicited. GAO upheld the agency's determination that although designated somewhat differently, the model offered met all the salient characteristics of the solicitation and was in essence the same brand-name item called for in the IFB. See also *GAF Corp.*, 53 Comp. Gen. 586, (B-179744), 74-1 CPD ¶ 68, reinstating a canceled IFB and permitted award to a brand name product that did not conform to all listed salient characteristics.

Nonconformities of bids that are merely a matter of form and not substance or that are immaterial or inconsequential variations from the exact requirements of an IFB may not properly be rejected as nonresponsive. FAR 14.405 requires minor informalities or irregularities to be corrected or waived if no prejudice will result to other bidders, or where the deviation has only a negligible effect on price, quality, quantity, or delivery when compared with the total cost or scope of supplies or work to be furnished. See, for example, *W.M. Schlosser Co.,* Comp. Gen. Dec. B-258284, 94-2 CPD ¶ 234 (bidder's failure to submit requested equipment history with bid that would not be used to evaluate bid waived as an immaterial deviation); *Universal Applicators, Inc.*, Comp. Gen. Dec. B-232670, 88-2 CPD ¶ 591 (failure to certify that bid price was not based on "spray painting" when IFB required a liquid roof sealant held to be an immaterial deviation); *Astrophysics Research Corp.*, 66 Comp. Gen. 211 (B-224532), 87-1 CPD ¶ 65 (10-pound discrepancy between 410-pound X-ray screening machine bid and 400-pound machine specified in IFB; IFB requirement waived as a minor informality where item met government need and there was no prejudice to other bidders); *Evans, Inc.*, Comp. Gen. Dec. B-216260.2, 85-1 CPD ¶ 535 (118.5-inch dryer minor deviation from 120-inch specification requirement); *Magnaflux Corp.*, Comp. Gen. Dec. B-211914, 84-1 CPD ¶ 4 (29.5-inch bath tank minor deviation to specification requiring 30-inch tank); *Champion Road Mach. Int'l Corp.*, Comp. Gen. Dec. B-200678, 81-2 CPD ¶ 27 (bid offering 168-horsepower road grader where solicitation specified 170 horsepower held responsive where deviation had no effect on price, quality, quantity, or delivery); and Comp. Gen. Dec. B-172227, May 13, 1971, *Unpub.* (bid offering uniform with five buttons and a scalloped pocket rather than the required four buttons and plain pocket held responsive since deviations were minor and did not affect quality, utility, or the cost of producing the uniform).

There are a few seemingly inconsistent decisions. See *Yale Materials Handling Corp.*, Comp. Gen. Dec. B-250208, 92-2 CPD ¶ 360 (bid offering forklift exceeding specified dimensions in the IFB by about one-half inch was a material deviation affecting the quality of the forklift and was rejected as nonresponsive); *Taylor-Forge Engineered Sys., Inc.*, 69 Comp. Gen. 54 (B-236408), 89-2 CPD ¶ 421 (bid offering delivery f.o.b. origin where IFB required f.o.b. destination constituted a material deviation); and 43 Comp. Gen. 209 (B-151968) (1963) (award of contract canceled where bid offered paper cutter that materially deviated from the IFB specifications by affecting price and quality, even though the product would better serve the agency's needs).

## 2. Failure to Agree to IFB Delivery Schedule

An IFB's delivery schedule is a material requirement of the solicitation, and any bid that fails to conform to the delivery schedule is nonresponsive and must be rejected, FAR 14.404-2(c). Thus, a bid offering a delivery period greater than the maximum delivery period permitted under the terms of the solicitation will be rejected as nonresponsive, *Chrysler Corp.*, Comp. Gen. Dec. B-249492, 92-2 CPD ¶ 253 (bid offering "shipments" within 90 days rejected as nonresponsive where IFB required "delivery" within 90 days); *Rhimco Indus., Inc.*, Comp. Gen. Dec. B-247600, 92-1 CPD ¶ 499 (IFB required delivery of all items within 120 days after award, but protester's bid offered delivery of one half of the requirements); *Delta Scientific Corp.*, Comp. Gen. Dec. B-233485, 88-2 CPD ¶ 516 (bid's delivery schedule of 120 days was rejected where IFB stated bidders could offer delivery schedule longer than the desired 60 days but within the required 90 days); *Meyer Tool & Mfg.*, Comp. Gen. Dec. B-222595, 86-1 CPD ¶ 537 (bid rejected as nonresponsive where numbers in proposed delivery period were transposed, due to a clerical error, from 120 days to 210 days, which exceeded the 180 days required by the IFB); *Mar-Mac Precision Corp.*, Comp. Gen. Dec. B-214604, 84-2 CPD ¶ 164 (failure to acknowledge an amendment that doubled the delivery requirements for the first 180 days of the contract rendered bid nonresponsive). Even a bid footnote objecting to and qualifying a required delivery schedule has rendered a bid nonresponsive, *Sunoptic, Inc.*, Comp. Gen. Dec. B-194722, 79-1 CPD ¶ 351. But see *TEREX Corp.*, Comp. Gen. Dec. B-212441, 84-1 CPD ¶ 330, where a bid that failed to offer delivery within 30 days was improperly rejected as nonresponsive because the IFB merely called for a "desired" delivery date of 30 days, and the offered delivery date was "reasonable."

The bid must indicate that the bidder is agreeing to meet the required date. In Comp. Gen. Dec. B-170287, Aug. 18, 1970, *Unpub.*, *recons. denied*, 50 Comp. Gen. 379 (1970), the invitation required delivery in 150 days and had a desired delivery date of 120 days. The bidder offered delivery in "approximately 120 days (as requested)." This deviation was found to be material and rendered the bid nonresponsive since no firm date was bid. But see Comp. Gen. Dec. B-175342, Mar. 27, 1972, *Unpub.*, where an approximate delivery date of 30 days did not render a bid nonresponsive when the required date was 90 days. GAO distinguished the earlier case by noting that the "approximate period of offered delivery is significantly greater in the instant case than in the earlier case both in terms of the absolute number of days between the approximate date and the deadline and the relative period involved."

When the IFB requires delivery within a certain time from date of contract award, bidders may specify delivery times starting from receipt of contract award documents. In such cases, FAR 11.403(e) requires that five calendar days (normal mail delivery time) be added to the bidder's date (one day if the notice of award is transmitted electronically), and if this date is later than the IFB required date, the bid is considered nonresponsive. See, for example, *AMP Inc.*, Comp. Gen. Dec. B-230120, 88-1 CPD ¶ 163 (bid offering a delivery schedule of 150 days after receipt of an order rejected as nonresponsive because it effectively added five days to the IFB required schedule as an allowance for delivery through ordinary mails); and *Discount Mach. & Equip.*, Comp. Gen. Dec. B-223048.2, 86-2 CPD ¶ 5 (bid offering a delivery period of 90 days after receipt of contract, where IFB required 90 days from contract award, in effect added five days for delivery of award documents through the mail and was rejected as nonresponsive).

A bid will also be nonresponsive if it indicates that the proposed schedule will result in unsatisfactory performance. See *Red John's Stone, Inc.*,Comp. Gen. Dec. B-280974, 98-2 CPD ¶ 135 (bidder's performance schedule required planting outside of growing season).

### 3. Conditions Altering the Invitation

Bids that impose conditions altering the requirements of the invitation or limiting the rights of the government must be rejected. FAR 14.404-2(d) states:

A bid shall be rejected when the bidder imposes conditions that would modify requirements of the invitation or limit the bidder's liability to the Government, since to allow the bidder to impose such conditions would be prejudicial to other bidders. For example, bids shall be rejected in which the bidder —

(1) Protects against future changes in conditions, such as increased costs, if total possible costs to the Government cannot be determined;

(2) Fails to state a price and indicates that price shall be "price in effect at time of delivery";

(3) States a price but qualifies it as being subject to "price in effect at time of delivery";

(4) When not authorized by the invitation, conditions or qualifies a bid by stipulating that it is to be considered only if, before date of award, the bidder receives (or does not receive) award under a separate solicitation;

(5) Requires that the Government is to determine that the bidder's product meets applicable Government specifications; or

(6) Limits rights of the Government under any contract clause.

## a. Modifying Material Requirements of the IFB

Any bid that imposes conditions that would modify the material requirements of the solicitation will be rejected as nonresponsive, *Fire-Trol Holdings, LLC v. United States*, 68 Fed. Cl. 281 (2005) (bid nonresponsive when it stated that government would be required to acquire material that bidder was required to furnish); *Antennas for Commc'ns*, Comp. Gen. Dec. B-253950, 93-2 CPD ¶ 48 (bid nonresponsive when it stated that government damages for delay "shall be billed at a rate of $1,000 per day"); *NR Vessel Corp.*, Comp. Gen. Dec. B-250925, 93-1 CPD ¶ 128 (bid conditioned on the government disposing of hazardous waste was rejected as nonresponsive where the IFB placed responsibility for disposal on the contractor); *Lathan Constr. Corp.*, Comp. Gen. Dec. B-250487, 93-1 CPD ¶ 107 (bid nonresponsive where document captioned "Contractor's Qualifications and Exclusions" excluded permit and engineering fees required by the IFB); *General Elec. Co.*, Comp. Gen. Dec. B-228191, 87-2 CPD ¶ 585 (bid rejected for taking exception to two parts of the IFB's warranty provision). See also *Garney Cos.*, Comp. Gen. Dec. 196075.2, 81-1 CPD ¶ 62 (bidder reserved right to use unacceptable pipe installation technique); *State Mut. Book & Periodical Serv., Ltd.*, Comp. Gen. Dec. B-191008.2, 78-1 CPD ¶ 264 (exception to specified delivery method); *National Ambulance Co.*, 55 Comp. Gen. 597 (B-184439), 75-2 CPD ¶ 413 (bid conditioned on receipt of local license); *Joy Mfg. Co.*, 54 Comp. Gen. 237 (B-181136), 74-2 CPD ¶ 183 (bid reserved the right to change prices if costs increase even though the IFB required a firm-fixed-price); and 43 Comp. Gen. 382 (B-152470) (1963) (bid stated that alignment of turbine and generator shafts would be accomplished at contractor's plant in Japan rather than in the United States as specified in the IFB).

If there is no prohibition in the IFB against conditions limiting the size of the award, the imposition of such a condition will not render the bid nonresponsive. In *Orvedahl Constr., Inc.*, 63 Comp. Gen. 288 (B-213408), 84-1 CPD ¶ 405, bids were entered on two line items at $781,000 and $622,000 respectively, along with a condition stipulating that no award over $1,000,000 would be accepted. The rejection of Orvedahl's bid was held improper because the bidder's obligation to perform according to the terms and conditions of the IFB was not affected in any way. See also FAR 14.404-5, which allows bidders to condition acceptance upon award of all or a specified group of items, unless the IFB expressly prohibits "all or none" or similarly restricted bids. See *Mansfield Assocs.*, Comp. Gen. Dec. B-242270, 91-1 CPD ¶ 284 (agency's failure to incorporate a provision expressly permitting "all or none" bids did not constitute an express prohibition of such bidding); and *Phillips Cartner & Co.*, 69 Comp. Gen. 105 (B-236416.2), 89-2 CPD ¶ 492 ("all or none" qualification did not render bid nonresponsive since the IFB did not expressly prohibit such bid qualifications).

A bid may be responsive in spite of a qualifying legend contained in the bid literature where it is reasonably clear from the bid that a "subject to change" legend is not intended to reserve the right to the bidder to change the offered product or to deviate from the material requirements of the invitation, *Syntrex Inc.*, 63 Comp. Gen. 360 (B-212781.2), 84-1 CPD ¶ 522. See also *Yale Materials Handling Corp.*, Comp. Gen. Dec. B-228974.2, 87-2 CPD ¶ 550, where, although the bid was held nonresponsive on other grounds, GAO stated that a handwritten statement, which immediately followed the "subject to change" clause, that all requirements will be met, effectively deleted the conditional language. Similarly, where a bid statement merely clarifies the bidder's understanding of the IFB without limiting any material provisions, the bid is responsive, *Westinghouse Elec. Corp.*, Comp. Gen. Dec. B-187487, 76-2 CPD ¶ 455.

### b. Limiting Rights of the Government

If a bid attempts to limit the rights of the government under any contract clause, the bid will be rejected as nonresponsive, *New Dimension Masonry, Inc.*, Comp. Gen. Dec. B-258876, 95-1 CPD ¶ 102 (bid rejected as nonresponsive where cover letter conditioned bid upon the use of a government storage area); *Municipal Leasing Sys., Inc.*, Comp. Gen. Dec. B-242648.2, 91-1 CPD ¶ 495 (bid language "after 12 months" limited the agency's right to exercise a purchase option within the first 12 months of the contract); *F.J. Dahill Co.*, Comp. Gen. Dec. B-235272, 89-2 CPD ¶ 103 (bid nonresponsive because it contained statement that bidder would not work on hazardous substances and would leave site if any were found); *Gelco Payment Sys., Inc.*, Comp. Gen. Dec. B-234957, 89-2 CPD ¶ 27 (bid stating that either party may cancel upon 30 days' notice attempted to limit the government's rights under the "termination for convenience" clause and was rejected as nonresponsive); *Integrated Research & Info. Sys.*, Comp. Gen. Dec. B-196456, 80-1 CPD ¶ 130 (bid specified that procuring agency rather than the bidder would pay shipping costs); *Kari-Vac, Inc.*, Comp. Gen. Dec. B-194202, 79-2 CPD ¶ 4 (bid conditioned upon payment by the government of 1% interest charge for payments made after 30 days). But see 48 Comp. Gen. 306 (B-164639) (1968), holding that a statement on one competitor's own bid form that "no withholding will be allowed without the prior written consent of the seller" did not affect the responsiveness of the bid, even though that it appeared to limit the government's rights. GAO stated at 310-11.

> In this instance we do not believe that the acceptance of the MSA bid, including the wording "no withholding will be allowed without the prior written consent of the seller," resulted in any diminution of the rights which the Government would have without that language. If the Government does withhold any or all of the contract price by reason of a claim against the contractor, we are not aware of any remedy available to the contractor except an action for the amount withheld, and in the event of such an action it is our opinion the Government could assert its claim either as a cross-claim or as a separate action.

## c.  Limiting Liability to the Government

A bid that attempts to limit the bidder's liability to the government as proposed in the invitation will be rejected as nonresponsive, *AAA Roofing Co.*, Comp. Gen. Dec. B-240852, 90-2 CPD ¶ 485 (form submitted with bid rendered bid nonresponsive since it imposed limitations on bidder's future liability to the government); *Contech Constr. Co.*, Comp. Gen. Dec. B-241185, 90-2 CPD ¶ 264 (bid nonresponsive when it included notation "impossible" next to two interim schedule requirements; argument that these were only estimator's notes rejected); *Roche Biomedical Labs., Inc.*, Comp. Gen. Dec. B-233123, 88-2 CPD ¶ 368 (bid claiming the right and privilege of terminating contract upon certain conditions limited bidder's liability to the government); *Southwest Marine of San Francisco, Inc.*, 66 Comp. Gen. 22 (B-224508), 86-2 CPD ¶ 388 (bid stating contractor "shall take every precaution to contain contaminate" from abrasive ship blasting rendered bid nonresponsive since statement attempted to limit its liability to the government for any environmental violations); *Dr. Beurt R. Servaas*, HUDBCA 83-780-B1, 83-2 BCA ¶ 16,690 (bid request for waiver of first 12 months' interest and principal payment found to be a material deviation from invitation thus requiring rejection); *Dubie-Clark Co.*, Comp. Gen. Dec. B-186918, 76-2 CPD ¶ 194 (exception to liquidated damages); 39 Comp. Gen. 259 (B-140236) (1959) (bid limiting contractor's liability for excess costs for failure or delay in making delivery rendered bid nonresponsive).

## d.  Barring Public Disclosure

Bids containing restrictions that prevent public disclosure are nonresponsive if they effectively keep competing bidders from knowing the essential nature and type of products offered or those elements of the bid that relate to quantity, price, and delivery terms, *Industrial Acoustics Co.*, Comp. Gen. Dec. B-255123.2, 94-1 CPD ¶ 220 (bid properly rejected as nonresponsive where bid restricted disclosure of required test data necessary to determine responsiveness of bid); *VACAR Battery Mfg. Co.*, Comp. Gen. Dec. B-223244.2, 86-2 CPD ¶ 21 (bid restricting public disclosure rejected as nonresponsive despite disclosure of the restricted bid price at bid opening); *Sperry-Univac*, Comp. Gen. Dec. B-200378, 81-1 CPD ¶ 38 (bid stamped "proprietary" properly rejected as nonresponsive because disclosure of price at bid opening was limited). But where the limitations on disclosure of a company's information relate solely to its ability to perform and not to price, quantity, or delivery, rejection is not required, *Tennessee Apparel Corp.*, Comp. Gen. Dec. B-253178.3, 94-1 CPD ¶ 104.

## 4.  Indefinite, Uncertain, or Ambiguous Bids

Bids that are indefinite, uncertain, or ambiguous are normally rejected as nonresponsive. The test is whether "the face of the bid indicates the bidder's intent to be bound" by the government's acceptance of the bid, *Orvedahl Constr., Inc.*, 63

Comp. Gen. 288 (B-213408), 84-1 CPD ¶ 405. See *Entwistle Co.*, Comp. Gen. Dec. B-192990, 79-1 CPD ¶ 112, stating:

> When determining the responsiveness of a bid, the controlling factor is not wheth-er the bidder intends to be bound, but whether this intention is apparent from the bid as submitted. 42 Comp. Gen. 502 (1963). Thus, if [the low bidder's] bid is am-biguous, as Entwistle seems to contend, then the intent to be bound is not apparent from the bid submitted and [the low bidder's] bid must be found nonresponsive. See *James W. Boyer Company*, B-187539, November 17, 1976, 76-2 CPD ¶ 433. In 48 Comp. Gen. 757 at 760 (1969), we stated:
>
> > The mere allegation that something is ambiguous does not make it so. Similarly, some factor in a written instrument may be somewhat confusing and puzzling without constituting an ambiguity, provided that an applica-tion of reason would serve to remove the doubt. In other words, an ambi-guity exists only if two or more *reasonable* interpretations are possible.

Thus, where a bid is subject to two reasonable interpretations, one of which would make it responsive and the other nonresponsive, the bid must be rejected as ambigu-ous, *Reid & Gary Strickland Co.*, Comp. Gen. Dec. B-239700, 90-2 CPD ¶ 222 (notation on bid schedule stating that bidder had "allowed" $ 500,000 for doors ambiguous because it could be interpreted as indicating an intent to offer something other than a firm-fixed-price contract); *Banks Ship Rigging Corp.*, Comp. Gen. Dec. B-239853, 90-2 CPD ¶ 181 (two reasonable interpretations concerning bidder's pro-posed delivery date); *Wasteco Container Servs., Inc.*, Comp. Gen. Dec. B-240309, 90-2 CPD ¶ 372 (bid notation that "prices are based on dumping fees of $26 per ton" created an ambiguity as to intended price under an IFB for a firm-fixed-price contract). The consideration of ambiguous bids for award would give the bidder an unfair competitive advantage by giving it the opportunity to withdraw or affirm the bid after seeing the bids of competitors. In this regard GAO, in *Fire & Technical Equip. Corp.*, Comp. Gen. Dec. B-192408, 78-2 CPD ¶ 91, stated:

> Only material available at bid opening may be considered by the contracting offi-cer when determining the responsiveness of the bid. To permit explanations after bid opening to render responsive a bid which is nonresponsive on its face would be tantamount to granting an opportunity to submit a new bid. 52 Comp. Gen. 602 (1973). Thus, a nonresponsive bid may not be corrected and it does not mat-ter whether the failure to comply with the requirements of the IFB was due to inadvertence, mistake or otherwise. 45 Comp. Gen. 433 (1966)

In *Don's Wheelchair & Ambulance Serv., Inc.*, Comp. Gen. Dec. B-216790, 85-1 CPD ¶ 82, a bid was found to be nonresponsive because it permitted the bidder to elect one of two prices, only one of which would result in award to the bidder. However, in *Hughes & Hughes*, 68 Comp. Gen. 194 (B-233624), 89-1 CPD ¶ 61, GAO found no ambiguity where the bidder submitted two conflicting bid sheets, reasoning that it was clear that the bid sheet with the later notations was the one that would be binding on the bidder.

## a. Conditioning the Offer

Bids that are ambiguous regarding whether they represent an unconditional offer to comply with the specifications are nonresponsive, *B&C Indus., Inc.*, Comp. Gen. Dec. B-244471.4, 91-2 CPD ¶ 314 (shipping information included with bid created an ambiguity as to whether bid would conform to the IFB's packaging requirement); *G.S. Link & Assocs.*, Comp. Gen. Dec. B-238600, 90-1 CPD ¶ 479 (statement that bid would comply with EPA guidelines rendered bid ambiguous with respect to whether the offered paper products would comply with the required waste paper content); *John C. Grimberg, Inc.*, Comp. Gen. Dec. B-218231, 85-1 CPD ¶ 305 (bidder's failure to unconditionally acknowledge referenced sketch created uncertainty concerning whether the bid was an unequivocal offer to meet material requirements of the solicitation). Bids also have been rejected when required descriptive literature submitted with them stated that specifications were "subject to change," *Air & Hydraulic Equip., Inc.*, Comp. Gen. Dec. B-250332, 93-1 CPD ¶ 54. However, if other language negates the "subject to change" provision, the bid has been held to be responsive. See *Yale Materials Handling Corp.*, Comp. Gen. Dec. B-228974.2, 87-2 CPD ¶ 550 (bid need not be rejected as nonresponsive where handwritten statement that all required specifications will be met immediately following the "subject to change" provision effectively deleted such language from bid); and *Waukesha Motor Co.*, Comp. Gen. Dec. B-178494, 74-1 CPD ¶ 329 (cover letter, stating that all equipment would meet specifications, negated the "subject to change" clause and did not render the bid nonresponsive).

If required bid literature — submitted to establish conformance to the specifications — does not clearly indicate such conformance, the bid is considered ambiguous and rejection will result, *AMSCO Scientific*, Comp. Gen. Dec. B-255313, 94-1 CPD ¶ 112. Similarly, where a bidder submits unsolicited bid literature that either takes exception to the specifications or renders the bid ambiguous as to whether or not the item offered will comply with the specifications, the bid will be rejected, *Nu-Lite Elec. Wholesalers, Inc.*, Comp. Gen. Dec. B-248383, 92-2 CPD ¶ 104.

The insertion of unsolicited part or model numbers in a bid, even where included only for a bidder's internal control purposes, creates an ambiguity regarding whether the bidder is offering to comply completely with the specifications, *IFR, Sys., Inc.*, Comp. Gen. Dec. B-222533, 86-2 CPD ¶ 224, *recons. denied*, 86-2 CPD ¶ 601. Thus, a bid containing unsolicited part numbers must be rejected as nonresponsive unless either the bid contains an express statement that the designated parts conform to the specifications or the contracting officer determines, from data available before bid opening, that the parts conform, *Infab Corp.*, Comp. Gen. Dec. B-238423, 90-1 CPD ¶ 506. In *Buckingham Mfg. Co.*, Comp. Gen. Dec. B-239999, 90-2 CPD ¶ 224, a bid ambiguity created by the unsolicited insertion of a part number resulted in rejection because the ambiguity could not be resolved by reference to the bid itself, commercial literature, or other data available at the time of bid opening. See also *Wright Tool Co.*, Comp. Gen. Dec. B-212343, 83-2 CPD ¶ 457; *Abbott*

*Labs.*, Comp. Gen. Dec. B-183799, 75-2 CPD ¶ 171; *Lift Power, Inc.*, Comp. Gen. Dec. B-182604, 75-1 CPD ¶ 13; and 50 Comp. Gen. 8 (B-169813) (1970). However, ambiguities created by unsolicited insertions of model numbers can be resolved by an express bid statement that the designated model numbers comply with the IFB specification, *Millipore Corp.*, Comp. Gen. Dec. B-234979, 89-2 CPD ¶ 31; *Carco Elecs.*, Comp. Gen. Dec. B-186747, 77-1 CPD ¶ 172; *Huey Paper & Material, Stacor Corp.*, Comp. Gen. Dec. B-185762, 76-1 CPD ¶ 382.

Although reference to commercially available literature or to documents that are submitted with the bid may clarify an otherwise ambiguous bid, this literature is to be used only to "fill in the gaps" and may not negate what is in the bid itself, *IFR, Inc.*, Comp. Gen. Dec. B-203391.4, 82-1 CPD ¶ 292. Note, also, that where the contracting agency obtained literature that detracted from the second low bidder's bid, the agency's refusal to consider contemporaneously available literature that showed the bid was in compliance was irrational, *Essex Electro Eng'rs, Inc. v. United States*, 3 Cl. Ct. 277 (1983).

## b.  Requests That Vary from the IFB

Bidders can also create uncertainty regarding their bids when they "request" additions to or variations from the IFB, because it is then not clear how such a request should be interpreted. In *National Oil & Supply Co.*, Comp. Gen. Dec. B-198321, 80-1 CPD ¶ 437, one bidder included the following provision:

> Please be advised that National Oil would like to be relieved against freight increases. Due to the unsteady trend of increasing freight rates by the common carriers, we are unable to predict an adequate freight rate. . . . We would wish to escalate our freight rates with verification along with those imposed upon us by carriers.

GAO upheld the agency's determination of nonresponsiveness, explaining:

> With regard to National's contention that the wording in its cover letter was merely precatory in nature, i.e., the expression of a request rather than taking exception to the terms of the invitation, the meaning of those words must be determined within the context of existing circumstances. Here, we do not find it unreasonable to view National's " request" as something more than a mere wish or desire, for if National's bid were accepted it could be argued that DLA would be legally bound, contrary to the IFB's cited clauses, to absorb unanticipated increases in freight costs above and beyond those which might be included in increases in posted prices.

> \* \* \*

> At best, National's bid, including its cover letter, is subject to two possible interpretations, under one of which it would be responsive and under the other nonresponsive. We have consistently held that the rejection of such a bid is required and that it would be prejudicial to other bidders to permit the bidder creating the ambiguity to select, after bid opening, the interpretation to be adopted.

See also *A & Z Eng'g Co.*, Comp. Gen. Dec. B-222806, 86-1 CPD ¶ 388 (bid containing a request to use a different type of alloy than required in the IFB was properly rejected as nonresponsive since the request indicated that without the deviation the bidder could not manufacture the item as specified in the invitation).

GAO has allowed bidders to "confirm" bids to a contracting officer who finds them ambiguous, stating that, in such situations, the low bidder is not given any advantage in being permitted to confirm its intended bid price because the confirmation is not inconsistent with the only reasonable interpretation of the bid, *Wismer & Becker Contracting Eng'rs*, Comp. Gen. Dec. B-198674, 80-2 CPD ¶ 170. See also 39 Comp. Gen. 653 (B-141591) (1960).

FAR 52.232-15 prescribes a standard solicitation clause for use when no progress payments are intended:

> PROGRESS PAYMENTS NOT INCLUDED (APR 1984)
>
> A progress payments clause is not included in this solicitation, and will not be added to the resulting contract at the time of award. Bids conditioned upon inclusion of a progress payment clause in the resulting contract will be rejected as nonresponsive.

In contrast, FAR 32.405(b) does not prohibit the request for advance payments:

> Bidders may request advance payments before or after award, even if the invitation for bids does not contain an advance payment provision. However, the contracting officer shall reject any bid requiring that advance payments be provided as a basis for acceptance.

Prior to GAO decision in *Canadian Commercial Corp.*, 62 Comp. Gen. 113 (B-207777), 83-1 CPD ¶ 16, *recons. denied*, 83-1 CPD ¶ 275, bids containing requests for advance payments were held responsive while bids requesting progress payments were held as conditions that rendered the bid nonresponsive. Compare *Potomac Iron Works, Inc.*, Comp. Gen. Dec. B-200075, 81-1 CPD ¶ 15 (bid "requesting" advance payments was not a condition or qualification, and rejection was improper) with 45 Comp. Gen. 809 (B-158915) (1966) (bid stating "Progress Payments are Requested" under an IFB that did not provide for progress payments renders bid nonresponsive, even though the word "request" is, in the ordinary sense, precatory in nature).

In *Canadian Commercial Corp.*, the distinction between progress payments and advance payments was held irrelevant. GAO stated that the issue is not whether a bidder requests advance or progress payments, but whether the request is a condition or a mere wish or desire. Whether a "request" is a condition or a mere wish or desire must be determined from the meaning of the words under the circumstances. GAO, relying primarily on the reasoning in *Potomac Iron Works, Inc.*, Comp. Gen. Dec. B-200075, 81-1 CPD ¶ 15, determined that the statement, "Progress payments, in accordance with governing U.S. procurement regulations, are requested" was a precatory request that did not affect the responsiveness of the bid. See also *GMI, Inc.*, 69 Comp. Gen. 557 (B-239064), 90-2 CPD ¶ 8, where a request for progress payments did not render a bid nonresponsive in the absence of circumstances showing that the request was more than a mere wish or desire.

### c. Uncertainties as to Price

If a total bid price is uncertain, the bid is not responsive, *Associated Mech., Inc.*, Comp. Gen. Dec. B-243892, 91-2 CPD ¶ 192 (telegram submitted prior to bid opening created uncertainty as to whether bidder proposed to deduct $311.00 from bid or $311,000 because it was unclear whether a comma or period preceded the zeros); *Harris Constr. Co.*, 64 Comp. Gen. 702 (B-218387.2), 85-2 CPD ¶ 92 (garbled telegraphic modification increasing bid price to an uncertain amount received prior to bid opening required rejection of bid). Similarly, a bid is nonresponsive if its intended price cannot be determined from all the bid documents submitted at the time of bid opening, *United States Coast Guard — Advance Decision*, Comp. Gen. Dec. B-252396, 93-1 CPD ¶ 286 (cover letter submitted with bid requesting additional charge of $1,000 per hour for government preacceptance tests rendered bid nonresponsive; the IFB provided no means of estimating the amount of testing and, thus, the bid price could not be calculated with any certainty). Note, however, that an ambiguity as to a low bidder's intended price does not render a bid nonresponsive if the bid would be low by a significant margin under all possible interpretations, *The Ryan Co.*, Comp. Gen. Dec. B-238932, 90-1 CPD ¶ 557. GAO holds that these ambiguities can be resolved without prejudice to other bidders, *Energy Maint. Corp.*, 64 Comp. Gen. 425 (B-215281.3), 85-1 CPD ¶ 341. Similarly, GAO has stated that when it is clear from the bid itself what price was intended, or where on the basis of logic and experience it can be determined that only one price makes sense, correction of a bid and displacement of another bidder is allowed, *J&J Maint., Inc.*, Comp. Gen. Dec. B-251355, 93-1 CPD ¶ 187. See also *R.R. Gregory Corp.*, Comp. Gen. Dec. B-217251, 85-1 CPD ¶ 449, holding that award to the bidder was proper even though the bid contained a price discrepancy because only one price could reasonably be regarded as the intended bid.

### d. Offers to Comply

Bidders often attempt to resolve ambiguities in their bids by including statements to the effect that they are offering to comply with all terms of the invitation. Overall offers to comply will cure bid discrepancies only if they are specific, resolve all doubts as to the bidder's intention, and remove any option to deviate from the invitation, Comp. Gen. Dec. B-179024, Oct. 30, 1973, *Unpub.* Successful offers to comply were present in *Millipore Corp.*, Comp. Gen. Dec. B-234979, 89-2 CPD ¶ 31 (insertion of a model number did not render bid ambiguous since the bid contained an express statement that the product identified conformed to the technical requirements of the IFB); *Syntrex Inc.*, Comp. Gen. Dec. B-212781.2, 84-1 CPD ¶ 522 (bidder's cover letter offering to comply with all material specifications overcame "subject to change" clause contained in bid literature); *Calma Co.*, Comp. Gen. Dec. B-209260.2, 83-2 CPD ¶ 31 (statement in bidder's descriptive literature indicating that it intends to supply processors with the 500,000 bytes of memory required by the IFB clarifies preprinted literature indicating that the processors have only 440,000 bytes of memory).

However, a "blanket" promise of compliance with the specifications of an IFB is not sufficient to establish the responsiveness of a bid that does not demonstrate compliance apart from that promise, *Electrophysics Corp.*, Comp. Gen. Dec. B-258674, 95-1 CPD ¶ 63 (bid rejected as nonresponsive where descriptive literature submitted with bid failed to demonstrate that the offered product would satisfy a salient characteristic in the IFB, despite a blanket statement of compliance); *Amjay Chems.*, Comp. Gen. Dec. B-252502, 93-1 CPD ¶ 426 (blanket offer in bid cover letter to comply with all IFB specifications was properly rejected as nonresponsive where unsolicited descriptive literature established noncompliance); *IRT Corp.*, Comp. Gen. Dec. B-233134, 89-1 CPD ¶ 216 (blanket statement in cover letter that bidder will meet specification requirements did not cure bid's failure to provide required descriptive literature); *JoaQuin Mfg. Corp.*, Comp. Gen. Dec. B-228515, 88-1 CPD ¶ 15 (bid rejected as nonresponsive where required descriptive literature demonstrated nonconformance with IFB requirement, despite blanket statement of compliance); *Eclipse Sys., Inc.*, Comp. Gen. Dec. B-216002, 85-1 CPD ¶ 267 (bidder's general reference to supplying item in accordance with military specification did not overcome ambiguity raised in cover letter). See also *Zero Mfg., Co.*, Comp. Gen. Dec. B-210123.2, 83-1 CPD ¶ 416 (bid that did not conform was not cured by statement that item would be equal to or better than that specified).

## 5.  *Failure to Furnish Required Items or Information*

Failure to furnish items or information required to be submitted with the bid can render a bid nonresponsive. However, if sufficient information is otherwise contained in the bid documents to determine the missing information, the bid will be responsive, *Inland Assocs.*, Comp. Gen. Dec. B-213579, 84-1 CPD ¶ 398 (registration status of modem is matter of FCC public record); *Abbot Power Corp.*, Comp. Gen. Dec. B-192792, 79-1 CPD ¶ 295 (failure to submit dimensions on drawing was a minor deviation since the information could be obtained from other information in the bid).

### a.  *Descriptive Literature and Bid Samples*

When descriptive literature or bid samples are necessary to determine if the items being offered meet the specifications, standard solicitation provisions are used to alert the bidders to this requirement. See the Bid Samples provision in FAR 52.214-20 and the Descriptive Literature provision in FAR 52.214-21. These provisions state that failure to furnish the literature or samples will require rejection of the bid. They are operative only when the IFB specifies the precise descriptive literature or bid samples that are required. Alternate provisions are to be used if there is a possibility that the requirement will be waived for some of the bidders. FAR 14.202-5(d) provides that an agency may waive the descriptive literature requirements for specific bidders. It states that:

> (1) The contracting officer may the requirement for descriptive literature if —
>
>> (i) The bidder states in the bid that the product being offered is the same as a product previously or currently being furnished to the contracting activity; and
>>
>> (ii) The contracting officer determines that the product offered by the bidder complies with the specification requirements of the current invitation for bids. When the contracting officer waives the requirement, see 14.201-6(p)(2).
>
> (2) When descriptive literature is not necessary and a waiver of literature requirements of a specification has been authorized, the contracting officer must include a statement in the invitation that, despite the requirements of the specifications, descriptive literature will not be required.
>
> (3) If the solicitation provides for a waiver, a bidder may submit a bid on the basis of either the descriptive literature furnished with the bid or a previously furnished product. If the bid is submitted on one basis, the bidder may not have it considered on the other basis after bids are opened.

FAR 14.202-4(e) contains a similar provision permitting the waiver of the requirement for bid samples. See *Entwistle Co.*, Comp. Gen. Dec. B-192990, 79-1 CPD ¶ 112, permitting waiver of a descriptive literature requirement where the bidder instead provided the contract number of a contract where it had supplied equipment that met the contract specifications. GAO affirmed the contracting officer's determination that this was an expression of intent to supply that equipment on the current contract.

Failure to furnish the descriptive literature called for by the IFB will result in a bid's rejection as nonresponsive, *TIMCO Elec. Power & Controls, Inc.*, Comp. Gen. Dec. B-248308, 92-2 CPD ¶ 84 (bid nonresponsive because it did not contain specific descriptive literature required by IFB); *BSC Indus., Inc.*, Comp. Gen. Dec. B-237299, 90-1 CPD ¶ 152 (bid nonresponsive because agency received only partial descriptive literature; bidder contention that far more literature had been provided with bid was unproven); *AMSCO Scientific*, Comp. Gen. Dec. B-255313, 94-1 CPD ¶ 112 (bid nonresponsive because descriptive literature was ambiguous). Even where the descriptive literature requirement is imprecise, a bid may be rejected for failure to include any of the required literature or if what was furnished evidences nonconformance with the specifications, *Baker Co.*, Comp. Gen. Dec. B-216220, 85-1 CPD ¶ 254; *Clackamas Commc'ns, Inc.*, Comp. Gen. Dec. B-209387, 83-1 CPD ¶ 549.

Imprecise requirements for descriptive data will be less likely to lead to a determination that a noncompliant submission is nonresponsive. For example, failure to furnish "drawings . . . showing overall dimensions of reactors" as required by the IFB did not render a bid nonresponsive in *Abbot Power Corp.*, Comp. Gen. Dec. B-192792, 79-1 CPD ¶ 295. In that case, GAO found that the agency reasonably determined that the purpose of the clause was "substantially met" by the material furnished, though the bidder did not state that the offered product was a previously furnished one. See also *Tri-Servs., Inc.*, Comp. Gen. Dec. B-245698, 92-1 CPD ¶ 75, stating that a bidder's failure to include required information regarding overhead and costs did not render the bid nonresponsive since the information was not material to bid evaluation or the bidder's obligation to perform.

Failure to provide bid samples as required by an invitation will also render a bid nonresponsive, *EEV, Inc.*, Comp. Gen. Dec. B-253061, 93-2 CPD ¶ 52; *Canon U.S.A., Inc.*, Comp. Gen. Dec. B-249521, 92-2 CPD ¶ 388, *recons. denied*, 93-1 CPD ¶ 219. Where an invitation requires that bid samples strictly comply with listed specifications, a sample that fails to demonstrate conformance renders a bid nonresponsive, *Aqua-Trol Corp.*, Comp. Gen. Dec. B-246473.2, 92-1 CPD ¶ 420; *ATD-American Co.*, Comp. Gen. Dec. B-227134, 87-2 CPD ¶ 58. Note, however, that bid samples need not meet every specification requirement that the items to be furnished under the contract must meet, but rather may be evaluated solely for the characteristics specified in the solicitation's bid sample provision, *LSL Indus., Inc.*, Comp. Gen. Dec. B-239486, Sept. 10, 1990, *Unpub.*; *Sherwood Med. Co.*, Comp. Gen. Dec. B-231184, 88-2 CPD ¶ 171; FAR 14.202 4(b)(3) and (d)(1)(ii). In addition, a bid is not necessarily nonresponsive for failing to include a bid sample "as part of the bid" as long as the sample is submitted to the agency in a responsive manner that identifies it with the procurement before bid opening, *Alan Scott Indus.*, Comp. Gen. Dec. B-200391.2, 81-1 CPD ¶ 525; *Unique Packaging, Inc.*, 54 Comp. Gen. 157 (B-181940), 74-2 CPD ¶ 125.

Submission of bid samples or descriptive literature not required by the IFB will generally not be considered as qualifying the bid and will be disregarded, FAR 14.202-4(f) and FAR 14.202-5(e). However, if the literature or sample indicates that the bidder is conditioning its bid, it will be rejected as nonresponsive, *Products for Indus.*, Comp. Gen. Dec. B-257463, 94-2 CPD ¶ 128.

### b. Bid Guarantees

FAR 14.404-2(j) states that when a bid bond or guarantee is required and a bidder fails to furnish it in accordance with the IFB, the bid shall be rejected as nonresponsive unless one of the stated exceptions in FAR 28.101-4, as discussed in A.3.b. of this section, is otherwise applicable, *Secur-Data Sys., Inc.*, Comp. Gen. Dec. B-255090, 94-1 CPD ¶ 68 (bid that did not include required bid guarantee was properly rejected despite the bidder's assertion that the guarantee was included in its bid package).

Submission of a defective bid bond or bid guarantee is as fatal to a bid as the total failure to submit a bid bond or guarantee. The determinative question as to the acceptability of bonds and guarantees containing defects is whether the bid documents submitted with the bid establish that the bond or guarantee is enforceable by the government should the bidder fail to meet its obligations, *A.W. & Assocs.*, 69 Comp. Gen. 737 (B-239740), 90-2 CPD ¶ 254; *F&F Pizano*, 64 Comp. Gen. 805 (B-219591.2), 85-2 CPD ¶ 234. For example, in *BW JV1, LLC*, Comp. Gen. Dec. B-401841, 2009 CPD ¶ 249, a bid bond executed by only member of a joint venture was defective when the joint venture agreement required the signature of both companies. Similarly, in *Interstate Rock Prods., Inc. v. United States*, 50 Fed. Cl. 349 (2001), a bid bond that omitted the penal sum was defective.

Copies of bid guarantees (rather than the original document) have not been accepted as proof that the signatory is bound. See *TJ's Marine Constr. LLC*, Comp. Gen. Dec. B-402227, 2010 CPD ¶ 19, stating:

> For the bid guarantee to be viewed as enforceable, the surety must appear to be clearly bound based on the information in the possession of the contracting officer at the time of bid opening. *Frank & Son Paving, Inc.*, B-272179, Sept. 5, 1996, 96-2 CPD ¶ 106 at 1. Copies of bid guarantee documents, whether transmitted electronically or hand-delivered, generally do not satisfy the requirement for a bid guarantee since there is no way, other than by referring to the original documents after bid opening, for the contracting agency to be certain that there had not been alterations to which the surety had not consented and could use as a basis to disclaim liability. *Excel Bldg. & Dev. Corp.*, B-401955, Dec. 23, 2009, 2009 CPD ¶ at 3. See *Jay-Brant Gen. Contractors*, B-274986, Jan. 10, 1997, 97-1 CPD ¶ 17 at 3; *G&A Gen. Contractors*, B-236181, Oct. 4, 1989, 89-2 CPD ¶ 308 at 1.

When the bid guarantee is signed by a person with a power of attorney the bidder must submit proof of the authenticity of the power of attorney. There has been considerable controversy as to the extent of proof required. Compare *Hawaiian Dredging Constr. Co. v. United States*, 59 Fed. Cl. 305 (2004) (computer-generated powers of attorney and certificates with mechanically applied signatures proof of authenticity), with *All Seasons Constr., Inc.*, Comp. Gen. Dec. B-291166.2, 2002 CPD ¶ 212, and *All Seasons Constr., Inc. v. United States*, 55 Fed. Cl. 175 (2003) (signatures generated as part of the power of attorney, as opposed to being affixed to the document after its generation, do not serve to validate the document). See also *Hydro Dredge Corp.*, Comp. Gen. Dec. B-214408, 84-1 CPD ¶ 400 (although penal amount listed on the bid bond was sufficient, the attorney-in-fact who signed the bond had the authority to bind the surety for only a fraction of the amount required by the IFB); *H.W. Houston Constr. Co.*, Comp. Gen. Dec. B-258581, 95-1 CPD ¶ 47 (bid properly rejected where the solicitation number on the bid bond was "whited out" and retyped without evidence of the surety's consent, and there was another ongoing procurement to which the altered number could refer); and *Pioneer Constr. Co.*, Comp. Gen. Dec. B-227948 , 87-2 CPD ¶279 (bid properly rejected where the penal amount was typed over "white out," and there was no evidence that the surety had consented to an alteration).

Failure to include a penal sum on a bond also results in a nonresponsive bid, *Allen County Bldrs. Supply*, 64 Comp. Gen. 505 (B-216647), 85-1 CPD ¶ 507. Failure to provide a bid bond or guarantee that is effective for the entire bid acceptance period also renders a bid nonresponsive, *J.C. & N. Maint., Inc.*, Comp. Gen. Dec. B-229556, 87-2 CPD ¶ 567; *McNamara – Lunz Warehouses, Inc.*, Comp. Gen. Dec. B-188100, 77-1 CPD ¶ 448, *recons. denied*, 77-2 CPD ¶ 149. However, where the government extends the bid acceptance period but fails to require extension of the bid bond, expiration of the bid bond prior to award does not render a bid nonresponsive, *Holk Dev., Inc.*, Comp. Gen. Dec. B-230830.2, 88-2 CPD ¶ 543; *Engle Acoustic & Tile, Inc.*, Comp. Gen. Dec. B-190467, 78-1 CPD ¶ 72.

FAR 28.101-2(b) requires bid guarantees to be for a minimum of 20% of the bid price but not to exceed $3 million. However, FAR 28.101-4(c)(2) requires waiver of the deficiency in the amount of the bid guarantee if the guarantee amount submitted is "equal to or greater than the difference between the offer price and the next higher acceptable offer." Such waiver has been accepted by GAO, *Centex-Great Sw. Corp.*, Comp. Gen. Dec. B-258578, 95-1 CPD ¶ 19, and waiver was required in one case, *Haag Elec. & Constr., Inc.*, 70 Comp. Gen. 180 (B-240974), 91-1 CPD ¶ 29. However, GAO has affirmed the exercise of discretion by a contracting officer that determined that the bid guarantee was not sufficient to equal the difference in bids in an indefinite-delivery, indefinite-quantity contract where the bids were stated in terms of multipliers, not dollar amounts, *Apex Servs., Inc.*, Comp. Gen. Dec. B-255118, 94-1 CPD ¶ 95. See also *P.B. Eng'g Co.*, Comp. Gen. Dec. B-244640, 91-2 CPD ¶ 80 (bid nonresponsive when bid guarantee 24% lower than required amount); and *Drill Constr. Co.*, Comp. Gen. Dec. B-239783, 90-1 CPD ¶ 538 (submission of bid bond for half the required penal amount rendered bid nonresponsive).

FAR 28.202 provides guidance on the use of corporate sureties for bid bonds and requires that only sureties listed in Department of Treasury Circular 570 will be acceptable. Thus, bids submitting bonds by other corporate sureties are nonresponsive, *Envirotox Techs., Inc.*, Comp. Gen. Dec. B-250091, 92-2 CPD ¶ 186 (bid bond executed by corporate surety not listed in Treasury Circular 570 rendered bid nonresponsive); *Siska Constr. Co.*, Comp. Gen. Dec. B-218428, 85-1 CPD ¶ 669, *recons. denied*, 85-2 CPD ¶ 102 (lack of notice in solicitation that unlisted surety was unacceptable is not an excuse for using unlisted surety, because the requirement for listed surety is in regulations and instructions to bond form).

Bid bonds may be furnished by individual sureties if the surety pledges assets equal to the amount of the bond, FAR 28.203. See *C. E. Wylie Constr. Co.*, Comp. Gen. Dec. B-234225, 89-1 CPD ¶ 427 (bid responsive where individual sureties demonstrated sufficient net worth to cover the penal amounts of the bonds); and *O.V. Campbell & Sons Indus., Inc.*, Comp. Gen. Dec. B-229555, 88-1 CPD ¶ 259 (completed SF 24 is proper "on its face" when executed by two individual sureties whose affidavits indicate that, subject to further investigation, they both have a net worth at least equal to the penal amount of the bond). A bid containing bid bonds furnished by individual sureties is responsive even if the sureties fail to file a pledge of assets, *Burtch Constr.*, Comp. Gen. Dec. B-240695, 90-2 CPD ¶ 423; *R.C. Benson & Sons, Inc.*, Comp. Gen. Dec. B-240251.2, 90-2 CPD ¶ 92. This is because a pledge of assets assists the contracting officer in determining the financial acceptability of individual sureties, which is a matter of responsibility, not responsiveness.

Where the bidder named on the bid form differs from the principal name on the bid bond, the bid must be rejected unless it can be established that the bidder is "the same legal entity as the principal," *Gem Eng'g Co.*, Comp. Gen. Dec. B-251644, 93-1 CPD ¶ 303; *Scotsman Group, Inc.*, Comp. Gen. Dec. B-245634, 92-1 CPD ¶ 57 (bid properly rejected where publicly available information submitted after bid opening did not demonstrate that the principal named on the bid bond and the named bidder were the same legal entity); *New Solid, Ltd.*, Comp. Gen. Dec. B-246357, 92-1 CPD ¶ 163 (bid properly rejected where bid bond identified "Eugene E. and Ingride Harmon" as principals, and the bidder identified in the bid form was "Eugene E. Harmon, owner"). See also *Tower Elevator Corp.*, Comp. Gen. Dec. B-192064, 78-2 CPD ¶ 188, stating that wholly owned subsidiaries and parent corporations are not "identical legal entities." Compare *Castle Floor Covering*, 70 Comp. Gen. 530 (B-242718), 91-1 CPD ¶ 510, where waiver of the defect was required because a cashier's check made out to "Farmers Home Bureau, U.S. Government" would be binding even though the procurement was by the "Farmers Home Administration."

The form of the bid guarantee may vary so long as the requisite monetary obligation by the surety is certain, *Niles Janitor Serv. & Supply, Inc.*, Comp. Gen. Dec. B-246575.3, 92-1 CPD ¶ 256 (bid properly rejected as nonresponsive where irrevocable letter of credit incorporated a force majeure provision of the Uniform Customs and Practices for Documentary Credits Act, which created uncertainty as to the liability of the issuing bank); *Central Mech., Inc.*, 61 Comp. Gen. 566 (B-206555), 82-2 CPD ¶ 150 (bidder's offer to assign funds allegedly due the bidder from the government was rejected because the amount actually owed was undetermined); *Colorado Elevator Serv., Inc.*, Comp. Gen. Dec. B-206950.2, 82-1 CPD ¶ 434 (letter of credit from a bank stating that it is subject to the bank's standard review process is not a firm commitment and renders bid nonresponsive). Where a bid guarantee does not list the United States as the obligee, an agency may waive the noncompliance since the guarantee correctly identified the offeror, the solicitation number, and the name of the location of the project involved, *S.J. Amoroso Constr. Co.*, Comp. Gen. Dec. B-240687, 90-2 CPD ¶ 432; *Nationwide Roofing & Sheet Metal, Inc.*, 64 Comp. Gen. 474 (B-216845), 85-1 CPD ¶ 454 (use of United States Postal Service bond form for a GSA procurement did not render bid nonresponsive where the intent of the surety and the principal to be bound to the government was clearly shown).

## c.  List of Subcontractors

Generally, a requirement to list subcontractors or suppliers in bids involves a matter of responsibility, because an agency utilizes these lists to evaluate subcontractor qualifications or the bidder's ability to meet equal employment opportunity requirements, *CDM Fed. Programs Corp.*, Comp. Gen. Dec. B-249022, June 23, 1992, *Unpub.*; *Norfolk Dredging Co.*, Comp. Gen. Dec. B-229572.2, 88-1 CPD ¶ 62; *A. Metz, Inc.*, Comp. Gen. Dec. B-213518, 84-1 CPD ¶ 386. However, if the requirement for bidders to list their proposed subcontractors is intended to prevent "bid shopping," the failure to furnish required subcontractor lists requires rejection of a bid as nonresponsive, *Industrial Structures, Inc.*, 64 Comp. Gen. 768 (B-219500), 85-2 CPD ¶ 165; *Lazos Constr. Co.*, Comp. Gen. Dec. B-211966, 83-2 CPD ¶ 201; *McCrory Constr. Co.*, Comp. Gen. Dec. B-192913, 79-1 CPD ¶ 64. A contractor who plans to do categories of work with its own employees must so indicate if required by the IFB, or the bid will be found nonresponsive for failure to list subcontractors, *Brisk Waterproofing Co. v. GSA*, Civ. Action No. 77-0659 (D.D.C. 1977). The listing of alternate subcontractors also renders a bid nonresponsive, *Burn Constr. Co.*, Comp. Gen. Dec. B-192196, 78-2 CPD ¶ 139. See also *Dawson Constr. Co.*, Comp. Gen. Dec. B-208547, 82-2 CPD ¶ 551, finding the rejection of a bid for failing to list all subcontractors improper because the IFB called only for a listing of those doing on-site work.

## 6.  Accurate Completion of Bids and Documents

Bids and accompanying documents must be accurately completed if they are to be considered responsive. FAR 14.301(d) states:

> Bids should be filled out, executed, and submitted in accordance with the instructions in the invitation. If a bidder uses its own bid form or a letter to submit a bid, the bid may be considered only if
>
> (1) The bidder accepts all the terms and conditions of the invitation; and
>
> (2) Award on the bid would result in a binding contract with terms and conditions that do not vary from the terms and conditions of the invitation.

This rule was applied in *J.C. Adams, Inc.*, Comp. Gen. Dec. B-252132, 93-1 CPD ¶ 394, where a bid was held nonresponsive because the bidder submitted a bid schedule that it had prepared itself, which varied from the material requirements of the solicitation's bid schedule. Similarly, in *Weber Constr.*, Comp. Gen. Dec. B-233848, 89-1 CPD ¶ 309, a bidder's omission of SF 1442, which contained material provisions of the solicitation, rendered the bid nonresponsive, because it was unclear whether the bidder would be unequivocally committed to all the material requirements of the invitation. See also *ATR Logistics Co. LLC*, Comp. Gen. Dec. B-402606, 2010 CPD ¶ 140 (bid nonresponsive when it failed to follow bidding schedule in amendment which it acknowledged); *Dillingham Ship Repair*, Comp. Gen. Dec. B-218653, 85-2 CPD ¶ 167 (bid nonresponsive for failure to include unit prices as required by the solicitation, even though the bid contained a lump sum for the total amount). In addition, a bid that contains uncertainties as to the identity of the bidder must be rejected as nonresponsive because, upon award, the bidder could avoid its obligations under the contract, *Sunrise Int'l Group, Inc.*, Comp. Gen. Dec. B-252735.2, 93-2 CPD ¶ 58 (award was improper where contracting officer concluded that the bid was submitted by T.B.F. Enterprises using Budget Inns of America (BIA) as a trade name without contemporaneous, publicly available evidence demonstrating that "BIA" was in fact "T.B.F. Enterprises" ); *Martin Co.*, Comp. Gen. Dec. B-178540, 74-1 CPD ¶ 234 (bid in the name of "Martin Co., Inc." was properly rejected as nonresponsive because the company bidding was in fact "Martin Co.," a sole proprietorship, and award to anyone other than the bidder named in the bid would be an improper substitution of entities).

Bids may be accepted despite a failure to complete the bid accurately if the deficiency is not material and the obligations of the parties are not altered, *J & K Plumbing & Heating Co.*, 71 Comp. Gen. 241 (B-246000), 92-1 CPD ¶ 174 (bidder's failure to return bid schedule was waived as a minor informality where bidder signed and submitted SF 1442, which incorporated the specifications of the IFB and therefore obligated the bidder to perform in accordance with the material requirements of the IFB); *Walker Constr.*, Comp. Gen. Dec. B-246759, 92-1 CPD ¶ 319 (failure to submit a bid for an alternate item does not render a bid nonresponsive where the alternate item was not awarded); *S.J. Amoroso Constr. Co.*, Comp. Gen. Dec. B-240687, 90-2 CPD ¶ 432 (bid guarantee that did not list the United States as the obligee was waived as a minor defect because the guarantee correctly identified the bidder, the solicitation number, and the name of the location of the project involved); *Hild Floor Mach. Co.*, Comp. Gen. Dec. B-217213, 85-1 CPD ¶ 456 (failure to furnish spare parts price list is waivable because bidders were not required to commit to specific prices).

Unsigned bids are generally nonresponsive, *FCC Constr., Inc.*, Comp. Gen. Dec. B-250304, 93-1 CPD ¶ 28; *Stafford Grading & Paving Co.*, Comp. Gen. Dec. B-245907, 92-1 CPD ¶ 66; *Loop to Loop Messenger Serv.*, Comp. Gen. Dec. B-241068, 90-2 CPD ¶ 519. Unsigned bids, even though accompanied by bid samples, must be considered nonresponsive, *Jonard Indus. Corp.*, Comp. Gen. Dec. B-192979, 79-1 CPD ¶ 5. See also Comp. Gen. Dec. B-148235, Mar. 23, 1962, *Unpub.*, stating that the presence of a bidder's representative at bid opening was not sufficient to overcome the lack of a signature on the bid or to indicate an intention to be bound to the material requirements of the solicitation.

If it can independently be established that the bidder submitting an unauthorized bid intended to be bound, the bid should be accepted. See FAR 14.405(c), which allows a bidder's failure to sign a bid to be waived as a minor informality only if:

(1) The unsigned bid is accompanied by other material indicating the bidder's intention to be bound by the unsigned bid (such as the submission of a bid guarantee or a letter signed by the bidder, with the bid, referring to and clearly identifying the bid itself); or

(2) The firm submitting a bid has formally adopted or authorized, before the date set for opening of bids, the execution of documents by typewritten, printed, or stamped signature and submits evidence of such authorization and the bid carries such a signature[.]

See *Micon Corp.*, Comp. Gen. Dec. B-249231, 92-2 CPD ¶ 293 (bidder's failure to sign SF 1442 waived where bid bond accompanying the bid was properly signed and referenced the solicitation); *Tomahawk Constr. Co.*, Comp. Gen. Dec. B-243582, 91-2 CPD ¶ 137 (failure to submit an originally signed bid held a minor informality because accompanying amendments, bid bond, and letter contained original signature of bidder); and *Wilton Corp.*, 64 Comp. Gen. 233 (B-218064), 85-1 CPD ¶ 128 (bidder's failure to sign bid waived as a minor informality where bid was accompanied by a signed amendment acknowledgment). However, an irrevocable letter of credit does not negate a bidder's failure to sign its bid in the same fashion as a properly executed bid bond, because it does not require the bidder's signature as a party to the instrument, *Cable Consultants, Inc.*, Comp. Gen. Dec. B-215138, 84-2 CPD ¶ 127.

The evidence of intent to be bound must be submitted prior to bid opening. To permit submission of this evidence after bid opening would give the bidder an improper advantage, *A & E Indus., Inc.*, Comp. Gen. Dec. B-239846, 90-1 CPD ¶ 527 (bid signed with a rubber stamp signature was properly rejected because there was no evidence that prior to bid opening, the use of a rubber stamp signature had been authorized); *Power Master Elec. Co.*, Comp. Gen. Dec. B-223995, 86-2 CPD ¶ 615 (bid that included typewritten signature does not evidence intent to be bound when typewritten signature was not authorized). In this regard, GAO stated in Comp. Gen. Dec. B-160856, Mar. 16, 1967, *Unpub.*:

> The reasoning behind this rule is that when a bid lacks a proper signature, and there is no other clear indication in the bid submission that the purported bidder intended to submit the bid, the contracting officer has no assurance that the bid was submitted by someone with authority to bind the bidder. For that reason, acceptance of such a bid would not have automatically obligated the named bidder to perform the contract advertised. The test in cases where bids are not manually signed is whether the bid as submitted will result in a binding contract upon acceptance of the bid by the Government without confirmation of the bidder's intention.

Bids must also be signed by authorized employees of the bidder. GAO has held that the level of evidence required to establish the authority of a particular person to sign and thus bind a corporation is for the contracting officer to determine, and that the burden of proof rests with the bidder, *Alpha Q, Inc.*, Comp. Gen. Dec. B-234403.2, 89-2 CPD ¶ 401; *Central Mech. Constr., Inc.*, Comp. Gen. Dec. B-220594, 85-2

CPD ¶ 730; *Dragon Servs., Inc.*, Comp. Gen. Dec. B-208081, 82-2 CPD ¶ 86. The evidence required to establish the authority of the signer to bind a corporation may be presented at any time prior to award. Failure to furnish such information at bid opening will not render a bid nonresponsive, *Southwest Maint. Serv.*, Comp. Gen. Dec. B-258178, 94-2 CPD ¶ 243; *Goss Fire Protection, Inc.*, Comp. Gen. Dec. B-253036, 93-2 CPD ¶ 97.

For other irregularities in the completion of the bid form that may be waived as minor informalities, see *Corbin Superior Composites, Inc.*, Comp. Gen. Dec. B-236777.2, 90-1 CPD ¶ 2 (bidder's failure to complete "contingent fee representation" clause); *Alpha Q, Inc.*, Comp. Gen. Dec. B-234403.2, 89-2 CPD ¶ 401 (failure to return SF 33, the cover sheet used in most government procurements, with signature); *O.V. Campbell & Sons Indus., Inc.*, Comp. Gen. Dec. B-229555, 88-1 CPD ¶ 259 (failure of surety to properly complete bid bonds); *All Star Maint., Inc.*, Comp. Gen. Dec. B-231618, 88-2 CPD ¶ 181 (bidder's failure to submit the required certifications and representations with bid at bid opening); *TCI, Ltd.*, 65 Comp. Gen. 23 (B-220578), 85-2 CPD ¶ 433 (failure to return the number of copies required by the invitation); *Bond Transfer & Storage Co.*, Comp. Gen. Dec. B-210251, 83-1 CPD ¶ 87 (failure to mark the solicitation number, date, and time of opening on the bid envelope); *Patterson Pump Co.*, Comp. Gen. Dec. B-200165, 80-2 CPD ¶ 453 (failure to return all specification pages where SF 33 was properly executed); *Johnson Auto Parts*, Comp. Gen. Dec. B-182102, 74-2 CPD ¶ 157 (submission of the bid on the addendum rather than on the IFB forms). See also *Excavation Constr., Inc. v. United States*, 204 Ct. Cl. 299, 494 F.2d 1289 (1974), which held that reference to an incorrect date for an addendum and the use of a superseded job number in the bid were waivable informalities.

## 7. *Accompanying Letter, Literature, and Other Material*

Letters, preprinted forms, descriptive literature, or other material submitted with a bid are considered part of the bid and can affect its responsiveness. Thus, if they condition the bid, they may render it nonresponsive. For example, bids accompanied by cover letters that conditioned the bid were found nonresponsive in *Air Prep Tech., Inc.*, Comp. Gen. Dec. B-252833, 93-1 CPD ¶ 459 (cover letter stating bidder's proposed conveyor system will be powered by a hydraulic motor rendered bid nonresponsive where IFB required a compressed air motor); *Perkin-Elmer Corp.*, 63 Comp. Gen. 27 (B-236175.2), 89-2 CPD ¶ 352 (bid was properly rejected as nonresponsive where cover letter offered a shorter bid acceptance period than required by the IFB); *Taylor-Forge Engineered Sys., Inc.*, 69 Comp. Gen. 54 (B-236408), 89-2 CPD ¶ 421 (bid was properly rejected because the cover letter and bid form contained conflicting delivery terms, thus rendering the bid ambiguous); *Northwest Ground Covers & Nursery*, Comp. Gen. Dec. B-201609, 81-1 CPD ¶ 81 (cover letter requested that bidder be allowed to withdraw bid if it was a successful bidder on another government contract).

FAR 14.202-5(e) provides that unsolicited descriptive literature will be treated under the same procedures set forth in FAR 14.202-4(f) for unsolicited bid samples:

> Bid samples furnished with a bid that are not required by the invitation generally will not be considered as qualifying the bid and will be disregarded. However, the bid sample will not be disregarded if it is clear from the bid or accompanying papers that the bidder's intention was to qualify the bid. (See 14.404-2(d) if the qualification does not conform to the solicitation.)

Thus, unsolicited descriptive literature will not be considered as qualifying a bid unless it is clear from the bid as a whole that it is intended as a qualification. In *Balantine's South Bay Caterers, Inc.*, Comp. Gen. Dec. B-250223, 93-1 CPD ¶ 39, GAO stated that unsolicited descriptive literature, which reasonably raised a question regarding whether the offered services complied with the material requirements of the IFB, could not be disregarded, because the cover letter referenced the solicitation number and described the literature as "pertinent information." See also *Delta Chem. Corp.*, Comp. Gen. Dec. B-255543, 94-1 CPD ¶ 175 (bid was properly rejected where unsolicited literature rendered uncertain the bidder's obligation to furnish the exact product called for under the IFB). However, unsolicited descriptive literature that takes exception to the IFB requirements to an immaterial extent only, will not render the bid nonresponsive, *Brown Boveri Elec., Inc.*, Comp. Gen. Dec. B-209338, 83-1 CPD ¶ 342.

When descriptive literature is required for bid evaluation, any statements reserving the right to alter or change the specifications generally will render the bid nonresponsive, *Air & Hydraulic Equip., Inc.*, Comp. Gen. Dec. B-250332, 93-1 CPD ¶ 54; *Erincraft, Inc.*, Comp. Gen. Dec. B-235829, 89-2 CPD ¶ 332 (uncontradicted legend on descriptive literature submitted with bid stating that "all specifications are subject to change" ); *Galaxy Distrib., Inc.*, Comp. Gen. Dec. B-220535, 85-2 CPD ¶ 441 ("subject to change" legend in required descriptive literature rendered bid nonresponsive because nothing else in the bid indicated that the legend was not intended to reserve the right to change or deviate from the material requirements of the IFB). However, when a bid contains sufficient assurances that the bidder intends to meet all contract requirements, despite the subject to change disclaimer, it may properly be held responsive, *Yale Materials Handling Corp.*, Comp. Gen. Dec. B-228974.2, 87-2 CPD ¶ 550; *Tektronix, Inc.*, 66 Comp. Gen. 704 (B-227800.2), 87-2 CPD ¶ 315 ("subject to change" legend included in unsolicited descriptive literature does not render bid nonresponsive where the bid otherwise indicates the bidder's intent to conform to the specifications); *Syntrex Inc.*, 63 Comp. Gen. 360 (B-212781.2), 84-1 CPD ¶ 522 (bid was properly viewed as responsive where there was sufficient indication in the bid that the bidder intended to meet all the contract requirements despite "subject to change" legend contained in the required descriptive literature); *Waukesha Motor Co.*, Comp. Gen. Dec. B-178494, 74-1 CPD ¶ 329 ("subject to change" legend in preprinted descriptive literature was effectively negated because cover letter stated that "all equipment and tests will be completed to specifications").

Other materials have resulted in findings of nonresponsiveness, even though the bid forms conformed exactly to the IFB. See *Star Brite Constr. Co.*, Comp. Gen. Dec. B-255206, 94-1 CPD ¶ 89 (notation in bid bond that stated bond was null and void if the "contract includes the removal of asbestos" rendered the bid nonresponsive); *Northwestern Motor Co.*, Comp. Gen. Dec. B-244334, 91-2 CPD ¶ 249 (bid properly rejected as nonresponsive where handwritten note on bid created an ambiguity regarding a material requirement of the IFB); and *Contech Constr. Co.*, Comp. Gen. Dec. B-241185, 90-2 CPD ¶ 264 (bid was properly rejected where notations in bid that the required performance schedule was "impossible" created uncertainty as to whether bidder agreed to the required performance terms).

## 8.  Failure to Acknowledge Amendments

The failure of a bidder to acknowledge receipt of an amendment containing a material requirement prior to bid opening renders a bid nonresponsive. In assessing whether a failure to acknowledge an amendment should have been waived, the issue is whether "something about the change . . . reflect[s] a legitimate need of the agency such that its requirements will not be met if the contractor performs to the unamended specifications," *Stanger Indus., Inc.*, Comp. Gen. Dec. B-279380, 98-1 CPD ¶ 157. See *T&S Maint. Servs.*, Comp. Gen. Dec. B-278598, 98-1 CPD ¶ 54 (an amendment is material, "even if it has only a trivial price impact, if it changes the legal relationship between the parties, such as by increasing or decreasing the contractor's obligation in a material manner"); *Overstreet Elec. Co.*, Comp. Gen. Dec. B-283830, 2000 CPD ¶ 8 ("An amendment is generally not material under this regulation where it has the effect of decreasing the price, quantity, quality, delivery, or the bidder's legal obligations, without materially increasing any of these matters."). There are many examples of nonresponsive bids because of failure to acknowledge a material amendment. See *Skyline ULTD, Inc.*, Comp. Gen. Dec. B-297800.3, 2009 CPD ¶ 128 (amendment added work to original requirement); *Hackney Group*, Comp. Gen. Dec. B-261241, 95-2 CPD ¶ 100 (amendment eliminated inconsistency in amount of work to be performed); *Farrar Aerospace*, Comp. Gen. Dec. B-259364, 95-1 CPD ¶ 165 (amendment required the manufacturing of parts stated in the specifications); *G.R. Spanaugle & Sons, Inc.*, Comp. Gen. Dec. B-257784, 94-2 CPD ¶ 178 (amendment limited the hours after regular work hours during which certain construction work could be performed), *Mike Vaneho*, 64 Comp Gen. 780 (B-219019), 85-2 CPD ¶ 184 (amendment required upward wage rate revision). This is because, absent acknowledgment of a material amendment, a bidder would not be obligated to the terms of the IFB as amended, *Jenness Woodkuts*, Comp. Gen. Dec. B-257345, 94-2 CPD ¶ 112. Even if the amendment was not acknowledged because it was never received, a bid must be rejected as nonresponsive unless the failure was the result of a deliberate and conscious effort to exclude the bidder from competing for the contract, *Southeastern Enters., Inc.*, Comp. Gen. Dec. B-245491.2, 92-1 CPD ¶ 88; *Shemya Constructors*, 68 Comp. Gen. 213 (B-232928.2), 89-1 CPD ¶ 108; or unless the record indicates that the agency did not make a reasonable effort to mail the amendment in accordance with regulatory requirements, *Andero Constr., Inc.*, 63 Comp. Gen. 253 (B-203898), 82-1 CPD ¶ 133 (agency compliance with a regulation is not established where three of four bidders appear not to have received the amendment in the mail).

FAR 14.405(d)(1) allows a bidder's failure to acknowledge receipt of an amendment to be waived as a minor informality if the bid demonstrates that the bidder received the amendment. Therefore, a bidder's failure to explicitly acknowledge receipt of an amendment may be waived if there is an implicit or constructive acknowledgment through submission of a bid reflecting some change made by the amendment. For examples of constructive acknowledgment of amendments, see *Bonded Maint. Co.*, Comp. Gen. Dec. B-235207, 89-2 CPD ¶ 51 (bid included a new pricing schedule established by an amendment); and *Professional Aviation Maint. & Mgmt. Servs., Inc.*, Comp. Gen. Dec. B-232078, 88-2 CPD ¶ 350 (bidder's cover letter included statements that it would perform in accordance with two unacknowledged amendments). But see *C Constr. Co.*, 67 Comp. Gen. 107 (B-228038), 87-2 CPD ¶ 534, stating that award to the bidder was improper because submission of the bid on the amended bid opening date is not sufficient to show that the bidder constructively acknowledged an amendment extending the bid opening date.

FAR 14.405(d)(2) also permits a bidder's failure to acknowledge an amendment to be waived if the amendment is trivial in nature. Thus, in *Pro Alarm Co.*, 69 Comp. Gen. 727 (B-240137), 90-2 CPD ¶ 242, GAO stated that a bidder's failure to acknowledge an amendment could be waived since the amendment had no effect or a negligible effect on quantity, quality, delivery, or price. See also *DBI Waste Sys., Inc.*, Comp. Gen. Dec. B-400687, 2009 CPD ¶ 15 (failure to acknowledge amendment substituting an item that cost the same as the originally specified item); *Lumus Constr., Inc.*, Comp. Gen. Dec. B-287480, 2001 CPD ¶ 108 (failure to acknowledge amendment that merely clarified specification requirements); *Wirco, Inc.*, 65 Comp. Gen. 255 (B-220327), 86-1 CPD ¶103 (failure to acknowledge amendment that added two containers to the previously scheduled deliveries waived as a minor informality because the bidder was obligated to provide the correct number of containers, and the effect on price, if any, was negligible).

In determining whether an amendment has a trivial impact, the increase in the cost of performance and the relative difference between the bid prices will be considered, *Marino Constr. Co.*, 61 Comp. Gen. 269 (B-204970), 82-1 CPD ¶ 167. Thus, a minimal cost increase will not be considered trivial if it represents a material difference between the two lowest bidders, *Gulf Elec. Constr. Co.*, 68 Comp. Gen. 719 (B-235635), 89-2 CPD ¶ 272 (failure to acknowledge amendment with an estimated cost impact of $650 rendered bid nonresponsive because that increase in price was double the difference between the low and second low bid, and 30% of the difference between the lowest bid and the protester's third lowest responsive bid); *Power Sys. Diesel Inc.*, Comp. Gen. Dec. B-224635, 86-2 CPD ¶ 599 (bidder's failure to acknowledge amendment rendered bid nonresponsive because the estimated increase in costs was 9.5% of the difference between the two lowest bids); *M. C. Hodom Constr. Co.*, Comp. Gen. Dec. B-209241, 83-1 CPD ¶ 440 (bidder's failure to acknowledge amendment that increased bid price only 0.25% rendered bid nonresponsive because that increase constituted 11.25% of the difference between the two low bidders); *Navaho Corp.*, Comp. Gen. Dec. B-192620, 79-1 CPD ¶ 24 (bid rejected as nonresponsive because bidder failed to acknowledge amendment that increased bid price by only 0.25% of low bid but was 13.34% of the difference between two lowest bidders).

However, in *K Servs.*, Comp. Gen. Dec. B-238744, 90-1 CPD ¶ 556, the procuring agency properly waived the failure to acknowledge an amendment with an estimated cost impact of $502.50, which was only 0.1% of the bidder's bid and 6.6 % of the difference between the low and second low bid. Similarly in *G.C. Smith Constr. Co.*, Comp. Gen. Dec. B-213525, 84-2 CPD ¶ 100, the low bidder's failure to acknowledge an amendment with an estimated increase in contractor costs of $2,390 should not have been rejected, because this was 0.262% of the bidder's bid and 4.92% of the difference between the two low bids. See also *Universal Contracting & Brick Pointing Co.*, Comp. Gen. Dec. B-188394, 77-1 CPD ¶ 347 (low bidder's failure to acknowledge an amendment with an estimated value of $820 was properly waived where the next lowest bid was $59,903 higher in price). The determination regarding the price impact of an amendment to an IFB may not be based on the value placed on it by the bidder seeking a waiver, but rather on the government's estimate, *Ira Gelber Food Servs., Inc.*, 55 Comp. Gen. 599, (B-184308) 75-2 CPD ¶ 415; 53 Comp. Gen. 64 (B-178640) (1973).

Generally, a bidder's failure to acknowledge an amendment that merely restates or clarifies the original solicitation and does not change the legal obligations it imposed, may be waived as a minor informality, *Cedar Elec., Inc.*, Comp. Gen. B-402284.2, 2010 CPD ¶ 79 (waiver proper when amendment made prior requirement more specific); *Futura Sys. Inc.*, 70 Comp. Gen. 365 (B-242060), 91-1 CPD ¶ 327 (rejection was improper where amendment made no substantial changes to the original warranty provision, and, by signing its bid, the bidder was bound to the original IFB); *Adak Commc'ns Sys., Inc.*, 67 Comp. Gen. 208 (B-228341), 88-1 CPD ¶ 74 (although bidder failed to acknowledge an amendment that changed line items for costs and required the use of manufacturer-approved parts and equipment, rejection of the bid was improper because the amendment merely clarified the bidder's obligations to provide parts for maintenance and repair work under the IFB). Compare *John D. Lucas Printing Co.*, Comp. Gen. B-285730, 2000 CPD ¶ 154 (agency should not have waived bidder's failure to acknowledge amendment which clarified patent ambiguity).

However, amendments that have more than a negligible effect on price, quantity, quality, or delivery are material, and the failure to acknowledge them may not be waived, *Specialty Contractors, Inc.*, Comp. Gen. Dec. B-258451, 95-1 CPD ¶ 38 (bidder's failure to acknowledge amendment that changed required color of roofing panels from "dark bronze" to " medium bronze" rendered bid nonresponsive under circumstances indicating that color was a material requirement); *MIBO Constr. Co.*, Comp. Gen. Dec. B-224744, 86-2 CPD ¶ 678 (failure to acknowledge amendment deleting the optional use of asbestos roofing materials significantly affected the quality of performance and rendered the bid nonresponsive); *Belfort Instrument Co.*, Comp. Gen. Dec. B-218561, 85-2 CPD ¶ 135 (bid properly rejected as nonresponsive where bidder failed to acknowledge amendment issued to correct defective and ambiguous technical specifications which affected the quality of the services solicited).

Failure to acknowledge an amendment revising wage rates generally cannot be waived because this would give the bidder the opportunity to become ineligible for award by not curing the defect, *Grade-Way Constr. v. United States*, 7 Cl. Ct. 263 (1985). See *Tri-Tech Int'l, Inc.*, Comp. Gen. Dec. B-246701, 92-1 CPD ¶ 304, where failure to acknowledge an amendment increasing wage rates made the bid nonresponsive even though the fringe benefit rate decreased more than the wages increased, and *Promethean Constr., Co.*, Comp. Gen. Dec. B-255222, 94-1 CPD ¶ 78, where failure to acknowledge an amendment increasing wage rates made the bid nonresponsive even though the rate increase impacted a class of workers that the bidder did not intend to use. Thus, failure to acknowledge a wage rate amendment can only be waived if the bidder can demonstrate that it was already obligated to pay the wages in the amendment, *ABC Project Mgmt., Inc.*, Comp. Gen. Dec. B-274796.2, 97-1 CPD ¶ 74. For example, if the bidder's employees are already covered by a collective bargaining agreement calling for wages as high as those in the revised wage determination, the failure to acknowledge an amendment containing that determination may be waived, *ABC Paving Co.*, 66 Comp. Gen. 47 (B-224408), 86-2 CPD ¶ 436; *Brutoco Eng'g & Constr., Inc.*, 62 Comp. Gen. 111 (B-209098), 83-1 CPD ¶ 9.

Oral rather than written acknowledgment of a material amendment is unacceptable and renders a bid nonresponsive, *Alcon, Inc.*, Comp. Gen. Dec. B-228409, 88-1 CPD ¶ 114; *Protex Sys., Inc.*, Comp. Gen. Dec. B-201146, 84-1 CPD ¶ 265. In *MET Elec. Testing, Inc.*, 60 Comp. Gen. 321 (B-201146), 81-1 CPD ¶ 202, GAO stated at 322-23:

> Permitting oral acknowledgment of a material amendment is detrimental to the competitive bidding process in two ways. First, it allows a bidder " two bites at the apple," by giving it the sole discretion to accept or reject the contract after bid opening, by affirming or denying that it intended to be bound by the amendment and, hence, the agreement. See *National Investigation Bureau, Inc.*, B-191759, July 18, 1978, 78-2 CPD ¶44. Second, because of the bidder's failure to timely acknowledge the amendment in writing, the terms of the resulting contract are not clear since the written bid acknowledges the terms of the solicitation, but not relevant amendments.

In *Construction Catering, Inc.*, Comp. Gen. Dec. B-207987, 82-2 CPD ¶ 49, GAO stated, referring to 33 Comp. Gen. 508 (B-119732) (1954), that oral acknowledgment of an immaterial amendment is permissible.

## III. EVALUATION AND AWARD

The CICA amended 10 U.S.C. § 2305(b)(3) and 41 U.S.C. § 253b(c) (now 41 U.S.C. § 3702) with respect to evaluation and award of sealed bids as follows:

Sealed bids shall be opened publicly at the time and place stated in the solicitation. The head of the agency shall evaluate the bids ... without discussions with the bidders and, except as provided in paragraph (2), shall award a contract with reasonable promptness to the responsible bidder whose bid conforms to the solicitation and is most advantageous to the United States, considering only price and the other price-related factors included in the solicitation. The award of a contract shall be made by transmitting, in writing or by electronic means, notice of the award to the successful bidder. Within three days after the date of contract award, the head of the agency shall notify, in writing or by electronic means, each bidder not awarded the contract that the contract has been awarded.

This language is substantially the same as was included in the prior statutes except that the term "the other price-related factors included in the solicitation" has been used in place of the term "other factors." This change continues the fundamental goal of sealed bid procurement — to base the award solely on objectively determined cost to the government, 47 Comp. Gen. 658 (B-163890) (1968).

The evaluation process necessary to determine which bidder is offering the lowest cost to the government can vary from the simple to the complex, depending on the circumstances of the procurement. For procurements involving the purchase of multiple items, indefinite quantities, or for an extended performance period, the evaluation process becomes more complicated, and evaluation criteria must be stated in the IFB. Price adjustment provisions such as discounts or economic price adjustment clauses can also become part of the evaluation process. The greatest complexity sometimes occurs when "other price-related factors" are introduced into the evaluation formula. All of these issues are addressed in this section.

The section also considers the procedures followed in awarding sealed bid contracts. Difficulties can arise when multiple awards are contemplated or when the contracting agency cannot make the award decision by the time the bids expire. Award based upon bids at below cost (so-called buy-ins) are also considered.

The section concludes with a discussion of cancellation of the procurement after bid opening. 10 U.S.C. § 2305(b)(2) and 41 U.S.C. § 3701(b) give broad discretion in the area, stating:

All sealed bids or competitive proposals received in response to a solicitation may be rejected if the head of the agency determines that such action is in the public interest.

However, cancellation is a serious matter because of the time and expense involved in preparing a bid and because bidders can be prejudiced if the competition is reopened after bids have been exposed. Thus, cogent and compelling reasons are usually required to support this course of action.

## A. Evaluation Process

The fundamental rule is that the bid evaluation process must be performed on the basis of the factors set forth in the IFB so that bidders are able to compete on a fair and equal basis, 36 Comp. Gen. 380 (B-127801) (1956).

### 1. Evaluation of Bid Prices

The solicitation must set forth the price evaluation method that will be used and the contracting officer must adhere to it. See *Jacobs Transfer, Inc.*, 53 Comp. Gen. 797 (B-180195), 74-1 CPD ¶ 213, where the invitation stated the evaluation would be on the basis of prices under Schedule A and B combined. However, just before bid opening the contracting officer orally stated that only the price of Schedule A would be evaluated. This was held improper because the contracting officer did not adhere to the price evaluation criteria set forth in the invitation. In *Southeastern Servs., Inc.*, 56 Comp. Gen. 668 (B-187872), 77-1 CPD ¶ 390, GAO stated the basic principle at 670:

> Revised evaluation criteria may not be used after bid opening to justify award, because bidders have not competed on that basis.

However, if the protester cannot show harm from the alteration of the price evaluation scheme, the IFB is not required to be cancelled. See *Williams Elevator Co.*, Comp. Gen. Dec. B-210049, 83-2 CPD ¶ 327, where the solicitation called for the evaluation of contract prices for a one-year period, but the contracting officer changed the evaluation method by tripling the prices to reflect the total cost to the government for the full three-year contract. The alteration was upheld because the disappointed bidder failed to show that its price would have been low had the IFB evaluation scheme been followed. Thus, it was not prejudiced by the different evaluation method.

### a. Accurate Reflection of Lowest Cost

The IFB evaluation criteria must reflect the lowest cost to the government based on the total work to be performed. If the evaluation scheme does not assure that award will be made to the bidder offering the lowest overall cost to the government during actual performance, cancellation of the IFB is required, *Maintenance Inc.*, Comp. Gen. Dec. B-208036, 83-1 CPD ¶ 631.

Agencies sometimes use evaluation criteria that preclude them from determining which bidder offers the lowest cost to the government. The most common error is overestimating the agency's needs. In *Southeastern Servs., Inc.*, 56 Comp. Gen. 668 (B-187872), 77-1 CPD ¶ 390, *recons. denied, Dyneteria, Inc.*, Comp. Gen. Dec. B-187872, 77-2 CPD ¶ 134, the solicitation for a food service contract calling for the evaluation of meal prices outside the contract range was held improper because it bore no relation to the agency's actual requirements. GAO stated at 670:

> Our office has held that the lowest bidder must be measured by the total and actual work to be awarded. Any measure which incorporates more or less than the work to be contracted in selecting the lowest bidder does not obtain the benefits of full and free competition required by the procurement statutes.

In this case the IFB evaluation method was based on more meals than the Air Force needed; it did not assure, therefore, that award would be made to the bidder offering the most favorable cost to the government. See also *Heritage Reporting Corp.*, Comp. Gen. Dec. B-248860.2, 92-2 CPD ¶ 276 (IFB for the base period of an option contract grossly overestimated quantities of transcripts needed by the government, and using those estimates would not assure award to the lowest bidder); and *W.H. Smith Hardware Co.*, Comp. Gen. Dec. B-228127, 87-2 CPD ¶ 556 (IFB listed a unit as four casters instead of one, which was an overstatement of the agency's needs; thus, there was a possibility of an award that would not result in the lowest cost to the government).

Sometimes the statement of estimated quantities for evaluation purposes is unclear, making it difficult to ascertain the lowest bidder. See *Duramed Homecare, Inc.*, Comp. Gen. Dec. B-260047, 95-1 CPD ¶ 257 (IFB failed to provide estimated quantities for some of the items); *Ferguson-Williams, Inc.*, Comp. Gen. Dec. B-258460, 95-1 CPD ¶ 39 (after bid opening, the agency determined that the three lowest bidders had misunderstood the estimated quantities); *MTL Sys., Inc.*, Comp. Gen. Dec. B-245363, 91-2 CPD ¶ 569 (IFB failed to include a price adjustment for accelerated delivery or the number of items that required the accelerated delivery); and *Robinson Mills & Williams*, Comp. Gen. Dec. B-236956.3, 90-1 CPD ¶ 156 (IFB failed to provide estimates for any of the specific services to be performed).

In some cases, the lowest bidder cannot be ascertained because the line items in the IFB do not include all factors that need to be considered in the evaluation equation. See, for example, *Bayfone of Tampa*, Comp. Gen. Dec. B-242925, 91-1 CPD ¶ 535 (the line item for telephone usage did not account for the number of telephones that would be using each type of service); and *Temps & Co.*, 65 Comp. Gen. 640 (B-221846), 86-1 CPD ¶ 535 (IFB calling for an assortment of personnel, but hourly wages excluded the amount of time that each temporary employee would work). In *Exclusive Temporaries of Ga.*, Comp. Gen. Dec. B-220331.2, 86-1 CPD ¶ 232, the line items included both full- and part-time work. It was unclear whether one or both line items should be filled out and what would be used to evaluate the bids. Thus, the IFB resulted in bids that "could not be evaluated on an equal basis" and would not necessarily render the lowest cost. In *S.W. Monroe Constr. Co.*,

Comp. Gen. Dec. B-256382, 94-1 CPD ¶ 362, the IFB failed to include a complete line item for a service that the government wanted performed and the quantity required on a different line item. Although some of the bidders did include the omitted item, the IFB did not elicit full and open competition, because it was unclear to the agency whether or not the other bids included the price for that item. In addition, there was no common basis for comparison on the omitted quantity, since "the relative standing of bidders could change depending on the number . . . and economies of scale used by each bidder."

In some instances an agency has used a mathematical method in the evaluation scheme that does not result in arriving at the actual lowest bid. In *Chemical Tech., Inc.*, Comp. Gen. Dec. B-187940, 77-1 CPD ¶ 126, the price evaluation entailed the averaging of five prices for varying quantities of monthly meals. However, historical data revealed that 50% of the time the meal service fell under only two of the five meal quantities. Since the method of evaluation gave no assurance that award would be made to the bidder offering the lowest cost to the government, GAO decided that the evaluation scheme was faulty. For another case where averaging was found not to discern the lowest bidder, see *Temps & Co.*, 65 Comp. Gen. 640 (B-221846), 86-1 CPD ¶ 535, where the IFB requested an assortment of personnel at different wage prices, and the agency attempted to average the wages to come up with a low bidder.

A defect in the evaluation scheme caused by a mistake by the agency may also make the lowest bidder difficult to determine. In *Earthworks of Sumter, Inc.*, Comp. Gen. Dec. B-232067.2, 89-1 CPD ¶ 9, bids were to be evaluated on a base period of four months. However, the Air Force mistakenly sent Earthworks a seven-month schedule, on which it consequently bid. The contracting officer tried to rectify the mistake by calculating a four-month bid out of Earthworks' estimate, but after protest, this method was deemed faulty. See also *Balva Financial Corp.*, Comp. Gen. Dec. B-235872, 89-2 CPD ¶ 263 (IFB called for evaluation of the price of one item two times, and therefore the lowest overall price to the government could not be calculated); and *R.P. Densen Contractors, Inc.*, 66 Comp. Gen. 31 (B-222627), 86-2 CPD ¶ 401 (evaluation clause used an algebraic sum of all adjustments applied to the base bid, which did not accurately measure the cost to the government).

As noted earlier, a defective evaluation scheme, such as those mentioned above, does not alone preclude award. Where award of the contract to the current lowest bidder under the defective IFB would serve the best interests of the government and the other bidders would not be prejudiced, award to the lowest bidder is permitted. In *Square Deal Trucking Co.*, Comp. Gen. Dec. B-183695, 75-2 CPD ¶ 206, *recons. denied*, 75-2 CPD ¶ 303, the invitation specified evaluation based on unit prices. One bidder's prices were low for monthly unit charges, but the price for the entire year of the contract was not low. GAO recommended award of the contract on the basis of the lowest overall price rather than on the basis of unit prices.

In cases where the award was unavoidably delayed for administrative reasons or due to protests, resulting in a shortened contract period, award is permitted to a bidder who was evaluated as low under the IFB performance period, even though that bidder's price was not low for the actual, shorter performance period, *Maintenance Pace Setters, Inc.*, Comp. Gen. Dec. B-208768.3, 83-2 CPD ¶ 514; *International Technical Servs. Corp.*, Comp. Gen. Dec. B-198314, 81-1 CPD ¶ 18. Even though the evaluation of bid prices did not reflect the actual work to be performed, award was sanctioned because bid prices had been exposed, and to resolicit would cost the government as much or more than it would cost to make the award to the current low bidder.

### b.  Unbalanced Bids

There are two aspects to unbalanced bidding — "mathematical" unbalancing and "material" unbalancing. A bid is not subject to rejection because of unbalancing unless it is found to be *both* mathematically and materially unbalanced. The first involves a mathematical evaluation to determine whether a bid is based upon understated prices for some work and inflated prices for other work. In this regard, it is necessary to show that a bid contains *both* understated and overstated prices in order to conclude that it is mathematically unbalanced. The second aspect — material unbalancing — involves an assessment of the cost impact of a mathematically unbalanced bid. A bid is materially unbalanced if there is a reasonable doubt that the acceptance of a mathematically unbalanced bid will result in the lowest ultimate cost to the government, *Continental Collection & Disposal, Inc.*, Comp. Gen. Dec. B-238842.2, 90-1 CPD ¶ 591. Unbalanced bidding is used for several reasons: (a) it may help a bidder to conceal its pricing strategy from its competitors; (b) it may permit a bidder to recover larger sums for earlier performed work, giving it both a monetary advance as well as shifting some of the risk of the contract to the government; (c) it may enable a bidder to become the lowest evaluated bidder through speculation on the accuracy of the government's quantity estimates in the invitation for bids; and (d) it may be used by bidders as a hedge against losses in cases where a program does not run to completion.

*Reliable Trash Serv.*, Comp. Gen. Dec. B-194760, 79-2 CPD ¶ 107, first established the two-pronged test to determine whether award may be made to an unbalanced bidder. Award may be made to a mathematically unbalanced bid, but not if the bid is also materially unbalanced. If a bid is both mathematically and materially unbalanced, then the government should reject it, FAR 14.404-2(g). In *Reliable*, GAO defined "materially unbalanced," stating:

> A bid is not materially unbalanced unless there is a reasonable doubt that award to the bidder submitting a mathematically unbalanced bid will not result in the lowest ultimate cost to the Government. Consequently, only a bid found to be materially unbalanced may not be accepted.

This test is set forth in the Contract Award — Sealed Bidding solicitation provision in FAR 52.214-10(e), which provides:

> The Government may reject a bid as nonresponsive if the prices bid are materially unbalanced between line items or subline items. A bid is materially unbalanced when it is based on prices significantly less than cost for some work and prices which are significantly overstated in relation to cost for other work, and if there is a reasonable doubt that the bid will result in the lowest overall cost to the Government even though it may be the low evaluated bid, or if it is so unbalanced as to be tantamount to allowing an advanced payment.

Another provision at FAR 9.306(j) requires contracting officers to warn offerors not to submit unbalanced offers for contracts that involve separately priced first articles. See also FAR 14.404-2. A bid can be found to be materially unbalanced if it creates a reasonable doubt as to whether award will be made to the lowest cost bid. GAO's view of what constitutes "reasonable doubt" has evolved over the years. In *Lear Siegler, Inc.*, Comp. Gen. Dec. B-205594.2, 82-1 CPD ¶ 632, GAO recognized that when a bid is front-loaded, so that it only becomes low "late" in the contracting period, and the program does not run to completion, the government will not be able to take advantage of the low prices, and therefore will pay more than would be the case if prices had been balanced over the total contracting period. In *Lear Siegler*, the IFB called for the operation of a transportation motor pool with one base period and three option periods. The contracting officer awarded the contract to SAE, and Lear Siegler protested, claiming that the bid was mathematically and materially unbalanced. GAO found that, "in view of SAE's front-loaded bid structure and the fact that it is not until well after the exercise of the third and final option year that SAE's total cost becomes low, there is reasonable doubt that award to SAE will result in the lowest ultimate cost to the Government."

GAO has sometimes determined that an agency's intent to exercise all options suffices to overcome an unbalancing situation. See *Rust Int'l Corp.*, Comp. Gen. Dec. B-256886.2, 94-2 CPD ¶ 84, finding that there was no doubt that the agency intended to have construction work completed over the option period of two years. However, other cases have made contractor reliance upon this logic dangerous. See, e.g., *Residential Refuse Removal, Inc.*, Comp. Gen. Dec. B-247198.6, 92-2 CPD ¶ 444, observing that despite "a contracting agency's intent to exercise all options, there is sufficient reason to doubt the low ultimate cost anticipated from a mathematically unbalanced bid where it does not become low until very late in a contract term." The effect of this rationale is to force contractors to allocate front-end costs across the option years of a long-term contract, with the commensurate risk to them that they will not recover their costs if the government does not fully exercise the options. This is discussed further below.

Another theory advanced by GAO for rejecting a materially unbalanced bid was that a grossly front-loaded bid is "tantamount to an advance payment," which is prohibited by 31 U.S.C. § 3324, except when otherwise expressly authorized by law, *Riverport Indus., Inc.*, 64 Comp. Gen. 441 (B-216707), 85-1 CPD ¶ 364. The rationale for rejection on this basis is that such an advance payment is analogous to an interest-free loan, thereby giving the bidder a competitive advantage, *F & E Erection Co.*, Comp. Gen. Dec. B-234927, 89-1 CPD ¶ 573 (bid should be rejected as materially unbalanced when the bidder would receive payment for inflated line items early in the contract); *Barnard-Slurry Walls*, Comp. Gen. Dec. B-274973, 97-1 CPD ¶ 23 (lump sum price for preparatory work line item was many multiples higher than the reasonable value of the work). See also *ACC Constr. Co.*, Comp. Gen. Dec. B-250688, 93-1 CPD ¶ 142, rejecting a low bid because the protester could receive progress payments on inflated prices for work performed early in the contract period — tantamount to an advance payment.

However, only *gross* front-loading was tantamount to an advance payment. See *Rust Int'l Corp.*, Comp. Gen. Dec. B-256886.2, 94-2 CPD ¶ 84, where GAO granted a protest where the agency had rejected a bid as being grossly front-loaded, but GAO found, on the basis of an analysis of the offeror's projected costs, that it was not. See also *Grumley Schlosser*, Comp. Gen. Dec. B-274012, 96-2 CPD ¶ 158, holding that a base bid that was less than two times greater than the government estimate or the protester's next low bid was not so grossly front-loaded as to be tantamount to an improper advance payment. See *Integrated Protection Sys., Inc.*, Comp. Gen. Dec. B-254457.2, 94-1 CPD ¶ 24, stating the rule as follows:

> Front-loaded bids that are not grossly front-loaded may be accepted, however. See *Aydin Corp.*, B-245461, Jan. 13, 1992, 92-1 CPD ¶ 51 (first article units priced approximately twice the production unit price); *Dodge Romig Tex Corp.*, B-241810, Mar. 5, 1991, 91-1 CPD ¶ 246 (first article priced two to three times production unit price).

> Here, [the awardee's] installation price is less than three times the government estimate and is not even two times greater than the protester's next low bid. We see no basis for finding gross front-loading in these circumstances.

GAO no longer applies the advance payment reasoning because FAR 14.408-1(b) calls for price analysis considering unbalanced bids to determine whether they are materially unbalanced using the risk analysis procedures in FAR 15.404-1(g). See *JND Thomas Co.*, Comp. Gen. Dec. B-402240, 2010 CPD ¶ 40; and *Reece Contracting, Inc.*, Comp. Gen. Dec. B-285666, 2000 CPD ¶ 135. See also *Fire-Trol Holdings, LLC v. United States*, 68 Fed. Cl. 281 (2005), agreeing with this procedure. Note, however, that the Contract Award — Sealed Bidding solicitation provision still embodies the advance payment concept. See *Enco Dredging*, Comp. Gen. Dec. B-284107, 2000 CPD ¶ 44, noting this discrepancy in the FAR but denying a protest where the contracting officer accepted a significantly unbalanced bid because they risk of overpayment was not perceived to be great — based on a payment provision that restricted payment of some costs until the end of the project.

## (1) Front-Loaded Construction Contracts

Front-loading of a construction contract follows the same general pattern found in all unbalancing situations, that is, a bidder will usually structure its bid to recover progress payments for early work in amounts significantly in excess of the cost of that work. For an example of a front-loaded construction bid, see *Dement Constr. Co.*, Comp. Gen. Dec. B-192794, 78-2 CPD ¶ 399, where the two low bidders for the construction job submitted the following figures for the first two items of work to be performed:

| Item | Universal | Dement | Government's Estimated Cost |
|---|---|---|---|
| 1. Mobilization | $2,749,318 | $30,000 | $22,600 |
| 2. Clearing & Grubbing | $120,505 | $1,192,000 | $202,860 |

Based on the government's estimated cost, GAO held that the bids must be rejected since "both bidders unbalanced their bids for these early items of work in an effort to recover the sums that must be expended for mobilization and preparation prior to actual commencement of construction." See also *L. W. Matteson, Inc.*, Comp. Gen. Dec. B-290224, 2002 CPD ¶ 89; and *Industrial Bldrs., Inc.*, Comp. Gen. Dec. B-283749, 99-2 CPD ¶ 114, finding rejection of grossly front-loaded bids proper.

To justify a front-loaded bid, the bidder will sometimes state that it included start-up costs in the progress payment schedule, *Jasper Painting Serv., Inc.*, Comp. Gen. Dec. B-251092, 93-1 CPD ¶ 204. In that case, GAO stated:

> Because start-up costs properly may be factored into an offer, a relatively front-loaded price does not automatically establish that an offer is unbalanced. However, the start-up costs may not carry a disproportionate share of the total contract price.

When start-up costs have been factored into the front end of a bid, award is generally not allowed, *ACC Constr. Co.*, Comp. Gen. Dec. B-250688, 93-1 CPD ¶ 142, unless the front-loading is so minor that it represents no more than a proportionate share of the contract work, *Cottrell Eng'g Corp.*, Comp. Gen. Dec. B-252891, 93-2 CPD ¶ 66 (bidder had unique mobilization costs because it was located far away, and prices were not deemed to be inflated). Another situation where some unbalancing has been found unobjectionable is in cases where a bidder intends to acquire unique equipment for which it will have no other use. See *Roan Corp.*, Comp. Gen. Dec. B-211228, 84-1 CPD ¶ 116. There have been no recent cases utilizing this concept. See also *Ken Leahy Constr., Inc.*, Comp. Gen. Dec. B-290186, 2002 CPD ¶ 93, permitting the inclusion of mobilization costs of option work in the cost of the base work because the costs were not "significantly overstated."

## (2) Quantity Estimates

Unbalancing can also occur in multiple item requirements and indefinite-quantity contracts. In these contracts, bids are evaluated on the basis of estimated quantities, and unbalancing can occur when a bidder believes that the actual quantities ordered by the government will vary from the estimates. In such cases, the bidder submits an unbalanced bid, with higher prices on items believed to have underestimated quantities and lower prices on items believed to have been overestimated.

For an example of such unbalanced bidding, see *Michael O'Connor, Inc.*, Comp. Gen. Dec. B-183381, 76-2 CPD ¶ 8, involving the installation of partitions in certain government buildings where the bidder submitted the following bids:

| IFB Item | IFB Estimated Quantities | Actual Prior Year Requirements | Bid |
|---|---|---|---|
| 5 | 16,000 | 0 | 0 (N/C) |
| 31 | 10 | 426 | $249 per unit |

The government based its estimates on an average of the previous years' requirements. The bidder based its bid on only the prior year's actual requirements. For Item 5, the IFB estimate significantly overstated the quantity, and the bidder took advantage of this by bidding "no charge." For Item 31, the bidder increased its unit bid price because the government had underestimated its needs. As a result, the bidder was evaluated low but would not have represented the actual lowest cost to the government. See also *Burney & Burney Constr. Co.*, Comp. Gen. Dec. B-292458.2, 2004 CPD ¶ 49; *Alice Roofing & Sheet Metal Works, Inc.*, Comp. Gen. Dec. B-275477, 97-1 CPD ¶ 86; and *Copy Graphics*, Comp. Gen. Dec. B-273028, 96-2 CPD ¶ 185.

GAO stated in *Robertson & Penn, Inc.*, Comp. Gen. Dec. B-234082, 89-1 CPD ¶ 365, that "a low bid for a requirements type contract is not materially unbalanced unless it can be shown that the Government's estimates are so unreliable that award to the low bidder will not result in the lowest cost to the Government." See *Belton Roofing & Remodeling Co.*, Comp. Gen. Dec. B-277651, 97-2 CPD ¶ 131; and *Ostrom Painting & Sandblasting, Inc.*, Comp. Gen. Dec. B-250827.2, 93-1 CPD ¶ 390, recommending that the IFB be canceled due to inaccurate government estimates. Thus, to determine that a mathematically unbalanced bid is not materially unbalanced, the government estimate must be sufficiently accurate to ensure that the mathematically unbalanced bid does not create a reasonable doubt that the government will be awarding to the lowest bidder. See *South Atlantic Constr. Co., LLC*, Comp. Gen. Dec. B-286592.2, 2001 CPD ¶ 63 (accuracy of estimates not in question and only few of many items unbalanced); *Beldon Roofing Co.*, Comp. Gen. Dec. B-283970, 2000 CPD ¶ 21 (accuracy of estimates not in question and work to be done at almost same time); *Adam II, Ltd.*, Comp. Gen. Dec. B-209194, 83-2 CPD ¶ 102 (Air Force estimates based on historical experience were sufficiently accurate). If the estimates in the IFB are not sufficiently accurate, the bids will be found unbalanced and the IFB will be canceled, *Edward B. Friel, Inc.*, 55 Comp. Gen. 231 (B-183381), 75-2 CPD ¶ 164. However, there is no requirement that the government's estimates be absolutely correct; they need only come from the best information available, thereby providing a reasonably accurate representation of the agency's needs, *Custom Envtl. Serv., Inc.*, 70 Comp. Gen. 184 (B-241052), 91-1 CPD ¶ 38.

## (3) Option Contracts

Unbalanced bidding occurs in option contracts when prices submitted for the base period are higher than the option year prices. As in other types of contracts, a two-step analysis is followed. First, it must be determined if a bid is mathematically unbalanced. If so, it must then be determined if the bid is materially unbalanced.

GAO has altered the analysis of mathematical unbalancing of option contracts in recent years. Originally, a bid with high base-year prices was found to be balanced if the base year contained only those costs chargeable to that year through normal accounting practices. Thus, a bid would be found to be mathematically balanced if it allocated all start-up costs to the base year or included a high base-year price because it used generally accepted accelerated techniques for allocating equipment costs. See *M & M Servs., Inc.*, Comp. Gen. Dec. B-228717, 87-2 CPD ¶ 382 (start-up and equipment costs make up high base-period cost); and *Professional Reprographic Servs.*, Comp. Gen. Dec. B-210608, 83-1 CPD ¶ 653 (high start-up costs accounted for the price differential). See *Fidelity Moving & Storage Co.*, Comp. Gen. Dec. B-222109.2, 86-1 CPD ¶ 476, stating that:

> [A]ssessment [of mathematical unbalancing] must go beyond the mere percentage differentials between base and option period prices to determine whether those prices are accurate reflections of the actual costs that will be borne by the bidder in performing each year of the contemplated contract. *See Integrity Management International, Inc.*, B-217016, Dec. 11, 1984, 84-2 CPD ¶ 654.

> While this Office has previously recognized that a 25 to 50 percent differential between base and option period prices does not necessarily constitute mathematical unbalancing ... these cases do not establish conclusively in this particular instance that Fidelity's bid, with 10 to 25 percent base/option period differentials, contains neither overstated nor understated prices. Rather, the determinative question is whether Fidelity's bid pricing structure is reasonably related to the actual costs to be incurred in each year.

However, in making this analysis GAO stated that a large pricing differential between the base year and option years, or between option years, would be prima facie evidence that the bid was mathematically unbalanced, *Howell Constr., Inc.*, 66 Comp. Gen. 413 (B-225766), 87-1 CPD ¶ 455. This placed the burden on the contractor to prove that the costs were allocated using generally accepted established accounting practices. When a contractor met this burden, award to the apparently unbalanced bid was sustained because it had been demonstrated that, in fact, the bid was not mathematically unbalanced, *Roan Corp.*, Comp. Gen. Dec. B-211228, 84-1 CPD ¶ 116; *Applicators, Inc.*, Comp. Gen. Dec. B-215035, 84-1 CPD ¶ 656.

In recent years GAO has rejected this reasoning and has held that a bid will be found to be mathematically unbalanced if the government pays more than "reasonable value" for the work even though the "high" prices are based upon the contractor's projected costs, *Eastex Maritime, Inc.*, Comp. Gen. Dec. B-256164, 94-1 CPD ¶ 340 (bid found unbalanced when it allocated all start-up costs to base bid). This rule has been applied to both start-up costs and equipment depreciation costs. See *Residential Refuse Removal*, 72 Comp. Gen. 68 (B-247198.6), 92-2 CPD ¶ 444, stating:

> An individual bidder's business decisions for front-loading costs, e.g., the bidder's use of a particular depreciation method, are not generally material to the issue of mathematical unbalancing. *Mitco Water Labs., Inc.*, B-249269, Nov. 2, 1992, 92-2 CPD ¶ (reasons for front-loading bid to cover equipment renovation costs are irrelevant); Government Leasing Corp., supra (accelerated depreciation method not considered for determination of mathematical unbalancing); *Westbrook Indus., Inc.*, [71 Comp. Gen. 139, 92-1 CPD ¶ 30] (reason for front-loading of equipment costs not considered for determination of mathematical unbalancing); *Professional Waste Sys., Inc.; Tri-State Servs. of Tex.*, [67 Comp. Gen. 68, 87-2 CPD ¶ 477] (method of financing a bidder's equipment costs not considered for determination of mathematical unbalancing). It is only where, because of the unique nature of the contract or of the equipment required to perform the contract, the equipment will have little or no value to the ordinary bidder in the event of early contract termination that we will consider a bidder's reasons for front-loading. See e.g., *Roan Corp.*, B-211228, Jan. 25, 1984, 84-1 CPD ¶ 116 (front-loading costs in the base year of a bid for a contract to lease a fleet of law enforcement vehicles did not mathematically unbalance the bid where, in the event of early termination, there was no market for leasing fleets of used law enforcement vehicles.) *Id.*

See also *Government Leasing Corp.*, Comp. Gen. Dec. B-245939, 92-1 CPD ¶ 117 (an admission that the bid was structured by factoring in depreciation and following other generally accepted accounting principles, which allowed the bidder to recover the greatest portion of its acquisition costs in the base year, is an admission that a front-loaded bid was submitted and that each price was not reflective of the value of the work it represented); *Inventory Accounting Serv.*, Comp. Gen. Dec. B-245906, 92-1 CPD ¶ 116 (even though business reasons existed for front-loading, the fact that it would result in advance payment and possibly a windfall to the bidder made bid mathematically unbalanced); *DGS Contract Servs., Inc.*, Comp. Gen. Dec. B-245400, 92-1 CPD ¶ 16 (offeror expected to "apportion" cost of generic equipment over entire contract period to avoid mathematical unbalancing); and *Omega One Co.*, Comp. Gen. Dec. B-251316.2, 93-1 CPD ¶ 254 (mathematically unbalanced when base was 31 to 46% higher than option prices, and work required no "unique or specialized" equipment). The rule has also been applied to unique performance techniques where an offeror justifies the high front-end costs by the cost of initiating "sophisticated" techniques, *McConico Inv. Mgmt. Corp.*, Comp. Gen. Dec. B-251895, 93-1 CPD ¶ 346. These decisions demonstrate that in order to escape the onus of mathematically unbalancing, option prices must be essentially the same as base year prices. This has been characterized as "value-based analysis" — meaning that GAO is insisting that the analysis be based upon "value" to the government not the costs to be incurred by the contractor.

As already noted, the determination of whether a mathematically unbalanced bid containing options is materially unbalanced has also changed. In early cases, if the government expected to exercise an option and there was a reasonable expectation that funds would be available, GAO held that a mathematically unbalanced bid was not materially unbalanced, *K.P. Food Servs., Inc.*, 60 Comp. Gen. 1 (B-198427.2), 82-1 CPD ¶ 289. However, in *Lear Siegler, Inc.*, Comp. Gen. Dec. B-205594.2, 82-1 CPD ¶ 632, and subsequent cases, GAO found that even if the government agency expected to exercise the options and funds were available, a bid would be found to be materially unbalanced if the government would not actually realize the cost advantage associated with the mathematically unbalanced bid until late in the contract term. GAO reasoned that there was a risk that the government would not realize such cost advantage if intervening events occurred, such as termination by default or failure to exercise an option, and the contractor would experience a windfall. See, for example, *Williams Elec. Co.*, Comp. Gen. Dec. B-275019, 97-1 CPD ¶ 25 (bid was materially unbalanced because the agency was unsure if it would exercise any of the options, and the protester's bid was low only if all three options were exercised); *Crown Laundry & Dry Cleaners, Inc.*, Comp. Gen. Dec. B-208795.2, 83-1 CPD ¶ 438 (bid was not low until fourth month of second option period, so despite the agency's intent to exercise all options, intervening events could cause a windfall); and *Westbrook Indus., Inc.*, 71 Comp. Gen. 139 (B-245019.2), 92-1 CPD ¶ 30 (when bid is not low until the thirty-fifth month, there is reason to believe intervening events could occur). GAO has held that a bid that does not become low until the final contract year is materially unbalanced on its face, *Fidelity Moving & Storage Co.*, Comp. Gen. Dec. B-222109.2, 86-1 CPD ¶ 476; *Inventory Accounting Serv.*, Comp. Gen. Dec. B-245906, 92-1 CPD ¶ 116. In other situations, GAO has determined that when the agency intends to use all of the option periods and there is no evidence to the contrary, there is no reasonable doubt, *MCI Constructors, Inc.*, Comp. Gen. Dec. B-274347, 96-2 CPD ¶ 210. This is more apt to occur when the bid will become low relatively early in the contract, *Grunley Schlosser*, Comp. Gen. Dec. B-274012, 96-2 CPD ¶ 158 (bid became low with the exercise of the first option); *Tri-Ark Indus.*, Comp. Gen. Dec. B-270756, 96-1 CPD ¶ 194 (bid became low in the second month of the first option period); *Integrated Protection Sys., Inc.*, Comp. Gen. Dec. B-254457.2, 94-1 CPD ¶ 24 (bid became low in first six months of first option year); *Omega One Co.*, Comp. Gen. Dec. B-251316.2, 93-1 CPD ¶ 254 (bid became low in second month of second option year, so no reasonable doubt existed); *Aquasis Servs., Inc.*, Comp. Gen. Dec. B-228044, 87-2 CPD ¶ 426 (bid became low in eighth month of first option year, so no reasonable doubt existed). But see *Storage Tech. Corp.*, GSBCA 9345-P, 88-2 BCA ¶ 20,667, where, although the bid did not become low until its fourth option year, the board held that because the contract was for maintenance, the Army would reasonably exercise all options since it intended to keep the equipment.

## (4) First Article Contracts

Unbalanced bidding may also occur in contracts requiring the delivery of first articles. In this situation, a contractor charges a large amount for the first article and lower amounts for production articles. GAO has followed the same reasoning as that used in contracts containing options, holding that, even if special equipment and tooling are needed for those first articles, it is improper not to amortize these costs over all of the articles when that tooling will be needed throughout the period of the contract, *Nebraska Aluminum Castings, Inc.*, Comp. Gen. Dec. B-222476, 86-1 CPD ¶ 582, *recons. denied*, 86-2 CPD ¶ 335, *recons. denied*, 86-2 CPD ¶ 515. Thus, if costs other than the unique costs of manufacturing and testing first articles are allocated to the first article, a mathematically unbalanced bid is likely to be found, *Star Dynamic Corp.*, Comp. Gen. Dec. B-248919.3, 93-1 CPD ¶ 63; *LBCO, Inc.*, Comp. Gen. Dec. B-254995, 94-1 CPD ¶ 57. When a first article price that is mathematically unbalanced is grossly front-loaded it cannot be accepted because that would be tantamount to allowing an advance payment. See *Riverport Indus., Inc.*, 64 Comp. Gen. 441 (B-218626), 85-1 CPD ¶ 364, *recons. denied*, 85-2 CPD ¶ 108 (first article unit prices were $185,000 and the production unit prices were $250); *Islip Transformer & Metal Co.*, Comp. Gen. Dec. B-225257, 87-1 CPD ¶ 327 (first article unit prices were $15,000 and the production unit prices were $408.90); *Nebraska Aluminum Castings*, Comp. Gen. Dec. B-222476, 86-1 CPD ¶ 582, *recons. denied*, 86-2 CPD ¶ 335, and 86-2 CPD ¶ 515 (first article unit prices were $22,510 and the production unit prices were $19.17); *Edgewater Mach. & Fabricators, Inc.*, Comp. Gen. Dec. B-219828, 85-2 CPD ¶ 630 (first article unit prices were $125,000 and the production unit prices were $301).

## (5) Alternative to Cancellation

GAO has suggested a number of alternatives to cancelling the invitation in the case of unbalanced bids. In *TWI Inc.*, 61 Comp. Gen 99 (B-202966), 81-2 CPD ¶ 424, GAO ruled that the Navy's estimate was not sufficiently accurate to assure that a mathematically unbalanced bid would represent the actual lowest cost to the government. It therefore recommended award to the next lowest mathematically balanced bid. In *Dement Constr. Co.*, Comp. Gen. Dec. B-192794, 78-2 CPD ¶ 399, GAO condoned negotiation with an unbalanced bidder to reduce the effect of the unbalancing. The Army originally canceled the IFB because award on the basis of the front-loaded bid would result in an advance payment of funds for work not yet performed. However, after "an understanding" was reached that payment for the item would be "over the life of the contract," the IFB was reinstated.

## c. Time Value of Money

In order to determine which bid represents the actual lowest cost to the government, the time value of money should be considered. See, for an explanation of this basic concept, *Linolex Sys., Inc.*, 53 Comp. Gen. 895 (B-179047), 74-1 CPD ¶ 296, stating at 901:

> A dollar received today is worth more than a dollar received next year, and conversely, to postpone spending a dollar until next year gives one the opportunity to earn interest on that dollar or otherwise productively use it for the 1-year period.

For procurements involving a considerable length of time, such as option contracts where base and several option years must be evaluated, good procurement practice would consider the time value of money to ensure that award is made to the bidder representing the "actual" lowest cost to the government. In order for the contracting agency to be able to consider the time value of money in the evaluation of bids, it must be itemized in the IFB as an evaluation factor, *General Tel. Co.*, 57 Comp. Gen. 89 (B-187793), 77-2 CPD ¶ 376 (not appropriate to consider present value in deciding whether to purchase or lease equipment in absence of IFB provision). Conversely, absent such a provision in the IFB, consideration of the time value of money is prohibited. Yet, neither the FAR nor most agency implementing regulations contain provisions for such consideration.

The government has included IFB provisions for the present value of money in the evaluation process in some procurements. See *Linolex Sys., Inc.*, 53 Comp. Gen. 895 (B-179047), 74-1 CPD ¶ 296, where the following paragraph was used in an ADPE procurement:

> A present value method will be used in calculation of all costs. The discount rate will be applied annually. The rate used will be current average market yield, rounded to the nearest one-eighth of one percent, on outstanding treasury marketable obligations with approximately five years remaining to maturity at the time proposals are received. As an example, if the rate were six percent, the factors would be:

| Year from Contract Award | Discount Factor |
| --- | --- |
| 1 | .943 |
| 2 | .890 |
| 3 | .840 |
| 4 | .792 |
| 5 | .747 |

This evaluation method could be used in the evaluation process for procurements where front-loading is expected to occur. However, it does not preclude other types of unbalancing. In future solicitations, the government might consider using the rate of interest established by the Secretary of the Treasury. For another example of a bid that took present value into consideration, see *Centurial Prods.*, 64 Comp. Gen. 858 (B-216517), 85-2 CPD ¶ 305 (guidelines established by the Water Resources Council required that agencies determine the present value of future expenditures before converting them to an annual equivalent cost).

Factoring in the time value of money in an evaluation removes much of the advantage that bidders attempt to gain through unbalanced bids, and it is proper to structure an IFB calling for such an evaluation, *Solon Automated Servs., Inc.*, Comp. Gen. Dec. B-206449.2, 82-2 CPD ¶ 548. However, absent a clause requiring consideration of the cost of money, GAO will not consider the additional cost to the government in interest expense that would result from award to a bidder that front-loaded its prices for earlier items, *Farrell Constr. Co.*, 57 Comp. Gen. 597 (B-191786), 78-2 CPD ¶ 45.

One means of quantifying the time value of money was the prompt payment discount. However, FAR 14.408-3 prohibits the consideration of prompt payment discounts for evaluation purposes. See *Alco Envtl. Servs., Inc.*, Comp. Gen. Dec. B-251053.6, 93-2 CPD ¶ 192; *IFR Sys., Inc.*, Comp. Gen. Dec. B-222533, 86-2 CPD ¶ 224; *Hayes Int'l Assocs.*, Comp. Gen. Dec. B-220471, 86-1 CPD ¶ 8; and *O.K. Tool & Die Co.*, Comp. Gen. Dec. B-219806, 85-2 CPD ¶ 398.

As a legislative agency, the Government Printing Office (GPO) is not subject to FAR 14.408-3, and the GPO may therefore consider prompt payment discounts in the evaluation of its bids, *Capitol Hill Blueprint Co.*, Comp. Gen. Dec. B-220354, 85-2 CPD ¶ 550. The IFB must provide that the discount will be used in evaluation, *Advanced Design Fabrication Corp.*, Comp. Gen. Dec. B-246341, 92-1 CPD ¶ 250; *Western Pub. Co.*, Comp. Gen. Dec. B-224376, 86-2 CPD ¶ 249.

### d.  Bids Including Price Adjustments

Since only contracts with fixed prices or fixed prices subject to economic adjustment can be used in sealed bid procurements, a bid stating that a price adjustment could be made if the cost of petroleum increased was required to be rejected as nonresponsive, *Re Con Paving, Inc.*, Comp. Gen. Dec. B-198294, 80-1 CPD ¶ 297. See also *Margaret Greenidge*, Comp. Gen. Dec. B-265979, 96-1 CPD ¶ 80, finding that an agency properly rejected a bid as nonresponsive when the protester included a handwritten notation on the bid schedule stating that "yearly increases is based on 3% or COLA, whichever is greater." Bids containing ceilings on such adjustments have been permitted but such bids must be evaluated at the ceiling. In the absence of a stated ceiling, practical considerations may permit consideration of the bid.

See *Copes-Vulcan Div., Blaw-Knox Co.*, 36 Comp. Gen. 259 (B-127372) (1956), where the low bidder stated that if more than three X-rays per valve were required, the price would be increased by $2.50 per X-ray. The IFB had stated that bids were to include the cost of all X-rays required but did not specify the number of X-rays. GAO held that rejection of the low bid was improper since 35 extra X-rays per unit would be necessary before the low bidder's price would be greater than the next low bid. There was no real possibility that such a large number would be required.

Bids based on economic price adjustment (EPA) provisions may be considered for award. FAR 14.408-4 gives the following guidance on the evaluation of EPA provisions:

(a) Bidder proposes economic price adjustment.

(1) When a solicitation does not contain an economic price adjustment clause but a bidder proposes one with a ceiling that the price will not exceed, the bid shall be evaluated on the basis of the maximum possible economic price adjustment of the quoted base price.

(2) If the bid is eligible for award, the contracting officer shall request the bidder to agree to the inclusion in the award of an approved economic price adjustment clause (see 16.203) that is subject to the same ceiling. If the bidder will not agree to an approved clause, the award may be made on the basis of the bid as originally submitted.

(3) Bids that contain economic price adjustments with no ceiling shall be rejected unless a clear basis for evaluation exists.

(b) Government proposes economic price adjustment.

(1) When an invitation contains an economic price adjustment clause and no bidder takes exception to the provisions, bids shall be evaluated on the basis of the quoted prices without the allowable economic price adjustment being added.

(2) When a bidder increases the maximum percentage of economic price adjustment stipulated in the invitation or limits the downward economic price adjustment provisions of the invitation, the bid shall be rejected as nonresponsive.

(3) When a bid indicates deletion of the economic price adjustment clause, the bid shall be rejected as nonresponsive since the downward economic price adjustment provisions are thereby limited.

(4) When a bidder decreases the maximum percentage of economic price adjustment stipulated in the invitation, the bid shall be evaluated at the base price on an equal basis with bids that do not reduce the stipu-

lated ceiling. However, after evaluation, if the bidder offering the lower ceiling is in a position to receive the award, the award shall reflect the lower ceiling.

This evaluation procedure gives a bid including an EPA clause no advantage, because the bid must be evaluated at the ceiling price. Most EPA clauses contain the required price ceiling since such ceilings are included in the standard clauses in FAR 52.216. For an example of a solicitation that contained a 15% ceiling on option-year prices, see *Echelon Serv. Co.*, 62 Comp. Gen. 542 (B-208720.2), 83-2 CPD ¶ 86. In *Phipps Products Corp.*, Comp. Gen. Dec. B-194840, 79-2 CPD ¶ 200, the solicitation included a 20% ceiling, but the bidder inserted an escalation clause without a price ceiling. GAO held that where a price ceiling cannot be determined with certainty, the bid must be rejected as nonresponsive.

A bid that fails to provide a base rate to which the economic rice adjustment clause applies is nonresponsive, *Galaxy Custodial Servs., Inc.*, 64 Comp. Gen. 593 (B-215738), 85-1 CPD ¶ 658. Similarly, if the IFB requires that prices be the same for all years, subject to an economic price adjustment clause, a bid that offers a fixed rate for price increases for later years is nonresponsive, *First Am. Engineered Solutions*, Comp. Gen. Dec. B-289051, 2001 CPD ¶ 207.

To allow for fair evaluation of bids, EPA clauses must reflect some objective standard, other than the bidder's own prices upon which price adjustments will be made, *Roarda, Inc.*, Comp. Gen. Dec. B-204524.5, 82-1 CPD ¶ 438 (IFB defective because it allowed the contractor to adjust prices for petroleum products based on its own price changes). Similarly, in *Hampton Metro. Oil Co.*, Comp. Gen. Dec. B-186509, 76-2 CPD ¶ 471, the solicitation for petroleum products allowed bidders to use their own posted prices in conjunction with the EPA provision. GAO concluded that the IFB was properly canceled because it was impossible to ensure that bidders would not indiscriminately raise their posted prices after contract award. It was therefore impossible for the government to determine which bids ultimately would result in the lowest cost to the government. For an example of the type of objective factor that can be used to determine price adjustments, see *American Transparents Plastics Corp.*, Comp. Gen. Dec. B-210898, 83-2 CPD ¶ 539 (Department of Labor's Producer Price Index for the market price of resin used to make plastic bags was upheld as a valid method for price adjustment).

The analysis used for EPA clauses also extends to other types of price adjustments. In *H. Edward Chozick*, 50 Comp. Gen. 733 (B-171938) (1971), the bid provided for 1½% interest per month on past due invoices, and GAO stated at 735:

> So far as concerns your position that the inclusion of the demand for interest on past due invoices should be treated as a reverse prompt payment, in addition to the fact that its consideration would be contrary to 5 Comp. Gen. 649, the solicitation form has no provision for reverse prompt payment discounts and to consider such

discounts could well add a substantial conjectural factor to the evaluation process to the detriment of the competitive bid system's integrity.

GAO would not allow this clause in a bid because it obligated the government to pay interest on unpaid invoices, and the contracting officer did not have the authority — at that time — to obligate the government for such payments.

## 2. Evaluation of "Other Price-Related Factors"

For many years the procurement statutes specified that award was to be made on the basis of "price and other factors." This was held to permit the use of any factor that could be assessed in terms of *cost to the government*, 37 Comp. Gen. 550 (B-132596) (1958). It was subsequently held that such "other factors" had to be directly related to the procurement. See 45 Comp. Gen. 59 (B-155725) (1965), stating at 68:

> Our Office has generally taken the position that a proper determination of the lowest responsible bidder under advertised procurements may properly include consideration of costs, over and above the bid price, which the Government would incur in the event of an award to each bidder, if the amount of such costs can be ascertained with reasonable certainty. . . . The economic impact or "ripple" effect of a particular procurement are not pertinent factors to be considered in making an award under competitive procedures especially where bidders are not requested to prepare their bids in the light of possible adverse effects their bids might have on a segment of the economy.

The CICA clarified this issue by requiring award on the basis of "price and other price-related factors."

While the contracting officer has considerable discretion in selecting which price-related factors will be evaluated, any factors chosen must be identified in the solicitation so that all bidders may prepare their bids on an equal and well-informed basis, *Hunot Fire Retardant Co.*, Comp. Gen. Dec. B-286679.2, 2001 CPD ¶ 94 (agency could not have evaluated clean-up costs after contract work because IFB did not specify such costs); *Respiratory & Convalescent Specialties Inc.*, Comp. Gen. Dec. B-255176, 94-1 CPD ¶ 101 (IFB failed to include oxygen rental charges as a price-related factor, failed to advise bidders how these rental charges would be evaluated, and gave no quantity estimate); *E & T Elecs., Inc.*, Comp. Gen. Dec. B-238099.2, 90-2 CPD ¶ 24 (evaluation factors including cost to government of shipping equipment, cost savings from using a local contractor, and a discount offered for certain repairs could not be utilized because they were not specified in the IFB); *Fairchild Weston Sys., Inc.*, Comp. Gen. Dec. B-211650, 83-2 CPD ¶ 347 (contracting officer was correct in not considering development risks and the cost of future modifications because these "other factors" were not stated in the IFB). See also *Old Dominion Sec.*, Comp. Gen. Dec. B-216534, 85-1 CPD ¶ 78, where the incumbent contractor argued that its bid ($52,560) was lower than a competing bid ($52,122) if the agency considered the cost of changing contractors. Such costs could not be considered because the IFB did not include transition costs as a factor in evaluating bids.

The evaluation method for price-related factors must permit objective determination of the cost to the government, as well as being described in the IFB with sufficient clarity that it can be understood by the bidders. In 36 Comp. Gen. 380 (B-127801) (1956), GAO stated at 385:

> The "basis" of evaluation which must be made known in advance to the bidders should be as clear, precise and exact as possible. Ideally, it should be capable of being stated as a mathematical equation. In many cases, however, that is not possible. At the minimum, the "basis" must be stated with sufficient clarity and exactness to inform each bidder prior to bid opening, no matter how varied the acceptable responses, of objectively determinable factors from which the bidder may estimate within reasonable limits the effect of the application of such evaluation factor on his bid in relation to other possible bids. By the term "objectively determinable factors" we mean factors which are made known to or which can be ascertained by the bidder at the time his bid is being prepared.

See *Envirotronics, Inc.*, Comp. Gen. B-215622, 84-2 CPD ¶ 18, where the protester contended that a competitor's past experience, its limited plant capacity and personnel, and its late deliveries on other government contracts were "other factors" (under the pre-CICA statute) that, when considered, should preclude award. In holding that all these factors relate to responsibility, not "other factors," GAO stated:

> The term "other factors" in the context of a formally advertised procurement concerns only objectively determinable elements of cost, such as shipping costs, that are identified in the IFB as factors to be evaluated in the selection of a contractor.

See also *Emerson Elec. Co.*, Comp. Gen. Dec. B-209272, 82-2 CPD ¶ 409 (usage of recovered materials held not to be an "objectively determinable" element of bid pricing and therefore should not have been included as an evaluation factor); and *Balimoy Mfg. Co.*, Comp. Gen. Dec. B-253287.2, 93-2 CPD ¶ 207 (even though solicitation was denoted as an IFB, it should have been clear to the bidders that it was not a sealed bid procurement because it stated that the agency would take non–price related factors into consideration, such as mobilization base consideration, contractor capacity, and premium cost).

A price-related factor must allow the government to arrive at a reasonable estimate of the actual cost impact on the government. See *Todd Pacific Shipyards Corp.*, Comp. Gen. Dec. B-281383, 99-1 CPD ¶ 28, sustaining a protest that the cost of moving a ship was grossly understated with the result that bidders at different locations could not be fairly evaluated and stating:

[W]hen a solicitation lacks accurate foreseeable costs, the agency cannot determine whether award to one firm versus another will result in a lower cost to the government. See *Hoechst Marion Roussel, Inc.*, B-279073, May 4, 1998, 98-1 CPD ¶ 127 at 3 (protest sustained where solicitation for drugs did not state accurate dosage estimates); *Beldon Roofing & Remodeling Co.*, B-277651, Nov. 7, 1997, 97-2 CPD ¶ 131 at 7 (protest sustained where solicitation for roofing work lacked accurate quantity estimates).

FAR 14.201-8 lists some of the price-related factors that may be considered in bid evaluation:

(a) Foreseeable costs or delays to the Government resulting from such factors as differences in inspection, locations of supplies, and transportation. If bids are on a f.o.b. origin basis (see 47.303 and 47.305), transportation costs to the designated points shall be considered in determining the lowest cost to the Government.

(b) Changes made, or requested by the bidder, in any of the provisions of the invitation for bids, if the change does not constitute a ground for rejection under 14.404.

(c) Advantages or disadvantages to the Government that might result from making more than one award (see 14.201-6(q)). The contracting officer shall assume, for the purpose of making multiple awards, that $ 500 would be the administrative cost to the Government for issuing and administering each contract awarded under a solicitation. Individual awards shall be for the items or combinations of items that result in the lowest aggregate cost to the Government, including the assumed administrative costs.

(d) Federal, State, and local taxes (see Part 29).

(e) Origin of supplies, and, if foreign, the application of the Buy American Act or any other prohibition on foreign purchases (see Part 25).

FAR 14.201-8 is not an inclusive list of price-related factors. In *Tek-Lite, Inc.*, Comp. Gen. Dec. B-230298, 88-1 CPD ¶ 241, GAO found an evaluation factor set forth in the solicitation for a value engineering royalty to be a proper evaluation factor even though it is not listed in FAR 14.201-8, stating:

[T]he cited language nowhere suggests that the listed factors were meant to be exclusive. . . . [S]ince the royalty fee evaluation factor allows consideration for what the actual cost to the Government would be if a bid based on the VECP alternate were accepted, we think the use of such an evaluation factor is appropriate.

## a. Transportation

The most common price-related factor is the cost of transportation. If the IFB provides that bids are to be made on an f.o.b. destination basis, the costs of transportation are included in the bid price and separate evaluation is not required. When bids are on an f.o.b. origin basis, FAR 14.201-8(a) requires consideration of transportation costs to the designated place of delivery. See *Marten C. Robb & Son*, B-256516, 94-1 CPD ¶ 392 (a reasonable estimate of the cost per mile was included in evaluating the bids to ensure that the government would obtain the lowest actual cost). If the exact destination is unknown at the time of the solicitation and the procuring agency is unable to predict even the general destination, transportation costs cannot be a factor in bid evaluation, *Wachtel, Wiener & Ross*, 52 Comp. Gen. 679 (B-177763) (1973). FAR 47.305-3 provides guidance on f.o.b. origin solicitations and requires the use of the Evaluation — F.O.B. Origin solicitation clause in FAR 52.247-47 to inform bidders that costs of transportation will be evaluated. If the exact destination is unknown at the time of solicitation but the general geographic locations can be reasonably established, the solicitation should include a tentative destination for the purposes of evaluation only, FAR 47.305-5(b). See *Entron, Inc.*, Comp. Gen. Dec. B-189362, 77-2 CPD ¶ 414, upholding the contracting agency's use of hypothetical delivery points for evaluation purposes since the actual destinations were unknown at the time of solicitation.

In order to evaluate transportation costs accurately, the procuring agency must require bidders to provide certain information with their bids such as minimum size of shipments, guaranteed shipping weights, and information regarding packing and crating, FAR 47.305-1. Part 52 of the FAR contains a number of standard solicitation provisions used to obtain this information. The most commonly used provision of this type is the Guaranteed Shipping Characteristics solicitation provision in FAR 52.247-60. This provision provides that if the specified information is not included in a particular bid, the government may include either the highest bidder's information or a government estimate to evaluate the bid. In *F&H Mfg. Corp.*, Comp. Gen. Dec. B-212254, 83-2 CPD ¶ 676, GAO affirmed the validity of using government estimates to evaluate bids where the bidders did not submit guaranteed maximum shipping weights and dimensions for shipments of Army vehicle parts. The clause also provides for a price adjustment as follows:

> If the item shipping costs, based on the actual shipping characteristics, exceed the item shipping costs used for evaluation purposes, the Contractor agrees that the contract price shall be reduced by an amount equal to the difference between the transportation costs actually incurred, and the costs which would have been incurred if the evaluated shipping characteristics had been accurate.

In *Kalyn Inc.*, Comp. Gen. Dec. B-237909, 90-1 CPD ¶ 331, GAO denied a protest contending that this solicitation provision permitted bidders to provide false information that reduced their evaluated transportation costs, thereby giving them an unfair competitive advantage, reasoning that the provision compensated for this problem by providing for a downward adjustment in price if the actual shipping costs were higher than those estimated because the bid's shipping

testing to the extent that such cost can be realistically estimated, FAR 9.306(i); and the cost that results from varying locations of performance, *Cascade Gen., Inc.*, Comp. Gen. Dec. B-272271, 96-2 CPD ¶ 52. See *Homexx Int'l Corp.*, Comp. Gen. Dec. B-192034, 78-2 CPD ¶ 219, where $70,000, the estimated cost of first article testing, was added to the bid price of any bidder that had not previously produced the procurement items. See also *Flexfab, Inc.*, Comp. Gen. Dec. B-221186, 86-1 CPD ¶ 188, where GAO determined that the agency properly considered the protester's price for first article testing when the IFB specifically required that bidders include a price for it, which would be evaluated. Government inspection costs may also be added to the bids for evaluation purposes, but in 52 Comp. Gen. 997 (B-177887) (1973), GAO stated that it was inappropriate to add such costs for evaluation purposes when there was already an inspector in residence in the contractor's plant. The reasoning is that "no actual cost to the Government is incurred nor can it be said at the time of evaluation of bids that any costs would, in fact, be incurred if the award were made to a prospective contractor with an inspector already in residence." In determining whether multiple awards would be less costly to the government than an aggregate award, FAR 14.201-8(c) requires that $ 500 be considered for evaluation purposes as the administrative cost to the government of issuing and administering each contract awarded. See *Weather Experts, Inc.*, Comp. Gen. Dec. B-255103, 94-1 CPD ¶ 93 (agency accepted the low aggregate bid, but should have accepted multiple bids, because even with the $500 administrative costs, the multiple bid option was lower); and *Patrick Loman*, B-254527, 93-2 CPD ¶ 340 (protest against aggregate award provision denied where IFB provided a reasonable method of assuring the lowest cost to the government).

### 3. *Evaluation of Equal Low Bids*

FAR 14.408-6 outlines the procedures that must be followed when two or more equal low bids are received:

(a) Contracts shall be awarded in the following order of priority when two or more low bids are equal in all respects:

(1) Small business concerns that are also labor surplus area concerns.

(2) Other small business concerns.

(3) Other business concerns.

(b) If two or more bidders still remain equally eligible after application of paragraph (a) above, award shall be made by a drawing by lot limited to those bidders. If time permits, the bidders involved shall be given an opportunity to attend the drawing. The drawing shall be witnessed by at least three persons, and the contract file shall contain the names and addresses of the witnesses and the person supervising the drawing.

(c) When an award is to be made by using the priorities under this 14.408-6, the contracting officer shall include a written agreement in the contract that the contractor will perform, or cause to be performed, the contract in accordance with the circumstances justifying the priority used to break the tie or select bids for a drawing by lot.

In *Randy Int'l, Ltd.*, 53 Comp. Gen. 466 (B-179880), 74-1 CPD ¶ 11, GAO stated that once a tie has occurred between two low evaluated bids, no other evaluation factors should be considered if not delineated in the IFB. Thus, additional factors such as past performance record, experience of a bidder's personnel, and shipment security may not be considered. Similarly, in *Richard A. Schwartz Assocs.*, Comp. Gen. Dec. B-214979, 84-1 CPD ¶ 695, the protester's greater technical competence was held an extraneous factor that could not be used to break the tie. Thus, lots must be drawn to determine the winner when there are tie bids, *Van Ben Indus., Inc.*, Comp. Gen. Dec. B-234875, 89-2 CPD ¶ 52; *Berklay Air Servs. Corp.*, Comp. Gen. Dec. B-179880, 74-1 CPD ¶ 115.

The tied bidders should be given the opportunity to attend the drawing to avoid raising doubts concerning its fairness. See *Alderson Reporting Co.*, Comp. Gen. Dec. B-205552.2, 82-1 CPD ¶ 128, criticizing the procuring agencies for performing the drawing by lot without inviting the tied bidders. Compare *Vetcorp, Inc.*, Comp. Gen. Dec. B-402519, 2010 CPD ¶ 114, accepting the drawing of lots without the offerors being present in a commercial item procurement that did not follow sealed bidding procedures. Note that since equal low bids may indicate price fixing, identical bids may be reported to the Department of Justice for investigation of possible collusive bidding practices. FAR 3.303(d) states:

Identical bids shall be reported under this section if the agency has some reason to believe that the bids resulted from collusion.

## B. Award

The following guidance on the award of contracts is provided in 10 U.S.C. § 2305(b)(3):

The head of the agency ... shall award a contract with reasonable promptness to the responsible bidder whose bid conforms to the solicitation and is most advantageous to the United States, considering only price and the other price-related factors included in the solicitation. The award of a contract shall be made by transmitting, in writing or by electronic means, notice of the award to the successful bidder. Within three days after the date of contract award, the head of the agency shall notify, in writing or by electronic means, each bidder not awarded the contract that the contract has been awarded.

Substantially the same guidance is set forth in 41 U.S.C.§ 3702. The major issues involved in awarding a sealed bid contract are the procedures to be followed, the determination of whether to make a single award or multiple awards, and the treatment of below-cost bids (also referred to as "buy-ins").

## 1.  Procedures

FAR 14.408-1 outlines the award procedures in sealed bid procurements as follows:

(a) The contracting officer shall make a contract award

(1) by written or electronic notice,

(2) within the time for acceptance specified in the bid or an extension (see 14.404-1(d)), and

(3) to that responsible bidder whose bid, conforming to the invitation, will be most advantageous to the Government, considering only price and the price-related factors (see 14.201-8) included in the invitation. Award shall not be made until all required approvals have been obtained and the award otherwise conforms with 14.103-2.

* * *

(c)(1) Award shall be made by mailing or otherwise furnishing a properly executed award document to the successful bidder.

(2) When a notice of award is issued, it shall be followed as soon as possible by the formal award.

(3) When more than one award results from any single invitation for bids, separate award documents shall be suitably numbered and executed.

(4) When an award is made to a bidder for less than all of the items that may be awarded to that bidder and additional items are being withheld for subsequent award, the award shall state that the Government may make subsequent awards on those additional items within the bid acceptance period.

(5) All provisions of the invitation for bids, including any acceptable additions or changes made by a bidder in the bid, shall be clearly and accurately set forth (either expressly or by reference) in the award document. The award is an acceptance of the bid, and the bid and the award constitute the contract.

### a.  Notice of Award

Award can be made by using the award portion of Standard Form 33, Solicitation, Offer and Award. FAR 14.408-1(d) provides that if "an offer leads to further changes," the resulting contract shall be prepared as a bilateral document on SF 26, Award/Contract. This regulation further provides that use of the award portion of SF 33 or SF 26 does not preclude the additional use of informal documents, including telegrams and notices of awards.

Notice of award must be in writing. Oral notice is not sufficient since the government's acceptance of an offer must be clear and unconditional, *James M. Smith, Inc.*, Comp. Gen. Dec. B-233877, 89-1 CPD ¶ 390 (low bidder sought and received assurances that it would be awarded the contract, but GAO held that retraction of the oral award was proper); *Phillip C. Clarke Elec. Constr. Inc.*, Comp. Gen. Dec. B-226594, 87-1 CPD ¶ 629 (low bidder was notified by telephone, but IFB was subsequently canceled and GAO held the oral notice ineffective). See also *R.J. Crowley, Inc.*, ASBCA 28730, 86-1 BCA ¶ 18,739, where oral notification without a follow-up ratification was held insufficient to establish award.

The award must be made on the basis of the IFB and the responsive bid. The contracting officer may not unilaterally impose different terms on the low bidder, *CRF v. United States*, 224 Ct. Cl. 312, 624 F.2d 1054 (1980). See Chapter 2 for further discussion of government acceptance issues.

## b.  Determining the Acceptance Period

As discussed earlier, bidders are subject to the firm bid rule if they include a promise in their bids to hold them open for a specified period of time. The standard cover sheets for sealed bid procurements, Standard Forms 33 and 1447, call for an acceptance period of 60 days but permit the bidder to insert a different period of time. In instances where neither of these forms is used, FAR 14.201-6(i) provides a Period for Acceptance of Bids solicitation provision in FAR 52.214-15 containing the same provisions. These provisions permit sealed bid procurements that will result in no minimum acceptance period if a bidder inserts "0 days" in the blank. See *Perkin-Elmer Corp.*, 69 Comp. Gen. 27 (B-236175.2), 89-2 CPD ¶ 352, holding that, even though the bidder had filled in "30 days" in another part of the bid, the bid's inclusion of the FAR 52.214-15 clause superseded that number because the bidder did not include its own 30-day period in the clause.

When the contracting officer determines that a minimum acceptance period "must be specified," FAR 14.201-6(j) provides a Minimum Bid Acceptance Period solicitation provision in FAR 52.214-16 to be used in all contracts except those for construction. The use of this provision is at the sole discretion of the contracting officer because the FAR contains no guidance as to its use. The provision allows the agency to designate a number of calendar days as the minimum acceptance period and permits bidders to enter a longer acceptance period, but warns that a bid with a shorter period will be rejected. See *Paragon Inv. Corp.* Comp. Gen. Dec. B-241715, 91-1 CPD ¶ 95, where a provision required a minimum acceptance period of 90 days, but the bidder entered 30 days. Although Paragon claimed that the insertion of "30 days" was a clerical error because it meant 30 days longer than the specified 60 days in Block 12 of SF 33, GAO held that the "error" was not a minor informality and the bid was nonresponsive. See also *Winsar Corp.*, Comp. Gen. Dec. B-226507, 87-1 CPD ¶ 585, where the bidder sent with the bid a standard letter containing a shorter acceptance period, and GAO held the bid nonresponsive. Similarly, in *Sundt Corp.*, Comp. Gen. Dec. B-274203, 96-2 CPD ¶ 171, GAO found a bid nonresponsive where the bidder acknowledged the solicitation amendment changing the minimum acceptance period from 90 to 120 calendar days, but inserted 90 in the bid form blank for proposing an acceptance period. In *Kim's Gen. Maint., Inc.*, Comp. Gen. Dec. B-275823, 97-1 CPD ¶ 128, GAO reasoned that because the protester failed to include SF 1447 with its bid, there was no way for the agency to verify whether the protester took exception to the 120-day minimum acceptance period and thus found the bid to be nonresponsive.

The FAR 52.214-16 provision provides that it supersedes any other provisions in the IFB dealing with the minimum acceptance period. However, care must be taken not to insert acceptance periods in these other provisions. See, for example, *Siems Rental & Sales Co.*, Comp. Gen. Dec. B-257773, 95-1 CPD ¶ 51, where the FAR 52.214-16 provision required an acceptance period of 60 days, but the bidder inserted "30 days" in Block 12 of SF 33. The bidder asserted that its insertion of "30 days" was of no consequence because SF 33 contained a note stating: "Item 12 does not apply if the solicitation includes the provisions at 52.214-16, Minimum Bid Acceptance Period." GAO rejected this argument holding that, at best, the bid was ambiguous and therefore nonresponsive. See also *Perkin-Elmer Corp.*, 69 Comp. Gen. 27 (B-236175.2), 89-2 CPD ¶ 352, where the IFB incorrectly contained both the FAR 52.214-15 and the FAR 52.214-16 provisions, calling for a 60-day bid acceptance period. GAO held that the insertion of "30 days" in the FAR 52.214-15 clause rendered the bid ambiguous and therefore nonresponsive.

## c.  Extensions from Bidders

The contracting officer frequently finds that award cannot be made within the time that the bids are firm. When this occurs, bidders are usually requested to extend the time for acceptance. FAR 14.404-1(d) provides:

> Should administrative difficulties be encountered after bid opening that may delay award beyond bidders' acceptance periods, the several lowest bidders whose bids have not expired (irrespective of the acceptance period specified in the bid) should be requested, before expiration of their bids, to extend in writing the bid acceptance period (with consent of sureties, if any) in order to avoid the need for resoliciting.

This practice gives bidders the opportunity to choose to remain in the competition or to withdraw. Since the low bidders make this decision with knowledge of how their bids compare to the other bids, they can assess the likely profitability of the contract and make a decision based on this assessment.

To remain in the competition, a bidder's extension must be unqualified and unconditional. In *Klein Constr. Co.*, Comp. Gen. Dec. B-201599, 81-1 CPD ¶ 158, an extension was rejected when the bidder also reserved the right to request additional time or money, even though that qualification was subsequently withdrawn. See *S.J. Groves & Sons Co.*, Comp. Gen. Dec. B-207172, 82-2 CPD ¶ 423, where, when the bidder conditioned an extension on an increase in its bid price, GAO interpreted this as a refusal to extend the bid "as originally submitted." See also *Dawson Constr. Co.*, Comp. Gen. Dec. B-244204, 91-1 CPD ¶ 523; and *GTA Containers, Inc.*, Comp. Gen. Dec. B-234395.3, 89-2 CPD ¶ 37 (bidder conditioned extension of bid acceptance period upon an increase in price and thus was ineligible for award).

Although the regulations only permit extension of bids before they expire, GAO has held that the government may accept *an expired bid* that has subsequently been revived through a bidder's actual or constructive waiver, provided that such waiver is not done with the intention of taking advantage of the other bidders. See *Mission Van & Storage Co.*, 53 Comp. Gen. 775 (B-180112), 74-1 CPD ¶ 195, stating at 778-79:

> In 46 Comp. Gen. 371 (1966), the low bidder extended its bid acceptance period when requested to do so 3 days after the original 60 day period had lapsed. We held that the bid properly could be accepted because the integrity of the competitive bidding system would not be compromised thereby and because there would be no prejudice to another bidder whose 60 day acceptance period had also expired. We distinguished that situation from the one in 42 Comp. Gen. 604, *supra*, in which the low bidder offered an acceptance period of only 20 days while the second low bidder offered the more customary 60 days. There we held that the low bid, which was not extended until more than 2 weeks after expiration of the original 20 day period, should not be accepted because the low bidder "sought and gained an advantage after bid opening in the nature of an option not sought by other bidders, of renewing its bid in short increments or allowing it to lapse as dictated by market conditions," and that "the integrity of the competitive bidding system would best be served by making an award to the second low bidder." 46 Comp. Gen. 371, 373.

\* \* \*

> We do not think that acceptance of DeWitt's bid would compromise the competitive bidding system. Unlike the bidders in 42 Comp. Gen. 604 and 48 *id.* 19, DeWitt did not seek any advantage over other bidders. It offered the standard 60 day acceptance period rather than an unusually short one. Furthermore, it is reasonably clear that DeWitt intended and considered its bid to be viable at least during the pendency of this protest. We have taken the position that a protest to this Office during a bidder's acceptance period could be viewed as tolling the bid acceptance period pending resolution of the protest, 50 Comp. Gen. 357 (1970). . . . Accordingly, we would not object to an award to DeWitt.

For cases involving prejudice to other bidders, see *MKB Mfg. Corp.*, Comp. Gen. Dec. B-208451, 83-1 CPD ¶ 204, where, when other bidders extended their bids before expiration of their 60-day acceptance period, it was held improper to allow MKB to revive its bid more than 15 days after expiration of its 60-day acceptance period because it would give MKB an unfair advantage over the other bidders; and *Esprit Int'l Corp.*, Comp. Gen. Dec. B-276294, 97-1 CPD ¶ 106, where allowing the protester to revive its bid after the expiration of its 14-day acceptance period would afford the protester an unfair advantage since its initial exposure to the risk of the marketplace was for a shorter period.

A waiver will be deemed to have occurred if, following expiration of the acceptance period, the bidder is still willing to accept award on the basis of the bid as submitted, *Cecile Indus., Inc.*, Comp. Gen. Dec. B-207277.3, 82-2 CPD ¶ 299. For an unusual case, see *Input Data, Inc.*, GSBCA 4937-R, 80-2 BCA ¶ 14,711, where the board found that the contractor was bound to perform a contract awarded after bid expiration, even though it had failed to execute a bid extension mailed to the contracting officer. Its failure to disavow a notice of award and the request for a modification delaying performance were "consistent with ratification of his bid and acceptance of the signed contract." The board distinguished *A.C. Ball Co.*, ASBCA 19375, 75-1 BCA ¶ 11,298, where a contractor fulfilled only the minimum quantity on an indefinite-quantity contract awarded after bid expiration. The board found that the contractor had accepted only a "counter-offer," the terms of which were limited to performance of the minimum quantity order, reasoning that the transaction lacked the strong evidence of communications and meetings between the parties which were consistent only with contract recognition.

GAO has also held that filing a protest tolls the acceptance period, *Phillips Cartner & Co.*, 69 Comp. Gen. 105 (B-236416.2), 89-2 CPD ¶ 492. Thus, where the award is made to another firm within the protester's shorter acceptance period, the protester's bid may be accepted if the protest is sustained, even though the acceptance period otherwise would have expired, *Professional Materials Handling Co.*, Comp. Gen. Dec. B-205969, 82-1 CPD ¶ 297. Similarly, award to the initial awardee after the protest is denied is proper without regard to the expiration of the awardee's bid, if the awardee actively participated in the protest, *Native Res. Dev., Inc.*, Comp. Gen. Dec. B-246597.2, 92-2 CPD ¶ 15; *Werres Corp.*, Comp. Gen. Dec. B-211870, 83-2 CPD ¶ 243. In effect, this prevents a protester from excluding the awardee by filing a protest by allowing tolling of the expiration period by participation in the protest. In *International Graphics v. United States*, 4 Cl. Ct. 515 (1984), the court extended the tolling concept by holding that "the bid acceptance period should remain open as long as the parties, through litigation or otherwise, have actually or constructively expressed their intent to accept the award."

Bids that have expired due to cancellation of a solicitation may generally be revived upon reinstatement of the solicitation, unless the bids have been returned and reinstatement would compromise the integrity of the competitive bidding system, *Baker Mfg. Co.*, 59 Comp. Gen. 573 (B-197016), 80-2 CPD ¶ 1. Even though the government has requested multiple extensions, it is not required to make an award, *Maceto Inc.*, Comp. Gen. Dec. B-216166, 84-2 CPD ¶ 277 (although Navy requested four extensions of the original bid acceptance period, Maceto had no legal right to require the Navy to award the contract).

## 2. Multiple versus Aggregate Awards

Considerable confusion has surrounded the award of contracts for multiple items. Part of the problem stems from the number of alternatives available to both the government and bidders when dealing with multiple items. The Contract Award — Sealed Bidding solicitation provision in FAR 52.214-10, used for all procurements except construction contracts, states:

> (c) The Government may accept any item or group of items of a bid, unless the bidder qualifies the bid by specific limitations. Unless otherwise provided in the Schedule, bids may be submitted for quantities less than those specified. The Government reserves the right to make an award on any item for a quantity less than the quantity offered, at the unit prices offered, unless the bidder specifies otherwise in the bid.

The Contract Award — Sealed Bidding — Construction solicitation provision in FAR 52.214-19 contains a slightly different provision:

> (c) The Government may accept any item or combination of items, unless doing so is precluded by a restrictive limitation in the solicitation or the bid.

Under these provisions awards may be made to one or more bidders for one or more items or to one bidder for all items, whichever is in the best interests of the government, Comp. Gen. Dec. B-149085, Aug. 28, 1962, *Unpub.;* 47 Comp. Gen. 233 (B-162092) (1967). See *Staab Constr. Corp.*, Comp. Gen. Dec. B-298454, 2006 CPD ¶ 136, agreeing that it was proper to award a contract for only one item of work where there were no bids within the funding limit for the other item of work and the IFB contained the FAR 52.214-19 provision.

Absent solicitation language requiring an aggregate award, the government must make multiple awards if different bidders offer the low evaluated price on each item to be awarded, *Action Mobile Transportation, Inc.*, Comp. Gen. Dec. B-275427.2, 97-1 CPD ¶ 132; *TAAS Israel Military Indus. Ltd.*, Comp Gen Dec. B 258039.3, 95-1 CPD ¶ 32; *Weather Experts, Inc.*, Comp. Gen. Dec. B-255103, 94-1 CPD ¶ 93; *HFS Inc.*, Comp. Gen. Dec. B-246018, 92-1 CPD ¶ 160. In this respect, GAO has required that in order to make an aggregate award, it must result in the lowest cost to the government, *S.J. Groves & Sons Co.*, 55 Comp. Gen. 936 (B-184260), 76-1 CPD ¶ 205; 47 Comp. Gen. 233 (B-162092) (1967) (aggregate award improper when based on considerations of centralized management and administration, when multiple awards would have resulted in a lower cost to the government). But if a bidder offers a low aggregate bid that is less than the sum of its bids on individual items, award should be made to the low aggregate bid. See 47 Comp. Gen. 658 (B-163890) (1968), upholding the agency's consideration of a combination bid for tractors and loaders that resulted in a lower overall cost to the government than on an item-by-item basis. In *Moir Ranch & Constr. Co.*, Comp. Gen. Dec. B-191616, 78-1 CPD ¶ 423, a bidder, offering an additional 10% discount if all eight of its bid items were accepted, was properly awarded the contract even though other bidders offered lower prices on individual items and without the discount, the total cost would have been lower under multiple awards.

If the solicitation notifies bidders that award will be made to the low aggregate bidder, then an aggregate award must be made even though such an award may be more costly to the government, *Northeast Constr. Co.*, 61 Comp. Gen. 317 (B-205246), 82-1 CPD ¶ 293. In *Northeast*, GAO sustained a protest because the agency split the base bid requirement between two bidders instead of making one aggregate award to the low bidder. However, it is proper to make a partial award if funds to make an aggregate award are not available. In *FBF Indus., Inc.*, Comp. Gen. Dec. B-252574, 93-1 CPD ¶ 477, the protester asserted that the agency should have evaluated bids on an item-by-item basis and made partial award. GAO denied the protest, stating that the solicitation provided that bids would be evaluated on an "all or none" basis for all items and did not contain a multiple awards clause. If the solicitation requires an aggregate award but multiple awards would serve the government's needs and there is no reasonable basis for an aggregate award, the solicitation must be canceled and the work reprocured, *Hawthorne Uniform Mfg. Co.*, Comp. Gen. Dec. B-200363, 81-1 CPD ¶ 68 (resolicitation recommended since there was no reason for the aggregate award restriction in the solicitation, and the contracting officer could have made multiple awards at a lower total cost to the government); *Roy's Rabbitry*, Comp. Gen. Dec. B-193628, 79-1 CPD ¶ 305 (resolicitation recommended because aggregate award restricted the competition unnecessarily to large producers, and multiple awards could meet the government's needs). See also *Com-Tran of Michigan, Inc.*, Comp. Gen. Dec. B-200845, 80-2 CPD ¶ 407. But see *Alcon Div. of Boyles Bros. Drilling Co.*, Comp. Gen. Dec. B-241058, 91-1 CPD ¶ 46, where a partial award was sustained where the only bidder submitting an aggregate bid within the agency funding limitation had bid some of the items at amounts exceeding the statutory funding limitations. GAO held that the aggregate award language did not preclude the agency from making an award to that bidder for all of the items that were within the statutory limitation.

In construction contracts, the agency frequently obtains bids on additive and deductive elements of the work and reserves the right to award to the lowest aggregate bidder on the combination of items that fall within the agency's funding limitation. See DFARS PGI 236.213 for guidance on the use of this technique.

The Additive or Deductive Items solicitation provision in DFARS 252.236-7007 states:

(a) The low offeror and the items to be awarded shall be determined as follows —

(1) Prior to the opening of bids, the Government will determine the amount of funds available for the project.

(2) The low offeror shall be the Offeror that —

(i) Is otherwise eligible for award; and

(ii) Offers the lowest aggregate amount for the first or base bid item, plus or minus (in the order stated in the list of priorities in the bid schedule) those additive or deductive items that provide the most features within the funds determined available.

(3) The Contracting Officer shall evaluate all bids on the basis of the same additive or deductive items.

(i) If adding another item from the bid schedule list of priorities would make the award exceed the available funds for all offerors, the Contracting Officer will skip that item and go to the next item from the bid schedule of priorities; and

(ii) Add that next item if an award may be made that includes that item and is within the available funds.

(b) The Contracting Officer will use the list of priorities in the bid schedule only to determine the low offeror. After determining the low offeror, an award may be made on any combination of items if—

(1) It is in the best interest of the Government;

(2) Funds are available at the time of award; and

(3) The low offeror's price for the combination to be awarded is less than the price offered by any other responsive, responsible offeror.

Under this clause the low bidder is determined by the low bid for the best combination of items within the funding limitation applicable *at the time of bid opening*, even if this amount varies from the funding limitation set forth in the solicitation, *Rodriguez & Del Valle, Inc.*, Comp. Gen. Dec. B-239224, 90-2 CPD ¶ 29 (award to bidder not low on base bid but low on base bid plus all additives sustained because agency budget officer certified prior to bid opening that sufficient funds were available); *Martz Constr. Corp.*, Comp. Gen. Dec. B-213320, 84-1 CPD ¶ 29 (award to bidder not low on base bid and all additives but low on base bid plus two additives sustained because that was all that could be awarded within the funding limitation); *Applicators, Inc.*, Comp. Gen. Dec. B-270162, 96-1 CPD ¶ 32 (award to bidder not low on base bid and additives but low on base bid sustained because that was all that could be awarded within the funding limitation); *Atherton Constr., Inc.*, Comp. Gen. Dec. B-266345, 96-1 CPD ¶ 51 (award made to low base bidder, without including additives, because funds available prior to bid opening were insufficient to cover even the lowest base bid). Once this low bidder has been determined, award can be made for more items if more funds become available thereafter — even if such award would not be to the low bidder for those items, *Sammy Garrison Constr. Co.*, Comp. Gen. Dec. B-215453, 84-2 CPD ¶ 545. In this case, the award was sustained even though the protester had submitted the low bid on the items included in the award — because the awardee was the low bidder on the items that could be included within the funding limitation. In one unusual case, there were no funds available at the time of bid opening, but GAO ruled that it was proper to award subsequently to the low bidder on the base bid minus all deductive items when funds became available for that amount of work, *Gartrell Constr., Inc.*, Comp. Gen. Dec. B-237032, 90-1 CPD ¶ 46. GAO rejected the protester's contention that it should have received the award because it was the low bidder on the base bid. An earlier solicitation provision gave the agency the flexibility to select the additive or deductive items after bid opening, but the funds available at the time of bid opening still controlled the determination of the low bidder, *Delta Indus. Contractors, Inc.*, Comp. Gen. Dec. B-226949, 87-1 CPD ¶ 569 (award to bidder not low on base bid but low on base bid plus additives sustained where such items were within the funding limitation); *Huntington Constr., Inc.*, 67 Comp. Gen. 499 (B-230604), 88-1 CPD ¶ 619 (protest sustained when agency determined low bidder based on lower figure than the funding limitation at the time of bid opening). It has been held improper to treat options the same as additive items when the solicitation does not call for the evaluation of options, *N-K Constr. Co.*, Comp. Gen. Dec. B-224534, 87-1 CPD ¶ 188.

When an agency uses an additive clause with somewhat ambiguous language, it will be interpreted to require award to the low bidder on the base price plus the additive items that are actually included in the award. For example, in *John C. Grimberg Co.*, Comp. Gen. B-284013, 2000 CPD ¶ 11, the IFB stated:

> The Government reserves the right to select all, none or any combination thereof of the Add Alternates listed above. A single award will be made to the lowest priced responsive and responsible bidder inclusive of the Base Bid and sum total of the Add Alternates.

> A single award will be made to the lowest priced responsive and responsible bidder.

GAO rejected the argument that this required award to the low bidder on the base bid plus all of the additives, ruling that it should be interpreted to require award to the low bidder on the base bid plus the additive work that was actually included in the award. See also *National Servs., Inc.*, Comp. Gen. B-400836.2, 2009 CPD ¶ 58, interpreting similarly ambiguous language to require award to the low bidder on the base bid plus the additives that were included in the award.

Prices may generally be submitted for individual items, for combinations of items, or on an "all or none" basis. An "all or none" bid precludes award to that bidder for less than the total number of items. FAR 14.404-5 provides:

> Unless the solicitation provides otherwise, a bid may be responsive notwithstanding that the bidder specifies that award will be accepted only on all, or a specified group, of the items. Bidders shall not be permitted to withdraw or modify "all or none" qualifications after bid opening since such qualifications are substantive and affect the rights of other bidders.

See *Steel King Indus., Inc.*, Comp. Gen. Dec. B-209239, 83-1 CPD ¶ 473, recommending award to an all or none bidder that submitted the lowest overall price for the items bid. In *Canova Moving & Storage Co.*, Comp. Gen. Dec. B-207168, 83-1 CPD ¶ 59, GAO stated that an "all or none" bidder does not have the option to decide after bid opening whether it will accept an award on less than the total number of items.

The Contract Award — Sealed Bidding solicitation provision in FAR 52.214-10 gives the government the right to make an award for less than the quantity advertised unless the bidder has restricted the government's right to do so by an "all or none" bid or by a provision limiting award for less than a stated quantity of any item. Awards for a lesser quantity of an item than that advertised could have a serious impact on the bidder's pricing. Thus, the government is only permitted to make such awards when the contracting officer learns of a reduced need after bid opening or has accepted a lower bid on a portion of the quantity, Comp. Gen. Dec. B-173666, Oct. 1, 1971, *Unpub.* If the contracting officer learns of a reduced need before award, FAR 14.208(a) requires an amendment to the IFB reflecting the reduction. Failure to follow this procedure would make it unconscionable to hold the bidder to the bid price, Comp. Gen. Dec. B-170808, May 14, 1971, *Unpub.* The government is not required to award for lesser quantities and may award the total quantity of an item or the entire group of items advertised even though a partial award would result in a lower cost to the government for the items awarded. See *General Fire Extinguisher Corp.*, 54 Comp. Gen. 416 (B-181796), 74-2 CPD ¶ 278, stating that "an all or none bid, lower in the aggregate than any combination of individual bids available, may be accepted by the Government even though a partial award could be made at a lower unit cost." See also *George C. Martin, Inc.*, 55 Comp. Gen. 100 (B-182175), 75-2 CPD ¶ 55, where the IFB called for separate bid prices for two facilities on Schedule A and B, respectively. X submitted the low total bid for both schedules and bid on an "all or none" basis, which was not precluded by the IFB. Y bid low on Schedule B. Had the government desired to award only on Schedule B (a partial award), it would have awarded that item to Y. However, since both schedules were being awarded, it was proper to make the award to X.

If a solicitation prohibits "all or none" offers, such offers are allowed as long as the offeror submits separate offers for each of the items called for, *Amerisource-Bergen Drug Corp. v. United States*, 60 Fed. Cl. 30 (2004). In this case, the court ruled that award at prices for all regions covered was proper because the offeror had also submitted offers for separate prices for several regions.

## 3. Award to Below-Cost Bidders

Receipt of a below-cost bid requires the contracting officer to exercise special care in the evaluation and award process. Such bids cannot be summarily rejected, because they offer the government a low price for obtaining the work. Yet they may pose the risk of default or poor contract performance such as deviating from the specifications to reduce costs. The actions the government should take depend on the circumstances underlying the bid.

There are several reasons a bidder may submit a below-cost bid: (1) by mistake, *Darwin Constr. Co.*, Comp. Gen. Dec. B-213314, 84-1 CPD ¶ 154; (2) through incompetence; (3) to eliminate competitors, *National Reporting Co.*, Comp. Gen. Dec. B-199497, 80-2 CPD ¶ 142; (4) to retain a team of employees within its organization; (5) to break into a new government market, *Flexible Metal Hose Mfg. Co. v. United States*, 4 Cl. Ct. 522 (1984); (6) to cover a portion of its fixed costs in a period of slow sales; or (7) to obtain work with the intention of recouping losses through future changes or contracts (known as "buying-in"); *Diemaster Tool, Inc.*, Comp. Gen. Dec. B-238877, 90-1 CPD ¶ 375.

The FAR does not contain comprehensive guidance on dealing with below-cost bids. However, the FAR coverage of improper business practices does address "buying-in," which FAR 3.501-1 defines as:

submitting an offer below anticipated costs, expecting to —

(a) Increase the contract amount after award (e.g., through unnecessary or excessively priced change orders); or

(b) Receive follow-on contracts at artificially high prices to recover losses incurred on the buy-in contract.

The regulations do not require that contracting officers reject such bids. FAR 3.501-2 cautions the contracting officer to be certain that possible losses are not recouped during performance or on follow-on contracts, stating:

(a) Buying-in may decrease competition or result in poor contract performance. The contracting officer must take appropriate action to ensure buying-in losses are not recovered by the contractor through the pricing of (1) change orders or (2) follow-on contracts subject to cost analysis.

(b) The Government should minimize the opportunity for buying-in by seeking a price commitment covering as much of the entire program concerned as is practical by using —

(1) Multiyear contracting, with a requirement in the solicitation that a price be submitted only for the total multiyear quantity; or

(2) Price options for additional quantities that, together with the firm contract quantity, equal the program requirements (see Subpart 17.2).

(c) Other safeguards are available to the contracting officer to preclude recovery of buying-in losses e.g., amortization of nonrecurring costs (see 15.408, Table 15-2, paragraph A, Column (2) under "Formats for Submission of Line Item Summaries") and treatment of unreasonable price quotations (see 15.405).

Although not likely, if the below-cost bid violates antitrust laws, such as predatory pricing, the procuring agency must report this practice to the Department of Justice, 41 U.S.C. § 3707; 10 U.S.C. § 2305(b)(5); and FAR 3.303(a).

The other major issues raised by below-cost bids are mistakes and nonresponsibility, which are more fully discussed in Section IV of this chapter and Chapter 4. An unusually low bid must be verified to assure that no mistake has been made, but upon such verification, award is proper. See *Associated Contractors & Renovators, Inc.*, HUDBCA 83-809-B4, 83-2 BCA ¶ 16,755, stating at 83,308:

There is no requirement that a contractor must submit a bid that provides for any profit, let alone a substantial profit. In fact, a bidder can even submit a negative profit "buy-in" so long as that bid is submitted with full knowledge of its cost implications and is not based on a mistake.

The contracting officer must also assure that the prospective contractor is responsible. See *TECOM Inc.*, Comp. Gen. Dec. B-215291, 84-1 CPD ¶ 644, stating:

The submission of a below-cost bid is not illegal and provides no basis for challenging the award of a government contract to a responsible prospective contractor. Whether the low bidder can perform the contract at the price bid is a matter of responsibility. Our office does not review protests concerning affirmative determinations of responsibility absent a showing that the contracting officer acted fraudulently or in bad faith or that definitive responsibility criteria in the solicitation have not been met.

See also *Seaton Van Lines, Inc.*, Comp. Gen. Dec. B-217298, 85-1 CPD ¶ 26.

## C. Cancellation after Bid Opening

While, as discussed earlier, agencies have considerable discretion to cancel a procurement prior to bid opening, cancellation after bid opening is a serious matter because it can give bidders an unfair advantage if they are later permitted to recompete with knowledge of the prior bids. FAR 14.404-1(a) permits such cancellation only for compelling reasons:

(1) Preservation of the integrity of the competitive bid system dictates that, after bids have been opened, award must be made to that responsible bidder who submitted the lowest responsive bid, unless there is a compelling reason to reject all bids and cancel the invitation.

(2) Every effort shall be made to anticipate changes in a requirement before the date of opening and to notify all prospective bidders of any resulting modification or cancellation. This will permit bidders to change their bids and prevent unnecessary exposure of bid prices.

(3) As a general rule, after the opening of bids, an invitation should not be cancelled and resolicited due solely to increased requirements for the items being acquired. Award should be made on the initial invitation for bids and the additional quantity should be treated as a new acquisition.

GAO has stated that the determination of whether a sufficiently compelling reason exists for bid cancellation is "primarily within the discretion of the administrative agency and will not be disturbed absent proof that the decision was clearly arbitrary, capricious, or not supported by substantial evidence," *Ace-Federal Reporters, Inc.*, Comp. Gen. Dec. B-237414, 90-1 CPD ¶ 144. In some cases GAO has sustained a cancellation because there was no showing of bad faith or fraud on the part of the agency, *J. Morris & Assocs.*, Comp. Gen. Dec. B-256840, 94-2 CPD ¶ 47 (cancellation was proper where the agency determined that prices were unreasonable and there was no showing of bad faith or fraud); *Moore's Cafeteria Servs., Inc.*, Comp. Gen. Dec. B-234063.4, 89-2 CPD ¶ 11 (cancellation of an IFB in order to initiate a solicitation under § 8(a) of the Small Business Administration Act was upheld because there was no showing of bad faith or fraud on the part of the agency). In cases where the agency erroneously cancels the solicitation after bid opening, reinstatement of the IFB may be proper if it would not prejudice other bidders and if the award under the original solicitation would serve the actual needs of the government, *Bilt-Rite Contractors, Inc.*, Comp. Gen. Dec. B-259106.2, 95-1 CPD ¶ 220.

When an agency cancels a solicitation after opening, all facts and circumstances will be considered in determining whether appropriate grounds for cancellation existed, *International Graphics, Div. of Moore Bus. Forms, Inc. v. United States*, 5 Cl. Ct. 100 (1984) (A-76 cost comparison was conducted after cancellation of a solicitation and was used to prove that the government had a compelling reason to cancel the solicitation); *McGhee Constr., Inc.*, Comp. Gen. Dec. B-250073.3, 93-1 CPD ¶ 379 (all relevant information was considered to determine that cancellation was appropriate); *I.T.S. Corp.*, Comp. Gen. Dec. B-242725, 91-1 CPD ¶ 518 (when agency's initial reason was inadequate, other information justified cancellation).

In most cases where an IFB is defective, GAO will recommend cancellation of the entire IFB. However, there may be certain situations where only partial cancellation of the solicitation is appropriate. In such a case, the government may cancel the defective portion of the IFB and award a contract for the remainder of the solici tation items to the bidder submitting the lowest bid for those items, *Adrian Supply Co.*, Comp. Gen. Dec. B-240871, 90-2 CPD ¶ 515.

The FAR offers guidance to determine when cancellation is proper. FAR 14.404-1(b) requires cancellation in only one circumstance — when the agency finds that it has not properly disclosed the identity or availability of the necessary specifications. In all other situations, cancellation is discretionary provided that there is a compelling reason. FAR 14.404-1(c) lists some compelling reasons:

Invitations may be canceled and all bids rejected before award but after opening when . . . the agency head determines in writing that —

(1) Inadequate or ambiguous specifications were cited in the invitation;

(2) Specifications have been revised;

(3) The supplies or services being contracted for are no longer required;

(4) The invitation did not provide for consideration of all factors of cost to the Government, such as cost of transporting Government-furnished property to bidders' plants;

(5) Bids received indicate that the needs of the Government can be satisfied by a less expensive article differing from that for which the bids were invited;

(6) All otherwise acceptable bids received are at unreasonable prices, or only one bid received and the contracting officer cannot determine the reasonableness of the bid price;

(7) The bids were not independently arrived at in open competition, were collusive, or were submitted in bad faith . . . ;

(8) No responsive bid has been received from a responsible bidder;

(9) A cost comparison as prescribed in the OMB Circular A-76 and Subpart 7.3 shows that performance by the Government is more economical; or

(10) For other reasons, cancellation is clearly in the public's interest.

## 1. Compelling Reasons for Cancellation

Cancellation is only proper if the interests of the government in canceling outweigh the expense and time of resolicitation and the impact on the competitive system resulting from disclosure of bidders and bid prices. This section discusses the major compelling reasons.

## a. Solicitation Defects

Failure to state proper evaluation criteria in the solicitation is a compelling reason to cancel, *Armco, Inc.*, Comp. Gen. Dec. B-210018, 83-1 CPD ¶ 553 (evaluation criteria inconsistent with other provisions of the solicitation). Where there is no assurance that compliance with a bid evaluation formula would result in the lowest cost to the government, the solicitation is materially defective, and cancellation is proper, *Dynamic Corp.*, Comp. Gen. Dec. B-296366, 2005 CPD ¶ 125 (IFB provisions on how to propose prices so ambiguous that bidders submitted different pricing information); *Paragon Van Lines, Inc.*, Comp. Gen. Dec. B-291820.2, 2003 CPD ¶ 79 (IFB contained inconsistent performance period and outdated Service Contract Act wage determination); *S.W. Monroe Constr. Co.*, Comp. Gen. Dec. B-256382, 94-1 CPD ¶ 362 (evaluation scheme did not set forth a common basis for evaluating offers); *Bayfone of Tampa*, Comp. Gen. Dec. B-242925, 91-1 CPD ¶ 535 (line item prices were based on defective criteria); *Earthworks of Sumter, Inc.*, Comp. Gen. Dec. B-232067.2, 89-1 CPD ¶ 9 (no basis for determining low bidder because IFB ambiguities permitted bids on different bases); *Reliable Reproductions, Inc.*, Comp. Gen. Dec. B-201137, 81-1 CPD ¶ 100 (defective evaluation method permitted bidders to submit materially unbalanced bids).

Solicitations have been properly canceled when it was apparent that a majority of bidders were misled by the solicitation, *Neals Janitorial Serv.*, Comp. Gen. Dec. B-276625, 97-2 CPD ¶ 6 (information in solicitation and ascertainable from site visit were inadequate for bidders to establish the actual work load requirements); *Ferguson-Williams, Inc.*, Comp. Gen. Dec. B-258460, 95-1 CPD ¶ 39 (three lowest bidders misunderstood the estimated quantities in the IFB); *P.J. Dick, Inc.*, Comp. Gen. Dec. B-259166, 95-1 CPD ¶ 131 (bidders were misled where conflicting terms in IFB caused some bidders to include sales taxes in price while others did not); *Hughes & Smith, Inc.*, Comp. Gen. Dec. B-245969, 91-2 CPD ¶ 530 (bidders were misled because Certification of Procurement Integrity in IFB contained no signature line); *A&P Surgical Co.*, 62 Comp. Gen. 256 (B-206111.2), 83-1 CPD ¶ 263 (IFB misled five out of six bidders to offer foreign melted specialty metals when the government required specialty metals melted in the United States); *Kleen-Rite Janitorial Servs., Inc.*, Comp. Gen. Dec. B-180345, 74-1 CPD ¶ 210 (bidding instructions were ambiguous causing the failure of three bidders (including two lowest bidders) to insert separate bid prices for a certain item).

Estimated quantities that are found to differ significantly from actual anticipated quantities provide a proper basis for cancellation, *C-Cubed Corp.*, Comp. Gen. Dec. B-289867, 2002 CPD ¶ 72; *Ferguson-Williams, Inc.*, Comp. Gen. Dec. B-258460, 95-1 CPD ¶ 39. See *Heritage Reporting Corp.*, Comp. Gen. Dec. B-248860.2, 92-2 CPD ¶ 276 (estimates for base period were exaggerated by 68%). See *Heuer, Inc.*, Comp. Gen. Dec. B-202017.2, 81-2 CPD ¶ 460, holding that cancellation was proper and stating:

Where there is a substantial variation between the IFB estimates and the actual estimated requirements, there is substantial doubt that award to any bidder will result in the lowest cost to the Government.

See also *Downtown Copy Ctr.*, 62 Comp. Gen. 65 (B-206999.6), 82-2 CPD ¶ 503, where the agency concluded that volume estimates were inaccurate and could have given an unfair advantage to the incumbent contractor. Cancellation is also proper where award is based on estimated quantities, but the solicitation failed to include estimated quantities for all items, *MTL Sys., Inc.*, Comp. Gen. Dec. B-245363, 91-2 CPD ¶ 569.

## b. Specification Defects

FAR 14.404-1(c)(1) states that "inadequate or ambiguous specifications" can be compelling reasons for cancellation. Use of specifications that do not adequately describe the government's actual needs generally provide a compelling reason for cancellation, *Brickwood Contractors, Inc.*, Comp. Gen. Dec. B-292171, 2003 CPD ¶ 120 (specification ambiguous and permitted bid that did not meet agency needs); *Cycad Corp.*, Comp. Gen. Dec. B-255870, 94-1 CPD ¶ 253 (IFB did not reflect the agency's needs where a requirement for commercial, off-the-shelf products was omitted); *Renic Gov't Sys.*, Comp. Gen. Dec. B-249484, Nov. 9, 1992, *Unpub.* (IFB failed to include the agency's requirement that work be done by a lawyer licensed in Texas); *United States Elevator Corp.*, Comp. Gen. Dec. B-225625, 87-1 CPD ¶ 401 (agency did not include specifications for major repairs and replacement parts); *Intercomp Co.*, Comp. Gen. Dec. B-213059, 84-1 CPD ¶ 540 (without revised weight and testing requirements for aircraft scales, specifications did not reflect the Navy's needs); *Heart of Am. Police Supply*, Comp. Gen. Dec. B-210911, 84-1 CPD ¶ 423 (specification failed to describe all required features of a brand-name product adequately which resulted in unacceptable bids); *Kings Point Mfg. Co.*, Comp. Gen. Dec. B-210757, 83-2 CPD ¶ 342 (design deficiencies in harness specifications resulted in harnesses that did not meet government's needs).

Vague and ambiguous specifications are another compelling reason for cancellation, *Meds Mktg., Inc.*, Comp. Gen. Dec. B-213352, 84-1 CPD ¶ 318 (specification was so vague that it was not clear what Meds' legal obligation would be if awarded the contract); *Commercial Envelope Mfg. Co.*, Comp. Gen. Dec. B-213272, 84-1 CPD ¶ 206 (specification was not specific enough to procure center-seam envelopes needed by the IRS). Preservation of the integrity of the competitive bidding system requires that an agency not award a contract if it intends to negotiate specifications after award. See *W.M. Grace, Inc.*, Comp. Gen. Dec. B-202842, 81-2 CPD ¶ 121, stating:

An attempt by the contracting officer to negotiate changes with the low bidder which amount to a substantial deviation from the original specifications would be prejudicial to the other bidders because the contract after negotiation would not be the same as that offered the other bidders under the invitation.

See also *Source AV, Inc.*, Comp. Gen. Dec. B-238017, 90-1 CPD ¶ 336, upholding cancellation of an IFB and denied the protester's argument that modification after award was appropriate, because an agency cannot award a contract with the intention of significantly modifying the terms of the solicitation.

A compelling reason for cancellation exists when an agency concludes that the government's needs can be satisfied by a less expensive design differing from that called for by the IFB, *Jarrett S. Blankenship Co.*, Comp. Gen. Dec. B-211582, 83-2 CPD ¶ 516 (specification of air-conditioning units with copper coils and fins properly canceled where aluminum coils could meet agency needs at a lesser cost); *Sunrise Int'l Group*, Comp. Gen. Dec. B-256912, 94-2 CPD ¶ 31 (cancellation of IFB for short-order meals was reasonable when full-course meals would meet government's needs at lesser cost); *Uffner Textile Corp.*, Comp. Gen. Dec. B-204358, 82-1 CPD ¶ 106 (specifications overstated minimum needs when smaller zipper and less restrictive batting specifications would be more cost effective and satisfy the needs of the government).

Cancellation is also appropriate if the agency determines that its specification is unduly restrictive, *Cummins Power Sys.*, LLC, Comp. Gen. Dec. B-402079.2, 2010 CPD ¶ 20 (requirement that bidder be a certified distributor of product); *Hroma Corp.*, Comp. Gen. Dec. B-285053, 2000 CPD ¶ 88 (requirement that bidder perform 60% of work with own forces); *Siemens Power Corp.*, Comp. Gen. Dec. B-257167, 94-2 CPD ¶ 160 (specifications overstated type of equipment needed); *Washex Mach. Corp.*, Comp. Gen. Dec. B-191224, 78-2 CPD ¶ 54 (specifications limited competition to one type of washing machine).

### c.  Alternate Performance by Government

When the services covered by the invitation could be performed by in-house personnel at a cost savings to the government, cancellation is proper, *Currents Constr., Inc.*, Comp. Gen. Dec. B-236735.2, 90-1 CPD ¶ 236. See also *Ameriko Maint. Co.*, Comp. Gen. Dec. B-243728, 91-2 CPD ¶ 191 (GSA determined that it could save nearly $3 million by maintaining in-house performance of the services required by the solicitation). In *Powertronic Sys., Inc.*, Comp. Gen. Dec. B-210283, 83-2 CPD ¶ 346, GAO stated that when the government can build an urgently needed item faster in-house than by contracting out, cancellation of an IFB that would not meet the urgency of the need is proper. See also *Bush-Herrick, Inc.*, Comp. Gen. Dec. B-209683, 83-1 CPD ¶ 669. Cancellation is also appropriate where a solicited item is available within the government at a lower cost, and the available item meets the agency's needs, *Nedlog Co.*, Comp. Gen. Dec. B-212665, 84-1 CPD ¶ 215 (Army's needs met by substituting in-house dry mix beverages for the solicited liquid beverages). See also *Essex Electro Eng'rs, Inc.*,

Comp. Gen. Dec. B-206012.3, 82-2 CPD ¶ 307, where solicitation for generator sets was canceled because adequate decommissioned generator sets were available within the government.

## d. Lack of Fair Competition

Cancellation is appropriate when competition on an equal basis has been thwarted, *Honeywell, Inc.*, Comp. Gen. Dec. B-210000, 83-1 CPD ¶ 445 (because Air Force did not make historical data or estimates of number of required service calls available, nonincumbent contractors lacked necessary information for intelligent bid preparation). See also *GS Elektro-Schewe GmbH*, Comp. Gen. Dec. B-259103.2, 95-1 CPD ¶ 196 (because agency sent a document to at least one bidder which required a specification that was not included in the IFB, competition on an equal basis was not assured); *HDL Research Lab, Inc.*, Comp. Gen. Dec. B-254863.3, 94-1 CPD ¶ 298 (specifications were biased in favor of the awardee and may have restricted competition when only three of the 66 bidders who were solicited submitted a bid); *Werres Corp.*, Comp. Gen. Dec. B-255379, 94-1 CPD ¶ 153 (solicitation was ambiguous and misled bidders because of an inconsistency between the pricing schedule and the specifications); *Air Inc.*, 69 Comp. Gen. 504 (B-238468), 90-1 CPD ¶ 533 (potential bidders had an unfair advantage where four bids were opened prematurely); *Jackson Marine Cos.*, Comp. Gen. Dec. B-212882, 84-1 CPD ¶ 402 (payment provision put undue economic risk on contractor and discouraged potential bidders from participating in the procurement); and *Downtown Copy Ctr.*, 62 Comp. Gen. 65 (B-206999.6), 82-2 CPD ¶ 503 (inaccurate estimated quantities gave incumbent contractor an unfair advantage). In *Mott Haven Truck Parts, Inc.*, Comp. Gen. Dec. B-210775, 83-2 CPD ¶ 189, untimely dispatch of a material IFB amendment (one day prior to bid opening) was a compelling reason for cancellation due to lack of adequate competition.

## e. Insufficient Funds

The contracting agency's determination that funds are not available for the contract is a compelling reason for cancellation, *Sea Box, Inc.*, Comp. Gen. Dec. B-400198, 2008 CPD ¶ 163; *First Enter.*, Comp. Gen. Dec. B-292967, 2004 CPD ¶ 11; *National Projects, Inc.*, Comp. Gen. Dec. B-283887, 2000 CPD ¶ 16; *Michelle F. Evans*, Comp. Gen. Dec. B-259165, 95-1 CPD ¶ 139; *Armed Forces Sports Officials, Inc.*, Comp. Gen. Dec. B-251409, 93-1 CPD ¶ 261; *Kato/Intermountain Elec. (J.V.)*, Comp. Gen. Dec. B-245807, 92-1 CPD ¶ 129; *Metric Constructors, Inc.*, Comp. Gen. Dec. B-229947, 88-1 CPD ¶ 311. See *First Enter. v. United States*, 61 Fed. Cl. 109 (2004), for a detailed analysis of the discretion afforded an agency in cancelling an IFB when the bids exceed its estimate. Where Congress passes legislation that prohibits obligating funds, cancellation is proper, *Consolidated Maint. Co.*, Comp. Gen. Dec. B-209766, 83-1 CPD ¶ 225 (Joint Continuing Resolution of Dec. 21, 1982, prohibited the agency from obligating funds for the custodial services involved in the solicitation). See also *Satellite Servs., Inc.*, Comp. Gen. Dec. B-225624, 87-1 CPD ¶ 314, finding that cancellation was proper where a congressional appropriations restriction created uncertainties concerning funding.

## f. Inaccurate Statement of Government Needs

FAR 14.404-1(c)(2) states that cancellation may be appropriate where specifications require revision. See, for example, *Corcel Corp.*, Comp. Gen. Dec. B-311332, 2008 CPD ¶ 125, where cancellation was permitted when the agency found that the specification permitted delivery of a valve that did not meet the agency's technical requirements. A compelling reason for cancellation exists where the other parts of the original IFB are inaccurate and must be revised to reflect the needs of the government, *Days Inn Marina*, Comp. Gen. Dec. B-254913, 94-1 CPD ¶ 23 (preaward surveys showed that the stated geographic restriction was insufficient to satisfy government's requirements); *McGhee Constr., Inc.*, Comp. Gen. Dec. B-250073.3, 93-1 CPD ¶ 379 (solicitation failed to reflect agency's need where additional construction services were required); *I.T.S Corp.*, Comp. Gen. Dec. B-242725, 91-1 CPD ¶ 518 (IFB for mail and message services omitting material duties and functions did not reflect agency's requirements); *News Printing, Inc.*, Comp. Gen. Dec. B-274773.2, 97-1 CPD ¶ 68 (significant decrease in estimated quantity provided compelling reason to cancel the IFB).

Changing the specifications of a procurement after bid opening to express the government's new needs constitutes sufficient reason for cancellation, *I.T.S. Corp.*, Comp. Gen. Dec. B-243223, 91-2 CPD ¶ 55 (deployment of troops to hostile area created a need for additional counseling services); *Holk Dev., Inc.*, Comp. Gen. Dec. B-236765.2, 90-1 CPD ¶ 65 (additional work required when asbestos was discovered); *Dyneteria, Inc.*, Comp. Gen. Dec. B-211525.2, 84-2 CPD ¶ 484 (Air Guard conversion from F-4 to F-16 fighters and C-130 to C-5A transports would significantly change manning requirements, aircraft servicing, and fuel consumption); *Tecom, Inc.*, Comp. Gen. Dec. B-213815.2, 84-2 CPD ¶ 152 (material workload changes caused IFB to fail to represent the government's needs); *Electric Maint. & Installation Co.*, Comp. Gen. Dec. B-213005, 84-1 CPD ¶ 292 (Army Corps of Engineers advised that change in river water level would require use of two motors involved in IFB earlier than the expected delivery time).

FAR 14.404-1(c)(3) states that cancellation is proper where supplies or services are no longer required. See *Orange Personnel Servs., Inc. — Recons.*, Comp. Gen. Dec. B-256164.2, 95-1 CPD ¶ 26 (cancellation of solicitation of layberthing services for two Ready Reserve Force ships proper where the ships were being repositioned and services were no longer needed); *International Typewriter Exch.*, Comp. Gen. Dec. B-205989.3, 82-2 CPD ¶ 279 (cancellation of solicitation for manual typewriters was proper where conversion to electric typewriters negated the requirement for solicited item).

## g.  Unreasonable Prices

Solicitations may properly be canceled if bid prices are unreasonable. FAR 14.404-1(c)(6) permits cancellation if the contracting officer determines in writing that "[a]ll otherwise acceptable bids received are at unreasonable prices." A determination of price unreasonableness may be based upon a comparison of bid prices with such factors as government estimates, past procurement history, current market conditions, or any other relevant factors, *Bay Cities Refuse Serv., Inc.*, Comp. Gen. Dec. B-250807, 93-1 CPD ¶ 151 (all bids were unreasonably high compared with the independent government estimate); *Omega Container, Inc.*, Comp. Gen. Dec. B-206858.2, 82-2 CPD ¶ 475 (agency properly compared Omega's small business bid prices with government estimates, the bid prices of an ineligible bidder, and past procurement prices of the item). Similarly, in *Logistics Int'l, Inc.*, Comp. Gen. Dec. B-254810, 94-1 CPD ¶ 28, a contracting officer properly compared an incumbent large business contractor's price for similar contracts with small business bids and found that the small business bids were unreasonable.

Cancellation is a proper exercise of agency discretion where bids exceed government estimates, even where the low responsible bid was as little as 7.2% greater than the government estimate, *Building Maint. Specialists, Inc.*, Comp. Gen. Dec. B-186441, 76-2 CPD ¶ 233. See *Overstreet Elec. Co.*, Comp. Gen. Dec. B-284691, 2000 CPD ¶ 79 (low bid price exceeded government estimate by 32%); *J. Morris & Assocs.*, Comp. Gen. Dec. B-256840, 94-2 CPD ¶ 47 (low bid exceeded the government estimate by 23%); and *Kinetic Structures Corp. v. United States*, 6 Cl. Ct. 387 (1984) (sole bidder's price was 27% above the government estimate). See also *Photo Data, Inc.*, Comp. Gen. Dec. B-208272, 83-1 CPD ¶ 281, where cancellation was found proper when Photo's bid was more than two times the government estimate for in-house performance, three times the bid prices received on the original solicitation, and well in excess of unit prices obtained for other comparable work.

A bid submitted by a commercial concern may be unreasonably high if the marketplace, which includes nonprofit associations, can satisfy the government's needs for substantially less, *International Alliance of Sports Officials*, 63 Comp. Gen. 162 (B-210491), 84-1 CPD ¶ 63 (nonprofit organization could perform for 30% less). GAO stated at 165:

> We agree with the Army that whether a bid is unreasonable does not depend on whether that bidder can account for every element in its bid price and can demonstrate that its price does not include exorbitant markups. In other words, a bidder's price may accurately reflect the costs unique to it plus a moderate profit and yet not be reasonable if the Government can obtain the same supplies or services from the marketplace for substantially less. Here, it is clear that officiating services are available from several sources other than IASO at prices substantially

less than what IASO bid. In determining what it reasonably should expect to pay in the Savannah area for sports officiating services, we do not see how the Army could ignore the existence of local organizations offering to perform the same services at IASO for approximately 30 percent less.

A determination of unreasonable price will be sustained barring bad faith or fraud, *California Shorthand Reporting*, Comp. Gen. Dec. B-250302.2, 93-1 CPD ¶ 202. In *Stewart-Thomas Indus., Inc.*, Comp. Gen. Dec. B-196295, 80-1 CPD ¶ 175, the contracting officer asked a prior supplier to explain its failure to bid. The supplier responded by offering a price 40% lower than the lowest bidder. In discussing the propriety of the contracting officer's cancellation of the invitation, GAO stated:

> Stewart-Thomas [low bidder] believes that any award to other than itself at its bid price would be improper because the actions of the contracting activity constituted an impermissible auction. After bids were opened and prices disclosed, the activity, in essence, allegedly attempted to find firms which could offer better prices, notwithstanding the fact that 80 firms had already been solicited on the original solicitation and only seven cared to bid. *Stewart-Thomas*, citing *Interscience Systems, Inc.*, 59 Comp. Gen. 68 (B-194497), 79-2 CPD ¶ 306, states the activity not only improperly permitted a potential bidder to possibly adjust its price knowing the prices offered by other parties, but it also gave a bidder who had not bothered to bid originally a second bite at the procurement.

> \* \* \*

> The contracting activity's purpose in contacting the prior contractor was not to require a bid from it, but only to ascertain the validity of the former prices in the current market. In the circumstances, we consider the action proper. Although any cancellation for unreasonable prices may result in nonbidders having another chance to bid (and with the knowledge of the prior bid prices), the competition the second time also provides those bidders who bid unreasonable prices the first time another opportunity to bid as well and this time at reasonable prices.

In some instances, rejected bids are used as the standard of reasonableness. See *Sigma West Corp.*, Comp. Gen. Dec. B-247916, 92-2 CPD ¶ 31 (nonresponsive bid was 12.5% lower and the defect of the nonresponsive bid had a negligible impact on price); *Dutra/AmClyde (J.V.)*, Comp. Gen. Dec. B-249364.2, 92-2 CPD ¶ 453 (government estimate and nonresponsive bid were used to determine that bid prices were unreasonable); *Colonial Ford Truck Sales, Inc.*, Comp. Gen. Dec. B-179926, 74-1 CPD ¶ 80 (nonresponsive bid was 13% lower even though the government had paid higher prices in three of five previous procurements); and *Hercules Demolition Corp.*, Comp. Gen. Dec. B-186411, 76-2 CPD ¶ 173 (even though the only responsive bid was within the government estimate, it was 36% higher than an "unacceptable" bid).

## h.  *Impossible to Perform Work Within Schedule*

Cancellation is proper when the agency determines that it is not possible to perform the work as called for by the schedule in the IFB, *Chenega Mgmt., LLC*, Comp. Gen. Dec. B-290598, 2002 CPD ¶ 143. See also *Gaffny Plumbing & Heating Corp.*, Comp. Gen. Dec. B-209815, 83-1 CPD ¶ 648 (delays in completing another construction project made installation of fire sprinkler system impractical); *Champion Structure Co.*, Comp. Gen. Dec. B-198863, 80-2 CPD ¶ 291 (inconsistent provisions rendered performance impossible); and 53 Comp. Gen. 92 (B-178106) (1973) (because of delay in award, the work could not be completed within the government preferred time).

## i.  *Miscellaneous*

Compelling reasons to cancel the IFB have been found where the agency discovered after bid opening that a similar item was on the Federal Supply Schedule from which the agency was required to make its purchases, *Raymond Corp.*, Comp. Gen. Dec. B-246410, 92-1 CPD ¶ 252; *Security Mgmt. Assocs.*, Comp. Gen. Dec. B-214186, 84-2 CPD ¶ 83; where the agency failed to include required wage determination provision in the solicitation, *Dismantlement & Envtl. Mgmt. Co.*, Comp. Gen. Dec. B-257632, 94-2 CPD ¶ 151 (Service Contract Act); *Sunspot Garden Ctr. & Country Craft Gift Shop*, Comp. Gen. Dec. B-237065.2, 90-1 CPD ¶ 224 (Davis-Bacon); *Logistical Support, Inc.*, Comp. Gen. Dec. B-212689.3, 84-1 CPD ¶ 191 (Service Contract Act); where the solicitation violates a statute, *Pavel Enters., Inc.*, Comp. Gen. Dec. B-249332, 92-2 CPD ¶ 330; where improper set-aside provisions were included in the IFB, *Midland Transp., Co.*, Comp. Gen. Dec. B-201319, 81-2 CPD ¶ 89; where the agency, although required to do so, did not set the procurement aside, *Baker Support Servs., Inc.*, Comp. Gen. Dec. B-256192.3, 95-1 CPD ¶ 75; *Ryon, Inc.*, Comp. Gen. Dec. B-256752.2, 94-2 CPD ¶ 163; where the completion of another construction project would allow the Air Force to continue its missions without disruption, *S. Sys. Corp.*, Comp. Gen. Dec. B-259827, 95-1 CPD ¶ 221; where the government was unable to timely furnish required government-furnished material and equipment, *Aul Instruments, Inc.*, Comp. Gen. Dec. B-195887, 80-1 CPD ¶ 98; *Monarch Enters., Inc.*, Comp. Gen. Dec. B-201688, 81-1 CPD ¶ 483; and where an "or equal" component of a "brand name or equal" clause was inadvertently omitted, *Scaward Int'l, Inc.*, Comp. Gen. Dec. B 199040, 81-1 CPD ¶ 23.

Occasionally bidders protest an agency's decision to go forward with the solicitation. If GAO agrees that a compelling reason exists and disagrees with the agency's decision not to cancel, it will recommend cancellation, *Gourmet Distribs.*, Comp. Gen. Dec. B-259083, 95-1 CPD ¶ 130 (agency misclassified the invitation in the *Commerce Business Daily* (CBD)); *Respiratory & Convalescent Specialties, Inc.*, Comp. Gen. Dec. B-255176, 94-1 CPD ¶ 101 (IFB failed to identify an evaluation factor and failed to provide estimates for an item); *Duramed Homecare*, 71 Comp. Gen. 193 (B-245766) 92-1 CPD ¶ 126 (requirements in the IFB were 12 times the amount of the agency's actual past use); *Bartomeli Co.*, 71 Comp. Gen. 237 (B-246060), 92-1 CPD ¶ 170 (protester's bid was prematurely opened and disclosed); *Elrich Constr. Co.*, Comp. Gen. Dec. B-187726, 77-1 CPD ¶ 105 (no quantity estimates were specified in a requirement-type IFB).

## 2. Reasons for Cancellation — Not Compelling

Even though competition is somewhat flawed, the defects may not be sufficiently compelling to call for cancellation. The Court of Federal Claims has emphasized the unfairness of cancellation after the bids have been exposed and has closely scrutinized the agency's basis for cancellation. See *Great Lakes Dredge & Dry Docks Co. v. United States*, 60 Fed. Cl. 350 (2004), rejecting the cancellation and holding that the agency's determination that the specifications were restrictive did not withstand analysis. See also *Overstreet Elec. Co. v. United States*, 47 Fed. Cl. 728 (2000) (cancellation based on high bid price compared to government estimate when court found that the government estimate was based on irrational assumptions); *California Marine Cleaning, Inc. v. United States*, 42 Fed. C. 281 (1998) (cancellation improper when it was based on a potential defect in the way bids were delivered to the agency but there was no evidence of an actual problem); *Vanguard Sec., Inc. v. United States*, 20 Cl. Ct. 90 (1990) (cancellation based on allegedly ambiguous IFB provisions improper when court found provisions clear).

### a. No Prejudice and Low Bidder Meets Agency's Needs

Cancellation after bid opening is generally inappropriate where an IFB or specification defect did not cause any competitive prejudice and an award under the solicitation would serve the actual needs of the government, *Massaro Co.*, Comp. Gen. Dec. B-280772.2, 98-2 CPD ¶ 123 (IFB pricing requirements subject to only one reasonable interpretation); *Canadian Commercial Corp.*, Comp. Gen. Dec. B-255642, 94-1 CPD ¶ 202 (no bidder prejudiced where an allegedly ambiguous provision only had one reasonable interpretation); *Sierra Forest Prods.*, Comp. Gen. Dec. B-245393, 92-1 CPD ¶ 4 (failure to send required form to prospective bidders did not prejudice bidders when they were on notice of the requirement and could have obtained a copy of the missing form); *Richard Hoffman Corp.*, Comp. Gen. Dec. B-212775.2, 83-2 CPD ¶ 656 (solicitation was ambiguous regarding pricing of informational items but no bidder was misled); *American Mut. Protective Bureau*, 62 Comp. Gen. 354 (B-209192), 83-1 CPD ¶ 469 (IFB ambiguous but no prejudice where all six bidders correctly computed their bids); *Tennessee Valley Serv. Co. — Recons.*, Comp. Gen. Dec. B-188771, 77-2 CPD ¶ 241 (no bidder prejudiced by having the contracting officer multiply the unit prices by the applicable estimated quantities to determine the low bidder). See also *Twehous Excavating Co.*, Comp.

Gen. Dec. B-208189, 83-1 CPD ¶ 42, where the solicitation did not fully describe the mathematical calculations for one of 32 items but the simple calculation was obvious. GAO stated:

> The fact that some terms of an invitation are in some way deficient does not, of itself, constitute a compelling reason to cancel. Our Office generally regards cancellation after opening as inappropriate when other bidders would not be prejudiced by an award under the ostensibly deficient solicitation.

In *Immigration & Naturalization Serv.*, Comp. Gen. Dec. B-182949, 75-1 CPD ¶ 165, GAO indicated that cancellation for ambiguous specifications would not be appropriate:

> if no prejudice would result from an award to an otherwise responsive bidder whose bid would meet the Government's actual needs, i.e., (1) where there was no reason to believe that additional firms would bid on revised specifications included in a resolicitation or that the original bidders would have offered any different equipment on a resolicitation . . . and (2) that there was in any event only one responsive bidder.

A solicitation was improperly canceled on the grounds of a purported ambiguity where evidence available from the offeror's cost proposals that tended to disprove the ambiguity was ignored, *Apex Int'l Mgmt. Servs., Inc.*, 60 Comp. Gen. 172 (B-200008), 81-1 CPD ¶ 24.

## b. *Potential Competitor Not Solicited*

Failure to solicit a potential competitor is not a compelling reason for cancellation if competition is otherwise adequate, prices are reasonable, the agency does not deliberately exclude a bidder, and it complies with all regulations governing the distribution and advertisement of a solicitation, *Eagle Creek Archaeological Servs., Inc.*, Comp. Gen. Dec. B-258480, 95-1 CPD ¶ 43 (agency did not deliberately exclude bidder, and the record showed there was adequate competition and reasonable prices); *Energy Mgmt. Sys.*, Comp. Gen. Dec. B-258391, 94-2 CPD ¶ 208 (no showing that agency deliberately excluded a bidder from competition where bidder failed to review the CBD and to apply for inclusion on the mailing list); *Cinema Color Group*, Comp. Gen. Dec. B-210666, 83-2 CPD ¶ 257 (advertising procurement under heading of "photographic equipment" not shown to be a deliberate attempt to preclude protester from bidding). In 52 Comp. Gen. 281 (B-176839) (1972), a potential supplier was precluded from bidding because the IFB amendment, which advanced the bid opening 10 days, was sent to San Benito, California, rather than San Benito, Texas. GAO stated at 283:

> We have also held that the propriety of a particular procurement must be determined from the Government's point of view upon the basis of whether adequate competition and reasonable prices were obtained, not upon whether every pos-

sible prospective bidder was afforded an opportunity to bid. . . . While it is un-
fortunate that your address was not correctly recorded on the bidders list, we do
not find anything in the record to indicate that the error was other than an inadvertent mistake, or that it was occasioned by any deliberate attempt on the part of
the procuring personnel to exclude you from participating in the procurement. In
such circumstances, although we recognize the resulting hardship which may be
experienced by your firm, it has been our consistent position that the nonreceipt
or delay in receiving bidding documents by a prospective bidder does not require
cancellation or amendment of the invitation.

However, where an agency fails to comply with the statutory and regulatory
requirements regarding distribution of solicitations, cancellation is appropriate,
*Goodway Graphics of Virginia, Inc.*, Comp. Gen. Dec. B-297789, 2006 CPD ¶ 54
(agency failed to solicit two incumbents and failed to post procurement on *fedbi-
zopps.gov*); *Kertzman Contracting, Inc.*, Comp. Gen. Dec. B-259461.2, 95-1 CPD
¶ 226 (agency failed to send amendment to a bidder on the mailing list); *Telos Field
Eng'g*, Comp. Gen. Dec. B-257747, 94-2 CPD ¶ 172 (agency failed to obtain "full
and open" competition when it only provided copies of the solicitation to four firms
considered to be industry leaders). In addition, an agency's failure to solicit an incumbent contractor may not satisfy "full and open" competition requirement, *Pratt
& Lambert, Inc.*, Comp. Gen. Dec. B-245537, 92-1 CPD ¶ 48; *Kimber Guard &
Patrol, Inc.*, Comp. Gen. Dec. B-248920, 92-2 CPD ¶ 220.

### c. Increases in Quantity Only

Where the government determines that additional quantities of the same item
are needed after bid opening, cancellation is not generally deemed compelling. FAR
14.404-1(a)(3) provides:

> As a general rule, after the opening of bids, an invitation should not be canceled
> and resolicited due solely to increased requirements for the items being acquired.
> Award should be made on the initial invitation for bids and the additional quantity
> should be treated as a new acquisition.

FAR 14.404-1(a)(3) only applies in cases where an agency is procuring products
and not where the agency is procuring services, *Bangar Contractors Corp.*, Comp.
Gen. Dec. B-240071, 90-2 CPD ¶ 295; *Bill McCann*, Comp. Gen. Dec. B-234199.2,
89-1 CPD ¶ 554. GAO has discussed this regulation on several occasions but has not
decided any case where increases in quantity alone were at issue, *Dyneteria, Inc.*,
Comp. Gen. Dec. B-211525.2, 84-2 CPD ¶ 484 (closely interrelated aspects of fuel
management operations made the above provision inapplicable). See *Genco Tool
& Eng'g Co.*, 61 Comp. Gen. 281 (B-204582), 82-1 CPD ¶ 175 (insufficient funds
were also at issue); and *ABC Demolition Corp.*, Comp. Gen. Dec. B-192111, 78-2
CPD ¶ 339 (change in agency needs involved additional performance of a different
nature than that required under the solicitation).

## 3. *Partial Cancellation*

There are situations after bid opening where partial cancellation of the solicitation is justified. See *Hampton Metropolitan Oil Co.*, Comp. Gen. Dec. B-186030, 76-2 CPD ¶ 471, stating:

> [W]e believe the provisions of ASPR 2-404.1(b) [now FAR 14.404-1(b)], which merely refer to cancellation of an IFB, must be read as permitting cancellation of either all or a portion of the IFB, as may be required by the circumstances, and not as requiring cancellation of the IFB *in toto* or not at all.

Where the solicitation includes, but is not limited to, work for an item that the agency does not need, or where there is a solicitation defect that directly affects only a portion of the invitation's bid items, and the government has the right under the solicitation to accept any item or groups of items, the contracting officer should cancel only the affected portion of the IFB, *Telemarc, Inc.*, Comp. Gen. Dec. B-242339, 91-1 CPD ¶ 375 (ambiguous specification for a line item of the solicitation justified cancellation of that one item); *Hartridge Equip. Corp.*, Comp. Gen. Dec. B-230039, 88-1 CPD ¶ 284 (cancellation proper for line item where specification for line item was defective); *Kan-Du Tool & Instrument Corp.*, Comp. Gen. Dec. B-210819, 83-2 CPD ¶ 12 (proper for Army to cancel 8,699 items and award 1,549 items to responsive bidders). See also *Adrian Supply Co.*, Comp. Gen. Dec. B-240871, 90-2 CPD ¶ 515 (partial cancellation appropriate where bid prices for line item exceeded government estimate by more than 100%); *Duracell, Inc.*, Comp. Gen. Dec. B-229538, 88-1 CPD ¶ 145 (partial cancellation proper where agency could not legally award 40% of the solicitation to bidder); and *McGregor Printing Corp.*, Comp. Gen. Dec. B-207084, 82-2 CPD ¶ 240 (proper for GSA to cancel portions of two solicitations because of decreased demand and amount of space available in certain depots).

## 4. *Reinstatement of the Solicitation*

Although the FAR does not directly address reinstatement of a procurement after cancellation, FAR 14.404-1 does contain the following guidance on "completion of the acquisition after cancellation":

> (e) Under some circumstances, completion of the acquisition after cancellation of the invitation for bids may be appropriate.
>
> (1) If the invitation for bids has been canceled for the reasons specified in subparagraphs (c) (6), (7), or (8) of this subsection, and the agency head has authorized, in the determination in paragraph (c) of this subsection, the completion of the acquisition through negotiation, the contracting officer shall proceed in accordance with 15.103.
>
> (2) If the invitation for bids has been canceled for the reasons specified in subparagraphs (c) (1), (2), (4), (5), or (10) of this subsection, or for the rea-

sons in subparagraphs (c) (6), (7), or (8) of this subsection and completion through negotiation is not authorized under subparagraph (e)(1) of this subsection, the contracting officer shall proceed with a new acquisition.

GAO has stated that this provision only prohibits reinstatement of a procurement that was properly canceled. See *KAL Maint., Inc.*, Comp. Gen. Dec. B-225429, 87-1 CPD ¶ 207, stating:

Although, as the protester points out, the FAR, 48 C.F.R. § 14.404-1(e)(2), does not expressly state that it applies only to IFB's which have been canceled properly, we think it logical to apply it only in that context, because the provision's purpose is to prescribe a second competition where the results of the first have been invalidated by some defect. It permits the government to set things right — through revising the specifications, for example — and obtain competition based upon an accurate statement of the government's needs. Here, the original IFB in fact was not defective (although for some time after bid opening the Air Force erroneously thought that it was) and it did result in competition from 17 bidders, including the protester. Since an award under the original IFB would serve the government's needs, a second competition would only prejudice those bidders whose prices have been exposed and afford the protester, the eighth low bidder, an opportunity to improve its competitive position. See *ADAK [Communications Sys., Inc.*, B-222546, July 24, 1986, 86-2 CPD ¶ 103]; *Woodson Construction Co. — Reconsideration*, B-221530.2, May 23, 1986, 86-1 CPD ¶ 483; *Suburban Industrial Maintenance Co.*, B-188179, June 28, 1977, 77-1 CPD ¶ 459. Reinstatement therefore is necessary to protect the integrity of the competitive procurement system by avoiding an unfair bidding situation after the bids were made public. See *ADAK, supra; Lanier Business Products, Inc.*, B-203977, Feb. 23, 1982, 82-1 CPD ¶ 159.

Thus, reinstatement is appropriate as a means of promoting the integrity of the bidding system when the cancellation was improper, *Bilt-Rite Contractors, Inc.*, Comp. Gen. Dec. B-259106.2, 95-1 CPD ¶ 220 (reinstatement was proper where IFB was erroneously canceled because agency incorrectly believed that low bid was nonresponsive); *U.S. Rentals*, 69 Comp. Gen. 395 (B-238090), 90-1 CPD ¶ 367 (IFB reinstated where apparent inconsistency in solicitation did not prejudice any bidder). However, where the agency's actual needs have changed since the issuance of the original solicitation, GAO will recommend resolicitation, rather than reinstatement, see *TWI Inc.*, Comp. Gen. Dec. B-202966.4, 82-2 CPD ¶ 487.

Upon reinstatement of the solicitation, bids may generally be revived, *U.S. Rentals*, 69 Comp. Gen. 395 (B-238090), 90-1 CPD ¶ 367; *Sac & Fox Indus., Ltd.*, Comp. Gen. Dec. B-231873, 88-2 CPD ¶ 250. This is appropriate even where bids have been returned to all offerors, if a record of the contents of the bids has been made. In *Baker Mfg. Co.*, 59 Comp. Gen. 573 (B-197016), 80-2 CPD ¶ 1, an abstract of bids provided suitable evidence of original bid prices and responsiveness. However, bids could not be revived in *L.V. Anderson & Sons, Inc.*, Comp. Gen. Dec. B-189835, 77-2 CPD ¶ 249, where no record of the contents of the bids was made prior to their return.

# IV. MISTAKES

Mistakes are a major exception to the firm bid rule used in sealed bidding, *Refining Assocs. v. United States*, 124 Ct. Cl. 115, 109 F. Supp. 259 (1953). The process of bid preparation and submission is frequently hectic. Specifications and drawings must be analyzed, subcontractors' and vendors' bids coordinated, and costs estimated — usually in a short period of time. In such an environment, mistakes are common. It has long been recognized that it would not be fair for the government to take advantage of a bid containing a mistake when the government knew or should have known of the mistake, *Chernick v. United States*, 178 Ct. Cl. 498, 372 F.2d 492 (1967). See also *Pavco, Inc.*, ASBCA 23783, 80-1 BCA ¶ 14,407; *Black Diamond Energies, Inc.*, Comp. Gen. Dec. B-241370, 91-1 CPD ¶ 119.

This exception has been exceedingly difficult to administer. Once bids are opened and announced, low bidders may be tempted to assert that mistakes have been made in order to increase their price or to avoid award. Bidders that are not low may identify mistakes that, if corrected, would make them low. In all such cases, the integrity of the bidding process may be threatened if correction of mistakes is too liberally permitted. Hence, a sophisticated set of rules has evolved to deal with mistakes in bids.

The first section analyzes the types of mistakes that are covered by these rules. The second section discusses the responsibility of the contracting officer when mistakes are suspected. Finally, the third section reviews the actions that can be taken after it has been ascertained that a mistake in bid has occurred.

## A. Defining Mistake

Relief is only provided for certain types of mistakes. Although the FAR is silent on this issue, the courts, boards, and GAO make a distinction between *ministerial errors* and *judgmental errors* in granting relief for mistakes in bids. In *Ruggiero v. United States*, 190 Ct. Cl. 327, 420 F.2d 709 (1970), the court stated at 335:

> The mistake . . . must be . . . a clear cut clerical or arithmetical error, or misreading of specifications, and the authorities cited do not extend to mistakes of judgment.

The court also ruled that negligence by the bidder was not a bar to relief since in most cases where relief had been granted the bidders had been "guilty of egregious blunders." See *BCM Corp. v. United States*, 2 Cl. Ct. 602 (1983), pointing out that "the reasonableness of the mistake is not relevant" to the rules relating to mistakes in bid.

### 1. Business Judgment

Bidders make numerous business judgments in the process of submitting bids. They must assess the complexity of the task, determine the amount of effort required to perform the work, and decide whether to perform the work with their own forces or by subcontract. If their judgments in these areas prove to be in error, relief will not be granted. Thus, when a bidder makes a business judgment, it assumes the responsibility that the judgment may be faulty and is "taking a conscious gamble with known risks," *Liebherr Crane Corp. v. United States*, 810 F.2d 1153 (Fed. Cir. 1987). See also *Giesler v. United States*, 232 F.3d 864 (Fed. Cir. 2000) (failure to read specification); *RQ Constr., Inc.*, ASBCA 52376, 01-2 BCA ¶ 31,627 (failing to determine the effort needed to use an arguably specified material); *Aydin Corp. v. United States*, 229 Ct. Cl. 309, 669 F.2d 681 (1982) (errors concerning the nature and costs of materials necessary to perform the work); *American Ship Bldg. Co. v. United States*, 228 Ct. Cl. 220, 654 F.2d 75 (1981) (not fully assessing the difficulty of the work); *National Line Co. v. United States*, 221 Ct. Cl. 673, 607 F.2d 978 (1979) (determinations of the adequacy of plant, equipment, personnel, and the attainable rate of production); *Wyodak Enters., Inc.*, VABCA 3678, 95-1 BCA ¶ 27,493 (underestimation of effort required to comply with contract requirements); *Franklin Pavkov Constr. Co.*, HUDBCA 93-C-C13, 94-3 BCA ¶ 27,078 (underestimation of square footage due to bidder's lack of site inspection); *Fan, Inc.*, GS-BCA 7836, 91-1 BCA ¶ 23,364 (using past experience to estimate the number of ventilation units needing adjustment); *EDC/MTI (J.V.)*, ENGBCA 5631, 90-2 BCA ¶ 22,669 (inaccurate assessments of the availability and cost of insurance); *Overhead Elec. Co.*, ASBCA 25656, 85-2 BCA ¶ 18,026 (neglecting to obtain prices from a supplier); *SCM Corp.*, ASBCA 26544, 85-1 BCA ¶ 17,783 (knowingly using a low overhead rate); and *Superior Servs.*, ASBCA 28300, 84-3 BCA ¶ 17,547 (failing to consider the costs of providing supplies and equipment).

A mistake that is neither a mistake in business judgment nor a misreading of the specifications but was inadvertent was held to be the type of mistake that is correctable, *Hall & Son, Inc. v. United States*, 54 Fed. Cl. 436 (2002). There the bidder had failed to read a caveat in a subcontractor's bid excluding required work. However, relief was denied because of lack of clear and convincing evidence of the intended bid.

## 2. Clerical or Arithmetical Errors

Clerical or arithmetical errors are the most common types of mistakes for which relief is granted. See, for example, *Paragon Energy Corp. v. United States*, 227 Ct. Cl. 176, 645 F.2d 966 (1981), *recons. denied*, 230 Ct. Cl. 884 (1982) (omission of one element of cost estimates); *McCarty Corp. v. United States*, 204 Ct. Cl. 768, 499 F.2d 633 (1974) (numbers transposed on bid document); *Government Micro Res., Inc. v. Department of the Treasury*, GSBCA 12364-TD, 94-2 BCA ¶ 26,680 (reversal of discount and cost rates in offer preparation); *Allen L. Bender, Inc.*, LBCA 80-BCA-103, 81-2 BCA ¶ 15,435 (cost of several items omitted from recap sheets); *Michaels Constr. Co.*, Comp. Gen. Dec. B-257764, 94-2 CPD ¶ 176 (using incorrect number of square feet to calculate the unit price); *Pipeline Constr., Inc.*, Comp. Gen. Dec. B-256799, 94-2 CPD ¶ 21 (omitting a zero when transcribing from worksheet to final bid); *C Constr. Co.*, Comp. Gen. Dec. B-253198.2, 93-2 CPD ¶ 198 (mistaken use of macro computer command resulted in a misleading screen); *Columbia Pac. Constr. Co.*, Comp. Gen. Dec. B-207313, 82-1 CPD ¶ 436 (dividing rather than multiplying in making metric conversion); and *PK Contractors, Inc.*, Comp. Gen. Dec. B-205482, 82-1 CPD ¶ 368 (error in pagination resulted in failure to include estimated costs on one page of estimating sheets).

Relief has also been given for clerical or arithmetical errors made by suppliers and subcontractors. See *R.P. Richards Constr. Co.* Comp. Gen. Dec. B-258923, 95-1 CPD ¶ 103, granting relief for a subcontractor's typographical error, stating that the error "precludes the bidder from making a knowing judgment about its actual intended bid." See also *Chemtronics, Inc.*, ASBCA 30883, 88-2 BCA ¶ 20,534, granting relief when the bidder relied on erroneous quotation from the only supplier of a particular commodity. But see *Triax Pac., Inc.*, ASBCA 41891, 94-1 BCA ¶ 26,380, denying relief because the subcontractor's price misquotation was obviously lower than any other quote received. The board reasoned that the bidder "assumed the risk of [the subcontractor's] mistaken . . . quote because it failed to investigate thoroughly the 'dramatically higher' . . . quote it received."

In some cases determining whether there is a clerical or arithmetical error or a mistake in judgment is very difficult. See, for example, *Ruggiero v. United States*, 190 Ct. Cl. 327, 420 F.2d 709 (1970), where the court concluded that failure to include an "all or none" stipulation in a multiple-item contract was a clerical mistake because the price of one item made no commercial sense without the other items; and *JAL Constr., Inc.*, AGBCA 80-117-3, 81-1 BCA ¶ 14,850, where an omission of work in a subcontractor's estimate due to a misunderstanding between the bidder and the subcontractor was held to be a clerical error. In *Rockwell Int'l Corp.*, ASBCA 41095, 95-1 BCA ¶ 27,459, the board found it unnecessary to determine whether the selection of the wrong algorithm was a clear-cut clerical or mathematical error or an error in judgment. Rather, it denied relief on the grounds that the "error" occurred in the use of a complex algorithm which was not "clear cut" and, therefore, did not meet the test for an arithmetical mistake.

### 3. *Misreading Specifications*

Misreading of specifications is not considered to be an error in business judgment when it involves the quantity or nature of the work rather than the effort required to perform the work. See *Walter Straga*, ASBCA 26134, 83-2 BCA ¶ 16,611, where the contractor's estimate was based upon an unreasonable but mistaken interpretation of the specifications. The board granted relief, finding the misreading of the specifications as to the quantity of items covered was not an error in business judgment. See also *Faulkner Corp.*, VABCA 2998, 90-1 BCA ¶ 22,507, where relief was granted when the contractor misread ambiguous plan headings and mistakenly substituted one for the other; and *BDF Tesa Corp.*, GSB-CA 8307, 89-3 BCA ¶ 21,925, where relief was granted when the contractor mistakenly believed its masking tape would meet the military's strict specifications. Similarly, in *BCM Corp. v. United States*, 2 Cl. Ct. 602 (1983), a contractor who unreasonably misinterpreted the contract specification obtained relief because a mistake in judgment had not occurred. When determining its bid price the bidder failed to include a particular, identifiable portion of work and had not underestimated the work it thought was included. See *Derek & Dana Contracting, Inc. v. United States*, 7 Cl. Ct. 627 (1985) (mistakenly believing that one part of the specified work would be included only when an addendum was issued); *WICO, Inc.*, EBCA 125-6-80, 80-2 BCA ¶ 14,790 (basing bid on obsolete drawings); and *Ralph Larsen & Son, Inc. v. United States*, 17 Cl. Ct. 39 (1989) ("unilateral mistake" when subcontractors misinterpreted specifications). For a case finding no mistake when the contractor's subcontractor misinterpreted the specifications, see *H. Fair Assocs.*, ASBCA 26950, 82-2 BCA ¶ 16,112. There the board concluded that the contractor had made a judgmental error in relying on the subcontractor and the subcontractor had made a judgmental error in "not examining all of the specifications and drawings" — apparently reasoning that they were so clear that the subcontractor would not have arrived at its interpretation if it had conducted a thorough examination.

No misreading of the specifications is found where the contractor makes a judgment as to the amount of effort or the cost that is required to perform the work. See *Aquila Fitness Consulting Sys., Ltd.*, Comp. Gen. Dec. B-286488, 2001 CPD ¶ 4 (decision to use part-time employees when specification required full-time employees); *Northern NEF, Inc.*, ASBCA 44996, 94-3 BCA ¶ 27,094 (decision to use an employee at a lower wage than permitted by Service Contract Act wage determination); *Boeing Computer Servs.*, ASBCA 42674, 94-3 BCA ¶ 27,114 (decision to use fewer employees than required to perform work); *Klinger Constructors, Inc.*, ASBCA 41006, 91-3 BCA ¶ 24,218 (failure to include state tax in price); *Dick & Kirkman, Inc.*, VABCA 1545, 84-3 BCA ¶ 17,662 (assumption, on advice of a supplier, that a portion of the specifications could be ignored); *Technology Chem., Inc.*, ASBCA 26304, 82-2 BCA ¶ 15,927 (deliberate choice to use a cheaper, nonconforming material).

Failure to read and consider the contract specifications does not constitute a "misreading," *Liebherr Crane Corp. v. United States*, 810 F.2d 1153 (Fed. Cir. 1987) (failure to read 94 of 98 specifications was a "conscious gamble with known risks" and treated as an error in business judgment). See also *Minority Enters., Inc.*, ASBCA 45549, 95-1 BCA ¶ 27,461 (contractor correctly read three golf course drawings but did not read fourth); *Electrical Sys. Eng'g Co.*, ASBCA 37147, 90-2 BCA ¶ 22,715 (reprocurement contractor used bill of materials of terminated contractor but did not read contract specifications); and *Universal Constr. Co.*, NASABCA 83-

1092, 93-3 BCA ¶ 26,173 (contractor failed to read drawings along with specifications as contract stipulated). But see *Minnesota Well Drillers*, ASBCA 26097, 82-1 BCA ¶ 15,539, where the board found a mistake where the contractor failed to read revised specifications describing harder material to be drilled than that called out in the original IFB. The board stated at 77,045:

> [The contractor's] stupidity in bidding without reading the revised specifications does not forfeit relief because such foolishness or a variation thereof is common to most bidders who err in bidding and such conduct is of diminished importance in deciding whether to reform a contract. *Chris Berg v. United States*, 192 Ct. Cl. 176, 426 F.2d 314 (1970).

The board reached this decision partially on the theory that there had not been a mistake in business judgment because most contractors in this area did not read specification revisions.

## B. Knowledge of Error and Verification

Although some mistakes are identified by the bidder, most of the controversy over mistakes revolves around the question of whether the government should have identified the mistake. The rationale underlying relief in this situation is that it would be unfair for the government to hold a bidder to a bargain when the government knew of or should have discerned the mistake and called it to the attention of the bidder. If the government appropriately notifies the bidder of a possible mistake or the bidder alleges a mistake, the bidder can request withdrawal or modification of the bid or can elect to stand by the bid as originally submitted.

If the government fails to notify the bidder of a suspected mistake, it may subsequently be subject to claims for price adjustment, or the contractor may use a claimed mistake as a basis for avoiding performance obligations. To eliminate these problems the regulations impose verification requirements on the contracting officer. FAR 14.407-1 provides the following guidance:

> After the opening of bids, contracting officers shall examine all bids for mistakes. In cases of apparent mistakes and in cases where the contracting officer has reason to believe that a mistake may have been made, the contracting officer shall request from the bidder a verification of the bid, calling attention to the suspected mistake. If the bidder alleges a mistake, the matter shall be processed in accordance with this section 14.407. Such actions shall be taken before award.

The verification process must be followed precisely in order to assure the bidder fair treatment. This section first discusses the circumstances under which the government obtains actual knowledge of a mistake or is held to have reason to know of it. It then deals with the adequacy of the verification process.

## 1. *Knowledge or Reason to Know*

There are relatively few litigated cases where the government actually knows of an error and awards without adequate verification. One example is *Walter Straga*, ASBCA 26134, 83-2 BCA ¶ 16,611, where the government project manager's actual knowledge of the contractor's error was imputed to the contracting officer. See also *Derek & Dana Contracting, Inc. v. United States*, 7 Cl. Ct. 627 (1985), where the bidder orally advised the bid opening official that certain costs were not included in the bid.

In determining whether the government *should have known* of the mistake, the general test is whether a reasonable person, knowing all the facts and circumstances, would have suspected a mistake. See *Chernick v. United States*, 178 Ct. Cl. 498, 372 F.2d 492 (1967), where the court stated at 504:

> The test of what an official in charge of accepting bids "should" have known must be that of reasonableness, *i.e.*, whether under the facts and circumstances of the case there were any factors which reasonably should have raised the presumption of error in the mind of the contracting officer; among such factors are obvious wide range of bids, and gross disparity between the price bid and the value of the article which was the subject of the bid.

The circumstances that can put the contracting officer on notice are more specifically detailed in *BCM Corp. v. United States*, 2 Cl. Ct. 602 (1983), at 610:

> An oft-cited article, Doke, *Mistakes in Government Contracts — Error Detection Duty of Contracting Officer*, 18 S.W.L.J. I (1964) ("Doke"), delineates these general categories: (1) facially apparent errors, such as multiplication errors made when computing unit prices into total price; (2) disparity in prices among the bids; (3) disparity between the bid and the private government estimate; (4) disparity between the bid and the cost of prior procurements of the same item; (5) disparity between the bid price and, if the contracting officer knows it, the market value for the goods.

These rules are not applied mechanically, and no single rule is either necessary or sufficient to impute knowledge of error. Thus, the government will properly be charged with knowledge only after a full consideration of all the circumstances, *Darwin Constr. Co.*, GSBCA 6590, 84-1 BCA ¶ 17,230, *recons. denied*, 84-2 BCA ¶ 17,356. See *Troise v. United States*, 21 Cl. Ct. 48 (1990), where the contractor purposely deviated from the contract specifications to arrive at its bid as it had done in a previous contract. The court held that since the bid was not out of line with the government estimate and the other bids, the contracting officer did not have to "speculate as to the basis of the contractor's bid" because to hold thus "would make the United States an insurer of its contractor's mistakes."

The most common situation putting the contracting officer on constructive notice of a possible error is a disparity between a favorable bid and the other bids or the government's estimate. In *Government Micro Res., Inc. v. Departmentt of the Treasury*, GSBCA 12364-TD, 94-2 BCA ¶ 26,680, constructive notice was imputed when the bidder's price of $864,482 was 62% less than the government's lowest estimate, 31% less than the supplier's schedule price, and 33% less than the other vendor's comparison quote. The board rejected the government argument that, based upon an audit report on a proposed contract of $130 million, it could expect large discounts on the supplier's list price. Constructive notice was also imputed in *L & D Indus., Inc.*, ASBCA 38239, 91-2 BCA ¶ 23,718, where there was an "obvious and substantial" disparity among the bidder's bid of $50.45, bids of $132.00 and $145.70 by the other low vendors, and a previous solicitation price of $15740 received for the same item; *George A. Harris Enters., Inc.*, GSBCA 9888, 90-1 BCA ¶ 22,405, where the bid was over 24% lower than the next lowest bid and "the contract was not large or particularly complex" so should not have produced the disparity that it did; *Figgie Int'l, Inc.*, ASBCA 27541, 83-1 BCA ¶ 16,421, where the bidder's failure to include costs for packaging should have been noted by the contracting officer because all other responsive bids were from 43% to 82% higher than the bid, and the bidder had not significantly increased its price from that of a prior contract with significantly less costly packaging requirements. GAO has found constructive notice when there was a disparity between the mistaken bid, the only other bid, and the prior year's contract price, *Ace Window Cleaning Co.*, Comp. Gen. Dec. B-183380, 75-1 CPD ¶ 379; a significant variation from the average of all other bids (127% higher) and from the next low bidder (59% higher), *American Food Serv. Equip., Inc.*, Comp. Gen. Dec. B-181878, 74-2 CPD ¶ 83; a variation from the bidder's general pattern of prior bids and the market prices for that item, *Calumet Y Farm Store*, Comp. Gen. Dec. B-181284, 74-2 CPD ¶ 11; and when the only bid received varied 21% over the government estimate, *Murphy Elevator Co.*, Comp. Gen. Dec. B-180607, 74-1 CPD ¶ 164.

Other factors in the bid may also place the contracting officer on notice that a mistake may have been made. See *Franklin Pavkov Constr. Co.*, HUDBCA 93-C-C13, 94-3 BCA ¶ 27,078 (bidder's estimate was based on 200 square feet of work and the contracting officer knew the need far exceeded that figure and the only other bid estimated 2,000 square feet); and *Carter Chevrolet Agency*, GSBCA 10142, 90-2 BCA ¶ 22,804 (bidder inconsistently priced vehicles with extra options the same or less than vehicles without options). Another example can be seen in *Con nelly Containers, Inc. v. United States*, 7 Cl. Ct. 423 (1985), where, while a bid was only 5% lower than the other lowest bid, the disparity of individual bid prices should have alerted the contracting officer to the possibility of mistake. In that instance, the prices for shipping identical containers were higher for shorter distances than for longer distances.

Constructive knowledge will not be found if the disparity is insufficiently wide and there are no other indications that a mistake has been made. Insufficient disparity has been found where the bid is far below the government estimate but is close to other bids, *Beyley Constr. Group Corp.*, ASBCA 55692, 08-2 BCA ¶ 33,999, *aff'd*, 351 Fed. App'x 446 (Fed. Cir. 2009) (bid 20.69% below government estimate but next low bid only 2.52% higher than contractor's bid); *Conner Bros. Constr. Co. v. United States*, 65 Fed. Cl. 657 (2005) (bid 90.3% of government estimate and approximately 12% under next low bidder); *R.J. Sanders, Inc. v. United States*, 24 Cl. Ct. 288 (1991) (bid 32% less than Navy's estimate but only 18% less than next low bid); *Electrical Sys. Eng'g Co.*, ASBCA 37147, 90-2 BCA ¶ 22,715 (bid 18.4% lower than government estimate and 6.7% away from next low bid). Insufficient disparity has also been found where the bid is far below all other bids but is close to the government estimate, *T.R. Orr, Inc.*, IBCA 3143, 94-2 BCA ¶ 26,865 (bid of $37,750 was much less than only other bid of $59,711, but government estimate was $41,100); *Triax Pac., Inc.*, ASBCA 41891, 94-1 BCA ¶ 26,380 (bid was 1.63% higher than government estimate, 13.78% lower than second low bid, and 14.94% lower than third low bid); *AQA Sys., Inc.*, ASBCA 45051, 93-3 BCA ¶ 25,996 (bid of $154,000 was close to government estimate of $167,450 even though the only other two bids were much higher at $274,700 and $600,000); *Edsall Constr. Co.*, IBCA 2450, 89-3 BCA ¶ 22,177 (disparity of $1,540,000, $1,678,010; and $1,712,000 in bids);and *C.E. Wylie Constr. Co.*, ASBCA 25587, 81-2 BCA ¶ 15,427 ($10,000 error on a $6 million procurement).

Even in instances where the disparity may be sufficiently wide, if the government can successfully explain the reasoning that led to a decision not to request verification, constructive notice will not be found. In *Hankins Constr. Co. v. United States*, 838 F.2d 1194 (Fed. Cir. 1988), a cluster of higher bids was explained with the theory of "high balling" from offerors that were not interested in receiving the job unless they would make a large profit. See also *Walsh Constr. Co. of Illinois*, ASBCA 52952, 02-1 BCA ¶ 32,024 (bid on one line item was quite low but total bid appeared close to other bids and government estimate); *Packard Constr. Corp.*, ASBCA 45996, 94-1 BCA ¶ 26,512 (bid was 13% less than government estimate but contracting officer knew that in a similar previous situation the same bidder had bid below the government estimate, had made no complaint of error, and had performed the contract); *Triax Pac., Inc.*, ASBCA 41891, 94-1 BCA ¶ 26,380 (government explained that it believed the bidder had bid low to "buy in" or because it did not make a site visit); *Wheeled Coach Indus. v. General Servs. Admin.*, GSBCA 10314, 93-1 BCA ¶ 25,245 (government's two-part price analysis search for errors was accepted even though a line item search would have discerned error); *Folgore Mobile Welding, Inc.*, ASBCA 33250, 88-3 BCA ¶ 21,172 (low bid partially explained because contracting officer knew the bidder was experienced, with excellent references, and that there had been a business slump in the oil industry); and *Singleton Contracting Co.*, ASBCA 26862, 82-2 BCA ¶ 15,994, *aff'd*, 723 F.2d 68 (Fed. Cir. 1983) (allegedly mistaken bid, only other bid, and government estimate were $123,460, $247,000, and $98,000, respectively, but variations did not place the contracting officer on notice of a mistake because (a) the contracting officer reasonably believed the high bid contained

---

errors, (b) the bidder "enjoyed a reputation of skill, integrity and competency in bidding and contracting," and (c) there was reason to believe that the government estimate was adequate, although low, while the bidder's bid was "exactly on target.") But see *James R. Sloss*, Comp. Gen. Dec. B-180402, 74-1 CPD ¶ 53, where GAO was concerned that some explanations had the appearance of being created after the fact to win the protest. In refusing to accept a farfetched government explanation, GAO stated:

> To rule otherwise would permit Government estimates to be rationalized away at any time a contractor made a substantial error, especially in a sole bidder situation, merely by evolving a possible hypothesis which might explain a lower bid. 48 Comp. Gen. 672, 676 (1969).

## 2. Adequacy of Verification Request

A contracting officer on notice of a possible mistake must not only request verification of the bid, but also disclose the particular reasons that led to the suspicion, FAR 14.407-3(g)(1). In *Klinger Constructors, Inc.*, ASBCA 41006, 91-3 BCA ¶ 24,218, the board summarized this concept, stating at 121,125:

> [T]he bid verification request should aim at informing the bidder of all the pertinent factors that indicate to the contracting officer that an error might have been made. The adequacy of verification will turn on an assessment of the reasonableness of the contracting officer's disclosure.

Absent such a disclosure, the request is inadequate, *United States v. Metro Novelty Mfg. Co.*, 125 F. Supp. 713 (S.D.N.Y. 1954). See *United States v. Hamilton Enters., Inc.*, 711 F.2d 1038 (Fed. Cir. 1983) (bidder not informed of large variation in manhours between its bid and government estimate, 1,941 versus 6,402 hours, respectively); *BCM Corp. v. United States*, 2 Cl. Ct. 602 (1983) (the third low bidder was told neither of the 18% variation between its bid price and the government estimate nor that the contracting officer was on notice of a possible misinterpretation of the solicitation); *BDF Tesa Corp.*, GSBCA 8307, 89-3 BCA ¶ 21,925 (verification request only stated that bid was too low without disclosing 70.7 to 79.3% disparity with other bids and a 10.3% to 36.3% disparity between bid and previous purchase prices for similar item); *Chemtronics, Inc.*, ASBCA 30883, 88-2 BCA ¶ 20,534 (form letter not adequate verification request where letter did not inform contractor of the gross disparity between its offer and that of the next lowest bidder or the government's funding estimate); *Ardmore Constr. Co.*, VABCA 2026, 85-1 BCA ¶ 17,743 (request for cost breakdown without advising bidder of suspected error not adequate); *Manistique Tool & Mfg. Co.*, ASBCA 29164, 84-3 BCA ¶ 17,599 (verification request did not state a mistake was suspected and did not disclose wide difference in bid prices); and *Walter Straga*, ASBCA 26134, 83-2 BCA ¶ 16,611 (verification request identifying price disparity was inadequate where government knew exact nature of error).

A verification request was found to be adequate in *Solar Foam Insulation*, ASBCA 46921, 94-2 BCA ¶ 26,901, where the contracting officer alerted the bidder to a disparity between its bid, the next two low bids, and the government estimate. The board found the verification request adequate even though the contracting officer failed to note that the error was found in a particular column of the bid and mistakenly said that the difference between the bid and the next lowest was $32,699, where it was really $113,669. See also *McClure Elec. Constructors, Inc. v. Dalton*, 132 F.3d 709 (Fed. Cir. 1997) (bidder not told error suspected but asked to verify its bid and given abstract showing that next low bid was almost 20% higher); *Fields Roof Serv., Inc.*, VABCA 3147, 90-3 BCA ¶ 23,232 (bidder told of difference between its bid of $417,545 and next lowest bid of $460,000); *Tri-States Serv. Co.*, ASBCA 31139, 90-3 BCA ¶ 23,059 (bidder told that its bid of $694,000 was less than the government's estimate of $779,983 for direct labor, and much less than the government's total estimate of $ 911,187); *W.B. & A., Inc.*, ASBCA 32524, 89-2 BCA ¶ 21,736 (bidder informed that its overall bid was low and attention called to five specific areas: edging, storm drainage, grass cutting, trash pickup, and tree removal); and *Central Mech., Inc.*, ASBCA 26543, 85-1 BCA ¶ 17,711 (bidder advised of disparity between its bid and the government estimate and that the bid was 10.2% under second low bid).

If verification is obtained but the contracting officer still has reason to believe a mistake has been made, a second verification request is required if the government has not revealed all of the information to the bidder, *United States v. Hamilton Enters., Inc.*, 711 F.2d 1038 (Fed. Cir. 1983). In *Hamilton*, the verification request pointed out a disparity with the other bids and asked for a manning chart. After verification, a contract was awarded. The court held that a second verification request was required because the government had not revealed that the bidder's estimate of man-hours was significantly lower than the government's estimate.

## C. Action after Mistake Identification

When a mistake in bid has been identified, the bidder must determine what course of action to follow. The easiest course is to request withdrawal of the bid. However, in many cases the bidder may attempt to persuade the agency to correct the mistake. If correction will maintain the status of a low bidder at a higher bid price, this is generally the bidder's most desirable course of action. However, it raises questions as to the integrity of the competitive bidding process. If correction results in the bid no longer being low, it is tantamount to withdrawal. In some cases, a low bidder may request correction but also be willing to accept award at the mistaken price if correction is denied. Finally, bidders that are not low may attempt to correct mistakes in order to become low. This course of action is the most controversial in terms of its effect on the integrity of the competitive bidding process. All of these courses of action are discussed below.

## 1. Withdrawal of Bid

The power to allow a bidder to withdraw its bid is vested in "an official above the contracting officer," FAR 14.407-3(c)(2). For many years, the regulations permitted withdrawal of a bid after bid opening if the bidder could prove the existence of a mistake by "clear and convincing" evidence, FPR 1-2.406-3(a)(3); DAR 2-406.3(a) (1). However, GAO followed a considerably more lenient policy concerning withdrawal after bid opening, generally permitting withdrawal even though there had been little more than a bare allegation of error by the bidder. For example, in 52 Comp. Gen. 258 (B-176111) (1972), GAO allowed withdrawal of the bid where the only evidence to support a mistake consisted of admittedly self-serving employee affidavits and unverified worksheets. This lenient withdrawal policy was apparently based on the rule that acceptance of a bid with knowledge of error does not consummate a valid and binding contract, *Alta Elec. & Mech. Co. v. United States*, 90 Ct. Cl. 466 (1940). See also 36 Comp. Gen. 441 (B-129736) (1956), stating at 444:

> In undertaking to bind a bidder by acceptance of a bid after notice of a claim of error by the bidder, the Government virtually undertakes the burden of proving either that there was no error or that the bidder's claim was not made in good faith.

In *Texas Turbo Jet, Inc.*, Comp. Gen. Dec. B-195303, 79-2 CPD ¶ 117, GAO stated that withdrawal would be permitted if the bidder is able to make a "prima facie" case in support of the alleged mistake. See also *Murphy Bros., Inc.*, 58 Comp. Gen. 185 (B-189756), 78-2 CPD ¶ 440.

FAR 14.407-3(c)(2) moved toward GAO's practice by permitting withdrawal of bids even if the evidence of mistake is less than clear and convincing but still "reasonably supports the existence of a mistake."

Recent GAO decisions have continued to follow this lenient withdrawal policy. See *H.A. Lewis, Inc.*, Comp. Gen. Dec. B-249368, 92-2 CPD ¶ 351 (withdrawal permitted where agency finds calculations used to allege mistake "make no sense under the circumstances"); *Weather Data Servs., Inc.*, Comp. Gen. Dec. B-241621, 91-1 CPD ¶ 185 (withdrawal allowed where bidder alleges mistake without any documentation showing how mistake was made); *McGeary Co.*, Comp. Gen. Dec. B-230713, 88-1 CPD ¶ 586, (withdrawal permitted even though Navy's allegation that "mistaken" price was a conscious choice to bid low is found reasonable), *Southwest Marine, Inc.*, Comp. Gen. Dec. B-225686, 87-1 CPD ¶ 510 (withdrawal granted even where the credibility of worksheet used to establish mistake is in doubt and the only testimony was from interested parties); and *C.T. Lighting, Inc.*, Comp. Gen. Dec. B-214462, 84-2 CPD ¶ 102 (withdrawal permitted despite contracting officer's contention that evidence of mistake was fabricated).

FAR 14.407-3(c)(1) also permits withdrawal of a bid if the evidence of the existence of a mistake is clear and convincing but the evidence of the intended bid is not. This is the typical case when withdrawal is the only possible course of action other than contract award. See, for example, *American Block Co.*, Comp. Gen. Dec. B-235053, 89-2 CPD ¶ 90, where evidence of a mistake was clear and convincing because the bidder clearly based its bid price on the wrong type of item, but a discrepancy in a worksheet prevented the establishment of the intended bid. See also *Northwest Builders*, 67 Comp. Gen. 278 (B-228555), 88-1 CPD ¶ 200, where discrepancies in computer-generated estimates and printouts established a mistake, but because of wide range of possibilities, the intended bid could not be established.

## 2. Rejection of Bid

Although the FAR does not deal directly with rejection of mistaken bids, where it is clear that a mistake in bid has been made, rejection of the bid is proper unless it is apparent that the bid both as submitted and intended will remain low. FAR 14.407-3(g)(5) indirectly recognizes the possibility of rejection of bids containing serious mistakes in providing the following guidance regarding when to evaluate a bid as submitted:

> Where the bidder fails or refuses to furnish evidence in support of a suspected or alleged mistake, the contracting officer shall consider the bid as submitted unless (i) the amount of the bid is so far out of line with the amounts of other bids received, or with the amount estimated by the agency or determined by the contracting officer to be reasonable, or (ii) there are other indications of error so clear, as to reasonably justify the conclusion that acceptance of the bid would be unfair to the bidder or to other bona fide bidders. Attempts made to obtain the information required and the action taken with respect to the bid shall be fully documented.

GAO has recognized that this provision provides authority for the rejection of bids containing mistakes. See *Orbas & Assocs.*, Comp. Gen. Dec. B-255276, 94-1 CPD ¶ 139, stating:

> A contracting officer's decision to reject an apparently mistaken bid under the authority of FAR 14.406-3(g)(5) is subject to question only where it is shown to be unreasonable. See *Pamfilis Painting, Inc.*, B-237968, Apr. 3, 1990, 90-1 CPD ¶ 355; *TLC Fin. Group*, [Comp. Gen. Dec;. B-237384, 90-1 CPD ¶ 116]. Where it is clear that a mistake has been made, the bid cannot be accepted, even if the bidder verifies the bid price, denies the existence of a mistake, or seeks to waive an admitted mistake, unless it is clear that the bid, both as submitted and intended, would remain low. *Trataros Constr., Inc.*, B-254600, Jan. 4, 1994, 94-1 CPD ¶ [1]; *Atlantic Serv., Inc.*, B-245763, Jan. 30, 1992, 92-1 CPD ¶ 125. Acceptance of such clearly erroneous bids would be unfair to other bidders. See 51 Comp. Gen. 498 (1972); *Atlantic Serv., Inc., supra; Panoramic Studios*, B-200664, Aug. 17, 1981, 81-2 CPD ¶ 144; FAR § 14.406-3(g)(5). Clearly erroneous bids requirements. See, e.g., *Atlantic Servs., Inc., supra; Innovative Refrigeration Concepts*, B-242515, Mar. 27, 1991, 91-1 CPD ¶ 332; *Martin Contracting*, B-241229.2, Feb. 6, 1991, 91-1 CPD ¶ 121.

In *Odyssey Int'l, Inc.*, Comp. Gen. Dec. B-296855.2, 2006 CPD ¶ 49, rejection was found improper because the low bidder had provided clear evidence of a mistake which increased its bid but kept it low.

However, rejection of mistaken low bids has been found proper in some circumstances even if the bidder verifies the bid price. See *Trataros Constr., Inc.*, Comp. Gen. Dec. B-254600, 94-1 CPD ¶ 1 (bid verified where bid price on item would not even cover the cost to produce that item); *Suffield Serv. Co.*, Comp. Gen. Dec. B-245579, 92-1 CPD ¶ 54 (bid verified where a group of percentage markups were obviously miscalculated); and *Prince Constr. Co.*, Comp. Gen. Dec. B-213496, 84-1 CPD ¶ 159 (bidder orally stated that an error had been made but refused to furnish evidence and later verified bid).

Rejection is also proper when the bidder denies the existence of a mistake. See *DGS Contract Servs., Inc.*, Comp. Gen. Dec. B-237157.2, 90-1 CPD ¶ 162 (bidder first claimed mistake based on subcontractor error and then claimed that there was no mistake); and *MTR, Inc.*, Comp. Gen. Dec. B-216685, 84-2 CPD ¶ 457, *recons. denied*, 84-2 CPD ¶ 624 (bidder refused to acknowledge mistake but contracting officer concluded, on convincing evidence, that bid was grossly low).

Rejection is proper even when the bidder seeks to waive an admitted mistake. See *Atlantic Servs. Inc.*, Comp. Gen. Dec. B-245763, 92-1 CPD ¶ 125, where the erroneous bid was rejected even though the bidder tried to "stand by" the bid and accept award. This decision was reached because award would be prejudicial to the other bidders if the bidder's mistaken bid would not have remained low after correction. See also *H. Martin Constr. Co.*, Comp. Gen. Dec. B-201352, 81-1 CPD ¶ 268, where GAO stated that the contracting officer "must reject" a clearly mistaken bid even though there had been no allegation of mistake.

The last basis for rejection would permit the contracting officer to reject the bid in those cases where award might result in an unfair contract. See *Southern Cal. Eng'g Co.*, Comp. Gen. Dec. B-255945, 94-1 CPD ¶ 271 (bid was much lower than all other bids and did not conform to specifications); and *Zeta Constr. Co.*, Comp. Gen. Dec. B-244672, 91-2 CPD ¶ 428 (bid based on major misinterpretation of the specifications).

An unstated reason for rejection of bids containing serious mistakes, even where there has been a proper verification, is to avoid the risk of a subsequent claim for reformation based on unconscionability. See, for example, *White Abstract Co.*, Comp. Gen. Dec. B-183643, 75-2 CPD ¶ 98 (would have cost $5,500 to perform item priced at $100); *Yankee Eng'g Co.*, Comp. Gen. Dec. B-180573, 74-1 CPD ¶ 333 ($106,000 mistake on $199,669 contract not discovered through verification); and 53 Comp. Gen. 187 (B-178795) (1973) (bid 74% below next low bid and only 1/12 of next low bid for first article unit).

## 3. Correction of Mistake

The most frequent request of a contractor after discovery of a mistake is that the mistake be corrected. The precise facts of the procurement determine the rules that apply to such requests. Unless the mistake is an apparent clerical error (discussed below), the power to allow a bidder to correct a mistake in its bid is vested in the agency head, FAR 14.407-3(a), and is subject to the following guidelines.

### a. Correction of Low Bid Upward

Where the low bidder seeks to correct the bid upward — but the corrected bid remains the low bid — both the existence of the mistake and the bid actually intended must be established by "clear and convincing evidence," FAR 14.407-3(a). The clear and convincing standard has been strictly adhered to in the case of correction. See 53 Comp. Gen. 232 (B-179084) (1973), stating that correction will be permitted if the bidder establishes by clear and convincing evidence:

1. That an error has occurred;

2. The manner in which the error occurred; and

3. The amount of the intended bid price.

This three-part standard has been used regularly by GAO. See, for example, *Pipeline Constr. Inc.*, Comp. Gen. Dec. B-256799, 94-2 CPD ¶ 21; *J. Schouten Constr., Inc.*, Comp. Gen. Dec. B-256710, 94-1 CPD ¶ 353; and *L.F. Leiker Constr. Co.*, Comp. Gen. Dec. B-238496, 90-1 CPD ¶ 453. FAR 14.407-3(g)(2) provides the following similar guidance:

> The request [of the contractor] must be supported by statements (sworn statements, if possible) and shall include all pertinent evidence such as the bidder's file copy of the bid, the original worksheets and other data used in preparing the bid, subcontractors' quotations, if any, published price lists, and any other evidence that establishes the existence of the error, the manner in which it occurred, and the bid actually intended.

Despite the skepticism evidenced by some contracting officers as to the accuracy of worksheets offered by bidders to prove the amount of a mistake, an agency cannot refuse a bidder an opportunity to demonstrate the amount of the intended bid by clear and convincing evidence, *Chris Berg, Inc. v. United States*, 192 Ct. Cl. 176, 426 F.2d 314 (1970); Comp. Gen. Dec. B-163284, Apr. 1, 1968, *Unpub.*

#### (1) TYPES OF EVIDENCE

Since the bidder must prove the amount of the intended bid price as well as the mistake, documentary evidence of the details of the original estimate must almost always be submitted. Such evidence is usually in the form of worksheets and other materials used during bid preparation. GAO has been quite liberal in accepting the validity of such materials. For example, a bidder was allowed to correct its bid despite erasures on the worksheets where the worksheet figures were corroborated by subcontractor bids and internal estimates for work intended to be done in-house, 51 Comp. Gen. 503 (B-174608) (1972). See also *IAP-Leopardo Constr., Inc.*, Comp. Gen. Dec. B-401923 2009 CPD ¶ 248 (worksheets showing misplaced decimals, subcontractor bids and affidavits stating authenticity of documents); *Cooper Constr., Inc.*, Comp. Gen. Dec. B-285880, 2000 CPD ¶ 153 (handwritten worksheets, although somewhat sloppy, clearly showed the mistake and the intended bid); *H.A. Sack Co.*, Comp. Gen. Dec. B-278359, 98-1 CPD ¶ 27 (computer diskette containing a spreadsheet file dated on the date of bid opening and a statement that these were the original documents used in preparing bid were sufficient evidence); *Black Diamond Energies, Inc.*, Comp. Gen. Dec. B-241370, 91-1 CPD ¶ 119 (worksheet confirmed the costs of omitted installation work and total corrected price for item (delivered and installed) was still less than government estimate and in line with other bids); *BAL/BOA Servs., Inc.*, Comp. Gen. Dec. B-233157, 89-1 CPD ¶ 138 (entry of one subcontractor quote for landscaping was erased and substituted by another lower quote when this price was omitted from final bid and it was very unlikely that this cost was included in any other cost); and *Vrooman Constructors, Inc.*, Comp. Gen. Dec. B-226965.2, 87-1 CPD ¶ 606 (numerous crossouts on the worksheet allowed because they were corrections of obvious arithmetic errors or erroneously repeated figures, and the worksheet was otherwise in good order).

When the prebid materials do not contain erasures or other evidence of modification, correction has been even more readily allowed. See *Huber, Hunt & Nichols, Inc.*, Comp. Gen. Dec. B-271112, 96-1 CPD ¶ 246 (worksheets and affidavits established clear and convincing evidence of the mistake and the intended bid); *Severino Trucking Co.*, Comp. Gen. Dec. B-259080.2, 95-1 CPD ¶ 160 (comparison between three worksheets revealed that two were calculated by adding a 25% profit/overhead factor but the third omitted this factor); *R.P. Richards Constr. Co.*, Comp. Gen. Dec. B-258923, 95-1 CPD ¶ 103 (bidder offered $48,200 instead of $148,200 because the worksheet was not made to accommodate six-digit numbers); *ACS Constr. Co.*, Comp. Gen. Dec. B-257775, 94-2 CPD ¶ 179 (worksheets and subcontractor quotes showed that bidder failed to include in final bid the price for steel hooks that were essential to contract requirements); *Southern Techs. Inc.*, Comp. Gen. Dec. B-256190, 94-1 CPD ¶ 321 (subcontractor facsimile demonstrated that bidder omitted costs for certain equipment by overlooking the relevant number on the facsimile); *Shoemaker & Alexander, Inc.*, Comp. Gen. Dec. B-241066, 91-1 CPD ¶ 41 (examination of worksheet and adding machine tape showed the bidder dropped a zero when transferring electrical work price from worksheet to final bid and bid $ 200,000 rather than $ 2,000,000); *Continental Heller Corp.*, Comp. Gen. Dec. B-230559, 88-1 CPD ¶ 571 (worksheets, project fee analysis, and adding machine tapes established transcription error of $ 450,000); *Riverport Indus., Inc.*, 64 Comp. Gen. 441 (B-216707), 85-1 CPD ¶ 364, *recons. denied*, 85-2 CPD ¶ 108 (worksheet showed that material costs had been calculated but not added to the bid price); and *Hughes & Smith, Inc.*, Comp. Gen. Dec. B-181140, 74-2 CPD ¶ 68 (presence of a mathematical error was plain on the worksheets).

In *Schoutten Constr. Co.*, Comp. Gen. Dec. B-215663, 84-2 CPD ¶ 318, a pro-tester questioned the validity of worksheets supporting the correction of a mistake placing the low bid within 1.9% of the second low bidder. In finding that the crimi-nal statutes partially protected the competitive bidding system from fraudulent evi-dence, GAO stated:

> Finally, Schoutten has, in essence, questioned the bona fides of the work-sheets and has pointed out in this regard that they are not accompanied by a sworn statement as required under FAR 14.406.3(g)(2), 48 Fed. Reg. 42181 (1983). This section of the FAR provides that correction requests "must be supported by statements (sworn statements if possible) and shall include all pertinent evidence such as . . . original worksheets." First, we point out that we have found that the penalties prescribed by 18 U.S.C. § 1001 (1982) could apply to false statements or representations by a bidder. *D.L. Draper Associates*, B-213177, Dec. 9, 1983, 83-2 CPD ¶ 662. In part because of this statutory protection, we have sanctioned the use of handwritten and computer printout worksheets which are readily susceptible to tampering. *D.L. Draper*, B-213177, *supra*. Moreover, we have explicitly accepted the agency consid-eration of handwritten worksheets which contained numerous erasures. 51 Comp. Gen. 503, 505 (1972). Schoutten's misgivings about the bona fide na-ture of the alleged mistake and the worksheets were not shared by the con-tracting officer. Nor do we find that they are supported by the record which appears to reflect only a rather elementary error in mathematics. Accordingly, we find that the protestor has failed to meet its burden of affirmatively proving its case in this respect. *Grandville Electric, Inc.*, B-213406, Feb. 22, 1984, 84-1 CPD ¶ 222.

See also *Ogden Allied E. States Maint.*, Comp. Gen. Dec. B-239550, 90-2 CPD ¶ 166, where the bidder did not use affidavits to prove mistake. GAO accepted this partially because the criminal code provided statutory protection against false state-ments or representations made by a bidder. But see *American Block Co.*, Comp. Gen. Dec. B-235053, 89-2 CPD ¶ 90, where correction was denied because the credibility of the bidder's evidence was in doubt. In that case, the bidder claimed the subcontractor gave a quote for the wrong item, the subcontractor claimed the bid-der solicited quotes for the wrong item, and there were unexplained discrepancies between the original and corrected worksheets.

Even if the credibility of the evidence submitted is not directly questioned, if the documents are found insufficient, correction will not be permitted. See *Big-horn Lumber Co.*, Comp. Gen. Dec. B-299906, 2007 CPD ¶ 173 (clear evidence of mistake but no clear evidence of intended bid); *Miramar Constr., Inc.*, Comp. Gen. Dec. B-298609, 2006 CPD ¶ 169 (explanation that person compiling bid "overrode" electronic spreadsheet illogical based on documents submitted); *Si-*

*Nor, Inc.*, Comp. Gen. Dec. B-288990, 2001 CPD ¶ 204 (worksheets undated and contained ambiguities); *CRK-JVC/Shockley*, Comp. Gen. Dec. B-265937, 96-1 CPD ¶ 85 (varying explanations for the mistake but two different base bid worksheets did not reflect the actual base bid); *Special Sys. Servs., Inc.*, Comp. Gen. Dec. B-259865.2, 95-1 CPD ¶ 241 (no explanation of how bid was prepared or how mistake occurred and the worksheets were not "in good order"); *U.S. Gen., Inc.*, Comp. Gen. Dec. B-245452, 92-1 CPD ¶ 8 (only evidence provided was an undated worksheet containing a series of previously unsubmitted line item prices and no backup documents to support the source of the numbers); *Imprints From the Past*, Comp. Gen. Dec. B-240447, 90-2 CPD ¶ 413 (uncertainty between two conflicting groups of worksheets); *Gunco, Inc.*, Comp. Gen. Dec. B-238910, 90-2 CPD ¶ 46 ("unexplained inconsistencies" between two worksheets that confirmed the bid price and a third worksheet that seemed to establish a $100,000 larger bid under the vague heading "Additional Costs"); and *Edmonds Elec. Co.*, Comp. Gen. Dec. B-214063, 84-1 CPD ¶ 615 ("worksheet" was prepared after bid opening to show the mistake that had been made).

GAO has treated computer evidence in the same manner as worksheets. In *Applied Constr. Tech. Inc.*, Comp. Gen. Dec. B-258426, 95-1 CPD ¶ 22, correction was allowed when the mistake was due to a computer spreadsheet program that had not been updated to account for an IFB amendment. See *Construction Tech. Group, Inc.*, Comp. Gen. Dec. B-283857, 2000 CPD ¶ 15 (mistake in formula in spreadsheet but mistake clear); *PLC Constructors Canada, Inc.*, Comp. Gen. Dec. B-274697, 96-2 CPD ¶ 239 (computer spreadsheet showed how bidder made a mistake when it attempted to substitute one subcontractor's quote for its own estimate); *Interstate Constr., Inc.*, Comp. Gen. Dec. B-248355, 92-2 CPD ¶ 86 (computer spreadsheet showed bid of $800 for electrical work instead of an intended $600,000); and *Price/CIRI Constr.*, Comp. Gen. Dec. B-230603, 88-1 CPD ¶ 500 (computer spreadsheet, including handwritten notations, demonstrated how bidder broke down the cost for 13 items and then failed to submit a price for one of them). However, when computer spreadsheets become very complicated, they can raise questions as to the sufficiency of the evidence to prove a mistake. See *Metric Constructors, Inc.*, Comp. Gen. Dec. B-285854, 2000 CPD ¶ 195, where the agency properly rejected correction because the spreadsheets made it impossible to determine exactly how an omitted subcontract price would have been added to the bid. Compare *D.L. Draper Assocs.*, Comp. Gen. Dec. B-213177, 83-2 CPD ¶ 662, following the same logic as in *Schoutten*, finding that the criminal statutes were applicable to computer-generated information and adequately protected the government from deception.

The most common failure in meeting the clear and convincing evidence standard occurs in proving the intended amount of the bid. For example, a bidder was not allowed to correct a bid where it could not substantiate the additional overhead and profit claimed as a result of having omitted several subcontract prices from the bid price, Comp. Gen. Dec. B-176357, Aug. 29, 1972, *Unpub.* The bidder omitted

$488,065 in subcontract items from the bid and substantiated that figure. It then added $20,000 for additional overhead and $30,000 for additional profit on the omitted figures. The bidder, however, did not normally use a fixed percentage rate in bidding overhead and profit, but rather derived those figures "after considering all of the other variable factors." Accordingly, the figures for overhead and profit were held to be arbitrary and not substantiated by the bidder's worksheets or records. A bid that indicated the bidder mistakenly bid on a quantity 24 times greater than that called for in the IFB could not be corrected by taking 1/24 of it because the bidder might well have included price reductions in its bid for the larger quantities, 49 Comp. Gen. 48 (B-165852) (1969). In *Three O Constr., S.E.*, Comp. Gen. Dec. B-255749, 94-1 CPD ¶ 216, correction was denied because the bidder gave inconsistent explanations of its intended bid price without supplying conclusive evidence to show which explanation was accurate. First, the bidder claimed a mistaken portion of the bid had to be increased by 40% for payroll tax; then the bidder claimed that the payroll tax had been accounted for, but that the mistaken portion needed to be marked up by 15% for workers' compensation. See also *4-S Constr., Inc.*, Comp. Gen. Dec. B-248090, 92-1 CPD ¶ 523 (worksheet indicates the price for mechanical work was omitted but presence of subcontractor quote for that item is not enough to establish intended bid because the bidder used different subcontractors for the job and might have done so again); and *L.F. Leiker Constr. Co.*, Comp. Gen. Dec. B-238496, 90-1 CPD ¶ 453 (blank line on worksheet for concrete work is evidence of mistake, but bidder's use of one cost analysis for concrete work at one site does not mean that the bidder would use same analysis to compute omitted price).

If there is a factor that prevents the intended bid from being established conclusively, but the bid would remain low even if that factor were included, the bid can be corrected. Where a bidder requests only the addition of direct costs and does not request the addition of overhead, profit, or other markups the bid may be so corrected, provided that the bid would have been low even if overhead, profit and other markups had been included, *IAP-Leopardo Constr., Inc.*, Comp. Gen. Dec. B-401923 2009 CPD ¶ 248 (subcontract amounts); 49 Comp. Gen. 480 (B-167068) (1970) (material cost); 51 Comp. Gen. 503 (B-174608) (1972) (subcontract addition). If the addition of overhead or profit might make the bid as corrected no longer low, then such correction (without overhead and profit) will not be allowed, *Camp Lewis Tent & Awning Co.*, Comp. Gen. Dec. B-182047, 74-2 CPD ¶ 174. In *Western Alaska Contractors*, Comp. Gen. Dec. B-220067, 86-1 CPD ¶ 66, correction was allowed to include a missing subcontractor quote because work papers showed that it was on the spreadsheet but not carried over to the final bid. However, markup on this omitted quote was not allowed because a formula for calculating this percentage was not on the worksheet and a pattern for calculating this percentage could not be derived from examining other subcontractor quotes. See also *Severino Trucking Co.*, Comp. Gen. Dec. B-259080.2, 95-1 CPD ¶ 160 (correction allowed where bidder rounded up final number in original bid, but did not attempt to do so in corrected bid when even rounded bid remained low); and *Avanti Constr. Corp.*, Comp. Gen. Dec. B-229839, 88-1 CPD ¶ 262 (correction allowed for error in transcription between worksheets, but overhead and profits were not allowed to be added because the bidder originally used an estimate rather than the final bid to calculate these numbers).

The clear and convincing test does not require absolute precision in ascertaining the amount the bidder could have bid. In *Chris Berg, Inc. v. United States*, 192 Ct. Cl. 176, 426 F.2d 314 (1970), the court stated that an "uncertainty within a relatively narrow range is not inconsistent with 'clear and convincing evidence' of what the bid would have been." In that case, the low bidder sought correction, but the government would not agree because the "rounding off" of numbers in the worksheets made it impossible to precisely ascertain the intended bid. The Court of Claims stated that the bidder had successfully established the intended bid price and that the "rounding off" was de minimis. GAO expanded this reasoning in *P.K. Painting Co.*, Comp. Gen. Dec. B-247357, 92-1 CPD ¶ 424, where the bidder was required to round down its corrected bid because it had done so with all numbers before correction, stating, "In [these] circumstances, correction is limited to increasing the contracting price only to the bottom end of the range of uncertainty." See *Roy Anderson Corp.*, Comp. Gen. Dec. B-292555, 2003 CPD ¶ 179 ("narrow" range of uncertainty ($86,000 in price of $39,498,340) not of concern); *Hampton Rds. Mech. Contractors, Inc.*, Comp. Gen. Dec. B-257908, 94-2 CPD ¶ 201 (range of $35 in $350,000 procurement is inconsequential); *Precon Constr. Co.*, Comp. Gen. Dec. B-255294.1, 94-1 CPD ¶ 239 (despite several discrepancies between the worksheet and bid price and despite an admitted mistake that bidder does not attempt to correct, correction was allowed because highest in range is still $80,000 low in $1 million procurement); and *Red Samm Constr., Inc.*, Comp. Gen. Dec. B-250891.2, 93-1 CPD ¶ 178 (rounding up and down in bid calculation prevented determination of exact number of intended bid, but correction was allowed when bid would remain low even if always rounded up). See also *Bromley Contracting Co. v. United States*, 219 Ct. Cl. 517, 596 F.2d 488 (1979), where a mistake of failing to add overhead and profit to a bid was remedied by assuming that these factors would have been computed at the same rates used on previous bids.

GAO has held that when an agency allows correction of bid based on evidence that is not totally clear and convincing, it will not override the decision unless it is unreasonable, *Gulf-Atlantic Constructors, Inc.*, Comp. Gen. Dec. B-289032, 2002 CPD ¶ 2. There, the decision was found reasonable even though there were "inconsistencies and gaps" in the evidence presented.

### (2) WHEN CORRECTED BID COMES VERY CLOSE TO NEXT BID

Sometimes the corrected bid price is extremely close to the next low bid. In this situation, there is a balancing required between the clarity of the evidence and the closeness of the bids. The closer the correction brings the bid to the next low bid, the greater the need for clear evidence, and the stricter the examination of that evidence, *Vrooman Constructors, Inc.*, Comp. Gen. Dec. B-226965.2, 87-1 CPD ¶ 606. This policy serves as a safeguard against bidders knowingly bidding low, declaring mistake, and fraudulently increasing their bid to an amount just under the second low bid by showing how the "error" was made, *R.H. Whelan Co.*, Comp. Gen. Dec. B-203248, 81-2 CPD ¶ 123. There is no specific percentage or dollar amount at which bids automatically become too close to be corrected, *International Serv. Corp.*, Comp. Gen. Dec. B-246159, 92-1 CPD ¶ 191.

If the evidence presented is sufficient, correction will be allowed even to the smallest of margins. In *J. Schouten Constr., Inc.*, Comp. Gen. Dec. B-256710, 94-1 CPD ¶ 353, correction was permitted to bring the bid within $ 700 of the next low bid in a $ 338,000 procurement because there was an obvious addition error on a worksheet, there was an affidavit from the worksheet compiler, and the worksheet was provided within 24 hours of the opening of bids. See also *Prudent Techs., Inc.*, Comp. Gen. Dec. B-401736.3, 2009 CPD ¶ 254 (correction allowed within 1% when arithmetic mistakes were clear on face of bid); *Odyssey Int'l, Inc.*, Comp. Gen. Dec. B-296855.2, 2006 CPD ¶ 49 (correction allowed within $2,584 of second low bid of $7,319,800 when spreadsheets clearly showed the mistake); *B&M Cillessen Constr. Co.*, Comp. Gen. Dec. B-287449.2, 2001 CPD ¶ 100 (correction allowed within $12,707 of second low bid of $4,855,000 when worksheets showed omission of state tax); *Pacific Components, Inc.*, Comp. Gen. Dec. B-252585, 93-1 CPD ¶ 478 (correction allowed to within 1% when mistake was obvious from review of erroneous quote from only subcontractor); *International Serv. Corp.*, Comp. Gen. Dec. B-246159, 92-1 CPD ¶ 191 (correction allowed to within 0.0235% when the worksheets showed that the bidder neglected to multiply unit price by quantity); *Vrooman Constructors, Inc.*, Comp. Gen. Dec. B-226965.2, 87-1 CPD ¶ 606 (correction allowed to 0.6% where 15 of 16 divisions were carried from a worksheet to the final bid, but one was not); and *Guardian Constr.*, Comp. Gen. Dec. B-220982, 86-1 CPD ¶ 224 (correction permitted to bring bid within 1% where misplaced decimal is obvious from adding machine tape); and *George C. Martin, Inc.*, Comp. Gen. Dec. B-187638, 77-1 CPD ¶ 39 (permitting correction of a bid to within $68,000 of the next lower bid in a $4.8 million procurement because the contractor's entire bid file of estimate sheets, subcontractor quotes, and personal testimony established the intended bid).

Even though correction would place the bid very close to the next bid, correction will almost always be permitted if the mistake is apparent on the face of the bid. See *Ogden Allied E. States Maint.*, Comp. Gen. Dec. B-239550, 90-2 CPD ¶ 166, where correction was allowed to within 1% where transcription error was apparent on the face of the bid. But see 48 Comp. Gen. 748 (B-166748) (1969), denying relief where correction would be within $613 in a $272,000 procurement. GAO stated at 750:

> The correction of mistakes in bid has always been a vexing problem. It has been argued that bid correction after bid opening and disclosure of prices quoted com-

promises the integrity of the competitive bidding system, and, to some extent at least, this is true. For this reason, it has been advocated that the Government should adopt a policy which would permit contractors to withdraw, but not to correct, erroneous bids. We do not agree completely with this position since we believe there are cases in which bid correction should be permitted. We do agree that, regardless of the good faith of the party or parties involved, correction should be denied in any case in which there exists any reasonable basis for argument that public confidence in the integrity of the competitive bidding system would be adversely affected thereby. The present case, it seems to us, falls in this category.

When correction would bring the bid close to the next low bid and the evidence of the mistake and the intended bid is not clear, correction will be denied. In *RJS Constructors*, Comp. Gen. Dec. B-257457, 94-2 CPD ¶ 130, correction was denied to within 0.13% of the next low bid even though the worksheet showed that if it had been added correctly the bid total should have been $375,960 rather than $276,379. Correction was denied because the credibility of the worksheet was in question, it did not contain entries for overhead and profit, and there were many inconsistencies between subcontractor quotes and the bid submitted. See also *Metric Constr. Co.*, Comp. Gen. Dec. B-259573, 95-1 CPD ¶ 197 (numerous discrepancies in addition and percentage calculation prevent correction to within 0.28%); *Northwest Bldrs.*, 67 Comp. Gen. 278 (B-228555), 88-1 CPD ¶ 200 (correction to within 1% not allowed because changes were undocumented and unexplained); and *Conner Bros. Constr. Co.*, Comp. Gen. Dec. B-228232.2, 88-1 CPD ¶ 103 (no correction to within 1% where worksheets and affidavits do not explain why certain costs were added and deducted from one subcontractor total, but not from two others). Similarly, correction was denied when the evidence was not clear in *Sam Gonzales, Inc.*, Comp. Gen. Dec. B-216728, 85-1 CPD ¶ 125 (amount of overhead not clear); and *D.L. Draper Assocs.*, Comp. Gen. Dec. B-213177, 83-2 CPD ¶ 662 (computer printout and unsworn statement not sufficiently strong evidence).

### b.  Displacement of Otherwise Low Bid

A stricter standard than the clear and convincing evidence standard applies if correction would reduce the bid price and displace the otherwise low bid. FAR 14.407-3(a) provides that mistakes cannot be corrected in such circumstances unless both the mistake and the bid actually intended are ascertainable substantially from the invitation and the bid itself. This requirement makes it very difficult to displace a low bidder through bid correction. See *Armstrong & Armstrong, Inc. v. United States*, 356 F. Supp. 514 (E.D. Wash. 1973), aff'd, 514 F.2d 402 (9th Cir. 1975), where a discrepancy between the sum of unit prices and the total bid price was found to be insufficient evidence to support a downward correction of the final price displacing the low bidder.

For cases were GAO denied correction, see *Nabholz Bldg. & Mgmt. Corp.*, Comp. Gen. Dec. B-274930, 96-2 CPD ¶ 196 (bidder claimed an ambiguity that let it to mistakenly include its bond costs under both a base bid line item and a bond costs line item); *Mallory Elec. Co.*, Comp. Gen. Dec. B-244699, 91-2 CPD ¶ 394 (clerical error apparent on the face of the bid was subject to two interpretations as to the intended bid, only one of which made the bid low); *Bullrun Mountain Honey Co.*, Comp. Gen. Dec. B-243325, 91-1 CPD ¶ 344 (bidder claimed a waiver of a 10% small business preference was an obvious mistake on the face of the bid); *R.C. Constr. Co.*, Comp. Gen. Dec. B-241176.2, 91-1 CPD ¶ 118 (bidder obviously overbid for an item, but it could not be determined whether the unit should be one square foot or 100 square feet); *Christos Painting & Contracting Corp.*, Comp. Gen. Dec. B-225647, 87-1 CPD ¶ 361 (bidder claimed line item entered in units of 100 as "19(19)" should be read as zero instead of $1,900); *Crystal Contracting Corp.*, Comp. Gen. Dec. B-223531, 86-2 CPD ¶ 433 (bid not corrected because "error" occurred in a schedule of deductions not appearing on the bid itself); and *Mayrant Constructors, Inc.*, Comp. Gen. Dec. B-215274, 84-1 CPD ¶ 617 (bidder claimed it was obvious that an entry of "449,668" was intended to be 49,668). GAO has used the same reasoning to refuse correction to break a tie bid, *W.G. James, Inc.*, 64 Comp. Gen. 561 (B-218230), 85-1 CPD ¶ 623.

GAO has permitted the use of rationales based upon past experience and other information in applying this high evidentiary standard. For example, in *Frontier Contracting Co.*, Comp. Gen. Dec. B-214260.2, 84-2 CPD ¶ 40, the bidder submitted an amendment to a bid as follows:

| **Base Bid** | | | |
|---|---|---|---|
| Item 1 | Add | Deduct | $133,752 |
| Item 2 | Add | Deduct | $60,000 |
| **Total Base Bid** | Add | Deduct | $193,752 |
| **Additive** | | | |
| Item 3 | Add | Deduct | $84,000 |
| **Total** | Add | Deduct | $277,752 |

GAO permitted the deduction of the figures, reasoning that the contracting officer had correctly concluded, based on the other bids and past experience with this contractor, that the only logical interpretation was that the figures were to be deducted rather than added. In *Allied Signal Avionics Inc.*, Comp. Gen. Dec. B-258457, 95-1 CPD ¶ 192, GAO permitted a line item for a two-year warranty to be changed from $50,268 to "no charge." This was allowed because the bidder had inserted "no charge" in four of five line items for the same warranty, had inserted "no charge" in five of five line items for the same warranty on an alternate bid, and the amount bid for that line item was the same as an item directly above on the bid sheet. See also *Concorde Battery Corp.*, 68 Comp. Gen. 523 (B-235119), 89-2 CPD ¶ 17 (correction allowed where bidder put total for line items 1 through 3 in line item 4 when line item 4 should have been an "inconsequential expense," and five out of seven bidders made this mistake); *George E. Failing Co.*, Comp. Gen

Dec. B-233207, 89-1 CPD ¶ 203 (bidder's entire bid package used to determine that bidder bid twice for three line items); and *Technical Support Servs., Inc.*, Comp. Gen. Dec. B-232488, 88-2 CPD ¶ 464 (correction allowed where bidder included a line item that was not supposed to be added to the total when five other bidders made this same error). But see *Electronic Space Sys. Corp.*, Comp. Gen. Dec. B-236006, 89-2 CPD ¶ 381, where correction was denied when the bidder offered two different prices on a basic and optional requirements schedule for the same item. Through prior dealings with contracts of this nature, the contracting officer determined that the higher price for the basic schedule was an often used bidding strategy.

In the case of errors in transmission by the telegraph company, GAO has relaxed the rule that the bid intended must be ascertainable substantially from the IFB and bid (where low bidders are displaced), 41 Comp. Gen. 165 (B-146295) (1960). However, the proof of the intended bid must come from the telegraph company's (not the bidder's) records, Comp. Gen. Dec. B-162627, Nov. 1, 1967, *Unpub.*; Comp. Gen. Dec. B-162740, Jan. 17, 1968, *Unpub.*

The most difficult application of this rule is in cases of a mistake in the extension of unit prices or the addition of subtotals. In most of these cases, it is not clear from the face of the bid whether the mistake is in the total price or in the subtotal or unit price. In *OTKM Constr., Inc.*, 64 Comp. Gen. 830 (B-219619), 85-2 CPD ¶ 273, *recons. denied*, 65 Comp. Gen. 202, 86-1 CPD ¶ 53, GAO permitted correction based on the internal consistency of the elements of the bid price, but stated the following general principles at 833-34:

> We have previously considered whether a bid may be corrected so as to displace an otherwise low bidder where there is a discrepancy between the correct mathematical total of lump sum and extended price items and the stated total of such items. In *DeRalco, Inc.*, B-205120, May 6, 1982, 82-1 CPD ¶ 430, we sustained a protest against the agency's determination to correct such a discrepancy as an apparent clerical error where neither the nature of the alleged mistake nor the bid actually intended could be determined without benefit of advice from the bidder. We noted that there was no one obvious or apparent explanation for the discrepancy. The difference did not suggest where the mistake might have been made and the stated total was not so grossly out of line with the other bid or with the government's estimate as to be patently erroneous. We found that the discrepancy could reasonably be attributed either to a mistake in totaling the items or to an incorrectly stated item.

See *Patterson Pump Co.*, Comp. Gen. Dec. B-200165, 80-2 CPD ¶ 453, permitting correction in such circumstances. Compare *Wilkinson & Jenkins Constr. Co.*, Comp. Gen. Dec. B-182687, 75-1 CPD ¶ 77, where the protesting bidder inadvertently entered a bid on the original bidding schedule rather than the amended bidding schedule, which had reduced the estimated quantity for one item. The bidder entered a unit price for the item and an extended price based on the larger estimated quantity. The IFB contained a statement that when there was a conflict between the unit price and the extension, the unit price would be considered to be the bid. Nevertheless, GAO did not permit correction of the extended price to reflect the smaller quantity of work because to do so would displace the low bidder, reasoning that the intended bid was not ascertainable from the bid documents since it was not clear that the bidder would not have bid a higher unit price for the lower quantity. See also *Argee Corp.*, 67 Comp. Gen. 421 (B-230165.3), 88-1 CPD ¶ 482, where correction was not allowed when a discrepancy existed between the unit prices and the extended prices because neither the unit prices nor the extended total was out of line with the other bids or the government estimate and there was no indication as to where the mistake occurred. Accord *Roy McGinnis & Co.*, Comp. Gen. Dec. B-239710, 90-2 CPD ¶ 251; and *Virginia Beach Air Conditioning Corp.*, 69 Comp. Gen. 132 (B-237172), 90-1 CPD ¶ 78. But see *J&J Maint., Inc.*, Comp. Gen. Dec. B-251355, 93-1 CPD ¶ 187, where correction of a unit price to reflect an extended price was allowed because the unit price total was clearly out of line with the government estimate and all other bids and the extended price was not. Further, dropping a zero from the unit price and multiplying by the stipulated 12-month period would result in the extended price See also *Marann Inventories, Inc.*, Comp. Gen. Dec. B-237467, 90-1 CPD ¶ 89, where correction was allowed where the uncorrected unit price, if extended, would result in a figure of $1.6 million above the next highest bid.

### c.  Correction of Nonresponsive Bids

FAR 14.407-3 precludes the use of mistake correction techniques to make nonresponsive bids responsive. However, GAO has permitted limited correction of nonresponsive bids if the same standards used to correct bids which displace low bids are satisfied, *United Food Servs.*, 65 Comp. Gen. 167 (B-218228.3), 85-2 CPD ¶ 727; and *Fujitsu Imaging Sys. of Am., Inc.*, Comp. Gen. Dec. B-241733.2, 91-1 CPD ¶ 243.

Most cases involving successful correction of nonresponsive bids have involved invitations containing a number of bid items where bidders have incorrectly entered or omitted prices for one or more of the items. In *Slater Elec. Co.*, Comp. Gen. Dec. B-183654, 75-2 CPD ¶ 126, GAO dealt with this kind of situation, stating:

> Basically, even though a bidder fails to submit a price for an item in a bid, that omission can be corrected if the bid, as submitted, indicates not only the probability of error but also the exact nature of the error and the amount intended. B-151332, June 27, 1963. The rationale for this exception is that where the consistency of the pricing pattern in the bidding documents establishes both the existence of the error and the bid actually intended, to hold that the bid is nonresponsive would be to convert what appears to be an obvious clerical error of omission to a matter of nonresponsiveness. B-157429, August 19, 1965.

See also *MKB Constructors, (J.V.)*, Comp. Gen. Dec. B-250413, 93-1 CPD ¶ 50; *Werres Corp.*, Comp. Gen. Dec. B-211870, 83-2 CPD ¶ 243; and *Lyon Shipyard, Inc.*, Comp. Gen. Dec. B-208978, 82-2 CPD ¶ 287, where a bid was considered to be responsive and the omitted item treated as a mistake when it was shown that the cost of the omitted bid item had been included in the contractor's total bid price. Compare *Automated Marketing Sys., Inc.*, Comp. Gen. Dec. B-230014, 88-1 CPD ¶ 289, denying a protest that contended that the contracting officer should have permitted correction when the protester included no bid prices in its bid.

In *Wellco Enters., Inc.*, Comp. Gen. Dec. B-237512, 90-1 CPD ¶ 196, the low bidder neglected to include option prices for two of its block bidding quantities. Correction was permitted because the bid included consistent percentage increases from base to option prices. Correction was allowed in *Burnside-Ott Aviation Training Ctr., Inc.*, Comp. Gen. Dec. B-228937, 87-2 CPD ¶ 461, even though the low bidder had not bid the same price for the omitted device everywhere on the bid. This was allowed because the bidder had bid "NC" (no charge) for all other subitems under which this device was grouped and for all work to be done in the transitional period when this work was to be done. Correction was also permitted on similar facts in *Slater Elec. Co.*, Comp. Gen. Dec. B-183654, 75-2 CPD ¶ 126, even though the bidder had not bid exactly the same price for the item everywhere in the bid. The price of the item wherever found in the bid had only varied by $.02, and GAO reasoned this was a de minimis variation. This case may be an unwarranted extension of the exception permitting correction of nonresponsive bids. As long as the exception is limited to situations where the mistake and the bid intended are plain on the face of the bid, the opportunities for abuse are small. Once the exception is enlarged to include situations where the intended bid is plainly within a de minimis range, abuses could increase. Bidders would be given the opportunity to press for correction of the bid if award would be advantageous or plead nonresponsiveness if they did not want the award.

### d.  Clerical Errors

Clerical errors not apparent on the face of the bid are correctable to the same extent as other errors as examined in this section. However, for many years, the regulations have treated apparent clerical errors as a separate class of mistake that can be corrected with less formal procedures than other types of mistakes. Apparent clerical errors are the only type of mistake that the contracting officer can correct without deferring to the agency head or any other higher officer. FAR 14.407-2 provides the following guidance:

(a) Any clerical mistake, apparent on its face in the bid, may be corrected by the contracting officer before award. The contracting officer first shall obtain from the bidder a verification of the bid intended. Examples of apparent mistakes are —

(1) Obvious misplacement of a decimal point;

(2) Obviously incorrect discounts (for example, 1 percent 10 days, 2 percent 20 days, 5 percent 30 days);

(3) Obvious reversal of the price f.o.b. destination and price f.o.b. origin; and

(4) Obvious mistake in designation of unit.

The difficulty with this guidance is that what is an obvious error to some may not be obvious to everyone. *McCarty Corp. v. United States*, 204 Ct. Cl. 768, 499 F.2d 633 (1974), illustrates the problem. The IFB called for itemized bids on three separate items of work and for a total bid. Bidders were instructed that they must bid on all three items. McCarty's president instructed his subordinate to bid $140,000 for item 1, $434,000 for item 2, $100,000 for item 3, and $674,000 for the total bid. However, the subordinate transposed two numbers on item 2 recording $443,000 rather than $434,000. All other figures, including the total, were recorded as instructed. Morris, another bidder, included $155,000 for item 1, $389,000 for item 2, $137,000 for item 3, and $690,000 for the total bid. The actual total of the bid prices for items 1, 2, and 3 was $681,000 rather than the $690,000 listed. In reviewing the bids, the government officials discovered the discrepancies in the bid totals and, without verifying the intended bid, treated these as apparent clerical errors, correcting the totals to reflect the sum of the individual items. This made the other bid total $681,000 and McCarty's bid $683,000. McCarty requested permission to correct its bid to show $434,000 as the amount quoted for item 2 and to leave the total at $674,000. This was denied, and the contract was awarded to Morris. McCarty protested to GAO and sought damages in the Court of Claims. The Court of Claims held that it was wrong to treat the mistakes in the McCarty and Morris bids as clerical mistakes apparent on the face of the bid. Instead, the mistakes involved a difference between the arithmetical sum of the amounts quoted on the three items comprising the bid and the amount listed as the total bid. It was impossible to tell from the face of the bid whether the bidder had made a mistake in entering one of the three item prices or in calculating the total. Correction of the Morris bid was not appropriate since the correction would have resulted in displacing the low bidder, and the "existence of the mistake and the bid actually intended" were not "ascertainable substantially from the invitation and the bid itself." On the other hand, the McCarty bid could have been corrected since the correction would not change its total price nor result in the displacement of the low bidder since the other bid would not be low without correction. See also *Armstrong & Armstrong, Inc. v. United States*, 356 F. Supp. 514 (E.D. Wash. 1973), *aff'd*, 514 F.2d 402 (9th Cir. 1975), reaching a similar result.

Even though the Court of Claims in the McCarty case stated that the mistake in that case was not an "apparent clerical error," GAO has continued to so label similar errors. See, for example, *Ace-Federal Reporters, Inc.*, 54 Comp. Gen. 340 (B-181451), 74-2 CPD ¶ 239, where one item of the bid was supposed to equal the difference between two other items but did not. The procuring agency and GAO treated this as an apparent clerical error and stated as a proposition that when one item is a function of arithmetic between two other items, the initial entries will be considered correct and the error will be in the arithmetic. This decision is inconsistent with both the letter and the spirit of the *McCarty* case. But see *North Landing Line Constr. Co.*, Comp. Gen. Dec. B-239662, 90-2 CPD ¶ 60, where correction in this situation was allowed to conform to the total price of two items. The intended bid for the mistaken item was ascertained by subtracting the price of the other item from the total price bid.

In *DeRalco, Inc.*, Comp. Gen. Dec. B-205120, 82-1 CPD ¶ 430, GAO sustained a protest against correction by a contracting officer and provided the following guidance:

> Prior decisions of our Office have stressed that, before the authority to correct a mistake under DAR § 2-406.2 may be invoked, the contracting officer must be able to ascertain the intended bid without the benefit of advice from the bidder. *See, e.g.,* 46 Comp. Gen. 77, 82 (1966) (only logical conclusion was that bidder had stated prices in reverse); 45 Comp. Gen. 682 (1966) (written words indicating a price 1,000 times the cost reflected in other bids and in prior contracts were patently in error; bid could be corrected based upon bidder's written figures); *Engle Acoustic & Tile, Inc.*, B-190467, January 27, 1978, 78-1 CPD 72 (obvious misplaced decimal point); *Edward E. Davis, Contracting, Inc.*, B-187132, November 17, 1976, 76-2 CPD 429 (obvious error in designation of unit). By contrast, we have held that, where the intended bid could not be determined from the bid alone, a mistake was not correctable as a clerical error under DAR § 2-406.2. *See, e.g., Western Equipment of Oregon*, B-204125, December 8, 1981, 81-2 CPD 447 (intended bid could not be determined from the bid alone where neither the unit price nor the extended price was grossly out of line; *Sundance Construction, Inc.*, B-182485, February 28, 1975, 75-1 CPD 123 (intended bid could not be determined by multiplying the quoted unit prices by the correct unit).

A good example of a true apparent clerical error is found in 52 Comp. Gen. 604 (B-177368) (1973), where the IFB required bidders to enter prices for an initial quantity of oscilloscopes and four follow-on order quantities, and bidders were required to enter prices for each quantity. The low bidder entered one price for the initial quantity and three of the four follow-on order quantities. However, the bidder failed to enter a price for follow-on order No. 3. Since the bidder had followed a consistent price pattern, bidding the same price for smaller as well as larger numbers of oscilloscopes, it was held that the mistake could be treated as an apparent clerical error and corrected. See *Action Serv. Corp.*, Comp. Gen. Dec. B-254861, 94-1 CPD ¶ 33, where an entry of "$ 5,0005" was allowed to be corrected to "$5,005" when $5,005 multiplied by 12 months equaled the submitted extended total; the extended total of $60,060, when added with the other extended totals, equaled the total bid; and $5,005 was in line with other bids for this item and $50,005 was not. See also *Cashman Dredging & Marine Contracting Co.*, Comp. Gen. Dec. B-401547, 2009 CPD ¶ 179 (correction of unit price of $425,000 to match extended price of $1,425,000 when the fact that the extended price was added to the total price demonstrated a clerical error); *SDV Constr. Group, LLC*, Comp. Gen. Dec. B-400703, 2009 CPD ¶ 11 (award at base price minus amount entered for deductive item or work proper even though IFB required deductive items to be bid at net amount); *Mid Eastern Bldrs., Inc.*, Comp. Gen. Dec. B-290717, 2002 CPD ¶ 164 (disregarding of price of $2,178,689 when other document showed that the 2 should be 7 and all other bids in range of $7 to $10 million); *Northwest Piping, Inc.*, Comp. Gen. Dec. B-233796, 89-1 CPD ¶ 333 (correction of discrepancy between unit and extended prices is allowed where only the unit price was logical in light of the government estimate and the other bids); *Technical Support Servs., Inc.* (correction allowed where bidder erroneously added $190,000 to bid for repair parts, and four other bidders made same mistake); *Military Waste Mgmt., Inc.*, Comp. Gen. Dec. B-228862, 87-2 CPD ¶ 424 (correction permitted where bidder inserted its unit price on a per-housing-unit basis instead of the proper per-month basis); and *S.C. Jones Servs., Inc.*, Comp. Gen. Dec. B-226972, 87-1 CPD ¶ 583 (bidder failed to add a certain portion of the work into the final bid).

The Preparation of Bids solicitation clause in FAR 52.214-12 contains the following curious statement in ¶ (c):

> In case of discrepancy between a unit price and an extended price, the unit price will be presumed to be correct, subject, however, to correction to the same extent and in the same manner as any other mistake.

No protest has been found where a contracting officer relied on this statement in determining that a clerical error should be corrected. However, this provision would not appear to give any stronger weight to the unit prices than would be obtained by a thorough analysis of the bid documents.

## 4. Award After Unsuccessful Request for Correction

One of the parties may desire award at the original bid price after a mistake has been alleged or suspected. The government may want to take advantage of the low bid, or the bidder may want to take the risk of performing the work at the original bid price.

### a. Award Required

The FAR is not clear on whether award is required on the basis of the bids as submitted when evidence does not establish that a mistake has been made. FAR 14.407-3(d) states that the agency head *"may* make a determination that the bid be neither withdrawn nor corrected" when the evidence does not establish the existence of a mistake or an intended bid. On the other hand, FAR 14.407-3(g)(2) states that the contracting officer *"shall* consider the bid as originally submitted" if the bidder verifies that there is no mistake. Similarly, FAR 14.407-3(g)(5) states that the "contracting officer *shall* consider the bid as submitted" if the bidder fails or refuses to submit evidence of the mistake. Gross errors are excepted from this requirement. While it is common practice to award the contract on the original bid after the bidder has verified the bid, it is much less common for the contracting officer to award the contract if the contractor requests withdrawal of the bid. Award in such cases conflicts with the liberal withdrawal policy of GAO. GAO has stated, however, that when the low responsible bidder submitting a responsive bid alleges error and seeks to withdraw its bid but is unable to make at least a prima facie showing of the existence of error, the firm bid rule prohibits the bidder from revoking the original bid, *Texas Turbo Jet, Inc.*, Comp. Gen. Dec. B-195303, 79-2 CPD ¶ 117. See also *Duro Paper Bag Mfg. Co.*, 65 Comp. Gen. 186 (B-217227), 86-1 CPD ¶ 6.

## b.  *Award Permitted*

In some cases, bidders desire to obtain the award even though a mistake has been established. The first section discusses the situation where the bidder seeks award of the contract at the original bid price if correction of an alleged mistake is denied. The second section discusses those cases where the bidder seeks award at the original bid price but reserves the right to assert a claim for reformation of the contract after award.

### (1) WAIVER

If a bidder seeks correction but is unable to prove the intended bid, it is ordinarily not permitted to then waive the mistake and be awarded the contract at the actual bid price. The rationale for this policy is that it would give such a bidder a competitive advantage if it could decide whether to accept the award after opening had exposed the other bids, 37 Comp. Gen. 579 (B-135272) (1958); 52 Comp. Gen. 706 (B-177482) (1973). Nevertheless, limited exceptions to the rule have developed. In early decisions, GAO ruled that if the bidder agreed to accept the award at the bid price notwithstanding that a mistake was established by clear and convincing evidence, the contract could be awarded at the bid price provided that the bid would remain low even if the correction were allowed, Comp. Gen. Dec. B-168673, Apr. 7, 1970, *Unpub.* However, the bidder had to request award at its original bid price if correction was not granted and the bid had to be clearly low before and after correction, 52 Comp. Gen. 706 (B-177482) (1973); *Teledyne McCormick Selph*, Comp. Gen. Dec. B-182026, 75-1 CPD ¶ 136. GAO reasoned in such cases that award of the contract to the bidder at the mistaken bid price would not result in prejudice to another bidder, *Arkay Prods. Corp.*, Comp. Gen. Dec. B-181596, 74-2 CPD ¶ 219. These cases did not make clear when the contractor was required to indicate its willingness to accept award at the original bid price if correction of the mistake was denied. However, it was clear that the contracting officer had no obligation to offer award at the original price if the bidder had remained silent on the issue. In a subsequent decision, GAO clarified this area by stating that when the bidder does not include with the request for correction a statement of willingness to accept the award at the original bid price, the contracting officer may either make award to another bidder or request the protesting bidder to accept award at the original bid price, *Guy F. Atkinson Co.*, 55 Comp. Gen. 546 (B-183842), 75-2 CPD ¶ 378. This policy permits the bidder to wait to see if the bid is corrected before deciding whether or not to accept the award at the bid price if it is willing to take the risk that the contracting officer will not offer award at the original price. See *Edmonds Elec. Co.*, Comp. Gen. Dec. B-214063, 84-1 CPD ¶ 615.

Clear evidence that the bid would remain low was found in *National Heat & Power Corp.*, Comp. Gen. Dec. B-212923, 84-1 CPD ¶ 125, where the requested correction, while not sufficiently clear to support correction, would have had to be tripled for the bid to cease being low. Compare *William G. Tadlock Constr.*, Comp. Gen. Dec. B-251996, 93-1 CPD ¶ 382, where waiver of a mistake was denied because the bidder's worksheets did not demonstrate the intended bid price and comparison of the allegedly mistaken item with the government estimate indicated that the bid as corrected might not have remained the low bid; *C Constr. Co.*, Comp. Gen. Dec. B-242717, 91-1 CPD ¶ 540, where waiver was denied because the requested correction would have brought the bid within 1.2% of the next low bidder; *LABCO Constr., Inc.*, Comp. Gen. Dec. B-219437, 85-2 CPD ¶ 240, where waiver was denied because the correction requested did not contain all potential costs of alleged mistake and inclusion of such costs would have raised bid against next low bidder; *DSG Corp.*, Comp. Gen. Dec. B-210818.3, 84-1 CPD ¶ 476, where waiver was held improper because two conflicting sets of worksheets made it unclear that the bid would have remained low; and *Hanauer Mach. Works*, Comp. Gen. Dec. B-196369, 80-1 CPD ¶ 178, where waiver was held improper because the addition of all potential costs of the alleged mistake brought the bidder very close to or even over the next low bid.

If a bidder decides not to request correction of a mistake after clear statements from the contracting officer that it has a right to pursue relief, it will be held to the ensuing contract, *Roy Case Constr. Co.*, ASBCA 52898, 02-1 BCA ¶ 31,665. There, the bidder had misinterpreted the specification but did not investigate the rights that it had under the regulations.

### (2) ACCEPTING AWARD WITH A RESERVATION OF RIGHT

Award without correction following an allegation of mistake may be permitted where the contractor agrees to accept award at the original price while reserving a right to seek reformation of the resulting contract. In *JAL Constr., Inc.*, AGBCA 80-117-3, 81-1 BCA ¶ 14,850, the board took jurisdiction of a contractor's claim for reformation under a contract that had been awarded at the original bid price with an understanding that the awardee would be permitted to present evidence in support of a claim for an increase in contract price attributable to an alleged mistake in bid. The board denied the claim for reformation, however, holding that the contractor had failed to establish the intended bid by clear and convincing evidence. See also *Fortec Constructors*, Comp. Gen. Dec. B-179204, 74-1 CPD ¶ 285, agreeing that this was a proper procedure.

## V. TWO-STEP SEALED BIDDING

Two-step sealed bidding is a procurement method that combines elements of sealed bidding and negotiation. The first step is flexible and resembles negotiation. In this step, the government agency initiates the purchase procedure by publishing a Request for Technical Proposals (RFTP), which outlines the government's requirements. Bidders then submit one or more unpriced technical proposals to satisfy these requirements, and discussions may be held with the offerors. Only those offerors who have submitted acceptable technical proposals are invited to submit step-two sealed bids on price. Offerors bid only on their own proposals, under rules similar to sealed bidding. Award is made to the low responsible bidder submitting a responsive bid.

Two-step formal advertising was suggested in 1957 during the course of the investigation of the Armed Services Procurement Act of 1947 by the House Armed Services Subcommittee for Special Investigations. The subcommittee recommended that the Air Force attempt a two-step procurement procedure in an effort to obtain more competition in military procurements. The Air Force agreed to test the procedure, and in 1959 the procedure was officially adopted by the Armed Services. In a series of decisions published in 1960, GAO concurred with the Armed Services Procurement Regulation (ASPR) on two-step formal advertising, 40 Comp. Gen. 35 (B-143277) (1960) and 40 Comp. Gen. 40 (B-143277) (1960). In 1963, similar provisions were incorporated in the Federal Procurement Regulations (FPR).

This procedure was adopted at a time when sealed bidding was the statutorily preferred method of procurement but negotiated procurement was more commonly used for major procurements, and there was some congressional dissatisfaction with this situation. Thus, two-step sealed bidding was seen as a means of satisfying the need for flexibility obtained through the use of negotiation while still selecting the winner through sealed bid procedures. The Competition in Contracting Act did away with much of the need for two-step sealed bidding by elevating negotiated procurement to the same status as sealed bidding procurement. However, the CICA still authorized the use of two-step sealed bidding by providing that the agencies "shall use the competitive procedure or combination of competitive procedures that is best suited under the circumstances of the procurement," 10 U.S.C. § 2304(a)(1) (B) and 41 U.S.C. § 253(a)(1)(B) (now 41 U.S.C. § 3301(a)(2)). The current regulations concerning two-step sealed bidding are set forth at FAR Subpart 14.5.

Two-step sealed bidding procedures offer certain advantages. First, it encourages competition for government contracts. Contractors that might not have competed under the more structured sealed bidding process may participate in the first step of this process because alternative approaches in the design specifications are encouraged. Second, the price competition of step two makes the award decision public and easily defendable because the decision is based on price alone. Third, the FAR provisions for two-step sealed bidding are the only regulations that explicitly authorize a procedure for the submission of multiple bids by an offeror, FAR 14.503-1(a)(10). Fourth, step one allows the government to take full advantage of industry's expertise and experience without the costly use of development or research contracts. In addition, the government hopes to develop adequate technical data packages through the two-step procedure to allow subsequent acquisitions to be made by conventional sealed bidding, FAR 14.501.

Two-step sealed bidding also has disadvantages. The process is generally time-consuming and costly for the government and for bidders who must draw up detailed technical proposals to meet the government's specifications. The two-step procedure also may result in the procurement of a product that is not the best or most cost-effective overall because, in contrast to competitive negotiation, there are no tradeoffs between technical performance and cost in either step. Thus, in step one the government might deem a less desirable proposal unacceptable because it is unable to evaluate how a cost savings would counterbalance the proposal's comparatively diminished performance or quality. Similarly, in step two an offeror will generally quote on its least costly design in order to maximize the chance of success even though a better value would be obtained if the government obtained the more expensive design. Since the government must accept the least costly proposal in step two, it may be compelled to turn down proposals that, though slightly higher priced, are markedly superior technically to the lowest-cost proposal. Finally, the system allows a bidder to forbid competitors from examining its technical proposal by including a restrictive legend on the proposal. This raises serious questions concerning the public nature of the procurement. Despite the disadvantages, two-step sealed bidding can be an effective procurement technique.

## A. Decision to Use Two-Step Sealed Bidding

The factors to be considered by an agency in selecting two-step sealed bidding are treated in FAR 14.502, which provides:

(a) Unless other factors require the use of scaled bidding, two-step sealed bidding may be used in preference to negotiation when all of the following conditions are present:

(1) Available specifications or purchase descriptions are not definite or complete or may be too restrictive without technical evaluation, and any necessary discussion, of the technical aspects of the requirement to ensure mutual understanding between each source and the Government.

(2) Definite criteria exist for evaluating technical proposals.

(3) More than one technically qualified source is expected to be available.

(4) Sufficient time will be available for use of the two-step method.

(5) A firm-fixed-price contract or a fixed-price contract with economic price adjustment will be used.

(b) None of the following precludes the use of two-step sealed bidding:

(1) Multi-year contracting.

(2) Government-owned facilities or special tooling to be made available to the successful bidder.

(3) A total small business set-aside (see 19.502-2).

(4) A first or subsequent production quantity is being acquired under a performance specification.

## 1. Sufficient Technical Data and Appropriate Specifications

The regulations, written before the passage of the CICA, provide that the nature of the available specifications is a major factor in determining whether to use two-step sealed bidding. The regulations permit its use when performance specifications ("criteria . . . for evaluating technical proposals") are available, FAR 14.502(a)(2), but the agency does not have detailed specifications or only has detailed specifications that are "too restrictive," FAR 14.502(a)(1). Thus, two-step procurement was devised for the situation where an agency sees a need for evaluating the detailed specifications before awarding a contract and wants to induce contractors to develop detailed specifications.

There are no objective guidelines for deciding whether the available specifications are too indefinite, incomplete, or restrictive to permit two-step procurement. Thus, the fulfillment of the prerequisite that detailed specifications are lacking has been granted wide agency discretion. See 52 Comp. Gen. 854 (B-177206) (1973) (two-step sealed bidding appropriate where the Air Force had detailed specifications for all aspects of a procurement of management services, except with respect to data processing and software operations); Comp. Gen. Dec. B-170135, Feb. 5, 1971, *Unpub.* (Navy's statement accepted that the required antenna coupler groups lacked detailed specifications although similar items were already used by Navy); 40 Comp. Gen. 514 (B-144432) (1961) (contracting officers found to be best qualified to review and evaluate the sufficiency of available technical data for procurement of diesel engine generators). Compare *ALS Elecs. Corp.*, Comp. Gen. Dec. B-181731, 74-2 CPD ¶ 214 (lack of experience of an agency in procuring a technical item was not a sufficient justification for using two-step procurement if the specification was sufficiently detailed to permit sealed bidding).

Although lack of detailed specifications may require the use of two-step sealed bidding, the contracting officer must have definite performance specifications providing criteria for the evaluation of the technical proposals, FAR 14.502(a)(2). Again, there are no objective guidelines for determining the adequacy of the available performance specifications, and fulfillment of the prerequisite of definite performance specifications has also been granted wide agency discretion, 50 Comp. Gen. 346 (B-170268) (1970) (determination of how to best satisfy Navy's requirement of ship hull blast cleaner is left to the discretion of contracting officer).

## 2. *Availability of Competition*

The availability of competition is the other major factor to be considered in deciding whether to use two-step sealed bidding, FAR 14.502(a)(3). If there is likely not to be any competition for the contract, GAO recommends using negotiation rather than two-step procurement, *Allen Osborne Assocs.*, Comp. Gen. Dec. B-235568.2, 89-2 CPD ¶ 279. The competition requirement is met if there is more than one technically qualified source at the end of the step-one competition, even if only one responsive bid is submitted in step two, *Exide Power Sys. Div. of ESB, Inc.*, Comp. Gen. Dec. B-186793, 76-2 CPD ¶ 140. However, if there is only one qualified source at the end of step one, two-step sealed bidding should be discontinued, and negotiated procurement should be used, *Exide Power Sys. Div., ESB, Inc.*, 57 Comp. Gen. 653 (B-191159), 78-2 CPD ¶ 106. It is proper to cancel a negotiated procurement and use two-step sealed bidding when the agency learns of the availability of competition through the submission of an unsolicited proposal, Comp. Gen. Dec. B-154070, June 24, 1964, *Unpub.* See also *Radionics, Inc.*, ASBCA 22727, 81-1 BCA ¶ 15,011, where two-step sealed bidding was used to develop a second source for an item that had been previously procured through sole source negotiation.

## 3. *Agency Discretion*

To date, no agency decision to use two-step procurement has been overturned — based on the reasoning that agencies have broad discretion in deciding whether to use this technique, 50 Comp. Gen. 346 (B-170268) (1970); 40 Comp. Gen. 514 (B-144432) (1961). The few cases concerning the selection of two-step sealed bidding that have found their way to the courts have been resolved in favor of the procuring agency. For example, in *Wheelabrator Corp. v. Chafee*, 455 F.2d 1306 (D.C. Cir. 1971), the court stated that the decision to use two-step formal advertising rather than negotiation was "an exercise of discretion which Congress committed solely to the discretion of the head of the agency, and which is not reviewable in court." For

surprising instances where two-step sealed bidding was used on procurements soliciting fixed labor rates for IDIQ contracts, see *AllWorld Language Consultants, Inc.*,
Comp. Gen. Dec. B-298831, 2006 CPD ¶ 198; and *SOS Int'l, Ltd.*, Comp. Gen. Dec.
B-295533.2, 2005 CPD ¶ 128. The protesters did not raise the argument that sealed
bidding can be used only for firm-fixed-price contracts and GAO did not comment on
this unusual use of the technique.

## B. Step One

FAR 14.501(a) contains the following description of step one:

Step one consists of the request for, submission, evaluation, and (if necessary)
discussion of a technical proposal. No pricing is involved. The objective is to
determine the acceptability of the supplies or services offered. As used in this
context, the word "technical" has a broad connotation and includes, among other
things, the engineering approach, special manufacturing processes, and special
testing techniques. It is the proper step for clarification of questions relating to
technical requirements. Conformity to the technical requirements is resolved in
this step, but not responsibility as defined in 9.1.

The focus in this step is on the preparation of the RFTPs, the evaluation of proposals, and discussions with offerors.

### 1. Request for Technical Proposals

FAR 14.503-1(a) requires that the RFTP contain the following information:

(1) A description of the supplies or services required.

(2) A statement of intent to use the two-step method.

(3) The requirements of the technical proposal.

(4) The evaluation criteria, to include all factors and any significant subfactors.

(5) A statement that the technical proposals shall not include prices or pricing
information.

(6) The date, or date and hour, by which the proposal must be received (see
14.201-6®)).

(7) A statement that (i) in the second step, only bids based upon technical proposals determined to be acceptable, either initially or as a result of discussions, will
be considered for awards and (ii) each bid in the second step must be based on the
bidder's own technical proposals.

(8) A statement that (i) offerors should submit proposals that are acceptable without additional explanation or information, (ii) the Government may make a final determination regarding a proposal's acceptability solely on the basis of the proposal as submitted, and (iii) the Government may proceed with the second step without requesting further information from any offeror; however, the Government may request additional information from offerors of proposals that it considers reasonably susceptible of being made acceptable, and may discuss proposals with their offerors.

(9) A statement that a notice of unacceptability will be forwarded to the offeror upon completion of the proposal evaluation and final determination of unacceptability.

(10) A statement either that only one technical proposal may be submitted by each offeror or that multiple technical proposals may be submitted. When specifications permit different technical approaches, it is generally in the Government's interest to authorize multiple proposals. If multiple proposals are authorized, see 14.201-6(s).

The RFTP may include delivery or "performance requirements," but these requirements are not considered evaluation factors under step one and are not binding on the government, FAR 14.503-1(b). In this context, the term "performance requirements" should be construed as factors unrelated to the technical competency of a proposal. For example, in *Diversified Contract Servs., Inc.*, Comp. Gen. Dec. B-234660, 89-1 CPD ¶ 590, GAO held that the government was not required to announce a bonding requirement in its RFTP because the bond was a performance requirement that did not affect the technical focus of step one. Additionally, quantities specified in the RFTP are not binding on the government, Comp. Gen. Dec. B-163050, Mar. 27, 1968, *Unpub.*

However, performance requirements (also known as "performance specifications") are considered evaluation factors under step one when the performance requirements state the needs of the government that must be met by the step one proposal. For example, in *Aerostat Servs. P'ship*, Comp. Gen. Dec. B-244939.2, 92-1 CPD ¶ 71, GAO upheld the Air Force's rejection of a technical proposal because the manning levels for the operation of a radar system did not fulfill the Air Force's performance requirements. See also *Halter Marine, Inc.*, Comp. Gen. Dec. B-239119, 90-2 CPD ¶ 95 (performance requirement of a patrol boat's speed a technical evaluation factor); and *HSQ Tech.*, Comp. Gen. Dec. B-227054, 87-2 CPD ¶ 77 (performance requirement of computer communications rate at 9600 baud a technical evaluation factor). While performance specifications in the RFTP should be relatively flexible in order to encourage varying proposals, the requirements must be sufficiently definite to state the government's needs accurately and to provide offerors with equal opportunities for submitting proposals. When the step-one evaluation is based upon requirements not set forth in the RFTP or ambiguously set forth, GAO has generally found that an unequal basis for competition has arisen. See *Federal Computer Corp.*, 66 Comp. Gen. 139

(B-223932), 86-2 CPD ¶ 665 (improper rejection of step-one proposal for failure to meet Navy's unstated requirements for automatic data processing system); *Tenavision, Inc.*, Comp. Gen. Dec. B-216274, 85-1 CPD ¶ 427 (rejection improper when based on GSA contract number listing requirement that was ambiguously set forth in RFTP); *Masstor Sys. Corp.*, Comp. Gen. Dec. B-206091, 82-2 CPD ¶ 262 (where solicitation provision has two reasonable interpretations and the ambiguity is not so obvious as to impose a duty on the offeror to seek clarification, it is improper for the agency to reject the offeror's proposal for failure to comply with the agency's interpretation); and *RCA Corp.*, 57 Comp. Gen. 809 (B-190247), 78-2 CPD ¶ 213 (camera sample not required by RFTP could not be used as evaluation factor).

GAO may also find an unequal basis for competition if the government significantly changes its requirements from the RFTP specifications, but does not issue an amendment to all bidders. For example, in 53 Comp. Gen. 47 (B-178192) (1973), the government was obligated to amend its RFTP before accepting a technical proposal with a ladder incorporated in the antenna rather than separate from the antenna as originally contemplated in the RFTP. See also *Helmets Ltd.*, 71 Comp. Gen. 281 (B-246301), 92-1 CPD ¶ 241 (proposal that represents a basic change in RFTP helmet design can only be accepted if Navy gives other offerors an opportunity to submit revised proposals); and *Irvin Indus. Canada, Ltd. v. Department of the Air Force*, 924 F.2d 1068 (D.C. Cir. 1990) (when no acceptable technical proposals were submitted, agency was not allowed to disregard material changes of its RFTP for only one offeror, but must negotiate with all offerors).

The determinative question regarding the adequacy of the specifications is whether the bidders are competing on a common basis, *Simulaser Corp.*, Comp. Gen. Dec. B-233850, 89-1 CPD ¶ 236, *recons. denied*, 89-2 CPD ¶ 65. However, absent a showing of prejudice to the protesting offeror, the mere existence of an improper evaluation of technical requirements does not provide a compelling reason to cancel or redo step one of the procurement.

Early GAO decisions treated late technical proposals with some leniency, 45 Comp. Gen. 24 (B-156466) (1965); Comp. Gen. Dec. B-160324, Feb. 16, 1967, *Unpub.* However, in 1973, GAO advised the General Services Administration "that in our view late proposals under step one should be treated in strict accordance with the terms of the solicitations" and heralded a shift toward more rigid adherence to deadlines, 52 Comp. Gen. 726 (B-177284) (1973). Currently, FAR 14.201-6(r) requires that the RFTP include the solicitation provision set forth at FAR 52.214-23. This provision provides that a late technical proposal will not be considered unless (1) the contracting officer determines that accepting it would not unduly delay the acquisition, and (2) any of the three following conditions is present:

(i) If it was transmitted through an electronic commerce method authorized by the request for technical proposals, it was received at the initial point of entry to the

Government infrastructure not later than 5:00 p.m. one working day prior to the date specified for receipt of proposals; or

(ii) There is acceptable evidence to establish that it was received at the Government installation designated for receipt of offers and was under the Government's control prior to the time set for receipt; or

(iii) It is the only proposal received and it is negotiated under part 15 of the Federal Acquisition Regulation.

This provision parallels the provision for late bids in sealed bidding, discussed earlier, where the late-is-late rule is strictly enforce. Accordingly, late technical proposals submitted under two-step procurement will be rejected unless they fall within one of the exceptions defined in the late proposal clause, *Baron & Assocs.*, Comp. Gen. Dec. B-213898, 84-1 CPD ¶ 80. Under the provision in effect until 1999, once a timely proposal was submitted that was acceptable or reasonably susceptible to being made acceptable, late responses to amendments of the RFTP or to agency requests for revisions could be accepted if further negotiations under step one were to be conducted. See *Control Central Corp.*, Comp. Gen. Dec. B-214466.2, 84-2 CPD ¶ 28 (failure to submit a timely revised proposal did not exclude bidder from further competition when negotiations are reopened by subsequent amendment); and *Angstrom, Inc.*, 59 Comp. Gen. 588 (B-193261), 80-2 CPD ¶ 20 (late response to amendment of RFTP allowed because subsequent amendments continued negotiations under step one). Additionally, there is no regulatory requirement for a common cutoff date for receipt of revised proposals after discussions, *J&J Maint., Inc.*, Comp. Gen. Dec. B-240802, 90-2 CPD ¶ 504, *recons. denied*, 91-1 CPD ¶ 396.

## 2. *Evaluation of First-Step Proposals*

FAR 14.503-1(e)(1) states that after proposals have been received, they are to be categorized as acceptable, unacceptable, or reasonably susceptible to being made acceptable. Offerors who submit unacceptable proposals are to be notified of that determination promptly and are to be advised that revisions will not be considered, FAR 14.503-1(g). However, failure to give prompt notice is a mere procedural irregularity and, therefore, does not invalidate the procurement, *Shughart & Assocs.*, Comp. Gen. Dec. B-226970, 87-2 CPD ¶ 56; 48 Comp. Gen. 349 (B-165050) (1968).

Contracting officers are given wide latitude in the evaluation of technical proposals, *Hughes Missile Sys. Co.*, Comp. Gen. Dec. B-257627.2, 94-2 CPD ¶ 256. Nevertheless, there have been a number of disputes between the offeror and the government regarding whether a proposal was properly evaluated — leading to delays in completing the two-step sealed bidding procurement. For example, in *Angstrom, Inc.*, 59 Comp. Gen. 588 (B-193261), 80-2 CPD ¶ 20, bidding disputes extended the procurement time of a commercial, off-the-shelf item to 33 months.

## a.  Acceptable Proposals

To be acceptable, a technical proposal must conform to the basic or essential requirements of the specifications, FAR 14.503-1(e)(2). However, variations from less significant details of the specifications are permissible in an acceptable proposal. See *Angstrom, Inc.*, 59 Comp. Gen. 588 (B-193261), 80-2 CPD ¶ 20, holding that a proposal need comply only with basic or essential requirements, not all details of specifications. The difficulty is that it is not always readily ascertainable which of the RFTP requirements are "basic" and, therefore, must be complied with and which are minor details that may be waived. Because there are few objective standards by which basic requirements of specifications may be differentiated from specification details, the contracting officer is given wide discretion in making this determination. See *Ricoh America's Corp.*, Comp. Gen. Dec. B-402239, 2010 CPD ¶ 55, finding no errors in concluding that all four proposals were acceptable, and *Hughes Missile Sys. Co.*, Comp. Gen. Dec. B-257627.2, 94-2 CPD ¶ 256, denying a protest of an agency's evaluation of a proposal as acceptable, even though one agency evaluator disagreed with the decision.

Once a proposal is classified as acceptable, it is permitted to compete in step two. There are no degrees of qualification within the acceptable category. Thus, superior and more costly proposals may compete with those that are minimally adequate and less costly, Comp. Gen. Dec. B-159469, Mar. 22, 1967, *Unpub.*

## b.  Proposals That Are Reasonably Susceptible to Being Made Acceptable

FAR 14.503-1(f) provides the following guidance on dealing with proposals that are reasonably susceptible to being made acceptable:

> (1) The contracting officer may proceed directly with step two if there are sufficient acceptable proposals to ensure adequate price competition under step two, and if further time, effort and delay to make additional proposals acceptable and thereby increase competition would not be in the Government's interest. If this is not the case, the contracting officer shall request bidders whose proposals may be made acceptable to submit additional clarifying or supplementing information. The contracting officer shall identify the nature of the deficiencies in the proposal or the nature of the additional information required. The contracting officer may also arrange discussions for this purpose. No proposal shall be discussed with any offeror other than the submitter.

Despite this guidance, GAO has stated that the first step of two-step sealed bidding contemplates the qualification of as many proposals as possible, *Hughes Missile Sys. Co.*, Comp. Gen. Dec. B-257627.2, 94-2 CPD ¶ 256. However, this goal of maximization of competition does not mean that an agency is required to classify a proposal as reasonably susceptible of being made acceptable if it fails to meet the basic requirements of the RFTP or can only be made acceptable through extensive revisions. See *Technology Research Int'l*, Comp. Gen. Dec. B-245174, 91-2 CPD ¶ 470 (agency is not required to afford an offeror an opportunity to revise its proposal if major rewrite is necessary); and *Infotec Dev., Inc.*, Comp. Gen. B-235568, 89-2 CPD ¶ 215 (although only one acceptable proposal was left after step one, agency was not required to consider other proposals that required major revisions). Although GAO will commonly defer to the government's decision to reject a proposal where substantial revision is necessary, *Network Sys. Solutions, Inc.*, Comp. Gen. Dec. B-249733, 92-2 CPD ¶ 410, GAO may overturn the decision if there is evidence that the government's evaluation was unreasonable and the proposal was susceptible to being made acceptable. See *Coastal Gov't Servs., Inc.*, Comp. Gen. Dec. B-250820, 93-1 CPD ¶ 167 (agency unreasonably determined that proposal was technically unacceptable based on minor informational deficiencies and proposal ambiguities); and *A.R.E. Mfg. Co.*, Comp. Gen. Dec. B-224086, 86-2 CPD ¶ 395 (decision unreasonable where Navy cannot explain how or why conclusion of unacceptability was reached).

The amount of discussion or clarification that is appropriate and which proposals are reasonably susceptible to being made acceptable are matters of agency discretion, *Ronnoc, Inc.*, Comp. Gen. Dec. 243729, 91-2 CPD ¶ 163. Although the step-one process is stated to be similar to negotiated procurement, when the government decides that a step one proposal is reasonably susceptible to being made acceptable, there is no requirement that the government hold "meaningful discussions" with the offeror, *Datron Sys., Inc.*, Comp. Gen. Dec. B-220423.2, 86-1 CPD ¶ 264. It is sufficient if the offeror is notified of deficiencies and afforded the opportunity to address them, *Lockheed Cal. Co.*, Comp. Gen. Dec. B-218143, 85-1 CPD ¶ 676. See also FAR 14.503-1(f)(1).

Discussions resulting in revised proposals that are classified as acceptable are regularly upheld as proper, Comp. Gen. Dec. B-179587, Sept. 27, 1973, *Unpub.* (modification effected in step one discussions substituted hydraulic actuators for mechanical ones); and *Guardian Elec. Mfg. Co.*, Comp. Gen. Dec. B-191871, 79-1 CPD ¶ 321 (extensive discussions needed to qualify proposal upheld). Additionally, protests alleging that a deficiency in discussions resulted in a proposal's rejection are generally denied. See *Applied Research Tech,*, Comp. Gen. Dec. B-240230, 90-2 CPD ¶ 358 (agency not required to conduct successive rounds of discussions and revisions of proposals); and *Anchor Conveyors, Inc.*, Comp. Gen. Dec. B-215624, 84-2 CPD ¶ 451 (FAA's effort to qualify proposal upheld as reasonable where agency identified deficient areas and afforded bidder an opportunity to correct those deficiencies in revised proposal).

GAO has found step-one discussions improper if there was evidence that technical transfusion (revealing a competitor's proprietary information) occurred and prior FAR provisions barred this technique. Current FAR no longer includes a prohibition of this technique but it is illegal under 18 U.S.C. § 1905. For examples of cases involving technical transfusion in two-step procurement, see *Aerial Image Corp.*, Comp. Gen. Dec. B-219174, 85-2 CPD ¶ 319, upholding an agency's decision not to hold discussions because of the danger of disclosing another offeror's innovative approach to an audio-video slide show, and *General Elec. Can., Inc.*, Comp. Gen. Dec. B-230584, 88-1 CPD ¶ 512, denying a protest alleging technical transfusion as being based on mere speculation by the protester.

The FAR does not explicitly ban technical leveling during step-one discussions and, as discussed in Chapter 6, this prohibition has been removed from the guidance on competitive negotiations. However, GAO applied the general prohibition on technical leveling during discussions found in FAR 15.610(d) (pre FAC 97-02, September 30, 1997 version). In *Applied Research Tech.*, Comp. Gen. Dec. B-240230, 90-2 CPD ¶ 358, GAO stated that successive rounds of discussion during step one are precluded because of the FAR 15.610(d) ban on technical leveling. See also *Essex Electro Eng'rs, Inc.*, Comp. Gen. Dec. B-210366, 83-1 CPD ¶ 650, holding that an agency is not required to engage in technical leveling to bring a proposal up to the level of other proposals.

Even when technical leveling was prohibited, GAO addressed the technical transfusion claim, which was easier to establish, and ignored the difficult technical leveling claim. See *J&J Maint., Inc.*, Comp. Gen. Dec. B-240802, 90-2 CPD ¶ 504, approving acceptance of revised proposal following discussions after finding no evidence of technical transfusion, but disregarded claims of technical leveling.

The amount of time to be allotted to discussion is also a discretionary matter. For example, in Comp. Gen. Dec. B-178071, May 22, 1973, *Unpub.*, GAO upheld the contracting officer's decision to allow 60 additional days to make a proposal acceptable after the date on which two other proposals qualified as acceptable.

### c.  Unacceptable Proposals

FAR 14.503-1(e)(2) states:

> Any proposal which modifies, or fails to conform to the essential requirements or specifications of, the request for technical proposals shall be considered nonresponsive and categorized as unacceptable.

A proposal may also be unacceptable because it contains insufficient information to permit a determination that the offeror possesses sufficient technical understanding of the work, *Radiation Sys., Inc.*, Comp. Gen. Dec. B-211732, 83-2 CPD ¶ 434. The cases uniformly follow the principle established in FAR 14.503-1(g) that the government does not have a duty to initiate or continue discussions with the offeror in order to clarify a clearly unacceptable proposal, that would require considerable time and effort to be made acceptable, *Network Sys. Solutions, Inc.*, Comp. Gen. Dec. B-249733, 92-2 CPD ¶ 410 (offeror should not have assumed that it would be afforded opportunity to make further clarifications); *Gichner Iron Works, Inc.*, Comp. Gen. B-230009, 88-1 CPD ¶ 459 (upholding rejection of proposal that would require substantial revisions); and *Colbar, Inc.*, Comp. Gen. Dec. B-227555.4, 88-1 CPD ¶ 168 (upholding evaluation team consensus upheld that proposal for food service would require total rewrite).

## d. Erroneous Evaluations

In reviewing protests of allegedly improper evaluations, GAO will not substitute its judgment for thatof the agency that retains wide discretion, but will examine the record to determine whether the evaluation was reasonable and in accord with listed criteria, and whether there were any violations of procurement statutes or regulations, *Anchor Conveyors, Inc.*, Comp. Gen. Dec. B-215624.2, 84-2 CPD ¶ 451. GAO lacks technical expertise to oversee the judgments of the procuring agencies and, therefore, is reluctant to review the step one evaluation process. Thus, the technical judgment of the agency is accepted unless it is shown to be erroneous, arbitrary, or not in good faith, *Kay & Assocs.*, Comp. Gen. Dec. B-234509, 89-1 CPD ¶ 567.

In contrast, GAO exercises judgment in matters considered to be legal in nature. See, e.g., Comp. Gen. Dec. B-170825.2, Mar. 12, 1971, *Unpub.*, where the meaning and effect of a specification as opposed to whether a product met the specification was declared to be a matter of law within the province of GAO to decide. See also *Federal Computer Corp.*, 66 Comp. Gen. 139 (B-223932), 86-2 CPD ¶ 665 (protest that evaluation factor was not set forth in RFTP); and *E.C. Campbell, Inc.*, Comp. Gen. Dec. B-205533, 82-2 CPD ¶ 34 (award overturned because agency improperly failed to consider awardee's noncompliance with material specification requirement).

Offerors that can demonstrate that a determination of unacceptability is improper are not foreclosed from further participation in the procurement. In 43 Comp. Gen. 255 (B-152261) (1963), a contractor revised a proposal and submitted a second-step bid based on the revised proposal within three days of learning that the proposal had been rejected. GAO permitted the contractor to participate in the second step, stating that the speed with which the proposal was made acceptable showed it had been erroneously rejected as unacceptable in the first instance. See also *Tenavision, Inc.*, Comp. Gen. Dec. B-218794, 85-2 CPD ¶ 62, awarding a protester bid preparation costs incurred in step one of a two-step sealed bid procurement because the offeror's proposal was improperly rejected in step one. However, if the unacceptable proposal is not corrected prior to the submission of the step-two bids, it may not be considered for award. Such proposals are still nonresponsive, and the strict rules of formal advertising applicable to the second step do not permit correction of the proposal at that stage. See 45 Comp. Gen. 487 (B-157084) (1966), holding improper the revision of a proposal during step two. Compare Comp. Gen. Dec. B-160324, Apr. 5,

1967, *Unpub.*, allowing a step-two bid on a proposal initially deemed unacceptable but made competitive before step two.

## C. Step Two

Generally, the second step of two-step sealed bidding is conducted in accordance with the procedures applicable to sealed bidding. See FAR 14.501(b), which states:

> Step two involves the submission of sealed priced bids by those who submitted acceptable technical proposals in step one. Bids submitted in step two are evaluated and the awards made in accordance with Subparts 14.3 and 14.4.

However, there are a number of unique aspects of the sealed bidding procedures used in step two.

Upon completion of step one, invitations for bids are issued to offerors whose technical proposals have been determined acceptable under step one. Limiting competition in step two to acceptable proposals is an exception to the normal sealed bid procedures but is an essential element of two-step sealed bidding. This limitation has been strictly enforced. See Comp. Gen. Dec. B-170175, Apr. 21, 1971, *Unpub.*, where a successful participant in the first step, unable to obtain the required bond, was prohibited from bidding in the second step under the name of a different company that could be bonded. But see *G&C Enters., Inc.*, Comp. Gen. Dec. B-186748, 76-2 CPD ¶ 367, *recons. denied*, 77-1 CPD ¶ 155, where an acceptable step one proposer was permitted to bid in a joint venture with an outside party in step two.

While participants in step two are limited to those submitting acceptable proposals in step one, step-one participants are not legally bound to participate in step two. The application of this rule could lead to the situation where only one bid is submitted in step two. However, this should not cause cancellation of the procurement unless the bidder was aware that the other successful step-one offerors did not intend to bid.

The regulations provide that the step-two invitation for bids shall "prominently state that the bidder shall comply with the specifications and the bidder's technical proposal," FAR 14.503-2(a)(3). This requirement has been strictly enforced. Products that vary from the RFTP and the accepted technical proposals in step one cannot be accepted in step two, *Qualimetrics, Inc.*, Comp. Gen. Dec. B-227044.3, 87-2 CPD ¶ 100. However, when the bidder deviates from the solicitation in the technical proposal, but would still be the lowest bidder, absent such deviation, the award is proper, *Lusardi Constr. Co.*, Comp. Gen. Dec. B-210276, 83-2 CPD ¶ 297 (price benefit of deviations from specifications did not affect relative standing of bidders); *Essex Electro Eng'rs, Inc.*, Comp. Gen. Dec. B-213892, 84-1 CPD ¶ 434 (relaxation of requirements found not to result in price advantage).

FAR 14.503-2(a)(4) states that it is unnecessary to publish and synopsize second-step IFBs. However, "names of firms which have submitted acceptable proposals in step one are required to be listed in *fedbizopps.gov* for the benefit of prospective subcontractors," FAR 14.503-2(b). Negligent failure to list the names of acceptable proposals before the second step has not been fatal to the procurement, *Bailey Controls Co.*, Comp. Gen. Dec. B-256189, 94-1 CPD ¶ 320. However, a failure to publish that is done in bad faith could require readvertisement if the government's interest in full competition has been affected or if the omitted bidder can establish prejudice, Comp. Gen. Dec. B-166315, Aug. 15, 1969, *Unpub.*

## 1. Responsiveness

There are two unique aspects of responsiveness in two-step sealed bidding. First, the bid must conform to all of the significant procurement documents. Second, GAO has sometimes stated that there is a presumption of responsiveness.

### a. Nonconforming Bids

In order to be eligible for award in two-step sealed bidding, bids must conform to the RFTP, to the technical proposal as approved by the procuring agency in step one, and to any additional requirements in the step two invitation for bids. However, it is not necessary for the bidder to physically incorporate the technical proposal in the second-step bid. The bid is considered responsive if it summarizes the technical proposal, as long as the summary is consistent with the acceptable technical proposal. Incorporation by reference or acknowledgment that the bid is in accordance with the accepted proposal is also sufficient, 52 Comp. Gen. 821 (B-177423) (1973).

An invitation to submit a second-step bid does not eliminate the possibility that the offeror will be found nonresponsive after receipt of second-step bids based on a nonconformity included in the step-one proposal. In *International Med. Indus., Inc.*, 62 Comp. Gen. 31 (B-208235), 82-2 CPD ¶ 386, an offeror's step-one proposal included a 30-day bid acceptance period rather than the 45-day period included in the RFTP and this wqs not altered in the step-two bid. Based upon this nonconformity the company was found nonresponsive in step two. See also *American Tel. & Tel. Co.*, Comp. Gen. Dec. B-193454, 79-1 CPD ¶ 365 and 52 Comp. Gen. 783 (B-177220) (1973). When GAO states that when such a bid is nonresponsive, it is tantamount to a finding that the procuring agency has made an erroneous determination of acceptability in step one.

Bidders can also be found nonresponsive by failing to comply with the requirements of the IFB. These requirements may include price schedules, delivery requirements and bid bond requirements. See *Tel-Instrument Elecs. Corp.*, Comp. Gen. Dec. B-291309, 2002 CPD ¶ 203 (cover letter required agency to provide equipment not called for in RFTP); *Parsons Precision Prods., Inc.*, Comp. Gen. Dec.

B-249940, 92-2 CPD ¶ 431 (cover letter to bid changing payment terms makes bid nonresponsive); *American Monorail, Inc.*, Comp. Gen. Dec. B-181226, 74-2 CPD ¶ 69 (bid with exception to required delivery schedule nonresponsive); and 52 Comp. Gen. 223 (B-176138) (1972). See generally *Metric Sys. Corp.*, Comp. Gen. Dec. B-256343, 94-1 CPD ¶ 360 (exception to indemnification clause); and *KW Control Sys., Inc.*, Comp. Gen. Dec. B-246963, 91-2 CPD ¶ 543 (total payment obligation inconsistent with IFB requirements). Compare *SOS Int'l, Ltd.*, Comp. Gen. Dec. B-295533.2, 2005 CPD ¶ 128, finding a step-two bid responsive when it contained tiered prices (based on the quantity of work ordered) which were not called for in the IFB — because all of the prices were low.

However, if a price for a certain item is not necessary for the agency's determination of the low bidder, failure to include the price in the step-two bid does not make the bidder nonresponsive, *Educational Computer Corp.*, Comp. Gen. Dec. B-227078, 87-2 CPD ¶ 156.

## b.  Presumption of Responsiveness

GAO has sometimes stated that bidders in the second step are entitled to a presumption of responsiveness. See *Spectrolab, Inc.*, Comp. Gen. Dec. B-180008, 74-1 CPD ¶ 321 (bid was ambiguous but GAO presumed offeror meant to be responsive); *Federal Aviation Admin.*, Comp. Gen. Dec. B-193238, 79-1 CPD ¶ 136 (offeror specifically addressed in step one an item that was omitted in step two). The rationale for this rule is that the time, effort, and money a bidder expends in participating in two-step sealed bidding would make it unlikely that the bidder would disqualify the bid by varying from the accepted proposal or the requirements of the specifications, 45 Comp. Gen. 221 (B-157454) (1965). Using this presumption of responsiveness, GAO has approved awards to firms despite deviations that would lead to determinations of nonresponsiveness in a regular sealed bid procurement. For example, in 45 Comp. Gen. 221 (B-157454), the bidder placed "N/A," indicating "not applicable," in the amount column of the item covering the furnishing of certain data related to the end item of the procurement. This created an ambiguity as to whether the bidder was refusing to provide the item or was offering to provide it at no cost. In similar situations in standard sealed bid procurements, such bids are routinely found nonresponsive. However, in this case GAO held that the bidder was responsive based on the asserted presumption of responsiveness. Similarly, in 50 Comp. Gen. 337 (B-169874) (1970), GAO found a bid responsive even though the bidder submitted descriptive literature that was not consistent with the government's requirements. See also *Spectrolab, Inc.*, Comp. Gen. Dec. B-180008, 74-1 CPD ¶ 321; and Comp. Gen. Dec. B-178764, June 27, 1973, *Unpub.*

The presumption of responsiveness is not applicable when the step-two bid takes specific exception to a material requirement that has a significant effect on price, *Universal Comm. Sys., Inc.*, Comp. Gen. Dec., B-205032, 82-2 CPD ¶ 236. See also

*Parsons Precision Prod., Inc.*, Comp. Gen. Dec. B-249940, 92-2 CPD ¶ 431 (conflict in payment terms); *Southwestern Bell Corp.*, GSBCA 10321-P, 90-1 BCA ¶ 22,545 (omission of cost of growth requirement); and *Abar Ipsen Indus.*, Comp. Gen. Dec. B-219499.2, 86-1 CPD ¶ 7 (delivery schedule and price terms in conflict).

While the Court of Federal Claims has not stated that there is a presumption of responsiveness, it has found a step two bid responsive when the bidder submitted a signed "back side" of the SF 1442 but did not submit the front side, *ECDC Envtl., L.C. v. United States*, 40 Fed. Cl. 236 (1998). The court concluded that the terms on the front side could be "inferred" from the fact that the bidder signed the back side.

## 2. Data Protection

The two-step regulations require the contracting officer to safeguard step-one proposals against disclosure to unauthorized persons. See FAR 14.503-1, which states:

> (c) Upon receipt, the contracting officer shall —
>
> (1) Safeguard proposals against disclosure to unauthorized persons;
>
> (2) Accept and handle data marked in accordance with 15.609 as provided in that section; and
>
> (3) Remove any reference to price or cost.

Thus, competitors have no way of determining whether the step-one proposal, as accepted by the government, varies from the RFTP. This conflicts with the public opening concept of sealed bidding. See FAR 14.404-4, which states that if a bidder restricts the disclosure of sufficient information to permit competing bidders to know the essential nature of the offer, the bid is nonresponsive. This special procedure has been accepted by GAO as a necessary part of two-step sealed bidding, 46 Comp. Gen. 34 (B-158865) (1966); Comp. Gen. Dec. B-164106, Nov. 8, 1968, *Unpub.* See also *Powers Regulator Co.*, Comp. Gen. Dec. B-181251, 74-2 CPD ¶ 98, rejecting a protester's contention that only a competitor's review of step-one proposals could protect the integrity of the competitive bidding system. GAO indicated that review by GAO was sufficient.

This rule does not apply to elements of the bid that are not included in the step-one proposal. Thus, the prices bid in step two must be disclosed. Therefore, a bid that restricts release of a price in a two-step sealed bid procurement must be found nonresponsive and be rejected, *Northern Telecom, Inc.*, Comp. Gen. Dec. B-209412, 83-1 CPD ¶ 382. Additionally, an agency may disclose prices for a similar prior contract so that potential bidders on the current contract have the same opportunity to bid competitively, *B.C. Cleaning & Maint. Corp.*, Comp. Gen. Dec. B-225909, 87-1 CPD ¶ 56.

## 3. Discontinuing Step Two

FAR 14.404-1 lists the circumstances under which cancellation of two-step sealed bid procurement is permitted after the step-two bids are opened. Cancellation at this stage most often results because the government has not obtained sufficient price competition, evidenced by the fact that the bid prices are too high. See *Aero Innovations, Ltd.*, Comp. Gen. Dec. B-227677, 87-2 CPD ¶ 332, upholding cancellation and resolicitation when restrictive specifications resulted in limited competition. The contracting officer has substantial discretion in concluding that lack of price competition justifies cancellation and may use the bid of a nonresponsive bidder in this determination of price unreasonableness, *McCarthy Mfg. Co.*, 56 Comp. Gen. 369 (B-186550), 77-1 CPD ¶ 116; Comp. Gen. Dec. B-168972, Apr. 14, 1970, *Unpub.* The procurement may also be canceled because the specifications failed to state or overstated the needs of the government. However, the presence of ambiguous specifications is a justification for cancellation only if there is a compelling reason, for instance, where an award would not meet the government's needs or a bidder would be prejudiced. See *Diversified Energy Sys.*, Comp. Gen. Dec. B-245593.3, 92-1 CPD ¶ 293, where cancellation was held to be appropriate because ambiguous specifications led to an overstatement of the agency's needs. Compare *Hydro Power Equip. Co.*, Comp. Gen. Dec. B-205263, 82-1 CPD ¶ 466, finding no compelling reason to cancel despite ambiguous specifications. Additionally, the procurement may be canceled if the agency determines from a cost comparison that it would be more advantageous to perform the services with agency personnel, *United Media Corp.*, Comp. Gen. Dec. B-259425.2, 95-1 CPD ¶ 289.

If the procurement is canceled in step two, the contracting agency may readvertise step two, initiate a new sealed bid procurement, or negotiate the contract. If negotiation is selected as the best means of obtaining the work, the competition may not be limited to the companies that submitted acceptable technical proposals, 46 Comp. Gen. 360 (B-159665) (1966). In one interesting case, GAO ruled that it was proper for an agency to obtain the item by negotiating a lease/purchase arrangement after cancellation of the two-step sealed bid procurement because the bids exceeded the funds available to the agency, 48 Comp. Gen. 471 (B-165013) (1968). Although GAO suggests cancellation of step two and initiation of negotiations when step one results in only one acceptable proposal, the contracting officer has the discretion to proceed to step two, *Allen Osborne Assocs.*, Comp. Gen. Dec. B-235568.2, 89-2 CPD ¶ 279.

# CHAPTER 6

# BASIC NEGOTIATION PROCEDURES

The term "negotiation" has been broadly used to refer to any procurement technique other than sealed bidding (previously known as formal advertising). In use since World War II, it was initially introduced into the procurement statutes by the Armed Services Procurement Act (ASPA) in 1948 and the Federal Property and Administrative Services Act (FPASA) in 1949 as an "exception" to procurement by formal advertising. Its use was authorized only if formal advertising was determined not to be "feasible and practicable" and one of a number of enumerated "exceptions" was present. As discussed in Chapter 3, both of these acts were amended by the Competition in Contracting Act (CICA) of 1984 to make competition the norm in federal procurement, placing competitive negotiation on an equal footing with sealed bidding.

The original ASPA and FPASA did not specify any procedures to be used in negotiating contracts and did not distinguish between sole source contracts and contracts arrived at competitively. However, subsequent statutes have incorporated various requirements aimed at insuring fair treatment when competition is used to select the contractor, while remaining silent on the procedures to be followed in sole source procurements (except for the truth in negotiation requirements discussed in Chapter 10).

With regard to sole source procurements, agencies have wide discretion as to the procedures to be used. FAR 15.002(a) appears to assume that agencies will issue an RFP to the selected contractor to initiate the negotiation process, but this is not mandatory. Hence, when the parties have a firm understanding of the contract requirements, such as with a follow-on contract, they can go directly into negotiations or the agency can issue an RFQ directing the contractor to submit a price proposal (the FAR is silent on this use of an RFQ). When the agency has not previously acquired the product or service but has determined through market research that only one source is available, the use of an RFP would be a sound way to inform the contractor of the agency's requirements on which a price proposal could be based. In neither instance is there any need for capability information, evaluation factors, or the other elements of a competitive negotiation. See FAR 15.300 stating that FAR Subpart 15.3 is only applicable to competitive negotiations. The key elements in such procurements is the detailed negotiation of the price or cost and reaching agreement on the terms and conditions. Once the parties have concluded this negotiation, the contracting officer will normally prepare an integrated contract document, obtain the contractors signature and then formalize the contract by signing the document.

In contrast, there are several mandatory procedures that apply to competitively negotiated procurements. The first Congressional effort to address these procedures occurred in 1962. Following complaints that noncompetitive practices were used by the Department of Defense (DoD) in negotiating contracts, the ASPA was amended by Pub. L. No. 87-653, to require "oral or written discussions" with all offerors submitting proposals within a "competitive range." Award without discussions was permitted only if the reasonableness of price could be determined through adequate competition or prior cost experience. These requirements were subsequently imposed on civilian agencies by the Federal Procurement Regulations. CICA restated and supplemented these requirements and made them statutorily applicable to civilian agency contracts. In addition, it introduced the term "competitive proposals" for negotiated contracts. Subsequent statutory changes, including the Federal Acquisition Streamlining Act of 1994 (FASA), Pub. L. No. 103-355, and the Clinger-Cohen Act of 1996, Pub. L. No. 104-106, required increased detail in stating evaluation factors and subfactors, removed restrictions on making awards without discussions, permitted limitation of the competitive range for purposes of efficiency, and required extensive debriefing of offerors. However, rather than specifying any single technique, the present statutes provide a framework within which procuring agencies have flexibility to devise varying strategies.

The purpose of competitive negotiation is to permit agencies to use more discretionary procedures than permitted in the sealed bidding process. As a result, proposals are not available for public inspection prior to award. The concept of responsiveness does not apply and proposals which vary from the RFP are not required to be rejected. Discussions and bargaining are permitted which can result in modifications of proposals by offerors to correct deficiencies or to enhance their offers. In selecting the contractor, the agency need not award to the low priced offeror but can make tradeoffs between cost or price and other factors. The flexibility of negotiation is reflected in FAR 15.306(d), stating:

> Negotiation are exchanges . . . between the Government and offerors, that are undertaken with the intent of allowing the offeror to revise its proposal. These negotiations may include bargaining. Bargaining includes persuasion, alteration of assumptions and positions, give-and-take, and may apply to price, schedule, technical requirements, type of contract, or other terms of a proposed contract.

The negotiation process gives contracting officials the option to seek proposal modifications but they are not required to do so if acceptance of the most favorable initial proposal(s) is in the best interests of the government. The options available in the most frequently used competitive negotiation procedure are shown in **Figure 6-1**.

Through the years much of the flexibility available in negotiated procurements became lost due to overly complex solicitations including unnecessarily large numbers of evaluation factors and subfactors. In an attempt to reverse this trend, FAR 15.002 establishes a policy aimed at minimizing the complexity of negotiated procurements as follows:

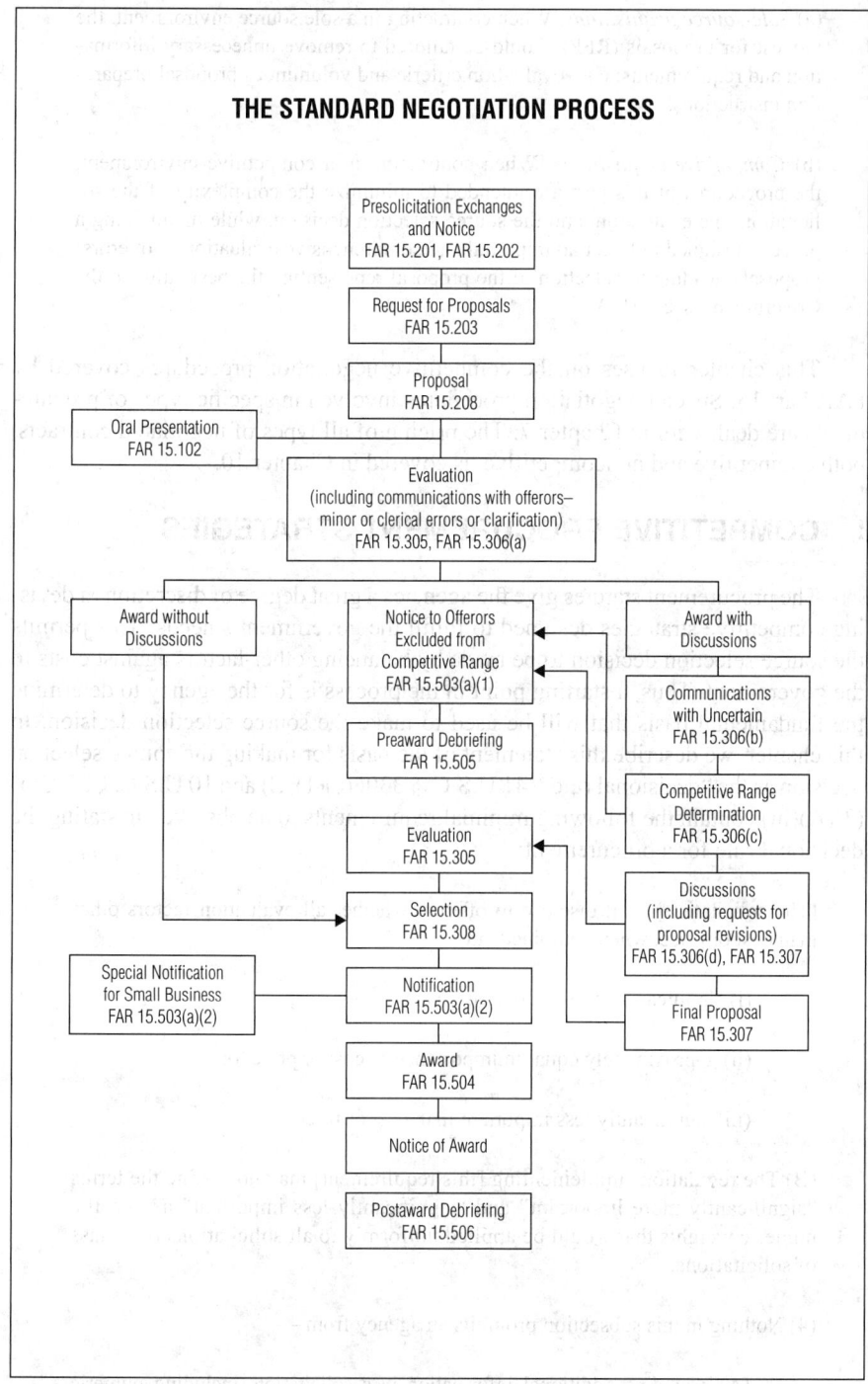

**Figure 6-1**

(a) *Sole-source acquisitions.* When contracting in a sole source environment, the request for proposals (RFP) should be tailored to remove unnecessary information and requirements; e.g., evaluation criteria and voluminous proposal preparation instructions.

(b) *Competitive acquisitions.* When contracting in a competitive environment, the procedures of this part are intended to minimize the complexity of the solicitation, the evaluation, and the source selection decision, while maintaining a process designed to foster an impartial and comprehensive evaluation of offerors' proposals, leading to selection of the proposal representing the best value to the Government (see 2.101).

This chapter focuses on the competitive negotiation procedures covered by FAR Part 15. Special negotiation procedures involved in specific types of procurements are dealt with in Chapter 7. The pricing of all types of negotiated contracts, both competitive and noncompetitive, is covered in Chapter 10.

# I.  COMPETITIVE PROCUREMENT STRATEGIES

The procurement statutes give the agencies a great degree of discretion in devising competitive strategies designed to fulfill the government's needs. This permits the source selection decision to be made by balancing other factors against costs to the government. Thus, a starting point in the process is for the agency to determine the fundamental basis that will be used to make the source selection decision. In this chapter, we describe this statement of the basis for making the source selection decision as the "decisional rule." 41 U.S.C. § 3306(c)(1)(C) and 10 U.S.C. § 2305(a)(3)(A)(iii) contain the following minimal requirements to be observed in stating the decisional rule for a procurement:

[The solicitation] shall disclose to offerors whether all evaluation factors other than cost or price, when combined, are —

(i) significantly more important than cost or price;

(ii) approximately equal in importance to cost or price; or

(iii) significantly less important than cost or price.

(B) The regulations implementing [this requirement] may not define the terms "significantly more important" and "significantly less important" as specific numeric weights that would be applied uniformly to all solicitations or a class of solicitations.

(4) Nothing in this subsection prohibits an agency from —

(A) providing additional information in a solicitation, including numeric weights for all evaluation factors and subfactors on a case-by-case basis; or

(B) stating in a solicitation that award will be made to the offeror that meets the solicitation's mandatory requirements at the lowest cost or price.

Although previous versions of FAR Part 15 did not use the term, procurements in which the selection was based on a tradeoff between price and other factors came to be known as "best value" procurements. However, the "Rewrite" of FAR Part 15, contained in FAC 97-02, 62 Fed. Reg. 51,224, Sept. 30, 1997, uses the term "best value" more broadly. It encompasses all procurement strategies, whether or not based on tradeoffs. FAR 15.302 states: "The objective of source selection is to select the proposal that represents the best value." The term is now defined in FAR 2.101 as follows:

"Best value" means the expected outcome of an acquisition that, in the Government's estimation, provides the greatest overall benefit in response to the requirement.

FAR 15.101, entitled "Best value continuum," elaborates on this concept as follows:

An agency can obtain best value in negotiated acquisitions by using any one or a combination of source selection approaches. In different types of acquisitions, the relative importance of cost or price may vary. For example, in acquisitions where the requirement is clearly definable and the risk of unsuccessful contract performance is minimal, cost or price may play a dominant role in source selection. The less definitive the requirement, the more development work required, or the greater the performance risk, the more technical or past performance considerations may play a dominant role in source selection.

Under this concept, procurement officials determine, in advance of soliciting proposals, what type of selection process will be best for the government. Where differences in non-cost factors will not materially impact the agency's needs, award on the basis of the lowest evaluated price would be appropriate. Where differences in non-cost factors will be material, a tradeoff process would be called for. The following material discusses these two processes. It also considers other potential strategies that are permissible under the ASPA and the FPASA.

## A. Tradeoff Process

As previously indicated, this strategy had previously been known as the best value technique. The hallmark of the system is that it permits the determination of best value to be made *after the receipt of proposals*. It is described in FAR 15.101-1 as follows:

(a) A tradeoff process is appropriate when it may be in the best interest of the Government to consider award to other than the lowest priced offeror or other than the highest technically rated offeror.

(b) When using the tradeoff process, the following apply:

(1) All evaluation factors and significant subfactors that will affect contract award and their relative importance shall be clearly stated in the solicitation; and

(2) The solicitation shall state whether all evaluation factors other than cost or price, when combined, are significantly more important than, approximately equal to, or significantly less important than cost or price.

(c) This process permits tradeoffs among cost or price and non-cost factors and allows the Government to accept other than the lowest priced proposal. The perceived benefits of the higher-priced proposal shall merit the additional cost, and the rationale for tradeoffs must be documented in the file in accordance with 15.406.

This process gives the source selection official very broad discretion when the offeror with the lowest cost to the government has not been evaluated best on the non-cost factors. There, the ultimate decision is made on a *subjective* judgment as to whether a higher cost to the government is worth the added value of the non-cost factors. See *TRW, Inc., v. Widnall*, 98 F.3d 1325 (Fed. Cir. 1996); *Environmental Chemical Corp.*, Comp. Gen. Dec. B-275819, 97-1 CPD ¶ 154. It is clear that this judgment as to the value of the non-cost factors need not be quantified, FAR 15.308. See *Widnall v. B3H Corp.*, 75 F.3d 1577 (Fed. Cir. 1996), stating that these tradeoff decisions must be based on a "reasoned explanation" of the decision but need not be based on quantification of the non-cost factors. The same result was reached by GAO in *Systems Mgmt., Inc.*, Comp. Gen. Dec. B-287032.5, 2002 CPD ¶ 29; *Kay & Assoc., Inc.*, Comp. Gen. Dec. B-258243.7, 96-1 CPD ¶ 266, and *EG&G Team*, Comp. Gen. Dec. B-259917.3, 95-2 CPD ¶ 175. If the agency does quantify some of the non-cost evaluation factors, GAO will not scrutinize the quantification for accuracy but will focus on the overall rationality of the best value decision, *DDD Co.*, Comp. Gen. Dec. B-276708, 97-2 CPD ¶ 44.

In the past, some agencies have attempted to devise numerical formulas to make this tradeoff appear to be *objective*. Some of these formulas have used a total point system by assigning points to the price, others have assigned dollar values to the non-price factors and a third have divided the price by the points assigned to non-price factors to come up with a dollars per point figure. Such techniques have been accepted as tools to be used in evaluating the relative merits of proposals. However, GAO has indicated that these are only evaluation techniques and that the source selection official should still exercise judgment in determining whether the merits of the highest scored proposal are worth paying a higher price. See *C&B Constr., Inc.,* Comp. Gen. Dec. B-401988.2, 2010 CPD ¶ 1, stating "a selection decision may not be made on point scores alone where the agency selection official has inadequate documentation on which to base a reasoned decision." See also *Harrison Sys., Ltd.*, 63 Comp. Gen. 244 (B-212675), 84-1 CPD ¶ 572 (recommending that a total point system not be used in combination with a statement that award will be made to the offeror receiving the highest number of points); *Storage Tech. Corp.*, Comp. Gen.

Dec. B-215336, 84-2 CPD ¶ 190 (dollar values assigned to non-price factors only to be used as a *guide* to the selection official); and *Moran Assocs.*, Comp. Gen. Dec. B-240564.2, 91-2 CPD ¶ 495 (cost/technical ratio formula only one tool to assure that the government was getting the best buy). In addition, a number of agencies have prohibited or strongly discouraged the use of such formulas.

## B. Lowest Price Technically Acceptable Source Selection Process

This strategy has been used for many years. The FAR now describes it as a "best value" procedure but the best value determination is made by the agency at the time the strategy is chosen, before receipt or analysis of proposals. Thus, when an agency has decided to use this strategy, it has decided that the best value will be obtained by paying the lowest price offered by any offeror that submits an acceptable "technical proposal" and has stated in the RFP that the decision will be made in this manner. The decision to use this process is highly discretionary, Comp. Gen. Dec. B-402530, 2010 CPD ¶ 117. A procurement is *not* a lowest price technically acceptable procurement if the RFP states that a tradeoff will be made but the source selection official concludes that the competitors are essentially equal on the non-price factors and awards to the offeror with the lowest price, *Apptis, Inc.*, Comp. Gen. Dec. B-403249, 2010 CPD ¶ 237.

FAR 15.101-2 describes this process as follows:

(a) The lowest price technically acceptable source selection process is appropriate when best value is expected to result from selection of the technically acceptable proposal with the lowest evaluated price.

(b) When using the lowest price technically acceptable process, the following apply:

(1) The evaluation factors and significant subfactors that establish the requirements of acceptability shall be set forth in the solicitation. Solicitations shall specify that award will be made on the basis of the lowest evaluated price of proposals meeting or exceeding the acceptability standards for non-cost factors. If the contracting officer documents the file pursuant to 15.304(c)(3)(iii), past performance need not be an evaluation factor in lowest price technically acceptable source selections. If the contracting officer elects to consider past performance as an evaluation factor, it shall be evaluated in accordance with 15.305. However, the comparative assessment in 15.305(a)(2)(i) does not apply. If the contracting officer determines that a small business' past performance is not acceptable, the matter shall be referred to the Small Business Administration for a Certificate of Competency determination, in accordance with the procedures contained in subpart 19.6 and 15 U.S.C. §637(b)(7).

(2) Tradeoffs are not permitted

       (3) Proposals are evaluated for acceptability but not ranked using the non-cost/price factors.

       (4) Exchanges may occur (see 15.306).

One important aspect of this technique is that the non-cost evaluation factors are all of equal importance. Thus, the failure of a proposal to meet any *one* of the factors will preclude award to the offeror submitting the proposal. See, for example, *Jungang Auto. Co.*, Comp. Gen. Dec. B-402623.2, 2010 CPD ¶ 144, where the protester was dropped from the procurement for failure to meet the experience requirement in the RFP; *Building Restoration Corp.*, Comp. Gen. Dec. B-402000, 2010 CPD ¶ 15, where the protester was dropped from the competition for an inadequate construction schedule and for having its safety officer also act as the quality control officer; *Synoptic Sys. Corp.*, Comp. Gen. Dec. B-290789.4, 2003 CPD ¶ 42, where two offerors were properly dropped from the competition after being scored unacceptable on two of a large number of factors; and *Dubinsky v. United States*, 44 Fed. Cl. 509 (1999), where an agency was precluded from awarding to an offer that had material failures to meet mandatory requirements. However, the offeror may be given an opportunity to cure the noncompliance through oral or written discussions if award on initial proposals will not be made and the proposal would otherwise be in the competitive range.

One major benefit of this strategy is that the agency can greatly shorten the evaluation process because, once the low price proposal has been found to be technically acceptable, there is no need to evaluate the acceptability of any of the other proposals. This streamlined process can be used as long as the agency has used the Instruction to Offerors — Competitive Acquisition solicitation provision in FAR 52.215-1 which states in ¶ (f)(4) that the agency intends to award without discussions.

The term "technically acceptable proposals" in the FAR refers to all non-cost factors. Thus, it includes factors dealing with the capability of the offerors as well as the technical details of the performance which is offered in the proposal. While FAR 15.101-2(b) refers only to "past performance" as requiring reference to Small Business Administration (SBA), the same rule would apply to other "capability" factors. See, e.g., *Vantex Serv. Corp.*, Comp. Gen. Dec. B-266199, 96-1 CPD ¶ 29, holding that when "traditional" responsibility factors such as "experience" are evaluated on a "go/no-go" basis, the matter must be referred to the SBA if the proposal is determined unacceptable because of such factors. See also *Dynamic Aviation — Helicopters*, Comp. Gen. Dec. B-274122, 96-2 CPD ¶ 166; and *Environsol, Inc.*, Comp. Gen. Dec. B-254223, 93-2 CPD ¶ 295.

This technique has been used extensively in the past. See, for example, *Weinschel Eng'g Co.*, 64 Comp. Gen. 524 (B-217202), 85-1 CPD ¶ 574, where GAO agreed with a source selection when the Navy awarded a fixed-price contract to the lowest priced offeror meeting the RFP's technical specifications. In *Saxon Corp.*,

Comp. Gen. Dec. B-216148, 85-1 CPD ¶ 87, the RFP provided for award to the offeror with the lowest overall price among those offers found acceptable in the technical and management areas. Technical and management factors were thus scored on a go/no-go basis. In *Computer Sciences Corp.*, Comp. Gen. Dec. B-213287, 84-2 CPD ¶ 151, the RFP for a data base management system called for award to the vendor with the lowest evaluated price offering a system judged to have a "user-friendly, English-like syntax." Award may also be made to the technically acceptable proposal with the lowest total discounted life cycle cost, *Hawaiian Tel. Co.*, Comp. Gen. Dec. B-187871, 77-1 CPD ¶ 298.

It has been held that "no narrative justifications" are required to support the assessment that an element of a technical proposal is unacceptable, *Al Ghanim Combined Group Co. Gen. Trad. & Cont. W.L.L. v. United States*, 56 Fed. Cl. 502 (2003) (evaluators merely circled "pass" or "fail" on an evaluation sheet). The court derived this rule from FAR 15.305(a)(3) stating that an "assessment of each offeror's ability to accomplish the technical requirements" was required only in tradeoff procurements. The court did not consider FAR 15.305(a) calling for documentation of "relative strengths, significant weaknesses, and risks."

The use of this method has on several occasions led to protests that sealed bidding was required for the procurement. In *Saxon Corp.*, Comp. Gen. Dec. B-216148, 85-1 CPD ¶ 87, GAO upheld the use of negotiation, finding that it was impossible to draft sufficiently precise specifications for a sealed bid procurement where a high level of technical and management competence was needed. Similarly, in *Essex Electro Eng'rs, Inc.*, 65 Comp. Gen. 242 (B-221114), 86-1 CPD ¶ 92, the use of negotiation was upheld because of the agency's need to conduct discussions with offerors. The protester's argument that the agency could have obtained the necessary information through a preaward survey was rejected, as the discussion process can be used to negotiate contractual terms as well as to obtain responsibility related information. See also *Vantex Serv. Corp.*, Comp. Gen. Dec. B-266199, 96-1 CPD ¶ 29, where the RFP listed three technical evaluation factors which the agency stated would be evaluated on a go/no-go basis to determine the acceptability of an offeror's proposal. Once technical acceptability was established based on the evaluation factors, price would become the determinative factor for award. GAO found proper the use of competitive negotiation because the agency reasonably determined that discussions were necessary.

## C. Combination of Tradeoff and Low Price Acceptable Processes

Although FAR Part 15 does not directly address the combination of these two processes, FAR 15.101 indicates that a "combination of source selection approaches" may be used. Thus an agency could subject some of the evaluation factors to a "go/no-go" test, while providing that others can be evaluated on the relative merits provided. This technique would enable tradeoffs to be made for those factors subject to evaluation on their relative merits while requiring rejection of the proposals not meeting the minimum requirements for those subject to the "go/no-go" test. Another strategy might be to subject all factors to a "go/no-go" test for the proposal to receive further consideration and then to evaluate the relative merits of those determined to be acceptable. These types of strategies were discussed in Chapter 2 of the GSA Handbook, Source Selection Procedures, APD P 2800.2, July 21, 1987, which provided the following guidance:

> [A] go, no-go approach can be applied to some or all of the major evaluation factors or subfactors identified in the solicitation. When all factors are go, no-go the process is equivalent to the lowest-priced acceptable proposal approach discussed above. When the "greatest value concept" is used, some evaluation factors may be used as discriminators and be evaluated on a go, no-go basis. An evaluation factor such as "management" may be used as a discriminator for evaluation on a go, no-go basis. If the "management" factor is scored adequate, it may, or may not, have further relevance in the evaluation process. . . . The evaluation process may be structured so that the factor has no further relevance . . . if it is scored adequate. On the other hand, the evaluation process may be structured so that the factor is scored and the merits of the proposal considered in the ultimate award decision. An adequate score in such an area is therefore a minimum requirement for selection. . . . This approach is frequently used in situations in which the product is subject to testing to establish whether it meets certain requirements outlined in the solicitation.

This method has been used in a number of situations and has not been questioned by either GAO or the Court of Federal Claims. See *Linc Gov't Servs., LLC v. United States*, 95 Fed. Cl. 155 (2010) (tradeoff between past performance and price among offerors that had submitted acceptable technical proposals); *Integrated Concepts & Research Corp.*, Comp. Gen. Dec. B-309803, 2008 CPD ¶ 117 (tradeoff of proposal risk, past performance and price among the acceptable technical proposals); *Utility Tool & Trailer, Inc.*, Comp. Gen. Dec. B-310535, 2008 CPD ¶ 1 (tradeoff of delivery, small business participation and price among the acceptable technical proposals); *Brewbaker White Sands JV*, Comp. Gen. Dec. B-295582.4, 2005 CPD ¶ 176 (tradeoff between past performance and price among offerors that had submitted acceptable technical proposals); *Sterling Servs., Inc.*, Comp. Gen. Dec. B-286326, 2000 CPD ¶ 208 (evaluation of past performance in a "Technically Acceptable — Performance/Price Tradeoff" procurement); and *ECI Telecom, Inc.*, 64 Comp. Gen. 688 (B-218533), 85-2 CPD ¶ 73 (go, no-go evaluation of all technical subfactors). See also *FMB Laundry, Inc.*, Comp. Gen. Dec. B-261837.2, 95-2 CPD ¶ 274, where the protester argued that the RFP was deficient because it failed to specify what weight would be accorded to the technical factors in relation to price. GAO stated that the fact that relative weight of acceptability verses price was not spelled out was irrelevant because the solicitation did not contemplate gradations in acceptability rankings as it was essentially a go/no-go determination. This procedure has been upheld in a procurement containing a "5000 round service life" requirement, *Smith & Wesson Div., Bangor Punta Corp. v. United States*, 782

F.2d 1074 (1st Cir. 1986), *reh'g and reh'g en banc denied, Unpub.* (1986), where a product was excluded from further consideration based on tests of samples which cracked before firing 5000 rounds. GAO has approved similar procedures where offerors had an opportunity to correct deficiencies found in initial testing, *Centennial Computer Prods., Inc.*, Comp. Gen. Dec. B-212979, 84-2 CPD ¶ 295.

## D. Negotiations After Source Selection

An "alternative source selection procedure" that had been identified in the earlier FAR 15.613 were the NASA "source evaluation board" and the DoD "Four-Step" procedures for use in contracting for research and development. The essential distinguishing element of these procedures was the selection of the winning offeror before the conduct of negotiations. These procedures are no longer alluded to in the FAR, but they appear to be acceptable procedures in contracting for technically complex work. This is explained in a comment by DoD in its promulgation of proposed revisions to the DFARS to implement the FAR Part 15 Rewrite, stating at 62 Fed. Reg. 63050, Nov. 26, 1997:

> DFARS guidance on the four-step source selection process and the alternate source selection process have been removed, as the new guidance at FAR 15.101, best value continuum, clearly allows such source selection processes.

For an example of the current use of this procedure, see *Veterans Tech., LLC*, Comp. Gen. Dec. B-310303.2, 2008 CPD ¶ 31.

Under the Four-Step procedure, technical and cost proposals were submitted sequentially. Preselection discussions were conducted only to permit clarification of proposals, restricted best and final offers were solicited and followed by full negotiation with the winner. The major differences in this technique from the conventional competitive negotiation technique are the amount of discussion permitted prior to source selection and the extent of negotiation that occurs after source selection. The major purpose of the Four-Step technique was to select the source based on its original proposal rather than on its proposal as enhanced by discussions. Its fundamental premise was that the most competent contractor was the one submitting the best original proposal. In order to ensure that the government ultimately got the best possible procurement, the Four-Step technique permitted full negotiation after source selection where the government agency had the opportunity to press for changes in the winner's proposal as long as they did not alter the basis for the source selection.

The original guidance on the procedure was contained in the 1970 NASA Procurement Directive 70-15, which stated in part:

> In cost-reimbursement type contracts and all research and development contracts, ambiguities and uncertainties in the proposals of such firms shall be pointed out during discussions by the contracting officer, but not deficiencies

Although GAO refused to rule that this original NASA procedure was in violation of the statutory requirement for discussions, it did find that it needed clarification, stating in 51 Comp. Gen. 621 (B-173677) (1972) at 622-23:

> We think the propriety of the prohibition in NASA Procurement Directive 70-15 against discussing "deficiencies" must be considered in the light of these problems. We think certain weaknesses, inadequacies, or deficiencies in proposals can be discussed without being unfair to other proposers. There well may be instances where it becomes apparent during the course of negotiations that one or more proposers have reasonably placed emphasis on some aspect of the procurement different from that intended by the solicitation. Unless this difference in the meaning given the solicitation is removed, the proposers are not competing on the same basis. Similarly, if a proposal is deemed weak because it fails to include substantiation for a proposed approach or solution, in the circumstance where the inadequacy appears to have arisen because of a reasonable misunderstanding of the amount of data called for, we believe the proposer should be given the opportunity, time permitting, to furnish such substantiation. Thus, it seems to us that the prohibition in NASA Procurement Directive 70-15 against discussing "deficiencies" needs clarification.

Subsequently, NASA made minor modifications to the policy. The complete regulatory statement was in NFS 18-15.613-71(b)(5):

> (ii) Cost-reimbursement contracts and all contracts for research and development.
>
>> (A) The contracting officer, in concert with or on behalf of the SEB, will conduct written and/or oral discussions of the effort to be accomplished and the cost of the effort with all offerors determined to be within the competitive range. The discussions are intended to assist the SEB or other evaluators (1) in understanding fully each offeror's proposal and its strengths and weaknesses based upon the individual efforts of each offeror; (2) in assuring that the meanings and the points of emphasis of RFP provisions have been adequately conveyed to the offerors so that all are competing equally on the basis intended by the Government; (3) in evaluating the personnel proposed by each firm; and (4) in presenting a report to the Source Selection Official that makes the discriminations among proposals clear and visible. In this process, prior to contractor selection, the Government's interests are not served by its assuming the role of an information exchange or clearinghouse.
>>
>> (B) In cost-reimbursement type contracts and all research and development contracts, the contracting officer shall point out instances in which the meaning of some aspect of a proposal is not clear and instances in which some aspects of the proposal failed to include substantiation for a proposed approach, solution, or cost estimate.
>>
>> (C) However, where the meaning of a proposal is clear and the Board has sufficient information to assess its validity and the proposal contains a

weakness which is inherent in an offeror's management, engineering, or scientific judgment, or which is the result of its own lack of competence or inventiveness in preparing its proposal, the contracting officer shall not point out the weaknesses. Discussions are useful in ascertaining the presence or absence of strengths and weaknesses. The possibility that such discussions may lead an offeror to discover that it has a weakness is not a reason for failing to inquire into a matter where the meaning is not clear or where insufficient information is available, since understanding of the meaning and validity of the proposed approaches, solutions, and cost estimates is essential to a sound selection. Offerors should not be informed of the relative strengths or weaknesses of their proposals in relation to those of other offerors.

This guidance was deleted from the regulation in 63 Fed. Reg. 44,408, Aug. 19, 1998.

GAO commented on the revised procedure in *Sperry Rand Corp.*, 54 Comp. Gen. 408 (B-181460), 74-2 CPD ¶ 276:

The NASA procedure represents one approach to meeting the statutory requirement for written and oral discussions, 10 U.S.C. § 2304(g) [now 10 U.S.C. § 2304(a)]. In part, at least, the underlying rationale is that to point out deficiencies during the discussions would compromise the competition, because weaker proposals would be improved, and a leveling effect would occur. To avoid this, discussions are limited to clarification of proposals; after selection, the agency then negotiates the best possible contract on terms most advantageous to the Government. Considered in the abstract, potential conflicts between the procedure and the statutory requirement can be envisioned; for instance, as appears to be contemplated by [the protester], a situation where the discussions are so limited in scope and content that they amount to little more than a ceremonial exercise, with the meaningful discussions transposed almost entirely into the final negotiations stage.

NASA decisions to limit discussions based on this policy were affirmed in *Program Res., Inc.*, Comp. Gen. Dec. B-192964, 79-1 CPD ¶ 281; *Pioneer Contract Servs., Inc.*, Comp. Gen. Dec. B-197245, 81-1 CPD ¶ 107; and *Taft Broad. Corp.*, Comp. Gen. Dec. B-222818, 86-2 CPD ¶ 125. However, discussions were not meaningful where NASA waived a regulation concerning interest rates for one offeror yet failed to inform the other offeror of the waiver during discussions, *Union Carbide Corp.*, 55 Comp. Gen. 802 (B-184495), 76-1 CPD ¶ 134. GAO held that discussions were required because this was not a question of technical transfusion.

DoD adopted a similar procedure for R&D procurements when it developed its Four-Step negotiation process, DFARS 215.613 (pre-Rewrite). Step one called for very limited discussions. DFARS 215.613-70(f) provided:

(2) In conducting step one — (i) Limit discussions to only what is necessary to ensure that both parties understand each other; (ii) Do not tell offerors about de-

ficiencies in their proposals; and (iii) Provide written clarifications to all offerors when it appears the Government's requirements have been misinterpreted.

The regulations concerning Four-Step negotiation did not cite technical transfusion as the reason for limiting discussions. Rather, this limitation on discussions was based on the premise that the competition was fairer if source selection was made on the basis of the initial position of the competitors rather than on their final position, which included modifications suggested or induced by the procuring agency through the process of discussions. The reason for not invoking technical transfusion as the reason for limiting discussions in step one may have been that the regulations anticipated that technical transfusion would take place with the selected offeror in step four. The DoD Four-Step procedure was challenged in *GTE Sylvania, Inc.*, 57 Comp. Gen. 715 (B-188272), 77-2 CPD ¶ 422, where GAO made an extensive analysis of the procedure and concluded that the limited discussions actually conducted met the statutory requirement. For a full evaluation of the Four-Step procedure, questioning whether it meets the statutory requirement for discussions, see Smith, *The New "Four Step" Source Selection Procedure: Is the Solution Worse Than the Problem?*, 11 Pub. Ct. L. Rev. 322 (1980).

EPA's version of the Four-Step procedure, PIN 77-15, was challenged in *Roy F. Weston, Inc.*, Comp. Gen. Dec. B-197949, 80-1 CPD ¶ 340. Although the protester contended that the items not brought up in discussion were deficiencies, GAO disagreed, stating:

> [W]e think a more accurate description would be that they were the differences in the relative merits of the proposals, as viewed by the [technical evaluation panel]. If they were truly weaknesses or deficiencies, then there would have been an obligation on the part of EPA to discuss the areas with Weston, assuming no danger of technical transfusion, notwithstanding PIN 77-15.

This would appear to indicate that the limitation on discussions in this type of procurement procedure will not be permitted in some circumstances.

## II. EVALUATION FACTORS AND SUBFACTORS

Evaluation factors and subfactors (often called "evaluation criteria") describe the matters which are to be considered in determining which proposal will be most advantageous to the government. See the following general guidance in FAR 15.304:

(a) The award decision is based on evaluation factors and significant subfactors that are tailored to the acquisition.

(b) Evaluation factors and significant subfactors must —

(1) Represent the key areas of importance and emphasis to be considered in the source selection decision; and

(2) Support meaningful comparison and discrimination between and among competing proposals.

While this general guidance is imprecise, it does provide a degree of assistance in selecting an appropriate number of evaluation factors. First, it indicates that the decision on the evaluation factors to be used should be made on each source selection. Thus, ¶ (a) calls for "tailoring" the factors to the acquisition. This precludes merely using the same factors that have been used in the past on similar acquisitions and suggests a new analysis for each new source selection. Second, ¶ (b)(1) calls for factors that focus on "key areas of importance" — with the implication that only major areas of importance should be evaluated. In following this guidance, contracting officers must point out to the other members of the acquisition team that, as a general proposition, *all* key areas of importance will be included in the specifications as mandatory requirements. Thus, when the contract is awarded, the contractor will be obligated to meet these requirements. Since this is the case, there is no necessity to evaluate all of the key areas of importance — only the major areas need be evaluated. This proposition is reinforced by ¶ (b)(2) requiring evaluation factors to "support meaningful comparison and discrimination." This required the acquisition team to review past acquisitions of the same or similar products or services to ascertain which evaluation factors have actually discriminated among the competitors. When it is found that a factor has not served this purpose — with the competitors being given similar scores or ratings — that factor should not be used in the new procurement. Following this analytical process, the acquisition team should be able to select a small number of evaluation factors that permit award to the offeror that will provide the best value to the government.

The specific number and types of evaluation factors and subfactors depend upon the nature of the procurement and the needs of the government. Procuring officials have broad discretion in selecting the factors and in determining their relative importance. See *Augmentation, Inc.*, Comp. Gen. Dec. B-186614, 76-2 CPD ¶ 235, where GAO stated:

> [I]t is well settled that a determination of an agency's minimum needs and the selection and weights of evaluation criteria to be used to measure how well offerors will meet those needs are within the broad discretion entrusted to agency procurement officials.

Within this broad authority, Congress has required that, as a minimum, the evaluation factors must include cost to the government and quality of the products or services and that all factors and significant subfactors and their relative importance must be disclosed in the solicitation, 10 U.S.C. § 2305(a)(3) and 41 U.S.C. § 33306(c)(1). FAR 15.304 implements these requirements (not reflecting the 2011 codification of Title 41), with additional factors, as follows:

> (c) The evaluation factors and significant subfactors that apply to an acquisition and their relative importance are within the broad discretion of agency acquisition officials, subject to the following requirements:

(1) Price or cost to the Government shall be evaluated in every source selection (10 U.S.C. 2305(a)(3)(A) (ii) and 41 U.S.C. 253a(c)(1)(B)) (also see part 36 for architect-engineer contracts);

(2) The quality of the product or service shall be addressed in every source selection through consideration of one or more non-cost evaluation factors such as past performance, compliance with solicitation requirements, technical excellence, management capability, personnel qualifications, and prior experience (10 U.S.C. 2305(a)(3) (A)(i) and 41 U.S.C. 253a(c) (1)(A)); and

(3)(i) Except as set forth in paragraph (c)(3)(iii) of this section, past performance shall be evaluated in all source selections for negotiated competitive acquisitions expected to exceed the simplified acquisition threshold.

(ii) For solicitations involving bundling that offer a significant opportunity for subcontracting, the contracting officer must include a factor to evaluate past performance indicating the extent to which the offeror attained applicable goals for small business participation under contracts that required subcontracting plans (15 U.S.C. 637(d)(4)(G)(ii)).

(iii) Past performance need not be evaluated if the contracting officer documents the reason past performance is not an appropriate evaluation factor for the acquisition.

(4) The extent of participation of small disadvantaged business concerns in performance of the contract shall be evaluated in unrestricted acquisitions expected to exceed $ 550,000 ($ 1,000,000 for construction) subject to certain limitations (see 19.201 and 19.1202).

(5) For solicitations involving bundling that offer a significant opportunity for subcontracting, the contracting officer must include proposed small business subcontracting participation in the subcontracting plan as an evaluation factor (15 U.S.C. 637(d)(4)(G)(i)).

(6) If telecommuting is not prohibited, agencies shall not unfavorably evaluate an offer that includes telecommuting unless the contracting officer executes a written determination in accordance with FAR 7.108(b).

The evaluation factors specified in a solicitation not only notify the offerors of what will be evaluated, they also state either the promises which must be included in each proposal or the issues that will be evaluated to assess the capability of the offeror. In this book we refer to these two types of evaluation factors as "offer factors" and "capability factors." Offer factors, which will be incorporated into the contract, include price or estimated cost and fee and any other features that will become part of the offeror's contractual undertaking, such as the precise product or service to be furnished, an offered delivery schedule, a specific warranty, or any other promise made by the offeror that will become part of the contract. Capability factors typically include past performance, experience, key personnel, and understanding of the work. Some capability factors, such as key personnel, can be treated as offer factors if the agency decides to incorporate the information submitted by the offeror into the contract. As far as evaluation and source selection is concerned, this classification is not relevant, but the solicitation should inform the offerors which factors will be made contractual promises and which will be used solely for evaluation purposes. This matter will be discussed in Section III, below. The following section deals with the types of evaluation factors and subfactors which might be used by an agency, the requirements for their disclosure, and the indication of their relative importance.

## A. Commonly Used Evaluation Factors

Neither the statutes nor the FAR deal coherently with the classification of evaluation factors. Both statutes combine non-cost factors dealing with the capability of the offeror with those describing offers solicited by the RFP under the broad category "quality." See 10 U.S.C. § 2305(a)(3)(A)(i) and 41 U.S.C. § 3306(c)(1)(A) specifying evaluation of the "quality of the product or services to be provided (including technical capability, management capability, prior experience, and past performance of the offeror)." FAR 15.304(c)(2) contains this same classification with the addition of "compliance with solicitation requirements" and "personnel qualifications."

Rather than combining non-cost factors under this general heading of quality, the following material distinguishes between factors dealing with the capability of the offeror and those which relate to offers solicited by the RFP.

### 1. Offer Factors

Offer factors are those factors that will result in contractual promises made by the contractor to the government beyond the promises embodied in the RFP. In the normal competitive procurement, the government spells out the greater portion of the offer it is soliciting in the RFP — including the contract specifications and the terms and conditions. If an offeror signs the proposal without taking exception to any mandatory element of the RFP, it has agreed to make the offer solicited by the government and those promises play no further role in the evaluation process. If an offeror takes exception to a mandatory element of the RFP, award to that offeror is precluded until the matter has been cleared up by amending the RFP or having the offeror withdraw the exception.

Thus, in this discussion, offer factors are additional promises that are solicited by the RFP and incorporated into the resulting contract, either by reference or, preferably, by specific contract terms that are agreed to by both parties.

## a.  Cost to the Government

The one offer evaluation factor that is present in every negotiated procurement is cost to the government. Offerors submit this offer by filling out Section B of the Uniform Contract Format when they submit their proposals. This discussion of cost to the government includes the amount to be paid to the contractor and other costs which the government might incur in procuring and using articles or services.

### (1) Amount to Be Paid to the Contractor

The amount to be paid to the contractor depends on the pricing arrangement to be used in the contract. When a firm-fixed-price contract is involved, the offeror's proposed price, not a mere estimate of the "realistic" cost, is the criterion which must be used in evaluating the proposal, *IBM Corp.*, Comp. Gen. Dec. B-299504, 2008 CPD ¶ 64; *Verestar Gov't Servs. Group*, Comp. Gen. Dec. B-291854, 2003 CPD ¶ 68; *Litton Sys., Inc.*, 63 Comp. Gen. 585 (B-215106), 84-2 CPD ¶ 317. This rule is followed because the contractor bears the risk of costs exceeding the price of a firm-fixed-price contract. If the agency doubts the offeror's ability to perform at the offered price, the problem should be treated in the evaluation of non-price factors, such as performance risk, or as a matter of responsibility, *Pemco Aeroplex, Inc.*, Comp. Gen. Dec. B-310372.3, 2008 CPD ¶ 126 (risk of low price properly evaluated because RFP called for evaluation of "proposal risk" by assessing "price realism"); *Alabama Aircraft Indus., Inc. — Birmingham v. United States*, 83 Fed. Cl. 666 (2008) (risk of low price in *Pemco Aeroplex* procurement not properly assessed because of flaws in agency reasoning); *Guam Shipyard*, Comp. Gen. Dec. B-311321, 2008 CPD ¶ 124 (low price properly assessed as "very high" risk when it was 23% under government estimate); *CSE Constr.*, Comp. Gen. Dec. B-291268.2, 2002 CPD ¶ 207 (where the RFP contains no relevant evaluation factor pertaining to price realism or understanding, a determination that an offeror's price on a fixed-price contract is a responsibility issue). Similarly, if the agency believes that the offeror's price indicates a lack of understanding of the work to be performed, this should be taken into consideration in the evaluation of capability or the determination of responsibility. See *Wackenhut Servs., Inc.*, Comp. Gen. Dec. B-286037, 2001 CPD ¶ 114 (low price of two offerors properly led to assessment of lack of understanding of the work but no requirement to make detailed assessment of elements of price of offeror with total price in line with other offerors); *Centech Group, Inc.*, Comp. Gen. Dec. B-278715, 98-1 CPD ¶ 108 (low option year prices indicated "an inherent lack of technical competence"). Furthermore, an agency may eliminate an offeror from the competitive range if it fails to submit information demonstrating that its low price is reasonable, *International Outsourcing Servs., LLC v. United States*, 69 Fed. Cl. 40 (2005). GAO has taken note of the fact that there is no regulatory requirement for a price realism analysis because FAR 15.305(a)(1) merely provides that cost realism analyses may be used "in exceptional cases, on other competitive fixed-price-type contracts (see 15.404-1(d)(3))," *Team BOS/Naples —*

*Gemmo S.p.A./DelJen*, Comp. Gen. Dec. B-298865.3, 2008 CPD ¶ 11. However, GAO appears to be holding that price realism analysis will be required when the RFP states that the agency "may" make such an analysis, *Al Qabandi United Co.*, Comp. Gen. Dec. B-310600.3, 2008 CPD ¶ 112; *Computer Sciences Corp.*, Comp. Gen. Dec. B-298494.2, 2007 CPD ¶ 103.

There has been considerable confusion over the evaluation of fixed-price incentive contracts and the FAR does not address this issue. In the past, GAO stated that target cost should be used to evaluate the proposed prices, *Televiso Elecs.*, 46 Comp. Gen. 631 (B-159922) (1967). In *Serv-Air, Inc.*, 58 Comp. Gen. 362, 79-1 CPD ¶ 212, GAO held that the target price of one offeror could be contrasted with the ceiling price of another offeror in a "best case/worst case" comparison. In *Motorola, Inc.*, Comp. Gen. Dec. B-236294, 89-2 CPD ¶ 484, GAO condoned the use of the ceiling price to evaluate cost to the government. The use of target prices alone might be logical if all offerors are proposing to use the same fixed-price incentive formula with the same ceiling. However, if the RFP permits the offerors to propose different formulas, it is better practice to use the ceiling price as the evaluation factor because this is the only element of the formula that is common to all offerors. With respect to realism of target cost proposals, FAR 15.305(a)(1) states that "Cost realism analyses may also be used on fixed-price incentive contracts" — apparently permitting use of probable target cost as an evaluation factor. GAO reached this conclusion in *Eurest Support Servs.*, Comp. Gen. Dec. B-285813.3, 2003 CPD ¶ 139, holding that an agency must assess the realism of proposed target costs and adjust them for evaluation purposes if they are unrealistic. See also *Allied-Signal Aerospace Co.*, Comp. Gen. Dec. B-250822, 93-1 CPD ¶ 201, finding an agency decision to adjust target cost to reflect unrealistically low estimate "a prudent exercise of agency discretion"; and *Universal Techs., Inc.*, Comp. Gen. Dec. B-241157, 91-1 CPD ¶ 63, finding that the agency properly compared a realistic proposed target cost of one offeror with the proposed ceiling price of a competitor in making the source selection tradeoff decision. If target price is used as the evaluation factor, the target profit should be adjusted if a cost realism analysis indicates an adjustment of the target cost. However, GAO has held that it is improper to adjust the ceiling price upward in connection with increasing the target cost based on a cost realism analysis, *Raytheon Co.*, Comp. Gen. Dec. B-242484.2 , 91-2 CPD ¶131.

In cost-reimbursement contracts, both the realistic expected cost of performance and the proposed fee should be used as evaluation factors. FAR 15.305(a)(1) requires that a cost realism analysis be conducted "to determine what the Government should realistically expect to pay for the proposed effort," and FAR 15.404-1(d)(2)(i) states that the probable cost "shall be used for purposes of evaluation to determine the best value." This is consistent with GAO decisions, 50 Comp. Gen. 739 (B-171663) (1971); *DOT Sys., Inc.*, Comp. Gen. Dec. B-185558, 76-2 CPD ¶ 186; *Boeing Sikorsky Aircraft Support*, Comp. Gen. Dec. B-277263.2, 97-2 CPD ¶ 91. GAO has held that where the RFP is amended to call for a cost-reimbursement rather than fixed-price contract, the agency should also amend the RFP to explicitly include cost realism as an evaluation factor and notify offerors that proposed costs may be adjusted accordingly, *Varian Assocs., Inc.*, Comp. Gen. Dec. B-209658, 83-1 CPD ¶ 658. In that case, the initial RFP had listed "Lowest Evaluated Cost to the Government" as a factor, but although the protest was denied GAO stated that the better practice was to amend the solicitation.

The evaluation of fee depends on what type of cost-reimbursement contract is used. In a cost-plus-fixed-fee contract, the proposed fixed-fee should be used as the evaluation factor, rather than a "realistic" estimate of the fee, since the former reflects a more reliable judgment, *Booz, Allen & Hamilton*, 63 Comp. Gen. 599 (B-213665), 84-2 CPD ¶ 329. In a cost-plus-award-fee contract, it is proper to use the offeror's proposed fee structure as the evaluation factor, *Management Servs., Inc.*, Comp. Gen. Dec. B-206364, 82-2 CPD ¶ 164. Thus, it is permissible to give a higher evaluation to an offeror that proposes a higher maximum fee on the theory that this will provide more incentive for good performance, *Boeing Sikorsky Aircraft Support*, Comp. Gen. Dec. B-277263.2, 97-2 CPD ¶ 91, or to an offeror that proposes to share its award fees with its employees on the theory that this will motivate them to perform better, *Cleveland Telecomm. Corp.*, 73 Comp. Gen. 303 (B-257294), 94-2 CPD ¶ 105. Compare *Research Triangle Inst.*, Comp. Gen. Dec. B-278254, 98-1 CPD ¶ 22, where an offeror was given a higher evaluation for proposing a low award fee.

The evaluation factors that can be used to determine the "price" in selecting contractors for variable quantity contracts are discussed in Chapter 9 in the discussion of these types of contracts.

## (2) OTHER COSTS TO THE GOVERNMENT

Products or services purchased by the government, on either a fixed-price or cost-reimbursement basis, may result in the government incurring costs of acquisition or ownership that are not included in the contract price or cost. There is little clear guidance on the consideration of such costs as evaluation factors. The procurement statutes might be interpreted to require that other costs to the government be specified as evaluation factors. They state that solicitations "shall at a minimum include" evaluation factors, "including cost or price, cost-related or price-related factors and subfactors," 10 U.S.C. § 2305(a)(2)(A)(i) and 41 U.S.C. § 3306(b)(1)(A). However, the FAR does not repeat this language, with FAR 15.304(c)(1) merely stating that "[p]rice or cost to the Government shall be evaluated in every source selection." GAO has not interpreted the statutes or the regulations as requiring the consideration of such costs in evaluating proposals, *Kastle Sys., Inc.*, Comp. Gen. Dec. B-231990, 88-2 CPD ¶ 415. See also *Sensis Corp.*, Comp. Gen. Dec. B-265790.2, 96-1 CPD ¶ 77 (life-cycle costs are not required to be evaluated as part of the cost/price evaluation). However, the failure to consider other costs to the government could lead to poor procurement decisions. As a matter of practice, other costs to the government are frequently used as evaluation factors or subfactors whether objectively quantified or subjectively determined.

The most common cost of acquisition used as an evaluation criterion is transportation costs. This is one of the few areas in which evaluation of costs incurred by the government is mandated. FAR 47.305-2 provides that a solicitation for supplies will specify that offers may be f.o.b. origin, f.o.b. destination, or both, and that they will be evaluated on the basis of the lowest overall cost to the government. In such cases, the solicitation must require the offeror to furnish the government with applicable data necessary to compute transportation costs.

Costs incurred as a result of owning an item are part of what is known as "life cycle" costs, and should be considered during acquisition planning, FAR 7.105(a)(3)(i). FAR 7.101 defines life cycle costs as "the total cost to the Government of acquiring, operating, supporting, and (if applicable) disposing of the items being acquired." The magnitude of the costs beyond the original acquisition costs can greatly exceed the item's purchase price or production cost. See, for example, *Lockheed Missiles & Space Co. v. Department of the Treasury*, GSBCA 11776-P, 93-1 BCA ¶ 25,401, *aff'd*, 4 F.3d 955 (Fed. Cir. 1993), in which such costs resulted in awarding the contract to an offeror whose price totaled $1.4 billion over others whose prices were $900 and $700 million. Extensive agency analysis, quantified in dollar figures, illustrated the differences between the technical proposals and justified paying the price premium.

Agencies are given broad discretion in selecting the life cycle costs that will be evaluated. In *ViON Corp.*, Comp. Gen. Dec. B-256363, 94-1 CPD ¶ 373, where the RFP contained a clear description of the factors that would be considered in determining life cycle costs, GAO denied the protest that environmental costs, such as cooling, electricity, and space should have been included. GAO concluded that the agency properly decided not to consider these factors because its prior experience indicated that they were not useful discriminators between technical solutions.

Quantification of life-cycle costs in dollar amounts in not required, *Raytheon Co.*, Comp. Gen. Dec. B-298626.2, 2007 CPD ¶ 185 (adjectival rating of life cycle costs permissible when RFP stated that such costs would not be a "driver" in the source selection process); *Ingalls Shipbuilding, Inc.*, Comp. Gen. Dec. B-275830, 97-1 CPD ¶ 180 (price premium justified because awardee's proposed life-cycle cost reduction *approach* provided the greatest probability of achieving the greatest life cycle cost savings). However, if the RFP requires the submission of specific life-cycle cost information, that information must be used in evaluating such costs, *Sikorsky Aircraft Co.*, Comp. Gen. Dec. B-299145, 2007 CPD ¶ 45. See also *Boeing Co.*, Comp. Gen. Dec. B-311344, 2008 CPD ¶ 114, sustaining a protest because the agency did not correctly use the data submitted by the protester to calculate the life cycle costs of proposed air tankers. Quantified life-cycle costs have been the critical element in several source selections. See, for example, *Sundstrand Corp.*,

Comp. Gen. Dec. B-227038, 87-2 CPD ¶ 83 (approving award to offeror with sub-stantially higher unit price on turbine engines due to superior life cycle cost sav-ings); and *American Airlines Training Corp.*, Comp. Gen. Dec. B-217421, 85-2 CPD ¶ 365 (finding that future flight training costs more than made up for the large price differential).

DFARS PGI 207.105(b)(13)(i) states that the acquisition plan should describe "the extent of integrated logistics support planning, including total life cycle system management and performance based logistics." However, this apparently does not require the use of life cycle costs as evaluation factors, as more definitive language was contained in DAR 1-335 and that regulation was not interpreted as imposing such a requirement, *Big Bud Tractors, Inc. v. United States*, 2 Cl. Ct. 188, *aff'd*, 727 F.2d 1118 (Fed. Cir. 1983); *Big Bud Tractors, Inc.*, Comp. Gen. Dec. B-209858, 83-1 CPD ¶ 127. GAO found that although the regulation "requires" that life cy-cle costs be considered as a factor during the procurement cycle, "we do not read the regulation as requiring that [life cycle costs] be an evaluation factor for each award." Accord *Prudential-Maryland Joint Venture Co. v. Lehman*, 590 F. Supp. 1390 (D.D.C. 1984). Whether to use life cycle costs as evaluation factors in defense procurements is thus left to the discretion of the contracting officer. Other deci-sions affirming an agency decision not to evaluate life-cycle costs include *General Tel. Co. Of California*, Comp. Gen. Dec. B-190142, Feb.22, 1978, *Unpub.* (evalua-tion of the cost of government self-insurance would have been too "indefinite" and "speculative"); *Hawaiian Tel. Co.*, Comp. Gen. Dec. B-187871, 77-1 CPD ¶ 298 (evaluation of possible termination costs would be too speculative); *General Elec. Aerospace Sys.*, Comp. Gen. Dec. B-250514, 93-1 CPD ¶ 101 (no requirement to evaluate cost of limited rights in technical data).

If life cycle costs are not identified as an evaluation factor, they may not be evaluated, *Marquette Medical Sys., Inc.*, Comp. Gen. Dec. B-277827.5, 99-1 CPD ¶ 90 (agency improperly evaluated the savings from receiving new equipment ver-sus the costs of receiving upgraded equipment). See also *Spectrum Sys., Inc.*, Comp. Gen. Dec. B-401130, 2009 CPD ¶ 110 (agency omitted life-cycle cost evaluation when RFQ contained no such evaluation factor); *Interspiro, Inc. v. United States*, 72 Fed. Cl. 672 (2006) (agency properly did not evaluate life cycle costs because the RFP contained no statement they would be evaluated). Compare *Engineered Air Sys., Inc.*, Comp. Gen. Dec. B-283011, 99-2 CPD ¶ 63, where GAO found that the agency properly evaluated extended warranties when the RFP merely stated that the agency would "give evaluation credit for proposed features that met or exceeded the stated objectives."

When life cycle costs are an evaluation factor, it is unclear whether a general statement in the solicitation informing offerors that such costs are to be evaluated is adequate, or whether it is necessary to specify the particular costs to be evaluated. In *Lanier Bus. Prods., Inc.*, 60 Comp. Gen. 306 (B-200695), 81-1 CPD ¶ 188, *recons. denied ex rel., Dictaphone Corp.*, Comp. Gen. Dec. B-200695.2, 81-2 CPD ¶ 511, resolicitation was recommended where the RFQ merely stated that life cycle costing would be employed and did not adequately inform offerors of the specific evaluation factors to be used. However, in *Southwestern Bell Tel. Co.*, Comp. Gen. Dec. B-200523.3, 82-1 CPD ¶ 203, GAO stated:

> Where an agency makes it clear that its evaluation will be based on an analysis of expected system life-cycle costs without qualification, offerors may reasonably expect that all determinable elements of cost will be taken into account.

These cases illustrate the difficulties created by vague language describing the life cycle costs that will be evaluated. The offerors clearly had difficulty ascertaining what costs would be evaluated, with the result that the ground rules of the competition were not clearly disclosed in the RFP. See also *AM Int'l*, Comp. Gen. Dec. B-200200 81-1 CPD ¶ 258, stating that "[w]hen life-cycle costs are to be evaluated, we believe that the solicitation should not only indicate the fact, but also the useful life period that will be utilized in the evaluation."

When the RFP states that life cycle costs are to be evaluated and requests data as to the costs that a proposed item will produce, the agency must use the data to assess the amount of life cycle costs to be attributed to each proposal, *Sikorsky Aircraft Co.*, Comp. Gen. Dec. B-299145, 2007 CPD ¶ 45. In that case, GAO sustained a protest because the agency had obtained maintenance data for each proposed helicopter but had used a normalized number attributing the same maintenance costs to different helicopters.

## b. Non-Cost Offer Factors

Where the contractor is merely required to comply with specifications furnished by the government and the terms and conditions in the RFP, there will be no non-cost offer evaluation factors and no need for technical or management proposals. However, in many procurements the government solicits or permits offerors to propose alterations to the specifications or terms and conditions and treats these offers as evaluation factors. When such alterations are used as evaluation factors, the agency is indicating to offerors that they are of value to the agency and that the agency will therefore consider paying a higher price to obtain that value. When this is done, the general practice is to subsequently amend the specifications and terms and conditions so that the awarded contract makes these offers contractually binding. However, agencies can treat these factors as capability factors and not incorporate them into the contract if they do not want to be contractually bound to them. See *DGR Assocs., Inc.*, Comp. Gen. Dec. B-285428, 2000 CPD ¶ 145, denying a protest asserting that the agency should not have assessed enhancements proposed by an offeror because they were not incorporated into the contract as promises.

The use of non-cost offer factors greatly complicates the task of offerors because they must attempt to anticipate the value that the agency will give to different amounts of enhanced performance or alteration of terms and conditions. To ease this problem, the best practice is for agencies to use such factors only when they can not specify their precise requirements in the RFP.

## (1) ENHANCEMENTS

Probably the most common type of non-cost offer factor is enhancements to the work or results called for by the specifications. In such cases the specification generally will call for a minimum level of performance and the RFP will indicate that the agency will evaluate greater performance. In such cases, the best practice is for the agency to clearly delineate the range of enhancements it is willing to consider so that offerors do not propose enhancements that are of no benefit to the agency. It is also good practice to obtain price proposals for different levels of enhancements to enable the agency to compare proposals at each level of performance. However, the use of general language stating that enhancements will be evaluated has been approved even when the offerors had to speculate as to the value of specific enhancements. See *Lexis-Nexis*, Comp. Gen. Dec. B-260023, 95-1 CPD ¶ 14, where GAO held that the RFP was sufficiently specific as to enhancements when it listed the areas where enhancements would be evaluated and gave some examples of features that were of value to the agency. When agencies state in the RFP that they are seeking enhancements, they must evaluate them. See *Boeing Co.*, Comp. Gen. Dec. B-311344, 2008 CPD ¶ 114 (statement requesting offerors to satisfy as many technical requirements as possible); *Humana Military Healthcare Servs.*, Comp. Gen. Dec. B-401652.2, 2009 CPD ¶ 219 (general requirement that offerors proposing enhancements "should describe and demonstrate its benefit, monetary or otherwise, to the Government").

General statements in the RFP indicating that the agency was seeking superior performance have also been found to be sufficient to alert offerors that the agency was going to evaluate enhancements. See, for example, *Northrop Grumman Info. Tech., Inc.*, Comp. Gen. Dec. B-400134.10, 2009 CPD ¶ 167 (agency required to consider enhancement when RFP stated that offerors would be evaluated on "extent to which" they exceeded a requirement); *IPlus, Inc.*, Comp. Gen. Dec. B-298020, 2006 CPD ¶ 90 (statement that award would be made to the "offeror whose proposal represented the best value" sufficient to alert offerors that agency would evaluate "innovations and creative approached"); *SGT, Inc.*, Comp. Gen. Dec. B-294722.4, 2005 CPD ¶ 151 (dedicated person to perform required job an enhancement when RFP evaluation factor was "comprehensiveness of the proposed approach, and likelihood of successfully meeting the solicitation requirements"); *Rome Research Corp.*, Comp. Gen. Dec. B-291162, 2002 CPD ¶ 209 (RFP sought "enhancements of value" in management proposals); *Moreland Corp.*, Comp. Gen. Dec. B-283685, 2002 CPD ¶ 4 (RFP statement that agency would evaluate "the quality of the building and the design concept" in a competition for a clinic); *Medical Dev. Int'l*, Comp. Gen. Dec. B-281484.2, 99-1 CPD ¶ 68 (RFP requirement for technical proposals indicated that enhancements would be evaluated); and *Engineering & Prof'l Servs., Inc.*, Comp. Gen. Dec. B-262179, 95-2 CPD ¶ 266 (RFP requirement that each offeror submit a matrix detailing where their systems met or exceeded the RFP requirements and desirable features alerted offeror that enhancements would be evaluated).

If the RFP does not call for evaluation of enhanced performance, an agency is free to disregard proposed enhancements that it concludes do not benefit the agency, *Team BOS/Naples-Gemmo S.p.A/DelJen*, Comp. Gen. Dec. B-298865.3, 2008 CPD ¶ 11; *U-Tech Servs. Corp.*, Comp. Gen. Dec. B-284183.3, 2002 CPD ¶ 78.

## (2) TECHNICAL SOLUTIONS

It has been common practice to request technical proposals providing solutions to meet a government requirement. This originated in competitions for development contracts where an agency wanted to evaluate proposed designs of a new system to assess which was most likely to meet its needs. The technique has been carried over into service contracts where competing solutions to a need are sought. These solutions can be an offer factor if the technical proposal is incorporated into the contract as a promise to perform in accordance with the proposal. More often they are a capability factor where the contract does not make the solution mandatory but uses it to assess the capability of the offeror.

Making technical proposals contractually binding has the effect of making them the baseline against which to measure the contractor's performance. This will arguably benefit the government if the proposal contains performance requirements that are more demanding than the original government specification. In that case, the government will be able to hold the contractor bound to perform in accordance with its proposal (assuming that it contains promissory language), but it will have deprived the contractor of some of the flexibility that it would have had if it was performing to a government performance requirement. Alternatively, making the proposal contractually binding will harm the government if the proposal contains performance requirements that are less demanding than the original government specification. In that case, effort demanded by the government to meet its original performance requirements may well be construed as a contractual change for which the government will be required to give an equitable adjustment. See, for example, *Northrop Grumman Corp. v. United States*, 47 Fed. Cl. 20 (2000), holding that the contractor was not entitled to equitable adjustments for work not required by its technical proposal because the proposal was not incorporated into the contract.

Agencies vary widely in their practice of incorporating these technical proposals into their contracts and the practice usually cannot be discerned from protests involving this type of evaluation factor. However, there are many examples of protests involving competing technical solutions. See, for example, *Northrop Grumman Sys.*

*Corp.*, Comp. Gen. Dec. B-298954, 2007 CPD ¶ 63 (evaluation of proposed radars in response to a government statement of objectives); *ViaSat, Inc.*, Comp. Gen. Dec. B-291152, 2002 CPD ¶ 211 (evaluation of proposed communication satellite terminals to meet stated performance requirements); and *DRS Sys., Inc.*, Comp. Gen. Dec. B-289928.3, 2002 CPD ¶ 192 (evaluation of proposed thermal imaging systems against an agency purchase description).

The best way to evaluate technical solutions is to conduct the procurement in two phases, selecting two or more contractors in the first phase to build sample products, testing the competing products, and awarding the second phase contract to the contractor with the best product. See, for example, *Northrop Grumman Space & Missile Sys. Corp.*, Comp. Gen. Dec. B-400837, 2009 CPD ¶ 52, where this technique was used to procure vehicles for the Army and Marine Corps, and *Textron, Inc. v. United States*, 74 Fed. Cl. 277 (2006), where this technique was used to procure ships for the Coast Guard. The advantage of this technique is that it allows the agency to evaluate the actual technical solution rather than the described technical solution (which may not be actually achieved during contract performance).

### (3) SPECIFIC PRODUCTS OR SERVICES

In some cases, an agency will use a performance specification and evaluate specific products or services that will meet that specification. This technique is most practicable when there are a variety of products or services in the marketplace that will meet the agency's performance requirements and the agency will benefit by obtaining competitive prices for each product or service in order to identify the best value at the time of contract award. See, for example, *MD Helicopters, Inc.*,Comp. Gen. Dec. B-298502, 2006 CPD ¶ 164 (commercially available helicopters); *Integrated Sys. Group*, Comp. Gen. Dec. B-272336, 96-2 CPD ¶ 144 (central processing units). This technique is more difficult to use when the offered product or service has not been sold or provided because, in such cases, the agency may have little ability to evaluate whether the offeror can actually deliver the product or perform the service and whether the product or service will actually meet the contract requirement. In such cases, the best practice is to perform a risk analysis in an attempt to ensure that the best value decision is based not only on the quality of the offered product or service but also on the risk that the offeror may not be able to perform as promised. See, for example, *Alliant Techs., Inc.*, Comp. Gen. Dec. B-276162, 97-1 CPD ¶ 141, where GAO denied a protest challenging the risk assessment of the technical feasibility of manufacturing the proposed product at the offered price. See also *Martin Marietta Corp.*, Comp. Gen. Dec. B-259823.4, 96-1 CPD ¶ 265, denying a protest that the agency had found that the protester's technical approach to meeting the specification was "unsatisfactory," and had awarded the contract to an offeror whose approach was rated "good."

## (4) Process or Techniques to Be Used

Another non-cost offer factor is the process or technique that the offeror intends to use to meet the government's performance requirements. This factor can be used in two ways. If it is used to evaluate the offeror's understanding of the work or capability to perform the work, it is a capability factor. However, if the agency intends to incorporate the technique or process into the contract, making it contractually binding, it will be an offer factor. In most instances, the best practice is to treat this as a capability factor — giving the contractor the freedom to meet the performance requirements using some other technique or process — but there are some instances where an agency has determined that the specific technique or process has an identified value that will not be achieved by the use of any other technique or process. In such cases, this should be treated as an offer factor.

When a proposed process or technique is used as an evaluation factor, it is good practice to evaluate the comparative risk of using different techniques. See, for example, *Robbins-Gioia, Inc.*, Comp. Gen. Dec. B-274318, 96-2 CPD ¶ 222, denying a protest that the agency had evaluated a proposal for the use of "state-of-the-art software architecture" as having moderate risk as compared to a proposal to use off-the-shelf software. In such cases, the agency is conducting a form of design competition requiring the evaluation of the potential effectiveness of the offered designs. See, for example, *AT&T Corp.*, Comp. Gen. Dec. B-261154.4, 96-1 CPD ¶ 232, where GAO agreed that the agency's evaluation of competing designs was performed effectively.

## (5) Terms and Conditions

A fifth type of non-cost offer factor is the enhanced or specific term or condition. Enhanced terms and conditions should be treated in the same manner as other enhancements — the agency should state a minimum acceptable level and the range of enhanced performance which it considers to be of potential value. Specific terms and conditions that the agency requires to be filled out with explicit information should be clearly stated so that the offerors clearly understand the information that will be incorporated in the contract.

A common enhanced term or condition is a warranty clause where the agency solicits better warranty coverage than the minimum specified in the RFP. See *Integrated Sys. Group*, Comp. Gen. Dec. B-272336, 96-2 CPD ¶ 144, where offers were obtained for "extended warranties" of one and two years. A warranty evaluation factor can also be stated as an open-ended factor, allowing each offeror to propose the warranty offered. See *Eomax Corp.*, Comp. Gen. Dec. B-311391, 2008 CPD ¶ 130 (protester properly downgraded for proposing only a one year warranty on a high price product); *Scot, Inc.*, Comp. Gen. Dec. B-295569, 2005 CPD ¶ 66 (proposed extended warranty properly evaluated as providing only a small advantage when equipment was going to be stored for long periods); *Landoll Corp.*, Comp. Gen. Dec. B-291381, 2003 CPD ¶ 40 (longer warranty properly evaluated as a strength) .

Another common example of a specific term or condition is the Key Personnel clause that is used in many service procurements. As discussed below, key personnel is a frequently used capability factor but when the names of the key personnel are incorporated into a Key Personnel clause, this factor becomes an offer factor because the contractor promises to use the specified personnel unless they become unavailable. While the evaluation of key personnel can be a strong predictor of performance, it is only completely valid if the personnel proposed by the offer actually work on the contract. Yet, that is not the effect of a Key Personnel clause. Almost all of the clauses in use call for the use of key personnel listed in the clause or equally qualified personnel approved by the contracting officer. This is, of course, a necessary part of the process because the contractor cannot guarantee that employees will stay with the company or be willing to work on the contract.

GAO has given contractors a substantial amount of freedom to operate under these clauses. See, for example, *Laser Power Techs., Inc.*, Comp. Gen. Dec. B-233369, 89-1 CPD ¶ 267, where GAO denied the protest that a competing offeror had to propose "permanent" employees to meet the key personnel requirements in the solicitation. GAO stated, "there is nothing unusual or inherently improper for an awardee to recruit and hire personnel employed by the incumbent contractor." On the other hand, GAO will intervene if there is a substitution of less qualified personnel. See *KPMG Peat Marwick, LLP*, Comp. Gen. Dec. B-259479.2, 95-2 CPD ¶ 13, *recons. denied*, 95-2 CPD ¶ 26, where GAO sustained a protest where the agency had ordered the winning contractor to substitute personnel less qualified than that required by the RFP. Thus, GAO will find that the competition has not been fairly conducted if the Key Personnel clause is not enforced as written and will require that the procurement be recompeted.

## (6) Delivery or Completion Schedule

In some instances, the agency will use the delivery or completion schedule as an offer factor. In such cases, the RFP will state the time of performance that the agency must have and will permit offerors to propose shorter times of performance. This technique should never be used unless the agency has determined that it will benefit from earlier performance, and, in such cases, the RFP should clearly state the amount of earlier performance that will be of value. See *Rotair Indus., Inc.*, Comp. Gen. Dec. B-276435.2, 97-2 CPD ¶ 17, finding that the agency's selection of a higher-priced vendor with a shorter delivery schedule was reasonable because the agency determined that a longer delivery schedule would have a detrimental impact on the continuing back-order status of the critical application item being procured. Like other enhancements, it is also good practice to obtain price proposals on a step ladder basis so that offers can be rationally compared. When delivery is listed as an evaluation factor, offerors should understand that the agency will favorably evaluate earlier delivery. See, for example, *Utility Tool & Trailer, Inc.*, Comp. Gen. Dec. B-310535, 2008 CPD ¶ 1 (proper to not pay significantly higher price for small delivery advantage); *Charles Kendall & Partners, Ltd.*, Comp. Gen. Dec. B-310093, 2007 CPD ¶ 210 (proper to pay significantly higher price for substantial delivery advantage); *American Material Handling, Inc.*, Comp. Gen. Dec. B-297536, 2006 CPD ¶ 28 (proper to pay somewhat higher price for delivery advantage).

## *2. Capability Factors*

"Capability factors" are those factors that will be used to evaluate the relative ability of the competing offerors to perform the contract. These factors are never made part of the contract because they do not constitute contractual promises made by the offeror. However, as discussed above, they frequently include enhancements, technical solutions, or descriptions of a process or technique to be used that are included in technical or management proposals that are required to be submitted by each offeror. Whether such evaluation factors are offer factors or capability factors depends entirely on whether the agency intends to incorporate them into the contract as promises or merely use them to evaluate capability. When they are treated as capability factors, they will be discussed below as part of the "understanding the work" factor.

The evaluation of capability is essentially an assessment of the risk that an offeror will not successfully perform the proposed contract. Thus, performance risk is an inherent evaluation factor even though it is undisclosed in the RFP, *AHNTECH, Inc.*, Comp. Gen. Dec. B-299806, 2007 CPD ¶ 213; *AIA Todini-Lotos*, Comp. Gen. Dec. B-294337, 2004 CPD ¶ 211. Performance risk is most frequently assessed with regard to past performance. See *Lockheed Martin MS2 Tactical Sys.*, Comp. Gen. Dec. B-400135, 2008 CPD ¶ 157 (high performance risk proper based on poor past performance of major subcontractor); *Midwest Metals*, Comp. Gen. Dec. B-299805, 2007 CPD ¶ 131 (risk determined from past performance data system); *Boersma Travel Servs.*, Comp. Gen. Dec. B-297986.2, 2006 CPD ¶ 175 (moderate risk because agency could not understand information submitted by protester); *TPL, Inc.*, Comp. Gen. Dec. B-297136.10, 2006 CPD ¶ 104 (moderately low risk because of "fair" past performance ratings on most comparable contracts). However, it can be used with regard to any evaluation factor. See, for example, *MCT JV*, Comp. Gen. Dec. B-311245.2, 2008 CPD ¶ 121, *recons. denied*, 2008 CPD ¶ 167 (significant risk from unrealistically capped overhead rates); *Fintrac, Inc.*, Comp. Gen. Dec. B-311462.2, 2008 CPD ¶ 191 (no perceived risk from lack of fixed fee in proposal); *Commercial Window Shield*, Comp. Gen. Dec. B-400154, 2008 CPD ¶ 134 (risk of vague staffing plan); *Global Solutions Network, Inc.*, Comp. Gen. Dec. B-298682.3, 2008 CPD ¶ 131 (risk of single person staffing two key positions); *Guam Shipyard*, Comp. Gen. Dec. B-311321, 2008 CPD ¶ 124 (high risk of unrealistically low price and mediocre past performance); *AT&T Corp.*, Comp. Gen. Dec. B-299542.3, 2008 CPD ¶ 65 (staffing plan created performance risk); *Raytheon Co.*, Comp. Gen. Dec. B-298626.2, 2007 CPD ¶ 185 (lack of data on product created high performance risk); *Savantage Fin. Servs., Inc.*, Comp. Gen. Dec. B-299798, 2007 CPD ¶ 214 (high performance risk based on evaluation of technical proposal submitted to demonstrate understanding of the work).

Air Force Mandatory Procedure 5315.305.5.2.2. describes this risk assessment as a "performance confidence assessment," which is applied to the evaluation of past performance using the evaluation technique described later in this chapter. This is an affirmative means of describing a risk assessment which has been accepted as rational, *CCITE/SC*, Comp. Gen. Dec. B-400782, 2008 CPD ¶ 216 (unknown confidence rating justified because of lack of relevant past performance); *United Paradyne Corp.*, Comp. Gen. Dec. B-297758, 2006 CPD ¶ 47 (technique acceptable but not used rationally). See also *Consolidated Eng'g Servs., Inc.*, Comp. Gen. Dec. B-311313, 2008 CPD ¶ 146, describing a Social Security Administration "confidence/performance risk" assessment covering both past performance and experience, and granting the protest because different assessments were given to the two final competitors even though they were both highly rated.

## a. Responsibility Determinations Distinguished

Since capability factors deal with the same matters that are considered in making responsibility determinations, it is important to distinguish between them. Agencies commonly evaluate factors and subfactors related to responsibility, notwithstanding the fact that a formal responsibility determination must ultimately be made before award of the contract. Such factors and subfactors frequently include experience, staffing, and past performance. This process does not officially constitute a responsibility determination as long as these factors are evaluated on a variable basis. Therefore, it does not conflict with the Small Business Administration's (SBA) authority to resolve questions concerning the responsibility of small businesses. In *Electrospace Sys., Inc.*, 58 Comp. Gen. 415 (B-192574), 79-1 CPD ¶ 264, GAO stated at 425:

> Since neither 10 U.S.C. §2304(g) nor applicable regulations in any way restrict the "other factors" that may be used by agencies in selecting the proposal having the greatest value to the Government, we have not prohibited procuring agencies from using responsibility-related factors in making *relative* assessments of the merits of competing proposals. There is no indication on the face of Public Law 95-89 or in the legislative history of the law that Congress intended to eliminate this long-standing practice as far as the evaluation of small business proposals are concerned. Thus, neither the cited precedent (40 Comp. Gen., *supra*) of advertised procurements nor the 1977 Public Law prevents the relative-assessment evaluation of responsibility-related information contained in small business proposals.

See also *Nomura Enters., Inc.*, Comp. Gen. Dec. B-277768, 97-2 CPD ¶ 148, where the protester, which was a small business concern, asserted that the evaluation of its past performance concerned a matter of its responsibility and was thus subject to SBA's Certificate of Competency (COC) procedures. GAO disagreed, stating:

> An agency may use traditional responsibility factors, such as experience or past performance, as technical evaluation factors, where, as here, a comparative evaluation of those areas is to be made. *Dynamic Aviation — Helicopters*, B-274122, Nov. 1, 1996, 96-2 ¶166 at 3. A comparative evaluation means that competing proposals will be rated on a scale relative to each other, as opposed to a pass/fail basis. *Id.* The record shows that the award here clearly was based on a comparative assessment of Nomura's and Defense's past performance records. Where a proposal is downgraded or found deficient pursuant to such an evaluation, the matter is one of relative technical merit, not nonresponsibility which would require a referral to the SBA.

In *T. Head & Co.*, Comp. Gen. Dec. B-275783, 97-1 CPD ¶ 169, GAO held that an evaluation of capability factors that resulted in the conclusion that the offeror's proposal was "unacceptable" was not a determination of nonresponsibility because the evaluation had been arrived at in the course of a best value procurement where past performance was being evaluated on a variable basis and "unacceptable" was merely the lowest adjectival rating available. Compare *Phil Howry Co.*, Comp. Gen. Dec. B-291402.3, 2003 CPD ¶ 33, where GAO ruled that refusing to award to the only company that had submitted a proposal because its past performance was rated "marginal/little confidence" was a nonresponsibility determination because there had been no comparative assessment (no other offeror to compare with). This appears to indicate that an agency will be required to allow a small business offeror to apply for a COC when it refuses to award to that offeror because of poor past performance when it is the only offer received.

It is improper to use responsibility-related factors or subfactors if the evaluation is merely to determine acceptability of a proposal, *Sanford & Sons Co.*, 67 Comp. Gen. 612 (B-231607), 88-2 CPD ¶ 266; *Angelo Warehouses Co.*, Comp. Gen. Dec. B-196780, 80-1 CPD ¶ 228. In *Sanford*, the agency determined that the small business offeror's past performance did not meet the minimum acceptable standard of performance. GAO ruled that since this was tantamount to a determination that the protester was not responsible, entitling it to request a Certificate of Competency from the SBA. See also *Federal Support Corp.*, 71 Comp. Gen. 152 (B-245573), 92-1 CPD ¶ 81, and *Clegg Indus., Inc.*, 70 Comp. Gen. 679 (B-242204.3), 91-2 CPD ¶ 145, finding that an agency had improperly used responsibility factors to determine technical acceptability and pointed out that responsibility factors should be used only to make a comparative evaluation of the proposals. These cases could be read as precluding the use of responsibility factors or subfactors in any procurement where the award was to be made to the offeror that submitted the lowest priced technically acceptable proposal since any negative evaluation of responsibility could only be used to disqualify the offeror. However, there are other decisions of GAO permitting rejection of proposals submitted by large businesses as being technically unacceptable based on responsibility-type factors related to the experience of the offeror, *Oak Ridge Associated Univ.*, Comp. Gen. Dec. B-245694, 92-1 CPD ¶ 86 (lack of experience required by RFP); *Aerostat Servs. Partner ship*, Comp. Gen. Dec. B-244939.2, 92-1 CPD ¶ 71 (failure to propose manning adequate to meet specifications); *Color Ad Signs & Displays*, Comp. Gen. Dec. B-241544, 91-1 CPD ¶ 154 (lack of required experience); *Sach Sinha & Assocs., Inc.*, 69 Comp. Gen. 108 (B-236911), 90-1 CPD ¶ 50 (personnel did not meet education and experience requirement of RFP). These decisions appear to indicate that responsibility-type factors may be used to determine lack of acceptability of proposals from large businesses, but not from small ones.

### b.  Past Performance

FASA amended 10 U.S.C. § 2305(a)(3)(A) and 41 U.S.C. § 253a(c) (now 41 U.S.C. § 3306(c)(1)(A) which does not contain a separate requirement to include past performance as an evaluation factor) to add past performance as one of the potential evaluation factors in source selection, and amended 41 U.S.C. § 401 (now 41 U.S.C. § 1126) to require the adoption of procedures "that encourage the consideration of the offerors' past performance in the selection of contractors." FAR 15.304(c)(3) makes past performance a mandatory factor as follows:

> (3)(i) Except as set forth in paragraph (c)(3)(iii) of this section, past performance shall be evaluated in all source selections for negotiated competitive acquisitions expected to exceed the simplified acquisition threshold.

> > (ii) For solicitations involving bundling that offer a significant opportunity for subcontracting, the contracting officer must include a factor to evaluate past performance indicating the extent to which the offeror attained applicable goals for small business participation under contracts that required subcontracting plans (15 U.S.C. 637(d)(4)(G)(ii)).

> > (iii) Past performance need not be evaluated if the contracting officer documents the reason past performance is not an appropriate evaluation factor for the acquisition.

See also the OFPP publication, *Best Practices for Collecting and Using Current and Past Performance Information*, May 2000 (*www.acqnet.gov/comp/seven_steps/library/OFPPbp-collecting.pdf)*, and the DoD publication, *A Guide to Collection and Use of Past Performance Information*, May 2003 (*www.acq.osd.mil/dpap/Docs/PPI_Guide_2003_final.pdf*).

The evaluation of past performance reduces the emphasis on merely writing good proposals in favor of focusing on actual performance on prior contracts. Past performance can be evaluated as a separate evaluation factor or as a subfactor. Even before the FAR requirement, there was no question that this was a proper factor in the evaluation process, *Ferranti Int'l Def. Sys., Inc.*, Comp. Gen. Dec. B-237555, 90-1 CPD ¶ 239, even though it may give the incumbent contractor with a good performance record an advantage in the competition, *Bendix Field Eng'g Corp.*, Comp. Gen. Dec. B-241156, 91-1 CPD ¶ 44; *Engineering & Computation, Inc.*, Comp. Gen. Dec. B-275180.2, 97-1 CPD ¶ 47.

While past performance can be used as either a factor or a subfactor, it is good practice to avoid using it in both situations simultaneously. For example, in *Center for Educ. & Manpower Res.*, Comp. Gen. Dec. B-191453, 78-2 CPD ¶ 21, it was held impermissible to evaluate past performance as a factor and also use past performance in the evaluation of technical and management factors. GAO reasoned that this gave a higher weight to past performance than was indicated in the RFP. A similar result was reached in *Metric Sys. Corp.*, Comp. Gen. Dec. B-210218.2, 83-2 CPD ¶ 394. Compare *Global Assocs., Ltd.*, Comp. Gen. Dec. B-275534, 97-1 CPD ¶ 129, rejecting a protest that undue weight had been given to past performance, and *United Ammunition Container, Inc.*, Comp. Gen. Dec. B-275213, 97-1 CPD ¶ 58, rejecting a protest asserting that past performance should have been evaluated separately and also in evaluating technical approach and management. See also *Halter Marine, Inc.*, B-255429, 94-1 CPD ¶ 161, finding the evaluation to be unreasonable because the agency gave overwhelming emphasis to past performance by repeated consideration of that factor in both the technical merit and quality control capability factors.

The FAR guidance on past performance contains several references to the importance of the relevance of past performance, including the following statements in FAR 15.305(a)(2):

(i) . . . The currency and relevance of the information, source of the information, context of the data, and general trends in contractor's performance shall be considered

(ii) . . . The source selection authority shall determine the relevance of similar past performance information.

GAO has interpreted these provisions are imposing a mandatory requirement on agencies to assess the relevance of past performance, *DRS C3 Sys., LLC*, Comp. Gen. Dec. B-310825, 2008 CPD ¶ 103; *Clean Harbors Envtl. Servs., Inc.*, Comp. Gen. Dec. B-296176.2, 2005 CPD ¶ 222.

While the regulation contains no explanation of the term "relevance of past performance information," it would appear to mean that an agency should give more weight to past performance on work that is like the work being procured (and conversely little or no weight to past performance of work that is dissimilar to the work being procured). Thus, the RFP should be clear that the offerors should refer their most relevant projects for consideration of past performance. This is particularly important because there are numerous instances where GAO has ruled that agencies properly downgraded an offeror because of lack of relevant past performance even though it had very good past performance on dissimilar projects. See *Commissioning Solutions Global, LLC* , Comp. Gen. Dec. B-403542, 2010 CPD ¶ 272, stating:

> [T]he RFQ provided for a qualitative assessment of vendors' past performance, and instructed vendors to identify "at least" two relevant contracts in the past 3 years. To the extent that [the protester] is complaining that the RFQ did not specifically state that the agency might credit a vendor for having a number of relevant contracts, we think such a consideration would be logically encompassed by or related to considering the quality of the vendor's past performance. *Birdwell Bros. Painting & Refinishing*, B-285035, July 5, 2000, 2000 CPD ¶ 129 at 6.

In effect, such reasoning allows an agency to consider lack of comparable experience in the evaluation of past performance. For example, NASA uses an evaluation scheme that rates offerors' past performance in accordance with the relevance of their experience. Thus, to receive an "excellent" past performance rating, an offeror must have experience that is "highly relevant." GAO has accepted this scheme without comment in many protests including *FN Mfg., LLC*, Comp. Gen. Dec. B-402059.4, 2010 CPD ¶ 104 (downgrading past performance proper when RFP stated relevance would be evaluated based on whether experience was comparable in complexity, size or value" of proposed effort); *ASRC Research & Tech. Solutions, LLC*, Comp. Gen. Dec. B-400217, 2008 CPD ¶ 202 (protest granted because scheme not followed); *Wackenhut Servs., Inc.*, Comp. Gen. Dec. B-400240, 2008 CPD ¶ 184 (protest denied because scheme followed). See also *Gonzales-McCaulley Inv. Group, Inc.*, Comp. Gen. Dec. B-402544, 2010 CPD ¶ 127 (agency reasonably downgraded past performance because protester lacked experience on agency work); *AT&T Corp.*, Comp. Gen. Dec. B-299542.3, 2008 CPD ¶ 65 (to obtain "excellent" past performance rating, offeror had to have "highly relevant" experience); *Sherrick Aerospace*, Comp. Gen. Dec. B-310359.2, 2008 CPD ¶ 17 (agency determination that winning offeror had relevant experience justified low risk past performance evaluation); *JWK Int'l Corp.*, Comp. Gen. Dec. B-297758.3, 2006 CPD ¶ 142 (agency rating of little confidence justified when offeror had very good past performance on contract that was "somewhat relevant").

Agencies must use care in stating in the RFP what projects are relevant to the current project because GAO has granted protests when an agency did not follow its own relevance guidelines. See, for example, *Clean Harbors Envtl. Servs., Inc.*, Comp. Gen. Dec. B-296176.2, 2005 CPD ¶ 222 (improper to fail to consider the lack of relevance of services that were smaller and less complex when RFP called for consideration of relevance); *Martin Elecs., Inc.*, Comp. Gen. Dec. B-290846.3, 2003 CPD ¶ 6 (improper to fail to consider late deliveries on incomplete contract when RFP called for consideration of performance "occurring within the past three years to the date of the solicitation closing"). Compare *All Phase Envtl., Inc.*, Comp. Gen. Dec. B-292919.2, 2004 CPD ¶ 62, agreeing that pest control work was relevant to ground maintenance when the RFP called for relevant performance on "contracts of a similar size, scope, dynamic environment, and complexity." GAO has also agreed that an agency is not bound by an experience relevance standard if the past performance relevance standard is stated in very general terms, *KIC Dev., LLC*, Comp. Gen. Dec. B-309869, 2007 CPD ¶ 184. In an unusual case, both GAO and the Court of Federal Claims agreed that an agency properly considered large contracts not relevant to a procurement where most of the work would be on projects in the range of $15,000 to $1.7 million, *J.C.N. Constr. Co. v. United States*, 60 Fed. Cl. 400 (2004); *J.C.N. Constr. Co.*, Comp. Gen. Dec. B-293063, 2004 CPD ¶ 12.

In using past performance as an evaluation factor, the agency should state the scope of the factor in the RFP. See FAR 15.305(a)(2), which states:

> (iii) The evaluation should take into account past performance information regarding predecessor companies, key personnel who have relevant experience, or subcontractors that will perform major or critical aspects of the requirement when such information is relevant to the instant acquisition.

In spite of the seemingly mandatory requirement to evaluate key personnel, GAO has ruled that it is proper to exclude key personnel from the evaluation of past performance, *JWK Int'l Corp.*, Comp. Gen. Dec. B-297758.3, 2006 CPD ¶ 142 (accepting explanation that information on skills of key personnel does not assist in evaluation of past performance of offeror). When an agency sees that two companies have the same key person (the operations manager), it can reasonably attribute the past performance of one company to the other, *Daylight Tree Serv. & Equip., LLC*, Comp. Gen. Dec. B-310808, 2008 CPD ¶ 22. In addition, an agency may reasonably determine that prior experience of key personnel does not overcome lack of corporate experience, *Blue Rock Structures, Inc.*, Comp. Gen. Dec. B-287960, 2001 CPD ¶ 184.

With regard to subcontractors to be used by the offeror, GAO has held that agencies can evaluate their past performance even though the RFP does not explicitly call for such evaluation, *AC Techs., Inc.*, Comp. Gen. Dec. B-293013, 2008 CPD ¶ 26; *Singleton Enters.*, Comp. Gen. Dec. B-298576, 2006 CPD ¶ 157; *Science & Tech., Inc.*, Comp. Gen. Dec. B-272748, 97-1 CPD ¶ 121. Thus, subcontractor performance is a frequent element of the past performance evaluation. See *Lockheed Martin MS2 Tactical Sys.*, Comp. Gen. Dec. B-400135, 2008 CPD ¶ 157 (high risk rating justified when 50% subcontractor had poor past performance); *STG, Inc.*, Comp. Gen. Dec. B-298543, 2006 CPD ¶ 166 (proper to limit subcontractor evaluations to work with government agencies); *Arora Group, Inc.*, Comp. Gen. Dec. B-297838.3, 2006 CPD ¶ 143 (proper to reduce performance rating because of mediocre subcontractor past performance); *Neal R. Gross & Co.*, Comp. Gen. Dec. B-275066, 97-1 CPD ¶ 30 (noting that the contractor always bears responsibility for the work of subcontractors); and *GZA Remediation, Inc.*, Comp. Gen. Dec. B-272386, 96-2 CPD ¶ 155 (good past performance rating properly based on a proposed subcontractor's prior contracts). Compare *USATREX Int'l, Inc.*, Comp. Gen. Dec. B-275592, 98-1 CPD ¶ 99, limiting past performance/experience to the offeror only. Agencies can properly assign a medium rating when a proposed subcontractor has excellent past performance/experience but the offeror has no relevant past performance/experience, *Iplus, Inc.*, Comp. Gen. Dec. B-298020, 2006 CPD ¶ 90.

The evaluation of past performance is essentially an evaluation of the risk that the offeror will not successfully perform the contract. This is best recognized by the Air Force Materiel Command (AFMC) that uses past performance as a specific risk assessment factor which is given to the source selection official to be used with the technical/management color codes and a technical proposal risk factor, AFMC-FARS Appendix BB, May 15, 1996. Performance risk is defined according to one of the following categories:

(1) High — Significant doubt exists, based on the offeror's performance record, that the offeror can perform the proposed effort.

(2) Moderate — Some doubt exists, based on the offeror's performance record, that the offeror can perform the proposed effort.

(3) Low — Little doubt exists, based on the offeror's performance record, that the offeror can perform the proposed effort.

(4) Not Applicable — No significant performance record is identified.

See *Universal Techs., Inc.*, Comp. Gen. Dec. B-241157, 91-1 CPD 63, *recons. denied*, Comp. Gen. Dec. B-241157.2, 91-1 CPD ¶ 505, fully displaying and affirming the use of these factors. In *Instrument Control Serv., Inc.*, Comp. Gen. Dec. B-247286, 92-1 CPD ¶ 407, GAO found proper a past performance risk assessment based upon information obtained from another agency regarding a default termination of the offeror. See also *Dragon Servs., Inc.*, Comp. Gen. Dec. B-255354, 94-1 CPD ¶ 151, an Army procurement, where GAO found proper a past performance risk assessment of "moderate" based upon unfavorable information received concerning the protester's performance under a similar contract at another agency.

## c. Experience

In most procurements the capability of an offeror cannot be determined accurately without considering the type and extent of its experience. FAR 15.304(c)(2) suggests that agencies evaluate "prior experience." It appears to be a common belief that an evaluation of relevant past performance entails an evaluation of experience, but this is only an indirect way of assessing experience. In fact, while past performance and experience are both components of a contractor's capability that involve inquires into the past, their evaluation requires asking entirely different questions. To determine a contractor's experience the questions are: What have you done? and How many times or for how long have you done it? The question for past performance is: How well have you done it? To further complicate this issue, the protest decisions contain conflicting statements on the relationship of experience and past performance. See, for example, *Telcom Sys. Servs., Inc. v. Department of Justice*, GSBCA 13272-P, 95-2 BCA ¶ 27,849, where the board stated that experience must be considered when evaluating past performance. In that case, the board stated that "[i]t is unreasonable to suggest that past performance does not encompass experience." In contrast, in *Hughes Georgia, Inc.*, Comp. Gen. Dec. B-272526, 96-2 CPD ¶ 151, GAO indicated that experience was not included in the evaluation of past performance. Other cases appear to indicate that there is a good deal of confusion on this issue. For example, many GAO decisions have allowed an agency to evaluate experience in the course of evaluating "relevant" past performance, *TPL, Inc.*, Comp. Gen. Dec. B-297136.10, 2006 CPD ¶ 104, while in *Ameriko, Inc.*, Comp. Gen. Dec. B-272989, 96-2 CPD ¶ 167, GAO did not object to the consideration of past performance when the evaluation factor in the RFP was "experience." It has also been acceptable to treat corporate experience as a subfactor to past performance and "client satisfaction," *McGoldrick Constr. Servs. Corp.*, Comp. Gen. Dec. B-310340.3, 2008 CPD ¶ 120. See, however, *United Paradyne Corp.*, Comp. Gen. Dec. B-297758, 2006 CPD ¶ 47, where GAO disapproved factoring an average of an offeror's experience into its past performance rating (in effect reducing the past performance rating for experience on work that was not similar to the work to be performed on the proposed contract).

Thus, it is highly desirable to evaluate past performance and experience separately. See *Executive Court Reporters, Inc.*, Comp. Gen. Dec. B-272981, 96-2 CPD ¶ 227, stating that past performance and experience should be separate factors and evaluated separately. See also *Smart Innovative Solutions*, Comp. Gen. Dec. B-400323.3, 2008 CPD ¶ 220 (lack of "relevant experience" properly considered); *Engineering Constr. Servs., Inc.*, Comp. Gen. Dec. B-310311.2, 2008 CPD ¶ 6 ("relevant experience" properly evaluated as separate subfactor); *Alpha Genesis, Inc.*, Comp. Gen. Dec. B-299859, 2007 CPD ¶ 167 (corporate experience and past performance evaluated properly); *JAVIS Automation & Eng'g, Inc.*, Comp. Gen. Dec. B-290434, 2002 CPD ¶ 140 (past performance and experience evaluated together); *PW Constr., Inc.*, Comp. Gen. Dec. B-272248, 96-2 CPD ¶ 130 (evaluation of both experience and past performance properly performed).

The RFP should state whether the agency intends to evaluate corporate experience, experience of key personnel, or both. There is a great deal of discretion in making this determination and GAO has held that the experience of key personnel can be evaluated under a "corporate experience" factor unless the RFP precludes such evaluation, *Data Mgmt. Servs. Joint Venture*, Comp. Gen. Dec. B-299702, 2007 CPD ¶ 139; *Dix Corp.*, Comp. Gen. Dec. B-293964, 2004 CPD ¶ 143. Nonetheless, it is better practice to state in the RFP precisely what experience is to be evaluated. See *Johnson Controls Sec. Sys., LLC*, Comp. Gen. Dec. B-296490.3, 2007 CPD ¶ 100 (corporate experience and experience of proposed staff); *Leader Commc'ns Inc.*, Comp. Gen. Dec. B-298734, 2006 CPD ¶ 192 (experience of key personnel and corporate experience); *KIC Dev., LLC*, Comp. Gen. Dec. B-297425.2,

2006 CPD ¶ 27 (RFP stated that experience requirement could be met by experience of key personnel or subcontractors); *Sigmatech, Inc.*, Comp. Gen. Dec. B-271821, 96-2 CPD ¶ 101 (corporate experience plus "sufficient personnel with ample qualifications"). It has also been held to be proper to evaluate corporate experience and key personnel experience separately, giving a low rating on corporate experience even though the key personnel have good experience, *Population Health Servs., Inc.*, Comp. Gen. Dec. B-292858, 2003 CPD ¶ 217.

Once it has been determined that experience is to be evaluated, the types of experience relevant to the procurement must be determined. Often, RFPs merely indicate that experience on "similar" projects will be considered. There are many factors to be considered in determining similarity, including dollar value, complexity, and nature of the work. Some RFPs go into great detail specifying the types of experience considered important and, in some cases, their relative importance, *Vox Optima, LLC*, Comp. Gen. Dec. B-400451, 2008 CPD ¶ 212 ("40,000 annual billable hours in public affairs work"); *Burns and Roe Servs. Corp.*, Comp. Gen. Dec. B-296355, 2005 CPD ¶ 150 ("similar in complexity (i.e., type of work, size (contracts in excess of $5,000,000 per year) and volume")); *Planning Sys., Inc.*, Comp. Gen. Dec. B-292312, 2004 CPD ¶ 83 ("similar or directly related work experience within the past five years of similar scope, magnitude or complexity to that detailed in the SOW"); *Telestar Corp.*, Comp. Gen. Dec. B-275855, 97-1 CPD ¶ 150 (experience required on projects "of similar size and scope related to this effort"). Furthermore, agencies have been permitted to specify very limited types of relevant experience, *SKE Int'l, Inc.*, Comp. Gen. Dec. B-311383, 2008 CPD ¶ 111 (construction of multiple vertical construction multi-discipline projects simultaneously); *Zolon Tech, Inc.*, Comp. Gen. Dec. B-299904.2, 2007 CPD ¶ 183 (experience in specific technology to be used in design of information system — consultant's experience properly downgraded because he was not a subcontractor); *MELE Assocs., Inc.*, Comp. Gen. Dec. B-299229.4, 2007 CPD ¶ 140 (experience in four tasks to be performed); *Systems Application & Techs., Inc.*, Comp. Gen. Dec. B-270672, 96-1 CPD ¶ 182 (experience with contracting agency); *CAN Indus. Eng'g, Inc.*, Comp. Gen. Dec. B-271034, 96-1 CPD ¶ 279 (experience with the agency's system that was to be tested under the contract).

Even where solicitations use terms such as "similar" or "relevant" in describing the nature of the experience, the cases have been quite liberal in permitting the government to use specific discriminators that are not stated in the solicitation. See *EastCo Bldg Servs., Inc.*, Comp. Gen. Dec. B-275334.2, 97-1 CPD ¶ 83, holding that the totality of the RFP will be considered in determining whether offerors were given appropriate notice of the factors to be considered. GAO concluded that offerors should have known what projects were "similar" from the fact that the RFP required each offeror to specify the "the type of facility, gross square footage, services performed, and duration" of its prior projects. See also *Aviate L.L.C.*, Comp. Gen. Dec. B-275058.6, 97-1 CPD ¶ 162 (a factor used was the awardee's experience on "performance based contracting" although the RFP did not specifically call for that type of experience). Compare *Omniplex World Servs. Corp.*, Comp. Gen. Dec.

B-290996.2, 2003 CPD ¶ 7, where GAO held that it was improper to eliminate an offeror from the competition for not having experience running a detention facility when the RFP called for the evaluation of "'guard/custody officer' experience similar in size, scope and complexity to the RFP work requirements."

Experience of major subcontractors is usually considered relevant to an evaluation of an offeror's experience, *Kellogg Brown & Root Servs., Inc.*, Comp. Gen. Dec. B-298694.7, 2007 CPD ¶ 124, even if the subcontractor has performed a large amount of the work, *ITT Corp.*, Comp. Gen. Dec. B-310102.6, 2010 CPD ¶ 12. If the RFP includes a statement to this effect, the experience of proposed subcontractors must be included in the evaluation, *KC Dev., LLC*, Comp. Gen. Dec. B-297425.2, 2006 CPD ¶ 27.

The critical question then is whether the agency can make a valid assessment of capability from these two factors alone or whether additional capability factors should be used. The answer depends on the specific procurement. For example, in some manufacturing contracts, the agency may believe that it is essential to evaluate the facilities of each offeror. In service contracts, some agencies believe it is crucial to evaluate key personnel. Most agencies believe it is advantageous in research and development contracts to evaluate understanding of the work. It is important to select an array of factors that provide a balanced assessment of the capability of each offeror to perform the work called for by the contract but to limit the number of capability factors as much as practicable.

### d.  Key Personnel

One of the most commonly used evaluation factors in best value procurements is the key personnel that the offeror intends to use to perform the contract. It is an especially useful means of assessing the capability of offerors in research and development and service contracts where the quality of the people will likely be a major determinant of the quality of the performance. However, this is only so if the contractor that wins the competition actually uses the key personnel that have been proposed. Many agencies attempt to make key personnel an offer factor by using Key Personnel clauses in solicitations requiring the offeror to use the personnel designated in the proposal (or equal personnel).

Key personnel can be a useful evaluation factor if an agency obtains sufficient information to make a meaningful assessment of the qualifications of the people that are proposed. This generally requires obtaining more than resumes that merely list academic and job experience. See, for example, *CIGNA Gov't Servs., LLC*, Comp. Gen. Dec. B-401068.4, 2010 CPD ¶ 230 (RFP contained generally stated education and experience requirements); *Resource Title Agency, Inc.*, Comp. Gen. Dec. B-402484.2, 2010 CPD ¶ 118 (detailed information on role of key personnel and whether they were committed to any other work); *Savannah River Alliance, LLC*,

Comp. Gen. Dec. B-311126, 2008 CPD ¶ 88 (RFP required resumes, references, letters of commitment and participation in oral presentation); *Systems Res. & Applications Corp.*, Comp. Gen. Dec. B-299818, 2008 CPD ¶ 28 (RFP required evidence that personnel had experience with type of work being procured); *Maden Techs.*, Comp. Gen. Dec. B-298543.2, 2006 CPD ¶ 167 (RFP required degree requirements and related experience for stated number of years); and *Advanced Tech. Sys., Inc.*, Comp. Gen. Dec. B-296493.5, 2006 CPD ¶ 147 (resumes had to identify when key personnel were also being proposed for another contract being competed at the same time). Nonetheless, agencies have been permitted to depend entirely on sketchy resumes. See *Powersolv, Inc.*, Comp. Gen. Dec. B-402534, 2010 CPD ¶ 206 (protest granted when agency evaluated qualifications of key person not called for by RFP); *D&J Enters., Inc.*, Comp. Gen. Dec. B-310442, 2008 CPD ¶ 8 (protester properly excluded from competition range when it submitted experience of key personnel in lieu of required resumes); *Operational Res. Consultants, Inc.*, Comp. Gen. Dec. B-299131.1, 2007 CPD ¶ 38 (protester properly downgraded because resume of proposed project manager did not clearly show required type of experience); *Critical Incident Solutions, LLC*, Comp. Gen. Dec. B-298077, 2006 CPD ¶ 88 (quotation unacceptable because resume did not show required experience and agency not required to review other material which allegedly showed experience); *Tessada & Assocs., Inc.*, Comp. Gen. Dec. B-293942, 2004 CPD ¶ 170 (proposal properly downgraded because resume did not clearly show that person met experience requirement); and *Aerotek Scientific LLC*, Comp. Gen. Dec. B-293089, 2004 CPD ¶ 21 (resume improperly evaluated with regard to experience requirement). In one instance, the agency was permitted to rely on resumes that were required to omit any reference to the name of the person or his or her work on the incumbent contract (depriving the agency of the ability to evaluate the most critical experience of the person), *SNAP, Inc.*, Comp. Gen. Dec. B-402746, 2010 CPD ¶ 165.

### e.    Facility to Be Used

Another evaluation factor that may be used in best value procurements is the evaluation of an offeror's proposed facility. See *Conrex, Inc.*, Comp. Gen. Dec. B-266060.2, 96-1 CPD ¶ 46 (proposal reasonably downgraded because offeror failed to adequately describe its facility); and *Bannum, Inc.*, Comp. Gen. Dec. B-270640, 96-1 CPD ¶ 167 (agency reasonably excluded protester from competitive range because the facility that the protester proposed would require major renovations which could not be completed within the 60-day commencement time frame). An offeror's facility may also be evaluated as a subfactor, *Schleicher Community Corrs., Inc.*, Comp. Gen. Dec. B-270499.3, 97-1 CPD ¶ 33.

### f.    Financial Capability

Earlier, there was considerable controversy over whether the financial ability of offerors should be used as an evaluation factor or subfactor. In *Delta Data Sys. Corp.*

*v. Webster*, 744 F.2d 197 (D.C. Cir. 1984), the court followed the general rule that factors related to responsibility could be used for comparative purposes and applied this rule to permit the comparative evaluation of the financial condition of the offerors in a long-term contract. In arriving at this result, the court reversed a contrary conclusion of GAO on the same case, *Delta Data Sys. Corp.*, Comp. Gen. Dec. B-213396, 84-1 CPD ¶ 430. GAO continued to adhere to the premise that financial condition should be used as an evaluation factor only when there is some special justification for doing so. See *Flight Int'l Group, Inc.*, 69 Comp. Gen. 741 (B-238953.4), 90-2 CPD ¶ 257, ruling that downgrading an offeror' management capabilities on the basis of financial weakness was actually a finding of nonresponsibility. See also *Velos, Inc.*, Comp. Gen. Dec. B-400500.8, 2010 CPD ¶ 13, holding that it is improper to find a performance risk because the protester did not submit a current Dun & Bradstreet report. However, there are cases where GAO has permitted the use of financial condition as a specific evaluation factor, *Greyback Concession*, Comp. Gen. Dec. B-239913, 90-2 CPD ¶ 278 (no discussion of special justification used to justify evaluation of financial condition); *E.H. White & Co.*, Comp. Gen. Dec. B-227122.3, 88-2 CPD ¶ 41 (competition between small businesses). In the normal procurement situation, there is little justification for making a comparative evaluation of financial condition and generally this should be left to the responsibility determination.

## g.  Understanding the Work/Soundness of Approach

A common means of evaluating capability of the offerors is to require the submission of technical and management proposals to assess each offeror's understanding of the work or the soundness of the approach of the offerors. As discussed above, such proposals can also be used to solicit non-cost elements of the offer such as enhancements, technical solutions, or processes or techniques to be used to perform the work. Some agencies make it mandatory to include such an evaluation factor. Thus, Air Force Mandatory Procedure 5315.304.4.4.1.1 requires the factor "Mission Capability" on all procurements of $1 million or more (to assess "the offeror's capability to satisfy the government's requirements"), and NASA Source Selection Guide 1815.304-70 requires the factor "Mission Suitability" on all procurements of $50 million or more (optional on smaller procurements).

The DoD Source Selection Procedures, March 2011, identify this factor, at 2.3.1.1., as a means of assessing the "quality of the product or services" that an offeror is proposing but soliciting technical proposals is only one of the means of addressing this issue (others being "past performance," "personnel qualifications," and "prior experience"). Moreover, in this context the term "technical" appears to include management issues. Thus, DoD agencies are permitted, but not required, to solicit technical and management proposals under this guidance. See the following statement when "technical" proposals are solicited:

2.3.1.2.1. Technical. The purpose of the technical factor(s) is to assess the offeror's approach, as detailed in its proposal, to satisfy the Government's requirements. There are many aspects which may affect an offeror's ability to meet the solicitation requirements. Examples include technical approach, risk, management approach, personnel qualifications, facilities, and others. The evaluation of risk is related to technical assessment.

This factor assumes that an offeror's capability can be evaluated by requiring it to submit a preliminary design or a technical/management plan that describes, at some specified level of detail, how the contract will be performed. To the extent that these written submissions are created by the personnel that will ultimately perform the contract, it is conceivable that this is a valid assumption. Thus, in research and development procurements, as well as in design-build competitions, where preliminary designs prepared by the offerors' own personnel are commonly used as a means of evaluating the capabilities of the competitors, the requirement for such designs may be a valid means of assessing the capability of the offerors. However, while such designs provide an agency with a considerable amount of information concerning the preliminary view of the offeror as to how the needs of the government can be best satisfied, they add a great amount of cost and time to the source selection process. In particular, the costs of the offerors are greatly increased because they are forced to create the preliminary design in order to participate in the competition, and the time required for the competition is greatly increased because the competitors must be given time to create the designs and the agency must allocate a significant period to evaluate the designs. Nonetheless, such design competitions have been accepted as a valid way of ascertaining the competence of the competitors. See, for example, *ITT Indus. Space Sys., LLC*, Comp. Gen. Dec. B-309964, 2007 CPD ¶ 217 (mission suitability properly evaluated in procurement of new land imaging instrument to be included in satellite); *Sikorsky Aircraft Co.*, Comp. Gen. Dec. B-299145, 2007 CPD ¶ 45 (mission capability properly evaluated but life-cycle cost improperly evaluated in procurement of new helicopter); *Compunetix, Inc.*, Comp. Gen. Dec. B-298489.4, 2007 CPD ¶ 12 (mission suitability properly evaluated in procurement of new mission voice systems). Unfortunately, procurements of this type frequently also call for technical and management plans to achieve other contract goals such as reliability and maintainability of the produce being designed. Such requirements add significantly to the cost and time required for the procurement with questionable added value.

In service contracting, this design-competition technique has been emulated by calling for the submission of technical and management plans to assess the offerors' understanding of the work. Here there is far greater doubt as to the validity of the process because it is far less likely that the plans will be written by the personnel that will ultimately perform the work. In fact, it is well understood that many technical/management plans are prepared by specialized proposal-writing personnel. Furthermore, it is doubtful if such plans are a valid means of assessing capability, since there are numerous instances where fully capable offerors were found to be incapable because of badly written plans. For example, in *ManTech Int'l Corp.*, Comp. Gen. Dec. B-311074, 2008 CPD ¶ 87, an incumbent contractor whose performance had been rated excellent was downgraded for not writing good responses to sample problems; in *HealthStar VA, PLLC*, Comp. Gen. Dec. B-299737, 2007 CPD ¶ 114, an incumbent contractor was downgraded because it left information out of its proposal; in *Management Tech. Servs.*, Comp. Gen. Dec. B-251612.3, 93-1 CPD ¶ 432, an incumbent contractor was downgraded in the scoring for failing to include in its plan the required information on how it intended to obtain and train its workforce, while in *Executive Sec. & Eng'g Techs., Inc.*, Comp. Gen. Dec. B-270518, 96-1 CPD ¶ 156, an incumbent contractor was downgraded for failing to provide information on its corporate experience. Successful incumbent contractors have also been excluded from the competitive range for poorly written technical/management plans, *Pedus Bldg. Servs., Inc.*, Comp. Gen. Dec. B-257271.3, 95-1 CPD ¶ 135 (sloppy technical proposal); *Premier Cleaning Sys., Inc.*, Comp. Gen. Dec. B-255815, 94-1 CPD ¶ 241 (omission of required documentation on capabilities of project manager currently managing the contract). See also *McAllister & Assocs., Inc.*, Comp. Gen. Dec. B-277029, 98-1 CPD ¶ 85, where an experienced contractor was dropped from the competitive range because it had submitted a poorly written technical proposal.

This type of assessment of understanding of the services to be performed through the use of technical/management plans is particularly questionable when the services being procured are routine, non-technical services. In these instances, even the most competent offerors are not likely to have personnel that can write good technical and management proposals and the ability to write such proposals gives little indication that they will be good performers. Nonetheless, there are numerous instances of offerors losing competitions for such services based on the evaluation of such plans. See, for example, *AHNTECH, Inc.*, Comp. Gen. Dec. B-299806, 2007 CPD ¶ 213 (food services); *Financial & Realty Servs., LLC*, Comp. Gen. Dec. B-299605.2, 2007 CPD ¶ 161 (warehouse operations and labor services); *Meeks Disposal Corp.*, Comp. Gen. Dec. B-299576, 2007 CPD ¶ 127 (refuse collection and recycling services set aside for small businesses); *Philadelphia Produce Mkt. Wholesalers, LLC*, Comp. Gen. Dec. B-298751, 2006 CPD ¶ 193 (fresh fruit and vegetable set aside for small businesses); *Leader Commc'ns Inc.*, Comp. Gen. Dec. B-298734, 2006 CPD ¶ 192 (business support services); *Advanced Fed. Servs. Corp.*, Comp. Gen. Dec. B-298662, 2006 CPD ¶ 174 (administrative support for government facility set aside for 8(a) businesses); *Kola Nut Travel, Inc.*, Comp. Gen. Dec. B-296090.4, 2005 CPD ¶ 184 (travel services set aside for small businesses); and *Cortez, Inc.*, Comp. Gen. Dec. B-292178, 2003 CPD ¶ 184 (facility logistics services).

It is proper to call for a risk assessment of the probability that a proposed management or technical plan will create performance problems. See Air Force Mandatory Procedure 5315.305.5.1.2. requiring the use of a "mission capability risk rating" and stating:

> The mission capability risk rating focuses on the weaknesses associated with an offeror's proposed approach. . . . Assessment of a mission capability risk considers potential for disruption of schedule, increased cost, or degradation of per-

formance, the need for increased government oversight, and the likelihood of unsuccessful contract performance. . . . For any weakness identified, the evaluation shall address the offeror's proposed mitigation . . . and document why that approach is or is not acceptable. Whenever a strength is identified as part of the mission capability technical rating, (see 5.5.1.1 above), the evaluation shall assess whether the offeror's proposed approach would likely cause an associated weakness which may impact schedule, cost, or performance.

See DoD Source Selection Procedures also calling for the assessment of technical risk:

2.3.1.2.1. Technical Risk. Risk assesses the degree to which the offeror's proposed technical approach for the requirements of the solicitation may cause disruption of schedule, increased costs, degradation of performance, the need for increased Government oversight, or the likelihood of unsuccessful contract performance. All evaluations that include a technical evaluation factor shall also consider risk. Risk can be evaluated in one of two ways:

- As one aspect of the technical evaluation, inherent in the technical evaluation factor or subfactor ratings (reference 3.1.2.1).

- As a separate risk rating assigned at the technical factor or subfactor level (reference 3.1.2.2).

This technique has been upheld in *Trend Western Tech. Corp.*, Comp. Gen. Dec. B-275395.2, 97-1 CPD ¶ 201 (denying a protest that the agency had assessed a plan as having "moderate risk" because the staffing level was low); *Sensis Corp.*, Comp. Gen. Dec. B-265790.2, 96-1 CPD ¶ 77 (agency properly found moderate risk because the protester did not have a mature software development process); and *Hydro Eng'g, Inc. v. United States*, 37 Fed. Cl. 448 (1997) (agency properly found specific elements of a technical and management proposal created a risk of timely performance and technical compliance).

## B. Unlisted Factors or Subfactors

FAR 15.304(d) required that the RFP state clearly "all factors and significant subfactors that will affect contract award." The best practice is to list in the RFP all evaluation factors and subfactors that the agency intends to evaluate. However, failure of the agency to specifically identify an evaluation factor will be excused if the solicitation fairly advises offerors that the factor will be considered. For example, in *Canadian Commercial Corp.*, Comp. Gen. Dec. B-276945, 97-2 CPD ¶ 48, the solicitation requested proposals for a commercial off-the-shelf boat with proven marine performance. The fact that the agency considered the failure of the protester to provide performance data or that the protester had not previously built the boat did not constitute the evaluation of unstated factors. These factors were held to be reasonably understood as related to and relevant to the agency's assessment of risk of whether the protester would successfully deliver a product conforming to the solicitation requirements. GAO has consistently held that innovations and creative approaches are an integral element of technical evaluation in a best value procurement, *ViroMed Labs., Inc.*, Comp. Gen. Dec. B-310747.4, 2009 CPD ¶ 32; *IAP World Servs., Inc.*, Comp. Gen. Dec. B-297084, 2005 CPD ¶ 199. There is also a tendency to broadly interpret evaluation factors to allow an agency to consider other elements of a proposal. See *USGC, Inc.*, Comp. Gen. Dec. B-400184.2, 2009 CPD ¶ 9 ("disincentive plan" forgoing profit for tasks not meeting performance work statement requirements fell within technical approach factor); *AT&T Corp.*, Comp. Gen. Dec. B-299542.3, 2008 CPD ¶ 65 (being manufacturer of equipment was related to factor assessing ability to provide equipment); *Apptis, Inc.*, Comp. Gen. Dec. B-299457, 2008 CPD ¶ 49 (proof of concept demonstration factor encompassed observations that company personnel were inefficient even though the demonstration was successful); *C. Young Constr., Inc.*, Comp. Gen. Dec. B-309740, 2007 CPD ¶ 198 (multiple-position personnel related to technical qualifications of key personnel factor); *Client Network Servs., Inc.*, Comp. Gen. Dec. B-297994, 2006 CPD ¶ 79 (knowledge of labor market related to staffing factor); *Ridoc Enter., Inc.*, Comp. Gen. Dec. B-292962.4, 2004 CPD ¶ 169 (management of subcontractors related to management plan factor); *Israel Aircraft Indus.*, Comp. Gen. Dec. B-274389, 97-1 CPD ¶ 41 (enhanced safety intrinsic to technical evaluation of equipment); *Myers Investigative & Security Servs., Inc.*, Comp. Gen. Dec. B-272947.2, 96-2 CPD ¶ 114 (solicitation clearly put offerors on notice that relevant experience would be evaluated under the past performance factor); and *Science & Tech., Inc.*, Comp. Gen. Dec. B-272748, 97-1 CPD ¶ 121 (offerors could not reasonably ignore factor left off the list of subfactors in section M but which was discussed in section L).

The requirement to list "significant subfactors" has been liberally interpreted to permit the nondisclosure of subfactors which are logically and reasonably related to the stated evaluation factors, *Buffalo Organization for Social & Tech. Innovation, Inc.*, Comp. Gen. Dec. B-196279, 80-1 CPD ¶ 107. See *Thomas G. Gebhard, Jr., P.E., Ph.D.*, Comp. Gen. Dec. B-196454, 80-1 CPD ¶ 115, where GAO stated:

> We have held that each evaluation subcriterion need not be disclosed in the solicitation so long as offerors are advised of the basic criteria. *Genasys Corporation*, 56 Comp. Gen. 835 (1977), 77-2 CPD ¶ 60. Additional factors may be used in an evaluation where there is sufficient correlation between an additional subcriterion and the generalized criteria in the RFP so that offerors are on reasonable notice of the evaluation criteria to be applied to their proposals. *Littleton Research and Engineering Corp.*, B-191245, June 30, 1978, 78-1 CPD ¶ 466.

See also *Hydro Eng'g, Inc. v. United States*, 37 Fed. Cl. 448 (1997).

In spite of this liberal interpretation, it is not good practice to omit subfactors. The best practice is to give the offerors as full an explanation of the factors that will be considered as is practicable. In addition, there are cases granting protests when a subfactor that is not logically related to the stated factor is used. See, for example, *Global Analytic Info. Tech. Servs., Inc.*, Comp. Gen. Dec. B-298840.2, 2007 CPD ¶ 57, finding that the incumbent contractors' methods of improving their performance was not related to the "management approach" factor because it was an "incumbent-specific factor" that could not have been foreseen by the incumbents. See also *American K-9 Detection Servs., Inc.*, Comp. Gen. Dec. B-400464.6, 2009 CPD ¶ 107 (GAO suggested that, in a corrective reopening of the competition, the agency should list the 10 subfactor "categories" to its evaluation of technical capability that had not been listed in the original competition); *PWC Logistics Servs. Co.*, Comp. Gen. Dec. B-400660, 2009 CPD ¶ 67 (agency required to include subfactor stating criteria for dividing work when two contracts were to be awarded).

There have been numerous protests where unlisted subfactors have been held to be logically related to a factor. For example, the requirement that the project director be available at the outset of the procurement was held to be logically related to the "Personnel Qualifications" evaluation factor, *Health Mgmt. Sys.*, Comp. Gen. Dec. B-200775, 81-1 CPD ¶ 255. See also *Building Restoration Corp.*, Comp. Gen. Dec. B-402000, 2010 CPD ¶ 15 (experience with work listed in specification sufficiently related to technical excellence subfactor); *RCL Components, Inc.*, Comp. Gen. Dec. B-400175, 2009 CPD ¶ 98 (relative amount of government contracting experience sufficiently related to "programmatic and logistical considerations" and "type of contract" factors); *Smart Innovative Solutions*, Comp. Gen. Dec. B-400323.3, 2008 CPD ¶ 220 (method of communication with offices sufficiently related to coordination with offices factor); *International Bus. & Tech. Consultants, Inc.*, Comp. Gen. Dec. B-310424.2, 2008 CPD ¶ 185 ("long-term, on-the-ground experience" sufficiently related to professional experience factor); *Cornell Cos.*, Comp. Gen. Dec. B-310548, 2007 CPD ¶212 (distance and remoteness of site of housing prisoners sufficiently related to site location factor); *SCS Refrigerated Servs., LLC*, Comp. Gen. Dec. B-298790, 2006 CPD ¶ 186 (location and evidence of firm contractual agreement with back-up sources sufficiently related to identification of back-up sources factor); *Client Network Servs., Inc.*, Comp. Gen. Dec. B-297994, 2006 CPD ¶ 79 (knowledge of job market in area sufficiently related to approach to managing staff and staffing fluctuations" factor); *Nicholson/Soletanche Joint Venture*, Comp. Gen. Dec. B-297011.3, 2006 CPD ¶ 70 (record of performing directional drilling sufficiently related to past performance factor); *Management Sys. Designers, Inc.*, Comp. Gen. Dec. B-244383.4, 91-2 CPD ¶ 518 ("Compliance with Stated Minimum Requirements," "Additional Experience/Qualifications of Key Personnel," and "Experience in the Topical Area" sufficiently related to the "Personnel Qualifications" factor). In *Telos Field Eng'g*, Comp. Gen. Dec. B-258805.2, 95-1 CPD ¶ 186, the protester contended that its proposal was improperly downgraded under the spare parts factor for proposing an inventory of older spare parts and on the ground that its current inventory did not consist of the optimal mix of equipment and was not organized in kits. The spare parts factor provided:

"[D]oes the contractor have the ability to supply spare parts when needed? Does the contractor have an adequate reserve of parts and the means to quickly deliver them to the site? Could the contractor replace a complete piece of equipment if need be to incur maximum equipment uptime?"

In finding the evaluation reasonable, GAO stated:

[T]he type of inventory and the mix of parts reasonably could be expected to affect the ability to furnish parts for certain equipment, as well as the speed with which the contractor can furnish a part for a newer piece of equipment. Similarly, making parts available in kits, rather than individually, reasonably relates to the speed with which parts necessary for a certain repair can be ordered.

In other cases, cost management was held to be clearly related to past performance even though the RFP only listed "technical performance" and "schedule performance" as subfactors, *Bendix Field Eng'g Corp.*, Comp. Gen. Dec. B-241156, 91-1 CPD ¶ 44, and specific experience was held to be reasonably related to general experience, *Technical Servs. Corp.*, 64 Comp. Gen. 245 (B-214634), 85-1 CPD ¶ 152. In *JoaQuin Mfg. Corp.*, Comp. Gen. Dec. B-275185, 97-1 CPD ¶ 48, GAO found that weight, number of footings, and visibility properly related to the suitability of design evaluation factor. In a very questionable decision, GAO held that performance of work by segments of the company rather than by subcontractors was clearly related to the factor "Offeror's Ability to Provide Additional Effort," *Specialized Tech. Servs., Inc.*, Comp. Gen. Dec. B-247489.2, 92-1 CPD ¶ 510.

Subfactors need not be included on a separate list if they are described in a narrative form in the description of the factor, *Moran Assocs.*, Comp. Gen. Dec. B-240564.2, 91-2 CPD ¶ 495. In that case, GAO apparently believed that a diligent offeror would identify the subfactors from the narrative description. See also *ITT Electron Tech. Div.*, Comp. Gen. Dec. B-242289, 91-1 CPD ¶ 383, holding that there was no need to disclose an evaluation "checklist" when the items on the list were reasonably related to the evaluation factors. In *Stone Webster Eng'g Corp.*, Comp. Gen. Dec. B-255286.2, 94-2 CPD ¶ 306, the protester contended that the evaluation was improper because the agency evaluated proposals on a basis of an evaluation factor, "general strategy," that was not listed as an evaluation factor in the RFP. The agency stated that general strategy was not a separate evaluation criterion but was, however, considered as part of the evaluation of several factors that were set forth in the RFP. GAO agreed, finding that the RFP did state that strategy formulation and selection of appropriate tactics would be a significant subfactor under the understanding the anticipated work evaluation factor.

If a subfactor will have an inordinate impact on the evaluation of a factor, it will be found to be a "significant" subfactor which must be identified in the RFP as having such impact. See *Lloyd H. Kessler, Inc.*, Comp. Gen. Dec. B-284693, 2000 CPD ¶ 96, requiring the listing of a very specific type of experience when that was the most important subfactor. See also *Devres, Inc.*, 66 Comp. Gen. 121 (B-224017), 86-2 CPD ¶ 652, where GAO required listing of a subfactor for specific experience even though it was related to the "general experience" that had been listed. The specific experience subfactor was 60% of the general experience factor and 25 % of the total scoring (it was larger than any other factor).

Listed subfactors must include only elements that bear a relationship to the subfactor. Thus, GAO has held that the financial condition of an offeror was not properly included in the subfactor "ability to meet the published schedule requirements of the Government at an acceptable level of risk," *Flight Int'l Group, Inc.*, 69 Comp. Gen. 741 (B-238953.4), 90-2 CPD ¶ 257.

## C. Relative Importance

There are two aspects of the statutory requirement to provide a statement of relative importance in the RFP. At the highest level, there must be a statement of the procurement strategy described in Section I, above. This is the relationship of cost/price to the non-cost/price factors required by 10 U.S.C. § 2305(a)(3)(iii) and 41 U.S.C. § 3306(c)(1)(C). Below that level, there must be some indication of the relative importance of the factors and subfactors within the non-cost or price areas, 10 U.S.C. § 2305(a)(2)(A)(ii) and 41 U.S.C. § (c)(1)(A).

### 1. Relationship of Cost/Price to Other Factors

At a minimum, the RFP must indicate the decisional logic that the agency intends to use to make the selection decision. See *Signatron, Inc.*, 54 Comp. Gen. 530 (B-181782), 74-2 CPD ¶ 386, where GAO stated at 535:

> We believe that each offeror has a right to know whether the procurement is intended to achieve a minimum standard at the lowest cost or whether cost is secondary to quality. Competition is not served if offerors are not given any idea of the relative values of technical excellence and price.

Thus, the solicitation must describe the procurement strategy that will be used to make the award.

If an agency has decided to use the lowest price, technically acceptable proposal decisional rule, the RFP should include a statement to that effect, FAR 15.101-2(b)(1). If the agency has decided to use a tradeoff decisional rule, it has a variety of ways to state that rule in the RFP. The following is provided, by way of illustration, as language that may be included in an RFP to convey essential information to the offerors:

> Award will be made to that offeror whose proposal contains the combination of those criteria offering the best overall value to the Government. This will be determined by comparing differences in the value of the non-cost criteria with dif-

ferences in cost to the Government. In making this comparison . . . (select the applicable alternative)

> No. 1 (Non-cost criteria most important) — non-cost criteria are significantly more important than cost to the Government because the Government is more concerned with obtaining superior performance than with making an award at the lowest overall cost to the Government. However, the Government will not make an award at a significantly higher overall cost to the Government to achieve slightly superior performance.

> No. 2 (Non-cost criteria and cost to the Government of equal importance) — non-cost criteria and cost to the Government are of equal importance because the Government is concerned with striking the most advantageous balance between the non-cost criteria and cost to the Government.

> No. 3 (Cost to the Government most important) — cost to the Government is significantly more important than non-cost criteria because the Government is more concerned with making an award at the lowest overall cost to the Government than with obtaining superior performance. However, the Government will not make an award based on a proposal with significantly inferior performance in order to achieve a small savings in cost to the Government.

This language attempts to tell offerors that the best value decision would ultimately be made on the basis of marginal differences between the competitors and that the agency would pay more for marginal differences in technical and management features but not a lot more for a small difference. This, of course, describes the essence of a tradeoff selection.

The shorter version of this rule in 10 U.S.C. § 2305(a)(3)(A)(iii) and 41 U.S.C. § 3306(c)(1)(C) is implemented in FAR 15.304(e) as follows:

> The solicitation shall also state, at a minimum, whether all evaluation factors other than cost or price, when combined, are —

>> (1) Significantly more important than cost or price;

>> (2) Approximately equal to cost or price; or

>> (3) Significantly less important than cost or price.

It is proper to state in the RFP that past performance is "more important" than price (rather than "significantly more important" than price) when that is a correct statement, *Braswell Servs., Group. Inc.*, Comp. Gen. Dec. B-276694, 97-2 CPD ¶ 18. However, when an agency uses the "more important" statement, it is improper to then treat the non-cost factors as significantly more important, *Johnson Controls Sec. Sys., LLC*, Comp. Gen. Dec. B-296490.3, 2007 CPD ¶ 100.

Failure to include any statement of relative importance of cost to the government versus non-cost factors is an issue apparent on the fact of the RFP which just be protested before the submission of proposals, *Cherokee Info. Servs., Inc.*, Comp. Gen. Dec. B-291718, 2003 CPD ¶ 49.

Since the ultimate source selection decisions is based on marginal differences between the offerors, the relationship of cost to the government and non-cost factors is actually variable. Agencies have included different types of statements in the RFP describing this fact. See, for example, *DLM&A, Inc. v. United States*, 6 Cl. Ct. 329 (1984), providing the following RFP statement at 330:

> [C]ost is not expected to be the controlling factor in the selection of a Contractor for this solicitation. The degree of importance of cost as a factor could become greater depending upon the equality of the proposals for other factors evaluated; where competing proposals are determined to be substantially equal, total cost and other cost factors would become the controlling factor.

Another example can be found in *EG&G Ortec*, Comp. Gen. Dec. B-213347, 84-1 CPD ¶ 182, *recons. denied*, 84-1 CPD ¶ 372, where the RFP contained the full point scoring system plus the following statement:

> You are advised that paramount consideration shall be given to the evaluation of technical proposals rather than cost or price. It is pointed out, however, that should technical competence between offerors be considered approximately the same, then cost or price could become paramount.

In some cases, GAO has held that this type of statement does not meet the requirement to state relative importance. See *Ogden Support Servs., Inc.*, Comp. Gen. Dec. B-270354, 96-1 CPD ¶ 175, where the RFP only stated that "cost would become more important as the difference in technical evaluation scores decreases and that cost 'may become' determinative when proposals are technically equal." GAO stated that this scheme failed to state the relative importance of the cost factor.

Some agencies have used the term "relative weight" to describe "relative importance," and in some cases they have used percentage weights to assign points in a numerical scoring system. Stating relative weights meets the requirement to state relative importance. See, for example, *GC Servs. Ltd. P'ship*, Comp. Gen. Dec. B-298102, 2006 CPD ¶ 96 (past performance and experience weighted at 45%, technical approach weighted at 30%, and management approach weighted at 25% of non-cost score); *Joint Mgmt. & Tech. Servs.*, Comp. Gen. Dec. B-294229, 2004 CPD ¶ 208 (technical approach — 35%, key/critical personnel — 25%, management approach — 20%, experience — 10%, past performance — 10%).

Failing to state relative "weights," when that term is used, will be found to be a failure to meet the requirement to state relative importance. See *ENCORP Int'l, Inc.*, Comp. Gen. Dec. B-258829, 95-1 CPD ¶ 100, where the agency had explicitly refrained from stating the relative weights of the "more important" technical factors listed in the RFP. Instead, the RFP stated:

> When making tradeoff decisions during proposal preparation, offerors should remember that the Government prefers to obtain better offeror experience, past performance, and better savings. However, the *relative influence* that any of these factors will have on the source selection decision will ultimately depend on the marginal differences among the competing offerors, which will not be known until the proposals have been analyzed and compared to one another. Therefore, the Government has not assigned *weights* to these factors. (emphasis added)

In a footnote GAO stated that this scheme failed to comply with the Competition in Contracting Act, which required, at a minimum, all evaluation factors and significant subfactors and their relative importance. See also *Bio-Rad Labs., Inc.*, Comp. Gen. Dec. B-297553, 2007 CPD ¶ 58 (no disclosure of relative weights of technical subfactors); and *SOS Interpreting, Ltd.*, Comp. Gen. Dec. B-293026, 2005 CPD ¶ 26 (no disclosure of relative weight of past performance or of technical subfactors).

## 2.  Relative Importance of Other Factors

There are a number of different methods of specifying the relative importance factors other than cost or price.

### a.  Listing Criteria

A questionable technique for disclosing the relative importance of non-cost factors is merely to list the factors that will be evaluated in the RFP with no statement of relative importance. In such cases the offerors are expected to assume that all evaluation criteria are of approximately equal importance. See, for example, *Carol Solomon & Assocs.*, Comp. Gen. Dec. B-271713, 96-2 CPD ¶ 28; *Computing & Software, Inc.*, 52 Comp. Gen. 686 (B-176763) (1973); *Dikewood Servs. Co.*, 56 Comp. Gen. 188 (B-186001), 76-2 CPD ¶ 520, where GAO applied the presumption of equality in the absence of a contrary indication of relative importance in the RFP.

### b.  Descending Order of Importance

Another inferior method of indicating relative order of importance is to list the non-cost factors and state that they are listed in descending order of importance. GAO has upheld use of this method where the evaluation scheme "reflects a reasonable downward progression of evaluation weights," *Optimum Tech., Inc.*, Comp. Gen. Dec. B-266339.2, 96-1 CPD ¶ 188. See also *Puglia Eng'g of California, Inc.*, Comp. Gen. Dec. B-297413, 2006 CPD ¶ 33; *A&W Maint. Servs., Inc.*, Comp. Gen. Dec. B-255711.2, 95-1 CPD ¶ 24; and *North-East Imaging, Inc.*, Comp. Gen. Dec. B-256281, 94-1 CPD ¶ 332. Thus, a mere statement that the evaluation factors are listed in the order of their relative importance, without specifically assigning a weight to each, is satisfactory so long as the difference between the importance assigned to any one factor and that assigned to the factor either immediately preceding or immediately following it is small. See *Sperry Rand Corp.*, Comp. Gen. Dec. B-179875, 74-2 CPD ¶ 158, stating that where one factor is to have predominant consideration over the other factors, this should be disclosed. In *BDM Servs. Co.*, Comp. Gen. Dec. B-180245, 74-1 CPD ¶ 237, GAO stated that a predominant factor should have been identified in the RFP and added:

> Moreover, we believe the general relationship of the remaining factors to each other could have been described in narrative without violating the prohibition against disclosure of precise numerical weights in ASPR 3-501(D)(i). As a matter of sound procurement policy, the fullest possible disclosure of all of the evaluation factors and their relative importance is to be preferred to reliance on the reasonableness of the offeror's judgment as to the relative significance of the various evaluation factors.

See also *Finlen Complex, Inc.*, Comp. Gen. Dec. B-288280, 2001 CPD ¶ 167, holding that the 5% weight of past performance was required to be disclosed because offerors could have expected this subfactor to have a higher weight.

Where a solicitation lists evaluation factors and subfactors in descending order of importance, such an evaluation scheme does not indicate that the subfactors of lower-weighted factors are necessarily of less individual weight than subfactors of higher-weighted factors, *Brown & Root, Inc.*, Comp. Gen. Dec. B-270505.2, 96-2 CPD ¶ 143. However, when technical factors are listed in descending order, it is improper to evaluate one of them on a pass/fail basis, *Helicopter Transport Servs. LLC*, Comp. Gen. Dec. B-400295, 2008 CPD ¶ 180.

## c. Adjectival Descriptions of Importance

Another technique for disclosing relative importance of the non-cost factors is to provide an adjectival description of the relationship of the factors. It has been common practice to use such descriptions when the agency actually has firm weights for the non-cost factors. See, for example, *ITT Federal Servs. Int'l Corp.*, Comp. Gen. Dec. B-296783, 2007 CPD ¶ 43, where the RFP stated:

> The RFP advised that the price/cost and business/management/technical approach factors were equal in importance, and that each was significantly more important than past performance, and further, that the past performance and business/management/technical approach factors together were more important than price/cost.

These adjectival statements are also commonly used to describe complex source selection schemes. See, for example, *MD Helicopters, Inc.*, Comp. Gen. Dec. B-298502, 2006 CPD ¶ 178, where GAO described the relationship of the factors as follows:

The RFP provided for a "best value" evaluation of [Federal Aviation Administration] certification (which was evaluated as a "go/no go" criteria) and five other evaluation factors: price, technical, producibility/management (P/M), logistics, and past performance. Price was stated to be more important than technical, technical more important than P/M, and price and technical combined were significantly more important than P/M, logistics, and past performance. P/M and logistics were stated to be of equal importance and each was more important than past performance.

While these types of statements are difficult to decipher, they have been found to convey sufficient information to the offerors as to the relative importance of the factors.

Prior to the statutory requirement for a statement of the relationship between cost/price factor and the non-cost factors, this type of adjectival description was permitted with regard to the entire evaluation. See *Bayshore Sys. Corp.*, Comp. Gen. Dec. B-184446, 76-1 CPD ¶ 146, finding a mere statement that technical factors were more important than price was proper where the undisclosed technical-to-price ratio was 3:1. See also *Kirk-Mayer, Inc.*, Comp. Gen. Dec. B-208582, 83-2 CPD ¶ 288, finding satisfactory a statement that the weights attached to the four factors did not differ significantly, where the weights used in the evaluation were 25, 25, 20, and 30 points; and *Technical Servs. Corp.*, 64 Comp. Gen. 245 (B-214634), 85-1 CPD ¶ 152, concurring with a statement that cost was "secondary" but "important" in a situation where cost was given a 20% weight and technical an 80% weight. However, GAO has agreed that an award should be cancelled and the RFP amended where the adjectival description is misleading as to the relative importance of a factor, *Unisys Corp.*, 67 Comp. Gen. 512 (B-230019.2), 88-2 CPD ¶ 35.

## d. Numerical Systems

The relative importance of factors and subfactors may also be indicated by disclosing the numerical point score or percentage for each evaluation criterion in the RFP. An agency's RFP disclosures of its numerical systems must be sufficient to inform prospective offerors of how the rating system will apply to their proposals. In *National Capital Med. Found. Inc.*, Comp. Gen. Dec. B-215303.5, 85-1 CPD ¶ 637, the RFP failed to inform offerors that proposals would receive zero points out of a possible 110 allocated to "admission objectives" and 200 allocated to "quality objectives" if any one of the subcriteria under these objectives was rated less than acceptable regardless of the merits of the others. GAO found that application of such an undisclosed scoring scheme was arbitrary and inconsistent with the RFP requirements.

## e. Subcriteria

As with primary areas of the evaluation, an offeror may assume that all subcriteria are of substantially equal importance in the absence of advice to the contrary, *North Am. Tel. Assoc.*, Comp. Gen. Dec. B-187239, 76-2 CPD ¶ 495; *Tracor, Inc.*,

56 Comp. Gen. 62 (B-186315), 76-2 CPD ¶ 386. However, if a subfactor is to play an important role in the source selection decision, that must be stated in the RFP. See, for example, *H. J. Group Ventures, Inc.*, Comp. Gen. Dec. B-246139, 92-1 CPD ¶ 203, where GAO found improper heavy reliance on past performance when that criterion had been listed as a "general consideration" but not included in the list of other criteria which were stated in relative order of importance. See also *J.A. Jones Mgmt. Servs., Inc.*, Comp. Gen. Dec. B-254941.2, 94-1 CPD ¶ 244, where the agency improperly had greatly exaggerated the weight the RFP assigned to the key personnel evaluation factor; and *University of Michigan*, 66 Comp. Gen. 538 (B-225756), 87-1 CPD ¶ 643, where it was improper to place heavy reliance on one criterion when the RFP appeared to indicate that four technical criteria were of relatively equal weight.

## 3.  Minimum Requirements

If an RFP provides that offerors must meet specified minimum requirements, award may not be made to an offeror that fails to meet the minimum requirements. Conversely, if the RFP does not clearly state a minimum requirement, the government may not reject a proposal which does not meet that requirement, *RJO Enters., Inc.*, Comp. Gen. Dec. B-260126.2, 95-2 CPD ¶ 93, nor drop a proposal from the competitive range for not meeting the requirement, *Omniplex World Servs. Corp.*, Comp. Gen. Dec. B-290996.2, 2003 CPD ¶ 7. Similarly if an agency uses a performance specification allowing an offeror to devise a solution, the agency is not required to inform other offerors that it intends to select an offeror with a desirable solution, *Cerner Corp.*, Comp. Gen. Dec. B-293093, 2004 CPD ¶ 34. In *ACS Sys. & Eng'g, Inc.*, Comp. Gen. Dec. B-275439.3, 97-1 CPD ¶ 126, GAO upheld an agency's corrective action allowing resubmission of BAFOs after its requirements had changed, stating that "[i]t is fundamental that offerors must be advised of a procuring agency's actual minimum requirements." See also *Lobar, Inc.*, Comp. Gen. Dec. B-247843.3, 92-2 CPD ¶ 139, where GAO required the agency to reopen the procurement and amend the RFP to state the minimum requirements that the agency was actually using in the evaluation of proposals. In *CNA Indus. Eng'g, Inc.*, Comp. Gen. Dec. B-271034, 96-1 CPD ¶ 279, the agency awarded a contract to an offeror who had similar experience with a similar software system. GAO held that the award was based on an improper relaxation of the agency's minimum requirement that offerors demonstrate expertise and experience with the agency's own software system. However, there is no need for an agency to formulate minimum requirements for each evaluation factor in order to satisfy minimum requirements disclosures, if objective measures are not relevant to the source selection, *W.B. Jolley*, 68 Comp. Gen. 443 (B-234490), 89-1 CPD ¶ 512.

Similarly, minimum requirements need not be stated if the agency is open to consideration of varying levels of performance, *Dismas Charities*, Comp. Gen. Dec. B-298390, 2006 CPD ¶ 131 (no minimum number of parking spaces although only a few spaces was considered a weakness); *National Beef Packing Co.*, Comp. Gen.

Dec. B-296534, 2005 CPD ¶ 168 (no minimum delivery requirement stated when RFP permitted offerors to propose alternate delivery schedules); *Carson & Assocs., Inc.*, GSBCA 9411-P, 88-2 BCA ¶ 20,778 (no need to state minimum staffing levels when agency considered staffing levels variable depending on proposed method of performing the work). Thus, an agency must only disclose in the RFP any minimum requirements that it intends to actually use in the evaluation.

If a minimum requirement is stated clearly in the RFP, there is no need to state additionally that it will be evaluated on a pass/fail basis, *OfficeMax, Inc.*, Comp. Gen. Dec. B-299340.2, 2007 CPD ¶ 158. Conversely, if the RFP states that a requirement will be evaluated on a pass/fail basis, offerors should assume that it is a minimum requirement, *National Shower Express, Inc.*, Comp. Gen. Dec. B-293970, 2004 CPD ¶ 140. However, some agencies include both statements in the RFP. See, for example, *Nu-Way, Inc.*, Comp. Gen. Dec. B-296435.5, 2005 CPD ¶ 195.

## III. REQUESTS FOR PROPOSALS

Once specifications have been adopted, a procurement strategy has been selected and evaluation factors and subfactors and their relative weights have been determined, the government must provide this information to potential offerors. In addition, offerors must be advised of the type of contract that will be used and the terms and conditions which it will contain. Finally, offerors must be given instructions on what must be submitted. The Request for Proposals (RFP) is the means by which these matters are communicated. See FAR 15.203(a):

> Requests for proposals (RFPs) are used in negotiated acquisitions to communicate Government requirements to prospective contractors and to solicit proposals. RFPs for competitive acquisitions shall, at a minimum, describe the —
>
> (1) Government's requirement;
>
> (2) Anticipated terms and conditions that will apply to the contract:
>
> > (i) The solicitation may authorize offerors to propose alternative terms and conditions, including the contract line item number (CLIN) structure; and
>
> > (ii) When alternative CLIN structures are permitted, the evaluation approach should consider the potential impact on other terms and conditions or the requirement (e.g., place of performance or payment and funding requirements) (see 15.206);
>
> (3) Information required to be in the offeror's proposal; and
>
> (4) Factors and significant subfactors that will be used to evaluate the proposal and their relative importance.

Thus, it can be seen that the RFP serves a number of functions and that a well-organized and well-drafted RFP is essential to achieving an effective and efficient procurement.

## A. Organization of the RFP

FAR 15.204 requires that RFPs be prepared using the Uniform Contract Format — specified in FAR 15.204-1(b) as follows:

### UNIFORM CONTRACT FORMAT

| SECTION | TITLE |
|---|---|
| **Part I—The Schedule** | |
| A | Solicitation/contract form |
| B | Supplies or services and prices/costs |
| C | Description/specifications/statement of work |
| D | Packaging and marking |
| E | Inspection and acceptance |
| F | Deliveries or performance |
| G | Contract administration data |
| H | Special contract requirements |
| **Part II—Contract Clauses** | |
| I | Contract clauses |
| **Part III—List of Documents, Exhibits, and Other Attachments** | |
| J | List of attachments |
| **Part IV—Representations and Instructions** | |
| K | Representations, certifications, and other statements of offerors or respondents |
| L | Instructions, conditions, and notices to offerors or respondents |
| M | Evaluation factors for award |

Parts I, II and III become part of the contract and Section K is to be incorporated into the contract by reference.

FAR 15.204 provides that the Uniform Contract Format "need not be used" for:

(a) Construction and architect-engineer contracts (see part 36).

(b) Subsistence contracts.

(c) Supplies or services contracts requiring special contract formats prescribed elsewhere in this part that are inconsistent with the uniform format.

(d) Letter requests for proposals (see 15.203(e)).

(e) Contracts exempted by the agency head or designee.

## B. Contract Provisions

The contract provisions in Parts I, II, and III of the Uniform Contract Format constitute a complete contract except for the prices or costs and fee in Part B, which the offeror must fill out when the proposal is submitted. Thus, as in the case of sealed bidding, the government normally writes an entire contract in the course of preparing the RFP. However, in negotiated procurement, the RFP may solicit additive or alternate offers which will vary the terms of the RFP and require rewriting of the contract after negotiation has occurred.

FAR 15.204-2(a) provides that Standard Form 33 (Solicitation, Offer and Award), FAR 53.301-33; or Optional Form 308 (Solicitation and Offer — Negotiated Acquisition) may be used as the cover sheet for the RFP and will constitute Section A of the contract. These forms contain a significant amount of key information, as well as blocks for the signatures of the prospective contractor. In addition, the SF 33 contains a block for the signature of the contracting officer, which permits it to be used as an award form. The most important information is the time by which the proposal must be submitted and the requirement for signature of the proposal by an authorized representative of the contractor. The information contained on these forms must be included in the RFP if these forms are not used. See FAR 15.203(e).

FAR 15.204-2(b) contains the following guidance on the information to be included in Section B of the RFP:

> Include a brief description of the supplies or services; e.g., item number, national stock number/part number if applicable, nouns, nomenclature, and quantities. (This includes incidental deliverables such as manuals and reports.)

The purpose of this section is to give offerors a summary description of the contract requirements and provide a place for offerors to submit their proposed prices. Thus, the descriptions of the work in this section are very brief — with details left to Section C.

The number of line items is discretionary with the procuring agency. However, it is normal practice to include a separate line item whenever a different source of funds is used for the supplies or services being procured. This can result in fragmentation of the same work (such as a single product) into a number of line items in instances where the agency is buying that work for a number of different users or in different years.

Section C contains the detailed description of the work to be performed under the contract. The contract specification is usually a detailed document that has evolved in an agency over a number of procurements or a new document written specifically for the procurement. In either case, the RFP must provide specific information to prospective offerors on the applicable specifications. However, the RFP need not actually contain the specifications except in certain situations. See FAR Subpart 11.2.

FAR 15.204-2(d) provides that Section D should contain packaging, packing, preservation, and marking provisions. Detailed guidance on this issue is left to agency regulations.

Section E should contain the special clauses that the agency will use in inspecting and accepting the work. In most cases, the procuring agency will include the appropriate standard inspection clause from FAR 52.246. FAR Subpart 46.2 contains detailed guidance on the selection of standard inspection clauses or other inspection clauses to minimize the costs to the government and utilize the contractor's inspection capabilities to the maximum extent consistent with obtaining the necessary quality of work.

Section F contains guidance on the time and place of contract performance in accordance with FAR Subpart 11.4. FAR 52.211-9 contains a number of alternate clauses to be used in specifying the time of delivery as either a firm contract requirement or a desired time. When the time is specified as a firm contract requirement, an offer may be rejected if it fails to comply with the requirement. Note, however, that offerors whose initial proposals do not comply with the required delivery schedules should still be considered for the competitive range. Unlike sealed bid procurements, negotiated procurements permit giving offerors the opportunity to satisfy government requirements through discussions. Therefore, an offeror in negotiated procurements that fails to comply with delivery times in its proposal should not be automatically labeled nonresponsive and rejected since this error could easily be corrected during discussions. See *Hollingsead Int'l*, Comp. Gen. Dec. B-227853, 87-2 CPD ¶ 372; *Xtek, Inc.*, Comp. Gen. Dec. B-213166, 84-1 CPD ¶ 264; *DPF Inc.*, Comp. Gen. Dec. B-180292, 74-1 CPD ¶ 303. These cases seem to contradict ¶ (b) of the Time of Delivery clause in FAR 52.211-8, which states that if the proposed delivery date is "later than the required delivery date, the offer will be considered nonresponsive and rejected." This language only applies to sealed bid procurements and should be deleted from the clause when it is used in negotiated procurements. Alternates I and II of the Time of Delivery clause in FAR 52.211-9 do not need to be altered in this way because they contain a ¶ (b) which omits such language.

In some cases, agencies use special time of performance clauses which make the time of performance, within a range, an evaluation factor. GAO has sanctioned the use of time of performance as an evaluation factor, especially when the procurement is urgent. See *Shirley Constr. Corp.*, 70 Comp. Gen. 62 (B-240357), 90-2 CPD ¶ 380 (total time of performance one of four evaluation criteria); and *Hydroscience*, Comp. Gen. Dec. B-227989, 87-2 CPD ¶ 501 (offeror's proposal properly devalued due to uncertainty as to time of performance when swift performance was crucial).

FAR 15.204-2(g) requires that Section G include accounting and appropriation data as well as contract administration information or instructions other than those pertaining to the solicitation. DFARS PGI 204.7107 requires contracting offices to use accounting classification reference numbers (ACRNs) in order to process certain contract data through the Military Standard Contract Administration Procedures (MILSCAP). MILSCAP utilizes the ACRNs to relate contract administration records to the long-line accounting classification used to obligate funds on the contract. NAPS 5232.792 repeats these requirements and adds that "accounting data shall also be shown on any change order or contract amendment to a contract that revises the accounting data for any item or increases or decreases the total amount of a contract."

FAR 15.204-2(h) provides that Section H may contain any special contract requirements that are not contained in Section I. While this gives procuring agencies almost total discretion on how to use this section, many agencies include clauses which are specially written for the procurement.

Section I contains most of the standard clauses for the proposed contract. Standard contract clauses are contained in FAR Part 52. The matrix in FAR Subpart 52.3 gives guidance on the clauses to be incorporated into the various types of contracts. Clauses are either (1) required, (2) required when applicable, or (3) optional. FAR 52.102(a) requires incorporation of clauses by reference to the "maximum practical extent" even if they —

(1) Are used with one or more alternates or on an optional basis;

(2) Are prescribed on a "substantially as follows" or "substantially the same as" basis, provided they are used verbatim;

(3) Require modification or the insertion by the Government of fill-in material (see 52.104); or

(4) Require completion by the offeror or prospective contractor. This instruction also applies to provisions completed as annual representations and certifications.

FAR 52.103 provides that when clauses are incorporated by reference they are to be identified by FAR number, title, and date or agency regulation number, title, and date.

The requirement to incorporate by reference clauses that must be filled in by one of the parties can result in an incomplete contract. See, for example, Alternate I of the Rights in Data — General clause in FAR 52.227-14 which specifies a blank space for the uses that a government agency can make of limited rights technical data which is frequently incorporated in contracts without filling in the uses. FAR 52.104 contains the following guidance on filling in such clauses:

(d) When completing blanks in provisions or clauses incorporated by reference, insert the fill-in information directly below the title of the provision or clause identifying to the lowest level necessary to clearly indicate the blanks being filled in.

If a clause that is incorporated by reference requires an offeror to fill in blanks, the offeror should print out the clause, fill in the blanks and submit the clause with its proposal. The only guidance on this procedure is the partial guidance in FAR 52.102(c) which requires contracting officers to identify, in special situations, such clauses in order to alert offerors that they must be filled in.

When an agency deviates from a standard clause, FAR 52.107(f) requires it to alert offerors to such deviation by including the following Authorized Deviation in Clauses clause from FAR 52.252-6 in the RFP:

(a) The use in this solicitation or contract of any Federal Acquisition Regulation (48 CFR chapter 1) clause with an authorized deviation is indicated by the addition of (DEVIATION) after the date of the clause.

(b) The use in this solicitation or contract of any [insert regulation name] (48 CFR) clause with an authorized deviation is indicated by the addition of (DEVIATION) after the name of the regulation.

Deviations are only effective if they are approved by an official with the authority to take such actions. See Chapter 1.

Section J contains all attachments and exhibits to the contract. FAR 15.204-4 requires that the title, date, and number of pages be listed for each of these documents. There is no provision dealing with the incorporation of these items by reference.

The requirements for certifications or representations by the offeror are contained in Section K. The government uses these provisions to determine the status of the offeror and to ensure that the offeror will be in compliance with the socio-economic requirements of the procurement. Thus, these provisions create a self-monitoring mechanism permitting offerors to establish their compliance by certification rather than by proving that certain requirements are met. In order to reduce the administrative burden on offerors, the government has adopted a policy of annual online representations and certifications using an Online Representations and Certifications Application (ORCA). All prospective contractors are required to participate in this system, FAR 4.1201. Offerors are alerted to this requirement be the inclusion in the RFP of the Annual Representations and Certifications solicitation provision in FAR 52.204-8 and the Central Contractor Registration clause in FAR 52.204-7. When this is done, FAR 4.1202 calls for the omission from the RFP of the separate clauses requiring certifications and representations — which are listed in that regulation.

## C. Solicitation Provisions

The solicitation provisions specify the ground rules under which proposals are to be submitted and evaluated and award is to be made. FAR 2.101 contains the following definition:

Solicitation provision or provision means a term or condition used only in solicitations and applying only before contract award.

These provisions will consist of standard terms or conditions dealing with the submission of proposals, specialized instructions relating to the specific procurement and a statement of the evaluation factors and subfactors and their relative importance. The RFP may be transmitted by electronic commerce or facsimile and may authorize the submission of proposals using electronic commerce or facsimiles, FAR 15.203(c) and (d).

### 1. Standard Provisions

FAR 15.209 requires the inclusion of a number of standard provisions in the RFP. FAR 15.209(a) requires that the FAR 52.215-1, Instructions to Offerors — Competitive Acquisition be included in all competitive solicitations where the government intends to award a contract without discussions. This provision does not prohibit conducting discussions if award without discussions is not feasible. Alternate I is to be added if the government has determined, in advance, that it will conduct discussions. When Alternate I is included, award without discussions is not permitted. This provision incorporates definitions and rules involving a number of matters, including modification and withdrawal of proposals, consideration of late proposals, acceptable restrictions on disclosure of information, and award. These matters were previously contained in twelve separate clauses. FAR 15.209(a)(2) also calls for the use of Alternate II to this solicitation provision when the government would be willing to accept alternate proposals. The use of this alternate allows the government to award a contract to an offeror submitting an alternate proposal without having to amend the RFP and provide all offerors the opportunity to compete on that alternate, *Litton Sys., Inc. v. Department of Transp.*, GSBCA 12911-P, 94-3 BCA ¶ 27,263. However, Alternate II "reserves the right" of the government to amend the RFP if the agency chooses to obtain competition on the alternate requirements.

FAR 15.209 also provides guidance on a number of additional provisions that are commonly used in RFPs. FAR 15.209(b) requires the use of the FAR 52.215-2, Audit and Records — Negotiation provision or one of its alternate provisions in all negotiated procurements except for simplified acquisitions, acquisition of utility services at established rates or acquisition of commercial items. FAR 15.209(e) requires the use of the FAR 52.215-5, Facsimile Proposals provision in all RFPs permitting the use of such proposals. FAR 15.209(f) requires use of the FAR 52.215-6,

Place of Performance provision in all RFPs where the place of performance is not specified by the government. FAR 15.209(h) requires the use of the FAR 52.215-8, Order of Precedence — Uniform Contract Format provision in all RFPs using the uniform contract format.

## 2. Specific Instructions — Section L

These instructions are the key to obtaining quality proposals. In the past, the failure to give clear and well organized guidance in Section L has been one of the most common defects in the competitive negotiation process. FAR 15.204-5(b) contains only the following brief discussion of this area, stating:

> Insert in this section solicitation provisions and other information and instructions not required elsewhere to guide offerors or respondents in preparing proposals or responses to requests for information. Prospective offerors or respondents may be instructed to submit proposals or information in a specific format or severable parts to facilitate evaluation. The instructions may specify further organization of proposal or response parts, such as —
>
> (1) Administrative;
>
> (2) Management;
>
> (3) Technical;
>
> (4) Past performance; and
>
> (5) Cost or pricing data (see Table 15-2 of 15.408) or information other than cost or pricing data.

This generalized coverage gives little advice to contracting officers as to the purpose of these specific instructions and the nature of the information which is to be furnished by offerors. It also does not deal with identification of the strategy which the agency has decided to use.

### a.  Procurement Strategy

Either Section M or the instructions in Section L should identify the procurement strategy that will be used in making the award. This entails the inclusion of a clear statement of whether the agency is using the tradeoff process, the lowest price, technically acceptable proposal process, some combination of these two, or any other strategy that the agency has selected. See Section I, above.

The instructions should also describe the type of contract that is to be used and the objectives that the agency has in the procurement. It is also helpful to include a description of the time that the agency intends to take to evaluate proposals and the intended date of award of the contract. Guidance of this nature is very beneficial to offerors in assisting them to allocate resources to the procurement.

It is also very helpful to offerors if the instructions include specific information on the evaluation process that will be followed. In particular, evaluation standards should be disclosed. See *Omniplex World Servs. Corp.*, Comp. Gen. Dec. B-290996.2, 2003 CPD ¶ 7; *RJO Enters., Inc.*, Comp. Gen. Dec. B-260126.2, 95-2 CPD ¶ 93; and *Sarasota Measurements & Controls, Inc.*, Comp. Gen. Dec. B-252406, 93-1 CPD ¶ 494, requiring the inclusion of evaluation standards in RFPs when they constituted government requirements. While GAO has not required the disclosure of evaluation standards that merely give guidance to evaluators in assessing the relative value of factors or subfactors, *Computer Assocs. Int'l, Inc.*, Comp. Gen. Dec. B-292077.3, 2004 CPD ¶ 163; *Lexis-Nexis*, Comp. Gen. Dec. B-260023, 95-2 CPD ¶ 14, the inclusion of such standards in the RFP is good practice because it provides fuller information on the agency's acquisition strategy.

### b.  *Required Submissions*

In the past, offerors have been requested to submit much information pertaining to their capability to perform in detailed technical and management "proposals." As discussed in Section II, above, much of this type of information comes under the category of "capability factors" to be used solely for evaluation purposes as opposed to "offer factors" to be incorporated into the contract. The RFP should make a clear distinction between these matters and should specify what information is to be furnished. "Technical proposals" should only be required where offerors are permitted to offer differing supplies or services than those specified in the RFP or where the government is requesting offerors to provide solutions to its needs.

Offerors should be provided detailed guidance on the information to be furnished for evaluation purposes. A well written RFP will contain a precise correlation between the information to be furnished and the evaluation factors and subfactors identified in Section M. Where different evaluation factors are to be evaluated by different personnel, the agency may wish to have the relevant information packaged in separate sections.

Data on past performance and experience will have to be obtained from each offeror in most procurements. This will normally entail the obtaining of information on a specified number of recent contracts where the offeror has performed similar types of work. Generally, agencies request the names of key people that can be called as references and data as to the work done on the contract and problems encountered in its performance. FAR 15.305(a)(2)(ii) contains guidance on obtaining information on past performance. It requires RFPs to "authorize offerors to provide information on problems encountered on the identified contracts and the offeror's corrective actions." This is most readily done by requiring that each offeror submit a short self-assessment of its performance on each of the referenced contracts.

The RFP should also specifically identify the cost or pricing information needed by the contracting officer to evaluate the cost/price proposal of the offeror. Since there are no standard solicitation provisions in the FAR for requesting such information, the contracting officer must draft a provision for each procurement detailing the information required. See Chapter 10 for a discussion of the types of information that should be requested.

### c. Oral Presentations

In recent years agencies have used oral presentations in lieu of written proposals to evaluate whether offerors fully understand the work that will be required to successfully perform the prospective contract. Such presentations have proved to be a superior means of assessing offerors' understanding because they permit the agency to communicate directly with the offeror's personnel that will perform the work rather than reading technical proposals that may have been written by professional proposal writers. FAR 15.102 provides the following guidance on the use of oral presentations:

(a) Oral presentations by offerors as requested by the Government may substitute for, or augment, written information. Use of oral presentations as a substitute for portions of a proposal can be effective in streamlining the source selection process. Oral presentations may occur at any time in the acquisition process, and are subject to the same restrictions as written information, regarding timing (see 15.208) and content (see 15.306). Oral presentations provide an opportunity for dialogue among the parties. Pre-recorded videotaped presentations that lack real-time interactive dialogue are not considered oral presentations for the purposes of this section, although they may be included in offeror submissions, when appropriate.

(b) The solicitation may require each offeror to submit part of its proposal through oral presentations. However, certifications, representations, and a signed offer sheet (including any exceptions to the Government's terms and conditions) shall be submitted in writing.

Although FAR 15.102(b) provides that offerors may be required to submit "part of its proposal" through oral presentations, FAR 15.102(f) precludes incorporation of oral statements in the contract by reference and provides that any information from an oral presentation that is to be incorporated in the contract must be put in writing.

FAR 15.102(c) indicates that such presentations are suitable for obtaining information, as follows:

Information pertaining to areas such as an offeror's capability, past performance, work plans or approaches, staffing resources, transition plans, or sample tasks (or other types of tests) may be suitable for oral presentations. In deciding what information to obtain through an oral presentation, consider the following:

(1) The Government's ability to adequately evaluate the information;

(2) The need to incorporate any information into the resultant contract;

(3) The impact on the efficiency of the acquisition; and

(4) The impact (including cost) on small businesses. In considering the costs of oral presentations, contracting officers should also consider alternatives to on-site oral presentations (e.g., teleconferencing, video teleconferencing).

FAR 15.102(d) requires that RFPs provide offerors with sufficient information to understand what is sought in the oral presentation. It suggests a description of the following issues:

(1) The types of information to be presented orally and the associated evaluation factors that will be used;

(2) The qualifications for personnel that will be required to provide the oral presentation(s);

(3) The requirements for, and any limitations and/or prohibitions on, the use of written material or other media to supplement the oral presentations;

(4) The location, date, and time for the oral presentations;

(5) The restrictions governing the time permitted for each oral presentation; and

(6) The scope and content of exchanges that may occur between the Government's participants and the offeror's representatives as part of the oral presentations, including whether or not discussions (see 15.306(d)) will be permitted during oral presentations.

There are several important issues that should be addressed in the RFP. First, it should state that the presentation is intended to address the key issues that are expected to arise during performance of the contract rather than the capability of the offeror. These key issues can be specifically identified in the RFP or chosen by each offeror, at the discretion of the agency. The RFP should also state that the offeror's personnel attending the oral presentation should be the people that will be managing the performance of the key issue areas — whether they be employees of the offeror or of a prospective subcontractor. The RFP should then state the time allocated to an initial presentation by the offeror and the time allocated to dialog between the parties

— in the form of a question-and-answer session, an interview, or the solution of a sample task. As a general proposition, it is good practice to devote more time to this dialog than to the initial presentation. It is implicit that when the RFP calls for an oral presentation, the subjects covered will be part of the evaluation process, *Brooks Range Contract Servs., Inc.*, Comp. Gen. Dec. B-401231, 2009 CPD ¶ 129.

The FAR makes it clear that agency officials may ask questions and seek further detail during the oral presentation, and this is consistent with prior decisions, *NAHB Research Found., Inc.*, Comp. Gen. Dec. B-219344, 85-2 CPD ¶ 248 (aggressive questioning permissible). However, both the Court of Federal Claims and GAO have rejected protests that the agency did not use the oral presentation to obtain full information on the capability of an offeror. See *Bean Stuyvesant, L.L.C. v. United States*, 48 Fed. Cl. 303 (2000) (offeror properly downgraded for not discussing an issue — with no agency effort to raise the issue in the dialog); *Oceaneering Int'l, Inc.*, Comp. Gen. Dec. B-287325, 2001 CPD ¶ 95 (agency didn't raise omitted issue with offeror). Agencies that conduct oral presentations in this manner lose the full benefit of the technique. While this is legally acceptable, it is not good practice to fail to explore areas where the offeror has omitted information that is necessary to determine its full capability to perform the work.

Agencies may adopt reasonable rules governing the nature of the presentations, including limitations on the length and nature of the presentations, *American Sys. Corp.*, 68 Comp. Gen. 475 (B-234449), 89-1 CPD ¶ 537. They may also require that offerors meet mandatory requirements in an RFP before being eligible to make an oral presentation, *Inte-Great Corp.*, Comp. Gen. Dec. B-272780, 96-2 CPD ¶ 159. Some agencies have followed the questionable practice of requiring offerors to submit the slides that they will use in the oral presentation at the time the proposal is submitted.

Agencies have identified two procedural requirements for oral presentations that have not enhanced the process. The first is the requirement that slides to be used must be submitted with the original proposal. While this requirement has been strictly enforced, *KSEND v. United States*, 69 Fed. Cl. 103 (2005), it is difficult to perceive how it reduces any advantage that might accrue to offerors that make their presentation later than other offerors. The second is the requirement restricting the nature of the media used in the presentation,. such as requiring only black and white slides. Such a requirement merely precludes the use of media that is most effective in demonstrating the offeror's ability to deal with a potential area of difficulty — such as a color slide of a pie chart. Requirements of these types should not be called for in the RFP.

Agencies may either preclude or permit discussions during the oral presentation, FAR 15.102(d)(6). However, if discussions occur, the agency must comply with the rules governing negotiations with all offerors in the competitive range, FAR 15.102(g). In *Sierra Military Health Servs., Inc.*, Comp. Gen. Dec. B-292780, 2004 CPD ¶ 55, GAO stated the rule as follows:

The FAR generally anticipates "dialogue among the parties" in the course of an oral presentation, FAR § 15.102(a), and we see nothing improper in agency personnel expressing their view about vendors' quotations or proposals, in addition to listening to the vendors' presentations, during those sessions. Once the agency personnel begin speaking, rather than merely listening, in those sessions, however, that dialogue may constitute discussions. As we have long held, the acid test for deciding whether an agency has engaged in discussions is whether the agency has provided an opportunity for quotations or proposals to be revised or modified. See, e.g., *TDS, Inc.*, B-292674, Nov. 12, 2003, 2003 CPD ¶ 204 at 6; *Priority One Servs., Inc.*, B-288836, B-288836.2, Dec. 17, 2001, 2002 CPD ¶ 79 at 5. Accordingly, where agency personnel comment on, or raise substantive questions or concerns about, vendors' quotations or proposals in the course of an oral presentation, and either simultaneously or subsequently afford the vendors an opportunity to make revisions in light of the agency personnel's comments and concerns, discussions have occurred. *TDS, Inc., supra*, at 6; see FAR § 15.102(g).

Compare *Development Alternatives, Inc.*, Comp. Gen. Dec. B-279920, 98-2 CPD ¶ 54, holding that requesting additional details concerning information in a proposal during an oral presentation did not constitute discussions, with *Global Analytic Info. Tech. Servs., Inc.*, Comp. Gen. Dec. B-298840.2, 2007 CPD ¶ 57, holding that allowing an offeror to submit revised pricing *after* an oral presentation was a discussion.

## 3. Evaluation Factors and Subfactors — Section M

The evaluation factors and subfactors to be used must be identified in Section M. FAR 15.204-5(c) provides minimal guidance, merely directing that the agency:

> Identify all significant factors and any significant subfactors that will be considered in awarding the contract and their relative importance (see 15.304(d)).

This provision also requires that the contracting officer insert one of the statements of relative importance in FAR 15.304(e) in the RFP (stating that non-price factors are "significantly more important," "approximately equal to," or "significantly less important" than the price factors). However, GAO has ruled that this requirement was met when the RFP contained an accurate statement that the non-price factor was "more important" than price, rather than "significantly more important," *Braswell Servs., Group*, Comp. Gen. Dec. B-276694, 97-2 CPD ¶ 18. As discussed in Section II., the relative importance of the non-price evaluation factors and subfactors should also be stated in this section.

## D. Method of Submission of Offers and Information

Traditionally, the offer and information were submitted together in paper media in a sealed envelope. However, there are a growing number of procurements where facsimile or electronic submission is permitted or required. In addition, part of or all the required information may be submitted in an oral presentation as discussed above.

## 1. *Paper Media*

Paragraph (c) of the Instructions to Offerors — Competitive Acquisition solicitation provision in FAR 52.215-1 provides guidance on the basic procedure to be followed in submitting offers and information:

(1) Unless other methods (e.g., electronic commerce or facsimile) are permitted in the solicitation, proposals and modifications to proposals shall be submitted in paper media in sealed envelopes or packages (i) addressed to the office specified in the solicitation, and (ii) showing the time and date specified for receipt, the solicitation number, and the name and address of the offeror. Offerors using commercial carriers should ensure that the proposal is marked on the outermost wrapper with the information in paragraphs (c)(1)(i) and (c)(1)(ii) of this provision.

(2) The first page of the proposal must show —

(i) The solicitation number;

(ii) The name, address, and telephone and facsimile numbers of the offeror (and electronic address if available);

(iii) A statement specifying the extent of agreement with all terms, conditions, and provisions included in the solicitation and agreement to furnish any or all items upon which prices are offered at the price set opposite each item;

(iv) Names, titles, and telephone and facsimile numbers (and electronic addresses if available) of persons authorized to negotiate on the offeror's behalf with the Government in connection with this solicitation; and

(v) Name, title, and signature of person authorized to sign the proposal. Proposals signed by an agent shall be accompanied by evidence of that agent's authority, unless that evidence has been previously furnished to the issuing office.

## 2. *Facsimile or Electronic Submission*

FAR 4.502(a) encourages the use of electronic commerce "whenever practicable or cost effective." FAR 15.203(c) provides that when electronic commerce is an authorized means of submission, the RFP must "specify the electronic commerce method(s) that offerors may use (see Subpart (d))." There is no standard FAR solicitation provision specifying the method to be used — with the result that agencies are permitted to adopt different methods. FAR 4.502(b) contains general guidance on the use of electronic commerce.

FAR 15.203(d) provides that proposals may be submitted by facsimile, depending on the following considerations:

(i) Anticipated proposal size and volume;

(ii) Urgency of the requirement;

(iii) Availability and suitability of electronic commerce methods; and

(iv) Adequacy of administrative procedures and controls for receiving, identifying, recording, and safeguarding facsimile proposals, and ensuring their timely delivery to the designated proposal delivery location.

FAR 15.209(e) requires the use of the FAR 52.215-5 Facsimile Proposals provision in an RFP when submission by facsimile is authorized. The instructions for handling unreadable portions of facsimile or electronic submissions contained in this provision are set forth in FAR 15.207(c).

Offerors assume the risk of nonreceipt of their facsimile transmissions, *S.W. Elecs. & Mfg. Corp.*, Comp. Gen. Dec. B-249308, 92-2 CPD ¶ 320; *Microscope Co.*, Comp. Gen. Dec. B-257015, 94-2 CPD ¶ 157; *International Garment Processors*, Comp. Gen. Dec. B-299674, 2007 CPD ¶ 130. Offerors also assume the risk of nonreceipt of electronic transmissions, *Joint Venture Penauillie Italia S.p.A.; Cofathec S.p.A.; SEB.CO S.a.s.; CO.PEL.S.a.s.*, Comp. Gen. Dec. B-298865, 2007 CPD ¶ 7 (e-mail received by agency lacked required data); *Seven Seas Eng'g & Land Surveying*, Comp. Gen. Dec. B-294424.2, 2004 CPD ¶ 236 (e-mail final proposal revisions received late); *Sea Box, Inc.*, Comp. Gen. Dec. B-291056, 2002 CPD ¶ 181 (e-mail proposal late when received at agency initial point of entry on time but not received by contracting office until after required time); *Comspace Corp.*, Comp. Gen. Dec. B-274037, 96-2 CPD ¶ 186 (quotation delivered to the offeror's government-approved Value Added Network but not transmitted to agency).

## E.  Amendment and Cancellation of the RFP

When needs or circumstances change or when new information or defects in the RFP are discovered, the agency may be required to amend or cancel the RFP. Cancellations resulting from the government no longer having a need for the procurement or from lack of funds are not at issue. However, where the government still intends to proceed with the procurement, the RFP must be amended. See FAR 15.206(a), which states:

When, either before or after receipt of proposals, the Government changes its requirements or terms and conditions, the contracting officer shall amend the solicitation.

Whether the amendment requires or permits cancellation and resolicitation or is such that the procurement is allowed to proceed depends upon the nature and timing of the changes. While both a cancellation followed by a resolicitation with an amended RFP and an amendment without cancellation involve amended RFPs, the latter action permits the government to continue on with the procurement. Thus, it may be more attractive to procurement officials since it saves both time and administrative effort. Conversely, resolicitation may expand the field of competition and result in a more advantageous deal for the government.

## 1. Cancellation and Resolicitation

The only FAR provision dealing with cancellation and resolicitation is FAR 15.206(e), which states:

> If, in the judgment of the contracting officer, based on market research or otherwise, an amendment proposed for issuance after offers have been received is so substantial as to exceed what prospective offerors reasonably could have anticipated, so that additional sources likely would have submitted offers had the substance of the amendment been known to them, the contracting officer shall cancel the original solicitation and issue a new one, regardless of the stage of the acquisition.

The pre-FAR 15 Rewrite version of this regulation had an additional provision which directed that the new solicitation be furnished to all firms originally solicited and any added to the original mailing list. Under current procedures, a new solicitation on the government-wide point of entry would be expected to alert all potential competitors to the procurement, but it would also seem appropriate for the agency to explicitly resolicit those companies that had responded to the original solicitation.

### a. Required Cancellation

Cancellation of an RFP after offerors have expended the effort to prepare proposals is not a desirable course of action. In *Loral Fairchild Corp.*, Comp. Gen. Dec. B-242957.2, 91-2 CPD ¶ 218, GAO stated that the changes would have to "significantly alter the purpose or nature of the contract" or change the "field of competition" in order to require a cancellation. See *Denwood Props. Corp.*, Comp. Gen. Dec. B-251347.2, 93-1 CPD ¶ 380, where the changes involved a reduction in the amount of space to be leased and the agency's desire to open the competition to consider build-to-suit facilities. GAO stated that "it would not have been proper" to simply amend the specifications because the changes were substantial and would likely increase the field of competition.

GAO has stated that generally cancellation is appropriate where changes to the solicitation are expected to result in increased competition or lower prices. See *Blue Rock Structures, Inc.*, Comp. Gen. Dec. B-400811, 2009 CPD ¶ 26 (rewriting specifications to obtain better prices through increased competition); *North Shore Medical Labs, Inc.*, Comp. Gen. Dec. B-311070, 2008 CPD ¶ 144 (original RFP did not promote effective competition); *SEI Group, Inc.*, Comp. Gen. Dec. B-299108, 2007

CPD ¶35 (agency decided to revise procurement strategy to reduce costs); *Glen/ Mar Constr., Inc.*, Comp. Gen. Dec. B-298355, 2006 CPD ¶ 117 (proposed prices were much higher than agency budget); *Goode Constr., Inc.*, Comp. Gen. Dec. B-288655.4, 2002 CPD ¶ 25 (adopting a different construction schedule); *Noelke GmbH*, Comp. Gen. Dec. B-278324.2, 98-1 CPD ¶ 46 (updating requirements and improving evaluation scheme to obtain increased competition); *Robertson Leasing Corp.*, Comp. Gen. Dec. B-275152, 97-1 CPD ¶ 49 (relaxing the specifications). Compare *Pro-Fab*, Comp. Gen. Dec. B-243607, 91-2 CPD ¶ 128, refusing to allow the contracting officer to cancel the solicitation because there was no reason to believe that any added competition would result from a resolicitation, nor was there any real prospect for additional cost savings.

Whether the field of competition would be increased by competition depends upon the facts and circumstances of each individual case. Thus, a number of cases have held that cancellation and resolicitation was not required even though significant changes were made. For example, in *Claude E. Atkins Enters., Inc*, Comp. Gen. Dec. B-241047, 91-1 CPD ¶ 42, a change from a 690-day, eight-phase construction schedule to one of 630 days with two phases was found not to be an appreciable change. See also *Defense Group, Inc.*, Comp. Gen. Dec. B-253795, 94-1 CPD ¶ 196, where a 12.3% increase in overall contract effort was not considered a substantial change to the basic nature of the contemplated contract. For other cases finding that cancellation of a solicitation was not required because the change was not substantial, see *Government Contract Servs. Co.*, Comp. Gen. Dec. B-294367, 2004 CPD ¶ 215 (amendment clarifying that alternate methods of performance were acceptable); *New Jersey & H St. Ltd. P'ship*, Comp. Gen. Dec. B-288026, 2001 CPD ¶ 125 (changing 15 year lease term to 14 years); *Cape Fear Paging Co.*, Comp. Gen. Dec. B-252160.2, 93-1 CPD ¶ 347 (elimination of separate line item and combining prices into remaining item); *SMS Data Prods. Group v. Austin*, 940 F.2d 1514 (Fed. Cir. 1991) (changing the solicitation by advancing the commercial availability date of laptop computers); *Di Frances Co.*, Comp. Gen. Dec. B-245492, 91-2 CPD ¶ 323 (5.9% decrease in the requirements); *Goodway Graphics of Virginia, Inc.*, Comp. Gen. Dec. B-236386, 89-2 CPD ¶ 491 (change affecting only five of 71 items); *Chromatics, Inc.*, Comp. Gen. Dec. B-224515, 87-1 CPD ¶ 171 (deletion of design requirements from specification); and *Hughes Aircraft Co.*, Comp. Gen. Dec. B-222152, 86-1 CPD ¶ 564 (elimination of one of two alternative technical approaches).

## b.  Discretionary Cancellation and Resolicitation

Although cancellation and resolicitation after the receipt of proposals subjects the competitors that responded to the solicitation to added cost and effort, because of the possibility of increased competition procurement officials have considerable discretion in making this decision. In this regard, the FAR 14.404-1(a) "compelling reason" basis for cancellation of an IFB after bid opening is not applicable. In *CFM*

*Equip. Co.*, Comp. Gen. Dec. B-251344, 93-1 CPD ¶ 280, GAO held that an agency needs only a "reasonable basis" to cancel an RFP. In discussing the difference between the standards for canceling an RFP or IFB, GAO stated:

> Under FAR 15.608 (b)(4), a procuring agency may reject all proposals received in response to an RFP if cancellation is clearly in the government's interest. Thus, as a general rule, in a negotiated procurement the contracting agency need only demonstrate a reasonable basis to cancel a solicitation after receipt of proposals, as opposed to the " cogent and compelling" reason required to cancel an IFB where sealed bids have been opened. *Xactex Corp.*, B-241739, May 5, 1992, 92-1 CPD ¶ 423. The standards differ because in procurements using sealed bids, competitive positions are exposed as a result of the public opening of bids, while in negotiated procurements there is no public opening. *ACR Elecs., Inc.*, B-232130.2; B-232130.3, Dec. 9, 1988, 88-2 CPD ¶ 577. The question presented by this protest is whether the agency's second thoughts about its procurement strategy have a reasonable basis.

Cancellation with the intent to resolicit is also proper if the agency finds that it had not done a good job in stating its requirements. See *Applied Res, Inc.*, Comp. Gen. Dec. B-400144.7, 2009 CPD ¶ 161 (prolonged protests led to reassessment of requirements); *Optimum Servs., Inc.*, Comp. Gen. Dec. B-401051, 2009 CPD ¶ 85 (program funding reduced after protest of original procurement); *Knight's Armament Co.*, Comp. Gen. Dec. B-299469, 2007 CPD ¶ 85 (offered products did not meet agency needs requiring revision of specifications); *ELEIT Tech., Inc.*, Comp. Gen. Dec. B-294193.2, 2004 CPD ¶ 203 (agency decided to bundle work into larger package); *Surgi-Textile*, Comp. Gen. Dec. B-289370, 2002 CPD ¶ 38 (specifications found to be inadequate); *Robertson Leasing Corp.*, Comp. Gen. Dec. B-275152, 97-1 CPD ¶ 49 (cancellation to recompete under relaxed specifications in order to increase competition and reduce costs to the government); *Nidek, Inc.*, Comp. Gen. Dec. B-272255, 96-2 CPD ¶ 112 (medical staff needed time to develop an accurate statement of its needs, when all firms could submit an offer); *Chant Eng'g Co.*, Comp. Gen. Dec. B-270149.2, 96-1 CPD ¶ 96 (government needs were overstated and the agency determined that enhanced competition would result from a relaxation of the requirements); and *JRW Mgmt. Co.*, Comp. Gen. Dec. B-260396.2, 95-1 CPD ¶ 276 (cancellation because agency received only one response and recognized that it could meet its needs with an alternate approach that presented an opportunity for increased competition).

Cancellation and resolicitation is also appropriate where necessary to ensure fair competition, *IT Corp.*, Comp. Gen. Dec. B-289517.3, 2002 CPD ¶ 123. In an unusual situation, cancellation was appropriate in order to avoid protests based on a disagreement between GAO and the Executive Branch over the priority that should be given the HUBZone contractors, *All Seasons Apparel, Inc.*, Comp. Gen. Dec. B-401805, 2009 CPD ¶ 221. See also *Kenco Assocs., Inc.*, Comp. Gen. Dec. B-297503, 2006 CPD ¶ 24, where cancellation was found a proper response to congressional criticism of the procurement.

Cancellation and resolicitation are also proper if an agency finds a better procurement strategy. See *Starlight Corp.*, Comp. Gen. Dec. B-297904.2, 2006 CPD ¶ 65 (RFP needed to be rewritten to clarify experience requirement); *Logistics Solutions Group, Inc.*, Comp. Gen. Dec. B-294604.7, 2005 CPD ¶ 141 (RFP no longer reflected agency needs); *VSE Corp.*, Comp. Gen. Dec. B-290452.2, 2005 CPD ¶ 111 (almost five years had passed since original proposals); *Best Foam Fabricators, Inc.*, Comp. Gen. Dec. B-259905.3, 95-1 CPD ¶ 275 (cancellation to obtain the items from the organization designated by the Committee for Purchase from the Blind and Other Severely Handicapped rather than another offeror under the solicitation); *General Projection Sys.*, 70 Comp. Gen. 345 (B-241418.2), 91-1 CPD ¶ 308 (cancellation because item was solicited in the RFP on a "brand name" rather than on a "brand name or equal" basis and an acceptable equal item was proposed); *Independent Bus. Servs., Inc.*, 69 Comp. Gen. 51 (B-235569.4), 90-1 CPD ¶ 207 (cancellation where no offerors proposed compliant products, and the agency determined that if it resolicited under less restrictive specifications, it would increase competition). However, cancellation was found unreasonable when the RFP had called for a price-only competition and the agency intended to reopen the competition on a sealed bidding basis, *Rand & Jones Enters. Co.*, Comp. Gen. Dec. B-296483, 2005 CPD ¶ 142.

## 2. *Amendment Without Cancellation*

Even if the agency decides not to cancel the RFP, an amendment is required if changes would have a significant impact on competition, *Joint Action in Community Serv., Inc.*, Comp. Gen. Dec. B-214564, 84-2 CPD ¶ 228; *Computek, Inc.*, 54 Comp. Gen. 1080 (B-182576), 75-1 CPD ¶ 384. A significant impact on competition occurs when (1) mandatory specifications or terms and conditions are changed, and (2) offerors not receiving notice of the changes would be prejudiced. This requirement is enforced even after the receipt of final proposal revisions, *Northrop Grumman Info. Tech., Inc.*, Comp. Gen. Dec. B-295526, 2005 CPD ¶ 45 (amendment required when agency requirements changed the day before award to the selected source); *Digital Techs., Inc.*, Comp. Gen. Dec. B-291657.3, 2004 CPD ¶ 235 (amendment proper when agency added quantities prior to award). In *Management Sys. Designers, Inc.*, Comp. Gen. Dec. B-244383.8, 92-1 CPD ¶ 496, prejudice was found where an offeror showed that it might have revised its proposal. Compare *NV Servs.*, Comp. Gen. Dec. B-284119.2, 2000 CPD ¶ 64, where no prejudice was found when the agency added somewhat less than ten percent more work after award but the protester did not prove that its costs would have materially changed.

FAR 15.206(d) requires an amendment to take advantage of an offer that deviates from the RFP as follows:

> If a proposal of interest to the Government involves a departure from the stated requirements, the contracting officer shall amend the solicitation, provided this can be done without revealing to the other offerors the alternate

solution proposed or any other information that is entitled to protection (see 15.207(b) and 15.306(e)).

See *Loral Terracom*, 66 Comp. Gen. 272 (B-224908), 87-1 CPD ¶ 182 (different technical approach suggested by an offeror).

An amendment is also called for where the relative importance of the evaluation factors is altered, *Hyperbaric Techs., Inc.*, Comp. Gen. Dec. B-293047.2, 2004 CPD ¶ 87 (adding the relative importance of factors when original RFP contained no such guidance); *Unisys Corp.*, 67 Comp. Gen. 512 (B-230019.2), 88-2 CPD ¶ 35 (clarifying the importance of cost), the standards for evaluating past performance have changed, *Cooperativa Muratori Riuniti*, Comp. Gen. Dec. B-294980.5, 2005 CPD ¶ 144, or the overall evaluation scheme is changed, *Galler Assocs., Inc.*, Comp. Gen. Dec. B-210204, 83-1 CPD ¶ 515 (changing from low cost acceptable offer scheme to best value scheme). See also *Lockheed Martin Sys. Integration-Owego*, Comp. Gen. Dec. B-299145.5, 2007 CPD ¶ 155, granting a protest because the agency did not allow the offerors to submit completely new proposals when the amendment made a major change in how support costs would be evaluation.

Amendments are not required if the claimed deviation is from a provision that is not mandatory, *Howard Cooper Corp. v. United States*, 763 F. Supp. 829 (1991). In *AEL Defense Corp.*, Comp. Gen. Dec. B-251376, 93-1 CPD ¶ 256, the protester alleged that the agency improperly awarded the contract to a firm whose proposal did not conform to a design referenced in a RFP document. The protester asserted that the design was mandatory and, therefore, the RFP should have been amended. GAO denied the protest, stating that the design was not mandatory under the hierarchy established in the specification. Similarly, a contracting officer was not required to issue an amendment to an RFP after changing specified computer systems where the government provided all equipment necessary for performance of the contract and the change brought about no cost savings to offerors, *Optimum Says., Inc.*, Comp. Gen. Dec. B-194984, 80-2 CPD ¶ 32.

## a. *Issuance of Amendments*

FAR 15.210(b) provides that Standard Form 30, Amendment of Solicitation/ Modification of Contract or Optional Form 309, Amendment of Solicitation "may be used to amend solicitations." Prior to the FAR 15 Rewrite, the use of Standard Form 30 was mandatory. Whether issued on these forms or otherwise in writing or electronically, the amendment must provide offerors sufficient information to determine the changed requirements. FAR 15.206(g) states that, "At a minimum, the following information should be included in each amendment":

(1) Name and address of issuing activity.

(2) Solicitation number and date.

(3) Amendment number and date.

(4) Number of pages.

(5) Description of the change being made.

(6) Government point of contact and phone number (and electronic or facsimile address, if appropriate).

(7) Revision to solicitation closing date, if applicable.

FAR 15.206(f) permits oral notice of the amendment when "time is of the essence." It states that, in such a case, "The contracting officer shall document the contract file and formalize the notice with an amendment." The importance of formalizing the notice in writing is illustrated in cases where the protester contends that it did not receive the notice that the agency claimed had been issued orally. In *Lockheed, IMS*, Comp. Gen. Dec. B-248686, 92-2 CPD ¶ 180, a protest was successful when the offeror denied that it received oral notice of the amendment, and the government did not follow up with an RFP amendment or other written confirmation. See also *CoMont, Inc.*, 65 Comp. Gen. 66 (B-219730), 85-2 CPD ¶ 555 (stressing that amendments must be made in writing); and *I.E. Levick & Assocs.*, Comp. Gen. Dec. B-214648, 84-2 CPD ¶ 695 (failure to issue a written amendment is a procedural defect whenever an offeror effectively denies having been advised orally). However, in *Family Stress Clinics of Am.*, Comp. Gen. Dec. B-270993, 96-1 CPD ¶ 223, an oral amendment extending the closing date for submission of proposals indefinitely was given full effect even though it was not confirmed in writing. GAO stated that the amendment was issued under exigent circumstances accompanying the shutdown of the contracting agency and the terms of the oral amendment were not in dispute.

In *Labat-Anderson Inc.*, 71 Comp. Gen. 252 (B-246071), 92-1 CPD ¶ 193, GAO suggested that notification of changes might be accomplished by either raising the issue in discussions with all offerors within the competitive range or issuing an amendment to the RFP. It would appear that the discussion method would only be appropriate for relatively simple changes.

### b. Actual Notice or No Prejudice

The failure to issue an amendment has been excused where the protesting offeror had actual notice of the change. See *General Offshore Corp.*, Comp. Gen. Dec. B-249601, 92-2 CPD ¶ 391, holding that the protester had received adequate notice of changed requirements through negotiations; and *Collins & Aikman Corp.*, Comp. Gen. Dec. B-247961, 92-2 CPD ¶ 41, stating in a footnote that an amendment was not required since the protester had knowledge of the change.

Failure to amend an RFP has also been excused where the protester was unable to demonstrate that it was prejudiced by the lack of notice. In *Saratoga Dev. Corp. v. United States*, 777 F. Supp. 29 (D.D.C. 1991), the court held that the test for prejudice is whether the protester would have altered its proposal to its competitive advantage, and further that the protester has the burden of showing how it would have responded to notice of the change. No prejudice was found in *Environmental Tectonics Corp.*, Comp. Gen. Dec. B-209423, 83-1 CPD ¶ 81, because the protester admitted that it could not have bettered its own proposed delivery time. Similarly, in *Canberra Indus.*, Comp. Gen. Dec. B-271016, 96-1 CPD ¶ 269, no prejudice was found for failing to amend a solicitation based on relaxed specifications because the protester did not present any evidence that it would have altered its proposal to its competitive advantage had it been given the opportunity to respond to the altered requirements. GAO will not overturn an award in which the agency has changed the evaluation criteria without notifying the offerors if the losers are not prejudiced by the change, *Akal Security, Inc.*, Comp. Gen. Dec. B-261996, 95-2 CPD ¶ 216; *Delta Dental Plan*, Comp. Gen. Dec. B-260461, 95-1 CPD ¶ 293; *FKW Inc. Says.*, Comp. Gen. Dec. B-235989, 89-2 CPD ¶ 370.

### c.  Firms to Be Notified

FAR 15.206 specifies that amendments must be furnished as follows:

(b) Amendments issued before the established time and date for receipt of proposals shall be issued to all parties receiving the solicitation.

(c) Amendments issued after the established time and date for receipt of proposals shall be issued to all offerors that have not been eliminated from the competition.

While an amendment may not be made after submission of proposals so as to intentionally preclude further competition, agencies may amend the solicitation after submission of proposals to take advantage of terms being offered by a particular offeror if other offerors are given the opportunity to respond to the change, *Cel-U-Dex Corp.*, Comp. Gen. Dec. B-195012, 80-1 CPD ¶ 102; *Sub-Sea Says, Inc.*, Comp. Gen. Dec. B-195741, 80-1 CPD ¶ 123. See *Zublin Delaware, Inc.*, Comp. Gen. Dec. B-227003.2, 87-2 CPD ¶ 149, in which an amendment containing new government needs was permitted even though it excluded some offerors since it was done in the public interest. Similarly, an agency may amend an RFP after the closing date to set aside the procurement exclusively for small business if such action has a reasonable basis, *Gill Mktg. Co.*, Comp. Gen. Dec. B-194414.3, 80-1 CPD ¶ 213. It has also been held that an agency need not issue an amendment after qualifying additional parties to a qualified products list (QPL), even though the RFP lists only one source on the QPL.

Once a competitive range has been established, agencies are not required to issue amendments to offerors outside the competitive range so long as the amendment is not directly related to the reason for the excluded offeror's rejection, *Amperif Corp.*, Comp. Gen. Dec. B-211992, 84-1 CPD ¶ 409. This is the case even where the change is significant, *Labat-Anderson Inc.*, B-246071, 92-1 CPD ¶ 193. For instance, no amendment is required where a contract is amended from a cost-type to a fixed-price contract, *Westinghouse Elec. Corp.*, Comp. Gen. Dec. B-197768, 80-1 CPD ¶ 378. See also *Loral Terracom, Marconi Italiana*, Comp. Gen. Dec. B-224908, 87-1 CPD ¶ 182, where an amendment recognizing alternative methods of satisfying the agency's requirements was properly limited to offerors within the competitive range. Compare *Information Ventures, Inc.*, Comp. Gen. Dec. B-232094, 88-2 CPD ¶ 443, where an amendment relaxing the specifications was required to be sent to an excluded offeror because it directly related to the reasons for exclusion. See also *Hamilton Tool Co.*, Comp. Gen. Dec. B-218260.1, 85-1 CPD ¶ 566, where resolicitation of all offerors was required when different requirements were arrived at with the only offeror in the competitive range. In *Lobar Inc.*, Comp. Gen. Dec. B-247843.3, 92-2 CPD ¶ 139, GAO found that the agency had acted properly when, after determining that the specifications exceeded the government's minimum needs, it amended the RFP and reopened with all offerors, both those within and outside the competitive range.

Even though the regulations provide that the amendment shall be sent to each prospective offeror, GAO has consistently held that the offeror bears the risk of not receiving an amendment, assuming that full and open competition has been found and it has not been shown that there was a conscious and deliberate effort by the agency to exclude the offeror from participating in the competition, *CardioMetrix*, Comp. Gen. Dec. B-270701, 96-1 CPD ¶ 149; *CDA Inc.*, Comp. Gen. Dec. B-224971, 87-1 CPD ¶ 163; *Maryland Computer Servs., Inc.*, Comp. Gen. Dec. B-216990, 85-1 CPD ¶ 187. The underlying theory is that the agency discharges its legal responsibility when it issues and dispatches an amendment in sufficient time to permit all offerors to consider the amendment in formulating their offers. In *LexisNexis, Inc.*, Comp. Gen. Dec. B-299381, 2007 CPD ¶ 73, an amendment posted on the FedBizOpps website hyperlinked to the agency website did not excuse the protester's failure to find it. In *CompuServe*, Comp. Gen. Dec. B-192905, 79-1 CPD ¶ 63, an amendment issued to the offeror, but addressed incorrectly, provided no basis for extending the closing date for initial proposals even though the offeror's late acknowledgment was prompted by late receipt of the amendment. However, in *Andero Constr., Inc.*, 61 Comp. Gen. 253 (B-203898), 82-1 CPD ¶ 133, GAO ignored the general rule that the offeror bears the risk of non-delivery of an amendment to the solicitation because the agency failed to affirmatively establish that it complied with DAR 2-208 (similar to FAR 14.208) where three of four offerors appeared not to have received the amendment in the mail. The agency never affirmatively stated that the amendments were mailed and thus GAO recommended that the agency cancel the solicitation and resolicit its requirements.

## IV. PREPARATION AND SUBMISSION OF PROPOSALS

In the past, the term proposal has been used broadly to refer to an offeror's entire submission in response to an RFP, consisting of both an offer which can be accepted by the government and information to be considered by the government in evaluating proposals. The term has also been used to describe separate parts of the submission. Thus, RFPs often requested offerors to organize submissions into separate portions called "Technical Proposals," "Management Proposals," and "Cost Proposals." Although the distinction between the offer and information was recognized in a number of provisions in drafts of FAR Part 15, the final Rewrite eliminated most of these distinctions. Thus, it is necessary to determine whether the final Rewrite's use of the term "proposal" in a particular provision is intended to refer to the offer or both the offer and the required information. Some contracting officers have recognized the distinction between these two portions of the submission and have drafted their RFPs so that the offer and information in the offeror's submission can be readily distinguished. The following discussion uses the term "proposal" to refer to the total submission in response to an RFP and the terms "offer" and "information" to distinguish between the two components of the submission.

### A. The Offer

The offer describes what the contractor is willing to agree to and its terms becomes part of the contract when accepted by the government. See FAR 2.101 which contains the following definition of the term "offer":

> "Offer" means a response to a solicitation that, if accepted, would bind the offeror to perform the resultant contract.

In the typical negotiated contract, the offer consists of the terms specified in the RFP (specifications, clauses, etc. contained in Parts I, II and III of the Uniform Contract Format) and the price specified by the offeror. FAR 15.204-2(a)(1) provides for the use of Optional Form (OF) 308, Solicitation and Offer — Negotiated Acquisition, or Standard Form (SF) 33, Solicitation, Offer and Award to prepare RFPs. These forms refer to the various sections of the RFP which will become part of the contract, refer to the prices "which are offered," and provide spaces for a signature and for the "offer date." FAR 15.204-2(a)(2)(ix) requires that the solicitation include the "offer expiration date" when the forms are not used.

#### 1. Intention to Be Bound

To be considered for award, the offer must evidence an intent to be bound to the terms and conditions in the RFP and any amendments. This is evidenced by the signature on SF 33 and OF 308, which bind the offeror to the terms and conditions of the RFP. In addition, the offeror must acknowledge receipt of any amendments to the RFP.

## a. Signature

Paragraph (c) of the Instructions to Offerors — Competitive Acquisition solicitation provision in FAR 52.215-1 contains the following guidance making signature of the proposal mandatory:

(2) The first page of the proposal must show —

* * *

> (v) Name, title, and signature of person authorized to sign the proposal. Proposals signed by an agent shall be accompanied by evidence of that agent's authority, unless that evidence has been previously furnished to the issuing office.

GAO has held that it is proper to reject a proposal which does not contain a signature if the RFP contemplates award on the basis of initial proposals, *SWR, Inc.*, Comp. Gen. Dec. B-278415, 97-2 CPD ¶ 166; *Valencia Tech. Servs., Inc.*, Comp. Gen. Dec. B-223288, 86-2 CPD ¶ 40. In these cases, GAO relied on cases dealing with unsigned sealed bids and found that it would be unfair to other offerors if a contracting officer permitted an offeror to sign its offer after the time proposals were opened. GAO also rejected the argument that lack of a signature was a minor informality. In effect, this is an application of the responsiveness requirement to competitive proposals even though this rule is generally not applicable in negotiated procurement. Neither decision contains any recognition of the significant differences between sealed bidding and competitive negotiation. It would appear that unsigned offers could be considered if the RFP included Alternate I to the Instructions to Offerors — Competitive Acquisition provision in FAR 52.215-1, precluding the agency from making an award on the basis of the initial proposals.

FAR 4.502(d) permits the use of electronic signatures when a proposal is to be submitted electronically. In *Tishman Constr. Corp.*, Comp. Gen. Dec. B-292097, 2003 CPD ¶ 94, the agency was required to honor a timely signed electronic proposal even though the required paper proposal was not submitted on time. GAO concluded that the late submission of the paper proposal was a "minor, immaterial deviation from the solicitation requirements."

GAO has also followed sealed bidding cases when competitive proposals are signed by agents. Thus, evidence of an agent's authority may be submitted after opening of proposals but proof that an offeror submitting a proposal in its own name was acting as an agent may not be submitted after opening. See *Hay-Holland Co.*, Comp. Gen. Dec. B-233002, 89-1 CPD ¶ 102, where the agency properly rejected an offer which was signed and subscribed by an agent without mention of the agent-principal relationship. GAO rejected the protester's contention that the incorrect signature was a clerical error which should have been corrected through discussions.

In *WorldWide Parts, Inc.*, Comp. Gen. Dec. B-244793, 91-2 CPD ¶ 156, GAO held that an agent who submits a proposal listing itself as the offeror may not submit evidence after the closing date for receipt of proposals to show the agent-principal relationship because to do so would constitute an improper transfer of a proposal. See also *American Material Handling, Inc.*, Comp. Gen. Dec. B-253818, 93-2 CPD ¶ 246 (award to an entity other than that named in original offer is improper).

A proposal which is properly signed by one offeror may be transferred or assigned to another firm only if such a transfer is affected by operation of law, which is interpreted to include a merger, a corporate reorganization, a sale of an entire business or that portion of a business embraced by a proposal, or other means not barred by anti-assignment statutes, *Numax Elecs., Inc.*, 54 Comp. Gen. 580 (B-181670), 75-1 CPD ¶ 21.

### b. Cover Letters

It is not good practice to include a cover letter with a proposal because any statements in the cover letter may be found to have conditioned the offer being made by the offeror. In this regard, GAO has followed the sealed bidding rule making conditioned bids nonresponsive. See, for example, *New Dimension Masonry, Inc.*, Comp. Gen. Dec. B-258876, 95-1 CPD ¶ 102. Thus, a contracting officer was found entitled to reject a proposal where a cover letter stating that its product was a "fit, form and function replacement" of the product described in the RFP, *Potomac Elec. Corp.*, Comp. Gen. Dec. B-311060, 2008 CPD ¶ 63. GAO concluded that the contracting officer had properly concluded that this statement could indicate that the product did not meet all of the salient characteristics that were included in the RFP. A similar result was reached in *INDUS Tech., Inc.*, Comp. Gen. Dec. B-297800.13, 2007 CPD ¶ 116, where cover letters accompanying the proposals provided for an acceptance period of 180 days, and the solicitation required a minimum acceptance period of 350 days and specifically stated that proposals providing less than the minimum acceptance period would be rejected.

### c. Acknowledge Receipt of Amendments

Offerors are required to acknowledge the receipt of amendments to the solicitation either upon receipt or on the cover sheet of the proposal. The Instructions to Offerors — Competitive Acquisition solicitation provision in FAR 52.215-1(b) provides:

> If this solicitation is amended, all terms and conditions that are not amended re main unchanged. Offerors shall acknowledge receipt of any amendment to this solicitation by the date and time specified in the amendment(s).

If a contracting officer posts a set of questions and answers to a solicitation on its website but does not designate them as an amendment, they will be treated as an amendment because they have a significant impact on the terms of the procurement, *Linguistic Sys., Inc.*, Comp. Gen. Dec. B-296221, 2005 CPD ¶ 104.

The failure to acknowledge receipt of a material amendment precludes award to that offeror on the basis of the initial proposal, *Nomura Enter., Inc.*, Comp. Gen. Dec. B-277768, 97-2 CPD ¶ 148. Agencies are also permitted to reject an offer where a material amendment has not been acknowledged, *ECI Def. Group*, Comp. Gen. Dec. B-400177, 2008 CPD ¶ 141; *Skyline ULTD, Inc.*, Comp. Gen. Dec. B-297800.3, 2006 CPD ¶ 128; *Integrated Bus. Solutions, Inc.* Comp. Gen. Dec. B-292239, 2003 CPD ¶ 122. However, a contracting officer may establish a competitive range and permit the offeror to acknowledge the amendment in negotiations, *Grove Res. Solutions, Inc.*, Comp. Gen. Dec. B-296228, 2005 CPD ¶ 133; *International Filter Mfg. Corp.*, Comp. Gen. Dec. B-235049, 89-1 CPD ¶ 586; *Galaxy Aircraft Instruments Co.*, Comp. Gen. Dec. B-194356, 80-1 CPD ¶ 364. The choice of which alternative to follow will depend upon the degree of competition and the value of the offer in relation to the other offers.

If the offeror shows that it has received the amendment by reflecting its terms in its offer, it will be found to have constructively acknowledged the amendment, *Language Servs. Assocs., Inc.*, Comp. Gen. Dec. B-297392, 2006 CPD ¶ 20 (quotation); *Pitney Bowes, Inc.*, Comp. Gen. Dec. B-294868, 2005 CPD ¶ 10 (quotation). Thus, the failure to acknowledge an amendment does not preclude award where "the offeror is otherwise obligated to perform in accordance with the terms of the solicitation," *E. Frye Enters., Inc.*, Comp. Gen. Dec. B-258699.2, 95-1 CPD ¶ 64.

If an amendment does not contain material provisions, failure to acknowledge it should be waived as a minor informality, *International Data Sys., Inc.*, Comp. Gen. Dec. B-277385, 97-2 CPD ¶ 96.

The mere fact that an offeror does not receive an amendment is no excuse for failure to acknowledge the amendment where full and open competition and reasonable prices are obtained and the agency did not deliberately exclude the offeror from competition, *CDA, Inc.*, Comp. Gen. Dec. B-224971, 87-1 CPD ¶ 163, and *O.J. Best Servs., Inc.*, Comp. Gen. Dec. B-276954, 97-1 CPD ¶ 231 (of 21 offers received, 19 acknowledged receipt of the amendments)

## 2. Offer Strategy

There are a number of strategies which may be available to an offeror. These include deciding on the pricing and other aspects of the offer, whether to make an offer on all the items covered by the RFP, and whether to submit alternate or multiple offers.

### a. Best Terms

One of the most difficult decisions to make is whether to submit an offer containing the best possible offer the firm can make or one reserving some improvements for the later stages of the process. The problem is that, in a competitive environment, the offeror may not get an opportunity to make concessions and improve the offer.

See *Advanced American Diving Serv., Inc.*, Comp. Gen. Dec. B-274766, 97-1 CPD ¶ 1, denying a protest that the agency should have established a competitive range to obtain better terms. In this regard, ¶ (f)(4) of the FAR 52.215-1 Instructions to Offerors — Competitive Acquisition provision warns offerors that:

> The Government intends to evaluate proposals and award a contract without discussions with offerors (except clarifications described in FAR 15.306 (a)). *Therefore, the offeror's initial proposal should contain the offeror's best terms from a cost or price and technical standpoint.* [Emphasis supplied.]

Even where the solicitation indicates that the government plans to undertake discussions with offerors within the competitive range, an offer at less than the best possible terms runs the risk of being found to be outside the competitive range. This leads to the conclusion that in many, if not most, acquisitions the best strategy is to submit the best offer initially.

### b.  Items Offered

Where the RFP calls for a number of severable items and the solicitation does not specifically require that offers be made on all the items, the offeror must decide whether to submit an offer on all the items or only some of them. The only FAR provision dealing with this issue is contained in ¶ (c)(4) of the FAR 52.215-1 Instructions to Offerors — Competitive Acquisition solicitation provision, stating, "Unless otherwise specified in the solicitation, the offeror may propose to provide any item or combination of items." If it decided to submit an offer covering all the items, the offeror should also consider whether to condition its offer on award of all the items. This condition, termed an "all or none" offer, would insure that the offeror would not receive partial awards. In such a case, the all-or-none prices will be compared with the price combinations for all the items offered by other offerors without an all-or-none condition, *Banknote Corp. of Am., Inc.*, Comp. Gen. Dec. B-245528.2, 92-1 CPD ¶ 53. If no such condition is contained in the offer, ¶¶ (f)(5) and (f)(6) of the FAR 52.215-1 Instructions to Offerors — Competitive Acquisition solicitation provision permit the government to award multiple contracts for all or a part of any contract line items. See Chapter 5, Section III for a further discussion of the rules for evaluating multiple item solicitations.

### c.  Alternate or Multiple Offers

Offerors may want to consider submitting more than one offer. This may be particularly desirable when the specifications permit the offeror to determine the way that the work will be performed such as in a performance or functional specification. See also FAR 11.002(e) permitting agencies to identify performance levels as targets rather than as fixed or minimum requirements. In other cases, an offeror may conclude that a non-specification offer will have sufficient advantages for the government that it might be persuaded to consider amending the specifications to permit its consideration. The term "alternate proposal" has sometimes been used to refer to these two different situations. It has been used to describe the case where an offeror submits two or more offers each meeting the RFP requirements. It has also been used to describe the case where the offeror submits one offer meeting the requirements and another which does not, or merely submits one offer which does not conform to the RFP. The FAR does not provide comprehensive directions as to the treatment to be given the offers when an offeror elects to follow one of these strategies, but it would appear that agencies have substantial discretion in evaluating such offers and conducting the procurement to obtain the best value for the government.

## (1) NONCONFORMING OFFERS

If an offeror submits an alternate offer that deviates from the requirements of the RFP, the government may not award to that offeror but must revise the RFP to permit other offerors to propose to the deviation, FAR 15.206(d). See *Labat-Anderson, Inc.*, 71 Comp. Gen. 252 (B-246071.5), 92-1 CPD ¶ 193, holding that it was improper to accept an offer which deviated from a staffing level required by the RFP. The proper course was followed in *Simmonds Precision Prods., Inc.*, Comp. Gen. Dec. B-244559.3, 93-1 CPD ¶ 483, where, upon the agency's receipt of a deviating offer containing terms that were more attractive than those required by the RFP, other offerors were given the opportunity to submit revised offers.

An offer is not nonconforming, however, if the RFP states that the agency reserves the right to award to a proposal that does not meet all of the mandatory requirements of the solicitation, *Litton Sys., Inc. v. Department of Transp.*, GSBCA 12911-P, 94-3 BCA ¶ 27,263. In that case, the board held that the agency was not required to amend the RFP to permit award to an alternate offer that did not conform to the mandatory requirements because all of the offerors had been informed that the agency might follow that procedure.

The only provision dealing with this issue is FAR 15.209(a)(2), which directs that language similar to the following Alternate II to the FAR 52.215-1 Instructions to Offerors — Competitive Acquisition provision be incorporated into the RFP if the government would be willing to accept "alternate proposals:"

> (9) Offerors may submit proposals that depart from stated requirements. Such proposals shall clearly identify why the acceptance of the proposal would be advantageous to the Government. Any deviations from the terms and conditions of the solicitation, as well as the comparative advantage to the Government, shall be clearly identified and explicitly defined. The Government reserves the right to amend the solicitation to allow all offerors an opportunity to submit revised proposals based on the revised requirements.

While the presence of this provision appears to indicate that nonconforming offers will be considered, such offers can only be accepted if the solicitation is amended to give other competitors the opportunity to make offers to the revised specifications.

The absence of the Alternate II language does not necessarily mean that offers which deviate from the RFP must be rejected. The sealed bid concept of "responsiveness," does not apply to negotiated procurements, *Gardiner, Kamya & Assocs., P.C.*, Comp. Gen. Dec. B-258400, 95-1 CPD ¶ 191. Thus, the contracting officer has the discretion to include such an offer in the competitive range and seek to have a nonconformity cured through discussions or to amend the solicitation as required by FAR 15.206(g). However, the offeror takes the risk that the offer will be rejected and the offeror excluded from the competitive range. See *Bencor-Petrifond*, Comp. Gen. Dec. B-254205, 93-2 CPD ¶ 208 (proposal departed from RFP's construction schedule); and *Discount Mach. & Equip., Inc.*, Comp. Gen. Dec. B-241444, 90-2 CPD ¶ 474 (offeror unable to meet technical provisions). Which course of action will be taken by the contracting officer will depend upon the number and nature of conforming offers received and the benefits offered by the nonconforming offer. However, an offer that is totally out of compliance with the RFP may not be considered, *Best W. Quantico Inn/Conference Ctr.*, Comp. Gen. Dec. B-209500, 83-1 CPD ¶ 164. In that case, the offeror responded to an RFP with only a "contract pricing proposal" when the RFP required a "technical proposal."

It is not improper to submit a noncompliant alternate offer to ensure that an agency does use ambiguous RFP language to award on a seemingly improper basis. See *Power Connector, Inc.*, Comp. Gen. Dec. B-285395, 2000 CPD ¶ 152, rejecting the contention that an alternate offer of a foreign product was unlawful when the RFP called for a domestic product but contained a description of how foreign products would be evaluated.

## (2) MULTIPLE CONFORMING OFFERS

The present FAR, like its predecessor, does not deal with the submission of multiple conforming offers. Nevertheless, GAO has held that there is no need for the solicitation to contain a provision authorizing multiple offers for them to be considered, *Educational Media, Inc.*, Comp. Gen. Dec. B-225457.2 , 87-1 CPD ¶ 498, and *Federal Computer Corp.*, 66 Comp. Gen. 139 (B-223932 ), 81-2 CPD ¶ 665. See also 33 Comp. Gen. 499 (B-119646) (1954); and 39 Comp. Gen. 892 (B-142957) (1960), holding that the submission of multiple offers are appropriate competitive techniques. For an instance where an alternate offer was selected for contract award, see *OK Produce*, Comp. Gen. Dec. B-299058 , 2007 CPD ¶ 31.

To be valid, alternate offers must conform to the terms of the solicitation. See *Aeroflex Test Solutions*, Comp. Gen. Dec. B-295380, 2005 CPD ¶ 51, holding that the contracting officer properly did not consider an alternate offer that did not contain fixed prices as required by the RFP. See also *P.G. Elecs., Ltd.*, Comp. Gen. Dec. B-261883, 95-2 CPD ¶ 202, where the agency could not evaluate an alternate offer of an extended warranty because its terms were unclear, and *Head, Inc.*, Comp. Gen. Dec. B-299523, 2007 CPD ¶ 109, where an alternate offer was not dealt with because of lack of supporting documentation. Compare *Citrus Coll.,* Comp. Gen. Dec. B-293543, 2004 CPD ¶ 104, where GAO rejected the contention that the agency accepted an alternate proposal that did not comply with the RFP requirements because the protester did not prove prejudice.

While the receipt of multiple offers can be of value to the government, they do require additional evaluation. This could be unduly burdensome in cases where substantial evaluation effort is required such as where a large number of different approaches are proposed or there are a large number of multiple proposals. See, for example, *Moreland Corp.,* Comp. Gen. Dec. B-291086, 2002 CPD ¶ 197, where five offerors submitted 14 offers and alternate offers, and *Banknote Corp. of Am., Inc.,* Comp. Gen. Dec. B-245528.2, 92-1 CPD ¶ 53, where the evaluation was complicated and delayed by the fact that one offeror submitted four separate price offers and another submitted ten. Thus, agencies can properly preclude multiple offers by including a provision in the solicitation prohibiting more than one offer, *ACS State Healthcare, LLC,* Comp. Gen. Dec. B-292981, 2004 CPD ¶ 57; *Dale Stevens Constr.,* Comp. Gen. Dec. B-242234, 91-1 CPD ¶ 354. However, such a provision will not necessarily prevent separate offers from being submitted by separate, but affiliated, firms. In *Robbins-Gioia, Inc.,* Comp. Gen. Dec. B-274318, 96-2 CPD ¶ 222, the RFP stated that (1) "an offeror may submit a maximum of one fully compliant proposal," (2) "no alternate proposals will be accepted," and (3) "if an offeror submits more than one proposal, all proposals will be returned without evaluation." GAO denied the protest against consideration of both offers, holding that the general rule is that contracting agencies may accept bids and offers from affiliated firms unless doing so would prejudice the government's interests or give the affiliated offerors an unfair advantage over other offerors.

### d. Unbalanced Offers

Where the solicitation contains multiple items, offerors may seek to obtain a competitive advantage by unbalancing the prices. Paragraph (f)(8) of the FAR 52.215-1 Instructions to Offerors — Competitive Acquisition provision warns offerors that their offers may be rejected if the prices are materially unbalanced, stating:

> The Government may determine that a proposal is unacceptable if the prices proposed are materially unbalanced between line items or subline items. Unbalanced pricing exists when, despite an acceptable total evaluated price, the price of one or more contract line items is significantly overstated or understated as indicated by the application of cost or price analysis techniques. A proposal may be rejected if the Contracting Officer determines that the lack of balance poses an unacceptable risk to the Government.

Although the majority of protests alleging unbalanced pricing occur in sealed bidding cases, the concept of unbalanced pricing has also been applied to negotiated procurements, *Litton Sys., Inc.,* Comp. Gen. Dec. B-239123.3, 90-2 CPD ¶ 276. GAO has

758       BASIC NEGOTIATION PROCEDURES

held that a proposed price may not be accepted by a contracting agency if the proposed price in the offer is found to be materially unbalanced, *International Transp., S.A.*, Comp. Gen. Dec. B-244853, 91-2 CPD ¶ 489. The contracting officer may reject such a proposal without discussions, *Ocean Habitability, Inc.*, Comp. Gen. Dec. B-227304, 87-2 CPD ¶ 265, or may seek to remedy the unbalanced price through discussions, *Dynamic Sci., Inc.*, Comp. Gen. Dec. B-270448.3, 96-1 CPD ¶ 236.

Prior to the FAR Part 15 Rewrite, unbalanced pricing in competitive proposals was treated in the same manner as in sealed bidding, requiring that to reject an offer it had to be both mathematically unbalanced and materially unbalanced. See Chapter 5, Section III. See *Astrosystems, Inc.*, Comp. Gen. Dec. B-260399.2, 95-2 CPD ¶ 18 (protester failed to show reasonable doubt for material unbalancing); *Laidlaw Envtl. Servs., Inc.*, Comp. Gen. Dec. B-261603, 95-2 CPD ¶ 171 (no evidence of enhanced prices); *Allstate Van & Storage, Inc.*, Comp. Gen. Dec. B-270744, 96-1 CPD ¶ 191 (no basis in record to conclude mathematical unbalancing).

The current FAR replaces this rule with a discretionary rule stating that an unbalanced offer may be rejected if the contracting officer determines that the lack of balance "poses an unacceptable risk to the Government," FAR 15.404-1(g)(3). For cases affirming the contracting officer's acceptance of unbalanced prices because of no unacceptable risk, see *Academy Facilities Mgmt. v. United States*, 87 Fed. Cl. 441 (2008) (detailed analysis indicated final prices not significantly unbalanced); *Accumark, Inc.*, Comp. Gen. Dec. B-310814, 2008 CPD ¶ 68 (estimated quantity of the high-priced line item was reasonably accurate); *Scot, Inc.*, Comp. Gen. Dec. B-295569, 2005 CPD ¶ 66 (price of most likely quantity to be purchased lower than competitors); and *Semont Travel, Inc.*, Comp. Gen. Dec. B-291179, 2002 CPD ¶ 200 (price of high-price base year was not out of line even if lower-priced option years were not exercised). See also *Cherokee Painting LLC*, Comp. Gen. Dec. B-311020.3, 2009 CPD ¶ 18, where no unacceptable risk was found by analyzing past prices which had not resulted in undue costs to the government, and *Citywide Managing Servs. of Port Washington, Inc.*, Comp. Gen. Dec. B-281287.12, 2001 CPD ¶ 6, rejecting a protest even though the agency had not analyzed the risk of unbalanced prices because the protester did not submit evidence that the government would pay higher prices. For a case agreeing that an offer should be rejected because of undue risk, see *L. W. Matteson, Inc.*, Comp. Gen. Dec. B-290224, 2002 CPD ¶ 89.

### 3. Modification, Revision and Withdrawal

The RFP forms specify the time within which the government may accept offers. Block 12 of SF 33 provides that the offeror agrees to perform the work "if this offer is accepted within *60 calendar days unless a different date is inserted by the offeror.*" Block 4 of OF 308, in turn, states, "Offers valid for 60 days unless a different period is entered here." Neither of these provisions prohibits the offeror from modifying, revising or withdrawing the offer prior to its acceptance. While the relevant FAR sections cited below speak in terms of modification, revision and withdrawal of "proposals," it is evident from the context that they are referring to "offers" and not "information." See, for example, FAR 15.208 which is titled, "Submission, modification, revision, and withdrawal of *proposal"* but which states in ¶ (a), "Offerors are responsible for submitting *offers*, and any revisions and modifications to them."

## a. *Modification*

FAR 15.001 defines a modification as follows:

> Proposal modification is a change made to a proposal before the solicitation closing date and time, or made in response to an amendment, or made to correct a mistake at any time before award.

This definition indicates that the term "proposal modification" is intended to cover the narrow situation where the offeror desires to modify its offer before it is contacted by the agency. By its terms, the definition precludes such modifications after the solicitation closing date and time unless the modification is made in response to an amendment to the solicitation. However, the definition also includes the situation where the offeror desires to correct a mistake in its offer after the closing date of the solicitation. This issue of mistake correction will be discussed in the following section dealing with Exchanges and Communications. FAR 15.508 provides that mistakes discovered after award are to be processed substantially in accordance with the mistake in bid procedures set forth in FAR 14.407-4.

## b. *Revision*

FAR 15.001 uses the term "revision" to cover the situation where an offeror changes the terms of its offer after the solicitation closing date and time. It defines a revision as follows:

> Proposal revision is a change to a proposal made after the solicitation closing date, at the request of or as allowed by a contracting officer, as the result of negotiations.

This definition permits offers to be "revised" only as a result of negotiations and negotiations will take place only after a competitive range has been established. See FAR 15.307. The subject of offer revisions will be covered in the discussion of competitive range below.

## c. *Withdrawal*

Offers may be withdrawn by an offeror at any time prior to acceptance. See ¶ (c) of the Instructions to Offerors — Competitive Acquisition solicitation provision at FAR 52.215-1, which states:

(3)(v) Proposals may be withdrawn by written notice received at any time before award. Oral proposals in response to oral solicitations may be withdrawn orally. If the solicitation authorizes facsimile proposals, proposals may be withdrawn via facsimile received at any time before award, subject to the conditions specified in the provision at 52.215-5, Facsimile Proposals. Proposals may be withdrawn in person by an offeror or an authorized representative, if the identity of the person requesting withdrawal is established and the person signs a receipt for the proposal before award.

\* \* \*

(8) Proposals may be withdrawn at any time before award. Withdrawals are effective upon receipt of notice by the Contracting Officer.

A similar provision is contained in FAR 15.208(e), which also contains the internal government procedures for disposing of withdrawn proposals, including electronically submitted proposals. Although this FAR 52.215-1 provision contains no guidance on the withdrawal of electronically submitted proposals, it can be assumed that they can be withdrawn electronically as long as the electronic transmission is received by the agency before acceptance of the proposal.

The broad right of withdrawal before award in the present FAR is consistent with previous FAR provisions and GAO has consistently accepted the FAR provision as governing and has held that a signed offer is revocable before acceptance and, therefore, is not a firm offer, *Pedestrian Bus Stop Shelters, Ltd.*, 63 Comp. Gen. 265 (B-212570), 84-1 CPD ¶ 331. The Armed Services Board of Contract Appeals has described an offeror's right to withdraw its offer prior to award as a "fundamental protection," *Toyad Corp.*, ASBCA 26785, 85-3 BCA ¶ 18,354.

## *4. Timely Submission Required*

Although earlier drafts had proposed liberalizing the rule concerning late proposals, the final FAR Part 15 Rewrite reestablished the "late is late" rule. Thus, offerors must use great care to ensure the timely submission of offers, modifications or revisions. This strict rule, with very limited exceptions, is contained in ¶ (c)(3) the FAR 52.215-1 Instructions to Offerors — Competitive Acquisition solicitation provision as follows:

(i) Offerors are responsible for submitting proposals, and any modifications or revisions, so as to reach the Government office designated in the solicitation by the time specified in the solicitation. If no time is specified in the solicitation, the time for receipt is 4:30 p.m., local time, for the designated Government office on the date that proposal or revision is due.

(ii)(A) Any proposal, modification, or revision received at the Government office designated in the solicitation after the exact time specified for receipt of proposals is "late" and will not be considered unless it is received before award is made, the Contracting Officer determines that accepting the late proposal would not unduly delay the acquisition; and —

(1) If it was transmitted through an electronic commerce method authorized by the solicitation, it was received at the initial point of entry to the Government infrastructure not later than 5:00 p.m. one working day prior to the date specified for receipt of proposals; or

(2) There is acceptable evidence to establish that it was received at the Government installation designated for receipt of proposals and was under the Government's control prior to the time set for receipt of proposals; or

(3) It is the only proposal received.

(B) However, a late modification of an otherwise successful proposal that makes its terms more favorable to the Government, will be considered at any time it is received and may be accepted.

(iii) Acceptable evidence to establish the time of receipt at the Government installation includes the time/date stamp of that installation on the proposal wrapper, other documentary evidence of receipt maintained by the installation, or oral testimony or statements of Government personnel.

(iv) If an emergency or unanticipated event interrupts normal Government processes so that proposals cannot be received at the office designated for receipt of proposals by the exact time specified in the solicitation, and urgent Government requirements preclude amendment of the solicitation, the time specified for receipt of proposals will be deemed to be extended to the same time of day specified in the solicitation on the first work day on which normal Government processes resume.

Essentially the same language is contained in FAR 15.208.

The government's determination of the time of receipt is binding unless it is clearly unreasonable. Thus, a contracting official's reliance on the time/date clock will generally be found to be reasonable, *Haskell Co.*, Comp. Gen. Dec. B-292756, 2003 CPD ¶202 (reasonable reliance on time/date clock that turned to 14:01 shortly after proposal received); *States Roofing Corp.*, Comp. Gen. Dec. B-286052, 2000 CPD ¶ 182 (reasonable reliance on time/date clock rather than wall clock in same room); *Pat Mathis Constr. Co.*, Comp. Gen. Dec. B-248979, 92-2 CPD ¶ 236 (reasonable reliance on time/date clock which showed offer's proposal to be one minute late rather than clock in conference room adjoining the proposal delivery point). If the agency does not record the time of receipt of proposals, a Federal Express receipt signed by an agency employee may be used to establish that a proposal was timely received, *MJS, Inc.*, Comp. Gen. Dec. B-244410, 91-2 CPD ¶ 344.

The late rule has been enforced strictly and the offer must be received by the government exactly on time and at the place specified in the RFP. See, for example, *Logistics Mgmt. Inst.*, Comp. Gen. Dec. B-276143, 97-1 CPD ¶ 186 (7 minutes late). See also *Med-National, Inc.*, Comp. Gen. Dec. B-277430, 97-2 CPD ¶ 67 (offeror could not show by a preponderance of evidence that its hand-carried proposal was "in the proper place by the proper time"); *Koba Assocs., Inc.*, Comp. Gen. Dec. B-265854, 95-2 CPD ¶ 212 (hand-carried proposal delivered to the depository office three minutes after time specified for receipt of proposals late); *Hallcrest Sys., Inc.*, Comp. Gen. Dec. B-215328, 84-2 CPD ¶ 334 (hand-carried proposal received one minute late rejected); and *Priest & Fine, Inc.*, Comp. Gen. Dec. B-213603, 84-1 CPD ¶ 358 (hand-delivered proposal received two minutes late not considered).

When submission of offers by facsimile is authorized by inclusion in the RFP of the Facsimile Proposals solicitation provision in FAR 52.215-5, the offeror must prove that the complete proposal was received by the closing time. See *GROH GmbH*, Comp. Gen. Dec. B-291980, 2003 CPD ¶ 53, holding that a proposal was late when the agency claimed it had not received the fax transmission and the RFP included the agency fax number but not the clause. Even if the fax is transmitted before opening, it must get to the place designated in the solicitation on time, *Instrument Assocs.*, Comp. Gen. Dec. B-256814, 94-2 CPD ¶ 52 (bid was rejected where both sender's and agency's fax activity reports showed fax was transmitted on time but did not get to opening on time); and *Microscope Co.*, Comp. Gen. Dec. B-257015, 94-2 CPD ¶ 157 (proposal was rejected even though offeror's telephone records showed timely transmission where agency provided sworn statement by contract specialist responsible for checking fax machine that proposal was not received on time). Further, the entire message must be received before the time for submission, *Cyber Digital, Inc.*, Comp. Gen. Dec. B-270107, 96-1 CPD ¶ 20; *Radar Devices, Inc.*, Comp. Gen. Dec. B-249118, 92-2 CPD ¶ 287 (where transmission began before closing but completed after closing, contracting officer could only consider preclosing transmission). However, the date/time notation on a facsimile has been used as evidence that a BAFO was timely received when the agency did not apply its own date/time stamp upon actual receipt, *Essex Electro Eng'rs, Inc.*, Comp. Gen. Dec. B-238207, 90-1 CPD ¶ 438. The fact that the government's fax machine is out of order, out of paper, or busy will not excuse the failure to meet the required time, *Brookfield Dev., Inc.*, Comp. Gen. Dec. B-255944, 94-1 CPD ¶ 273 (BAFO due at 4 p.m. rejected where transmission began at 3:50 but was not completed until 4:16 because the government's fax machine was busy).

When the RFP required submission of both paper and electronic proposals, failure of the paper version to arrive on time after timely receipt of the electronic version was a minor informality that should have been waived by the contracting officer, *Tishman Constr. Corp.*, Comp. Gen. Dec. B-292097, 2003 CPD ¶ 94.

## 5. Circumstances Permitting Acceptance of Late Offers

GAO ruled for a number of years that contracting officers could avoid the late-is-late rule by extending the closing time for proposals or final proposal revisions when they found out that a late proposal or revision was about to be submitted or had been submitted. See *Ivy Mech. Co.*, Comp. Gen. Dec. B-272764, 96-2 CPD ¶ 83; *Geo-Seis Helicopters, Inc.*, Comp. Gen. Dec. B-299175, 2007 CPD ¶ 135. However, in *Geo-Seis Helicopters, Inc. v. United States*, 77 Fed. Cl. 633 (2007), the Court of Federal Claims ruled that the FAR late-is-late provision pertaining to both proposals and final proposal revisions is binding on the contracting officer and prohibits extending the closing time after the time has passed. In *Allied Materials & Equip. Co. v. United States*, 81 Fed. Cl. 448 (2008), the court held that this decision does not preclude extending the closing time before it has occurred. Thus, it appears that the only grounds for accepting a late proposal are those stated in the FAR. Compare *Watterson Constr. Co.. v. United States.*, 98 Frd. Cl. 84 (2011) reaching the opposite result from *Sea Box.*

### a. Electronic Submission

The FAR has adopted a special rule for a late electronically submitted proposals, stating that they will only be acceptable if they are "received at the initial point of entry to the Government infrastructure not later than 5:00 p.m. one working day prior to the date specified for receipt of proposals." There is no explanation for this unusually strict rule but GAO has held that the correct reading of the FAR is that this rule is the exclusive rule for electronically submitted proposals, *Sea Box, Inc.*, Comp. Gen. Dec. B-251056, 2002 CPD ¶ 181. Thus, it held in that case that the rule on government mishandling of proposals and revisions did not apply when they were submitted electronically.

The late-is-late rule is strictly enforced with regard to electronically submitted proposals or final proposal revisions. See *Symetrics Indus., LLC*, Comp. Gen. Dec. B-298759, 2006 CPD ¶ 154, where proposals were due by 3:00 p.m., Symetrics' electronically submitted final proposal revision was received by the agency's server at 2:57:41 p.m. but did not reach the contracting office until 3:01 p.m. Because the contracting office was the designated place for submission of proposals, GAO ruled that the late-is-late rule applied and the contracting officer was correct in rejecting the proposal. Further, GAO ruled that the exception for government mishandling of proposals did not apply. See also *Urban Title, LLC*, Comp. Gen. Dec. B-311437.3, 2009 CPD ¶ 31 (electronically submitted final proposal revision late even though it was transmitted 12 minutes before closing time because it arrived at agency five weeks later); *Conscoop — Consorzia Fra Coop. Di Prod. E Lavoro v. United States*, 62 Fed. Cl. 219 (2004) (electronically submitted proposal late even though it was transmitted two minutes before the closing time because it arrived at agency over an hour later);

*PMTech, Inc.*, Comp. Gen. Dec. B-291082, 2002 CPD ¶ 172 (electronically submitted proposal late even though it was transmitted 13 minutes before closing time). In *Integrated Bus. Solutions, Inc.*, Comp. Gen. Dec. B-292239, 2003 CPD ¶ 122, an electronically submitted proposal was late when it was received two minutes late and the RFP did not permit the submission of proposals electronically. The same result was reached in *Integrated Bus. Solutions, Inc. v. United States*, 58 Fed. Cl. 420 (2003). Similarly, in *Adirondack Constr. Co.*, Comp. Gen. Dec. B280015 .2, 98-2 CPD ¶ 55, the electronically submitted proposal was found to be late because it was not received by the agency by the closing time and had been transmitted only 13 minutes before that time. In *Labatt Food Serv., Inc. v. United States*, 84 Fed. Cl. 50 (2008), the court overlooked the late electronic submission of a final proposal revision and ruled that the procurement should be redone because the RFP required proposals to be submitted by fax and all business had been conducted electronically. GAO had reached the opposite result in *Labatt Food Serv., Inc.*, Comp. Gen. Dec. B-310939.6, 2008 CPD ¶ 162.

Once electronic commerce is adopted as the means for publicizing RFPs and submitting proposals, offerors are responsible for monitoring the website for RFPs and amendments. Thus, failure to see an RFP when it is posted is not an excuse for late submission of a proposal, *Optelec U.S., Inc.*, Comp. Gen. Dec. B-400349, 2008 CPD ¶ 192. In that case, the protester had registered on the FedBizOpps website and applied for automatic notification of proposals but had failed to notice that the website had discontinued this practice, resulting in late receipt of the RFP and late submission of the proposal.

### b. Offers Submitted By Other Means That Are "Under the Control" of the Government

The only excuse for offers, revisions and modifications that do not arrive at the designated office by the closing time is provided in FAR 52.215-1(c)(3)(ii)(A)(2), which indicates that they can be accepted if they are "received at the Government installation designated for receipt" and "under the Government's control" by the closing time. This appears to be a less stringent test than under the prior regulation which provided that offers, revisions and modifications submitted by regular mail, by facsimile, or hand carried that did not arrive at the designated office by the closing time could be considered only if the lateness was due primarily to government mishandling. However, in order to avail itself of the current rule an offeror must show that the proposal was both "received" and "under the control." Thus, a proposal delivered to the agency at the wrong address would be "under the control" of the agency but would not have been "received" because it was not delivered to the "designated" office, *Shirlington Limousine & Transp., Inc.*, Comp. Gen. Dec. B-299241.2, 2007 CPD ¶ 68. Similarly, a proposal that was time-stamped by a security guard and then taken to the contracting office by the offeror was not "under the control" of the government until final delivery, *Immediate Sys. Res., Inc.*, Comp. Gen. Dec. B-292856, 2003 CPD ¶ 227.

Under the prior rule, mishandling by the U.S. Postal Service did not constitute "Government mishandling," *California State Univ., Fullerton*, Comp. Gen. Dec. B-243020.2, 91-1 CPD ¶ 452. See also *Northwest Heritage Consultants*, Comp. Gen. Dec. B-299547, 2007 CPD ¶ 93, where, under the current rule, GAO found that a Postal Service tracking record was found to be insufficient proof of delivery.

Causes for late delivery that are outside of the government's control have never been recognized as an excuse for late delivery of an offer. See, for example, *Ironhorse Ltd.*, Comp. Gen. Dec. B-256582, 94-1 CPD ¶ 76 (severe weather); *University of Kansas*, Comp. Gen. Dec. B-222329, 86-1 CPD ¶369 (bad weather and congested air traffic); *Unitron Eng'g Co.*, 58 Comp. Gen. 748 (B-194707), 79-2 CPD ¶ 155 (common carrier closed its offices during emergency at nearby nuclear electric power generating plant).

An offeror can not meet the requirement that the government has "received" the proposal on time if it is partially at fault for the late delivery. See, for example, *Sector One Security Solution*, Comp. Gen. Dec. B-400728, 2008 CPD ¶ 224, where the agency refused delivery of a proposal sent by UPS messenger. GAO denied the protest because the offeror had not made special arrangements for hand-carried proposals as required by the RFP. See also *U.S. Aerospace, Inc.*, Comp. Gen. Dec. B-403464, 2010 CPD ¶ 225 (offeror's messenger went to wrong gate); *Castle Group*, Comp. Gen. Dec. B-297853, 2006 CPD ¶ 55 (offeror did not use the full address required by the RFP); *InfoGroup Inc.*, Comp. Gen. Dec. B-294610, 2004 CPD ¶ 190 (offeror failed to use room number provided in RFP); *Environmental, Inc.*, Comp. Gen. Dec. B-294057, 2004 CPD ¶ 138 (offerors delivered courier-delivered proposals to address for mailed proposals). The same result was reached under prior regulations. See *Social Eng'g Tech.*, Comp. Gen. Dec. B-187194, 77-1 CPD ¶ 234, where the offer was found to be late even though it had been delivered to the HUD mail room on time. GAO reached this conclusion because the mail room was not the office designated for hand-delivered proposals. The same result was arrived at in *CSLA, Inc.*, Comp. Gen. Dec. B-255177, 94-1 CPD ¶ 63.

When government actions prior to the receipt of the bid or proposal cause the lateness, the current regulation permits consideration of the offer. See *Weeks Marine, Inc.*, Comp. Gen. Dec. B-292758, 2003 CPD ¶ 183, holding that it was proper to accept a late bid when the IFB listed the wrong room for delivery of the bid and the bid was delivered one minute late. Compare *O.S. Sys., Inc.*, Comp. Gen. Dec. B-292827, 2003 CPD ¶ 211, holding that a late proposal was properly rejected even though the delivery instructions in the RFP did not indicate the difficulty that was encountered because of base security.

Under the prior "mishandling" rule it was extremely difficult for offerors to establish that the lateness was due to improper government action. In *Vikonics, Inc.*, Comp. Gen. Dec. B-222423, 86-1 CPD ¶ 419, a protester alleged that its hand-carried proposal was late because it was delayed in getting a base pass and the receptionist gave incorrect directions. GAO denied the protest stating that delays in gaining access to government buildings are not unusual and should be expected. See also *Einhorn Yaffee Prescott*, Comp. Gen. Dec. B-259552, 95-1 CPD ¶ 153, where the protester's BAFO was logged in at 1:05, five minutes after the time set for receipt. In denying the protester's claim of improper government action, GAO reasoned that the paramount cause of the lateness was that the offeror's messenger attempted to make the delivery only five minutes before the closing time. This same reasoning is used by GAO in ruling on protests under the new rule. See, for example, *Kesser Int'l*, Comp. Gen. Dec. B-296294, 2005 CPD ¶ 127, holding that a 20 minute security delay on a military base should have been foreseen by the offeror and was not the "paramount" cause of the late delivery, and *Hospital Klean of Texas, Inc.*, Comp. Gen. Dec. B-295836, 2005 CPD ¶ 185, holding that the fact that the designated building was locked was the "paramount" cause of the protester's inability to deliver the proposal.

Government mishandling was found in *Brazos Roofing, Inc.*, Comp. Gen. Dec. B-275113, 97-1 CPD ¶ 43 (lateness caused by inoperable government equipment); *Timber-Mart Southwest, Inc.*, Comp. Gen. Dec. B-274677, 97-1 CPD ¶ 38 (failure to check mailbox until after time for receipt); *Wand Elec.*, Comp. Gen. Dec. B-250576, 93-1 CPD ¶ 59 (bid depository was not checked within a reasonable time before offers were due); and *Space Ordnance Sys.*, 63 Comp. Gen. 482 (B-214079), 84-2 CPD ¶ 61 (telegraphic proposal modification received two and one-half hours prior to closing, but not delivered to the proper office until two days later).

Mishandling was generally not found if the proposal did not contain the time and date specified for receipt and the solicitation number, as required by FAR 52.215-1(c)(3)(iii). Thus, no mishandling was found in *Human Res. Consulting Serv.*, Comp. Gen. Dec. B-232338, 88-2 CPD ¶ 340, where a proposal not containing the solicitation number or time for receipt was delivered over eight hours before submission time but was misrouted by the agency. GAO concluded the primary cause of the lateness was the contractor's lack of diligence. In *Alpha Tech. Servs., Inc.*, Comp. Gen. Dec. B-243322, 91-2 CPD ¶ 56, proposals were delivered via U.S. mail's express mail delivery service two hours before time set for receipt of proposals. However, the proposals were not routed to the contracting officer until after closing time. GAO held that lack of identification markings rather than agency mishandling caused the late deliveries. See also *Secure Applications, Inc.*, Comp. Gen. Dec. B-261885, 95-2 CPD ¶ 190, finding no government mishandling where the offeror had failed to identify its submission as a proposal or otherwise mark the submission with an identifying solicitation number or closing date deadline and time; and had allowed only one day for delivery.

GAO would not consider the government mishandling exception to the late proposal rule until the offeror established, with documented evidence, that the proposal was actually received by the government prior to the closing date *Southeastern CAD/CAM*, 71 Comp. Gen. 78 (B-244745), 91-2 CPD ¶ 453 (drawings were allegedly transmitted by facsimile but no proof of receipt); *Microscope Co.*, Comp. Gen. Dec. B-257015, 94-2 CPD ¶ 157 (revised proposal was allegedly transmitted by facsimile but no proof of receipt).

### c.  Modifications to "Otherwise Successful" Proposals

Under FAR 15.208(b)(2), the contracting officer can accept a modification to an "otherwise successful" proposal if it makes the terms of the offer more favorable to the government. However, this rule deals only with modifications to offers that have already been determined to be winning offers. Thus, the rule cannot be used to accept a final proposal revision that is late. See *Sunrise Medical HHG, Inc.*, Comp. Gen. Dec. B-310230, 2008 CPD ¶ 7, precluding an offeror from making itself the "otherwise successful offeror" by submitting a late proposal modification. See also *Omega Sys., Inc.*, Comp. Gen. Dec. B-298767, 2006 CPD ¶ 170, where the protester's late proposal revisions were properly rejected because it had been told in discussions that it was not in line for award; and *Masai Techs. Corp. v. United States*, 79 Fed. Cl. 433 (2007), where the protester's late proposal modifications were properly rejected because it had been told previously that its proposal was unacceptable. Compare *NCR Govt. Sys. LLC*, Comp. Gen. Dec. B-297959, 2006 CPD ¶ 82, holding that it was proper to accept a late addition to the winning offeror's final proposal revisions because the addition was not instrumental in the award decision.

### d.  Emergencies or Unanticipated Events

The "emergency or unanticipated event" exception in ¶ (3)(iv) applies only if the event impacts the operations of the government agency. See *Conscoop — Consorzia Fra Coop. Di Prod. E Lavoro v. United States*, 62 Fed. Cl. 219 (200 (government electronic mail system fully functional and five proposals received in spite of regional power failure); *Educational Planning & Advice, Inc.*, Comp. Gen. Dec. B-274513, 96-2 CPD ¶ 173 (four bidders submitted timely bids and agency proceeded to bid opening in spite of hurricane emergency); and *Unitron Eng'g Co.*, 58 Comp. Gen. 748 (B-194707), 79-2 CPD ¶ 155 (Mail deliveries were normal and five bids received in spite of blizzard).

## B.  Information

The typical RFP will require the offeror to furnish a considerable amount of information. Much of the information will deal with the offeror's capability to perform, including such subjects as past performance, experience, facilities and equipment, financial capacity and key personnel. Requests for information dealing with how the offeror intends to perform the work and what techniques it will use in managing the work often call for the offeror to include this information in what have been called "technical proposals" and "management proposals." Such requests for information have been criticized as creating "essay contests" and some agencies have stopped requiring them. They should be distinguished from RFP provisions which require the offeror to include in the offer details of the work or explanations of the offer which may or may not be incorporated into the contract. When such technical information is to be incorporated into the contract, it should be accomplished through negotiations and included in a revised offer or in the final contract document.

## 1. Technical Information

Offerors may be required to furnish technical information which will be used in assessing the offeror's "know how" or the degree of risk involved in the way the offeror intends to perform. When such information is required, offerors should devote full attention to ensuring that their information describes sound technical solutions and contains thorough documentation. Proposals with significant informational deficiencies are excluded as a matter of course, *AHNTECH, Inc.*, Comp. Gen. Dec. B-299806, 2007 CPD ¶ 213; *Kahn Instruments, Inc.*, Comp. Gen. Dec. B-277973, 98-1 CPD ¶ 11; *McAllister & Assocs., Inc.*, Comp. Gen. Dec. B-277029.3, 98-1 CPD ¶ 85; *Integrated Microcomputer Sys., Inc.*, Comp. Gen. Dec. B-239126.4, 90-2 CPD ¶ 195; and submissions that are not supported with sufficient technical information may be excluded from the competitive range, *Hamilton Sundstrand Power Sys. v. United States*, 75 Fed. Cl. 512 (2007); *Hamilton Sundstrand Power Sys.*, Comp. Gen. Dec. B-298757, 2006 CPD ¶ 209; *LaBarge Prods., Inc.*, Comp. Gen. Dec. B-287841, 2001 CPD ¶ 177; *Millar Elevator Indus., Inc.*, Comp. Gen. Dec. B-250992.2, 93-1 CPD ¶ 212; *KCI, Inc.*, Comp. Gen. Dec. B-244690, 91-2 CPD ¶ 395; *Wyle Lab.*, Comp. Gen. Dec. B-239671, 90-2 CPD ¶ 231. Page limitations on the length of technical proposals are not accepted as an excuse for insufficient technical information, *Professional Performance. Dev. Group, Inc.*, Comp. Gen. Dec. B-311273, 2008 CPD ¶ 101 (35-page limitation).

If the RFP calls for a specific description of how the work will be performed, the offeror can be downgraded for not supplying such information, *Northwestern Travel Agency, Inc.*, Comp. Gen. Dec. B-244592, 91-2 CPD ¶ 363. Merely repeating portions of the RFP (termed " parroting" the RFP) is a poor strategy, *Paragon Dynamics, Inc.*, Comp. Gen. Dec. B-251280, 93-1 CPD ¶ 248. See *Government Telecommc'ns, Inc.*, Comp. Gen. Dec. B-299542.2, 2007 CPD ¶ 136; *Bannum, Inc.*, Comp. Gen. Dec. B-271075, 96-1 CPD ¶ 248, and *Supreme Automation Corp.*, Comp. Gen. Dec. B-224158, 87-1 CPD ¶ 83, where offerors were eliminated from the competitive range because they repeated back portions of the specification without affirmatively demonstrating the merits of their technical approach. Parroting solicitation language almost always leads to downgrading of the technical proposal, *DEI Consulting*, Comp. Gen. Dec. B-401258. 2009 CPD ¶ 151. Similarly, merely promising to meet the requirements in the RFP will almost invariably lead to a poor evaluation, *IVI Corp.*, Comp. Gen. Dec. B-310766, 2008 CPD ¶ 21 (blanket offer to submit an "equal" product not sufficient to show that it would meet salient characteristics); *Hubbell Elec. Heater Co.*, Comp. Gen. Dec. B-289098, 2002 CPD ¶ 15 (blanket promise to conform to ISO 9000 insufficient to demonstrate ability to do so); *Bannum, Inc.*, Comp. Gen. Dec. B-271075, 96-1 CPD ¶ 248 (exclusion from competitive range proper where the protester merely paraphrased the statement of work requirements); *Eastern Tech. Enters., Inc.*, Comp. Gen. Dec. B-259844, 95-1 CPD ¶ 232 (blanket offers of compliance are not adequate substitutes for detailed technical information); *Inter-Con Sec. Sys., Inc.*, Comp. Gen. Dec. B-235248, 89-2 CPD ¶ 148 (exclusion from competitive range proper when proposal merely made a "blanket promise" to comply with RFP). Compare *Moxon, Inc.*, Comp. Gen. Dec. B-179160, 74-1 CPD ¶ 134, where GAO held that discussions should have been held to determine what the protester was offering.

If the RFP requires the submission of test data to show that an offered product meets the specifications, an offer can be rejected for failing to submit compete test data, *General Dynamics C4 Sys., Inc.*, Comp. Gen. Dec. B-299675.2, 2008 CPD ¶ 122. Technical information may also be necessary to instruct an agency on how to conduct the test of a sample. See *L-3 Commc'ns EOTech, Inc.*, Comp. Gen. Dec. B-311453, 2008 CPD ¶ 139, denying a protest where an agency did not properly use a sample because of lack of information on how to tighten a locking nut.

If an RFP calls for the submission of a sample task response, care must be used to submit a full description of the offeror's approach to performing the task. See *Veterans Tech., LLC*, Comp. Gen. Dec. B-310303.2, 2008 CPD ¶ 31 (response failed to include technical approach or demonstration of competence of personnel).

A misrepresentation as to the technical capabilities of a proposed product can be construed as a false statement under 31 U.S.C. § 1001, subjecting the offeror to civil liability under the False Claims Act, 31 U.S.C. § 3729, *United States ex rel. Westrick v. Second Chance Body Armor, Inc.*, No 04-280 (RWR) (D.D.C. 2010). See *Harrison v. Westinghouse Savannah River Co.*, 176 F.3d 776 (4th Cir. 1999), holding that false statements about how a contract will be performed could be false claims.

## 2. *Management Information*

The offeror may be called upon to explain how it plans to manage the work to attain the promised technical solution. While technical information focuses on how the work will be performed, management information focuses on whether the offeror's organization will manage its resources to achieve those results. The offeror will be required to show the government what personnel and material resources it will use and how it will organize and control those resources to bring the contract work to a successful conclusion. As is the case with technical proposals, lack of detail in management proposals will generally result in lower scores and general statements will not suffice, *Kuhana-Spectrum*, Comp. Gen. Dec. B-401270, 2010 CPD ¶ 61 (management proposal did not discuss how the responsibilities, experience and qualifications of major officials would contribute to successful contract performance); *SPAAN Tech, Inc.*, Comp. Gen. Dec. B-400406, 2009 CPD ¶ 46 (management proposal contained little rationale for proposed organizational structure); *DIY, Inc.*, Comp. Gen. Dec. B-293105.13, 2005 CPD ¶ 50 (insufficient description of methods of conducting management and marketing services for homes); *Science & Tech., Inc.*, Comp. Gen. Dec. B-272748, 97-1 CPD ¶ 121 (lower grade justified when management proposal contains statements such as " our managers who are incumbent personnel understand Fort Huachuca's mission"). See also *Joint Threat Servs.*, Comp. Gen. Dec. B-278168, 98-1 CPD ¶ 18 (staffing cuts in option years were only implied in protester's management proposal, notwithstanding fact that cost proposal promised an in-depth analysis of the reduction plan in its management proposal); *Global Eng'g & Constr. (J.V.)*, Comp. Gen. Dec. B-275999.4, 97-2 CPD ¶ 125 (agency reasonably downgraded offeror's management proposal because it did not submit a clear management structure); and *Quality Elevator Co.*, Comp. Gen. Dec. B-271899, 96-2 CPD ¶ 89 (lower grade justified because protester's management proposal failed to describe the differing management needs of the various work tasks). In *Avue Techs. Corp.*, Comp. Gen. Dec. B-298380.4, 2008 CPD ¶ 182, a proposal was rejected for failing to demonstrate that the offeror was agreeing to the agency's requirements regarding proprietary information.

### 3. Representations and Certifications

Section K of the RFP will contain a number of representations and certifications that must be filled out by the offeror. Offerors are properly excluded from the competition if they submit a false representation or certification, *Southwestern Bell Tel. Co.*, Comp. Gen. Dec. B-292476, 2003 CPD ¶ 177; *Hedgecock Elec., Inc.*, Comp. Gen. Dec. B-274776.2, 97-1 CPD ¶ 51. See *Universal Techs. Inc.*, Comp. Gen. Dec. B-248808.2, 92-2 CPD ¶ 212, holding that a firm need not be disqualified if the agency determines that the false certification was not made in bad faith. Compare *Tiger Enters., Inc.*, Comp. Gen. Dec. B-292815.3, 2004 CPD ¶ 19, recommending immediate termination of a contract that was awarded based on a false certification that the offeror met the small business size standard. However, the contracting agency is not required to investigate a certification to determine if it is false unless it has information so indicating, *E.D.I., Inc.*, Comp. Gen. Dec. B-251750, 93-1 CPD ¶ 364.

### 4. Capability Information

Most RFPs call for the submission of information showing the offeror's capabilities as part of the technical or management proposal or as separate information. The most important types of capability information deal with experience, past performance, and the personnel who will perform the contract. As a general rule, submission of specific information is far more effective than the mere inclusion of general statements on the abilities of the organization, *Honolulu Marine, Inc.*, Comp. Gen. Dec. B-245329, 91-2 CPD ¶ 586; *EAP Consultants*, Comp. Gen. Dec.

B-238103, 90-1 CPD ¶ 358. See *Capitol Drywall Supply, Inc.*, Comp. Gen. Dec. B-400721, 2009 CPD ¶ 17, where a proposal was correctly downgraded because it did not include specific information showing experience and relevant past performance, *Prudent Techs., Inc.*, Comp. Gen. Dec. B-297425, 2006 CPD ¶ 16, where a proposal was correctly rated unacceptable because the protester did not furnish specific capability information in the form required by the RFP, and *MIL Corp.*, Comp. Gen. Dec. B-297508, 2006 CPD ¶ 34, and *Carpetmaster*, Comp. Gen. Dec. B-294767, 2004 CPD ¶ 226, where proposals were downgraded for failure to submit specific information as requested by the solicitation.

Offerors should exercise care in the assertions that they make concerning their capability. See *United States ex rel. Longhi v. Lithium Power Techs., Inc.*, 530 F. Supp.2d 888 (S.D. Tex. 2008), *aff'd*, 575 F.3d 458 (5th Cir. 2009), *cert. denied*, 130 Sup. Ct. 2092 (2010), assessing triple the contract price as damages because the contractor misrepresented its prior experience, its arrangements with another firm and the extent of its facilities in its proposal. See also *Dual, Inc.*, Comp. Gen. Dec. B-280719, 98-2 CPD ¶ 133, where the protester argued that the winning offeror had been guilty of misrepresentation by stating that it would perform the work at a particular division when, in fact, it was negotiating the sale of that division to another company while the procurement was being conducted. GAO sustained the protest, agreeing with the protester that Dual had an obligation to advise the Air Force of its negotiations and that its failure to do so was a misrepresentation which affected the evaluation process. See also *Greenleaf Constr. Co.*, Comp. Gen. Dec. B-293105.18, 2006 CPD ¶ 19, sustaining a protest because the winning offeror had not informed the agency that two of the designated key personnel had stated they would not work on contract.

### a. Experience and Past Performance

Information concerning an offeror's experience and past performance record will be required to be furnished in almost all procurements. Experience deals with the types of work which the offeror or its employees have performed and past performance deals with how well the work has been performed. While the request may not clearly distinguish between the two, information on both types of background will be important. See *Telcom Sys. Servs., Inc. v. Department of Justice*, GSBCA 13272-P, 95-2 BCA ¶ 27,849 ("unreasonable to suggest that past performance does not encompass experience").

In addition to complying with the RFP's specific requests for past performance information, the offeror should offer additional information which would explain or supplement the information furnished. Thus, the offeror should provide a thorough analysis of its past performance on contracts that are similar to the procurement in question and should demonstrate that those contracts are relevant to the evaluation of its performance for the current effort. If the RFP requires offerors to obtain questionnaires from references, it is the offeror's responsibility to ensure that the questionnaires are submitted, *Capitol Drywall Supply, Inc.*, Comp. Gen. Dec. B-400721, 2009 CPD ¶ 17; *American Floor Consultants, Inc.*, Comp. Gen. Dec. B-294530.7, 2006 CPD ¶ 97, and that they are submitted by an independent source, *Metro Mach. Corp.*, Comp. Gen. Dec. B-295744, 2005 CPD ¶ 112 (evaluation by offeror of subcontractors did not meet RFP requirement for independent evaluation). Where there have been instances of poor or unsuccessful past performance, the offeror should provide any factual information which would establish extenuating circumstances. In addition, factual information on steps taken to correct or avoid such occurrences should be included. See *Del-Jen Int'l Corp.*, Comp. Gen. Dec. B-297960, 2006 CPD ¶ 81 (protest denied when protester did not demonstrate that it had corrected past deficiencies in performing as incumbent contractor); *Hanley Indus., Inc.*, Comp. Gen. Dec. B-295318, 2005 CPD ¶ 20 (low rating of past performance justified when protester did not take opportunity to submit evidence of corrective action); *Si-Nor, Inc.*, Comp. Gen. Dec. B-292748.2, 2004 CPD ¶ 10 (low rating of past performance justified when agency was given only partial evidence of corrective action). The past performance of a parent company may be used if the offeror can show that the parent will participate in performing the prospective contract, *Frontier Sys. Integrators, LLC*, Comp. Gen. Dec. B-298872.3, 2007 CPD ¶ 46.

When information on experience is requested, a detailed description of past efforts should be provided, *M. Erdal Kamisli, Ltd.*, Comp. Gen. Dec. B-291522, 2003 CPD ¶ 19; *Sunbelt Props., Inc.*, Comp. Gen. Dec. B-245729.3, 92-1 CPD ¶ 278. In some cases, the RFP may require information on the experience of both the offeror and its personnel, *General Physics Fed. Sys., Inc.*, Comp. Gen. Dec. B-275934, 97-1 CPD ¶ 171 (personnel experience and corporate experience); and *Global Assocs., Ltd.*, Comp. Gen. Dec. B-275534, 97-1 CPD ¶ 129 (corporate experience and personnel qualifications and experience). Where an offeror has not had the specific experience required, the lack of corporate experience may be overcome by the experience of employees, *Consultants on Family Addiction*, Comp. Gen. Dec. B-274924.2, 97-1 CPD ¶ 80 (nothing improper in evaluating an offeror's capacity to perform services based on the experience of those who will perform those services); and *EBA Eng'g, Inc.*, Comp. Gen. Dec. B-275818, 97-1 CPD ¶ 127 (a competitor for a service contract was entitled to use the experience of the incumbent employees).

### b.  Key Personnel

The personnel that the offeror intends to use in performing the contract are of prime importance. Thus, resumes of key personnel are frequently required and probably should be submitted even when they have not been requested. The importance of complying with resume requirements is demonstrated by *Verizon Fed., Inc.*, Comp. Gen. Dec. B-293527, 2004 CPD ¶ 186, where an offeror was rated unacceptable because of missing and incomplete resumes even though it was rated outstanding in past performance. See also *Inter-Con Sec. Sys., Inc.*, Comp. Gen. Dec.

B-235248, 89-2 CPD ¶ 148, where an incumbent contractor was properly omitted from the competitive range of the follow-on procurement because it failed to provide resumes of key personnel and other requested information. For similar results, see *Lakeside Escrow & Title Agency, Inc.*, Comp. Gen. Dec. B-310331.3, 2008 CPD ¶ 14; and *Pyramid Servs., Inc.*, Comp. Gen. Dec. B-257085.2, 94-2 CPD ¶ 79. See also *DEI Consulting*, Comp. Gen. Dec. B-401258. 2009 CPD ¶ 151, where the protester was properly downgraded because it did not specify which of its offered engineers would be the senior engineer. In *Client Network Servs., Inc.*, Comp. Gen. Dec. B-297994, 2006 CPD ¶ 79, the protester was properly downgraded because the resumes it submitted did not meet the page limitations or format requirements in the RFP. Compare *Global Solutions Network, Inc.*, Comp. Gen. Dec. B-298682.3, 2008 CPD ¶ 131, denying a protest that the agency allowed the winning offeror to submit resumes exceeding the RFP page limitation — because the protester was not prejudiced. GAO used similar reasoning in granting a protest where the agency had improperly downgraded a proposal because the resumes did not include information that it had learned during discussions, *Arora Group*, Comp. Gen. Dec. B-293102, 2004 CPD ¶ 61.

Offerors have also been disqualified from the competition because of inaccuracies in listing key personnel, *Electronic Data Sys. Fed. Corp.*, GSBCA 9869-P, 89-2 BCA ¶ 21,655, *recons. denied*, 89-2 BCA ¶ 21,778, *aff'd in part, vacated in part sub. nom. Planning Research Corp. v. United States*, 971 F.2d 736 (Fed. Cir. 1992) (submission of 101 resumes with no intention to use the personnel); *Ultra Tech. Corp.*, Comp. Gen. Dec. B-230309.6, 89-1 CPD ¶ 42 (proposing person as "lead technician" without obtaining his permission); *ManTech Advanced Sys. Int'l., Inc.*, Comp. Gen. Dec. B-255719.2, 94-1 CPD ¶ 326 (misrepresenting availability of incumbent personnel). Compare *Patriot Contract Servs., LLC v. United States*, 388 F. Supp. 2d 1010 (N.D. Cal. 2005), holding that the winning offeror had not clearly known that most of the key personnel would not be available when the contract was awarded a year after their names had been submitted, and *Orion Int'l Techs. v. United States*, 66 Fed. Cl. 569 (2005), holding that there was no misrepresentation when an employee of the incumbent contractor had signed a noncompete agreement but appeared willing to work for the offeror. In *CBIS Fed., Inc.*, 71 Comp. Gen. 319 (B-245844.2), 92-1 CPD ¶ 308, and *Greenleaf Constr. Co.*, Comp. Gen. Dec. B-293105.18, 2006 CPD ¶ 19, GAO stated that when an offeror finds that proposed personnel are no longer available the offeror should withdraw the names and propose substitutes in the best and final offer.

In many cases, the offeror will be required to furnish evidence that the listed key personnel will be available for performance if the offeror receives the award. In such cases, GAO has ruled that award would be improper if the offeror does not supply information ensuring that key personnel would be available to perform the contract, *ManTech Field Eng'g Corp.*, Comp. Gen. Dec. B-245886.4, 92-1 CPD ¶ 309. Thus, failure to do so will result in the submission being held to be unacceptable or downgraded, *Native American Indus. Distribs., Inc.*, Comp. Gen. Dec.

B-310737.3, 2008 CPD ¶ 76 (signed nondisclosure agreements not substitutes for required letters of commitment); *Xeta Int'l Corp.*, Comp. Gen. Dec. B-255182, 94-1 CPD ¶ 109 (failure to provide required letters of commitment for proposed key personnel). Compare *Science Applications Int'l Corp.*, Comp. Gen. Dec. B-290971, 2002 CPD ¶ 184, holding that a commitment statement on signed resumes met the requirement for a letter of commitment. In *Scientific Mgmt. Assocs., Inc.*, Comp. Gen. Dec. B-238913, 90-2 CPD ¶ 27, the RFP stated that proposed personnel with nonbinding hiring agreements would not be evaluated as highly. GAO held that the protester was properly excluded from the competitive range because of conditional hiring agreements for several key personnel. Similarly, in *IMR Servs. Corp.*, Comp. Gen. Dec. B-230586, 88-1 CPD ¶ 548, the proposed program manager was also committed to work as a site manager at another location. GAO held that it was not unreasonable for the agency to downgrade a proposal in which a proposed manager would be stationed at a location different from the center of contract activity.

## C. Rules Governing Submission

The RFP will specify the method of submitting offers and information and the format that must be observed. The failure to follow these instructions may result in the submission being rejected. See *Environmental Control Div., Inc.*, Comp. Gen. Dec. B-255181, 94-1 CPD ¶ 115, where GAO found that the agency properly rejected a protester's BAFO which was transmitted by facsimile in response to the agency's facsimile transmitted request for BAFOs because the solicitation did not allow for offers or modifications to be transmitted by facsimile.

### 1. Method of Submission

The basic method of submission of offers and information is in paper media in a sealed envelope. However, there are a growing number of procurements where facsimile or electronic submission is permitted or required. In addition, part or all of the required information may be submitted in an oral presentation.

#### a. Paper Media

Paragraph (c) of the Instructions to Offerors — Competitive Acquisition solicitation provision in FAR 52.215-1 provides guidance on the basic procedure to be followed in submitting offers and information:

> (1) Unless other methods (e.g., electronic commerce or facsimile) are permitted in the solicitation, proposals and modifications to proposals shall be submitted in paper media in sealed envelopes or packages (i) addressed to the office specified in the solicitation, and (ii) showing the time and date specified for receipt, the solicitation number, and the name and address of the offeror. Offerors using commercial carriers should ensure that the proposal is marked on the outermost wrapper with the information in paragraphs (c)(1)(i) and (c)(1)(ii) of this provision.

(2) The first page of the proposal must show —

(i) The solicitation number;

(ii) The name, address, and telephone and facsimile numbers of the offeror (and electronic address if available);

(iii) A statement specifying the extent of agreement with all terms, conditions, and provisions included in the solicitation and agreement to furnish any or all items upon which prices are offered at the price set opposite each item;

(iv) Names, titles, and telephone and facsimile numbers (and electronic addresses if available) of persons authorized to negotiate on the offeror's behalf with the Government in connection with this solicitation; and

(v) Name, title, and signature of person authorized to sign the proposal. Proposals signed by an agent shall be accompanied by evidence of that agent's authority, unless that evidence has been previously furnished to the issuing office.

## b. Facsimile or Electronic Submission

FAR 15.203(c) provides that when electronic commerce is an authorized means of submission, the RFP must "specify the electronic commerce method(s) that offerors may use (see Subpart 4.5)." FAR 15.209(e) requires the contracting officer to include the Facsimile Proposals solicitation provision in FAR 52.215-5 in an RFP when submission by facsimiles is authorized. The instructions for handling unreadable portions of facsimile or electronic submissions contained in this provision are set forth in FAR 15.207(c).

Offerors assume the risk of having their facsimile or electronic transmissions considered, *S.W. Elecs. & Mfg. Corp.*, Comp. Gen. Dec. B-249308, 92-2 CPD ¶ 320. For electronic transmission, delivery to the offeror's government approved Value Added Network (VAN) was not sufficient, *Comspace Corp.*, Comp. Gen. Dec. B-274037, 96-2 CPD ¶ 186 (involving a request for quotations).

## c. Oral Presentations

Oral presentations, as discussed earlier, have been used for some time to enable procurement officials to obtain information leading to additional understanding of the offerors' capability and features of their offers. However, it was not until the FAR Part 15 Rewrite that comprehensive coverage was adopted for these procedures. FAR 15.102 provides detailed guidance on obtaining information, but not offers, through this process. This regulatory provision for obtaining information through the presentation process is consistent with prior practice. See *Intermagnetics Gen.*

*Corp.*, Comp. Gen. Dec. B-255741.2, 94-1 CPD ¶ 302, holding that while an agency may limit its evaluation to information contained in written submissions, it also may decide to use other information, including that obtained in oral presentations. The RFP should identify the process that the agency will require offerors to follow in making the oral presentation. See FAR 15.102(d). If there is any ambiguity in the RFP as to the precise process to be followed, an offeror should request more detail from the contracting officer. Agencies may require that offerors meet mandatory requirements in an RFP before being eligible to make an oral presentation, *Inte-Great Corp.*, Comp. Gen. Dec. B-272780, 96-2 CPD ¶ 159, and it is very common practice to conduct oral presentations with only those offerors in the competitive range.

The offeror should use the oral presentation to demonstrate that it is fully capable of performing the critical tasks on the proposed contract. This is usually best done by discussing these tasks and identifying key problems that are anticipated and proposed methods of dealing with those problems. Lengthy discussion of the general capabilities of the offeror is generally not as effective as specific identification of the capability to perform key tasks. See *Client Network Servs., Inc.*, Comp. Gen. Dec. B-297994, 2006 CPD ¶ 79, where an offeror was downgraded because it covered general capability in the oral presentation rather than addressing the issues involved in the procurement for which it was competing. It is also important that all of the designated tasks be addressed during the oral presentation. See *T Square Logistics Servs. Corp.*, Comp. Gen. Dec. B-291851, 2003 CPD ¶ 160, requiring the downgrading of an oral presentation that did not address some of the specified subelements of the work.

Offerors should ensure that the key personnel that they propose to use will be available to attend the oral presentation. See *Sandi Group, Inc.*, Comp. Gen. Dec. B-401218, 2009 CPD ¶ 123, holding that the protester was properly denied the opportunity to make an oral presentation (or to compete for the work) when its project manager left the company after the proposal had been submitted and the agency refused to permit substitution of another person because that would constitute a late proposal revision.

Offerors should exercise care in the assertions that they make in their oral presentations. See *Johnson Controls Sec. Sys.*, Comp. Gen. Dec. B-296490, 2007 CPD ¶102, where an offeror was faced with potential disqualification because it misrepresented in its oral presentation that it was taking required actions to qualify its personnel. Compare *EBA Eng'g, Inc.*, Comp. Gen. Dec. B-275818, 97-1 CPD ¶ 127, where the protester argued that the winning offeror had been guilty of misrepresentation by stating that it would hire all necessary incumbent employees to perform the service contract that was the subject of the competition. GAO held that this was not a defect in the procurement because the offeror had inserted a statement in its BAFO correcting this overly broad statement.

The offeror's team should be composed of key personnel who will perform or personally direct the work if awarded the contract, such as project managers, task leaders, and other in-house staff. If a significant amount of the work will be subcontracted, members of the subcontractor staff should make the relevant presentation. The offeror's team must demonstrate that it has the expertise to satisfy the requirement. Compare *ARTEL, Inc.*, Comp. Gen. Dec. B-248478, 92-2 CPD ¶ 120, where the agency concluded from an oral presentation that there were serious doubts as to the quality and availability of the offeror's key personnel, and *Planning & Dev. Collaborative Int'l*, Comp. Gen. Dec. B-299041, 2007 CPD ¶ 28, where an offeror was downgraded because its team did not work well together during an oral presentation, with *Savannah River Alliance, LLC*, Comp. Gen. Dec. B-311126, 2008 CPD ¶ 88, where the agency selected a contractor based, to large measure, on the fact that its team functioned very well in solving problems during the oral presentation,. It can be seen that one of the most important aspects of an oral presentation is the ability of the offeror's participants to function well as a team. As another example, in *Labat-Anderson, Inc.*, 71 Comp. Gen. 252 (B-246071), 92-1 CPD ¶ 193, the oral presentation resulted in a determination that the offeror lacked capability.

The present regulations make it clear that agency officials may ask questions and seek further detail. This is consistent with prior decisions, *NAHB Research Found., Inc.*, Comp. Gen. Dec. B-219344, 85-2 CPD ¶ 248 (aggressive questioning permissible). Offerors have been properly downgraded because they did not give convincing responses to questions during an oral presentation. See *Zolon Tech, Inc.*, Comp. Gen. Dec. B-299904.2, 2007 CPD ¶ 183 (no member of offeror's team could answer a question about a critical aspect of the proposed work); *Advanced Tech. Sys., Inc.*, Comp. Gen. Dec. B-296493.5, 2006 CPD ¶ 147, (team responded that it had not yet decided on what management tool to use). See also *Systems Research & Applications Corp.*, Comp. Gen. Dec. B-299818, 2008 CPD ¶ 28, where a protest was granted, in part, because the agency failed to ask the protester to explain a term used in the oral presentation and then downgraded the protester because it did not understand the term.

Agencies may also adopt reasonable rules governing the nature of the presentations, including limitations on the length and nature of the presentations, *American Sys. Corp.*, 68 Comp. Gen. 475 (B-234449), 89-1 CPD ¶ 537. They may also require that offerors meet mandatory requirements in an RFP before being eligible to make an oral presentation, *Inte-Great Corp.*, Comp. Gen. Dec. B-272780, 96-2 CPD ¶ 159.

Agencies may either preclude or permit discussions during the oral presentation, FAR 15.102(d)(6). However, if discussions occur, the agency must comply with the rules governing negotiations with all offerors in the competitive range, FAR 15.102(g). See *Global Analytic Info. Tech. Servs., Inc.*, Comp. Gen. Dec. B-298840.2, 2007 CPD ¶ 57, holding that a discussion had occurred when an agency asked to more detailed pricing information during the oral presentation and the offeror subsequently submitted the information using revised pricing logic. See also

*General Physics Fed. Sys., Inc.*, Comp. Gen. Dec. B-275934, 97-1 CPD ¶ 171, where no ruling on this issue was made because there was no prejudice to the protester when the agency sought information on the commitment of proposed key personnel from all of the offerors during the oral presentations. Most protests on this issue have found that no discussions occurred during the oral presentation, *Sierra Military Health Servs., Inc.*, Comp. Gen. Dec. B-292780, 2004 CPD ¶ 55 (probing staffing information in original presentation not discussion); *Development Alternatives, Inc.*, Comp. Gen. Dec. B-279920, 98-2 CPD ¶ 54 ( question and answer session not discussions).

It has been common practice for agencies to require the submission of slides to be used in the oral presentation at the time the original proposal is submitted. This requirement has been strictly enforced, *KSEND v. United States*, 69 Fed. Cl. 103 (2005) (proposal properly rejected when transparencies were not submitted with offer). See also *Innovative Mgmt., Inc.*, Comp. Gen. Dec. B-291375, 2003 CPD ¶ 11, finding no basis for a protest when the agency lost the transparencies with the result that the protester had to use copies during the presentation.

## 2. Format and Style

The format and style of a submission are intangible considerations in winning competitions. A good submission is organized and written so that it can be read by government evaluators of many different functional and technical disciplines such as management, contracting, engineering, legal, accounting, and others. Some features the offeror will want to consider in developing its are:

- Inclusion of an *executive summary* to highlight the salient aspects. A good summary may be read by the source selection official and other agency officials too busy to read the entire document.

- An *index* which cross-references the statement of work to the information and the offer. This can be valuable in showing the government exactly how the offer matches the evaluation factors expressed in the RFP.

- The *organization* of the submission should indicate that the offeror is orderly, thorough, and effective. It should be made easy to break out into component parts for evaluation by technical, business, and pricing personnel.

The way in which a submission is presented can have a significant effect on its evaluation. See *Professional Software Eng'g, Inc.*, Comp. Gen. Dec. B-272820, 96-2 CPD ¶ 193 (proposal downgraded for typographical errors); *Engineering & Envt., Inc.*, Comp. Gen. Dec. B-271868.3, 96-2 CPD ¶ 182 ("many typographical errors and misspelling" and "inattention to detail"); and *Pannesma Co.*, Comp. Gen. Dec. B-251688, 93-1 CPD ¶ 333 ("sloppy proposal" reflecting a "casual approach").

It is the offeror's responsibility to ensure its submission is, in all respects, a complete document, *Westvold & Assocs.*, Comp. Gen. Dec. B-201032, 81-1 CPD ¶ 354. It should also be a coherent document — both within each section and among sections. One of the most common failings is the inclusion of conflicting data and information in the technical, management, and cost sections. See, for example, *Earle Palmer Brown Cos.*, 70 Comp. Gen. 667 (B-243544) 91-2 CPD ¶ 134, where the agency properly adjusted the contractor's price upward upon determining that the contractor could not pay the salary of required personnel for the cost offered in its proposal; and *AmerInd, Inc.*, Comp. Gen. Dec. B-248324, 92-2 CPD ¶ 85, where the agency properly determined that the costs offered by the protester bore no relation to the cost of personnel for whom the protester submitted resumes.

Whenever data can be summarized in graphic form, it is good practice to include such charts and graphs. They are particularly important when page limitations make it necessary to present information in the most concise form. However, such charts and graphs should be simple and direct. Although the FAR Part 15 Rewrite eliminated the Unnecessarily Elaborate Proposals or Quotations solicitation provision, it is still sound advise not to submit unnecessarily elaborate brochures or other presentations beyond those sufficient to present a complete and effective response to a solicitation. In *Professional Data Servs., Inc.*, Comp. Gen. Dec. B-220002, 33 Cont. Cases Fed. (CCF) ¶ 74,331, Dec. 13, 1985, the agency rejected the protester's offer because it was overly elaborate and GAO upheld that decision, stating:

> [O]ne reason that [the protester] did not receive higher scores for Technical Understanding and Approach was because [the protester] submitted an unnecessarily elaborate proposal that in part was confusing regarding what was being offered. An offeror has the burden of submitting an adequately written proposal permitting the agency to make an intelligent evaluation, and failure to do so justifies lowering the proposal's score.

Conversely, when a proposal has been rejected because it lacks detail or specifics, GAO has routinely rejected the argument that the proposal could not be more detailed without violating the unnecessarily elaborate proposal prohibition. In *TLC Sys.*, Comp. Gen. Dec. B-243220, 91-2 CPD ¶ 37, GAO stated that none of the unnecessarily elaborate provisions "can be read to obviate the clearly expressed requirements to submit specified information with the proposal." See also *Global Valuation Serv.*, Comp. Gen. Dec. B-230753, 88-1 CPD ¶ 604, rejecting the protester's assertion that its "rather limited proposal" was justified by the RFP's caution against submitting overly elaborate proposals. Thus, offerors must strike a balance between clear and coherent explanation of their proposed method of performance and unduly elaborate detailing.

Another formal requirement in many solicitations is a page limitation for some or all of the sections of the proposal. Page limitations are strictly enforced, *Client Network Servs., Inc.*, Comp. Gen. Dec. B-297994, 2006 CPD ¶ 79 (agency properly downgraded proposal that did not follow formatting requirements in RFP); *Electronic Design, Inc.*, Comp. Gen. Dec. B-279662.2, 98-2 CPD ¶ 69 (agency improperly permitted offeror to include material greatly exceeding page limitations in BAFO without informing other offerors); *Management & Indus. Techs. Assocs.*, Comp. Gen. Dec. B-257656, 94-2 CPD ¶ 134 (agency properly rejected pages in excess of limitation); *U.S. Envtl. & Indus., Inc.*, Comp. Gen. Dec. B-257349, 94-2 CPD ¶ 51 (smaller typeface created excess pages and improper competitive advantage); *All Star Maint., Inc.*, Comp. Gen. Dec. B-244143, 91-2 CPD ¶ 294 (single space, instead of double space created excess pages and improper competitive advantage). However, GAO has ruled that it is proper to exclude the cover sheet and table of contents from the page limitation requirement, *Trident Sys., Inc.*, Comp. Gen. Dec. B-243101, 91-1 CPD ¶ 604. GAO has also ruled that it is not proper to evaluate a long appendix to a proposal which exceeded the page limitation in the RFP, *ITT Electron Tech. Div.*, Comp. Gen. Dec. B-242289, 91-1 CPD ¶ 383. In *Macfadden & Assocs., Inc.*, Comp. Gen. Dec. B-275502, 97-1 CPD ¶ 88, GAO reasoned that an agency can automatically reject an entire proposal that exceeds a page limit rather than evaluate only the proposal pages within the limit when the language of the solicitation explicitly states that this course of action will be followed. In *HSQ Tech.*, Comp. Gen. Dec. B-277048, 97-2 CPD ¶ 57, the RFP stated that noncompliance with the stated page limitation "could result in elimination of the offer from the proposal process." GAO followed the logic in *Macfadden* stating that "could" meant that such a proposal could not automatically be rejected but rather may properly be rejected only if there was a reasonable basis for the rejection. GAO found that the agency reasonably concluded that the proposal without the excess pages was unacceptable since it lacked material sections of the technical proposal and the entire price proposal.

Paragraph (c)(iv) of the Instructions to Offerors — Competitive Acquisition solicitation provision in FAR 52.215-1 contains a further formal requirement — that offerors must provide the names, titles, and telephone and facsimile numbers of persons authorized to negotiate on the offeror's behalf. While there is no indication that a proposal can be rejected for failure to comply with this requirement, the information should be furnished as a matter of course in each proposal.

### 3. *Proprietary Data*

FAR 15.207(b) provides that proposals must be "safeguarded from unauthorized disclosure throughout the source selection process." This provision merely instructs the contracting officer on the protections that are required to be used in handling the data. Offerors are permitted to place proprietary markings on their proposals to ensure that such protection is given. The following ¶ (e) in FAR 52.215-1 implements this regulation:

> Offerors that include in their proposals data that they do not want disclosed to the public for any purpose, or used by the Government except for evaluation purposes, shall —

(1) Mark the title page with the following legend:

> This proposal includes data that shall not be disclosed outside the Government and shall not be duplicated, used, or disclosed — in whole or in part — for any purpose other than to evaluate this proposal. If, however, a contract is awarded to this offeror as a result of — or in connection with — the submission of this data, the Government shall have the right to duplicate, use, or disclose the data to the extent provided in the resulting contract. This restriction does not limit the Government's right to use information contained in this data if it is obtained from another source without restriction. The data subject to this restriction are contained in sheets *[insert numbers or other identification of sheets]*; and

(2) Mark each sheet of data it wishes to restrict with the following legend:

> Use or disclosure of data contained on this sheet is subject to the restriction on the title page of this proposal.

This provision permits offerors to mark all data in the proposal — whether technical, management, or financial data — with the prescribed legend, and requires government agencies to protect such data during the source selection process, and thereafter for the losing offerors. However, if the contract is awarded, this provision states that the government's obligation to protect the data of the winning offeror ceases, and, thereafter, the government's right to disclose the information is governed by the clauses of the contract. FAR 27.407 permits civilian agencies to use the following Rights in Proposal Data clause in FAR 52.227-23:

> Except for data contained on pages ____, it is agreed that as a condition of award of this contract, and notwithstanding the conditions of any notice appearing thereon, the Government shall have unlimited rights (as defined in the Rights in Data — General clause contained in this contract) in and to the technical data contained in the proposal dated , upon which this contract is based.

When this clause is included in the contract, the offeror should be careful to fill in the pages where there is proprietary data. See *General Atronics Corp.*, ASBCA 49196, 02-1 BCA ¶ 31,798, where the contractor was held to have given the government unlimited rights to software submitted without proprietary legends even though it had inserted "all" in the clause. With regard to properly marked technical data submitted to civilian agencies, protection would be determined by the terms of the Rights in Data — General clause in FAR 52.227-14 when it is included in the resulting contract. If this clause is not included in the contract, there may well be no government promise to protect proprietary technical data. Even if the clause is included in the contract, it contains no government promise to protect management and financial data. Thus, offerors dealing with civilian agencies desiring to protect such data should request that a clause be included in the contract for that purpose.

With regard to proposal data submitted to the Department of Defense, DFARS 227.7103-6(e)(1) and DFARS 227.7203-6(b) require the inclusion of the Rights in Bid or Proposal Information clause in DFARS 252.227-7016 in all contracts for noncommercial items. This clause provides:

> (c) Government rights subsequent to contract award — The Contractor agrees —
>
> > (1) Except as provided in paragraphs (c)((2), (d), and (e) of this clause, the Government shall have the rights to use, modify, reproduce, release, perform, display, or disclose information contained in the Contractor's bid or proposal within the Government. The Government shall not release, perform, display, or disclose such information outside the Government without the Contractor's written permission.
>
> > (2) The Government's right to use, modify, reproduce, release, perform, display, or disclose information that is technical data or computer software required to be delivered under this contract are determined by the Rights in Technical Data-Noncommercial Items, Rights in Noncommercial Computer Software and Noncommercial Computer Software Documentation, or Rights in Noncommercial Technical Data and Computer Software-Small Business Innovative Research (SBIR) Program clause(s) of this contract.

The clauses specified in ¶ (2) give protection to all properly marked technical data pertaining to items, components, or processes developed at private expense and all computer software developed at private expense as well as to all such data developed with mixed funding. However, the clause does not cover management and financial data. Thus, such data that is submitted with the prescribed proprietary legends would appear to be protected.

Both 10 U.S.C. § 2305(g) and 41 U.S.C. § 4702(b) prohibits disclosure of proposal data pursuant to requests under the Freedom of Information Act, 5 U.S.C. § 552, unless it is incorporated in the contract by reference. These statutes would appear to override the above contract language limiting the protection for the winning contractor.

FAR 15.309 provides additional instructions concerning the protection of data in unsolicited proposals. This procedure directs contracting officers to protect data in proposals even though legends are omitted and advises contracting officers to attempt to persuade offerors to delete legends that are different from the prescribed legend. This procedure also authorizes contracting officers to reject proposals with deviating legends. See, however, *Xerxe Group, Inc. v. United States*, 278 F.3d 1357 (Fed. Cir. 2002), where the court ignored the FAR language calling for the protection of unmarked data and held that the offeror gave up all rights by not marking the data. This decision requires companies submitting unsolicited proposals to carefully follow the FAR marking instructions. See also FAR 15.609(e), noting that the provisions of the Freedom of Information Act override this government promise to protect information — as was established in *Petkas v. Staats*, 501 F.2d 887, 163 U.S. App. D.C. 327 (D.C. Cir. 1974).

## V.  COMMUNICATIONS TO FACILITATE EVALUATION

Following the submission of offers, there are many occasions when communications between the government and one or more of the offerors would facilitate the evaluation process. After the receipt of initial offers, such communications can assist the government in determining whether to make an award on initial proposals or in deciding which offerors should be included in the competitive range. Communications can also be helpful if questions arise after the submission of final revised offers. In these situations, communications may also be necessary when mistakes are suspected or alleged. However, if any of these communications become "discussions," the government loses the right to award without conducting discussions with all offerors in the competitive range.

This limitation on the ability of an agency to communicate with offerors during proposal evaluation places contracting officials in a dilemma. To maximize efficiency, they want to award contracts on the basis of the initial proposals as frequently as possible, and if they establish a competitive range and conduct discussions, they want to award a contract based on the final proposal revisions that are received thereafter. Yet, in both of these situations, they do not want to award a contract without fully understanding the proposals of the competitors. Thus, they may need to communicate with one or more offerors during evaluation of the proposals of final proposal revisions. Limited communications, called "clarifications," are permissible, but contracting officials must always be conscious of the need to avoid conducting discussions. Unfortunately, the statutes, regulations and decisions in this area have not been very helpful in assisting them in deciding what communications with one or more offerors would preclude award without discussions or would require reopening discussion with all other offerors within the competitive range.

An attempt to permit more robust communications was made in the FAR Part 15 Rewrite effort in 1996-97. However, there was criticism of the initial rule, relaxing the rules on communications, because of its perceived potential for unfair treatment of the competitors. This concern was addressed in the comments explaining the final rule, which backed off of the initial rule, at 62 Fed. Reg. 51226 (1997):

> Some respondents expressed concerns that the increased exchanges between the Government and industry throughout the acquisition process increased the risk of unfair practices. The final rule encourages earlier and more meaningful exchanges of information between the Government and potential contractors to achieve a better understanding of the Government's requirements and the offerors' proposals. This rule contains limits on exchanges that preclude favoring one offeror

over another, revealing offerors' technical solutions, revealing prices without the offerors' permission, and knowingly furnishing source selection information.

The result has been that the current rule in FAR 15.306 has not encouraged "more meaningful exchanges" but has left contracting officials in the same dilemma that they faced before the FAR Rewrite.

There has never been any doubt that fair treatment of the competitors was the key consideration in determining whether a communication with one offeror required similar communications with other offerors. See *General Physics Fed. Sys., Inc.*, Comp. Gen. Dec. B-275934, 97-1 CPD ¶ 171, stating:

> Our decisions sustaining protests that an agency held discussions with only one offeror — a scenario found in a minority of our meaningful discussions cases, which usually present distinctions between clarifications and discussions or challenges to the adequacy of discussions the agency intended to hold — have generally focused on the inherent unfairness of agency actions that fail to provide unsuccessful offerors the same opportunity as the awardee to improve their relative standing in a negotiated competition. *Raytheon Co.*, B-261959.3 , Jan. 23, 1996, 96-1 CPD ¶37, at 11-12; *Paramax Sys. Corp.*; *CAE-Link Corp.*, B-253098.4 ; B-253098.5 , Oct. 27, 1993, 93-2 CPD ¶282, at 6. In such cases, we generally conclude that if the protester had been given the opportunity to address evaluator concerns during discussions it would have submitted a materially revised proposal, and the outcome of the competition might have been changed. *Raytheon Co.*, *supra*, at 12, n.11.

Thus, it appears that in close questions as to the classification of communications, the decision will be based upon considerations of whether an offeror has been treated unfairly or whether another offeror has been given favorable unequal treatment.

## A.  Development of Statutory and Regulatory Language

At the center of the confusion over the effect of communications are the statutory terms "discussions" and "clarification," neither of which are defined in the statutes. The term " discussions" was originally incorporated into 10 U.S.C. § 2304 by Pub. L. No. 87-653 on Sept. 10, 1962, providing for oral or written discussions with all offerors within the competitive range and award on initial proposals without discussions. GAO interpreted these provisions as requiring "discussions" with all offerors in the competitive range "if negotiations (i.e., discussions) be conducted with one of the offerors," 46 Comp. Gen. 191 (B-158686), 1966 CPD ¶ 76. The regulations did not attempt to define "discussions" until the FAR was published in April 1984. At that time the term "clarification" was also defined as a communication distinct from a "discussion." Shortly thereafter, the Competition in Contracting Act, Pub. L. No. 98-369, provided that "discussions conducted for the purpose of minor clarification" would not prohibit award without discussions. The same terminology is now contained in 10 U.S.C. § 2305(b)(4)(A), as follows:

The head of an agency shall evaluate competitive proposals in accordance with paragraph (1) and may award a contract —

> (i) after discussions with the offerors, provided that written or oral discussions have been conducted with all responsible offerors who submit proposals within the competitive range; or

> (ii) based on the proposals received, without discussions with the offerors (other than discussions conducted for the purpose of minor clarification) provided that the solicitation included a statement that proposals are intended to be evaluated, and award made, without discussions, unless discussions are determined to be necessary.

Essentially the same language is contained in 41 U.S.C. § 3703(a).

The following definitions of "clarification" and "discussion" remained in FAR 15.601 until they were removed by the FAR Part 15 Rewrite:

> "Clarification," as used in this subpart, means communication with an offeror for the sole purpose of eliminating minor irregularities, informalities, or apparent clerical mistakes in the proposal. It is achieved by explanation or substantiation, either in response to Government inquiry or as initiated by the offeror. Unlike discussion (see definition below), clarification does not give the offeror an opportunity to revise or modify its proposal, except to the extent that correction of apparent clerical mistakes results in a revision.

> "Discussion," as used in this subpart, means any oral or written communication between the Government and an offeror (other than communications conducted for the purpose of minor clarification), whether or not initiated by the Government, that (a) involves information essential for determining the acceptability of a proposal, or (b) provides the offeror an opportunity to revise or modify its proposal.

In addition, FAR 15.607 contained detailed provisions dealing with mistakes disclosed before award. That entire section was also removed in the Rewrite.

Post-submission communications are now addressed under FAR 15.306 titled, "Exchanges with offerors after receipt of proposals." Three types of exchanges are covered: (1) communications and award without discussion, (2) communications prior to establishing the competitive range, and (3) negotiations with offerors within the competitive range. This section discusses the first two types of communications. It also discusses the treatment of mistakes alleged before award. Negotiations with offerors within the competitive range will be discussed in a following section.

## B. Communications and Award Without Discussions

FAR 15.306(a) contains the following coverage of communications (termed clarifications) prior to award without discussions:

(a) *Clarifications and award without discussions.* (1) Clarifications are limited exchanges, between the Government and offerors, that may occur when award without discussions is contemplated.

> (2) If award will be made without conducting discussions, offerors may be given the opportunity to clarify certain aspects of proposals (e.g., the relevance of an offeror's past performance information and adverse past performance information to which the offeror has not previously had an opportunity to respond) or to resolve minor or clerical errors.

The comments accompanying its publication indicate that the deletion of the previous definitions and the adoption of the above language were intended to permit increased exchanges of information while still complying with the statutory requirements for award without discussions. See 62 Fed. Reg. 51228-29 (1997), stating:

> (1) *Clarifications.* We drafted the rule to allow as much free exchange of information between offerors and the Government as possible, while still permitting award without discussions and complying with applicable statutes. The proposed rule did not differentiate between exchanges of information when award without discussions was contemplated versus when a competitive range would be established. Public comment pointed out that the proposed rule language may allow exchanges beyond what is permitted by applicable statute when making award without discussions. In drafting the second proposed rule, we limited these exchanges. The resulting language still permits more exchange of information between offerors and the Government than the current FAR. This policy is expected to help offerors, especially small entities that may not be familiar with proposal preparation, by permitting easy clarification of limited aspects of their proposals.

An earlier draft would have enabled the government to obtain "relevant information (in addition to that submitted in the offeror's proposal) needed to understand and evaluate the offeror's proposal." It further provided that "[t]he nature and extent of communications between the Government and offerors is a matter of contracting officer judgment."

The statutory term "minor clarification" and the FAR term "limited exchanges" are not in themselves meaningful. Relatively small bits of information can result in an offer being revised. Thus, in determining the extent to which the final Rewrite "permits more exchange of information" than the prior FAR rules, it is necessary to consider the purpose of the exchange. If the exchange is intended to obtain a revision in the offer, oral or written discussions and final revised offers will be required. Conversely, it would appear that information exchanges which are conducted with all offerors that are similarly situated and do not vary the terms of their offers should not preclude award without discussions. Some decisions of GAO and the Court of Federal Claims have looked outside of FAR 15.306(a) to arrive at this interpretation of the permissible scope of clarifications. See *Antarctic Support Assocs. v. United States*, 46 Fed. Cl. 145 (2000); *Cubic Def. Sys., Inc. v. United States*, 45 Fed. Cl. 450 (1999); and *MG Indus.*, Comp. Gen. Dec. B-283010.3, 2000 CPD ¶ 17, looking to the FAR 15.306(d) rule on "discussions" and reasoning that if a discussion pursuant to that definition did not occur, the agency must have been conducting clarifications. Using different reasoning, the court in *Information Tech. & Applications Corp. v. United States*, 51 Fed. Cl. 340 (2001), affirmed in a 2 to 1 decision, 316 F. 3d 1312 (Fed. Cir. 2003), held that the additional information sought by the contracting officer was better described by the rule in FAR 15.306(b) but that, since it did not fall within the rule in FAR 15.306(d), it was a permissible clarification. This reasoning is understandable because exchanges that occur during the initial evaluation of proposals are simultaneously covered by the rules in both FAR 15.306(a) and (b). However, GAO decisions discussed below do not always follow this seemingly logical distinction between "clarifications" and "discussions."

## 1. Communications Concerning Offer Revisions

A major problem with the statutory and regulatory coverage of discussions and clarifications has been the ambiguous use of the word "proposal" — sometimes referring to the entire submission of each offeror (the offer plus information solicited by the RFP) and other times referring only to the offer. While any changes or additions to information will result in a revision to the information that was included in the proposal, such changes or additions should be distinguished from offer revisions. Revisions are defined in FAR 15.001, as follows:

> "Proposal revision" is a change to a proposal made after the solicitation closing date, at the request of or as allowed by a contracting officer, as the result of negotiations.

While the word "proposal" is used in this definition, a reasonable interpretation is that it refers to offers only without including the information that has been submitted in response to the RFP. This interpretation makes the most sense because the definition indicates that these revisions result from "negotiations" and it is not likely that the contracting officer would negotiate over information. Generally, negotiations are conducted over the terms of the offer, which will be incorporated into the contract. Such revisions would result from changes in the price, time for performance, description of the work or other terms of the contract.

However the word "proposal" is interpreted, it is clear that changes to the offer made in a proposal can not be considered to be clarifications. See, for example, *General Dynamics One Source LLC*, Comp. Gen. Dec. B-400340.5, 2010 CPD ¶ 45 (mandatory percentage of costs at which award fee had to be proposed could only have been corrected during discussions); *Manthos Eng'g., LLC*, Comp. Gen. Dec. B-401751, 2009 CPD ¶ 216 (mandatory option prices could not be obtained through a clarification); *Kellogg Brown & Root Servs., Inc.*, Comp. Gen. Dec. B-400614.3, 2009 CPD ¶ 50 (offeror's "assumption" attached to its cost proposal that raised question whether it would comply with mandatory technical specification could only be cleared up by discussions); *Tiger Truck, LLC*, Comp. Gen. Dec. B-400685, 2009

CPD ¶ 19 (obtaining revised prices constituted discussions); *C. Young Constr., Inc.*, Comp. Gen. Dec. B-309740, 2007 CPD ¶ 198 (offeror's proposal to staff job that did not comply with mandatory specification could only be cleared up by discussions); *Nu-Way, Inc.*, Comp. Gen. Dec. B-296435.5, 2005 CPD ¶ 195 (ambiguity in offeror's proposal as to whether its equipment met mandatory requirement could only be resolved by discussions); *Cooperativa Maratori Riuniti-Anese*, B-294747, 2004 CPD ¶ 210 (allowing offeror to revise offer to meet required completion data could only be done through discussions); *DynCorp Int'l LLC*, Comp. Gen. Dec. B-294232, 2004 CPD ¶ 187 (allowing offeror to explain inadequacies in mandatory staffing plan would have required discussions); *Priority One Servs., Inc.*, Comp. Gen. Dec. B-288836, 2002 CPD ¶ 79 (changes to cost proposal); *International Res. Group*, Comp. Gen. Dec. B-286663, 2001 CPD ¶ 35 (email containing a list of "technical and cost comments"); *Dubinsky v. United States*, 43 Fed. Cl. 243 (1999) (telephone call discussion to "clear up" specification compliance and warranties); and *Wellco Enters., Inc.*, Comp. Gen. Dec. B-282150, 99-1 CPD ¶ 107 (allowing offeror to clear up proposed deviations to the contract specifications would have been a discussion). Compare *S4, Inc.*, Comp. Gen. Dec. B-299817, 2007 CPD ¶ 164, holding that a request that the offeror confirm that it would comply with contract requirement was not a discussion because it did not allow the offeror to alter the offer.

In *Language Servs. Assocs., Inc.*, Comp. Gen. Dec. B-297392, 2006 CPD ¶ 20, GAO did not follow this reasoning but held that a "clarification" of the quoted prices stating that the offeror "would like to reserve the right to negotiate with the [agency] an adjustment in pricing" if the agency's estimated quantities were incorrect was not a discussion.

## 2. Communications Concerning Information

While it is clear that communications concerning revisions to offers are not permitted, information exchanges which do not concern changes to offers may be appropriate in the clarification process. However, it is useful to distinguish between information concerning the capability of the offeror and information relating to the features of the offer. While the former should clearly fall under the FAR 15.206(a) "minor clarification" category, past decisions dealing with information relating to the offer make inclusion of this type of communication more problematic.

As noted above, the distinction between clarifications and discussions is particularly difficult because the decisions use the ambiguous word "proposal" in ruling on this issue. For many years, GAO has stated, as in *Government Telecomms., Inc.*, Comp. Gen. Dec. B-299542.2, 2007 CPD ¶ 136:

> The "acid test" for deciding whether discussions have been held is whether it can be said that an offeror was provided the opportunity to modify its proposal. *National Beef Packing Co.*, B-296534, Sept. 1, 2005, 2005 CPD ¶ 168 at 11; *Park Tower Mgmt. Ltd.*, B-295589, B-295589.2, Mar. 22, 2005, 2005 CPD ¶ 77 at 7.

As discussed below, the question of whether the communication gave the offeror an "opportunity to modify its proposal" is decided on a case-by-case basis. While GAO decisions are somewhat confusing, they generally indicate that obtaining information to make a proposal "acceptable" is a discussion, while information supporting a proposal that has already been determined to be "acceptable" is a clarification.

### a. Capability Information

Capability information deals with the offeror's ability to perform as promised, as opposed to information pertaining to what has been promised. FAR 15.306(a)(2) recognizes that this is an appropriate area of communication, identifying past performance information as an example of the class of information which should be subject to "clarification." This distinction was also recognized under prior regulations when offerors were determined to be capable because they were "responsible" companies. In *Hercules, Inc.*, Comp. Gen. Dec. B-167643, Jan. 20, 1970, *Unpub.*, GAO stated:

> [W]e conclude that an offeror's responsibility or ability to perform may be discussed without foreclosing the right of the contracting officer to invoke the exception to the requirement for conducting written or oral discussions. Any other conclusion would either deprive the government of the right to make award on the basis of initial proposals or allow such an award only at the peril of dealing with nonresponsible contractors.

Subsequently, however, GAO reached the curious conclusion that determining responsibility and assessing capability were different functions that should be subject to different rules. See *Edgewater Mach. & Fabricators, Inc.*, Comp. Gen. Dec. B-219828, 85-2 CPD ¶ 630, stating:

> Although we recognize that a successful negotiated procurement requires both an acceptable proposal and a capable contractor, we find no substance to Edgewater's argument that the determination of the acceptability of the proposal and the capability of the prospective contractor are inextricably intertwined. The FAR, at 48 C.F.R. §§ 15.610 and 15.611, clearly relates to the discussions necessary to determine the acceptability of a proposal and the best and final offers that must follow such discussions. FAR, 48 C.F.R. § 9.100, clearly indicates that the purpose of a preaward survey is to evaluate the capability of the prospective contractor to perform the contract. See *Saxon Corp.*, B-216148, Jan. 23, 1985, 85-1 CPD ¶ 87. Thus, the determinations as to the acceptability of a proposal and the capability of an offeror involve distinct functions for different purposes usually performed at different times by different people. Moreover, the record here demonstrates that the survey team did not step outside the bounds of its responsibility evaluation. This is illustrated by Edgewater's statement that the survey included:
>
> > " . . . a physical survey of the manufacturing facilities, its equipment, the quality control program, what subcontracting programs were envisaged, inquiries as to quotations from seller of long lead items and all of the other

matter which go into a sound manufacturing operation. Before and after the actual day of this visit of the pre-award survey team, [Edgewater] had been supplying financial data to DCAAS in Orlando as a part of the pre-award survey."

These are all appropriate matters on which to base a responsibility determination and are consistent with the requirements of FAR, 48 C.F.R. § 9.104, that set forth the general and special standards to be applied by the survey team in its evaluations.

Thus, the typical actions during responsibility determinations where not found to be discussions, *Kitco, Inc.*, Comp. Gen. Dec. B-221386, 86-1 CPD ¶ 321 (requesting and furnishing information regarding background and capability of proposed subcontractor did not preclude award without discussions); *Dynamic Res., Inc.*, Comp. Gen. Dec. B-277213, 97-2 CPD ¶ 100 (preaward survey not improper discussions); *Unicco Gov't Servs., Inc.*, Comp. Gen. Dec. B-277658, 97-2 CPD ¶ 134 (site visit to offeror's facility and inspection of equipment did not constitute discussions); and *McKissacki + Delcan JV II*, Comp. Gen. Dec. B-401973.2, 2010 CPD ¶ 28 (determining whether offeror had compliant accounting system). The same rule is followed with regard to exchanges the determine whether an offeror's plan to mitigate an organizational conflict of interest is satisfactory, *Cahaba Safeguard Administrators, LLC* Comp. Gen. Dec. B-401844.2, 2010 CPD ¶ 39 ("such exchanges are more closely related to matters concerning the offeror's responsibility"). The same result was reached in *C2C Solutions, Inc.*, Comp. Gen. Dec. B-401106.6, 2010 CPD ¶ 145.

FAR 15.306(a) is not clear as to whether these decisions allowing communications to determine responsibility of the offeror as part of the clarification process permit the same amount of communication when an agency intends to evaluate the capability of the offerors on a relative basis, as is normally done in a tradeoff procurement. However, the Federal Circuit appears to have concluded that similar reasoning should be followed in ascertaining the scope of FAR 15.306(a). See *Information Tech. & Applications Corp. v. United States*, 316 F.3d 1312 (Fed. Cir. 2003), holding that requests for information about the qualifications of subcontractors and the amount of work they would perform were clarifications not discussions because the information did not "change the terms of its proposal to make it more appealing to the government." This decision indicates that weight should be given to the intent of the agency in communication with the offerors. Hence, when an agency intends to probe capability information in the clarification process, this should be clearly stated in the RFP. Furthermore, all offerors should be treated in the same manner when this type of clarification is conducted. This will ensure that no offeror is given a preference prior to award without discussions by being given the opportunity to supplement or explain its capability while a competitor is not given the same opportunity.

GAO had reached the same result as the court in *Information Tech. & Applications Corp.*, B-288510, 2002 CPD ¶ 28, reasoning that this subcontractor information pertained to the relevance of the offeror's past performance. Several court decisions have also followed similar reasoning. See *Antarctic Support Assocs. v. United States*, 46 Fed. Cl. 145 (2000) (the names of references to vouch for the fact that a proposed subcontractor would continue to operate in the face of a declaration of bankruptcy); and *Forestry Surveys & Data v. United States*, 44 Fed. Cl. 493 (1999) (several offerors queried about aspects of their performance on prior contracts). See also *Griffy's Landscape Maint., LLC v. United States*, 46 Fed. Cl. 257 (2000), holding that an agency was *obligated* to verify a lack of required information relating to an offeror's insurance coverage in its proposal. The court reasoned that not including such information was a mistake that was apparent to the contracting officer and, therefore, should have led to a verification request. The court held that such a verification request was in the nature of a clarification not a discussion.

Subsequent GAO decisions have not followed the broad reasoning of the court in *Information Technology*. See, for example, *Computer Scis. Corp.*, Comp. Gen. Dec. B-298494.2, 2007 CPD ¶ 103, where GAO explicitly rejected the argument that subcontracting plans could be made acceptable through the clarification process. In reaching this conclusion, it stated that its prior decisions holding that improvement of a subcontracting plan during an assessment of responsibility of the offeror was not a discussion did not apply when capability of the offerors was to be determined on a comparative basis. However, GAO has sometimes found that capability information can be obtained through the clarification process. See, for example, *SOS Int'l, Ltd.*, Comp. Gen. Dec. B-402558.3, 2010 CPD ¶ 131 (determining whether joint venturer would be used on contract); *Kuhana-Spectrum Joint Venture, LLC*, Comp. Gen. Dec. B-400803, 2009 CPD ¶ 36 (missing certifications and representations can be corrected during clarification); *USGC, Inc.*, Comp. Gen. Dec. B-400184.2, 2009 CPD ¶ 9 (explanations of composition of labor in acceptable technical proposals properly obtained through clarifications); *United Med. Sys.-DE, Inc.*, Comp. Gen. Dec. B-298438, 2006 CPD ¶ 148 (obtaining information showing that offeror had necessary equipment to perform work promised by the offer was proper clarification); *Park Tower Mgmt. Ltd.*, Comp. Gen. Dec. B-295589, 2005 CPD ¶ 77, and *Park Tower Mgmt. Ltd. v. United States*, 67 Fed. Cl. 548 (2005) (checking with offeror to determine whether it still intended to hire incumbent contractor's personnel was proper clarification); *AHNTECH, Inc.*, Comp. Gen. Dec. B-293582, 2004 CPD ¶ 113 (52 "clarification requests" seeking more information on how offeror would perform the work were proper clarifications); and *Citrus Coll.*, Comp. Gen. Dec. B-293543, 2004 CPD ¶ 104 (obtaining explanation of manning chart a proper clarification).

Other GAO decisions reach the opposite conclusion holding that capability information can only be obtained through discussions when the information is obtained to determine the "acceptability" of a proposal. See *General Injectables & Vaccines, Inc.*, Comp. Gen. Dec. B-298590, 2006 CPD ¶ 173 (clearing up inadequate responses to a significant number of the system security plan questions not proper clarification when offeror had to submit an acceptable plan to qualify for award); *T.J. Lambrecht Constr., Inc.*, Comp. Gen. Dec. B-294425, 2004 CPD ¶ 198 (obtaining experience information that offeror had omitted from proposal could not be done through clarification process); *Verizon Fed., Inc.*, Comp. Gen. Dec. B-293527, 2004 CPD ¶ 186 (obtaining resumes required to be submitted with proposal would have constituted discussions); *ACS State Healthcare, LLC*, Comp. Gen. Dec. B-292981, 2004 CPD ¶ 57 (amplifying poorly written aspects of technical proposal could not have been done through obtaining clarifications); *Ballast Ham Dredging BV*, Comp. Gen. Dec. B-291848, 2003 CPD ¶ 76 (obtaining required information on capability to schedule work would have constituted discussions); *Priority One Servs., Inc.*, Comp. Gen. Dec. B-288836, 2002 CPD ¶ 79 (allowing offeror to substitute key personnel for those that were unavailable or unacceptable was a discussion); and *J.A.Jones/IBC J.V.*, Comp. Gen. Dec. B-285627, 2000 CPD ¶ 161 (obtaining additional information about the qualifications of offeror's design team would have been a discussion).

Allowing an offeror to provide required representations and certifications that have been omitted from a proposal is a clarification, *Kuhana-Spectrum Joint Venture, LLC*, Comp. Gen. Dec. B-400803, 2009 CPD ¶ 36; *Doty Bros. Equip. Co.*, Comp. Gen. Dec. B-274634 96-2 CPD ¶ 234. GAO reasoned that such an omission is a "minor irregularity" which can be corrected through the clarification process.

The provision in FAR 15.306(a)(2) that offerors "may" be given an opportunity to comment on adverse past performance information is permissive and, hence, a contracting officer may award without discussions to another offeror without obtaining such comments, *NMS Mgmt., Inc.*, Comp. Gen. Dec., B-286335, 2000 CPD ¶ 197; *U.S. Constructors, Inc.*, Comp. Gen. Dec. B-282776, 99-2 CPD ¶ 14; *Inland Servs. Corp.*, Comp. Gen. Dec. B-282272, 99-1 CPD ¶ 113; *Rohmann Servs., Inc.*, Comp. Gen. Dec. B-280154.2, 98-2 CPD ¶ 134. See *A.G. Cullen Constr., Inc.*, Comp. Gen. Dec. B-284049.2, 2000 CPD ¶ 45, holding that clarifications would be required in this situation if there was a clear abuse of discretion such as where there were obvious inconsistencies between a reference's narrative comments and the actual ratings the reference gives the offeror. See *United Coatings*, Comp. Gen. Dec. B-291978.2, 2003 CPD ¶ 146, applying this standard but finding no abuse of discretion because the agency had no reason to question the validity of the adverse information; *General Dynamics-Ordnance & Tactical Sys.*, Comp. Gen. Dec. B-295987, 2005 CPD ¶ 114, finding no abuse of discretion because agency had firsthand knowledge of the adverse information; and *Bannum, Inc.*, Comp. Gen. Dec. B-298281.2, 2006 CPD ¶ 163, finding no prejudice in failing to discuss adverse past performance information because protester had received high rating in spite of adverse information.

## b.  Offer Information

Early decisions dealing with offer information made a distinction between obtaining information explaining the features of an offer and revisions to the offer which would preclude award without discussions. See *Amram Nowak Assocs., Inc.,* Comp. Gen. Dec. B-187253, 76-2 CPD ¶ 454, stating:

> The question of what constitutes discussions depends on whether an offeror has been given a chance to revise or modify its proposal. 51 Comp. Gen. 479, 481, *supra.* Thus, we have held that a requested " clarification" which resulted in a price reduction constituted discussions. 48 Comp. Gen. 663 (1969). However, an explanation by an offeror of the basis of its price reduction without an opportunity to change its proposal was held not to constitute discussions. B-170989, B-170990, November 17, 1971.

See also *Keco Indus., Inc.,* Comp. Gen. Dec. B-170990, Nov. 17, 1971, *Unpub.,* stating:

> In B-167643, November 14, 1969, we stated that the discussions contemplated by the statute relate to proposals within the competitive range but not to discussions relating to an offeror's responsibility or the ability to perform. In B-170751, September 23, 1970, 50 Comp. Gen. [202], cited by Keco's counsel, one of the offerors failed to acknowledge an addendum which changed the specifications and thereby affected the price. This offeror orally acknowledged the amendment subsequent to the closing time for receipt of proposals. In the written confirmation of the oral acknowledgment requested by the procuring activity, the offeror confirmed that the price offered was based on the specifications as changed by the amendment. It was held that this exchange constituted negotiations and that award could no longer be made on the basis of the initial proposals.

> The meeting with Trane on August 21, 1970, was intended only as an opportunity for Trane to explain its price reductions and was in fact so limited. Presumably there was no opportunity for Trane to make any change in its proposal or for the government representatives to effect any change in the solicitation provisions. Therefore, we do not believe that the meeting constitutes a basis for invalidating the award.

However, following the adoption of the definition of "discussion" in the former FAR 15.601, communications were found to be discussions even though the terms of the offer were not changed. Those holdings were based on the language in the definition stating that discussion "involves information essential for determining the acceptability of a proposal." See *Integration Tech. Group, Inc.,* Comp. Gen. Dec. B-274288.5, 97-1 CPD ¶ 214 (identification of components to be furnished); *Integration Tech. Group,* Comp. Gen. Dec. B-274288, 97-1 CPD ¶ 214 (identification of components to be furnished); *Strategic Analysis, Inc.,* Comp. Gen. Dec. B-270075.4, 96-1 CPD ¶ 41 (inquiry of employment status of designated key employee where RFP required letters of intent for proposed key personnel not current employees). Compare *Houston Air, Inc.,* Comp. Gen. Dec. 292382, 2003 CPD ¶ 144, finding no discussions where agency sought corrections to weight and balance information; *SRS Techs.,* Comp. Gen. Dec. B-291618.2, 2003 CPD ¶ 70, finding no discussions where the agency obtained information on how accounting systems accounted for uncompensated overtime; *WECO Cleaning Specialists, Inc.,* Comp. Gen. Dec.

B-279305, 98-1 CPD ¶ 154, finding no discussions where the agency obtained cost or pricing data to ensure that the offeror's price was realistic; and *Robotic Sys. Tech.*, Comp. Gen. Dec. B-278195.2, 98-1 CPD ¶ 20, finding no discussions where the offeror explained its cost proposal but did not add any information that was not included in the original proposal.

There continues to be a variety of decisions under the current FAR 15.306(a). In general, obtaining information to explain an offeror's proposed costs or prices has been held to be a proper clarification as long as the offeror does not alter the proposed cost or price. See *Environmental Quality Mgmt., Inc.*, Comp. Gen. Dec. B-402247.2, 2010 CPD ¶ 75 (request to show that "fringe rate" had been applied to labor rates when rate was "hidden" in spreadsheet); *Allied Tech. Group, Inc.*, Comp. Gen. Dec. B-402135, 2010 CPD ¶ 152 (explanation that offeror would be bound by pricing of a line item that it had denoted as "n/a" in its proposal and that costs excluded by terms of proposal would not be required to perform work); *VMD Sys. Integrators, Inc.*, Comp. Gen. Dec. B-401037.4, 2009 CPD ¶ 252 (question whether proposed rates had been audited by DCAA); *Career Training Concepts, Inc. v. United States*, 83 Fed. Cl. 215 (2008), and *Career Training Concepts, Inc.*, Comp. Gen. Dec. B-311429, 2009 CPD ¶ 97 (request for the elements of the offeror's price and an explanation of the escalation rate used to determine the price); *Colson Servs. Corp.*, Comp. Gen. Dec. B-310971, 2008 CPD ¶ 85 (request as to whether offered rebates were on a monthly or annual basis a proper clarification because it did not represent "a meaningful opportunity to revise pricing"); *NCR Gov't Sys. LLC*, Comp. Gen. Dec. B-297959, 2006 CPD ¶ 82 (request for a revised catalog of prices when the offer contained all of the required prices with the catalog being merely a backup document); *SecureNet Co. v. United States*, 72 Fed. Cl. 800 (2006) (obtaining price realism analysis from DCAA was not a discussion); *SRS Techs.*, Comp. Gen. Dec. B-291618.2, 2003 CPD ¶ 70 (request for information on how accounting system dealt with uncompensated overtime); *Northeast MEP Servs., Inc.*, Comp. Gen. Dec. B-285963.9, 2001 CPD ¶ 66 (obtaining assurance that estimated costs covered all required services when some government evaluators thought the technical proposal might have indicated otherwise); and *MG Indus.*, Comp. Gen. Dec. B-283010.3, 2000 CPD ¶ 17 (obtaining assurance that proposed price covered solicitation requirements). These decisions frequently stated that the exchange is a clarification because the information was not required to determine the acceptability of the proposal.

The decisions vary with regard to obtaining information as to other elements of an offer. Most decisions hold that obtaining explanations about an offered product or service is a discussion. See *4D Security Solutions, Inc.*, Comp. Gen. Dec. B-400351.2, 2009 CPD ¶ 5 (explanation of characteristics of offered product could not be obtained during clarifications because this would allow the company to "materially alter or explain its quotation by having the agency consider information not contained within the four corners of its initial quotation"); *Government Telecomms., Inc.*, Comp. Gen. Dec. B-299542.2, 2007 CPD ¶ 136 (obtaining information to determine whether offered products were available on the market could not be done through clarifications because this "would have involved material changes to the offeror's proposal"); *Gemmo-CCC*, Comp. Gen. Dec. B-297447.2, 2006 CPD ¶ 182 (obtaining required information describing the offered product would consti-tute discussions because it "would involve submission of information necessary to make the proposal acceptable"); *Southern California Eng'g, Inc.*, Comp. Gen. Dec. B-296244, 2005 CPD ¶ 134 (obtaining missing pump specifications needed to deter-mine acceptability of product could only be done through discussions); *QuickHire, LLC*, Comp. Gen. Dec. B-293098, 2004 CPD ¶ 33 (clearing up vague or incomplete technical description of product offered would have required discussions); *ProMar*, Comp. Gen. Dec. B-292409, 2003 CPD ¶ 187 (obtaining missing product litera-ture showing compliance with specifications would have required discussions); and *eMind*, Comp. Gen. Dec. B-289902, 2002 CPD ¶ 82 (obtaining required course de-scriptions nor permissible through clarifications). Compare *Houston Air, Inc.*, Comp. Gen. Dec. B-292382, 2003 CPD ¶ 144 (obtaining updated information on product not a discussion when offeror had already submitted acceptable information); *Fire-arms Training Sys., Inc. v. United States*, 41 Fed. Cl. 743 (1998) (demonstration of offered computer-operated simulator does not bar award without discussions).

GAO has also held that obtaining information to clear up a "material propos-al deficiency" cannot be done through the clarification process, *URS Group, Inc.*, Comp. Gen. Dec. B-402820, 2010 CPD ¶ 175. In that case, the "deficiency" was naming the parent company, without the required security clearance, as the offeror while stating in the technical proposal that the work would be performed by a part of the company that had the required clearance. Similarly, in *Professional Performance Dev. Group, Inc.*, Comp. Gen. Dec. B-311273, 2008 CPD ¶ 101, GAO held that clarifications could not be used to clear up "informational deficiencies [that] would have required major revisions to the . . . proposal." See also *Sletten Cos./Sletten Constr. Co.*, Comp. Gen. Dec. B-402422, 2010 CPD ¶ 97; *Superior Gunite*, Comp. Gen. Dec. B-402392.2, 2010 CPD ¶ 83; and *eMind*, Comp. Gen. Dec. B-289902, 2002 CPD ¶ 82, stating that clarifications may not be used "to cure proposal defi-ciencies or material omissions, materially alter the technical or cost elements of the proposal, or otherwise revise the proposal." The quoted language is from the rule on communications prior to establishing a competitive range in FAR 15.306(b) — indi-cating that GAO is applying this test to determine when a clarification is precluded under FAR 15.306(a).

It can be seen that there is a lack of clarity in the decisions regarding the distinc-tion between clarifications and discussions when the government obtains additional information regarding offers. With the deletion of the FAR 15.601 definitions of discussions and clarification, and the stated intent of the drafters of the FAR Part 15 Rewrite, it is arguable that agencies should be permitted to seek explanations of of-fers before award without discussions. This would be in accord with earlier holdings of GAO prior to the adoption of the FAR.

If an agency adopts this interpretation of the FAR Part 15 Rewrite, it should clearly state in the RFP that it reserves the right to seek information clarifying any element of an offer prior to award without discussions. Thereafter, in following this procedure, it should exercise great care to ensure that all offerors are treated even-handedly. Thus, if any offeror is permitted to clarify its offer, all other offerors whose offers are not fully understood should also be given an opportunity to clarify or explain their offers.

### 3. The Permissive Nature Of Clarifications

Because FAR 15.306(a) is permissive rather than mandatory, most decisions hold that contracting officers have a great deal of discretion in determining whether to ask for clarification of some element of a proposal. See *Gulf Group, Inc. v. United States*, 61 Fed. Cl. 338 (2004), where the agency evaluation team stated that clarification of the protester's experience was necessary but the source selection official proceeded to award to a competitor without obtaining the clarification. The court denied the protest, stating at 360:

> In support of its argument that the Corps's failure to exercise its discretionary authority was itself an abuse of discretion, Gulf Group notes the announced goal of the clarifications policy: "This policy is expected to help offerors, especially small entities that may not be familiar with proposal preparation, by permitting easy clarification of limited aspects of their proposals." Gulf Group argues that it is exactly the sort of business this regulation was intended to benefit. But the benefit that was created, if it could even be characterized as such, was not the *right* to clarify information in proposals. The benefit, instead, is that whenever the contracting officials think a clarification of certain aspects of a proposal would be helpful, *they* have the discretion to seek such a clarification, even when discussions with all bidders would not occur. The FAR allows, but does not require, such exchanges to take place. As this Court has found, "an agency representative has broad discretion to decide whether to communicate with a firm concerning its performance history." *JWK International Corp v United States*, 52 Fed Cl 650, 661 (2002).

See also *Hi-Tec Sys., Inc.*, Comp. Gen. Dec. B-402590, 2010 CPD ¶ 156, holding that agencies have "broad discretion as to whether to seek clarification from offerors." Compare *L-3 Communications Eotech, Inc. v. United States*, 83 Fed. Cl. 643 (2008), granting a protest when the agency did not seek clarification of unclear information on conducting a test procedure but established a competitive range of one with a competitor with the intention of allowing that company to work out issues of noncompliance with the specifications during discussions. In contrast, in *JBlanco Enters., Inc.*, Comp. Gen. Dec. B-402905, 2010 CPD ¶ 186, a protest that a "minor" error in completing a demonstration project should have been clarified was denied on the grounds that allowing correction of the error would have defeated the purpose of the demonstration (to prove capability).

The discretionary clarification rule has resulted in a number of decisions holding that an agency is not required to permit an offeror to submit information explaining or rebutting adverse past performance information on which it has had no previous opportunity to comment. See *SKE Int'l, Inc.*, Comp. Gen. Dec. B-311383, 2008 CPD ¶ 111; *JWK Int'l Corp. v. United States*, 52 Fed. Cl. 650 (2002); *NMS Mgmt., Inc.*, Comp. Gen. Dec. B-286335, 2000 CPD ¶ 197. In *General Dynamics — Ordnance & Tactical Sys.*, Comp. Gen. Dec. B-295987, 2005 CPD ¶ 114, GAO indicated that giving an offeror such an opportunity would be required "where there clearly is a reason to question the validity of the past performance information" being used by the agency.

The discretionary clarification rule has also resulted in a number of decisions holding that clarifications can be conducted with only one offeror. See *DynCorp Int'l LLC v. United States*, 76 Fed. Cl. 528, 540 (2007), holding that it was proper to clear up minor issues with one offeror without clarifying the information submitted by the protester. See also *General Dynamics — Ordinance & Tactical Sys.*, Comp. Gen. Dec. B-295987, 2005 CPD ¶ 114, stating:

> [C]larifications, in contrast to discussions, do not trigger a requirement that the agency seek clarifications from other offerors. See *Landoll Corp.*, B-291381 et al., Dec. 23, 2002, 2003 CPD ¶ 40 at 8; *Priority One Servs., Inc.*, B-288836, B-288836.2, Dec. 17, 2001, 2002 CPD ¶ 79 at 5; *Global Assocs. Ltd.*, B-271693, B-271693.2, Aug. 2, 1996, 96-2 CPD ¶ 100 at 4. While we recognize that there may be a rare situation where it would be unfair to request clarification from one offeror but not from another, the mere fact that an agency requests clarification from one offeror and not another, does not constitute unfair treatment.

Similarly, in *INDUS Tech., Inc.*, Comp. Gen. Dec. B-297800.13, 2007 CPD ¶ 116, it was proper to not clarify whether a cover letter statement was intended to indicate that the offeror would not comply with a mandatory requirement even though the agency had clarified issues in other proposals, and in *Landoll Corp.*, Comp. Gen. Dec. B-291381, 2003 CPD ¶ 40, it was proper not to clarify issues because such action would not have changed the protester's competitive position. Thus, only when clarification with only one offeror is perceived as resulting in unfair treatment to another offeror, will such action be held to be improper.

## C. Communications Prior to Establishing the Competitive Range

The previous FAR did not deal with the subject of communications with parties prior to the establishment of the competitive range. The following detailed provisions were incorporated into FAR 15.306(b) by the FAR Part 15 Rewrite:

> (b) *Communications with offerors before establishment of the competitive range.* Communications are exchanges, between the Government and offerors, after re-

ceipt of proposals, leading to establishment of the competitive range. If a competitive range is to be established, these communications —

(1) Shall be limited to the offerors described in paragraphs (b)(1)(i) and (b)(1)(ii) of this section and —

(i) Shall be held with offerors whose past performance information is the determining factor preventing them from being placed within the competitive range. Such communications shall address adverse past performance information to which an offeror has not had a prior opportunity to respond; and

(ii) May only be held with those offerors (other than offerors under paragraph (b)(1)(i) of this section) whose exclusion from, or inclusion in, the competitive range is uncertain;

(2) May be conducted to enhance Government understanding of proposals; allow reasonable interpretation of the proposal; or facilitate the Government's evaluation process. Such communications shall not be used to cure proposal deficiencies or material omissions, materially alter the technical or cost elements of the proposal, and/or otherwise revise the proposal. Such communications may be considered in rating proposals for the purpose of establishing the competitive range;

(3) Are for the purpose of addressing issues that must be explored to determine whether a proposal should be placed in the competitive range. Such communications shall not provide an opportunity for the offeror to revise its proposal, but may address —

(i) Ambiguities in the proposal or other concerns (e.g., perceived deficiencies, weaknesses, errors, omissions, or mistakes (see 14.407)); and

(ii) Information relating to relevant past performance; and

(4) Shall address adverse past performance information to which the offeror has not previously had an opportunity to comment.

The promulgation comments indicate that these provisions were adopted to assuage the concerns of small business commenters. See 62 Fed. Reg. 51229 (1997):

Public comments indicated that the second proposed rule did not establish a "bright line" distinction between when communications conducted in order to establish a competitive range end, and when discussions begin. Small businesses were concerned that the Government may conduct inappropriate communications with selected offerors prior to the establishment of the competitive range to the detriment of small businesses. We revised the final rule to accommodate this concern by clearly defining when discussions begin. We adopted this alternative to preclude the occurrence of the inappropriate communications that concerned small businesses.

While these provisions seem unnecessary, they appear to give the contracting officer considerable discretion in seeking both offer and capability information on offers when their inclusion in the competitive range is uncertain. Seeking such information permits the agency to make the competitive range determination based on a full understanding of the proposal — furthering the goal of establishing a competitive range consisting of only those offerors that are most highly rated. The only limitation on such communications is that the offers may not be revised, FAR 15.306(b)(2) and (3). The only way to carry out the intent of this provision of facilitating the competitive range determination is to interpret the term "proposal" to mean "offer."

Where the evaluation indicates, with certainty, that an offer is outside the competitive range, communication is required for adverse past performance information which the offeror has not had an opportunity to address, FAR 15.306(b)(1)(i); *Americom Gov't Servs., Inc.*, Comp. Gen. Dec. B-292242, 2003 CPD ¶ 163 136. However, communications concerning other issues with the proposal are discretionary with the agency. See *L-3 Commc'ns EOTech, Inc.*, Comp. Gen. Dec. B-311453, 2008 CPD ¶ 139 (no requirement that agency ask offeror whether its test procedure was correctly written when the offered product had failed the procedure); *Professional Performance Dev. Group, Inc.*, Comp. Gen. Dec. B-311273, 2008 CPD ¶ 101 (no requirement that agency give protester the opportunity to correct significant informational deficiencies); *Government Telecomms., Inc.*, Comp. Gen. Dec. B-299542.2, 2007 CPD ¶ 136 (no requirement that agency allow offeror to cure "proposal deficiencies or material omissions"); and *The Cmty. P'ship LLC*, Comp. Gen. Dec. B-286844, 2001 CPD ¶ 38 (protester properly excluded from competitive range without communication because decision not uncertain and past performance not determining factor). With respect to offers that are clearly within the competitive range, there is no need for communications prior to the conduct of negotiations.

## D. Oral Presentations

As discussed earlier, oral presentations were incorporated into FAR 15.102 by the Rewrite. FAR 15.102(a) states that oral presentations can occur at any time during the acquisition process. Presentations that occur during the discussion process following the establishment of the competitive range will be controlled by the negotiation rules in FAR 15.306(d), which will be discussed in a later section. This section is concerned with communications during presentations prior to award without discussions and prior to the establishment of the competitive range.

FAR 15.102 appears to indicate that oral presentations conducted prior to award without discussions can encompass both capability information and information explaining offers but may not be used to permit an offeror to alter its offer. It is clear that this regulation authorizes broadened exchange of information when oral presentations are conducted. FAR 15.102 does not use the term "clarification" and the FAR 15.102(c) suggested subjects for presentations consist of both capability and offer information. FAR 15.102(a) indicates that such presentations may "substitute for, or augment, written information," and that they are "subject to the same restrictions as written information." Thus, is appears that oral presentations should be subject to the same rules as written information. See also FAR 15.102(g) stating:

> If, during an oral presentation, the Government conducts discussions (see 15.306(d)), the Government must comply with 15.306 and 15.307.

This provision, by its reference to FAR 15.306(d), indicates that award on initial offers would be precluded only where the communications are the negotiations described in FAR 15.306(d).

The very nature of oral presentations involves obtaining additional information as to the capability of each offeror making a presentation. See FAR 15.102(a) and (b) describing oral presentations as a means for each offeror to submit "portions" or "part" of its proposal through such presentations. In such circumstances, the entire oral presentation process can be regarded as the initial obtaining of information to be used for evaluation of each offeror's capability and there can be no issue of proposal revision since all information submitted would be initial proposal information. This interpretation will be effective as long as the agency does not elicit information during the oral presentation that significantly varies information contained in the written proposal. See *Aliron Int'l, Inc.*, Comp. Gen. Dec. B-285048.2, 2000 CPD ¶ 125, denying a protest that discussions had occurred during an oral presentation. The dialog during an oral presentation also inevitably involves the exchange of information. Thus, it should be expected that a broader range of communications would be permitted where the presentations involve all offerors submitting acceptable offers. The government made this argument in *General Physics Fed. Sys., Inc.*, Comp. Gen. Dec. B-275934, 97-1 CPD ¶ 171. There, award was made after oral presentations, including a question and answer session, without a call for best and final offers. The protester provided information which was used by the government in downgrading its ranking. It argued that the oral presentations process constituted discussions and that it should have been given an opportunity to submit a best and final offer. GAO found that the protester was not prejudiced because the presentation process conducted by the government did not result in unfair treatment and resolved the protest on those grounds. However, it declined to rule on the issue of whether the oral presentation process should be treated differently from other communications. Subsequently, in *Sierra Military Health Servs., Inc.*, Comp. Gen. Dec. B-292780, 2004 CPD ¶ 55, GAO found that information provided in an oral presentation before the agency personnel had asked any questions "could not have been the result of discussions." In addition, GAO held that a question about the scope of the offeror's experience was a clarification request not a discussion. See also *Synoptic Sys. Corp.*, Comp. Gen. Dec. B-290789.4, 2003 CPD ¶ 42, where GAO treated an oral presentation as a means of obtaining information about the lines of communication within the offeror's organization On the other hand, allowing an offeror to change its offer as a result of the exchange during an oral presentation has been held to be a discussion, *Global Analysis Info. Tech. Servs., Inc.*, Comp. Gen. Dec. B-298840.2, 2007 CPD ¶ 57 (offeror changed option prices); *TDS, Inc.*, Comp. Gen. Dec. B-2988402, 2003 CPD ¶ 204 (offeror changed price and technical proposal). In any event, it is clear that agencies will be required to follow the procedure for an oral presentation described in the RFP and will also be required to treat all offerors evenhandedly in conducting oral presentations.

If any agency has decided to establish a competitive range, it does not appear likely that oral presentations would occur until after the range had been established. Then oral presentations would be conducted only with those offerors in the competitive range, and it would not matter if discussions occurred during the oral presentation or later in the process. See, for example, *L&M Techs., Inc.*, Comp. Gen. Dec. B-278044.5, 98-1 CPD ¶ 131, finding that the agency had followed proper procedures in conducting an oral presentation with offerors in the competitive range, conducting discussions immediately thereafter, obtaining and evaluating best and final offers, and obtaining another set of best and final offers without conducting additional oral presentations. See also *RTF/TCI/EAI J.V.*, Comp. Gen. Dec. B-280422.3, 98-2 CPD ¶ 162, where oral presentations were conducted only with offerors in the competitive range. If oral presentations were conducted in order to determine which offerors should be placed in the competitive range, the rules in FAR 15.306(b) would apply, but there would appear to be little or no harm if discussions occurred at this time since the offerors would be requested to submit final proposal revisions after the conclusion of discussions. See, e.g., *Dynamic Res., Inc.*, Comp. Gen. Dec. B-277213.2, 97-2 CPD ¶ 100.

FAR 15.102 contains the following additional guidance on the procedures to be followed when oral presentations are required:

> (e) The contracting officer shall maintain a record of oral presentations to document what the Government relied upon in making the source selection decision. The method and level of detail of the record (e.g., videotaping, audio tape recording, written record, Government notes, copies of offeror briefing slides or presentation notes) shall be at the discretion of the source selection authority. A copy of the record placed in the file may be provided to the offeror.

> (f) When an oral presentation includes information that the parties intend to include in the contract as material terms or conditions, the information shall be put in writing. Incorporation by reference of oral statements is not permitted.

While this regulation gives the contracting officer the choice of the method of documentation, GAO has granted protests when the documentation did not indicate the content of the presentation that led to a reduced score for the protester, *Checchi & Co. Consulting, Inc.*, Comp. Gen. Dec. B-285777, 2001 CPD ¶ 132. In that case there was conflicting evidence as to what subjects the protester had covered in its presentation and no "contemporaneous record" of the presentation. See also *Johnson Controls Sec. Sys.*, Comp. Gen. Dec. B-296490, 2007 CPD ¶ 102 (agency criticized for lack of any documentation or presentation); *e-LYNXX Corp.*, Comp. Gen. Dec. B-292761, 2003 CPD ¶ 219 (lack of documentation required hearing that produced conflicting testimony which did not resolve protest); *J & J Maint., Inc.*, Comp. Gen. Dec. B-284708.2, 2000 CPD ¶ 106 (evaluators' notes on the presentation insufficient because they did not summarize the presentation), and *Future-Tec Mgmt. Sys., Inc.*, Comp. Gen. Dec. B-283793.5, 2000 CPD ¶ 59 (lack of any documentation led to granting of protest). These cases indicate that some recording of the presentation should be made in order to create the type of evidence required by GAO. See *Resource Dimensions, LLC*, Comp. Gen. Dec. B-404536, 2011 CPD ¶ 50, granting a protest when the agency's notes on a question and answer session conflicted with the technical evaluation. The agency had videotaped the initial presentation of the protester but had not recorded the question and answer session with the result that the agency prepared notes and allowed the protester to edit the notes to reflect its answers to the agency's questions.

## E. Mistakes

The statutes do not deal with the subject of mistakes discovered or alleged prior to award. Prior to the FAR Rewrite, FAR 15.607 contained detailed procedures directing contracting officers to examine proposals for mistakes. Where communications were considered to prejudice "the interest of other offerors" or where correction of a mistake would require reference "to documents, worksheets, or other data outside the solicitation and proposal," the mistake could be corrected only through oral or written discussions with all offerors within the competitive range. These provisions were removed in the final Rewrite and the FAR now contains only fragmentary procedures for correction of mistakes.

Under the FAR Rewrite as was the case under the prior regulations, allegations of error and requests for *verification* and subsequent verifications that mistakes have not been made are not discussions but may be conducted as necessary to clarify whether a mistake has been made, *U.S. Facilities, Inc.*, Comp. Gen. Dec. B-293029, 2004 CPD ¶ 17; *R&B Rubber & Eng'g, Inc.*, Comp. Gen. Dec. B-214299, 84-1 CPD ¶ 595. Similarly, since a proposal may be *withdrawn* freely, communications resulting in withdrawal do not require discussions with all offerors. However, the FAR contains no explicit requirement that a contracting officer request verification when a mistake is suspected (as is the case in sealed bidding under FAR 14.407-1) and it is not clear whether GAO will impose such a requirement. Compare *CSE Constr.*, Comp. Gen. Dec. B-291268.2, 2002 CPD ¶ 207, holding that verification that a low price was not mistaken was required, with *FedSys, Inc.*, Comp. Gen. Dec. B-401453, 2009 CPD ¶ 181, holding that the agency was not permitted to verify whether seemingly irrational labor rates were mistaken because that would have been a discussion. See also *Griffy's Landscape Maint. LLC v. United States*, 46 Fed. Cl. 257 (2000), requiring a contracting officer to verify whether a mistake had been made when the offeror failed to provide the name and telephone number of a point of contact for its insurer — a failure which the court concluded was a "clerical mistake."

The deletion of the pre-Rewrite FAR 15.607 and its requirements for *correction* of mistakes through the discussion process raises the question of what types of mistakes may be corrected without requiring discussions with all offerors in the competitive range. It appears that the authors of the FAR Part 15 Rewrite intended to adopt the rule applicable to sealed bidding when they indicated in FAR 15.001 that a "Proposal modification" is a change made to a proposal "to correct a mistake at any time before award." This would allow correction of mistakes prior to award without discussions as is done in sealed bidding procurements. See FAR 14.407 and the discussion in Chapter 5, Section IV. Application of these rules would require that the contracting officer request verification of an offer whenever a mistake was suspected and would permit correction of a mistake at any time that it met the requirements of the regulation. This would permit the contracting officer to deal with mistakes as they were identified or disclosed without losing the right to award the contract without discussions. See *U.S. Facilities, Inc.*, Comp. Gen. Dec. B-293029, 2004 CPD ¶ 17, holding that asking the offeror to verify its price or request correction of a mistake did not constitute discussions. Thus, logically correction of a mistake to an *offer* should not be treated as a clarification but as a distinct process that should routinely occur as an agency is evaluating a proposal. Stated differently, correction of a mistake in an offer should be considered to be the only alteration to an offer that can properly occur prior to award without discussions — as occurs regularly in the sealed bidding process.

However, FAR 15.306(a) includes communications to "resolve minor or clerical errors" as an element of "clarifications" with the result that decisions have focused on whether a mistake was a "minor or clerical error." Court decisions have been willing to give this term a relatively broad construction. See *Galen Med. Assocs., Inc. v. United States*, 369 F.3d 1324 (Fed. Cir. 2004), permitting an offeror to raise its price to correct an "obvious" mathematical error prior to award without discussions, and *International Res. Recovery, Inc. v. United States*, 64 Fed. Cl. 150 (2005), permitting an offeror to correct a tonnage capacity when the contracting officer concluded from the proposal that it had stated a monthly capacity when it meant to state an annual capacity.

In contrast, GAO has held that a mistake cannot be a minor or clerical error, correctable in the clarification process, unless it is apparent on the face of the proposal. See *Environmental Quality Mgmt., Inc.*, Comp. Gen. Dec. B-402247.2, 2010 CPD ¶ 75 (transposition of percentage of work to be done by team members not reasonably identifiable in proposal); *Joint Venture Penauillie Italia S.p.A.; Cofathec S.p.A.; SEB.CO S.a.s.; CO.PEL.S.a.s.*, Comp. Gen. Dec. B-298865, 2007 CPD ¶ 7 (omission of option year pricing not a correctable mistake during the clarification process, because the existence of the mistake and the amount intended by the offeror was not clear from the face of the proposal); *Paraclete Contracts*, Comp. Gen. Dec. B-299883, 2007 CPD ¶ 153 (improper to obtain clarification of ambiguous prices by using mistake correction procedures because the prices were not "apparent on the face of its offer"); *Battelle Mem'l Inst.*, Comp. Gen. Dec. B-299533, 2007 CPD ¶ 94 (decision not to obtain clarification of omitted option prices by using mistake correction procedures proper because the prices "were not apparent on the face of the proposal"); *CIGNA Gov't Servs., LLC*, Comp. Gen. Dec. B-297915.2, 2006 CPD ¶ 74 (improper to obtain clarification of level of effort in final proposal revision when correct level was not apparent on revision's face); and *Omega World Travel, Inc.*, Comp. Gen. Dec. B-283218, 2002 CPD ¶ 5 (correcting erroneous application of discount rate could only be done through discussions). In a few cases, errors have been found to be correctable because they were minor or clerical, *EMS Ice, Inc.*, Comp. Gen. Dec. B-401688.3, 2009 CPD ¶ 211 (line item prices had not been carried forward correctly to "Net" amount for each line item); *IPlus, Inc.*, Comp. Gen. Dec. B-298020, 2006 CPD ¶ 90 (contract line item prices corrected to match sub line item prices and to delete the price from a contract line item that called for no price); *National Beef Packing Co.*, Comp. Gen. Dec. B-296534, 2005 CPD ¶ 168 (labeling of a product (changing "case ready ground beef" to "coarse ground beef") corrected because the specifications clearly called for coarse ground beef).

FAR 15.306(b)(3)(i) includes "errors, omissions, or mistakes (see 14.407)" as items which might be addressed prior to the establishment of the competitive range. This appears to indicate that there is more discretion to correct mistakes prior to establishing the competitive range — permitting an agency to correct a mistake that kept an offeror out of the competitive range. However, there are several decisions holding that agencies have the discretion to refuse to allow an offeror to correct mistakes at this stage of the process. See *Battelle Mem'l Inst.*, Comp. Gen. Dec. B-299533, 2007 CPD ¶ 94 (alleged mistake held to be a "proposal deficiency" which should not be cleared up under this rule); *Aeronautical Instrument & Radio Co.*, Comp. Gen. Dec. B-298582.2, 2007 CPD ¶ 10 (protester did not furnish required evidence of mistake); and *U.S. Reconstruction & Dev. Corp.*, Comp. Gen. Dec. B-296195, 2005 CPD ¶ 126 (proposing nonconforming work not type of mistake that fell within rule).

# VI. EVALUATION OF PROPOSALS

Evaluation is an ongoing process that starts upon the receipt of proposals, continues during communications and negotiations, and concludes with the evaluation of final proposal revisions. The purpose of evaluation is to assess the quality of each offer and to determine the capability of each offeror. However, this may be done only by evaluating proposals in terms of the evaluation factors set forth in the RFP. The results of proposal evaluation are explained in narrative comments of the evaluators and are generally summarized in some type of scoring system. FAR 15.305(a) states the basic rules for proposal evaluation as follows:

> Proposal evaluation is an assessment of the proposal and the offeror's ability to perform the prospective contract successfully. An agency shall evaluate competitive proposals and then assess their relative qualities solely on the factors and subfactors specified in the solicitation. Evaluations may be conducted using any rating method or combination of methods, including color or adjectival ratings, numerical weights, and ordinary rankings. The relative strengths, deficiencies, significant weaknesses, and risks supporting proposal evaluation shall be documented in the contract file.

## A. The Evaluation Process

Because there is no guidance in the FAR on the methodology used by agencies to evaluate proposals, they are free to perform the evaluation in any manner that ensures fairness and objectivity. See FAR 1.102-2(c)(3) stating that "[a]ll . . . prospective contractors shall be treated fairly and impartially but need not be treated the same." This requires that, after receipt, all proposals must be evaluated, FAR 15.306(c)(1), and such evaluation should be done with the same degree of care. Thereafter, agencies may drop excessively deficient proposals from the evaluation process. See *Douglass Colony/Kenny Solar, JV*, Comp. Gen. Dec. B-402649, 2010 CPD ¶ 142 (required information not included in technical proposal); *Mike Kessler Enters.*, Comp. Gen. Dec. B-401633, 2009 CPD ¶ 205 (unacceptable technical proposal); *L-3 Commc'ns EOTech, Inc.*, Comp. Gen. Dec. B-311453, 2008 CPD ¶ 139 (product failed to meet test); *USIA Underwater Equip. Sales Corp.*, Comp. Gen. Dec. B-292827.2, 2004 CPD ¶ 32 (sample product failed test); *Pride Mobility Prods. Corp.*, Comp. Gen. Dec. B-291878, 2003 CPD ¶ 80 (poor rating on one test requirement); *Sun Chem. Corp.*, Comp. Gen. Dec. B-288466, 2001 CPD ¶ 185 (sample product that did not meet safety standard); *LaBarge Prods., Inc.*, Comp. Gen. Dec. B-287841, 2001 CPD ¶ 177 (lack of "support and elaboration" on system to be furnished); *Good Food Serv., Inc.*, Comp. Gen. Dec. B-277145, 98-1 CPD ¶ 102 ("numerous and extensive informational deficiencies"); *Advanced Design Corp.*, Comp. Gen. Dec. B-275928, 98-1 CPD ¶ 100 (completely nonconforming proposal); *W&D Ships Deck Works, Inc. v. United States*, 39 Fed. Cl. 638 (1997) ("grossly deficient" proposal); *Inte-Great Corp.*, Comp. Gen. Dec. B-272780, 96-2 CPD ¶ 159 (proposal did not furnish information demonstrating compliance with mandatory requirements); *Dimensions Int'l/QSOFT, Inc.*, Comp. Gen. Dec. B-270966, 96-1 CPD ¶ 257 (proposal with inadequate response to sample task).

When an agency intends to separate the cost and technical evaluations, this procedure is usually facilitated by requiring the offerors to submit their cost and technical proposals in separate packages. In this situation, it has been common practice to withhold the cost information from technical personnel with the result that the technical package describes the work to be done but may not include a description of the resources (labor hours of the contractor and its major subcontractors) needed to perform the various tasks on the contract. Without such resource information, the technical evaluation will be imprecise at best. The FAR Part 15 Rewrite addresses this problem by providing in FAR 15.305(a)(4) that "[c]ost information may be provided to members of the technical evaluation team." A well-written RFP requires that such information be included in the technical package. If the RFP does not contain this requirement, the agency should extract the resource information (labor hours but not labor or indirect cost rates) from the cost proposal and provide it to the technical evaluators. This will permit them to arrive at an accurate assessment of the offerors' technical understanding of the requirements as well as their ability to perform the work described in the RFP. See *AmerInd, Inc.*, Comp. Gen. Dec. B-248324, 92-2 CPD ¶ 85, where GAO affirmed the contracting officer's adjustment of an offeror's cost proposal to reflect the salaries of personnel discussed in the technical proposal. See also *Satellite Servs., Inc.*, Comp. Gen. Dec. B-286508, 2001 CPD ¶ 30, where a protest was sustained because the winning offeror's low estimate of resources in its price proposal was not used by the technical evaluators to assess its understanding of the work.

Objectivity is generally sought by having the same evaluators review each proposal or portion of a proposal. However, if it is impractical to do so, proposals can be evaluated by different personnel. See *Design Concepts, Inc.*, Comp. Gen. Dec. B-186125, 76-2 CPD ¶ 365 (30 proposals divided among the evaluators); *T.V. Travel, Inc.*, 65 Comp. Gen. 109 (B-218198), 85-2 CPD ¶ 640 (37 proposals evaluated in six groups); and *Innovative Logistics Techniques, Inc.*, Comp. Gen. Dec. B-275786.2, 97-1 CPD ¶ 144 (one evaluator reviewed both proposals and two evaluators each reviewed one proposal). Oral presentations can also be evaluated by different personnel, *Quality Elevator Co.*, Comp. Gen. Dec. B-276750, 97-2 CPD ¶ 28. The key question is whether the evaluation fairly reflects the strengths and weaknesses of each proposal.

Agencies may change evaluators during the course of a procurement. For example, initial proposals may be evaluated by one set of evaluators, and final proposal revisions by another, *Data Flow Corp.*, 62 Comp. Gen. 506 (B-209499), 83-2 CPD ¶ 57. Similarly, an agency may re-evaluate proposals using a more experienced group of evaluators, *WR Sys., Ltd*, Comp. Gen. Dec. B-287477, 2001 CPD ¶ 118; *SOS Interpreting, Ltd.*, Comp. Gen. Dec. B-287505, 2001 CPD ¶ 104; *Pro-Mark, Inc.*, Comp. Gen. B-247248, 92-2 CPD ¶ 124. New evaluations may also be used after the agency has lost a protest, *LIS, Inc.*, Comp. Gen. B-400646.4, 2010 CPD ¶ 18; *Burchick Constr. Co.*, Comp. Gen. B-400342.3, 2009 CPD ¶ 102; *PRC, Inc.*, Comp. Gen. Dec. B-233561.8, 92-2 CPD ¶ 215, or has decided to take corrective action to forestall a protest, *Domain Name Alliance Registry*, Comp. Gen. B-310803.2, 2008 CPD ¶ 168. Occasionally, the agency will be ordered to create a new evaluation team, *Wackenhut Servs., Inc. v. United States*, 85 Fed. Cl. 273 (2008). See *Matrix Int'l Logistics, Inc.*, Comp. Gen. Dec. B-277208, 97-2 CPD ¶ 94, for a case where GAO did not object to the fact that a different team of evaluators arrived at significantly different evaluations. However, most agencies attempt to use the same evaluation personnel throughout the procurement.

## 1.  Disparate Evaluations

Frequently, the same factors are evaluated by a number of evaluators who arrive at a different assessment of the merits of the proposals and different scores. GAO has stated "[s]ince evaluating proposals involves subjective as well as objective judgments, it is not unusual for individual evaluators to reach disparate conclusions," *Mounts Eng'g*, 65 Comp. Gen. 476 (B-218489.4), 86-1 CPD ¶ 358. Similarly, in *Systems Research & Applications Corp.*, Comp. Gen. Dec. B-299818, 2008 CPD ¶ 28, GAO stated: "We recognize that it is not unusual for individual evaluator ratings to differ from one another, or to differ from the consensus ratings eventually assigned." In *Group GPS Multimedia*, Comp. Gen. Dec. B-310716, 2008 CPD ¶ 34, it was proper for the source selection official to make the final evaluation when two technical evaluators could not agree, and in *EBA Ernest Bland Assocs.*, Comp. Gen. Dec. B-270496, 96-1 CPD ¶ 148, GAO found nothing unusual or improper in the fact that two individual agency evaluators gave widely divergent scores to the same proposal. Therefore, disparities in evaluator scores alone do not suffice to show improper or irrational evaluation schemes, even if the final scores are averaged. See *Cube-All Star Servs. (J.V.)*, Comp. Gen. Dec. B-291903, 2003 CPD ¶ 145 (all evaluators did not identify same technical deficiencies); *Arsenault Acquisition Corp.*, Comp. Gen. Dec. B-276959, 97-2 CPD ¶ 74 (low score of one of four evaluators based on different assessment); *Arthur Anderson & Co.*, 71 Comp. Gen. 233 (B-245903), 92-1 CPD ¶ 168 (consensus score of 27 after initial scores of 25, 25, and 30); *Syscon Servs.*, 68 Comp. Gen. 698 (B-235647), 89-2 CPD ¶ 258 (evaluations ranged from unacceptable to acceptable to better than acceptable); and *Monarch Enters., Inc.*, Comp. Gen. Dec. B-233303, 89-1 CPD ¶ 222 (scores from different evaluation panels varied significantly). On the other hand, if factor scores are averaged or added, the agency must make sure that offers are not unreasonably downgraded for notations which are meant to be neutral. See *Inlingua Sch. of Language*, Comp. Gen. Dec. B-229784, 88-1 CPD ¶ 340, finding unfairness in a point adding system which scored questions answered as "not applicable" with zeros, thereby penalizing the protester for meaningless data. Similarly, consensus evaluations must be supported by rational conclusions, *Magnum Med. Personnel, A Joint Venture,* Comp. Gen. Dec. B-297687.2, 2006 CPD ¶ 99.

There is no requirement that agencies develop consensus scores in order to reconcile disparate evaluations, *Smart Innovative Solutions*, Comp. Gen. Dec. B-400323.3, 2008 CPD ¶ 220. Nonetheless, whenever possible the agency should attempt to reconcile disparate scores to ensure that the evaluators have not made obvious mistakes in their evaluation. See *Resource Applications, Inc.*, Comp. Gen. Dec. B-274943.3, 97-1 CPD ¶ 137, where GAO described the flexibility given consensus procedures to achieve this result:

There is nothing inherently objectionable in an agency's decision to develop a consensus rating. *Appalachian Council, Inc.,* B-256179, May 20, 1994, 94-1 CPD ¶ 319. The fact that the evaluators individually rated TechLaw's proposal for [certain] subfactors less favorably than they did on a consensus basis for those subfactors, and individually rated RAI's proposal for [certain] subfactors more favorably than they did on a consensus basis for those subfactors does not, by itself, warrant questioning the final evaluation results. See *Syscon Servs., Inc.,* 68 Comp. Gen. 698 (1989), 89-2 CPD ¶ 258; *Dragon Servs., Inc.,* B-255354, Feb. 25, 1994, 94-1 CPD ¶ 151. Agency evaluators may discuss the relative strengths and weaknesses of proposals in order to reach a consensus rating, which often differs from the ratings given by individual evaluators, since such discussions generally operate to correct mistakes or misperceptions that may have occurred in the initial evaluation. *Schweizerr Aircraft Corp.,* B-248640.2; B-248640.3, Sept. 14, 1992, 92-2 CPD ¶ 200; *The Cadmus Group, Inc.,* B-241372.3, Sept. 25, 1991, 91-2 CPD ¶ 271. Thus, a consensus score need not be the score of the majority the evaluators initially awarded — the score may properly be determined after discussions among the evaluators. *GZA Remediation, Inc.,* B-272386, Oct. 3, 1996, 96-2 CPD ¶ 155 (note 3). In short, the overriding concern in the evaluation process is that the final score assigned accurately reflect the actual merits of the proposals, not that it be mechanically traceable back to the scores initially given by the individual evaluators. *Id.*; *Dragon Servs., Inc., supra.*

See *James Constr.,* Comp. Gen. Dec. B-402429, 2010 CPD ¶ 98 (proper consensus of "acceptable" when evaluators had ratings of "good," "good," and "good/acceptable"); *Robbind-Gioia, LLC,* Comp. Gen. Dec. B-402199, 2010 CPD ¶ 67 (proper for consensus report to reflect views of only one evaluator); *Bering Straits Tech. Servs., LLC,* Comp. Gen. Dec. B-401560.3, 2009 CPD ¶ 201 (proper consensus of "good" when three evaluators rated proposal "excellent" and one rated it "good"); *Domain Name Alliance Registry,* Comp. Gen. Dec. B-310803.2, 2008 CPD ¶ 168 (proper consensus of "minor weakness" when two evaluators found no weakness and one found major weakness); *Systalex Corp.,* Comp. Gen. Dec. B-400109, 2008 CPD ¶ 148 (strength found by one evaluator need not be reflected in consensus score); *Veterans Tech., LLC,* Comp. Gen. Dec. B-310303.2, 2008 CPD ¶ 31 (consensus evaluation can vary from evaluation of all evaluators); *General Injectables & Vaccines, Inc.,* Comp. Gen. Dec. B-298590, 2006 CPD ¶ 173 ("pressure" on evaluators to reach consensus did not demonstrate irrational evaluation).

Consensus evaluations have been held to be rational and reliable even when the agency has destroyed the evaluation records of individual evaluators, *Government Acquisitions, Inc.,* Comp. Gen. Dec. B-401048, 2009 CPD ¶ 137; *Alliance Tech. Servs., Inc.,* Comp. Gen. Dec. B-311329, 2008 CPD ¶ 108; *Joint Mgmt. & Tech. Servs.,* Comp. Gen. Dec. B-294229, 2004 CPD ¶ 208, merely averaged the individual scores, *Trusted Base, LLC,* Comp. Gen. Dec. B-401670, 2009 CPD ¶ 218; or permitted the individual evaluators to not record their evaluations, *Dellew Corp.,* Comp. Gen. Dec. B-298233.2, 2006 CPD ¶ 144.

In *United Int'l Investigative Servs., Inc. v. United States*, 41 Fed. Cl. 312 (1998), the court held that the agency had acted improperly in failing to permit the evaluators to discuss their evaluations in an effort to arrive at a consensus when the source selection plan called for such a "group discussion." This decision is unusual because it has generally been held that agencies are not bound by their internal source selection plans.

## 2. Retention of Evaluation Documents

Agencies should retain all of the evaluation documents created during the evaluation process. FAR 4.801(a) requires agencies to establish contract files "containing the records of all contractual transactions." FAR 4.801(b) requires these filed "constitute a complete history of the transaction for the purpose of — (4) Furnishing essential facts in the event of litigation or congressional inquiries." In *Pitney Bowes Gov't Solutions, Inc. v. United States*, 93 Fed. Cl. 327 (2010), the court held that destruction of evaluators' worksheets violated this requirement, stating at 335:

> [T]he destruction of the individual TEP [technical evaluation panel] members' score sheets is barred by the FAR provisions. The current contract file for the challenged procurement does not "constitute a *complete* history of the transaction," FAR § 4.801(b) (emphasis added), nor does it "[f]urnish[] essential facts in the event of litigation. FAR § 4.801(b)(4). FAR § 4.801(b) expressly refers to § 4.803, which provides "examples of the records normally contained . . . in contract files." FAR § 4.803. Specifically, the record as submitted does not contain all "[s]ource selection documentation," as required by FAR § 4.803(a)(13). It was foreseeable that the individual rating sheets could well become relevant to issues arising in a bid protest, particularly in a situation where, as here, the bias of one or more of the panel members is alleged. No preturnatural clairvoyance would be required to envision that possibility. Although the ratings of the individual members of the TEP presumably were taken into account by, and wrapped into, the consensus report of the TEP, without the separate score sheets of the individual panel members, the court is unable to assess any divergence in the ratings which produced that consensus, or in turn, determine whether there existed personal bias in favor of [the winning contractors] on the part of one or more of the panel members. The argument by the government and the intervenor that the individual members' rating sheets were in effect no more than drafts of the final consensus report of the [TEP] is not supportable. The consensus report necessarily represented an amalgam of the views of the panel members and would have tended to suppress individual views.

In this case, the court ruled that the protester could depose each member of the evaluation panel in order to determine his or her individual views in the initial evaluation. It also noted that the contracting officer responsible for destroying the worksheets might be subject to sanctions for spoilation of evidence.

GAO has reached the opposite conclusion, holding in numerous decisions that it does not object to the destruction of the worksheets of individual evaluators as long as a consensus evaluation supports the source selection decision. See *Joint Mgmt. & Tech. Servs.*, Comp. Gen. Dec. B-294229, 2004 CPD ¶ 208, stating:

> Where, as here, the agency has destroyed individual evaluation materials, its actions are unobjectionable provided that the consensus evaluation materials relied on by the agency support the agency's judgments regarding the relative merits of the proposals. *Global Eng'g and Constr., LLC*, B-290288.3, B-290288.4, Apr. 3, 2003, 2003 CPD ¶ 180 at 3 n.3.

Nonetheless, on occasion GAO has held a hearing in order to determine the substantive conclusions reached by each individual evaluator. See *Dynalantic Corp.*, Comp. Gen. Dec. B-274944.2, 97-1 CPD ¶ 101, where such a hearing was held and the agency was directed to pay the protester for the cost of the hearing when the protest was granted on other grounds.

## B.  Agency Discretion

Just as the procuring agency has great discretion in selecting evaluation factors, its evaluation will not be disturbed unless it is arbitrary or in violation of procurement statutes or regulations, *Pacific Consultants*, Comp. Gen. Dec. B-198706, 80-2 CPD ¶129. See *Buffalo Org. for Soc. & Tech. Innovation, Inc.*, Comp. Gen. Dec. B-196279, 80-1 CPD ¶ 107, where GAO stated its traditional position in this area:

> The determination of the relative merits of proposals is the responsibility of the procuring agency since it must bear the burden of any difficulties incurred by reason of a defective evaluation. In light of this, we have held that procuring officials enjoy a reasonable degree of discretion in the evaluation of proposals and such discretion must not be disturbed unless shown to be arbitrary or in violation of the procurement statutes and regulations.

More recently, GAO summarized its position *Lakeside Escrow & Title Agency, Inc.*, Comp. Gen. Dec. B-310331.3, 2008 CPD ¶ 14:

> In reviewing [protests of an agency's evaluation], we do not conduct a new evaluation or substitute our judgment for that of the agency, but examine the record to determine whether the agency's judgment was reasonable and in accordance with the terms of the solicitation and applicable procurement statutes and regulations. *Wahkontah Servs., Inc.*, B-292768, Nov. 18, 2003, 2003 CPD ¶ 214 at 4. An offeror's mere disagreement with the agency's evaluation is not sufficient to render the evaluation unreasonable. *Ben-Mar Enters., Inc.*, D-295781, Apr. 7, 2005, 2005 CPD ¶ 68 at 7.

See *Matrix Int'l Logistics, Inc.*, Comp. Gen. Dec. B-272388.2, 97-2 CPD ¶ 89; *PRC, Inc.*, Comp. Gen. Dec. B-274698.2, 97-1 CPD ¶ 115; *Main Bldg. Maint, Inc.*, Comp. Gen. Dec. B-260945, 95-2 CPD ¶ 214.

Thus, agencies have broad discretion in the evaluation process. In spite of this broad discretion, however, evaluations must be able to withstand scrutiny as to their reasonableness and must be made in accordance with the evaluation scheme described in the RFP. Thus, agency evaluations have been overturned if they are irrational, not in compliance with the RFP, arbitrary, or not based on evidence in the record.

## 1. Irrational Evaluations

Irrational evaluations involve evaluation decisions which are inherently erroneous and could not be used even if specifically outlined in the RFP. For example, in *Dynalantic v. United States*, 945 F.2d 416 (Fed. Cir. 1991), the offeror's significantly less expensive bid was rejected based on an unreasonable assumption that Dynalantic was ignorant of industry standards. Expert testimony illustrated that the Air Force itself lacked such knowledge. In *Programmatics, Inc.*, Comp. Gen. Dec. B-228916.2, 88-1 CPD ¶ 35, GAO deemed an evaluation irrational where two of five evaluators significantly reduced the protester's technical scores during a second evaluation without having any reason for doing so. See also *PMO P'ship Joint Venture*, Comp. Gen. Dec. B-401973.3, 2010 CPD ¶ 29 (joint venture's proposed overhead rate structure rejected based on CAS criteria when offeror was not subject to CAS); *Humana Military Healthcare Servs.*, Comp. Gen. Dec. B-401652.2, 2009 CPD ¶ 219 (protester's prior practice of obtaining discounts not rejected in evaluation of cost proposal); *Engineering Mgmt. & Integration, Inc.*, Comp. Gen. Dec. B-400356.4, 2009 CPD ¶ 114 (offeror downgraded for not providing required percentage of certified employees when it provided the raw number of such employees); *Honeywell Tech. Solutions, Inc.*, Comp. Gen. Dec. B-400771, 2009 CPD ¶ 49 (past performance on a very small contract was relevant to work called for by contract being competed); *Sikorsky Aircraft Co.*, Comp. Gen. Dec. B-299145, 2007 CPD ¶ 45 (life-cycle cost evaluation normalized when RFP called for data from each offeror on past costs); *Systronics, Inc.*, Comp. Gen. Dec. B-293102, 2006 CPD ¶ 15 (noncomplying quotation given a high score); *Arora Group*, Comp. Gen. Dec. B-297346, 2004 CPD ¶ 61 (offeror downgraded because required certifications were not listed on resume when they were included in response to discussion question); *T Square Logistics Servs. Corp.*, Comp. Gen. Dec. B-291851, 2003 CPD ¶ 160 (high scores given to areas not covered in oral presentation); *Eurest Support Servs.*, Comp. Gen. Dec. B-285813.3, 2003 CPD ¶ 139 (unreasonable evaluation of realism of quantity of labor needed to perform fixed price incentive contract); *Dismas Charities, Inc.*, Comp. Gen. Dec. B-292091, 2003 CPD ¶ 125 (failure to consider all information submitted in proposal); *M&S Farms, Inc.*, Comp. Gen. Dec. B-290599, 2002 CPD ¶ 174 (high past performance score based on receipt of more questionnaires); *PADCO, Inc. — Costs*, Comp. Gen. Dec. B-289096.3, 2002 CPD ¶ 135 (acceptance, without analysis, of proposed indirect cost rates far below incurred rates); *Perini/Jones, (J.V.)*, Comp. Gen. Dec. B-285906, 2002 CPD ¶ 68 (giving company credit for experience for affiliated company that would not perform work on contract); *OSI Collection Servs.*, Inc.,

Comp. Gen. Dec. B-286597, 2001 CPD ¶ 18 (past performance evaluation based on numerical scores detailing number of failures where offerors had disparate amount of work); *Summit Research Corp.*, Comp. Gen. Dec. B-287523, 2001 CPD ¶ 176 (exclusion of small business offeror from evaluation of small business participation); *Green Valley Transp., Inc.*, Comp. Gen. Dec. B-285283, 2000 CPD ¶ 133 (assessing number of performance problems when offerors had disparate amounts of work); *AIU N. Am., Inc.*, Comp. Gen. Dec. B-283743.2, 2000 CPD ¶ 39 (failing to consider resources of corporation that acquired offeror when evaluating such resources); *Consolidated Eng'g Servs., Inc.*, Comp. Gen. Dec. B-279565.2, 99-1 CPD ¶ 75 (offeror downgraded because of inadequate description of subcontractor's experience when another offeror provided information on same subcontractor); *SCIENTECH, Inc.*, Comp. Gen. Dec. B-277805.2, 98-1 CPD ¶ 33 (exclusion from the past performance evaluation of offeror's efforts as the incumbent contractor and its major subcontractors); *HG Props. A, L.P.*, Comp. Gen. Dec. B-277572, 97-2 CPD ¶ 123 (giving awardee 225 points of the 250 points available for efficient layout when the awardee's layout was inconsistent with the stated evaluation factors); *Technology Servs. Int'l, Inc.*, Comp. Gen. Dec. B-276506, 97-2 CPD ¶ 113 (giving awardee the highest rating under a significant quality control technical subfactor when it did not submit a detailed work scheduling scheme as contemplated by this subfactor); *ST Aerospace Engines Pte., Ltd.*, Comp. Gen. Dec. B-275725, 97-1 CPD ¶ 161 (evaluating negative past performance of affiliate when it will play no role in contract performance); *International Bus. Sys., Inc.*, Comp. Gen. Dec. B-275554, 97-1 CPD ¶ 114 (ignoring past performance of incumbent contractor because the agency technical person had not filled out the past performance questionnaire); *PMT Servs., Inc.*, Comp. Gen. Dec. B-270538.2, 96-2 CPD ¶ 98 (evaluating only the size of prior projects when the evaluation factor called for a review of projects with "similar complexity" to the subject procurement); *Safeguard Maint. Corp.*, Comp. Gen. Dec. B-260983.3, 96-2 CPD ¶ 116 (giving a low score to a proposal for not furnishing required information when the evaluators had personal knowledge of the information); and *DynCorp*, Comp. Gen. Dec. B-232999, 89-1 CPD ¶ 152 (scoring proposals technically equal where awardee's proposal contained many obvious weaknesses not apparent in protester's proposal). Similarly, in *Inlingua Schs. of Languages*, Comp. Gen. B-229784, 88-1 CPD ¶ 340, questions answered by an offeror's reference as "not applicable" were irrationally scored as zeros, and in *SDA, Inc.*, Comp. Gen. Dec. B-248528.2, 93-1 CPD ¶ 320, rating past experience by the percentage of past projects that were similar in size to the contract work was inherently irrational. In the latter case, GAO commented that the rating scheme gave the highest rating to the offeror that listed the fewest irrelevant past projects. Such a system was seen to be inherently illogical and the protest was sustained.

## 2. Evaluations Not in Compliance with the RFP

Evaluations will be found to be improper if the evaluators do not comply with the evaluation scheme set forth in the RFP. This requires that the evaluation process be completed during the source selection — issues cannot be left for resolution after contract award, *Sabreliner Corp.*, Comp. Gen. Dec. B-290515, 2003 CPD ¶ 4.

In most best value procurements, the RFP will call for a comparative assessment of various aspects of the proposals and this requires the agency evaluators to identify and assess the relative merits of the proposals. Thus, merely finding that disparate proposals are satisfactory or acceptable will be found to fail to comply with the RFP requirements. See, for example, *Systems Research & Applications Corp.*, Comp. Gen. Dec. B-299818, 2008 CPD ¶ 28, where GAO stated:

> Where, as here, the RFP states a best value evaluation plan — as opposed to selection of the lowest priced, technically acceptable offer — evaluation of proposals is not limited to determining whether a proposal is merely technically acceptable; rather, proposals should be further differentiated to distinguish their relative quality under each stated evaluation factor by considering the degree to which technically acceptable proposals exceed the stated minimum requirements or will better satisfy the agency's needs. See *The MIL Corp.*, B-294836, Dec. 30, 2004, 2005 CPD ¶ 29 at 8; *Johnson Controls World Servs., Inc., Meridian Mgmt. Corp.*, B-281287.5 et al., June 21, 1999, 2001 CPD ¶ 3 at 8.

Agencies must also perform the evaluation in accordance with the procedures in the RFP. See *Milani Constr., LLC*, Comp. Gen. Dec. B-401942, 2010 CPD ¶ 87, improperly determining that the protester's price was unreasonably low when there was no indication in the RFP that price realism would be considered. See also *PMO P'ship Joint Venture*, Comp. Gen. Dec. B-403214, 2010 CPD ¶ 256 (requiring cost data in accordance with Table 15-2 of FAR 15.408 when no such requirement in RFP); *General Dynamics One Source, LLC*, Comp. Gen. Dec. B-400340.5, 2010 CPD ¶ 45 (accepting incentive fee lower than fee specified in RFP); *Ashbury Int'l Group, Inc.*, Comp. Gen. Dec. B-401123, 2009 CPD ¶ 140 (agency had not tested the product sample of the selected offeror as required by the RFP); *General Dynamics Info. Tech.*, Comp. Gen. Dec. B-299873, 2007 CPD ¶ 194 (agency used labor rates proposed by an offeror in one table when the RFP stated that the rates in another table would be used if there was an inconsistency); *KIC Dev., LLC*, Comp. Gen. Dec. B-297425.2, 2006 CPD ¶ 27 (agency determined offeror did not meet experience requirement when RFP allowed subcontractor experience to meet requirement); *Clean Harbors Envt'l Servs., Inc.*, Comp. Gen. Dec. B-296176.2, 2005 CPD ¶ 222 (agency treated all past performance as equally relevant when RFP called for assessing varying degrees of relevance); *Lockheed Martin Corp.*, Comp. Gen. Dec. B-293679, 2004 CPD ¶ 115 (agency determined that proposal met RFP requirement to fully describe design features of product based on evaluator's knowledge of subcontractor's competence); *Computer Info. Specialist, Inc.*, Comp. Gen. Dec. B-293049, 2004 CPD ¶ 1 (agency relied on blanket statements of compliance when RFP called for submission of specific information showing compliance); *Johnson Controls World Servs., Inc.*, Comp. Gen. Dec. B-281287.5, 2001 CPD ¶ 3 (agency gave no credit for proposals with greater technical merit); *Saco Defense Corp.*, Comp. Gen. Dec. B-283885, 2000 CPD ¶ 34 (rating proposal low risk when offeror did not provide detailed information required by RFP to make the assessment); *HG Props. A, L.P.*, Comp. Gen. Dec. B-277572, 97-2 CPD ¶ 123 (agency gave the awardee 225 points of the 250 points available for efficient layout even though the awardee's layout was inconsistent with the RFP requirement); *Technology Servs. Int'l, Inc.*, Comp. Gen. Dec. B-276506, 97-2 CPD ¶ 113 (agency gave the highest rating under a significant quality control technical subfactor even though the awardee's proposal did not submit a detailed work scheduling scheme as contemplated for this subfactor); *Ogden Support Servs., Inc.*, Comp. Gen. Dec. B-270012.2, 96-1 CPD ¶ 177, Comp. Gen. Dec. B-270012.4, 96-2 CPD ¶ 137 (agency evaluated past performance on dissimilar work although the RFP called for "successful performance on similar efforts"); *RJO Enters., Inc.*, Comp. Gen. Dec. B-260126.2, 95-2 CPD ¶ 93 (agency downgraded a proposal for not furnishing sufficient resumes but the resumes were not called for in the RFP); See *also University of Michigan*, 66 Comp. Gen. 538 (B-225756), 87-1 CPD ¶ 643 (agency gave almost total weight to one of four criteria listed in the RFP); *H. J. Group Ventures, Inc.*, Comp. Gen. Dec. B-246139, 92-1 CPD ¶ 203 (agency gave heavy weight to a criterion which was listed as a "general consideration" but not included in the list of relative order of importance of criteria); *SIMCO, Inc.*, Comp. Gen. Dec. B-229964, 88-1 CPD ¶ 383 (cost evaluation overturned for using an "all or nothing" point system not specified in the RFP and for failing to weigh price as 20% of the total score as promised); *T.V. Travel, Inc.*, 65 Comp. Gen. 323 (B-221526.2), 86-1 CPD ¶ 172 (agency failed to deduct points for certain deficiencies in awardee's proposal as set forth in the RFP); *National Capital Med. Found., Inc.*, Comp. Gen. Dec. B-215303.5, 85-1 CPD ¶ 637 (technical evaluation scheme giving no credit for partially unsatisfactory proposals noncompliant because such a grading system was not outlined in the RFP).

Evaluations have been found not to comply with the RFP even when the agency had no knowledge of the noncompliance. See, for example, *CBIS Fed., Inc.*, 71 Comp. Gen. 319 (B-245844.2), 92-1 CPD ¶ 308, where the agency gave high scores to proposed personnel to perform the work and later found that the contractor had no "letters of commitment" with two of the key personnel. GAO granted the protest because the evaluation was not in accord with the RFP requirement that each offeror furnish the names of key personnel that would actually be used to perform the contract.

In some instances, a detailed analysis of the RFP is required to determine whether the agency has followed the evaluation scheme. For example, in *University of New Orleans*, 55 Comp. Gen. 1281 (B-184194), 76-1 CPD ¶ 22, the RFP stated that primary emphasis in the evaluation of proposals would be placed on the analysis of "the effects of a particular pollutant on various environmental media," but the actual evaluation rated proposals in terms of whether they treated each of the environmental media equally. The evaluation was held to be improper. In *Safeguard Maint. Corp.*, Comp. Gen. Dec. B-260983.3, 96-2 CPD ¶ 116, GAO reviewed the entire scoring of the protester's proposal and found that the evaluation was improper because a number of the low scores were based on noncompliance with agency requirements that were not stated in the RFP. See also *Lithos Restoration, Ltd.*, 71 Comp. Gen. 367 (B-247003.2), 92-1 CPD ¶ 379, where the RFP stated that technical factors were more important than price, technical subfactors were listed in descending order of importance, and the first of four technical subfactors listed would be evaluated on a go/no-go basis. GAO held that failing to score the first evaluation subfactor in these circumstances was a violation of the RFP evaluation scheme because the evaluation procedure could only be reasonably interpreted as requiring point scoring of the most important technical subfactor in making the price/technical tradeoff.

### 3. Arbitrary Evaluations

Evaluations are found to be arbitrary when offerors are not treated equally in the evaluation process. Such situations develop when decisions to award or deduct points are made without rational justification. *J.M. Cashman, Inc.*, Comp. Gen. Dec. B-233733, 89-1 CPD ¶ 380, is a good example of such arbitrary decision-making. In that case, GAO found that downgrading one offeror's score due to a lack of experience without doing the same for a similar offeror was unjustified. Similarly, in *United Int'l Eng'g, Inc.*, 71 Comp. Gen. 177 (B-245448.3), 92-1 CPD ¶ 122, an evaluation was found to be arbitrary for treating offerors differently. There, the contracting officer raised one offeror's labor cost estimate without doing the same for a competitor with a similar estimate. Likewise, in *Contingency Mgmt. Group, LLC*, Comp. Gen. Dec. B-309752, 2008 CPD ¶ 83, unequal treatment was found where one offeror was permitted to base its proposal on assumptions about a sample task scenario that did not match the RFP and were not available to the other offerors. See also *Brican, Inc.*, Comp. Gen. Dec. B-400760.4, 2010 CPD ¶ 32 (crediting one offeror with experience of subcontractor when protester given no credit in spite of proposing same subcontractor); *AINS, Inc.*, Comp. Gen. Dec. B-402602, 2010 CPD ¶ 141 (giving negative evaluation to product capability when same evaluation not given to winning offeror's product that also did not meet the requirement); *Ahtna Support & Training Servs., LLC*, Comp. Gen. Dec. B-400947.2, 2009 CPD ¶ 119 (crediting only one offeror with experience of subcontractor); *ITT Federal Servs. Int'l Corp.*, Comp. Gen. Dec. B-296783, 2007 CPD ¶ 43 (using one competitor's staffing approach to adjust the costs of protester an unfair practice); *Magnum Med. Personnel, A Joint Venture*, Comp. Gen. Dec. B-297687.2, 2006 CPD ¶ 99 (disparate evaluations of capability); *BAE Tech. Servs., Inc.*, Comp. Gen. Dec. B-296699, 2006 CPD ¶ 91 (using different standard to evaluate offerors' proposed initiatives to reduce staffing); *PGBA, LLC v. United States*, 60 Fed. Cl. 196 (2004) (downgrading one offeror for lack of specificity without applying same standard to other offerors); *Ashe Facility Servs., Inc.*, Comp. Gen. Dec. B-292218.3, 2004 CPD ¶ 80 (giving credit for experience of key personnel in evaluating corporate experience only to awardee); *Southwestern Bell Tel. Co.*, Comp. Gen. Dec. B-292476, 2003 CPD ¶ 177 (equal evaluations when awardee had ethical problems); *Preferred Sys. Solutions, Inc.*, Comp. Gen. Dec. B-292322, 2003 CPD ¶ 166 (same ratings where evaluation showed differences); *Kathryn Huddleston & Assocs., Ltd.*, Comp. Gen. Dec. B-289453, 2002 CPD ¶ 57 (different treatment of quotations failing to meet solicitation requirement); *Myers Investigations & Sec. Servs., Inc.*, Comp. Gen. Dec. B-288468, 2001 CPD ¶ 189 (different evaluations of past performance when data was similar); *York Bldg. Servs., Inc.*, Comp. Gen. Dec. B-282887.10, 2000 CPD ¶ 141 (key personnel not meeting requirement rated differently); *Saco Defense Corp.*, Comp. Gen. Dec. B-283885, 2000 CPD ¶ 34 (winning offeror given same score as protester when it submitted very sparse information on its quality system); *CRAssocs., Inc.*, Comp. Gen. Dec. B-282075.2, 2000 CPD ¶ 63 (disparate scores when two offerors made same statement); *Electronic Design, Inc.*, Comp. Gen. Dec. B-279662.2, 98-2 CPD ¶ 69 (one offeror permitted to add to its BAFO 1,700 page attachment to initial proposal that exceeded page limitation although no other offerors were told that such detailed information was permissible for inclusion in BAFO); *Aerospace Design & Fabrication, Inc.*, Comp. Gen. Dec. B-278896.2, 98-1 CPD ¶ 139 (one offeror permitted to submit more past performance references than another offeror); *U.S. Property Mgmt. Serv. Corp.*, Comp. Gen. Dec. B-278727, 98-1 CPD ¶ 88 (two offerors with a similar lack of experience given very disparate scores); *New Breed Leasing Corp.*, Comp. Gen. Dec. B-259328, 96-2 CPD ¶ 84 (evaluation comments indicated that protester had addressed all of the agency's concerns in its BAFO and had "enhanced" its proposal but the protester's scores were not raised); *Main Bldg. Maint., Inc.*, Comp. Gen. Dec. B-260945.4, 95-2 CPD ¶ 214 (one offeror evaluated as having none of the six "strengths" of the winning offeror when the protester had four of the six strengths); *Deployable Hosp. Sys., Inc.*, Comp. Gen. Dec. B-260778, 95-2 CPD ¶ 65 (two technical proposals rated as equal because both offerors had the same experience when protester had significantly more experience); and *Arco Mgmt. of Washington, D.C., Inc.*, Comp. Gen. Dec. B-248653, 92-2 CPD ¶ 173 (winning offeror's BAFO scores were increased based on very "conclusionary" information while the protester's BAFO scores were not increased after the submission of substantive responses to issues raised in discussions).

An extreme form of arbitrary evaluation is evident in situations where the procuring agency purposely favors one offeror over another. For example, in *Xerox Corp. v. United States*, 21 Cl. Ct. 278 (1990), the agency displayed an unethical and even criminal bias toward the awardee. It changed the RFP to omit a requirement that the awardee could not satisfy. It also met secretly with the awardee to allow it to improve its evaluation by correcting a mistake in its proposal, after BAFOs had been submitted, without allowing other offerors to change their proposals. The entire procurement was eventually voided and Xerox obtained reimbursement for all costs. See also *Lockheed Martin Corp.*, Comp. Gen. Dec. B-295402, 2005 CPD ¶ 24, where the source selection official changed the RFP technical requirements to favor a contractor with which she was negotiating future employment. Similarly, in *Lockheed Martin Corp.*, Comp. Gen. Dec. B-295401, 2005 CPD ¶ 41, the source selection official pressured the evaluators into changing their evaluations and then awarded the contract to the contractor with which she was negotiating future employment.

## 4. Evaluation Not Based on Evidence

Evaluation decisions must be based on tangible evidence to support an agency's decision. In *Amtec Corp.*, Comp. Gen. Dec. B-240647, 91-2 CPD ¶ 211, *recons. denied*, 91-2 CPD ¶ 473, GAO overturned a "marginal" technical evaluation because the agency record contained no evidence supporting such a rating. Similarly, in *Radiation Oncology Group of WNY, PC*, Comp. Gen. Dec. B-310354.2, 2009 CPD ¶ 136, GAO sustained a protest because the agency concluded two proposals were technically equal but had no evidence demonstrating that their unequal evaluations were incorrect. See also *Irving Burton Assocs., Inc.*, Comp. Gen. Dec. B-401983.3, 2010 CPD ¶ 92 (evaluation of transition plan not supported by proposal after surplus pages were removed); *Cahaba Safeguard Admins., LLC*, Comp. Gen. Dec. B-401842.2, 2010 CPD ¶ 39 (agency accepted OCI mitigation plan containing no detailed implementation information); *Spherix, Inc.*, Comp. Gen. Dec. B-2945723, 2005 CPD ¶ 3 (agency "projected" offeror's staffing level with no evidence to support projection); *National City Bank of Indiana*, Comp. Gen. Dec. B-287608.3, 2002 CPD ¶ 190 (no evidence to support conclusion low staffing was adequate); *DynCorp Int'l, LLC*, Comp. Gen. Dec. B-289863, 2002 CPD ¶ 83 (no evidence to support rejection of technical evaluators' concern of inadequate staffing); *Meredian Mgmt.*, Comp. Gen. Dec. B-281287.10, 2001 CPD ¶ 5 (inadequate staffing not factored into evaluation); *SWR, Inc.*, Comp. Gen. Dec. B-286161.2, 2001 CPD ¶ 32 (lack of experience not demonstrated by information provided by protester); *OneSource Energy Servs., Inc.*, Comp. Gen. Dec. B-283445, 2000 CPD ¶ 109 (report of telephone conversation with references not a fair reflection of conversation); *Maritime Berthing, Inc.*, Comp. Gen. Dec. B-284123.3, 2000 CPD ¶ 89 (evaluation that offeror met specification requirement when evidence in proposal and known to agency proved otherwise); *Future-Tec Mgmt. Sys., Inc.*, Comp. Gen. Dec. B-283793.5, 2000 CPD ¶ 59 (cost realism adjustment based on misunderstanding of the cost proposal); *L-3 Commc'ns Corp.*, Comp. Gen. Dec. B-281784.3, 99-1 CPD ¶ 81 (cost realism analysis using unaudited indirect cost information which was rescinded by protester); *Matrix Int'l Logistics, Inc.*, Comp. Gen. Dec. B-272388.2, 97-2 CPD ¶ 89 (no evidence to support changing of winning contractor's scores from "good" to "excellent" in evaluating BAFO); *JW Assoc., Inc.*, Comp. Gen. Dec. B-275209, 97-1 CPD ¶ 57 (no evidence to support evaluation of technical proposals); *TRESP Assoc.*, Comp. Gen. Dec. B-258322.5, 96-1 CPD ¶ 8 (contracting officer relied on three supposed discriminators, none of which accurately reflected terms of protester's proposal); *Eng'g Computation, Inc.*, Comp. Gen. Dec. B-261658, 95-2 CPD ¶ 176 (no evidence to support evaluation that protester's proposal posed performance risks); *Telos Field Eng'g*, Comp. Gen. Dec. B-253492.6, 94-2 CPD ¶ 240 (no evidence to support higher scores for winning offeror's BAFO); *TRW, Inc.*, Comp. Gen. Dec. B-254045.2, 94-1 CPD ¶ 18 (high evaluation of selected offeror not supported when questions raised by lower-level evaluators regarding the selected firm's technical proposal and substantial "unquantified" concerns about that firm's evaluated cost were not resolved); *HSI-CCEC*, Comp. Gen. Dec. B-240610, 90-2 CPD ¶ 465 (low evaluation of skills of subcontractors not supported by information submitted by the offeror; low evaluation of minority subcontracting unjustified when offeror stated intention to use minority firms that were part of its joint venture); *Asbestos Mgmt., Inc.*, Comp. Gen. Dec. B-237841, 90-1 CPD ¶ 325 (evaluation of key consultant improper when agency had lost qualification statement submitted with proposal); and *Coastal Science & Eng'g, Inc.*, 69 Comp. Gen. 66 (B-236041), 89-2 CPD ¶ 436 (evaluation not substantiated by the record when two competitors received relatively equal technical scores even though one was found to be "sufficiently technically superior to warrant payment of [a significant] cost premium").

Evaluations will also be held to be improper if the agency ignores evidence. See, for example, *Intercon Assocs., Inc.*, Comp. Gen. Dec. B-298282, 2006 CPD ¶ 121, where GAO sustained a protest because the "evaluation judgments are, in many instances, either factually incorrect, internally contradictory, or so cryptic that we are unable to discern the basis for the evaluators' concerns." See also *Contrack Int'l, Inc.*, Comp. Gen. Dec. B-401871.5, 2010 CPD ¶ 126 (evaluation of "excellent" past performance ignoring adverse information); *Velos, Inc.*, Comp. Gen. Dec. B-400500.8, 2010 CPD ¶ 13 (source selection decision based on consultant's report that ignored technical panel report); *MMI Fed. Mktg. Serv. Corp.*, Comp. Gen. Dec. B-297537, 2006 CPD ¶ 38 (evaluation that offeror met Berry Amendment requirement when evidence indicated it did not); *Cogent Sys., Inc.*, Comp. Gen. Dec. B-295990.4, 2006 CPD ¶ 179 (evaluators ignored different product offered in final proposal revision); and *Locus Tech., Inc.*, Comp. Gen. Dec. B-293012, 2004 CPD ¶ 16 (evaluators ignored significant portion of final proposal revision).

Evaluations will also be overturned when it becomes apparent that the evaluators do not understand the data available to them. For example, in *Mine Safety Appliance Co.*, 69 Comp. Gen. 562 (B-238597.2), 90-2 CPD ¶ 11, the evaluation was overturned when the evaluators "extrapolated" successful performance after the offeror had failed the required tests. GAO concluded that the agency should not have proceeded with the procurement without determining why the item did not perform properly. See also *Haworth, Inc.*, Comp. Gen. Dec. B-297077, 2005 CPD ¶ 215 (evaluators did not see that descriptive literature concerning product indicated that it did not meet specifications).

## C.  Using Factors Contained in the RFP

The FAR follows the language in 10 U.S.C. § 2305(b)(1) and 41 U.S.C. § 3701(a), stating that evaluation shall be based solely on the factors specified in the RFP. Thus, GAO has stated that it is generally improper to add or substitute evaluation criteria after proposals have been submitted and reviewed by government evaluators. See *Grey Advertising, Inc.*, 55 Comp. Gen. 1111 (B-184825), 76-1 CPD ¶ 325, stating that "once offerors are informed of the criteria against which proposals will be evaluated, it is incumbent upon the procuring activity to adhere to those criteria." Thus, unless the solicitation has been amended, the entire evaluation must be based on the stated factors throughout the competitive negotiation process.

## 1. Scope of Evaluation

Notwithstanding the requirement that only stated factors may be evaluated, agencies have been permitted to broaden the scope of the evaluation by considering all issues that are related to a factor and to narrow the scope of the evaluation by only considering those issues that are perceived to be relevant to the factor.

### a. Broadening the Scope

Agencies may evaluate any issue that is logically related to a stated evaluation factor. See *Bank St. Coll. of Educ.*, 63 Comp. Gen. 393 (B-213209), 84-1 CPD ¶ 607, where GAO stated at 400:

> As far as consistency with the evaluation criteria is concerned, while the source selection official may not judge the merits of the proposals based on criteria that offerors were not advised would be considered, the official may properly take into account specific, albeit not expressly identified, matters that are logically encompassed by or related to the stated criteria.

This relationship will be found if a consideration is not listed in Section M but is discussed in Section L of the RFP, *J.A. Jones Grupo de Servicios, SA*, Comp. Gen. Dec. B-283234, 99-2 CPD ¶ 80; *Science & Tech., Inc.*, Comp. Gen. Dec. B-272748, 97-1 CPD ¶ 121. See also *NEQ, LLC v. United States*, 88 Fed. Cl. 38 (2009), where it was found proper to evaluate the presence of the offerors' personnel in listed cities when they were required to submit charts and maps showing the location of their personnel, and *Forestry, Surveys & Data*, Comp. Gen. Dec. B-276802.3, 97-2 CPD ¶ 46, where experience was properly evaluated when it was not listed as a factor in the solicitation but experience questionnaires were required to be submitted.

Agency evaluation personnel are given considerable discretion in determining which considerations are within the scope of an evaluation factor. This discretion has been very broad when factors involving the capability of the offerors are being evaluated. For example, in *Homequity, Inc.*, Comp. Gen. Dec. B-223997, 86-2 CPD ¶ 685, it was held proper for evaluators to consider the cumulative experience of the offerors' key personnel in evaluating the " organization and experience" factor, and in *Cygnus Corp.*, Comp. Gen. Dec. B-275957, 97-1 CPD ¶ 202, evaluation of the experience of key personnel was proper when the evaluation factor was " corporate experience." See also *NEQ, LLC v. United States*, 88 Fed. Cl. 38 (2009) (metropolitan presence of offerors' offices properly considered in evaluating quick response time requirement); *Professional Perf. Dev. Group, Inc.*, Comp. Gen. Dec. B-311273, 2008 CPD ¶ 101 ("tested relationships" with required personnel properly considered under RFP calling for evaluation of how offeror would respond to "temporary staffing surges"); *Savannah River Alliance, LLC*, Comp. Gen. Dec. B-311126, 2008 CPD ¶ 88 (diverse experience of key personnel properly considered in evaluating innovative approaches and broad experience); *Matthews Mfg., Inc.*, Comp. Gen. Dec. B-299518, 2007 CPD ¶ 110 (producing the identical product properly considered in evaluating "existing manufacturing capabilities"); *Base Techs., Inc.*, Comp. Gen. Dec. B-293061.2, 2004 CPD ¶ 31 (length of relevant experience of key personnel properly considered in evaluating "qualifications" of key personnel); *Network Eng'g, Inc.*, Comp. Gen. Dec. B-292996, 2004 CPD ¶ 23 (use of incumbent personnel properly considered in evaluating "relevant staff experience"); *Gentex Corp. — Western Ops.*, Comp. Gen. Dec. B-291793, 2003 CPD ¶ 66 (funding profile properly considered in evaluating offeror's ability to meet program objectives including development effort "within cost and schedule constraints"); *IBP, Inc.*, Comp. Gen. Dec. B-289296, 2002 CPD ¶ 39 (special consideration for performance as incumbent contractor considered under "experience" factor); *NCLN20, Inc.*, Comp. Gen. Dec. B-287692, 2001 CPD ¶ 136 (organizational structure and transaction plan considered under staffing plan); *Oceaneering Int'l, Inc.*, Comp. Gen. Dec. B-287325, 2001 CPD ¶ 95 (contingency of lack of availability of mobilization port considered under mobilization factor); *MCA Research Corp.*, Comp. Gen. Dec. B-278268.2, 98-1 CPD ¶ 129 (number of employees with security clearances and retention rates of personnel properly considered under management and personnel factors); *EastCo Bldg. Servs., Inc.*, Comp. Gen. Dec. B-275334, 97-1 CPD ¶ 83 (past performance of only contracts of a similar size considered proper even though the RFP did not mention this limitation); *American Dev. Corp.*, Comp. Gen. Dec. B-251876.4, 93-2 CPD ¶ 49 (relevance of prior contracts proper when the evaluation factor was past performance); *AWD Techs., Inc.*, Comp. Gen. Dec. B-250081.2, 93-1 CPD ¶ 83 (experience in specific work called for by the contract properly given heavy weight when the evaluation factor was "past project experience"); *Western Med. Pers., Inc.*, 66 Comp. Gen. 699 (B-227991), 87-2 CPD ¶ 310 (past performance properly evaluated when RFP contained an evaluation factor entitled "references"); and *S.C. Jones Servs., Inc.*, Comp. Gen. Dec. B-223155, 86-2 CPD ¶ 158 (experience of predecessor firm with the same key personnel properly used to evaluate the factor "organizational experience and past performance"). Similarly, in *Quantum Research, Inc.*, Comp. Gen. Dec. B-242020, 91-1 CPD ¶ 310, it was held proper to downgrade a proposal calling for extended work weeks when the evaluation factors called for evaluation of the quality of personnel and their ability to provide services.

An evaluation issue has also been found to be within the scope of the RFP because it was raised during discussions with the offerors, *Intermagnetics Gen. Corp.*, Comp. Gen. Dec. B-286596, 2001 CPD ¶ 10. There, GAO held that the agency had properly evaluated the compatibility of offered products with other products because this question had been asked during discussions. See also *Interstate Elec. Corp.*, Comp. Gen. Dec. B-286466, 2001 CPD ¶ 29, where an unlisted evaluation factor was found proper because it was identified in an oral presentation as well as in Section L of the RFP.

Considerable discretion has also been granted to agencies in determining which considerations are related to offers. For example, in *International Bus. Machs. Corp. v. Department of the Treasury*, GSBCA 11777-P, 92-3 BCA ¶ 25,401, *aff'd, Lockheed Missiles & Space Co. v. Bentsen*, 4 F.3d 955 (Fed. Cir. 1993), the board held that the agency properly evaluated the productivity of the proposed computer systems in the technical and cost evaluation even though productivity was not mentioned in the list of factors. The board stated that the protesters should not have been surprised that the agency would be concerned about productivity because it was inherent in the evaluation of computer systems for use by government agencies. In this regard, agencies can evaluate the extent that an offeror proposes to exceed the agency's requirement when it evaluates the offer. See *IAP World Servs., Inc.*, Comp. Gen. Dec. B-297084, 2005 CPD ¶ 199, stating:

> [In a best value procurement,] the agency is not limited to determining whether a proposal is merely technically acceptable; rather, proposals may be evaluated to distinguish their relative quality by considering the degree to which they exceed the minimum requirements or will better satisfy the agency's needs. *Israel Aircraft Indus., Ltd., MATA Helicopters Div.*, B-274389 et al., Dec. 6, 1996, 97-1 CPD ¶ 41 at 5-6; *Meridian Corp.*, B-246330.3, July 19, 1993, 93-2 CPD ¶ 29 at 6-7.

See also *USGC, Inc.*, Comp. Gen. Dec. B-400184.2, 2009 CPD ¶ 9 (innovative disincentive plan offered agency a way to reduce risk); *Cerner Corp.*, Comp. Gen. Dec. B-293093, 2004 CPD ¶ 34 (selection of approach that agency evaluated as best meeting RFP's performance goals); *Preferred Sys. Solutions*, Comp. Gen. Dec. B-291750, 2003 CPD ¶ 56 (transition plan and resumes of key personnel demonstrated that management plan offered lower risk even though such information was not required by RFP); *Israel Aircraft Indus., Ltd.*, Comp. Gen. Dec. B-274389, 97-1 CPD ¶ 41 (enhanced safety of aircraft subsystem intrinsic to stated evaluation factors covering performance and usability of subsystem); *Hydro Eng'g, Inc. v. United States*, 37 Fed. Cl. 448 (1997) (efficiency, reliability and maintainability of equipment properly considered in evaluating design of equipment); and *JoaQuin Mfg. Corp.*, Comp. Gen. Dec. B-275185, 97-1 CPD ¶ 48 (weight, number of footings, and visibility properly related to the suitability of design evaluation factor).

Also inherent in the evaluation of technical and management factors is the *risk* involved in successfully carrying out the proposed management or technical approach to be performed under the prospective contract. Thus, the scoring can account for such risks even though the RFP does not describe this aspect of the evaluation process. See, for example, *S-Tron*, Comp. Gen. Dec. B-244767.2, 92-1 CPD ¶ 409 (possibility that protester could not meet expedited delivery schedule was a proper reason to deduct points from the proposal); *Honeywell, Inc.*, Comp. Gen. Dec. B-238184, 90-1 CPD ¶ 435 (proposed reverse engineering of software created the risk of a failure to meet required schedules and costs); *AT&T Techs., Inc.*, Comp. Gen. Dec. B-237069, 90-1 CPD ¶ 114 (inability to test computerized system until in actual use created great technical and scheduling risks); *Raytheon Support Servs. Co.*, 68 Comp. Gen. 566 (B-234920), 89-2 CPD ¶ 84 (insufficient staff and organization needed to meet program requirements created risk of failure to meet contract requirements); and *Kaiser Elecs.*, 68 Comp. Gen. 48 (B-232175), 88-2 CPD ¶ 448 (new design approach created technical risk of malfunction).

In spite of the breadth of the rules permitting significant leeway in interpreting the scope of the listed evaluation factors, an agency may not evaluate an issue that has no relationship to the factors contained in the RFP. GAO has stated that there must be a "clear nexus between the stated (evaluation) criteria and the unstated criteria," *Global Analytic Info. Tech. Servs., Inc.*, Comp. Gen. Dec. B-298840.2, 2007 CPD ¶ 57. See *T-C Transcription*, Comp. Gen. Dec. B-401470, 2009 CPD ¶ 172 (improper to downgrade proposal for lack of resumes when RFP did not call for their submission); *Consolidated Eng'g Servs., Inc.*, Comp. Gen. Dec. B-311313, 2008 CPD ¶ 146 (improper to evaluate whether offeror had performed all services in a single past contract when factor was experience of "size, scope and complexity" of proposed work); *Meridian Mgmt. Corp.*, Comp. Gen. Dec. B-285127, 2000 CPD ¶ 121 (maintenance and repair of specialized laboratory equipment not within scope of services for laboratories when offerors were not permitted to see laboratories before proposing and no specialized equipment mentioned in RFP); *NITCO*, Comp. Gen. Dec. B-246185, 92-1 CPD ¶ 212 (improper to evaluate past experience in manufacturing a product when there was no indication in the RFP that this would be a consideration); *Flight Int'l Group, Inc.*, 69 Comp. Gen. 741 (B-238953.4), 90-2 CPD ¶ 257 (financial condition was not within the scope of subfactor "ability to meet the published schedule requirements of the government at an acceptable level of risk"); and *J.M. Cashman, Inc.*, Comp. Gen. Dec. B-233733, 89-1 CPD ¶ 380 (improper to downgrade an offeror for proposing to subcontract work when there was no mention of the issue in the evaluation factors).

Agencies have encountered problems in attempting to include price realism as a consideration when it is not listed as a factor. See *Possehn Consulting*, Comp. Gen. Dec. B-278579, 98-1 CPD ¶ 10, where GAO held that price realism did not fall within the past performance, experience, or key personnel factors. GAO stated that price realism would have been a legitimate consideration if there had been a factor encompassing the offerors' understanding of the work. Compare *SEEMA, Inc.*, Comp. Gen. Dec. B-277988, 98-1 CPD ¶ 12, where consideration of price realism was found to be within the scope of the factors because the RFP included a factor evaluating management. GAO found that price realism was within the scope of this factor because the RFP description of what would be evaluated in the management area included the evaluation of understanding of the work. Price realism has also been held to fall under other factors, *Centech Group, Inc.*, Comp. Gen. Dec. B-278715, 98-1 CPD ¶ 108 (technical competence factor); and *Arora Group, Inc.*, Comp. Gen. Dec. B-277674, 98-1 CPD ¶ 64 (proposal risk factor).

## b. Narrowing the Scope

Agencies have also been permitted to evaluate only those considerations that they perceive to be relevant to an evaluation factor. See, for example, *EastCo Bldg. Servs., Inc.*, Comp. Gen. Dec. B-275334, 97-1 CPD ¶ 83, where evaluation of past performance of only contracts of a similar size was considered proper even though the RFP did not mention this limitation, and *AVIATE L.L.C.*, Comp. Gen. Dec. B-275058.6, 97-1 CPD ¶ 162, where a factor used in selecting the source was the awardee's experience on performance-based contracting although the RFP did not specifically call for that type of experience. See also *AWD Techs., Inc.*, Comp. Gen. Dec. B-250081.2, 93-1 CPD ¶ 83 (experience in the specific work called for by the contract was properly given heavy weight when the evaluation factor was denominated "past project experience").

## 2. Failure to Evaluate a Stated Factor

Once an evaluation factor has been included in the RFP, the agency may not ignore that factor. In *Cardkey Sys., Inc.*, Comp. Gen. Dec. B-239433, 90-2 CPD ¶ 159, an evaluation was found improper because it did not consider a feature of the system being procured that had been designated as "desirable" in the RFP. GAO found that the protester had increased its price to provide the feature and was prejudiced by the fact that the feature was not considered during the evaluation. See also *General Dynamics Info. Tech.*, Comp. Gen. Dec. B-299873, 2007 CPD ¶ 194 (agency used labor rates proposed by an offeror in one table when the RFP stated that the rates in another table would be used if there was an inconsistency); *Advanced Sys. Dev., Inc.*, Comp. Gen. Dec. B-298411, 2006 CPD ¶ 137 (agency did not evaluate price proposals for "completeness" of supporting data when RFP stated it would be evaluated); Comp. Gen. Dec. B-297444.2, 2006 CPD ¶ 76 (RFP on-site performance requirement ignored in evaluation); *KIC Dev., LLC*, Comp. Gen. Dec. B-297425.2, 2006 CPD ¶ 27 (agency determined offeror did not meet experience requirement when RFP allowed subcontractor experience to meet requirement); *EPW Closure Servs., LLC*, Comp. Gen. Dec. B-294910, 2006 CPD ¶ 3 (agency failed to assess stated factor in evaluation); *Lockheed Martin Corp.*, Comp. Gen. Dec. B-293679, 2004 CPD ¶ 115 (agency determined that proposal met RFP requirement to fully describe design features of product based on evaluator's knowledge of subcontractor's competence); *Computer Info. Specialist, Inc.*, Comp. Gen. Dec. B-293049, 2004 CPD ¶ 1 (agency relied on blanket statements of compliance when RFP called for submission of specific information showing compliance); *CSE Constr.*, Comp. Gen. Dec. B-291268.2, 2002 CPD ¶ 207 (evaluation of understanding of work when that was not a stated factor); *Priority One Servs., Inc.*, Comp. Gen. Dec. B-288836, 2002 CPD ¶ 79 (no determination of probable cost of offers in cost reimbursement contract); *Wackenhut Int'l, Inc.*, Comp. Gen. Dec. B-286193, 2001 CPD ¶ 8 (failure to make "comprehensive review of compensation plans" as called for by RFP); *Saco Def. Corp.*, Comp. Gen. Dec. B-283885, 2000 CPD ¶ 34 (rating proposal low risk when offeror did not provide detailed information required by RFP to make the assessment); *ENMAX Corp.*, Comp. Gen. Dec. B-281965, 99-1 CPD ¶ 102 (rating proposal acceptable when offeror did not submit required information); *E.L. Hamm & Assocs., Inc.*, Comp. Gen. Dec. B-280766.3, 99-1 CPD ¶ 85 (failure to adjust labor rates in cost realism analysis to conform to wage determination); *Labat-Anderson*, 71 Comp. Gen. 252 (B-246071), 92-1 CPD ¶ 193 (institutional experience and quality of proposal not evaluated); and *Cenci Powder Prods., Inc.*, 68 Comp. Gen. 387 (B-234030), 89-1 CPD ¶ 381 (seven factors not considered).

The same rule applies to past performance. When it is designated as an evaluation factor, a source selection official may not ignore information regarding poor past performance of an offeror, *G. Marine Diesel*, 68 Comp. Gen. 577 (B-236622), 89-2 CPD ¶ 101 (agency failed to use data within agency regarding poor performance of ongoing contract), or good past performance, *Univox California, Inc.*, Comp. Gen. Dec. B-210941, 83-2 CPD ¶ 395 (agency failed to use data furnished by offeror); *Inlingua Schs. of Languages*, Comp. Gen. Dec. B-229784, 88-1 CPD ¶ 340 (agency failed to use data within agency relating to performance as incumbent contractor). Neither may it treat all past performance as equally relevant when RFP called for assessing varying degrees of relevance, *Clean Harbors Envt'l Servs., Inc.*, Comp. Gen. Dec. B-296176.2, 2005 CPD ¶ 222.

### 3. Subfactors

When a subfactor is specified in the RFP, it is subject to the same rule applying to factors — it may not be ignored in the evaluation. Thus, it was improper for an agency to fail to consider six of twelve specified evaluation subfactors where the effect was to increase the relative importance of price from 30% to 50%, *Dynalectron Corp.*, Comp. Gen. Dec. B-187057, 77-1 CPD ¶ 95. If subfactors are listed without any indication of relative importance, they will be treated as equally important. Thus, giving such a subfactor "predominant" importance is improper, *Isratex, Inc. v. United States*, 25 Cl. Ct. 223 (1992). See also *Lloyd H. Kessler, Inc.*, Comp. Gen. Dec. B-284693, 2000 CPD ¶ 96, sustaining a protest where a subfactor was given very heavy importance without notice in the RFP.

When a subfactor is not specified in the RFP, it may be used in the evaluation of offers if it meets the relationship rule discussed above. GAO has been liberal in applying this rule. See, for example, *Bendix Field Eng'g Corp.*, Comp. Gen. Dec. B-241156, 91-1 CPD ¶ 44, where the past performance factor listed two subfactors, "technical performance" and "schedule performance," yet GAO ruled that it was proper to downgrade past performance because of a cost overrun on a prior contract. See also *Barnes & Reinecke, Inc.*, Comp. Gen. Dec. B-236622, 89-2 CPD ¶ 572, where past efforts in designing tracked vehicles were found to be reasonably related to a subfactor covering "knowledge of Tracked Armored Vehicles." In *Stewart-Warner Elecs. Corp.*, Comp. Gen. Dec. B-235774.3, 89-2 CPD ¶ 598, GAO permitted the evaluation of 31 technical subfactors where the RFP called for "paying appropriate premiums for measured increments of quality."

Subfactors need not be included on a separate list if they are described in a narrative form in the description of the factor, *Moran Assocs.*, Comp. Gen. Dec. B-240564.2, 91-2 CPD ¶ 495. In that case GAO apparently believed that a diligent offeror would identify the subfactors from the narrative description. See also *ITT Electron Tech. Div.*, Comp. Gen. Dec. B-242289, 91-1 CPD ¶ 383, holding that there was no need to disclose an evaluation checklist when the items on the list were reasonably related to the evaluation factors. In *Stone Webster Eng'g Corp.*, Comp. Gen. Dec. B-255286.2, 94-2 CPD ¶ 306, the protester contended that the evaluation was improper because the agency evaluated proposals on a basis of "general strategy," which was not listed as an evaluation factor in the RFP. The agency stated that general strategy was not a separate evaluation criterion but was, however, considered as part of the evaluation of several factors that were set forth in the RFP. GAO agreed, finding that the RFP did state that strategy formulation and selection of appropriate tactics would be a significant subfactor under the understanding the anticipated work evaluation factor.

## 4. Changing Factors or Subfactors

As discussed earlier, FAR 15.206 provides specific guidance governing changes to overnment requirements. These rules also apply to changes to the evaluation factors. Thus, if an agency determines during the evaluation process that different evaluation factors will yield a more sound source selection decision, it may amend the RFP to ensure that the offerors have an opportunity to respond to the new evaluation factors. For example, GAO has held that changes in evaluation factors are ordinarily permitted during the course of a negotiated procurement so long as the offerors are given the opportunity to respond to them, *Consulting & Program Mgmt.*, 66 Comp. Gen. 229 (B-225369), 87-1 CPD ¶ 229. Similarly, in *H.J. Group Ventures, Inc.*, Comp. Gen. Dec. B-246139.3, 92-2 CPD ¶ 116, it was found proper to add an evaluation factor for performance risk and permit new proposals.

One result of this rule is that a relaxation of requirements for the winning offeror without informing the other competitors is improper, *Courtland Mem'l Hosp.*, Comp. Gen. Dec. B-286890, 2001 CPD ¶ 48 (disregard of "preferences" in RFP); *ACS Gov't Solutions Group, Inc.*, Comp. Gen. Dec. B-282098, 99-1 CPD ¶ 106 (relaxation of specification guidance on use of in-house system); *Barents Group, L.L.C.*, Comp. Gen. Dec. B-276082, 97-1 CPD ¶ 164 (relaxation of requirement to submit resumes in specific labor category); *Armour of Am., Inc.*, Comp. Gen. Dec. B-237690, 90-1 CPD ¶ 304 (relaxation of technical specifications); *MTS Sys. Corp.*, Comp. Gen. Dec. B-238137, 90-1 CPD ¶ 434 (relaxation of domestic source requirement). In *Minnesota Mining & Mfg. Co. v. Shultz*, 583 F. Supp. 184 (D.D.C. 1984), the court found an improper deviation from the technical requirements by the offeror that had been selected for award and noted that any change in factors must be communicated to every offeror. See also *Paper Corp. of the U.S.*, Comp. Gen. Dec. B-229785, 88-1 CPD ¶ 388, where the agency was found to have improperly relaxed a testing requirement in evaluating the sample submitted by the awardee, and *Management Sys. Designers, Inc.*, Comp. Gen. Dec. B-244383.4, 91-2 CPD ¶ 518, where the agency was required to inform offerors of a significant change in quantity. In extreme cases, substantial and significant changes in the evaluation factors will require an amended solicitation in order to allow other offerors the opportunity to submit proposals, *United Tel. Co.*, Comp. Gen. Dec. B-246977, 92-1 CPD ¶ 374.

The requirement that offerors be advised of changes in evaluation factors does not apply to changes in subfactors that are reasonably related to stated evaluation factors but which are not themselves listed in the RFP, *Dynalectron Corp.*, Comp. Gen. Dec. B-199741, 81-2 CPD ¶ 70. In that case, GAO reasoned that the unlisted subcriterion which was changed "was devised in order to assist the technical evaluators in their internal deliberations."

The same procedures must be used when an agency changes the evaluation scheme. Thus, it is not improper for an agency to issue an amended solicitation altering the relative importance of the evaluation factors, *Unisys Corp.*, 67 Comp. Gen. 512 (B-230019.2), 88-2 CPD ¶ 35 (clarifying the importance of cost), or the overall evaluation scheme, *Galler Assocs., Inc.*, Comp. Gen. Dec. B-210204, 83-1 CPD ¶ 515 (changing from low cost acceptable offer scheme to best value scheme), *American Lawn Serv., Inc.*, Comp. Gen. Dec. B-267715, 95-2 CPD ¶ 278 (changing from best value scheme to lowest priced, technically acceptable basis). It is also proper to amend the evaluation scheme in the solicitation to accommodate a method of performance suggested by an offeror, *Loral Terracom*, 66 Comp. Gen. 272 (B-224908), 87-1 CPD ¶ 182 (different technical approach). Of course, such changes are only permissible if all offerors still under consideration are informed of the change, *Labat-Anderson Inc.*, 71 Comp. Gen. 252 (B-246071), 92-1 CPD ¶ 193 (change required by issuance of amendment to RFP or by raising issue in discussions).

GAO will not overturn an award in which the agency has changed the evaluation criteria without notifying the offerors if the losers are not prejudiced by the change, *FKW Inc. Sys.*, Comp. Gen. Dec. B-235989, 89-2 CPD ¶ 370; *Akal Security, Inc.*, Comp. Gen. Dec. B-261996, 96-1 CPD ¶ 33; *Mc Rae Indus., Inc.*, Comp. Gen. Dec. B-287609.2, 2001 CPD ¶ 127.

## D. Disqualification of an Offeror

There is a growing body of law holding that an offeror should be disqualified from the procurement if the agency learns during the evaluation that the offeror has violated a criminal statute or committed some other serious impropriety. Such disqualification is not a determination of lack of responsibility and thus need not be referred to the Small Business Administration if the offeror is a small business, *NKF Eng'g, Inc. v. United States*, 805 F.2d 372 (Fed. Cir. 1986); *Compliance Corp. v. United States*, 22 Cl. Ct. 193 (1990), *aff'd*, 960 F.2d 157 (Fed. Cir. 1992). The result of this rule is that an offeror may be immediately dropped from the evaluation when the agency learns of the impropriety.

One type of violation that has led to such disqualification is fraud in the form of material misrepresentation. See, for example, *ACS Gov't Servs., Inc.*, Comp. Gen. Dec. B-293014, 2004 CPD ¶ 18, where GAO ruled that an offeror should be disqualified when it falsely represented that three key personnel had agreed to work for the firm. Other cases disqualifying offerors for material misrepresentation include *Patriot Contract Servs. — Advisory Opinion*, Comp. Gen. Dec. B-294777.3, 2005 CPD ¶ 97 (submission of resumes without discussing salary as required by RFP and misstatements as to reasons why they subsequently rejected employment); *S.C. Myers & Assocs., Inc.*, Comp. Gen. Dec. B-286297, 2001 CPD ¶ 16 (submission of name of key person with knowledge that that person would only remain on job during initial phase of contract); *ManTech Advanced Sys. Int'l, Inc.*, Comp. Gen. Dec. B-255719.2, 94-1 CPD ¶ 326 (submission of resumes of personnel with no intent to use those workers); *PPATHI, Inc.*, Comp. Gen. Dec. B-249182.4, 93-1 CPD ¶ 64 (multiple nondisclosures and false certifications); *Electronic Data Sys. Fed. Corp.*, GSBCA 9869-P, 89-2 BCA ¶ 21,655, *recons. denied*, 89-2 BCA ¶ 21,778, *aff'd sub. nom. Planning Research Corp. v. United States*, 971 F.2d 736 (Fed. Cir. 1992) (submission of resumes of 101 personnel to be employed on contract with no intent to use those workers); *Ultra Tech. Corp.*, Comp. Gen. Dec. B-230309.6, 89-1 CPD ¶ 42 (proposing person as "lead technician" without obtaining his permission); and *Informatics, Inc.*, 57 Comp. Gen. 217 (B-188566), 78-1 CPD ¶ 53 (misstating the availability of proposed personnel). See also *Biospherics, Inc.*, Comp. Gen. Dec. B-253891.2, 93-2 CPD ¶ 333, where GAO agreed that an offeror should be disqualified when it did not disclose that a number of the personnel proposed for the contract had also been proposed for another contract being competed at the same time.

Disqualification is not proper when the misrepresentation is inadvertent rather than intentional, *Johnson Controls Sec, Sys.*, Comp. Gen. Dec. B-296490, 2007 CPD ¶ 102 (no recommendation to disqualify offeror when agency recorded false statement but record of oral presentation did not clearly indicate that statement had been made); *Integration Techs. Group, Inc.*, Comp. Gen. Dec. B-291657, 2003 CPD ¶ 55 (no recommendation to disqualify offeror that had misrepresented the role of important subcontractor); *Tucson Mobilephone, Inc.*, Comp. Gen. Dec. B-258408.3, 95-1 CPD ¶ 267 (record did not support a finding that offeror intentionally misrepresented that it had lead technician's permission to use his credentials); and *Universal Techs., Inc.*, Comp. Gen. Dec. B-248808.2, 92-2 CPD ¶ 212 (false certification not made in bad faith). In *Mantech Field Eng'g Corp.*, Comp. Gen. Dec. B-245886.4, 92-1 CPD ¶ 309, *recons. denied*, 92-2 CPD ¶ 89, although the offeror made no attempt to determine whether personnel were available prior to submitting its BAFO,

GAO did not find an intentional misrepresentation and recommended that discussions be reopened.

GAO has held that the degree of misrepresentation will establish whether an offeror must be barred from the procurement. See *Aerospace Design & Fabrication, Inc.*, Comp. Gen. Dec. B-278896.2, 98-1 CPD ¶ 139, holding that the agency was not required to disqualify an offeror that had falsely stated that it had commitments from three of its five key personnel because the misrepresentation was not "pervasive."

It is unlikely that a misrepresentation will be found when an offeror makes statements about events that will occur in the future. For example, no misrepresentation was found when an offeror stated that its product was a nondevelopmental item but numerous changes were required to meet requirements, *Northrop Grumman Corp. v. United States*, 50 Fed. Cl. 443 (2001). See also *R&D Maint. Servs., Inc.*, Comp. Gen. Dec. B-292342, 2003 CPD ¶ 162 (disqualification not required when company subcontracted work that was proposed to be performed in-house); *Ann Riley & Assocs., Ltd*, Comp. Gen. Dec. B-271741.3, 97-1 CPD ¶ 122 (violation of subcontracting limitation due to events during performance).

The Court of Federal Claims has held that there is no misrepresentation if the offeror learns after submission of its final proposal revisions that its key personnel will not be available but does not inform the government, *OAO Corp. v. United States*, 49 Fed. Cl. 478 (2001). The court reasoned that it was not clear that there was a legal duty to update a proposal in this manner. Compare *Dual, Inc.*, Comp. Gen. Dec. B-280179, 98-2 CPD ¶ 133, holding that there had been a misrepresentation when an offeror sold a division employing the listed personnel after submitting its proposal but did not inform the agency of the sale.

Offerors have also been disqualified for violating or appearing to violate the conflict of interest laws barring retired government employees from participating in certain government procurements, 18 U.S.C. § 207 (representation of contractor in matter where there has been substantial prior involvement). See, for example, *Guardian Techs. Int'l*, Comp. Gen. Dec. B-270213, 96-1 CPD ¶ 104 (recommending disqualification of company whose president had access to inside information because he was former employee of procuring agency); and *Naddaf Int'l Trading Co.*, Comp. Gen. Dec. B-238768.2, 90-2 CPD ¶ 316 (ruling that the contracting officer had properly disqualified an offeror that employed a retired military officer who had contacted the Small Business Administration to argue for the issuance of a Certificate of Competency). Compare *CNA Corp. v. United States*, 81 Fed. Cl. 722 (2008), holding that a company should not be disqualified because its principal investigator had not participated "substantially" in program before he left the agency.

Offerors have also been disqualified for conducting employment discussions with a current government employee, 18 U.S.C. § 208 (engaging in discussion of future employment with government official); 41 U.S.C. § 423 (engaging in any discussion of future employment with a procurement officer). For example, in *NKF Eng'g, Inc. v. United States*, 805 F.2d 372 (Fed. Cir. 1986), the court ruled that the contracting officer had properly disqualified an offeror who hired a member of the Navy source selection board after the initial evaluation and prior to the submission of the best and final offer. The contracting officer had concluded that this gave an appearance of impropriety even though the offeror claimed that the government employee had been carefully screened from the people in the company handling the procurement.

Conflicts of interest involving current government employees will disqualify offerors from the procurement, 18 U.S.C. § 208 (participation in procurement involving offeror in which employee had financial interest); FAR Subpart 3.6 (award of contract to company owned or controlled by government employee). For example, in *United Tel. Co.*, GSBCA 10031-P, 89-3 BCA ¶ 22,108, an offeror was disqualified because its subcontractor had used a government employee participating in the procurement as a consultant during the competition. Similarly, in *Revnet Env't & Analytical Lab., Inc.*, Comp. Gen. Dec. B-221002.2, 86-2 CPD ¶ 102, the contracting officer disqualified an offeror that had submitted an offer developed by a government employee who had attempted to disassociate himself from his company by turning it over to his wife.

The responsibility for determining whether an offeror should be disqualified due to a conflict of interest rests with the agency and will be upheld by GAO so long as the decision is reasonable. See *Cygnus Corp.*, Comp. Gen. Dec. B-275957, 97-1 CPD ¶ 202, where the protester asserted that the offeror should have been disqualified from the competition because the offeror's spouse was a government employee. The protester argued that by virtue of having vested marital property rights, the government employee possessed substantial ownership or control of the offeror such that the matter constituted a conflict of interest. GAO denied the protest finding no evidence of substantial control or interest such as to warrant disqualification.

Offerors are also properly disqualified because of an organizational conflict of interest, *DSD Lab., Inc. v. United States*, 46 Fed. Cl. 467 (2000). There the court sustained a disqualification because the company had given advice to the agency on structuring the procurement and participated in writing the work statement. See also *Lucent Techs. World Servs. Inc.*, Comp. Gen. Dec. B-295462, 2005 CPD ¶ 55 (protester properly disqualified because it prepared specification for commercial-type item); *Aetna Gov't Health Plans, Inc.*, Comp. Gen. Dec. B-254397.15, 96-2 CPD ¶ 129 (protester should have been disqualified because of impaired objectivity); *QualMED, Inc. v. Office of Civilian Health & Med. Program of the Uniformed Servs.*, 934 F. Supp. 1227 (D. Col. 1996) (agreeing that GAO had power to make recommendation in *Aetna*). In *L-3 Servs., Inc.*, Comp. Gen. Dec. B-400134.11, 2009 CPD ¶ 171, GAO recommended that a subcontractor with an OCI be excluded from the competition but that the agency could reopen the competition allowing the contractor to obtain a new subcontractor.

Improperly obtaining information during the procurement process will also serve as a grounds for disqualify offerors. For example, in *Kellogg Brown & Root Servs., Inc.*, Comp. Gen. Dec. B-400787.2, 2009 CPD ¶ 54, the protester was properly disqualified from competing for two task orders when its employee had received an email from the contracting officer containing proprietary information and had not immediately deleted it from his computers. GAO held that the contracting officer had cause to disqualify the protester because of an appearance of impropriety even though the employee stated that he had not read the document. See also *Computer Tech. Assocs., Inc.*, Comp. Gen. Dec. B-288622, 2001 CPD ¶ 187 (reasonable to disqualify protester whose employees had seen transcripts of competitors' oral presentations); *Litton Sys., Inc.*, 68 Comp. Gen. 422 (B-234060), 89-1 CPD ¶ 450, *recons. denied*, 68 Comp. Gen. 677 (B-234060.2) 89-2 CPD ¶ 228 (contractor disqualified for obtaining government information through a marketing consultant); *AT&T Commc'ns, Inc.*, GSBCA 9252-P, 88-2 BCA ¶ 20,805 (offeror disqualified when it had been given the range of its competitor's prices by a government employee with whom it had conducted employment discussions and to whom it had given gratuities). Similarly, in *Compliance Corp.*, Comp. Gen. Dec. B-239252, 90-2 CPD ¶ 126, *recons. denied*, Comp. Gen. Dec. 239252.3, 90-2 CPD ¶ 435, the contracting officer properly disqualified an offeror who had obtained government information from an incumbent service contractor through the use of "industrial espionage." The Federal Circuit agreed with this decision in *Compliance Corp. v. United States*, 22 Cl. Ct. 193 (1990), *aff'd*, 960 F.2d 157 (Fed. Cir. 1992), holding that industrial espionage was a valid ground for disqualification (even though no government personnel were involved) because such activity puts the integrity of the procurement system at risk.

In reviewing the reasonableness of an agency's decision on disqualification, GAO will examine both the nature of the information to which the offeror had access, *Textron Marine Sys.*, Comp. Gen. Dec. B-255580.3, 94-2 CPD ¶ 63 (information disclosed did not give an unfair competitive advantage), and the conditions under which access was gained, *KPMG Peat Marwick*, Comp. Gen. Dec. B-251902.3, 93-2 CPD ¶ 272, *recons. denied*, 94-1 CPD ¶ 201 (information received through Freedom of Information Act). For example, in *IGIT, Inc.*, Comp. Gen. Dec. B-271823, 96-2 CPD ¶ 51, GAO sustained a protest challenging a contracting officer's decision to disqualify the protester from the competition on the basis that the protester had possessed a page from the installation's solicitation register which included a lump-sum government estimate for the cost of the solicited work, finding that there was no basis to conclude that the offeror obtained the information improperly. The information was taped to the offeror's door apparently to advise IGIT of the agency's decision to resolicit the laundry services rather than to exercise the options. GAO also found that the information could be given to the other offerors to ameliorate any competitive advantage.

Offerors that give bribes or gratuities to government employees will also be disqualified. See *Litton Sys., Inc.*, 68 Comp. Gen. 422 (B-234060), 89-1 CPD ¶ 450, *recons. denied*, 68 Comp. Gen. 677 (B-234060.2), 89-2 CPD ¶ 228, ordering termination of a major contract due to bribery of a high-ranking government employee by the awardee. See also *Howema Bau-GmbH*, Comp. Gen. Dec. B-245356, 91-2 CPD ¶ 214 (excluding protester from contract consideration due to suspected bribery of government officials); and *National Roofing & Painting Corp.*, ASBCA 36,551, 90-2 BCA ¶ 22,936 (voiding contract because it was "tainted with fraud from its inception as well as during performance").

## E. Assessment of Strengths, Weaknesses and Risks

The most important part of the evaluation process is the assessment of the strengths, deficiencies, significant weaknesses and risks of each proposal and the assessment of their relative qualities, FAR 15.305(a). This is the critical information that is used to make the source selection decision and serves as the documentation supporting that decision. The FAR contains no guidance on the timing of these assessments but it has been common practice to direct the evaluators to make their initial evaluation by only assessing each proposals' quality in meeting the requirements of the RFP and its evaluation factors and then to have the evaluators or some other group make the assessment of the relative merits of the competing proposals. In a case where the Air Force regulation required this two-step procedure, the Court of Federal Claims held that permitting the evaluators to make the comparative assessment was a "harmless regulatory violation," *Aero Corp. v. United States*, 38 Fed. Cl. 237 (1997). See also *Food Servs. of Am.*, Comp. Gen. Dec. B-276860, 97-2 CPD ¶ 55, and *ASR Mgmt. & Tech. Servs.*, Comp. Gen. Dec. B-244862.3, 92-1 CPD ¶ 383, where GAO noted that comparative assessments were made by technical evaluators but did not comment on the use of the procedure. Thus, it appears that agencies can use a two-step evaluation process or evaluate the proposals by making a comparative assessment in the initial evaluation. Whatever system is used, it should be clear that the end result of the evaluation process is a comparative assessment of the relative merits of the proposals because that must be the basis for the ultimate source selection decision, FAR 15.308.

## 1. Documenting the Assessment

FAR 15.305(a) requires documentation as follows:

> The relative strengths, deficiencies, significant weaknesses, and risks supporting proposal evaluation shall be documented in the contract file.

This documentation is generally prepared in narrative form simultaneously with some notation of a rating or scoring and describes the reasons that the evaluators have assigned the scores to each proposal. Thus, these narratives identify the "strengths, weaknesses, and risks" of each proposal that have led to the score that has been assigned. A fully documented evaluation will contain such narratives for each score — generally at the lowest level of scoring in the evaluation scheme. It is very helpful if these narratives contain a reference to the specific pages of the proposal that contain the information on which the evaluation is based.

These narrative statements can be prepared by each individual evaluator or as a summary evaluation by all of the evaluators that have assessed the element of the proposals being evaluated. Preparation of these narratives at the same time the proposals are scored provides an excellent discipline for the evaluators because it forces them to justify their scores. If the narratives are prepared by the entire evaluation team, this will also force evaluators to reconcile disparate scores or at least to focus on the reason for the disparities. Thus, this part of the narratives can improve the scoring as well as flow valuable information to the source selection official. When a consensus evaluation document is prepared, it is important that it include sufficient explanation of the assessment so that it can be reviewed in the event of a protest, *DGR Assocs., Inc.*, Comp. Gen. Dec. B-285428, 2000 CPD ¶ 145.

Although the FAR gives no guidance on the extent of documentation required, it is clear that GAO demands sufficient documentation to permit consideration of a protest asserting that the agency has not followed the evaluation scheme in the RFP. See *Satellite Servs., Inc.*, Comp. Gen. Dec. B-286508, 2001 CPD ¶ 30, stating:

> In reviewing an agency's evaluation of proposals and source selection decision, we examine the record to determine whether the agency acted reasonably and consistent with the stated evaluation factors as well as applicable statutes and regulations. *PRC, Inc.*, B-274698.2, B-274698.3, Jan. 23, 1997, 97-1 CPD ¶ 115 at 4. Implicit in the foregoing is that the evaluation must be documented in sufficient detail to show that it was reasonable and bears a rational relationship to the announced evaluation factors. FAR §§ 15.305(a), FAR 15.308 .

This appears to be a flexible requirement based on the complexity of each source selection. In *Champion-Alliance, Inc.*, Comp. Gen. Dec. B-249504, 92-2 CPD ¶ 386, GAO held that relatively little documentation was required from the agency because the requirements under the RFP were fairly unambiguous and the proposals were very similar. See also *Quality Elevator Co.*, Comp. Gen. Dec. B-276750, 97-2 CPD ¶ 28, where inadequate documentation was overlooked because the proposals were very similar. In *Apex Marine Ship Mgmt. Co., LLC*, Comp. Gen. Dec. B-278276.25, 2000 CPD ¶ 164, GAO stated that there was "no absolute requirement that evaluation records must include narrative explanations for every score assigned." It has also been held that there is no need for narrative statements when the proposal was acceptable with no notable advantages or disadvantages, *PRC, Inc.*, Comp. Gen. Dec. B-274698.2, 97-1 CPD ¶ 115. See also *Delta Dental Plan v. Perry*, F. Supp. (N.D. Cal. 1996) (no need for narrative supporting a rating of "satisfactory").

When the technical scores of the two top offerors were within one percentage point of each other, GAO sustained a protest because the scores were not adequately supported by written narratives, *Universal Shipping Co.*, Comp. Gen. Dec B-223905.2, 87-1 CPD ¶ 424. For other protests that have been sustained because of insufficient documentation, see *LIS, Inc.*, Comp. Gen. Dec. B-4002646.2, 2010 CPD ¶ 5 (documents contain no discussion of "relative proposal strengths, deficiencies, significant weaknesses, and risks"); *Radiation Oncology Group of WNY, PC*, Comp. Gen. Dec. B-310354.2, 2009 CPD ¶ 136 (agency record contained no "comprehensive assessment or listing of the proposals' strengths and weaknesses"); *Panacea Consulting, Inc.*, Comp. Gen. Dec. B-299307.4, 2007 CPD ¶ 141 (no statement of strengths or weaknesses supporting numerical scores); *Pemco Aeroplex, Inc.*, Comp. Gen. Dec. B-310372, 2007 CPD ¶ 2, *recons. denied*, 2008 CPD ¶ 24 (no documentation supporting element of price realism analysis); *Systems Research & Applications Corp.*, Comp. Gen. Dec. B-299818, 2008 CPD ¶ 28 (evaluators worksheets contained no explanation of scoring); *Intercon Assocs., Inc.*, Comp. Gen. Dec. B-298282, 2006 CPD ¶ 121 (evaluator documents "factually incorrect, internally contradictory," or "cryptic"); *Keeton Corrs., Inc.*, Comp. Gen. Dec. B-293348, 2005 CPD ¶ 44 (no evidence that source selection official was presented with details of evaluation); *National City Bank of Indiana*, Comp. Gen. Dec. B-287608.3, 2002 CPD ¶ 190 (no documentation explaining why staffing reductions would allow offeror to meet technical requirements); *Bank of Am.*, Comp. Gen. Dec. B-287608, 2001 CPD ¶ 137 ("virtually no evaluator worksheets" showing the basis for cost realism calculations and adjustments); *BAE Sys.*, Comp. Gen. Dec. B-287189, 2001 CPD ¶ 86 (no indication that a "potential strength" included in the protester's technical proposal was considered by the agency evaluators); *J & J Maint., Inc.*, Comp. Gen. Dec. B-284708.2, 2000 CPD ¶ 106 (no narratives showing how numerical scores were reconciled); *Future-Tec Mgmt., Sys., Inc.*, Comp. Gen. Dec. B-283793.5, 2000 CPD ¶ 59 (insufficient documentation of evaluation to understand source selection decision); *MCR Fed., Inc.*, Comp. Gen. Dec. B-280969, 99-1 CPD ¶ 8 (no documentation showing that technical proposals were equal when they were scored differently); *Matrix Int'l Logistics, Inc.*, Comp. Gen. Dec. B-272388.2, 97-2 CPD ¶ 89 (summary evaluation results with no narrative supporting changed scores on BAFOs); *JW Assocs., Inc.*, Comp. Gen. Dec. B-275209, 97-1 CPD ¶ 57 (one-paragraph summary of each proposal with no supporting narrative for low scores); *Engineering & Computation, Inc.*, Comp. Gen. Dec. B-261658, 95-2 CPD ¶ 176 (summary decision memorandum but no narrative for individual subfactors where significant risks had been found); *Deployable Hosp. Sys., Inc.*, Comp. Gen. Dec. B-260778, 95-2 CPD ¶ 65 (preaward survey showed significant distinctions between the two offerors that did not support an equal rating on their quality control factors and subfactors and the ratings were not otherwise explained or justified*)*; *Arco Mgmt. of Washington, D.C., Inc.*, Comp. Gen. Dec. B-248653, 92-2 CPD ¶ 173 (no narratives supporting point scores); *Northwest EnviroService, Inc.*, 71 Comp. Gen. 453 (B-247380.2), 92-2 CPD ¶ 38 (no documentation to support evaluation that competing offerors were equal in past performance); and *Beckman Instruments, Inc.*, Comp. Gen. Dec. B-246195.3, 92-1 CPD ¶ 365 (no documentation showing that agency evaluated changes in BAFO). When the agency's source selection apparently deviates in any way from the stated evaluation criteria, GAO will require comprehensive documentation explaining the apparent deviation, *Dewberry & Davis*, Comp. Gen. Dec. B-247116, 92-1 CPD ¶ 421 (award to low priced, technically acceptable offer where evaluation scheme provided that technical merit was more important than price).

In a rare case, *Helicopter Transport Servs. LLC*, Comp. Gen. Dec. B-400295, 2008 CPD ¶ 180, where the agency arrived at an evaluation of an offeror's past performance by a discussion by a group of evaluators providing their experience working with the offerors, GAO granted the protest because of lack of documentation, stating:

> In an evaluation that takes into account the agency's own knowledge of offerors' performance, the fundamental requirement that evaluation judgments be documented in sufficient detail to show that they are reasonable and not arbitrary must still be met. *Omega World Travel, Inc.*, B-271262.2, July 25, 1996, 96-2 CPD ¶ 44 at 4.

It appears to be relatively common practice for agencies to destroy evaluators worksheets when consensus evaluations are arrived at. However, this practice was held improper in *Pitney-Bowes Gov't Solutions, Inc. v. United States*, 93 Fed. Cl. 327 (2010), based on the record retention requirements in FAR Subpart 4.8. No sanctions were imposed on the agency for spoilation of evidence because backup copies of the documents were recovered and supplied to the protester, *Pitney-Bowes Gov't Solutions, Inc. v. United States*, 94 Fed. Cl. 1 (2010).

GAO had not sanctioned agencies for destroying evaluator worksheets, *Government Acquisitions, Inc.*, Comp. Gen. Dec. B-401048, 2009 CPD ¶ 137; *Joint Mgmt. & Tech. Servs.*, Comp. Gen. Dec. B-294229, 2004 CPD ¶ 208; *The Cmty. P'ship LLC*, Comp. Gen. Dec. B-286844, 2001 CPD ¶ 38; *Structural Pres. Sys., Inc.*, Comp. Gen. Dec. B-285085, 2000 CPD ¶ 131. See, however, *Dynalantic Corp.*, Comp. Gen. Dec. B-274944.2, 97-1 CPD ¶ 101, where GAO permitted the agency to attempt to justify the evaluation of the protester in a hearing after it had destroyed the evaluators' work papers. In sustaining the protest because of the lack of rationale supporting the decision, GAO granted protest costs and noted that they were higher because of the need for a hearing. It was also noted that the agency had decided to discontinue the practice of destroying work papers.

## 2. Comparison of Proposals

The other part of the narratives is the statement of the "relative qualities of the proposals." As noted above, this comparison of the proposals has generally been done as a second step in the evaluation process and is frequently done by the evaluation board or the evaluation team leaders. In many ways, this is the most important part of the narratives because it summarizes the information needed by the source selection official to make the selection decision.

This comparison of proposals should be prepared in sufficient detail to identify each area where there is a significant difference between proposals. Ideally, the narrative will contain a concise description of the difference and an assessment of the *value of the difference* or the *impact* that the difference will have on the procuring agency. This value/impact statement in the areas of technical and management provides the key information needed by the source selection official in making the tradeoff with the cost/price differences among offerors. Thus, such narratives provide the source selection official clear information concerning the relative advantages or disadvantages of proposals in a way that scores, such as numbers, colors, or adjectives obviously cannot.

Agencies are permitted considerable discretion in identifying the values and impacts of competing proposals during this comparative assessment. See *Alliant Techsystems, Inc.*, Comp. Gen. Dec. B-276162, 97-1 CPD ¶ 141, stating:

> Evaluating the relative merits of competing proposals is a matter within the discretion of the contracting agency since the agency is responsible for defining its needs and the best method of accommodating them, and it must bear the burden resulting from a defective evaluation. *Advanced Tech. and Research Corp.*, B-257451.2, Dec. 9, 1994, 94-2 CPD ¶230 at 3. Consequently, in reviewing an evaluation we will not reevaluate proposals but instead will examine the agency's evaluation to ensure that it was reasonable and consistent with the stated evaluation criteria.

See also *Suncoast Assocs., Inc.*, Comp. Gen. Dec. B-265920, 95-2 CPD ¶ 268, holding that the agency's explanation of why it determined two proposals to be technically equivalent, despite the protester's two-point advantage in technical scoring, was reasonable and consistent with the documentation which showed the relative strengths and weaknesses of the proposals. Compare *Northwest EnviroService, Inc.*, 71 Comp. Gen. 453 (B-247380.2), 92-2 CPD ¶ 38, sustaining a protest because the record lacked sufficient documentation to show that the source selection was reasonably based on the announced evaluation criteria.

## F. Scoring

After assessment of proposals, agencies generally score some or all of the evaluation factors as a means of summarizing the evaluations to assist the source selection official in making the tradeoff decision between the competing proposals. Thus, scoring systems are notational devices which provide a rough means of measuring differences between proposals. However, it is clear that, in almost all cases, the scores alone will not support a source selection decision. See *JW Assocs., Inc.*, Comp. Gen. Dec. B-275209, 97-1 CPD ¶57, stating:

> While both adjectival ratings and point scores are useful as guides to decision-making, they generally are not controlling, but rather, must be supported by documentation of the relative differences between proposals, their weaknesses and risks, and the basis and reasons for the selection decision.

In general, an agency's scoring system cannot be challenged, *MINACT, Inc.*, Comp. Gen. Dec B-400951, 2009 CPD ¶ 76 (adjectival rating permissible when RFP called for numerical scoring); *Trajen, Inc.*, Comp. Gen. Dec. B-296334, 2005 CPD ¶ 153 (use of three adjective system instead of five called for by RFP not grounds for protest); *BRC Assocs., Inc.*, Comp. Gen. Dec. B-237156, 90-1 CPD ¶ 145 (numerical scoring of subfactors permitted even though the RFP stated that subfactors did not have assigned points).

In addition, agency evaluators are given considerable discretion in assigning scores to proposals. See *MiTech, Inc.*, Comp. Gen. Dec. B-275078, 97-1 CPD ¶ 208, stating:

> The evaluation and scoring of proposals is a matter primarily within the discretion of the contracting activity since it is responsible for defining its needs and for determining the best methods of accommodating those needs, and technical evaluators have considerable latitude in assigning ratings which reflect their subjective judgments of a proposal's relative merits. *Bunker Ramo Corp.*, 56 Comp. Gen. 712 (1977), 77-1 CPD ¶ 427; *Met-Pro Corp.*, B-250706.2, Mar. 24, 1993, 93-1 CPD ¶ 263; *Abt Assocs., Inc.*, B-237060.2, Feb. 26, 1990, 90-1 CPD ¶ 223. In reviewing an agency's technical evaluation, we will not rescore proposals but rather will review the agency's evaluation to ensure that it was reasonable and in accordance with the RFP criteria. *Abt Assocs., Inc.*, *supra*. A protester's mere disagreement with the particular point scores awarded to its proposal does not render the evaluation unreasonable. *DBA Sys., Inc.*, B-241048, Jan. 15, 1991, 91-1 CPD ¶ 36.

Thus, when source selection decisions are based on the strengths, weakness, and risks in the proposals, protests of incorrect scoring are routinely denied. See, for example, *Blackwater Lodge & Training Ctr., Inc. v. United States*, 86 Fed. Cl. 488 (2009) ("Courts should look beyond the adjectival ratings because proposals awarded the same adjectival ratings are not necessarily equal in quality."); *Karrar Sys. Corp.*, Comp. Gen. Dec. B-310661.3, 2008 CPD ¶ 55 ("focus on the adjectival ratings . . . misplaced"); *GAP Solutions, Inc.*, Comp. Gen. Dec. B-310564, 2008 CPD ¶ 26 ("Where the evaluators and source selection official reasonably consider the underlying bases for the ratings . . . a protester's disagreement over the actual adjectival or numeric ratings assigned essentially is inconsequential"); *Pemco Aeroplex, Inc.*, Comp. Gen. Dec. B-310372, 2008 CPD ¶ 2 (proposals with same adjectival rating "not necessarily of equal quality"); *Raymond Assocs., LLC*, Comp. Gen. Dec. B-299496, 2007 CPD ¶ 107 (purportedly irrational averaging of subfactor ratings not relevant when decision considered strengths and weaknesses); *DeTekion Sec. Sys., Inc.*, Comp. Gen. Dec. B-298235, 2006 CPD ¶ 130 ("adjectival ratings and point scores are . . . tools to assist source selection officials in evaluating proposals; they do not mandate automatic selection of a particular proposal"); *Mechanical Equip. Co.*, Comp. Gen. Dec. B-292789.2, 2004 CPD ¶ 192 ("the protesters' disagreement over the actual adjectival ratings is essentially inconsequential"). This reasoning has been followed by GAO even when the protester had alleged that the scoring system called for by the RFP misled the protester in deciding what effort to propose, *Northrop Grumman Tech. Servs., Inc.*, Comp. Gen. Dec. B-291506, 2003 CPD ¶ 25. There the agency had used a computerized system that gave the same point score to "good" and "excellent" but had not actually relied on the system in making the final source selection decision.

Most scoring systems do not score all of the factors and subfactors. Technical factors appear to be the most frequently scored while price or cost is the least frequently scored. This is logical because the marginal difference in price or cost between the proposals, which will be used to make the source selection decision, is clearly apparent in dollar amounts and scoring tends to obscure rather than illuminate this difference. However, GAO has held that it is proper to give adjectival scores to life cycle costs, *Raytheon Co.*, Comp. Gen. Dec. B-298626.2, 2007 CPD ¶ 185.

Scoring systems are particularly useful when there are a large number of evaluation factors and subfactors. However, as the number of factors decreases, there is less need for scoring. For example, there have been a number of procurements were the only factors were past performance and price. In that case, there would appear to be no need to score the proposals.

Any system can be used as long as it provides meaningful differentiation among proposals of various merit. The most frequently used systems are adjectival rating systems, color coding, numerical scoring, and ranking. These are the systems identified in FAR 15.305(a).

## 1. *Adjectival Ratings*

Adjectival rating systems are widely used and generally call for the use of four or five ratings such as excellent, good, fair and poor or outstanding, highly acceptable, acceptable, marginally acceptable and unacceptable. They have the disadvantage of providing very few gradations to distinguish between proposals — making the scoring somewhat imprecise as a tool to measure the marginal differences between proposals. However, GAO has accepted the use of these systems — finding that they can give the source selection official a clear understanding of the relative merit of the proposals, *Dynamics Research Corp.*, Comp. Gen. Dec. B-240809, 90-2 CPD ¶ 471. See also *Metropolitan Contract Servs., Inc.*, Comp. Gen. Dec. B-191162, 78-1 CPD ¶ 435, *recons. denied*, 78-2 CPD ¶ 43, rejecting the argument that the use of an adjectival rating system precluded offerors from access to the rationale employed in the decision-making process. The acceptance of such systems is justified because they do not form the basis for the ultimate source selection decisions. See *Able-One Refrigeration, Inc.*, Comp. Gen. Dec. B-244695, 91-2 CPD ¶ 384, where GAO commented that adjectival scores "are useful only as guides to intelligent decision making, and are not generally controlling for award because they often reflect the disparate, subjective judgments of the evaluators." This reasoning has appeared in numerous decisions such as *Stateside Assocs., Inc.*, Comp. Gen. Dec. B-400670.2, 2009 CPD ¶ 120.

Some of these decisions indicate that evaluators must exercise care in providing narrative comments, noting instances where the same adjectival rating has been given to proposals of different merit. See *Command Mgmt. Servs., Inc.*, Comp. Gen. Dec. B-310261, 2008 CPD ¶ 29, stating:

> The evaluation of proposals and assignment of adjectival ratings should generally not be based upon a simple count of strengths and weaknesses, but on a qualitative assessment of the proposals consistent with the evaluation scheme; thus, to the extent that CMS's arguments are based on merely counting weaknesses, they do not provide a basis to challenge the reasonableness of the evaluation. *Kellogg Brown & Root Servs., Inc.*, B-298694.7, June 22, 2007, 2007 CPD ¶ 124 at 5. . . . The more important consideration is whether the evaluation record and source selection decision show that the agency reasonably assessed the relative merits of the proposals in accordance with the stated evaluation criteria.

Adjectival rating will not be accepted if the system distorts the relationship between the proposals. See, for example, *Redstone Tech. Servs.*, Comp. Gen. Dec. B-259222, 95-1 CPD ¶ 181, sustaining a protest finding that the contracting officer had mechanically applied the adjectival scoring system without documenting whether the relative differences represented any meaningful qualitative differences justifying award to higher technically rated, significantly higher cost offeror. See also *Deployable Hosp. Sys., Inc.*, Comp. Gen. Dec. B-260778, 95-2 CPD ¶ 65, sustaining a protest when two offerors with significantly different levels of experience were scored as "acceptable." Compare *Wackenhut Servs., Inc.*, Comp. Gen. Dec. B-400240, 2008 CPD ¶ 184, denying a protest that the agency had not given it a higher rating because it had more good adjectival scores, stating that such scores "should not be mechanically derived or applied." The opposite result was reached in *Wackenhut Servs., Inc. v. United States*, 85 Fed. Cl. 273 (2009), where the court enjoined the procurement, in part because the agency had been arbitrary and capricious in scoring the proposals without adequate documentation of how the scores were arrived at. See also *Femme Comp Inc. v. United States*, 83 Fed. Cl. 704 (2008), where the court found that the agency's scoring was flawed but that the flaw amounted to "harmless error." Similarly, in *Information Scis. Corp. v. United States*, 80 Fed. Cl. 759 (2008), the court granted a protest, in part because of inaccurate scoring.

## 2. Color Coding

Most color rating systems are very similar to adjectival scoring in the fact that they have very few scores. Thus, the notational system, in itself, does not provide very clear gradations between proposals. See, for example, the Air Force system discussed earlier which distinguishes categories only as blue, green, yellow, and red. The DoD Source Selection Procedures requires all defense agencies to use a color coding system consisting of blue, purple, green yellow and red when scoring the "technical" evaluation factor.

In spite of the minimal gradation in color coding systems, GAO has agreed with the use of color coding, holding that such a system does not produce "an artificial equality in the ratings," *Ferguson-Williams, Inc.*, 68 Comp. Gen. 25 (B-231827), 88-2 CPD ¶ 344. GAO has also held that a color rating system does not prevent the agency from gaining a clear understanding of the relative merits of the proposals, *Gracon Corp.*, Comp. Gen. Dec. B-293009, 2004 CPD ¶ 58, and *Bendix Field Eng'g Corp.*, Comp. Gen. Dec. B-241156, 91-1 CPD ¶ 44. See also *Peterson Bldrs., Inc.*, Comp. Gen. Dec. B-244614, 91-2 CPD ¶ 419, denying a protest that the color coding system obscured the fact that the technical proposals were essentially equal, and *Hogar Crea, Inc.*, Comp. Gen. Dec. B-311265, 2008 CPD ¶ 107, denying a protest that since the offerors were given the same color scores, they should have been treated as equal.

These decisions are based on the view that the color coding will not be the basis of the source selection decision, but that the source selection official will be provided with an analysis of the relative strengths and weaknesses of the proposals. See *Precision Mold & Tool*, Comp. Gen. Dec. B-400452.4, 2009 CPD ¶ 84, stating that, when strengths and weaknesses are used to make the source selection decision, "the color rating assigned is inconsequential in the analysis." See also *Cherry Road Techs.*, Comp. Gen. Dec. B-296915, 2005 CPD ¶ 197, rejecting the argument that the color rating scheme "lacked coherent standards" and that the assigned colors were inconsistent with the evaluation. Thus, when such scoring does not differentiate between proposals of unequal merit, great care should be exercised to ensure that the differences between the proposals are documented. See *Trijicon, Inc.*, 71 Comp. Gen. 41 (B-244546), 91-2 CPD ¶ 375, rejecting the use of a green-yellow-red scoring system that was used without differentiating between proposals that were merely acceptable and those with superior technical features — thus converting a tradeoff decisional scheme into a low-price, technically acceptable proposal scheme.

## 3.  Numerical Systems

Numerical systems have typically assigned 100 or 1000 points to the factors being scored numerically. Most agencies that have used numerical scoring have scored only the technical and management factors. However, a few agencies have used total numerical systems — scoring price or cost as well as the other factors.

### a.  Partial Systems

The advantage of numerical scoring systems is that they generally contain a large number of gradation which permits greater differentiation between proposals. However, GAO has approved systems which reduce the number of gradations by prohibiting the use of certain scores. See *Hoffman Mgmt., Inc.*, 69 Comp. Gen. 579 (B-238752), 90-2 CPD ¶ 15 (10-5-0 scoring system with 0 points given for meeting minimum requirements); *American Sys. Corp.*, Comp. Gen. Dec. B-247923.3, 92-2

CPD ¶ 158 (10-4-2-0 system); and *Fox & Co.*, Comp. Gen. Dec. B-197272, 80-2 CPD ¶ 340 (10-8-5-2-0 system). These systems tend to distort the differences between proposals but GAO has not seen the distortion as a serious problem — probably because the scores are not used as the basis of the source selection decision.

The apparent accuracy of numerical scoring can mislead source selection officials into believing that the total scores provide a precise overall assessment of the relative strengths and weaknesses of the proposals. See, for example, *Serco Inc. v. United States*, 81 Fed. Cl. 463 (2008), where the court granted a protest because the agency had used a point scoring system that resulted in "false statistical precision." The flaw detected by the court was that the agency had scored subfactors adjectivally, converted these scores into whole numbers, averaged the whole number to arrive at a numerical value for each offeror that went to three decimal places, and then used this data to make the source selection decision. Similarly, in *Midland Supply, Inc.*, Comp. Gen. Dec. B-298720, 2007 CPD ¶ 2, GAO sustained a protest because the source selection official had based the decision on "a mechanical comparison of the offerors' total point scores." Compare *GAP Solutions, Inc.*, Comp. Gen. Dec. B-310564, 2008 CPD ¶ 26, where the source selection official properly ignored minor differences in numerical scores, determined that the offerors were "technically equal," and awarded to the low price offeror.

Protests have been granted when numerical scoring does not provide similar scores for similar proposals. See, for example, *Century Envtl. Hygiene, Inc.*, Comp. Gen. Dec. B-279378, 98-1 CPD ¶ 164, granting a protest because the agency identified weaknesses in proposals but gave different scores to the competitors without any explanation of the differences. See also *Ogden Servs., Inc.*, Comp. Gen. Dec. B-270012.2, 96-1 CPD ¶ 177 (no explanation of why awardee received a near perfect score under past performance factor when proposal did not demonstrate mail/ service or similar experience as required by RFP); *Engineering & Computation, Inc.*, Comp. Gen. Dec. B-261658, 95-2 CPD ¶ 176 (no documentation explaining protester's low scores where it appeared to have addressed a perceived weakness in its BAFO); *DNL Props., Inc.*, Comp. Gen. Dec. B-253614.2, 93-2 CPD ¶ 301 (no explanation of different scores for different proposals that appear to be similar); *Arco Mgmt. of Washington, D.C., Inc.*, Comp. Gen. Dec. B-248653, 92-2 CPD ¶ 173. See also *SDA, Inc.*, Comp. Gen. Dec. B-248528.2, 93-1 CPD ¶ 320, granting a protest because the numerical scores given for experience were irrational. The agency had used a system where an offeror was given a zero score if over half of the prior projects it listed were under an undisclosed size — even if many of the projects indicated substantial experience.

## b. Totally Numerical Systems

Some agencies have used totally numerical systems to select sources. There are three systems of this nature that have been commonly used.

## (1) TOTAL POINT SCORING

This system assigns point scores to each evaluation factor and makes the source selection decision based on the total point scores. In such a system all criteria, including price or cost, are numerically scored. Generally, price is scored by giving the lowest price proposal the total points assigned to the criteria and computing the number of points for the other proposals in accordance with their relationship to the lowest price. Although this evaluation technique totally obscures the tradeoff between price and the other evaluation factors, GAO has ruled that an evaluation that one offeror has achieved the highest number of points will validly support the selection of that offeror for award. See *Barnard Constr. Co.*, Comp. Gen. Dec. B-271644, 96-2 CPD ¶ 18, stating:

> Our Office has specifically recognized the propriety of using such a formula in selecting an offeror. See *Stone & Webster Eng'g Corp.*, B-255286.2, Apr. 12, 1994, 94-1 CPD ¶ 306; *Management Sys. Designers, Inc.*, B-244383.3, Sept. 30, 1991, 91-2 CPD ¶ 310. Because the awardee's proposal earned the highest combined price/technical score under the specified formula, the agency was not required to perform price/technical tradeoff analysis to justify the selection decision.

The same result was reached in *Tulane Univ.*, Comp. Gen. B-259912, 95-1 CPD ¶ 210, and *Securigard, Inc.*, Comp. Gen. Dec. B-248584, 92-2 CPD ¶ 156.

An illustration of the difficulties created by this system is found in *Harrison Sys., Ltd.*, 63 Comp. Gen. 379 (B-212675), 84-1 CPD ¶ 572, where price was assigned 30 points and the proposals were:

A     $1,150,782

B     $1,392,293

Offeror A was given 30 points and Offeror B was given 24.79 points derived from the following formula:

$$\frac{\$1,150,782}{\$1,392,293} \times 30 = 24.79 \text{ points}$$

After completing the technical evaluation, the agency computed the results of the total evaluation as follows:

| Proposal | Cost | Technical | Total |
|---|---|---|---|
| A | 30 points | 59.88 points | 89.88 points |
| B | 24.79 points | 70 points | 94.79 points |

However, the source selection official was unwilling to blindly follow the RFP and award to Offeror B on the basis of the highest point score. The source selection official made an independent analysis and determined that the technical proposals were of equal merit. The contract was therefore awarded to Offeror A based on its low price. GAO upheld this decision but stated that it would have granted the protest if the source selection official had independently analyzed whether the difference in technical merit was worth the difference in price. This example demonstrates the pitfalls inherent in the total point evaluation system. The simple summation of points to obtain a total score gives the appearance of mathematical exactitude but there is no assurance that points assigned to one set of criteria have the same value to the government as points assigned to another set of criteria. Thus, award on the sole basis of the total points may not provide the government with the best value.

Some agencies have used the total point evaluation system but have not stated in the RFP that award would be made to the offeror earning the most points. In that situation, it is proper to make a normal tradeoff analysis and award to the offeror with the best value, *DATEX, Inc.*, Comp. Gen. Dec. B-270268.2, 96-1 CPD ¶ 240; *Paxson Elec. Co. v. United States*, 14 Cl. Ct. 634 (1988). See *Midland Supply, Inc.*, Comp. Gen. Dec. B-298720, 2007 CPD ¶ 2, holding that the use of a normal tradeoff is required in this situation. Thus, it is not clear what is added to the evaluation process by giving point scores to price when a full tradeoff analysis is going to be made.

The use of numerical scoring methods which produce "distorted" scores has been discouraged. In *Custom Janitorial Serv.*, Comp. Gen. Dec. B-205023, 82-2 CPD ¶ 163, GAO criticized the use of "spread scoring," in which the proposal with the lowest realistic cost received the maximum number of points and that with the highest cost received zero, concluding that this system produced distorted results when applied to the two offerors in the competitive range. See also *Tennessee Wholesale Drug Co.*, Comp. Gen. Dec. B-243018, 91-2 CPD ¶ 9, holding that a system which improperly reduced the importance of price as an evaluation factor unfairly distorted the scores. In *Lingtec, Inc.*, Comp. Gen. Dec. B-208777, 83-2 CPD ¶ 279, a form of mathematical analysis in which prices closest to the government estimate received maximum points and deviations from the estimate were penalized was held improper, as it penalized lower prices more than higher ones. It can be argued that any system which assigns scores by formula will potentially produce distorted results and thus should not be used.

## (2) CONVERSION TO DOLLAR VALUES

Another completely numerical system determines the relative value of all evaluation factors according to their expected impact on the life cycle cost of the item being procured. An example of this method is found in *Storage Tech. Corp.*, Comp. Gen. Dec. B-215336, 84-2 CPD ¶ 190, in which GAO described the method as follows:

Section IV.3 of the RFP, " Evaluation of Proposals" . . . states that award will be " made to that responsible offeror whose proposal is in the best interests of the VA, cost and other factors considered." Section H.1.3 of the RFP lists the additional factors that the VA would consider. These factors were ranked in order of importance based on their maximum dollar impact on ESLC and listed in descending order of importance . . . . For each of these factors, the VA assigned a dollar credit or assessment commensurate with the cost savings/avoidance or added cost to be incurred by the VA with each proposal system. The VA indicates that the technical evaluation " dollars" are not intended to be precise indicators of actual value, but, rather, like a point score, will serve as a guide to the selecting official. The VA states that the dollar figures arrived at for these additional factors will be compared to the ESLC to determine which proposal is in the VA's best interests and award will be made on that basis.

See also *C.M.P., Inc.*, Comp. Gen. Dec. B-216508, 85-1 CPD ¶ 156, where the agency made the entire evaluation in dollars by assigning dollar amounts for the value of three years of previous performance, guarantee of performance, and remedial and preventive maintenance services.

Assigning dollar values to all evaluation factors is an extremely rare form of proposal evaluation. However, it is not uncommon to assign dollar values to some of the evaluation factors. See, for example, *Cessna Aircraft Co.*, Comp. Gen. Dec. B-261953.5, 96-1 CPD ¶ 132, where this occurred. GAO indicated that it would accept the judgment of the agency in such cases stating that life-cycle cost analysis "involves the exercise of informed judgment and . . . [its use] will not [be] question[ed] . . . unless it clearly lacks a reasonable basis." See also *Global Assocs., Ltd.*, Comp. Gen. Dec. B-275534, 97-1 CPD ¶ 129 (quantified values of non-price factors properly used to determine best value*); Continential Airlines, Inc.*, Comp. Gen. Dec. B-258271.4, 97-1 CPD ¶ 81 (adjusted prices based on monetary benefits of non-price factors properly used in making selection decision).

### (3) DOLLARS PER POINT

The third numerical system is the dollars per point system. In this system all of the criteria other than cost are scored numerically and the prices proposed are used to compute a mathematical relationship. An earlier version of DARCOM Pamphlet 1715-3 described this system as follows:

(3) *Evaluation of lowest dollar per technical quality point ($/q.p.).* The concept of selecting the best technical proposal for the dollar is supportable by the dollar/technical point relationships. This factor can be determined by dividing the cost of the proposal by the total unweighted raw score developed for " technical." With the knowledge contained in the RFP that this relationship will be given consideration and will force offerors to tradeoff between cost and technical factors in order to prepare the best possible proposal at a fair and reasonable price, $/q.p. relationship by itself is not justification for selection; but is only considered an additional factor to offer to the SSA in making the decision. An example area is below:

In some instances, a dollar per quality point system has been used as the sole basis for source selection. GAO has approved this method even when a losing competitor submitted a lower priced proposal that was technically acceptable, *Shapell Gov. Hous., Inc.*, 55 Comp. Gen. 839 (B-183830), 76-1 CPD ¶ 161. See *Management Sys. Designers, Inc.*, Comp. Gen. Dec. B-244383.3, 91-2 CPD ¶ 310, where GAO accepted the use of this technique as the sole basis for the source selection even though the RFP reserved the right to make an independent cost/technical tradeoff decision. See also *Frank E. Basil, Inc.*, Comp. Gen. Dec. B-208133, 83-1 CPD ¶ 91, allowing such an award even though the protester's price was significantly lower.

This technique gives an appearance of greater precision than is justified by the point scores assigned because point scoring inherently is less precise than price, yet the use of a ratio between the scores assumes that they are of equal precision. Thus, it is better to use this technique as one method of evaluating the merits of the proposals. See *Moran Assocs.*, Comp. Gen. Dec. B-240564.2, 91-2 CPD ¶ 495, where the agency did this and GAO stated:

> We have recognized that such a cost/technical ratio formula can be a proper tool for the government to utilize in determining which proposal is the most advantageous to the government. See *Morrison-Knudsen Co., Inc.*, B-237800.2 , 90-1 CPD ¶443. Here, the ratio was only one tool utilized to assure that the government was getting the best buys, given relative technical rankings and costs. The record shows that awards were not made to the offerors with the best ratios.

### 4. Ranking

The direct ranking of proposals, without the aid of scores, has also been upheld, as numerical scoring does not "transform the technical evaluation into a more objective process," *Development Assocs., Inc.*, Comp. Gen. Dec. B-205380, 82-2 CPD ¶ 37. GAO has even stated that "ranking proposals may be a more direct and meaningful method" than numerical scoring, *Maximus*, Comp. Gen. Dec. B-195806, 81-1 CPD ¶ 285. However, ranking is infrequently used because it bypasses the scoring of proposals in terms of how well they meet the RFP requirements. To overcome this potential difficulty, an agency can use initial scoring but then provide overall ranking to the source selection official to aid in the decision, *Cerner Corp.*, Comp. Gen. Dec. B-293093, 2004 CPD ¶ 34. However, ranking is done, it does not overcome the necessity of identifying the strengths, weaknesses and risks in the proposals.

## G. Evaluation of Specific Factors

A number of evaluation factors are commonly used in most competitively negotiated procurements. These factors have been subject to such numerous protests that there is extensive guidance on the pitfalls that can be encountered in their evaluation.

## 1. Price or Cost to the Government

In every procurement, price or cost to the government is an evaluation factor. In fixed-price contracts, the agency must make a price reasonableness determination as part of the evaluation process. In cost-reimbursement contracts, the evaluation factor must be probable cost to the government which must be determined by making a cost realism analysis. This critical part of the evaluation process is discussed in detail in Chapter 10.

## 2. Past Performance

Past performance has become a major evaluation factor, and it has become common to see agencies using only two evaluation factors — price and past performance. See *USA Elecs.*, Comp. Gen. Dec. B-275389, 97-1 CPD ¶ 75, where GAO agreed that it was rational to award to an offeror with a good past performance but a higher price. Thus, a fair and even-handed assessment of the past performance of each offeror is vital, *Myers Investigative & Security Servs., Inc.*, Comp. Gen. Dec. B-288468, 2001 CPD ¶ 189 (similar data on two offerors treated differently); *Beneco Enters., Inc.*, Comp. Gen. Dec. B-283512, 2000 CPD ¶ 175, B-283512.3, 2000 CPD ¶ 176 (ratings did not correspond to information in the contract file).

In the numerous protests of past performance evaluations GAO has accorded agencies considerable discretion. See *HLC Indus., Inc.*, Comp. Gen. Dec. B-274374, 96-2 CPD ¶214, stating:

> Evaluation of an offeror's past performance is a matter within the discretion of the contracting agency, and we will not substitute our judgment for the agency's, so long as the rating is reasonably based and documented. *PMT Servs., Inc.*, B-270538.2 , Apr. 1, 1996, 96-2 CPD ¶98. Mere disagreement with the agency's evaluation does not itself render the evaluation unreasonable, *Macon Apparel Corp.*, B-272162 , Sept. 4, 1996, 96-2 CPD ¶95.

This broad discretion permits agencies to refuse to accept an offeror's explanation for a poor past performance rating, *H.F. Henderson Indus.*, Comp. Gen. Dec. B-275017, 97-1 CPD ¶ 27; and *Continental Serv. Co.*, Comp. Gen. Dec. B-274531, 97-1 CPD ¶ 9. In *Precision Echo, Inc.*, Comp. Gen. Dec. B-276740, 97-2 CPD ¶ 114, GAO found that the agency had properly concluded that difficulties in using the offeror's equipment, although primarily due to user error, were also due to the design of the equipment. See also *Master Lock Co., LLC*, Comp. Gen. Dec. B-309982.2, 2009 CPD ¶ 2 (denying protest that contractor with highly satisfactory past performance had only been rated "good"); *ITT Indus. Space Sys.*, LLC, Comp. Gen. Dec. B-309964, 2007 CPD ¶ 217 (denying protest that agency had not properly considered a variety of performance information); *S3 Ltd.*, Comp. Gen. Dec. B-288195, 2001 CPD ¶ 164 (agency acted properly in finding some performance risk after evaluating somewhat conflicting assessments of several people that had worked on a contract where the protester had encountered problems); *KELO, Inc.*, Comp. Gen. Dec. B-284601.2, 2000 CPD ¶ 110 (agency rejected explanations of performance problems); and *MAC's General Contractor*, Comp. Gen. Dec. B-276755, 97-2 CPD ¶ 29 (agency could give a poor evaluation based on a default termination that was still in litigation — stating that such an evaluation may be based on a "reasonable perception of inadequate prior performance"). Agencies may also exercise their discretion to downgrade an offeror that does not submit the past performance information called for by the RFP, *Al Andalus Gen. Contracts Co. v. United States*, 86 Fed. Cl. 252 (2009). However, this broad discretion does not permit use of an irrational evaluation system. See *Shaw-Parsons Infrastructure Recovery Consultants, LLC*, Comp. Gen. Dec. B-401679.8, 2010 CPD ¶ 211 (agency used numerical scoring system that penalized protester for references on less relevant contracts); *Green Valley Trans, Inc.*, Comp. Gen. Dec. B-285283, 2000 CPD ¶ 133 (agency used the total number of instances of defective performance without regard to the volume of work of the competitors).

A similar degree of discretion is accorded by the Court of Federal Claims, *Akal Sec.y, Inc. v. United States*, 87 Fed. Cl. 311 (2009); *Gulf Group Inc, v. United States*, 61 Fed. Cl. 338 (2004); *Maint. Eng'rs v. United States*, 50 Fed. Cl. 399 (2001).

One of the major tasks in evaluating contractor past performance information is to distinguish between a few inconsequential problems and a significant record of inferior performance. For example, in *Marinette Marine Corp.*, Comp. Gen. Dec. B-400697, 2009 CPD ¶ 16, the agency closely reviewed a single case of inferior performance and concluded that it would not impact the work on the contract to be awarded. See also *MCT JV*, Comp. Gen. Dec. B-311245.2, 2008 CPD ¶ 121 (agency reasonably found "outstanding" past performance even though offeror had encountered some problems in the past); *BFI Waste Sys. of Nebraska, Inc.*, Comp. Gen. Dec. B-278223, 98-1 CPD ¶ 8 (contracting officer reasonably found that awardee's performance overall during the past five to six years overcame alleged deficiencies its performance under the incumbent contract); and *Cubic Applications, Inc.*, Comp. Gen. Dec. B-274768, 97-1 CPD ¶ 98 (contracting officer reasonably evaluated the performance reports on the competitors, considered the negative comments, but concluded that the overall positive nature of the reports indicated that the winning offeror was entitled to an excellent rating). However, when contracting officers received a significant number of negative comments on an offeror's past performance, they have properly been given lower ratings. See, for example, *AAC Assocs., Inc.*, Comp. Gen. Dec. B 274928, 97-1 CPD ¶ 55, where the contracting officer gave a moderate past performance rating based on a number of negative comments from references; and *SEAIR Transport Servs., Inc.*, Comp. Gen. Dec. B-274162, 96-2 CPD ¶ 198, where the contracting officer concluded that the overall ratings given by references adequately reflected the severity of the problems that they had identified. In *Quality Fabricators, Inc.*, Comp. Gen. Dec. B-271431, 96-2 CPD ¶ 22, there were so many past performance problems that the contracting officer properly dropped the offeror out of the competitive range.

Care must also be exercised in determining responsibility for past performance problems. See *CDA Inv. Techs., Inc.*, Comp. Gen. Dec. B-272093, 97-1 CPD ¶ 102, affirming the evaluation of a prime contractor and a subcontractor on a prior contract that were competing for a new contract and there had been performance problems on the prior contract. The evaluators took the time to make a careful analysis of which problems should be attributable to each of the two companies and gave them past performance ratings in accordance with this assignment of responsibility. Similarly, in *Pemco Aeroplex, Inc.*, Comp. Gen. Dec. B-310372, 2008 CPD ¶ 2, the agency properly gave an offeror a rating of "satisfactory confidence" after carefully assessing the cause of prior performance difficulties, and in *Sumaria Sys., Inc.*, Comp. Gen. Dec. B-299517, 2007 CPD ¶ 122, the agency properly rechecked with the personnel on a referenced contract to obtain more current information on the cause of the problem. Compare *Sikorsky Aircraft Co.*, Comp. Gen. Dec. B-299145.4, 2007 CPD ¶ 78, where the protester was downgraded based on a negative report from the program manager on an ongoing contract where significant problems had been encountered. Although GAO ruled that this was proper, there was little indication that the agency had investigated to determine whether the problems were caused by the government or the contractor and four other customers of the protester reported very good past performance. It is also proper to defer the assessment of responsibility for a prior problem when an agency investigation is still underway, *Metson Marine Servs., Inc.*, Comp. Gen. Dec. B-299705, 2007 CPD ¶ 159.

### a. Sources and Reliability of Past Performance Information

Past performance information is obtained in several ways. Most agencies have obtained the information from offerors and from references submitted by the offerors or other organizations that have dealt with the offeror. FAR 15.305(a)(2)(ii) requires that offerors be permitted to identify all such organizations to whom they have sold similar goods or services. While there may be some question as to the reliability of such information, the practice of calling references and other organizations for whom the offeror has worked has not been challenged. However, care must be exercised to ensure that offerors are given the same opportunity to submit reference information. See *Aerospace Design & Fabrication, Inc.*, Comp. Gen. Dec. B-278896.2, 98-1 CPD ¶ 139, sustaining a protest because one offeror had been permitted to submit more reference information than was permitted by the RFP. In *Serco, Inc. v. United States*, 81 Fed. Cl. 463 (2008), the court held that this method of data collection was unreliable because the surveys were taken using a set of questions that did not correspond to the evaluation considerations used in the selection process. See also *Cooperativa Muratori Riuiniti*, 2005 CPD ¶ 21 (survey that was not geared to the evaluation criteria held to be arbitrary and capricious); *Dismas Charities, Inc.*, Comp. Gen. Dec. B-292091 2003 CPD ¶ 125 (questionnaires were "materially flawed" and contrary to the FAR when the agency did not provide references with instructions on how to score offeror's past performance).

In using references, random sampling has been permitted, *MilTech, Inc.*, Comp. Gen. Dec. B-275078, 97-1 CPD ¶ 208, and there is no requirement that strenuous efforts be made to contact references, *Guam Shipyard*, Comp. Gen. Dec. B-311321, 2008 CPD ¶ 124, or that all references given by the offeror be contacted, *Sunrise Med. HHG, Inc.*, Comp. Gen. Dec. B-310230, 2008 CPD ¶ 7; *U.S. Tech. Corp.*, Comp. Gen. Dec. B-278584, 98-1 CPD ¶ 78. Furthermore, agencies may contact a different number of sources for different offerors, *IGIT, Inc.*, Comp. Gen. Dec. B-275299.2, 97-2 CPD ¶ 7. Although contacting only a single reference would not appear to yield an inadequate sample, this questionable practice has also been permitted, *Neal R. Gross & Co.*, Comp. Gen. Dec. B-275066, 97-1 CPD ¶ 30; *HLC Indus., Inc.*, Comp. Gen. Dec. B-274374, 96-2 CPD ¶ 214. Thus, adverse past performance assessments have been considered to be reliable when they were based on a single contract, *Compania De Asesoria Y Comercio, S.A.*, Comp. Gen. Dec. B-278358, 98-1 CPD ¶ 26 (seven deficiency reports on prior contract); *ECC Int'l Corp.*, Comp. Gen. Dec. B-277422, 98-1 CPD ¶ 45 (significant difficulties on prior production contract). If the references can not be contacted with reasonable efforts, an agency may give an offeror a poor past performance rating, *Consolidated Eng'g Servs., Inc.*, Comp. Gen. Dec. B-277273, 97-2 CPD ¶ 86.

Some agencies have used questionnaires to obtain past performance information and this practice has been approved by GAO, *Continental Serv.*, Co., Comp. Gen. Dec. B-274531, 97-1 CPD ¶ 9; *SWR, Inc.*, Comp. Gen. Dec. B-276878, 97-2 CPD ¶ 34. Although this is a questionable practice, use of scores on questionnaires without supporting information or commentary has also been approved, *Pacific Ship Repair & Fabrication, Inc.*, Comp. Gen. Dec. B-279793, 98-2 CPD ¶ 29; *Boeing Sikorsky Aircraft Support*, Comp. Gen. Dec. B-277263.2, 97-2 CPD ¶ 91.

It is proper to use the ratings on cost-plus-award-fee contracts in the assessment of past performance, *Oceaneering Int'l, Inc.*, Comp. Gen. Dec. B-278126, 98-1 CPD ¶ 133.

Another way to obtain past performance information is through data collection systems. FAR 42.1502(a) requires the preparation of performance evaluation reports on all contracts over $150,000. FAR 42.1503(e) limits the retention and use of the information to three years after the completion of contract performance. Under this regulation, contractors are given a minimum of 30 days to submit comments, rebut statements, or provide additional information. The completed evaluated information cannot be released to other than government personnel and the contractor whose performance is being evaluated during the period the information is being used for source selection purposes. These evaluations are then available for use by all agencies, FAR 42.1503(c), and there is little question that such information can be used in the evaluation process, *American Constr. Co.*, Comp. Gen. Dec. B-401493.2, 2009 CPD ¶ 214; *Precision Mold & Tool*, Comp. Gen. Dec. B-400452.4, 2009 CPD ¶ 84. In *Contrack Int'l, Inc.*, Comp. Gen. Dec. B-401871.5, 2010 CPD ¶ 126, GAO granted a protest because the agency did not factor in the information in the DoD rating system. The Department of Defense has implemented these requirements by adopting a detailed performance rating system. See "A Guide to Collection and Use of Past Performance Information," May 2003. This system classifies contracts into eight areas: systems, services, information technology, operations support, health care, fuels, construction and architect-engineer services, and science and technology. In each of these areas, specified elements of performance will be assessed and placed in an automated data bank for use in the source selection process. FAR 36.201 also requires the collection of performance information on all construction contracts over $650,000, while FAR 36.604 requires the collection of performance information on all architect-engineer contracts over $30,000.

Another source of past performance information is agency personnel that have dealt with the offeror in the past. FAR 15.305(a)(2)(ii) states that the agency "shall consider . . . information obtained from any other sources, when evaluating past performance." In *Paragon Sys., Inc.*, Comp. Gen. Dec. B-299548.2, 2007 CPD ¶ 178, GAO rejected the contention that such information should not be used, finding it proper to contact personnel on a referenced contract that were not included in the offeror's information, stating:

> [A]n agency is generally not precluded from considering any relevant information, and is not limited to considering only the information provided within the "four corners" of vendor's quotation when evaluating past performance. See FAR § 15.305(a)(2)(ii); *Weidlinger Assocs., Inc.*, [B-299433, B-299433.2, May 7, 2007, 2007 CPD ¶ 91]; *Forest Regeneration Servs.* B-290998, Oct. 30, 2002, 2002 CPD ¶ 187 at 6.

Thus, agencies can seek information from a variety of sources in order to assess the past performance of an offeror. It is proper to use information within the government as well as the information obtained from references, *PHT Supply Corp. v. United States*, 71 Fed. Cl. 1 (2006). Thus, it is proper to consider a past default termination of the offeror, *Precision Prosthetics, Inc.*, Comp. Gen. Dec. B-401023, 2009 CPD ¶ 83. In rating past performance with the same agency, it is proper for the evaluators to use their personal knowledge of an offeror's performance of contracts with the agency. See *TEAM Support Servs., Inc.*, Comp. Gen. Dec. B-279379.2, 98-1 CPD ¶ 167; *Omega World Travel, Inc.*, Comp. Gen. Dec. B271262.2, 96-2 CPD ¶ 44; and *HLC Indus., Inc.*, Comp. Gen. Dec. B-274374, 96-2 CPD ¶ 214. In these cases GAO commented that the agency was, in effect, using itself as a reference.

The subjectivity of some past performance information has led to questions about its reliability. FAR 42.1501 defines "past performance information" as follows:

> Past performance information is relevant information, for future source selection purposes, regarding a contractor's action under previously awarded contracts. It includes, for example, the contractor's record of conforming to contract requirements and to standards of good workmanship; the contractor's record of forecasting and controlling costs; the contractor's adherence to con-

tract schedules, including the administrative aspects of performance; the contractor's history of reasonable and cooperative behavior and commitment to customer satisfaction; and generally, the contractor's business-like concern for the interest of the customer.

Although the elements of this definition dealing with "reasonable and cooperative behavior" and "customer satisfaction" allow a great deal of subjectivity in the evaluations, GAO has denied a protest that these elements permit contracting officers to rely on "gossip and innuendo," *RMS Indus.*, Comp. Gen. Dec. B-247229, 92-1 CPD ¶ 451. In that procurement the agency used the FAR definition but changed "history of" to " reputation for." GAO stated:

> [W]e find nothing unlawful in the agency's taking into account, as one element of past performance, an offeror's reputation for reasonable and cooperative behavior and commitment to customer satisfaction. In the context of this [Request for Proposals], we understand the term " reputation" to refer to fact-based evaluations rather than mere hearsay. We note that [the protester] does not challenge the propriety of the agency's seeking references from prior contracts. Indeed, where, as here, the solicitation informs offerors that the references will be considered as part of the evaluation process, relying on such references is a common and proper part of proposal negotiation.

### b. Relevance of the Data

FAR 15.305(a)(2)(i) requires agencies to consider the relevance of past performance information. Thus, it is improper to give performance on less relevant work the same weight as performance on highly relevant work. See *United Paradyne Corp.*, Comp. Gen. Dec. B-297758, 2006 CPD ¶ 47, granting a protest because the agency had averaged the past performance evaluations for highly relevant work and far less relevant work. Similarly, in *Shaw-Parsons Infrastructure Recovery Consultants, LLC; Vanguard Recovery Assistance, Joint Venture*, Comp. Gen. Dec. B-401679.8, 2010 CPD ¶ 211, GAO granted a protest because the agency reduced the score of past performance that was less relevant, reasoning that this penalized an offeror for submitting such references. See also *Ne. Milkitary Sales, Inc.*, Comp. Gen. Dec. B-404153, 2011 CPD ¶ 2 (failure to consider adverse information on same type work); *ASRC Research & Tech. Solutions, LLC*, Comp. Gen. Dec. B-400217, 2008 CPD ¶ 202 (failure to consider the substantial difference in size between the awardee's past performance references and the size of the contemplated contract, as required by the solicitation); *DRS C3 Sys., LLC*, Comp. Gen. Dec. B-310825, 2008 CPD ¶ 103 (ignoring assessment of poor performance on highly relevant contract); *Harbors Envtl. Servs., Inc.*, Comp. Gen. Dec. B-296176.2, 2005 CPD ¶ 222 (giving incumbent contractor and awardee identical ratings, although awardee's references were for services smaller and less complex than service being procured); *KMR, LLC*, Comp. Gen. Dec. B-292860, 2003 CPD ¶ 233 (using references for different work when solicitation stated evaluation would be based on performance of "same or similar" work).

Agencies have considerable discretion in determining what prior work will yield a meaningful assessment of the competence of the offeror to perform the contract being awarded, *ManTech Int'l Corp.*, Comp. Gen. Dec. B-311074, 2008 CPD ¶ 87; *Roy F. Weston, Inc.*, Comp. Gen. Dec. B-274945, 97-1 CPD ¶ 92. See *Jason Assocs. Corp.*, Comp. Gen. Dec. B-278689, 98-1 CPD ¶ 67, holding that the source selection official had acted properly in reading reference questionnaires to ascertain which work was relevant. It has been held proper to base the entire past performance evaluation on the single most relevant contract, ignoring other work, *Braswell Servs. Group, Inc.*, Comp. Gen. Dec. B-278921.2, 98-2 CPD ¶ 10. GAO has also denied protests when the agency determined that dissimilar work was relevant, *All Star Maint., Inc.*, Comp. Gen. Dec. B-271119, 96-1 CPD ¶ 278; *Hughes Missile Sys. Co.*, Comp. Gen. Dec. B-272418, 96-2 CPD ¶ 221. Similarly, a protest was denied when the agency considered the quality of prior work more relevant than the small size of the contracts on which the work was done, *SP Sys., Inc. v. United States*, 86 Fed. Cl. 1 (2009). Compare *Ogden Support Servs., Inc.*, Comp. Gen. Dec. B-270012.2, 96-1 CPD ¶ 137, granting a protest where the agency had considered dissimilar work relevant but the RFP had used an evaluation factor of "demonstrated successful performance on similar efforts," and *PMT Servs., Inc.*, Comp. Gen. Dec. B-270538.2, 96-2 CPD ¶ 98, granting a protest when the agency found the protester had no prior contracts of the same size as the current procurement but GAO found that complexity of the work on prior contracts was more important than dollar value of the contracts. In one unusual situation, an agency properly determined that work on smaller projects was more relevant than work on larger projects because the contract to be awarded would require work on small projects, *J.C.N. Constr. Co. v. United States*, 60 Fed. Cl. 400 (2004); *J.C.N. Constr Co.*, Comp. Gen. Dec. B-293063, 2004 CPD ¶ 12.

GAO has required that agencies consider past performance on work that is "too close at hand" to the current procurement. This requires an agency to obtain information on a contract with the agency for the same services, *International Bus. Sys., Inc.*, Comp. Gen. Dec. B-275554, 97-1 CPD ¶114. GAO granted the protest in part because of the fact that the contracting officer had also been the contracting officer on the prior contract and had recently written a letter stating that the offeror's performance on the prior contract had been "exemplary." GAO stated the rule that "some information is simply too close at hand to require offerors to shoulder the inequities that spring from an agency's failure to obtain, and consider, the information." The same result was reached in *East-West Indus., Inc.*, Comp. Gen. Dec. B-297391.2, 2006 CPD ¶ 161 (prior contract with agency); *International Res. Recovery, Inc. v. United States*, 64 Fed. Cl. 150 (2005) (settlement agreement with agency replacing a default termination); *Seattle Sec. Servs., Inc. v. United States*, 45 Fed. Cl. 560 (2000), and *SCIENTECH, Inc.*, Comp. Gen. Dec. B-277805.2, 98-1 CPD ¶ 33. The "too close at hand" rule was also applied to reference information on past contracts that the agency had required but did not use, *Shaw-Parsons Infrastructure Recovery Consultants, LLC*, Comp. Gen. Dec. B 401679.4, 2010 CPD ¶ 77. This rule will not apply if the agency personnel conducting the procurement do not know of the offeror's past performance, *MIL Corp.*, Comp. Gen. Dec. B-297508, 2006 CPD ¶ 34. See also *Shaw-Parsons Infrastructure Recovery Consultants, LLC; Vanguard Recovery Assistance, Joint Venture*, Comp. Gen. Dec. B-401679.4, 2010 CPD ¶ 77 (rule was not violated when the evaluators did not know about incumbent's performance, even though the COTR for the incumbent contract was an advisor to the evaluation board); *Firestorm Wildfire Suppression, Inc.*, Comp. Gen. Dec. B-3120136, 2007 CPD ¶ 218 (rule did not apply when evidence did not show evaluators knew of report prepared by different agency, even though the report was provided to official of their own agency); and *Paragon Sys., Inc.*, Comp. Gen. Dec. B-299548.2, 2007 CPD ¶ 178 (rule did not apply where comments written by agency inspectors critical of selectee's performance under previous task order had been lost, were not referred to in evaluation file, and were unknown to source selection authority, although known to the evaluators).

It is common practice to describe what work is relevant in the RFP and agencies are required to follow that description in the evaluation process. In numerous procurements, the RFP states that references should be provided for "the same or similar work" as that being procured with guidance on the size of contracts that were performed. When such a description is included in the RFP, the agency will be required to apply it in the evaluation process. See *Honeywell Tech. Solutions, Inc.*, Comp. Gen. Dec. B-400771, 2009 CPD ¶ 49 (evaluation unreasonable when agency gave "excellent" rating when prior contracts were much smaller than proposed contract and RFP called for evaluation of "similar" work); *Continental RPVs*, Comp. Gen. Dec. B-292768.2, 2004 CPD ¶ 56 (evaluation unreasonable when agency gave the awardee the same low risk rating for past performance as it gave the incumbent, even though it appeared that the awardee had not done as much of the "same or similar" work as the incumbent); *Southwestern Bell Tel. Co.*, Comp. Gen. Dec. B-292476, 2003 CPD ¶ 177 (evaluation unreasonable when agency failed to consider awardee's record of integrity and business ethics, as required by RFP, and the awardee's record was problematical); *Martin Elecs., Inc.*, Comp. Gen. Dec. B-290846.3, 2003 CPD ¶ 6 (evaluation unreasonable when agency failed to consider negative past performance information with respect to contracts that were "recent" as defined by RFP); *Sonetronics, Inc.*, Comp. Gen. Dec. B-289459.2, 2002 CPD ¶ 48 (evaluation unreasonable when RFP contemplated evaluation on basis of "at least" three completed contracts for similar work and agency gave awardee perfect score for past performance based on only one completed contract for similar work); *Finlen Complex, Inc.*, Comp. Gen. Dec. B-288280, 2001 CPD ¶ 167 (agency gave past performance far less weight than indicated in solicitation); and *Meridian Mgmt. Corp.*, Comp. Gen. Dec. B-285127, 2000 CPD ¶ 121 (agency downgraded offeror for failure to submit references that were not required by RFP). However, "same or similar" description does not require agency to review only identical work, *Tiger Truck LLC*, Comp. Gen. Dec. B-310759, 2008 CPD ¶ 44; *DGR Assocs., Inc.*, Comp. Gen. Dec. B-285428, 2000 CPD ¶ 145.

It is proper to give heavier weight to work for the same agency than work for private buyers, *Court Copies & Images, Inc.*, Comp. Gen. Dec. B-277268, 97-2 CPD ¶ 85. In *Systems Integration & Dev., Inc.*, Comp. Gen. Dec. B-271050, 96-1 CPD ¶ 273, GAO also denied a protest that using the past performance of an incumbent gave the incumbent an unfair competitive advantage.

FAR 15.305(a)(2)(iii) states that agencies "should take into account . . . predecessor companies, key personnel . . . or subcontractors" when assessment of their performance is relevant. Prior to this regulation GAO permitted agencies to include key personnel on the past performance assessment, *Technical Res., Inc.*, Comp. Gen. Dec. B-253506, 93-2 CPD ¶ 176, or to exclude them from the assessment, *Hard Bodies, Inc.*, Comp. Gen. Dec. B-279543, 98-1 CPD ¶ 172. Under the current regulation key personnel can be evaluated even when this is not listed as an evaluation factor, *SDS Int'l v. United States*, 48 Fed. Cl. 742 (2001); *DRA Software Training*, Comp. Gen. Dec. B-289128, 2002 CPD ¶ 11. It is proper to evaluate a new company solely on the basis of the past performance of its key personnel, *JSW Maint., Inc.*, Comp. Gen. Dec. B-400581.5, 2009 CPD ¶ 182. See also *Lynwood Mach. & Eng'g, Inc.*, Comp. Gen. Dec. B-287652, 2001 CPD ¶ 138 (proper to evaluate past performance of "special project manager"); *General Atomics*, Comp. Gen. Dec. B-287348, 2001 CPD ¶ 169 (proper to evaluate past performance of a group of key personnel that had worked on project when the contract was held by another company); *SDS Int'l*, Comp. Gen. Dec. B-285822, 2000 CPD ¶ 167 (proper to evaluate past performance of one key person of newly formed company). On the other hand, it is also proper not to evaluate key personnel separately, *KIRA, Inc.*, Comp. Gen. Dec. B-287573, 2001 CPD ¶ 152, 43 GC ¶ 367; *Urban-Meridian Joint Venture*, Comp. Gen. Dec. B-287168, 2001 CPD ¶ 91; *SWR, Inc.*, Comp. Gen. Dec. B-286044.2, 2000 CPD ¶ 174.

It has also been held proper to evaluate past performance of subcontractors in evaluating a contractor, *Triad Logistics Servs. Corp.*, Comp. Gen. Dec. B-296511.3, 2005 CPD ¶ 189 (proper to rate contractor with no past performance record "very good" when major subcontractor had excellent ratings); *Information Tech. & Applications Corp. v. United States*, 51 Fed. Cl. 340 (2001) (even subcontractors performing minor elements of work may be evaluated); *Neal R. Gross & Co.*, Comp. Gen. Dec. B-275066, 97-1 CPD ¶ 30 (adverse performance rating proper even though poor performance was attributable to some extent to subcontractors, because the prime contractor always bears responsibility for the work of subcontractors); *Battelle Memorial Inst.*, Comp. Gen. Dec. B-278673, 98-1 CPD ¶ 107 (good past performance rating proper even though good performance was entirely the result of subcontractor effort).

Although the FAR is silent on the issue, agencies have also been permitted to evaluation the performance of parent companies and affiliates when their resources will be used to perform the contract, *Humana Military Healthcare Servs.*, Comp. Gen. Dec. B-401652.2, 2009 CPD ¶ 219; *Ecompex, Inc.*, Comp. Gen. Dec.

B-292865.4, 2004 CPD ¶ 149. See also *Daylight Tree Serv.& Equip., LLC*, Comp. Gen. Dec. B-310808, 2008 CPD ¶ 23 (information on affiliated company at same address as offeror is relevant). Compare *Health Net Fed. Servs., LLC*, Comp. Gen. Dec. B-401652.3, 2009 CPD ¶ 220, granting a protest because the agency gave credit for past performance of a parent company and affiliates without proof of what prior contracts they had performed or what work they would do on current contract. If the agency finds no evidence that the resources of the parent or affiliate organization will be used and there is not other relevant past performance, it is proper to assign a neutral rating to the offeror, *Bering Straits Tech. Servs. LLC*, Comp. Gen. Dec. B-401560.3, 2009 CPD ¶ 201.

A number of agencies have used the questionable logic of treating the relevance of past performance as an assessment of the offeror's experience by giving offerors without much relevant work lower scores on their past performance evaluation, and this has been accepted by GAO. See *Gonzales-McCaulley Inv. Group. Inc.*, Comp. Gen. Dec. B-402544, 2010 CPD ¶ 127 ("weakness" given for less relevant work); *ACS State Healthcare, LLC*, Comp. Gen. Dec. B-292981, 2004 CPD ¶ 57 (lower past performance rating justified by less relevant experience); *Five-R Co.*, Comp. Gen. Dec. B-288190, 2001 CPD ¶ 163 (proper to give only "satisfactory/confidence" score to protester because its past projects were not like work being procured); *Gulf Group, Inc.*, Comp. Gen. Dec. B-287697, 2001 CPD ¶ 135 (score lowered because relevance of past work was "limited"); *J.A. Jones Mgmt. Servs., Inc.*, Comp. Gen. Dec. B-284909.5, 2001 CPD ¶ 64 (assessment reduced because of less relevant past performance); *Birdwell Bros. Painting & Refinishing*, Comp. Gen. Dec. B-285035, 2000 CPD ¶ 129 (score lowered because no past work of the size and complexity of the instant contract); *Marathon Constr. Corp.*, Comp. Gen. Dec. B-284816, 2000 CPD ¶ 94 (score lowered because no work of the type called for by the instant contract); *Molina Eng'g, Ltd./Tri-J Indus., Inc. Joint Venture*, Comp. Gen. Dec. B-284895, 2000 CPD ¶ 86 (score of "amber/high risk" based on lack of contracts of similar size and scope as instant contract); *Dellew Corp.*, Comp. Gen. Dec. B-284227, 2000 CPD ¶ 52 (assessment of higher performance risk than winning offeror because of lack of relevant work); *Clean Venture, Inc.*, Comp. Gen. Dec. B-284176, 2000 CPD ¶ 47 (score of "fair" for very good performance on contracts of less complexity than instant contract); *Champion Serv. Corp.*, Comp. Gen. Dec. B-284116, 2000 CPD ¶ 28 (higher performance risk because of less relevant work than winning contractor). Compare *Airwork Limited-Vinnell Corp. (a Joint Venture)*, Comp. Gen. Dec. B-285247, 2000 CPD ¶ 150, where GAO agreed with the agency that it was not required to give the protester a higher past performance rating because it had more relevant work experience. A clearer way to evaluate the amount of experience of an offeror is to treat "experience" as a separate evaluation factor.

One way to ensure relevance is to evaluate past performance on only those contracts that were performed by the group that is proposed for the current procurement and that were for similar work. In *Robbins-Gioia, Inc.*, Comp. Gen. Dec. B-274318, 96-2 CPD ¶ 222, the agency only considered contracts performed by the same division of the company. In *TESCO*, Comp. Gen. Dec. B-271756, 96-1 CPD ¶ 284, the scope of work was narrowly defined. Similarly, in *Israel Aircraft Indus.*, Comp. Gen. Dec. B-274389, 97-1 CPD ¶ 41, the RFP stated that the agency would focus its evaluation of past performance risk on the offerors' and proposed subcontractors' histories of past performance relevant to the proposed effort, and stated detailed instructions regarding the information that offerors were to provide. In *EastCo Bldg. Servs., Inc.*, Comp. Gen. Dec. B-275334, 97-1 CPD ¶ 83, GAO denied a protest where the agency had limited its evaluation of past performance to contracts of a comparable size to the procurement being undertaken. Compare *Computer Sys. Dev. Co.*, Comp. Gen. Dec. B-275356, 97-1 CPD ¶ 91, denying a protest where the agency gave the winning offeror high past performance ratings based on much smaller contracts than the one under consideration.

### c. Corrective Action

FAR 15.305(a)(2)(ii) requires that offerors be permitted to submit information on corrective action that has been taken to overcome past performance problems, and agencies have lost protests for failure to tell an offeror that corrective action is necessary to cure a past performance problem, *Alliant Techsystems, Inc.*, Comp. Gen. Dec. B-260215.4, 95-2 CPD ¶ 79.

Agencies have been given broad discretion in assessing whether corrective action will overcome prior performance problems. See, for example, *Lockheed Martin MS2 Tactical Sys.*, Comp. Gen. Dec. B-400135, 2008 CPD ¶ 157, and *Parmatic Filter Corp.*, Comp. Gen. Dec. B-285288.3, 2001 CPD ¶ 71, where the agency determined that the corrective action of one offeror was more effective than the corrective action of the protester. There are numerous instances where the refusal to adjust past performance ratings to reflect corrective action has been upheld. See *Day & Zimmermann Pantex Corp.*, Comp. Gen. Dec. B-286016, 2001 CPD ¶ 96 (agency discounted protester's claim that it had rectified poor prior performance); *GEC-Marconi Elec. Sys. Corp.*, Comp. Gen. Dec. B-276186, 97-2 CPD ¶ 23 (evaluators not convinced that on-time delivery on recent contracts demonstrated that offeror had corrected problems that led to late delivery on earlier contracts); *Laidlaw Envtl. Servs. (GS), Inc.*, Comp. Gen. Dec. B-271903, 96-2 CPD ¶ 75 (evaluators not convinced that corrective action would be effective); *Macon Apparel Corp.*, Comp. Gen. Dec. B-272162, 96-2 CPD ¶ 95 (evaluators not convinced that corrective action was sufficient to solve problems). In *Hughes Missile Sys. Co.*, Comp. Gen. Dec. B-272418, 96-2 CPD ¶ 221, GAO denied a protest where the agency had adjusted a rating of one competition based on corrective action but had refused to adjust the rating of another competitor that had overcome some of the problems encountered on a development contract by taking action on a follow-on productions contract. Compare *Trifax Corp.*, Comp. Gen. Dec. B-279561, 98-2 CPD ¶ 24, where a protest was granted because the agency had not properly rescored a proposal after it learned that prompt corrective action had been taken by the protester.

GAO and the Court of Federal Claims have also affirmed agency decisions to accept the corrective action taken by an offeror as curing the performance problems. See *Blackwater Lodge & Training Ctr., Inc. v. United States*, 86 Fed. Cl. 488 (2009), where the agency had assessed the performance risk as "low" after considering the offeror's new procedures to correct safety problems on past contracts. See also *CWIS, LLC*, Comp. Gen. Dec. B-287521, 2001 CPD ¶ 119 (winning offeror's score was reasonably increased based on corrective action); *Proteccion Total/Magnum Sec., S.A.*, Comp. Gen. Dec. B-278129.4, 98-1 CPD ¶ 137 (agency had found that an offeror's prompt response to a cure notice demonstrated that its past performance was good); and *Chemical Demilitarization Assocs.*, Comp. Gen. Dec. B-277700, 98-1 CPD ¶ 171 (agency had found that past poor performance was based on poor specifications and the offeror had no further problems after the specifications were corrected).

### d.  Offerors With No Past Performance

41 U.S.C. § 1126(b) states the following rule with regard to evaluating offerors where the agency has no past performance information:

> If there is no information on past contract performance of an offeror or the information on past contract performance is not available, the offeror may not be evaluated favorably or unfavorably on the factor of past contract performance.

After originally requiring a "neutral" rating in these circumstances, FAR 15.305(a)(2)(iv) now contains essentially the same language as the statute.

This rule covers not only offerors with no past performance but also offerors where the agency is unable to obtain data. See *Advanced Data Concepts, Inc.*, Comp. Gen. Dec. B-277801.4, 98-1 CPD ¶ 145, holding that it was proper to give an offeror a "neutral" rating when offices in the same agency failed to complete reference questionnaires, stating:

> [T]here is no legal requirement that all past performance references be included in a valid review of past performance. *Dragon Servs., Inc.*, B-255354, Feb. 25, 1994, 94-1 CPD ¶ 151 at 8; *Questech, Inc.*, B-236028, Nov. 1, 1989, 89-2 CPD ¶ 407 at 3. For our Office to sustain a protest challenging the failure to obtain or consider a reference's assessment of past performance, a protestor must show unusual factual circumstances that convert the failure to a significant inequity for the protester. *International Bus. Sys., Inc.*, B-275554, Mar. 3, 1997, 97-1 CPD ¶ 114 at 5. The record here shows that the agency contacted each of [the protester's] references, and made at least an initial attempt to obtain the information properly identified by [the protester] in its proposal. When the agency did not receive responses, the agency followed the RFP-described procedure of assigning a neutral rating in this area.

There are numerous cases affirming an agency's assigning a "neutral" rating because the offeror has no contracts or similar size or complexity. See, for example,

*Commissioning Solutions Global, LLC*, Comp. Gen. Dec. B-401553, 2009 CPD ¶ 210 (all three referenced contracts much smaller than instant procurement); *CMC & Maint., Inc.*, Comp. Gen. Dec. B-292081, 2003 CPD ¶ 107 (referenced contracts smaller and dissimilar from instant procurement); *Kalman & Co.*, Comp. Gen. Dec. B-287442.2, 2002 CPD ¶ 63 (no contracts of similar size or similarity with instant procurement); *MCS of Tampa, Inc.*, Comp. Gen. Dec. B-288271.5, 2002 CPD ¶ 52 (two referenced contracts were smaller and no information could be obtained on only similar contract). Similarly, GAO has affirmed "neutral" ratings when an offeror has no contracts that have been completed within a reasonable time of the competition. See *Futurecom, Inc.*, Comp. Gen. Dec. B-400730.2, 2009 CPD ¶ 42 ("neutral" rating appropriate when offeror has no relevant contracts that have been completed in last three years). In a questionable decision, GAO affirmed the use of a "neutral" rating on one reference for which no information could be obtained although information was received from two other references, *Chicataw Constr., Inc.*, Comp. Gen. Dec. B-289592, 2002 CPD ¶ 62.

This rule covers not only offerors with no relevant past performance but also offerors where the agency is unable to obtain data. See *Advanced Data Concepts, Inc.*, Comp. Gen. Dec. B-277801.4, 98-1 CPD ¶ 145, holding that it was proper to give an offeror a "neutral" rating when offices in the same agency failed to complete reference questionnaires, and *Bering Straits Tech. Servs., LLC*, Comp. Gen. Dec. B-401560.3, 2009 CPD ¶ 201, affirming a "neutral" rating when the protester did not show that affiliated companies would perform any part of the work and proposed a project manager that had only worked on a small contract that required similar work to the instance procurement. See also *Herley Indus., Inc.*, Comp. Gen. Dec. B-400736.2, 2009 CPD ¶ 48, holding it proper to give an offeror a "neutral" rating when it had not furnished past performance information on two of the three elements of the work. However, a neutral rating should not be assigned if an offeror intentionally fails to submit required past performance information, *Forest Regeneration Servs. LLC*, Comp. Gen. Dec. B-290998, 2002 CPD ¶ 187.

GAO has accorded agencies wide discretion in implementing this rule. Thus, GAO has agreed that an "excellent" rating on past performance can be considered superior to a "neutral" rating, *Engineering & Computation, Inc.*, Comp. Gen. Dec. B-275180.2, 97-1 CPD ¶ 47. GAO also stated that an evaluation of "good" past performance may be considered to be superior to an evaluation of "neutral" past performance, *Excalibur Sys., Inc.*, Comp. Gen. Dec. B-272017, 96-2 CPD ¶ 13. GAO has also affirmed giving an offeror with no performance record a "good" rating when that rating connoted "adequately sufficient," *Oceaneering Int'l, Inc.*, Comp. Gen. Dec. B-278126, 98-1 CPD ¶ 133. GAO explained that "good" in the rating scheme was not substantively different from "neutral" when it meant merely adequate. However, it is clearly improper to give an offeror with no performance record a "red" rating, *MIL Corp.*, Comp. Gen. Dec. B-294836, 2005 CPD ¶ 29. Furthermore, GAO has rejected the contention that a contract should not be awarded to an offeror with a neutral rating based on no relevant past performance, *M&M Ret. Enters., LLC*, Comp. Gen. Dec. B-297282, 2005 CPD ¶ 224.

When agencies evaluate past performance in terms of performance risk, there is some question as to how an offeror with no record of past performance should be scored. See *Phillips Indus., Inc.*, Comp. Gen. Dec. B-280645, 98-2 CPD ¶ 74, where the protester questioned the legality of a finding that such an offeror posed a performance risk but GAO denied the protest because the contract had been awarded to a slightly higher-priced offeror with excellent past performance.

## 3. Experience

As noted above, the experience of the offerors is evaluated either as part of the evaluation of past performance or as a separate evaluation factor. The latter practice is superior because it allows the agency to make a separate assessment of whether the offeror's have performed work that is similar to the work being procured and to use the fact that they have such experience in determining the risk that they will not successfully accomplish the work. When experience is stated as a separate factor, the agency must demonstrate that it actually evaluated this factor, *Bio-Rad Labs., Inc.*, Comp. Gen. Dec. B-297553, 2007 CPD ¶ 58. However, if an offeror fails to provide the information on experience requested by the RFP, the agency can drop the offeror from the competition, *Prudent Techs., Inc.*, Comp. Gen. Dec. B-297425, 2006 CPD ¶16. See also *Sam Facility Mgmt., Inc.*, Comp. Gen. Dec. B-292237, 2003 CPD ¶ 147, where the agency properly downgraded the protester because it had no provided the required details on past contracts in the experience section of its proposal — even though the details were in the past performance section. GAO commented that "agencies evaluating one section of a proposal are not obligated to go in search of needed information." See also *JAVIS Automation & Eng'g, Inc.*, Comp. Gen. Dec. B-290434, 2002 CPD ¶ 140 (offeror downgraded for lack of details required by RFP).

When experience is to be evaluated, the standard to be used is normally stated in the RFP and agencies must adhere to this description. See *Consolidated Eng'g Servs., Inc.*, Comp. Gen. Dec. B-311313, 2008 CPD ¶ 146, sustaining a protest where the agency downgraded the protester because it had not obtained its experience on a single contract when the RFP contained no "one contract" standard. Protests have also been sustained in *Doyon-Am. Mech., JV; NAJV, LLC*, Comp. Gen. Dec. B-310003, 2008 CPD ¶ 50 (agency evaluated experience of parent/affiliated companies when RFP stated only projects on which offeror served as prime contractor or teaming partner would be considered); *GlassLock, Inc.*, Comp. Gen. Dec. B-299931, 2007 CPD ¶ 216 (agency gave double credit for good experience by including it in the evaluation of a proposed project plan factor as well as the experience factor); *Data Mgmt. Servs. Joint Venture*, Comp. Gen. Dec. B-299702, 2007 CPD ¶ 139 (agency improperly considered experience on smaller projects when

RFP required experience of projects of "similar" magnitude but protest denied for lack of prejudice; Court of Federal Claims held agency interpreted RFP properly in *Data Mgmt. Servs. Joint Venture v. United States*, 78 Fed. Cl. 366 (2007)); *L-3 Commc'ns Titan Corp.*, Comp. Gen. Dec. B-299317, 2007 CPD ¶ 66, *recons. denied*, 2007 CPD ¶ 121 (agency concluded offerors had equal experience when one had more and the RFP stated that more credit would be given "the greater the extent" of experience); *KIC Dev., LLC*, B-297425.2, 2006 CPD ¶ 27 (agency did not evaluate the experience of subcontractors and key personnel as permitted by RFP); *Myers Investigative & Sec. Servs., Inc.*, Comp. Gen. Dec. B-288468, 2001 CPD ¶ 189 (agency evaluated only experience with agency when there was no such RFP statement); *Mechanical Contractors, S.A.*, Comp. Gen. Dec. B-277916, 97-2 CPD ¶ 121 (agency gave no weight to industry certifications as demonstrating experience although the RFP required information as to such certifications). This requirement to follow the RFP description is enforced loosely by reading the description broadly. See *RCL Components, Inc.*, Comp. Gen. Dec. B-400175, 2009 CPD ¶ 98, finding the agency had properly evaluated experience because the RFP description of the past performance evaluation included a statement that relevancy would be determined by the "magnitude of effort and complexities."

As in the case of past performance, agencies are accorded considerable discretion in assessing the relevance of past work to the work to be performed on the contract, *K-Mar Indus., Inc.*, Comp. Gen. Dec. B-400487, 2009 CPD ¶ 159. See *Zolon Tech, Inc.*, Comp. Gen. Dec. B-299904.2, 2007 CPD ¶ 183, where GAO denied a protest when the agency surprisingly downgraded the protester on experience because it intended to use a consultant with experience rather than having employees with the requisite experience. See also *Alpha Genesis, Inc.*, Comp. Gen. Dec. B-299859, 2007 CPD ¶ 167 (agency was free to evaluate only the amount of experience not the quality of the experience when the RFP narrowly stated the evaluation factor); *Financial & Realty Services, LLC*, Comp. Gen. Dec. B-299605.2, 2007 CPD ¶ 161 (agency properly downgraded protester because it did not comply with RFP requirement to match its experience with each contract task); *MarLaw-Arco MFPD Mgmt.*, Comp. Gen. Dec. B-291875, 2003 CPD ¶ 85 (agency properly did not give experience with agency work higher value that experience with other comparable work); *M. Erdal Kamisli, Ltd.*, Comp. Gen. Dec. B-291522, 2003 CPD ¶ 19 (agency permitted to give higher experience rating to offeror that listed the most projects on which it had comparable experience). However, GAO will grant a protest if the evaluation is irrational. See, for example, *Cooperativa Muratori Riuniti*, Comp. Gen. Dec. B-294980, 2005 CPD ¶ 21, where GAO granted a protest when the agency downgraded the protester because no single referenced contract was of the magnitude of the current procurement but that procurement called for multiple items of work and the protester had numerous prior contracts whose work cumulated to the magnitude being procured. Similarly, in *Olympus Bldg. Servs., Inc.*, Comp. Gen. Dec. B-285351, 2000 CPD ¶ 178, a protest was granted when the agency gave experience ratings on the basis of the size of buildings that had been managed and averaged the ratings, but did not inform the offerors of this scoring method, with the result that the protester submitted more projects than required, yielding a lower experience assessment.

Agencies frequently evaluate the experience of prospective subcontractors and this is proper when there is some indication in the RFP that it will be done, *PAI Corp. v. United States*, 2009 U.S. Claims LEXIS 320 (2009). GAO has gone further and held that subcontractor experience can be evaluated even when the RFP does not provide for such evaluation as long as the RFP permits the use of subcontractors, *Kellogg Brown & Root Servs., Inc.*, Comp. Gen. Dec. B-298694.7, 2007 CPD ¶ 124. This reasoning has also been applied to the evaluation of the experience of key personnel when the RFP does not specifically state that such information would be considered in the evaluation of the offeror's experience, *Dix Corp.*, Comp. Gen. Dec. B-293964, 2004 CPD ¶ 143. However, there is no requirement that an agency evaluate key personnel as part of the evaluation of corporate experience, *Blue Rock Structures, Inc.*, Comp. Gen. Dec. B-287960.2, 2001 CPD ¶ 184.

When an offeror has no experience but intends to use subcontractors with good experience, an agency can reach a balanced evaluation of the overall experience, *IPlus, Inc.*, Comp. Gen. Dec. B-298020, 2006 CPD ¶ 90. This same reasoning applies when a agency is evaluating the experience of key personnel that is gained working for another contractor. See *STEM Int'l, Inc.*, Comp. Gen. Dec. B-295471, 2005 CPD ¶ 19, where GAO concurred with the agency's balancing of good experience of key personnel with no experience of the protester.

Where a solicitation indicates that experience will be evaluated, the agency may evaluate the extent to which an offeror's specific experience is directly related to the work required by the contract even when there is no statement in the RFP to that effect. See *International Bus. & Tech. Consultants, Inc.*, Comp. Gen. Dec. B-310424.2, 2008 CPD ¶ 185, where the agency properly considered whether the offerors had experience performing the precise work called for by the contract. See also *American Artisan Prods., Inc.*, B-293801.2, 2004 CPD ¶ 127 (proper to evaluate whether offerors had experience in setting up specific types of exhibits called for by RFP); *High Country Contracting*, Comp. Gen. Dec. B-278649, 98-1 CPD ¶ 39 (contracting officer reasonably determined that the protester's proposal posed a moderate risk because it had limited relevant construction experience); *Dual, Inc.*, Comp. Gen. Dec. B-279295, 98-1 CPD ¶ 146 (agency reasonably determined that protester did not have relevant corporate experience in a required area); *ECG, Inc.*, Comp. Gen. Dec. B-277738, 97-2 CPD ¶ 153 (agency reasonably determined that although experience on one small project was not similar in size, scope, or complexity to that described in the RFP, experience of proposed subcontractors had corporate experience on projects similar in size, scope, and complexity to that described in the RFP). See also *WECO Cleaning Specialists, Inc.*, Comp. Gen. Dec. B-279305, 98-1 CPD ¶ 154 (protester's proposal failed to elaborate on the scope and complexity of its prior experience, and the information provided "was very vague"); *Centra Tech., Inc.*, Comp. Gen. Dec. B-274744, 97-1 CPD ¶ 35 (protester's experience was rated as only "fair" and awardee's rating was "excellent" because protester and its proposed subcontractors had limited experience compared to the incumbent awardee); *EastCo Bldg. Servs., Inc.*, Comp. Gen. Dec. B-275334, 97-1 CPD ¶ 83 (protester's proposal downgraded based on lack of certain experience under three-year contracts); *Engineering & Computation, Inc.*, Comp. Gen. Dec. B-275180.2, 97-1 CPD ¶ 47 (incumbent contractor was rated "excellent" for relevant corporate experience as opposed to the protester, a new corporate entity, which was rated "neutral" for this evaluation factor because it had no prior corporate experience).

Proposals must be treated equally under the experience evaluation factor. Unequal treatment was found in *Ahtna Support & Training Servs., LLC*, Comp. Gen. Dec. B-400947.2, 2009 CPD ¶ 119 (agency assessed the experience of subcontractor of one offeror but not of protester); *Ashe Facility Servs., Inc.*, Comp. Gen. Dec. B-292218.3, 2004 CPD ¶ 80 (agency assessed the experience of key personnel of one offeror, but not the protester, in its evaluation of experience); and *U.S. Prop. Mgmt. Serv. Corp.*, Comp. Gen. Dec. B-278727, 98-1 CPD ¶ 88 (agency unequally evaluated the experience of the protester and the awardee where both firms were newly formed corporations). In *Aerospace Design & Fabrication, Inc.*, Comp. Gen. Dec. B-278896.2, 98-1 CPD ¶ 139, GAO found that ambiguous terms in the solicitation resulted in an unequal competition. Based on RFP limitations of five pages discussing the offeror's relevant experience and past performance and two references on forms supplied within the solicitation for each prime and subcontractor participating in the proposal, the protester included two references for itself and two references for each of its subcontractors and used its five-page discussion to expand on the information related to its two references and those of its subcontractors. In contrast, the awardee, which did not propose to use subcontractors, included the two required references but used its five-page discussion to expand on those two references and on its experience with six other related contracts.

## 4. Key Personnel

When an agency decides to evaluate key personnel as a separate factor, it should assess the experience of the personnel rather than merely reviewing resumes. See, for example, *Savannah River Alliance, LLC*, Comp. Gen. Dec. B-311126, 2008 CPD ¶ 88, where the agency evaluated resumes, made reference checks, reviewed letters of commitment and then required the key personnel to attend an oral presentation where they worked sample tasks. GAO rejected the protester's contention that the evaluation was not correctly done when the agency concluded that the protester's personnel were not as experienced as the winning offeror. See also *PAI Corp.*, Comp. Gen. Dec. B-298349, 2006 CPD ¶ 124, where GAO agreed with the agency's determination that certain experience of a key person did not qualify as the type of experience required by the RFP; and *Base Techs., Inc.*, Comp. Gen. Dec. B-293061.2, 2004 CPD ¶ 31, where GAO denied a protest arguing that the experience of key personnel should not have been considered because it was not explicitly stated in the RFP. The disadvantage of only reviewing resumes is seen in *DEI Consulting*, Comp. Gen. Dec. B-401258, 2009 CPD ¶ 151, where the agency downgraded the protester because of lack of full information in the resume. GAO denied a protest of this procedure but it is apparent that the agency acted without adequate information as to the qualifications of the key person in arriving at this result. Compare *Trammell Crow Co.*, Comp. Gen. Dec. B-311314.2, 2008 CPD ¶ 129, holding that the agency was required to disclose the downgrading of key personnel in discussions because they were significant weaknesses.

It is proper to evaluate a key person even if the agency knows that he will not be assigned to the contract for its full duration, *U.S. Facilities, Inc.*, Comp. Gen. Dec. B-293029, 2004 CPD ¶ 17 (project manager had been promoted but was committed to stay with project until a suitable replacement was found). Conversely, it is within the discretion to drop a competitor when an agency finds that the project manager will leave the company after the contract work has commenced successfully, *S. C. Myers & Assocs., Inc.*, Comp. Gen. Dec. B-286297, 2001 CPD ¶ 16. See also *MCR Eng'g Co.*, Comp. Gen. Dec. B-287164, 2001 CPD ¶ 82, where it was found proper to ignore the fact that former key employees had assisted the offeror in achieving good past performance because it had continued to perform well after they left the company.

### 5. Technical and Management Plans

Agencies have very broad discretion in evaluating technical and management plans. See *Hernandez Eng'g, Inc.*, Comp. Gen. Dec. B-286336, 2001 CPD ¶ 89, stating:

> The evaluation of technical proposals is primarily the responsibility of the contracting agency. Our Office will not make an independent determination of the merits of technical proposals; rather, we will examine the record to ensure that the agency's evaluation was reasonable and consistent with the stated evaluation criteria. *Litton Sys., Inc.*, B-237596.3, Aug. 8, 1990, 90-2 CPD ¶ 115 at 8. A protester's mere disagreement with the agency's evaluation does not render the evaluation unreasonable. *SWR Inc.*, B-286044.2, B-286044.3, Nov. 1, 2000, 2000 CPD ¶ 174 at 3.

As discussed earlier, there are two distinct types of technical and management plans that are used as evaluation factors. The first type is the description of the work that is being *offered* to meet the agency's needs. The second type is the description of the processes that will be used that demonstrates that the offeror has the *capability* to perform the work. This latter type of plan is generally submitted under an evaluation factor described as "understanding the work" or "soundness of approach."

### a. Description of Work

The evaluation of the work that an offeror proposes to do to meet the requirements of the RFP is primarily within the province of the technical staff of the agency. Thus, neither GAO nor the Court of Federal Claims will overturn such a technical evaluation unless it is clearly irrational. See, for example, *Robbins-Gioia, LLC*, Comp. Gen. Dec. B-402199, 2010 CPD ¶ 67 (lack of detailed explanation of how contract goal would be achieved); *Savannah River Tank Closure, LLC*, Comp. Gen. Dec. B-400953, 2009 CPD ¶ 78 (winner proposed superior technical approach); *Savannah River Alliance, LLC*, Comp. Gen. Dec. B-311126, 2008 CPD ¶ 88 (winner offered superior key personnel); *Wackenhut Int'l, Inc.*, Comp. Gen. Dec. B-299022, 2007 CPD ¶ 44 (excessively long workweek); *Smiths Detection, Inc.*, Comp. Gen. Dec. B-298838, 2007 CPD ¶ 5 (inferior software design); *Gemma-CCC*, Comp. Gen. Dec. B-297447.2, 2006 CPD ¶ 182 (failure to submit required data showing that proposed product met agency requirements); *Integrate, Inc.*, Comp. Gen. Dec. B-296526, 2005 CPD ¶ 154 (failure to show that proposed software met RFP requirements); *TDF Corp.*, Comp. Gen. Dec. B-288392, 2001 CPD ¶ 178 (inadequate staffing); *SOS Interpreting, Ltd.*, Comp. Gen. Dec. B-287505, 2001 CPD ¶ 104 (inadequate system for handling sensitive information); *United Def. LP*, Comp. Gen. Dec. B-286925.3, 2001 CPD ¶ 75 (offered product inferior in a number of ways to that of competitor); *ABIC, Ltd.*, Comp. Gen. Dec. B-286460, 2001 CPD ¶ 46 (insufficient staffing and inadequate staff coverage of key work); *Coastal Drilling, Inc.*, Comp. Gen. Dec. B-285085.3, 2000 CPD ¶ 130 (offered product did not meet a mandatory requirement); *AMS Mech. Sys., Inc.*, Comp. Gen. Dec. B-281136, 99-2 CPD ¶ 59 (offered product did not appear to meet requirements and offeror did not furnish supporting information to demonstrate that it did); *Joint Threat Servs.*, Comp. Gen. Dec. B-278168, 98-1 CPD ¶ 18 (inadequate staffing). In contrast, protests were sustained in Compare *Meridian Mgmt. Corp.*, Comp. Gen. Dec. B-281287.10, 2001 CPD ¶ 5 (agency gave high rating to technical proposal that did not contain employees with skills necessary for the job); *OneSource Energy Servs., Inc.*, Comp. Gen. Dec. B-283445, 2000 CPD ¶ 109 (low rating for inadequate staffing was based on the agency's estimate of staffing needs without analysis of the proposal to determine if it was based on a "unique approach" or skilled staff); *ATA Def. Indus., Inc.*, Comp. Gen. Dec. B-282511, 99-2 CPD ¶ 33 (agency gave winning offeror high technical rating not supported by the facts); and *Consolidated Eng'g Servs., Inc.*, Comp. Gen. Dec. B-279565.2, 99-1 CPD ¶ 75 (agency did not give the protester credit for beneficial features in its technical proposal).

It is proper to make a risk assessment of the probability that a proposed management or technical approach will create performance problems. See, for example, *Trend W. Tech. Corp.*, Comp. Gen. Dec. B-275395.2, 97-1 CPD ¶ 201, denying a protest that the agency had assessed a plan as having moderate risk because the staffing level was low. In *TEAM Support Servs., Inc.*, Comp. Gen. Dec. B-279379.2, 98-1 CPD ¶ 167, the agency downgraded the protester's proposal because the protester did not propose to use permanent employees for general on-site labor. GAO found reasonable the evaluator's assessment that the management approach created the risk that maintenance and operation tasks would be unacceptably delayed because the local construction industry would be competing for the same laborers and the evaluator believed it unlikely that the protester could obtain local labor in a timely manner. See also *Ultra Elecs. Ocean Sys., Inc.*, Comp. Gen. Dec. B-400219, 2008 CPD ¶ 183 (proposed revisions to the design of product created potential performance risk); *Compunetix, Inc.*, Comp. Gen. Dec. B-298489.4, 2007 CPD ¶ 12 (significant modification needed for product posed a technical risk); *Sensis Corp.*, Comp. Gen. Dec. B-265790.2, 96-1 CPD ¶ 77 (moderate risk because the protester did not have a mature software development process); and *Hydro Eng'g, Inc. v. United States*, 37 Fed. Cl. 448 (1997) (specific elements of a technical and management proposal created a risk of timely performance and technical compliance).

When an agency evaluates the actual product to be delivered, it is highly unlikely that a protest will be successful. See, for example, *MD Helicopters, Inc.*, Comp. Gen. Dec. B-298502, 2006 CPD ¶ 164, denying a protest where the agency based its technical evaluation on four hours of flight testing of competitive helicopters.

### b.  Understanding the Work

A less rational, but common, type of evaluation of technical and management plans assesses whether the offeror has proven that it has the requisite capability by demonstrating an understanding of the work in the way the plan is written. Agencies also have wide latitude in making this subjective type of evaluation. See, for example, *Cylab, Inc.*, Comp. Gen. Dec. B-402716, 2010 CPD ¶ 163 (program management approach general, not addressing specific program requirements); *Government Acquisitions, Inc.*, Comp. Gen. Dec. B-401048, 2009 CPD ¶ 137 (offeror failed to submit resumes required in management plan); *Kuhana-Spectrum Joint Venture, LLC*, Comp. Gen. Dec. B-400803, 2009 CPD ¶ 36 (management plan misdescribed mentor/protégé program and omitted key personnel); *LOGMET, LLC*, Comp. Gen. Dec. B-400355.2, 2008 CPD ¶ 175 (proposed staffing plan showed lack of understanding of requirements); *Professional Performance Dev. Group, Inc.*, Comp. Gen. Dec. B-311273, 2008 CPD ¶ 101 (numerous informational deficiencies in plans); Comp. Gen. Dec. B-309964, 2007 CPD ¶ 217 (inadequate coverage of required technical maturation plans); *Operational Res. Consultants, Inc.*, Comp. Gen. Dec. B-299131.1, 2007 CPD ¶ 38 (technical proposal failed to discuss some required areas); *Bernard Cap Co.*, Comp. Gen. Dec. B-297168, 2005 CPD ¶ 204 (manufacturing approach not as sound as winning offeror); *TekStar, Inc.*, Comp. Gen. Dec. B-295444, 2005 CPD ¶ 53 (technical and management proposals did not demonstrate capability); *LifeCare, Inc.*, Comp. Gen. Dec. B-291672, 2003 CPD ¶ 95 (poorly written and incomplete technical proposal); *Chart Indus., Inc.*, Comp. Gen. Dec. B-288248, 2001 CPD ¶ 174 (technical plan very general, lacking sufficient detail); *Strategic Res., Inc.*, Comp. Gen. Dec. B-287398, 2001 CPD ¶ 131 (management plan lacked detail in dealing with staffing issues); *Fisherman's Boat Shop, Inc.*, Comp. Gen. Dec. B-287592, 2001 CPD ¶ 123 (required network schedule omitted option items and merely added start and finish dates to items listed in RFP); *Evolving Res., Inc.*, Comp. Gen. Dec. B-287178, 2001 CPD ¶ 83 (management plan failed to adequately describe its process for managing task orders); *ITT Fed. Sys.*

*Int'l Corp.*, Comp. Gen. Dec. B-285176.4, 2001 CPD ¶ 45 (lack of sufficient detail in technical proposal); *Calian Tech. (US), Ltd.*, Comp. Gen. Dec. B-284814, 2000 CPD ¶ 85 (technical plan showed lack of understanding of work to be performed); *Rotech Med. Corp.*, Comp. Gen. Dec. B-283295.2, 99-2 CPD ¶ 86 (technical proposal "disorganized, confusing, and largely bereft of narrative detail"); *Scientific & Commercial Sys. Corp.*, Comp. Gen. Dec. B-283160, 99-2 CPD ¶ 78 (technical proposal lacked detail in discussion of one task); *Manufacturing Eng'g Sys., Inc.*, Comp. Gen. Dec. B- 287074, 99-2 CPD ¶ 58 (technical proposal lacked complete explanation of approach); *Johnson Controls, Inc.*, Comp. Gen. Dec. B-282326, 99-2 CPD ¶ 6 (some pages of proposal unreadable); *Companie De Asesoria Y Comercio, S.A.*, Comp. Gen. Dec. B-278358, 98-1 CPD ¶ 26 (technical proposal lacked specific details and descriptions); *Intown Props., Inc.*, Comp. Gen. Dec. B-272524, 96-2 CPD ¶ 149 (management plan merely repeated solicitation without providing specific information); *Quality Elevator Co.*, Comp. Gen. Dec. B-271899, 96-2 CPD ¶ 89 (management plan lacked detail).

The great latitude accorded to the agency in this area is demonstrated by the cases that deny protests even though the agency has awarded the contract to a company that did not submit a plan with the detail required by the RFP. See, for example, *GTE Hawaiian Tel. Co.*, Comp. Gen. Dec. B-276487.2, 97-2 CPD ¶ 21, where the agency had required each offeror to address compliance with more than 1,300 technical requirements but had imposed an 800-page limit on technical proposals. GAO denied a protest that the winning offeror had not addressed all the requirements. See also *JW Assocs., Inc.*, Comp. Gen. Dec. B-275209, 97-1 CPD ¶ 57, where GAO initially granted a protest, in part because the agency had not documented its evaluation of a technical plan, but subsequently denied the protest when the agency reevaluated the technical plan of the winning offeror and determined that it was adequate even though it contained far less detail than the plan of the protester, and *SDS Int'l, Inc.*, Comp. Gen. Dec. B-279361, 98-2 CPD ¶ 7, affirming an agency's evaluation of a technical proposal as acceptable even though it did not describe the technical approach to be used as called for in the RFP, reasoning that the offeror had complied with the RFP by stating that it was capable of performing and that the contract specification was so detailed that there was little room for describing a technical approach different from that specification.

Disparate scoring has not generally been grounds for protest. See *Matrix Int'l Logistics, Inc.*, Comp. Gen. Dec. B-272388.2, 97-2 CPD ¶ 89, where the agency had evaluated one proposal as "excellent" and "clearly superior" to another in the initial procurement but had evaluated the same proposal as "good" and the other proposal as "excellent" in a resolicitation following a sustained protest. GAO did not comment on the disparity in evaluations in denying the protest on the resolicitation. Compare *Dynalantic Corp.*, Comp. Gen. Dec. B-274944.2, 97-1 CPD ¶ 101, where GAO made a detailed review of the agency's evaluation of the protester's technical and management proposal and determined that the identified deficiencies were easily correctable and, thus, that the protester should not have been dropped from the competitive range. See also *ITT Fed. Servs. Int'l Corp.*, Comp. Gen. Dec. B-29783, 2007 CPD ¶ 43 (protest granted where staffing plan was downgraded because it had less staff than irrational government estimate); *Engineering Mgmt. & Integration, Inc.*, Comp. Gen. Dec. B-291672, 2003 CPD ¶ 95 (protest granted where offeror was rejected for not furnishing required staffing information but had actually furnished more complete information in a different form).

In some cases, this type of evaluation drops offerors that are known to be capable from the competition. See, for example, *Raloid Corp.*, Comp. Gen. Dec. B-297176, 2005 CPD ¶ 205, denying a protest by a company that had successfully manufactured a product in the past but was downgraded because it did not state precisely how the product would be manufactured as required by the RFP. Similarly, in *Ideamatics, Inc.*, Comp. Gen. Dec. B-297791.2, 2006 CPD ¶ 87, the company that had created a computerized system was determined to have only had a fair understanding of that system and a fair ability to maintain and enhance the system because of its inadequate description of these functions in its technical proposal. Successful incumbents (where the agency has explicit knowledge of their capabilities) frequently lose competitions for failure to write good technical or management proposals. See *ManTech Int'l Corp.*, Comp. Gen. Dec. B-311074, 2008 CPD ¶ 87 (poor response to sample task); *HealthStar VA, PLLC*, Comp. Gen. Dec. B-299737, 2007 CPD ¶ 114 (incomplete information because of page limitations); *BAE Sys. Norfolk Ship Repair, Inc.*, Comp. Gen. Dec. B-297879, 2006 CPD ¶ 75 (downgrading of management approach satisfactory even though offeror had successfully managed prior projects); *International Res. Recovery, Inc. v. United States*, 60 Fed. Cl. 1 (2004) (failure to submit mobilization plan for work it was currently performing); *Executive Sec. & Eng'g Techs., Inc.*, Comp. Gen. Dec. B-270518, 96-1 CPD ¶ 156 (no information on corporate experience); *Pedus Bldg. Servs., Inc.*, Comp. Gen. Dec. B-257271.3, 95-1 CPD ¶ 135 (sloppily written technical proposal); *Management Tech. Servs.*, Comp. Gen. Dec. B-251612.3, 93-1 CPD ¶ 432 (minimal information on obtaining and training workforce).

Protests have been granted when the agency does not evenhandedly evaluate such proposals. See, for example, *Northrop Grumman Info. Tech., Inc.*, Comp. Gen. Dec. B-400134.10, 2009 CPD ¶ 167, granting a protest where the agency had given the same evaluation to proposals offering different levels of subcontracting. See also *Tidewater Homes Realty, Inc.*, Comp. Gen. Dec. B-274689, 96-2 CPD ¶ 241 (agency had given the protester low scores for lack of detail but had given the winning offeror high scores for a proposal containing a similar level of detail). In *Electronic Design, Inc.*, Comp. Gen. Dec. B-279662.2, 98-2 CPD ¶ 69, a protest was sustained on the basis that the agency conducted the competition on an unequal basis by permitting the awardee to include in its BAFO a 1,700-page appendix that had been rejected initially because it exceeded the page limitation on the management/technical proposals. GAO found that this was unfair to the protester who had no way of determining that such an extensive addition to its management/technical plan would be accepted or expected.

## VII.     DECISION TO AWARD

Upon the completion of the evaluation of offers, the agency must decide, circumstances permitting, whether to make an award without negotiations or to establish a competitive range and conduct negotiations with all the offerors within the competitive range. Whether award without negotiations is permissible depends upon a number of factors, including the provisions included in the solicitation, the offers received, and the nature of communications between the agency and the offerors. Within these parameters, the agency has broad discretion in deciding whether to award or to negotiate. It also has broad discretion in establishing the competitive range. The statutory and regulatory requirements concerning the exercise of these discretionary determinations have evolved over the years.

Although the statutes use the phrase "award without discussions," the phrase "award without negotiations" is more descriptive of the concept and avoids use of the same term to describe two different types of communications. The statutory provisions authorizing award "based on the proposals received," give two different meanings to the word "discussions." It is used to describe both the communications which are permitted prior to award on the basis of proposals received and the communications which are to occur after the competitive range is established. See 10 U.S.C. § 2305(b)(4)(A)(ii) and 41 U.S.C. § 3703(a)(2) stating that award can be made on the basis of proposals received "without discussions with the offerors (other than discussions conducted for the purpose of minor clarifications)." The same different meanings of "discussions" are contained in 10 U.S.C. § 2305(a)(2)(B)(ii)(I) and 41 U.S.C. § 3306(b)(2)(B)(i). In addition, the FAR Part 15 Rewrite removed the definition of "discussions" which had previously appeared in the FAR. It envisions that the exchanges between the agency and the offerors after establishment of the competitive range will constitute "negotiations" which "may include bargaining," FAR 15.306(d).

## A. Background

The government policy concerning whether to award without negotiations or to establish a competitive range and conduct discussions has changed several times over the years. The original statutory standard permitted award on an "initial proposal . . . where it can be clearly demonstrated from the existence of adequate competition or accurate prior cost experience that acceptance of an initial proposal without discussion would result in fair and reasonable prices," 10 U.S.C. § 2304(g) (1964). However, CICA changed the standard substituting "full and open competition" for "adequate competition" and "lowest overall cost to the Government" for "fair and reasonable prices." These changes were interpreted by GAO to mean that award would have to be made on the basis of the lowest evaluated price unless the proposal was technically unacceptable and that price/quality/capability tradeoffs where not permitted. See, e.g., *Information Spectrum, Inc.*, Comp. Gen. Dec. B-233208, 89-1

CPD ¶ 187. In 1990, recognizing that the "lowest overall cost" standard was too restrictive, causing unnecessary competitive range determinations thereby increasing the cost and time of procurements, Congress removed the "lowest overall cost" language and made related changes for defense contracts, § 802 of the National Defense Authorization Act for 1991, Pub. L. No. 101-510. Four years later, the same changes were adopted for non-defense agencies by the Federal Acquisition Streamlining Act of 1994, Pub. L. No. 103-355.

## B. Solicitation Provisions

While recognizing that award without negotiations would be preferable in many situations, Congress was concerned that competitors would not submit their best offers if they believed that the agency would likely conduct negotiations. Thus, 10 U.S.C. § 2305(a)(2)(B)(ii)(I) and 41 U.S.C. § 3306(b)(2)(B)(i) require that the solicitation indicate whether the agency intends to award without negotiations or intends to conduct negotiations, stating that the solicitation shall include:

> [E]ither a statement that the proposals are intended to be evaluated with, and award made after, discussions with the offerors, or a statement that the proposals are intended to be evaluated, and award made, without discussions with the offerors (other than discussions conducted for the purpose of minor clarification) unless discussions are determined to be necessary.

Neither the statute nor the regulations provide any directions related to selecting the appropriate provision. FAR 15.209(a) merely requires that once this determination is made, the appropriate solicitation provision is to be adopted.

### 1. Award Without Negotiations Intended

Paragraph (f)(4) of the standard FAR 52.215-1 Instructions to Offerors — Competitive Acquisition solicitation provision permits award without negotiations as follows:

> The Government intends to evaluate proposals and award a contract without discussions with offerors (except clarifications as described in FAR 15.306 (a)). Therefore, the offeror's initial proposal should contain the offeror's best terms from a cost or price and technical standpoint. The Government reserves the right to conduct discussions if the Contracting Officer later determines them to be necessary. If the Contracting Officer determines that the number of proposals that would otherwise be in the competitive range exceeds the number at which an efficient competition can be conducted, the Contracting Officer may limit the number of proposals in the competitive range to the greatest number that will permit an efficient competition among the most highly rated proposals.

While indicating that award without negotiation is intended, this provision gives the agency the option to conduct negotiations when they are determined to be "necessary." However, FAR 15.306(a)(2) requires that when such a determination is made, "the rationale for doing so shall be documented in the contract file." This provision apparently reflects the congressional concern that offerors might not make their best offers in their original submission if they expect negotiations to take place. Thus, the government should not avail itself of this option as a matter of course.

Incorporation of the substance of this notice into solicitations has been held to put offerors on notice that they should not expect to have an opportunity to revise their offers. See, e.g., *Robotic Sys. Tech.*, Comp. Gen. Dec. B-278195.2, 98-1 CPD ¶ 20, stating:

> [S]ince the RFP advised offerors that the agency intended to make award without discussions, RST could not reasonably presume that it would have a chance to improve its proposal through discussions. *Scientific-Atlanta, Inc.*, B-255343.2, B-255343.4, Mar. 14, 1994, 94-1 CPD ¶ 325 at 8-9.

An offeror does not have a *right* to award on the basis of an initial proposal, *Kisco Co.*, Comp. Gen. Dec. B-216953, 85-1 CPD ¶ 334.

## 2. Negotiations Intended

When the agency has determined that it intends to conduct negotiations, the following Alternate I to the FAR 52.215-1 ¶ (f)(4) solicitation provision is to be used:

> The Government intends to evaluate proposals and award a contract after conducting discussions with offerors whose proposals have been determined to be within the competitive range. If the Contracting Officer determines that the number of proposals that would otherwise be in the competitive range exceeds the number at which an efficient competition can be conducted, the Contracting Officer may limit the number of proposals in the competitive range to the greatest number that will permit an efficient competition among the most highly rated proposals. Therefore, the offeror's initial proposal should contain the offeror's best terms from a price and technical standpoint.

When this provision is used, the government may not make award without negotiations, *American Native Med, Transp., LLC*, Comp. Gen. Dec. B-276873, 97-2 CPD ¶ 73.

## C. Deciding Whether or Not to Negotiate

Neither the statutes nor the FAR specify criteria for determining whether or not to hold negotiations. 10 U.S.C. § 2305(b)(4)(A) merely states:

> The head of an agency shall evaluate competitive proposals in accordance with paragraph (1) and may award a contract —

(i) after discussions with the offerors, provided that written or oral discussions have been conducted with the responsible offerors who submit proposals within the competitive range; or

(ii) based on the proposals received, without discussions with the offerors (other than discussions conducted for the purpose of minor clarification) provided that the solicitation included a statement that proposals are intended to be evaluated, and award made, without discussions, unless discussions are determined necessary.

Substantially the same language is contained in 41 U.S.C. § 3703(a)(2).

Under the CICA standard, negotiations appeared to have been the favored procedure. However, the statutory changes have served to make award without negotiations at least an equally appropriate procedure. House Report 101-665, 101st Cong., 2d Sess. (accompanying Pub. L. No. 101-510) discussed some of the factors to consider in making the selection. However, it did not go so far as indicating a preference for either procedure, stating, "The committee does not recommend a preference for conducting discussions or not conducting discussions, believing that this is more appropriately dealt with in regulation." The FAR has not adopted any guidance implementing these statutes. Thus, the lack of statutory or regulatory direction leaves the agency with broad discretion in determining whether or not negotiations should be conducted either in advance or after offers are received. See, however, the DoD Source Selection Procedures stating at 3.3.1. that the source selection official "may choose, in rare circumstances, to award a contract on the basis of the initial proposals received without conducting discussions." This appears to state a policy that award without negotiations should be used infrequently.

## 1. Award Without Negotiations

Award without negotiations is one of the most important techniques that agencies have adopted to streamline their procurements. House Report 101-665 recognized the advantages of this process by noting the following benefits of making awards without negotiations:

- Significant reduction of acquisition lead-time

- Permitting award on technical superiority when discussions are not needed

- Lessening the chances of wrongful disclosure of source selection information

- Reduction of the government's overall acquisition costs by reducing the amount a contractor is spending on bid and proposal costs

An additional benefit is the avoidance of final proposal revisions which include arbitrary price reductions. Such reductions have resulted in excessively low prices which can create serious difficulties during contract performance.

## a. Agency Discretion

There are numerous protest decisions recognizing the broad discretion given to agencies to make the decision to award without discussions. See, e.g., *Synectic Solutions, Inc.*, Comp. Gen. Dec. B-299086, 2007 CPD ¶ 36; *Colmek Sys. Eng'g*, Comp. Gen. Dec. B-291931.2, 2003 CPD ¶ 123; *J.A. Jones/IBC J.V.*, Comp. Gen. B-285627, 2000 CPD ¶ 161; *Bulova Techs. LLC*, Comp. Gen. Dec. B-281384, 99-1 CPD ¶ 99; and *International Data Prods. Corp.*, Comp. Gen. Dec. B-274654.5, 97-1 CPD ¶ 34.

The mere possibility that lower prices or better technical solutions might result from negotiations is not sufficient to overcome the agency's determination that negotiations are not "necessary." Agency decisions to award without negotiations were found to be reasonable in the following cases: *Richard M. Milburn High School*, Comp. Gen. Dec. B-277018, 97-2 CPD ¶ 53 (award on initial proposals reasonable given deficiencies in protester's proposal and overall technical superiority of awardee's proposal); *Harry A. Stroh Assocs., Inc.*, Comp. Gen. Dec. B-274335, 97-1 CPD ¶ 18 (award on initial proposals to offeror submitting technically superior proposal at a fair price reasonable even though protester argued that a possibility existed that its inferior proposal could become best value through discussions); *Lloyd-Lamont Design, Inc.*, Comp. Gen. Dec. B-270090.3, 96-1 CPD ¶ 71 (award on initial proposals reasonable where awardee was best value and agency had advised offerors of intent to award without conducting discussions); *Cornet, Inc.*, Comp. Gen. Dec. B-270330, 96-1 CPD ¶ 189 (award on initial proposals reasonable given technical superiority of awardee's proposal and determination that no other offeror could improve its proposal to the level of awardee's); and *Southwest Marine, Inc.*, Comp. Gen. Dec. B-265865.3, 96-1 CPD ¶ 56 (award on initial proposals reasonable where proposal was evaluated as clearly best value).

## b. Lack of Discussions

The rule was established many years ago that once a discussion was held with one offeror, the agency could no longer award on the basis of initial proposals but was required to establish a competitive range and conduct discussions with all offerors within the range, 50 Comp. Gen. 202 (B-170751) (1970). However, communications in the form of clarifications were permissible prior to award on the basis of the initial proposals, *CompuServe Data Sys., Inc.*, 60 Comp. Gen. 468 (B-195982.2), 81-1 CPD ¶ 374. In applying this rule, it does not appear to matter which party initiated the communication that led to a discussion. See, for example, *CDA Inv. Techs., Inc.*, Comp. Gen. Dec. B-272093, 97-1 CPD ¶ 102, *recons. denied*, 97-1 CPD ¶ 103, where the agency selected one of the offerors on the basis of its initial proposal and sent it a contract document incorporating the full proposal by reference. The offeror signed the document and returned it to the agency with a cover letter noting that it would perform the contract using a few personnel and subcontractors different from those it had proposed. In several subsequent exchanges, the contracting officer stated that the offeror could not change its proposal and the offeror stated that it would abide by the "material terms and conditions" of its original proposal. GAO concluded that award on the basis of the original proposal was proper because there had been no discussion. See also *Environmental Quality Mgmt., Inc.*, Comp. Gen. Dec. B-402247.2, 2010 CPD ¶ 75, where GAO found award without discussions proper after the agency had sent evaluation notices to clarify past performance information and minor issues in 28 proposals but failed to allow the protester to explain or correct a "material error" in its proposal.

### c.  Best Value Determination

Award without negotiations should be made when the agency can determine that one of the offerors has submitted a proposal that clearly represents the best value to the government. GAO has denied protests of awards on the basis of initial proposals when the agency can demonstrate that the award was made to the offeror that offered the best value. In such cases the mere possibility that lower prices or better technical solutions might result from negotiations is not sufficient to overcome the agency's determination that negotiations are not necessary. See, for example, *Bannum, Inc.*, Comp. Gen. Dec. B-400928.2, 2009 CPD ¶ 144 (reasonable to award without discussions to technically superior offeror with slightly higher price); *Chem-Spray-South, Inc.*, Comp. Gen. Dec. B-298281.2, 2006 CPD ¶ 163 (reasonable to award without discussions to lower priced proposal even when higher technically rated offeror stated informally that it would lower its price); *HDL Research Lab, Inc.*, Comp. Gen. Dec. B-294959, 2005 CPD ¶ 8 (reasonable to drop protester that had numerous informational deficiencies when award was made without negotiations); *ACC Constr. Co.*, Comp. Gen. Dec. B-288934, 2001 CPD ¶ 190 (reasonable to award without discussions to technically superior offeror with 3.8% higher price); *Olympus Bldg. Servs., Inc.*, Comp. Gen. Dec. B-285351.3, 2001 CPD ¶ 115 (award on initial proposals reasonable when offeror has low price and best technical evaluation); *Carlson WagonLit Travel*, Comp. Gen. Dec. B-287016, 2001 CPD ¶ 49 (award to only acceptable proposal); *PEMCO World Air Servs.*, Comp. Gen. Dec. B-284240.3, 2000 CPD ¶ 71 (award could not be made to protester because of questions as to whether it could meet contract requirements); *Sabreliner Corp.*, Comp. Gen. Dec. B-284240.2, 2000 CPD ¶ 68 (award to acceptable offeror when protester's 25% lower price was unrealistically low); *Inland Servs. Corp.*, Comp. Gen. Dec. B-282272, 99-1 CPD ¶ 113 (award without discussions even though protester had no opportunity to comment on adverse past performance information); *TEAM Support Servs., Inc.*, Comp. Gen. Dec. B-279379.2, 98-1 CPD ¶ 167 (reasonable to award to technically superior proposal even though protester's technically unacceptable proposal had lower price); *Robotic Sys. Tech.*, Comp. Gen. Dec. B-278195.2, 98-1 CPD ¶ 20 (reasonable to award to offeror with superior technical proposal even though protester's unacceptable proposal was capable of being made acceptable and its price was one half of price of awardee); *Richard M. Milburn High School*, Comp. Gen. Dec. B-277018, 97-2 CPD ¶ 53 (reasonable to award without negotiations to offeror whose proposal contains a reasonable price and is technically superior); *Harry A. Stroh Assocs., Inc.*, Comp. Gen. Dec. B-274335, 97-1 CPD ¶ 18 (award without negotiations to offeror submitting technically superior proposal at a fair price reasonable even though protester argued that a possibility existed that its inferior proposal could become best value through discussions); *Lloyd-Lamont Design, Inc.*, Comp. Gen. Dec. B-270090.3, 96-1 CPD ¶ 71 (award without negotiations to offeror with technically superior proposal at slightly higher cost reasonable where awardee was best value); *Cornet, Inc.*, Comp. Gen. Dec. B-270330, 96-1 CPD ¶ 189 (award without negotiations reasonable given technical superiority of awardee's proposal and determination that no other offeror could improve its proposal to the level of awardee's); *Southwest Marine, Inc.*, Comp. Gen. Dec. B-265865.3, 96-1 CPD ¶ 56 (award without negotiations reasonable where proposal was evaluated as clearly best value); *Facilities Mgmt. Co.*, Comp. Gen. Dec. B-259731.2, 95-1 CPD ¶ 274 (award without negotiations reasonable when awardee with lowest probable cost was highest ranked technically); and *Information Spectrum, Inc.*, Comp. Gen. Dec. B-256609.3, 94-2 CPD ¶ 251 (award without negotiations to offeror with best technical proposal at higher price reasonable when agency determined it constituted the best value). In *Battelle Mem'l Inst.*, Comp. Gen. Dec. B-299533, 2007 CPD ¶ 94, GAO held that the agency properly dropped the protester from the competition without discussing lack of required option year prices when the RFP stated that a competitive range would be established on the basis of only the technical proposals. GAO reasoned that since the agency had decided to award without negotiations, the RFP provision reserving price negotiations to offerors in the competitive range did not come into play.

GAO has also recognized that an agency may consider the need for early commencement of performance and the cost of continuing the procurement process in deciding to award without negotiations. See *Charleston Marine Containers, Inc.*, Comp. Gen. Dec. B-283393, 99-2 CPD ¶ 84, denying a protest where the contracting officer awarded the contract to the best value offeror without discussions in order to ensure that the delivery schedule would be met, and *Tomco Sys., Inc.*, Comp. Gen. Dec. B-275551, 97-1 CPD ¶ 130, denying a protest where the agency had cited these considerations in awarding to a technically strong proposal at a slightly higher price than the protester had proposed.

GAO has also denied protests of award without negotiations when the award was to be made to the lowest-priced technically acceptable proposal, *Advanced Am. Diving Serv., Inc.*, Comp. Gen. Dec. B-274766, 97-1 CPD ¶ 1. In that case it was held that the agency was not required to conduct discussions with an offeror that had submitted an unacceptable proposal even though its price was the lowest. Award to a reasonably priced acceptable proposal was sustained. See also *LOGMET, LLC*, Comp. Gen. Dec. B-400355.2, 2008 CPD ¶ 175 (award without negotiations proper when there were a number of acceptable proposals); and *Integrated Techs. Group, Inc.*, Comp. Gen. Dec. B-274288.5, 97-1 CPD ¶ 214 (award without negotiations proper where there were two technically acceptable proposals and discussions would have been required to correct an obvious mistake in the protester's proposal that could not be corrected through clarifications).

Award without negotiations has been held to be improper if the agency cannot make a clear determination as to which offeror has proposed the best value without discussions. See, for example, *Jonathan Corp.*, Comp. Gen. Dec. B-251698.3, 93-2 CPD ¶ 174, *recons. denied*, 93-2 CPD ¶ 233, where the agency had determined that competing technical proposals were essentially equal and had awarded without negotiations to the offeror with the lowest probable cost. GAO found that the agency's cost realism analysis was flawed, with the result that it was unclear which proposal represented the best value to the government. Where negotiations were necessary to ascertain the probable costs of the competing offerors, GAO held that award without negotiations was improper. This reasoning was followed by the Court of Federal Claims in *Day & Zimmermann Servs. v. United States*, 38 Fed. Cl. 591 (1997), where the agency had conducted a flawed cost realism analysis in a procurement where the competing offerors had been evaluated as being very close on the other evaluation factors. The court held that it was improper to award without negotiations when discussions were needed to determine an accurate probable cost in order to make a rational tradeoff decision. Compare *Silynx Commc'ns, Inc.*, Comp. Gen. Dec. B-310667, 2008 CPD ¶ 36, holding that award without negotiations was proper because there was a clear basis for distinguishing between the technical merits of the proposals.

## 2. Decision to Negotiate

The nature of the specifications and the extent to which technical merit is to be considered in a tradeoff strategy procurement will be critical in determining whether to indicate in the solicitation that negotiations are intended. This was noted in H.R. Rep. 101-665, which stated:

> The committee believes that when technical characteristics that cannot be quantified in cost terms are so critical that they are weighed more than lowest overall cost, the government may need discussions to ensure a clear understanding by both the government and the contractor of what the government truly needs and can get.

Where the solicitation indicates that award without negotiations is anticipated, the decision to negotiate will depend on the facts and circumstances of the procurement. Even though the criteria for such an award are present, negotiations would be called for if circumstances indicate that the government could obtain a significantly better bargain. This would be the case where one or more otherwise favorable offers contain defects. This is particularly so where the defects are readily correctable. See *Day & Zimmermann Servs. v. United States*, 38 Fed. Cl. 591 (1997), where the court questioned the decision to award without discussions when the competitors were very close and the agency made a speculative cost realism determination that could have been verified through discussions. In *Veda Inc. v. United States*, Civ. Action No. 93-0518-LFO (D.D.C. 1993), the court found that the decision to conduct discussions was reasonable because the contracting officer had serious problems with Veda's Small Business and Small Business Subcontracting Plan and deemed it unacceptable. Negotiations may also be called for when offers vary substantially from government estimates, *Jonathan Corp.*, Comp. Gen. Dec. B-251698.3 , 93-2 CPD ¶174. In deciding whether to negotiate in such situations, the agency should balance the delay and expense involved in conducting negotiations with the potential benefits which might be obtained. It should also consider the effect on competitors, such as unduly increasing bid and proposal expense.

## D. Determining the Competitive Range

Prior to 1996, many agencies had included a large number of companies in the competitive range — resulting in unduly high bid and proposal costs and excessively long evaluation periods. In one case, this resulted in the recovery of the costs of remaining in the competition because the protester was placed in the competitive range without any real chance for award, *SMS Data Prods., Group, Inc.*, GSBCA 8589-P, 87-1 BCA ¶19,496. These negative effects of broad inclusion of offerors in the competitive range were recognized as detrimental to the competitive negotiation process; and, in 1995, Congress was requested to amend the procurement statutes to permit more limited competitive range determinations.

### 1. Standards for Inclusion

The current standard for inclusion in the competitive range and for determining its size were established by the Clinger-Cohen Act of 1996, Pub. L. No. 104-106, and the promulgation of the FAR Part 15 Rewrite.

#### a. Statutory Changes

In passing the Clinger-Cohen Act, Congress recognized that the inclusion of large numbers of offers in the range can unnecessarily increase the time and cost of procurements and considered a number of ways in which the size of the range could be limited. Alternatives aimed at replacing the requirement for "full and open competition" were rejected because of concerns that they would lead to noncompetitive practices. However, two provisions were adopted which the FAR Council has relied upon to change the standards for determining inclusion in the competitive range. First, 10 U.S.C. § 2304(j) and 41 U.S.C. § 3301(c) require that "full and open competition" be conducted "efficiently" as follows:

The Federal Acquisition Regulation shall ensure that the requirement to obtain full and open competition is implemented in a manner that is consistent with the need to efficiently fulfill the Government's requirements.

More specifically, 10 U.S.C. § 2305(b)(4)(B) and 41 U.S.C. § 3703(b) permit the contracting officer to limit the competitive range:

> If the contracting officer determines that the number of offerors that would other-wise be included in the competitive range . . . exceeds the number at which an efficient competition can be conducted, the contracting officer may limit the number of proposals in the competitive range, in accordance with the criteria specified in the solicitation, to the greatest number that will permit an efficient competition among the offerors rated most highly in accordance with the criteria.

### b.  FAR Part 15 Rewrite

The FAR implementation of these statutes appears to call for a two-step process. First, the agency is required to establish a competitive range which is to include, "all of the most highly rated proposals," FAR 15.306(c)(1). Then, the agency must decide if the number of such proposals is too large for an "efficient competition." If so, FAR 15.306(c)(2) permits the number to be limited as follows:

> After evaluating all proposals in accordance with 15.305(a) and paragraph (c) (1) of this section, the contracting officer may determine that the number of most highly rated proposals that might otherwise be included in the competitive range exceeds the number at which an efficient competition can be conducted. Provided the solicitation notifies offerors that the competitive range can be limited for purposes of efficiency (see 52.215-1(f)(4)), the contracting officer may limit the number of proposals in the competitive range to the greatest number that will permit an efficient competition among the most highly rated proposals (10 U.S.C. §2305(b)(4) and 41 U.S.C. §253b(d)).

### c.  Most Highly Rated Offers and
### Efficient Competition

Neither the statutes nor the FAR attempt to define these terms. Draft versions of the FAR Part 15 Rewrite had listed factors to be considered in limiting the competitive range but these were deleted from the final Rewrite to permit "the facts of the instant acquisition to guide the contracting officer" in limiting the competitive range, 62 Fed. Reg. 51228 (1997). Similarly, the Rewrite does not contain a definition of "efficiency." However, the promulgation comments make it clear that the cost and time involved in conducting negotiations were the primary factors in rejecting the prior "when in doubt leave them in" rule.

The determination of which offers are the "most highly rated" will depend upon the facts and circumstances of each procurement. Under the current FAR, as under the prior regulations, the determination will be based on a comparison of the proposals. Thus, a break or gap in the evaluation scores might be the basis for determining the most highly rated offerors. See *Community P'ship LLC*, Comp. Gen. Dec. B-286844, 2001 CPD ¶ 38, and *Arsenault Acquisition Corp.*, Comp. Gen. Dec. B-276959, 97-2 CPD ¶ 74, affirming the use of this technique. For other protests denying exclusion from the competitive range, see *Cylab, Inc.*, Comp. Gen. Dec. B-402716, 2010 CPD ¶ 163 (three technically weak proposals excluded, four proposals included); *Orion Mgmt., LLC*, Comp. Gen. Dec. B-400680.2, 2009 CPD ¶ 21 (lowest rated of three proposals excluded); *Computer & Hi-Tech Mgmt., Inc.*, Comp. Gen. Dec. B-293235.4, 2004 CPD ¶ 45 (agency has discretion to determine which proposals are most highly rated); *Aliron Int'l, Inc.*, Comp. Gen. Dec. B-285048.2, 2000 CPD ¶ 125 (lowest rated of four proposals excluded); *Northwest Procurement Inst., Inc.*, Comp. Gen. Dec. B-286345, 2000 CPD ¶ 192 (two highly rated proposals included — protester's lower-rated proposal excluded); and *Wilson 5 Servs. Co.*, Comp. Gen. Dec. B-285343.2, 2000 CPD ¶ 157 (top two offerors included based on break in scores even though excluded protester had lower price). Compare *ABIC Ltd.*, Comp. Gen. Dec. B-286460, 2001 CPD ¶ 46, where an agency included six offerors in the range even though there was a clear gap after the third offeror.

The comparative approach to determining the competitive range generally precludes the use of a predetermined cut-off score as a means of determining the range, *DOT Sys., Inc.*, Comp. Gen. Dec. B-186192, 76-2 CPD ¶ 3. In 50 Comp. Gen. 59 (B-169645) (1970), the RFP contained a minimum score, 75, below which proposals would be deemed outside the competitive range. As a result of this cut-off score, five proposals with point scores between 71.4 and 74.8 were excluded. GAO held that these five proposals could not be excluded from the competitive range solely because of failure to meet the cut-off score. In *National Veterans Law Ctr.*, 60 Comp. Gen. 223 (B-198738), 81-1 CPD ¶ 58, the contracting agency established an evaluation score of 80 points, arguing that the score was only a "qualifying score" meant to inform the offerors of the relative importance of each area of evaluation. GAO found no difference between this "qualifying score" and a "predetermined cut-off score . . . used to establish the competitive range" and reiterated the impropriety of its use. Nevertheless, GAO has upheld the exclusion of an offeror based on a predetermined cut-off score when the score of the excluded proposal was so low in comparison with scores on other proposals that no prejudicial effect could be said to exist, 52 Comp. Gen. 382 (B-174870) (1972); *PRC Computer Ctr., Inc.*, 55 Comp. Gen. 60 (B-178205), 75-2 CPD ¶ 35; *Monarch Enters., Inc.*, Comp. Gen. Dec. B-233303, 89-1 CPD ¶ 222.

Reduction of the competitive range on the basis for efficiency is more problematic. The FAR Councils appear to have concluded that, as a general rule, no more than three offerors should be included in the competitive range. See 62 Fed. Reg. 51226 stating that "award is nearly always made to one of the three most highly rated offerors." Nonetheless, the FAR contains no such guidance. See, however, NFS 1815.306, which contains the following statement:

(c)(2) A total of no more than three proposals shall be a working goal in establishing the competitive range. Field installations may establish procedures for approval of competitive range determinations commensurate with the complexity or dollar value of an acquisition.

It seems clear that elimination of proposals that have been determined to be among those most highly rated would be likely to subject an agency to protests of unfair treatment. Thus, elimination of such proposals should be done very cautiously. Where negotiations are not anticipated to be complex or time consuming, a relatively large number of offerors might not result in inefficiency. In contrast, where the nature of the procurement and the offers require substantial negotiations and complex offer revisions, limiting the competitive range would be desirable. In such cases the agency should carefully document the differences between the proposals and endeavor to eliminate those proposals that do not have a good chance of winning the competition. If, as the FAR seems to indicate, reduction requires the elimination of "most highly rated" offers, it is difficult to see what rationale would support the elimination of offerors from the competitive range when other offerors that had similar evaluations were included in the range. It would be sounder practice to include all of the most highly rated offerors in the range. See, however, *Kathpal Techs., Inc.*, Comp. Gen. Dec. B-283137.3, 2000 CPD ¶ 6, where GAO suggested that using this technique might have been a way to limit the number of competitors in a situation where the agency had received over 200 proposals. Compare *Meridian Mgmt. Corp.*, Comp. Gen. Dec. B-285127, 2000 CPD ¶ 121, granting a protest where the agency achieved an efficient number of competitors by dropping all proposals with low scores or high prices. GAO reasoned that the agency had not considered the protester's low prices in dropping it because of a questionable poor evaluation of its non-price factors.

## 2. Discretion to Include or Exclude

Under the current FAR, as under the prior regulations, the agencies continue to have broad discretion in determining whether to include or exclude an offer within the competitive range. Thus, it can be anticipated that their decisions will not be disturbed unless they are clearly shown to be arbitrary or unreasonable. See, for example, *W&D Ships Deck Works, Inc. v. United States*, 39 Fed. Cl. 638 (1997), where the court stated that it would not overrule a competitive range decision unless it was "clearly unreasonable," and *L&M Techs., Inc.*, Comp. Gen. Dec. B-278044.5, 98-1 CPD ¶ 131, stating that "[t]he determination of whether a proposal is in the competitive range is principally a matter within the contracting agency's discretion." Accord, *Impresa Construzioni Geom. Domenico Garufi v. United States*, 44 Fed. Cl. 540 (1999), *aff'd*, 238 F.3d 1324 (Fed. Cir. 2001). This same broad discretion is being accorded under the new "most highly rated" standard, *Medical Staffing Joint Venture, LLC*, Comp. Gen. Dec. B-400705.2, 2009 CPD ¶ 71; *EAA Capital Co., L.L.C.*, Comp. Gen. Dec. B-287460, 2001 CPD ¶ 107. See also *NAE-TECH*

*Remediation Servs.*, Comp. Gen. Dec. B-402158, 2010 CPD ¶ 89, where GAO emphasized the great discretion in this area and summarily rejected the protester's contention that it should not have been excluded from the competitive range because it had intended to correct its defects during discussions.

Nonetheless, contracting officers must treat all offerors fairly. Thus, they are not free to treat similarly situated offerors differently. See *Isometrics, Inc. v. United States*, 5 Cl. Ct. 420 (1984), where the exclusion of a proposal that might legitimately have been excluded due to a failure to comply with RFP requirements was held to be improper because a similarly situated offeror was included in the competitive range and given an opportunity to cure the problems. See also *Columbia Research Corp.*, Comp. Gen. Dec. B-284157, 2000 CPD ¶ 158, holding that an offeror was improperly excluded when comparison of its technical proposal to the higher scored proposals revealed no material differences in either the quantity or magnitude of the weaknesses and its cost proposal was the lowest. Compare *Outdoor Venture Corp.*, Comp. Gen. Dec. B-401351.2, 2009 CPD ¶ 194, finding no unequal treatment when one offeror with deficiencies in its technical proposal was included and the protester with deficiencies in its technical proposal was excluded because its deficiencies were "of greater significance."

The discretion to include or exclude offerors from the competitive range permits agencies to include marginal proposals in the competitive range in order to broaden the competition. See, for example, *440 E. 62d St. Co.*, Comp. Gen. Dec. B-276058.2, 98-1 CPD ¶ 73, denying a protest asserting that it should have been excluded from the competitive range because it was weak on several evaluation factors.

### a.   *Factors to be Considered*

The statutes require that the competitive range be established "solely on the factors specified in the solicitation," 10 U.S.C. § 2305(b)(1) and (4)(A) or "considering only cost or price and the other factors included in the solicitation," 41 U.S.C. § 3703(c). This requirement is repeated in FAR 15.306(c)(1) and FAR 15.305(a). Previously, the regulations required that "cost or price and other factors, be considered" in establishing the competitive range, pre-Rewrite FAR 15.609(a). The same language was also included in an earlier draft of FAR 15.306(c)(1) but it was removed in the final draft.

The deletion of the language concerning consideration of cost does not necessarily mean that cost is not to be considered. Cost, with all the other evaluation factors would ordinarily be considered in establishing the range. However, in some instances a complete evaluation of each element of each offer would not appear to be necessary prior to determining the competitive range. If one or more aspects of an offer is so inferior to other offers as to make it unlikely that it could be improved through negotiations, it would not be reasonable to invest more time and effort into evaluating other aspects of the offer. See NFS 1815.305-70, Identification of Unacceptable Proposals, stating:

(a) The contracting officer shall not complete the initial evaluation of any proposal when it is determined that the proposal is unacceptable because:

(1) It does not represent a reasonable initial effort to address the essential requirements of the RFP or clearly demonstrates that the offeror does not understand the requirements;

(2) In research and development acquisitions, a substantial design drawback is evident in the proposal, and sufficient correction or improvement to consider the proposal acceptable would require virtually an entirely new technical proposal; or

(3) It contains major technical or business deficiencies or omissions or out-of-line costs which discussions with the offeror could not reasonably be expected to cure.

(b) The contracting officer shall document the rationale for discontinuing the initial evaluation of a proposal in accordance with this section. While an offeror has a right to have its offer fairly evaluated, the government should not be required to perform expensive and useless exercises.

There is support for this interpretation in decisions under the prior rules. Under the pre-Rewrite rules (requiring consideration of cost) it was held to be proper to exclude offers without considering price or cost when the technical proposal is clearly unacceptable, *Regional Envtl. Consultants*, 66 Comp. Gen. 67 (B-223555), 86-2 CPD ¶ 476, *recons. denied*, 66 Comp. Gen. 388 (B-223555.2), 87-1 CPD ¶ 428; *Aid Maint. Co.*, Comp. Gen. Dec. B-255552, 94-1 CPD ¶ 188; *Telestar Corp.*, Comp. Gen. Dec. B-275855, 97-1 CPD ¶ 150. For an analysis of this rule, see *Paul & Gordon*, 52 Comp. Gen. 382 (B-174870) (1972), where GAO explained that the procedure was compatible with the prior statutory requirement in 10 U.S.C. § 2304(g) that "proposals, including price, shall be solicited." However, technically inferior but acceptable proposals may not be rejected without considering cost or price, *Arc-Tech, Inc.*, Comp. Gen. Dec. B-400325.3, 2009 CPD ¶ 53; *Femme Comp, Inc. v. United States*, 83 Fed. Cl. 704 (2008); *Information Scis. Corp. v. United* States, 73 Fed. Cl. 70 (2006); *Global, A 1" Flagship Co.*, Comp. Gen. Dec, B-297235, 2006 CPD ¶ 14; *Columbia Research Corp.*, Comp. Gen. Dec. B-284157, 2000 CPD ¶ 158; *Kathpal Techs., Inc.*, Comp. Gen. Dec. B-283137.3, 2000 CPD ¶ 6.

A technically acceptable proposal may be properly determined to be outside the competitive range because the contracting officer believes that the prospective costs of performance are too high and cannot be reduced sufficiently without detracting from the proposal's technical acceptability, *Tracor Marine, Inc.*, Comp. Gen. Dec. B-222484, 86-2 CPD ¶ 150 (denying protest even though protester's technical score was highest). See also *Radio Sys., Inc.*, Comp. Gen. Dec. B-255080, 94-1 CPD ¶ 9 (price 350% higher than the low offeror); *Everpure, Inc.*, Comp. Gen. Dec. B-226395.2, 88-2 CPD ¶ 264 (sustaining exclusion of higher priced proposal even though that left only one offeror in the competitive range); *Systems Integrated*, Comp. Gen. Dec. B-225055, 87-1 CPD ¶ 114 (30 % higher proposed costs); and *Jack Faucett Assocs.*, Comp. Gen. Dec. B-224414, 86-2 CPD ¶ 310 (35% higher costs).

A technically acceptable proposal may also be properly determined to be outside the competitive range because the contracting officer believes that the proposed price is unrealistically low, *International Outsourcing Servs., LLC*, Comp. Gen. Dec. B-295959, 2006 CPD ¶ 6.

The lower the technical rating, the less the cost differential must be to properly exclude an offeror from the competitive range. See, for example, *Bollam, Sheedy, Torani & Co.*, Comp. Gen. Dec. B-270700, 96-1 CPD ¶ 185 (protester properly excluded from the competitive range because it was ranked tenth out of 34 and its price was higher than seven of the eight proposals with higher technical scores that were included in the competitive range); and *Emerald Maint., Inc.*, Comp. Gen. Dec. B-221353, 86-1 CPD ¶ 308 (offeror only 14% higher in probable cost properly excluded when its technical rating was 30% lower).

A low cost proposal is not guaranteed inclusion in the competitive range by virtue of its low cost. See, for example, *DS, Inc.*, Comp. Gen. Dec. B-289676, 2002 CPD ¶ 58 (proposal contained insufficient costs to perform the work); *Molina Eng'g, Ltd./Tri-J Indus., Inc. J.V.*, Comp. Gen. Dec. B-284895, 2000 CPD ¶ 86 (proposal with unrealistically low price); *McDonald Constr. Servs., Inc.*, Comp. Gen. Dec. B-285980, 2000 CPD ¶ 183 (proposal was approximately 10% lower in price but was much lower rated on technical factors); and *Hydroscience, Inc.*, Comp. Gen. Dec. B-227989, 87-2 CPD ¶ 501 (proposal with three major technical deficiencies properly excluded even though it was considerably lower in cost than the four proposals placed in the competitive range).

## b. Inclusion of Defective or Unacceptable Offers

Because negotiations are conducted for the purpose of giving offerors the opportunity to cure weaknesses or deficiencies or to modify other aspects of their proposals, an offer need not be excluded from the competitive range solely because it fails to conform to the RFP. In this respect, the competitive range decision is very different from the "nonresponsiveness" determination in sealed bid contracting. See *Carahsoft Tech. Corp. v. United States*, 86 Fed. Cl. 325 (2009), where the court stated "a technically unacceptable proposal may be considered for award if the proposal would otherwise be competitive and if its technically unacceptable terms can be cured by the offeror in a revised proposal," and *Construcciones Aeronauticas, S.A.*, Comp. Gen. Dec. B-244717, 91-2 CPD ¶ 461, where GAO stated that "the concept of competitive range — whether the proposal is or can be readily made acceptable — is incompatible with responsiveness." See also *DeMat Air, Inc. v. United States*, 2 Cl. Ct. 197 (1983). In *National Ass'n of State Directors of Special Educ., Inc.*, Comp. Gen. Dec. B-227989, 89-1 CPD ¶ 189, GAO affirmed a contracting officer's decision to keep a technically unacceptable proposal in the competitive range because it was only one of two proposals. See also *Grove Res. Solutions, Inc.*, Comp. Gen. Dec. B-296228, 2005 CPD ¶ 133; and *SWR, Inc.*, Comp. Gen. Dec. B-286229, 2000 CPD ¶ 196, noting that the purpose of establishing a competitive range is to cure deficiencies. In one decision, which is at variance with the regulatory and decisional principles for establishing the competitive range, GAO held that the Army should have rejected a proposal which substantially failed to conform to the RFP, *Computer Mach. Corp.*, 55 Comp. Gen. 1151 (B-185592), 76-1 CPD ¶ 358. In that decision, GAO stated that when an agency uses the term "responsive" in its RFP, the offeror should understand that any terms referenced thereby are considered to be material requirements, and that a proposal failing to conform to such terms will be considered unacceptable.

### c.  *Exclusion for Offer Deficiencies*

While proposals with significant offer deficiencies may be included in the competitive range, they may also be excluded if the contracting officer determines that the offeror does not stand a chance of winning the competition. Contracting officers have been given broad discretion in making this determination. Thus, exclusion has been found proper in *All Computer Consulting, Inc.*, Comp. Gen. Dec. B-401204, 2009 CPD ¶ 132 (proposal did not demonstrate that proposed product met specification requirements); *L-3 Commc'ns. EOTech, Inc.*, Comp. Gen. Dec. B-311453, 2008 CPD ¶ 130 (bid sample failed tests — Court of Federal Claims reached opposite result in *L-3 Commc'ns. EOTech, Inc. v. United States*, 83 Fed. Cl. 643 (2008)); *Pacific Lock Co.*, Comp. Gen. Dec. B-309982, 2007 CPD ¶ 191 (proposal did not clearly prove that product was "U.S. made"); *Kolob Canyons Air Serv.*, Comp. Gen. Dec. B-398240.2, 2006 CPD ¶ 106 (proposal did not demonstrate that aircraft contained required avionics); *Integration Techs. Group, Inc.*, Comp. Gen. Dec. B-295958, 2005 CPD ¶ 99 (offered product did not meet specifications); *CliniComp, Int'l*, Comp. Gen. Dec. B-294059, 2004 CPD ¶ 209 (product not commercially available as required by RFP); *Wahkontah Servs., Inc.*, Comp. Gen. Dec. B-292768, 2003 CPD ¶ 214 (proposal merely parroted back RFP requirements); *Americom Gov't Servs., Inc.*, Comp. Gen. Dec. B-292242, 2003 CPD ¶ 163 (proposal included conditions on contract requirements); *B.E. Meyers & Co.*, Comp. Gen. Dec. B-283796, 2000 CPD ¶ 9 (proposal was very short and incomplete); *Novavax, Inc.*, Comp. Gen. Dec. B-286167, 2000 CPD ¶ 202 (offeror took exception to important requirement of RFP); *Wirt Inflatable Specialists, Inc.*, Comp. Gen. Dec. B-282554, 99-2 CPD ¶ 34 (product failed test even though offeror could have easily corrected problem); *Clean Serv. Co.*, Comp. Gen. Dec. B-281141.3, 99-1 CPD ¶ 36 (winning proposal was subsequently reevaluated without pages exceeding page limitation and found unacceptable); and *Cache Box, Inc.*, Comp. Gen. Dec. B-279892, 98-2 CPD ¶ 146 (proposal offered product that either did not meet specification or was ambiguous as to its ability to meet specification). It is clearly proper to exclude from the competitive range a proposal that could be made acceptable only if major modifications or revisions were undertaken, *Orincon Corp.*, Comp. Gen. Dec. B-276704, 97-2 CPD ¶ 26 (failure to propose small business subcontractors sufficient to meet the contractual subcontracting requirement); *Orbit Advanced Techs., Inc.*, Comp. Gen. Dec. B-271293, 96-1 CPD ¶ 254 (numerous deficiencies in explaining how its proposed product met the contract specifications and in justifying its costs); *Hines-Ike Co.*, Comp. Gen. Dec. B-270693, 96-1 CPD ¶ 158 (proposed technique of performing one segment of work that did not meet the specifications plus numerous informational deficiencies). A proposal was also properly excluded where the offeror informed the agency that it needed more time to resolve a zoning deficiency with the local authorities, *Dismas Charities, Inc.*, Comp. Gen. Dec. B-284754, 2000 CPD ¶ 84.

A proposal was also found properly excluded when the offeror did not respond to a request for clarification of the technically unacceptable proposal in a timely manner, *Data Res., Inc.*, 65 Comp. Gen. 125 (B-220079), 85-2 CPD ¶ 670. The exclusion of a proposal which was not "grossly deficient" was upheld where inclusion would not have enhanced competition, as the protester was the sole offeror, *Magnavox Advanced Prods. & Sys. Co.*, Comp. Gen. Dec. B-215426, 85-1 CPD ¶146. The agency decided to exclude the proposal from the competitive range and resolicited with relaxed specifications.

## d. Informational Deficiencies

Many RFPs require the submission of information relating to the offeror's capability to perform or to establish that the products or services offered meet the specifications. In the past, the contracting agency has been permitted to exclude offers from the competitive range for material failures to provide the information requested. In determining whether an informational deficiency is "material," GAO has considered (1) the detail called for in the RFP, (2) whether the omissions make the proposal unacceptable or merely inferior, (3) the scope and range of omissions, and (4) whether the proposal offers significant cost savings, *XYZTEK Corp.*, Comp. Gen. Dec. B-214704, 84-2 CPD ¶ 204. Offerors have been held to bear the risk of submitting proposals which do not comply with the RFP's informational requirements, *Pace Data Sys., Inc.*, Comp. Gen. Dec. B-236083, 89-2 CPD ¶ 429. Compare *Birch & Davis Int'l, Inc. v. Christopher*, 4 F.3d 970 (Fed. Cir. 1993), finding an offeror improperly excluded from the competitive range based on informational deficiencies because it had a reasonable chance for award.

Proposal page limitations are not excuses for failing to provide required information. In *Infotec Dev., Inc.*, Comp. Gen. Dec. B-238980, 90-2 CPD ¶ 58, a proposal was properly excluded for lack of information after the agency rejected 49 pages of the proposal which exceeded the page limitations in the RFP. Similarly, in *Management & Indus. Techs. Assocs.*, Comp. Gen. Dec. B-257656, 94-2 CPD ¶ 134, an RFP had a 20-page limit and the protester submitted over 200 pages of material. The agency removed the pages which exceeded the page limit and found the remaining pages deficient and excluded the protester from the competitive range. See also *HSQ Tech.*, Comp. Gen. Dec. B-277048, 97-2 CPD ¶ 57, finding it proper to exclude a proposal that exceeded the overall 300-page limitation with the result that none of its price proposal was included in the evaluation; and *Integrated Tech. Works, Inc. — Telara, Inc.*, Comp. Gen. Dec. B-286769.5, 2001 CPD ¶ 141, where the refusal to evaluate pages exceeding the 30-page limitation made an offeror technically unacceptable.

Where the information that is not submitted is for the purpose of verifying whether the offered products or services conform to specifications, exclusion from the competitive range has been held to be justified. See *Hamilton Sundstrand Poser Sys. v. United States*, 75 Fed. Cl. 512 (2007) (lack of narrative description as to how product complies with purchase description); *TMC Design Corp.*, Comp. Gen. Dec. B-296194.3, 2005 CPD ¶ 158 (lack of details about product's capabilities — exclusion proper even though testing of product was to be conducted prior to award decision); *Consultants in Continual Improvement*, Comp. Gen. Dec. B-289351, 2002 CPD ¶ 40 (proposal did not give details of the offeror's proprietary method of performing the work); *Speegle Constr., Inc.*, Comp. Gen. Dec. B-286063, 2000 CPD ¶ 190 (offeror that had not provided the technical solutions required by the RFP); and *Working Alternatives, Inc.*, Comp. Gen. Dec. B-276911, 97-2 CPD ¶ 2 (offeror failed to provide mandatory documentation demonstrating that it had a right to use its proposed prison facility)

Information related to the capability of the offeror has also been held to be material, and the failure to furnish such information has been held to be a valid reason for exclusion from the competitive range. Thus, informational deficiencies in technical or management proposals used to assess the offerors' understanding of the work also constitute valid reasons for exclusion of an offeror from the competitive range. See *D&J Enters., Inc.*, Comp. Gen. Dec. B-310442, 2008 CPD ¶ 8 (insufficient information on key personnel and organizational structure); *Professional Performance Dev. Group. Inc.*, Comp. Gen. Dec. B-311273, 2008 CPD ¶ 101 (information provided either parroted back RFP's requirements or stated intent to comply with RFP); *Femme Comp, Inc. v. United States*, 83 Fed. Cl. 704 (2008) (information was in wrong volume of proposal as delineated in RFP); *C. Martin Co.*, Comp. Gen. Dec. B-299382, 2007 CPD ¶ 74 (proposal appeared to use old information not responding to current requirements); *B&S Transp., Inc.*, Comp. Gen. Dec. B-299144, 2007 CPD ¶ 16 (insufficient information on management and operational approach); *Sigma One Corp.*, Comp. Gen. Dec. B-294719, 2005 CPD ¶ 49 ("overly general" treatment of required information); *Wahkontah Servs., Inc.*, Comp. Gen. Dec. B-292768, 2003 CPD ¶ 214 (information provided either parroted back in whole or part RFP's requirements or lacked sufficient information and detail to determine that offeror understood work required); *DSC Cleaning, Inc.*, Comp. Gen. Dec. B-292125, 2003 CPD ¶ 118 (no references provided); *LaBarge Prod., Inc.*, Comp. Gen. Dec. B-287841, 2001 CPD ¶ 177 (insufficient information on experience and qualifications as well as insufficient technical information); and *EAA Capital Co., L.C.C.*, Comp. Gen. Dec. B-287460, 2001 CPD ¶ 107 (insufficient information on management capability, technical plan and prior experience).

Offerors have been properly excluded from the competitive range for informational deficiencies demonstrating their understanding of the work even when the agency knows that they are fully capable of performing, *HealthStar VA, PLLC*, Comp. Gen. Dec. B-299737, 2007 CPD ¶ 114. Thus, incumbent contractors have been excluded from the competitive range for informational deficiencies, *SPAAN Tech, Inc.*, Comp. Gen. Dec. B-400406, 2009 CPD ¶ 46 (failure to provide information on quality assurance plan); *International Res. Recovery, Inc. v. United States*, 60 Fed. Cl. 1 (2004) (failure to submit mobilization plan for work currently being performed); *Interactive Communication Tech., Inc.*, Comp. Gen. Dec. B-271051, 96-1 CPD ¶ 260 (incumbent's technical proposal lacked detailed information on technical approach and staffing); *Pedus Bldg. Servs., Inc.*, Comp. Gen. Dec. B-257271.3, 95-1 CPD ¶ 135 (sloppy technical proposal did not demonstrate that incumbent contractor understood how to perform the work). An incumbent contractor has also been excluded from the competitive range for failing to meet an RFP requirement as to how the work is to be performed even though they have successfully performed the work a different way, *Saftey-Kleen (Pecatonica), Inc.*, Comp. Gen. Dec. B-290838, 2002 CPD ¶ 176.

### e.  Competitive Range of One

Prior to the new rules on establishing the competitive range, an agency's decision to include only one offeror in the competitive range was subject to close scrutiny due to the elimination of competition, *Birch & Davis Int'l, Inc. v. Christopher*, 4 F.3d 970 (Fed. Cir. 1993); and *Besserman Corp.*, Comp. Gen. Dec. B-237327, 90-1 CPD ¶ 191. A competitive range of one was overturned in a number of cases. See *Dynalantic Corp.*, Comp. Gen. Dec. B-274944.2, 97-1 CPD ¶ 101 (deficiencies of eliminated proposal were minor and easily correctable and price was lower); *Coastal Gov't Servs., Inc.*, Comp. Gen. Dec. B-250820, 93-1 CPD ¶ 167 (inadequacies were minor and could have been easily resolved during discussions); *Stay, Inc.*, Comp. Gen. Dec. B-247606, 92-1 CPD ¶ 481 (reasons for exclusion of protester were minor and some deficiencies were also found in awardee's proposal); *Corporate Strategies, Inc.*, Comp. Gen. Dec. B-239219, 90-2 CPD ¶ 99 (lower priced proposals that were eliminated were rated excellent or good and had weaknesses that could have been resolved by discussions).

Based on the new competitive range rules, GAO no longer follows this rule. Thus, since the FAR now uses the term "most highly rated proposals," an agency is permitted to include only one proposal in the competitive range if no other proposal has a reasonable chance of being selected for award, *TekStar, Inc.*, Comp. Gen. Dec. B-295444, 2005 CPD ¶ 53; *Information Sys. Tech. Corp.*, Comp. Gen. Dec. B-291747, 2003 CPD ¶ 72; *SDS Petroleum Prods., Inc.*, Comp. Gen. Dec. B-280430, 98-2 CPD ¶ 59, or if all other proposals have deficiencies, *General Atomics Aeronautical Sys., Inc.*, Gen. Dec. B-311004, 2008 CPD ¶ 105 (protester's proposal would have required major revisions); *M&M Investigations, Inc.*, Gen. Dec. B-299369.2, 2007 CPD ¶ 200 (protester's proposal was 30% higher in price and not rated best technically); *SOS Interpreting, Ltd.*, Comp. Gen. Dec. B-287505, 2001 CPD ¶ 104 (TEP rated proposal conditionally acceptable overall, which meant proposal did not meet all requirements); *Clean Serv. Co.*, Comp. Gen. Dec. B-281141.3, 99-1 CPD ¶ 36 (protester's proposal exceeded page limitations); *Wirt Inflatable Specialists, Inc.*, Comp. Gen. Dec. B-282554, 99-2 CPD ¶ 34 (protester's product leaked during preaward test). In the *SDS* decision, GAO rejected the argument that the agency was required to keep the top rated proposals in the competition because of the new language in the FAR and the deletion of the prior language stating that the competitive range should include "all proposals with a reasonable chance for award." See also *Firearms Training Sys., Inc. v. United States*, 41 Fed. Cl. 743 (1998), where the court held that the new FAR language permitted a competitive range of one. In that case, the court also held that the new FAR gave the agency broad discretion in determining when to establish the competitive range — allowing the agency to conduct a demonstration of proposed products before establishing the competitive range. Compare *Bean Stuyvesant, L.L.C. v. United States*, 48 Fed. Cl. 303 (2000), upholding a determination that only one offeror was in the competitive range but stating that "strict scrutiny" should continue to be given to such determinations under the new FAR.

## 3. Changes in the Competitive Range

The competitive range is dynamic rather than static. Thus, as an agency learns more about an offer, through communications, negotiations or reevaluation, the competitive range may be altered to reflect the current status of the offerors.

### a. Removal from the Competitive Range

Procuring agencies are not bound by initial determinations to include offers within the competitive range, *Intown Properties, Inc.*, Comp. Gen. Dec. B-250232, 93-1 CPD ¶ 43. In this regard, FAR 15.306(c)(3) provides that an offer originally included in the competitive range may be removed, as follows:

> If the contracting officer, after complying with paragraph (d)(3) of this section, decides that an offeror's proposal should no longer be included in the competitive range, the proposal shall be eliminated from consideration for award. Written notice of this decision shall be provided to unsuccessful offerors in accordance with 15.503.

If during or after discussions it becomes clear that a proposal should not have been included in the competitive range or no longer belongs in that range, the offeror may be precluded from further written or oral discussions, *Shel-Ken Props., Inc.*, Comp. Gen. Dec. B-277250, 97-2 CPD ¶ 79; *MAR Inc.*, Comp. Gen. Dec. B-246889, 92-1 CPD ¶ 367; *Scientific Mgmt. Assocs., Inc.*, Comp. Gen. Dec. B-238913, 90-2 CPD ¶ 27. In *Travel Co.*, Comp. Gen. Dec. B-249560.2, 93-1 CPD ¶ 76, the protester was initially found to be within the competitive range but after the agency requested and received supplementary and clarifying information, it determined that the protester was only at a minimally acceptable level and therefore no longer within the competitive range. Similarly, in *Hamilton Sundstrand Power Sys.*, Comp. Gen. Dec. B-298757, 2006 CPD ¶ 194; *Worldwide Primates, Inc.*, Comp. Gen. Dec. B-294481, 2004 CPD ¶ 206; *Outdoor Venture Corp.*, Comp. Gen. Dec. B-288894.2, 2002 CPD ¶ 13, *PeopleSoft USA, Inc.*, Comp. Gen. Dec. B-283497, 2000 CPD ¶ 25, and *Novavax, Inc.*, Comp. Gen. Dec. B-286167, 2000 CPD ¶ 202, proposals with significant deficiencies were included in the competitive range but dropped when discussions did not clear up the deficiencies. Compare *Symtech Corp.*, Comp. Gen. Dec. B-289332, 2002 CPD ¶ 43, holding that the agency had no reasonable basis for dropping a proposal from the competitive range because of its response to discussion questions. See also *Impresa Construzioni Geom. Domenico Garufi v. United States*, 44 Fed. Cl. 540 (1999), *aff'd*, 238 F.3d 1324 (Fed. Cir. 2001) (proper to exclude offeror from competitive range when answers to discussion questions show lack of understanding of work); *Dismas Charities, Inc.*, Comp. Gen. Dec. B-284754, 2000 CPD ¶ 84 (proper to drop an offeror when necessary information was not included in BAFO); *Labat — Anderson, Inc. v. United States*, 42 Fed. Cl. 806 (1999) (proper exclusion when BAFO was technically unacceptable); and *Magnum Prods., Inc.*, Comp. Gen. Dec. B-277917, 97-2 CPD ¶ 160 (offeror properly dropped after its BAFO did not cure a major deficiency pointed out during discussions). Compare *Voith Hydro, Inc.*, Comp. Gen. Dec. B-277051, 97-2 CPD ¶ 68, holding that an offeror was improperly dropped from the competitive range based on deficiencies in its BAFO when the deficiencies had been apparent in a question and answer session during oral presentations but had not been identified by the agency during negotiations.

An offer also may be dropped from the competitive range once negotiations have begun without affording the offeror an opportunity to submit a revised offer. See FAR 15.306(d)(4) stating:

> If, after discussions have begun, an offeror originally in the competitive range is no longer considered to be among the most highly rated offerors being considered for award, that offeror may be eliminated from the competitive range whether or not all material aspects of the proposal have been discussed, or whether or not the offeror has been afforded an opportunity to submit a proposal revision (see 15.307(a) and 15.503(a)(1)).

Conducting discussions with a group of offerors does not obligate the agency to conduct further discussions with all offerors in the group or to allow all to submit proposal revisions, *All State Boiler Work, Inc.*, Comp. Gen. Dec. B-277362, 97-2 CPD ¶ 144; *ALM, Inc.*, Comp. Gen. Dec. B-217284, 85-1 CPD ¶ 433; *Informatics Gen. Corp.*, Comp. Gen. Dec. B-210709, 83-2 CPD ¶ 47, *recons. denied*, 83-2 CPD ¶ 580. In *A. T. Kearney, Inc.*, Comp. Gen. Dec. B-237731, 90-1 CPD ¶ 305, an offeror was properly dropped from the competitive range when additional cost realism analysis indicated that its probable costs were not as low as originally thought and its technical score was far below the other offeror. In *Systems Integrated*, Comp. Gen. Dec. B-225055, 87-1 CPD ¶ 114, it was held proper to drop one of two competitors with almost equal technical scores from the competitive range because its cost proposal was almost 30% higher. See also *DuVall Servs. Co.*, Comp. Gen. Dec. B-265698.2, 96-1 CPD ¶ 133, where GAO found proper an agency's decision to drop a protester from the revised competitive range because it did not have a reasonable chance for award. The protester's explanation and analysis of the staffing requirement during discussions indicated to the contracting officer that it would not be likely to perform well.

### b.  Addition or Reinstatement to the Competitive Range

Offerors excluded or removed from the competitive range are required to be given prompt " preaward" notice of exclusion, FAR 15.503 (a)(1) and may request a " preaward debriefing," FAR 15.505. Following notice or debriefing the agency may discover that the offer was mistakenly excluded. Under such circumstances, it would be appropriate for the agency to include or reinstate the offer in the range. However, the inclusion would have to be based on the offer as originally submitted. FAR 15.307 (a) prohibits the agency from accepting or considering revisions to offers once they are excluded:

> If an offeror's proposal is eliminated or otherwise removed from the competitive range, no further revisions to that offeror's proposal shall be accepted or considered.

A similar provision was in the pre-Rewrite FAR (FAR 15.603 ). While this provision affords the agency protection against having to cope with a flurry of proposal revisions and a never-ending evaluation process, there may be circumstances where consideration of a revision would be desirable. It is difficult to see the harm in considering an unsolicited revision which did not require significant evaluation effort and did not result in unfair treatment of the other offerors.

## VIII.   NEGOTIATIONS

The procurement statutes require written or oral discussions with all offerors in the competitive range, but do not indicate the purpose of the discussion process, the matters to be discussed, or the procedures to be followed in conducting negotiations. The pre-Rewrite FAR was also silent on the purpose of discussions. In addition, under the pre-Rewrite rules, contracting agencies were significantly limited in the type of exchanges which could take place in the discussion process (former FAR 15.610). The Rewrite made a number of substantial changes in the rules for discussions and recognized that discussions means negotiation which includes bargaining with the view to "allowing the offeror to revise its proposal," 62 Fed. Reg. 51229 (1997). FAR 15.306(d) states:

> *Exchanges with offerors after establishment of the competitive range.* Negotiations are exchanges, in either a competitive or sole source environment, between the Government and offerors, that are undertaken with the intent of allowing the offeror to revise its proposal. These negotiations may include bargaining. Bargaining includes persuasion, alteration of assumptions and positions, give-and-take, and may apply to price, schedule, technical requirements, type of contract, or other terms of a proposed contract. When negotiations are conducted in a competitive acquisition, they take place after establishment

This new description of the process of discussions with offerors in the competitive range encourages contracting officers to conduct in-depth negotiations with each offeror. However, if such negotiations alter the contract requirements or terms and conditions included in the RFP, all offerors still in the competition must be informed of the alteration by an amendment to the RFP, FAR 15.206(a) and (c). Protests for not doing this have been sustained in *Red River Holdings, LLC v. United States*, 87 Fed. Cl. 768 (2009) (agency relaxed mandatory specification requirements); *Trammell Crow Co.*, Comp. Gen. Dec. B-311314.2, 2008 CPD ¶ 129 (agency altered key evaluation factor); *OTI Am., Inc. v. United States*, 68 Fed. Cl. 646 (2005) (agency used internal evaluation criteria inconsistently without amending RFP to inform offerors of criteria); *Northrop Grumman Info. Tech., Inc.*, Comp. Gen. Dec. B-295526, 2005 CPD ¶ 45 (agency significantly changed its approach to exercising options after receipt of final proposal revisions); *Systems Mgmt., Inc.*, Comp. Gen. Dec. B-287032, 2001 CPD ¶ 85 (agency relaxed mandatory solicitation requirement); *Mangi Envtl. Group, Inc. v. United States*, 47 Fed. Cl. 10 (2000) (agency relaxed mandatory requirements); *International Data Sys., Inc.*, Comp. Gen. Dec. B-277385, 97-2 CPD ¶ 96 (winning offeror permitted to furnish product with newer technology than that in specifications); *Symetrics Indus., Inc.*, Comp. Gen. Dec. B-274246.3, 97-2 CPD ¶ 59 (agency made significant changes to the estimated quantities in an IDIQ solicitation); and *Dairy Maid Dairy, Inc.*, Comp. Gen. Dec. B-251758.3, 93-1 CPD ¶ 404 (agency changed proposed requirements contract to definite quantity contract prior to award). Furthermore, if the alteration is "so substantial as to exceed what prospective offerors reasonably could have anticipated," the contracting officer must cancel the solicitation and issue a new one, FAR 15.206(e). See *AirTrak Travel*, Comp. Gen. Dec. B-292101, 2003 CPD ¶ 117, recommending reopening the competition to all vendors when the agency had issued an amendment to the RFP that significantly altered the risk imposed on contractors by the original RFP. Compare *The New Jersey & H St. Ltd. P'ship*, Comp. Gen. Dec. B-288026, 2001 CPD ¶ 125, ruling that an offeror that had been excluded from the competitive range was not entitled to receive an amendment to the RFP because the amendment was not substantial, and *Government Contract Servs. Co.*, Comp. Gen. Dec. B-294367, 2004 CPD ¶ 215, ruling that an offeror that had not competed was not entitled to cancellation of the solicitation because the amendment to the RFP did not substantially alter it.

## A. Purpose of Negotiations

Among the stated purposes of the Rewrite were to increase the "scope of discussions," 62 Fed. Reg. 51225 (1997), and to "require a more robust exchange of information during discussions," 62 Fed. Reg. 51229 (1997). Implementing the policy favoring enhanced discussions, FAR 15.306(d)(2) states that the primary purpose of negotiations is to obtain best value for the government:

> The primary objective of discussions is to maximize the Government's ability to obtain best value, based on the requirement and the evaluation factors set forth in the solicitation.

See DoD Source Selection Procedures repeating this statement at 3.4.1.and adding: "Discussions are highly recommended for source selections."

This is consistent with the view expressed by GAO that discussions should be conducted "to the end that competition is maximized and the Government is assured of receiving the most favorable contract," 51 Comp. Gen. 621 (B-173677) (1972). See also 52 Comp. Gen. 466 (B-177008) (1973), stating at 468:

> Since one of the primary purposes of conducting negotiations with offerors is to raise to an acceptable status those proposals which are capable of being made acceptable, and thereby increase competition for the procurement, we believe it is incumbent upon Government negotiators to be as specific as practical considerations will permit in advising offerors of the corrections required in their proposals.

Although there is no express statement requiring the agencies to "assist" an offeror in improving an offer, other changes in the FAR support the propriety of appropriately assisting an offeror to improve its offer. See FAR 15.306(d) stating:

> (3) . . . The contracting officer . . . is encouraged to discuss other aspects of the offeror's proposal that could, in the opinion of the contracting officer, be altered or explained to enhance materially the proposal's potential for award.

> (4) In discussing other aspects of the proposal, the Government may, in situations where the solicitation stated that evaluation credit would be given for technical solutions exceeding any mandatory minimums, negotiate with offerors for increased performance beyond any mandatory minimums, and the Government may suggest to offerors that have exceeded any mandatory minimums (in ways that are not integral to the design), that their proposals would be more competitive if the excesses were removed and the offered price decreased.

Furthermore, under the pre-Rewrite rules, agencies were prohibited from "helping an offeror" to improve its proposal under certain conditions (former FAR 15.610(d)). Such coaching was labeled "technical leveling." However, this prohibition was removed in the Rewrite. Thus, it would appear that assistance would be appropriate if all offerors are treated fairly, the rules against improper disclosure of source selection information are observed, and the assistance is not a response to an offeror's incompetence. See *First Preston Hous. Initiatives, LP*, Comp. Gen. Dec. B-293105.2, 2004 CPD ¶ 221, recognizing that helping offerors improve their proposals is proper because "such improvement is precisely what the discussion process envisions."

A careful reading of the above FAR provisions indicates that they *do not* state a mandatory rule requiring contracting officers to engage in robust negotiations with offerors in the competitive range. Rather, they are *permissive* — presumably to keep them from being grounds for protest. This is clear from the additional language in FAR 15.306(d)(3):

> However, the contracting officer is not required to discuss every area where the proposal could be improved. The scope and extent of discussions are a matter of contracting officer judgment.

The result is that the *mandatory* requirement for discussion is narrowly stated in FAR 15.306(d)(3) as follows:

> At a minimum, the contracting officer must, subject to paragraphs (d)(5) and (e) of this section and 15.307(a), indicate to, or discuss with, each offeror still being considered for award, deficiencies, significant weaknesses, and adverse past performance information to which the offeror has not yet had an opportunity to respond.

In spite of this narrow description of the mandatory discussion rule, conducting limited discussions is not sound policy. Particularly, attempting to draw distinctions between "deficiencies" and "weaknesses" and to determine when a "weakness" is "significant," would be difficult, at best, and of questionable benefit. Furthermore, GAO and court decisions in this area are somewhat unpredictable. Thus, contracting officers should fully explore the offers that are in the competitive range and conduct meaningful negotiations on all elements of the proposal which could be altered to improve the chance of the offeror winning the competition.

## B. Negotiating to Obtain Best Value

Negotiations are not an end in themselves. The purpose of the policy favoring robust negotiations is to obtain the most favorable contract for the government. Obtaining best value does not necessarily mean negotiating the lowest possible price and imposing the greatest possible risk on the contractor. While the contracting officer is required to ensure that the government does not pay a higher price than is necessary, it is also incumbent on the contracting officer to make certain that the price is not so low as to impede performance. See FAR 9.103(c) which indicates the various problems that can result from a price which is too low:

> The award of a contract to a supplier based on lowest evaluated price alone can be false economy if there is subsequent default, late deliveries, or other unsatisfactory performance resulting in additional contractual or administrative costs. While it is important that Government purchases be made at the lowest price, this does not require an award to a supplier solely because that supplier submits the lowest offer.

It is also important that the appropriate contract type be selected so that too great a risk is not imposed on the contractor. See FAR 16.103(a):

> Selecting the contract type is generally a matter for negotiation and requires the exercise of sound judgment. Negotiating the contract type and negotiating prices are closely related and should be considered together. The objective is to negotiate a contract type and price (or estimated cost and fee) that will result in reasonable contractor risk and provide the contractor with the greatest incentive for efficient and economical performance.

The following material contains a detailed analysis of the legal rules distinguishing between mandatory and permissive negotiations, which are identified in GAO and Court of Federal Claims decisions as the requirement for "meaningful discussions." Contracting officer must be aware of these rules but should recognize that they do not identify a clear line of demarcation. In the face of this lack of clarity, it is not good business practice to attempt to limit the issues raised during negotiations to the smallest number that will satisfy the legal rules. Rather, contracting officers should err on the side of robust negotiations where all elements of a proposal that have been downgraded are identified and explained to each offeror in the competitive range.

## 1. Deficiencies and Weaknesses

The terms "deficiency" and "weakness" have been at the center of much confusion in the discussion process. Prior to the FAR Part 15 Rewrite, when the only mandatory discussion requirement was that the agency address deficiencies, GAO had found inadequate discussions where the contracting officer failed to discuss "weaknesses" in an offeror's technical and management proposals where it had received low scores because of lack of detail in the proposal, *Eldyne, Inc.*, Comp. Gen. Dec. B-250158, 93-1 CPD ¶ 430. GAO explained this ruling in *Department of the Navy — Recons.*, Comp. Gen. Dec. B-250158.4, 93-1 CD ¶ 422, as follows:

> The Navy's contention that contracting officers are never required to discuss aspects of a proposal that do not make it unacceptable is simply wrong. As we stated in our decision sustaining Eldyne's protest, discussions conducted with offerors in the competitive range must be meaningful. FAR 15.610; *Jaycor, B-240029.2*

*et al.,* Oct. 31, 1990, 90-2 CPD ¶ 354. The FAR explicitly recognizes that, in conducting meaningful discussions, a contracting officer must use his or her judgment based on the facts of each acquisition (except that deficiencies and other matters listed in FAR 15.610(c) must always be discussed). Substitution of the mechanical approach suggested by the Navy for this exercise of judgment can, as it did in this case, frustrate the fundamental requirement of the Competition in Contracting Act of 1984 (CICA), 41 U.S.C. § 253b(d)(2) (1988), for meaningful discussions. As reflected in FAR 15.610, CICA effectively requires agencies to point out weaknesses, deficiencies or excesses in proposals necessary for an offeror to have a reasonable chance of being selected for award, which is, after all, the basis for including a proposal in the competitive range in the first place.

* * *

Regardless of the agency's description of its concerns with Eldyne's proposal as constituting a weakness rather than a deficiency, the record shows that Eldyne's proposal was significantly downgraded in these areas of its proposal. We believe the agency was required to discuss the matter with Eldyne; the firm should have been allowed the opportunity to amplify its approach to confirm its understanding of the RFP's requirements and satisfy the agency's serious concerns.

When the Rewrite was issued, this rule appeared to have been adopted in FAR 15.306(d)(3), requiring the disclosure in negotiations of not only "deficiencies" but also "significant weaknesses" and "other aspects of its proposal that could . . . be altered or explained to enhance materially the proposal's potential for award." However, in *MCR Fed., Inc.,* Comp. Gen. Dec. B-280969, 99-1 CPD ¶ 8, a protest was denied where the agency had failed to discuss the fact that a technical evaluation was scored as "acceptable" because it met all of the solicitation requirements. GAO stated, "We do not read the revised Part 15 language to change the legal standard so as to require discussion of all proposal areas where ratings could be improved." Similarly, in *Du & Assocs., Inc.,* Comp. Gen. Dec. B-280283.3, 98-2 CPD ¶ 156, GAO stated that it did not view the Rewrite "as having changed the prior legal requirements governing discussions." Subsequently, in 2001 the language "other aspects of its proposal that could . . . be altered or explained to enhance materially the proposal's potential for award" was removed from the mandatory rule, FAC 2001-02, 66 Fed. Reg. 65347, Dec. 18, 2001.

The result is that the current rule requires the discussion of "deficiencies" and "significant weaknesses." These terms are defined in FAR 15.001:

*Deficiency*, as used in this subpart, is a material failure of a proposal to meet a Government requirement or a combination of significant weaknesses in a proposal that increases the risk of unsuccessful contract performance to an unacceptable level.

*Weakness*, as used in this subpart, is a flaw in the proposal that increases the risk of unsuccessful contract performance. A "significant weakness" in the proposal is a flaw that appreciably increases the risk of unsuccessful contract performance.

Subsequent decisions provide little confidence that deficiencies and significant weaknesses can be distinguished from other matters that must be discussed. For example, some cases held that only "material" problems need be discussed. See *Cube Corp. v. United States*, 46 Fed. Cl. 368 (2000), where the court reasoned at 384:

> Plaintiff has not convinced the court that the disadvantages which were not shared with Cube meet these somewhat stringent definitions [of "deficiency" and "significant weakness"]. The disadvantages listed above do not rise to the level of "material failures," rendering the risk of unsuccessful contract performance unacceptable, or constitute flaws of such magnitude that appreciably increase the risk of unsuccessful contract performance, or even provide an opportunity to enhance "materially" the chance for award. Plaintiff has not demonstrated how disadvantages on the order of [DELETED] would have improved materially Cube's chance for award.

Lack of discussion of material issues has been found in a few instances. See *CRAssociates, Inc.*, Comp. Gen. Dec. B-282075.2, 2000 CPD ¶ 63, where two unidentified material deficiencies were not discussed and the protester won. See also *Dismas Charities, Inc.*, Comp. Gen. Dec. B-284754, 2000 CPD ¶ 84, where lack of proof of zoning for a building was identified as a material deficiency but the protest was denied because of lack of proof of prejudice, and *ACS Gov't Solutions Group, Inc.*, Comp. Gen. Dec. B-282098, 99-1 CPD ¶ 106, finding a lack of adequate discussions where the agency did not inform the protester that it was concerned with the fact that option year prices were higher than the base year price. This latter decision relied on GAO's pre-FAR Part 15 Rewrite rule rather than the FAR language. Similarly, in *Cotton & Co., LLP*, Comp. Gen. Dec. B-282808, 99-2 CPD ¶ 48, GAO found a lack of meaningful discussions when the agency did not inform the protester of the major deficiency in its technical proposal as well as its concern regarding the qualifications and experience of its proposed staff. See also *OMV Med., Inc.*, Comp. Gen. Dec. B-281388, 99-1 CPD ¶ 53, implying that failing to tell the protester that its labor rates are high is an inadequate discussion but denying the protest because there was no prejudice from such failure.

The agency must disclose any matters which would result in the proposal not be considered for award, *Columbia Research Corp.*, Comp. Gen. Dec. B-247631, 92-1 CPD ¶ 539. A failure to hold meaningful discussions was found where several offerors were not told during discussions that various proposed personnel were considered unqualified, 52 Comp. Gen. 466 (B-177008) (1973). See also *ACS Gov't Solutions Group, Inc.*, Comp. Gen. Dec. B-280098, 99-1 CPD ¶ 106 (agency did not inform offeror of concern over high prices in option years); *CitiWest Props., Inc.*, Comp. Gen. Dec. B-274689.4, 98-1 CPD ¶ 3 (agency failed to inform protester of its deficiency in not submitting required form); *International Data Sys., Inc.*, Comp. Gen. Dec. B-277385, 97-2 CPD ¶ 96 (agency failed to tell an offeror that it had proposed a noncompliant delivery schedule); *Delta Data Sys. Corp. v. Webster*, 240 App. D.C. 182, 744 F.2d 197 (D.C. Cir. 1984) (agency did not inform the offeror that it had concluded that the proposal evidenced insufficient financing for the contract);

and *General Elec. Co. v. Seamans*, 340 F. Supp. 636 (D.D.C. 1972) (offeror was not informed that its price was considered unrealistically low).

A number of protests have been denied because the issue was minor or it did not appear that it would change the outcome of the competition. See *DMS-All Star Joint Venture*, Comp. Gen. Dec. B-310932.6, 2009 CPD ¶ 212 (concerns about labor rates and other costs not significant weaknesses); *Ryder Move Mgmt., Inc. v. United States*, 48 Fed. Cl. 380 (2001) (interpretation of data that could not be altered in another proposal); *J.A. Jones/Bell, J.V.*, Comp. Gen. Dec. B-286458, 2001 CPD ¶ 17 (one area of concern that protester did not show how it could have improved its proposal); *Arctic Slope World Servs., Inc.*, Comp. Gen. Dec. B-284481, 2000 CPD ¶ 75 (two areas of concern that were viewed by the agency "simply as weaknesses"); *Consolidated Eng'g Servs., Inc.*, Comp. Gen. Dec. B-279565.5, 99-1 CPD ¶ 76 (offered "optional initiative" was of no value to the agency because it did not have an impact on price); and *ACRA, Inc. v. United States*, 44 Fed. Cl. 288 (1999) (although it was a "close question," no requirement to tell an offeror that it's failure to propose an "enhancement" had led to a reduced score). GAO has frequently stated that an agency "is under no obligation to discuss every aspect of the proposal which received less than the maximum score," *ADP Network Servs., Inc.*, Comp. Gen. Dec. B-200675, 81-1 CPD ¶ 157; *Communications Int'l, Inc.*, Comp. Gen. Dec. B-246076, 92-1 CPD ¶ 194; *ManTech Sec. Techs. Corp.*, Comp. Gen. Dec. B-297133.3, 2006 CPD ¶ 77. The Court of Federal Claims is in accord with this view, *Structural Assocs., Inc./Comfort Sys. USA (Syracuse) Joint Venture v. United States*, 89 Fed. Cl. 735 (2009); *WorldTravelServ. v. United States*, 49 Fed. Cl. 431 (2001); *Dynacs Eng'g Co. v. United States*, 48 Fed. Cl. 124 (2000). See also *SEAIR Transport Servs.*, Inc., Comp. Gen. Dec. B-274436, 96-2 CPD ¶ 224, holding that the protester was not entitled to discussions which would essentially have been conducted solely to permit it to achieve a perfect score in all areas. In *TRW, Inc.*, Comp. Gen. Dec. B-243450.2, 91-2 CPD ¶ 160, GAO stated this rule very liberally holding that the agency was required to disclose deficiencies in subfactors only when the subfactor had received a score of less than four on a ten point rating scale. This ruling was based on the fact that the agency defined a score of four as "satisfactory." Compare *Technical & Mgmt. Servs. Corp.*, Comp. Gen. Dec. B-242836.3, 91-2 CPD ¶ 101, where the protester was rated unacceptable in several subcategories, but received acceptable ratings in every category because high scores in other subcategories raised the averages. GAO held that the agency must discuss every rating that is less than acceptable, and hence was required to discuss these inadequate ratings. Minor weaknesses were also found in *International Bus. & Tech. Consultants, Inc.*, Comp. Gen. Dec. B-310424.2, 2008 CPD ¶ 185 (weakness that agency itself considered minor in the evaluation); *Cornell Cos.*, Comp. Gen. Dec. B-310548, 2007 CPD ¶ 212 (weakness that did not prevent protester from having a reasonable chance to win); *PWC Logistics Servs., Inc.*, Comp. Gen. Dec. B-299820, 2007 CPD ¶ 162 (criticisms of risk management plan when it was rated "at the low end" of "highly acceptable"); *IAP World Servs., Inc.*, Comp. Gen. Dec. B-297084, 2005 CPD ¶ 199 (agency not required to discuss all areas where protester did not receive "highest possible rating"); *American Ordnance, LLC*, Comp. Gen. Dec. B-292847, 2004 CPD ¶ 3 (only minor weaknesses when proposal was rated "good"); *4-D Neuroimaging*, Comp. Gen. Dec. B-286155.2, 2001 CPD ¶ 183 (relative disadvantages in comparison to competitor); *KIRA, Inc.*, Comp. Gen. Dec. B-287573, 2001 CPD ¶ 152 (lack of experience of subcontractor that was not considered material); *SDOS Interpreting, Ltd.*, Comp. Gen. Dec. B-287477.2, 2001 CPD ¶ 84 (higher price that was considered reasonable); *Digital Sys. Group, Inc.*, Comp. Gen. Dec. B-286931, 2001 CPD ¶ 50 (two marginal past performance ratings that were not considered significant weaknesses); *AJT & Assocs., Inc.*, Comp. Gen. Dec. B-284305, 2000 CPD ¶ 60 (higher price that was believed to have resulted from technical approach of protester); *PRB Assocs., Inc.*, Comp. Gen. Dec. B-277994, 98-1 CPD ¶ 13 (proposal areas were rated "good" but not "excellent"); *American Combustion Indus., Inc.*, Comp. Gen. Dec. B-275057.2, 97-1 CPD ¶ 105 (issues that did not "strongly influence" the source selection decision); *Software Eng'g, Inc.*, Comp. Gen. Dec. B-272820, 96-2 CPD ¶ 193 (instances that result from the offeror's own lack of diligence, such as typographical errors in the proposal); and *TRI-COR Indus., Inc.*, Comp. Gen. Dec. B-259034.2, 95-1 CPD ¶ 143 (instances in which the protester's proposal exhibited a lack of technical understanding). There is also no requirement to discuss minor weaknesses that later become critical to the source selection decision, *Volmar Constr., Inc.*, Comp. Gen. Dec. B-270364, 96-1 CPD ¶ 139.

It can be seen that the distinction between "deficiencies" and "weaknesses" is problematic. Attempting to draw distinctions between these terms and to determine when a "weakness" is "significant," would be difficult, at best, and of questionable benefit. Thus, contracting officers should fully explore the offers which are in the competitive range and conduct meaningful negotiations on all elements of the proposal which could be altered to improve the chance of the offeror winning the competition.

## 2. Offer Information

In many cases, there is uncertainty as to exactly what performance is being offered. This may result from an offeror's failure to provide required information or from questions as to the meaning of terms in the offer. To the extent that these matters were not cleared up in pre-competitive range communications and the offeror is included in the competitive range, they should be addressed in the negotiation. When an agency finds that it needs information to evaluate the proposal but that information was not explicitly called for by the RFP, it must request that information, *Ashbury Int'l Group, Inc.*, Comp. Gen. Dec. B-401123, 2009 CPD ¶ 140. Similarly, when such an informational inadequacy results from a lack of clarity in the RFP, discussion of the matter is required. In *Logistic Sys. Inc.*, 59 Comp. Gen. 548 (B-196254), 80-1 CPD ¶ 442, *recons. denied*, 80-2 CPD ¶ 313, the GAO stated at 553:

> Where, as here, a proposal in the competitive range is informationally inadequate so that the agency evaluators cannot determine the extent of the offeror's compli-

ance with its requirements, the agency should use the discussion process to attempt to ascertain exactly what the offeror is proposing. In this connection, we have recognized that where a solicitation specifically calls for certain information, the agency should not be required to remind the offeror to furnish the necessary information with its final proposal. *Value Engineering Company*, Comp. Gen. Dec. B-182421, July 3, 1975, 75-2 CPD ¶10. But here the solicitation was not so specific in calling for information on the offeror's personnel and laboratory facilities.

See also *Bank of Am.*, Comp. Gen. Dec. B-287608, 2001 CPD ¶ 137 (agency required to discuss numerous instances of lack of detail where protester could have improved proposal); *CRAssociates, Inc.*, Comp. Gen. Dec. B-282075.2, 2000 CPD ¶ 263 (agency required to identify missing information and information it did not understand); and *Mechanical Contractors, S.A.*, Comp. Gen. Dec. B-277916.2, 98-1 CPD ¶ 68 (perceived informational gaps in proposal). Since it is frequently difficult to determine whether an informational deficiency is due to lack of clear guidance in the RFP, contracting officers should normally point out such deficiencies during discussions.

When information in the proposal is readily correctable, a required discussion will likely be found. See *Sperry Corp.*, 65 Comp. Gen. 195 (B-220521), 86-1 CPD ¶ 28, where discussions of price alone were held improper because there were correctable informational deficiencies in lower priced offers. See also *Bank of Am.*, Comp. Gen. Dec. B-287608, 2001 CPD ¶ 137 (agency required to discuss numerous instances of lack of detail where protester could have improved proposal); *CRAssociates, Inc.*, Comp. Gen. Dec. B-282075.2, 2000 CPD ¶ 263 (agency required to identify missing information and information it did not understand); and *Mechanical Contractors, S.A.*, Comp. Gen. Dec. B-277916.2, 98-1 CPD ¶ 68 (perceived informational gaps in proposal).

Inadequate discussions have also been found when the agency needs additional information to fully evaluate an offeror's proposal. See *Tiger Truck, LLC*, Comp. Gen. Dec. B-400685, 2009 CPD ¶ 19 (agency failed to obtain sufficient information to determine whether offered product complied with the Trade Agreements Act); *Cogent Sys., Inc.*, Comp. Gen. Dec. B-295990.4, 2005 CPD ¶ 179 (agency failed to seek information on whether product met requirements); *Cotton & Co. LLP*, Comp. Gen. Dec. B-282808, 99-2 CPD ¶ 48 (agency did not clear up issues where it was clear protester misunderstood solicitation); *Voith Hydro, Inc.*, Comp. Gen. Dec. B-277051, 97-2 CPD ¶ 68 (agency determined that the protester's plan to use a new plant to manufacture the required items was an unacceptable risk but failed to discuss this deficiency with the protester); *Boeing Sikorsky Aircraft Support*, Comp. Gen. Dec. B-277263.2, 97-2 CPD ¶ 91 (request for verification of proposed costs not sufficiently specific when the agency had a detailed concern with the format used to display the costs); *American Combustion Indus.*, Comp. Gen. Dec. B-275057.2, 97-1 CPD ¶ 105 (agency improperly downgraded the protester when the agency, without discussing the matter with the protester, assumed that one of the protester's personnel would initially substitute for the proposed project manager); and *Peter N.G. Schwartz Cos. Judiciary Square Ltd.*, Comp. Gen. Dec. B-239007.3, 90-2 CPD ¶ 353, *aff'd*, Civ. Action No. 90-2951 (D.D.C. 1991) (improper to downgrade a proposal based on a lack of clarity of the role of certain employees when the matter could have been cleared up through discussions).

When the solicitation contains a clear requirement for information, the agency has a very low disclosure requirement in the negotiation process. See, for example, *Wade Perrow Constr.*, Comp. Gen. Dec. B-255332.2, 94-1 CPD ¶ 266, finding no requirement to identify missing information when Section L of the RFP contained a clear requirement for the information. See also *Trajen, Inc.*, Comp. Gen. Dec. B-296334, 2005 CPD ¶ 153, finding adequate discussions when the agency requested the submission of information already required by the RFP. Compare *Burchick Constr. Co.*, Comp. Gen. Dec. B-400342, 2008 CPD ¶ 203, sustaining a protest where the agency did not discuss weaknesses in a technical proposal that were based on inadequate information that was required by the RFP. GAO reasoned that the informational deficiencies were significant weaknesses that could have been corrected if the protester had been informed of them.

Agencies have also been required to conduct discussions in order to ascertain whether an offeror is submitting an alternate proposal. See *Peirce-Phelps, Inc.*, Comp. Gen. Dec. B-238520.2, 91-1 CPD ¶ 385, stating:

> Where there are uncertainties with respect to proposals, attempts should be made to resolve the problem with meaningful discussions which point out the uncertainties and give the offeror an opportunity to resolve them. . . . The requirement for meaningful discussions extends to alternate, acceptable proposals within the competitive range. *San/Bar Corp.*, B-219644.3, Feb. 21, 1986, 86-1 CPD ¶ 183.

## 3.  Capability Information

Most of the protests concerning capability information deal with past performance. Prior to the December 2001 revision, FAR 15.306(d)(3) required discussion of such adverse past performance information only if it was a "significant weakness" or a "deficiency." This led to GAO denying protests of lack of discussion of such information, *Digital Sys. Group, Inc.*, Comp. Gen. Dec. B-286931, 2001 CPD ¶ 50 ("marginal" ratings), *ITT Fed. Servs. Int'l Corp.*, Comp. Gen. Dec. B-283307, 99-2 CPD ¶ 76 ("good" rating). The Court of Federal Claims followed this reasoning and permitted very limited discussions of past performance issues, *JWK Int'l Corp. v. United States*, 49 Fed. Cl. 371 (2001), *aff'd*, 279 F.3d 985 (2002) (sufficient discussion when contracting officer identified an "unsatisfactory" rating in a "discussion letter").

However, the current FAR requires that, to the extent that past performance information has not been discussed with an offeror prior to establishing the competitive range, negotiations must address adverse past performance information to which the offeror has not previously had an opportunity to comment, FAR 15.306(b)(4). Once such a discussion occurs, the agency must follow the requirement that meaningful discussions be held with all offerors in the competitive range, *Gulf Copper Ship Repair, Inc.*, Comp. Gen. Dec. B-293706.5, 2005 CPD ¶ 108.

Discussions have been found inadequate where the agency did not inform the offeror of adverse past performance information, *Dismas Charities, Inc.*, Comp. Gen. Dec. B-292091, 2003 CPD ¶ 125, and *Biospherics, Inc.*, Comp. Gen. Dec. B-278278, 98-1 CPD ¶ 161. See also *ST Aerospace Engines Pte. Ltd.*, Comp. Gen. Dec. B-275725, 97-1 CPD ¶ 161 (agency improperly downgraded protester's proposal based on the protester's affiliate company's poor past performance when the agency should have verified the relationship between the two companies during discussions with the firm). In contrast, adequate discussions have been found in a number of cases. See *JWK Int'l Corp. v. United States*, 49 Fed. Cl. 371 (2001), *aff'd*, 279 F.3d 985 (2002) (an "unsatisfactory" rating was identified in a discussion letter); *Davies Rail & Mech. Works, Inc.*, Comp. Gen. Dec. B-283911.2, 2000 CPD ¶ 48 (past problems were listed in a discussion letter); *Cubic Def. Sys., Inc. v. United States*, 45 Fed. Cl. 450 (1999) (agency stated there were reported management deficiencies without identifying the contracts where they were reported); and *IGIT, Inc.*, Comp. Gen. Dec. B-275299.2, 97-2 CPD ¶ 7 (agency sent the protester a discussion question asking if it had any information from a contractor showing that its subcontract had not been terminated for poor performance).

When past performance issues are "well documented," no discussion of adverse past performance information is necessary. See *Stateside Assocs., Inc.*, Comp. Gen. Dec. B-400670.2, 2009 CPD ¶ 120 (adverse performance had been addressed during performance of task orders); *Del-Jen Int'l Corp.*, Comp. Gen. Dec. B-297960, 2006 CPD ¶ 81 (adverse performance had been addressed during contract administration); *PharmChem, Inc.*, Comp. Gen. Dec. B-292408.2, 2004 CPD ¶ 60 (adverse performance had been addressed during contract administration). Neither is there a requirement to discuss such information when it was not material in deciding not to award to the company. See *Standard Commc'ns, Inc.*, Comp. Gen. Dec. B-296972, 2005 CPD ¶ 200 (no requirement to discuss relevance of information when it is clear to the agency); *Maytag Aircraft Corp.*, Comp. Gen. Dec. B-287589, 2001 CPD ¶ 121 (discussions would not have changed the facts); *Digital Sys. Group, Inc.*, Comp. Gen. Dec. B-286931, 2001 CPD ¶ 50 (marginal ratings would not have enhanced potential for award); *ABIC, Ltd.*, Comp. Gen. Dec. B-286460, 2001 CPD ¶ 46 (low ratings were not the determinative factor in eliminating protester from competitive range); *ITT Fed. Servs. Int'l Corp.*, Comp. Gen. Dec. B-283307, 99-2 CPD ¶ 76 ("good" ratings were not significant weaknesses).

When the offeror is told of adverse past performance information, the agency may not reveal the names of individuals providing the adverse information, FAR 15.306(e)(4). This prohibition does not appear to preclude revealing the name of the contractor or government agency from whom the information was obtained or the contract or project that the information relates to, and indeed, such information would be necessary in order to permit the offeror to provide its comments rebutting the information or explaining the steps that it had taken to ensure that the problem would not recur.

When capability is being assessed by requiring a technical proposal to demonstrate understanding of the work required to meet the agency's needs, the requirement for identification of a deficiency is reduced. See *ITT Fed. Sys. Int'l Corp.,* Comp. Gen. Dec. B-285176.4, 2001 CPD ¶ 45, stating:

> [T]he requirement for meaningful discussions does not require [giving] the offeror the opportunity to learn each and every weakness associated with its proposal during discussions, particularly where as here one aspect of the evaluation was to test the offerors' technical understanding.

## 4. Cost and Price Negotiations

Under the pre-Rewrite FAR, there was a hesitancy on the part of some agencies to conduct meaningful cost or price negotiations. This was caused partly by the admonition in pre-Rewrite FAR 15.610(e)(2) that the contracting officer not use:

> Auction techniques, such as —
>
> > (i) Indicating to an offeror a cost or price that it must meet to obtain further consideration;
> >
> > (ii) Advising an offeror of its price standing relative to another offeror (however, it is permissible to inform an offeror that its cost or price is considered by the Government to be too high or unrealistic); and
> >
> > (iii) Otherwise furnishing information about other offerors' prices.

The reference to auction techniques and subsections (i) and (ii) were removed in the Rewrite and replaced with the following language in FAR 15.306(e):

> Government personnel engaged in the acquisition shall not engage in conduct that
>
> > (3) Reveals an offeror's price without that offeror's permission. However, the contracting officer may inform an offeror that its price is considered by the Government to be too high, or too low, and reveal the results of the analysis supporting that conclusion. It is also permissible, at the Government's discretion, to indicate to all offerors the cost or price that the Government's price analysis, market research, and other reviews have identified as reasonable (41 U.S.C. 423(h)(1)(2)).

In addition FAR 15.306(d)(3) includes cost and price among examples of "other aspects of [a] proposal" which might be enhanced through negotiations. Thus, the FAR now permits full price negotiation with each offeror in the competitive range. The best guidance has been issued by NASA in NFS 1815.306, stating:

(d)(3)(A) The contracting officer shall identify any cost/price elements that do not appear to be justified and encourage offerors to submit their most favorable and realistic cost/price proposals, but shall not discuss, disclose, or compare cost/price elements of any other offeror. The contracting officer shall question inadequate, conflicting, unrealistic, or unsupported cost information; differences between the offeror's proposal and most probable cost assessments; cost realism concerns; differences between audit findings and proposed costs; proposed rates that are too high/low; and labor mixes that do not appear responsive to the requirements. No agreement on cost/price elements or a "bottom line" is necessary.

See *MCT JV*, Comp. Gen. Dec. B-311245.2, 2008 CPD ¶ 121, holding that the agency was required to indicate to the protester that there was a significant disparity between the allocation of the labor hours in its cost and technical proposals. See also *Price Waterhouse*, 65 Comp. Gen. 205 (B-220049), 86-1 CPD ¶ 54, sustaining a protest because the agency failed to inform the protester during discussions that its estimated level of effort and proposed price were considered unreasonably high. Compare *Metro Mach. Corp.*, Comp. Gen. Dec. B-295744, 2005 CPD ¶ 112, where an adequate discussion occurred when the agency asked for an explanation of the proposed labor rates without telling the protester that it concluded they were unrealistically low, and *Engineering Servs. Unlimited, Inc.*, Comp. Gen. Dec. B-291275, 2003 CPD ¶ 15, where no violation of the FAR was found when the agency told the protester that its labor rates were significantly lower than incumbent rates.

Under the pre-Rewrite rules, agencies could reveal their own conception of price reasonableness to all offerors. See *M.W. Kellogg Co./Siciliana Appalti Costruzioni, S.p.A., J.V. v. United States*, 10 Cl. Ct. 17 (1986) (disclosing the amount of funds available for the project); *Bethlehem Steel Corp., Baltimore Marine Div.*, Comp. Gen. Dec. B-231923 , 88-2 CPD ¶ 438 (disclosing current contract prices). In *Ikard Mfg. Co.*, 63 Comp. Gen. 239 (B-213891), 84-1 CPD ¶266, GAO held that it was proper for the contracting officer to reopen negotiations after both best and final offers contained prices considered too high and tell both offerors that the Army's negotiating goal was a $1,740 unit price. See also *Printz Reinigung GmbH*, Comp. Gen. Dec. B-241510, 91-1 CPD ¶ 143, where GAO considered the disclosure of a desired price range to be a permissible negotiation tool for achieving a fair and reasonable price.

The government may have different price objectives for each offer. See *Racal Guardata, Inc.*, 71 Comp. Gen. 218 (B-245139.2), 92-1 CPD ¶ 159, where GAO reasoned that no unfairness occurred where the disclosed price objectives were based on the technical proposals of each competitor and were not stated as mandatory figures. See also *Griggs & Assocs., Inc.*, Comp. Gen. Dec. B-205266, 82-1 CPD ¶ 458, upholding the agency's disclosure of individual cost objectives developed for each offeror's proposal based on separate appraisals of each offeror's costs as a valid basis for negotiations, and *Newport News and Drydock Co.*, Comp. Gen. Dec. B-254969, 94-1 CPD ¶ 198, finding it proper to disclose the approximate percentages that an offeror's prices were below the government estimate.

Agencies must disclose unreasonably high prices in discussions, *Gas Turbine Engines, Inc.*, Comp. Gen. Dec. B-401868.2, 2009 CPD ¶ 257; *Tiger Truck, LLC*, Comp. Gen. Dec. B-400685, 2009 CPD ¶ 19; *Creative Info. Tech., Inc.*, Comp. Gen. Dec. B-293073.10, 2005 CPD ¶ 110. However, GAO has *not* required agencies to discuss price with offerors whose prices are not "unreasonably" high (even though they are considerably higher), *DB Consulting Group. Inc.*, Comp. Gen. Dec. B-401543.2, 2010 CPD ¶ 109 (price approximately 40 % higher than winning offeror); *Integrated Concepts & Research Corp.*, Comp. Gen. Dec. B-309803, 2008 CPD ¶ 117 (estimated cost of sample task triple that of competitor due to different solution); *DeTekion Sec. Sys,, Inc.*, Comp. Gen. Dec. B-298235, 2006 CPD ¶ 130 (price 22% higher than winning offeror); *MarLaw-Arco MFPD Mgmt.*, Comp. Gen. Dec. B-291875, 2003 CPD ¶ 85 (although price was "significantly" higher than awardee, it was "reasonable" and only somewhat higher than government estimate); *Cherokee Info. Servs.*, Comp. Gen. Dec. B-287270, 2001 CPD ¶ 77 (although price was over 15 % over winning offeror, it was "competitive and not unrealistically high"); *Hydraulics Int'l, Inc.*, Comp. Gen. Dec. B-284684, 2000 CPD ¶ 149 (although price was 70% higher than winning offeror, it was not "inherently unreasonable" when the technical proposal was considered); *Biospherics, Inc.*, Comp. Gen. Dec. B-285065, 2000 CPD ¶ 118 (although price was considerably higher, it was within 200 % of winning offeror and thus not subject to discussion under agency's rule); *AJT & Assocs.*, Inc., Comp. Gen. Dec. B-284305, 2000 CPD ¶ 60 (contracting officer did not consider 24% higher price too high). In other cases, very limited discussion of a high price have been held to be sufficient, *WorldTravelService*, Comp. Gen. Dec. B-284155.3, 2001 CPD ¶ 68 (protester told that is should "take a look" at its prices because they were "way too high"); *Wackenhut Int'l, Inc.*, Comp. Gen. Dec. B-286193, 2001 CPD ¶ 8 (suggestion that protester "revise its price to make it more favorable"); *WinStar Fed. Servs.*, Comp. Gen. Dec. B-284617, 2000 CPD ¶ 92 (protester told to "review sharpening [its] pencil" and that numerous prices "significantly exceed" the government's estimate).

The Court of Federal Claims has followed GAO reasoning on this issue. See *DMS All-Star Joint Venture v. United States*, 90 Fed. Cl. 653 (2010), stating at 669:

> As to discussions regarding an offeror's costs, unless an offeror's costs constitute a significant weakness or deficiency in its proposal, the contracting officer is not required to address in discussions costs that appear to be higher than those proposed by other offerors. *SOS Interpreting, Ltd.*, B-287477.2, 2001 CPD ¶ 84, at 3 (Comp. Gen. May 16, 2001) (citation omitted). In other words, "if an offeror's costs are not so high as to be unreasonable and unacceptable for contract award, the agency may conduct meaningful discussions without raising the issue of the offeror's

costs." *Yang Enters., Inc.; Santa Barbara Applied Research, Inc.,* B-294605.4, B-294605.5, B-294605.6, 2005 CPD ¶ 65, at 9 (Comp. Gen. April 1, 2005) (citation omitted). In essence, it is mandatory for the agency to discuss costs or pricing when the prices submitted in a firm's proposal "would preclude award to the firm." *Gen. Dynamics-Ordnance & Tactical Sys.,* B-401658, B-401658.2, 2009 CPD ¶ 217, at 5 (Comp. Gen. Oct. 26, 2009) (*General Dynamics*) (citation omitted).

Compare *WorldTravelServ. v. United States,* 49 Fed. Cl. 431 (2001), holding that an agency must disclose during discussions that it has concluded that a price is "too high." The court made it clear, however, that there was no requirement to tell the offeror how much it was too high.

Neither has GAO required that offerors be specifically told that their price was unrealistically low as long as they were informed that the agency was looking at this issue. See *SEEMA, Inc.,* Comp. Gen. Dec. B-277988, 98-1 CPD ¶ 12, denying a protest where the agency did not tell the protester that its price was considered unrealistic but told it that its price was significantly below the government estimate and not supported by the cost-savings data included in its proposal. Compare *Robinson's Lawn Servs., Inc.,* Comp. Gen. Dec. B-299551.5, 2009 CPD ¶ 45, denying a protest that the price discussions had induced the protester to raise its prices resulting in loss of the competition where the agency told both offerors that their prices were unrealistically low. In contrast, in *Advanced Sys. Dev., Inc.,* Comp. Gen. Dec. B-298411, 2006 CPD ¶ 137, GAO held that an unfair discussion had occurred when the agency induced a competitor to lower its price by not disclosing that it corrected an error to raise the price and telling the competitor that its price violated a price target — resulting in award to the competitor.

## 5. Sample Tasks

An agency may limit discussions of a deficiency when the deficient score relates to the offeror's general understanding of the technical aspects of the work as demonstrated by its submission of a solution to a sample task, *Syscon Servs., Inc.,* 68 Comp. Gen. 698 (B-235647), 89-2 CPD ¶ 258. In *Technology Applications, Inc.,* Comp. Gen. Dec. B-238259, 90-1 CPD ¶ 451, GAO stated:

> Where an offeror's responses to sample tasks are used to test its understanding of the technical requirements of a contemplated contract, as opposed to being used to evaluate the adequacy of its technical approach to the contract work, an agency need not specify during discussions all identified deficiencies in the offeror's approach to the tasks.

GAO reasoned that if the purpose of the task is to determine whether the offeror has the background and understanding to identify and resolve the technical issues that would arise during contract performance, to require the agency to discuss weak sample task results would defeat the purpose of using the response to a sample task to determine the offeror's understanding of the work. See also *Fluor Daniel, Inc.*, Comp. Gen. Dec. B-262051, 95-2 CPD ¶ 241, finding no need to discuss weakness in "limited scenerio" submitted by offerors to show understanding of work; *Delany, Siegel, Zorn & Assocs., Inc.*, Comp. Gen. Dec. B-258221.2, 95-2 CPD ¶ 7, finding no need to discuss "sample report;" and *NDI Eng'g Co.*, Comp. Gen. Dec. B-245796, 92-1 CPD ¶ 113, upholding the agency's decision not to discuss low scores on responses to a sample task when the responses were used to determine the offerors' understanding of the contract work. In *MCR Fed., Inc.*, Comp. Gen. Dec. B-280969, 99-1 CPD ¶ 8, GAO found no requirement to discuss an "acceptable" sample task rating when the agency had discussed a "marginal" sample task rating with the winning offeror.

Although discussions of sample task responses are not generally required, an agency may open discussions in order to better understand the response. However, if that occurs, the discussions must be meaningful. See *Integrated Concepts & Research Corp.*, Comp. Gen. Dec. B-309803, 2008 CPD ¶ 117 (informing offeror that amount of labor in sample task appeared high sufficient to alert protester that its price was high); *Serco, Inc.*, Comp. Gen. Dec. B-298266, 2006 CPD ¶ 120 (discussions elicited more information from offerors but agency misused information in evaluation process); *Delphinus Eng'g, Inc.*, Comp. Gen. Dec. B-298266, 2006 CPD ¶ 7 (discussions requested explanation of low price but protester provided in explanation in final proposal revision); *American Sys. Corp.*, Comp. Gen. Dec. B-292755, 2003 CPD ¶ 225 (evaluation notice sufficient to alert protester to issues even though it was misunderstood).

### 6. *Product Demonstrations*

When the agency requires offerors to demonstrate their product as part of the evaluation and then conducts discussions with the offerors still in the competitive range, it must discuss any perceived weaknesses revealed in the demonstration. In *Apptis, Inc.*, Comp. Gen. Dec. B-299457, 2008 CPD ¶ 49, the agency claimed that there was no such requirement because the demonstration revealed difficulty in using the product which could not be corrected (arguing that the sample task reasoning applied). GAO rejected this argument, stating:

> [E]ven though Apptis could not change the events that transpired at its . . . demonstration, the agency was nevertheless required to point out the weaknesses it observed and provide the firm with an opportunity to address them. Thus, for example, Apptis's discussion responses and/or FPR could have refuted the agency's purported observations, provided explanations as to why the events occurred, or proposed methods by which to address the agency's associated concerns.

Compare *Cerner Corp.*, Comp. Gen. Dec. B-293093, 2004 CPD ¶ 34, holding that there was no requirement that a contractor be advised that its product used an approach that was considered to be less effective than a competing product, and *SeaArk Marine, Inc.*, Comp. Gen. Dec. B-292195, 2003 CPD ¶ 108, holding that there was no requirement for discussions after a product demonstration when the RFP precluded such discussions.

## 7. Correction of Mistakes

Prior to the FAR Rewrite, most mistakes in proposals were corrected during oral or written discussions. See pre-Rewrite FAR 15.607(c). The Rewrite deleted this guidance and covered mistakes in a very cursory way, mentioning that they could be corrected prior to establishing a competitive range with offerors whose exclusion or inclusion in the competitive range was uncertain. The FAR is silent on correction of mistakes during negotiations, but it seems apparent that the contracting officer should notify offerors of suspected mistakes if they have not been identified previously.

In *Fidelity Techs. Corp.*, Comp. Gen. Dec. B-276425, 97-1 CPD ¶ 197, the protest was sustained where the protester's proposal included an apparently erroneous small disadvantaged business (SDB) certification and the contracting officer failed to provide the protester an opportunity to correct it. In refuting the Navy's argument that it did not have to provide the protester notice of possible error during negotiations, GAO stated:

> The Navy argues that it could only consider information within the four corners of that proposal. This argument is unpersuasive, both because the inconsistencies within the proposal itself put the contracting officer on notice of the apparent error and because an agency may take into account its knowledge in evaluating proposals and making an award. *TRESP Assocs., Inc.*; *Advanced Data Concepts, Inc.*, B-258322.5; B-258322.6, Mar. 9, 1995, 96-1 CPD ¶ 8 at 6–7. Indeed, some information is simply too close at hand for the agency not to consider it. *International Bus. Sys., Inc.*, B-275554, Mar. 3, 1997, 97-1 CPD ¶ 114 at 5.

> Here, the Navy made no attempt to resolve the protester's SDB status, even though it could have done so through the clarification process. *See Jimmy's Appliance*, 61 Comp. Gen. 4444, 446 (1982), 82-1 CPD ¶ 542 at 2-4. Moreover, despite conducting discussions with the offerors, it did not mention the SDB status question in its discussions with Fidelity. Because discussions were held, we need not decide whether the agency would have been required to clarify Fidelity's SDB status if award had been made on the basis of initial proposals. When discussions are held, they are required to be meaningful. *See Ashland Sales & Serv., Inc.*, B-255159, Feb. 14, 1994, 94-1 CPD ¶ 108 at 3. Here, this meant that the Navy had an obligation to raise the SDB status question in its discussions with Fidelity, in light of the inconsistencies within the firm's proposal, the significance of the 10% evaluation preference under the program whose purpose is to assist small disadvantaged firms, and the agency's apparent knowledge of the inaccuracy of the SDB representations in the proposal. See FAR § 15.610(c)(4) (FAC 90-44) (during discussions, contracting officer shall resolve any suspected mistakes by calling them to offeror's attention). Accordingly, we conclude that, because of the specific circumstances present in this instance, the agency acted improperly by not resolving the question of Fidelity's SDB status before award.

See also *American Mgmt. Sys., Inc.*, Comp. Gen. Dec. B-215283, 84-2 CPD ¶ 199, sustaining a protest where the offeror's proposal indicated a unit charge for tape storage of $2.50 per tape per day in one area and $2.50 per tape per year in another and the contracting officer failed to resolve the discrepancy during discussions. Similarly, in *Department of the Air Force*, 67 Comp. Gen. 372 (B-229059.2), 88-1 CPD ¶ 357, GAO modified its recommendation of an earlier opinion, admitting that it had overlooked the fact that a contracting officer had failed to clarify or correct a significant price error in one offeror's BAFO that increased the offered price significantly. In the earlier opinion, *Centel Bus. Sys.*, 67 Comp. Gen. 156 (B-229059), 87-2 CPD ¶ 629, GAO sustained the protest and recommended that the offer be reevaluated as if the protester had not made the error. In this case GAO looked at the facts again and conceded that some ambiguity in Centel's price proposal still existed. Recommending that discussions be reopened, GAO stated at 375:

> Although to reopen negotiations at this juncture would create an auction situation, in our view, the importance of correcting the error through further negotiations overrides any harmful effect on the integrity of the competitive procurement system.

Compare *American Elec. Lab., Inc.*, 65 Comp. Gen. 62 (B-219582), 85-2 CPD ¶ 545, holding that prohibition of price auctioning outweighs benefits of reopening discussions. See also *Contel Info. Sys., Inc.*, Comp. Gen. Dec. B-220215, 86-1 CPD ¶ 44, finding that an agency had no obligation to correct a mistake that was the fault of the offeror and could not be easily detected by the contracting officer.

If the contracting officer resolves a potential mistake through a reasonable interpretation of the proposal, there will be no obligation to raise the issue during discussions with the offeror. In *Timeplex, Inc.*, Comp. Gen. Dec. B-220069, 85-2 CPD ¶ 651, there was a large discrepancy between the B- and L-tables. The Air Force assumed that the protester had merely miscalculated the various cost summaries in the L-table, which served only as a summary of the prices listed in the B-table, and therefore did not request verification of the protester's bid. The protester, however, had calculated the L-table first and then had intended to structure those cost summaries back into the B-table. GAO held that the government's assumption was reasonable, given that the normal procedure would have been to calculate the L-table summaries from the various pricing elements in the B-table. Compare *PAE GmbH Planning & Constr.*, 68 Comp. Gen. 358 (B-233823), 89-1 CPD ¶ 336, holding that minor irregularities or clerical errors apparent on the face of the proposal had to be corrected during discussions if the agency opened discussions.

There is no obligation to correct mistakes in discussions if an offeror could not win the competition with the corrected offer. See *Engineering & Prof'l Servs.*, Comp. Gen. Dec. B-219657, 85-2 CPD ¶ 621, holding that failure to reopen discussions was not prejudicial because the protester would not have been found responsible.

## C.  Conduct of Negotiations

Contracting agencies have broad discretion in conducting negotiations. See FAR 15.306(d)(3) stating that "the scope and extent of discussions are a matter of contracting officer judgment." See also *Dimensions Travel Co.*, Comp. Gen. Dec. B-224214, 87-1 CPD ¶ 52 (agency is given broad discretion in determining content of discussions because it is most familiar with its needs); and *Pioneer Contract Servs., Inc.*, Comp. Gen. Dec. B-197245, 81-1 CPD ¶ 107 (discussions are "essentially a matter of judgment primarily for decision by the agency"). However, within this discretion, negotiations must be meaningful and must be conducted in a way that offerors are treated fairly. See 51 Comp. Gen. 621 (B-173677) (1972); and *Wetlands Research Assocs., Inc.*, Comp. Gen. Dec. B-246342 , 92-1 CPD ¶251. The "burden to conduct meaningful discussions is on the contracting officer and not on individual offerors," *Teledyne Lewisburg Okl. Aerotronics, Inc.*, Comp. Gen. Dec. B-183704, 75-2 CPD ¶ 228. In evaluating whether there has been sufficient disclosure of deficiencies, the primary focus is on whether there has been a reasonable communication of specific deficiencies rather than requiring any specific form of communication. Thus, discussions must fairly and reasonably lead an offeror into areas of its offer requiring change or amplification, *Creative Mgmt. Tech., Inc.*, Comp. Gen. Dec. B-266299, 96-1 CPD ¶ 61; *Research Analysis & Maint., Inc.*, Comp. Gen. Dec. B-242836.4, 91-2 CPD ¶ 387.

## 1. *Form of Negotiations*

The descriptions in FAR 15.306(d) of negotiation as including bargaining and in FAR 15.307(b) of negotiating until the parties reach understanding make it clear that the FAR Councils believed that discussions would include more face-to-face meetings where the contracting officer and the offeror conduct negotiations until they reach an understanding of the best offer that each offeror can make. However, it does not appear from the description in protest decisions that this has occurred. Rather, there continue to be numerous instances of pro forma discussions where the agency merely sends offerors a list of deficiencies and significant weaknesses. While it is doubtful whether this type of negotiation is a satisfactory communication device, it has not been questioned by either GAO or the Court of Federal Claims. See, for example, *Fort Carson Support Servs. v. United States*, 71 Fed. Cl. 571 (2006), finding a list of discussion questions designated either "weaknesses" or "deficiencies" adequate to inform protester of areas to be addressed in its final proposal revisions. See also *Kerr Contractors, Inc. v. United States*, 89 Fed. Cl. 312 (2009) (discussion letters sent to all offerors); *DRS C3 Sys., LLC*, Comp. Gen. Dec. B-310825, 2008 CPD ¶ 103 (letter listing "discussion questions" and calling for written response); *Korrect Optical, Inc.*, Comp. Gen. Dec. B-288128, 2001 CPD ¶ 171 (letter with list of "significant deficiencies"); *Interstate Elec. Corp.*, Comp. Gen. Dec. B-286466, 2001 CPD ¶ 29 (telecopied "evaluation notices" identifying specific concerns); *Davies Rail & Mech. Works, Inc.*, Comp. Gen. Dec. B-283911.2, 2000 CPD ¶ 48 (letter with list of "deficiencies and weaknesses"); *Gutierrez-Palmenberg, Inc.*, Comp. Gen. Dec. B 255797.3, 94-2 CPD ¶ 158 (written list of items); *Johnson, Basin & Shaw, Inc.*, Comp. Gen. Dec. B-240265, 90-2 CPD ¶ 371 (written questions submitted to the offeror); and *American Dist. Tel. v. Dep't of Energy*, 555 F. Supp. 1244 (D.D.C. 1983) (list of requested "explanations" and "clarifications"). See also *KPMG Peat Marwick*, Comp. Gen. Dec. B-258990, 95-1 CPD ¶ 116, holding that there was no requirement that the agency conduct face-to-face discussions in addition to, or in lieu of, written discussions; and *Austin Elecs.*, 54 Comp. Gen. 60 (B-180690), 74-2 CPD ¶ 61, rejecting the protester's assertion that the agency was required to conduct give-and-take oral discussions. GAO held that the agency's decision to disclose deficiencies by letter was not an abuse of discretion.

The DoD Source Selection Procedures describes the discussion process at 3.4.3:

> This is accomplished through the release of Evaluation Notices (ENs). ENs are prepared by the SSEB and reviewed by the PCO and Legal Council. All ENs shall clearly indicate the type of exchange being conducted (e.g. clarification, communication, etc). Any EN addressing a proposal deficiency or weakness shall clearly indicate that a deficiency/weakness exists.

In spite of the numerous decisions permitting written discussions, it is doubtful that this procedure is an adequate form of communication when there are significant deficiencies or weaknesses. See *Logistic Sys., Inc.*, 59 Comp. Gen. 548 (B-196254), 80-1 CPD ¶ 442, finding that there had been inadequate communication of the deficiencies when the agency sent the offeror an elaborate list of deficiencies and conducted no oral discussions. See also *Hughes STX Corp.*, Comp. Gen. Dec. B-278466, 98-1 CPD ¶ 52, where very brief written discussion questions were held to have misled the offeror as to the level of concern the agency had as to the realism of the proposed labor costs, and *Gas Turbine Engines, Inc.*, Comp. Gen. Dec. B-401868.2, 2009 CPD ¶ 257, criticizing the agency for sending the same form letter to each offeror in the competitive range.

Oral discussions can be held over the telephone, Comp. Gen. Dec. B-157156, Nov. 8, 1965, *Unpub.*, by teleconference, *ITT Corp., Sys. Div.*, Comp. Gen. Dec. B-310102.6, 2010 CPD ¶ 12, or in a face-to-face meeting. However, meetings are normally called for in procurements where there are significant deficiencies or weaknesses. The information conveyed orally should be carefully documented to ensure that the offeror fully understands the issue. See *New Jersey & H St., LLC*, Comp. Gen. Dec. B-311314.3, 2008 CPD ¶ 133, sustaining a protest when the protester asserted that it had never been told of a weakness that the agency claimed it had disclosed. When meetings are held, there is no requirement that agreement be reached on each issue, 52 Comp. Gen. 161 (B-176223) (1972).

## 2. *Meaningful Negotiations*

The FAR Rewrite emphasizes that negotiations with each offeror in the competitive range includes bargaining to obtain the best offer. Thus, FAR 15.306(d)(4) permits bargaining about the optimum technical solution that can be offered by each offeror as well as price and the terms and conditions of the contract. Furthermore, FAR 15.307(b) implies that negotiations will be conducted to reach "understandings." The goal is clearly to encourage agencies to conduct in-depth negotiations to fulfill the obligation to conduct meaningful negotiations.

Prior to the FAR Rewrite the emphasis was on *the minimum standards* that a contracting officer had to meet to conduct meaningful negotiations. In *Boeing Sikorsky Aircraft Support*, Comp. Gen. Dec. B-277263.3, 97-2 CPD ¶91, GAO made the following observations concerning meaningful negotiations:

> Discussions cannot be meaningful unless they lead an offeror into those aspects of its proposal that must be addressed in order for it to have a reasonable chance of being selected for award, and afford an offeror an opportunity to revise its proposal to satisfy the government's requirements. *Global Indus., Inc.*, B-270592.2 et al, Mar. 29, 1996, 96-2 CPD ¶85 at 4-5; *Stone & Webster Eng'g Corp.*, B-255286.2, Apr. 12, 1994, 94-1 CPD ¶306 at 10-11. An agency may not consciously coerce or mislead an offeror during discussions (see *Eagle Tech., Inc.*, B-236255, Nov. 16, 1989, 89-2 CPD ¶468 at 3-4), nor may it inadvertently mislead an offeror through the framing of discussion questions into responding in a manner that does not address the agency's concerns. *Peckham Vocational Indus., Inc.*, B-257100, Aug. 26, 1994, 94-2 CPD ¶81 at 6.

## a. Specific Identification

GAO has stated that "it is incumbent upon Government negotiators to be as specific as practical considerations will permit in advising offerors of the corrections required in their proposals," 52 Comp. Gen. 466 (B-177008) (1973). Thus, at a minimum, discussions must lead the offeror "into the areas of [its] proposal which require amplification," *Price Waterhouse*, Comp. Gen. Dec. B-222562, 86-2 CPD ¶ 190. In *International Underwriters, Inc.*, Comp. Gen. Dec. B-198109, 80-2 CPD ¶ 410, the deficiency in question, lack of details of the offeror's experience, was held to be "particularly suitable to cure through discussions." The protest was granted because the agency had not informed the offeror that it was unable to contact the offeror's references.

When a competitive range offeror's proposal indicates that it does not understand the evaluation scheme, the agency must raise this issue, *Lockheed Martin Corp.*, Comp. Gen. Dec. B-293679, 2004 CPD ¶ 115. There the agency did not inform the protester that it had rejected proposed manufacturing cost savings if a product the protester was proposing to design was manufactured in its facilities because it planned to compete the production work.

Vague statements that do not identify a specific issue have also been held to be inadequate discussions. In *Matrix Int'l Logistics, Inc.*, Comp. Gen. Dec. B-272388.2, 97-2 CPD ¶ 89. inadequate discussions were found when the agency identified a particular material line item whose price was either grossly excessive or mistaken but only gave the offeror a general statement that its overall price was too high. See also *AMEC Earth & Envtl., Inc.*, Comp. Gen. Dec. B-401961, 2010 CPD ¶ 151 (asking questions about functions of software did not indicate that agency had determined software was inadequate for job); *AINS, Inc.*, Comp. Gen. Dec. B-400760.4, 2010 CPD ¶ 32 (request for new schedule did not convey agency concern that proposed schedule was too aggressive); *New Jersey & H St., LLC*, Comp. Gen. Dec. B-311314.3, 2008 CPD ¶ 133 (general statement to all competitors that evaluation factor was important but no indication to protester of specific issues with its compliance); *AT&T Corp.*, Comp. Gen. Dec. B-299542.3, 2008 CPD ¶ 65 (reference to lack of information on staffing plan but no indication that agency believed it contained too few personnel); *Creative Info. Tech., Inc.*, Comp. Gen. Dec. B-293073.10, 2005 CPD ¶ 110 (agency's statement that price was "overstated" did not inform protester that it had grossly overestimated the level of effort anticipated by the agency); *Lockheed Martin Simulation, Training & Support*, Comp. Gen. Dec. B-292836.8, 2005 CPD ¶ 27 (statement that protester was responsible for making proposal "responsive, clear and accurate" and that responses should be "strategic, not just tactical" insufficient to alert protester to specific weaknesses). In *Advanced Sys. Dev., Inc.*, Comp. Gen. Dec. B-298411, 2006 CPD ¶ 137, the agency's statement that the offeror had violated the RFP's price target led the protested to reduce its price when the agency's concern was that the price was too low. GAO sustained the protest after the protester had been awarded the contract at the low price.

GAO has also stated that, in general, once discussions are opened, the agency is required to point out all deficiencies in the offeror's proposal, not merely selected areas, *Checchi & Co.*, 56 Comp. Gen. 473 (B-187982), 77-1 CPD ¶ 232; *TM Sys., Inc.*, Comp. Gen. Dec. B-228220, 87-2 CPD ¶ 573; *CRAssociates, Inc.*, Comp. Gen. Dec. B-282075.2, 2000 CPD ¶ 63. Thus, partial discussions have also been found inadequate. For example, in *Multimax, Inc.*, Comp. Gen. Dec. B-298249.6, 2006 CPD ¶ 165, offerors were misled when agency identified some labor rates as high but did not identify other labor rates that were also high. See also *Tracor Marine, Inc.*, Comp. Gen. Dec. B-207285, 83-1 CPD ¶ 604, finding it improper to disclose to the offeror that its proposed schedule was unrealistic, while disclosing only one out of five bases for this conclusion. Offerors should not be left with the impression that there are no remaining problem areas. See *Dynalectron Corp.*, Comp. Gen. Dec. B-193604, 79-2 CPD ¶ 50, finding that Dynalectron had not been sufficiently alerted to remaining deficiencies in its proposal when, after revisions had been made, it was shown a list of five deficiencies with the words "cleared by amendment" written after the first three deficiencies. Dynalectron misinterpreted this to mean these deficiencies had been cleared up by its revisions and made no further changes in these areas.

### b. Lack of Identification Excused

In a number of cases, GAO has found that factors surrounding a procurement may excuse the agency from specifically identifying areas where offers should be amplified or changed. However, it would seem that agencies should err on the side of greater communication rather than relying on these rulings to win a protest.

A lack of specific identification will not be fatal if the offeror has been given sufficient information to provide notice of the deficiency. In *Broomall Indus., Inc.*, Comp. Gen. Dec. B-193166, 79-1 CPD ¶ 467, GAO found that a broad request that the offeror "discuss in detail" one aspect of the required work was sufficient to disclose that the proposal was deficient in that area, stating:

> We have held that requests for clarification or amplification or other statements made during discussions which lead offerors into areas of their proposals that are unclear are sufficient to alert offerors to deficiencies in their proposals. *Serv-Air, Inc.*, B-189884, September 25, 1978, 78-2 CPD ¶223; *Houston Films, Inc.*, B-184402, December 22, 1975, 75-2 CPD ¶404.

Similarly, where the agency was concerned about the analytic model used by the protester, and questioned the protester's low proposed level of effort which was primarily attributable to the model, this was enough to alert the protester of the real concern, *CRC Sys., Inc.*, Comp. Gen. Dec. B-207847, 83-1 CPD ¶ 462. See also *Kerr Contractors, Inc. v. United States*, 89 Fed. Cl. 312 (2009) (asking protester to address "risk" of work at proposed level sufficient to indicate that agency considered level too low); *Academy Facilities Mgmt. v. United States*, 87 Fed. Cl. 441 (2009) (use of term "overstated" when price appeared high and "significantly overstated" when price appeared both high and unbalanced was sufficient indication of government concerns); *SelectTech Bering Straits Solutions JV*, Comp. Gen. Dec. B-400964, 2009 CPD ¶ 100 (statement that staffing levels were low sufficient without identifying that only some were low and others were high); *New Breed, Inc.*, Comp. Gen. Dec. B-400554, 2009 CPD ¶ 4 (no requirement to identify specific weaknesses when protester told that its risk management and quality control plans were weak); *Karrar Sys. Corp.*, Comp. Gen. Dec. B-310661, 2008 CPD ¶ 51 (request to confirm that prices were based on RFP data sufficient to indicate that prices were considered high); *Mechanical Equip. Co.*, Comp. Gen. Dec. B-292789.2, 2004 CPD ¶ 192 (statement that manning was "inadequate" sufficient without indicating how low the estimate was); *Hanford Envtl. Health Found.*, Comp. Gen. Dec. B-292858.2, 2004 CPD ¶ 164 (no need to tell protester staffing was considered high when agency told it to more effectively describe staffing); *T-L-C Sys.*, Comp. Gen. Dec. B-287452, 2001 CPD ¶ 106 (general warning that proposal did not meet RFP requirement for full documentation sufficient to alert protester to lack of clarity of product literature); *J.A. Jones/Bell, J.V.*, Comp. Gen. Dec. B-286458, 2001 CPS ¶ 17 (request for reasoning to support use of technique sufficient to indicate that agency was critical of technique); *Information Network Sys., Inc.*, Comp. Gen. Dec. B-284854, 2000 CPD ¶ 104 (question as to adequacy of labor rates sufficient to indicate concern with workforce retention risk); *Professional Performance Dev. Group, Inc.*, Comp. Gen. Dec. B-279561.2, 99-2 CPD ¶ 29 (question as to responsibilities of two levels of management sufficient to indicate view that they were redundant); *SEEMA, Inc.*, Comp. Gen. Dec. B-277988, 98-1 CPD ¶ 12 (stating that price was significantly below the government estimate and that its cost savings measures were not supported by data sufficient to lead the protester into the area of the deficiency); *Centech Group, Inc.*, Comp. Gen. Dec. B-278715, 98-1 CPD ¶ 108 (advising protester that composite labor category prices for services contract were either too high or two low sufficient even though the agency did not specify which categories were high and which were low); *EastCo Bldg. Servs., Inc.*, Comp. Gen. Dec. B-275334, 97-1 CPD ¶ 83 (advising protester that staffing for mechanical requirements appear to be inadequate sufficient without detailed analysis because the RFP contained detailed specifications covering all work required to be performed); and *Quachita Mowing, Inc.*, Comp. Gen. Dec. B-276075, 97-1 CPD ¶ 167 (pointing out that protester's work year was based on 1,992 hours rather than the standard 2,080 hours sufficient to indicate the agency's general concern that proposed hours were too low).

## 3. *Reaching Agreement on Final Proposals*

In adopting the term "negotiations" to describe the discussion process, the FAR Rewrite appears to have embraced the concept that negotiations should result in agreement between the parties as to the final proposal that will be submitted by the offeror. Thus, FAR 15.307(b) calls for proposal revisions to "document understandings reached during negotiations." FAR 15.001 amplifies this concept with the following definition:

> Proposal revision is a change to a proposal made after the solicitation closing date, at the request of or as allowed by a contracting officer, as the result of negotiations.

This concept has been adopted by the Army in *Contracting for Best Value: A Best Practices Guide to Source Selection*, AMC-P 715-3 (Jan. 1, 1998), which states:

> During discussions, our objective should be to reach complete agreement between and understanding by the Government and the offeror regarding all of the basic requirements in the solicitation. In essence, obtaining a contract that demonstrates the greatest promise of meeting the solicitation's requirements and no surprises after award is the goal of both the Government and the offeror.

Similar guidance is contained in NFS 1815.306(d)(3):

> (B) The contracting officer shall discuss contract terms and conditions so that a "model" contract can be sent to each offeror with the request for final proposal revisions. If the solicitation allows, any proposed technical performance capabilities above those specified in the RFP that have value to the Government and are considered proposal strengths should be discussed with the offeror and proposed for inclusion in that offeror's "model" contract. These items are not to be discussed with, or proposed to, other offerors. If the offeror declines to include these

strengths in its "model" contract, the Government evaluators should reconsider their characterization as strengths.

The goal of reaching agreement with each competing offeror during the negotiation places a significant burden on the contracting officer because such "agreements" can not guarantee to any offeror that it will win the competition. During negotiations of this type, the agency personnel must work with each offeror to assist it to make the best offer it is capable of but, at the same time, must alert each offeror to the fact that the ultimate selection decision will be based on analysis of the relative merits of the competing offers. Throughout such negotiations, the offerors must be treated in an evenhanded fashion with regard to the information revealed. Furthermore, agency personnel must exercise great care not to reveal elements of one offer to any other offeror.

Care must be exercised to ensure that interim revisions to offers are documented in writing and are understood to supersede the original offer. See *CCL, Inc.*, Comp. Gen. Dec. B-251527, 93-1 CPD ¶ 354, *recons. denied*, 93-2 CPD ¶ 178, ruling that although revised prices submitted by an offeror during negotiations revoked the original offer, they were not new offers that served the purpose of keeping the offer open for 60 days as called for by the Standard Form 33 cover sheet of the original offer. GAO reached this conclusion because the letter submitting the revised prices contained no indication that the offeror intended to keep them open for 60 additional days.

## 4. Fairness

Fair treatment of offerors is a cornerstone of effective competition. Thus, assuring that all offerors are treated fairly is a major concern when conducting negotiations. See FAR 1.102-2 stating:

> (1) An essential consideration in every aspect of the [Federal Acquisition] System is maintaining the public's trust. Not only must the System have integrity, but the actions of each member of the Team must reflect integrity, fairness, and openness. The foundation of integrity within the System is a competent, experienced, and well-trained, professional workforce. Accordingly each member of the Team is responsible and accountable for the wise use of public resources as well as acting in a manner which maintains the public's trust. Fairness and openness require open communication among team members, internal and external customers, and the public.

GAO identified fairness during the discussion process as a fundamental requirement in 51 Comp. Gen. 621 (B-173677) (1972), stating at 622:

> [T]he statute [now 10 U.S.C. § 2305(b)(4)(A)] should not be interpreted in a manner which discriminates against or gives preferential treatment to any competitor. Any discussion with competing offerors raises the question as to how to avoid unfairness and unequal treatment.

The Court of Federal Claims identified the fact that fairness continues to be an integral part of the negotiation/discussion process in *Dynacs Eng'g Co. v. United States*, 48 Fed. Cl. 124 (2000), where it found unfair discussions when, during reopened discussions, the agency identified "weaknesses" that had been identified in the first round of discussions, but not addressed, with one offeror but not with the protester.

## a. Even-handed Treatment

Fairness requires the agency to ensure that offerors compete on an equal basis. Thus, offerors must be treated even-handedly. One of the most common examples of lack of even-handed treatment is where the agency gives information to one or more offerors but fails to provide the same information to other offerors who might be able to use it to their advantage. See *Kerr Contractors, Inc. v. United States*, 89 Fed. Cl. 312 (2009), stating at 329:

> The government, when conducting discussions with offerors in the competitive range, may not "engage in conduct that . . . [f]avors one offeror over another." 48 C.F.R. § 15.306(e) (2008). This regulation does not permit a procuring agency to engage in unequal discussions, where a crucial and advantageous piece of information is withheld from some but not all offerors remaining in the competition. *See, e.g., Metcalf Constr. Co. v. United States,* 53 Fed. Cl. 617, 634-35 (2002) (holding, in that case, that "the bidders were treated unequally where one bidder was advised, in no uncertain terms, not to exceed the budget ceilings, and a second bidder under identical circumstances was not"). Nonetheless, "agencies are not required to conduct identical discussions with each offeror." *Femme Comp [Inc. v. United States]*, 83 Fed. Cl. [704 (2008)] at 735 (citing *WorldTravelService v. United States,* 49 Fed. Cl. 431, 440 (2001)). Rather, the procuring agency should tailor discussions to each offeror's proposal. *WorldTravelService,* 49 Fed. Cl. at 440.

See, for example, *SeaSpace*, 70 Comp. Gen. 268 (B-241564), 91-1 CPD ¶ 179, where the agency improperly suggested that one offeror use a more powerful computer that had recently come on the market without providing the same suggestion to other offerors. See also *Ashbury Int'l Group, Inc.*, Comp. Gen. Dec. B-401123, 2009 CPD ¶ 140 (improper to tell only one offeror that management plan should be submitted); *TDS, Inc.*, Comp. Gen. Dec. B-292674, 2003 CPD ¶ 204 (agency gave two competitors far more detailed questions than those given protester); *CitiWest Props., Inc.*, Comp. Gen. Dec. B-274689.4, 98-1 CPD ¶ 3 (unfair to point out insufficient information in a prescribed form to one offeror but not to another); and *Cylink Corp.*, Comp. Gen. Dec. B-242304, 91-1 CPD ¶ 384 (improper to inform only one competitor that the agency would accept performance that seemed to be out of compliance with the specifications).

Unfairness was found where an agency asked one offeror to demonstrate that an affiliated company's experience should be attributed to it without informing the protester that it had informational deficiencies in its experience information, *Core Tech Int'l Corp. — Costs*, Comp. Gen. Dec. B-400047.2, 2009 CPD ¶ 59. See also

*American K-9 Detection Servs., Inc.*, Comp. Gen. Dec. B-400464.6, 2009 CPD ¶ 107 (agency allowed one offeror to correct deficiency making proposal technically acceptable without telling protester that its option prices created a "performance risk"); *Boeing Co.*, Comp. Gen. Dec. B-311344, 2008 CPD ¶ 114 (in continuing discussions, agency told protester it had met requirement and did not reveal that it had altered this conclusion while continuing to work with competitor to ensure that it met the requirement); *Advanced Sys. Dev., Inc.*, Comp. Gen. Dec. B-298411, 2006 CPD ¶ 137 (agency induced competitor to lower its price by misleading discussions and then selected competitor based on low price); *Martin Elecs., Inc.*, Comp. Gen. Dec. B-290846.3, 2003 CPD ¶ 6 (agency discussed delivery deficiencies with only one offeror); *Morrison Knudsen Corp.*, Comp. Gen. Dec. B-270703, 96-2 CPD ¶ 86 (agency did not adequately inform the protester that it needed to list the equipment that would be used but explicitly told the awardee that it should list such equipment); *Management Sys. Designers, Inc.*, Comp. Gen. Dec. B-244383.4, 91-2 CPD ¶ 518 (agency told only one offeror that it had decided to delete a significant portion of the work); *EMS Dev. Corp.*, 70 Comp. Gen. 459 (B-242484), 91-1 CPD ¶ 427, *recons. denied*, 91-2 CPD ¶ 131 (agency provided clarifications of the solicitation requirements to an offeror under a sole source solicitation but did not provide the same clarifications to the protester when the solicitation was resolicited on a competitive basis); and *Grumman Data Sys. Corp. v. Stone*, 37 Cont. Cas. Fed. (CCH) ¶ 76,179 (D.D.C. 1991) (agency answered questions of one offeror but disclosed answers without the corresponding questions to the other offerors).

While fairness requires even-handed treatment of offerors with similar deficiencies, it does not require the agency to spend an equal amount of time with all offerors, or to discuss the same areas. See FAR 15.306(d)(1) stating that discussions "are tailored to each offeror's proposal." The Court of Federal Claims has recognized that the content and extent of negotiations with each offeror will be determined by the deficiencies in the particular proposal, *Drexel Heritage Furnishings, Inc. v. United States*, 7 Cl. Ct. 134 (1984). See *Lockheed Martin Corp.*, Comp. Gen. Dec. B-293679, 2004 CPD ¶ 115, where GAO responded to an agency evaluator's statement that he was told that, to be fair, he had to ask the same questions of each offeror by stating:

> This advice is directly contrary to the FAR, which provides that discussions should be "tailored to each offeror's proposal." FAR § 15.306(d)(1).

See also *Trident Sys., Inc.*, Comp. Gen. Dec. B-243101, 91-1 CPD ¶ 604, where GAO made the following observations concerning tailoring the negotiations:

> [I]nsofar as Trident alleges the Navy did not hold equal discussions because the offerors were not asked the same questions, the only additional question Trident was asked concerned its relationship with its subcontractor; SPA was not asked this question because SPA did not propose to use a subcontractor. In any case, in order for discussions to be meaningful, contracting agencies must furnish information to all offerors in the competitive range as to the areas in which their proposals are believed to be deficient so that the offerors have a chance to revise

their proposals to fully satisfy the agency requirements. *Pan Am World Servs., Inc.*; *Base Maintenance Support Group; Holmes & Narver Servs, Inc.*, B-231840 et al., Nov. 7, 1988, 88-2 CPD ¶ 446. In other words, since the number and type of proposal deficiencies will vary among offerors the agency should tailor the discussions for each offeror, based on the offerors' evaluated deficiencies. *Holmes & Narver, Inc.*, B-239469.2; B-239469.3, Sept. 14, 1990, 90-2 CPD ¶ 210.

Thus, an agency may properly conduct "extensive discussions with offerors whose initial proposals contain technical deficiencies while conducting more limited discussions with offerors whose proposals contain fewer weaknesses or deficiencies," *Pacific Architects & Eng'rs, Inc.*, Comp. Gen. Dec. B-236432, 89-2 CPD ¶ 494. Hence, it is proper to conduct detailed discussions with offerors whose proposals contain technical deficiencies while affording those with technically acceptable proposals only an opportunity to submit a final proposal, *Weinschel Eng'g Co.*, 64 Comp. Gen. 524 (B-217202), 85-1 CPD ¶ 574. The agency may also reveal the government's cost estimate to an offeror proposing a cost considered too high without disclosing the estimate to an offeror submitting an acceptable proposed cost, *Bank St. Coll. of Educ.*, 63 Comp. Gen. 393 (B-213209), 84-1 CPD ¶ 607, *recons. denied*, 84-2 CPD ¶ 445. See also *Biospherics, Inc.*, Comp. Gen. Dec. B-285065, 2000 CPD ¶ 118, finding no unequal discussions where the agency discussed low price with one offeror but did not discuss high price with the protester, and *Ralph G. Moore & Assocs.*, Comp. Gen. Dec. B-270686, 96-1 CPD ¶ 118, holding that an agency did not conduct unequal discussions when it discussed the awardee's unreasonably low price and did not discuss the protester's reasonable price. See also *Pharm-Chem, Inc.*, Comp. Gen. Dec. B-291725.3, 2003 CPD ¶ 148 (clearing up role of one required employee proper when no such discussion was necessary with incumbent protester); *WorldTravelService*, Comp. Gen. Dec. B-284155.3, 2001 CPD ¶ 68 (proper to identify technical deficiencies with one offeror only when the other offerors have no such deficiencies); *Ann Riley & Assocs., Ltd.*, Comp. Gen. Dec. B-271741.2, 97-1 CPD ¶ 120, *recons. denied*, 97-1 CPD ¶ 122 (more discussion with one offeror proper because its proposal contained more weaknesses); *Quality Elevator Co.*, Comp. Gen. Dec. B-271899, 96-2 CPD ¶ 89 (more questions posed to higher-rated offeror proper when questions were tailored to proposals); *CBIS Fed. Inc.*, 71 Comp. Gen. 319 (B-245844.2), 92-1 CPD ¶ 308 (more extensive discussions with one offeror proper because that offeror's proposal contained more deficiencies); *Holmes & Narver, Inc.*, Comp. Gen. Dec. B-239469.2, 90-2 CPD ¶ 210 (issues to be discussed vary among proposals).

When the procurement is conducted on a low-price, technically acceptable basis, there is no requirement for discussion with an offeror that has submitted a technically acceptable proposal, *Commercial Design Group, Inc.*, Comp. Gen. Dec. B-400923.4, 2009 CPD ¶ 157. GAO reasoned that there was no value in helping such an offeror improve its proposal.

Under the FAR Part 15 Rewrite the rules regarding fairness were somewhat altered. Thus, in *Synetics, Inc. v. United States*, 45 Fed. Cl. 1 (1999), the court ruled that it was fair to tell an offeror a precise way to improve its proposal, citing the removal of the prohibition of technical leveling in FAR 15.306(e) as well as the encouragement to "enhance materially the proposal's potential for award," in FAR 15.306(d)(3). See also *Mantech Telecomms. & Info. Sys. Corp. v. United States*, 49 Fed. Cl. 57 (2001), where the court held that it was fair to conduct multiple rounds of discussions, noting that the FAR Part 15 Rewrite had eliminated the limitations on multiple rounds as well as the prohibition of technical leveling.

### b.  Misleading Negotiations

In addition to treating offerors even-handedly, an agency may not mislead an offeror during negotiations, *Hughes STX Corp.*, Comp. Gen. Dec. B-278466, 98-1 CPD ¶ 52. In that case the discussions suggested two separate cost concerns and appear to have induced Hughes not only to escalate its first-year direct labor rates, but also to then increase these rates across the board. GAO found that the discussion questions materially overstated the agency's relatively limited concern about the Hughes rates and were thus misleading. Other decision finding misleading discussions include *Velos, Inc.*, Comp. Gen. Dec. B-400500, 2010 CPD ¶ 3 (agency agreed to terms in software license and then rejected revised proposal including those terms); *Multimax, Inc.*, Comp. Gen. Dec. B-298249.6, 2006 CPD ¶ 165 (agency identified only some labor rates that were higher than government estimate); *Spherix, Inc.*, Comp. Gen. Dec. B-294572.3, 2005 CPD ¶ 183 (agency implied that RFP requirements were firm while accepting an alternate solution from a competitor); *Cygnus Corp.*, Comp. Gen. Dec. B-292649.3, 2004 CPD ¶ 162 (agency stated that the discussions "resulted in agreement of all technical and cost issues raised during negotiations" when it had identified a number of undiscussed weaknesses); *Biospherics, Inc.*, Comp. Gen. Dec. B-278278, 98-1 CPD ¶ 161 (agency failed to inform it that its cost/pricing was considered unrealistically low and, instead, twice encouraging protester to reduce its proposed price); *SRS Techs.*, Comp. Gen. Dec. B-254425.2, 94-2 CPD ¶ 125 (agency considered the protester's initial proposal to be deficient for proposing cost discounts without adequate supporting information and not only failed to advise the protester of this deficiency during discussions but instructed the protester not to discount costs); and *Price Waterhouse*, Comp. Gen. Dec. B-254492.2, 94-1 CPD ¶ 168 (agency questioned level pricing of options in the initial discussions, inducing the offeror to propose lower levels of effort for option years, and subsequently did not inform the offeror that it had determined internally lower levels of effort in option years were not called for). Compare *American Med. Prof'ls, Inc.*, Comp. Gen. Dec. B-275784, 97-1 CPD ¶ 134 (not misleading to ask offeror to verify that it could perform at the quoted prices); *Analytical & Research Tech., Inc.*, Comp. Gen. Dec. B-276064, 97-1 CPD ¶ 200 (protester unreasonably interpreted agency's explanation regarding staffing requirements as permitting an approach that was inconsistent with the solicitation requirements); *Ideal Elec. Sec. Co.*, Comp. Gen. Dec. B-298221, 98-2 CPD ¶ 14 (agency had not misled the protester into offering only a small price reduction by stating that its price was competitive and its escalation ratios appeared reasonable); and *DMS All-Star Joint Venture v. United States*, 90 Fed. Cl. 653 (2010) (not misleading to point out only one of several pricing issues when protester given opportunity to revise prices).

### c. Prohibited Conduct

The FAR Part 15 Rewrite made significant changes in specifying the conduct which is proper. FAR 15.306(e) provides the following limitations on communications:

Government personnel involved in the acquisition shall not engage in conduct that —

(1) Favors one offeror over another;

(2) Reveals an offeror's technical solution, including unique technology, innovative and unique uses of commercial items, or any information that would compromise an offeror's intellectual property to another offeror;

(3) Reveals an offeror's price without that offeror's permission. However, the contracting officer may inform an offeror that its price is considered by the Government to be too high, or to low, and reveal the results of the analysis supporting that conclusion. It is also permissible, at the Government's discretion, to indicate to all offerors the cost or price that the Government's price analysis, market research, and other reviews have identified as reasonable (41 U.S.C. 423(h)(1)(2));

(4) Reveals the names of individuals providing reference information about an offeror's past performance; or

(5) Knowingly furnishes source selection information in violation of 3.104 and 41 U.S.C. 423(h)(1)(2).

The first three prohibitions were substantially rewritten in the FAR Part 15 Rewrite to reduce their scope. Thus, as discussed earlier, the "technical leveling" prohibition was eliminated and the "auction" prohibition was narrowed. The second prohibition of revealing another offeror's technical solution, previously described as "technical transfusion," was not significantly altered from the prior FAR. The fourth prohibition was added by the Rewrite. The fifth prohibition refers to a portion of the Procurement Integrity Act.

In addition to these prohibitions, there are criminal statutes broadly prohibiting disclosure of certain types of information, such as 18 U.S.C. § 1905. Thus, violation of these statutory provisions could result in criminal liability. See *Panafax Corp.*, Comp. Gen. Dec. B-201176, 81-1 CPD ¶ 515, *recons. denied*, 81-2 CPD ¶ 220, where a disclosure to another offeror of Panafax's identity as an offeror and the fact that Panafax was offering a newly developed machine enabled the offeror to lower its price 27%, $1 below Panafax's price. A referral was made to the Department of Justice and GAO sustained the protest, stating that the disclosure of information enabled the other of-feror to determine what equipment its competitor was offering and at approximately what price. See Chapter 1, Section VII for a discussion of these statutory provisions.

## (1) FAVORING ONE OFFEROR

The first prohibition covered "technical leveling" in the pre-Rewrite FAR. Thus, prior to the Rewrite, agencies were prohibited from coaching offerors to bring them up to the level of a competitor. However, there were no protests finding that such coaching had actually occurred. As discussed earlier, such coaching is now encouraged as long as it does not involve providing information from a competitor's proposal. GAO is now citing the first prohibition barring favoring one offeror in holding that agencies have engaged in unfair treatment, *Boeing Co.*, Comp. Gen. Dec. B-311344, 2008 CPD ¶ 114 (agency misled protester into believing that it had met performance objective); *Sytronics, Inc.*, Comp. Gen. Dec. B-297346, 2006 CPD ¶ 15 (winning offeror was told its price was "excessive" while protester with similar price was told that its price was "high"); *Martin Elecs., Inc.*, Comp. Gen. Dec. B-290846.3, 2003 CPD ¶ 6 (winning offeror was "favored" because its poor past performance was probed while the protester's was not) and *Chemonics Int'l, Inc.*, Comp. Gen. Dec. B-282555, 99-2 CPD ¶ 61 (personnel which the agency believed were unsuitable were probed in one offer but not the other). See also *Knightsbridge Constr.*, Comp. Gen. Dec. 291475.2, 2003 CPD ¶ 5, finding unfair treatment in providing information to only one offeror but dismissing the protest for lack of prejudice.

## (2) TECHNICAL TRANSFUSION

Helping an offeror to improve its proposal through the use of information gained from another offer was described in the pre-FAR Rewrite as "technical trans-fusion." It is now described in the second prohibition as revealing information that is "unique" or "intellectual property." In addition to being illegal, there is a pro-curement policy reason for refraining from such conduct. In 51 Comp. Gen. 621 (B-173677) (1972), GAO enunciated this reason for avoidance of this practice, stat-ing that if the government disclosed technical innovations to other offerors, offerors would tend to hold back technical innovation from the negotiation process. Thus, the government would lose the benefits accruing from contractor innovation during negotiation. See also 52 Comp. Gen. 870 (B-177542) (1973), stating at 872:

> [I]1 Comp. Gen. 621 (1972), we recognized that the statute should not be inter-preted in a manner which discriminates against or gives preferential treatment to a competitor and that the disclosure to other offerors of one offeror's innovative solution to a problem is unfair. Thus, where there is a research and development procurement and the offeror's independent approach to solving a problem is the essence of the procurement, technical negotiations must be curtailed to the extent necessary to avoid technical "transfusion."

It has been very difficult for a protester to establish that technical transfusion has taken place because GAO requires proof "that the contracting agency either directly or indirectly disclosed one offeror's technical approach to another offeror," *Northwest Reg'l Educ. Lab.*, Comp. Gen. Dec. B-222591.3, 87-1 CPD ¶ 4. Thus, even if the protester can prove similarities to its technical approach in a competitor's BAFO, the lack of actual evidence of disclosure will lead to a denial of the protest, *Le Don Computer Servs., Inc.*, Comp. Gen. Dec. B-225451.2, 87-1 CPD ¶ 441. Similarly, speculative protests of possible technical transfusion are summarily denied, *Sparta, Inc.*, Comp. Gen. Dec. B-228216, 88-1 CPD ¶ 37. A lack of technical transfusion has been found in *Ashe Facility Servs., Inc.*, Comp. Gen. Dec. B-292218.3, 2004 CPD ¶ 80 (asking about equipment to be used for ground maintenance work); *WorldTravelServ.*, Comp. Gen. Dec. B-284155.3, 2001 CPD ¶ 68 (asking about use of interpreters where RFP required special treatment for patients speaking different languages); *Voith Hydro, Inc.*, Comp. Gen. Dec. B-277051, 97-2 CPD ¶ 68 (advising offeror to use proven manufacturing facility); *Creative Mgmt. Tech., Inc.*, Comp. Gen. Dec. B-266299, 96-1 CPD ¶ 61 (asking offeror to provide specific documents showing capability when such documents were not called for by RFP but had been provided by competitor). In *Gentex Corp. — Western Operations*, Comp. Gen. Dec. B-291793, 2003 CPD ¶ 66, the protester contended that since its initial proposal contained variation in quantity and warranty clauses and its competitor's did not, transfusion occurred when the clauses appeared in the competitor's revised proposal. The protester argued that the transfusion resulted when the agency asked the competitor whether it would "consider putting a variation clause in the contract" and what were its "[t]houghts on warranty." GAO ruled that "technical transfusion" had not occurred since there was not a "disclosure of a unique or ingenious technical solution from a competitor's proposal." It also ruled that the questions were not improper because they were "neutral."

If one offeror proposes a technical approach not permitted by the RFP but which the agency would like to consider, it is not improper to disclose to other offerors that the agency is willing to consider alternative approaches (as long as the specific technical approach proposed is not disclosed), *Rix Indus., Inc.*, Comp. Gen. Dec. B-241498, 91-1 CPD ¶ 165; *Loral Terracom*, 66 Comp. Gen. 272 (B-224908), 87-1 CPD ¶ 182. In addition, if the procuring agency is aware of a technical concept prior to the submission of a proposal incorporating that concept, conveying the concept to another offeror is not technical transfusion, *Dynalectron Corp.*, Comp. Gen. Dec. B 216201, 85-1 CPD ¶ 525. See also *Litton Sys., Inc.*, Comp. Gen. Dec. B-239123, 90-2 CPD ¶ 114, finding no technical transfusion when the procuring agency discussed with all offerors the need for testing which was first identified by the protester. GAO accepted the procuring agency's explanation that all the offerors had identified the need to verify that the various proposed techniques met the contract requirement and the discussions of specific testing flowed from this mutual identification of a gap in the RFP. It is also not improper to permit an offeror for a follow-on service contract to visit the government site where the incumbent contractor is performing the work, *Contact Int'l Corp.*, 70 Comp. Gen. 115 (B-237122.3), 90-2 CPD ¶ 442.

## (3) REVEALING PRICES

Prior to the FAR Rewrite, the third prohibition banned "auctions." However, it was narrowed considerably in the Rewrite so that it now prohibits only the disclosure of prices without consent. See *Strand Hunt Constr., Inc.*, Comp. Gen. Dec. B-292415, 2003 CPD ¶ 167, noting that the auction prohibition was removed from the FAR. In addition, this provision permits disclosure of government estimates of reasonable costs or prices. This rewritten language has been interpreted to allow agencies to reveal a considerable amount of pricing information to offerors. There is general agreement that it allows an agency to tell an offeror that its price is considered to be "high," *Dynacs Eng'g Co. v. United States*, 48 Fed. Cl. 124 (2000). Other decisions permitting disclosure of information include *Chenega Fed. Sys., LLC*, Comp. Gen. Dec. B-299310.2, 2007 CPD ¶ 196 (revealing detailed government analysis of offeror's probable costs); *Kaneohe Gen. Servs., Inc.*, Comp. Gen. Dec. B-293097.2, 2004 Comp. Gen. ¶ 50 (disclosing government estimate to all offerors in second round of discussions); *Engineering Servs. Unlimited, Inc.*, Comp. Gen. Dec. B-291275, 2003 CPD ¶ 15 (questioning the low level of labor rates in proposal); *Korrect Optical, Inc.*, Comp. Gen. Dec. B-288128, 2001 CPD ¶ 171 (revealing average prices of five offerors in competitive range); and *OMV Med., Inc. v. United States*, 219 F.3d 1337 (Fed. Cir. 2000) (stating that proposed salaries were below "current average annual salaries").

It might be argued that this provision precludes the use of reverse auction procedures where prices are electronically posted without disclosing the company submitting the price. There is no decision on whether FAR 15.306(e)(3) bears on this issue, but GAO ruled in *MTB Group, Inc.*, Comp. Gen. Dec. B-295463, 2005 Comp. Gen. ¶ 40, that reverse auctions do not violate the procurement statutes when used in simplified acquisitions, stating:

> Regarding MTB's specific objection — that the reverse auction here is impermissible because it will result in disclosure of its price — we find no basis for objecting to the agency's approach. MTB is correct that the Act prohibits government officials and those acting on behalf of the government from knowingly disclosing contractor quotation or proposal information before award. 41 U.S.C. § 423(a). However, that prohibition is not absolute. Rather, the Act specifically provides that it does not "restrict the disclosure of information to, or its receipt by, any person or class of persons authorized in accordance with applicable agency regulations or procedures, to receive the information," 41 U.S.C. § 423(h)(1), and does not "restrict a contractor from disclosing its own quote or proposal information or the recipient from receiving that information." 41 U.S.C. § 423(h)(2). We think the price disclosure under HUD's reverse auction procedures falls within the exception language, although we are aware of no judicial or other authoritative interpretation of these provisions. First, under the procedure the agency has established, vendors actually will disclose their own prices — albeit, as a condition of competing — by entering the prices on the auction website; as noted, a vendor's disclosing its own price is not prohibited under the Act. Moreover, even

922  **BASIC NEGOTIATION PROCEDURES**

if the price disclosure were considered to be by government officials due to its nature as a precondition to a vendor's competing, the disclosure is pursuant, and integral, to the reverse auction procurement procedures established by the agency; we thus would view the disclosure as being to persons authorized by agency procedures to receive the information, consistent with the exception language. See generally *DGS Contract Serv., Inc. v. United States*, 43 Ct. Cl. 227, 236 (1999); *Ocean Servs., LLC.*, B-292511.2, Nov. 6, 2003, 2003 CPD ¶ 206 at 5 (neither the Act nor the FAR establishes an absolute prohibition against disclosure of price information, and both make clear that prices can be disclosed under certain circumstances) [FN omitted].

### (4) NAMES OF REFERENCE INDIVIDUALS

While it is clear that offerors will know the references that they provide to an agency to ascertain their past performance and experience, the FAR prohibits revealing the names of the individuals working for the referenced agency or company that have provided the information. The intent of this prohibition is not clear and there is no indication of the harm that is done by revealing these names. Perhaps the goal is to obtain a more forthright appraisal of the performance of the offeror providing the reference.

### (5) PROCUREMENT INTEGRITY

The reference to the Procurement Integrity Act (implemented in FAR 3.104) only prohibits the release of source selection information. However, the Act also prohibits the release of contractor bid or proposal information — which should have been included in this segment of the regulation. See Chapter 1 for a discussion of the scope of this Act.

## d. Procedure Following Improper Disclosure

When there has been an improper disclosure of pricing or technical information, the contracting officer must decide on a course of action to minimize the harm. The general rule stated by GAO is that the requirement for full and open competition overrides the prohibitions against improper disclosure — with the result that the proper course of action may be to reopen the competition permitting all offerors to compete. See *Pan Am Support Servs., Inc.*, 66 Comp. Gen. 457 (B-225964.2), 87-1 CPD ¶ 512, stating at 460:

[C]oncerns as to technical leveling or technical transfusion do not necessarily overcome the need to remedy a procurement which has failed to satisfy the statutory requirement for full and open competition. See *Roy F. Weston, Inc. — Request for Reconsideration*, B-221863.3, Sept. 29, 1986, 86-2 CPD ¶324. Similarly, the risk of an auction is generally viewed as secondary to the preservation of the integrity of the competitive procurement system through the taking of appropriate corrective action. *Environmental Tectonics Corp. — Reconsideration*, B-225474.2 et al., Apr. 9, 1987, 87-1 CPD ¶ [96].

This rule has been followed in *Logicon, Inc. v. United States*, 22 Cl. Ct. 776 (1991), and *IMS Servs., Inc. v. United States*, 33 Fed. Cl. 167 (1995). In both cases, the court emphasized the difficult burden — not met by either plaintiff — of showing that an offeror's individual prejudice resulting from the disclosure of pricing information outweighed the harm to the procurement process that would occur if the agency were denied the ability to take corrective action by reopening the solicitation. However, there is generally no requirement to disclose the prices submitted by all offerors when the competition is reopened. See *SYMVIONICS, Inc.*, Comp. Gen. Dec. B-293824.2, 2004 CPD ¶ 204, and *Alatech Healthcare, LLC*, Comp. Gen. Dec. B-289134.3, 2002 CPD ¶ 73, where the protesters argued that they should be provided with a competitor's unit prices since their unit prices had been disclosed in a debriefing. GAO noted that while such a technique might be acceptable where prices have been *improperly* disclosed, it was not required in these cases because disclosure of prices in a debriefing is *not* improper. See also *BNF Techs., Inc.*, Comp. Gen. Dec. B-254953.4, 94-2 CPD ¶ 258 (stating that "the possibility that a contract may not be awarded based upon true competition is more harmful to the integrity of the competitive procurement system than the risk of an auction"); *Unisys Corp.*, 67 Comp. Gen. 512 (B-230019.2), 88-2 CPD ¶ 35 (holding that "where the reopening of negotiations is properly required, the prior disclosure of an offeror's proposal does not preclude reopening"); and *Faxon Co.*, 67 Comp. Gen. 39 (B-227835.3), 87-2 CPD ¶ 425 (reopening negotiations after an improper award was neither technical leveling nor an improper auction, although original awardee's proposal had been disclosed). An exception to this rule occurs when the offeror obtains information by illegal means. See *Litton Sys., Inc.*, 68 Comp. Gen. 422 (B-234060), 89-1 CPD ¶ 450, *recons. denied*, 68 Comp. Gen. 677, 89-2 CPD ¶228, where GAO ordered the termination of a contract because of evidence that the contractor had obtained proprietary information concerning the procurement through bribery of a government official.

In following the general rule, GAO has approved actions in which the agency did not attempt to remedy the effects of the improper disclosure. For example, in *Computer Scis. Corp.*, Comp. Gen. Dec. B-231165, 88-2 CPD ¶ 188, negotiations were continued with an offeror that had inadvertently been given access to another's costing data. GAO stated that the agency would be justified in removing the offeror from the procurement if its BAFO indicated that it had made use of the data. See also *Lockheed Martin Maritime Sys. & Sensors*, Comp. Gen. Dec. B-299766, 2008 CPD ¶ 116, where GAO approved of the agency's reopening of the competition including the offeror that had received a competitor's technical information.

In contrast to the rule on pricing information, an agency is required to disclose to all competitors detailed information on solicitation requirements that has been disclosed to one offeror in the debriefing process, *SYMVIONICS, Inc.*, Comp. Gen. Dec. B-293824.2, 2004 CPD ¶ 204.

When prices have been revealed to one offeror, several methods have been used to avert an unfair competitive advantage. A commonly used method is for the agency to make an award on the basis of initial proposals and permit no modifications, Comp. Gen. Dec. B-171015, July 13, 1971, *Unpub.* For instance, in *M. Bennett, Ltd.*, Comp. Gen. Dec. B-198316, 80-1 CPD ¶ 363, GAO recommended that an award on initial proposals be made where the offerors' prices were improperly revealed at a public opening of proposals. See also *American Elec. Labs., Inc.*, 65 Comp. Gen. 62 (B-219582), 85-2 CPD ¶ 545, concurring with award on BAFOs where pricing information had been revealed in a protest because reopening negotiations would constitute auctioning, which would impugn the integrity of the competitive system.

Another method of averting unfairness is to solicit revisions to the non-price aspects of the competing proposals but to deny the opportunity to revise prices. This is appropriate when the new negotiations are necessary to correct some aspect of the procurement that is not likely to have an impact on the competing prices. See *ST Aerospace Engines Pte., Ltd.*, Comp. Gen. Dec. B-275725.3, 97-2 CPD ¶ 106 (correcting past performance evaluation); *Krueger Int'l, Inc.*, Comp. Gen. Dec. B-260953.4, 96-1 CPD ¶ 235 (curing informational deficiencies).

Another technique is to conduct another round of final proposal revisions. This occurred in *ManTech Telecomms. & Info. Sys. Corp. v. United States*, 49 Fed. Cl. 57 (2001), *aff'd*, 30 Fed. App'x 995 (Fed. Cir. 2002), where the court agreed that totally new final proposal revisions were justified, carefully reviewed the competitor's pricing information that had been revealed to the protester, and enjoined the agency from undertaking the corrective action of revealing the protester's price. The court held that the information that was proposed to be revealed was broader and that a fair round of final proposal revisions could be conducted without revealing any more pricing information. See also *American K-9 Detection Servs., Inc.*, Comp. Gen. Dec. B-400464.6, 2009 CPD ¶ 107, granting a protest because the agency conducted another round of discussions and final proposal revisions but did not disclose all of the protester's deficiencies and significant weaknesses.

Another technique is to cancel the RFP after an improper disclosure has been made, *Neomed, Inc.*, Comp. Gen. Dec. B-186930, 76-2 CPD ¶ 434; *Ford Aerospace & Commc'ns Corp.*, Comp. Gen. Dec. B-224421.2, 86-2 CPD ¶ 582. Compare *Apex Int'l Mgmt. Servs., Inc.*, 60 Comp. Gen. 172 (B-200008), 81-1 CPD ¶ 24, finding it improper for the agency to have cancelled a solicitation due to an improper award, but, because low prices had been disclosed, recommending reinstatement of the solicitation and award based on a new responsibility determination. In *Franklin Inst.*, 55 Comp. Gen. 280 (B-182560), 75-2 CPD ¶ 194, an employee of one competitor was allowed to sit in on discussions conducted with another offeror. GAO recommended that the agency either revise its RFP to eliminate possible advantages or, if a revision would be detrimental to the agency's needs, to exclude the recipient of the information from the competition.

GAO has also approved remedies which attempt to eliminate an improper advantage one offeror may have as a result of the disclosure, although not averting an auction. For instance, in *T M Sys., Inc.*, 55 Comp. Gen. 1066 (B-185715), 76-1 CPD ¶ 299, one offeror submitted a revised price, claiming a mistake on its initial proposal, after it was erroneously informed of the only other offeror's initial price. It was held that it was proper for the contracting officer to disclose both offerors' proposed prices and call for BAFOs. See also *Federal Data Corp.*, GSBCA 9732-P, 89-1 BCA ¶ 21,414 , *aff'd*, 911 F.2d 699 (Fed. Cir. 1990), finding that the government's disclosure of all competitors' prices after one offeror's price was prematurely disclosed was a good faith effort to place all competitors on an equal footing during the second round of BAFOs, and any auction concerns were overridden by the need for such corrective action. It is highly questionable whether this type of mass disclosure of pricing information is proper in view of the Procurement Integrity Act, 41 U.S.C. § 423(a).

## D. Proposal Revisions

Under the pre-Rewrite FAR, changes to offers following negotiations were termed "best and final offers" (BAFOs). The Rewrite changed this terminology to deal with both "proposal revisions" and "final proposal revisions." FAR 15.001 defines "proposal revision" as a revision that occurs "as a result of negotiations:"

> "Proposal revision" is a change to a proposal made after the solicitation closing date, at the request of or as allowed by a contracting officer, as the result of negotiations.

Thus, such revisions of proposals will occur only during or after negotiations with offerors within the competitive range. FAR 15.307(b) contains the following coverage of such proposal revisions and also addresses "final proposal revisions:"

> The contracting officer may request or allow proposal revisions to clarify and document understandings reached during negotiations. At the conclusion of discussions, each offeror still in the competitive range shall be given an opportunity to submit a final proposal revision. The contracting officer is required to establish a common cut-off date only for receipt of final proposal revisions. Requests for final proposal revisions shall advise offerors that the final proposal revisions shall be in writing and that the Government intends to make award without obtaining further revisions.

Thus, this guidance deals with two types of proposal revisions: those agreed to during the negotiation process and final proposal revisions.

The first type of proposal revision is made to "clarify and document understandings reached during negotiations." This language appears to deal with alterations to the original *offer* made by the offeror since it is unlikely that the contracting officer would reach an "understanding" regarding information submitted by the offeror to demonstrate its capability or to support its offer. Thus, this new FAR appears to permit contracting agencies to request an offeror to put revisions to its offer in writing in order to ensure that the parties have reached a clear understanding on the terms of the potential contract they have negotiated. This practice has been followed by some contracting agencies in the past — especially on relatively complex procurements. See NFS 1815.306(d)(3)(C), calling for reaching agreement on a "model contract" with each offeror during negotiations. Under the FAR Rewrite, contracting agencies may adopt this procedure if they believe that it will enhance the competitive negotiation process.

The second type of proposal revision is the "final proposal revision." Obtaining such revisions is mandatory, and all offerors remaining in the competitive range must be permitted to submit their proposal revisions on a common cutoff date. In the initial draft of the FAR Rewrite, obtaining such revisions was permissive and no common cutoff date was required. However, there were major objections to this change to the process, with the result that the FAR Councils withdrew the proposal and adopted a final rule essentially the same as the prior BAFO rule. Because the protest decisions in this area had focused on this mandatory BAFO process, they are equally applicable to the new rule.

Final proposal revisions, like BAFOs, can include alterations to the original offer as well as revisions to any part of the original proposal. Thus, offerors can submit additional information to enhance their capability assessment or to support their offers. For example, it has been common practice to propose different personnel or to revise a technical proposal that is being used to assess the offeror's understanding of the work. BAFOs have also included additional information supporting offered prices or technical performance. The amount of information submitted will depend on the number of weaknesses and deficiencies identified in the negotiations, but it should be clear that the offeror has the full opportunity to address all such weaknesses and deficiencies in its proposal revision.

## 1. Requesting Final Proposal Revisions

If the negotiations with the offerors in the competitive range have not been carried to the point of agreement between the parties, the request for final proposal revisions will be essentially the same as a request for BAFOs. Assuming that the negotiations have been thorough and meaningful, all that is required is that the offeror be clearly informed of the common cutoff date for submission of the final proposal. There is no need for a statement that negotiations are concluded or for a statement that award may be made without further discussions, *Spectrum Scis. & Software, Inc.*, Comp. Gen. Dec. B-282373, 99-1 CPD ¶ 114. It is good practice to warn offerors that significant changes in their proposals that have not been discussed may lead to a rescoring of the proposal to their detriment and will not generally require additional negotiations. See *Jacobs Serv. Co.*, Comp. Gen. Dec. B-262088.3, 97-1 CPD ¶ 220, finding that the agency had not misled an offeror when it warned that changes to the staffing allocations could result in a finding that the proposal was unacceptable.

Oral requests may be necessary on some procurements and are not prohibited by the FAR. However, they should be followed up in writing, to ensure that there is no misunderstanding. See *Woodward Assocs., Inc.*, Comp. Gen. Dec. B-216714, 85-1 CPD ¶274, where, under prior regulations, the protester misinterpreted an ambiguous oral request for a second round of BAFOs as a request for reconfirmation of its price. GAO ruled that another round of discussions should be held to correct the confusion that had occurred as a result of the unclear nature of the oral request and the lack of a written confirmation. When oral requests for BAFOs were followed up by a written confirmation, no relief was granted if the offeror misconstrued the request, *KMS Fusion, Inc.*, Comp. Gen. Dec. B-242529, 91-1 CPD ¶ 447; *Israel Aircraft Indus., Ltd.*, Comp. Gen. Dec. B-239211, 90-2 CPD ¶ 84. It was also held that when an amendment did not specifically request offerors to submit BAFOs, "language giving notice to all offerors of a common cutoff date for receipt of offers has the intent and effect of a request for BAFOs," *Cleveland Telecomms. Corp. v. National Aeronautics & Space Admin.*, GSBCA 12586-P, 94-2 BCA ¶ 26,620.

If the negotiations have been carried to the point of agreement with each offeror in the competitive range, the agency may expect the final proposal revisions to reflect that agreement. However, under FAR 15.307(b), offerors can submit a final offer that varies from such agreement in any way that they desire. Final offers that vary substantially from the prior agreement can lead to difficulties in the procurement process because they require the agency to expend resources in evaluating the new offer and create the risk of misunderstandings between the parties. In some cases they have led to the need for additional negotiations and a new set of final proposals. Thus, some agencies have attempted to reduce the number of unforeseen changes to the offers by including specific guidance in the request for final revisions, including the agreement that has been reached. See, for example, NFS 1815.307, stating:

> (b)(i) The request for final proposal revisions (FPRs) shall also:
>
>> (A) Instruct offerors to incorporate all changes to their offers resulting from discussions, and require clear traceability from initial proposals;
>>
>> (B) Require offerors to complete and execute the "model" contract, which includes any special provisions or performance capabilities the offeror proposed above those specified in the RFP;
>>
>> (C) Caution offerors against unsubstantiated changes to their proposals; and
>>
>> (D) Establish a page limit for FPRs.

For a case agreeing that it is proper to require offerors to substantiate changes to their proposals that alter prices, as required by subparagraph (C) above, see *Cessna*

*Aircraft Co.*, Comp. Gen. Dec. B-261953.5, 96-1 CPD ¶ 132. See also *Sutron Corp.*, Comp. Gen. Dec. B-270456, 96-1 CPD ¶ 143, agreeing with an agency's evaluation that an unexplained BAFO price reduction posed a high performance risk that rendered the protester's proposal unacceptable.

In any case, the aim should be to receive a proposal from each competitor that the agency fully understands and can accept if it is determined to be most advantageous to the government. This is achievable under the FAR Rewrite because full communication is permitted in the negotiation process.

Generally, the request for proposal revisions is open-ended in permitting alterations to the original proposals. However, in limited circumstances it is permissible to limit the scope of such revisions. Thus, GAO will review the record to see if the agency has a "reasonable basis for restricting the scope of revisions," *Computer Assocs. Int'l, Inc.*, Comp. Gen. Dec. B-292077.2, 2003 CPD ¶ 157. See *Honeywell Tech. Solutions, Inc.*, Comp. Gen. Dec. B-400771.6, 2009 CPD ¶ 240 (limiting revisions to past performance information needed to overcome prior protest); *Rel-Tek Sys. & Design, Inc.*, Comp. Gen. Dec. B-280463.7, 99-2 CPD ¶ 1 (limiting revisions to areas that had been identified in prior protest as being ambiguous); *Krueger Int'l, Inc.*, Comp. Gen. Dec. B-260953.4, 96-1 CPD ¶ 235 (limiting revisions to the submission of samples and additional technical information but prohibited new prices); and *Metron Corp.*, Comp. Gen. Dec. B-227014, 87-1 CPD ¶ 642 (limiting revisions to only costs and prices). When a request for final proposals contains restrictions on the permissible alterations, the agency must abide by those restrictions and not consider additional alterations submitted by offerors, *DynaLantic Corp.*, 68 Comp. Gen. 413 (B-234035), 89-1 CPD ¶ 421 (technical alterations should not have been considered when agency had called for "best and final price and delivery schedule" and had stated "negotiations have been concluded").

## a. Reasonable Time

To foster fair competition, the established common cut-off date should allow sufficient time for all offerors in the competitive range to submit their final offer revisions. When discussions are conducted sequentially, this means that the closing date should give adequate time to the last offeror with whom discussions were conducted. However, the amount of time is highly dependent on the circumstances. See *Morris Guralnick Assocs., Inc.*, Comp. Gen. Dec. B-218353, 85-2 CPD ¶ 50 (allowing one day for submission of BAFOs reasonable when both competitors were able to submit proposals within that time period); *Evergreen Landscaping, Inc.*, Comp. Gen. Dec. B-239241, 90-2 CPD ¶ 36 (six days reasonable for submission of BAFOs where both offerors were given the same amount of time and both offerors were located in the same city); *FRC Int'l, Inc.*, Comp. Gen. Dec. B-255345, 94-1 CPD ¶ 125 (two hours and fifteen minutes reasonable for submission of BAFOs where there was decreasing availability and increasing price of the item needed and the offerors' proposals were scheduled to expire within two days).

When negotiations have been carried to the point of agreement with each of the competitors, it would appear that less time is required for the preparation of final proposal revisions. In that case each offeror might need to do no more than verify that its negotiated agreement is still valid. However, additional time should be allowed if it is clear that offerors will submit proposal revisions dealing with informational deficiencies or weaknesses.

## b.  Common Cut-off Date

The FAR 15.307(b) requirement for a common cut-off date for the receipt of final revisions has been justified as necessary to preserve the integrity of the competition in order to minimize the possibility of information in one proposal "leaking" to another offeror with a later closing date. See *Federal Data Corp.*, Comp. Gen. Dec. B-236265.4, 90-1 CPD ¶ 504; and *Kleen-Rite Corp.*, Comp. Gen. Dec. B-209474, 83-1 CPD ¶ 512, stressing the need for such a common cutoff date as an essential part of the competitive negotiation process. The purpose of establishing a common cutoff date is to prevent offerors from being treated unfairly or being prejudiced. See *Comprehensive Health Servs., Inc. v. United States*, 70 Fed. Cl. 700 (2006), stating at 730-31:

> Had NASA considered new information supplied after the cut-off date, as a revision to the offeror's proposal, the agency would have violated FAR 15.307(b) and such conduct reasonably could have been viewed as according CHS with preferential treatment. *See Integrated Bus. Solutions v. United States*, 58 Fed. Cl. 420, 428 (Fed. Cl. 2003) ("Here, as GAO recognized, it would have been unfair to require the other offerors to submit FRPs by the March 13 deadline but permit IBS to confirm its initial proposal days later."); *Dubinsky v. United States*, 43 Fed. Cl. 243, 263-64 (Fed. Cl. 1999) ("[B]y providing a common cut-off date, it sets a level playing field on which [the offerors] may compete for the contract.") . . .

However, prejudice does not necessarily occur because there is no common cutoff date. See *Gas Turbine Corp.*, Comp. Gen. Dec. B-251265, 93-1 CPD ¶ 400, denying a protest because there was no actual prejudice in allowing one competitor "an additional few days." See also *Atlantic Terminal Co.*, Comp. Gen. Dec. B-160976, May 29, 1967, *Unpub.*, finding no prejudice, although the successful offeror was permitted to revise its price on February 6, and the unsuccessful offeror was last contacted regarding its price on January 31; *Canaveral Port Servs., Inc.*, Comp. Gen. Dec. B-211627.3, 84-2 CPD ¶ 358, finding no prejudice where the agency used staggered closing dates but kept all offers sealed until a common opening date; and *Special Operations Group, Inc.*, Comp. Gen. Dec. B-287013, 2001 CPD ¶ 73, noting lack of common date but not citing it as basis for sustaining protest. Mistaken notification to one offeror of a common closing date one week in advance of the date supplied to other offerors was not prejudicial since the government offered to extend the offeror's time to enable resubmission of the BAFO, *Alan-Craig, Inc.*, Comp. Gen. Dec. B-202432, 81-2 CPD ¶ 263. In *B.F. Goodrich Co.*, Comp. Gen. Dec. B-230674, 88-1 CPD ¶ 471, GAO criticized the agency for not establishing a common cutoff date but denied the protest. In *Amcare Med. Servs., Inc.*, Comp. Gen. Dec. B-271595, 96-2 CPD ¶ 10, GAO ruled that a protest claiming the lack of a common cutoff date was untimely because it was apparent on the face of the RFP. The common cutoff date applies to written offers, or written confirmation of oral offers, unless oral BAFOs are authorized in the RFP, *Gregory A. Robertson*, Comp. Gen. Dec. B-213351, 84-1 CPD ¶ 592.

The contracting officer may extend the closing date for receipt of final proposal revisions if such extension will enhance competition, *Solar Res., Inc.*, Comp. Gen. Dec. B-193264, 79-1 CPD ¶ 95. In *Institute for Advanced Safety Studies*, Comp. Gen. Dec. B-221330.2, 86-2 CPD ¶ 110, it was held proper to extend the closing date for BAFOs three days after the closing date because none of the offerors were prejudiced by this extension. In addition, an agency may extend the closing date for BAFOs upon request of an offeror. See also *Fort Biscuit Co.*, Comp. Gen. Dec. B-247319, 92-1 CPD ¶ 440, where extension of the closing date was proper to permit a competitor to submit a proposal that would not have otherwise been submitted, and *TRS Design & Consulting Servs.*, Comp. Gen. Dec. B-218668.2, 85-2 CPD ¶ 370, where the agency properly extended the closing date after it misinformed one of two offerors, causing it to miss the original closing date.

### c.  Late Final Revisions

The Instructions to Offerors — Competitive Acquisition solicitation provision at FAR 52.215-1 defines "late" proposals, modifications, or final revisions as those received after the designated time for receipt. Thus, late final proposal revisions are normally rejected unless they meet one of the exceptions to these rules — discussed earlier.

GAO has strictly construed the FAR definition of lateness. For example, GAO held that a BAFO which was received six minutes late was properly rejected where none of the exceptions to the late offer rule applied, *Potomac Sys. Res., Inc.*, Comp. Gen. Dec. B-219896, 85-2 CPD ¶ 393. See *Einhorn Yaffee Prescott*, Comp. Gen. Dec. D-259552, 95-1 CPD ¶ 153 (no agency mishandling when a courier arrived at the agency at five minutes before the closing time but could not make contact with agency personnel until five minutes after the closing time); *Fishermen's Boat Shop, Inc.*, Comp. Gen. Dec. B-223366, 86-2 CPD ¶ 389 (BAFO received in the agency's central mail depot 25 minutes before the closing time properly rejected as late because receipt at the mail depot does not constitute receipt at the designated contracting facility, and an agency cannot reasonably be expected to convey the mail to the contracting facility in 25 minutes).

When a final proposal submitted by facsimile transmission, the facsimile must be received in its entirety by the government with a reasonable time remaining for the government to carry it from the facsimile room to the contracting office, *Phoenix Research Group, Inc.*, Comp. Gen. Dec. B-240840, 90-2 CPD ¶ 514. Thus, an offer which is received in the facsimile room several minutes before the deadline may still be rejected if the government could not reasonably relay it to the contracting office before the deadline. See also *Cyber Digital, Inc.*, Comp. Gen. Dec. B-270107, 96-1 CPD ¶20 (where entire BAFO was not received until after deadline, agency was not required to consider that portion of the BAFO received before the deadline since it did not constitute the entire offer).

When a final proposal is submitted electronically, it must arrive at the designated office within the time specified, *Symetrics Indus., LLC*, Comp. Gen. Dec. B-298759, 2006 CPD ¶ 154. In that case, the final proposal arrived at the agency server on time but was delayed in arriving at the contracting office. GAO held that the rule in FAR 15.215-1(c)(3)(ii)(A)(2), permitting acceptance if it arrived at the government installation on time, did not apply to electronically submitted final proposal revisions.

GAO has applied the late proposal revision rule to a situation where the agency called for the submission of responses to "items for negotiation" by a specified date even though the request did not use the term "final proposal revision," *Seven Seas Eng'g & Land Surveying*, Comp. Gen. Dec. B-294424.2, 2004 CPD ¶ 236.

FAR 52.215-1(c)(6) allows offers to submit modifications "at any time before award" if the modification is made in response to an amendment or for the purpose of correcting a mistake. Thus, the government was allowed to consider a late BAFO which modified an otherwise acceptable low offer, *Woodward Assocs., Inc.*, Comp. Gen. Dec. B-216714, 85-1 CPD ¶ 274. GAO reasoned that other offerors could not complain because their relative standing was not affected.

Although a late final offer generally may not be considered for award, it has been held to be a revocation of the original offer precluding award on the basis of the original offer, *Touchstone Textiles, Inc.*, Comp. Gen. Dec. B-272230.4, 96-2 CPD ¶ 107 (higher-priced late BAFO manifested intent to modify and replace original offer); *Department of the Army — Recons.*, Comp. Gen. Dec. B-251527.3, 93-2 CPD ¶ 178 (late BAFO was "evidence that [offeror] no longer intended [its earlier prices] to be available for acceptance"). In *Integrated Bus. Solutions, Inc.*, Comp. Gen. Dec. B-292239, 2003 CPD ¶ 122, the submission of an unauthorized electronic revision and a late hard copy revision operated to revoke the initial offer.

## 2. Procedure Following Receipt of Final Revision

After receipt of final proposal revisions, the agency must reevaluate the proposals as quickly as possible. It is then in a position to proceed to source selection and award of a contract. However, under some circumstances, it may be necessary to reopen negotiations. An agency can obtain clarification of final proposal revisions, *VMD Sys. Integrators, Inc.*, Comp. Gen. Dec. B-401037.4, 2009 CPD ¶ 252; *IPlus, Inc.*, Comp. Gen. Dec. B-298020, 2006 CPD ¶ 90; *Antarctic Support Assocs. v. United States*, 46 Fed. Cl. 145 (2000), or correct a mistake in a final proposal revision, *Joint Threat Servs.*, Comp. Gen. Dec. B-178168, 98-1 CPD ¶ 18, but, if it enters into negotiations/discussions with one offeror, it must reopen discussions with all offerors in the competitive range, *International Res. Group*, Comp. Gen. Dec. B-286663, 2001 CPD ¶ 35, unless there has been no prejudice to the protester, *USATREX Int'l, Inc.*, Comp. Gen. Dec. B-275592, 98-1 CPD ¶ 99.

## a. Reevaluation

The first step after receipt of final proposal revisions is the reevaluation of each proposal to determine its current status in the competition. The failure to correctly assess the changes an offeror made in a proposal can lead to the granting of a protest, *Jaycor*, Comp. Gen. Dec. B-240029.2, 90-2 CPD ¶ 354. See, for example, *Ashbury Int'l Group, Inc.*, Comp. Gen. Dec. B-401123, 2009 CPD ¶ 140 (agency failed to test article submitted with final proposal revisions); *Contingency Mgmt. Group, LLC*, Comp. Gen. Dec. B-309752, 2008 CPD ¶ 83 (agency's acceptance of nonconforming assumption of requirements in offeror's final proposal revision gave it unfair advantage over others); *Johnson Controls Sec. Sys.*, Comp. Gen. Dec. B-296490, 2007 CPD ¶ 102 (agency based award on material misrepresentation in final proposal revisions); *ITT Fed. Servs. Int'l Corp.*, Comp. Gen. Dec. B-296783, 2007 CPD ¶ 43 (agency ignored requirement that offeror explain basis for reduced labor hours); *Advanced Sys. Dev., Inc.*, Comp. Gen. Dec. B-298411, 2006 CPD ¶ 137 (agency lack of understanding of awardee's revised prices led to irrational decision); *YORK Bldg. Servs., Inc.*, Comp. Gen. Dec. B-296948.2, 2005 CPD ¶ 202 (agency only evaluate final proposal revisions for acceptability); *Spherix, Inc.*, Comp. Gen. Dec. B-294572.3, 2005 CPD ¶ 183 (unfair evaluation of final proposal revisions); *Lockheed Martin Info. Sys.*, Comp. Gen. Dec. B-292836, 2003 CPD ¶ 230 (significant evaluation errors); *Matrix Int'l Logistics, Inc.*, Comp. Gen. Dec. B-272388.2, 97-2 CPD ¶ 89 (agency could not explain its rationale for upgrading one offeror from good to excellent and finding technical equality with protester); *Intown Props., Inc.*, Comp. Gen. Dec. B-262236.2, 96-1 CPD ¶ 89 (agency did not consider qualifications of different personnel in BAFO); and *Jack Faucett Assocs.*, Comp. Gen. Dec. B-233224, 89-1 CPD ¶ 115, *recons. denied*, 89-1 CPD ¶ 551 (agency could not explain its failure to upgrade a BAFO when the offeror included more manpower in response to an agency statement that too little manpower was a deficiency). This reevaluation must, of course, follow the original evaluation criteria in the RFP, *Hattal & Assocs.*, 70 Comp. Gen. 632 (B-243357), 91-2 CPD ¶ 90.

Agency evaluators have the same discretion in evaluating final proposal revisions that they have in evaluating original proposals. Thus, an agency may use information in a cost proposal to downgrade a technical proposal, *Cygna Project Mgmt.*, Comp. Gen. Dec. B-236839, 90-1 CPD ¶ 21. Similarly, a BAFO may be downgraded for failing to specifically elaborate on how the work will be performed, *Northwestern Travel Agency, Inc.*, Comp. Gen. Dec. B-244592, 91-2 CPD ¶ 363, or how its costs have been estimated, *Labat-Anderson, Inc.*, Comp. Gen. Dec. B-287091, 2001 CPD ¶ 79. In *Fintrac, Inc.*, Comp. Gen. Dec. B-311462.2, 2008 CPD ¶ 191, GAO found that the agency had properly altered the weights of evaluation subfactors to correct an error in the original evaluation. Final proposal revision changes may also be disregarded if the agency concludes that they do not effect the initial evaluation, *Cobra Techs., Inc.*, Comp. Gen. Dec. B-280475, 98-2 CPD ¶ 98. In *SelectTech Bering Straits Solutions JV*, Comp. Gen. Dec. B-400964, 2009 CPD ¶ 100, the agency properly downgraded an offeror when it did not include initially proposed enhancements in the model contract submitted with its final proposal revisions, the agency correctly reasoning that the enhancement would not be contractually binding.

In assessing the impact of final proposal revisions, the agency can totally reevaluate the proposals, *Information Sys. Tech. Corp.*, Comp. Gen. Dec. B-288490.2, 2002 CPD ¶ 120, or reevaluate only the changes from the original proposal, *Ecology & Env't, Inc.*, Comp. Gen. Dec. B-277061.2, 97-2 CPD ¶ 65. It has been found proper for agency evaluators to assess the changes that revisions have made to the original proposal and report them to the source selection official, *Northwest Reg'l Educ. Lab.*, Comp. Gen. Dec. B-222591.3, 87-1 CPD ¶ 74; *VSE Corp.*, Comp. Gen. Dec. B-224397, 86-2 CPD ¶ 392, or to take the changes into consideration when making the source selection decision, *Marinette Marine Corp.*, Comp. Gen. Dec. B-400697, 2009 CPD ¶ 16; *Palmetto GBA, LLC*, Comp. Gen. Dec. B-298962, 2007 CPD ¶ 25; *Ebon Research Sys.*, Comp. Gen. Dec. B-261403.2, 95-2 CPD ¶ 152; *Scientex Corp.*, Comp. Gen. Dec. B-238689, 90-1 CPD ¶ 597. See also *Aircraft Porous Media, Inc.*, Comp. Gen. Dec. B-241665.2, 91-1 CPD ¶ 356, *recons. denied*, 91-1 CPD ¶ 613, finding that it was proper for an agency not to bother rescoring because the changes in the BAFO could not have altered the original determination that two proposals were technically equal; *Cygnus Corp.*, Comp. Gen. Dec. B-275957, 97-1 CPD ¶ 202, finding that the agency had acted properly in deciding that no technical rescoring was necessary when the competitors had made only minor changes to proposals that had been evaluated as excellent in the original scoring; and *Health Mgmt. Res., Inc.*, Comp. Gen. Dec. B-270185, 96-1 CPD ¶ 23, finding that rescoring was not required because the agency found that each offeror "had improved to the same degree." However, a lack of documentation showing that BAFOs have been evaluated will lead to a sustained protest, *Biospherics, Inc.*, Comp. Gen. Dec. B-278508.4, 98-2 CPD ¶ 96.

There is no requirement that the final proposals be evaluated by the same evaluators that scored the original proposals, *Data Flow Corp.*, 62 Comp. Gen. 506 (B-209499), 83-2 CPD ¶ 57. However, the reevaluation must be reasonable in applying the evaluation criteria, *Bauer Assocs., Inc.*, Comp. Gen. Dec. B-229831.6, 88-2 CPD ¶ 549. GAO has stated that the fact that new evaluators reached different conclusions than the original evaluators does not automatically indicate an impropriety, *Chemonics Int'l*, Comp. Gen. Dec. B-222793, 86-2 CPD ¶ 161. See also *Magnavox Advanced Prods. & Sys. Co.*, Comp. Gen. Dec. B-215426, 85-1 CPD ¶ 146 (finding differences among individual evaluators as insufficient to discredit a technical evaluation).

## b.  Reopening Negotiations

Reopening negotiations is not a desirable course of action. It adds time and expense to the procurement and extends the time when information may be improperly disclosed. See *Mine Safety Appliances Co.*, Comp. Gen. Dec. B-242379.5, 92-2 CPD ¶ 76, holding that the conduct of another round of negotiations in the absence of a valid reason tends to undermine the integrity of the competitive negotiation process. Pre-Rewrite FAR 15.611(c) stated that negotiations should not be reopened "unless it is clearly in the Government's best interests to do so." In addition, DFARS 215.611 prohibited contracting officers from reopening negotiations unless higher-level approval was obtained. However, the FAR Part 15 Rewrite removed this coverage, leaving the matter to the contracting officer's discretion under the circumstances surrounding each procurement. In *Dynacs Eng'g Co.*, Comp. Gen. Dec. B-284234, 2000 CPD ¶ 50, GAO noted this change in holding that the agencies use of multiple rounds of discussions was not improper. Similarly, DoD requirement for higher approval has been deleted from the DFARS. See, however, NFS 1815.307(b)(ii), requiring the approval of the Associate Administrator for Procurement to reopen discussions on procurements of $50 million or more and the approval of the procurement officer of the procuring activity to reopen discussions on smaller procurements.

Agencies are required to reopen discussions if the evaluation of the offeror's final proposal identifies significant weaknesses or deficiencies that were not identified in the original evaluation and hence not discussed in the original discussion, *Al Long Ford*, Comp. Gen. Dec. B-297807, 2006 CPD ¶ 68; *Consolidated Eng'g Servs., Inc. v. United States*, 64 Fed. Cl. 617 (2005); *DevTech Sys., Inc.*, Comp. Gen. Dec. B-284860.2, 2001 CPD ¶ 11. See *Carahsoft Tech. Corp. v. United States*, 86 Fed. Cl. 325 (2009), holding that it is proper to reopen discussions in such circumstances even if the deficiency makes the proposal unacceptable. Furthermore, if discussions are reopened with one offeror in the competitive range, they must be reopened with all other offerors still in the range, *Cigna Gov't Servs., LLC*, Comp. Gen. Dec. D-297915.2, 2006 CPD ¶ 74; *Lockheed Martin Aeronautics Co.*, Comp. Gen. Dec. B-295401, 2005 CPD ¶ 41.

It is proper to reopen discussions if questions are not resolved in one offeror's proposal revisions, *General Dynamics — Ordnance & Tactical Sys.*, Comp. Gen. Dec. B-401658, 2009 CPD ¶ 217; substantial questions requiring discussions are raised by one of the BAFOs, *Ocean Tech., Inc.*, Comp. Gen. Dec. B-183749, 75-2 CPD ¶ 262; previously existing ambiguities are not discovered until after submission of BAFOs, 52 Comp. Gen. 409 (B-176913) (1973); *Swedlow, Inc.*, 53 Comp. Gen. 564 (B-178212), 74-1 CPD ¶ 55; additional technical information is needed to evaluate the proposals, *Introl Corp.*, Comp. Gen. Dec. B-194570, 80-1 CPD ¶ 41; government estimates are discovered to be in error, *Dyneteria, Inc.*, Comp. Gen. Dec. B-181707, 75-1 CPD ¶ 86; government requirements change, *ACS Sys. & Eng'g, Inc.*, Comp. Gen. Dec. B-275439.2, 97-1 CPD ¶ 126; *Simulators Ltd., Inc.*, Comp. Gen. Dec. B-208418, 82-2 CPD ¶ 473; incorrect information was provided to one offeror during discussions, *Computer Related Servs., Inc.*, Comp. Gen. Dec. B-244638, 91-2 CPD ¶ 420; specifications were not clear, *ES, Inc.*, Comp. Gen. Dec. B-258911.2, 95-1 CPD ¶ 168; or deficiencies in initial BAFO prevented offeror's acceptance, *Dube Travel Agency & Tours, Inc.*, Comp. Gen. Dec. B-270438, 96-1 CPD ¶ 141. Also upheld was a decision to reopen discussions and request a second round of BAFOs after the recommended awardee's place of performance had become unavailable and the quality of materials required by the government had changed, *Hayes Int'l Corp. v. United States*, 7 Cl. Ct. 681 (1985). See also *M.W. Kellogg Co./Siciliana Appalti Costruzioni S.p.A. (J.V.) v. United States*, 10 Cl. Ct. 17 (1986), and *Meridian Mgmt. Corp.*, Comp. Gen. Dec. B-278099, 97-2 CPD ¶ 157, permitting multiple BAFOs.

If discussions are reopened, it is proper to raise issues that were brought to an offeror's attention in the initial discussions, *Dynacs Eng'g Co.*, Comp. Gen. Dec. B-284234, 2000 CPD ¶ 50. GAO stated that this was an acceptable means of "maximizing the Government's ability to obtain best value" as called for by FAR 15.306(d)(2) in the FAR Rewrite. GAO also noted that there had been previous rulings to this effect, stating:

> We note that, even under the prior version of the FAR, a procuring agency properly could reopen discussions to discuss a previously raised item when the agency felt such action was necessary to resolve its concerns before making an award. See *Telos Corp.*, B-279493.3, July 27, 1998, 98-2 CPD ¶ 30 at 9-11; *Prospective Computer Analysts, Inc.*, B-275262.2, Feb. 24, 1997, 97-2 CPD ¶ 22 at 3-5.

While the agency has the discretion to call for another round of proposals, it also has the discretion to refuse to do so. See *Textron, Inc. v. United States*, 74 Fed. Cl. 277 (2006), where the agency was not required to reopen negotiations when it asked for additional test data during the original discussions and concluded that the new data indicated a deficiency in the proposed ship without giving the protester the opportunity to explain the data. Thus, the agency is not obligated to bring up deficiencies remaining from the initial proposal when the offeror has already been informed of the deficiency, *LIS, Inc.*, Comp. Gen. Dec. B-400646.4, 2010 CPD ¶ 18; *ITT Indus. Space Sys., LLC,* Comp. Gen. Dec. B-309964, 2007 CPD ¶ 217; *Ideamatics, Inc.*, Comp. Gen. Dec. B-297791.2, 2006 CPD ¶ 87; *Si-Nor, Inc.*, Comp. Gen. Dec. B-290150.4, 2003 CPD ¶ 45; *Metcalf Constr. Co.*, Comp. Gen. Dec. B-289100, 2002 CPD ¶ 31; *Phoenix Safety Assocs., Ltd.*, Comp. Gen. Dec. B-216504, 84-2 CPD ¶ 621.

It is also proper not to conduct further negotiations to clarify or amplify newly introduced aspects of its final proposal revision. See *Sabre Sys., Inc.*, Comp. Gen. Dec. B-402040.2, 2010 CPD ¶ 128 (incomplete data in response to weakness in original proposal); *Akal Sec., Inc.*, Comp. Gen. Dec. B-401469, 2009 CPD ¶ 183 (reduced staffing was a weakness); *Honeywell Tech. Solutions, Inc.*, Comp. Gen. Dec. B-400771, 2009 CPD ¶ 49 (protester demonstrated lack of understanding of requirement in responding to prior discussed weaknesses); *DRS C3 Sys., LLC*, Comp. Gen. Dec. B-310825, 2008 CPD ¶ 103 (design submitted in response to discussions inferior); *L-3 Commc'ns Corp.*, Comp. Gen. Dec. B-299227, 2007 CPD ¶ 83 (substitution of another product indicated a lack of technical competence); *MD Helicopters, Inc.*, Comp. Gen. Dec. B-298502, 2006 CPD ¶ 164 (level pricing over long contract posed a risk); *Air Prods. Healthcare*, Comp. Gen. Dec. B-298293, 2006 CPD ¶ 123 (new information on sufficiency of services did not to meet agency requirements); *Mechanical Equip. Co.*, Comp. Gen. Dec. B-292789.2, 2004 CPD ¶ 192 (lack of supporting data in final proposal revisions); *Cube-All Star Servs., Joint Venture*, Comp. Gen. Dec. B-291903, 2003 CPD ¶ 145 (proposal revision made proposal unacceptable); *NLX Corp.*, Comp. Gen. Dec. B-288785, 2001 CPD ¶ 198 (significantly reduced price imposed a risk); *Litton Sys., Inc., Amecon Div.*, Comp. Gen. Dec. B-275807.2, 97-1 CPD ¶ 170 (probable cost properly adjusted without further discussions when it increased the labor hours estimated to be necessary to perform the work); *Serv-Air, Inc.*, Comp. Gen. Dec. B-258243, 96-1 CPD ¶ 267 (deficiency or weakness introduced in the BAFO); and *Saco Def., Inc.*, Comp. Gen. Dec. B-252066, 93-1 CPD ¶ 395 (new tests on a redesigned item not required). See also *Joint Threat Servs.*, Comp. Gen. Dec. B-278168, 98-1 CPD ¶ 18, where it was held proper not to reopen negotiations to point out a staffing deficiency in the BAFO that had not been made a part of the original discussions because it had been considered a minor weakness. GAO found that the agency had acted correctly because it was the staff reductions in the BAFO that turned the weakness into a deficiency. Thus, an offeror takes the risk that aspects of its proposal included in the final proposal revisions for the first time will be found unacceptable by the agency, *Global Solutions Network, Inc.*, Comp. Gen. Dec. B-298682.3, 2008 CPD ¶ 131 (single employee filling two key positions); *Suntron Corp.*, Comp. Gen. Dec. B-270456, 96-1 CPD ¶ 143 (unexplained cost reduction); *Logicon RDA*, Comp. Gen. Dec. B-261714.2, 95-2 CPD ¶ 286 (unsupported cost reduction introduced for first time in BAFO); *Aircraft Porous Media, Inc.*, Comp. Gen. Dec. B-241665.2, 91-1 CPD ¶ 356 (reduced cost adjusted upward because not realistic and rationale for reduction not sufficiently explained); *Management & Tech. Servs. Co.*, Comp. Gen. Dec. B-209513, 82-2 CPD ¶ 571 (new management technique).

This rule has been carried to the extreme in holding that an agency need not reopen discussions to permit correction of a mistake in the BAFO, *Standard Mfg. Co.*, 65 Comp. Gen. 451 (B-220455), 86-1 CPD ¶ 304; *American Elec. Lab., Inc.*, 65 Comp. Gen. 62 (B-219582), 85-2 CPD ¶ 545. Compare *FCC.O&M, Inc.*, Comp. Gen. Dec. B-238610.2, 91-1 CPD ¶ 26, where it was found proper to conduct another round of discussions in order to correct a mistake in the winning offeror's proposal. Thus, an agency may, but is not required to, reopen discussions after submission of final proposal revisions and the agency's decision will not be disturbed unless it is found to be unreasonable.

The rule permitting the contracting officer not to reopen discussions when an offeror has included newly introduced material in a final proposal does not apply to information which the agency learns from other sources that appears to modify the proposal. See *AAA Eng'g & Drafting, Inc.*, Comp. Gen. Dec. B-250323, 93-1 CPD ¶ 287, where the contracting officer gave a BAFO a low evaluation based on a manning table obtained in a preaward survey which appeared to conflict with the manning table that had been included in the BAFO. GAO ruled that the contracting officer should have sought clarification since the offeror did not state that the new manning table modified its BAFO.

# IX. SOURCE SELECTION

Upon completion of the evaluation of the proposals, the agency is prepared to select the winning contractor(s). FAR 15.302 states: "The objective of source selection is to select the proposal that represents the best value." When the FAR 15.101-2 lowest-price technically acceptable source selection process is used, the selection decision can be made quite quickly because it does not involve tradeoffs. The only matters for determination are whether the lowest priced offer is technically acceptable and whether that offeror is responsible. Thus, there is not even a need to evaluate the technical acceptability of higher priced offerors. In FAR 15.101-2 tradeoff procurements, offers other than the lowest priced or other than the highest technically rated may be selected. Depending upon the evaluation factors and the evaluation scheme, this can be a more difficult decision requiring a significant degree of judgment to be exercised in selecting the source.

## A. Source Selection Authority

While the procurement statutes provide that the "agency," 41 U.S.C. § 253b(d) (3), or the "executive agency," 10 U.S.C. § 3703(c), shall award the contract, the FAR provisions focus on the individual who will make the selection and award decisions. This individual is called the source selection authority (SSA). FAR 15.303 (a) provides that the contracting officer is the SSA "unless the agency head appoints another individual for a particular acquisition or group of acquisitions." In many agencies, particularly in large dollar value procurements, the SSA is a high level agency official.

### 1. Responsibilities

The source selection responsibilities of the SSA are set out in FAR 15.303 (b), as follows:

(4) Ensure that proposals are evaluated based solely on the factors and subfactors contained in the solicitation (10 U.S.C. 2305(b)(1) and 41 U.S.C. 253b(d)(3));

(5) Consider the recommendations of advisory boards or panels (if any); and

(6) Select the source or sources whose proposal is the best value to the Government (10 U.S.C. 2305(b)(4)(B) and 41 U.S.C. 253b(d)(3)).

In addition, the SSA must make a determination of whether to award without negotiation or whether to award after receiving final offer revisions or to call for further revisions.

Another responsibility of the SSA is to determine whether to cancel the solicitation. Under some circumstances, it would not be appropriate to continue a procurement and make an award. In this regard, the procurement statutes provide that "all . . . proposals . . . may be rejected if the head of the agency determines that such action is in the public interest," 10 U.S.C. § 2305(b)(2) and 41 U.S.C. § 3701(b). FAR 15.305 vests the authority to make this determination in the SSA. Pre-Rewrite FAR 15.608 (b) dealt with this subject and contained a number of examples where rejection of all offers would be justified. It also required a determination, in writing, that one of the identified factors was present. However, this provision was deleted in the Rewrite which merely authorizes rejection if the SSA determines rejection to be in the "public interest." The SSA has broad discretion in making such determinations. Hence, cancellations have been found appropriate in *FFTF Restoration Co. LLC v. United States*, 86 Fed. Cl. 226 (20090 (agency encountered delays in awarding the contract, faced budget limitations and concluded that the remaining work could be more effectively performed by the incumbent contractor); *Lasmer Indus., Inc.*, Comp. Gen. Dec. B-400866.2, 2009 CPD ¶ 77 (it was more advantageous to procure the part from an existing contract); *Atlantic Scientific & Tech. Corp.*, Comp. Gen. Dec. B-276334.2, 97-2 CPD ¶ 116 (protest led agency to reassess its needs); and *Rotary Furnishing Co.*, Comp. Dec. B-277704, 97-2 CPD ¶ 140 (one offeror submitted a high price and the other offeror was nonresponsible). Thus, rejection of all proposals and cancellation is appropriate when it is determined that it is not in the best interest of the government to award to any of the offerors. See *North Shore Med. Labs, Inc.*, Comp. Gen. Dec. B-311070, 2008 CPD ¶ 144 (no acceptable proposals and stringent RFP requirement limited competitors); *DCMS-ISA, Inc. v. United States*, 84 Fed. Cl. 501 (2008) (small business set aside cancelled because none of the competitors had sufficient experience); *Knight's Armament Co.*, Comp. Gen. Dec. B 299469, 2007 CPD ¶ 85 (none of the offered products met agency needs); *Glen/Mar Constr., Inc.*, Comp. Gen. Dec. B-298355, 2006 CPD ¶ 117 (all offered prices much higher than agency budget); *Sunshine Kids Serv. Supply Co.*, Comp. Gen. Dec. B-292141, 2003 CPD ¶ 119 (only HUBZone competitor submitted unacceptable proposal); *Nutech Laundry & Textiles, Inc.*, B-291739, 2003 CPD ¶ 34 (small business price was much higher than government estimate); *D&K Constr. Co.*, Comp. Gen. Dec. B-281244.3, 99-2 CPD ¶ 57 (protester's final proposal was noncompliant and other offeror's final proposal was submitted late); and *Rotary Furnishing Co.*, Comp. Dec. B-277704, 97-2 CPD ¶ 140 (one offeror submitted a high price and the other offeror was nonresponsible). Cancellation and resolicitation is also proper where the lowest price can not be determined to be reasonable, *Razorcom Teleph & Net, LLC v. United States*, 56 Fed. Cl. 140 (2003); *Process Control Techs. v. United States*, 53 Fed. Cl. 71 (2002), and *Interstate Rock Prods., Inc. v. United States*, 50 Fed. Cl. 349 (2001). Another proper basis for cancellation is when the agency determines that there is another source for the product or service. See *Klinge Corp. v. United States*, 83 Fed. Cl. 773 (2008) (agency used Federal Supply Schedule after mistakenly concluding that protester's offer was noncompliant with the Trade Agreements Act); *Borenstein Group, Inc.*, Comp. Gen. Dec. B-309751, 2007 CPD ¶ 174 (agency found that existing contract could be used); *Management Solutions, L.C.*, Comp. Gen. Dec. B-298883, 2006 CPD ¶ 197 (agency found item was required to be procured from Federal Prison Industries); and *CAT Flight Servs., Inc.*, Comp. Gen. Dec. B-294186, 2004 CPD ¶ 178 (agency found existing contract). However, rejection of all offers and requiring resubmission or cancellation of the solicitation is a serious matter, particularly where substantial effort is required in the submission and evaluation of offers. Thus, rejection and cancellation would not be appropriate where concerns with the procurement could be addressed through negotiations, *A&W Flamar GmbH*, Comp. Gen. Dec. B-278486, 98-1 CPD ¶ 40. Cancellation was held to be improper where prices had been disclosed and the agency intended to move to a sealed bid procurement, *Rand & Jones Enters. Co.*, Comp. Gen. Dec. B-296483, 2005 CPD ¶ 142, where the winning small business was found nonresponsible without referring the matter to the Small Business Administration, *Phil Howry Co.*, Comp. Gen. Dec. B-291402.3, 2003 CPD ¶ 33, where a determination of excessive price was not warranted, *Nutech Laundry & Textile, Inc. v. United States*, 56 Fed. Cl. 588 (2003), and where the sole reasons were to avoid contracting with an offeror, *Parcel 49C Ltd. P'ship v. United States*, 31 F.3d 1147 (Fed. Cir. 1994), and *126 Northpoint Plaza Ltd. P'ship v. United States*, 34 Fed. Cl. 105 (1995).

## 2. *Independent Judgment*

FAR 15.308 requires that, while the SSA may use the analyses of other participants in the process, the source selection decision must represent the SSA's independent judgment:

> The source selection authority's (SSA) decision shall be based on a comparative assessment of proposals against all source selection criteria in the solicitation. While the SSA may use reports and analyses prepared by others, the source selection decision shall represent the SSA's independent judgment.

The information furnished to the SSA can vary in nature and detail. It may consist only of evaluation results or may also contain further analyses and recommendations for award. The SSA must make an assessment of the information and determine whether it conforms to the evaluation factors specified in the solicitation and whether it is sufficient to make a rational selection for award. If not, the SSA must see that corrective action is taken.

In fulfilling his or her obligations, the SSA can become deeply involved in all aspects of the procurement. See *Digital Sys. Group, Inc.*, Comp. Gen. Dec. B-286931, 2001 CPD ¶ 50, rejecting a protest that the contracting officer, acting as the SSA, had approved the source selection plan, conducted discussions, served as a member of the evaluation board and the cost team. The decision states that "While it is conceivable that a CO's active participation in multiple stages of the evaluation process could compromise that process, that clearly is not the case here." See also *JW Holding Group & Assocs., Inc.*, Comp. Gen. Dec. B-285882.3, 2003 CPD ¶ 126, denying a protest that the SSA served as the head of the price evaluation team. Compare *Wackenhut Servs., Inc. v. United States*, 85 Fed. Cl. 273 (2008), suggesting that it may have been improper for the SSA to influence the evaluators during the evaluation process.

A suggestion from the contracting officer that the SSA "beef up" the explanations for arriving at the source selection decision did not indicate that the SSA had not exercised independent judgment, *Microware Outsourcing, Inc. v. United States*, 72 Fed. Cl. 694 (2006).

### a. Evaluations or Recommendations

In smaller procurements the SSA (generally the contracting officer) may participate in the entire evaluation process with the result that there is no need to communicate the results of the evaluation to the SSA. However, in larger procurements there will be such a need because the SSA has not participated in the evaluation. In that situation agencies generally require the preparation of written documentation summarizing the results of the evaluation and often require briefings of the SSA. See DoD Source Selection Procedures containing extensive guidance at 1.4 on the roles of the various participants (SSA, SSAC, SSEB, PCO) in this process. See also NFS 1815.370 requiring the following procedure when source evaluation boards (SEBs) have done the evaluation:

(h) SEB presentation. (1) The SEB Chairperson shall brief the SSA on the results of the SEB deliberations to permit an informed and objective selection of the best source(s) for the particular acquisition.

(2) The presentation shall focus on the significant strengths, deficiencies, and significant weaknesses found in the proposals, the probable cost of each proposal, and any significant issues and problems identified by the SEB. This presentation must explain any applicable special standards of responsibility; evaluation factors, subfactors, and elements; the significant strengths and significant weaknesses of the offerors; the Government cost estimate, if applicable; the offerors' proposed cost/price; the probable cost; the proposed fee arrangements; and the final adjectival ratings and scores to the subfactor level.

(3) Attendance at the presentation is restricted to people involved in the selection process or who have a valid need to know. The designated individuals attending the SEB presentation(s) shall:

(i) Ensure that the solicitation and evaluation processes complied with all applicable agency policies and that the presentation accurately conveys the SEB's activities and findings;

(ii) Not change the established evaluation factors, subfactors, elements, weights, or scoring systems; or the substance of the SEB's findings. They may, however, advise the SEB to rectify procedural omissions, irregularities or inconsistencies, substantiate its findings, or revise the presentation.

(4) The SEB recorder will coordinate the formal presentation including arranging the time and place of the presentation, assuring proper attendance, and distributing presentation material.

Procedures such as these that communicate summaries of the evaluations to the SSA have been sustained as fully adequate to ensure rational source selection decisions. See, for example, *Sabreliner Corp.*, Comp. Gen. Dec. B-242023, 91-1 CPD ¶ 326, where GAO stated:

The SSA is not required to personally review the proposals or the complete evaluation documentation, but can rely upon a briefing that presents the results of the proposal evaluation. *See Systems & Processes Eng'g Corp.*, B-234142, May 10, 1989, 89-1 CPD ¶ 441. Here, the SSA, in addition to receiving a technical evaluation briefing, reviewed the proposal analysis report, which set forth, among other things, a description of the evaluation standards and criteria; a description of the competing proposals; a comparative evaluation analysis of the proposal; the offerors' proposed prices/costs; and the performance risk assessment.

In most cases the SSA can rely on the assessments of the evaluators and the evaluation board's conclusions. See *Wyle Labs., Inc.*, Comp. Gen. Dec. B-311123, 2009 CPD ¶ 96 (SSA based decision on SSEB's overriding of evaluators judgment of risk); *MD Helicopters, Inc.*, Comp. Gen. Dec. B-298502, 2006 CPD ¶ 164 (SSA based decision detailed discussions with SSEB, SSAC and users or product being procured); *Metro Mach. Corp.*, Comp. Gen. Dec. B-295744, 2005 CPD ¶ 112 (SSA accepted evaluation assessments of three evaluation committees); *Computer Scis. Corp. v. United States*, 51 Fed. Cl. 297 (2001) (SSA based decision on evaluators comparative assessment of offerors' past performance); *Keane Fed. Sys., Inc.*, Comp. Gen. Dec. B-280595, 98-2 CPD ¶ 132 (SSA based decision on detailed comparison of offers by "best value working group"); *Development Alternatives, Inc.*, Comp. Gen. Dec. B-279920, 98-2 CPD ¶ 54 (SSA relied on assessment of majority of evaluators); *KRA Corp.*, Comp. Gen. Dec. B-278904, 98-1 CPD ¶ 147 (SSA based decision on oral and written evaluation reports plus questions of evaluators); *International Data Prods. Corp.*, Comp. Gen. Dec. B-274654, 97-1 CPD ¶ 34 (SSA based selection decision on detailed analysis in SSEB report); *Allied Tech. Group, Inc.*, Comp. Gen. Dec. B-271302, 96-2 CPD ¶ 4 (SSA based selection decision on contract evaluation board findings and discussion with board); *ICF Kaiser Engr's*,

Comp. Gen. Dec. B-271079, 96-2 CPD ¶ 15 (source selection official based award decision on information set forth in the SEB and TEP reports). It is also proper for the SSA to obtain and rely on legal advice from an agency lawyer, *Creative Apparel Assocs.*, Comp. Gen. Dec. B-275139, 97-1 CPD ¶ 65.

When there is disagreement among the evaluators or within an evaluation board, the SSA may have a heightened responsibility to explain his or her reliance on the evaluation report. See *Information Scis. Corp. v. United States*, 73 Fed. Cl. 70 (2006), *amended*, 75 Fed. Cl. 406 (2007), sustaining a protest where the SSA adopted a minority report almost verbatim in the source selection decision. The court held that this did not demonstrate the exercise of independent judgment — apparently because the SSA did not explain why the minority view was correct.

### b. Reliance Not Justified

The SSA is not entitled to rely upon faulty evaluations. Thus, the SSA is ultimately responsible for any mistakes made in the evaluation process. In *J.A. Jones Mgmt. Servs., Inc.*, Comp. Gen. Dec. B-276864, 97-2 CPD ¶ 47, GAO observed:

> While an agency's initial review of proposals may be done independently, it is necessary for the agency at some point to make a rational comparison of the relative merits of directly competing proposals. The agency's SSA cannot make a rational comparison where the evaluators' point scores do not accurately reflect the relative strengths and weaknesses of the competing proposals and the record lacks adequate documentation in support of such technical point scores. Here, the dearth of evaluation narratives or other explanations in this evaluation record and the SSA's summary reliance on the point scores, which have been sufficiently shown by the protester to be inaccurate in numerous areas, lead us to the conclusion that the SSA could not and did not make a reasonable selection decision. *See Adelaide Blomfield Management Co.*, [Comp. Gen. Dec. B-253128.2, 93-2 CPD ¶ 197], at 4-6. In sum, on the evaluation record furnished to our Office — consisting of point scores and cursory narratives — we find the absence of a consistent, reasonable and accurate evaluation scoring as well as the absence of supporting narrative documentation; moreover, the agency has offered no substantive response to the protester's concerns in response to the protest, and our review shows none. Here, we simply are unable to assess the reasonableness of the agency's selection decision. Accordingly, we sustain the protest.

Thus, protests have been granted when the SSA made the selection decision based on the conclusions of the evaluators but it was later determined that the conclusions were unsupported by the evaluation documentation. See *Health Net Fed. Servs., LLC*, Comp. Gen. Dec. B-401652.3, 2009 CPD ¶ 220 (SSA relied on evaluator's conclusion that corporate parent of offeror met experience requirement when neither had investigated role of parent); *Contingency Mgmt. Group, LLC*, Comp. Gen. Dec. B-309752, 2008 CPD ¶ 83 (decision based on responses to scenario in RFP where evaluators did not consider impact of proposals that altered the assumptions in the scenario with the result that they were able to propose lower prices); *Apptis, Inc.*, Comp. Gen. Dec. B-299457, 2008 CPD ¶ 49 (SSA relied on SSEB's improper use of past performance to evaluate risk of technical solution); *Keeton Corrs., Inc.*, Comp. Gen. Dec. B-293348, 2005 CPD ¶ 44 (SSA relied on misleading narrative supporting contracting officer's evaluation of past performance); *SDS Int'l, Inc.*, Comp. Gen. Dec. B-291183, 2003 CPD ¶ 137 (SSA based decision on evaluators' misreading of technical proposal); *Ashland Sales & Serv. Co.*, Comp. Gen. Dec. B-291206, 2003 CPD ¶ 36 (SSA relied on contracting officer document that contained factual errors); *Shumaker Trucking & Excavating Contractors, Inc.*, Comp. Gen. Dec. B-290732, 2002 CPD ¶ 169 (SSA endorsed contracting officer's conclusion that was based on higher point score with no consideration of strengths and weaknesses); *Green Valley Trans., Inc.*, Comp. Gen. Dec. B-285283, 2000 CPD ¶ 133 (SSA followed the evaluators' theory that past performance should be rated on the basis of the number of late deliveries without considering the volume of shipments); *CRAssociates, Inc.*, Comp. Gen. Dec. B-282075.2, 2000 CPD ¶ 63 (SSA relied on faulty technical evaluation and mathematical scoring mistakes); *Saco Def. Corp.*, Comp. Gen. Dec. B-283885, 2000 CPD ¶ 34 (SSA relied on an evaluation that the prospective winning offeror had furnished sufficient information to demonstrate that its quality system was adequate); *ITT Fed. Servs. Int'l Corp.*, Comp. Gen. Dec. B-283307, 99-2 CPD ¶ 76 (SSA determined that the protester's costs were unrealistic when the cost evaluation team had made no cost realism analysis to determine the probable costs of performance); and *JW Assocs., Inc.*, Comp. Gen. Dec. B-275209, 97-1 CPD ¶ 57 (evaluation report contained only the prices, point scores of the non-price evaluation factors, and a one-paragraph narrative giving summary conclusions without explaining the different scores given to the competing offerors).

## c. Ordering Reevaluation

The SSA can order a complete reevaluation if there are doubts about the validity of the initial evaluation, *PRC, Inc.*, Comp. Gen. Dec. B-233561.8, 92-2 CPD ¶ 215. In that case, a new evaluation panel was constituted after questions were raised about the propriety of the initial evaluation. GAO stated:

> Contracting officials in negotiated procurements have broad discretion to take corrective action where the agency determines that such action is necessary to ensure fair and impartial competition. *Oshkosh Truck Corp.; Idaho Norland Corp.*, B-237058.2; B-237058.3, Feb. 14, 1990, 90-1 CPD ¶ 274. An agency may convene a new selection board and conduct a new evaluation where the record shows that the agency made the decision in good faith, without the specific intent of changing a particular offeror's technical ranking or avoiding an award to a particular offeror. *Burns & Roe Servs. Corp.*, B-248394, Aug. 25, 1992, 92-2 CPD ¶ [124]; *Loschky, Marquardt & Nesholm*, B-222606, Sept. 23, 1986, 86-2 CPD ¶ 336. We will not object to proposed corrective action where the agency concludes that award was not necessarily made on a basis most advantageous to the government, so long as the corrective action taken is appropriate to remedy the impropriety.

See also *Team BOS/Naples — Gemmo S.p.A./DelJen*, Comp. Gen. Dec. B-298865.3, 2008 CPD ¶ 11 (not questioning reevaluation when SSA found errors in initial evaluation); *East/West Indus., Inc.*, Comp. Gen. Dec. B-278734.4, 98-1 CPD ¶ 143 (not questioning reconvening the evaluators to perform a more detailed evaluation of the proposals); and *EBA Eng'g, Inc.*, Comp. Gen. Dec. B-275818, 97-1 CPD ¶ 127 (finding proper agency's decision to replace panel members in order to avoid the appearance of impropriety).

## d.  *Rescore or Conduct Own Evaluation*

The SSA is not bound by the rankings, scores, or recommendations of either the evaluators, boards or other intermediate groups, as long as the official has a rational basis for the differing evaluation. In some cases, source selection officials merely ignore the scores and make the source selection decision based on the narratives. However, in most instances, an attempt is made to make the scores an accurate reflection of the merits of the proposals.

There have been numerous protest decisions upholding rescoring by source selection officials, either explicitly or implicitly. See *Grey Advertising, Inc.*, 55 Comp. Gen. 1111 (B-184825), 76-1 CPD ¶ 325, stating at 1120:

> [W]hile point scores, technical evaluation narratives, and adjective ratings may well be indicative of whether one proposal is technically superior to another and should therefore be considered by source selection officials, see *EPSCO, Incorporated*, B-183816, November 21, 1975, 75-2 CPD ¶ 338, we have recognized that selection officials are not bound by the recommendations made by evaluation and advisory groups. *Bell Aerospace Company*, 55 Comp. Gen. 244 (1975), 75-2 CPD ¶ 168; *Tracor Jitco, Inc.*, *supra*; 51 Comp. Gen. 272 (1971); B-173137(1), *supra*. This is so even though it is the working level procurement officials and evaluation panel members who may normally be expected to have the technical expertise relevant to the technical evaluation of proposals. Accordingly, we have upheld source selection officials' determinations that technical proposals were essentially equal despite an evaluation point score differential of 81 out of 1000, see 52 Comp. Gen. 686, *supra*, and despite contracting officer recommendations that award be made to the offeror with the highest technical rating. See 52 Comp. Gen. 738, *supra*.

Reevaluation or rescoring is often performed by the SSA to correct errors or poor judgment of subordinate evaluation personnel. In *Grey Advertising*, for instance, Navy officials determined that two proposals were technically equal, although the evaluation panel rated the protester's technical proposal 47 points higher — on a scale of 1000 points. GAO found this judgment had a rational basis, as the officials had concluded that the protester's higher score was based too much on the advantages of incumbency rather than actual technical superiority. See also *TPL, Inc.*, Comp. Gen. Dec. B-297136.10, 2006 CPD ¶ 104 (SSA disagreed with evaluators' assessment of program management subfactor); *University Research*

*Co.*, Comp. Gen. Dec. B-294358.6, 2005 CPD ¶ 83 (contracting officer disregarded assessments of evaluator and found technical proposals equal); *Synoptic Sys. Corp.*, Comp. Gen. Dec. B-290789.4, 2003 CPD ¶ 42 (SSA reevaluated proposals after outcome prediction by GAO); *Sayed Hamid Behbehani & Sons, WLL*, Comp. Gen. Dec. B-288818.6, 2002 CPD ¶ 163 (SSA reevaluated proposals without reference to original evaluations); *R.C.O. Reforesting*, Comp. Gen. Dec. B-280774.2, 98-2 CPD ¶ 119 (contracting officer properly reduced past performance score because of default termination not known to evaluators); and *Pro-Mark, Inc.*, Comp. Gen. Dec. B-247248, 92-1 CPD ¶448 (contracting officer lowered incongruous quality control scores as given by an inexperienced review panel).

When an SSA makes an independent assessment, it will be subject to scrutiny for reasonableness. See *Consolidated Eng'g Servs.Inc.*, Comp. Gen. Dec. B-311313, 2008 CPD ¶ 146 (SSA changed experience evaluation based on issues not in RFP); *AT&T Corp.*, Comp. Gen. Dec. B-299542.3, 2008 CPD ¶ 65 (no explanation of how SSA arrived at different conclusion than evaluators regarding the impact of over-staffing); *IDEA Int'l, Inc. v. United States*, 74 Fed. Cl. 129 (2006) (SSA awarded to low price without considering evaluators' conclusion that protester had "slightly stronger proposal"); *DynCorp Int'l LLC*, Comp. Gen. Dec. B-289863, 2002 CPD ¶ 83 (SSA discounted weaknesses in awardee's proposal without explaining ratio-nale for decision); *AIU North Am., Inc.*, Comp. Gen. Dec. B-283743.2, 2000 CPD ¶ 39 (SSA's determination that technical proposals were equal was neither supported by contemporaneous documentation nor satisfactorily explained during the protest); *Chemical Demilitarization Assocs.*, Comp. Gen. Dec. B-277700, 98-1 CPD ¶ 171 (SSA made improper determination that two technical proposals were of equal tech-nical merit when the evaluation documentation rated the protester's proposal con-siderably higher in merit and the SSA could not explain why this assessment of the evaluators was inaccurate); *Morrison Knudsen Corp.*, Comp. Gen. Dec. B-270703, 96-2 CPD ¶ 86 (SSA's conclusion that selected offeror had superior subcontract approach unreasonable when the two proposals were not fundamentally different in this regard); *TRESP Assocs., Inc.*, Comp. Gen. Dec. B-258322.5, 96-1 CPD ¶ 8 (SSA's independent assessment of the capability of the offeror not backed up by any specific facts but based on general impressions).

In a number of cases, a source selection decision has been upheld on the basis that the SSA implicitly rescored some aspect of the evaluation. For example, in *PRC Kentron, Inc.*, Comp. Gen. Dec. B-230212, 88-1 CPD ¶ 537, rescoring was permitted to overcome the over reliance on incumbency by the evaluators, but "no formal rescoring was performed." See also *GTE Hawaiian Tel. Co.*, Comp. Gen. Dec. B-276487.2, 97-2 CPD ¶ 21 (SSA acted rationally in ignoring a significant difference in technical scores that seemed to greatly overstate the actual difference between the offerors); *NKF Eng'g, Inc.*, Comp. Gen. Dec. B-232143, 88-2 CPD ¶ 497 (contracting officer properly considered the protester's score an exaggera-tion of its technical superiority because the evaluation committee did not consider relevant factors in management and employee transition when giving the scores);

and *CRC Sys., Inc.*, Comp. Gen. Dec. B-207847, 83-1 CPD ¶ 462 (contracting officer implicitly lowered the protester's high score because its offer did not satisfy all the RFP requirements). In an unusual case, *Bank St. Coll. of Educ.*, 63 Comp. Gen. 393 (B-213209), 84-1 CPD ¶ 607, *recons. denied*, 84-2 CPD ¶ 445, the agency director overturned a finding of technical superiority made by a technical evaluation panel without actually altering the technical scores. GAO approved this intervention into the selection process finding that the director properly concluded that the awardee's proposal was actually technically superior because the level of effort in the protester's proposal deviated significantly from the RFP's estimated level of effort. Implicit rescoring is not sound practice and should be avoided. When the source selection official concludes that rescoring is necessary, the contract file should contain a clear indication of the rescoring that has occurred and the justification for that rescoring.

The SSA is also permitted to conduct a completely independent evaluation if the original evaluation is not acceptable. See *Benchmark Sec., Inc.*, Comp. Gen. Dec. B-247655.2, 93-1 CPD ¶ 133, where GAO affirmed the decision of the SSA after he completely altered the evaluation of the offerors, determined that the two best proposals were technically equal and that costs of performance would be equivalent, and selected the incumbent contractor — commenting that the evaluation and source selection were well reasoned and thoroughly documented. See also *Fort Carson Support Servs. v. United States*, 71 Fed. Cl. 571 (2006) (upholding SSA's reassessment of past performance of protester); *Jason Assocs. Corp.*, Comp. Gen. Dec. B-278689, 98-1 CPD ¶ 67 (upholding SSA's reevaluation of sample writings when it became known that they had been previously accepted by the agency); *EBA Eng'g, Inc.*, Comp. Gen. Dec. B-275818, 97-1 CPD ¶ 127 (upholding SSA's independent assessment when the evaluation panel was severely divided); *LTR Training Sys., Inc.*, Comp. Gen. Dec. B-274996, 97-1 CPD ¶ 71 (upholding SSA's decision to bypass the evaluations and make a completely independent assessment of the proposals determining that they were technically equal in merit); and *Ryan Assocs., Inc.*, Comp. Gen. Dec. B-274194, 97-1 CPD ¶ 2 (upholding SSA's independent cost/technical tradeoff differing from the technical evaluators' tradeoff analysis based on criticism of the contracting officer).

The SSA is permitted to use information in one of the segments of a proposal to alter an evaluation of another segment. For example, in a procurement which precluded the technical evaluators from seeing the pricing proposal, the source selection evaluation board made substantial adjustments to the technical evaluation based on information in the pricing proposal. GAO denied a protest — ruling that this procedure was entirely proper, *Cygna Project Mgmt.*, Comp. Gen. Dec. B-236839, 90-1 CPD ¶ 21. Failure to correlate the information in the segments of an offeror's proposal can lead to an irrational evaluation or at least to a poor selection of the source. Hence, SSAs should ensure that such correlation is made, with commensurate adjustments to the scores, before the source selection decision is made.

## 3. Allegations of Bias

Offerors are entitled to fair and impartial treatment in the source selection process and have a right to an unbiased determination of which source should receive the award. In a number of cases, charges have been made that the selection was based upon favoritism. However, it has been very difficult to overcome a decision through the allegation of bias of the SSA. In *Avtel Servs., Inc. v. United States*, 70 Fed. Cl. 173 (2005), the court held that a protester must overcome the presumption that government officials act in good faith in order to prove bias. In *Conax Fla. Corp. v. United States*, 641 F. Supp. 408 (D.D.C. 1986), *aff'd*, 824 F.2d 1124 (D.C. Cir. 1987), the court held that even if a protester establishes some degree of bias, it cannot win unless it can show that the source selection decision was unreasonable. In addition, in *Howard Cooper Corp. v. United States*, 763 F. Supp. 829, 841 (E.D. Va. 1991), the court, quoting *Arrowhead Metals, Ltd. v. United States*, 8 Cl. Ct. 703, 712 (1985), stated that claims of bias must be established by "well-nigh irrefragable proof." In *GE Gov't Servs., Inc. v. United States*, 788 F. Supp. 581 (D.D.C. 1992), a protester attempted to establish bias by providing statements about the SSA that demonstrated he was prejudiced against the protester. The protester also submitted evidence of sexual improprieties with a contractor employee. The court denied any relief because there was no proof that the source selection decision was affected by any alleged bias. It based its decision, to a large extent, on the fact that other agency officials that had participated in the procurement had also arrived at the decision that the selected contractor had offered the "best value" to the government.

GAO also requires very clear evidence of bias, *Crescent Helicopters*, Comp. Gen. Dec. B-283469.2, 99-2 CPD ¶ 107. For example, in *Centra Tech., Inc.*, Comp. Gen. Dec. B-274744, 97-1 CPD ¶ 35, GAO found no evidence that the personal relationship between the director of the Johnson Space Center and the president of the awardee firm improperly influenced the SSA's decision because the SSA was in a subordinate position to the director. GAO pointed out that although the director appointed the SSA, the director was not involved in the evaluation nor was there any evidence that the director had any contact with the source selection team during the course of the procurement. See also *TruLogic, Inc.*, Comp. Gen. Dec. B-297252.3, 2006 CPD ¶ 29 (failure to follow recommendation of evaluation panel not evidence of bias); *Millar Elevator Serv. Co.*, Comp. Gen. Dec. B-284870.5, 2001 CPD ¶ 34 (no proof of bias in letter written to a competitor by the project manager on a previous project, who was serving as an evaluator, suggesting that it could win this procurement by performing well on that project); and *J.A. Jones Grupo d Servicios, SA*, Comp. Gen. Dec. B-283234, 99-2 CPD ¶ 80 (no bias when contracting officer advised the incumbent contractor to make its oral presentation as if it were a new contractor and not rely on fact that it was the incumbent).

In several instances GAO has dealt with source selection decision effected by bias when the SSA admitted bias toward the Boeing Co. See *Lockheed Martin Aero-*

*nautics Co.*, Comp. Gen. Dec. B-295401, 2005 CPD ¶ 41 (protest sustained when biased SSA required technical ratings be changed and discussions to be reopened to favor Boeing); *Lockheed Martin Corp.*, Comp. Gen. Dec. B-295402, 2005 CPD ¶ 24 (protest sustained when biased senior procurement official deleted a requirement and its evaluation factor to favor Boeing). See also *Ball Aerospace & Techs. Corp.*, Comp. Gen. Dec. B-298522, 2006 CPD ¶ 113, rejecting a protest because it was not timely filed after the public admission of bias.

Although GAO normally rejects allegations of bias, it has recommended, in the face of protests of unfair treatment of an offeror, that the agency appoint a new source selection team to reevaluate the proposals. See, for example, *Meridian Mgmt. Corp.*, Comp. Gen. Dec. B-281287.10, 2001 CPD ¶ 5 (unequal treatment of offerors "makes it advisable to convene a new source selection team"). Agencies have also appointed new personnel as a means of overcoming allegations of bias. See *U-Tech Servs. Corp.*, Comp. Gen. Dec. B-284183.3, 2002 CPD ¶ 78 (entirely new team); *RTF/TCI/EAI J.V.*, Comp. Gen. Dec. B-280422.3, 98-2 CPD ¶ 162 (new evaluators); and *EBA Eng'g, Inc.*, Comp. Gen. Dec. B-275818, 97-1 CPD ¶ 127 (chairman of evaluation panel).

## B. Selection Decision

Neither the procurement statutes nor the FAR specify detailed standards for the source selection decision. The statutes merely require that the award is to be made "to the responsible source whose proposal is most advantageous to the United States, considering only cost or price and the other factors included in the solicitation," 10 U.S.C. § 2305(b)(4)(C) or "based solely on the factors specified in the solicitation," 41 U.S.C. § 3701(a). The FAR adds little, simply stating that the selection decision "shall be based upon a comparative assessment of proposals against all source selection criteria in the solicitation," FAR 15.308. Thus, the rules governing the source selection decision have been derived from decisions in contract award controversies.

The elements of the source selection decision are the comparative assessment of the proposals against the evaluation criteria and the ultimate tradeoff decision if the lowest price proposal is not rated most highly on the nonprice factors. The SSA has broad discretion in making the tradeoff decision but must make the decision consistent with the description of the evaluation factors and evaluation scheme in the solicitation.

### *I. Broad Discretion In Tradeoff Decision*

If the selection decision is based on the evaluation factors enumerated in the RFP, the selection official has broad discretion in determining which offer is most advantageous to the government. See *Lockheed Missiles & Space Co. v. Bentsen*, 4 F.3d 955 (Fed. Cir. 1993), stating that "effective contracting demands broad discretion." Thus, the selection will be upheld so long as there is a coherent and reasonable explanation for the selection, *Latecoere Int'l, Inc. v. Department of the Navy*, 19

F.3d 1342 (11th Cir. 1994). To be successful, a protester must show the selection to be "irrational or unreasonable," *Analytical & Research Tech., Inc. v. United States*, 39 Fed. Cl. 34 (1997). In *Brisk Waterproofing Co.*, Comp. Gen. Dec. B-276247, 97-1 CPD ¶ 195, GAO stated:

> [S]ource selection officials in negotiated procurements have broad discretion in determining the manner and extent to which they will make use of the technical and price results subject only to the tests of rationality and consistency with the RFP's evaluation factors. *Grey Advertising, Inc.*, 55 Comp. Gen. 1111, 1120-1121 (1976), 76-1 CPD ¶325 at 12.

See also *Research Triangle Inst.*, Comp. Gen. Dec. B-278254, 98-1 CPD ¶ 22; and *LTR Training Sys., Inc.*, Comp. Gen. Dec. B-274996, 97-1 CPD ¶ 71.

## 2.  Consistency With the Solicitation

Despite having a great deal of discretion in making the ultimate tradeoff decision, the SSA must follow the guidance in the RFP as to the way the selection decision will be made. However, the majority of decisions hold that there is no requirement that the SSA comply with the source selection plan adopted by the agency in formulating the procurement, *Manson Constr. Co. v. United States*, 79 Fed. Cl. 16 (2007); *Delta Dental of Cal.*, Comp. Gen. Dec. B-296307, 2005 CPD ¶ 152; DTH Mgmt. JV, Comp. Gen. Dec. B-283239, 99-2 CPD ¶ 68; *Allied Signal, Inc.*, Comp. Gen. Dec. B-272290, 96-2 CPD ¶ 121; *Johnson Controls World Servs., Inc.*, 72 Comp. Gen. 91 (B-249643.2), 93-1 CPD ¶ 72. Compare *Fort Carson Support Servs. v. United States*, 71 Fed. Cl. 571 (2006), holding that an agency's failure to adhere to its source selection plan made its source selection decision arbitrary, and *USFalcon, Inc. v. United States*, 92 Fed. Cl. 436 (2010), reasoning that a failure to follow the source selection plan without the approval of the SSA could be evidence of an erroneous evaluation.

### a.  Consideration of All Factors

The SSA must consider all evaluation factors as called for by the RFP and may not introduce new factors or subfactors into the process. See *Halter Marine, Inc.*, 73 Comp. Gen. 99 (B-255429), 94-1 CPD ¶ 161, sustaining a protest because the agency failed to consider a number of the enumerated evaluation factors. See also *Navistar Def., LLC*, Comp. Gen. Dec. B-401865, 2009 CPD ¶ 258 (improper to fail to consider risk of lack of key tooling when RFP stated that existing production capability would be evaluated for risk); *Apptis, Inc.*, Comp. Gen. Dec. B-299457, 2008 CPD ¶ 49 (past performance improperly used to evaluate risk of technical solution); *ProTech Corp.*, Comp. Gen. Dec. B-294818, 2005 CPD ¶ 73 ("betterments" not given consideration called for by RFP); *KIRA, Inc.*, Comp. Gen. Dec. B-287573, 2001 CPD ¶ 152 (improper to consider possible bankruptcy of subcontractor because financial ability was not a factor); *Courtland Mem'l Hosp.*, Comp. Gen. Dec. B-286890, 2001 CPD ¶ 48 (one factor not given the importance stated in the RFP and another factor ignored); *Wackenhut Int'l, Inc.*, Comp. Gen. Dec. B-286193, 2001 CPD ¶ 8 (improper to not consider full compensation plan when RFP called for comprehensive review of plans); *Meridian Mgmt. Corp*, Comp. Gen. Dec. B-285127, 2000 CPD ¶ 121 (improper to consider experience in performing specialized work when RFP gave no indication that such work was required); *Lloyd H. Kessler, Inc.*, Comp. Gen. Dec. B-284693, 2000 CPD ¶ 96 (improper to consider undesignated special experience that was treated as 40% of total nonprice evaluation); *AIU North Am., Inc.*, Comp. Gen. Dec. B-283743.2, 2000 CPD ¶ 39 (agency did not consider the "availability of corporate resources" factor); and *Marquette Med. Sys., Inc.*, Comp. Gen. Dec. B-277827.5, 99-1 CPD ¶ 90 (improper to consider agency's internal savings for use of items when no indication of life cycle cost factor in RFP).

The evaluation criteria in the RFP must be followed even if this produces an irrational result. See *Unified Indus., Inc.*, Comp. Gen. Dec. B-237868, 90-1 CPD ¶ 346, *recons. denied*, 90-2 CPD ¶ 120, where the agency was required to follow the RFP statement that all offerors would be evaluated using "the same number of hours" even though this meant evaluating the incumbent contractor on labor hours that it would not incur in performing the proposed contract. GAO dismissed the Navy's argument that this would be "irrational and unrealistic" holding that the rule requiring evaluation in accordance with the RFP was firm. Clearly, in this case, the agency should have amended the evaluation criteria in the RFP when it found that the stated criteria produced an irrational result.

As discussed in Section II, this rule does not prevent evaluation using any matters within the scope of the factors and subfactors set forth in the RFP, and there are numerous cases giving a broad interpretation of scope.

### b. Follow Selection Scheme

The SSA must follow the decisional scheme described in the RFP. For example, if the RFP states that award will be made to the proposal with the best value based on a tradeoff analysis, the agency may not select the lowest-priced offer among those proposals that are technically acceptable, *Special Operations Group, Inc.*, Comp. Gen. Dec. B-287013, 2001 CPD ¶ 73; *Technical Support Serv., Inc.*, Comp. Gen. Dec. B-279665, 98-2 CPD ¶ 126; and *DynCorp*, 71 Comp. Gen. 129 (D-245289), 91-2 CPD ¶ 575. Neither may an agency evaluate one of the non-price factors on a pass/fail basis when the RFP lists it as a factor to be used in making a tradeoff decision, *Helicopter Transport Servs., LLC*, Comp. Gen. Dec. B-400295, 2008 CPD ¶ 180. See also *Beacon Auto Parts*, Comp. Gen. Dec. B-287483, 2001 CPD ¶ 116, where a protest was sustained because the agency awarded to the offeror with the best technical score after determining that it had proposed a "fair and reasonable" price. GAO concluded that no tradeoff had been made in these circumstances even though the source selection decision stated that the winning offeror's proposal was "considered the best value to the government based on past performance and technical capability."

In a tradeoff procurement, an SSA may not select the offeror with the best technical proposal from among only those offerors that submitted good prices. See *Electronic Design, Inc.*, Comp. Gen. Dec. B-279662.2, 98-2 CPD ¶ 69, where the agency chose the best technical offer from those that were priced within the agency budget. GAO granted the protest, stating:

> An evaluation and source selection which fails to give significant consideration to cost or price is inconsistent with CICA and cannot serve as a reasonable basis for award. . . . Cost or price has not been accorded significant consideration if the agency's evaluation and source selection decision so minimizes the potential impact of cost or price as to make it a nominal evaluation factor. *Coastal Science and Eng'g, Inc.*, B-236041, Nov. 7, 1989, 89-2 CPD ¶ 436 at 3.

> Here, the agency states that price was considered only to determine whether a proposal was eligible for award. Proposals with prices greater than the budget were not eligible for, nor considered for award. Once three of the proposals were determined eligible for award based on price, the Navy states that it did not consider the relative differences in price among the proposals, and did not perform a price/technical tradeoff; rather, technical merit was the sole consideration in the selection decision. Thus, to the extent the agency did consider price in this procurement, it was solely to determine basic eligibility for award. Such a consideration of price is nominal; indeed, anything less would be to ignore price completely.

Conversely, an agency must include in its tradeoff analysis any lower-priced offeror that submits an acceptable proposal, *Finlen Complex, Inc.*, Comp. Gen. Dec. B-288280, 2001 CPD ¶ 167. See also *Coastal Env'ts, Inc.*, Comp. Gen. Dec. B-401889, 2009 CPD ¶ 261 (improper tradeoff between the two offerors that had been rated "good" on the non-price factors, omitting consideration of lower offerors that had been rated "acceptable"); *T-C Transcription, Inc.*, Comp. Gen. Dec. B-401470, 2009 CPD ¶ 172 (improper tradeoff between offeror rated "excellent" on non-price factors and lowest priced offeror rated "good" — omitting other offerors rated "good"); *Universal Bldg. Maint., Inc.*, Comp. Gen. Dec. B-282456, 99-2 CPD ¶ 32 (improper consideration of only the four highest ranked technical proposals with the result that no tradeoff analysis was made of the protester's lowest price proposal). See also *A & D Fire Protection, Inc.*, Comp. Gen. Dec. B-288852, 2001 CPD ¶ 201, where a protest was sustained when the agency made no tradeoff analysis on proposals that were not "sufficiently technical capable to perform the project." GAO found that the agency had determined that the protester's proposal was technically acceptable and therefore was required to include it in the tradeoff analysis. This rule does not apply to technically unacceptable proposals, which need not be subjected to a tradeoff analysis, *SBC Fed. Sys.*, Comp. Gen. Dec. B-283693, 2000 CPD ¶ 5.

When making multiple awards, an agency must perform a tradeoff analysis between all of the offerors with acceptable offers. Thus, it is improper to drop the highest rated technical proposal because it contains such a high price that it does not win against the lowest price proposal, *Beneco Enters., Inc.*, Comp. Gen. Dec. B-283154, 2000 CPD ¶ 69. GAO reasoned that the protester might have won against the two other awardees that had higher prices even though they had higher technical evaluations than the lowest price proposal. See also *Boeing Sikorsky Aircraft Support*, Comp. Gen. Dec. B-277263.2, 97-2 CPD ¶ 91, ruling that probable cost was a mandatory element of the source selection decision in a procurement involving a cost-reimbursement contract, and *Geo-Centers, Inc.*, Comp. Gen. Dec. B-276033, 97-1 CPD ¶ 182, holding that the offerors' costs to perform sample tasks had to be considered in making a source selection decision on a cost-reimbursement contract. In *MIS Farms, Inc.*, Comp. Gen. Dec. B-290599, 2002 CPD ¶ 174, GAO held that it was improper to deduct points when an offeror met a mandatory minimum requirement.

### c.   Use of Scores

In tradeoff procurements, the SSA is required to make the source selection decision by comparing the differences in non-price factors with the differences in prices. See FAR 15.308 calling for a "comparative assessment of proposals against all source selection criteria in the solicitation." In almost all cases this means that the scores assigned to the proposals should not be used, by themselves, to make the source selection decision. See *JW Assocs., Inc.*, Comp. Gen. Dec. B-275209, 96-2 CPD ¶ 18, stating:

> While both adjectival ratings and point scores are useful as guides to decision-making, they generally are not controlling, but rather, must be supported by documentation of the relative differences between proposals, their weaknesses and risks, and the basis and reasons for the selection decision.

See *Allied Signal, Inc.*, Comp. Gen. Dec. B-272290, 96-2 CPD ¶ 121, stating that "a selection should reflect the procuring agency's considered judgment of whether significant technical differences exist in the proposals that identify a particular proposal as technically superior regardless of close scores or ratings among proposals." See also *Wackenhut Servs., Inc. v. United States*, 85 Fed. Cl. 273 (2008) (no tradeoff between price and non-price factors); *Shumaker Trucking & Excavating Contractors, Inc.*, Comp. Gen. Dec. B-290732, 2002 CPD ¶ 169 (higher point score on technical not justification for selection of higher price offer), *DevTech Sys., Inc.*, Comp. Gen. Dec. B-284879, 2000 CPD ¶ 200 (based on detailed analysis, 6% higher technical score does not indicate superior technical proposal). In *Computer Tech. Servs., Inc.*, Comp. Gen. Dec. B-271435, 96-1 CPD ¶ 283, GAO approved the SSA's probing of the evaluation team to determine the significance of differences in point scores, stating:

> Selection officials must decide whether the point scores show technical superiority and what that difference may mean in terms of contract performance. *See Grey Advertising, Inc.*, 55 Comp. Gen. 1111 (1976) 76-1 CPD ¶ 325.

* * *

Source selection officials in appropriate circumstances properly may conclude that a numerical scoring advantage based primarily on incumbency does not indicate an actual technical superiority that would warrant paying a higher price, *Sparta, Inc.*, B-228216, Jan. 15, 1988, 88-1 CPD ¶ 37; *see also Northern Virginia Serv. Corp.*, B-258036.2; B-258036.3, Jan. 23, 1995, 95-1 CPD ¶ 36, n. 5 (citing *NUS Corp.; The Austin Co.*, B-221863; B-221863.2, June 20, 1986, 86-1 CPD ¶ 574), and we see nothing unreasonable about the SSA's conclusion here. Accordingly, we think that the SSA's conclusion that [the protester's] numerical rating advantage did not reflect an actual technical superiority that would warrant paying its higher price also was a reasonable exercise of the SSA's discretion.

This logic was approved by the Federal Circuit in *Lockheed Missiles & Space Co. v. Bentsen*, 4 F.3d 955 (Fed. Cir. 1993), where the court stated at 960:

Neither the FAR nor the broad language of the RFP requires that evaluation points be proportional to cost. Accordingly, a proposal which is one point better than another but costs millions of dollars more may be selected if the agency can demonstrate within a reasonable certainty that the added value of the proposal is worth the higher price. Here, as we have already noted, the [agency] tradeoff analysis revealed that the dollar value of the two technical subfactors together with the value of the nonquantified discriminators justified the additional price to the [winning offeror's] proposal.

Accord, *Grumman Data Sys. v. Dalton*, 88 F. 3d 990 (Fed. Cir. 1996). Thus, the selection will be upheld so long as there is a coherent and reasonable explanation for the selection, *Latecoere Int'l, Inc. v. Department of the Navy*, 19 F.3d 1342 (11th Cir. 1994).

### (1) IMPROPER RELIANCE ON SCORES

Since the tradeoff decision must be made on the basis of the relative strengths, weaknesses and risks of the proposals, a bare comparison of point scores will not demonstrate that the agency has made a rational source selection decision. See *Shumaker Trucking & Excavating Contractors, Inc.*, Comp. Gen. Dec. B-290732, 2002 CPD ¶ 169, where the source selection decision stated:

It was the recommendation of the technical evaluation board that the URS Group has presented the best value based on its overall technical evaluation and price. It received the highest technical evaluation, scoring 134 points, verses 93 points for Shumaker Trucking. This represents a technical difference of 44 percent (134/93=1.44). Also the difference on item 3, which is the technical approach to perform the work, the difference was even greater, being 20 points for Shumaker Trucking and 43 points for URS. This represents over 100 percent difference in this important aspect.

The URS Group's bid, while being below the Government Estimate, is within 2 percent. The URS Group was selected for recommendation of award as they offer the best overall value to the Government. This is based on their technical score and the price being fair and reasonable. While they are somewhat higher than the second rated firm (Shumaker Trucking) the Technical Evaluation Board and the Contracting Officer felt the difference in cost of $395,739.05 is justified based on the superior scoring on past performance and technical approach provided in their proposal.

GAO sustained the protest, stating:

> The record contains no evidence that the agency compared the advantages of the awardee's proposal to those of Shumaker's proposal, or considered why any advantages of the awardee's proposal were worth the approximately $400,000 higher price. As we have previously stated, point scores are but guides to intelligent decision making. *Ready Transp., Inc.*, B-285283.3, B-285283.4, May 8, 2001, 2001 CPD ¶ 90 at 12. In this case the [agency's] tradeoff is inadequate because its mechanical comparison of the offerors' point scores was not a valid substitute for a qualitative assessment of the technical differences between the offers from URS and Shumaker, so as to determine whether URS's technical superiority justified the price premium involved.

There are several GAO decisions finding a source selection unreasonable because it was based on a "mechanical comparison" of scores. See *Midland Supply, Inc.*, Comp. Gen. Dec. B-298720, 2007 CPD ¶ 2 (decision based on total points without any tradeoff analysis); *Johnson Controls World Servs., Inc.*, Comp. Gen. Dec. B-289942, 2002 CPD ¶ 88 (decision based solely on number of "outstanding" and "highly satisfactory" ratings); *Opti-Lite Optical*, Comp. Gen. Dec. B-281693, 99-1 CPD ¶ 61 (decision based solely on point scores for technical and price when RFP did not state award would be made to offeror with most points); and *Teltara Inc.*, Comp. Gen. Dec. B-280922, 98-2 CPD ¶ 124 (decision based on percentage differences in price and technical scores). In *Wackenhut Servs., Inc.*, Comp. Gen. Dec. B-400240, 2008 CPD ¶ 184, the protester argued that its proposal was superior because it received more "strengths" than the winning offeror. GAO denied the protest concluding that the protester was asking for a "mathematical or mechanical consideration" of the scores which was not the correct way to make the source selection decision. The Court of Federal Claims reached the opposite conclusion in *Wackenhut Servs., Inc. v. United States*, 85 Fed. Cl. 273 (2008), concluding that the source evaluation board's increase of point scores was arbitrary because it was not adequately justified. This may indicate that the court is more willing to grant relief when there are disparities in scoring — even though the scores are not the ultimate basis for the source selection decision.

## (2) GENERAL STATEMENTS

General statements as to the merits of the various proposals are also insufficient to demonstrate that a satisfactory tradeoff analysis has been made. See *Serco, Inc. v. United States*, 81 Fed. Cl. 463 (2008), stating at 496-97:

[FAR 15.308] requires the agency to make a business judgment as to whether the higher price of an offer is worth the technical benefits its acceptance will afford. *See, e.g., TRW, Inc.*, 98 F.3d at 1327; *Dismas Charities, Inc.*, 61 Fed. Cl. at 203. Doing this, the decisional law demonstrates, obliges the agency to do more than simply parrot back the strengths and weaknesses of the competing proposals — rather, the agency must dig deeper and determine whether the relative strengths and weaknesses of the competing proposals are such that it is worth paying a higher price. Second, in performing the tradeoff analysis, the agency need neither assign an exact dollar value to the worth associated with the technical benefits of a contract nor otherwise quantify the non-cost factors. FAR § 15.308 ("the documentation need not quantify the tradeoffs that led to the decision"); *Widnall v. B3H Corp.*, 75 F.3d 1577, 1580 (Fed. Cir. 1996). But, this is not to say that the magnitude of the price differential between the two offers is irrelevant — logic suggests that as that magnitude increases, the relative benefits yielded by the higher-priced offer must also increase. *See Beneco Enters., Inc.*, 2000 CPD ¶ 69 at 5 (1999). To conclude otherwise, threatens to "minimize[] the potential impact of price" and, in particular, to make "a nominal technical advantage essentially determinative, irrespective of an overwhelming price premium." *Coastal Sci. and Eng'g, Inc.*, 89-2 CPD ¶ 436 at 2 (1989); *see also Lockheed Missiles & Space Co.*, 4 F.3d at 959-60. Finally — and many cases turn on this point — the agency is compelled by the FAR to document its reasons for choosing the higher-priced offer. Conclusory statements, devoid of any substantive content, have been held to fall short of this requirement, threatening to turn the tradeoff process into an empty exercise. Indeed, apart from the regulations, generalized statements that fail to reveal the agency's tradeoff calculus deprive this court of any basis upon which to review the award decisions. *See Johnson Controls World Servs.*, 2002 CPD ¶ 88 at 6; *Satellite Servs., Inc.*, 2001 CPD ¶ 30 at 9-11; *Si-Nor, Inc.*, 2000 CPD ¶ 159 at 3 (1999).

See also *Blue Rock Structures, Inc.*, Comp. Gen. Dec. B-293134, 2004 CPD ¶ 63, sustaining a protest where the source selection decision merely concluded that the protester's higher rated proposal was essentially equal to the winning proposals without any discussion or analysis of the differences in the proposals. GAO stated:

> A tradeoff analysis that fails to furnish any explanation as to why a higher-rated proposal does not in fact offer technical advantages or why those technical advantages are not worth a price premium does not satisfy the requirement for a documented tradeoff rationale, particularly where, as here, price is secondary to technical considerations under the RFP's evaluation scheme.

See also *LIS, Inc.*, Comp. Gen. Dec. B-400646.2, 2010 CPD ¶ 5 (general statement that selected offeror addressed all agency concerns without any analysis of strength, weaknesses or risks in proposals); *Systems Research & Applications Corp.*, Comp. Gen. Dec. B-299818, 2008 CPD ¶ 28 (no qualitative assessment of strengths of competing proposals to satisfy agency requirements using different approaches); *Preferred Sys. Solutions, Inc.*, Comp. Gen. Dec. B-292322, 2003 CPD ¶ 166 (general statement that the proposals had "nearly equivalent ratings in non-cost areas" inadequate explanation of why protester's highly rated proposal was not worth its higher costs and prices); *Johnson Controls World Servs., Inc.*, Comp. Gen. Dec. B-289942, 2002 CPD ¶ 88 (general statement that higher scored proposal contained "no discernible benefits" inadequate demonstration of tradeoff analysis); *Si-Nor, Inc.*, Comp. Gen. Dec. B-282064, 2000 CPD ¶ 159 (bare statement that better past performance was worth over 10% more); *Lloyd H. Kessler, Inc.*, Comp. Gen. Dec. B-284693, 2000 CPD ¶ 96 (mere statement that "concerns arising from reports of adverse past performance" justified paying a higher cost); *Beneco Enters., Inc.*, Comp. Gen. Dec. B-283154, 2000 CPD ¶ 69 (statement that "the benefits and advantages" of the protester's higher-rated technical proposal did not justify "payment of the significant additional price" and is not "in the best interest of the Government" insufficient proof of rational tradeoff analysis); and *TRW, Inc.*, 68 Comp. Gen. 511 (B-234558), 89-1 CPD ¶ 584 ("Monte Carlo" risk analysis, computing potential costs of improving proposal with low ratings not a demonstration that tradeoff analysis considered differences in evaluations).

### (3) DETERMINATIONS OF EQUALITY

There are a large number of cases where the SSA properly exercises discretion by ignoring differences in technical scoring by evaluators and determining that the technical merit of competing offers is relatively equal, thus allowing contracts to be awarded to the lower-cost offeror. In *Verify, Inc.*, 71 Comp. Gen. 158 (B-244401.2), 92-1 CPD ¶ 107, for example, the contracting personnel and evaluators agreed that the original technical scores given to Verify were an overstatement of merit and that rescoring was necessary to achieve accuracy. The final score given by the contracting officer was actually lower than the original score and supported a finding of technical equality between Verify and the lower cost awardee. Similarly, in *Resource Mgmt. Int'l, Inc.*, Comp. Gen. Dec. B-278108, 98-1 CPD ¶ 29, the SSA made a careful assessment of the evaluations and determined that the slightly higher technical score of the protester was not significantly different from that of a lower-priced offeror.

In most cases such determinations of equality are made without explicitly rescoring the proposals. For example, in *Jack Faucett Assocs. — Request for Recons.*, Comp. Gen. Dec. B-233224.2, 89-1 CPD ¶ 551, the contracting officer properly awarded the contract to the low-priced offeror after concluding that Faucett's higher-price offer, with a technical score of 8.63 out of 10 points, was substantially equal to the lower-priced offeror's technical score of 8.22. See also *RONCO Consulting Corp.*, Comp. Gen. Dec. B-280113, 98-2 CPD ¶ 41 (technical evaluation committee advised the contracting officer that it had no preference among three offerors with different technical scores); *EBA Eng'g, Inc.*, Comp. Gen. Dec. B-275818, 97-1 CPD ¶ 127 (SSA determined that the technical proposals were basically equal even though the source selection panel rated the protester higher on every evaluation factor); *LTR*

*Training Sys., Inc.*, Comp. Gen. Dec. B-274996, 97-1 CPD ¶ 71 (contracting officer found the proposals technically equal although the evaluators had scored the protester's proposal substantially higher); *Juarez & Assocs., Inc.*, Comp. Gen. Dec. B-265950.2, 96-1 CPD ¶ 152 (contracting officer found the proposals technically equal when the evaluators had scored the protester's proposal somewhat higher); *General Offshore Corp.*, Comp. Gen. Dec. B-246824, 92-1 CPD ¶ 335 (contracting officer properly found that a nine percent higher technical score did not represent any actual technical superiority and awarded to the lower-cost offeror); and *Systems Integrated*, Comp. Gen. Dec. B-225055, 87-1 CPD ¶ 114 (low-priced awardee's technical score of 66.7 out of 80 points was properly considered by the contracting officer to be equal to the 68.1 technical score of the higher-priced offer).

Such a determination of equality has also been supported in a case where the RFP called for precise numerical scores for technical and cost factors and stated that award would be made to the offeror with the highest number of points. GAO stated that the source selection official would not have been permitted to alter the cost/technical tradeoff announced in the RFP but was entitled to rescore the proposals by determining that the technical proposals were equal, *Harrison Sys., Ltd.*, 63 Comp. Gen. 379 (B-212675), 84-1 CPD ¶ 572. See also *Crowley Maritime Salvage*, Comp. Gen. Dec. B-234555, 89-1 CPD ¶ 555 (award to lower point total permissible where contracting officer determined that a 14.4 % difference in technical score was not significant).

GAO has permitted determinations of equality even though the technical factors are weighted more heavily than cost, *E.J. Richardson Assocs., Inc.*, Comp. Gen. Dec. B-250951, 93-1 CPD ¶ 185 (technical scores of 93.3 and 90.0 found substantially equal when technical factor "slightly more important" than cost); *WB, Inc.*, Comp. Gen. Dec. B-250954, 93-1 CPD ¶ 173 (technical scores of 88 and 87 found essentially equal when technical factor was "primary" and price/cost was "least important"); *Systems Research Corp.*, Comp. Gen. Dec. B-237008, 90-1 CPD ¶ 106 (technical scores of 48.15 and 54.63 found equal where technical factors had weight of 60%); *DDL Omni Eng'g*, Comp. Gen. Dec. B-220075, 85-2 CPD ¶ 684 (technical scores of 6.61 and 6.96 found equal where the technical score was "of paramount importance" but variable).

A finding of equality of technical scores is frequently upheld where technical evaluators can give no cogent reasons explaining the technical point differential between two proposals. This was permitted in *DLM&A, Inc. v. United States*, 6 Cl. Ct. 329 (1984), where the selection official determined on this basis that the proposals were "substantially equal" and, therefore, awarded to the low cost proposal.

Determinations of equality will be overturned if they are not supported by reasoned analysis. See, for example, *Radiation Oncology Group of WNY, PC*, Comp. Gen. Dec. B-310354.2, 2009 CPD ¶ 136 (no support for contracting officer's conclusion that offerors with different point scores were equal); *DynCorp*, Comp. Gen.

Dec. B-232999, 89-1 CPD ¶ 152 (no rational explanation for ignoring evaluators' concerns); *University Found., California State Univ., Chico*, Comp. Gen. Dec. B-200608, 81-1 CPD ¶ 54 (no indication given as to why the evaluation point scores were not followed in awarding the contract). See also *Tracor Jitco, Inc.*, 54 Comp. Gen. 896 (B-182213), 75-1 CPD ¶ 253, where the source selection was based on the conclusion of one evaluator that the proposals were technically equal, but no reasoning was advanced to support the conclusion and it conflicted with the factually supported views of two other evaluators and the technical evaluation committee. The selection decision was later found to be supportable, after a review of the selection process by the procuring agency showed that the evaluator had judged the proposals technically equal on the basis of additional information from the awardee that cleared up deficiencies, *Tracor Jitco, Inc.*, 55 Comp. Gen. 499 (B-182213), 75-2 CPD ¶ 344.

The selection official is not required to find the proposals equal when the point differential is small. See *Super Teams Operating Co.*, Comp. Gen. Dec. B-260100, 95-1 CPD ¶ 246, where the protester received a technical score of 83.3, the awardee received a score of 86.7, and a third (high-cost) offeror received a technical score of 91.1. The source selection official considered the 86.7 and 91.1 scores to be technically equal. The protester argued that if difference of 4.4 points makes two proposals technically equal, the smaller difference of 2.9 points must make its proposal equal to the awardee's technical proposal. GAO denied the protest, stating that "closeness of point scores does not necessarily indicate that proposals are essentially equal." The source selection official determined that there were significant differences in the technical merit between the proposals and this difference was reflected in the narrative summaries. See also *Bell & Howell Corp.*, Comp. Gen. Dec. B-196165, 81-2 CPD ¶ 49, upholding the decision that close technical scores were not equal, stating "[t]he dispositive element in a case such as this is not the technical scores per se but the considered judgment of the procuring agency concerning the significance of that difference."

## d.  Impact of Statement of Relative Importance

. In procurements where the source selection official is given discretion to select the offeror proposing the best value, the statement of relative importance in the RFP does not play a significant rule in the source selection decision. This is because the tradeoff between price/cost and non-price/cost factors made by the selection official must still be based on the established criteria and the ultimate decision will be based on an assessment of whether the difference in the non-price/cost factors is worth the difference in price/cost. For example, if the RFP states that non-price factors are significantly more important than price/cost, award would rationally be made to the low price/cost offer when the difference in the non-price factors was small. Conversely, if the RFP states that price/cost is significantly more important than the non-price/cost factors, award would rationally be made to the a higher priced/

cost offer when there was a significant difference in the non-price/cost factors. Thus, as illustrated below, whatever the statement of relative importance, a reasonable tradeoff between price/cost and the other factors will be supported.

## (1) NON-PRICE/COST MORE IMPORTANT THAN PRICE/COST

If the RFP states that the non-price/cost factors are more important than price/cost, the SSA is permitted to select an offeror that has proposed a significantly higher price if the benefits in the non-price/cost factors can be identified. See, for example, *Comprehensive Health Servs., Inc.*, Comp. Gen. Dec. B-310553, 2008 CPD ¶ 9 (RFP stated that technical approach, management capability and past performance significantly more important than price); *Textron, Inc. v. United States*, 74 Fed. Cl. 277 (2006) (RFP stated that management, systems engineering, mission effectiveness, and support significantly more important than price in contract to design and manufacture boats); *Puglia Eng'g of California, Inc.*, Comp. Gen. Dec. B-297413, 2006 CPD ¶ 33 (RFP stated that five non-price factors were significantly more important than price); *Remington Arms Co.*, Comp. Gen. Dec. B-297374, 2006 CPD ¶ 32 (RFP stated that bid sample and technical proposal significantly more important than price); *Standard Commc's, Inc.*, Comp. Gen. Dec. B-296972, 2005 CPD ¶ 200 (RFP stated that mission capability, past performance and risk significantly more important than price); *Chenega Tech. Prods., LLC*, Comp. Gen. Dec. B-295451.5, 2005 CPD ¶ 123 (RFP stated that past performance significantly more important than price); *Continental RPVs*, Comp. Gen. Dec. B-292768.6, 2004 CPD ¶ 103 (RFP made non-price factors more important than price); and *Information Network Sys., Inc.*, Comp. Gen. Dec. B-284854, 2000 CPD ¶ 104 (better prospect of workforce retention worth slightly higher probable cost). In contrast, award to the higher-priced offeror has been overturned in a few cases where the benefits could not be demonstrated. See *Sturm, Ruger & Co.*, Comp. Gen. Dec. B-250193, 93-1 CPD ¶ 42, overturning a $1,366,550 award to an offeror receiving a technical score of 94 points when the protester had received a score of 89 points and had proposed a price of $768,012. GAO rejected the agency's contention that price should only be considered when the technical scores were equal and held that, in such a best value procurement, award to the higher-priced offer "should be supported by a specific, documented determination that the technical superiority of the higher-priced offer warrants the additional cost involved, even where, as here, cost is stated to be the least important factor." See also *ITT Fed. Servs. Int'l Corp.*, Comp. Gen. Dec. B-296783, 2007 CPD ¶ 43 (unreasonable evaluation made decision to pay higher price questionable); *YORK Bldg. Servs., Inc.*, Comp. Gen. Dec. B-296948.2, 2005 CPD ¶ 202 (flawed evaluation made decision to pay higher price questionable); *Spherix, Inc.*, Comp. Gen. Dec. B-294572.3, 2005 CPD ¶ 183 (failure to consider relative similarities and differences in the two proposals made decision to pay higher price questionable); *Beautify Prof'l Servs. Corp.*, Comp. Gen. Dec. B-291954.3, 2003 CPD ¶ 178 (award to highest rated past performance without considering that it was 25% higher in price not proper); and *CRAssocs., Inc.*, Comp. Gen. Dec. B-282075.2, 2000 CPD ¶ 63 (inadequate documentation and potential evaluation errors made decision to pay significantly higher costs questionable).

Selection of a lower priced proposal is justified if the SSA determines that the benefits in the non-price/cost factors offered by the high priced offeror are not worth the higher cost. See, for example, *United Eng'rs & Constructors, Inc.*, Comp. Gen. Dec. B-240691, 90-2 CPD ¶ 490, agreeing with a decision to award to an offeror that was $11 million lower in probable cost even though a competitor had submitted a clearly superior technical and management proposal. The RFP had stated that management and technical factors were more important than cost but that award would be made to the most advantageous proposal. GAO stated:

> [E]ven if cost is the least important evaluation criterion, an agency may properly award to a lower-cost, lower-scored offeror if it determines that the cost premium involved in awarding to a higher-rated, higher-cost offeror is not justified given the acceptable level of technical competence available at the lower cost. *Carrier Joint Venture*, B-233702, Mar. 13, 1989, 89-1 CPD ¶ 268, *aff'd*, B-233702.2, June 23, 1989, 89-1 CPD ¶ 594. The determining element is not the difference in technical merit, per se, but the contracting agency's judgment concerning the significance of the difference. *Dayton T. Brown, Inc.*, B-229664, Mar. 30, 1988, 88-1 CPD ¶ 321. Cost/technical tradeoffs may be made, and the extent to which one may be sacrificed for the other is governed only by the test of rationality and consistency with the established evaluation criteria.

See also *Karrar Sys. Corp.*, Comp. Gen. Dec. B- 310661.3, 2008 CPD ¶ 55 (rational to award at significantly lower price when non-price differential between offerors was small); *First Preston Housing Initiatives, LP,* Comp. Gen. Dec. B-293105.2, 2004 CPD ¶ 221 (award at lower price justified when non-price factors were evaluated as essentially equal); *Mechanical Equip. Co.*, Comp. Gen. Dec. B-292789.2, 2004 CPD ¶ 192 (rational to award at significantly lower price when either company could perform contract); *E.L. Hamm & Assocs., Inc.*, Comp. Gen. Dec. B-280766.5, 2000 CPD ¶ 13 (rational to award to lower cost because technical benefits not worth difference); *Randolph Eng'g Sunglasses*, Comp. Gen. Dec. B-280270, 98-2 CPD ¶ 39 (reasonable to award at lower price to offeror evaluated as "good" on past performance rather than to higher-priced offeror evaluated as "excellent"); and *East/West Indus., Inc.*, Comp. Gen. Dec. B-278734.4, 98-1 CPD ¶ 143 (reasonable to award to low priced proposal with medium risk rather than to the higher-priced proposal with low risk). In contrast, award to a lower-priced offeror will be overturned if the source selection official cannot state a reasonable basis for giving up the non-price/cost benefits offered by the higher priced offeror with such benefits. For instance, in *Dewberry & Davis*, Comp. Gen. Dec. B-247116, 92-1 CPD ¶ 421, a protest was sustained because the agency did not provide justification of its selection of the lower-priced proposal where the RFP had stated that technical was more important than cost. GAO stated that it would uphold such a decision only if the agency provided a "cogent rationale" in the documentation for such a decision. See also *PharmChem Lab., Inc.*, Comp. Gen. Dec. B-244385, 91-2 CPD ¶ 317 (not reasonable to save a small difference in cost when high-cost offeror was clearly superior); *Hattal & Assocs.*, 70 Comp. Gen. 632 (B-243357 ), 91-2 CPD ¶90 (not reasonable to award to lower-cost offeror when the two competitors were both determined to be "technically acceptable"). In some cases involving cost-reimbursement contracts, GAO has stressed the "extremely strong justification" necessary to support award to a lower cost proposal which is ranked lower in the non-price/cost factors, *DLI Eng'g Corp.*, Comp. Gen. Dec. B-218335, 85-1 CPD ¶742, *recons. denied*, 65 Comp. Gen. 34 (B-218335.2), 85-2 CPD ¶468; *RCA Serv. Co.*, Comp. Gen. Dec. B-219406.2, 86-2 CPD ¶278; *AAA Eng'g & Drafting, Inc.*, Comp. Gen. Dec. B-202140, 81-2 CPD ¶16.

## (2) Price/Cost More Important Than Non-Price/Cost

When the RFP states that price is more important than the other factors, the SSA can award the contract to the offeror with the lowest price as long as the price advantage outweighs the technical advantage of higher-priced offerors, *GTE Hawaiian Tel. Co.*, Comp. Gen. Dec. B-276487.2, 97-2 CPD ¶ 21. See also *Geo-Seis Helicopters, Inc.*, Comp. Gen. Dec. B-299175, 2007 CPD ¶ 135 (rational to award at lower price when price was more important than past performance and difference in past performance was "exceptional" versus "neutral"); *MD Helicopters, Inc.*, Comp. Gen. Dec. B-298502, 2006 CPD ¶ 164 (rational to award at lower price when price was more important than non-price factors). In contrast, the SSA is also permitted to award the contract to an offeror with a higher price if the differences in the non-price/cost factors are worth paying the higher costs. Thus, in *Frequency Eng'g Lab. Corp.*, Comp. Gen. Dec. B-225606 , 87-1 CPD ¶393, award at a price of $57.6 million was permitted when the protester had offered a price of $51.2 milion but had proposed to use less qualified personnel whom the agency evaluated as posing a much higher risk that performance would not be successfully accomplished. See also *Centex Constr. Co.*, Comp. Gen. Dec. B-238777, 90-1 CPD ¶ 566 (award to offeror with slightly higher price justified by strong technical rating); *Oklahoma Aerotronics, Inc.*, Comp. Gen. Dec. B-237705.2, 90-1 CPD ¶ 337 (award to an offeror with 2% higher price justified by the lower technical risk obtained); and *F.A.S. Sys. Corp.*, Comp. Gen. Dec. B-236344, 89-2 CPD ¶ 512 (award to offeror with $1,100,000 higher price justified when detailed agency evaluation indicated significantly stronger technical ability).

## (3) Price and Non-Price/Cost Equally Important

When the price/cost factor and the non-price/cost factors are stated to be equal, the source selection official probably has the greatest discretion to make a "best value" source selection decision. In *440 East 62d Street Co.*, Comp. Gen. Dec. B-276058.2, 98-1 CPD ¶ 73, and *EER Sys. Corp.*, 69 Comp. Gen. 207 (B-237054),

90-1 CPD ¶ 123, selection decisions for a higher priced, higher technically rated offeror were affirmed because they provided the best value to the government. See also *J.C.N. Constr. Co.*, Comp. Gen. Dec. B-293063, 2004 CPD ¶ 12 (award at higher price because of higher technical rating); *Kay & Assocs., Inc.*, Comp. Gen. Dec. B-291269, 2003 CPD ¶ 12 (award at higher price because of better past performance); *Dawco Constr., Inc.*, Comp. Gen. Dec. B-278048.2, 98-1 CPD ¶ 32 (award at "somewhat" higher price to offeror with a much higher-rated proposal); *SWR, Inc.*, Comp. Gen. Dec. B-276878, 97-2 CPD ¶ 34 (award to a higher-priced offer to obtain better past performance); and *Martech USA, Inc.*, Comp. Gen. Dec. B-250284.2, 93-1 CPD ¶ 110 (award at 15% higher price when protester had been rated lowest technically because of poor past performance). However, the tradeoff that is made between cost and non-price/cost must still be justified as being rational. See, for example, *Kempter-Rossman Int'l*, Comp. Gen. Dec. B-220772, 86-1 CPD ¶ 127, finding it unreasonable to award to a 2% lower-priced offer when the competitive offer had a 25% technical superiority and the RFP gave equal weight to the price and technical factors.

## 3. Documentation

Agencies must prepare documentation demonstrating that the source selection decision was reasonable and consistent with the solicitation. Prior to the FAR Rewrite, the FAR was somewhat unclear as to the documentation required to support selection decisions. However, GAO required agencies to submit documentation when awards were protested. See *Quality Elevator Co.*, Comp. Gen. Dec. B-276750, 97-2 CPD ¶ 28, stating:

> While judgments concerning the evaluation of proposals are by their nature subjective, they must be reasonable; such judgments must bear a rational relationship to the announced criteria upon which proposals were to be evaluated. *Management Technology, Inc.*, B-257269.2, Nov. 8, 1994, 95-1 CPD ¶ 248 at 6-7. Implicit in the foregoing is that the rationale for these judgments must be documented in sufficient detail to show that they are not arbitrary and that there was a reasonable basis for the selection decision. . . . Where there is inadequate supporting documentation for an award decision, we cannot conclude that the agency had a reasonable basis for the decision. *Hattal & Assocs.*, 70 Comp. Gen. 632, 637 (1991), 91-2 CPD ¶ 90 at 7.

The FAR Rewrite adopted a more rigorous documentation requirement following the guidance established by GAO. See FAR 15.308 stating the following requirement:

> The source selection decision shall be documented, and the documentation shall include the rationale for any business judgments and tradeoffs made or relied on by the SSA, including benefits associated with additional costs. Although the rationale for the selection decision must be documented, that documentation need not quantify the tradeoffs that led to the decision.

See also FAR 15.305(a) requiring documentation of the evaluations:

> (3) *Technical evaluation.* When tradeoffs are performed (see 15.101-1), the source selection records shall include —
>
> > (i) An assessment of each offeror's ability to accomplish the technical requirements; and
> >
> > (ii) A summary, matrix, or quantitative ranking, along with appropriate supporting narrative, of each technical proposal using the evaluation factors.

The documentation need not be contained in the ultimate award decision, but it must be present in the record. See *All Star-Cabaco Enter. (JV)*, Comp. Gen. Dec. B-290133, 2002 CPD ¶ 127, and *Allied Tech. Group, Inc.*, Comp. Gen. Dec. B-282739, 99-2 CPD ¶ 45, where the SSA accepted the recommendation of the Source Selection Evaluation Board, and the qualitative tradeoff documentation in the Board's recommendation was held to be sufficient. However, merely accepting evaluators' recommendations that do not contain such tradeoff analyses is insufficient, *Universal Bld'g Maint., Inc.*, Comp. Gen. Dec. B-282456, 99-2 CPD ¶ 32.

## a.  Rationale for Business Judgment

If an agency's documentation does not demonstrate that the source selection decision is rational, a protest will be granted. See *Matrix Int'l Logistics, Inc.*, Comp. Gen. Dec. B-272388.2, 97-2 CPD ¶ 89, where the determination of the SSA that two technical proposals were "essentially equal" was not supported in the documentation submitted by the agency. GAO sustained the protest, stating:

> An agency which fails to adequately document its evaluation of proposals or [the] source selection decision bears the risk that its determinations will be considered unsupported, and absent such support, our Office may be unable to determine whether the agency had a reasonable basis for its determinations.

See also *Navistar Def., LLC*, Comp. Gen. Dec. B-401865, 2009 CPD ¶ 258 (no documentation to support rating of "good" past performance (rather than "excellent") which agency stated was based on negative comments that had been inadvertently destroyed); *Radiation Oncology Group of WNY, PC*, Comp. Gen. Dec. B-310354.2, 2009 CPD ¶ 136 (no documentation showing that contracting officer considered strengths and weaknesses of competing proposals — merely a statement that offerors with different point scores were equal); *ACCESS Sys., Inc.*, Comp. Gen. Dec. B-400623.3, 2009 CPD ¶ 56 (no documentation showing that agency made meaningful tradeoff analysis); *AT&T Corp.*, Comp. Gen. Dec. B-299542.3, 2008 CPD ¶ 65 (no documentation showing how SSA arrived at different conclusion than evaluators regarding the impact of overstaffing); *Apptis, Inc.*, Comp. Gen. Dec. B-299457, 2008 CPD ¶ 49 (no documentation to support findings regarding demonstration of proposed solution); *Systems Research & Applications Corp.*, Comp. Gen. Dec. B-299818, 2008 CPD ¶ 28 (no documentation showing that SSA made a qualitative assessment of strengths of competing proposals to satisfy agency requirements using different approaches); *Panacea Consulting, Inc.*, Comp. Gen. Dec. B-299307.4, 2007 CPD ¶ 141 (no documentation showing that agency made meaningful tradeoff analysis — only numerical scores); *Bank of Am.*, Comp. Gen. Dec. B-287608, 2001 CPD ¶ 137 (documents contained multiple errors and reflected various mistakes and/or omissions); *Beacon Auto Parts*, Comp. Gen. Dec. B-287483, 2001 CPD ¶ 116 (documentation contained no indication that a cost/technical tradeoff had been made); *Cortland Mem'l Hosp.*, Comp. Gen. Dec. B-286890, 2001 CPD ¶ 48 (documentation did not show that agency followed evaluation criteria); *J&J Maint., Inc.*, Comp. Gen. Dec. B-284708.2, 2000 CPD ¶ 106 (no adequate documentation of oral presentation or strengths, weaknesses or risks of proposals); *Opti-Lite Optical*, Comp. Gen. Dec. B-281693, 99-1 CPD ¶ 61 (point scores alone inadequate to explain tradeoff decisions); *MCR Fed., Inc.*, Comp. Gen. Dec. B-280969, 99-1 CPD ¶ 8 (no documentation showing a comparison of the proposals or a discussion of their technical differences); *J.A. Jones Mgmt. Servs., Inc.*, Comp. Gen. Dec. B-276864, 97-2 CPD ¶ 47 (inadequate documentation to support decision when agency submitted "point scores and cursory narratives" with no "consistent, reasonable and accurate evaluation scoring" nor "supporting narrative documentation"); *J.W. Assocs., Inc.*, Comp. Gen. Dec. B-275209, 97-1 CPD ¶57 (point scores plus one paragraph " evaluation summary" inadequate to explain the evaluation of technical proposals); and *Cygnus Corp.*, Comp. Gen. Dec. B-275181, 97-1 CPD ¶63 (documentation contained only point scores for technical factors with no explanation of basis for scores).

GAO has not demanded that the documentation cover every element of the selection decision as long as it supports the overall rationale used by the SSA. See *SEAIR Transport Servs., Inc.*, Comp. Gen. Dec. B-274436, 96-2 CPD ¶ 224, stating:

SEAIR challenges the agency's documentation of its award decision, characterizing the record as "devoid of any real rationale for the decision to award the contract to EAST," and alleging that the source selection decision does not address the relative differences between SEAIR's and EAST's proposals. While the selection official's judgment must be documented in sufficient detail to show it is not arbitrary, *KMS Fusion, Inc.*, B-242529, May 8, 1991, 91-1 CPD ¶ 447, a source selection official's failure to specifically discuss every detail regarding the relative merit of the proposals in the selection decision document does not affect the validity of the decision if the record shows that the agency's award decision was reasonable. See *McShade Gov't Contracting Servs.*, B-232977, Feb. 6, 1989, 89-1 CPD ¶ 118. Here, the record documents the evaluation process, the color coding, and the risk assessments, concluding with the agency's determination that SEAIR's and EAST's proposals were essentially equal technically. The source selection document refers to this determination and concludes that, taking price into consideration, EAST's lower-priced offer represented the best overall value to the government. We see no basis to object to the source selection document, which very clearly sets forth the basis for the agency's award decision.

The documentation need not comply literally with the requirement of the FAR that it contain a statement of the "strengths, weaknesses and risks" as long as it explains the selection decision. See *Matrix Int'l Logistics, Inc.,* Comp. Gen. Dec. B-272388.2, 97-2 CPD ¶ 89, stating:

> The form of the documentation is not important if it supports the source selection decision. Thus, sketches of proposed designs were adequate documentation in lieu of narratives where aesthetics was a relevant factor in the construction of a scenic footbridge, *Bell Free Contractors, Inc.,* Comp. Gen. Dec. B-227576, 87-2 CPD ¶ 418.

See also *PRC, Inc.,* Comp. Gen. Dec. B-274698.2, 97-1 CPD ¶ 115, where the documentation was found adequate because it identified all of the "significant discriminators" between the proposals even though it did not record strengths and weaknesses of the individual proposals.

## b.  Post-Protest Documentation

While documentation compiled contemporaneously with the evaluation and the source selection decision is required by the FAR, the lack of contemporaneous documentation will not be fatal in a protest if the evaluation and selection can be shown to be reasonable and in conformance with the evaluation criteria. Thus, documentation supporting the source selection decision may be created by the agency after the filing of a protest. See *Remington Arms Co.,* Comp. Gen. Dec. B-297374, 2006 CPD ¶ 32, stating:

> While we generally give little weight to reevaluations prepared in the heat of the adversarial process, post-protest explanations that provide a detailed rationale for contemporaneous conclusions, as is the case here, simply fill in previously unrecorded details, and will generally be considered in our review of the rationality of selection decisions, so long as those explanations are credible and consistent with the contemporaneous record. *NWT, Inc.: PharmChem Labs., Inc.,* B-280988, B-280988.2, Dec. 17, 1998, 98-2 CPD ¶ 158 at 16.

Thus, documentation supporting the source selection decision may be provided by the agency after the filing of a protest as long as that documentation is consistent with the rationale used in making the original decision, *Ideal Elec. Sec. Co.,* Comp. Gen. Dec. B-283398, 99-2 CPD ¶ 87; *MCR Fed., Inc.,* Comp. Gen. Dec. B-280969, 99-1 CPD ¶ 8. See also *TLT Constr. Corp.,* Comp. Gen. Dec. B-286226, 2000 CPD ¶ 179 (agency's post-protest explanation of its determination to use negotiated procedures held to be consistent with the evaluation plan); *Pickering Firm, Inc.,* Comp. Gen. Dec. B-277396, 97-2 CPD ¶ 99 (source selection decision affirmed based on evaluator worksheets and consensus ratings created after protest to support a "sparse" memorandum prepared at time of selection decision), *Environmental Affairs Mgmt., Inc.*, Comp. Gen. Dec. B-277270, 97-2 CPD ¶ 93 (source selection decision affirmed based on "legal brief, a contracting officer's statement, and declarations made by the SSA and the chairman of the [source evaluation committee]," all prepared after the protest was filed); *AT&T Corp.*, Comp. Gen. Dec. B-260447.4, 96-1 CPD ¶ 200 (source selection decision affirmed based on the agency protest report, which presented extensive and detailed narratives concerning the strengths of the awardee's technical and management proposals when this information was consistent with the less detailed contemporaneous documentation); *Sociometrics, Inc.*, Comp. Gen. Dec. B-261367.2, 95-2 CPD ¶ 201 (although the details of the cost realism analysis were not spelled out in a contemporaneous document, the contracting officer adequately explained the details of the analysis in an agency protest report); and *Hydraudyne Sys. & Eng'g B.V.*, Comp. Gen. Dec. B-241236, 91-1 CPD ¶ 88 (source selection decision sustained based on its after-the-fact explanations of the scoring of individual evaluators after the documentation created by these evaluators had been discarded).

GAO has refused to rely on post-protest explanations of the source selection decision that have been prepared by the agency's legal counsel, *Radiation Oncology Group of WNY, PC*, Comp. Gen. Dec. B-310354.2, 2009 CPD ¶ 136. In that case the SSA had only stated that she determined the offerors were "essentially technically equal" with no further explanation.

The Court of Federal Claims has also admitted documentation filed after the plaintiff has lost a GAO protest, *Wackenhut Servs., Inc. v. United States*, 85 Fed. Cl. 273 (2008).

A common technique for remedying insufficient documentation has been for GAO to hold a hearing where agency officials can explain the evaluation and source selection decision. A number of protests have been denied on the basis of such information. See *Manassas Travel, Inc.*, Comp. Gen. Dec. B-294867.3, 2005 CPD ¶ 113 (testimony providing more details regarding strengths of winning offeror); *SOS Interpreting, Ltd.*, Comp. Gen. Dec. B-287505, 2001 CPD ¶ 104 (testimony providing detailed rationale for selection decision held to be credible and consistent with contemporaneous record); *Northeast MEP Servs., Inc.*, Comp. Gen. Dec. B-285963.5, 2001 CPD ¶ 28 (chairman of evaluation board explained the basis for determining that protester had weaknesses); *Draeger Safety, Inc.*, Comp. Gen. Dec. B-285366, 2000 CPD ¶ 139 (testimony of evaluator after evaluation documentation was destroyed accepted as providing acceptable contemporaneous documentation supporting selection decision); *Simborg Dev., Inc.*, Comp. Gen. Dec. B-283538, 2000 CPD ¶ 12 (testimony gave credible explanation of selection decision); *NWT, Inc.*, Comp. Gen. Dec. B-280988.2, 98-2 CPD ¶ 158 (based on transcript and hearing, GAO concluded that "while not recorded at the time, the agency did compare performance levels"); *Pacifica Servs., Inc.*, Comp. Gen. Dec. B-280921, 98-2 CPD ¶ 137 (detailed rationale given in declaration and hearing was held to "simply fill in unrecorded details") and *Jason Assocs. Corp.*, Comp. Gen. Dec. B-278689, 98-1 CPD ¶ 67 (source selection affirmed based on testimony). GAO has even permitted such later explanations in the extreme case where the agency has destroyed the original documentation, *Southwest Marine, Inc.*, Comp. Gen. Dec. B-265865.4, 96-1 CPD ¶ 56. In contrast, the hearing may confirm that the agency has made a flawed source selection decision, *Keeton Corrs., Inc.*, Comp. Gen. Dec. B-293348, 2005 CPD ¶ 44 (hearing showed SSA had been given faulty information on past performance); *Preferred Sys. Solutions, Inc.*, Comp. Gen. Dec. B-292322, 2003 CPD ¶ 166 (hearing showed that SSA did not make independent decision); *Sabreliner Corp.*, Comp. Gen. Dec. B-288030, 2001 CPD ¶ 170 (testimony repeated "errors" and "inconsistencies" in documentation supporting sole source procurement).

There is some disagreement on the weight to be accorded to documentation that is created after a protest has been filed. One judge in the Court of Federal Claims has stated that it should be accorded the "same deference" given to documentation created at the time the selection decision was made, *Tech Sys., Inc. v. United States*, 50 Fed. Cl. 216 (2001). Another judge treated such documentation as mere "argument," *Cubic Applications, Inc. v. United States*, 37 Fed. Cl. 339 (1997). GAO accords "greater weight to contemporaneous source selection materials rather than documents . . . prepared in response to protest contentions," *DynCorp*, 71 Comp. Gen. 129 (B-245289), 91-2 CPD ¶ 575. Thus, documentation that offers new justifications for the selection decision rather than amplifying the original justification will be highly suspect. See *Boeing Sikorsky Aircraft Support*, Comp. Gen. Dec. B-277263.2, 97-2 CPD ¶ 91, refusing to rely on the agency's mock source selection decision based on the assumption that all the protester's complaints were valid, stating:

> While we consider the entire record, including statements and arguments made in response to a protest in determining whether an agency's selection decision is supportable, we accord greater weight to contemporaneous source selection materials rather than judgments, such as the selection officials' reevaluation here, made in response to protest contentions. *Dyncorp*, 71 Comp. Gen. 129, 134 n.12 (1991), 91-2 CPD ¶ 575 at 7 n.13; *Southwest Marine, Inc.; American Sys. Eng'g Corp.*, B-265865.3, B-265865.4, Jan. 23, 1996, 96-1 CPD ¶ 56 at 10. As pointed out above, the agency does not acknowledge that it erred. Rather, we are faced with an agency's efforts to defend, in the face of a bid protest, its prior source selection through submission of new analyses, which the agency itself views as merely hypothetical and which are based on information that the agency continues to argue is not accurate. The lesser weight that we accord these post-protest documents reflects the concern that, because they constitute reevaluations and redeterminations prepared in the heat of an adversarial process, they may not represent the fair and considered judgment of the agency, which is a prerequisite of a rational evaluation and source selection process.

This logic was followed in *United Int'l Eng'g, Inc.*, 71 Comp. Gen. 177 (B-245448.3), 92-1 CPD ¶ 122, in which the source selection official's post-selection testimony regarding his reluctance to award to the protester was inconsistent with the evaluation criteria and contemporaneous evidence. GAO sustained the protest "giving due weight to the contemporaneous source selection documents." In *Man-Tech Envt'l Research Servs. Corp.*, Comp. Gen. Dec. B-292602, 2003 CPD ¶ 221, GAO rejected post-protest reevaluation because it was performed by the same personnel defending the protest. See also *Systems Research & Applications Corp.*, Comp. Gen. Dec. B-299818, 2008 CPD ¶ 28 (granting protest because agency officials showed at hearing that they did not qualitatively assess the merits of the proposals); *Si-Nor, Inc.*, Comp. Gen. Dec. B-292748.2, 2004 CPD ¶ 10 (rejecting argument that dissimilar prior contract was not used to evaluate experience); *Dis-mas Charities, Inc.*, Comp. Gen. Dec. B-292091, 2003 CPD ¶ 125 (rejecting post-protest reevaluation of past performance); *Johnson Controls World Servs., Inc.*, Comp. Gen. Dec. B-289942, 2002 CPD ¶ 88 (rejecting sufficiency of post-protest addendum that still did not contain comparative assessment of strength of pro-tester's technical proposal); *Wackenhut Servs., Inc.*, Comp. Gen. Dec. B-286037, 2001 CPD ¶ 114 (rejecting justification for selection decision that was not reflect-ed in contemporaneous record); *BAE Sys.*, Comp. Gen. Dec. B-287189, 2001 CPD ¶ 86 (rejecting explanation of evaluation that was inconsistent with record); *Farm-land Nat'l Beef*, Comp. Gen. Dec. B-286607, 2001 CPD ¶ 31 (rejecting undocu-mented testimony that telephone call occurred); *CRAssociates, Inc.*, Comp. Gen. Dec. B-282075.2, 2000 CPD ¶ 63 (post-protest documentation does not overcome contemporaneous record showing improper evaluation); *Maritime Berthing, Inc.*, Comp. Gen. Dec. B-284123.3, 2000 CPD ¶ 89 (rejecting documentation using new date from offeror not contained in original proposal); *Possehn Consulting*, Comp. Gen. Dec. B-278579.2, 98-2 CPD ¶ 33 (rejecting argument that if agency had included protester's proposal in the competitive range, it still would not have won the competition); *Arora Group, Inc.*, Comp. Gen. Dec. B-277674, 98-1 CPD ¶ 64 (rejecting post-protest justifications of clearly erroneous price realism analy-sis); and *Mechanical Contractors, S.A.*, Comp. Gen. Dec. B-277916, 97-2 CPD ¶ 121 (rejecting statement in protest report that agency had given favorable con-sideration to a certification of a subcontractor because there was no indication of such consideration in contemporaneous evaluation documents).

### c.  Quantification of Non-Price Factors

Quantification of technical ratings is not required when a tradeoff decision is made, FAR 15.308. This rule was established by the Court of Appeals for the Federal Circuit in *Lockheed Missiles & Space Co. v. Bentsen*, 4 F.3d 955 (Fed. Cir. 1993). See also *EG&G Team*, Comp. Gen. Dec. B-259917, 95-2 CPD ¶ 175, stating that "the source selection authority has discretion to determine how to balance cost and techni-cal advantages in making an award decision in a best value procurement." Quantifi-cation was not required in *MD Helicopters, Inc.*, Comp. Gen. Dec. B-298502, 2006 CPD ¶ 164; *Basic Contracting Servs., Inc.*, Comp. Gen. Dec. B-284649, 2000 CPD ¶ 120; *A.G. Cullen Constr., Inc.*, Comp. Gen. Dec. B-284049.2, 2000 CPD ¶ 45; *Allied*

*Tech. Group, Inc.*, Comp. Gen. Dec. B-282739, 99-2 CPD ¶ 45; *KRA Corp.*, Comp. Gen. Dec. B-278904, 98-1 CPD ¶ 147; *Research Triangle Inst.*, Comp. Gen. Dec. B-278254, 98-1 CPD ¶ 22; *Sudath Van Lines, Inc.*, Comp. Gen. Dec. B-274285.2, 97-1 CPD ¶ 204; *Ingalls Shipbuiding, Inc.*, Comp. Gen. Dec. B-275830, 97-1 CPD ¶ 180; and *Kay & Assocs., Inc.*, Comp. Gen. Dec. B-258243.7, 96-1 CPD ¶ 266.

When quantification of the benefit of making an award to a higher-priced offer is practical, the tradeoff should be justified in terms of dollars. See, for example, *Continental Airlines, Inc.*, Comp. Gen. Dec. B-258271.4, 97-1 CPD ¶ 81, holding that the agency had made a valid tradeoff decision by quantifying most of the non-price evaluation factors; and *Global Assocs., Ltd.*, Comp. Gen. Dec. B-275534, 97-1 CPD ¶ 129, where quantification of many of the non-price factors was found to be proper. See *Satellite Servs., Inc.*, Comp. Gen. Dec. B-286508, 2001 CPD ¶ 30, stating:

> While quantification of the value of technical differences is not required, a source selection official may quantify the value of technical differences in dollar terms as part of a cost/technical tradeoff; the quantification, however, must be rationally based and consistent with the RFP. *University of Kansas Med. Ctr.*, B-278400, Jan. 26, 1998, 98-1 CPD ¶ 120 at 6.

See *Olin Corp.*, Comp. Gen. Dec. B-283401, 99-2 CPD ¶ 88, finding that the SSA properly rejected the quantification of one offeror's litigious record of past performance because there was no way to accurately predict its future behavior.

It is also proper to quantify in-house costs necessitated by an offeror's proposed method of performance in order to determine the full cost of award to that offeror, *Cerner Corp.*, Comp. Gen. Dec. B-293093, 2004 CPD ¶ 34 (additional costs in using protester's software and following protester's deployment schedule).

## C. Post Selection Communication

Neither the procurement statutes nor the FAR deal with the subject of communications between the agency and the selected offeror after selection has been made and before award. However, in many cases, it is necessary to clear up uncertainties or to resolve remaining issues before award can be made. In other cases the agency may wish to negotiate more favorable terms or prices with the selected source. Thus, it is essential to determine whether such communications constitute negotiations which would require the agency to negotiate with all those who submitted offers (if award was being made on the basis of initial proposals) or with all those remaining in the competitive range if final offer revisions have been requested.

### 1. Negotiations Not Permitted

The general rule is that negotiation with only one offeror is prohibited. Such negotiations would occur if an offeror were given the opportunity to revise its offer to establish that the offer is acceptable. See *SmitKline Beecham Pharms., N.A.*, Comp. Gen. Dec. B-252226.2, 93-2 CPD ¶ 79, stating:

> It is a fundamental principle of federal procurement that all offerors must be treated equally. *Loral Terracom; Marconi Italiana*, 66 Comp. Gen. 272 (1987), 87-1 CPD ¶ 182. Thus, the conduct of discussions with one offeror generally requires that discussions be conducted with all offerors whose offers are within the competitive range and that offerors have an opportunity to submit revised offers. *Microlog Corp.*, B-237486, Feb. 26, 1990, 90-1 CPD ¶ 227. This rule applies even to post-selection negotiations that do not directly affect the offerors' relative standing, because all offerors are entitled to an equal opportunity to revise their proposals. *PRC Information Sciences Co.*, 56 Comp. Gen. 768 (1977), 77-2 CPD ¶ 11.

See also *Priority One Servs., Inc.*, Comp. Gen. Dec. B-288836, 2002 CPD ¶ 79 (offeror required to replace personnel not found to be acceptable and raising salary levels for some personnel); *The Futures Group Int'l*, Comp. Gen. Dec. B-281274.5, 2000 CPD ¶ 148 (agreeing to cap on indirect cost rates during a protest a material change in offer requiring discussions with all competitors in competitive range); and *Global Assocs., Ltd.*, Comp. Gen. Dec. B-271693.2, 96-2 CPD ¶ 100 (offer as received could not have been accepted). *In Matrix Int'l Logistics, Inc.*, Comp. Gen. Dec. B-272388.2, 97-2 CPD ¶89, GAO held that correction of a mistake in awardee's price after receipt of best and final offers required "discussions" with all offerors where the intended price was not ascertainable from the offer and the solicitation. In assessing the post selection communication cases, GAO focuses on whether there is a "reasonable possibility of prejudice" to the other offerors, *Labat-Anderson Inc.*, 71 Comp. Gen. 252 (B-246071.2), 92-1 CPD ¶ 193.

## 2.  *Clarifications and Nonmaterial Changes*

Communications in the nature of clarifications that would be permissible under FAR 15.306(a) do not require communications with other offerors. See Section V, above for a discussion of this type of communications. Thus, "touch up negotiations" have been permitted, *Medical Care Dev., Inc.*, Comp. Gen. Dec. B-227848.3, 87-2 CPD ¶ 371. In addition, discussing or requiring changes in nonmaterial aspects of an offer would not require negotiations with other offerors. See *Acepex Mgmt. Corp.*, Comp. Gen. Dec. B-283080, 99-2 CPD ¶ 77 (obtaining comments on the validity of a protest not a change to the offer); *Assets Recovery Sys., Inc.*, Comp. Gen. Dec. B-275332, 97-1 CPD ¶ 67 (change in payment provision did not increase or decrease overall value of offer); *Optimum Sys., Inc.*, Comp. Gen. Dec. B-194984, 80-2 CPD ¶ 32 (substitution of computer would have had same effect on all offerors); and *Information Sys. & Networks Corp.*, Comp. Gen. Dec. B-220661, 86-1 CPD ¶ 30 (negotiations to obtain a small reduction in price). See also *L.G. Lefler v. United States*, 6 Cl. Ct. 514 (1984), where the offer would have been lowest even without the negotiated price change.

It appears that communications of this type are contemplated by the guidance in FAR 15.504, which states:

> The contracting officer shall award a contract to the successful offeror by furnishing the executed contract or other notice of the award to that offeror.
>
> > (a) If the award document includes information that is different than the latest signed proposal, as amended by the offeror's written correspondence, both the offeror and the contracting officer shall sign the contract award.

This provision apparently permits the contracting officer to include information in the final contract that is different from the prior documentation in the proposal and proposal revisions. Such information would be the likely result of post-selection communications to clear up minor problems.

## 3. Negotiations Permitted

There are several situations in which negotiations with only the selected source will be permitted.

### a. Alternate Source Selection Procedures

Prior to 1997, pre-Rewrite FAR 15.613 permitted agencies to adopt alternate source selection procedures. Several agencies, including DoD and NASA adopted a procedure which permitted a degree of negotiation with only the selected offeror. Under the NASA procedure and the DoD "Four-Step" procedure set forth in pre-Rewrite DFARS 215.613-70, the agency conducted limited communications with all offerors within the competitive range and then negotiated the final contract price, terms, and conditions with the selected offeror. However, the negotiations could not permit any changes in the government's requirements or the offer which would affect the source selection decision. GAO recognized that such procedures met the statutory requirements for conducting oral or written discussions with all offerors within the competitive range, *Ogden Logistics Servs.*, Comp. Gen. Dec. B-257731.3, 95-1 CPD ¶ 3; *Taft Broad. Corp.*, Comp. Gen. Dec. B-222818, 86-2 CPD ¶ 125; *Support Sys. Assocs., Inc.*, Comp. Gen. Dec. B-215421, 84-2 CPD ¶ 249; *Program Res., Inc.*, Comp. Gen. Dec. B-192964, 79-1 CPD ¶ 281; *GTE Sylvania*, 57 Comp. Gen. 715 (B-188272), 77-2 CPD ¶ 422; *Management Servs., Inc.*, 55 Comp. Gen. 715 (B-184606), 76-1 CPD ¶ 74; *Dynalectron Corp.*, 54 Comp. Gen. 562 (B-181738), 75-1 CPD ¶ 17; and *Sperry Rand Corp.*, 54 Comp. Gen. 408 (B-181460), 74-2 CPD ¶ 276.

GAO has also recognized the validity of similar procedures adopted by the Department of Energy, *Holmes & Narver, Inc.*, Comp. Gen. Dec. B-239469.2, 90-2 CPD ¶ 210, *recons. denied*, 91-1 CPD ¶ 51. Compare *Airco, Inc. v. Energy Res. & Dev. Admin*, 528 F.2d 1294 (7th Cir. 1975), rejecting the contention that these procedures should be applied retroactively.

The Department of Health and Human Services alternate procedure at HHSAR 315.670 provided:

> (a) After selection of the successful proposal, the Contracting Officer may finalize details with the selected offeror, if necessary. However, the Contracting Officer shall not introduce any factor that could have an effect on the selection process after the common cutoff date for receipt of final proposal revisions, nor shall the finalization process in any way prejudice the competitive interest or rights of the unsuccessful offerors. The Contracting Officer shall restrict finalization of details with the selected offeror to definitizing the final agreement on terms and conditions, assuming none of these factors were involved in the selection process.

In *Prospect Assocs., Inc.,* Comp. Gen. Dec. B-260696, 95-2 CPD ¶ 53, the agency, using this procedure, conducted negotiations with the selected offeror on labor and indirect cost rates and other "minor issues." The negotiations resulted in a "relatively minor reduction" in the offered cost. GAO held that there was no need to negotiate with other offerors since the purpose of the negotiation was to "definitize" the terms "not to obtain more competitive pricing." That case should be contrasted with *SmithKline Beecham Pharms., N.A.,* Comp. Gen. Dec. B-252226.2, 93-2 CPD ¶ 79, where the agency negotiated a "concession" from the selected offeror and GAO held that this required negotiations with other offerors. GAO's rationale was that the agency was "reluctant" to award a contract to the selected source without the concession.

The former FAR 15.613 authorizing these alternative procedures was removed in the FAR Part 15 Rewrite. However, FAR 15.101 permits agencies considerable latitude in designing source selection methods:

> An agency can obtain best value in negotiated acquisitions by using any one or a combination of source selection approaches.

The Department of Defense has indicated that FAR 15.101 permits contracting agencies to develop selection procedures which permit negotiation after source selection. See 62 Fed. Reg. 63050 (1997), stating:

> DFARS guidance on the four-step source selection process and the alternate source selection process have been removed, as the new guidance at FAR 15.101, best value continuum, clearly allows such source selection processes.

The removal of the four-step procedure indicates that alternative procedures can be adopted by contracting officers without the necessity of regulatory coverage. However, in doing so the procedures to be followed must be spelled out in the solicitation so that offerors will be able to compete on a common basis. In addition, negotiations must not (1) change the government's requirements, (2) make an unacceptable offer acceptable, (3) change the basis for selection or (4) otherwise prejudice other offerors. See *SAMS El Segundo, LLC,* Comp. Gen. Dec. B-291620.3, 2003 CPD ¶ 48, where the agency adopted a phased selection procedure calling for negotiations with the selected offeror. See also *Northrop Grumman Tech. Servs., Inc.*, Comp. Gen. Dec. B-291506, 2003 CPD ¶ 25, where the agency added an item of government-furnished property before award — following a procedure specified in the RFP.

## b. Competitive Range of One

Post selection negotiations have been held to be appropriate where only one offeror was found to be in the competitive range. See *HITCO*, 68 Comp. Gen. 10 (B-232093), 88-2 CPD ¶ 337 (all but one offeror excluded from the competitive range when others were found to have deficiencies); *Rice Servs., Ltd.*, 68 Comp. Gen. 112 (B-232610), 88-2 CPD ¶ 514 (the sum of both major and minor deficiencies in the protester's offer justified its exclusion from the competitive range, which was narrowed to one); and *Regional Envtl. Consultants*, 66 Comp. Gen. 67 (B-223555), 86-2 CPD ¶ 476, *recons. denied*, 66 Comp. Gen. 388 (B-22355.2), 87-1 CPD ¶ 428 (one of two offerors excluded from the competitive range because of its undesirable approach to the contracted-for work). However, in these cases, GAO made it clear that source selection decisions that result in competitive ranges of one would be carefully scrutinized in the interest of achieving full and open competition.

The statutory and regulatory changes in describing the competitive range have made competitive ranges of one more acceptable. See *Clean Serv. Co.*, Comp. Gen. Dec. B-281141.3, 99-1 CPD ¶ 36, stating:

> [T]he FAR Part 15 rewrite provides that "based on the ratings of each proposal against all evaluation criteria, the contracting officer shall establish a competitive range comprised of all of the most highly rated proposals." FAR 15.306(c)(1); see *SDS Petroleum Prods., Inc.*, [B-280430, Sept. 1, 1998, 98-2 CPD ¶ 59]. We have concluded that the Part 15 rewrite does not require that agencies retain a proposal in the competitive range simply to avoid a competitive range of one; conducting discussions and requesting best and final offers from offerors with no reasonable chance of award would benefit neither the offerors nor the government. *Id.* at 6; see also 62 Fed. Reg. 51,224, 51,226 (1997) (retaining marginal offers in competitive range imposes additional and largely futile effort and cost on government and industry).

See also *L-3 Commc'ns EOTech, Inc.*, Comp. Gen. Dec. B-311453, 2008 CPD ¶ 139 (protester eliminated for failing to meet essential requirement); *General Atomics Aeronautical Sys., Inc.*, Comp. Gen. Dec. B-311004, 2008 CPD ¶ 105 (protester eliminated based on significant deficiencies); *M&M Investigations, Inc.*, Comp. Gen. Dec. B-299369.2, 2007 CPD ¶ 200 (protester did not have reasonable chance for award); *Brian X. Scott*, Comp. Gen. Dec. B-298568, 2006 CPD ¶ 156 (protester required change in contract terms); *TekStar, Inc.*, Comp. Gen. Dec. B-295444, 2005 CPD ¶ 53 (protester eliminated based on materially deficient proposal); *National Shower Express, Inc.*, Comp. Gen. Dec. B-293970, 2004 CPD ¶ 140 (protester's proposal stated only that it would comply with requirements); *Information Sys. Tech. Corp.*, Comp. Gen.

Dec. B-291747, 2003 CPD ¶ 72 (protester did not have reasonable chance for award); *SOS Interpreting, Ltd.*, Comp. Gen. Dec. B-287505, 2001 CPD ¶ 104 (protester eliminated based on several deficiencies); *Novavax, Inc.*, Comp. Gen. Dec. B-286167, 2000 CPD ¶ 202 (offeror eliminated from second round of discussions); *Dismas Charities, Inc.*, Comp. Gen. Dec. B-284754, 2000 CPD ¶ 84; and *Firearms Training Sys., Inc. v. United States*, 41 Fed. Cl. 743 (1998). In *Outdoor Venture Corp.*, Comp. Gen. Dec. B-401351.2, 2010 CPD ¶ 194, GAO concurred with the agency decision to put one unacceptable offeror in the competitive range while excluding another unacceptable offeror that had more deficiencies. Compare *Global, A 1st Flagship Co.*, Comp. Gen. Dec. B-297235, 2006 CPD ¶ 14, finding an improper competitive range of one where the agency included awardee's technically unacceptable proposal and excluded protester's "highly acceptable" technical proposal, on the basis that protester's evaluated cost/price was 15% higher than the awardee's. These cases indicate that a competitive range of one is appropriate when one offeror is clearly superior.

# X.  AWARD

Once a source selection decision has been made, the contracting officer is to make the award with "reasonable promptness" by transmitting the notice of award "in writing or by electronic means," 10 U.S.C. § 2305(b)(4)(C) and 41 U.S.C. § 3703(d). Additional procedures for making awards are outlined in FAR 15.504:

> The contracting officer shall award a contract to the successful offeror by furnishing the executed contract or other notice of the award to that offeror.
>
> (a) If the award document includes information that is different than the latest signed proposal, as amended by the offeror's written correspondence, both the offeror and the contracting officer shall sign the contract award.
>
> (b) When an award is made to an offeror for less than all of the items that may be awarded and additional items are being withheld for subsequent award, each notice shall state that the Government may make subsequent awards on those additional items within the proposal acceptance period.

In some cases the notice of award might constitute an acceptance by the government of an offer contained in a final proposal revision or initial proposal. This would occur, for example, in a situation where the government was fully in agreement with all the terms of that offer and merely desired to enter into a binding contract immediately. However, in many cases the contracting officer will want to prepare an integrated contractual document and obtain the signature of both parties to that document, as described in FAR 15.504(a) above. In such cases the notice of award may merely notify the offeror that it has been selected for award and that the integrated document will be forwarded in due course. Offerors should be aware that there are varying procedures used in this area and should ensure that they have a legally binding document before beginning work.

Statutory and regulatory requirements for a notice of award to be "in writing or by electronic means" raise the question of whether the contracting officer can form a contract by giving an oral notice of award. There is sparse litigation dealing with this subject, but the cases that do exist suggest strongly that an oral notice would not be effective. See, for example, *R.J. Crowley, Inc.*, ASBCA 28730, 86-1 BCA ¶ 18,739. In addition, GAO has enforced the FAR requirement that award of the contract be in written form. See *Litton Sys., Inc.*, Comp. Gen. Dec. B-229921, 88-1 CPD ¶ 448, holding that the protester's argument that partial award had been made orally over the phone was irrelevant in light of an actual written award made to another offeror, as was required. In *G. McMillan & Co.*, Comp. Gen. Dec. B-239805, 90-2 CPD ¶ 214, GAO stated, in reference to an argument that a protester was due expenses it incurred in anticipation of receiving a contract award, that "[s]ince the law and regulations require written notice of award, we think it unlikely that the protester could establish that a contract resulted from the alleged oral advice." GAO generally will not consider protests as to the "adequacy" of the award because that is a "procedural matter,"*Al Hamra Kuwait Co.*, Comp. Gen. Dec. B-288970, 2001 CPD ¶ 208.

When award is made by obtaining the signature of both of the parties, it is usually made on one of the standard forms prescribed by the government. If the government is merely accepting an offer without alteration by awarding on the basis of the initial proposals or final proposal revisions that have not changed the original offer, it can accomplish this by signing Standard Form (SF) 33, FAR 53.301-33, or SF 1442, FAR 53.301-1442, if these have been used as the cover page for the solicitation.

If Optional Form (OF) 308, FAR 53.302-308, has been used in transmitting the solicitation, this is not possible because that form has no place for signature by the contracting officer. If there have been alterations to the RFP during the procurement process, the agency can use either SF 26, FAR 53.301-26, or OF 307, FAR 53.302-307, as the cover page to the integrated contract. Alternatively, an agency can create its own award cover page as long as it complies with FAR 15.504 as follows:

(c) If the Optional Form (OF) 307, Contract Award, Standard Form (SF) 26, Award/Contract, or SF 33, Solicitation, Offer and Award, is not used to award the contract, the first page of the award document shall contain the Government's acceptance statement from Block 15 of that form, exclusive of the Item 3 reference language, and shall contain the contracting officer's name, signature, and date. In addition, if the award document includes information that is different than the signed proposal, as amended by the offeror's written correspondence, the first page shall include the contractor's agreement statement from Block 14 of the OF 307 and the signature of the contractor's authorized representative.

Merely signing the cover page to an RFP can lead to confusion if there have been alterations to the RFP during the procurement process. See *F & F Lab., Inc.*, ASBCA 33007, 89-1 BCA ¶21,207, where the contracting officer signed Standard

Form (SF) 26 after the contractor had stated in its offer that it would supply a candy bar at variance with that called for by the specifications. The board held the government bound on the theory that the offer was incorporated by reference into the contract by the terms of the standard form. The listing of provisions on the standard form can also have consequences when these forms are used for acceptance. For example, in *Codex Corp.*, GSBCA 8186-P, 86-1 BCA ¶ 18,590, the contracting officer and the awardee signed the cover page of SF 26, where the table of contents indicated which sections of the contract were to be incorporated. In actuality, one of the sections was missing from the contract due to a clerical error. The board found that the parties had entered into a binding contract and that, despite its absence from the actual contract, the section in question was incorporated into the contract by reference on the cover page.

Telegraphic notices of award were frequently used by the government to speed up the award process. In 49 Comp. Gen. 295 (B-167473) (1969), where an offeror was notified of award of a negotiated contract telegraphically and only later sent the formal contract documents, GAO remained silent on the issue as to what point the government was bound. In many cases involving sealed bidding, however, GAO has explicitly held that the government was bound by telegraphic notices of award. In *S.J. Groves*, 55 Comp. Gen. 936 (B-184260), 76-1 CPD ¶ 205, GAO held that because Groves protested after the agency had sent a telegraphic notice of award to the winner, its protest was a postaward protest. In *Wolverine Diesel Power Co.*, 57 Comp. Gen. 468 (B-189789), 78-1 CPD ¶ 375, telegraphic notices of award of two contracts were sent several days before the awardee attempted to withdraw its erroneous bids. GAO held that the telegrams made the contract effective and, therefore, that the awardee had made its allegations of mistake in bidding after award. See also *Niedenthal Corp.*, ASBCA 48159, 96-2 BCA ¶ 28,572, where the agency sent notice of award to the offeror on July 20, 1994, via facsimile transmission. Niedenthal informed the agency of a mistake in its bid on July 26, and later tried to claim that award could not be made by facsimile. The board held that the mistake-in-bid claim was a postaward claim under the Contract Disputes Act. Although these cases primarily refer to sealed bid procurements, their reasoning would be applicable to negotiated procurements where the telegraphic notice was framed in terms of acceptance of an offeror's initial proposal or final proposal revisions with no alteration in terms.

As a general rule, when written or oral discussions have been held and new offers requested, award is made by acceptance of the new offer (in one of the forms described above). However, award has been permitted on the basis of an original offer where the offeror did not submit a BAFO in response to the request for BAFOs, *MR&S/AME*, Comp. Gen. Dec. B-250313.2, 93-1 CPD ¶ 245. In this case, GAO reasoned that the offeror had agreed to an extension that kept its original offer open beyond the award date and the submission of a BAFO was permissible, not mandatory. GAO also ruled that contacting the offeror to find out why no BAFO had been submitted was not a post-BAFO discussion. Award has not been permitted on the basis of the initial offer where the offeror submitted its BAFO late, *Touchstone Textiles, Inc.*, Comp. Gen. Dec. B-272230.4, 96-2 CPD ¶ 107. In that case GAO reasoned that the agency could not ignore the intent conveyed by the submission of a modified proposal and, thus, the late BAFO constituted a revocation of the initial offer. Revocation of the original offer was also found when an offeror submitted its final proposal revisions in unauthorized electronic form that arrived late, *Integrated Bus. Solutions, Inc.*, Comp. Gen. Dec. B-292239, 2003 CPD ¶ 122; *Integrated Bus. Solutions, Inc. v. United States*, 58 Fed. Cl. 203 (2003).

## A. Contents of Contract

The contracting parties should ensure that the award document is clear as to the contents of the contract. If award is made by signing SF 33 or SF 1442, the parties will have agreed that the contract consists of the documents referred to on those forms plus any amendments to the solicitation. This would appear to exclude any parts of the offeror's proposal that were submitted in separate documents, including any cover letter to the proposal. However, if the contractor includes contract language conflicting with the RFP, it may create an ambiguity which should be cleared up. See, for example, *Catel, Inc.*, ASBCA 52224, 02-1 BCA ¶ 31,731, holding the contractor bound when it attempted to exclude work that was required by the specifications but was held bound to the specifications because its language was vague. See also *Ferguson-Williams, Inc.*, ENGBCA 6482, 99-1 BCA ¶ 30,731, where the contractor's statement in Part B that home office overhead was included in its price conflicted with a special contract clause in Part I. The board ruled that the contractor was not entitled to be reimbursed its home office overhead because a solicitation provision stated that "financial data submitted with an offer . . . will [not] form a part of the resulting contract." Apparently, in neither case did either party recognize their lack of agreement on the terms of the contract — with the contractor being penalized for not clearly up the problem.

When SF 33 or SF 1442 are used and an offeror conditions the offer by altering the solicitation requirements in a material way, the award would not be binding on the offeror because the government's acceptance would not match the offer. Thus, the issue must be addressed before award. When the agency wants to incorporate material in the contract that is not part of the solicitation, then SF 26, OF 307, or an agency form should be used. In such cases the contracting officer should clearly indicate what documents are part of the contract. When SF 26 is used, the contracting officer can rewrite the contract documents, check block 17 on the form, and send the new contract to the offeror for signature. The offeror's proposal will not be part of the contract unless it is specifically listed, *Loral Aerospace Corp.*, ASBCA 46373, 97-2 BCA ¶ 29,128, but, if it is listed, it will be part of the contract, *Ervin & Assocs., Inc. v. United States*, 59 Fed. Cl. 267 (2004), *aff'd*, 120 Fed. App'x 353 (Fed. Cir. 2005). Alternatively, the contracting officer can incorporate the offeror's proposal in the contract, sign the form, and check block 18. In either case the form should clearly identify what is part of the contract in order to avoid confusion on this issue. See the discussion of *F & F Lab., Inc.* and *Codex Corp.*, above.

OF 307 ameliorates the problem of potential confusion in using SF 26 by omitting blocks 17 and 18 and providing in block 14 that the contract will consist of "this document and any documents attached or incorporated by reference." However, the clarity of the document is still dependent on a clear statement of the contents of the contract.

The most troublesome issue in determining what is part of the contract is the question of whether proposals are part of the contract. Because the typical proposal contains considerable material that is in the nature of information or other non-promissory type material, it is generally not good practice to incorporate the entire proposal in the contract. Furthermore, the proposal may contain detailed data that conflicts with the contract specifications. The lack of clarity as to the contents of the contract can easily lead to litigation. See *Singer-General Precision, Inc.*, ASBCA 13241, 73-2 BCA ¶ 10,258, where the board had to resolve the question of whether the specifications or the conflicting technical proposal embodied the agreement of the parties. It gave no general rule but stated:

> [The contractor] was not free to ignore clearly-stated contractual requirements merely because the Government found the technical proposal acceptable and incorporated it into the contract. On the other hand, the Government could not with immunity require [the contractor] to perform work which was contrary to stated details, design and concepts in the proposal. When consideration is given to the specific claims, we will if applicable and necessary to decide a particular claim give further consideration to the contentions of the parties as presented in this general issue.

The board then analyzed each claim of the contractor for an equitable adjustment to determine what the parties had agreed to. See also *TRW, Inc.*, ASBCA 27299, 87-3 BCA ¶ 19,964, where the contracting officer incorporated the proposal into the contract to the extent it did not deviate from the government specifications. The board held that one aspect of the proposal was binding because it was promissory and another aspect was not binding because it was not promissory. Compare *Omni Corp. v. United States*, 41 Fed. Cl. 585 (1998), holding that a contractor was not bound to perform work in accordance with a technique described in its technical proposal which was not incorporated (the agency had unsuccessfully attempted to bind the contractor to perform such work by vague language in Section M of the RFP).

Silence on the status of proposals has also led to difficulties. See, for example, *Johnson Controls, Inc.*, ASBCA 25714, 82-1 BCA ¶ 15,779, holding the government bound to the terms of a technical proposal that was not clearly incorporated into the contract because it clearly stated that the contractor was offering to perform the work in a way that deviated with a detailed specification statement. In contrast, in *Northrop Grumman Corp. v. United States*, 47 Fed. Cl. 20 (2000), the court held that the contractor's proposal was not the baseline for determining whether constructive changes had occurred because the proposal was not incorporated into the contract. See also *Consolidated Sec. Servs. Corp.*, GSBCA 7714, 86-1 BCA ¶ 18,597, holding that the details of a pricing proposal were not part of a contract. This result conformed with the Contract Award solicitation provision in FAR 52.215-16, which stated that neither financial data nor representations concerning facilities or financing would "form part of the resulting contract." This helpful language was removed from the FAR by the FAR Part 15 Rewrite.

There have also been problems with contractual statements that do not contain clear promissory language. See, for example, *Hamilton Secs. Advisory Servs., Inc. v. United States*, 60 Fed. Cl. 144 (2004), denying a government claim that the contractor breached the contract because it could find no clear promise, stating at 158-59:

> The United States Court of Appeals for the Federal Circuit has advised that the "requirement of certainty in contracts serves two purposes. One is the need to determine whether the parties in fact intended to contract at all, and the other relates to the ability of a court to determine when a breach has occurred and to formulate any appropriate remedy." *Aviation Contractor Employees, Inc.* v. *United States*, 945 F.2d 1568, 1572 (Fed. Cir. 1991) (citing RESTATEMENT § 33) ("The terms of a contract are reasonably certain if they provide a basis for determining the existence of a breach and for giving an appropriate remedy.") and *Neeley* v. *Bankers Trust Co.*, 757 F.2d 621 (5th Cir. 1985), wherein the United States Court of the Fifth Circuit held that:
>
>> the entire contract falls with the failure of indefinite promises. . . . Like most questions of contract law, whether a promise or other term forms an essential part of an agreement depends primarily upon the intent of the parties. Thus, an *"essential" promise denotes one that the parties reasonably regarded, at the time of contracting,* as a vitally important ingredient in their bargain. Failure to fulfill such a promise, in other words, would seriously frustrate the expectations of one or more of the parties as to what would constitute sufficient performance of the contract as a whole. *Courts refuse to enforce agreements that contain indefinite promises or terms they deem essential precisely because judicial clarification of the uncertainty entails great danger of creating intentions and expectations that the parties themselves never entertained.*
>
> *Id.* at 628 (emphasis added); *see also Ace-Federal Reporters, Inc.* v. *Barram*, 226 F.3d 1329, 1332 (Fed. Cir. 2002); *Modern Sys. Tech. Corp.* v. *United States*, 979 F.2d 200, 202 (Fed. Cir. 1992); *Brookhaven Hous. Coalition* v. *Solomon*, 583 F.2d 584, 593 (2d Cir. 1978) (holding that "a court cannot decree performance of an agreement unless it can discern with reasonable certainty and particularity what the terms of the agreement are. *To consummate an enforceable agreement, the parties must not only believe that they have made a contract, they must also have expressed their intent in a manner that is susceptible of judicial interpretation.*") (emphasis added).

In *United Techs. Corp.*, ASBCA 46880, 97-1 BCA ¶ 28,818, the board interpreted nonpromissory language as promissory because the Secretary of the Navy had made a firm promise to the contractor but the contracting officer had used nonpromissory language in the contract (using the terms "intends to permit the Contractor to compete" for future work when the Secretary had guaranteed the right to compete). The board based its decision to a large degree on the fact that the contractor had sought to obtain promissory language and had been told by a number of officials that "intends" would be interpreted to mean "agrees."

## B. Time for Acceptance

Once an offer expires the government loses the power to form a contract by acceptance. The Instructions to Offerors — Competitive Acquisition solicitation provision in FAR 52.215-1 specifies the time that an offeror holds its offer open:

> (d) *Offer expiration date.* Proposals in response to this solicitation will be valid for the number of days specified in the solicitation cover sheet (unless a different period is proposed by the offeror).

Block 4 of OF 308 follows this provision by stating that offers will be valid for 60 days unless a different period is entered in the block. The standard solicitation forms, SF 33 and SF 1442, used to solicit both sealed bids and competitive proposals, contain statements that offerors agree to be bound by their offers if they are accepted within a stated number of days. While these provisions were written to require bidders on sealed bid procurements to submit firm bids, they also appear to limit the time in which a competitive proposal can be accepted. GAO has ruled, however, that, although these provisions contain dates when the offers expire, the agency can accept an expired offer after all offers have expired if the offeror waives the expiration date. See *Fletcher Constr. Co.*, Comp. Gen. Dec. B-248977, 92-2 CPD ¶ 246, reasoning:

> Even assuming that protester's interpretation of the acceptance period clause on the SF 1442 on which BAFOs were submitted is correct, and that all offers including the protester's had expired by the time of award, it is not improper for an agency to accept an expired offer for a proposed award without reopening negotiations. *Protective Materials Co., Inc.*, B-225495, Mar. 18, 1987, 87-1 CPD ¶ 303. Where the acceptance period has expired on all offers, the contracting officer may allow the successful offeror to waive the expiration of its proposal acceptance period without reopening negotiations to make an award on the basis of the offer as submitted, since waiver under these circumstances is not prejudicial to the competitive system. *Sublette Elec., Inc.*, B-232586, Nov. 30, 1988, 88-2 CPD ¶ 540.

This rule has been followed in *Scot, Inc.*, Comp. Gen. Dec. B-295569, 2005 CPD ¶ 66 (procurement with expiration date in RFP); *Pride Mobility Prod. Corp.*, Comp. Gen. Dec. B-292822.5, 2005 CPD ¶ 72 (procurement with expiration date in RFP amendment); and *CDA Investment Techs., Inc.*, Comp. Gen. Dec. B-272093.3, 97-1

CPD ¶ 102, *recons. denied*, 97-1 CPD ¶ 103 (procurement using SF 33). In *Krug Life Scis., Inc.*, Comp. Gen. Dec. B-258669.2, 95-1 CPD ¶ 111, GAO permitted waiver of the expiration date when the protester had kept its acceptance period open by sending in unsolicited extensions but the winning offeror had permitted its offer to expire. See also *BioGenesis Pacific, Inc.*, Comp. Gen. Dec. B-283738, 99-2 CPD ¶ 109, rejecting a contention that the agency improperly issued an amendment to the RFP extending the expiration date after it expired.

If an offeror submits an offer with an expiration date shorter than that required by the RFP, it will not be permitted to waive the expiration date after its offer has expired because that is prejudicial to the competitive system. See *Camden Shipping Corp. v. United States*, 89 Fed. Cl. 433 (2009), stating at 440:

> Permitting revival of an offer would compromise the integrity of the competitive process if the offeror designated a shorter acceptance period than that requested by the solicitation, and other offerors specified the longer period. *Espirit Int'l Corp.*, [Comp. Gen. Dec. B-276294, 97-1 CPD ¶ 106], at 1; *The Vemo Co.*, [Comp. Gen. Dec. B-243390, 91-2 CPD ¶ 443], at 2; *Fred Rutledge*, [63 Comp. Gen. 253 (B-213474),] 84-1 CPD ¶ 297, at 1; . . . If an offeror shortens the length of time its offer is open, it faces less exposure to the market risk of price fluctuation than other offerors. *Postmaster Gen.*, at 4; *see also Espirit Int'l Corp.*, at 1. Permitting an offeror to revive its offer after the shorter acceptance period has expired would be unfair, because it would allow the offeror to take its risk in increments, assessing after its offer expired whether the market situation had changed, while other offerors have no such opportunity.

The same result was reached in *Data Express*, Comp. Gen. Dec. B-234468, 89-1 CPD ¶ 507, where the protester had allowed its offer to expire by not acknowledging an amendment to the RFP that extended the expiration date of offers. See also *NECCO Inc.*, Comp. Gen. Dec. B-258131, 94-2 CPD ¶ 218, following the same reasoning in a case where the bidder on a sealed bid procurement responded to a request for an extension of the expiration date of a bid with an agreement to extend the date for a shorter length of time and then had its bid expire.

If neither the RFP nor the offer contain an expiration date, to be valid an award must be made within a reasonable time after receipt of a proposal or final proposal revisions. However, once a reasonable time has expired, the offer will no longer be open for award. See *Western Roofing Serv.*, 70 Comp. Gen. 323 (B-232666.4), 91-1 CPD ¶ 242, *recons. denied*, 91-1 CPD ¶ 566, where the agency had delayed action on a procurement for over a year and then reopened the procurement by requesting another round of BAFOs. When one of the original offerors protested because it had never received the request for a BAFO, GAO denied the protest holding that the agency was correct in assuming that the earlier BAFO had expired and, hence, award could be made only to an offeror that had submitted a new BAFO. GAO reasoned that the offer had expired in view of the statutory mandate for agencies to award promptly, 41 U.S.C. § 253b(d)(4), and the *Uniform Commercial Code* rule that offers without expiration dates remain open only for a reasonable time, U.C.C. § 2-205. GAO found that the 13 months that had passed between the submission of the BAFO and the award was too long a period to constitute a reasonable time. See *M.J.S., Inc.*, Comp. Gen. Dec. B-244410, 91-2 CPD ¶ 344, holding that a BAFO with no expiration date could clearly be accepted one month after submission.

Generally, contracting officers obtain proposal extensions from offerors when they find that there will be substantial delays in awarding the contract. GAO has found this to be proper when the agency has valid reasons for extending the time of award, *Saco Def., Inc.*, Comp. Gen. Dec. B-240603, 90-2 CPD ¶ 462 (11-month delay to permit a small business reasonable time to cure a responsibility problem and to conduct discussions); *Trim-Flite, Inc.*, 67 Comp. Gen. 550 (B-229926.4), 88-2 CPD ¶ 124 (eight-month delay to correct agency errors); *American Identification Prods., Inc.*, Comp. Gen. Dec. B-227599, 87-2 CPD ¶ 42 (six-month delay to evaluate samples). In *Ocean Tech., Inc.*, Comp. Gen. Dec. B-236470, 89-2 CPD ¶ 189, GAO denied a protest claiming that the proposal extension had been signed by an unauthorized employee of the offeror because the award could have been made even if the offer expired.

If an offeror agrees to hold its offer open and is later awarded the contract, it takes the risk of cost increases that may have occurred in the intervening period. See *Magna Enters., Inc.*, ASBCA 51188, 02-1 BCA ¶ 31660, stating at 156,419-20:

> Magna voluntarily extended its offer repeatedly, and used that time to resolve the Government's serious concerns over Magna's ability to perform. Although the offer remained open for a protracted period, that time was not shown to be unreasonable under the circumstances. Magna assumed the risk in this fixed-price supply contract that potential subcontractors or suppliers might become unavailable, or that prices could increase. *Consolidated Airborne Systems, Inc. v. United States*, 348 F.2d 941 (Ct. Cl. 1965); *D.W. Clark, Inc.*, ASBCA No. 45562, 94-3 BCA ¶ 27,132. A contractor is properly terminated for default when it fails to perform due to price increases during an extended offer period.

See also *Ordnance Parts & Eng'g Co.*, ASBCA 44327, 93-2 BCA ¶ 25,690, where the contractor was properly terminated for default when it failed to perform because of significant price increases that had occurred in the year that it held its offer open.

## C. Delay of Award By Protest

When a preaward protest is filed, the award is generally delayed until the protest is resolved. This imposes the burden on the winning offeror if such delayed award increases its costs of performance or otherwise makes it more difficult to perform the work. However, a winning offeror is not required to remain available for award in the face of a protest.

If an agency decides to withhold award pending the outcome of a protest, the selected offeror, as well as other offerors that might be in line for award, will normally be requested to keep their offers open. In addition, the protester's offer will be held to have remained open by virtue of the protest, 50 Comp. Gen. 357 (B-170178) (1970). Thus, upon conclusion of the protest, the agency will normally be able to make award in accordance with the original procurement if that is the proper course of action. GAO has permitted this outcome by holding that expiration dates may be waived and offers revived by the offeror in negotiated procurements because the only right conferred by expiration dates is upon the offeror, *Riggins & Williamson Mach. Co.*, 54 Comp. Gen. 783 (B-182801), 75-1 CPD ¶ 168. GAO has specified that revival of offers or waiver of expiration dates for the purpose of awarding the contract must be done "on the basis of the offer as submitted," *Donald N. Humphries & Assocs.*, 55 Comp. Gen. 432 (B-183292), 75-2 CPD ¶ 275. Under these circumstances, GAO has repeatedly held that, because the offer was not altered, no reopening of negotiations was necessary as it was not prejudicial to the competitive system. See *Sublette Elec., Inc.*, Comp. Gen. Dec. B-232586, 88-2 CPD ¶ 540; *Protective Materials Co.*, Comp. Gen. Dec. B-225495, 87-1 CPD ¶ 303; and *Medical Coaches, Inc.*, Comp. Gen. Dec. B-196339.2, 79-2 CPD ¶ 308, where the offers were not altered and, therefore, no further discussions were found to have been held by the agency. In *Ocean Tech., Inc.*, Comp. Gen. Dec. B-236470, 89-2 CPD ¶ 189; and *Data Tech. Indus., Inc.*, Comp. Gen. Dec. B-197858, 80-2 CPD ¶ 2, GAO specifically noted that the actual request that an offeror waive the expiration date of its offer did not constitute discussions requiring the reopening of negotiations with all offerors. See also *Rentfrow, Inc.*, Comp. Gen. Dec. B-243215, 91-2 CPD ¶ 25, holding that it was proper to request a waiver of the expiration date only from the winning offeror.

Offerors that elect to keep their offers open during the protest period and are subsequently awarded the contract have no recourse thereafter. GAO has refused to grant delay damages in such circumstances. See *Trim-Flite, Inc.*, 67 Comp. Gen. 550 (B-229926.4), 88-2 CPD ¶ 124, stating at 550:

> A delay in meeting procurement milestones generally is a procedural deficiency which does not provide a basis of protest because it has no effect on the validity of the procurement. *American Identification Products, Inc.*, B-227599 , July 13, 1987, 87-2 CPD ¶42. While an agency is required to award a contract with reasonable promptness, the 8-month period here from closing date to award is not unreasonable per se given the attempts by the agency to correct the matters raised in offerors' complaints and protests through reevaluations. See *Id.* The fact that the delays may have been the result of initial agency errors in the procurement is irrelevant; once the errors occurred . . . the [agency's] proper course of action was to take steps to correct the errors. The award delay was merely an unfortunate, but necessary, by-product of the [agency's] proper action.

Subsequently, GAO ruled that delay in award of a contract is not a protestable issue, *Federal Sales Serv., Inc.*, Comp. Gen. Dec B-237978, 90-1 CPD ¶ 249. See also *M.A. Mortenson Co. v. United States*, 843 F.2d 1360 (Fed. Cir. 1988), where the court denied a price adjustment when the contractor had extended its bid expiration date by 77 days and later claimed additional compensation to reflect the fact that this time extension had forced it to perform in winter weather. Similarly, in *DeMatteo Constr. Co. v. United States*, 220 Ct. Cl. 579, 600 F.2d 1384 (1979), the contractor was denied compensation for a suspension of work when it extended its expiration date pending the outcome of a protest. On the other hand, if performance is stayed after award, the contractor is entitled to compensation under the Protest After Award clause in FAR 52.233-3.

## D.  Date of Award

There has been controversy on the date that an award through government acceptance of a firm's offer creates a binding contract. This issue can be important when a firm attempts to withdraw its offer before it has received the government's acceptance but finds that the acceptance was place in the mail before the withdrawal. The traditional common-law rule was that the contract was binding when acceptance of the offer is dispatched (the "mailbox" rule). However, this rule was rejected by the Court of Claims in *Emeco Indus., Inc. v. United States*, 202 Ct. Cl. 1006, 485 F.2d 652 (1973), and *Rhode Island Tool Co. v. United States*, 130 Ct. Cl. 698, 128 F. Supp. 417 (1955), where the court, relying on postal regulations allowing the retrieval of mailed documents from the mail by the sender, reasoned that award does not occur until the offeror receives the mailed document. See also *Titan Atlantic Constr. Corp./The Gallegos Corp., a Joint Venture*, ASBCA 26007, 83-2 BCA ¶ 16,791, following this rule in determining that acceptance of a government offer by the contractor was not binding until the government received the acceptance. This decision contains a complete history of the evolution of this rule. Following the *Emeco* decision, some of the government forms stated that acceptance was effective when placed in the mail (adopting the old "mailbox" rule), and several appeals boards held that these forms governed. See *Adaptive Concepts, Inc.*, ASBCA 73123, 96-1 BCA ¶ 28,248; *G.E. Sales & Rentals v. General Servs. Admin.*, GSBCA 13304, 1995 GSBCA LEXIS 409; *Singleton Contracting Corp.*, IBCA-1770-1-84, 86-2 BCA ¶ 18,800; *Computer Wholesale Corp.*, GSBCA 4217, 76-1 BCA ¶ 11,859; and *IMCO Precision Prods., Inc.*, ASBCA 17572, 73-2 BCA ¶ 10,250. GAO also concluded that the language in these forms was controlling in making the "mailbox" rule applicable, *Wolverine Diesel Power Co.*, 57 Comp. Gen. 468 (B-189789), 78-1 CPD ¶ 375 (telegraphic acceptance effective when dispatched). Although no decisions have been found on this issue, since the Instruction to Offerors — Competitive Acquisition solicitation provision in FAR 52.215-1 contains language essentially the same as that construed by the board and GAO decisions, it would appear that acceptance will be effective when the government mails the signed SF 33, SF 1442 or OF 307. The solicitation provision states in ¶ (f):

> (10) A written award or acceptance of proposal mailed or otherwise furnished to the successful offeror within the time specified in the proposal shall result in a binding contract without further action by either party.

The parties may agree to an effective date of the contract other than the date of execution of the contract document. In *Northrop Worldwide Aircraft Servs., Inc.*, ASBCA 45216, 96-2 BCA ¶ 28,574, the agency amended Standard Form 26 to read "conditional/award," whereby the parties agreed that the contract effective date would be the date on which it received approval from the secretary of the agency. The approval occurred subsequent to the date the form was executed, and it was this later date that the board recognized as the effective date of the contract.

# XI. NOTICES AND DEBRIEFINGS

Agencies are required to notify offerors when they are eliminated from the competition and to provide debriefings when requested. Section 1014 of FASA, amending 10 U.S.C. § 2305(b), and § 1064 of FASA, amending 41 U.S.C. § 253b, added new guidance on postaward debriefings. Section 4104 of the Clinger-Cohen Act of 1996, further amended 10 U.S.C. § 2305(b) and 41 U.S.C. § 253b (now 41 U.S.C. § 3704 and § 3705) to add a new provision on preaward debriefings. These statutes are implemented in FAR 15.605 and FAR 15.606.

## A. Preaward Notices and Debriefings

Preaward notices and debriefings serve a number of purposes. Early notice of exclusion from the competition will permit excluded offerors to turn their attention to other contracting opportunities. It will also conserve resources since offerors will be on notice that investing further expense on the procurement would not be productive. These purposes were noted in the promulgation comments of the FAR Part 15 Rewrite at 62 Fed. Reg. 51226 (1997):

> This final rule insures that offerors with little probability of success are advised early on that their competitive position does not merit additional expense in a largely futile attempt to secure the contract.

> This knowledge will benefit both large and small entities, but will be especially beneficial to small entities that have constrained budgets. These entities will be able to conserve scarce bid and proposal funds and employ their resources on more productive business opportunities.

Another function of the preaward notice is that it provides an offeror an opportunity to challenge its elimination from the competition by requesting a preaward debriefing and determining whether to file a preaward protest or request alternative dispute resolution of its objection to the exclusion. While additional effort may be required of procurement personnel and delays in the procurement result if protests are filed, early resolution will be to the public's advantage if the exclusion was not appropriate. Corrective action is less time consuming and expensive to all parties if undertaken while the procurement is in process than after award.

## 1. *Preaward Notices*

Although the procurement statutes do not specifically state that preaward notice of exclusion from competition is to be given, the requirement for such notice is implicit in the offeror's right to request a preaward debriefing. Thus, FAR 15.503(a) requires preaward notices of exclusion as follows:

Preaward notices — (1) Preaward notices of exclusion from competitive range. The contracting officer shall notify offerors promptly in writing when their proposals are excluded from the competitive range or otherwise eliminated from the competition. The notice shall state the basis for the determination

The term "or otherwise eliminated from the competition" is not defined. It apparently is meant to implement the statutory phrase "or otherwise excludes such an offeror from further consideration prior to the final source selection decision" providing for preaward debriefing, 10 U.S.C. § 2305(b)(6)(A) and 41 U.S.C. § 3705(a). Determinations of exclusion which would qualify for such notice would include determinations that an offeror is not responsible or otherwise not eligible for award or that an offer is inexcusably late (FAR 15.208(c)) or is unacceptable. It might also be argued that an offeror is "eliminated from the competition" when another offeror is selected for award. Contradicting such an interpretation is the statutory language providing for preaward debriefing for an excluded offeror "prior to the final source selection decision." While the FAR would be free to go beyond the statutory mandate, it is doubtful if this is the correct interpretation because FAR 15.503(a)(2) specifically provides for post-selection, preaward notice for small business setasides, as follows:

Preaward notices for small business set-asides. In addition to the notice in paragraph (a)(1) of this section, when using a small business set-aside (see Subpart 19.5), upon completion of negotiations and determinations of responsibility, but prior to award, the contracting officer shall notify each offeror in writing of the name and location of the apparent successful offeror. The notice shall also state that

(i) The Government will not consider subsequent revisions of the offeror's proposal; and

(ii) No response is required unless a basis exists to challenge the small business size status of the apparent successful offeror. The notice is not required when the contracting officer determines in writing that the urgency of the requirement necessitates award without delay or when the contract is entered into under the 8(a) program (see 19.805-2).

## 2. *Preaward Debriefings*

The statutory provisions for preaward debriefings at 10 U.S.C. § 2305(b)(6)(A) and 41 U.S.C. § 3705(a) are implemented in FAR 15.505, as follows:

Offerors excluded from the competitive range or otherwise excluded from the competition before award may request a debriefing before award (10 U.S.C. 2305(b)(6)(A) and 41 U.S.C. 253b(f)-(h)).

(a)(1) The offeror may request a preaward debriefing by submitting a written request for debriefing to the contracting officer within 3 days after receipt of the notice of exclusion from the competition.

(2) At the offeror's request, this debriefing may be delayed until after award. If the debriefing is delayed until after award, it shall include all information normally provided in a postaward debriefing (see 15.506(d)). Debriefings delayed pursuant to this paragraph could affect the timeliness of any protest filed subsequent to the debriefing.

(3) If the offeror does not submit a timely request, the offeror need not be given either a preaward or a postaward debriefing. Offerors are entitled to no more than one debriefing for each proposal.

(b) The contracting officer shall make every effort to debrief the unsuccessful offeror as soon as practicable, but may refuse the request for a debriefing if, for compelling reasons, it is not in the best interests of the Government to conduct a debriefing at that time. The rationale for delaying the debriefing shall be documented in the contract file. If the contracting officer delays the debriefing, it shall be provided no later than the time postaward debriefings are provided under 15.506. In that event, the contracting officer shall include the information at 15.506(d) in the debriefing.

(c) Debriefings may be done orally, in writing, or by any other method acceptable to the contracting officer.

(d) The contracting officer should normally chair any debriefing session held. Individuals who conducted the evaluations shall provide support.

(e) At a minimum, preaward debriefings shall include —

(1) The agency's evaluation of significant elements in the offeror's proposal;

(2) A summary of the rationale for eliminating the offeror from the competition; and

(3) Reasonable responses to relevant questions about whether source selection procedures contained in the solicitation, applicable regulations, and other applicable authorities were followed in the process of eliminating the offeror from the competition.

(f) Preaward debriefings shall not disclose —

(1) The number of offerors;

(2) The identity of other offerors;

(3) The content of other offerors' proposals;

(4) The ranking of other offerors;

(5) The evaluation of other offerors; or

(6) Any of the information prohibited in 15.506(e).

(g) An official summary of the debriefing shall be included in the contract file.

Because ¶ (a)(3) limits offerors to a single debriefing and ¶ (a)(2) permits offerors to request a postaward debriefing in lieu of a preaward debriefing, they must exercise care in deciding the type of debriefing to request when they have been excluded from the competition prior to the award decision. If they believe that they have been unfairly eliminated from the competition, they will undoubtedly elect a preaward debriefing to determine the basis for the agency's action. However, because the procurement is ongoing, ¶ (f) severely limits the amount of information that can be given to the offeror in this type of debriefing. Thus, in cases where the offeror does not intend to challenge its exclusion from the competition but desires to learn how to improve its competitive position in future procurements, a postaward debriefing is a sensible election because far more information can be obtained in a postaward debriefing. This election also benefits the procuring agency because it permits debriefing at a time when the workload of the source selection team is likely to be smaller than it would be prior to award. The safe procedure to follow in requesting a postaward debriefing is to request a preaward debriefing, including a request that it be deferred until postaward. See 10 U.S.C. § 2305(b)(6)(B), and 41 U.S.C. § 3705(c) stating that postaward debriefings are required in this situation *only* if a preaward debriefing has been requested and refused.

Great care should be exercised by offerors in this regard because if they learn in a postaward debriefing that they were excluded from the competitive range because of deficiencies in their proposal, a protest of faulty evaluation may be held to be untimely. This occurred in *United Int'l Investigative Servs., Inc.*, Comp. Gen. Dec. B-286327, 2000 CPD ¶ 173, where GAO rejected the protest as being untimely, stating that, since postaward debriefings were only "required" if the agency refused the preaward debriefing, the protester's free choice to delay the debriefing made the protest untimely.

GAO will not review an agency's decision to delay the debriefing until after award, *Global Eng'g & Constr.*, Comp. Gen. Dec. B-275999.3, 97-1 CPD ¶ 77. In that case, Global requested a preaward debriefing after the agency excluded its proposal from the competitive range. The agency denied Global's request on the ground that preaward debriefings in the procurement would not be in the government's best interest. The agency also stated that a preaward debriefing would require redirecting the agency's resources "which would not best serve our customers' needs or be a wise expenditure of U.S. tax dollars." GAO stated that the offeror would not be prejudiced by the denial of the preaward debriefing because it would be entitled to receive a postaward debriefing and, if it filed a protest after award, work on the procurement would be stayed. In GAO's view, an agency postponing the debriefing "may find it difficult to marshall the resources to defend its earlier decision" and that "simply may prejudice the agency in defending the protest." Although GAO found that Global presented several valid reasons why preaward debriefings should be encouraged, it still denied the protest.

The same agency indicated its intention not to grant a preaward debriefing in another decision, *Siebe Envtl. Controls*, Comp. Gen. Dec. B-275999.2, 97-1 CPD ¶ 70. In denying relief GAO stated that the protest process was not to be used to determine why a contractor had been eliminated from the procurement and suggested that the information could be obtained by seeking information under the Freedom of Information Act. GAO's refusal to review such actions would appear to permit the agency to arbitrarily deny a preaward debriefing. Whether that is consistent with the intent of the statute is questionable.

GAO has ruled on the requirement that a preaward debriefing be requested within three days of receipt of the notice of exclusion from the competitive range. See *International Res. Group*, Comp. Gen. Dec. B-286663, 2001 CPD ¶ 35, holding that when the notice of exclusion is sent by the agency electronically after business hours, the first day for the computation should be the first business day after the day that the notice was sent.

## B. Postaward Notices and Debriefings

Postaward notices and debriefings serve a number of functions in addition to those served by preaward notices and debriefings. In addition to advising offerors that their offers are no longer under consideration and providing them with information to challenge the selection, postaward debriefings can provide offerors with "an indication of how those offerors can improve their chances for success in future procurements," Sen. Rep. 103-258 accompanying FASA, Pub. L. No. 103-355. By identifying the source selected, postaward notices also provide information which other offerors may use for subcontracting opportunities.

### 1. Postaward Notices

The procurement statutes require notice of contract award to be given to "all other offerors within 3 days after date of contract award in writing or by electronic means of the rejection of their proposals," 10 U.S.C. § 2305(b)(4)(C) and 41 U.S.C. § 3704(a). This requirement is implemented in FAR 15.503(b) as follows:

*Postaward notices.* (1) Within 3 days after the date of contract award, the contracting officer shall provide written notification to each offeror whose proposal was in the competitive range but was not selected for award (10 U.S.C. 2305(b) (5) and 41 U.S.C. 253b(c)) or had not been previously notified under paragraph (a) of this section. The notice shall

(i) The number of offerors solicited;

(ii) The number of proposals received;

(iii) The name and address of each offeror receiving an award;

(iv) The items, quantities, and any stated unit prices of each award. If the number of items or other factors makes listing any stated unit prices impracticable at that time, only the total contract price need be furnished in the notice. However, the items, quantities, and any stated unit prices of each award shall be made publicly available, upon request; and

(v) In general terms, the reason(s) the offeror's proposal was not accepted, unless the price information in paragraph (b)(1)(iv) of this section readily reveals the reason. In no event shall an offeror's cost breakdown, profit, overhead rates, trade secrets, manufacturing processes and techniques, or other confidential business information be disclosed to any other offeror.

(2) Upon request, the contracting officer shall furnish the information described in paragraph (b)(1) of this section to unsuccessful offerors in solicitations using simplified acquisition procedures in Part 13.

(3) Upon request, the contracting officer shall provide the information in paragraph (b)(1) of this section to unsuccessful offerors that received a preaward notice of exclusion from the competitive range.

## 2. Postaward Debriefings

The statutory requirements for postaward debriefings, 10 U.S.C. § 2305(b)(5) and 41 U.S.C. § 3704, are implemented in FAR 15.506 which provides:

(a)(1) An offeror, upon its written request received by the agency within 3 days after the date on which that offeror has received notification of contract award in accordance with 15.503(b), shall be debriefed and furnished the basis for the selection decision and contract award.

(2) To the maximum extent practicable, the debriefing should occur within 5 days after receipt of the written request. Offerors that requested a postaward debriefing in lieu of a preaward debriefing, or whose debriefing was delayed for compelling reasons beyond contract award, also should be debriefed within this time period.

(3) An offeror that was notified of exclusion from the competition (see 15.505(a)), but failed to submit a timely request, is not entitled to a debriefing.

(4)(i) Untimely debriefing requests may be accommodated.

(ii) Government accommodation of a request for delayed debriefing pursuant to 15.505(a)(2), or any untimely debriefing request, does not automatically extend the deadlines for filing protests. Debriefings delayed pursuant to 15.505(a)(2) could affect the timeliness of any protest filed subsequent to the debriefing.

(iii) Debriefings of successful and unsuccessful offerors may be done orally, in writing, or by any other method acceptable to the contracting officer.

(c) The contracting officer should normally chair any debriefing session held. Individuals who conducted the evaluations shall provide support.

(d) At a minimum, the debriefing information shall include —

(1) The Government's evaluation of the significant weaknesses or deficiencies in the offeror's proposal, if applicable;

(2) The overall evaluated cost or price (including unit prices) and technical rating, if applicable, of the successful offeror and the debriefed offeror, and past performance information on the debriefed offeror;

(3) The overall ranking of all offerors, when any ranking was developed by the agency during the source selection;

(4) A summary of the rationale for award;

(5) For acquisitions of commercial items, the make and model of the item to be delivered by the successful offeror; and

(6) Reasonable responses to relevant questions about whether source selection procedures contained in the solicitation, applicable regulations, and other applicable authorities were followed.

(e) The debriefing shall not include point-by-point comparisons of the debriefed offeror's proposal with those of other offerors. Moreover, the debriefing shall not reveal any information prohibited from disclosure by 24.202 or exempt from release under the Freedom of Information Act (5 U.S.C. 552) including —

(1) Trade secrets;

(2) Privileged or confidential manufacturing processes and techniques;

(3) Commercial and financial information that is privileged or confidential, including cost breakdowns, profit, indirect cost rates, and similar information; and

(4) The names of individuals providing reference information about an offeror's past performance.

(f) An official summary of the debriefing shall be included in the contract file.

Congress has given protesters more rights by making the stay from proceeding with performance of an awarded contract in the event of a protest dependent on the debriefing. Prior to the FASA, this stay was put in effect (absent urgency) only if the protest was received no more than 10 days from contract award. Under § 1402 of the FASA, the stay will go into effect if a protest is received within five days after the debriefing is conducted. This provision penalizes agencies that do not conduct their postaward debriefings in a timely fashion. Although agencies can wait, by doing so they lengthen the time that a protester has to evaluate the merits of any projected protest.

A debriefing must be timely requested and acted upon in order to preserve the offeror's rights. First, the right to the statutory stay from proceeding with performance after award will be lost if the protest is not filed within five days after a debriefing date *offered* by the agency, FAR 33.103(f)(3), not the actual date of the debriefing. Second, the right to protest to GAO will be lost entirely if the protest is not filed within 10 days of the date a debriefing is *offered* by the agency. See *Pentec Envtl., Inc.*, Comp. Gen. Dec. B-276874.2, 97-1 CPD ¶ 199, where a protest was found untimely because the protester delayed the debriefing one month after the date offered by the agency in order to obtain information through a Freedom of Information Act request. See also *Professional Rehabilitation Consultants, Inc.*, Comp. Gen. Dec. B-275871, 97-1 CPD ¶ 94, dismissing a postaward debriefing protest because the protester waited two months to request a debriefing after it was informed that it had not received the award.

Inadequate debriefings have not, in the past, created a protestable issue, *Thermolten Tech., Inc.*, Comp. Gen. Dec. B-278408, 98-1 CPD ¶ 35; *McShade Enters.*, Comp. Gen. Dec. B-278851, 98-1 CPD ¶ 90; *CACI Field Servs., Inc.*, Comp. Gen. Dec. B-234945, 89-2 CPD ¶ 97; *Haworth, Inc.*, Comp. Gen. Dec. B-215638.2, 84-2 CPD ¶ 461. However, an inadequate debriefing can extend the time that an offeror has to protest even if the time to stay the performance of the contract has passed. For example, in *Geo-Centers, Inc.*, Comp. Gen. Dec. B-276033, 97-1 CPD ¶ 182, GAO sustained a protest that was filed three months after contract award and two months after a debriefing that did not contain sufficient details to disclose the basis for the protest, ruling that the protest was timely because it was filed within 10 days after the protester learned of the grounds for protest in a response to a request for the information pursuant to the Freedom of Information Act. Similarly, in *Bio-*

*spherics, Inc.*, Comp. Gen. Dec. B-278278, 98-1 CPD ¶ 161, the protester asserted that the agency failed to inform it of adverse past performance information during discussions. The agency countered that this argument was not timely because it had informed the protester during debriefing that the protester had been ranked lower than the awardee under the past performance factor and it did not receive a perfect score on this factor. GAO held that the protest filed more than 10 days of the debriefing was timely because the protester was not informed during the debriefing of the degree to which its proposal was downgraded under this factor and did not know the specific adverse past performance information being considered by the agency.

A losing firm may obtain more relief in the Court of Federal Claims, where the protest timeliness requirements are not as strict. See, for example, *Tin Mills Props., LLC v. United States*, 82 Fed. Cl. 584 (2008), where the court ordered the contracting officer to inform the protester of the precise reasons for its exclusion from the competitive range when the debriefing had been extremely cursory, even after repeated requests by the protester for detailed information.

# CHAPTER 7

# SPECIAL NEGOTIATION PROCEDURES

In addition to the standard negotiation procedure discussed in Chapter 6, a number of special procedures are used in various classes of negotiated procurements. The procurement statutes contain provisions permitting the use of these special procedures in order to simplify the procurement process or adapt it to the unique conditions that are encountered in specific markets. This chapter covers seven such procedures. The first is the procurement of supplies or services that are designated as "commercial items." The second is the procurement of work with a value of $150,000 or less following simplified acquisition procedures. The following two procedures cover the procurement of architect-engineer services and the use of a two-step design-build contract for the procurement of construction work. Next, the chapter addresses the broad agency announcement procedures used to procure research work in general and under the small business innovative research program. This is followed by a discussion of special procedures for the procurement of information technology. The chapter concludes with a discussion of the major special procedures that have been adopted by specific agencies to enhance their ability to carry out their procurement missions.

## I. COMMERCIAL ITEMS

In recent years, there have been a number of initiatives in government procurement designed to take advantage of products and services available in the commercial marketplace. These initiatives have focused on the use of commercial product or service descriptions rather than government-unique specifications. They have also been aimed at using commercial buying practices and eliminating statutory and regulatory provisions that either discourage commercial firms from competing for government business or unnecessarily increase the costs of performance. As a result, a number of provisions were adopted by the Federal Acquisition Streamlining Act of 1994 (FASA), Pub. L. No. 103-355, and the Clinger-Cohen Act of 1996, Pub. L. No. 104-106. These provisions, designed to promote and facilitate the procurement of commercial items, include 10 U.S.C. § 2377(b) which requires that:

> The head of an agency shall ensure that procurement officials in that agency, to the maximum extent practicable —
>
> (1) acquire commercial items or nondevelopmental items other than commercial items to meet the needs of the agency;
>
> (2) require prime contractors and subcontractors at all levels under the agency contracts to incorporate commercial items or nondevelopmental

items other than commercial items as components of items supplied to the agency;

(3) modify requirements in appropriate cases to ensure that the requirements can be met by commercial items or, to the extent that commercial items suitable to meet the agency's needs are not available, nondevelopmental items other than commercial items;

(4) state specifications in terms that enable and encourage bidders and offerors to supply commercial items or, to the extent that commercial items suitable to meet the agency's needs are not available, nondevelopmental items other than commercial items in response to the agency solicitations;

(5) revise the agency's procurement policies, practices, and procedures not required by law to reduce any impediments in those policies, practices, and procedures to the acquisition of commercial items; and

(6) require training of appropriate personnel in the acquisition of commercial items.

Substantially the same requirements are included in 41 U.S.C. § 3307(c). Congress also granted special authority to use commercial item procurement procedures in 41 U.S.C. § 428a (now 41 U.S.C. § 1903(c)) and § 437 (pre-2011 codification). In addition, agency competition advocates are responsible for "promoting the acquisition of commercial items," 41 U.S.C. § 1705(c). Other provisions dealing with the procurement of commercial items are scattered throughout various statutes that are discussed in the following material.

FAR Part 12 is the primary regulation implementing the commercial item statutes, while FAR Subpart 13.5 covers the test program for procurement of commercial items using simplified acquisition procedures. In addition, a number of different FAR Parts deal with commercial items. For example, requirements for market research, the drafting of specifications, and the solicitation of offers are covered in FAR Parts 10, 11, and 5, respectively. The rules applicable to pricing commercial items are contained in FAR Part 15. See Chapter 10. This section deals with the special rules applicable to contracts for commercial items excluding procurements under the special test program using simplified acquisition procedures in FAR Subpart 13.5. This test program permits the use of simplified acquisition procedures on procurements not in excess of $6,500,000, or $12,000,000 if the procurement is in support of a contingency operation or to facilitate the defense against or recovery from nuclear, biological, chemical, or radiological attack, FAR 13.500(e). Procurements under this test program are covered in the following section dealing with simplified acquisition procedures.

Although commercial item procedures permit agencies to adopt commercial practices to the greatest possible extent, they do not alter the basic rules of contracting as discussed in Chapters 2 and 3. See *Altos Fed. Group*, ASBCA 53523, 07-2 BCA ¶ 33,657, rejecting the government's argument that the commercial item procedures precluded a contractor's claim for a mistake in its offer that should have been seen by the contracting officer, and stating at 166,673:

> The Board considered a similar argument in *Orion Technology, Inc.*, ASBCA No. 54608, 06-1 BCA ¶ 33,266, wherein appellant sought contract reformation based upon a unilateral mistake discovered after award. The government defended against the claim by asserting that FAR 14.407 Mistakes in Bids did not apply to awards made under FAR subpart 13.5 Test Program for Certain Commercial Items, and argued that simplified acquisition procedures imposed only the duty of reasonableness upon the contracting officer. The Board disagreed, and distinguished facilitating the procurement process by avoiding unnecessarily constrictive procedures from precluding contractors from obtaining relief due to government error, and held that "While [FAR 13.106-2 Evaluation of Quotations or Offers ¶ (b)(1)] gives the contracting officer flexibility as to evaluation procedures, it does not affect the principles applicable to remedies for mistakes disclosed after award," *Orion*, 06-1 BCA at 164,853. *Accord, Finlen Complex, Inc.*, B-288280, 2001 WL 1198650 (Comp. Gen) at 7 ("the labeling of a procurement as 'simplified' does not absolve the agency from its obligation to treat vendors fairly").

## A. Definitions

The term "commercial item," as defined in 41 U.S.C. § 103(12) and FAR 2.101, includes both commercial supplies and commercial services. However, supplies and services are given disparate treatment, with the definition of commercial supplies being much broader than the definition of commercial services. The terminology is further complicated by the fact that when used alone, the term "item" most often refers to supplies only. In addition, nondevelopmental items and.commercial off-the-shelf items are distinct subcategories of commercial supplies. The following material deals with the definitions of the various types of commercial items and the critical elements of the definition of services and commercial off-the-shelf items.

The definition of supplies or services as a "commercial item" cannot be successfully protested unless the protester can show that it has been prejudiced by that classification, *Johnson Controls World Servs., Inc.*, Comp. Gen. Dec. B-285144, 2000 CPD ¶ 108; *Global Solutions Network, Inc.*, Comp. Gen. Dec. B-298682, 2006 CPD ¶ 179.

### 1. Supplies

The statutes and the FAR contain a general definition of commercial supplies and special definitions of nondevelopmental items and commercial off-the-shelf items.

## a.  General Definition

The following general definition of commercial supplies is contained in FAR 2.101, which is identical to the definition contained in 41 U.S.C. § 103 except that additional language has been added to ¶ (3)(ii) of the FAR definition:

Commercial item means —

(1) Any item, other than real property, that is of a type customarily used by the general public or by nongovernmental entitles for purposes other than governmental purposes, and —

(i) Has been sold, leased, or licensed to the general public; or

(ii) Has been offered for sale, lease, or license to the general public;

(2) Any item that evolved from an item described in paragraph (1) of this definition through advances in technology or performance and that is not yet available in the commercial marketplace, but will be available in the commercial marketplace in time to satisfy the delivery requirements under a Government solicitation;

(3) Any item that would satisfy a criterion expressed in paragraphs (1) or (2) of this definition, but for —

(i) Modifications of a type customarily available in the commercial marketplace; or

(ii) Minor modifications of a type not customarily available in the commercial marketplace made to meet Federal Government requirements. Minor modifications means modifications that do not significantly alter the nongovernmental function or essential physical characteristics of an item or component, or change the purpose of a process. Factors to be considered in determining whether a modification is minor include the value and size of the modification and the comparative value and size of the final product. Dollar values and percentages may be used as guideposts, but are not conclusive evidence that a modification is minor;

This broad definition of commercial items includes a large number of supplies, as long as they meet the key test of being "of a type customarily used for nongovernmental purposes." Thus, under ¶ (2), the government can be the first purchaser of such an item even though it is not being sold commercially at the time of the procurement. The definition also includes in ¶ (3) modified products as long as they are of the type customarily available in the marketplace or the modifications are minor. Under prior DoD policy, certifications from offerors that their products met the definition were sufficient to justify award using the commercial item procedures, *Coherent, Inc.*, Comp. Gen. Dec. B-270998, 96-1 CPD ¶ 214 (product had been offered for sale); *Canberra Indus., Inc.*, Comp. Gen. Dec. B-271016, 96-1 CPD ¶ 269 (modifications in offered product were minor). Under the current definition, GAO has held that the determination that a product meets the commercial item definition "is largely within the discretion of the contracting agency," *NLB Corp.*, Comp. Gen. Dec. B-286846, 2001 CPD ¶ 67. Although the determination that a product meets the commercial item definition is usually made by evaluating literature submitted in response to an RFP or RFQ, it can be made during market research, *GIBBCO LLC*, Comp. Gen. Dec. B-401890, 2009 CPD ¶ 255 (housing units were commercial even though they were required to meet two special government requirements); *Firearms Training Sys., Inc.*, Comp. Gen. Dec. B-292819.2, 2004 CPD ¶ 107 (weapon simulators, as an entire system, were commercial); *NABCO, Inc.*, Comp. Gen. Dec. B-293027, 2004 CPD ¶ 15 (modifications were both of a type customarily offered in the commercial marketplace and minor), or by evaluating samples of the product, *Premier Eng'g & Mfg., Inc.*, Comp. Gen. Dec. B-283028, 99-2 CPD ¶ 65 (modifications were both of a type customarily offered in the commercial marketplace and minor).

### b. Nondevelopmental Items

Nondevelopmental items were covered by the statutes and regulations in two different ways. However, these were codified into a single definition in 41 U.S.C. § 110. FAR 2.101 breaks this definition into two segments. First, a nondevelopmental item is considered to be a commercial item if it meets the following requirements contained in the definition of "commercial item:"

> (8) A nondevelopmental item, if the procuring agency determines that the item was developed exclusively at private expense and sold in substantial quantities, on a competitive basis, to multiple State and local governments.

Second, nondevelopmental items are treated as a separate category of item subject to the congressional policies encouraging the purchase of commercial items *or* nondevelopmental items discussed earlier. For this purpose, the term "nondevelopmental item" is given a narrower definition in FAR 2.101 as follows:

> (a) Any previously developed item of supply *used exclusively for governmental purposes* by a Federal agency, a State or local government, or a foreign government with which the United States has a mutual defense cooperation agreement;

> (b) Any item of supply described in paragraph (a) of this definition that requires only minor modification or modifications of a type customarily available in the commercial marketplace in order to meet the requirements of the procuring department or agency; or

> (c) Any item of supply being produced that does not meet the requirements of paragraph (a) or (b) solely because the item is not yet in use. (Italics added)

Under the first definition, an item will qualify even if it has also been sold commercially. However, under the second definition, it can only have been sold to governmental entities. See *Lucent Techs. World Servs., Inc.*, Comp. Gen. Dec. B-295462, 2005 CPD ¶ 55, discussing these definitions.

Care must be exercised in using these two definitions because some of the policies discussed in this section apply only to commercial items, while other policies apply as well to nondevelopmental items (as defined in the narrower sense). If a solicitation permits proposals for either commercial items or nondevelopmental items, the second definition will be used and minor modifications will be acceptable, *Trimble Navigation, Ltd.*, Comp. Gen. Dec. B-271882, 96-2 CPD ¶ 102 (award on the basis of a proposed nondevelopmental item improper because modifications were major). When an agency called for a "NDI commercial item," GAO agreed with the agency that either a commercial item or an NDI item would meet the requirements of the solicitation, *Avtron Mfg., Inc.*, Comp. Gen. Dec. B-280758, 98-2 CPD ¶ 148. If the solicitation calls for the use of COTS/NDI components "to the maximum extent practicable," it will not be subject to the NDI procurement procedures, *Recon-Optical, Inc.*, Comp. Gen. Dec. B-286529, 2001 CPD ¶ 14.

### c.  Commercially Available Off-the-Shelf Items

The following definition was inserted in 41 U.S.C. § 431(c) (now 41 U.S.C. § 104) in 1996 by Pub. L. No. 104-106:

In this subtitle the term "commercially available off-the-shelf item"

(1) means an item that —

(A) is a commercial item (as described in [41 U.S.C. § 103(1)];

(B) is sold in substantial quantities in the commercial marketplace; and

(C) is offered to the Government, without modification, in the same form in which it is sold in the commercial marketplace; but

(2) does not include bulk cargo, as defined in [46 U.S.C. § 30102(4)], such as agricultural products and petroleum products.

Substantially the same definition is set forth in FAR 2.101.

Although this definition requires that a COTS item be "without modification," GAO has permitted an agency to use its discretion in determining that software met the definition even though it would require "minimal configuration," *Cerner Corp.*, Comp. Gen. Dec. B-293093, 2004 CPD ¶ 34. See also *SAP Public Servs., Inc.*, Comp. Gen. Dec. B-297535.2, 2006 CPD ¶ 39, denying a protest that the COTS requirement was not met when interfaces between COTS software modules did not meet the COTS requirement. Compare *Chant Eng'g Co.*, Comp. Gen. Dec. B-281521, 99-1 CPD ¶ 45, holding that a product did not meet the COTS definition when the offeror stated that it would use COTS components "to the fullest extent possible;" and *Clini-Comp, Int'l*, Comp. Gen. Dec. B-294059, 2004 CPD ¶ 209, holding that software "still in testing" did not meet the COTS definition. In *Dynamic Access Sys.*, Comp. Gen. Dec. B-295356, 2005 CPD ¶ 34, GAO denied a protest of a procurement calling for COTS software even though it excluded the protester's software that had been written for a government agency but had not been sold commercially.

## 2. Services

The statute and the FAR include two types of services within the definition of commercial items.

### a. Services in Support of Commercial Supplies

FAR 2.101 contains the following definition, which is substantially the same as the definition included in 41 U.S.C. § 103:

> (5) Installation services, maintenance services, repair services, training services, and other services if—
>
> > (i) Such services are procured for support of an item referred to in paragraphs (1), (2), (3), or (4) of this definition, regardless of whether such services are provided by the same source or at the same time as the item; and
> >
> > (ii) The source of such services provides similar services contemporaneously to the general public under terms and conditions similar to those offered to the Federal Government;

This definition was amended to its present language in 1999 by § 805 of Pub. L. No. 106-65, Oct. 5, 1999, to make it clear that this type of services did not have to be provided by the company that supplied the product the services were supporting.

### b. Stand-alone Services

The stand-alone services that constitute commercial items are defined in FAR 2.101 as follows:

> (6) Services of a type offered and sold competitively in substantial quantities in the commercial marketplace based on established catalog or market prices for specific tasks performed and under standard commercial terms and conditions. This does not include services that are sold based on hourly rates without an

established catalog or market price for a specific service performed. For purposes of these services —

> (i) Catalog price means a price included in a catalog, price list, schedule, or other form that is regularly maintained by the manufacturer or vendor, is either published or otherwise available for inspection by customers, and states prices at which sales are currently, or were last, made to a significant number of buyers constituting the general public; and

> (ii) Market prices means current prices that are established in the course of ordinary trade between buyers and sellers free to bargain and that can be substantiated through competition or from sources independent of the offerors.

The first sentence of this definition substantially adopts the definition contained in 41 U.S.C. § 103 except that it adds the term "of a type." The second sentence is not contained in the statute but is derived from the legislative history, House Conf. Rep. 103-712. The third sentence, including the definitions, was added by Federal Acquisition Circular 2001-01, 66 Fed. Reg. 53483, Oct. 22, 2001. This definition has been very difficult to understand because of the ambiguity of some of its language. However, it seems clear that to fall within this category of services, the precise services need not have been specifically sold but merely must be "*of a type* offered and sold competitively . . . in the commercial marketplace." In addition, such sales must have been based on "prices for *specific tasks.*" There is no guidance on the breadth of a specific task under this definition, but some agencies have interpreted it to include all the work called for under a contract, such as performing janitorial services on a building. Nor is there any guidance as to whether fixed hourly rates can constitute "prices" if the services are sold commercially on that basis and the rates can be established through catalogs, market research or competition.

With regard to services being "of a type" sold commercially, see *Aalco Forwarding, Inc.*, Comp. Gen. Dec. B-277241.8, 97-2 CPD ¶ 110, where GAO held that an agency properly determined that household goods moving services for military personnel could be acquired under commercial item procedures because such services were a "type" offered and sold in the commercial marketplace. See also *SHABA Contracting*, Comp. Gen. Dec. B-287430, 2001 CPD ¶ 105, holding that tree thinning services were commercial because they were widely sold in the commercial marketplace; and *Crescent Helicopters*, Comp. Gen. Dec. B-284706, 2000 CPD ¶ 90, holding that helicopter flight services were commercial even though they were custom tailored for the government. Other GAO decisions, not challenging that the services were commercial but dealing with the procedures used, provide an indication of the variety of types of services that have been treated as commercial, *Global Solutions Network, Inc.*, Comp. Gen. Dec. B-298682.3, 2008 CPD ¶ 131 (task order management and financial support); *ABF Freight Sys., Inc.*, Comp. Gen. Dec. B-291185, 2002 CPD ¶ 201 (motor-carrier freight services); *Daly Assocs.*, Comp. Gen. Dec. B-287908, 2001 CPD ¶ 139 (training of Army spouses in facilitating, leadership, and group skills); *Lynwood Mach. & Eng'g, Inc.*, Comp. Gen. Dec. B-285696, 2001 CPD ¶ 113 & Comp. Gen. Dec. B-287652, 2001 CPD ¶ 138 (weighing, banding, crimping, and relocation of lead); *Rockwell Elec. Commerce Corp.*, Comp. Gen. Dec. B-286201, 2001 CPD ¶ 65 (telephone call answering service); *Cortland Mem. Hosp.*, Comp. Gen. Dec. B-286890, 2001 CPD ¶ 48 (community-based outpatient medical clinic); *Symtech Corp.*, Comp. Gen. Dec. B-285358, 2000 CPD ¶ 143 (technical and administrative support of offices dealing with administration, resources management, financial management, acquisition, and technical publications as well as the research library and the reproduction center); and *Birdwell Bros. Painting & Refinishing*, Comp. Gen. Dec. B-285035, 2000 CPD ¶ 129 (maintenance of military housing). Compare *Carr's Wild Horse Ctr.*, Comp. Gen. Dec. B-285833, 2000 CPD ¶ 210, where the contracting officer determined that support of a program promoting the adoption of animals was not a commercial service; and *C.W. Gov't Travel, Inc.*, Comp. Gen. Dec. B-283408, 99-2 CPD ¶ 89, where the contracting officer determined that travel services were not commercial because several of the tasks being required were not sold commercially.

The most difficult interpretative problem with this definition is determining when a market price is "substantiated through competition or from sources independent of the offeror." The terminology seems to recognize that many market prices are obtained through competition for a specific project, such as constructing or cleaning a building. But the requirement that such commercial market prices be "substantiated" can be interpreted to require the contracting officer to ascertain what prices were obtained. A more sensible reading is that what must be substantiated is that competition is the normal way to obtain market prices for the specific type of commercial service being procured.

## 3. Combinations

The statute and FAR 2.101 permit combinations of supplies and services in support of commercial supplies as follows:

> (4) Any combination of items meeting the requirements of paragraphs (1), (2), (3), or (5) of this definition that are of a type customarily combined and sold in combination to the general public.

## 4. Transfers Between Organizations

The statute and FAR 2.101 permit transfers between organizations with a contractor to be treated as commercial items as follows:

> (7) Any item, combination of items, or service referred to in paragraphs (1) through (6) of this definition, notwithstanding the fact that the item, combination of items, or service is transferred between or among separate divisions, subsidiaries, or affiliates of a contractor.

## 5.  Key Terms

The statutory and regulatory definitions of commercial items use a number of key terms that are not defined. The following definitions of these terms and related terms were previously incorporated into FAR 15.804-3, but were removed from the FAR by Federal Acquisition Circular 90-32, Sept. 18, 1995.

### a.  General Public

The term "general public" is used in the definition of commercial supplies and services supporting such supplies. It is defined in DFARS 202.101 as follows:

> *General public and non-governmental entities*, as used in the definition of *commercial item* at FAR 2.101, do not include the Federal Government or a State, local, or foreign government (Pub. L. 110-181, section 815(b)).

The previous FAR definition stated:

> (5) The "general public" is a significant number of buyers other than the Government or affiliates of the offeror; the item involved must not be for Government end use. For the purpose of this subsection 15.804-3, items acquired for "Government end use" include items acquired for foreign military sales.

### b.  Substantial Quantities

The phrase "sold in substantial quantities" is applicable only to stand-alone services and commercially available off-the-shelf supplies. The previous FAR definition stated:

> (4) An item is "sold in substantial quantities" only when the quantities regularly sold are sufficient to constitute a real commercial market. Nominal quantities, such as models, samples, prototypes, or experimental units, do not meet this requirement. For services to be sold in substantial quantities, they must be customarily provided by the offeror, using personnel regularly employed and equipment (if any is necessary) regularly maintained solely or principally to provide the services.

## B.  Solicitation, Evaluation, and Award

The statutory goal is to use procurement procedures that "reduce any impediments . . . to the acquisition of commercial items," 10 U.S.C. § 2377(b)(5) and 41 U.S.C. § 3307(c)(5). Such impediments should be identified by the contracting officer in the course of performing the required market research to determine the availability of commercial items as discussed in Chapter 3. See FAR 12.202. In general, it can be expected that the major impediments will be excessive requirements for proposal information and data during contract performance. See, for example, *Worldwide Pri-*

*mates, Inc.*, Comp. Gen. Dec. B-294481, 2004 CPD ¶ 206, where the agency required detailed technical proposals and found only two of the nine proposals received were satisfactory, and *Phantom Prods., Inc.*, Comp. Gen. Dec. B-283882, 2000 CPD ¶ 7, denying a protest that the agency had not sufficiently specified the detailed information needed for the evaluation of technical and management proposals. Based on an understanding of the impact of such requirements on the government's ability to attract offers from commercial sellers, the procurement should be structured to minimize the affect of such impediments by streamlining the source selection process. The procedural guidance discussed in this section contains sufficient flexibility to permit contracting with commercial sources in most situations.

## 1. Type of Contract

Section 8002 of the Federal Acquisition Streamlining Act, Pub. L. No. 103-355, contained the following provision on the appropriate type of contract for the procurement of commercial items:

> (d) Use of firm, fixed price contracts.The Federal Acquisition Regulation shall include, for acquisitions of commercial items —
>
> > (1) a requirement that firm, fixed price contracts or fixed price with economic price adjustment contracts be used to the maximum extent practicable; and
> >
> > (2) a prohibition on use of cost type contracts.

This statute was implemented in FAR 12.207 requiring that contracts for commercial items be either firm-fixed-price or fixed-price with economic price adjustment and prohibiting the use of any other type of contract. This provision also provided that indefinite-delivery contracts could be used if they call for the establishment of prices on one of these two bases. The effect of this implementation was that time-and-materials and labor-hour contracts could not be used to procure commercial items even though they would have been permissible under the statute. Congress clarified the guidance on this issue in § 1432 of the National Defense Authorization Act for Fiscal Year 2004, Pub. L. No. 108-136. That section amended § 8002 to expressly authorize the use of time-and-materials and labor-hour contracts for the procurement of commercial services. See 41 U.S.C. § 3307(e)(4)(B). As a result, FAR 12.207 was amended to permit limited use of such contracts:

> (b)(1) A time-and-materials contract or labor-hour contract (see Subpart 16.6) may be used for the acquisition of commercial services when —
>
> > (i) The service is acquired under a contract awarded using —
> >
> > > (A) Competitive procedures (e.g., the procedures in 6.102, the set-aside procedures in Subpart 19.5, or competition conducted in accordance with Part 13);

(B) The procedures for other than full and open competition in 6.3 provided the agency receives offers that satisfy the Government's expressed requirement from two or more responsible offerors; or

(C) The fair opportunity procedures in 16.505, if placing an order under a multiple award delivery-order contract; and

(ii) The contracting officer —

(A) Executes a determination and findings (D&F) for the contract, in accordance with paragraph (b)(2) of this section (but see paragraph (c) of this section for indefinite-delivery contracts), that no other contract type authorized by this subpart is suitable;

(B) Includes a ceiling price in the contract or order that the contractor exceeds at its own risk; and

(C) Authorizes any subsequent change in the ceiling price only upon a determination, documented in the contract file, that it is in the best interest of the procuring agency to change the ceiling price.

(2) Each D&F required by paragraph (b)(1)(ii)(A) of this section shall contain sufficient facts and rationale to justify that no other contract type authorized by this subpart is suitable. At a minimum, the D&F shall —

(i) Include a description of the market research conducted (see 10.002(e));

(ii) Establish that it is not possible at the time of placing the contract or order to accurately estimate the extent or duration of the work or to anticipate costs with any reasonable degree of certainty;

(iii) Establish that the requirement has been structured to maximize the use of firm-fixed-price or fixed-price with economic price adjustment contracts (e.g., by limiting the value or length of the time-and-material/labor-hour contract or order; establishing fixed prices for portions of the requirement) on future acquisitions for the same or similar requirements; and

(iv) Describe actions planned to maximize the use of firm-fixed-price or fixed-price with economic price adjustment contracts on future acquisitions for the same requirements.

(3) See 16.601(d)(1) for additional approval required for contracts expected to extend beyond three years.

Several other provisions can be added to these basic contract types. For example, FAR 12.301(e)(2) permits the use of options in commercial item procurements. In addition, FAR 12.207(d) was added by FAC 2001-13, 68 Fed. Reg. 13201, March 18, 2003, to permit the use of award fees and incentives based on factors other than cost.

The National Defense Authorization Act for Fiscal Year 2008, Pub. L. No. 110-181, adds a special rule for DoD contracts. This is implemented in DFARS 212.207 as follows:

> (b) In accordance with section 805 of the National Defense Authorization Act for Fiscal Year 2008 (Pub. L. 110-181), use of time-and-materials and labor-hour contracts for the acquisition of commercial items is authorized only for the following:
>
>> (i) Services acquired for support of a commercial item, as described in paragraph (5) of the definition of commercial item at FAR 2.101 (41 U.S.C. 403(12)(E)).
>>
>> (ii) Emergency repair services.
>>
>> (iii) Any other commercial services only to the extent that the head of the agency concerned approves a written determination by the contracting officer that —
>>
>>> (A) The services to be acquired are commercial services as defined in paragraph (6) of the definition of commercial item at FAR 2.101 (41 U.S.C. 403(12)(F));
>>>
>>> (B) If the services to be acquired are subject to FAR 15.403-1(c)(3)(ii), the offeror of the services has submitted sufficient information in accordance with that subsection;
>>>
>>> (C) Such services are commonly sold to the general public through use of time-and-materials or labor-hour contracts; and
>>>
>>> (D) The use of a time-and-materials or labor-hour contract type is in the best interest of the Government.

## 2.  Specifications

FAR 12.202(b) provides the following guidance on specifications for commercial item procurements:

> (b) The description of agency need must contain sufficient detail for potential offerors of commercial items to know which commercial products or services may be suitable. Generally, for acquisitions in excess of the simplified acquisition threshold, an agency's statement of need for a commercial item will describe the type of product or service to be acquired and explain how the agency intends to use the product or service in terms of function to be performed, performance

requirement or essential physical characteristics. Describing the agency's needs in these terms allows offerors to propose methods that will best meet the needs of the Government.

The preference for the acquisition of commercial items may significantly weaken the general rule that specifications may not be unduly restrictive. Thus, when an agency decides to use a commercial item, it will be difficult for a competitor to argue that it should have opened up the competition to noncommercial items. See, for example, *Dynamic Access Sys.*, Comp. Gen. Dec. B-295356, 2005 CPD ¶ 34, finding that requiring a COTS product was not unduly restrictive when the agency had determined that use of such a product would reduce its life-cycle costs.

In the case of products, the description can be a brand name but the agency must follow the requirement in FAR 11.104 that the salient characteristics of the product be provided, *Elementar Americas, Inc.*, Comp. Gen. Dec. B-289115, 2002 CPD ¶ 20. However, the agency is not required to provide the brand name of a product that meets its requirements if it provides all of its functional requirements, *Omega World Travel, Inc.*, Comp. Gen. Dec. B-280456.2, 98-2 CPD ¶ 73. See also *Access Logic, Inc.*, Comp. Gen. Dec. B-274748, 97-1 CPD ¶ 36, *recons. & mod.*, 97-1 CPD ¶ 159, holding that, while the use of functional or performance specifications is appropriate, the agency must advise offerors of its "specific ideas" of what features would satisfy its needs. See also *Candle Corp. v. United States*, 40 Fed. Cl. 658 (1998), holding that when an agency relaxes a specification requirement for a commercial item, the solicitation must be amended to permit all competitors an equal opportunity to compete for the relaxed requirement.

## 3. Solicitation

The FAR contains general guidance on the solicitation procedures to be followed in acquiring commercial items, as well as a "streamlined" solicitation procedure. The contracting officer has complete discretion as to the procedure to be used.

### a. General Guidance

The initial guidance states in FAR 12.203 that the contracting officer "shall use" the policies in FAR Part 12 "in conjunction with the policies and procedures" in FAR Parts 13, 14, and 15 "as appropriate for the particular acquisition." This appears to give the contracting officer complete freedom in selecting the solicitation procedure — including the use of sealed bidding or competitive negotiation procedures. See *Johnson Controls World Servs., Inc.*, Comp. Gen. Dec. B-285144, 2000 CPD ¶ 108 (sealed bidding appropriate procedure for base operations and maintenance services).However, the balance of the guidance makes it clear that simplification is desirable. Thus, sealed bidding or standard negotiation procedures should be used very rarely in the procurement of commercial items. However, as discussed below, the protests to GAO indicate that agencies frequently structure their commercial item acquisitions like competitively negotiated procurements with multiple evaluation factors.

Unless the streamlined procedure is used, the contracting officer must use Standard Form 1449, Solicitation/Contract/Order for Commercial Items, when issuing written solicitations and awarding contracts and placing orders for commercial items. This form may also be used for documenting receipt, inspection, and acceptance of commercial items, FAR 12.204. FAR 12.205 provides the following guidance for solicitations for commercial items:

(a) Where technical information is necessary for evaluation of offers, agencies should, as part of market research, review existing product literature generally available in the industry to determine its adequacy for purposes of evaluation. If adequate, contracting officers shall request existing product literature from offerors of commercial items in lieu of unique technical proposals.

(b) Contracting officers should allow offerors to propose more than one product that will meet a Government need in response to solicitations for commercial items. The contracting officer shall evaluate each product as a separate offer.

(c) Consistent with the requirements at 5.203(b), the contracting officers may allow fewer than 30 days response time for receipt of offers for commercial items, unless the acquisition is subject to NAFTA or the Trace Agreements Act (see 5.203(h))..

FAR 12.301(b) provides two standard solicitation provisions, described as follows:

Insert the following provisions in solicitations for the acquisition of commercial items, and clauses in solicitations and contracts for the acquisition of commercial items:

(1) *The provision at 52.212-1, Instructions to Offerors — Commercial Items.* This provision provides a single, streamlined set of instructions to be used when soliciting offers for commercial items and is incorporated in the solicitation by reference (see Block 27a, SF 1449). The contracting officer may tailor these instructions or provide additional instructions tailored to the specific acquisition in accordance with 12.302.

(2) *The provision at 52.212-3, Offeror Representations and Certifications — Commercial Items.* This provision provides a single, consolidated list of certifications and representations for the acquisition of commercial items and is attached to the solicitation for offerors to complete and return with their offer. This provision may not be tailored except in accordance with Subpart 1.4.

FAR 12.302 provides the following guidance on the permissible tailoring of the FAR 52.212-1 solicitation provision:

The provision and clauses established in this subpart are intended to address, to the maximum extent practicable, commercial market practices for a wide range of potential Government acquisitions of commercial items. However, because of the broad range of commercial items acquired by the Government, variations in commercial practices, and the relative volume of the Government's acquisitions in the specific market, contracting officers may, within the limitations of this subpart, and after conducting appropriate market research, tailor the provision at 52.212-1, Instructions to Offerors — Commercial Items, . . .

DFARS 212.301(f) requires the use of additional solicitation provisions in Department of Defense procurements.

## b.  Pricing Information

Contracting officers are prohibited from requiring certified cost or pricing data when they acquire commercial items, FAR 15.403-1(c)(3)(i). However, this prohibition applies only if the contracting officer determines in writing "that the offeror has submitted sufficient information to evaluate, through price analysis, the reasonableness of the price of such services," FAR 15.403-1(c)(3)(ii)(A). FAR 15.403-1(c)(3)(ii) provides the following guidance on the information that would be sufficient:

(B) In order to make this determination, the contracting officer may request the offeror to submit prices paid for the same or similar commercial items under comparable terms and conditions by both Government and commercial customers; and

(C) If the contracting officer determines that the information described in paragraph (c)(3)(ii)(B) of this section is not sufficient to determine the reasonableness of price, other relevant information regarding the basis for price or cost, including information on labor costs, material costs and overhead rates may be requested.

See Chapter 10 for a more detailed discussion of pricing commercial item contracts.

## c.  Streamlined Procedures

The FAR also contains a "test program" permitting the use of simplified acquisition procedures for procurements of commercial items in amounts not exceeding $6,500,000. A higher threshold is applicable to procurements not exceeding $12,000,000 as prescribed by FAR 13.500(e) as follows:

(1) The acquisition is for commercial items that, as determined by the head of the agency, are to be used in support of a contingency operation or to facilitate the defense against or recovery from nuclear, biological, chemical, or radiological attack; or

(2) The acquisition will be treated as an acquisition of commercial items in accordance with 12.102(f)(1).

FAR 12.102(f)(1) states:

(f)(1) Contracting officers may treat any acquisition of supplies or services that, as determined by the head of the agency, are to be used to facilitate defense against or recovery from nuclear, biological, chemical, or radiological attack, as an acquisition of commercial items.

If an agency conducts a procurement under the test program when it has no reasonable evidence that the threshold will not be exceeded, the procurement will be held to be improper, *Global Communications Solutions, Inc.*, Comp. Gen. Dec. B-299044, 2007 CPD ¶ 30.

The major advantage of this "test program" is the streamlined procedure described in FAR Subpart 12.6. This permits the combining of the synopsis and solicitation into a single document with a response time no longer than is necessary to give potential offerors a reasonable opportunity to respond to the solicitation. This allows greatly shortening the statutory requirements for standard procurement that require a 15-day synopsis period and a 30-day offer period. The guidance on the use of this fast procedure is set forth in FAR 12.603, as follows:

(a) When a written solicitation will be issued, the contracting officer may use the following procedure to reduce the time required to solicit and award contracts for the acquisition of commercial items. This procedure combines the synopsis required by 5.203 and the issuance of the solicitation into a single document.

(b) When using the combined synopsis/solicitation procedure, the SF 1449 is not used for issuing the solicitation.

(c) To use these procedures, the contracting officer shall —

(1) Prepare the synopsis as described at 5.207.

(2) In the Description, include the following additional information:

(i) The following statement:

This is a combined synopsis/solicitation for commercial items prepared in accordance with the format in FAR Subpart 12.6, as supplemented with additional information included in this notice. This announcement constitutes the only solicitation; proposals are being requested and a written solicitation will not be issued.

(ii) The solicitation number and a statement that the solicitation is issued as an invitation to bid (IFB), request for quotation (RFQ) or request for proposal (RFP).

(iii) A statement that the solicitation document and incorporated provisions and clauses are those in effect through Federal Acquisition Circular ___.

(iv) A notice regarding any set-aside and the associated NAICS code and small business size standard. Also include a statement regarding the Small Business Competitiveness Demonstration Program, if applicable.

(v) A list of contract line item number(s) and items, quantities and units of measure, (including option(s), if applicable).

(vi) Description of requirements for the items to be acquired.

(vii) Date(s) and place(s) of delivery and acceptance and FOB point.

(viii) A statement that the provision at 52.212-1, Instructions to Offerors — Commercial, applies to this acquisition and a statement regarding any addenda to the provision.

(ix) A statement regarding the applicability of the provision at 52.212-2, Evaluation — Commercial Items, if used, and the specific evaluation criteria to be included in paragraph (a) of that provision. If this provision is not used, describe the evaluation procedures to be used.

(x) A statement advising offerors to include a completed copy of the provision at 52.212-3, Offeror Representations and Certifications — Commercial Items, with its offer.

(xi) A statement that the clause at 52.212-4, Contract Terms and Conditions — Commercial Items, applies to this acquisition and a statement regarding any addenda to the clause.

(xii) A statement that the clause at 52.212-5, Contract Terms and Conditions Required To Implement Statutes Or Executive Orders — Commercial Items, applies to this acquisition and a statement regarding which, if any, of the additional FAR clauses cited in the clause are applicable to the acquisition.

(xiii) A statement regarding any additional contract requirement(s) or terms and conditions (such as contract financing arrangements or warranty requirements) determined by the contracting officer to be necessary for this acquisition and consistent with customary commercial practices.

(xiv) A statement regarding the Defense Priorities and Allocations System (DPAS) and assigned rating, if applicable.

(xv) The date, time and place offers are due.

(xvi) The name and telephone number of the individual to contact for information regarding the solicitation.

(3) Allow response time for receipt of offers as follows:

(i) Because the synopsis and solicitation are contained in a single document, it is not necessary to publish a separate synopsis 15 days before the issuance of the solicitation.

(ii) When using the combined synopsis and solicitation, contracting offerors shall establish a response time in accordance with 5.203(b) (but see 5.203(h)).

(4) Publish amendments to solicitations in the same manner as the initial synopsis and solicitation.

This procedure permits a 15 day combined synopsis and response time. See *GIBBCO LLC*, Comp. Gen. Dec. B-401890, 2009 CPD ¶ 255, denying a protest that a 22 day response time was unreasonable, and *American Artisans Prods., Inc.*, Comp. Gen. Dec. B-281409, 98-2 CPD ¶ 155, denying a protest that 15 days was too short when five offers were received within that time.

## d.  Late Proposals

Paragraph (f) of the FAR 52.212-1 solicitation provision contains the same strict late offer provision that is included in sealed bid and negotiated procurements. This requirement is strictly enforced, *Labatt Food Serv., Inc.*, Comp. Gen. Dec. B-310939.6, 2008 CPD ¶ (time specified in solicitation governs over default time in the provision); *Kesser Int'l*, Comp. Gen. Dec. B-296294, 2005 CPD ¶ 127 (proposal rejected because it was two minutes late). Obtaining additional information to support an offeror's technical proposal was held to violate the late proposal rule, *Radiation Oncology Group of WNY, PC*, Comp. Gen. Dec. B-310354.2, 2009 CPD ¶ 136. In *Labatt* GAO denied an additional grounds of protest asserting that none of the proposal revisions should have been accepted because they were sent by email which was not allowed by the solicitation. GAO reasoned that there was no prejudice when all offerors followed the same procedure. The Court of Federal Claims disagreed, enjoining the award of the contract in *Labatt Food Serv., Inc. v. United States*, 84 Fed. Cl. 50 (2008).

Although this provision permits acceptance of late offers from an "otherwise successful offeror," GAO agreed that it was proper to reject a late modification lowering the price from an offeror that had not yet been determined to be the successful offeror. See *Sunrise Med. HHG, Inc.*, Comp. Gen. Dec. B-310230, 2008 CPD ¶ 7, stating:

[A]n offeror cannot make itself the "otherwise successful offeror" by submitting a late proposal modification; instead the offeror must already be the offeror in line for award prior to the time the late proposal modification is submitted. *Phyllis M. Chestang*, B-298394.3, Nov. 20, 2006, 2006 CPD ¶ 176 at 5 n.3. In this regard, an offeror cannot avail itself of the late proposal submission provision where the agency has not already identified an "otherwise successful offeror." *Global Analytic Info. Tech. Servs., Inc.*, B-298840.2, Feb. 6, 2007, 2007 CPD ¶ 57 at 5-6.

In *M. Braun, Inc.*, Comp. Gen. Dec. B-298935.2, 2007 CPD ¶ 96, GAO assumed that this provision also applied to late quotations (even though it used the term "proposal") because the agency had made that assumption.

## 4. Evaluation Scheme

The general guidance on the evaluation scheme to be used in the acquisition of commercial items indicates that the contracting officer has broad latitude in selecting the evaluation factors and may conduct commercial item procurement without evaluation factors. This would entail the procurement of commercial items on the basis of price alone. However, FAR 12.206 states that past performance "should be an important element in every evaluation." The balance of the guidance on evaluation factors is directed to supply contracts where agencies are urged not to solicit technical proposals. See FAR 12.205 stating:

(a) Where technical information is necessary for evaluation of offers, agencies should, as part of market research, review existing product literature generally available in the industry to determine its adequacy for purposes of evaluation. If adequate, contracting officers shall request existing product literature from offerors of commercial items in lieu of unique technical proposals.

See also FAR 12.602(b) stating:

For many commercial items, the criteria need not be more detailed than technical (capability of the item offered to meet the agency need), price and past performance. Technical capability may be evaluated by how well the proposed products meet the Government requirement instead of predetermined subfactors. Solicitations for commercial items do not have to contain subfactors for technical capability when the solicitation adequately describes the item's intended use. A technical evaluation would normally include examination of such things as product literature, product samples (if requested), technical features and warranty provisions. Past performance shall be evaluated in accordance with the procedures in section 13.106 or subpart 15.3, as applicable.

In spite of this sound guidance, agencies tend to ignore the FAR and call for technical proposals in commercial item procurements for relatively straightforward supplies and services. See, for example, *Command Mgmt. Servs., Inc.*, Comp. Gen. Dec. B-310261, 2008 CPD ¶ 29 (lodging, meal and transportation services); *OK Produce*, Comp. Gen. Dec. B-299058, 2007 CPD ¶ 31 (fresh fruit and vegetables);

*Philadelphia Produce Market Wholesalers, LLC*, Comp. Gen. Dec. B-298751, 2006 CPD ¶ 193 (fresh fruit and vegetables); *NCR Gov't Sys. LLC*, Comp. Gen. Dec. B-297959, 2006 CPD ¶ 82 (computer system for retail stores); *Cogent Sys., Inc.*, Comp. Gen. Dec. B-295990.4, 2005 CPD ¶ 179 (fingerprint identification system). Such practices, of course, deprive the agency of the benefit of streamlining that the FAR suggests.

The agency is not required to state how a product will be tested and may use any rational test procedure, *IMLCORP LLC*, Comp. Gen. Dec. B-310582, 2008 CPD ¶ 15 (subjective test of acoustical properties of device by Navy personnel satisfactory). It is also proper to evaluate a product by using the results of studies of the product and field reports from users even though the offer has submitted samples of a modified product. See *Silynx Commc'ns, Inc.*, Comp. Gen. Dec. B-310667, 2008 CPD ¶ 36, stating:

> We find that the agency's determination was reasonable. First, nothing in the solicitation contemplated or required the agency to conduct product inspection or testing, or to permit product demonstrations; in fact, the RFP's instructions called for submission of product samples only where such samples were otherwise required under the terms of the solicitation, and there was no such requirement for product samples in the RFP. Rather, the RFP contemplated that offerors would include product literature or other information — for example, test data or feedback from prior or current users of their product — to demonstrate compliance with the RFP's requirements, and that, after award, the contractor would conduct first article testing and field user evaluation demonstrations to verify compliance of its product with the performance characteristics proposed in the firm's offer. Thus, there was nothing improper in the agency's declining to conduct an inspection or to perform testing of the Silynx product, or to permit demonstrations as part of the evaluation process.

> Second, we find no basis to object to the agency's reliance on the informal inquiry of operational force members and the audiologist's opinion. While the inquiry of the operational forces was informal in nature, there is no indication in the record that it did not accurately reflect the users' opinions. Silynx has submitted no information — for example, its own user feedback information or test data for either of its proposed earpieces — showing different results from the information obtained by the agency.

When evaluation factors are used, FAR 12.301(c) provides a standard solicitation provision in FAR 52.212-2. This provision calls for the insertion of the evaluation factors and their relative importance. Agencies are also permitted to use a different solicitation provision if they are using the procedures of FAR Parts 13, 14 or 15, FAR 12.301(c)(2). If the agency chooses to use simplified acquisition procedures, no statement of relative importance is required, FAR 12.602. However, the agency may not mislead competitors as to the relative importance of a factor. See *Finlen Complex, Inc.*, Comp. Gen. Dec. B-288280, 2001 CPD ¶ 167, granting a protest in a procurement of commercial services using simplified procedures contained multiple evaluation factors because past performance was given very little importance. If an agency conducts the procurement using FAR Part 15 procedures, GAO will disregard the FAR permitting no statement of relative importance and apply the normal rule giving equal weight to evaluation factors where no relative importance statement is included in the solicitation, *Bio-Rad Labs., Inc.*, Comp. Gen. Dec. B-297553, 2007 CPD ¶ 58.

As with all other types of procurement, evaluation must be based on the factors stated in the solicitation, FAR 12.602(b). The basic standard is that "an agency must conduct the procurement consistent with a concern for fair and equitable competition and must evaluate quotations [or offers] in accordance with the terms of the solicitation," *DOER Marine*, Comp. Gen. Dec. B-295087, 2004 CPD ¶ 252. See also *Access Logic, Inc.*, Comp. Gen. Dec. B-274748, 97-1 CPD ¶ 36, *recons. & mod.*, 97-1 CPD ¶ 159 (proposed commercial product may not be rejected on the basis of technical requirements not set forth in the solicitation). Compare *InterOcean Sys., Inc.*, Comp. Gen. Dec. B-290916, 2002 CPD ¶ 178, agreeing that an agency properly evaluated proposals in accordance with unspecified subfactors as permitted by the FAR. It is permissible to cancel the procurement after receipt of proposals if the evaluation factors are inadvertently omitted from the solicitation, *Nidek, Inc.*, Comp. Gen. Dec. B-272255, 96-2 CPD ¶ 112.

## 5. Communications After Receipt of Quotations or Offers

FAR Part 12 contains no guidance on communications with competitors after the receipt of quotations or offers. Thus, it can be expected that the rules pertaining to the type of procedure adopted will be applied to the procurement. This would mean that the contracting officer would be free to conduct open communications after receipt of quotations but would be very restricted in the permissive communications after receipt of bids. See *American Recycling Sys., Inc.*, Comp. Gen. Dec. B-292500, 2003 CPD ¶ 143, where extensive communication with the potential vendor and the manufacturer of the quoted product was permitted. See also *United Marine Int'l LLC*, Comp. Gen. Dec. B-281512, 99-1 CPD ¶ 44 (negotiation with only company with best quotation permitted). With regard to procurements using competitive negotiation procedures, it would be expected that the rules pertaining to clarifications and discussions, discussed in Chapter 6, would be followed. Exchanges have been found to be clarifications not discussions in *MG Indus.*, Comp. Gen. Dec. B-283010.3, 2000 CPD ¶ 17 (request for explanation of the pricing terms of the quotation); and *National Beef Packing Co.*, Comp. Gen. Dec. B-296534, 2005 CPD ¶ 168 (description of product). However, the controlling factor will probably be the way the procurement is actually conducted. See, for example, *Kathryn Huddleston & Assocs., Ltd.*, Comp. Gen. Dec. B-289453, 2002 CPD ¶ 57, where the agency solicited quotations but then conducted the procurement as if it were a competitive negotiation. GAO held that rules governing the establishment of a competitive range and discussions were applicable, stating:

> Although an agency is not required to establish a competitive range or conduct discussions under simplified acquisition procedures, we think that where an agency avails itself of these negotiated procurement procedures, the agency should fairly and reasonably treat quoters in establishing the competitive range and conducting discussions. See *Finlen Complex, Inc.*, B-288280, Oct. 10, 2001, 2001 CPD ¶ 167 at 8-10.

* * *

> Under [FAR Part 15] rules, the determination of whether a proposal is in the competitive range is principally a matter within the discretion of the procuring agency. *Dismas Charities, Inc.*, B-284754, May 22, 2000, 2000 CPD ¶ 84 at 3. FAR § 15.306(c) allows an agency to establish a competitive range consisting of only the most highly-rated proposals. Under the regulation, agencies properly may eliminate proposals that are deemed to have no realistic prospect for award. *SDS Petroleum Prods., Inc.*, B-280430, Sept. 1, 1998, 98-2 CPD ¶ 59 at 5-6. Judgments regarding which proposals are included in the competitive range must be made in a relatively equal manner. An agency cannot reasonably exclude a proposal from the competitive range where the strengths and weaknesses found in that proposal are similar to those found in proposals included in the competitive range. *Columbia Research Corp.*, B-284157, Feb. 28, 2000, 2000 CPD ¶ 158 at 4; *Nations, Inc.*, B-280048, Aug. 24, 1998, 99-2 CPD ¶ 94 at 6-10.

See also *Dubinsky v. United States*, 43 Fed. Cl. 243 (1999), where the court found that FAR Part 15 procedures had been used and ruled that the agency had not complied with those procedures when it conducted discussions with only the awardee. Compare *Paraclete Contracts*, Comp. Gen. Dec. B-299883, 2007 CPD ¶ 153, holding that no clarification of a mistake was required when the agency used simplified procedures.

## 6. Source Selection and Award

The only guidance on source selection and the award of contracts for commercial items is found in FAR 12.602(c), as follows:

> Select the offer that is most advantageous to the Government based on the factors contained in the solicitation. Fully document the rationale for selection of the successful offeror including discussion of any tradeoffs considered.

Award on the basis of the initial proposals is permissible when there is a reasonable basis for distinguishing between the proposals because ¶ (g) of the FAR 52.212-1 solicitation provision calls for such award, *Chem-Spray-South, Inc.*, Comp. Gen. Dec. B-400928.2, 2009 CPD ¶ 144 (significant price differential led agency to conclude that there was a clear winner); *Silynx Commc'ns, Inc.*, B-310667, 2008 CPD ¶ 36 (awardee was only offeror with acceptable technical proposal).

As in other types of procurement, award to an offeror that does not comply with the solicitation is improper, *Wyse Tech., Inc.*, Comp. Gen. Dec. B-297454, 2006 CPD ¶ 23 (failure to submit required Trade Agreements Act certificate).

When evaluation factors other than price are used, the source selection must be based on a reasoned trade-off analysis. See *General Dynamics C4 Sys., Inc.*, Comp. Gen. Dec. B-299675.2, 2008 CPD ¶ 122, agreeing that award to a higher priced offeror was proper when the protester did not meet the mandatory requirements of the solicitation; and *BTC Contract Servs., Inc.*, Comp. Gen. Dec. B-295877, 2005 CPD ¶ 96, confirming an award to a higher priced offeror based on better past performance. See also *Midland Supply, Inc.*, Comp. Gen. Dec. B-298720, 2007 CPD ¶ 2, granting a protest because the agency used a point scoring system (including point scoring price) and, without further analysis, selected the offeror with the highest number of points. GAO stated:

> While this is a commercial-item procurement, it was conducted using negotiated procedures, at least in terms of the substance of the agency's actions. n5 Specifically, the solicitation provided that the combination of technical evaluation factors — past performance and delivery — would be considered significantly more important than price in determining the proposals that were most advantageous to the government. Under this type of evaluation scheme, an agency has the discretion to determine whether the technical advantage associated with an offeror's proposal is worth its higher price. The propriety of a price/technical tradeoff turns not on the difference in the technical scores or ratings per se, but on whether the agency's judgment concerning the significance of the difference is reasonable and adequately justified in light of the evaluation scheme. *Opti-Lite Optical*, B-281693, Mar. 22, 1999, 99-1 CPD ¶ 61 at 4.
>
> In order for our Office to perform a meaningful review of an agency's award determination, the agency is required to have adequate documentation to support its evaluation of proposals and its award decision. *Century Envtl. Hygiene, Inc.*, B-279378, June 5, 1998, 98-1 CPD ¶ 164 at 4; *Biospherics, Inc.*, B-278508.4 et al., Oct. 6, 1998, 98-2 CPD ¶ 96 at 4; *Arco Mgmt. of Wash., D.C., Inc.*, B-248653, Sept. 11, 1992, 92-2 CPD ¶ 173 at 3. An award decision is not reasonable where there is no documentation or explanation to support the price/technical tradeoff and where the agency makes its award decision based strictly on a mechanical comparison of the offerors' total point scores. *Universal Bldg. Maint., Inc.*, B-282456, July 15, 1999, 99-2 CPD ¶ 32 at 4; see also FAR §§ 12.602(c), 15.308.

## C. Special Authority

In 41 U.S.C. § 428a and § 437 (now 41 U.S.C. § 1903(c)), Congress granted special authority to use commercial item procurement procedures for certain classes of procurement. When this authority is exercised, a few special procedures are applicable. This authority and the special procedures are described in FAR 12.102 as follows:

(f)(1) Contracting officers may treat any acquisition of supplies or services that, as determined by the head of the agency, are to be used to facilitate defense against or recovery from nuclear, biological, chemical, or radiological attack, as an acquisition of commercial items.

(2) A contract in an amount greater than $18 million that is awarded on a sole source basis for an item or service treated as a commercial item under paragraph (f)(1) of this section but does not meet the definition of a commercial item as defined at FAR 2.101 shall not be exempt from —

(i) Cost accounting standards (see Subpart 30.2); or

(ii) Cost or pricing data requirements (see 15.403).

(g)(1) In accordance with section 1431 of the National Defense Authorization Act for Fiscal Year 2004 (Pub. L. 108-136) (41 U.S.C. 437), the contracting officer also may use Part 12 for any acquisition for services that does not meet the definition of commercial item in FAR 2.101, if the contract or task order —

(i) Is entered into on or before November 24, 2013;

(ii) Has a value of $30 million or less;

(iii) Meets the definition of performance-based contracting at FAR 2.101;

(iv) Includes a quality assurance surveillance plan;

(v) Includes performance incentives where appropriate;

(vi) Specifies a firm-fixed price for specific tasks to be performed or outcomes to be achieved; and

(vii) Is awarded to an entity that provides similar services to the general public under terms and conditions similar to those in the contract or task order.

(2) In exercising the authority specified in paragraph (g)(1) of this section, the contracting officer should tailor paragraph (a) of the clause at FAR 52.212-4 as may be necessary to ensure the contract's remedies adequately protect the Government's interests.

## D.  Terms and Conditions

One of the major elements of the policy favoring the procurement of commercial items was the elimination of as many contract clauses as was practicable. The

FASA amended a number of laws to state that they did not apply to the procurement of commercial items and added 41 U.S.C. § 430 (now 41 U.S.C. § 1906) requiring the FAR to include a list of laws that were not applicable to contracts and subcontracts for commercial items. Subsequently, § 4203 of the Clinger-Cohen Act of 1996 enacted 41 U.S.C. § 431 (now 41 U.S.C. § 1907) requiring that the FAR list laws that are not applicable to the procurement of commercial off-the-shelf items.

## 1. *Standard Commercial Items*

There are two standard clauses for commercial item procurements. The first contains the operating clauses for contract performance while the second covers the statutory and executive order provisions applicable to government procurement in general.

### a. *Operating Provisions*

FAR 52.212-4 provides a standard contract clause, Contract Terms and Conditions — Commercial Items, which contains 20 specific provisions to be used in contracts for commercial items. Many of these provisions are greatly shortened versions of the standard clauses used in the procurement of supplies such as the termination clauses, the inspection clauses, the changes clause, and the disputes clause. An Alternate I clause is provided for use in time-and-materials and labor-hour contracts. This clause includes an elaborate Payments provision (¶ (i)).

The contracting officer is authorized to "tailor" certain of these provisions, but only to reflect commercial practices, FAR 12.302(a). However, FAR 12.302(b) provides that the following clauses, which implement statutory requirements, may not be tailored:

(1) Assignments;

(2) Disputes;

(3) Payment (except as provided in subpart 32.11);

(4) Invoice;

(5) Other compliances; and

(6) Compliance with laws unique to government contracts.

FAR 12.213 contains the following guidance to contracting officers on the subject of tailoring:

It is a common practice in the commercial marketplace for both the buyer and seller to propose terms and conditions written from their particular perspectives.

The terms and conditions prescribed in this Part 12 seek to balance the interests of both the buyer and seller. These terms and conditions are generally appropriate for use in a wide range of acquisitions. However, market research may indicate other commercial practices that are appropriate for the acquisition of the particular item. These practices should be considered for incorporation into the solicitation and contract if the contracting officer determines them appropriate in concluding a business arrangement satisfactory to both parties and not otherwise precluded by law or Executive order.

FAR 12.302 permits tailoring of clauses that does not follow customary commercial practice if a waiver is obtained:

> (c) *Tailoring inconsistent with customary commercial practice.* The contracting officer shall not tailor any clause or otherwise include any additional terms or conditions in a solicitation or contract for commercial items in a manner that is inconsistent with customary commercial practice for the item being acquired unless a waiver is approved in accordance with agency procedures. The request for waiver must describe the customary commercial practice found in the marketplace, support the need to include a term or condition that is inconsistent with that practice and include a determination that use of the customary commercial practice is inconsistent with the needs of the Government. A waiver may be requested for an individual or class of contracts for that specific item.

Inclusion of a clause not in accordance with commercial practice is improper if no waiver is obtained, *Smelkinson Sysco Food Servs.*, Comp. Gen. Dec. B-281631, 99-1 CPD ¶ 57 (clause requiring disclosure of internal profit data). Compare *American Coll. of Physicians Servs., Inc.*, Comp. Gen. Dec. B-294881, 2005 CPD ¶ 1, denying a protest where the protester could not identify a specific clause that had been tailored.

Since the FAR 52.212-4 clause contains provisions reflecting supply contracting practices, tailoring may be required when it is used for other types of contracts such as procurements of services and construction. See the July 3, 2003 memorandum from the Administrator of the Officer of Federal Procurement Policy (*http://www.whitehouse.gov/omb/procurement/far/far_part12.pd*) noting that FAR Part 12 is not equipped to handle "differing site conditions, change orders, and suspension of work" that are likely to arise during new construction or non-routine alteration and repair services. Instead of recommending tailoring, the memorandum states that Part 12 procedures should not be used for this type of work.

There have been a number of contract appeals requiring the board to interpret the FAR 52.212-4 clause and the decisions indicate that they will generally apply the same legal principles to this clause as have been applied to the standard contract clauses. However, following commercial practice, this clause gives the government greater rights than the standard inspection clause with regard to post-acceptance rights. See the following provisions:

(a) *Inspection/Acceptance.* The Contractor shall only tender for acceptance those items that conform to the requirements of this contract. The Government reserves the right to inspect or test any supplies or services that have been tendered for acceptance. The Government may require repair or replacement of nonconforming supplies or reperformance of nonconforming services at no increase in contract price. If repair/replacement or reperformance will not correct the defects or is not possible, the Government may seek an equitable price reduction or adequate consideration for acceptance of nonconforming supplies or services. The Government must exercise its postacceptance rights (1) within a reasonable time after the defect was discovered or should have been discovered; and (2) before any substantial change occurs in the condition of the item, unless the change is due to the defect in the item.

\* \* \*

(o) Warranty. The Contractor warrants and implies that the items delivered hereunder are merchantable and fit for use for the particular purpose described in this contract.

See *John Snow, Inc. v. United States*, 78 Fed. Cl. 763 (2007), discussing these differences in a dispute involving a contract that contained both the FAR 52.212-4 clause and standard clauses. The above inspection provision was interpreted in *Fischer Imaging Corp.*, VABCA 6125-6127, 02-2 BCA ¶ 32,003, and VABCA 6343, 02-2 BCA ¶ 32,048, to require government final inspection within a reasonable time after delivery and use of the commercial product in order to preserve the post-acceptance rights given to the government by the clause. In *Bay Shipbuilding Co.*, DOTBCA 4153, 03-1 BCA ¶ 32,256, the board held that this provision required the contractor to bear the cost of reinspecting government property that might have been damaged by defectively performed services.

The changes paragraph in the FAR 52.212-4 clause (¶ (c)) is unique in the fact that it does not permit the government to issue unilateral changes — with the result that it is questionable whether there can be constructive changes. Nonetheless, in *SAWADI Corp.*, ASBCA 53073, 01-1 BCA ¶ 31,357, the board, without citing the contract clause, decided four constructive changes claims for extra work, two constructive suspension of work claims, and one constructive acceleration claim. The boards have ruled on constructive changes claims without citing the clause in *Keller Mech. Servs., Inc.*, ASBCA 56318, 09-1 BCA ¶ 34,111 (claim for extra work granted based on ambiguous specifications); *Service Rodriguez Barragan, S.L.*, ASBCA 54622, 08-1 BCA ¶ 33,812 (claim for extra work denied because of patent ambiguity); *Arcadis U.S., Inc. v. Department of Interior*, CBCA 918, 08-1 BCA ¶ 33,807 (claim for extra work denied based on interpretation of unilateral modification); *California Bus Tels. v. Department of Agriculture*, CBCA 135, 07-1 BCA ¶ 33,553 (claim for extra work denied because no contracting officer ordered it); *Range Tech.* Corp., ASBCA 51943, 06-2 BCA ¶ 33,371 (claim for extra work denied because contractor voluntarily performed extra work); *Bradford E. Englander, Liquidating Trustee for*

*Dulles Networking Assocs., Inc.*, VABCA 6473, 01-2 BCA ¶ 31,466 (claim for extra work granted). These cases may be instances where the board found jurisdiction in the Disputes paragraph of the clause. See also *Madison Lawrence, Inc.*, ASBCA 56551, 09-2 BCA ¶ 34,235, where the board found that the contractor had filed a proper Disputes clause claim for reformation based on alleged government misstatements of the amount of work to be performed. In contrast, in *Hawaii CyberSpace*, ASBCA 54065, 04-2 BCA ¶ 32,744, the board noted the difference in the changes language but ruled that the contractor should be compensated for extra work because it had been directed by the contracting officer. Compare *Bridget Allen*, ASBCA 54696, 05-1 BCA ¶ 32,871, *aff'd*, 177 Fed. Appx. 977 (Fed. Cir.), *cert. denied*, 549 U.S. 903 (2006), where the board denied a constructive changes claim but the contract contained a standard Changes clause as well as the FAR 52.212-4 clause.

A number of appeals have sustained terminations for cause (¶ (m)). In *Double B Enter., Inc.*, ASBCA 52010, 01-1 BCA ¶ 31,396, the board rejected a claim of excusable delay and held that a termination for cause was valid even though it occurred the day after delivery was required. See also *ZIOS Corp.*, ASBCA 56626, 2010 BCA ¶ 34,344 (termination for cause proper when contractor failed to perform on time);*Thomson & Pratt Ins. Assocs., Inc. v. Department of State*, GSBCA 15979-ST, 05-1 BCA ¶ 32,944 (termination for cause proper when contractor refused to provide disputed insurance coverage); *Falls Mfg., Inc.*, DOTBCA 4149, 04-2 BCA ¶ 32,632 (valid termination when less than 50% of the commercial products had been delivered by the delivery date); *Sigma Tech Enter., Inc.*, ASBCA 52774, 04-1 BCA ¶ 32,484 (termination for cause proper when product did not meet specification requirements); *Specialty Trans., Inc. v. United States*, 57 Fed. Cl. 1 (2003) (termination for cause proper when contractor refused to continue performance); *Aerobotics Corp.*, ASBCA 52134, 02-2 BCA ¶ 31,974 (termination for cause for nonperformance of a purchase order for the design, fabrication, and demonstration of three models of an unmanned aircraft proper because contractor had assumed the risk of commercial impracticability by accepting a performance specification); *Ultimate Labs., Inc.*, VABCA 6641, 02-1 BCA ¶ 31,663 (nondelivery a valid grounds for termination — rejecting contractor's argument that it properly refused to deliver eyeglasses because it believed that they were going to be prescribed improperly); *Integrated Sys. Group, Inc. v. Social Security Admin.*, GSBCA 14054-SSA, 98-2 BCA ¶ 29,848 (termination for cause proper when contractor refused to deliver a domestic product as required by the contract's Buy American clause). Compare *Free & Ben, Inc.*, ASBCA 56129 09-1 BCA ¶ 34,127, denying the government's motion for summary judgment because there was evidence that its failure to cooperate with the contractor caused the contractor's failure to perform the contract, *ALKAI Consultants, LLC*, ASBCA 55581, 09-1 BCA ¶ 34,058, holding that a termination for cause was improper because the contractor was excusably delayed when the government failed to cooperate and the contractor encountered unforeseen conditions during performance, and *Trinity Installers, Inc.*, AGBCA 2004-139-1, 05-1 BCA ¶ 32,868, ruling that a termination for cause was improper because the contractor had substantially completed performance of the construction work. It has also been held that the agency need not permit the terminated contractor to compete for the reprocurement contract, *Essan Metallix Corp.*, Comp. Gen. Dec. B-310357, 2008 CPD ¶ 5.

The termination for cause paragraph does not contain the requirement for a cure notice prior to terminations for causes other than late delivery. However, FAR 12.403(c)(1) requires a cure notice in such cases and one board has indicated that it would apply this requirement, *Business Mgmt. Research Assocs., Inc. v. General Servs. Admin.*, CBCA 464, 07-1 BCA ¶ 33,486. See also *KSC-TRI Sys., USA, Inc.*, ASBCA 54638, 06-1 BCA ¶ 33,145, holding that the procedures in FAR Part 49 do not apply when this clause is used and that cure notices need not allow ten days to cure, and *Geo-Marine, Inc. v. General Servs. Admin.*, GSBCA 16247, 05-2 BCA ¶ 33,048, holding that no cure notice is required if the contractor repudiated the contract.

Although the excusable delays provision (¶ (f)) is much shorter than the standard provision and does not mention subcontractor delays, it has been held that a contractor is responsible for delays that are the fault of subcontractors, *General Injectables & Vaccines, Inc. v. Gates*, 527 F.3d 1375 (Fed. Cir. 2008); *Wellington House v. General Servs. Admin.*, GSBCA 14665, 99-1 BCA ¶ 30,279. In contrast, in *The NTC Group, Inc.*, ASBCA 53720, 04-2 BCA ¶ 32,706, the board found an excusable delay when a service contractor could not hire the critical incumbent employees because their employers (the incumbent contractors) conspired to prevent their employment.

The termination for convenience paragraph (¶ (l)) gives the government the right to terminate all or any part of the contract but contains no provision granting an equitable adjustment to reprice the unterminated work when there is a partial termination. Thus, such an equitable adjustment was denied in *Individual Dev. Assocs., Inc.*, ASBCA 53910, 04-2 BCA ¶ 32,740, *recons. denied*, ASBCA 55174, 06-2 BCA ¶ 33,349. In *Individual Dev. Assocs., Inc.*, ASBCA 55174, 08-1 BCA ¶ 33,754, the board held that a contract line item terminated after it had commenced was properly treated as a partial termination. The right to partially terminate a commercial item contract was also upheld in *Dehdari General Trading & Contracting EST,* ASBCA 53987, 03-1 BCA ¶ 32,249, and *Hermes Consolidated, Inc.*, ASBCA 52308, 02-1 BCA ¶ 31,767. In *Hermes* the agency significantly reduced the guaranteed minimum quantity of an indefinite delivery/indefinite quantity contract eight days before the end of the one-year ordering period but the board rejected the contractor's argument that it was entitled to be paid the price of the unordered quantity in accordance with *Maxima Corp. v. United States*, 847 F.2d 1549 (Fed. Cir. 1988), citing *Montana Refining Co.*, ASBCA 50515, 00-1 BCA ¶ 30,694, for the proposition that "the expiration of the basic performance period is the demarcation line for retroactive terminations." A constructive termination for convenience was found in *Praecomm, Inc. v. United States*, 78 Fed. Cl. 5, aff'd 296 Fed. App'x 929 (Fed. Cir. 2008), where the agency accepted delivery of radios but modified the provision requiring the contractor to install them. The court rejected the contractor's argument that this action was a constructive change or a breach of contract (thus denying compensation).

The termination for convenience paragraph provides that the contractor will be paid a percentage of the contract price which reflects "the percentage of the work performed" and the "reasonable charges [it] can demonstrate...have resulted from the termination." In *Red River Holdings, LLC*, ASBCA 56316, 09-2 BCA the board held that, in accordance with FAR 12.403(a), FAR Part 49 did not apply to commercial item terminations and that, therefore, the contractor was only entitled to a percentage of the contract price corresponding to the percentage of the work completed. Thus, the board rejected the contractor's claim for preparatory and insurance costs. Similarly, in *Corners & Edges, Inc. v. HHS*, CBCA 762, 08-2 BCA ¶ 33,961, the board held that the contractor had been paid on a percentage of work basis for services when the government had paid the monthly amount for services rendered up to the time of the termination. The board also accepted a broad interpretation of the "reasonable charges" provision, including unamortized costs and settlement expenses, although it found that the contractor had incurred no such charges. In *Individual Dev. Assocs., Inc.*, ASBCA 55174, 08-1 BCA ¶ 33,754, the board held that the amount of settlement expenses incurred to pursue a total cost claim were not "reasonable charges" because recovery of total costs in not a proper computation of a percentage of the work performed.

## b.  Statutory and Executive Order Provisions

FAR 52.212-5 provides a standard clause, Contract Terms and Conditions Required to Implement Statutes or Executive Orders — Commercial Items, that sets forth the mandatory clauses that must be included in these procurements. An additional clause is prescribed for use on Department of Defense procurements in DFARS 252.212-7001. The contracting officer must check the appropriate provisions in these clauses in accordance with the instructions in FAR 12.503 and DFARS 212.503, respectively. The FAR 52.212-5 clause also contains a list of the four statutes and executive orders that must be passed down to subcontractors. See the guidance in FAR 12.504 which includes a list of the statutes that are not applicable to subcontractors. DFARS 212.504 contains a list of additional statutes that are not applicable to subcontractors.

Contractors should be aware that there are other statutes that are of general applicability in the United States that are also not listed in this clause. See ¶ (r) of the FAR 52.212-4 clause, stating:

> (r) Compliance with laws unique to Government contracts. The Contractor agrees to comply with 31 U.S.C. 1352 relating to limitations on the use of appropriated funds to influence certain Federal contracts; 18 U.S.C. 431 relating to officials not to benefit; 40 U.S.C. 327, et seq., Contract Work Hours and Safety Standards Act; 41 U.S.C. 5158, Anti-Kickback Act of 1986; 41 U.S.C. 265 and 10 U.S.C. 2409 relating to whistleblower protections; 49 U.S.C. 40118, Fly American; and 41 U.S.C. 423 relating to procurement integrity.

See **Figure 7-1** for a comprehensive list giving the applicability of these statutes and executive orders and the standard FAR clause that is used to implement them.

## 2. *Commercial Off-the-Shelf Items*

The Clinger-Cohen Act of 1996 also required a FAR list of provisions not applicable to commercial off-the-shelf items. See 41 U.S.C. § 1907:

(a) Inclusion in Federal Acquisition Regulation.

(1) In general. The Federal Acquisition Regulation shall include a list of provisions of law that are inapplicable to contracts for the procurement of commercially available off-the-shelf items. A provision of law properly included on the list pursuant to paragraph (2) does not apply to contracts for the procurement of commercially available off-the-shelf items. This section does not render a provision of law not included on the list inapplicable to contracts for the procurement of commercially available off-the-shelf items.

(2) Laws to be included. A provision of law described in subsection (b) shall be included on the list of inapplicable provisions of law required by paragraph (1) unless the Administrator makes a written determination that it would not be in the best interest of the Federal Government to exempt contracts for the procurement of commercially available off-the-shelf items from the applicability of the provision.

(3) Other authorities or responsibilities not affected. This section does not modify, supersede, impair, or restrict authorities or responsibilities under —

(A) section 15 of the Small Business Act (15 U.S.C. 644); or

(B) bid protest procedures developed under the authority of —

(i) [31 U.S.C. §§ 3551 et seq.];

(ii) section 2305(e) and (f) of title 10; or

(iii) [41 U.S.C. §§ 3706 and 3707].

(b) Covered law. Except as provided in subsection (a)(3), a provision of law referred to in subsection (a)(1) is a provision of law that the Administrator determines imposes Federal Government-unique policies, procedures, requirements, or restrictions for the procurement of property or services on persons whom the Federal Government has awarded contracts for the procurement of commercially available off-the-shelf items, except for a provision of law that —

(1) provides for criminal or civil penalties; or

(2) specifically refers to this section and provides that, notwithstanding this section, it shall be applicable to contracts for the procurement of commercially available off-the-shelf items.

This provision is implemented in FAR 12.505, stating:

COTS items are a subset of commercial items. Therefore, any laws listed in sections 12.503 and 12.504 are also inapplicable or modified in their applicability to contracts or subcontracts for the acquisition of COTS items. In addition, the following laws are not applicable to contracts for the acquisition of COTS items:

(a)(1) 41 U.S.C. 10a, portion of first sentence that reads "substantially all from articles, materials, or supplies mined, produced, or manufactured, as the case may be, in the United States," Buy American Act — Supplies, component test (see 52.225-1 and 52.225-3).

(2) 41 U.S.C. 10b, portion of first sentence that reads "substantially all from articles, materials, or supplies mined, produced, or manufactured, as the case may be, in the United States," Buy American Act — Construction Materials, component test (see 52.225-9 and 52.225-11).

(b) 42 U.S.C. 6962(c)(3)(A), Certification and Estimate of Percentage of Recovered Material.

## II.  SIMPLIFIED ACQUISITION PROCEDURES

Known for many years as "small purchases," simplified acquisition procedures now encompass three different classes of procurement — micro-purchases, simplified acquisition, and purchases of commercial items over the simplified acquisition threshold but not in excess of $6,500,000, or $12,000,000 as discussed below. The rules governing these procurements are promulgated in the FAR under authority granted by the Federal Acquisition Streamlining Act of 1994 (FASA), Pub. L. No. 103-355, and the Clinger-Cohen Act of 1996, Pub. L. No. 104-106. Neither the statutes nor the regulations provide any detailed procedures for these purchases. Rather, they relieve contracting officers from most of the procedures required for sealed bidding and conventional negotiated procurement.

The statutory provisions mandating the use of simplified acquisition procedures are contained in 41 U.S.C. §§ 1901-05. Directions for agencies to use them are provided in 10 U.S.C. § 2302b and 41 U.S.C. § 3305(a). The major thrust of these statutes was to allow the government efficiently to issue contracts for smaller acquisitions with simpler terms and conditions. The government's policy is that simplified acquisition procedures are to be used to the "maximum extent practicable," Executive Order 12931, 59 Fed. Reg. 52,387, Oct. 13, 1994; FAR 13.003(a). Purchases over the micro-purchase threshold but not more than the simplified acquisition threshold must be set aside exclusively for small business concerns in accordance with FAR Subpart 19.5, FAR 13.003(b)(1). The authority to use simplified acquisition procedures does not relieve agencies of their obligation to use the required sources of supply specified in Part 8 of the FAR.

FAR 13.002 specifies the following purposes of simplified acquisition procedures:

(a) Reduce administrative costs;

(b) Improve opportunities for small, small disadvantaged, women-owned, veteran-owned, HUB Zone, and service-disabled veteran-owned small business concerns to obtain a fair proportion of Government contracts;

(c) Promote efficiency and economy in contracting; and

(d) Avoid unnecessary burdens for agencies and contractors.

## A. Thresholds

The original thresholds for simplified acquisitions and micro-purchases in FASA have been modified by the adoption of 42 U.S.C. § 193 to grant greater authority in times of emergency. The threshold applies to the entire price of the procurement including options. See FAR 13.106-1(e) stating:

(e) *Use of options*. Options may be included in solicitations, provided the requirements of subpart 17.2 are met and the aggregate value of the acquisition and all options does not exceed the dollar threshold for use of simplified acquisition procedures.

FAR Subpart 17.2 requires that a solicitation state whether an option will be evaluated in awarding a contract, *Seaborn Health Care, Inc. v United States*, 55 Fed. Cl. 520 (2003). See also *SMS Sys. Maint. Servs., Inc.*, Comp. Gen. Dec. B-284550.2, 2000 CPD ¶ 127 (options must be included in determining whether micro-purchase threshold is exceeded).

### 1. Simplified Acquisition

The original upper threshold for simplified acquisition was $100,000, 41 U.S.C. § 403(11). However, the statutes have been amended several times to increase that threshold in specific circumstances. In addition, the threshold has been raised, pursuant to 41 U.S.C. § 1908, to account for escalation. The current thresholds are prescribed in FAR 2.101 as follows:

*Simplified acquisition threshold* means $150,000, except for acquisitions of supplies or services that, as determined by the head of the agency, are to be used to support a contingency operation or to facilitate defense against or recovery from nuclear, biological, chemical, or radiological attack (41 U.S.C. 428a), the term means —

(1) $300,000 for any contract to be awarded and performed, or purchase to be made, inside the United States; and

(2) $1 million for any contract to be awarded and performed, or purchase to be made, outside the United States.

The threshold for simplified acquisitions under the test program for commercial items is $6,500,000 or $12,000,000 if the contract is to support a contingency operation or to facilitate defense against or recovery from nuclear, biological, chemical, or radiological attack, FAR 13.500.

## 2. Micro-Purchases

The original threshold for micro-purchases was $2,500. However, this amount has been adjusted for inflation and the statutes have been amended several times to increase that threshold in specific circumstances. FAR 2.101 implements these statutes by prescribing the following thresholds:

*Micro-purchase threshold* means $3,000, except it means —

(1) For construction subject to the Davis-Bacon Act, $2,000;

(2) For acquisitions of services subject to the Service Contract Act, $2,500; and

(3) For acquisitions of supplies or services that, as determined by the head of the agency, are to be used to support a contingency operation or to facilitate defense against or recovery from nuclear, biological, chemical, or radiological attack, as described in 13.201(g)(1), except for construction subject to the Davis-Bacon Act (41 U.S.C. 428a) —

(i) $15,000 in the case of any contract to be awarded and performed, or purchase to be made, inside the United States; and

(ii) $30,000 in the case of any contract to be awarded and performed, or purchase to be made, outside the United States.

## 3. Thresholds Applicable to Both Solicitation Estimates and Award Values

The dollar values apply to *both* the amount estimated for the procurement as well as resulting contract values, FAR 13.003(c). Thus, if a procurement is begun using other than simplified procedures based on an estimate that exceeds the ap plicable threshold, simplified procedures may not be used even though the price of the source selected is lower than the threshold, *Global Commc'ns Solutions, Inc.*, Comp. Gen. Dec. B-299044, 2007 CPD ¶ 30 (commercial item test program threshold). Conversely, even though a solicitation was issued under simplified procedures, award may not be made above the applicable threshold. However, award on the basis of simplified procedures would be proper if the selected source reduced its price to come within the threshold.

Once an award is properly made using simplified acquisition procedures, there is no requirement that the actual amount paid under the contract be below the threshold. The contract may be modified to an amount above the threshold to cover unforeseen circumstances such as a change order or an unexpected overrun in the quantity of work, *Jones Seeding & Sprigging Co.*, 63 Comp. Gen. 497 (B-215260), 84-2 CPD ¶ 87.

### 4.  Breaking Down Purchases to Fit Within Thresholds Prohibited

Agencies are prohibited from "breaking down" procurements that aggregate more than the thresholds to permit use of the procedures within the applicable threshold, 41 U.S.C. § 1901(b) and FAR 13.003(c). Thus, an $175,000 procurement could not be properly acquired using seven $25,000 purchase orders. Similarly, if an agency has an identified recurring need for supplies or services, it is improper to enter into a series of small purchases to fulfill this need. In *L.A. Sys. v. Department of the Army*, GSBCA 13472-P, 96-1 BCA ¶ 28,220, the board held that the determination of whether a "fragmentation" or breaking down of a quantity occurs depends upon the knowledge of the user, not the contracting officer. The board stated at 140,915-16:

> That the contracting officer had no "advance knowledge of the megacenter's total requirements" is not dispositive of the issue. The prohibition in FAR 13.103(c) against breaking down requirements into several purchases that are less than the simplified acquisition threshold does not excuse fragmentation merely because the contracting officer is unaware that a series of orders is actually one requirement. To read the regulation as respondent suggests would allow a contracting officer to receive orders for a fragmented requirement and circumvent the regulation as long as the contracting officer is not told of the true nature of the requirement by individuals who had such knowledge.

See also *Critical Process Filtration, Inc.*, Comp. Gen. Dec. B-400746, 2009 CPD ¶ 25, holding it improper to issue a purchase order for an indefinite quantity with a limitation on orders to the amount of the simplified acquisition threshold when the estimated quantity was greater than the threshold.

Fragmentation has been permitted when an agency issued monthly purchase orders to the incumbent contractor for services during the resolution of a protest,

*Keeton Corr., Inc. v. United States*, 59 Fed. Cl. 753 (2004). The court reasoned that such fragmentation was a proper balancing of the requirement for full and open competition above the simplified acquisition threshold with the beneficial purpose of the stay of the award of a new contract during a protest. Similarly, fragmentation has been permitted while an agency is establishing the grounds for full and open competition above the simplified acquisition threshold, *Petchem, Inc. v. United States*, 99 F. Supp. 2d 50 (D.D.C. 2000) (permissible to make spot purchases of tugboat services after a competitively negotiated procurement did not yield offers at prices comparable to local market prices); *Master Sec., Inc.*, Comp. Gen. Dec. B-274990, 97-1 CPD ¶ 21 (permissible to use small purchase procedures to make month-to-month procurements of critically needed services until a "a fully competitive award is possible"); *Mas-Hamilton Group, Inc.*, 72 Comp. Gen. 6 (B-249049), 92-1 CPD ¶ 259 (permissible to use small purchase procedures to make "short-term, filler buys" of urgently needed product until a fully competitive award could be completed).

FAR 13.003(c) states that requirements should not be broken down "merely" to take advantage of the threshold. While that language is not contained in 41 U.S.C. § 1901(b), it appears that fragmentation would be appropriate if there were a valid reason to do so. One reason might be to permit small businesses to take advantage of the procurement. Another possible reason might be lack of funding. In *L.A. Systems*, the government argued that it could not "consolidate" the procurement because of a lack of available funding and that to allow funds to accumulate would result in a loss of funding. However, the board found that sufficient funds were available for the total requirement before the first order was placed.

## B. Micro-Purchases

Purchases under the micro-purchase threshold may be conducted using any of the simplified acquisition procedures in FAR Subpart 13.3. Micro-purchases do not require the incorporation of provisions or clauses.

The authority to make micro-purchases is frequently delegated to nonprocurement personnel. See FAR 1.603-3, stating:

> (b) Agency heads are encouraged to delegate micro-purchase authority to individuals who are employees of an executive agency or members of the Armed Forces of the United States who will be using the supplies or services being purchased. Individuals delegated this authority are not required to be appointed on an SF 1402, but shall be appointed in writing in accordance with agency procedures.

A contractor must exercise care to ensure that government employees without contracting officer authority do no exceed their delegated authority to make micro-purchases. See, however, *Healthcare Practice Enhancement Network, Inc.*, VABCA 5864, 01-1 BCA ¶ 31,383, holding that a purchase above the micro-purchase threshold was ratified by a contracting officer that did not take action after learning of the unauthorized use of micro-purchase authority.

These purchases are generally made using the governmentwide commercial purchase card. See FAR 13.201(b) stating that these cards are "the preferred method to purchase and to pay for micro-purchases." Sparse guidance on the use of purchase cards is contained in FAR 13.301. Additional guidance is contained in DFARS 213.301.

## 1. Sources

Micro-purchases are not reserved exclusively for small businesses, and the Buy American Act is not applicable. However, the requirements in FAR Part 8, Required Sources of Supplies and Services, apply to purchases within the micro-purchase threshold, FAR 13.201(e).

## 2. Procedures

Based on the authority granted in 41 U.S.C. § 1902, the following purchase guidelines are set forth in FAR 13.202:

(a) *Solicitation, evaluation of quotations, and award.* (1) To the extent practicable, micro-purchases shall be distributed equitably among qualified suppliers.

(2) Micro-purchases may be awarded without soliciting competitive quotations if the contracting officer or individual appointed in accordance with 1.603-3(b) considers the price to be reasonable.

(3) The administrative cost of verifying the reasonableness of the price for purchases may more than offset potential savings from detecting instances of overpricing. Therefore, action to verify price reasonableness need only be taken if —

(i) The contracting officer or individual appointed in accordance with 1.603-3(b) suspects or has information to indicate that the price may not be reasonable (e.g., comparison to the previous price paid or personal knowledge of the supply or service); or

(ii) Purchasing a supply or service for which no comparable pricing information is readily available (e.g., a supply or service that is not the same as, or is not similar to, other supplies or services that have recently been purchased on a competitive basis).

(b) *Documentation.* If competitive quotations were solicited and award was made to other than the low quoter, documentation to support the purchase may be limited to identification of the solicited concerns and an explanation for the award decision.

See *Michael Ritschard*, Comp. Gen. Dec. B-276820, 97-2 CPD ¶ 32 (protest that agency improperly refused to solicit a potential source denied where agency conducted the acquisition in accordance with micro-purchase procedures), and *Navistar Marine Instrument Corp.*, Comp. Gen. Dec. B-278075, 97-2 CPD ¶ 168 (acquisition was micro-purchase not subject to competition requirements and therefore unpriced purchase order was properly awarded on a sole source basis).

A vendor cannot appeal a directive from a contracting officer to agency personnel with micro-purchase authority to reduce their use of a single vendor in order to distribute such purchases "equitably among qualified suppliers," *Tom & Tony's Auto Wrecker Serv. v. General Servs. Admin.*, GSBCA 15698, 03-1 BCA ¶ 32,161. The board concluded that it had no jurisdiction to hear such an appeal because the vendor had no contract covering more that the numerous single orders that it had received.

## C.  Simplified Acquisition

The rules for conducting simplified acquisitions apply to procurements over the micro-purchase threshold. FAR 13.003(a) requires that the procedures prescribed in FAR Part 13 be used "to the maximum extent practicable." See *Southeast Tech. Servs.*, Comp. Gen. Dec. B-272374.2, 97-1 CPD ¶ 107, requesting that a contracting officer justify why simplified procedures are not practicable. These procedures are not required to be followed if the agency obtains the supplies or services by issuing an order against an existing indefinite delivery/indefinite quantity contract, FAR 13.003(a)(2).

### 1.  *Competition Requirements*

In contrast to micro-purchases, agencies are expected to obtain competition on simplified acquisitions.

#### a.  *Degree of Competition*

The statutes and regulations require that competition be promoted "to the maximum extent practicable," 41 U.S.C. § 1901(c) and FAR 13.104. As long as the agency makes a reasonable effort to obtain competition and does not intentionally and improperly exclude an interested source from competing, it will be found to have met this standard. In *S.D.M. Supply, Inc.*, Comp. Gen. Dec. B-271492, 96-1 CPD ¶ 288, *recons. denied*, 96-2 CPD ¶ 203, GAO indicated that this encompasses both the obtaining and consideration of quotations, stating:

> In meeting this requirement, agencies must make reasonable efforts, consistent with efficiency and economy, to afford all eligible and interested vendors an opportunity to compete. *RMS Indus.*, B-247074, Mar. 18, 1992, 92-1 CPD ¶ 290. Agencies have a fundamental obligation to have procedures in place not only to receive quotations, but also to reasonably safeguard quotations

actually received and to give them fair consideration. *East West Research, Inc.*, B-239565, B-239566, Aug. 21, 1990, 90-2 CPD ¶ 147, *aff'd, Defense Logistics Agency — Recons.*, B-239565.2, B-239566.2, Mar. 19, 1991, 91-1 CPD ¶ 298.

GAO found that the agency failed to meet this standard when it lost quotations due to a previously identified "systemic" failure of its computer system. In doing so, GAO distinguished those cases where "the occasional negligent loss of a quotation by an agency does not entitle the supplier to any relief." For example, in *Shubhada, Inc.*, Comp. Gen. Dec. B-292437, 2003 CPD ¶ 161, a protest was denied when the protester claimed that the agency had lost a part of its quotation but there was no systemic failure in the agency's procedures. See also *American Material Handling, Inc.*, Comp. Gen. Dec. B-281556, 99-1 CPD ¶ 46, where the protest was denied when the agency did not receive an electronically submitted quotation because its computer malfunctioned.

FAR 13.104(b) provides that when electronic solicitation procedures are not used, maximum practicable competition ordinarily can be obtained by soliciting quotations or offers from at least three sources within the local trade area. However, if the contracting officer is aware of additional sources that wish to participate in the competition, they should be accorded an opportunity to submit offers or quotations. See *Military Agency Servs. Pty., Ltd.*, Comp. Gen. Dec. B-290414, 2002 CPD ¶ 130, stating:

> We have recognized that while the solicitation of three vendors may be sufficient to satisfy the statutory requirement to promote competition to maximum extent practicable where there is no synopsis requirement, see *SF & Wellness*, B-272313, Sept. 23, 1996, 96-2 CPD ¶ 122 at 2; *Omni Elevator Co.*, B-246393, Mar. 6, 1992, 92-1 CPD ¶ 264 at 2, an agency may not, consistent with this requirement, deliberately fail to solicit a responsible source which expressed interest in competing. *Bosco Contracting, Inc.*, B-270366, Mar. 4, 1996, 96-1 CPD ¶ 140 at 3; *Kahn Indus., Inc.; Midwest Dynamometer & Eng'g Co.*, B-251777, B-251777.2, May 3, 1993, 93-1 CPD ¶ 356 at 4-5.

It is difficult to demonstrate that an agency "deliberately excluded" a prospective vendor. In *Omni Elevator Co.*, 71 Comp. Gen. 308 (B-246393), 92-1 CPD ¶ 264, GAO concluded that the failure to solicit Omni was an "unintentional oversight that resulted from VA's use of a bidders list based upon an informal market survey conducted by the contracting officer, instead of the standard bidders list on which Omni was included." GAO found that this was a reasonable method of identifying prospective offerors and the fact that four firms (two of which responded) were solicited satisfied the maximum practicable competition standard. See also *GMA Cover Corp.*, Comp. Gen. Dec. B-288018, 2001 CPD ¶ 144 (lack of knowledge of vendor not deliberate exclusion when vendor was not in local database); *The Source*, Comp. Gen. Dec. B-266362, 96-1 CPD ¶ 48 (failure of agency supply officer to advise the contracting officer of the protester's interest in the procurement not deliberate exclusion); *SF & Wellness*, Comp. Gen. Dec. B-272313, 96-2 CPD ¶ 122 (purchasing agent's statements that she left a message on the incumbent's answering machine indicated that the incumbent had been solicited). In contrast, improper exclusion was found in *Solutions Lucid Group, LLC*, Comp. Gen. Dec. B-400967, 2009 CPD ¶ 198 (agency knew protester was interested in competing); and *Bosco Contracting, Inc.*, Comp. Gen. Dec. B-270366, 96-1 CPD ¶ 140 (exclusion based on an alleged record of poor past performance which was not supported by the record).

### b. Sole Source

Sole source procurement is authorized if the contracting officer makes a determination that "only one source is reasonably available," FAR 13.106-1(b)(1). The decision will be supported if the contracting officer makes a reasonable attempt to find other sources. See *Information Ventures, Inc.*, Comp. Gen. Dec. B-290785, 2002 CPD ¶ 152 (access to proprietary membership list needed to carry out contract work); *Flowlogic*, Comp. Gen. Dec. B-289173, 2002 CPD ¶ 22 (after failed competitive procurement, contracting officer contacted known source of urgently needed software); *Midwest Dynamometer & Eng'g Co.*, Comp. Gen. Dec. B-252168, 93-1 CPD ¶ 408 (contracting officer contacted three sources and found that only one would meet the government's needs). However, it is improper to issue sole source purchase orders to selected companies holding blanket purchase agreements, *Envirosolve LLC*, Comp. Gen. Dec. B-294974.4, 2005 CPD ¶ 106.

Sole source procurement can also be justified on the basis of urgency. See *Aleman & Assocs., Inc.*, Comp. Gen. Dec. B-287275, 2001 CPD ¶ 93, holding that it was proper to issue a three-month sole source contract to the incumbent contractor during the resolution of a protest. However, urgency is not a proper justification if the agency is not diligent in conducting market research to identify sources, *Europe Displays, Inc.*, Comp. Gen. Dec. B-297099, 2005 CPD ¶ 214.

## 2. Solicitation and Procurement Notices

Agencies are given broad discretion in determining whether to solicit quotes or offers and in choosing techniques to use for the solicitation.

### a. Quote or Offer

The traditional method of solicitation for small purchases has been the Request for Quotations (RFQ), and this method is preserved in the simplified acquisition regulations. This technique places the government in the position of being the offeror with the quoter having the right either to accept or reject the offer. FAR 13.004(a) states:

A quotation is not an offer and, consequently, cannot be accepted by the Government to form a binding contract. Therefore, issuance by the Government of an order in response to a supplier's quotation does not establish a contract. The order is an offer by the Government to the supplier to buy certain supplies or services upon specified terms and conditions. A contract is established when the supplier accepts the offer.

Using an RFQ presents a substantially lower risk for the supplier than that which would be incurred if the supplier were making an offer. If the quote contains judgmental errors or costs go up, the supplier can escape a loss contract by simply refusing to accept the government's offer or by making a counteroffer, *Bloch Lumber Co.*, ASBCA 23512, 79-2 BCA ¶ 14,167. This reduced risk could reduce contingencies and result in lower quoted prices. Alternatively, a company could agree to perform only part of the quoted work. See *Howell It Is*, AGBCA 2003-137-2, 03-1 BCA ¶ 32,244, where the quoter rejected the award of the full quantity but stated that it would perform a portion of the work. When the contracting officer agreed to this, the board held that the contract was for only that portion of the work.

Using an RFQ also gives the agency more flexibility in conducting a procurement. See, for example, *Computer Assocs. Int'l, Inc.*, Comp. Gen. Dec. B-292077.3, 2004 CPD ¶ 163, *recons. denied*, 2004 CPD ¶ 110, where GAO held that it was proper to award a contract to a quoter whose quotation had "expired," reasoning:

> A quotation . . . is not a submission for acceptance by the government to form a binding contract; rather, vendor quotations are purely informational, *Zarc Int'l, Inc.*, B-292708, Oct. 3, 2003, 2003 CPD ¶ 172 at 2. In the RFQ context, it is the government that makes the offer, albeit generally based on the information provided by the vendor in its quotation, and no binding agreement is created until the vendor accepts the offer. Federal Acquisition Regulation (FAR) § 13.004(a). A vendor submitting a price quotation therefore could, the next moment, reject an offer from the government at its quoted price. Because vendors in the RFQ context hold the power of acceptance and their submissions are purely informational, there is nothing for vendors to hold open; thus, it simply does not make sense to apply the acceptance period concept or the attendant rules regarding expiration of bids or offers to RFQs. As a consequence, notwithstanding the statement in Serena's revised price quotation that "this offer is valid through June 31 [sic], 2003," Serena's discounted price was "valid," or not, at Serena's option, both before and after the date mentioned in the quotation — on whatever date the agency might present an offer to the firm.

Under the broad discretion afforded by FAR Part 13, an agency could request offers (either proposals or bids) rather than quotations. However, the regulations give no suggestions as to when it would be advantageous to do so. One reason might be that timing is critical and it is essential to have the contract formed at the time the government makes the award decision. In *Seaborn Health Care, Inc. v United States*, 55 Fed. Cl. 520 (2003), the contracting officer's mistaken "acceptance" of a quotation was found not to be a determinative indication that the agency intended to use competitive negotiation procedures in FAR Part 15 in conducting the procurement.

## b. Method of Solicitation

Solicitations may be made orally, on paper, or electronically. FAR 13.106-1(c) calls for the use of oral solicitations "to the maximum extent practicable" when the procurement does not exceed the simplified acquisition threshold. However, it warns that oral solicitation may not be practicable for procurements over $30,000. In that case, FAR 13.003 (e) and (f) favor the use of electronic commerce. FAR 13.106-1(d) then states:

> Written solicitations. If obtaining electronic or oral quotations is uneconomical or impracticable, the contracting officer should issue paper solicitations for contract actions likely to exceed $30,000. The contracting officer shall issue a written solicitation for construction requirements exceeding $2,000.

It is not clear when obtaining electronic quotations would be impracticable or why that would call for a written solicitation.

When electronic commerce is used, the agency may make the material available only on the Internet and post amendments to the solicitation on the web site, allowing potential competitors to register for e-mail notification of such amendments, *USA Info. Sys., Inc.*, Comp. Gen. Dec. B-291488, 2002 CPD ¶ 205. Such electronic amendments are adequate to inform offerors of changes to the solicitation, *Linguistic Sys., Inc.*, Comp. Gen. Dec. B-296221, 2005 CPD ¶ 104. Although agencies are required to make Internet postings accessible, they need not be posted on regional listings as long as potential offerors can find the solicitation by a reasonable search, *Jess Bruner Fire Suppression*, Comp. Gen. Dec. B-296533, 2005 CPD ¶ 163. See also *NuWestern USA Contractors, Inc.*, Comp. Gen. Dec. B-275514, 97-1 CPD ¶ 90, holding that the issuance of a solicitation only in electronic form (CD-ROM) is not unduly restrictive of competition.

## c. Procurement Notices

The requirements for public notice of procurements depends upon the estimated dollar value. The regulations do not prescribe any public notice requirements for procurements not in excess of $15,000. For procurements expected to exceed $15,000 but not exceed $25,000, a notice must be publicly displayed or posted electronically, FAR 5.101(a)(2). For procurements in excess of $25,000, a notice must be published in the governmentwide point of entry (*http://www.fedbizopps.gov*) at least 15 days before issuance of a solicitation, FAR 5.203(a). However, solicitation for commercial items can be combined with the notice, thus eliminating the 15-day waiting period, FAR 12.603. Exceptions to this notice requirement are contained in FAR 5.202. Detailed guidance on the preparation of notices is contained in FAR 5.207(a).

Notices must contain a "clear and concise description" of the supplies or services being acquired, FAR 5.207(c). See *TMI Mgmt. Sys., Inc.*, Comp. Gen. Dec.

B-401530, 2009 CPD ¶ 191 (notice insufficient when it misclassified of a procurement for facilities support services under a "miscellaneous" product classification code); *M.D. Thompson Consulting, LLC*, Comp. Gen. Dec. B-297616, 2006 CPD ¶ 41 (notice of sole source contract extension insufficient when it did not describe precise services required); *Information Ventures, Inc.*, Comp. Gen. Dec. B-293518, 2004 CPD ¶ 76 (notice insufficient when it did not match the requisition for the services sent to the contracting office). Agencies are generally expected to notify potential quoters of changes in their requirements. However, if a quoter is aware that the agency is willing to consider alternate products, no formal notice is required, *Aqua-Flo, Inc.*, Comp. Gen. Dec. B-283944, 99-2 CPD ¶ 116.

## d. Submission of Quotes or Offers

Contracting officers are given broad discretion to determine the time and manner for the submission of responses. Deadlines for responses to solicitations are required to be set to afford suppliers a reasonable opportunity to respond, FAR 13.003(h)(2). The amount of time should be sufficient to permit competitors to submit quotations, *Pacific Sky Supply, Inc.*, B-225420, 87-1 CPD ¶ 206. Short response times have been held to be inadequate, *Information Ventures, Inc.*, Comp. Gen. Dec. B-293541, 2004 CPD ¶ 81 (less than two days); *Sabreliner Corp.*, Comp. Gen. Dec. B-288030, 2001 CPD ¶ 170 (three hours); *Jack Faucett Assocs., Inc.*, Comp. Gen. Dec. B-279347, 98-1 CPD ¶ 155 (one day). However, when price is the only evaluation factor and the need is urgent, short response times have been permitted, *Military Agency Servs. Pty., Ltd.*, Comp. Gen. Dec. B-290414, 2002 CPD ¶ 130.

Responses may be required to be oral, on paper, or submitted by electronic means. The needs of the agency will be considered in determining whether the time and method selected is reasonable. See *Arcy Mfg. Co.*, Comp. Gen. Dec. B-261538, 95-2 CPD ¶ 283, where the agency stated that it would consider quotations only if submitted on its electronic bulletin board (EBB). The protester claimed that this placed an undue burden on small businesses. However, GAO denied the protest based upon the agency's claim that the large volume of purchases it processed made the use of the electronic method cost effective, stating:

> With regard to the burden imposed on the protesters by the requirement that quotes be electronically transmitted, the essential difference between the electronic method of responding to RFQs and the paper method is that under the electronic method the protester is required to have access to a personal computer, certain telecommunications, and .communications software, and a modem. These items are readily available for purchase in the commercial marketplace, or, as the record demonstrates, should a vendor not desire to purchase such equipment, access to the EBB can be obtained by contacting an EDI service provider. As such, we fail to see how requiring access to the EBB can be considered overly burdensome to a prospective DISC supplier.

In our view, the record establishes that the agency has a reasonable basis for requiring that quotes be submitted electronically and that this requirement is not overly burdensome on the vendor community. In this regard, we note that no potential vendor is precluded from submitting quotes; only the format of quotes is being restricted. *See Essex Electro Eng'rs, Inc.*, B-252288.2, 93-2 CPD ¶ 47 (protest that proposal format instructions were overly burdensome because they required an unnecessary amount of desktop publishing capabilities was denied where the formatting requirements were determined reasonable and could easily be met using a personal computer). In sum, under the circumstances here, DISC's requirement that quotes be submitted electronically is reasonable and consistent with the mandate that it promote competition to the maximum extent practicable for small purchase acquisitions.

See also *Commonwealth Indus. Specialties, Inc.*, Comp. Gen. Dec. B-277833, 97-2 CPD ¶ 151, finding proper an agency's requirement that responses to a simplified acquisition request for quotations be submitted electronically through the agency's electronic bulletin board.

## e. *Standing Quotations*

FAR 13.103 permits the use of "standing price quotations" in lieu of the solicitation of specific quotations as follows:

Authorized individuals do not have to obtain individual quotations for each purchase. Standing price quotations may be used if—

(a) The pricing information is current; and

(b) The Government obtains the benefit of maximum discounts before award.

This procedure is used extensively by the Department of Veterans Affairs.

There is no definition in the FAR of a standing price quotation but generally an agency would call for vendors to submit prices that remain open for a designated period of time — against which orders can be placed without further solicitation. However, in *Southeast Tech. Servs.*, Comp. Gen. Dec. B-289065, 2001 CPD ¶ 206, the agency awarded a contract to a company that had submitted a quotation in response to the agency's contact during market research after it concluded that the responses to its RFQ were unsatisfactory. GAO held that this was a proper use of the standing price quotation procedure, stating:

Southeast asserts that MGC's quotation should not have been considered because it was not submitted in response to the RFQ. However, there is no requirement that agencies consider only quotations in response to an RFQ; under FAR § 13.103, a standing quotation properly may be considered in a simplified acquisition if it is current. As noted above, MGC's quotation, received in connection with the agency's earlier attempt to have the laboratory furniture installed, was current, with an acceptance period of 45 days after September 5. Southeast claims that MGC gained an unfair competitive advantage by submitting its quotation before the solicitation was advertised. However, both MGC's and Southeast's quotations were evaluated on the same basis, and the award decision had nothing to do with the times at which the quotations were submitted. There thus is no basis for finding that MGC enjoyed an unfair advantage.

## 3. Procedures

FAR 13.003(g) gives wide latitude in the procedures that can be used for simplified acquisitions by allowing "any appropriate combination" of the procedures in other parts of the FAR and encouraging the use of "innovative approaches, to the maximum extent practicable." This has been held to permit the use of reverse auction procedures where the participants are required to allow the agency to reveal their prices, *MTB Group, Inc.*, Comp. Gen. Dec. B-295463, 2005 CPD ¶ 40; *MTB Group, Inc. v. United States*, 65 Fed. Cl. 516 (2005).

The absence of statutory or regulatory procedures does not permit agencies to use arbitrary or unfair selection procedures. See *General Metals, Inc.*, 72 Comp. Gen. 54 (B-249259), 92-2 CPD ¶ 319, stating that simplified acquisition procedures must be conducted "consistent with the concern for fair and equitable treatment that is inherent in any federal procurement."

### a. Evaluation Factors

The factors to be evaluated may be price alone or price and other factors, but "best value" is encouraged, FAR 13.106-1(a)(2). Solicitations must state the basis upon which award is to be made, but the relative importance of evaluation factors is not required to be stated in the solicitation and subfactors need not be included, FAR 13.106-1(a)(2). See, however, *Finlen Complex, Inc.*, Comp. Gen. Dec. B-288280, 2001 CPD ¶ 167, holding that relative importance must be disclosed when the agency requires the submission of "detailed proposals addressing unique government requirements." GAO has indicated that where relative importance is not indicated, it will be presumed that the factors will be given "approximately equal weight," *Bio-Rad Labs., Inc.*, Comp. Gen. Dec. B-297553, 2007 CPD ¶ 58 (protest granted when agency used subfactors in descending order of importance); *Carol Soloman & Assocs.*, Comp. Gen. Dec. B-271713, 96-2 CPD ¶ 28. However, the FAR does not contain such a statement.

There appears to be considerable flexibility in the amount of information on the evaluation process that must be disclosed in the solicitation. See, for example, *General Metals, Inc.*, 72 Comp. Gen. 54 (B-249259), 92-2 CPD ¶ 319, and *Essner Metal Works, Inc.*, Comp. Gen. Dec. B-251599, 93-1 CPD ¶ 285, holding that the fact that the agency would add or deduct an amount from quoted prices when quot-

### c. Discussions and Consideration of Noncompliant Responses

The contracting officer is not required to establish a competitive range nor to conduct oral or written discussions, FAR 13.106-3(b)(2). Neither is there any requirement to afford quoters an opportunity to submit additional information. See *Rotair Indus., Inc.*, Comp. Gen. Dec. B-219994, 85-2 CPD ¶ 683, stating:

> [T]he solicitation was issued under the small purchase procedures, which do not contemplate the type of discussions or the opportunity to submit revised proposals that occur in a full scale negotiated procurement. In this context, we do not believe that the agency acted improperly by rejecting Rotair's offer without affording it an opportunity to submit additional information. See *M.F. Services, Inc.*, B-210954, Jan. 20, 1984, 84-1 CPD ¶ 87.

See also *United Marine Int'l, LLC*, Comp. Gen. Dec. B-281512, 99-1 CPD ¶ 44 (negotiation with only the selected low-price quoter to obtain minor additional work acceptable procedures); *Metropolitan Fed. Network*, Comp. Gen. Dec. B-232096, 88-2 CPD ¶ 495 (small purchase procedures "do not contemplate the type of discussions that occur in a full scale negotiated procurement"). The lack of a requirement to conduct discussions allows a contracting officer to use negative past performance information without verifying it with the quoter, *John Blood*, Comp. Gen. Dec. B-290593, 2002 CPD ¶ 151; *Lynwood Mach. & Eng'g, Inc.*, Comp. Gen. Dec. B-285696, 2001 CPD ¶ 113, or to use a clearly mistaken price in the evaluation without asking for verification of the price, *Paraclete Contracts*, Comp. Gen. Dec. B-299883, 2007 CPD ¶ 153.

Although oral or written discussions are not required, the contracting officer is not prohibited from conducting discussions and obtaining modifications of offers or quotations, provided that all offerors are treated fairly and equitably and are not prejudiced. See *Ann Riley & Assocs., Ltd.*, Comp. Gen. Dec. B-241309.2, 91-1 CPD ¶ 142 (improper to inform only one quoter that bonus bid was acceptable). Thus, if the contracting officer does establish a competitive range, quoters with substantially similar quotations must be included in the range and the discussions, *Kathryn Huddleston & Assocs., Ltd.*, Comp. Gen. Dec. B-289453, 2002 CPD ¶ 57. This does not mean that discussions must be conducted with all quoters, *Oregon Innovative Prods.*, Comp. Gen. Dec. B-231767, 88-2 CPD ¶ 110. See *Data Vault Corp.*, Comp. Gen. Dec. B-248664, 92-2 CPD ¶ 166, where GAO stated:

> The government's small purchase procedures establish abbreviated, competitive requirements designed to minimize administrative costs that might otherwise equal or exceed the cost of relatively inexpensive items. An RFQ, unlike an invitation for bids (IFB) or request for proposals (RFP), does not seek offers that can be accepted by the government to form a contract. Rather, the government's purchase order is the offer which the proposed supplier may accept through performance or by a formal acceptance document. FAR 13.108. It

follows that, generally, the government may seek and consider revisions to a quotation under small purchase procedures any time prior to the government's issuance of a purchase order. See *Instruments & Controls Serv. Co.*, 65 Comp. Gen. 685 [B-222122] (1986), 86-2 CPD ¶ 16; *Oregon Innovative Prods.*, B-231767, Aug. 2, 1988, 88-2 CPD ¶ 110. Here, since the Army could properly seek additional information regarding a quotation up to the time the purchase order was issued, we find nothing improper in the agency's issuance of a purchase order to FFC after determining that FFC would comply with the RFQ vault temperature requirements.

The contracting officer also has considerable discretion in working with quoters to bring their quotations into compliance with the solicitation requirements. Since the concept of responsiveness is not applicable, *Memoir, Inc.*, GSBCA 8264-P, 86-1 BCA ¶ 18,702, the contracting officer is free to consider responses that deviate from the solicitation. See *Williams-Trane Co.*, Comp. Gen. Dec. B-283522, 99-2 CPD ¶ 91, permitting several contacts with noncompliant quoters. However, if a substantial specification change is made, all quoters should be advised, *Unite Mfg. Co.*, Comp. Gen. Dec. B-208324, 82-2 CPD ¶ 483. Conversely, the contracting officer may decide to reject responses that are technically unacceptable and not to permit modification of the response, *Huntington Valley Indus.*, Comp. Gen. Dec. B-272321, 96-2 CPD ¶ 126. It is also proper to require a data package demonstrating that a product meets the specifications if the agency cannot determine that it has been previously accepted, *Viking, Inc. — USA*, Comp. Gen. Dec. B-401528, 2009 CPD ¶ 176. Compare *SKJ & Assocs., Inc.*, Comp. Gen. Dec. B-291533, 2003 CPD ¶ 3, holding that it was improper to reject a proposal for an inadequate technical proposal when the solicitation gave no guidance on the contents of the proposal.

### d. Late Quotations

Late quotations must be considered unless the solicitation contains a late quotations clause, other bidders would be prejudiced, or the agency has begun the award process. See *John Blood*, Comp. Gen. Dec. B-274624, 96-2 CPD ¶ 233, stating:

> Under simplified acquisition procedures, agencies generally may seek and consider revisions to a quotation any time prior to award. See *Data Vault Corp.*, B-248664, Sept. 10, 1992, 92-2 CPD ¶ 166. Where, as here, an RFQ does not contain a late quotations provision — but merely requests quotations by a certain date — that date is not considered to be a firm closing deadline; consequently, so long as the award process has not begun, an agency is not precluded from considering a quotation received after that date. *AFT Constr. Co., Inc.*, B-260829, July 18, 1995, 95-2 CPD ¶ 29.

In *Instruments & Controls Serv. Co.*, 65 Comp. Gen. 685 (B-222122), 86-2 CPD ¶ 16, GAO stated that the "failure to do so would be inconsistent with the statutory requirement for competition to the maximum extent practicable." See also *Payne Constr.*, Comp. Gen. Dec. B-291629, 2003 CPD ¶ 46; *G.E.G. Sugar Blues & Noe's*

*Colors*, Comp. Gen. Dec. B-284117, 2000 CPD ¶ 29, granting a protest because the agency did not consider a late quotation. Two exceptions to this requirement were noted in *Compspace Corp.*, Comp. Gen. Dec. B-274037, 96-2 CPD ¶ 186. Late quotations would not have to be considered if substantial activity had transpired in evaluating quotations or if other firms would be prejudiced. GAO explained:

> When, as here, the RFQ does not contain a late quotations clause, but merely requests quotations by a certain date, that date is not considered a firm date for purposes of determining whether a quotation may form the basis for an award. *A&B Trash Serv.*, B-250322, Jan. 22, 1993, 93-1 CPD ¶ 53. Rather, the agency is not precluded from considering a quotation received after the announced due date provided that no substantial activity has transpired in evaluating quotations, and the other firms submitting quotations would not be prejudiced. *Id.* Activity is deemed substantial where the agency has begun the award process prior to receiving the late quotation. *Adrian Supply Co.*, 68 Comp. Gen. 575 (1989), 89-2 CPD ¶ 99.

See also *Joint Sys., Inc.*, Comp. Gen. Dec. B-298573, 2006 CPD ¶ 150 (proper to reject information submitted after evaluation had been completed); *RMG Indus. Sales*, Comp. Gen. Dec. B-281632, 99-1 CPD ¶ 58 (proper to reject late amended final quotation after "substantial activity" in evaluating quotations had occurred).

Because a late quotations clause is not prescribed by the regulations, it is unlikely that purchasing agents and contracting officers will include such a clause in a solicitation. GAO decisions indicate that a late quotations provision must expressly provide that quotations must be received by the specified date to be considered. See, for example, *Instruments & Controls Serv. Co.*, 65 Comp. Gen. 685 (B-222122), 86-2 CPD ¶ 16. Thus, language that "merely suggests" the submission of quotes by a specified date would not qualify. Neither would language that advises quoters that failure to submit a quote by a specified date "may result in your quotation not being considered for award," *Adrian Supply Co.*, 68 Comp. Gen. 575 (B-235352), 89-2 CPD ¶ 99.

If a late quotations clause is included, it will be strictly enforced, *Data Integrators, Inc.*, Comp. Gen. Dec. B-310928, 2008 CPD ¶ 27; *Zebra Techs. Int'l, LLC*, Comp. Gen. Dec. B-296158, 2005 CPD ¶ 122. See also *Alpha Executive Servs., Inc.*, Comp. Gen. Dec. B-246173, 92-1 CPD ¶ 197, where GAO held that the agency "acted reasonably" in declining to consider a late proposal when the solicitation had included a late quotations clause. Compare *Williams-Trane Co.*, Comp. Gen. Dec. B-283522, 99-2 CPD ¶ 91, denying a protest of acceptance of late information from the winning vendor when the clause was included because the agency had allowed all of the quoters to submit information after the quotation date.

Some simplified acquisitions use the standard clauses for commercial items. In that case, the Instructions to Offerors — Commercial Items clause at FAR 52.212-1 states:

> (f) *Late submissions, modifications, revisions, and withdrawals of offers.* (1) Offerors are responsible for submitting offers, and any modifications, revisions, or

withdrawals, so as to reach the Government office designated in the solicitation by the time specified in the solicitation. If no time is specified in the solicitation, the time for receipt is 4:30 p.m., local time, for the designated Government office on the date that offers or revisions are due.

> (2)(i) Any offer, modification, revision, or withdrawal of an offer received at the Government office designated in the solicitation after the exact time specified for receipt of offers is "late" and will not be considered unless it is received before award is made, the Contracting Officer determines that accepting the late offer would not unduly delay the acquisition; and —
>
>> (A) If it was transmitted through an electronic commerce method authorized by the solicitation, it was received at the initial point of entry to the Government infrastructure not later than 5:00 p.m. one working day prior to the date specified for receipt of offers; or
>>
>> (B) There is acceptable evidence to establish that it was received at the Government installation designated for receipt of offers and was under the Government's control prior to the time set for receipt of offers; or
>>
>> (C) If this solicitation is a request for proposals, it was the only proposal received.

This is a confusing provision when it is incorporated into an RFQ because it refers to "offers" which are not submitted in response to an RFQ. Nonetheless, it was strictly enforced to bar the award based on a late quotation in *M. Braun, Inc.*, Comp. Gen. Dec. B-298935.2, 2007 CPD ¶ 96. GAO "assumed" the clause applied to quotations because the agency had cited the clause in defending the protest.

When electronic quotations are submitted, the quote is considered received on the date it is received by the agency, not the date the quoter submits it to a Value Added Network (VAN), *Comspace Corp.*, Comp. Gen. Dec. B-274037, 96-2 CPD ¶ 186. There, the only evidence of government receipt showed that the quote was received by the government after award, too late to be considered.

### e. Disclosure of Prices

There are no rules in FAR Part 13 prohibiting the disclosure of prices during a competition. However, the Procurement Integrity Act, 41 U.S.C. §§ 2101-07, prohibits the disclosure of vendor prices, with certain exceptions. See *MTB Group, Inc.*, Comp. Gen. Dec. B-295463, 2005 CPD ¶ 40, ruling that disclosure of prices in a reverse auction was permissible, stating:

[T]he Act prohibits government officials and those acting on behalf of the government from knowingly disclosing contractor quotation or proposal information before award. 41 U.S.C. § 423(a) [now § 2102]. However, that prohibition is not absolute. Rather, the Act specifically provides that it does not "restrict the disclosure of information to, or its receipt by, any person or class of persons authorized in accordance with applicable agency regulations or procedures, to receive the information," 41 U.S.C. § 423(h)(1) [now § 2107(1)], and does not "restrict a contractor from disclosing its own quote or proposal information or the recipient from receiving that information." 41 U.S.C. § 423(h)(2)) [now § 2107(2)]. We think the price disclosure under HUD's reverse auction procedures falls within the exception language, although we are aware of no judicial or other authoritative interpretation of these provisions. First, under the procedure the agency has established, vendors actually will disclose their own prices — albeit, as a condition of competing — by entering the prices on the auction website; as noted, a vendor's disclosing its own price is not prohibited under the Act. Moreover, even if the price disclosure were considered to be by government officials due to its nature as a precondition to a vendor's competing, the disclosure is pursuant, and integral, to the reverse auction procurement procedures established by the agency; we thus would view the disclosure as being to persons authorized by agency procedures to receive the information, consistent with the exception language. See generally *DGS Contract Serv., Inc. v. United States*, 43 Ct. Cl. 227, 236 (1999); *Ocean Servs., LLC.*, B-292511.2, Nov. 6, 2003, 2003 CPD ¶ 206 at 5 (neither the Act nor the FAR establishes an absolute prohibition against disclosure of price information, and both make clear that prices can be disclosed under certain circumstances).

See also *MTB Group, Inc. v. United States*, 65 Fed. Cl. 516 (2005), reaching the same conclusion.

## f.   Award

Although the FAR contains no provision on failure to meet mandatory requirements, award cannot be made to a quoter that does not agree to meet such requirements. See *CAMS, Inc.*, Comp. Gen. Dec. B-292546, 2003 CPD ¶ 191, stating:

> A quote that fails to conform to material terms and conditions of the solicitation should be considered unacceptable and may not form the basis for an award. *United Coatings*, B-291978.2, July 7, 2003, 2003 CPD ¶ 146; see *Rel-Tek Sys., & Design, Inc.*, B-280463.3, Nov. 25, 1998, 99-1 CPD ¶ 2 at 3. The terms in a solicitation governing inspection and acceptance are material requirements that must be met without qualification — regardless of whether the solicitation sets them out as minimum requirements — because they affect the government's rights under the resulting contract.

See also *Multi-Spec Products Corp.*, Comp. Gen. Dec. B-287135, 2001 CPD ¶ 72, denying a protest that the selected contractor did not meet a mandatory delivery date because the RFQ allowed later dates. Had the delivery date been mandatory, award would have been improper. See *Muddy Creek Oil & Gas, Inc.*, Comp. Gen. Dec. B-296836, 2005 CPD ¶ 143 (agency properly rejected quotation that altered terms in the statement of work); *American Floor Consultants & Installations, Inc.*, Comp.

Gen. Dec. B-294934, 2004 CPD ¶ 248 (agency properly rejected quotation that did not contain descriptive literature to support the offered "equal" item); *Elementar Americas, Inc.*, Comp. Gen. Dec. B-282698, 99-2 CPD ¶ 17 (proper to reject quotation that did not furnish required descriptive literature to show that the technical requirements were met); and *CDS Network Sys., Inc.*, Comp. Gen. Dec. B-281200, 98-2 CPD ¶ 154 (proper to reject a quotation that did not provide required documentation).

Award need not be made to the firm submitting the lowest quotation if the contracting officer makes a good faith finding that award to a different firm is in the best interests of the government and that the price is reasonable, *Environmental Tectonics Corp.*, Comp. Gen. Dec. B-280573, 98-2 CPD ¶ 140 (superior past performance justified paying higher price); *University of Kansas Med. Ctr.*, Comp. Gen. Dec. B-278400, 98-1 CPD ¶ 120 (technical superiority justified paying higher price); *Creative Elecs., Inc.*, Comp. Gen. Dec. B-206684, 83-2 CPD ¶ 95 (assumed better warranty service justified paying higher price). However, the decision to award to a higher priced quoter in order to obtain best value must be rational, *e-LYNXX Corp.*, Comp. Gen. Dec. B-292761, 2003 CPD ¶ 219. See *National Aerospace Group, Inc.*, Comp. Gen. Dec. B-281958, 99-1 CPD ¶ 82, holding that it was not reasonable to pay a significantly higher price merely because the low quoter had no prior performance record. In that case the contracting officer had made no comparative assessment of the risk involved in dealing with a new vendor. Compare *Northwest Mgmt., Inc.*, Comp. Gen. Dec. B-277503, 97-2 CPD ¶ 108, finding an award to a slightly higher priced quoter to be rational when the contracting officer assessed the lower priced quoter as posing more risk.

Agencies may make either a single ("all-or-none") award or multiple award if vendors are so advised in the solicitation, FAR 13.101(b)(1). If the solicitation is silent, multiple awards must be made if that yields the lowest total price to the government after considering administrative cost savings, *Para Scientific Co.*, Comp. Gen. Dec. B-299046.2, 2007 CPD ¶ 37.

Where price was identified as the only evaluation factor, it was improper not to award to the quoter that took no exception to the RFQ and submitted the lowest price, *Cromartie Constr. Co.*, Comp. Gen. Dec. B-271788, 96-2 CPD ¶ 48. GAO also indicated that where price is the only evaluation factor, the quote of a small business may not be rejected because the agency believes that it is too low. In such a situation, the matter is one of responsibility, requiring reference to the Small Business Administration. The same result was reached in *Possehn Consulting*, Comp. Gen. Dec. B-278579, 98-1 CPD ¶ 10.

If an agency has solicited offers, award will be made by accepting the offer in the same way that this is accomplished in standard negotiated procurement. If an agency has solicited quotations, award will be made by issuance of a purchase order. In such cases, the contracting officer must determine whether the contractor will be required to provide a written acceptance of the purchase order — forming a bilateral contract, FAR 13.302-3(a). Alternatively, FAR 13.004(b) states:

[T]he supplier may indicate acceptance by furnishing the supplies or services ordered or by proceeding with the work to the point where substantial performance
has occurred.

If the latter procedure is adopted, the government is not contractually bound until
substantial performance has occurred. Thereafter, it may terminate or cancel the
order, FAR 13.004(c), but it will be subject to compensate the contractor in accordance with FAR 13.302-4. However, if the contractor does not deliver the products
at the time specified in the RFQ, the government's offer will be considered to have
lapsed with the result that the government is not liable to compensate the contractor
for costs incurred to that time, *Smart Bus. Machs. v. United States*, 72 Fed. Cl. 706
(2006); *Rex Sys., Inc.*, ASBCA 45,301, 93-3 BCA ¶ 26,065.

## g. Documentation

FAR 13.106-3 contains the following requirement for very minimal documentation:

(b) *File documentation and retention.* Keep documentation to a minimum. Purchasing offices shall retain data supporting purchases (paper or electronic) to the
minimum extent and duration necessary for management review purposes (see
subpart 4.8). The following illustrate the extent to which quotation or offer information should be recorded:

(1) Oral solicitations. The contracting office should establish and maintain
records of oral price quotations in order to reflect clearly the propriety of
placing the order at the price paid with the supplier concerned. In most
cases, this will consist merely of showing the names of the suppliers contacted and the prices and other terms and conditions quoted by each.

(2) Written solicitations (see 2.101). For acquisitions not exceeding the simplified acquisition threshold, limit written records of solicitations or offers
to notes or abstracts to show prices, delivery, references to printed price lists
used, the supplier or suppliers contacted, and other pertinent data.

(3) Special situations. Include additional statements —

(i) Explaining the absence of competition (see 13.106-1 for brand
name purchases) if only one source is solicited and the acquisition does not exceed the simplified acquisition threshold (does
not apply to an acquisition of utility services available from only
one source); or

(ii) Supporting the award decision if other than price-related factors were considered in selecting the supplier.

In *Universal Bldg. Maint., Inc.*, Comp. Gen. Dec. B-282456, 99-2 CPD ¶ 32, GAO
granted a protest because the agency provided no documentation to support a price/

technical tradeoff. This would indicate that agencies should include a short description of the basis for determining the winning quoter in the contract file.

### h.  Notice and Debriefing

FAR 13.106-3(c) states that notice to "unsuccessful suppliers shall be given only if requested or required." However, this would not appear to preclude the agency from giving notice as a courtesy. Furthermore, a notice of award is required to be published electronically if the award is over $25,000 and "if there is likely to be any subcontract," 41 U.S.C. § 1708(a)(3); FAR 5.301(a). Once notification is requested an agency's failure to respond in a timely fashion is improper, *Professional Data Sys.*, GSBCA 8475-P, 86-3 BCA ¶ 19,083.

If a supplier requests information on an award that was based on factors other than price alone, FAR 13.106-3(d) provides that a brief explanation of the basis for the contract award decision must be provided.

## D.  Commercial Item Test Procedure

FAR 13.500(a) authorizes contracting agencies to use the simplified procedures of Part 13 "as a test program" if the contracting officer "reasonably expects, based on the nature of the supplies or services sought, and on market research, that offers will include only commercial items." Such procedures may be used for procurements not exceeding $6,500,000, or $12,000,000 if the procurement is "in support of a contingency operation or to facilitate the defense against or recovery from nuclear, biological, chemical, or radiological attack," FAR 13.500(e). The simplified procedures are to be used to the "maximum extent practicable," FAR 13.500(b). The authority to use the "test program" expires periodically, FAR 13.500(d), and contracting officers may award contracts after the expiration of this authority only for solicitations issued before this date.

FAR 13.501 requires special documentation when sole source contracts are awarded under the commercial item test program. This documentation must meet the requirements of FAR 6.303-2 in justifying the solicitation of only one source, FAR 13.501(a)(1)(ii). For proposed contracts over $150,000, but not exceeding $650,000, the contracting officer must certify that the justification for sole source procurement is accurate and complete, FAR 13.501(a)(2)(i). For proposed contracts in excess of $650,000, but not exceeding $13,000,000, the approval must be by the competition advocate of the procuring activity on a non-delegable basis, FAR 13.501(a)(2)(ii). For proposed contracts in excess of $13,000,000, but not exceeding $64,000,000 (for DoD, NASA, and the Coast Guard $87,000,000), the approval must be by the head of the procuring activity on a non-delegable basis, FAR 13.501(a)(2)(iii). For proposed contracts in excess of $64,000,000 (for DoD, NASA, and the Coast Guard

$87,000,000), the approval must be by the senior procurement executive head of the agency on a nondelegable basis (except for DoD), FAR 13.501(a)(2)(iv).

For all procurements conducted under the test program, the contract file is to include a brief description of the procedures used, the number of offers received, the basis for the award, and any justification required for a sole source procurement, FAR 13.501(b).

## E. Blanket Purchase Agreements

Blanket purchase agreements (BPAs) are a "simplified method of filling anticipated repetitive needs for supplies or services by establishing 'charge accounts' with qualified sources of supply," FAR 13.303-1(a). In entering into a BPA, the parties agree to a set of terms and conditions that will be applicable to future purchases but do not agree to any specific purchase.

BPAs are recommended for use by FAR 13.303-2(a) in implementing the simplified acquisition procedures in the following circumstances:

(1) There is a wide variety of items in a broad class of supplies or services that are generally purchased, but the exact items, quantities, and delivery requirements are not known in advance and may vary considerably.

(2) There is a need to provide commercial sources of supply for one or more offices or projects in a given area that do not have or need authority to purchase otherwise.

(3) The use of this procedure would avoid the writing of numerous purchase orders.

(4) There is no existing requirements contract for the same supply or service that the contracting activity is required to use.

The major advantage of BPAs is that they permit a vendor to respond to a number of orders and to submit consolidated invoices on a regular basis. FAR 13.303-3(a)(6) provides guidance on the invoicing provisions that can be included in BPAs. A BPA is also a convenient way for a contracting officer to negotiate an across-the-board discount for all of the supplies or services furnished by a single supplier, FAR 13.303-2(d).

BPAs are established by contracting officers when they find that repetitive purchases are being made from a supplier. There is no need for a requisition for any specific supplies or services to initiate a BPA, FAR 13.303-2(d).

## 1. Number and Effect of BPAs

BPAs may be established with a single supplier or with multiple suppliers depending on the needs of the agency, FAR 13.303-2(c). However, the existence of a

BPA does not justify purchasing from the holder of a single BPA on a sole source basis or avoiding any required small business set-aside, FAR 13.303-5(c). FAR 13.303-5(d) contains the following guidance:

> (d) If, for a particular purchase greater than the micro-purchase threshold, there is an insufficient number of BPAs to ensure maximum practicable competition, the contracting officer shall —
>
>> (1) Solicit quotations from other sources (see 13.105) and make the purchase as appropriate; and
>>
>> (2) Establish additional BPAs to facilitate future purchases if —
>>
>>> (i) Recurring requirements for the same or similar supplies or services seem likely;
>>>
>>> (ii) Qualified sources are willing to accept BPAs; and
>>>
>>> (iii) It is otherwise practical to do so.

In *Envirosolve LLC*, Comp. Gen. Dec. B-294974.4, 2005 CPD ¶ 106, GAO held that it was improper to award BPAs without competition and then issue orders against them on a noncompetitive basis, interpreting this competition requirement as follows:

> Agencies are not required to request proposals or to conduct a competition before establishing BPAs. *Information Sys. Tech. Corp.*, B-280013.2, Aug. 6, 1998, 98-2 CPD ¶ 36 at 3. After a BPA is established, however, otherwise applicable competition requirements still apply to all procurements under the BPA. FAR § 13.303-5(a) (BPA to be used only for purchases that are otherwise authorized by law or regulation); *Information Sys. Tech. Corp., supra.* Moreover, the existence of a BPA does not justify purchasing from only one source. FAR § 13.303-5(c). If, for a procurement in excess of $2,500 there is an insufficient number of established BPAs to ensure maximum practicable competition, the contracting officer must solicit quotations from other sources. FAR § 13.303-5(d)(1).

GAO subsequently ruled that there is no requirement for competition among holders of multiple BPAs because the agency conducted competition in selecting these BPA contractors, *Logan, LLC*, Comp. Gen. Dec. B-294974.6, 2006 CPD ¶ 188 (agency rotated awards and excluded protester from award during investigation of improprieties). In contrast, it is proper under this FAR guidance to compete non-BPA holders against BPA holders. See *AudioCARE Sys.*, Comp. Gen. Dec. B-283985, 2000 CPD ¶ 24, discussing a procurement where this occurred.

When an agency conducts a competition among BPA holders, it's award decision will be subject to protest, *C&B Constr., Inc.*, Comp. Gen. Dec. B-401988.2, 2010 CPD ¶ 1. In that case, the protest was sustained because the agency did not document its tradeoff decision sufficiently to demonstrate that the higher priced quotation was the best value.

The late quotation rules, discussed earlier, apply to quotations for BPAs, *Zebra Techs. Int'l, LLC*, Comp. Gen. Dec. B-296158, 2005 CPD ¶ 122.

A BPA is not a contract because the government is not obligated to issue any orders. See *Production Packaging*, ASBCA 53662, 03-2 BCA ¶ 32,338, holding that a supplier with a BPA has "no legal expectation to receive exclusive orders" and stating at 159,972:

> It is well established that a BPA is not a contract. Rather, a BPA is nothing more than an agreement of terms by which the Government could purchase. See, e.g., *Mid-America Officials Ass'n*, ASBCA No. 38678, 89-3 BCA ¶ 22,231 at 111,775-76. Until the Government places an order under a BPA, no contract is formed for lack of consideration. *Julian Freeman*, ASBCA No. 46675, 94-3 BCA ¶ 27,280 at 135,906.

Even if an order is issued under a BPA, that order can still be terminated if the BPA includes a Termination for the Convenience of the Government clause, *Dehdari General Trading & Contracting EST.*, ASBCA 53987, 03-1 BCA ¶ 32,249. In that case, the order for a one-year lease was terminated after one month with no liability for the government to pay the rental for the remaining eleven months. See also *Zhengxing v. United States*, 71 Fed. Cl. 732, *aff'd*, 204 Fed. Appx. 885 (2006), where failure to issue orders was held not to be an improper termination, and *Janice L. Cox*, ASBCA 50587, 03-1 BCA ¶ 32,205, where reassigning the work to another supplier after work had commenced was treated as a termination for convenience not a breach of the order.

## *2. Terms and Conditions*

FAR 13.303-3(a) requires that BPAs contain, at a minimum, terms and conditions covering the following matters:

(1) *Description of agreement.* A statement that the supplier shall furnish supplies or services, described in general terms, if and when requested by the contracting officer (or the authorized representative of the contracting officer) during a specified period and within a stipulated aggregate amount, if any.

(2) *Extent of obligation.* A statement that the Government is obligated only to the extent of authorized purchases actually made under the BPA.

(3) *Purchase limitation.* A statement that specifies the dollar limitation for each individual purchase under the BPA (see 13.303-5(b)).

(4) *Individuals authorized to purchase under the BPA.* A statement that a list of individuals authorized to purchase under the BPA, identified either by title of

position or by name of individual, organizational component, and the dollar limitation per purchase for each position title or individual shall be furnished to the supplier by the contracting officer.

(5) *Delivery tickets.* A requirement that all shipments under the agreement, except those for newspapers, magazines, or other periodicals, shall be accompanied by delivery tickets or sales slips that shall contain [prescribed] minimum information.

\* \* \*

(6) *Invoices.* One of the following statements shall be included [prescribing the use of either summary invoices or itemized invoices submitted at least monthly].

BPAs must also contain the applicable clauses for simplified acquisitions that are discussed below, FAR 13.303-4. They can also include the optional Terms and Conditions — Simplified Acquisitions (Other Than Commercial Items) clause in FAR 52.213-4 when appropriate, FAR 13.303-8.

## F.  Laws and Clauses Not Applicable

In carrying out the objective of reducing the number of contract clauses applicable to simplified acquisitions, FASA made certain laws inapplicable to these procurements. Thess laws are listed in FAR 13.005. FAR 13.006 lists additional provisions and clauses that are inapplicable to contracts and subcontracts at or below the simplified acquisition threshold even though the provision or clause is merely for the purpose of informing contractors that they are subject to the statute. Contractors performing simplified acquisitions must be independently aware that they are subject to these statutes.

The list of provisions and clauses set forth in FAR 13.005 as inapplicable is not an exclusive list. **Figure 7-1** is a complete list of all socioeconomic clauses from FAR Parts 19-26 and their applicability to simplified acquisitions. See also the Terms and Conditions — Simplified Acquisitions (Other Than Commercial Items) clause at FAR 52.213-4 which may be used in simplified acquisitions over the micro-purchase threshold that are not for commercial items, FAR 13.302-5(d). This clause lists the statutory and regulatory provisions that are applicable to simplified acquisitions as well some of the standard provisions covering inspection/acceptance, excusable delays, termination for convenience, termination for cause and warranty. It may be tailored to fit the needs of the procuring agency, FAR 13.302-5(d)(2)(ii), pursuant to the following guidance:

Modifications (i.e., additions, deletions, or substitutions) must not create a void or internal contradiction in the clause. For example, do not add an inspection and acceptance or termination for convenience requirement unless the existing requirement is deleted. Also, do not delete a paragraph without providing for an appropriate substitute.

While this clause is not mandatory, a clause of this nature is necessary to inform the contracting parties of the basic terms of their contract.

When the simplified acquisition is for commercial items, the clauses applicable to such procurement, as discussed in the preceding section, should be used.

| Collateral Policy | Simplified Procedures | Commercial (Less than $150,000) | Commercial (Greater than $150,000 and less than $6.5 million) | Standard (over $150,000 and not commercial) |
|---|---|---|---|---|
| **Small Business and Socially Disadvantaged** | | | | |
| Women-Owned Business (52.204-5) | No | No | Yes | Yes |
| Small Business Program Representations (52.219-1) | Yes | Yes | Yes | Yes |
| Utilization of Small, Small Disadvantaged and Women-Owned Small Business Concerns (52.219-8) | No | No | Yes | Yes |
| Small, Small Disadvantaged and Women-Owned Small Business Subcontracting Plan (52.219.9) | No | No | Yes | Yes over $500,000 |
| Incentive Subcontracting Program (52.219-10) | No | No | Yes | Yes over $500,000 |
| Utilization of Indian Organizations and Indian-Owned Economic Enterprises (52.226-1) | No | No | Yes | Yes over $500,000 |
| Historically Black College or University and Minority Institution (52.226-2) | Yes | Yes | Yes | Yes |
| **Labor and Equal Opportunity** | | | | |
| Convict Labor (52.222-3) | Yes | Yes | Yes | Yes |
| Contract Work Hours and Safety Standards (52.222-4) | No | No | No | Yes |
| Balance of Payments Program — Construction Materials — NAFTA (52.225-22) | Yes | Yes | Yes | Yes |

**Figure 7-1 (cont'd on next page)**

| Collateral Policy | Simplified Procedures | Commercial (Less than $150,000) | Commercial (Greater than $150,000 and less than $6.5 million) | Standard (over $150,000 and not commercial) |
|---|---|---|---|---|
| Preference for U.S.-Flag Air Carriers (52.247-63 | No | No | No | Yes |
| Preference for Privately Owned U.S.-Flag Commercial Vessels (52.247.64) | Yes | Yes | Yes | Yes |
| Davis-Bacon Act (52.222-6) | Yes | Yes | Yes | Yes |
| Walsh-Healey Act (52.222-20) | Yes | No | No | Yes |
| Certification of Nonsegregated Facilities (52.222-21) | Yes | Yes | Yes | Yes |
| Affirmative Action Compliance (52.222.25) | Yes | Yes | Yes | Yes |
| Equal Opportunity (52.222-26) | Yes | Yes | Yes | Yes |
| Affirmative Action Compliance Requirements for Construction (52.222-27) | Yes | Yes | Yes | Yes |
| Equal Opportunity Preaward Clearance of Subcontracts (52.222-28) | No | No | No | Yes over $1m |
| Affirmative Action for Special Disabled and Vietnam-Era Veterans (52.222-35) | Yes | Yes | Yes | Yes |
| Affirmative Action for Handicapped Workers (52.222.36) | Yes | Yes | Yes | Yes |
| Service Contract Act (52.222-41) | Yes | Yes | Yes | Yes |
| Fair Labor Standards Act and Service Contract Act — Price Adjustment (Multiple Year and Option Contracts (52.222-43) | No | No | Yes | Yes |
| Fair Labor Standards Act and Service Contract Act — Price Adjustment (52.222-44) | No | No | Yes | Yes |
| **Protection of the Environment** | | | | |
| Clean Air and Water Certification (52.223-1) | No | No | No | Yes |
| Clean Air and Water (52.223-2) | No | No | No | Yes |

**Figure 7-1 (cont'd from previous page)**

| Collateral Policy | Simplified Procedures | Commercial (Less than $150,000) | Commercial (Greater than $150,000 and less than $6.5 million) | Standard (over $150,000 and not commercial) |
|---|---|---|---|---|
| Hazardous Material Identification and Material Safety Data (52.223-3) | Yes | Yes | Yes | Yes |
| Recovered Material Certification (52.223-4) | Yes | Yes | Yes | Yes |
| Pollution Prevention Right-to-know Information (52.223-5) | Yes | Yes | Yes | Yes |
| Drug-Free Workplace (52.223-6) | No | No | No | Yes |
| Notice of Radioactive Materials (52.223-7) | Yes | Yes | Yes | Yes |
| Certification of Percentage of Recovered Material Content for EPA-Designated Items Used in Performance of the Contract (52.223-9) | No | No | Yes | Yes |
| Waste Reduction Program (52.223-10) | Yes | Yes | Yes | Yes |
| Ozone-Depleting Substance (52.223-11) | Yes | Yes | Yes | Yes |
| Refrigeration Equipment and Air Conditioners (52.223-12) | Yes | Yes | Yes | Yes |
| Certification of Toxic Chemical Release Reporting (52.223-13) | No | No | Yes | Yes |
| Toxic Chemical Release (52.223-14) | No | No | Yes | Yes |
| **Preferences** | | | | |
| Buy American Act Certificate (52.225-1) | Yes | Yes | Yes | Yes |
| Balance of Payments Program Certificate (52.225-6) | No | No | Yes | Yes |
| Balance of Payments Program (52.225-7) | No | No | Yes | Yes |
| Buy American Act — Trade Agreements — Balance of Payments Certificate (52.225-8) | Yes | Yes | Yes | Yes |

**Figure 7-1 (cont'd from previous page)**

| Collateral Policy | Simplified Procedures | Commercial (Less than $150,000) | Commercial (Greater than $150,000 and less than $6.5 million) | Standard (over $150,000 and not commercial) |
|---|---|---|---|---|
| Buy American Act — Trade Agreements — Balance of Payments Program (52.225-9) | Yes | Yes | Yes | Yes |
| Duty-Free Entry (52.225-10) | No | No | Yes | Yes |
| Restrictions on Certain Foreign Purchases (52.225-11) | Yes | Yes | Yes | Yes |
| Buy American Act — North American Free Trade Agreement Implementation Act — Balance of Payments Program (52.225-20) | Yes | Yes | Yes | Yes |
| Buy American Act — North American Free Trade Agreement Implementation Act — Balance of Payments Certificate (52.225-21) | Yes | Yes | Yes | Yes |

**Figure 7-1 (cont'd from previous page)**

## G. Forms

There are a number of forms that are available, but not mandatory, when using simplified acquisition procedures. FAR 13.307(a) calls for the use of the SF 1449, Solicitation/Contract/Order for Commercial Items, in most instances where commercial items are being procured. For noncommercial items, FAR 13.307(b) provides:

(1) Except when quotations are solicited electronically or orally, the SF 1449; SF 18, Request for Quotations; or an agency form/automated format may be used. Each agency request for quotations form/automated format should conform with the SF 18 or SF 1449 to the maximum extent practicable.

(2) Both SF 1449 and OF 347, Order for Supplies or Services, are multipurpose forms used for negotiated purchases of supplies or services, delivery or task orders, inspection and receiving reports, and invoices. An agency form/automated format also may be used.

FAR 13.307(c) provides that three forms can be used for both commercial and noncommercial items — the OF 336, Continuation Sheet, the OF 348, Order for Supplies or Services Schedule — Continuation, and the SF 30, Amendment of Solicitation/Modification of Contract. Alternatively, agency regulations may prescribe their own forms or an automated format.

FAR 13.306 prescribes the use of the SF 44, Purchase Order — Invoice — Voucher, which is a multipurpose pocket-size purchase order form designated primarily for on-the-spot, over-the-counter micro-purchases.

FAR 13.307(e) prescribes the use of the SF 1165, Receipt for Cash — Subvoucher, for purchases using imprest funds or third party drafts.

For military departments, DD Form 1155, Orders for Supplies or Services, must be used for purchases made using the simplified acquisition procedures of FAR Part 13, DoD PGI 213.307-1(b). This guidance prohibits the use of Optional Forms 347 and 348. Civilian agencies may also use special forms when using simplified acquisition procedures. For example, the General Services Administration uses GSA Form 300, Order for Supplies or Services; GSA Form 3186, Order for Supplies or Services; or GSA Form 3186B, Order for Supplies or Services (EDI) when making simplified acquisitions, GSA Acquisition Manual 513.302-70(c). The Department of Agriculture uses Form AD-838, Purchase Order, in lieu of Optional Forms 347 and 348, AGAR 453.213. The Environmental Protection Agency permits the use of Form 1900-8, Procurement Request/Order, in lieu of Optional Forms 347 and 348 for simplified acquisitions, EPAAR 1513.505. DOE provides that Optional Forms 347 and 348 or DOE F 4250.3, Order for Supplies or Services, may be used for purchase orders using simplified acquisition procedures, DEAR 913.307(b).

## III. ARCHITECT-ENGINEER CONTRACTS

Architectural or engineering services must be procured in accordance with the procedures set forth in the Brooks Act. This statute was originally enacted as 40 U.S.C. §§ 541-44 and codified in Pub. L. No. 107-217, Aug. 21, 2002, as 40 U.S.C. §§ 1102-04. It is implemented in FAR Subpart 36.6. These procedures meet the Competition in Contracting Act mandate to use "competitive procedures," 10 U.S.C. § 2302(2)(A); 41 U.S.C. § 152(1). The Brooks Act was passed in 1972 after GAO notified Congress in 46 Comp. Gen. 556 (B-152306), 1966 CPD ¶ 110, that the existing practices in awarding architect-engineer (A-E) contracts "represent a deviation from the statutory requirements expressed in 10 U.S.C. § 2304(g) that proposals from a maximum number of qualified sources shall be solicited and that written or oral discussions be conducted with all responsible offerors who submit proposals within a competitive range, price and other factors considered." The Act amended the Federal Property and Administrative Services Act by ratifying the longstanding practice of procuring A-E services without price competition. The Act states that the government's policy is to "negotiate a contract for architectural and engineering services at compensation which the agency head determines is fair and reasonable," 40 U.S.C. § 1104(a).

The Act only applies if the prospective contract is primarily for A-E services. See FAR 36.601-3 stating:

(c) When the contract statement of work includes both architect-engineer services and other services, the contracting officer shall follow the procedures in this subpart if the statement of work, substantially or to a dominant extent, specifies performance or approval by a registered or licensed architect or engineer. If the statement of work does not specify such performance or approval, the contracting officer shall follow the procedures in Parts 13, 14, or 15.

These procedures must be used for task orders as well as for new procurements, § 1427 of the Services Acquisition Reform Act of 2003, Pub. L. No. 108-136. See FAR 8.403(c) stating:

(8) In accordance with section 1427(b) of Public Law 108-136, for requirements that substantially or to a dominant extent specify performance of architect-engineer services (as defined in 2.101), agencies —

(i) Shall use the procedures at Subpart 36.6; and

(ii) Shall not place orders for such requirements under a Federal Supply Schedule.

Although A-E services are an integral part of a design-build contract, it does not appear that these procedures are required to be used on such contracts. FAR Subpart 36.3 is silent on this issue. See *Fluor Enters., Inc. v. United States*, 64 Fed. Cl. 461 (2005), concluding that the Brooks Act does not apply to design-build contracts. See also *Neeser Constr., Inc./Allied Bldrs. Sys., A Joint Venture*, Comp. Gen. Dec. B-285903, 2000 CPD ¶ 207, where Brooks Act procedures were not followed on a design-build procurement without protest, and *Tyler Constr. Group v. United States*, 83 Fed. Cl. 94 (2008), *aff'd*, 570 F.3d 1329 (Fed. Cir. 2009), rejecting the argument that indefinite delivery/indefinite quantity contracts could not be used for design-build projects without discussing the applicability of the Brooks Act.

## A. Definition of Architect-Engineer Services

In 1988, Pub. L. No. 100-656 and Pub. L. No. 100-679 amended the Brooks Act definition of A-E services to establish three independent categories of A-E services. See 40 U.S.C. § 1102(2). This definition is implemented in FAR 2.101 as follows:

Architect-engineer services, as defined in 40 U.S.C. 1102, means —

(1) Professional services of an architectural or engineering nature, as defined by State law, if applicable, that are required to be performed or approved by a person licensed, registered, or certified to provide those services;

(2) Professional services of an architectural or engineering nature performed by contract that are associated with research, planning, development, design, construction, alteration, or repair of real property; and

(3) Such other professional services of an architectural or engineering nature, or incidental services, that members of the architectural and engineering professions (and individuals in their employ) may logically or justifiably perform, including studies, investigations, surveying and mapping, tests, evaluations, consultations, comprehensive planning, program management, conceptual designs, plans and specifications, value engineering, construction phase services, soils engineering, drawing reviews, preparation of operating and maintenance manuals, and other related services.

In *Forest Serv., Dep't of Agriculture*, 68 Comp. Gen. 555 (B-233987), 89-2 CPD ¶ 47, GAO discussed the reason for the amendment to the A-E services definition, as follows:

The legislative history of Pub. L. No. 100-656, § 42, 102 Stat. 3853 (1988), indicates that the amendment is intended to clarify the definition of A-E services in response to the General Accounting Office decisions issued since the enactment of the Brooks Act, "which have had the effect of narrowing the application of the law, particularly in the field of surveying and mapping." 134 Cong. Rec. H10058 (daily ed. Oct. 12, 1988) (statement of Mr. Myers).

GAO stated that the amendment required a modification of the two-prong test enunciated in prior decisions, stating:

Clause (C) of the 1988 amendment includes in the definition "other professional services of an architectural or engineering nature, or incidental services, which members of the architectural and engineering professions (and individuals in their employ) may logically or justifiably perform . . . ." The statute then lists services such as surveying and mapping which fall into this category. Thus, the revised definition now makes it clear that "incidental services" means types of services which are incidental to (part of) A-E services, and not, as we previously have held, incidental to an A-E project. The test to be applied in making this determination, then, is not whether the service is incidental to a traditional A-E project; rather, it is first, whether the service is the type which is incidental to professional services of an architectural or engineering nature, and if so, whether the service is one which members of the architectural and engineering profession may logically or justifiably perform.

Thus, even though services are not connected with the design of a structure, they will be defined as A-E services if they are the type normally performed by A-E firms. See *White Shield, Inc.*, 68 Comp. Gen. 696 (B-235522), 89-2 CPD ¶ 257 (cadastral surveying and mapping services); *Fodrea Land Surveys*, Comp. Gen. Dec. B-236413, 89-2 CPD ¶ 364 (traditional surveying and mapping of land). See, however, FAR 36.601-4(a)(4) stating:

[M]apping services that are not connected to traditionally understood or accepted architectural and engineering activities, are not incidental to such architectural and engineering activities or have not in themselves been considered architectural and engineering services shall be procured pursuant to Parts 13, 14, and 15.

See *Management Ass'n for Private Photogrammetric Surveyors v. United States*, 492 F. Supp. 2d 540 (E.D. Va. 2007), rejecting a challenge to this interpretation of the statute.

Other types of A-E services include computer-assisted design and drafting services, *EBA Ernest Bland Assocs.*, Comp. Gen. Dec. B-270496, 96-1 CPD ¶ 148; conducting flood studies, *Northwest Hydraulic Consultants, Inc.*, Comp. Gen. Dec. B-266211, 95-2 CPD ¶ 229; inspection and maintenance of work on towers and an antenna, *Fantozzi Co.*, Comp. Gen. Dec. B-265631, 95-2 CPD ¶ 255; and comprehensive long-term environmental services, *ABB Envtl. Servs., Inc.*, Comp. Gen. Dec. B-258258.2, 95-1 CPD ¶ 126. Compare *Photo Science, Inc.*, Comp. Gen. Dec. B-296391, 2005 CPD ¶ 140 (services to identify, measure and analyze natural resource habitats and cultural resource sites, using Global Positioning System services and Geographic Information Systems data management services not A-E services); and *Terra Surveys*, Comp. Gen. Dec. B-294015, 2004 CPD ¶ 155 (services requiring installation of equipment to monitor water levels not A-E services).

## B. Gathering Qualification Data

Each agency that procures A-E services is required to maintain files containing current data on the qualifications of A-E firms that desire contracts with the agency. FAR 36.603 contains the following guidance:

(a) *Establishing offices.* Agencies shall maintain offices or permanent evaluation boards, or arrange to use the offices or boards of other agencies, to receive and maintain data on firms wishing to be considered for Government contracts. Each office or board shall be assigned a jurisdiction by its parent agency, making it responsible for a geographical region or area, or a specialized type of construction.

(b) *Qualifications data.* To be considered for architect-engineer contracts, a firm must file with the appropriate office or board the Standard Form 330, "Architect-Engineer Qualifications," Part II, and when applicable, SF 330, Part I.

(c) *Data files and the classification of firms.* Under the direction of the parent agency, offices or permanent evaluation boards shall maintain an architect-engineer qualifications data file. These offices or boards shall review the SF 330 filed, and shall classify each firm with respect to:

(1) Location;

(2) Specialized experience;

(3) Professional capabilities; and

(4) Capacity, with respect to the scope of work that can be undertaken. A firm's ability and experience in computer-assisted design should be considered, when appropriate.

The Standard Form 330 contains two parts. Part II lists the general qualifications of a firm, consisting of a list of the key personnel and projects performed in the last five years. Part I lists the team that will be used to perform a specific prospective project with information on their experience on prior projects, with the result that this part of the form can only be submitted when a specific project is identified. A-Es and agencies should update Part II of the form on a regular basis, FAR 36.603(d). See *Dhillon Eng'rs., Inc.*, Comp. Gen. Dec. B-209687, 83-1 CPD ¶ 268, criticizing a six-month lag in recording information on prior contract awards and recommending that the agency update the information before the selection board's final recommendation.

Agencies are also required to prepare performance reports at the conclusion of each A-E project with a value of $30,000 or more, FAR 36.604 and 42.1502(f). These reports are submitted electronically to the Past Performance Information Retrieval System (PPIRS) at *www.ppirs.gov* and are required to be used in making the decision as to the qualification of specific A-E firms, FAR 42.1503(e). DFARS 236.604 requires Department of Defense activities to make this report using DD Form 2631.

# C. Announcement of Requirements

The Brooks Act originally provided that the agency was required to "publicly announce all requirements for architectural and engineering services," 40 U.S.C. § 542. When the Act was codified in 2002, this requirement was revised in 40 U.S.C. § 1103(d) to state that the selection of an A-E firm "shall be based on criteria established and published by the agency head." FAR 36.601-1 implements this requirement by calling for a public announcement of all requirements for A-E services. This policy is implemented in FAR 5.205(d)(1) which requires posting a synopsis on the governmentwide point of entry for any proposed A-E contract expected to exceed $25,000. FAR 5.207(c)(12) states that the synopsis should contain the following information:

For architect-engineer projects and other projects for which the supply or service codes are insufficient, provide brief details with respect to: location, scope of services required, cost range and limitations, type of contract, estimated starting and completion dates, and any significant evaluation factors.

This synopsis serves as a solicitation — alerting firms that want to compete for a project that they should submit a SF 330 to the agency. See *Wadell Engr'g Corp.*,

60 Comp. Gen. 11 (B-199171), 80-2 CPD ¶ 269, noting that no other solicitation is used in this form of procurement. Therefore, after publishing the synopsis, agencies must allow a 30-day response time from the date of publication before taking further action if the procurement exceeds the simplified acquisition threshold, FAR 5.203(d). A firm that does not respond to this notice is not necessarily excluded from consideration, as A-E firms are selected based on forms on file with the agency. However, the synopsis allows interested firms that have not done so to file the proper forms or to update data already on file. The synopsis also alerts firms which might wish to protest some aspect of the procurement. An agency may refuse to consider a firm that has not submitted the information by the time required by the synopsis, *Northwest Heritage Consultants*, Comp. Gen. Dec. B-299547, 2007 CPD ¶ 93.

If the agency prepares a preliminary conceptual design, it is not required to release it to the A-E firms. See *Hack v. Department of Energy*, 538 F. Supp. 1098 (D.D.C. 1982), rejecting a request for such a design pursuant to the Freedom of Information Act. 5 U.S.C. § 552.

## D. Evaluation Criteria

The policy of the Brooks Act is to award A-E contracts on the basis of competence and qualifications. This involves a two-step process: (1) selection based upon demonstrated competence and qualifications, and (2) post-selection negotiation of a fair and reasonable price.

Each contractor is evaluated in terms of professional qualifications, specialized experience in the type of work required, capacity to perform on time, past performance, location in the area of the project (provided this criterion leaves an appropriate number of qualified firms), and acceptability under other appropriate evaluation criteria, FAR 36.602-1(a). Firms may be evaluated on the basis of the project design as well. FAR 36.602-1(b) provides that design competitions may be used, with the approval of the agency head or a designee, when unique situations exist involving prestige projects, sufficient time is available for the production and evaluation of designs, and the design competition will benefit the project after considering its costs. There is no requirement that A-E work be equitably distributed among competing firms, *Fantozzi Co.*, Comp. Gen. Dec. B-265631, 95-2 CPD ¶ 255, *recons. denied*, 96-1 CPD ¶ 220.

These criteria are applied at two stages. The information submitted or on file with the agency is reviewed and not less than three firms are chosen for discussions "regarding concepts and the relative utility of alternative methods of furnishing the required services," FAR 36.602-3(c). There is no requirement that the A-E firm be advised of weaknesses or deficiencies that are perceived during the discussions, *HydroGeoLogic, Inc.*, Comp. Gen. Dec. B-311263, 2008 CPD ¶ 218 (weaknesses found during oral presentation); *Metcalf & Eddy Servs., Inc.*, Comp. Gen. Dec.

B-298421.2, 2007 CPD ¶ 61 (Brooks Act discussion requirement different from FAR Part 15 requirement). Neither is there any requirement that the full board participate in the discussions with the selected firms. See *Pickering Firm, Inc.*, Comp. Gen. Dec. B-277396, 97-2 CPD ¶ 99, finding it proper to have subordinates attend the discussions as long as one board member was present. After these discussions, the top three firms are ranked according to the evaluation criteria as well as the merit of each firm's concepts. In some cases, firms have been called upon to make oral presentations and it is proper to require their submitted materials to match their presentations, *Metcalf & Eddy Servs., Inc.*, Comp. Gen. Dec. B-298421.2, 2007 CPD ¶ 61.

When a source selection official is unable to choose between offerors on the basis of the established factors, other "rationally related" factors may be considered, *Group Hosp. Serv., Inc.*, 58 Comp. Gen. 263 (B-190401), 79-1 CPD ¶ 245. However, under no circumstances is cost or price to be considered. In *Mounts Eng'g; Dep't of the Interior — Request for Advance Decision*, 64 Comp. Gen. 772 (B-218489), 85-2 CPD ¶ 181, because the agency found two A-E firms "equally preferred," it requested cost proposals prior to selection. GAO sustained the protest, stating at 777:

> [G]iven the legislative mandate to rank A-E firms without reference to compensation, we believe that the fee proposed by a firm is not a factor rationally related to deciding which A-E firm is most highly qualified . . . .

One factor previously used by the Department of Defense, but now absent from the DFARS, was the equitable distribution of work. GAO sustained a protest when the Navy failed to consider this factor, *Randolph Eng'g, Inc.*, Comp. Gen. Dec. B-192375, 79-1 CPD ¶ 465. However, where equitable distribution of work was an evaluation factor, it was still permissible to find that it was outweighed by other performance- and qualification-based factors, *Liberty Assocs., Inc.*, Comp. Gen. Dec. B-232650, 89-1 CPD ¶ 29. In *ABB Envtl. Servs., Inc.*, Comp. Gen. Dec. B-258258.2, 95-1 CPD ¶ 126, the fact that equitable distribution of work was not a listed evaluation factor but was nonetheless used to resolve a tie, was deemed not to have prejudiced the protester because (1) it was applied equally to all offerors and (2) it was implausible to believe that the protester would not have competed had it known that this factor would be used.

Since most factors considered in the Brooks Act evaluation process are responsibility-related, determinations of no responsibility are rare in this type of procurement. In *Richard Sanchez Assocs.*, 64 Comp. Gen. 603 (B-218404.2), 85-1 CPD ¶ 661, after the firm had been tentatively selected, negotiations were terminated due to the firm having fewer employees than the agency had believed. GAO held that since A-E selection procedures concern a firm's capabilities and qualifications relative to other firms rather than minimal responsibility, no referral to SBA for a Certificate of Competency was required when assessing relative capability. See also *Nomura Enters., Inc.*, Comp. Gen. Dec. B-236217, 89-2 CPD ¶ 437, holding that, although certain evaluation criteria encompassed traditional elements of responsibility, this did not convert a technical finding that the protester was less qualified and experienced than other firms into a finding of nonresponsibility.

Although neither the Brooks Act nor the FAR contain a requirement for a statement of relative importance of the evaluation criteria, such a statement is frequently included in the synopsis. A statement of relative importance is required to be included in the synopsis by DFARS 236.602-1. See *Mounts Eng'g*, 65 Comp. Gen. 476 (B-218489.4), 86-1 CPD ¶ 358, rejecting a protest challenging the importance given to the distance of the offerors' offices from the project site.

## E.  Source Selection Personnel

Evaluation boards are made up of professional personnel, from the government or A-E firms, who are capable of appraising the qualifications of the prospective A-Es. FAR 36.602-2 provides:

(a) When acquiring architect-engineer services, an agency shall provide for one or more permanent or ad hoc architect-engineer evaluation boards (which may include preelection boards when authorized by agency regulations) to be composed of members who, collectively, have experience in architecture, engineering, construction, and Government and related acquisition matters. Members shall be appointed among highly qualified professional employees of the agency or other agencies, and if authorized by agency procedure, private practitioners of architecture, engineering, or related professions. One Government member of each board shall be designated as the chairperson.

(b) No firm shall be eligible for award of an architect-engineer contract during the period in which any of its principals or associates are participating as members of the awarding agency's evaluation board.

GAO will not grant a protest that board members were not qualified unless the protester can show "possible fraud, bad faith, or a conflict of interest," *Geographic Res. Solutions*, Comp. Gen. Dec. B-260402, 95-1 CPD ¶ 278; *IDG Architects*, 68 Comp. Gen. 683 (B-235487), 89-2 CPD ¶ 236.

## F.  Appraising Firms' Qualifications

The first step in the selection process is to appraise each firm's qualifications using SF 330 and the reports in the PPIRS. In deciding which firms to hold discussions with, agencies are permitted but not required to use information not included in these data systems. See *FACE Assocs., Inc.*, Comp. Gen. Dec. B-211877, 83-2 CPD ¶ 643, finding that the Brooks Act, which provides that firms should be encouraged to submit statements of qualifications and performance data annually, evidenced a legislative intent to avoid burdensome investigations into the firms' qualifications for each procurement.

Some agencies also gather past performance information from recent clients of the A-E firms. See *Shaw-Parsons Infrastructure Recovery Consultants, LLC*, Comp. Gen. Dec. B-401679.4, 2010 CPD ¶ 77, holding that when an agency requires the submission of questionnaires from recent clients, it must include that information in the evaluation of a firm's past performance because it is too close at hand to ignore. See also *SEI Group, Inc.*, Comp. Gen. Dec. B-400829, 2009 CPD ¶ 51, where an agency properly sought and relied on questionnaires from recent clients when it found that one potential A-E firm had no data in the PPIRS.

It is proper to include in the appraisal the qualifications of subcontractors and consultants that will be used on the project, *Foundation Eng'g Scis., Inc.*, Comp. Gen. Dec. B-292834, 2003 CPD ¶ 229.

When an agency learns that information on the standard forms is misleading or inaccurate, it may terminate negotiations with a firm that has been tentatively selected, *Veterans Design Assocs.*, Comp. Gen. Dec. B-242080, 91-1 CPD ¶ 265; *Richard Sanchez Assocs.*, 64 Comp. Gen. 603 (B-218404.2), 85-1 CPD ¶ 661; *Paul F. Pugh & Associated Professional Eng'rs.*, Comp. Gen. Dec. B-198851, 80-2 CPD ¶ 171. The evaluation board is also free to change its ranking upon receipt of new information, *Henderson Design Group*, Comp. Gen. Dec. B-248973.3, 92-2 CPD ¶ 406; *Harding Lawson Assocs., Inc.*, Comp. Gen. Dec. B-230219, 88-1 CPD ¶ 483; *Arix Corp.*, Comp. Gen. Dec. B-195503, 79-2 CPD ¶ 331.

## G. Selection and Ranking of Firms

After the discussions with at least three of the most highly qualified firms, the evaluation board prepares a selection report recommending the top three firms in order of preference, FAR 36.602-3(c). The selection report must include a narrative of the board's discussions and evaluation in order to allow the selection authority to review the recommendation. GAO sustained a protest where no documentation of the board's reasoning was created, rejecting the contention that because architects and engineers "are called upon to exercise their professional judgment . . . the process is necessarily a highly subjective one which does not lend itself to reasoned statements of the basis on which the selection is made," *Wadell Eng'g Corp.*, 60 Comp. Gen. 11 (B-199171), 80-2 CPD ¶ 269. However, in *ABB Envtl. Servs., Inc.*, Comp. Gen. Dec. B-258258.2, 95-1 CPD ¶ 126, the fact that the evaluation board was orally advised that its report was inadequate and was instructed to revise it (rather than rejecting the report outright and stating the reasons therefor in writing) was deemed to be a deficiency of form that did not affect the validity of the selection decision. See also *Pickering Firm, Inc.*, Comp. Gen. Dec. B-277396, 97-2 CPD ¶ 99, where supplemental documentation was accepted to bolster "sparse" original documentation.

The final ranking is made by the agency head or another designated selection authority. The selection official reviews the board's recommendations with the advice of staff and technical representatives and selects the most qualified firms in order of preference. The selection official may select from only those firms on the board's list, FAR 36.602-4, but exercises an independent evaluation function, *SRG Partnership, PC*, 56 Comp. Gen. 721 (B-188444), 77-1 CPD ¶ 438. However, if the highest-ranked firm is not the firm most highly rated by the evaluation board, a written explanation must be provided, FAR 36.602-4(b).

GAO has consistently held that it will not upset the A-E selection decision as long as the record shows that the agency reasonably evaluated the protester's qualifications in accordance with the stated evaluation criteria. See *URS Consultants*, Comp. Gen. Dec. B-27506, 97-1 CPD ¶ 100; *Geographic Resource Solutions*, Comp. Gen. Dec. B-260402, 95-1 CPD ¶ 278; *CH2M Hill, Ltd.*, Comp. Gen. Dec. B-259511, 95-1 CPD ¶ 203; *Environmental Tech. Assessment Compliance Serv.*, Comp. Gen. Dec. B-258093, 94-2 CPD ¶ 239; *Shah & Assocs.*, Comp. Gen. Dec. B-257405, 94-2 CPD ¶ 123; *Conseco Eng'g, Inc.*, Comp. Gen. Dec. B-250666, 93-1 CPD ¶ 98. GAO has also denied a protest that the agency materially altered the project requirements without permitting new conceptual designs to be submitted, *Kerry Lindale*, Comp. Gen. Dec. B-276057, 97-1 CPD ¶ 165.

FAR 36.602-5 allows two "short selection processes," consisting of selection by the board or by the chairperson of the board, when the contract is not expected to exceed the simplified acquisition threshold. The agency may also use a longer process including "reselection boards" if it desires.

In other cases agencies may use more elaborate procedures. In *URS Consultants*, Comp. Gen. Dec. B-275068, 97-1 CPD ¶ 100, the agency followed a two-stage procedure to make its selection. The process was described as follows:

> The CBD synopsis indicated that GSA would select a contractor through a two-stage process. Stage I would establish the architectural, mechanical and electrical engineering, and industrial hygienist design capabilities of interested A/E firms and their key designers. During Stage I, interested firms were to submit standard forms (SF) 254 and 255 for the A/E design firm only and additional information including: 8 X 10 graphics and written descriptions of relevant prior completed projects; a statement from their key designers regarding the firm's design philosophy and the parameters that apply specifically to the modernization of buildings; their key designers' portfolios; and biographical profiles of their key designers. After the qualifications statements and related materials were evaluated, a short list of at least three firms would be selected for participation in Stage II. The synopsis stated that, during Stage II, each short-list offeror's entire project team — including the A/E design firm, its key designers, and all the consultants that will work on the project — would be evaluated. This evaluation was to be based upon submission of Sis 254 and 255 which reflected the entire project team and would include a face-to-face interview with each project team.

See also *Gene Corp.*, Comp. Gen. Dec. B-274390-2, 97-1 CPD ¶ 225, where the selection procedure involved site visits, live-test demonstrations, and oral presentations. The solicitation contained 18 evaluation criteria and 38 sub criteria.

## H. Negotiations

Final ranking by the selection official authorizes the contracting officer to begin negotiations with the most highly rated firm, FAR 36.606(a). The contracting officer should ordinarily request a proposal from the firm "ensuring that the solicitation does not inadvertently preclude the firm from proposing the use of modern design methods," FAR 36.606(b). Such methods, such as computer-assisted design, should be discussed in negotiations if not covered in the firm's proposal, FAR 36.606(d).

The negotiation process differs significantly from discussions in standard competitive procurement. This is primarily because 40 U.S.C. § 1104(a) requires the agency to negotiate a contract at a "fair and reasonable" price although the statute does not permit the agency to consider price in selecting the contractor. FAR 36.606(a) states that these negotiations "shall be conducted in accordance with Part 15" without explaining the meaning of this statement.

If the contracting officer is unable to negotiate a reasonable price or is otherwise unable to negotiate a satisfactory contract, negotiations should be formally terminated and negotiations should begin with the second-ranked firm, 40 U.S.C. § 1104(b); FAR 36.606(f). In *Drowsy Assocs.*, Comp. Gen. Dec. B-248216, 92-1 CPD ¶ 533, the contracting officer's decision to terminate negotiations when, after 10 months, the parties could not come to a mutually acceptable agreement was not arbitrary or unreasonable. FAR 36.606(f) provides that the contracting officer should request a written final proposal revision from a firm prior to terminating negotiations. This procedure continues until a satisfactory contract is negotiated. See *Inca Engrs., Inc.*, 69 Comp. Gen. 34 (B-236406), 89-2 CPD ¶ 371.

Negotiation may involve matters other than price. See FAR 36.606(e) calling for the negotiation of subcontractors that will be used on the project because the standard clause Subcontractors and Outside Consultants (Architect-Engineer Services) at FAR 52.244-4 requires that only such subcontractors be used on the project. In contrast, when a design competition is held as a basis for selection, the government will not be bound to the design proposed by the selected firm unless the solicitation so provides, *Kerry Lindale*, Comp. Gen. Dec. B-276057, 97-1 CPD ¶ 165.

## I. Fee Limitations

There are a number of statutory provisions requiring A-E contracts to contain limitations on the amount that can be paid for A-E services. The statute applicable to most civilian agencies, 41 U.S.C. § 254(b), contained the following provisions applicable to A-E contracts:

> [I]n the case of a cost-plus-a-fixed-fee contract the fee shall not exceed 10 percent of the estimated cost of the contract, exclusive of the fee, as determined by the agency head at the time of entering into such contract (except . . . that a fee inclusive of the contractor's costs and not in excess of 6 percent of the estimated cost, exclusive of fees, as determined by the agency head at the time of entering into the contract, of the project to which such fee is applicable is authorized in contracts for architectural or engineering services relating to any public works or utility project).

In the 2011 codification, Pub. L. No. 111-350, the meaning of this provision was changed to state in 41 U.S.C. § 3905(b):

> (3) Architectural or engineering services. The fee in a cost-plus-a-fixed-fee contract for architectural or engineering services relating to any public works or utility project may include the contractor's costs and shall not exceed 6 percent of the estimated cost, not including the fee, as determined by the agency head at the time of entering into the contract, of the project to which the fee applies.

This codification would apply the fee restriction only to cost-plus-fixed-fee contracts whereas the prior statute was applicable to all types of A-E contracts. Since codification are not intended to substantively alter the law, this language should not be literally followed.

The statute applicable to DoD, NASA, and the Coast Guard, 10 U.S.C. § 2306(d), contains different language, stating:

> The fee for performing a cost-plus-a-fixed-fee contract for architectural or engineering services for a public work or utility plus the cost of those services to the contractor may not be more than 6 percent of the estimated cost of that work or project, not including fees. The fee for performing any other cost-plus-a-fixed-fee contract may not be more than 10 percent of the estimated cost of the contract, not including the fee.

In addition, each of the military services has fee limitation provisions in 10 U.S.C. § 4540(b) (Army), 10 U.S.C. § 7212(b) (Navy), and 10 U.S.C. § 9540(b) (Air Force). These provisions state:

> The fee for any service under this section may not be more than 6 percent of the estimated cost, as determined by the Secretary, of the project to which it applies.

The statutory limitation of 6% applies to all A-E contracts, whether they are fixed-price or cost-reimbursement. See FAR 15.404-4(c) stating:

> (4)(i) The contracting officer shall not negotiate a price or fee that exceeds the following statutory limitations, imposed by 10 U.S.C. 2306(d) and 41 U.S.C. 254(b):

\* \* \*

(B) For architect-engineer services for public works or utilities, the contract price or the estimated cost and fee for production and delivery of designs, plans, drawings, and specifications shall not exceed 6 percent of the estimated cost of construction of the public work or utility, excluding fees.

This 6% limitation is computed as a percentage of the estimated cost of construction of the project being designed. In order to comply with this requirement, the agency must have a sufficient definition of the work to be designed to permit it to arrive at a reasonable estimate of this cost of the construction. See FAR 36.605(a) requiring the agency to prepare an independent cost estimate for contracts over $25,000 based on a detailed analysis of the work, "as though the Government were submitting a proposal," and provide it to the contracting officer prior to negotiations. See also *Fluor Enters., Inc. v. United States*, 64 Fed. Cl. 461 (2005), holding that, since under the civilian agency fee limitation statute an agency had no authority to issue a contract calling for A-E services without a project estimate, such a contract was unenforceable. The court rejected the government's argument that the 6% limitation should be imposed on the actual costs of construction and remanded to the agency to determine and pay, under a quantum meruit theory, the reasonable value of the A-E services based on its best judgment of what the estimated cost of the construction would have been when the A-E contract was issued (even though the court accepted the fact that the work had not been defined at that time because part of the work of the A-E was to define the construction that was needed).

In *Fluor* the court held that these statutory limitations apply to any portion of a contract that calls for A-E work. The court reasoned at 479:

§ 254(b) indicates that a fee not in excess of 6% of the estimated cost is "authorized in *contracts for architectural or engineering services* related to any public works." § 254(b) (emphasis added). At least facially, there is nothing ambiguous about this language that might suggest that its applicability should only extend to contracts *primarily* or *substantially* for A&E services or, alternatively, that A&E services to be rendered as part of a broad professional services contract like Fluor's might somehow be exempt from the statute's purview.

The court supported its interpretation as follows at 481:

That interpretation of the fee limitation — that it only applies to a limited range of services despite the variety of services called for in the contract — is consistent with opinions from administrative bodies that have interpreted the statute. The Comptroller General has expressed the opinion that "the codifications of the 1939 statutes *apply to all types of contracts* and that costs which do not relate to the preparation of designs, plans, drawings, and specifications may be regarded as not subject to the 6-percent limitation imposed by those statutes." 46 Comp. Gen. 556, 560 (Dec. 12, 1966) (emphasis added). "In light of the legislative history of the Brooks Act, we have held that the Act applies to the procurement of services which uniquely or to a substantial or dominant extent logically requires performance by a professionally licensed and qualified A-E firm." *In re Assoc. of Soil and Foundation Engs.*, 61 Comp. Gen. 377, 378 (May 6, 1982). Logically, if services that do not properly fall within the Brooks Act's circumspection of "architectural or engineering services" or, even more apparent, are not architectural or engineering services at all, then the fees for those services are not rightly subject to the § 254(b) fee limitation. However, the presence of such services — even if they represent a substantial or predominant portion of the contract — does not exempt from the fee limitation the fees for those services that are properly within the scope of the Brooks Act provisions.

This rule is stated in DFARS 236.606-70 as follows:

(c) The six percent limit applies only to that portion of the contract (or modification) price attributable to the preparation of designs, plans, drawings, and specifications. If a contract or modification also includes other services, the part of the price attributable to the other services is not subject to the six percent limit.

The 6% limitation also applies to contract modifications. DFARS 236.6-6-70 gives the following guidance:

(b) The six percent limit also applies to contract modifications, including modifications involving —

(1) *Work not initially included in the contract.* Apply the six percent limit to the revised total estimated construction cost.

(2) *Redesign.* Apply the six percent limit as follows —

(i) Add the estimated construction cost of the redesign features to the original estimated construction cost;

(ii) Add the contract cost for the original design to the contract cost for redesign; and

(iii) Divide the total contract design cost by the total estimated construction cost. The resulting percentage may not exceed the six percent statutory limitation.

In *Fluor* the court also held that 41 U.S.C. § 254(b) (now § 3905(b)(3)) calls for a dual limitation when an agency procures A-E services using a cost-reimbursement contract. In that case, the 6% limitation applies to the total of the estimated cost and the fixed fee of the contract and the 10% limitation applies to the fixed fee as a percentage of the estimated costs. The court illustrated this rule as follows at 473-74:

To illustrate these concepts, a hypothetical construction project is helpful. If the government were to procure A&E services for a building whose estimated total cost was $2 million . . . , then the 6% fee limitation applicable to A&E services under § 254(b) would limit the A&E contractor's allowable costs and fixed fee to no more than $120,000 (6% of $2 million is $120,000). However, if the estimated costs of the A&E contractor's services — those actual costs for which the contractor would be reimbursed under the cost-plus-fixed-fee scenario — were only $80,000, then the fixed fee that the contractor would receive could be no more than $8,000 because the 10% fee limitation applicable to all cost-plus-fixed-fee contracts under § 254(b) would apply (10% of $80,000 is $8,000).

Under that scenario, the A&E contractor's total fee, including both his reimbursable costs and his fixed-fee, would be no more than $88,000. This total fee would not run afoul of the 6% fee limitation because it is less than $120,000. On the other hand, if the same A&E contractor's estimated costs were not $80,000, but instead were $115,000, the maximum fixed-fee that the A&E contractor could receive would be $5,000. Even though 10% of $115,000 (the reimbursable costs) is $11,500, the 6% fee limitation would restrict the A&E contractor to no more than $120,000 for both reimbursable costs and fixed-fee.

This makes the use of a cost-reimbursement contract for A-E services a risky venture because once the A-E contractor reaches the estimated cost, it is no longer require to perform — with the result that the agency would have no way to require the A-E to complete the design and would be unable to provide additional funding above the 6% limitation. It is questionable whether 10 U.S.C. § 2306(d) leads to the same result because that statute appears to apply the 10% fee limitation to contracts other than A-E contracts. However, these statutes are so badly written that it is difficult to predict how they will be interpreted.

## J. Contract Clauses

There are three mandatory clauses for A-E contracts, FAR 36.609. The first, the Responsibility of the Architect-Engineer Contractor clause at FAR 52.236-23 requires the A-E contractor to "correct or revise any errors or deficiencies in its designs, drawings, specifications and other services" without additional compensation. This clause also states that this remedy is "in addition to any other rights and remedies provided by law." In *Parsons Main, Inc.*, ASBCA 51355, 02-2 BCA ¶ 31,886 the board enumerated the elements that the government must prove to require the contractor to redesign under this clause at 157,537:

> To prevail in a defective design claim under the FAR 52.236-23 Responsibility of the Architect-Engineer Contractor clause, the Government has the burden of establishing three elements of proof: (1) Did the construction contractor substantially comply with the A-E's design in the manner intended by the A-E? (2) Did the A-E exercise its skill, ability and judgment negligently, instead of with reasonable care, with respect to the design? (3) Was the A-E's defective design the proximate cause of damage to the Government? *See Brunson Associates, Inc.*, ASBCA No. 41201, 94-2 BCA ¶ 26,936 at 134,152; *Ralph M. Parsons Co.*, ASBCA No.

24347, 85-1 BCA ¶ 17,787 at 88,901-02, *recon. denied.* 85-2 BCA ¶ 18,112; *Benjamin S. Notkin & Associates,* ASBCA No. 29336, 86-1 BCA ¶ 18,535 at 93,123 (Gov't has burden of proof of negligent A-E design claim).

In *Gee & Jenson Eng'rs, Architects & Planners v. United States,* 2008 U.S. Claims LEXIS 504 (Fed. Cl. 2008), the A-E was held liable for faulty design when it did not provide for roof flashing that was clearly required by the specifications. In *Brunson Assocs., Inc.,* ASBCA 41201, 94-2 BCA ¶ 26,936, the A-E was held to have negligently designed a building that did not survive snow loads that could have been anticipated. In that case, the board also rejected the defense that the government had been negligent in accepting the design. Compare *C. H. Guernsey & Co. v. United States,* 65 Fed. Cl. 582 (2005) (no negligence when A-E demonstrated that its design could be complied with).

The Work Oversight in Architect-Engineer Contracts clause at FAR 52.236-24 provides that the work is subject to the "general oversight, supervision, direction, control and approval" of the contracting officer.

The Requirements for Registration of Designers clause at FAR 52.236-25 requires that the preparation, review and approval of the design be performed by architects and engineers registered to practice in a state, the District of Columbia or an "outlying area of the United States."

There is also a standard clause provided when the agency decides to impose funding limitations on the project costs. This clause, Design Within Funding Limitations at FAR 52.236-22, requires the A-E firm to redesign the project without an increase in price if the construction cost exceeds the funding limitation in the contract. The requirement is not applicable to increases in price outside of the control of the A-E firm. FAR 36.609-1(c) requires the use of this clause except when —

(1) the head of the contracting activity or a designee determines in writing that cost limitations are secondary to performance considerations and additional project funding can be expected, if necessary,

(2) the design is for a standard structure and is not intended for a specific location, or

(3) there is little or no design effort involved.

This clause does not require the A-E to prepare a design that results in an ultimate project cost within the budget, only to permit contract award within the budget, *Parsons Main, Inc.,* ASBCA 51355, 02-2 BCA ¶ 32,051. The clause was strictly enforced in *Anlauf Ingenieur-Consulting,* ASBCA 37361, 90-1 BCA ¶ 22,352.

A-E contracts also generally include the Changes clause provided in FAR 52.243-1, Alternate III. See *Taylor & Partners, Inc.,* VABCA 4898, 97-1 BCA

¶ 28,970, holding that alterations called for in the 75% design review were not changes but rather were normal alterations in the course of project design. Similarly, no changes were found because of additional work required in design reviews in *DMJM H&N, Inc.*, ASBCA 56557, 09-2 BCA ¶ 34,173, and *Planned Envtl. Design Corp.*, ASBCA 47599, 96-1 BCA ¶ 28,001. See also *GBQC Architects v. General Servs. Admin.*, GSBCA 15578, 02-1 BCA ¶ 31,846, finding no changes when an A-E allegedly accelerated its performance of construction phase services but could not prove that the government ordered such acceleration. Compare *Wyatt/Rhodes Architects, Inc.*, ASBCA 38938, 90-1 BCA ¶ 22,476, finding a contract change when the A-E was required to attend an extra meeting, and *Lenz GmbH Architect-Engineer*, ASBCA 36819, 90-3 BCA ¶ 23,220, finding contract changes when the government failed to cooperate with the A-E during the design process. For a case discussing the interrelationship of the Changes clause and the Design Within Funding Limitations clause, see *Fanning, Phillips & Molnar*, VABCA 3856, 96-1 BCA ¶ 28,214.

# IV. TWO-PHASE DESIGN-BUILD SELECTION PROCEDURES

Traditionally, the federal government has obtained new buildings and other civil works by contracting with an architect-engineering firm (A-E) for design of the project, soliciting competitive bids or proposals for the construction of the project, and awarding a contract to the successful offeror. This is known as the design-bid-build delivery system. Although this system has worked satisfactorily in many instances, it is relatively slow and it has the disadvantage of separating design responsibility from construction responsibility. Thus, the system has been criticized for not bringing sufficient consideration of constructibility into the design process and for subjecting the government to claims of the construction contractor for design defects. This has imposed considerable liability on the government because, in using detailed construction drawings, the government is liable to the contractor on a standard that approaches strict liability yet its claims against the A-E for defective design are generally judged by a standard of negligence.

Private owners, finding themselves in this same situation, have increasingly turned to a delivery system known as design-build. Under this system, the owner contracts initially with a single entity for both the design and the construction of the project. This entity is selected by a careful interview process, and the owner then proceeds to work with the design-build contractor for the remainder of the project. Usually, after the full scope of the project is determined (but before the detailed design is developed), the design-build contractor will agree to deliver the entire project within a guaranteed maximum price. The design-build contractor is not a construction contractor. It is a team composed of A-Es and constructors that work together from the beginning of design to the completion of construction to ensure that the owner receives the most cost-effective project that the team is capable of producing.

Federal agencies such as the Postal Service, the General Services Administration, and the Army Corps of Engineers began using the design-build system in the 1980s but they concluded that the contractor should be selected using a competitive negotiation process. See the General Services Administration publication "Design-Build Request for Proposals Guide" (Nov. 1991) and the Corps of Engineers publication "Design-Build Instructions for Military Construction" (Sept. 26, 1994) *http:// www.wbdg.org/ccb/ARMYCOE/DBI/cemp_ea.pdf*. This procedure placed a heavy burden on offerors because these agencies generally required extensive design work as a part of an initial competitive proposal with the result that the losing offerors received little or no compensation for this design effort.

Section 4105 of the Clinger-Cohen Act of 1996 amended 10 U.S.C. § 2305a and 41 U.S.C. § 253m (now § 3309) to include new "design-build selection procedures." This section of the Act establishes a series of new acquisition rules — known as two-phase selection procedures — that must be followed when an agency decides to use the design-build delivery system and concludes that extensive design proposals will be required. The regulatory implementation added a new FAR Subpart 36.3.

## A.  Authorization and Criteria for Use

The following statement on when the new procedure should be used is set forth in 10 U.S.C. § 2305a:

> *Authorization* — Unless the traditional acquisition approach of design-bid build established under the Brooks Architect-Engineers Act (41 U.S.C. § 541 et seq.) is used or another acquisition procedure authorized by law is used, the head of an agency shall use the two-phase selection procedures for entering into a contract for the design and construction of a public building, facility, or work when a determination is made that the procedures are appropriate for use.

Substantially the same language is used in 41 U.S.C. § 3309(a). FAR 36.104 uses virtually the same language but also includes the following sentence:

> Other acquisition procedures authorized by law include the procedures established in this part and other parts of this chapter and, for DoD, the design-build process described in 10 U.S.C. 2862.

The "chapter" referred to is the entire Federal Acquisition Regulation, including Part 15 covering competitive negotiation procedures. Thus, there are essentially two delivery systems for construction projects — design-bid-build and design-build. If design-bid-build is chosen, the design effort must be done using the Brooks Act procedures discussed above. Thereafter, the construction can be procured using sealed bidding, negotiation, or construction management. If design-build is chosen, either a one-step or two-step procedure may be used. The one-step procedure would follow normal competitive negotiation procedures. The two-step procedure would follow this new statutory two-phase procedure.

Contracting officers must consider the following criteria set forth in 10 U.S.C. § 2305a to determine whether the two-phase procedure is appropriate:

> (b) *Criteria for use.* — A contracting officer shall make a determination whether two-phase selection procedures are appropriate for use for entering into a contract for the design and construction of a public building, facility, or work when the contracting officer anticipates that three or more offers will be received for such contract, design work must be performed before an offeror can develop a price or cost proposal for such contract, the offeror will incur a substantial amount of expense in preparing the offer, and the contracting officer has considered information such as the following:
>
>> (1) The extent to which the project requirements have been adequately defined.
>>
>> (2) The time constraints for delivery of the project.
>>
>> (3) The capability and experience of potential contractors.
>>
>> (4) The suitability of the project for use of the two-phase selection procedures.
>>
>> (5) The capability of the agency to manage the two-phase selection process.
>>
>> (6) Other criteria established by the agency.

Substantially the same guidance is in 41 U.S.C. § 3309(b). These criteria are repeated in FAR 6.301(b)(3). The key criteria are the requirement for design work and the resulting incurrence of cost by offerors. If extensive design work will be required with commensurate high proposal costs, the two-phase design-build procedure should be used. If little design work or proposal costs will be required, the normal competitive negotiation procedure will likely be the most efficient procedure.

Neither the FAR nor the statutes contain any guidance on when the design-build delivery system should be used in preference to the design-bid-build delivery system. Thus, this decision is left entirely to the discretion of each contracting agency. However, if the agency is considering the use of a design-build procedure, FAR 36.301(b) requires the use of the two-phase procedure if:

> (1) Three or more offers are anticipated.
>
> (2) Design work must be performed by offerors before developing price or cost proposals, and offerors will incur a substantial amount of expense in preparing offers.
>
> (3) The following criteria have been considered:

(i) The extent to which the project requirements have been adequately defined.

(ii) The time constraints for delivery of the project.

(iii) The capability and experience of potential contractors.

(iv) The suitability of the project for use of the two-phase selection method.

(v) The capability of the agency to manage the two-phase selection process.

(vi) Other criteria established by the head of the contracting activity.

# B. Procedures

The agency develops, either in-house or by contract, a scope of work statement for inclusion in the solicitation that defines the project and provides prospective offerors with sufficient information regarding the government's requirements (which may include criteria and preliminary design, budget parameters, and schedule or delivery requirements) to enable the offerors to submit proposals that meet the government's needs. If the agency contracts for development of this work statement, it must contract for A-E services in accordance with the Brooks Architect-Engineers Act, 40 U.S.C. § 1102 et seq. In that case, the A-E that drafts the work statement will be disqualified from the competition because of an organizational conflict of interest, *Energy Sys. Group*, Comp. Gen. Dec. B-402324, 2010 CPD ¶ 73 (protester drafted report that was used to create work statement); *B.L. Harbert-Brasfield & Gorrie, JV*, Comp. Gen. Dec. B-402229, 2010 CPD ¶ 69 (protester assisted in preparation of agency design concept and in evaluating technical proposals).

A two-phase procurement can utilize a single solicitation covering both phases or sequential solicitations, FAR 36.303. In either case, FAR 36.303-1 provides the following guidance on the solicitation instructions covering phase one:

(a) Phase One of the solicitation(s) shall include —

(1) The scope of work;

(2) The phase-one evaluation factors, including —

(i) Technical approach (but not detailed design or technical information);

(ii) Technical qualifications, such as —

(A) Specialized experience and technical competence;

(B) Capability to perform;

(C) Past performance of the offeror's team (including the architect-engineer and construction members); and

(iii) Other appropriate factors (excluding cost or price related factors, which are not permitted in Phase One);

(3) Phase-two evaluation factors (see 36.303-2); and

(4) A statement of the maximum number of offerors that will be selected to submit phase-two proposals. The maximum number specified shall not exceed five unless the contracting officer determines, for that particular solicitation, that a number greater than five is in the Government's interest and is consistent with the purposes and objectives of two-phase design-build contracting).

The intent of this guidance is to ensure that the phase one competition will not be unduly expensive. Thus, detailed design work and cost or price proposals are *prohibited.* The result is that the phase one competition is primarily based on the evaluation of the capabilities of the competing teams. This is appropriate because success of the entire technique depends on selecting a highly competent team. Two things must be evaluated here — the competence of the individual members of the team (as well as their key employees) and the ability of the team members to work together. The key data that should be used to perform this evaluation are information on the experience and past performance records of both the members of the team and the team itself. An agency may evaluate the amount of experience each offeror has in performing design-build contracts, *J.C.N. Constr. Co.*, Comp. Gen. Dec. B-293063, 2004 CPD ¶ 12, in designing projects similar to the proposed project, *Neeser Constr., Inc./Allied Builders Sys., A Joint Venture*, Comp. Gen. Dec. B-285903, 2000 CPD ¶ 207; or in constructing similar projects, *CTI-NAN JV, LLC*, Comp. Gen. Dec. B-400979, 2009 CPD ¶ 118.

The second phase of this procedure is conducted with the most highly qualified offerors in phase one, FAR 36.303-1(b). In order to carry out the intent of the statute, the number of offerors should be limited to three in most cases (the guidance is no more than five). In this phase, standard competitive negotiation procedures are used. See FAR 36.303-2, which states:

(a) Phase Two of the solicitation(s) shall be prepared in accordance with Part 15, and include phase-two evaluation factors, developed in accordance with 15.304. Examples of potential phase-two technical evaluation factors include design concepts, management approach, key personnel, and proposed technical solutions.

(b) Phase Two of the solicitation(s) shall require submission of technical and price proposals, which shall be evaluated separately, in accordance with part 15.

The key evaluation factors in this phase will be the proposed design, the capability of the offerors, and the price. In accordance with FAR Part 15, the solicitation is required to identify all significant subfactors and the relative importance of the factors. The agency has considerable discretion in deciding to award to an offeror with a higher price in order to obtain desirable design features, *Nippo Corp.*, Comp. Gen. Dec. B-402363.2, 2010 CPD ¶ 112; *JVSCC*, Comp. Gen. Dec. B-311303.2, 2009 CPD ¶ 138. While the proposed designs will almost always be a significant evaluation factor, the agency need not evaluate whether the design proposal demonstrates compliance with every element of the specification, *Medlin Constr. Group*, Comp. Gen. Dec. B-286166, 2000 CPD ¶ 199.

While the price will normally be an important factor, the solicitation should make it clear that the agency will not give a high value to a price that is too low to permit the contractor to give the agency the level of quality that it needs. Thus, the RFP should state that the agency is looking for a reasonable price and will perform a price realism analysis to ensure that no award will be made at a price that is unrealistically low. Price realism must be explicitly stated as an evaluation factor in order to make such assessment. See *CSE Constr.*, Comp. Gen. Dec. B-291268.2, 2002 CPD ¶ 207 (improper to assess price realism when the evaluation factor in the RFP was price reasonableness); *SAMS El Segundo, LLC*, Comp. Gen. Dec. B-291620.3, 2003 CPD ¶ 48 (price realism also used to assess understanding of the work). An agency may want to include its estimate of the price range of the project in the RFP in order to avoid this problem.

In the past, offerors have been required to include detailed information on all aspects of the proposed project, including conceptual designs, and agencies have then evaluated and scored the numerous elements of each proposal. This has resulted in a lengthy evaluation process. The process can be conducted more efficiently if the design information called for in the phase-two RFP is limited to the amount of design effort necessary to arrive at a guaranteed maximum price. There is no need to evaluate the details of the proposed design if the performance specification is adequately written and the capability of the offerors is an important evaluation factor.

Following evaluation of the proposals, the agency can select a contractor without discussions or conduct discussions to enable offerors to enhance their proposals. The agency has considerable discretion in proceeding directly to award when there is a clear superior proposal, *Sletten Cos./Sletten Constr. Co.*, Comp. Gen. Dec. B-402422, 2010 CPD ¶ 97.

## C. Multiple Awards

Some agencies have procured design-build work on smaller projects by awarding indefinite delivery/indefinite quantity contracts to multiple contractors. This enables the agency to enter into contracts with two or more companies and then obtain the design-build work by individual task orders which are issued after a competition between those companies. For protests involving this technique, see *Dorado Servs.*,

*Inc.*, Comp. Gen. Dec. B-402244. 2010 CPD ¶ 71; *ICON Consulting Group, Inc.*, Comp. Gen. Dec. B-310431.2, 2008 CPD ¶ 38; and *Doyon-American Mech., JV; NAJV, LLC*, Comp. Gen. Dec. B-310003, 2008 CPD ¶ 50.

## D. Type of Contract

The most difficult problem in using the two-phase design-build procedure is determining the type of contract that will be used. Most government agencies have been unwilling to use the commercial technique of awarding the contract and establishing a guaranteed maximum price after the contractor has performed sufficient design work to obtain reasonable estimates of the actual construction costs that will be incurred. As a result, in order to award a fixed-price type contract, they have adopted techniques that require a significant amount of design effort prior to the award of the contract resulting from the phase-two competition. When this is done as part of the phase-two competition, it places a significant financial burden on the competitors unless the agency compensates them for all or a part of this effort. Some agencies have reduced this burden by employing another A-E to undertake preliminary design effort and included these preliminary drawings and specifications in the design-build RFP. When this is done, that A-E will not be permitted to compete for the design-build contract because it will have an organizational conflict of interest, *SSR Eng'rs, Inc.*, Comp. Gen. Dec. B-282244, 99-2 CPD ¶ 27.

Providing detailed requirements, of course, partially negates one of the advantages of the design-build technique — the transferring of full liability for defective design to the contractor. See *Donohue Elec., Inc.*, VABCA 6618, 03-1 BCA ¶ 32,129 (government liable for contract change when it required equipment not called for in 50% design furnished to design-build offerors "for information"). Compare *United Excel Corp.*, VABCA 6937, 04-1 BCA ¶ 32,485 (contractor denied recovery for ambiguous preliminary specification because it knew of the ambiguity at the time it submitted its phase-two price); *Fire Sec. Sys., Inc.*, VABCA 5559-63, 02-2 BCA ¶ 31,977 (government not liable for accuracy of drawings furnished "for information only" when specification required contractor to make its own measurements of the spaces being renovated). The inclusion of design details in the design-build RFP also imposes detailed requirements on the contractor which can be enforced by the government. See *WPC, Inc.*, ASBCA 53964, 04-1 BCA ¶ 32,476 (enforcing a specification requirement covering a method of performance of the work), and *FSEC, Inc.*, ASBCA 49509, 99-2 BCA ¶ 30,512 (enforcing "prescriptive" specification requirement). Furthermore, if the work performed is necessary to meet the performance requirements of the design-build specification, the contractor is not entitled to additional compensation when the government insists on such work, *Wade Perrow Constr., Inc.*, ASBCA 53021, 03-1 BCA ¶ 32,156.

Another alternative is to use a cost-reimbursement contract for the design-build effort. FAR Subpart 36.3 contains no guidance on this possibility but it is clearly appropriate under FAR Part 16. When this type of contract is chosen, the agency is required to evaluate cost realism and to use probable cost of performance (not estimated cost) as an evaluation factor, FAR 15.404-1(d)(2). See *Pueblo Envtl. Solution, LLC*, Comp. Gen. Dec. B-291487, 2003 CPD ¶ 14, holding that the contracting officer properly adjusted the protester's cost estimate upward to reflect too few manhours to perform the work.

## E.  Source Selection and Contract Award

Selection of the contractor on the basis of the proposal with the best value to the government and award of the contract will be done following the procedures for standard competitive negotiations. See Chapter 6 for a full discussion of these procedures.

In a number of instances, the agency has incorporated the winning offeror's design proposal in the contract by reference. This, in effect, freezes the design to the extent that such a proposal includes detailed materials or performance techniques. This reduces the flexibility of the contractor to provide the best value project to the government and makes the elements of the design proposal mandatory performance requirements to the extent that they constitute firm promises. See *Sherman R. Smoot Corp.*, ASBCA 52150, 03-1 BCA ¶ 32,073, rejecting the contractor's argument that it was entitled to provide an "equal" product when it included a specific type of lighting fixture in its design proposal. The board reasoned that since the contractor had not included salient characteristics of the fixture in its design proposal, all significant elements of the fixture had to be met by any substituted fixture. See also *Elam Woods Constr. Co.*, ASBCA 52448, 01-1 BCA ¶ 31,305, holding the contractor bound to perform the work included in its technical proposal even though its price did not appear to include that work. The board reasoned that the work described in the proposal was a contemporaneous interpretation of the RFP requirements. In that procurement, the contracting officer had attempted to deal with the potential problem of a conflict between the performance specifications and the contractor's proposed design by including the following provision in the RFP:

> The criteria specified in this RFP are binding contract criteria and in cases of any conflict, subsequent to award, between RFP criteria and Contractor's proposal, design, and submittals, the RFP criteria shall govern unless there is a written agreement between the Contracting Officer and the Contractor waiving the specific requirement or accepting a specific condition pertaining to the offer.

This provision was not relied on by the board in deciding the dispute. Compare *Medlin Constr. Group*, Comp. Gen. Dec. B-286166, 2000 CPD ¶ 199, where the RFP made it clear that the contract specifications controlled by stating:

Final design submissions found to be not in compliance with the requirements of the RFP will be returned to the Contractor for correction and resubmission. The Contractor shall make such modifications as may be necessary to bring the design into compliance at no change in contract price and schedule. . . .

See also *PGDC/Teng Joint Venture*, ASBCA 56573, 10-1 BCA ¶ 34,423, holding, under the contract provisions, that the RFP specification overroad a conflicting provision in the contractor's proposal even though the proposal was part of the contract. Compare *ADT Constr. Group, Inc.*, ASBCA 55307, 09-2 BCA ¶ 34,200, holding that the contractor's proposal clarified the RFP's ambiguous language on whether the project would be performed on a fast-track basis.

# V.  BROAD AGENCY ANNOUNCEMENT PROCEDURE

Research contracts or grants can be awarded through a "broad agency announcement" (BAA) procedure that meets the requirement for full and open competition. See 10 U.S.C. § 2302(2)(B) and 41 U.S.C. § 152(2) which recognize that this procedure is a "competitive procedure," described as follows:

the competitive selection for award of basic research proposals resulting from a general solicitation and the peer review or scientific review (as appropriate) of such proposals.

See the following definition in FAR 2.101:

Broad agency announcement means a general announcement of an agency's research interest including criteria for selecting proposals and soliciting the participation of all offerors capable of satisfying the Government's needs (see 6.102(d)(2)).

This competitive procedure differs significantly from sealed bid or competitive proposal procedures. Here research organizations propose to undertake different research tasks in response to periodic announcements of broad areas of research interest by the various contracting agencies. The agencies then sequentially review these proposals and award contracts until funds run out in a particular area.

The nomenclature for BAAs varies from agency to agency. One common term is the Program Research and Development Announcement (PRDA) used by the Department of Energy and the Department of the Air Force. NASA uses the terms "Announcement of Opportunity," " NASA Research Announcements" and "NASA Acquisition of Investigations."

Agencies have considerable discretion in fashioning the specific procedure to the used in this form of procurement. However, basic rules are set forth in FAR 35.016. Some agencies have issued guides on proposal preparation. See NFS 1852.235-72 and the NASA *NRA Proposers Guidebook* (*http://www.hq.nasa.gov/*

*office/procurement/nraguidebook*); and the Department of the Air Force *BAA and PRDA: A Guide for Industry* and *BAA and PRDA Proposal Preparation Instructions* (*http://www.rl.af.mil/div/IFK/prda/prda-main.html*).

## A.  Nature of Work

Although the statutes permit the use of this procedure for "basic research," the FAR implementation of the statute permits the use of this procedure for a broader classification of work by including "applied research" and "development not related to the development of a specific system or hardware procurement" within the description of this "competitive procedure," FAR 6.102(d)(2). The legislative history of this provision, H. Rep. 861, 98th Cong., 2d Sess. 7517, *reprinted in* 1984 U.S.C.C.A.N. 1445, 2111, indicates that the drafters of the statute considered basic research as research "directed toward increasing knowledge of a subject apart from any clear or necessary practical application of that knowledge." It is questionable whether "applied research" and "development," as defined in FAR 31.205-18 and FAR 35.001, fall within the scope described in the legislative history. Nevertheless, in response to a request from the FAR Secretariat, GAO indicated that it had no objection to the inclusion of "applied research" in the proposed FAR implementation, Comp. Gen. Dec. B-227314, Aug. 6, 1987. However, there was no mention of "development" by GAO.

FAR 35.016(a) contains the following guidance on the type of work than can be procured using the BAA procedure:

> This paragraph prescribes procedures for the use of the broad agency announcement (BAA) with Peer or Scientific Review (see 6.102(d)(2)) for the acquisition of basic and applied research and that part of development not related to the development of a specific system or hardware procurement. BAA's may be used by agencies to fulfill their requirements for scientific study and experimentation directed toward advancing the state-of-the-art or increasing knowledge or understanding rather than focusing on a specific system or hardware solution. The BAA technique shall only be used when meaningful proposals with varying technical/scientific approaches can be reasonably anticipated.

The Department of Energy has more specific guidance on when PRDAs should be used. See DEAR 917.7301-1 stating:

> (b) The PRDA should not replace existing acquisition procedures where a requirement can be sufficiently defined for solicitation under standard advertised or negotiated acquisition procedures. Similarly, it should not inhibit or curtail the submission of unsolicited proposals. However, a proposal which is submitted as though it were unsolicited but is in fact germane to an existing PRDA shall be treated as though submitted in response to the announcement or returned without action to the proposer, at the proposer's option. Further, the PRDA is not to be used in a competitive situation where it is appropriate to negotiate a study contract to obtain analysis and recommendations to be incorporated in the subsequent request for proposals.

The NASA guidance in NFS 1835.016-71 states:

An NRA [NASA Research Announcement] is used to announce research interests in support of NASA's programs, and, after peer or scientific review using factors in the NRA, select proposals for funding. Unlike an RFP containing a statement of work or specification to which offerors are to respond, an NRA provides for the submission of competitive project ideas, conceived by the offerors, in one or more program areas of interest. An NRA shall not be used when the requirement is sufficiently defined to specify an end product or service.

Agencies have used these procedures for a wide variety of efforts, including the procurement of new products. See, for example, *Land O'Frost*, ASBCA 52012, 03-2 BCA ¶ 32,395 (production of chicken breast fillets as part of the Meals Ready to Eat program); *Gamut Elec., LLC*, Comp. Gen. Dec. B-292347, 2003 CPD ¶ 150 (state-of-the-art counterdrug equipment); *Energy Conversion Devices, Inc.*, Comp. Gen. Dec. B-260514, 95-2 CPD ¶ 121 (improvements in manufacturing technology); *TRW, Inc.*, Comp. Gen. Dec. B-258347, 95-1 CPD ¶ 15 (development and flight test of a gel propellant divert and attitude control system); *Golden Mfg. Co.*, Comp. Gen. Dec. B-255347, 94-1 CPD ¶ 183, *recons. denied*, 94-2 CPD ¶ 28 (manufacturer field coats using commercial processes).

## B. Announcements

In this form of procurement, an agency publishes its areas of interest and private organizations submit proposals for specific projects within a specified area. Awards are made to proposals that are judged to be promising until the funds have been utilized. Thus, the competition is for funding within an area of interest rather than to perform a task that has been specified by the agency. However, the area of interest may be very narrowly defined, making the procedure much like a normal competitive procurement. See *TRW, Inc.*, Comp. Gen. Dec. B-258347, 95-1 CPD ¶ 15, sustaining a best value type award decision in a narrowly defined area.

The FAR treats broad agency announcements (BAAs) as another type of solicitation. Thus, FAR 35.016(c) states:

The availability of the BAA must be publicized through the Governmentwide point of entry (GPE) and, if authorized pursuant to subpart 5.5, may also be published in noted scientific, technical, or engineering periodicals. The notice shall be published no less frequently than annually.

Following this guidance, many agencies publish a list of areas of interest semi-annually or annually. In such cases, many awards for different subjects of research within the general area may be made under a single BAA — doing away with the need for the issuance of a large number of individual RFPs. In contrast, some agencies also issue narrowly focused BAAs calling for proposals to perform a specific type of project. These BAAs are almost indistinguishable from RFPs that are issued in the competitive negotiation process. A challenge to the use of a BAA in lieu of an RFP must be submitted to GAO before the closing time for receipt of proposals, *Gamut Elec., LLC*, Comp. Gen. Dec. B-292347, 2003 CPD ¶ 150.

FAR 35.016(f) provides that BAAs need not be synopsized pursuant to FAR Subpart 5.2. In effect, this makes the BAA a combined synopsis/solicitation with no mandatory waiting period between the two.

There is no mandatory late proposal rule associated with BAAs. See NFS 1852.235-72 covering proposals submitted in response to NASA Research Announcements:

> (g) *Late Proposals.* Proposals or proposal modifications received after the latest date specified for receipt may be considered if a significant reduction in cost to the Government is probable or if there are significant technical advantages, as compared with proposals previously received.

### 1. Contracts or Other Instruments

Not all BAAs result in the award of contracts. Agencies issuing BAAs usually retain the option of funding the research under a contract or using a grant, cooperative agreement, or other form of assistance agreement. The requirements of the procurement statutes and the FAR apply only if a contract is used. As discussed in Chapter 1, when the agency decides to use another funding instrument, different statutory or regulatory requirements may be prescribed. See *Energy Conversion Devices, Inc.*, Comp. Gen. Dec. B-260514, 95-2 CPD ¶ 121, concluding that the principal purpose of the contract was not the acquisition of supplies or services and, therefore, use of an "other transaction" in lieu of a procurement contract was justified.

In the case of the Air Force, NASA, and DOE, the general policy is to use contracts for profit-making organizations and grants for nonprofit organizations and universities. However, contracts may be used for nonprofit organizations and universities to obtain tighter control over research projects involving substantial acquisition of equipment or considerable subcontracting. Classified research is also usually done under a contract.

### 2. Requirement for Competition

The legislative history, H. Rep. 861, 98th Cong., 2d Sess. 7517, *reprinted in* 1984 U.S.C.C.A.N. 1445, 2111, makes it clear that the authority of 10 U.S.C. § 2302(2)(B) and 41 U.S.C. § 152(2) may not be used if the general solicitation precludes the participation of capable individuals or firms:

> By recognizing such procurement of basic research as competitive, the conferees intend to promote the participation of all individuals or companies capable of

supporting the government's needs in this important area. Any agency procurement which cannot meet this standard and, in fact, restricts participation, must be justified and approved under the requirements in this substitute for other than competitive procurement procedures.

Thus, if a BAA limits the submission of proposals to certain firms or individuals, procurement on the basis of other than full and open competition must be justified. See, for example, *Right Away Foods/Shelf Stable Foods*, Comp. Gen. Dec. B-259859.3, 95-2 CPD ¶ 34 (limitation of competition justified on the need to maintain the mobilization base). See DFARS 235.016 encouraging agencies to reserve "discrete or severable areas of research interest" in BAAs for "exclusive competition among historically black colleges and universities and minority institutions."

### 3.  Content

FAR 35.016 specifies the following requirements for BAAs:

(b) The BAA, together with any supporting documents, shall—

(1) Describe the agency's research interest, either for an individual program requirement or for broadly defined areas of interest covering the full range of the agency's requirements;

(2) Describe the criteria for selecting the proposals, their relative importance, and the method of evaluation;

(3) Specify the period of time during which proposals submitted in response to the BAA will be accepted; and

(4) Contain instructions for the preparation and submission of proposals.

Agencies are free to add other requirements as necessary. See, for example, *HMX, Inc.*, Comp. Gen. Dec. B-291102, 2003 CPD ¶ 52, where the agency added a requirement for the submission of "certifiable" cost or pricing data in all proposals over $550,000. GAO denied the protest that HMX's proposal had not been selected for negotiations because it refused to submit the data — ruling that this protest was not timely because since the problem was apparent when the BAA was posted, the protest was required prior to the submission of proposals. See also *Spaltudaq Corp.*, Comp. Gen. Dec. B-400650, 2009 CPD ¶ 1, where the agency required cost proposals that were "auditable" by the Defense Contract Audit Agency.

## C.  Discussions With Proposers

Agency discussions with proposers occur in several stages. Prior to submitting a proposal the researcher is encouraged to talk informally with agency scientists in order to ascertain the degree of interest in the proposed research. Some agencies will also consider a preliminary proposal or a brief outline of a proposal. These contacts must be initiated by the proposer. The appropriate scientist is usually identified in the BAA. After a proposal has been submitted, the agency may contact a representative of the proposing institution, usually the principal investigator, for any necessary clarification.

The contacts between the agency and proposer differ considerably from the type of contacts allowed in the standard procedures. There is no guidance on the type or extent of assistance that should be provided during this process. Such guidance is less necessary in this context, as proposers are generally proposing to do different tasks, and it is proper to make the selection based on the original proposals with no discussion with the proposers, *Energy & Envtl. Research Corp.*, Comp. Gen. Dec. B-261422, 95-2 CPD ¶ 81. However, when proposals are being compared, the basic rule of fair treatment of all offerors in FAR 1.102-2(c) applies even though it is not mentioned in FAR 35.016. In addition, when the agency uses the BAA procedure to obtain head-to-head competition against a specific requirement, GAO will impose the "meaningful discussion" rule that is used in competitively negotiated procurements, *Interstate Elecs. Corp.*, Comp. Gen. Dec. B-286466, 2001 CPD ¶ 29.

When a proposal has been selected based on its technical merit, the agency may have to negotiate the terms and conditions before award of a contract. In such cases, the agency has considerable discretion in deciding that it cannot reach agreement on the terms and conditions. See *Spaltudaq Corp.*, Comp. Gen. Dec. B-400650, 2009 CPD ¶ 1, stating:

> Although we find that [the agency] had no obligation to follow the specific requirements for discussions set forth in FAR Part 15, agencies may not conduct themselves in an arbitrary manner, and they must negotiate in good faith and in a manner consistent with the BAA. See *Health Servs. Mktg. & Dev. Corp.*, B-241830, Mar. 5, 1991, 91-1 CPD ¶ 247 at 7.

* * *

> [T]he BAA provided for post-selection negotiations with firms that were selected for award. The BAA permitted the agency to discontinue discussions if an offeror failed to provide necessary information in a timely manner, or if the parties failed to reach agreement on contract terms within a reasonable time. Here, the record shows that over a 4-month period, the parties engaged in good faith negotiations in an attempt to reach agreement over the parties' rights to intellectual property, but that no agreement could be reached. The record shows that Spaltudaq proposed a number of approaches that limited or restricted the government's rights, and the agency repeatedly objected to these approaches. The agency articulated its "final negotiation position" regarding intellectual property in its August 7, 2008 letter and unambiguously stated that "the Government is unwilling to consider" recent proposal changes that would limit or restrict the government's rights to data or inventions. Despite this admonition, Spaltudaq responded with a revised statement of work that included previously submitted proposal revisions to restrict the intellectual property

rights granted to the agency. In our view, the agency reasonably determined that the parties had failed to reach agreement within a reasonable time, and the agency could discontinue negotiations on this basis alone.

## D. Evaluation of Proposals

FAR 35.016(d) specifies the following requirements for evaluating BAA proposals:

> Proposals received as a result of the BAA shall be evaluated in accordance with evaluation criteria specified therein through a peer or scientific review process. Written evaluation reports on individual proposals will be necessary but proposals need not be evaluated against each other since they are not submitted in accordance with a common work statement.

This is generally consistent with the rule applicable to conventional negotiated procurement. The following discussion focuses on some of the unique aspects of this type of contracting, including the requirement for peer or scientific review.

### 1. Evaluation Factors

FAR 35.016(e) prescribes the following factors and states the primary basis for the evaluation of proposals:

> The primary basis for selecting proposals for acceptance shall be technical, importance to agency programs, and fund availability. Cost realism and reasonableness shall also be considered to the extent appropriate.

The use of unstated criteria is not permitted in evaluating proposals, but criteria that are reasonably related to stated criteria may be used, *Avogadro Energy Sys.*, Comp. Gen. Dec. B-244106, 91-2 CPD ¶ 229. There, GAO reviewed and approved the evaluation criteria in a BAA for basic research, finding that, to the extent that unstated criteria were present, they were reasonably related to stated criteria and so caused no prejudice to the selection process. See also *Interstate Elec. Corp.*, Comp. Gen. Dec. B-286466, 2001 CPD ¶ 29 (proper to evaluate whether proposal met a "minimum" requirement in PRDA); *ABB Lummus Crest, Inc.*, Comp. Gen. Dec. B-244440, 91-2 CPD ¶ 252 (allegation of evaluation based upon an unstated criterion — access to rights in proprietary data — not proved).

Although a formal responsibility determination is not made, responsibility-related factors are taken into account. Particularly important in contracting for basic research are the qualifications of the principal investigator and other key personnel, as the success of the endeavor is likely to depend more on these individuals than on the characteristics of the sponsoring institution.

## 2. Peer or Scientific Review

Peer or scientific review is a process of proposal review that utilizes a group of experts in the field represented by the proposal to evaluate the proposal merit. Peer or scientific review can be done by government or outside scientists and can take a number of forms. The evaluation can be done by assembling panels of scientists, by receiving evaluations by mail, or by hiring a contractor to evaluate all proposals.

The use of outside evaluators is probably the most controversial element of this process. When this is done, there are two major issues that must be addressed. First, steps must be taken to ensure that outside evaluators do not disclose proprietary information that they have received in the review process. DEAR 915.207-70 contains the most complete coverage of this issue. It permits marking of all proposals with a prescribed proprietary legend and requires outside evaluators to sign the following nondisclosure agreement prior to receipt of the proposal:

Nondisclosure Agreement

Whenever DOE furnishes a proposal for evaluation, I, the recipient, agree to use the information contained in the proposal only for DOE evaluation purposes and to treat the information obtained in confidence. This requirement for confidential treatment does not apply to information obtained from any source, including the proposer, without restriction. Any notice or restriction placed on the proposal by either DOE or the originator of the proposal shall be conspicuously affixed to any reproduction or abstract thereof and its provisions strictly complied with. Upon completion of the evaluation, it is agreed all copies of the proposal and abstracts, if any, shall be returned to the DOE office which initially furnished the proposal for evaluation. Unless authorized by the Contracting Officer, I agree that I shall not contact the originator of the proposal concerning any aspect of its elements.

Recipient: _____

Date: _____

The second issue is the potential conflict of interest of outside reviewers. Such reviewers should not be permitted to participate in the review of proposals submitted in response to an area covered by the BAA in which they have some other interest.

The most complete guidance on this issue is in the regulations of the Public Health Service at 42 C.F.R. § 52h.5 as follows:

(b) A reviewer with a real conflict of interest must recuse him/herself from the review of the application or proposal, except as otherwise provided in this section.

(1) A reviewer who is a salaried employee, whether full-time or part-time, of the applicant institution, offeror, or principal investigator, or is negotiat-

ing for employment, shall be considered to have a real conflict of interest with regard to an application/proposal from that organization or principal investigator, except that the Director may determine there is no real conflict of interest or an appearance of a conflict of interest where the components of a large or multicomponent organization are sufficiently independent to constitute, in effect, separate organizations, provided that the reviewer has no responsibilities at the institution that would significantly affect the other component.

(2) Where a reviewer's real conflict of interest is based upon the financial or other interest of a close relative or professional associate of the reviewer, that reviewer must recuse him/herself, unless the Director provides a waiver in accordance with paragraph (b)(4) of this section.

(3) For contract proposal reviews, an individual with a real conflict of interest in a particular proposal(s) is generally not permitted to participate in the review of any proposals responding to the same request for proposals. However, if there is no other qualified reviewer available having that individual's expertise and that expertise is essential to ensure a competent and fair review, a waiver may be granted by the Director to permit that individual to serve as a reviewer of those proposals with which the reviewer has no conflict, while recusing him/herself from the review of any particular proposal(s) in which there is a conflict of interest.

(4) The Director may waive any of the requirements in paragraph (b) of this section relating to a real conflict of interest if the Director determines that there are no other practical means for securing appropriate expert advice on a particular grant or cooperative agreement application, contract project, or contract proposal, and that the real conflict of interest is not so substantial as to be likely to affect the integrity of the advice to be provided by the reviewer.

(c) Any appearance of a conflict of interest will result in recusal of the reviewer, unless the Director provides a waiver, determining that it would be difficult or impractical to carry out the review otherwise, and the integrity of the review process would not be impaired by the reviewer's participation.

See *Herdon Sci. & Software, Inc.*, Comp. Gen. Dec. B-245505, 92-1 CPD ¶ 46 (allegation of conflict of interest unfounded where evaluators were excluded from review or discussion of any proposal which they submitted as a principal or collaborator or which was supported by an institutional affiliate).

# E. Award

After the technical and cost evaluations are completed, a designated agency official reviews the information and decides whether to accept the proposal for negotiation. The award decision is discretionary. See, for example *AEC-ABLE Eng'g Co.*, Comp. Gen. Dec. B-257798.2, 95-1 CPD ¶ 37, reviewing a number of allegations that the agency had improperly selected two other proposals but holding that the agency was justified in awarding to those companies. See also *INRAD, Inc.*, Comp. Gen. Dec. B-284021, 2000 U.S. Comp. Gen. LEXIS 39, finding that the agency's decision not to fund a proposal was consistent with the terms of the PRDA. Challenges to technical evaluations are almost always denied because GAO defers to the agency's technical assessment of the merits of a proposal. See *Tamper Proof Container Sys. Corp.*, Comp. Gen. Dec. B-402191, 2010 CPD ¶ 46, stating:

> In reviewing a protest of an agency's proposal evaluation, it is not our role to reevaluate proposals. Rather, we will consider only whether the evaluation was reasonable and consistent with the terms of the solicitation and applicable procurement statutes and regulations. *Gamut Elecs., LLC*, B-292347, B-292347.2, Aug. 7, 2003, 2003 CPD ¶ 150 at 4; *HMX, Inc.*, B-291102, Nov. 4, 2002, 2003 CPD ¶ 52 at 7. An offeror's mere disagreement with an agency's judgment is not sufficient to establish that the agency acted unreasonably. *HMX, Inc., supra.*

See also *Microcosm, Inc.*, Comp. Gen. Dec. B-277326, 97-2 CPD ¶ 133.

FAR 35.016(d) provides that in making awards, there is no need to evaluate proposals against each other. However, this may not be the case when proposals are required to be submitted on a common date. NASA provides the following guidance on selecting proposals submitted in response to its Research Announcements in NFS 1852.235-72:

> (j) Evaluation Techniques. Selection decisions will be made following peer and/or scientific review of the proposals. Several evaluation techniques are regularly used within NASA. In all cases proposals are subject to scientific review by discipline specialists in the area of the proposal. Some proposals are reviewed entirely in-house, others are evaluated by a combination of in-house and selected external reviewers, while yet others are subject to the full external peer review technique (with due regard for conflict-of-interest and protection of proposal information), such as by mail or through assembled panels. The final decisions are made by a NASA selecting official. A proposal which is scientifically and programmatically meritorious, but not selected for award during its initial review, may be included in subsequent reviews unless the proposer requests otherwise.

> (k) Selection for Award.

>> (1) When a proposal is not selected for award, the proposer will be notified. NASA will explain generally why the proposal was not selected. Proposers desiring additional information may contact the selecting official who will arrange a debriefing.

>> (2) When a proposal is selected for award, negotiation and award will be handled by the procurement office in the funding installation. The proposal is used as the basis for negotiation. The contracting officer may re-

quest certain business data and may forward a model award instrument and other information pertinent to negotiation.

# VI. SMALL BUSINESS INNOVATIVE RESEARCH PROGRAM

Another special procedure permitted by 10 U.S.C. § 2302(2)(E) and 41 U.S.C. § 152(5) is competitive selection of research proposals resulting from a general solicitation and peer or scientific review solicited pursuant to § 9 of the Small Business Act, 15 U.S.C. § 638. This section of the Small Business Act, known as the Small Business Innovation Development Act, Pub. L. No. 97-219, became effective in October 1982 and created the Small Business Innovation Research (SBIR) program. This section of the Act was substantially amended in 2002 by the Small Business Innovation Research Program Reauthorization Act of 2000, Pub. L. No. 106-554. A small program administered along with the SBIR program is the Small Business Technology Transfer Program (STTR) created by Pub. L. No. 102-564 in 1992. The purposes of these programs are to increase participation in government-funded research and development by small innovative firms and to provide incentives for the conversion of research into commercial applications. Firms owner or controlled by United States entities with 500 or fewer employees are eligible for participation in the program, 13 C.F.R. § 121.702. These statutes are not permanent legislation and reauthorization of the programs has not passed Congress. However, temporary extensions have been passed. See Pub. L. No. 112-17 extending the programs through September 30, 2011.

SBIR-STTR contracts have significant benefit to small businesses because they allow the contractor to maintain proprietary rights in technical data developed in the course of performing the contract. 15 U.S.C. § 638(j)(2)(A) requires that small businesses under this program be permitted to "retain rights to data generated by the concern in the performance of an SBIR award for a period of not less than 4 years." This requirement is implemented by the use of two clauses — the FAR Rights in Data — SBIR Program (DEC 2007) clause in FAR 52.227-20 (maintaining proprietary rights for four years "after acceptance of all items to be delivered under this contract") and the DFARS Rights in Noncommercial Technical Data and Computer Software — Small Business Innovative Research (SBIR) Program (June 1995) clause in DFARS 252.227-7018 (maintaining proprietary rights for five years "after completion of the project from which such data were generated").

## A. Description of SBIR Program

Section 638(f) of the Small Business Act requires each agency with an "extramural budget" for research and development of over $100 million to expend 2.5% of its R&D funds on SBIR contracts, grants or cooperative agreements with small businesses. Section 638(n) requires each agency with an "extramural budget" for research and development of over $1 billion to expend 0.3% of its R&D funds on

STTR contracts, grants or cooperative agreements with small businesses. Statutory requirements for this program are contained in 15 U.S.C. § 638(o). This program provides for the awarding of contracts to small business concerns for the purpose of conducting cooperative research and development with a nonprofit research institution, such as a university. The agencies with this mandate run the two programs as joint programs with SBIR/STTR regulations and websites.

The law directed the SBA to issue a SBIR/STTR Program Policy Directive to be used as guidance by the participating agencies. The current directive, 67 Fed. Reg. 60072, September 24, 2002, constitutes the main source of guidance in this area. GAO has held that in the absence of an express statutory provision, the policy directive's terms (in this case, providing for payment of a profit) will take precedence over an agency's regulations, *Appropriations/Financial Mgmt.*, 71 Comp. Gen. 310 (B-245032) (1992). The SBA maintains a website providing full information on the program at http://*www.sba.gov/sbir/*.

The three phases of the program are designed to take an idea through the stages of research, development and demonstration, and commercial application. Phase I primarily involves awards of $100,000 or less to support up to six months of effort to demonstrate the scientific and technical merit and feasibility of a proposed innovation. Only Phase I awardees are eligible to compete for Phase II funding. Phase II awards generally involve a maximum of $750,000 to support up to two years of work to further develop the innovation. Projects with commercial potential receive special consideration for a Phase II award. Phase III is for the commercialization of Phase II results and does not involve SBIR/STTR funding. Private or non-SBIR/STTR federal funds must be used for this purpose. The dollar amounts for NASA are slightly less, $100,000 for Phase I and $600,000 for Phase II contracts, *http://sbir.gsfc.nasa.gov/SBIR/SBIR.html*.

The program is designed to assist small businesses by establishing simplified and fairly uniform procedures, while also allowing sufficient flexibility to the participating agencies. Thus, the SBA's Office of Technology establishes certain guidelines, primarily concerning the timing and content of SBIR solicitations. The individual procuring agencies unilaterally determine the categories of research to be included in the SBIR/STTR program, issue solicitations, evaluate and select projects, and administer the resulting agreements. Agencies are free to choose the SBIR/STTR funding instrument, consistent with the Grants and Cooperative Agreements Act. They are generally expected to make Phase I and Phase II awards within the $100,000 and $750,000 guidelines, but they may make larger awards when necessary.

The SBIR/STTR program is not intended to replace research awards to small businesses authorized under statutes or regulations. Thus, unsolicited proposals from small businesses, or any other proposals not submitted in response to the SBIR/STTR solicitations, are ineligible for SBIR-STTR awards, SBIR Program Policy Directive § 5(g)(3).

## B. Phase I SBIR Announcement

Section 4 of the SBIR Program Policy Directive describes the Phase I solicitation as follows:

(a) *Phase I.* Phase I involves a solicitation of contract proposals or grant applications (hereinafter referred to as proposals) to conduct feasibility-related experimental or theoretical R/R&D related to described agency requirements. These requirements, as defined by agency topics contained in a solicitation, may be general or narrow in scope, depending on the needs of the agency. The object of this phase is to determine the scientific and technical merit and feasibility of the proposed effort and the quality of performance of the [Small Business Concern] with a relatively small agency investment before consideration of further Federal support in Phase II.

(1) Several different proposed solutions to a given problem may be funded.

(2) Proposals will be evaluated on a competitive basis. Agency criteria used to evaluate SBIR proposals must give consideration to the scientific and technical merit and feasibility of the proposal along with its potential for commercialization. Considerations may also include program balance or critical agency requirements.

(3) Agencies may require the submission of a Phase II proposal as a deliverable item under Phase I.

The solicitation process used in this phase is essentially the same as that used for broad agency announcements. Each procuring agency is required to issue a "program solicitation" at least once a year setting forth the categories of research in which Phase I proposals are to be solicited. These solicitations are incorporated into an SBA "Master Schedule" which spaces the solicitations throughout the year in order to permit small businesses to participate to the maximum practicable extent. Section 5 of the SBIR Program Policy Directive describes the solicitation process as follows:

(b) The Act requires issuance of SBIR (Phase I) Program solicitations in accordance with a Master Schedule coordinated between SBA and the SBIR agency. The SBA office responsible for coordination is: Office of Technology, Office of Government Contracting, Office of Government Contracting and Business Development, U.S. Small Business Administration, 409 Third Street, SW., Washington, DC 20416. Phone: (202) 205-6450. Fax: (202) 205-7754. E-mail: technology@sba.gov. Internet site: *www.sba.gov/sbir.*

\* \* \*

(d) *Master Schedule.* SBA posts an electronic Master Schedule of release dates of program solicitations with links to Internet web sites of agency solicitations.

Agencies must post on their Internet web sites the following information regarding each program solicitation:

(1) The list of topics upon which R/R&D proposals will be sought.

(2) Agency address, phone number, or email address from which SBIR Program solicitations can be requested or obtained, especially through electronic means.

(3) Names, addresses, and phone numbers of agency contact points where SBIR-related inquiries may be directed.

(4) Release date(s) of program solicitation(s).

(5) Closing date(s) for receipt of proposals.

(6) Estimated number and average dollar amounts of Phase I awards to be made under the solicitation.

Agency SBIR solicitations must follow a uniform format established by the SBA to minimize the burden on participating businesses. Instructions for the preparation of these solicitations are contained in Appendix I to the SBIR Program Policy Directive. Solicitations must contain a cover sheet, a table of contents and the following sections in the order shown:

1. Program Description

2. Definitions

3. Proposal Preparation Instructions and Requirements

4. Methods of Selection and Evaluation Criteria

5. Considerations

6. Submission of Proposals

7. Scientific and Technical Information Sources

8. Submission Forms and Certifications

9. Research Topics

The agency solicitations basically contain all the information and forms a firm needs in order to submit a proposal. The solicitation must indicate if external review is to be used as part of the evaluation process. The main body of the solicitation is the description of research topics for which proposals are being solicited. Appendix I of the Policy Directive also contains guidance on the terms and conditions that should be included in the solicitation.

A research topic can be canceled at any time, *Pike Creek Computer Co.*, Comp. Gen. Dec. B-290329, 2002 CPD ¶ 106 (irrelevant that company had expended proposal funds prior to cancellation).

Firms submitting proposals must be careful to provide accurate information about their capabilities and resources. See *United States ex rel. Longhi v. Lithium Power Techs, Inc.*, 575 F.3d 458 (5th Cir. 2009), *cert. denied*, 130 S. Ct. 2092 (2010), holding a recipient of an SBIR contract liable under the Civil False Claims Act, 31 U.S.C. § 3729. The firm had misrepresented the extent of its facilities and the relationships it had with other organizations and had failed to disclose its prior work on SBIR grants.

## C. Evaluation and Selection of Phase I Proposals

Agencies have considerable freedom to develop evaluation and selection procedures under the SBIR program. Section 7 of the SBIR Program Policy Directive contains the following minimal guidance:

> (b) *Review of SBIR Proposals*. SBA encourages SBIR agencies to use their routine review processes for SBIR proposals whether internal or external evaluation is used. A more limited review process may be used for Phase I due to the larger number of proposals anticipated. Where appropriate, "peer" reviews external to the agency are authorized by the Act. SBA cautions SBIR agencies that all review procedures must be designed to minimize any possible conflict of interest as it pertains to applicant proprietary data. The standardized SBIR solicitation advises potential applicants that proposals may be subject to an established external review process and that the applicant may include company designated proprietary information in its proposal.

Although this regulation cautions only against conflicts of interest relating to proprietary data, financial conflicts must also be avoided. See *R&D Dynamics Corp.*, Comp. Gen. Dec. B-285979.2, 2000 CPD ¶ 193, finding no conflict when agency evaluators had dealt with a winning contractor on earlier projects.

Paragraph (b)(1) of Appendix I to the SBIR Program Policy Directive requires the use of the following evaluation factors at a minimum:

> (i) The technical approach and the anticipated agency and commercial benefits that may be derived from the research.

> (ii) The adequacy of the proposed effort and its relationship to the fulfillment of requirements of the research topic or subtopics.

(iii) The soundness and technical merit of the proposed approach and its incremental progress toward topic or subtopic solution.

(iv) Qualifications of the proposed principal/key investigators, supporting staff, and consultants.

(v) Evaluations of proposals require, among other things, consideration of a proposal's commercial potential as evidenced by:

> (A) the SBC's record of commercializing SBIR or other research,

> (B) the existence of second phase funding commitments from private sector or non-SBIR funding sources,

> (C) the existence of third phase follow-on commitments for the subject of the research, and,

> (D) the presence of other indicators of the commercial potential of the idea.

Most agencies limit contact with proposers during the proposal preparation and evaluation stage. For example, the DoD website, *http://www.acq.osd.mil/osbp/sbir/solicitations/index.htm* contains the following guidance:

> During the pre-release period, you may talk directly with the Topic Authors to ask technical questions about the topics. Their names, phone numbers, and e-mail addresses are listed within each solicitation topic above. For reasons of competitive fairness, direct communication between proposers and topic authors is not allowed when DoD begins accepting proposals for each solicitation. However, proposers may still submit written questions about solicitation topics through the SBIR/STTR Interactive Topic Information System (SITIS), in which the questioner and respondent remain anonymous and all questions and answers are posted electronically for general viewing until the solicitation closes. All proposers are advised to monitor SITIS during the solicitation period for questions and answers, and other significant information, relevant to the SBIR/STTR topic under which they are proposing.

These limitations are not required by the SBA Policy Directive.

The selection of proposals for award of contracts is a highly discretionary process. In *Systems Research Co.*, Comp. Gen. Dec. B-260280.2, 95-2 CPD ¶ 62, GAO confirmed that, in conducting an SBIR procurement, agencies have wide discretion and, absent a violation of applicable regulations or solicitation provisions or a finding of fraud or bad faith, the agency's decision of which proposals it will fund will not be disturbed. Winning a protest of a Phase I selection is particularly difficult because there are frequently a large number of proposals submitted against each research topic. See *NW Sys.*, Comp. Gen. Dec. B-401352, 2009 CPD ¶ 152 (omitted information led to failure to award contract); *Nautical Control*

*Solutions, LP*, Comp. Gen. Dec. B-299918, 2007 CPD ¶ 215 (evaluation based on inadequate data reasonable); *Fantastic Data*, Comp. Gen. Dec. B-299076, 2007 CPD ¶ 32 (bias of evaluators not demonstrated); *Quimba Software*, Comp. Gen. Dec. B-299000, 2007 CPD ¶ 14 (agency evaluation of proposal reasonable); *Glatz Aeronautical Corp.*, Comp. Gen. Dec. B-293968.2, 2004 CPD ¶ 160 (selection of more innovative proposals reasonable); *Noble Solutions*, Comp. Gen.. Dec. B-294393, 2004 CPD ¶ 197 (proposal technically unacceptable); *Glatz Aeronautical Corp.*, Comp. Gen. Dec. B-293968.2, 2004 CPD ¶ 160 (proposal contained no innovative work; *Higher Power Eng'g*, Comp. Gen. Dec. B-278900, 98-1 CPD ¶ 84 (proper to downgrade a proposal for failure to submit required information); *Virginia Accelerators Corp.*, Comp. Gen.. Dec. B-271066, 97-2 CPD ¶ 13 (selection of evaluators a discretionary decision); *Bostan Research, Inc.*, Comp. Gen. Dec. B-274331, 96-2 CPD ¶ 209 (page limitation not an excuse for failure to submit required information); *Deborah Bass Assocs.*, Comp. Gen. Dec. B-257958, 94-2 CPD ¶ 180 (failure to hold discussions or request BAFOs is unobjectionable); and *Noise Cancellation Techs., Inc.*, Comp. Gen. Dec. B-246476, 92-1 CPD ¶ 269 (no basis for the contention that agency failed to apply the evaluation criteria properly). Compare *Celadon Labs., Inc.*, Comp. Gen. Dec. B-298533, 2006 ¶ CPD 158, granting a protest because the agency had used outside evaluators that had a conflict of interest with the protester because they worked for firms that were promoting competitive technology.

## D. Phase II Selection Procedures

Small businesses that have received Phase I contracts can request continuation of the project through the award of a Phase II contract. Section 4 of the SBIR Program Policy Directive describes the Phase II procedure as follows:

(b) *Phase II.* The object of Phase II is to continue the R/R&D effort from the completed Phase I. Only SBIR awardees in Phase I are eligible to participate in Phases II and III. This includes those awardees identified via a "novated" or "successor in interest" or similarly-revised funding agreement, or those that have reorganized with the same key staff, regardless of whether they have been assigned a different tax identification number. Agencies may require the original awardee to relinquish its rights and interests in an SBIR project in favor of another applicant as a condition for that applicant's eligibility to participate in the SBIR Program for that project.

(1) Funding must be based upon the results of Phase I and the scientific and technical merit and commercial potential of the Phase II proposal. Phase II awards may not necessarily complete the total research and development that may be required to satisfy commercial or Federal needs beyond the SBIR Program. The Phase II funding agreement with the awardee may, at the discretion of the awarding agency, establish the procedures applicable to Phase III agreements. The Government is not obligated to fund any specific Phase II proposal.

(2) The SBIR Phase II award decision process requires, among other things, consideration of a proposal's commercial potential. Commercial potential includes the potential to transition the technology to private sector applications, Government applications, or Government contractor applications. Commercial potential in a Phase II proposal may be evidenced by:

(i) the SBC's record of successfully commercializing SBIR or other research;

(ii) the existence of Phase II funding commitments from private sector or other non-SBIR funding sources;

(iii) the existence of Phase III, follow-on commitments for the subject of the research; and

(iv) other indicators of commercial potential of the idea.

Agencies have substantial discretion in deciding whether a project should be continued by the award of a Phase II contract. The decision is made on a case-by-case basis and can be dependent on the amount of funds available to the agency for SBIR work. Thus, protests of such awards are unlikely to succeed. See *R&D Dynamics Corp.*, Comp. Gen. Dec. B-298766, 2006 CPD ¶ 195 (reasonable to award to only those 19 contractors evaluated highest when that used up available funds); *RDAS Corp.*, Comp. Gen. Dec. B-294848, 2004 CPD ¶ 253 (no support for protester's contention that agency decision not to fund work was based on erroneous technical conclusion); *U S Positioning Group, LLC*, Comp. Gen. Dec. B-294027, 2004 CPD ¶ 133 (not unreasonable to consider deliverables when agency only has sufficient funds to award one Phase II contract); *R&D Dynamics Corp.*, Comp. Gen. Dec. B-285979.3, 2000 CPD ¶ 201 (not unreasonable to award to highest evaluated proposal when funds were only available to award one Phase II contract); *I.S. Grupe, Inc.*, Comp. Gen. Dec. B-278839, 98-1 CPD ¶ 86 (technical evaluation of outside evaluator reasonable); *Quantum Magnetics, Inc.*, Comp. Gen. Dec. B-257968, 94-2 CPD ¶ 215 (technical evaluation of a competing Phase II proposal reasonable). See also *InkiTiki Corp.*, Comp. Gen. Dec. B-291823.4, 2003 CPD ¶ 104, where GAO denied a protest that the Phase I contractor had not been invited to submit a Phase II proposal. GAO held that the agency had properly based its decision not to invite a proposal on the review of the work during Phase I. Compare *Intellectual Props., Inc.*, Comp. Gen. Dec. B-280803, 98-2 CPD ¶ 115, where GAO granted a protest of failure to award a Phase II contract because the decision was based on lack of private sector funding — a factor not specified in the solicitation. In *Intellectual Properties, Inc.*, Comp. Gen. Dec. B-280803.2, 99-1 CPD ¶ 83, GAO granted a second protest after the agency decided again not award a Phase II contract. That decision was based on the fact that the denial of the contract was based on reasons that were not supported by the comments of the evaluators that had reviewed the Phase II proposal in detail. See also *R&D Dynamics Corp. v. United States*, 80 Fed. Cl. 715 (2007), where the Court of Federal Claims inexplicably ruled that it had no jurisdiction to hear this type of protest because SBIR procurements were not procurements.

If the negotiations for a Phase II contract require effort beyond the funding of the Phase I effort, the contractor bears the risk that such costs will not be recoverable from the government, *RADCON Radar Control Sys.*, ASBCA 50022, 99-2 BCA ¶ 30,571. In that case, the board also ruled that it had no jurisdiction over a claim that the government had prevented obtaining private financing for a continuation of the project by misrepresenting the level of success of the Phase II work. See also *California Consulting Eng'rs*, ASBCA 50355, 98-2 BCA ¶ 29,995, denying a claim for additional money spent to build a prototype to support its Phase II proposal (which did not lead to the award of a contract). Compare *Applied Tech. Assocs., Inc.*, ASBCA 49200, 98-1 BCA ¶ 29,633, where the board held that the government was obligated to pay an amount exceeding the funds provided for a fixed-price Phase II contract because the unique Limitation of Government Obligation clause in the contract did not contain a statement that the contractor could cease working when it had expended all of the funds allotted to the contract.

Paragraph 7(d) of the SBIR Program Policy Directive allows cost sharing in SBIR contracts but states that cost sharing may not be an evaluation factor. Nonetheless, the Department of Defense has adopted a "fast track" procedure that permits Phase I contractors to submit proposals for Phase II contracts for consideration on an expedited basis — based on the agreement of an outside investor to provide 50% of the funding of the Phase II project. See DoD Fast Track Guidance, *http://www.acq.osd.mil/osbp/sbir/fasttrack/index.htm,* advising that such proposals have a far greater likelihood of award. In *R&D Dynamics Corp.*, Comp. Gen. Dec. B-285979.2, 2000 CPD ¶ 193, GAO denied a protest that agency officials had discouraged the protester from submitting a fast-track proposal based on lack of evidence plus the clear statement in the regulations that fast track proposals were encouraged and that they had a far greater chance of obtaining funding.

## E. Phase III Selection Procedures

Phase III contracts are awarded when the agency decides to use non-SBIR funds to continue the project. They are unique in the fact that they can be awarded to a contractor that is not a small business. Section 4 of the SBIR Program Policy Directive describes the Phase III procedure as follows:

(c) *Phase III.* SBIR Phase III refers to work that derives from, extends, or logically concludes effort(s) performed under prior SBIR funding agreements, but is funded by sources other than the SBIR Program. Phase III work is typically oriented towards commercialization of SBIR research or technology.

(1) Each of the following types of activity constitutes SBIR Phase III work:

(i) commercial application of SBIR-funded R/R&D financed by non-Federal sources of capital (**Note:** The guidance in this Policy Directive regarding SBIR Phase III pertains to the non-SBIR federally-funded work described in (ii) and (iii) below. It does not address the nature of private agreements the SBIR firm may make in the commercialization of its technology.);

(ii) SBIR-derived products or services intended for use by the Federal Government, funded by non-SBIR sources of Federal funding;

(iii) continuation of R/R&D that has been competitively selected using peer review or scientific review criteria, funded by non-SBIR Federal funding sources.

(2) A Phase III award is, by its nature, an SBIR award, has SBIR status, and must be accorded SBIR data rights. (*See* Section 8(b)(2) regarding the protection period for data rights.) If an SBIR awardee wins a competition for work that derives from, extends, or logically concludes that firm's work under a prior SBIR funding agreement, then the funding agreement for the new, competed work must have all SBIR Phase III status and data rights. A Federal agency may enter into a Phase III SBIR agreement at any time with a Phase II awardee. Similarly, a Federal agency may enter into a Phase III SBIR agreement at any time with a Phase I awardee. An agency official may determine, using the criteria set forth in the Directive as guidance, whether a contract or agreement is a Phase III award.

(3) The competition for SBIR Phase I and Phase II awards satisfies any competition requirement of the Armed Services Procurement Act, the Federal Property and Administrative Services Act, and the Competition in Contracting Act. Therefore, an agency that wishes to fund an SBIR Phase III project is not required to conduct another competition in order to satisfy those statutory provisions. As a result, in conducting actions relative to a Phase III SBIR award, it is sufficient to state for purposes of a Justification and Approval pursuant to FAR 6.302-5, that the project is a SBIR Phase III award that is derived from, extends, or logically concludes efforts performed under prior SBIR funding agreements and is authorized under 10 U.S.C. 2304(b)(2) or 41 U.S.C. 253(b)(2).

(4) Phase III work may be for products, production, services, R/R&D, or any combination thereof.

(5) There is no limit on the number, duration, type, or dollar value of Phase III awards made to a business concern. There is no limit on the time that may elapse between a Phase I or Phase II award and Phase III award, or between a Phase III award and any subsequent Phase III award.

If an agency is going to pursue the technology that has been developed under an SBIR contract, there is a strong preference that a contract be awarded to the SBIR contractor. See ¶ 4(c)(8) of the SBIR Program Policy Directive requiring notice to the SBA of the intent to award such a contract to another firm and stating that the SBA may appeal such decision to the head of the contracting activity. Upon receipt of an appeal, the head of the contracting activity must issue a written decision within 30 days and the agency must suspend the award pending the decision.

In spite of this strong preference for award of a Phase III contract to the SBIR contractor, award to a subcontractor on the Phase II work was sustained in *Night Vision Corp. v. United States*, 469 F.3d 1369 (Fed. Cir. 2006), *cert. denied*, 550 U.S. 934 (2007). In that instance, the agency conducted a competitive procurement for the Phase III work, giving potential offerors access to the prototype delivered on the Phase II contract but not disclosing the data delivered by the Phase II contractor. The court held that the statutory preference conferred no rights on the Phase II contractor, stating at 1373-74:

> The only specific requirement that § 638(j)(2)(C) imposes is that the Administrator "modify the policy directives issued pursuant to this subsection to provide for . . . (C) procedures to ensure, to the extent practicable, that an agency which intends to pursue . . . a technology developed by a small business concern under an SBIR program enters into follow-on, non-SBIR funding agreements with the small business concern for such research, development or production." The Administrator has done so. *See SBIR Research Program Policy Directive*, 67 Fed. Reg. 60,072, 60,075-076 (Sept. 24, 2002) (noting that the special acquisition preference given to SBIR awardees is "a preference and is not mandatory" and that "[i]t is clear that Congress intends, to the greatest extent practicable, that agencies issue Phase III awards to the SBIR awardees that developed the technology"); *SBIR Research Program Policy Directive,* 58 Fed. Reg. 42,607, 42,612 (Aug. 10, 1993) ("A Federal agency may enter into a third phase agreement with a small business concern for additional work to be performed during or after the second phase period. . . . Agencies which intend to pursue research, research and development or production of a technology developed by a small business concern under the STTR [Small Business Technology Transfer] Program will give special acquisition preference . . . to the STTR company which developed the technology").

> \* \* \*

> Nothing in § 638(j), however, bars the government from [choosing to use competitive procedures to select the follow-on contractor] or requires it to (1) select a Phase III procurement and (2) award the contract therefor to the small business concern that performed the Phase I and II contracts. We decline to read into those contracts such a requirement for, and commitment by, the government. Whatever may be the policy favoring small business in the present situation, there is simply no valid basis for reading such a requirement into the contract.

## VII. INFORMATION TECHNOLOGY

Another new acquisition procedure established by the Clinger-Cohen Act of 1996, Pub. L. No. 104-106, 40 U.S.C. § 11302, relates to information technology. The Act repealed the Brooks Act, 40 U.S.C. § 759, giving the General Services Administration (GSA) central authority over the purchase of information technology for the federal government, and gave each agency the authority to procure information technology to meet its needs, 40 U.S.C. § 11314. This effectively abolished the Federal Information Resources Management Regulation (FIRMR), which was the primary regulation on the acquisition of information technology. This type of procurement is now done using normal procurement procedures following a few special rules in FAR Part 39.

The Director of the Office of Management and Budget (OMB) has major responsibilities with regard to the government's information technology investments. See 44 U.S.C. § 3504(h) stating:

(h) With respect to Federal information technology, the Director shall —

(1) in consultation with the Director of the National Institute of Standards and Technology and the Administrator of General Services —

(A) develop and oversee the implementation of policies, principles, standards, and guidelines for information technology functions and activities of the Federal Government, including periodic evaluations of major information systems; and

(B) oversee the development and implementation of standards under section 11331 of title 40;

(2) monitor the effectiveness of, and compliance with, directives issued under subtitle III of title 40 [40 USC § 11101 et seq.] and directives issued under section 322 of title 40;

(3) coordinate the development and review by the Office of Information and Regulatory Affairs of policy associated with Federal procurement and acquisition of information technology with the Office of Federal Procurement Policy;

(4) ensure, through the review of agency budget proposals, information resources management plans and other means —

(A) agency integration of information resources management plans, program plans and budgets for acquisition and use of information technology; and

(B) the efficiency and effectiveness of inter-agency information technology initiatives to improve agency performance and the accomplishment of agency missions; and

(5) promote the use of information technology by the Federal Government to improve the productivity, efficiency, and effectiveness of Federal programs, including through dissemination of public information and the reduction of information collection burdens on the public.

See also 40 U.S.C. § 11302(b) stating:

> *Use of information technology in Federal programs.* The Director shall promote
> and improve the acquisition, use, security, and disposal of information technology
> by the Federal Government to improve the productivity, efficiency, and effective-
> ness of Federal programs, including through dissemination of public information
> and the reduction of information collection burdens on the public.

This authority has been implemented by the issuance of OMB Circular A-130, *http://
www.whitehouse.gov/omb/circulars/a130/a130trans4.html.* This circular was last updated by Transmittal Memorandum No. 4, 65 Fed. Reg. 77677, December 12, 2000.

FAR 2.101 defines information technology as follows:

> Information technology means any equipment, or interconnected system(s) or
> subsystem(s) of equipment, that is used in the automatic acquisition, storage,
> manipulation, management, movement, control, display, switching, interchange,
> transmission, or reception of data or information by the agency.
>
>> (1) For purposes of this definition, equipment is used by an agency if the
>> equipment is used by the agency directly or is used by a contractor under
>> a contract with the agency that requires —
>>
>>> (i) Its use; or
>>>
>>> (ii) To a significant extent, its use in the performance of a service
>>> or the furnishing of a product.
>>
>> (2) The term "information technology" includes computers, ancillary
>> equipment, software, firmware and similar procedures, services (including
>> support services), and related resources.
>>
>> (3) The term "information technology" does not include any equipment that —
>>
>>> (i) Is acquired by a contractor incidental to a contract; or
>>>
>>> (ii) Contains imbedded information technology that is used as an
>>> integral part of the product, but the principal function of which
>>> is not the acquisition, storage, manipulation, management, move-
>>> ment, control, display, switching, interchange, transmission, or
>>> reception of data or information. For example, HVAC (heating,
>>> ventilation, and air conditioning) equipment, such as thermostats
>>> or temperature control devices, and medical equipment where in-
>>> formation technology is integral to its operation, are not informa-
>>> tion technology.

Each agency is required to have a Chief Information Officer to oversee the entire information technology program of the agency, 40 U.S.C. § 11315.

## A. Planning Information Technology Procurements

Because of the large amount that the government invests in information technology, there are special requirements that must be met in planning such procurements. 40 U.S.C. § 11312(b) requires that each agency implement a process for acquiring information technology that:

(1) provide[s] for the selection of investments in information technology (including information security needs) to be made by the executive agency, the management of those investments, and the evaluation of the results of those investments;

(2) [is] integrated with the processes for making budget, financial, and program management decisions in the executive agency;

(3) include[s] minimum criteria to be applied in considering whether to undertake a particular investment in information systems, including criteria related to the quantitatively expressed projected net, risk-adjusted return on investment and specific quantitative and qualitative criteria for comparing and prioritizing alternative information systems investment projects;

(4) identif[ies] information systems investments that would result in shared benefits or costs for other federal agencies or state or local governments;

(5) identif[ies] quantifiable measurements for determining the net benefits and risks of a proposed investment; and

(6) provide[s] the means for senior management personnel of the executive agency to obtain timely information regarding the progress of an investment in an information system, including a system of milestones for measuring progress, on an independently verifiable basis, in terms of cost, capability of the system to meet specified requirements, timeliness, and quality.

Paragraph 8.b.(4) of OMB Circular A-130 implements these requirements with regard to acquisition policies as follows:

Agencies must:

(a) Make use of adequate competition, allocate risk between government and contractor, and maximize return on investment when acquiring information technology;

(b) Structure major information systems into useful segments with a narrow scope and brief duration. This should reduce risk, promote flexibility and interoperability, increase accountability, and better match mission need with current technology and market conditions;

(c) Acquire off-the-shelf software from commercial sources, unless the cost effectiveness of developing custom software is clear and has been documented through pilot projects or prototypes; and

(d) Ensure accessibility of acquired information technology pursuant to the Rehabilitation Act of 1973, as amended (Pub. L. 105-220, 29 U.S.C. 794d).

FAR 39.102 provides further guidance as follows:

(a) Prior to entering into a contract for information technology, an agency should analyze risks, benefits, and costs. (See part 7 for additional information regarding requirements definition.) Reasonable risk taking is appropriate as long as risks are controlled and mitigated. Contracting and program office officials are jointly responsible for assessing, monitoring and controlling risk when selecting projects for investment and during program implementation.

(b) Types of risk may include schedule risk, risk of technical obsolescence, cost risk, risk implicit in a particular contract type, technical feasibility, dependencies between a new project and other projects or systems, the number of simultaneous high risk projects to be monitored, funding availability, and program management risk.

(c) Appropriate techniques should be applied to manage and mitigate risk during the acquisition of information technology. Techniques include, but are not limited to: prudent project management; use of modular contracting; thorough acquisition planning tied to budget planning by the program, finance and contracting offices; continuous collection and evaluation of risk-based assessment data; prototyping prior to implementation; post implementation reviews to determine actual project cost, benefits and returns; and focusing on risks and returns using quantifiable measures.

# B. Performance-Based and Results-Based Management

40 U.S.C. § 11303 provides that the Director of OMB is required to encourage performance-based and results-based management for agency information technology programs, and 40 U.S.C. § 11302(b) requires the Director to promote the efficient acquisition and use of information technology through the capital planning process. The Director is required to review an agency's management practices based on the performance and results of its information technology programs and investments, and to issue clear and concise directions to ensure that agencies have effective and efficient capital planning processes that are used to select, control, and evaluate the results of major information systems investments and to ensure that agency information security is adequate. Agencies are required to follow these procedures by 40 U.S.C. § 11312 and § 11313.

These requirements are implemented in OMB Circular A-130. Paragraph 8.b.(1) states the basic procedures as follows:

> Agencies must establish and maintain a capital planning and investment control process that links mission needs, information, and information technology in an effective and efficient manner. The process will guide both strategic and operational IRM, IT planning, and the Enterprise Architecture by integrating the agency's IRM plans, strategic and performance plans prepared pursuant to the Government Performance and Results Act of 1993, financial management plans prepared pursuant to the Chief Financial Officer Act of 1990 (31 U.S.C. 902a5), acquisition under the Federal Acquisition Streamlining Act of 1994, and the agency's budget formulation and execution processes. The capitalplanning and investment control process includes all stages of capital programming, including planning, budgeting, procurement, management, and assessment.

## C. Modular Contracting

41 U.S.C. § 2308 requires agencies to use modular contracting to the maximum extent practicable for acquisition of information technology major systems. Under modular contracting, an agency's need for a system is satisfied by successive acquisitions of interoperable increments. Each increment complies with common or commercially accepted standards applicable to information technology so that the increments are compatible with other increments of information technology comprising the system.

This statute is implemented in FAR 39.103 as follows:

(a) . . . . Modular contracting is intended to reduce program risk and to incentivize contractor performance while meeting the Governments need for timely access to rapidly changing technology. Consistent with the agency's information technology architecture, agencies should, to the maximum extent practicable, use modular contracting to acquire major systems (see 2.101) of information technology. Agencies may also use modular contracting to acquire non-major systems of information technology.

(b) When using modular contracting, an acquisition of a system of information technology may be divided into several smaller acquisition increments that —

> (1) Are easier to manage individually than would be possible in one comprehensive acquisition;

> (2) Address complex information technology objectives incrementally in order to enhance the likelihood of achieving workable systems or solutions for attainment of those objectives;

> (3) Provide for delivery, implementation, and testing of workable systems or solutions in discrete increments, each of which comprises a system or

solution that is not dependent on any subsequent increment in order to perform its principal functions;

(4) Provide an opportunity for subsequent increments to take advantage of any evolution in technology or needs that occur during implementation and use of the earlier increments; and

(5) Reduce risk of potential adverse consequences on the overall project by isolating and avoiding custom-designed components of the system.

(c) The characteristics of an increment may vary depending upon the type of information technology being acquired and the nature of the system being developed. The following factors may be considered:

(1) To promote compatibility, the information technology acquired through modular contracting for each increment should comply with common or commercially acceptable information technology standards when available and appropriate, and shall conform to the agency's master information technology architecture.

(2) The performance requirements of each increment should be consistent with the performance requirements of the completed, overall system within which the information technology will function and should address interface requirements with succeeding increments.

(d) For each increment, contracting officers shall choose an appropriate contracting technique that facilitates the acquisition of subsequent increments. Pursuant to Parts 16 and 17 of the Federal Acquisition Regulations, contracting officers shall select the contract type and method appropriate to the circumstances (e.g., indefinite delivery, indefinite quantity contracts, single contract with options, successive contracts, multiple awards, task order contracts). Contract(s) shall be structured to ensure that the Government is not required to procure additional increments.

(e) To avoid obsolescence, a modular contract for information technology should, to the maximum extent practicable, be awarded within 180 days after the date on which the solicitation is issued. If award cannot be made within 180 days, agencies should consider cancellation of the solicitation in accordance with 14.209 or 15.206(e). To the maximum extent practicable, deliveries under the contract should be scheduled to occur within 18 months after issuance of the solicitation.

GSA issued an *Acquisition White Paper on Modular Contracting*, July 25, 1997 (*http://www.estrategy.gov/documents/white_paper_on_modular_contracting.html*) giving additional guidance on this type of contracting. This paper warns that there are risks in using modular contracting because the modules may not be fully compatible. To overcome this problem, the paper recommends that prior to undertaking modular contracting the agency should formulate agencywide information technology architecture based on common and commercial standards.

# 1110 SPECIAL NEGOTIATION PROCEDURES

Section 804 of the National Defense Authorization Act for Fiscal Year 2010, Pub. L. No. 111-84, contains the following additional requirements for DoD acquisitions of information technology:

> (a) NEW ACQUISITION PROCESS REQUIRED.— The Secretary of Defense shall develop and implement a new acquisition process for information technology systems. The acquisition process developed and implemented pursuant to this subsection shall, to the extent determined appropriate by the Secretary—
>
> > (1) be based on the recommendations in chapter 6 of the March 2009 report of the Defense Science Board Task Force on Department of Defense Policies and Procedures for the Acquisition of Information Technology; and
> >
> > (2) be designed to include —
> >
> > > (A) early and continual involvement of the user;
> > >
> > > (B) multiple, rapidly executed increments or releases of capability;
> > >
> > > (C) early, successive prototyping to support an evolutionary approach; and
> > >
> > > (D) a modular, open-systems approach.

## D. Share-In-Savings Contracts

There was temporary authority for agencies to enter into share-in-savings contracts for information technology in 41 U.S.C. § 266a. This statute was never implemented nor used. See *Federal Contracting: Share-In-Savings Initiative Not Yet Tested*, GAO-05-736, July 26, 2005. This statute was allowed to expire in 2005.

## E. Governmentwide Acquisition Contracts

The Clinger-Cohen Act required the Director of OMB to designate one or more agencies as "executive agent" for governmentwide acquisitions of information technology, 40 U.S.C. § 11302(e). When so designated, heads of agencies are authorized to award such contracts, 40 U.S.C. § 11314(a)(2). These governmentwide acquisition contracts (GWACs) are indefinite delivery/indefinite quantity contracts that permit any agency to issue task orders for information technology without complying with the requirements of the Economy Act, 31 U.S.C. § 1535. See FAR 17.500(b)(2). See Chapter 8 for a discussion of these contracts.

## F. Federal Supply Schedule Orders

A large number of information technology procurements are accomplished using contractors on Schedule 70 of the GSA multiple award schedules issued as part of the Federal Supply Schedule. This schedule contains over 5000 contracts cover-ing a wide span of information technology supplies and services. The 14 catego-ries, called "special item numbers" (SINs) are listed at *www.gsa.gov/Portal/gsa/ ep/channelView.do?pageTypeId=81998channelId=13472.* The procedures used to issue task orders against these contracts are covered in Chapter 8.

## VIII.   OTHER AGENCY PROCEDURES

In addition to the "other procedures" specified in 10 U.S.C. § 2302(2) and 41 U.S.C. § 152, some agencies have statutory authority to use special procurement procedures in an effort to streamline the acquisition process. The procedures de-scribed below provide the affected agencies with considerably greater latitude to conduct their procurements following more business-like practices.

### A.  Federal Aviation Administration

Pub. L. No. 104-50 exempted the Federal Aviation Administration (FAA) from the Federal Property and Administrative Services Act, the Federal Acquisition Reg-ulation and a number of other designated statutes, 49 U.S.C. § 40110(d)(2). As a result, on April 1, 1996, the FAA issued a separate procurement regulation entitled the Federal Aviation Administration Acquisition Management System (AMS). The AMS was issued in June 1997 and has been revised several times — the last revision being in October 2008. It is not published in the Federal Register but is available at http://fast.faa.gov/.

The AMS differs from the FAR in that it is a combined contracting and program management system. It also differs in that it confers considerably greater discre-tion on contracting personnel — with fewer prescriptive rules than the FAR. For a critique of the system, see *Air Traffic Control: FAA's Acquisition Management Has Improved, but Policies and Oversight Need Strengthening to Help Ensure Results*, GAO-05-23, December 2004.

Under the AMS, there are two competitive procurement methods available for obtaining products and services through the FAA contracting process. The first method is described under "Complex and Noncommercial Source Selection" and is used for complex, large-dollar, developmental, and noncommercial items and ser-vices. The second method is described under "Commercial and Simplified Purchase Method" and is typically used for commercial items that are less complex, small in dollar value, and shorter term.

### 1.  Complex and Noncommercial Source Selection

AMS 3.2.2.3 provides that there are five phases in complex and noncommercial source selection:

- Planning

- Screening

- Selection

- Debriefing (as requested)

- Lessons Learned

Procurement planning is required for all FAA procurements except for those procurements using the commercial and simplified purchasing methods and those for real property and utilities, AMS 3.2.1.1. The planning can be accomplished by the preparation of a formal written procurement plan, AMS 3.2.1.2.2, or by a procurement strategy meeting, AMS 3.2.1.2.3. Independent government cost estimates are required for all procurements over $100,000, with a few exceptions, AMS 3.2.1.2.4.

The screening process is the fundamental method used by the FAA to select a contractor that will provide the best value to the FAA. It consists of one to three steps in limiting the competition depending on the complexity of the procurement. The document issued to potential competitors to carry out this process is called a screening information request (SIR). AMS 3.2.2.3.1.2.1 describes this process as follows:

> The purpose of the SIR is to obtain information, which will ultimately allow the FAA to identify the offeror that provides the best value, make a selection decision, and award the contract to conclude the competitive process. A SIR is a request by the FAA for documentation, information, presentations, proposals, or binding offers. Three categories of SIRs (see below) may be used according to the procurement strategy adopted by the service organization. Once the public announcement has been released, the SIR may be released to start the competitive process. The service organization will determine the type(s) of SIR(s) that are appropriate for each procurement.

> For a given procurement, the FAA may make a selection decision after one SIR, or the FAA may have a series of SIRs (with a screening decision after each one) to arrive at the selection decision. This will depend on the types of products and services to be acquired and the specific source selection approach chosen by the service organization. When it is desired to make a selection decision after one SIR, that SIR should be a request for offer (see below). In general when multiple SIRs are contemplated, the initial SIR should request general information, and future SIRs should request successively more specific information.

AMS 3.2.2.3.1.2.1 describes three potential categories of SIRs. The first category is a request for only "qualification information" in order to screen out those companies that do not meet the FAA's minimum qualification requirements. The end result of this step is the establishment of a qualified vendor list (QVL). When this is done, only qualified vendors may compete for future procurements of the product or service with the result that no other companies are notified of the procurement.

The second category of SIR requests "screening information" from potential contractors. This information is essentially the same information that is included in the normal RFP — consisting of all information that the agency determines to be necessary to select the source. Thus, it should focus on information that directly relates to the key discriminators for the procurement. Types of information that may form the basis of a screening request include equipment/products for FAA testing, capability statements, draft/model contracts, technical proposals (including oral presentations, if appropriate), commercial pricing information, financial information, cost or price information, and cost or price proposals. Each SIR requesting screening information must include some cost or pricing information appropriate to the specific SIR level of detail.

The last category of SIR is the "request for offer," which is a request for an offeror to commit formally to provide the products or services required by the acquisition. The request for offer may take the form of an SIR, a proposed contract, or a purchase order. The response to the request for offer is a binding offer and will become a binding contract if signed by the contracting officer. If this type of SIR is used, the agency can request an offer from only the offeror that has been selected as a result of the evaluation of the second category SIR.

The AMS encourages open communication with the potential contractors without imposing the formalized clarification/discussion logic of the FAR. See AMS 3.2.2.3.1.2.2 stating:

> Communications with all potential offerors should take place throughout the source selection process. During the screening, selection, and debriefing phases of source selection, communications are coordinated with the CO. Communications may start in the planning phase and continue through contract award. All SIRs should clearly inform offerors how communications will be handled during the initial screening phase.

> The purpose of communications is to ensure there are mutual understandings between the FAA and the offerors about all aspects of the procurement, including the offerors' submittals/ proposals. Information disclosed as a result of oral or written communication with an offeror may be considered in the evaluation of an offeror's submittal(s).

AMS 3.2.2.3.1.2.3 encourages the use of a flexible evaluation methodology as follows:

> The evaluation methodology should be set up to allow for maximum flexibility in selecting the offeror(s) providing the best value. To facilitate such flexibility, the following should be considered in setting up evaluations:
>
> • Relative importance between criteria is not required (when relative importance is used, the relative order of importance between criteria should be disclosed).

- Each SIR may incorporate separate and/or distinct criteria that relate to the specific SIR discriminators.

- The use of either adjectival or numerical ratings is acceptable.

- Comparative evaluations between offerors' proposals/products are acceptable.

- The service organization should be selective/inventive concerning the screening requirements for document submissions (e.g., oral presentations, sample tests, plant visits, etc.).

- Communications with offerors during the evaluation may help clarify submittals, allow a fuller understanding of the offeror submittals, and provide a more comprehensive evaluation.

- Testing of products is encouraged to the maximum extent practical ("try before you buy").

- Award based on initial offers to other than the low cost or price offer is allowed.

The selection decision is based on the stated evaluation criteria, including cost or price considerations, and the source selection official must document the selection decision in a decision memorandum including the rational basis supporting the screening or selection decision, AMS 3.2.2.3.1.3. The contracting officer then transmits a proposed contract to the selected offeror, AMS 3.2.2.3.1.3.

All offerors that participated in the competitive process are notified of the award and given three working days from receipt of the notification to request a debriefing, AMS 3.2.2.3.1.4.

The last phase in this method is the preparation of a lessons learned memorandum, AMS 3.2.2.3.1.5. The purpose of this memorandum is to relay the agency's procurement experiences to other FAA personnel. The memorandum should highlight those issues that had a significant impact on their procurement.

## 2. Commercial and Simplified Purchase Method

This method permits the FAA to acquire commercial products and services from the marketplace using a simplified purchase method and best commercial practices. AMS 3.2.2.5.1 calls for procurement planning to —

- determine whether commercial items meet the FAA's needs;

- identify potential commercial sources; and

- publicly announce requirements in excess of $100,000.

Under this method, the contracting officer "should solicit an appropriate number of vendors to ensure quality products and services are delivered in a timely manner at a fair and reasonable price," and should state requirements in commercial terms, AMS 3.2.2.5.2.

AMS 3.2.2.5.3 gives maximum flexibility in selecting an efficient procurement process, as follows:

> The CO should determine the appropriate screening approach and format for vendor's responses (e.g., electronic, written, oral, use of standard commercial or FAA forms). The CO may also conduct communications with individual offerors, as appropriate, to address offeror understanding of the requirement, performance capability, prices, and other terms and conditions. For commercially available products, the CO is encouraged to use "commercial competition techniques" such as continuing market research throughout the process by using vendor proposals as the source of prices and commercially available capabilities and sharing that information with other vendors.

The contracting officer's selection decision is to be based on the FAA's stated evaluation criteria, AMS 3.2.2.5.4. The selection criteria should include such factors as price, functional specifications, delivery capability, warranty, and payment terms, AMS 3.2.2.5.4. The method of selection and rationale for awards should be documented, as well as a determination that the price is fair and reasonable, AMS 3.2.2.5.4.1.

## 3. Protests

Protests of FAA procurements may not be taken to GAO, 49 U.S.C. § 40110(d)(2)(F). Rather, they are handled by the FAA Office of Dispute Resolution for Acquisition (ODRA), 14 C.F.R. § 17.5. Procedures for such protests are published at 14 C.F.R. Part 17, Subparts A and B. See also AMS 3.9. These procedures are similar to those followed by GAO except that they contain greater emphasis on using the alternative disputes resolution procedures prescribed in Subpart D. Decisions of the ODRA can be appealed to the Court of Appeals for the District of Columbia Circuit or any other circuit having jurisdiction over the protester, 49 U.S.C. § 46110(d)(4). See also *J.A. Jones Mgmt. Servs. v. FAA*, 225 F.3d 761 (D.C. Cir. 2000); and *Multimax, Inc. v. FAA*, 231 F.3d 882 (D.C. Cir. 2000).

## B. Postal Service

The Postal Reorganization Act of 1970, Pub. L. No. 91-375, codified at 39 U.S.C. § 101 et seq., abolished the old Post Office Department and in its place created the U.S. Postal Service as an independent establishment of the executive branch. Under the Act, Congress exempted the Postal Service from most statutes and regulations relating to government procurement, 39 U.S.C. § 410(a). The Postal Service follows special procedures that were set forth in the *U.S. Postal Service Procurement Manual* until 1997. That was followed by the *U.S. Postal Service Purchasing Manual* that was issued in several editions between 1997 and 2005. These manuals were canceled with the issuance of very general policies in 39 C.F.R. Part 601 in May 2005, with revisions in October 2007. Pending the issuance of new detailed procedures, interim procedures were set forth in the *U.S. Postal Service Interim Internal Purchasing Guidelines*, May 19, 2005. Subsequently, on May 1, 2006 the agency published *Postal Service Supplying Principles and Practices* (SPs and Ps). These SPs and Ps are not published in the Federal Register but are available at *http://www.usps.com/cpim/ftp/manuals/spp/spp.pdf.* Since they are not referenced in 39 C.F.R. Part 601, it is likely that they do not have the force and effect of law and therefore are not binding on the agency. See *Asia Pacific Airlines v. United States*, 68 Fed. Cl. 8 (2005), *appeal dismissed*, 171 Fed. Appx. 837 (Fed. Cir. 2006), holding that the Purchasing Manual had the force and effect of law because it was referenced in 39 C.F.R. Part 601 and granting injunctive relief because the agency did not follow the procedures in the manual.

The basic policy set forth in 39 C.F.R. § 601.105(b) is that the Postal Service "may decline to accept or consider proposals when a person or organization exhibits unacceptable conduct or business practices that do not meet reasonable business expectations or does not provide a high level of confidence about the entity's current or future business relations." The regulation contains illustrations of the kinds of conduct that will be sanctioned and provides guidance on how such decisions can be contested.

The Postal Service SPs and Ps contain detailed discussion of procurement policies and procedures which are stated to be "advisory and illustrative" and "for internal use only." Thus, they confer broad discretion on procurement officials to adopt procedures that will attain "best value." They are in the nature of a purchasing manual, containing far more guidance on the conduct of the acquisition process than is contained in the Federal Acquisition Regulation. They place a heavy emphasis on thoroughly planning procurements by conducting market research, communications with industry, risk analysis, and preparation of requirement documents.

The Postal Service SPs and Ps do not require full and open competition, but rather require only "adequate competition," stating:

> Competitive purchases should be made on the basis of adequate competition whenever feasible. Adequate competition means the solicitation of a sufficient number of the best qualified suppliers to ensure that the required quality and quantity of goods and services are obtained when needed and that the price that is fair and reasonable.

The guidance emphasizes, much like the FAA, that it is highly beneficial to prequalify suppliers before a competition is actually conducted.

Publicizing procurements is done on the governmentwide point of entry (*www. fedbizopps.gov*) but such publication is discretionary. Offers are solicited using Requests for Proposal and contracting officers are encouraged to make RFPs available to any company that requests one. The competitive negotiation process used is much like FAR Part 15 except that it gives contracting officers far more freedom to use commercial practices. Thus, there is no firm rule on the time allowed for submission of proposals, late proposals may be accepted, evaluators are permitted to make comparative evaluations of proposals, and communications are encouraged at any time during the procurement process to obtain a better value from the competitors. All communications are called "discussions" and the following broad guidance is given:

> During the evaluation process, including during oral presentations, discussions may be held with any supplier to clear up misunderstandings or uncertainties or to gain a better understanding of the supplier's proposal (including price) in order to obtain a more informed comparison of the relative value of individual proposals.

> After proposal comparisons have been made, further discussions may be held to address any outstanding matters. Suppliers whose offers are the subject of discussion at any stage must be given sufficient time to revise their proposals in light of those discussions.

The guidance distinguishes between "discussions" and "negotiations," and recommends negotiations as the final step in the process of selecting the winning offeror:

> Discussions and negotiations are not the same. . . . Generally, negotiations are held with one or more suppliers after [the team] has determined that . . . [their] proposal has the best chance of providing the Postal Service the best value. The goal of negotiations is to come to final agreement on contract terms and conditions, including contract type and price.

> \* \* \*

> Before opening negotiations, [the team] must clearly categorize negotiation objectives that are either *must* points (terms and conditions that are essential to desired contract performance that the Postal Service must obtain), or *give* points (terms and conditions that are not central to the Postal Service obtaining best value). . . . In order to avoid deadlock, the Contracting Officer will have to properly balance what is given and what is taken, especially as final agreement becomes more imminent, while focusing on obtaining the *must* points.

This provision is significantly different from the FAR Part 15 process in that there is no competitive range determination, no mandatory discussions with offerors in the competitive range, no final proposal revisions and the contracting officer is permitted to negotiate with the winning offeror after selection of the source.

The Postal Service also has special procedures for purchasing architect-engineer services, construction, design-build contracting, construction management services, mail transportation, professional/technical and consultant services, and information technology.

Protests may not be taken to GAO, *Falcon Sys., Inc.*, 65 Comp. Gen. 584 (B-222549), 86-1 CPD ¶ 462, *recons. denied*, 86-1 CPD ¶ 526, but they may be taken to the Court of Federal Claims, *Hewlett-Packard Co. v. United States*, 41 Fed. Cl. 99 (1998); *Emery Worldwide Airlines, Inc. v. United States*, 49 Fed. Cl. 211, *aff'd*, 264 F.3d 1071 (Fed. Cir. 2001). 39 C.F.R. § 601.107(b) also provides for internal procedures to consider protests as follows:

> (b) *Policy*. It is the policy of the Postal Service and in the interest of suppliers to resolve disagreements by mutual agreement between the supplier and the responsible contracting officer. All disagreements arising in connection with the purchasing process must be lodged with the responsible contracting officer in writing via facsimile, e-mail, hand delivery, or U.S. Mail, within ten days of the date the supplier received notification of award or ten days from the date the supplier received a debriefing. During the supplier-contracting officer ten-day resolution period, the responsible contracting officer's management may help to resolve the disagreement. At the conclusion of the ten-day resolution period, the contracting officer must communicate, in writing, to the supplier his or her resolution of the disagreement.

> (c) *Alternative dispute resolution*. Alternative dispute resolution (ADR) procedures may be used, if agreed to by all interested parties. The use of ADR to resolve the disagreement must be considered, regardless of the nature of the disagreement or when it occurred during the purchasing process. If the use of ADR is agreed upon, the ten-day limitation is suspended; if the parties cannot reach an agreement under ADR, the supplier has ten days to lodge its disagreement with the [Supplier Disagreement Resolution] Official.

39 C.F.R. § 601.108 attempts to narrow the extent of judicial resolution of these protests by the following provisions relating to resolution of protests by the Supplier Disagreement Resolution (SDR) Official:

> (b) *Scope and applicability*. In order to resolve expeditiously disagreements that are not resolved at the responsible contracting officer level, to reduce litigation expenses, inconvenience, and other costs for all parties, and to facilitate successful business relationships with Postal Service suppliers, the supplier community, and other persons, the following procedure is established as the sole and exclusive means to resolve disagreements. All disagreements will be lodged with and resolved, with finality, by the SDR Official under and in accordance with the sole and exclusive procedure established in this section.

\* \* \*

*(f) Guidance.* In considering and in resolving a disagreement, the SDR Official will be guided by the regulations contained in this part and all applicable public laws enacted by Congress. Non-Postal Service procurement rules or regulations and revoked Postal Service regulations will not apply or be taken into account in resolving disagreements. Failure of any party to provide requested information may be taken into account by the SDR Official in the decision.

(g) *Binding decision.* A decision of the SDR Official will be final and binding on the person or organization lodging the disagreement, other interested parties, and the Postal Service. However, the person or organization that lodged the disagreement or another interested person may appeal the decision of the SDR Official to a federal court with jurisdiction over such claims, but only on the grounds that the decision was procured by fraud or other criminal misconduct, or was obtained in violation of the regulations contained in this part or an applicable public law enacted by Congress.

These procedures were adopted in 70 Fed. Reg. 20,292, April 19, 2005, and amended slightly in 72 Fed. Reg. 58,251, Oct. 15, 2007. No reported judicial decision has been found challenging their validity.

# CHAPTER 8

# INTERAGENCY ACQUISITIONS

## I. USE OF INTERAGENCY ACQUISITION

Interagency acquisition is a process in which one agency acquires supplies or services by placing an order against a contract awarded by another agency or by asking another agency to award a contract or place an order on its behalf. It permits agencies to benefit from the efficiencies achievable through the use of contracts already in existence and from the specialized expertise of other agencies with respect to certain types of purchases. Rules and guidance for the conduct of interagency acquisitions are in the FAR and agency FAR supplements, in a publication of the Office of Federal Procurement Policy, *Interagency Acquisitions*, June 2008 (*http://www.whitehouse.gov/sites/default/files/omb/assets/omb/procurement/interagency_acq/iac_revised.pdf*), and in publications and at websites of the agencies that provide interagency acquisition services.

Interagency acquisitions are conducted mainly through the use of three types of "vehicles" contracts established under various statutes:

- General Services Administration (GSA) schedule contracts under 40 U.S.C. § 501 and 41 U.S.C. § 153(3) and schedule contracts awarded by other agencies;

- Governmentwide Acquisition Contracts (GWACs) for information technology under 40 U.S.C. § 11302(e); and

- Multiagency Contracts (MACs) under the Economy Act, 31 U.S.C. § 1535.

These vehicles are indefinite-delivery indefinite-quantity (IDIQ) contracts that contain (a) lists of available items of supply and unit prices, or (b) broad statements of work for services and hourly labor rates that include contractor G&A and profit (often referred to as "fully burdened" or "loaded" rates). In the case of services, detailed specification of requirements can be deferred until the time at which orders are issued. Those features make such contracts readily adaptable to the various needs of different requesting agencies and analogous to shopping malls. Large numbers of such contracts have been awarded that overlap in their coverage — so many of them that the government has had to establish a website to list them. This has given rise to a paradox of choice — with so many possibilities and no readily available comparative data, requesting agencies sometimes cannot determine which vehicle offers the best value for any given requirement without undertaking considerable administrative effort.

In addition to the three types of contract vehicles, Congress has established "franchise funds" — organizations within Executive departments and independent agencies that are set up to function like commercial service providers of common administrative services and that are funded by revolving funds. The franchise funds were authorized as a pilot program by S. 403 of the Government Management Reform Act of 1994, Pub. L. No. 103-356, 108 Stat. 3410, and have been subsequently reauthorized.

## A. Definitions

FAR 2.101 contains the following definitions:

"Interagency acquisition" means a procedure by which an agency needing supplies or services (the requesting agency) obtains them from another agency (the servicing agency), by an assisted acquisition or a direct acquisition. The term includes —

> (1) Acquisitions under the Economy Act (31 U.S.C. 1535); and

> (2) Non-Economy Act acquisitions completed under other statutory authorities, (e.g., General Services Administration Federal Supply Schedules in subpart 8.4 and Governmentwide acquisition contracts (GWACs)).

"Assisted acquisition" means a type of interagency acquisition where a servicing agency performs acquisition activities on a requesting agency's behalf, such as awarding and administering a contract, task order, or delivery order.

"Direct acquisition" means a type of interagency acquisition where a requesting agency places an order directly against a servicing agency's indefinite-delivery contract. The servicing agency manages the indefinite-delivery contract but does not participate in the placement or administration of an order.

"Requesting agency" means the agency that has the requirement for an interagency acquisition.

"Servicing agency" means the agency that will conduct an assisted acquisition on behalf of the requesting agency.

"Governmentwide acquisition contract (GWAC)" means a task-order or delivery-order contract for information technology established by one agency for Governmentwide use that is operated —

> (1) By an executive agent designated by the Office of Management and Budget pursuant to 40 U.S.C. 11302(e); or

> (2) Under a delegation of procurement authority issued by the General Services Administration (GSA) prior to August 7, 1996, under authority

granted GSA by former section 40 U.S.C. 759, repealed by Pub. L. 104-106. The Economy Act does not apply to orders under a Governmentwide acquisition contract.

"Multi-agency contract (MAC)" means a task-order or delivery-order contract established by one agency for use by Government agencies to obtain supplies and services, consistent with the Economy Act (see 17.502-2). Multi-agency contracts include contracts for information technology established pursuant to 40 U.S.C. 11314(a)(2).

# B. Background

## 1. Controversies

Although agencies have engaged in interagency acquisitions for many years, the number of such acquisitions surged in the mid-1990s as agencies sought ways to compensate for shortages in contracting personnel, to avoid unnecessarily duplicative administrative costs, to circumvent limits on their own acquisition authority, and to extend the time available for obligating appropriated funds. The process has been referred to as "offloading." As early as 1993 GAO, agency inspectors general, and Congress expressed concerns about the ways in which agencies conducted such transactions. Those concerns were summarized by Senator William S. Cohen at a hearing conducted on July 30, 1993, by the Senate Committee on Governmental Affairs, Subcommittee on Oversight of Government Management:

> Mr. Chairman, I would like to commend you for holding this hearing to examine problems that arise when one agency of the government uses another agency's contract to buy goods and services. This practice, known as off-loading, is permitted under the Economy Act of 1932, and has created a significant loophole in the safeguards established for federal procurement. This loophole enables contracting officers to by-pass important safeguards and makes taxpayers vulnerable to waste and abuse.

> In 1984, Congress passed the Competition in Contracting Act (CICA) to create checks and balances in a procurement system that brought us $640 toilet seats and $435 claw hammers. It has taken almost a decade but a number of contracting offices have discovered off-loading as a way to sidestep the procurement safeguards — safeguards we included in CICA to ensure the integrity of the procurement process and protect taxpayer dollars.

> As commonly practiced, off-loading permits circumvention of competition and results in the unchecked expenditure of billions of taxpayer dollars. Despite the potential for abuse, agencies and contractors alike defend the off-loading loophole saying it provides a win-win situation — the contractors get the business and the government gets it's [sic] goods in a timely manner, all without having to go through the "arduous" process of competition. However, what you don't hear is that the big loser when off-loading is abused is the taxpayer. In one example of

an off-load arrangement constructed specifically to avoid competition, the Army actually instructed NASA's Jet Propulsion Laboratory to award the contract to a specific vendor the Army wanted.

There is also little incentive for agencies to curb offloading activity. It has become a fast way to obligate funds and receive goods and services. Another contributing factor is that agencies make money by charging fees for allowing other agencies to buy off of their existing contracts. These fees which range between one and 30 percent for each contract action, are ostensibly used to cover overhead costs. However, GAO has recently reported that off-loading fees charged by NASA's Jet Propulsion Laboratory bear little relation to the actual cost of overhead or contract office performance. In addition, there is little or no accountability of the fees agencies charge for off-loading.

Off-loading is pervasive throughout government and is growing.

In other testimony at the same hearing, the Deputy Under Secretary of Defense (Acquisition Reform) acknowledged the problem, stating:

I agree with the [Department of Defense Inspector General] that some program officials, in what I believe to be an earnest effort to achieve positive results and to accomplish their missions in a timely manner, have violated our regulations for placing orders under the Economy Act. Under the regulation, a DoD contracting officer must make a determination that it is in the best interest of the government to place an order under the Economy Act. I believe the main reason for this disregard of our contracting procedures is the mounting frustration of program officials with the increasing time it takes to make a contract award. Organizations such as the Library of Congress and the TVA [Tennessee Valley Authority] are able to conduct their contracting activities in a shorter period of time than DoD because they are not subject to all of the laws governing DoD. These laws have increased lead times on many non-major system awards to an average of six to eight months in DoD. The Library of Congress and the TVA were able to issue the orders in question in a few days.

I am not condoning this behavior, but I understand that pressures to get the job done may lead some program officials to take short cuts in an acquisition process that must be simplified and streamlined.

## 2.  The MAC/GWAC Program Managers Compact

In 1997, in response to rising concerns, the Administrator of the Office of Federal Procurement Policy negotiated an agreement among agency managers of MACs and GWACs — the Multiagency/GWAC Program Managers Compact, which provided in part as follows:

III. PRINCIPLES

Judicious management of multiagency contracts and GWACs requires adherence to the following principles.

A. Structuring Multiagency Contracts and GWACs

We agree to assess the potential magnitude of interagency orders to ensure that we have or will have adequate resources to properly administer the combined resultant workload. We further agree to consider, if necessary, placing limits on the size of individual orders, as well as initial limits on the amount of interagency usage, subject to periodic adjustment based on our demonstrated ability to adequately manage the contract in light of the volume of orders received.

We agree to provide electronic access to sufficient information to minimize the burden of using these contracts. We have placed or will consider placing this information on our Websites along with a link to the Acquisition Reform Network (ARNet).

We agree that the functions we perform will be limited to those that are inherently governmental. If fees are established to recover the costs of performing these functions, they shall be at the level necessary to cover actual costs for managing and administering the multiagency contract or GWAC. We agree that fees should be established so that the projected total revenue generated by the use of these contracts do not exceed projected actual costs. We further agree that fees should be adjusted so that total revenues do not exceed actual costs.

We commit to use, to the maximum extent practicable, small businesses (including small disadvantaged and women-owned businesses) at the prime or subcontract levels.

We agree to define ordering processes that are easy to understand and that emphasize streamlined procedures and electronic processes. We further agree to explain our approach for ensuring that all contractors are given a fair opportunity to be considered for individual task orders.

B. Accepting Tasks

We agree to remind the requesting agency of its obligation to determine the economy and efficiency of using those contracts to meet its needs. We further agree to remind the requesting agency that it must follow the requirements set forth in OMB Circular A-76 when applicable.

We agree to remind the requesting agency of its obligation to perform quality reviews of work statements to ensure that tasks are within the scope of the multiagency contract or GWAC, and that they reflect specific requirements.

We agree to remind the requesting agencies of their obligation to ensure that tasks satisfy their internal requirements, such as architectural standards for information technology. We will further remind requesting agencies that their use of multiagency contracts or GWACs does not relieve them of their responsibility to comply with applicable laws, regulations, and policies governing federal procurement.

We agree to encourage the requesting agency to use performance-based work statements to the maximum extent practicable. We further agree, for services that would be in the highest demand, to develop performance-based service contracting (PBSC) templates that could be used by the requesting agency to develop PBSC task orders.

We agree that contracts or GWACs should not be used for the sole purpose of obligating expiring funds at the end of a fiscal year. The requesting agency should have a bona fide need in the fiscal year to which funds are being obligated and follow all other appropriation law requirements.

C. Processing Orders

We agree to ensure that contractors are given a fair opportunity to be considered and that the exceptions to fair opportunity recognized in FAR 16.505 are used appropriately.

We agree to incorporate a best value approach and use past performance in determining contractors for individual tasks.

We will strive to minimize contractor costs associated with preparing proposals for orders. Where appropriate, we will consider limiting the size of written proposals, or encouraging the use of oral proposals. We further agree that proposal detail should be tailored to the minimum level necessary for adequate evaluation and selection for award.

D. Administering Orders

We agree to record information regarding contractor performance on orders and make it available to source selection officials to facilitate maximum practical consideration of past performance in awarding subsequent tasks.

E. Recompeting or Establishing New Multiagency Contracts

We agree to recompete or establish our own multiagency contract only after we determine that such a vehicle is in the best interest of the government and the most cost effective means of satisfying our requirements. In making this decision, we will consider (1) the economies and efficiencies to be gained by establishing our own multiagency contract, in light of the existence and feasibility of having our needs met through another agency, or multiagency contracts and (2) if the requirements are generally within our mission or competency to award.

### 3.  The Services Acquisition Reform Act Advisory Panel

Much of the concern about interagency acquisition arose from its use in the acquisition of services. In 2003, Congress enacted the Services Acquisition Reform Act, Title XIV of the National Defense Authorization Act of 2004, Pub. L. No. 108-136. Section 1423 of the Act directed the Administrator of the Office of Federal Procurement Policy to appoint an advisory panel to review acquisition laws and regulations governing the acquisition of services. One of the topics to be investigated was "performance of acquisition functions across agency lines of responsibility and the use of Governmentwide contracts." The panel devoted Chapter 3 of its January 2007 report to interagency acquisition. See *Report of the Acquisition Advisory Panel to the Office of Federal Procurement Policy and the United States Congress, https://www.acquisition.gov/comp/aap/24102_GSA.pdf.* The panel introduced the topic as follows:

> The performance of acquisition functions across agency lines is almost exclusively accomplished through the use of interagency contract vehicles described in detail in the next section. The significant increase in the use of these vehicles by agencies over the last ten years has raised a number of complex policy issues and has been the subject of extensive oversight by Congress, the Government Accountability Office ("GAO"), the inspectors general ("IGs") of various federal agencies, outside organizations, and the media. This attention has highlighted significant benefits in award efficiencies these vehicles provide to the federal government and the taxpayer. It has also uncovered past deficiencies in their creation and administration and continuing risks associated with their use.
>
> Several critical observations have been made regarding the creation and use of interagency contract vehicles. In its January 2005 High Risk Update, GAO observed that a number of factors contribute to making these vehicles high risk in certain circumstances:
>
> > 1) they are attracting rapid growth of taxpayer dollars;
> >
> > 2) they are being used and administered by some agencies with limited expertise in this contracting method; and
> >
> > 3) they contribute to a significantly more complex environment in which accountability has not always been clearly established.

After making several findings, the panel concluded:

> There is little doubt that interagency contracts can and do provide significant benefits and efficiencies, but these efficiencies have been narrowly viewed primarily as transaction efficiencies such as reduced pre-award lead time and protest risk. Interagency contracts broadly defined are important to the operation of the federal acquisition process. Witnesses speaking on the subject before the Panel identified

the benefits of interagency contracts and several remarked that they viewed them as essential for meeting mission needs. However, the focus on transaction-based value hides the even greater efficiencies to be gained if interagency contracts are employed toward the goal of creating strategic governmentwide efficiencies. Unfortunately, the lack of readily available, reliable and timely data on the use and management of interagency contracts has hampered the government's ability to realize the more strategic value of these contracts. This lack of data is a barrier to strategic planning as well as oversight, on both an enterprise-wide and government-wide basis.

The Panel believes that meaningful improvements to interagency contracting practices can be achieved by agencies focusing their efforts on a sound and consistent process that provides oversight during the creation and the continuation (or reauthorization) of these contracts. Many of the issues identified by GAO and agency IGs dealing with the misuse of these vehicles are related to the internal controls, management and oversight, and division of roles and responsibilities between the vehicle holder and ordering agency. These issues can best be addressed with a government-wide policy that requires agencies to specifically and deliberately address these matters at the point of creation and continuation rather than attempting to remedy these problems at the point of use. The current lack of an established process and limited transparency allows for the proliferation of these vehicles in a largely uncoordinated, bottom-up fashion, focusing attention on the short term, transaction-based benefits of reduced procurement lead time. The Panel and the Working Group received testimony from government witnesses who stated that interagency vehicles are often utilized when an agency does not have ample time to fully define its acquisition requirements. Establishing guidelines for the creation and continuation of these vehicles will help to ensure they are used as an effective tool for enterprise-wide and government-wide strategic sourcing.

See *Oversight Plan Needed to Help Implement Acquisition Advisory Panel Recommendations*, GAO-08-160 (2007).

## 4.  The Duncan Hunter National Defense Authorization Act

In 2009, Congress enacted the Duncan Hunter National Defense Authorization Act for Fiscal Year 2009, Pub. L. No. 110-417. Section 865 was entitled, "Preventing Abuse of Interagency Contracts" and provided as follows:

(a) Office of Management and Budget Policy Guidance-

(1) REPORT AND GUIDELINES- Not later than one year after the date of the enactment of this Act, the Director of the Office of Management and Budget shall —

(A) submit to Congress a comprehensive report on interagency acquisitions, including their frequency of use, management controls, cost-effectiveness, and savings generated; and

(B) issue guidelines to assist the heads of executive agencies in improving the management of interagency acquisitions.

(2) MATTERS COVERED BY GUIDELINES- For purposes of paragraph (1)(B), the Director shall include guidelines on the following matters:

(A) Procedures for the use of interagency acquisitions to maximize competition, deliver best value to executive agencies, and minimize waste, fraud, and abuse.

(B) Categories of contracting inappropriate for interagency acquisition.

(C) Requirements for training acquisition workforce personnel in the proper use of interagency acquisitions.

(b) Regulations Required —

(1) IN GENERAL- Not later than one year after the date of the enactment of this Act, the Federal Acquisition Regulation shall be revised to require that all interagency acquisitions —

(A) include a written agreement between the requesting agency and the servicing agency assigning responsibility for the administration and management of the contract;

(B) include a determination that an interagency acquisition is the best procurement alternative; and

(C) include sufficient documentation to ensure an adequate audit.

(2) MULTI-AGENCY CONTRACTS — Not later than one year after the date of the enactment of this Act, the Federal Acquisition Regulation shall be revised to require any multi-agency contract entered into by an executive agency after the effective date of such regulations to be supported by a business case analysis detailing the administration of such contract, including an analysis of all direct and indirect costs to the Federal Government of awarding and administering such contract and the impact such contract will have on the ability of the Federal Government to leverage its purchasing power.

(c) Agency Reporting Requirement — The senior procurement executive for each executive agency shall, as directed by the Director of the Office of Management and Budget, submit to the Director annual reports on the actions taken by the executive agency pursuant to the guidelines issued under subsection (a).

(d) Definitions — In this section:

(1) The term "executive agency" has the meaning given such term in section 4(1) of the Office of Federal Procurement Policy Act (41 U.S.C. 403(1)), except that, in the case of a military department, it means the Department of Defense.

(2) The term "head of executive agency" means the head of an executive agency except that, in the case of a military department, the term means the Secretary of Defense.

(3) The term "interagency acquisition" means a procedure by which an executive agency needing supplies or services (the requesting agency) obtains them from another executive agency (the servicing agency). The term includes acquisitions under section 1535 of title 31, United States Code (commonly referred to as the "Economy Act"), Federal Supply Schedules above $500,000, and Governmentwide acquisition contracts.

(4) The term "multi-agency contract" means a task or delivery order contract established for use by more than one executive agency to obtain supplies and services, consistent with section 1535 of title 31, United States Code (commonly referred to as the "Economy Act").

The regulations promulgated to implement S. 865 were added to FAR by Federal Acquisition Circular 2005-47, Item III, 75 Fed. Reg. 77733-37, Dec. 13, 2010, which added definitions of interagency acquisition, direct acquisition, assisted acquisition, requesting agency, and servicing agency to FAR 2.101; revised FAR 8.404, Use of Federal Supply Schedules; added new Subpart 17.5, and made minor changes to several other parts. These are the core rules for interagency contracting.

## C. Policy and Procedure

FAR Subpart 17.5 states general policies and procedures for the conduct of interagency acquisitions, which are designed to ensure compliance with applicable laws and regulations and proper use of appropriations. FAR 17.500 applies those policies and procedures to all prospective interagency acquisitions except those valued at $500,000 or less that are conducted through the GSA Federal Supply Schedule program. FAR 17.501 states the general policy for interagency acquisitions as follows:

(a) Interagency acquisitions are commonly conducted through indefinite-delivery contracts, such as task- and delivery-order contracts. The indefinite-delivery contracts used most frequently to support interagency acquisitions are Federal Supply Schedules (FSS), Governmentwide acquisition contracts (GWACs), and multi-agency contracts (MACs).

(b) An agency shall not use an interagency acquisition to circumvent conditions and limitations imposed on the use of funds.

(c) An interagency acquisition is not exempt from the requirements of subpart 7.3, Contractor Versus Government Performance.

(d) An agency shall not use an interagency acquisition to make acquisitions conflicting with any other agency's authority or responsibility (for example, that of the Administrator of General Services under title 40, United States Code, "Public Buildings, Property and Works" and title III of the Federal Property and Administrative Services Act of 1949).

# 1. *Determination of Best Procurement Approach*

FAR 17.502-1(a) requires that before proceeding with an interagency acquisition, an agency must determine the best procurement approach:

(a) Determination of best procurement approach.

(1) Assisted acquisitions. Prior to requesting that another agency conduct an acquisition on its behalf, the requesting agency shall make a determination that the use of an interagency acquisition represents the best procurement approach. As part of the best procurement approach determination, the requesting agency shall obtain the concurrence of the requesting agency's responsible contracting office in accordance with internal agency procedures. At a minimum, the determination shall include an analysis of procurement approaches, including an evaluation by the requesting agency that using the acquisition services of another agency —

(i) Satisfies the requesting agency's schedule, performance, and delivery requirements (taking into account factors such as the servicing agency's authority, experience, and expertise as well as customer satisfaction with the servicing agency's past performance);

(ii) Is cost effective (taking into account the reasonableness of the servicing agency's fees); and

(iii) Will result in the use of funds in accordance with appropriation limitations and compliance with the requesting agency's laws and policies.

(2) Direct acquisitions. Prior to placing an order against another agency's indefinite-delivery vehicle, the requesting agency shall make a determination that use of another agency's contract vehicle is the best procurement approach. At a minimum, the determination shall include an analysis, including factors such as:

(i) The suitability of the contract vehicle;

(ii) The value of using the contract vehicle, including —

(A) The administrative cost savings from using an already existing contract;

(B) Lower prices, greater number of vendors, and reasonable vehicle access fees; and

(iii) The expertise of the requesting agency to place orders and administer them against the selected contract vehicle throughout the acquisition lifecycle.

The best procurement approach presumably will be the one most likely to yield the best combination of price, quality, delivery, and administrative convenience. In order to make such a determination, a prospective requesting agency should conduct market research to discover what is available under existing contracts and what is available on the open market. In order to prevent the bypassing of internal contracting policy, procedure, and limitations, a decision to proceed with an assisted acquisition, turning the acquisition over to another contracting office, must be approved by the requesting agency's contracting office. Presumably, this decision will be made because the agency contracting office does not have the capacity or expertise to conduct the acquisition with its own resources. Alternatively, the agency contracting office can obtain the required supplies or services through a direct acquisition. Any decision to proceed with an interagency acquisition, assisted or direct, must take into account the expertise of the servicing agency.

The proliferation of interagency vehicles since the mid-1990s has greatly complicated market research, made price comparisons for similar products and services difficult, and has caused considerable confusion. In order to assist market researchers, the government has established an Internet Interagency Contract Directory, *https://www.contractdirectory.gov/contractdirectory/*, which is based on information obtained from the Federal Procurement Data System — Next Generation from 1979 through the present. The database may be searched for any indefinite-delivery contract signed on or after October 1, 2006. Searches may be made by product or service description. The database includes information about each contract, such as the types of supplies and services that may be acquired under the contract, whether the contract is available for interagency acquisition, the awarding agency, the pricing arrangements that may be used, the contractor's socioeconomic status, the capacity remaining in the indefinite-delivery vehicle maximum quantity, and the last date on which orders may be placed. The database is updated every 24 hours. In addition to this general database, there are specialized databases, such as the National Interagency Fire Center Forest Service Contracting Directory, *http://www.fs.fed.us/ fire/contracting/directory/directory.htm*. Many contractors maintain websites in order to advertise their availability through interagency vehicles. As is the case for all Internet sources, these sources are subject to change at any time.

## 2. Interagency Agreements for Assisted Acquisitions

If an agency decides to proceed with an assisted acquisition, FAR 17.502-1 requires that the requesting agency and the servicing agency enter into an interagency agreement:

(b) Written agreement on responsibility for management and administration.

(1) Assisted acquisitions.

(i) Prior to the issuance of a solicitation, the servicing agency and the requesting agency shall both sign a written interagency agreement that establishes the general terms and conditions governing the relationship between the parties, including roles and responsibilities for acquisition planning, contract execution, and administration and management of the contract(s) or order(s). The requesting agency shall provide to the servicing agency any unique terms, conditions, and applicable agency-specific statutes, regulations, directives, and other applicable requirements for incorporation into the order or contract; for patent rights, see 27.304-2. In preparing interagency agreements to support assisted acquisitions, agencies should review the Office of Federal Procurement Policy guidance, *Interagency Acquisitions*, available at *http://www.whitehouse.gov/omb/assets/procurement/iac_revised.pdf*.

(ii) Each agency's file shall include the interagency agreement between the requesting and servicing agency, and shall include sufficient documentation to ensure an adequate audit consistent with 4.801(b).

(2) Direct acquisitions. The requesting agency administers the order; therefore, no written agreement with the servicing agency is required.

FAR 17.502-1(b) prescribes only general requirements for interagency agreements. However, *Interagency Acquisitions* contains detailed guidance.

An interagency agreement may cover a single acquisition or multiple acquisitions that may be conducted during a specified period of time. Interagency agreements contain two key parts: A. General Terms and Conditions and B. Requirements and Funding Information. Part A states the overall agreement between the agencies and specifies roles and responsibilities — who will do what. It may cover a single acquisition or a number of acquisitions to be conducted within a specific period of time. *Interagency Acquisitions* prescribes the following elements for Part A:

Purpose

Authority

Identifying number or other reference

Scope

Period

Roles & responsibilities

Billing & payment

Small business credit

Contract termination, disputes, & appeals

Interpretation of the agreement

Signatures

Part B must contain the details of a specific acquisition, such as the specification or statement of work, the source and identification of funds, billing and payment instructions, and restrictions. Each acquisition under an interagency agreement must be covered by its own Part B, which serves as the basis for and for authorization of the transfer of funds from the requesting agency to the servicing agency and the obligation of funds by the requesting agency. The requesting agency incurs and must record an obligation of funds when the servicing agency accepts each individual Part B, which must be prepared in sufficient detail to ensure that the funds are being used for the purpose and for the period of time for which they were appropriated. When an assisted interagency acquisition is to be incrementally funded, its Part B may be supplemented by addendum in order to document the transfer of an increment to the servicing agency. *Interagency Acquisitions* specifies the following elements for Part B:

Purpose

Authority

Identifying number or other reference

General terms & conditions

Project title

Description of products or services/bona fide need

Projected milestones

Billing & payment

Description of acquisition assistance

Fees

Obligation information

Requesting agency funding information

Servicing agency funding information

Description of requesting agency specific restrictions

Small business credit

Amendment procedure

Contact information

Signatures

Some agencies have published actual agreements or models for use as guidance. See, for example, Department of Defense, Memorandum from the Director, Defense Procurement, *Standard Interagency Agreement Part A for DOD Components and All DOE Components in FY 2011*, Dec. 16, 2010, which contains detailed guidance for agreements between the Department of Defense and the Department of Energy. *http://www.acq.osd. mil/dpap/policy/policyvault/USA006586-10-DPAP.pdf.* See also Department of Energy, Acquisition Letter AL 2011-03, *Interagency Acquisitions*, January 13, 2011. *http:// management.energy.gov/documents/AttachmentFlash2011-31AL_2011-03.pdf.* Several interagency agreements may be found by searching the Internet.

## 3. Economy Act Determinations and Findings

If there is no specific statutory authority for an interagency acquisition, such as the statutes authorizing the Federal Supply Schedule and GWACs, agencies can conduct such acquisitions under the Economy Act, 31 U.S.C. § 1535. FAR 17.502-2 states additional prerequisites for the conduct of such interagency acquisitions. FAR 17.502-2(b) requires preparation and approval of a determination and findings (D&F) for all Economy Act acquisitions, whether assisted or direct. The D&F must state that (1) use of interagency acquisition is in the best interests of the government and (2) acquisition of the supplies or services directly from a commercial source cannot be done as conveniently or economically.

If the servicing agency must award a contract or issue an order for the requesting agency, FAR 17.502-2(b)(2) requires that the D&F include a statement that at least one of the following circumstances applies:

(i) The acquisition will appropriately be made under an existing contract of the servicing agency, entered into before placement of the order, to meet the requirements of the servicing agency for the same or similar supplies or services.

(ii) The servicing agency has the capability or expertise to enter into a contract for such supplies or services that is not available within the requesting agency.

(iii) The servicing agency is specifically authorized by law or regulation to purchase such supplies or services on behalf of other agencies.

The D&F must be approved (signed) by a contracting officer of the requesting agency with authority to conduct the procurement or by another official designated by the agency head. If the servicing agency is not required to conduct its acquisitions in accordance with the FAR, e.g., the Bonneville Power Administration or the Federal Aviation Administration, the D&F must be approved by the requesting agency's Senior Procurement Executive or a higher level official. The requesting agency must furnish a copy of the D&F to the servicing agency.

## 4. *Establishment of Multiagency Contracts Under the Economy Act*

In order to control the proliferation of interagency vehicles, FAR 17.502-2 requires that agencies wanting to establish a multiagency contract for use by other agencies under the Economy Act prepare a "business-case analysis," which must include the following:

(d) Business-case analysis requirements for multi-agency contracts. In order to establish a multi-agency contract in accordance with Economy Act authority, a business-case analysis must be prepared by the servicing agency. The business-case analysis shall —

(1) Consider strategies for the effective participation of small businesses during acquisition planning (see 7.103(s));

(2) Detail the administration of such contract, including an analysis of all direct and indirect costs to the Government of awarding and administering such contract;

(3) Describe the impact such contract will have on the ability of the Government to leverage its purchasing power, e.g., will it have a negative effect because it dilutes other existing contracts;

(4) Include an analysis concluding that there is a need for establishing the multi-agency contract; and

(5) Document roles and responsibilities in the administration of the contract.

## D. Obligation of Appropriated Funds in Assisted Acquisition

When an agency conducts a direct acquisition by issuing an order against a GSA schedule contract, a GWAC, or a MAC, the rules for obligation of funds are the same as for non-interagency acquisitions — an obligation is made and must be recorded when the agency issues the order. However, when agencies conduct assisted acquisitions, the rules become more complex. There are three key issues: first, the authority to transfer appropriated funds and the limitations on the use of funds, second, the standard for recording an obligation, and third, the bona fide needs rule.

### 1. Transfer and Use of Funds

The transfer of appropriated funds within an agency or from one agency to another must be authorized by statute, such as the Economy Act, 31 U.S.C. § 1535. Unless otherwise authorized by statute, transferred funds continue to be available only for the purpose for which they were appropriated and only for the specified period of availability for obligation, 31 U.S.C. § 1532. This is true even when the funds are transferred for deposit in a revolving fund that is not subject to fiscal year limitations on availability. Thus, requesting agencies cannot "park" or "bank" funds by transferring them to servicing agencies in order to avoid restrictions on their use. This rule applies also to canceled unexpended balances of funds properly obligated within the period of availability, *United States Capitol Police — Advances to Volpe Center Working Capital Fund*, Comp. Gen. Dec. B-319349, June 4, 2010, *Unpub.*; *Implementation of the Library of Congress FEDLINK Revolving Fund*, Comp. Gen. Dec. B-288142, Sept. 6. 2001, *Unpub.*

### 2. Standard for Recording Obligations

The rules that govern the obligation of funds under interagency acquisitions are in 31 U.S.C. § 1501(a)(1) and (a)(3), 2 *Principles of Federal Appropriations Law* 3d, 7-28 to 7-29. 31 U.S.C. § 1501(a)(1) applies to transactions in which the requesting agency chooses to proceed through interagency acquisition. GAO refers to such transactions as "voluntary orders." 31 U.S.C. § 1501(a)(3) applies to those transactions in which the requesting agency is required by law to place the order with the servicing agency.

31 U.S.C. § 1501(a)(1) states:

(a) An amount shall be recorded as an obligation of the United States Government only when supported by documentary evidence of —

(1) a binding agreement between an agency and another person (including an agency) that is

(A) in writing, in a way and form, and for a purpose authorized by law; and

(B) executed before the end of the period of availability for obligation of the appropriation or fund used for specific goods to be delivered, real property to be bought or leased, or work or service to be provided. . . .

Thus, when a requesting agency enters into a binding agreement with a servicing agency, it must record an obligation of funds.

In order to be binding and properly recordable as an obligation under 31 U.S.C. § 1501(a)(1), an interagency agreement for a voluntary order must specify the supplies or services to be acquired in enough detail to establish the responsibilities of the servicing agency. In the absence of sufficient specificity, the agreement between the agencies is not binding and the requirement for documentary evidence of a binding agreement is not met. There is no obligation, and the recording of an obligation with the intent to complete the description of required supplies or services after the expiration of the period of funds availability would constitute improper "banking" or "parking" of funds, *Expired Funds and Interagency Agreements between GovWorks and the Dep't of Defense*, Comp. Gen. Dec. B-308944, July 17, 2007, *Unpub.* (descriptions of supplies in Military Interdepartmental Purchase Request too vague to establish binding agreement between requesting agency and servicing agency). Any attempt by the servicing agency or the requesting agency to complete the specification and obligate the funds after the last day of availability would violate the bona fide needs rule and might violate the Antideficiency Act.

An additional condition applies to interagency acquisitions governed by the Economy Act. 31 U.S.C. § 1535(d) states:

(d) An order placed or agreement made under this section obligates an appropriation of the ordering agency or unit. The amount obligated is deobligated to the extent that the agency or unit filling the order has not incurred obligations, before the end of the period of availability of the appropriation, in —

(1) providing goods or services; or

(2) making an authorized contract with another person to provide the requested goods or services.

Thus, while the requesting agency must record an obligation upon placing its order with the servicing agency, the servicing agency must subsequently obligate the funds by awarding a contract or placing an order before the period of funds availability has expired, otherwise the requesting agency must deobligate the funds, 2 *Principles of Federal Appropriations Law* 3d, 7-29 to 7-30, 12-43 to 12-46.

However, the deobligation requirement of the Economy Act does not apply to transactions carried out under other statutes. Thus, if proceeding under a different statute, and if the requesting agency validly recorded an obligation when it entered into an interagency agreement with a servicing agency, then the funds remain obligated and available for payment even if the servicing agency does not award a contract or place an order prior to the expiration of the period of funds availability. The servicing agency's contract or order must, however, fulfill a bona fide need of the requesting agency in the year for which the funds were appropriated, 2 *Principles of Federal Appropriations Law* 3d, 7-30 to 7-31. This will not violate the prohibition against "banking" or "parking" of funds as long as the interagency agreement is sufficiently specific in its description of the supplies or services required so as to constitute a binding agreement with the servicing agency.

For interagency transactions that are required by law, 31 U.S.C. § 1501(a)(3) requires only documentary evidence of "an order required by law to be placed with an agency." The deobligation rule of the Economy Act does not apply in such cases. See *Comptroller General Campbell to the Administrator, General Servs. Admin.*, 34 Comp. Gen. Dec. 705 (B-184830), June 28, 1955 (obligation by agency required by law to place order with GSA for building management operations was valid even though GSA does not award contract before last day of funds availability). However, the requesting agency's order still must be for a bona fide need of the year for which the funds were appropriated. See *Chemical Safety and Hazard Investigation Board — Interagency Agreement with the Gen. Servs. Admin.*, Comp. Gen. Dec. B-218425, Dec. 8, 2009, *Unpub.*; *Natural Res. Conservation Serv. — Obligating Orders with GSA's AutoChoice Summer Program*, Comp. Gen. Dec. B-317249, July 1, 2009, *Unpub.*

## E. Fees and Revenues

Servicing agencies must recover the costs of the supplies and services acquired and their administrative expenses. As a general rule, agencies may not augment their appropriations without statutory authorization. To charge more than costs would augment the servicing agency's appropriation; to charge less would augment the requesting agency's appropriation, 2 *Principles of Federal Appropriations Law* 3d, 6-162.

## 1. Reasonableness of Fees

In 2002 GAO found that servicing agencies were charging more than enough to cover their costs, in some cases substantially more. See *Contract Management: Interagency Contract Program Fees Need More Oversight*, GAO-02-734 (July 2004):

> Most of the contract service programs we reviewed reported an excess of revenues over costs in at least one year between fiscal years 1999 and 2001. The exceptions were the GWACs at Commerce and Transportation, which reported losses each year during this period. The [GSA] Schedules program has produced

exceptionally high earnings, with revenues exceeding costs by more than 53 percent — for a total of $151 million during the 3-year period.

OMB guidance directs agencies with GWACs or franchise fund programs to account for and recover fully allocated actual costs and to report on their financial results. Agencies are supposed to identify all direct and indirect costs and to charge fees to ordering agencies based on these costs. However, some GWAC programs have not identified or accurately reported the full cost of providing interagency contract services. Thus, there is no assurance that their fees accurately reflect their costs. Because OMB has not required agencies to submit annual financial reports summarizing program results that include a description of the agencies. indirect cost allocation methodologies, it was unaware that not all agencies are following its guidance.

OMB's guidance further directs that agencies transfer GWAC earnings to the miscellaneous receipts account of the U.S. Treasury's General Fund. However, the way agencies operate their revolving funds conflicts with OMB's guidance. Agencies that operate their GWACs under revolving funds have used GWAC earnings to support other programs within the revolving fund or to maintain fund operations. They have not transferred any GWAC earnings to the Treasury. These revolving funds were established by statutes that allow retention of earnings. Agency officials believe their revolving funds' statutory provisions prevail over OMB's guidance to GWAC agencies. OMB officials view this as an important issue that needs review.

The Schedules program has generated hefty earnings, largely because of the rapid growth of information technology sales. Rather than adjust the fee, however, GSA has used the earnings primarily to support GSA's stock program and fleet program. Both of these uses are permitted by the revolving fund in which the Schedules program resides. However, the significant amount of earnings means that Schedules program customers are, in effect, being consistently overcharged for the contract services they are buying. (Footnotes omitted.)

## 2. Fees Under the Economy Act

The Economy Act, 31 U.S.C. § 1535(b), expressly limits the amounts to be charged by servicing agencies to "estimated or actual cost as determined by the agency or unit filling the order." The servicing agency is entitled to invoice for payment in advance without prior audit or certification of its invoice.

## 3. GSA's Industrial Funding Fee

GSA's schedule program, which is carried out by its Federal Acquisition Service, is paid for through its Acquisition Services Fund, authorized by 40 U.S.C. § 303 and § 321. Pursuant to that authority, GSA establishes an "industrial funding fee." The rate is established annually and is set to recover the direct and indirect costs of GSA's operations. The fee is included in the schedule contract prices and is collected by the contractors and then reported and paid to GSA in accordance with a clause inserted in all schedule contracts, 48 C.F.R. § 552.238-74, Industrial Funding Fee and Sales Reporting, which states:

(a) Reporting of Federal Supply Schedule Sales. The Contractor shall report all contract sales under this contract as follows:

(1) The Contractor shall accurately report the dollar value, in U.S. dollars and rounded to the nearest whole dollar, of all sales under this contract by calendar quarter (January 1-March 31, April 1-June 30, July 1-September 30, and October 1-December 31). The dollar value of a sale is the price paid by the Schedule user for products and services on a Schedule task or delivery order. The reported contract sales value shall include the Industrial Funding Fee (IFF). The Contractor shall maintain a consistent accounting method of sales reporting, based on the Contractor's established commercial accounting practice. The acceptable points at which sales may be reported include —

(i) Receipt of order;

(ii) Shipment or delivery, as applicable;

(iii) Issuance of an invoice; or

(iv) Payment.

(2) Contract sales shall be reported to FSS within 30 calendar days following the completion of each reporting quarter. The Contractor shall continue to furnish quarterly reports, including "zero" sales, through physical completion of the last outstanding task order or delivery order of the contract.

(3) Reportable sales under the contract are those resulting from sales of contract items to authorized users unless the purchase was conducted pursuant to a separate contracting authority such as a Governmentwide Acquisition Contract (GWAC); a separately awarded FAR Part 12, FAR Part 13, FAR Part 14, or FAR Part 15 procurement; or a non-FAR contract. Sales made to state and local governments under Cooperative Purchasing authority shall be counted as reportable sales for IFF purposes.

(4) The Contractor shall electronically report the quarterly dollar value of sales, including "zero" sales, by utilizing the automated reporting system at an Internet website designated by the General Services Administration (GSA)'s Federal Supply Service (FSS). Prior to using this automated system, the Contractor shall complete contract registration with the FSS Vendor Support Center (VSC). The website address, as well as registration instructions and reporting procedures, will be provided at the time of award. The Contractor shall report sales separately for each National Stock Number (NSN), Special Item Number (SIN), or sub-item.

(5) The Contractor shall convert the total value of sales made in foreign currency to U.S. dollars using the "Treasury Reporting Rates of Exchange" issued by the U.S. Department of Treasury, Financial Management Service. The Contractor shall use the issue of the Treasury report in effect on the last day of the calendar quarter. The report is available from Financial Management Service, International Funds Branch, Telephone: (202) 874-7994, Internet: *http://www.fms.treas.gov/intn.html*.

(b) The Contractor shall remit the IFF at the rate set by GSA's FSS.

(1) The Contractor shall remit the IFF to FSS in U.S. dollars within 30 calendar days after the end of the reporting quarter; final payment shall be remitted within 30 days after physical completion of the last outstanding task order or delivery order of the contract.

(2) The IFF represents a percentage of the total quarterly sales reported. This percentage is set at the discretion of GSA's FSS. GSA's FSS has the unilateral right to change the percentage at any time, but not more than once per year. FSS will provide reasonable notice prior to the effective date of the change. The IFF reimburses FSS for the costs of operating the Federal Supply Schedules Program and recoups its operating costs from ordering activities. Offerors must include the IFF in their prices. The fee is included in the award price(s) and reflected in the total amount charged to ordering activities. FSS will post notice of the current IFF at *http://72a.fss.gsa.gov/* or successor website as appropriate.

(c) Within 60 days of award, an FSS representative will provide the Contractor with specific written procedural instructions on remitting the IFF. FSS reserves the unilateral right to change such instructions from time to time, following notification to the Contractor.

(d) Failure to remit the full amount of the IFF within 30 calendar days after the end of the applicable reporting period constitutes a contract debt to the United States Government under the terms of FAR Subpart 32.6. The Government may exercise all rights under the Debt Collection Improvement Act of 1996, including withholding or setting off payments and interest on the debt (see FAR clause 52.232-17, Interest). Should the Contractor fail to submit the required sales reports, falsify them, or fail to timely pay the IFF, this is sufficient cause for the Government to terminate the contract for cause.

## 4. Fees Charged by Franchise Funds and Other Revolving Funds

The amounts that may be charged by franchise funds and other revolving or working capital funds depends on their authorizing legislation. The franchise funds that provide assisted acquisition services pursuant to 31 U.S.C. § 501, note, and other authority may charge a fee of 4% above costs for acquisition of capital equipment and for the improvement and implementation of department financial management, information technology, and other support systems, and may receive payment in advance. See *Budget Issues: Franchise Fund Pilot Review*, GAO-03-1069, Aug. 2003.

## 5. *Interagency Agreement on Payment by Requesting Agency*

The amount, method, and timing of payment of the servicing agency by the requesting agency should be agreed upon in advance and stated in the interagency agreement. The following is an example of such a statement from a model agreement by the Department of the Interior:

B.10.  Service Charge

Services charges will be determined as follows: [insert description on how service charges will be accrued and collected.]

Example 1: The Servicing Agency shall earn a service charge upon the execution of any award or modification under this IA in the amount of [insert percentage] of the total funds obligated under that award or modification, in consideration of acquisition services rendered by the Servicing Agency on behalf of the Requesting Agency.

In the event that an award or modification under this IA is canceled by the Requesting Agency prior to award but after pre-award acquisition services have been rendered by the Servicing Agency on behalf of the Requesting Agency, the Servicing Agency shall earn a service charge in the amount of [insert percentage] of the Requesting Agency's estimated cost of the acquisition, in consideration of these services.

Example 2: The Servicing Agency shall earn a service charge equal to the total estimated cost to AQD to provide services to the Requesting Agency for a period of one year. For the first year of this IA, this service charge shall be [insert specific dollar amount].

## II.  GSA SCHEDULE CONTRACTS

GSA provides access by federal agencies and, in some cases, by state and local government agencies and other organizations, to contracts for a wide variety of commercial products and services through its schedules program. The program is interchangeably referred to as Federal Supply Schedules (FSS) and Multiple Award Schedules (MAS). FAR 38.101 describes the program in general terms:

(a) The Federal Supply Schedule program, pursuant to 41 U.S.C. 259(b)(3)(A), provides Federal agencies with a simplified process of acquiring commercial supplies and services in varying quantities while obtaining volume discounts. Indefinite-delivery contracts are awarded using competitive procedures to firms. The firms provide supplies and services at stated prices for given periods of time, for delivery within a stated geographic area such as the 48 contiguous states, the District of Columbia, Alaska, Hawaii, and overseas. The schedule contracting office issues Federal Supply Schedule publications that contain a general overview of the Federal Supply Schedule (FSS) program and address pertinent topics.

(b) Each schedule identifies agencies that are required to use the contracts as primary sources of supply.

(c) Federal agencies not identified in the schedules as mandatory users may issue orders under the schedules. Contractors are encouraged to accept the orders.

(d) Although GSA awards most Federal Supply Schedule contracts, it may authorize other agencies to award schedule contracts and publish schedules. For example, the Department of Veterans Affairs awards schedule contracts for certain medical and nonperishable subsistence items.

(e) When establishing Federal Supply Schedules, GSA, or an agency delegated that authority, is responsible for complying with all applicable statutory and regulatory requirements (e.g., Parts 5, 6, and 19). The requirements of Parts 5, 6, and 19 apply at the acquisition planning stage prior to issuing the schedule solicitation and do not apply to orders and BPAs placed under resulting schedule contracts (see 8.404).

A GSA schedule is a list of product and service items and of indefinite-delivery indefinite-quantity contracts for a particular class of products or services against which agencies may issue task and delivery orders. A complete list of all GSA schedules is available online at *http://www.gsaelibrary.gsa.gov/ElibMain/ scheduleList.do*. A schedule contains a list of Special Item Numbers (SINs) for groups of generically similar products and services. For example, Schedule 871, Professional Engineering Services, consists of seven SINs, 871-1, Strategic Planning for Technology Programs/Activities, through 871-7, Construction Management. Schedule 70, General Purpose Commercial Information Technology Equipment, Software, and Services consists of 22 SINs, such as 132-62, Homeland Security Presidential Directive 12 Product and Service Components; 132-9, Purchase of Used or Refurbished Equipment; and 132-32, Term Software Licenses. There are multiple contractors for each SIN and each contractor publishes its own price list. Each schedule has its own webpage, where users can view the solicitation for the schedule and the standard contract clauses. Contractors for each of the SINs can be identified by clicking on the SIN number. Clicking on the contractor name will take the user to contact information and links to item price lists at the "GSA Advantage!" webpage, where authorized users can make purchases after logging in, which requires a user ID and password.

Schedule contracts are awarded by GSA's Federal Acquisition Service (FAS) in accordance with the FAR and with the General Services Administration Acquisition

Manual (GSAM), which contains the General Services Administration Acquisition Regulation (GSAR) and non-regulatory guidance. Procedures for placing orders against GSA schedule contracts are in FAR Subpart 8.4, but GSA provides extensive additional guidance to contractors and to schedule users at its website. GSA administers its contracts, but the issuing agencies (referred to as "ordering activities") administer the orders that they place. FAS's Office of Assisted Acquisition Services provides assisted acquisition services to agencies upon request.

## A. Eligible Users

Eligibility to use GSA Schedules is established by GSA Order ADM-4800.2G, *Eligibility to Use GSA Sources of Supplies and Services*, Feb. 16, 2011. Generally, use of the schedules is open to Executive agencies, including Executive Departments as defined by 5 U.S.C. § 101, wholly owned government corporations as defined by 31 U.S.C. § 9101(3), and independent establishments as defined by 5 U.S.C. § 104. In addition, a large number of other federal agencies, mixed-ownership government corporations, the District of Columbia, qualified nonprofit agencies, and state and local governments may use them as permitted by law. Government contractors and subcontractors may use them under some circumstances, see FAR Subpart 51.1 "Contractor Use of Government Supply Sources." See Appendices A through C of the GSA order for a complete list of eligible users. Organizations other than those listed in the GSA order may use the schedules based on case-by-case determinations by GSA.

## B. Solicitation, Offer, and Award of Schedule Contracts

### 1. Solicitation

GSA announces the availability of schedule contract solicitations at the Government-wide Point of Entry, *www.fedbizopps.gov*, and at its own website. Prospective offerors must identify the schedule under which they wish to offer products and services, go to GSA's webpage for that schedule, identify and read the appropriate solicitation, and then submit offers. Schedule solicitations are open-ended. There is no specific deadline for submitting offers, which may be submitted at any time while the solicitation is available. Solicitations are periodically "refreshed" to incorporate new regulations and policies and each edition describes the changes made since the last edition. After March 2011, GSA requires the electronic submission of all offers through its eOffer/eMod website, *http://eoffer.gsa.gov/*. See solicitation provision A-FSS-11, "Consideration of Offers Under Standing Solicitation (DEC 2000)":

> (a) This solicitation is a standing solicitation from which the Government contemplates award of contracts for supplies/services listed in the Schedule of Items. This solicitation will remain in effect unless replaced by an updated solicitation.

(b) There is no closing date for receipt of offers; therefore, offers may be submitted for consideration at any time.

(c) An offer may be rejected if an offeror fails to meet timeframes established by the Contracting Officer either to address deficiencies in the offer or to submit a final proposal revision. A resubmission(s) is permitted; however, it may be rejected immediately if it is still deficient in the area(s) that caused its initial rejection.

(d) Contracts awarded under this solicitation will be in effect for 5 years from the date of award, unless further extended, pursuant to clause I-FSS-164, Option to Extend the Term of the Contract (Evergreen), canceled pursuant to the Cancellation clause, or terminated pursuant to the termination provisions of the contract.

(e) Current contractors may submit a new offer as early as 9 months prior to the expiration of the existing contract.

The content of GSA schedule solicitations includes solicitation provisions and contract clauses from FAR, GSAM/GSAR, and an unpublished document called the FSS (FAS) clause manual. The latter are usually identified by a heading that includes the abbreviation "FSS." On January 26, 2009, GSA announced its intention to incorporate the texts in the clause manual into GSAM/GSAR Part 538, 74 Fed. Reg. 4596. This was not done and the clause manual is no longer available. However, GSA contracting officers copy the provisions and clauses that had once been in the clause manual from old solicitations and paste them into new ones, sometimes tailoring the text. The result is diverse and inconsistent use of the old provisions and clauses among schedule solicitations. GSA contracting officers continue to use some of the clauses even though they are clearly out of date.

GSA schedule solicitations follow a general format, as follows:

Cover Page

I.    Goods and Services

II.   Contract Terms and Conditions

III.  Vendor Instructions

IV.   Evaluation Factors for Contract Award

V.    Offeror Representations & Certifications

The cover "page" is actually several pages long and includes detailed information about the solicitation and instructions for submission of offers. See, for example, SCP-FSS-001, "General Proposal Submission Instructions (Dec 2010) (Alternate I — Dec 2010)":

(a) Read the entire solicitation document prior to preparation of your offer.

(b) All information provided by the offeror shall be current concise, specific, and complete, and shall demonstrate a thorough understanding of the requirements described in the Statement of Work in Part I. By signing the offer, the offeror attests to the fact that there have been no changes to the text of this solicitation, unless otherwise stated.

(c) All offers must include the following. Omission of any section or substantial deficiencies within any section will result in rejection of the offer.

    (1) Section I Administrative/Contract Data

    (2) Section II Technical Proposal

    (3) Section III Price Proposal

(d) Offers will be rejected if they do not meet all of the following criteria:

    (1) Submit "Pathway to Success" training certificate.

    (2) Submit a signed Standard Form 1449 (unless submitting an eOffer).

    (3) If a consultant or an agent, other than an employee of the company, is being used during or after award, submit an agent authorization letter.

    (4) Submit a completed Vendor Response Document (Vendor Information document if submitting an eOffer).

    (5) The offeror currently has an up to date registration in Central Contractor Registry (CCR).

    (6) The offeror has completed the Online Representations and Certifications Application (ORCA) in its entirety. The information is current, accurate, and complete, and reflects the North American Industrial Classification System (NAICS) code(s) for this solicitation.

    (7) Submit a completed Open Ratings, Inc. (ORI) Past Performance Evaluation and Order Form (references).

    (8) Submit a completed Commercial Sales Practices (CSP) Format.

    (9) Submit a complete Small Business Subcontracting Plan, as applicable.

(e) Withdrawal of Offer: An offeror may withdraw its offer at any time prior to award by submitting a written withdrawal request to the GSA Contract Specialist evaluating the offer. If the offer is withdrawn, it can be resubmitted as a new offer at a later date.

(f) Electronic submission of offers via eOffer is mandatory via *http://eOffer.gsa. gov*, unless otherwise stated in the electronic submission standards and requirements at the Vendor Support Center website (*http://vsc.gsa.gov*).

This is typically followed by a much longer provision entitled, "Specific Proposal Submission Instructions." Yet more instructions are in Part III, Vendor Instructions.

## 2.  *Proposal Review and Negotiation*

Because solicitations are open-ended, offerors do not compete on a head-to-head basis and contract award does not entail offer-to-offer comparisons or tradeoff analyses. GSA does not follow the procedures in FAR Subpart 15.3, "Source Selection." GSA describes its process at its website, *http://www.gsa.gov/portal/content/202577*, as follows:

**Offer Review Process**

GSA's offer review process usually takes between 30 and 120 days. A complete and accurate offer will help speed the process — a majority of offers are returned to the vendor for correction or clarification. The review is handled by a GSA Procurement Contracting Officer (PCO), who evaluates the offer based on the following criteria:

1. **Responsibility** — You should be in a healthy financial state and have a good record of positive past performance.

2. **Responsiveness** — Follow all instructions and include the necessary documentation.

3. **Scope** — Ensure your offered products or services match the Schedule / SIN descriptions.

4. **Subcontracting plan** — Large businesses are required to have a plan in place for subcontracting a percentage of their work towards socioeconomic goals. This requirement applies if anticipated sales exceed $650,000. Contact the Small Business Administration (SBA) Commercial Marketing Representative (CMR) with questions about the subcontracting program and for help locating resources.

5. **Pricing Analysis and Review of Terms** — Prices should be fair and reasonable, with appropriate data supporting and explaining the pricing structure.

**Negotiation and Contract Award**

Once the PCO completes a review of the offer, if necessary, a meeting with you will be scheduled to discuss terms and negotiate pricing. If additional information is needed prior to awarding a contract, the PCO will send a deficiency letter that explains what is needed. The goal of negotiations is to create a discount ratio in regards to your Most Favored Customer (MFC). Your MFC is the customer or class of customers who obtain your best pricing and discounts. After negotiations, a final version of the offer will be prepared, including discounts or concessions.

If an offer fails to meet the evaluation criteria or offer fair and reasonable pricing, it may be rejected. If an offer is rejected, you may request a meeting with the PCO for an explanation. You may alter and re-submit the offer based on feedback received in this meeting.

If the offer is accepted, you will receive a Schedules contract and will be eligible to start doing business with the government through the Schedules program.

Offeror capabilities are evaluated on the basis of nonprice factors such as experience, past performance, and others relevant to the subject matter of the contract. Offerors must propose the prices that they give to their most favored customers. GSA contracting officers analyze the prices and may then engage in price negotiations. See the instruction to GSA personnel at GSAM/GSAR 538.270:

> **538.270  Evaluation of Multiple Award Schedule (MAS) Offers.**
>
> (a) The Government will seek to obtain the offeror's best price (the best price given to the most favored customer). However, the Government recognizes that the terms and conditions of commercial sales vary and there may be legitimate reasons why the best price is not achieved.
>
> (b) Establish negotiation objectives based on a review of relevant data and determine price reasonableness.
>
> (c) When establishing negotiation objectives and determining price reasonableness, compare the terms and conditions of the MAS solicitation with the terms and conditions of agreements with the offeror's commercial customers. When determining the Government's price negotiation objectives, consider the following factors:
>
> > (1) Aggregate volume of anticipated purchases.
> >
> > (2) The purchase of a minimum quantity or a pattern of historic purchases.
> >
> > (3) Prices taking into consideration any combination of discounts and concessions offered to commercial customers.
> >
> > (4) Length of the contract period.
> >
> > (5) Warranties, training, and/or maintenance included in the purchase price or provided at additional cost to the product prices.

(6) Ordering and delivery practices.

(7) Any other relevant information, including differences between the MAS solicitation and commercial terms and conditions that may warrant differentials between the offer and the discounts offered to the most favored commercial customer(s). For example, an offeror may incur more expense selling to the Government than to the customer who receives the offeror's best price, or the customer (e.g., dealer, distributor, original equipment manufacturer, other reseller) who receives the best price may perform certain value-added functions for the offeror that the Government does not perform. In such cases, some reduction in the discount given to the Government may be appropriate. If the best price is not offered to the Government, you should ask the offeror to identify and explain the reason for any differences. Do not require offerors to provide detailed cost breakdowns.

(d) You may award a contract containing pricing which is less favorable than the best price the offeror extends to any commercial customer for similar purchases if you make a determination that both of the following conditions exist:

(1) The prices offered to the Government are fair and reasonable, even though comparable discounts were not negotiated.

(2) Award is otherwise in the best interest of the Government.

Contracts are awarded to qualified offerors that propose prices that the contracting officer determines to be fair and reasonable. Once an award has been made, the contractor must publish a price list for its contract. Head-to-head price competition does not occur during the contract award process. To the extent that it will occur, it will happen when agencies place orders.

## C. Schedule Contracts Terms

GSA schedule contracts are indefinite-delivery indefinite-quantity contracts for commercial items, written in accordance with FAR Part 12 and other instructions in FAR and in GSAM/GSAR. Each contract is organized into two parts: Part I — Goods and Services and Part II — Contract Terms and Conditions. Part I lists and describes the special item numbers (SINs) for each contract. It also contains estimates of predicted annual sales for each SIN, which are based on historical data. Part II contains the clause at FAR 52.212-4, Contract Terms and Conditions — Commercial Items, which applies to firm-fixed-price orders and 52.212-4 Alternate I, which applies to time-and-materials orders. Part II also contains FAR 52.212-5, Contract Terms and Conditions Required to Implement Statutes or Executive Orders — Commercial Items, Alternate I, additional clauses from FAR and GSAM/GSAR, and clauses that had formerly been contained in the FSS clause manual. GSA has approved deviations from the texts of some of the standard FAR clauses. Such clauses are identified by the parenthetical "Deviation" in the clause title.

Several clauses unique to GSA schedule contracts warrant special mention. GSAM/GSAR 552.538-78, Scope of Contract (Eligible Ordering Activities) (SEP 2008), identifies the organizations authorized to place orders, as follows:

(a) This solicitation is issued to establish contracts which may be used on a nonmandatory basis by the agencies and activities named below, as a source of supply for the supplies or services described herein, for domestic and/or overseas delivery. For Special Item Number 132-53, Wireless Services ONLY, limited geographic coverage (consistent with the Offeror's commercial practice) may be proposed.

(1) Executive agencies (as defined in FAR Subpart 2.1) including non-appropriated fund activities as prescribed in 41 CFR 101-26.000;

(2) Government contractors authorized in writing by a Federal agency pursuant to FAR 51.1;

(3) Mixed ownership Government corporations (as defined in the Government Corporation Control Act);

(4) Federal Agencies, including establishments in the legislative or judicial branch of government (except the Senate, the House of Representatives and the Architect of the Capitol and any activities under the direction of the Architect of the Capitol).

(5) The District of Columbia;

(6) Tribal governments when authorized under 25 USC 450j(k);

(7) Qualified Nonprofit Agencies as authorized under 40 USC 502(b); and

(8) Organizations, other than those identified in paragraph (d) of this clause, authorized by GSA pursuant to statute or regulation to use GSA as a source of supply.

\* \* \*

(d) The following activities may place orders against Schedule 70 contracts, and Consolidated Schedule contracts containing information technology Special Item Numbers, and Schedule 84 contracts, on an optional basis; PROVIDED, the Contractor accepts order(s) from such activities: State and local government, includes any state, local, regional or tribal government or any instrumentality thereof (including any local educational agency or institution of higher learning).

(e) Articles or services may be ordered from time to time in such quantities as may be needed to fill any requirement, subject to the Order Limitations thresholds which will be specified in resultant contracts. Overseas activities may place orders directly with schedule contractors for delivery to CONUS port or consolidation point.

(f) (1) The Contractor is obligated to accept orders received from activities within the Executive branch of the Federal Government.

(2) The Contractor is not obligated to accept orders received from activities outside the Executive branch; however, the Contractor is encouraged to accept such orders. If the Contractor elects to accept such orders, all provisions of the contract shall apply, including clause 552.232-79, Payment by Credit Card. If the Contractor is unwilling to accept such orders, and the proposed method of payment is not through the Credit Card, the Contractor shall return the order by mail or other means of delivery within 5 workdays from receipt. If the Contractor is unwilling to accept such orders, and the proposed method of payment is through the Credit Card, the Contractor must so advise the ordering activity within 24 hours of receipt of order. (Reference clause 552.232-79, Payment by Credit Card.) Failure to return an order or advise the ordering activity within the time frames of this paragraph shall constitute acceptance whereupon all provisions of the contract shall apply.

(g) The Government is obligated to purchase under each resultant contract a guaranteed minimum of $2,500 (two thousand, five hundred dollars) during the contract term.

Note that ordering eligibility notwithstanding, a schedule contractor is obligated to accept orders only from Executive branch organizations.

Clause I-FSS-106, Guaranteed Minimum (JUL 2003), states:

The minimum that the Government agrees to order during the period of this contract is $2,500. If the Contractor receives total orders for less than $2,500 during the term of the contract, the Government will pay the difference between the amount ordered and $2,500.

(a) Payment of any amount due under this clause shall be contingent upon the Contractor's timely submission of GSA Form 72A reports (see GSAR 552.238-74 "Industrial Funding Fee and Sales Reporting") during the period of the contract and receipt of the close-out sales report pursuant to GSAR 552.238-74.

(b) The guaranteed minimum applies only if the contract expires or contract cancellation is initiated by the Government. The guaranteed minimum does not apply if the contract is terminated for cause or if the contract is canceled at the request of the Contractor.

Clause I-FSS-163, Option to Extend the Term of the Contract (Evergreen) (APR 2000), provides:

(a) The Government may require continued performance of this contract for an additional 5 year period when it is determined that exercising the option is advantageous to the Government considering price and other factors. The option clause may not be exercised more than three times. When the option to extend the term of this contract is exercised the following conditions are applicable:

(1) It is determined that exercising the option is advantageous to the Government considering price and the other factors covered in (2 through 4 below).

(2) The Contractor's electronic catalog/pricelist has been received, approved, posted, and kept current on GSA Advantage!TM in accordance with clause I-FSS-600, Contract Price Lists.

(3) Performance has been acceptable under the contract.

(4) Subcontracting goals have been reviewed and approved.

(b) The Contracting Officer may exercise the option by providing a written notice to the Contractor within 30 days, unless otherwise noted, prior to the expiration of the contract or option.

(c) When the Government exercises its option to extend the term of this contract, prices in effect at the time the option is exercised will remain in effect during the option period, unless an adjustment is made in accordance with another contract clause (e.g., Economic Price Adjustment Clause or Price Reduction Clause).

In addition to the termination for convenience and termination for cause articles in FAR 52.212-4, schedule contracts include GSAM/GSAR 552.238-73, Cancellation (SEP 1999), which provides as follows:

Either party may cancel this contract in whole or in part by providing written notice. The cancellation will take effect 30 calendar days after the other party receives the notice of cancellation. If the Contractor elects to cancel this contract, the Government will not reimburse the minimum guarantee.

## D.  Contract Pricing

FAR 8.404(d) describes the pricing of schedule contracts:

Supplies offered on the schedule are listed at fixed prices. Services offered on the schedule are priced either at hourly rates, or at a fixed price for performance of a specific task (e.g., installation, maintenance, and repair). GSA has already determined the prices of supplies and fixed-price services, and rates for services offered at hourly rates, under schedule contracts to be fair and reasonable. Therefore, ordering activities are not required to make a separate determination of fair and reasonable pricing, except for a price evaluation as required by 8.405-2(d). By placing an order against a schedule contract using the procedures in 8.405, the ordering activity has concluded that the order represents the best value (as defined in FAR 2.101) and results in the lowest overall cost alternative (considering price, special features, administrative costs, etc.) to meet the Government's needs. Although GSA has already negotiated fair and reasonable pricing, ordering activities may seek additional discounts before placing an order (see 8.405-4).

Although GSA maintains that it has determined that the prices in schedule contracts are fair and reasonable, FAR 8.404(d), GAO has long complained that schedule contract prices are not as advantageous as they could be if GSA made greater use of pre-award and postaward contract audits. See *Contract Management: Opportunities Continue for GSA to Improve Pricing of Multiple Award Schedules Contracts*, GAO-05-229, Feb. 2005:

> Contract negotiators at the four MAS acquisition centers that GAO reviewed use a variety of tools for obtaining most favored customer pricing — that is, the prices vendors offer their best customers. However, the GAO analysis of GSA's review of selected fiscal year 2004 MAS contract files found that nearly 60 percent lacked the documentation needed to establish clearly that the prices were effectively negotiated. Specifically, the contract documentation did not establish that negotiated prices were based on accurate, complete, and current vendor information; adequate price analyses; and reasonable price negotiations. GSA's efforts to ensure most favored customer pricing have been hindered by the significant decline in the use of pre-award and postaward audits of pre-award pricing information, two independent pricing tools that have helped GSA avoid or recover hundreds of millions of dollars in excessive pricing. In fiscal year 1995, GSA conducted 154 pre-award audits; by 2004 the number of pre-award audits fell to 40. Postaward audits — which resulted in an average annual recovery of $18 million in the early 1990s — were discontinued in 1997 when GSA revised its MAS contract audit policies to increase the use of pre-award audits — an increase that has not materialized.

Notwithstanding GSA's declaration that schedule prices are fair and reasonable, FAR 8.405-4, states that agencies may seek a price reduction whenever placing an order and must seek a price reduction when placing an order valued in excess of the simplified acquisition threshold. Contractors that agree to give a price reduction to an individual agency are not obligated to give the same reduction to other agencies. Thus, each contracting officer must bargain for better prices to the best of his or her ability.

GSA schedule contracts contain two clauses that provide for price reductions under specified circumstances. GSAM/GSAR 552.215-72, Price Reduction — Failure to Provide Accurate Information (Aug 1997), states:

(a) The Government, at its election, may reduce the price of this contract or contract modification if the Contracting Officer determines after award of this contract or contract modification that the price negotiated was increased by a significant amount because the Contractor failed to:

(1) Provide information required by this solicitation/contract or otherwise requested by the Government; or

(2) Submit information that was current, accurate, and complete; or

(3) Disclose changes in the Contractor's commercial pricelist(s), discounts or discounting policies which occurred after the original submission and prior to the completion of negotiations.

(b) The Government will consider information submitted to be current, accurate and complete if the data is current, accurate and complete as of 14 calendar days prior to the date it is submitted.

(c) If any reduction in the contract price under this clause reduces the price for items for which payment was made prior to the date of the modification reflecting the price reduction, the Contractor shall be liable to and shall pay the United States—

(1) The amount of the overpayment; and

(2) Simple interest on the amount of such overpayment to be computed from the date(s) of overpayment to the Contractor to the date the Government is repaid by the Contractor at the applicable underpayment rate effective each quarter prescribed by the Secretary of Treasury under 26 U.S.C. 6621(a)(2).

(d) Failure to agree on the amount of the decrease shall be resolved as a dispute.

(e) In addition to the remedy in paragraph (a) of this clause, the Government may terminate this contract for default. The rights and remedies of the Government specified herein are not exclusive, and are in addition to any other rights and remedies provided by law or under this contract.

GSAM/GSAR 552.238-75, Price Reductions (May 2004), provides:

(a) Before award of a contract, the Contracting Officer and the Offeror will agree upon (1) the customer (or category of customers) which will be the basis of award, and (2) the Government's price or discount relationship to the identified customer (or category of customers). This relationship shall be maintained throughout the contract period. Any change in the Contractor's commercial pricing or discount arrangement applicable to the identified customer (or category of customers) which disturbs this relationship shall constitute a price reduction.

(b) During the contract period, the Contractor shall report to the Contracting Officer all price reductions to the customer (or category of customers) that was the basis of award. The Contractor's report shall include an explanation of the conditions under which the reductions were made.

(c) (1) A price reduction shall apply to purchases under this contract if, after the date negotiations conclude, the Contractor—

> (i) Revises the commercial catalog, pricelist, schedule or other document upon which contract award was predicated to reduce prices;

> (ii) Grants more favorable discounts or terms and conditions than those contained in the commercial catalog, pricelist, schedule or other documents upon which contract award was predicated; or

> (iii) Grants special discounts to the customer (or category of customers) that formed the basis of award, and the change disturbs the price/discount relationship of the Government to the customer (or category of customers) that was the basis of award.

(2) The Contractor shall offer the price reduction to the Government with the same effective date, and for the same time period, as extended to the commercial customer (or category of customers).

(d) There shall be no price reduction for sales—

> (1) To commercial customers under firm, fixed-price definite quantity contracts with specified delivery in excess of the maximum order threshold specified in this contract;

> (2) To Federal agencies;

> (3) Made to State and local government entities when the order is placed under this contract (and the State and local government entity is the agreed upon customer or category of customer that is the basis of award); or

> (4) Caused by an error in quotation or billing, provided adequate documentation is furnished by the Contractor to the Contracting Officer.

(e) The Contractor may offer the Contracting Officer a voluntary Governmentwide price reduction at any time during the contract period.

(f) The Contractor shall notify the Contracting Officer of any price reduction subject to this clause as soon as possible, but not later than 15 calendar days after its effective date.

(g) The contract will be modified to reflect any price reduction which becomes applicable in accordance with this clause.

Schedule contracts also include the GSAM/GSAR 552.216-70, Economic Price Adjustment — FSS Multiple Award Schedule Contracts (Sep 1999) clause, which permits contractors to submit price decreases at any time and to request price increases under specified circumstances.

Contract prices must include the industrial funding fee that GSA charges to agencies that use schedule contracts. Contractors must report sales and remit the fees to GSA. See the GSAM/GSAR 552.238-74, Industrial Funding Fee and Sales Reporting (Jul 2003) clause:

(a) Reporting of Federal Supply Schedule Sales. The Contractor shall report all contract sales under this contract as follows:

(1) The Contractor shall accurately report the dollar value, in U.S. dollars and rounded to the nearest whole dollar, of all sales under this contract by calendar quarter (January 1-March 31, April 1-June 30, July 1-September 30, and October 1-December 31). The dollar value of a sale is the price paid by the Schedule user for products and services on a Schedule task or delivery order. The reported contract sales value shall include the Industrial Funding Fee (IFF). The Contractor shall maintain a consistent accounting method of sales reporting, based on the Contractor's established commercial accounting practice. The acceptable points at which sales may be reported include—

(i) Receipt of order;

(ii) Shipment or delivery, as applicable;

(iii) Issuance of an invoice; or

(iv) Payment.

(2) Contract sales shall be reported to FSS within 30 calendar days following the completion of each reporting quarter. The Contractor shall continue to furnish quarterly reports, including "zero" sales, through physical completion of the last outstanding task order or delivery order of the contract.

(3) Reportable sales under the contract are those resulting from sales of contract items to authorized users unless the purchase was conducted pursuant to a separate contracting authority such as a Governmentwide Acquisition Contract (GWAC); a separately awarded FAR Part 12, FAR Part 13, FAR Part 14, or FAR Part 15 procurement; or a non-FAR contract. Sales made to state and local governments under Cooperative Purchasing authority shall be counted as reportable sales for IFF purposes.

(4) The Contractor shall electronically report the quarterly dollar value of sales, including "zero" sales, by utilizing the automated reporting system at an Internet website designated by the General Services Administration (GSA)'s Federal Supply Service (FSS). Prior to using this automated system, the Contractor shall complete contract registration with the FSS Vendor Support Center (VSC). The website address, as well as registration instructions and reporting procedures, will be provided at the time of award. The Contractor shall report sales separately for each National Stock Number (NSN), Special Item Number (SIN), or sub-item.

(5) The Contractor shall convert the total value of sales made in foreign currency to U.S. dollars using the "Treasury Reporting Rates of Exchange" issued by the U.S. Department of Treasury, Financial Management Service. The Contractor shall use the issue of the Treasury report in effect on the last day of the calendar quarter. The report is available from Financial Management Service, International Funds Branch, Telephone: (202) 874-7994, Internet: *http://www.fms.treas.gov/intn.html.*

(b) The Contractor shall remit the IFF at the rate set by GSA's FSS.

(1) The Contractor shall remit the IFF to FSS in U.S. dollars within 30 calendar days after the end of the reporting quarter; final payment shall be remitted within 30 days after physical completion of the last outstanding task order or delivery order of the contract.

(2) The IFF represents a percentage of the total quarterly sales reported. This percentage is set at the discretion of GSA's FSS. GSA's FSS has the unilateral right to change the percentage at any time, but not more than once per year. FSS will provide reasonable notice prior to the effective date of the change. The IFF reimburses FSS for the costs of operating the Federal Supply Schedules Program and recoups its operating costs from ordering activities. Offerors must include the IFF in their prices. The fee is included in the award price(s) and reflected in the total amount charged to ordering activities. FSS will post notice of the current IFF at *http://72a.fss.gsa.gov/* or successor website as appropriate.

(c) Within 60 days of award, an FSS representative will provide the Contractor with specific written procedural instructions on remitting the IFF. FSS reserves the unilateral right to change such instructions from time to time, following notification to the Contractor.

(d) Failure to remit the full amount of the IFF within 30 calendar days after the end of the applicable reporting period constitutes a contract debt to the United States Government under the terms of FAR Subpart 32.6. The Government may exercise all rights under the Debt Collection Improvement Act of 1996, including withholding or setting off payments and interest on the debt (see FAR clause 52.232-17, Interest). Should the Contractor fail to submit the required sales reports, falsify them, or fail to timely pay the IFF, this is sufficient cause for the Government to terminate the contract for cause.

After award, contractors are required to publish price lists containing the agreed-upon SIN prices. See the GSAM/GSAR 552.238-71, Submission and Distribution of Authorized FSS Schedule Pricelists (Sep 1999) clause:

(a) Definition. For the purposes of this clause, the Mailing List is [Contracting officer shall insert either: "the list of addressees provided to the Contractor by the Contracting Officer" or "the Contractor's listing of its Federal Government customers"].

(b) The Contracting Officer will return one copy of the Authorized FSS Schedule Pricelist to the Contractor with the notification of contract award.

(1) The Contractor shall provide to the GSA Contracting Officer:

(i) Two paper copies of Authorized FSS Schedule Pricelist; and

(ii) The Authorized FSS Schedule Pricelist on a common-use electronic medium.

The Contracting Officer will provide detailed instructions for the electronic submission with the award notification. Some structured data entry in a prescribed format may be required.

(2) The Contractor shall provide to each addressee on the mailing list either:

(i) One paper copy of the Authorized FSS Schedule Price List; or

(ii) A self-addressed, postage-paid envelope or postcard to be returned by addressees that want to receive a paper copy of the pricelist. The Contractor shall distribute price lists within 20 calendar days after receipt of returned requests.

(3) The Contractor shall advise each addressee of the availability of pricelist information through the on-line Multiple Award Schedule electronic data base.

(c) The Contractor shall make all of the distributions required in paragraph (c) at least 15 calendar days before the beginning of the contract period, or within 30 calendar days after receipt of the Contracting Officer's approval for printing, whichever is later.

(d) During the period of the contract, the Contractor shall provide one copy of its Authorized FSS Schedule Pricelist to any authorized schedule user, upon request. Use of the mailing list for any other purpose is not authorized.

## E. Use of GSA Schedule Contracts by Federal Agencies

### 1. Requirement for Use

Unless an agency is listed in a schedule as a mandatory user, agencies may use GSA schedule contracts at their discretion. Although FAR 8.002 places schedule contracts ahead of other commercial sources in the prescribed order of priorities for the acquisition of supplies and services, GAO has held that agencies that are not identified in a schedule as mandatory users are not required to order supplies or services from the schedule contract. See *Murray-Benjamin Elec. Co., LP*, Comp. Gen. Dec. B-298481, 2006 CPD ¶ 129:

> [W]hile the list of required sources found in FAR sect. 8.002 places non-mandatory FSS contracts above commercial sources in priority, it does not require an agency to order from the FSS. Further, although an agency's placement of an FSS order indicates that the agency has concluded that the order represents the best value (FAR § 8.404(d)), the regulation does not establish a presumption that all FSS contractors represent the best value, such that the agency would be required to purchase from an FSS contractor.

In Footnote 4 of that decision, GAO reported that it sought the opinion of GSA, which confirmed that use of a schedule contract is voluntary unless a statute or regulation mandates use of the contract. Thus, an agency is not required to place an order against a schedule contract if it can obtain a better value from a non-schedule contractor. See also *ATA Defense Indus., Inc. v. United States*, 38 Fed. Cl. 489 (1997) (agency may choose competitive procedure that is best suited to the circumstances).

### 2. Applicability of Small Business Programs

Small business programs raise two similar but distinct issues with respect to GSA schedule contracts: (1) whether agencies must consider making an "open market" small business set-aside before deciding to place an order against a GSA schedule contract and (2) whether agencies placing an order against schedule contracts must consider setting the order aside for competition among small business schedule contractors. The first issue is addressed by FAR 8.002:

> (a) Except as required by 8.003, or as otherwise provided by law, agencies shall satisfy requirements for supplies and services from or through the sources and publications listed below in descending order of priority —
>
> > (1) Supplies.
> >
> > > (i) Agency inventories;

(ii) Excess from other agencies (see Subpart 8.1);

(iii) Federal Prison Industries, Inc. (see Subpart 8.6);

(iv) Supplies which are on the Procurement List maintained by the Committee for Purchase From People Who Are Blind or Severely Disabled (see Subpart 8.7);

(v) Wholesale supply sources, such as stock programs of the General Services Aministration (GSA) (see 41 CFR 101-26.3), the Defense Logistics Agency (see 41 CFR 101-26.6), the Department of Veterans Affairs (see 41 CFR 101-26.704), and military inventory control points;

(vi) Mandatory Federal Supply Schedules (see Subpart 8.4);

(vii) Optional use Federal Supply Schedules (see Subpart 8.4); and

(viii) Commercial sources (including educational and nonprofit institutions).

(2) Services.

(i) Services which are on the Procurement List maintained by the Committee for Purchase From People Who Are Blind or Severely Disabled (see Subpart 8.7);

(ii) Mandatory Federal Supply Schedules (see Subpart 8.4);

(iii) Optional use Federal Supply Schedules (see Subpart 8.4); and

(iv) Federal Prison Industries, Inc. (see Subpart 8.6), or commercial sources (including educational and nonprofit institutions).

(b) Sources other than those listed in paragraph (a) of this section may be used as prescribed in 41 CFR 101-26.301 and in an unusual and compelling urgency as prescribed in 6.302-2 and in 41 CFR 101-25.101-5.

See also FAR 19.502-1, which states:

(a) The contracting officer shall set aside an individual acquisition or class of acquisitions for competition among small businesses when —

(1) It is determined to be in the interest of maintaining or mobilizing the Nation's full productive capacity, war or national defense programs; or

(2) Assuring that a fair proportion of Government contracts in each industry category is placed with small business concerns; and the circumstances described in 19.502-2 or 19.502-3(a) exist.

(b) This requirement does not apply to purchases of $3,000 or less ($15,000 or less for acquisitions as described in 13.201(g)(1)), or purchases from required sources of supply under Part 8 (e.g., Committee for Purchase From People Who are Blind or Severely Disabled, and Federal Supply Schedule contracts).

Thus, when buying supplies or services contracting officers must consider the use of schedule contracts before considering "open market" set-asides among "commercial sources."

This issue was considered in *K-LAK Corp. v. United States*, 98 Fed. Cl. 1 (2011), where a small business which had held a contract with an agency to provide credit reports protested when, after its contract had expired, the agency decided to procure future credit services from a large business under a GSA schedule contract. The court held that the agency was not required to consider setting aside procurements before ordering under the schedules program, stating at 5 - 6:

Much of the plaintiff's argument rests on the validity of the government's determination that K-LAK and other small businesses were incapable of supplying the credit reports the Air Force needed at a "fair market price." K-LAK argues that the Air Force did not conduct a proper study of market prices under FAR Part 19 (regarding small business set-asides)… This so-called "Rule of Two" requires a contracting officer to make a determination as to whether at least two small businesses could provide the relevant good or service at a fair market price before proceeding with the procurement process with a larger business.

[The government] argues that it was not necessary for the Air Force to evaluate price under FAR Part 19 when it decided to use the FSS, because, by law, the price comparison provisions of Part 19 do not apply when an agency decides to meet its mission requirements through the FSS. In support of this contention, the government points to several FAR provisions, including FAR Part 8, which provides, "Parts 13 … 14, 15, and 19 [regarding small business set-asides] (except for the requirement at 19.202-1(e)(1)(iii) [regarding bundling]) do not apply to [blanket purchase agreements ("BPAs")] or orders placed against Federal Supply Schedules contracts …," FAR 8.404(a); FAR Part 38, which states with regard to FSS contracting, "The requirements of parts 5, 6, and 19 apply at the acquisition planning stage prior to issuing the schedule solicitation and do not apply to orders and BPAs placed under resulting schedule contracts (see 8.404)," FAR 38..101(e); and FAR Part 19 on set-asides for small businesses, which states that requirements for setting aside acquisitions do not apply to "purchases from required sources of supply under Part 8 (e.g., . . . Federal Supply Schedule Contracts)," FAR 19.502-1(b).

The court agrees with the government and concludes . . . that because the Air Force decided to use the FSS after K-LAK's contract expired, the Air Force was not required to comply with the Rule of Two or any of the other regulations applicable to small businesses

See also *Edmond Computer Co.; Edmond Scientific Co.*, Comp. Gen. Dec. B-402863, 2010 CPD ¶ 200:

> Nothing in the Small Business Act suggests or requires that the Rule of Two-which is set forth in the regulations that implement that Act (but is not found in the Act itself), see *Delex Sys., Inc.*, B-400403, Oct. 8, 2008, 2008 CPD ¶ 181 at 6-7-takes precedence over the FSS program. To the contrary, and as noted above, the implementing regulations for the small business set-aside program and the FSS program expressly provide that set-aside requirements for the program do not apply to FSS buys. See FAR sections 8.404(a), 19.502-1(b), 38.101(e). Accordingly, we conclude that the Small Business Act and its implementing regulations do not impose a requirement on agencies to first evaluate whether a solicitation should be set-aside for small businesses before purchasing the goods or services through the FSS program.

See also *Future Solutions, Inc.*, Comp. Gen. Dec. B-293194, 2004 CPD ¶ 39, and *Information Ventures, Inc.*, Comp. Gen. Dec. B-291952, 2003 CPD ¶ 101. Reliance on FAR 8.404(a) in those cases seems misplaced, since that paragraph appears to address the applicability of small business programs in the placement of orders *after* a decision has already been made to conduct the acquisition through the use of a schedule contract. Nevertheless, both the Court of Federal Claims and GAO have cited it as the basis for finding that contracting officers need not consider small business programs before deciding whether to use a schedule contract.

The second issue — whether small business programs apply in the issuance of orders or the establishment of BPAs — is addressed by FAR 8.404(a), which provides in part that FAR Part 19 (except for 19.202-1(e)(1)(iii)) does not apply "to BPAs or orders placed against Federal Supply Schedules contracts. . . ." See also FAR 8.405-5 which states:

> (a) Although the mandatory preference programs of Part 19 do not apply, orders placed against schedule contracts may be credited toward the ordering activity's small business goals. For purposes of reporting an order placed with a small business schedule contractor, an ordering agency may only take credit if the awardee meets a size standard that corresponds to the work performed. Ordering activities should rely on the small business representations made by schedule contractors at the contract level.

> (b) Ordering activities may consider socio-economic status when identifying contractor(s) for consideration or competition for award of an order or BPA. At a minimum, ordering activities should consider, if available, at least one small business, veteran-owned small business, service disabled veteran-owned small business, HUBZone small business, women-owned small business, or small disadvantaged business schedule contractor(s). GSA Advantage! and Schedules e-

Library at *http://www.gsa.gov/fss* contain information on the small business representations of Schedule contractors.

(c) For orders exceeding the micro-purchase threshold, ordering activities should give preference to the items of small business concerns when two or more items at the same delivered price will satisfy the requirement.

Thus, agencies need not set aside competitions for the placement of orders or for the establishment of BPAs. See *Global Analytic Information Tech. Servs., Inc.*, Comp. Gen. Dec. B-297200.3, 2006 CPD ¶ 53 (agency's withdrawal of small business set-aside in schedule competition unobjectionable because FAR Part 19 did not apply to schedule competitions).

Despite the inapplicability of FAR Part 19 to competitions for orders and BPAs under schedule contracts, an agency may limit a competition for an order or for the establishment of a BPA to small business schedule contractors. If it does so, it may require competing contractors to certify their small business status for purposes of the particular competition, even if they previously certified their status for purposes of competing for the GSA schedule contract. See *CMS Information Servs., Inc.*, Comp. Gen. Dec. B-290541, 2002 CPD ¶ 132.

## 3. Responsibility Determinations

The requirements of FAR Subpart 9.1 regarding determinations of the responsibility of prospective contractors does not apply when agencies place orders or establish BPAs under schedule contracts. See *Advanced Tech. Sys., Inc.*, Comp. Gen. Dec. B-296493.6, 2006 CPD ¶ 151:

Responsibility is a contract formation term that refers to the ability of a prospective contractor to perform the contract for which it has submitted an offer; by law, a contracting officer must determine that an offeror is responsible before awarding it a contract. See 41 U.S.C. § 253b(c), (d); FAR § 9.103(a), (b). The concept of responsibility expressly applies to "prospective contractors" — not "current" or "existing" contractors — a limitation that is repeated throughout the applicable statutes and regulations, and that indicates that the requirement for a responsibility determination applies before award of a contract. See, e.g., 41 U.S.C. § 403 ("As used in this Act . . . the term 'responsible source' means a prospective contractor. . . ."), FAR 9.100 ("This subpart prescribes policies, standards, and procedures for determining whether prospective contractors . . . are responsible"); FAR s 9.102(a) ("This subpart applies to all proposed contracts with any prospective contractor. . . ."); and FAR s 9.103(c) ("A prospective contractor must affirmatively demonstrate its responsibility. . . .").

Consistent with this statutory and regulatory framework, once an offeror is determined to be responsible and is awarded a contract, there is no requirement that an agency make additional responsibility determinations during contract performance. *E. Huttenbauer & Son, Inc.*, B-258018.3, Mar. 20, 1995, 95-1 CPD ¶ 148 at 2 (holding that a contracting officer was not required to make a new responsibility determination before deciding whether to exercise an option because the concept of responsibility has no applicability with respect to a contract once that contract has been awarded). Contrary to the protester's position, the extent of the requirement for a determination of responsibility is not tied to the type of contracting vehicle that the government elects to use for an acquisition; thus, there is no basis to conclude that the requirement for a responsibility determination is broader for orders placed under FSS contracts. In this regard, we note that FAR s 8.405 and s 8.406 set forth the ordering procedures and ordering activity's responsibilities, respectively, with regard to FSS contracts; there is no requirement in these provisions to make a responsibility determination. In sum, we conclude that the initial responsibility determination made by GSA in connection with the award of the underlying FSS contract satisfies the requirement for a responsibility determination regarding that vendor and that there is no requirement that an ordering agency perform separate responsibility determinations when placing orders under that contract. (Footnotes omitted)

## F. Ordering

Agencies may issue individual orders and may establish a "blanket purchase agreement" (BPA) under schedule contracts against which orders may be placed. Procedures for placing orders and establishing BPAs against schedule contracts are in FAR 8.405. FAR 8.405-1 states procedures for ordering supplies and for services at fixed prices for a specific task that do not require a statement of work; FAR 8.405-2 states procedures for ordering services that are priced at hourly rates and that require a statement of work; and FAR 8.405-3 states procedures for establishing BPAs. GSA provides additional procedural guidance at a webpage: Ordering Guidelines, *http://www.gsa.gov/portal/category/100639* and in an online publication entitled *GSA Multiple Award Schedules Program Desk Reference*, which is available at *http://www.gsa.gov/portal/content/226369*. (The discussion which follows is based on the interim rule in FAC 2005-50, Item II, 76 Fed. Reg. 14548, March 16, 2011, which took effect on May 16, 2011 and applies to orders issued and BPAs established on and after that date, regardless of when the underlying schedule contract was awarded. The interim rule was promulgated to implement § 863 of Pub. L. No. 110-417, the Duncan Hunter National Defense Authorization Act for Fiscal Year 2008.)

### 1. General Rules

#### a. Acquisition Planning

FAR 8.404(c) states that contracting officers must engage in acquisition planning when issuing schedule orders:

(c) *Acquisition planning.* Orders placed under a Federal Supply Schedule contract—

(1) Are not exempt from the development of acquisition plans (see Subpart 7.1), and an information technology acquisition strategy (see Part 39);

(2) Must comply with all FAR requirements for a bundled contract when the order meets the definition of "bundled contract" (see 2.101(b)); and

(3) Must, whether placed by the requiring agency, or on behalf of the requiring agency, be consistent with the requiring agency's statutory and regulatory requirements applicable to the acquisition of the supply or service.

## b. Limiting the Number of Sources to Be Considered

### (1) CIRCUMSTANCES PERMITTING LIMITATION OF SOURCES

The issuance of orders against schedule contracts is not subject to the full and open competition requirement in 10 U.S.C. § 2304, 41 U.S.C § 3301, and FAR Subpart 61. See FAR 8.405-6:

Orders placed or BPAs established under Federal Supply Schedules are exempt from the requirements in part 6. However, an ordering activity must justify its action when restricting consideration in accordance with paragraphs (a) or (b) of this section[.]

Nonetheless, agencies are subject to special notice and competition requirements, 41 U.S.C. § 3302. These requirements are implemented in FAR 8.405-1, 8.405-2, and 8.405-3, as discussed below, and when these requirements are met any limitations on competition are accepted. If these requirements are not met, FAR 8.405-6(a)(1) describes other circumstances that would justify limiting sources when the order or BPA will exceed the micro-purchase threshold:

(a) *Orders or BPAs exceeding the micro-purchase threshold based on a limited sources justification.*

(1) Circumstances justifying limiting the source.

(i) For a proposed order or BPA with an estimated value exceeding the micro-purchase threshold not placed or established in accordance with the procedures in 8.405-1, 8.405-2, or 8.405-3, the only circumstances that may justify the action are —

(A) An urgent and compelling need exists, and following the procedures would result in unacceptable delays;

(B) Only one source is capable of providing the supplies or services required at the level of quality required because the supplies or services are unique or highly specialized; or

(C) In the interest of economy and efficiency, the new work is a logical follow-on to an original Federal Supply Schedule order provided that the original order was placed in accordance with the applicable Federal Supply Schedule ordering procedures. The original order or BPA must not have been previously issued under sole-source or limited-sources procedures.

(ii) See 8.405-6(c) for the content of the justification for an order or BPA exceeding the simplified acquisition threshold.

FAR 8.405-6(b)(1) states an additional restriction on the use of brand name specifications:

(b) *Items peculiar to one manufacturer.* An item peculiar to one manufacturer can be a particular brand name, product, or a feature of a product, peculiar to one manufacturer. A brand name item, whether available on one or more schedule contracts, is an item peculiar to one manufacturer.

(1) Brand name specifications shall not be used unless the particular brand name, product, or feature is essential to the Government's requirements, and market research indicates other companies' similar products, or products lacking the particular feature, do not meet, or cannot be modified to meet, the agency's needs.

## (2) REQUIREMENT FOR WRITTEN JUSTIFICATION

FAR 8.405-6(b)(2) requires that contracting officers document the basis for using a brand name specification in an order or BPA valued at less than the simplified acquisition threshold. This document is distinct from the justification described in FAR 8.405-6(c). When using a brand name specification in an order or BPA valued in excess of the simplified acquisition threshold, contracting officers must prepare a limited sources justification and obtain its approval in accordance with FAR 8.405-6(c).

FAR 8.405-6(c) requires preparation and approval of a written justification for limiting sources for orders or BPAs that exceed the simplified acquisition threshold. The justification must state that the acquisition is conducted under the authority of the "Multiple-Award Schedule Program" and must, at a minimum, include the following information:

(i) Identification of the agency and the contracting activity, and specific identification of the document as a ``Limited-Sources Justification.''

(ii) Nature and/or description of the action being approved.

(iii) A description of the supplies or services required to meet the agency's needs (including the estimated value).

(iv) The authority and supporting rationale (see 8.405-6(a)(1)(i) and (b)(1)) and, if applicable, a demonstration of the proposed contractor's unique qualifications to provide the required supply or service.

(v) A determination by the ordering activity contracting officer that the order represents the best value consistent with 8.404(d).

(vi) A description of the market research conducted among schedule holders and the results or a statement of the reason market research was not conducted.

(vii) Any other facts supporting the justification.

(viii) A statement of the actions, if any, the agency may take to remove or overcome any barriers that led to the restricted consideration before any subsequent acquisition for the supplies or services is made.

(ix) The ordering activity contracting officer's certification that the justification is accurate and complete to the best of the contracting officer's knowledge and belief.

(x) Evidence that any supporting data that is the responsibility of technical or requirements personnel (e.g., verifying the Government's minimum needs or requirements or other rationale for limited sources) and which form a basis for the justification have been certified as complete and accurate by the technical or requirements personnel.

(xi) For justifications under 8.405-6(a)(1), a written determination by the approving official identifying the circumstance that applies.

### (3) Justification Approval Levels

**Figure 8-1** displays the requirements for approval of justifications for limiting sources for orders and BPA's exceeding the simplified acquisition threshold (SAT);

**LIMITED SOURCES JUSTIFICATION APPROVAL AUTHORITIES**

| Dollar Value of Order or BPA | | | | |
|---|---|---|---|---|
| | > SAT < $650,000 | > $650,000 < $12.5M | > $12.5M < $62.5M or $85.5M for DoD, NASA, and Coast Guard | > $62.5M or $85.5M for DoD, NASA, and Coast Guard |
| **Approving Official** | Contracting officer, unless agency procedures require a higher-level official | Competition Advocate (authority may not be delegated) | Head of the procuring activity placing the order or a designee who is a general or flag officer, a civilian in a grade above GS-15, or the Senior Procurement Executive | Senior Procurement Executive (authority may not be delegated except for the Under Secretary of Defense for Acquisition, Technology, and Logistics acting as the Senior Procurement Executive) |

**Figure 8-1**

## (4) REQUIREMENT TO POST JUSTIFICATION

FAR 8.405-6(b)(3)(i) requires that when an agency uses a brand name specification in an order or BPA valued in excess of $25,000 but not exceeding the simplified acquisition threshold, the agency must post the document explaining the basis for that decision at *e-Buy* along with any RFQ. FAR 8.405-6(b)(3)(ii) establishes three exceptions to the posting requirement:

(A) Disclosure would compromise the national security (e.g., would result in disclosure of classified information) or create other security risks. The fact that access to classified matter may be necessary to submit a proposal or perform the contract does not, in itself, justify use of this exception;

(B) The nature of the file (e.g., size, format) does not make it cost-effective or practicable for contracting officers to provide access through e-Buy; or

(C) The agency's senior procurement executive makes a written determination that access through e-Buy is not in the Government's interest.

Generally, FAR 5.301(a)(2)(i) and 8.405-6(a)(2) require that agencies post approved justifications for limiting sources at the Governmentwide Point of Entry, *www.fedbizopps.gov*, within 14 days after placing an order or establishing a BPA unless the limitation was based on an unusual or compelling urgency, in which case the justification must be posted within 30 days. Contracting officers must screen justifications and remove proprietary information and information protected pursuant to FAR 24.202. FAR 5.301(a)(3) and 8.405-6(a)(2)(iii) state that justifications need not be posted if to do so would compromise national security or create other security risks.

In reviewing an agency's justification for limiting sources, GAO will apply "logical scrutiny," and will require supporting analyses and documentation, *NCS Techs., Inc.*, Comp. Gen. Dec. B-403435, 2010 CPD ¶ 281 (protest sustained in absence of analyses and documentation supporting restriction specifications based on need for standardization). An agency's judgment will stand as long as it is reasonable, *Systems Integration & Mgmt., Inc.*, Comp. Gen. Dec. B-402785.2, 2010 CPD ¶ 207 (mere disagreement with agency's limitation of sources based on "compelling need" does not show agency's judgment was unreasonable); *Computers Universal, Inc.*, Comp. Gen. Dec. B-296536, 2005 CPD ¶ 160 (agency reasonably extended FSS order for short period until pending protest resolved).

### c.  Contractor Teams

GSA allows schedule contractors to form teams to submit quotes for orders or BPAs. Contractor team arrangements (CTAs) are private relationships in which the government does not participate. A CTA is not a prime-subcontractor relationship, in which the prime remains wholly responsible for performance. Under a CTA, all team members must be schedule contractors and are to be in privity with the government under the order or BPA. GSA describes CTAs as follows at its website: *http:// www.gsa.gov/portal/content/202257*:

> A GSA Schedule Contractor Team Arrangement (CTA) is an arrangement between two or more GSA Schedule contractors to work together to meet agency requirements. The CTA document is a written agreement between team members detailing the responsibilities of each team member.
>
> The CTA allows the contractor to meet the government agency needs by providing a total solution that combines the supplies and/or services from the team members' separate GSA Schedule contracts. It permits contractors to complement each other's capabilities to compete for orders for which they may not independently qualify. A customer benefits from a CTA by buying a solution, rather than making separate buys from various contractors.

Schedule contracts include the I-FSS-40, Contractor Team Arrangements (Jul 2003) clause, which provides as follows:

> Contractors participating in contractor team arrangements must abide by all terms and conditions of their respective contracts. This includes compliance with contract clause 552.238-74, Industrial Funding Fee and Sales Reporting, i.e., each contractor (team member) must report sales and remit the IFF for all products and services provided under its individual contract.

### d. Bid Protests

Unlike the award of orders against delivery order and task order contracts pursuant to FAR Subpart 16.5, which may be protested to GAO, but not to the Court of Federal Claims, when in excess of $10 million, the award of orders and BPAs under schedule contracts may be protested to GAO and to the Court of Federal Claims regardless of dollar value. GAO has found that such protests fall within the jurisdiction granted it by the Competition in Contracting Act. See *Panacea Consulting, Inc.*, Comp. Gen. Dec. B-299307.4, 2007 CPD ¶ 141 (note 1):

> The agency, citing 41 U.S.C. § 253j(d) (2000) (which generally prohibits protests against the issuance of a task or delivery order under indefinite-delivery, indefinite-quantity contracts), asserts that our Office lacks jurisdiction to consider these protests because it is placing task orders against blanket purchase agreements entered into between the agency and vendors pursuant to the vendors' FSS contracts. The agency is incorrect. The task orders ultimately are to be placed against the successful vendor's FSS contract. The limitation on our jurisdiction to consider task/delivery order protests does not extend to orders issued under the FSS. Thus, the protests here are subject to our jurisdiction. *Severn Cos., Inc.*, B-275717.2, Apr. 28, 1997, 97-1 CPD ¶ 181 at 2-3 n.1; see also *CMS Info. Servs., Inc.*, B-290541, Aug. 7, 2002, 2002 CPD ¶ 132 at 4 n.7 (no basis to distinguish between issuance of task orders and blanket purchase agreements under the FSS since, in both cases, the acquiring activity ultimately is placing orders against a vendor's FSS contract).

See also *Savantage Financial Servs., Inc.*, Comp. Gen. Dec. B-292046, 2003 CPD p 113; and *Labat-Anderson, Inc.*, Comp. Gen. Dec. B-287081, 2001 CPD ¶ 79. Similarly, the Court of Federal Claims has held that such protests fall within its jurisdiction. See *Data Mgmt. Servs. Joint Venture v. United States*, 78 Fed. Cl. 366 (2007), stating at 370-71:

> We have jurisdiction pursuant to the Tucker Act, 28 U.S.C. § 1491(b)(1) (2000), as amended by the Administrative Dispute Resolution Act of 1996, Pub.L. No. 104-320, § 12, 110 Stat. 3870, 3874-75 (1996), to consider an action by an interested party objecting to an award of a contract and any alleged violation of a statute or regulation in connection with a procurement. We may provide any relief, including declaratory and injunctive relief, we deem proper. 28 U.S.C. § 1491(b)(2). The court's protest jurisdiction extends to protests of task or delivery orders placed against a GSA schedule contract. See *IDEA Int'l, Inc. v. United States*, 74 Fed.Cl. 129, 135-37 (2006).

In a footnote, the court addressed what had appeared to be past inconsistencies in its reasoning about jurisdiction:

> Although the government does not question jurisdiction, it is worth clarifying a past inconsistency in the court's treatment of the issue. In *Group Seven Assocs., LLC v. United States*, 68 Fed.Cl. 28 (2005), the court suggested that

"jurisdiction [was] doubtful" with respect to protests of task orders placed against a GSA schedule contract. *Id.* at 32. That conclusion was based on the fact that the court's protest jurisdiction does not extend to the issuance of all task and delivery orders. The Federal Acquisition Streamlining Act ("FASA") of 1994, Pub.L. No. 103-355, 108 Stat. 3243 (codified in scattered sections of Title 10 and 41 of the United States Code), authorized a new type of multiple award contract called either a "task order contract" or "delivery order contract," defined at 41 U.S.C. § 253k. See 41 U.S.C. § 253h(a) (2000). Under this new authority, any executive agency may issue task and delivery order contracts for the procurement of services or property. These contracts are different from GSA schedule contracts, however, even though both types of contracts utilize task or delivery orders to trigger performance or delivery. One of the ways in which FASA sought to streamline the government's acquisition of supplies and services was to prohibit protests on the issuance of task or delivery orders, except in limited circumstances. See 41 U.S.C. § 253j(d). This limitation on protests only applies to orders issued under the newly authorized "task order contracts" or "delivery order contracts" (i.e., contracts authorized under 41 U.S.C. § 253h or 253i), see 41 U.S.C. § 253f, not orders placed against GSA schedule contracts. See *IDEA Int'l*, 74 Fed.Cl. at 135-37. The court's reservations with respect to jurisdiction in *Group Seven* were therefore unfounded.

## 2.  Specific Ordering Procedures

### a.  General

FAR 8.405-1(b) and 8.405-2(c)(1) state that agencies may place orders valued at or below the micro-purchase threshold with any contractor and prescribe no particular method of selection. Procedures for orders valued in excess of the micro-purchase threshold generally fall into two broad categories: (a) procedures in FAR 8.405-1 for ordering supplies and services at fixed prices for specific tasks that do not require a statement of work and (b) procedures in FAR 8.405-2 for ordering services priced at hourly rates that require a statement of work. The latter procedures are more demanding and time-consuming when the value of services exceeds the simplified acquisition threshold. The key procedural distinctions are: (a) how many schedule contractors an agency must consider or solicit and (b) whether the agency may make a selection simply by reviewing information or must solicit head-to-head competition by issuing an RFQ.

### b.  Orders Requiring a Statement of Work

Whenever an agency seeks to buy a service that is not described in a schedule contract as a task that can be procured for a fixed price, it must describe the service that it wants to buy in sufficient detail to permit prospective contractors to prepare quotes and to establish a basis for quality assurance.

## (1) Preparing the Statement of Work

If an agency's needs are generic, it might be able to describe the service that it wants in a few words or short paragraphs. However, if the agency's needs are custom, specific, and detailed, it may need to write a more extensive description. Such a detailed description is called a "statement of work." FAR does not define the term statement of work or work statement, nor does it prescribe the organization or content of statements of work in any detail except in FAR 35.005 for research and development. The term statement of work appears only once in FAR Part 37, where it is mentioned in the definition of "performance based contracting." A "performance work statement," as defined in FAR 2.101, is a type of statement of work:

> "Performance Work Statement (PWS)" means a statement of work for performance-based acquisitions that describes the required results in clear, specific and objective terms with measurable outcomes.

FAR 37.602 provides the following minimal guidance:

> (a) A Performance work statement (PWS) may be prepared by the Government or result from a Statement of objectives (SOO) prepared by the Government where the offeror proposes the PWS.
>
> (b) Agencies shall, to the maximum extent practicable —
>
>> (1) Describe the work in terms of the required results rather than either "how" the work is to be accomplished or the number of hours to be provided (see 11.002(a)(2) and 11.101);
>>
>> (2) Enable assessment of work performance against measurable performance standards;
>>
>> (3) Rely on the use of measurable performance standards and financial incentives in a competitive environment to encourage competitors to develop and institute innovative and cost-effective methods of performing the work.
>
> (c) Offerors use the SOO to develop the PWS; however, the SOO does not become part of the contract. The SOO shall, at a minimum, include —
>
>> (1) Purpose;
>>
>> (2) Scope or mission;
>>
>> (3) Period and place of performance;
>>
>> (4) Background;

(5) Performance objectives, i.e., required results; and

(6) Any operating constraints.

Thus, it is not clear when a description of services becomes sufficiently detailed to warrant being called a statement of work. That being the case, it may not always be clear when an agency must use the more demanding ordering procedures in FAR 8.405-2. *If* an agency must use a statement of work, FAR 8.405-2(b) states:

> Statements of Work (SOWs). All Statements of Work shall include the work to be performed; location of work; period of performance; deliverable schedule; applicable performance standards; and any special requirements (e.g., security clearances, travel, special knowledge). To the maximum extent practicable, agency requirements shall be performance-based statements (see Subpart 37.6).

## (2) ORDERING PROCEDURES

The procedures in FAR 8.405-2 apply when an agency must write a statement of work to describe the services that it wants to buy. FAR 8.405-2 requires that agencies solicit head-to-head competition by issuing an RFQ. FAR 8.405-2(a) states:

> Ordering activities shall use the procedures in this subsection when ordering services priced at hourly rates as established by the schedule contracts. The applicable services will be identified in the Federal Supply Schedule publications and the contractor's pricelists.

The introductory paragraph in FAR 8.405-2(c) states:

> *Request for Quotation procedures.* The ordering activity must provide the Request for Quotation (RFQ), which includes the statement of work and evaluation criteria (e.g., experience and past performance), to schedule contractors that offer services that will meet the agency's needs. The RFQ may be posted to GSA's electronic RFQ system, e-Buy (see 8.402(d)).

FAR 8.405-2(e) requires the following minimum documentation:

> (1) The schedule contracts considered, noting the contractor from which the service was purchased;
>
> (2) A description of the service purchased;
>
> (3) The amount paid;
>
> (4) The evaluation methodology used in selecting the contractor to receive the order;
>
> (5) The rationale for any tradeoffs in making the selection;

(6) The price reasonableness determination required by paragraph (d) of this subsection;

(7) The rationale for using other than —

(i) A firm-fixed price order; or

(ii) A performance-based order; and

(8) When an order exceeds the simplified acquisition threshold, evidence of compliance with the ordering procedures at 8.405-2(c).

Following award, losing contractors must be notified and given "a brief explanation of the basis for the award decision," FAR 8.405-2(d).

### (A) ORDERS EXCEEDING THE MICRO-PURCHASE THRESHOLD BUT NOT THE SIMPLIFIED ACQUISITION THRESHOLD

When the services are valued in excess of the micro-purchase threshold, but at or below the simplified acquisition threshold, FAR 8.405-2(c)(2)(ii) requires that the agency provide its RFQ to at least three schedule contractors that offer services that will meet its needs. The agency must prepare a written explanation if it is unable to provide the RFQ to at least three contractors. The agency must specify the desired pricing arrangement — e.g., firm-fixed-price or time-and-materials.

### (B) ORDERS EXCEEDING THE SIMPLIFIED ACQUISITION THRESHOLD

When an order will exceed the simplified acquisition threshold, FAR 8.405-2(c)(3)(iii) requires that the agency either post the RFQ at the *e-Buy* website or provide it to as many schedule contractors as practicable to ensure receipt of at least three quotes from capable contractors. An agency that chooses the latter course of action and receives fewer than three quotes must prepare a written statement that, despite its efforts, no other contractors could be found, and it must describe the efforts that it undertook to find at least three schedule contractors to submit quotes. The agency must evaluate quotes received in accordance with the terms of the RFQ.

## c.  Compliance with Other FAR Procedures

FAR 8.404(a) states that agencies need not comply with FAR Parts 13, 14, or 15 when placing orders or establishing BPAs:

(a) General. Parts 13 (except 13.303-2(c)(3)), 14, 15, and 19 (except for the requirement at 19.202-1(e)(1)(iii)) do not apply to BPAs or orders placed against Federal Supply Schedules contracts (but see 8.405-5). BPAs and orders placed against a MAS, using the procedures in this subpart, are considered to be issued using full and open competition (see 6.102(d)(3)). Therefore, when establishing a BPA (as authorized by 13.303-2(c)(3)), or placing orders under Federal Supply Schedule contracts using the procedures of 8.405, ordering activities shall not seek competition outside of the Federal Supply Schedules or synopsize the requirement; but see paragraph (e) for orders (including orders issued under BPAs) funded in whole or in part by the American Recovery and Reinvestment Act of 2009 (Pub. L. 111-5).

Thus, unless otherwise stated in agency-specific rules or in the RFQ, there is no requirement to reject late quotes, conduct a public bid opening, prepare a source selection plan, establish a proposal evaluation board, establish a competitive range, conduct discussions with all offerors in the competitive range, request final proposal revisions from all offerors in the competitive range, or provide a debriefing. See *Ellsworth Assocs., Inc. v. United States,* 45 Fed. Cl. 388 (1999), stating at 395-96:

> The purpose of the FSS program is to provide federal agencies with a simplified process for obtaining certain goods and services. See FAR § 8.401, § 8.404(a). When agencies take this approach, no requirement mandates that contractors receive any advance notice of the agency's needs or the selection criteria. See FAR § 8.404(a). Because Part 8 contemplates agencies ordering off the schedule, no regulations govern the proper procedure for selecting contractors. See FAR § 8.401. This is consistent with the simplified and flexible approach Part 8 takes toward procurements. To be sure, within the FSS program an agency may choose, for any number of reasons, to engage in a more comprehensive selection process than contemplated by the scheme. When that occurs, a frustrated bidder may still challenge the agency award under the arbitrary and capricious standard articulated in 5 U.S.C. § 706(2)(A). However, the protester will not be able to prevail on the theory that the procurement procedure involved a clear and prejudicial violation of applicable statutes and regulations, because no applicable procedural regulations are contained in Part 8. A protester instead must rely on establishing that the government officials involved in the procurement process were without a rational and reasonable basis for their decision.

See also *Holloway & Co., PLLC v. United States*, 87 Fed. Cl. 381 (2009) (agency not required to comply with Part 15 procedures for evaluation price); *Systems Plus, Inc. v. United States*, 68 Fed. Cl. 206 (2005) (schedule ordering procedure not a "competitive proposals" requiring compliance with FAR Part 15 debriefing requirement). Accord, *Source Diversified, Inc.*, Comp. Gen. Dec. B-403437.2, 2010 CPD ¶ 297; *Digital Solutions, Inc.*, Comp. Gen. Dec. B-402067, 2010 CPD ¶ 26; *Carahsoft Tech. Corp.*, Comp. Gen. Dec. B-401169, 2009 CPD ¶ 134; *OPTIMUS Corp.*, Comp. Gen. Dec. B-400777, 2009 CPD ¶ 33.

When an agency issues an RFQ and solicits head-to-head competition based on stated evaluation criteria, it will place an extra procedural burden upon itself if it adopts procedures similar to the competitive negotiation procedures in FAR Part 15. In the event of a protest, GAO may apply its standards of review for source selections under Part 15, which otherwise would not apply. See *CourtSmart Digital Sys., Inc.*, Comp. Gen. Dec. B-292995.2, 2004 CPD ¶ 79:

> [U]nder the FSS program, FAR Subpart 8.4 anticipates that an agency will review vendors' schedules and place an order with the vendor whose goods or services represent the best value and meet the agency's needs at the lowest overall cost. *KPMG Consulting LLP*, B-290716, B-290716.2, Sept. 23, 2002, 2002 CPD ¶ 196 at 10-11; *OSI Collection Servs. Inc.; C.B. Accounts, Inc.*, B-286597.3 *et al.*, June 12, 2001, 2001 CPD ¶ 103 at 4. If, however, the agency issues an RFQ and thus shifts the burden to the vendors for selecting the items from their schedules, the agency must provide guidance about its needs and selection criteria sufficient to allow the vendors to compete intelligently. Where, as here, the agency intends to use the vendors' responses as the basis of a detailed technical evaluation and selection decision, the agency has elected to use an approach that is more like a competition in a negotiated procurement than a simple FSS buy, and the RFQ is therefore required to provide for a fair and equitable competition. *COMARK Fed. Sys.*, B-278343, B-278343.2, Jan. 20, 1998, 98-1 CPD ¶ 34 at 4-5. While we recognize that the FAR Part 15 procedures, for contracting by negotiation, do not govern the FSS program, *Computer Prods., Inc.,* B-284702, May 24, 2000, 2000 CPD ¶ 95 at 4, where, as here, the agency has conducted such a competition and a protest is filed, we will review the record to ensure that the evaluation is reasonable and consistent with the terms of the solicitation and with standards generally applicable to negotiated procurements. *KPMG Consulting LLP, supra.*

See also *USCG, Inc.*, Comp. Gen. Dec. B-400184.2, 2009 CPD ¶ 9; *Advanced Tech. Sys., Inc.*, Comp. Gen. Dec. B-298854, 2007 CPD ¶ 22.

If an agency adopts a FAR Part 15 approach, the Court of Federal Claims will apply the "arbitrary and capricious" standard of the Administrative Procedures Act. See *Labat-Anderson, Inc. v. United States*, 50 Fed. Cl. 99 (2001), stating at 103-04:

> The INS adopted many of the procedures specified in FAR Part 15 for negotiated procurements, including: 1) price analysis techniques prescribed by FAR § 15.404; 2) post-award debriefing prescribed by FAR § 15.506; and 3) technical evaluation definitions prescribed by FAR § 15.001 (formerly codified at 48 C.F.R. § 15.301 (1999)). While this Court has held that FSS acquisitions are not transformed into negotiated procurements simply because an agency chooses to utilize in its evaluation process more formal elements typically used in a negotiated procurement, where an agency engages in a more comprehensive selection process than contemplated by the FSS scheme, a frustrated bidder may still challenge the agency award under the arbitrary and capricious standard articulated in 5 U.S.C. § 706(2)(A). *Ellsworth Assocs., Inc. v. United States*, 45 Fed.Cl. 388, 395-96 (1999).

Agencies should take these considerations into account before requiring the submission of detailed "technical" or "management" proposals and establishing a formal evaluation board, and before mentioning in its RFQ the establishment of a "competitive range," the conduct of "discussions," and the submission of "final proposal revisions" or using any of those procedures. Adopting the terminology and using the procedures of FAR Part 15 may diminish the advantages of the relative simplicity and informality of schedule ordering procedures.

## d.  Orders Not Requiring a Statement of Work

FAR 8.405-1 prescribes procedures for ordering supplies or for ordering services that do not require a statement of work. In this situation, there is no need for a statement of work because the supplies are specifically defined in the schedule contract or the services are defined by task in the schedule contract — both at fixed prices. FAR 8.405-1(f) states that when determining best value agencies must consider price and may consider additional factors, including but not limited to the following factors:

- Past performance.

- Special features of the supply or service required for effective program performance.

- Trade-in considerations.

- Probable life of the item selected as compared with that of a comparable item.

- Warranty considerations.

- Maintenance availability.

- Environmental and energy efficiency considerations.

- Delivery terms.

Note that these factors are directed toward orders for supplies. When the agency is ordering services defined by specific tasks, it must select appropriate factors to ensure the selection of contractor offering the best value.

### (1) Orders Exceeding the Micro-Purchase Threshold but not the Simplified Acquisition Threshold

FAR 8.405-1(c) states that when placing orders valued in excess of the micro-purchase threshold, but at or below the simplified acquisition threshold, agencies need consider only "reasonably available" information at *GSA Advantage!* about the products or services of at least three schedule contractors as described in online catalogs and price lists. Agencies may request quotations instead of using *GSA Advantage!* If the agency restricts consideration to fewer than three contractors, it must document which of the circumstances listed in FAR 8.405-6 applies.

### (2) ORDERS EXCEEDING THE SIMPLIFIED ACQUISITION THRESHOLD

FAR 8.405-1(d) states that when placing orders valued in excess of the simplified acquisition threshold agencies must seek competition among schedule contractors by issuing an RFQ. The RFQ must describe the required supplies or services and the basis for selecting the contractor to which the order will be issued. The RFQ either must be posted at GSA's *e-Buy* website or provided to as many schedule contractors as practicable to reasonably ensure receipt of quotes from at least three capable contractors. If an agency chooses the latter course of action and receives fewer than three quotes, it must make a reasonable effort to find additional sources. If it cannot find additional sources it must include in the order file a written description of its efforts to do so.

## 3. Order Pricing

GSA maintains that its contracting officers have determined the fairness and reasonableness of schedule prices and that contracting officers issuing orders need not make a separate determination in that regard. However, contracting officers are required to request a price reduction on all orders and BPAs exceeding the simplified acquisition threshold. See FAR 8.405-4 stating:

> Ordering activities may request a price reduction at any time before placing an order, establishing a BPA, or in conjunction with the annual BPA review. However, the ordering activity shall seek a price reduction when the order or BPA exceeds the simplified acquisition threshold.

Seeking a price reduction is particularly desirable when the agency is ordering supplies or services at fixed prices for specified tasks following the FAR 8.405-1 procedures because the schedule price may not reflect the quantities being ordered or the conditions of the marketplace at the time the order is placed.

In addition, FAR 8.405-2(d) provides as follows concerning the evaluation of quotes for orders that require a statement of work:

> *Evaluation.* The ordering activity shall evaluate all responses received using the evaluation criteria provided to the schedule contractors. The ordering activity is responsible for considering the level of effort and the mix of labor proposed to perform a specific task being ordered, and for determining that the total price is

reasonable. Place the order with the schedule contractor that represents the best value (see 8.404(d) and 8.405-4). After award, ordering activities should provide timely notification to unsuccessful offerors. If an unsuccessful offeror requests information on an award that was based on factors other than price alone, a brief explanation of the basis for the award decision shall be provided.

In short, nothing prevents an ordering agency contracting officer from bargaining for a better deal that otherwise offered under a schedule contract. GSA considers the pursuit of lower prices in all cases a "best practice." See the GSA webpage, Price Reductions, *www.gsa.gov/schedulespricereductions*. Notwithstanding the obvious advantages of bargaining for better prices, GAO has found that contracting officers often do not do so. See *Contract Management: Not Following Procedures Undermines Best Pricing Under GSA's Schedule*, GAO-01-125.

Contractors may be deterred from offering lower prices by a misreading of the price reduction clause in schedule contracts, GSAM 552.238-75, Price Reductions (MAY 2004), which may lead to the perception that a discount offered to one agency will obligate the contractor to provide the same discount to other agencies. That is not the case. FAR 8.405-4 states: "Schedule contractors are not required to pass on to all schedule users a price reduction extended only to an individual ordering activity for a specific order or BPA."

## 4. Content of Orders

### a. General Contents

FAR 8.406-1 provides that agencies may issue orders orally if they are for (1) supplies and services not requiring a statement of work and not exceeding the simplified acquisition threshold, or (2) orders containing brand-name specifications not exceeding $25,000. Otherwise, orders must be issued in writing on Optional Form 347 (FAR 53.302-347), an agency form, or in electronic format. At a minimum, orders must include the following information in addition to any information required by the schedule contract:

(a) Complete shipping and billing addresses.

(b) Contract number and date.

(c) Agency order number.

(d) F.o.b. delivery point; i.e., origin or destination.

(e) Discount terms.

(f) Delivery time or period of performance.

(g) Special item number or national stock number.

(h) A statement of work for services, when required, or a brief, complete description of each item (when ordering by model number, features and options such as color, finish, and electrical characteristics, if available, must be specified).

(i) Quantity and any variation in quantity.

(j) Number of units.

(k) Unit price.

(l) Total price of order.

(m) Points of inspection and acceptance.

(n) Other pertinent data; e.g., delivery instructions or receiving hours and size-of-truck limitation.

(o) Marking requirements.

(p) Level of preservation, packaging, and packing.

Note that this list is addressed to orders for supplies and must be tailored when services are being ordered.

## b.  Additional Clauses

GSA allows agencies to include their own agency-specific clauses in orders and BPAs as long as they are not inconsistent with the terms and conditions of the GSA schedule contract. See *GSA Multiple Award Schedule Program Desk Reference* 28:

The GSA Schedules program is designed to assist government customers in achieving their goals. The terms and conditions, including all clauses, are available for viewing for each Schedule through GSA eLibrary. While GSA will not alter the terms and conditions of a Schedule contract in violation of CICA, nor alter the scope of a contract to meet an individual ordering activity's unique needs, an ordering activity may add terms to an order that do not conflict with the Schedule contract terms and conditions.

## c.  Options in Orders and BPAs

Agencies may include options in orders to extend the term of the order or to purchase additional quantities. See GSA Ordering Guidelines, Item 25, "Options on Orders Placed Against GSA Multiple Award Schedule Contracts":

Options may be included on orders placed against GSA Multiple Award Schedule (MAS) contracts, provided that the options are clearly stated in the requirement and are evaluated as part of the ordering activity's best value determination. Such options may be exercised on GSA Schedule contract orders, provided that:

- Funds are available;

- The requirement covered by the option fulfills an existing government need;

- Prior to exercising an option, the ordering activity ensures that it is still in the government's best interest, i.e., that the option is the most advantageous method of fulfilling the government's need, price and other factors considered; and

- The options do not extend beyond the period of the Schedule contract, including option year periods.

Under the preceding conditions, Blanket Purchase Agreements (BPAs) under Schedule contracts may be established with options that extend beyond the end of the basic Schedule contract period, so long as there are option periods in the GSA contract that, if exercised, will cover the BPA's period of performance. The length of the order and the risk to the ordering activity could be considered as part of the overall evaluation of best value.

## 5.  Items Not on Schedule

Since the Court of Federal Claims' decision in *ATA Defense Indus., Inc., v. United States*, 38 Fed. Cl. 489 (1987), it has become well-established that agencies may not place orders that include non-schedule items ("open market items" or "incidental items") valued in excess of the micro-purchase threshold unless they first comply with all applicable laws and regulations. See *CourtSmart Digital Sys., Inc.*, Comp. Gen. Dec. B-292995.2, 2004 CPD ¶ 79:

The FSS program, directed and managed by the General Services Administration (GSA), gives federal agencies a simplified process for obtaining commonly used commercial supplies and services. FAR § 8.401(a). Orders placed using the procedures established for the FSS program satisfy the statutory and regulatory requirement for full and open competition. FAR § 6.102(d)(3), § 8.404(a). Non-FSS products and services may not be purchased using FSS procedures; instead, their purchase requires compliance with the applicable procurement laws and regulations, including those requiring the use of competitive procedures. *Simplicity Corp.*, B-291902, Apr. 29, 2003, 2003 CPD ¶ 89 at 4; see *ATA Def. Indus., Inc. v. United States*, 38 Fed. Cl. 489, 504 (1997). Therefore, where, as here, an agency solicits quotations from vendors for purchase from the FSS, the issuance of a purchase order to a vendor whose quotation includes a non-FSS item priced above the micro-purchase threshold is improper. *Simplicity Corp.*, *supra*, at 4-5; *T-L-C Sys.*, B-285687.2, Sept. 29, 2000, 2000 CPD ¶ 166 at 4.

See also FAR 8.402(f):

(f) For administrative convenience, an ordering activity contracting officer may add items not on the Federal Supply Schedule (also referred to as open market items) to a Federal Supply Schedule blanket purchase agreement (BPA) or an individual task or delivery order only if—

(1) All applicable acquisition regulations pertaining to the purchase of the items not on the Federal Supply Schedule have been followed (e.g., publicizing (Part 5), competition requirements (Part 6), acquisition of commercial items (Part 12), contracting methods (Parts 13, 14, and 15), and small business programs (Part 19));

(2) The ordering activity contracting officer has determined the price for the items not on the Federal Supply Schedule is fair and reasonable;

(3) The items are clearly labeled on the order as items not on the Federal Supply Schedule; and

(4) All clauses applicable to items not on the Federal Supply Schedule are included in the order.

See *Marine Group Boat Works, LLC*, Comp. Gen. Dec. B-404277, 2011 CPD ¶ 23:

Where an agency announces its intention to purchase using FSS procedures, all items evaluated and ordered are generally required to be within the scope of the vendor's FSS contract.

See also *Rapiscan Sys., Inc.*, Comp. Gen. Dec. B-401773.2, 2010 CPD ¶ 60:

The sole exception to this requirement is for items that do not exceed the micropurchase threshold of $3,000, since such items properly may be purchased outside the normal competition requirements in any case.

When an order is for services, a contractor's contract must include all labor categories and items required to perform the work, *Tarheel Specialties, Inc.*, Comp. Gen. Dec. B-298197, 2006 CPD ¶ 140 (labor needed to support operations of firearms tactical training unit not included in schedule contract for security consulting services). However, the Court of Federal Claims has held that agencies may make "common sense identification of overlapping, related labor categories." See *HomeSource Real Estate Asset Servs., Inc. v. United States*, 94 Fed. Cl. 466 (2010), stating at 486:

An agency that orders services against a schedule contract "shall not seek competition outside the Federal Supply Schedules." [FAR 8.404(a)]. In this case, HUD restricted competition to those vendors offering services on Schedule 520. "Where an agency announces an intention to order from an existing GSA Schedule contractor, it means that the agency intends to order all items using GSA FFS procedures and that all items are required to be within the scope of the vendor's FSS contract. " *IDEA Int'l, Inc. v. United States* (IDEA Int'l), 74 Fed.Cl. 129, 139 (2006).

Although the government is required to order items that fall "within the scope of the vendor's FSS contract," id., there is "no prohibition [ ] on the government's common sense identification of overlapping, related labor categories," *Career Training Concepts, Inc. v. United States* (*Career Training*), 83 Fed. Cl. 215, 227 (2008). In *Career Training* the court rejected plaintiff's protest based on its finding that the awardee's job category was "sufficiently close to the [FSS labor category] to be compliant with the solicitation." Id. at 228. Although job titles and qualifications may differ between an offeror's FSS contract and the solicitation, a government agency may find that the services offered are within the scope of an offeror's FSS contract if the function of the two job positions is "sufficiently close." *Career Training*, 83 Fed. Cl. at 228; see *Data Mgmt. Servs. Joint Venture v. United States*, 78 Fed. Cl. 366, 378 (2007).

See also *Mobile Medical Int'l Corp. v. United States*, 95 Fed. Cl. 706 (2010) (mobile trailer required by order not included in awardee's schedule contract).

## G. Blanket Purchase Agreements

Agencies may use the procedures in FAR 8.405-3 to establish BPAs with schedule contractors in order to simplify ordering and reduce administrative costs. GSA describes the benefits of BPAs at its webpage: Blanket Purchase Agreements, *http://www.gsa.gov/portal/category/100643.*

**Benefits and Advantages of BPAs**

BPAs offer an excellent option for federal agencies and Schedule contractors alike, providing convenience, efficiency, and reduced costs. Contractual terms and conditions are contained in GSA Schedule contracts and are not to be re-negotiated for GSA Schedule BPAs. Therefore, as a purchasing option, BPAs eliminate such contracting and open market costs as the search for sources, the need to prepare solicitations, and the requirement to synopsize the acquisition.

BPAs also:

- Provide opportunities to negotiate improved discounts;

- Satisfy recurring requirements;

- Reduce administrative costs by eliminating repetitive acquisition efforts;

- Permit ordering activities to leverage buying power through volume purchasing;

- Enable ordering activities streamlined ordering procedures;

- Permit ordering activities to incorporate Contractor Team Arrangements (CTAs);

- Reduce procurement lead time; and

- Permit ordering activities the ability to incorporate terms and conditions not in conflict with the underlying contract.

A BPA can be set up for field offices across the nation, thus allowing them to participate in a customer's BPA and place orders directly with GSA Schedule contractors. In doing so, the entire agency reaps the benefits of additional discounts negotiated into the BPA.

A multi-agency BPA is also permitted if the BPA identifies the participating agencies and their estimated requirements at the time the BPA is established.

## FAR 8.405-3 provides as follows:

(a)(1) *Establishment.* Ordering activities may establish BPAs under any schedule contract to fill repetitive needs for supplies or services. BPAs may be established with one or more schedule contractors. The number of BPAs to be established is within the discretion of the ordering activity establishing the BPAs and should be based on a strategy that is expected to maximize the effectiveness of the BPA(s). In determining how many BPAs to establish, consider —

(i) The scope and complexity of the requirement(s);

(ii) The need to periodically compare multiple technical approaches or prices;

(iii) The administrative costs of BPAs; and

(iv) The technical qualifications of the schedule contractor(s).

(2) Establishment of a single BPA, or multiple BPAs, shall be made using the same procedures outlined in 8.405-1 or 8.405-2. BPAs shall address the frequency of ordering, invoicing, discounts, requirements (e.g. estimated quantities, work to be performed), delivery locations, and time.

(3) When establishing multiple BPAs, the ordering activity shall specify the procedures for placing orders under the BPAs.

(4) Establishment of a multi-agency BPA against a Federal Supply Schedule contract is permitted if the multi-agency BPA identifies the participating agencies and their estimated requirements at the time the BPA is established.

(b) *Ordering from BPAs* —

(1) *Single BPA.* If the ordering activity establishes one BPA, authorized users may place the order directly under the established BPA when the need for the supply or service arises.

(2) *Multiple BPAs.* If the ordering activity establishes multiple BPAs, before placing an order exceeding the micro-purchase threshold, the ordering activity shall —

(i) Forward the requirement, or statement of work and the evaluation criteria, to an appropriate number of BPA holders, as established in the BPA ordering procedures; and

(ii) Evaluate the responses received, make a best value determination (see 8.404(d)), and place the order with the BPA holder that represents the best value.

(3) *BPAs for hourly rate services.* If the BPA is for hourly rate services, the ordering activity shall develop a statement of work for requirements covered by the BPA. All orders under the BPA shall specify a price for the performance of the tasks identified in the statement of work.

(c) *Duration of BPAs.* BPAs generally should not exceed five years in length, but may do so to meet program requirements. Contractors may be awarded BPAs that extend beyond the current term of their GSA Schedule contract, so long as there are option periods in their GSA Schedule contract that, if exercised, will cover the BPA's period of performance.

(d) *Review of BPAs.*

(1) The ordering activity that established the BPA shall review it at least once a year to determine whether —

(i) The schedule contract, upon which the BPA was established, is still in effect;

(ii) The BPA still represents the best value (see 8.404(d)); and

(iii) Estimated quantities/amounts have been exceeded and additional price reductions can be obtained.

(2) The ordering activity shall document the results of its review.

GSA provides additional guidance at its webpage: BPA Frequently Asked Questions, *http://www.gsa.gov/portal/content/200549#1*, where a sample format is provided.

A standard clause used in schedule contracts, I-FSS-646, Blanket Purchase Agreements (MAY 2010), stipulates the contractor's agreement to enter into BPAs:

> Blanket Purchase Agreements (BPA's) can reduce costs and save time because individual orders and invoices are not required for each procurement but can instead be documented on a consolidated basis. The Contractor agrees to enter into BPA's with ordering activities provided that:
>
> (a) The period of time covered by such agreements shall not exceed the period of the contract including option year period(s);
>
> (b) Orders placed under such agreements shall be issued in accordance with all applicable regulations and the terms and conditions of the contract; and
>
> (c) BPAs may be established to obtain the maximum discount (lowest net price) available in those schedule contracts containing volume or quantity discount arrangements.

BPAs against GSA schedule contracts should not be confused with the BPAs used for simplified acquisitions and described at FAR 13.303. A more apt term for schedule contract BPAs would be blanket orders. Such agreements allow agencies to select a contractor and then issue orders during an agreed-upon period of time without further consideration of other schedule contractors or further price negotiations. The contracting officer can delegate ordering under the BPA to other offices in the agency.

GAO has ruled that a BPA is not itself a contract and that orders issued against it are issued against the underlying schedule contract. *AINS, Inc.*, Comp. Gen. Dec. B-400760.2, 2009 CPD ¶ 142. Accordingly, BPAs are not stand-alone agreements and orders can no longer be issued against a BPA once the underlying schedule contract has expired. See *Canon USA, Inc.*, Comp. Gen. Dec. B-311254.2, 2008 CPD ¶ 113:

> We agree with Canon that an FSS BPA is a separate agreement from its associated FSS contract. Nevertheless, we conclude that when Canon's FSS contract expired, Canon's BPA ceased to be a valid procurement vehicle for the placement of new orders because, as explained below, an FSS BPA is in effect solely a pass-through to the BPA holder's FSS contract and does not provide an independent foundation for issuing orders.
>
> In order for any procurement to be valid, it must be conducted in accordance with the competition requirements set forth in the Competition in Contracting Act of 1984 (CICA), 10 U.S.C. § 2304(a)(1)(A) (2000), and FAR part 6. Under 10 U.S.C. § 2303(2)(c), contracts awarded under the FSS program pursuant to FAR part 8 satisfy the requirements for full and open competition. As relevant here,

FAR § 8.405-3(a)(1) authorizes the establishment of BPAs under FSS contracts as a means to fill "repetitive needs for supplies or services." It is well-settled, however, that a BPA itself is not a contract; rather, a contract is formed by the subsequent placement of a valid order against the BPA, or by the incorporation of the basic agreement into a new contract. [1]See *Envirosolve LLC*, B-294974.4, June 8, 2005, 2005 CPD ¶ 106 at 3 n.3, citing *Modern Sys. Tech. Corp. v. United States*, 24 Cl. Ct. 360, 363 (1991).

As with any contract, orders placed under an FSS BPA must satisfy the applicable statutory requirements for competition.

In this case, the record shows that the BPA was issued pursuant to Canon's FSS contract, the plain language of Canon's BPA states that it is established "[p]ursuant to GSA Federal Supply Schedule (FSS) Contract Number GS-25F-0023M," Motion to Dismiss, Tab 1, Canon BPA, at 1, and Canon itself does not dispute that the BPAs here were all "initially awarded to vendors based on their then current GSA copier schedule contracts." Protest at 5. It is therefore clear that Canon's BPA is an FSS BPA, established under FAR part 8.4.

Because use of the FSS procedures constitutes full and open competition under 10 U.S.C. § 2303(2)(c), orders placed under a valid FSS contract, whether directly or via a BPA, meet the CICA competition requirements. Conversely, in the absence of a valid FSS contract, any order placed under a BPA must independently satisfy the statutory competition requirements; that is, to be a valid ordering vehicle independent from an FSS contract, the BPA itself would have to have been established using procedures that satisfy the statutory requirements for competition. That clearly is not the case here, or in any FSS BPA of this type, given that the pool of vendors that could receive a BPA was limited to FSS contract holders, as directed by FAR sect. 8.404(a) ("ordering activities shall not seek competition outside of the Federal Supply Schedules"). Consistent with this interpretation, we have stated that an FSS BPA is not established with the contractor directly, but rather is established under the contractor's FSS contract, such that FSS BPA orders "ultimately are to be placed against the successful vendor's FSS contract." *Panacea Consulting, Inc.*, B-299307.4, B-299308.4, July 27, 2007, 2007 CPD ¶ 141 at 1-2 n.1; see also *CMS Info. Servs., Inc.*, B-290541, Aug. 7, 2002, 2002 CPD ¶ 132 at 4 n.7. Thus, in our view, when, as in this case, an agency intends to place an order under an FSS BPA, the vendor must have a valid FSS contract in place because that contract is the means by which the agency satisfies the competition requirements of CICA in connection with any orders issued under the BPA.

However, the term of a BPA can extend beyond the term of the schedule contract if the contract itself has options to extend its term. See BPA Frequently Asked Questions, Question No. 12, *http://www.gsa.gov/portal/content/200549.*

## III. GOVERNMENTWIDE ACQUISITION CONTRACTS, MULTIAGENCY CONTRACTS, AND ENTERPRISEWIDE CONTRACTS

### A. Definitions

Governmentwide Acquisition Contracts (GWACs), Multiagency Contracts (MACs), and Enterprisewide Contracts are multiple-award indefinite-delivery indefinite-quantity (IDIQ) contracts awarded by agencies for use by other agencies. They differ mainly in the authority for their establishment. GWACs are authorized pursuant to 40 U.S.C. § 11302(e) (formerly, 40 U.S.C. ¶ 759), and are for the acquisition of information technology. See the definition in FAR 2.101:

> *Governmentwide acquisition contract (GWAC)* means a task-order or delivery-order contract for information technology established by one agency for Governmentwide use that is operated—
>
> (1) By an executive agent designated by the Office of Management and Budget pursuant to 40 U.S.C. 11302(e); or
>
> (2) Under a delegation of procurement authority issued by the General Services Administration (GSA) prior to August 7, 1996, under authority granted GSA by former section 40 U.S.C. 759, repealed by Pub. L. 104-106. The Economy Act does not apply to orders under a Governmentwide acquisition contract.

Orders placed against GWACs are not subject to the Economy Act, 31 U.S.C. § 1535.

MACs are authorized for the acquisition of all kinds of supplies and services pursuant to the Economy Act, or for the acquisition of information technology by 40 U.S.C. § 11314(a)(2). See the definition in FAR 2.101:

> *Multi-agency contract (MAC)* means a task-order or delivery-order contract established by one agency for use by Government agencies to obtain supplies and services, consistent with the Economy Act (see 17.502-2). Multi-agency contracts include contracts for information technology established pursuant to 40 U.S.C. 11314(a)(2).

All orders placed against MACs, regardless of the authority for establishment of the contract, are subject to the Economy Act. Enterprisewide Contracts are established within an agency for its own use. However, awarding agencies may make such contracts available for other agencies to use, in which case the contracts are MACs and orders placed against them are subject to the Economy Act. GWACs, MACs, and Enterprisewide Contracts are similar in concept, structure, and procedure to GSA Multiple Award Schedule Contracts.

# B. Establishment of GWACs and MACs

## 1. *Planning, Management, and Inventory*

The principle issues concerning these contracts have been their proliferation and management. See Report of the Acquisition Advisory Panel to the Office of Federal Procurement Policy and the United States Congress (January 2007), 246-247:

The pressures and incentives to create and use these vehicles, coupled with inconsistent or lacking oversight and little transparency has created an environment biased towards the uncoordinated proliferation of interagency contracts. GAO has noted that they are attracting rapid growth of taxpayer dollars with Fiscal Year 2004 FPDS-NG data showing total obligations of $142 Billion or 40 percent of the total government-wide spend for the year.

\* \* \*

Certainly, uncoordinated proliferation without adequate transparency into the establishment or use of these vehicles creates serious challenges for those organizations responsible for oversight. While GWACs, franchise funds, and schedules are readily identifiable, the significant number of other interagency vehicles such as non-GWAC multi-agency contracts and the emerging trend in the proliferation of enterprise-wide contracts presents an obstacle for oversight both in terms of sheer numbers and difficulty in identification. Lack of transparency in both the use and management of these vehicles severely hampers the government's ability to maximize their effectiveness.

In order to establish a GWAC an agency must prepare a business case and submit it to the Office of Management and Budget for approval and authorization. The Court of Federal Claims described the process in *Knowledge Collections, Inc. v. United States*, 79 Fed. Cl. 750 (2007), stating at 753:

In February 2005, GSA sent OMB the Veterans Technology Service [VETS] business case, a proposal to establish the VETS GWAC. See GSA Determination Pursuant to Remand Order, July 25, 2007 ("Remand Determination") *754 at 10; FN8 AR 16-50 (GSA, VETS (Veterans Technology Services) Business Case For a Service-Disabled Veteran-Owned Small Business (SDVOSB) Government-Wide Acquisition Contract (GWAC) (Feb. 3, 2005)) ("Business Case"). GSA described the VETS GWAC as "a streamlined acquisition vehicle" through which GSA would "offer a pre-qualified group of SDVOSB information technology ["IT"] firms the opportunity to compete for government IT services orders from [government agencies]." AR 18 (Business Case). GSA stated that "[e]valuation criteria [would], at a minimum, focus on technical expertise, successful past performance and price." AR 21 (Business Case). GSA ascribed importance to "building brand awareness" by "forg[ing] strategic partnerships with the SBA [and] VA ["Veterans Administration"]" and noted that "frequent and consistent messaging by GSA and any strategic partners (SBA, Veterans Administration, and Department of

Defense) is mandatory in order to properly explain the recent statute and Executive Order in addition to managing the expectations of both industry and federal communities." AR 33 (Business Case).

OMB has the statutory obligation to direct and oversee the federal government's "acquisition and use of information technology," 44 U.S.C. § 3504(a)(1)(B)(vi), and federal agencies are required to comply with policies established by OMB in that regard. 44 U.S.C. § 3506(a)(1)(B). Correlatively, the Director of OMB is authorized by the Clinger-Cohen Act, Pub.L. No. 104-106, § 5112(e), 110 Stat. 186, 681 (Feb. 10, 1996) (codified at 40 U.S.C. § 11302(e)) (enacted as part of the National Defense Authorization Act for Fiscal Year 1996), to designate heads of executive agencies as "executive agent[s] for [g]overnment-wide acquisitions of information technology." Id. Heads of executive agencies, in turn, have authority to enter into "contract[s] that provide[ ] for multiagency acquisitions of information technology in accord[ ] with guidance issued by [OMB]." 40 U.S.C. § 11314(a)(2). "Executive agents" have "discretion on matters of procurement planning, implementation, administration, and management, subject to any terms and conditions that OMB includes in the designation." Def.'s Opp'n to Pl.'s Mot. .... and Cross-Mot. ("Def.'s Cross-Mot."), attached Decl. of Michael Gerich, General Attorney, OFPP, OMB (Sept. 13, 2007) ("Gerich Decl.") at 2.

OMB reviewed the Business Case submitted by GSA and designated GSA as the "executive agent" for the VETS GWAC on July 5, 2005. AR 85 (Letter from Joshua B. Bolten, Director, OMB, to Stephen A. Perry, Administrator, GSA (July 5, 2005)) ("OMB Designation"). The grant of authority embraced two primary functional areas: information systems engineering and systems operations and maintenance. AR 89 (OMB Designation, Encl. A). In designating GSA as the executive agent for the VETS GWAC, OMB stated that "[t]he GWAC would fulfill GSA's responsibilities under Executive Order 13360, which requires the agency to 'establish a Government-wide Acquisition Contract reserved for participation by service-disabled veteran businesses.' " AR 92-93 (OMB Designation, Encl. B). OMB also made the designation subject to certain terms, reporting requirements, and understandings. AR 90 (OMB Designation, Encl. B). Specifically, the designation was granted with "the expectation that contracts under this GWAC w[ould] be awarded to the most highly qualified service-disabled veteran owned small businesses. Potential contractors should not be excluded from being GWAC holders based on their lack of experience as a government contractor." AR 93 (OMB Designation, Encl. B). Thirteen months later, in August 2006, OMB extended the executive-agent designation until the completion of the VETS GWAC contract period. AR 96, 99 (Letter *755 from Rob Portman, Director, OMB, to Lurita A. Doan, Administrator, GSA (Aug. 9, 2006)).

An agency awarding a GWACs contract must do so in accordance with the terms of OMB's grant of executive agent designation. *Knowledge Connections, Inc. v. U.S.*, 76 Fed. Cl. 6 (2007) (judgment for plaintiff where record insufficient to show that agency evaluation was consistent with OMB grant of executive designation).

To date, OMB has authorized only five agencies to award GWACs: Department of Commerce, Environmental Protection Agency, General Services Administration, Department of Health and Human Services, and National Aeronautics and Space Administration. Collectively, they have established 13 GWACs. OMB maintains a list of GWACs at *http://www.whitehouse.gov/sites/default/files/omb/assets/procurement/gwacs.pdf*.

In 1997, OMB issued Memorandum M-97-07, *Multiagency Contracts under the Information Technology Management Reform Act of 1996*. The memorandum authorized agencies to establish MACs and provided guidance for doing so. In December 2010, the Federal Acquisition Regulation councils published an interim rule amending FAR Subpart 17.5 to require that agencies prepare a business-case analysis in order to establish a MAC. See FAR 17.502-2 stating:

> (d) *Business-case analysis requirements for multi-agency contracts.* In order to establish a multi-agency contract in accordance with Economy Act authority, a business-case analysis must be prepared by the servicing agency. The business-case analysis shall —
>
>> (1) Consider strategies for the effective participation of small businesses during acquisition planning (See 7.103(s));
>>
>> (2) Detail the administration of such contract, including an analysis of all direct and indirect costs to the Government of awarding and administering such contract;
>>
>> (3) Describe the impact such contract will have on the ability of the Government to leverage its purchasing power, e.g., will it have a negative effect because it dilutes other existing contracts;
>>
>> (4) Include an analysis concluding that there is a need for establishing the multi-agency contract; and
>>
>> (5) Document roles and responsibilities in the administration of the contract.

However, there is no requirement that the analysis be reviewed or approved outside of the agency. A number of agencies have established MACs, including Department of Commerce, Defense of Defense, Department of the Interior, Environmental Protection Agency, General Services Administration, Department of Health and Human Services, Department of the Treasury, and Department of Veterans Affairs. There is no specific authority or procedure for establishing Enterprisewide Contracts for use only by offices of the awarding agency.

OMB maintains a list of MACs at *http://www.whitehouse.gov/sites/default/files/omb/assets/procurement/macs.pdf*. In addition to the lists of GWACs and MACs, the government maintains a searchable inventory of interagency contracts at *https://*

*www.contractdirectory.gov/contractdirectory/*. Many of the links on the lists and obtained through the inventory do not work. Another source is the *Where In Federal Contracting?* website: *http://www.wifcon.com/quickit.htm*.

GWACs and MACs may encompass very broad scopes of work, making them virtual shopping malls for wide varieties of supplies and services. See, for example, the description of the scope of the Naval Sea Systems Command's SeaPort MAC at *http://www.seaport.navy.mil/SeaPort/MAC%20Scope.aspx*:

> SeaPort Multiple Award Contracts (MACs) are designed to include all aspects of professional support services (SeaPort-I MAC) and Engineering, Technical, & Programmatic Support Services (SeaPort-e MAC) as required by the Virtual Systems Command, its related Program Executive Offices (PEOs) and field affiliates. These contracts are not intended to nor will they be used to procure any personal services or services which are inherently governmental.

> Generally, SeaPort MACs provide vehicles to procure engineering, technical, programmatic, and professional support services for authorized users through all phases of ship and weapon system life cycle — technology development, concept exploration, design, specification development, construction/production, test and evaluation, certification, operation, maintenance, improvement/modernization, overhaul and refueling, salvage and disposal. The scope of the contracts also includes professional support services to assist in the development, review and execution of search and salvage, diving, underwater ship husbandry, and pollution control program areas.

> The objective of the MACs is to provide government managers with timely high quality services for a reasonable price maximizing innovation and cost reduction initiatives. All Task Orders placed against a MAC contract must fall within the general scope defined in the basic MAC contracts.

## 2. Competition and Award Controversies

As is the case in virtually all acquisitions of services under IDIQ contracts, competition is usually based on proposed labor rates that include direct costs, indirect costs, and profit. This reduces or even eliminates any real chance for real price competition, which may not take place until the conduct of a competition for the award of a task order.

Perhaps the most unique feature of competitions for GWACs and MACs has been the fact that the prospect of multiple awards prompts a large response, resulting in large numbers of proposals being submitted and forcing agencies to find ways to streamline the source selection process. This can be risky if not done properly. See, for example, GAO's comments in *Kathpal Techs., Inc.*, Comp. Gen. Dec. B-283137.3, 2000 CPD ¶ 6, sustaining the protest in part because the agency did not consider price when screening proposals to select candidates for more in-depth evaluation:

At the outset, we appreciate the difficulty faced by [Department of] Commerce in needing to evaluate more than 200 proposals, particularly given the RFP requirement for oral presentations. The agency may well have believed that the way it conducted this procurement showed that it was implementing recent reforms in the procurement system. It is true that government-wide acquisition contracts, such as the COMMITS program, are largely the creatures of recent procurement reform. See Clinger-Cohen Act of 1996, Pub. L. No. 104-106, § 5124, 110 Stat. 642, 684 (1996). It is also true that recent reforms have given contracting agencies greater discretion to more effectively and efficiently conduct procurements. For example (and of some relevance here, as discussed below), Congress has given agencies the authority to limit the number of offers included in a competitive range to the greatest number that would permit an efficient competition. See 41 U.S.C. § 253b(d)(2); FAR § 15.306(c). Our Office believes that the government procurement system can benefit substantially from the increased flexibility inherent in recent procurement reform. In this procurement, however, we are persuaded, as explained below, that the agency's conduct violated applicable law and regulations in several significant ways.

[W]e disagree with the agency that it could ignore price in its initial screening evaluation. Cost or price to the government must be included in every RFP as an evaluation factor, and agencies must consider cost or price to the government in evaluating competitive proposals. 41 U.S.C. § 253a(c)(1)(B) (1994); FAR § 15-304(c)(1); *S.J. Thomas Co., Inc.*, B-283192, Oct. 20, 1999, 99-2 CPD ¶ at 3. [Footnote omitted.]

In denying the agency's request to modify this decision, Comp. Gen. Dec. B-283137.7, 2000 CPD ¶ 27, GAO did agree that oral presentations could be limited to "highly rated offerors" if that procedure was spelled out in the RFP.

One solution has been to award contracts to all competitors, as happened in the General Services Administration's 2009 award of its Alliant GWAC, where the agency awarded contracts to 59 out of 59 offerors after an initial decision to make only 29 awards was followed by a protest that was upheld by the Court of Federal Claims, *Serco, Inc. v. U.S.*, 81 Fed. Cl. 463 (2008). This tactic, while it may reduce the chances of a protest, may effectively neutralize the presumably beneficial effects of true competition, since all but the most incompetent firms can be expect to be successful, regardless of the prices offered. In such cases, real competition is deferred until the conduct of competition for orders, and contracting officers should negotiate aggressively for fair and reasonable prices before placing an order. Some agencies provide for "rolling admissions" to a GWAC or MAC during its term. In this way, additional contractors may be added from time to time. Agencies may also cull contractors from the pool by not exercising options to extend a contract's life.

## C. Ordering

Some interagency contracts permit only the awarding agency to place orders, necessitating an assisted acquisition. Others permit using agencies to order directly.

Regardless of which agency places an order, the ordering process is governed by FAR 16.505. FAR 16.505(a) provides:

(7) Orders placed under a task-order contract or delivery-order contract awarded by another agency (i.e., a Governmentwide acquisition contract, or multi-agency contract) —

(i) Are not exempt from the development of acquisition plans (see subpart 7.1), and an information technology acquisition strategy (see part 39);

(ii) May not be used to circumvent conditions and limitations imposed on the use of funds (e.g., 31 U.S.C. 1501(a)(1)); and

(iii) Must comply with all FAR requirements for a bundled contract when the order meets the definition of "bundled contract" (see 2.101(b)).

(8) In accordance with section 1427(b) of Public Law 108-136, orders placed under multi-agency contracts for services that substantially or to a dominant extent specify performance of architect-engineer services, as defined in 2.101, shall —

(i) Be awarded using the procedures at Subpart 36.6; and

(ii) Require the direct supervision of a professional architect or engineer licensed, registered or certified in the State, Federal District, or outlying area, in which the services are to be performed.

## 1. Competition

GWACs, MACs, and enterprisewide contracts are subject to the same fair opportunity procedures for awarding orders as all other multiple award IDIQ contracts. These procedures have become more stringent as discussed in Chapter 9.

The agencies with GWACs have established websites for their contracts that provide information about ordering procedures. See, for example, the National Aeronautics and Space Administration's website for its Solutions for Enterprise-Wide Procurement (SEWP) GWAC, *http://www.sewp.nasa.gov/*. See also the Naval Sea System Command's website for its SeaPort MAC for engineering, financial management, and program management support services, *http://www.seaport.navy.mil/default.aspx*. Agencies need not seek full and open competition when placing orders, FAR 16.505(b)(1)(ii). Instead, agencies must give contract holders a "fair opportunity" to be considered for award of an order. When placing an order valued at or below the simplified acquisition threshold, agencies need not contact each of the contract holders if the contracting officer has enough information to give each a fair opportunity to be considered. When placing orders valued in excess of the simplified acquisition threshold, agencies must give "fair notice" to all contract holders of their intention to place an order, and ensure that all proposals received are "fairly considered," FAR 16.505(b)(1)(iii). The notice must include a description of the supplier or services to be acquired and the basis on which selection of the awardee is to be made. Agencies may provide notice to fewer contractors if notice is provided to as many "as practicable." However, in such cases, an award cannot be made unless quotes or proposals are received from at least three of the contractors or the contracting officer determines no other qualified contractors could be identified.

## 2. Exceptions to the Requirement for Competition

FAR 16.505(b)(2) lists the exceptions to the requirement for "fair opportunity" competition:

1. urgent need precludes competition;

2. only one contractor is capable of doing the work;

3. sole source award is in the interest of economy and efficiency as a logical follow-on to a competitively awarded order;

4. sole source award is necessary to meet minimum purchase requirement; and

5. for orders exceeding the simplified acquisition threshold, as authorized or required by statute.

The rules in FAR 16.505(b)(2)(ii) about documenting justification for use of an exception are lengthy and complex. Use of any of the exceptions for an order valued in excess of $3,000 requires preparation of a written justification. For orders exceeding the simplified acquisition threshold, FAR lists ten specific requirements:

(1) Identification of the agency and the contracting activity, and specific identification of the document as a "Justification for an Exception to Fair Opportunity."

(2) Nature and/or description of the action being approved.

(3) A description of the supplies or services required to meet the agency's needs (including the estimated value).

(4) Identification of the exception to fair opportunity (see 16.505(b)(2)) and the supporting rationale, including a demonstration that the proposed contractor's unique qualifications or the nature of the acquisition requires use of the exception cited. If the contracting officer uses the logical follow-on exception, the rationale shall describe why the relationship between the initial order and the follow-on is logical (e.g., in terms of scope, period of performance, or value).

(5) A determination by the contracting officer that the anticipated cost to the Government will be fair and reasonable.

(6) Any other facts supporting the justification.

(7) A statement of the actions, if any, the agency may take to remove or overcome any barriers that led to the exception to fair opportunity before any subsequent acquisition for the supplies or services is made.

(8) The contracting officer's certification that the justification is accurate and complete to the best of the contracting officer's knowledge and belief.

(9) Evidence that any supporting data that is the responsibility of technical or requirements personnel (e.g., verifying the Government's minimum needs or requirements or other rationale for an exception to fair opportunity) and which form a basis for the justification have been certified as complete and accurate by the technical or requirements personnel.

(10) A written determination by the approving official that one of the circumstances in (b)(2)(i)(A) through (E) of this section applies to the order.

Contracting officers may approve justifications for orders at $650,000 by certifying that the justification is accurate and complete to the best of the contracting officer's knowledge and belief. Justifications valued in excess of $650,000 require approval by higher level officials in accordance with FAR 16.505(b)(2)(ii)(C). In accordance with FAR 16.505(b)(2)(ii)(D), for orders exceeding the simplified acquisition threshold the contracting officer must, within 14 days after issuing the order, post a notice at the Governmentwide Point of Entry in accordance with FAR 5.301 and make the justification publicly available. The posting requirement may be waived in the interests of national security. See FAR 16.505(b)(2)(ii)(D)(5).

## 3. Competitive Procedures

Neither the statutes nor the regulations prescribe procedures for the conduct of competitions for orders. Agencies are not required to follow the source selection procedures in FAR Subpart 15.3, but contracting officers must develop fair placement procedures and may not allocate orders among contractors or permit designation of a preferred awardee. FAR counsels contracting officers to tailor the procedures to each acquisition, FAR 16.505(b)(2)(ii)(A) through (E). Contracting officers must describe their procedures in the solicitation for the order competition and must consider proposed price or cost when selecting awardees. See Chapter 9 for more detail on these procedures.

Protests are not permitted against the award of orders valued at $10 million or less, except on grounds that the order increases the scope, period, or maximum value of the underlying contract. However, protests on any grounds may be filed with GAO against the award of orders valued in excess of $10 million, FAR 16.505(a)(9).

# CHAPTER 9

# TYPES OF CONTRACTS

There are two basic types of pricing arrangements used in government contracts — the cost-reimbursement contract, where the contractor is reimbursed for the allowable costs incurred in performance of the contract, and the fixed-price contract, where the contractor is paid a price for performing the work. In their purest form, these types of contracts are distinguished by the degree of risk of the cost of performance which is allocated to the contractor. In the firm-fixed-price contract, the contractor must complete the work to receive the price, which is preestablished and is not influenced by the cost of performance (except for price adjustments under contract clauses). Thus, if the costs are greater than the price and no price adjustments are warranted, the contractor will suffer a loss; conversely, the lower the costs the greater the profits. Further, if the work is not satisfactorily completed on time, the contractor will be liable to the government for default termination or breach. In contrast, under a cost-plus-fixed-fee contract, the contractor's profit is not affected by the cost of performance because incurred costs will be reimbursed and the amount of the fee is predetermined. Equally as important, if the costs of performance are higher than estimated, the contractor is not obligated to complete the work if the government does not continue to furnish additional funds. Further, it is extremely unlikely that the contractor would be held liable for defective or untimely work.

Fixed-price and cost-reimbursement contracts are also distinguished by the method of payment of the contractor. Under the fixed-price contract, payment is made for completed and delivered work. If this method of payment imposes financial burdens on the contractor, the government may agree to provide financing in the form of progress payments. In either case, contractors incur significant financing costs in performing most fixed-price contracts. In contrast, payment is made on cost-reimbursement contracts on the basis of costs incurred during contract performance. Under these contracts, the contractor is assured of reimbursement of costs on a regular basis and needs to provide only a minimal amount of financing.

Refinements and sophistication in contracting techniques have resulted in a variety of types of fixed-price and cost-reimbursement contracts that alter the normal risk distribution and blur the distinctions between these basic contract types. The major category of contract types that fall in this middle ground are called incentive contracts. In these contracts, the parties share the risk by negotiating arrangements that alter the contractor's profit based on the cost or quality of performance. Another means of sharing the risk is the fixed-price contract with economic price adjustment, where the costs of labor and material are adjusted if there are fluctuations in market conditions which affect the contractor's costs. In another category of contracts, the government relieves the contractor of risk by contracting for a level-of-effort or for labor-hours rather than for a completed job or task. These contracts are called time-and-materials, labor-hour, or level-of-effort contracts.

The government also uses several different types of variable quantity forms of contracts. In some of these instances, the government uses a form of contract where the contractor is bound to perform but the government is free to order some or all of the work from another party. Examples of this type of arrangement are simple options and indefinite-quantity contracts with minimum quantities. Other forms of variable quantity contracts bind the government as firmly as the contractor. The most commonly used contracts of this type are requirements contracts and multiyear contracts. All of these types of contracts are discussed in this chapter.

# I.  BASIC POLICIES

The statutory guidance on the selection of contracts is simple and direct. 10 U.S.C. § 2306(a) and 41 U.S.C. § 3901(a) and § 3905(a) give broad discretion to use any appropriate type of contract on negotiated procurements but prohibit the use of a cost-plus-a-percentage-of-cost (CPPC) system of contracts. FAR 16.102 implements these statutes by restricting the types of contracts considered appropriate to those described in Part 16, as follows:

(a) Contracts resulting from sealed bidding shall be firm-fixed-price contracts or fixed-price contracts with economic price adjustment.

(b) Contracts negotiated under Part 15 may be of any type or combination of types that will promote the Government's interest, except as restricted in this part (see 10 U.S.C. § 2306(a) and 41 U.S.C. § 254(a)). Contract types not described in this regulation shall not be used, except as a deviation under Subpart 1.4.

(c) The cost-plus-a-percentage-of-cost system of contracting shall not be used (see 10 U.S.C. § 2306(a) and 41 U.S.C. § 254(b)) [pre-2011 codification]. Prime contracts (including letter contracts) other than firm-fixed-price contracts shall, by an appropriate clause, prohibit cost-plus-a-percentage-of-cost subcontracts (see clauses prescribed in Subpart 44.2 for cost-reimbursement contracts and Subparts 16.2 and 16.4 for fixed-price contracts).

This section addresses several general issues that must be considered in selecting the appropriate type of contract. The first issue is the *broad discretion* granted to contracting officers in selecting the type of contract in negotiated procurements. Second is the scope of the prohibition of CPPC systems of contracting. Finally, the section reviews the policies on undefinitized contractual actions such as letter contracts or letters of intent.

## A. Discretion

The amount of discretion afforded to agencies in selecting the type of contract depends on the procurement technique that is used. The least discretion is conferred when sealed bidding is used because in that situation the agency is required to use either firm-fixed-price contracts or fixed-price contracts with economic price adjustment, FAR 14.104; FAR 16.102(a).

Somewhat more discretion is granted in contracts for commercial items. There FAR 12.207 provides:

(a) Except as provided in paragraph (b) of this section, agencies shall use firm-fixed-price contracts or fixed-price contracts with economic price adjustment for the acquisition of commercial items.

(b)(1) A time-and-materials contract or labor-hour contract (see Subpart 16.6) may be used for the acquisition of commercial services when —

(i) The service is acquired under a contract awarded using —

(A) Competitive procedures (e.g., the procedures in 6.102, the set-aside procedures in Subpart 19.5, or competition conducted in accordance with Part 13);

(B) The procedures for other than full and open competition in 6.3 provided the agency receives offers that satisfy the Government's expressed requirement from two or more responsible offerors; or

(C) The fair opportunity procedures in 16.505, if placing an order under a multiple award delivery-order contract; and

(ii) The contracting officer —

(A) Executes a determination and findings (D&F) for the contract, in accordance with paragraph (b)(2) of this section (but see paragraph (c) of this section for indefinite-delivery contracts), that no other contract type authorized by this subpart is suitable;

(B) Includes a ceiling price in the contract or order that the contractor exceeds at its own risk; and

(C) Authorizes any subsequent change in the ceiling price only upon a determination, documented in the contract file, that it is in the best interest of the procuring agency to change the ceiling price.

(2) Each D&F required by paragraph (b)(1)(ii)(A) of this section shall contain sufficient facts and rationale to justify that no other contract type authorized by this subpart is suitable. At a minimum, the D&F shall —

(i) Include a description of the market research conducted (see 10.002(e));

(ii) Establish that it is not possible at the time of placing the contract or order to accurately estimate the extent or duration of the work or to anticipate costs with any reasonable degree of certainty;

(iii) Establish that the requirement has been structured to maximize the use of firm-fixed-price or fixed-price with economic price adjustment contracts (e.g., by limiting the value or length of the time-and-material/labor-hour contract or order; establishing fixed prices for portions of the requirement) on future acquisitions for the same or similar requirements; and

(iv) Describe actions planned to maximize the use of firm-fixed-price or fixed-price with economic price adjustment contracts on future acquisitions for the same requirements.

The stringent requirements allowing the use of time-and-materials or labor-hour contracts in procuring commercial services were added to the FAR in 2006 by Federal Acquisition Circular 2005-15, 71 Fed. Reg. 74,667, Dec. 12, 2006. They implement § 1432 of the National Defense Authorization Act for FY 2004, Pub. L. No. 108-136, which explicitly authorized to use of these types of contracts under limited circumstances.

The greatest discretion is granted in selecting the type of contract to be used in negotiated procurements. There FAR 16.103 balances the need to impose *reasonable risks* on the contractor with the need to use a type of contract that *motivates effective performance*, stating:

(a) Selecting the contract type is generally a matter for negotiation and requires the exercise of sound judgment. Negotiating the contract type and negotiating prices are closely related and should be considered together. The objective is to negotiate a contract type and price (or estimated cost and fee) that will result in reasonable contractor risk and provide the contractor with the greatest incentive for efficient and economical performance.

(b) A firm-fixed-price contract, which best utilizes the basic profit motive of business enterprise, shall be used when the risk involved is minimal or can be predicted with an acceptable degree of certainty. However, when a reasonable basis for firm pricing does not exist, other contract types should be considered, and negotiations should be directed toward selecting a contract type (or combination of types) that will appropriately tie profit to contractor performance.

FAR 16.104 provides a list of factors to be considered in selecting the contract type with guidance as to the application of each factor. The factors are listed as follows:

- Price competition

- Price analysis

- Cost analysis

- Type and complexity of the requirement

- Urgency of the requirement

- Period of performance or length of production run

- Contractor's technical capability and financial responsibility

- Adequacy of the contractor's accounting system

- Concurrent contracts

- Extent and nature of proposed subcontracting

- Acquisition history

The guidance in this paragraph of the FAR makes it quite clear that the basic policy of the government is to use the type of contract that imposes sufficient risk on the contractor to motivate good performance yet relieves the contractor of unduly high risks over which it has no control and that are unpredictable.

The contracting officer has broad discretion in selecting the contract type. See, for example, *PCL Constr. Servs., Inc. v. United States*, 47 Fed. Cl. 745 (2000), *aff'd*, 96 Fed. App'x 672 (Fed. Cir. 2004), where the court denied the contractor's claim that the agency had illegally used a firm-fixed-price contract when there was substantial pricing risk, stating at 807-08:

> [T]he solicitation and contract made no secret of the variables to be encountered by the contractor selected which would require design efforts and likely modifications using the changes clause procedures. If plaintiff believed that these variables were so uncertain that it was improper to use an FFP contract, and that the scope of the contract, was, therefore, ambiguous; it had a duty to inquire as to the true nature of the contract before submitting a bid. See *Triax Pac., Inc. v. West*, 130 F.3d at 1474-75; see also *Ryan Co. v. United States*, 43 Fed. Cl. 646, 654 (1999) ("When a solicitation presents conflicting signals, a contractor is under an affirmative duty to call the ambiguity to the attention of the contracting official."). Moreover, the contractor is assumed to understand the risks inherent in the type of contract it signs at the time of execution. Among the distinguishing characteristics between the various types of contracts is the degree of risk allocated to the contractor. In addition, even if the plaintiff had an argument regarding the

choice of contract type, when a statutory or regulatory restriction is designed for the protection and benefit of the government and the taxpayers, a contract made in violation of that restriction and relied on by the government is binding upon the contractor unless repudiated by the government. The plaintiff cannot gain an advantage from regulations not designed for its benefit. See *National Elec. Lab. v. United States*, 148 Ct. Cl. 308, 314, 180 F. Supp. 337, 340-41 (1960). The solicitation clearly identified the contract to be awarded as an FFP contract. PCL willingly bid on an FFP contract, and willingly signed an FFP contract, thereby assuming the risks attendant to an FFP contract.

See also *Master Sec., Inc.*, Comp. Gen. Dec. B-232263, 88-2 CPD ¶ 449, denying a protest where the contracting officer had used a firm-fixed-price contract for three years of work. The protester argued that such a contract imposed an inordinate risk of higher labor costs, but GAO accepted the contracting officer's reasoning that competition would keep the prices from containing too high a contingency and that "practical individual financial considerations would dissuade offerors from proposing unrealistically low prices." See also *Surface Techs. Corp.*, Comp. Gen. Dec. B-288317, 2001 CPD ¶ 147, where a protest was denied when the contracting officer chose a cost-reimbursement contract instead of a fixed-price contract. GAO accepted the reasoning that there were sufficient unknowns in ship preservation work to justify the use of a cost-reimbursement contract.

Historically, this broad discretion in the selection of the contract type has occasionally been used to impose very high risks on contractors undertaking major development programs. Congress reacted to this practice by limiting the use of fixed-price contracts in the following section of the Omnibus Appropriations Act of 1988, Pub . L. No. 100-202:

> Section 8118. None of the funds provided for the Department of Defense in this Act may be obligated or expended for fixed-price-type contracts in excess of $10,000,000 for the development of a major system or subsystem unless the Under Secretary of Defense for Acquisition determines, in writing, that program risk has been reduced to the extent that realistic pricing can occur, and that the contract type permits an equitable and sensible allocation of program risk between the contracting parties.

This provision was implemented in DFARS 235.006. In *American Tel. & Tel. Co. v. United States*, 177 F.3d 1368 (Fed. Cir. 1999) (en banc), the court held that violating this statute did not result in a void contract, while in *American Tel. & Tel. Co. v. United States*, 307 F.3d 1374 (Fed. Cir. 2002), *cert. denied*, 540 U.S. 937 (2003), the court held that the contractor was entitled to no relief when the government violated this statute because the statute was not intended to create a private cause of action. See also *Northrop Grumman Corp. v. United States*, 63 Fed. Cl. 38 (2004), reaching the same result.

Congress altered this policy in 2006. Section 818 of the National Defense Authorization Act for FY 2007, Pub. L. No. 109-364, states a preference for the use of fixed-price type contracts for development work on major systems by requiring a written determination by the "Milestone Decision Authority" whenever a cost-type contract is used for a "major defense acquisition program." This requirement is implemented in DFARS 234.004 as follows:

(2) In accordance with Section 818 of the National Defense Authorization Act for Fiscal Year 2007 (Pub. L. 109-364), for major defense acquisition programs as defined in 10 U.S.C. 2430 —

(i) The Milestone Decision Authority shall select, with the advice of the contracting officer, the contract type for a development program at the time of Milestone B approval or, in the case of a space program, Key Decision Point B approval;

(ii) The basis for the contract type selection shall be documented in the acquisition strategy. The documentation —

(A) Shall include an explanation of the level of program risk; and

(B) If program risk is determined to be high, shall outline the steps taken to reduce program risk and the reasons for proceeding with Milestone B approval despite the high level of program risk; and

(iii) If a cost-type contract is selected, the contract file shall include the Milestone Decision Authority's written determination that —

(A) the program is so complex and technically challenging that it would not be practicable to reduce program risk to a level that would permit the use of a fixed-rice type contract; and

(B) the result of a failure to meet the requirements established in section 2366a of title 10, United States Code.

Another provision showing the congressional attempt to limit the use of cost-reimbursement contracts is § 864 of the National Defense Authorization Act for FY 2009, Pub. L. No. 110-417, requiring the revision of the FAR on the use of cost-reimbursement contracts and calling for a review of the use of such contracts by agency Inspectors General and an annual report on use of such contracts by the Officer of Management and Budget. The first annual OMB report indicated that in fiscal year 2008 the major agencies issued $135 billion in cost-reimbursement contracts, constituting 25% of their procurement dollars (*www.whitehouse.gov/omb/assets/procurement/cost_contracting_report_031809.pdf*). See also *Contract Management: Extent of Federal Spending Under Cost-Reimbursment Contracts Unclear and Key Controls Not Always Used*, GAO-09-921, Sept. 30, 2009, for an assessment of the amount of cost type contracting in major agencies.

The broad discretion with regard to negotiated procurement has also been used, on occasion, to impose very low risks on contractors by using cost-reimbursement contracts in situations where fixed-price contracts could be used. This can occur, for example, when the following guidance in FAR 16.103 is not followed:

> (c) In the course of an acquisition program, a series of contracts, or a single long-term contract, changing circumstances may make a different contract type appropriate in later periods than that used at the outset. In particular, contracting officers should avoid protracted use of a cost-reimbursement or time-and-materials contract after experience provides a basis for firmer pricing.

One example of failure to follow this guidance was in the case of support service contracts awarded by the National Aeronautics and Space Administration (NASA) on a cost-plus-award-fee basis for many years. This policy was criticized by Congress in the early 1990s, and NASA was ordered in § 401 of the NASA Authorization Act for FY 1993, Pub. L. No. 102-588, to review its policies to allocate the risk more equitably.

Thus, the discretion conferred on the contracting officer in this area must be exercised with great care — taking into account the interests of both the government and the contractor. The number of contract types included in the regulations permit the striking of a fair balance between these interests in virtually all contracting situations.

## B. Cost-Plus-a-Percentage-of-Cost Contracts

The two major procurement statutes prohibit CPPC contracts. Both 10 U.S.C. § 2306(a) and 41 U.S.C. § 3905(a) state simply, with no further statutory guidance, that a "cost-plus-a-percentage-of-cost system of contracting shall not be used." This prohibition applies to both cost-reimbursement and fixed-price contracts. The Supreme Court explained the basis for this statutory prohibition in *Muschany v. United States*, 324 U.S. 49 (1944), at 61-62:

> The purpose of Congress was to protect the Government against the sort of exploitation so easily accomplished under cost-plus-a-percentage-of-cost contracts under which the Government contracts and is bound to pay costs, undetermined at the time the contract is made and to be incurred in the future, plus a commission based on a percentage of these future costs. The evil of such contracts is that the profit of the other party to the contract increases in proportion to that other party's costs expended in the performance. The danger guarded against by the Congressional prohibition was the incentive to a government contractor who already had a binding contract with the Government for payment of undetermined future costs to pay liberally for reimbursable items because higher costs meant a higher fee to him, his profit being determined by a percentage of cost.

In view of the clear statutory prohibition, explicit CPPC contracts are not likely to be encountered. Since, however, the statutory language prohibits a "system of contracting" and not merely a type of contract, numerous sorts of contractual arrangements may become subject to this prohibition. Generally, any contractual arrangement where the contractor is assured of greater profits by incurring additional costs will be held illegal. GAO has enunciated general criteria for ascertaining whether a contract violates this proscription. These criteria were adopted by the Federal Circuit in *Urban Data Sys., Inc. v. United States*, 699 F.2d 1147 (Fed. Cir. 1983), at 1150:

> We accept, at the outset, the general criteria (adopted by the Board) which were developed by the Comptroller General for determining whether a contract is a cost-plus-a-percentage-of-cost contract: (1) payment is on a predetermined percentage rate; (2) the predetermined percentage rate is applied to actual performance costs; (3) the contractor's entitlement is uncertain at the time of contracting; and (4) the contractor's entitlement increases commensurately with increased performance costs. 55 Comp. Gen. 554, 562 (1975). These standards incorporate the common understanding of the "cost-plus-a-percentage-of-cost system of contracting," an understanding which was undoubtedly in Congress's mind when it enacted the prohibition.

In spite of these clear criteria, there is still some confusion as to the arrangements that will constitute such a system of contracting. See, for example, *General Eng'g & Mach. Works v. O'Keefe*, 991 F.2d 775 (Fed. Cir. 1993), where the court affirmed a board holding that the recovery of a separate material handling charge and the inclusion of material handling costs in the hourly rate of a time-and-materials contract would constitute a violation of the CPPC prohibition because it was double recovery. The board had stated in *General Eng'g & Mach. Works*, ASBCA 38788, 92-3 BCA ¶ 25,055, at 124,872:

> If [the contractor] has already received compensation for its effort in handling material as part of its general overhead, further compensation in the form of a material handling charge would constitute additional profit. The payment of that additional profit, in an amount dependent upon the amount of material costs incurred, would constitute a cost-plus-a-percentage-of-cost contractual payment, and thus be illegal.

Neither the board nor the court found that payment of material handling costs as a percentage of material costs was proscribed as long as the material handling costs were excluded from the contractor's overhead. The current contract provisions are silent on this matter. See the Payments under Time-and-Materials and Labor-Hour Contracts clause in FAR 52.232-7, which permits the inclusion of "applicable indirect costs" in charges for material without specifying whether such costs could be charged at a predetermined rate.

Similar confusion occurred in *Information Sys. & Networks Corp. v. United States*, 64 Fed. Cl. 599 (2005). There the court correctly ruled that a contractor was not entitled to additional fee when its state taxes were increased. However, in responding to the contractor's argument that it would have negotiated a higher fee if the parties had known about the higher taxes, the court stated that awarding such fees would be a clear violation of the cost-plus-a-percentage-of-cost prohibition. In so holding, the court rejected the contractor's argument that there was no such violation because it could not have increased the state tax in order to obtain more profit.

## 1. Percentage Compensation

To fall within the definition of a CPPC arrangement, the agreement must provide that some element of the contractor's compensation will be computed as a *percentage* of some of the costs of performance. Such an arrangement meets the first, second, and fourth elements of the above criteria. When the element of compensation established on a percentage basis is profit or fee, it is easy to determine that a violation has occurred. See *Alisa Corp.*, AGBCA 84-193-1, 94-2 BCA ¶ 26,952, where the board found a CPPC contract where it was stated to be an "actual cost + fixed fee" contract with the fee to be paid at 10% of actual costs. Compare *Michael Weller, Inc.*, GSBCA 10627-NHI, 94-2 BCA ¶ 26,849, where a time-and-materials contract that authorized reimbursement for cost of subcontracts was held not to be a CPPC contract because the profit paid was not computed as a percentage of costs.

A violation is somewhat more difficult to see when one element of cost is paid as a percentage of another cost element. However, this is the more common form of violation. Thus, payment of indirect costs on a percentage basis has been held to violate the CPPC proscription. Such violations were found when a contract called for the payment of overhead rates at predetermined percentages of direct costs, 35 Comp. Gen. 434 (B-126794) (1956); 35 Comp. Gen. 63 (B-120714) (1955); *Decision of Assoc. Gen. Counsel Kepplinger*, Comp. Gen. Dec. B-252378, Sept. 21, 1993, *Unpub.*, and when a material handling charge was to be paid at a percentage of subcontract and material costs, *Systems Eng'g Assocs. Corp.*, ASBCA 21846, 77-2 BCA ¶ 12,740. Similarly, a time-and-materials contract calling for payment of overhead and profit at 15% and 10% of cost, respectively, was held to be unenforceable, 46 Comp. Gen. 612 (B-159713) (1967). The problem created by contracts where one type of costs is paid on a percentage basis is that such compensation may be greater than the actual costs incurred by the contractor, with the result that a part of this compensation will be additional profit. Hence, these contracts contain the same improper motivation — to increase the base costs in order to increase the potential amount of profit that is derived from the cost element that is paid as a percentage of the base costs.

The most unusual element of cost included under this proscription is an executive bonus. In *Air Repair, GmbH.*, ASBCA 10288, 67-1 BCA ¶ 6115, a contractor working under a cost-reimbursement contract agreed to pay its principal officer a bonus computed at a percentage of gross billings. The board found that this was a CPPC arrangement since the officer of the company had the ability to increase the amount of the bonus by increasing the costs of performing the contract.

In most cases finding this type of violation, the percentage has been applied evenly to some of the costs of performance. However, a "stepladder" compensation arrangement has also been held to be a violation. For example, in *Department of State Method of Payment Provisions*, Comp. Gen. Dec. B-196556, 80-2 CPD ¶ 87, GAO found a violation where the contractor was to be paid a management fee based on a sliding scale of actual costs incurred, as follows:

| Monthly Total Actual Cost | Management Fee |
|---|---|
| $0    –    5,000 | $250 |
| 5,001    –   10,000 | 750 |
| 10,001    –   15,000 | 1,250 |
| 15,001    –   20,000 | 1,750 |
| above   20,001 | 1,750 plus $500 for each additional $5,000 of invoiced costs |

GAO rejected the argument of the agency that this formula was merely a series of fixed fees. A similar result was reached in *Marketing Consultants Int'l, Ltd.*, 55 Comp. Gen. 554 (B-183705), 75-2 CPD ¶ 384. In contrast, no violation was found in *Grey Advertising, Inc.*, 55 Comp. Gen. 1111 (B-184825), 76-1 CPD ¶ 325, where the contract provided for interim fee payments based on "costs being paid" but the total fee was fixed at the inception of the contract.

Violation can be avoided by removing the percentage basis of compensation. When fee is involved, the remedy is to use a cost-reimbursement contract with a fixed or target fee. When overhead is involved, the remedy is accomplished by compensating contractors at negotiated billing rates until the close of an accounting period, FAR 42.704, at which time final rates are negotiated on the basis of actual cost data and costs are adjusted to reflect these final rates, FAR 42.705. One statutory exception to this rule permits educational institutions to be compensated based on predetermined overhead rates, 41 U.S.C. § 4708, FAR 42.705-3. Another means of removing the percentage relationship is to include overhead and profit in fixed rates for labor. This is done in time-and-materials and labor-hour contracts where the contractor is paid a single rate for each hour of labor performed, FAR 16.601, FAR 16.602. Since this type of arrangement contains an incentive, similar to the CPPC contract, to increase costs, the regulations require close government surveillance of such contracts, FAR 16.601(b)(1).

## 2. Uncertain Entitlement

To fall within the statutory proscription, a contractor's entitlement to compensation must also be uncertain *at the time of contracting*. Conversely, when the amount of entitlement is established at the time of contracting, even though it was computed on a percentage basis, the contract will not be viewed as a CPPC contract. For example, in *Muschany v. United States*, 324 U.S. 49 (1944), the Supreme Court ruled that an arrangement permitting a broker, acquiring land on behalf of the government, to charge vendors of the land a 5% commission was not a violation of the statute. The Court reasoned that since the 5% was part of the price of the land, certain at the time of purchase, the government was fully able to determine whether it should pay that price. Thus, it concluded that the arrangement did not motivate the broker to increase its fee by increasing the cost of the land. The Court stated at 63:

> The arrangement may have been improvident from the point of view of the Government. But that question goes to the quality of management by its procurement officers. The fact that the procurement system is improvident obviously does not make it illegal. Illegality does not emerge from inadequate supervision of prices by the Real Estate Branch. Such official failures are not chargeable to a third party dealing with the Government in good faith. It may be unwise for the Government to pay its purchasing agent a commission which is figured on cost of purchases to the Government but there is no statutory prohibition.

*Marketing Consultants Int'l Ltd.*, 55 Comp. Gen. 554 (B-183705), 75-2 CPD ¶ 384, addresses a similar situation. In that case, the contractor was buying work from subcontractors on behalf of the government, under an agreement providing for a percentage markup to compensate the contractor. For some of the purchases, where the government reviewed the subcontract prices prior to award of the subcontracts by the contractor, GAO ruled that there was no violation of the statute. For other purchases, where the contractor was authorized to award the subcontract without prior government review and approval, GAO found a violation because the amount of subcontractor compensation was uncertain "at the time of contracting." See also *Tero Tek Int'l, Ltd.*, Comp. Gen. Dec. B-228548, 88-1 CPD ¶ 132, where a contract that provided for reimbursement of travel expenses based on actual cost plus an agreed percentage thereof subject to a regulatory guideline was held not to be a CPPC contract because the contractor's entitlement was not uncertain at the time of contracting.

## 3. Ceilings

The inclusion of a ceiling price in an arrangement that otherwise violates the statute will not cure the violation, 38 Comp. Gen. 38 (B-120546) (1958); *Federal Aviation Admin. — Request for Advance Decision*, 58 Comp. Gen. 654 (B-195173), 79-2 CPD ¶ 34. In these cases, GAO reasoned that there was a violation because the contractor had the same improper motivation to increase profit by increasing the costs up to the amount of the ceiling. *Urban Data Sys., Inc. v. United States*, 699 F.2d 1147 (Fed. Cir. 1983), follows this reasoning in a more complex transaction. There the parties had agreed to a fixed-price contract that included a clause calling for a downward price adjustment computed as the difference between actual costs and anticipated costs, plus 5%. The court reasoned that this was no different from paying actual costs plus 5% profit up to a ceiling price. This holding was buttressed by the fact that the parties negotiated the fixed price using the anticipated costs plus the same 5% profit rate.

In *Department of Labor — Request for Advance Decision*, 62 Comp. Gen. 337 (B-211213), 83-1 CPD ¶ 429, GAO applied this rule on ceilings in an unusual way. The agreement provided for markups of a "maximum of . . . 7.5 percent . . . to cover overhead and profit." GAO reasoned that limiting the markup to a maximum amount was the same as providing for a ceiling price and was thus a statutory violation. This is a highly questionable decision because the contract language can be interpreted more logically as calling for a markup to be negotiated by the parties at the time of pricing new work, with a ceiling on that amount. Such an arrangement would not be a violation of the proscription since the government would not have agreed to a fixed percentage rate of compensation.

In *Fluor Enters., Inc. v. United States*, 64 Fed. Cl. 461 (2005), the court discussed the possibility that a contract permitting an A-E firm to prepare the construction cost estimate might violate the statute because that estimate would constitute the base for determining the 6% fee limitation applicable to A-E firms under 41 U.S.C. § 254(b).

## 4. Pricing After Incurrence of Costs

After-the-fact pricing is quite common in government contracting and presents the appearance of CPPC contracting because the profit policy of most government agencies, adopted pursuant to FAR 15.404-4(b), computes profit largely on the basis of costs of performance. See Chapter 10. Such pricing does not violate the statute, however, when there is no agreement between the contracting parties that any fixed percentage will be applied to incurred costs in negotiating the price. Further, the policy is generally construed as calling for a lower rate of profit if substantial costs have been incurred prior to pricing, because the contractor's risk has been reduced, and contractor risk is one of the key elements considered in arriving at the government's profit position.

The courts and boards have generally agreed that after-the-fact pricing is not a statutory violation. The Court of Claims held that a contract calling for price revision after completion did not violate the CPPC prohibition; the court concluded that the contract more closely resembled a cost-plus-fixed-fee (CPFF) contract than a CPPC contract, *National Elec. Labs., Inc. v. United States*, 148 Ct. Cl. 308, 180 F. Supp. 337 (1960). In *United Food Servs., Inc.*, 64 Comp. Gen. 880 (B-217211), 85-2 CPD ¶ 326, it was held that a CPAF contract was not a CPPC contract because the amount of fee to which the contractor was entitled decreased as costs increased. In *MIG Corp.*, ASBCA 54451, 05-1 BCA ¶ 32,979, it was held that paying termination costs did not violate the statute. In *Digicon Corp. v. Department of Commerce*, GSBCA 14257-COM, 98-2 BCA ¶ 29,988; *Rex Sys., Inc.*, ASBCA 49065, 98-2

BCA ¶ 29,926; *E.V. Lane Corp.*, ASBCA 9741, 65-2 BCA ¶ 5076; and *J.G. Watts Constr. Co.*, ASBCA 9454, 1964 BCA ¶4171, it was held that the pricing of changes following completion of work did not violate the rule. See also *Allison Div., General Motors Corp.*, ASBCA 15528, 72-1 BCA ¶ 9343, stating at 43,382-83:

> The Government also contends that to grant an increase in fixed fee for a "comparatively minor" change in the contract would transform the contract into a cost-plus-percentage-of-cost contract which is prohibited by law. 10 U.S.C. 2306. No argument or reasoning, other than the bare assertion, has been advanced by the Government in support of its contention. The change here, as we have concluded, was not minor. It substantially increased appellant's work under the contract. The fixed fee was earned when appellant had exerted the level of effort specified in the contract (i.e., 173,200 hours) in performing the work called for. ASPR 3-405.6(d)(2). In cost-plus-fixed-fee contracts, the fixed fee once negotiated does not vary with actual cost, but it may be adjusted as a result of any subsequent changes in the work or services to be performed under the contract. ASPR 3-405.6(a), cf. *Martin Marietta Corporation*, ASBCA 10062, 65-2 BCA ¶ 4973. The granting of additional profit in connection with increased work under change orders has never been considered, to our knowledge, a violation of the cost-plus-a-percentage-of-cost system of contracting.

A few questionable cases reach the opposite result. GAO has held that the conversion of a letter contract to a definitive contract, after the work was substantially completed, violated the rule, 33 Comp. Gen. 291 (B-110609) (1954). See also *Program Res., Inc.*, ASBCA 21656, 78-1 BCA ¶ 12,867, where the board concluded that allowing the contractor an additional fee for an increase in labor rates, when there was no "change" in the nature of the work, would violate the CPPC proscription. In one unusual case, the Court of Claims held that payment of any profit on government-caused delay costs would constitute a violation of the CPPC prohibition, *Laburnum Constr. Corp. v. United States*, 163 Ct. Cl. 339, 325 F.2d 451 (1963).

### 5. *Quantum Meruit Compensation*

While contracts violating the CPPC proscription are illegal and thus unenforceable, GAO has sometimes permitted contractors to recover the fair value of goods and services provided to the government on a quantum meruit or quantum valebant basis despite the use of a CPPC contract, *Federal Aviation Admin. — Request for Advance Decision*, 58 Comp. Gen. 654 (B 195173), 79-2 CPD ¶ 34; 33 Comp. Gen. 533 (B-118109) (1954); Comp. Gen. Dec. B-167790, Apr. 12, 1973, *Unpub.* See also *Yosemite Park & Curry Co. v. United States*, 217 Ct. Cl. 360, 582 F.2d 552 (1978), where the Court of Claims granted quantum meruit relief because the agency had entered into an invalid contract when the fee exceeded the 10% statutory limitation. In *Alisa Corp.*, AGBCA 84-193-1, 94-2 BCA ¶ 26,952, the board awarded quantum meruit relief in the amount the contractor paid to a supplier for the supplies delivered to the government, stating that it was the lowest price the contractor could have negotiated.

## C. Undefinitized Contractual Actions

Government agencies sometimes encounter situations where they must issue a contract on very short notice with too little time to negotiate all of the terms and conditions or the price. In such cases, it has been common practice to issue a "letter contract" firmly binding the government to pay for the work but calling for the negotiation of a firm contract at a later date. See FAR 16.603-1, stating:

> A letter contract is a written preliminary contractual instrument that authorizes the contractor to begin immediately manufacturing supplies or performing services.

Congress has placed limitations on "undefinitized contractual actions" by the Department of Defense in 10 U.S.C. § 2326. This statute is implemented by DFARS Subpart 217.74, which contains the following definition in DFARS 217.7401(d):

> *Undefinitized contract action* means any contract action for which the contract terms, specifications, or price are not agreed upon before performance is begun under the action. Examples are letter contracts, orders under basic ordering agreements, and provisioned item orders, for which the price has not been agreed upon before performance has begun.

### 1. *Restrictions on Use*

The general policy has been to greatly restrict the use of such transactions because they are open-ended arrangements that place the risk of excessive costs largely on the government. FAR 16.603-2(a) permits the use of letter contracts when —

> (1) the Government's interests demand that the contractor be given a binding commitment so that work can start immediately and

> (2) negotiating a definitive contract is not possible in sufficient time to meet the requirement.

FAR 16.603-3 places the following limitations on the use of such contracts:

> A letter contract may be used only after the head of the contracting activity or a designee determines in writing that no other contract is suitable. Letter contracts shall not —
>
>> (a) Commit the Government to a definitive contract in excess of the funds available at the time the letter contract is executed;
>>
>> (b) Be entered into without competition when competition is required by Part 6; or

(c) Be amended to satisfy a new requirement unless that requirement is inseparable from the existing letter contract. Any such amendment is subject to the same requirements and limitations as a new letter contract.

Similar limitations are contained in 10 U.S.C. § 2326 as implemented by DFARS 217.7404. Sole source letter contracts have been approved when properly justified in accordance with the standards discussed in Chapter 3, *Space Vector Corp.*, Comp. Gen. Dec. B-253295.2, 93-2 CPD ¶ 273 (only one company capable of meeting agency needs within time requirements); *Essex Electro Eng'rs, Inc.*, Comp. Gen. Dec. B-250437, 93-1 CPD ¶ 74 (only one firm capable of quickly supplying product needed urgently for military program); *Greenbrier Indus.*, Inc., Comp. Gen. Dec. B-241304, 91-1 CPD ¶ 92 (only one company capable of meeting urgent need); *Mil-Com Elecs. Corp. v. Aldridge*, 712 F. Supp. 232 (D.D.C. 1989). Compare *Jervis B. Webb Co.*, Comp. Gen. Dec. B-211724, 85-1 CPD ¶ 35, holding that a sole source award of a letter contract was improper because the agency had conducted inadequate acquisition planning.

## 2. Terms and Conditions

A letter contract should contain the terms and conditions appropriate for the type of contract that the contracting officer believes will be used for the definitive contract, FAR 16.603-4(a). In addition, special contract clauses must be used in these contracts.

### a. Expenditure Limitations and Ceiling Prices

FAR 52.216-24 contains a standard clause limiting the government's obligations prior to definitization:

LIMITATION OF GOVERNMENT LIABILITY (APR 1984)

(a) In performing this contract, the Contractor is not authorized to make expenditures or incur obligations exceeding _____ dollars.

(b) The maximum amount for which the Government shall be liable if this contract is terminated is _____ dollars.

The amount to be inserted in this clause is the amount of costs expected to be incurred before definitization, and generally, this amount should not be greater than 50% of the estimated cost of the contract, FAR 16.603-2(d). The government is not obligated to pay more than the amount included in the clause, *Magnavox Co.*, ASBCA 17455, 74-1 BCA ¶ 10,495.

Agencies normally obligate the amount of funds set forth in these expenditure limits from current year appropriations and may not obligate any greater amount from an annual appropriation if the contract is definitized in a subsequent fiscal year. Rather, the balance of the contract amount must be obligated from the appropriations current at the time of the contract definitization, *Obligating Letter Contracts*, Comp. Gen. Dec. B-197274, 84-1 CPD ¶ 90. This rule applies even if the work called for by the letter contract is nonseverable because the only amount of work that was a bona fide need of the first fiscal year was the amount covered by the expenditure limit, with the balance of the work a bona fide need of the fiscal year in which the contract was definitized.

The Department of Defense is subject to statutory rules calling for the negotiation of a ceiling price on undefinitized contractual actions and limiting expenditures to 50% of that ceiling, 10 U.S.C. § 2326(b)(2). DFARS 252.217-7027 provides a modified Contract Definitization clause to implement this requirement. FAR 16.603-4(b)(3) also requires the insertion of a ceiling price in letter contracts that are awarded on the basis of competition. This is to ensure that the contractor is held to the price that was the basis of the source selection. Such ceilings impose a significant risk on a contractor because they necessarily must be determined before all of the elements of the contract have been negotiated. See, for example, *Litton Sys., Inc.*, ASBCA 36976, 93-2 BCA ¶ 25,705, where a contractor that had agreed to a letter contract that was to become a firm-fixed-price contract was bound by the ceiling price even though its costs were substantially higher than that price. In that case, the board also ruled that the ceiling price was to be adjusted to reflect changes to the work, both additive and deductive.

The DoD procedure also permits the contracting officer to raise the level of the government's limitation of obligations to 75% of the ceiling price if the contractor has submitted a "qualifying proposal" prior to reaching the 50% limitation, DFARS 217.7404-4. DFARS 217.7401(c) contains the following definition:

> *Qualifying proposal* means a proposal containing sufficient information for the DoD to do complete and meaningful analysis aqnd audits of the —
>
> > (1) Information in the proposal; and
> >
> > (2) Any other information that the contracting officer has determined DoD needs to review in connection with the contract.

## b. Definitization Schedule

FAR 52.216-25 provides the following clause setting forth the procedures for contract definitization:

CONTRACT DEFINITIZATION (OCT 2010)

(a) A [*insert specific type of contract*] definitive contract is contemplated. The Contractor agrees to begin promptly negotiating with the Contracting Officer the terms of a definitive contract that will include (1) all clauses required by the Federal Acquisition Regulation (FAR) on the date of execution of the letter contract, (2) all clauses required by law on the date of execution of the definitive contract, and (3) any other mutually agreeable clauses, terms, and conditions. The Contractor agrees to submit a _____ [*insert specific type of proposal (e.g., fixed-price or cost-and-fee)*] proposal, including data other than cost or pricing data, and certified cost or pricing data, in accordance with FAR 15.408, Table 15-2, supporting its proposal.

(b) The schedule for definitizating this contract is [*insert target date for definitization of the contract and dates for submission of proposal, beginning of negotiations, and, if appropriate, submission of make-or-buy and subcontracting plans and cost or pricing data*]:

(c) If agreement on a definitive contract to supersede this letter contract is not reached by the target date in paragraph (b) of this section, or within any extension of it granted by the Contracting Officer, the Contracting Officer may, with the approval of the head of the contracting activity, determine a reasonable price or fee in accordance with Subpart 15.4 and Part 31 of the FAR, subject to Contractor appeal as provided in the Disputes clause. In any event, the Contractor shall proceed with completion of the contract, subject to only to the Limitation of Government Liability clause.

(1) After the Contracting Officer's determination or price or fee, the contract shall be governed by —

(i) All clauses required by the FAR on the date of execution of this letter contract for either fixed-price or cost-reimbursement contracts, as determined by the Contracting Officer under this paragraph (c);

(ii) All clauses required by law as of the date of the Contracting Officer's determination; and

(iii) Any other clauses, terms, and conditions mutually agreed upon.

(2) To the extent consistent with subparagraph (c)(1) of this section, all clauses, terms, and conditions included in this letter contract shall continue in effect, except those that by their nature apply only to a letter contract.

FAR 16.603-2(c)(3) requires that the schedule for definitization call for completion of the process "within 180 days after the date of the letter contract or before completion of 40 percent of the work to be performed, whichever occurs first." It permits the granting of additional time "in extreme cases." These provisions reflect the strong policy of the government to preclude letter contracts from running indefinitely without being firmly priced. If the parties cannot agree to the definitization, the clause permits unilateral action by the contracting officer with appeal under the Disputes clause. In *Litton Sys., Inc.*, ASBCA 36976, 93-2 BCA ¶ 25,705, the board considered such an appeal and ruled that the unilaterally definitized price should have included the costs of extra work performed by the contractor. Earlier versions of the clause did not contain this procedure, but the Court of Claims ruled that it had jurisdiction to make a decision as to the proper definitization of a letter contract where the contractor had completed the work but the parties had been unable to agree to a final price, *Sanders Assocs., Inc. v. United States*, 191 Ct. Cl. 157, 423 F.2d 291 (1970).

The clause also binds the parties to the mandatory contract clauses in effect at the time the letter contract was issued and the statutory clauses in effect on the date of definitization, unless the parties agree to other clauses. Thus, a contractor must be sure to obtain agreement prior to contract execution for any variances from FAR clauses or other modifications to the language that may be desired. See *Teledyne Continental Motors*, ASBCA 22571, 85-3 BCA ¶ 18,472, where the government was bound to a clause that it had included in the modification definitizing the letter contract even though that clause increased the costs chargeable to the contract.

Paragraph (a) of the clause requires the submission of certified cost or pricing data — a requirement that will substantially increase the time necessary for definitization. FAR 16.603-4(b)(3) permits deletion of this requirement if "at the time of entering into the letter contract, the contracting officer knows that the definitive contract will be based on adequate price competition or will otherwise meet the criteria of 15.403-1 for not requiring submission of certified cost or pricing data."

## c. Payment

In letter contracts contemplating a cost-reimbursement contract, FAR 16.603-4(c) requires the use of the Payments of Allowable Costs Before Definitization clause in FAR 52.216-26. This clause is intended to motivate the contractor to definitize the contract quickly by limiting reimbursement as follows:

(a)(1) One hundred percent of approved costs representing financing payments to subcontractors under fixed-price subcontracts; *provided*, that the Government's payments to the Contractor will not exceed 80 percent of the allowable costs of those subcontractors.

(2) One hundred percent of approved costs representing cost-reimbursement subcontracts; *provided*, that the Government's payments to the Contractor shall not exceed 85 percent of the allowable costs of those subcontractors.

(3) Eighty-five percent of all other approved costs.

There is no such clause to be used for letter contracts contemplating fixed-price contracts. Thus, if the contractor desires progress payments during performance of a fixed-price letter contract, one of the standard clauses should be used. See Progress Payments, FAR 52.232-16 (fixed-price supply or service contracts) or Payment under Fixed-Price Construction Contracts, FAR 52.232-5 (fixed-price construction contracts).

## II.  FIXED-PRICE CONTRACTS

One of the basic types of contract is the fixed-price contract. Such contracts can be either firm-fixed-price or fixed-price subject to adjustment by formula during or after performance. All fixed-price contracts are also subject to adjustment under a variety of contract clauses such as the Changes clause. These contracts all have the common characteristic of binding the contractor to complete the work at a fixed amount of compensation, once adjusted, regardless of the costs of performance. To obtain the benefit of the fixed price, the government must draft and administer the contract in a manner that avoids significant claims for price adjustment. If these conditions exist, the firm-fixed-price contract places the risk of incurring unforeseen costs on the contractor rather than on the government. Conversely, it provides the contractor the greatest opportunity to earn higher profits by devising ways to reduce the costs of performance.

Since there are many situations where the work can be reasonably well defined but it is unwise to place the entire cost risk on the contractor, a number of variations on the firm-fixed-price contract are used. These variations are of three types: (i) fixed-price contracts with *formula repricing*, such as the fixed-price incentive (FPI) and the fixed-price with economic price adjustment contracts, (ii) fixed-price contracts with subjective repricing (using award fees), and (iii) fixed-price contracts with repricing *after some costs have been incurred*, such as the fixed-price redeterminable contracts. Descriptions of the firm-fixed-price contract and its variations follow. FPI contracts and fixed-price contracts with award fees are dealt with in the section on incentive contracts.

## A.  Firm-Fixed-Price Contracts

The purest form of fixed-price contract is the firm-fixed-price contract. There the bargain is stated in terms of a fixed amount of compensation with no formula or technique for varying the price in the event of unforeseen contingencies. FAR 16.202-1 describes this type of contract as follows:

> A firm-fixed-price contract provides for a price that is not subject to any adjustment on the basis of the contractor's cost experience in performing the contract. This contract type places upon the contractor maximum risk and full responsibility for all costs and resulting profit or loss. It provides maximum incentive for the contractor to control costs and perform effectively and imposes a minimum administrative burden upon the contracting parties.

The first sentence of this description is misleading in that it fails to recognize that firm-fixed-price contracts contain a number of clauses that call for price adjustments to compensate the contractor when specified events occur.

FAR 16.202-2, recognizing that the use of this type contract might place the risk of *too high* a price on the government, contains the following guidance:

A firm-fixed-price contract is suitable for acquiring commercial items (see Parts 2 and 12) or for acquiring other supplies or services on the basis of reasonably definitive functional or detailed specifications (see Part 11) when the contracting officer can establish fair and reasonable prices at the outset, such as when —

(a) There is adequate price competition;

(b) There are reasonable price comparisons with prior purchases of the same or similar supplies or services made on a competitive basis or supported by valid certified cost or pricing data;

(c) Available cost or pricing information permits realistic estimates of the probable costs of performance; or

(d) Performance uncertainties can be identified and reasonable estimates of their cost impact can be made, and the contractor is willing to accept a firm fixed price representing assumption of the risks involved.

Firm-fixed-price contracts must be used with caution because both parties can lose if the actual costs of performance are greatly at variance with the contract price. If the costs greatly exceed the price, the contractor will incur a substantial loss and may be financially unable or unwilling to complete the work at the contract price. See *Ball Bros. Research Corp.*, NASABCA 1277-6, 80-2 BCA ¶ 14,526, where the government converted a fixed-price contract to a cost-plus-fixed-fee (CPFF) contract in order to obtain completion of the work. See also *General Dynamics Corp. v. United States*, 229 Ct. Cl. 399, 671 F.2d 474 (1982), where a similar "conversion" to a cost-type contract occurred after the contractor encountered great difficulties in performing a fixed-price-type contract. If the costs are far under the price, the government will have paid substantially more for the work than might have been possible under some other form of contract. When there is adequate information to assure the parties that the costs are predictable, however, the firm-fixed-price contract is the simplest form of contract to accomplish the work.

Firm-fixed-price contracts are also of questionable value if the work is not well defined and stable in nature. If the scope of the work is unclear or subject to change during performance, the contractor will inevitably assert its entitlement to price adjustments during performance and contract administration will be very complex. These issues are dealt with in detail in Cibinic, Nash & Nagle, *Administration of Government Contracts* (4th ed., 2005).

## B. Fixed-Price Contract with Economic Price Adjustment

This type of contract provides for upward or downward adjustment of the fixed price or incentive target price if economic conditions change during contract performance. Usually, such adjustments are based on changes in material costs or labor rates (reflected by actual costs or indexes) but they can be based on changes to a contractor's prices if such prices are subject to market forces.

The use of economic price adjustment clauses (frequently called "escalation" clauses) is a major means of risk allocation. Such clauses place on the government some or all of the risk of increases in the cost of labor or material or of the contractor's prices. Absent such a clause, these risks are allocated to the contractor by virtue of entering into a firm-fixed-price contract, *Office Automation & Training Consultants*, ASBCA 56779, 11-1 BCA ¶ 34,666 (no mutual mistake as to applicability of Service Contract Act when parties used firm-fixed-price contract); *McNamara Constr. of Manitoba, Ltd. v. United States*, 206 Ct. Cl. 1, 509 F.2d 1166 (1975) (no mutual mistake as to labor rates when parties used firm-fixed-price contract); *Charles H. Siever Co.*, ASBCA 23968, 80-1 BCA ¶ 14,390, *recons. denied*, 80-2 BCA ¶ 14,589 (contractor not entitled to increase price of firm-fixed-price contract when escalation clause was not included in the contract). See *Southern Dredging Co.*, ENGBCA 5843, 92-2 BCA ¶ 24,886, denying reformation of a contract to account for increased fuel prices where fixed-price contract did not include a price escalation clause, and stating at 124,116:

> "It is black letter law that the risk of performance costs in a firm fixed-price contract, absent a clause stating otherwise, are on the contractor." *Chevron U.S.A., Inc.*, ASBCA No. 32323, 90-1 BCA ¶ 22,602. See *Nedlog Co.*, ASBCA No. 26034, 82-1 BCA ¶15,519 ; *D.K.'s Precision and Manufacturing*, ASBCA No. 39616, 90-2 BCA ¶ 22,830. Further, neither abnormal price increases nor unusual trade conditions change this basic principle regarding a contractor's assumption of the risk of increased performance costs in a fixed-price contract. *Anthony P. Miller, Inc. v. United States* [9 CCF ¶ 72,218 ], 161 Ct. Cl. 455, *cert. denied*, 375 U.S. 879 (1963); *Jalaprathan Cement Co., Ltd.*, ASBCA No. 21248, 79-2 BCA ¶ 13,927.

See also *Cobra, S.A.*, ASBCA 28146, 84-3 BCA ¶ 17,535, denying reformation of a contract to include an escalation clause. These cases demonstrate the general understanding that this matter is covered by specific contract language, and absent such specific language, the risk of upward economic fluctuations is on the contractor.

These clauses benefit the government in the unlikely event of downward economic fluctuations. See FAR 16.203-1 describing these clauses as leading to "price adjustments [which] are based on increases or decreases" in the costs of materials and labor or in the contractor's prices.

## 1. *Use of Economic Price Adjustment Clauses*

FAR 16.203-2 provides the following brief guidance on the use of this type of contract:

A fixed-price contract with economic price adjustment may be used when

(i) there is serious doubt concerning the stability of market or labor conditions that will exist during an extended period of contract performance, and

(ii) contingencies that would otherwise be included in the contract price can be identified and covered separately in the contract. Price adjustments based on established prices should normally be restricted to industry-wide contingencies. Price adjustments based on labor and material costs should be limited to contingencies beyond the contractor's control. For use of economic price adjustment in sealed bid contracts, see 14.408-4.

(a) In establishing the base level from which adjustment will be made, the contracting officer shall ensure that contingency allowances are not duplicated by inclusion in both the base price and the adjustment requested by the contractor under economic price adjustment clause.

(b) In contracts that do not require submission of certified cost or pricing data, the contracting officer shall obtain adequate data to establish the base level from which adjustment will be made and may require verification of data submitted.

FAR 16.203-3 prohibits the use of economic price adjustment clauses that do not meet certain standards:

A fixed-price contract with economic price adjustment shall not be used unless the contracting officer determines that it is necessary either to protect the contractor and the Government against significant fluctuations in labor or material costs or to provide for contract price adjustment in the event of changes in the contractor's established prices.

This prohibition has led to considerable litigation regarding economic price adjustment clauses for petroleum products that were based on a government report of average sales prices of such products. In *Mapco Alaska Petroleum, Inc. v. United States*, 27 Fed. Cl. 405 (1992), the court held that such an economic price adjustment clause was illegal because it was not based on either the contractor's established prices or the contractor's cost of labor and material. This reasoning was accepted in *Barrett Refining Corp. v. United States*, 242 F.3d 1055 (Fed. Cir. 2001), where the court affirmed a decision that, after striking the illegal economic price adjustment clause from the contract, the contractor had an implied-in-fact contract for the fair market value of the fuel it had delivered. The court remanded the case to determine the amount that the government should recover on contracts where the illegal clause had led to overpayment for the fuel — the recovery being based on the theory that these were "unauthorized payments." Subsequently, a different panel of the court held that the clause was not illegal because the FAR did not require that economic price adjustment clauses be based on the *contractor's* established prices but, rather, it permitted such a clause to be based on any other measure of established prices, *Tesoro Hawaii Corp. v. United States*, 405 F.3d 1339 (Fed. Cir. 2005). Another panel later ruled that the compilation of sales prices used as the basis for economic price adjustment complied with the FAR requirement that such adjustments had to be based on "published or otherwise established prices." See *ConocoPhillips, Conoco, Inc. v. United States*, 501 F.3d 1374 (Fed. Cir. 2007), stating at 1378:

> The [sales price compilation's] use of an amalgamation of related products does not render [it] ineligible to serve as the basis for a price adjustment clause under the regulations. The language of FAR § 16.203-1(a), which allowed the contract price to be adjusted based on increases or decreases "in published or otherwise established prices" for particular items, gave the contracting parties substantial freedom to use "market-based references to identify 'established prices.'" *Tesoro*, 405 F.3d at 1347. Under that standard, it was permissible to use a published weighted average of multiple reference items if the reference items are sufficiently similar to the contract items that it was reasonable, at the time the parties entered into the contract, to expect the index to approximate the change in the market price of the contract item. The regulations did not require the use of particular vendors' prices, and they also did not require the use of any particular measure of the market. In such a setting, it is not surprising that the regulations gave the parties some flexibility in choosing how market-based price adjustments would be calculated. Absent some degree of flexibility, contractual agreements would constantly be subject to second-guessing through litigation over whether the method chosen in advance for price adjustment turned out after the fact to correlate sufficiently closely to what each party regards as the correct measure of market price.

The court therefore concluded that the fact that the chosen measure for determining economic price adjustment did not reflect the amount of price variation that actually occurred in the market was not a mistake because the contractor voluntarily agreed to the measure and could have protected itself by bargaining for a better measure of price variation. The court distinguished *Beta Sys., Inc. v. United States*, 838 F.2d 1179 (Fed. Cir. 1988), which had granted reformation on the basis of mutual mistake when an index did not include the major material used on the contract. These decisions indicate that the Federal Circuit interprets the FAR as giving the contracting parties considerable leeway in selecting a measure to be used as the basis for economic price adjustment.

Although most economic price adjustment clauses are used in firm-fixed-price contracts, they may also be used in any fixed-price-type contract, including incentive or redeterminable contracts. On major systems contracts, economic price adjustment provisions have frequently been used in fixed-price incentive contracts. In such cases, the government bears the risk of increases in labor rates and material prices and the parties share the risk of increases in cost due to other factors.

If there is the possibility of significant economic fluctuation during contract performance, the use of an economic price adjustment clause will probably encourage more companies to participate in the competition and will permit contracting at a price free of the contingencies that would otherwise be included to compensate for such fluctuations. However, the contracting officer may conclude that there is sufficient competition to minimize contingencies in pricing and therefore use firm-fixed-price contracting. If large fluctuations in the economy are possible, it can be argued that it is not in the government's best interests to contract without economic price adjustment clauses even if it is likely that competition will limit price contingencies. In such cases, a loss contract may result with all of its inherent difficulties.

The contracting officer has substantial discretion to determine whether to use an economic price adjustment clause, and challenges to a decision to omit an economic price adjustment clause from a procurement will invariably fail. See, for example, *B & P Refuse Disposal, Inc.*, Comp. Gen. Dec. B-253661, 93-2 CPD ¶ 177 (contracting officer told offerors of prior increases in price and forced them to include such a contingency in bid to protect against risk); *Master Sec., Inc.*, Comp. Gen. Dec. B-232263, 88-2 CPD ¶ 449 (contracting officer determined market conditions were sufficiently stable to enable offerors to make realistic estimates of future costs); *Sentinel Elecs., Inc.*, Comp. Gen. Dec. B-212770, 84-1 CPD ¶ 5 (contracting officer determined that there were sufficient capable producers that could reasonably price work even though last delivery was 43 months after award); *Barker & Williamson*, Comp. Gen. Dec. B-208236, 82-2 CPD ¶ 454 (omission of clause in basic quantity in first year of contract upheld even though it was included in option quantities in subsequent years because contracting officer determined that pricing was sufficiently stable to permit bidders to assume risks for initial requirement); and *Tri-Wall Containers*, Comp. Gen. Dec. B-200702, 81-1 CPD ¶ 277 (omission of clause upheld because market price had been stable for eight months and three bids were received although prior-year pricing had been very volatile). See also *Argus Servs., Inc.*, Comp. Gen. Dec. B-234016.2, 89-2 CPD ¶ 227, holding that the contracting officer had the discretion not to use an economic price adjustment provision in order to have "minimum administrative burdens" even though it imposed "maximum risks" on the prospective contractor.

The government can run a competition allowing offerors to select the provisions that will mitigate long-term risk. See, for example, *American States Utils. Servs. Inc.*, Comp. Gen. Dec. B-291307.3, 2004 CPD ¶ 150, holding that it was proper to select an offeror that proposed fixed prices with economic price adjustment as posing less risk for the government than an offeror that proposed periodic price redetermination.

## 2. Types of Economic Price Adjustment Provisions

FAR 16.203-1 describes three general types of economic price adjustment provisions: (1) adjustments based on established prices, (2) adjustments based on the contractor's actual costs of labor and material, and (3) adjustments based on cost indexes of labor and material.

FAR 16.203-4 provides standard clauses for use with the first two types. However, there is no standard clause for economic price adjustment based on indexes — requiring each agency to draft its own clause in this area. In addition, FAR 16.203-4 permits the use of "agency prescribed" clauses with the result that great latitude is given in drafting special clauses for different contracting situations. Generally, such specially drafted economic price adjustment clauses should use some basis of measurement of the fluctuations in the contractor's prices or costs of material and labor that is not under the control of the contractor. See FAR 16.203-2 stating that such clauses should cover contingencies that are "industry-wide" or "beyond the contractor's control." This protects the government from price increases due to contractor inefficiency or intentional overspending and permits evaluation of competitive prices. For example, an economic price adjustment clause providing that the price would be adjusted in an amount equal to higher prices charged by the contractor for a component that was not being sold in substantial quantities to other customers would be improper because there would be no market constraints limiting the ability of the contractor to manipulate its prices. See *Roarda, Inc.*, Comp. Gen. Dec. B-204524.5, 82-1 CPD ¶ 438, where GAO found a clause improper because it permitted the contractor to increase the contract price if its market price increased. GAO objected that the agency had not included any mechanism in the procurement to ascertain that the contractor's price reflected "some objective standard," with the result that the price could be varied at will. In that case, consequently, there was no assurance in a sealed bid procurement that the contractor was actually the low bidder. See also *American Transparents Plastic Corp.*, Comp. Gen. Dec. B-210898, 83-2 CPD ¶ 539, stating the same "objective standard" rule.

In a sealed bid procurement, it is also important that all bidders use substantially the same basis for price adjustment so that the low price can be determined. Thus, a clause should not be used that allows the bidder to select the basis for price adjustment. See *Steuart Petroleum Co. v. United States*, 438 F. Supp. 527 (D.D.C. 1977), enjoining the performance of a contract awarded to a bidder that had selected a volatile basis for price adjustment, which cast great doubt on whether its low bid would actually lead to the low price after economic price adjustment. See also *Galaxy Custodial Servs., Inc.*, 64 Comp. Gen. 593 (B-215738), 85-1 CPD ¶ 658, criticizing an Invitation For Bids (IFB) permitting each bidder to establish a base rate because that produced an incentive to bid a base rate lower than the rate used to compute the bid. In *Amarillo Aircraft Sales & Servs., Inc.*, 63 Comp. Gen. 568 (B 214225), 84-2 CPD ¶ 269, GAO concurred in the termination of a procurement after the procuring agency determined that the contractor had used a basis for price adjustment that was not comparable to that used by other bidders and was subject to the control of the contractor. See FAR 14.408-4(b) requiring that bids that take exception to government imposed economic price adjustment clauses be found nonresponsive. In *First Am. Engineered Solutions*, Comp. Gen. Dec. B-289051, 2001 CPD ¶ 207, GAO held that it was proper to declare a bid nonresponsive when the bidder did not agree to base all option year prices on the economic price adjustment clause as required by the IFB. If the bidder inserts a price adjustment provision in a bid where the IFB does not call for a clause, an even more restrictive rule will apply. If the clause contains no ceiling, the bid will be held to be nonresponsive, *Joy Mfg. Co.*, 54 Comp. Gen. 237 (B-181136), 74-2 CPD ¶ 183. If the clause contains a ceiling, the bid will be evaluated at the ceiling price, FAR 14.408-4(a)(1). This rule removes all of the bidding advantage that would be obtained from including a clause in the bid.

In negotiated procurement, the government will be bound if it accepts an offer containing a price adjustment clause. See *United States Steel Corp.*, ASBCA 29111, 85-1 BCA ¶ 17,761, *recons. denied*, 85-1 BCA ¶ 17,921, holding the government to a provision in a letter responding to a negotiated RFP stating the price would be that "in effect at the time of shipment, subject to a 10 percent maximum escalation" from the price in effect at the time of award. The board reasoned that this type of bargain was permitted in negotiated procurement.

### a. Adjustments Based on Contractor's Established Prices

The first type of economic price adjustment provision provided for in FAR 16.203-1 uses established catalog or market prices as the basis for price adjustment. Standard contract clauses are provided for standard supplies, FAR 52.216-2, and semi-standard supplies, FAR 52.216-3. Standard supplies are those with established catalog or market prices, while semi-standard supplies are those whose "prices can be reasonably related to the prices of nearly equivalent standard supplies," FAR 16.203-4(b)(1)(ii). In the latter situation, the clause requires that the related catalog or market item be identified in the schedule of the contract. Both clauses contain the same provisions calling for upward or downward price adjustments on a pro rata basis following changes in catalog or market prices. The clause for standard supplies provides:

ECONOMIC PRICE ADJUSTMENT — STANDARD SUPPLIES (JAN 1997)

(a) The Contractor warrants that the unit price stated in the Schedule for [*offeror insert Schedule line item number*] is not in excess of the Contractor's applicable established price in effect on the contract date for like quantities of the same item. The term "unit price" excludes any part of the price directly resulting from requirements for preservation, packaging, or packing beyond standard commercial practice. The term "established price" means a price that —

(1) Is an established catalog or market price for a commercial item sold in substantial quantities to the general public; and

(2) Is the net price after applying any standard trade discounts offered by the Contractor.

(b) The Contractor shall promptly notify the Contracting Officer of the amount and effective date of each decrease in any applicable established price. Each corresponding contract unit price shall be decreased by the same percentage that the established price is decreased. The decrease shall apply to those items delivered on and after the effective date of the decrease in the Contractor's established price, and this contract shall be modified accordingly.

(c) If the Contractor's applicable established price is increased after the contract date, the corresponding contract unit price shall be increased, upon the Contractor's written request to the Contracting Officer, by the same percentage that the established price is increased, and the contract shall be modified accordingly, subject to the following limitations:

> (1) The aggregate of the increases in any contract unit price under this clause shall not exceed 10 percent of the original contract unit price.

> (2) The increased contract unit price shall be effective —

>> (i) On the effective date of the increase in the applicable established price if the Contracting Officer receives the Contractor's written request within 10 days thereafter; or

>> (ii) If the written request is received later, on the date the Contracting Officer receives the request.

> (3) The increased contract unit price shall not apply to quantities scheduled under the contract for delivery before the effective date of the increased contract unit price, unless failure to deliver before that date results from causes beyond the control and without the fault or negligence of the Contractor, within the meaning of the Default clause.

> (4) No modification increasing a contract unit price shall be executed under this paragraph (c) until the Contracting Officer verifies the increase in the applicable established price.

> (5) Within 30 days after receipt of the Contractor's written request, the Contracting Officer may cancel, without liability to either party, any undelivered portion of the contract items affected by the requested increase.

(d) During the time allowed for the cancellation provided for in subparagraph (c) (5) above, and thereafter if there is no cancellation, the Contractor shall continue deliveries according to the contract delivery schedule, and the Government shall pay for such deliveries at the contract unit price, increased to the extent provided by paragraph (c) above.

Note that this clause addresses *the contractor's established price* not established prices of other contractors. Nonetheless, the Federal Circuit held that a clause of this nature basing adjustments on market prices in the petroleum industry were of the same nature as this clause, *Tesoro Hawaii Corp. v. United States*, 405 F.3d 1339 (Fed. Cir. 2005).

DFARS 216.203-4 -70 provides two additional bases of price adjustment of this type. See the clauses at DFARS 252.216-7000 for basic steel, aluminum, brass, bronze, or copper mill products and DFARS 252.216-7001 for nonstandard steel products.

These clauses provide the necessary "objectivity" by using catalog or market prices for items that are sold by the contractor to the general public in "substantial quantities." Elaborate tests for establishing that items fall within this category were removed from FAR 15.804-3(c) in 1995 with the result that there is no current guidance on what constitutes "substantial quantities." The other terms are defined in the definition of "commercial item" in FAR 2.101 as follows:

(i) Catalog price means a price included in a catalog, price list, schedule, or other form that is regularly maintained by the manufacturer or vendor, is either published or otherwise available for inspection by customers, and states prices at which sales are currently, or were last, made to a significant number of buyers constituting the general public; and

(ii) Market prices means current prices that are established in the course of ordinary trade between buyers and sellers free to bargain and that can be substantiated through competition or from sources independent of the offerors.

The theory is that if an item meets these tests, its price will be determined by market forces and the contractor will be unable to manipulate the price to increase the amount paid under the contract containing the economic price adjustment clause.

### b. Adjustment Based on Contractor's Actual Costs

The second type of economic price adjustment provision in FAR 16.203-1 uses the actual costs of the contractor as the basis for the adjustment. A standard contract clause is provided in FAR 52.216-4:

ECONOMIC PRICE ADJUSTMENT — LABOR AND MATERIAL (JAN 1997)

(a) The Contractor shall notify the Contracting Officer if, at any time during contract performance, the rates of pay for labor (including fringe benefits) or the unit prices for material shown in the Schedule either increase or decrease. The Contractor shall furnish this notice within 60 days after the increase or decrease, or within any additional period that the Contracting Officer may approve in writing, but not later than the date of final payment under this contract. The notice shall include the Contractor's proposal for an adjustment in the contract unit prices to be negotiated under paragraph (b) below, and shall include, in the form required by the Contracting Officer, supporting data explaining the cause, effective date, and amount of the increase or decrease and the amount of the Contractor's adjustment proposal

(b) Promptly after the Contracting Officer receives the notice and data under paragraph (a) above, the Contracting Officer and the Contractor shall negotiate a price adjustment in the contract unit prices and its effective date. However, the Contracting Officer may postpone the negotiations until an accumulation of increases and decreases in the labor rates (including fringe benefits) and unit prices of material shown in the Schedule results in an adjustment allowable under subparagraph (c)(3) below. The Contracting Officer shall modify this contract (1) to include the price adjustment and its effective date and (2) to revise the labor rates (including fringe benefits) or unit prices of material as shown in the Schedule to reflect the increases or decreases resulting from the adjustment. The Contractor shall continue performance pending agreement on, or determination of, any adjustment and its effective date.

(c) Any price adjustment under this clause is subject to the following limitations:

(1) Any adjustment shall be limited to the effect on unit prices of the increases or decreases in the rates of pay for labor (including fringe benefits) or unit prices for material shown in the Schedule. There shall be no adjustment for —

(i) Supplies or services for which the production cost is not affected by such changes,

(ii) Changes in rates or unit prices other than those shown in the Schedule, or

(iii) Changes in the quantities of labor or material used from those shown in the Schedule for each item.

(2) No upward adjustment shall apply to supplies or services that are required to be delivered or performed before the effective date of the adjustment, unless the Contractor's failure to deliver or perform according to the delivery schedule results from causes beyond the Contractor's control and without its fault or negligence, within the meaning of the Default clause.

(3) There shall be no adjustment for any change in rates of pay for labor (including fringe benefits) or unit prices for material which would not result in a net change of at least 3 percent of the then-current total contract price. This limitation shall not apply, however, if, after final delivery of all contract line items, either party requests an adjustment under paragraph (b) above.

(4) The aggregate of the increases in any contract unit price made under this clause shall not exceed 10 percent of the original unit price. There is no percentage limitation on the amount of decreases that may be made under this clause.

(d) The Contracting Officer may examine the Contractor's books, records, and other supporting data relevant to the cost of labor (including fringe benefits) and material during all reasonable times until the end of 3 years after the date of final payment under this contract or the time periods specified in Subpart 4.7 of the Federal Acquisition Regulation (FAR), whichever is earlier.

When this clause is used, FAR 16.203-4(c)(3) requires that a clause be inserted in the schedule of the contract describing the specific types of labor and material subject to price adjustment, the labor rates and material prices to be increased or decreased, and the quantities of labor and material allocable to each contract unit. In the 1980s, DFARS 216.203-4(c)(3) contained a sample provision that contained useful guidance:

The following types of labor and material are subject to price adjustment pursuant to the "Economic Price Adjustment — Labor and Material" clause of this contract.

| Type of Labor and Material | Contract Item No. 1 Rates of Pay and Material Prices | Quantities and Direct Costs Per Unit of Procurement |
|---|---|---|
| Drill Press Operator | $3.00/hour<br>no fringe benefits included<br>———<br>$3.00 | 20 min. — $1.00 |
| Welder | $2.75/hour<br>.05/hour — vacation pay<br>.20/hour — pension plan<br>———<br>$3.00 | 10 min. — $ .50 |
| Copper Sheet | $ .40/lb. | 2 lb. — $ .80 |
| Purchased Parts:<br>(1) ABC tube X5721<br>(2) XYZ part #9348 | $1.00 each<br>$ .50 each | 3 ea. — $3.00<br>10 ea. — $5.00 |

This schedule provision is of critical importance because adjustments are made only for listed elements of the price. Thus, no adjustment was granted for a profit-sharing plan that did not appear among the fringe benefits in the labor rates listed in the schedule, *Optic-Electronic Corp.*, ASBCA 24962, 83-2 BCA ¶ 16,677, *recons. denied*, 84-3 BCA ¶ 17,565. Similarly, it was held that this type of economic price adjustment clause applied only to items added to a contract by amendment rather than to all contract items, because the schedule listed only the added items, *Minowitz Mfg. Co.*, ASBCA 23784, 83-1 BCA ¶ 16,324. See also *Arcadia Mfg. Co.*, ASBCA 20764, 76-2 BCA ¶ 12,058, where the board found, in a sealed bid procurement, that the bidder's failure to include the required schedule of items covered eliminated the clause even though it was designated in the IFB. Compare *Transportes Especiales de Automoviles, S.A.*, ASBCA 43851, 93-2 BCA ¶ 25,745, ordering reformation of a negotiated contract because the contract contained the standard economic price adjustment clause but did not have the schedule required by the FAR and illustrated by the DFARS to set rates and quantities of labor. The board concluded that the parties intended to have escalation but had mistakenly omitted the schedule.

At first glance, this type of economic price adjustment appears to contain no objective basis for price increases. However, FAR 16.203-2 states that this technique should "normally be restricted to industry-wide contingencies" and "limited to contingencies beyond the contractor's control." To meet this requirement, the clause should only be used in those situations where the labor covered by the clause is used for a mix of work, some of which is not subject to economic price adjustment or reimbursement of costs, and the material covered by the clause is material bought in a competitive market. In such cases, there would be outside pressures limiting the amount of increases the contractor could pay and subsequently recover under the clause. It is clear when this clause is included that changes in quantity of items or amount of effort will not lead to escalation — only changes in labor rates or material prices, *Nuclear Components, Inc.*, ASBCA 22884, 79-2 BCA ¶ 14,006.

This clause is not well suited for use in sealed bid contracts because it requires each bidder to furnish the schedule as part of the bid. This makes evaluation rather speculative, *VBM Corp.*, Comp. Gen. Dec. B-182225, 75-1 CPD ¶ 130, and may motivate bidders to include rates in the schedule that are lower than those actually used in order to obtain greater price adjustments. See *Galaxy Custodial Servs., Inc.*, 64 Comp. Gen. 594 (B-215738), 85-1 CPD ¶ 658, suggesting that if the agency found the data inaccurate, the bid should be rejected. GAO has agreed to the use of this type provision in two-step sealed bidding, *Norris Indus.*, Comp. Gen. Dec. B-182921, 75-2 CPD ¶ 31.

### c.  Adjustments Based on Cost Indexes

The third type of economic price adjustment provision in FAR 16.203-1 uses national indexes as the basis for price adjustment. The procurement regulations contain no standard clauses for this type of price adjustment, and the FAR contains virtually no guidance on the structuring of such a clause. However, the drafting of such a clause is highly complex. GSAR 516.203-4(c) gives brief guidance on the preparation of such a clause and requires approval of the "contracting director." DFARS PGI 216.203-4 contains the following elaborate guidance on drafting a clause of this type:

(1) Do not make the clause unnecessarily complex.

(2) Normally, the clause should not provide either a ceiling or a floor for adjustment unless adjustment is based on indices below the four digit level of the Bureau of Labor Statistics —

(i) Producer Price Index;

(ii) Employment Cost Index for wages and salaries, benefits, and compensation costs for aerospace industries; or

(iii) Wage and Income Series by Standard Industrial Classification (Labor).

(3) Normally, the clause should cover all potential economic fluctuations within the original contract period of performance.

(4) The clause must accurately identify the index(es) upon which adjustments will be based.

(i) It must provide for a means to adjust for appropriate economic fluctuation in the event publication of the movement of the designated index is discontinued. This might include the substitution of another index if the time remaining would justify doing so and an appropriate index is reasonably available, or some other method for repricing the remaining portion of work to be performed.

(ii) Normally, there should be no need to make an adjustment if computation of the identified index is altered. However, it may be appropriate to provide for adjustment of the economic fluctuation computations in the event there is such a substantial alteration in the method of computing the index that the original intent of the parties is negated.

(iii) When an index to be used is subject to revision (e.g., the Bureau of Labor Statistics Producer Price Indexes), the economic price adjustment clause must specify that any economic price adjustment will be based on a revised index and must identify which revision to the index will be used.

(5) Construct the index to encompass a large sample of relevant items while still bearing a logical relationship to the type of contract costs being measured. The basis of the index should not be so large and diverse that it is significantly affected by fluctuations not relevant to contract performance, but it must be broad enough to minimize the effect of any single company, including the anticipated contractor(s).

(6) Construction of an index is largely dependent upon three general series published by the U.S. Department of Labor, Bureau of Labor Statistics (BLS). These are the —

(i) Industrial Commodities portion of the Producer Price Index;

(ii) Employment Cost Index for wages and salaries, benefits, and compensation costs for aerospace industries; and

(iii) Wage and Income Series by Standard Industrial Classification (Labor).

Since there is no BLS published series currently available that relates directly to total prices of delivered DoD aircraft, ships, missiles, electronics, etc., it will be necessary to construct composite indices from major portions of the three series identified.

(7) Normally, do not use more than two indices, i.e., one for labor (direct and indirect) and one for material (direct and indirect).

(8) The clause must establish and properly identify a base period comparable to the contract periods for which adjustments are to be made as a reference point for application of an index.

(9) The clause should not provide for an adjustment beyond the original contract performance period, including options. The start date for the adjustment may be the beginning of the contract or a later time, as appropriate, based on the projected rate of expenditures.

(10) The expenditure profile for both labor and material should be based on a predetermined rate of expenditure (expressed as the percentage of material or labor usage as it relates to the total contract price) in lieu of actual cost incurred.

(i) If the clause is to be used in a competitive acquisition, determine the labor and material allocations, with regard to both mix of labor and material and rate of expenditure by percentage, in a manner which will, as nearly as possible, approximate the average expenditure profile of all companies to be solicited so that all companies may compete on an equal basis.

(ii) If the clause is to be used in a noncompetitive acquisition, the labor and material allocations may be subject to negotiation and agreement.

(iii) For multiyear contracts, establish predetermined expenditure profile tables for each of the annual increments in the multiyear buy. Each of the second and subsequent year tables must be cumulative to reflect the total expenditures for all increments funded through the latest multiyear funding.

(11) The clause should state that percentage of the contract price subject to price adjustment.

(i) Normally, do not apply adjustments to the profit portion of the contract.

(ii) Examine the labor and material portions of the contract to exclude any areas that do not require adjustment. For example, it may be possible to exclude —

(A) Subcontracting for short periods of time during the early life of the contract which could be covered by firm-fixed-priced subcontracting,

(B) Certain areas of overhead, e.g., depreciation charges, prepaid insurance costs, rental costs, leases, certain taxes, and utility charges;

(C) Labor costs for which a definitive union agreement exists; and

(D) Those costs not likely to be affected by fluctuation in the economy.

(iii) Allocate that portion of the contract price subject to adjustment to specific periods of time (e.g., quarterly, semiannually, etc.) based on the most probable expenditure or commitment basis (expenditure profile).

(12) The clause should provide for definite times or events that trigger price adjustments. Adjustments should be frequent enough to afford the contractor appropriate economic protection without creating a burdensome administrative effort. The adjustment period should normally range from quarterly to annually.

(13) When the contract contains cost incentives, any sums paid to the contractor on account of economic price adjustment provisions must be subtracted from the total of the contractor's allowable costs for the purpose of establishing the total costs to which the cost incentive provisions apply. If the incentive arrangement is cited in percentage ranges, rather than dollar ranges, above and below target costs, structure the economic price adjustment clause to maintain the original contract incentive range in dollars.

(14) The economic price adjustment clause should provide that once the labor and material allocations and the portion of the contract price subject to price adjustment have been established, they remain fixed through the life of the contract and shall not be modified except in the event of significant changes in the scope of the contract. The clause should state that pricing actions pursuant to the Changes clause or other provisions of the contract will be priced as though there were no provisions for economic price adjustment. However, subsequent modifications may include a change to the delivery schedule or significantly change the amount of, or mix of, labor or material for the contract. In such cases, it may be appropriate to prospectively apply economic price adjustment coverage. This may be accomplished by —

(i) Using an economic price adjustment (EPA) clause that applies only to the effort covered by the modification;

(ii) Revising the baseline data or period in the EPA clause for the basic contract to include the new work; or

(iii) Using an entirely new EPA clause for the entire contract, including the new work.

(15) Consistent with the factors in paragraphs (1) through (14) of this subsection, it may also be appropriate to provide in the prime contract for similar economic price adjustment arrangements between the prime contractor and affected subcontractors to allocate risks properly and ensure that those subcontractors are provided similar economic protection.

(16) When economic price adjustment clauses are included in contracts that do not require submission of cost or pricing data as provided in FAR 15.403-1, the

contracting officer must obtain adequate information to establish the baseline from which adjustments will be made. The contracting officer may require verification of the data submitted to the extent necessary to permit reliance upon the data as a reasonable baseline.

This type of economic price adjustment is normally the most objective since it is usually based on national indexes prepared by the Bureau of Labor Statistics of the Department of Labor. When a national index is used, the effect of an economic price adjustment clause need not be evaluated in selecting the source since the index will have the same effect on all prices, *California Microwave, Inc.*, Comp. Gen. Dec. B-202317, 81-1 CPD ¶ 505.

A clause of this type is very difficult to negotiate and draft. First, the parties must agree on an index or a weighted group of indexes that match, with reasonable accuracy, the work on the contract. Second, the parties must agree on an expenditure profile that represents the expenditure of funds in performing the contract. This is to prevent the contractor from influencing the recovery under the clause by varying the incurrence of actual costs. Third, the parties must agree on those portions of the work subject to price adjustment. All of these factors require a detailed analysis of the work called for by the contract. Yet it should be anticipated that the clause finally arrived at will cover no more than a portion of the risk of fluctuations in the economy. This is especially true since the guidance suggests that no adjustments be made for deliveries beyond the scheduled delivery date. This requires the contractor to bear the risk of price fluctuations due to delays for which the government is not responsible. As a result, the contractor will seek to assure that the contract price reflects the residual pricing risk assumed by the contractor. See *American Transparents Plastic Corp.*, Comp. Gen. Dec. B-210898, 83-2 CPD ¶ 539, for a case upholding the use of a clause based on a national index even though it did not relieve the contractor of many of the risks of fluctuations in the economy. The use of a national index was also approved in *Utah LP Gas, Inc. v. General Servs. Admin.*, GSBCA 12472, 96-1 BCA ¶ 27,960, where the contracting officer chose to use the index in the contract even though the clause permitted amendment "to substitute a more appropriate index" if the contractually specified index did not reflect market conditions. The board reviewed the contracting officer's analysis of the situation and concluded that there had been no abuse of discretion in deciding not to alter the national index.

Contracting officers in the DoD have been held bound to the DFARS guidance on the proper structuring of economic price adjustment clauses using indexes. See *Beta Sys., Inc. v. United States*, 838 F.2d 1179 (Fed. Cir. 1988), where the court ordered reformation of an index in a clause that did not match the work under the contract, and *Craft Mach. Works, Inc.*, ASBCA 35167, 90-3 BCA ¶ 23,095, where the board reformed the portion of the clause that based the price adjustment in each period on the baseline of the prior period. In both cases, it was held that the intent of the DFARS was to provide a price adjustment that fairly compensated the contractor for fluctuations in the economy and that clauses that significantly deviated from this intent were not binding on the contractor because they did not comply with regulations that had the force and effect of law. Compare *Glopak Corp. v. United States*, 851 F.2d 334 (Fed. Cir. 1988), where the court refused to reform a General Services Administration contract that contained an index that did not match the contractor's costs. In that case, there was no regulation, such as the DFARS, that bound the contracting officer, and the court reasoned that reformation was only available if the resulting contract was "unconscionable." See also *Hydraulics Int'l, Inc.*, ASBCA 50325, 00-2 BCA ¶ 30,921, where the board refused to grant a contractor's motion for summary judgment that a clause did not comport with the DFARS guidance.

### 3. Common Problems in Structuring Economic Price Adjustment Clauses

Most economic price adjustment clauses are tailored to the individual procurement as permitted or required by the regulations. This places a large burden on the contracting parties to analyze the situation fully and draft a contract clause that provides the intended protection from economic fluctuations. The litigated cases in this area indicate that there are numerous instances where specially drafted clauses do not achieve this goal.

### a. Clarity in Contract Language

Probably the most common problem encountered is vague or ambiguous contract language. In most cases, these ambiguities appear to result from a failure of the parties to understand fully the intricacies of the arrangement they have negotiated. For example, in *Firestone Tire & Rubber Co. v. United States*, 195 Ct. Cl. 21, 444 F.2d 547 (1971), an index price adjustment clause called for the use of a Steel Products index without specifying any subcategories of the index. The court found that it was not reasonable to use the main index since its fluctuations did not match the fluctuations in the price of the steel components used in the contract. The court therefore "interpreted" the clause to require the use of subcategories of the index that matched the actual work. Interpretation was more appropriately used in several cases where the question was whether the cost was covered by the clause. In *Optic-Electronic Corp.*, ASBCA 24962, 83-2 BCA ¶ 16,677, *recons. denied*, 84-3 BCA ¶ 17,565, the board looked to the negotiations of the parties to determine if they might have intended to include profit-sharing as a fringe benefit even though it had been omitted from the contract schedule in a labor and material adjustment clause. The board found no evidence of such intent and therefore interpreted the contract as omitting the benefit from the price adjustment formula. Similarly, in *ITT Arctic Servs., Inc. v. United States*, 207 Ct. Cl. 743, 524 F.2d 680 (1975), the contractor was denied recovery for increased "labor cost" under the price escalation clause since the increases were due to currency fluctuation. In *Merritt-Chapman & Scott Corp.*, IBCA 240, 61-2 BCA ¶3193, the escalation clause provided for increases in wages but not subsistence payments, and the government unsuccessfully claimed that the portion of the hourly wage paid on a "remote" project in excess of the state average was actually a subsistence payment.

Interpretation was also used to determine the correct method of computing the price adjustment in *Brunswick Corp. v. United States*, 951 F.2d 334 (Fed. Cir. 1991). There the court affirmed the board decision at 91-1 BCA ¶ 23,458 that the government was correct in adjusting the base for the price adjustment by the factors included in a table in the contract. The contractor had argued that the proper adjustment was the amount it had used in computing its bid, but the court held that this was not in accord with the contract language and would give it an undue advantage over other bidders. See also *United States Steel Corp.*, ASBCA 29111, 85-1 BCA ¶ 7,761, *recons. denied*, 85-1 BCA ¶ 17,921, where the government was held bound to a contractor's brief description in the proposal of the price adjustment technique to be used even though the RFP had included one of the standard economic price adjustment clauses. Perhaps the most egregious example of lack of clarity is found in *Holland Oil Co.*, ASBCA 26603, 82-2 BCA ¶ 15,908, where the government was bound to a questionable price due to its inartful draftsmanship and lack of attention to detail in analyzing bids. Compare *Barry L. Miller Eng'g, Inc.*, ASBCA 20554, 75-2 BCA ¶ 11,567, where an unambiguous response in the contractor's proposal was held to bind the government to pay costs over the escalation ceiling in the RFP.

### b. Ceilings

One of the most troublesome elements of economic price adjustment clauses is the ceiling on the total amount of the adjustment. The three FAR clauses all contain a ceiling of 10% of the total contract price, with the provision that this ceiling may be modified when drafting the contract with the approval of the "chief of the contracting office," FAR 52.216-2, -3, and -4. The current DoD guidance on index adjustment clauses provides that normally no ceiling will be used although ceilings have been used in the past in such clauses. Whenever a ceiling is used, the parties should carefully review the economic situation to ascertain whether the clause provides the necessary protection since these ceilings are enforced literally. See, for example, *Martin-Copeland Co.*, ASBCA 26551, 83-2 BCA ¶ 16,752, where a 10% ceiling covered only one third of the price fluctuation in the price of gold encountered by the contractor. The board held that the parties were bound to the contract agreement and that no further recovery was warranted. See also *American Transparents Plastic Corp.*, Comp. Gen. Dec. B-210898, 83-2 CPD ¶ 539, dismissing a protest that a 30% ceiling was inadequate to cover the risk of price fluctuations. GAO stated that there was no statutory or regulatory requirement that economic price adjustment clauses fully protect the contractor. In one curious case, the parties left the ceiling provision blank in the executed contract and the contracting officer subsequently inserted 25% in the blank, *American Optical Corp. v. United States*, 219 Ct. Cl. 131, 592 F.2d 1149 (1979). The court concluded that the basic guidance in the ASPR called for the ceiling to be "reasonable" and that 25% was reasonable in a situation where the escalation provision covered the price of gold over a one-year period.

The use of ceilings creates a problem in price adjustment clauses where the contractor is required to warrant that the contract price does not include any contingency for items subject to escalation. See, for example, the Economic Price Adjustment — Standard Supplies clause set forth above. In *Echelon Serv. Co.*, Comp. Gen. Dec. B-208720.2, 83-2 CPD ¶ 86, GAO concurred with the agency's use of a ceiling and a warranty against allowances for increased costs in the original contract price and appeared to concur with the agency's view that the warranty did not prevent the inclusion of a contingency for cost elements not covered by the clause. See also *International Bus. Invs., Inc.*, Comp. Gen. Dec. B-213723, 84-1 CPD ¶ 668, reaching the same conclusion on the validity of the two provisions without discussion of whether a contingency was permitted.

### c. Pricing Elements Subject to Adjustment

The specific elements of the contractor's price that are subject to adjustment must be carefully and accurately described to avoid controversy in the application of economic price adjustment provisions. For example, in *VBM Corp.*, ASBCA 23268, 79-2 BCA ¶ 14,037, the clause called for escalation of "direct labor cost" defined as "the hours of work as of the contract date of non-supervisory employees required for the manufacture of each unit of contract supplies times the hourly rate." The board ruled that the tooling costs were within this definition since they had been treated as direct costs by the contractor in its proposal and met accounting definitions of direct costs. See also *Fermont Div., Dynamics Corp.*, ASBCA 21949, 79-1 BCA ¶ 13,774, where the board concluded that an escalation clause covering "delivered items" applied to option quantities. The board held that such escalation was warranted even though the option prices were higher than the base price for the items on the contract. Apparently, the evidence indicated that the contractor had not included a contingency in the option prices to cover higher labor or material costs. The board distinguished *F.W. Faxon Co.*, ASBCA 20925, 76-2 BCA ¶ 12,103, in which the board refused to apply an escalation clause where the government had exercised an option to extend the performance period of the contract. In that case the board concluded that the clause was clear and that it only applied to the first calendar year of performance of the work.

### d. Timing of Price Adjustments

It has been common practice to limit adjustments for economic fluctuations to price changes prior to the adjusted delivery or completion dates set forth in the contract. See the standard FAR clauses containing such a provision. Such provisions do not involve substantial risk in stable market periods but can impose unreasonable risks when markets are volatile. See, for example, *Stanwick Corp.*, ASBCA 24010, 80-1 BCA ¶ 14,252, denying any adjustment because the price increase occurred after the contract delivery date. The difficulty with this provision is that the parties are agreeing to such risks without a very clear approximation of the amount of risk that may be encountered. In instances of large inflationary increases, the resulting costs of such agreements may be greater than the contractor can sustain, while in periods of deflation, the government may pay excessive prices.

There have also been interpretation problems in contract language describing the timing of the adjustment. A contract providing for price adjustment "as of the date of delivery" was interpreted as allowing adjustment based on the scheduled delivery date rather than the actual date of late delivery, *Deloro Smelting & Refining Co. v. United States*, 161 Ct. Cl. 489, 317 F.2d 382 (1963). In *Sears Petroleum & Transp. Corp.*, ASBCA 41401, 94-2 BCA ¶ 26,414, the board held that a clause in which the price was to be that in effect on the "date of delivery" meant the price was to be determined at the date on which the product was actually delivered and not the date when the contractor gave notice of readiness to deliver. Similarly, in *Ssangyong Trading Co.*, ASBCA 21614, 79-1 BCA ¶ 13,810, the board held that a clause calling for price adjustment on all items delivered "on and after" the date of a price change was to be applied literally to the specified delivery dates of items under the contract. In one case, an economic price adjustment clause provided for price increases under the contract to become effective on the date of the issue of the trade journal in which the price increases were published rather than on the date the prices were reported to have become effective, *Sterling Oil Terminal Corp.*, ASBCA 3704, 57-1 BCA ¶ 1265. See also *St. Louis Refrigerator Car Co.*, ASBCA 10837, 65-2 BCA ¶ 5161, in which the board held that the earliest date of price adjustment was the date of delivery of the price adjustment demand to the government and not before. In *Allis-Chalmers Corp.*, Comp. Gen. Dec. B-186693, 76-2 CPD ¶ 48, GAO held that the term "latest available indices" meant published indexes rather than preliminary figures available from the Department of Labor. In *Libby Corp.*, ASBCA 40765, 96-1 BCA ¶ 28,255, the board accepted the argument that the government could not recover a price reduction based on the contract delivery date if it had been responsible for a delay but found no proof of government responsibility. See also *ECC Int'l Corp. v. United States*, 43 Fed. Cl. 359 (1999), denying cross motions for summary judgment and remanding to the contracting officer to issue a final decision on whether a contract modification permitted economic price adjustment during a period of delayed performance.

### e. Effect of Changes

Changes affecting the amount or type of labor or material must be carefully analyzed to determine whether they require modifications to the economic price adjustment provisions. If such changes substantially alter the cost elements subject to price adjustment, the structure of a composite economic price adjustment formula can be significantly impacted. The ASBCA has held that because the government issues a change order that distorts or destroys the adjustment formula, it is not excused from its basic agreement to escalate, *Babcock & Wilcox Co.*, ASBCA 7531, 1962 BCA ¶ 3575. The most appropriate method of overcoming this problem would be for the parties to agree on separate price escalation provisions in any major contract amendments or supplemental agreements, Sharp, *Pricing and Contracting for Inflation*, 5 Nat. Cont. Mgt. J. 87 (1971). The parties may also agree that a change requires an economic price adjustment clause even though none had been included in the basic contract, *Minowitz Mfg. Co.*, ASBCA 23784, 83-1 BCA ¶ 16,324.

### f.   Notice Requirements

Almost all economic price adjustment clauses require that the contractor notify the contracting officer, within a specified period of time, when a price adjustment is due. Such requirements have generally been held to be enforceable only when the government is prejudiced by lack of notice, and such prejudice has been difficult to demonstrate, *Chemray Coatings Corp.*, GSBCA 10117, 91-1 BCA ¶ 23,356; *Sky Top Plastics*, GSBCA 7000, 91-1 BCA ¶ 23,350; *Interlog Corp.*, ASBCA 21212, 77-1 BCA ¶ 12,362. However, in *Bataco Indus., Inc. v. United States*, 29 Fed. Cl. 318 (1993), *aff'd*, 31 F.3d 1176 (Fed. Cir. 1994), the court held that a notice provision was a "time-bar" provision that should be strictly enforced. The clause stated:

(d) Price increases shall be subject to the following limitations:

* * *

(2) The contractor's entitlement to price increases shall be waived, unless the contractor's written request therefor is received by the contracting officer within 180 days after the date of final shipment of supplies under the contract.

The same result was reached in *Universal Dev. Corp. v. General Servs. Admin.*, GSBCA 12138, 93-3 BCA ¶ 26,100. This strict interpretation of the clause is completely dependent on the language setting forth the notice provision. Thus, some of these provisions may be interpreted to impose only a notice requirement (that will be waived absent prejudice to the government) while others may be interpreted to bar contractor claims for price adjustment.

## C.  Fixed-Price Redeterminable

FAR 16.205 and 206 provide for two types of redeterminable contracts where the prices are established during or after performance. Contracts of this type were widely used in the past but are now infrequently used since they provide very little incentive for the contractor to control the costs of performance. Thus, the current guidance calls for their use in quite narrow circumstances.

## *1. Prospective Price Redetermination*

This type of redeterminable contract calls for an initial amount of work at a firm fixed price followed by subsequent amounts of work with prices to be determined prior to the beginning of each period. FAR 16.205-2 contains the following guidance:

A fixed-price contract with prospective price redetermination may be used in acquisitions of quantity production or services for which it is possible to negotiate a fair and reasonable firm fixed price for an initial period, but not for subsequent periods of contract performance.

(a) The initial period should be the longest period for which it is possible to negotiate a fair and reasonable firm fixed price. Each subsequent pricing period should be at twelve months.

(b) The contract may provide for a ceiling price based on evaluation of the uncertainties involved in performance and their possible cost impact. This ceiling price should provide for assumption of a reasonable proportion of the risk by the contractor and, once established, may be adjusted only by operation of contract clauses providing for equitable adjustment or other revision of the contract price under stated circumstances.

FAR 16.205-3 contains the following limitations on the use of this type of contract:

This contract type shall not be used unless —

(a) Negotiations have established that —

(1) The conditions for use of a firm-fixed-price contract are not present (see 16.202-2), and

(2) A fixed-price incentive contract would not be more appropriate;

(b) The contractor's accounting system is adequate for price redetermination;

(c) The prospective pricing periods can be made to conform with operation of the contractor's accounting system; and

(d) There is reasonable assurance that price redetermination actions will take place promptly at the specified times.

This is a very difficult type of contract to use because it requires great diligence on the part of both the contractor and the government agency to meet the goal of completing the annual price redetermination before the work for the next year is begun. The Price Redetermination — Prospective clause in FAR 52.216-5, which is required to be used for this type of contract, must specify the number of days before the beginning of the prospective redetermination period that the contractor must submit its proposal for the prices for that period, and Note 2 to that clause contains the following instruction:

> (2) Insert the number of days chosen so that the Contractor's submission will be late enough to reflect recent cost experience (taking into account the Contractor's accounting system), but early enough to permit review, audit (if necessary), and negotiation before the start of the prospective period.

The requirement that the pricing periods be at least 12 months in duration reflects the need for a significant amount of time to arrive at a redetermined price and attempts to ensure that such price be based on prior actual cost experience. Yet to arrive at firm fixed prices before the beginning of each pricing period will require the agency to complete the review, audit, negotiation and internal clearance process in a period of three to six months. This is a challenging task for many agencies.

## 2. Retroactive Redetermination

An infrequently used type of redetermination is the retroactive redetermination type contract with a ceiling price where the final price is negotiated after completion of the work. FAR 16.206-2 provides the following guidance:

> A fixed-ceiling-price contract with retroactive price redetermination is appropriate for research and development contracts estimated at $150,000 or less when it is established at the outset that a fair and reasonable firm fixed price cannot be negotiated and that the amount involved and short performance period make the use of any other fixed-price contract type impracticable.
>
> (a) A ceiling price shall be negotiated for the contract at a level that reflects a reasonable sharing of risk by the contractor. The established ceiling price may be adjusted only if required by the operation of contract clauses providing for equitable adjustment or other revision of the contract price under stated circumstances.
>
> (b) The contract should be awarded only after negotiation of a billing price that is as fair and reasonable as the circumstances permit.
>
> (c) Since this contract type provides the contractor no cost control incentive except the ceiling price, the contracting officer should make clear to the contractor during discussion before award that the contractor's management effectiveness and ingenuity will be considered in retroactively redetermining the price.

Because of the obvious lack of incentive in this type of contract, FAR 16.206-3 permits its use only on research and development contracts under the simplified acquisition threshold and requires the approval of the head of the contracting activity or a higher level authority if required by agency procedures. A standard clause for this type of contract is contained in FAR 52.216-6. As discussed in Section I, this type of contract has been held to be a violation of the prohibition against a cost-plus-percentage-of-cost system of contracting.

## III. COST-REIMBURSEMENT CONTRACTS

When it has been decided that the nature of the work or the unreliability of the cost estimate makes it necessary to use a cost-reimbursement contract, the contracting officer and the contractor have several choices. This section discusses three types of cost-reimbursement contracts. First, the basic type of cost-reimbursement contract — the CPFF contract — will be reviewed. The section then considers the various types of cost-sharing contracts that have been used when the parties desire to share the risks of the contract by entering into an agreement that provides for cost-sharing throughout performance of the work. The section concludes with a discussion of the cost-no-fee contract. Cost-plus-incentive-fee (CPIF), cost-plus-award-fee (CPAF), and cost-plus-award-term (CPAT) contracts are dealt with in the next section on incentive contracts. Cost-reimbursement term type contracts are covered in the section on level-of-effort contracts.

FAR 16.301-2 contains the following basic guidance on the use of cost-reimbursement contracts:

> Cost-reimbursement contracts are suitable for use only when uncertainties involved in contract performance do not permit costs to be estimated with sufficient accuracy to use any type of fixed-price contract.

FAR 16.301-3 provides limitations on the use of any cost-reimbursement contract as follows:

> (a) A cost-reimbursement contract may be used only when —
>
> > (1) The contractor's accounting system is adequate for determining costs applicable to the contract; and
> >
> > (2) Appropriate Government surveillance during performance will provide reasonable assurance that efficient methods and effective cost controls are used.
>
> (b) The use of cost-reimbursement contracts is prohibited for the acquisition of commercial items (see parts 2 and 12).

There has been considerable recent criticism of the over-use of cost-reimbursement contracts. As a result, § 864 of the National Defense Authorization Act for Fiscal Year 2009, Pub. L. No. 110-417, (codified at 41 U.S.C. § 3906) requires the revision of this FAR provision to contain at a minimum, guidance regarding:

(1) when and under what circumstances cost-reimbursement contracts are appropriate;

(2) the acquisition plan findings necessary to support a decision to use cost- reimbursement contracts; and

(3) the acquisition workforce resources necessary to award and manage cost-reimbursement contracts.

This statute also requires review of the use of cost-reimbursement contracts by agency Inspectors General and submission of an annual report on such contract by the Office of Management and Budget. The first annual report from OMB (*www.whitehouse. gov/omb/assets/procurement/cost_contract_report_031809.pdf*) indicated in fiscal year 2008 the government issued cost-reimbursement contracts in the amount of $135 billion, constituting 25% of the total dollars obligated for contracts in that year. See also *Contract Management: Extent of Federal Spending Under Cost-Reimbursement Contracts Unclear and Key Controls Not Always Used*, GAO-09-921, Sept. 30, 2009, characterizing cost-reimbursement contracts as "high risk" and criticizing agencies for not documenting their decision to use such contracts. The report contains data indicating that agencies with research and development missions are making great use of cost-reimbursement contracts and that they are also used extensively to obtain professional services and for management and operation of government facilities.

The statutory requirement for additional guidance on the use of cost-reimbursement contracts was implemented in FAR 16.103(d):

(1) Each contract file shall include documentation to show why the particular contract type was selected. This shall be documented in the acquisition plan, or if a written acquisition plan is not required, in the contract file.

(i) Explain why the contract type selected must be used to meet the agency need.

(ii) Discuss the Government's additional risks and the burden to manage the contract type selected (e.g., when a cost-reimbursement contract is selected, the Government incurs additional cost risks, and the Government has the additional burden of managing the contractor's costs). For such instances, acquisition personnel shall discuss —

(A) How the Government identified the additional risks (e.g., pre-award survey, or past performance information);

(B) The nature of the additional risks (e.g., inadequate contractor's accounting system, weaknesses in contractor's internal control, non-compliance with Cost Accounting Standards, or lack of or inadequate earned value management system); and

(C) How the Government will manage and mitigate the risks.

(iii) Discuss the Government resources necessary to properly plan for, award, and administer the contract type selected (e.g., resources needed and the additional risks to the Government if adequate resources are not provided).

(iv) For other than a firm-fixed price contract, at a minimum the documentation should include —

(A) An analysis of why the use of other than a firm-fixed-price contract (e.g., cost reimbursement, time and materials, labor hour) is appropriate;

(B) Rationale that detail the particular facts and circumstances (e.g., complexity of the requirements, uncertain duration of the work, contractor's technical capability and financial responsibility, or adequacy of the contractor's accounting system), and associated reasoning essential to support the contract type selection;

(C) An assessment regarding the adequacy of Government resources that are necessary to properly plan for, award, and administer other than firm-fixed-price contracts; and

(D) A discussion of the actions planned to minimize the use of other than firm-fixed-price contracts on future acquisitions for the same requirement and to transition to firm-fixed-price contracts to the maximum extent practicable.

In addition, FAR 16.301-2(b) requires that an acquisition plan calling for the use of a cost-reimbursement contract by approved "one level above the contracting officer" in accordance with FAR 7.103(j).

The feature that all cost-reimbursement contracts have in common is the Limitation of Cost clause, FAR 52.232-20. This clause overrides all of the contract requirements by providing that when the contractor has fully expended the funds included in the contract, there is no further obligation to continue performance or incur costs, but that when the government provides additional funds, the contractor must continue performance as long as funds are available until completion of the specified work. The clause provides, in addition, that the contractor must give notice of overruns and that the government has no obligation to provide such additional funding or to reimburse the contractor for costs incurred in excess of the contractual amount. This latter provision has been quite strictly enforced to deny contractors' reimbursement of cost overruns not approved in writing by the contracting officer, *ITT Def. Commc'ns Div.*, ASBCA 14270, 70-2 BCA ¶ 8370; *American Standard, Inc.*, ASBCA 15660, 71-2 BCA ¶ 9109. In the most liberal case on this issue, the Court of Claims found that an overrun had been funded when a contracting officer indicated approval of the funding on an internal memorandum that was not communicated to the contractor, *General Elec. Co. v. United States*, 188 Ct.

Cl. 620, 412 F.2d 1215, *mot. for reh'g denied*, 189 Ct. Cl. 116, 416 F.2d 1320 (1969). In making the decision on whether to fund the overrun, the contracting officer has great discretion. Hence, a choice can be made either to fund or not to fund the overrun after the costs have been incurred, *Eyler Assocs., Inc.*, ASBCA 16804, 75-1 BCA ¶ 11,320; *ARINC Research Corp.*, ASBCA 15861, 72-2 BCA ¶ 9721. However, a decision not to fund the overrun based entirely on the failure of the contractor to give notice of the overrun as required by the clause may lead to difficulty. It has been held to be an abuse of discretion to make such a decision in a situation where the contractor could not have known of the overrun, *General Elec. Co. v. United States*, 194 Ct. Cl. 678, 440 F.2d 420 (1971). In contrast, a stringent test has been used to determine if the contractor could have learned of the overrun in such circumstances, and it has been held that it can meet this test only by showing that a fully adequate accounting system would not have revealed the overrun, *Stanwick Corp.*, ASBCA 14905, 71-1 BCA ¶ 8777, *recons. denied*, 71-2 BCA ¶ 9115. The government has also been estopped from denying overrun funding where it told the contractor funds were available and observed the occurrence of the overrun, *American Elec. Labs., Inc. v. United States*, 774 F.2d 1110 (Fed. Cir. 1985). For a complete discussion of the Limitation of Cost clause see Cibinic & Nash, *Cost-Reimbursement Contracting* 978-1018 (3d ed. 2004).

It has also become quite common practice to include ceiling amounts at the inception or during performance of cost-reimbursement contracts. If such provisions are carefully drafted to provide that they establish ceiling prices and that the contractor is obligated to complete the work, they will be enforced, *LSi Serv. Corp. v. United States*, 191 Ct. Cl. 185, 422 F.2d 1334 (1970); *National Civil Serv. League v. United States*, 226 Ct. Cl. 478, 643 F.2d 768 (1981); *CRC Sys. Inc. v. General Servs. Admin.*, GSBCA 11173, 93-2 BCA ¶ 25,842. However, in less clearly drafted clauses, the contractor has been permitted to avoid the ceiling, *Singer — General Precision, Inc. v. United States*, 192 Ct. Cl. 435, 427 F.2d 1187 (1970) (cost allocated to overhead as bidding expense); *General Dynamics Corp. v. United States*, 229 Ct. Cl. 399, 671 F.2d 474 (1982) (termination clause with ceiling interpreted to permit reimbursement of costs up to ceiling after default termination but making contractor responsible for excess costs of reprocurement). Overhead rate ceilings have also been strictly enforced when clearly drafted, *Metro Mach. Corp.*, ASBCA 47005, 97-1 BCA ¶ 28,723; *General Dynamics Corp., Elec. Boat Div.*, ASBCA 21737, 83-2 BCA ¶ 16,907, 84-2 BCA ¶ 17,394. For a complete discussion of ceilings see Cibinic & Nash, *Cost-Reimbursement Contracting* 1019-24 (3d ed. 2004).

## A. Cost-Plus-Fixed-Fee Contracts

In the CPFF contract, the parties negotiate an estimated cost of performance and preestablish the fee to be paid to the contractor for performing the work. This fixed fee is stated as a set amount of dollars that will vary only as the contractor is required to perform additional work not included in the original contract or less work than required by the contract. Thus, the contractor bears the risk of the adequacy of the fee while the government bears the risk of the incurrence of additional costs to permit full performance of the work. FAR 16.306(a) describes this type of contract as follows:

> A cost-plus-fixed-fee contract is a cost-reimbursement contract that provides for payment to the contractor of a negotiated fee that is fixed at the inception of the contract. The fixed fee does not vary with actual cost, but may be adjusted as a result of changes in the work to be performed under the contract. This contract type permits contracting for efforts that might otherwise present too great a risk to contractors, but it provides the contractor only a minimum incentive to control costs.

The CPFF contract is typically used for small jobs and those involving the early stages of research and development. FAR 16.306(b)(1) describes two situations where a CPFF contract is appropriate:

> (i) The contract is for the performance of research or preliminary exploration or study, and the level of effort required is unknown; or
>
> (ii) The contract is for development and test, and using a cost-plus-incentive-fee contract is not practical.

This guidance greatly restricts the use of the CPFF contract. Furthermore, the procurement regulations indicate that the government's policy is to use, whenever feasible and practical, a type of cost-reimbursement contract imposing some of the cost risk on the contractor. For example, FAR 16.306(b)(2) states:

> A cost-plus-fixed-fee contract normally should not be used in development of major systems (see Part 34) once preliminary exploration, studies, and risk reduction have indicated a high degree of probability that the development is achievable and the Government has established reasonably firm performance objectives and schedules.

In the CPFF contract, the estimated cost and the fixed fee are stated separately and, thus, must be negotiated separately. The estimated cost will, ideally, be the amount that the parties agree represents their best estimate of the amount that will be spent in accomplishing the work called for by the contract. It is not uncommon, however, for the estimated cost to be set at an amount less than the best estimate. Two factors appear to account for this practice. First, in a number of government procurements, agencies have not had sufficient funds in the budget to cover the cost estimate submitted by the contractor. In such cases, contractors have frequently been willing to agree to a lower cost estimate in order to obtain the immediate award of the contract. This will generally result in a somewhat lower fixed fee than would have been used if a higher estimated cost had been included. This lower fixed fee has been seen as a small concession compared to the risk of not being awarded the contract.

The second factor that has led to low estimated costs is the presence of competition in the contract award process. In most competitive procurements, the cost of performance is a significant evaluation factor in the source selection decision. As a result, offerors are motivated to make very optimistic estimates of the costs of performance. Although such estimates are adjusted to reflect "probable cost," through cost-realism analysis, for the purpose of selecting the winning contractor, FAR 15.404-1(d)(2), contracting officers generally award contracts based on the cost estimate submitted by the contractor in the competitive process rather than any higher probable cost that was arrived at by the cost-realism analysis. This is a questionable procedure because it results in a contract funded at too low a level to permit accomplishment of the work. A much better procedure is to include an estimated cost at a level representing the contracting officer's appraisal of the realistic cost of performance. However, it appears that only a minority of contracting officers follow this procedure, with the result that many CPFF contracts contain estimated costs that are unreasonably low.

The fixed fee in a CPFF contract is established in one of two ways. If the contract is awarded using a competitive negotiation process, the contracting officer may provide in the solicitation that each offeror propose the fixed fee that it will accept to perform the work and that this fixed fee be evaluated in the source selection process. This, of course, will induce some of the offerors to propose low fees and may result in a fixed fee that is quite low, perhaps in the range of 2% to 5%. Alternatively, most often in sole source procurements, the contracting officer may provide for the fixed fee to be established using the profit formula established in the agency's regulations (see Chapter 10). In this case, the offeror will normally submit an analysis of the elements of the fee, following the agency profit formula, and the fee will be negotiated during written or oral discussions or negotiations depending on the amount of competition. In such cases, fixed fees in the range of 6% to 10% can be anticipated. In addition, contractors with unique capabilities have been able in a few instances to negotiate, on a sole source basis, fee levels significantly higher than this range.

## B. Cost-Sharing Contracts

When contracting parties expect to receive mutual benefit from the performance of a contract, the most equitable arrangement may be to enter into an agreement at the outset providing for a sharing of costs. There are numerous ways to share costs of government work. One of the most common is to enter into a fixed-price contract at a price below anticipated costs. Another technique is to enter into a cooperative agreement or "other transaction" as discussed in Chapter 1. Grants also can be used as cost-sharing vehicles. This text discusses cost-sharing only in the context of procurement contracts where a cost-reimbursement contract is used with an agreement by the contractor to bear some portion of the incurred costs. FAR 16.303 describes this type of contract giving the following minimal guidance:

(a) *Description.* A cost-sharing contract is a cost-reimbursement contract in which the contractor receives no fee and is reimbursed only for an agreed-upon portion of its allowable costs.

(b) *Application*. A cost-sharing contract may be used when the contractor agrees to absorb a portion of the costs, in the expectation of substantial compensating benefits.

Some agencies have additional guidance. For example, the Environmental Protection Agency policy specifies that cost-sharing should be used "where the principal purpose is ultimate commercialization and utilization of technologies by the private sector" and where "future economic benefits" are expected for the government as well as the contractor, EPAAR 1516.303-72(a).

FAR 35.003(b) states further that cost sharing on research and development contracts should be in accordance with agency procedures and FAR 42.707(a) provides that cost sharing may be accomplished by the negotiation of indirect cost rates lower than anticipated actual rates. FAR 31.205-23 provides that the costs of the contractor's contributed portion under cost-sharing contracts are unallowable.

Prior to issuance of the FAR in April 1984, there was considerably greater guidance on this type of contract. Both the Federal Procurement Regulation and the Defense Acquisition Regulation contained substantive provisions, and the Office of Management and Budget had issued Federal Management Circular 73-3 on this topic. The last significant policy initiative in this area occurred in December 1980 when the Office of Federal Procurement Policy circulated a proposed policy letter suggesting significant changes to the cost-sharing policy of the federal government, 45 Fed. Reg. 86952 (Dec. 1980). This policy letter would have prohibited cost-sharing on all R&D contracts. It was accompanied, however, by a policy letter suggesting recoupment of R&D costs on contracts where a clear potential for commercial sales resulted from performance of the contract, 45 Fed. Reg. 86953 (1980). Industry objection to these policies apparently resulted in a lack of further action, and no governmentwide guidance has been issued since that time.

There has also been sporadic congressional activity in this area. For many years, the Department of Labor — Health and Human Services Appropriation Act contained a provision requiring cost sharing on research grants. This provision is no longer included in the Act. But since 1970, the Department of Housing and Urban Development — Independent Agencies Appropriation Act has contained a similar provision. See the Consolidated Appropriations Act for FY 2005, Pub. L. No. 108-477, § 404:

> None of the funds provided in this Act may be used for payment, through grants or contracts, to recipients that do not share in the cost of conducting research resulting from proposals not specifically solicited by the Government: *Provided*, That the extent of cost sharing by the recipient shall reflect the mutuality of interest of the grantee or contractor and the Government in the research.

Since this provision was included in a consolidated appropriations act, it appeared to apply to all departments and agencies of the government except the Department of Homeland Security and the Department of Defense. In recent years, these appropriations have been included in Continuing Resolutions or Consolidated Appropriations Acts which have not contained such a provision.

This section discusses three aspects of cost-sharing contracts: their use on research contracts, the recovery of research and development costs through recoupment, and use of cost-sharing contracts for development of commercial products.

## 1. Research Contracts

Congressional interest in cost-sharing has focused on research contracts, and prior to the FAR, the major procurement regulations gave guidance in this area. These regulations generally stated that cost sharing was appropriate when the contractor was expected to derive a significant commercial benefit from the research work. This policy has now been withdrawn, and the only significant guidance in the area is in separate agency regulations. Several agencies have broad policy guidance encouraging the use of cost-sharing contracts. See, for example, the following guidance in HHSAR 335.070-1(a):

> Contracting activities shall encourage performing organizations to contribute to the cost of performing R & D, through the use of cost-sharing contracts, where there is a probability that the contractor will receive present or future benefits from participation, such as increased technical know-how, training for employees, acquisition of equipment, and use of background knowledge in future contracts. Cost-sharing is intended to serve the mutual interests of the Government and the performing organization by helping to ensure efficient utilization of the resources available for the conduct of R & D projects and by promoting sound planning and prudent fiscal policies of the performing organization. The Contracting Officer shall use a cost-sharing contract, unless the Contracting Officer determines that a request for cost-sharing would not be appropriate because of the following circumstances:
>
> > (1) The particular R & D objective or scope of effort for the project is specified by the Government rather than proposed by the performing organization. This would usually include any formal Government solicitation for a specific project.
> >
> > (2) The R & D effort has only minor relevance to the non-Federal activities of the performing organization, and the organization is proposing to undertake the R & D primarily as a service to the Government.
> >
> > (3) The organization has little or no non-Federal sources or funds from which to make a cost contribution. Organizations which are predominantly engaged in R & D and have little or no production or other service activities may not be in a favorable position to make a cost contribution.

Accordingly, the Contracting Officer shall normally not request cost-sharing, if cost-sharing would require the Government to provide funds through some other means (such as fees) to enable the organization to cost-share.

This regulation provides that the amount of cost sharing should be proportional to the benefit to be derived by the contractor, HHSAR 335.070-2, and that it can be accomplished either by negotiating percentages of costs or elements of cost to be borne by the contractor, HHSAR 335.070-3.

Other agencies with policies encouraging cost sharing on research contracts include the Department of Energy, DEAR 917.7001 (primarily on projects to develop commercial technology), the Environmental Protection Agency, EPAAR 1516.303 (when purpose is commercialization of technology), and the Department of Homeland Security, HSAR 3035.003 (discretionary cost sharing and recoupment). Of these agencies, only the EPA has guidance on the implementation of the policy — including the provision in EPAAR 1516.303-73 that cost sharing may include "cash outlays, real property or interest therein, personal property or services, cost matching, or other in-kind contributions."

Some agencies have restricted their policy to contracts resulting from unsolicited proposals. For example, NASA requires cost sharing in research contracts resulting from unsolicited proposals from "for-profit organizations" unless no nongovernmental benefit will be derived from the project, NFS 1816.303-70. In contrast, no cost sharing is required if the proposal is submitted by a nonprofit organization unless there will be nongovernmental benefit. Under this policy NASA requires that the costs be shared as a minimum percentage of the total allowable costs to be determined by assessing the relative benefits of the work but not to exceed 10% in the case of contracts with nonprofit organizations. A standard clause is provided in NFS 1852.216-73 for this purpose:

ESTIMATED COST AND COST SHARING (DEC 1991)

(a) It is estimated that the total cost of performing the work under this contract will be $ ____.

(b) For performance of the work under this contract, the Contractor shall be reimbursed for not more than ____ percent of the costs of performance determined to be allowable under the Allowable Cost and Payment clause. The remaining ____ percent or more of the costs of performance so determined shall constitute the Contractor's share, for which it will not be reimbursed by the Government.

(c) For purposes of the ____ [insert " Limitation of Cost" or " Limitation of Funds" ] clause, the total estimated cost to the Government is hereby established as $ ____ (insert estimated Government share); this amount is the maximum Government liability.

(d) The Contractor shall maintain records of all contract costs claimed by the Contractor as constituting part of its share. Those records shall be subject to audit by the Government. Cost contributed by the Contractor shall not be charged to the Government under any other grant, contract, or agreement (including allocation to other grants, contracts, or agreements as part of an independent research and development program).

Several other agencies have adopted this policy of requiring cost sharing on research contracts resulting from unsolicited proposals. See DEAR 915.605(b)(5) (Department of Energy); HUDAR 2415.605-70 (Department of Housing and Urban Development); DOLAR 2915.605 (Department of Labor).

It is also possible to share costs by having the contractor agree to pay all or a part of specified costs. See, for example, *Shale Dev. Corp.*, IBCA 1256-3-79, 81-1 BCA ¶ 15,128, where the board held that a cost-sharing contract existed because the parties had agreed that the government would pay direct costs and the contractor would pay indirect costs. However, cost-sharing provisions must be carefully drafted to ensure that they carry out the parties' intent. See *Jacobs Eng'g Group, Inc. v. United States*, 434 F.3d 1378 (Fed. Cir. 2006), holding that cost sharing did not apply to costs paid as a result of a termination for convenience of the government because the termination clause called for the payment of "all cost reimbursable under this contract." A subsequent decision held that this holding did not call for the reimbursement of "foregone fee" which the parties had agreed could be counted as part of the contractor's share of costs, *Jacobs Eng'g Group, Inc. v. United States*, 75 Fed. Cl. 752 (2007), *aff'd*, 263 Fed. Appx. 875 (Fed. Cir. 2008). See also *Interstate Electronics Corp.*, ASBCA 55064, 07-2 BCA ¶ 33,643, involving a dispute over whether contract language precluded charging its share of costs as independent research and development costs, and *General Am. Research Div., Gen. Am. Transp. Corp.*, PSBCA 91, 77-1 BCA ¶ 12,732, where the board held that a CPFF contract with a special clause providing for cost sharing on overruns did not require sharing of costs incurred in a convenience termination settlement.

## 2. Recoupment of Development Costs

Another method of sharing costs, after the fact, is recoupment. Recoupment is the recovery of nonrecurring costs of developing and preparing a product for manufacture from other buyers of that product. Recoupment was a standard practice of the DoD from the 1950s until 1992. However, on June 19, 1992, the White House issued a press report announcing that the President had abolished recoupment fees on all products other than "major defense equipment" (MDE) exported for military uses. As a result, recoupment is now only utilized by DoD as required by statute in contracts for foreign military sales (FMS). However, FAR 35.003(c) permits recoupment "in accordance with agency procedures." See HSAR 3035.003 setting forth the Department of Homeland Security's recoupment policy as follows:

(c) Recoupment shall be determined on a case-by-case basis. Recoupment not otherwise required by law should be structured to address factors such as recovering the Department's fair share of its investment in nonrecurring costs related to the items acquired. Advice of legal counsel shall be obtained prior to establishing cost sharing policies and recoupment mechanisms under (FAR) 48 CFR 35.003(b) and (c).

Recoupment has been implemented by DoD in two ways. First, DoD recovers a recoupment charge directly from a foreign government if a product is sold to a foreign government under a FMS arrangement. Second, a contractor adds a recoupment charge to the contract and pays it to the government if a product is sold by the contractor directly to a foreign or domestic customer, or if a foreign company is licensed to manufacture the product.

DoD first issued a written policy on recoupment in 1967 — DoD Directive 2140.2, Recovery of Nonrecurring Costs Applicable to Foreign Sales. This directive applied to sales of MDE to foreign buyers. MDE was defined as equipment that had been developed and produced with an expenditure of Research, Development, Test, and Evaluation (RDT&E) funds in excess of $25 million or a production investment in excess of $100 million. The thresholds for MDE doubled in 1972. Subsequently, in 1974, the Directive was revised to split the recoupment charge into two segments, one for nonrecurring development costs and the other for nonrecurring production costs.

Congress first adopted the recoupment policy in the Arms Export Control Act of 1976, Pub. L. No. 94-329. The Act contains a provision at 22 U.S.C. § 2761(e)(1) (B), requiring that FMS agreements include:

> a proportionate amount of any nonrecurring costs of research, development, and production of major defense equipment (except for equipment wholly paid for either from funds transferred under section 503(a)(3) of the Foreign Assistance Act of 1961 [22 U.S.C. §2311(a)(3)] or from funds made available on a nonrepayable basis under section 23 of this Act [22 U.S.C. §2763]).

The Office of Federal Procurement Policy subsequently determined that recoupment was not a sound policy because it had a negative impact on the competitiveness of American industry in international markets— resulting in the 1992 presidential action. In response to the new policy, DoD issued a revised Directive 2140.2, Jan. 13, 1993, which states that a "recoupment charge shall be imposed for sales of MDE only as required by Act of Congress." See 32 C.F.R. § 165.4(a). In 1996, § 4303 of the Clinger-Cohen Act, Pub. L. No. 104-106, added 22 U.S.C. § 2761(e)(2), which provides for Presidential waiver of recoupment on FMS sales to obtain standardization of military equipment by allied countries, to prevent loss of the sale or to obtain savings on procurement of equipment for the United States, and to correct prior estimates of the amount of sales. Waiver procedures are set forth in 32 C.F.R. § 165.7.

Recoupment clauses have created some difficult contractual issues. See, for example, *BMY, Div. of Harsco Corp.*, ASBCA 38172, 93-2 BCA ¶ 25,704, where the board held that the government was entitled to recoupment of nonrecurring costs only in connection with the second of two commercial sales because the government's investment in the R&D of the product at the time of the first sale was less than the $5 million required for reimbursement in the DAR clause in the contract. In *Hughes Aircraft Co.*, ASBCA 30570, 90-2 BCA ¶ 22,780, the board found the contractor liable for R&D expenditures following a commercial sale of weapons to the United Kingdom despite a subsequent international agreement between the United States and the United Kingdom that stated such costs would be paid by the United Kingdom. The board concluded the contractor was not relieved of its responsibility to pay because the agreement had not been made for the purpose of absolving the contractor of liability. In *General Elec. Co.*, ASBCA 20930, 79-2 BCA ¶ 13,956, the board held that the government was not entitled to recoupment for nonrecurring program and R&D costs because the original contractor sold the product to another contractor for use in a separate government contract. The board reasoned that no commercial sale warranting recoupment had occurred because the government would ultimately be the end user in both contracts. See also *Lockheed Martin Corp. v. United States*, 210 F.3d 1366 (Fed. Cir. 2000), holding that recoupment provisions did not divest a contractor from having "substantial rights" in the intellectual property flowing from government R&D contracts — with the result that the contractor was entitled to the research tax credit under 26 U.S.C. § 41.

## 3. *Support of Commercial Development*

The most obvious type of agreement where cost sharing should be required is the agreement used when the government supports the work of an organization to develop a product for the commercial market. The Department of Energy (DOE) has issued the most helpful regulation dealing with this type of contract, which requires "cost participation." DEAR 917.7001(a) states:

> When DOE supports performer research, development, and/or demonstration efforts, where the principal purpose is ultimate commercialization and utilization of the technologies by the private sector, and when there are reasonable expectations that the performer will receive present or future economic benefits beyond the instant contract as a result of performance of the effort, it is DOE policy to obtain cost participation. Full funding may be provided for early phases of development programs when the technological problems are still great.

This regulation gives full discretion in establishing the type of cost sharing required on each contract. DEAR 917.7001(b) gives the following guidance on the amount of "cost participation":

> In making this determination to obtain cost participation, and evaluating present and future economic benefits to the performer, DOE will consider the technical feasibility, projected economic viability, societal and political acceptability

of commercial application, as well as possible effects of other DOE-supported projects in competing technologies.

The Environmental Protection Agency has also issued a cost-sharing policy. EPAAR 1516.303-72 states:

(a) The Agency shall use cost-sharing contracts where the principal purpose is ultimate commercialization and utilization of technologies by the private sector. There should also be a reasonable expectation of future economic benefits for the contractor and the Government beyond the Government's contract.

EPAAR 1516.303-75 gives the following guidance on the amount of cost-sharing:

(a) Contractors should contribute a reasonable amount of the total project cost covered under the contract. The ratio of cost participation should correlate to the apparent advantages available to performers and the proximity of implementing commercialization, i.e., the higher the potential for future profits, the higher the contractor's share should be.

\* \* \*

(c) The Contracting Officer, with the input of technical experts, may consider the following factors in determining reasonable levels of cost sharing:

(1) The availability of the technology to competitors;

(2) Improvements in the contractor's market share position;

(3) The time and risk necessary to achieve success;

(4) If the results of the project involve patent rights which could be sold or licensed;

(5) If the contractor has non-Federal sources of funds to include as cost participation; and

(6) If the contractor has the production and other capabilities to capitalize the results of the project.

(d) A contractor's cost participation can be provided by other subcontractors with which it has contractual arrangements to perform the contract as long as the contractor's cost-sharing goal is met.

EPAAR 1516.303-74 also contains guidance on in-kind contributions, which can be accepted as part of a contractor's cost sharing. EPAAR 1552.216-76 contains a standard clause for cost-sharing contracts.

The Department of Defense has used similar reasoning in requiring cost sharing in contracts issued under its "manufacturing technology program" where one of the military services supports a contractor's development of improved manufacturing processes. However, § 216 of the FY 2000 National Defense Authorization Act, Pub. L. No. 106-65, adopted 10 U.S.C. § 2521(d) deleting the prior requirement for mandatory cost sharing and substituting a provision calling for the amount of cost sharing proposed by competitive offerors to be used as an evaluation factor in selecting the winning contractor. This procedure has been implemented in DFARS 235.006-70(b).

## C. Cost-No-Fee Contracts

Perhaps the least used cost-reimbursement contract is the cost-no-fee contract. This contract is recognized in FAR 16.302 as a cost contract," but the only guidance given is that such contracts "may be appropriate for research and development work, particularly with nonprofit educational institutions, or other nonprofit organizations, and for facilities contracts." Since most contractors incur disallowed costs of 1% to 3%, a cost-no-fee contract is actually a loss contract.

In order to avoid losing money in the performance of a research and development contract, most nonprofit organizations are permitted to earn a fee on such contracts. See, for example, DFARS 215.404-75 stating:

For nonprofit organizations that are [Federally Funded Research and Development Centers], the contracting officer —

> (a) Should consider whether any fee is appropriate. Considerations shall include the FFRDC's —
>
>> (1) Proportion of retained earnings (as established under generally accepted accounting methods) that relates to DoD contracted effort;
>>
>> (2) Facilities capital acquisition plans;
>>
>> (3) Working capital funding as assessed on operating cycle cash needs; and
>>
>> (4) Provision for funding unreimbursed costs deemed ordinary and necessary to the FFRDC.
>
> (b) Shall, when a fee is considered appropriate, establish the fee objective in accordance with FFRDC fee policies in the DoD FFRDC Management Plan.

See also DFARS 215.404-72 providing for the use of a modified weighted guidelines approach to calculate fees for other nonprofit organizations which are "entities that have been identified by the Secretary of Defense or a Secretary of a Department as receiving sustaining support." Thus, the use of cost-no-fee contracts with nonprofit organizations is relatively rare. When such a contract is negotiated for research and development work, agencies are required to use the Cost Contract—No Fee clause in FAR 52.216-11. NASA has a special clause, Estimated Cost, NFS 1852.216-81, for such contracts.

Contracts paying a contractor to acquire facilities in order to perform government work have traditionally been cost-no-fee contracts. Prior to June 2007, FAR 45.302-2(c) required that no fee be paid on such contracts. This was implemented in the mandatory Allowable Cost and Payment — Facilities clause in FAR 52.216-13. All of this guidance on facilities contracts was removed when the rewrite of FAR Part 45 was issued in 72 Fed. Reg. 27,364, May 15, 2007.

## IV. INCENTIVE CONTRACTS

Incentive contracts are used when the pricing risk is not sufficiently large to justify the use of a cost-plus-fixed-fee contract but is too great to support the use of a firm fixed-price contract. Thus, they provide a middle alternative that the contracting parties can use to impose some risk on the contractor without requiring a full assumption of pricing risk. There are two distinct types of incentive contracts: the "objective" incentive, where the parties include a *formula* in the contract to determine the profit earned by the contractor based on the actual performance results achieved; and the "subjective" incentive, where the parties agree that the profit earned on the contract will be *determined by the government* based on an appraisal of the contractor's performance. The two objective incentive contracts are the cost-plus-incentive-fee (CPIF) contract and the fixed-price incentive (FPI) contract. The subjective incentive contracts are the cost-plus-award-fee (CPAF) contract and the cost-plus-award-term (CPAT).

FAR 16.401 contains the following basic guidance on these forms of contract:

> (a) Incentive contracts as described in this subpart are appropriate when a firm-fixed-price contract is not appropriate and the required supplies or services can be acquired at lower costs and, in certain instances, with improved delivery or technical performance, by relating the amount of profit or fee payable under the contract to the contractor's performance. Incentive contracts are designed to obtain specific acquisition objectives by —
>
>> (1) Establishing reasonable and attainable targets that are clearly communicated to the contractor; and
>
>> (2) Including appropriate incentive arrangements designed to —
>
>>> (i) Motivate contractor efforts that might not otherwise be emphasized; and
>
>>> (ii) Discourage contractor inefficiency and waste.

Numerous kinds of incentives are included in these types of contracts. In all cases, they must include incentives or constraints on the cost of performance, FAR 16.402-1(a). Incentives on technical performance and time of performance may be included at the discretion of the procuring agency. This section first discusses the major types of objective incentive contract focusing on the cost incentives. It then addresses technical and delivery incentives. The section concludes with a discussion of CPAF and CPAT contracts.

## A. Cost-Plus-Incentive-Fee Contracts

The CPIF contract is an objective incentive where the parties include a formula in the contract to determine the profit earned by the contractor based on the actual performance results achieved. FAR 16.405-1(a) describes this type of contract, as follows:

> The cost-plus-incentive-fee contract is a cost-reimbursement contract that provides for the initially negotiated fee to be adjusted later by a formula based on the relationship of total allowable costs to total target costs. This contract type specifies a target cost, a target fee, minimum and maximum fees, and a fee adjustment formula. After contract performance, the fee payable to the contractor is determined in accordance with the formula. The formula provides, within limits, for increases in fee above target fee when total allowable costs are less than target costs, and decreases in fee below target fee when total allowable costs exceed target costs. This increase or decrease is intended to provide an incentive for the contractor to manage the contract effectively. When total allowable cost is greater than or less than the range of costs within which the fee-adjustment formula operates, the contractor is paid total allowable costs, plus the minimum or maximum fee.

FAR 16.405-1(b)(1) indicates that this type of contract is particularly appropriate for services or development and test programs, but it has been used in many other contracting situations as well. DoD PGI 216.104-70 suggests the use of incentive contracts on contracts for research and exploratory development and for advanced development. To use CPIF contracts effectively the parties must have sufficient knowledge of the work to establish a target cost with some reasonable degree of accuracy yet not have such firm data as to make a fixed-price type contract appropriate. If the parties misjudge the problems that will be encountered in performing the contract, with the result that the target cost does not accurately reflect the costs of performance, the contractor will be paid a fee that is not commensurate with the true worth of its performance because the CPIF contract pays an incentive fee based on the relationship of actual costs to target costs without regard to unforeseen problems which may have caused the discrepancy between the target and actual costs.

CPIF contracts can include incentives only on the costs of performance or can include multiple incentives covering, in addition, technical performance and delivery. In this regard, DoD PGI 216.104-70(3)(iii) contains the following limitations on the use of only cost incentives on contracts for advanced development work:

Contracting officers should not use contracts with only cost incentives where —

(A) There will be a large number of major technical changes; or

(B) Actions beyond the control of the contractor may influence the contractor's achievement of cost targets.

This section addresses cost incentives in the CPIF contract. Incentives on performance and delivery are addressed in a later section.

## 1. Elements of the Contract Formula on Costs

There are five elements in the basic formula for CPIF contracts covering the costs of performance:

- Target Cost
- Target Fee
- Maximum Fee
- Minimum Fee
- Sharing Arrangement

The formula is expressed in contract language in the Incentive Fee clause in FAR 52.216-10, as follows:

(e) *Fee Payable.* (1) The fee payable under this contract shall be the target fee increased by _____ [*Contracting Officer insert Contractor's participation*] cents for every dollar that the total allowable cost is less than the target cost or decreased by _____ [*Contracting Officer insert Contractor's participation*] cents for every dollar that the total allowable cost exceeds the target cost. In no event shall the fee be greater than _____ [*Contracting Officer insert percentage*] percent or less than _____ [*Contracting Officer insert percentage*] percent of the target cost.

The essence of the cost-incentive formula is that the contractor's actual fee *varies inversely* with the amount of costs incurred as long as the actual costs incurred fall within the range of sharing established by the points where the maximum and minimum fees take effect. Once these points are reached, the contract becomes a CPFF contract at either the maximum or minimum fee depending on the circumstances. The range in which the sharing arrangement is effective is commonly called the "range of incentive effectiveness" (RIE). **Figure 9-1** is a graphic illustration of the relationship of these elements of the CPIF contract where the following elements have been negotiated:

| | |
|---|---|
| Target Cost | $100 |
| Target Fee | $8 |
| Maximum Fee | 15% ($15) |
| Minimum Fee | 2% ($2) |
| Sharing Arrangement | 80/20 |

In this incentive formula, the RIE where sharing occurs is between incurred costs of $65 and $130. If the work is performed at a cost of $65 or less, the contractor is paid the maximum fee of $15, while the minimum fee of $2 is paid if the total costs of performance are $130 or more. This formula is the simplest possible with a single sharing percentage for the entire RIE.

**Figure 9-1** presents the CPIF contract in terms of variations in earned fee against variations in incurred cost. This is the normal form of presentation used to depict the outcome of incentives on cost. Both cost and fee are expressed in terms of dollars rather than percentages, although the target fee is commonly negotiated in terms of a percentage. The graphic presentation is easy to work with because it clearly shows the extent of the sharing and the outcomes at any projected level of cost incurrence.

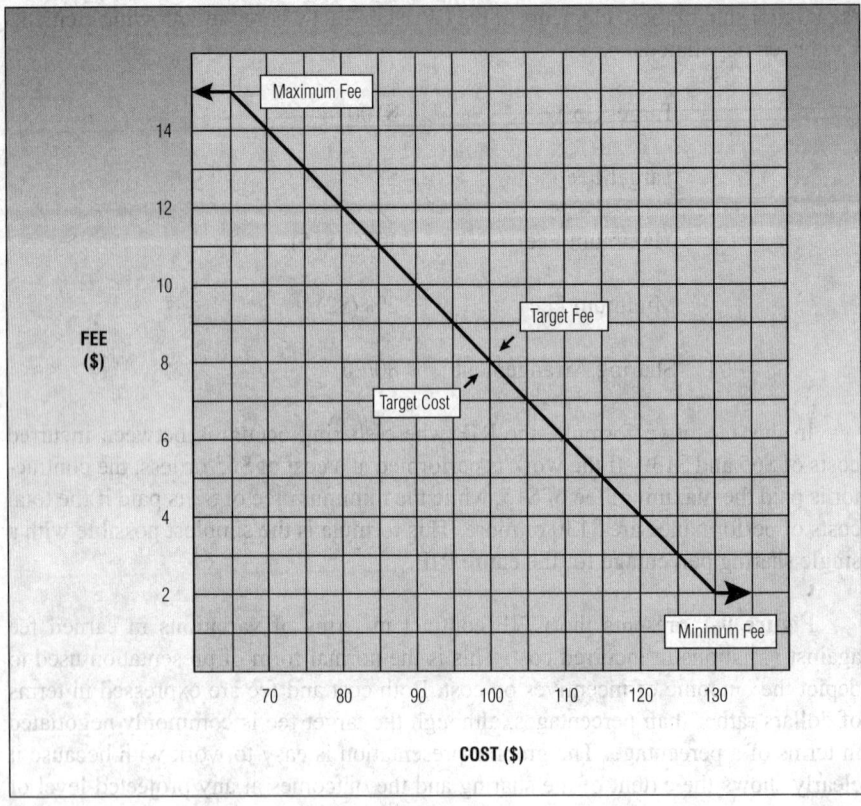

**Figure 9-1**

## 2. *Negotiating the Cost Incentive Formula*

Little general guidance is available on procedures for negotiating the elements of an incentive formula, although a good discussion of some of the factors is included in the DoD and NASA Incentive Contracting Guide, October 1969 (*https://acc. dau.mil/GetAttachment.aspx?id=189615&pname=file&aid=32537&lang=en-US*). In practice, it appears that the most common method of establishing these formulas is to follow past practice in the specific procuring agency negotiating the contract. In this sense, local practice is the major determinant in establishing the elements of the formula. Historically, the range of these elements for most CPIF contracts has been as follows:

| | |
|---|---|
| Target Cost | $100 |
| Target Fee | 6.5% to 9% |
| Maximum Fee | 10% to 15% |

Minimum Fee                0% to 4%

Sharing Arrangement        90/10 to 70/30

## a. Guidance on Cost Incentive Elements

While the incentive formula is probably best viewed as a single, unified formula for risk allocation, the formula can be established in different ways. In some instances, particularly in procurements with limited or no competition, the contracting officer will follow the guidance of FAR 16.103(a) and establish the elements of the formula through negotiation with the contractor. In such cases, the parties usually conduct negotiations using a step-by-step process beginning with the establishment of the target cost, proceeding to the negotiation of the target fee, and finally factoring in the other elements of the formula. In contrast, when the source is selected competitively, the government agency may prescribe the elements of the incentive formula in the RFP, permitting the competitors to propose the target cost but maintaining the other elements of the formula at specified percentages or amounts in order to ease the problem of evaluating the proposals. In either case, the tendency has been to arrive at a formula on a mechanical basis without regard to whether the formula is a realistic reflection of the possible outcome of the performance of a contract. For example, in the formula depicted in **Figure 9-1** the maximum fee is reached only when actual costs incurred are $65, implying that an underrun of 35% is possible. However, the facts of the procurement, including the practices used in establishing the target cost of $100, would almost always show that an underrun of this magnitude would be unlikely, if not impossible. Thus, in this formula, the maximum fee is set at an unrealistic level.

Although the elements of the incentive formula may be established in a variety of ways, the following guidance is provided on the considerations applicable to each element.

## (1) TARGET COST

The target cost is usually the focal point of the negotiation process since it is the baseline around which the other elements of the formula revolve. This cost is established through the competitive process or after detailed analysis of the contractor's proposal, as discussed in Chapter 10. In either case, the target cost must be subjected to cost-realism analysis to ensure that it is realistic, *Teledyne Ryan Aeronautical*, 56 Comp. Gen. 635 (B-187325, 77-1 CPD ¶ 352. If it is unrealistically low in a competitive procurement, the agency should adjust it to the probable cost of performance in order to evaluate the proposal — with a commensurate downward adjustment to the proposed target fee to reflect the incentive-sharing formula. See *Bechtel Hanford, Inc.*, Comp. Gen. Dec. B-292288, 2003 CPD ¶ 199, where this was done with the awardee but the agency did not then take into consideration the fact that this contractor had little margin between the most probable cost and the cost that would result in minimum fee. GAO granted the protest because the agency had not taken into consideration that award to that contractor would result in very little application of the incentive formula to motivate the contractor to control overrun costs (because it would reach the cost level where minimum fee applied very quickly after it exceeded the probable cost amount).

Although the CPIF contract places greater risk on the contractor than does the CPFF contract, it is generally believed that the target cost should be estimated using the same basic methodology that is used to arrive at the estimated cost in the CPFF contract. In competitive procurements, this would require that it be set at the probable cost of performance when cost-realism analysis indicates that the proposed target cost is unrealistically low. However, as discussed earlier with regard to CPFF contracts, most contracting officers probably do not make such adjustment with the result that numerous contracts contain a target cost level lower than probable cost — resulting in a target fee that will be unlikely to be achieved if the probable cost assessment is correct. Even in a noncompetitive environment, the target cost may be negotiated to an unduly low level because of the guidance given to contracting officers that contingencies should not be included in target costs unless they "may arise from presently known and existing conditions, the effects of which are foreseeable within reasonable limits of accuracy," FAR 31.205-7(c)(1). Another influence working to produce a low target cost is the generally optimistic view of program and technical personnel concerning the level of effort needed to accomplish R&D contracts. Such personnel may not fully recognize or anticipate the pitfalls that are frequently encountered during the course of performance; as a result, they use a low estimate of labor-hours in establishing the target cost.

The same factors that may lead to a low target cost also make it difficult for the contractor and contracting officer to reach agreement on the target cost. When the contractor and contracting officer have such difficulty, the other elements of the formula provide a means of compromise. A common compromising technique is the use of a "plateau" in the sharing formula, whereby the parties agree that in a certain range of cost no sharing will take place. For example, if the contracting officer will agree to a target cost of no more than $95 and the contractor is adamant that a figure of no less than $105 is the most valid prediction of the costs of performance, the contract could provide for no sharing between these two amounts. The parties would still have to agree on an intermediate target cost for purposes of making the fee calculation, but this too is susceptible to compromise at a target cost of $100. The result would be that the middle segment of the formula would contain a CPFF plateau, which would keep either party from encountering windfall profits or losses. Another possible means of compromise is for the contracting officer to accept the contractor's position on the target cost while both parties agree that the target fee will be established using the government's anticipated target cost as the base. This reduces the target fee somewhat and gives the government some protection from excessive profits if the contractor performs the contract at a low cost. Thus, the process of establishing the target cost provides the parties with considerable flexibility in arriving at a mutually acceptable incentive formula.

## (2) Target Fee

There are two major factors that come into play in establishing the target fee — the competitive situation and the profit policy of the procuring agency, as discussed in Chapter 10. In a procurement with little or no competition, the contracting officer will generally use the agency profit formula as the starting point for negotiation of the fee. Most contractors are willing to use these profit formulas as the basis for negotiation of the target fee and many will submit their analysis in their original proposal (although FAR 15.404-4(c)(5) prohibits contracting officers from requiring such submission). However, their analysis may well result in a considerably higher fee than that arrived at by the contracting officer. In such cases, the target fee will be determined by vigorous negotiations. In contrast, in highly competitive procurements, some contractors are likely to propose lower target fees in an effort to win the competition, and contracting officers are prone to accept such fees.

Use of the agency profit formula will result in varying levels of target fee in CPIF contracts, depending primarily on the factors of performance risk and investment in facilities in DoD contracts and on contractor effort in contracts with other agencies. In addition, these formulas provide for a small increment of fee for a CPIF contract based on cost risk. The major factor determining this risk in the incentive formula is the sharing arrangement. Thus, a high contractor share should lead to a higher target fee than a low contractor share.

## (3) Maximum Fee

The maximum fee should be established at a level that provides a sufficiently wide RIE to reward the contractor for all realistic levels of cost that might be incurred to perform the contract. Thus, assuming that the parties have negotiated a target cost of $100 and have concluded that the lowest possible cost of performance is $85, the maximum fee should be established at a level so that incentive bonuses will be earned in the full range between $85 and $100. If they have agreed to a 70/30 share for underruns and a target fee of 7%, this would require a maximum fee of 11½%. Any lower maximum fee would provide no incentive for the contractor to strive to perform the contract for costs of $85.

Prior to 1997, the limiting factor in establishing the maximum fee was the statutory fee limitation on CPFF contracts — 15% on R&D contracts and 10% on all other contracts. While it was generally agreed that the statutory fee limitations were not applicable to CPIF contracts, FAR 15.903(d)(2) required a deviation from the FAR before the maximum fee on a CPIF contract could exceed the CPFF level. FAC 97-02, September 30, 1997, eliminated this provision from the FAR, with the result that contracting officers are now authorized to negotiate maximum fees that provide the necessary incentive to the contractor to reduce the costs of performance.

## (4) Minimum Fee

The minimum fee is probably the most contentious element in the CPIF formula because in negotiating this element the parties' goals are diametrically opposed. The contracting officer generally wants a low minimum fee in order to ensure that the sharing continues over a wide range of cost overruns, while the contractor wants a high minimum fee in order to protect against the possibility of a loss contract. It is generally accepted that a minimum fee set between 2% and 3% of target cost will yield little or no profit because this amount of profit is necessary to cover *disallowed costs.* Hence, the contractor will normally argue that the minimum fee should be no less than this amount. In some cases, the government has agreed to this figure, but there have been many instances where a minimum fee under 2% has been used. There are even a few instances where the contracting parties have negotiated a minimum fee of less than 0%. As with the target fee, the negotiation of the minimum fee will depend on the competitive situation and the bargaining skills of the parties.

It has been quite common for the minimum and maximum fees to be equally distant from the target fee, and FAR 16.405-1(b)(3) requires a low minimum fee when a high maximum fee is negotiated. It is commonly believed that this is the fairest arrangement because it permits the contractor to earn as much in incentive bonuses as it risks losing in incentive penalties. However, this is not necessarily the case. If a uniform sharing arrangement is used for the entire contract, it is possible that the maximum fee will never be attainable, whereas reaching the minimum fee may be quite possible. For example, with the 80/20 sharing arrangement in **Figure 9-1** the contractor could earn $6 of additional fee by performing the work at $70 but would lose $6 of the fee by performing at $130. In most development contracting situations, where such a formula would be found, it is far more likely that the actual results will reach $130 than $70 since it is very difficult to achieve significant cost underruns. Thus, it is important that the parties analyze the true potential outcomes of minimum and maximum fees within the sharing arrangement rather than merely negotiate theoretical formulas that have the appearance of symmetry.

## (5) Sharing Arrangement

The amount of motivation provided by a CPIF contract is controlled primarily by the level of sharing agreed to by the parties. Clearly, a contract where the contractor shares at a rate of 30% of costs incurred over the entire RIE is a more powerful tool than a contract where the contractor's share is only 10%. Thus, the sharing arrangement is the major element of the formula reflecting the cost risk imposed by the contract, and the contractor's share will be established, to a large extent, by the parties' appraisal of the amount of risk the procurement entails. If the work is well defined and the cost outcome relatively predictable, imposing more risk by using a higher contractor share would be expected. Conversely, if the work statement is vague and the field of technology not well defined, a lower contractor share would be appropriate. There is very little guidance on which sharing levels are proper in varying circumstances, but it is usually agreed that a contractor share of less than 10% is relatively ineffective and a contractor share of over 30% is somewhat unusual, with the result that almost all CPIF contracts contain sharing levels within this range. Further, the great majority of the contracts in existence use shares in the middle of the range, from 15% to 25%. These practices are probably best understood and explained in terms of the traditions within procuring agencies rather than logic. Nevertheless, the establishment of the sharing level is the subject of hard negotiation in many cases and does provide the parties an opportunity to tailor the incentive formula to fit the nature and difficulty of the work called for by the contract.

Widely divergent sharing arrangements have been used in CPIF contracts. The most common is probably the single, straight-line share depicted in **Figure 9-1**, but multiple-line arrangements such as that depicted in **Figure 9-2** have also been quite common. The rationale for this arrangement is that the sharing should increase, with commensurately greater rewards and penalties, as the contractor deviates from the norm of the target cost. This recognizes that the target cost estimate may not be too accurate and that deviations close to target may be desirable as the work progresses. Of course, any other sharing structure that accomplishes the objectives of the parties is equally acceptable, and the contracting officer and the contractor are expected to negotiate a sharing structure that best serves the needs of the specific procurement.

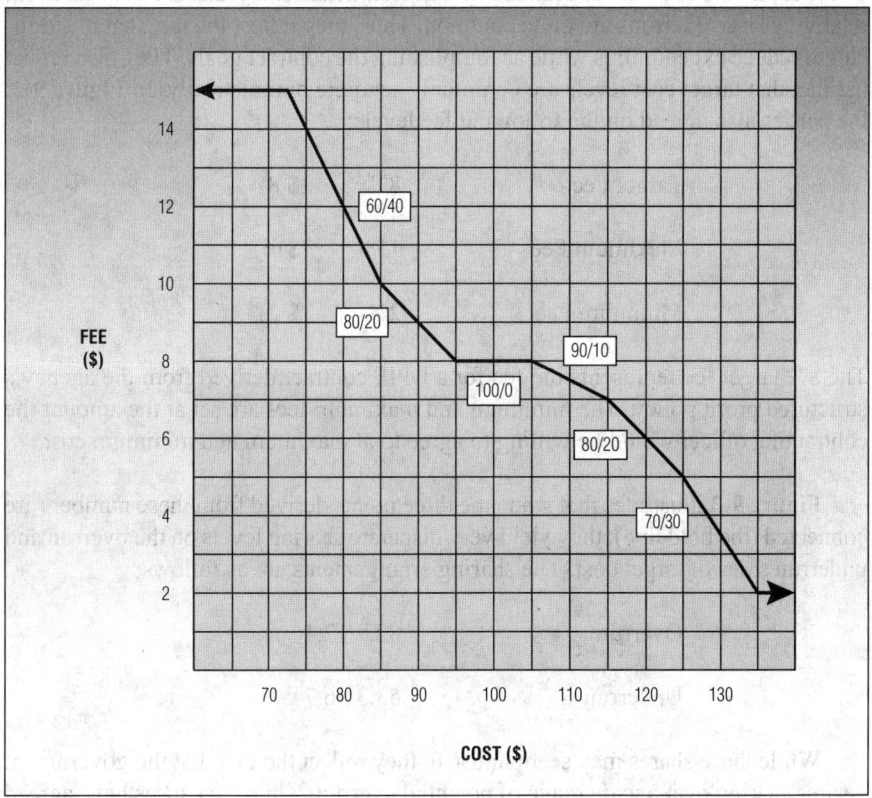

**Figure 9-2**

## b. Use of Range of Incentive Effectiveness

An alternate, and far more realistic, method of arriving at the elements of the CPIF contract, suggested in the DoD and NASA Incentive Contracting Guide, is to use the RIE as the major controlling element in establishing the formula. This technique is depicted in **Figure 9-3**, which reflects parties negotiating three levels of cost: the most likely cost outcome, the best foreseeable cost outcome, and the worst foreseeable cost outcome. The parties also negotiate three levels of profit, reflecting the reasonable profits that a contractor should earn at each of the three cost outcomes. They then structure the sharing arrangement as an outcome of these cost and fee amounts.

For example, in **Figure 9-3** the parties agreed on the following cost levels:

|  |  |
|---|---|
| Target Cost | $ 100 |
| Minimum Possible Cost | $  85 |
| Maximum Probable Cost | $ 135 |

These levels are reasonably realistic in that significant underruns are very rare, but relatively large overruns are quite common. Thus, they reflect the fact that it is difficult to reduce expenditures while accomplishing the contract goals. They also reflect the fact that target cost levels are commonly set quite optimistically. In **Figure 9-3**, the parties also agreed on the following fee levels:

|  |  |  |
|---|---|---|
| Target Fee | 8% | ($ 8) |
| Maximum Fee | 15% | ($15) |
| Minimum Fee | 2% | ($ 2) |

The 8% target fee represents the fee for a CPIF contract derived from the agency's structured profit policy. The minimum and maximum fees are set at the amount the contracting officer would be willing to agree to at maximum and minimum cost.

**Figure 9-3** illustrates that when the three points derived from these numbers are connected (the bold line), they yield very disparate sharing levels on the overrun and underrun sides of target cost. The sharing arrangements are as follows:

|  |  |
|---|---|
| Overrun | 82.9/17.1 |
| Underrun | 53.3/46.7 |

While these shares may seem unusual, they reflect the fact that the government desires sharing over a wide range of potential overrun, while the parties have agreed that sharing is not realistic over nearly such a wide range of underrun. One way to reduce this disparity is to reduce the maximum fee as depicted in the alternate formula in **Figure 9-3** (the thin line). Another way to modify this formula is to reduce the overrun sharing for the first part of the overrun and to increase it as the contractor approaches minimum fee. This is also depicted in the alternate formula in **Figure 9-3**. Either of these formulas is a far more realistic reflection of the realities of the normal R&D procurement than the formula in **Figure 9-1**, and the contracting officer should not be disturbed by the higher shares for underruns, since great effort is demanded of contractors to accomplish such cost savings, and the rewards for such efforts should be substantial.

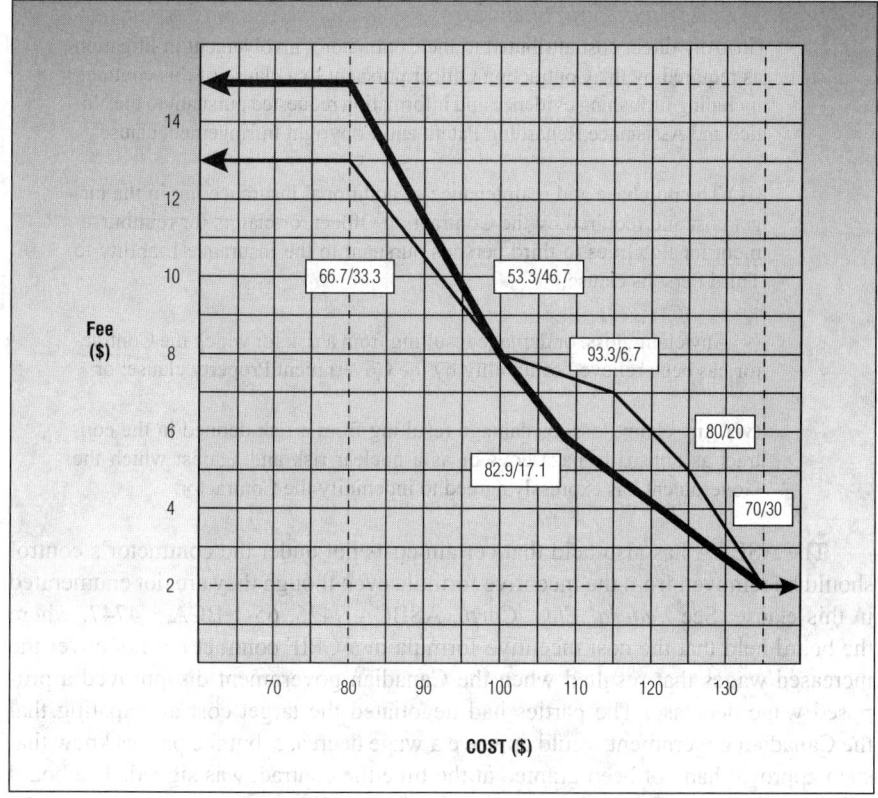

**Figure 9-3**

## c. *Costs Subject to Incentive Sharing*

Consistent with the theory of the CPIF contract that transferring a portion of the cost risk to the contractor will motivate more efficient performance, the contract language has been carefully drafted to remove certain costs not under the contractor's control from the sharing formula. See the following paragraph in the Incentive

Fee clause in FAR 52.216-10:

> (e)(4) For the purpose of fee adjustment, "total allowable cost" shall not include allowable costs arising out of —
>
> > (i) Any of the causes covered by the Excusable Delays clause to the extent that they are beyond the control and without the fault or negligence of the Contractor or any subcontractor;
> >
> > (ii) The taking effect, after negotiating the target cost, of a statute, court decision, written ruling, or regulation that results in the Contractor's being required to pay or bear the burden of any tax or duty or rate increase in a tax or duty;
> >
> > (iii) Any direct cost attributed to the Contractor's involvement in litigation as required by the Contracting Officer pursuant to a clause of this contract, including furnishing evidence and information requested pursuant to the Notice and Assistance Regarding Patent and Copyright Infringement clause;
> >
> > (iv) The purchase and maintenance of additional insurance not in the target cost and required by the Contracting Officer, or claims for reimbursement for liabilities to third persons pursuant to the Insurance-Liability to Third Persons clause;
> >
> > (v) Any claim, loss, or damage resulting from a risk for which the Contractor has been relieved of liability by the Government Property clause; or
> >
> > (vi) Any claim, loss, or damage resulting from a risk defined in the contract as unusually hazardous or as a nuclear risk and against which the Government has expressly agreed to indemnify the Contractor.

The ASBCA has also held that certain costs not under the contractor's control should be removed from the incentive formula even though they are not enumerated in this clause. See *Federal Elec. Corp.*, ASBCA 9476, 65-1 BCA ¶ 4747, where the board held that the cost incentive formula in a CPIF contract did not cover the increased wages that resulted when the Canadian government disapproved a proposed wage decrease. The parties had negotiated the target cost anticipating that the Canadian government would approve a wage decrease, but the parties knew that such approval had not been granted at the time the contract was signed. The board adjusted the target cost of the contract to reflect the increased wages based on the following questionable reasoning found at 22,573:

> In arriving at these terms, the parties must have been aware of the fact that one of the cost elements — the wage rates to be paid the DEW line employees — was to some extent beyond their control, because it depended on the approval of the Canadian Department of Labour. While the witnesses for the parties at the hearing asserted that they did not doubt that the reduced wage rates would be approved, other testimony in the record leads to the conclusion that they must have been

aware of the fact that such approval was not a certainty and might be denied. In any event, the record is clear that both parties negotiated on the basis of the wage rates proposed by the [contractor]. In the light of the goal inherent in incentive contracting it does not seem, therefore, likely or believable that two highly so-phisticated parties, such as [the contractor] and ROAMA as representative of the Government, intended to, and did, enter into a cost-plus-incentive-fee contract, which would, upon the occurrence of a particular event beyond the control of either party and prior to commencement of the contract term deprive appellant automatically of a large portion of its proposed target fee.

### d.  Relationship of Cost Incentives to Other Clauses

Cost incentives are subject to adjustment pursuant to the Changes clause of the contract if the work is altered during performance of the contract. See *Northrop Grumman Corp. v. United States*, 41 Fed. Cl. 645 (1998), where the government waived a number of the specification requirements in order to complete the work on schedule and within funding limitations. The court held that ¶ (d) of the Incentive Fee clause in FAR 52.216-10 allowed the contracting officer to unilaterally restructure the incentive formula to account for the reduced work performed by the contractor. The court rejected the contractor's argument that the proper course of action for the government was to provide additional funds to complete the work (as if it were cor-recting defects) and to apply the original incentive formula to the higher costs.

## B.  Fixed-Price Incentive Contracts

The FPI contract is very similar in concept to the CPIF contract except that it contains a ceiling price in lieu of the minimum and maximum fees. FAR 16.403(a) describes this type of contract as follows:

> A fixed-price incentive contract is a fixed-price contract that provides for adjust-ing profit and establishing the final contract price by application of a formula based on the relationship of total final negotiated cost to total target cost. The final price is subject to a price ceiling, negotiated at the outset. The two forms of fixed-price incentive contracts, firm target and successive targets, are further described in 16.403-1 and 16.403-2 below.

Because the ceiling price requires the contractor to complete performance no matter how high the cost, this type of contract should be used only when the contracting parties can predict the costs of performance with a reasonable degree of accuracy. The FAR provides that FPI contracts are normally used to place more cost risk on contractors in order to motivate them to control costs more vigorously than they would on cost-reimbursement contracts. Thus, these regulations discuss the use of the "profit motive" as a fundamental means of inducing lower costs of performance. However, there is another use of the FPI contract — that of protecting the govern-ment from excessive profits when a contractor will not agree to a firm-fixed-price contract at a level that the government believes represents a fair sharing of the cost

**1270    TYPES OF CONTRACTS**

risk. See *Televiso Elecs.*, 46 Comp. Gen. 631 (B-159922) (1967), where GAO upheld a contracting officer's decision to use a FPI contract when a contractor would not agree to a firm-fixed-price at a level deemed to be fair to the government. In both situations, the incentive contract gives the parties a means of sharing the cost risk so that neither will be seriously impacted by a degree of cost fluctuations from those costs projected at the outset.

The FPI contract is similar to the CPIF contract in that both provide for sharing of costs on a predetermined percentage basis. However, the FPI contract uses fixed-price clauses and contains no Limitation of Cost clause, with the result that the government is legally obligated to pay all cost up to the ceiling price without prior notification, and the contractor is obligated to complete the work and is subject to default termination which entails an assessment of excess costs of reprocurement and repayment of progress payments or other damages if it does not. The final price of the FPI contract is established by negotiation after incurrence and audit of substantially all costs of performance, while the final costs in a CPIF contract are paid through audit determination.

There are two types of FPI contracts: the fixed-price incentive with a firm target price (FPIF) and the fixed-price incentive with successive targets (FPIS).

## 1. *Elements of the Formula*

The elements of the basic formula covering the costs of performance in the FPIF contract are:

- Target Cost
- Target Profit
- Ceiling Price
- Sharing Arrangement

The formula is expressed in contract language in the Incentive Price Revision — Firm Target clause in FAR 52.216-16, as follows:

> (a) *General.* The supplies or services identified in the Schedule as Items [*Contracting Officer Insert Schedule line item numbers*] are subject to price revision in accordance with this clause; *provided,* that in no event shall the total final price of these items exceed the ceiling price of _____ dollars ($_____). Any supplies or services that are to be (1) ordered separately under, or otherwise added to, this contract and (2) subject to price revision in accordance with the terms of this clause shall be identified as such in a modification to this contract.

\* \* \*

*(d) Price revision.* Upon the Contracting Officer's receipt of the data required by paragraph (c) above, the Contracting Officer and the Contractor shall promptly establish the total final price of the items specified in (a) above by applying to final negotiated cost an adjustment for profit or loss, as follows:

(1) On the basis of the information required by paragraph (c) above, together with any other pertinent information, the parties shall negotiate the total final cost incurred or to be incurred for supplies delivered (or services performed) and accepted by the Government and which are subject to price revision under this clause.

(2) The total final price shall be established by applying to the total final negotiated cost an adjustment for profit or loss, as follows:

(i) If the total final negotiated cost is equal to the total target cost, the adjustment is the total target profit.

(ii) If the total final negotiated cost is greater than the total target cost, the adjustment is the total target profit, less [*Contracting Officer insert percent*] percent of the amount by which the total final negotiated cost exceeds the total target cost.

(iii) If the final negotiated cost is less than the total target cost, the adjustment is the total target profit plus [*Contracting Officer insert percent*] percent of the amount by which the total final negotiated cost is less than the total target cost.

\* \* \*

*(k) Equitable adjustment under other clauses.* If an equitable adjustment in the contract price is made under any other clause of this contract before the total final price is established, the adjustment shall be made in the total target cost and may be made in the maximum dollar limit on the total final price, the total target profit, or both. If the adjustment is made after the total final price is established, only the total final price shall be adjusted.

As in the CPIF contract, the contracting officer has significant discretion in establishing the elements of this FPIF formula. The range of these elements most commonly encountered is:

| | |
|---|---|
| Target Cost | $ 100 |
| Target Profit | 9% to 12% |
| Ceiling Price | $115 to $135 |
| Sharing Arrangement | 80/20 to 60/40 |

Two formulas are compared in **Figure 9-4**. Guidance on negotiating formulas is contained in the DoD and NASA Incentive Contracting Guide. See also Nash, *Incentive Contracting*, Government Contracts Monograph 7 (1963).

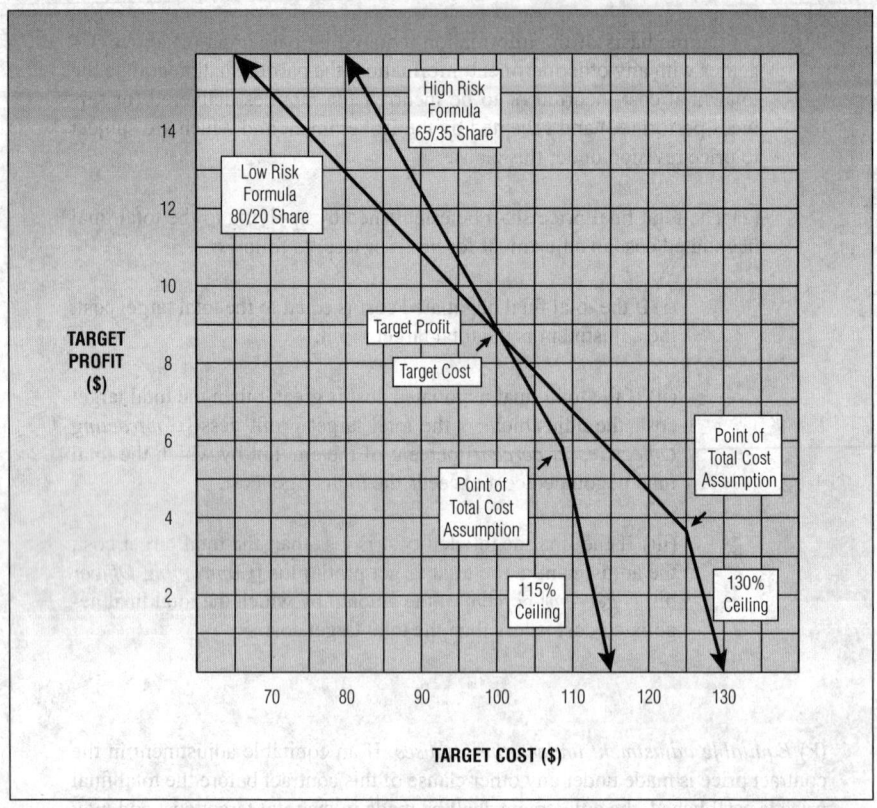

**Figure 9-4**

## 2. Negotiation and Analysis of Formulas

The procurement regulations imply that incentive formulas are established by negotiation, and this is generally the case in noncompetitive situations. The regulations contain no guidance on the techniques that should be used in competitive procurements. Hence, contracting officers are free to allow the competitors to propose their own incentive formulas or include a required formula (specifying the target profit rate, sharing percentages, and ceiling percentage above target cost) in the RFP if they conclude that proper evaluation is not otherwise possible. This latter technique is a means of overcoming the difficulty that is encountered in comparing FPI contract proposals with different sharing formulas and ceilings. This forces all competitors to propose the same basic incentive formula and allows a valid comparison of target costs proposed by the competitors. Notwithstanding the contrary views of GAO in *Televiso Elecs.*, 46 Comp. Gen. 631 (B-159922) (1967), without such similarity, the use of target costs as the comparative number can greatly distort the comparison and lead to the selection of a contractor that is taking less cost risk than, for example, another company that has proposed a higher target cost but a lower ceiling price. In such cases where the agency permits each offeror to propose the entire incentive formula, it is more rational to evaluate the ceiling prices. See *General Elec. Co.*, Comp. Gen. Dec. B-186372, 76-2 CPD ¶ 269, for a case recognizing the validity of the agency's giving more weight in the competitive evaluation to the proposed ceiling prices than to proposed targets. See also *DRS C3 Sys., LLC*, Comp. Gen. Dec. B-310825, 2008 CPD ¶ 103, holding that it is improper for an agency to adjust the target cost for evaluation purposes if it unrealistically low (as would be done in a CPIF situation) but that it is proper to evaluate the risk that the contractor cannot perform at that cost. In *Eurest Support Servs.*, Comp. Gen. Dec. B-285813.3, 2003 CPD ¶ 139, GAO granted a protest because the agency did not assess the risk of an unrealistically low target price when the RFP called for an assessment of price realism.

Whether the contractor or the government establishes the formula independently or they establish it through negotiation, the pertinent considerations are essentially the same as those discussed above in considering CPIF contracts. Thus, the elements of the formula should be determined by an analysis of the risk of the specific procurement on which the formula is used. Guidance from the Under Secretary of Defense in 2010, however, indicated that the "norm, or starting point" for FPIF contracts should be a 120% ceiling and a 50/50 sharing arrangement. See 76 Fed. Reg. 11410, March 2, 2011 including this guidance in a proposed amendment to the DFARS. The use of such a formula imposed a very high risk on the contractor.

The unique element in FPIF contracts is the ceiling price, and this, of course, is the critical element. The first aspect of this ceiling that must be recognized is that it is a ceiling *price* — combining both cost and profit. Thus, except for price adjustments under contract clauses, it imposes an ultimate limitation on the amount the contractor will be paid for the work. As such, it should be established at a level commensurate with the ability of the parties to accurately estimate the costs of performance. In the past, ceiling prices have been negotiated as high as 150% of target costs in contracts where the parties had very little confidence in the accuracy of their cost estimates. However, in that situation, use of the CPIF contract is more appropriate. Thus, in normal circumstances, ceiling prices would be expected to range from 115% to 135% of the target cost. **Figure 9-4** depicts two FPI formulas — a high-risk formula with a ceiling price of $115, and a low-risk formula with a ceiling of $130.

In some cases, contracts have used different ceiling prices for different elements of the work. See, for example, *Reflectone, Inc.*, ASBCA 34891, 89-3 BCA ¶ 21,962, *aff'd*, 891 F.2d 299 (Fed. Cir. 1989), where the board ruled that the proper interpretation of contract ceiling prices was that a ceiling on the base work and another ceiling on option work were separate ceilings that were separately enforceable. Compare *Aerojet-General Corp.*, ASBCA 13548, 70-1 BCA ¶ 8245, where the board found that the contract contained a single ceiling for both development and production work. See also *CTA, Inc.*, ASBCA 47062, 00-2 BCA ¶ 30,946, holding that the government cannot unilaterally create separate line item ceiling prices in a contract that originally contained a single ceiling and that such action is a change entitling the contractor to an equitable adjustment. When the contract contains work using two different appropriations, as in *Aerojet-General*, it is better practice to use separate ceilings for those different elements in order to avoid any possibility that work in one area might be charged to the other appropriation.

If the contractor must incur costs exceeding the target cost to complete performance of the contract, the initial overrun will be subject to the sharing arrangement — as is the case in the CPIF contract. This is clearly stated in the standard Incentive Price Revision clause which is not subject to any other interpretation. See *Southwest Marine, Inc.*, ASBCA 54550, 09-1 BCA ¶ 34,116, rejecting the contractor's argument that when it agreed to 0% target profit, it believed that the contracting officer was agreeing that there would be no profit (loss) sharing of overruns up to the ceiling.

At some point, the ceiling price will force the contractor to bear *all of the extra costs* being incurred. This point is called the *point of total cost assumption* — and it is generally at a point lower than the ceiling price. This occurs because the ceiling price is usually negotiated as a percentage of target cost, not a percentage of target price. Hence, in a FPI contract such as the high-risk contract in **Figure 9-4**, the ceiling price is 115% of target cost but only 105.5% of the target price of $109. This provides very little room for the incurrence of unanticipated costs before the contractor will bear the entire burden of overruns. In this formula, the point where the agreed sharing percentage ceases to operate and all additional costs of performance are treated as they would be in a firm-fixed-price contract is at approximately 109% of target cost. If the parties do not have the ability to predict costs within a high degree of accuracy, the use of such a formula would impose an inordinate risk on the contractor.

The point of total cost assumption is the most important feature in the FPIF contract because it identifies the point at which the contractor's risk changes from the incentive sharing that has been negotiated to a fixed-price risk — 100% responsibility for costs incurred. As depicted on **Figure 9-4**, this point occurs where the share line and the ceiling line intersect, because this is the point where the ceiling overrides the sharing arrangement. Hence, the amount of ceiling is the key determinant of the point of total cost assumption. For example, in the low-risk formula in **Figure 9-4**, the point of total cost assumption occurs much further from target cost — at approximately 126% of target cost.

If a contractor is performing the work at costs less than target cost, ¶ (g) of the Incentive Price Revision — Firm Target clause requires it to adjust its billings if they has exceeded the costs incurred for delivered supplies or services plus the target profit attributable to those supplies or services. See *Kearfott Guidance & Navigation Corp.*, ASBCA 49271, 04-2 BCA ¶ 32,757, rejecting the contractor's arguments that this provision should not be enforced and that earned performance incentives should be included in the calculation of the adjustment and ruling on the proper allowable costs that should be included in the adjustment.

## 3. Successive Targets

A less frequently used form of FPI contract is the FPIS contract. This type of contract is described in FAR 16.403-2 as follows:

(a) *Description.* (1) A fixed-price incentive (successive targets) contract specifies the following elements, all of which are negotiated at the outset:

(i) An initial target cost.

(ii) An initial target profit.

(iii) An initial profit adjustment formula to be used for establishing the firm target profit, including a ceiling and floor for the firm target profit. (This formula normally provides for a lesser degree of contractor cost responsibility than would a formula for establishing final profit and price.)

(iv) The production point at which the firm target cost and firm target profit will be negotiated (usually before delivery or shop completion of the first item).

(v) A ceiling price that is the maximum that may be paid to the contractor, except for any adjustment under other contract clauses providing for equitable adjustment or other revision of the contract price under stated circumstances.

(2) When the production point specified in the contract is reached, the parties negotiate the firm target cost, giving consideration to cost experience under the contract and other pertinent factors. The firm target profit is established by the formula. At this point, the parties have two alternatives, as follows:

(i) They may negotiate a firm fixed price, using the firm target cost plus the firm target profit as a guide.

(ii) If negotiation of a firm fixed price is inappropriate, they may negotiate a formula for establishing the final price using the firm target cost and firm target profit. The final cost is then negotiated at completion, and the final profit is established by formula, as under the fixed-price incentive (firm target) contract (see 16.403-1 above).

This type of contract is used when the parties do not have adequate costing or pricing information to establish firm prices at the outset but they believe that sufficiently accurate information will be available early in performance to permit the negotiation of a firm-fixed-price or a FPIF contract, FAR 16.403-2(b). The use of this type of contract is limited since it requires a significant administrative effort to conduct the two or three negotiations required. However, it does provide some flexibility in pricing long-term contracts whose performance period will extend over two or more years. The initial formula in this contract is established using the same logic as that used in negotiating the FPIF contract with a firm target but it is expected that the ceiling price would be quite high and the initial sharing arrangement would impose a modest share on the contractor, to reflect that the parties do not have the ability to accurately predict the cost of performance at the outset.

FAR 16.406(b) calls for the use of the Incentive Price Revision — Successive Targets clause in FAR 52.216-17 in all contracts of this type.

## C. Performance and Delivery Incentives

Objective incentives have also been applied to contract performance requirements (such as the weight of an item, thrust of an engine, or speed of a vehicle) and to contract delivery requirements (such as the date of delivery or the date of meeting a contract milestone for some intermediate task). These incentives have been most frequently used on incentive contracts, which meet the requirement that a contract containing such incentives must contain an incentive or a constraint on cost, FAR 16.402-1(a). Since any fixed-price type contract contains a constraint on cost, these incentives can also be used in firm-fixed-price contracts, fixed-price contracts with economic price adjustment or redeterminable fixed price contracts. There is no guidance on whether time-and-material or labor-hour contracts provide a sufficient constraint on cost to permit the use of performance or delivery incentives on those type contracts.

Objective performance and delivery incentives were originally used by the military services and NASA on development contracts. However, their use has spread to contracts for many types of services. See FAR 37.601(b)(3) calling for the use of "performance incentives" "where appropriate." NASA uses such incentives in all hardware contracts over $25 million which are "based on performance-oriented documents" except commercial items, NFS 1816.402-270. Such incentives are both positive and negative based on the following guidance in NFS 1816.402:

> When considering the use of a quality, performance, or schedule incentive, the following guidance applies.
>
> (1) A positive incentive is generally not appropriate unless —
>
> > (i) Performance above the target (or minimum, if there are no negative incentives) level is of significant value to the Government;

(ii) The value of the higher level of performance is worth the additional cost/fee;

(iii) The attainment of the higher level of performance is clearly within the control of the contractor; and

(iv) An upper limit is identified, beyond which no further incentive is earned.

(2) A negative incentive is generally not appropriate unless —

(i) A target level of performance can be established, which the contractor can reasonably be expected to reach with a diligent effort, but a lower level of performance is also minimally acceptable;

(ii) The value of the negative incentive is commensurate with the lower level of performance and any additional administrative costs; and

(iii) Factors likely to prevent attainment of the target level of performance are clearly within the control of the contractor.

(3) When a negative incentive is used, the contract must indicate a level below which performance is not acceptable.

Objective performance and delivery incentives of this type should be contrasted with other types of provisions used by government agencies to motivate technical or schedule performances. These other types of provisions are most frequently called "liquidated damages," requiring fixed compensation to the government for a contractor's failure to meet contract requirements — usually specified delivery or completion dates. See FAR Subpart 11.5 for guidance on the use of such clauses pertaining to the time of delivery or performance. While not termed "incentives," bonuses or rewards are also occasionally used in contracts that may or may not contain required compensation for inferior performance.

FAR 16.402-2 gives the following guidance on the use of technical performance incentives:

(a) Performance incentives may be considered in connection with specific product characteristics (e.g., a missile range, an aircraft speed, an engine thrust, or a vehicle maneuverability) or other specific elements of the contractor's performance. These incentives should be designed to tailor profit or fee to results achieved by the contractor, compared with specified targets.

(b) To the maximum extent practicable, positive and negative performance incentives shall be considered in connection with service contracts for performance of objectively measurable tasks when quality of performance is critical and incentives are likely to motivate the contractor.

(c) Technical performance incentives may be particularly appropriate in major systems contracts, both in development (when performance objectives are known and the fabrication of prototypes for test and evaluation is required) and in production (if improved performance is attainable and highly desirable to the Government).

FAR 16.402-3 provides guidance on the use of delivery incentives:

(a) Delivery incentives should be considered when improvement from a required delivery schedule is a significant Government objective. It is important to determine the Government's primary objectives in a given contract (e.g., earliest possible delivery or earliest quantity production).

Performance and delivery incentives have been used in many contracts. In some instances, they have been used to balance cost incentives, attempting to ensure that the contractor does not overemphasize low costs to the detriment of performance. The FAR emphasizes the use of incentives for a different purpose: to focus attention on specific important performance and delivery objectives of the government.

## 1. Enforceability of Clauses

Traditionally, liquidated damages clauses have been enforceable only if they do not assess a "penalty" for nonperformance. See *Priebe & Sons, Inc. v. United States*, 332 U.S. 407 (1947), applying this rule to a government contract and stating that such clauses would not be enforced where they were "included not to make a fair estimate of damages to be suffered but to serve only as an added spur to performance." This rule has been uniformly applied to provisions specifically termed "liquidated damages" clauses. The fundamental test that has been used to determine whether the clause provides for a "penalty" is whether the amount assessed was a reasonable forecast of damages at the time of entering into the contract, *DJ Mfg. Corp. v. United States*, 86 F.3d 1130 (Fed. Cir. 1996); *Southwest Eng'g Co. v. United States*, 341 F.2d 998 (8th Cir.), *cert. denied*, 382 U.S. 819 (1965); *International Elec. Corp. v. United States*, 227 Ct. Cl. 208, 646 F.2d 496 (1981).

These principles would appear to be directly applicable to any performance or delivery incentive clause written in terms of a penalty for failure to meet the contract requirement, since in very few cases would the government be able to show that such penalties were a reasonable approximation of actual damage. No court or board decision has considered this issue concerning performance incentives. However, in *Fairchild Camera & Instrument Corp.*, ASBCA 12291, 68-2 BCA ¶ 7327, the board ruled that a delivery incentive clause has a "distinct legal identity" from a liquidated damages clause. The board stated that no reasonable forecast of damages was necessary and that the clause was enforceable as a binding agreement between the parties.

The penalty rule has been applied to contract clauses that are not termed liquidated damages clauses but that assess compensation for delinquent performance. For example, in *JMNI, Inc. v. United States*, 4 Cl. Ct. 310 (1984), the court refused to enforce a clause calling for a "payment adjustment factor" that reduced the contract payment on a pro rata basis for units of work up to 15% delinquent and provided for no payment for a unit that was more than 15% delinquent. The court found that this clause was in the nature of a liquidated damages clause and that the nonpayment for over 15% delinquency was a penalty and not a reasonable forecast of damages. The same result was reached in *Charley O. Estes*, IBCA 1198-7-78, 84-1 BCA ¶ 17,073. See also *Maintenance Engrs., Inc.*, VABCA 5350, 99-2 BCA ¶ 30,513, rejecting as a penalty an interpretation of a clause that would allow multiple deductions for payment for services which could result in no payment even though the contractor performed some of the work, and *Wackenhut Corp.*, IBCA 2311, 91-1 BCA ¶ 23,318, finding a clause assessing a "penalty" of 1% of the price per day unenforceable. Compare *Work Force Reforestation, Inc.*, AGBCA 90-132-3, 90-3 BCA ¶ 22,233, holding that a clause that payment on a proportional basis for reduced coverage in a tree planting contract was not a penalty; and *Double E Reforestation, Inc.*, AGBCA 85-109-1, 86-2 BCA ¶ 18,764, holding that nonpayment for coverage of less than 80% in a tree planting contract was not a penalty because the government would likely reperform the work in that circumstance.

GAO has also sustained protests of contracts which impose penalties for partially completed performance. See *Linda Vista Indus., Inc.*, Comp. Gen. Dec. B-214447, 84-2 CPD ¶ 380, applying the liquidated damages rule to a Contractor's Failure to Perform clause that called for nonpayment for an entire cleaning item if the contractor failed to perform any part of the cleaning services required for that item. See also *D. J. Findley*, Comp. Gen. Dec. B-215230, 85-1 CPD ¶ 197, and *Environmental Aseptic Servs. Admin.*, 62 Comp. Gen. 219 (B-207771), 83-1 CPD ¶ 194, finding a Performance Requirements Summary clause to be a penalty clause because it permitted nonpayment for an entire task when only part of the task was poorly performed.

## 2. *Structuring Practices*

The procurement regulations contain no specific guidance on the structuring of performance and delivery incentives. FAR 16.402-2 contains the following general guidance on writing technical performance incentives:

(d) Technical performance incentives may involve a variety of specific characteristics that contribute to the overall performance of the end item. Accordingly, the incentives on individual technical characteristics must be balanced so that no one of them is exaggerated to the detriment of the overall performance of the end item.

(e) Performance tests and/or assessments of work are generally essential in order to determine the degree of attainment of performance targets. Therefore, the contract must be as specific as possible in establishing test criteria (such as testing conditions, instrumentation precision, and data interpretation) and performance standards (such as the quality levels of services to be provided).

(f) Because performance incentives present complex problems in contract administration, the contracting officer should negotiate them in full coordination with Government engineering and pricing specialists.

(g) It is essential that the Government and contractor agree explicitly on the effect that contract changes (e.g., pursuant to the Changes clause) will have on performance incentives.

(h) The contracting officer must exercise care, in establishing performance criteria, to recognize that the contractor should not be rewarded or penalized for attainments of Government-furnished components.

FAR 16.402-3 contains only the following provision on delivery incentives:

(b) Incentive arrangements on delivery should specify the application of the reward-penalty structure in the event of Government-caused delays or other delays beyond the control, and without the fault or negligence, of the contractor or subcontractor.

See also DoD PGI 216.402-2, stating that such incentives "should relate to specific performance areas or milestones, such as delivery or test schedules, quality controls, maintenance requirements, and reliability standards."

Since performance and delivery incentives are always used in conjunction with cost incentives, they are usually written in terms of dollar bonuses and penalties for deviations from contractually specified targets. Such a formula is depicted in **Figure 9-5** using the following factors:

| | |
|---|---|
| Target Weight | 100 lbs. |
| Maximum Bonus | $3 |
| Maximum Penalty | $3 |
| Sharing Arrangement | $1 for each 3 lb. Weight |

In this case, the sharing occurs over a range of 18 pounds of weight (from 91 pounds to 109 pounds), and the bonus or penalty earned is added to or deducted from the profit or fee that results from the application of the incentive formula on costs of performance.

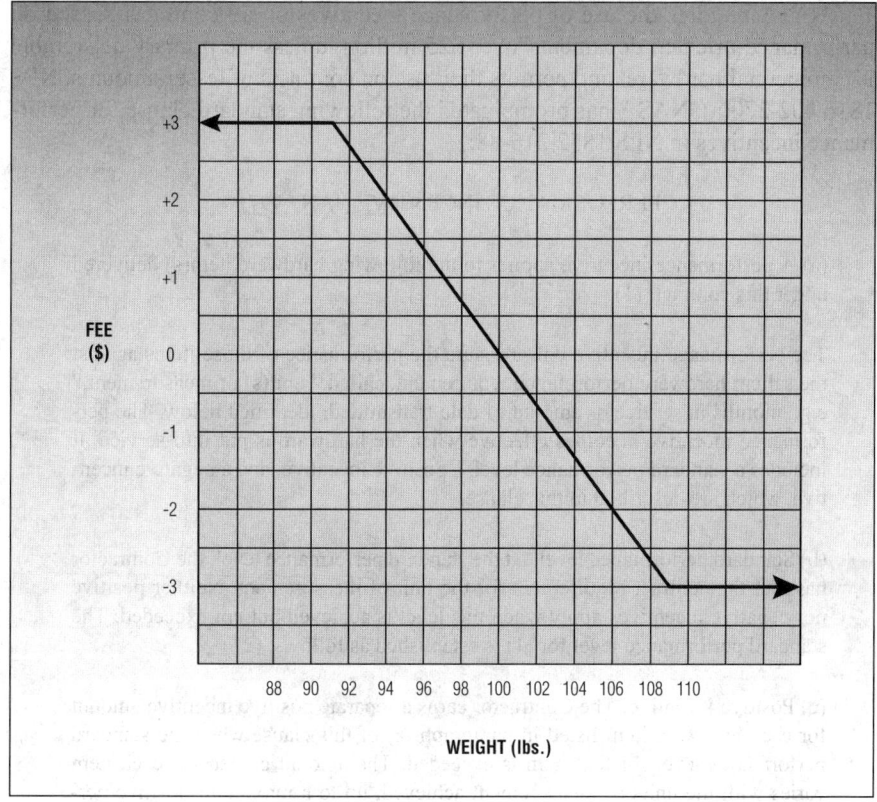

**Figure 9-5**

The DFARS no longer contains any detailed guidance on the structuring of performance and delivery incentives. Prior to 1991, however, DFARS 16.402-2(S-70) contained the following guidance on the levels of performance that should be used to set the fee levels:

> "Performance," as used in this paragraph, refers not only to the performance of the article being procured, but to the performance of the contractor as well. Performance which is the minimum which the Government will accept shall be mandatory under the terms of the Completion form contract and shall warrant only the minimum profit or fee related thereto. Performance which meets the stated targets will warrant the "target" profit or fee. The incentive feature (providing for increases or decreases, as appropriate) is applied to performance targets rather than performance requirements.

Following this guidance, performance and delivery incentives should never be used in ranges of performance and delivery *that the government is not willing to accept* as meeting the contract requirements.

NASA requires the use of performance incentives on all contracts "based on performance-oriented documents"over $25 million, unless the primary deliverable is commercial hardware, and permits their use on contracts of lesser amounts, NFS 1816.402-270(a). NASA has promulgated the following standard clause for performance incentives in NFS 1852.216-88:

PERFORMANCE INCENTIVE (JAN 1997)

(a) A performance incentive applies to the following hardware item(s) delivered under this contract: (1).

The performance incentive will measure the performance of those items against the salient hardware performance requirement, called " unit(s) of measurement," e.g., months in service or amount of data transmitted, identified below. The performance incentive becomes effective when the hardware is put into service. It includes a standard performance level, a positive incentive, and a negative incentive, which are described in this clause.

(b) Standard performance level. At the standard performance level, the Contractor has met the contract requirement for the unit of measurement. Neither positive nor negative incentives apply when this level is achieved but not exceeded. The standard performance level for (1) is established as follows: (2).

(c) Positive incentive. The Contractor earns a separate positive incentive amount for each hardware item listed in paragraph (a) of this clause when the standard performance level for that item is exceeded. The amount earned for each item varies with the units of measurement achieved, up to a maximum positive performance incentive amount of $ (3) per item. The units of measurement and the incentive amounts associated with achieving each unit are shown below: (4).

(d) Negative incentive. The Contractor will pay to the Government a negative incentive amount for each hardware item that fails to achieve the standard performance level. The amount to be paid for each item varies with the units of measurement achieved, up to the maximum negative incentive amount of $ (5) . The units of measurement and the incentive amounts associated with achieving each unit are shown below: (6).

(e) The final calculation of positive or negative performance incentive amounts shall be done when performance (as defined by the unit of measurement) ceases or when the maximum positive incentive is reached.

(1) When the Contracting Officer determines that the performance level achieved fell below the standard performance level, the Contractor will either pay the amount due the Government or credit the next payment voucher for the amount due, as directed by the Contracting Officer.

(2) When the performance level exceeds the standard level, the Contractor may request payment of the incentive amount associated with a given

level of performance, provided that such payments shall not be more frequent than monthly. When performance ceases or the maximum positive
incentive is reached, the Government shall calculate the final performance
incentive earned and unpaid and promptly remit it to the contractor.

(f) If performance cannot be demonstrated, through no fault of the Contractor,
within (*insert number of months or years*) after the date of hardware acceptance
by the Government, the Contractor will be paid (*insert percentage*) of the maximum performance incentive.

(g) The decisions made as to the amount(s) of positive or negative incentives are
subject to the Disputes clause.

(1) Insert applicable item number(s) and/or nomenclature.

(2) Insert a specific unit of measurement for each hardware item listed in
(1) and each salient characteristic, if more than one.

(3) Insert the maximum positive performance incentive amount (see
1816.402-270(e)(1) and (2)).

(4) Insert all units of measurement and associated dollar amounts up to the
maximum performance incentive.

(5) Insert the appropriate amount, in accordance with 1816.402-270(e).

(6) Insert all units of measurement and associated dollar amounts up to the
maximum negative performance incentive.

NFS 1816.402-270 provides the following guidance on structuring such performance incentives:

(b) When a performance incentive is used, it shall be structured to be both positive and negative based on hardware performance after delivery and acceptance.
In doing so, the contract shall establish a standard level of performance based on
the salient hardware performance requirement. This standard performance level
is normally the contract's minimum performance requirement. No incentive
amount is earned at this standard performance level. Discrete units of measurement based on the same performance parameter shall be identified for performance both above and below the standard. Specific incentive amounts shall be
associated with each performance level from maximum beneficial performance
(maximum positive incentive) to minimal beneficial performance or total failure
(maximum negative incentive). The relationship between any given incentive,
both positive and negative, and its associated unit of measurement should reflect
the value to the Government of that level of hardware performance. The contractor should not be rewarded for above-standard performance levels that are of no
benefit to the Government.

(c) The final calculation of the performance incentive shall be done when performance, as defined in the contract, ceases or when the maximum positive incentive is reached. When the performance ceases below the standard established in the contract, the Government shall calculate the amount due and the contractor shall pay the Government that amount. Once hardware performance exceeds the standard, the contractor may request payment of the incentive amount associated with a given level of performance, provided that such payments shall not be more frequent than monthly. When hardware performance ceases above the standard level of performance, or when the maximum positive incentive is reached, the Government shall calculate the final performance incentive earned and unpaid and promptly remit it to the contractor. The exclusion at FAR 16.405 (e)(3) does not apply to decisions made as to the amount(s) of positive or negative incentive.

(d) When the deliverable hardware lends itself to multiple, meaningful measures of performance, multiple performance incentives may be established. When the contract requires the sequential delivery of several hardware items (e.g., multiple spacecraft), separate performance incentive structures may be established to parallel the sequential delivery and use of the deliverables.

(e) In determining the value of the maximum performance incentives available, the contracting officer shall follow the following rules:

(1) For a CPFF contract, the sum of the maximum positive performance incentive and fixed fee shall not exceed the limitations in FAR 15.404-4(c)(4)(i).

(2) For an award fee contract.

(i) The individual values of the maximum positive performance incentive and the total potential award fee (including any base fee) shall each be at least one-third of the total potential contract fee. The remaining one-third of the total potential contract fee may be divided between award fee and the maximum performance incentive at the discretion of the contracting officer.

(ii) The maximum negative performance incentive for research and development hardware (e.g., the first and second units) shall be equal in amount to the total earned award fee (including any base fee). The maximum negative performance incentives for production hardware (e.g., the third and all subsequent units of any hardware items) shall be equal in amount to the total potential award fee (including any base fee). Where one contract contains both cases described above, any base fee shall be allocated reasonably among the items.

(3) For cost reimbursement contracts other than award fee contracts, the maximum negative performance incentives shall not exceed the total earned fee under the contract.

It is also possible to create performance and delivery incentives in terms of a single bonus or penalty to be paid or deducted upon the meeting or missing of a target. This type of incentive is used most frequently in the case of performance milestones where the contract contains a series of bonuses to be paid upon the meeting of each milestone. Such an incentive combines both performance and delivery incentives because the bonus is paid only if the contractor performs the required work in accordance with the specifications at the time called for. There has been some criticism of this type of incentive because it gives the contractor additional profit when performance is no better than that called for by the contract. If contract requirements are demanding, however, and if the performance and delivery incentive motivates the contractor to perform well, there should be no objection to this type of incentive.

When performance or delivery incentives are used, the contract should include specific provisions defining conditions that must be met for the contractor to earn the bonus or suffer the loss called for by an incentive clause. One issue that should be addressed is the effect on performance incentives of government failure to fund an overrun on a CPIF contract. In such a case, for example, the contractor may not be able to conduct a test program to demonstrate that a performance incentive has been earned. See, for example, *North Am. Rockwell Corp.*, ASBCA 14329, 72-1 BCA ¶ 9207, where the board held that because the contractor submitted convincing evidence that the product met the weight requirement earning the maximum bonus on a weight incentive, a pro rata share of that bonus, commensurate with the percentage of completion of the contract, should be paid. The board reasoned at 42,724:

> We find no merit in the Government's argument that the performance incentive provision does not come into operation unless and until the Government accepts the tank as meeting all contract requirements. The performance incentive provision was written in contemplation of full contract performance and does not cover the situation where the contractor exercises its right to stop work before full performance because of the Government's refusal to allot the additional funds necessary for full performance. When the contractor exercises its right to stop work after failure of the Government to add funds necessary for the completion of the contract, this has the practical effect of terminating the contract for the convenience of the Government as to any work remaining to be done under the contract. Under the standard termination clause included in the contract, when the contract is terminated for the convenience of the Government before completion, the contractor is entitled to be paid " the percentage of the fee equivalent to the percentage of the completion of the work contemplated by the contract." The performance incentive provision should be interpreted in conjunction with the termination clause when the contract work is stopped before completion due to the failure of the Government to add sufficient funds for its completion.

There may also be difficulties in specifying the precise tests to be used to determine when each performance incentive has been met. This was an issue in *Western Elec. Co.*, ASBCA 16110, 73-1 BCA ¶ 10,013, where the bonus was to be paid if a missile passed through a point under guidance control. The board ruled that the contractor had earned the bonus even though the missile engine failed prior to reaching the specified point, since the missile did in fact pass through the point and the guidance system functioned sufficiently well before engine failure.

## 3. Relationship of Incentive to Other Provisions

In drafting incentive contracts with performance and delivery incentives, great care must be exercised to ensure that the relationship of these incentives to other contract provisions is clearly defined. Thus, the relationship of performance incentives to the inspection and warranty clauses in the contract must be stated. Contractors failing to meet performance goals may also fail to meet specification requirements, but the penalties for these two failures are quite different. The performance incentive formula calls for a profit or fee reduction when performance goals are not met, while other provisions of the contract allow the contracting officer to reject the work, require rework until specifications are met, or even terminate the contract for default. Many contracts containing performance incentives do not spell out the rights of the parties, but in most contracting situations it is clear that the parties do not intend to provide a double remedy for the government. This issue should be addressed and resolved by specific contract language. In general, such language would state that the *sole remedy* to be assessed when the performance falls in the RIE would be the penalty under the performance incentive clause. This is logical when, as in the case of the DoD, the government does not include unacceptable ranges of performance within the incentive provision. If, as in the case of NASA, the performance incentive includes failure of an item of hardware, it is logical to conclude that the negative incentive has been calculated to include the damages that the government will suffer. See *Maintenance Engrs., Inc.*, VABCA 5350, 99-2 BCA ¶ 30,513, where the board discussed the parallel remedies of penalty provisions for nonperformance and the government's rights under the Inspection of Services clause in FAR 52.246-4 to reperform work and charge the cost to the contractor. The board decision is not clear as to whether these are alternate remedies or duplicative remedies.

In the case of delivery incentives, the contract should include explicit language stating the relationship of the incentive to excusable delays. FAR 16.402-3(b) requires that this issue be addressed in the contract but gives no guidance as to the preferred agreement. In many cases, contracting officers have included contract language providing that the date for calculation of the delivery incentive will be extended for excusable delays. In CPIF contracts, this is generally accomplished by keying the incentive bonus or penalty to the Excusable Delays clause in FAR 52.249-14, which is included in all cost-reimbursement contracts. This clause provides for schedule adjustments for excusable delays; and the contract language would state that such adjustments would occur prior to the computation of the incentive bonus or penalty. In FPI contracts, the incentive bonus or penalty must be keyed to ¶ (c) of the Default (Fixed-Price Supply and Service) clause in FAR 52.249-8, and the special contract clause should explicitly provide that the contractor will be granted a time extension for excusable delays (the Default clause contains no such language). Even if there is no such contract provision, it may be held that such is the proper interpretation of the total contract, *North Am. Aviation, Inc.*, ASBCA 11603, 68-1 BCA ¶ 6998 (CPIF contract); *General Precision, Inc.*, ASBCA 11071, 66-2 BCA ¶ 5904 (FPI contract). See, however, *Sosedil-Pizzarotti*, ASBCA 31135, 89-2 BCA ¶ 21,807, where the board enforced clear contract language stating that "no time extensions shall be allowed for the purpose of payment under the bonus clause provisions."

## 4. Interrelationship With Cost Incentives

When performance and delivery incentives are used in incentive contracts, any increased costs incurred to achieve better performance or avoid a performance and delivery penalty will be chargeable to the contract and subject to sharing. Thus, if the contractor incurs more labor-hours or uses more expensive labor or material in attempting to enhance performance, such costs will be shared by the government to the extent that the costs are reasonable and within the RIE. In addition, the contractor has considerable latitude in selecting techniques to motivate employees. See *Celesco Indus., Inc.*, ASBCA 20569, 77-1 BCA ¶ 12,445, *sustained on other grounds*, 77-2 BCA ¶ 12,585, where the contractor established an internal incentive program to motivate its employees that used the entire performance incentive bonus for successful missile flights. After earning $70,500, which was distributed to the employees, the contractor claimed the amount as an allowable cost. The government argued that the cost was unallowable since it was a distribution of profit, but the board ruled that the employee bonuses were reasonable compensation under the Cost Principles. Compare *Petroleum Operations & Support Servs., Inc.*, EBCA 291-6-83, 85-2 BCA ¶ 18,037, denying the allowability of bonuses paid on a CPAF contract because they did not comply with the Cost Principles.

One important aspect of performance and delivery incentives is that they create a value structure, within the incentive formula, that states the value of each performance and delivery factor in the formula. For example, if the weight incentive in **Figure 9-5** is used on a contract containing the cost incentive in **Figure 9-1**, the two sharing arrangements tell the contractor the value of weight savings. The value is determined by equating each incentive to the fee bonus or penalty to be derived from the formula. Thus, the contractor will incur a fee bonus or penalty of $1 for each three pounds of weight variance and each $5 of cost variance. The result is that the incentive formula tells the contractor that the government places a value of $5 on a three-pound weight savings, as long as each expenditure or savings occurs within the RIE. From this information the contractor could be expected to make decisions on weight reduction efforts based on the cost of the reduction. If it was probable that a weight reduction of three pounds could be achieved at a cost of less than $5, the contractor would be expected to spend the funds (in an attempt to achieve the weight reduction) and increase its total fee on the contract. Thus, the formula contains an unexpressed tradeoff for each performance and delivery incentive, where fee can be maximized by spending or saving money. In some cases, this tradeoff situation is not fully thought through at the time the formula is written, with the result that the contractor may take actions during contract performance that are not desired by the government.

FAR 16.402-4 recognizes this issue but gives the following minimal guidance:

A properly structured multiple-incentive arrangement should —

(a) Motivate the contractor to strive for outstanding results in all incentive areas; and

(b) Compel tradeoff decisions among the incentive areas, consistent with the Government's overall objectives for the acquisition. Because of the interdependency of the Government's cost, the technical performance, and the delivery goals, a contract that emphasizes only one of the goals may jeopardize control over the others. Because outstanding results may not be attainable for each of the incentive areas, all multiple-incentive contracts must include a cost incentive (or constraint) that operates to preclude rewarding a contractor for superior technical performance or delivery results when the cost of those results outweighs their value to the Government.

This requirement is generally implemented in one of two ways. First, in the ideal situation, performance and delivery incentives are structured on the basis of the government's tradeoff analysis. For example, in the weight incentive discussed above, the contracting officer determines from consultation with agency technical personnel that the value of weight savings is at least $5 for three pounds. The incentive arrangement is then structured to reflect this government tradeoff judgment. Second, special contract clauses are used to prevent incentive awards when they are not desired by the government. For example, if the contracting officer has determined that weight savings are of value only if the contractor does not overrun the target cost of the contract, a special clause will provide that no bonuses will be paid for the performance incentive on weight if there is a cost overrun. These clauses should be used judiciously, however, since they cancel out the performance and delivery incentives in the specified range of cost.

Better regulatory guidance would permit use of performance and delivery incentives only when the government can identify the specific value of enhanced performance or avoidance of performance reductions and has determined that such results are worth additional costs. If this policy were followed, the government would be assured that the contractor was not being motivated to overrun the contract in situations where the government did not desire enhanced performance.

## D.  Cost-Plus-Award-Fee Contracts

The CPAF contract is used when the agency wants to include some profit motivation in the contract but does not have sufficient information to establish firm, objectively-stated cost, performance, or delivery targets at the beginning of contract performance. Thus, the CPAF contract provides that the contractor's fee will be determined largely by an award given periodically by a "fee determining official" (FDO) in the procuring agency. While the basic elements to be evaluated in arriving at this award and the evaluation mechanism itself are usually disclosed to the contractor prior to performance, this type of contract is known as a "subjective" incentive since the award official has a significant amount of discretion in establishing the precise amount of award. This subjectivity has led some contractors to question the use of this type of incentive, but experience gathered over the past four decades indicates that CPAF contracts are quite effective in situations where it is not possible to write a contract specification or work statement that contains a precise description of the work the contractor is expected to perform. FAR 16.405-2 describes this type of contract as follows:

> A cost-plus-award-fee contract is a cost-reimbursement contract that provides for a fee consisting of (1) a base amount fixed at inception of the contract, if applicable and at the discretion of the contracting officer, and (2) an award amount that the contractor may earn in whole or in part during performance and that is sufficient to provide motivation for excellence in the areas of cost, schedule, and technical performance.

CPAF contracts have been used primarily in service contracts and research and development contracts. Beginning in the 1960s, NASA used this type of contract in order to provide incentives for its major support service contractors, and it was NASA that provided the early guidance on CPAF contracts in the NASA Cost-Plus-Award-Fee Contracting Guide, NHB 5104.4, August 1967. Subsequently, the military services, NASA, and the Department of Energy (DOE) broadened the use of the CPAF contract to include R&D contracting. See ¶ 1.3 of the NASA Award-Fee Contracting Guide, December 1997 and DEAR 916.404-2. Note that DFARS 216.405-2(3) places limitations on use of CPAF contracts for certain types of development. Other agencies have used CPAF contracts extensively, as the advantages of CPAF contracts have become known throughout the government.

Beginning in 2005 there was considerable criticism of the use and implementation of CPAF contracts. A series of GAO reports indicated that unduly high award fees were being paid on CPAF contracts. See *Defense Acquisitions: DoD Has Paid Billions in Award and Incentive Fees Regardless of Acquisition Outcomes*, GAO-06-66, Dec. 19, 2005; *Defense Acquisitions: DoD Wastes Billions of Dollars Through Poorly Structured Incentives*, GAO-06-409T, Apr. 6, 2006; and *NASA Procurement: Use of Award Fees for Achieving Program Outcomes Should Be Improved*, GAO-07-58, Jan. 2007. As a result, there has been considerable congressional activity giving guidance on when and how these contracts should be used — including language adopting GAO recommendation that award fees be based on program *outcomes* rather than subjective appraisals of the procedures followed by the contractor. The first statute adopting this GAO recommendation was § 814 of the National Defense Authorization

Act for FY 2007, Pub. L. No. 109-364, requiring the issuance of regulations to "ensure that all new contracts using award fees link such fees to acquisition outcomes (which shall be defined in terms of program cost, schedule, and performance)" and providing relatively detailed criteria governing the award fees to be paid. This was followed up by provisions in the Consolidated Security, Disaster Assistance, and Continuing Appropriations Act, 2009, Pub. L. No. 110-329, which reiterates these requirements for the Department of Defense in § 8105 of the Department of Defense Appropriations Act, 2009 (Division C of the Consolidated Act), and for the Department of Homeland Security in § 533 of the Department of Homeland Security Appropriations Act, 2009 (Division D of the Consolidated Act). Finally, the National Defense Authorization Act for FY 2009, Pub. L. No. 110-417, adopted similar requirements for all civilian agencies. See 41 U.S.C. § 4711.

These statutes were implemented by Federal Acquisition Circular 2005-37, 74 Fed. Reg. 52856, Nov. 14, 2009 — revising FAR 15.401.

## 1.  *Advantages and Disadvantages of CPAF Contracts*

The major advantage of the CPAF contract is improved communication between the parties. In the course of making periodic awards, the government gives the contractor a detailed evaluation of performance, pointing out perceived deficiencies and weaknesses. As a result, the contractor is able to improve performance as work proceeds or persuade the government that it's analysis is incorrect. In either case, the contracting parties are forced to analyze performance on a regular basis and communicate with each other regarding any problems. From the contractor's point of view, the CPAF contract has also been advantageous in that it has frequently yielded higher fees than the CPFF contract.

The major disadvantage of the CPAF contract is that substantial administrative costs are incurred through the continual evaluations and the processing of award decisions. Increasing the length of the evaluation periods can ameliorate this situation, but the CPAF contract inherently calls for a significant amount of paperwork. It has been suggested that the internal evaluation effort is not significantly greater than the work a well-staffed program management office does in its regular evaluation of a development contractor's performance, but even when the evaluation is done by a program management office, the paperwork is increased substantially. Of course, this added paperwork leads to the enhanced communication that is the strength of the CPAF contract. An agency should recognize, however, the demands that this type of contract places on its staff and limit the use of CPAF contracts to situations where the size and importance of the work justify the expenditure of such resources.

Another disadvantage noted by some commentators is the potential for the CPAF contractor to follow government directions without challenge. Evaluators are normally the government personnel monitoring the contractor's performance, and the contractor's reaction may be to follow an evaluator's direction in order to earn a higher award fee. This disadvantage can be overcome by carefully selecting government evaluators, ensuring that they have sufficient technical and management expertise and judgment to make sound decisions. Full participation of the contractor in the award process is also helpful in ensuring that sound decisions are made in evaluating the contractor's performance.

A disadvantage identified in recent studies of CPAF contracts was the tendency of some government evaluators to give high ratings to contractors that had not met the goals of the program being implemented by the contract. In some instances, this apparently occurred on long-standing CPAF contracts where the evaluators had become accustomed to working with the contractor over a number of years. This disadvantage may result from the burdensome nature of the administrative effort demanded by this type of contract. One result of this disadvantage was NASA's adoption of more stringent requirements for the use of this type of contract, NFS 1816.404-270. Under this regulation, award fee provisions may be used only when a contractor's effort cannot "be objectively measured in terms of technical and quality achievement, schedule progress or cost performance." In addition, such provisions are to be used only in contracts over $2 million per year with the approval by the procurement officer.

## 2. Guidance on Use of CPAF Contracts

The regulatory guidance on the use of CPAF contracts has always emphasized that they should be used only when objectively-stated criteria cannot be established. In spite of the statutory requirement that such contracts link award fees to "acquisition outcomes (which shall be defined in terms of program cost, schedule, and performance)," this regulatory guidance has not changed. See FAR 16.401(e)(1) stating that the CPAF contract is suitable for use in the following circumstances:

> (i) The work to be performed is such that it is neither feasible nor effective to devise predetermined objective incentive targets applicable to cost, technical performance, or schedule;

> (ii) The likelihood of meeting acquisition objectives will be enhanced by using a contract that effectively motivates the contractor toward exceptional performance and provides the Government with the flexibility to evaluate both actual performance and the conditions under which it was achieved; and

> (iii) Any additional administrative effort and cost required to monitor and evaluate performance are justified by the expected benefits as documented by a risk and cost benefit analysis to be included in . . . Determinations and Findings [required by FAR 15.401(d)].

See also DoD PGI 216.405-2(3) stating that the CPAF contract is suitable for level-of-effort contracts for services "where mission feasibility is established but measurement of achievement must be by subjective evaluation rather than objective measurement."

The clearest indication that "acquisition outcomes" need not be defined by using objective criteria is in DFARS 216.401-71 making it clear that when objective criteria can be established, a CPAF contract should not be used, stating:

> (1) Contracting officers shall use objective criteria to the maximum extent possible to measure contract performance. Objective criteria are associated with cost-plus-incentive-fee and fixed-price-incentive contracts.

> (2) When objective criteria exist but the contracting officer determines that it is in the best interest of the Government also to incentivize subjective elements of performance, the most appropriate contract type is a multiple-incentive contract containing both objective incentives and subjective award-fee criteria (*e.g.*, a cost-plus-incentive-fee/award fee or fixed-price-incentive/award fee).

The statutes contain additional guidance that appears to be resulting in greatly reduced use of CPAF contracts. They require additional regulations on when award fees can be earned including a provision to "ensure that no award fee may be paid for contractor performance that is judged to be below satisfactory performance or performance that does not meet the basic requirements of the contract." See FAR 16.401(e)(2) stating:

> Award fee shall not be earned if the contractor's overall cost, schedule, and technical performance is below satisfactory. The basis for all award-fee determinations shall be documented in the contract file to include, at a minimum, a determination that overall cost, schedule and technical performance is or is not at a satisfactory level. This determination and the methodology for determining the award fee are unilateral decisions made solely at the discretion of the Government.

It is not clear how an agency official will determine whether "overall" performance is unsatisfactory but this requirement creates a considerable risk for a contractor that it will earn no award fee if it fails to meet one of the performance objectives of the contract.

## 3.  *Award Fee Plan*

FAR 16.401(e)(3) requires that CPAF contracts must be supported by an award fee plan as follows:

> All contracts providing for award fees shall be supported by an award-fee plan that establishes the procedures for evaluating award fee and an Award-Fee Board for conducting the award-fee evaluation. Award-fee plans shall —

> (i) Be approved by the FDO unless otherwise authorized by agency procedures;

(ii) Identify the award-fee evaluation criteria and how they are linked to acquisition objectives which shall be defined in terms of contract cost, schedule, and technical performance. Criteria should motivate the contractor to enhance performance in the areas rated, but not at the expense of at least minimum acceptable performance in all other areas;

(iii) Describe how the contractor's performance will be measured against the award-fee evaluation criteria;

(iv) Utilize the adjectival rating and associated description as well as the award-fee pool earned percentages shown below in Table 16-1. Contracting officers may supplement the adjectival rating description. The method used to determine the adjectival rating must be documented in the award-fee plan;

(v) Prohibit earning any award fee when a contractor's overall cost, schedule, and technical performance is below satisfactory;

(vi) Provide for evaluation period(s) to be conducted at stated intervals during the contract period of performance so that the contractor will periodically be informed of the quality of its performance and the areas in which improvement is expected (e.g. six months, nine months, twelve months, or at specific milestones); and

(vii) Define the total award-fee pool amount and how this amount is allocated across each evaluation period.

These mandatory elements of the plan cover most of the aspects of the CPAF contract that are discussed below (including a discussion of the application of the rating system in Table 16-1). They also require the plan to cover the procedures that the agency will use to determine the amount of the award fee. Thus, they require agencies to obtain high level approval of CPAF contracts before they are used.

Agencies have followed varying practices in determining whether the plan should be made part of the contract or furnished to the contractor separately. While there is no requirement that the entire award fee plan be made available to offerors or contractors, it is clear that they must be informed of the criteria and rating system. Whether or not the plan is part of the contract, it is subject to prospective revision by the government. See the clause in DFARS 252.216-7005:

AWARD FEE (FEB 2011)

The Contractor may earn award fee from a minimum of zero dollars to the maximum amount stated in the award-fee plan in this contract. In no event will award fee be paid to the Contractor for any evaluation period in which the Government rates the Contractor's overall cost, schedule, and technical performance below satisfactory. The Contracting Officer may unilaterally revise the award-fee plan prior to the beginning of any rating period in order to redirect contractor emphasis.

## 4. Structuring the Award Fee

The elements of a CPAF contract are as follows:

- Estimated Cost

- Base Fee

- Award Fee Pool

- Award Periods

The amount of fee in the award fee pool is allocated to the award periods, and each award is made in accordance with the criteria provided in the contract. The estimated cost in the CPAF contract is established in the competitive process or negotiated based on a detailed analysis of the proposed costs in the same manner as the target cost in the CPIF contract, as discussed in Chapter 10. The other elements of the CPAF contract are established through negotiation, if the contract is awarded as a sole source contract, or on the basis of competitive proposals, if the contract is awarded under competitive procedures. In the latter case, it is quite common for the government to permit offerors to propose CPAF structures and consider the adequacy of the proposed structures in evaluating competing sources. It has been held proper for an agency to downgrade a proposal for offering a structure that does not meet the agency's needs as stated in the RFP, *Boeing Sikorsky Aircraft Support*, Comp. Gen. Dec. B-277263.2, 97-2 CPD ¶ 91 (proposed base fee too high and maximum fee too low); *Management & Tech. Servs. Co.*, Comp. Gen. Dec. B-209513, 82-2 CPD ¶ 571 (proposed base fee and maximum fee too high); *Management Servs., Inc.*, Comp. Gen. Dec. B-206364, 82-2 CPD ¶ 164 (proposed awards too high for levels of performance, and proposed employee bonuses for very high levels of performance found to be a disincentive for such performance). It has also been held proper for an agency to request assurances of "cost containment," which induced the competitors to propose cost ceilings, *Hughes Space & Commc'ns Co.*, Comp. Gen. Dec. B-266225.6, 96-1 CPD ¶ 199.

### a. Base Fee

The base fee is the minimum dollar amount of fee that a contractor can earn on a CPAF contract. By using the concept of a base fee rather than a target fee, the government has made the decision that all the incentive will be in the form of awards (no penalties). Thus, the base fee is comparable to the minimum fee in the CPIF contract. There is no guidance in the FAR on the level of base fee or its relationship to the award fees. However, DFARS 216.405-2(3)(iii) states that the base fee shall not exceed 3% of estimated cost. NASA used base fees for many years; but in 1993 NFS 1816.405-271 was issued prohibiting base fees where the award fee evaluation was "final," such as on service contracts (in effect, requiring a zero base fee). This regulation further states that on other CPAF contracts, "such as those for hardware or software development," the base fee cannot exceed 3% and must be refunded if the final award fee evaluation is "poor/unsatisfactory." EPAAR 1516.404-273(b) provides that base fees should not exceed 3% of the estimated costs. DEAR 915.404-4-72(a)(1) permits base fees from 0% to 50% of the fee amount for a CPFF contract, arrived at by using the agency's profit policy. The regulations of other agencies contain no maximum amount for the base fee, and in the past, base fees have ranged from 0% to 5%. Many contracts have used base fees of 2% of estimated cost but a number of recent contracts have contained base fees of 0%.

Base fees in the range of 2% to 3% do little more than guarantee the contractor against loss, since such base fees are roughly equivalent to normal cost disallowances. In practice, significant awards have usually been earned on CPAF contracts, with the result that there has been only modest risk that the contractor will be required to perform the work for the base fee. However, as discussed above, there has been significant congressional pressure to ensure that no award fees would be earned for performance that is "below satisfactory." This places considerable pressure on prospective contractors to negotiated higher base fees.

## b. Award Fee Pool

Prior to 1997, the controlling requirement with regard to the award fee pool in a CPAF contract was that this fee plus the base fee could not exceed the statutory limitation on CPFF contracts. This requirement was deleted from the FAR by Federal Acquisition Circular 97-02, September 30, 1997, with the result that the contracting officer is now permitted to negotiate any amount of award fee necessary to accomplish the purpose of the contract. FAR 16.401(e)(2) contains the following minimal guidance:

> *Award-fee amount.* The amount of award fee earned shall be commensurate with the contractor's overall cost, schedule, and technical performance as measured against contract requirements in accordance with the criteria stated in the award-fee plan.

The most complete guidance is contained in DEAR 915.404-4-72(a) as follows:

> (2) The base fee plus the amount included in the award fee pool should normally not exceed the fixed fee (as subjectively determined or as developed from the fee schedule) by more than 50%. However, in the event the base fee is to be less than 50% of the fixed fee, the maximum potential award fee may be increased proportionately with the decreases in base fee amounts.

(3) The following maximum potential award fees shall apply in award fee contracts: (percent is stated as percent of fee schedule amounts).

| Base fee percent | Award fee percent | Maximum total percent |
|:---:|:---:|:---:|
| 50 | 100 | 150 |
| 40 | 120 | 160 |
| 30 | 140 | 170 |
| 20 | 160 | 180 |
| 10 | 180 | 190 |
| 0 | 200 | 200 |

In *CACI, Inc.-Fed.*, 64 Comp. Gen. 439 (B-216516.2), 85-1 CPD ¶ 363, GAO ruled that the maximum fee should be computed as a percentage of contract estimated cost and not realistic cost as determined by the agency. In *CACI*, the realistic cost was lower, but the agency did not negotiate down the estimated cost to match the realistic cost.

Whether the procurement is sole source or competitive, the base fee and the award fee pool can be established by the procuring agency's either specifying precise percentages in the RFP or permitting the offeror to propose the levels. For example, in *Holmes & Narver, Inc.*, Comp. Gen. Dec. B-196832, 80-1 CPD ¶ 134, GAO affirmed the propriety of an RFP provision permitting offerors to propose any base fee plus award fee pool up to 10%. The total potential fee, of course, is an important competitive factor since it places a ceiling on the government's expenditures in this part of the contract. In theory, a low award fee pool is disadvantageous to the government because, by reducing the amount of fee available for award purposes, the contractor's incentive to better its performance is also reduced; GAO did not, however, consider this aspect of the situation. In contrast, in *Boeing Sikorsky Aircraft Support*, Comp. Gen. Dec. B-277263.2, 97-2 CPD ¶ 91, and *Management & Tech. Servs. Co.*, Comp. Gen. Dec. B-209513, 82-2 CPD ¶ 571, GAO agreed with the agency's negative evaluation of proposed award fee pools, which were too low to provide sufficient incentive. Compare *CACI, Inc.-Fed.*, Comp. Gen. Dec. B-216516, 84-2 CPD ¶ 542, where the agency also permitted the offerors to propose any level of base fee and award fee pool within the regulatory maximum but stated that fee levels would not be evaluated in the source selection process. GAO affirmed this procedure even though the competitors offered different base and award fee pool levels. Not surprisingly, all of the competitors proposed a base fee plus award fee pool of 10% since the level was not to be evaluated. This gave the agency the maximum amount of incentive fee on the contract and provided significant award fees for the competing contractors.

## c.  Award Periods

FAR 16.401(e)(3) contains the following guidance on the evaluation periods incorporated in the award fee plan:

> (vi) Provide for evaluation period(s) to be conducted at stated intervals during the contract period of performance so that the contractor will periodically be informed of the quality of its performance and the areas in which improvement is expected (e.g. six months, nine months, twelve months, or at specific milestones)[.]

Originally, NASA used three-month evaluation periods, but the administrative effort necessary for evaluations was too great to be performed satisfactorily in such short periods. Subsequently, agencies have normally used either four or six-month evaluation periods. See, for example, NFS 1816.405-272(a), calling for periods of at least six months but permitting shorter periods when the "additional administrative costs . . . are balanced by benefits accruing to the Government." Clearly, the period should be long enough to permit fee award well before the end of the next evaluation period. This permits the contractor to use the agency evaluation of its performance to better its performance in the following period. It is also possible to use award periods of varying length if the amount of work done in some periods of performance is substantially less than in others. For example, in an R&D contract where the initial effort is small, the contracting officer might specify a six-month award period for the initial period, followed by four-month periods thereafter. In service contracts, since the work is usually level over the life of the contract, the award periods are generally of the same duration.

Evaluation periods can also be established in terms of contractual milestones rather than calendar periods. See NFS 1816.405-272(a), suggesting this technique but stating that such periods must be no longer than 12 months. This would be appropriate in a situation where the contractor was performing critical tests or design reviews on the work under the contract and the evaluation would not be accurate until completion of the tests or reviews.

## d.  Allocation of Award Fee

The award fee pool must be allocated to award periods to provide a maximum award fee for each period. See NFS 1816.405-272(b), stating:

> A portion of the total available award fee shall be allocated to each of the evaluation periods. This allocation may result in either an equal or unequal distribution of fee among the periods. The contracting officer should consider the nature of each contract and the incentive effects of fee distribution in determining the appropriate allocation structure.

The Department of Defense requires that a large percentage of the award fee be allocated to the final evaluation of contract performance. See DFARS 216.405-2(1) stating:

The contracting officer shall perform an analysis of appropriate fee distribution to ensure that at least 40 percent of the award fee is available for the final evaluation so that the award fee is appropriately distributed over all evaluation periods to incentivize the contractor throughout the performance of the contract. The percentage of award fee available for the final evaluation may be set below 40 percent if the contracting officer determines that a lower percentage is appropriate, and this determination is approved by the head of the contracting activity (HCA). The HCA may not delegate this approval authority.

Several agencies have adopted clauses on this issue. See the following clause at TAR 1252.216-73:

### DISTRIBUTION OF AWARD FEE (APR 2005)

(a) The total amount of award fee available under this contract is assigned according to the following evaluation periods and amounts:

Evaluation Period:

Available Award Fee: (insert appropriate information)

(b) After the contractor has been paid 85 percent of the base fee and potential award fee, the Government may withhold further payment of the base fee and award fee until a reserve is set aside in an amount that the Government considers necessary to protect its interest. This reserve shall not exceed 15 percent of the total base fee and potential award fee or $100,000, whichever is less. Thereafter, base fee and award fee payments may continue.

(c) In the event of contract termination, either in whole or in part, the amount of award fee available shall represent a prorata distribution associated with evaluation period activities or events as determined by the Government.

(d) The Government will promptly make payment of any award fee upon the submission by the contractor to the contracting officer's authorized representative, of a public voucher or invoice in the amount of the total fee earned for the period evaluated. Payment may be without using a contract modification.

A similar clause, without the withholding provision, is included in HUDAR 2452.216-74 and was included in DFAR 916 405(e) until 1996.

The total award fee has generally been distributed to the award periods in rough proportion to the amount of costs to be spent in each period. However, the importance of the work in each period should also be considered in making this allocation. The NASA Guidance on Award Fee Contracting, June 1989 (NASA 1989 Guidance), suggested that a portion of the award fee pool could be allocated to specific events such as tests or demonstrations and that this portion need not be put in a specific award period:

Tests, demonstrations, and other milestones or events are subject to possible slippage. To eliminate the need for a reallocation of award fee potential, it may be a good idea to allocate any portion of the award fee earmarked for such milestones or events to whatever evaluation periods the milestones or events ultimately occur, rather than allocating to a specific period.

This guidance has been removed from the current NASA Guide, which states, at ¶ 3.5.2, that award periods containing critical milestones should be allocated a larger portion of the award fee pool.

Some agencies have followed a practice of supplementing the award fee pool by adding award fees not earned in earlier periods to the pool available for awards in later periods. The NASA 1989 Guidance called this technique "rollover" or "rollforward" and gave the following guidance:

> The determination whether to permit a rollover of unearned award fee should be based upon an analysis of the work effort, the planned allocation of the award fee potential, and the likely effect on contractor motivation. Generally speaking, an automatic rollover of unearned award fee from one evaluation period to the next should be avoided, because it tends to reduce the effectiveness of the incentive in the current period. Instead, when rollover authority is desired, consideration should be given to providing in the evaluation plan for the exercise of that authority at the discretion of the designated Fee Determination Official.

The use of this technique in service contracts was prohibited by NASA in 1997, NFS 1816.405-273(a), and is now prohibited on all contracts by FAR 16.401(e)(4). Authority to use it was provided in the Determination of Award Fee Earned clause (used by DOT and HUD), which is discussed below. Section 814 of the National Defense Authorization Act for FY 2007, Pub. L. No. 109-364, required the issuance of regulations that "provide specific direction on the circumstances, if any, in which it may be appropriate to roll over award fees" but the FAR implemented this provision with a blanket prohibition of rollover.

When the contract calls for an "end item," NASA requires that the award fee be determined by the performance of that end item. Thus, award fees are made on an interim basis but are provisional until the final performance outcome is determined. See NFS 1816.405-273, stating:

> (b) *End item contracts.* On contracts such as those for end item deliverables where the true quality of contractor performance cannot be measured until the end of the contract, only the last evaluation is final. At that point, the total contract award fee pool is available, and the contractor's total performance is evaluated against the award fee plan to determine total earned award fee. In addition, interim evaluations are done to monitor performance prior to contract completion, provide feedback to the contractor on the Government's assessment of the quality of its performance, and establish the basis for making interim award fee payments (see

1816.405-276(a)). These interim evaluations and associated interim payments are superseded by the fee determination made in the final evaluation at contract completion. The Government will then pay the contractor, or the contractor will refund to the Government, the difference between the final award fee determination and the cumulative interim fee payment.

These provisional award fees are implemented in the Award Fee for End Item Contracts clause in NFS 1852.216-77. Less specific guidance of this nature is given in DEAR 916.404-2 stating that the award fee "should be concentrated on the end product of the contract."

### e.  Payment of Fee

No standard FAR or DFARS clauses governs the payment of base and award fees. However, FAR 16.406(e) directs agencies to use "appropriate" award fee clauses. Thus, the agencies follow different policies on the payment of these fees. The NASA Award Fee for Service Contracts clause at NFS 1852.216-76 allows the contracting officer to insert the method of award fee payment. The NASA Award Fee for End Item Contracts clause at NFS 1852.216-77 provides for payment of the base fee on a monthly (or less) basis and of award fees after each interim evaluation. The Distribution of Award Fee clause at TAR 1252.216-73 provides for payment of the base and award fees upon receipt of an invoice from the contractor for the "total fee earned" (with potential withholding after payment of 85% of the fees). The Payment of Base and Award Fee clause at HUDAR 2452.216-71 provides for payment of the base and award fees in accordance with a schedule to be included in the contract by the contracting officer.

DFARS 216.405-2 allowed provisional payment of award fees until 2011. That provision now states:

(2) *Award-fee evaluation and payments.* Award-fee payments other than payments resulting from the evaluation at the end of an award-fee period are prohibited. (This prohibition does not apply to base-fee payments.) The fee-determining official's rating for award-fee evaluations will be provided to the contractor within 45 calendar days of the end of the period being evaluated. The final award-fee payment will be consistent with the fee-determining official's final evaluation of the contractor's overall performance against the cost, schedule, and performance outcomes specified in the award-fee plan.

### 5.  Performance Evaluation Plan

Although the CPAF contract has always been intrinsically subjective, the evaluation has been done in a very methodical way. Agencies have carefully spelled out in a performance evaluation plan the areas of performance that will be evaluated, the rating system that will be used, and the way in which these ratings will be translated into fee awards. Some agencies have adopted contract clauses describing this process. See TAR 1252.216-72 prescribing the use of the following clause:

PERFORMANCE EVALUATION PLAN (OCT 1994)

(a) A Performance Evaluation Plan shall be unilaterally established by the Government based on the criteria stated in the contract and used for the determination of award fee. This plan shall include the criteria used to evaluate each area and the percentage of award fee (if any) available for each area. A copy of the plan shall be provided to the contractor _____ (insert number) calendar days prior to the start of the first evaluation period.

(b) The criteria contained within the Performance Evaluation Plan may relate to (1) Technical (including schedule) requirements if appropriate; (2) Management; and (3) Cost.

(c) The Performance Evaluation Plan may, consistent with the contract, be revised unilaterally by the Government at any time during the period of performance. Notification of such changes shall be provided to the contractor (insert number) calendar days prior to the start of the evaluation period to which the change will apply.

A similar clause is set forth in HUDAR 2452.216-73.

These clauses are explicit in giving the agency full flexibility to issue and change the evaluation plan during contract performance. This is a major advantage to both parties because, particularly in the case of R&D contracts being performed over a period of time, the parties may learn of changed circumstances, making it advisable to redirect the contractor's efforts and, thus, bringing about changes in award criteria. Of course, if such changes are made, the contractor should be fully informed of the new evaluation plan prior to the beginning of the award period. See *URS Consultants, Inc.*, IBCA 4285-2000, 02-1 BCA ¶ 31,812, *recons. denied*, 02-2 BCA ¶ 31,917, holding that ¶ (c) of the Performance Evaluation Plan clause prohibits retroactive changes to the plan.

### a.  *Award Criteria*

The award criteria set forth elements of the contractor's performance that will be evaluated by the agency in determining the amount of award fees and the relative weight of these fees.

### (1) SELECTING THE CRITERIA

A great deal of flexibility is given to contracting officers in selecting the award criteria, and it is important that the criteria be tailored to the specific procurement. See FAR 16.401(e)(3), stating that the award fee plan must:

Identify the award-fee evaluation criteria and how they are linked to acquisition objectives which shall be defined in terms of contract cost, schedule, and technical performance. Criteria should motivate the contractor to enhance performance in the areas rated, but not at the expense of at least minimum acceptable performance in all other areas;

While, as discussed above, the statutes call for the award fees to be made on the basis of "outcomes," it seems clear from this FAR language that the criteria can be subjective as long as they are "linked to acquisition objectives." There has been a long-standing debate among the agencies as to whether award criteria should focus on *contractual results* (called "output" criteria) or *methods of performance* (called "input" criteria). See DEAR 916.404-2 stating:

The goals and evaluation criteria should be results-oriented. The award fee should be concentrated on the end product of the contract, that is, output, be it hardware, research and development, demonstration or services, together with business management considerations. However, input criteria such as equal employment opportunity, small business programs, functional management areas, such as safety, security, etc., should not be disregarded and may be appropriate criteria upon which to base some part of the award fee.

In contrast, the NASA 1989 Guidance gave considerable discretion in this area, as follows:

Depending upon the procurement situation, performance evaluation factors may include outputs, inputs or a combination of both. Output factors relate to the end results of contract performance, such as the quality of the end items delivered or services rendered, the actual time of their delivery or completion, and the actual costs incurred. Their use has obvious advantages, but there are potential disadvantages as well. In certain situations, end results of this type may not be discernible until it is too late for an award fee evaluation process to have any appreciable effect on the direction in which the results are heading. Also, given the uncertainties that made it necessary to use a cost reimbursement contract, an evaluation limited to output factors may not provide a true or complete picture of actual accomplishments. To illustrate, the incurrence of a cost underrun or overrun may reflect less on the contractor's cost control accomplishments than on the uncertainties existing at the time the contract cost estimate was negotiated.

For these reasons, input factors often are used instead of or as a supplement to the use of output factors. Input factors relate to those intermediate processes, procedures, actions or techniques that experience and analysis indicate will be key elements influencing successful contract performance.

Following this reasoning, output criteria call for assessment of the contractor's performance in meeting the end objectives of the contract. However, such assessment can be quite subjective in some instances. Hence, output criteria frequently do not assess only whether the contractor met an objective standard, such as an estimated cost or a scheduled completion date. See, for example, the current NASA regulation, NFS 1816.404-274, which does not contain the above guidance but rather states that in evaluating "cost control" (an input criteria), the contractor should "normally" be given a score of 0 if it incurs a significant overrun (an output criteria). However, the regulation goes on to allow scoring using a subjective evaluation of how well the contractor controlled costs, without regard to whether there was an overrun of the original estimated cost.

As a general rule, the better the work is defined, the more desirable it is to evaluate output criteria, and when contract objectives can be established by setting clear targets for cost, schedule or performance, a CPIF formula would be the proper type of arrangement for that element of the work. Even when the parties cannot agree on firm targets, output criteria are probably desirable because they call for less subjectivity than input criteria. Thus, output criteria would likely be used on service contracts for repetitive services. Input criteria would more likely be used on R&D contracts where the parties are not sure of their projections of end results and the government desires to encourage the best performance, even if the parties have originally agreed to erroneous goals.

It can be seen that the difference between output criteria and input criteria is a matter of degree not a clear distinction. See the NASA Guide at ¶ 3.4.1, giving the following specific examples of the types of output award criteria:

a. *Technical Performance* — Accomplishment achieved in the areas of:

- Design: Approach in design concepts, analysis, detailed execution, and low cost design and manufacturing. Design of test specimens, models, and prototypes.

- Development: Conception/execution of manufacturing process, test plans, and techniques. Effectiveness of proposed hardware changes.

- Quality: Quality assurance, e.g., appearance, thoroughness and accuracy, inspections, customer surveys.

- Technical: Meeting technical requirements for design, performance and processing, e.g., weight control, quality assurance, maintainability, reliability design reviews, test procedures, equipment, performance.

- Processing Documentation: Timely and efficient preparation, implementation and closeout.

- Facilities/GFE: Operation and maintenance of assigned facilities and Government Furnished Equipment.

- Schedule: Meeting program key milestones and contractual delivery dates; anticipating and resolving problems; recovery from delays; reaction time and appropriateness of response to changes.

- Safety: Providing a safe work environment; conducting annual inspections of all facilities; maintaining accident/incident files; timely reporting of mishaps; providing safety training for all personnel.

- Information Management: Ability of computer system to provide adequate, timely and cost effective support; meets security requirements; management information systems ensure accurate, relevant and timely information.

- Material Management: Efficient and effective processing of requisitions, with emphasis on priority requisitions; responsiveness to changes in usage rates.

b. *Project Management* — Accomplishment achieved in the areas of:

- Program Planning/Organization/Management: Assignment and utilization of personnel; recognition of critical problem areas; cooperation and effective working relationships with other contractors and Government personnel to assure integrated operation efficiency; support to interface activities; technology utilization; effective use of resources; labor relations; planning, organizing, and managing all program elements; management actions to achieve and sustain a high level of productivity; response to emergencies and other unexpected situations.

- Compliance with contract provisions: Effectiveness of property and material control, Equal Employment Opportunity Program, Minority Business Enterprise Program, system and occupational safety and security. Effectiveness in meeting or exceeding small business and small disadvantaged business subcontracting goals.

- Subcontracting: Subcontract direction and coordination. Purchase order and subcontractor administration.

- Timely and accurate financial management reporting

c. *Cost Control* — The contractor's ability to control, adjust, and accurately project contract costs (estimating contract costs, not budget or operating plan costs) through:

- Control of indirect and overtime costs. Control of direct labor costs.

- Economies in use of personnel, energy, materials, computer resources, facilities, etc.

- Cost reduction through use of cost saving programs, cost avoidance programs, alternate designs and process methods, etc. "Make versus buy" program decisions.

- Reduced purchasing costs through increased use of competition, material inspection, etc.

The NASA Guide also contains, at ¶ 3.4.2, a few examples of commonly used input criteria:

*Staffing*: Optimal allocation of resources; adequacy of staffing; qualified and trained personnel; identification and effective handling of employee morale problems; etc.

*Planning*: Adequate, quality, innovative, self-initiated and timely planning of activities; effective utilization of personnel; quality of responses; etc.

See also Table 16-1, after DoD PGI 216.470, illustrating both output and input criteria.

The NASA 1989 Guidance contained the following suggestion aimed at limiting the number of award criteria:

Fragmentation of the award fee potential over a large number of performance areas and factors dilutes emphasis. Instead, broad performance areas should be selected, such as technical and business management, supplemented by a limited number of subfactors describing significant evaluation elements over which the contractor has effective management control. Project history and past performance can be helpful in identifying those key problem or improvement areas that should be subject to award fee evaluations.

There is some disagreement as to whether the award criteria should be made a part of the contract document. Prior to 1991, DFARS 216.404-2(b)(S-72)(ii) stated that this information should be set forth in the contract (there is no statement on this issue in the current DFARS), but a number of agencies reserve the right to unilaterally issue the criteria to the contractor after contract award.

## (2) Weighting the Criteria

In most CPAF contracts, the award criteria are assigned relative weights as a means of establishing the priorities of the agency in the elements of performance. Most weighting systems assign points to each evaluation criterion, generally using a total of 100 points. See Table 16-2, after DoD PGI 216.470, illustrating a comprehensive weighting system.

The NASA Guide provides, at ¶ 3.4.3, that weighting of the factors need not be done and that, when it is done, it does not control the awards, as follows:

[T]he detailed performance evaluation plan should indicate the relative priorities assigned to the various performance areas and evaluation factors and subfactors. This may be accomplished through the use of narrative phrases such as "more important," "important," and "less important" or through the use of percentage weights. When percentages are used, the plan should state that they are for the sole purpose of communicating relative priorities, and in no way imply an arithmetical precision to the judgmental determinations of overall performance quality and the amount of award fee earned.

The NASA Guide suggests, at ¶ 3.4.3, that when weighting is done, a two-step process should be used. First, the major areas of performance are given relative weights in accordance with the agency's priorities. Thus, the agency might decide, on an R&D contract, that the weights should be as follows:

| Factor | Assigned Weight |
|---|---|
| Technical | 55 |
| Business Management | 35 |
| Cost Control | 10 |

The NASA Guide then suggests weighting the subfactors within each factor in the same manner. Thus, within the technical factor there might be three subfactors:

| Subfactor | Assigned Weight |
|---|---|
| Design | 55 |
| Quality | 30 |
| Schedule | 15 |

After the subfactors for business management and cost control are weighted in a similar manner, the agency has a complete matrix of relative weights. For most agencies other than NASA, this matrix is used for calculating the final evaluation of the award fee.

## b. Rating System

The rating system that will be used is the key determinate of whether the CPAF contract will yield a reasonable profit for the contractor. Most agencies disclose the grading system to the contractor but it has been held proper to use an undisclosed grading system, *Burnside-Ott Aviation Training Ctr.*, ASBCA 43184, 96-1 BCA ¶28,102, *aff'd*, 107 F.3d 854 (Fed. Cir. 1997). However, the FAR now prescribes a mandatory rating scheme which presumably will be used on all CPAF contracts. This rating system appears as Table 16-1 of FAR 16.401(e), and is set forth in **Figure 9-6**.

| Award-Fee Adjectival Rating | Award-Fee Pool Available To Be Earned | Description |
|---|---|---|
| Excellent | 91% — 100% | Contractor has exceeded almost all of the significant award-fee criteria and has met overall cost, schedule, and technical performance requirements of the contract in the aggregate as defined and measured against the criteria in the award-fee plan for the award-fee evaluation period. |
| Very Good | 76% — 90% | Contractor has exceeded many of the significant award-fee criteria and has met overall cost, schedule, and technical performance requirements of the contract in the aggregate as defined and measured against the criteria in the award-fee plan for the award-fee evaluation period. |
| Good | 51% — 75% | Contractor has exceeded some of the significant award-fee criteria and has met overall cost, schedule, and technical performance requirements of the contract in the aggregate as defined and measured against the criteria in the award-fee plan for the award-fee evaluation period. |
| Satisfactory | No Greater Than 50% | Contractor has met overall cost, schedule, and technical performance requirements of the contract in the aggregate as defined and measured against the criteria in the award-fee plan for the award-fee evaluation period. |
| Unsatisfactory | 0% | Contractor has failed to meet overall cost, schedule, and technical performance requirements of the contract in the aggregate as defined and measured against the criteria in the award-fee plan for the award-fee evaluation period. |

**Figure 9-6**

The key problem in this rating system is that it is not keyed to the base fee and the award fee but, rather, appears to be mandatory without regard to those elements of the award fee plan. Thus, it does not ensure the contractor that it yields awards commensurate with its actual performance. For example, assume that the contractor has "exceeded" a few criteria and has met almost all of the "requirements" — which the fee determination official concludes yields a score of satisfactory and a fee award of 50%. This would yield fees on two hypothetical contracts as follows:

|  | Contract A | Contract B |
|---|---|---|
| Base Fee | 3% | 0% |
| Award Fee Pool | 12% | 10% |
| Fee Earned | 9% (3% + 6%) | 5% (0% + 5%) |

This illustrates the inequity of applying this mandatory rating system on contracts with low base fees and low award fee pools. It yields a fair result on contract A but not on contract B.

Another problem with this rating system is that it does not define the terms "criteria" and "requirements." In requiring that awards will only be made when a contractor has met the requirements, it identifies those requirements as they are "defined and measured against the criteria."As discussed above, some criteria are and have been established to match the contract requirements, such as performing within the estimated cost, while others are highly subjective evaluations of the way the contractor has performed the work. Thus, the FAR rating system creates great doubt as to how it will be applied in determining whether criteria have been "exceeded" and requirements "met." Yet the scoring system appears to yield significant awards only when the contractor has exceeded the criteria and met the "overall" requirements. This raises the possibility that a contractor performing development work could complete the work within the schedule and estimated cost yet only earn a 50% award because it has not exceeded the criteria. In addition, the scoring system calls for no award if the contractors "has failed to meet overall, cost, schedule, and performance requirements." This raises the specter of a very low fee if that language is interpreted harshly.

To be fair to contractors, CPAF contracts should be structured in a way that allows a contract to earn the same fee on a CPAF contract that it would earn for the same level of performance on a CPFF contract. Thus, if an agency would normally negotiate a 7% fixed fee it should structure its CPAF contract to yield at least 7% for satisfactory performance. Yet in its reports on CPAF contracts, GAO appears to have disagreed with systems that gave substantial awards for average performance. This GAO criticism was based, in part, on the description of CPAF contracts in FAR 16.405-2 stating:

> A cost-plus-award-fee contract is a cost-reimbursement contract that provides for a fee consisting of (1) a base amount fixed at inception of the contract and (2) an award amount that the contractor may earn in whole or in part during performance and that is *sufficient to provide motivation for excellence* in such areas as quality, timeliness, technical ingenuity, and cost-effective management. (Emphasis added.)

GAO reports apparently interpret this language are requiring that award fees only be given for performance that is at least above average.

## c.  Award Procedure

The amount of the award is usually determined by a three-step procedure within the contracting agency. The first step consists of evaluation and preliminary scoring of the contractor's performance by personnel within the procuring agency who are familiar with the contractor's performance. Generally, the personnel used for this task are the technical and business personnel who are monitoring the contractor's work on a regular basis. In cases where there is a government program manager, this function will be performed primarily by personnel in the program office. The goal of this part of the process is to obtain an evaluation by the most knowledgeable people in the agency on each aspect of the contractor's performance. Most of the guidance on CPAF contracting contains instructions calling for very detailed monitoring of contractor performance and full documentation of perceived strengths and weaknesses. Detailed documentation is essential because these evaluations form the basis of the entire award process.

The second step consists of a review of these evaluations by a board of higher-level personnel. While this step should be unnecessary on smaller procurements, FAR 16.401(e)(3) requires agencies to establish such boards on all procurements. This step ensures that the evaluations are internally consistent and that they reflect an overall view of the contractor's accomplishments. A board of this type would be expected to discern, for instance, not only that one evaluator has unreasonably downgraded a contractor, but also that the contractor's performance was marginal because of a conscious decision to devote effort to some other important task.

The third step is the award by the award official, generally called the "fee determination official." In major procurements, this official should be at the management level of the procuring agency, while in small contracts, the contracting officer might perform this task. The contract clauses generally provide that awards are purely discretionary decisions. See the following clause in TAR 1252.216-71:

DETERMINATION OF AWARD FEE EARNED (APR 2005)

(a) The Government shall evaluate contractor performance at the end of each specified evaluation period to determine the amount of award. The contractor agrees that the amount of award and the award fee methodology are unilateral decisions to be made at the sole discretion of the Government.

(b) Contractor performance shall be evaluated according to a Performance Evaluation Plan. The contractor shall be periodically informed of the quality of its performance and areas in which improvements are expected.

(c) The contractor shall be promptly advised, in writing, of the determination and reasons why the award fee was or was not earned. The contractor may submit a performance self-evaluation for each evaluation period. The amount of award is at the sole discretion of the Government but any self-evaluation received within (insert number) days after the end of the current evaluation period will be given such consideration, as may be deemed appropriate by the Government.

(d) The amount of award fee which can be awarded in each evaluation period is limited to the amounts set forth at (identify location of award fee amounts). Award fee which is not earned in an evaluation period cannot be reallocated to future evaluation periods.

A similar clause is included in HUDAR 2452.216-72.

If the fee determination official is designated by a specific position within the agency, it will be an abuse of discretion for another official to dictate the amount of the award fee. See *Boeing Co. v. United States*, 75 Fed. Cl. 34 (2007), stating at 46-47:

> An agreement that "designate[s] a particular [g]overnment official to make a certain factual determination must be strictly observed." *Southern, Waldrip [& Harvick Co. v. United States]*, 334 F.2d [245 (Ct. Cl. 1964)] at 249-50; see also *General Elec. Co. v. United States*, 412 F.2d 1215, 1220, 188 Ct. Cl. 620 (Ct. Cl. 1969) ("[T]he internal administrative scheme whereby the Boston Procurement District was to defer to the Army Weapons Command concerning funding cannot diminish . . . authority" provided by the contract to the contracting officer.); *New York Shipbuilding Corp. v. United States*, 385 F.2d 427, 433-34, 180 Ct. Cl. 446 (Ct. Cl. 1967) (Where "the parties expressly chose and named a specific official . . . as the initial decider . . . [,] the [g]overnment could not unilaterally substitute another official."); *Williams Eng'g & Contr. Co. v. United States*, 55 Ct. Cl. 349, 365, 382-83 (1920) (holding that a contract was breached when the Secretary of Navy made a decision that the contract had entrusted to the Chief of the Bureau of Yards and Docks).

The court noted that the agency could have replaced the individual holding the designated job, stating at 46:

> [T]he contract did not purport to abrogate the Secretary's authority over personnel decisions or prevent him from formally removing or replacing Mr. Twining as Manager, Albuquerque Operations. *New York Shipbuilding*, 385 F.2d at 434 (suggesting that contractual designation of the Nuclear Projects Officer "would not mean that the Maritime Administration could not change . . . the occupant of that post"). However, the Secretary was not permitted by the contract to displace the AFDO by informally "invest[ing] [AFDO] authority in himself . . . or in others of his choice," *Fischbach & Moore Int'l Corp. v. United States*, 617 F.2d 223, 226 n.7, 223 Ct. Cl. 119 (Ct. Cl. 1980) ("[W]here the contract or controlling regulations designate (without qualification) a specific officer or body as the one to render a contractual decision . . ., other persons (including higher officials) cannot displace the designated decision maker.").

A provision precluding appeal of award fee determinations under the Disputes clause is not enforceable under the Contract Disputes Act of 1978, *Burnside-Ott Aviation Training Ctr. v. Dalton*, 107 F.3d 854 (Fed. Cir. 1997). However, the review of an award decision is a very narrow one, focusing only on whether it is arbitrary or capricious. Thus, the court affirmed *Burnside-Ott Aviation Training Ctr.*, ASBCA 43184, 96-1 BCA ¶ 28,102, where the board ruled that the use of a conversion table was not arbitrary or capricious but was within the contracting officer's discretion even though its use was not disclosed to the contractor. The ASBCA has also taken jurisdiction over a dispute concerning the "availability" of the award fee. See *Technical Support Servs., Inc.*, ASBCA 37976, 89-2 BCA ¶ 21,861, where the board noted that it was not ruling that it had jurisdiction over the "amount" of the award. The sufficiency of awards was considered in *Nash Janitorial Servs., Inc.*, GSBCA 6390, 84-1 BCA ¶ 17,135, *recons. denied*, 84-2 BCA ¶ 17,355, where the board found that a contract modification agreeing to a total amount of cost and fee (including award fees) due on a services contract was void because of economic duress by the contracting officer. The conduct constituting duress was the manner in which the contracting officer administered the contract, including granting very low award fees that penalized the contractor for government actions.

The most significant review of an award fee occurred in *URS Consultants, Inc.*, IBCA 4285-2000, 02-2 BCA ¶ 31,812, where the contracting officer determined that a retroactive downward recalculation of award fees paid over nine years was appropriate to correct an "error" in the calculation. The board rejected this reduction in the award fees that had already been paid, holding that the unilaterally determined award fees were binding on the government because they were based on the award fee plan in place at the time of the awards and the Award Fee clause in the contract provided that the plan could only be adjusted prospectively.

One major issue in the award process is the degree of participation that should be granted to the contractor. In the past, some contracts have greatly limited the contractor's participation, giving the contractor no opportunity to submit information or see evaluations and limiting its role to a thorough debriefing after the award has been made. Earlier versions of the DFARS provided that evaluations should be furnished to the contractor for comment, but DoD PGI 216.405-2(4)(ii) now states that the agency "may . . . afford the contractor an opportunity to present information on its own behalf." The DOT/HUD clauses discussed above and the NASA Award Fee clauses in NFS 1852.216-76 and -77 also provide that the contractor is entitled to submit a self-evaluation as part of the evaluation process. Another option is to permit the contractor to make an independent presentation to the board or award official, either in writing or orally. This was included in an earlier edition of the DFARS but has been removed from the current version of the regulation. Whatever system is selected, the agency must eventually give the contractor detailed information on the basis of the award so that it can fully understand what aspects of performance were downgraded and how performance can be improved in subsequent award periods.

Since the CPAF contract will function best when the contractor has a high degree of confidence in the reliability, accuracy, and fairness of the evaluations and awards, the process selected should engender such confidence.

## 6. Relationship of Award Fee to Other Provisions

As with CPIF contracts, it is important that CPAF contracts state the relationship of the award fee provisions to other provisions of the contract that provide the government with remedies for less than specified performance. Since most award fee provisions call for awards only if the performance reaches the minimally acceptable level, it would be logical to state that the government could make fee adjustments under no other contract clauses as long as the award fee provisions were in effect. Similarly, clauses providing remedies other than fee adjustment, such as the Termination clause, would be applied without regard to the award fee provisions. This is a reasonable interpretation of the standard clauses, if the relationship between clauses is not well stated in the contract, since it is not reasonable to conclude that the government is providing itself a choice of remedies or overlapping remedies. The best solution, of course, is to include clear language in the contract.

Unfortunately, this issue is not adequately addressed in many CPAF contracts. A good example of the problems that can ensue is found in *Holmes & Narver Servs., Inc.*, ASBCA 33025, 88-3 BCA ¶ 20,932, where the contract contained an award fee provision on cost and technical performance and an Inspection of Services clause similar to the clause in FAR 52.246-5. The Inspection of Services clause gave the government the right to "reduce any fee payable" if the services were defective and could not be corrected. The contracting officer's attempt to reduce the base fee because of poor cost control was held to be improper because cost control was not a specified service under the contract. The board would have faced a more difficult issue if the reduction in base fee had occurred because of poor performance of the technical work called for by the contract, but it would seem that a proper interpretation would be that the award fee provisions are the stated mechanism for making such fee reductions. See also *UNC Nuclear Indus., Inc.*, EBCA 412-4-88, 90-1 BCA ¶ 22,463, interpreting a DOE contract clause stating that "in the event of contract termination . . . the amount of award fee available shall represent a pro rata distribution associated with evaluation period activities or events, and allowable costs." The board ruled that the government was wrong in using a share of the base and award fees computed by prorating (based on the number of days of performance prior to the convenience termination) the fee assigned to the evaluation period. Here the government attempted to draft a clause dealing with the possibility of convenience termination but failed to state the result with sufficient clarity. Contrast *Textron Def. Sys. v. Widnall*, 143 F.3d 1465 (Fed. Cir. 1998), where the court held that the contractor was not entitled to a pro-rata share of the award fee because the contract stated that the award fee was "not subject to" the Termination clause. The court also held that, even without the clause, the contractor would not have been entitled to a pro rata share of the entire award fee because "it had no reasonable expectation of ever receiving the total award fee." See also *Northrop Grumman Corp. v. Goldin*, 136 F.3d 1479 (Fed. Cir. 1998), where the parties omitted any contract language on the effect of a convenience termination on award fee that had been accumulated over the total period of contract performance and was to be awarded based on ultimate success. The court ruled that the contractor was entitled to an award based on the proportionate share of this fee in the pool at the time of termination.

The contract should also spell out the consequences of any plan to give employee bonuses if high levels of award fee are earned. As noted in the discussion of CPIF contracts, such bonuses are potentially allowable costs of performance, if they comply with the cost principle in FAR 31.205-6(f). See *Petroleum Operations & Support Servs., Inc.*, EBCA 291-6-83, 85-2 BCA ¶ 18,037, denying compensation of the cost of an award fee–based bonus because it was not given in accordance with a "good faith agreement" between the contractor and its employees. If the bonuses had been recognized as allowable costs, the contractor's costs would have been higher, with the possibility that its award fee would have been lower. It is this interrelationship that should be addressed in the negotiation of the contract.

## 7. CPAF/CPIF Contracts

It has become quite common practice to combine CPAF and CPIF contracting techniques in a single contract. Although this practice is not covered in the FAR, it is discussed in NFS 1816.405-270(b). See also DEAR 916.405-2 stating:

> [T]he award fee arrangement shall include both technical performance (including scheduling as appropriate) and business management considerations tailored to the needs of the particular situation. In addition, in a situation where cost estimating reliability and other factors are such that the negotiation of a separate predetermined incentive sharing arrangement applicable to cost performance is determined both feasible and advantageous, cost incentives may be added. The resulting contract would then be identified as a cost-plus-incentive-fee/award-fee combination type.

As indicated, the CPAF/CPIF contract usually involves using a CPIF formula for the cost incentive and adding CPAF awards in the areas of performance and delivery. The fee is then generally divided into its constituent parts and the incentive provisions structured accordingly. For example, if it were decided to assign 40 % of the fee to cost incentives and the balance to the award areas, the cost incentive would be structured at this level. Thus, if the normal CPIF contract would have a target fee of 8%, with minimum and maximum fees of 2% and 14%, the parties would use 40% of the total fee pool (12 percentage points of fee) to structure the cost incentive in the CPAF/CPIF contract. This would yield:

| | |
|---|---|
| Target Fee | 4.4% |
| Minimum Fee | 2.0% |
| Maximum Fee (on costs) | 6.8% |

The balance of the total fee pool (7.2 percentage points of fee) would be assigned to the award fee pool available for awards in the performance and delivery areas, and the maximum fee on the total contract would be set at 14%.

There are many variations of this structuring technique. For example, the government might decide that the above formula did not provide sufficient incentive in the cost area. In that case, it is possible to overlap the different areas using, for example, CPIF elements as follows:

| | |
|---|---|
| Target Fee | 6% |
| Minimum Fee | 2% |
| Maximum Fee (on costs) | 10% |

The award fee pool for performance and delivery would be kept at 7.2 percentage points, and the maximum fee for the total contract would be kept at 14%. This might result in no fee being available for awards in the final periods of contract performance, but it would increase the motivation for reducing costs and would allow the cost incentive to be spread over a broader RIE.

## 8.  Award Fee Provisions in Fixed-Price Contracts

FAR 16.404 provides the following minimal guidance on including award fee provisions in fixed-price contracts:

> Award-fee provisions may be used in fixed-price contracts when the Government wishes to motivate a contractor and other incentives cannot be used because contractor performance cannot be measured objectively. Such contracts shall establish a fixed price (including normal profit) for the effort. This price will be paid for satisfactory contract performance. Award fee earned (if any) will be paid in addition to that fixed price.

This technique was proper prior to adoption of the FAR language. See *Diversified Contract Servs., Inc.*, Comp. Gen. Dec. B-224152, 86-2 CPD ¶ 675, where an agency used a stand-alone award fee provision to motivate the contractor to increase the quality of the services being performed. GAO ruled that this was well within the power of an agency and was a valid method of obtaining the quality of work required. For another case where an award fee provision was included in a fixed-price contract, see *Technology Applications, Inc.*, Comp. Gen. Dec. B-238259, 90-1 CPD ¶ 451.

DoD PGI 216.470 contains rather cryptic guidance on "other applications of award fees," as follows:

> The *award amount* portion of the fee may be used in other types of contracts under the following conditions —
>
>> (1) The Government wishes to motivate and reward a contractor for —
>>
>>> (i) Purchase of capital assets (including machine tools) manufactured in the united States, on major defense acquisition programs; or
>>>
>>> (ii) Management performance in areas which cannot be measured objectively and where normal incentive provisions cannot be used. For example, logistics support, quality, timeliness, ingenuity, and cost effectiveness are areas under the control of management which may be susceptible only to subjective measurement and evaluation.
>>
>> (2) The "base fee" (fixed amount portion) is not used.
>>
>> (3) The chief of the contracting office approves the use of the "award amount."
>>
>> (4) An award review board and procedures are established for conduct of the evaluation.
>>
>> (5) The administrative costs of evaluation do not exceed the expected benefits.

Although this guidance appears to permit evaluation of "cost effectiveness," the areas of evaluation for award in this situation would normally include only performance and delivery because the contractor would be motivated to control costs by the use of a fixed-price type contract.

The determination of whether a contractor had earned the bonuses attached to these types of performance and delivery incentives would be made in the same manner as described above for the CPAF contract. See *Lockheed Martin Info. Sys.*, Comp. Gen. Dec. B-292836, 2003 CPD ¶ 230, involving a procurement where the agency included the "financial incentives" that could be earned for "enhanced performance" of a fixed-price contract in a separate contract line item. In *DGR Assocs., Inc.*, Comp. Gen. Dec. B-285428, 2000 CPD ¶ 145, GAO ruled that the agency properly gave an enhanced rating to an offeror that intended to give its employees bonuses from part of its award fee for better performance.

## E.  Cost-Plus-Award-Term Contracts

A new type of contract that has not yet be identified in the FAR is the cost-plus-award-term (CPAT) contract. This contract is similar to the CPAF contract in that the award decision is subjectively made by the agency based on its periodic evaluation of the contractor's performance. However, the contract provides that if the contractor is evaluated as having achieved a specified level of performance, it will be awarded another period of performance. Agencies have varied in writing these contracts as to whether they (1) make a binding promise to add one or more years, subject to the availability of appropriations and a continuing requirement, or (2) merely promise to add one or more option years, which gives the contractor no *right* to additional years. This new type of contract is described in the Office of Federal Procurement Policy publication, Seven Steps to Performance-Based Services Acquisition at *http://www.acquisition.gov/sevensteps/index.html*. See also the Defense Acquisition Guidebook providing guidance on entering into long-term life-cycle support contracts with contractors and stating at 5.1.5.1:

> Award term contracts should be used where possible to incentivize industry to provide optimal support. Incentives should be tied to metrics tailored to reflect the DoD Component's specific definitions and reporting processes. Award and incentive contracts should include tailored cost reporting to enable appropriate contract management and to facilitate future cost estimating and price analysis.

The typical CPAT contract calls for performance of services for a period of two to five years with an evaluation period after several years of contractually required performance. If the contractor is awarded an additional term, the contract will generally call for subsequent evaluations with the possibility of earning further periods of performance. In some cases, such contracts have made it possible for the contractor to continue working under the contract for 15 to 20 years. See, however, § 813 of the National Defense Authorization Act for Fiscal Year 2005, Pub. L. No. 108-375, applicable to DoD, NASA and the Coast Guard, placing a limitation of five years of work on task and delivery order contracts with five years of options unless the head of the agency determines that exceptional circumstances justify a longer period of time. This statute is implemented in DFARS 217.204 to provide that this statutory restriction applies to "ordering periods" not performance periods. Neither the statute nor the DFARS implementation discuss the application of these rules to award term periods.

Since there is no regulatory guidance on this type of contract, the process used has varied considerably. Many agencies have structured the initial period of performance with an award of a base period of one or two years followed by several years of options before the award term years go into effect. The award term periods have also varied — from one to three years. A few of these contracts have also included negative award term incentives with the agency deducting years of performance for evaluations of below average performance. See *Pitney Bowes Gov't*

*Solutions, Inc. v. United States*, 93 Fed. Cl. 327 (2010) (less-than-one-year base period, four option years, and two one-year award term options); *2B Brokers*, Comp. Gen. Dec. B-298651, 2006 CPD ¶ 178 (three-year contract with four award term options); *Spherix, Inc.*, Comp. Gen. Dec. B-294572, 2005 CPD ¶ 3 (three-year requirements contract with six one-year award terms); *Bannum, Inc.*, Comp. Gen. Dec. B-298281.2, 2006 CPD ¶ 163 (three-year base period and seven one-year award terms); *Orion Int'l Tech., Inc.*, Comp. Gen. Dec. B-293256, 2004 CPD ¶ 118 (base period of three years with 12 "option" years — not specifying which were options and which were award term years); *Research Analysis & Maint., Inc.*, Comp. Gen. Dec. B-292587.4, 2004 CPD ¶ 100 (base period of three years with six two-year award terms); *Cortez, Inc.*, Comp. Gen. Dec. B-292178, 2003 CPD ¶ 184 (base period of three years with two option years and five award term years); *NLX Corp.*, Comp. Gen. Dec. B-288785, 2001 CPD ¶ 198 (base period of 39 months with two three-year award term periods).

The most difficult problem in structuring CPAT contracts is determining the pricing of award periods that are subject to unknown economic conditions years after the award of the contract. These periods have generally been included in the contract with pricing arrangements matching those used on periods with firm requirements. Thus, on a cost-plus-incentive-fee contract, the award terms would have a target cost and a target fee. On a contract with firm fixed prices for early years, later option years and award term years would usually contain fixed prices subject to economic price adjustment or price redetermination up to ceiling amounts. Some award term contracts have made the award conditional on a government determination that the price applicable to the award terms is a reasonable price. Some of these contracts have also contained provisions allowing the contractor to cancel an award term provision or an award term award with appropriate notice to the government.

CPAT contracts have also included evaluation plans that are essentially the same as the evaluation plans used on CPAF contracts. Thus, they inform the contractor of the elements of performance that will be evaluated and the level of performance necessary to achieve high scores.

## V. LEVEL-OF-EFFORT CONTRACTS

The standard types of contracts discussed above generally describe the work in terms of the end product to be delivered or the services to be performed. This section covers an alternate method of describing the work — in terms of the level of effort to be expended by the contractor. In this type of contract, the contractor receives the compensation called for by the contract upon expenditure of the required hours of effort, regardless of whether the anticipated work is completed. As a result, this type of contract is used sparingly since it imposes significantly less risk on the contractor than contracts calling for completion of a specified task.

In these types of contracts, the government is primarily buying hours of labor from a contractor. Hence, the most important consideration is the quality of the labor, and negotiated procurement procedures are generally used to permit the evaluation of the capabilities of each offerors' employees. See, for example, *ManTech Envtl. Research Servs. Corp.*, Comp. Gen. Dec B-292602, 2003 CPD ¶ 221, where the technical evaluation factors in a CPFF level of effort procurement were, in descending order of importance, demonstrated qualifications of assigned personnel, past performance, demonstrated corporate experience, quality of proposed program management plan, and appropriateness of the proposed quality management plan. Frequently, agencies evaluate an offeror's relative experience, *Wickman Spacecraft & Propulsion Co.*, Comp. Gen. Dec. B-219675, 85-2 CPD ¶ 690 (1985) (failure to include a small, new firm in competitive range for fixed-price level of effort contract was acceptable); *DDL Omni Eng'g*, Comp. Gen. Dec. B-220075.2, 85-2 CPD ¶ 684 (an agency was allowed to take into consideration personnel and corporate experience in evaluating the proposals). Agencies need not choose a contractor with the most specific experience but may infer that the contractor has the ability to perform the work, *U.S. Defense Sys., Inc.*, Comp. Gen. Dec. B-260702, 95-2 CPD ¶ 22 (award of a contract concerning guard services at embassies given to a contractor with comparable, but not the specific, guard experience); *Research Analysis & Maint., Inc.*, Comp. Gen. Dec. B-239223, 90-2 CPD ¶ 129 (award to contractor without experience on the specific missile at issue). An agency cannot, however, require experience to the extent that it is "unduly restrictive." See *Daniel H. Wagner, Assocs., Inc.*, 65 Comp. Gen. 305 (B-220633), 86-1 CPD ¶ 166, where the Navy had to revise its solicitation because its requirements for experience were so restrictive that competition was limited to a sole source of supply. GAO also noted that sealed bidding would be appropriate when routine services were being acquired.

There are two techniques used to contract for a level of effort. First, the parties can agree to fixed hourly rates for specified classes of labor with payment based on the number of actual hours incurred. These rates include the contractor's indirect costs and profit. If this type of contract calls for labor only, it is called a "labor-hour" contract, FAR 16.602. If it includes the purchase of materials as well as the incurrence of labor effort, it is called a " time-and-materials" contract, FAR 16.601. The second technique provides a stated amount of compensation for the incurrence of a specified number of labor-hours over a fixed period of time. This type of contract is generally called a "term" type contract and can be written as a "firm-fixed-price, level-of-effort term contract," FAR 16.207, or a cost-reimbursement term contract, FAR 16.306(d). In the former contract, the contractor is paid the price upon the incurrence of the labor-hours, while in the latter contract, the contractor is paid the fixed fee plus the costs upon the incurrence of the labor-hours.

# A. Time-and-Materials and Labor-Hour Contracts

Although time-and-materials and labor-hour contracts have been used for many years, they are not regarded as contracts that are beneficial to the government since they provide "no positive profit incentive to the contractor for cost control or labor efficiency," FAR 16.601(c)(1). This lack of incentive is due to the difficulty of controlling the number of hours that will be expended to perform any assigned task. Thus, FAR guidance on how to use these types of contracts is minimal. However, FAR 52.301 does include these types of contracts in the matrix of contract clauses — providing guidance as to the clauses that are appropriate for these types of contract.

FAR 16.601(d) contains the following limitations on the use of time-and-materials contracts:

A time-and-materials contract may be used only if —

(1) The contracting officer prepares a determination and findings that no other contract type is suitable. The determination and finding shall be —

(i) Signed by the contracting officer prior to the execution of the base period or any option periods of the contracts; and

(ii) Approved by the head of the contracting activity prior to the execution of the base period when the base period plus any option periods exceeds three years; and

(2) The contract includes a ceiling price that the contractor exceeds at its own risk. The contracting officer shall document the contract file to justify the reasons for the amount of any subsequent change in the ceiling price. Also see 12.207(b) for further limitations on use of Time-and-Materials or Labor Hour contracts for acquisition of commercial items.

These same requirements are applicable to labor-hour contracts, FAR 16.602. The determination and findings supporting the use of these contracts is not required by statute but is an additional safeguard called for by the regulation.

DFARS 216.601 contains the following additional provisions intended to limit the use of time-and-material and labor-hour contracts:

(i) The determination and findings shall contain sufficient facts and rationale to justify that no other contract type is suitable. At a minimum, the determination and findings shall—

(A) Include a description of the market research conducted;

(B) Establish that it is not possible at the time of placing the contract or order to accurately estimate the extent or duration of the work or to anticipate costs with any reasonable degree of certainty;

(C) Establish that the requirement has been structured to minimize the use of time-and-materials requirements (e.g., limiting the value or length of the time-and-materials portion of the contract or order; establishing fixed prices for portions of the requirement); and

(D) Describe the actions planned to minimize the use of time-and-materials contracts on future acquisitions for the same requirements.

FAR 16.601(c)(1) also requires "appropriate Government surveillance" of contractor performance of these types of contract "to give reasonable assurance that efficient methods and effective cost controls are being used." See *Midwest Maint. & Constr. Co.*, GSBCA 6225, 85-1 BCA ¶ 17,716, commenting on the use of this type of contract without adequate government surveillance.

The additional limitations when these type of contracts are used to procure commercial services are prescribed in FAR 12.207(b) as follows:

(1) A time-and-materials contract or labor-hour contract (see Subpart 16.6) may be used for the acquisition of commercial services when —

(i) The service is acquired under a contract awarded using —

(A) Competitive procedures (e.g., the procedures in 6.102, the set-aside procedures in Subpart 19.5, or competition conducted in accordance with Part 13);

(B) The procedures for other than full and open competition in 6.3 provided the agency receives offers that satisfy the Government's expressed requirement from two or more responsible offerors; or

(C) The fair opportunity procedures in 16.505, if placing an order under a multiple award delivery-order contract; and

(ii) The contracting officer

(A) Executes a determination and findings (D&F) for the contract, in accordance with paragraph (b)(2) of this section (but see paragraph (c) of this section for indefinite-delivery contracts), that no other contract type authorized by this subpart is suitable;

(B) Includes a ceiling price in the contract or order that the contractor exceeds at its own risk; and

(C) Authorizes any subsequent change in the ceiling price only upon a determination, documented in the contract file, that it is in the best interest of the procuring agency to change the ceiling price.

DFARS 212.207 contains the following additional constraints on using these types of contracts for commercial services:

(b) In accordance with Section 805 of the National Defense Authorization Act for Fiscal Year 2008 (Pub. L. 110-181), use of time-and-materials and labor-hour contracts for the acquisition of commercial items is authorized only for the following:

(i) Services acquired for support of a commercial item, as described in paragraph (5) of the definition of commercial item at FAR 2.101 (41 U.S.C. 403(12)(E)).

(ii) Emergency repair services.

(iii) Any other commercial services only to the extent that the head of the agency concerned approves a written determination by the contracting officer that —

(A) The services to be acquired are commercial services as defined in paragraph (6) of the definition of commercial item at FAR 2.101 (41 U.S.C. 403(12)(F));

(B) If the services to be acquired are subject to FAR 15.403-1(c)(3)(ii), the offeror of the services has submitted sufficient information in accordance with that subsection;

(C) Such services are commonly sold to the general public through use of time-and-materials or labor-hour contracts; and

(D) The use of a time-and-materials or labor-hour contract type is in the best interest of the Government.

Contractors bear very little risk in these types of contract because they will be paid for labor hours even though they are not used productively. See *CACI, Inc.-Federal v. General Servs. Admin.*, GSBCA 15588, 03-1 BCA ¶ 32,106, rejecting the government's contention that the contractor should not be paid for labor hours expended because it "failed to deliver a usable product." The board granted summary judgment for the contractor reasoning at 158,754-55:

Appellant is correct that it was not required to deliver a usable program, and that it is entitled to be paid for services performed and goods purchased and delivered under the contract even if the contract requirements were not fully met by CACI. Respondent's allegations concerning CACI's failure to [take a step necessary to

1322 **TYPES OF CONTRACTS**

successfully perform] and complete the project are simply not germane, given the legal standard governing recovery in the context of a time and materials endeavor. In essence, these disputed facts are not material to appellant's entitlement to recover. See *Barmag Barmer Maschinenfabrik AG v. Murata Machinery, Ltd.*, 731 F.2d 831, 836 (Fed. Cir. 1984). The outcome is clear — respondent would not prevail even if we were to find these facts in its favor.

See also *E.I.L. Instruments, Inc.*, GSBCA 4459, 76-1 BCA ¶ 11,909, holding that a contractor was entitled to be paid for time spent in unsuccessfully attempting to repair government instruments.

Furthermore, the "ceiling price" in these types of contracts is not a binding contractual requirement but, rather, a limitation of cost — with the result that the contractor is no longer required to perform work when it reaches the ceiling until the government increases the ceiling. See the Payments Under Time-and-Materials and Labor-Hour Contracts clause in FAR 52.232-7, stating:

> (d) *Total cost.* It is estimated that the total cost to the Government for the performance of this contract shall not exceed the ceiling price set forth in the Schedule and the Contractor agrees to use its best efforts to perform the work specified in the Schedule and all obligations under this contract within such ceiling price.

> \* \* \*

> (e) *Ceiling price.* The Government will not be obligated to pay the Contractor any amount in excess of the ceiling price in the Schedule, and the Contractor shall not be obligated to continue performance if to do so would exceed the ceiling price set forth in the Schedule, unless and until the Contracting Officer notifies the Contractor in writing that the ceiling price has been increased and specifies in the notice a revised ceiling that shall constitute the ceiling price for performance under this contract. When and to the extent that the ceiling price set forth in the Schedule has been increased, any hours expended and material costs incurred by the Contractor in excess of the ceiling price before the increase shall be allowable to the same extent as if the hours expended and material costs had been incurred after the increase in the ceiling price.

This provision contains notice requirements similar to those in the cost-reimbursement contract Limitation of Cost clause. Thus, the same legal rules barring contractor recovery for unreported overruns apply to this type of contract, *Abacus Tech. Corp. v. General Servs. Admin.*, GSBCA 16634, 06-1 BCA ¶ 33,250; *Tyrone Shanks*, ASBCA 54538, 06-1 BCA ¶ 33,155; *Corbett Tech. Co.*, ASBCA 49478, 00-1 BCA ¶ 30,801, *recons. denied*, 00-2 BCA ¶ 31.049; *Ragsdale, Beals, Hooper & Seigler v. Department of the Treasury*, GSBCA 13142-TD, 96-1 BCA ¶ 27,930. See also *Dawkins Gen. Contractors & Supply, Inc.*, ASBCA 48535, 03-2 BCA ¶ 32,305, stating this rule and noting that, when the ceiling is reached, the contractor is also permitted to stop work until additional funding is provided. A claim for a constructive change in the work would permit a price adjustment to the ceiling under the

FAR 52.243-3 Changes clause for time-and-materials or labor-hour contracts. See *Bendix Field Eng'g Corp.*, ASBCA 10124, 66-2 BCA ¶ 5959.

The contract clauses used in time-and-materials and labor-hour contracts also place little risk on the contractor. The Inspection — Time-and-Material and Labor-Hour clause in FAR 52.246-6 requires in ¶ (f) that the contractor "replace or correct services or materials that at the time of delivery failed to meet contract requirements," but calls for compensation for such work under normal payment procedures except that the hourly rates are to be reduced by the amount of profit in the rate. The only limitation on this payment is in ¶ (h) which states that correction or replacement will be "without cost to the government" if due to "fraud, lack of good faith, or willful misconduct on the part of the Contractor's managerial personnel" or as a result of conduct of an employee "selected or retained" by the contractor when managerial personnel had "reasonable grounds to believe that the employee is habitually careless or unqualified. The Termination (Cost-Reimbursement), Alternate IV in FAR 52.249-6 provides that, in the event of a default termination, the contractor will be paid the hourly rate for materials and services delivered and accepted by the government. For those materials and services not delivered and accepted, the clause requires exclusion from the hourly rate of that portion "allocable to profit." Neither clause indicates how that amount of profit in the hourly rate is to be determined.

Time-and-materials and labor-hour contracts can be awarded for a single specified amount of work, but they are more frequently used as the basis for pricing tasks to be specified after contract award. In that situation, they are subject to the limitations imposed on "task order contracts" — as discussed in the following section on indefinite-delivery contracts.

The initial step required in preparing a time-and-materials or labor-hour contract is to determine the classes or types of labor that will be required to perform the work and the qualification standards that each type of labor must meet. Agreed rates are required to be included in the contract for each category of labor provided by the contractor and its subcontractors (the term "subcontractor" is not defined). When a contract for noncommercial services is awarded after obtaining adequate price competition, the Time-and-Materials/Labor-Hour Proposal Requirements — Non-Commercial Item Acquisition With Adequate Price Competition solicitation provision in FAR 52.216-29 allows offerors to propose "blended rates" for either contractor or subcontractor employees. However, DoD does not permit blended rates. This is accomplished by requiring the use of an Alternate I to the FAR 52.216-29 provision which is set forth in DFARS 252.216-7002. When such a contract is awarded without adequate price competition, the rates must be separate rates for the contractor and its subcontractors. See FAR 16.601(c) stating:

> (2) *Fixed hourly rates.* (i) The contract shall specify separate fixed hourly rates that include wages, overhead, general and administrative expenses, and profit for each category of labor (see 16.601(e)(1)).

(ii) For acquisitions of noncommercial items awarded without adequate price competition (see 15.403-1(c)(1)), the contract shall specify separate fixed hourly rates that include wages, overhead, general and administrative expenses, and profit for each category of labor to be performed by —

(A) The contractor;

(B) Each subcontractor; and

(C) Each division, subsidiary, or affiliate of the contractor under a common control.

(iii) For contract actions that are not awarded using competitive procedures, unless exempt under paragraph (c)(2)(iv) of this section, the fixed hourly rates for services transferred between divisions, subsidiaries, or affiliates of the contractor under a common control —

(A) Shall not include profit for the transferring organization; but

(B) May include profit for the prime contractor.

(iv) For contract actions that are not awarded using competitive procedures, the fixed hourly rates for services that meet the definition of commercial item at 2.101 that are transferred between divisions, subsidiaries, or affiliates of the contractor under a common control may be the established catalog or market rate when —

(A) It is the established practice of the transferring organization to price interorganizational transfers at other than cost for commercial work of the contractor or any division, subsidiary or affiliate of the contractor under a common control; and

(B) The contracting officer has not determined the price to be unreasonable.

If a contract does not specify subcontractor hourly rates (such as when a new subcontractor is obtained after award of the contract), the contractor must either obtain a contract amendment adding the rates or bill the subcontract costs as material costs constituting "subcontracts for . . . incidental services for which there is not a labor category specified in the contract" pursuant to ¶ (b)(1)(ii)(B) of the Payments Under Time-and-Materials and Labor-Hour Contracts clause in FAR 52.232-7. In the latter case, the contractor would be precluded from including its profit as part of the subcontractor billing.

Contractors and subcontractors must exercise great care to ensure that they only use employees that meet the labor qualifications for their category of labor that are described in the contract because the Payments Under Time-and-Materials and

Labor-Hour Contracts clause in FAR 52.232-7 provides for payment for only such labor. The clause is silent with regard to payment for labor that does not meet the labor qualifications. Paragraph (a) of the clause contains the following guidance on payment for labor:

> (2) The amounts shall be computed by multiplying the appropriate hourly rates prescribed in the Schedule by the number of direct labor hours performed.

> (3) The hourly rates shall be paid for all labor performed on the contract that meets the labor qualifications specified in the contract. Labor hours incurred to perform tasks for which labor qualifications were specified in the contract will not be paid to the extent the work is performed by employees that do not meet the qualifications specified in the contract, unless specifically authorized by the Contracting Officer.

> (4) The hourly rates shall include wages, indirect costs, general and administrative expense, and profit. Fractional parts of an hour shall be payable on a prorated basis.

> \* \* \*

> (8) Unless the Schedule prescribes otherwise, the hourly rates in the Schedule shall not be varied by virtue of the Contractor having performed work on an overtime basis. If no overtime rates are provided in the Schedule and overtime work is approved in advance by the Contracting Officer, overtime rates shall be negotiated. Failure to agree upon these overtime rates shall be treated as a dispute under the Disputes clause of this contract. If the Schedule provides rates for overtime, the premium portion of those rates will be reimbursable only to the extent the overtime is approved by the Contracting Officer.

See *Dawkins Gen. Contractors & Supply, Inc.*, ASBCA 48535, 03-2 BCA ¶ 32,305, where, although missing from the contract, this clause was included in a time-and-materials contract by operation of law.

When competitive proposals are received for these types of contract, the contracting officer should closely analyze the elements of the proposal to determine that the price and estimated costs are fair and reasonable. However, the contracting officer need not obtain cost or pricing data and perform a detailed cost analysis if adequate competition has been obtained, *Milcom Sys. Corp.*, Comp. Gen. Dec. B-255448.2, 94-1 CPD ¶ 339; *Research Mgmt. Corp.*, 69 Comp. Gen. 368 (B-237865), 90-1 CPD ¶ 352.

Lack of clarity in the contract can lead to serious disputes over the proper billing of labor-hours. See *Software Research Assocs.*, ASBCA 33578, 88-3 BCA ¶ 21,046, where the contractor was permitted to bill the hourly rates for consultants. The government had argued that consultants were in the nature of material to be paid at actual cost, but the board reasoned that the consultants did the same work as employees of the contractor. See also *Emerson-Sack-Warner Corp.*, Comp. Gen. Dec. B-206123, 82-2 CPD ¶ 488, where the original IFB was unclear as to whether the contractor could bill the hourly rate for travel time. The procurement was canceled and readvertised under a solicitation that made it clear that such time was not to be reimbursed. A contractor may not recover underestimated indirect costs by billing for extra hours, *Progressive Mach. Works, Inc.*, ASBCA 28785, 85-2 BCA ¶ 18,018. Contractors must also have adequate records to substantiate the hours billed, *JANA, Inc. v. United States*, 936 F.2d 1265 (Fed. Cir. 1991), *cert. denied*, 502 U.S. 1030 (1992) (government recovered payments made to contractor that could not be substantiated in subsequent audit).

Prior to 2007 the Payments Under Time-and-Materials and Labor-Hour Contracts clause in FAR 52.232-7 clause appeared to require that subcontractor effort by treated as material costs with the result that the contractor could not include profit on such work. Two major issues arose under this clause. The first was the proper treatment of subcontracts. Some contractors argued that when the direct work on the contract was performed by subcontractors, that work should be paid for at the contractual hourly rates. This did not appear to be the correct interpretation of the clause unless the contractual schedule of rates specifically includes rates for subcontractor employees. See *Serco, Inc. v. Pension Benefit Guaranty Corp.*, CBCA 1695, 11-1 BCA ¶ 34,662, rejecting the argument that the contractor could add indirect costs and profit to subcontractor costs. See also *Compliance Corp.*, ASBCA 35317, 89-2 BCA ¶ 21,832, rejecting the contractor's claim that it was entitled to bill for overhead on these subcontractor costs because the contract contained no provision calling for the payment of such costs.

The other major issue was the treatment of material handling costs. Since the clause permitted contractors to include such costs in labor rates or as material costs in accordance with their usual accounting practices, GAO held that an unequal bidding situation is created. See *Beta Indus., Inc.*, 60 Comp. Gen. 487 (B-200121), 81-1 CPD ¶ 391, suggesting that bidders be required to state in the bid which method they would use. There was no FAR guidance on this issue. See also *Ray Serv. Co.*, 64 Comp. Gen. 528 (B-217218), 85-1 CPD ¶ 582, holding that there is nothing intrinsically improper about including material handling costs in the hourly rate. In *General Eng'g & Mach. Works v. Sean C. O'Keefe*, 991 F.2d 775 (Fed. Cir. 1993), the court affirmed a board decision at 92-3 BCA ¶ 25,055 that the contractor was not entitled to charge a 15% material handling rate because it did not collect its material handling costs in a separate cost pool, as required by the contract. The court reasoned that this was a proper interpretation in order to avoid the possibility that the contractor could obtain double compensation for material handling in both the labor and material charges. Similarly, in *Bemol Corp. v. Department of the Treasury*, GS-BCA 16374-TD, 05-1 BCA ¶ 32,897, the contractor's claim for material handling costs was denied because it did not collect the costs separately and did not present evidence convincing the board that the costs were not included in the indirect costs that were part of its labor rates.

## B.  Cost-Reimbursement Term Contracts

The cost-reimbursement term type contract describes the work to be performed in terms of a level of effort. FAR 16.306(d) provides the following guidance on this form of contract:

(2) The term form describes the scope of work in general terms and obligates the contractor to devote a specified level of effort for a stated time period. Under this form, if the performance is considered satisfactory by the Government, the fixed fee is payable at the expiration of the agreed-upon period, upon contractor statement that the level of effort specified in the contract has been expended in performing the contract work. Renewal for further periods of performance is a new acquisition that involves new cost and fee arrangements.

* * *

(4) The term form shall not be used unless the contractor is obligated by the contract to provide a specific level of effort within a definite time period.

When an agency adds hours of effort and extends the contract period into a new fiscal year, the appropriation for that year should be used, *Funding for Air Force Cost Plus Fixed Fee Level of Effort Contract*, Comp. Gen. Dec. B-277165, 2000 CPD ¶ 54.

Although this FAR guidance on term type contracts pertains explicitly only to CPFF contracts, agencies have commonly used term form contracts on all types of cost-reimbursement contracts. See EPAAR 1552.211-73 prescribing a Level of Effort — Cost Reimbursement Term Contract clause for cost-no-fee, cost sharing, CPFF, CPIF and CPAF contracts. This clause provides for no fee adjustment if the level of effort falls within 90% and 110% of the prescribed amount.

FAR 35.005(c) provides the following guidance on work statements for level of effort research contracts:

In reviewing work statements, contracting officers should ensure that language suitable for a level-of-effort approach, which requires the furnishing of technical effort and a report on the results, is not intermingled with language suitable for a task-completion approach, which often requires the development of a tangible end item designed to achieve specific performance characteristics. The wording of the work statement should also be consistent with the type and form of contract to be negotiated (see 16.207 and 16.306(d)). For example, the work statement for a cost-reimbursement contract promising the contractor's best efforts for a fixed term would be phrased differently than a work statement for a cost-reimbursement completion contract promising the contractor's best efforts for a defined task. Differences between work statements for fixed-price contracts and cost-reimbursement contracts should be even clearer.

Contracting agencies have a great deal of latitude in deciding how to express the required level of effort. The principal objective should be to state the desired effort in sufficient detail so as to assure that the government gets the type and amount of effort it wants while leaving contractors enough flexibility to adjust to new circumstances without the need for repeated contract amendments. The required effort can be expressed in the amount of time to be devoted to performance through the use of terms such as labor-hours, labor-days, or labor-months. In addition, different types of effort can be specified by stating that amount of effort required of different categories of personnel. However, too much detail may greatly limit the flexibility of the contractor in performing the work. Maximum flexibility is achieved under clauses that specify a range of required effort as in the following:

Level of Effort

Recognizing that this contract is a term form within the meaning of DAR 3-405.6(d)(2), the contractor shall devote to the research hereunder not less than 1,250,000 direct man-hours nor more than 1,360,000 direct man-hours.

The government also builds flexibility into Level of Effort clauses through provisions stating that deviations in effort up to certain limits will be acceptable and will not effect other contract provisions.

Most cost type level of effort contracts are for specified work, but some of these contracts may call for work to be done as tasks are ordered up to a ceiling number of labor-hours. Such contracts are subject to the limitations on task order contracts discussed below in the section on indefinite-delivery contracts.

When a cost-reimbursement level of effort contract is awarded competitively, the contracting officer must make a cost realism analysis, as discussed in Chapter 10, to determine the probable costs of performance of the contract. See, for example, *SRS Techs.*, Comp. Gen. Dec. B-291618.2, 2003 CPD ¶ 70, holding that adjusting the protester's labor rates upward to account for uncompensated overtime was improper when the rates were based on average rates including uncompensated overtime. See also *Advanced Commc'n Sys., Inc.*, Comp. Gen. Dec. B-283650, 2000 CPD ¶ 3, and *Telos Corp.*, Comp. Gen. Dec. B-279493.3, 98-2 CPD ¶ 30, sustaining the contracting officer's determination that the winning offeror's labor rates were realistic, and *Delta Research Assocs., Inc.*, Comp. Gen. Dec. B-254006.2, 94 1 CPD ¶ 47, sustaining the contracting officer's determination that the most realistic probable cost of performance was at the proposed indirect cost rates rather than at the ceiling on those rates that had been proposed by the offeror.

Since this type of level of effort contract is a cost-reimbursement contract, the contract will contain a Limitation of Cost clause providing that the contractor need not expend effort when its actual costs reach the cost estimate, and the government is not bound to compensate for costs incurred above the estimate. If the contract is incrementally funded, the contract will contain a Limitation of Funds clause. These clauses will be enforced in the same manner that they would in completion type cost-reimbursement contracts, with the contractor being denied overrun funding if the required notices are not given, *JJM Sys., Inc.*, ASBCA 51152, 03-1 BCA ¶ 32,192. However, the Level of Effort clause is controlling as to the fee to be paid and can be controlling as to the contractor's entitlement to incurred costs. See *Space Tech. Labs., Inc.*, ASBCA 7676, 1962 BCA ¶ 3609, where the board disallowed costs attributable to labor-hours in excess of the stated monthly maximum level of effort. In *Booz, Allen & Hamilton, Inc.*, EBCA 116-3-80, 80-2 BCA ¶ 14,796, the board held that the fact that the government added funds to the contract in order to permit the contractor to continue to provide labor-hours up to the stated maximum level of effort did not entitle the contractor to additional fee. In reaching this result, the board relied upon the following clause:

> In the event that during the period of this contract, the Contracting Officer shall issue Task Assignments requiring an effort of greater than *48,635* DPMH but less than *59,440* DPMH, the fixed fee of this contract shall not be adjusted. However, in the event that the contractor shall be required to furnish effort greater than *59,440* DPMH or less than *48,635* the estimated cost and fixed fee shall be adjusted.

Compare *International Space Corp.*, ASBCA 13883, 70-2 BCA ¶ 8519, where the board found that the only "practicable effect" of a generally worded level-of-effort clause was to establish the minimum effort that the contractor had to expend in order to earn the contract's fixed fee. See also *Falcon Research & Dev. Co.*, ASBCA 26678, 83-1 BCA ¶ 16,437, where the board granted a pro rata reduction in fee when the level of effort was not attained, and *PRC Info. Scis. Co.*, EBCA 171-5-81, 82-2 BCA ¶ 15,866, where the board disagreed with the contractor's contention that the full fee was earned when the estimated costs were fully expended.

The government has been held liable when its estimate of the number of labor hours to be procured is far higher than the number of hours required. Thus, in *Sanford Cohen & Assocs., Inc.*, IBCA 4239/00, 04-2 BCA ¶ 32,738, the board held that the government was liable for a negligently prepared estimate of the number of labor hours. As a result, the board rejected the government's claim for a pro rata reduction in the fixed fee as called for by the contract's level of effort provisions and remanded the case to the parties "for a determination of damages based on an equitable adjustment in the price of hours delivered." Similarly, in *SocioTechnical Research Applications, Inc.*, IBCA 3969, 03-1 BCA ¶ 32,214, the board awarded damages to a contractor that had retained staff anticipating that the agency would order the estimated number of labor hours. Compare *RJO Enter., Inc.*, ASBCA 50981, 03-1 BCA ¶ 32,137, holding that the government had not breached the a cost-reimbursement level of effort contract by not ordering the estimated hours because the contract was for an indefinite delivery/indefinite quantity (IDIQ) term type CPFF contract under which the government had ordered far more than the minimum amount of work.

## C. Fixed-Price, Level-of-Effort Term Contract

While a fixed-price, level of effort term contract is listed as a fixed-price type contract in the FAR, it is similar to a cost-reimbursement term type contract except that, rather than paying for the costs of a specified number of labor hours, the agency pays the price upon the incurrence of the labor hours. Thus, this type of contract imposes little risk on the contractor. When a solicitation requests firm fixed-price offers or quotations, the agency can reject fixed-price level of effort offers or quotations because they do not require the pricing risk entailed by firm fixed prices, *Mangi Envtl. Group, Inc.*, Comp. Gen. Dec. B-294597, 2004 CPD ¶ 238.

FAR 16.207-2 provides the following guidance:

A firm-fixed-price, level-of-effort term contract is suitable for investigation or study in a specific research and development area. The product of the contract is usually a report showing the results achieved through application of the required level of effort. However, payment is based on the effort expended rather than on the results achieved.

FAR 16.207-3 places the following limitations on the use of this type of contract:

This contract type may be used only when —

    (a) The work required cannot otherwise be clearly defined;

    (b) The required level of effort is identified and agreed upon in advance;

    (c) There is reasonable assurance that the intended result cannot be achieved by expending less than the stipulated effort; and

    (d) The contract price is $150,000 or less, unless approved by the chief of the contracting office.

Since this is a fixed-price type contract, no cost realism or price realism analysis is required although an agency can assess performance risk if it chooses to, *AllWorld Language Consultants, Inc.*, Comp. Gen. Dec. B-291409, 2003 CPD ¶ 13.

No clauses are included in the FAR for this type of contract. However, the contract should contain a schedule of the types of effort required. Failure to expend the effort should lead to a pro rata reduction in payment while complete expenditure of the required labor-hours should result in full payment without regard to the level of accomplishment of the work called for by the contract.

# VI. VARIABLE QUANTITY CONTRACTS

Variable quantity contracts obligate the contractor to furnish articles or services in quantities to be ordered by the government within specified maximum amounts. While the contractor is firmly obligated, the government's obligation is more malleable and depends upon the technique used. The techniques discussed in this section are contained in two parts of the procurement regulations. FAR 16.5 describes the requirements contract and the indefinite delivery/indefinite quantity (IDIQ) contract with stated minimum and maximum quantities. FAR 17.1 permits the use of the multi-year contract providing for firm contractual commitments over a number of years if there are both continued need and appropriations to cover the later years. FAR 17.2 permits the use of options by government procuring activities.

These types of contracts, permitting the government to vary the quantity of the work, can use any of the pricing arrangements previously discussed in this chapter. Thus, they can be fixed-price, cost-reimbursement, incentive, time-and-materials or labor-hours. See FAR 16.501-2(c). For a case where the distinction between the ordering arrangement and the pricing arrangement was not clear, see *Sociotechnical Research Applications, Inc.*, IBCA 3969-98, 01-1 BCA ¶ 31,235.

The common characteristic of these types of contracts is that they permit government agencies to enter into binding arrangements for supplies or services that have not yet been identified as firm requirements or for which funds have not yet been appropriated. One advantage of such arrangement is that it allows the government to buy supplies or services in sufficient quantities over longer periods in order to induce contractors to introduce techniques that promote more efficient performance of the contract at reduce prices. This policy of using contracts that call for economic quantities of supplies is contained in 10 U.S.C. § 2384a and 41 U.S.C. § 3310(a) and implemented in FAR Subpart 7.2. The latter statute states:

> Each executive agency shall procure supplies in such quantities as (A) will result in the total cost and unit cost most advantageous to the United States, where practicable, and (B) does not exceed the quantity reasonably expected to be required by the agency.

The use of variable quantity contracts greatly increases an agency's ability to meet the objectives of these statutes when an agency has not identified current requirements supported by appropriated funds sufficient to support an immediate procurement of economic quantities yet it may be aware, from past experience, that such requirements will become available over time.

Another advantage of these types of contract is that they reduce the administrative costs of issuing numerous contracts as requirements become firm. Prior to the 1990s it was common practice to procure supplies and services annually as appropriated funds because available. However, as agencies adopted less streamlined procurement practices (see Chapter 6) and contracting offices were reduced in size, annual buying became less practicable. The result was a massive increase in the use of variable quantity contracts — often covering many years of supplies or services. While this has led to reduced administrative costs and a more stable flow of work under contracts, it has the significant disadvantage of depriving government agencies of access to new companies that might be able to fulfill their requirements more effectively or at lower prices. It also deprives the government of any benefits that might derive from regular competition for a product or a service. Contracting agencies should weigh the advantages and disadvantages of long-term variable quantity contracts in making the decision to use these types of contract.

In some of the forms of contract discussed below, the government legally binds itself to purchase the goods or services during a given period of time if the need materializes and is funded. In others, the government obligates itself to purchase an initial quantity or minimum quantity but makes no further legally binding commitment to the contractor. The basic ordering agreement, FAR 16.703, is not discussed in this section since neither party is contractually bound in this arrangement. Such agreements can constitute open offers which would form a contract upon acceptance by the government but which have no legal effect until that time.

It can be argued that a lower price will be obtained when the government is obligated to buy a significant amount from the contractor. However, since almost all government contracts contain a Termination for the Convenience of the Government clause, giving the government the right to terminate the contract virtually at will, there is much less distinction among the actual government obligation under the various forms of variable quantity contract than would appear at first glance. Thus, any given agency will use one variable quantity form of contract in preference to another primarily because it has used that form successfully in the past and secondarily because that form may be well adapted to dealing with that agency's peculiar problems such as fiscal or administrative requirements.

## A. Statutory Requirements

Almost all variable quantity contracts state the contractor's obligation in terms of open-ended commitments to perform work in the future upon the issuance of a task or delivery order (FAR 16.502 describes another type of task or delivery order contract, the little-used indefinite delivery/definite quantity contract, which is not discussed in this section.) Such a provision makes them subject to the provisions of the Federal Acquisition Streamlining Act of 1994 (FASA), Pub. L. No. 103-355, dealing with "task order contracts" and "delivery order contracts," 10 U.S.C. §§ 2304a-2304d and 41 U.S.C. §§ 4101-06. The following definitions are contained in 10 U.S.C. § 2304d and 41 U.S.C. § 4101:

(1) The term "task order contract" means a contract for services that does not procure or specify a firm quantity of services (other than a minimum or maximum

quantity) and that provides for the issuance of orders for the performance of tasks during the period of the contract.

(2) The term "delivery order contract" means a contract for property that does not procure or specify a firm quantity of property (other than a minimum or maximum quantity) and that provides for the issuance of orders for the delivery of property during the period of the contract.

These statutory provisions are implemented in FAR Subpart 16.5, covering indefinite-delivery/indefinite-quantity contracts. Other types of contracts, such as requirements contracts or level-of-effort contracts, may also provide for the ordering of work by tasks without calling for a "firm quantity" of work. If so, they would be subject to these statutes even though the FAR does not specify that they are covered.

One major purpose of these statutes is to ensure that these types of contracts will be sufficiently precise to enable offerors to ascertain the scope of the work to be ordered so that they can submit meaningful offers. See 10 U.S.C. § 2304a and 41 U.S.C. § 4103(b), stating:

(b) *Solicitation*. The solicitation for a task or delivery order contract shall include the following:

(1) The period of the contract, including the number of options to extend the contract and the period for which the contract may be extended under each option, if any.

(2) The maximum quantity or dollar value of the services or property to be procured under the contract.

(3) A statement of work, specifications, or other description that reasonably describes the general scope, nature, complexity, and purposes of the services or property to be procured under the contract.

See *Valenzuela Eng'g, Inc.*, Comp. Gen. Dec. B-277979, 98-1 CPD ¶ 51, containing letters from GAO to the Secretaries of the Air Force and the Army criticizing their services for using and issuing a contract with a statement of work that was so broad that it did not comply with this statute. GAO described the overly broad work statement as follows:

[The] request for proposals (RFP) [called for] "Operation and Maintenance (O&M) and incidental repair and replacement services for Government facilities." The RFP's work statement identifies no specific facilities or locations at which these services are to be performed. It provided that the services being acquired "will include operation, preventive maintenance, commissioning, management, and incidental repair and replacement of all systems, equipment, and components inherent in Government facilities such as but not limited to medical, non-medical, training, administrative, plants, labs and storage facilities." These facilities were initially limited by location "in the continental United States, Hawaii and Alaska," but this was subsequently modified to add the words "and outside the continental United States."

Compare *CW Gov't Travel, Inc.*, Comp. Gen. Dec. B-295530.2, 2005 CPD ¶ 139 (procurement of worldwide military transportation services not too broad); *Phoenix Scientific Corp.*, Comp. Gen. Dec. B-286817, 2001 CPD ¶ 24 (IDIQ contract to provide unplanned maintenance services for all Air Force-managed weapons systems not too broad where Air Force placed concrete reviewable limits on availability of contract). In *Computers Universal, Inc.*, Comp. Gen. Dec. B-293548, 2004 CPD ¶ 78, GAO did not object to a very broad "statement of objectives" as the basis for a procurement, noting, however, its "concern about whether the use of such broad long-term IDIQ contracts undermines the efficiencies that full and open competition would produce."

In order to ensure that competition is maximized, these statutes favor the award of *multiple contracts* over single contracts for a designated series of task orders or delivery orders. See 10 U.S.C. § 2304a(d) which grants authority to make single awards but states:

(3)(A) No task or delivery order contract in an amount estimated to exceed $ 100,000,000 (including all options) may be awarded to a single source unless the head of the agency determines in writing that—

(i) the task or delivery orders expected under the contract are so integrally related that only a single source can reasonably perform the work;

(ii) the contract provides only for firm, fixed price task orders or delivery orders for—

(I) products for which unit prices are established in the contract; or

(II) services for which prices are established in the contract for the specific tasks to be performed;

(iii) only one source is qualified and capable of performing the work at a reasonable price to the government; or

(iv) because of exceptional circumstances, it is necessary in the public interest to award the contract to a single source.

(B) The head of the agency shall notify the congressional defense committees within 30 days after any determination under clause (i), (ii), (iii), or (iv) of subparagraph (A).

(4) The regulations implementing this subsection shall—

(A) establish a preference for awarding, to the maximum extent practicable, multiple task or delivery order contracts for the same or similar services or property under the authority of paragraph (1)(B); and

(B) establish criteria for determining when award of multiple task or delivery order contracts would not be in the best interest of the Federal Government.

41 U.S.C. § 4103(d)(3) contains substantially the same language except that the congressional notification requirement is only applicable when the ¶ (A)(iv) justification for a single source is used. This multiple award preference is implemented in FAR 16.504(c) with regard only to IDIQ contracts.

10 U.S.C. § 2304b(e) and 41 U.S.C. § 4105 contain special limitations on task order contracts for "advisory and assistance services" if the contract period exceeds three years and the estimated contract amount is over $10 million. In such cases, a single contract can be awarded only if the head of the executive agency determines that because the services required under the contract are unique or highly specialized, it is not practicable to award more than one contract. "Advisory and assistance services" are defined in 31 U.S.C. § 1105(g)(2)(A) as follows:

[T]he term "advisory and assistance services" means the following services when provided by nongovernmental sources:

(i) Management and professional support services.

(ii) Studies, analyses, and evaluations.

(iii) Engineering and technical services.

A more complete definition of advisory and assistance services is included in FAR 2.101. See *Nations, Inc.*, Comp. Gen. Dec. B-272455, 96-2 CPD ¶ 170, holding that, pursuant to this expansive FAR definition, training services were included in management and professional support services. See also *Cubic Applications, Inc. v. United States*, 37 Fed. Cl. 345 (1997), holding that a procurement to conduct "computer driven battle simulation exercises" was a procurement of advisory and assistance services.

10 U.S.C. § 2304a(f) imposes limits on the length of the ordering period in task and delivery order contracts awarded by DoD, NASA and the Coast Guard. The original limit of five years was adopted in § 843 of the National Defense Authorization Act for Fiscal Year 2004, Pub. L. No. 108-136, Nov. 24, 2003. The statute was amended the following year to lengthen the ordering period to ten years with a five years limit on the initial contract, § 813 of the National Defense Authorization Act for Fiscal Year 2005, Pub. L. No. 108-375, Oct. 28, 2004. These statutes are implemented in DFARS 217.204(e). The limitations do not apply to other agencies of the government. See, however, FAR 17.204(e) containing a general five-year limitation

on the length of all contracts except those for information technology. See also 10 U.S.C. § 2304b(b) and 41 U.S.C. § 4105(c) limiting the ordering period of advisory and assistance service contracts to five years with a permissible extension of six months if necessary to award a follow-on contract. See FAR 16.505(c).

## B. Requirements Contracts

A requirements contract is a contract where one party promises to buy all or a designated part of its requirements from another party. FAR 16.503(a) contains the following narrow definition:

> A requirements contract provides for filling all actual purchase requirements of designated Government activities for supplies or services during a specified contract period, with deliveries or performance to be scheduled by placing orders with the contractor.

This definition only contemplates requirements contracts covering *the entire government quantity* for some class of supplies or services. However, as discussed below, requirements contracts can also be used for designated parts of a government requirement.

FAR 16.506(d) instructs contracting officers to include the Requirements clause at FAR 52.216-21, or one of its four alternates, in all requirements contracts. The basic clause states:

REQUIREMENTS (OCT 1995)

> (a) This is a requirements contract for the supplies or services specified, and effective for the period stated, in the Schedule. The quantities of supplies or services specified in the Schedule are estimates only and are not purchased by this contract. Except as this contract may otherwise provide, if the Government's requirements do not result in orders in the quantities described as " estimated" or " maximum" in the Schedule, that fact shall not constitute the basis for an equitable price adjustment.

> (b) Delivery or performance shall be made only as authorized by orders issued in accordance with the Ordering clause. Subject to any limitations in the Order Limitations clause or elsewhere in this contract, the Contractor shall furnish to the Government all supplies or services specified in the Schedule and called for by orders issued in accordance with the Ordering clause. The Government may issue orders requiring delivery to multiple destinations or performance at multiple locations.

> (c) Except as this contract otherwise provides, the Government shall order from the Contractor all the supplies or services specified in the Schedule that are required to be purchased by the Government activity or activities specified in the Schedule.

(d) The Government is not required to purchase from the Contractor requirements in excess of any limit on total orders under this contract.

(e) If the Government urgently requires delivery of any quantity of an item before the earliest date that delivery may be specified under this contract, and if the Contractor will not accept an order providing for the accelerated delivery, the Government may acquire the urgently required goods or services from another source.

(f) Any order issued during the effective period of this contract and not completed within that period shall be completed by the Contractor within the time specified in the order. The contract shall govern the Contractor's and Government's rights and obligations with respect to the order to the same extent as if the order were completed during the contract's effective period; *provided*, that the Contractor shall not be required to make any deliveries under this contract after [insert date].

If the contract is for less than the full requirements of the government, as discussed below, the clause must be tailored to fit the precise circumstances of the procurement.

FAR 52.216-18 provides an Ordering clause to be inserted in all requirements contracts as well as other indefinite-delivery contracts. In addition to stipulating the time period during which orders may be issued, the clause provides that the order is binding when issued:

(c) If mailed, a delivery order or task order is considered " issued" when the Government deposits the order in the mail. Orders may be issued orally, by facsimile, or by electronic commerce methods only if authorized in the Schedule.

Boards have ruled that, in accordance with this provision, orders are binding when deposited in the mail, *Canadian Commercial Corp.*, ASBCA 20067, 75-2 BCA ¶ 11,441, and *Victory Container Corp.*, GSBCA 5596, 81-2 BCA ¶ 15,346. Note that the clause permits oral, facsimile and electronic orders only if called for by a separate schedule clause. In *General Dynamics C4 Sys., Inc.*, ASBCA 54988, 08-1 BCA ¶ 33,779, the requirement was strictly enforced by ruling that the contractor was not bound by electronically issued orders sent to the contractor on the last days of the final ordering period. This decision was reversed by *Mabus v. General Dynamics C4 Sys., Inc.*, 633 F.3d 1356 (Fed. Cir. 2011), on the grounds that the contractor was estopped from asserting that the clause was binding because it had accepted electronic orders for over four years.

## 1. *Nature of Requirements Contracts*

A requirements contract provides the contractor with both the legal right and the legal duty to supply goods or services in an amount that is determined by *the government's need* rather than by a fixed quantity. See *Torncello v. United States*, 231 Ct. Cl. 20, 681 F.2d 756 (1982); and *Mason v. United States*, 222 Ct. Cl. 436,

615 F.2d 1343 (1980). The consideration of the government that makes this a legally binding contract is *its promise to satisfy its needs by buying only from the contractor or contractors with contracts.* A contract containing language that abrogates this promise is not an enforceable requirements contract, *Satellite Servs., Inc.*, Comp. Gen. Dec. B-280945, 98-2 CPD ¶ 125 (statement that agency could order from others when "in the best interests of the Government" precludes a requirements contract); *Sea-Land Serv., Inc.*, Comp. Gen. Dec. B-266238, 96-1 CPD ¶ 49 (Limitation of Government Liability clause giving government the blanket right to obtain the services from other companies overrides requirements promise).

Any contract under which an agency of the government undertakes to order all, or any specified portion, of its needs for a product or service during a designated period of time from a single contractor will be classified as a requirements contract. The key feature is that the legal obligation of the government is defined by its *needs* rather than by a fixed amount. See *East Bay Auto Supply, Inc.*, ASBCA 25542, 81-2 BCA ¶ 15,204, stating that the "good faith duty to order all requirements from the contractor renders the contract enforceable, and not illusory." Accord *A-Transport Nw. Co. v. United States*, 27 Fed. Cl. 206 (1992), *aff'd*, 36 F.3d 1576 (1994); *Hilton's Cleaners, Inc.*, ASBCA 18213, 74-1 BCA, ¶ 10,433; *Export Packing & Crating Co.*, ASBCA 16133, 73-2 BCA ¶ 10,066. Under this type of contract, the government is bound to order its requirements from the contractor but is under no obligation to have requirements as long as the absence of requirements is in good faith.

Whether a contract is in fact a requirements contract depends not upon the label attached to it by the parties but, rather, upon the nature of the rights and duties created by the contract, *Ceredo Mortuary Chapel, Inc. v. United States*, 29 Fed. Cl. 346 (1993); *Ralph Constr., Inc. v. United States*, 4 Cl. Ct. 727 (1984). See, for example, *Centurion Elecs. Serv.*, ASBCA 51956, 03-1 BCA ¶ 32,097, finding that a contract was a requirements contract despite absence of the FAR 52.216-21 clause because the contract required the contractor to perform all repairs of specified equipment. In the event that the issue is litigated, the court or board will look first to the terms of the contract to determine its type. For example, in *Torncello v. United States*, 231 Ct. Cl. 20, 681 F.2d 756 (1982), the court held that when the Navy contracted for an indefinite quantity of ground maintenance services, with no guaranteed minimum amount, implicit in the terms was a promise to forgo diverting work to other contractors. Accord *Myers Investigative & Sec. Servs., Inc. v. United States*, 47 Fed. Cl. 605 (2000). In *Local Communications Network, Inc.*, ASBCA 55154, 08-1 BCA ¶ 33,734, the board held that since the parties clearly intended to enter into a requirements contract, the FAR 52.216-21 clause was incorporated into the contract by operation of law. In contrast, in *Maintenance Eng'rs. v. United States*, 749 F.2d 724 (Fed. Cir. 1984), the court held that all of the language in the contract indicated that it was not a requirements contract even though it included the Requirements clause stating explicitly that it was a requirements contract. See also *Modern Sys. Tech. Corp. v. United States*, 24 Cl. Ct. 360 (1991), *aff'd*, 979 F.2d 200 (Fed. Cir. 1992), holding that a Basic Purchasing Agreement was not a requirements contract because it contained no express promise by the government to obtain its needs from the contractor. Similarly, in *Ann Riley & Assocs.*, DOTBCA 2418, 93-3 BCA ¶ 25,963, the board found that an indefinite-quantity contract was not a requirements contract because it did not include the "essential ingredient of a requirements contract, a statement that the [agency] was obligated to satisfy all of its requirements . . . from this source and no other." The board rejected government testimony that it had intended to enter into a requirements contract and had used such contracts for these services in the past.

The court or board may also consider both facts known to the parties at the time of contracting and prior course of dealing between the parties, even where these are not explicitly mentioned in the contract, *Stanley F. Horton*, DOTCAB 1231, 82-2 BCA ¶ 15,967. In *Crown Laundry & Dry Cleaners, Inc. v. United States*, 29 Fed. Cl. 506 (1993), the court looked to the intentions of the parties to determine that the contract was a requirements contract — even though the contract was labeled an indefinite-quantity contract (with no stated minimum quantity) and did not contain the Requirements clause in FAR 52.216-21. See also *Jez Enter., Inc.*, ASBCA 51851, 00-2 BCA ¶ 30,939, where the board ruled that it could not determine the nature of the contract from its language but was required to hold a hearing to assess the facts underlying the transaction.

Requirements contracts should be distinguished from variable quantity contracts where the amount of work may vary but can be identified by some independent criterion other than the needs of the government. In *Brawley v. United States*, 96 U.S. 168 (1877), the Supreme Court held that a requirements contract resulted when the contractor was obligated to deliver 880 cords of wood, "more or less, as shall be determined to be necessary . . . for the regular supply . . . of the troops." The Court stated at 171-72:

> Where a contract is made to sell or furnish certain goods identified by reference to independent circumstances, such as an entire lot deposited in a certain warehouse, or all that may be manufactured by the vendor in a certain establishment, or that may be shipped by his agent or correspondent in certain vessels, and the quantity is named with the qualification of " about," or " more or less," or words of like import, the contract applies to the specific lot; and the naming of the quantity is not regarded as in the nature of a warranty, but only as an estimate of the probable amount, in reference to which good faith is all that is required of the party making it. . . .

> If, however, the qualifying words are supplemented by other stipulations or conditions which give them a broader scope or a more extensive significancy, then the contract is to be governed by such added stipulations or conditions. As, if it be agreed to furnish so many bushels of wheat, more or less, according to what the party receiving it shall require for the use of his mill, then the contract is not governed by the quantity named, nor by that quantity with slight and unimportant variations, but by what the receiving party shall require for the use of his mill; and the variation from the quantity named will depend upon his discretion and requirements, so long as he acts in good faith.

The most common form of variable quantity contracts where the quantity is identified by "independent circumstances" is the construction contract with unit prices to be paid on the basis of actual work performed. See FAR 36.207 permitting the procurement of construction work on the basis of fixed-unit prices. Although both contracts obligate the government to pay only for the work that is done, the requirements contract is for needs that may arise in the future and will be ordered as they are identified, while the unit-price contract covers work that can be identified by a physical description such as excavation within specified boundaries (requiring no subsequent orders). In other respects, these contracts are quite similar. Although this section is directed to requirements contracts, it uses cases dealing with unit price contracts when the legal principles are the same.

*Brawley* also distinguishes another form of contract that indicates that the quantity of work may vary from a stated amount using terms such as "more or less" or "about." If the contract specifies no other criteria for determining quantity, such as requirements or a physical description, the contract will be construed to permit only slight variation. See *Brawley*, stating at 171-72:

> But when no such independent circumstances are referred to, and the engagement is to furnish goods of a certain quality or character to a certain amount, the quantity specified is material, and governs the contract. The addition of the qualifying words, "about," " more or less," and the like, in such cases, is only for the purpose of providing against accidental variations arising from slight and unimportant excesses or deficiencies in number, measure, or weight.

In determining which form of contract has been entered into, the court will look to all surrounding circumstances as well as the contract language. Thus, a contract to supply "six hundred thousand pounds, more or less, of oats . . . or such other quantity, more or less, as may be required . . . for the wants of said station" was found not to be a requirements contract because the contractor knew that another contract for oats had been awarded simultaneously, *Merriam v. United States*, 107 U.S. 437 (1883). In *Shader Contractors, Inc. v. United States*, 149 Ct. Cl. 535, 276 F.2d 1 (1960), the court looked to the contract terms to find a requirements contract where the contract called for the contractor to collect the amount ordered by the contracting officers as "may be needed." The contract contained an estimated quantity of coal of 5,500 tons and an estimated quantity of refuse of 4,000 tons and contained the provision, "The quantity may vary from 75 percent to 125 percent of the figure." The court ruled that the variation provision did not override the requirements language.

## 2. Use of Requirements Contracts

FAR 16.503(b) contains very general guidance stating that it is appropriate to use a requirements contract —

for acquiring any supplies or services when the Government anticipates recurring requirements but cannot predetermine the precise quantities of supplies or services that designated Government activities will need during a definite period.

While it is clearly less burdensome for a government agency to issue a single requirements contract than to conduct a series of small, individual purchases, the requirements contract is not always preferable to a definite-quantity contract. Thus, although the regulations give no guidance on this issue, the contracting officer should carefully review the agency's needs before issuing a requirements contract. If those needs can be accumulated into an economic ordering quantity, a definite-quantity contract is usually preferable. See FAR Subpart 7.2 implementing 10 U.S.C. § 2384a and 41 U.S.C. § 3310(a), which require the use of economic quantities in purchasing supplies. See also *A.G. Schoonmaker, Inc.*, Comp. Gen. Dec. B-170544, 1971 CPD ¶ 3, where GAO recommended to the DoD that where appropriated funds were available and the agency's needs had been ascertained with reasonable certainty, with only the allocation of funds remaining, the regulations should express a preference for a more definite type of contract in order to achieve more realistic and reasonable bid prices.

While it is clear that a requirements contract is a task order or delivery order contract, the FAR contains no general guidance on the statutory preference for multiple requirements contracts — which could be achieved by issuing two or more requirements contracts for shares of the agency's requirements. The working group that drafted the present FAR explained this omission as follows:

The working group believes multiple awards are inconsistent with the requirements contracts which require a contractor to receive the buyer's entire requirement to establish legal consideration for the contract. See *Appeal of R.C. Swanson Printing & Typesetting Company*, GPOBCA No. 15-90, 1993 WL 668317 (1973). The working group is aware of no legal authority that recognizes the legitimacy of multiple award requirements contracts where a requirement is continuously competed. However, the working group is also aware that some individuals advocate the use of "multiple award requirements contracts."

The prior draft rule attempted to reach a compromise position by including certain elements of secs 1004 and 1054 of FASA in 16.503 while remaining silent on the issue of whether multiple awards may be made. That draft rule was criticized for its ambiguity.

The proposed rule has been revised to essentially retain the current FAR language in 16.503. The proposed rule also includes a limitation on the use of requirements contracts for advisory and assistance services in excess of 3 years and $10,000,000. This limitation is necessary to close a "loophole" so that agencies cannot escape the mandate to make multiple awards for CAAS in excess of the threshold by defining the acquisition as a requirements contract.

Although the proposed rule does not apply the multiple award preference to requirements contracts, the proposed rule does not preclude agencies from experimenting with a multiple award requirements contract if the agency believes it can overcome the legal problems (i.e. illusory promise) related to a multiple award requirements contract.

This intentional ambiguity in the FAR raises the possibility that issuing a single requirements contract may be a statutory violation when the multiple award preference applies. See *Nations, Inc.*, Comp. Gen. Dec. B-272455, 96-2 CPD ¶ 170, where GAO found such a violation when the agency proposed to issue a single requirements contract for simulation training services with a value of over $10 million.

The limitation in FAR 16.503 for advisory and assistance services recognizes that the task and delivery order statutes apply to requirements contracts by stating:

(d) *Limitations on use of requirements contracts for advisory and assistance services.* (1) Except as provided in paragraph (d)(2) of this section, no solicitation for a requirements contract for advisory and assistance services in excess of three years and $13 million (including all options) may be issued unless the contracting officer or other official designated by the head of the agency determines in writing that the services required are so unique or highly specialized that it is not practicable to make multiple awards using the procedures in 16.504.

(2) The limitation in paragraph (d)(1) of this section is not applicable to an acquisition of supplies or services that includes the acquisition of advisory and assistance services, if the contracting officer or other official designated by the head of the agency determines that the advisory and assistance services are necessarily incident to, and not a significant component of, the contract.

### 3. Pricing Arrangement

FAR 16.501-2(c) provides that requirements contracts may use any "cost or pricing arrangement" permitted by the FAR. Thus, these contracts can use any fixed-price, cost-reimbursement, or incentive arrangement or can be a time-and-materials or labor-hour contract. FAR 16.501-2(c) warns:

Cost or pricing arrangements that provide for an estimated quantity of supplies or services (e.g., estimated number of labor hours) must comply with the appropriate procedures of this subpart.

If the government's requirements are for well-defined supplies or tasks, arrangements with fixed unit prices are the most desirable. This permits the most balanced competition and assures the government that it will obtain performance of the contract at the costs that it anticipated. If the contract is for supplies that are not well defined, cost-reimbursement or incentive contracts can be used to ensure that undue risk is not being placed on the contractor. If the contract is for services that are not well defined, a time-and-materials or labor-hour contract can be used to hold the contractor to fixed labor rates while permitting flexibility as to the amount of work that needs to be done to meet the government requirement. Alternatively, a cost-reimbursement contract can be used in these circumstances. These latter types of pricing arrangements, of course, place much of the risk of increased costs on the government.

## 4. Length of Requirements Contracts

As discussed above, there are statutory limitations of ten years on task and delivery order contracts issued by DoD. FAR 17.204(e) also contains a general five year limitation on all contracts. 10 U.S.C. § 2304(d)(3) and 41 U.S.C. § 3304(c)(1) (B) contain a one year limitation on contracts over the simplified acquisition threshold that are awarded without full and open competition based on urgency, unless the head of the agency determines that exceptional circumstances apply.

Requirements contracts may be for a single year or for multiple years. In most cases, requirements contracts for more than one year include options for a specified number of additional years where appropriations are not available at the time of contracting. See, for example, *Free State Reporting, Inc.*, Comp. Gen. Dec. B-259650, 95-1 CPD ¶ 199 (requirements for support services for base year and two option years); *Tulane Univ.*, Comp. Gen. Dec. B-259912, 95-1 CPD ¶ 210 (requirements for services for two base years and three option years). Multiple-year requirements contracts could also be issued as a single document, including later years not covered by current appropriations, if there is no possibility that the contractor could obligate the government by performing work prior to the issuance of a requirement. See 42 Comp. Gen. 272 (B-144641) (1962), where GAO ruled that a requirements contract was in violation of appropriations law because the government would be obligated to pay for work in a later year not covered under the contract. See also 67 Comp. Gen. 190 (B-224081) (1988), and 48 Comp. Gen. 494 (B-164908) (1969). In cases where a requirement contract is used in this way, an agency will normally include an "availability of funds" clause stating that the government will not be liable to pay the contractor until funds for future years have been made contractually available. See *Funding of Maint. Contract Extending Beyond Fiscal Year*, Comp. Gen. Dec. B-259274, 96-1 CPD ¶ 247, where GAO approved a requirements contract where the requirement covered two fiscal years with the second year restricted by an Availability of Funds clause, stating that "a naked contractual obligation that carries with it no financial exposure to the government does not violate the Anti-Deficiency Act." In contrast, the GAO publication *Principles of Federal Appropriations Law (Volume 1)*, January 2004 (*http://www.gao.gov/legal/redbook.html*), states at 5-41 that, in order to comply with appropriations law, such contracts must contain a "renewal option" calling for the government to renew the contract at the beginning of each fiscal year.

Agencies have also used multiyear requirements contracts when multiyear or no-year funds are being used for the procurement. This practice was explicitly permitted by FAR 17.104-4 until 1996, when the provision was deleted from the regulation. It is still legally permissible even though the FAR is silent on the subject. For examples of multiyear requirements contracts, see *Liebert Corp.*, 70 Comp. Gen. 448 (B-232234.5), 91-1 CPD ¶ 413 (agency issued firm-fixed-price requirements contract for services and materials over a five-year period); and *CDI Marine Co.*, Comp. Gen. Dec. B-219934.2, 86-1 CPD ¶ 242 (agency issued a CPFF requirements contract for services performed over a three-year period). In *Mills Mfg. Corp.*, Comp. Gen. Dec. B-224004, 86-2 CPD ¶ 679, *recons. denied*, 87-1 CPD ¶ 393, GAO denied a protest arguing that a three-year requirements contract was improper because the protester could not obtain firm prices from its suppliers for the second and third year.

## 5.  *Structuring the Requirement*

The contracting officer has great flexibility in tailoring a requirements contract to fit the circumstances of each procurement. The government attempts to obtain the best possible price by defining the requirement in such a way that competition can be maximized and risks to the contractor minimized. The government also endeavors to structure such contracts to provide maximum assurance that its needs will be met in a timely manner and that it has the operating flexibility that it needs. The most important aspect of a requirements contract is the statement of the "requirement."

There are a number of ways in which the requirement can be stated to achieve these purposes. FAR 16.503(a) gives the following guidance on limitations on the requirement:

> (2) The contract shall state, if feasible, the maximum limit of the contractor's obligation to deliver and the Government's obligation to order. The contract may also specify maximum or minimum quantities that the Government may order under each individual order and the maximum that it may order during a specified period of time.

There is no guidance on limitations on the timing of ordering requirements, and the contractor bears the risk if the government clusters its orders in one period, *Asfaltos Panamenos, S.A.*, ASBCA 41657, 92-3 BCA ¶ 25,141, or at the end of the contract, *Victory Container Corp.*, GSBCA 5596, 81-2 BCA ¶ 15,346.

The government may also wish to obtain only a part of its overall requirements from one contractor and to obtain the balance from others either through another requirements contract or some other form of contract. In some cases, the requirement may be structured to accommodate performance by government personnel.

### a.  *Limiting the Requirement*

Two types of limitations are commonly used in requirements contracts. First, minimum and maximum order limitations are included in almost all such contracts.

Second, limitations are sometimes included to divide the work between among two or more contractors.

## (1) MINIMUMS AND MAXIMUMS

The government includes minimums and maximums on individual orders and maximums for specified periods of time, FAR 16.503(a)(2). FAR 16.506(b) instructs contracting officers to insert a clause in all requirements contracts that is substantially the same as the following Order Limitations clause at FAR 52.216-19:

(a) *Minimum order.* When the Government requires supplies or services covered by this contract in an amount of less than [*insert dollar figure or quantity*], the Government is not obligated to purchase, nor is the Contractor obligated to furnish, those supplies or services under the contract.

(b) *Maximum order.* The Contractor is not obligated to honor —

(1) Any order for a single item in excess of [*insert dollar figure or quantity*];

(2) Any order for a combination of items in excess of [*insert dollar figure or quantity*]; or

(3) A series of orders from the same ordering office within days that together call for quantities exceeding the limitation in subparagraph (1) or (2) above.

(c) If this is a requirements contract (i.e., includes the Requirements clause at subsection 52.216-21 of the Federal Acquisition Regulation (FAR)), the Government is not required to order a part of any one requirement from the Contractor if that requirement exceeds the maximum-order limitations in paragraph (b) above.

(d) Notwithstanding paragraphs (b) and (c) above, the Contractor shall honor any order exceeding the maximum order limitations in paragraph (b), unless that order (or orders) is returned to the ordering office within days after issuance, with written notice stating the Contractor's intent not to ship the item (or items) called for and the reasons. Upon receiving this notice, the Government may acquire the supplies or services from another source.

Although inartfully drafted, this clause appears to cover only individual orders in the case of minimums, and both individual orders and a series of orders within a specified period in the case of maximums. The FAR contains no guidance on how to determine maximum or minimum order limitations. However, it is clear that the major advantage of minimum order limitations is to assure the contractor that orders will not be placed in such a manner as to be administratively burdensome. These minimum order limitations should not be confused with guaranteed minimums which are used in indefinite-quantity contracts.

Maximum order limitations are apparently intended to permit the contractor to determine the maximum resources that must be committed to the contract at any time during performance. These limitations are essential if performance is required within a short period of time after placement of orders. If more flexibility in the time of performance is granted, these limitations should be stated in terms of a maximum amount of work over a period of time rather than in terms of individual orders or a series of orders. Maximum order limitations also permit the government to avoid its requirements obligation if "one requirement" exceeds the limitations in the clause. Neither the clause nor the FAR provides any guidance as to how to determine when one requirement exists. The government has been permitted to program its requirements to issue orders within a monthly maximum order limitation. In *Victory Container Corp.*, GSBCA 5596, 81-2 BCA ¶ 15,346, the contracting officer ordered the maximum quantity permitted each month in order to build the inventory of the items called for by the contract. The board held that this practice was a good faith use of the requirements contract since the contractor was aware that the items were normally carried in inventory by the government.

While the Order Limitations clause contains no provision for total contract maximum quantities, FAR 16.503(a)(2) instructs the contracting officer to state the maximum quantity or dollar value of the entire contract. Such a contract maximum defines the scope of the original competition and assists the contractor by placing an outside limit on the resources it must commit to the contract. It also benefits the government by permitting it the freedom to seek lower prices after the maximum is reached. Such provisions must be included in the contract schedule or by separate clause. Note, however, that orders placed in excess of the maximum order limitation are not necessarily considered to be outside the scope of the contract. See *Exide Corp.*, Comp. Gen. Dec. B-276988, 97-2 CPD ¶ 51, holding that a delivery order issued under an existing requirements contract for a quantity in excess of the maximum order limitation was not beyond the scope of the contract because the contract permitted orders in excess of maximum quantity and the total quantity ordered under the contract did not significantly exceed the estimated quantity.

## (2) DIVIDING THE REQUIREMENT

In some cases the government can obtain more competition by dividing the requirement among two or more contractors. This technique is particularly useful when the goods or services are normally furnished by smaller contractors and the government's requirements are large. FAR 52.216-21 contains Alternate III for the Requirements clause that covers the situation where the contracting officer decides to divide the requirement between a small business set-aside contractor and a non-set-aside contractor. This provision states, in part:

> The Government may choose between the set-aside Contractor and the non-set-aside Contractor in placing any particular order. However, the Government shall allocate successive orders, in accordance with its delivery requirements, to main-

tain as close a ratio as is reasonably practicable between the total quantities ordered from the two Contractors.

See *Valley Forge Flag Co.*, VABCA 4667, 97-2 BCA ¶ 29,246, holding the government liable for a change outside of the scope of the contract when it ordered a larger percentage of its requirements from a contractor with a requirements contract for 60% of the government's requirements. In reaching this decision, the board stated at 145,486:

> [M]ultiple awards of separate contracts for Government requirements are not uncommon. For example, there may be awards of separate requirements contracts for certain services in separate geographical locations, or requirements for supplies may be split up based on the sizes of the orders. *Property Analysts, Inc.,* Unpub. B-259853, 95-1 CPD ¶ 270; *Pro-Mark, Inc., Unpub.* B-247248, May 18, 1992; *City Wide Press, Inc.,* Unpub. B-231469, 88-2 CPD ¶ 127.

The FAR does not address the potential advantages of dividing requirements between contractors without using set-aside techniques. However, there is no prohibition of such practice, and it is clear that the government might benefit in some circumstances by dividing a requirement geographically, mathematically, or by prescribing the mode of competition to be used in selecting the contractor for each requirement. Dividing the requirement and issuing two or more requirements contracts would also meet the statutory preference for multiple task order or delivery order contracts. For an example of this type of requirements contract, see *Ace-Federal Reporters, Inc. v. Barram*, 226 F.3d 1329 (Fed. Cir. 2000), holding that the government had breached six mandatory Federal Supply Schedule contracts for reporting services that required designated agencies to order all of their reporting requirements for administrative hearings from one of the contractors. The decision does not restrict its reasoning to this unique type of requirements contract but would appear to be applicable to any requirements contracts awarded to multiple contractors that will share the requirement. In *Ace-Federal Reporters, Inc. v. General Servs. Admin.*, GSBCA 13298-REM, 02-2 BCA ¶ 31,913, the board awarded damages for this breach by calculating the profits lost on the work ordered from other contractors and allocating those lost profits to the six contractors based on their share of orders.

## b. Allowing In-House Work

The government may structure the requirement by limiting it to only those requirements in excess of the quantities that the government activity may itself furnish within its own capabilities. The government is thereby obligated to obtain from the contractor only that work "required to be purchased." Alternate I of the Requirements clause at FAR 52.216-21 provides the following provision for this purpose:

> (c) The estimated quantities are not the total requirements of the Government activity specified in the Schedule, but are estimates of requirements in excess

of the quantities that the activity may itself furnish within its own capabilities. Except as this contract otherwise provides, the Government shall order from the Contractor all of that activity's requirements for supplies and services specified in the Schedule that exceed the quantities that the activity may furnish within its own capabilities.

The failure to include this alternate is not dispositive as to whether the government has the right to perform some of the work with its own forces. See *Datalect Computer Servs., Ltd. v. United States*, 40 Fed. Cl. 28 (1997), *aff'd*, 215 F.3d 1344 (Fed. Cir. 1999), *cert. denied*, 529 U.S. 1037 (2000), where the court read ¶ (c) of the Requirements clause in FAR 52.216-21 to permit in-house work. That clause states, "the Government shall order from the Contractor all the supplies or services specified in the Schedule that are required to be purchased by the Government activity . . ." The court concluded that the term "required to be purchased" permitted the government to do work in-house.

The government can also structure such a contract to provide for specific situations where government employees will perform the work. For example, in *Tucson Mobilephone, Inc.*, Comp. Gen. Dec. B-247685, 92-1 CPD ¶ 487, GAO approved a requirements contract that provided for work by government employees when the contractor's personnel were not available or when the work could be done by agency personnel with the equipment on hand.

There is discord among the various courts and boards concerning both the adequacy of consideration where the government retains the right to perform work in-house and the degree of discretion that the government may exercise in performing under such contracts. The confusion stems, in part, from the language in FAR 16.503(a) which states, "A requirements contract provides for filling all actual purchase requirements of designated government activities for specific supplies or services." This occasionally leads to the incorrect conclusion that a requirements contract must obligate the government to buy all of its needs from the contractor. For example, in *Ralph Constr., Inc. v. United States*, 4 Cl. Ct. 727 (1984), the court ruled that because a requirements contract gives the contractor the right to "fill all of the government's needs," and yet the instant contract permitted the government to assign work in-house, the contract was unenforceable because of a lack of mutuality of consideration. This analysis begs the question of what the "requirements" were. The contract itself clearly stated that the supplies and services covered by the contract were not all the government needs but only those "in excess of the quantities which the activity may itself furnish within its own capabilities." Because the contract bound the government to order from the contractor if it ordered at all, there appears to have been sufficient consideration to support the contractor's promise to perform. See also *Modern Sys. Tech. Corp. v. United States*, 24 Cl. Ct. 360 (1991), *aff'd*, 979 F.2d 200 (Fed. Cir. 1992), and *Coyle's Pest Control, Inc. v. Cuomo*, 154 F.3d 1302 (Fed. Cir. 1998), stating that a requirements contract is one calling for the contractor to fulfill *all* of the government's requirements. GAO has followed this view in *Satellite Servs., Inc.*, Comp. Gen. Dec. B-280945, 98-2 CPD ¶ 125, finding a proposed contract illusory because it promised multiple contractors the right to compete for services unless they were "unique" or it was in "the best interest of the Government" to award sole source. See also *JRS Mgmt.*, Comp. Gen. Dec. B-4010524.2, 2010 CPD ¶ 25, where GAO repeated the holding in *Modern Systems* that a requirements contract must call for the government to buy "exclusively" from one contractor.

Some appeals boards have declined to follow the view adopted by the Claims Court in *Ralph Construction*. See *Dynamic Sci., Inc.*, ASBCA 29510, 85-1 BCA ¶ 17,710, holding that such a contract was legally binding. After noting that the government's only obligation was to procure, from the contractor alone, "such requirements as did arise during the contract term that were not to be satisfied by in-house capabilities," the board followed its holding in *Maya Transit Co.*, ASBCA 20186, 75-2 BCA ¶ 11,552, discussing that decision at 88,383:

> We characterized the contract as a "limited form" requirements type. The limitation of the requirement to that portion that the Government did not choose to meet from its own capabilities did not render the promise illusory particularly because the Government was precluded from expanding its capabilities during contract performance at the expense of the contractor.

See also *Operational Serv. Corp.*, ASBCA 37059, 93-3 BCA ¶ 26,190, where the board again reviewed a "limited form" requirements contract, stating that it did not agree with the *Ralph Construction* reasoning and did not believe that the affirmance of the Federal Circuit in the *Modern Systems* decision was an adoption of that reasoning. In *D.M. Summers, Inc.*, VABCA 2750, 89-3 BCA ¶ 22,123, the board held that the government had not breached a requirements contract by using some in-house services because the contractor was aware of this practice when it entered into the contract.

After entering into such a requirements contract, the government may use its discretion in making ordering decisions, subject to a duty to act in good faith. See *Henry Angelo & Sons, Inc.*, ASBCA 15082, 72-1 BCA ¶ 9356, *recons. denied*, 72-2 BCA ¶ 9493, where the contract was for painting services beyond the capability of the Army's own forces, but because of budgetary considerations, the government decided to apply funds to other projects even though the painting was still needed. Further, the government expanded the painting work that was to be accomplished by its own forces. The board held that these actions constituted arbitrary reasons for not placing orders, did not comply with the government's duty of good faith, and constituted a partial termination. See also *Maya Transit Co.*, ASBCA 20186, 75-2 BCA ¶ 11,552, where, although the government undertook to buy only those bus services "in excess of the quantities which the activity may itself furnish within its own capabilities," it was not permitted to reduce the services ordered by reordering its budget priorities and redistributing its capabilities to assume more bus routes for its own drivers. In contrast, in *Export Packing & Crating Co.*, ASBCA 16133, 73-2 BCA ¶ 10,066, the government's decision to assign work to civilian employees, rather than order from the contract, was approved and the contract for services "which are required to be purchased by the Government" was upheld. In *Arcon-Pacific Contractors*, ASBCA 25057, 82-2 BCA ¶ 15,838, the board held that "[a]bsent bad faith, the government had discretion to determine what painting was required to be purchased." In exercising that discretion, the government was permitted to consider the most economical way of meeting its needs and to assign work in-house in a cost-effective manner.

### c.  Measuring the Work Required

Another aspect of structuring the requirement is selecting the units of measure that will be used in ordering. When the government procures goods, choosing the appropriate measure is simple. When the government structures a requirements contract for services, however, it may choose to order by either unit of work actually completed or by unit of time. This choice affects the risks that each party bears.

The most common approach is to estimate, order, and pay for services on the basis of units of work supplied. The government may, for example, contract for painting services on a per-square-foot basis, *Arcon-Pacific Contractors*, ASBCA 25057, 82-2 BCA ¶ 15,838; for renovation services based on multiple descriptions of renovation work with separate prices, *MDP Constr., Inc.*, ASBCA 49527, 96-2 BCA ¶ 28,525; or for motor vehicle maintenance on a per-vehicle-serviced basis, *S & W Tire Servs., Inc.*, GSBCA 6376, 82-2 BCA ¶ 16,048. Under this type of contract, the contractor assumes the risk that each unit of work can be performed profitably at the contract unit prices without regard to variations between actual and estimated quantities. In addition, both parties assume the risk of quantity variations when such variations increase or decrease the unit costs of performance.

The government also contracts for services by unit of time. One way to do this is on an hourly basis using a labor-hour or time-and-materials pricing arrangement. For example, in *Stanley F. Horton*, DOTCAB 1231, 82-2 BCA ¶ 15,967, the government ordered snow removal services at an hourly rate. The consequences of structuring the requirement on an hourly basis are similar to those of the unit of work situation except that there is significantly less contractor risk since the contractor is paid for the hours actually incurred in performing the work. Nevertheless, this type of contract is useful in situations where the work is not easily quantifiable in other units and is also subject to fluctuation in requirements.

## 6.  Government Estimates

To provide equal information to all offerors as to the expected amount of supplies or services required and to provide a basis for evaluating the proposed prices, the government includes estimated quantities of the work in the solicitation and uses these estimates to evaluate the offers. FAR 16.503(a) states:

(1) For the information of offerors and contractors, the contracting officer shall state a realistic estimated total quantity in the solicitation and resulting contract. This estimate is not a representation to an offeror or contractor that the estimated quantity will be required or ordered, or that conditions affecting requirements will be stable or normal. The contracting officer may obtain the estimate from records of previous requirements and consumption, or by other means, and should base the estimates on the most current information available.

GAO has ruled that it is improper merely to evaluate units prices or fixed labor rates without the use of estimates, *R&G Food Serv., Inc.*, Comp. Gen. Dec. B-296435.4, 2005 CPD ¶ 194, *recons. denied*, 2005 CPD ¶ 201. See the discussion below of evaluation of IDIQ contract prices.

Paragraph (a) of the Requirements clause in FAR 52.216-21 indicates that the government is not liable for incorrect estimates as follows:

> Except as this contract may otherwise provide, if the Government's requirements do not result in orders in the quantities described as "estimated" or "maximum" in the Schedule, that fact shall not constitute the basis for an equitable price adjustment.

## a. Liability for Incorrect Estimate

Notwithstanding the above language in the Requirements clause, the government is obligated to use care in calculating estimated quantities. However, a variation between the estimated quantity and the actual quantity does not in itself establish a basis for contractor relief, *Bannum, Inc. v. Department of Justice*, DOTBCA 4450, 05-2 BCA ¶ 33,049; *Special Waste, Inc.*, ASBCA 36775, 90-2 BCA ¶ 22,935; *Standard-Southern Corp.*, ASBCA 20964, 77-1 BCA ¶ 12,359, *aff'd*, 223 Ct. Cl. 669 (1980). See also *Willamette Indus., Inc.*, Comp. Gen. Dec. B-188548, 79-2 CPD ¶ 338, holding that discrepancies between estimated and actual quantities of up to 80% were insufficient to afford a legal basis for relief. The government's estimate of its needs is not generally regarded as a warranty that such amounts will be required, *Shader Contractors, Inc. v. United States*, 149 Ct. Cl. 535, 276 F.2d 1 (1960).

The decisions granting relief to contractors for faulty government estimates have varied in their statement of the standard of conduct to which the government is to be held. Some early cases stated that the government's only obligation was to use good faith in its estimates, *Wheeler Bros.*, ASBCA 13089, 69-2 BCA ¶ 7861 (good faith error in estimating spare parts on hand); *Sponge Fishing Co.*, GSBCA 1386, 65-1 BCA ¶ 4627 (22,000 estimated, 53,967 ordered, but no recovery because estimate made in good faith). Thus, it was believed that in order to support recovery for an incorrect estimate, the government's estimate had to be made in bad faith. See Comp. Gen. Dec. B-169037, May 4, 1970, *Unpub.*, approving the contracting officer's settlement of a breach of contract claim based on bad faith.

More recently, the government has been held to a somewhat higher degree of care. The rationale supporting these decisions is based upon *Womack v. United States*, 182 Ct. Cl. 399, 389 F.2d 793 (1968), which, although not involving a requirements contract, held the government liable on a misrepresentation theory for faulty estimates furnished for bidding purposes. Following the reasoning of *Womack*, the Federal Circuit has held that the contractor is not required to prove bad faith in order to recover, *Rumsfeld v. Applied Cos.*, 325 F.3d 1328 (Fed. Cir.), *cert. denied*, 540 U.S. 981 (2003). Earlier decisions had also concluded that the government should be held to a *negligence* standard. See *Clearwater Forest Indus., Inc. v. United States*, 227 Ct. Cl. 386, 650 F.2d 233 (1981) (stating that in making estimates, the government "must act in good faith and use reasonable care"); and *Integrity Mgmt. Int'l, Inc.*, ASBCA 18289, 75-1 BCA ¶ 11,235, *recons. denied*, 75-2 BCA ¶ 11,602 (reviewing prior decisions and granting relief because of government negligence in preparing estimates). See also *Datalect Computer Servs., Ltd. v. United States*, 40 Fed. Cl. 28 (1997) (relief granted because government was negligent in that it knew of several facts that would likely affect estimate); *Crown Laundry & Dry Cleaners, Inc. v. United States*, 29 Fed. Cl. 506 (1993) (relief granted because government was negligent in not checking estimates whose accuracy had been questioned by government personnel during preparation of solicitation); *Travel Centre v. General Servs. Admin.*, GSBCA 14057, 98-1 BCA ¶ 29,422, *recons. denied*, 98-1 BCA ¶ 29,541 (relief granted because GSA knew or should have known that the estimates provided were vastly overstated); *Ambulance Serv. & Transp. of Marlin*, VABCA 3485, 94-2 BCA ¶ 26,729 (relief granted because government failed to adequately utilize available information when making estimate); *Viktoria Fit Internationale Spedition*, ASBCA 39703, 92-2 BCA ¶ 24,968 (relief granted when contracting officer provided no convincing rationale for arriving at the estimate); *McCotter Motors, Inc.*, ASBCA 30498, 86-2 BCA ¶ 18,784 (relief granted when government used disproportionately high prior-year quantity without determining whether that figure was an accurate forecast); *Pied Piper Ice Cream, Inc.*, ASBCA 20605, 76-2 BCA ¶ 12,148 (adopting reasonable care standard and finding government grossly negligent); *American Maint. & Mgmt. Servs., Inc.*, ASBCA 18756, 75-2 BCA ¶ 11,407, *recons. denied*, 75-2 BCA ¶ 11,572 (stating contractor is entitled to honest and informed estimate, but finding no negligence). In *Atlantic Garages, Inc.*, GSBCA 5891, 82-1 BCA ¶ 15,479, where the government's solicitation for large-scale engine repair was restricted to contractors in a geographical area where large-scale organizations could not be expected to be operating, the government was held to an enhanced duty to consider the potential effect of faulty estimates on smaller contractors. Compare *Medart, Inc.*, GSBCA 8939, 91-2 BCA ¶ 23,741, *aff'd*, 967 F.2d 579 (Fed. Cir. 1992), finding no liability for very inaccurate estimates because the agency had used the prior-year quantities, as suggested by FAR 16.503(a)(1), as the basis for the estimate. In affirming, the Federal Circuit stated at 582:

> The government may go beyond the requirements of the regulations, of course. And it might be well advised to do so if it wants to secure the best prices and avoid

contractors raising their bids to cover the uncertainties. But we are in no position to impose such a requirement either in this case or as a general proposition in the face of the regulations promulgated by competent authority. The regulations explicitly say that estimates may be based on the most current information about previous requirements available; Medart knew this, as well as who bore the risks of variances in quantity. It should have factored the risks into its bid . . . just as the regulation was factored into the contract.

See also *Apex Int'l Mgmt. Servs., Inc.*, ASBCA 37813, 94-1 BCA ¶ 26,299, where the board found no negligence because the agency had used historical workload figures to compile its estimates; *American Marine Decking Servs., Inc.*, ASBCA 44440, 97-1 CPD ¶ 28,821, where the board found no negligence where the agency had based its estimate on work in another location because it had no experience at the location covered by the contract; and *Federal Group,, Inc. v. United States*, 67 Fed. Cl. 87 (2005), where the court found no negligence where the agency disclosed that its estimate was subject to change because of government downsizing.

Where the government acts in good faith and without negligence but the estimate is grossly inaccurate, the contractor may be entitled to relief if the resulting contract is unconscionable. That result was reached in *Operational Serv. Corp.*, ASBCA 37059, 93-3 BCA ¶ 26,190.

The most common type of faulty estimate occurs when the agency fails to consider all relevant, available information, *Grover Contracting Corp.*, GSBCA 4115, 75-2 BCA ¶ 11,550. See *Hi-Shear Tech. Corp. v. United States*, 53 Fed. Cl. 420 (2002), *aff'd*, 356 F.3d 1372 (Fed. Cir. 2004) (estimate of quantities of spare parts did not reflect returned parts that could be repaired); *National Salvage & Serv. Corp.*, ASBCA 53750, 04-2 BCA ¶32,654 (estimate was not adjusted to reflect internal decisions on likelihood of ordering work); *Contract Mgmt., Inc.*, ASBCA 44885, 95-2 BCA ¶ 27,886 (estimate was not adjusted for anticipated budget shortfall); *Pruitt Energy Sources, Inc.*, ENGBCA 6134, 95-2 BCA ¶ 27,840 (estimate was not adjusted for shorter contract base period than those of prior contracts); *Fa. Kammerdiener GmbH & Co., KG*, ASBCA 45248, 94-3 BCA ¶27,197 (government had information rendering its estimate inaccurate well before award); and *Crown Laundry & Dry Cleaners, Inc.*, ASBCA 28889, 85-2 BCA ¶ 18,003 (government ignored available workload figures in estimating its requirements). GAO has also stated that relief in the form of contract reformation can be granted when the government has not based its estimate "on all relevant information that is reasonably available to it," *Lone Star Energy Co.*, Comp. Gen. Dec. B-199049, 80-2 CPD ¶ 98; *Union Carbide Corp.*, Comp. Gen. Dec. B-188426, 77-2 CPD ¶ 204, and that the estimates must be "reasonably accurate representations of anticipated actual needs," *CardioMetrix*, Comp. Gen. Dec. B-252758.3, 94-1 CPD ¶ 316; *Richard M. Walsh Assocs.*, Comp. Gen. Dec. B-216730, 85-1 CPD ¶ 621; *Yamas Constr. Co.*, Comp. Gen. Dec. B-217459, 85-1 CPD ¶ 599.

The Court of Claims held that, in making its estimate, the government must give consideration to all potential work, whether or not "firm" requirements exist, *Chemical Tech., Inc. v. United States*, 227 Ct. Cl. 120, 645 F.2d 934 (1981). A possible way for the government to avoid this problem is to provide estimates based on firm data and to inform the offerors of additional data that may indicate greater or fewer requirements. See *International Bus. Invs., Inc.*, Comp. Gen. Dec. B-215081, 85-1 CPD ¶ 228, where GAO denied a protest alleging that workload estimates in the IFB were not based upon the best available information, reasoning, in part, that because the information that the protester asserted to be more accurate was provided by letter to all of the bidders prior to their response to the solicitation, no prejudice had occurred to the protester.

Where the contractor fills government orders far exceeding the estimates without objecting to the validity of the estimates, the contractor will be estopped from later challenging the estimates, *Standard-Southern Corp.*, ASBCA 20964, 77-1 BCA ¶ 12,359, *aff'd*, 223 Ct. Cl. 669 (1980).

### b.  Contractor Obligation to Fulfill Requirements Exceeding Government Estimate

Subject to any contract or order maximums in the schedule, the requirements contractor must supply the full requirement regardless of the extent to which it may exceed the estimate, *Kasehagen Sec. Servs., Inc.*, ASBCA 25629, 86-2 BCA ¶ 18,797; *Sponge Fishing Co.*, GSBCA 1386, 65-1 BCA ¶ 4627. Where the contractor fails to fulfill that obligation, it will be held liable for excess costs incurred by the government in reprocurement of any items that the government would have been entitled to order under the contract, irrespective of whether orders had actually been placed with the defaulted contractor, *Interroyal Corp.*, GSBCA 5439, 83-1 BCA ¶ 16,339.

This same result would not be reached under the *Uniform Commercial Code* (U.C.C.) § 2-306(1), which states that a contractor has no obligation to provide quantities "unreasonably disproportionate to any stated estimate." In *Miltex Indus., Inc.*, ASBCA 19449, 77-2 BCA ¶ 12,768, the board rejected the application of this provision, holding that federal precedent in this area consistently limited contractor liability only when the government made a bad faith estimate. Accord *Machlett Labs., Inc.*, ASBCA 16194, 73-1 BCA ¶ 9929.

Commercial impracticability has been used to avoid the contractor's obligation to supply required services. In *Selectronix Commc'ns*, ASBCA 20981, 77-1 BCA ¶ 12,547, a default termination was converted to a termination for the convenience of the government when the inventory requirements necessary for contractor compliance with an Air Force communications system repair schedule were deemed commercially impracticable.

## c.  Relief for Faulty Government Overestimate

Contractors have frequently submitted claims for relief when quantity under-runs were the result of faulty estimates. While the promulgation of such estimates are breaches of contract, *Atlantic Garages, Inc.*, GSBCA 5891, 82-1 BCA ¶ 15,479, the boards have sometimes dealt with such claims as terminations for convenience, *Integrity Mgmt. Int'l, Inc.*, ASBCA 18289, 75-1 BCA ¶ 11,235, *recons. denied*, 75-2 BCA ¶ 11,602; *Pied Piper Ice Cream, Inc.*, ASBCA 20605, 76-2 BCA ¶ 12,148. It has now been determined that such breaches of contract do not permit the recovery of lost profit on the incorrect estimated quantity but should be remedied by repricing the contract to pay the contractor the price that it would have offered had it known the amount of a correct estimate, *Rumsfeld v. Applied Cos.*, 325 F.3d 1328 (Fed. Cir.), *cert. denied*, 540 U.S. 981 (2003). See *Hi-Shear Tech. Corp. v. United States*, 356 F.3d 1372 (Fed. Cir. 2004), holding that a proper computation of this repricing was the award of "fixed overhead" on the lost sales plus G&A on that overhead. The court also held that reliance damages were not a proper measure of damages in this instance. See also *Admiral Elevator v. Soc. Sec. Admin.*, CBCA 470, 08-2 BCA ¶ 33,884, where the amount for a faulty estimate was determined by computing the difference between the amount the contractor was paid and the amount it would have been paid had the estimate been correct minus the cost of material not needed and the price for work not performed. Compare *Datalect Computer Servs., Ltd. v. United States*, 56 Fed. Cl. 178 (2003), *aff'd*, 97 Fed. Appx. 333 (Fed. Cir. 2004), where the court rejected a repricing claim because the contractor could not submit sufficient proof to permit computation of the amount of the repricing. *Applied Cos* also held that the situation should be treated as a termination for convenience if the government ordered no quantities as a result of the faulty estimate.

## 7.  Variations in Estimated Quantities Clauses

The government often uses clauses that provide for price adjustment when government requirements vary from the estimate by more than stated percentages. There is no standard variation in quantity clause prescribed for requirements contracts, but FAR 52.211-18 provides a Variations in Estimated Quantities clause for use in construction contracts. Many requirements contracts contain similar clauses calling for price adjustments for quantities varying from the estimate by more than a stated percentage. The Variations in Estimated Quantities clause is applicable to the entire contract not the delivery or task orders issued under the contract, *Emerson Constr. Co.*, ASBCA 55165, 06-2 BCA ¶ 33,382.

The government has unsuccessfully argued that these clauses protect it from liability for faulty estimates or improper actions during performance. In *Integrity Mgmt. Int'l, Inc.*, ASBCA 18289, 75-1 BCA ¶ 11,235, *recons. denied*, 75-2 BCA ¶ 11,602, the board found that the government had made a faulty estimate and reasoned that the clause did not bind the contractor to assume the burden of the first

25% of the government's negligence. In *Chemical Tech., Inc. v. United States*, 227 Ct. Cl. 120, 645 F.2d 934 (1981), the court granted relief even though the deviation from the estimated quantity fell within the range of the Volume Variation clause, stating, "In its dealings with contractors, the government cannot provide inaccurate data in this manner and then be allowed to bar an equitable recovery by arguing that the resulting damages . . . fall within the 25% Volume Variation clause." It has also been held that a variation in quantity clause will not apply if the original government estimate is negligently made, *Marine Constr. & Dredging, Inc.*, ASBCA 38538, 95-1 BCA ¶ 27,286; *John Murphy Constr. Co.*, AGBCA 418, 79-1 BCA ¶ 13,836.

Clauses of this type will not prevent the contractor from obtaining a price adjustment under the Differing Site Conditions clause when the variation in quantity occurs because of a condition that falls within the bounds of that clause. For example, in *Continental Drilling Co.*, ENGBCA 3455, 75-2 BCA ¶ 11,541, a changed condition was found when the contractor had to use a substantially larger quantity of a drill hole casing than the estimated quantity. The board reasoned that the government estimate of a small amount of drill hole casing was an indication that a certain type of subsurface material would be encountered, whereas the need to use a large quantity of the casing indicated that a different type of material was actually present at the site. In *A.S. Horner, Inc.*, ASBCA 76-145, 79-1 BCA ¶ 13,561, a changed condition was found when the contractor had to use different methods to excavate a trench deeper than had been anticipated, and in *Brezina Constr., Inc.*, ENGBCA 3215, 75-1 BCA ¶ 10,989, a changed condition was found where the contractor was required to dispose of a large amount of material off-site although the parties had anticipated that there would be an approximate balance between the excavated material and the material used for fill. In *Brezina*, the board found a changed condition rather than a variation in quantity because the contractor had encountered an "entirely different job" than anticipated. Similarly, in *United Contractors v. United States*, 177 Ct. Cl. 151, 368 F.2d 585 (1966), the court held that the Differing Site Conditions clause was applicable when unforeseen conditions were encountered, stating at 171:

> The [VEQ] clause is a ready vehicle for adjusting, with a minimum of haggling, the compensation received by contractors who are called upon in the course of performance to do, within limits, more or less work than could be estimated. But we have held that clauses of this type do not control when the cost of doing the extra work greatly differs from the stated unit-price because of factors not foreseen by either party. In that event, the [Differing Site Conditions] clause comes into play and overrides the [VEQ] clause.

This rule has been followed in *Met-Pro Corp.*, ASBCA 49694, 98-2 BCA ¶ 29,776 (very large variation from estimated quantity due to incorrect analysis of conditions at site); *Continental Drilling Co.*, ENGBCA 3455, 75-2 BCA ¶ 11,541 (very large variation from estimated quantity because of cave in due to unforeseen soil condition).

The Changes clause has also been held to override the Variations in Estimated Quantities clause in situations where the government orders the contractor to perform unit priced work in excess of that contemplated when the quantity estimates were established. For example, in *Morrison-Knudsen Co. v. United States*, 184 Ct. Cl. 661, 397 F.2d 826 (1968), the court found the contractor entitled to a price adjustment under the Changes clause when the government overcame unforeseen conditions by ordering the contractor to perform the work in a different manner. Similarly, in *ThermoCor, Inc. v. United States*, 35 Fed. Cl. 480 (1996), the court held that the Changes clause could override the Variations in Estimated Quantities clause but denied summary judgment in order to conduct a trial to determine whether the overrun in quantities had been caused by changes. See also *Flat Head Contractors, LLC v. Department of Agriculture*, CBCA 118, 07-1 BCA ¶ 33,556, where the need to construct a wall higher than indicated in the specifications was found to be a change that overrode the variation in quantity clause; and *C.H. Leavell & Co.*, ENGBCA 3492, 75-2 BCA ¶ 11,596, where a contracting officer's order to change the concrete mixtures was held to be a change rather than a variation in quantity of the contract's unit price for cement. Compare *Luedtke Eng'g Co.*, ASBCA 54226, 05-2 BCA ¶ 32,971, and *CEMS, Inc. v. United States*, 59 Fed. Cl. 168 (2003), rejecting the contractor's contention that changes had occurred which would have overridden the Variations in Quantity clause. In *Maya Transit Co.*, ASBCA 20186, 75-2 BCA ¶ 11,552, the board held that the clause was not intended to apply to a constructive change.

Normally, variation in quantity clauses provide that the unit prices set forth in the contract are to apply to all quantities of work within the range specified in the clause. Thus, price adjustments on overruns will be made only to that quantity above the stated percentage. In *N. Fiorito Co. v. United States*, 189 Ct. Cl. 215, 416 F.2d 1284 (1969), it was held that this type of clause binds the parties to the unit prices for quantities of work up to the full extent of the variation range (110% of the estimated quantity in the clause in question) with repricing to occur only as to the quantities in excess of the range.

These clauses do not provide for complete repricing of the work above or below the range. The clause in FAR 52.212-11 provides that any equitable adjustment under the clause will be based on increases or decreases in cost "due solely to the variation." In *Victory Constr. Co. v. United States*, 206 Ct. Cl. 274, 510 F.2d 1379 (1975), the court held that the party demanding the adjustment had the burden of proof that the costs had varied because of the difference in quantity. The court further stated that the amount of the equitable adjustment was to be determined solely on the basis of differences in cost because of the larger or smaller quantity rather than on a complete repricing of the work based on actual incurred costs for the excess quantity. The Federal Circuit followed and more fully explained this reasoning in *Foley Co. v. United States*, 11 F.3d 1032 (Fed. Cir. 1993). See also *ThermoCor, Inc. v. United States*, 35 Fed. Cl. 480 (1996); *Clement-Mtarri Cos.*, ASBCA 38170, 92-3 BCA ¶ 25,192, *aff'd*, 11 F.3d 1072 (Fed. Cir. 1993). Compare *Burnett Constr.*

*Co. v. United States*, 26 Cl. Ct. 296 (1992); *Bean Dredging Corp.*, ENGBCA 5507, 89-3 BCA ¶ 22,034, and *Carvel Walker*, ENGBCA 3744, 78-1 BCA ¶ 13,005, decided before *Foley* and interpreting *Victory* as calling for adjusting the price of an overrun quantity based on the total costs of the additional quantity rather than the increased costs due to the additional quantity. These cases have been effectively overruled by *Foley*.

One of the most common reasons for a price adjustment is that the increase or decrease in quantity will alter the amount of fixed costs allocable to each unit. In *Henry Angelo & Co.*, ASBCA 43669, 94-1 BCA ¶ 26,484, the board included in the adjustment for a severe underrun in estimated quantity an amount for indirect costs that would have been recovered if the estimated quantity had been ordered. Compare *P.R. Contractors, Inc. v. United States*, 76 Fed. Cl. 621 (2007), rejecting a claim for unrecovered overhead, profit, bond and taxes due to an underrun in quantities because the contractor did not prove "increased costs" of the underrun. In *Cottrell Eng'g Corp.*, ENGBCA 3038, 70-2 BCA ¶ 8462, the board found a difference in cost due to the larger quantity based on the full recovery of nonrecurring costs in the unit prices for the estimated quantity. The board therefore granted a downward equitable adjustment removing the nonrecurring costs from the unit prices for the purposes of paying for the overrun quantity. In *S & T Enters.*, AGBCA 2001-159-1, 03-2 BCA ¶ 32,282, the board denied a price increase for overrun quantities because the contractor did not prove that its increased costs were caused by the overrun. A dissenting judge argued that there should have been an adjustment because there was proof that the cost of the overrun quantity was higher than the cost of the quantity within the clause. In *KiSKA Constr. Corp.-USA and Kajima Eng'g & Constr., Inc., A Joint Venture*, ASBCA 54613, 09-1 BCA ¶ 34,089, the board granted compensation for increased quantities outside the variation range at the contract unit prices because the contractor did not claim that higher costs were incurred. In *Ronald Adams Contractor, Inc.*, AGBCA 91-155-1, 94-3 BCA ¶ 27,018, the board denied a price adjustment for either party because neither had proved that the significant overrun had altered the contractor's costs of performance.

## 8.  Government Failure to Order Its Requirements Under the Contract

The contractor is not entitled to compensation if the government's failure to place orders results from either risks assumed by the contractor or good faith decisions of the government to reduce its activity because of unanticipated changes in its situation. See *Technical Assistance Int'l, Inc. v. United States*, 150 F.3d 1369 (Fed. Cir. 1998), rejecting the argument that the contractor should be entitled to relief if the government's requirements changed because the facts underlying the estimate changed. In that decision, the court equated lack of good faith with bad faith, stating at 1373:

[I]n a requirements contract case in which the seller alleges that the buyer breached the contract by reducing its requirements, the burden of proof is on the seller to prove that the buyer acted in bad faith, for example, by reducing its requirements solely in order to avoid its obligations under the contract. In the absence of such a showing, the buyer will be presumed to have varied its requirements for valid business reasons, *i.e.*, to have acted in good faith, and will not be liable for the change in requirements.

See also *Lockheed Martin Aircraft Center*, ASBCA 55164, 08-1 BCA ¶ 33,832, requiring the contractor to prove bad faith when the government performed part of the requirement with its own forces. It is not clear whether intentional diversion of work constitutes bad faith but most of the decisions discussed below have granted relief on that basis.

### a.  Obtaining Needs from Alternate Source

Relief has been granted to contractors when the government has improperly failed to order its requirements under the contract and has obtained its needs from another source or has accomplished the work in-house. In *C&S Park Serv., Inc.*, ENGBCA 3624, 78-1 BCA ¶ 13,134, the contractor was allowed to recover for losses incurred due to the reduction in work caused by government personnel performing the lawn maintenance services covered by a contract that made no allowances for in-house performance. See also *Datalect Computer Servs., Ltd. v. United States*, 56 Fed. Cl. 178 (2003), *aff'd*, 97 Fed. Appx. 333 (Fed. Cir. 2004) (agency obtained maintenance work by extending warranty of original supplier); *Vehicle Maint. Servs. v. General Servs. Admin.*, GSBCA 11663, 94-2 BCA ¶ 26,893 (work diverted to other vendors); *Erwin v. United States*, 19 Cl. Ct. 47 (1989) (work bought from other vendors); *Arcon-Pacific Contractors*, ASBCA 25057, 82-2 BCA ¶ 15,838 (government ordered another contractor to do work); *North Chicago Disposal Co.*, ASBCA 25535, 82-1 BCA ¶ 15,488 (government had no right to retroactively recoup an amount paid to a contractor where the bulk of the job was actually performed by Navy personnel ignorant of the contract); *Inland Container, Inc. v. United States*, 206 Ct. Cl. 478, 512 F.2d 1073 (1975) (government requisitioned most of the goods from the GSA); *Maya Transit Co.*, ASBCA 20186, 75-2 BCA ¶ 11,552 (government performed work in-house because of budget considerations); and *Pacific Tech. Enters., Ltd.*, ASBCA 17087, 74-2 BCA ¶ 10,679 (government diverted some of its requirements to another contractor). In *MDP Constr., Inc.*, ASBCA 49527, 96-2 BCA ¶ 28,525, the government breached a requirements contract for renovation of bathrooms by including bathroom renovation in a larger contract for renovation of total buildings. Similarly, in *S & W Tire Servs., Inc.*, GSBCA 6376, 82-2 BCA ¶ 16,048, the board held that the government was in breach of a requirements contract for tire recapping when, during the contract period, it hired a new contractor to run its entire motor pool, thereby depriving the original contractor of the recapping business. But where the contractor had actual knowledge, prior to bidding, of the government's capacity for performing work in-house and of its intent to do so, the contractor was held to have bid in full realization that it would only be called upon to perform in the event that the government's capability proved inadequate to meet its requirements, *Stanley F. Horton*, DOTCAB 1231, 82-2 BCA ¶ 15,967. See also *Pegasus Aviation, Inc. v. General Servs. Admin.*, GSBCA 10112, 93-3 BCA ¶ 25,944, where the board held that the government had not diverted work where the contract provided six exceptions in which services would be sought elsewhere.

In determining whether a breach has occurred, the court or board will review the specification to ensure that the work obtained from another contract is the same work as that under the requirements contract. In *Cleek Aviation v. United States*, 19 Cl. Ct. 552 (1990), the court found no breach of a requirements contract for supplying aviation fuel directly into airplanes when the agency ordered aviation fuel for storage tanks from another contractor. The court reasoned that the two types of services were essentially different. See also *Eastern Ambulance Servs., Inc.*, VABCA 2078, 86-2 BCA ¶ 18,852, where the board found that award of a contract with a company to transport "stretcher" patients did not violate a requirements contract to provide ambulance services. The board compared the two types of services and found them dissimilar even though the "stretcher" patients could receive some medical services in transit. Compare *T&M Distributors, Inc.*, ASBCA 51279, 01-2 BCA ¶ 31,442, making numerous findings on the scope of a requirements contract and holding that supplying parts for vehicles included supplying parts for components of those vehicles.

Another factor in the interpretation of the requirements covered by the contract is the contemporaneous interpretation of the contract by the parties. In *Metropolitan Area Transit, Inc.*, VABCA 7022, 05-2 BCA ¶ 32,970, this evidence was used to deny recovery because the contractor had not contended that the contract covered services that it subsequently claimed were within its scope.

Contractors have been required to submit evidence of specific transactions that have amounted to diversions of work from the contract, *United Med. Supply Co. v. United States*, 63 Fed. Cl. 430 (2005). However, the government must preserve the evidence in its possession that will prove that work was diverted. In *United Med. Supply Co. v. United States*, 77 Fed. Cl. 257 (2007), the court sanctioned the government for destroying such evidence — by precluding the cross-examination of the contractor's expert witness that reconstructed the evidence to fill in the gaps that had been destroyed, by precluding the government from presenting expert testimony on those gaps, and by assessing the contractor's costs of this effort to the government.

### b.  Government Change in Work

The contractor may also be entitled to relief on a theory that a government change in work has occurred. In *Desco Serv. Contractors*, ASBCA 21856, 77-2 BCA ¶ 12,752, a change occurred when the government decreased the frequency of vehicle maintenance inspections under the contract. See also *California Bus Lines*, ASBCA 19732, 75-2 BCA ¶ 11,601 (change in work plan reducing amount of work necessary to meet government's unchanged requirements constituted a constructive change); and *Del Rio Flying Serv.*, ASBCA 15304, 71-1 BCA ¶ 8744 (government change in definition of "students," resulting in decreased work is compensable if increased costs result).

The changes theory will not cover reductions in the government's needs that occur because of changed circumstances, *Padilla v. United States*, 58 Fed. Cl. 585 (2003) (reduced work because of Congressional moratorium on project requiring work); *East Bay Auto Supply, Inc.*, ASBCA 25542, 81-2 BCA ¶ 15,204 (reduction of fleet at base contractor was servicing caused a decline in demand for spare vehicle parts); *Solano Aircraft Serv., Inc.*, ASBCA 20677, 77-2 BCA ¶ 12,584 (military commitments in Southeast Asia reduced the number of available domestic aircraft to be serviced); *Gulf Coast Aviation Co.*, ASBCA 10189, 65-2 BCA ¶ 4928 (base closing eliminated the requirement for food services). Neither is it a change if the government cancels an order after it is issued, *California Bus Lines, Inc.*, ASBCA 42181, 91-3 BCA ¶ 24,341. However, the contractor will be entitled to compensation for costs incurred if the cancellation order is received too late to permit it to avoid the costs, *California Bus Lines, Inc.*, ASBCA 19571, 76-1 BCA ¶ 11,655.

It is not a change to the contract when the government orders uneven quantities, *Asfaltos Panamenos, S.A.*, ASBCA 41657, 92-3 BCA ¶ 25,141. The board held that the contractor should not have relied on even ordering because there was no contract clause requiring orders to be placed uniformly. See also *Tennessee Valley Auth. v. Imperial Prof'l Coatings*, 599 F. Supp. 436 (E.D. Tenn. 1984), where construction of nuclear power plants was deferred because demand for electricity was less than anticipated. The court held that the requirements contractor for painting services had assumed the risk of a good faith decision to cancel the construction of the plant.

### c. Measuring Contractor Relief

As discussed above, the government's failure to perform its obligations under a requirements contract has been alternatively treated as a breach of contract or a constructive change. In general, government breaches have been treated as constructive terminations for convenience when the contract contains a Termination for Convenience clause, *Nesbitt v. United States*, 170 Ct. Cl. 666, 345 F.2d 583 (1965); *Inland Container, Inc. v. United States*, 206 Ct. Cl. 478, 512 F.2d 1073 (1975); *Kalvar Corp. v. United States*, 211 Ct. Cl. 192, 543 F.2d 1298 (1976), *cert. denied*, 434 U.S. 830 (1977). Traditionally, this rule has not been applied if the failure to order was in bad faith, *Kalvar Corp. v. United States*, 211 Ct. Cl. 192, 543 F.2d 1298 (1976), *cert. denied*, 434 U.S. 830 (1977), or if it was based on circumstances known to the government at the time of award, *Torncello v. United States*, 231 Ct. Cl. 20, 681 F.2d 756 (1982). In *Torncello*, the government obtained a requirement at a lower price about which it had known at the time of award of the contract. The court reasoned that the Termination for Convenience clause was not properly usable in such circumstances. See also *S & W Tire Servs., Inc.*, GSBCA 6376, 82-2 BCA ¶ 16,048, where the board found that contracting out an entire operation, of which the requirements contract was a part, was a breach and not a constructive termination, because the government knew of the decision to contract out at the time of award of the requirements contract. In *Erwin v. United States*, 19 Cl. Ct. 47 (1989), the court refused to find a constructive termination when the government ordered all of the services from other vendors because the Termination for Convenience clause limited compensation to the price of completed work. The court reasoned that use of this clause would amount to "illusory consideration" for the requirements contract. In *Viktoria Transp. GmbH & Co.*, ASBCA 30371, 88-3 BCA ¶ 20,921, the board treated a failure to order all requirements as a constructive termination for convenience rather than as a breach because there was no bad faith. This rule will also prevent the agency from issuing a termination for convenience order to avoid a requirements contract when no changed circumstances are present, *Tamp Corp.*, ASBCA 25692, 84-2 BCA ¶ 17,460. However, termination for convenience is proper when the government finds that it had significantly underestimated the requirement, *T & M Distribs., Inc. v. United States*, 185 F.3d 1279 (Fed. Cir. 1999).

Recent cases have indicated that diversion of requirements should be treated as a breach of contract, *Rumsfeld v. Applied Cos.*, 325 F.3d 1328 (Fed. Cir.), *cert. denied*, 540 U.S. 981 (2003); *Ace-Federal Reporters, Inc. v. Barram*, 226 F.3d 1329 (Fed. Cir. 2000). This will allow the recovery of lost profits if they can be proven with some degree of certainty. See *T&M Distribs., Inc.*, ASBCA 51279, 01-2 BCA ¶ 31,442, where the board awarded profits on diverted sales. See also *Tamp Corp.*, ASBCA 25692, 84-2 BCA ¶ 17,460, stating that changes must be calculated to put the contractor in "as good a position as if it had been permitted to fully perform the contract." The board held that this required compensation for profits that would have been earned plus "expenses reasonably incurred as the result of the premature termination."

Alternatively, contractors may be able to assert such claims as terminations for convenience. If so, they will forego recovery of anticipated profits, but will be able to use the special cost principle in FAR 31.205-42 applicable to this type pricing. The major advantage in characterizing the claim as one for termination is the ability to recover settlement costs incurred after the termination. See *Kalvar Corp. v. United States*, 211 Ct. Cl. 192, 543 F.2d 1298 (1976), *cert. denied*, 434 U.S. 830 (1977), where the prohibition of anticipated profits was broadly construed to preclude recovery for the difference between the contract price and a profitable resale price and for higher unit costs on subsequent sales of terminated items. The court also disallowed financing costs and administrative costs associated with the alleged breach on the theory that these were not recoverable under termination cost principles. The court did permit the recovery of some of the contractor's legal fees as settlement costs. Appeals boards have been somewhat more liberal in computing termination costs. See *Drain-A-Way Sys.*, GSBCA 7022, 84-1 BCA ¶ 16,929, where the board held that the unit prices should be recomputed to reflect lower volumes because of the termination. Similarly, in *Wheeler Bros.*, ASBCA 20465, 79-1 BCA ¶ 13,642, where there was a partial termination for convenience, the board permitted repricing to include the entire increase in overhead costs resulting from the reduced volume. See also *Inland Container, Inc. v. United States*, 206 Ct. Cl. 478, 512 F.2d 1073 (1975), where the court permitted recovery of losses incurred in running a manufacturing plant for six months awaiting government orders under the requirements contract. The court reasoned that this loss was a reasonable approximation of initial and preparatory expenses since the plant would probably not have incurred losses had the government properly issued orders. However, profits have been limited to those earned on the completed work. See *Adams Mfg. Co.*, GSBCA 5747, 82-1 BCA ¶ 15,740, *aff'd*, 714 F.2d 161 (Fed. Cir. 1983), precluding anticipated profits where failure to order constituted a total termination for convenience, and *Arcon-Pacific Contractors*, ASBCA 25057, 82-2 BCA ¶ 15,838, where the board limited recovery to actual incurred costs plus profit on those costs in the case of a constructive partial convenience termination.

A different pricing theory applies when the government's failure to honor its requirements obligation is construed as a constructive change. There, the proper measure of the equitable adjustment is the difference between the cost of the work originally called for and the changed work. See *Desco Serv. Contractors*, ASBCA 21856, 77-2 BCA ¶ 12,752, using this technique to compute the adjustment. In *Maya Transit Co.*, ASBCA 20186, 75-2 BCA ¶ 11,552, the board stated that the unit prices of the work should be recomputed following this theory. See also *Pacific Tech. Enters., Ltd.*, ASBCA 17087, 74-2 BCA ¶ 10,679, where the equitable adjustment was computed by granting the contractor payment for work diverted to another company.

## C. Multiyear Contracts

The multiyear contract is a specialized type of requirements contract that creates a slightly different relationship between the contractor and the government. It is defined in FAR 17.103 as follows:

> *Multi-year* contract means a contract for the purchase of supplies or services for more than 1, but not than 5, program years. A multi-year contract may provide that performance under the contract during the second and subsequent years of the contract is contingent upon the appropriation of funds, and (if it does so provide) may provide for a cancellation payment to be made to the contractor if appropriations are not made. The key distinguishing difference between multi-year contracts and multiple year contracts is that multi-year contracts, defined in [10 U.S.C. § 2306b and 41 U.S.C. § 254c], buy more than 1 year's requirement (of a product or service) without establishing and having to exercise an option for each program year after the first.

Thus, the FAR distinguishes between the multi-year contract and the other types of variable quantity contracts (requirements contracts and indefinite-quantity contracts) that frequently cover multiple years as part of the basic contract requirement or by including option clauses for additional years. See *Innovative (PBX) Tel. Servs., Inc. v. Department of Veterans Affairs*, CBCA 122, 08-1 BCA ¶ 33,854, and *Bureau of Customs and Border Protection — Automated Commercial Env't Contract*, Comp. Gen. Dec. B-302358, 2004 U.S. Comp. Gen. LEXIS 271, holding that an IDIQ contract with option years contained no indicia of a multiyear contract.

This form of contract was devised by the DoD in the 1960s to allow its contracting activities to procure supplies for several years in spite of the fact that appropriated funds were available for such supplies for only one year. The goal was to achieve lower unit prices by permitting the contractor to spread start-up costs over more work, to introduce cost-saving methods of performing the work, and to realize the economies of continuous manufacture of goods. In 1969, the regulations were amended to include service contracts. See FAR 17.105-2, which lists the following objectives for both types of multiyear contracting:

Use of multi-year contracting is encouraged to take advantage of one or more of the following:

(a) Lower costs.

(b) Enhancement of standardization.

(c) Reduction of administrative burden in the placement and administration of contracts.

(d) Substantial continuity of production or performance, thus avoiding annual startup costs, preproduction testing costs, make-ready expenses, and phaseout costs.

(e) Stabilization of contractor work forces.

(f) Avoidance of the need for establishing quality control techniques and procedures for a new contractor each year.

(g) Broadening the competitive base with opportunity for participation by firms not otherwise willing or able to compete for lesser quantities, particularly in cases involving high startup costs.

(h) Providing incentives to contractors to improve productivity through investment in capital facilities, equipment, and advanced technology.

GAO has made numerous assessments of the effectiveness over the years that this technique has been in use. Its latest assessment, *DoD's Practices and Processes for Multiyear Procurement Should Be Improved*, GAO-08-298, February 2008, contains the following criticism:

> Multiyear contracting is big business and promises savings at some risk to the government, yet DoD's management direction and process for justifying multiyear programs to the Congress is limited, raising questions about the appropriateness of some approved multiyear programs and the cost effectiveness of investments made for the risks assumed. We identified concerns about the relative stability and savings potential of two recently approved programs, the F-22A Raptor and V-22 Osprey. We found differences in how officials interpreted and applied the statutory criteria and in the methods and data used to compute contract cost and savings. Further, few records are kept to document decisions and supporting evidence. The statutory criteria establish requirements for stable, low risk programs with realistic cost and savings estimates, but DoD has not provided sufficient guidance and a rigorous, disciplined process to ensure high quality, consistent decisions supported by strong empirical evidence.

> Although it is difficult to precisely determine the impact of multiyear contracting on actual procurement costs, our case studies of completed multiyear contracts for the C-17A Globemaster, F/A-18E/F Super Hornet, and Apache Longbow Helicopter identified significant unit cost growth, ranging from 10 to 30 percent compared to the original estimates provided to Congress. All three programs — presumably approved based on their stability — were significantly impacted during contract execution by labor and material cost increases, changes in requirements and funding, and other factors that helped drive up total contract costs much beyond original projections. Savings also do not appear to have materialized as expected in the budget justifications submitted to the Congress and ultimately more funding was needed to buy the systems. In two of the three cases, actual costs for multiyear procurement exceeded original estimates for annual contracts. While both annual and multiyear contracting are prone to the underestimation of costs and overstatement of benefits as we have noted in our prior body of work on defense acquisitions, the stakes are arguably higher for multiyear programs because of the increased up-front investment required, considerable cost increases if a program is significantly restructured, and the greater liabilities incurred if multiyear programs are cancelled.

GAO has held that multiyear contracting is not unduly prejudicial to small business, 43 Comp. Gen. 657 (B-152766) (1964). See also 46 Comp. Gen. 749 (B-160815) (1967).

In order to use multiyear procurement, an agency must comply with the Anti-Deficiency Act, 31 U.S.C. § 1341, which prohibits the making of contracts in advance of appropriations. This is accomplished by entering into a firm commitment for one year and making the government's liability for future years' quantities contingent on funds becoming available. The contractor is protected in the event the government fails to order all of the program years' quantities by the inclusion of a Cancellation under Multiyear Contracts clause in FAR 52.217-2, providing for reimbursement of unrecovered start-up costs. Since these are long term contracts, the use of economic price adjustment provisions is also permitted, FAR 17.109(b). The proper funding for these contractual commitments is discussed below.

## 1.  *Legal Authority*

There has been considerable confusion over the legal authority of agencies to use multiyear contracts. However, it seems clear that agencies have the inherent authority to use multiyear contracts because, for a number of years, Congress acquiesced to the DoD's use of multiyear contracts for the procurement of *supplies* without statutory authority when multiyear or no-year funds were being used. Ultimately, a limit was imposed on cancellation ceilings of $5 million, § 810 of the DoD Authorization Act of 1976, Pub. L. No. 94-106. This effectively precluded the use of multiyear procurements on major systems. Subsequently, in 1982, the Armed Services Committees concluded that multi-year contracts were a means of obtaining lower prices for major weapon systems. The Armed Services Procurement Act was therefore amended to encourage the DoD to use multiyear contracting under the surveillance of Congress, 10 U.S.C. § 2306(h) (pre-1994). This provision is codified at 10 U.S.C. § 2306b and is applicable to DoD, NASA, and the Coast Guard. It contains a limitation on such contracts by requiring notification of Congress and a 30-day waiting period before contract award if a cancellation ceiling of more than $100 million is included in such a contract, 10 U.S.C. § 2306b(g), as well as many other limitations. Thus, there is congressional oversight on the use of this technique on all major systems. These oversight provisions are currently found in 10 U.S.C. § 2306b(i) as well as in specific Appropriations Acts. The National Defense Authorization Act for Fiscal Year 1988, Pub. L. No. 105-85, added additional approval requirements to § 2306b(l) for defense multiyear contracts or advance procurements leading to a multi-year contract that employ economic order quantity procurement in excess of $20 million, or that include an unfunded contingent liability in excess of $20 million.

During this same period, Congress authorized the DoD, NASA, and the Coast Guard to enter into multiyear contracts for *services*. This was permitted for contracts outside of the United States by the enactment of 10 U.S.C. § 2306(g) in 1968. This statute was broadened in 1981 to permit such contracts within the United States. This statute is now in 10 U.S.C. § 2306c, permitting multiyear contracts using any type of funds if they are for the following types of services:

(1) operation, maintenance, and support of facilities and installations;

(2) maintenance or modification of aircraft, ships, vehicles, and other highly complex military equipment;

(3) specialized training necessitating high quality instructor skills (for example, pilot and aircrew members; foreign language training); and

(4) base services (for example, ground maintenance; in-plane refueling; bus transportation; refuse collection and disposal);

(5) Environmental remediation services for —

    (A) an active military installation;

    (B) a military installation being closed or realigned under a base closure law; or

    (C) a site formerly used by the Department of Defense.

This statute also contains limitations similar to those in 10 U.S.C. § 2306b.

DoD has obtained the required congressional authorizations by submitting detailed justifications on each system to the Armed Services Committees of the Congress, which obtain assistance in reviewing such proposed actions from the Government Accountability Office. See, for example, GAO Reports, GAO/NSIAD-90-270BR, Aug. 1990, GAO/NSIAD-89-224BR, Sept. 1989, GAO/NSIAD-86-1, Nov. 1985, GAO/NSIAD-85-9, Oct. 1984. DoD requests for congressional approvals are submitted in the budget process. See DFARS 217.170 as follows:

(d)(1) DoD must receive authorization from, or provide notification to, Congress before entering into a multiyear contract for certain procurements, including those expected to —

    (i) Exceed $500 million for supplies (see 217.172(c) and 217.172(e)(4)) or $572.5 million for services (see 217.171(a)(6));

    (ii) Employ economic order quantity procurement in excess of $20 million in any one year (see 217.174(a)(1));

    (iii) Employ an unfunded contingent liability in excess of $20 million (see 217.171(a)(4)(i) and 217.172(d)(1));

    (iv) Involve a contract for advance procurement leading to a multiyear contract that employs economic order quantity procurement in excess of $20 million in any one year (see 217.174(a)(2)); or

    (v) Include a cancellation ceiling in excess of $100 million (see 217.171(a)(4)(ii) and 217.172(d)(2)).

(2) A DoD component must submit a request for authority to enter into multiyear contracts described in paragraphs (d)(1)(i) through (iv) of this section as part of the component's budget submission for the fiscal year in which the multiyear contract will be initiated. DoD will include the request, for each candidate it supports, as part of the President's Budget for that year and in

the Appendix to that budget as part of proposed legislative language for the appropriations bill for that year (Section 8008(b) of Public Law 105-56).

(3) If the advisability of using a multiyear contract becomes apparent too late to satisfy the requirements in paragraph (d)(2) of this section, the request for authority to enter into a multiyear contract must be —

    (i) Formally submitted by the President as a budget amendment; or

    (ii) Made by the Secretary of Defense, in writing, to the congressional defense committees. (Section 8008(b) of Public Law 105-56)

(4) Agencies must establish reporting procedures to meet the congressional notification requirements of paragraph (d)(1) of this section. The head of the agency must submit a copy of each notice to the Director of Defense Procurement and Acquisition Policy, Office of the Under Secretary of Defense (Acquisition, Technology, and Logistics) (OUSD(AT&L)DPAP), and to the Deputy Under Secretary of Defense (Comptroller) (Program/Budget) (OUSD (C) (P/B)).

When the FAR was issued in 1984, FAR 17.102-1 reflected the fact that multiyear contracting could be used on both supply and service contracts containing multiyear or no-year funds without statutory authority by stating:

(a) Multiyear contracting may be used when no-year or multiyear funds are available or, in the case of 1-year funds, when multiyear contracting is specifically authorized by statute. (Specific statutory authority is needed for an agency to make financial commitments for amounts greater than those appropriated annually by the Congress. See 31 U.S.C. § 1341(a)(1).)

(b) The multiyear contracting method may be used for the acquisition of services or supplies (including, but not limited to systems, subsystems, major equipment, components, parts, materials, supplies, and the advance acquisition thereof, and commercial and noncommercial items).

The perceived necessity of statutory authority for multiyear contracting using annual ("1-year") funds was based on the fear that such contracting would be construed as a procurement of more than the bona fide needs of the government for the single year for which the funds were appropriated, in violation of 31 U.S.C. § 1341, 43 Comp. Gen. 657 (B-152766) (1964). See also *Defense Logistics Agency Multiyear Contract for Storage & Rotation of Sulfadiazine Silver Cream*, 67 Comp. Gen. 190 (B-224081) (1987), and 42 Comp. Gen. 272 (B-144641) (1962), discussing this issue. In *Army's Multiple Launch Rocket Sys. Multiyear Contract*, 64 Comp. Gen. 163 (B-215825) (1984), GAO implied that the bona fide needs rule, 31 U.S.C. § 1502, also precludes multi-year contracts using multiyear funds without explaining the reasoning.

The Federal Acquisition Streamlining Act of 1994, Pub. L. No. 103-355, broadened the statutory coverage of multiyear contracting. First, it moved the provision on multiyear contracting for *supplies* in 10 U.S.C. § 2306(h) to 10 U.S.C. § 2306b and brought the NASA and the Coast Guard within its coverage. In so doing, Congress imposed some of the restrictive provisions in the prior statute on these two agencies and continued to impose some special requirements on the DoD. This statute also stated that it was inapplicable to contracts under 40 U.S.C. § 759 for information resource management supplies, 10 U.S.C. §2306b(k). This provision was deleted from the Act in 1996, Pub. L. No. 104-106, but 40 U.S.C. § 759 still provides special rules for those types of procurements. See FAR 17.102. Second, the Act added a new multi-year statute for both *supplies and services* procured by civilian agencies, 41 U.S.C. § 3903. This is a short statute that permits the use of multiyear contracts with any type of funds (annual, multiyear, or no-year) with fewer congressional restrictions. This statute is implemented in FAR Subpart 17.1.

These new statutes giving authority to use multi-year contracts without regard to the type of funds provide legal authority to use multiyear contracts with annual funds. The FAR is now silent on this issue.

## 2. *Use*

The statutes give agencies considerable discretion in deciding whether to use a multiyear contract or a multiple year contract, *Prisoner Transp. Servs., LLC*, Comp. Gen. Dec. B-292179, 2003 CPD ¶ 121. However, a multiyear contract can only be used when specified criteria are met. Different criteria are contained in 10 U.S.C. § 2306b(a), 41 U.S.C. § 254c(a), and 10 U.S.C. 2306c(a). FAR 17.105-1 states these criteria for the first two statutes as follows:

(a) Except for DoD, NASA and the Coast Guard, the contracting officer may enter into a multi-year contract if the head of the contracting activity determines that —

(1) The need for the supplies or services is reasonably firm and continuing over the period of the contract; and

(2) A multi-year contract will serve the best interests of the United States by encouraging full and open competition or promoting economy in administration, performance, an operation of the agency's programs.

(b) For DoD, NASA, and the Coast Guard, the head of the agency may enter into a multi-year contract for supplies if—

(1) The use of such a contract will result in substantial savings of the total estimated costs of carrying out the program through annual contracts;

(2) The minimum need to be purchased is expected to remain substantially unchanged during the contemplated contract period in terms of production rate, procurement rate, and total quantities;

(3) There is a stable design for the supplies to be acquired, and the technical risks associated with such supplies are not excessive;

(4) There is a reasonable expectation that, throughout the contemplated contract period, the head of the agency will request funding for the contract at a level to avoid contract cancellation; and

(5) The estimates of both the cost of the contract and the cost avoidance through the use of a multi-year contract are realistic.

The guidance in ¶ (b) applies only to contracts for supplies — implementing 10 U.S.C. § 2306b. The FAR contains no guidance on the criteria applicable to the separate statute for services, 10 U.S.C. § 2306c. However, DFARS 217.171(a) contains the following guidance:

(3) Before entering into a multiyear contract for services, the head of the agency must make a written determination that —

(i) There will be a continuing requirement for the services consistent with current plans for the proposed contract period;

(ii) Furnishing the services will require —

(A) A substantial initial investment in plant or equipment; or

(B) The incurrence of substantial contingent liabilities for the assembly, training or transportation of a specialized work force; and

(iii) Using a multiyear contract will promote the best interests of the United States by encouraging effective competition and promoting economies in operations.

The FAR provisions reflect the fact that the civilian agency statute imposes very few limitations on use of multiyear contracts. For example, it contains no requirement for an estimate of savings in order to justify the use of a multiyear contract, whereas the statute applying to DoD, NASA, and the Coast Guard requires "substantial" savings. Under the prior statute, GAO stated that savings should be "significant," but no fixed standard was adopted. In deciding whether projected savings were significant enough to justify multi-year procurement, cost savings were balanced against added risks. See GAO Report, GAO/NSIAD-86-1, Nov. 1985, stating at 6:

Each proposed multiyear contract should be evaluated on its own merits, weighing the margin of savings against added risks and any other uncertainties. The savings should be high enough to offset any additional risks of entering into a multiyear contract. For example, a candidate with no risks in terms of requirement, funding, or design stability, and in which a high degree of confidence in the cost estimate does exist, may provide only a small percentage or amount of savings. If the savings are essentially ensured, they may be judged substantial enough to take advantage of them. In contrast, a candidate with high projected savings may be inappropriate for multiyear contracting if the design, funding, and/or requirement is unstable or if the cost estimate is not based on sound information and logic.

Accordingly, savings should be assessed in relation to the risk or absence of risk which is reflected in (1) the confidence in the cost estimate, (2) requirement stability, (3) funding stability, and (4) configuration or design stability.

Congress has been less than clear in enunciating the required degree of cost savings for multiyear procurement of weapons systems. The 1986 DoD Authorization Act, Pub. L. No. 99-145, 99 Stat. 583, declared that multi-year contracts authorized for the Army "may not be entered into unless the total anticipated cost over the period of the contract is no more than 90 percent of the total anticipated cost of carrying out the same program through annual contracts," 99 Stat. 591. The Act simultaneously authorized the Army to enter into multi-year contracts for both Bradley fighting vehicle transmissions and M1A1 tank chassis for which the estimated contract cost savings were 8.9% and 9.5% respectively, GAO Report, GAO/NSIAD-86-1, Nov. 1985. The 1986 Authorization Act contained no parallel provision for minimum cost savings for Navy multiyear contracts, 99 Stat. 594. The Act did, however, bar the use of multiyear contracting for the procurement of P-3C aircraft following GAO's report that "savings are relatively small at 5.5 percent and there is a risk that cost estimates are not sound," GAO Report, GAO/NSIAD-86-1, Nov. 1985. Both the DoD and GAO discount to present value when projecting cost savings for multiyear candidates, though different interest rates are applied in calculating present value, GAO Report, GAO/NSIAD-90-270BR, Aug. 1990, at 8.

In some cases, the savings associated with multiyear procurement are achieved by entering into multiyear subcontracts under multiyear contracts. See discussion of "Source of Savings" in GAO Reports, GAO/NSIAD-86-1, Nov. 1985, at 13; and GAO/NSIAD-88-125, May 1988, at 42. FAR 17.106-3 encourages the use of multiyear subcontracts by contractors of DoD, NASA and the Coast Guard in order to "broaden the defense industrial base, to the maximum extent practicable."

Two of the criteria for the use of multiyear procurement deal with program stability in the areas of the government requirement and the design. Program stability has been considered to be a necessary element of multiyear procurement because significant changes during contract performance jeopardize the projected savings. Both GAO Analysis of Multiyear Candidates and the DoD Appropriations Acts have stressed that multi-year contracting should be used only for systems with stable designs. GAO report states that implementation of multi-year procurement should not occur until successful R&D, operational tests and evaluation, and one or two production runs have been completed. See also *Multiyear Procurement Authority for the Virginia Class Submarine Program*, GAO-03-895R, June 23, 2003, and *F/A-18E/F Aircraft Does Not Meet All Criteria for Multiyear Procurement*, GAO/NSIAD-00-158, May 2000, questioning the stability of design of weapon systems proposed for multiyear contracts. A contractor, however, has no legal right to a stable design when it enters into a multi-year contract, *Gould, Inc. v. United States*, 66 Fed. Cl. 253 (2005) (contractors not intended beneficiaries under multi-year contract statute).

The final criterion listed in FAR 17.105-1(b)(5) for the use of multi-year contracts by DoD, NASA and the Coast Guard is a measure of confidence in estimates of costs and savings. The report on 1986 Multiyear Candidates, GAO/NSIAD-86-1, stated:

> Confidence in the cost estimates may be increased by receiving firm proposals . . . on an annual and multiyear basis, and then comparing and analyzing these proposals. . . . However, this is not always practical, and DoD officials stated that the additional administrative effort and the cost to negotiate both proposals must be considered.

Cost-savings estimates are usually based on prior history, information received informally from contractors, or in-house estimates by the procuring activity, GAO Report, GAO/NSIAD-85-9, Oct. 1984, Appendix II at 5.

The use of multiyear contracts is further limited by restricting their term to a maximum of five years, absent specific statutory authority, 10 U.S.C. § 2306b(k); 10 U.S.C. § 2306c(f); 41 U.S.C. § 3903(a); FAR 17.104(a). Because of the five-year limitation on multiyear contracting, the exercise of an option for advance procurement of economic order quantities to be ordered in the sixth or seventh program year has been held to be unauthorized, *Multiple Launch Rocket Sys. Multiyear Contract*, 64 Comp. Gen. 163 (B-215825) (1984). Compare *Freightliner Corp.*, ASBCA 42982, 94-1 BCA ¶ 26,538, where the board held that an option in the fifth year of a multiyear contract could be used to require the contractor to furnish items that were included in the agency's sixth budget year. Similarly, when the multi-year services statute allowed options in additional years (since repealed), options for additional services in program years six through eight were treated as proper options in *Cessna Aircraft Co.*, ASBCA 43196, 93-3 BCA ¶ 25,912.

The statutes also contain monetary restrictions on the use of multiyear contracts. 10 U.S.C. § 2306b(g) and 10 U.S.C. § 2306c(d)(4) require notification and a 30-day waiting period before award of a multi-year contract for supplies or services with a cancellation ceiling over $100 million. The civilian agency statute, 41 U.S.C. § 3903(d), contains a similar notice and waiting period requirement for any supply or service contract with a cancellation ceiling over $10 million. FAR 17.108 has adjusted these amounts for inflation to be $125 million and $12.5 million respectively.

GAO has upheld the use of multiple award schedule (MAS) multiyear agreements because, unlike multiyear contracts, the MAS agreement does not obligate the government to purchase the items on the schedule, *GSA — Multiple Award Schedule Multiyear Contracting*, 63 Comp. Gen. 129 (B-199079), 84-1 CPD ¶ 46. Thus, even though funds for the purchase of MAS agreement items are generally one-year appropriations, there is no violation of the Anti-Deficiency Act since each agency must make a specific determination that funds are available before issuing an order under the schedule contract.

## 3. Procurement Technique

The multiyear contract is probably the most complex contract used by the government. This requires that the solicitation be carefully structured to ensure that the parties fully understand their respective rights and obligations.

### a. Sharing the Risk

In the past, almost all multiyear supply contracts have been written on a fixed-price basis. Multi-year service contracts have been written using a variety of types of pricing arrangements, including cost-reimbursement contracts. When fixed-price contracts are used, the contractor can be expected to incur costs in the first year of performance to reduce the overall contract costs but to allocate some or all of these costs to the full contract period. This means that if the contract is not carried to its full term, the contractor will have not recovered such "nonrecurring costs," defined in FAR 17.103 as follows:

> "Nonrecurring costs" means those costs which are generally incurred on a one-time basis and include such costs as plant or equipment relocation, plant rearrangement, special tooling and special test equipment, preproduction engineering, initial spoilage and rework, and specialized work force training.

See also FAR 17.106-1(c)(2), which describes nonrecurring costs to include:

> initial rework, . . . pilot runs, allocable portions of the costs of facilities to be acquired or established for the conduct of the work, costs incurred for the assembly training and transportation to and from the job site of a specialized work force, and unrealized labor learning.

This risk of nonrecovery is mitigated by the inclusion in the multi-year contract of a Cancellation Under Multiyear Contracts clause in FAR 52.217-2 which promises the contractor reimbursement, up to a cancellation ceiling, for enumerated costs if the government does not order the full quantities called for by the contract. This provision is the major distinguishing feature of the multiyear contract and is discussed in full below.

Also inherent in fixed-price multiyear contracts is the risk of changes in the cost of materials and labor over the extended period of contract performance. To mitigate this risk, FAR 17.106-1(b) suggests the use of economic price adjustment clauses. FAR 17.109(b) contains the following guidance on the clauses to be used:

> *Economic price adjustment clauses.* Economic price adjustment clauses are adaptable to multiyear contracting needs. When the period of production is likely to warrant a labor and material costs contingency in the contract price, the contracting officer should normally use an economic price adjustment clause (see 16.203). When contracting for services, the contracting officer —
>
>> (1) Shall add the clause at FAR 52.222-43 , Fair Labor Standards Act and Service Contract Act-Price Adjustment (Multiple Year and Option Contracts), when the contract includes the clause at FAR 52.222-43, Service Contract Act of 1965, as amended;
>>
>> (2) May modify the clause at FAR 52.222-43 in overseas contracts when laws, regulations, or international agreements require contractors to pay higher wage rates; or
>>
>> (3) May use an economic price adjustment clause authorized by FAR 16.203, when potential fluctuations require coverage and are not included in cost contingencies provided for by the clause at FAR 52.222-43.

In selecting the clause to be used in service contracts, the issue is whether the work includes a significant amount of material and whether the contractor is willing to take the risk that its labor rates will fluctuate at the same rates of fluctuation as the prevailing wages determined by the Department of Labor. The clause at FAR 52.222-43 only includes such fluctuations in prevailing wages, whereas an economic price adjustment clause can use indexes or other measures of wage fluctuation and can also include fluctuations in material prices.

The use of an economic price adjustment clause is at the contracting officer's discretion. Thus, GAO rejected a protest that the contracting officer was arbitrary in not including such a clause in a solicitation, *Kings Point Mfg. Co.*, Comp. Gen. Dec. B-220224, 85-2 CPD ¶ 680.

## b. Ensuring Government Flexibility

Although multiyear contracts are generally not used unless there is a reasonable belief that the requirements for the multiyear period will remain in effect, there is always a significant risk that program requirements will change. Reduced requirements can be implemented by use of the Termination for the Convenience of the Government clause, as discussed below. Increased requirements are frequently dealt with by the inclusion of options for additional quantities in the contract. See FAR 17.107, which states:

> Benefits may accrue by including options in a multi-year contract. In that event, contracting officers must follow both the requirements of subpart 17.2. Options

should not include charges for plant and equipment already amortized, or other nonrecurring charges which were included in the basic contract.

This guidance is to ensure that the contractor does not obtain double recovery for nonrecurring costs that have already been fully included in the base prices and would be paid in cancellation charges if all of the base quantities were not ordered. Inclusion of option quantities is a discretionary decision of the contracting officer, *Kings Point Mfg. Co.*, Comp. Gen. Dec. B-220224, 85-2 CPD ¶ 680.

Options are generally included for each year of the multiyear contract. However, the fact that they are identified as an option for a designated year does not preclude the government from using an option for one year to buy quantities needed to meet the requirements of the next year, *Freightliner Corp.*, ASBCA 42982, 94-1 BCA ¶ 26,538. In that case, the board ruled that a fifth-year option could be used to buy products needed to meet the sixth year's requirements. This imposes some pricing risk on the contractor since the price of the subsequent year may be higher due to costs increases during that year. See also *Freightliner Corp.*, ASBCA 42982, 98-2 BCA ¶ 30,026, holding that fifth-year options were not limited to products that could be manufactured within the completion date of the contract. Similarly, in *Cessna Aircraft Co.*, ASBCA 43196, 93-3 BCA ¶ 25,912, the board held that the government could properly exercise an option for three additional years of services at the end of a five-year multiyear contract even though the funds for the second and third years had not been appropriated. The board reasoned that, in accordance with the legislative history of 10 U.S.C. § 2306(g) (now 2306b), this was *renewing* the multiyear contract for three years, not ordering the work for three years.

Options in multiyear contracts would normally not be evaluated as part of the initial award. Thus, the solicitation should include the Evaluation Exclusive of Options clause in FAR 52.217-3. In one unique instance the government evaluated the options and included a complex repricing clause in the contract to allow higher prices if all of the options were not exercised, *ITT Def. Commc'ns Div.*, ASBCA 44791, 98-1 BCA ¶ 29,590. When many of the option quantities were not ordered, the board resolved a dispute on the correct interpretation of the repricing clause in the contractor's favor and remanded the case to the parties to negotiate the price adjustment.

### c. Competition Requirements

Multiyear contracting may be accomplished on a competitive or noncompetitive basis, and competition may be obtained through sealed bidding, two-step sealed bidding, or negotiation, FAR 17.106-1(a). However, as in the case of any other type of procurement, the use of noncompetitive procurement must be justified. Thus, where competitive procurement would have been feasible in two to three years, a protest of a noncompetitive award of a five-year contract for telephone services was sustained, *Rolm Intermountain Corp.*, Comp. Gen. Dec. B-206327.4, 82-2 CPD ¶ 564. Similarly, in *Lear Siegler Inc.*, Comp. Gen. Dec. B-209524, 83-2 CPD ¶ 285, the fact that a limited initial quantity of F-16 fuel tanks was urgently needed and could only be obtained from a particular contractor did not justify the award of a multiyear contract for more items than were urgently needed at the time of the award. See also *Command, Control & Commc'ns Corp.*, Comp. Gen. Dec. B-210100, 83-2 CPD ¶ 448.

After submission of proposals, if a contracting officer finds that more competition is available on a multiyear procurement, it is proper to cancel the procurement and resolicit, *JRW Mgmt. Co.*, Comp. Gen. Dec. B-260396.2, 95-1 CPD ¶ 276; *Maytag Aircraft Corp.*, Comp. Gen. Dec. B-250628, 93-1 CPD ¶ 93. On reconsideration of the *Maytag* case, GAO rejected the protester's contention that the proper course of action was to have contracted for the single year's quantity and recompeted for the future years, Comp. Gen. Dec. B-250628.2, 93-1 CPD ¶ 456.

### d.  Evaluation of Offers

On multiyear contracts the government solicits offers on a single-year basis as well as on a multiyear basis in order to ensure that it will obtain lower prices by buying on a multiyear basis. Administrative costs of buying annually can be included in this evaluation if they are included in the solicitation. If multiyear unit prices are not lower than single-year prices, award for a single year could be anticipated. FAR 17.106-2 provides the following general guidance on the solicitation provisions alerting offerors to these procedures:

Solicitations for multi-year contracts shall reflect all the factors to be considered for evaluation, specifically including the following:

(a) The requirements, by item of supply or service, for the —

(1) First program year; and

(2) Multi-year contract including the requirements for each program year.

(b) Criteria for comparing the lowest evaluated submission on the first program year requirements to the lowest evaluated submission on the multi-year requirements.

(c) A provision that if the Government determines before award that only the first program year requirements are needed, the Government's evaluation of the price or estimated cost and fee shall consider only the first year.

(d) A provision specifying a separate cancellation ceiling (on a percentage or dollar basis) and dates applicable to each program year subject to a cancellation (see 17.106-1 (c) and (d)).

(e) A statement that award will not be made on less than the first program year requirements.

(f) The Government's administrative costs of annual contracting may be used as a factor in the evaluation only if they can be reasonably established and are stated in the solicitation.

(g) The cancellation ceiling shall not be an evaluation factor.

FAR 17.106-3 permits the DoD, NASA, and the Coast Guard to solicit only multi-year prices, as follows:

(f) *Annual and multi-year proposals.* Obtaining both annual and multi-year offers provides reduced lead time for making an annual award in the event that the multi-year award is not in the Government's interest. Obtaining both also provides a basis for the computation of savings and other benefits. However, the preparation and evaluation of dual offers may increase administrative costs and workload for both offerors and the Government, especially for large or complex acquisitions. The head of a contracting activity may authorize the use of a solicitation requesting only multi-year prices, provided it is found that such a solicitation is in the Government's interest, and that dual proposals are not necessary to meet the objectives in 17.105-2.

When the government selects the contractor by comparing multi-year unit prices with single-year unit prices, it has no assurance that buying single-year quantities will actually be cheaper even when the single-year price is lowest because it cannot prevent yearly price increases when buying one year at a time. Nevertheless, this evaluation procedure has been approved by GAO, *Mil-Tech Sys., Inc.*, Comp. Gen. Dec. B-212385.4, 84-1 CPD ¶ 632. GAO has also rejected a protest that it was irrational to evaluate the first year against a five-year price without including an inflation factor for future years if the award is made for only the single year, *Engineered Air Sys., Inc.*, Comp. Gen. Dec. B-220392.4, 86-2 CPD ¶ 43. In one case, the low offeror on the first-year quantity challenged the right of the government to award the contract to the low offeror on the multi-year (three-year) quantity on the grounds that to do so would be the same as evaluating option quantities. GAO held that multi-year quantities were not like options in that they did not create the same degree of uncertainty since the government was binding itself to buy the second and third-year quantities if funds were available, 43 Comp. Gen. 215 (B-152286) (1963). In another case, a disappointed offeror argued that the decision to use the multi-year alternative, based on the price comparison, was improper since some of the offerors had deliberately overpriced their single-year bids, 46 Comp. Gen. 749 (B-160815) (1967). In denying the protest, GAO noted that offerors were not precluded from submitting noncompetitive prices on the single-year part of a solicitation to ensure that they did not receive a single-year award. That decision also held that in this case, the multi-year offers were, in fact, competitive. In another case, GAO held that it was proper for a contracting officer to award on a single-year basis since the IFB permitted the government to select either the multi-year or single-year offer, *VBM Corp.*, Comp. Gen. Dec. B-182225, 75-1 CPD ¶ 130.

The evaluation process becomes even more involved if the multi-year contract is also a small business or labor-surplus area set-aside, or involves application of the Buy American Act. See 45 Comp. Gen. 735 (B-158525) (1966).

## *4. Level Pricing Requirement*

In the early use of multiyear contracting, the DoD adopted a policy of requiring that unit prices be the same for all program years in order to eliminate the evaluation difficulties created by unbalanced bidding, as discussed in Chapter 5. When the FAR was adopted in 1984, this requirement was included in FAR 17.103-2(e). It has been deleted from the general guidance in the FAR implementing the FASA but is discussed as follows in the special procedures applicable to the DoD, NASA, and the Coast Guard in FAR 17.106-3:

> (g) *Level unit prices.* Multi-year contract procedures provide for the amortization of certain costs over the entire contract quantity resulting in identical (level) unit prices (except when the economic price adjustment terms apply) for all items or services under the multi-year contract. If level unit pricing is not in the Government's interest, the head of a contracting activity may approve the use of variable unit prices, provided that for competitive proposals there is a valid method of evaluation.

Thus, all agencies appear to have discretion to require level unit pricing or to permit offerors to propose variable unit prices for the program years covered by the procurement. The major advantage of requiring level pricing is that it greatly simplifies the evaluation of offers by eliminating the possibility of unbalancing the prices between the program years.

There are several disadvantages to level pricing. The most serious is that a contractor must incur higher financing costs on such multi-year contracts because it cannot invoice for the high costs in early years, such as starting and learning costs, which must be spread over the entire quantity of supplies or services covered in the procurement. This may be counterbalanced by the fact that high costs of later years, such as the estimated costs of inflation in labor rates and material prices, would also be spread over the prices of all years. However, the government generally avoids this by using economic price adjustment provisions, FAR 17.109(b). Another disadvantage is that level pricing forces a large amount of costs into the cancellation cost pool, which can lead to difficulties in establishing the cancellation ceiling, as discussed below.

Under the prior mandatory level pricing requirement, contracting officers were permitted to waive the requirement where there was no prejudice to other offerors. In *Keco Indus., Inc.*, 54 Comp. Gen. 967 (B-183114), 75-1 CPD ¶ 301, variable prices were permitted in a case where the IFB contained no warning to offerors that failure to comply with the level pricing requirement would result in a nonresponsive bid. In

*International Harvester Co.*, Comp. Gen. Dec. B-212341, 83-2 CPD ¶ 313, variable prices were permitted in a procurement where the IFB contained an explicit warning. See also *InterTrade Indus., Ltd.*, Comp. Gen. Dec. B-225702, 87-1 CPD ¶ 567; and *Everett Dykes Grassing Co.*, Comp. Gen. Dec. B-210223.4, 84-1 CPD ¶ 176.

Some difficulties have been encountered in determining whether the level pricing requirement applies to preproduction items. In one case where a bid was rejected because of higher prices for preproduction items, GAO ruled that the bid was responsive but that the procurement was ambiguous and should be canceled, Comp. Gen. Dec. B-169205, May 22, 1970, *Unpub.* Taking the case to the district court, the bidder obtained an order directing that it be awarded the contract, *A.G. Schoonmaker Co. v. Resor*, 319 F. Supp. 933 (D.D.C. 1970). This decision was reversed by the circuit court on the grounds that the procuring agency had not acted arbitrarily or capriciously in following the view of GAO that it should reject all bids and resolicit, *A.G. Schoonmaker Co. v. Resor*, 445 F.2d 726 (D.C. Cir. 1971). In *Keco Indus., Inc.*, 64 Comp. Gen. 48 (B-216396.2), 84-2 CPD ¶ 491, GAO ruled that the contracting officer properly waived a failure to level price a bid by submitting a lower price on two preproduction items, finding no prejudice to other bidders.

Options in multiyear contracts are not normally subject to the level pricing requirement because it is expected that they will exclude nonrecurring costs. See FAR 17.107, warning that option prices should not include "charges for plant and equipment already amortized, or other nonrecurring charges which were included in the basic contract." In *Keco Indus., Inc.*, 64 Comp. Gen. 48 (B-216396.2), 84-2 CPD ¶ 491, the IFB explicitly stated that although unit prices for base quantities in the multiyear procurement had to be level priced, varying prices could be offered for option quantities.

## 5. Orders for Future Years

Since the multiyear contract is funded one year at a time, it should contain a provision establishing the procedure that will be used to order quantities of work subsequent to the first year and the limitations on the obligations of the parties. However, the FAR contains no such provision. Thus, contracting officers will have to include special provisions in each multiyear contract covering these issues. FAR 17.106-1 contains the following partial guidance:

(g) *Payment limit.* The contracting officer shall limit the Government's payment obligation to an amount available for contract performance. The contracting officer shall insert the amount for the first program year in the contract upon award and modify it for successive program years upon availability of funds.

(h) *Termination payment.* If the contract is terminated for the convenience of the Government in whole, including requirements subject to cancellation, the Government's obligation shall not exceed the amount specified in the Schedule as available for contract performance, plus the cancellation ceiling.

The prior FAR contained a Limitation of Price and Contractor Obligations clause in FAR 52.217-1 for use in this type of contract. This clause made it clear that the government was making no legal obligation for quantities not covered by firm contractual orders. It also required the contracting officer to notify the contractor, in writing, when additional funds became available for the full requirements of the next succeeding program year. Conversely, this clause provided that the contractor was only obligated to honor the contract as to future-year quantities if the government gave written notification by the contractually specified date. The Court of Claims held that the clause should be interpreted to require strict compliance, *International Tel. & Tel. v. United States*, 197 Ct. Cl. 11, 453 F.2d 1283 (1972) (written order received several hours after stated cutoff date did not bind the contractor even thought oral notice was given before the cutoff date). The same result obtains when the government exercises options for additional quantities, *Cessna Aircraft Co.*, ASBCA 43196, 96-1 BCA ¶ 27,966. There the board held that the option was validly exercised when the contractor received a facsimile on the last day permitted.

## 6. Cancellation of Items

The major legal problems in multi-year procurements arise in formulating and administering the cancellation provisions of this type of contract.

### a. Costs Included in Ceiling

The initial use of multiyear contracts included only nonrecurring costs in the cancellation ceiling. The original DoD multiyear contracting statute, 10 U.S.C. § 2306(h)(2)(B), recognized the use of such cancellation provisions and also permitted the inclusion of recurring costs:

> [R]egulations may provide for cancellation provisions in such multiyear contracts to the extent that such provisions are necessary and in the best interests of the United States. Such cancellation provisions may include consideration of both recurring and nonrecurring costs of the contractor associated with the production of the items to be delivered under the contract.

Since there was no similar statute applicable to civilian agencies, there was some question as to whether they could include recurring costs in the ceiling. FAR 17.102-3(d)(3) (pre-1996) restricted the inclusion of recurring costs in cancellation ceilings by stating:

> The inclusion of recurring costs in cancellation ceilings is an exception to normal contract financing arrangements and requires approval by the agency head or a designee.

This provision permitted civilian agencies to include recurring costs in ceilings if the proper approvals were obtained. However, the issue was largely resolved by including a very broad definition of "nonrecurring costs" in the standard Cancellation of Items clause of FAR 52.217-2 (which only provided for the recovery of nonrecurring costs). This confusing use of terminology has been continued under the current provisions of the statutes and FAR. 10 U.S.C. § 2306b(c) continues to permit recovery of "both recurring and nonrecurring costs," while 41 U.S.C. § 3903 is silent on the subject. The Cancellation under Multiyear Contracts clause in FAR 52.217-2 resolves this issue by giving detailed guidance on the costs that may be included in the cancellation claim. Paragraphs (f) and (g) of the clause state:

> (f) The Contractor's claim may include —
>
> > (1) Reasonable nonrecurring costs (see Subpart 15.4 of the Federal Acquisition Regulation) which are applicable to and normally would have been amortized in all supplies or services which are multiyear requirements;
> >
> > (2) Allocable portions of the costs of facilities acquired or established for the conduct of the work, to the extent that it is impracticable for the Contractor to use the facilities in its commercial work, and if the costs are not charged to the contract through overhead or otherwise depreciated;
> >
> > (3) Costs incurred for the assembly, training, and transportation to and from the job site of a specialized work force; and
> >
> > (4) Costs not amortized solely because the cancellation had precluded anticipated benefits of Contractor or subcontractor learning.
>
> (g) The claim shall not include —
>
> > (1) Labor, material, or other expenses incurred by the Contractor or subcontractors for performance of the canceled work;
> >
> > (2) Any cost already paid to the Contractor;
> >
> > (3) Anticipated profit or unearned fee on the canceled work; or
> >
> > (4) For service contracts, the remaining useful commercial life of facilities. Useful commercial life means the commercial utility of the facilities rather than their physical life with due consideration given to such factors as location of facilities, their specialized nature, and obsolescence.

In spite of this broad coverage, FAR 17.106-3 contains the following special procedure applicable to DoD, NASA, and the Coast Guard:

> (e) *Recurring costs in cancellation ceilings.* The inclusion of recurring costs in cancellation ceilings is an exception to normal contract financing arrangements and requires approval by the agency head.

The ASBCA has followed the principle that costs included in cancellation ceilings should be broadly construed. For example, in *Continental Elecs. Mfg. Co.*, ASBCA 14749, 71-2 BCA ¶ 9108, the board held that cancellation costs properly included (i) higher costs of early units (computed with the use of a learning curve), (ii) costs charged to a preproduction unit above the contract unit price, and (iii) engineering costs incurred and measured after cancellation. In dealing with this issue, the board took a broad view of the matter since the contractor was forced to bid the same price for all units and had no means of recovering uneven costs other than through the cancellation charge. See also *Bermite Div. of Tasker Indus.*, ASBCA 18280, 77-1 BCA ¶ 12,349, *modified on recons.*, 77-2 BCA ¶ 12,731.

### b.  Computation of Ceiling

A separate cancellation ceiling is included in the contract for each program year after the first year, FAR 17.106-1(c)(1). Thus, the ceiling decreases in amount as each year's requirement is ordered. The cancellation ceiling is estimated by the contracting officer and included in the solicitation to be applicable to all competitors, FAR 17.106-2(d). It must be established based upon a reasonable estimate of nonrecurring costs (broadly defined) of an "average" contractor, FAR 17.106-1(c)(2). The regulations permit the contracting officer to adjust the cancellation ceiling prior to award "if necessary," FAR 17.106-1(d). In a sealed bid procurement, this would be done by amendment to the solicitation, while in a negotiated procurement, it could be done during the negotiation process. Such adjustment would appear to be mandatory since the Court of Claims reformed a cancellation ceiling that was not reasonable in *Applied Devices Corp. v. United States*, 219 Ct. Cl. 109, 591 F.2d 635 (1979). The court concluded that the regulations calling for inclusion of a reasonable ceiling were for the benefit of potential contractors and increased the ceiling to a reasonable amount in spite of the fact that the contractor had not protested the inadequacy of the ceiling before bid opening. A similar adjustment to the cancellation ceiling was made in *Technical & Mgmt. Servs. Corp.*, ASBCA 39999, 93-2 BCA ¶ 25,681, *aff'd*, 16 F.3d 420 (Fed. Cir. 1993).

Because the purpose of the cancellation charge is normally to reimburse the contractor for unamortized costs in the event the contract is canceled, where no such costs are involved in the procurement there is no need to include a cancellation ceiling. See FAR 17.104(b), permitting agency heads to modify cancellation terms to fit the conditions of an individual procurement. In *Big Bud Tractors, Inc.*, Comp. Gen. Dec. B-209858, 83-1 CPD ¶ 127, GAO held that the Army's RFP for the multiyear procurement of a standard commercial unit of equipment was not defective despite the fact that it did not include a cancellation ceiling where there were no unamortized nonrecurring costs.

### c.  Failure to Order Full Quantity

The Cancellation Under Multiyear Contracts clause provides that cancellation may occur when *funds are not available* for "contract performance for any subsequent program year." If the government does not order the full requirement for some other reason, a termination for convenience will have occurred and the contractor will be entitled to compensation without regard to the cancellation ceiling. However, in *Varo, Inc.*, ASBCA 13739, 70-1 BCA ¶ 8099, the board construed the "funds available" provision broadly, holding that the cancellation provisions of the contract applied not only when funds were not appropriated but also when the agency decided that it no longer had a requirement for the items. The board reached this conclusion by looking to the agency's records documenting the formulation of the multiyear contracting policy. This reasoning was subsequently adopted by the Court of Claims in *Applied Devices Corp. v. United States*, 219 Ct. Cl. 109, 591 F.2d 635 (1979). The court held that the Cancellation of Items clause was properly used in a situation where the agency obtained the funds necessary for the procurement from Congress but decided, based on an analysis of agency needs, that the requirement should be met by procuring different equipment. The court reasoned that in such a case, the requirement no longer existed. The court further concluded that lack of funding included a lack of requirements, stating that it "is a fallacy to suppose that requirements and funds availability exist in two separate universes of discourse." This questionable reasoning deprives the contractor of the benefits of the Termination for the Convenience of the Government clause when the government agency makes an internal decision to alter its requirements.

Contractors have been given the protection of the Termination for the Convenience of the Government clause in other circumstances. Thus, when an agency ordered the items from another contractor, a termination for convenience was found, *Maxson Elecs. Corp.*, ASBCA 12983, 72-2 BCA ¶ 9543. This result might not occur under the current clause because it also includes in the definition of "cancellation" the situation where the contracting officer "fails to notify the Contractor that funds are available for performance of the succeeding program year requirement."

A termination for convenience will also be found if work is deleted during a program year. See FAR 17.104(d), stating:

> The termination for convenience procedure may apply to any Government contract, including multiyear contracts. As contrasted with cancellation, termination can be effected at any time during the life of the contract (cancellation is effected between fiscal years) and can be for the total quantity or a partial quantity (whereas cancellation must be for all subsequent fiscal years' quantities).

See *Aeronca, Inc.*, ASBCA 13040, 70-1 BCA ¶ 8278, where the board held that a partial termination for convenience had occurred when the government funded only some of the items in the second and third program years. Similarly, the ceiling was held not to apply to a future year when the government did not completely order all prior years' quantities. In *Conaec Corp.*, ASBCA 14234, 73-1 BCA ¶ 9808, the government issued a notice of convenience termination during the second year and argued that the contract price for purposes of computing the termination costs was the price for two years' quantity (with the third-year quantity being subject to the cancellation ceiling). The board disagreed, holding that the government had not proved that there was no requirement for the third year's quantity and that its action therefore constituted a termination of the total multiyear quantity. It has been suggested that this holding obligates the government agency with reduced requirements to order those requirements under the multiyear contract and to reprice as if there had been a partial termination of the year's quantity, Latham, *Multi-Year Procurement*, Federal Publications Briefing Paper 73-2 (1973).

## d.  Legal Validity of Cancellation Provisions

Under normal appropriations law, agencies would be required to obligate current-year funds to cover cancellation costs within the contractual ceiling. However, 10 U.S.C. § 2306b(f) provides:

> In the event funds are not made available for the continuation of a contract made under this subsection into a subsequent fiscal year, the contract shall be canceled or terminated. The costs of cancellation or termination may be paid from —
>
> > (A) appropriations originally available for the performance of the contract concerned;
> >
> > (B) appropriations currently available for procurement of the type of property concerned, and not otherwise obligated; or
> >
> > (C) funds appropriated for those payments.

See also 10 U.S.C. § 2306c(e), which includes substantially the same language applying to service contracts.

These provisions were apparently written to permit DoD, NASA and the Coast Guard to incur the legal liability for paying cancellation costs without obligating funds to cover that liability. However, it appears that the statutory language was written omitting any reference to a firm obligation of the government covering cancellation costs in order to avoid any implication that Congress was granting "contract authority" pursuant to the Anti-Deficiency Act. This was in recognition that 31 U.S.C. § 1341 precludes the creation of contract authority for procurement. See House Report 97-311, the Conference Committee Report on the 1982 Defense Authorization Act (including this language in the provision giving multi-year contracting authority for major systems), stating at 126:

> The provisions agreed to by the conferees limit the authority to enter into multi-year contracts to cases where "funds are otherwise available for obligation." This language was adopted to make clear that the provision does not, by itself, provide contract authority. Rather the authority to enter into contracts is provided subject to funds being available for obligation through other actions of the Congress or

other provisions of law. In adopting this language, the conferees did not intend to restrict the authority to enter into multiyear contracts solely to those cases where funds are appropriated for that purpose. On the contrary, the conferees envision that funds could be available for obligation for a multiyear contract from, for example, annually made appropriations, including funds made available through reprogramming or transfer; proceeds from sales of goods and services which under current provision of law would be available for obligation; and funds available for obligation in connection with foreign military sales.

In spite of this confusing situation, which seems to require agencies to violate the Anti-Deficiency Act, funds have not been obligated by the military services to cover cancellation ceilings. See DoD Authorization Act, 1985, Pub. L. No. 98-525, 98 Stat. 2492, directing this course of action at 2498:

> [Multiyear] contracts may include an unfunded cancellation ceiling. If funds are not made available for the continuation of such a contract in subsequent fiscal years, the contract shall be cancelled and the costs of cancellation shall be paid as provided in section 2306(h)(5) of title 10, United States Code.

Since 41 U.S.C. § 3903 contains no language similar to 10 U.S.C. § 2306b(f), it would appear that civilian agencies are required to obligate funds to cover cancellation ceilings or termination costs. See 41 U.S.C. § 3903(c), stating:

> Termination Clause — A multiyear contract entered into under the authority of this section shall include a clause that provides that the contract shall be terminated if funds are not made available for the continuation of such contract in a fiscal year covered by the contract. Funds available for paying termination costs shall remain available for that purpose until the costs associated with termination of the contract are paid.

See *Bureau of Customs and Border Protection — Automated Commercial Env't Contract*, Comp. Gen. Dec. B-302358, 2004 U.S. Comp. Gen. LEXIS 271, holding that since a multiple-year IDIQ contract was not a multiyear contract, the agency was not required to obligate funds to cover termination costs if later years' work was not procured.

FAR 17.104(c) appears to ignore the legislative history of the DoD statutes. It requires that funds covering cancellation costs be obligated at the time of contracting, as follows:

> Agency funding of multi-year contracts shall conform to the policies in OMB Circulars A-11 (Preparation and Submission of Budget Estimates) and A-34 (Instructions on Budget Execution) and other applicable guidance regarding the funding of multi-ear contracts. As provided by that guidance, the funds obligated for multi-year contracts must be sufficient to cover any potential cancellation and/or termination costs; and multi-year contracts for the acquisition of fixed assets should be fully funded or funded in stages that are economically or programmatically viable.

## 7. *Distinguishing Requirements Contracts*

Requirements contracts are used to procure supplies or services where precise quantities are not fully known. They may be entered into for several years without following the procedures prescribed for multiyear contracts, *Mills Mfg. Corp.*, Comp. Gen. Dec. B-224004, 86-2 CPD ¶ 679, *recons. denied*, 87-1 CPD ¶ 393. The fact that a requirements contract contemplates performance over a period of years will not transform it into a multi-year contract, *Solar Turbines Int'l v. United States*, 3 Cl. Ct. 489 (1983). In *Solar Turbines*, the government used a requirements contract containing a Cancellation Ceiling Cost clause entitling the contractor to increased compensation for shortfalls in actual orders. The contractor unsuccessfully argued that Best Estimated Quantities (BEQ) were actually firm orders for minimum quantities under a multiyear contract.

Prior to the enactment of the FASA, FAR 17.104-4 (pre-1996) set forth procedures for the multi-year acquisition of supplies and services under modified requirements contracts, to be used only when anticipated annual requirements could be projected with reasonable certainty. Anticipated requirements expressed as BEQ were set forth in the contract. Nonrecurring costs were to be amortized over the BEQ, FAR 17.104-4(a)(2). If actual orders fell short of the BEQ, the contractor was to be reimbursed in accordance with the Cancellation of Items clause. In *Viktoria Transport GmbH & Co., KG*, ASBCA 30371, 88-3 BCA ¶ 20,921, the board held that the contractor should recover under the Termination for Convenience clause instead of the Cancellation of Items clause because the government did not order all of its requirements from the contractor.

The current FAR is silent on these issues.

## D. Indefinite-Quantity Contracts

The indefinite-quantity contract is the other form of variable quantity, indefinite-delivery contract in Subpart 16.5 of the FAR. This type of contract is commonly called an IDIQ contract. In the IDIQ contract, the government obligates itself to buy at least a stated minimum quantity of the goods or services, and the contract will also contain a maximum quantity beyond which the contractor is not bound, FAR 16.504(a)(1). This type of contract is very similar to a contract for a firm quantity with options for additional quantities, the major difference being that the IDIQ contract can be issued initially without any firm orders being placed as long as the government is obligated to order an adequate minimum quantity.

When an agency awards an IDIQ contract, it must immediately obligate an amount of funds that corresponds to the minimum quantity. See *Bureau of Customs and Border Protection — Automated Commercial Environment Contract*, Comp. Gen. Dec. B-302358, 2004 Comp. Gen. LEXIS 271, stating:

When an agency executes an indefinite-quantity contract such as an IDIQ contract, the agency must record an obligation in the amount of the required minimum purchase. In an IDIQ contract, the government commits itself to purchase only a minimum amount of supplies or services. FAR § 16.501-2(b)(3). At the time of award, the government has a fixed liability for the minimum amount to which it committed itself. *See* FAR § 16.504(a)(1) (specifying that an IDIQ contract must require the agency to order a stated minimum quantity). An agency is required to record an obligation at the time it incurs a legal liability. 65 Comp. Gen. 4, 6 (1985); B-242974.6, Nov. 26, 1991. Therefore, for an IDIQ contract, an agency must record an obligation for the minimum amount at the time of contract execution.

See also *Interagency Agreements — Obligation of Funds under an Indefinite Delivery, Indefinite Quantity Contract*, Comp. Gen. Dec. B-308969, 2007 CPD ¶ 120.

The following Indefinite Quantity clause in FAR 52.216-22 is used in all indefinite-quantity contracts:

INDEFINITE QUANTITY (OCT 1995)

(a) This is an indefinite-quantity contract for the supplies or service specified, and effective for the period stated, in the Schedule. The quantities of supplies and services specified in the Schedule are estimates only and are not purchased by this contract.

(b) Delivery or performance shall be made only as authorized by orders issued in accordance with the Ordering clause. The Contractor shall furnish to the Government, when and if ordered, the supplies or services specified in the Schedule up to and including the quantity designated in the Schedule as the "maximum." The Government shall order at least the quantity of supplies or services designated in the Schedule as the "minimum."

(c) Except for any limitations on quantities in the Order Limitations clause or in the Schedule, there is no limit on the number of orders that may be issued. The Government may issue orders requiring delivery to multiple destinations or performance at multiple locations.

(d) Any order issued during the effective period of this contract and not completed within that period shall be completed by the Contractor within the time specified in the order. The contract shall govern the Contractor's and Government's rights and obligations with respect to that order to the same extent as if the order were completed during the contract's effective period; *provided*, that the Contractor shall not be required to make any deliveries under this contact after [*insert date*].

## 1. *Adequate Minimum Quantity*

As discussed in Chapter 2, to be binding on the contractor, an IDIQ contract must contain a minimum quantity that is more than "nominal," FAR 16.504(a)(2). In

*Tennessee Soap Co. v. United States*, 130 Ct. Cl. 154, 126 F. Supp. 439 (1954), a $10 minimum order was held to be nominal. See also *Goldwasser v. United States*, 163 Ct. Cl. 450, 325 F.2d 722 (1963), where the court found that a contract with a minimum quantity of $100 compared to an estimated price of $40,000 "would have been a one-sided bargain, bordering upon lack of mutuality." The court did not decide this issue since it held the contract to be a requirements contract. GAO has stated that the analysis of whether a minimum is nominal should be based on "the nature of the acquisition as a whole," *CW Gov't Travel, Inc.*, Comp. Gen. Dec. B-295530, 2005 CPD ¶ 59. In that case, a minimum of $2,500 in transaction fees was not nominal although the contract permits orders up to $150,000,000. GAO reasoned that since each transaction fee would approximate $5, the minimum represented a significant number of transactions. See also *Library of Congress — Obligation of Guaranteed Minimums for Indefinite-Delivery, Indefinite-Quantity Contracts under the FEDLINK Program*, Comp. Gen. Dec. B-318046, 2009 Comp. Gen. LEXIS 126 (minimum of $500 not nominal when purchases could be as high as $15 million but no reliable data available to judge amount of orders); *ABF Freight Sys., Inc.*, Comp. Gen. Dec. B-291185, 2002 CPD ¶ 201, and *ABF Freight Sys., Inc. v. United States*, 55 Fed. Cl. 392 (2003) (minimums of approximately 5% of work not nominal); *Carr's Wild Horse Center*, Comp. Gen. Dec. B-285833, 2000 CPD ¶ 210 (minimum of 100 animals not nominal in contract to handle up to 100,000 animals); *Aalco Forwarding, Inc.*, Comp. Gen. Dec. B-277241.15, 98-1 CPD ¶ 87 ($25,000 minimum per contract in multiple award contracts for moving goods not nominal even though $75,000,000 work anticipated). A nominal minimum amount for each task will not invalidate an IDIQ contract if it contains a non-nominal minimum for the entire contract, *C.W. Over & Sons, Inc.*, Comp. Gen. Dec. B-274365, 96-2 CPD ¶ 223.

The minimum quantity need not be ordered at the time the contract is issued as long as the government promises to buy a meaningful minimum amount of goods or services, *Federal Elec. Corp.*, ASBCA 11726, 68-1 BCA ¶ 6834; Comp. Gen. Dec. B-160063, Feb. 10, 1967, *Unpub.* In *Federal Elec. Corp. v. United States*, 202 Ct. Cl. 1028, 486 F.2d 1377 (1973), the Court of Claims upheld the board decision but stated that the contractor was bound to the contract because the minimum quantity had been ordered at the same time the parties entered into the contract. Since the minimum was a substantial quantity, the time the first order was placed would appear to be irrelevant to the issue of whether the contractor was bound to perform the contract.

When an IDIQ contract contains options for additional items or years of services, there is no requirement that there be a minimum quantity supporting each option, *Varilease Tech. Group, Inc. v. United States*, 289 F.3d 795 (Fed. Cir. 2002). This is based on the reasoning that the minimum for the base year is consideration for the options. See also *EFG Assocs., Inc.*, ASBCA 50342, 99-2 BCA ¶ 30,525.

If an IDIQ contract contains no specified minimum quantities, the court or board may find a means of furnishing a minimum in order to prevent the contract from failing for lack of consideration. For example, in *Howell v. United States*, 51 Fed. Cl. 516 (2002), the court found that the parties intended to enter into a binding contract and concluded that it could furnish a reasonable minimum of $1,000 per contract using its power to supply a "missing essential term" under Restatement (Second) of Contracts § 204. In another case where an IDIQ contract contained no minimum, the contractor was held to be entitled to assume that the estimated quantities were the minimum quantities that would be ordered, *Apex Int'l Mgmt. Servs., Inc.*, ASBCA 38087, 94-2 BCA ¶ 26,842. The standard Indefinite Quantity clause in FAR 52.216-22 calls for the inclusion in the contract schedule of both minimum quantities and estimated quantities, but the board held that the absence of minimum quantities was an ambiguity for which the government was responsible as the drafter of the contract. Compare *Delfour, Inc.*, PSBCA 3333, 95-1 BCA ¶ 27,524, *recons. denied*, 95-2 BCA ¶ 27,908, *aff'd*, 95 F.3d 1163 (Fed. Cir. 1996), where a contract stating that it was an IDIQ contract and containing a minimum quantity of $10,000 was held to constitute an IDIQ contract even though it also stated that it had an "initial contract value" of $1 million.

IDIQ contracts contain a Termination for the Convenience of the Government clause which permit the government to terminate the contract before ordering the minimum quantity. In *Southwest Lab. of Oklahoma, Inc.*, Comp. Gen. Dec. B-251778, 93-1 CPD ¶ 368, GAO held that a special clause stating this proposition did not destroy the consideration supporting the contract because the promise of the government to pay termination costs and profit was sufficient consideration. GAO ruled, however, that a further provision of the clause making a failure to order the minimum an automatic termination for convenience was improper because it was an attempt to convert a government breach into a termination for convenience — in conflict with the holding in *Maxima Corp. v. United States*, 847 F.2d 1549 (Fed. Cir. 1988).

When a combination fixed-price/IDIQ contract specifies that the fixed-price component is to be used as the guaranteed minimum, the government is not obligated to guarantee an additional minimum amount of work under the indefinite-quantity component, *Mac's Cleaning & Repair Serv.*, ASBCA 49652, 97-1 BCA ¶ 28,748, *aff'd*, 132 F.3d 51 (Fed. Cir. 1997). Similarly, in a contract with some indicia of an IDIQ contract calling for reimbursement of costs, the initial funding of costs was held to meet the requirement for a non-nominal minimum, *Sociotechnical Research Applications, Inc.*, IBCA 3969-98, 01-1 BCA ¶ 31,235.

## 2. Distinguishing Requirements Contracts

There have been a number of disputes as to whether a contract is a requirements contract or an IDIQ contract. In such cases, the courts and boards have carefully analyzed the contract language to determine the type of contract intended. In *Goldwasser v. United States*, 163 Ct. Cl. 450, 325 F.2d 722 (1963), the court resolved a conflict between the Indefinite Quantity clause and the specifications listing the items to be procured by concluding that the latter showed an intent to create a requirements contract. In contrast, in *Mason v. United States*, 222 Ct. Cl. 436, 615 F.2d 1343 (1980), the court found that the stated minimum quantity in the contract indicated that the parties had entered into an IDIQ contract because otherwise that clause was superfluous. In *Maintenance Eng'rs v. United States*, 749 F.2d 724 (Fed. Cir. 1984), a conflict between a term in the solicitation identifying the contract as one for an indefinite quantity and a term in the General Provisions stating "this is a requirements contract" was resolved by the Order of Precedence clause giving priority to the solicitation language. In *Stanley F. Horton*, DOTCAB 1231, 82-2 BCA ¶ 15,967, the board considered both course of dealing and the knowledge of the parties at the time of contract formation and found that the contract was a requirements contract despite the absence of an explicit term barring the government from obtaining snow removal services elsewhere. In contrast, in *Ann Riley & Assocs.*, DOTBCA 2418, 93-3 BCA ¶ 25,963, the board found an IDIQ contract based on the contract language even though the government argued that it intended to create a requirements contract. Where course of dealing or other circumstances do not imply a requirements contract, the absence of a government obligation to satisfy all needs under the contract will render the contract an IDIQ contract, *Hemet Valley Flying Serv. Co. v. United States*, 7 Cl. Ct. 512 (1985). In *Hemet Valley*, the court was able to find a binding IDIQ contract despite the fact that no stated minimum quantity of flying hours was promised because the government paid a non-nominal amount for contractor's promise to maintain "availability" to fly. In *Export Packing & Crating Co.*, ASBCA 16133, 73-2 BCA ¶ 10,066, the board looked to the underlying contractual relationship to find a requirements contract and stated that there was no ambiguity despite clauses identifying the contract as both an IDIQ and requirements contract.

In *J. Cooper & Assocs., Inc. v. United States*, 53 Fed. Cl. 8 (2002), *aff'd*, 65 Fed. App'x 731 (Fed. Cir. 2003), the government issued a letter contract containing a minimum dollar amount of work and calling for the submission of a price proposal for an IDIQ contract. The court rejected the contractor's argument that when the letter contract was never converted to a firm contract, it became a requirement contract, holding that the correct interpretation of the transaction was that the parties intended to enter into an IDIQ contract.

In *Varilease Tech. Group, Inc. v. United States*, 289 F.3d 795 (Fed. Cir. 2002), the contractor argued that the options in its IDIQ contract were for all of the government's requirements because the only minimum quantity was for the base contract. The court rejected this argument holding that the clear language of the contract indicated that it was an IDIQ contract and there was "no basis in either the relevant regulations or case law for treating option periods of an IDIQ contract as separate contracts." See also *RJO Enter., Inc.*, ASBCA 50981, 03-1 BCA ¶ 32,137, where the board held that the contractor had no recourse when the government exercised its options for additional years' services on an IDIQ contract but stopped issuing orders after it had awarded a successor contract to another contractor.

Where a contract contains neither a guaranteed minimum quantity nor the Requirements clause in FAR 52.216-21, it will be held to be a requirements contract if it contains language leading to the interpretation that the government will not deal with other contractors in obtaining the work. See *Rowe, Inc. v. General Servs. Admin.*, GSBCA 15217, 03-1 BCA ¶ 32,162, *recons. denied*, 03-1 BCA ¶ 32,215 (requirements contract based on language stating agency would purchase quantities of vehicles needed "to fill any requirements determined in accordance with applicable procurement regulations and supply procedures."); and *Centurion Elecs. Serv.*, ASBCA 51956, 03-1 BCA ¶ 32,097 (requirements contract because it called for contractor to furnish "all per call repairs" of designated equipment). Compare *Coyle's Pest Control, Inc. v. Cuomo*, 154 F.3d 1302 (Fed. Cir. 1998), where the court found that such a contract was not a requirements contract because of conflicting language, stating at 1305-06:

> The contract does include terms that suggest exclusivity. For instance, the contract obligates Coyle "to furnish *all* labor, service, equipment, transportation, materials and supplies to provide subterranean termite control and related services on *assigned* properties by [HUD]." (emphasis added). While the contract states that Coyle will provide all labor and services for a given property, the clause does not require HUD to assign Coyle *all* properties in the region. Thus, this contract language falls short of the exclusivity language necessary for a requirements contract.

## 3. *Estimated Quantities*

In order to evaluate prices or costs in IDIQ contracts, the government frequently includes estimated quantities of work. The price or cost evaluation is then performed by multiplying the quoted unit prices or costs times the estimated quantities to arrive at the total price or cost. Paragraph (a) of the Indefinite Quantities clause in FAR 52.216-22 warns offerors that these estimates are not ordered quantities but merely estimates.

In contrast to the rule governing requirements contracts, the estimates in IDIQ contracts impose no liability on the government if they are negligently arrived at, *Travel Centre v. Barram*, 236 F.3d 1316 (Fed. Cir. 2001). The court reached this conclusion following the questionable reasoning that the contractor could not reasonably rely on these estimates because the only legal obligation of the government was to order the minimum quantity of work. The court stated at 1319:

> Regardless of the accuracy of the estimates delineated in the solicitation, based on the language of the solicitation for the IDIQ contract, Travel Centre could not have had a reasonable expectation that any of the government's needs beyond the minimum contract price would necessarily be satisfied under this contract.

This reasoning ignores the fact that the contractor had to rely on the estimates because it was well aware of the fact that they would be used to evaluate its proposed prices. Nonetheless, the rule that the government is not liable for negligent estimates in IDIQ contracts has been followed in *Transtar Metals, Inc.*, ASBCA 55039, 07-1 BCA ¶ 33,482; *White Sands Constr., Inc.*, ASBCA 51875, 02-2 BCA ¶ 31,858 (the board stated "how the estimates were determined is simply not relevant"); and *Abatement Constr. Corp. v. United States*, 58 Fed. Cl. 594 (2003) (no government liability for negligent estimate prepared when agency intended to issue a requirements contract but subsequently issued an IDIQ contract).

If the agency explicitly directs offerors to rely on government estimates in arriving at their prices, the agency will be liable for inaccurate estimates without regard to whether they have been negligently prepared, *Admiral Elevator v. Social Sec. Admin.*, CBCA 470 07-2 BCA ¶ 33,676. In that case the offerors were required to provide two on-site personnel at all times but had to allocate their costs to unit priced maintenance work which was estimated to be sufficient to permit recovery of those costs. The board reasoned at 166,730:

> [The agency's] response [to inquiries from potential offerors] makes clear that SSA intended that offerors use the agency's estimates as a basis for their contract pricing and additionally expected offerors to construct their pricing on the assumption that the costs of the mandated on-site personnel would be recovered, under the per-unit, per-month pricing structure, no matter how many elevators were to be maintained in any particular month. Internal communications among SSA employees involved in the procurement and the deposition testimony of an SSA contracting officer confirm the agency's expectations as to use of the estimates by offerors. This case is consequently like several others in which the Court of Appeals for the Federal Circuit and its predecessor Court of Claims found an agency responsible for the losses which a contractor suffered because, in pricing the contract, it reasonably relied on material, incorrect agency representations in solicitations. Among these cases are *Brown [Constructors, Inc. v. Pena]*, 132 F.3d [724 (Fed. Cir. 1997)] at 729 (erroneous representation as to soil content, due to incorrect washed sieve analysis); *Summit Timber Co. v. United States*, 677 F.2d 852 (Ct. Cl. 1982) (erroneous representation as to boundaries within which timber could be cut, due to incorrect markings); *Everett Plywood & Door Corp. v. United States*, 419 F.2d 425 (Ct. Cl. 1969) (erroneous representation as to volume of timber available for cutting in oddly-shaped area, due to incorrect estimates by inexperienced personnel); and *United Contractors v. United States*, 368 F.2d 585 (Ct. Cl. 1966) (erroneous representation as to subsurface conditions, due to incorrect soil borings). Indeed, the contractor's position is even stronger in this case than it was in those, because here the contractor not only was expected to rely on the key information, but also was told to rely on that information.

## 4.  Multiple Award Preference

The statutory multiple award preference for task order and delivery order contracts, discussed at the beginning of this section, has been incorporated in the FAR coverage of IDIQ contracts. See FAR 16.504(c), which states:

*Multiple award preference —*

(1) *Planning the acquisition.* (i) Except for indefinite-quantity contracts for advisory and assistance services as provided in paragraph (c)(2) of this section, the contracting officer must, to the maximum extent practicable, give preference to making multiple awards of indefinite-quantity contracts under a single solicitation for the same or similar supplies or services to two or more sources.

(ii) (A) The contracting officer must determine whether multiple awards are appropriate as part of acquisition planning. The contracting officer must avoid situations in which awardees specialize exclusively in one or a few areas within the statement of work, thus creating the likelihood that orders in those areas will be awarded on a sole-source basis; however, each awardee need not be capable of performing every requirement as well as any other awardee under the contracts. The contracting officer should consider the following when determining the number of contracts to be awarded:

(1) The scope and complexity of the contract requirement.

(2) The expected duration and frequency of task or delivery orders.

(3) The mix of resources a contractor must have to perform expected task or delivery order requirements.

(4) The ability to maintain competition among the awardees throughout the contracts' period of performance.

(B) The contracting officer must not use the multiple award approach if —

(1) Only one contractor is capable of providing performance at the level of quality required because the supplies or services are unique or highly specialized;

(2) Based on the contracting officer's knowledge of the market, more favorable terms and conditions, including pricing, will be provided if a single award is made;

(3) The expected cost of administration of multiple contracts may outweighs the expected benefits of making multiple awards;

(4) The projected orders are so integrally related that only a single contractor can reasonably perform the work;

(5) The total estimated value of the contract is less than the simplified acquisition threshold; or

(6) Multiple awards would not be in the best interests of the Government.

(C) The contracting officer must document the decision whether or not to use multiple awards in the acquisition plan or contract file. The contracting officer may determine that a class of acquisitions is not appropriate for multiple awards (see subpart 1.7).

(D)(1) No task or delivery order contract in an amount estimated to exceed $ 103 million (including all options) may be awarded to a single source unless the head of the agency determines in writing that —

(i) The task or delivery orders expected under the contract are so integrally related that only a single source can reasonably perform the work;

(ii) The contract provides only for firm-fixed price (see 16.202) task or delivery orders for —

(A) Products for which unit prices are established in the contract; or

(B) Services for which prices are established in the contract for the specific tasks to be performed;

(iii) Only one source is qualified and capable of performing the work at a reasonable price to the Government; or

(iv) It is necessary in the public interest to award the contract to a single source due to exceptional circumstances.

(2) The head of the agency must notify Congress within 30 days after any determination under paragraph (c)(1)(ii)(D)(1)(iv) of this section.

(3) The requirement for a determination for a single-award contract greater than $103 million:

(i) Is in addition to any applicable requirements of Subpart 6.3.

(ii) Is not applicable for architect-engineer services awarded pursuant to Subpart 36.6.

(2) *Contracts for advisory and assistance services.* (i) Except as provided in paragraph (c)(2)(ii) of this section, if an indefinite-quantity contract for advisory and assistance services exceeds 3 years and $11.5 million, including all options, a contracting officer must make multiple awards unless —

(A) The contracting officer or other official designated by the head of the agency determines in writing, as part of acquisition planning, that multiple awards are not practicable. The contracting officer or other official must determine that only one contractor can reasonably perform the work because either the scope of work is unique or highly specialized or the tasks so integrally related;

(B) The contracting officer or other official designated by the head of the agency determines in writing, after the evaluation of offers, that only one offeror is capable of providing the services required at the level of quality required; or

(C) Only one offer is received.

(ii) The requirements of paragraph (c)(2)(i) of this section do not apply if the contracting officer or other official designated by the head of the agency determines that the advisory and assistance services are incidental and not a significant component of the contract.

The criteria for not issuing multiple IDIQ contracts give the contracting officer considerable discretion. However, when an agency is obtaining a significant amount of supplies or services over long periods of time through the use of such contracts, there are substantial benefits to be obtained through the issuance of more than one contract. The major benefits of the continuous competition that can be achieved under multiple contracts are the ability to control the prices of individual task and delivery orders and the ability to award such orders based on the past performance of the contractors. Multiple contracts also permit the agency to award IDIQ contracts to contractors with varying skills — giving the government access to a broader range of competence than would be possible with only a single contract. It has been held permissible to restrict multiple awards to affiliates when there was a risk that failure of performance of affiliated contractors would jeopardize the agency's program, *District Moving & Storage, Inc.*, Comp. Gen. Dec. B-272070, 96-2 CPD ¶ 60.

Determinations to make a single award have been held not to be properly based on the factors set forth in the FAR. See *Information Ventures, Inc.*, Comp. Gen. Dec. B-403321, 2010 CPD ¶ 223 (fact that when multiple contracts were issued, some contractors did not provide acceptable products not a justification for single award); *One Source Mech. Servs., Inc.*, Comp. Gen. Dec. B-293692, 2004 CPD ¶ 112 (administrative cost and time required to conduct competitions between multiple awardees not a justification for single award); *WinStar Commc'ns, Inc. v. United States*, 41 Fed. Cl. 748 (1998) (failure to consider the benefits of multiple awards); and *Nations, Inc.*, Comp. Gen. Dec. B-272455, 96-2 CPD ¶ 170 (single requirements contract not proper for advisory and assistance services over dollar threshold requiring multiple awards). Compare *Outdoor Venture Corp.*, Comp. Gen. Dec. B-288894.2, 2002 CPD ¶ 13 (single award justified when only one acceptable proposal received); *SmithKline Beecham Pharms.*, Comp. Gen. Dec. B-277253.4, 97-2 CPD ¶ 78 (single award justified by belief of contracting officer that more favorable terms will be achieved by a single requirements contract); *Cubic Applications, Inc. v. United States*, 37 Fed. Cl. 345 (1997) (single award justified because advisory and assistance services being procured are so integrally related that they could not be performed by more than one contractor). See also *R.C.O. Reforesting*, Comp. Gen. Dec. B-280774.2, 98-2 CPD ¶ 119, agreeing that it was proper to award only two contracts when the agency had insufficient administrative support to deal with more contractors.

Congress enacted additional provisions to motivate agencies to award multiple award contracts in § 843 of the National Defense Authorization Act for FY 2008, adding the following provision to 10 U.S.C. § 2304a(d) and 41 U.S.C. § 4103(d):

(3)(A) No task or delivery order contract in an amount estimated to exceed $100,000,000 (including all options) may be awarded to a single source unless the head of the agency determines in writing that —

> (i) the task or delivery orders expected under the contract are so integrally related that only a single source can reasonably perform the work;

> (ii) the contract provides only for firm, fixed price task orders or delivery orders for —

>> (I) products for which unit prices are established in the contract; or

>> (II) services for which prices are established in the contract for the specific tasks to be performed;

> (iii) only one source is qualified and capable of performing the work at a reasonable price to the government; or

> (iv) because of exceptional circumstances, it is necessary in the public interest to award the contract to a single source.

(B) The head of the agency shall notify Congress within 30 days after any determination under subparagraph (A)(iv).

This provision is implemented in FAR 16.504, quoted above.

When the agency intends to award multiple contracts, the following Single or Multiple Awards solicitation provision in FAR 52.216-27 is used to alert offerors of this intention:

SINGLE OR MULTIPLE AWARDS (OCT 1995)

The Government may elect to award a single delivery order contract or task order contract or to award multiple delivery order contracts or task order contracts for the same or similar supplies or services to two or more sources under this solicitation.

## 5.  *Structuring the Contract*

The major elements of the indefinite-quantity contract are the minimum quantities, the maximum quantities, the inclusion of multiple years, and the ordering procedures. The minimums and maximums can be stated in dollars or units of work, FAR 16.504(a).

### a.  *Minimum Quantities*

As discussed above, the minimum quantity must be more than a nominal quantity to ensure that the contract is legally binding. The only other guidance contained in FAR 16.504(a)(2) is that the minimum quantity should not exceed the amount "that the Government is fairly certain to order." The minimum order limitation is to be included in ¶ (a) of the mandatory Order Limitations clause in FAR 52.216-19. All other information on minimum quantities must be included in the contract schedule.

There appears to be a tendency for contracting officers to specify very low contract minimums in order to limit the government's liability in the event its requirements change during the life of the contract and to avoid obligating significant amounts of funds at the inception of the contract. However, better prices may be obtained if higher minimum quantities are specified. When multiple contracts are awarded and orders will be placed competitively, the ordering process should control the prices, and there will be little need for concern about the impact of low minimum quantities.

In multiple item, indefinite-quantity contracts, minimum quantities can also be stated for each item or type of services. This gives the offerors assurance that the government intends to order each item and may provide some inducement for the offerors to avoid unbalanced pricing. However, it is proper to use only a single contract minimum, *C.W. Over & Sons, Inc.*, Comp. Gen. Dec. B-274365, 96-2 CPD ¶ 223; *Sunbelt Props., Inc.*, Comp. Gen. Dec. B-249307, 92-2 CPD ¶ 309.

### b.  *Maximum Quantities*

FAR 16.504(a)(1) provides that the contract should contain a maximum quantity that should be "reasonable" and "based on market research, trends on recent contracts for similar supplies or services, survey of potential users, or any other rational basis." It also permits maximum quantities for any single task or delivery order and maximum quantities that may be ordered during any specified period of time. The Order Limitations clause in FAR 52.216-19 contains the following paragraph, which is to be filled in by the contracting officer to specify such maximums:

(b) *Maximum order.* The Contractor is not obligated to honor —

(1) Any order for a single item in excess of [*insert dollar figure or quantity*];

(2) Any order for a combination of items in excess of [*insert dollar figure or quantity*]; or

(3) A series of orders from the same ordering office within . . . . days that together call for quantities exceeding the limitation in subparagraph (1) or (2) above.

This paragraph should be carefully tailored to fit the circumstances of each procurement. In addition, the contract maximum quantity should be stated in the contract schedule.

Paragraph (d) of the Order Limitations clause requires the contractor to honor an order above the maximums stated in the clause if timely notice is not given of its intention not to fill the order. In *General Cutlery v. General Servs. Admin.*, GSBCA 13154, 96-1 BCA ¶ 27,957, the board affirmed the default termination of a contractor that had not filled an order above the maximum quantity but had not given notice of its intention not to fill the order.

Where the IDIQ contract fails to set maximum amounts for a portion of the work to be performed, the government may not order unlimited quantities of work, and the amount ordered will be measured by the standard of reasonableness under the circumstances, *Computer Scis. Corp.*, ASBCA 24035, 82-2 BCA ¶ 15,923.

## c.  Length of the Contract

As discussed above, there are statutory limitations of ten years on task and delivery order contracts issued by DoD. FAR 17.204(e) also contains a general five year limitation on all contracts. 10 U.S.C. § 2304(d)(3) and 41 U.S.C. § 3304(c)(1)(B) contain a one year limitation on contracts over the simplified acquisition threshold that are awarded without full and open competition based on urgency, unless the head of the agency determines that exceptional circumstances apply.

FAR 16.504(a)(4) requires an IDIQ contract to

(i) Specify the period of the contract, including the number of options and the period for which the contract may be extended under each option;

This would imply that all such contracts for a period of longer than one year would be written as a contract for the base year plus a series of options. However, the same result can be achieved by writing the contract for a minimum quantity in the first year and for additional quantities, as called for by the government, subject to the availability of appropriations. This would avoid the need to follow the regulatory rules on the exercise of options.

If the IDIQ contract is written for a period longer than one year by the inclusion of options, the contracting officer has the choice of several standard clauses — the Option for Increased Quantities clause in FAR 52.217-6, the Option to Extend Services clause in FAR 52.217-8, or the Option to Extend the Term of the Contract clause in FAR 52.217-9. If this last clause is used, exercise of the option does not procure additional work but merely extends the period when work can be ordered, *Five Star Elecs., Inc.*, ASBCA 44984, 96-2 BCA ¶ 28,421. Contracting officers must exercise care is including these clauses because they confer different rights on the government, as discussed in the next section.

If the contract is for a period of longer than one year without options, ¶ (a) of the mandatory Ordering clause in FAR 52.216-18 will include an end date for ordering that corresponds to the final day of the last year covered by the contract. If such a contract contains firm prices, the contracting officer should ensure that the prices are still in line with current prices that are available from other vendors. This would not be of concern if multiple contracts have been awarded and the prices of each task or delivery order are to be established by competition between the contractors.

The Indefinite Quantity clause in FAR 52.216-22 also provides for the insertion in ¶ (d) of a date after which no "deliveries" are to be made. When this clause is used for services, this is presumably the final date that services may be performed.

There is no general guidance on the permissible length of indefinite-quantity contracts. However, 10 U.S.C. § 2304b(b) and 41 U.S.C. § 4105(c) limit task or delivery order contracts for advisory and assistance services to five years, unless a specific statute permits a longer period.

## 6. *Evaluation and Award*

The FAR gives very little guidance on the evaluation and award of IDIQ contracts. However, it would be expected that normal best value techniques would be used in most cases. The evaluation of prices is the most difficult part of the evaluation process. If only one type of supplies or services is included in the contract, evaluation would be based on the unit prices quoted. If more than one type of supplies or services is included in the contract, the FAR gives no guidance as to the basis for evaluation. However, GAO has ruled that the mere evaluation of unit prices or fixed labor rates without multiplying these rates by estimated quantities to arrive at an estimated "price" is improper, *KISS Eng'g Corp.*, 65 Comp. Gen. 549 (B-221356), 86-1 CPD ¶ 425 (rejecting the use of an average labor rate, including indirect costs, profit, and material, because there was "no necessary relationship between this rate and the likely actual cost of the contract"); *West Coast Copy, Inc.*, Comp. Gen. Dec.

B-254044, 93-2 CPD ¶ 283 (rejecting the comparison of unit prices for various types of copying without factoring-in the quantities of labor that would be used to perform the work); *SCIENTECH, Inc.*, Comp. Gen. Dec. B-277805.2, 98-1 CPD ¶ 33 (rejecting comparison of fixed labor rates and fee ceilings); *S.J. Thomas Co.*, Comp. Gen. Dec. B-283192, 99-2 CPD ¶ 73 (rejecting the comparison of "mark-up rates" (excluding labor rates and material) for construction work); *AirTrak Travel*, Comp. Gen. Dec. B-292101, 2003 CPD ¶ 117 (rejecting the averaging of travel service area "transaction fees" when usage will vary between areas); and *R&G Food Serv., Inc.*, Comp. Gen. Dec. B-296435.4, 2005 CPD ¶ 194 (rejecting comparison of unit prices for meals, mileage and handwashing because they were not multiplied by estimated quantities). Compare *Linc Gov't Servs., LLC v. United States*, 95 Fed. Cl. 155 (2010), where the court denied a protest that the agency had compared unit prices without multiplying them by estimated quantities. In that procurement the agency had provided estimated quantities in the RFP and had used them to check the proposed unit prices to ensure that they were not unbalanced. See also *Bristol-Myers Squibb Co.*, Comp. Gen. Dec. B-294944.2, 2005 CPD ¶ 16, and *SmithKline Beecham Corp.*, Comp. Gen. Dec. B-283939, 2000 CPD ¶ 19, where comparing unit prices of drug dosages was proper because the expected dosage per day was the major use of the drug and the agency had no way to estimate other uses.

This leaves agencies with two possible techniques of evaluating price — using estimated quantities stated in the RFP to arrive at a total "price" for proposed unit prices or fixed labor rates or obtaining prices for sample tasks. GAO has endorsed the use of estimated quantities, *LexisNexis*, Comp. Gen. Dec. B-402114, 2010 CPD ¶ 17; *Bering Straits Tech./Servs., LLC*, Comp. Gen. Dec. B-401560.3, 2009 CPD ¶ 201; *Health Servs. Int'l, Inc.*, Comp. Gen. Dec. B-247433, 92-1 CPD ¶ 493. It has also endorsed the use of sample tasks when offerors are required to propose "binding" fixed unit prices or labor rates and to use such prices or rates in arriving at their price for the sample task(s) that are proposed, *CW Gov't Travel, Inc.*, Comp. Gen. Dec. B-295530.2, 2005 CPD ¶ 139. In addition, the sample tasks must be representative of the type of work that is expected to be performed on the contract, *Dayton T. Brown, Inc.*, Comp. Gen. Dec. B-402256, 2010 CPD ¶ 72 (sample task encompassed many of the anticipated labor categories); *Information Ventures, Inc.*, Comp. Gen. Dec. B-299255, 2007 CPD ¶ 80 ("Although the sample task here is not reflective of the full range of services that the agency may order under the contracts to be awarded, we are not persuaded that it is not sufficiently typical of the work to be performed"); *Metro Mach. Corp.*, Comp. Gen. Dec. B-297879.2, 2006 CPD ¶ 80 (cost realism analysis flawed because "notational" tasks were not sufficiently representative of work). However, when an agency has no reasonable method to prepare a representative sample task, a hypothetical sample task has been approved when the protester could not show that its use led to an unreasonable evaluation of the actual costs of performance, *High Point Schaer*, 70 Comp. Gen. 524 (B-242616), 91-1 CPD ¶ 509; *Aalco Forwarding, Inc.*, Comp. Gen. Dec. B-277241.15, 98-1 CPD ¶ 87.

There have also been instances where the solicitation called for evaluation at the maximum quantity level, *Radionics, Inc.*, ASBCA 20796, 77-1 BCA ¶ 12,448. In that case, the maximum quantity was set at the government's estimated requirement, and the contractor claimed a price adjustment when the government failed to order the maximum quantity. The board recognized that evaluation at the maximum had a tendency to induce the offerors to submit lower prices but held that no recovery was appropriate under the facts of the case, because no negligence was found in preparing the estimate.

## 7. Ordering Work Under Indefinite-Quantity Contracts

The ordering of work under indefinite-quantity contracts is subject to different rules than the award of contracts. The general procedures for ordering are contained in the following mandatory Ordering clause in FAR 52.216-18:

ORDERING (OCT 1995)

(a) Any supplies and services to be furnished under this contract shall be ordered by issuance of delivery orders or task orders by the individuals or activities designated in the Schedule. Such orders may be issued from through [insert dates].

(b) All delivery orders or task orders are subject to the terms and conditions of this contract. In the event of conflict between a delivery order or task order and this contract, the contract shall control.

(c) If mailed, a delivery order or task order is considered "issued" when the Government deposits the order in the mail. Orders may be issued orally, by facsimile, or by electronic commerce methods only if authorized in the Schedule.

The contract schedule should contain a detailed description of the procedures that will be followed in issuing task or delivery orders under the contracts. In particular, agencies that intend to issue orders electronically or by facsimile must explicitly include this procedure in the schedule. See *General Dynamics C4 Sys., Inc.*, ASBCA 54988, 09-2 BCA ¶ 34,150, finding electronic orders invalid in accordance with ¶ (c) of the clause because there was no schedule language calling for the use of this technique. This decision was reversed in *Mabus v. General Dynamics C4 Sys., Inc.*, 633 F.3d 1356 (Fed. Cir. 2011), on the grounds that the contractor was estopped from asserting its rights under the clause because it had accepted orders for over four years.

### a. Verification of Prices

Although the regulations contain no guidance on whether the contracting officer should verify the reasonableness of prices before placing orders under indefinite-quantity contracts, it would appear that, as in the case of options, such orders should not be placed until a determination has been made that it is the most advantageous course of action available to the government. This determination will be relatively straightforward when multiple award contracts are being used and competitive prices are obtained on each task or delivery order. In the case of single award contract, the determination will become more difficult as market conditions change. Certainly, if market research revealed that better prices were available, the continued use of an indefinite-quantity contract would be questionable.

It can be argued that there should be no testing of the market until the government has honored its promise to purchase the minimum quantity of work specified in the contract. Thereafter, market testing would be legally permissible because indefinite-quantity contracts contain no promise to purchase additional quantities from the contractor. However, there is no requirement for obtaining competition by means of a solicitation. In addition, orders under indefinite-quantity contracts are not subject to the synopsis requirement, FAR 5.202(a)(6).

## b.  Ordering Under Multiple Award Contracts

The basic requirement for issuing orders under multiple award contracts is that holders of such contracts be given a "fair opportunity" to compete for awards, FAR 16.505. However, substantial criticism of the effectiveness of this rule has led to the congressional imposition of more stringent requirements on agencies. The first statute of this nature was § 803 of the National Defense Authorization Act for FY 2002, applicable only to the Department of Defense and implemented in DFARS 216.505-70. This was followed by § 843 of the National Defense Authorization Act for FY 2008, Pub. L. No. 110-181, adding the following provision to 10 U.S.C. § 2304c and 41 U.S.C. § 4106(d):

> (d) Enhanced Competition for Orders in Excess of $5,000,000 — In the case of a task or delivery order in excess of $5,000,000, the requirement to provide all contractors a fair opportunity to be considered under subsection (b) is not met unless all such contractors are provided, at a minimum —
>
> > (1) a notice of the task or delivery order that includes a clear statement of the agency's requirements;
> >
> > (2) a reasonable period of time to provide a proposal in response to the notice;
> >
> > (3) disclosure of the significant factors and subfactors, including cost or price, that the agency expects to consider in evaluating such proposals, and their relative importance;
> >
> > (4) in the case of an award that is to be made on a best value basis, a written statement documenting the basis for the award and the relative importance of quality and price or cost factors; and

(5) an opportunity for a post-award debriefing consistent with the requirements of section 2305(b)(5) of this title.

Subsequently, § 863 of the National Defense Authorization Act for FY 2009, Pub. L. No. 110-417, requires the issuance of regulations calling for notification of all contractors with task or delivery order contracts of potential task or delivery orders of any size. There is an exception to this requirement if it is impracticable and at least three offers have been received from qualified contractors. This section also calls for public notice of all sole source task or delivery orders. These provisions went into effect on Sept. 28, 2009. The act repeals § 803 of the National Defense Authorization Act for FY 2002 (containing similar notice requirements).

Prior to the enactment of § 843 of the National Defense Authorization Act for FY 2008, protests of task or delivery orders were not permitted but 10 U.S.C. §2304c(e) and 41 U.S.C. §253j(e) (now § 4106(f)) required agencies to have a task and delivery order ombudsman. However, that statute amended these provisions to allow protests to GAO as follows:

(f) Protests. . . . (1) A protest is not authorized in connection with the issuance or proposed issuance of a task or delivery order except for —

(A) a protest on the ground that the order increases the scope, period, or maximum value of the contract under which the order is issued; or

(B) a protest of an order valued in excess of $10,000,000.

(2) Notwithstanding section 3556 of title 31, the Comptroller General of the United States shall have exclusive jurisdiction of a protest authorized under paragraph (1)(B).

(3) This subsection shall be in effect for three years, beginning on the date that is 120 days after January 28, 2008.

Task and delivery order ombudsmen are now required by 10 U.S.C. § 2304c(f) and 41 U.S.C. §4106(g).

### c.  Time of Effectiveness

The Ordering clause in FAR 52.216-18 states that orders will be effective when deposited in the mail. If this clause is not used, the legal rules for issuing orders under indefinite-quantity contracts will likely be governed by the law of options. For example, *Dynamics Corp. of Am. v. United States*, 182 Ct. Cl. 62, 389 F.2d 424 (1968), involved a dispute as to whether certain orders, placed under a fixed-price, indefinite-quantity contract with a specified minimum and maximum, were issued within the time period specified in the contract. The court stated at 74:

In analyzing this contract, it cannot be seriously disputed that the portion in question is most accurately characterized as an option contract. As related above, Part VIII ("Orders") of the Special Provisions provides:

> The Contractor agrees to furnish to the Government, when ordered, the supplies or services set forth in the Schedule up to and including the quantity designated in the Schedule as the " maximum quantity."

The court concluded that orders were effective only if they were received within the time specified in the contract.

### d.  Failure to Order Minimum Quantity

Unless the government terminates the minimum quantity before the end of the performance period, its failure to order the minimum quantity will constitute a breach of contract with compensation based on appropriate damages reflecting the injury to the contractor. In *Maxima Corp. v. United States*, 847 F.2d 1549 (Fed. Cir. 1988), the court held that the government was not permitted to recoup its payment of the minimum dollar amount of the contract by retroactively terminating for convenience. This appeared to entitle the contractor to the entire minimum amount of the contract even though it had not incurred the costs of the unordered work — which some commentators interpreted as a holding that the correct calculation of damages for the unordered elements of the minimum quantity was the entire minimum price on the theory that this minimum dollar amount had been promised in return for the contractor's maintenance of the capability to perform the minimum quantity. See, for example, *Mid-Eastern Indus., Inc.*, ASBCA 53016, 02-1 BCA ¶ 31,657. However, in *PHP Healthcare Corp.*, ASBCA 39207, 91-1 BCA ¶ 23,647, the board refused to award the entire price for the unordered work, holding that the contract was not for the maintenance of a capability. Thus, it required the contractor to prove damages — the amount of costs incurred plus anticipated profits on the minimum quantity. See also *Apex Int'l Mgmt. Servs., Inc.*, ASBCA 38087, 94-2 BCA ¶ 26,842; and *Golden West Bldrs.*, PSBCA 3378, 93-3 BCA ¶ 26,195, following the same reasoning.

In contrast, in *Merrimac Mgmt. Inst., Inc.*, ASBCA 45291, 94-3 BCA ¶ 27,251, the board stated that damages should be computed by deducting the costs that would have been incurred from the price of the minimum quantity. This was confirmed as the correct method of calculating damages in *White v. Delta Constr. Int'l, Inc.*, 285 F.3d 1040 (Fed. Cir. 2002), stating at 1044-45:

> All that the court held in *Maxima* was that the government could not retroactively terminate the contract for convenience after the contract had been fully performed. *Cf. Krygoski Constr. Co. v. United States*, 94 F.3d 1537, 1542 n.2 (Fed. Cir. 1996) ("*Maxima* stands for the proposition the Government cannot retroactively create a breach in order to change the Government's obligations under a completed contract."). The court did not purport to and did not decide any question concerning the proper measure of damages in that situation. The court

discussed and rejected the various theories upon which the government sought to justify its retroactive termination and to uphold the Board's direction that the contractor refund to the government the balance of the contractual minimum. The court did so, however, only in connection with its conclusion that the retroactive termination was improper.

To be sure, the result of the court's decision in *Maxima* was that the contractor would retain the amount the government had paid it, representing the difference between the guaranteed minimum and the amount of work the government had ordered. That resulted, however, not because the court approved the basis of payment (it did not address that issue), but because the court found improper the method the government used to recapture the payment (retroactive termination for convenience). *Maxima* did not decide anything about the propriety of the basis of calculating damages that the Board used in this case. Fairly and carefully read, *Maxima* cannot properly be understood to hold that where there is an indefinite-quantity contract with a guaranteed minimum and the contractor is obligated to be ready to perform a certain amount of work, the contractor is entitled to receive the amount by which the government falls short of the guaranteed minimum.

Thus, the correct measure of damages would be the minimum dollar amount minus the costs that would have been incurred had the minimum amount been ordered. See, however, *Admiral Elevator v. Social Sec. Admin.*, CBCA 470, 07-2 BCA ¶ 33,676, stating that the board would accept "any workable, sensible approach" which calculates damages that put the contractor in the same position it would have been in had the minimum quantity been ordered; *Greenlee Constr. Co. v. General Servs. Admin.*, CBCA 415, 07-2 BCA ¶ 33,619, stating that "Any costs the contractor might have incurred from performing work valued at the guaranteed minimum amount must be subtracted from that amount to reach the correct figure for damages"; and *Jim Phillips Contracting, Inc.* IBCA 4319, 04-1 BCA ¶ 32,416, awarding an amount of profits that the contractor would have earned when the government ordered no work (determined on the basis of a "jury verdict" based on conflicting evidence). See *Admiral Elevator v. Social Sec. Admin.*, CBCA 470, 08-2 BCA ¶ 33,884, where the board awarded damages on a unique IDIQ contract by reducing the price for work not done by the cost of materials required for that work and the price for work that it should have anticipated would not be ordered (under a contract clause warning that some work would not be needed).

Prior to *Maxima*, damages for not ordering the minimum quantity had been limited by the Termination for the Convenience of the Government clause if it was in the contract, *Manuals, Inc.*, ASBCA 24123, 80-2 BCA ¶ 14,579; *Charles Bainbridge, Inc.*, ASBCA 19949, 75-2 BCA ¶ 11,414. This rule was also applied to each item in a multiple item, indefinite-quantity contract, *Unified Eng'g, Inc.*, ASBCA 21565, 81-1 BCA ¶ 14,940. These cases are no longer applicable to situations where the government lets the contract run out without ordering the minimum quantity. They are still applicable if the government orders a termination for convenience during the contract performance period, *ITT Commc'ns Servs., Inc.*, GSBCA 9072, 91-3 BCA ¶ 24,337 (short form Termination for the Convenience of the Government clause yields no recovery). In that case, the compensation should include repricing of unit prices necessary to recover fixed costs that were spread over the minimum quantity, *SteelCare, Inc.*, GSBCA 5491, 81-1 BCA ¶ 15,143. In *Montana Refining Co.*, ASBCA 44250, 94-2 BCA ¶ 26,656, the board remanded the case to the parties to compute " damages" even though the contracting officer had issued a termination for convenience for most of the unordered minimum quantity 18 days before the end of the contract period. The board did not discuss whether such "damages" should include anticipated profit. In contrast, in *Montana Refining Co.*, ASBCA 50515, 00-1 BCA ¶ 30,694, the board found a valid partial termination for convenience when the termination order was issued four months before the end of the contract period.

## 8. Termination for Convenience

Once the government has ordered the minimum quantity, it is not required to order additional quantities and no further action is required to end the contract. However, since all IDIQ contracts contain a Termination for Convenience clause, it can also terminate the contract under that clause. In *Int'l Data Prods. Corp. v. United States*, 492 F.3d 1317 (Fed. Cir. 2007), the court held that the government was not obligated to pay either termination costs or warranty and upgrade costs after termination because the clause limited the government's obligation to the contract price. The court reasoned that the contract price was the $ 35 million that the agency had paid for the ordered equipment, and, since the contractor had been paid that amount in full, it had no further rights under the Termination for Convenience clause (or under any other legal theory).

## E. Options

Another method of obtaining firm commitments from contractors to perform additional work is the inclusion of option clauses in contracts procuring the initial quantities. Options can be for additional quantities of work or for longer periods of performance. FAR 2.101 contains the following definition:

"Option" means a unilateral right in a contract by which, for a specified time, the Government may elect to purchase additional supplies or services called for by the contract, or may elect to extend the term of the contract.

The major difference between options and requirements contracts or multiyear contracts is that the government makes *no binding commitment* when an option provision is used. Thus, the key characteristic of option clauses is that they give the government a unilateral right to order the additional quantities or services if that order is issued by a prescribed time. An option for additional quantities of work is very similar to an indefinite-quantity contract, but the obligation of the government is stated differently. Option clauses state that the government has the right to order specified additional quantities, while indefinite-quantity contracts state that the government has the right to purchase quantities within a specified range. It has been held that regulations pertaining to indefinite-quantity contracts are not applicable to options, *International Transducer Corp. v. United States*, 30 Fed. Cl. 522 (1994); *Schmid Labs., Inc.*, Comp. Gen. Dec. B-214333, 84-2 CPD ¶411.

There is no question that validly exercised options are binding on the contractor. Thus, refusal to perform an option is a proper grounds for default termination, *Specialty Transp., Inc. v. United States*, 57 Fed. Cl. 1 (2003). Conversely, the contractor has no rights if the government fails to exercise an option, unless that failure "was a product of bad faith or so arbitrary and capricious as to be an abuse of discretion," *Blackstone Consulting, Inc. v. General Servs. Admin.*, CBCA 718, 08-1 BCA ¶ 33,770, citing *Greenlee Constr., Inc. v. General Servs. Admin.*, CBCA 416, 07-1 BCA ¶ 33,514; *Nova Express*, PSBCA 5102, 08-1 BCA ¶ 33,763; and *IMS-Engineers-Architects, PC*, ASBCA 53471, 06-1 BCA ¶ 33,231. See also *Continental Collection & Disposal, Inc. v. United States*, 29 Fed. Cl. 644 (1993), apparently recognizing a bad faith exception to the rule giving contractors no rights to options, but finding that no bad faith was present in the situation at hand.

## 1. Use

Options were infrequently used in the 1960s and 1970s and an effort was made by GAO in 1962 to strictly limit their use. See 41 Comp. Gen. 682 (B-148019) (1962), where GAO stated that option quantities should be limited to 25% of the contract quantity and should be exercisable no more than 90 days after award. However, as part of the acquisition streamlining efforts of the 1990s, options came into wide use in government procurement — primarily as a means of avoiding the need to issue new contracts each year for supplies and services. Thus, at the current time options for additional years' work are the norm in government procurement.

Because the government is not bound by options for additional quantities of supplies or services, there are no fiscal or legal impediments to their use. See Volume 1 of *Principles of Federal Appropriations Law*, January 2004, as updated in March 2010, stating at 5-41:

If an agency is contracting with fiscal year appropriations and does not have multiyear contracting authority, one course of action, apart from a series of separate fiscal year contracts, is a fiscal year contract with renewal options, with each renewal option (1) contingent on the availability of future appropriations and (2) to be exercised only by affirmative action on the part of the government (as opposed to automatic renewal unless the government refuses). *Leiter v. United States*, 271 U.S. 204 (1926); 66 Comp. Gen. 556 (1987); 36 Comp. Gen. 683 (1957); 33 Comp. Gen. 90 (1953); 29 Comp. Gen. 91 (1949); 28 Comp. Gen. 553 (1949); B-88974, Nov. 10, 1949. The inclusion of a renewal option is key; with a renewal option, the government incurs a financial obligation only for the fiscal year, and incurs no financial obligation for subsequent years unless and until it exercises its right to renew. The government records the amount of its obligation for the first fiscal year against the appropriation current at the time it awards the contract. The government also records amounts of obligations for future fiscal years against appropriations current at the time it exercises its renewal options.

FAR Subpart 17.2 prescribes general policies for the use of options, stating in FAR 17.200 that these regulations do not apply to contracts for construction, architect-engineer services, or R&D services; but that options may be used for such procurements. FAR 17.202 provides:

(a) Subject to the limitations of paragraphs (b) and (c) of this section, for both sealed bidding and contracting by negotiation, the contracting officer may include options in contracts when it is in the Government's interest. When using sealed bidding, the contracting officer shall make a written determination that there is a reasonable likelihood that the options will be exercised before including the provision at 52.217-5, Evaluation of Options, in the solicitation. (See 17.207(f) with regard to the exercise of options.)

(b) Inclusion of an option is normally not in the Government's interest when, in the judgment of the contracting officer —

(1) The foreseeable requirements involve —

(i) Minimum economic quantities (i.e., quantities large enough to permit the recovery of startup costs and the production of the required supplies at a reasonable price); and

(ii) Delivery requirements far enough into the future to permit competitive acquisition, production, and delivery.

(2) An indefinite quantity or requirements contract would be more appropriate than a contract with options. However, this does not preclude the use of an indefinite quantity contract or requirements contract with options.

(c) The contracting officer shall not employ options if —

(1) The contractor will incur undue risks; e.g., the price or availability of necessary materials or labor is not reasonably foreseeable;

(2) Market prices for the supplies or services involved are likely to change substantially; or

(3) The option represents known firm requirements for which funds are available unless —

(i) The basic quantity is a learning or testing quantity; and

(ii) Competition for the option is impracticable once the initial contract is awarded.

(d) In recognition of —

(1) The Government's need in certain service contracts for continuity of operations; and

(2) The potential cost of disrupted support, options may be included in service contracts if there is an anticipated need for a similar service beyond the first contract period.

The regulations also provide that, unless approved in accordance with agency procedures, the total coverage of a contract with options, including the initial quantity and the option quantities, shall not exceed the requirements of the agency for five years, FAR 17.204(e). Information technology contracts are excluded from this requirement.

The guidance in FAR 17.202 is highly discretionary, with the result that there is little likelihood that offerors can successfully protest the use of options. See *Pool's Moving & Storage*, Comp. Gen. Dec. B-233563, 89-1 CPD ¶ 141, stating:

The regulations provide that contracting officers may include options in service contracts if there is an anticipated need for a similar service beyond the first contract period. Federal Acquisition Regulation (FAR) § 17.202(d); see *Key Air*, B-227893, Aug. 20, 1987, 87-2 CPD ¶188. Here, the agency made the requisite determination to include the option because it anticipated the need for services beyond the current year due to the constant relocation of military personnel at the base. We do not believe Pool's concern with unstable insurance and other operational costs is relevant to a determination to use an option in a service contract like the one involved here. The only requirement in the regulations is that the agency anticipate a need for similar services in the future. The agency did so and protester does not dispute this. In any event, the risks cited by the protester appear to fall well within the normal type of risks associated with bidding; agencies are not obligated to eliminate these risks. See *Triple P Servs., Inc.*, B-220437.3, Apr. 3, 1986, 86-1 CPD ¶ 318.

A similar conclusion was arrived at in *Information Ventures, Inc.*, Comp. Gen. Dec. B-241441, 91-1 CPD ¶ 83; and *Canon U.S.A., Inc.*, Comp. Gen. Dec. B-232262, 88-2 CPD ¶ 538.

The most important limitation on the use of options is the provision in ¶ (b)(1)(ii) that they should not be used if adequate competition can be obtained when the future requirements are ascertained. Many agencies do not comply with this recommendation and there is no apparent means of inducing compliance. There were a few attempts by GAO to apply such a rule. See *Altron Iron Works, Inc.*, Comp. Gen. Dec. B-179212, 74-1 CPD ¶ 121, where GAO urged the procuring agency to go forward with a new procurement of standard commercial supplies rather than using option provisions. See also *Safemasters Co.*, 58 Comp. Gen. 255 (B-192941), 79-1 CPD ¶ 38, where options were found improper when realistic competition was available for subsequent procurements.

Another important limitation in ¶ (c)(3) is that options cannot be used to procure known requirements for which funds are available. In *East Wind Indus., Inc.*, 58 Comp. Gen. 586 (B-193720), 79-1 CPD ¶ 404, GAO held that this provision precluded the testing of a currently available option by the addition of an option for the same quantity to a new procurement. GAO suggested that the proper technique was to test the option by advertising the entire new requirement as a fixed quantity.

Contractors have been unsuccessful in using ¶ (c)(1), precluding the use of options that impose undue risk on the contractor, as the basis for protests or claims. See *Madison Servs., Inc.*, Comp. Gen. Dec. B-278962, 98-1 CPD ¶ 113, holding that there was no imposition of undue risk in requiring offerors to propose variable options for from one to twelve months, and *LBM, Inc.*, 70 Comp. Gen. 493 (B-242664), 91-1 CPD ¶ 476, finding no undue risk in requiring fixed price bids for options for four years of maintenance and repair of family housing. See also *General Dynamics C4 Sys., Inc.*, ASBCA 54988, 08-1 BCA ¶ 33,779, where the contractor argued that this provision should preclude the government from exercising an option knowing that it imposed risk on the contractor. The board rejected the argument, noting that the rule applied at the time of issuing the contract not at the time of option exercise. See also *Loral Fairchild Corp.*, ASBCA 45719, 97-1 BCA ¶ 28,905, holding that technical, cost, and schedule risks were not the type of risks that precluded the use of option provisions.

## 2. *Advantages and Disadvantages of Options*

The major advantage of options is that they allow the government to obtain additional quantities of supplies or services if agency needs change after the contract has been awarded. Thus, options can be used to cover potential additional quantities during the year of the original contract, during subsequent years of multiple-year contracts, and for additional years on a contract for a limited number of years. The latter type of options (for additional years) is probably the most frequently used at the current time.

Options for additional years' work have proved to be a major means of reducing the workload of acquisition personnel in contracting agencies. This occurs because, as a general rule, agencies tend to exercise such options rather than conduct a new procurement for the quantities covered by the options because it is almost always far easier to exercise an option than to conduct a new procurement. Thus, in a contract for one year of services with options for five additional years, the agency would not have to conduct a new procurement for six years.

A major disadvantage of options for additional years' work is that they are difficult to price accurately. If they are at fixed prices, they may impose a significant risk on the contractor or, conversely, induce the contractor to include a contingency in the price to protect against the risk. This makes them problematic for the government with the result that contracting officers may need to add economic price adjustment clauses to the contract (with the risk that they will not cover the pricing risk because of the way they are structured) and to move to a less risky type of contract such as a cost-reimbursement contract or a time-and-materials or labor-hour contract. In recent years, the use of these latter types of contract appears to have resulted from the extensive use of options for additional years' work.

Another disadvantage of options for additional years' work is that they allow agencies to avoid taking steps to conduct procurements in an efficient fashion. One of the major reasons agencies have resorted to such frequent use of such options is that conducting a new procurement takes from six months to a year. When an agency follows such inefficient procedures, the use of options for additional years almost becomes imperative. On the other hand, if an agency could conduct a new procurement in two to three months, options for additional years' work would be less attractive and the advantage of obtaining new prices each year more manifest. The ready availability of these options has appeared to provide many agencies with the ability to continue to use inefficient procurement procedures, whereas restrictions on the use of options might well motivate agencies to search for more efficient procedures to conduct new procurements.

## 3. Standard Option Clauses

There are four standard option clauses in the FAR and two additional clauses in the DFARS. These clauses are quite narrow in their application with the result that an agency may have to tailor them to fit its needs. This is accommodated in the guidance on their use in FAR 17.208 which requires the use of clauses that are "substantially the same" as the standard FAR clauses. See *C. Martin Co.*, ASBCA 54182, 04-2 BCA ¶ 32,637, finding that a tailored clause with significant differences from the FAR 52.217-9 clause was substantially the same as that clause.

Many contracts contain option clauses that vary from the standard clauses. Government agencies must exercise care to ensure that tailored clauses accomplish their purpose. For example, in *Wackenhut Servs., Inc.*, ASBCA 55691, 08-1 BCA ¶ 33,831, the agency included the FAR 52.217-8 clause as well as a tailored option clause permitting extension of the contract for up to six years. The board held that the government could not hold the contractor to the option prices for part of the work called for by exercising an option under the tailored clause because that clause did not call for ordering "any services" as was permitted by the FAR 52.217-8 clause.

The first two standard FAR clauses are for use in contracts for supplies. The first is for use when the agency structures the option quantity as a percentage of the basic contract line(s) or as additional quantities of the basic contract line item(s). See FAR 52.217-6 providing:

OPTION FOR INCREASED QUANTITY (MAR 1989)

The Government may increase the quantity of supplies called for in the Schedule at the unit price specified. The Contracting Officer may exercise the option by written notice to the Contractor within .... [*insert in the clause the period of time in which the Contracting Officer has to exercise the option*]. Delivery of the added items shall continue at the same rate as the like items called for under the contract, unless the parties otherwise agree.

Note that this clause calls for delivery of additional products after delivery of the basic contract units has ended. Thus, it must be modified if an agency needs an option for additional supplies within the contract delivery period. The clause also requires the option prices to be the same as the prices of the basic contract prices. The difficulties that this requirement imposes are discussed below.

The second supply contract clause is for use when the agency structures the options as separate contract line items. See FAR 52.217-7 providing:

OPTION FOR INCREASED QUANTITY — SEPARATELY PRICED LINE ITEM (MAR 1989)

The Government may require the delivery of the numbered line item, identified in the Schedule as an option item, in the quantity and at the price stated in the Schedule. The Contracting Officer may exercise the option by written notice to the Contractor within .... [*insert in the clause the period of time in which the Contracting Officer has to exercise the option*]. Delivery of added items shall continue at the same rate that like items are called for under the contract, unless the parties otherwise agree.

This clause also deals only with option quantities to be delivered after completion of delivery the basic contract units. Thus, it must be modified if an agency needs an option for additional supplies within the contract delivery period. The clause does, however, allow an agency to include option prices that are different from the prices of the basic contract units.

The other two FAR clauses are for use in service contracts. The first is to allow the agency to obtain additional services for a period up to six months if the award of a follow on contract is delayed. See FAR 37.111 stating:

Award of contracts for recurring and continuing service requirements are often delayed due to circumstances beyond the control of contracting offices. Examples of circumstances causing such delays are bid protests and alleged mistakes in bid. In order to avoid negotiation of short extensions to existing contracts, the contracting officer may include an option clause (see 17.208(f)) in solicitations and contracts which will enable the Government to require continued performance of any services within the limits and at the rates specified in the contract. However, these rates may be adjusted only as a result of revisions to prevailing labor rates provided by the Secretary of Labor. The option provision may be exercised more than once, but the total extension of performance thereunder shall not exceed 6 months.

The following clause is provided in FAR 52.217-8:

OPTION TO EXTEND SERVICES (NOV 1999)

The Government may require continued performance of any services within the limits and at the rates specified in the contract. These rates may be adjusted only as a result of revisions to prevailing labor rates provided by the Secretary of Labor. The option provision may be exercised more than once, but the total extention of performance hereunder shall not exceed 6 months. The Contracting Officer may exercise the option by written notice to the Contractor within [*insert the period of time within which the Contracting Officer may exercise the option*].

This clause is appropriate only when fully priced labor rates are specified in the contract. In such cases, it binds the contractor to those rates even if its costs have increased. See *JWK Int'l Corp.*, ASBCA 54153, 04-2 BCA ¶ 32,783 (barring recovery of bonuses that accrued during option period), and *Tecom, Inc.*, ASBCA 51880, 00-2 BCA ¶ 30,944 (barring recovery of payments in lieu of vacation time that could not be granted because of exercise of option). When using this clause, the agency must justify the sole source procurement when the additional services ordered have not been evaluated in the original competition (as is normally the case), *Major Contracting Servs., Inc.*, Comp. Gen. Dec. B-401472, 2009 CPD ¶ 170, *recons. denied*, 2009 CPD ¶ 250.

Although FAR 37.111 states that this clause is to be used to cover procurement delays "due to circumstances beyond the control of contracting offices," the clause contains no such limitation with the result that agencies have been permitted to use it for other purposes. See *Petchem, Inc.*, ASBCA 53792, 05-1 BCA ¶ 32,870 (clause used after missing notice date in FAR 52.217-9 clause but option period limited to six months); *Griffin Servs., Inc.*, ASBCA 52280, 02-2 BCA ¶ 31,943 (clause properly used when agency missed the time to extend the contract under the FAR 52.217-9 clause); and *American Contract Servs., Inc.*, ASBCA 46788, 94-2 BCA ¶26,855, *recons. denied*, 94-3 BCA ¶ 27,025, *aff'd*, 53 F.3d 348 (Fed. Cir. 1995) (clause properly used in lieu of FAR 52.217-9 clause in order to obtain lower option prices). The result is that this clause can impose significant pricing risk on the contractor — particularly when it is used in conjunction with the FAR 52.217-9 clause. In that case, the requirement that the contractor accept up to six months of additional work at "the rates specified in the contract" binds the contractor to the rates paid for the last option that has been exercised under the FAR 52.217-9 clause.

There is another clause that can be used to obtain additional services from a contractor when a contract has been awarded to a follow-on contractor. The Continuity of Services clause in FAR 52.237-3 allows the agency to order the contractor to provide "phase-in training" and transition services to a new contractor for a period of up to 90 days after award. In *Arko Exec. Servs., Inc. v. United States*, 78 Fed. Cl. 420 (2007), the court held that the agency properly used the FAR 52.217-8 clause to extend the contract for two months beyond the expiration of all of the FAR 52.217-9 options, rejecting the contractor's argument that the services should have been ordered under the FAR 52.237-3 clause. The court reasoned that the FAR 52.217-8 clause had been used for the specific purpose for which it was intended, as stated in FAR 37.111. See also *Konitz Contracting, Inc.*, ASBCA 52299, 01-2 BCA ¶ 31,572; and *Storage Tech. Corp. v. CCL Serv. Corp.*, 94 F. Supp. 2d 697 (D. Md. 2000), holding that the FAR 52.217-8 clause permits the government to exercise options beyond the time limitation for options under the FAR 52.217-9 clause.

The second services contract clause allows the government to obtain the services for additional periods of time. The following clause is provided in FAR 52.217-9:

> OPTION TO EXTEND THE TERM OF THE CONTRACT (MAR 2000)
>
> (a) The Government may extend the term of this contract by written notice to the Contractor within [*insert the period of time within which the Contracting Officer may exercise the option*]; provided that the Government gives the Contractor a preliminary written notice of its intent to extend at least ___ days [*60 days unless a different number of days is inserted*] before the contract expires. The preliminary notice does not commit the Government to an extension.
>
> (b) If the Government exercises this option, the extended contract shall be considered to include this option clause.
>
> (c) The total duration of this contract, including the exercise of any options under this clause, shall not exceed _____ (months) (years).

This clause contains no coverage of the labor rates that will be paid in option years. Thus, it is appropriate for use in cost-reimbursement contracts but should be supplemented to state the basis of payment if it is used in contracts with fixed prices or fixed labor rates.

The two DFARS clauses are an open-ended clause to be used to fulfill foreign military sales commitments in DFARS 252.217-7000 and a surge option clause in DFARS 252.217-7001 that allows the agency to order increased deliveries to a "maximum sustainable rate." These clauses generally call for pricing after the option is exercised although the latter clause permits prepricing if the parties have included prices in the original contract.

## 4.  *Structuring and Evaluation of Options*

Option provisions must be carefully structured to induce offerors to propose the most advantageous prices. The key considerations are the time the option can be exercised and whether the option prices will be evaluated in the selection of the winning offeror. Agencies must include a provision in the solicitation stating whether they will or will not evaluate options, *Golden N. Van Lines, Inc.*, 69 Comp. Gen. 610 (B-238874), 90-2 CPD ¶ 44. See the guidance in FAR 17.208. The absence of such a provision is a solicitation defect that must be protested before the submission of an offer, *Home Care Med., Inc.*, Comp. Gen. Dec. B-245189, 91-2 CPD ¶ 186.

The period during which an option may be exercised must be stated in the contract, FAR 17.204(b). In the case of supply contracts, it must be set "so as to provide the contractor adequate lead time to ensure continuous production," FAR 17.204(c). In *Aerojet Techsys. Co.*, Comp. Gen. Dec. B-220033, 85-2 CPD ¶ 636, GAO reasoned that because this regulation ensures the contractor's continuous production, the government erred in rejecting as nonresponsive a bid that conditioned third-year option prices on exercise of second-year options. In the case of service contracts, continuity of services should also be provided for, but the FAR is silent on this requirement. The Option to Extend Services clause in FAR 52.217-8 permits the contracting officer to select a period during which that option can be exercised, and this period should be clearly stated. See *American Contract Servs., Inc.*, ASBCA 46788, 94-2 BCA ¶ 26,855, *recons. denied*, 94-3 BCA ¶ 27,025, *aff'd*, 53 F.3d 348 (Fed. Cir. 1995), where the contracting officer used the ambiguous phrase "within 15 days," and the board held that this had to mean within 15 days of contract expiration.

FAR 17.204(d) permits the period for exercise of the option to "extend beyond the contract completion date" when funds would not be available on the completion date. This allows the contracting officer to structure the option to permit its exercise on the first day of the fiscal year (or year when funds are available) when the period of services ends on the previous day. It should not be used to permit longer gaps in service. See *Cessna Aircraft Co.*, ASBCA 43196, 96-1 BCA ¶ 27,966, *aff'd*, 126 F.3d 1442 (Fed. Cir. 1997), *cert. denied*, 525 U.S. 818 (1998), where the board held that a clause permitting exercise of an option on the first day of the fiscal year was legally binding even though it extended beyond the contract completion date.

The other key consideration in structuring options is the determination of whether option prices will be evaluated. The goal is to give the offerors the greatest possible incentive to propose prices that are realistic and competitive. If the option quantities are included in the evaluation, the offerors will have the incentive to offer competitive prices but may be inclined to unbalance the prices between the years. This could lead to unnecessarily high prices for early years if the later years' requirements do not materialize. If the option quantities are not included in the evaluation, offerors may be inclined to inflate option prices in the hope that the agency will be forced by circumstances to exercise the options. While the FAR contains some minimal guidance on evaluation of options, it contains no guidance on structuring options to achieve the best prices. Methods of structuring and evaluation are dealt with in this section.

## *a. Evaluation of Option Quantities*

The regulations call for the evaluation of options when the government is likely to exercise them in the course of the contract. FAR 17.206 provides:

(a) In awarding the basic contract, the contracting officer shall, except as provided in paragraph (b) of this section, evaluate offers for any option quantities or periods contained in a solicitation when it has been determined prior to soliciting offers that the Government is likely to exercise the options. (See 17.208.)

(b) The contracting officer need not evaluate offers for any option quantities when it is determined that evaluation would not be in the best interests of the Government and this determination is approved at a level above the contracting officer. An example of a circumstance that may support a determination not to evaluate offers for option quantities is when there is a reasonable certainty that funds will be unavailable to permit exercise of the option.

When the options are to be evaluated, the Evaluation of Options clause in FAR 52.217-5 is used, and GAO has upheld this method of evaluation, *S.A.F.E. Export Corp.*, Comp. Gen. Dec. B-204718, 82-1 CPD ¶ 62. This clause permits the government not to evaluate the options when it is "not . . . in the Government's best interests." In *Solon Automated Servs., Inc. v. United States*, 658 F. Supp. 28 (D.D.C. 1987), the court found an abuse of discretion in selecting an offeror that had submitted an unbalanced bid by greatly front-loading the initial year price. In *Foley Co.*, Comp. Gen. Dec. B-245536, 92-1 CPD ¶ 47, GAO concurred with a decision not to evaluate options when the base price of the low bidder including the options exceeded the available funding. This permitted the agency to award the contract to the bidder whose base price was within the government funding limit. However, GAO has found that the FAR states a "clear preference" for the evaluation of options, *Crowley Co.*, Comp. Gen. Dec. B-258967, 95-1 CPD ¶ 105, and has affirmed the propriety of evaluating options after the contracting officer confirmed that funds would likely be available for their exercise, *Marshall Co.*, Comp. Gen. Dec. B-311196, 2008 CPD ¶ 78 (contracting officer found agency was assembling additional funding); *Building Constr. Enters., Inc.*, Comp. Gen. Dec. B-294784, 2004 CPD ¶ 251 (contracting officer believed that necessary funding "might be available"); *Merlo, Inc.*, Comp. Gen. Dec. B-277384, 97-2 CPD ¶ 39 (contracting officer was advised that sufficient funding would be included in later year appropriations). See also *Thermal Combustion Innovators, Inc.*, Comp. Gen. Dec. B-279602.2, 98-2 CPD ¶ 94, where GAO rejected the protester's argument that it was unreasonable for the agency to pay higher prices in the first two years in order to obtain lower prices in later years because the agency could ensure better prices later by conducting another competition.

If the solicitation unequivocally states that options will be evaluated, the agency has no discretion to decide not to evaluate them, *Global Commc'ns Solutions, Inc.*, Comp. Gen. Dec. B-291113, 2002 CPD ¶ 194. There the solicitation stated that "the evaluation period" would be the entire period of the contract including the option periods.

If the solicitation contains options for work that can be exercised in the alternative, it is improper to add the prices of both alternates to the evaluated price, *Kruger Constr., Inc.*, Comp. Gen. Dec. B-286960, 2001 CPD ¶ 43.

When the clause calling for evaluation of options is used in an IFB, bidders must submit unequivocal offers. In *Sess Constr. Co.*, 64 Comp. Gen. 355 (B-216924), 85-1 CPD ¶ 319, a bid in which prices for option periods included the statement "plus rate of inflation, fuel, labor and gravel" was properly rejected for failure to offer a firm-fixed-price. It is also proper to refuse to evaluate a bid where the prices are conditioned upon exercise of the options. Thus, option price bids should not include separate "all or none" price discounts for option items. In *Telex Commc'ns, Inc.*, Comp. Gen. Dec. B-211236, 83-2 CPD ¶ 122, GAO concluded that where an IFB reserves the right to exercise only a portion of the options, to require evaluation of options at the bidder's "all or none" discounted price would improperly introduce uncertainty as to whether the bid was actually the lowest received.

The regulations state that the government may reject unbalanced bids if they pose an unacceptable risk to the government, FAR 14.404-2; FAR 15.404-1(g)(3), and this right of the government is stated in the standard solicitation provisions in FAR 52.214-10 and FAR 52.215-1. Guidance on determining whether an unbalanced bid poses such a risk states only that the contracting officer should consider "whether award of the contract will result in paying unreasonably high prices," FAR 15.404-1(g)(2)(ii). See Chapter 5 and Chapter 6 for a detailed discussion of unbalanced bidding.

### b. Nonevaluation of Option Quantities

Although FAR 17.206(a) states that the normal procedure is to structure options so that both the base quantity and option quantities are evaluated in making the initial award, FAR 17.206(b) states that a contracting officer may decide not to evaluate option quantities when that is "in the best interests of the Government" and is approved by a superior. GAO has also held that "[t]here is no legal or regulatory requirement that an agency evaluate options in a particular procurement," *International Bus. Invs., Inc.*, 63 Comp. Gen. 463 (B-215530), 84-1 CPD ¶ 693. This is consistent with the reasoning of GAO that bid bonds or bid guarantees should cover only base quantities, *Madison Servs., Inc.*, Comp. Gen. Dec. B-245420, 91-2 CPD ¶ 345; *Pacific Coast Utils. Serv., Inc.*, Comp. Gen. Dec. B-209003.2, 83-1 CPD ¶ 73; *Consolidated Techs., Inc.*, Comp. Gen. Dec. B-215723, 84-2 CPD ¶ 639.

When it is decided not to evaluate options, the Evaluation Exclusive of Options clause at FAR 52.217-3 is used. The regulations give no guidance on how to deal with unusually high option prices where the option quantities are not to be evaluated, but it has been held that significantly higher unevaluated option prices, as compared to prices offered on the basic quantity, are not a sufficient reason for rejecting a bid, *R&R Inventory Serv., Inc.*, 54 Comp. Gen. 206 (B-181264), 74-2 CPD ¶ 163 (prices for second- and third-year options were 700% to 900% more than basic quantity prices, but bid was accepted as lowest on basic quantity). See also *SeaArk Marine, Inc.*, Comp. Gen. Dec. B-248755, 92-2 CPD ¶ 193, where it was held that the agency was not required to consider unevaluated option quantity prices when deciding whether a bid was materially unbalanced. Compare *Gracon Corp. v. United States*, 6 Cl. Ct. 497 (1984), holding that the contracting officer had discretion to accept or reject a bid containing significantly higher unevaluated option prices in accordance with a solicitation provision permitting the rejection of materially unbalanced bids. In *Gracon*, the court agreed with the contracting officer's decision to award the contract to the low bidder on the base quantity assuming that the government would not exercise the option but would meet its requirements in some other way. If a subsequent separate procurement was not possible, the proper course of action would arguably have been to reject the bid and award to the next low bidder. In solicitations calling for nonevaluation of options and containing no clause permitting rejection of materially unbalanced bids, the contracting officer would have to cancel the solicitation to avoid awarding to the low base bid with a high option price. The FAR contains no guidance on this issue.

In *Occu-Health, Inc.*, Comp. Gen. Dec. B-270228.3, 96-1 CPD ¶ 196, *recons. denied*, 96-2 CPD ¶ 80, GAO ruled that an agency was required to inform offerors that it was not going to evaluate options if it made that decision prior to the submission of best and final offers, stating:

> To read FAR 17.206(a) as broadly as [the agency] suggests — as granting an agency essentially unfettered discretion to decide not to evaluate options without advising offerors of this change under the circumstances when the agency could reasonably provide that advice — would be inconsistent with the agency's fundamental obligations to allow offerors the opportunity to respond to the government's actual needs and to obtain the offer that is most advantageous to the government.

See *ACC Constr. Co.*, Comp. Gen. Dec. B-289167, 2002 CPD ¶ 21, holding that this rule has no application to the situation where the agency finds out about a lack of funding after bid opening.

### c. Limited Evaluation

Another technique is to evaluate only those options that are exercised at the time of award. FAR 17.208(b) requires the use of the following clause at FAR 52.217-4 when this technique is used:

EVALUATION OF OPTIONS EXERCISED AT TIME OF CONTRACT
AWARD (JUN 1988)

Except when it is determined in accordance with FAR 17.206(b) not to be in the Government's best interests, the Government will evaluate the total price for the basic requirement together with any option(s) exercised at the time of award.

This is the one method provided in the regulations that does not give the bidder definite information as to whether options will be evaluated. The result may be that it is the technique most likely to result in balanced bidding. In *National Council for Urban Econ. Dev., Inc.*, Comp. Gen. Dec. B-213434, 84-2 CPD ¶ 140, GAO held that where the government's RFP both provided for evaluation of option quantities and stated that options could not be exercised at the time of award, the government's decision to nevertheless exercise options at the time of award, in light of unexpected availability of funds, was valid. See also *Contractors Nw., Inc.*, Comp. Gen. Dec. B-293050, 2003 CPD ¶ 232, holding that the government was not precluded from evaluating options that would not be exercised at the time of award, as called for by the FAR 52.217-4 clause, when it also included the FAR 51.217-5 clause in the contract.

## d.  Level Pricing

Another technique used to avoid unbalanced bidding is to require that option prices be the same as base prices. This technique is used in multiyear procurement, but the regulations are silent on its use in options. See, however, the FAR 52.217-6 clause which requires such level pricing. The FAR also permits the use of a solicitation clause preventing unbalanced bidding by low base prices. FAR 17.203 states:

(f) Solicitations may, in unusual circumstances, require that options be offered at prices no higher than those for the initial requirement, *e.g.*, when —

(1) the option cannot be evaluated under 17.206; or

(2) future competition for the option is impracticable.

(g) Solicitations that require the offering of an option at prices no higher than those for the initial requirement shall —

(1) Specify that the Government will accept an offer containing an option price higher than the base price only if the acceptance does not prejudice any other offeror; and

(2) Limit option quantities for additional supplies to not more than 50 percent of the initial quantity of the same contract line item. In unusual circumstances, an authorized person at a level above the contracting officer may approve a greater percentage of quantity.

GAO has permitted award to a bidder that violated the IFB by bidding option prices higher than the base price but was the low bidder on both the base and option prices, 44 Comp. Gen. 581 (B-155847) (1965). See also Comp. Gen. Dec. B-176356, Nov. 8, 1972, *Unpub*. In cases where prejudice to other bidders has been found, however, GAO has agreed with decisions to reject the bids. See 51 Comp. Gen. 439 (B-172978) (1972), and *Bristol Elecs., Inc.*, 54 Comp. Gen. 16 (B-180247), 74-2 CPD ¶ 23, where the low bidder on the base quantity violated the solicitation instructions on level pricing, and the aggregate prices (base price plus all options) were higher than another bidder whose option prices did not exceed the base price; GAO ruled that it was improper to award to the low bidder on the base quantity. See also *Keco Indus., Inc.*, Comp. Gen. Dec. B-216396.2, 84-2 CPD ¶ 491. In *ABL Gen. Sys. Corp.*, 54 Comp. Gen. 476 (B-182066), 74-2 CPD ¶ 318, GAO ruled that a bid that was low on the base quantity, high on the option prices, but low in the aggregate should not be considered since it had violated the level bidding requirement and it was not clear that it would have been low had other bidders been permitted to submit higher option prices. Additionally, where the IFB advised prospective bidders that offers "containing an option price higher than the lowest basic price for the same item may be accepted only if such acceptance does not prejudice any other offeror," GAO upheld the rejection of a bid that was low on the base quantity but scaled option prices according to volumes ordered so that exercise of the entire option quantity would have resulted in level option pricing, but limited exercise of the option would have resulted in higher prices, *Numax Elecs. Inc.*, Comp. Gen. Dec. B-206127.2, 82-2 CPD ¶ 317.

In cases where there are significant nonrecurring costs, the contractor takes a large risk when level pricing is required. See *Contact Int'l Corp.*, ASBCA 44636, 95-2 BCA ¶ 27,887, *aff'd*, 106 F.3d 426 (Fed. Cir. 1997), where the board rejected a claim that the failure to exercise the options on a five-year requirements contract was a termination for convenience of the government. The board found that the government had full rights not to exercise the options and that the contractor "bears the attendant risks" of spreading nonrecurring costs over the five-year period. The same result was reached in *D&S Mfg. Co.*, ASBCA 32865, 87-1 BCA ¶ 19,351. See also *Metro Mach. Corp.*, ASBCA 47005, 97-1 BCA ¶ 28,723, where the contractor had agreed to overhead rate ceilings on cost-reimbursement contract with multiple options because it assumed that the options would be ordered and that it could spread its overhead costs over the large quantity of work covered by the options. When no options were ordered, the board ruled that the contractor has assumed the risk of this type of pricing and was bound by the ceilings.

### e. Prohibition of Nonrecurring Costs in Option Prices

Another method of controlling the pricing of options is to attempt to prohibit the inclusion of nonrecurring start-up costs in option prices. This forces the inclusion of all such costs in the base price. This can readily be accomplished in negotiated procurement. However, it may not be feasible in sealed bidding. See *Hitachi Denshi Am., Ltd.*, Comp. Gen. Dec. B-212925, 84-1 CPD ¶ 342, where GAO held that a bid that contained the same price for base and option quantities was responsive to such a prohibition because bidders were not required to submit cost breakdowns, and inflation during the five-year period could account for the fact that the option prices were the same as the base price.

## f. Discounting to Present Value

The most straightforward technique that could be used for evaluating options is to provide that all option-year prices be discounted to present value. This would remove most of the incentive for offerors to front-load their prices in order to obtain the free use of the money in the early years. However, the FAR is silent on the use of this technique. The government previously used a Present Value Method (PVM) of evaluation on ADPE procurements, having recognized a necessity to consider the time value of money in evaluating bids, Federal Information Resources Management Regulations, 41 C.F.R. § 201-32.205-3. However, this regulation is no longer extant. See also *Linolex Sys., Inc.*, 53 Comp. Gen. 895 (B-179047), 74-1 CPD ¶ 296. There appears to be no reason why this evaluation method could not be used in evaluating options on other types of procurement. See Chapter 5 for a discussion of the time value of money.

## 5. Failure to Bid Options

If option prices are not to be evaluated, failure to bid option prices will not result in the bid being nonresponsive unless such failure deprives the government of a "substantive and valuable right," 51 Comp. Gen. 528 (B-174575) (1972). GAO reasoned that there was no such deprivation in a case where the solicitation contained no requirement limiting the amount of option prices since the bidder could have bid excessive option prices and been eligible for award if it was low bidder on the base quantity. Compare 46 Comp. Gen. 434 (B-160051) (1966), where GAO sustained the rejection of a bid omitting an unevaluated option quantity because the IFB required all options to be bid. GAO reasoned that the government was deprived of a valuable right.

If option quantities are to be evaluated, failure to bid an option will result in rejection of the bid, *Areawide Servs., Inc.*, Comp. Gen. Dec. B-240134.4, 90-2 CPD ¶ 182; *Huff & Huff Serv. Corp.*, Comp. Gen. Dec. B-233740.5, 90-1 CPD ¶ 167; *Rozier, Sidbury & Co.*, Comp. Gen. Dec. B-216741, 85-1 CPD ¶ 58; *Ainslie Corp.*, Comp. Gen. Dec. B-190878, 78-1 CPD ¶ 340. In *E.H. Morrill Co.*, 63 Comp. Gen. 348 (B-214556), 84-1 CPD ¶ 508, GAO held that a bid that did not provide prices for option work added by an amendment and whose receipt was acknowledged was nonresponsive. Subsequently, in a case that did not involve options, GAO explicitly clarified the *E.H. Morrill* decision and stated that "where an omitted item is divisible from the contract requirements, is de minimis as to total cost, and would not affect the competitive standing of the bidders, it may be waived," *Leslie & Elliott Co.*, 64 Comp. Gen. 279 (B-216676), 85-1 CPD ¶ 212.

There is another limited exception to this rule, stating that the omission of the option price can be corrected by the contracting officer if it can be determined from the face of the bid that the omission is the result of a clerical error, *Con-Chen Enters.*, Comp. Gen. Dec. B-187795, 77-2 CPD ¶ 284; 52 Comp. Gen. 604 (B-187795) (1973). In both of these cases, GAO reasoned that a clerical error was apparent because, while some options were omitted, the final option was priced in each case. Further, the pricing pattern was uniform, indicating the amount that the bidder had intended to bid. In contrast, in *Ainslie Corp.*, Comp. Gen. Dec. B-190878, 78-1 CPD ¶ 340, it was found that correction was not possible since no option prices had been bid. See also *Goldco Int'l*, Comp. Gen. Dec. B-248059, 92-2 CPD ¶ 59, where the government properly accepted a bid including a fifth option year when only four years were called for in the IFB.

## 6. Exercise of Options

If the government can fulfill its needs by exercise of an option, significant savings in time and administrative costs can be realized. However, exercise of an option could be very disadvantageous to the government if the work can be obtained from another source at a lower price. Traditionally, the contracting officer has been given broad discretion in deciding whether to exercise an option, *National Cash Register Co.*, Comp. Gen. Dec. B-179045, 74-1 CPD ¶ 116; 36 Comp. Gen. 62 (B-128449) (1956) ("options . . . purely for the interest and benefit of the Government"). Thus, a bankruptcy court has refused to order a government agency to exercise an option when it was demonstrated that the decision not to exercise was not based on the fact the company was bankrupt, *In re Plum Run Serv. Corp.*, 159 B.R. 496 (S.D. Ohio 1993). Similarly, the ASBCA has held that it will not review a decision not to exercise an option unless it is demonstrated that the decision is made in bad faith or is an abuse of discretion, *Pennyrile Plumbing, Inc.*, ASBCA 44555, 96-1 BCA ¶ 28,044; *Sample Enters.*, ASBCA 44564, 94-3 BCA ¶ 27,105.

GAO will no longer consider contractor contentions that their options should be exercised, *C.G. Ashe Enters.*, 56 Comp. Gen. 387 (B-188043), 77-1 CPD ¶ 166; *Lanson Indus., Inc.*, 60 Comp. Gen. 661 (B-202942), 81-2 CPD ¶ 176; *Digital Sys. Group, Inc.*, Comp. Gen. Dec. B-252080.2, 93-1 CPD ¶ 228. In *Albert G. Gricoski Private Detective Agency*, Comp. Gen. Dec. B-214179, 84-1 CPD ¶ 157, GAO reiterated this rule and noted that the contractor's need to be reimbursed for costs not included in base prices did not require the government to exercise options. GAO will consider cases where the contracting officer is selecting among options in the contracts of competing firms, *Fjellestad, Barrett & Short*, Comp. Gen. Dec. B-248391, 92-2 CPD ¶ 118; *Mine Safety Appliance Co.*, 69 Comp. Gen. 562 (B-238597.2 ), 90-2 CPD ¶ 11.

It would be poor business practice to lose the opportunity of an advantageous purchase by failure to exercise an option. Thus, in all cases, the contracting officer should check market prices before failing to exercise an option. See *A.C. Elecs., Inc.*, Comp. Gen. Dec. B-185553, 76-1 CPD ¶ 295, where a decision not to exercise an option was upheld because there had been recent procurements at prices lower than the option price.

## a. Determining That Exercise Is Advantageous to the Government

Before exercising an option, the contracting officer must analyze the situation and make a number of determinations. FAR 17.207 provides:

(b) When the contract provides for economic price adjustment and the contractor requests a revision of the price, the contracting officer shall determine the effect of the adjustment on prices under the option before the option is exercised.

(c) The contracting officer may exercise options only after determining that —

(1) Funds are available;

(2) The requirement covered by the option fulfills an existing Government need;

(3) The exercise of the option is the most advantageous method of fulfilling the Government's need, price and other factors (see paragraphs (d) and (e) below) considered;

(4) The option was synopsized in accordance with Part 5 unless exempted by 5.202(a)(11) or other appropriate exemptions in 5.202; and

(5) The contractor is not listed on the Excluded Parties List System (EPLS) (see FAR 9.405-1).

(d) The contracting officer, after considering price and other factors, shall make the determination on the basis of one of the following:

(1) A new solicitation fails to produce a better price or a more advantageous offer than that offered by the option. If it is anticipated that the best price available is the option price or that this is the more advantageous offer, the contracting officer should not use this method of testing the market.

(2) An informal analysis of prices or an examination of the market indicates that the option price is better than prices available in the market or that the option is the more advantageous offer.

(3) The time between the award of the contract containing the option and the exercise of the option is so short that it indicates the option price is the lowest price obtainable or the more advantageous offer. The contracting officer shall take into consideration such factors as market stability and comparison of the time since award with the usual duration of contracts for such supplies or services.

(e) The determination of other factors under (c)(3) of this section —

(1) Should take into account the Government's need for continuity of operations and potential costs of disrupting operations; and

(2) May consider the effect on small business.

(f) Before exercising an option, the contracting officer shall make a written determination for the contract file that exercise is in accordance with the terms of the option, the requirements of this section, and Part 6. To satisfy requirements of Part 6 regarding full and open competition, the option must have been evaluated as part of the initial competition and be exercisable at an amount specified in or reasonably determinable from the terms of the basic contract, *e.g.* —

(1) A specific dollar amount;

(2) An amount to be determined by applying provisions (or a formula) provided in the basic contract, but not including renegotiation of the price for work in a fixed-price type contract;

(3) In the case of a cost-type contract, if —

(i) The option contains a fixed or maximum fee; or

(ii) The fixed or maximum fee amount is determinable by applying a formula contained in the basic contract (but see 16.102(c));

(4) A specific price that is subject to an economic price adjustment provision; or

(5) A specific price that is subject to change as the result of changes to prevailing labor rates provided by the Secretary of Labor.

(g) The contract modification or other written document which notifies the contractor of the exercise of the option shall cite the option clause as authority.

This regulation incorporated two changes reflecting the requirements of the Competition in Contracting Act of 1984 (CICA). First, ¶ (c)(4) was added to require synopses of all prospective option exercises unless the original contract was synopsized with sufficient clarity to inform offerors of that possibility. Second, ¶ (f) was amended to cross-reference Part 6 of the FAR, calling for "full and open competition." This regulation has been regarded as an internal operating procedure which contractors cannot use to avoid the exercise of an option within the terms of the option provision in the contract, *Freightliner Corp. v. Caldera*, 225 F.3d 1361 (Fed. Cir. 2000).

The requirement for full and open competition applies to the exercise of options that have not been evaluated in the award, since such exercise can be considered to be a form of sole source contracting. See *Major Contracting Servs., Inc.*, Comp. Gen. Dec. B-401472, 2009 CPD ¶ 170, *recons. denied*, 2009 CPD ¶ 250, holding that exercising the option to extend services under the FAR 51.217-8 clause was improper because it had not been evaluated in the original competition. GAO rejected the argument that the option implicitly had been evaluated because the clause required the contractor to perform at the current contract rates. This same logic may be applicable to the FAR 52.237-3 clause. See also *Kollsman Instrument Co.*, 68 Comp. Gen. 303 (B-233759), 89-1 CPD ¶ 243, where GAO denied a protest that an option had been exercised without competition on a contract where the option prices had not been evaluated. GAO found that the agency had properly justified the lack of competition on the basis of urgency and also found that the agency had performed a sufficient check of market conditions before exercising the option.

It appears that the competition requirement does not apply to evaluated options, because they were part of the original competition. However, FAR 17.207(d) requires some analysis of the reasonableness of the price before exercising options, *Ross & McDonald Contracting, GmbH*, ASBCA 38154, 94-1 BCA ¶ 26,316 (improper to exercise option on reprocurement contract without checking validity of prices); *Banknote Corp. of Am.*, Comp. Gen. Dec. B-250151, 92-2 CPD ¶ 413 (improper to rely on original bid prices, especially when quantities were increasing); *AAA Eng'g & Drafting, Inc.*, Comp. Gen. Dec. B-236034.2, 92-1 CPD ¶ 307 (current market price must be checked to ensure that option price is reasonable). GAO has been quite lenient in enforcing this requirement. See *Sippican, Inc.*, Comp. Gen. Dec. B-257047.2, 95-2 CPD ¶ 220, where the protester, a firm that had lost the competition, had informed the agency that it could offer the option quantities at lower prices because it had reduced its costs. GAO held that the contracting officer had properly exercised his discretion in failing to conduct a competition for the option quantity, stating:

> As a general rule, option provisions in a contract are exercisable at the discretion of the government. See Far 17.201. An informal analysis of prices or an examination of the market which indicates " that the option price is better than prices available in the market or that the option is the more advantageous offer" is one of three methods specifically set forth in FAR 17.207(d) as a basis for determining whether to exercise an option. *Person-System Integration, Ltd.*, B-246142; B-246142.2, Feb. 19, 1992, 92-1 CPD ¶ 204. The form of such examination is largely within the discretion of the contracting officer, so long as it is reasonable. See *Kollsman Instrument Co.*, 68 Comp. Gen. 303 (1989), 89-1 CPD ¶ 243; *Action Mfg. Co.*, 66 Comp. Gen. 463 (1987), 87-1 CPD ¶ 518. The FAR also per-

mits a determination that the option price is the most advantageous based upon a finding that the time between contract award and option exercise is short enough and the market stable enough that the option price remains most advantageous. FAR 17.207(d).

Our Office will not question an agency's exercise of an option under an existing contract unless the protester shows that the agency failed to follow applicable regulations or that the determination to exercise the option, rather than conduct a new procurement, was unreasonable. *Tycho Technology, Inc.*, B-222413.2, May 25, 1990, 90-1 CPD ¶ 500. The intent of the regulations is not to afford a firm that offered high prices under an original solicitation an opportunity to remedy this business judgment by undercutting the option price of the successful offeror. *Person-System Integration, Ltd., supra.* We find no basis to question the agency's determination to exercise the option.

The record shows that the contracting officer considered (1) the prices offered in the original competition and the fact that [the contractor's] high technical score and low price had made its proposal more advantageous than the protester's proposal; (2) that only a relatively short period of time had passed since the original competition and the agency's requirements for the third option year remained the same as stated in the original competition; (3) that agency information showed that [the protester] had recently charged substantially more for EMATT units in a foreign procurement than [the contractor's] option price; (4) that there was no known change in the current EMATT market; (5) that since [the protester] did not provide any financial data to support its allegations of more advantageous pricing, and since prior prices known to the agency for required materials were substantial, it remained unlikely that [the protester] could reduce its material costs to the extent stated to be below those of [the contractor]; and (6) the need for continuity of operations and the cost of disruption, as well as the costs of a new competition (which would involve additional costs of proposal evaluation, start-up costs and the possible requalification of a vendor or qualification of a new contractor).

The same result was reached in *Antmarin, Inc.*, Comp. Gen. Dec. B-296317, 2005 CPD ¶ 149; *Bulova Techs., Inc.*, Comp. Gen. Dec. B-252660, 93-2 CPD ¶ 23, and *Valentec Wells, Inc.*, Comp. Gen. Dec. B-239499, 90-2 CPD ¶ 177.

It is proper to test the market before exercising an option by conducting a competition and evaluating the option holder's product at its option price, *Beretta USA Corp.*, Comp. Gen. Dec. B-232681, 88-2 CPD ¶ 395, *recons. denied*, 89-1 CPD ¶ 16. However, it is improper to add significant costs involved in procuring a duplicate product to the costs of the competitors, *Smith & Wesson*, Comp. Gen. Dec. B-232681.2, 89-1 CPD ¶ 134.

Even if option prices have been evaluated in the original competition, it is not proper to exercise an option unless the dollar amount can be determined from the original contract, FAR 17.207(f). In *Magnum Opus Techs., Inc. v. United States*, 94 Fed. Cl. 553 (2010), the court held that the agency had violated this requirement when it had waived the not-to-exceed labor rates in the original contract, with the result that there was no binding rates at the time the option was exercised.

Since option prices are generally a matter of public record, they should be disclosed when examining the market or soliciting offers. GAO has held that disclosure of the option price in a solicitation is permissible, *Grant's Janitorial & Food Serv., Inc.*, Comp. Gen. Dec. B-244170, 91-1 CPD ¶ 512; *JL Assocs.*, Comp. Gen. Dec. B-239790, 90-2 CPD ¶ 261; *Milwaukee Valve Co.*, Comp. Gen. Dec. B-206249, 82-1 CPD ¶ 135. See, however, *Canadian Commercial Corp. v. Department of the Air Force*, 514 F.3d 37 (D.C. Cir. 2007), holding that it was a violation of the Freedom of Information Act 5 U.S.C. § 552(b)(4), to release option prices because they were proprietary information.

FAR 17.207(c)(5) now prohibits the exercise of an option if the contractor is on the suspension of debarment list. This prohibition was added to the FAR in 2009 by Federal Acquisition Circular 2005-34, 74 Fed. Reg. 31,557. DFARS 217.207 also requires ensuring that the contractor's record in the Central Contractor Registration database is accurate before option exercise.

Under the prior statutes and regulations, GAO held that where option prices have been evaluated in the initial award, the requirement that the exercise of options be advantageous to the government was not intended to require a new solicitation that would permit a firm that had an opportunity to compete under the original solicitation to displace the incumbent contractor by undercutting the option price, *Jaxon, Inc.*, Comp. Gen. Dec. B-213998, 84-2 CPD ¶ 33; *A.J. Fowler Corp.*, Comp. Gen. Dec. B-205062, 82-1 CPD ¶ 582. In addition, the contracting officer was permitted to consider the satisfactory performance of the incumbent contractor and administrative budget constraints that might cause lack of personnel to process a new solicitation, *Humanics, Ltd.*, Comp. Gen. Dec. B-202418.2, 82-1 CPD ¶ 514. Note that FAR 17.207(e) still permits consideration of continuity of operations and disruption costs. GAO has affirmed the exercise of an option where, "due to time constraints, procuring competitively would disrupt services and create substantial costs to the Government," *A. Lee Parker*, Comp. Gen. Dec. B-206735, 82-2 CPD ¶ 259. See also *Cerberonics, Inc.*, Comp. Gen. Dec. B-199924, 81-1 CPD ¶ 351, holding that a contracting officer had properly decided to exercise an option rather than conduct a new competition in a case where the option was on a cost-reimbursement basis and the agency determined that it needed the continuity of the contractor that was performing the job well. In this case, the protesting competitor had submitted an unsolicited proposal to perform the work for less than the option price. See also *Silent Hoist & Crane Co.*, Comp. Gen. Dec. B-186006, 76-1 CPD ¶ 392 (exercise of option upheld when repeated IFBs for additional quantity did not result in lower prices); and *Oscar Holmes & Sons, Inc.*, Comp. Gen. Dec. B-183897, 75-2 CPD ¶ 339 (survey of market supported exercise of option even though other firms claimed that competitive bidding would result in lower prices).

The GSA has adopted special procedures calling for the contractor's past performance to be one of the considerations in deciding whether to exercise an option, GSAR Subpart 517.2. This procedure is intended to motivate the contractor to give better performance in an effort to induce the government to exercise an option. However, comparative prices are still a major consideration in the exercise of such options.

Prior to CICA, GAO limited the discretion of the contracting officer in instances where the option prices were not evaluated in the original procurement. See *KET Inc.*, 58 Comp. Gen. 38 (B-191949), 78-2 CPD ¶ 305, holding that the procedures followed in determining whether to exercise the option should "comport, as much as possible, with the competitive norm of federal procurement." GAO has also held that where an option is included in a sole source contract, it may be exercised despite the possibility that competition may become feasible at a future date; GAO did also advise that exercise should be delayed where practicable, *Bird Elecs. Corp.*, Comp. Gen. Dec. B-205155, 82-1 CPD ¶ 519. However, where options were not evaluated and prior to exercise of the option a competitor unambiguously declared that it was willing to perform at a price lower than the option price, the government may not renegotiate any terms of the option without issuing a new solicitation, *Department of the Army-Recons.*, Comp. Gen. Dec. B-208281.2, 83-2 CPD ¶ 78.

Where an option contract has been awarded under the Small Business Administration's 8(a) program, the government may exercise options, subject to other regulatory requirements, irrespective of the fact that the company outgrows its small business status during the time of the contract, *Vantex Serv. Corp.*, Comp. Gen. Dec. B-251102, 93-1 CPD ¶ 221; *Gallegos Research Corp.*, Comp. Gen. Dec. B-209992.2, 83-2 CPD ¶ 597.

It has been held that the government may exercise an option as part of a litigation settlement, even when a minor increase in price was allowed and the agency relied on an informal market survey in its determination that exercise was in the best interests of the government, *Gulton Indus., Inc.*, Comp. Gen. Dec. B-203265, 82-2 CPD ¶ 59.

## b.  Negotiation of Options

In some cases, the contracting officer has negotiated with the contractor extending the option to obtain more favorable terms. GAO has held that this is permissible if it is done as part of a negotiated procurement to test the option price, *Interscience Sys., Inc.*, Comp. Gen. Dec. B-194497, 79-2 CPD ¶ 306, *recons. denied*, 81-1 CPD ¶ 61. However, an incumbent contractor may not undermine the integrity of the competitive bidding system by reducing the option price subsequent to bid opening if the option-testing competition is accomplished using sealed bid procedures, Comp. Gen. Dec. B-173504, Sept. 12, 1972, *Unpub.*

GAO has also held that negotiation of the terms of the option prior to testing the market is, in effect, a new procurement requiring negotiation with all competitors, *Varian Assocs., Inc.*, Comp. Gen. Dec. B-208281, 83-1 CPD ¶ 160, *modified on other grounds*, 83-2 CPD ¶ 78. However, it is proper to test the market by soliciting firm prices against an option price that has to be negotiated by the agency, *Smith & Wesson*, Comp. Gen. Dec. B-232681.2, 89-1 CPD ¶ 134. In circumstances where the market included only two eligible contractors, informal negotiations on price and delivery schedules were sufficient because both eligible offerors were afforded an equal opportunity to compete, *Nuclear Metals, Inc.*, 64 Comp. Gen. 290 (B-216319), 85-1 CPD ¶ 217.

## c. Method of Exercising an Option

The government must exercise options in a timely manner and in exact compliance with the option terms, *Lockheed Martin IR Imaging Sys., Inc. v. West*, 108 F.3d 319 (Fed. Cir. 1997); *New England Tank Indus. of New Hampshire, Inc. v. United States*, 861 F.2d 685 (Fed. Cir. 1988); *Chemical Tech., Inc.*, ASBCA 21863, 80-2 BCA ¶ 14,728; *Holly Corp.*, ASBCA 24975, 83-1 BCA ¶ 16,327.

### (1) STRICT COMPLIANCE

The strict compliance requirement governing the exercise of options has been imposed because options give the party with the right to exercise unique power over the other party. FAR 17.207 provides minimal guidance in this regard, stating:

(a) When exercising an option, the contracting officer shall provide written notice to the contractor within the time period specified in the contract.

However, it has consistently been held that for the government's exercise of an option to be effective, the election must be positive, unambiguous, and in exact compliance with the terms of the option, 51 Comp. Gen. 119 (B-172586) (1971). Thus, exercise of an option is invalid if the option reduces the quantity of work, *Grumman Tech. Servs., Inc.*, ASBCA 46040, 95-2 BCA ¶ 27,918, unless the option contains flexible quantities, *Raven Indus., Inc.*, Comp. Gen. Dec. B-185052, 76-1 CPD ¶ 90 (clause permitting option "up to" 100% enables government to order partial quantity). Adding new contract clauses in conjunction with an option exercise will also invalidate the exercise, *Varo, Inc.*, ASBCA 47945, 96-1 BCA ¶ 28,161. An option exercise is also improper if it is sent to an official of the contractor without authority to receive such communications, *Western States Mgmt. Servs., Inc.*, ASBCA 37490, 89-2 BCA ¶ 21,803.

Exercise of an option before funds are made available, contingent of the availability of funds, is an invalid exercise, *J.E.T.S., Inc.*, ASBCA 26135, 82-2 BCA ¶ 15,986, *Lear Siegler Inc.*, ASBCA 30224, 86-3 BCA ¶ 19,155. However, exercise of an option contingent on the availability of funds is proper if that is called for in the option clause of the contract, *Western States Mgmt. Servs., Inc.*, ASBCA 37504, 92-1 BCA ¶ 24,663. Similarly, exercise of the option on the date an appropriations act is signed by the President is proper, *Cessna Aircraft Co.*, ASBCA 43196, 93-3 BCA ¶ 25,912, *aff'd*, 126 F.3d 1442 (Fed Cir. 1997). See also *Freightliner Corp.*, ASBCA 42982, 94-1 BCA ¶ 26,538, 98-2 BCA ¶ 30,026, *aff'd*, 225 F.3d 1361 (Fed. Cir. 2000), where the board held that the agency could obtain its requirements for a sixth year by exercising an option on the fifth year of a multiyear contract.

If a contractor leads the government to believe that it can exercise the option without strictly complying with the clause, it will be estopped from asserting the strict compliance rule, *Ampex Corp.*, GSBCA 5913, 82-1 BCA ¶ 15,738, *recons. denied*, 82-2 BCA ¶ 15,858 (authorized contractor employee told the government that the option notice could be sent by TWX). For another case not requiring strict compliance with the terms of the option exercise, see *Contel Page Servs., Inc.*, ASBCA 32100, 87-1 BCA ¶ 19,540. There, the board found that an option was properly exercised when the contracting officer sent the contractor an unsigned bilateral modification exercising the option. The board reasoned that the cover letter, signed by the contracting officer, was a proper exercise of the option. In *TECOM, Inc.*, IBCA 2970 A-1, 95-2 BCA ¶ 27,607, the board required exact compliance with the option terms distinguishing *Contel Page Services* and holding that the mailing of a draft bilateral modification was not a proper option exercise. Where the period for option exercise is established by reference to the date of final delivery, amendments changing that date should specify whether the option period is also changed. See *Damascus Hosiery Mills, Inc.*, ASBCA 18776, 74-2 BCA ¶ 10,961; and Comp. Gen. Dec. B-176386, Oct. 24, 1972, *Unpub.* (contractor allowed to recover for untimely exercise of the option where a modification of the delivery schedule was the direct result of government-caused delay).

Although the strict compliance rule is generally adhered to closely, there are a few cases allowing less strict compliance when there are ambiguous option clauses. See, for example, *International Transducer Corp. v. United States*, 30 Fed. Cl. 522 (1994), where the court interpreted an option for "a part of" any line item to include an option to order parts of subline items — finding that this was a patent ambiguity for which the contractor should have sought clarification. In *Griffin Servs., Inc.*, ASBCA 52280, 04-2 BCA ¶ 32,745, where the option clause called for exercise "within the period specified in the Schedule" but the schedule contained no date, the board found that the option could be exercised at any time during the period of contract performance specified in the Schedule then in effect. See also *BMY-Combat Sys.*, ASBCA 39495, 95-2 BCA ¶ 27,809, where the board permitted exercise of an option after the full documentation of the results of the "testing process" when the contract called for exercise of the option "within 30 days after completion of initial production testing." The board used contract interpretation principles to give the government additional time to exercise the option.

There are also cases finding proper exercise of options where the language purporting to exercise the option is not completely clear. For example, in *Technical Servs. Corp.*, ASBCA 36505, 93-1 BCA ¶ 25,310, the board found a proper option exercise where a letter stated that "the Government shall exercise the second option year" and contained an incorrect line item number and an incorrect initial date for the option work. Similarly, in *Mills Mfg. Corp.*, ASBCA 10416, 66-1 BCA ¶ 5450, the board found a proper exercise where a telegram stated that "the government proposes to exercise the option." In both cases, the board found that the total import of the communications was that the option was being exercised and that it would not require the government to be grammatically correct.

## (2) PRELIMINARY NOTICE REQUIREMENT

The FAR 52.217-9 option clause requires the government to give the contractor a "preliminary written notice of its intent to extend" the contract at least 60 days "before the contract expires" (unless the contracting officer inserts a different date). Since this date is usually before the option exercise date, it places two notice requirements on the government. This preliminary notice requirement must be strictly complied with the have a valid option exercise, *White Sands Constr., Inc.*, ASBCA 51875, 04-1 BCA ¶ 32,598. In reaching this conclusion, the board reasoned that "[t] he preliminary notice is an integral component of the process by which the government binds the contractor to another contract term."

## (3) SEQUENTIAL OPTIONS

If options are sequential, failure to exercise the option properly for one year will preclude the government from exercising future year options, *Grumman Tech. Servs., Inc.*, ASBCA 46040, 95-2 BCA ¶ 27,918. There the board reasoned that the contract "came to an end" when an annual option was not exercised; in effect, no options then remained for future years. Similarly, where a contract contained several options that both parties understood were priced on a learning curve, they were required to be exercised sequentially, *Motorola, Inc.*, ASBCA 39782, 93-3 BCA ¶ 26,081 (exercise of second option improper when first option had been permitted to expire). The same reasoning was followed in *Texas Instruments, Inc.*, ASBCA 25942, 88-1 BCA ¶ 20,421 (parties understood options were based on continuous production). However, in *Loral Fairchild Corp.*, ASBCA 45719, 97-1 BCA ¶ 28,905, exercise of an option after expiration of a prior option was found proper because the FAR 52.217-7 clause permitted such exercise and there was no evidence that the parties had discussed the fact that the option prices were based on a learning curve. Prior to 1990, the FAR 52.217-7 clause calling for options for "separately priced line items" stated that such items were "independent of each other" and that the government could exercise the options independently. See *Knights' Piping, Inc.*, ASBCA 46989, 94-3 BCA ¶ 27,023, following this clause. This language has now been omitted from the FAR clause, but it appears that the contractor would be bound to "independent" options if the contract clearly gave the government this right.

### (4) TIME OF EFFECTIVITY

The time of exercise of an option is calculated based on the time of *receipt* of the notice not on the time of transmission. Thus, one aspect of the strict compliance rule is that, to be timely, a notice of exercise of an option must be received prior to the expiration of the contractual time for exercise. Comment f. of *Restatement, Second, Contracts* § 63, states:

> Option contracts are commonly subject to a definite time limit, and the usual understanding is that the notification that the option has been exercised must be received by the offeror before that time. Whether or not there is such a time limit, in the absence of a contrary provision in the option contract, the offeree takes the risk of loss or delay in the transmission of the acceptance and remains free to revoke the acceptance until it arrives. Similarly, if there is such a mistake on the part of the offeror as justifies the rescission of his unilateral obligation, the right to rescind is not lost merely because a letter of acceptance is posted.

Thus, exercise of an option is effective upon receipt unless a contrary intent is shown, *Dynamics Corp. of Am. v. United States*, 182 Ct. Cl. 62, 389 F.2d 424 (1968); *Jim Phillips Contracting, Inc.*, IBCA 4319, 04-1 BCA ¶ 32,416. In *Cessna Aircraft Co.*, ASBCA 43196, 96-1 BCA ¶ 27,966, *aff'd*, 126 F.3d 1442 (Fed Cir. 1997), *cert. denied*, 525 U.S. 818 (1998), the board found receipt of a facsimile on the nonworking day it was sent, even though no contractor employee picked it up for two days. When a contract provision alters the basic rule, that provision will govern. See *USD Techs., Inc.*, ASBCA 31305, 87-2 BCA ¶ 19,680, where the contract contained a special provision stating that the option would be "considered to have been exercised at the time the Government deposits [it] in the mails." The board held that the government had the burden of proof that the option exercise was actually mailed before the option expired.

There have been a number of instances where the contract clause is rather vague as to the final date for exercising the option. In such cases, the boards have looked to the entire agreement to determine the date. For example, in *TECOM, Inc.*, IBCA 2970 A-1, 94-2 BCA ¶ 26,787, the board interpreted a clause calling for exercise of an option "within 30 calendar days of expiration date" to require exercise of the option at least 30 days *before* the final date of contract performance. See also *American Contract Servs., Inc.*, ASBCA 46788, 94-2 BCA ¶ 26,855, *recons. denied*, 94-3 BCA ¶ 27,025, *aff'd*, 53 F.3d 348 (Fed. Cir. 1995), where the board held that "within 15 days" inserted in the Option to Extend the Term of the Contract clause in FAR 52.217-9 meant within 15 days of the expiration of the contract, not within 15 days of contract award.

## (5) Requirement for Written Notice

Almost all option clauses call for exercise of the option by written notice, and it has been held that oral notice will not suffice, *International Tel. & Tel. v. United States*, 197 Ct. Cl. 11, 453 F.2d 1283 (1972) (exercise of right to purchase quantities in a subsequent program year under multiyear procurement where the court decided the case using the legal principles applicable to options); *Maintenance, Inc.*, Comp. Gen. Dec. B-215619.3, 84-2 CPD ¶ 263 (oral advice that an option will be exercised is not binding on the government). See, however, *American Mach. & Foundry Co.*, ASBCA 8862, 65-1 BCA ¶ 4654, where the government was held bound to an oral agreement extending the date on which the option could be exercised. In *Diversified Marine Tech, Inc.*, DOTBCA 2455, 93-2 BCA ¶ 25,720, the board refused to compensate the contractor for work done on an option that had been orally discussed with the captain of a ship (indicating a high probability that the option would be exercised) but which had not been exercised in writing.

## (6) Performing after Improper Option Exercise

There have been a number of instances where a contractor has asserted that an option was not properly exercised but has agreed to perform the option work "under protest." In such cases, relief for the added costs of option work done pursuant to untimely exercises of options has been granted on the theory that a constructive change has occurred, *Lockheed Martin Ir Imaging Sys., Inc. v. West*, 108 F.3d 319 (Fed. Cir. 1997); *Lear Siegler Inc.*, ASBCA 12164, 69-1 BCA ¶ 7563; *Keco Indus., Inc.*, ASBCA 16645, 73-2 BCA ¶ 10,056. See also *Holly Corp.*, ASBCA 24975, 83-1 BCA ¶ 16,327, where the exercise of an option without adequate funds was held to be a constructive change order because a government employee stated funds were available and the contractor could not reasonably have known of the lack of funds. GAO has refused to consider such allegations because they are "appropriate for handling under the Disputes clause," *Murdock Mach. & Eng'g Co.*, Comp. Gen. Dec. B-183098, 75-1 CPD ¶ 98.

If the contractor honors an improper option exercise by performing without objection, it is normally estopped from later contesting the validity of the option exercise. In *E. Walters & Co. v. United States*, 217 Ct. Cl. 254, 576 F.2d 362 (1978), the court held that the contractor had lost the right to an equitable adjustment for improper exercise of an option because it had performed the option work without challenge and had not raised the issue until six months after completion of performance. See also *CARAM v. General Servs. Admin.*, GSBCA 12773, 95-1 BCA ¶ 27,488, where the contractor was estopped from asserting an improper option exercise when it failed to raise the issue at any time during the option year. Similarly, in *USD Techs., Inc.*, ASBCA 31305, 87-2 BCA ¶ 19,680, the board found that the contractor was estopped from denying that an option was properly exercised when it had signed a bilateral modification "restating" the terms of the option exercise. In

*TECOM, Inc.*, IBCA 2970 A-1, 95-2 BCA ¶ 27,607, the board found no estoppel where the contractor performed the option work for four and one-half months without protest but did not realize that the option had been improperly exercised until it hired an attorney.

## (7) UNCONSCIONABILITY

The ASBCA has considered allegations of unconscionability in the government's decision to exercise options, but these protests have been unsuccessful, *United Serv. Corp.*, ASBCA 25786, 82-2 BCA ¶ 15,985; *Mercantile Servs., Ltd.*, ASBCA 26386, 82-1 BCA ¶ 15,767, absent evidence that the entire contract had become commercially senseless and that the government had superior knowledge regarding inflation at the time it exercised the options. In *McGrail Equip. Co.*, ASBCA 20555, 76-1 BCA ¶ 11,723, where prices had increased substantially after a government price freeze had been lifted, the exercise of an option was held not to be unconscionable. GAO has stated that the concept of unconscionability is inapplicable to the exercise of options since the exercise of an option does not constitute the making of a new contract, *Heirs of Kim Xum*, Comp. Gen. Dec. B-189121, 83-1 CPD ¶ 408.

## 7. Soft Options

The traditional option used in government contracts has been on a firm-fixed-price basis with definitive specifications and a firm delivery schedule. Such options have been referred to as "hard" options. Procuring agencies also use options with less definite terms, referred to as "soft" options. See, for example, *Aviation Contractor Employees, Inc. v. United States*, 945 F.2d 1568 (Fed. Cir. 1991), holding that such an option to extend the contract period with no agreement on how additional work would be priced was not invalid for lack of certainty because it required the parties to negotiate in good faith to establish the price. See also *Fox Int'l, Inc.*, Comp. Gen. Dec. B-181675, 75-1 CPD ¶ 126, finding no lack of good faith when government terminated the negotiations when it found a cheaper method of fulfilling its requirements. In *North Star Steel Co. v. United States*, 477 F.3d 1324 (Fed. Cir. 2007), the court held that to prove that the government breached such a good faith obligation, the contractor would have to prove "bad faith." The decision is not clear on what conduct would constitute bad faith but it does indicate that failure to disclose vital information pertinent to the pricing would "constitute a failure to negotiated in good faith." Compare *England v. Systems Mgmt. Am. Corp.*, 38 Fed. Appx. 567 (Fed. Cir. 2002), where the court reversed a board decision holding that the government had been arbitrary and capricious in delaying finalization of option pricing until after the contractor was ineligible to received the options (because it lost its small business status). There the court found four bases for a holding that the government had acted improperly, (1) whether the government official acted with "subjective bad faith," (2) whether the official had "no reasonable basis" supporting the decision at issue, a factor closely associated with the bad faith test stated above (3) the amount of discretion vested in the government official who rendered the decision under scrutiny and (4) whether a proven violation of the relevant statutes or regulations can alone render a decision arbitrary and capricious and thus provide a basis for recovery. In reversing the board decision on the basis that the government action was reasonable, the court recognized that an agreement to negotiate in good faith might "actually require something more than simply not negotiating in bad faith" and made the following comment on what might constitute good faith at 573:

> "Good faith" ordinarily refers to "'that state of mind denoting honesty of purpose, freedom from intention to defraud, and, generally speaking, . . . faithfulness to one's duty or obligation.'" *Arnold M. Diamond, Inc.* [*v. Dalton*], 25 F.3d [1006 (Fed. Cir. 1994)] at 1010 (quoting *People v. Nunn*, 46 Cal. 2d 460, 296 P.2d 813, 818 (Cal. App. 1956) and discussing "good faith" as used in the Contract Disputes Act).

Thus, it is not clear what standard should be applied to determine whether a party has negotiated the price of a soft option in good faith.

Because the contractor's obligations under such soft options are uncertain, the major purpose for using options — that of protecting the government from future uncertainties — is absent. It appears that the major benefits to be gained by the government from such options are administrative convenience in the option procurement and any advantage accruing from the contractor's obligation to negotiate in good faith. In *Electronic Sys. USA, Inc.*, ASBCA 26063, 82-1 BCA ¶ 15,521, the board held that performance of work in accordance with the government's exercise of an unpriced option is compensable as a constructive change.

The Department of Homeland Security has prohibited the use of "unpriced options," HSAR 3017.202.

# CHAPTER 10

# CONTRACT PRICING

The government's policy is to purchase supplies and services at reasonable prices. In this regard, FAR 14.408-2 requires the contracting officer to determine that bid prices are reasonable before awarding the contract, and FAR 14.404-1(c)(6) permits cancellation of sealed bid solicitations if all acceptable bids are at unreasonable prices or if only one bid is received and the reasonableness of the price cannot be established. With respect to negotiated procurement, FAR 15.402(a) requires the contracting officer to "[p]urchase supplies and services . . . at fair and reasonable prices." Reasonableness of price is also a concept applicable to contract modifications. Thus, in the vast majority of contract actions, the contracting officer is required to determine that the proposed contract price is reasonable before an award is made.

The primary focus of these requirements is to ensure that the government does not pay unreasonably high prices. However, prices that are *unreasonably low* should also be dealt with before an award is made. Such prices may place the contracting officer on notice of a possible mistake in the bid or proposal. When there is a perceived mistake in a bid received in a sealed bid procurement, the offeror must be requested to verify the price, FAR 14.407-1. The FAR contains no similar requirement for requesting verification of perceived mistakes in prices submitted in negotiated procurements, but it is good practice to follow this procedure. See *Griffy's Landscape Maint., LLC v. United States*, 46 Fed. Cl. 257 (2000) (request for verification of perceived mistake in proposal mandatory); and *C.W. Over & Sons, Inc. v. United States*, 54 Fed. Cl. 514 (2002) (no blanket rule requiring request for verification). Unreasonably low prices may also constitute evidence that the offeror is not responsible, FAR 9.103(c). In negotiated procurement, an unreasonably low price may indicate that the offeror does not understand the work, FAR 15.305(a)(1), resulting in a reduced scoring of the offeror's technical proposal. Similarly, an unreasonably low price may be perceived as creating a high risk that the offeror cannot perform the work in a satisfactory manner. Finally, proposing an unreasonably low price that is below cost may constitute "buying in," alerting the contracting officer to take precautions to prevent the contractor from obtaining improper relief from the underpricing. See FAR 3.501.

This chapter considers the process that is followed by the contracting parties in establishing the contract price or cost and fee. The first step in this process is the submission of proposed prices or estimated costs and a proposed fee by offerors. The contracting officer is then charged with the evaluation of those prices or costs and fees to determine reasonableness and/or realism. The techniques used by the government to determine reasonableness of price are price analysis and cost analysis. Price analysis looks at an offeror's proposed unit or total prices and uses data external to the offeror's anticipated costs of performance to make a judgment as to their reasonableness. In contrast, cost analysis reviews the offeror's proposed estimated costs to ascertain the reasonableness of each cost element. The first section of this chapter describes the various techniques that may have been used by offerors to arrive at their submitted prices or cost estimates. The second section deals with the contracting officer's selection of the analytical technique to be used to assess such proposals and the data necessary to use that technique. The third section considers the roles and functions of the various government personnel involved in cost analysis and price analysis. The fourth section covers the process of price analysis, while the fifth section deals with the process of cost analysis. The sixth section addresses the methods prescribed for the negotiation of profit where the parties have negotiated the costs of performance. The last section reviews the procedures to be followed in price negotiations.

# I.  OFFEROR PRICE OR COST ESTIMATING TECHNIQUES

Companies use a variety of techniques to arrive at a proposed price or cost estimate. In proposing firm fixed prices where competition is expected, offerors have much greater leeway in deciding what price to propose because they generally do not have to disclose any detailed cost information in their proposals. Hence, they can factor in the impact of competition and the condition of the market as well as the expected cost of performance in arriving at a proposed fixed price. In contrast, in cost-reimbursement and incentive contracting situations, costs will have to be proposed separately, with a commensurate need to provide some detailed cost information. There the offeror will be expected to justify the cost estimate that is submitted. Volume 1 of the DoD Contract Pricing Reference Guide (CPRG) describes two basic type of pricing used by companies — "cost-based pricing" and "market-based pricing."

In cost-based pricing, the company makes its best estimate of the cost of performing the work and then adds a profit to arrive at the price. The profit is determined by various methods — generally either by a percentage of the cost or a percentage of the investment needed to perform the prospective contract. The estimated costs are arrived at based on the amount of data that is available to the offeror from past work or industry norms that will indicate the amount of resources that will be necessary to perform the work. Thus, cost estimates for repetitive tasks will tend to be quite precise whereas cost estimates for new work will be highly judgmental. The Defense Contract Audit Manual (DCAM) describes three types of estimating techniques at 9-303:

> d. There are various methods of preparing cost estimates. The most frequently
> used are the detailed, comparison, and roundtable methods or a combination of
> the three.

(1) The detailed method requires the accumulation of detailed information to arrive at estimated costs and typically uses cost data derived from the accounting system, adjunct statistical records, and other sources. The information often includes specifications; drawings; bills of material; statements of production quantities and rates; machine and work-station workloads; manufacturing processes, including the analysis of labor efficiency, setup and rework, and material scrap, waste, and spoilage; data determining plant layout requirements; analysis of tooling and capital equipment, labor, raw material and purchased parts; special tools and dies; and composition of the indirect cost pools.

(2) The comparison method is used when specifications for the item being estimated are similar to other items already produced or currently in production and for which actual cost experience is available. Under this method, requirements for the new item are compared with those for a past or current item, the differences are isolated, and cost elements applicable to the differences are deleted from or added to experienced costs. Adjustments are also made for possible upward or downward cost trends.

(3) The roundtable method is used to estimate the cost of a new item where there is no cost experience or detailed information regarding specifications, drawings, or bills of material. Under this method, representatives of the engineering, manufacturing, purchasing, and accounting departments (among others) develop the cost estimate by exchanging views and making judgments based on knowledge and experience. This method has the advantage of speed of application and is relatively inexpensive, but may not produce readily supportable or reliable cost estimates. When this method is used, technical assistance may be required to evaluate the resultant cost estimates.

It can be seen that these descriptions relate to arriving at a cost estimate for a manufactured product. However, the same techniques are used in making estimates of the cost of construction work or other types of services. The critical issue is whether the offeror has sound information regarding the cost of performing the same or similar work. DCAM 9-303 suggests that there are a number of factors influencing the amount of detail that an offeror should consider in arriving at its cost estimate:

b. Contractors may employ uniform procedures to prepare prospective price proposals or may justifiably use a variety of method and procedures. Special problems may require a deviation from established procedures. It may be desirable in certain instances, from both the cost and time standpoints, to use overall or broad estimating procedures, rather than more precise, detailed methods; or it may be necessary to rely on the judgment of qualified personnel in design, production or other fields. Variations in estimating procedures employed may be attributable to such factors as:

(1) the relative dollar amount of each estimate,

(2) the contractor's competitive position,

(3) the degree of firmness of specifications related to the new item, and

(4) the available cost data applicable to the same or related products/services previously furnished.

Market-based pricing is very different than cost-based pricing because it is arrived at by establishing a price in order to maximize the company's position in the market. The CPRG describes seven market-based pricing strategies at I.1.4:

I.1.4.1 Profit-Maximization Pricing

I.1.4.2 Market-Share Pricing

I.1.4.3 Market Skimming

I.1.4.4 Current-Revenue Pricing

I.1.4.5 Promotional Pricing

I.1.4.6 Demand-Differential Pricing

I.1.4.7 Market-Competition Pricing

Some of these strategies are used in open commercial markets where prices are known to competitors and are not very applicable to sealed bidding or competitive negotiation procurements where prices are not known until after an offer has been submitted. However, they might be applicable to Federal Supply Schedules or other types of procurement where prices are posted and thus available to all competitors. For example, in profit-maximization pricing the company sets the price at a level that yields the highest total profit for the quantity sold. This might be a price higher than its competitors but one that will yield sufficient sales to generate the best total profit. Similarly, in the market skimming strategy, the price is set at a high level to skim off those few customers that are willing to pay that price. The same result would occur in current-revenue pricing where the seller sets a high price on the assumption that it is unlikely that there will be long-term sales.

Strategies more applicable to sealed bidding or competitive negotiation procurements are promotional pricing and market-competition pricing. The CPRG indicates that promotional pricing may occur on task order or delivery order contracts and describes some of its implications as follows at ¶ I.1.4.5:

- Bait-and-switch pricing can be particularly attractive to a firm preparing an offer for a delivery-order contract with multiple line items. An offeror using this strategy lures the buyer using a low-priced item (e.g., a low labor rate for a particular labor category) and then switches the buyer to a "better" item (e.g., a higher priced category of labor) during the sale.

- Loss-leader pricing can be attractive in situations where many items are commonly bought from the same source. An offeror using this strategy reduces the price of one item, or a group of items, to near cost, or even below. Customers are attracted to buy the low-priced items and buy other related items at the same time (e.g., set the price of a system low and the price of supplies for the system high).

- Prestige pricing uses a high-quality, high-priced item to enhance the image of an entire product line and attract more buyers. For example, many consultants feel that buyers are reluctant to buy from firms that do not charge enough. In other words, it can be almost impossible to evaluate qualifications so high price equals high quality.

Perhaps the most common form of commercial pricing found in government procurement is market-competition pricing. The CPRG contains the following coverage at I.1.4.7:

[In this strategy] different companies may set prices at a level that keeps pace with competitors' prices. When employing this strategy, the seller considers the following points:

- Determine competitor prices and/or anticipated prices.

- Set price to keep pace with competitor prices.

Major strategy applications include sealed-bid and going-rate pricing. Sealed bid pricing forces the seller to:

- Estimate what competitors will bid.

- Determine what the seller can profitably bid.

- Submit the bid knowing that it will be accepted or rejected without further discussion.

Going-rate pricing requires the seller to:

- Determine what competitors are charging.

- Establish product price within an established range of the competition.

This government guidance makes it clear that offerors factor the competitive situation into their pricing. However, it does not include any discussion of two major influences on contractor pricing decisions. The first of these influences is the relative optimism that can influence competitive pricing of work where there is no good cost experience. In this sort of "roundtable" pricing, the various experts in a company are prone to arrive at estimates of the optimal way of performing the work without sufficiently taking into account the pitfalls that may be encountered in performing a new task. Thus, their original estimates of the cost of performance may be low.

Subsequently, the company's management may reduce these estimates in order to arrive at a price that will win the competition. This phenomenon is probably the explanation for the fact that many, if not most, weapon system development contracts have been awarded at prices or estimated costs that could not be met during actual contract performance. See *Defense Acquisitions: Major Weapon Systems Continue To Experience Cost and Schedule Problems Under DoD's Revised Policy,* GAO-06-368, Apr. 13, 2006. See also *Strong Leadership Is Key to Planning and Executing Stable Weapon Programs*, GAO-10-522, May 2010, reporting that 21% of DoD's major programs were "stable and on track with original cost and schedule goals."

The second influence on pricing that is not discussed in the government guidance is below-cost pricing. In times when there is not much work being acquired, companies are tempted to propose prices that cover all of their anticipated direct costs plus only some of their indirect costs. This permits them to retain key employees that they might otherwise have to release and to cover some of the fixed costs of the business. This can be a viable short-term business strategy but imposes significant risk on the contractor if such prices cover a very long period. Some government employees might consider this a form of "buying-in" which is listed in the FAR as "an improper business practice" but is not prohibited by FAR 3.501.

## II. GOVERNMENT SELECTION OF THE ANALYTICAL TECHNIQUE

Analysis of prices by the contracting officer to determine that they are fair and reasonable is *required* in all procurement actions, FAR 14.408-2 and FAR 15.404-1(a). Thus, the contracting officer must select the analytical technique that will be used to make this determination. The major techniques are price analysis and cost analysis.

The contracting officer should obtain data to permit the use of one of these analytical techniques on all procurements. However, as discussed in Section IV, these data need not necessarily be obtained from offerors because it may be available in the agency or obtainable through market research.

Cost analysis must be conducted when it is necessary to examine individual cost elements, such as estimated labor hours or material prices, to determine the reasonableness of price, FAR 15.404-1(a)(3). Traditionally, cost analysis was performed by obtaining cost element breakdowns and supporting factual data. This factual data is referred to by the statutes and regulations as "cost or pricing data" and is required to be submitted and certified by contractors and subcontractors in certain specified types of procurement actions over the statutory threshold ($700,000 at the current time), 10 U.S.C. § 2306a and 41 U.S.C. §§ 3501-09 (called the "Truth in Negotiations Act" or "TINA"). Cost analysis can also be performed by obtaining cost element breakdowns or other information regarding the estimated costs of performance of the contract with limited or no cost or pricing data. This type of cost analysis is frequently called *cost realism analysis*. Such analysis is required when awarding a cost-reimbursement contract, FAR 15.404-1(d)(2). Cost analysis is *never* performed on sealed bid procurements, but on negotiated procurements the contracting officer must determine whether cost analysis is necessary and, if so, what type of data are necessary to perform such analysis.

Cost analysis is *required* to be performed on all procurement actions where certified cost or pricing data are required, FAR 15.404-1(a)(3). However, GAO has made it clear that this requirement applies only when applicable statutes require obtaining certified cost or pricing data. Thus, in those instances where offerors have been required to submit certified cost or pricing data by an RFP but it is later determined that one of the statutory exceptions applies, cost analysis is not required, *Research Mgmt. Corp.*, 69 Comp. Gen. 368 (B-237865), 90-1 CPD ¶ 352 (adequate price competition precluded need for cost analysis). Prior to 1994, contracting officers had substantial discretion to require the submission of certified cost or pricing data and to perform detailed cost analysis using those data. However, the Federal Acquisition Streamlining Act of 1994 (FASA), Pub. L. No. 103-355, as amended by the Clinger-Cohen Act of 1996, Pub. L. No. 104-106, *prohibited* obtaining certified cost or pricing data when one of the statutory exceptions applies. See 10 U.S.C. § 2306a(b) stating:

> (1) In General. — Submission of certified cost or pricing data shall not be required under subsection (a) in the case of a contract, a subcontract, or modification of a contract or subcontract —
>
> > (A) for which the price agreed upon is based on —
> >
> > > (i) adequate price competition; or
> > >
> > > (ii) prices set by law or regulation.
> >
> > (B) for the acquisition of a commercial item; or
> >
> > (C) in an exceptional case when the head of the procuring activity, without delegation, determines that the requirements of this section may be waived and justifies in writing the reasons for such determination.
>
> (2) Modifications of Contracts and Subcontracts for Commercial Items. — In the case of a modification of a contract or subcontract for a commercial item that is not covered by the exception to the submission of cost or pricing data in paragraph (1)(A) or (1)(B), submission of certified cost or pricing data shall not be required under subsection (a) if —
>
> > (A) the contract or subcontract being modified is a contract or subcontract for which submission of certified cost or pricing data may not be required by reason of paragraph (1)(A) or (1)(B); and

(B) the modification would not change the contract or subcontract, as the case may be, from a contract or subcontract for the acquisition of a commercial item to a contract or subcontract for the acquisition of an item other than a commercial item.

Substantially the same provision is set forth in 41 U.S.C. § 3503. The following provision was added to 10 U.S.C. § 2306a(b) by Pub. L. No. 108-375, Oct. 24, 2004:

(3) Noncommercial modifications of commercial items.

(A) The exception in paragraph (1)(B) does not apply to cost or pricing data on noncommercial modifications of a commercial item that are expected to cost, in the aggregate, more than the amount specified in subsection (a)(1)(A)(i), as adjusted from time to time under subsection (a)(7), or 5 percent of the total price of the contract (at the time of contract award), whichever is greater.

(B) In this paragraph, the term "noncommercial modification", with respect to a commercial item, means a modification of such item that is not a modification described in section 4(12)(C)(i) of the Office of Federal Procurement Policy Act (41 U.S.C. 403(12)(C)(i)).

(C) Nothing in subparagraph (A) shall be construed —

(i) to limit the applicability of the exception in subparagraph (A) or (C) of paragraph (1) to cost or pricing data on a noncommercial modification of a commercial item; or

(ii) to require the submission of cost or pricing data on any aspect of an acquisition of a commercial item other than the cost and pricing of noncommercial modifications of such item.

Under this statutory mandate, the contracting officer must determine whether any of these exceptions applies and, if so, select the appropriate technique to be used and the data to be obtained. FAR 15.402 contains the following guidance — suggesting that contracting officers should obtain only the minimum amount of data necessary to make a determination of price reasonableness when certified cost or pricing data are not required:

Contracting officers shall —

(a) Purchase supplies and services from responsible sources at fair and reasonable prices. In establishing the reasonableness of the offered prices, the contracting officer —

(1) Shall obtain certified cost or pricing data when required by 15.403-4, along with data other than certified cost or pricing data as necessary to establish a fair and reasonable price; or

(2) When certified cost or pricing data are not required by 15.403-4, obtain data other than certified cost or pricing data as necessary to establish a fair and reasonable price, generally using the following order of preference in determining the type of data required:

(i) No additional data from the offeror, if the price is based on adequate price competition, except as provided by 15.403-3(b).

(ii) Data other than certified cost or pricing data such as —

(A) Data related to prices (e.g., established catalog or market prices, sales to non-governmental and governmental entities), relying first on data available within the Government; second, on data obtained from sources other than the offeror; and, if necessary, on data obtained from the offeror. When obtaining data from the offeror is necessary, unless an exception under 15.403-1(b)(1) or (2) applies, such data submitted by the offeror shall include, at a minimum, appropriate data on the prices at which the same or similar items have been sold previously, adequate for evaluating the reasonableness of the price.

(B) Cost data to the extent necessary for the contracting officer to determine a fair and reasonable price.

(3) Obtain the type and quantity of data necessary to establish a fair and reasonable price, but not more data than is necessary. Requesting unnecessary data can lead to increased proposal preparation costs, generally extend acquisition lead time, and consume additional contractor and Government resources. Use techniques such as, but not limited to, price analysis, cost analysis, and/or cost realism analysis to establish a fair and reasonable price. If a fair and reasonable price cannot be established by the contracting officer from the analyses of the data obtained or submitted to date, the contracting officer shall require the submission of additional data sufficient for the contracting officer to support the determination of the fair and reasonable price.

This guidance combines both price information and cost information (other than certified cost or pricing data) into a broad category of data called "data other than certified cost or pricing data." FAR 2.101 defines this category of data:

*Data other than certified cost or pricing data* means pricing data, cost data, and judgmental information necessary for the contracting officer to determine a fair and reasonable price or to determine cost realism. Such data may include the identical types of data as certified cost or pricing data, consistent with Table 15-2 of 15.408, but without the certification. The data may also include, for example, sales data and other information reasonably required to explain the offeror's estimating process, including, but not limited to —

(1) The judgmental factors applied and the mathematical or other methods used in the estimate, including those used in projecting from known data; and

(2) The nature and amount of any contingencies included in the proposed price.

The result of this statutory and regulatory scheme is that the contracting officer is given broad discretion to select the analytical technique to be used on a procurement but is encumbered with numerous limitations on the information that can be obtained to make the analysis. The critical first step is to determine whether TINA applies and, if so, whether the procurement falls under the monetary threshold or within one of the statutory exceptions. The contracting officer can then decide on the analytical technique that will be used and the data that will be needed to carry out the necessary analysis. This section discusses these issues separately for each of the categories of procurement described in TINA.

## A. Where Certified Cost or Pricing Data Are Required

The mandatory requirement for the submission of certified cost or pricing data was placed in the Armed Services Procurement Act in 1962 by Pub. L. No. 87-653. It was later applied to civilian agencies by the Federal Procurement Regulation. Subsequently, the Competition in Contracting Act (CICA), Pub. L. No. 98-369, added the requirement to the Federal Property and Administrative Services Act in 1984. The submission requirements for certified cost or pricing data are now contained in very similar language in 10 U.S.C. § 2306a(a) and 41 U.S.C. § 3502.

### 1. When Obtaining Certified Cost or Pricing Data Is Mandatory

Obtaining certified cost or pricing data is required and cost analysis is mandatory when the procurement action (a) is a negotiated contract or contract modification or a subcontract or subcontract modification under such a contract or contract modification; (b) is over the $700,000 threshold; and (c) is not within one of the statutory exceptions. Since each of the statutory exceptions is a separate class of procurement action, they will be dealt with individually in the following subsections.

#### a. Type of Procurement Action

The statutes require the submission of certified cost or pricing data only on negotiated procurement actions. Thus, no cost or pricing data are submitted in the initial award of a sealed bid contract or a subcontract under such a contract. However, amendments or modifications to sealed bid contracts, as well as those to negotiated contracts, are covered because they are negotiated procurement actions, FAR 15.403-4(a)(1)(iii). This regulation provides that final negotiated pricing actions, such as termination settlements or final pricing of fixed-price incentive or redeterminable contracts, are contract modifications to which the procedures apply. Prior regulations applied this rule to final negotiated overhead rate settlements, but the current regulations are silent on this issue.

Subcontracts under negotiated contracts are covered by the statute as long as the contract and all higher-tier subcontracts are not exempted from coverage, FAR 15.403-4(a)(1)(ii). Amendments to such subcontracts are also covered, FAR 15.403-4(a)(1)(iii).

## b.  Dollar Threshold

The original Truth in Negotiations Act in 1962 contained a $100,000 threshold. In 1981, this threshold in the Armed Services Procurement Act was raised to $500,000, Pub. L. No. 97-86. This change was effective on December 1, 1981, but was not implemented in the Defense Acquisition Regulation until December 27, 1982. CICA reduced the threshold to $100,000, effective with solicitations issued after March 31, 1985. This Act also added this requirement to the Federal Property and Administrative Services Act — with a $100,000 threshold. In 1990, the threshold in the Armed Services Procurement Act was again raised to $500,000, effective December 5, 1990, Pub. L. No. 101-510. This Act called for the threshold to revert to $100,000 on December 31, 1995. However, the FASA repealed this reversion and raised the threshold in the Federal Property and Administrative Services Act to $500,000. This increased threshold became effective October 13, 1994, but was not incorporated in the FAR until December 5, 1994, Federal Acquisition Circular (FAC) 90-22, 59 Fed. Reg. 62498 (1994).

10 U.S.C. § 2306a(a)(7) and 41 U.S.C. § 3502(g) call for the adjustment of the TINA threshold every five years to account for inflation. This resulted in raising the threshold to $ 550,000 in 2000, FAC 97-20, 65 Fed. Reg. 60542 (effective Oct. 11, 2000); to $650,000 in 2006, FAC 2005-15, 71 Fed. Reg. 57363 (effective Sept. 28, 2006); and to $700,000 in 2010, FAC 2005-45, 75 Fed. Reg. 53135 (effective Aug. 18, 2010).

With these numerous changes in the threshold and the accompanying delays in implementation of the statutes, it can be expected that some contracts will contain contract requirements that differ from the statutory requirements. Generally, the contract provisions dealing with contract modifications will govern over statutory provisions. However, the FASA contained a provision, 41 U.S.C. § 254b(a)(6) (now § 3502(f)), permitting contractors to obtain contract amendments adopting the new $500,000 threshold for civilian agency contracts:

On the request of a contractor that was required to submit cost or pricing data . . . in connection with a prime contract entered into on or before October 13, 1994, the head of the executive agency that entered into the contract shall modify the contract to [change the threshold to $500,000]. All those modifications shall be made without requiring consideration.

The FAR did not implement this provision. However, FAR 43.102(c) contains an omnibus provision permitting the inclusion of any part of FASA or the Clinger-Cohen Act into an existing contract without consideration, pursuant to § 4402 of the Clinger-Cohen Act of 1996. Thus, new statutory provisions can be implemented by inserting the new contract clauses into particular contracts and providing that such clauses are applicable only to contract modifications and subcontracts for which agreement on price was reached after the date of their enactment.

For the purpose of applying the statute, the dollar value of a price adjustment is calculated by totaling the costs added and the costs deleted by the adjustment, FAR 15.403-4(a)(1)(iii). Thus, a modification adding $400,000 and deleting $300,000 would be subject to the statutory requirement. The regulation notes that this rule should not be followed when "unrelated and separately priced" changes are included in the modification "for administrative convenience."

## 2. Obtaining the Data

When the contracting officer determines that a procurement will be over the $700,000 threshold and none of the exceptions apply, FAR 15.403-5(a) requires the contracting officer to specify that certified cost or pricing data must be submitted. However, the standard solicitation provisions allow the contractor to object to this requirement. Thus, the Requirements for Certified Cost or Pricing Data or Data Other Than Certified Cost or Pricing Data solicitation provision in FAR 52.215-20 gives the offeror the opportunity to defer the submission of cost or pricing data by claiming that either the Commercial Item exception or the Prices Set By Law or Regulation exception applies. Paragraph (a) of the provision states that if the offeror believes that it qualifies for either of these exceptions to the requirement for the submission of cost or pricing data, it may submit a written request for exception with the data pertinent to that exception. The provision is silent as to what action an offeror may take if it believes that the adequate price competition exception applies or if it wants the agency to grant a statutory waiver. However, offerors would be well advised to request either of these exceptions if they believe they are applicable. Paragraph (b) of the provision states that the offeror must submit certified cost or pricing data if it "is not granted an exception." In addition, if no exception applies — as in the case of a sole source procurement of an item or service that is not a commercial item — the offeror should submit the applicable cost or pricing data with the proposal (with the intention of certifying it at the conclusion of negotiations) and the provision requires that it be submitted in accordance with the instructions in Table 15-2 in FAR 15.408. FAR 52.215-20 also provides for four alternate provisions that can be used to (1) require the data to be delivered in a format other than required by Table 15-2, (2) require copies of the offeror's proposal to be submitted to the Administrative Contracting Officer and the contract auditor, (3) require the data to be submitted by electronic media, and (4) specify the type of data other than certified cost or pricing data that is required. See the instructions in FAR 15.408(l).

Similar procedures are prescribed for contract modifications. FAR 15.408(m) permits the contracting officer to insert the Requirements for Certified Cost or Pricing Data or Data Other Than Certified Cost or Pricing Data — Modifications clause in FAR 52.215-21 in contracts "if it is reasonably certain that [such] data will be required for modifications" to the contract. This clause also permits the contractor to apply for an exception in lieu of submitting certified cost or pricing data to support a modification over the statutory threshold and contains the same alternate provisions for varied submissions of data. Since some data will be required for modifications over the statutory threshold, it is anticipated that this clause will be used in all contracts where there is any possibility that a modification over $700,000 might be issued.

## B. Where Certified Cost or Pricing Data Are Not Required

10 U.S.C. § 2306a(d)(1) and 41 U.S.C. § 3505(a) state that when certified cost or pricing data are not required, "the contracting officer shall require submission of data other than certified cost or pricing data to the extent necessary to determine the reasonableness of the price" and "shall require that the data submitted include, at a minimum, appropriate information on prices at which the same or similar items have previously been sold." This is implemented in FAR 15.403-3 as follows:

(a)(1) In those acquisitions that do not require certified cost or pricing data, the contracting officer shall —

(i) Obtain whatever data are available from Government or other secondary sources and use that data in determining a fair and reasonable price;

(ii) Require submission of data other than certified cost or pricing data, as defined in 2.101, from the offeror to the extent necessary to determine a fair and reasonable price (10 U.S.C. 2306a(d)(1) and 41 U.S.C. 254b(d) (1)) if the contracting officer determines that adequate data from sources other than the offeror are not available. This includes requiring data from an offeror to support a cost realism analysis;

(iii) Consider whether cost data are necessary to determine a fair and reasonable price when there is not adequate price competition;

(iv) Require that the data submitted by the offeror include, at a minimum, appropriate data on the prices at which the same item or similar items have previously been sold, adequate for determining the reasonableness of the price unless an exception under 15.403-1(b)(1) or (2) applies; and

(v) Consider the guidance in section 3.3, chapter 3, volume I, of the Contract Pricing Reference Guide cited at 15.404-1(a)(7) to determine the data an offeror shall be required to submit.

(2) The contractor's format for submitting the data should be used (see 15.403-5(b)(2)).

(3) The contracting officer shall ensure that data used to support price negotiations are sufficiently current to permit negotiation of a fair and reasonable price. Requests for updated offeror data should be limited to data that affect the adequacy of the proposal for negotiations, such as changes in price lists.

(4) As specified in section 808 of the Strom Thurmond National Defense Authorization Act for Fiscal Year 1999 (Pub. L. 105-261), an offeror who does not comply with a requirement to submit data for a contract or subcontract in accordance with paragraph (a)(1) of this subsection is ineligible for award unless the HCA determines that it is in the best interest of the Government to make the award to that offeror, based on consideration of the following:

> (i) The effort made to obtain the data.

> (ii) The need for the item or service.

> (iii) Increased cost or significant harm to the Government if award is not made.

Note that the definition of "data other than certified cost or pricing data" (set forth above) was rewritten by FAC 2005-45, 75 Fed. Reg. 53135, Aug. 30, 2010, to include "identical types of data as certified cost or pricing data, consistent with Table 15-2 of 15.408, but without the certification." This was intended to make it clear to contracting officers that they have the discretion to call for the submission of uncertified cost or pricing data if they conclude that such data is needed to ensure a fair and reasonable price.

The guidance on what data to call for is followed by specific guidance on each type of procurement where certified cost or pricing data may not be required. These will be discussed separately in the material below.

## C. Actions Under the Dollar Threshold

The contracting officer has considerable discretion in selecting the analytical technique and calling for appropriate data when the procurement action is under the $700,000 threshold for the submission of certified cost or pricing data. However, FAR 15.403-4(a)(2) permits heads of contracting activities, without the power of delegation, to authorize the contracting officer to obtain certified cost or pricing data on procurements under the threshold but over the simplified acquisition threshold of $150,000 when it is not prohibited by statute. In this case or when the uncertified cost or pricing data were obtained, the contracting officer would perform cost analysis. In other cases, the contracting officer would be expected to use the same analytical technique for procurements in this category as would be appropriate for larger procurements of the same type. Thus, if, for example, a procurement was for a commercial item with a contract price of less than $700,000, it could be anticipated that the contracting officer would use the same analytical techniques that would be appropriate for procurement of commercial items over $700,000.

The statutes permit the obtaining of certified cost or pricing data in procurements under the threshold in *extremely limited circumstances.* See 10 U.S.C. § 2306a(c) and 41 U.S.C. § 3504 as follows:

> Cost or Pricing Data on Below Threshold Contracts. —
>
> (1) *Authority to Require Submission.* — Subject to paragraph (2), when certified cost or pricing data are not required to be submitted . . . for a contract, subcontract, or modification of a contract or subcontract, such data may nevertheless be required to be submitted by the head of the procuring activity, but only if the head of the procuring activity determines that such data are necessary for the evaluation by the agency of the reasonableness of the price of the contract, subcontract, or modification of a contract or subcontract. In any case in which the head of the procuring activity requires such data to be submitted under this subsection, the head of the procuring activity shall justify in writing the reason for such requirement.
>
> (2) *Exception.* — The head of the procuring activity may not require certified cost or pricing data to be submitted under this paragraph for any contract or subcontract, or modification of a contract or subcontract, covered by the exceptions [for adequate price competition, prices set by law or regulation or commercial items].
>
> (3) *Delegation of Authority Prohibited.* — The head of a procuring activity may not delegate the functions under this paragraph.

FAR 15.403-1(a) prohibits obtaining certified cost or pricing data on acquisitions at or below the $150,000 simplified acquisition threshold. Although FAR 15.403-4(a)(2) implements this statutory provision for acquisitions between $150,000 and $700,000, since it precludes contracting officers from obtaining certified cost or pricing data without getting the approval of the head of the contracting activity and may not be used when the major exceptions apply, it will probably be used sparingly. Its major application will be to contract modifications where there is little or no pricing information. Under the prior statute, agencies frequently required the submission of certified cost or pricing data when the price was determined to be unreasonable. See *Sperry Rand Corp. v. United States,* 212 Ct. Cl. 329, 548 F.2d 915 (1977), where the court affirmed the exercise of this discretion under the Defense Acquisition Regulation (which gave considerably greater discretion to the contracting officer). In contrast, when the contracting officer did not request the data because it was determined that an exemption applied, the board held that no submission was required, *J.W. Bateson Co.,* GSBCA 4133, 76-1 BCA ¶ 11,751, *recons. denied,* 76-2 BCA ¶ 12,109.

## D. Actions Where There Is Adequate Price Competition

The statutes and the regulations prohibit the obtaining of certified cost or pricing data for this type of procurement action. Thus, when adequate price competition exists, the contracting officer is generally expected to rely heavily on the competitive prices to ascertain the reasonableness of the price. See FAR 15.404-1(a)(2) stating that "[p]rice analysis shall be used when cost or pricing data are not required."

### 1.  Definition of Adequate Price Competition

The statute does not define "adequate price competition," but FAR 15.403-1(c) contains the following guidance to be used in determining whether there is adequate price competition:

(1) Adequate price competition. A price is based on adequate price competition if —

(i) Two or more responsible offerors, competing independently, submit priced offers that satisfy the Government's expressed requirement and if —

(A) Award will be made to the offeror whose proposal represents the best value (see 2.101) where price is a substantial factor in source selection; and

(B) There is no finding that the price of the otherwise successful offeror is unreasonable. Any finding that the price is unreasonable must be supported by a statement of the facts and approved at a level above the contracting officer;

(ii) There was a reasonable expectation, based on market research or other assessment, that two or more responsible offerors, competing independently, would submit priced offers in response to the solicitation's expressed requirement, even though only one offer is received from a responsible offeror and if —

(A) Based on the offer received, the contracting officer can reasonably conclude that the offer was submitted with the expectation of competition, e.g., circumstances indicate that —

(1) The offeror believed that at least one other offeror was capable of submitting a meaningful offer; and

(2) The offeror had no reason to believe that other potential offerors did not intend to submit an offer; and

(B) The determination that the proposed price is based on adequate price competition, is reasonable, and is approved at a level above the contracting officer; or

> (iii) Price analysis clearly demonstrates that the proposed price is reasonable in comparison with current or recent prices for the same or similar items, adjusted to reflect changes in market conditions, economic conditions, quantities, or terms and conditions under contracts that resulted from adequate price competition.

This regulation was revised in 1995 to permit a finding of adequate price competition, under limited circumstances, when *only one offer* is received by the government. Prior regulations required that at least two responsible offerors compete independently for the award. Under this earlier, more restrictive rule, determinations of adequate price competition were upheld even though only a small number of competitors were involved in serious consideration for award. See *Ogden Plant Maint. Co.*, Comp. Gen. Dec. B-255156.2, 94-1 CPD ¶ 275 (adequate price competition when two offerors were in competitive range; offeror downgraded on capability factors not a nonresponsible offeror); *Family Realty*, Comp. Gen. Dec. B-247772, 92-2 CPD ¶ 6 (adequate price competition where two offerors were in competitive range); *Adrian Supply Co.*, Comp. Gen. Dec. B-241502, 91-1 CPD ¶ 138 (adequate price competition on second solicitation when two price-competitive proposals received; no adequate price competition on first solicitation when only one proposal received); *D-K Assocs., Inc.*, Comp. Gen. Dec. B-213417, 84-1 CPD ¶ 396 (adequate price competition where only two of seven proposals were technically acceptable); and *Uniflite, Inc.*, ASBCA 27818, 85-1 BCA ¶ 17,813 (determination of adequate price competition based upon prices of three offerors and government estimate). In one case, the contracting officer's determination of adequate price competition was found to be reasonable, although one of two offerors thought that the government might not receive any other proposals, *ABA Electromechanical Sys., Inc.*, NASABCA 1081-13, 85-3 BCA ¶ 18,225. The other proposal and the government estimate were held to have demonstrated the reasonableness of the proposed price. However, in *Akin, Gump, Strauss, Hauer & Feld*, 53 Comp. Gen. 5 (B-177847) (1973), it was held that price competition did not exist when only one acceptable proposal was received. In *Litton Sys., Inc.*, ASBCA 35914, 96-1 BCA ¶ 28,201, the board rejected a motion for summary judgment based on the argument that the contractor had no liability for defective data because there had been adequate price competition. The board ruled that the presence of only one "responsive" offeror precluded the applicability of the exception.

In best value procurements, where there are multiple evaluation factors, adequate price competition will be found where price is a *substantial evaluation factor* and is so evaluated. This rule applies to both fixed-price contracts and cost-reimbursement contracts. It is derived from decisions of GAO and has now been incorporated in FAR 15.403-1(c)(1)(i)(A). See *Serv-Air, Inc. — Recons.*, 58 Comp. Gen. 362 (B-189884), 79-1 CPD ¶ 212, where cost to the government was held to be a "substantial" factor even though it was considerably less important than the other factors. The case involved the award of a fixed-price incentive contract where price was stated to be 30% of the total evaluation, with 15% for the comparative level of the price (which increased the score for prices that were low) and 15% for "cost realism" (which reduced the score for prices that were considered to be too low). GAO ruled that price was a substantial factor even though the components of the evaluation might cancel out the factor. In *Dynalectron Corp.*, 52 Comp. Gen. 346 (B-176217) (1972), cost to the government was found to be a substantial factor in a cost-plus-award-fee contract even though it was 20% of the total evaluation. In *U.S. Nuclear, Inc.*, 57 Comp. Gen. 185 (B-187716), 77-2 CPD ¶ 511, adequate price competition was found on a cost-plus-fixed-fee contract. The contracting officer also has the discretion to determine that price is not a substantial factor in these circumstances. See *Cubic Defense Sys.*, Comp. Gen. Dec. B-229884, 88-1 CPD ¶ 395, where GAO affirmed such a decision where price on a fixed-price contract was a minor factor (stating that *Serv-Air* holds that "the contracting officer has broad discretion to make that determination"). See also *United Techs. Corp.*, ASBCA 51410, 04-1 BCA ¶ 32,556, *aff'd*, 463 F.3d 1261 (Fed. Cir. 2006), holding that the contracting officer did not abuse his discretion in finding that competition was not adequate when two companies competed on a best value procurement and questioning the reasoning in *Serv-Air*. In spite of the *United Technologies* implication that adequate price competition could not exist in a best value procurement, when the final award decision is made by a tradeoff analysis between the differences in price and the difference in the other factors (as is the case in almost all best value procurements), it would appear that price would always be a substantial factor and the contracting officer would have little discretion in this regard.

Adequate price competition also exists when the RFP provides for award on the basis of the "lowest-priced, technically acceptable offer," *D-K Assocs., Inc.*, Comp. Gen. Dec. B-213417, 84-1 CPD ¶ 396. This rule is now included in FAR 15.403-1(c)(1)(i)(A) because the broad definition of "best value" in FAR 2.101 would include this type of procurement.

Adequate price competition can exist where offerors propose to furnish different products to satisfy a government performance specification. See *Prudential-Maryland (J.V.) Co. v. Lehman*, 590 F. Supp. 1390 (D.D.C. 1984), where the contracting officer's determination that adequate price competition existed was found to be reasonable in a procurement of hospital ships in which the competitors were proposing different designs. Similarly, in *ABA Electromechanical Sys., Inc.*, NASABCA 1081-13, 85-3 BCA ¶ 18,225, the board found the contracting officer's determination that adequate price competition existed to be reasonable. In that procurement, two offerors submitted proposals for different hardware configurations in response to the government's performance specification.

The fact that oral and written discussions are conducted does not preclude a finding of adequate price competition. See *UTL Corp.*, Comp. Gen. Dec. B-185832, 76-1 CPD ¶ 209, holding that conducting oral and written discussions and calling for "best and final offers" supported a finding of adequate price competition because competition was, in fact, enhanced. Further, adequate price competition can exist even though "full and open competition" does not occur, *International Sys. Mktg., Inc.*, GSBCA 7948-P, 85-3 BCA ¶ 18,196.

FAR 15.403-1(c)(1)(iii) allows a contracting officer to find adequate price competition by comparing the price submitted to "current or recent prices for the same or similar items." In the one litigated case on a similar statement in a prior regulation, the board held that the procurement did not meet the test, *Norris Indus., Inc.*, ASBCA 15442, 74-1 BCA ¶ 10,482. In *Norris*, the contractor argued that its prices were based on adequate price competition in view of two prior competitive procurements of the items. The board held that the two prior procurements provided too meager a basis for price comparison under the circumstances.

Adequate price competition can also be found when a split award to dual sources is contemplated. See DFARS 215.403-1(c)(1) giving the following additional guidance:

(B) Adequate price competition normally exists when —

(i) Prices are solicited across a full range of step quantities, normally including a 0-100 percent split, from at least two offerors that are individually capable of producing the full quantity; and

(ii) The reasonableness of all prices awarded is clearly established on the basis of price analysis (see FAR 15.404-1(b)).

In the past the determination of whether adequate price competition existed had been held to be a discretionary decision of the contracting officer. A contracting officer's determination that adequate price competition exists was not disturbed if it was reasonably based, *Fraass Surgical Mfg. Co. v. United States*, 215 Ct. Cl. 820, 571 F.2d 34 (1978). See also *Sperry Rand Corp. v. United States*, 212 Ct. Cl. 329, 548 F.2d 915 (1977), recognizing that sound pricing depends upon the exercise of sound judgment. The contracting officer was required first to determine whether adequate price competition existed before the mandatory exemption would apply. However, see *Libby Welding Co.*, ASBCA 15084, 73-1 BCA ¶ 9859, holding that a contracting officer's internal notation that there was adequate price competition could have no effect when there was actually no competition at all in the procurement.

## 2.  Technique and Data

In most cases when there is adequate price competition, the contracting officer will be able to determine that the price is reasonable by making a price analysis. When there are two or more competitors that have submitted competitive prices, the prices submitted will frequently be sufficient to demonstrate that the award price is fair and reasonable. If the supplies or services have been procured in the past, the contracting officer will also have those prices to be used in a price analysis. Normally, such data would be sufficient in fixed-price contracting situations. In contrast, in cost-reimbursement contracts where there is adequate price competition, the contracting officer will generally need some cost data to evaluate the cost realism of the proposals. FAR 15.403-3(b) gives the following guidance on these issues:

> When adequate price competition exists (see 15.403-1(c)(1)), generally no additional information is necessary to determine the reasonableness of price. However, if there are unusual circumstances where it is concluded that additional information is necessary to determine the reasonableness of price, the contracting officer shall, to the maximum extent practicable, obtain the additional information from sources other than the offeror. In addition, the contracting officer may request information to determine the cost realism of competing offers or to evaluate competing approaches.

Obtaining pricing information from an offeror, such as the prices charged to other customers, is viewed by the statutes and regulations as a circumstance that will occur rarely. When cost data are required in order to perform a cost realism analysis in these situations, the contracting officer is *prohibited* from obtaining certified cost or pricing data.

When the contracting officer decides to obtain data in these circumstances, FAR 15.408(l)(4) calls for the use of an alternate solicitation provision to obtain "data other than certified cost or pricing data." This provision (Alternate IV in FAR 52.215-20) provides:

> (a) Submission of cost or pricing data is not required.

> (b) Provide information described below: [Insert description of the information and the format that are required, including access to records necessary to permit an adequate evaluation of the proposed price in accordance with 15.403-3.]

## E.  Actions Where There Are Prices Set by Law or Regulation

FAR 15.403-1(c)(2) contains the following brief statement on this exception:

> *Prices set by law or regulation.* Pronouncements in the form of periodic rulings, reviews, or similar actions of a governmental body, or embodied in the laws, are sufficient to set a price.

The Requirements for Cost or Pricing Data or Information Other Than Cost or Pricing Data solicitation provision in FAR 52.215-20 requires that offerors submit supporting data when this exception applies:

> (a) Exceptions from cost or pricing data. (1) In lieu of submitting cost or pricing data, offerors may submit a written request for exception by submitting the

information described in the following subparagraphs. The Contracting Officer may require additional supporting information, but only to the extent necessary to determine whether an exception should be granted, and whether the price is fair and reasonable.

> (i) Identification of the law or regulation establishing the price offered. If the price is controlled under law by periodic rulings, reviews, or similar actions of a governmental body, attach a copy of the controlling document, unless it was previously submitted to the contracting office.

This guidance appears to allow the use of this exception and a determination of price reasonableness if the data submitted demonstrates that the proposed price meets the requirements of the law or regulation by which it is governed. However, FAR 15.403-3(a)(1) gives the contracting officer discretion to seek additional information to determine price reasonableness or cost realism. The contracting officer is prohibited from obtaining certified cost or pricing data in these circumstances.

## F.  Actions Where There Are Commercial Items

The FASA added a new prohibition to obtaining cost or pricing data under the Truth in Negotiations Act to permit the government to follow commercial buying practices with a wide variety of commercial items. This created considerable confusion because there was already an exception for "catalog or market price items." The Clinger-Cohen Act of 1996 clarified this situation by deleting the "catalog or market price items" exception. Thus, there is now a single prohibition to the obtaining of cost or pricing data when procuring a commercial item, 10 U.S.C. § 2306a(b)(1)(B); 41 U.S.C. § 3503(a)(2). Under 41 U.S.C. § 1903(c), noncommercial products or service may be treated as a commercial item if they are "used (1) in support of a contingency operation; or (2) to facilitate the defense against or recovery from nuclear, biological, chemical, or radiological attack against the United States." This extended authority does not apply to sole source procurements of such products or services with a price of over $17.5 million. See FAR 15.403-1(c)(3)(iv).

The term "commercial item" is defined in 41 U.S.C. §103 and FAR 2.101 to include both products and services. See the discussion and analysis in Chapter 7. The guidance on the data that may be obtained when procuring commercial items is varied and confusing — particularly with regard to the amount of data an offeror must submit on prior sales of the item to its commercial customers. 10 U.S.C. § 2306a(d)(1) and 41 U.S.C. § 3505(a) contains the following mandatory requirement to obtain data:

> *Authority to Require Submission.* When certified cost or pricing data are not required to be submitted under this section for a contract, subcontract, or modification of a contract or subcontract, the contracting officer shall require submission of data other than certified cost or pricing data to the extent necessary to determine

the reasonableness of the price of the contract, subcontract, or modification of the contract or subcontract. Except in the case of a contract or subcontract covered by the exceptions [for adequate price competition and prices set by law or regulation], the data submitted shall include, at a minimum, appropriate information on the prices at which the same item or similar items have previously been sold that is adequate for evaluating the reasonableness of the price for the procurement.

This requirement is implemented in FAR 15.403-3(c)(1) as follows:

(1) At a minimum, the contracting officer must use price analysis to determine whether the price is fair and reasonable whenever the contracting officer acquires a commercial item (see 15.404-1(b)). The fact that a price is included in a catalog does not, in and of itself, make it fair and reasonable. If the contracting officer cannot determine whether an offered price is fair and reasonable, even after obtaining additional data from sources other than the offeror, then the contracting officer shall require the offeror to submit data other than certified cost or pricing data to support further analysis (see 15.404-1). This data may include history of sales to non-governmental and governmental entities, cost data, or any other information the contracting officer requires to determine the price is fair and reasonable. Unless an exception under 15.403-1(b)(1) or (2) applies, the contracting officer shall require that the data submitted by the offeror include, at a minimum, appropriate data on the prices at which the same item or similar items have previously been sold, adequate for determining the reasonableness of the price.

This guidance was significantly revised in 2010 (FAC 2005-45) to permit the contracting officer to call for the submission of uncertified cost or pricing data. In response to numerous comments that this revision would induce contracting officers to request such data when procuring commercial items, the FAR councils stated at 75 Fed. Reg. 53136-37:

Such an outcome would be contrary to the intent of the rule, which does not alter the current intent of the FAR regarding the type and quantity of data to determine if the price of a commercial item is fair and reasonable. FAR 15.403-1(c)(3) specifically exempts commercial items from certified cost or pricing data requirements, and this rule does not change that exception. Also, FAR 15.403-3(c)(2) sets limitations on the type of cost data or pricing data that can be requested regarding commercial items. When contracting officers determine that they can use price analysis to determine the price to be fair and reasonable, the order of preference at FAR 15.402 means cost data will generally not be obtained for pricing commercial items. Contracting officers are to obtain only that information needed to determine a fair and reasonable price, which, in some cases, may include contractor cost data (without certification) for commercial items.

10 U.S.C. § 2306a(d)(2) and 41 U.S.C. § 3505(b) also require that the regulations contain limitations on the data that can be obtained when procuring a commercial item. These limitations are set forth in FAR 15.403-3(c)(2) as follows:

(i) The contracting officer shall limit requests for sales data relating to commercial items to data for the same or similar items during a relevant time period.

(ii) The contracting officer shall, to the maximum extent practicable, limit the scope of the request for information relating to commercial items to include only information that is in the form regularly maintained by the offeror as part of its commercial operations.

(iii) The Government shall not disclose outside of the Government information obtained relating to commercial items that is exempt from disclosure under 24.202(a) or the Freedom of Information Act (5 U.S.C. 552(b)).

In addition, the Requirements for Certified Cost or Pricing Data or Data Other Than Certified Cost or Pricing Data solicitation provision at FAR 52.215-20 contains the following guidance on the type of data that should be submitted to support a request for application of the commercial item exception:

(a)(1)(ii) *Commercial item exception.* For a commercial item exception, the offeror shall submit, at a minimum, information on prices at which the same item or similar items have previously been sold in the commercial market that is adequate for evaluating the reasonableness of the price for this acquisition. Such information may include —

(A) For catalog items, a copy of or identification of the catalog and its date, or the appropriate pages for the offered items, or a statement that the catalog is on file in the buying office to which the proposal is being submitted. Provide a copy or describe current discount policies and price lists (published or unpublished), e.g., wholesale, original equipment manufacturer, or reseller. Also explain the basis of each offered price and its relationship to the established catalog price, including how the proposed price relates to the price of recent sales in quantities similar to the proposed quantities.

(B) For market-price items, the source and date or period of the market quotation or other basis for market price, the base amount, and applicable discounts. In addition, describe the nature of the market.

(C) For items included on an active Federal Supply Service Multiple Award Schedule contract, proof that an exception has been granted for the schedule item.

Alternatively, the contracting officer can use the Alternate IV provision in FAR 52.215-20 and describe the specific data that each offeror is required to provide.

It would appear that the key issue in ascertaining the reasonableness of prices of commercial items is the amount of competition that will be achieved. If there will be significant competition, the competitive prices should provide sufficient information without the need for additional data. On the other hand, if the commercial item is a sole source item or the competition is very limited, the contracting officer will need additional data. FAR 15.403-1(c)(3)(ii)(A) addresses this problem by stating that the prohibition on obtaining certified cost or pricing data for commercial items only applies if the contracting officer determines in writing "that the offeror has submitted sufficient information to evaluate, through price analysis, the reasonableness of the price of such services." FAR 15.403-1(c)(3)(ii) contains the following guidance:

> (B) In order to make this determination, the contracting officer may request the offeror to submit prices paid for the same or similar commercial items under comparable terms and conditions by both Government and commercial customers; and

> (C) If the contracting officer determines that the information described in paragraph (c)(3)(ii)(B) of this section is not sufficient to determine the reasonableness of price, other relevant information regarding the basis for price or cost, including information on labor costs, material costs and overhead rates may be requested.

If such data are available through market research, there may be no need to require offerors to submit the data. If not, sales data or cost data will have to be obtained from offerors. The goal of the statutes and regulations is to obtain necessary data in the least burdensome manner possible in the circumstances of each procurement. While the guidance in the FAR is not clear, it is sufficiently permissive to permit the contracting officer to obtain necessary information while still minimizing the data submission requirements.

The Department of Defense has issued detailed guidance on obtaining sufficient data to determine that commercial item prices are fair and reasonable – particularly when there is little or no competition or the item has not yet been sold to commercial customers. DFARS PGI 215.403-1(c)(3)(A)(2) directs contracting officers to obtain "prior non-government sales data" on the precise item or the predecessor item if the item being procured has not yet been sold commercially but has evolved from a commercial item. PGI 215.403-3(1) states:

> Sales data must be comparable to the quantities, capabilities, specifications, etc. of the product or service proposed. Sufficient steps must be taken to verify the integrity of the sales data, to include assistance from the Defense Contract Management Agency, the Defense Contract Audit Agency, and/or other agencies if required.

PGI 215.404-1(b)(i) points out that sometimes these types of sales data can be obtained through market research that finds data on commercial sales or in published catalogs or prices.

DFARS PGI 215.404-1(b)(ii) calls for obtaining "cost information" when sales data are not sufficient to demonstrate that the price is fair and reasonable:

In some cases, commercial sales are not available and there is no other market information for determining fair and reasonable prices. This is especially true when buying supplies or services that have been determined to be commercial but have only been "offered for sale" or purchased on a sole source basis with no prior commercial sales upon which to rely. In such cases, the contracting must require the offeror to submit whatever cost information is needed to determine price reasonableness.

The DoD guidance then makes it clear at PGI 215.404-1(c)(iii) that such "cost information" need not be submitted in accordance with the instructions in Table 15-2 of FAR 15.408 dealing with the submission of cost or pricing data but can be submitted in the contractor's format.

DFARS PGI 215.403-3(4) also contains a warning about relying on prior prices paid by the government:

Before relying on a prior price paid by the Government, the contracting officer must verify and document that sufficient analysis was performed to determine that the prior price was fair and reasonable. Sometimes, due to exigent situations, supplies and services are purchased even though an adequate price or cost analysis could not be performed. The problem is exacerbated when other contracting officers assume these prices were adequately analyzed and determined to be fair and reasonable. The contracting officer also must verify that the prices previously paid were for quantities consistent with the current solicitation. Not verifying that a previous price analysis was performed, or the consistencies in quantity, has been a recurring issue on sole source commercial items reported by oversight organizations. Sole source commercial items require extra attention to verify that previous prices paid on Government contracts were sufficiently analyzed and determined to be fair and reasonable. At a minimum, a contracting officer reviewing price history shall discuss the basis of previous prices paid with the contracting organization that previously bought the item. These discussions shall be documented in the contract file.

## G. Actions Where There Are Agency Waivers

Originally, this exception permitted the waiver of the requirement for submission of certified cost or pricing data by the agency head. The FASA granted this waiver authority to "the head of the procuring activity, without delegation." The statutes require that waivers be supported by written documentation. FAR 15.403-1(c) provides the following guidance on the use of waivers:

(4) *Waivers.* The head of the contracting activity (HCA) may, without power of delegation, waive the requirement for submission of certified cost or pricing data in exceptional cases. The authorization for the waiver and the supporting rationale shall be in writing. The HCA may consider waiving the requirement if the price can be determined to be fair and reasonable without submission of certified cost or pricing data. For example, if certified cost or pricing data were furnished on

previous production buys and the contracting officer determines such data are sufficient, when combined with updated information, a waiver may be granted. If the HCA has waived the requirement for submission of certified cost or pricing data, the contractor or higher-tier subcontractor to whom the waiver relates shall be considered as having been required to provide certified cost or pricing data. Consequently, award of any lower-tier subcontract expected to exceed the certified cost or pricing data threshold requires the submission of certified cost or pricing data unless —

(i) An exception otherwise applies to the subcontract; or

(ii) The waiver specifically includes that subcontract and the rationale supporting the waiver for that subcontract.

While the above waiver guidance is stated in permissive language, prior to 2010 FAR 15.402(a)(3) appeared to encourage the use of waivers by stating that contracting officers should "use every means available to ascertain whether a fair and reasonable price can be determined before requesting cost or pricing data." This guidance was deleted from the FAR by FAC 2005-45.

DoD has provided additional guidance on waivers in DFARS 215.403-1(c)(4) as follows:

(A) The head of the contracting activity may, without power of delegation, apply the exceptional circumstances authority when a determination is made that —

(1) The property or services cannot reasonably be obtained under the contract, subcontract, or modification, without the granting of the waiver;

(2) The price can be determined to be fair and reasonable without the submission of certified cost or pricing data; and

(3) There are demonstrated benefits to granting the waiver. Follow the procedures at PGI 215.403-1(c)(4)(A) for determining when an exceptional case waiver is appropriate, for approval of such waivers, for partial waivers, and for waivers applicable to unpriced supplies or services.

* * *

(C) DoD has waived the requirement for submission of cost or pricing data for the Canadian Commercial Corporation and its subcontractors.

(D) DoD has waived cost or pricing data requirements for nonprofit organizations (including education institutions) on cost-reimbursement-no-fee contracts. The contracting officer shall require —

(1) Submission of information other than cost or pricing data to the extent necessary to determine reasonableness and cost realism; and

(2) Cost or pricing data from subcontractors that are not nonprofit organizations when the subcontractor's proposal exceeds the cost or pricing data threshold at FAR 15.403-4(a)(1).

Initially, GAO permitted an informal waiver, *Televiso Elecs.*, 46 Comp. Gen. 631 (B-159922) (1967), but subsequent decisions stated that this requirement must be formally complied with to justify not obtaining data, Comp. Gen. Dec. B-161448, Feb. 7, 1968, *Unpub.*; *Akin, Gump, Strauss, Hauer & Feld*, 53 Comp. Gen. 5 (B-177847) (1973). It has also been held that an agency may refuse to waive the cost or pricing data requirement and contract with another offeror on a sole source basis, *Telectro-Mek, Inc.*, Comp. Gen. Dec. B-185892, 76-2 CPD ¶ 81.

In *M-R-S Mfg. Co. v. United States*, 203 Ct. Cl. 551, 492 F.2d 835 (1974), the Court of Claims held that the contracting officer could not agree to nonsubmission of data. The court stated at 562:

Since the Government chose to ignore any data developed between March 23 and August 17, the plaintiff says the obligation to furnish accurate, complete, and current data was waived. The most basic flaw in this argument is the assumption that the obligation to furnish proper data can be waived by a Government agent. The duty to furnish accurate, complete, and current data is a duty imposed on Government contractors by a statute, and, therefore, that duty cannot be waived by a Government agent. *United States v. Stewart*, 311 U.S. 60 (1940); *Utah Power & Light Co. v. United States*, 243 U.S. 389 (1917); *see Federal Crop Ins. Corp. v. Merrill*, 332 U.S. 380 (1947); *Montilla v. United States*, 198 Ct. Cl. 48, 457 F.2d 978 (1972).

The court omitted any discussion of statutory waiver by the agency head since that was not an issue in the case. The same result was reached in *Conrac Corp. v. United States*, 214 Ct. Cl. 561, 558 F.2d 994 (1977), where the court noted that a "reasonable" cutoff date for establishing the timeliness of data submissions would not have constituted an improper waiver. In *Numax Elecs., Inc.*, ASBCA 29186, 85-3 BCA ¶ 18,396, the board found that the submission of data could not be waived by the contracting officer. See also *Southwest Marine, Inc.*, DOTBCA 1577J, 95-2 ¶ 27,760, where the board held that the contracting officer's failure to request cost and pricing data did not waive the government's right to reduce the contract proceeds for defective pricing. The board stated that the contractor had a statutory duty to disclose and certify all relevant cost and pricing data regardless of whether the contracting officer asked for them.

## H. Modifications to Commercial Items

10 U.S.C. § 2306a(b)(2) and 41 U.S.C. § 3503(b) prohibit the obtaining of cost or pricing data for modifications to contracts for commercial items. FAR 15.403-1(c)(3)(i) implements this prohibition with regard to any modification "that does not change the item from a commercial item to a noncommercial item." As discussed

in Chapter 7, modifications that meet this requirement must be either "minor" or "customarily available in the commercial marketplace." The FAR contains no guidance on the explicit data that should be obtained to ascertain that the price for such modifications is fair and reasonable. However, FAR 52.215-21 contains a standard contract clause for modifications that permits the contractor to request an exception to the submission of cost or pricing data and submit information on prices at which the same or similar items have been sold to demonstrate that the modification is reasonably priced. This appears to assume that the prices for such modifications can be evaluated without the use of cost or pricing data and that obtaining cost or pricing data would be done only in unusual cases.

Section 818 of the National Defense Authorization Act for FY 2005, Pub. L. No. 108-375, amended 10 U.S.C. § 2306a to provide that the commercial item modification exception to the requirement for submission of cost or pricing data does not apply to modifications that are expected to cost, in the aggregate, more than $500,000 or 5% of the total price of the contract, whichever is greater, for contracts funded by the DoD, NASA, or the Coast Guard. This limitation on the exception is implemented in FAR 15.403-1(c)(3)(ii)(C) (revising the dollar threshold) as follows:

> (B) For acquisitions funded by DoD, NASA, or Coast Guard, such modifications of a commercial item are exempt from the requirement for submission of certified cost or pricing data provided the total price of all such modifications under a particular contract action does not exceed the greater of the threshold for obtaining certified cost or pricing data in 15.403-4 or 5 percent of the total price of the contract at the time of contract award.

> (C) For acquisitions funded by DoD, NASA, or Coast Guard such modifications of a commercial item are not exempt from the requirement for submission of certified cost or pricing data on the basis of the exemption provided for at 15.403-1(c)(3) if the total price of all such modifications under a particular contract action exceeds the greater of the threshold for obtaining certified cost or pricing data in 15.403-4 or 5 percent of the total price of the contract at the time of contract award.

## III. ROLES OF GOVERNMENT PERSONNEL

The regulations provide that the determination of the reasonableness of the contract price is the responsibility of the contracting officer. FAR 15.402 states that the contracting officer "must . . . [p]urchase supplies and services . . . at fair and reasonable prices." See also FAR 14.408-2(a) stating that the "contracting officer shall determine . . . that prices offered are reasonable before awarding the contract." Thus, the contracting officer has the primary responsibility for performing the analysis of the contract price or estimated/target cost on all procurements. However, FAR 15.404-1(a) provides that the contracting officer may obtain assistance as follows:

> (5) The contracting officer may request the advice and assistance of other experts to ensure that an appropriate analysis is performed.

Although contracting officers have one or more specialists that participate in the analysis of costs or prices, the regulations have always made it clear that the ultimate responsibility for the adequacy of the price analysis or cost analysis rested with the contracting officer and his or her immediate staff. However, initial analysis is done by many other employees, depending on the agency and the resources available. In many instances, the initial assistance that is available is from employees working at locations close to the contractor's place of business or the site of the work. FAR 15.404-2(a) provides the following guidance on obtaining this "field pricing assistance:"

(1) The contracting officer should request field pricing assistance when the information available at the buying activity is inadequate to determine a fair and reasonable price. Such requests shall be tailored to reflect the minimum essential supplementary information needed to conduct a technical or cost or pricing analysis.

(2) The contracting officer must tailor the type of information and level of detail requested in accordance with the specialized resources available at the buying activity and the magnitude and complexity of the required analysis. Field pricing assistance is generally available to provide

(i) Technical, audit, and special reports associated with the cost elements of a proposal, including subcontracts;

(ii) Information on related pricing practices and history;

(iii) Information to help contracting officers determine commerciality and a fair and reasonable price, including —

(A) Verifying sales history to source documents;

(B) Identifying special terms and conditions;

(C) Identifying customarily granted or offered discounts for the item;

(D) Verifying the item to an existing catalog or price list;

(E) Verifying historical, data for an item previously not determined commercial that the offeror is now trying to qualify as a commercial item; and

(F) Identifying general market conditions affecting determinations of commerciality and a fair and reasonable price.

(iv) Information relative to the business, technical, production, or other capabilities and practices of an offeror.

(3) When field pricing assistance is requested, contracting officers are encouraged to team with appropriate filed experts throughout the acquisition process, including negotiations. Early communication with these experts will assist in determining the extent of assistance required, the specific areas for which assistance is needed, a realistic review schedule, and the information necessary to perform the review.

(4) When requesting field pricing assistance on a contractor's request for equitable adjustment, the contracting officer shall provide the information listed in 43.204(b)(5).

(5) Field pricing information and other reports may include proprietary or source selection information (see 3.104-4(j) and (k)). Such information shall be appropriately identified and protected accordingly.

DFARS PGI 215.404-2(a) gives the following additional guidance to DoD contracting officers:

(i) The contracting officer should consider requesting field pricing assistance for —

(A) Fixed-price proposals exceeding the cost or pricing data threshold;

(B) Cost-type proposals exceeding the cost or pricing data threshold from offerors with significant estimating system deficiencies (see DFARS 215.407-5-70(a)(4) and (c)(2)(i)); or

(C) Cost-type proposals exceeding $10 million from offerors without significant estimating system deficiencies.

(ii) The contracting officer should not request field pricing support for proposed contracts or modifications in an amount less than that specified in paragraph (a) (i) of this subsection. An exception may be made when a reasonable pricing result cannot be established because of —

(A) A lack of knowledge of the particular offeror; or

(B) Sensitive conditions (e.g., a change in, or unusual problems with, an offeror's internal systems).

The FAR guidance gives the contracting officer broad discretion on obtaining field pricing assistance but the DFARS guidance appears, in general, to limit the discretion to cases where cost analysis is necessary. The prior FAR guidance had made the obtaining of field pricing support mandatory for procurement over $500,000 when cost or pricing data was obtained. It also contained considerable guidance on the types of information that was generally obtained from field pricing personnel.

These provisions assume that agencies have fully staffed field offices capable of providing the type of analysis discussed in this regulation. However, most civilian agencies have no such capability, with the result that such assistance cannot be obtained. See, for example, DEAR 915.404-2(a)(1), stating that field pricing assistance is not required in the Department of Energy because "pricing support" is expected to be provided by internal DOE personnel.

## A. Field Contracting Offices

Some agencies, such as DoD and NASA, have fully staffed field offices that are available to provide field pricing support when requested. Other agencies can obtain such assistance from field personnel on only a portion of their acquisitions. These agencies can often obtain assistance from the field offices of other agencies that are familiar with the offeror. Field pricing assistance is also available from government auditors familiar with the offeror's organization, as discussed below.

FAR 15.404-2(b) encourages contracting officers to use informal means to obtain assistance from field contracting offices:

> (1) Depending upon the extent and complexity of the field pricing review, results, including supporting rationale, may be reported directly to the contracting officer orally, in writing, or by any other method acceptable to the contracting officer.
>
> > (i) Whenever circumstances permit, the contracting officer and field pricing experts are encouraged to use telephonic and/or electronic means to request and transmit pricing information.

In many cases, the factual data supporting the offeror's estimate are submitted to these personnel in the field rather than to the contracting officer negotiating the contract. Since it is expected that the data will be subsequently transmitted to the contracting officer, such submission meets the statutory requirements for the submission of certified cost or pricing data, *Singer Co. v. United States*, 217 Ct. Cl. 225, 576 F.2d 905 (1978). In *Singer*, however, the court noted that submission required physical delivery of the data and disclosure of their significance to the pricing action. Thus, the furnishing of monthly reports of labor cost information to government field personnel was held not to be an adequate submission of data to support a specific pricing action. See also *Sylvania Elec. Prods., Inc. v. United States*, 202 Ct. Cl. 16, 479 F.2d 1342 (1973), where the court held that submission of relevant data on another contract pricing action was not an adequate submission. In *M-R-S Mfg. Co. v. United States*, 203 Ct. Cl. 551, 492 F.2d 835 (1974), the court clarified this requirement by stating that the submission requirement could be met by either physically submitting the data or making known its significance to the pricing action. In *M-R-S*, the submission requirement was not met by giving the government auditor the bill of materials and open access to all of the offeror's purchasing records. This requirement is spelled out in Table 15-2, Instructions for Submitting Cost or Pricing Data, in FAR 15.408, which states:

Note 1: There is a clear distinction between submitting certified cost or pricing data and merely making available books, records, and other documents without identification. The requirement for submission of certified cost or pricing data is met when all accurate certified cost or pricing data reasonably available to the offeror have been submitted, either actually or by specific identification, to the Contracting Officer or an authorized representative. As later information comes into your possession, it should be submitted promptly to the Contracting Officer in a manner that clearly shows how the information relates to the offeror's proposal. The requirement for submission of certified cost or pricing data continues up to the time of agreement on price, or an earlier data agreed upon between the parties if applicable.

A proper submission was found in *Texas Instruments, Inc.*, ASBCA 30836, 89-1 BCA ¶ 21,489, where the offeror submitted data correcting an error in the previous data to the administrative contracting officer one day before it signed its certificate, and in *FMC Corp.*, ASBCA 30069, 87-1 BCA ¶ 19,544, where the offeror followed a standard practice of submitting supporting data for its incurred labor rates to the administrative contracting officer. See also *McDonnell Douglas Corp.*, ASBCA 12786, 69-2 BCA ¶ 7897, and *Boeing Co.*, ASBCA 32753, 90-1 BCA ¶ 22,270, *recons. denied*, 90-1 BCA ¶ 22,426, stating that the submission requirement would be met if government field personnel had "actual knowledge" of the data.

When the personnel providing field pricing assistance find that the offeror is unable to provide sufficient information to permit them to provide the necessary assistance to the contracting officer, they must address this problem immediately. FAR 15.404-2 states:

(d) *Deficient proposals.* The ACO or the auditor, as appropriate, shall notify the contracting officer immediately if the data provided for review is so deficient as to preclude review or audit, or if the contractor or offeror has denied access to any records considered essential to conduct satisfactory review or audit. Oral notifications shall be confirmed promptly in writing, including a description of deficient or denied data or records. The contracting officer immediately shall take appropriate action to obtain the required data. Should the offeror/contractor again refuse to provide adequate data, or provide access to necessary data, the contracting officer shall withhold the award or price adjustment and refer the contract action to a higher authority, providing details of the attempts made to resolve the matter and a statement of the practicability of obtaining the supplies or services from another source.

## B. Auditors

All contracting agencies have access to audit services and can therefore obtain prepricing audit reviews of proposals even when they have no field contracting personnel. The contracting officer has considerable discretion in determining when to request audit, *Del-Jen Inc.*, Comp. Gen. Dec. B-216589, 85-2 CPD ¶ 111. The major contract audit agency is the Defense Contract Audit Agency (DCAA), which performs all contract audit work for the DoD and NASA, Defense Contract Audit Manual (DCAM) 1-201, 15-106. Other agencies can sometimes obtain audit assistance from their Inspectors General who have this responsibility pursuant to the Inspector General Act of 1978, 5 U.S.C. App. § 1-11. When a contracting officer cannot obtain audit assistance within the agency, assistance can be obtained from another audit group under a cross-servicing arrangement. See OMB Circular A-73 and DCAM 1-303 for guidance in this area.

FAR 15.404-2 contains the following guidance on prepricing audits:

(c) *Audit   assistance for prime contracts or subcontracts.* (1) The contracting officer may contact the cognizant audit office directly, particularly when an audit is the only field pricing support required. The audit office shall send the audit report, or otherwise transmit the audit recommendations, directly to the contracting officer.

(i) The auditor shall not reveal the audit conclusions or recommendations to the offeror/contractor without obtaining the concurrence of the contracting officer. However, the auditor may discuss statements of facts with the contractor.

(ii) The contracting officer should be notified immediately of any information disclosed to the auditor after submission of a report that may significantly affect the audit findings and, if necessary, a supplemental audit report shall be issued.

(2) The contracting officer shall not request a separate preaward audit of indirect costs unless the information already available from an existing audit, completed within the preceding 12 months, is considered inadequate for determining the reasonableness of the proposed indirect costs (41 U.S.C. 254d and 10 U.S.C. 2313).

(3) The auditor is responsible for the scope and depth of the audit. Copies of updated information that will significantly affect the audit should be provided to the auditor by the contracting officer.

(4) General access to the offeror's books and financial records is limited to the auditor. This limitation does not preclude the contracting officer or the ACO, or their representatives from requesting that the offeror provide or make available any data or records necessary to analyze the offeror's proposal.

See DCAM Chapter 9 for detailed guidance on audits evaluating pricing proposals. This manual emphasizes the need to tailor the extent of the audit in order to allow the DCAA to provide service in a timely manner. Contracting officers should take advantage of the fast service that DCAA can provide by requesting assistance on specific cost elements when that is sufficient to permit analysis of a proposal. See DCAM 9-107.1 containing the following guidance on processing such requests:

a. In connection with a pricing action, a PCO may request specific information concerning a contractor's costs without requesting an audit or evaluation of the contractor proposal. Data to be provided should already be determined. Examples of such information include recent costs for specific production items or lots; established pricing formulas such as for spare parts or other logistics items; established prices for standard components; and current rates for labor, indirect costs, per diem, etc. However, auditors may also respond to any request (telephone or written) from a customer as a telephone request for specific cost information when effort can be accomplished in 4 hours or less. When a PCO requests a complete audit and the auditor determines that there is sufficient information available in the [field audit office] files to meet the PCO's request, the auditor should explain the available options to the PCO and make an appropriate recommendation. (See 9-103.1d.). The PCO has the final decision in determining if a full audit is needed to determine cost reasonableness.

b. The PCO may request specific cost information by telephone, mail, fax, or electronically directly from the field auditor. Such requests should receive timely attention. Written requests are sometimes desirable for clarity, but will not be required.

FAR 15.404-2(b) requires coordination between auditors and ACOs when written audit reports are requested, stating:

(ii) When it is necessary to have written technical and audit reports, the contracting officer shall request that the audit agency concurrently forward the audit report to the requesting contracting officer and the administrative contracting officer (ACO). The completed field pricing assistance results may reference audit information, but need not reconcile the audit recommendations and technical recommendations. A copy of the information submitted to the contracting officer by field pricing personnel shall be provided to the audit agency.

FAR 15.404-3 makes the contracting officer responsible for the reasonableness of subcontract prices and provides the following guidance on the responsibility of the contractor or higher-tier subcontractor:

(a) The contracting officer is responsible for the determination of price reasonableness for the prime contract, including subcontracting costs. The contracting officer should consider whether a contractor or subcontractor has an approved purchasing system, has performed cost or price analysis of proposed subcontractor prices, or has negotiated the subcontract prices before negotiation of the prime contract, in determining the reasonableness of the prime contract price. This does not relieve the contracting officer from the responsibility to analyze the contractor's submission, including subcontractor's certified cost or pricing data.

(b) The prime contractor or subcontractor shall —

(1) Conduct appropriate cost or price analyses to establish the reasonableness of proposed subcontract prices;

(2) Include the results of these analyses in the price proposal; and

(3) When required by paragraph (c) of this subsection, submit subcontractor certified cost or pricing data to the Government as part of its own cost or pricing data.

The FAR has no explicit statement as to when audits of subcontractor pricing should be requested. However, DFARS PGI 215.404-3 contains the following guidance:

(a) The contracting officer should consider the need for field pricing analysis and evaluation of lower-tier subcontractor proposals, and assistance to prime contractors when they are being denied access to lower-tier subcontractor records.

(i) When obtaining field pricing assistance on a prime contractor's proposal, the contracting officer should request audit or field pricing assistance to analyze and evaluate the proposal of a subcontractor at any tier (notwithstanding availability of data or analyses performed by the prime contractor) if the contracting officer believes that such assistance is necessary to ensure the reasonableness of the total proposed price. Such assistance may be appropriate when, for example —

(A) There is a business relationship between the contractor and subcontractor not conducive to independence and objectivity;

(B) The contractor is a sole source and the subcontract costs represent a substantial part of the contract cost;

(C) The contractor has been denied access to the subcontractor's records; or

(D) The contracting officer determines that, because of factors such as the size of the proposed subcontract price, audit or field pricing support for a subcontract or subcontracts at any tier is critical to a fully detailed analysis of the prime contract proposal.

(E) The contractor or higher-tier subcontractor has been cited for having significant estimating system deficiencies in the area of subcontract pricing, especially the failure to perform adequate cost analyses of proposed subcontract costs or to perform subcontract analyses prior to negotiation of the prime contract with the Government; or

(F) A lower-tier subcontractor has been cited as having significant estimating system deficiencies.

(ii) It may be appropriate for the contracting officer or the ACO to provide assistance to a contractor or subcontractor at any tier, when the contractor or higher-tier subcontractor has been denied access to a subcontractor's records in carrying out the responsibilities at FAR 15.404-3 to conduct price or cost analysis to determine the reasonableness of proposed subcontract prices. Under these circumstances, the contracting officer or the ACO should consider whether providing audit or field pricing assistance will serve a valid Government interest.

(iii) When DoD performs the subcontract analysis, DoD shall furnish to the prime contractor or higher-tier subcontractor, with the consent of the subcontractor reviewed, a summary of the analysis performed in determining any unacceptable costs included in the subcontract proposal. If the subcontractor withholds consent, DoD shall furnish a range of unacceptable costs for each element in such a way as to prevent disclosure of subcontractor proprietary data.

The current FAR gives the contracting officer complete discretion as to when prepricing audits are required on major contracts. This should obviate the problem under the prior FAR where a waiver was required when certain audits were not obtained. Under such regulations, it was held that a settlement agreed to by the parties was not binding because the contracting officer did not obtain a mandatory prepricing audit and did not follow the waiver procedure, *Bromley Contracting Co.*, DOTCAB 1284, 84-2 BCA ¶ 17,233.

When government auditors work with contractors on a regular basis, they become very conversant with contractors' estimating and pricing practices. In such cases, they can be expected to know the impact of cost or pricing data given to them during prepricing audits, with the result that a contractor may meet the submission requirement more easily than when data are submitted to less experienced personnel. There are a number of cases where data submitted to an auditor was found to meet the submission requirement. See, for example, *Motorola, Inc.*, ASBCA 48841, 96-2 BCA ¶ 28,465 (subcontractor submitted its data to a DCAA auditor); *Motorola, Inc.*, ASBCA 41528, 94-2 BCA ¶ 26,596 (subcontractor disclosed data to its cognizant DCAA auditor with whom the prime contractor was conferring); *Litton Sys., Inc.*, ASBCA 34435, 93-2 BCA ¶ 25,707 (contractor submitted monthly actuals of indirect cost data to resident DCAA auditor); *Texas Instruments, Inc.*, ASBCA 23678, 87-3 BCA ¶ 20,195 (contractor submitted detailed data on the costs incurred in manufacturing parts to the DCAA auditor and to a government price analyst); *Hardie-Tynes Mfg. Co.*, ASBCA 20717, 76-2 BCA ¶ 12,121 (offeror gave the auditor the file containing the record of purchases of a part without stating which purchases were relevant to the current procurement); and *Whittaker Corp.*, ASBCA 17267, 74-2 BCA ¶ 10,938 (a purchase order was available to an auditor during a prepricing audit and the auditor specifically knew of its relevance to the audit through prior correspondence). The contractor cannot, however, mislead the auditor and escape liability. For example, in *Aerojet-General Corp.*, ASBCA 16988, 73-2 BCA ¶ 10,242, a failure of submission was found where the contractor gave the auditor all of the current factual data but incorrectly told him it would be fruitless to analyze them because they were commingled with other data. In addition, submission to an auditor may not suffice if the offeror later finds that the auditor has not included the data in the audit report, *American Mach. & Foundry Co.*, ASBCA 15037, 74-1 BCA ¶ 10,409. There the offeror learned during contract negotiations that the contracting officer did not know of an additional quotation that had been received from a vendor and furnished to the auditor. The board held that the offeror had a duty to inform the contracting officer about the quotation even though it had been submitted to the auditor.

Auditors obtain access to a firm's books and records in several ways. If the offeror has had no previous negotiated contracts with the government, it is generally believed that the auditor has no legal right of access to the firm's books and records. See, however, *Aerospatiale Helicopter Corp.*, DOTCAB 1981, 89-1 BCA ¶ 21,559, where the board granted access to the contractor's books and records to audit data submitted to support a contract modification — based on the board's interpretation of the contract's Audit clause. Generally, offerors permit access to their records voluntarily because failure to cooperate can result in the contracting officer's refusal to negotiate with the firm. In addition, Table 15-2, Instructions for Submitting Cost or Pricing Data, in FAR 15.408 contains the following statement:

> Note 2: By submitting your proposal, you grant the Contracting Officer or an authorized representative the right to examine records that formed the basis for the pricing proposal. That examination can take place at any time before award. It may include those books, records, documents, and other types of factual information (regardless of form or whether the information is specifically referenced or included in the proposal as the basis for pricing) that will permit an adequate evaluation of the proposed price.

The enforceability of this regulatory statement is subject to question because there is no contractual agreement at the time an offer is submitted.

Offerors that have had negotiated government contracts are generally required to give access to their books and records. While no contract clause gives the government the specific right to audit for purposes of determining reasonableness of proposed prices on a new contract, information relating to incurred costs or other data under existing contracts would frequently be subject to audit and could be useful in analyzing proposed costs. The Audit and Records — Negotiation clause in FAR 52.215-2 gives the procuring agency the right to audit costs on all but firm-fixed-price contracts, certified cost or pricing data submitted to support contract modifications, and reports as follows:

> (b) *Examination of costs.* If this is a cost-reimbursement, incentive, time-and-materials, labor-hour, or price redeterminable contract, or any combination of these, the Contractor shall maintain and the Contracting Officer, or an authorized representative of the Contracting Officer, shall have the right to examine and audit

all records and other evidence sufficient to reflect properly all costs claimed to have been incurred or anticipated to be incurred directly or indirectly in performance of this contract. This right of examination shall include inspection at all reasonable times of the Contractor's plants, or parts of them, engaged in performing the contract.

(c) *Certified cost or pricing data.* If the Contractor has been required to submit certified cost or pricing data in connection with any pricing action relating to this contract, the Contracting Officer, or an authorized representative of the Contracting Officer, in order to evaluate the accuracy, completeness, and currency of the certified cost or pricing data, shall have the right to examine and audit all of the Contractor's records, including computations and projections, related to —

   (1) The proposal for the contract, subcontract, or modifications;

   (2) The discussions conducted on the proposal(s), including those related to negotiating;

   (3) Pricing of the contract, subcontract, or modification; or

   (4) Performance of the contract, subcontract or modification.

* * *

(e) *Reports.* If the Contractor is required to furnish cost, funding, or performance reports, the Contracting Officer or an authorized representative of the Contracting Officer shall have the right to examine and audit the supporting records and materials, for the purpose of evaluating (1) the effectiveness of the Contractor's policies and procedures to produce data compatible with the objectives of these reports and (2) the data reported.

This clause implements the audit requirements of 10 U.S.C.§ 2313 and 41 U.S.C. § 3508. Note that, as amended by FAC 2005-45, it does not give the government the right to audit uncertified cost or pricing data.

A broad right to audit negotiated contracts is also granted to GAO in the Audit and Records — Negotiation clause in FAR 52.215-2 as follows:

(d) *Comptroller General* — (1) The Comptroller General of the United States, or an authorized representative, shall have access to and the right to examine any of the Contractor's directly pertinent records involving transactions related to this contract or a subcontract hereunder.

   (2) This paragraph may not be construed to require the Contractor or subcontractor to create or maintain any record that the Contractor or subcontractor does not maintain in the ordinary course of business or pursuant to a provision of law.

This clause is required to be included in all negotiated contracts by 10 U.S.C. § 2313(c) and 41 U.S.C. § 4706(d). However, GAO is not normally involved in prepricing audits. When using this audit authority, GAO is permitted to audit "directly pertinent records involving transactions related to this contract." In *Hewlett-Packard Co. v. United States*, 385 F.2d 1013 (9th Cir. 1967), *cert. denied*, 390 U.S. 988 (1968), the court interpreted this provision to include production costs of a catalog-priced item for which the government had not required the submission of cost or pricing data. In *United States, v. McDonnell Douglas Corp.*, 751 F.2d 220 (8th Cir. 1984), GAO was granted access to estimates of tooling and design engineering costs. *Bowsher v. Merck & Co.*, 460 U.S. 824 (1983), held that records relating to costs of independent research and development, marketing and promotion, distribution and administration are not directly pertinent records unless the contractor "allocated these costs as attributable to the particular contract." The court was apparently distinguishing between situations where a contractor allocates these general costs of overhead to individual contracts or products, in which case they would be directly pertinent, and those cases where the costs are collected in a general pool and charged against total sales for the year. See also *Bristol Labs. Div. of Bristol-Myers Co. v. Staats*, 428 F. Supp. 1388 (S.D. N.Y. 1977), *aff'd*, 620 F.2d 17 (2d Cir. 1980), *aff'd*, 451 U.S. 400 (1981).

Inspectors General have the right to subpoena books and records necessary to carry out their functions, Inspector General Act of 1978, 5 U.S.C. App. § 6; 41 U.S.C. § 4706(c). This broad right is available in the civilian agencies to support an agency's analysis of proposed costs. Because the DoD Inspector General's duties do not include contract pricing audits (5 U.S.C. App. § 8), there is some question whether that organization's subpoena powers can be used for such purposes. See *United States v. Westinghouse Elec. Corp.*, 788 F.2d 164 (3d Cir. 1986), where the DoD Inspector General issued a subpoena to obtain records for the DCAA. The court held that the subpoena was valid based on the district court's finding that the Inspector General had an independent investigative purpose in issuing the subpoena. The court also held that this subpoena power is extremely broad, extending to documents such as a company's internal audit reports.

The DCAA has subpoena powers of its own, 10 U.S.C. § 2313(b). This power is granted only for books and records subject to audit under the FAR 52.215-2 Audit and Records — Negotiation clauses. In *United States v. Newport News Shipbuilding & Dry Dock Co.*, 837 F.2d 162 (4th Cir. 1988), the court denied access to reports by the company's internal auditors because they were not "cost or financial data." However, in *United States v. Newport News Shipbuilding & Dry Dock Co.*, 862 F.2d 464 (4th Cir. 1988), the court granted access to a wide variety of financial data, including state and federal income tax returns, because they were "objective factual material useful in verifying actual costs." Subsequently, access was granted for estimates, projections, and accompanying work papers on the ground that they would assist in verifying claimed costs, *United States v. Newport News Shipbuilding & Dry Dock Co.*, 737 F. Supp. 897 (E.D. Va. 1989), *aff'd*, 900 F.2d 257 (4th Cir. 1990).

## IV. PRICE ANALYSIS

FAR 15.404-1(b)(1) defines "price analysis" as follows:

Price analysis is the process of examining and evaluating a proposed price without evaluating its separate cost elements and proposed profit.

The most desirable method of determining that the price of a negotiated firm-fixed-price contract is fair and reasonable is price analysis without a detailed analysis of its cost and profit elements. This technique is faster and requires much less accumulation of detailed data by both parties. See *Gap Solutions, Inc.*, Comp. Gen. Dec. B-310564, 2008 CPD ¶ 26; and *Citywide Managing Servs. of Port Washington, Inc.*, Comp. Gen. Dec. B-281287.12, 2001 CPD ¶ 6, rejecting the contention that the agency was required to evaluate the cost elements of each offerors' proposal in order to determine that the prices were reasonable and realistic.

Price analysis is generally based on data obtained from sources other than the prospective contractor. See the preferences set forth in FAR 15.403-3. This information is gathered by the government negotiating team from as many sources as possible and should be accumulated as a product or service is repeatedly purchased. Generally, a sound price analysis will be based on several different types of data. See, for example, *Navistar Def., LLC*, Comp. Gen. Dec. B-401865, 2009 CPD ¶ 258, where the agency used a variety of techniques to make a thorough analysis to determine that seemingly low prices were realistic. However, when strong competition is obtained, the primary element of price analysis will be the competitive prices that have been submitted to the agency.

There is a large degree of discretion when a contracting officer does a thorough price analysis and determines that a price is reasonable in spite of its being higher than other prices. See, for example, *Ashland Sales & Serv. Co./Macon Garment, Inc., a Joint Venture*, Comp. Gen. Dec. B-400466, 2008 CPD ¶ 196, denying a protest that a HUBZone set-aside should have been withdrawn because the price was 30% higher than the price of the small business protester. GAO reasoned:

Here, the record indicates that the contracting officer conducted a thorough price analysis of [the HUBZone contractor's] offer. This price analysis explicitly made a comparison between [that] price and the price offered by [the protester] on [an earlier] small business set-aside, and noted the 30.7 percent price differential. The price analysis also considered that there was adequate price competition in the HUBZone set-aside solicitation in the form of offers from five different HUBZone firms, three of which were included in the competitive range; during discussions, all three firms were advised to review their proposed prices. Ultimately, the contracting officer determined that [the HUBZone contractor's] price was fair and reasonable based on adequate price competition, and discounted the price differential between [the two companies] as a product of the three times greater quantity under the small business set-aside solicitation.

Based on our review of the record, we cannot conclude that the contracting officer's conclusion was unreasonable. That all offers received in response to the HUBZone set-aside solicitation were higher in price than the offer submitted by the protester on the prior solicitation can reasonably be interpreted (as the contracting officer did) to indicate that the difference in volume between the two solicitations had a material impact on price. In light of that factor, we find the contracting officer's decision to discount the differential between solicitations in determining reasonable price, relying on the price competition achieved on the particular solicitation at issue, to be unobjectionable.

## A. Uses of Price Analysis

The major use of price analysis is to determine that a proposed price is fair and reasonable. As discussed earlier, this determination is required in sealed bidding, FAR 14.408-2(a), and in negotiated procurement, FAR 15.404-1(a). It is also required when procuring commercial items, FAR 12.209, and when using simplified acquisition procedures, FAR 13.106-3(a). There are a considerable number of protests where the contracting officer has used price analysis to make a determination as to the reasonableness of the price. Almost all of these cases deny the protest that the agency has performed an improper price analysis, finding instead that there is great discretion in this area. See *Family Realty*, Comp. Gen. Dec. B-247772, 92-2 CPD ¶ 6, stating that "[t]he depth of an agency's price analysis is a matter within the sound exercise of the agency's discretion." But see *Crawford Labs.*, Comp. Gen. Dec. B-277069, 97-2 CPD ¶ 63, where GAO sustained a protest finding that the agency provided no rational basis for its determination of price reasonableness of contract awards for primer coatings at prices more than double the award prices under the prior procurement for the same items.

Price analysis can also be used to determine price realism — whether the price is so low that it will impose an undue risk on the government. This use of price analysis is addressed only peripherally in FAR 15.404-1(d)(3), stating that "cost realism analysis" can be used on fixed-price incentive contracts, or "in exceptional cases, on other competitive fixed-price type contracts," but that, if it is used, prices cannot be adjusted upwards as a result of the analysis. See *IBM Corp.*, Comp. Gen. Dec. B-299504, 2008 CPD ¶ 64, granting a protest when the agency increased a contractor's prices in the evaluation process as a result of its price realism analysis.

In spite of the sparse FAR coverage, price realism analysis is a common practice with some procuring agencies. This use is limited by decisions of GAO holding that price realism can only be assessed if the solicitation contains an evaluation factor indicating that a proposal will be downgraded if the price is unrealistically low, *Possehn Consulting*, Comp. Gen. Dec. B-278579, 98-1 CPD ¶ 10 (where there is no RFP statement on the issue, price realism can only be used to evaluate responsibility of the offeror); *CSE Constr.*, Comp. Gen. Dec. B-291268.2, 2002 CPD ¶ 207 (price realism analysis not permitted when evaluation factor was "unbalanced or unreasonable price"

— reasonableness indicates price is too high); *J.A. Farrington Janitorial Servs.*, Comp. Gen. Dec. B-296875, 2005 CPD ¶ 187 (price realism analysis not permitted when evaluation factor was "unreasonable as to price"); *Indtai, Inc.*, Comp. Gen. Dec. B-298432.3, 2007 CPD ¶ 13 (price realism analysis not permitted if not called for by RFP). Compare *DMS All-Star Joint Venture v. United States*, 90 Fed. Cl. 653 (2010), permitting price realism analysis under a solicitation with very vague language as to whether such analysis would be conducted, and *Afghan Am. Army Servs. Corp. v. United States*, 90 Fed. Cl. 341 (2009), requiring an adequate price realism analysis when the solicitation stated that proposals that had "an unreasonable (high or low) price may be deemed to be unacceptable." See *Pemco Aeroplex, Inc.*, Comp. Gen. Dec. B-310372.3, 2008 CPD ¶ 126, recognizing the need for price realism analysis to evaluate the "negative impacts . . . that may result from an offeror's overly optimistic proposal."

Although the contracting officer has considerable discretion in determining that a contractor's low price constitutes a performance risk, GAO will grant a protest if the risk is minimal. See, for example, *Joint Venture Penauille/BMAR & Assocs., LLC*, Comp. Gen. Dec. B-311200, 2008 CPD ¶ 118. Compare *Team BOS/Naples — Gemmo S.p.A./DelJen*, Comp. Gen. Dec. B-298865.3, 2008 CPD ¶ 11, upholding a contracting officer's analysis indicating that a low price did not constitute a performance risk.

Evaluation factors that have supported the use of price realism analysis are "performance risk," *Trauma Serv. Group*, Comp. Gen. Dec. B-242902.2, 91-1 CPD ¶ 573; *Sabreliner Corp.*, Comp. Gen. Dec. B-284240.2, 2000 CPD ¶ 68; *Guam Shipyard*, Comp. Gen. Dec. B-311321, 2008 CPD ¶ 124, "management," *SEEMA, Inc.*, Comp. Gen. Dec. B-277988, 98-1 CPD ¶ 12 (low price indicated lack of understanding of the work by the offeror's management), and "understanding the requirements," *Consolidated Servs., Inc.*, Comp. Gen. Dec. B-276111.4, 98-1 CPD ¶ 14. A direct statement that price realism will be used to evaluate offers is also satisfactory. See *Centech Group, Inc.*, Comp. Gen. Dec. B-278715, 98-1 CPD ¶ 108, approving the price realism analysis and describing the RFP language as follows:

> The RFP emphasized that any proposal that was "unrealistically low in cost(s) and/or price [would] be deemed reflective of an inherent lack of technical competence [or] failure to comprehend the complexity and risk" of the requirements, justifying "rejection of the proposal."

Price analysis is also useful in detecting mistakes. See FAR 14.407-1 requiring contracting officers to examine all bids for mistakes immediately after bid opening and requiring a request for verification of the bid if a mistake is suspected. FAR Part 15 has no similar explicit requirement when conducting a negotiated procurement but it is good practice to follow the same procedure. See, however, *University of Dayton Research Inst.*, Comp. Gen. Dec. B-296946.6, 2006 CPD ¶ 102, holding that a significant mistake could not be corrected during clarifications.

Price analysis can be done at different levels of work depending on the complexity of the procurement. In the case of procurements with multiple contract line items, prices will usually be solicited for each line item and price analysis will be performed for each line item. See, for example, *Academy Facilities Mgmt. — Advisory Opinion*, Comp. Gen. Dec. B-401094.3, 2009 CPD ¶ 139; and *Comprehensive Health Servs., Inc.*, Comp. Gen. Dec. B-310553, 2008 CPD ¶ 9, upholding the price analysis of line item prices. It is improper, however, to determine that an offeror's proposed prices are unreasonable because a single line item price is high when its total price is similar to other total prices, *R&G Food Serv., Inc.*, Comp. Gen. Dec. B-296435.4, 2005 CPD ¶ 194 (high mileage rate for delivering food not dispositive when food prices are reasonable). In procurements for complex work, prices can be required to be submitted for segments of the work — allowing price analysis for each segment. This is commonly done on construction contracts where prices are required for each element of a building, using standard construction breakdowns of the work (excavation, foundations, structure, electrical, plumbing, etc.).

Although price analysis is also done to evaluate fixed-price labor hour rates — particularly in evaluating proposals for IDIQ contracts — it is of questionable value in this area. The difficulty is that, while price analysis can indicate whether the proposed labor rate is high or low in comparison with other rates, it cannot account for the productivity of the labor that is being offered. Thus, the use of price analysis to evaluate fixed labor rates can lead to a false assessment of the costs that the government will actually pay for work that is awarded to an offeror with low labor rates on a cost-reimbursement of time-and-materials basis.

## B. Price Analysis Techniques

The price analysis techniques that are usable in this process are described in FAR 15.404-1(b)(2):

The Government may use various price analysis techniques and procedures to ensure a fair and reasonable price, given the circumstances surrounding the acquisition. Examples of such techniques include, but are not limited to the following:

(i) Comparison of proposed prices received in response to the solicitation. Normally, adequate price competition establishes price reasonableness (see 15.403-1(c)(1)).

(ii) Comparison of previously proposed prices and previous Government and commercial contract prices with current proposed prices for the same or similar end items, if both the validity of the comparison and the reasonableness of the previous price(s) can be established.

(iii) Use of parametric estimating methods/application of rough yardsticks (such as dollars per pound or per horsepower, or other units) to highlight significant inconsistencies that warrant additional pricing inquiry.

(iv) Comparison with competitive published price lists, published market prices of commodities, similar indexes, and discount or rebate arrangements.

(v) Comparison of proposed prices with independent Government cost estimates.

(vi) Comparison of proposed prices with prices obtained through market research for the same or similar items.

(vii) Analysis of pricing information provided by the contractor.

See also FAR 13.106-3(a)(2) containing a similar list of price analysis techniques to be used when using simplified acquisition procedures.

## 1. Competitive Prices

Prices proposed by competitors are the most important data used in price analysis. They are based on the identical specifications for the work and are submitted in the same time period, thus reflecting current economic conditions. Competitors' prices are particularly useful when the contract will be firm-fixed-price or fixed-price with economic price adjustment. In these cases, the competitors are motivated to estimate their costs accurately, yet are subject to competitive pressures to propose a price that is low enough to win the competition. Thus, reliance on comparison of the competitive prices to ensure reasonableness of the price may be all that is necessary. See, for example, *HSG-SKE*, Comp. Gen. Dec. B-274769, 97-1 CPD ¶ 20, where GAO denied a protest alleging inadequate price analysis when the contracting officer had compared the competitive prices for each contract line item and had checked these prices against the independent government estimate. See also *Cube Corp.*, Comp. Gen. Dec. B-277353, 97-2 CPD ¶ 92 (price analysis fully adequate when contracting officer used competitive prices, independent government estimate and limited cost data); *Ameriko-OMSERV*, Comp. Gen. Dec. B-252879.5, 94-2 CPD ¶ 219 (price analysis adequate where agency performed a line-item-by-line-item comparison of awardee's prices to those of its competitors); and *Management Tech. Servs.*, Comp. Gen. Dec. B-251612.3, 93-1 CPD ¶ 432 (no basis to question the agency's price analysis where agency compared awardee's price to the government estimate and to the prices submitted by the other offerors).

Competitive prices have also been used to determine that a price was unreasonable. For example, it is proper to cancel an IFB based on unreasonableness of prices (1) when the price of a nonresponsive bidder was significantly lower than the lowest responsive bid, *McCarthy Mfg. Co.*, 56 Comp. Gen. 369 (B-186550), 77-1 CPD ¶ 116; and (2) when the prices in a post-bid opening quotation were lower than the timely bids, *Mil-Base Indus.*, Comp. Gen. Dec. B-218015, 85-1 CPD ¶ 421. In *Mil-Base*, GAO recognized that such a situation could establish price unreasonableness but questioned the reliability of the quote under the facts of that case. Similarly, it is proper to cancel an RFP when only one proposal is received and there was no other information available to ensure that the price was reasonable, *Adrian Supply Co.*, Comp. Gen. Dec. B-241502, 91-1 CPD ¶ 138. Prices from small businesses have also been found unreasonable (and set-asides canceled) based on proposed prices from large business firms, *Nutech Laundry & Textiles, Inc.*, Comp. Gen. Dec. B-291739, 2003 CPD ¶ 34; *Hughes & Sons Sanitation*, Comp. Gen. Dec. B-270391, 96-1 CPD ¶ 119; *Western Filter Corp.*, Comp. Gen. Dec. B-247212, 92-1 CPD ¶ 436; *Stacor Corp.*, 57 Comp. Gen. 234 (B-189987), 78-1 CPD ¶ 68; on proposed prices from other small businesses, *Frontier Transp., Inc.*, Comp. Gen. Dec. B-400345, 2008 CPD ¶ 165 (HUBZone preference not followed in cascaded set-aside); and on prices from foreign companies, *General Metals, Inc.*, Comp. Gen. Dec. B-248446.3, 92-2 CPD ¶ 256. But see *Airborne Servs., Inc.*, Comp. Gen. Dec. B-221894, 86-1 CPD ¶ 523, holding that an informal telephone quotation from a firm was not sufficiently reliable to support a determination of unreasonable price.

The mere presence of competition is not always adequate to ensure that the prices proposed are fair and reasonable. For example, if the low offeror has such a decided advantage gained from past performance of the work that it is practically immune from competition, other competitive prices would not provide a valid basis for comparison. Similarly, competitive prices may be suspect when there are a very limited number of competitors. In such cases, the relative experience and sophistication of the offerors must be closely scrutinized. The contracting officer must also assess whether the market conditions are the same for the various competitors. In a period of high economic activity when the competitors are working close to their levels of capacity, competitive prices are not nearly as good an indicator of reasonable price as are prices submitted when competitors are actively seeking more work.

Much less credence should be given to estimated costs and fees submitted in a competitive environment. While the sum of the estimated cost and fee might be considered to be a "price," the fact that offerors are not bound to the estimated cost in a cost-reimbursement contract makes such a "price" inherently unreliable. In such cases, the cost estimates of the various competitors may be established with very different goals in mind than predicting the actual costs of performance. Because the government will bear the risk of underestimates of the performance costs, competitors are not as fully motivated to predict the costs accurately. This is why cost realism analysis is required for such procurements. Comparisons of cost-reimbursement proposals are made in cost realism analysis, but they must be done very carefully, as discussed below.

## 2. Prior Pricing Information

The second type of information that can be used to assess proposed prices is pricing information from prior procurements. Both contract prices and other available price information should be reviewed. See, for example, *General Dynamics — Ordnance & Tactical Sys.*, Comp. Gen. Dec. B-401658, 2009 CPD ¶ 217 (prior prices paid by agency showed prices were realistic); *Paraclete Contracts*, Comp. Gen. Dec. B-299883, 2007 CPD ¶ 153 (prior prices paid by agency showed price was reasonable); *Crawford Labs.*, Comp. Gen. Dec. B-277069, 97-2 CPD ¶ 63 (prices double those of prior procurement unreasonable); *TAAS Israel Indus., Ltd.*, Comp. Gen. Dec. B-260733, 95-2 CPD ¶ 23 (prior prices paid to other contractors on recent competitive procurements showed that price was reasonable); *California Scaffold Corp.*, Comp. Gen. Dec. B-220082.2, 85-2 CPD ¶ 729 (prior prices of an incumbent contractor were used to show unreasonable price); and *Century Metal Parts Corp.*, Comp. Gen. Dec. B-194421.3, 79-2 CPD ¶ 437 (past procurement history demonstrated that price was reasonable). In some cases, prior prices have been used along with the government estimate to demonstrate that the price was unreasonable, *Quality Inn & Suites Conference Center*, Comp. Gen. Dec. B-283468, 99-2 ¶ 72; *Western Filter Corp.*, Comp. Gen. Dec. B-247212, 92-1 CPD ¶ 436; *Freund Precision, Inc.*, Comp. Gen. Dec. B-207426, 82-2 CPD ¶ 509; *Society Brand, Inc.*, 55 Comp. Gen. 475 (B-183963), 75-2 CPD ¶ 327.

There are several variables that must be accounted for when using prior pricing information. One of the most important of these variables is changes in economic conditions between the times of the prior procurements and the current procurement. See *Honolulu Disposal Serv., Inc. — Recons.*, 60 Comp. Gen. 642 (B-200753.2), 81-2 CPD ¶ 126, finding a price unreasonable because it was 14% higher than prior years' prices, whereas the agency believed a 3% inflation adjustment was reasonable. This type of adjustment is particularly important in a period of sharply rising prices. Another important variable is differences in quantity. As a general rule, it is expected that higher quantities will yield lower prices, but this may not hold true when a company is working at full capacity. It is also important to determine the total quantities involved when the product or service is being produced or performed for other customers as well as the procuring agency. A third factor is the inclusion of nonrecurring costs in the prices. If the offeror has been forced to discontinue the work since the performance of the prior contract, startup costs may necessarily be included in the new price. This also raises the question of whether nonrecurring costs have been included in the prior prices. In order to make a fair comparison, such nonrecurring costs should be removed from both prices and assessed separately. See *General Fire Extinguisher Corp.*, 54 Comp. Gen. 416 (B-181796), 74-2 CPD ¶ 278, where prior prices from a contractor were used to demonstrate reasonableness of prices including startup costs. The source of the prior price may also be a factor. See *W.H. Compton Shear Co.*, Comp. Gen. Dec. B-208626.2, 83-2 CPD ¶ 404, where the fact that the prior price was obtained from a foreign company was validly considered in finding reasonableness of price.

If the same work has not been done in the past, comparative prices of *similar work* can be used as a rough means of price analysis. In such cases, adjustments must be made to account for the dissimilarities between the two types of work. If the differences in the work are minor, such adjustments may not be too difficult to determine. However, at a minimum, this will require a detailed analysis of the product to ascertain its specific differences from prior products. See *Family Realty*, Comp. Gen. Dec. B-247772, 92-2 CPD ¶ 6, where prices received on another solicitation for similar services were used, along with the competitive prices on the instant procurement and the government estimate, to determine that the proposed price was reasonable.

When data is available for several years, price analysis can be very valuable. Detailed analysis will disclose pricing trends that may indicate that significant learning has occurred and should be expected to continue through the current purchase. This type of information is a valuable cross-check for the competitive pricing information discussed above.

### 3.  Parametric Data

Some industries compile and use very general data relating prices of products to characteristics of the product such as weight, electrical or electronic circuits, or other units of measurement. One of the oldest types of parametric information is the data compiled by the aircraft manufacturing industry relating labor hours in manufacturing to aircraft weight. Such data is a useful tool in making a price analysis — especially if the database is sufficiently large to demonstrate a consistent relationship. There is very little published guidance on the use of parametric data. However, the DCAA Contract Audit Manual contains five criteria for judging the reliability of this type of data when submitted by a contractor at DCAM 9-1003.2:

1. Do the procedures clearly establish guidelines for when parametric techniques would be appropriate?

2. Are there guidelines for the consistent application of estimating techniques?

3. Is there proper identification of sources of data and the estimating methods and rationale used in developing cost estimates?

4. Do the procedures ensure that relevant personnel have sufficient training, experience, and guidance to perform estimating tasks in accordance with the contractor's established procedures?

5. Is there an internal review of and accountability for the adequacy of the estimating system, including the comparison of projected results to actual results and an analysis of any differences?

If these criteria are met, parametric data submitted by contractors can provide another indication of the reasonableness of a proposed price. Such data can also be compiled and used by government agencies in analyzing prices. Supplementary guidance on parametric cost estimating is contained in the NASA *Parametric*

*Cost Estimating Handbook* (2d ed. 2009) (*http://cost.jsc.nasa.gov/pcehg.html*).
See also the International Society of Parametric Analysts' *Parametric Estimating Handbook* (4th ed. 2008) (*www.galorath.com/images/uploads/ISPA_PEH_4th_ed_Final.pdf*).

Agencies have also used statistical techniques to evaluate prices. See, for example, *PWC Logistics Servs., Inc.*, Comp. Gen. Dec. B-299820, 2007 CPD ¶ 162, upholding the use of a "best case" and "worst case" analysis of material prices based on changes in prices over the past ten years. Compare *Boeing Co.*, Comp. Gen. Dec. B-311344, 2008 CPD ¶ 114, where a protest was granted because the agency improperly used a "Monte Carlo" simulation to adjust prices for realism. The defect identified by GAO was that the agency used data on government costs of total weapon systems to determine possible variations in costs of nonrecurring engineering (only one small element of total cost variations). See also *EPW Closure Servs., LLC*, Comp. Gen. Dec. B-294910, 2006 CPD ¶ 3, criticizing an agency for accepting a contingency allowance included in a proposed price based on a "Monte Carlo" simulation performed by the offeror.

## 4. Published Prices

If the product or service is sold to the public, the offeror may have published prices or standard pricing techniques that are used for these sales. Such information will frequently demonstrate that the price is reasonable — especially if the product or service is sold in a competitive market. For example, in *Logics, Inc.*, Comp. Gen. Dec. B-237412, 90-1 CPD ¶ 189, a protest was sustained where the agency failed to consider pricing information contained in a government catalog which indicated that the fair market prices of an item in question were much higher than the agency estimates. When using this type of information, care must be used in determining what discounts are given for quantity purchases and what other types of special arrangements are made for preferred customers. See *Interscience Sys., Inc.*, 59 Comp. Gen. 658 (B-195773), 80-2 CPD ¶ 106, finding that discounts were not sufficiently large to permit a determination of reasonableness based on market prices. The volume of sales to the general public will also be a factor in assessing the validity of this type of data. Thus, a large volume of sales at a published price in a competitive market would make such data highly reliable, while a low volume of sales in a narrow market would render the data less reliable.

Published prices for similar products or services may also be useful in performing a price analysis. Of course, adjustments have to be made to reflect dissimilarities, but if the differences are minor, this may be a valid source of information. See, for example, *Eclipse Sys., Inc.*, Comp. Gen. Dec. B-216002, 85-1 CPD ¶ 267, where reasonableness of price was determined based on a "market survey" of prices of comparable products.

## 5. Independent Government Cost Estimates

Although the current FAR contains no requirement that agencies prepare an independent cost estimate for each procurement, this has been very common practice. Prior to FAC 97-02, Sept. 30, 1997, FAR 15.803(b) required the development of such an estimate as follows:

> Before issuing a solicitation, the contracting officer shall (when it is feasible to do so) develop an estimate of the proper price level or value of the supplies or services to be purchased. Estimates can range from simple budgetary estimates to complex estimates based on inspection of the product itself and review of such items as drawings, specifications, and prior data.

The only mandatory requirements for the preparation of such estimates are in FAR 36.203 (construction procurements) and FAR 36.605 (architect/engineering services).

Paragraph 4.5.1 of DoD Instruction 5000.2-R, *Mandatory Procedures for Major Defense Acquisition Programs and Major Automated Information System Acquisition Programs*, March 15, 1996, also required "life-cycle cost estimates" for all major programs in the Department of Defense.

Such independent estimates are based on all of the types of data that are discussed above plus any cost or pricing data that may be available from past procurements. They represent the agency's best estimate of the most reasonable current price for the products or services being procured. Thus, they can serve as a sound basis for finding a price unreasonable, *Division Laundry & Cleaners, Inc.*, Comp. Gen. Dec. B-311242, 2008 CPD ¶ 97 (upholding cancellation of set-aside when two small businesses were over 35% above government estimate); *Overstreet Elec. Co.*, Comp. Gen. Dec. B-284691, 2000 CPD ¶ 79 (approving cancellation of solicitation when low bid exceeded government estimate by 32%); *Trebor Indus., Inc.*, Comp. Gen. Dec. B-228906, 87-2 CPD ¶ 446 (denying protest of cancellation when the sole bidder's price was 38% higher than a government estimate based on data from a reliable incumbent supplier); *Kinetic Structures Corp. v. United States*, 6 Cl. Ct. 387 (1984) (permitting cancellation of IFB because all prices were unreasonable when compared to government estimate); *Northern Va. Van Co. v. United States*, 3 Cl. Ct. 237 (1983) (approving cancellation of solicitation because of a large discrepancy between the bid and the government estimate because the cancellation would prevent "a misapplication of public funds"); *Clark Bros. Contractors*, Comp. Gen. Dec. B-189625, 78-1 CPD ¶ 11 (upholding cancellation of IFB because sole bid was 13.67% higher than government estimate). When offerors propose different products to meet an agency's requirements, it is reasonable for the agency to make a separate independent cost estimate for each product and determine that a higher priced product is reasonably priced based on that estimate, *Marinette Marine Corp.*, Comp. Gen. Dec. B-400697, 2009 CPD ¶ 16.

Because government estimates are made early in the procurement process, it may be necessary to update them for use in the price analysis. See, for example, *Legacy Mgmt. Solutions, LLC*, Comp. Gen. Dec. B-299981.2, 2007 CPD ¶ 197, where the government estimate was revised downward in order to determine that seemingly low prices were realistic. See also *Adam Elec. Co.*, Comp. Gen. Dec. B-207782, 82-2 CPD ¶ 576, where all bid prices were determined to be unreasonable based on a government estimate that was revised after bid opening. GAO upheld the cancellation of the IFB even though the bid prices were lower than the original government estimate. Of course, the competitive prices that are proposed may also demonstrate that market conditions have overridden the basic logic used in making the government estimate. The proper procedure is to consider both the government estimates and other proposed prices. See *Francis & Jackson, Assocs.*, 57 Comp. Gen. 244 (B-190023), 78-1 CPD ¶ 79 (price found reasonable by comparing it to both the government estimate and competitive prices); *Mid-Atlantic Forestry Servs., Inc.*, Comp. Gen. Dec. B-217334, 85-2 CPD ¶ 279 (competitive prices and the government estimate used to demonstrate that the proposed price was not only reasonable but also quite low); *Hughes Advanced Sys. Co.*, GSBCA 9601-P, 89-1 BCA ¶ 21,276 (government estimate used to suggest price reasonableness, and competitive prices supported the decision); *Mindleaf Techs., Inc.*, Comp. Gen. Dec. B-294242, 2004 CPD ¶ 157 (price realistic because, although it was somewhat lower than competitors' prices, it was higher than government estimate); *Synectic Solutions, Inc.*, Comp. Gen. Dec. B-299086, 2007 CPD ¶ 36 (three acceptable proposals were lower than the government estimate); *Hawkeye Glove Mfg., Inc.*, Comp. Gen. Dec. B-299237, 2007 CPD ¶ 49 (government estimate and other small business prices used to determine price reasonableness); and *Academy Facilities Mgmt. — Advisory Opinion*, Comp. Gen. Dec. B-401094.3, 2009 CPD ¶ 139 (government estimates, competitive prices and analysis of some cost data used to determine price realism). Compare *National Projects, Inc.*, Comp. Gen. Dec. B-283887, 2000 CPD ¶ 16, where all five competitive prices significantly exceeded the government estimate but the agency still concluded that the government estimate was accurate, cancelled the IFB and conducted a negotiated procurement. In one interesting case, an agency was allowed to cancel a procurement after a specification change rendered the government estimate unreliable and left the contracting officer uncertain as to the reasonableness of the protester's price, *Adrian Supply Co.*, Comp. Gen. Dec. B-241502, 91-1 CPD ¶ 138. Verifying the price would have required an audit which could not have been completed before the end of the fiscal year, when the funds for the project expired.

### 6. Market Prices

Prices of the same or similar items that are available in the commercial market provide an excellent comparison to prices proposed for government contracts. See *Tiger Truck, LLC*, Comp. Gen. Dec. B-400685, 2009 CPD ¶ 19, where GAO rejected the contention that the agency should not have used the price of foreign-made vehicles in determining whether a price was fair and reasonable. See also *Operational Support & Servs.*, Comp. Gen. Dec. B-299660.2, 2007 CPD ¶ 183, upholding a determination of fair market price based on the labor rates on Federal Supply Schedule contracts and salaries listed on websites, and *Sea-Land Serv., Inc.*, Comp. Gen. Dec. B-246784.6, 93-2 CPD ¶ 84, where GAO agreed with the use of this type of information for price analysis before this category was added to the FAR in 1995.

Care must be exercised in using this type of information because of the large differences that may exist between commercial transactions and government procurements. In some cases, the undue complexity of government procurements may justify a significantly higher price than that being offered in the commercial market. On the other hand, there may be situations where the government is buying such large quantities of the supplies or services that it will expect to pay a lower price than the commercial market price.

### 7. Information Submitted by Offeror

Occasionally, the solicitation will require offerors to submit detailed pricing information and a price can be determined unreasonable if that information demonstrates such unreasonableness. For example, in *Concepts Bldg. Sys., Inc.*, Comp. Gen. Dec. B-281995, 99-1 CPD ¶ 95, the agency solicited information on the markup that vendors would add to commercial prices. GAO agreed that the agency properly rejected a proposal calling for a markup of 13% because the agency's negotiation objective was a 7% markup.

Information in a technical proposal as to how an offeror will perform the work can also bear on the validity of a price analysis if the details of the offeror's pricing information do not match the technical proposal. See *Resource Consultants, Inc.*, Comp. Gen. Dec. B-293073.3, 2005 CPD ¶ 131, granting a protest on the basis that the winning offeror's price was not in line with its proposed method of accomplishing the work — which had unfairly earned it a high technical evaluation.

## V.  COST ANALYSIS

FAR 15.404-1(c)(1) defines "cost analysis" as follows:

> Cost analysis is the review and evaluation of the separate cost elements and profit or fee in an offeror's or contractor's proposal, as needed to determine a fair and reasonable price or to determine cost realism, and the application of judgment to determine how well the proposed costs represent what the cost of the contract should be, assuming reasonable economy and efficiency.

Cost analysis differs intrinsically from price analysis in that cost analysis focuses on the reasonableness of the estimated costs of performance, not the reasonableness of the contract price. Thus, cost analysis reviews each element of cost to ascertain whether the contractor's estimate contains an accurate and reasonable prediction of the costs that will be incurred during performance of the work. The contract price is then arrived at by adding a rate of profit that is determined to be fair in accordance with the profit guidelines that will be discussed in the next section. The fundamental theory of pricing using cost analysis is that a price is fair if it includes all reasonable costs of performance plus a fair profit. This theory, of course, ignores the fact that such a price may be far out of line with the market value or intrinsic value of the work. FAR 15.404-1(f)(1) recognizes this problem, to some extent, by precluding the inclusion of costs other than manufacturing or acquisition costs in unit prices if such costs would result in unit prices greatly out of line with the "intrinsic value" of the item.

The fact that costs and profit are analyzed separately does not mean that they must be negotiated separately when the parties are agreeing on firm-fixed prices. See the basic guidance in FAR 15.405(a), which states:

> The purpose of performing cost or price analysis is to develop a negotiation position that permits the contracting officer and the offeror an opportunity to reach agreement on a fair and reasonable price. A fair and reasonable price does not require that agreement be reached on every element of cost, nor is it mandatory that the agreed price be within the contracting officer's initial negotiation position. Taking into consideration the advisory recommendations, reports of contributing specialists, and the current status of the contractor's purchasing system, the contracting officer is responsible for exercising the requisite judgment needed to reach a negotiated settlement with the offeror and is solely responsible for the final price agreement. However, when significant audit or other specialist recommendations are not adopted, the contracting officer should provide rationale that supports the negotiation result in the price negotiation documentation.

Thus, in firm-fixed-price contracts and fixed-price contracts with economic price adjustment clauses, the parties merely need to agree on a price to consummate the negotiation. In cost-reimbursement and fixed-price incentive contracts, this is not true. There the estimated cost or target cost and the fee or profit are stated separately in the contract document and must therefore be separately negotiated. However, even in these types of contracts, there is no need for the parties to agree on each element of the costs. Compromises are frequently made among elements of cost in order to arrive at an agreement on the estimated cost of performing the contract. Note that FAR 15.405(a) does not reflect 10 U.S.C. § 2324(f)(4) and 41 U.S.C. § 256(f)(4) (now § 4305(c)(3)) which require identification of the treatment accorded specific costs included in indirect cost proposals that have been questioned by auditors, as follows:

> The Federal Acquisition Regulation shall require that all categories of costs designated in the report of the contract auditor as questioned with respect to a proposal

for settlement [of indirect costs] be resolved in such a manner that the amount of the individual questioned costs that are paid will be reflected in the settlement.

See FAR 42.705-1(b)(4) implementing this requirement. While this provision requires internal documentation of the results of negotiations of indirect cost rates, it does not appear to require specific agreement on individual costs. The codified provision in 41 U.S.C. § 4305(c)(3) could be interpreted to impose this requirement on all costs not just indirect costs but this was not the interpretation of the prior statute.

Cost analysis requires a complete review of the offeror's proposed costs to ensure that they reflect an accurate projection of the costs of performance of the work to be placed under the contract. The elements of cost analysis are described in FAR 15.404-1(c) as follows:

(2) The Government may use various cost analysis techniques and procedures to ensure a fair and reasonable price, given the circumstances of the acquisition. Such techniques and procedures include the following:

(i) Verification of cost or pricing data and evaluation of cost elements, including —

(A) The necessity for, and reasonableness of, proposed costs, including allowances for contingencies;

(B) Projection of the offeror's cost trends, on the basis of current and historical cost or pricing data;

(C) Reasonableness of estimates generated by appropriately calibrated and validated parametric models or cost-estimating relationships; and

(D) The application of audited or negotiated indirect cost rates, labor rates, and cost of money or other factors.

(ii) Evaluating the effect of the offeror's current practices on future costs. In conducting this evaluation, the contracting officer shall ensure that the effects of inefficient or uneconomical past practices are not projected into the future. In pricing production of recently developed complex equipment, the contracting officer should perform a trend analysis of basic labor and materials, even in periods of relative price stability.

(iii) Comparison of costs proposed by the offeror for individual cost elements with —

(A) Actual costs previously incurred by the same offeror;

(B) Previous cost estimates from the offeror or from other offerors for the same or similar items;

(C) Other cost estimates received in response to the Government's request;

(D) Independent Government cost estimates by technical personnel; and

(E) Forecasts or planned expenditures.

(iv) Verification that the offeror's cost submissions are in accordance with the contract cost principles and procedures in Part 31 and, when applicable, the requirements and procedures in 48 CFR Chapter 99 (Appendix of the FAR loose-leaf edition), Cost Accounting Standards.

(v) Review to determine whether any cost data or pricing data, necessary to make the offeror's proposal suitable for negotiation, have not been either submitted or identified in writing by the contractor. If there are such data, the contracting officer shall attempt to obtain and use them in negotiations or make satisfactory allowance for the incomplete data.

(vi) Analysis of the results of any make-or-buy program reviews, in evaluating subcontract costs (see 15.407-2).

The following material discusses three types of cost analysis: (1) analysis of the offeror's proposed costs using cost or pricing data, (2) analysis of the proposed costs without using cost or pricing data, and (3) should-cost analysis. While the above FAR guidance is primarily concerned with the first type of cost analysis, it also recognizes the other two types. Thus, ¶ (iii) reflects the analysis of the cost elements proposed by an offeror using data other than cost or pricing data. Similarly, ¶ (ii) reflects the need for should-cost analysis.

## A. Analysis of Proposed Costs Using Cost or Pricing Data

The basic cost analysis techniques were formulated by the government (principally in the Department of Defense) when *certified* cost or pricing data was required to be submitted on many, if not most, procurements. While this requirement has been reduced by the adoption of a $700,000 threshold and the prohibition of requiring such data on procurements with adequate price competition and for commercial items, FAC 2005-45 has amended the FAR to permit contracting officers to obtain *uncertified* cost or pricing data in some instances and to follow the same procedures when calling for the submission of such data as when certified cost or pricing data are required. This section therefore addresses the analytical techniques that will be used when cost or pricing data (whether certified or uncertified) is obtained from an offeror.

While the Truth in Negotiations Act requires submission of certified cost or pricing data in specified circumstances, this is a disclosure requirement not a use requirement. Thus, the offeror is entitled to arrive at its offered price without using the cost or pricing data that it has submitted. See *United Techs. Corp.*, ASBCA 51410, 04-1 BCA ¶ 32,556, *modified*, 05-1 BCA ¶ 32,860, *aff'd*, 463 F.3d 1261 (Fed. Cir. 2006), stating at 161,024:

> The plain language of the Act does not obligate a contractor to use any particular *cost or pricing data to put together its proposal. Indeed, TINA does not instruct a* contractor in any manner regarding the manner or method of proposal- preparation.

> TINA is a disclosure statute. It requires a contractor under certain circumstances to disclose and to furnish cost or pricing data to the government and to certify that the *data are accurate, current and complete. This disclosure and certification obligation is not* limited to that data actually used or relied upon by the contractor to prepare its proposal. Under the regulatory definition, the data to be provided consists of "all facts existing up to the time of agreement on price which prudent buyers and sellers would reasonably expect to have a significant effect on price negotiations . . . . " On the other hand, once a contractor has furnished accurate, current and complete data, it has fulfilled its TINA obligations. The statute does not require that all or any of that data be used to prepare the proposal. One would think that any contractor with the desire to obtain a contract award would use credible, historical cost data so as to demonstrate to the government that its proposed price is consistent therewith. However this is a matter for the contractor to decide, and for the Government to evaluate as part of the proposal review process, and is not a mandate under TINA.

In affirming this decision, the Federal Circuit addressed the government's contention that it was entitled to recover for defective data that it had not relied on because the contractor used the defective data in arriving at its proposed price. The court ruled that proof of contractor reliance on defective cost or pricing data does not overcome lack of proof of government reliance, citing *Universal Restoration, Inc. v. United States*, 798 F.2d 1400 (Fed. Cir. 1986).

In this type of cost analysis, the contracting officer has full cost or pricing data to assist in the review the offeror's cost estimate to ensure that the proposed costs are as accurately projected as is possible under the circumstances of the procurement. Summaries of cost estimates (cost element breakdowns) are submitted in a format that depicts the manner that the offeror accumulates costs, and cost or pricing data is submitted to support this summary information. Detailed guidance on the required submission is set forth in Table 15-2 of FAR 15.408. The General Instructions in Table 15-2 call for the submission of separate cost element breakdowns for each contract line item as follows:

> D. You must show the relationship between contract line item prices and the total contract price. You must attach cost-element breakdowns for each proposed line item, using the appropriate format prescribed in the "Formats for Submission of

Line Item Summaries" section of this table. You must furnish supporting break-downs for each cost element, consistent with your cost accounting system.

These instructions also call for the submission of certified cost or pricing data as follows:

B. In submitting your proposal, you must include an index, appropriately refer-enced, of all the certified cost or pricing data and information accompanying or identified in the proposal. In addition, you must annotate any future additions and/or revisions, up to the date of agreement on price, or an earlier date agreed upon by the parties, on a supplemental index.

C. As part of the specific information required, you must submit, with your proposal —

    (1) Certified cost or pricing data (as defined at FAR 2.101). You must clearly identify on your cover sheet that certified cost or pricing data are included as part of the proposal.

    (2) Information reasonably required to explain your estimating process, including —

        (i) The judgmental factors applied and the mathematical or other methods used in the estimate, including those used in projecting from known data; and

        (ii) The nature and amount of any contingencies included in the proposed price.

* * *

F. Whenever you have incurred costs for work performed before submission of a proposal, you must identify those costs in your cost/price proposal.

G. If you have reached an agreement with Government representatives on use of forward pricing rates/factors, identify the agreement, including a copy, and describe its nature.

While these instructions apply by their own terms only when certified cost or pricing data are required to be submitted, the definition of "data other than certified cost or pricing data" in FAR 2.101 states that such data "may include the identical types of data as certified cost or pricing data, consistent with Table 15-2 of 15.408." Thus, the FAR allows contracting officers to require offerors to submit uncertified cost or pricing data following these instructions.

The cost or pricing data will vary in amount depending on the element of cost being considered and the work being procured; and, typically, the parties will use this data as the basis for the negotiation of the price or estimated/target cost. However, the key issue in such negotiations will be the projections of cost submitted by the offeror and made by the government negotiators. In many cases, the government cost analysts and negotiators will explore the reasonableness of the offeror's projections, including the questioning of their validity, during negotiations. Thus, it is good practice for offerors to submit a detailed explanation of why the methodology they have used in making their projections is logical and reasonable, although there is no penalty under the Truth in Negotiations Act if the methodology is faulty or even if it is not submitted to the government since it is not cost or pricing data. (See, however, the discussion in Chapter 1 regarding the treatment of false statements about estimating methodology as fraud under the False Claims Act.) The government team will also make independent projections in most cases, and much of the ultimate price negotiation will consist of a comparison and evaluation of these different projections.

The offeror's estimate is normally broken down into categories of cost, such as labor, material, and indirect costs, which are listed in the cost element breakdowns. In accordance with Cost Accounting Standard 401, 48 C.F.R. § 9904.401, each contractor's estimating practices must be consistent with its cost accounting practices used in accumulating and reporting actual costs. Thus, while each contractor has substantial freedom in establishing its cost accounting system, the costs accumulated must be directly relatable to the cost elements in estimates. Table 15-2 reflects this freedom by prescribing no specific cost breakdown by elements of cost. The following discussion addresses the requirement for the submission of cost or pricing data, the broad types of costs that are common to almost all systems, and the requirement that certified cost or pricing data be certified at the conclusion of negotiations.

## 1.  Cost or Pricing Data

The statutes require that, when required, offerors must submit certified cost or pricing data that are *"accurate, complete, and current."* There is no such explicit requirement that is attached to uncertified cost or pricing data but contractors must recognize that such a requirement would likely be applied if suit for defective data was brought under the False Claims Act, 31 U.S.C. § 3729. Thus, contractors must know what data fall within the definition of "cost or pricing data," what will constitute "complete" data, and how recent their records must be in order to comply fully with the requirement that the data be "current."

The submission requirement for certified cost or pricing data is a strict requirement. Hence, available data that are significant must be submitted even if the offeror does not use the data in arriving at the proposed price of the contract, *Rosemount, Inc.*, ASBCA 37520, 95-2 BCA ¶ 27,770; *Hardie-Tynes Mfg. Co.*, ASBCA 20717, 76-2 BCA ¶ 12,121. However, the government has the burden of proving that the data was reasonably available to the contractor before the close of negotiations, *Litton Sys., Inc.,* ASBCA 34435, 93-2 BCA ¶ 25,707.

## a. Definition of Cost or Pricing Data

The regulations contain a comprehensive definition of "cost or pricing data," emphasizing that such data are factual in nature but including some illustrations that are less than clear. See FAR 2.101, which states:

> *Cost or pricing data* (10 U.S.C. 2306a(h)(1) and 41 U.S.C. 254b) means all facts that, as of the date of price agreement or, if applicable, an earlier date agreed upon between the parties that is as close as practicable to the date of agreement on price, prudent buyers and sellers would reasonably expect to affect price negotiations significantly. Cost or pricing data are factual, not judgmental; and are verifiable. While they do not indicate the accuracy of the prospective contractor's judgment about estimated future costs or projections, they do include the data forming the basis for that judgment. Cost or pricing data are more than historical accounting data; they are all the facts that can be reasonably expected to contribute to the soundness of estimates of future costs and to the validity of determinations of costs already incurred. They also include such factors as —
>
> (1) Vendor quotations;
>
> (2) Nonrecurring costs;
>
> (3) Information on changes in production methods and in production or purchasing volume;
>
> (4) Data supporting projections of business prospects and objectives and related operations costs;
>
> (5) Unit-cost trends such as those associated with labor efficiency;
>
> (6) Make-or-buy decisions;
>
> (7) Estimated resources to attain business goals; and
>
> (8) Information on management decisions that could have a significant bearing on costs.

The statutes contain a much shorter definition at 10 U.S.C. § 2306a(i) and 41 U.S.C. § 3501(2):

> [T]he term "cost or pricing data" means all facts that, as of the date of agreement on the price of a contract (or the price of a contract modification) or, if applicable consistent with [the requirement that the data to be as close to the data of agreement on price " as is practicable" ], another date agreed upon between the parties,

a prudent buyer or seller would reasonably expect to affect price negotiations significantly. Such term does not include information that is judgmental, but does include the factual information from which a judgment was derived.

It has been very difficult to arrive at a precise distinction between factual data and judgmental information. However, it is very clear that recorded costs are factual — with the result that they are cost or pricing data. Thus, the term includes labor rates paid in prior periods, *Boeing Co.*, ASBCA 32753, 90-1 BCA ¶ 22,270, *recons. denied*, 90-1 BCA ¶ 22,426; *Kaiser Aerospace & Elecs. Corp.*, ASBCA 32098, 90-1 BCA ¶ 22,489, *recons. denied*, 90-2 BCA ¶ 22,695; incurred labor hours, *Grumman Aerospace Corp.*, ASBCA 35188, 90-2 BCA ¶ 22,842; and incurred indirect costs, *Norris Indus., Inc.*, ASBCA 15442, 74-1 BCA ¶ 10,482. Information in the offeror's purchasing department relating to the prices of materials is also factual in nature. Thus, the term includes purchase orders, *Grumman Aerospace Corp.*, ASBCA 35188, 90-2 BCA ¶ 22,842, and vendor quotations, *Cutler-Hammer, Inc. v. United States*, 189 Ct. Cl. 76, 416 F.2d 1306 (1969). Accounting adjustments to actual cost data are also cost or pricing data, *Hughes Aircraft Co.*, ASBCA 46321, 97-1 BCA ¶ 28,972.

Accounting information on the costs of prior work on different projects may also be cost or pricing data if the information is sufficiently relevant to be usable in the analysis of proposed costs. Thus, prices paid for "similar" items were held to be cost or pricing data, *Hardie-Tynes Mfg. Co.*, ASBCA 20717, 76-2 BCA ¶ 12,121.

In some cases, a mixture of factual data and judgmental information has been held to be cost or pricing data. For example, in *Lambert Eng'g Co.*, ASBCA 13338, 69-1 BCA ¶ 7663, labor-hour estimates derived from actual information were held to be cost or pricing data even though they were not technically "actual" cost data. In *Aerojet-General Corp.*, ASBCA 12264, 69-1 BCA ¶ 7664, *modified*, 70-1 BCA ¶ 8140, the underlying factual data in an internal company report analyzing a subcontractor's pricing proposal were held to be cost or pricing data. See also *Grumman Aerospace Corp.*, ASBCA 27476, 86-3 BCA ¶ 19,091, holding that an internal company report analyzing a subcontractor's proposal was cost or pricing data; *Texas Instruments, Inc.*, ASBCA 23678, 87-3 BCA ¶ 20,195, holding that a computer-generated report containing an estimate of the costs of future work that was derived from actual cost data but manipulated using complex estimating formulas was cost or pricing data; and *United Techs. Corp.*, ASBCA 51410, 04-1 BCA ¶ 32,556, *modified*, 05-1 BCA ¶ 32,860, *aff'd*, 463 F.3d 1261 (Fed. Cir. 2006), holding that two documents summarizing the costs that "flowed into" the proposed price were cost or pricing data. All of these cases seem to find that a document is cost or pricing data because it is of material assistance in showing how the cost or pricing data relates to the proposed price. In most cases, these documents also contain some factual data.

A contractor's management decisions are cost or pricing data if (1) they have a substantial relationship to a cost element and (2) they are made by an official with the authority to approve the action under consideration, *Lockheed Corp.*, ASBCA

36420, 95-2 BCA ¶ 27,722. In *Lockheed*, the board found that a decision to adopt a new strategy in collective bargaining negotiations met the first test because it would have a substantial effect on wage rates to be paid in the future. The board found, however, that this decision did not meet the second test because it had not been approved by senior corporate management as required by the policies of the company. In *Motorola, Inc.*, ASBCA 41528, 94-2 BCA ¶ 26,596, and *Motorola, Inc.*, ASBCA 48841, 96-2 BCA ¶ 28,465, a manufacturing policy memorandum directing that certain costs not be charged to government contracts was held to be cost or pricing data. In *Aerojet Ordnance Tenn.*, ASBCA 36089, 95-2 BCA ¶ 27,922, a management decision to proceed "with all possible haste" to close a waste containment pond was not cost or pricing data because the cost consequences of the decision could not be determined until the action was approved by the state of Tennessee. In contrast, *Millipore Corp.*, GSBCA 9453, 91-1 BCA ¶ 23,345, held that a decision to change the company's discount policy did constitute cost or pricing data. The board did not address the question of whether a decision to alter the discount policy had been made at a level of management with the authority to approve the decision. It would seem that, to fall within the scope of this rule, the decision would have to impact the resources expected to be used to perform the work, such as a decision to change work methods or to buy from a different vendor. Thus, it is doubtful that a management decision to project costs differently would fall within this rule since such a decision is purely judgmental.

Factual data submitted by a subcontractor on a prior contract to support the prices of "long lead" items were held to be cost or pricing data on a current contract because the items were transferred to the current contract, *General Dynamics Corp.*, ASBCA 39866, 94-1 BCA ¶ 26,339. Similarly, a cost analysis made by a subcontractor to test the validity of the price of a sub-subcontractor was cost or pricing data when it demonstrated that the subcontractor's quoted price, that had been submitted to the government, was too high, *McDonnell Aircraft Co.*, ASBCA 44504, 97-1 BCA ¶ 28,977.

Data containing only judgments are not cost or pricing data. In *Litton Sys., Inc.*, ASBCA 36509, 92-2 BCA ¶ 24,842, the board held that the estimated standard labor hours (ESLH) used by the contractor were not cost or pricing data even though there were internal reports listing these hours for parts manufactured by the contractor. The board found that the reports were not in themselves factual in nature because they contained no facts. The board distinguished these reports from documents containing mixed fact and judgment, stating at 123,944-45:

> The ESLH report is not mixed fact and judgment. In this appeal, we have no underlying document that is verifiable. The ESLH report is based on estimates made by [the contractor's] industrial engineers or test engineers and, as we have found above, no two industrial engineers or test engineers would estimate either the task or the frequency of the task the same. The ESLH report is therefore pure judgment and is, accordingly, not data and need not be disclosed.

## b.  Insignificant Data

In a few cases, contractors have escaped liability for nonsubmission of cost or pricing data by demonstrating that the data were not the type that prudent buyers and sellers would have believed to have a significant effect on the pricing. For example, in *Plessey Indus., Inc.*, ASBCA 16720, 74-1 BCA ¶ 10,603, a rejected vendor quotation was found not to be significant, and in *Boeing Co.*, ASBCA 20875, 85-3 BCA ¶ 18,351, incurred labor costs at the beginning of the contract were held to be the type of information that would not have been used by prudent buyers and sellers in the pricing process. The same logic would apply to old information in the nature of cost or pricing data. For example, contractors have labor rate and overhead rate information going back many years. Only the data relating to recent years are useful in estimating future costs. Reasonable buyers and sellers might disagree over how many years' information is significant, but all would agree that obsolete information would be of no use.

The rule that all significant data must be disclosed has on occasion been interpreted very strictly. In *Sylvania Elec. Prods., Inc. v. United States*, 202 Ct. Cl. 16, 479 F.2d 1342 (1973), the Court of Claims held that if there is a "logical nexus between the nondisclosed pricing data and the possibility of a lower negotiated contract price, then the data is to be considered significant and subject to disclosure." Offerors should exercise care in deciding to use this logic to withhold data that the government may believe are necessary to evaluate the proposed costs.

## c.  Submission Techniques

A note in Table 15.2 provides that there are two techniques for the submission of cost or pricing data: *physical submission* or *specific identification*:

> Note 1: There is a clear distinction between submitting certified cost or pricing data and merely making available books, records, and other documents without identification. The requirement for submission of certified cost or pricing data is met when all accurate cost or pricing data reasonably available to the offeror have been submitted, either actually or by specific identification, to the Contracting Officer or an authorized representative. As later information comes into your possession, it should be submitted promptly to the Contracting Officer in a manner that clearly shows how the information relates to the offeror's proposal. The requirement for submission of certified cost or pricing data continues up to the time of agreement on price, or an earlier data agreed upon between the parties if applicable.

There is little guidance in the regulations or the litigated cases as to how specific identification of data is accomplished. See *M-R-S Mfg. Co. v. United States*, 203 Ct. Cl. 551, 492 F.2d 835 (1974), requiring communication of the specific data that are relevant to the pricing action. Volume 1 of the Armed Services Pricing Manual

(ASPM) (1986) (*http://www.library.dau.mil/ASPM_v1_1986.pdf*) contains the following guidance to contracting officers at 3-39:

> The requirement for submission of cost or pricing data is met when all accurate cost or pricing data reasonably available to the offeror have been submitted, either actually or by specific identification, to the contracting officer or *an authorized representative. As later information comes into the offeror's* possession, it should be promptly submitted to the contracting officer. The requirement for submission of cost or pricing data continues up to the time of final agreement on price.

> *Comment.* The requirement to submit is an expression of your right, need, and obligation to be an informed buyer, to know the facts that shape the offer. Specific identification is authorized to reduce the burden of proposing and to tell you where to look for data to help you understand and evaluate significant parts of the proposal.

> This instruction covers the aspect of identification and is the key to trackability. For accounting data, the authorized representative referred to likely will be the auditor; for information relating to engineering and production it probably will be the ACO (and any of the ACO's team of specialists).

> The identified data will be the details behind the proposal. There will he several layers of data, each more detailed than the preceding, and you will be faced with deciding what you have to see and what you can rely on auditor and ACO to look at. Your decision will not always be the same, even with the same company, auditor, and ACO.

This would indicate that the specific identification requirement is met if the offeror includes a matrix of all data related to each element of performance. This matrix should contain specific information on where the data are located at the offeror's site and which of the offeror's employees have custody of the data. General Instruction 2 in Table 15-2 contains guidance on the preparation of an index of data that may meet part or all of this requirement, as follows:

> B. In submitting your proposal, you must include an index, appropriately referenced, of all the certified cost or pricing data and information accompanying or identified in the proposal. In addition, you must annotate any future additions and/or revisions, up to the date of agreement on price, or an earlier date agreed upon by the parties, on a supplemental index

While these specific identification requirements are somewhat cryptic, there is a clear rule that merely making the data available without specific identification is insufficient. Thus, giving complete access to all contractor data does not meet the submission requirement, *Hughes Aircraft Co.*, ASBCA 46321, 97-1 BCA ¶ 28,972 (making cost ledgers available for audit); *Aerojet-General Corp.*, ASBCA 12873, 69-1 BCA ¶ 7585 (submitting data to the government plant representative); *McDonnell Douglas Corp.*, ASBCA 12786, 69-2 BCA ¶ 7897 (making data available to the government auditor and resident price analyst); *Grumman Aerospace Corp.*, ASBCA 35188, 90-2 BCA ¶ 22,842 (giving contractor complete access to subcontractor data but not identifying relevant data). However, if the government pricing personnel have actual knowledge of the data, the submission requirement is satisfied, *Texas Instruments, Inc.*, ASBCA 23678, 87-3 BCA ¶ 20,195; *Boeing Co.*, ASBCA 32753, 90-1 BCA ¶ 22,270, *recons. denied*, 90-1 BCA ¶ 22,426. In one case, *Motorola, Inc.*, ASBCA 41528, 94-2 BCA ¶ 26,596, the board inferred that current indirect cost data of a subcontractor had been submitted to a resident auditor because that auditor gave the contractor a recommendation for an overhead rate that was apparently based on knowledge of that data.

## d. Explaining the Significance of the Data

In a number of cases, submission of cost or pricing data without an explanation of their significance has been held to be a failure to meet the statutory requirement. Thus, a contractor must make efforts to tell the government pricing personnel how the data are relevant to the cost estimate in instances when this is not readily apparent. This obligation occurs in two distinct situations — when the data are complex or unusual in nature and when they are submitted to update previously submitted data.

Complexity of the data is determined on a case-by-case basis. For example, in *Grumman Aerospace Corp.*, ASBCA 35188, 90-2 BCA ¶ 22,842, the subcontractor had not explained the significance of labor-hour data submitted to the contractor in computerized form. The board determined that the relevance of the data was not readily apparent to the contractor's pricing personnel and that the subcontractor had failed to meet the submission requirement when it did not explain the data. See also *United Techs. Corp.*, ASBCA 51410, 04-1 BCA ¶ 32,556, *modified*, 05-1 BCA ¶ 32,860, *aff'd*, 463 F.3d 1261 (Fed. Cir. 2006), holding that two documents summarizing the costs that "flowed into" the proposed price were required to be submitted. Apparently, the board concluded that without these documents the government personnel could not fully understand the relationship of the factual cost data to the proposed price. In contrast, in *Boeing Co.*, ASBCA 32753, 90-1 BCA ¶ 22,270, *recons. denied*, 90-1 BCA ¶ 22,426, the contractor was found to have met the submission requirement when it submitted raw data on labor rates without explanation. The board found that the government personnel were fully able to use the data in their raw form and, therefore, that no further explanation of the data was required. Similarly, in *Rosemount, Inc.*, ASBCA 37520, 95-2 BCA ¶ 27,770, the contractor was found to have met the submission requirement when it gave the government its incurred labor hours for the product being procured. The board rejected the argument that the contractor was required to plot the hours on a learning curve in order to meet the submission requirement, finding that the agency's negotiators could easily have plotted the data. These latter cases illustrate the basic proposition that the Truth in Negotiations Act does not require the offeror to perform routine analysis of cost or pricing data for the government.

This rule requiring explanation of the data will also apply if the data contain information that is unusual in nature. For example, in the *Grumman* case, the subcontractor submitted information on an interdivisional order but did not disclose that the price of the order included profit. The board ruled that this nondisclosure was a failure to meet the submission requirement because the subcontractor knew that the inclusion of profit in such orders was generally against government policy.

The rule is also applied in cases where the contractor updates prior data. For example, in *Singer Co. v. United States*, 217 Ct. Cl. 225, 576 F.2d 905 (1978), the court held that the contractor's mailing of monthly labor-hour reports to government field pricing personnel and auditors did not meet the submission requirement. The court was critical of the offeror's failure to specifically identify the relationship of this information to the cost estimate. Similarly, cost or pricing data submitted in connection with other procurements do not meet the submission requirement on a contract to which the data have not been related, *Sylvania Elec. Prods., Inc. v. United States*, 202 Ct. Cl. 16, 479 F.2d 1342 (1973).

### e.  Currency of the Data

Until 1995, the certificate required to be executed by the offeror before award of the contract stated that the date of currency of the data was to be the date when price negotiations were concluded. See *Arral Indus., Inc.*, ASBCA 41493, 96-1 BCA ¶ 28,030, where the board found that the date when price negotiations were concluded was best determined by the date on the certificate. This made the data used in the negotiation defective because they had not been updated.

To preclude this result offerors began to perform "sweeps" making a total review of their cost or pricing data after the conclusion of price negotiations and submitting all new data to the contracting officer. This delayed the award of the contract and led to difficult decisions as to what the government should do with the new data.

In 1995, the FAR was revised to permit the parties to agree on variable dates of currency. This is now relocated in Table 15-2 as quoted above. The Certificate of Current Cost or Pricing Data, in FAR 15.406-2(a) was also revised to contain the following instruction on the date of currency of the data:

> ** Insert the day, month, and year when price negotiations were concluded and price agreement was reached or, if applicable, an earlier date agreed upon between the parties that is as close as practicable to the date of agreement on price.

In addition, FAR 15.406-2(c) contains the following guidance:

> The contracting officer and contractor are encouraged to reach a prior agreement on criteria for establishing closing or cutoff dates when appropriate in order to minimize delays associated with proposal updates. Closing or cutoff dates should

be included as part of the data submitted with the proposal and, before agreement on price, data should be updated by the contractor to the latest closing or cutoff dates for which the data are available. Use of cutoff dates coinciding with reports is acceptable, as certain data may not be reasonably available before normal periodic closing dates (e.g., actual indirect costs). Data within the contractor's or a subcontractor's organization on matters significant to contractor management and to the Government will be treated as reasonably available. What is significant depends upon the circumstances of each acquisition.

This policy reflects the fact that in order to be in compliance with the currency requirement, the offeror must continually update the data until the price is agreed upon, and this requirement may not be waived by a government employee, *Singer Co. v. United States*, 217 Ct. Cl. 225, 576 F.2d 905 (1978). If there is insufficient time to compile the data in a usable form, the requirement can arguably be met by submitting raw data as they exist in the contractor's records, *Conrac Corp. v. United States*, 214 Ct. Cl. 561, 558 F.2d 994 (1977); *Lambert Eng'g Co.*, ASBCA 13338, 69-1 BCA ¶ 7663.

The best way to ensure that the currency requirement is met is for the contracting officer and the offeror to reach a written agreement on the closing dates for various types of data at the conclusion of the negotiation, to reference this agreement on the face of the certificate and to attach the agreement to the certificate. In most cases, these closing dates correspond to the labor rate and indirect cost rate information already furnished to the government. The contractor should then conduct a "sweep" to check for any material cost or labor-hour information that has been accumulated during the negotiation. Such information would be furnished to the contracting officer with the signed certificate. By following this procedure, the contractor fully complies with the currency requirement of the Truth in Negotiations Act.

In the absence of an agreement on cutoff dates, there is a significant question as to whether an offeror is permitted any "lag time" for the transmission of cost or pricing data within the corporate structure. In *Sylvania Elec. Prods., Inc. v. United States*, 202 Ct. Cl. 16, 479 F.2d 1342 (1973), the Court of Claims established a strict rule that the data must be "current" as of the time of the price negotiation. The court held that data received by the contractor's purchasing department approximately one week prior to price negotiations were required to be furnished to the government. This decision raises the question as to whether any period of time is permitted for processing the information through a company. The original board decisions allowed such a time lag, *American Bosch Arma Corp.*, ASBCA 10305, 65-2 BCA ¶ 5280, and one later case permitted a substantial time lag (as much as six months) in a situation where the contracting officer concurred in the nonsubmission of current data, *LTV Electrosystems, Inc.*, ASBCA 16802, 73-1 BCA ¶ 9957, *recons. denied*, 74-1 BCA ¶ 10,380. However, it is clear from the language in *Sylvania* that the court will not tolerate a time lag of any significant length. See, however, *Boeing Co.*, ASBCA 20875, 85-3 BCA ¶ 18,351, where the board permitted a three-week lag in the preparation of labor-cost data because this was the period required by the contractor's accounting system. In *Aerojet Ordnance Tenn.*, ASBCA 36089, 95-2 BCA ¶ 27,922, labor-hour information through the month of February was required to be submitted for a negotiation completed on March 2, 1983.

## 2. *Types of Costs*

The types of data provided and the analytical techniques available vary considerably depending on the types of cost being evaluated.

### a. *Material Costs*

This category encompasses all work purchased by the contractor from raw materials to major subcontracts. Table 15-2 contains guidance on the information desired for each purchased item, including the degree of competition or other information demonstrating the reasonableness of the price. In all cases, the critical information necessary to estimate the costs of any material category is the past purchases, if any, of the material, the anticipated source(s) of the material for the proposed procurement, and any pricing information that has been obtained from those sources.

#### (1) Vendor Data

If the work to be performed on a contract is reasonably understood, the offeror will have decided which part of that work will be purchased. Generally, the offeror also will have prepared a list of such items or services. For manufacturing contracts involving items that are fully designed, the contractor normally prepares a bill of materials that lists each material item with quantities, estimated prices, and source data. A typical bill of materials is set forth in **Figure 10-1**. See *Sylvania Elec. Prods., Inc. v. United States*, 202 Ct. Cl. 16, 479 F.2d 1342 (1973), where the court held that, in spite of the fact that the Truth in Negotiations Act does not normally require contractor's to create data, a bill of materials must be submitted because it is the basic factual tool necessary for estimating and analyzing the cost of materials. See also *Lockheed Aircraft Corp. v. United States*, 193 Ct. Cl. 86, 432 F.2d 801 (1970), where a subcontractor had furnished raw data containing all of the purchasing records of the company but had not created a bill of materials indicating which purchased items were applicable to the contract being negotiated.

The prices of material items frequently consists of a combination of factual data and projections. The most reliable data would be fully negotiated.

## SCHEDULE A
### (See Bill of Materials 1523, June 19X2)

| PART NO. | NOMENCLATURE | QUANTITY PER ITEM | SCRAP FACTOR* (%) | TOTAL QUANTITY | UNIT PRICE | TOTAL |
|---|---|---|---|---|---|---|
| 9876543 | Housing casting. (Vendor — Pic Corp. PO 351522, issued 12/20 to lowest three proposals.) | 1 | 4 | 468 | $84.72 | $39,648.96 |
| 9876542 | Bearing, X design. (Vendor — Sun Co. PO 351480, issued 12/5 to only qualified source. Cost analysis performed.) | 2 | 4 | 936 | 14.89 | 13,937.04 |
| 9876541 | Gear, 14-tooth. (Vendor — Autoco. Two proposals. Autoco's the lower and its price used here. Bid file BB 442.) | 4 | 4 | 1,872 | 418.00 | 7,824.96 |
| 9876540 | Cable assembly. (Vendor — Rockaway Corp. Only proposal received. Completed 1411 attached.) | 1 | 4 | 468 | 328.00 | 153,504.00 |
| 9876539 | Bracket, main. (Vendor — Cee Cee Corp. Bracket is same as that used on earlier model of this system. Prior price was $22.19 each (PO 341110). 8% added in making estimate, two years since last buy.) | 3 | 4 | 1,404 | 23.97 | 33,653.88 |
| 9876538 | Race assembly. (Similar assembly bought 5/25 from Hup, Inc., for $150 each. Engineering estimates P/N 9876538 will cost 1/3 more to make.) | 1 | 4 | 468 | 200.00 | 93,600.00 |
| 9876537 | Solenold. (Engineer estimate (estimate file — Eng-47).) | 1 | 4 | 468 | 90.00 | 42,120.00 |
| 9876536 | Gear, drive. (Engineer estimate, review of drawing (estimate file — Eng-487).) | 1 | 4 | 468 | 24.00 | 11,232.00 |
|  | TOTAL MATERIAL |  |  |  |  | $395,520.84 |

**Figure 10-1**

The court held that this was an inadequate submission because it did not factually relate the data to the pricing action at hand. *Compare Conrac Corp. v. United States*, 214 Ct. Cl. 561, 558 F.2d 994 (1977), where the contractor argued that *Lockheed* stood for the proposition that when there was insufficient time to prepare a bill of material, raw data need not be furnished. The court rejected this argument, holding that raw purchasing data must be submitted if there is no time to prepare a bill of materials, stating at 569-70:

> The rule in *Lockheed* is that the best price data must be furnished, not that data in less than prime form, because of time or other constraints, may handily be hidden from the Government.

Thus, the contractor is normally expected to furnish the material data in the form of a priced bill of materials referencing all of the available cost or pricing data relevant to the items listed, yet must present the raw data if the bill of materials cannot be compiled for some reason.

The quantities on a bill of materials are derived from an analysis of the detailed drawings for the item, and any mistake in the quantities will constitute defective cost or pricing data. In the *Sylvania* case, discussed above, a defective submission was found when an offeror duplicated the quantities of two items on the bill of materials. The court dismissed the contractor's contention that the contracting officer should have recognized the error by comparing the bill of materials with other data.

The prices of material items frequently consist of a combination of factual data and projections. The most reliable data would be fully negotiated purchase orders or subcontracts for the work under the contract. However, FAR 15.404-3(a) does not permit a determination that prices are fair and reasonable on the basis of that fact alone. Thus, contracting officers must analyze such prices before making a determination.

Normally, an offeror will not have entered into purchase orders or subcontracts with prospective vendors at the time of negotiation with the government; such prices will therefore not be available. If there have been past purchases of an item, however, the price paid will be available and will almost always be considered to be cost or pricing data, *Grumman Aerospace Corp.*, ASBCA 35188, 90-2 BCA ¶ 22,842. Similarly, quotations from vendors for the current work are generally held to be facts that must be disclosed to the government, *Cutler-Hammer, Inc. v. United States*, 189 Ct. Cl. 76, 416 F.2d 1306 (1969); *Bell & Howell Co.*, ASBCA 11999, 68-1 BCA ¶ 6993. See also *Aydin Monitor Sys.*, NASABCA 381-1, 84-2 BCA ¶ 17,297, holding that a vendor quote for a quantity greater than that to be supplied under the contract was factual data and was therefore required to be submitted. The board reasoned that the quote was significant since its total price, including the greater quantity, was less than the contractor's estimated total price for the smaller quantity actually being purchased. Similarly, the cost of items held in inventory that have a reasonable chance of being used on the contract must be disclosed, *Hardie-Tynes Mfg. Co.*, ASBCA 20367, 76-1 BCA ¶ 11,827. See also *Etowah Mfg. Co.*, ASBCA 27267, 88-3 BCA ¶ 21,054, where the board granted a price reduction when the contractor submitted vendor quotations but failed to submit subsequent purchase orders entered into with the vendors at the quoted prices. The board reasoned that there had been a violation of the submission requirement and that the purchase orders provided a more certain basis for estimating the costs of performance.

If the offeror is actively negotiating with a proposed vendor at the same time it is negotiating the contract price with the government, any significant changes of position by the vendor are cost or pricing data and must be disclosed. See *TGS Int'l, Inc.*, ASBCA 31120, 87-2 BCA ¶ 19,683, *recons. denied*, 87-3 BCA ¶ 19,989, where the contractor failed to submit information specifying that the vendor had agreed to alter the work to be done and had failed to give the subcontractor's new proposal to the contracting officer. See also *McDonnell Aircraft Co.*, ASBCA 44504, 97-1 BCA ¶ 28,977, where nondisclosure of cost or pricing data was found when a subcontractor developed additional information about the validity of the price of a sub-subcontractor but did not disclose it to the contractor in time for it to be disclosed to the government. Changes in the offeror's negotiating position with a subcontractor may also be cost or pricing data. See *Boeing Military Airplane Co.*, ASBCA 33168, 87-2 BCA ¶ 19,714, where the company was held liable for failing to furnish all of the information relating to a dispute with a vendor on the proper price of work that had already been performed on a letter contract.

Vendor quotations and other vendor data must be included in the submission of cost or pricing data only if they would have a significant effect on the pricing action. Thus, outdated data or data not relevant to the pricing action need not be submitted or evaluated. For example, a contractor was permitted to omit data pertaining to a vendor quotation that had been rejected although the contractor subsequently decided to purchase the item from that vendor, *Chu Assocs., Inc.*, ASBCA 15004, 73-1 BCA ¶ 9906, *recons. denied*, 73-2 BCA ¶ 10,120. Similarly, in *Plessey Indus., Inc.*, ASBCA 16720, 74-1 BCA ¶ 10,603, the contractor was not required to submit a vendor quotation when the contractor had decided prior to price negotiation to manufacture the item in-house. See also *Boeing Co.*, ASBCA 20875, 85-3 BCA ¶ 18,351, where the board held that the price of an undisclosed purchase order signed after data submission but before negotiation of the price was so close to the price of a submitted quotation from another vendor that the undisclosed data did not have a significant effect on price.

If the parties have agreed that the pricing should be based on data other than the cost or pricing data accumulated by the contractor, the requirement for submission of the data will not be enforced. See *Texas Instruments, Inc.*, ASBCA 30836, 89-1 BCA ¶ 21,489, where all of the current vendor data — purchase order prices, quotations, and subcontractor negotiations — were found not to constitute cost or pricing data because the parties had agreed that material costs would be computed using average prices of each item based on accumulated costs after the material had been used in the manufacturing process. The board found that since this pricing system made no use of the normal vendor data, the data could have no significant effect on the pricing.

The projections from the factual data are much more difficult to evaluate. If vendor quotations for the instant procurement are being used, the projection is relatively simple. There the key issue is whether the quotation was obtained under conditions that assure that it reflects a reasonable price. Normal price analysis techniques can be used to make this judgment. In most material pricing, however, the offeror is not required to obtain vendor quotes. In such cases, the data will consist of past purchase prices and the analysis will have to consider the length of time between purchases, the number of items purchased, the economic trends, and other relevant data in order to arrive at an appraisal of the reasonableness of the projection of the estimated price. See Chapter 5 of the ASPM for detailed guidance on the techniques that should be used in making this analysis.

## (2) MAJOR SUBCONTRACTS

There is one special situation where offerors are required to submit detailed cost or pricing data relating to material purchases. FAR 15.404-3(c) requires contractors to submit certified subcontractor cost or pricing data for each subcontract cost estimate that is (1) $11.5 million or more or (2) both more than the cost or pricing data threshold ($700,000 at the current time) and more than 10% of the total price. Failure to submit such data will constitute a violation of the statutory submission requirement, *Martin Marietta Corp.*, ASBCA 48223, 96-2 BCA ¶ 28,270. In addition, the contracting officer is authorized by these regulations to require the submission of subcontractor data for subcontracts of lesser amounts if it is "necessary for adequately pricing the prime contract." When such data is submitted, it becomes the offeror's data with consequent liability for price reduction if it is inaccurate, incomplete, or not current, *Lockheed Aircraft Corp. v. United States*, 193 Ct. Cl. 86, 432 F.2d 801 (1970); *EDO Corp.*, ASBCA 41448, 93-3 BCA ¶ 26,135. The offeror is also required to conduct and submit an analysis of the subcontractor's certified cost or pricing data in these circumstances, FAR 15.404-3(b).

Subcontractor cost or pricing data above the thresholds need not be submitted if the subcontract falls within one of the statutory exceptions to the submission of data, FAR 15.404-3(c). The regulation contains no guidance on whether the contractor or the contracting officer is empowered to decide whether an exception applies. Prior to the issuance of FAC 97-02, September 30, 1997, FAR 15.806-2(c) appeared to state that the contracting officer had to make this determination.

When a subcontractor is a competitor of the contractor, contracting officers have permitted the subcontractor to submit required cost or pricing data directly to the government. In such cases, a government administrative contracting officer or auditor will analyze the data and, in most instances, provide the analysis to the contractor. See *Motorola, Inc.*, ASBCA 41528, 94-2 BCA ¶ 26,596, where the board found that a subcontractor had properly submitted data to a government auditor because the auditor gave the contractor up-to-date information on an indirect cost rate that was applicable to the subcontract.

### (3) NEW ITEMS

When work that has not previously been performed is purchased, cost estimating and analysis are much less precise. The specific material that will be used on the contract may not have been fully ascertained, yet the contractor will be forced to make the best possible estimate of material costs. In this situation, the most relevant data may be prices for similar work, and this information may be determined to be factual data which must be submitted to the government. See *Hardie-Tynes Mfg. Co.*, ASBCA 20717, 76-2 BCA ¶ 12,121, where the board found that the price of items similar to those that were to be designed for the contract were cost or pricing data. The board also held that a vendor quote for an item that the offeror was considering using on the contract had to be submitted as part of the proposal. The contractor had made its own estimate on a very broad basis without regard to prior data, but the board held, nonetheless, that the data, if available, had to be furnished to the government so that it could be used in the cost analysis. See also *Aerojet-General Corp.*, ASBCA 12264, 69-1 BCA ¶ 7664, *modified*, 70-1 BCA ¶ 8140, where the board held that a contractor's analysis of a subcontractor proposal was cost or pricing data.

## b. Direct Labor Costs

This category covers all of the types of labor — manufacturing, engineering, tooling, etc. — that will be directly charged to the contract. The contractor is free to group labor in any categories that assist in managing the company, as long as the costs are accumulated for the same categories that are used for estimating purposes. The instructions to Table 15-2 calls for a "time-phased breakdown" of labor-hours and labor rates, reflecting the fact that the process of estimating and analyzing labor costs normally considers hours and rates separately.

### (1) LABOR-HOURS

Labor-hours present the greatest difficulty in the analysis of costs. In cases where the contractor has performed the same or similar work in the past, the number of labor-hours incurred will be factual data which must be presented in the proposal or disclosed during the negotiations. See *McDonnell Douglas Corp.*, ASBCA 12786, 69-2 BCA ¶ 7897 (tapes containing labor-hours incurred in months prior to price negotiation); *Singer Co. v. United States*, 217 Ct. Cl. 225, 576 F.2d 905 (1978) (labor-hour data adjusting standard labor-hour information to actual costs incurred in prior period); *Grumman Aerospace Corp.*, ASBCA 35188, 90-2 BCA ¶ 22,842 (reports of labor-hour lot costs containing data collected prior to conclusion of negotiations); and *Limpiezas Corona S.A.*, ASBCA 45504, 96-1 BCA ¶ 28,137 (number of employees on current janitorial services contract). When the contractor must analyze the data in order to use it for estimating purposes, it is entitled to the time necessary to make the analysis, *Litton Sys., Inc.*, ASBCA 34435, 93-2 BCA ¶ 25,707. Even if the offeror does not record labor-hours, derivative data providing approximate labor-hours must be disclosed, *Lambert Eng'g Co.*, ASBCA 13338, 69-1 BCA ¶ 7663. In *Lambert*, the board held that an offeror must disclose labor-hour information derived by dividing the recorded labor dollars by average labor rates to arrive at the approximate labor hours used by the offeror on past work. Internal company work authorizations permitting departments to incur a specified number of labor-hours of work need not be disclosed to the government because they are not factual in content, *Kaiser Aerospace & Elecs. Corp.*, ASBCA 32098, 90-1 BCA ¶ 22,489, *recons. denied*, 90-2 BCA ¶ 22,695. Similarly, pure estimates made by industrial engineers or test engineers need not be disclosed because they contain no factual element, *Litton Sys., Inc.*, ASBCA 36509, 92-2 BCA ¶ 24,842.

If an offeror uses an estimating system that factors actual labor-hours through pricing formulas, it may be necessary to disclose the entire system to the government. See *Texas Instruments, Inc.*, ASBCA 23678, 87-3 BCA ¶ 20,195, where the board found that such a system was cost or pricing data because disclosure was necessary for the government to fully understand the labor-hour data contained in the estimating system. However, there is no requirement to disclose a learning curve analysis of labor-hours because this technique is so well understood that any competent price analyst can plot the curve using the raw data, *Rosemount, Inc.*, ASBCA 37520, 95-2 BCA ¶ 27,770. Further, there is no requirement to present the labor-hour data in the form of a learning curve when the contractor does not use learning curve analysis, *Aerojet Ordnance Tenn.*, ASBCA 36089, 95-2 BCA ¶ 27,922.

If the contractor has begun work on the contract before the price is negotiated, incurred labor-hours would be factual data that would be expected to be disclosed, *Aerojet Ordnance Tenn.*, ASBCA 36089, 95-2 BCA ¶ 27,922; *University of California., San Francisco*, VABCA 4661, 97-1 BCA ¶ 28,642. Nondisclosure might not create contractor liability, however, if the data are so incomplete that they are not helpful in arriving at a meaningful estimate of the price. See *Boeing Co.*, ASBCA 20875, 85-3 BCA ¶ 18,351, holding that labor-hours incurred early in the performance of a developmental contract would not have been useful to the negotiators even if such data had been disclosed.

The projections made from labor-hours from prior contracts present far more difficult problems. In some cases, the offeror will use an accepted technique for projecting labor-hours, such as a learning curve analysis, and the government will in turn analyze this projection technique using its own calculations. In other cases, an offeror will base the projection on an estimate of the variance that can be expected from standard costs. In all cases, volume and continuity of work will be major factors affecting the projection. See Chapters 5.2 and 5.3 of ASPM for a discussion of the various techniques that can be used to analyze labor-hour estimates. The most difficult situation occurs when the offeror has no previous experience in performing the work to be purchased. In such cases, the estimate of labor-hours must be made by breaking down the projected work into its constituent parts and estimating the labor-hours necessary to perform each part of the work. In most cases, each part of the work can be compared to similar work that the contractor has performed in the past, and this data can be used to support the estimate. Nevertheless, this process requires the application of a large amount of judgment, and analysis of this judgmental process is quite difficult. In such cases, parametric estimating techniques may be useful in checking the estimate.

## (2) LABOR RATES

Labor rate determination is considerably easier. Even if the offeror has never performed the specific work being contracted for, there will be factual information regarding the labor rates that have been paid to the various categories of employees to be used on the contract. This information must be included as part of the offeror's cost or pricing data and must be updated as new data are accumulated, *Boeing Co.*, ASBCA 32753, 90-1 BCA ¶ 22,270, *recons. denied*, 90-1 BCA ¶ 22,426; *Kaiser Aerospace & Elecs. Corp.*, ASBCA 32098, 90-1 BCA ¶ 22,489, *recons. denied*, 90-2 BCA ¶ 22,695. Management decisions affecting labor rates must also be disclosed, *Lockheed Corp.*, ASBCA 36420, 95-2 BCA ¶ 27,722. There the board ruled that a management decision to utilize a new bargaining strategy in collective bargaining negotiations would have been cost or pricing data if it had been made by a corporate officer with authority to adopt the policy.

Based on the historical data on labor rates and any decisions as to future plans affecting the workforce, the cost analyst can make a projection of the rates that will be paid during contract performance. This projection involves determining the rate of increase or decrease in the wages or salaries and the length of time between the date of the actual data and the time of contract performance. The estimate usually will be based on the midpoint of projected contract performance, which can be determined by analyzing the rate of usage of labor over the contract performance period. The changes in labor rate are dependent on economic conditions over the long run and may be easily determinable by reviewing the terms of the offeror's labor agreements. The other factor that must be assessed is the number of workers the contractor expects to employ during the contract performance period. If the number is increasing, average labor rates will normally decrease, while a reduction in the number of employees will normally increase the rate. See Chapter 7 of the ASPM for a discussion of techniques for analyzing labor rate projections.

### c.  Other Direct Costs

Contractors charge a variety of costs directly to contracts to obtain more accurate cost allocation. Such costs are frequently sporadic in nature varying greatly from one contract to another. They are therefore difficult to analyze based on past incurred costs. It is clear, however, that offerors must submit past data on such costs. The contracting officer will usually have to assess each type of direct cost in terms of its relationship to the work on the contract to determine if the offeror is estimating a level of cost that is reasonable under the circumstances. See Chapter 5.5 of the ASPM for a discussion of this area.

### d.  Indirect Costs

Contractors maintain pools of indirect costs in a variety of categories depending on the nature of their work and the size of the organization. Common groupings of indirect costs are manufacturing overhead, engineering overhead, and general and administrative (G&A) expense. However, any logical grouping is proper, FAR 31.203(c). A typical indirect cost pool for manufacturing overhead is set forth in **Figure 10-2**. Indirect costs are accumulated over a period of time, usually the contractor's fiscal year, and are uniformly charged as a percentage of an allocation base to all of the contractor's work during that period. See Cost Accounting Standard 406, 48 C.F.R. § 9904.406, for guidance on the selection of these accounting periods. Cost Accounting Standards 410, 48 C.F.R. § 9904.410, and 418, 48 C.F.R. § 9904.418, provide guidance on the selection of allocation bases and allocation methods. Normally, allocation bases for manufacturing and engineering overhead are direct labor dollars in these categories, while the allocation base for G&A expense is total costs before G&A. However, the contractor has significant discretion to select an accounting system that most accurately allocates indirect costs to work being performed, *Ford Aerospace & Commc'ns Corp.*, ASBCA 23833, 83-2 BCA ¶ 16,813.

| EXHIBIT 1 — MANUFACTURING OVERHEAD | | | |
|---|---|---|---|
| ACCOUNT TITLE | YEAR ENDED DEC 31,   X3 | YEAR ENDED DEC 31,   X4* | PROJECTED YEAR ENDING DEC 31,   X5 |
| Salaries and wages: | | | |
| Indirect labor | $1,338,330 | $1,395,245 | $1,472,160 |
| Additional compensation | 80,302 | 83,950 | 88,000 |
| Overtime premium | 13,214 | 11,296 | 4,500 |
| Sick leave | 63,575 | 67,742 | 72,130 |
| Holidays | 79,164 | 83,006 | 87,080 |
| Suggestion awards | 310 | 423 | 500 |
| Vacations | 140,272 | 147,891 | 154,3000 |
| Personnel expense: | | | |
| Compensation insurance | 25,545 | 26,304 | 27,500 |
| Unemployment insurance | 50,135 | 52,692 | 51,500 |
| FICA tax | 70,493 | 73,907 | 77,850 |
| Group insurance | 153,755 | 161,401 | 169,130 |
| Travel expense | 11,393 | 12,725 | 13,900 |
| Dues and subscriptions | 175 | 175 | 175 |
| Recruiting and relocation — new employees | 897 | 574 | 250 |
| Relocation — transferees | 4,290 | 3,562 | 1,825 |
| Employees pension fund: | | | |
| Salary | 25,174 | 26,350 | 27,500 |
| Hourly | 62,321 | 65,497 | 64,200 |
| Training, conferences, and technical meetings | 418 | 539 | 575 |
| Educational loans and scholarships | 400 | 400 | 400 |
| Supplies and services: | | | |
| General operating | 495,059 | 509,839 | 545,000 |
| Maintenance | 9,102 | 12,318 | 15,700 |
| Stationary, printing, and office supplies | 23,052 | 24,125 | 25,500 |
| Material O/H on supplies | 56,566 | 62,071 | 62,500 |
| Maintenance | 9,063 | 10,875 | 15,000 |
| Rearranging | 418 | 3,523 | 500 |
| Other | 3,314 | 2,653 | 2,500 |
| Heat, light, and power | 470,946 | 489,123 | 517,200 |
| Telephone | 32,382 | 33,874 | 35,000 |
| Fixed charges: | | | |
| Depreciation | 187,118 | 175,641 | 439,850 |
| Equipment rental | 7,633 | 7,633 | 7,633 |
| Total manufacturing expense (A) | $3,416,816 | $3,545,336 | $3,979,858 |
| Total manufacturing direct labor dollars (B) | $1,340,887 | $1,407,931 | $1,267,200 |
| Manufacturing overhead rate (A) ÷ (B) | 254.8% | 251.8% | 314.1% |
| *Includes budgetary estimate for last two months | | | |

Figure 10-2

Analysis of indirect costs involves analysis of the individual costs in the overhead pool and the allocation base. Except in the case of new businesses, there will always be a substantial amount of factual data on the costs in each indirect cost pool. The offeror's accounting system will contain such data for past years, and if the estimate is for work commencing during the year, there will be some data for that current year. See *Rose, Beaton & Rose*, PSBCA 459, 80-1 BCA ¶ 14,242, where incorrect inclusion of an item of cost in the indirect cost pool was held to be a violation of the obligation to disclose accurate cost or pricing data, and *Norris Indus., Inc.*, ASBCA 15442, 74-1 BCA ¶ 10,482, where failure to submit past indirect costs was a violation of the obligation to submit complete cost or pricing data. See also *PAE Int'l*, ASBCA 20595, 76-2 BCA ¶ 12,044, where inclusion of other direct costs in a G&A pool was held to be a violation of the requirement to disclose accurate data. Contractors normally collect indirect cost data on a monthly or quarterly basis, and FAR 15.406-2(c) encourages agreement on closing or cutoff dates for submission of cost or pricing data that match these periodic cost collection dates. All of this actual cost data serves as the base for evaluation of the offeror's projection of the costs in the indirect cost pool for the years of contract performance. Each cost element of the pool should be analyzed to assure that the projection is reasonable in view of the current and projected business situation of the offeror. See Section 9-700 of DCAM for further discussion of this evaluation process.

Analysis of the indirect cost allocation bases is considerably more difficult. These bases are estimated by forecasting the sales that the offeror will make in the accounting periods during which the contract work will be performed. Such forecasting is inherently imprecise although some of the sales will be factual, i.e., in accordance with signed contracts. See *Universal Restoration, Inc. v. United States*, 798 F.2d 1400 (Fed. Cir. 1986), where newly recorded sales were held to be cost or pricing data required to be disclosed during negotiations. Current negotiation of contracts with other customers might also be thought to be factual information which must be furnished by the offeror. See *E-Systems, Inc.*, ASBCA 17557, 74-2 BCA ¶ 10,782, *recons. denied*, 74-2 BCA ¶ 10,943, for a case dealing with this type of information and holding that an offeror's study of this type of data was not cost or pricing data because the underlying factual information had been furnished to the government. In addition to the factual data on sales during the contract performance period, an estimate must be made of other sales that will be booked. Analysis of this estimate is very difficult, but information can often be obtained from other procuring activities on future contracts that will likely be awarded to the offeror.

## 3. *Certification*

When certified cost or pricing data is required to be furnished by statute, the offeror is required to certify that the data is accurate, current, and complete. The certificate is furnished after completion of negotiations, *not at the time of submission of the data*. FAR 15.406-2(a) contains the following certificate to be used in such cases:

CERTIFICATE OF CURRENT COST OR PRICING DATA

This is to certify that, to the best of my knowledge and belief, the cost or pricing data (as defined in section 15.201 of the Federal Acquisition Regulation (FAR) and required under FAR subsection 15.403-4) submitted, either actually or by specific identification in writing, to the Contracting Officer or to the Contracting Officer's representative in support of _____* are accurate, complete, and current as of _____**. This certification includes the cost or pricing data supporting any advance agreements and forward pricing rate agreements between the offeror and the Government that are part of the proposal.

    Firm _____

    Signature _____

    Name _____

    Title _____

    Date of Execution*** _____

*Identify the proposal, request for price adjustment, or other submission involved, giving the appropriate identifying number (e.g., RFP No.).

**Insert the day, month, and year when price negotiations were concluded and price agreement was reached or, if applicable, an earlier date agreed upon between the parties that is as close as practicable to the date of agreement on price.

***Insert the day, month, and year of signing, which should be as close as practicable to the date when the price negotiations were concluded and the contract price was agreed to.

This certificate is to be furnished as soon as practicable after price agreement is reached. In order to avoid major updating of data after the conclusion of negotiations (with resulting delay in furnishing the certificate), FAR 15.406-2(c) encourages reaching agreement on cutoff dates for specific categories of data.

In some cases, certified cost or pricing data may be called for by an RFP, but it may be subsequently determined that there is an exception to the submission requirement, such as adequate price competition or a commercial item. In such cases, cost or pricing data may have already been submitted by the offeror and reviewed by the government. Under these circumstances, the question arises as to whether the data must be certified by the successful offeror. FAR 15.406-2(e) states that such data "shall not be considered certified cost or pricing data . . . and shall not be certified." This regulatory policy follows *ABA Electromechanical Sys., Inc.*, NASABCA 1081-13, 85-3 BCA ¶ 18,225, where data were submitted and audited but not certified because the contracting officer determined that adequate price competition was present, and *Intermountain Research*, Comp. Gen. Dec. B-209827, 83-2 CPD ¶ 103, where neither cost analysis nor a certificate was necessary since adequate price competition was present even though cost and pricing data were required to be submitted by the RFP.

## B. Cost Analysis Without Cost or Pricing Data

A significant amount of cost analysis can be performed on proposals submitted in negotiated procurements without obtaining full cost or pricing data. FAR 15.403-3(a)(1) recognizes that "data other than certified cost or pricing data" may be requested, but advises contracting officers to obtain cost data from "Government or other secondary sources" in preference to requiring the offeror to submit such data. See also FAR 15.402(a)(3) stating that the contracting officer should not obtain "more data than is necessary." Thus, as discussed above, in almost all negotiated procurements where competition is expected or obtained, there will be no need for cost analysis and hence no need for cost data. The result is that the major situation where cost analysis will be required is on competitive cost-reimbursement contracts where *cost realism analysis* will be required — with the result that the contracting officer will need to have some cost data. The contracting officer can specify the type of information needed for the analysis by including in the RFP the Requirements for Certified Cost or Pricing Data or Data Other Than Certified Cost or Pricing Data clause, FAR 52.215-20, with Alternate IV. No further guidance is provided on how the data should be used.

The most common form of cost information that will have to be obtained from offerors in order to perform a cost realism analysis will be *cost element breakdowns* for the work that is required by the contract. These breakdowns show the types of cost (material, labor, indirect costs, etc.) that the offeror anticipates will be required to perform the work. They are not cost or pricing data but are merely summary estimates that have been made by the offeror. However, they provide sufficient information to allow the contracting officer to perform a cost realism analysis — obtaining additional information (such as prior labor or indirect cost rates) from government auditors or from internal files documenting prior negotiations with the offeror. There are numerous protests holding that a cost realism analyses was properly performed using information obtained from sources other than the offeror. See, for example, *ASRC Research & Tech Solutions, LLC*, Comp. Gen. Dec. B-400217, 2008 CPD ¶ 202 (agency used labor rates of incumbent contractor when offeror was proposing to use that work force), *NHIC Corp.*, Comp. Gen. Dec. B-310801, 2008 CPD ¶ 67 (agency obtained rate analysis from DCAA and evaluated labor hours with internal personnel); *ITT Indus. Space Sys., LLC*, Comp. Gen. Dec. B-309964, 2007 CPD ¶ 217 (agency obtained rate analysis from DCAA and evaluated labor hours and other direct costs with internal personnel); and *CIGNA Gov't Servs., LLC*, Comp. Gen. Dec. B-297915, 2006 CPD ¶ 73 (agency personnel evaluated past efficiency information on all offerors to assess labor hours used to perform tasks).

When contracting officers include a requirement for cost element breakdowns in the RFP, they should specify the level in the "work breakdown structure" that should be supported by such cost breakdowns. A work breakdown structure separates the contract work into its separate parts in a logical manner in order to ensure that all necessary tasks are considered in planning the job. See MIL-Handbook-881, *Work Breakdown Structures for Defense Materiel Items*, July 30, 2005, (*www. acq.osd,mil/pm/currentpolicy/wbs/MIL_HDBK-881A/MILHDBK881A/WebHelp3/ MILHDBK881A.htm*) containing the following definition:

1.6.3 Work Breakdown Structure (WBS)

This term is defined as:

a. A product-oriented family tree composed of hardware, software, services, data, and facilities. The family tree results from systems engineering efforts during the acquisition of a defense materiel item.

b. A WBS displays and defines the product, or products, to be developed and/or produced. It relates the elements of work to be accomplished to each other and to the end product. In other words the WBS is an organized method to breakdown a product into subproducts at lower levels of detail.

c. A WBS can be expressed down to any level of interest. Generally, the top three levels are sufficient unless the items identified are high cost or high risk. Then, is it important to take the WBS to a lower level of definition.

The Handbook describes the three levels of the work breakdown structure as follows at 1.6.5:

a. Level 1 is the entire defense materiel item, a program element, project or subprogram, for example, an electronic system. An "electronic system" might be a command and control system, a radar system, a communications system, a management information system, a sensor system, navigation or guidance system, or electronic warfare system.

b. Level 2 elements are the major elements subordinate to the Level 1 major elements, for example, an air vehicle of a missile or aircraft system, or the complete round of an ordnance system. These major elements are prime mission products, which include all hardware and software elements. Level 2 elements also include aggregations of system level services (like system test and evaluation, or systems engineering and program management), and data.

c. Level 3 elements are elements subordinate to Level 2 major elements, including hardware and software and services. For example, the radar data processor of the fire control radar or, the Developmental Test and Evaluation (DT&E) subordinate element of System Test and Evaluation, or technical publications element of Technical Data. Lower levels follow the same process.

It can be seen that Level 1 corresponds, in general, to an entire contract, while Level 2 is normally used to identify the specific line items in a contract. Contractual documents do not normally contain any breakdowns that correspond to Level 3 in the DoD cost breakdown structure.

Cost breakdowns can be obtained for any level in the cost breakdown structure — with the understanding that the lower the level the more detailed the information that will be available to the contracting officer to use for evaluation purposes. In general, the size of the procurement will indicate which level is appropriate. Level 1 — providing only a single cost element breakdown for the entire contract — will generally be sufficient for contracts with one major task. Level 2 — providing cost element breakdowns for each contract line item – will be sufficient for many contracts. Level 3 or lower — providing cost element breakdowns for parts of the work — will be called for in contracts for major systems or complex services.

## 1. *Cost Realism Analysis*

Cost realism analysis is required on cost-reimbursement contracts to determine *the probable cost of performance* that will be used as the evaluation factor, FAR 15.404-1(d)(2); *KPMG Peat Marwick, LLP*, Comp. Gen. Dec. B-259479, 95-2 CPD ¶ 13. It's fundamental purpose is to ensure that an offeror has not submitted a cost estimate that unrealistically low. See the following definition in FAR 15.404-1(d):

> (1) Cost realism analysis is the process of independently reviewing and evaluating specific *elements* of each offeror's proposed cost estimate to determine whether the estimated proposed cost elements are realistic for the work to be performed; reflect a clear understanding of the requirements; and are consistent with the unique methods of performance and materials described in the offeror's technical proposal. (Emphasis added)

While this description of cost realism analysis is somewhat cryptic, it can be seen as describing three reasons why an offeror's cost estimate might be perceived to be lower than is realistic. First, the offeror might be intentionally proposing a low cost in order to win the competition. The government is protected against this practice by adjusting the offeror's estimate to the probable cost when making the source selection decision. Second, the offeror's estimate might be low because it does not understand the work required to carry out the contract tasks. Such a low estimate is generally factored into the assessment of the offeror's management or technical capability — as well as by adjusting it to the probable cost. The third reason for a low estimate might be that the offeror has a more efficient or effective way to carry out the work. This type of seemingly low estimate should not be adjusted upward and should reflect favorably on the assessment of the offeror's management or technical capability. The difficulty faced by the contracting officer making the cost realism analysis is in determining which of these reasons explains the apparently low cost estimate that has been submitted by an offeror. Until a sound determination in this regard is made, a successful cost realism analysis has not been conducted.

It is very clear that cost realism analysis is mandatory on cost-reimbursement contracts. See *Tidewater Constr. Corp.*, Comp. Gen. Dec. B-278360, 98-1 CPD ¶ 103, where the agency merely compared the costs proposed by the competing offerors. GAO granted the protest stating that this was a price analysis not a cost realism analysis because the agency did not analyze the individual cost elements of the offerors for realism. Neither may an agency avoid updating the cost realism analysis if the procurement is extended as a result of a sustained protest, *The Futures Group Int'l*, Comp. Gen. Dec. B-281274.5, 2000 CPD ¶ 148, or when an offeror has altered its proposed costs in its best and final offer, *ITT Fed. Servs. Int'l Corp.*, Comp. Gen. Dec. B-283307, 99-2 CPD ¶ 76. Further, an agency risks being found to have conducted an improper cost realism analysis if the contracting officer makes an adjustment based on a guess as to the cost methodology used by the offeror and the guess proves to be incorrect, *Future-Tec Mgmt. Sys., Inc.*, Comp. Gen. Dec. B-283793.5, 2000 CPD ¶ 59. An agency must also adequately document its cost realism analysis or risk having an award overturned, *National City Bank of Indiana*, B-287608.3, 2002 CPD ¶ 190.

Cost realism analysis is accomplished by determining the amount of resources (labor-hours and material) that the offeror proposes to use to accomplish each contract task and by ascertaining whether this amount of resources is a realistic estimate of the amount of and cost of the resources that will actually be required. The contracting officer must specify in the solicitation the data which offerors are required to submit to permit a sound cost realism analysis, FAR 15.403-3(a)(1)(ii). See, however, FAR 15.403-5(b)(2) stating that such data "may be submitted in the offeror's own format unless the contracting officer decides that use of a specific format is essential for evaluating and determining that the price is fair and reasonable and the format has been described in the solicitation." The key information that is needed is estimated labor hours and material costs for designated elements of the work. In order to compare offerors, labor hours of both the offeror and its major subcontractors should be requested (in order to account for the fact that different offerors will make different allocation of the contract tasks between their own employees and subcontractors). Generally, each offeror should be permitted to identify the labor categories to be used and the specific material to be acquired, and it is good practice to request the offerors to submit information on how they intend to perform the contract tasks with these proposed resources. Labor rate and indirect cost rate information is also needed but data supporting the accuracy of such estimates should not be obtained from the offerors if it can be readily obtained from the cognizant government auditor. It is also possible that such information will be available in the contracting agency. All available information should be used in this type of analysis.

While, as discussed earlier, cost realism analysis can be effectively used in assessing risk or competence when a fixed-price contract is contemplated, it must be used in the selection of cost-reimbursement contractors, where it has been regularly challenged by losing offerors. In these protests, GAO, and the Court of Federal Claims, in determining whether the agency has followed a rational process in arriving at the probable cost of performance, have reviewed the analytical processes used by contracting officers. The standard of review was described in *Palmetto GBA, LLC*, Comp. Gen. Dec. B-298962, 2007 CPD ¶ 25, as follows:

> An agency is not required to conduct an in-depth cost analysis, see FAR § 15.404-1(c), or to verify each and every item in assessing cost realism; rather, the evaluation requires the exercise of informed judgment by the contracting agency. *Cascade Gen., Inc.*, B-283872, Jan. 18, 2000, 2000 CPD ¶ 14 at 8. Further, an agency's cost realism analysis need not achieve scientific certainty; rather, the methodology employed must be reasonably adequate and provide some measure of confidence that the rates proposed are reasonable and realistic in view of other cost information reasonably available to the agency as of the time of its evaluation. See *SGT, Inc.*, B-294722.4, July 28, 2005, 2005 CPD ¶ 151 at 7; *Metro Mach. Corp.*, B-295744; B-295744.2, Apr. 21, 2005, 2005 CPD ¶ 112 at 10-11. Because the contracting agency is in the best position to make this determination, we review an agency's judgment in this area only to see that the agency's cost realism evaluation was reasonably based and not arbitrary. *Hanford Envtl. Health Found.*, B-292858.2, B-292858.5, Apr. 7, 2004, 2004 CPD ¶ 164 at 8-9.

Thus, agencies are accorded substantial discretion in making a cost realism analysis but they must meet the test of rationality, *Science Applications Int'l Corp.*, Comp. Gen. Dec. B-238136.2, 90-1 CPD ¶ 517. See also *Westech Int'l, Inc. v. United States*, 79 Fed. Cl. 272 (2007); and *Halifax Tech. Servs., Inc. v. United States*, 848 F. Supp. 240 (D.D.C. 1994), following the same standard. Thus, a cost realism analysis need not identify every adjustment that might be made to an offeror's cost of performance. However, adjustments must be made if an offeror includes no cost estimate for work that is required by the contract work statement, *NV Servs.*, Comp. Gen. Dec. B-284119.2, 2000 CPD ¶ 64. In that case, the agency made no adjustments when the winning offeror left out costs for employee training, safety equipment and phaseout costs. Similarly, an adjustment was required where an offeror had included significant costs that were not necessary for contract performance, *Priority One Servs., Inc.*, Comp. Gen. Dec. B-288836, 2002 CPD ¶ 79. Furthermore, when cost realism adjustments are made, offerors must be afforded equal treatment, *DynCorp Int'l LLC*, Comp. Gen. Dec. B-289863, 2002 CPD ¶ 83. Furthermore, the adjustments that are made must be supported by sufficient data to permit analysis of the validity of the adjustments, *Day & Zimmermann Servs. v. United States*, 38 Fed. Cl. 591 (1997). In *Raytheon Support Servs. Co.*, 68 Comp. Gen. 566 (B-234920 ), 89-2 CPD ¶ 84, GAO found that the agency's cost realism analysis was satisfactory even though it did not make some possible adjustments, stating in a footnote:

> We find no merit to Raytheon's argument that the Navy should have made downward adjustments to its cost proposal for Raytheon's " inadvertent" failure to take into consideration any "productivity" or " learning curve" reductions in its cost

proposal. The burden is on the offeror to submit a cost proposal that takes into consideration all aspects of its technical approach and the agency has no duty to prepare or revise an offeror's proposal.

See also *PAE GmbH Planning & Constr.*, 68 Comp. Gen. 358 (B-233823), 89-1 CPD ¶ 336, denying a protest that the contracting officer should have seen a mistake in the offeror's cost proposal in the process of making the cost realism analysis. GAO concluded that the mistake was neither readily apparent in the data included in the protester's proposal nor made any clearer by comparison with other proposals.

Neither must the cost realism analysis use all of the data requested from offerors. See, for example, *Allied-Signal Aerospace Co.*, Comp. Gen. Dec. B-249214.4, 93-1 CPD ¶ 109, where GAO held that an agency was not required to make a comparative analysis of each element of each offeror's detailed cost estimates. GAO stated that instructing the offerors to submit cost estimates at a specified work breakdown level did not obligate the agency to analyze that information "in any greater detail than was necessary to assure the realism of the cost proposals." See also *Communications Int'l, Inc.*, Comp. Gen. Dec. B-246076, 92-1 CPD ¶ 194, where the sum of work element cost estimates, rather than the total cost estimate, was properly used in the evaluation and the contracting officer was not required to reopen discussions to reconcile disparity between the two.

In order to be rational, the cost realism analysis has to be performed on a contractor-by-contractor basis. The contracting officer must consider both the way the contractor proposes to do the work and the contractor's cost structure in order to determine whether the proposed costs are an accurate projection of the costs of that work. Thus, a mechanical approach that applies the same factors to all offerors is likely to fail the test of rationality (generally called "normalization"). In *Jonathan Corp.*, Comp. Gen. Dec. B-251698.3, 93-2 CPD ¶ 174, the protesters argued that the Navy's cost realism analysis was arbitrary and irrational because it mechanically adjusted the offerors' proposed labor-hour and material cost estimates based on an undisclosed government estimate. GAO summarized the Navy approach as follows:

> The computer was programmed to accept an offeror's labor hour and material costs for a work item if the number was within plus or minus [deleted] percent of the government's estimate for that item.

> For those work items where an offeror's proposed labor hour and material cost estimates were outside the [deleted] percent range, the source selection plan proposed a two-pronged approach. The first approach provided that if an "offeror's estimate is not adequately supported with data and rationale," the estimate would be rejected and the government's labor hour or material cost estimate would be used instead to calculate the projected cost to the government. The second approach provided that if an "offeror's estimate is well supported with an equal probability of [g]overnment or [o]fferor being correct," the following predeter-

mined mathematical formula would be used to determine an adjusted labor hour or material cost estimate:

> "One half of the difference between the [g]overnment estimate and the offeror's proposed cost [will be] added to (or subtracted from) the offeror's estimate after first reducing or increasing the [g]overnment estimate by [deleted] % in the direction of the difference (reduce the difference) in order to establish projected cost and adjustment dollars."

In other words, the computer program approximately "split the difference" between the government's labor hour or material cost estimate and the offeror's proposed labor hours and material cost for each of the 100 work items in the notional package.

GAO sustained the protest, finding that the agency failed to consider each offeror's individualized approach and instead mechanically adjusted costs, stating that the agency's cost evaluation "did not satisfy the requirement for an independent analysis of each offeror's cost proposal based upon its particular approach, personnel, and other circumstances." The Court of Claims reached the same conclusion in *Day & Zimmermann*. See also *Metro Mach. Corp.*, Comp. Gen. Dec. B-297879.2, 2006 CPD ¶ 80; *Information Ventures, Inc.*, Comp. Gen. Dec. B-297276.2, 2006 CPD ¶ 45; and *Honeywell Tech. Solutions, Inc.*, B-292354, 2005 CPD ¶ 107, granting protests when the agency used the its own estimate of labor hours to adjust the offered labor hours without evaluating the techniques the offerors proposed to perform the work. Similarly, in *SRS Techs.*, Comp. Gen. Dec. B-291618.2, 2003 CPD ¶ 70, GAO held that it was unreasonable to increase the rates for the protester who planned to use uncompensated overtime when the other offeror did not plan to use uncompensated overtime, reasoning that the protester was entitled to use the advantage of the lower rates since there was no prohibition on the use of uncompensated overtime and there was no indication that the protester would not use uncompensated overtime.

Normalization is proper if there is no logical reason to believe that the offerors' costs will be different for some element of the work. See *Univ. Research Co., LLC v. United States*, 65 Fed. Cl. 500 (2005), stating at 509:

> This Court and GAO have recognized that normalization is appropriate when there is no logical basis for differences in approach, or there is insufficient information available in the proposals. See, e.g., [*Computer Sciences Corp. v. United States*, 51 Fed. Cl. 297, 316 (2002)] at 316; *General Research Corp.*, 70 Comp Gen. 279, B-241569 (1991). Thus, in general, the purpose of the cost realism analysis "is to segregate cost factors which are 'company unique' — depending on variables resulting from dissimilar company policies – from those which are generally applicable to all offerors and therefore subject to normalization." *Computer Sciences Corp.*, 51 Fed. Cl. at 316 (citing *SGT, Inc.*, B-281773 (1999)).

See also *ASRC Research & Tech. Solutions, LLC*, Comp. Gen. Dec. B-400217, 2008 CPD ¶ 202, holding that it was proper to use the same fixed labor rates for all offerors that intended to hire the incumbent workforce (a normalization logic). However, GAO granted the protest because the agency had increased the protester's probable cost with no proof that it's proposed fixed labor rates were lower than the incumbent's rates. GAO also ruled that it was improper to downgrade the protester in the evaluation of its management plan because it had proposed low labor costs when the agency did not have precise data on the incumbent's labor rates.

Cost realism adjustments are also improper if they alter an offeror's standard accounting practices. See *Kellogg Brown & Root Servs., Inc.*, Comp. Gen. Dec. B-298694, 2006 CPD ¶ 160, granting a protest when the agency deleted an element of cost from the offeror's indirect costs, thereby not accepting the offeror's approved accounting system. GAO reasoned that Cost Accounting Standards 401 and 402 required that the offeror to follow the allocation of costs that it proposed.

If an offeror places a contractually binding "cap" on an element of cost, that amount can be determined by a cost realism analysis to be the probable cost of performance, *BNF Techs., Inc.*, Comp. Gen. Dec. B-254953.3, 94-1 CPD ¶ 274 (contracting officer improperly adjusted capped overhead and G&A costs above the amount of the cap); *Unisys Corp. v. National Aeronautics & Space Admin.*, GSBCA 13247-P, 95-2 BCA ¶ 27,818 (contracting officer properly used cap on phase-out costs but was entitled to adjust cap on overhead based on information in proposal); *Halifax Tech. Servs., Inc. v. United States*, 848 F. Supp. 240 (D.D.C. 1994) (contracting officer properly used capped labor costs in making cost realism analysis). However, if the contracting officer concludes that a realistic estimate of the rates to be incurred is below the cap, that estimate can be used in lieu of the cap, *Delta Research Assocs., Inc.*, Comp. Gen. Dec. B-254006.2, 94-1 CPD ¶ 47. Similarly, if the contracting officer reasonably concludes that the cap will only be partially effective, other costs can be adjusted to a realistic amount, *University Research Co., LLC*, Comp. Gen. Dec. B-294358.8, 2006 CPD ¶ 66. When the capped costs are used as the probable costs, the contracting officer must still consider whether the amount imposes a constraint on the offeror significant enough to hamper its ability to perform the work under contract, *MCT JV*, Comp. Gen. Dec. B-311245.2, 2008 CPD ¶ 121, *recons. denied*, 2008 CPD ¶ 167; *Cubic Field Servs., Inc.*, Comp. Gen. Dec. B-247780, 92-1 CPD ¶ 525.

The cost realism analysis is normally done by analyzing each major cost element: material, direct labor, indirect costs, and other direct costs.

### a.  Material

This category encompasses all work to be purchased by the offeror from raw materials to major subcontracts. Most of the cost realism analysis of material costs appears to occur in reviewing the proposed subcontracts in competing offers. See, for example, *BAF Sys. Norfolk Ship Repair, Inc.*, Comp. Gen. Dec. B-297879, 2006

CPD ¶ 75, agreeing that it was reasonable to use prior labor costs rather than fixed-price quotations from subcontractors to determine the realistic costs of performance. The contracting officer had concluded that the quotations were not a good indication of the price that would ultimately be paid to the subcontractors. See also *Electronic Data Sys. Fed. Corp.*, Comp. Gen. Dec. B-207311, 83-1 CPD ¶ 264, where the offeror's proposed subcontract costs were found to be too low because they did not reflect the need for a subcontractor during the entire life of the contract. Subcontractors' labor and indirect cost rates should also be checked for cost realism when the subcontracts will be performed on a cost-reimbursement basis, *General Marine Indus. of N.Y., Inc.*, Comp. Gen. Dec. B-240059, 90-2 CPD ¶ 311; *OptiMetrics, Inc.*, 68 Comp. Gen. 714 (B-235646), 89-2 CPD ¶ 266. See also *Dayton T. Brown, Inc.*, Comp. Gen. Dec. B-229664, 88-1 CPD ¶ 321, where material costs were determined to be realistic even though they appeared low; the reasoning was that the material costs would not impact the ultimate cost to the government because they were included in indirect costs of performance. In *GEC-Marconi Elec. Sys. Corp.*, Comp. Gen. Dec. B-276186, 97-2 CPD ¶ 23, GAO found reasonable an agency's determination that the protester's proposed material costs were unrealistically low. The agency had found 30 material cost deviations. The agency considered 17 of the deviations to be substantiated by the protester's explanation that the reduction in material costs was due to a new source of supply or an increase in quantity to be ordered. The agency rejected as unsubstantiated those reductions that the protester stated were due merely to an audit or correction to the pricing bill of material without further explanation. Similarly, in *Litton Sys., Inc., Amecom Div.*, Comp. Gen. Dec. B-275807.2, 97-1 CPD ¶ 170, GAO found it proper to add subcontract labor hours where the offeror had included no labor hours because the subcontractors had stated that they would perform the work at no cost. The agency's rationale was that the offeror had no binding agreement with the subcontractors.

### b.  Direct Labor

Cost realism analysis of direct labor costs is performed by reviewing the labor-hours proposed by the offeror, as well as the labor rates that will be applied to the various categories of direct labor to be used.

Perhaps the major area where discrepancies are found in proposals is the estimated number of labor hours required for performance. One cost realism analysis technique that is commonly used is to compare the labor-hours in the cost proposal with the labor hours in the technical proposal. If they vary, it is logical to adjust costs upward, concluding that the cost proposal is incorrect and relying on the hours in the technical proposal, *TechDyn Sys. Corp.*, Comp. Gen. Dec. B-237618, 90-1 CPD ¶ 264; *Complere, Inc.*, Comp. Gen. Dec. B-227832, 87-2 CPD ¶ 254. In *Earl Indus., LLC*, Comp. Gen. Dec. B-309996, 2007 CPD ¶ 203, a protest was granted when the agency used the hours in the cost proposal rather than adjusting them upwards to reflect the technical proposal. See, however, *DLM&A, Inc. v. United States*, 6 Cl.

Ct. 329 (1984), where this type of discrepancy in the two proposals was resolved during the analysis. In *ITT Fed. Servs. Int'l Corp.*, Comp. Gen. Dec. B-289863.4, 2002 CPD ¶ 216, GAO held that the cost realism analysis was defective because the agency did not resolve the discrepancy between the effort described in the technical proposal and the quoted labor costs. See also *Frank A. Bloomer — Agency Tender Official*, Comp. Gen. Dec. B-401482.2, 2009 CPD ¶ 203, where GAO sustained a protest because the agency had accepted the offeror's estimate that it could institute a 10 % reduction in the labor hours without any explanation of how that could be accomplished, and *ITT Fed. Servs. Int'l Corp.*, Comp. Gen. Dec. B-283307, 99-2 CPD ¶ 76, where GAO sustained a protest because the agency had failed to analyze the technical approach of the offeror in concluding that the labor costs were too low.

Cost realism adjustments are required if an analysis of the offeror's proposal indicates that no labor hours have been included for required elements of the work, *NV Servs.*, Comp. Gen. Dec. B-284119.2, 2000 CPD ¶ 64. Numerous cases have sustained discretionary decisions that labor-hour estimates are incorrect. See, for example, *Lumetra v. United States*, 84 Fed. Cl. 542 (2008) (prior performance of work with substantially more hours required upward adjustment of labor hours); *Westech Int'l, Inc. v. United States*, 79 Fed. Cl. 272 (2007) (hours added based on agency judgment that they were needed to provide sufficient staff to perform required tasks); *ITT Indus. Space Sys., LLC*, Comp. Gen. Dec. B-309964, 2007 CPD ¶ 217 (proposed techniques for performing work required adjusting labor hours); *EDO Corp.*, Comp. Gen. Dec. B-296861, 2005 CPD ¶ 196 (lack of explanation of low amounts of labor for specific tasks justified upward adjustment); *United Payors & United Providers Health Servs., Inc. v. United States*, 55 Fed. Cl. 323 (2003) (underestimate of required work led to adjusted costs); *Hernandez Eng'g, Inc.*, Comp. Gen. Dec. B-286336, 2001 CPD ¶ 89 (unsubstantiated labor hours lower than "historical" levels not realistic); *Scientific & Commercial Sys. Corp.*, Comp. Gen. Dec. B-283160, 99-2 CPD ¶ 78 (staffing level low because past attempts to reduce staff had failed); *Joint Threat Servs.*, Comp. Gen. Dec. B-278168, 98-1 CPD ¶ 18 (reduced labor hours for option years not realistic when no work reduction was anticipated in those years); *TRW Inc.*, Comp. Gen. Dec. B-234558.2, 89-2 CPD ¶ 560 (use of new personnel would require more labor-hours than estimated); and *Range Tech. Servs.*, 68 Comp. Gen. 81 (B-231968), 88-2 CPD ¶ 474 (past staffing levels indicated that the labor-hours were underestimated). See also *Aircraft Porous Media, Inc.*, Comp. Gen. Dec. B-241665.2, 91-1 CPD ¶ 356, holding it proper to conclude that the estimate of labor-hours was too low when the offeror had reduced the labor-hours in its best and final offer (BAFO) because of savings that could be achieved through simultaneous performance of similar work on another contract. GAO found that the contracting officer had the discretion to question the offeror's ability to achieve such savings. In *Fairchild Weston Sys., Inc.*, Comp. Gen. Dec. B-229568.2, 88-1 CPD ¶ 394, the agency was permitted to make major changes in the labor-hours proposed by both offerors based on the technical expertise of agency personnel. See, however, *Aurora Assocs., Inc.*, Comp. Gen. Dec. B-215565, 85-1 CPD ¶ 470, finding improper an assumption that all offerors' direct costs would be the same, despite the agency's claim that this assumption was necessary: the contracts were indefinite-quantity contracts for the design and evaluation of agricultural projects, and the agency did not know what tasks each contractor would be asked to perform and for what period of time. See also *Univ. Research Co., LLC v. United States*, 65 Fed. Cl. 500 (2005), finding it improper to normalized reproduction costs when offerors proposed methods for reducing these costs.

A number of cases support an agency's decision not to adjust low estimates of labor-hours because it has determined that the offeror's approach to the work will likely require fewer hours than have been used in the past, *Honeywell Tech. Solutions, Inc.*, Comp. Gen. Dec. B-400771, 2009 CPD ¶ 49; *Palmetto GBA, LLC*, Comp. Gen. Dec. B-298962, 2007 CPD ¶ 25; *Cascade Gen., Inc.*, Comp. Gen. Dec. B-283872, 2000 CPD ¶ 14; *Consolidated Safety Servs., Inc.*, Comp. Gen. Dec. B-252305.2, 93-2 CPD ¶ 225; *Research Analysis & Maint., Inc.*, Comp. Gen. Dec. B-239223, 90-2 CPD ¶ 129; *SRS Techs.*, Comp. Gen. Dec. B-238403, 90-1 CPD ¶ 484; *Opti-Metrics, Inc.*, 68 Comp. Gen. 714 (B-235646.2), 89-2 CPD ¶ 266. See *TrailBlazer Health Enters., LLC*, Comp. Gen. Dec. B-402751, 2010 CPD ¶ 183, where GAO agreed that the agency had properly accepted the low labor hours based on the offeror's explanation of the innovative methods it intended to use to perform the work. See also *CIGNA Gov't Servs., LLC*, Comp. Gen. Dec. B-297915, 2006 CPD ¶ 73, where GAO agreed that the agency properly did not adjust seemingly low labor hours because the agency's review of past performance of the offeror indicated that it had done the work more efficiently than other contractors. Compare *PRC Kentron, Inc.*, Comp. Gen. Dec. B-230212, 88-1 CPD ¶ 537, where GAO did not object to a solicitation provision calling for automatic adjustment of labor-hours that did not conform to the agency's prescribed staffing levels, with *ELS, Inc.*, Comp. Gen. Dec. B-283236, 99-2 CPD ¶ 92, where GAO agreed that the agency was not required to adjust a proposal to reflect the amount of effort that the agency had included in its budget estimate. However, it is improper to accept low labor hour estimates that are based on performance of the work using methods that do not meet the contract requirements, *M. Stoller Corp.*, Comp. Gen. Dec. B-400937, 2009 CPD ¶ 193.

Labor rates can also be questioned when the rates included in a proposal are not realistic. For example, in *ASRC Research & Tech. Solutions, LLC*, Comp. Gen. Dec. B-400217, 2008 CPD ¶ 202 ; *Hernandez Eng'g, Inc.*, Comp. Gen. Dec. B-286336, 2001 CPD ¶ 89; and *Computer Sciences Corp.*, Comp. Gen. Dec. B-210800, 84-1 CPD ¶ 422, the agency properly concluded that the offeror's proposed labor rates were too low because they were below the rates being paid by an incumbent service contractor. The agency assumed that the winning contractor would hire most of the incumbent employees at their current salaries. In *A. T. Kearney, Inc.*, Comp. Gen. Dec. B-237731, 90-1 CPD ¶ 305, rates were properly analyzed as being low because they were under the current average rates being paid on a similar contract, while in *Associates in Rural Dev., Inc.*, Comp. Gen. Dec. B-238402, 90-1 CPD ¶ 495, both salaries and fringe benefits were properly found to be low by comparing them to earlier costs. Similarly, in *Booz-Allen & Hamilton, Inc.*, Comp. Gen. Dec. B-275934.2,

97-1 CPD ¶ 222, an upward adjustment of labor rates was sustained even though the offeror based its proposed rates on actual averages. The agency concluded that the offeror could not retain competent personnel at the proposed rates. In *E.L. Hamm & Assocs., Inc.*, Comp. Gen. Dec. B-280766.3, 99-1 CPD ¶ 85, a protest was granted when the agency failed to make an upward adjustment to labor rates that were for personnel that were not qualified to perform the proposed work. In *Magellan Health Servs.*, Comp. Gen. Dec. B-298912, 2007 CPD ¶ 81, and *ManTech Envtl. Tech., Inc.*, Comp. Gen. Dec. B-271002, 96-1 CPD ¶ 272, protests were granted when the agency failed to adjust very low labor rates and it was doubtful the offeror would be able to hire qualified personnel at those rates. See also *ITT Fed. Servs. Int'l Corp.*, B-289863.4, 2002 CPD ¶ 216. In *Radian, Inc.*, Comp. Gen. Dec. B-256313.2, 94-2 CPD ¶ 104, it was proper to make an upward adjustment in labor rates based on a "rate check" furnished by the cognizant DCAA auditors. See also *Sabre Sys., Inc.*, Comp. Gen. Dec. B-255311, 94-1 CPD ¶ 129, and *NKF Eng'g, Inc.*, Comp. Gen. Dec. B-232143, 88-2 CPD ¶ 497, where labor rates after the first year of performance were found to be low because they did not reflect normal escalation, and *Bendix Field Eng'g Corp.*, Comp. Gen. Dec. B-230076, 88-1 CPD ¶ 437, where rates were found low because they were under the rates prescribed by the Service Contract Act. See also *Westech Int'l, Inc. v. United States*, 79 Fed. Cl. 272 (2007), where it was found proper to escalate Service Contract Act labor rates by 3% per year based on past experience. In *Unified Indus. Inc.*, Comp. Gen. Dec. B-237868, 90-1 CPD ¶ 346, it was held improper not to question proposed wages that were less than the required wage rates under the Service Contract Act.

When an offeror satisfactorily explains why seemingly low labor rates are an accurate prediction of the rates that will be paid, no adjustment is warranted. See *ITT Corp.*, Comp. Gen. Dec. B-310102.6, 2010 CPD ¶ 12 (offeror presented evidence that current employees were accepting lower rates than in the past); *Information Network Sys., Inc.*, Comp. Gen. Dec. B-284854, 2000 CPD ¶ 104 (agency concluded that the offeror could probably hire employees at labor rates that were lower than those of the incumbent contractor); *Advanced Commc'ns Sys., Inc.*, Comp. Gen. Dec. B-283650, 2000 CPD ¶ 3 (the impact of a few of the labor rates that were slightly lower than Bureau of Labor Statistics rates in the area was less than 1%). See also *Ares Corp.*, Comp. Gen. Dec. B-275321, 97-1 CPD ¶ 82, where an adjustment of only 1% for future years was found to be reasonable based on analysis of the specific company.

It is improper to question labor rates based on past experience without making a detailed analysis of the offeror's specific approach to performance and the personnel expected to be hired, *United Int'l Eng'g, Inc.*, 71 Comp. Gen. 177 (B-245448.3), 92-1 CPD ¶ 122. In that case, the contracting officer had mechanically questioned the labor rates without making such an analysis. See *Bendix Field Eng'g Corp.*, Comp. Gen. Dec. B-246236, 92-1 CPD ¶ 227, where GAO also ruled that a labor rate adjustment was improper when the agency's application of a projected inflation factor resulted in labor rates in excess of those called for by the collective bargaining agreement that the offeror had with its union. GAO also rejected adjustments to management salaries because they were made "mechanically" without considering the specifics of the offeror's situation. It is proper to accept rates that appear to be low when the agency determines that they are the rates being paid by the incumbent offeror that is competing for the work, *Kalman & Co.*, Comp. Gen. Dec. B-287442.2, 2002 CPD ¶ 63, are the rates currently being paid by the offeror and its major subcontractor, *Advanced Commc'ns Sys., Inc.*, Comp. Gen. Dec. B-283650, 2000 CPD ¶ 3, are supported by commitments from personnel to work at those rates, *Telos Corp.*, Comp. Gen. Dec. B-279493.3, 98-2 CPD ¶ 30, or are the rates being currently paid to employees that will work on the contract, *ATLIS Fed. Servs., Inc.*, Comp. Gen. Dec. B-275065.2, 97-1 CPD ¶ 84.

When labor rates are questioned, the contracting officer must be certain that the adjustments are based on the offeror's accounting practices. For example, an adjustment of rates to reflect a 40-hour workweek was overturned in *General Research Corp.*, Comp. Gen. Dec. B-241569, 91-1 CPD ¶ 183, because the offeror had an established accounting practice (disclosed in its Cost Accounting Standards Disclosure Statement) that charged for labor based on the full hours worked by each employee. GAO stated that the contracting officer should not have relied on the incorrect advice of the Defense Contract Audit Agency (DCAA) auditor, who stated that the Disclosure Statement did not deal with this issue, but should have been familiar with the offeror's accounting practices. Compare *PAI, Inc.*, 67 Comp. Gen. 516 (B-230610), 88-2 CPD ¶ 36, sustaining a protest that the contracting officer had not adjusted labor rates to comply with a solicitation provision prohibiting use of rates based on uncompensated overtime. GAO did not address the issue of whether such rates were in accordance with the offeror's accounting practices. Similarly, in *Hardman J.V.*, Comp. Gen. Dec. B-224551, 87-1 CPD ¶ 162, GAO agreed with an adjustment to remove the effect of uncompensated overtime, pursuant to a solicitation provision, without addressing the accounting practices of the offeror. Compare *Systems Integration & Research, Inc.*, Comp. Gen. Dec. B-279759.2, 99-1 CPD ¶ 54, where labor rates based on uncompensated overtime were properly accepted where the solicitation did not prohibit the use of such rates, and *SRS Techs.*, Comp. Gen. Dec. B-291618.2, 2003 CPD ¶ 70, where it was improper to adjust the rates for uncompensated overtime since the solicitation did not prohibit its use.

In *Compuware Corp.*, GSBCA 9533-P, 88-3 BCA ¶ 21,109, the board rejected an upward adjustment of labor rates that conflicted with the findings of the auditor reviewing the proposals. The auditor had determined that the contractor reasonably concluded that an imminent turnover in employees would lower its labor costs because the new workers would be paid less than those with seniority. The board found that the contracting officer had no evidence that the audit finding was incorrect. Compare *SGT, Inc.*, Comp. Gen. Dec. B-294722.4, 2005 CPD ¶ 151, where GAO held that the agency properly made an independent analysis of labor rates when the DCAA audit of the rates was inconclusive.

## c. Indirect Costs

Contracting officers also frequently question proposed indirect costs. In *Polaris, Inc.*, Comp. Gen. Dec. B-220066, 85-2 CPD ¶ 669, GAO held that an agency was correct in concluding that the offeror's proposed overhead rates were too low. The offeror had projected a gradual reduction in overhead rates over a five-year period, but the agency had rejected this possibility based on the recommendations of the DCAA. See also *Mandex, Inc.*, Comp. Gen. Dec. B-241841, 91-1 CPD ¶ 253, *recons. denied*, 91-2 CPD ¶ 83, where an offeror's G&A rate was found to be low because it was based on an accounting system change that had not been fully approved by the administrative contracting officer at the time of award (the change had been approved by the DCAA subject to correction of deficiencies in the accounting system). Similarly, in *Hanford Envtl. Health Found.*, Comp. Gen. Dec. B-292858.2, 2004 CPD ¶ 164, acceptance of a fringe benefit rate that was lower than the incumbent contractor's rate was proper when the lower rate was comparable to local rates. Compare *Aurora Assocs., Inc.*, Comp. Gen. Dec. B-215565, 85-1 CPD ¶ 470, where a conclusion that the rate was too low was found to be improper because the agency used only the highest indirect cost multiplier when three different multipliers, corresponding to different categories of employees, were applicable to the proposed costs.

Some contracting officers have avoided the detailed analysis of indirect costs by merely comparing proposed overhead rates to prior rates. While this is a rather imprecise technique, it has been affirmed as a proper basis for a cost realism analysis. See *Signal Corp.*, Comp. Gen. Dec. B-241849, 91-1 CPD ¶ 218, and *Purvis Sys., Inc.*, Comp. Gen. Dec. B-245761, 92-1 CPD ¶ 132, where it was held proper to determine a probable cost using prior-year indirect cost rates when the offeror had included substantially lower rates in the proposal based on its theory that additional work would reduce its rates but had failed to submit sufficient evidence to support this theory. Protests have been granted because the contracting officer did not adjust rates that were below current rates, *E.L. Hamm & Assocs., Inc.*, Comp. Gen. Dec. B-280766.3, 99-1 CPD ¶ 85 (rate substantially below the DCAA approved rate); *The Futures Group Int'l*, Comp. Gen. Dec. B-281274.2, 2000 CPD ¶ 147 (rates were significantly below the most recent rates). Compare *Booz-Allen & Hamilton, Inc.*, Comp. Gen. Dec. B-275934.2, 97-1 CPD ¶ 222, where it was found proper to use the five months experienced rates to project annual rates when the offeror had revised its accounting system. In that case, the contracting officer had rejected the DCAA auditor's analysis that suggested using average rates.

If an offeror agrees to place a "cap" on its indirect cost rates, it is proper to use the cap rates in determining the probable cost in making the cost realism analysis, *E.L. Hamm & Assocs., Inc.*, Comp. Gen. Dec. B-280766.5, 2000 CPD ¶ 13 (capped G&A rate); *MAR, Inc.*, Comp. Gen. Dec. B-255309.4, 94-2 CPD ¶ 19 (capped overhead rate); *Technical Res., Inc.*, Comp. Gen. Dec. B-253506, 93-2

CPD ¶ 176 (capped overhead rate); *Vitro Corp.*, Comp. Gen. Dec. B-247734.3, 92-2 CPD ¶ 202 (capped G&A rate). It has also been held that it is improper to disregard capped rates in determining the probable cost, *Veda, Inc.*, Comp. Gen. Dec. B-278516.2, 98-1 CPD ¶ 112 (contracting officer improperly disregarded proposed overhead cap in determining probable cost); *BNF Techs., Inc.*, Comp. Gen. Dec. B-254953.3, 94-1 CPD ¶ 274 (contracting officer improperly adjusted capped overhead and G&A costs above the amount of the cap). However, if the contracting officer concludes that a realistic estimate of the rates to be incurred is below the cap, that estimate can be used in lieu of the cap, *Delta Research Assocs., Inc.*, Comp. Gen. Dec. B-254006.2, 94-1 CPD ¶ 47. If the capped rates are unrealistically low, the agency should consider the risk that performing at a low will impact the contractor's financial condition, *MCT JV*, Comp. Gen. Dec. B-311245.2, 2008 CPD ¶ 121 (protest granted because agency did not consider risk of capped rates when RFP warned of such risk).

In making the cost realism analysis of indirect costs, the contracting officer may rely entirely on the computations of the cognizant auditor, *Summit Research Corp.*, Comp. Gen. Dec. B-287523, 2001 CPD ¶ 176; *ELS, Inc.*, Comp. Gen. Dec. B-283236, 99-2 CPD ¶ 92; *SRS Techs.*, Comp. Gen. Dec. B-238403, 90-1 CPD ¶ 484. See also *Geo-Centers, Inc.*, Comp. Gen. Dec. B-276033, 97-1 CPD ¶ 182, where an agency correctly accepted a new overhead structure that had been approved by the DCAA, and *Polaris, Inc.*, Comp. Gen. Dec. B-220066, 85-2 CPD ¶ 669, where an agency was found to have correctly concluded that the offeror's projected gradual reduction in overhead rates over a five-year period led to unduly low overhead rates, based on the recommendations of the DCAA. Conversely, an auditor's recommendations may be disregarded entirely if the contracting officer believes that the information is invalid, *Electronic Warfare Integration Network*, Comp. Gen. Dec. B-235814, 89-2 CPD ¶ 356.

A cost realism adjustment will not be sustained if it is based on incorrect advice from the DCAA, *General Research Corp.*, Comp. Gen. Dec. B-241569, 91-1 CPD ¶ 183. In addition, reliance on unaudited information obtained from a government auditor has been found to be unjustified where the information proves to be unreliable, *L-3 Commc'ns Corp.*, Comp. Gen. Dec. B-281784.3, 99-1 CPD ¶ 81. Compare *Intermetrics, Inc.*, Comp. Gen. Dec. B-259254.2, 95-1 CPD ¶ 215, and *Radian, Inc.*, Comp. Gen. Dec. B-256313.2, 94-2 CPD ¶ 104, sustaining cost realism adjustments based on unaudited rate checks by DCAA auditors that were based on current data.

FAR 15.407-3(b) requires contracting officers to use forward pricing rates as the basis for pricing "all contracts" during the period an agreement on such rates is in effect, unless the ACO determines that a "changed condition invalidates the agreement." See FAR 42.1701 specifying the procedures for negotiation of forward pricing rates. It is proper to use such labor and indirect cost rates in performing a cost realism analysis, *Hoboken Shipyards, Inc.*, Comp. Gen. Dec. B-219428, 85-2

CPD ¶ 416, *recons. denied*, 85-2 CPD ¶ 582. In *Jonathan Corp.*, Comp. Gen. Dec. B-230971, 88-2 CPD ¶ 133, the contracting officer used such rates in concluding that the estimated costs were too low even though the offeror attempted to demonstrate that the forward pricing rates were invalid due to changed conditions. GAO agreed with the contracting officer's conclusion, finding that the offeror had not clearly demonstrated that the rates were invalid. Similarly, in *Coleman Research Corp.*, Comp. Gen. Dec. B-278793, 98-1 CPD ¶ 111, the contracting officer properly relied on recently negotiation forward pricing rates as well as rates incurred on a prior contract in rejecting low proposed rates.

### d. Other Direct Costs

Cost realism analysis has also been used to question other direct costs proposed by offerors. For example, in *Amtec Corp.*, Comp. Gen. Dec. B-240647, 90-2 CPD ¶ 482, the contracting officer properly found the estimate of travel costs too low because the discount fares proposed by an offeror would probably not be obtainable during performance. Similarly, in *CWIS, LLC*, Comp. Gen. Dec. B-287521, 2001 CPD ¶ 119, travel costs were properly adjusted upward to reflect a requirement for trips on short notice, and in *Centra Tech., Inc.*, Comp. Gen. Dec. B-274744, 97-1 CPD ¶ 35, travel costs were properly adjust upward to reflect the costs that had been incurred by the incumbent contractor. See also *Priority One Servs., Inc.*, Comp. Gen. Dec. B-288836, 2002 CPD ¶ 79, sustaining a protest where the agency failed to reduce costs of equipment which protester had included in its estimate because it misunderstood the requirements. Compare *Abt Assocs.*, Comp. Gen. Dec. B-294130.2, 2004 CPD ¶ 220, where the agency made no adjustments to travel and per diem costs because they were in line with past experience. In *Science Applications Int'l Corp.*, Comp. Gen. Dec. B-238136.2, 90-1 CPD ¶ 517, it was found proper to accept a low rate for other direct costs when the agency, after discussions, agreed with the offeror's rationale for the low rate.

### e. Use of Analysis

As discussed above, the most common use of cost realism analysis is to determine the probable cost of performance of a cost-reimbursement contract in order to use that cost in the evaluation of the proposals and the selection of the source. It is also proper to use such analysis to reduce the probable cost of performance in a cost-reimbursement contract by negotiating a cap on G&A expenses where the cost realism analysis indicates that this element of the costs is far below expected costs, *Vitro Corp.*, Comp. Gen. Dec. B-247734.3, 92-2 CPD ¶ 202.

The cost realism analysis can also be used as a negotiating tool. If the analysis indicates that the proposed price of a fixed-price contract or the estimated cost of a cost-reimbursement contract is low, the offeror can be alerted to the problem in the written or oral discussion. This provides a better understanding of the basis for the price or estimated cost and may identify problems such as mistakes or lack of understanding of the requirements of the RFP. It may also lead to a revised price or estimated cost in the offeror's BAFO. See *Abt Assocs. Inc.*, Comp. Gen. Dec. B-295449, 2005 CPD ¶ 54, where the contracting officer followed this procedure with the result that the winning offeror revised its cost proposal to meet the agency's realism criteria — leading to GAO denying a protest claiming that the cost realism analysis was not reasonable.

When a cost realism analysis indicates that the probable costs of performance are significantly higher that the offeror's estimate, the agency can also downgrade the technical or management evaluation, *Fort Carson Support Servs. v. United States*, 71 Fed. Cl. 571 (2006). The low cost estimate might demonstrate a lack of understanding of the work, *Chesapeake & Potomac Tel. Co.*, GSBCA 9297-P, 90-1 BCA ¶ 22,335. It could also signal significant risks in terms of future performance, *Cubic Field Servs., Inc.*, Comp. Gen. Dec. B-247780, 92-1 CPD ¶ 525 (proposed cap on costs of performance of cost-reimbursement contract created risk of nonperformance); *Modern Techs. Corp.*, Comp. Gen. Dec. B-236961.4, 90-1 CPD ¶ 301 (extended workweek created substantial risk offeror would be unable to hire and retain stable workforce); *Culver Health Corp.*, Comp. Gen. Dec. B-242902, 91-1 CPD ¶ 556 (low rates of compensation of proposed employees created risk of poor performance). Compare *Harris Corp. v. United States*, 628 F. Supp. 813 (D.D.C. 1986), where the court held that it was improper to downgrade a proposal merely because the offeror had made a decision to absorb some costs of performance. See also *VSE Corp.*, Comp. Gen. Dec. B-247610.2, 92-2 CPD ¶ 81, where GAO held that the contracting officer had acted properly in not downgrading an offeror's technical and management proposal; the proposed labor rates were lower than the government's estimate, but analysis indicated that they did not detract from the offeror's ability to perform the work. On the other hand, GAO granted a protest in *Serco, Inc.*, Comp. Gen. Dec. B-298266, 2006 CPD ¶ 120, because the agency had not considered whether the low number of labor hours proposed by an offeror indicated that it did not understand the work.

## 2. Determining Price Reasonableness

Cost analysis using cost element breakdowns and other data on the offeror's prospective costs of performance can also be used to determine if the price of a fixed-price contract is fair and reasonable. The analysis in these circumstances is substantially the same as that made for cost realism. Here, however, the focus is on whether the price is too high. See *TAAS Israel Indus., Ltd.*, Comp. Gen. Dec. B-260733, 95-2 CPD ¶ 23, agreeing that a valid price reasonableness determination was made when the contracting officer used detailed cost element breakdowns from two competitors to perform the analysis. A similar result was reached in *Family Realty*, Comp. Gen. Dec. B-247772, 92-2 CPD ¶ 6. Cost data can also be used to make a performance risk assessment. See *General Elec. Co.*, 55 Comp. Gen. 1450 (B-

186372), 76-2 CPD ¶ 269, where the source selection official concluded that there was performance risk because the contractor had not submitted detailed cost data supporting the reduced price in its BAFO, and *Systems & Processes Eng'g Corp.*, Comp. Gen. Dec. B-234142, 89-1 CPD ¶ 441, where cost data indicated a low price and, thus, a risk of inability to perform.

The contracting officer enjoys considerable discretion in deciding how much cost data to obtain and how to make use of such cost data in these circumstances. See, for example, *Allied-Signal Aerospace Co.*, Comp. Gen. Dec. B-249214.4, 93-1 CPD ¶ 109, where GAO held that an agency was not required to make a comparative analysis of each element of each offeror's detailed cost estimates. GAO stated that instructing the offerors to submit cost estimates at the work breakdown level did not obligate the agency to analyze that information "in any greater detail than was necessary to assure the realism of the cost proposals." See also *Communications Int'l, Inc.*, Comp. Gen. Dec. B-246076, 92-1 CPD ¶ 194, where the sum of work element cost estimates, rather than the total cost estimate, was properly used in the evaluation and the contracting officer was not required to reopen discussions to reconcile disparity between the two.

## C. Should-Cost Analysis

A selective form of cost analysis used primarily on major procurements is should-cost analysis. This process is described in FAR 15.407-4(a), as follows:

> (1) Should-cost reviews are a specialized form of cost analysis. Should-cost reviews differ from traditional evaluation methods because they do not assume that a contractor's historical costs reflect efficient and economical operation. Instead, these reviews evaluate the economy and efficiency of the contractor's existing workforce, methods, materials, facilities, operating systems, and management. These reviews are accomplished by a multi-functional team of Government contracting, contract administration, pricing, audit, and engineering representatives. The objective of should-cost reviews is to promote both short and long-range improvements in the contractor's economy and efficiency in order to reduce the cost of performance of Government contracts. In addition, by providing rationale for any recommendations and quantifying their impact on cost, the Government will be better able to develop realistic objectives for negotiation.

See also DFARS PGI 215.407-4(b)(2) stating that should-cost reviews should be considered on major systems acquisitions. Should-cost analysis has been used most often on major contracts for the manufacture of high-priced equipment. It requires a detailed industrial engineering analysis of the specific methods used by the contractor to manufacture the product and a determination of more cost-effective methods that will reduce the costs. In this regard, it is significantly different than conventional cost analysis because it challenges not the offeror's projections of current costs but, rather, the necessity for incurring those costs. Congress has occasionally expressed interest in increasing the use of should-cost analysis. See § 915 of the

Defense Procurement Improvement Act of 1985, Pub. L. No. 99-145, requiring a report to Congress on the amount of should-cost analysis performed on sole source manufacturing contracts for weapon systems.

## D.  Methods for Expediting Analysis

In the case of contractors performing numerous government contracts, proposals are being submitted and analyzed on a regular basis. Since many of the elements of cost, such as labor and indirect cost rates, are the same regardless of the contract for which the costs are incurred, repetitive analysis is unnecessary. An agency's cost analysis can also be greatly expedited if the parties are in agreement on the basic estimating system used by the contractor. The regulations give guidance on these techniques for expediting cost analysis.

### 1.  Forward Pricing Rate Agreements

FAR 15.407-3 recognizes that major contractors frequently enter into forward pricing rate agreements with elements of the Department of Defense. These agreements are negotiated by administrative contracting officers and may cover indirect cost rates or labor rates. FAR 15.407-3(b) requires contracting officers to use the rates in these agreements "as bases for pricing all contracts, modifications, and other contractual actions" and to report conditions that would affect the agreement's validity to the administrative contracting officer. DFARS 215.407-3(b) recognizes that such agreements can be "waived" by the head of a contracting activity but requires that such waivers be reported to the cognizant administrative contracting officer.

Because the labor and indirect cost rates covered by these agreements are subject to fluctuation at any time based on the costs being incurred by the contractor, these agreements must be closely monitored to ensure that they contain valid rates. However, if the administrative contracting officer and the cognizant auditor regularly monitor them and renegotiate the rates quickly when new data call for such modification, these agreements can greatly reduce the effort needed to complete a cost analysis and negotiate a price. If the agreement covers all labor and indirect cost elements of the contractor's estimating system, only direct labor hours and material will require analysis on an individual basis. This can greatly expedite the procurement process.

### 2.  Estimating System Reports

FAR 15.407-5 provides that "cognizant audit activities" will establish regular programs for reviewing estimating systems used by contractors. The purpose of such a review is to identify deficiencies in contractor's estimating systems so that they can be addressed and corrected. Ultimately, this process is intended to lead to complete agreement on an estimating system with resultant reduction in the audit necessary on any proposal. Each estimating system review is to be documented by a report from the audit activity.

FAR 15.407-5(b) calls for the following procedure:

> The auditor shall send a copy of the estimating system survey report and a copy of the official notice of corrective action required to each contracting office and contract administration office having substantial business with that contractor. Significant deficiencies not corrected by the contractor shall be a consideration in subsequent proposal analyses and negotiations.

DFARS 215.407-5-70(b)(2)(i) requires all large business contractors with DoD prime contracts or subcontracts totalling $ 50 million or more for which cost or pricing data are required to meet detailed estimating system requirements. The details of this program are contained in the Cost Estimating System Requirements clause in DFARS 252.215-7002 . The intent of this requirement is to ensure that such contractors have estimating systems that produce accurate, documented estimates of the cost of future work. See DCAM 5-1200 for additional guidance in this area.

A deficiency in an offeror's estimating system would logically require the contracting officer to make a more thorough cost realism analysis of the area where the system is found to be deficient. See *Metro Mach. Corp.*, Comp. Gen. Dec. B-402567, 2010 CPD ¶ 132, denying a protest where the agency performed a detailed review of the indirect cost rates that had been based on an estimating system that had been reported by DCAA as a failed system.

### 3. Purchasing System Reviews

FAR 44.305-1 makes administrative contracting officers responsible for approving contractors' purchasing systems based on reviews of such systems. FAR 44.301 states the objective of purchasing system reviews as follows:

> The objective of a contractor purchasing system review (CPSR) is to evaluate the efficiency and effectiveness with which the contractor spends Government funds and complies with Government policy when subcontracting. The review provides the administrative contracting officer (ACO) a basis for granting, withholding, or withdrawing approval of the contractor's purchasing system.

The cognizant administrative contracting officer is also required to "ensure that the contractor is effectively managing its purchasing program," FAR 44.304(a). Detailed guidance on the procedures to be followed in making purchasing system reviews is contained in DFARS 244.305-70.

If a procuring agency determines that a prospective contractor has an approved purchasing system, there is less need to delve into how effectively that offeror performs the purchasing function in making a cost analysis. This, of course, does not relieve the contracting officer in that agency from the necessity to analyze the proposed costs of material and subcontracts on a specific acquisition.

## VI. NEGOTIATION OF PROFIT

In negotiated procurements where cost is negotiated separately, the parties must also negotiate the profit that will be included in the price. This occurs primarily in situations where no significant competition has been obtained. In cost-reimbursement contracts, this profit will be stated separately in the contract as a fixed fee (in a CPFF contract), a base fee (in a CPAF contract), or a target fee (in a CPIF contract). In fixed-price contracts, this profit will either be included in the price or stated as a target fee (in an FPI contract). In agencies with major procurement programs, the contracting officer is subject to specific regulatory guidance on the techniques that are to be used to determine the government's negotiation position with regard to profit.

### A. Fee Limitations

There are similar statutory limitations on the rates of fee that can be negotiated in CPFF contracts in both the Armed Services Procurement Act, 10 U.S.C. § 2306(d), and the Federal Property and Administrative Services Act, 41 U.S.C. § 3905(b). They prohibit fees greater than 10% of the estimated cost of all CPFF contracts except those for "experimental, developmental, or research work" where the limitation is 15%. They also contain limitations on the amount an architect-engineers can be paid as discussed in Chapter 7.

These statutes have several features. First, the statutes apply to the rate of fee *negotiated*, not the rate of fee actually *earned* by the contractor through performance of the contract. In this regard, the rate is limited in terms of a percentage of the estimated cost of the contract as determined by the "agency head" at the outset, *Fluor Enters., Inc. v. United States*, 64 Fed. Cl. 461 (2005); *CACI, Inc. — Federal*, Comp. Gen. Dec. B-216516, 85-1 CPD ¶ 363. GAO has ruled that when a settlement of an aborted cost-reimbursement contract is negotiated, the statute must be applied to limit the total fee paid in settlement, but the agency is not required to impose the percentage limitation on each part of the work performed, *National Visitors Ctr.*, Comp. Gen. Dec. B-158792, 80-1 CPD ¶ 121. Second, the statutes apply by their precise terms to only CPFF contracts and not to other types of cost-reimbursement contracts. Thus, the provisions do not apply to CPIF contracts. This rule is set forth in DoD/NASA Incentive Contracting Guide, October 1969 (*https://acc.dau. mil/GetAttachment.aspx?id=189615&pname=file&aid=32537&lang=en-US*). For many years, the FAR imposed 10% and 15% limitations on the maximum fees computed as a percentage of estimated or target cost of CPAF and CPIF contracts but these limitations were deleted by FAC 97-02, Sept. 30, 1997.

In one case, the Court of Claims applied this statute in an unusual way in holding that the government was not bound by a contract containing a fee arrangement that violated the statute. In *Yosemite Park & Curry Co. v. United States*, 217 Ct. Cl. 360, 582 F.2d 552 (1978), the parties had entered into a transportation contract that compensated the contractor for the cost of providing bus service plus a fee at the rate of 12% of the contractor's gross investment in equipment to perform the contract. The court held that the contract was a CPFF contract that was invalid because the fee resulted in an amount greater than 10 % of the estimated costs of performance of the contract. Thus, a fee not based directly on costs of performance but yielding a rate higher than permitted by the statute may be found to be in violation of the statute. In *Yosemite Park*, the court further held that the contractor was entitled to be paid for the value of the services rendered to the government not exceeding "the entire, total, provable costs" of performance plus 10% of these costs. It is interesting to note that this judgment permitted a larger payment than is permitted by the fee limitation statute.

## B. Profit Negotiation Techniques

The techniques used to establish the government's negotiating position on profit have varied among the procuring agencies. In the 1950s and 1960s, contracting officers were given complete discretion to negotiate profits with contractors; the regulations merely contained a list of the factors that should be considered in such negotiation. In 1964, the DoD adopted the "weighted guidelines" approach to profit negotiation, requiring their contracting officers to follow a prescribed formula in analyzing the profit to be negotiated and arriving at a prenegotiation position. The weighted guidelines formula was revised extensively in the 1970s to give greater recognition to facilities employed by contractors in the performance of contracts. During this period, the civilian agencies continued to give their contracting officers greater latitude. In December 1980, OFPP issued Policy Letter 80-7, 45 Fed. Reg. 82,593, requiring that all agencies making noncompetitive awards over $100,000 adopt a "structured approach" to profit negotiation when these awards total $50 million or more each year. This policy letter was subsequently canceled, but the policy is now included in FAR 15.404-4. This policy requires all agencies with significant procurement functions to follow an approach similar to the DoD's weighted guidelines but permit each agency to tailor its formula to the particular programs of the agency. The DoD subsequently conducted another profit study, the Defense Financial and Investment Review (DFAIR), June 1985, and adopted a new weighted guidelines formula in August 1987. This newer formula departs from the FAR guidance in significant ways but has never been challenged.

### 1. Goal of Structured Approach

The original weighted guidelines approach was based on a detailed study of the negotiation of profit in the DoD. The study found that the rates of profit and fee negotiated were almost the same regardless of the complexity of the work, the past performance of the contractor, or variations in other elements that might be considered relevant to the amount of profit included in the contract. It was concluded that a new procedure was needed to force contracting officers to use a profit negotiation process that recognized these different aspects of procurements. A major goal was to use profit to encourage good performance and penalize bad performance. FAR 15.404-4(a) now contains the following general guidance:

> (1) Profit or fee prenegotiation objectives do not necessarily represent net income to contractors. Rather, they represent that element of the potential total remuneration that contractors may receive for contract performance over and above allowable costs. This potential remuneration element and the Government's estimate of allowable costs to be incurred in contract performance together equal the Government's total prenegotiation objective. Just as actual costs may vary from estimated costs, the contractor's actual realized profit or fee may vary from negotiated profit or fee, because of such factors as efficiency of performance, incurrence of costs the Government does not recognize as allowable, and the contract type.

> (2) It is in the Government's interest to offer contractors opportunities for financial rewards sufficient to stimulate efficient contract performance, attract the best capabilities of qualified large and small business concerns to Government contracts, and maintain a viable industrial base.

> (3) Both the Government and contractors should be concerned with profit as a motivator of efficient and effective contract performance. Negotiations aimed merely at reducing prices by reducing profit, without proper recognition of the function of profit, are not in the Government's interest. Negotiation of extremely low profits, use of historical averages, or automatic application of predetermined percentages to total estimated costs do not provide proper motivation for optimum contract performance.

Since each structured approach imposes a formula on contracting officers, their discretion is significantly limited. The goal is to make profit determination considerably more objective than it has been in the past. However, there is no indication in any of the regulations that the objective is binding on either the contractor or the government. The profit or fee to be used in the contract is subject to free bargaining and is ultimately determined in the negotiation process, where the contracting officer has a substantial amount of discretion. Some regulations require that contracting officers document their profit analysis in the contract file. See, for example, DFARS 215.404-4 (c)(2)(E), NFS 1815.404-4(c)(2), and DEAR 915.404-4-70-3.

Agencies also retain considerable flexibility under the FAR policy. Thus, they may accommodate different policy objectives by varying the elements of their formula and the weights given to each element.

## 2. Applicability of Structured Approach

Although FAR 15.404-4(b)(1)(i) states that agencies must use a structured approach to fee determination in all procurements where cost analysis is required, agencies generally do not use such approach when the agency is conducting a competitive procurement where the only significant analysis is a cost realism analysis. See DFARS 215.404-4(b)(1) stating that the approach must be used when cost or pricing data is obtained, DFARS 215.404-4(c)(1) stating that the approach should not be used when making a cost realism analysis on competitive procurements, and NFS 1815.404-4(b)(1)(i)(a)(1) stating that the structured approach should be used when the contract is "awarded on the basis of other than full and open competition."

From the outset, it has been recognized that a structured approach is not applicable to all types of procurements, and FAR 15.404-4(b)(1)(ii) permits agencies to make exceptions to their policies. DFARS 215.404-4(c)(2)(C) states that the contracting officer may use an alternate structured approach (see 215.404-73) when

(1) The contract action is —

(i) At or below the cost or pricing data threshold (see FAR 15.403-4(a)(1);

(ii) For architect-engineer or construction work;

(iii) Primarily for delivery of material from subcontractors; or

(iv) A termination settlement; or

(2) The weighted guidelines method does not produce a reasonable overall profit objective and the head of the contracting activity approves use of the alternate approach in writing.

A similar list of exceptions is included in NFS 1815.404-4(b)(1)(ii), and DEAR 915.404-4-70-4(b).

## 3. Procedure

The structured approach to profit determination is a procedure used by the contracting officer to arrive at a "prenegotiation objective" on the profit that will be used in negotiations with the contractor, FAR 15.404-4(a). The regulations require the contracting officer to calculate this objective but contain very little guidance on the procedures to be used to obtain the information necessary to make this calculation. See DEAR 915.404-4(d), which states:

> The contracting officer's analysis of these prescribed factors is based on information available prior to negotiations. Such information is furnished in proposals, audit data, performance reports, preaward surveys and the like.

See also DFARS 215.404-4(c)(5) which permits contractors to furnish specific information in proposals:

[T]he contracting officer may encourage the contractor to —

(1) Present the details of its proposed profit amounts in the weighted guidelines format or similar structured approach; and

(2) Use the weighted guidelines format in developing profit objectives for negotiated subcontracts.

See, however, FAR 15.404-4(c)(5), which prohibits contracting officers from *requiring* contractors to submit such information.

In all of the structured profit approaches, the profit objective is determined by separately analyzing each factor in the formula and computing the dollars of profit for that factor. The contracting officer then totals the dollars of profit for each factor to arrive at the profit objective. When these policies were implemented in the 1980s, a number of agencies adopted forms in their FAR supplements with accompanying short explanations. However, most of the forms have been taken out of the procurement regulations and placed in agency acquisition manuals. The Departments of Energy has removed its form entirely but has placed detailed guidance on applying the factors in the Department of Energy Acquisition Guide (*management.energy. gov/policy_guidance/Acquisition_Guide.htm*). The current forms are:

| AGENCY | FORM |
|---|---|
| Department of Defense | DD Form 1547 |
| National Aeronautics & Space Admin. | NASA Form 634 |
| General Services Administration | GSA Form 1766 |
| Department of Homeland Security | DHS Form 700-17 |
| Department of Transportation | DOT Form 4220.32 |

Most of the computations in the structured approaches that have been used in the past are based on the anticipated costs of performance of the work. FAR 15.404-4(c)(3) provides that the contracting officer will use the government prenegotiation cost objective amounts as the basis for calculating the profit objective. The result is that the contracting officer's profit objective is based on the government's analysis of the costs of performance rather than the contractor's proposed costs. If the costs are changed significantly during negotiation, an adjustment in the government's negotiated profit objective is appropriate.

## 4.  Profit Factors

While the FAR contains no prescribed formula, FAR 15.404-4(d)(1) does require all agencies to include, at a minimum, six factors in their structured approach:

(1) contractor effort;

(2) contract cost risk;

(3) federal socioeconomic programs;

(4) capital investments;

(5) cost control and other past accomplishments; and

(6) independent development.

These were the factors in the original DoD weighted guidelines formula which were adopted by the civilian agencies that implemented the OFPP Policy Letter and the FAR in the 1980s. The civilian agencies that still prescribe the use of most of these factors are the Department of Energy, the Department of Homeland Security, the Department of Transportation, and the General Services Administration. See DEAR 915.404-4-70-2(d) and the Department of Energy Acquisition Guide; the Homeland Security Acquisition Manual (HSAM) 3015.404-4, Appendix A (*www.uscg.mil/hq/cg9/procurement/pdf/Consolidated HSAMDEC2006withNotice07-01.pdf*); the Transportation Acquisition Manual (TAM) (*www.dot.gov/ost/m60/earl/tam.htm*); and the GSA Acquisition Manual (GSAM) 515.404-4(d) (*www.acquisition.gov/gsam/gsam.html*). The following detailed explanation of the proper implementation of these requirements uses material from the Armed Services Pricing Manual (ASPM) that was issued in 1986 because it contains the best explanation of how these factors should be utilized. However, the policy of each civilian agency must be carefully scrutinized to determine when it has adopted some element of the current DoD weighted guidelines technique.

The current DoD profit policy, adopted in 1987, dropped a number of these techniques and substituted new techniques. This policy is set forth in DFARS 215.404-71. See DFARS 215.404-4(d)(1) explaining that the "common factors (the six FAR factors) are embodied in the DoD structured approaches and need not be further considered by the contracting officer." In late 1999, NASA adopted a new profit policy that uses the first two elements of the DoD policy and some elements of the old policy. See NFS 1815.404-471. The following detailed explanation of the proper implementation of these requirements uses material from these regulations because they contain the best guidance on the application of the factors.

| RECORD OF WEIGHTED GUIDELINES APPLICATION | | | | | | | REPORT CONTROL SYMBOL DD-AT&L(Q)1751 | |
|---|---|---|---|---|---|---|---|---|

| 1. REPORT NO. | 2. BASIC PROCUREMENT INSTRUMENT IDENTIFICATION NO. | | | | 3. SPIIN | 4. DATE OF ACTION | |
|---|---|---|---|---|---|---|---|
| | a. PURCHASING OFFICE | b. FY | c. TYPE PROC INST CODE | d. PRISN | | a. YEAR | b. MONTH |

| 5. CONTRACTING OFFICE CODE | ITEM | COST CATEGORY | OBJECTIVE |
|---|---|---|---|
| 6. NAME OF CONTRACTOR | 13. | MATERIAL | |
| | 14. | SUBCONTRACTS | |
| 7. DUNS NUMBER / 8. FEDERAL SUPPLY CODE | 15. | DIRECT LABOR | |
| | 16. | INDIRECT EXPENSES | |
| 9. DOD CLAIMANT PROGRAM / 10. CONTRACT TYPE CODE | 17. | OTHER DIRECT CHARGES | |
| | 18. | SUBTOTAL COSTS (13 thru 17) | 0 |
| 11. TYPE EFFORT / 12. USE CODE | 19. | GENERAL AND ADMINISTRATIVE | |
| | 20. | TOTAL COSTS (18 + 19) | 0 |

**WEIGHTED GUIDELINES PROFIT FACTORS**

| ITEM | CONTRACTOR RISK FACTORS | ASSIGNED WEIGHTING | ASSIGNED VALUE | BASE (Item 20) | PROFIT OBJECTIVE |
|---|---|---|---|---|---|
| 21. | TECHNICAL | % | | | |
| 22. | MANAGEMENT/COST CONTROL | % | | | |
| 23. | PERFORMANCE RISK (COMPOSITE) | | | | |
| 24. | CONTRACT TYPE RISK | | | | |

| | | COSTS FINANCED | LENGTH FACTOR | INTEREST RATE | |
|---|---|---|---|---|---|
| 25. | WORKING CAPITAL | | | % | |

| | CONTRACTOR FACILITIES CAPITAL EMPLOYED | ASSIGNED VALUE | AMOUNT EMPLOYED | |
|---|---|---|---|---|
| 26. | LAND | | | |
| 27. | BUILDINGS | | | |
| 28. | EQUIPMENT | | | |

| | | ASSIGNED VALUE | BASE (Item 20) | |
|---|---|---|---|---|
| 29. | COST EFFICIENCY FACTOR | % | | |

| 30. | TOTAL PROFIT OBJECTIVE | 0.00 |
|---|---|---|

**NEGOTIATED SUMMARY**

| | | PROPOSED | OBJECTIVE | NEGOTIATED |
|---|---|---|---|---|
| 31. | TOTAL COSTS | | | |
| 32. | FACILITIES CAPITAL COST OF MONEY (DD Form 1861) | | | |
| 33. | PROFIT | | | |
| 34. | TOTAL PRICE (Line 31 + 32 + 33) | 0 | 0.00 | 0 |
| 35. | MARKUP RATE (Line 32 + 33 divided by 31) | % | % | % |

**CONTRACTING OFFICER APPROVAL**

| 36. TYPED/PRINTED NAME OF CONTRACTING OFFICER (Last, First, Middle Initial) | 37. SIGNATURE OF CONTRACTING OFFICER | 38. TELEPHONE NO. | 39. DATE SUBMITTED (YYYYMMDD) |
|---|---|---|---|

**OPTIONAL USE**

| 96. | 97. | 98. | 99. |
|---|---|---|---|

**DD FORM 1547, JUL 2002**     PREVIOUS EDITION IS OBSOLETE.     Reset

**Figure 10-3**

| ![NASA] National Aeronautics and Space Administration | **Structured Approach Profit/Fee Objective** | |
|---|---|---|
| 1. CONTRACTOR | 4. RFP/CONTRACT NUMBER | |
| 2. BUSINESS UNIT | 5. CONTRACT TYPE | |
| 3. ADDRESS | | |

| CONTRACTOR EFFORT | | |
|---|---|---|
| **COST CATEGORY** | | **OBJECTIVE** |
| 6. MATERIAL (Less direct charged contractor acquired property categorized as equipment. See FAR 15.404-4(c)(3)) | | $ |
| 7. SUBCONTRACTS | | |
| 8. DIRECT LABOR | | |
| 9. INDIRECT EXPENSES | | |
| 10. OTHER DIRECT CHARGES | | |
| 11. SUBTOTAL COSTS | | $ |
| 12. GENERAL AND ADMINISTRATIVE | | $ |
| 13. SUBTOTAL (Base used to calculate Profit/Fee) | | $ |
| 14. COST OF MONEY | | $ |
| 15. TOTAL COST OBJECTIVE | | $ |

| WEIGHTED GUIDELINE PROFIT FACTORS | | | | | |
|---|---|---|---|---|---|
| **PERFORMANCE RISK FACTOR** | **(a) ASSIGNED WEIGHTING** | **(b) ASSIGNED VALUE** (Range = 4% to 8% normal = 6%) | **(c) CALCULATED %** | **(d) BASE** (From Block 13) | **(e) PROFIT/FEE OBJECTIVE** |
| 16. TECHNICAL | | | | | |
| 17. MANAGEMENT | | | | | |
| 18. COST CONTROL | | | | | |
| TOTAL ASSIGNED WEIGHT (100%) | | | | | |
| 19. COMPOSITE PERFORMANCE RISK | Line above must = 100% | | | $ | $ |
| 20. CONTRACT TYPE RISK (See Instructions for range) | | | ASSIGNED VALUE | | |
| | | | | $ | $ |
| 21. WORKING CAPITAL (See Instructions for range) | COSTS FINANCED | | LENGTH FACTOR | INTEREST FACTOR | |
| | $ | | | | $ |

| OTHER CONSIDERATIONS | | WEIGHT RANGE (Max of 5% Total) | WEIGHT DESIGNATED | BASE | |
|---|---|---|---|---|---|
| 22. PAST PERFORMANCE (within last 3 yrs) | | -1% TO +1% | | | |
| 23. SOCIO-ECONOMIC, ENVIRONMENTAL, PUBLIC POLICY IMPLEMENTATION | | -.5% TO +.5% | | | |
| 24. CORPORATE CAPITAL INVESTMENT | | 0% TO +1% | | | |
| 25. UNUSUAL UNPLANNED GFP USEAGE | | -1% TO 0% | | | |
| 26. OTHER INNOVATIONS & EFFICIENCIES | | DISCRETIONARY | | | |
| SUBTOTAL OTHER CONSIDERATIONS | | MAX TOTAL = 5% | | $ | $ |
| | | | | 27. TOTAL PROFIT OBJECTIVE | $ |

| COMPOSITE COMPARISONS | |
|---|---|
| 28. FEE % OF TOTAL COST | |
| 29. FEE % OF TOTAL COST (Without cost of money) | |

**NASA FORM 634** APR 11  PREVIOUS EDITIONS ARE OBSOLETE.                    NRRS 5/1A1(a)

Figure 10-4 (cont'd on next page)

## INSTRUCTIONS

**PERFORMANCE RISK: Normal Value: 6% Range: 4% to 8%.**

### TECHNICAL

**ABOVE NORMAL CONDITIONS:**
A. Developing or applying advanced technologies;
B. Manufacturing specifications with stringent tolerance limits;
C. Use of highly skilled personnel or state-of-the-art machinery;
D. Important services/analytical efforts with exacting standards;
E. Independent development/investment reduces risk or cost;
F. Accelerated delivery schedule; or
G. Warranty provisions add risk.

**MAXIMUM VALUE CONDITIONS:**
A. Personnel with exceptional abilities, experience, professional credentials for extremely complex, vital efforts with difficult technical obstacles
B. New item development/initial production, esp. with tight performance/ quality specifications;
C. High degree of development or production concurrency.

**BELOW NORMAL CONDITIONS:**
A. Acquisition is for off-the-shelf items;
B. Requirements are relatively simple;
C. Technology is not complex;
D. Efforts do not require highly skilled personnel;
E. Efforts are routine;
F. Follow-on or repetitive type acquisition.

**MINIMUM VALUE CONDITIONS:**
A. Routine services;
B. Production of simple items;
C. Rote entry or routine integration of Govt-furnished information; or
D. Simple operations with Govt-furnished property.

### MANAGEMENT

**ABOVE NORMAL CONDITIONS:**
A. Considerable & reasonably difficult value added;
B. High degree of integration & coordination.

**MAXIMUM VALUE CONDITIONS:**
A. Large scale integration of most complex nature;
B. Major international activities with significant management coordination; or
C. Critically important milestones.

**BELOW NORMAL CONDITIONS:**
A. Mature program with many end item deliveries completed;
B. Contractor adds minimum value;
C. Efforts routine & require minimal supervision;
D. Inadequate analysis of subcontractor costs; or
E. Uncooperative in evaluation & negotiation of proposal.

**MINIMUM VALUE CONDITIONS:**
A. Field administration office reviews disclose unsatisfactory management & internal control systems; or
B. Unusually low degree of management involvement required.

### COST CONTROL

**ABOVE NORMAL CONDITIONS:**
A. Aggressive cost reduction program with demonstrable benefits;
B. High degree of subcontract competition (e.g., aggressive dual sourcing); or
C. Proven record of cost tracking & control.

**BELOW NORMAL CONDITIONS:**
A. Marginal cost estimating system;
B. Minimal effort to initiate cost reduction programs;
C. Inadequate cost proposal; or
D. Record of cost overruns, indication of unreliable cost estimates or lack of cost control.

## CONTRACT TYPE RISK

| | Notes | Normal Value (%) | Designation Range % |
|---|---|---|---|
| Firm-fixed-price (FFP), no financing | (1) | 5.00 | 4 to 6 |
| FFP w/ performance-based payments | (6) | 4.00 | 2.5 to 5.5 |
| FFP w/ progress payments (2) 4 3 to 5 | (2) | 3.00 | 2 to 4 |
| Fixed-price-incentive (FPI), no financing | (1) | 3.00 | 2 to 4 |
| FPI w/ performance-based payments | (6) | 2.00 | .5 to 3.5 |
| Fixed-price, redeterminable | (3) | | |
| FPI w/ progress payments | (2) | 1.00 | 0 to 2 |
| Cost-plus-incentive-fee | (4) | 1.00 | 0 to 2 |
| Cost-plus-award-fee | (4) | 0.75 | 0 to 1.5 |
| Cost-plus-fixed-fee | (5) | 0.50 | 0 to 1 |
| Time-and-materials | (5) | 0.50 | 0 to 1 |
| Labor-hour | (5) | 0.50 | 0 to 1 |
| FFP, level-of-effort, term | (5) | 0.50 | 0 to 1 |

(1) "No financing" means none or limited progress or performance based payments. Do not compute working capital adjustment.
(2) When progress payments are present, compute a working capital adjustment.
(3) Treat as FPI with below normal provisions
(4) Cost-plus contracts - no working capital adjustment.
(5) Treat as CPFF for assigning profit values.
(6) Do not compute working capital adjustment w/ performance-based payments.

### EVALUATION CRITERIA

**MANDATORY:** Extent of costs incurred prior to definitization. If substantial, a value as low as 0 may be assigned regardless of contract type.

**ABOVE NORMAL CONDITIONS:**
I. Minimal cost history;
II. Long-term contracts without provisions protecting contractor, esp. when there is considerable economic uncertainty;
III. Incentive provisions which place high degree of risk on contractor;
IV. Performance-based payments total less than maximum allowable amount; or
V. Aggressive performance-based payment schedule that increases risk.

**BELOW NORMAL CONDITIONS:**
I. Very mature product line with extensive cost history;
II. Relatively short-term contracts;
III. Contractual provisions substantially reduce contractor risk;
IV. Incentive provisions place a low amount of risk on contractor; or
V. Routine performance-based payment schedule w/ minimal risk.

### WORKING CAPITAL ADJUSTMENT
(Applies to FFP w/ progress Payments ONLY)

**COSTS FINANCED:** Equals total costs multiplied by % of costs financed.

**CONTRACT LENGTH FACTOR:** Time necessary to complete substantive portion of work versus time between contract award & final delivery.

| Performance Period (months) | Contract Length Factor |
|---|---|
| 21 or less | 0.40 |
| 22 to 27 | 0.65 |
| 28-33 | 0.90 |
| 34 to 39 | 1.15 |
| 40 or more | 1.40 |

NOTE: Adjustment must not exceed 2%.

**Figure 10-4 (cont'd from previous page)**

## STRUCTURED APPROACH PROFIT/FEE OBJECTIVE

| CONTRACTOR | RFP/CONTRACT NO. |
|---|---|
| BUSINESS UNIT | CONTRACT TYPE |
| ADDRESS | |

### CONTRACTOR EFFORT

| 1. COST CATEGORY | GOVERNMENT'S COST OBJECTIVE (a) | WEIGHT RANGE (b) | ASSIGNED WEIGHT (c) | WEIGHTED PROFIT/FEE ((a) x (c)) (d) |
|---|---|---|---|---|
| MATERIAL ACQUISITION | | 1% TO 4% | | |
| DIRECT LABOR | | 4% TO 12% | | |
| OVERHEAD | | 3% TO 8% | | |
| OTHER COSTS | | 1% TO 3% | | |
| GENERAL MANAGEMENT (G & A) | | 4% TO 8% | | |
| 1A. TOTAL | | | | |

### OTHER FACTORS

| 2. FACTOR | MEASUREMENT BASE (a) | WEIGHT RANGE (b) | ASSIGNED WEIGHT (c) | WEIGHT PROFIT/FEE 1.A (a) x (c) (d) |
|---|---|---|---|---|
| COST RISK | | 0 TO 7% | | |
| INVESTMENT | | -2% TO +2% | | |
| PERFORMANCE | TOTAL COST OBJECTIVE 1. A (a) | -2% TO +2% | | |
| SOCIO-ECONOMIC PROGRAMS | | -.5% TO + 5% | | |
| SPECIAL SITUATIONS | | -2% TO +2% | | |
| 2A TOTAL OTHER FACTORS | | | | |
| 3. SUBTOTAL PROFIT/FEE LINES (1.A) + (2.A) | | | | |
| 4. LESS FACILITIES CAPITAL COST OF MONEY | | | - | |
| 5. TOTAL PROFIT/FEE OBJECTIVE LINE (3) - (4) | | | | |

| | |
|---|---|
| GENERAL SERVICES ADMINISTRATION | GSA FORM 1766 (11-82) |

Figure 10-5

DEPARTMENT OF HOMELAND SECURITY
## WEIGHTED GUIDELINES PROFIT/FEE OBJECTIVE
(See Instructions in HSAM
Chapter 3015, Appendix J)

| 1. CONTRACTOR IDENTIFICATION | a. COMPANY NAME | | | b. DIVISION NAME *(If Any)* | |
|---|---|---|---|---|---|
| | c. STREET ADDRESS | | d. CITY | e. STATE | f. ZIP CODE |

| 2. WEIGHTED GUIDELINES CATEGORY *(Check One)* | 3. TYPE OF CONTRACT |
|---|---|
| ☐ MANUFACTURING  ☐ RESEARCH & DEVELOPMENT  ☐ SERVICES | |

| 4. BASIC PROCUREMENT INSTRUMENT IDENTIFICATION NO. | | | | 5. SPECIALIST NAME |
|---|---|---|---|---|
| a. PURCHASING OFFICE | b. FISCAL YEAR | c. C/S PROD/SVCS CODE | d. PR NO. | |

**6. WEIGHTED GUIDELINES PROFIT FACTORS**

| PROFIT/FEE FACTOR OR SUBFACTOR (a) | MEASURE-MENT BASE (b) | PROFIT WAGE RANGES | | | ASSIGNED WEIGHT (%) (f) | PROFIT/FEE DOLLARS (g) |
|---|---|---|---|---|---|---|
| | | MFG (%) (c) | R&D (%) (d) | SVCS (%) (e) | | |
| **PART 1 - CONTRACTOR EFFORT** | | | | | | |
| 7. MATERIAL ACQUISITION a. SUBCONTRACTED ITEMS | | 1 TO 5 | 1 TO 5 | 1 TO 5 | | |
| b. PURCHASED PARTS | | 1 TO 4 | 1 TO 4 | 1 TO 4 | | |
| c. OTHER MATERIAL | | 1 TO 4 | 1 TO 4 | 1 TO 4 | | |
| 8. ENGINEERING a. DIRECT LABOR | | 9 TO 15 | 9 TO 15 | | | |
| b. OVERHEAD | | 0 TO 9 | 6 TO 9 | | | |
| 9. MANUFACTURING a. DIRECT LABOR | | 5 TO 9 | 5 TO 9 | | | |
| b. OVERHEAD | | 4 TO 7 | 4 TO 7 | | | |
| 10. SERVICES a. DIRECT LABOR | | | | 5 TO 15 | | |
| b. OVERHEAD | | | | 4 TO 8 | | |
| 11. OTHER COSTS | | | | | | |
| 12. GENERAL MGMT - G & A | | 6 TO 8 | 6 TO 8 | 6 TO 8 | | |
| 13. TOTAL EFFORT | | | | | | |
| **PART II - CONTRACTOR RISK** | | | | | | |
| 14. COST RISK | (Total from Col. b) | 0 TO 8 | 0 TO 7 | 0 TO 4 | | |
| **PART III - FACILITIES INVESTMENT** | | | | | | |
| 15. CAPITAL EMPLOYED | HSAM 3015, APP J | 16 TO 20 | | | | |
| 16. BASIC PROFIT/FEE OBJECTIVE | *(Items 13 + 14 + 15, Col. g)* | | | | | |
| **PART IV - SPECIAL FACTORS** | | | | | | |
| 17. SPECIAL PROFIT/FEE OBJECT a. PRODUCTIVITY | | | | | | |
| b. INDEPENDENT DEVELOPMENT | | 1 TO 4 | 1 TO 4 | | | |
| c. OTHER | (Total from Item 16) | -5 TO +5 | -5 TO +5 | -5 TO +5 | | |
| d. TOTAL SPECIAL PROFIT/FEE OBJECTIVE | | | | | | |
| 18. SUBTOTAL PROFIT/FEE OBJECTIVE | *(Items 16 + 17, Col. g)* | | | | | |
| **PART V - COST OF MONEY OFFSET** *(Applicable to Research and development and Services Weighted Guidelines only.)* | | | | | | |
| 19. LESS: FACILITIES CAPITAL COST OF MONEY | | | | | | |
| 20. TOTAL PROFIT/FEE OBJECTIVE | *(Items 18 - 19, Col. g)* | | | | | |

DHS Form 700-17 (2/11)                                     AUTHORIZED FOR LOCAL REPRODUCTION

**Figure 10-6**

## WEIGHTED GUIDELINES PROFIT/FEE OBJECTIVE
### (See Instructions on Reverse)

| 1 CONTRACTOR IDENTIFICATION | a. COMPANY NAME | | | b. DIVISION NAME (IF ANY) | |
|---|---|---|---|---|---|
| | c. STREET ADDRESS | | d. CITY | e. STATE | f. ZIP CODE |

| 2. WEIGHTED GUIDELINES CATEGORY (CHECK ONE) | 3. TYPE OF CONTRACT |
|---|---|
| a. ☐ MANUFACTURING   b. ☐ RESEARCH AND DEVELOPMENT   c. ☐ SERVICES | |

| 4. BASIC PROCUREMENT INSTRUMENT IDENTIFICATION NO. | | | | 5. SPECIALIST NAME |
|---|---|---|---|---|
| a. PURCHASING OFFICE | b. FY | c. C/S PROD/SVCS CODE | d. PR NO. | |

**6    WEIGHTED GUIDELINES PROFIT FACTORS**

| PROFIT/FEE FACTOR OR SUBFACTOR (a) | MEASUREMENT BASE (b) | PROFIT WAGE RANGES | | | ASSIGNED WEIGHT (%) (f) | PROFIT/FEE DOLLARS (g) |
|---|---|---|---|---|---|---|
| | | MFG (%) (c) | R&D (%) (d) | SVCS (%) (e) | | |
| **PART I - CONTRACTOR EFFORT** | | | | | | |
| 7. MATERIAL ACQUISITION a. SUBCONTRACTED ITEMS | | 1 TO 5 | 1 TO 5 | 1 TO 5 | | |
| b. PURCHASED PARTS | | 1 TO 4 | 1 TO 4 | 1 TO 4 | | |
| c. OTHER MATERIAL | | 1 TO 4 | 1 TO 4 | 1 TO 4 | | |
| 8. ENGINEERING a. DIRECT LABOR | | 9 TO 15 | 9 TO 15 | | | |
| b. OVERHEAD | | 6 TO 9 | 6 TO 9 | | | |
| 9. MANUFACTURING a. DIRECT LABOR | | 5 TO 9 | 5 TO 9 | | | |
| b. OVERHEAD | | 4 TO 7 | 4 TO 7 | | | |
| 10. SERVICES a. DIRECT LABOR | | | | 5 TO 15 | | |
| b. OVERHEAD | | | | 4 TO 8 | | |
| 11. OTHER COSTS | | | | | | |
| 12. GENERAL MGMT - G & A | | 6 TO 8 | 6 TO 8 | 6 TO 8 | | |
| 13. TOTAL EFFORT | | | | | | |
| **PART II - CONTRACTOR RISK** | | | | | | |
| 14. COST RISK | (Total from Col. b) | 0 TO 8 | 0 TO 7 | 0 TO 4 | | |
| **PART III - FACILITIES INVESTMENT** | | | | | | |
| 15. CAPITAL EMPLOYED | (Line 8 of DOT F 4220.34) | 16 TO 20 | | | | |
| 16. BASIC PROFIT/FEE OBJECTIVE | (Items 13 + 14 + 15, Col. g) | | | | | |
| **PART IV - SPECIAL FACTORS** | | | | | | |
| 17. SPECIAL PROFIT/FEE OBJECTIVE a. PRODUCTIVITY | | | | | | |
| b. INDEPENDENT DEVELOPMENT | | 1 TO 4 | 1 TO 4 | | | |
| c. OTHER | (Total from Item 16) | -5 TO +5 | -5 TO +5 | -5 TO +5 | | |
| d. TOTAL SPECIAL PROFIT/FEE OBJECTIVE | | | | | | |
| 18. SUBTOTAL PROFIT/FEE OBJECTIVE | (Items 16 + 17, col. g) | | | | | |
| **PART V - COST OF MONEY OFFSET** (Applicable to Research and Development and Services Weighted Guidelines only.) | | | | | | |
| 19. LESS: FACILITIES CAPITAL COST OF MONEY | | | | | | |
| 20. TOTAL PROFIT/FEE OBJECTIVE | (Items 18-19, col. g) | | | | | |

Form DOT F 4220.32 (REV. 11/04) (EXCEL)          PREVIOUS EDITION OBSOLETE          AUTHORIZED FOR LOCAL REPRODUCTION

**Figure 10-7**

## a.  Contractor Effort

The first major element in the profit computation measures the value of the work to be performed on the contract. Intrinsic to this valuation process is the concept that a contractor is entitled to a higher rate of profit on its own efforts than on the efforts of others. In addition, the formulas provide higher profits on managerial and technological effort than on other more routine types of work. FAR 15.404-4(d)(1) gives the following guidance:

(i) *Contractor effort.* This factor measures the complexity of the work and the resources required of the prospective contractor for contract performance. Greater profit opportunity should be provided under contracts requiring a high degree of professional and managerial skill and to prospective contractors whose skills, facilities, and technical assets can be expected to lead to efficient and economical contract performance. The subfactors in paragraphs (d)(1)(i)(A) through (D) of this subsection shall be considered in determining contractor effort, but they may be modified in specific situations to accommodate differences in the categories used by prospective contractors for listing costs —

(A) *Material acquisition.* This subfactor measures the managerial and technical effort needed to obtain the required purchased parts and material, subcontracted items, and special tooling. Considerations include the complexity of the items required, the number of purchase orders and subcontracts to be awarded and administered, whether established sources are available or new or second sources must be developed, and whether material will be obtained through routine purchase orders or through complex subcontracts requiring detailed specifications. Profit consideration should correspond to the managerial and technical effort involved.

(B) *Conversion direct labor.* This subfactor measures the contribution of direct engineering, manufacturing, and other labor to converting the raw materials, data, and subcontracted items into the contract items. Considerations include the diversity of engineering, scientific, and manufacturing labor skills required and the amount and quality of supervision and coordination needed to perform the contract task.

(C) *Conversion-related indirect costs.* This subfactor measures how much the indirect costs contribute to contract performance. The labor elements in the allocable indirect costs should be given the profit consideration they would receive if treated as direct labor. The other elements of indirect costs should be evaluated to determine whether they merit only limited profit consideration because of their routine nature, or are elements that contribute significantly to the proposed contract.

(D) *General management.* This subfactor measures the prospective contractor's other indirect costs and general and administrative (G&A) expense, their composition, and how much they contribute to contract performance. Considerations include how labor in the overhead pools would be treated if it were direct labor, whether elements within the pools are routine expenses or instead are elements that contribute significantly to the proposed contract, and whether the elements require routine as opposed to unusual managerial effort and attention.

This FAR guidance reflects the logic in the original DoD weighted guidelines. However, the 1987 DoD weighted guidelines adopted an entirely different approach to calculating this element of the formula and NASA followed suit in 1999. The other civilian agencies continue to use the old approach set forth in the DoD weighted guidelines (with variation of the ranges of profit to be applied). The following discussion reviews the approaches separately and uses the prior DoD guidance when it provides the most helpful explanation of how the computation should be made.

## (1) CIVILIAN AGENCY CALCULATION

The weighted guidelines "value added" approach is implemented in the agencies' profit formulas by assigning varying weights to the elements of cost in the government's estimate of the cost of performance. See DEAR 915.404-4-70-2(d) and the forms set forth in **Figures 10-5** through **10-7**. In this procedure, purchased effort (purchased parts, subcontracted items and other material) is given a weight of 1% to 3% or 4%, and direct labor is given weights of 4% to 20% (GSAM ¶ 515.404-4(d) prescribes 4% to 12%). Except for GSA, the agencies give the following weights for the different types of direct labor:

| | |
|---|---|
| Scientific | 10% to20% |
| Project management/administration | 8% to 20% |
| Engineering | 8% to 14% |
| Manufacturing | 4% to 8% |
| Support services | 4% to 14% |

These weights reflect the higher value given technological and management effort. Indirect costs are assigned weights by analyzing the specific elements of cost in the contractor's indirect cost pools and applying a weight to each element of cost in accordance with the general value-added theory. Each agency's policy must be examined to determine the specific percentages that are prescribed. In some cases, it is necessary to look to guidance from other sources because an agency's guidance may be sparse. The most detailed explanation of the application of these weights is contained in the DOE Acquisition Guide ¶ 15.4-2B and the ASPM.

Chapter 4 of the ASPM suggested at 4-7 that indirect cost pools not be analyzed for each procurement since the weight would not change until the composition of the pool changed significantly. While the ranges of weights to be used for each cost element are prescribed by the profit formula of the agency issuing the contract, the contracting officer is given considerable discretion in selecting the weight within the range. The ASPM gave the following guidance on assigning weights to material costs at 4-4:

> Weight ranges for material are lower than the ranges for other costs because material represents the lowest investment of resources per sales dollar. Analysis of direct material costs will show variations in the managerial and technical effort needed to obtain the material. A direct material cost of $1 million could represent a single subcontract with an established source for standard material, or it could include several subcontracts that require the contractor to find suppliers to develop difficult items to complex performance specifications. Obviously, the amount of managerial and technical effort is much greater in the second case than in the first.

> The contractor that obtains maximum competition in procuring direct materials exerts greater effort than the contractor that routinely places repeat orders with established vendors. Subcontracts for professional or consulting services should be assigned a weight commensurate with the management liaison involved.

> The normal low weight for direct materials is 2 percent. A lesser weighting should be used only in unusual circumstances where the contractor makes only a minimum contribution. You might use a weighting of less than 2 percent, for instance, if the material represents a large part of the total contract costs, is a follow-on order with an existing vendor, and is to be shipped directly from the vendor to the Government.

The ASPM guidance on labor costs is set forth at 4-5 as follows:

> There are two basic rules in assigning weights to the labor categories. First, all labor must be rated within minimum and maximum DFARS weights. For instance, all engineering labor must carry weights within the 9-to-15 percent range, and services labor must carry weights within ranges of 5-to- 15 percent for direct labor and 4 to 8 percent for overhead. Second, except for services, labor carries the same weight whether it is classified as direct or indirect.

> One way to arrive at an appropriate weight is to use the contractor's job designations to classify labor into the categories shown in [the following table:]

| Engineering | Manufacturing | Administrative |
|---|---|---|
| Top scientist or engineer | Department head | Top management |
| Senior engineering or project manager | Supervisor | Executive assistants |
| Engineer | Engineer | Professional staff |
| Junior engineer | Skilled | Clerical |
| Draftsman | Semi-skilled | Support |
| Technical writer | Unskilled | |
| Clerical | Support | |
| Support | | |

Next, [an agency] might assign weights to the classes of labor. The assigned weights remain the same whether the salary cost represented by the job designation is treated as a direct or an indirect cost. [The agency] would determine the approximate dollar amounts attributable to salaries of personnel with these job designations and would multiply the amounts by the assigned weights.

Assignment by job designations is only one method of arriving at an appropriate weight assignment. Another is to find the total scale of labor rates within the labor pool of the contractor's organization, determine the average labor rate for the particular contract, and assign the weight that bears the same relationship to the DFARS range of weights that the average labor rate for the contract bears to the total scale of labor rates in the labor pool.

For example, if the scale of labor rates within the contractor's engineering organization is from $5 to $20 per hour, and the average engineering labor in the particular contract is $12 per hour, [an agency] could determine that $12 falls within the scale of $5 to $20 as 11.8 percent falls within the 9-to-15 percent range. As a result, [an agency] might assign a weight of 11.8 percent to the direct engineering labor input.

The same technique is used for indirect costs, except that the contracting officer has the discretion to assign weights to individual items of cost outside the prescribed ranges as long as the final weight given to the total indirect cost pool falls within the range in the formula, ASPM at 4-6.

All costs of performance are included in the cost base for purposes of making this profit calculation, except that the facilities capital cost of money provided for in FAR 31.205-10(a) is specifically required to be excluded from this base, FAR 15.404-4(c)(3).

## (2) DoD and NASA Calculation

In the DoD and NASA profit calculation, the contractor effort factor is now called the "performance risk" factor. See DFARS 215.404-71-2(a), which states:

This profit factor addresses the contractor's degree of risk in fulfilling the contract requirements. The factor consists of two parts —

(1) Technical — the technical uncertainties of performance.

(2) Management/cost control — the degree of management effort necessary –

(i) To ensure that contract requirements are met; and

(ii) To reduce and control costs.

NASA uses the same logic but it separates the management and cost control factors into two separate factors, NFS 1815.404-471-2.

This calculation is accomplished by applying gross percentages (rather than percentages by cost element) to the government's estimate of the costs of performance excluding facilities capital cost of money, DFARS 215.404-71-2(b)(4). The DFARS contains two ranges of percentages to be applied in this calculation:

| Calculation | Normal Value | Designated Range |
|---|---|---|
| Standard Calculation | 5% | 3% to 7% |
| Alternate Calculation | 9% | 7% to 11% |

The standard calculation is used in most types of procurements. The alternate calculation is provided for those research and development and service contracts where the contractor has made a relatively low capital investment in facilities. It provides the 4% higher profit on the technical factor in lieu of the facilities-capital-employed factor. See DFARS 215.404-71-2(c) stating:

> (2) *Technology incentive.* For the technical factor only, contracting officers may use the technology incentive range for acquisitions that include development, production, or application of innovative new technologies. The technology incentive range does not apply to efforts restricted to studies, analyses, or demonstrations that have a technical report as their primary deliverable.

See also DFARS 215.404-71-2(d)(4)(i) giving the following additional guidance on the use of this incentive:

> Use the technology incentive range only for the most innovative contract efforts. Innovation may be in the form of—
>
> (A) Development or application of new technology that fundamentally changes the characteristics of an existing product or system and that results in increased technical performance, improved reliability, or reduced costs; or
>
> (B) New products or systems that contain significant technological advances over the products or systems they are replacing.

NASA does not provide for an alternate calculation to cover technology innovations. It has adopted a normal value of 6% and a range of 4% to 8% as the sole basis for its calculation, NFS 1815.404-471-2(c).

The DoD profit calculation is made separately on the two different criteria — technical and management/cost control. The first step in the calculation is the determination by the contracting officer of the weight to be assigned to each of these criteria. These weights are determined on the basis of the importance of the criteria to the government in the performance of the contract. For example, if the contract is for research and development work requiring the use of new technology on a CPFF contract, the following weights might be appropriate:

Technical                          60%

Management/Cost Control            40%

In contrast, if the contract is for the manufacture of an item with a stable design on a fixed-price type contract, the contracting officer might assign weights as follows:

Technical                          20%

Management/Cost Control            80%

The next step in the calculation is the assignment of values to each criterion. The DoD and NASA FAR Supplements contain considerable guidance on the logic of assigning these values. With regard to the technical criterion, values are assigned on the basis of the difficulty and risk of the task in the specific contract. Thus, if the contract requires the contractor to perform development work using advanced technologies that require highly skilled personnel, a value above normal would be assigned. In contrast, a contract calling for routine technical effort would be assigned a value below normal. When DoD uses the technology incentive factor, the value is assigned on the basis of the amount of innovation required by the contract in comparison with the entire contract effort. With regard to the management/cost control criterion, the focus is more on past performance of the contractor in managing and controlling costs on prior work. However, the complexity of the tasks on the contract is also taken into consideration. In the NASA formula, management and cost control are dealt with as separate criteria.

The final step in the calculation is to arrive at a composite percentage. This is done using the assigned weights and values. For example, in the research and development contract calling for use of proven technology, the calculation might be as follows:

| Criterion | Weight Assigned | Value Assigned | Weighted Value |
|---|---|---|---|
| Technical | 55% | 5.2% | 2.86% |
| Management/ Cost Control | 45% | 5.6% | 2.52% |
| Composite Value | | | 5.38% |

If it were determined that the contract called for the use of highly innovative technology, the alternate calculation would be used. Such a calculation might be as follows:

| Criterion | Weight Assigned | Value Assigned | Weighted Value |
|---|---|---|---|
| Technical | 60% | 9.6% | 5.76% |
| Management/ Cost Control | 40% | 5.4% | 2.16% |
| Composite Value | | | 7.92% |

If NASA was awarding this same contract, the calculation might be as follows:

| Criterion | Weight Assigned | Value Assigned | Weighted Value |
|---|---|---|---|
| Technical | 60% | 7.2% | 4.32% |
| Management | 20% | 6.2% | 1.24% |
| Cost Control | 20% | 6.2% | 1.24% |
| Composite Value | | | 6.80% |

## b.  Contract Cost Risk

The second major factor included in structured approaches to profit is the risk assumed by the contractor in the pricing arrangement. This factor *does not measure economic risk* assumed by the contractor in undertaking the contract, but merely the pricing risk as determined by the pricing arrangement. FAR 15.404-4(d)(1) contains the following discussion of this factor:

(ii) *Contract cost risk.* (A) This factor measures the degree of cost responsibility and associated risk that the prospective contractor will assume as a result of the contract type contemplated and considering the reliability of the cost estimate in relation to the complexity and duration of the contract task. Determination of contract type should be closely related to the risks involved in timely, cost-effective, and efficient performance. This factor should compensate contractors proportionately for assuming greater cost risks.

Since the government assumes almost all of the risk of cost overruns on cost-reimbursement contracts, this factor is insignificant on such contracts. In contrast, it is quite significant on fixed-price contracts where the contractor assumes much of this risk. However, it varies somewhat between the profit policies of the different agencies. The normal values and the designated ranges used by the DoD are set forth in DFARS 215.404-71-3(c), as follows:

| Contract type | Notes | Normal value (percent) | Designated range (percent) |
|---|---|---|---|
| Firm-fixed-price, no financing | (1) | 5.0 | 4 to 6. |
| Firm-fixed-price, with performance-based payments | (6) | 4.0 | 2.5 to 5.5 |
| Firm-fixed-price, with progress payments | (2) | 3.0 | 2 to 4. |
| Fixed-price incentive, no financing | (1) | 3.0 | 2 to 4. |
| Fixed-price incentive, with performance-based payments | (6) | 2.0 | 0.5 to 3.5. |
| Fixed-price with redetermination provision | (3) | | |
| Fixed-price incentive, with progress payments | (2) | 1.0 | 0 to 2. |
| Cost-plus-incentive-free | (4) | 1.0 | 0 to 2. |
| Cost-plus-fixed-fee | (4) | 0.5 | 0 to 1. |
| Time-and-materials (including overhaul contracts priced on time-and-materials basis) | (5) | 0.5 | 0 to 1. |
| Labor-hour | (5) | 0.5 | 0 to 1. |
| Firm-fixed-price, level-of-effort | (5) | 0.5 | 0 to 1. |

NASA uses these same levels but adds a category for CPAF contracts with a normal value of .75% and a range of .5% to 1.5%, NFS 1815.404-471-3(c).

DFARS 215.404-71-3(d) provide detailed guidance on the elements of the prospective contract that should be considered when determining whether to assign a profit factor at the upper or lower end of the prescribed range. These elements are length of contract, adequacy of cost data for projections, economic environment, nature and extent of subcontracting activity, protection provided to the contractor under contract provisions (e.g., economic price adjustment clauses), the ceilings and share lines contained in incentive provisions, risks associated with contracts for foreign military sales not funded by U.S. appropriations, the extent and type of performance-based payments, and the amount of costs that have been incurred on a undefinitized contract before definitization. See NFS 1815.404-471-3(d) for similar guidance.

Civilian agencies tend to use different weightings for this factor depending on the type of procurement but the guidance varies from agency to agency. For example, the DOE Acquisition Guide ¶ 15.4-2C calls for higher amounts for "equipment and supply contracts," slightly lesser amounts for research and development contracts, and even lower amounts for contracts for services. These latter amounts are quite low, as follows:

| | |
|---|---|
| Cost-Plus-Fixed-Fee | 0 to 0 .5% |
| Cost-Plus-Incentive-Fee | 1 to 2% |
| Fixed-Price-Incentive | 2 to 3% |
| Firm-Fixed-Price | 3 to 4% |

DHS Form 700-17 and DOT Form 4220.32 follow this same logic with lower profit rates for research and development and service contracts. GSAM ¶ 515.404-4(h)(3) merely specifies a range of 0 to 7% with broad guidance that cost-reimbursement type contracts should receive 0 to 3% and fixed-price type contracts 3% to 7% — with lower rates for service contracts.

The regulations and manuals of the civilian agencies contain a varied amount of guidance on how these ranges should be applied. However, the reliability of the cost estimate, the amount of risk that has been transferred to subcontractors, and whether the pricing action has occurred after work has commenced are all relevant to establishing the profit objective within these ranges.

## c.  Federal Socioeconomic Programs

This factor has been included in the weighted guidelines since its inception. FAR 15.404-4(d)(1) contains the following guidance:

> (iii) *Federal socioeconomic programs.* This factor measures the degree of support given by the prospective contractor to Federal socioeconomic programs, such as those involving small business concerns, small business concerns owned and controlled by socially and economically disadvantaged individuals, women-owned small business concerns, handicapped sheltered workshops, and energy conservation. Greater profit opportunity should be provided contractors that have displayed unusual initiative in these programs.

This factor is not considered separately in the DoD formula but is made a part of the management evaluation in the performance risk area. In NASA the factor is not included in the performance risk evaluation but is weighted at -0.5% to 0.5% of the costs used as the base for the performance risk factor, NFS 1815.404-471-4(c)(2). In the formulas of the other civilian agencies, it is treated as a separate factor and handled in one of two ways. In the Department of Energy the factor has a range of -5% to 5% of the basic profit objective derived from adding all of the other profit factors. In the Department of Homeland Security and the GSA, the factor is weighted at -0.5% to 0.5% of the costs used as the base for the contractor effort factor. In either case, the guidance generally provides that "merely satisfactory" effort in implementing these programs is entitled to no weight, that "unusual" support is entitled to a plus weight, and that "failure or unwillingness" to support these programs should receive a minus weight. See the DOE Acquisition Guide ¶ 15.4-2F. In either case, the regulations provide that "unusual initiative" or "extraordinary steps" in supporting these programs is entitled to positive weight and that "nonparticipation in or violation of" these programs should receive a minus weight. See NFS 1815.404-471-4(c)(2).

### d. Capital Investments

Originally, OFPP Policy Letter 80-7 required that all structured profit approaches consider capital investment in *both facilities and working capital*. However, the DoD weighted guidelines never included investment in working capital because the DoD did not agree with this guidance. As a result, FAR 15.404-4(d)(1), issued in 1984, states this requirement in very general language, as follows:

(iv) *Capital Investments.* This factor takes into account the contribution of contractor investments to efficient and economical contract performance.

Agencies have adopted a wide variety of techniques to calculate the amount of profit/fee under this factor. They have also adopted different approaches to the correlation of this profit factor to the allowability of the cost of facilities capital (imputed interest on the cost of facilities).

### (1) PRECISE MEASUREMENT OF FACILITIES CAPITAL

In 1987, the DoD weighted guidelines adopted a rather precise mathematical method of determining the amount of profit to be given for facilities capital. This approach is now being followed by a number of agencies with significantly less guidance on its implementation.

The approach is spelled out in DFARS 215.404-71-4(f) calling for use of a factor that is computed based on the following percentages of the net book value of capital equipment employed on the contract:

| Normal Value | Designated Range |
|---|---|
| 17.5% | 10% to 25% |

Note that this computation does not include the value of land or buildings which have been capitalized.

The goal of this relatively large profit factor is to motivate the contractor to invest in labor-saving equipment. Thus, DFARS 215.404-71-4(g) provides the following guidance on selection of the percentage within the designated range:

(2) *Above normal conditions.* (i) The contracting officer may assign a higher than normal value if the facilities capital investment has direct, identifiable, and exceptional benefits. Indicators are —

(A) New investments in state-of-the-art technology which reduce acquisition cost or yield other tangible benefits such as improved product quality or accelerated deliveries;

(B) Investments in new equipment for research and development applications..

(ii) The contracting officer may assign a value significantly above normal when there are direct and measurable benefits in efficiency and significantly reduced acquisition costs on the effort being priced. Maximum values apply only to those cases where the benefits of the facilities capital investment are substantially above normal.

(3) *Below normal conditions.* (i) The contracting officer may assign a lower than normal value if the facilities capital investment has little benefit to DoD. Indicators are —

(A) Allocations of capital apply predominantly to commercial product lines;

(B) Investments are for such things as furniture and fixtures, home or group level administrative offices, corporate aircraft and hangars, gymnasiums; or

(C) Facilities are old or extensively idle.

(ii) The contracting officer may assign a value significantly below normal when a significant portion of defense manufacturing is done in an environment characterized by outdated, inefficient, and labor-intensive capital equipment.

The net book value of facilities employed on the contract is calculated using a two-step process. The first step is to compute the cost of money factors for each overhead pool of the contractor's organizations performing work on the contract. This calculation is made using Form CASB-CMF and following the procedures set forth in CAS 414, 48 CFR § 9904.414. Form CASB-CMF is set forth in **Figure 10-8**. These cost-of-money factors are percentages (like overhead rates) reflecting the ratio of the imputed cost of capital (imputed interest) to the cost base (normally direct labor dollars) for the overhead pool for any fiscal period. They provide a mechanism for allocating the imputed cost of capital to any specific contract, and they are also used to calculate the net book value of assets employed in the performance of a contract. This second step of the profit calculation is made using DD Form 1861, set forth in **Figure 10-9**. Here the imputed cost of interest attributable to each overhead pool is calculated by multiplying the cost-of-money factor for each pool by the estimated expenditure of effort on the contract in that pool (direct labor dollars in most cases). The total imputed cost of capital obtained from this calculation is divided by the cost of money rate (interest rate) to provide the net book value of facilities used on the contract. This amount is then entered on DD Form 1547 (see **Figure 10-3**) as the measurement base, and the weight determined to be applicable for equipment is applied to compute this profit factor.

Form CASB-CMF

**TABLE XI**

**FACILITIES CAPITAL**
**COST OF MONEY FACTORS COMPUTATION**
("Regular" Method – Cost of Money Excluded from Total Cost Input)

CONTRACTOR: **ABC Corp.**
BUSINESS UNIT: **A Division**
ADDRESS:
COST ACCOUNTING PERIOD: Y.E. 12/31/75

| | 1. APPLICABLE COST OF MONEY RATE 8 % | 2. ACCUMULATION & DIRECT DISTRIBUTION OF N.B.V. | 3. ALLOCATION OF UNDISTRIBUTED — BASIS OF ALLOCATION | 4. TOTAL NET BOOK VALUE — COLUMNS 2+3 | 5. COST OF MONEY FOR THE COST ACCOUNTING PERIOD — COLUMNS 1 × 4 | 6. ALLOCATION BASE FOR THE PERIOD — IN UNIT(S) OF MEASUREMENT | 7. FACILITIES CAPITAL COST OF MONEY FACTORS — COLUMNS 5 ÷ 6 |
|---|---|---|---|---|---|---|---|
| **BUSINESS UNIT FACILITIES CAPITAL** | | | WORKSHEET TABLE X | | | TABLE VII | |
| RECORDED | Table IX | 8,270,000 | | | | | |
| LEASED PROPERTY | | | | | | | |
| CORPORATE OR GROUP | Table VI | 450,000 | | | | | |
| TOTAL | | 8,720,000 | | | | | |
| UNDISTRIBUTED | | 3,450,000 | | | | | |
| DISTRIBUTED | | 5,270,000 | | | | | |
| **OVERHEAD POOLS** | | | | | | | |
| Engineering | Table IX | 320,000 | 756,000 | 1,076,000 | 86,080 | $2,000,000 | .04304 |
| Manufacturing | Table IX | 4,500,000 | 2,250,000 | 6,750,000 | 540,000 | $3,000,000 | .18 |
| Technical Computer | | | 444,000 | 444,000 | 35,520 | 2,280 hr | 15.57895 |
| **G & A EXPENSE POOLS** | | | | | | | |
| G & A Expense | Table VI | 450,000 | | 450,000 | 36,000 | $36,700,000 | .00098 |
| TOTAL | | 5,270,000 | 3,450,000 | 8,720,000 | 679,600 | //////////// | //////////// |

**Figure 10-8**

Defense Federal Acquisition Registration Supplement

Part 253 — Forms

| CONTRACT FACILITIES CAPITAL COST OF MONEY | Form Approved<br>OMB No. 0704-0267<br>Expires Feb 28, 1995 |
|---|---|

Public reporting burden for this collection of information is estimated to average 10 hours per response, including the time for reviewing instructions, searching existing data sources, gathering and maintaining the data needed, and completing and reviewing the collection of information. Send comments regarding this burden estimate or any other aspect of this collection of information, including suggestions for reducing this burden, to Washington Headquarters Services, Directorate for Information Operations and Reports, 1215 Jefferson Davis Highway, Suite 1204, Arlington, VA 22202-4302, and to the Office of Management and Budget, Paperwork Reduction Project (0704-0267), Washington, DC 20503.

**PLEASE DO NOT RETURN YOUR COMPLETED FORM TO EITHER OF THESE ADDRESSES.**
**RETURN COMPLETED FORM TO YOUR CONTRACTING OFFICIAL.**

| 1. CONTRACTOR NAME | 2. CONTRACTOR ADDRESS |
|---|---|

**3. BUSINESS UNIT**

| 4. RFP/ CONTRACT PIN NUMBER | 5. PERFORMANCE PERIOD |
|---|---|

**6. DISTRIBUTION OF FACILITIES CAPITAL COST OF MONEY**

| POOL<br>a. | ALLOCATION BASE<br>b. | FACILITIES CAPITAL COST OF MONEY<br>c. | |
|---|---|---|---|
| | | FACTOR<br>(1) | AMOUNT<br>(2) |
| | | | |
| | | | |
| | | | |
| | | | |
| | | | |
| | | | |
| | | | |
| | | | |
| | | | |
| d. TOTAL | | | % |
| e. TREASURY RATE | | | |
| f. FACILITIES CAPITAL EMPLOYED<br>(TOTAL DIVIDED BY TREASURY RATE) | | | |

**7. DISTRIBUTION OF FACILITIES CAPITAL EMPLOYED**

| | PERCENTAGE<br>a. | AMOUNT<br>b. |
|---|---|---|
| (1) LAND | % | |
| (2) BUILDINGS | % | |
| (3) EQUIPMENT | % | |
| (4) FACILITIES CAPITAL EMPLOYED | 100% | |

DD Form 1861, MAR 93          PREVIOUS EDITION IS OBSOLETE

DAC 91-6          253.3-79

**Figure 10-9**

The Department of Energy has adopted the DoD policy with regard to facilities capital, DOE Acquisition Guide ¶ 15.4-2D, using a range of 5% to 20% of facilities capital employed on the contract. The Department Homeland Security has also adopted this technique in DHS Form 700-17 (see **Figure 10-6**) using a range of 16% to 20% of the net book value of facilities capital employed on the contract. The Department of Transportation also uses the range of 16% to 20% of the net book value of facilities capital employed on the contract, DOT Form 4220.32 (see **Figure 10-7**). In order to apply this factor, contracting officers in these civilian agencies may need to review DFARS 215.404-71-4 which contains the most detailed guidance on this issue.

## (2) DISCRETIONARY DETERMINATION

NASA and GSA follow discretionary approaches to this factor. NASA provides that a weight of -1% to 1% of the cost base may be included in the profit for this factor. The following guidance is provided at NFS 1815.404-471-4(c):

(3) Consideration of up to 1 percent should be given when contract performance requires the expenditure of significant corporate capital resources.

4) Unusual requests for use of government facilities and property may merit a downward adjustment of as much as - 1 percent.

See also GSAM ¶ 515.404-4(d) which calls for a range of -2% to 2% with minimal guidance.

## (3) WORKING CAPITAL TECHNIQUES

The DoD has adopted a "working capital adjustment" factor to compensate for the use of working capital in fixed-price type contracts with a very long period of performance and providing for progress payments, DFARS 215.404-71-3(f). This factor also compensates for unusual increases in interest rates. The factor is only applicable when cost-based progress payments are included in a fixed-price type contract and is computed by the following calculation:

costs financed × contract length factor × current interest rate

The costs financed are the amount of costs not paid through progress payments. Thus, if the contract contains a provision for progress payments at the rate of 75% of costs incurred, the costs financed would be 25% of the total estimated costs of performance excluding facilities capital cost of money, DFARS 215.404-71-3(e). This regulation calls for reduction of this amount "as appropriate" in the following circumstances:

(i) The contractor has little cash investment (e.g., subcontractor progress payments liquidated late in period of performance);

(ii) Some costs are covered by special financing provisions, such as advance payments; or

(iii) The contract is multiyear and there are special funding arrangements.

The contract length factor is computed using the following table:

| Period to perform substantive portion (in months) | Contract length factor |
|---|---|
| 21 or less | .40 |
| 22 to 27 | .65 |
| 28 to 33 | .90 |
| 34 to 39 | 1.15 |
| 40 to 45 | 1.40 |
| 46 to 51 | 1.65 |
| 52 to 57 | 1.90 |
| 58 to 63 | 2.15 |
| 64 to 69 | 2.40 |
| 70 to 75 | 2.65 |
| 76 or more | 2.90 |

DFARS 215.404-71-3(f) provides that the contract period should exclude periods where only minimum performance is called for (usually at the beginning of the contract) and should average the end date of contract performance when multiple deliveries are required. It also provides for exclusion from the calculation of option years and multiyear contract years beyond the initial program year. The interest rate to be used is the rate established by the Secretary of the Treasury that is used to calculate the cost of facilities capital.

As an example of this calculation, assume a $10 million fixed-price contract calls for progress payments of 75% and deliveries of three aircraft in months 36, 38, and 40 after award of the contract (yielding an average contract period of 38 months). This factor would be derived by the following calculation:

| Costs Financed | | Contract Length Factor | | Interest Rate | | Factor |
|---|---|---|---|---|---|---|
| $ 2,500,000 | × | 1.15 | × | 5% | = | $ 143,750 |

NASA uses this same factor following the DoD guidance. See NFS 1815.404-471-3(f).

The Department of Energy has a much broader factor for working capital, requiring the discretionary consideration of the amount of "operating capital" needed to perform the contract under a broad factor called "other considerations," DOE Acquisition Guide ¶ 15.4-2G.3. This guide suggests that a negative profit rate would be appropriate for cost-reimbursement contracts. GSAM ¶ 515.404-4(d) calls for the consideration of the amount of working capital needed to finance the contract without any detailed guidance as to the amount of profit adjustment.

## e.  Cost Control and Other Past Accomplishments

FAR 15.404-4(d)(1) gives the following guidance on cost control and other past accomplishments:

> (v) *Cost-control and other past accomplishments.* This factor allows additional profit opportunities to a prospective contractor that has previously demonstrated its ability to perform similar tasks effectively and economically. In addition, consideration should be given to measures taken by the prospective contractor that result in productivity improvements, and other cost-reduction accomplishments that will benefit the Government in follow-on contracts.

It can be seen that this factor covers several different aspects of the contractor's past or prospective performance. Contractor performance, in general, was a factor in the original weighted guidelines adopted by the DoD in 1964 but was deleted from the formula in 1976. The remaining elements of this factor were deleted from the DoD weighted guidelines in 1987.

### (1) CIVILIAN AGENCY APPROACHES

The civilian agencies have adopted a broad factor called "other considerations" or "other" where a number of the FAR factors are merged and other issues are included. The NASA "other considerations" factor contains some evaluations of the contractor's performance. See NFS 1815.404-471-4(c) stating:

> (1) Consistent demonstration by the contractor of excellent past performance within the last three years, with a special emphasis on excellence in safety, may merit an upward adjustment of as much as 1 percent. Similarly, an assessment of poor past performance, especially in the area of safety, may merit a downward adjustment of as much as -1 percent. This consideration is especially important when negotiating modifications or changes to an ongoing contract.
>
> (5) Cost efficiencies arising from innovative product design, process improvements, or integration of a life cycle cost approach for the design and development of systems that minimize maintenance and operations costs, that have not been recognized in Performance Risk or Contract Type Risk, may merit an upward adjustment. This factor is intended to recognize and reward improvements resulting from better ideas and management that will benefit the Government in the contract and/or program.

The Department of Energy has also adopted a broad factor called "other considerations" with a weight of -5% to 5% of the basic profit objective. This factor includes (1) cost control and other past accomplishments, (2) complexity of research and development or services assignment, and (3) operating capital. The DOE Acquisition Guide ¶ 15.4-2G.1 provides the following guidance on the cost control element of this factor:

> This factor benefits a prospective contractor that has previously performed similar tasks effectively and economically. In addition, consideration is given to: measures taken by the prospective contractor that result in productivity improvements and other cost-reduction accomplishments that will benefit Government contracts. Among other things, consideration is given to the contractor's efforts to explore additional production opportunities or to improve or develop new product, manufacturing or performance technologies to reduce production cost.

The Department of Homeland Security includes a similar factor on DHS Form 700-17 (see the discussion in Appendix A of the HSAM) and the Department of Transportation includes a similar factor on DOT Form 4220.32.

GSAM ¶ 515.404-4(d) has a separate factor covering cost control and other past accomplishments with a weight of -2 % to 2 % of the cost base. However, the manual contains no guidance on the application of this factor.

### f.  Independent Development

FAR 15.404-4(d)(1) contains the following guidance on independent development:

> (vi) *Independent development.* Under this factor, the contractor may be provided additional profit opportunities in recognition of independent development efforts relevant to the contract end item without Government assistance. The contracting officer should consider whether the development cost was recovered directly or indirectly from Government sources.

The original DoD weighted guidelines contained this factor with a weight of 1% to 4% of the cost base, but it was deleted from the DFARS in 1987. NASA has also deleted any reference to the independent development factor from its regulations. However, NFS 1815.404-471-4(b) permits the inclusion in the formula of an amount based on the contractor's "unusual and innovative actions."

This factor is still included in most of the civilian agency policies. The Department of Energy has two factors in this category. The DOE Acquisition Guide ¶ 15.4-2E provides for a factor for a "viable" independent research and development program at a weight of 5% to 7% of allowable independent research and development costs allocable to the contract. It also provides for an independent development factor with a weight of 0 to 20% of the basic profit dollars when contractors develop "items with energy program applications on their own initiative with no direct Government assistance and little or no indirect Government assistance."

GSAM ¶ 515.404-4(d) has a factor for "independent development and additional factors" with a weight of -2% to 2% of the cost base. The manual contains no guidance on the application of this factor. The Department of Transportation (DOT Form 4220.32) and the Department of Homeland Security (DHS Form 700-17) have a factor of 1% to 4% for independent development, which is applicable to manufacturing and research and development contracts (not service contracts).

### g. Other Factors

FAR 15.404-4(d)(2) also permits agencies to include additional factors in their structured approaches to profit. Several of the civilian agencies have included such factors. For example, the NFS 1815.404-471-4(a) "other considerations" factor provides for additional profit for "unusual acceptance of contractual or program risks." See also DOE Acquisition Guide ¶ 15.4-2H which provides for a "productivity/performance adjustment" to be added to the profit objective for follow-on contracts in cases where the contractor has taken special steps to reduce the costs of performance of an entire program. This factor is designed to overcome the reluctance of contractors to reduce costs when they anticipate follow-on contracts that would benefit from such cost reductions but would yield commensurately lower profits. The Department of Homeland Security also discusses this factor in Appendix A of the HSAM. The Department of Transportation also uses this factor in DOT Form 4220.32.

## 5. Facilities Capital Cost of Money Adjustment

FAR 31.205-10(b)(3) provides that the facilities capital cost of money will be an allowable cost of performance of government contracts if it is "specifically identified or proposed in cost proposals," but FAR 15.404-4(c)(3) provides that it will not be included in the cost base for computation of the fee. FAR 15.404-4 also provides that a contractor can waive this cost, and FAR 52.215-16 provides a Waiver of Facilities Capital Cost of Money clause to be used when the contractor makes this election.

If the contractor does not waive this cost, the FAR is silent on any profit adjustment for this cost element. However, OFPP Policy Letter 80-7 (canceled in 1984 but replaced by FAR policy) addressed this issue as follows:

> (2) Agencies shall ensure that contractors are not compensated for facilities capital cost of money both as a direct or indirect cost and in profit or fee. Before the allowability of facilities capital cost of money, this cost was included in profits and fees. Therefore, profit and fee prenegotiation objectives shall be reduced if necessary to reflect this refinement in cost accounting practices. This reduction may be accomplished by means of offsets; that is, by (i) using a dollar-for-dollar offset in the Government's prenegotiation profit or fee objective or (ii) incorporating a common offset factor under an agency's structured approach. No offset

is necessary when the profit rates applied to the profit analysis factors under an agency's structured approach already take into account the allowability of facilities capital cost of money.

The agencies have split on which of these two techniques to use. NASA uses the "dollar-for-dollar offset" technique by providing that any facilities capital cost of money included in the estimated cost will be deducted from the profit objective, NFS 1815.404-471-5. GSAM ¶ 515.404-4(f) contains the same requirement. The Department of Transportation (DOT Form 4220.32) and the Department of Homeland Security (DHS Form 700-17) require the "dollar-for-dollar" adjustment only on research and development and service contracts.

The Departments of Defense and Energy require no such reduction because *they have incorporated the offset into the standard profit formula.* In such cases, it would be improper for the contracting officer to take any additional offset when recognizing the cost of facilities capital cost of money. Similarly, it would be unwise for the contractor to waive the recovery of such costs in these circumstances since no profit offset is required. Unfortunately, most of the agency regulations are silent on this issue. See, however, DFARS 215.404-73(b)(2), which permits contracting officers to use alternate formulas in lieu of the weighted guidelines formula but requires such alternate formulas to include an offset in the amount of the facilities capital cost of money. The regulation explains the need for this adjustment as follows:

> (ii) This adjustment is needed for the following reason: The values of the profit factors used in the weighted guidelines method were adjusted to recognize the shift in facilities capital cost of money from an element of profit to an element of contract cost (FAR 31.205-10 ) and reductions were made directly to the profit factors for performance risk. In order to ensure that this policy is applied to all DoD contracts which allow facilities capital cost of money, similar adjustments shall be made to contracts which use alternate structured approaches.

DFARS 215.404-74(c) also requires contracting officers to apply this offset to the base fee on CPAF contracts.

## 6. *Application to Nonprofit Organizations*

Although the structured profit approaches currently in use were devised to determine the profits negotiated with commercial organizations, a number of agency regulations provide that they will also be used to calculate the profits paid to nonprofit organizations with certain prescribed adjustments. For example, DFARS 215.404-72(b) calls for the following adjustments:

> (1) Modifications to performance risk (Blocks 21-23 of the DD Form 1547). (i) If the contracting officer assigns a value from the standard designated range (see 215.404-71-2(c)), reduce the fee objective by an amount equal to 1 percent of the

costs in Block 20 of the DD Form 1547. Show the net (reduced) amount on the DD Form 1547.

(ii) Do not assign a value from the technology incentive designated range.

(2) Modifications to contract type risk (Block 24 of the DD Form 1547). Use a designated range of - 1 percent to 0 percent instead of the values in 215.404-71-3. There is no normal value.

Since the alternate performance risk factor would be used in almost all contracts with nonprofit organizations, the net result of this policy is the use of a profit factor that is 3% (of the cost base) lower than that used with profit-making organizations. Similar guidance is contained in Appendix A of the HSAM.

Similarly, NFS 1815.404-471-6 provides for the use of a structured approach for nonprofit organizations other than educational institutions. This regulation states:

(b) For contracts with nonprofit organizations under which profit or fee is involved, an adjustment of up to 3 percent of the costs in Block 13 of NASA Form 634 must be subtracted from the total profit/fee objective. In developing this adjustment, it is necessary to consider the following factors:

(1) Tax position benefits;

(2) Granting of financing through letters of credit;

(3) Facility requirements of the nonprofit organization; and

(4) Other pertinent factors that may work to either the advantage or disadvantage of the contractor in its position as a nonprofit organization.

See also GSAM ¶ 515.404-70 containing the same guidance.

DEAR 915.404-4-70-5(c) calls for the payment of fees to nonprofit organizations other than educational institutions using the structured profit approach reduced by at least 25%.

# VII.  PRICE NEGOTIATION PROCEDURES

The extent of negotiation will vary from one procurement to another depending on the nature of the procurement, the type of analysis done by the government, and the past business dealings of the parties. If price analysis is used on a commercial item, there may be little need for negotiation. In contrast, if cost analysis is done on a new item where the government agency has had little experience with the contractor, protracted negotiations may be necessary to permit the contracting officer to gain confidence in the offeror's estimating system and the price to be paid. In all cases, sufficient negotiations must be conducted to permit the contracting officer to determine that the price to be paid is fair and reasonable, FAR 15.404-1(a).

While the extent of negotiation is left to the discretion of the contracting officer, there are two procedures relating to the negotiation process that are mandatory. First, prior to entering into a price negotiation, the contracting officer must establish a prenegotiation objective. Second, after completing the negotiation, the contracting officer must prepare and circulate a price negotiation memorandum (PNM). These procedures are discussed in this section.

## A. Prenegotiation Objectives

FAR 15.406-1 requires the determination of prenegotiation objectives as follows:

(a) The prenegotiation objectives establish the Government's initial negotiation position. They assist in the contracting officer's determination of fair and reasonable price. They should be based on the results of the contracting officer's analysis of the offeror's proposal, taking into consideration all pertinent information including field pricing assistance, audit reports and technical analysis, fact-finding results, independent Government cost estimates and price histories.

(b) The contracting officer shall establish prenegotiation objectives before the negotiation of any pricing action. The scope and depth of the analysis supporting the objectives should be directly related to the dollar value, importance, and complexity of the pricing action. When cost analysis is required, the contracting officer shall document the pertinent issues to be negotiated, the cost objectives, and a profit or fee objective.

This process forces the contracting officer to assimilate all of the data prepared by the offeror, the government auditor, the administrative contracting officer, and all other specialists who have reviewed the proposed pricing action. The result should be a government negotiating position that represents the government's best estimate of a fair and reasonable price.

A number of agencies require the contracting officer to obtain approval from a higher authority before the negotiation of major contracts. See, for example, NFS 1815.406-171, requiring each field center to establish a formal system for the review of prenegotiation memoranda, and NFS 1815.406-172, requiring approval of the prenegotiation position by the assistant administrator for procurement before negotiations on any procurement action selected for headquarters review.

## B. Negotiation

The contracting officer is the key government person in the negotiation process. FAR 15.404-1(a)(1) provides that the contracting officer is "responsible for evaluating the reasonableness of the offered prices," and FAR 15.306(d)(3) states "the scope and extent of discussions are a matter of contracting officer to judgment." See also FAR 15.405 providing the following guidance on price negotiation:

(a) The purpose of performing cost or price analysis is to develop a negotiation position that permits the contracting officer and the offeror an opportunity to reach agreement on a fair and reasonable price. A fair and reasonable price does not require that agreement be reached on every element of cost, nor is it mandatory that the agreed price be within the contracting officer's initial negotiation position. Taking into consideration the advisory recommendations, reports of contributing specialists, and the current status of the contractor's purchasing system, the contracting officer is responsible for exercising the requisite judgment needed to reach a negotiated settlement with the offeror and is solely responsible for the final price agreement. However, when significant audit or other specialist recommendations are not adopted, the contracting officer should provide rationale that supports the negotiation result in the price negotiation documentation.

(b) The contracting officer's primary concern is the overall price the Government will actually pay. The contracting officer's objective is to negotiate a contract of a type and with a price providing the contractor the greatest incentive for efficient and economical performance. The negotiation of a contract type and a price are related and should be considered together with the issues of risk and uncertainty to the contractor and the Government. Therefore, the contracting officer should not become preoccupied with any single element and should balance the contract type, cost, and profit or fee negotiated to achieve a total result-a price that is fair and reasonable to both the Government and the contractor.

The General Services Administration directs contracting officers to "refer the matter to one level above the contracting officer for resolution" if a contractor "insists on a price or demands a profit or fee that you consider unreasonable," GSAM 515.405.

While this guidance merely provides that the contracting officer should take "into consideration"the recommendations of other government specialists such as auditors, price analysts, technical personnel, or lawyers, FAR 15.404-2(a)(3) provides that when "field pricing assistance" is obtained, the contracting officer is "encouraged to team with appropriate field experts throughout the acquisition process, including negotiations." Auditors are required to be included in DoD negotiations involving indirect costs by 10 U.S.C. § 2324(f)(3), stating:

The Federal Acquisition Regulation shall provide that, to the maximum extent practicable, the contract auditor be present at any negotiation or meeting with the contractor regarding a determination of the allowability of indirect costs of the contractor.

DFARS PGI 215.404-2(c)(i) suggests obtaining audit assistance on procurements (both contractor and subcontractor) over $ 10 million if they are fixed-price and over $ 100 million if they are cost-reimbursement. The Department of Energy requires audit assistance in DEAR 915.404-2-70 as follows:

(a) When a contract price will be based on cost or pricing data submitted by the offerors, the DOE contracting officer or authorized representative shall request a review by the cognizant Federal audit activity prior to the negotiation of any contract or modification including modifications under advertised contracts in excess of:

(1) $500,000 for a firm fixed-price contract or a fixed-price contract with economic price adjustment provisions; or adjustment provisions; or

(2) $1,000,000 for all other contract types, including initial prices, estimated costs of cost-reimbursement contracts, interim and final price redeterminations, and target and settlement of incentive contracts.

(b) The requirement for auditor reviews of proposals which exceed the thresholds specified in paragraph (a) of this section may be waived at a level above the contracting officer when the reasonableness of the negotiated contract price can be determined from information already available. The contract file shall be documented to reflect the reason for any such waiver, provided, however, that independent Government estimates of cost or price shall not be used as the sole justification for any such waiver.

## C. Price Negotiation Memorandum

FAR 15.406-3 requires the preparation of a PNM on each negotiated procurement as follows:

(a) The contracting officer shall document in the contract file the principal elements of the negotiated agreement. The documentation (e.g., price negotiation memorandum (PNM)) shall include the following:

(1) The purpose of the negotiation.

(2) A description of the acquisition, including appropriate identifying numbers (e.g., RFP No.).

(3) The name, position, and organization of each person representing the contractor and the Government in the negotiation.

(4) The current status of any contractor systems (e.g., purchasing, estimating, accounting, and compensation) to the extent they affected and were considered in the negotiation.

(5) If cost or pricing data were not required in the case of any price negotiation exceeding the cost or pricing data threshold, the exception used and the basis for it.

(6) If cost or pricing data were required, the extent to which the contracting officer —

(i) Relied on the cost or pricing data submitted and used them in negotiating the price;

(ii) Recognized as inaccurate, incomplete, or noncurrent any cost or pricing data submitted; the action taken by the contracting officer and the contractor as a result; and the effect of the defective data on the price negotiated; or

(iii) Determined that an exception applied after the data were submitted and, therefore, considered not to be cost or pricing data.

(7) A summary of the contractor's proposal, any field pricing assistance recommendations, including the reasons for any pertinent variances from them, the Government's negotiation objective, and the negotiated position. Where the determination of price reasonableness is based on cost analysis, the summary shall address the amount of each major cost element. When determination of price reasonableness is based on price analysis, the summary shall include the source and type of data used to support the determination.

(8) The most significant facts or considerations controlling the establishment of the prenegotiation objectives and the negotiated agreement including an explanation of any significant differences between the two positions.

(9) To the extent such direction has a significant effect on the action, a discussion and quantification of the impact of direction given by Congress, other agencies, and higher-level officials (i.e., officials who would not normally exercise authority during the award and review process for the instant contract action).

(10) The basis for the profit or fee prenegotiation objective and the profit or fee negotiated.

(11) Documentation of fair and reasonable pricing.

(b) Whenever a field pricing assistance has been obtained, the contracting officer shall forward a copy of the negotiation documentation to the office(s) providing assistance. When appropriate, information on how advisory field support can be made more effective should be provided separately.

See DFARS PGI 215.406-3 altering ¶ (a)(7) above to state:

(a)(7) Include the principal factors related to the disposition of findings and recommendations contained in preaward and postaward contract audit and other advisory reports.

This provision was adopted to implement a policy memorandum from the Director, Defense Procurement and Acquisition Policy on December 4, 2009, requiring contracting officers to resolve differences with prenegotiation audit reports by the DCAA on acquisitions over $10 million. See also Air Force Informational Guidance 5315.406-3 *(farsite.hill.af.mil/reghtml/regs/far2afmcfars/af_afmc/affars/5315.htm)* for a very detailed checklist covering many aspects of a PNM. See also NFS 1815.406-3(a)(2)(ii) stating that no PNM is required when a contract is awarded "under competitive negotiated procedures."

Contractors should also prepare a memorandum of negotiations in at least as great detail as is required of the contracting officer. This memorandum should compare the original price or cost proposed and the price or cost agreed to with an explanation of the justification for the variations. It should also describe the results of any negotiations of the profit or fee with a similar explanation of any significant differences that were agreed to.

As stated in FAR 15.405(a), the parties to the negotiation are not required to agree on each element of cost in the ultimate negotiated price. As a result, it is very likely that the memorandum of each party will contain a different explanation of the way the final cost estimate was calculated. If there is a subsequent dispute over the adequacy of the contractor's submission of cost or pricing data, it would be expected that the memorandum of the contracting officer would be the best evidence of whether the price was significantly altered by the data deficiency, *McDonnell Douglas Corp.*, ASBCA 12786, 69-2 BCA ¶ 7897; and *Sperry Corp. Computer Sys., Def. Sys. Div.*, ASBCA 29525, 88-3 BCA ¶ 20,975. See, however, *Sperry Rand Corp.*, DOTCAB 1144, 82-2 BCA ¶15,812, *recons. denied*, 84-1 BCA ¶ 16,968, where the contractor was able to persuade the board that no price reduction should be made because its negotiation memorandum reflected the fact that it had reduced its negotiating position to reflect the undisclosed data. Compare *McDonnell Douglas Helicopter Co.*, ASBCA 41378, 92-1 BCA ¶ 24,655, where the board denied a contractor's motion for summary judgment based on its price reduction where there was no evidence that the contracting officer knew that the reduction was based on undisclosed price concessions from subcontractors. See 10 U.S.C. § 2306a(e)(3)(C) and 41 U.S.C. § 3506(c)(3), stating that it is not a defense to a government claim for a price reduction because of defective cost or pricing data that "the contract was based on an agreement between the contractor and the United States about the total cost of the contract and there was no agreement about the cost of each item procured under such contract." Of course, if the parties do negotiate and agree on specific costs, they will be the basis for the price adjustment for defective cost or pricing data, *Grumman Aerospace Corp.*, ASBCA 35188, 90-2 BCA ¶ 22,842.

# CHAPTER 11

# COLLATERAL POLICIES

The primary focus of this book is on how the federal government achieves the primary goal of any procurement: obtaining timely satisfaction of its needs at fair prices under fair terms and conditions. However, the government also uses the acquisition process to implement policies that have little or no direct relationship to, and are often in tension with, the primary goals of procurement. For example, in choosing a contractor, the government may give weight to the size of the contractor (i.e., is it a small business?); the place of performance (i.e., is work being done in an area of high unemployment?); the ownership of the contractor (i.e., is it women-owned?); and the compliance of the contractor with a variety of other federal standards (e.g., minimum wage and hour requirements). This chapter examines the major collateral policies, particularly those that have social or economic goals as their primary focus.

Implementing these collateral policies through the acquisition process sometimes conflicts with the government's policy of full and open competition and may increase the total costs of a procurement. However, the prevailing view is that these negative features are offset by the benefits that flow to many contractors that would otherwise be excluded from the process.

There are a number of ways in which collateral policies impact on the government procurement function. First, the contract price may be increased by excluding from award an offeror with a potentially lower price. For example, to implement a collateral policy, an agency may specify that award will be made only to offerors in a preferred group, even though entities outside that group may be able to offer lower prices. Contractors' administrative costs of implementing collateral programs also lead to higher overall prices. Second, agencies also incur additional costs in implementing the policies. They need to prepare, maintain, and enforce extensive regulations and may become involved in "bid protests" over whether particular awards are consistent with the rules concerning collateral policies. Some observers have also suggested that collateral policies sometimes result in awards to firms that are more likely to default, thereby seriously impeding the procurement process and ultimately causing added expense and delays to the involved agencies.

In view of these factors, there has been constant debate over whether the government should use the procurement process to implement collateral policies. Proponents of implementation argue that it is reasonable and effective to use the government's purchasing power to carry out policies aiding disadvantaged persons, reducing unemployment, reducing pollution, conserving energy, and accomplishing other beneficial purposes. These proponents also argue that the policies broaden the base of suppliers, thereby ultimately increasing competition for federal contracts.

Opponents contend that since the costs of implementing collateral policies are high and may be hidden, there rarely is any conclusive determination that the costs are justified by the benefits. They argue further that the collateral policies are often difficult to reconcile with one another and frequently become outmoded, that the acquisition process is slowed and made more complicated by the collateral policies, and that some potentially excellent contractors become discouraged by the preferences and by the complex regulations that their enforcement requires. This view has prevailed, to some extent, by the adoption in the Federal Acquisition Streamlining Act of provisions calling for the inapplicability of some of the collateral policies when the government uses simplified acquisition procedures or procures commercial items. See Chapter 7 for a discussion of this relaxation of the collateral policies.

There is a view that collateral policies can be implemented only when authorized by statute. GAO has ruled that an executive agency needs a clear grant of authority from Congress to implement a collateral policy that limits those who are eligible for award of contracts, 10 Comp. Gen. 294 (A-34106) (1931); 42 Comp. Gen. 1 (B-148930) (1962). GAO also has held that a particular executive agency's rules for collateral policies must be consistent with higher-level executive branch regulations, *Educational Servs. Group (ESG)*, 62 Comp. Gen. 353 (B-210420), 83-1 CPD ¶ 466.

Statutory authority for collateral policies may be explicit or implicit. Examples of explicit statutory authority are the Buy American Act, 41 U.S.C. § 8301 et seq., and the Small Business Act, 15 U.S.C. § 631 et seq. Implicit authority can be found in the general language of the procurement statutes, particularly in the Federal Property and Administrative Services Act (FPASA), 40 U.S.C. § 481(a) (now § 501), which requires procurement of goods and services in a manner "advantageous to the Government in terms of economy, efficiency, or service." See *American Fed'n of Labor & Congress of Indus. Orgs. v. Kahn*, 618 F.2d 784 (D.C. Cir.), *cert. denied*, 443 U.S. 915 (1979), where the court sustained the power of the President to deny contract awards to companies that were in violation of presidentially imposed wage and price standards; and *Contractors Ass'n of E. Pa. v. Secretary of Labor*, 442 F.2d 159 (3d Cir.), *cert. denied*, 404 U.S. 854 (1971), where the court sustained equal employment contract provisions promulgated under Executive Order 11,246. Compare *Liberty Mut. Ins. Co. v. Friedman*, 639 F.2d 164 (4th Cir. 1981), where the court held that this statutory authority did not authorize the imposition of equal employment obligations on a workers' compensation insurer. In *Chamber of Commerce v. Reich*, 74 F.3d 1322 (D.C. Cir. 1996), the court reversed the district court's finding that the President had authority under the FPASA to issue an executive order authorizing the Secretary of Labor to disqualify workers with federal contracts exceeding $100,000 who hire permanent replacement workers during a lawful economic strike. The court stated that although the broad contract management authority under the FPASA generally permits the President to draw on policy views directed beyond immediate concerns with the quality and price of purchased goods, labor relations are viewed differently because of the NLRA and its broad field of preemption.

GAO also has upheld some collateral policies where authorization was found in broad statutory language, *Fairplain Dev. Co.*, 59 Comp. Gen. 409 (B-192483), 80-1 CPD ¶ 293 (policy dealing with preference for location of federal facilities in urban areas).

# I.  POLICIES ASSISTING SMALL BUSINESSES

Congress has authorized a number of programs the are designed to assist small businesses in the procurement process. These programs are under the general supervision and control of the Small Business Administration (SBA) and are promulgated by the Small Business Act, 15 U.S.C. § 631 et seq. Under this Act, the SBA establishes small business size standards, rules on size appeals, and is solely authorized to make determinations that a small business is not a responsible contractor. The Act also establishes a number of business preferences for small businesses, including "set-aside" programs and programs to assist in small business subcontracting. These various programs are discussed in this section.

## A.  Size Determination

The Small Business Act defines a "small business concern" as one that is independently owned and operated and that is not dominant in its field of operation, 15 U.S.C. § 632(a)(1). The statute provides that a concern's number of employees and dollar business volume criteria determine whether it qualifies as a small business. The SBA has established size criteria for numerous classes of businesses, as classified in the North American Industry Classification System (NAICS). The NAICS Manual is at *www.census.gov/eped/www/naics.html*. See 13 C.F.R. § 121.201 for a listing of size standards by industry, NAICS code, and description. When a procurement is directed to small businesses, the contracting officer is required to identify the appropriate NAICS code in the solicitation, FAR 19.303(a). If different products or services are included in a procurement, the solicitation must state the appropriate NAICS code for each product or service, FAR 19.303(b). The contracting officer's determination of the appropriate NAICS code is "final," FAR 19.303(c), but if appealed to the SBA, the contracting officer must follow the decision of the SBA, *Eagle Home Medical Corp.*, Comp. Gen. Dec. B-402387, 2010 CPD ¶ 82. SBA decisions on the appropriate NAICS code are also binding on GAO, *DynaLantic Corp.*, Comp. Gen. Dec. B-402326, 2010 CPD ¶ 103. If a contracting officer awards a contract based on the SBA's determination of the appropriate NAICS code, the agency is not required to terminate the contract if that determination is reversed by the SBA Office of Hear-

ings and Appeals, *ONS21 Security Servs.*, Comp. Gen. Dec. B-403067, 2010
CPD ¶ 218.

Most size determinations are based on average gross receipts or number of employees, 15 U.S.C. § 632(a)(2), 13 C.F.R. Part 121. The standards vary from one
industry to another, depending on the number and sizes of firms within the industry,
but they "may utilize number of employees, dollar volume of business, net worth,
net income, a combination thereof, or other appropriate factors," 15 U.S.C. § 632(a)
(2)(B). A company whose stock is publicly traded, as opposed to a corporation
whose stock is privately held, can qualify as a small business concern if it meets the
size standard designated in the solicitation, *Geo-Seis Helicopters, Inc.*, SIZ-94-3-
23-32, 1994 SBA LEXIS 29.

In terms of determining annual receipts, 13 C.F.R. § 121.104 states:

> (1) Receipts means "total income" (or in the case of a sole proprietorship, "gross
> income") plus the "cost of goods sold" as these terms are defined or reported on
> Internal Revenue Service (IRS) Federal tax return forms (such as Form 1120 for
> corporations; Form 1120S and Schedule K for S corporations; Form 1120, Form
> 1065 or Form 1040 for LLCs; Form 1065 and Schedule K for partnerships; Form
> 1040, Schedule F for farms; Form 1040, Schedule C for other sole proprietor-
> ships). Receipts do not include net capital gains or losses, taxes collected for and
> remitted to a taxing authority if included in gross or total income, such as sales or
> other taxes collected from customers and excluding taxes levied on the concern
> or its employees; proceeds from transactions between a concern and its domestic
> or foreign affiliates; and amounts collected for another by a travel agent, real es-
> tate agent, advertising agent, or conference management service provider, freight
> forwarder or customs broker. For size determination purposes, the only exclu-
> sions from receipts are those specifically provided for in this paragraph. All other
> items, such as subcontractor costs, reimbursements for purchases a contractor
> makes at a customer's request, and employee-based costs such as payroll taxes,
> may not be excluded from receipts.

A concern must prove that it acted as an agent if it is seeking to exclude amounts
"collected for others," *Social Impact, Inc.*, SIZ-5090, 2009 SBA LEXIS 109. See
also *Crown Moving & Storage Co.* SIZ-4872, 2007 SBA LEXIS 57 (rent paid by affiliated firm is not included in computation); *Kittrell Garlock & Assocs.*, SIZ-94-10-
26-142, 1995 SBA LEXIS 32 (consultants' fees of an architectural and engineering
firm must be included in calculating average annual receipts).

Annual receipts for a concern that has been in business for three or more
completed fiscal years means the receipts of the concern over its last three completed fiscal years divided by three, 13 C.F.R. § 121.104(c)(1). For a concern that
has been in business for less than three completed fiscal years, annual receipts
means the receipts for the period the concern has been in business divided by the
number of weeks in business, multiplied by 52, 13 C.F.R. § 121.104(c)(2). Re-

ceipts are determined from the concern's federal tax returns and the SBA is not obligated to analyze the returns to determine whether sales have been reported for the correct year, *J.M. Waller Assocs., Inc.*, SIZ-5108, 2010 SBA LEXIS 8.

## 1. Affiliates

An offeror's size is determined by considering not only the offeror itself, but by aggregating the annual receipts and number of employees of the offeror and all "affiliates," regardless of industrial classification. FAR 19.101 provides that "[b]usiness concerns are affiliates of each other if, directly or indirectly, either one controls or has the power to control the other, or another concern controls or has the power to control both." In determining affiliation, all pertinent facts may be considered, including common ownership, common management, and contractual relationships, 13 C.F.R. § 121.103; FAR 19.101. Note that not all affiliation factors need be considered — only those appropriate or relevant under the specific facts of the case. Moreover, equal weight need not be given to each factor; the presence of one or more of these factors may be sufficient to constitute affiliation, *Agrigold Juice Prods.*, SIZ-95-7-19-72, 1996 SBA LEXIS 7. In addition, these factors are not intended to be exhaustive. Affiliation has been a controversial issue, particularly where a finding of affiliation has the effect of disqualifying a concern that would otherwise be able to compete as a small business, *Aloha Dredging & Constr. Co. v. Heatherly*, 661 F. Supp. 738 (D.D.C. 1987). See also Reeder and Vergilio, *Small Business Set-Asides and Corporate Affiliation — A Billion Dollar Business*, 15 Pub. Cont. L.J. 279 (1985).

If an affiliate dissolves itself, its sales need not be counted as long as the dissolution is completed prior to the beginning of the first year in the calculation of annual sales, *Hallmark-Phoenix 8, LLC*, SIZ-5046, 2009 SBA LEXIS 57 (sales required to be counted because dissolution not complete).

Common ownership is often considered in determining affiliation. For instance, affiliation has been found to exist among firms owned by brothers and a cousin and uncle, based not on family ties but rather on the common investments and ownership, *Agrigold Juice Prods.*, SIZ-95-7-19-72, 1996 SBA LEXIS 7. See also *Vortec Dev. Inc.*, SIZ-4866, 2007 SBA LEXIS 58, finding firms owner by a brother and sister to be affiliates. Similarly, where a franchiser controlled 60% of the franchisee's voting stock, the franchiser's chairman of the board was also the franchisee's chairman of the board, the franchiser provided ongoing management and assistance to the franchisee, and there were excessive restrictions on the sale of the franchisee's stock, the two firms were considered affiliates, *ERM-South, Inc.*, SIZ-95-4-12-33, 1995 SBA LEXIS 139. On the other hand, in *ROH, Inc.*, SIZ-94-11-25-156, 1995 SBA LEXIS 59, the SBA found no affiliation between firms where the challenged firm's owner had sold all its stock in a large firm and divested any interest prior to the challenged firm's self-certification as a small business, and there was no evidence to show that any ties remained between the two firms. See also *Shiloh Indus. Contractors, Inc.*, SIZ-95-9-22-90, 1996 SBA LEXIS 9 (although both firms were owned by the same family, no affiliation existed because the alleged large firm had no ownership or other interest in the other firm, and the firms did not share officers, directors, shareholders, employees, or facilities); and *Griffin Servs., Inc.*, SIZ-95-10-28-110, 1996 SBA LEXIS 4 (no affiliation where alleged affiliates no longer shared family ties, and the challenged firm's owner had given up his executive position and sold his stock in the alleged affiliate nine years prior to the challenge). See FAR 19.101(4) and (5) for guidance on the impact of stock options, convertible debentures and voting trusts in determining common ownership.

Common management is another factor often considered when examining affiliation. For example, where the overall management of a contract is only nominally in the control of the prime contractor and actual control resides in a large subcontractor and there is no demarcation of the tasks that would be performed by each participant, the relationship will be regarded as a joint venture and the firms will be considered affiliates, *Fortier & Assocs., Inc.*, SIZ-95-2-22-15, 1995 SBA LEXIS 88. Similarly, where the ostensible subcontractor will perform the vital and primary requirements of the solicitation, the relationship will be regarded as a joint venture and the firms will be considered affiliates under the solicitation, *CardioMetrix, Inc.*, SIZ-95-1-11-4, 1995 SBA LEXIS 84. See FAR 19.101(6) for guidance on the impact of interlocking management, common facilities and newly organized concerns on the determination of common management. See *Sabre88, LLC*, SIZ-5161, 2010 SBA LEXIS 82, holding that a newly organized firm was affiliated with a firm from which the founders came and which provided most of the new firm's work.

Affiliation may be found based upon a contractual relationship between parties. For example, where an agreement between the challenged firm and a large firm provides that the large firm has total management authority over the challenged firm's contracts, the businesses will be considered affiliates, *Picazo Constructors, Inc.*, SIZ-94-7-19-95, 1994 SBA LEXIS 66. See FAR 19.101(7) for guidance on this determination.

A determination of affiliation through stock ownership is provided in 13 C.F.R. § 121.103(c). This provision states that an individual, concern or other entity is an affiliate of a concern if it "owns, or has the power to control, 50 percent or more of a concern's voting stock, or a block of voting stock which is large compared to other outstanding blocks of voting stock." Similar guidance is provided in FAR 19.101(3). If a single person owns over 50% of the stock of two companies, they will be found to be affiliates even though the person does not actually exercise control, *DMS Facility Servs., LLC*, SIZ-4913, 2008 SBA LEXIS 31. See *McLane Advanced Techs., LLC*, SIZ-474, 2005 SBA LEXIS 79, for a discussion of the application of these rules to limited liability companies.

An affiliation may arise where officers, directors, or other key employees serve as the majority or otherwise as the controlling element of another concern. See *SA Techs., Inc.*, SIZ-95-4-28-40, 1995 SBA LEXIS 143, where because key employees of a large firm organized a new firm in the same industry and the large firm's purchase orders amounted to 80% of the new firm's annual receipts, the two firms were considered affiliated. But see *Ferg-N-Sons Plastics, Inc.*, SIZ-94-2-22-12, 1994 SBA LEXIS 4 (individual was the comptroller but not an officer or director of the business entity and thus not considered a key employee).

Joint venturers will be held to be affiliates if they are "awarded more than three contracts over a two year period, starting from the date of the award of the first contract," 13 C.F.R. § 121.103(h). Subcontractors have been held to fall under this rule if they are "ostensible subcontractors," *B&M Constr., Inc.*, SIZ-2006-06-05-40, 2006 SBA LEXIS 60; *STA Techs., Inc.*, SIZ-2006-04-24-28, 2006 SBA LEXIS 38.

13 C.F.R. § 121.103(b) excludes from affiliation coverage:

(1) Business concerns owned in whole or substantial part by investment companies licensed, or development companies qualifying, under the Small Business Investment Act of 1958, as amended, are not considered affiliates of such investment companies or development companies.

(2)(i) Business concerns owned and controlled by Indian Tribes, Alaska Native Corporations (ANCs) organized pursuant to the Alaska Native Claims Settlement Act (43 U.S.C. 1601 et seq.), Native Hawaiian Organizations (NHOs), Community Development Corporations (CDCs) authorized by 42 U.S.C. 9805, or wholly-owned entities of Indian Tribes, ANCs, NHOs, or CDCs are not considered affiliates of such entities.

(ii) Business concerns owned and controlled by Indian Tribes, ANCs, NHOs, CDCs, or wholly-owned entities of Indian Tribes, ANCs, NHOs, or CDCs are not considered to be affiliated with other concerns owned by these entities because of their common ownership or common management. In addition, affiliation will not be found based upon the performance of common administrative services, such as bookkeeping and payroll, so long as adequate payment is provided for those services. Affiliation may be found for other reasons.

(3) Business concerns which are part of an SBA approved pool of concerns for a joint program of research and development or for defense production as authorized by the Small Business Act are not affiliates of one another because of the pool.

(4) Business concerns which lease employees from concerns primarily engaged in leasing employees to other businesses or which enter into a co-employer arrangement with a Professional Employer Organization (PEO) are not affiliated with the leasing company or PEO solely on the basis of a leasing agreement.

(5) For financial, management or technical assistance under the Small Business Investment Act of 1958, as amended, an applicant is not affiliated with the investors listed in paragraphs (b)(5) (i) through (vi) of this section.

(i) Venture capital operating companies, as defined in the U.S. Department of Labor regulations found at 29 CFR 2510.3-101(d);

(ii) Employee benefit or pension plans established and maintained by the Federal government or any state, or their political subdivisions, or any agency or instrumentality thereof, for the benefit of employees;

(iii) Employee benefit or pension plans within the meaning of the Employee Retirement Income Security Act of 1974, as amended (29 U.S.C. 1001, et seq.);

(iv) Charitable trusts, foundations, endowments, or similar organizations exempt from Federal income taxation under section 501(c) of the Internal Revenue Code of 1986, as amended (26 U.S.C. 501(c));

(v) Investment companies registered under the Investment Company Act of 1940, as amended (1940 Act) (15 U.S.C. 80a-1, et seq.); and

(vi) Investment companies, as defined under the 1940 Act, which are not registered under the 1940 Act because they are beneficially owned by less than 100 persons, if the company's sales literature or organizational documents indicate that its principal purpose is investment in securities rather than the operation of commercial enterprises.

(6) An 8(a) BD Participant that has an SBA-approved mentor/protege agreement is not affiliated with a mentor firm solely because the protege firm receives assistance from the mentor under the agreement. Similarly, a protege firm is not affiliated with its mentor solely because the protege firm receives assistance from the mentor under a Federal Mentor-Protege program where an exception to affiliation is specifically authorized by statute or by SBA under the procedures set forth in § 121.903. Affiliation may be found in either case for other reasons.

(7) The member shareholders of a small agricultural cooperative, as defined in the Agricultural Marketing Act (12 U.S.C. 1141j), are not considered affiliated with the cooperative by virtue of their membership in the cooperative.

Where a different party is involved in a later protest involving that firm, the doctrines of res judicata and collateral estoppel do not apply, and a regional office or area office may reach a contrary result as to affiliation as long as it adequately explains the legal and factual basis for that result, *Agrigold Juice Prods.*, SIZ-95-7-19-72, 1996 SBA LEXIS 7. In this case, an area office determined that Agrigold was other than a small business based on affiliation. Agrigold argued that the area office failed to give proper weight to the prior regional office determination that it was small. The SBA stated that because the regional office determination was not appealed, the Office of Hearings and Appeals had no opportunity to consider the question and, thus, the prior regional office determination did not constitute precedent.

## 2. Subcontracts to Large Firms

15 U.S.C. § 644(o) limits the amount of subcontracting by small businesses as follows:

(1) A concern may not be awarded a contract under subsection (a) as a small business concern unless the concern agrees that— —

    (A) in the case of a contract for services (except construction), at least 50 percent of the cost of contract performance incurred for personnel shall be expended for employees of the concern; and

    (B) in the case of a contract for procurement of supplies (other than procurement from a regular dealer in such supplies), the concern will perform work for at least 50 percent of the cost of manufacturing the supplies (not including the cost of materials).

(2) The Administrator may change the percentage under subparagraph (A) or (B) of paragraph (1) if the Administrator determines that such change is necessary to reflect conventional industry practices among business concerns that are below the numerical size standard for businesses in that industry category.

(3) The Administration shall establish, through public rulemaking, requirements similar to those specified in paragraph (1) to be applicable to contracts for general and specialty construction and to contracts for any other industry category not otherwise subject to the requirements of such paragraph. The percentage applicable to any such requirement shall be determined in accordance with paragraph (2).

This statute is implemented in 13 C.F.R. § 125.6 which states that the 50% rule applies to full or partial small business set-aside contracts, 8(a) contracts, WOSB or EDWOSB contracts, or unrestricted procurements where a concern has claimed a 10% small disadvantaged business price evaluation preference. This regulation adopts a 15% rule for construction contracts. FAR 52.219-14 contains a Limitation on Subcontracting clause for use on procurements over the simplified acquisition threshold when this requirement applies. When an agency uses this clause for a contract for both supplies and services, it must specify which work is the predominant work to which the clause will apply, *TFab Mfg., LLC*, Comp. Gen. Dec. B-401190, 2009 CPD ¶ 127. The result of this interpretation is that the less predominant work will not be subject to the 50 % limitation. When the clause is used on a contract with option years, the contractor can perform less than 50% of the work during the early years as long as it performs 50% of the work over the entire contract, *Spectrum Security Servs., Inc.*, Comp. Gen. Dec. B-297320.2, 2005 CPD

¶ 227. GAO will not rule on a protest that the winning offeror will not comply with this clause unless that lack of compliance if apparent on the fact of the offer, *Chant Eng'g Co.*, Comp. Gen. Dec. B-402054 2010 CPD ¶ 16; *TYBRIN Corp.*, Comp. Gen. Dec. B-298364.6, 2007 CPD ¶ 51.

In a total small business set-aside, service-disabled veteran-owned small business set-aside, WOSB or EDWOSB set-aside, or an 8(a) procurement for products, a small business that is not a manufacturer but is a regular dealer is permitted to offer a product that is totally manufactured by another small business, 13 C.F.R. § 121.406. This "nonmanufacturer" rule is explained in FAR 19.102(f) and 19.502-3(c). A nonmanufacturer must be a small business under the applicable size standard, FAR 19.001. Waivers to the requirement that the manufacturing subcontractor be a small business are issued by the SBA on an individual or class basis, FAR 19.102(f)(4). The nonmanufacturer rule is implemented by including the FAR 52.219-6 Notice of Small Business Set-Aside clause in solicitations, FAR 19.508(c). If a waiver has been issued, Alternate I is used. See *Controlled Sys.*, SIZ-5039, 2009 SBA LEXIS 46. affirming the issuance of a contract to a nonmanufacturer obtaining the product from a large business when a class waiver had been issued. When no waiver had been issued, a bid that indicated that the end item would not be manufactured or produced by a small business was considered nonresponsive, *American Amplifier & Tel. Corp.*, 53 Comp. Gen. 463 (B-179149), 74-1 CPD ¶ 10. If a small business offers the product of a large business and no class waiver has been issued by the SBA, the contracting officer must reject the offer or seek a waiver from the SBA in accordance with FAR 19.102(f)(5), *Hydroid, LLC*, Comp. Gen. Dec. B-299072, 2007 CPD ¶ 20 (termination of contract recommended). There has been considerable controversy as to whether the nonmanufacturer rule applies to contracts that call for services along with products. See *Rotech Healthcare, Inc. v. United States*, 71 Fed. Cl. 393 (2006) (interpreting 15 U.S.C. § 637(a)(17) to require application of the rule to all contracts calling for products). The SBA regulation at 13 C.F.R. § 121.406(b) states:

> (3) The nonmanufacturer rule applies only to procurements that have been assigned a manufacturing or supply NAICS code. The nonmanufacturer rule does not apply to contracts that have been assigned a service, construction, or specialty trade construction NAICS code.

> (4) The nonmanufacturer rule applies only to the supply component of a requirement classified as a manufacturing or supply contract. If a requirement is classified as a service contract, but also has a supply component, the nonmanufacturer rule does not apply to the supply component of the requirement.

See *Eagle Home Med. Corp.*, Comp. Gen. Dec. B-402382, 2010 CPD ¶ 82, following the SBA regulation and distinguishing *Rotech* after the SBA ruled that a contract for mixed products and services should be classified as a contract for rental of equipment with the result that no manufacturing was called for by the contract (making the nonmanufacturer rule inapplicable). See also *B&B Med. Servs., Inc.,* Comp. Gen. Dec. B-404241, 2011 CPD ¶ 24, holding that the nonmanufacturer rule does not apply to procurements set aside for HUBZone concerns.

GAO has consistently held that subcontracting up to 49% of the contract dollar volume is not against the policy of the Small Business Act, *M.D. Oppenheim & Co.,* 70 Comp. Gen. 213 (B-241252), 91-1 CPD ¶ 98; *Science Sys. & Applications, Inc.,* Comp. Gen. Dec. B-240311, 90-2 CPD ¶ 381. See also *Tonya, Inc. v. United States,* 28 Fed. Cl. 727 (1993), *aff'd without op.,* 31 F.3d 1176 (Fed. Cir. 1994), where the court held that an agency's expectation that a prospective contractor would subcontract a portion of its work to a large contractor did not violate the Small Business Act.

## 3. Self-Certification

The initial determination of size is made by the small business, which is required to "self-certify" with its offer that it is small, 13 C.F.R. § 121.405(a). Thus, each offeror must determine whether it qualifies as a small business. In order to facilitate self-certification, federal procuring agencies are required to classify the NAICS code applicable to the products and services being procured and specify an applicable size standard in each solicitation, FAR 19.102(b) and FAR 19.303. The self-certification is made by checking the appropriate blank(s) in the Small Business Program Representations solicitation provision in FAR 52.219-1, thereby representing and certifying whether the offeror is a small business concern. If a concern has submitted an Online Representation and Certification Applications (ORCA) for the same NAICS code, it can use that to meet the certification requirement, FAR 4.1201, but offerors should take care that their status has not changed at the time of submitting the offer. In sealed bid procurement, failure to self-certify at the time of bidding may not be cured after opening, *Covenant Indus., Inc.,* Comp. Gen. Dec. B-218091.2, 85-1 CPD ¶ 372; *Julie Cades,* Comp. Gen. Dec. B-248218, 92-2 CPD ¶ 18. Further, the failure of a bidder to self-certify is not cured by completion of the Place of Performance clause, which relates to responsibility of the bidder and not responsiveness of the bid, *Delta Concepts, Inc.,* 67 Comp. Gen. 522 (B-230632), 88-2 CPD ¶ 43.

FAR 19.309(d) requires the inclusion of the Post-Award Small Business Representation clause in FAR 52.219-28 in all contracts above the micro-purchase threshold. This clause requires recertification after execution of a novation agreement, the finalization of a merger of acquisition or prior to the end of a "long term" contract (a contract of more than 5 years duration, including options. See 13 C.F.R. § 121.404(g) stating that "long term" contracts include "Multiple Award Schedule (MAS) Contracts, Multiple Agency Contracts (MACs) and Government-wide Acquisition Contracts (GWACs),." See also *Enterprise Info. Servs., Inc.,* Comp. Gen. Dec. B-403028, 2010 CPD ¶ 213, holding that a contracting officer properly required recertification when issuing a task order under a seven year GWAC and noting that this was a discretionary rule.

An offeror may represent that it is "small" if it meets the definition of a small business concern in the solicitation and the SBA has made no adverse determination regarding its size status, FAR 19.301(a). The certification must be current at the time the small business submits an offer including price, 13 C.F.R. § 121.404(a). Thus, a self-certification at the time of a phase 1 proposal (excluding price) was not effective when the concern was not a small business at the time it submitted its phase 2 proposal which included price. See *Cox Constr. Co.*, SIZ-5070, 2009 SBA LEXIS 76, rejecting the arguments that the ORCA procedure in FAR 4.1201, calling only for annual updates, overrode the SBA regulation and that the fact that the contracting officer did not call for a new representation with the phase 2 proposal freed the offeror from the SBA requirement.

This certification must be made in accordance with a high standard of good faith because of the potential for abuse inherent in a self-certification procedure, *Bancroft Cap Co.*, 55 Comp. Gen. 469 (B-182569), 75-2 CPD ¶ 321. Lack of good faith is "not necessarily limited to an incident of intentional misrepresentation" but can also be found in a failure to exercise prudence and care in ascertaining size under prescribed guidelines, 51 Comp. Gen. 595 (B-174807) (1972). A bidder's self-certification was held to be not prepared in good faith when it certified itself as small although it knew the SBA had questioned that status, 41 Comp. Gen. 47 (B-144621) (1961). However, in 49 Comp. Gen. 369 (B-167353) (1969), GAO found no basis for imputing bad faith even though the successful bidder changed its management structure between the filing of the protest and the SBA size determination and it was held not to be a small business at the time of award. In *Vantex Serv. Corp.*, Comp. Gen. Dec. B-251102, 93-1 CPD ¶ 221, a contractor properly certified as a small business was awarded a contract and later was acquired by a large business. GAO found that the agency was not required to reexamine the contractor's size status in order to exercise an option under the contract because the size determination at the time of self-certification controls.

A knowingly false certification of small business status is a crime under 15 U.S.C. § 645(d), punishable by a fine up to $500,000 or imprisonment for up to ten years. It can also be the basis for a civil false claims suit. See also *United States ex re Longi v. Lithium Power Techs, Inc.*, 530 F. Supp. 2d 888 (S.D. Tex. 2008), *aff'd*, 575 F.3d 458 (5th Cir. 2009), assessing treble damages under the False Claims Act, 31 U.S.C. § 3729 et seq., requiring repayment of three times the prices of four SBIR contracts that had been obtained by falsely certifying that the firm was a small business. Compare *Ab-Tech Const., Inc. v. United States*, 31 Fed. Cl. 429 (1994), *aff'd*, 57 F.3d 1084 (Fed. Cir. 1995), finding a false certification that the contractor was an 8(a) firm. There the court granted statutory damages under the False Claims Act of $10,000 per invoice submitted on the contract but did not grant treble damages because the contractor had fully performed the contract. The Small Business Jobs Act of 2010, Pub. L. No. 111-240, Sept. 27, 2010, added a provision to 15 U.S.C. § 632 making it a presumption that the loss to the United States for false certification is the entire contract price (establishing a right to treble damages). This provision states:

(w) Presumption. — (1) In general — In every contract, subcontract, cooperative agreement, cooperative research and development agreement, or grant which is set aside, reserved, or otherwise classified as intended for award to small business concerns, there shall be a presumption of loss to the United States based on the total amount expended on the contract, subcontract, cooperative agreement, cooperative research and development agreement, or grant whenever it is established that a business concern other than a small business concern willfully sought and received the award by misrepresentation. (2) Deemed certifications — The following actions shall be deemed affirmative, willful, and intentional certifications of small business size and status:

(A) Submission of a bid or proposal for a Federal grant, contract, subcontract, cooperative agreement, or cooperative research and development agreement reserved, set aside, or otherwise classified as intended for award to small business concerns.

(B) Submission of a bid or proposal for a Federal grant, contract, subcontract, cooperative agreement, or cooperative research and development agreement which in any way encourages a Federal agency to classify the bid or proposal, if awarded, as an award to a small business concern.

(C) Registration on any Federal electronic database for the purpose of being considered for award of a Federal grant, contract, subcontract, cooperative agreement, or cooperative research agreement, as a small business concern.

(3) Certification by signature of responsible official. —

(A) In general. — Each solicitation, bid, or application for a Federal contract, subcontract, or grant shall contain a certification concerning the small business size and status of a business concern seeking the Federal contract, subcontract, or grant.

(B) Content of certifications. — A certification that a business concern qualifies as a small business concern of the exact size and status claimed by the business concern for purposes of bidding on a Federal contract or subcontract, or applying for a Federal grant, shall contain the signature of an authorized official on the same page on which the certification is contained.

In addition, state law may provide a remedy for fraud, unjust enrichment, or interference with a business relationship caused by a lowest bidder that misrepresents itself as a small business, See, for example, *Tectonics, Inc. v. Castle Constr. Co.*, 753 F.2d 957 (11th Cir.), *cert. denied*, 474 U.S. 848 (1985), and *Iconco v. Jensen Constr. Co.*, 622 F.2d 1291 (8th Cir. 1980), where losing offerors recovered against contractors that falsely certified their status. Obviously, to receive such a remedy, the plaintiff must demonstrate that the firm that received the award does not qualify as a small business under the Act, *Ferguson-Williams, Inc. v. BAMSI, Inc.*, 782 F.2d 940 (11th Cir. 1986) (SBA determined that low bidder qualified as a small business; therefore, no recovery was allowed).

An offeror's self-certification is normally accepted without any further inquiry, unless it is challenged, FAR 19.301(b); *Otis Steel Prods. Corp. v. United States*, 161 Ct. Cl. 694, 316 F.2d 937 (1963). Challenges may be made by the contracting officer, offerors in the same procurement, or other interested parties. Although such challenges are often filed with the procuring agency, the investigation and determination of whether the offeror is in fact "small" will be made by the SBA, FAR 19.302(c). An initial determination is ordinarily made by a regional office of the SBA. Any appeal must be taken to the SBA Office of Hearings and Appeals in Washington, D.C., "within the time limits and in strict accordance with the procedures contained in 13 C.F.R. Part 134," FAR 19.302(i). The procedures for protesting the self-certification of an offeror are set forth in 13 C.F.R. §§ 121.1001-1010.

Where a timely size protest is filed after a small business award, and the awardee is found by the SBA to be other than small, the agency, in the absence of legitimate countervailing reasons, should terminate the contract. In *Diagnostic Imaging Tech. Educ.*, Comp. Gen. Dec. B-257590, 94-2 CPD ¶ 148, the protester timely protested the size status of the awardee to the contracting officer, who referred the matter to the SBA. The SBA found the awardee to be other than a small business. In spite of this finding, the agency did not terminate the contract. GAO held that the agency should not have permitted the award to stand when it was apprised by the SBA that the awardee was not small, stating:

> While FAR § 19.302(j) treats post-award size protests as having no applicability to the current contract, awards under set-aside procurements to other than small businesses should be terminated if possible, and SBA's regulations provide that such timely-filed size protests "shall apply to the procurement in question even though the contracting officer may have awarded the contract prior to receipt of the protest." 13 C.F.R. § 121.1603(a)(2); *see also* FAR § 19.302(d)(1)(ii). Further, RSTI did not defend its adverse size certification by appealing SBA's determination. Thus, in the absence of countervailing reasons, it would be inconsistent with the integrity of the competitive procurement system, and the intent of the Small Business Act, to permit a large business, which under the terms of the solicitation was ineligible for award, to continue to perform the contract. *American Mobilphone Paging, Inc.*, [69 Comp. Gen. 392 (B-238027), 90-1 CPD ¶ 366].

See *Hydroid, LLC*, Comp. Gen. Dec. B-299072, 2007 CPD ¶ 20, describing the breadth of this rule as follows:

In prior cases where, as here, a contracting agency's improper actions led to an award before a size protest could be filed — typically, where the agency failed to provide the required pre-award notice of the intended awardee — and SBA determined after award that the awardee was not an eligible small business, we have sustained the protests and recommended termination of the contracts. See, e.g., *Spectrum Sec. Servs., Inc.*, B-297320.2, B-297320.3, Dec. 29, 2005, 2005 CPD ¶ 227 at 4; *Tiger Enters., Inc.*, B-292815.3, B-293439, Jan. 20, 2004, 2004 CPD ¶ 19 at 4-5.

GAO views the SBA as having conclusive authority to determine whether a particular business is "small" for purposes of federal procurement, *Arbor Indus., Inc.*, Comp. Gen. Dec. B-231515, 88-1 CPD ¶ 564. Therefore, GAO will not make such a determination, or review SBA determinations, *NJCT Corp.*, Comp. Gen. Dec. B-216919, 85-1 CPD ¶ 33. Once an offeror has been found not to be small, the offeror may not, unless the SBA has issued a later decision finding the firm to be small, certify itself as small under the same or lower standards as those under which it had been found not to be small, 13 C.F.R. § 121.1009(g)(5); *Choctaw Mfg. Co. v. United States*, 761 F.2d 609 (11th Cir. 1985); *Propper Int'l, Inc.*, 55 Comp. Gen. 1188 (B-185302), 76-1 CPD ¶ 400. See *Timothy S. Graves*, Comp. Gen. Dec. B-253813, 93-2 CPD ¶ 244, *recons. denied*, 94-1 CPD ¶ 19, where award was denied to a firm that was in fact small at the time of award. In this case, the bidder on a timber sale had been determined not to be a small business by the SBA regional office. The bidder appealed the determination to the SBA's Office of Hearings and Appeals (OHA), and while the matter was being considered by the OHA, the bidder submitted a bid on a subsequent timber sale and certified itself to be a small business. Subsequently, the OHA reversed the regional office's determination on the previous contract, and the agency proposed to award the contract to the bidder. However, the award was appealed to the OHA, which held that the bidder could not qualify as small because the regional office determination had not been reversed at the time that the bidder signed its self-certification, even though by OHA's own determination, the bidder was small at the time. GAO denied the subsequent protest on the grounds that the SBA size determination was conclusive.

Once a business is found to be other than small, it is required to be recertified by SBA prior to bidding on any government procurement, 13 C.F.R. § 121.1010. In *Evans Cooperage Co.*, SIZ-94-11-2-145, 1995 SBA LEXIS 55, the appellant was found to be other than small for the applicable 500-employee size standard in a particular solicitation. The appellant did not recertify but stated that it had intended to do so and that it now had fewer than 500 employees. The SBA found that this argument had no merit.

## B. Certificates of Competency

The SBA has the authority to issue certificates of competency (COCs) for all elements of responsibility of small businesses. In the original Small Business

Act, Congress authorized the SBA to certify as to the "capacity and credit" of small businesses to perform particular contracts. If a small business were found by a contracting officer not to be responsible, the firm could seek a COC from the SBA. If granted, such a certificate was conclusive on the procuring agency as to the "capacity and credit" of the small business for performance of the particular contract. However, GAO later ruled that since "responsibility" determinations included elements — such as perseverance, integrity, and tenacity — that were separable from "capacity and credit," contracting officers could still find a small business not responsible, even though the SBA had issued a COC, 43 Comp. Gen. 257 (B-151121) (1963).

As a result of complaints about this "dilution" of the COC authority, Congress expanded the reach of such certificates in 1977 to cover "all elements of responsibility, including, but not limited to, capability, competency, capacity, credit, integrity, perseverance, and tenacity," 15 U.S.C. § 637(b)(7). Such a certificate is conclusive on a procuring agency, *J.R. Youngdale Constr. Co.*, Comp. Gen. Dec. B-219439, 85-2 CPD ¶ 473; *International Bus. Invs., Inc.*, 60 Comp. Gen. 275 (B-198894), 81-1 CPD ¶ 125. The scope of the SBA's review authority is not limited to those factors specified by a contracting officer as deficient in a referral letter, but rather includes all elements of responsibility, *C & G Excavating, Inc. v. United States*, 32 Fed. Cl. 231 (1994) (contracting officer based nonresponsibility finding on capacity, whereas SBA based nonresponsibility on financial condition). Neither the SBA nor the procuring agency may create exceptions to the statutory requirement for referral to the SBA for determination regarding whether a COC should be issued, 15 U.S.C. § 637(b)(7); *Sess Constr. Co.*, 64 Comp. Gen. 355 (B-216924), 85-1 CPD ¶ 319; *Small Business Admin. — Request for Recons.*, Comp. Gen. Dec. B-219654.3, 86-1 CPD ¶ 420.

COCs are issued on a contract-by-contract basis. If a contracting officer determines that a small business that submitted the most favorable acceptable offer lacks responsibility, contract award must be withheld and the matter referred to the "cognizant SBA Regional Office," FAR 19.602-1(a)(2). The SBA then offers the small business an opportunity to apply for a COC, FAR 19.602-2(a)(1). If the small business provides the detailed information required by the application, the SBA will investigate the matter and issue or deny issuance of the COC. If the SBA has not issued a COC within 15 business days, or a longer period agreed to by the contracting officer, the agency proceeds with the acquisition, FAR 19.602-4(c). See *General Painting Co.*, Comp. Gen. Dec. B-219449, 85-2 CPD ¶ 530, holding that award should have been made when the SBA delayed issuing a COC without an agreement with the contracting officer. If an agency rejects a proposal as technically unacceptable on the basis of factors not related to responsibility as well as responsibility-related ones, the agency is not required to refer the matter to the SBA under its COC procedure, *Paragon Dynamics, Inc.*, Comp. Gen. Dec. B-251280, 93-1 CPD ¶ 248.

Prior to issuance of a COC, the SBA is required to notify the contracting officer, FAR 19.602-2(d). If the contracting officer disagrees with the proposed issuance of a COC, and the controversy cannot be resolved through further communications, the procuring agency may request referral of the matter to the SBA Central Office, FAR 19.602-3. A contractor otherwise eligible for the COC program is entitled to have the involved agency notify the SBA prior to terminating negotiations, so that the contractor could have the SBA's assistance in responding to the deficiencies perceived by the agency, *CelTech, Inc. v. United States*, 24 Cl. Ct. 269 (1991).

The Court of Federal Claims will review the denial of a COC, *United Enter. & Assocs. v. United States*, 70 Fed. Cl. 1 (2006) (action of the SBA in denying COC was not arbitrary or capricious); *CSE Constr., Inc. v. United States*, 58 Fed. Cl. 230 (2003) (action of the SBA in denying COC was arbitrary and capricious because it did not consider full past performance of offeror). On the other hand, GAO will not review the denial of a COC unless the procurement agency makes a showing of fraud or bad faith, for example, where information vital to the determination of responsibility has not been considered, or where the SBA has disregarded its own published regulations, *West State, Inc.*, Comp. Gen. Dec. B-255692, 94-1 CPD ¶ 211; *Tomko, Inc.*, 63 Comp. Gen. 218 (B-210023.2), 84-1 CPD ¶ 202; *Skillens Enters.*, 61 Comp. Gen. 142 (B-202508.2), 81-2 CPD ¶ 472.

FAR 19.602-1(a)(2) provides that the COC procedure does not apply to issues of eligibility covered in FAR 9.104-1(g) or to suspended or debarred contractors. See *Aardvark Keith Moving, Inc.*, Comp. Gen. Dec. B-290565, 2002 CPD ¶ 134 (affiliated firm proposed for debarment). GAO has held that the COC procedure does not apply to an agency's determination that certain technical requirements are essential even though the effect of such a determination may be to exclude a small business from the procurement, *Aero Corp.*, 59 Comp. Gen. 146 (B-194445.3), 79-2 CPD ¶ 430. In addition, the COC procedure does not apply to findings that a proposal is technically unacceptable, *Light-Pod, Inc.*, Comp. Gen. Dec. B-401739, 2009 CPD ¶ 238, or that a bid is nonresponsive, *Trading Atlanta Ltd.*, Comp. Gen. Dec. B-238978, 90-2 CPD ¶ 52; *Vac-Hyde Corp.*, 64 Comp. Gen. 658 (B-216840), 85-2 CPD ¶ 2; *Pacific Sky Supply, Inc.*, 64 Comp. Gen. 194 (B-215189), 85-1 CPD ¶ 53. Neither does the COC procedure apply when an agency determines that the offer has not submitted sufficient information to demonstrate that it met the solicitation's experience requirement, *Eagle Aviation Servs. & Tech., Inc.*, Comp. Gen. Dec. B-403341, 2010 CPD ¶ 242, or that the offeror's low price creates a risk of nonperformance, *Zolon Tech, Inc.*, Comp. Gen. Dec. B-299904.2, 2007 CPD ¶ 183 (price was only one element in best value determination). Compare *J2Aû JV, LLC*, Comp. Gen. Dec. B-401663.4, 2010 CPD ¶ 102, recommending that an agency allow an offeror to attempt to obtain a COC determining that it met a definitive experience requirement.

The COC procedure does not apply when an agency is evaluating offers in a negotiated procurement if the evaluation factors are scored on a comparative basis, *J. Womack Enters., Inc.*, Comp. Gen. Dec. B-299344, 2007 CPD ¶ 69; *Smith of Galeton Gloves, Inc.*, Comp. Gen. Dec. B-271686, 96-2 CPD ¶ 36. However, if there is only one technical evaluation factor, past performance, a determination that a contractor does not have sufficient past performance is a responsibility determination, *Phil Howry Co.*, Comp. Gen. Dec. B-291402.3, 2003 CPD ¶ 33. However, the COC procedure is not applicable in deciding whether a small business concern comes within the "competitive range" in a negotiated procurement, even if some of the factors used in determining the "competitive range" are related to responsibility, *Electro-Methods, Inc. v. United States*, 7 Cl. Ct. 755 (1985); *C.M.P. Corp.*, Comp. Gen. Dec. B-211371, 83-2 CPD ¶ 238; *Electrospace Sys., Inc.*, 58 Comp. Gen. 415 (B-192574), 79-1 CPD ¶ 264. However, the COC procedure does apply if an agency determines that the offeror's price is unrealistically low, *Milani Constr., LLC*, Comp. Gen. Dec. B-401942, 2010 CPD ¶ 87 (low price is a matter of responsibility).

If an agency is evaluating offers on a go/no go basis, and the solicitation includes a criterion that is traditionally a responsibility-type factor, then the matter must be referred to the SBA, *Tri-Servs., Inc.*, Comp. Gen. Dec. B-256196.4, 94-2 CPD ¶ 121. GAO explained this rule in *Federal Support Corp.*, 71 Comp. Gen. 152 (B-245573), 92-1 CPD ¶ 81, stating:

> While traditional responsibility factors may be used as technical evaluation criteria in a negotiated procurement, *see, e.g., CORVAC, Inc.*, B-244766, Nov. 13, 1991, 91-2 CPD ¶ 454; and 87-1 CPD ¶ 292, the factors may be used only if circumstances warrant a comparative evaluation of those areas. *Flight Int'l Group, Inc.*, 69 Comp. Gen. 741 (1990), 90-2 CPD ¶ 257; *Sanford and Sons Co.*, 67 Comp. Gen. 612 (1988), 88-2 CPD ¶ 266. Otherwise, an agency effectively would be determining the responsibility of an offeror under the guise of making a technical evaluation of proposals. Under the Small Business Act, agencies may not find that a small business is nonresponsible without referring the matter to the SBA, which has the ultimate authority to determine the responsibility of small business concerns. See *Clegg Indus., Inc.*, B-242204.3, Aug 14, 1991, 70 Comp. Gen. 679, 91-2 CPD ¶ 145; 52 Comp. Gen. 47 (1972); *Antenna Prods. Corp.*, B-227116.2, Mar. 23, 1988, 88-1 CPD ¶ 297.

> Here, the Air Force did not use the responsibility-related technical evaluation criterion "corporate experience" for the purpose of making a comparative evaluation of proposals received; rather, it determined technical acceptability solely on a "go-no go" basis, and the record shows that FSC's proposal was found technically unacceptable and incapable of being made acceptable solely because of the firm's purported lack of 3 years of corporate experience in the area of operating civil engineering supply stores. Thus, regardless of how the corporate experience criterion was characterized in the RFP or the evaluation, the determination that FSC was technically unacceptable was, in effect, a determination by the

contracting officer that FSC was not a responsible contractor and the rejection of FSC's proposal without a referral to SBA for complete consideration under the COC procedures was improper.

SBA issuance of a COC was reversed because the bidder lacked the personnel, space, and equipment needed to produce marine propulsion systems; the overwhelming portion of the assembly work was subcontracted; and the bidder's leases were not binding within the meaning of Walsh-Healey regulations, *Ulstein Maritime, Ltd. v. United States*, 646 F. Supp. 720 (D.C. R.I. 1986). The court concluded that no COC should have been issued because both the Navy and the SBA failed to make a sincere inquiry into whether the bidder was capable of complying with the contract specifications.

## C. Business Preferences

It is federal policy that a "fair proportion" of government contracts and subcontracts be placed with small businesses, 15 U.S.C. § 631(a). See also 41 U.S.C. § 3104, and 50 U.S.C. App. § 468(a). In order to assure that small businesses receive a "fair proportion" of federal procurements, it has been recognized that small businesses must receive more smaller dollar contracts than they would obtain in full and open competition with large businesses since major systems contracts require greater funds and capability than small businesses possess. In seeking comment on a regulation dealing with small businesses, the Office of Federal Procurement Policy (OFPP) has stated at 49 Fed. Reg. 40135 (1984) that:

> The bulk of Federal expenditures are for major systems which, at the prime contract level, are unavailable to small business. Therefore, ensuring that small business receives a fair proportion of the total Government contracts practically dictates that a disproportionate share must be awarded to small business outside of the major systems.

A court of appeals has stated that Congress has sought to protect small business from unlimited competition, and that the term "fair proportion" of federal contracts is to be determined on the basis of total awards, not awards within a particular industry, *J.H. Rutter Rex Mfg. Co. v. United States*, 706 F.2d 702 (5th Cir.), *cert. denied*, 464 U.S. 1008 (1983).

Advocates of small business interests have periodically urged Congress to establish by statute the percentage of contract awards that would constitute a "fair proportion." Congress has made the President responsible for establishing annual government-wide goals for participation by small business concerns. 15 U.S.C. § 644(g)(1) provides that these goals may not fall below the congressionally mandated minimums of 23% of the total value of all prime contract awards for small businesses, and the percentages for various classes of small businesses set forth in **Figure 11-1**:

| Class of Small Business | Percentage |
|---|---|
| Concerns owned and controlled by socially and economically disadvantaged individuals | 5% |
| Concerns owned and controlled by women (WOSBs) | 5% |
| Concerns owned and controlled by service-disabled veterans (SDVOs) | 3% |
| HUBZone concerns | 3% |

**Figure 11-1**

Each agency is assigned goals which are to be set jointly by the head of the procuring agency and the SBA. If the procuring agency and SBA disagree, the Administrator of OFPP is empowered to resolve the dispute, 15 U.S.C. § 644(g)(2).

After each fiscal year, the procuring agency must inform the SBA of the extent to which the goals have been met; and the SBA must forward the information, along with any SBA comments, to the President who, in turn, includes the information in the annual report to Congress on the state of small business, 15 U.S.C. § 644(h).

These goals are achieved by setting aside procurements for small businesses, directing procurements to small businesses, giving small businesses a percentage evaluation preference and encouraging subcontracting with small businesses. Each of these techniques is discussed below. Following this discussion of the basic techniques used, the unique aspects of each of the special classes of small businesses is briefly discussed.

## 1. Set-Asides

The major form of preference given to small businesses in the award of federal contracts is through "set-asides," a term applied to the reservation of contracts for award only to a designated group. Congress has authorized federal agencies to restrict entire procurements ("total set-asides") or portions of procurements ("partial set-asides") for award to small businesses, 15 U.S.C. § 644(a). The primary responsibility for determining which procurements should be set aside is vested in the contracting officer, FAR 19.501(a), but SBA Procurement Center Representatives (PCRs) also review procurements not set aside to determine whether they should be set aside. See 13 C.F.R. § 125.2(b) requiring contracting officers to cooperate with PCRs in the acquisition planning process. When PCR recommendations are adopted, the set-asides are called "joint set-asides," FAR 19.501(b).

The Federal Acquisition Streamlining Act of 1994 (FASA), Pub. L. No. 103-355, § 7101, eliminated those sections of the Small Business Act that established the priority for award of partial and total set-asides. Contracting officers are required to set aside individual acquisitions or classes of acquisitions in order to assure that a fair proportion of government contracts in each NAICS category is placed with small business concerns. A contract may not be awarded under a small business set-aside if the cost of that contract exceeds a fair market price (15 U.S.C. § 644(a)) as determined by the price analysis techniques set forth in FAR 15.404-1(b), FAR 19.202-6(a).

Procurements above the micro-purchase threshold and within the simplified acquisition threshold are automatically set aside for small business unless the contracting officer determines that there is no reasonable possibility of obtaining two competitive offers, FAR 19.502-2. For procurements above the simplified acquisition threshold, the major contracting agencies do not use set-aside procedures for classes of work that have been determined to yield sufficient small business participation through open competition. This is called the Small Business Competitiveness Demonstration Program, FAR Subpart 19.10. See FAR 19.1005(a) for a list of the classes of procurement to which this program applies. The program also calls for these agencies to specify 10 classes of work where special efforts are necessary to attract small business participation because of past under-participation, FAR 19.1005(b). For a sample list, see DFARS 219.1005(b).

For procurements over the simplified acquisition threshold, set-asides to SDVOs, WOSBs, HUBZone concerns and procurements reserved for disadvantaged businesses through the 8(a) program are in parity with each other but take priority over set-asides to other small businesses, FAR 19.203(c). There is very little guidance on which class of small business should be selected for a set-aside, but contracting officers need to take a balanced approach to select a class of small businesses that can meet the agency needs and that will fulfill the agency's goals for each class. See 13 C.F.R. § 125.2(f)(2) stating:

> (ii) SBA believes that Progress in fulfilling the various small business goals, as well as other factors such as the results of market research, programmatic needs specific to the procuring agency, anticipated award price, and the acquisition history, will be considered in making a decision as to which program to use for the acquisition.

## a.  Total Set-Aside Procedures

Total set-asides are required if there is a reasonable expectation that offers will be made by at least two responsible small businesses, offering the products of differ ent small business concerns, and award will be made at "fair market prices," FAR 19.502-2(b). This "rule of two" has no basis in the statutes but is a product of an agreement between the SBA and the contracting agencies. See the SBA statement of the rule in 13 C.F.R. § 125.2(f)(2). Both the FAR and the SBA regulation call for application of the "rule of two" to all "acquisitions," which has generally been interpreted to mean that it applies when an agency is awarding a new contract. However, GAO has ruled that the "rule of two" applies to task and delivery orders being competed under multiple award IDIQ contracts, *Delex Sys., Inc.*, Comp. Gen. Dec. B-400403, 2008 CPD ¶ 181. However, the "rule of two" does not apply in awarding task or delivery orders under the Federal Supply Schedule, *Edmond Computer Co.*, Comp. Gen. Dec. B-402863, 2010 CPD ¶ 200 (citing FAR 8.404(a) stating that FAR Part 19 does not apply to FSS procurements). In this decision, GAO indicated that the SBA does not agree with this exclusion of efforts to assist small businesses from FSS procurements.

The "fair market price" need not be as low as the price obtainable in full and open competition, *Society Brand, Inc.*, 55 Comp. Gen. 475 (B-183963), 75-2 CPD ¶ 327. GAO has ruled that receipt of only one reasonable bid is not a valid basis to challenge a set-aside because there was a reasonable expectation of at least two reasonable bids, *NJCT Corp.*, Comp. Gen. Dec. B-219455, 85-2 CPD ¶ 70. In making this determination, the past acquisition history of the item or items being procured, while important, is not the only factor to be considered. For example, in making research and development (R&D) set-asides, there must also be a reasonable expectation of obtaining from small businesses the best scientific and technical sources consistent with the requirements of the acquisition, FAR 19.502-2(b).

Contracting officers have broad discretion in determining whether particular procurements should be set aside for small businesses or whether set-asides that have been established should be withdrawn, *Louisiana-Pacific Corp. v. Block*, 694 F.2d 1205 (9th Cir. 1982); *Kinnett Dairies, Inc. v. Farrow*, 580 F.2d 1260 (5th Cir. 1978); *McGhee Constr., Inc.*, B-249235, 92-2 CPD ¶ 318; *FACE Assocs., Inc.*, 63 Comp. Gen. 86 (B-211877), 83-2 CPD ¶ 643; *Fermont Div., Dynamics Corp. of Am.*, 59 Comp. Gen. 533 (B-195431), 80-1 CPD ¶ 438. In *Peterson Bldrs., Inc.*, Comp. Gen. Dec. B-251695, 93-1 CPD ¶ 342, GAO found that an agency's determination not to set aside a procurement was reasonable where it involved the development of a craft that had never been attempted by the shipbuilding industry, stating that the agency could not reasonably expect to receive the best mix of cost, performance, and schedules from the small business shipbuilding community. For other decisions affirming agency conclusion that two small business competitors were not available, see *Metasoft, LLC*, Comp. Gen. Dec. B-402800, 2010 CPD ¶ 170 (analysis of sources sought replies indicated that companies couldn't perform 50 % of work with own forces); *EMMES Corp.*, Comp. Gen. Dec. B-402245, 2010 CPD ¶ 53 (analysis of sources sought replies and market research); *Information Ventures, Inc.*, Comp. Gen. Dec. B-400604, 2008 CPD ¶ 232 (analysis of sources sought replies plus prior procurement history); *Protective Group, Inc.*,

Comp. Gen. Dec. B-310018, 2007 CPD ¶ 208 (analysis of responses at industry day conference); *Marketing & Mgmt. Info., Inc.*, Comp. Gen. Dec. B-283399.4, 2000 CPD ¶ 82 (market research); *CardioMetrix*, Comp. Gen. Dec. B-261327, 95-2 CPD ¶ 96 (analysis of prior procurement history for the solicited services). For decisions affirming the agency decision to set a procurement aside, see *Ceradyne, Inc.*, Comp. Gen. Dec. B-402281, 2010 CPD ¶ 70 (analysis of production capacity of two firms with IDIQ contracts); *ViroMed Labs.*, Comp. Gen. Dec. B-298931, 2007 CPD ¶ 4 (sources sought responses and contact with prospective offerors indicated at least three small businesses could submit offers).

Protests have been sustained if it is determined that an agency's decision not to set aside is unreasonable. In *Rhinocorps, Ltd. v. United States*, 86 Fed. Cl. 642 (2009), an injunction was granted when an agency decided not to set aside a follow-on procurement when the prior work had been performed by a small business. Similarly, in *Thermal Solutions, Inc.*, Comp. Gen. Dec. B-259501, 95-1 CPD ¶ 178, GAO found that an agency's decision not to set aside a procurement for small disadvantaged business (SDB) was unreasonable, stating that the agency received expressions of interest from five undisputed SDBs. The decision not to set aside the procurement was based on prior SDB set-aside procurements for dissimilar work, and prior procurements for similar work that were not set aside for SDBs. GAO stated that SDBs often cannot effectively compete with non-SDB firms, and thus may not bid on contracts that they are otherwise capable of performing. See also *Kato Corp.*, 69 Comp. Gen. 374 (B-237965), 90-1 CPD ¶ 354 (agency made no effort to ascertain SDB interest and capabilities, and the agency reasonably should have expected offers from at least two responsible SDBs); *Bollinger Mach. Shop & Shipyard, Inc.*, Comp. Gen. Dec. B-258563, 95-1 CPD ¶ 56 (agency expected bids from at least two small businesses and did not have a reasonable basis for concluding that award at a fair market price could not be expected); *ACCU-Lab Med. Testing*, Comp. Gen. Dec. B-270259, 96-1 CPD ¶ 106 (agency improperly withdrew set-aside by relying on the prior procurement history instead of investigating the numerous small business responses to the CBD announcement and performing a current market study); *Information Ventures, Inc.*, Comp. Gen. Dec. B-294267, 2004 CPD ¶ 205 (agency performed inadequate market research and knew that there were three capable small businesses). However, GAO may object to a set-aside when the evidence strongly indicates that only one small business is likely to submit an offer, *DISA Elecs.*, 62 Comp. Gen. 271 (B-206798), 83-1 CPD ¶ 306.

## b.  *Partial Set-Asides*

An agency may determine that small businesses cannot furnish the entire quantity that is needed but may be able to supply a portion. FAR 19.502-3 provides that a partial set-aside is appropriate when:

(1) A total set-aside is not appropriate (see 19.502-2);

(2) The requirement is severable into two or more economic production runs or reasonable lots;

(3) One or more small business concerns are expected to have the technical competence and productive capacity to satisfy the set-aside portion of the requirement at a fair market price;

(4) The acquisition is not subject to simplified acquisition procedures; and

(5) A partial set-aside shall not be made if there is a reasonable expectation that only two concerns (one large and one small) with capability will respond with offers unless authorized by the head of a contracting activity on a case-by-case basis. Similarly, a class of acquisitions, not including construction, may be partially set aside. Under certain specified conditions, partial set-asides may be used in conjunction with multiyear contracting procedures.

A "partial set-aside" reserves for award to small businesses only a portion — called the "set-aside" portion — of the quantity being procured. Any firm, regardless of size, is eligible for award of the balance — the non-set aside portion. Partial small business set-asides may be conducted using sealed bids or competitive proposals, FAR 19.502-4(a). The small business portion must be for an economic amount of the work, *Aalco Forwarding, Inc.*, Comp. Gen. Dec. B-277241.16, 98-1 CPD ¶ 75.

Both small and large offerors may submit offers on the non-set-aside portion, which is awarded first, following normal contracting procedures, FAR 19.502-3(c)(1). The set-aside portion is then awarded through negotiation with small business offerors that submitted responsive offers on the non-set-aside portion. The priority in which small business offerors will be asked to negotiate on the set-aside portion is determined by the terms of the solicitation, FAR 19.502-3(c)(2)(i). Under the standard Notice of Partial Small Business Set-Aside solicitation provision in FAR 52.219-7, negotiations are conducted first with the small business concern that submitted the lowest responsive offer on the non-set-aside portion. If the negotiations are not successful or if only part of the set-aside portion is awarded to that concern, negotiations are conducted with the concern that submitted the second low responsive offer. This process continues until a contract (or contracts) are awarded for the entire set-aside portion.

The set-aside portion is awarded at the highest unit price(s) on which the non-set-aside portion was awarded, adjusted to reflect transportation and similar factors. For example, assume that an agency needs 1 million units and believes that small businesses may be able to supply at least 400,000 units but not the entire requirement, and that 100,000 units is a reasonable production run. The agency should use a small business partial set-aside, with 600,000 units as the non-set-aside portion and 400,000 units reserved for award to small businesses. As stated above, both large and small offerors may bid on the non-set-aside portion. Assume the following simplified results of bidding:

| Offeror | Size | Price | No. of Units |
|---------|------|-------|--------------|
| A | Large | $1.00 | 400,000 max. |
| B | Large | 1.03 | unlimited |
| C | Large | 1.05 | unlimited |
| D | Small | 1.06 | unlimited |
| E | Large | 1.08 | unlimited |
| F | Small | 1.09 | unlimited |
| G | Small | 1.11 | 500,000 max. |

Assume further that all offers are responsive, that all offerors are responsible. The non-set-aside portion would be awarded as follows:

| A | Large | 400,000 at $1.00 each |
|---|-------|-----------------------|
| B | Large | 200,000 at $1.03 each |

The agency should then ask D, whose offer was the lowest small-business offer on the non-set-aside portion, whether it is willing to accept award for all or any portion of the 400,000 set-aside units at $1.03, the maximum price paid on the non-set-aside units. If D will accept award at $1.03 each, award should be made to it. If D will not take all 400,000 units, any remaining units should be offered to F, and then, if necessary, to G, at $1.03 per unit. If any of the 400,000 set-aside units cannot be awarded through this procedure, they may only be awarded through negotiation or sealed bidding in an entirely new procurement.

### c.  Small Business Innovation Research Set-Asides

Congressional hearings produced evidence that small businesses are the nation's most efficient innovators, but that only a small proportion of federal R&D funds go to them, S. Rep. No. 97-194, 97th Cong., 1st Sess. (1984). As a result, Congress passed the Small Business Innovation Development Act, Pub. L. No. 97-219 (1982). Under that Act, federal agencies with budgets over certain amounts for outside R&D must direct specified percentages of such funds to small businesses, 15 U.S.C. § 638(f). The program has been reauthorized periodically since that time. See Chapter 7 for a discussion of the procedures for such procurements.

## 2.  Sole Source Contracting and Evaluation Preferences

Several of the small business programs for designated classes of small businesses permit sole source contracting or call for percentage evaluation preferences. These will be discussed below in the coverage of the specific programs where they are applied.

## 3.  Subcontracting to Small Businesses

The government recognizes that many of its acquisitions require resources that are beyond the capability of any small business to serve as the prime contractor. However, small businesses may be able to participate as subcontractors. There are mechanisms designed to increase awards of subcontracts to small businesses.

Under procedures established in 1978 by Pub. L. No. 95-507, most federal contracts that exceed the simplified acquisition threshold must contain a clause stating that it is federal policy that small businesses have the "maximum practicable opportunity to participate in the performance of" federal contracts, 15 U.S.C. § 637(d)(1). Under the Utilization of Small Business Concerns clause in FAR 52.219-8 the contractor agrees "to carry out this policy in the awarding of subcontracts to the fullest extent consistent with efficient contract performance," and the contractor also agrees to cooperate with the contracting agency and the SBA in studies to determine the extent of compliance with the statute.

There are far more extensive requirements for contracts of $650,000 or more ($1.5 million or more for contracts for construction of a public facility) awarded to any entity other than a small business, 15 U.S.C. §637(d)(4). See FAR 19.702. The Small Business Subcontracting Plan clause in FAR 52.219-9 requires that the contractor must provide a subcontracting plan that, as approved by the contracting officer, is incorporated into the contract. Paragraph (k) of the clause provides that failure to comply in good faith with the plan is a material breach. See also 15 U.S.C. § 637(d)(8). FAR 19.704(a) provides that each such plan must include:

(1) Separate percentage goals for using small business (including ANCs and Indian tribes), veteran-owned small business, service-disabled veteran-owned small business, HUBZone small business, small disadvantaged business (including ANCs and Indian tribes) and women-owned small business concerns as subcontractors;

(2) A statement of the total dollars planned to be subcontracted and a statement of the total dollars planned to be subcontracted to small business (including ANCs and Indian tribes), veteran-owned small business, service-disabled veteran-owned small business, HUBZone small business, small disadvantaged business (including ANCs and Indian tribes) and women-owned small business concerns;

(3) A description of the principal types of supplies and services to be subcontracted and an identification of types planned for subcontracting to small business (including ANCs and Indian tribes), veteran-owned small business, service-disabled veteran-owned small business, HUBZone small business, small disadvantaged business (including ANCs and Indian tribes), and women-owned small business concerns;

(4) A description of the method used to develop the subcontracting goals;

(5) A description of the method used to identify potential sources for solicitation purposes;

(6) A statement as to whether or not the offeror included indirect costs in establishing subcontracting goals, and a description of the method used to determine the proportionate share of indirect costs to be incurred with small business (including ANCs and Indian tribes), veteran-owned small business, service-disabled veteran-owned small business, HUBZone small business, small disadvantaged business (including ANCs and Indian tribes), and women-owned small business concerns;

(7) The name of an individual employed by the offeror who will administer the offeror's subcontracting program, and a description of the duties of the individual;

(8) A description of the efforts the offeror will make to ensure that small business, veteran-owned small business, service-disabled veteran-owned small business, HUBZone small business, small disadvantaged business, and women-owned small business concerns have an equitable opportunity to compete for subcontracts;

(9) Assurances that the offeror will include the clause at 52.219-8, Utilization of Small Business Concerns (see 19.708(a)), in all subcontracts that offer further subcontracting opportunities, and that the offeror will require all subcontractors (except small business concerns) that receive subcontracts in excess of $650,000 ($1.5 million for construction) to adopt a plan that complies with the requirements of the clause at 52.219-9, Small Business Subcontracting Plan (see 19.708(b));

(10) Assurances that the offeror will —

(i) Cooperate in any studies or surveys as may be required;

(ii) Submit periodic reports so that the Government can determine the extent of compliance by the offeror with the subcontracting plan;

(iii) Submit the Individual Subcontract Report (ISR), and the Summary Subcontract Report (SSR) using the Electronic Subcontracting Reporting System (eSRS) (*http://www.esrs.gov*), following the instructions in the eSRS;

(A) The ISR shall be submitted semi-annually during contract performance for the periods ending March 31 and September 30.

A report is also required for each contract within 30 days of contract completion. Reports are due 30 days after the close of each reporting period, unless otherwise directed by the contracting officer. Reports are required when due, regardless of whether there has been any subcontracting activity since the inception of the contract or the previous reporting period.

(B) The SSR shall be submitted as follows: For DoD and NASA, the report shall be submitted semi-annually for the six months ending March 31 and the twelve months ending September 30. For civilian agencies, except NASA, it shall be submitted annually for the twelve-month period ending September 30. Reports are due 30 days after the close of each reporting period.

(iv) Ensure that its subcontractors with subcontracting plans agree to submit the ISR and/or the SSR using the eSRS;

(v) Provide its prime contract number, its DUNS number, and the e-mail address of the offeror's official responsible for acknowledging receipt of or rejecting the ISRs to all first-tier subcontractors with subcontracting plans so they can enter this information into the eSRS when submitting their ISRs; and

(vi) Require that each subcontractor with a subcontracting plan provide the prime contract number, its own DUNS number, and the e-mail address of the subcontractor's official responsible for acknowledging receipt of or rejecting the ISRs, to its subcontractors with subcontracting plans.

(11) A description of the types of records that will be maintained concerning procedures adopted to comply with the requirements and goals in the plan, including establishing source lists; and a description of the offeror's efforts to locate small business, veteran-owned small business, service-disabled veteran-owned small business, HUBZone small business, small disadvantaged business, and women-owned small business concerns and to award subcontracts to them.

In negotiated procurements, the successful offeror must submit a proposed plan and negotiate its terms with the contracting officer, and "[i]f the apparently successful offeror fails to negotiate a subcontracting plan acceptable to the contracting officer within the time limit prescribed by the contracting officer, the offeror will be ineligible for award," FAR 19.702(a)(1). Such negotiation is required to ensure that the plan included in the contract provides "the maximum practicable opportunity" for small businesses to participate in the performance of the contract. See *Columbia Research Corp.*, 61 Comp. Gen. 194 (B-202762), 82-1 CPD ¶ 8, where GAO approved a plan stating "zero percent of the estimated costs would be subcontracted to small business." GAO noted that the statute required only the offeror's best efforts in subcontracting to small business. Raising issued during discussion is a sufficient negotiation of the plan, *A P Logistics, LLC*, Comp. Gen. Dec. B-401699, 2010 CPD

¶ 179 (offeror that did not address issues in final proposal revisions properly rejected for unsatisfactory plan).

The acceptability of a subcontracting plan in a negotiated procurement is generally a matter of responsibility, with the result that negotiation of the plan is not a "discussion." However, if subcontracting plans are evaluated comparatively as part of the best value decision, the negotiation of the plan is a discussion. For a detailed analysis of this issue, see *Computer Scis. Corp.*, Comp. Gen. Dec. B-298494, 2007 CPD ¶ 103.

In sealed bid procurements, the firm selected for award must submit its plan regarding subcontract awards to small businesses, FAR 19.702(a)(2), but the plan is not subject to negotiation because such negotiation would be inconsistent with sealed bidding. Subcontracting plans are a matter of responsibility, not responsiveness, and thus may be submitted after bids are received and opened, *Devcon Sys. Corp.*, 59 Comp. Gen. 614 (B-197935), 80-2 CPD ¶ 46; *CH2M Hill, Ltd.*, Comp. Gen. Dec. B-259511, 95-1 CPD ¶ 203.

Contractors may establish, for either plants or divisions, a master subcontracting plan that, after approval by the contracting officer, can be incorporated into individual contracts, eliminating the need for separate plans for each individual contract, FAR 19.704(b). These plans are effective for three years but they must be updated when required.

Agencies have authority to include in negotiated contracts an Incentive Subcontracting Program clause under which the contractor may increase its profit by a percentage based upon the extent to which the actual awards to small businesses exceed the percentage negotiated and included in the clause, 15 U.S.C. § 637(d); FAR 19.708(c)(1). FAR 52.219-10 provides a clause for this purpose.

15 U.S.C. § 637(d)(4)(F) directs that liquidated damages shall be paid by the contractor if it does not make a good faith effort to meet the goals in its plan. This requirement is implemented by the insertion in contracts that require subcontracting plans of the Liquidated Damages — Subcontracting Plan clause at FAR 52.219-16. Guidance on the use of this clause is in FAR 19.705-7.

## D.  Programs for Special Classes of Small Business

Congress has established a substantial number of classes of small businesses that are entitled to preferential treatment — with different rules and procedures applicable to each class. The major procedure applicable to all of the classes is the set-aside procedure. As noted earlier, for procurements over the simplified acquisition threshold, set-asides to SDVOs, WOSBs, HUBZone concerns and procurements reserved for disadvantaged businesses through the

8(a) program are in parity with each other but take priority over set-asides to other small businesses, FAR 19.203(c). The other special procedures are discussed in this section.

## 1. Small Disadvantaged Businesses

Starting in the late 1960s, the executive branch of the government began several programs to increase awards of federal contracts to "minority-owned" businesses. In 1978, most of those programs were revised and expanded by amendments to the Small Business Act, Pub. L. No. 95-507. Those amendments used the expression "small businesses owned and controlled by socially and economically disadvantaged persons" to describe the businesses aided by such programs. The shortened expression, "small disadvantaged businesses" (SDBs), and the older term, "minority-owned businesses" are used interchangeably.

A 1995 Supreme Court decision has cast a cloud over the entire SDB program. In *Adarand Constructors, Inc. v. Pena*, 515 U.S. 200 (1995), the Supreme Court significantly limited the federal government's authority to implement programs that favor racial minorities. In this decision, the Supreme Court held that federal affirmative action programs that use racial classifications are subject to a high level of judicial scrutiny, must serve a compelling government interest, and must be narrowly tailored to further that interest. The impact of *Adarand* on government contracting programs designed to assist SDBs has not yet been fully determined. Reacting to *Adarand*, the President issued a directive to federal agencies ordering officials to review existing affirmative action programs and to eliminate or reform any program that creates a quota, creates preferences for unqualified individuals, creates reverse discrimination, or continues even after its equal opportunity purposes have been achieved, Memorandum for Heads of Executive Departments and Agencies, Evaluation of Affirmative Action Programs 1, July 19, 1995.

GAO has dismissed bid protest challenges to the constitutionality of the DoD's SDB set-aside program based on *Adarand*, citing a lack of clear judicial precedent, *Elrich Contracting Inc.*, Comp. Gen. Dec. B-262015, 95-2 CPD ¶ 71. Noting that *Adarand* set forth the standard to be applied by the federal courts in determining the constitutionality of such programs but did not actually decide whether the challenged program was unconstitutional, GAO stated that "[t]here must be clear judicial precedent before we will consider a protest based on the asserted unconstitutionality of the procuring agency's actions."

As a result of the *Adarand* decision, in October 1995, the DoD issued a directive suspending its SDB set-aside program. The directive provided that until further notice, contracting officers should not set aside acquisitions for SDBs. It further ordered that contracting officers should amend already issued solicitations to remove set-asides that were based on the suspended sections of the DFARS "where the amendment of the solicitation will not unduly delay a procurement." GAO concluded that deletion of an SDB preference provision from an Air Force RFP in accordance with the DoD's directive was proper even though proposals had already been received and evaluated, *PI Constr. Corp.*, Comp. Gen. Dec. B-270576.2, 95-2 CPD ¶ 270.

The result is that there is no set-aside program for SDBs but there are three program that assist them: the "8(a)" program, a participation encouragement program, and a price evaluation adjustment program applicable to the Department of Defense, the National Aeronautics and Space Administration and the Coast Guard.

## a. Qualification as an SDB

15 U.S.C. § 637(a)(4) provides:

(A) For purposes of this section, the term "socially and economically disadvantaged small business concern" means any small business concern which meets the requirements of subparagraph (B) and —

    (i) which is at least 51 per centum unconditionally owned by —

        (I) one or more socially and economically disadvantaged individuals,

        (II) an economically disadvantaged Indian tribe (or a wholly owned business entity of such tribe), or

        (III) an economically disadvantaged Native Hawaiian organization, or

    (ii) in the case of any publicly owned business at least 51 per centum of the stock of which is unconditionally owned by —

        (I) one or more socially and economically disadvantaged individuals,

        (II) an economically disadvantaged Indian tribe (or a wholly owned business entity of such tribe), or

        (III) an economically disadvantaged Native Hawaiian organization.

(B) A small business concern meets the requirements of this subparagraph if the management and daily business operations of such small business concern are controlled by one or more —

(i) socially and economically disadvantaged individuals described in sub-paragraph (A)(i)(I) or subparagraph (A)(ii)(I),

(ii) members of an economically disadvantaged Indian tribe described in subparagraph (A)(i)(II) or subparagraph (A)(ii)(II), or

(iii) Native Hawaiian organizations described in subparagraph (A)(i)(m) or subparagraph (A)(ii)(III).

The statute also contains separate definitions of "socially disadvantaged" and "economically disadvantaged" individuals, 15 U.S.C. § 637(a)(5) and (6). Participation requires that the individuals meet both of these tests, *Autek Sys Corp.*, 835 F. Supp. 13 (D.D.C. 1993), *aff'd*, 43 F.3d 712 (D.C. Cir. 1994). 13 C.F.R. § 124.103 provides the following definition of "socially disadvantaged:"

(a) General. Socially disadvantaged individuals are those who have been subjected to racial or ethnic prejudice or cultural bias within American society because of their identities as members of groups and without regard to their individual qualities. The social disadvantage must stem from circumstances beyond their control.

(b) Members of designated groups. (1) There is a rebuttable presumption that the following individuals are socially disadvantaged: Black Americans; Hispanic Americans; Native Americans (Alaska Natives, Native Hawaiians, or enrolled members of a Federally or State recognized Indian Tribe); Asian Pacific Americans (persons with origins from Burma, Thailand, Malaysia, Indonesia, Singapore, Brunei, Japan, China (including Hong Kong), Taiwan, Laos, Cambodia (Kampuchea), Vietnam, Korea, The Philippines, U.S. Trust Territory of the Pacific Islands (Republic of Palau), Republic of the Marshall Islands, Federated States of Micronesia, the Commonwealth of the Northern Mariana Islands, Guam, Samoa, Macao, Fiji, Tonga, Kiribati, Tuvalu, or Nauru); Subcontinent Asian Americans (persons with origins from India, Pakistan, Bangladesh, Sri Lanka, Bhutan, the Maldives Islands or Nepal); and members of other groups designated from time to time by SBA according to procedures set forth at paragraph (d) of this section. Being born in a country does not, by itself, suffice to make the birth country an individual's country of origin for purposes of being included within a designated group.

The regulation contains detailed guidance on the application of this definition, means of challenging the determination of social disadvantage and procedures that can be used by other individuals to demonstrate that they are socially disadvantaged.

13 C.F.R. § 124.104 provides the following definition of "economically disadvantaged:"

(a) General. Economically disadvantaged individuals are socially disadvantaged individuals whose ability to compete in the free enterprise system has been impaired due to diminished capital and credit opportunities as compared to others in the same or similar line of business who are not socially disadvantaged.

The regulation contains detailed guidance on the information that must be submitted to meet this definition and the factors that are considered (including the key factor that the individual's net worth and adjusted gross income must each be less than $ 250,000). The size standards discussed earlier are used to determine whether these businesses qualify as small businesses, 13 C.F.R. § 124.102. There are special requirements for Indian tribes in 13 C.F.R. § 124.109(b), except that Alaskan Native Corporations are not subject to these requirements because they are deemed economically disadvantaged under 43 U.S.C. § 1626(e) and have special size requirements, 13 C.F.R. § 124.109(a). Special requirements for Native Hawaiian Organizations are set forth in 13 C.F.R. § 124.110(b). Key definitions are set forth in 13 C.F.R. § 124.13.

Small businesses that desire to take advantage of SDB status generally apply to the SBA to participate in the 8(a) program (discussed below) following the procedures in 13 C.F.R. § 124.201 - 207. Small businesses that do not want to participate in the 8(a) program can apply for separate certification as SDBs in accordance with 13 C.F.R. § 124.1003.

The SBA has reasonable discretion to deny participation in the 8(a) program to clearly unqualified firms as long as applications receive thorough and careful review. See *Neuma Corp. v. Abdnor*, 713 F. Supp. 1 (D.D.C. 1989).

SBA responsibility determinations for SDBs seeking contracts under the 8(a) program are covered exclusively by 15 U.S.C. § 637(a)(16) and do not involve the COC procedures required by § 637(b)(7). In *DAE Corp. v. Small Bus. Admin.*, 958 F.2d 436 (D.C. App. 1992), the court distinguished § 637(a) and § 637(b), stating at 439:

> Section 637(b)(7) no doubt does mean what it plainly says — but only where it applies. It is part of the § 8(b) program, and any small business proceeding under § 8(b) is entitled to its protections and its disadvantages. As the Comptroller General has affirmed, § 637(b)(7) is designed to help small businesses overcome the hesitance a procuring agency may have in awarding an ordinary contract to a small business. See *Custom Research, Inc.*, Comp. Gen. Dec. B-238976.2, 90-1 Comp. Gen. Dec. ¶ 567 (1990) (explaining that the COC process "is provided by law to protect small businesses from arbitrary nonresponsibility determinations made by procurement agencies.").

> The disadvantaged small business seeking a sole source contract under § 8(a), such as DAE, faces a vastly different situation. There, the procuring agency has asked the SBA to obtain the services of a specified disadvantaged small business — no passport is necessary because the contractor has already been admitted.

### b.  The "8(a)" Program

The primary program designed to assist SDBs is commonly known as the "8(a)" program. The program takes its name from Section 8(a) of the Small Business Act.

Section 8(a) authorizes the SBA to enter into contracts with other federal agencies and to perform such contracts by subcontracting to small businesses, 15 U.S.C. § 637(a). Beginning in the late 1960s, the SBA employed the 8(a) procedure to increase the amount of federal contract work performed by minority-owned businesses by taking contracts from procuring agencies and awarding subcontracts to minority-owned businesses. The SBA invested considerable resources in the 8(a) program, and it grew quickly. By the late 1970s, contracts valued at hundreds of millions of dollars were being awarded annually under the 8(a) program. The program has withstood challenges that it discriminated in favor of minority-owned small businesses, *Ray Baillie Trash Hauling, Inc. v. Kleppe*, 477 F.2d 696 (5th Cir. 1973), *cert. denied*, 415 U.S. 914 (1974). In one instance, nonminority competing contractors were granted declaratory relief because a total set-aside of all 1981 Corps of Engineers small business contracts in the Mississippi market was found to be an overly broad exercise of statutory power and, therefore, discriminatory to non-SDBs in violation of 42 U.S.C. § 2000d, *Fordice Constr. Co. v. Marsh*, 773 F. Supp. 867 (S.D. Miss. 1990).

In 1988, Congress enacted the Business Opportunity Development Reform Act, Pub. L. No. 100-656, which sought to curb abuses in the 8(a) program and make SDBs more competitive. The Act included reforms of the program which (1) require competition among 8(a) firms for manufacturing contracts exceeding $5 million and for service contracts and nonmanufacturing contracts exceeding $3 million, (2) require the SBA to establish business activity targets for businesses that have been in the program for five years, (3) authorize contracting officers to assess "liquidated damages" against prime contractors that fail to meet SDB subcontracting goals, and (4) prohibit SBA employees from holding stock in 8(a) firms for two years after leaving the SBA.

Firms participating in the 8(a) program must have an approved business plan, 15 U.S.C. § 636(j)(10)(D); 13 C.F.R. § 124.402. The maximum period of time a disadvantaged firm can remain in the program is nine years, 13 C.F.R. § 124.2. This is divided into a four-year developmental stage and a five-year transitional stage. See 13 C.F.R. § 124.404 for guidance on the assistance provided by SBA in each of these stages. The SBA regulations limiting the period that firms can participate in the 8(a) program were upheld in *Minority Bus. Legal Def. & Educ. Funds, Inc. v. Small Bus. Admin.*, 557 F. Supp. 37 (D.D.C. 1982). A court did not abuse its discretion by refusing to extend an 8(a) contractor's eligibility beyond nine years, even though the SBA had acted unlawfully in preventing the contractor from receiving full 8(a) benefits, *Woerner v. United States*, 934 F.2d 1277 (App. D.C. 1991).

GAO will not review SBA decisions on a firm's eligibility for the 8(a) program, unless there are strong allegations of fraud, bad faith, or the SBA's violation of its own regulations, *Forway Indus.*, Comp. Gen. Dec. B-217046, 84-2 CPD ¶ 573. One court has also ruled that egregious procedural violations by SBA of its own regulations in terminating a firm's participation in the 8(a) program justify court review, *Oklahoma Aerotronics, Inc. v. United States*, 661 F.2d 976 (D.C. Cir. 1981).

## (1) Obtaining Contracts

FAR 19.803 describes three ways that contracting agencies determine to award contracts under the 8(a) program:

(a) The SBA advises an agency contracting activity through a search letter of an 8(a) firm's capabilities and asks the agency to identify acquisitions to support the firm's business plans.

(b) The SBA identifies a specific requirement for a particular 8(a) firm or firms and asks the agency contracting activity to offer the acquisition to the 8(a) Program for the firm(s).

(c) Agencies may also review other proposed acquisitions for the purpose of identifying requirements which may be offered to the SBA.

The regulation contains guidance on the information that it to be provided by the SBA when it uses either of the first two procedures. See also 13 C.F.R. § 124.501(e) urging contractors to "market their capabilities to appropriate procuring activities to increase their prospects of receiving sole source 8(a) contracts."

When an agency has determined that the 8(a) process should be used, it "offers" the procurement to the SBA with a description of the work and a recommendation of the type of procurement to be used, FAR 19.804-2. The SBA then determines whether to "accept" the requirement for the 8(a) program, FAR 19.804-3. The SBA will not accept a requirement if it has an adverse impact on a small business with a contract to perform the work, 13 C.F.R. § 124.504(c). The adverse impact rule does not apply if the requirement is changed, *Klett Consulting Group, Inc.*, Comp. Gen. Dec. B-404023, 2010 CPD ¶ 301 (agency had expanded the work from four states to seven states); *ANTECH, Inc.*, Comp. Gen. Dec. B-401092, 2009 CPD ¶ 91 (agency intended to use a facility in a different manner).

## (2) Competition Requirement

Procurements over specified dollar thresholds are subject to a competition requirement when possible. See FAR 19.805-1 stating:

(a) Except as provided in paragraph (b) of this subsection, an acquisition offered to the SBA under the 8(a) Program shall be awarded on the basis of competition limited to eligible 8(a) firms if —

(1) There is a reasonable expectation that at least two eligible and responsible 8(a) firms will submit offers and that award can be made at a fair market price; and

(2) The anticipated total value of the contract, including options, will exceed $6.5 million for acquisitions assigned manufacturing North Ameri-

can Industry Classification System (NAICS) codes and $4 million for all other acquisitions.

(b) Where an acquisition exceeds the competitive threshold, the SBA may accept the requirement for a sole source 8(a) award if —

(1) There is not a reasonable expectation that at least two eligible and responsible 8(a) firms will submit offers at a fair market price; or

(2) SBA accepts the requirement on behalf of a concern owned by an Indian tribe or an Alaska Native Corporation.

Agencies may also request the SBA to approve a competitive procurement below the competitive threshold, FAR 19.805-1(d).

As noted above, the competition thresholds do not apply to Indian tribes and Alaska Native Corporations. However, 13 C.F.R.§ 124.506(b) has limited this rule by stating that it will not approve such a sole source after it has agreed to a competitive procurement. See *JXM, Inc.*, Comp. Gen. Dec. B-402643, 2010 CPD ¶ 158, agreeing that it was proper for an agency to change a competitive 8(a) procurement to a sole source 8(a) procurement with an Alaska Native Corporation when the requirement had substantially changed.

### (3) ENTERING INTO THE CONTRACT

Although the 8(a) arrangement is technically a contract between the procuring agency and the SBA, and a subcontract between the SBA and the SDB, the procuring agency and the disadvantaged small business normally deal directly with each other. With respect to the contract with the procuring agency, 15 U.S.C. § 637(a)(3) (A) provides that, when practicable, the concern shall "participate in any negotiation of the terms and conditions of such contract."

In competitive 8(a) procurements, the contracting agency solicits offers from those firms that have been selected by the SBA, FAR 19.805-2(a). If sealed bidding procedures have been used, it evaluates the bids and sends the SBA a list of the bidders and its determination of fair market price for a determination of eligibility of the low bidder, FAR 19.805-2(b)(1). The contracting agency then determines whether to award to the successful bidder "in accordance with normal contracting procedures." If negotiation procedures have been used, the agency selects the winning offeror, obtains a determination of eligibility from the SBA and awards the contract, FAR 19.805-2(b)(2) and 19.808-2. See 13 C.F.R. § 124.507 for a description of the eligibility determination process.

In sole source 8(a) procurements, the agency uses standard negotiation procedures with the participation of the SBA "whenever practicable," FAR 19.808-1. Such procurements are subject to the requirements for obtaining certified cost or pricing data, FAR 19.806(a). The contracting agency is required to obtain concurrence of the SBA on the final price that is negotiated, FAR 19.806(d).

FAR 19.811-1 requires a contract between the agency and the SBA and a subcontract between the SBA and the SDB concern when the award has been made using sole source procedures. In contrast, "tripartite" contracts, where the contracting agency, the SBA and the SDB concern sign the document, are used when the award has been made using competitive procedures, FAR 19.811-2. See FAR 19.811-3 for guidance on the clauses to be used in these contracts. In either case, contract administration is normally delegated to the contracting activity, 13 C.F.R. § 124.512. The SBA does not "insure" performance of its 8(a) subcontractors, *ATC Petroleum, Inc. v. Sanders*, 860 F.2d 1104 (D.C. Cir. 1988). The subcontract between the 8(a) firm and the SBA contains a clause stating that the SBA has delegated responsibility for administering the subcontract to the procuring agency, which will act for the government, FAR 52.219-12. In such circumstances, the procuring agency may properly terminate an 8(a) contract for default and the termination need not come from the SBA, *Philadelphia Regent Builders, Inc. v. United States*, 225 Ct. Cl. 234, 634 F.2d 569 (1980).

### c.  Other Aids to SDBs

There are two other programs that have been established to assist SDBs — a "participation" evaluation factor, including a monetary incentive, and a price evaluation factor.

### (1) THE "PARTICIPATION" PROGRAM

The SDB participation program is described in FAR Subpart 19.12. It provides for the use of an evaluation factor in best value negotiated procurements exceeding $650,000 ($1.5 million for conmstruction) where agencies can give a competitor credit for offering to use SDBs to perform a significant amount of the work, FAR 19.1202-2. It does not apply to set-aside procurements, 8(a) procurements, low price technically acceptable procurements, or foreign procurements.

Agencies are given full discretion to develop the evaluation factor following the guidance in FAR 19.1202-3. When it is used, the solicitation must require offerors to propose percentage targets for the amount of SDB participation in the performance of the contract and to list the concerns that will participate, FAR 19.1202-4. The Small Disadvantaged Business Participation Program — Targets solicitation provision in FAR 52.219-24 is used to implement this factor. It states:

> The targets may provide for participation by a prime contractor, joint venture partner, teaming arrangement member, or subcontractor; however, the targets for subcontractors must be listed separately.

The Small Disadvantaged Business Participation Program—Disadvantaged Status and Reporting clause in FAR 52.219-25 is included in contracts utilizing this program. It requires representations as to the status of the SDBs listed and reports of their use.

This program also permits agencies to use the Small Disadvantaged Business Participation Program – Incentive Subcontracting clause in FAR 52.219-26 providing monetary awards to contractors that exceed their SDB subcontracting target. Contracting officers have almost total discretion in this aspect of the program. See FAR 19.1203. See also DFARS 219.1203 stating that contracting officers "shall" provide these monetary incentives.

### (2) THE "PRICE EVALUATION ADJUSTMENT" FACTOR PROGRAM

FAR Subpart 19.11 provides guidance on the use of a monetary price adjustment in the evaluation of procurements where SDBs compete against other contractors. Only the Department of Defense, NASA and the Coast Guard are authorized to use this technique, FAR 19.1102(a). FAR 19.1102(b) provides that it does not apply to simplified acquisitions, set-aside procurements, 8(a) procurements, architect/engineer procurements and multiple award schedule procurements.

Contracting officers are required to give a 10% price adjustment advantage to SDBs when they are in industry segments that SBA has determined have under-representation of SDBs, FAR 19.1103. See FAR 19.201 for guidance on the determination of the applicable segments and the way the factor is to be used. The Notice of Price Evaluation Adjustment for Small Disadvantaged Business Concerns clause in FAR 52.219-23 is used to implement this process. The adjustment is not applicable if the price of the SDB exceeds a fair market price, FAR 19.1103(c). SDB concerns can waive this adjustment if they desire to use the SDB participation program.

## 2. HUBZone Concerns

Contractors in HUBZones are one of the types of small businesses that are given preference over other small businesses. Thus, if there are two HUBZone contractors a set aside would be required, FAR 19.1305. However, HUBZone contractors are in parity with SDVOSBs and WOSBs — with the result that if there are also two small businesses in one or both of those categories, the contracting officer has the choice of which class of business the procurement should be set aside for. HUBZone contractors are also in parity with 8(a) concerns — giving the contracting officer a choice when there is a qualified 8(a) concern and two HUBZone contractors. However, a HUBZone set-aside is not proper if an 8(a) contractor is currently performing the requirement or the requirement has been accepted by the SBA for 8(a) participation, FAR 19.1304(d). See FAR 19.1305 for procedures to be followed when the contracting officer decides to set aside a procurement for HUBZone contractors. When this type of set-aside is made, agencies must use the Notice of Total HUBZone Set-Aside clause in FAR 52.219-3.

There are two other program to assist HUBZone contractors — the sole source contracting program and the evaluation preference program.

## a.  Certification of HUBZone Concerns

The requirements to qualify as a HUBZone concern are set forth in 13 C.F.R. § 126.200 as follows:

(1) Ownership. (i) The concern must be at least 51% unconditionally and directly owned and controlled by persons who are United States citizens;

(2) Size. The concern, together with its affiliates, must qualify as a small business under the size standard corresponding to its primary industry classification as defined in part 121 of this chapter.

(3) Principal office. The concern's principal office must be located in a HUBZone.

(4) Employees. At least 35% of the concern's employees must reside in a HUB-Zone. When determining the percentage of employees that reside in a HUBZone, if the percentage results in a fraction, round up to the nearest whole number;

(5) Contract Performance. The concern must represent, as provided in the application, that it will "attempt to maintain" (see § 126.103) having 35% of its employees reside in a HUBZone during the performance of any HUBZone contract it receives.

(6) Subcontracting. The concern must represent, as provided in the application, that it will ensure that it will comply with certain contract performance requirements in connection with contracts awarded to it as a qualified HUBZone SBC, as set forth in § 126.700.

There are special requirements for Indian Tribal Governments, Alaska Native Corporations, Community Development Corporations, and small agricultural cooperatives.

A small business that wants to participate in the HUBZone program must apply to the SBA for certification and receive that certification as a prerequisite to participation, 13 C.F.R. § 126.300. The procedures followed to obtain certification are set forth in 13 C.F.R. § 126.301-126.309.

## b.  Sole Source Contracts

When there is only one HUBZone contractor and there are not two SDVOSBs or WOSBs, the contracting agency may, in some circumstances, award a sole source HUBZone contract. See 19.1306 stating:

(a) A contracting officer may award contracts to HUBZone small business concerns on a sole source basis (See 6.302-5(b)(5)) before considering small business set-asides (See 19.203 and subpart 19.5), provided none of the exclusions at 19.1304 apply; and —

(1) The contracting officer does not have a reasonable expectation that offers would be received from two or more HUBZone small business concerns;

(2) The anticipated price of the contract, including options, will not exceed —

(i) $ 6.5 million for a requirement within the North American Industry Classification System (NAICS) codes for manufacturing; or

(ii) $ 4 million for a requirement within all other NAICS codes;

(3) The requirement is not currently being performed by an 8(a) participant under the provisions of subpart 19.8 or has been accepted as a requirement by SBA under subpart 19.8.

(4) The acquisition is greater than the simplified acquisition threshold (see part 13);

(5) The HUBZone small business concern has been determined to be a responsible contractor with respect to performance; and

(6) Award can be made at a fair and reasonable price.

There is no guidance on the procedures to be followed when a sole source contract is awarded to a HUBZone contractor but, since the contracting officer is required to ensure that the price is fair and reasonable, normal contracting procedures should apply. This would require the submission of certified cost or pricing data when the procurement is over the $700,000 threshold and the negotiation of the price before award.

## c.  Price Evaluation Preference

When a procurement is open to all firms, both large and small, HUBZone contractors are given a 10% evaluation preference. FAR 19.1307 contains the following guidance:

(c) The factor of 10 percent shall be applied on a line item basis or to any group of items on which award may be made. Other evaluation factors, such as transportation costs or rent-free use of Government property, shall be added to the offer to establish the base offer before adding the factor of 10 percent.

(d) A concern that is both a HUBZone small business concern and a small disadvantaged business concern shall receive the benefit of both the HUBZone small business price evaluation preference and the small disadvantaged business price evaluation adjustment (see subpart 19.11). Each applicable price evaluation preference or adjustment shall be calculated independently against an offeror's base offer. These individual preference and adjustment amounts shall both be added to the base offer to arrive at the total evaluated price for that offer.

This preference is implemented by inclusion of the Notice of Price Evaluation Preference for HUBZone Small Business Concerns clause in FAR 52.219-4.

## 3.  Service-Disabled Veterans-Owned Small Businesses

SDVOSBs are one of the types of small businesses that are given preference over other small businesses. Thus, if there are two SDVOSBs a set-aside would be required, FAR 19.1405. However, SDVOSBs are in parity with HUBZone contractors and WOSBs — with the result that if there are also two small businesses in one or both of those categories, the contracting officer has the choice of which class of business the procurement should be set aside for. SDVOSBs are also in parity with 8(a) concerns —.giving the contracting officer a choice when there is a qualified 8(a) concern and two SDVOSBs. However, an SDVOSB set-aside is not proper if an 8(a) contractor is currently performing the requirement or the requirement has been accepted by the SBA for 8(a) participation, FAR 19.1404(d). See FAR 19.1405 for procedures to be followed when the contracting officer decides to set aside a procurement for SDVOSBs. When this type of set-aside is made, agencies must use the Notice of Total Service-Disabled Veteran-Owned Set-Aside clause in FAR 52.219-27.

There is one other program to assist SDVOSBs — the sole source contracting program.

### a.  Determination of SDVOSB Status

13 C.F.R. § 125.8 sets forth the following definitions:

(g) SBC owned and controlled by service-disabled veterans (also known as a Service-Disabled Veteran-Owned SBC) is a concern —

(1) Not less than 51% of which is owned by one or more service-disabled veterans or, in the case of any publicly owned business, not less than 51% of the stock of which is owned by one or more service-disabled veterans;

(2) The management and daily business operations of which are controlled by one or more service-disabled veterans or, in the case of a service-disabled veteran with permanent and severe disability, the spouse or permanent caregiver of such veteran; and

(3) That is small as defined by § 125.11.

(f) Service-disabled veteran is a veteran with a disability that is service-connected.

FAR 19.1403 requires that a SDVOSB must represent that it is such a concern at the time it submits an offer and provides that a joint venture can qualify if one member is a SDVOSB and it meets other specified conditions.

## b. *Sole Source Contracts*

When there is only one SDVOSB and there are not two HUBZone contractors or WOSBs, the contracting agency may, in some circumstances, award a sole source SDVOSB contract. See 19.1406 stating:

(a) A contracting officer may award contracts to service-disabled veteran-owned small business concerns on a sole source basis (See 6.302-5(b)(6)), before considering small business set-asides (See 19.203 and subpart 19.5) provided none of the exclusions of 19.1404 apply and —

(1) The contracting officer does not have a reasonable expectation that offers would be received from two or more service-disabled veteran-owned small business concerns;

(2) The anticipated award price of the contract, including options, will not exceed —

(i) $6 million for a requirement within the NAICS codes for manufacturing; or

(ii) $3.5 million for a requirement within any other NAICS code;

(3) The requirement is not currently being performed by an 8(a) participant under the provisions of subpart 19.8 or has been accepted as a requirement by SBA under subpart 19.8;

(4) The service-disabled veteran-owned small business concern has been determined to be a responsible contractor with respect to performance; and

(5) Award can be made at a fair and reasonable price.

## 4. *Women Owned Businesses*

WOSBs are one of the types of small businesses that are given preference over other small businesses. Thus, if there are two WOSBs a set-aside would be required, FAR 19.1505. However, WOSBs are in parity with HUBZone contractors and SD-VOSBs — with the result that if there are also two small businesses in one or both of those categories, the contracting officer has the choice of which class of business the procurement should be set aside for. WOSBs are also in parity with 8(a) concerns — giving the contracting officer a choice when there is a qualified 8(a) concern and two WOSBs. However, an WOSB set-aside is not proper if an 8(a) contractor is currently performing the requirement or the requirement has been accepted by the SBA for 8(a) participation, FAR 19.1504(a). There are two types of set-asides for WOSBs but no other programs to assist them.

## a.   *Determination of WOSB Status*

There are two categories of WOSBs — economically disadvantaged WOSBs (EDWOSBs) and WOSBs. WOSBs are defined in 13 C.F.R. § 127.200 as follows:

(b) Qualification as a WOSB. To qualify as a WOSB, a concern must be:

(1) A small business as defined in part 121 of this chapter; and

(2) Not less than 51 percent unconditionally and directly owned and controlled by one or more women who are United States citizens.

To be an EDWOSB the women must be economically disadvantaged, defined in 13 C.F.R. § 127.203(a) as follows:

A woman is economically disadvantaged if she can demonstrate that her ability to compete in the free enterprise system has been impaired due to diminished capital and credit opportunities as compared to others in the same or similar line of business. SBA does not take into consideration community property laws when determining economic disadvantage when the woman has no direct, individual or separate ownership interest in the property.

This regulation contains detailed guidance on the determination of economic disadvantage.

Rules on ownership and control are contained in 13 C.F.R. § 127.201 and § 127.202.

WOSBs and EDWOSBs can self-certify and be certified by third party certifiers approved by the SBA. See FAR 19.1503 and 13 C.F.R. § 127.303 - § 127.305.

## b.   *Set-Aside Procedures*

Set-aside procedures are set forth in FAR 19.1505. They provide that when the SBA determines in which NAICS codes WOSBs are underrepresented and substantially underrepresented:

(a) The contracting officer may set-aside acquisitions exceeding the micro-purchase threshold for competition restricted to EDWOSB or WOSB concerns eligible under the WOSB Program in those NAICS codes in which SBA has determined that women-owned small business concerns are underrepresented or substantially underrepresented in Federal procurement, as specified on SBA's Web site at *http://www.sba.gov/WOSB*.

(b) For requirements in NAICS codes designated by SBA as underrepresented, a contracting officer may restrict competition to EDWOSB concerns if the contracting officer has a reasonable expectation based on market research that—

(1) Two or more EDWOSB concerns will submit offers for the contract;

(2) The anticipated award price of the contract (including options) does not exceed $6.5 million, in the case of a contract assigned an NAICS code for manufacturing; or $4 million, for all other contracts; and

(3) Contract award will be made at a fair and reasonable price.

(c) A contracting officer may restrict competition to WOSB concerns eligible under the WOSB Program (including EDWOSB concerns), for requirements in NAICS codes designated by SBA as substantially underrepresented if there is a reasonable expectation based on market research that —

(1) Two or more WOSB concerns (including EDWOSB concerns), will submit offers;

(2) The anticipated award price of the contract (including options) will not exceed $ 6.5 million, in the case of a contract assigned an NAICS code for manufacturing, or $ 4 million for all other contracts; and

(3) Contract award may be made at a fair and reasonable price.

(d) The contracting officer may make an award, if only one acceptable offer is received from a qualified EDWOSB or WOSB concern.

(e) The contracting officer must check whether the apparently successful offeror filed all the required eligibility documents, and file a status protest if any documents are missing. See 19.1503(d)(2).

# II.  DOMESTIC PREFERENCE POLICIES

The government has a variety of policies favoring the acquisition of articles of domestic origin or acquisition from domestic sources. The major policies are the Buy American Act and the Trade Agreements Act, but there are numerous additional policies that also favor the use of domestic products or sources.

## A.  Buy American Act

The Buy American Act establishes a general preference for the acquisition of domestic "articles, materials, and supplies" when they are being acquired for public use in the United States, 41 U.S.C. §§ 8301-05. The Act was passed during the Depression of the 1930s and was designed to save and create jobs for American workers. The central consideration under the BAA has consistently been the place of manufacture; the nationality of the contractor is not relevant, *E-Systems, Inc.*, 61 Comp. Gen. 431 (B-206209), 82-1 CPD ¶ 533; *Patterson Pump Co.*, Comp. Gen. Dec. B-200165, 80-2 CPD ¶ 453. The term "acquired for public use" applies to leases as well as purchases, *National Office Equip. Co.*, Comp. Gen. Dec. B-191003, 78-1 CPD ¶ 413.

The BAA has separate provisions governing supply and construction contracts. The rules for determining whether articles, materials, or supplies are foreign or domestic are the same for both types of procurement, the differences being the terminology used and the juncture in the total manufacturing or construction process at which the test is applied. Under supply contracts, the proscriptions of the BAA fall on the articles, materials, or supplies delivered to the government; whereas, under construction contracts, they apply to the articles, materials, and supplies used by the contractor and subcontractors in constructing, altering, or repairing the building or work.

The articles, materials, and supplies covered by the BAA are discussed in the FAR using different nomenclature for supply and construction contracts. FAR 25.101 restricts the purchase of supplies that are not domestic "end products," while FAR 25.201 requires the use of only domestic "construction materials." Items delivered to the construction site simply for the use of the contractor that are not to be incorporated into the building or work, such as construction shacks and trailers, are not construction materials subject to the Buy American Act, *Mico Mobile Sales & Leasing Co.*, 51 Comp. Gen. 538 (B-174851) (1972).

The BAA applies similar distinct requirements to unmanufactured and manufactured articles, materials, or supplies.

## 1.  *Unmanufactured Articles*

For unmanufactured articles, materials, or supplies acquired by the government for use in the United States, the BAA requires that they must have been "mined" or "produced" in the United States, unless one of the exceptions discussed below applies, 41 U.S.C. § 8302(a)(1) (supply contracts)and § 8303(a)(1) (construction contracts).

## 2.  *Manufactured Articles*

The BAA requires that manufactured articles, materials, or supplies acquired by the government for public use in the United States or incorporated into domestic construction projects must have been manufactured in this country "substantially all" (more than 50%) from components that have themselves been "mined, produced, or manufactured" within the United States, unless one of the exceptions discussed below is applicable, 41 U.S.C. § 8302(a)(2) (supply contracts) and § 8303(a)(2) (construction contracts). Hence, for a manufactured end product or a manufactured construction material to be domestic, it must meet two tests: it must have been manufactured in the United States, and more than 50% of its components must have been mined, produced, or manufactured in the United States. In contrast, components must meet only one test — manufacture in the United States. For example, a watch movement that was domestically manufactured (assembled) entirely from foreign-made parts is a domestic component of the watch into which it is incorporated, *Hamilton Watch Co.*, Comp. Gen. Dec. B-179939, 74-1 CPD ¶ 306. Thus, a manufactured end product or construction material is of domestic origin only (1) if manufactured domestically and (2) if the costs of the foreign components do not exceed 50% of the costs of all the components. A component, however, qualifies as being of domestic origin if it has been manufactured domestically.

The three major issues concerning manufactured products are (a) what constitutes manufacturing, (b) the distinction between end products and construction materials versus components, and (c) the application of the "substantially all" rule.

## a.  Manufacturing

The meaning of "manufacturing" is important because it will determine whether an end product, construction material, or component is domestic. The term "manufacture" has been interpreted broadly to include the assembly of parts, *Hamilton Watch Co.*, Comp. Gen. Dec. B-179939, 74-1 CPD ¶ 306, but does not include packaging, testing, and evaluation operations, 48 Comp. Gen. 727 (B-166008) (1969). However, GAO has also held that disassembly and reassembly in the United States of a product that was manufactured outside the United States to a condition almost ready to use before the disassembly do not constitute domestic "manufacture," *Ampex Corp.*, Comp. Gen. Dec. B-203021, 82-1 CPD ¶ 163. Compare *Textron, Inc. v. Adams*, 493 F. Supp. 824 (D.D.C. 1980), where foreign disassembly and domestic reassembly was held to constitute domestic manufacture. In *DynAmerica, Inc.*, Comp. Gen. Dec. B-248237, 92-2 CPD ¶ 210, GAO held that the packing in Mexico of domestically manufactured ammunition links into feeder sleeve cartons was merely packaging that made the end product easier to use and did not constitute manufacturing. "Processing" of magnetic tape for computer use was held not to constitute manufacturing since it was a service analogous to translation, *Blodgett Keypunching Co.*, 54 Comp. Gen. 18 (B-153751), 76-2 CPD ¶ 331. GAO has drawn some fine distinctions in this area resulting in considerable confusion. Compare 45 Comp. Gen. 658 (B-158869) (1966) with 48 Comp. Gen. 727 (B-166008) (1969), both involving sequential manufacturing processes, from which GAO drew different conclusions. The basic test is whether the operations performed on the foreign item create a basically new material or result in a fundamental change in the item. See *A. Hirsh, Inc.*, Comp. Gen. Dec. B-237466, 90-1

CPD ¶ 247, ruling that domestic processing of foreign-bought horsehair — including sterilization, sorting, cutting, inspecting, blending with oil, wrapping, and trimming — was not "manufacturing," because after all the processing, the horsehair was still horsehair. See also *TRS Research*, Comp. Gen. Dec. B-285514, 2000 CPD ¶ 128, ruling that "refurbishing" foreign containers was not manufacturing because it did not "transform or alter the essential nature of the containers."

Construction cases are equally fact-sensitive. For example, where contract specifications required the construction of a water pump unit, and the complete, operable unit was delivered to the construction site, the entire unit, rather than simply its motor, was considered to be the construction material, 46 Comp. Gen. 813 (B-161061) (1967). In contrast, where circuit breakers and switchgear were brought to the site separately and installed in a building as a unit, they were each held to be construction material, *George Hyman Constr. Co.*, ASBCA 13777, 69-2 BCA ¶ 7830.

Once it is determined that an end product, construction material, or component has been "manufactured," the actual place the "manufacturing" occurred — not the relative costs of manufacturing — will control the BAA determination. Thus, if an end product is assembled (manufactured) outside of the United States from domestic components, it is not a domestic product even though substantially all of the costs of the product are incurred domestically, 52 Comp. Gen. 13 (B-175526) (1972). In this case, GAO reasoned that manufacture had occurred outside of the United States, even though only 3% of the costs were incurred for foreign work. An interesting controversy over the application of this rule occurred where a company performed final assembly and testing in the United States after 85 to 90 % of the manufacture was accomplished in Mexico using American components, *Cincinnati Elecs. Corp.*, 55 Comp. Gen. 1479 (B-185842), 76-2 CPD ¶ 286. GAO denied a protest against this procedure because this issue was under consideration at a policy level in the agency. However, the regulations are still silent on whether early stages of the final assembly process can be performed outside of the United States within the requirement for domestic manufacture.

GAO has noted that the meaning of "manufacture" is difficult to ascertain and has recommended that the procurement regulations be amended to provide a precise definition, *Davis Walker Corp.*, Comp. Gen. Dec. B-184672, 76-2 CPD ¶ 182. GAO suggested that a procuring agency formulate a general definition of "manufacture." The agency replied that such a rigid approach to a fluid concept was undesirable, 654 FCR A-5 (1976). The FAR does not provide a general definition of "manufacture" for BAA purposes.

### b. *End Products and Construction Materials versus Components*

FAR 25.003 contains the following definitions:

*End product* means those articles, materials, and supplies to be acquired for public use.

*Component* means an article, material, or supply incorporated directly into an end product or construction material.

*Construction material* means an article, material, or supply brought to the construction site by a contractor or subcontractor for incorporation into the building or work. The term also includes an item brought to the site preassembled from articles, materials, or supplies. However, emergency life safety systems, such as emergency lighting, fire alarm, and audio evacuation systems, that are discrete systems incorporated into a public building or work and that are produced as complete systems, are evaluated as a single and distinct construction material regardless of when or how the individual parts or components of those systems are delivered to the construction site. Materials purchased directly by the Government are supplies, not construction material.

These definitions provide little guidance regarding the distinctions between supply and construction contracts. Yet this is a major issue, since the origin of parts assembled into components need not be domestic, 45 Comp. Gen. 658 (B-158869) (1966). In view of the lack of regulatory guidance, the definitions primarily rest on the exercise of procurement judgment, 48 Comp. Gen. 384 (B-165634) (1968).

There have sometimes been conflicting results. In *Bell Helicopter Textron*, 59 Comp. Gen. 158 (B-195268), 79-2 CPD ¶ 431, GAO ruled that the end product was a helicopter rather than the total work performed on the contract including the helicopter. In *Textron, Inc. v. Adams*, 493 F. Supp. 824 (D.D.C. 1980), the court disagreed, ruling that the contract end product was a helicopter system consisting of five components: a helicopter, system test and evaluation, system engineering/management, data, and integrated logistics support. The court reasoned that deference should be given to the agency's contractual statement of its need for a "system" without regard to the fact that the helicopter constituted the predominant element of the procurement. This decision concludes that an end product may be composed of various discrete products, so long as it is being procured as, and will be used as, a single unit, such as a "tool kit," *Imperial Eastman Corp.*, 53 Comp. Gen. 726 (B-177865), 74-1 CPD ¶ 153, or a modification kit, 47 Comp. Gen. 21 (B-161325) (1967). Occasionally, a solicitation will specify what items will be considered end products for BAA purposes. Compare *Ampex Corp.*, Comp. Gen. Dec. B-203021, 82-1 CPD ¶ 163, where operation and maintenance manuals were held not to be components. This follows the more prevalent GAO view that an end product is the item being manufactured, in the form in which it is required by the government, as distinguished from such things as packaging and services or tests performed after the item has been manufactured, *Patterson Pump Co.*, Comp. Gen. Dec. B-200165, 80-2 CPD ¶ 453. See also 46 Comp. Gen. 784 (B-160627) (1967), where sulfa tablets, not the bottled sulfa tablets actually delivered, were held to be the end products.

## c.  "Substantially All" Rule

An end product or a manufactured construction material is considered to have been manufactured "substantially all" from components of domestic origin if the cost of all components mined, manufactured, or produced in the United States is more than 50% of the cost of all of its components, FAR 25.101(a)(2); Executive Order 10582, 19 Fed. Reg. 8723 (1954). In applying the over-50% test, the boards and GAO have addressed two issues: what constitutes a component and what costs are included in the computation.

The term "component" is applied only to those articles, materials, and supplies directly used in the manufacture of the end product or construction material. For example, in the procurement of clothing, yarn used in the manufacture of the cloth was not considered a component because it was not directly incorporated into the clothing, 45 Comp. Gen. 658 (B-158869) (1966). See also *Ampex Corp.*, Comp. Gen. Dec. B-203021, 82-1 CPD ¶ 163 (operation and maintenance manuals were merely tools to provide instructions and not components incorporated into the end product).

In *General Kinetics, Inc.*, 70 Comp. Gen. 473 (B-242052.2), 91-1 CPD ¶ 445, the government was purchasing both "Tempest" (used for secure messages) and "non-Tempest" fax systems. The major component of each system was a commercial fax machine of foreign origin. Each of the fax machines was disassembled in the United States, certain operations were conducted, and the machines were reassembled in the United States. GAO found that the operations conducted on the Tempest fax machine, which included replacement of the programmable memory chips, addition of Tempest-required insulation, and the addition and integration of a protocol converter, were sufficient to make it a domestic component, and the "Tempest" system a domestic end product. However, the operations conducted on the non-Tempest machine, which consisted of disassembly, removal of circuit board and replacement of memory chips, and reassembly, were not sufficient to alter the essential nature of the machine, so that it remained a foreign component. Thus, the non-Tempest system was a foreign end item subject to the BAA's evaluation differential. See *Leisure-Lift, Inc.*, Comp. Gen. Dec. B-291878.3, 2003 CPD ¶ 189, holding that only the "shell" or "base unit" that cost 47.7% of the components of a motor scooter was foreign with the result that the scooter was a domestic end item. See also *City Chem. LLC*, Comp. Gen. Dec. B-296135.2, 2005 CPD ¶ 120, describing the analysis of whether a component was manufacturer in the United States as follows:

> [W]here it is alleged that a foreign material has been manufactured into a component domestically and the component in turn manufactured into an end item domestically, we have . . . looked at whether the manufacturing process consists of two distinct phases, the first yielding a component that is distinguishable from the original material and the second yielding an end item that is distinguishable from the component.

In applying the substantially-all test, only the cost of components is considered. FAR 25.003 contains the following definition:

> Cost of components means —
>
>> (1) For components purchased by the contractor, the acquisition cost, including transportation costs to the place of incorporation into the end product or construction material (whether or not such costs are paid to a domestic firm), and any applicable duty (whether or not a duty-free entry certificate is issued); or
>
>> (2) For components manufactured by the contractor, all costs associated with the manufacture of the component, including transportation costs as described in paragraph (1) of this definition, plus allocable overhead costs, but excluding profit. Cost of components does not include any costs associated with the manufacture of the end product.

Domestic component costs are comprised of the purchase price of the component or the full cost of manufacture if the contractor manufactured the component, *Avantek, Inc.*, 50 Comp. Gen. 697 (B-170498) (1973). The total cost of the end product — what it would sell for, minus profit — is irrelevant, since that figure includes cost elements other than components. For example, labor, packaging, testing, and evaluation costs incurred in manufacturing the end product would not be included as part of the costs of the components of the end product. Thus, transportation costs of ready mixed concrete were not assignable as a cost of the components because the concrete was an identifiable end item at the time it was transported to the job site, *Dick Hollan, Inc.*, ASBCA 21304, 77-1 BCA ¶ 12,540. Similarly, in 53 Comp. Gen. 259 (B-179029) (1973), engineering costs were excluded from the computation because such services were not directly incorporated into the end product.

## 3. Solicitation and Contract Provisions

The procuring agency is required to include BAA provisions in each solicitation and contract that is determined to be subject to the Act, FAR 25.1101 (supplies) and FAR 25.1102 (construction). For supply contracts the required clauses are the Buy American Act - Supplies clause in FAR 52.225-1, the Buy American Certificate solicitation provision in FAR 52.225-2, and the Place of Manufacture solicitation provision in FAR 52.225-18. For construction contracts valued at less than $7,443,000 the required clauses are the Buy American Act — Construction Materials clause in FAR 52.225-9 and the Notice of Buy American Act Requirements solicitation provision in FAR 52.225-10. See DFARS 225.1101 for different clauses and solicitation provisions used in DoD contracts.

The Buy American Certificate provision requires the offeror to certify that each end product, other than those specifically identified in the certificate, is of domestic origin, and that components of unknown origin have been considered to have been mined, produced, or manufactured outside the United States. If the offeror leaves the certificate blank, the offeror will be deemed to be offering only products of domestic origin, *Consolidated Devices, Inc.*, Comp. Gen. Dec. B-214469, 84-1 CPD ¶ 383; *Lanier Bus. Prods., Inc.*, Comp. Gen. Dec. B-196736, 81-1 CPD ¶ 186. See *Designware, Inc.*, Comp. Gen. Dec. B-221423, 86-1 CPD ¶ 181, where the fact that a listed product was manufactured only in Korea was held irrelevant where the bidder left the certificate blank and the contracting officer did not know that the product was foreign. See, however, *Airpro Equip., Inc.*, 62 Comp. Gen. 154 (B-209612), 83-1 CPD ¶ 105, where the product was treated as foreign when the bidder left the certificate blank but identified the country of manufacture as "USA/ England" in the schedule.

The standard BAA contract clauses for supply and construction require that the contractor deliver domestic end products or domestic construction materials, unless one of the specified exceptions to the Act's provisions is applicable, FAR 52.225-1 and FAR 52.225-9. If an offeror certifies that it will comply with the BAA, the contracting officer can rely on that certification unless there is reason to believe that it is not correct. See *General Kinetics, Inc.*, 70 Comp. Gen. 473 (B-242052.2), 91-1 CPD ¶ 445, stating:

> As a general matter, a contracting agency should go beyond a firm's self-certification for Buy American Act purposes, and not automatically rely on the validity of that certification, where the agency has reason to believe, prior to award, that a foreign end product will be furnished. See *Cryptek, Inc.*, B-241354, Feb. 4, 1991, 91-1 CPD ¶ 111; *American Instrument Corp.*, B-239997, Oct. 12, 1990, 90-2 CPD ¶ 287.

If the contractor does not comply with the BAA, the contract may be terminated for default, *Sunox, Inc.*, ASBCA 30025, 85-2 BCA ¶ 18,077.

## 4. Exceptions

Congress has recognized that application of the BAA might severely restrict an agency's ability to meet its needs. For example, many specific products are not manufactured, mined, or produced in the United States or, if they are available domestically, their prices might be far higher than the price of equivalent items of foreign origin. Congress has established a number of exceptions to give procuring agencies flexibility.

### a. Unreasonable Costs

The head of an agency is authorized to permit procurement of foreign items if the cost of the lowest-priced domestic item is "unreasonable," 41 U.S.C. § 8302(a) (1) and § 8303(b)(2). The President has established uniform standards for agencies to use in determining when prices of foreign supplies are considered "unreasonable," and those standards have been incorporated into the FAR, Executive Order 10582, 19 Fed. Reg. 8723 (1954); FAR 25.105.

Under these standards, agencies add a percentage to the price, inclusive of duty, of the low acceptable offer of a foreign item and then compare that increased price to the price for an item of domestic origin, FAR 25.105(a). The percentage is 6% for large businesses and 12% for small businesses, FAR 25.105(b). If, for example, the low responsive bid offering a foreign item is $100, the 6% differential would be $6, and the agency would, solely for evaluation purposes, treat the price of the offeror of a foreign item as $106. If the low responsive offeror of a domestic item is a small business, the differential would be 12%, and the evaluated price of the offeror of the foreign item would be treated as $112. DoD uses an evaluation factor of 50% in lieu of the above factors, DFARS 225.104(b).

The differential is applied only to the material delivered under the contract and not necessarily to the total bid price. Thus, post-delivery services such as installation, testing, and training are exempted from the surcharge applicable to foreign end products, *Dynatest Consulting, Inc.*, Comp. Gen. Dec. B-257822.4, 95-1 CPD ¶ 167. See *STD Research Corp.*, 72 Comp. Gen. 211 (B-252073.2), 93-1 CPD ¶ 406 (agency should not apply the surcharge to an offeror's total evaluated price for a high-technology power generator, which included not only the price of foreign hardware but also post-delivery services); and *Allis-Chalmers Corp. v. Friedkin*, 635 F.2d 248 (3d Cir. 1980) (costs of installation and post-delivery services were excluded from the price of the foreign item to which the 12% differential was applied).

The evaluation procedure ordinarily is applied on an item-by-item basis, or to any group of items on which award may be made as specifically provided in the solicitation, FAR 25.501(a). Absent such a provision, each item or group of closely related items will be treated separately for evaluation purposes, even though award may be made on an all-or-nothing basis, 47 Comp. Gen. 676 (B-163740) (1968); *Essex Assocs., Inc.*, 63 Comp. Gen. 503 (B-213279), 84-2 CPD ¶ 97. FAR Subpart 25.5 contains more detailed guidance on the evaluation of foreign offers on supply contracts.

This evaluation process does not apply to procurements under the Trade Agreements Act, FAR 25.105(a)(2). A separate evaluation process applies to procurements subject to the Caribbean Basin Trade Initiative, FAR 25.405 and 25.504.2, or the Israeli Trade Act, FAR 25.406 and 25.504-3.

## b.  Unavailability

The requirements of the BAA do not apply to products that have been determined not to be reasonably available in commercial quantities and of a satisfactory quality, 41 U.S.C. § 8302(a)(2)(B) and § 8303(b)(1)(B); FAR 25.103(b). A list of such products is set forth in FAR 25.104(a). See *Midwest Dynamometer & Eng'g Co.*, Comp. Gen. Dec. B-252168, 93-1 CPD ¶ 408, where GAO held that the BAA was not applicable to the purchase of a dynamometer from a foreign firm because the item was not manufactured in the United States in sufficient and reasonably available commercial quantities.

### c. Use Abroad

The BAA exempts articles purchased "for use outside the United States," 41 U.S.C. § 8302(a)(2)(A) and § 8303(b)(1)(A). See *Systems & Def. Servs. Int'l*, Comp. Gen. Dec. B-254254.2, 94-1 CPD ¶ 91 (contract not subject to BAA because the work was to be performed outside the United States); and *Maremont Corp.*, 55 Comp. Gen. 1362 (B-186276), 76-2 CPD ¶ 181 (BAA held not to apply to the purchase of machine guns for installation in vehicles deployed outside the United States, or to the procurement of steel towers for installation as part of a communications system in West Germany). This exception permits any foreign-made product to be offered for such procurements and does not require the furnishing of products manufactured in the country of use.

### d. Public Interest

The BAA allows the head of a procuring agency to waive application of the Act upon a determination that such application would be "inconsistent with the public interest," 41 U.S.C. § 8302(a)(1) and § 8303(b)(3). FAR 25.202(a)(1) calls for the use of this exception when an agency has an agreement with a foreign government. DoD has used this authority to grant a broad exemption from foreign acquisition restrictions for procurements of defense equipment from certain countries with which the United States has entered into Memoranda of Understanding (MOU) or other relevant agreements, DFARS Subpart 225.8. See *Self-Powered Lighting, Ltd. v. United States*, 492 F. Supp. 1267 (S.D.N.Y. 1980), where the court ruled that a MOU created a blanket exemption for all United Kingdom defense products and *American Hosp. Supply, Equipping & Consulting*, Comp. Gen. Dec. B-221357, 86-1 CPD ¶ 70, where GAO found proper use of an exemption under a MOU with Italy. Such exemptions extend to nondefense products procured by the DoD, *Allis-Chalmers Corp. v. Arnold*, 619 F.2d 44 (9th Cir. 1980). See also *Air Plastics, Inc.*, Comp. Gen. Dec. B-199307, 80-2 CPD ¶ 141 (exemption for Denmark by MOU); and *Baganoff Assocs., Inc.*, 54 Comp. Gen. 44 (B-179607), 74-2 CPD ¶ 56 (broad Canadian exemption).

The head of a procuring agency has considerable discretion in determining whether to invoke the public interest exception. GAO has held that this exception may be invoked after bid opening, *E-Systems, Inc.*, 61 Comp. Gen. 431 (B-206209), 82-1 CPD ¶ 533. An agency has also been permitted to invoke this exception after contract award when the only domestic price is unreasonable, *John T. Brady & Co. v. United States*, 693 F.2d 1380 (Fed. Cir. 1982). In *John T. Brady & Co.*, VACAB 1300, 84-1 BCA ¶ 16,925, *recons. denied*, 84-1 BCA ¶ 17,161, the board, on remand, held that the failure of the agency to grant the exception was an abuse of discretion since the government would have incurred no additional costs by granting the exception. The board, therefore, granted the contractor a price adjustment for the difference in price between the domestic and foreign material. However, a contractor should generally request waiver of the BAA before contract award or at least before contract performance, *C. Sanchez & Son, Inc. v. United States*, 24 Cl. Ct. 14 (1991), *aff'd in part, vacated in part*, 6 F.3d 1539 (Fed. Cir. 1993). In *C. Sanchez*, a contractor sought an equitable adjustment to compensate for certain increased costs in using domestic wire and cable. Although the contractor complained during performance about the cost to a contracting officer's technical representative (COTR), it never submitted a waiver of the BAA. The Claims Court held that the contractor should have requested a waiver of the BAA before contract performance, and since it did not do so, it was not entitled to an equitable adjustment.

### e.  Commercial Items

The requirements of the BAA do not apply to information technology that is a commercial item when it is an element of construction material, FAR 25.202(a)(4). This exception is derived from § 535(a) of the FY 2004 Consolidated Appropriations Act and subsequent appropriations acts. It does not apply to information technology that is an element of an end product furnished on a supply contract.

The requirements of the BAA do not apply to the components test when the agency is procuring commercial off-the-shelf items, FAR 25.101(a)(2); FAR 12.505(a). Thus, if a manufactured end item or construction material is manufactured in the United States, the components can be 100% foreign products (not meeting the over-50% test). This rule has been adopted under the authority of 41 U.S.C. § 1907(a)(1).

## B.  Trade Agreements

There have been a number of "free trade" agreements entered into over the years that apply special procedures to the procurement of foreign products and services. An early effort of this type was the "Tokyo Round" of international trade negotiations during the 1970s to reduce "nontariff barriers," such as the BAA, to international trade. The Tokyo Round resulted in a series of "international codes," one of which is known as the "Government Procurement Code." That code includes provisions designed to reduce the effect of buy-national practices of the signatory nations.

The United States joined in the agreements that resulted from the Tokyo Round, including the Government Procurement Agreement (WTO GPA). To implement those agreements, Congress enacted the Trade Agreements Act (TAA) of 1979, 19 U.S.C. § 2501 et seq. This was followed by the Uruguay Round Agreements Act, 19 U.S.C. § 3501 et seq. One provision of the TAA authorized the President to waive any otherwise applicable "law, regulation, procedure or practice regarding Government procurement" that would accord foreign products less favorable treatment than that given to domestic products, 19 U.S.C § 2511(a). That provision of the TAA was implemented by the President, Executive Order 12260, 46 Fed. Reg. 1653 (1981). Thus, the BAA and at least some other federal restrictions favoring domestic products have been superseded as to the specific products and countries covered by the President's action, FAR Subpart 25.4.

The United States has entered into a number of other "free trade" agreements that supersede the BAA to some extent. These are listed in FAR 25.400(a), describing the coverage of FAR Subpart 25.4 as follows:

(2) Free Trade Agreements (FTA), consisting of —

(i) NAFTA (the North American Free Trade Agreement, as approved by Congress in the North American Free Trade Agreement Implementation Act of 1993 (19 U.S.C. 3301 note));

(ii) Chile FTA (the United States-Chile Free Trade Agreement, as approved by Congress in the United States-Chile Free Trade Agreement Implementation Act (Pub. L. 108-77));

(iii) Singapore FTA (the United States-Singapore Free Trade Agreement, as approved by Congress in the United States-Singapore Free Trade Agreement Implementation Act (Pub. L. 108-78) (19 U.S.C. 3805 note));

(iv) Australia FTA (the United States-Australia Free Trade Agreement, as approved by Congress in the United States-Australia Free Trade Agreement Implementation Act (Pub. L. 108-286) (19 U.S.C. 3805 note));

(v) Morocco FTA (The United States--Morocco Free Trade Agreement, as approved by Congress in the United States--Morocco Free Trade Agreement Implementation Act (Pub. L. 108-302) (19 U.S.C. 3805 note));

(vi) CAFTA-DR (The Dominican Republic-Central America-United States Free Trade Agreement, as approved by Congress in the Dominican Republic-Central America-United States Free Trade Agreement Implementation Act (Pub. L. 109-53) (19 U.S.C. 4001 note));

(vii) Bahrain FTA (the United States-Bahrain Free Trade Agreement, as approved by Congress in the United States-Bahrain Free Trade Agreement Implementation Act (Pub. L. 109-169) (19 U.S.C. 3805 note));

(viii) Oman FTA (the United States-Oman Free Trade Agreement, as approved by Congress in the United States-Oman Free Trade Agreement Implementation Act (Pub. L. 109-283) (19 U.S.C. 3805 note)); and

(ix) Peru FTA (the United States-Peru Trade Promotion Agreement, as approved by Congress in the United States-Peru Trade Promotion Agreement Implementation Act (Pub. L. 110-138) (19 U.S.C. 3805 note));

(3) The least developed country designation made by the U.S. Trade Representative, pursuant to the Trade Agreements Act (19 U.S.C. 2511(b)(4)), in acquisitions covered by the WTO GPA;

(4) The Caribbean Basin Trade Initiative (CBTI) (determination of the U.S. Trade Representative that end products or construction material granted duty-free entry from countries designated as beneficiaries under the Caribbean Basin Economic Recovery Act (19 U.S.C. 2701, et seq.), with the exception of Panama, must be treated as eligible products in acquisitions covered by the WTO GPA);

(5) The Israeli Trade Act (the U.S.-Israel Free Trade Area Agreement, as approved by Congress in the United States-Israel Free Trade Area Implementation Act of 1985 (19 U.S.C. 2112 note)); or

(6) The Agreement on Trade in Civil Aircraft (U.S. Trade Representative waiver of the Buy American Act for signatories of the Agreement on Trade in Civil Aircraft, as implemented in the Trade Agreements Act of 1979 (19 U.S.C. 2513)).

FAR 25.401(a) provides that these agreements (including the WTO GPA) do not cover:

(1) Acquisitions set aside for small businesses;

(2) Acquisitions of arms, ammunition, or war materials, or purchases indispensable for national security or for national defense purposes;

(3) Acquisitions of end products for resale;

(4) Acquisitions from Federal Prison Industries, Inc., under Subpart 8.6, and acquisitions under Subpart 8.7, Acquisition from Nonprofit Agencies Employing People Who Are Blind or Severely Disabled; and

(5) Other acquisitions not using full and open competition, if authorized by Subpart 6.2 or 6.3, when the limitation of competition would preclude use of the procedures of this subpart; or sole source acquisitions justified in accordance with 13.501(a).

See also DFARS 225.401-70 for a list of products subject to these trade agreements. In addition, the trade agreements do not cover specified services. FAR 25.401(b) contains the following table:

| The service (Federal Service Codes from the Federal Procurement Data System Product/Service Code Manual are indicated in parentheses for some services.) | WTO GPA | Bahrain FTA, CAFTA–DR, Chile FTA, NAFTA, Oman FTA and Peru FTA | Singapore FTA | Australia and Morocco FTA |
|---|---|---|---|---|
| (1) All services purchased in support of military services overseas. | X | X | X | X |
| (2) (i) Automatic data processing (ADP) telecommunications and transmission services (D304), except enhanced (*i.e.*, value-added) telecommunications services. | X | X | | |
| (ii) ADP teleprocessing and timesharing services (D305), telecommunications network management services (D316), automated news services, data services or other information services (D317), and other ADP and telecommunications services (D399) | X | X | | |
| (iii) Basic telecommunications network services (*i.e.*, voice telephone services, packet-switched data transmission services, circuit-switched data transmission services, telex services, telegraph services, facsimile services, and private leased circuit services, but not information services, as defined in 47 U.S.C. 153(20)). | * | * | X | X |
| (3) Dredging | X | X | X | X |
| (4) (i) Operation and management contracts of certain Government or privately owned facilities used for Government purposes, including Federally Funded Research and Development Centers | X | | X | |
| (ii) Operation of all Department of Defense, Department of Energy, or the National Aeronautics and Space Administration facilities; and all Government-owned research and development facilities or Government-owned environmental laboratories | * * | X | * * | X |
| (5) Research and development | X | X | X | X |
| (6) Transportation services (including launching services, but not including travel agent services—V503) | X | X | X | X |
| (7) Utility services | X | X | X | X |
| (8) Maintenance, repair, modification, rebuilding and installation of equipment related to ships (J019) | | X | | X |
| (9) Nonnuclear ship repair (J998) | | X | | X |

Supplies and services covered by the trade agreements must be procured without regard to application of the BAA when they exceed specified dollar thresholds. These thresholds are revised periodically. FAR 25.402(b) contains a table stating the thresholds as of March 16, 2011, 76 Fed. Reg. 14570:

| Trade agreement | Supply contract (equal to or exceeding) | Service contract (equal to or exceeding) | Construction contract (equal to or exceeding) |
|---|---|---|---|
| WTO GPA | $203,000 | $203,000 | $7,804,000 |
| FTAs: | | | |
|     Australia FTA | 70,079 | 70,079 | 7,804,000 |
|     Bahrain FTA | 203,000 | 203,000 | 9,110,318 |
|     CAFTA–DR (Costa Rica, El Salvador, Dominican Republic, Guatemala, Honduras, and Nicaragua) | 70,079 | 70,079 | 7,804,000 |
|     Chile FTA | 70,079 | 70,079 | 7,804,000 |
|     Morocco FTA | 203,000 | 203,000 | 7,804,000 |
| NAFTA: | | | |
|     —Canada | 25,000 | 70,079 | 9,110,318 |
|     —Mexico | 70,079 | 70,079 | 9,110,318 |
| Oman FTA | 203,000 | 203,000 | 9,110,318 |
| Peru FTA | 203,000 | 203,000 | 7,804,000 |
| Singapore FTA | 70,079 | 70,079 | 7,804,000 |
| Israeli Trade Act | 50,000 | | |

For protests involving these trade agreements, see *Presto Lock, Inc.*, Comp. Gen. Dec. B-218766, 85-2 CPD ¶ 183 (padlocks from Hong Kong); and *Qualimetrics, Inc.*, Comp. Gen. Dec. B-222726, 86-1 CPD ¶ 519 (use of Finnish components raises no BAA issue since Trade Agreement Act applies). See also *Olympic Container Corp.*, Comp. Gen. Dec. B-250403, 93-1 CPD ¶ 89 (no application of the BAA's differential to offers of products from non-designated countries is permitted); *Trading Atlanta Ltd.*, Comp. Gen. Dec. B-239056, 90-2 CPD ¶ 88 (since the TAA prohibits the acceptance of South African products, the protester was not prejudiced by the award to a higher-priced domestic competitor); and *Puerto Rico Marine Mgmt., Inc.*, Comp. Gen. Dec. B-247975.5, 92-2 CPD ¶ 275 (items indispensable to the national defense is not subject to the TAA; in such cases the BAA applies).

## 1.  Trade Agreements End Products

An article is considered to be a trade agreements country "end product" under the TAA if it is "wholly the growth, product, or manufacture of the designated country," or, "if it consists in whole or in part of materials from another country, has been substantially transformed" in the trade agreements country "into a new and different article of commerce with a name, character, or use distinct article or articles from which it was transformed." See the definitions of "WTO GPA country end product,'"Free Trade Agreement country end product," "Canadian end product,"and "Caribbean Basin country end product" in FAR 25.003.

There is no other guidance in the FAR as to the meaning of "substantial transformation." However, in *Klinge Corp. v. United States*, 82 Fed. Cl. 127 (2008), the court held that additional work on a refrigeration unit in the United States did not constitute substantial transformation because the unit had passed functional tests in a nonqualifying country. The court reasoned that the work in the United States did not make the unit a "new and different article." GAO had reached the opposite conclusion in *Klinge Corp.*, Comp. Gen. Dec. B-309930.2, 2008 CPD ¶ 102. In a subsequent decision, *Klinge Corp. v. United States*, 83 Fed. Cl. 773 (2008) the court apparently agreed that when a company sells spare parts, each part is subject to the substantial transformation test. See also *Pacific Lock Co.*, Comp. Gen. Dec. B-309982, 2007 CPD ¶ 191, sustaining an agency determination that padlocks that were assembled in the United States from noncompliant country components were not substantially transformed in the United States because there was no substantial content of domestic components. The agency had relied on international trade rulings that locks did not meet the substantial transformation test if the components were mainly of foreign origin. No substantial transformation was also found in *CSK Int'l, Inc.*, Comp. Gen. Dec. B-278111.2, 97-2 CPD ¶ 178 (assembling handle to tool head); *Ran-Paige Co. v. United States*, 35 Fed. Cl. 117 (1996) (attaching handles to pots); *Becton Dickinson AcuteCare*, Comp. Gen. Dec. B-238942, 90-2 CPD ¶ 55 (assembly of parts manufactured and sterilized in the United States).

The concept of substantial transformation is derived from U.S. Customs Regulations. These regulations are entitled to be given considerable deference in deciding ruling of the Customs Service, *United States v. Haggar Apparel Co.*, 526 U.S. 380 (1999). There are a number of Customs cases dealing with the matter. See *Ferrostaal Metals Corp. v. United States*, 664 F. Supp. 535 (N.D. Ill. 1987) (full-hard cold rolled steel sheet substantially transformed by continuous annealing and hotdip galvanizing operation); *Superior Wire v. United States*, 669 F. Supp. 472 (1987 Ct. Intl. Trade), *aff'd*, 867 F.2d 1409 (Fed. Cir. 1989) (wire rod made into wire did not constitute substantial transformation); *Madison Galleries, Ltd. v. United States*, 688 F. Supp. 1544 (1988 Ct. Intl. Trade), *aff'd*, 870 F.2d 627 (Fed. Cir. 1989) (blank porcelain pieces substantially transformed by decoration); *Bestfoods v. United States*, 1653 F.3d 1371 (Fed. Cir. 1999) (making peanut butter not substantial transformation of peanut slurry); *Crawfish Processors Alliance v. United States*, 483 F.3d 1358 (Fed. Cir. 2007) (making crawfish etouffee substantial transformation of crawfish tail meat); and *Ugine & Alz Belgium v. United States*, 551 F.3d 1339 (Fed. Cir. 2009) (cold rolling of steel did not substantially transform hot rolled steel).

## 2. *Procedures*

FAR 25.502 provides for the following evaluation procedures for foreign supplies:

(a) Unless otherwise specified in agency regulations, perform the following steps in the order presented:

(1) Eliminate all offers or offerors that are unacceptable for reasons other than price; e.g., nonresponsive, debarred or suspended, or a prohibited source (see Subpart 25.7).

(2) Rank the remaining offers by price.

(3) If the solicitation specifies award on the basis of factors in addition to cost or price, apply the evaluation factors as specified in this section and use the evaluated cost or price in determining the offer that represents the best value to the Government.

(b) For acquisitions covered by the WTO GPA (see Subpart 25.4) —

(1) Consider only offers of U.S.-made or designated country end products, unless no offers of such end products were received;

(2) If the agency gives the same consideration given eligible offers to offers of U.S.-made end products that are not domestic end products, award on the low offer. Otherwise, evaluate in accordance with agency procedures; and

(3) If there were no offers of U.S.-made or designated country end products, make a nonavailability determination (see 25.103(b)(2)) and award on the low offer (see 25.403(c)).

GAO has held that these procedures do not allow award to a WTO GPA foreign product unless the price is fair and reasonable, *Tiger Truck*, LLC, Comp. Gen. Dec. B-400685, 2009 CPD ¶ 19. In this decision, GAO also held that if there are no domestic products or compliant foreign products, award cannot be made to the low price non-compliant foreign product until the head of the contracting activity has made a nonavailability determination in accordance with FAR 25.502(b)(3).

In procurements over $203,000 covered by the WTO GPA, agencies are required to use the Trade Agreements clause in FAR 52.225-5 and the Trade Agreements Certificate solicitation provision in FAR 52.225-6. The certificate states that the products to be supplied will be from compliant countries and requires listing of products from noncompliant countries. See DFARS 225.1101 for different clauses and solicitation provisions used in DoD contracts.

In *Master Lock Co., LLC*, Comp. Gen. Dec. B-309982.2, 2009 CPD ¶ 2, GAO ruled that not listing any noncompliant products allowed the agency to award to the company, providing the following guidance on the procedure to be followed:

> When a bidder or offeror represents that it will furnish end products of designated or qualifying countries (including domestic end products) in accordance with the TAA, it is obligated under the contract to comply with that representation. That is, where a bidder or offeror leaves the certificate blank and does not exclude any end product from the certificate, and does not otherwise indicate that it is offering anything other than a TAA-compliant end product, acceptance of the offer will result in an obligation on the offeror's or bidder's part to furnish a TAA-compliant end product. *Wyse Tech., Inc.*, B-297454, Jan. 24, 2006, 2006 CPD ¶ 23 at 6. If prior to award an agency has reason to believe that a firm will not provide compliant products, the agency should go beyond the firm's representation of compliance with the Act; however, where the agency has no information prior to award that would lead to such a conclusion, the agency may properly rely upon an offeror's representation without further investigation. *Leisure-Lift, Inc.*, B-291878.3; B-292448.2, Sept. 25, 2003, 2003 CPD ¶ 189 at 8. Where an agency is required to investigate further, we will review the evaluation and resulting determination regarding compliance with the requirements of the Act to ensure that they were reasonable. *Pacific Lock Co.*, B-309982, Oct. 25, 2007, 2007 CPD ¶ 191 at 4.

See also *Klinge Corp. v. United States*, 82 Fed. Cl. 127 (2008), holding that if a proposal contains information on its face indicating that the certificate is inaccurate, the agency must "make reasonable inquiry and satisfy itself that the product offered meets the terms of the act."

## C. Other Domestic Preferences

The government has a number of policies, besides the BAA and the trade agreements acts, favoring acquisition of articles of domestic origin. These policies either impose restrictions on the purchase of specific articles or services or require the use of price differentials in evaluating the price of foreign articles or services.

### 1. Statutory Restrictions

There are a number of statutory restrictions. The oldest originated in 1941 when the military services were prohibited from using appropriated funds to procure foreign food or clothing, *A&P Surgical Co.*, 62 Comp. Gen. 256 (B-206111.2), 83-1 CPD ¶ 263. DFARS Subpart 225.70 contains detailed guidance on Appropriation or Authorization Act restrictions applying to food, clothing, fabrics, hand or measuring tools, specialty metals, buses, chemical weapons antidotes, naval air circuit breakers, anchor and mooring chain, ball and roller bearings, carbon alloy and armor steel plate, supercomputers, shipyard construction or repair of vessels, overseas A/E services, and ballistic missile defense R&D. See also DFARS 225.7102-1 placing limitations on the various types of foreign forgings. DFARS Subpart 252.225 contains special clauses and solicitation provisions for many of these items.

Additional restrictions are found in the transportation field. See FAR Subpart 47.4, implementing the statutes giving preference to U.S. flag air carriers for the transportation of freight and persons. See also FAR Subpart 47.5, implementing the numerous statutes giving preference to U.S. flag vessels for the transportation of supplies.

The provisions of such specific statutes may bar purchase of foreign materials even if the BAA would not, *Penthouse Mfg. Co.*, Comp. Gen. Dec. B-217480, 85-1 CPD ¶ 487; 49 Comp. Gen. 606 (B-168791)(1970).

### 2. *Balance of Payments Differentials*

DoD has adopted an additional technique favoring domestic supplies and services called the Balance of Payments Program. DFARS Subpart 225.75 makes this program applicable to acquisitions of supplies, services, or construction for use outside the United States. However, DFARS 225.7501(a) contains a long list of exceptions to the application of this program. See also DFARS 225.7501(b) for guidance on the relationship of this program to trade agreements and application of a 50% evaluation factor for price reasonableness determinations. Examples of the proper evaluation of offers subject to the balance of payment procedures are set forth in DFARS PGI 225.504.

## III. POLICIES ON THE ENVIRONMENT AND ENERGY

Since the 1960s, Congress has passed a number of statutes concerning the environment and energy. These statutes and the regulations implementing them contain a variety of provisions that use federal contracts to foster the policies established for environment and energy.

### A. National Environmental Policy Act

The National Environmental Policy Act, passed in 1969, "authorizes and directs that, to the fullest extent possible    the policies, regulations and public laws of the United States" shall be interpreted and administered in accordance with the environmental policies set out in the Act, 42 U.S.C. § 4332. The Act also requires that an environmental impact statement be prepared in connection with all "major Federal actions significantly affecting the quality of the human environment," 42 U.S.C. § 4332(2)(C). Examples of regulations implementing this requirement include 24 C.F.R. Part 50 (Department of Housing and Urban Development) and 14 C.F.R. Part 1216.3 (National Aeronautics and Space Administration). In certain circumstances, award of a federal contract might be a "major federal action" that triggers the need for an environmental impact statement. Sometimes contract award acts as a signal that prompts opponents of a federal project (e.g., a dam or new military installation) to seek an injunction delaying the project on grounds that no environmental impact statement, or an inadequate one, has been prepared; see Nash & Linden, "Federal Procurement and the Environment, in Environmental Law Institute," Federal Environmental Law 476-87 (1974).

## B. Energy and Water Efficiency

The Energy Policy and Conservation Act, Pub. L. No. 94-163, codified at 42 U.S.C. § 6361(a)(1), passed in 1975, directs that

[t]he President shall, to the extent of his authority under other law, establish or coordinate Federal agency actions to develop mandatory standards with respect to energy conservation and energy efficiency to govern the procurement policies and decisions of the Federal Government and all Federal agencies, and shall take such steps as are necessary to cause such standards to be implemented.

The National Energy Conservation Policy Act, Pub. L. No. 95-619, codified at 42 U.S.C. § 8201 et seq., passed in 1978, calls for a number of energy and water conservation programs with regard to federal buildings. These statutes are implemented in FAR Subpart 23.2.

FAR 23.202 contains the following broad statement of policy:

The Government's policy is to acquire supplies and services that promote energy and water efficiency, advance the use of renewable energy products, and help foster markets for emerging technologies. This policy extends to all acquisitions, including those below the simplified acquisition threshold.

## 1. Energy-Efficient Products

The first technique that has been adopted to implement this policy is the requirement that agencies must procure energy-saving products unless the head of the agency determines that no product is reasonably available or cost effective over the life of the product, FAR 23.204. Guidance is provided in FAR 23.203(a) as follows:

(1) When acquiring energy-consuming products listed in the ENERGY STAR [REGISTERED TRADEMARK] Program (*http://www.energystar.gov/products*) or Federal Energy Management Program (FEMP) (*http://www1.eere.energy.gov/ femp/procurement/eep*) —

    (i) Agencies shall purchase ENERGY STAR [REGISTERED TRADE-MARK] or FEMP-designated products; and

(ii) For products that consume power in a standby mode and are listed on FEMP's Low Standby Power Devices product listing, agencies shall —

(A) Purchase items which meet FEMP's standby power wattage recommendation or document the reason for not purchasing such items; or

(B) If FEMP has listed a product without a corresponding wattage recommendation, purchase items which use no more than one watt in their standby power consuming mode. When it is impracticable to meet the one watt requirement, agencies shall purchase items with the lowest standby wattage practicable; and

(2) When contracting for services or construction that will include the provision of energy-consuming products, agencies shall specify products that comply with the applicable requirements in paragraph (a)(1) of this section.

When an agency is procuring products using energy or such products will be required to perform the contract, it is required to use the Energy Efficiency in Energy-Consuming Products clause in FAR 52.223-15.

## 2. *Energy-Savings Performance Contracts*

The other technique that is called for to implement the energy-savings policy is the use of energy-savings performance contracts that are permitted by 42 U.S.C. § 8287. These contracts can turn over one or more of the energy systems in a government facility to a private company for up to 25 years in order to allow the contractor to provide an energy-savings system and to be compensated by a negotiated share of the savings. These contracts are a type of multiyear contract with cancellation ceilings allowing the recovery of capital expenditures made by the contractor in the event that the contract is not allowed to run to its full term. See 10 C.F.R. § 436.34:

(a) Subject to paragraph (b) of this section, Federal agencies may enter into a multiyear energy savings performance contract for a period not to exceed 25 years, as authorized by 42 U.S.C. 8287, without funding of cancellation charges, if:

(1) The multiyear energy savings performance contract was awarded in a competitive manner using the procedures and methods established by this subpart;

(2) Funds are available and adequate for payment of the scheduled energy cost for the first fiscal year of the multiyear energy savings performance contract;

(3) Thirty days before the award of any multiyear energy savings performance contract that contains a clause setting forth a cancellation ceiling in excess of $750,000, the head of the awarding Federal agency gives written

notification of the proposed contract and the proposed cancellation ceiling for the contract to the appropriate authorizing and appropriating committees of the Congress; and

(4) Except as otherwise provided in this section, the multiyear energy savings performance contract is subject to 48 CFR part 17, subpart 17.1, including the requirement that the contracting officer establish a cancellation ceiling.

(b) Neither this subpart nor any provision of the Act requires, prior to contract award or as a condition of a contract award, that a Federal agency have appropriated funds available and adequate to pay for the total costs of an energy savings performance contract for the term of such contract.

The Department of Energy has specified the procedures, selection method and terms and conditions that must be used in awarding energy-savings contracts. See 10 C.F.R. Part 436. These contracts are issued to prequalified contractors in one of two ways. First, DOE issues a list of prequalified contractors each year, 10 C.F.R. § 436.32, and other agencies have followed the same procedure. See *Strategic Resource Solutions Corp.*, Comp. Gen. Dec. B-278732, 98-1 CPD ¶ 74, holding that it was proper to exclude a contractor not on the list from the competition even though it had been added to the subsequent year's list. Second, DOE and other agencies award multiple "Super ESPCs" which are IDIQ contracts calling for the issuance of energy-savings delivery orders for work at a specific facility. See *http://www1.eere.energy.gov/femp/index.html*. When an agency conducts a competition to award a number of Super ESPCs, a protest by an offeror that is not awarded a contract is decided on the same basis as any protest of a best value negotiation procurement, *Johnson Controls, Inc.*, Comp. Gen. Dec. B-282326, 99-2 CPD ¶ 6.

The energy-savings contract or delivery order for a specific facility must be negotiated on the basis of projections of the capital expenditure the contractor will make and the savings that are anticipated over the life of the contract. The goal is to arrive at a savings share to be paid to the contractor that will permit recovery of its investment, including interest, and some reasonable profit. Guidance on analysis and negotiation of these elements of the savings formula is provided in 10 C.F.R. Subpart A. See also Introduction to Measurement and Verification for DOE Super ESPC Projects, June 2007 (*http://www1.eere.energy.gov/femp/pdfs/intro_mv.pdf*). Some agencies have agreed to pay for some or all of the work to be performed by the contractor. See the delivery order issued under a DOE Super ESPC discussed in *AmerescoSolutions, Inc.*, ASBCA 56824, 11-1 BCA ¶ 34,705. Under 42 U.S.C. § 8287 agencies are allowed to return 50% of the savings (after sharing with the contractor) to their appropriation for future use, *Issues related to share-in-savings contract authorities of the National Energy Conservation Policy Act . . .*, Comp. Gen. Dec. B-287488, 2001 U.S. Comp. Gen. LEXIS 217.

An energy-savings contract or delivery order for a specific facility can include all of the energy sources being used at the facility and offerors not approved by the state or local government are entitled to compete for these contracts, *Virginia Elec. & Power Co.*, Comp. Gen. Dec. B-285209, 2000 CPD ¶ 134.

Because these contracts are generally long-term contracts, agencies must work with the contractor to ensure performance. See *Biomass One Operating Co.*, ASBCA 41972, 94-1 BCA ¶ 27,051, converting a default termination to one for convenience because the agency terminated the contract early in performance and had delayed performance.

## C. Promoting the Use of Non-Polluting Products or Processes

Several statutes require federal procuring agencies to give preference to products that are "environmentally friendly." These policies are implemented, in a general manner in FAR 23.703, requiring agencies to:

(a) Implement cost-effective contracting preference programs promoting energy-efficiency, water conservation, and the acquisition of environmentally preferable products and services; and

(b) Employ acquisition strategies that affirmatively implement the following environmental objectives:

(1) Maximize the utilization of environmentally preferable products and services (based on EPA-issued guidance).

(2) Promote energy-efficiency and water conservation.

(3) Eliminate or reduce the generation of hazardous waste and the need for special material processing (including special handling, storage, treatment, and disposal).

(4) Promote the use of nonhazardous and recovered materials.

(5) Realize life-cycle cost savings.

(6) Promote cost effective waste reduction when creating plans, drawings, specifications, standards, and other product descriptions authorizing material substitutions, extensions of shelf-life, and process improvements.

(7) Promote the use of biobased products.

(8) Purchase only plastic ring carriers that are degradable (7 USC 8102(c)(1), 40 CFR part 238).

FAR Subpart 23.7 focuses specifically on computers requiring them to meet industry standards. See the IEEE 1680 Standard for the Environmental Assessment of Personal Computer Products clause at FAR 52.223-16 which is used for this purpose.

In the Resource Conservation and Energy Act of 1976, 42 U.S.C. § 6901 et seq., Congress required procuring agencies to modify their traditional policy of "buying new." Congress required that agencies examine their specifications and remove requirements for "new" materials to the extent such requirements could not be justified, 42 U.S.C. § 6962(c)(1). Congress also required that the Office of Federal Procurement Policy designate items that can be produced with "recovered material" and whose procurement would carry out the objectives of the Act. Agencies are required to procure such items "composed of the highest percentage of recovered material practicable . . . consistent with maintaining a satisfactory level of competition," 42 U.S.C. § 6962. The term "recovered material" includes most material recovered from "any garbage, refuse, sludge from a waste treatment plant, water supply treatment plant, or air pollution control facility and other discarded material," 42 U.S.C. § 6903(19) and (27). Agencies must require vendors to certify that the percentage of "recovered materials" to be used in contract performance will be at least the amount required by applicable specifications or contract requirements, 42 U.S.C. § 6962(d)(2). Agencies may decide not to procure items composed of the highest percentage of recovered materials practicable consistent with maintaining a satisfactory level of competition if they determine that such items are not reasonably available in a reasonable time, or that they will not meet applicable performance standards, or are available only at an unreasonable price, 42 U.S.C. § 6962(c)(1). Similar requirements are included in the Farm Security and Rural Investment Act of 2002, 7 U.S.C. § 8102, dealing with "biobased" materials. FAR 23.404 requires agencies to establish an "affirmative procurement program" within one year after either EPA or the Department of Agriculture has designated an item that can be made using recovered or biobased materials. Solicitation provisions and clauses to carry out there requirements are called for in FAR 23.406.

The Emergency Planning and Community Right-to-Know Act of 1986, 42 U.S.C. § 11023, and the Pollution Prevention Act of 1990, 42 U.S.C. § 13106, require owners and operators of manufacturing facilities to provide EPA and the states with information on toxic chemical releases and waste management activities. Executive Order 13148, April 21, 2000, implements these requirements for all competitive contracts over $100,000 and competitive 8(a) contracts, excluding contracts for commercial items, FAR 23.903. This reporting requirement is implemented by the use of the Certification of Toxic Chemical Release Reporting solicitation provision in FAR 52.223-13, and the Toxic Chemical Release Reporting clause in FAR 52.223-14.

Under the Noise Control Act of 1972, 42 U.S.C. § 4901 et seq., federal agencies must give preference to products that meet several prerequisites. The Environmental Protection Agency must determine through appropriate testing that the product is a "low-noise emission" product, 42 U.S.C. § 4914(b). The product must be found to be a "suitable substitute" for articles that the government is procuring. The General Services Administration must determine that the cost of the product is not more than 125% of the retail price of the least expensive article for which it is a substitute, 42 U.S.C. § 4914(c)(1). There is no implementation of this policy in the FAR.

## D.  Clean Air and Water

The Clean Air Amendments of 1970, 42 U.S.C. § 7401 et seq., and the Water Pollution Control Act Amendments of 1972, 33 U.S.C. § 1251 et seq., establish a procedure to use federal contract awards to help implement the pollution control aspects of those statutes. The Environmental Protection Agency is authorized to list facilities if they are found liable for violations of air and water pollution standards. Prior to 2000, offerors on certain federal contracts were required to certify that their performance would not take place at any of these listed facilities, FAR Subpart 23.1. This requirement was deleted from the FAR by FAC 97-15, 64 Fed. Reg. 72,414, Dec. 27, 1999. The policy is now implemented by including such facilities in the Excluded Parties List System discussed in Chapter 4.

# IV. EQUAL EMPLOYMENT OPPORTUNITY

Nondiscrimination provisions have been required in government contracts by a series of executive orders commencing with Executive Order 8802, 6 Fed. Reg. 3109 (1941). This section deals first with the current executive orders requiring equal opportunity in employment. It then reviews other sources of equal employment policies.

## A.  Executive Order 11246

The major source of the equal employment opportunity requirements for federal contractors is Executive Order 11246, 30 Fed. Reg. 12319 (1965), as amended by Executive Order 11375, 32 Fed. Reg. 14303 (1967); Executive Order 11478, 34 Fed. Reg. 12985 (1969); Executive Order 12086, 43 Fed. Reg. 46501 (1978); Executive Order 13279, 67 Fed. Reg. 76819 (2002); and Executive Order 13403, 71 Fed. Reg. 28543 (2006). These orders provide that the Secretary of Labor will administer this program and promulgate regulations. This is done through the Office of Federal Contract Compliance Programs (OFCCP). See 41 C.F.R. Part 60. At the same time, Executive Order 11246, as amended, makes each contracting agency primarily responsible for ensuring that its contractors comply with the applicable regulations, rules, and orders. FAR Subpart 22.8 contains the general regulations for these procedures.

The legal authority of the President to issue Executive Order 11246, has been sustained. See *Contractors Ass'n of E. Pa. v. Secretary of Labor*, 442 F.2d 159 (3d Cir.), *cert. denied*, 404 U.S. 854 (1971). But note that the two grounds on which the court in *Contractors Association* based its decision were questioned by another court in *AFL-CIO v. Kahn*, 618 F.2d 784 (D.C. Cir.), *cert. denied*, 443 U.S. 915 (1979). See also *Regents of the Univ. of California. v. Bakke*, 438 U.S. 265 (1978), stating at 302:

> Every decision upholding the requirement of preferential hiring under the authority of Exec. Order No. 11246, . . . has emphasized the existence of previous discrimination as a predicate for the imposition of a preferential remedy.

Other cases supporting the executive order's validity include *Farkas v. Texas Instruments, Inc.*, 375 F.2d 629 (5th Cir.), *cert. denied*, 389 U.S. 977 (1967); *Legal Aid Soc'y of Alameda County v. Brennan*, 381 F. Supp. 125 (N.D. Cal. 1974), *aff'd in part*, 608 F.2d 1319 (9th Cir. 1979), *cert. denied*, 447 U.S. 921 (1980); and *United States v. Local 189, United Papermakers & Paperworkers*, 282 F. Supp. 39 (E.D. La. 1968). GAO has held that including nondiscrimination provisions in a federal contract does not violate the requirements of statutes requiring maximum feasible competition, 40 Comp. Gen. 592 (B-145475) (1961).

## 1. Equal Opportunity Clause

Executive Order 11246 prescribes a clause that is mandatory in all contracts exceeding $10,000, absent a special exemption from the Secretary of Labor. The clause is also required for contracts under $10,000 if the contractor has, or reasonably can expect to have, contracts or subcontracts with the government with an aggregate value exceeding $10,000 in a 12-month period, FAR 22.807(b)(1). The required Equal Opportunity clause is set forth in FAR 52.222-26. The clause can be applicable even if it is not included in a contract. See *United States v. New Orleans Pub. Serv., Inc.*, 553 F.2d 459 (5th Cir. 1977), *vacated & remanded on other grounds*, 436 U.S. 942 (1978), where the court held that a utility supplying electricity to the government was subject to the provisions of the executive order even though the company had refused to sign a contract because of the inclusion of this clause. Compare *Liberty Mut. Ins. Co. v. Friedman*, 639 F.2d 164 (4th Cir. 1981), invalidating Labor Department regulations requiring sureties to comply with the requirements of the executive order. The court reasoned that a surety could not reasonably be construed to be a subcontractor.

Under the Equal Opportunity clause, the contractor agrees not to discriminate against any employee or applicant for employment because of race, color, religion, sex, or national origin. Paragraph (c)(2) of the clause further requires that "[t]he Contractor shall take affirmative action to ensure that applicants are employed, and that employees are treated during employment, without regard to their race, color, religion, sex, or national origin." The clause also commits the contractor to furnish certain information and reports and to permit access to records by the contracting agency and the Department of Labor to ascertain compliance with the applicable requirements. Unless an exemption applies, ¶ (c)(10) of the clause provides that a contractor must flow down the requirements of the clause in its subcontracts and purchase orders.

Affirmative action is described in detail in 41 C.F.R. Part 60-2. Initially the contractor must make a utilization analysis to determine if the composition of its workforce is in conformity with the composition of people living in its labor area. This requires a determination of the appropriate labor area serving the contractor, the availability of minority groups and women in categories of labor in that area, and the number of minority employees and women working in each job category. If this analysis indicates that the contractor's percentage of minority employment or women is less than those available in any labor category, "underutilization" is required to be found. In such cases, the contractor must establish a series of "placement goals" to assist in attaining percentages of minority and women employment comparable to the availability of minorities and women in the labor area. 41 C.F.R. § 60-2.16(e) states the following principles applicable to these goals:

> (1) Placement goals may not be rigid and inflexible quotas, which must be met, nor are they to be considered as either a ceiling or a floor for the employment of particular groups. Quotas are expressly forbidden.

> (2) In all employment decisions, the contractor must make selections in a nondiscriminatory manner. Placement goals do not provide the contractor with a justification to extend a preference to any individual, select an individual, or adversely affect an individual's employment status, on the basis of that person's race, color, religion, sex, or national origin.

> (3) Placement goals do not create set-asides for specific groups, nor are they intended to achieve proportional representation or equal results.

> (4) Placement goals may not be used to supersede merit selection principles. Affirmative action programs prescribed by the regulations in this part do not require a contractor to hire a person who lacks qualifications to perform the job successfully, or hire a less qualified person in preference to a more qualified one.

The contractor must also adopt policies for recruitment and training that will aid in achieving these goals. It is proper to consider the need to meet the goal in a hiring decision as long as the basic consideration is the qualification of the potential employees, *Sharkey v. Dixie Elec. Membership Corp.*, 262 Fed. Appx. 598 (5th Cir. 2008). The affirmative action requirement applies to promotion as well as employment. See *Legal Aid Soc'y of Alameda County v. Brennan*, 381 F. Supp. 125 (N.D. Cal. 1974), *aff'd in part*, 608 F.2d 1319 (9th Cir. 1979), *cert. denied*, 447 U.S. 921 (1980), for a decision analyzing and finding deficient an agency's efforts to ensure that its contractors are complying with the affirmative action requirement.

## 2. Affirmative Action Programs

Each nonconstruction contractor or subcontractor with 50 or more employees and a contract or subcontract for $50,000 or more (or cumulatively expected to total $50,000 or more in any 12-month period) is required to develop a written affirmative action program, FAR 22.804-1. These programs are reviewed and approved by the OFCCP regional office and must be developed within 120 days from the commencement of the first contract or subcontract for $50,000 or more. The regulations require an affirmative action program for each establishment of a contractor, 41 C.F.R. § 60-2.1 (containing detailed guidance on the application of this rule). This requirement has been interpreted as applying to every establishment of a contractor regardless of whether such establishment performs work for the government. However, the Deputy Assistant Secretary of Labor may exempt a "facility" that is separate and distinct from the activities called for by the contract, FAR 22.807(b)(5), pursuant to a request from a contracting officer, FAR 22.807(c). An OFCCP Policy Interpretation issued in the 1970s contained the following statement regarding the meaning of "establishment":

> Revised Order No. 4 requires that a written affirmative action program be developed for each of the contractor's establishments. The question has arisen as to whether this means that a contractor must develop such plans for an "establishment" where it may have a few employees, such as a sales outlet. We have defined "establishment" for purposes of Revised Order No. 4 as a facility at which hiring takes place and/or personnel actions are instituted. If such authority exists at the facility, it would be required to have a written affirmative action program as specified in Revised Order No. 4. If such authority does not exist at the facility, the location that has the hiring authority and handles personnel actions for the facility would have to develop and implement an affirmative action plan. In the latter case, the personnel at the facility would be covered by the plan maintained at the hiring and personnel location.

A subsidiary not performing government work is considered an "establishment" only if the parent exercises actual control, 50 Comp. Gen. 627 (B-170536) (1971).

When the Equal Opportunity clause is required to be included in a contract, the agency must also include the Affirmative Action Compliance solicitation provision in FAR 52.222-25, requiring the offeror to represent whether it has an affirmative action program. The lack of an approved affirmative action program by a nonconstruction concern is grounds for a determination that the company is not a responsible offeror, *William Dixon Co.*, Comp. Gen. Dec. B-235241, 89-2 CPD ¶ 114. However, the OFCCP regulations do not require the contracting officer to ascertain whether such a program exists in smaller procurements. For example, the regulations provide that if "it comes to the contracting officer's attention" in the preaward period that there is no approved affirmative action program, the offeror must be declared nonresponsible unless the contracting officer "otherwise affirmatively determines that the contractor is able to comply with the equal employment obligations," 41 C.F.R. § 60-2.2(b).

Requirements become more stringent as dollar amounts increase. For instance, contracts or subcontracts over $10 million (excluding construction contracts) may not be awarded unless a compliance review of the contractor has been conducted within 24 months prior to the award and the contractor is found to be in compliance, 41 C.F.R. §60-1.20(d). See FAR 22.805(a), providing that compliance reviews should be requested from OFCCP in such circumstances and award should be withheld for 45 days while the review is conducted. This procedure is intended to prevent the award of major contracts without an affirmative determination by the compliance agency that the contractor's program meets the affirmative action requirements. A prospective contractor may be determined nonresponsible twice without a hearing, but is entitled to a hearing after the second determination of nonresponsibility, 41 C.F.R. § 60-2.2(b). In *Commercial Envelope Mfg. Co. v. Dunlop*, 21 Cont. Cas. Fed. (CCH) ¶ 84,097 (S.D.N.Y. 1975), the court held that this procedure did not violate any of the prospective contractor's rights and found that a contractor was properly determined nonresponsible a fifth time based on employment practices, even though the four prior determinations were based on other grounds. GAO has stated that similar procedures violate the requirement for open and competitive bidding because they do not contain sufficiently definitive requirements to enable all bidders to compete on an equal basis, *Illinois Equal Employment Opportunity Regulations for Public Contracts*, 54 Comp. Gen. 6 (B-167015), 74-2 CPD ¶ 1.

Construction contractors are not required to develop affirmative action programs since many do not perform work in fixed geographic areas. However, they must comply with any "hometown plan" covering a geographic area in which they work, FAR 22.804-2(a). These hometown plans are affirmative action programs covering specific geographic areas that have been agreed to by unions, contractor associations, and governmental units in that area. See 41 C.F.R. § 60-4.5. Each contracting agency is required to maintain a list of such plans, FAR 22.804-2(b), and contracting officers are required to include the goals and timetables from such plans in solicitations for work to be performed in geographic areas with plans in effect. The Notice of Requirements for Affirmative Action to Ensure Equal Employment Opportunity for Construction solicitation provision used for this purpose is set forth in FAR 52.222-23. If the construction is to be performed in an area not covered by a plan, the contractor is not obligated to attempt to meet any goals and timetables. However, all construction contracts over $10,000 must contain the Affirmative Action Compliance Requirements for Construction clause at FAR 52.222-27, which contains 16 affirmative action steps that the contractor must take during contract performance.

All of the affirmative action program requirements are matters of responsibility not responsiveness. Thus, bidders can furnish information demonstrating that they are in compliance after bid opening, *A&C Bldg. & Indus. Maint. Corp.*, Comp. Gen. Dec. B-218035, 85-1 CPD ¶ 195.

## 3. Compliance Procedures

If an individual employee has a grievance regarding a contractor's compliance with Executive Order 11246, requirements, the employee may file a complaint with

OFCCP within 180 days of the violation, 41 C.F.R. § 60-1.21. Complaints filed with the contracting officer are required to be immediately forwarded to the OFCCP, FAR 22.808. That office may investigate and may, in appropriate circumstances, refer the complaint to the Equal Employment Opportunity Commission, 41 C.F.R. § 60-1.24. Procedures for consideration of complaints by OFCCP are set forth in 41 C.F.R. § 60-1.26. Executive Order 11246 gives private parties no cause of action against employers, *Utley v. Varian Assocs., Inc.*, 811 F.2d 1279 (9th Cir.), *cert. denied*, 484 U.S. 824 (1987); *Rogers v. Frito-Lay*, 611 F.2d 1074 (5th Cir.), *cert. denied*, 449 U.S. 889 (1980).

The OFCCP may without any complaint by an employee or applicant review a contractor's compliance with executive order requirements. If it concludes that a violation exists, the OFCCP will ordinarily seek to resolve the matter through discussions and a "conciliation agreement" with the contractor. The OFCCP may institute administrative enforcement proceedings and may refer the matter to the Department of Justice for initiation of a lawsuit, 41 C.F.R. 60-1 Subpart B. The government may sue seeking an order barring the defendant from violating or interfering with rights of employees under the order, *United States v. Local 189, United Papermakers & Paperworkers*, 301 F. Supp. 906 (E.D. La.), *aff'd*, 416 F.2d 980 (5th Cir. 1969), *cert. denied*, 397 U.S. 919 (1970).

## 4. Sanctions

Among the sanctions available for violation of the requirements of the order are cancellation of the contract and debarment of the contractor from eligibility for future government contracts, FAR 22.809. In *Timken Co. v. Vaughan*, 413 F. Supp. 1183 (N.D. Ohio 1976), the government's efforts to debar a contractor for an alleged violation of the order were unsuccessful. Upon consideration of the population surrounding the contractor's facility, the court held that the failure of the contractor's affirmative action program to include a city with a higher minority population did not violate the executive order. The court reasoned that, although the city was within a reasonable commuting distance, the population's habits indicated that residents were unlikely to seek work in the contractor's facility.

## B. Equal Opportunity for Veterans

The Vietnam Era Veterans' Readjustment Assistance Act of 1972, 38 U.S.C. § 4211 and § 4212, as amended, requires that contractors not discriminate against and take affirmative action with regard to "qualified covered veterans." Unless exempted by the Secretary of Labor, contractors awarded contracts for supplies or services, including construction, of $100,000 or more must agree to these requirements, FAR 22.1303(a). Guidance on the implementation of this policy is contained in 41 C.F.R. 60-250 and FAR Subpart 22.13. This policy does not apply to contracts to be performed outside the United States. However, it does apply to all facilities of the contractor unless a waiver is granted, *Trinity Indus., Inc. v. Herman*, 173 F.3d 527 (4th Cir. 1999). A standard Equal Opportunity for Veterans clause on this subject is prescribed for contracts and subcontracts over $100,000, FAR 52.222-35.

The veterans covered by this policy are defined in FAR 52.222-35 as:

> Disabled veteran means (1) A veteran of the U.S. military, ground, naval, or air service, who is entitled to compensation (or who but for the receipt of military retired pay would be entitled to compensation) under laws administered by the Secretary of Veterans Affairs; or (2) A person who was discharged or released from active duty because of a service-connected disability.

> Recently separated veteran means any veteran during the three-year period beginning on the date of such veteran's discharge or release from active duty in the U.S. military, ground, naval or air service.

> Other protected veterans means a veteran who served on active duty in the U.S. military, ground, naval, or air service, during a war or in a campaign or expedition for which a campaign badge has been authorized under the laws administered by the Department of Defense.

> Armed Forces service medal veteran means any veteran who, while serving on active duty in the U.S. military, ground, naval, or air service, participated in a United States military operation for which an Armed Forces service medal was awarded pursuant to Executive Order 12985 (61 FR 1209).

The clause provides that if a veteran is disabled, he or she is "qualified" if the veteran has "the ability to perform the essential functions of the employment positions with or without reasonable accommodation."

Contracts subject to the Act are also required to contain the Employment Reports on Veterans clause in FAR 52.222-37 which calls for annual reports containing data on the veterans in the contractor's workforce and its employment activity. Solicitations must contain the Compliance with Veterans' Employment Reporting Requirements provision in FAR 52.222-38 representing that the offeror has submitted the most recent report. Contracting officers are expected to verify that these reports have been filed, FAR 22.1304. Entering into a contractor after failing to submit reports or submitting false reports is grounds for a false claim under 31 U.S.C. § 3729 et seq., *United States ex rel. Kirk v. Schindler Elevator Corp.*, 601 F.3d 92 (2d Cir. 2010), *rev'd on other grounds*, 131 S. Ct. 1885 (2011).

Complaint procedures under these requirements are handled by the OFCCP in the same manner as equal opportunity complaints, FAR 22.1308. Courts will not review decisions of the OFCCP as to a company's practices under this statute because such decisions are committed to agency discretion, *Greer v. Chao*, 492 F.3d 962 (8th Cir. 2007). There is no private cause of action against a contractor under this statute,

*Wikberg v. Reich*, 21 F.3d 88 (7th Cir. 1994); *Barron v. Nightingale Roofing, Inc.*, 842 F.2d 20 (1st Cir. 1988).

Contracting officers are required to implement any sanctions ordered by the Department of Labor, including withholding of progress payments and termination or suspension of a contract, FAR 22.1309; 41 C.F.R. § 60-300.66. Debarment of a contractor for noncompliance would result on its listing on the Excluded Parties List System.

## C. Other Sources of Equal Employment Opportunity Requirements

Most contractors and subcontractors are likely to be subject to some of the provisions of the Civil Rights Act of 1964, as amended by the Equal Employment Opportunity Act of 1972, 42 U.S.C. § 2000e - § 2000e(17). Title VII of this Act prohibits employers with 15 or more employees and employment entities of labor organizations affecting interstate commerce from discriminating because of race, color, religion, sex, or national origin. An aggrieved employee or applicant for employment may sue the employer in a district court. The Equal Employment Opportunity Commission has power to investigate charges of discrimination under the Act and to sue if efforts to secure voluntary compliance fail.

Under Executive Order 11141, federal contractors and subcontractors may not discriminate against employees or potential employees based on age, except upon the basis of a bona fide occupational qualification, retirement plan, or statutory requirement, 29 Fed. Reg. 2477 (1964). FAR 22.901(c) provides that agencies are to bring this policy to the attention of contractors, but that no implementing contract clause is required.

All federal contracts and subcontracts over $15,000 for supplies and services, including construction, except where the Secretary of Labor grants a waiver, must include requirements barring discrimination against any employee or applicant because of physical or mental handicaps. Contractors under such contracts and subcontracts are also required to agree to take affirmative action with respect to such individuals, 29 U.S.C. § 793; Executive Order 11758, 39 Fed. Reg. 2075 (1974); 41 C.F.R. 60-741; FAR Subpart 22.14. The Affirmative Action for Workers with Disabilities clause prescribed for use is set forth at FAR 52.222-36.

# V. LABOR STANDARDS

For many years there has been extensive statutory coverage of the labor standards to be observed by federal government contractors. These statutes have imposed minimum wage levels, overtime wage restrictions, and provisions governing working conditions on various classes of work. This section considers the minimum wage provisions governing contracts for construction, supplies, and services.

## A. Davis-Bacon Act

The Davis-Bacon Act, 40 U.S.C. § 3141 et seq., establishes minimum wages, including fringe benefits, to be paid to laborers and mechanics on contracts of over $2,000 for the construction, alteration, or repair of public buildings and public works. Department of Labor regulations implementing this statute are found in 29 C.F.R. Part 5. FAR regulations are contained in Subpart 22.4.

The purpose of this Act is not to guarantee contractors that specified wage levels will be applicable, but rather to protect employees from substandard earnings by fixing a minimum wage on government projects, *United States v. Binghamton Constr. Co.*, 347 U.S. 171, *reh'g denied*, 347 U.S. 940 (1954). Therefore, the contractor has no right under the Act for recovery if the wage that must be paid to obtain employees is higher than the prevailing wage rate set forth in the contract. But see *Sunswick Corp. v. United States*, 109 Ct. Cl. 772, 75 F. Supp. 221, *cert. denied*, 334 U.S. 827 (1948), where a contractor was allowed recovery for payment of wages higher than the wage determination when the higher payment was the result of a directive and the contract clause prohibited payment of more or less than the wage determination.

### 1. Determination That Contract Is a Construction Contract

It is the procuring agency's responsibility to determine initially whether the Davis-Bacon Act is applicable to a particular contract, 29 C.F.R. § 5.5(a). GAO has held that the procuring agency's good faith determination should not be overturned, 44 Comp. Gen. 498 (B-150828) (1965).

The Act applies only to federal contracts that essentially or substantially contemplate construction, alteration, or repair, 40 Comp. Gen. 565 (B-144901) (1961). Contracting officers must determine the extent of construction, alteration, or repair work that will be involved, *D.E. Clarke*, Comp. Gen. Dec. B-146824, 75-1 CPD ¶ 317. FAR 22.402 contains the following guidance:

(a) Contracts for construction work. (1) The requirements of this subpart apply —

> (i) Only if the construction work is, or reasonably can be foreseen to be, performed at a particular site so that wage rates can be determined for the locality, and only to construction work that is performed by laborers and mechanics at the site of the work;

> (ii) To dismantling, demolition, or removal of improvements if a part of the construction contract, or if construction at that site is anticipated by another contract as provided in subpart 37.3;

> (iii) To the manufacture or fabrication of construction materials and components conducted in connection with the construction

and on the site of the work by the contractor or a subcontractor under a contract otherwise subject to this subpart; and

(iv) To painting of public buildings or public works, whether performed in connection with the original construction or as alteration or repair of an existing structure.

(2) The requirements of this subpart do not apply to —

(i) The manufacturing of components or materials off the site of the work or their subsequent delivery to the site by the commercial supplier or materialman;

(ii) Contracts requiring construction work that is so closely related to research, experiment, and development that it cannot be performed separately, or that is itself the subject of research, experiment, or development (see paragraph (b) of this section for applicability of this subpart to research and development contracts or portions thereof involving construction, alteration, or repair of a public building or public work);

(iii) Employees of railroads operating under collective bargaining agreements that are subject to the Railway Labor Act; or

(iv) Employees who work at contractors' or subcontractors' permanent home offices, fabrication shops, or tool yards not located at the site of the work. However, if the employees go to the site of the work and perform construction activities there, the requirements of this subpart are applicable for the actual time so spent, not including travel unless the employees transport materials or supplies to or from the site of the work.

(b) Nonconstruction contracts involving some construction work. (1) The requirements of this subpart apply to construction work to be performed as part of nonconstruction contracts (supply, service, research and development, etc.) if —

(i) The construction work is to be performed on a public building or public work;

(ii) The contract contains specific requirements for a substantial amount of construction work exceeding the monetary threshold for application of the Davis Bacon Act (the word substantial relates to the type and quantity of construction work to be performed and not merely to the total value of construction work as compared to the total value of the contract); and

(iii) The construction work is physically or functionally separate from, and is capable of being performed on a segregated basis from, the other work required by the contract.

(2) The requirements of this subpart do not apply if —

(i) The construction work is incidental to the furnishing of supplies, equipment, or services (for example, the requirements do not apply to simple installation or alteration at a public building or public work that is incidental to furnishing supplies or equipment under a supply contract; however, if a substantial and segregable amount of construction, alteration, or repair is required, such as for installation of heavy generators or large refrigerator systems or for plant modification or rearrangement, the requirements of this subpart apply); or

(ii) The construction work is so merged with nonconstruction work or so fragmented in terms of the locations or time spans in which it is to be performed, that it is not capable of being segregated as a separate contractual requirement.

A contract for the furnishing and installing of a mechanized materials handling system for which 30% of the work and 40% of the dollar value of the equipment represented construction work was properly subject to the provisions of the Davis-Bacon Act, Comp. Gen. Dec. B-178159, June 6, 1973, *Unpub.*

It is sometimes difficult to ascertain whether the contract is for construction, services, or manufacturing. In one situation, the Secretary of Labor held that the construction of a mobile nuclear reactor was work covered by the Act while GAO held it was not, Opinion Letter of the Solicitor of Labor, Oct. 14, 1966, DB-52, C.C.H. Labor Law Transfer Binder, Wages, Hours and Administrative Rulings, ¶ 30,997.49; 47 Comp. Gen. 192 (B-161858) (1967). See also *American Warehouse Sys.*, Comp. Gen. Dec. B-402292, 2010 CPD ¶ 41 (free-standing mezzanine structure delivered to site and bolted to floor not construction); and *Voith Hydro, Inc.*, Comp. Gen. Dec. B-401244.2, 2009 CPD ¶ 239 (improvement of generators and excitation system in power plant construction not services).

## 2. Employees Covered

The Act covers the minimum wages "to be paid various classes of laborers and mechanics." FAR 22.401 defines laborers or mechanics as workers "whose duties are manual or physical in nature (including those workers who use tools or who are performing the work of a trade), as distinguished from mental or managerial." The definition includes apprentices, trainees, and helpers, but not workers whose duties are primarily executive, supervisory, administrative, or clerical.

The Act applies to all "mechanics and laborers employed directly upon the site of the work." 29 C.F.R. § 5.2(k)(1)(2) defines the "site of the work" as follows:

(1) The site of the work is the physical place or places where the building or work called for in the contract will remain; and any other site where a significant por-

tion of the building or work is constructed, provided that such site is established specifically for the performance of the contract or project;

(2) Except as provided in paragraph (l)(3) of this section, job headquarters, tool yards, batch plants, borrow pits, etc., are part of the site of the work, provided they are dedicated exclusively, or nearly so, to performance of the contract or project, and provided they are adjacent or virtually adjacent to the site of the work as defined in paragraph (l)(1) of this section;

(3) Not included in the site of the work are permanent home offices, branch plant establishments, fabrication plants, tool yards, etc., of a contractor or subcontractor whose location and continuance in operation are determined wholly without regard to a particular Federal or federally assisted contract or project. In addition, fabrication plants, batch plants, borrow pits, job headquarters, tool yards, etc., of a commercial or material supplier, which are established by a supplier of materials for the project before opening of bids and not on the site of the work as stated in paragraph (l)(1) of this section, are not included in the site of the work. Such permanent, previously established facilities are not part of the site of the work, even where the operations for a period of time may be dedicated exclusively, or nearly so, to the performance of a contract.

This definition conforms to *Ball, Ball & Brosamer v. Secretary of Labor*, 24 F.3d 1447 (D.C. Cir. 1994), where the court held that a contractor was not obligated to pay Davis-Bacon Act wages to workers at a batch plant and borrow pit two miles from the construction site because those locations were not directly on the site of the work within the meaning of the Act. See also *L.P. Cavett Co. v. Department of Labor*, 101 F.3d 1111 (6th Cir. 1996), reversing a Department of Labor Wage Appeals Board ruling that the subcontractor's truck drivers hauling asphalt from a batch plant approximately three miles from the work site should have been paid Davis-Bacon Act wages because the plant was located on "the site of the work." In *Building & Constr. Trades Dept., AFL-CIO v. Department of Labor Wage Appeals Bd.*, 932 F.2d 985 (D.C. Cir. 1991), the court held that material delivery truck drivers were not covered under the Act because the truck drivers came on to the site only to deliver materials. The court stated that the truck drivers spent 90% of their workday on the highway driving to and from commercial supply sources and stayed on the work site only long enough to drop off their loads, usually for not more than 10 minutes. In *Bechtel Constructors*, DOL-ARB, No. 95-45A, July 15, 1996, the board held that workers at sites providing concrete for a nearby federal project were subject to Davis-Bacon wage requirements. The board stated that the D.C. Circuit's ruling in *Ball, Ball & Brosamer* does not bar application of prevailing rates for all off-site plants and that "work performed in actual or virtual adjacency to one portion of a long continuous project is to be considered adjacent to the entire project."

The Federal Acquisition Streamlining Act amended the Davis-Bacon Act by waiving the application of prevailing wage-setting requirements to volunteer workers. The purpose of this waiver is to promote and provide opportunities for volunteers to provide their services in the construction, repair, or alteration of public buildings and works, 40 U.S.C. § 3161. Under 40 U.S.C. § 3162, Davis-Bacon wage-setting provisions are waived for persons who perform services directly to a "state or local government, a public agency, or a public or private nonprofit recipient of federal assistance" as long as these persons do not work directly for a contractor, subcontractor, or government agency. Payment of expenses and nominal fees to such volunteers is authorized.

### 3. *Obtaining Wage Determinations*

The Department of Labor is responsible for issuing wage determinations reflecting prevailing wages, including fringe benefits, FAR 22.404. There are two types of wage determinations — general and project.

A general wage determination contains prevailing wage rates for the types of construction designated in the determination and is used in contracts performed within a specified geographical area, FAR 22.404-1. General wage determinations are published on the WDOL website (*www.wdol.gov*), and are effective on the publication date of the notice or upon receipt by the contracting agency, whichever occurs first, FAR 22.404-1(a)(1). Such wage determinations contain no expiration date and are valid until modified, superseded, or canceled. If there is a general wage determination applicable to the project, the agency may use it without notifying the Department of Labor, FAR 22.404-3(a). Once incorporated into a contract, a general wage determination normally remains effective for the life of the contract unless the contract contains options to extend the period of the contract, FAR 22.404-1(a)(1). These determinations must be used whenever possible.

A project wage determination is issued at the specific request of a contracting agency, FAR 22.404-1(b). It is used only when no general wage determination applies. A contracting officer must submit requests for project wage determinations on SF 308 to the Department of Labor, FAR 22.404-3(b). The contracting officer must include a sufficiently detailed description of the work to indicate the type of construction involved, FAR 22.404-3(b). The wage determination is effective for 180 calendar days from the date of issuance and applies only to contract awards made within that time period, FAR 22.404-1(b). Once incorporated into a contract, a project wage determination is normally effective for the entire contract.

If it appears that a project wage determination may expire between bid opening and contract award, the contracting officer must request a new wage determination sufficiently in advance of bid opening, FAR 22.404-5(b)(1). If a wage determination expires after opening but prior to award, the contracting officer should request that the administrator extend the expiration date, FAR 22.404-5(b)(2). If the request is granted, the contracting officer will award the contract and modify it to apply the extended expiration date to the already incorporated project wage determination, FAR 22.404-5(b)(2). If the request is denied, the administrator will issue a new project wage determination. If a new determination changes any wage rates for classifications to be used in the contract, the contracting officer may cancel the solicitation only in accordance with FAR 22.404-5(b)(2)(i). Otherwise, the contracting officer must award the contract and incorporate the new wage determination. The new determination is to be effective on the date of contract award. The contractor must equitably adjust the contract price for any increased or decreased cost of performance resulting from any changed wage rates, FAR 22.404-5(b)(2)(i). If the new determination does not change any wage rates, the contracting officer must award the contract and modify it to include the number and date of the new determination, FAR 22.404-5(b)(2)(ii).

## 4. Procedures for Making Wage Determinations

The Act requires that the minimum wages included in wage determinations be based upon the "prevailing wages" paid to various classes of employees on projects of a similar character in the "city, town, village or other civil subdivision of the state in which the work is to be performed." The prevailing wage is the wage paid to more than 50% of the laborers or mechanics in the classification on similar projects in the area during the period in question, 29 C.F.R. § 1.2(a)(1). If the same wage is not paid to a majority in the class, the wage is calculated by taking the average wage paid to all the employees, 29 C.F.R. § 1.2(a)(1). The Labor Secretary's authority to make wage determinations in such a manner is based on the broad language employed in the Act delegating the authority, *Building & Constr. Trades Dep't, AFL-CIO v. Donovan,* 712 F.2d 611 (D.C. Cir. 1983), *cert. denied,* 464 U.S. 1069 (1984). The geographic reference point for wage determinations is normally the county in which the work is to be performed, 29 C.F.R. § 1.7(a). If there has not been sufficient similar construction in the area within the past year, the wage determination may be based upon wages paid on similar construction sites in surrounding counties, 29 C.F.R. § 1.7(b). However, the wages paid on projects in metropolitan counties may not be used as a source of data to be paid on projects in rural counties and vice versa, 29 C.F.R. § 1.7(b). In *Building & Constr. Trades Dep't,* the court upheld this regulation as furthering the intention of the statute. If no similar construction in the surrounding counties or in the state was performed within the past year, wages paid on projects completed more than one year prior to the beginning of the survey period may be considered, 29 C.F.R. § 1.7(c).

The Secretary of Labor's wage determinations are final and unreviewable by GAO, unless they are found to be arbitrary, capricious, or not supported by substantial evidence, 50 Comp. Gen. 103 (B-160778) (1970). The courts are also precluded from reviewing wage determinations, *United States v. Binghamton Constr. Co.,* 347 U.S. 171, *reh'g denied,* 347 U.S. 940 (1954). Thus, questions about the applicability or interpretation of a wage determination must be submitted to the Secretary of Labor, *North Ga. Bldg. & Constr. Trades Council v. Goldschmidt,* 621 F.2d 697 (5th Cir. 1980). However, "conformance" determinations of the Secretary of Labor that certain workers not included in an issued wage determination should or should not be classified as other workers are subject to judicial review, *Mistick PBT v. Chao*, 440 F.3d 503 (D.C. Cir. 2006).

## 5. Contract Clauses

Construction contracts must include the Davis Bacon Act clause in FAR 52.222-6. This clause requires the payment of employees' wages at "rates not less than those contained in the wage determination of the Secretary of Labor which is attached hereto and made a part hereof." If the Davis-Bacon provisions are omitted from the contract but are included in the IFB, they are incorporated in the contract by reference, *International Bhd. of Elec. Workers*, Comp. Gen. Dec. B-183271, 75-1 CPD ¶ 201. The wage rate may be corrected after award if they contain clerical errors, FAR 22.404-7. In such cases, the contractor is entitled to an equitable adjustment, FAR 22.404-6(b)(5); *W.G. Yates & Sons Constr. Co. v. General Servs. Admin.*, CBCA 11-1 BCA ¶ 34,638 (Davis-Bacon Act — Price Adjustment clause in FAR 52.222-32 not applicable). If a wage rate is incorrect through an error in judgment, the contract should not be corrected, *Dawson Constr. Co.*, Comp. Gen. Dec. B-189036, 78-1 CPD ¶ 108.

When a construction contract contains options, the contracting officer must ensure that the most current wage determination is applied at the time the option is exercised, FAR 22.404-12(a). One of three Davis-Bacon Act — Price Adjustment clauses in FAR 52.222-30, -31, and -32 must be included in the contract depending on the method selected by the contracting officer to determine how the change in wage rates will be applied. See the guidance in FAR 22.404-12. The FAR 52.222-30 clause provides for no price adjustment because the contractor has been allowed to include higher wage rates in its prices for option years. The FAR 52.222-31 and -32 clauses provide for price adjustments on different bases but do not allow the contractor to receive profit on the increased amounts.

Construction contracts must also include nine other clauses listed in FAR 22.407. These clauses describe the procedures that must be followed by the contractor, the sanctions for noncompliance, and special dispute resolution procedures. The Withholding of Funds clause in FAR 52.222-7 permits the withholding of a reasonable amount to compensate for not paying the full amount of wages required See *Copeland v. Veneman*, 350 F.3d 1230 (Fed. Cir. 2004), and *Overstreet Elec. Co.*, ASBCA 51653, 01-2 BCA ¶ 31,646, finding that contracting officers had acted reasonably under this clause.

## 6. Enforcement

The contracting agency is responsible for enforcement of these labor requirements, including periodic review of the contractors and its subcontractors records, FAR 22.406-1(a). The Department of Labor also conducts independent investigations of compliance, 29 C.F.R. § 5.6(a)(5) and (b), and the contracting agency is required to cooperate in such investigations, FAR 22.406-12. If enforcement issues cannot be resolved by agreement with the contractor, they are subject to the Disputes Concerning Labor Standards clause in FAR 52.222-14, which calls for resolution by the Department of Labor. Such disputes are not subject to the Contract Disputes Act, *Emerald Maint., Inc. v. United States*, 925 F.2d 1425 (Fed. Cir. 1991); *Trataros Constr., Inc. v. United States*, 51 Fed. App'x 10 (Fed. Cir. 2002).

Workers that believe that they have not been paid in accordance with the Act can file a complaint with the contracting officer or the Department of Labor. However, they have no private cause of action against the contractor, *Operating Eng'rs Health & Welfare Trust Fund v. JWJ Contracting Co.*, 135 F.3d 671 (9th Cir. 1998); *Chan v. City of New York*, 1 F.3d 96 (2d Cir. 1993); *Weber v. Heat Control Co.*, 728 F.2d 599 (3d Cir. 1984). Neither do they have a cause of action under state law, *Grochowski v. Phoenix Constr.*, 318 F.3d 80 (2d Cir. 2003). Compare *Cox v. NAP Constr. Co.*, 861 N.Y. 2d 238 (N.Y. 2008), finding a state cause of action for not paying Davis-Bacon wages. See also *United States ex rel. Wall v. Circle C Constr., LLC*, 700 F. Supp. 2d 926 (M.D. Tenn. 2010), holding that a qui tam False Claims Act suit was proper and assessing treble damages against a contractor that did not flow down the Davis-Bacon requirements to a subcontractor. Contractor employees that falsely certify compliance with the Act are also subject to criminal penalties under 18 U.S.C. § 1001, *United States v. Shafer*, 23 Fed. Appx. 380 (6th Cir. 2001) (24 months prison sentence and monetary fine).

## B. Service Contract Act

The Service Contract Act of 1965, 41 U.S.C. §§ 6701-07, establishes minimum wage rates and fringe benefits based on those prevailing in the locality to be paid service employees for contracts over $2,500 which are principally for services which are furnished by service employees, 41 U.S.C. § 6703(1) and (2). It prohibits employment under hazardous or unsanitary working conditions and requires the contractor to provide notice of required compensation to all covered service employees on the first day of employment, 41 U.S.C. § 6703(3). The Act also provides remedies for noncompliance including debarment (§ 6706), contract termination ("cancellation") (§ 6705(c)), and withholding of contract funds (§ 6705(b)(1)).

The Act applies only when the services are performed in the United States, 41 U.S.C. § 6702(a)(3). Both contractors and subcontractors are subject to the Act, 41 U.S.C. § 6703.

41 U.S.C. § 6704(a) requires all contractors and subcontractors subject to the Act to pay their service employees no less than the minimum wage specified by the Fair Labor Standards Act, 29 U.S.C. § 206(a)(1). This requirement applies to contracts under $2,500 where no wage determination is required and to contracts

over $2,500 where no wage determination has been issued. This requirement is applicable even though the contract contains no applicable contract clause, Comp. Gen. Dec. B-167287, Sept. 4, 1969, *Unpub.*

The Secretary of Labor has responsibility for administering and implementing the Act, 41 U.S.C. § 6707(a). Enforcement authority is vested in both the Secretary of Labor and the head of the procuring agency, 41 U.S.C. § 6705. Pursuant to this authority, the Secretary has issued regulations governing the administration and interpretation of the Act in 29 C.F.R. Part 4. In addition, the Secretary has established the Administrative Review Board to provide administrative appellate review of Department of Labor (DOL) decisions regarding the Service Contract Act, 29 C.F.R. Part 8. FAR regulations are contained in Subpart 22.10. A supplementary regulation is provided by FAR 37.301 for the contracts involving dismantling, demolition, or removal of improvements.

## 1.  Scope of the Act

Rulings by the DOL on coverage of the Act are binding on the procuring agencies and GAO, 48 Comp. Gen. 22 (B-164338) (1968). See also 57 Comp. Gen. 501 (B-190505) (1978) (an agency must comply with the DOL's regulations implementing the Act unless the regulation is clearly contrary to law). However, the procuring agency makes the initial determination as to whether a contract falls within the Act; it has been held that if the contracting officer believes in good faith that the Act is not applicable, there is no duty to notify DOL or to include the Service Contract Act provisions in the contract, 53 Comp. Gen. 412 (B-178773) (1973); *Curtiss-Wright Corp. v. McLucas*, 381 F. Supp. 657 (D.N.J. 1974). GAO subsequently modified this ruling, finding that if the contracting officer is on notice that DOL may regard the procurement as subject to the Act, the matter must be referred to DOL whose decision on the question will be binding, *Hewes Eng'g Co.*, Comp. Gen. Dec. B-179501, 74-1 CPD ¶ 112. FAR 22.1003-7 requires a contracting officer that has a question as to the applicability of the Act to request advice of the "agency labor advisor" and to refer unresolved questions to DOL. A contractor cannot rely on the statement of a contracting officer that the Act does not apply when the statute is clear, *Shawview Cleaners, LLC*, ASBCA 56938, 10-2 BCA ¶ 34,550.

In general, the Service Contract Act is construed liberally by DOL. Thus, the Act has been applied to a referral service even though the service contractor had neither control over its nominal employees nor interest in the work they performed, *Menlo Serv. Corp. v. United States*, 765 F.2d 805 (9th Cir. 1985).

### a.  Services Covered

The Act does not define the type of service that it covers, but DOL regulations at 29 C.F.R. § 4.130 provide examples of the types of services covered. Such services include repair and maintenance, aircraft flight services, stenographic reporting, food service, trash and garbage removal, and warehousing or storage services. See also FAR 22.1003-5. In addition, interpretations regarding the coverage of the Act are issued by the Wage and Hour Administrator of DOL. The Act's apparent legislative intent, according to 29 C.F.R. § 4.111(b), was to include "those contracts which have as their principal purpose the procurement of something other than the construction activity described in the Davis-Bacon Act or the materials, supplies, articles, and equipment described in the Walsh-Healey Act." If a contract involves both end products and services, it will be covered by the Act as long as the facts demonstrate that the contract is chiefly for services and that the furnishing of products is secondary, 29 C.F.R. § 4.131(a).

Department of Labor regulations interpret "principal purpose" to mean that the Act applies to all contracts that are primarily for services unless the contractor's use of service employees is incidental to the performance of the contract, 29 C.F.R. § 4.111(a) and § 4.113(a)(3). See 29 C.F.R. § 4.111(a) stating:

[N]o hard and fast rule can be laid down as to the precise meaning of the term principal purpose. This remedial Act is intended to be applied to a wide variety of contracts, and the Act does not define or limit the types of services which may be contracted for under a contract the principal purpose of which is to furnish services. Further, the nomenclature, type, or particular form of contract used by procurement agencies is not determinative of coverage. Whether the principal purpose of a particular contract is the furnishing of services through the use of service employees is largely a question to be determined on the basis of all the facts in each particular case. Even where tangible items of substantial value are important elements of the subject matter of the contract, the facts may show that they are of secondary import to the furnishing of services in the particular case. This principle is illustrated by the examples set forth in § 4.131.

Although the regulation fails to define "incidental," DOL has considered the use of service employees incidental only when they have constituted less than 20% of the contract's workforce, 48 Fed. Reg. 49743 (1983). This broad interpretation of "principal purpose" has prevailed, as evidenced by DOL's rejection of a proposed change to its regulations that would have limited the scope of the Act to contracts that were principally for services and principally performed by service employees, 48 Fed. Reg. 49743 (1983).

Confusion has arisen concerning whether the Act applies to specific tasks within a contract where the contract as a whole is not principally for services. Until 1983, DOL applied the Act to any line item for services in a contract, such as maintenance and repair of automated data processing equipment. After persistent objections by the GSA and the computer industry and recommendations by GAO (Comp. Gen. Report Nos. HRD-80-102, Sept. 16, 1980, and HRD-80-102(A), Mar. 25, 1981) DOL revised its regulations to provide that the Act applies only if services are the principal part of the contract as a whole. Thus, such contracts with distinct line items should contain the appropriate labor provisions for each line item when the principal purpose it to furnish services. See 29 C.F.R. § 4.132 stating:

> If the principal purpose of a contract is to furnish services through the use of service employees within the meaning of the Act, the contract to furnish such services is not removed from the Act's coverage merely because, as a matter of convenience in procurement, the service specifications are combined in a single contract document with specifications for the procurement of different or unrelated items. In such case, the Act would apply to service specifications but would not apply to any specifications subject to the Walsh-Healey Act or to the Davis-Bacon Act. With respect to contracts which contain separate specifications for the furnishing of services and construction activity, see § 4.116(c).

FAR 22.1003-6 contains extensive guidance on the distinction between repair, which is subject to the Act, and remanufacturing, which is subject to the Walsh-Healey Act. Remanufacturing occurs when major overhaul or major modification of "an item, piece of equipment, or material" is "completely or substantially torn down," parts are replaced as needed, the item or equipment is rebuilt, and the delivered work is usable like a new item. See *Sabreliner Corp.*, Comp. Gen. Dec. B-275163, 96-2 CPD ¶ 244, holding that a contract for overhaul and repair of jet engines was properly classified as a supply contract not subject to the Service Contract Act.

### b. Service Employees

Although the Act originally applied only to blue collar workers, *Descomp, Inc. v. Sampson*, 377 F. Supp. 254 (D. Del. 1974); *Federal Elec. Corp. v. Dunlop*, 419 F. Supp. 221 (M.D. Fla. 1976), Congress amended the Act in 1976 to include some white collar workers, Pub. L. No. 94-489, 90 Stat. 2358 (1976). 41 U.S.C. § 357(b) states:

> The term "service employee" means any person engaged in the performance of a contract entered into by the United States and not exempted under section 7 [41 U.S.C. § 356], whether negotiated or advertised, the principal purpose of which is to furnish services in the United States (other than any person employed in a bona fide executive, administrative, or professional capacity, as those terms are defined in part 541 of title 29, Code of Federal Regulations, as of July 30, 1976, and any subsequent revision of those regulations); and shall include all such persons regardless of any contractual relationship that may be alleged to exist between a contractor or subcontractor and such persons

The Department of Labor has found several classes of white collar workers to be service employees. For example, 29 C.F.R. § 4.152 considers stenographers to be service employees, and wage determinations have been issued covering marine engineers, priests, ministers, librarians, and radio announcers.

The Act applies if some of the services will be performed by service employees. See 29 C.F.R. § 4.113 stating:

(2) The coverage of the Act does not extend to contracts for services to be performed exclusively by persons who are not service employees, i.e., persons who are bona fide executive, administrative or professional personnel as defined in part 541 of this title (see paragraph (b) of this section). A contract for medical services furnished by professional personnel is an example of such a contract.

The principal issue in determining who is a "service employee" is in distinguishing such employees from "executive, administrative or professional" employees. 29 C.F.R. Part 541 contains extensive guidance on making this distinction.

## 2. Wage Determinations

The principal purpose of the Act is to specify the minimum wages and benefits to be paid to service employees in accordance with prevailing rates in the locality, 41 U.S.C. § 351. When a procuring agency determines that a prospective contract is subject to the Act, the contracting officer must obtain a wage determination, FAR 22.1007. Initially, this entails searching the WDOL website to find an applicable determination posted by DOL. This website contains a register of wage determinations for various types of services in different localities in the United States, 29 C.F.R. § 4.3. If the contract is to be performed in one of these localities, the contracting officer is authorized to select the appropriate class of service employees from the descriptions and wage rate determinations provided by DOL, *IBI Sec. Servs., Inc.*, Comp. Gen. Dec. B-218565, 85-2 CPD ¶ 7, *recons. denied*, 85-2 CPD ¶ 136. If no wage determination is found, the contracting officer must request a wage determination using DOL'S e98 electronic process — giving DOL adequate time to process the request. See the instructions in FAR 22.1008-1. Contracting officers are responsible for selecting the correct wage determination from the WDOL website but they can rely on DOL wage determinations furnished by DOL in answering specific requests, FAR 22.1008-1(d). If there is a delay of over 60 days in bid opening or commencement of work under a negotiated contract, the contracting officer is required to recheck the WDOL website or obtain a new wage determination using the e98 process, FAR 22.1014. See *Office Automation & Training Consultants*, ASBCA 56779, 11-1 BCA ¶ 34,666, where the contractor was held responsible for determining the correct wage determinations when the solicitation referred to the WDOL website. See also *Beyley Constr. Group Corp.*, ASBCA 55692, 08-2 BCA ¶ 33,999, *aff'd*, 351 Fed. Appx. 446 (Fed. Cir. 2009), denying a claim for reformation of a contract where the contractor had not included some of the fringe benefits in its price. The board found that the agency had no reason to know of the unilateral mistake.

DOL revises wage determinations periodically and agencies are responsible for ensuring that their contracts contain current wage determinations. See 29 C.F.R. § 4.5(a)(2) requiring contracts to contain wage determination that were revised prior to award with the following exceptions:

(i) However, revisions received by the Federal agency later than 10 days before the opening of bids, in the case of contracts entered into pursuant to competitive bidding procedures, shall not be effective if the Federal agency finds that there is not a reasonable time still available to notify bidders of the revision.

(ii) In the case of procurements entered into pursuant to negotiations (or in the case of the execution of an option or an extension of the initial contract term), revisions received by the agency after award (or execution of an option or extension of term, as the case may be) of the contract shall not be effective provided that the contract start of performance is within 30 days of such award (or execution of an option or extension of term). Any notice of a revision received by the agency not less than 10 days before commencement of the contract shall be effective, if:

(A) The contract does not specify a start of performance date which is within 30 days from the award; and/or

(B) Performance of such procurement does not commence within this 30-day period.

See also FAR 22.1012-1. A contractor can rely on a wage determination for the life of the contract, but new wage determinations are required in the event of a modification or change to the contract or use of an option clause, 29 C.F.R. § 4.143.

There are two major issues that have to be addressed in determining the proper wage determination: (1) defining the "locality" of the work and (2) deciding between prevailing wages and higher wages under a collective bargaining agreement.

## a. Determining Locality

Wage determinations must include wages for the "locality" where the work will be performed. When a contract requires services to be performed at a government site, locality has been defined as the area in which the facility is located. However, early in the implementation of the Act there was controversy as to the meaning of "locality" when the work was to be performed at a contractor's facility. DOL defined locality as the site of the procuring activity, 41 Fed. Reg. 5388 (1976), but this was overturned in *Southern Packaging & Storage Co. v. United States*, 458 F. Supp. 726 (D.S.C. 1978), *aff'd*, 618 F.2d 1088 (4th Cir. 1980). As a result, DOL has adopted a two-step procedure for making wage determinations, 29 C.F.R. § 4.3(c) and § 4.4(a)(2)(I).

Initially, the contracting agency attempts to identify the prospective offerors and their localities during the acquisition planning process. See FAR 22.1009-2 stating:

The contracting officer should attempt to identify the specific places or geographical areas where the services might be performed. The following may indicate possible places of performance:

(a) Locations of previous contractors and their competitors.

(b) Databases available via the Internet for lists of prospective offerors and contractors.

(c) Responses to a presolicitation notice (see 5.204).

A wage determination is then included in the solicitation for each locality. If the contracting officer subsequently learns that another offeror may participate in the competition, a wage determination must be obtained and included in the solicitation, FAR 22.1009-3. There is no solicitation provision informing offerors of this procedure, but an offeror that intends to compete for the work should immediately notify the contracting officer of the need for a wage determination for its locality. If the contracting officer determines initially that there may be offerors competing which are unknown, the Service Contract Act — Place of Performance Unknown solicitation provision in FAR 52.222-49 is included in the solicitation, FAR 22.1009-4. This informs offerors of the need to obtain a wage determination for their locality and places the risk of being bound by a post-contract wage determination if they do not inform the contracting officer of a need for the determination within a specified period (generally 10 to 15 days after receipt of the solicitation). In either instance, the resulting contract must contain a wage determination for the locality of the winning contractor.

## b. Collective Bargaining Agreements

The Service Contract Act originally allowed DOL to find a prevailing wage lower than the wage being paid by an incumbent contractor under a collective bargaining agreement. This provision was amended at 41 U.S.C. § 353(c), making the prior collective bargaining agreement rates applicable to subsequent contracts without regard to any wage determination that had been issued unless one of the statutory exceptions applies. See *Eastern Serv. Mgmt. Co.*, SCA-352-355, 22 WH Cases 796 (1975). DOL has issued procedures to implement this requirement in 29 C.F.R. § 4.1b(b). Under these procedures, the contracting officer, during acquisition planning, must determine whether there is an incumbent contractor subject to the Act that has a collective bargaining agreement with its service employees, FAR 22.1008-2. If so, the contracting officer is required to give the incumbent contractor and the collective bargaining representative of the incumbent's employees prior written notice of the proposed procurement at least 30 days before issuance of a solicitation, FAR 22.1010. If the contracting officer does not receive timely notice of a collective bargaining agreement, the procurement is allowed to proceed without regard to the wage rates in the collective bargaining agreement, FAR 22.1012-2. Otherwise, such wages are binding on the new contractor. The procedure for incorporating the provisions of a collective bargaining agreement into the wage determination attached to the contract are set forth in FAR 22.1008-2(d).

This "successor" contract rule does not apply if DOL makes a determination that a collective bargaining agreement was not entered into as a result of arm's-length negotiations, or the negotiated wages and benefits substantially vary from those prevailing in the locality. Determination that the predecessor contractor's collective bargaining agreement resulted from arm's-length negotiations may be made through investigation, hearing, or pursuant to the Secretary's authority, FAR 22.1002-3(a). The regulations are also quite complete in setting forth the procedures to be followed for making a determination that the rates in the collective bargaining agreement are substantially at variance with prevailing rates, 29 C.F.R. § 4.10. In the past, if a substantial variance decision was made after the contract had been awarded, DOL applied the new wage determination retroactively to the start of contract performance if it increased the workers' wages, but applied the determination prospectively when it decreased those wages. Since 1983, DOL has made these determinations solely on a prospective basis, 48 Fed. Reg. 49737 (1983).

This "successor" contract rule also does not apply if the incumbent contractor enters into the collective bargaining agreement for the first time and the agreement does not become binding until its contract has ended, FAR 22.1008-2(c)(1). Neither does the rule apply if the collective bargaining agreement is not implemented by the predecessor contractor and the union, *Upshaw v. Akal Security, Inc.*, 2008 U.S. Dist. LEXIS 22856 (N.D. Ill. 2008). In addition, the rule does not apply if the incumbent contractor enters into the collective bargaining agreement during contract performance but fails to give timely notice. See FAR 22.1008-2(c)(2) describing late notice as follows:

> (i)(A) In sealed bidding, the contracting agency receives notice of the terms of the collective bargaining agreement less than 10 days before bid opening and finds that there is not reasonable time still available to notify bidders (see 22.1012-2(a)); or

>> (B) For contractual actions other than sealed bidding, the contracting agency receives notice of the terms of the collective bargaining agreement after award, provided that the start of performance is within 30 days of award (see 22.1012-2(b)); and

> (ii) The contracting officer has given both the incumbent contractor and its employees' collective bargaining agent timely written notification of the applicable acquisition dates (see 22.1010).

### 3.  *Exemptions to Service Contract Act*

The Secretary of Labor has authority to exempt contracts from the Service Contract Act under 41 U.S.C. § 353(c). Exempted from the provisions of the Act are contracts for transportation (§ 356(3)), communications (§ 356(4)), public utilities (§ 356(5)), individual personal services (§ 356(6)), and contracts with the Postal Service (§ 356(7)).

Contracts covered by the Walsh-Healey Act are also exempt from the Act (§ 356(2)), but DOL has ruled that the Act will cover some contracts that would otherwise be subject to Walsh-Healey but for the fact that they are for amounts less than $10,000, SCA Op. 303.4, 302.4, 302.3, Feb. 1, 1968. For example, the Act has been held to apply to storage of household goods, SCA Op. 401, May 21, 1969, and a contract to furnish, stock, and maintain vending machines, SCA Op. 302.3, 303.4, Jan. 22, 1968. See also *Williams v. Department of Labor*, 697 F.2d 842 (8th Cir. 1983), where military "pack and crate" contracts were not exempted from the Act because the contracts were not primarily for carriage of freight.

Similarly, contracts subject to the Davis-Bacon Act are exempt (§ 356(1)). For dismantling, demolition, or removal of improvements contracts, FAR 37.301 requires the use of the Davis-Bacon Act only if "further work which will result in the construction, alteration, or repair of a public building or public work at that location is contemplated." Otherwise, the Service Contract Act applies. See also 29 C.F.R. § 4.131(f). For other contracts containing both services and construction, GAO has permitted broad discretion by contracting officers, loosely following the rule that the Davis-Bacon Act will apply if the contract contains substantial amounts of construction work, *D.E. Clarke*, Comp. Gen. Dec. B-146824, 75-1 CPD ¶ 317.

In 1983, DOL promulgated 29 C.F.R. § 4.123(e)(1) which permits exemption of contracts for the maintenance and repair of automated data processing equipment and office information systems, office and business machines, and high technology scientific and medical apparatus. See also FAR 22.1003-4(c). To qualify for the exemption, the contractor is required to certify that it will maintain the same compensation plan for employees on both government and commercial equipment contracts. See *AFL-CIO v. Donovan*, 757 F.2d 330 (D.C. Cir. 1985), where the court found proper an exemption for contracts for commercial products support services of high-technology companies in view of the industry's established merit pay systems and the significant impairment of government operations which would result if computers were not available because manufacturers refused to accept service contracts. See *Savantage Fin. Servs., Inc. v. United States*, 86 Fed. Cl. 700 (2009), finding reasonable a determination that a contract for an integrated system solution" was not subject to the Act.

Contracts with commercial contractors are also exempt. See FAR 22.1003-4(d) listing the type of services covered by this exemption and the conditions that must be met. To meet this requirement the contractor's employees must "spend only a small portion of his or her time (a monthly average of less than 20 percent of the available hours on an annualized basis, or less than 20 percent of available hours during the contract period if the contract period is less than one month) servicing the Government contract." The major conditions are that the services are sold regularly to nongovernment customers in substantial quantities and are furnished at prices at, or based on, established catalog or market prices.

DOL has declined a proposal to exempt R&D contracts from the Act after concluding that such an exemption is unnecessary and would be extremely difficult to define, 48 Fed. Reg. 49751 (1983).

## 4.  *Contract Clauses*

The Service Contract Act of 1965 clause in FAR 52.222-41 is used in all contracts where the Act applies. Detailed instructions on the use of this clause are set forth in FAR 22.1006(a). The Statement of Equivalent Rates for Federal Hires clause in FAR 52.222-42 is also required to be included in these contracts. See FAR 22.1016 for instructions on the use of this clause. When service contracts cover multiple years, FAR 22.1006(c)(1) requires use of the Fair Labor Standards Act and Service Contract Act — Price Adjustment (Multiple Year and Option Contracts) clause in FAR 52.222-43. When service contracts do not cover multiple years, FAR 22.1006(c)(2) requires use of the Fair Labor Standards Act and Service Contract Act — Price Adjustment clause in FAR 52.222-44. These price adjustment clauses allow compensation for higher wages resulting from new wage determinations but do not permit the inclusion of indirect costs or profit. They require notice to the contracting officer of claimed increased amounts within 30 days of receipt of a new wage determination. See *DTS Aviation Servs., Inc.*, ASBCA 56352, 09-2 BCA ¶ 34,288, discussing the enforceability of this notice requirement. These clauses also contain a warranty that the prices in the contract do not contain any contingency for higher wages in later periods. See *JDD, Inc.*, ASBCA 55282, 06-2 BCA ¶ 33,345, granting a price adjustment under the FAR 52.222-43 clause even though the solicitation directed the offerors to include an amount in their option year prices to cover higher wages. The board concluded that the warranty in the clause precluded such a contingency. See also *Lear Siegler Servs., Inc.*, ASBCA 54449, 05-1 BCA ¶ 32,937, for an in depth discussion of the application of these price adjustment provisions.

## 5.  *Enforcement*

Both the contracting agency and DOL have enforcement powers. Both DOL and the contracting officer can withhold funds when it is found that a contractor has not paid the correct wages, 29 C.F.R. § 187. See ¶ (k) of the Service Contract Act of 1965 clause and FAR 22.1022. Noncompliance with the Act is also grounds for default termination, FAR 22.1023, or "cancellation," 29 C.F.R. § 190. Placing a contractor in the Excluded Parties List System is adequate grounds for default termination, *Webco Transp. Corp.*, PSBCA 5276, 09-1 BCA ¶ 34,042.

DOL also conducts hearings and reaches decisions which are binding on "all agencies of the Government," 29 C.F.R. § 189, and the contracting agency is required to cooperate in all DOL investigations, FAR 22.1024. If enforcement issues cannot be resolved by agreement with the contractor, they are subject to ¶ (t) of the Service Contract Act of 1965 clause, which calls for resolution by the Department of Labor.

The Act requires contractor that violate its provisions to be debarred for three years unless DOL finds that there are "unusual circumstances." See 29 C.F.R. § 188(b) stating:

(3)(i) The Department of Labor has developed criteria for determining when there are unusual circumstances within the meaning of the Act. See, e.g., Washington Moving & Storage Co., Decision of the Assistant Secretary, SCA 68, August 16, 1973, Secretary, March 12, 1974; Quality Maintenance Co., Decision of the Assistant Secretary, SCA 119, January 11, 1974. Thus, where the respondent's conduct in causing or permitting violations of the Service Contract Act provisions of the contract is willful, deliberate or of an aggravated nature or where the violations are a result of culpable conduct such as culpable neglect to ascertain whether practices are in violation, culpable disregard of whether they were in violation or not, or culpable failure to comply with recordkeeping requirements (such as falsification of records), relief from the debarment sanction cannot be in order. Furthermore, relief from debarment cannot be in order where a contractor has a history of similar violations, where a contractor has repeatedly violated the provisions of the Act, or where previous violations were serious in nature.

(ii) A good compliance history, cooperation in the investigation, repayment of moneys due, and sufficient assurances of future compliance are generally prerequisites to relief. Where these prerequisites are present and none of the aggravated circumstances in the preceding paragraph exist, a variety of factors must still be considered, including whether the contractor has previously been investigated for violations of the Act, whether the contractor has committed recordkeeping violations which impeded the investigation, whether liability was dependent upon resolution of a bona fide legal issue of doubtful certainty, the contractor's efforts to ensure compliance, the nature, extent, and seriousness of any past or present violations, including the impact of violations on unpaid employees, and whether the sums due were promptly paid.

Courts give considerable deference to debarment decisions, *Karawia v. Department of Labor*, 627 F. Supp. 2d 137 (S.D.N.Y. 2009) (debarment proper when contractor had been subject to 57 DOL enforcement actions).

GAO will not hear challenges that a competitor will not comply with the Act, *K-Mar Indus., Inc.*, Comp. Gen. Dec. B-400487, 2009 CPD ¶ 159; *SAGE Sys. Techs., LLC*, Comp. Gen. Dec. B-310155, 2007 CPD ¶ 219.

Workers that believe that they have not been paid in accordance with the Act can file a complaint with the contracting officer or the Department of Labor, 29 C.F.R. § 4.191. However, they have no private cause of action against the contractor, *Miscellaneous Serv. Workers, Drivers & Helpers v. Philco-Ford Corp.*, 661 F.2d 776 (9th Cir. 1981). Some courts have held that there is a state cause of action for additional compensation, *Inkrote v. Protection Strategies, Inc.*, 2009 U.S. Dist. LEXIS 101070 (N.D. W.Va. 2009); *Naranjo v. Spectrum Sec. Servs., Inc.*, 91 Cal. Rptr. 3d 393 (Cal. App. 2009). See also *United Gov't Sec. Officers of Am. v. Chert-*

*off*, 587 F. Supp. 2d 209 (D.D.C. 2008), holding that the court could order an agency to incorporate a new wage DOL determination into its contract.

Aggrieved workers can file a qui tam False Claims Act suit for a contractor's flase statement that it was in complaince with the Act, *United States. ex rel. Sutton v. Double Day Office Servs., Inc.*, 121 F.3d 531 (9th Cir. 1997).

## C. Contract Work Hours and Safety Standards Act

The Contract Work Hours and Safety Standards Act, 40 U.S.C. § 3701 et seq., requires that laborers and mechanics be paid overtime for all hours over 40 hours in a week. It applies to all construction contracts of $150,000 or more that are not for commercial items, transportation, the transmission of intelligence, or are not to be performed outside of the United States, FAR 22.305. See *Dingell v. Halliburton Co.*, 2006 U.S. Dist. LEXIS 68616 (S.D. Tex. 2006), holding that the clause was improperly included in a contract calling for performance outside of the United States.

The Act also applies to certain service contract employees. See 29 C.F.R. § 4.181(b)(1) stating:

> The Contract Work Hours and Safety Standards Act (40 U.S.C. 327-332) applies generally to Government contracts, including service contracts in excess of $150,000, which may require or involve the employment of laborers and mechanics. Guards, watchmen, and many other classes of service employees are laborers or mechanics within the meaning of such Act. However, employees rendering only professional services, seamen, and as a general rule those whose work is only clerical or supervisory or nonmanual in nature, are not deemed laborers or mechanics for purposes of the Act. The wages of every laborer and mechanic for performance of work on such contracts must include compensation at a rate not less than 1 1/2 times the employees' basic rate of pay for all hours worked in any workweek in excess of 40. Exemptions are provided for certain transportation and communications contracts, contracts for the purchase of supplies ordinarily available in the open market, and work, required to be done in accordance with the provisions of the Walsh-Healey Act.

Contracts subject to the Act must contain the Contract Work Hours and Safety Standards Act — Overtime Compensation clause in FAR 52.222-4. This clause not only requires the payment of overtime to workers but also the payment of liquidated damages to the government in the event of nonpayment. These damages are assessed at the rate of $10 per day per worker. FAR 22.302(c) permits agency heads to waive or reduce liquidated damages if the violation was inadvertent. See *Myers Investigative & Sec. Servs., Inc. v. Environmental Protection Agency*, CBCA 16587-EPA, 05-2 BCA ¶ 32,983, holding that the issue of whether liquidated damages were properly assessed is a Contract Disputes Act issue not a labor standards issue (requiring resolution by the Department of Labor under the Fair Labor Standards Act and Service Contract Act — Price Adjustment clause).

The clause also calls for withholding of funds to cover insufficient payments to workers. See *Overstreet Elec. Co.*, ASBCA 51653, 01-2 BCA ¶ 31,646, finding that contracting officers had acted reasonably under this clause and that this was a Contract Disputes Act issue not a labor standards issue (requiring resolution by the Department of Labor under the Davis-Bacon Act — Price Adjustment clause).

## D. Walsh-Healey Act

The Walsh-Healey Act, 41 U.S.C. § 6501 et seq., is the supply contract counterpart of the Davis-Bacon Act. It establishes "minimum" wages for contracts in excess of $15,000 for the manufacturing or furnishing of materials, supplies, articles, and equipment. Department of Labor regulations implementing this statute are found in 41 C.F.R. Part 50-201. The Walsh-Healey Act was part of a package of New Deal legislation in the 1930s. The Act sought to provide worker protection in order to alleviate two major problems faced by workers during the Depression — the number of hours worked and minimum wages. The protections of the Act have been superseded by the Fair Labor Standards Act, 29 U.S.C. § 207.

FAR 22.604-1 provides that specified supplies are statutorily exempt from the Act:

(a) Any item in those situations where the contracting officer is authorized by the express language of a statute to purchase "in the open market" generally (such as commercial items, see part 12); or where a specific purchase is made under the conditions described in 6.302-2 in circumstances where immediate delivery is required by the public exigency.

(b) Perishables, including dairy, livestock, and nursery products.

(c) Agricultural or farm products processed for first sale by the original producers.

(d) Agricultural commodities or the products thereof purchased under contract by the Secretary of Agriculture.

FAR 22.604-2 provides that specified supplies are exempt by regulation from the Act:

(1) Public utility services.

(2) Supplies manufactured outside the United States, Puerto Rico, and the U.S. Virgin Islands.

(3) Purchases against the account of a defaulting contractor where the stipulations of the Act were not included in the defaulted contract.

(4) Newspapers, magazines, or periodicals, contracted for with sales agents or publisher representatives, which are to be delivered by the publishers thereof.

Contracts subject to the Act must contain the Walsh-Healey Public Contracts Act clause in FAR 52.222-20. This clause incorporates the regulations of the Department of Labor at 41 C.F.R. Chapter 50 into the contract and requires the contractor to pay the minimum wages prescribed by the Fair Labor Standards Act.

## VI. OTHER EMPLOYEE-RELATED STATUTES

Congress has enacted other statutes that have direct impact on the manner in which contractor employees are treated at the workplace. This section discusses statutes giving rights to persons with disabilities and the statute aimed at ensuring that contractors establish a drug-free workplace. Although the main purposes of these laws are not related, they share the common goals of attempting to make the contract work environment more accessible to all qualified personnel, more acceptable as a "good" place to work, and more productive.

### A. Workers With Disabilities

There are two statutes providing rights to persons with disabilities. Detailed guidance on determining whether a person has a disability and whether such a person is qualified for a job is contained in 29 C.F.R. § 1630.2 and § 1630.3.

### 1. The Rehabilitation Act

The Rehabilitation Act of 1973, 29 U.S.C. § 793, requires contractors to take affirmative action with regard to hiring and promotion of "qualified individuals with disabilities." The Act is implemented by Executive Order 11758, DOL regulations in 41 C.F.R. Part 60-741; and FAR Subpart 22.14.

FAR 22.1402 requires all contracts over $15,000 to contain the Affirmative Action for Workers with Disabilities clause at FAR 52.222-36. FAR 22.1403 provides for waivers to "any or all" of the terms of this clause as follows:

(a) The agency head, with the concurrence of the Deputy Assistant Secretary for Federal Contract Compliance of the U.S. Department of Labor (Deputy Assistant Secretary), may waive any or all of the terms of the clause at 52.222-36, Affirmative Action for Workers with Disabilities, for —

(1) Any contract if a waiver is deemed to be in the national interest; or

(2) Groups or categories of contracts if a waiver is in the national interest and it is —

(i) Impracticable to act on each request individually; and

(ii) Determined that the waiver will substantially contribute to convenience in administering the Act.

(b)(1) The head of a civilian agency, with the concurrence of the Deputy Assistant Secretary, or, (2) the Secretary of Defense, may waive any requirement in this subpart when it is determined that the contract is essential to the national security, and that its award without complying with such requirements is necessary to the national security. Upon making such a determination, the head of a civilian agency shall notify the Deputy Assistant Secretary in writing within 30 days.

The clause was properly omitted from a solicitation to select insurance carrier to furnish contractors with Defense Base Act workers' compensation insurance coverage because the acquisition was not subject to the FAR, *Fidelity & Cas. Co. of New York*, Comp. Gen. Dec. B-281281, 99-1 CPD ¶ 16.

Complaints of violation of the clause are handled by the DOL Office of Federal Contract Compliance, 41 C.F.R. § 60-741.61, and, if received by an agency should be forwarded to that office, FAR 22.1406. DOL can impose the sanctions of withholding of payment, termination or suspension of a contract or debarment of a contractor, 41 C.F.R. § 60-741.66; FAR 22.1407.

## 2. *The Americans with Disabilities Act*

The Americans with Disabilities Act of 1990 (ADA), 42 U.S.C. § 12101 et seq., seeks to protect "individuals with a disability" if they are qualified to perform job requirements. It defines an "individual with a disability" as someone with a physical or mental impairment that substantially limits one or more major life activities, 42 U.S.C. § 12102(2). It prohibits discrimination against such individuals and requires "reasonable accommodation" for them, 42 U.S.C. § 12112. The Act is implemented in 29 C.F.R. 1630. It is not covered in the FAR.

### a. *Prohibited Discrimination*

The ADA prohibits all employers (not only government contractors) from discriminating in all aspects of employment against any "qualified individual with a disability" because of that person's disability. The ADA specifically bars discrimination in job application procedures, hiring, promotion, termination, compensation, training, and other "terms, conditions, and privileges of employment," 42 U.S.C. § 12112(a).

The statute defines the term "qualified individual with a disability" to mean an "individual with a disability who, with or without reasonable accommodation, can perform the essential functions of the employment position that such individual holds," 42 U.S.C. § 12111(8). In *Floyd E. McDaniel v. AlliedSignal, Inc.*, 896 F. Supp. 1482 (1995), the court found that a security clearance was an essential function of an individual's employment position. An employee of AlliedSignal claimed that the company was obligated under the ADA to provide him a reasonable accommodation that would cure or mitigate his disability so that his required security clearance would not be revoked by the government. The court stated that to make a prima facie case under the ADA, an employee must be able to perform the essential functions of the job in spite of the disability with no need for accommodation or with reasonable accommodation. The employee conceded that he could not perform the essential functions of the job unless AlliedSignal provided some sort of accommodation. The court held that because the decision to revoke a security clearance is solely the government's, no amount of accommodation by AlliedSignal would render the employee able to perform the essential functions of the position.

The ADA expressly forbids any preemployment medical examination or other inquiry of a job applicant about the existence or extent of any disability, 42 U.S.C. § 12112(d). However, if all employees are subject to a medical examination, then an individual with a disability can properly be subject to the same requirement so long as the results are maintained in confidence and used only as otherwise permitted under the statute, 42 U.S.C. § 12112(d)(3). Employers are further forbidden from discriminating against an otherwise qualified individual because of the disability of another person with whom the qualified individual has a relationship, 42 U.S.C. § 12112(b)(4). Finally, the ADA requires that the job application process be accessible to people with different disabilities, and it prohibits the use of standards or tests if they tend to screen out individuals with disabilities, unless the selection criteria are job related for the position in question and consistent with business necessity, 42 U.S.C. § 12112(b)(6).

### b.  Reasonable Accommodation

The ADA requires employers to make "reasonable accommodation" for the physical or mental impairments of the employee or applicant, that is, changes in the work environment or in the way things are customarily done that enable a person with a disability to enjoy equal employment opportunities, 29 C.F.R. Part 1630 App. § 1630(2)(o).

Employers are required to make only accommodations that are reasonable. An accommodation is not reasonable if the employer can demonstrate that it would impose undue hardship on the conduct of its business. This would include accommodations that are unduly costly, extensive, substantial, or disruptive, or that would fundamentally alter the nature or operation of the business, 29 C.F.R. Part 1630 App. 1630(2)(o)

### c.  Defenses

Employers have several defenses available. First, accommodations need not be made if they would impose an undue hardship on the employer's business. Second, qualification standards may be used, even those that tend to screen out people with disabilities, if the standards are job related and consistent with business necessity. Furthermore, employers are not obligated to hire anyone who poses a direct threat to the health or safety of himself or herself or to others in the workplace, 42 U.S.C. § 12113(b). Protection under the ADA does not extend to any employee or applicant who is currently engaging in the illegal use of drugs, 42 U.S.C. § 12114(a).

## d.  Enforcement

The ADA is enforced by the EEOC in the same manner used to enforce Title VII of the Civil Rights Act of 1964, 42 U.S.C. § 12117(a). Any job applicant or employee who believes that discrimination has occurred can file a charge with the nearest EEOC office. The complaining party, once its administrative remedies have been exhausted, is free to file suit in federal court.

The remedies available to a successful complainant in an ADA proceeding are the same remedies available under Title VII of the Civil Rights Act of 1964, 42 U.S.C. § 12117(a). Available remedies may include hiring, reinstatement, promotion, back or front pay, reasonable accommodation, attorney fees, expert witness fees, and court costs, 42 U.S.C. § 1981a(a). Compensatory and punitive damages also may be available where intentional discrimination is found, 42 U.S.C. § 1981a(a). These damages are capped at a level corresponding to the size of the employer. For example, employers of between 15 and 100 employees will not pay damages in excess of $ 50,000, 42 U.S.C. § 1981a(b)(3).

The ADA expressly prohibits retaliation against an individual who makes a charge of discrimination or who participates in any resulting investigation, proceeding, or hearing, 42 U.S.C. § 12203.

## B.  Drug-Free Workplace Act of 1988

The Drug-Free Workplace Act of 1988 (DFWA), 41 U.S.C. § 701, requires most government contractors to establish and maintain a drug-free workplace as a condition of their current contracts and in order to maintain eligibility for future contracts. This Act is implemented in FAR Subpart 23.5. It is also implemented with regard to grants, cooperative agreements and other financial assistance in 29 C.F.R. Part 94.

## 1.  Policy

The Act prohibits award of contracts except those under the simplified acquisition threshold or for commercial items, unless the contractor has certified that it will provide a drug-free workplace and adhere to several specific practices, FAR 23.504. Contractors must:

- Publish a policy statement that prohibits any unlawful activity involving controlled substances in the workplace and specifying the actions that will be taken with respect to violations of the policy.

- Establish a drug-free awareness program that will inform employees about the drug-free workplace, the availability of counseling and employee assistance programs, and the sanctions that will be imposed for drug abuse violations occurring in the workplace.

- Notify the contracting agency in writing of any employee conviction for a drug statute violation within 10 calendar days after being made aware of the conviction.

- Impose sanctions (up to and including termination) on the involved employee or require the employee to participate in an approved drug abuse assistance or rehabilitation program.

- Make a "good faith" effort to maintain a drug-free workplace.

The Act is implemented by a Drug-Free Workplace clause at FAR 52.223-6.

## 2.  Drug Testing

The Act does not require drug testing of employees by contractors. However, Executive Order 12564, issued by President Reagan in 1986, did provide for random drug testing in sensitive positions. The FAR is silent on drug testing procedures. Individual agencies have issued drug testing procedures that vary depending upon the duties of the agency and the "sensitivity" of the work being performed by contractors. The DoD and NASA offer representative examples of these rules.

The drug testing protocol required of DoD contractors is found in the Drug-Free Work Force clause, DFARS 252.223-7004. This clause requires as part of a contractor's drug-free program "provisions for identifying illegal drug users on a controlled and carefully monitored basis." The clause goes on to discuss the extent of and criteria for such testing. As important considerations it lists the nature of the work being performed; the employee's duties; the efficient use of contractor resources; and the risks to health, safety, and national security that could result from the failure of employees to adequately perform their work. In addition, the clause provides that testing is appropriate (1) when there is a reasonable suspicion that an employee uses illegal drugs, (2) when an employee has been involved in an accident or unsafe practice, (3) as part of a follow-up to counseling or rehabilitation, or (4) as part of a voluntary employee drug testing program.

NASA has adopted a drug and alcohol testing program to implement the Civil Space Employee Testing Act of 1991, NFS 1823.5. This requires the use of the Drug- and Alcohol-Free Workforce clause in NFS 1852.223-74 in contracts for critical missions or contract over $5 million where employees "in a sensitive position" will perform work. Among other things, the clause requires NASA contractors to provide preemployment, reasonable suspicion, random, postaccident, and periodic follow-up testing of contractor employees "in sensitive positions."

The Department of Health and Human Services has issued "Guidelines for Federal Workplace Drug Testing Programs," 59 Fed. Reg. 29908, June 6, 1994, which, as revised, became effective in September 1994. Among other things, these Guidelines seek to establish (1) scientific and technical rules for federal agencies' workplace drug testing programs, and (2) a certification program for laboratories engaged in urine drug testing for federal agencies.

## 3. Sanctions

FAR 23.504(a) provides that no offeror will be considered a responsible source in the absence of an agreement regarding a drug-free workplace. Similarly, under FAR 23.504(b), an individual will be denied award of a contract of any dollar amount unless that individual agrees that he or she "will not engage in the unlawful manufacture, distribution, dispensing, possession, or use of a controlled substance while performing the contract."

FAR 23.506 provides that the contracting officer may suspend contract payments if a contractor has failed to comply with the Drug-Free Workplace clause, or if the number of contractor employees convicted of criminal drug violations indicates that the contractor has failed to make a good faith effort to provide a drug-free workplace. The contracting officer also has the discretion to terminate a contract for default, FAR 23.506(b), and must refer a contractor for debarment or suspension when payments are suspended or the contract is terminated, FAR 23.506(c).

# CHAPTER 12

# CONTRACT AWARD CONTROVERSIES

Contract award controversies have become a substantial part of the procurement process. Disappointed offerors often seek to challenge procurement actions. For many years, these challenges were heard without specific statutory authority. However, beginning in 1982, Congress began to take an active role in formalizing the process by adopting a number of statutes dealing with award controversies. Presently, there are three forums where contract award controversies may be heard — the procuring agencies, the Comptroller General (the head of the Government Accountability Office (GAO)), and the Court of Federal Claims. **Figure 12-1** summarizes the major features of each of these forums.

The boards of contract appeals have not generally been involved in contract award controversies. See *Coastal Corp. v. United States*, 713 F.2d 728 (Fed. Cir. 1983), holding that the board's jurisdiction under the Contract Disputes Act of 1978, 41 U.S.C. § 601 - § 613, does not extend to implied contracts to consider bids and proposals fairly. A notable exception was the General Services Administration Board of Contract Appeals (GSBCA). In 1984 the GSBCA was granted authority to hear protests on Brooks Act automatic data processing equipment (now, information technology) procurements, 40 U.S.C. § 759(h). However,§ 5101 of the Clinger-Cohen Act of 1996, Pub. L. No. 104-106, repealed this authority. During this time, the board rendered numerous decisions dealing with the award process. Those decisions and the decisions of the Court of Appeals for the Federal Circuit dealing with them can be helpful in resolving current award controversies.

Except for the time period between 1970 and 2001, the district courts have not been an available forum for protesters. The Supreme Court ruled in 1940 in *Perkins v. Lukens Co. v. United States*, 310 U.S. 113 (1940), that no one had a right to a government contract; as a result, it was held that disappointed bidders were not entitled to have their protests heard in court. Then, in *Scanwell Labs., Inc. v. United States*, 424 F.2d 859 (D.C. Cir. 1970), the court held that the Administrative Procedure Act (APA), 5 U.S.C. § 702, gave offerors a right to bring an action challenging agency action in the process of awarding contracts. The jurisdiction of the district courts over protests was affected by the passage of the Federal Courts Improvement Act of 1982, Pub. L. No. 97-164. This Act established the Claims Court (renamed the Court of Federal Claims by the Federal Courts Administrative Act of 1992, Pub. L. No. 102-572) and provided the court jurisdiction over preaward protests. The Act allowed the Claims Court "to afford complete relief on any contract claim brought before the contract is awarded." This Act created confusion as to whether the Claims Court possessed exclusive jurisdiction to hear preaward protests. Postaward judicial authority remained with the district courts. Section 12(d) of the Administrative Dispute Resolution Act (ADRA) of 1992, Pub. L. No. 104-320, resolved the issue by granting the Court of Federal Claims and the district courts concurrent jurisdiction to hear both preaward and postaward protests. The ADRA, however, provided that bid protest jurisdiction in the district courts would expire on January 1, 2001, unless extended by Congress. Congress did not renew the jurisdiction of the district courts over bid protests with the result that the Court of Federal Claims is now the exclusive judicial forum over preaward and postaward bid protests.

This chapter first deals with the distinction between contract award controversies that may be brought by a third party and contract performance disputes. It then considers, in detail, the features of each of the three forums.

| Forum | Procuring Agency | Court of Federal Claims (COFC) | GAO |
|---|---|---|---|
| Who May Protest | Interested parties | Non-procurement contract offerors with implied contract for good faith consideration of offer and procurement contract offerors that are interested parties | Interested parties |
| Jurisdiction | FAR 33. 103 | 28 U.S.C. § 1491(a)(1) and (b)(2) | 31 U.S.C. § 3551, with deference to actions in other forums |
| Time for Protest | Pre- and postaward | Pre- and postaward | Pre- and postaward |
| Time of Decision | No designated time | No designated time | 100 calendar days (65 calendar days — express option) |
| Procedures | Various agency procedures; Informal in nature | Evidentiary trial, including limited discovery | Submission of written reports and optional hearing |
| Burden of Proof | Probably same as GAO | Clear and convincing evidence of violation | Presumption of correctness of agency action |
| Standards of Review | Probably same as GAO | No rational basis or clear violation of statute or regulation | No rational basis or clear violation of statute or regulation |
| Interim Remedies | Agency must delay award or suspend performance unless CICA override | Discretionary temporary restraining order or preliminary injunction | Agency must delay award or suspend performance unless CICA override |
| Remedies | Any appropriate actions | Injunction or declaratory judgment if consistent with national defense; bid or proposal costs | Recommend that agency recompete, terminate, or award; contract costs; attorneys' fees; bid or proposal costs |
| Appeals | If within jurisdictional time period, begin action again in either GAO or COFC | Federal Circuit | Indirectly through suit in the COFC |

**Figure 12-1**

# I.  AWARD VERSUS PERFORMANCE CONTROVERSIES

Contract award controversies must be distinguished from controversies arising during contract performance. As a general rule, performance controversies occur between the parties to a contract, and third parties cannot challenge actions that occur during the performance of a contract. See, for example, *Gull Airborne Instruments, Inc. v. Weinberger*, 694 F.2d 838 (D. C. Cir. 1982), denying a competitor a right to obtain an injunction ordering the contracting officer to terminate the contract for default based on the contractor's alleged failure to perform as proposed. This rule has been incorporated in the protest regulations of GAO at 4 C.F.R. § 21.5(a), which states: "The administration of an existing contract is within the discretion of the contracting agency." In *Data Monitor Sys., Inc. (DMS) v. United States*, 74 Fed. Cl. 66 (2006), the court held that it lacked jurisdiction to enjoin termination of a contract and refused to enjoin resolicitation. The matter arose after the agency had issued a convenience termination shortly after award of a contract to DMS as a result of a protest by a competitor. The Court of Federal Claims denied jurisdiction, stating that such issues were reviewable only under the Contract Disputes Act. Other court cases denying protest jurisdiction because the issue was a matter involving contract administration include *Gonzalez-McCaulley Inv. Group. Inc. v. United States*, 93 Fed. Cl. 710 (2010) (breach of "implied contract" after agency issued notice of award but "withdrew" award); *Griffy's Landscape Maint. LLC v. United States*, 51 Fed. Cl. 667 (2001) (termination of contract in response to protest); *Control Data Sys., Inc. v. United States*, 32 Fed. Cl. 520 (1994) (decision not to exercise an option); *C. M. P., Inc. v. United States*, 8 Cl. Ct. 743 (1985) (exercise of an option in competitor's contract); and *Willow Beach Resort, Inc. v. United States*, 5 Cl. Ct. 241 (1984) (refusal of agency to treat "preferential right" in contract as a promise to buy only from protester). In *Davis/HRGM Joint Venture v. United States*, 50 Fed. Cl. 539 (2001), the court explained that a contractor's challenge to a termination for convenience "does not fall within the express language of [28 U.S.C.] § 1491(b) because it does not relate to an interested party's objection to a solicitation, a proposed award, or an award." If an offeror that originally won the competition, but has its contract terminated as a result of a protest, merely challenges the resolicitation of offers, the court will take protest jurisdiction, *Delaney Constr. Corp. v. United States*, 56 Fed. Cl. 470 (2003).

GAO decisions finding the matter involved contract administration include *Training Mgmt. Solutions, Inc.*, Comp. Gen. Dec. B-403461.2, 2010 CPD ¶ 224 (whether awardee was able to begin timely performance); *Crewzers Fire Crew Transport, Inc.*, Comp. Gen. Dec. B-402530, 2010 CPD ¶ 117 (whether agency will allow defective performance by awardees); *CES Indus., Inc.*, Comp. Gen. Dec. B-401427, 2010 CPD ¶ 43 (whether awardee will infringe a patent); *Solar Plexus, LLC*, Comp. Gen. Dec. B-402061, 2009 CPD ¶ 256 (whether awardee complies with RFP requirements); *Petro Star, Inc.*, Comp. Gen. Dec. B-401108, 2009 CPD ¶ 92 (seeking contract reformation); *Nilson Van & Storage, Inc.*, Comp. Gen. Dec.

B-310485, 2007 CPD ¶ 224 (whether awardee complies with performance work statement standard to conduct background check on prospective employees); *Murray-Benjamin Elec. Co., LP*, Comp. Gen. Dec. B-298481, 2006 CPD ¶ 129 (whether agency violated its obligation to procure items under one of the contractor's existing vehicles); *Catapult Tech., Ltd.*, Comp. Gen. Dec. B-294936, 2005 CPD ¶ 14 (exercise of an option); *Public Facility Consortium I, LLC*, Comp. Gen. Dec. B-295911, 2005 CPD ¶ 170 (whether awardee will perform in accordance with solicitation requirements); *Shinwha Elec.*, Comp. Gen. Dec. B-291064, 2002 CPD ¶ 154 (debarment of suspension of protester); *Military Agency Servs., Pty,. Ltd.*, Comp. Gen. Dec. B-290414, 2002 CPD ¶ 130 (whether services were required to be ordered under contractor's multiple award schedule); *Magney Grande Distrib., Inc.*, Comp. Gen. Dec. B-286981, 2001 CPD ¶ 56 (whether awardee will be held to the RFP's performance testing requirements); *AT&T Corp.*, Comp. Gen. Dec. B-270344, 96-1 CPD ¶ 117 (challenge to the termination of its contract); *Digital Sys. Group, Inc.*, Comp. Gen. Dec. B-252080.2, 93-1 CPD ¶ 228, and *AVW Elec. Sys., Inc.*, Comp. Gen. Dec. B-252399, 93-1 CPD ¶ 386 (exercise of an option); *Anderson Columbia Co.*, Comp. Gen. Dec. B-249475.3, 92-2 CPD ¶ 288 (whether awardee may violate contract requirement for use of U.S. flag vessels); *Sierra Techs., Inc.*, Comp. Gen. Dec. B-251460, 92-2 CPD ¶ 427 (failure to continue making dual awards on acquisition program); *RGI, Inc.*, Comp. Gen. Dec. B-243387.2, 91-2 CPD ¶ 572 (use of less qualified individuals by the awardee than originally proposed to fill positions under the contract); and *American Instrument Corp.*, Comp. Gen. Dec. B-239997, 90-2 CPD ¶ 287 (whether awardee complies with Buy American Act certification).

## A. Actions Compromising Competition

Where the contract action is considered to clearly compromise the competition that led to the award, it will be considered a contract award controversy, *Webcraft Packaging, Div. of Beatrice Foods Co.*, Comp. Gen. Dec. B-194087, 79-2 CPD ¶ 120 (agency should have resolicited rather than relax specifications in contract for specialty product produced by only a few sources). Thus, the contract award controversy process will be available where a contract modification alters the contract requirement to the extent that the modified contract is outside the scope of the original competition, *AT&T Commc'ns, Inc. v. Wiltel, Inc.*, 1 F.3d 1201 (Fed. Cir. 1993). This is determined by analyzing the entire contract to determine whether the original competitors would have anticipated that the modification would be issued under the contract. See *Cardinal Maint. Serv., Inc. v. United States*, 63 Fed. Cl. 98 (2004) (changes not of the type that were specifically authorized or even foreseen in original contract); *CW Gov't Travel v. United States*, 61 Fed. Cl. 559 (2004), *reh'g denied*, 63 Fed. Cir. 459 (2005), *aff'd*, 163 Fed. App'x 853 (2005) (new services so far removed from the original requirements that they should have been independently solicited through full and open competition); and *CCL, Inc. v. United States*, 39 Fed. Cl. 780 (1997) (increasing the number of locations where computer maintenance services were to be performed). For GAO decision, see *DynCorp Int'l*

*LLC*, Comp. Gen. Dec. B-402349, 2010 CPD ¶ 59 (training, facilities and logistics support services not related to contract for counter-narcoterrorism support services); *Poly-Pacific Techs.*, Comp. Gen. Dec. B-296029, 2005 CPD ¶ 105 (RFP did not anticipate that contractor could be relieved of the recycling requirement or that a disposal effort could be ordered in lieu of recycling); *Sprint Commc'ns Co.*, Comp. Gen. Dec. B-278407.2, 98-1 CPD ¶ 60 (modification adding transmission services were outside the scope because the initial procurement had stated that such services were not required); *MCI Telecomms. Corp.*, Comp. Gen. Dec. B-276659.2, 97-2 CPD ¶ 90 (modification permitting contractor to design, operate, and maintain customized networks beyond the scope of FTS 2000 contract for telecommunications services because this was a different type of service than those called for in original contract); *Marvin J. Perry & Assocs.*, Comp. Gen. Dec. B-277684, 97-2 CPD ¶ 128 (modification of Federal Supply Schedule to substitute stained ash for red oak furniture beyond scope because ash was substantially cheaper); *Neil R. Gross & Co.*, Comp. Gen. Dec. B-237434, 90-1 CPD ¶ 212 (modification adding new court reporting services with substantial increased costs was outside scope of original competition); *Avtron Mfg., Inc.*, 67 Comp. Gen. 404 (B-229972), 88-1 CPD ¶ 458 (modifying the speed drive of the equipment would materially alter the terms of the original contract); and *American Air Filter Co.*, 57 Comp. Gen. 567 (B-188408), 78-1 CPD ¶ 443 (modification requiring units to operate on diesel fuel rather than gasoline was outside scope of original competition).

Cases finding that the modification did not violate the competition requirements include *Emergent BioSolutions, Inc.*, Comp. Gen. Dec. B-402576, 2010 CPD ¶ 136 (changes in "processes and activities" in research contract did not change basic contract objectives); *Overseas Lease Group, Inc.*, Comp. Gen. Dec. B-402111, 2010 CPD ¶ 34 (solicitation's differentiating between "non-tactical" and "up-armored" vehicles was sufficient to put protester on notice that term "non-tactical" was intended to refer to unarmored vehicles); *Lasmer Indus., Inc.*, Comp. Gen. Dec. B-400866.2, 2009 CPD ¶ 77 (part was specifically included in contract, and contract allowed the agency to order the part under a negotiated delivery schedule); *Armed Forces Hospitality*, Comp. Gen. Dec. B-298978.2, 2009 CPD ¶ 192 (lack of definitiveness in the original SOW provided the Army with additional contractual flexibility and latitude to reduce the number of rooms to be renovated and extend performance); *Chapman Law Firm Co. v. United States*, 81 Fed. Cl. 323 (2008) (geographic expansion of service and possibility of new pricing were changes clearly contemplated in the contracts); *Sallie Mae, Inc.*, Comp. Gen. Dec. B-400486, 2008 CPD ¶ 221 (statement of objective clearly placed offerors on notice that the agency intended to award contract for the management of all types of student loans); *CWT/Alexander Travel, Ltd. v. United States*, 78 Fed. Cl. 486 (2007) (given the nature of services required under the contract, price changes were viewed as inevitable); *DOR Biodefense, Inc.*, Comp. Gen. Dec. B-296358.3, 2006 CPD ¶ 35 (RFP advised offerors that the government reserves the right to change the list of vaccine sertoypes to add or delete products as need may arise); *HDM Corp. v. United States*, 69 Fed. Cl. 243 (2005) (consolidating responsibility for the crossover function was consistent with the broad objectives of the original contract); *CESC Plaza Ltd. P'ship v. United States*, 52 Fed. Cl. 91 (2002) (modifications did not materially alter contract's cash flow features or shift the risk of performance); *HG Props. A, LP*, Comp. Gen. Dec. B-290416, 2002 CPD ¶ 128 (changing location of site for construction of offered building space within the scope of the underlying lease where the property location requirements were only general in nature and scope with wide location boundaries); *VMC Behavioral Healthcare Servs., Div. of Vasquez Group, Inc. v. United States*, 50 Fed. Cl. 328 (2001) (level of effort contract for employee assistance services was subject to modification as additional agencies were added to the contract's coverage); *Hughes Space & Commc'ns Co.*, Comp. Gen. Dec. B-276040, 97-1 CPD ¶ 158 (addition of "system preemptible" satellite transponder leases to a satellite communications services contract, which previously specified only "non-preemptible" transponder leases, did not change fundamental nature and purpose of contract); and *Arjay Elecs. Corp.*, Comp. Gen. Dec. B-243080, 91-2 CPD ¶ 3 (contract price not adjusted, period of time for delivery not extended, and no evidence that changes in the item descriptions were significant).

## B. Task and Delivery Orders

The Federal Acquisition Streamlining Act of 1994 (FASA), Pub. L. No. 103-355, task and delivery order authority precluded protests concerning the issuance of orders under task and delivery order contracts except for a protest on the ground that the order increases the scope, period, or maximum value of the contract under which the order is issued. Section 843 of the National Defense Authorization Act (NDAA) of Fiscal Year 2008, Pub. L. No. 110-181, modified FASA's prior limitations on task order protests, providing that, in addition to previously permitted task order protests on the ground that the order increases the scope, period, or maximum value of the contract, a protest at GAO is also authorized to decide protests of "an order valued in excess of $10,000,000." This grant of jurisdiction was subject to a three-year sunset provision, expiring on May 27, 2011, 41 U.S.C. § 253j(e); however, 10 U.S.C. § 2304c(e) was amended to state:

(1) A protest is not authorized in connection with the issuance or proposed issuance of a task or delivery order except for

    (A) a protest on the ground that the order increases the scope, period, or maximum value of the contract under which the order is issued; or

    (B) a protest of an order valued in excess of $10,000,000.

(2) Notwithstanding section 3556 of title 31, the Comptroller General of the United States shall have exclusive jurisdiction of a protest authorized under paragraph (1)(B).

(3) Paragraph (1)(B) and paragraph (2) of this subsection shall not be in effect after September 30, 2016.

The rule is implemented in FAR 16.505. Costs of equipment and services furnished to the contractor by the government are not considered in calculation the $10 million value of the order, *Quest Gov't Servs., Inc.,* Comp. Gen. Dec. B-404845, 2011 CPD ¶ 77.

There is a possibility that agencies might issue separate task orders in order to evade the $10 million threshold. See, for example, *Armorworks Enters., LLC,* Comp. Gen. Dec. B-401671.3, 2009 CPD ¶ 225, where the agency issued three task orders totaling $21 million. GAO held that it would not aggregate separate task orders in order to take jurisdiction "absent a clear showing that the agency's decision to issue separate orders was made solely to evade our protest jurisdiction." GAO denied the protest based on the agency's reasonable explanation for issuing separate task orders. In *ESCO Marine, Inc.,* Comp. Gen. Dec. B-401438, 2009 CPD ¶ 234, for purposes of determining whether the $10 million threshold has been met, GAO held that it was not limited to consideration of the offerors' proposed prices, but properly included consideration of the estimated ship scrap values when the prospective contractors were required to sell the scrap resulting from the ship dismantling and retain the scrap sale proceeds. Essentially, the task order provided the contractor with two different forms of payment — the price and payment-in-kind (the right to keep the scrap sale proceeds).

The $10 million threshold is not applicable to a blanket purchase agreement (BPA), since a BPA is not a task or delivery order contract, *C&B Constr., Inc.,* Comp. Gen. Dec. B-401988.2, 2010 CPD ¶ 1. See also *Envirosolve LLC,* Comp. Gen. Dec. B-294974.4, 2005 CPD ¶ 106 (sustaining protest against orders placed under multiple-award BPAs where orders were valued under $100,000).

Protests of task and delivery orders at GAO are decided following the same rules that apply to other protests, *Triple Canopy, Inc.,* Comp. Gen. Dec. B-310566.4, 2008 CPD ¶ 207; *Bay Area Travel, Inc.,* Comp. Gen. Dec. B-400442, 2009 CPD ¶ 65. Thus, protests objecting to the terms of the task order solicitation are subject to GAO timeliness rules. In *Innovative Tech. Corp.,* Comp. Gen. Dec. B-401689, 2009 CPD ¶ 235, GAO dismissed as untimely the protest of alleged improprieties apparent on the face of the task order solicitation, filed after issuance of the task order, because the protester knew or should have known, upon receipt and review of the RFP, that the task order would be issued for an amount in excess of $10 million, given that it was the incumbent contractor and its initial proposal price exceeded $10 million.

Agencies are required to have a task and delivery order ombudsman to review complaints from contractors holding multiple-award task order or delivery order contracts to ensure that they are afforded a fair opportunity to be considered for task or delivery orders. 10 U.S.C. § 2304c(f) and 41 U.S.C. § 253j(f) provide:

Each head of an agency who awards multiple task or delivery order contracts pursuant to section 2304a(d)(1)(B) or 2304b(e) of this title shall appoint or designate a task and delivery order ombudsman who shall be responsible for reviewing complaints from the contractors on such contracts and ensuring that all of the contractors are afforded a fair opportunity to be considered for task or delivery orders when required under subsection (b). The task and delivery order ombudsman shall be a senior agency official who is independent of the contracting officer for the contracts and may be the agency's competition advocate.

FAR 16.505(b)(6) incorporates this requirement with slightly different wording. While the statute appears to limit the ombudsman's role to multiple-award situations, the FAR appears to extend it to all aspects of all task and delivery order contracts, whether single or multiple award.

Task and delivery orders, regardless of the dollar value, can be challenged through the contract award controversy process if they increase the scope, period, or maximum value of the contract under which the order is issued. See *Global Computer Enters., Inc. v. United States*, 88 Fed. Cl. 350 (2009), *modified*, 88 Fed. Cl. 466 (2009) (provision and maintenance of audit not within scope of technical services task order); *Anteon Corp.*, Comp. Gen. Dec. B-293523, 2004 CPD ¶ 51 (physical deliverables under the task order request not reasonably within the scope of GSA's smart card contract); *Floro & Assocs.*, Comp. Gen. Dec. B-285451.3, 2000 CPD ¶ 172 (task order beyond the scope of a contract for noncomplex integration services of commercially available off-the-shelf hardware and software where it required the contractor to provide management services to assist in support of distance learning product lines); *Ervin v. Assocs., Inc.*, Comp. Gen. Dec. B-278850, 98-1 CPD ¶ 89 (task order beyond the scope when the work was not mentioned in the original solicitation); *Dynamac Corp.*, Comp. Gen. Dec. B-252800, 93-2 CPD ¶ 37 (order for support of a computerized information system outside the scope of a contract that was intended to provide engineering support for an agency's information resources management systems); *Data Transformation Corp.*, Comp. Gen. Dec. B-274629, 97-1 CPD ¶ 10 (operation of a nationwide debt collection system outside the scope of a litigation support contract); and *Comdisco, Inc.*, Comp. Gen. Dec. B-277340, 97-2 CPD ¶ 105 (agency exceeded the scope of its task orders for computer equipment and related services by permitting computer hardware/software to constitute more than its allotted share of a contract).

Task orders were found to be within the scope of the underlying contract in *Outdoor Venture Corp.*, Comp. Gen. Dec. B-401628, 2009 CPD ¶ 260 (delivery order requirement for full concealment covers within scope since the SOW listed variations of Ultra Lightweight Camouflage Net Systems to be procured and noted that other versions not specifically identified could also be procured); *Morris Corp.*, Comp. Gen. Dec. B-400336, 2008 CPD ¶ 204 (logical connection between the broad scope of food service operations delineated in the IDIQ contract — the feeding of individuals housed within a specified Iraqi training camp and/or coalition base — and the food service operations required to feed detainees located within the camp); *Colliers Int'l*, Comp. Gen. Dec. B-400173, 2008 CPD ¶ 147 (task order to conduct feasibility study within scope of IDIQ contract which was broad and specifically provided for unidentified "special studies"); *Relm Wireless Corp.*, Comp. Gen. Dec. B-298715, 2006 CPD ¶ 190 (tactical radio within scope of IDIQ contract because RFP's definition of Land Mobile Radio covered similar assets designated for contingency, tactical or war ready material purposes); *Specialty Marine, Inc.*, Comp. Gen. Dec. B-293871, 2004 CPD ¶ 130 (SOW language encompassed a broad category of ships without limitation to size); *Symetrics Indus., Inc.*, Comp. Gen. Dec. B-289606, 2002 CPD ¶ 65 (retrofitting reasonably falls within definition of depot level maintenance); *Ervin & Assocs., Inc.*, Comp. Gen. Dec. B-279083, 98-1 CPD ¶ 126 (relevant language in the solicitation's SOW sets forth the anticipated services in broad, general, and flexible terms); *Techno-Sciences, Inc.*, Comp. Gen. Dec. B-277260.3, 98-1 CPD ¶ 138 (tasks within scope where the contract specifically contemplated that operations, maintenance, and technical support would include whatever was necessary to support mission); *Exide Corp.*, Comp. Gen. Dec. B-276988, 97-2 CPD ¶ 51 (delivery orders in excess of maximum order limitation and to be delivered after contract expiration within scope when its terms provided for such flexibility); *Master Sec., Inc.*, Comp. Gen. Dec. B-274990.2, 97-1 CPD ¶ 21 (addition of number of hours and contract sites not a material change); *LDDS WorldCom*, Comp. Gen. Dec. B-266257, 96-1 CPD ¶ 50 (the added services could have been anticipated from the face of the contract and were not materially different than the services currently rendered under the contract); *Liebert Corp.*, Comp. Gen. Dec. B-232234.5, 91-1 CPD ¶ 413 (work within scope but quantity beyond maximum stated in contract outside scope); and *Information Ventures, Inc.*, Comp. Gen. Dec. B-240458, 90-2 CPD ¶ 414 (tasks "logically related to the overall purpose" of the agreement).

## II. PROCURING AGENCIES AND OMBUDSMEN

Persons seeking to contest a procurement have always had the option of lodging a complaint with the procuring agency, and some agencies have adopted procedures to handle these protests. Until the mid-1990s, however, there were no governmentwide regulations dealing with agency protests. On October 25, 1995, President Clinton issued Executive Order 12979, 60 Fed. Reg. 55171, requiring all agencies to establish administrative procedures for resolving bid protests. These procedures are required to:

(a) emphasize that whenever conduct of a procurement is contested, all parties should use their best efforts to resolve the matter with agency contracting officers;

(b) to the maximum extent practicable, provide for inexpensive, informal, procedurally simple, and expeditious resolution of protests, including where appropriate and as permitted by law, the use of alternative dispute resolution techniques, third party neutrals, and another agency's personnel;

(c) allow actual or prospective bidders or offerors whose direct economic interests would be affected by the award or failure to award the contract to request a review, at a level above the contracting officer, of any decision by a contracting officer that is alleged to have violated a statute or regulation and, thereby, caused prejudice to the protester.

The provisions of the executive order are implemented in FAR 33.103. This section considers the various ways in which the agencies have responded to the executive order and the FAR.

## A. Jurisdiction

There are no jurisdictional limitations on agency protests because any agency of the government has inherent authority to consider a protest alleging some defect in one of its procurements. The agency protest procedures mandated by FAR Subpart 33.1 apply to all "executive agencies," FAR 2.101. The meaning of this term is discussed in the next section on protests to GAO.

## B. Who May Protest

The FAR contains no rule limiting the parties that may file a protest with an agency. Agencies may consider protests from any party that raises legitimate concerns about the conduct of a procurement; and it is clear that some agency officials, such as the NASA ombudsman, will consider such protests. To determine the scope of an agency's protest procedures, each agency regulation must be reviewed.

FAR 33.102(e) does "encourage" an "interested party" wishing to protest to seek resolution within the procuring activity. FAR 33.101 defines "interested party" as "an actual or prospective offeror whose direct economic interest would be affected by the award of a contract or by the failure to award a contract." This is the same definition as used by GAO.

## C. Time for Protest

FAR 33.103(e) states very formal rules, patterned on GAO rules, on the time for submitting protests to an agency. Protests based on alleged apparent improprieties in a solicitation must be filed prior to bid opening or the closing date for receipt of proposals. In all other cases protests must be filed not later than ten days after the basis of the protest is known or should have been known, whichever is earlier. The agency may, for good cause shown or where the protest raises issues significant to the agency's acquisition system, consider the merits of any protest that is not timely filed. In addition, there is nothing in the FAR that precludes an agency from considering untimely protests on other bases.

The FAR provides some assurance to protesters that an executive agency will not moot a protest by permitting contract performance during the consideration of the protest. FAR 33.103(f)(1) provides that if an agency protest is filed before award, award will not be made unless it is justified in writing for "urgent and compelling reasons or is determined, in writing, to be in the best interests of the Government." This decision to award in the face of a protest must be made "at a level above the contracting officer, or by another official pursuant to agency procedures." With respect to agency protests received within 10 days after award, or within 5 days after a debriefing, whichever is later, the contracting officer must immediately suspend performance unless continued performance is justified for urgent and compelling reasons or is determined to be in the best interest of the government, FAR 33.103(f)(3). Such justification or determination must be approved at a level above the contracting officer, or by another official pursuant to agency procedures, FAR 33.103(f)(3).

Pursuing an agency protest does not extend the time for obtaining a stay at GAO. Agencies may, however, include as part of the agency protest process, a voluntary suspension period when agency protests are denied and the protester subsequently files at GAO. See, for example, DOLAR 2933.103(m):

> If the protest is denied, and contract performance has been suspended under paragraph (i) of this section, the contracting officer will not lift such suspension until five (5) days after the protest decision has been issued, to allow the protester to file a protest with the General Accounting Office, unless the HCA makes a new finding under FAR 33.103(f)(3). The contracting officer shall consider allowing such suspension to remain in effect pending the resolution of any GAO proceeding.

## D. Procedures

Protests to the contracting agency should be submitted to the person designated in the solicitation. Under the standard Service of Protest clause in FAR 52.233-2, this is generally expected to be the contracting officer, but each agency may designate the official to which protests may be sent. When the protester sends in its protest, it may "request an independent review at a level above the contracting officer," FAR 33.103(d)(4).

Agency-level protests should include a complete statement of the complaint that the protester has with the procurement. In adopting procedures for agency-level protests, FAR 33.103(d) sets forth the following legalistic guidance modeled on GAO protest procedures:

> The following procedures are established to resolve agency protests effectively, to build confidence in the Government's acquisition system, and to reduce protests outside of the agency:
>
> > (1) Protests shall be concise and logically presented to facilitate review by the agency. Failure to substantially comply with any of the require-

ments of paragraph (d)(2) of this section may be grounds for dismissal of the protest.

(2) Protests shall include the following information:

(i) Name, address, and fax and telephone numbers of the protester.

(ii) Solicitation or contract number.

(iii) Detailed statement of the legal and factual grounds for the protest, to include a description of resulting prejudice to the protester.

(iv) Copies of relevant documents.

(v) Request for a ruling by the agency.

(vi) Statement as to the form of relief requested.

(vii) All information establishing that the protester is an interested party for the purpose of filing a protest.

(viii) All information establishing the timeliness of the protest.

Agencies are encouraged to resolve agency protests within 35 days after the protest is filed, FAR 33.103(g). Written protest decisions should be sent to the protester and should be well reasoned and explain the agency position, FAR 33.103(h).

The Army Materiel Command (AMC) has successfully used agency-level protests since 1991. Under the AMC's protest procedures, a protest may be filed with either the contracting officer or the AMC Office of Command Counsel. Within ten working days after the protest is filed, the contracting officer, with the assistance of legal counsel, is required to file an administrative report responsive to the protest to the AMC Office of Command Counsel. The AMC protest decision authority will issue a written decision within 20 working days after the filing of the protest. For good cause, the AMC protest decision authority may grant an extension of time for filing the administrative report and for the issuance of the written decision. The written decision is binding on the AMC and its contracting activities. See Office of Command Counsel at *www. amc.army.mil/pa*.

The Department of Energy also has detailed guidance on agency-level protests. See DOE Acquisition Guide, Chapter 33.1 (October 2008). Generally the protest will be decided by the head of the contracting activity, but it may be decided by the Senior Procurement Executive under certain circumstances. Decisions are issued within 35 calendar days, unless a longer period of time is needed. The guidance provides that the contracting officer should make every attempt to resolve the protest through direct negotiations with the offeror with due regard for the need to take corrective action, if appropriate.

One technique used to resolve an agency protest is to appoint an ombudsman. NASA has created an ombudsman program, NFS Subpart 1815.70. The contracting officer must insert a clause substantially the same as the one at NFS 1852.215-84, Ombudsman, in all solicitations (including draft solicitations) and contracts:

(a) An ombudsman has been appointed to hear and facilitate the resolution of concerns from offerors, potential offerors, and contractors during the preaward and postaward phases of this acquisition. When requested, the ombudsman will maintain strict confidentiality as to the source of the concern. The existence of the ombudsman is not to diminish the authority of the contracting officer, the Source Evaluation Board, or the selection official. Further, the ombudsman does not participate in the evaluation of proposals, the source selection process, or the adjudication of formal contract disputes. Therefore, before consulting with an ombudsman, interested parties must first address their concerns, issues, disagreements, and/or recommendations to the contracting officer for resolution.

(b) If resolution cannot be made by the contracting officer, interested parties may contact the installation ombudsman, _____ [Insert name, address, telephone number, facsimile number, and e-mail address]. Concerns, issues, disagreements, and recommendations which cannot be resolved at the installation may be referred to the NASA ombudsman, the Director of the Contract Management Division, at 202-358-0422, facsimile 202-358-3083, e-mail sthomps1@ hq. nasa. gov. Please do not contact the ombudsman to request copies of the solicitation, verify offer due date, or clarify technical requirements. Such inquiries shall be directed to the Contracting Officer or as specified elsewhere in this document.

The scope of this ombudsman's duties extends beyond protests orders — covering all matters concerning contracts with the agency.

## E. Alternative Dispute Resolution

Another procedure for resolving a protest in lieu of either protesting with GAO or litigation is alternative dispute resolution. Alternative dispute resolution includes any procedure or combination of procedures voluntarily used to resolve issues in controversy. These techniques are now recognized and encouraged by the Administrative Dispute Resolution Act, 5 U.S.C. § 571 - § 584. FAR 33.103(c) provides:

The agency should provide for inexpensive, informal, procedurally simple, and expeditious resolution of protests. Where appropriate, the use of alternative dispute resolution techniques, third party neutrals, and another agency's personnel are acceptable protest resolution methods.

## F. Standards of Review

The FAR is not clear on the standards of review that will be used in dealing with agency-level protests. Its initial guidance is the broad statement that contracting officers "shall consider all protests," FAR 33.102(a). See also FAR 33.103(b), which states:

> Prior to submission of an agency protest, all parties shall use their best efforts to resolve concerns raised by an interested party at the contracting officer level through open and frank discussions.

This guidance indicates that a potential offeror can obtain the contracting officer's review of any concern regarding the procurement. In particular, this type of protest would be appropriate when a potential offeror has questions about the meaning of a solicitation or concerns that a solicitation is not properly drafted.

If the more formal "agency protest" procedure is used, FAR 33.102(b) states that the standard of review will be whether a solicitation, proposed award, or award complies with "the requirements of law and regulation." It appears that this is too narrow a statement of the standard of review that will be applied to formal agency protests, because such protests will also consider whether the actions of the contracting agency are reasonable (as that requirement is construed by GAO and the courts). In addition, agencies may adopt broader standards of review in accordance with their own internal procedures.

## G. Prejudice

As discussed below, GAO and the courts have refused to grant relief on a protest unless they find that the protester has been prejudiced by the improper agency action. There is no reason why this rule should be followed in an agency protest, because agencies should correct a problem that has occurred in the procurement process as soon as they are aware of the problem.

## H. Remedies

The contracting officer or an agency protest authority with broad powers, such as the NASA ombudsman, can take any action necessary to resolve a protest that is brought to it. If a protest is brought to the head of an agency using the FAR agency protest procedures, the FAR provides that the agency can take any action that could have been recommended by GAO had the protest been filed there. FAR 33.102(b) states:

> (b) If, in connection with a protest, the head of an agency determines that a solicitation, proposed award, or award does not comply with the requirements of law or regulation, the head of the agency may —
>
> > (1) Take any action that could have been recommended by the Comptroller General had the protest been filed with the Government Accountability Office;

(2) Pay appropriate costs as stated in 33.104(h); and

(3) Require the awardee to reimburse the Government's costs, as provided in this paragraph, where a postaward protest is sustained as the result of an awardee's intentional or negligent misstatement, misrepresentation, or miscertification. In addition to any other remedy available, and pursuant to the requirements of Subpart 32.6, the Government may collect this debt by offsetting the amount against any payment due the awardee under any contract between the awardee and the Government.

(i) When a protest is sustained by GAO under circumstances that may allow the Government to seek reimbursement for protest costs, the contracting officer will determine whether the protest was sustained based on the awardee's negligent or intentional misrepresentation. If the protest was sustained on several issues, protest costs shall be apportioned according to the costs attributable to the awardee's actions.

(ii) The contracting officer shall review the amount of the debt, degree of the awardee's fault, and costs of collection, to determine whether a demand for reimbursement ought to be made. If it is in the best interests of the Government to seek reimbursement, the contracting officer shall notify the contractor in writing of the nature and amount of the debt, and the intention to collect by offset if necessary. Prior to issuing a final decision, the contracting officer shall afford the contractor an opportunity to inspect and copy agency records pertaining to the debt to the extent permitted by statute and regulation, and to request review of the matter by the head of the contracting activity.

(iii) When appropriate, the contracting officer shall also refer the matter to the agency debarment official for consideration under Subpart 9.4.

Because this provision is permissive, there appear to be no restrictions preventing the agency from granting other requested relief following review of an agency-level protest. This includes the authority to allow correction or withdrawal in mistake cases, *Unico Constr. Co.,* Comp. Gen. Dec. B-258862, 95-1 CPD ¶ 42; *National Heat & Power Corp.,* Comp. Gen. Dec. B-212923, 84-1 CPD ¶ 125. However, the granting of relief from mistakes in sealed bid procurements is subject to a number of restrictions within the executive agencies. Contracting officers are permitted to correct clerical mistakes apparent on the face of the bid, FAR 14.407-2, but relief for other types of mistakes must be granted by the agency heads who may delegate their authority to a limited number of central authorities, FAR 14.407-3(e). In all such mistake cases, the concurrence of legal counsel within the agency is required before a determination is made, FAR 14.407-3(f). Numerous subsidiary regulations implement the FAR and contain delegations of authority to grant relief for mistakes prior to award. See, e.g., DFARS 214.407-3, NFS 1814.407, and GSAR 514.407-3.

The current FAR guidance on mistakes in negotiated procurements is unclear. See the discussion in Chapter 6.

## III. GOVERNMENT ACCOUNTABILITY OFFICE

For many years the only forum to consider contract award controversies was GAO, headed by the Comptroller General of the United States. It began to hear protests from disappointed bidders early in its existence, 10 Comp. Gen. 480 (A-36067) (1931); 11 Comp. Gen. 220 (A-39095) (1931). GAO took these protests and issued decisions under the predecessors of 31 U.S.C. § 3526 and § 3529. These statutes give GAO the authority to settle and adjust the accounts of accountable officers and the obligation to render advance decisions to certifying and disbursing officers on questions concerning the legality of payments. The procuring agencies generally acquiesced in the decisions, with the result that GAO protest procedure became firmly embedded in the procurement process.

It was not until 1984 that GAO was given specific statutory authority to hear protests, 31 U.S.C. § 3551 et seq. As originally enacted, this statute gave GAO the authority to order a stay of performance longer than the period specified in the statute, 31 U.S.C. § 3554(a)(1). This raised questions as to the constitutionality of the provision given that GAO is an office in the legislative branch and procurement is an executive function. However, this provision was deleted by § 8139 of the 1989 Department of Defense Appropriations Act, Pub. L. No. 100-463. As a result, *United States Army Corps of Eng'rs v. Ameron, Inc.,* 809 F.2d 979 (3d Cir. 1986), *cert. granted,* 485 U.S. 958 (1988), *motion denied,* 488 U.S. 809 (1988), *cert. dismissed,* 488 U.S. 918 (1988), which had been scheduled for argument to determine the constitutionality of the statute, was dismissed at the request of the Solicitor General.

### A. Jurisdiction

GAO has slightly different authority to hear protests under 31 U.S.C. § 3551 et seq. than under its prior nonstatutory authority.

#### 1. Statutory Authority

The jurisdiction of GAO under its statutory authority depends on the status of the agency conducting the procurement and the nature of the transaction. 31 U.S.C. § 3551 defines "protest" as a written objection to a "procurement of property or services" by a "federal agency" as defined in 40 U.S.C. § 472.

##### a. Status of Agency

The term "federal agency" covers virtually all agencies of the government that operate with appropriated funds. Protests have been taken on procurements of the Tennessee Valley Authority, *Monarch Water Sys., Inc.,* 64 Comp. Gen. 756 (B-218441), 85-2 CPD ¶ 146, *recons. denied,* 85-2 CPD | 335; the Federal Housing Administration Fund, *CoMont, Inc.,* 65 Comp. Gen. 66 (B-219730), 85-2 CPD ¶ 555; the Bonneville Power Administration, *International Line Bldrs.,* 67 Comp. Gen. 8 (B-227811), 87-2 CPD ¶ 345, *recons. denied,* 87-2 CPD ¶ 472; the Federal Reserve Board, *Computer Support Sys., Inc.,* 69 Comp. Gen. 644 (B-239034), 90-2 CPD ¶ 94; the Overseas Private Investment Corporation, *MFM Lamey Group, LLC,* Comp. Gen. Dec. B-402377, 2010 CPD ¶ 81; and Federal Prison Industries, *USA Fabrics,* Comp. Gen. Dec. B-295737, 2005 CPD ¶ 82. See, however, *P.O.M., Inc.,* 64 Comp. Gen. 488 (B-218178), 85-1 CPD ¶ 467, where GAO held that the District of Columbia government is not a federal agency for purposes of the statute, citing 40 U.S.C. § 472, and *United Way of Nat'l Capital Area,* Comp. Gen. Dec. B-311235, 2008 CPD ¶ 96, holding that a Local Fund Campaign Committee is not a federal agency. Mixed-ownership corporations are not considered federal agencies, *Kennan Auction Co.,* Comp. Gen. Dec. B-248965, 92-1 CPD ¶ 503 (Resolution Trust Corporation); *Chas. G. Stott & Co.,* Comp. Gen. Dec. B-220302, 85-2 CPD ¶ 333 (Federal Deposit Insurance Corporation). Nonappropriated fund instrumentalities, as well, are not considered federal agencies, *LDDS Worldcom,* Comp. Gen. Dec. B-270109, 96-1 CPD ¶ 45. The House of Representatives also is not considered to be a federal agency, *Court Reporting Servs., Inc.,* Comp. Gen. Dec. B-259492, 94-2 CPD ¶ 236.

GAO's protest jurisdiction does not depend on the intended use of the items being acquired or on the source of the funds for the acquisition, *CPT Text-Computer GmbH,* Comp. Gen. Dec. B-222037.2, 86-2 CPD ¶ 29. The key factor in determining applicability is that the procurement is conducted by a federal agency. See *Artisan Bldrs.,* 65 Comp. Gen. 240 (B-220804), 86-1 CPD ¶ 85, holding that the statutory bid protest authority is applicable to a procurement that the Air Force conducted for a base golf course, a nonappropriated fund activity. In *Professional Pension Termination Assocs.,* Comp. Gen. Dec. B-230007.2, 88-1 CPD ¶ 498, GAO found that it had jurisdiction over a protest even though the procurement was partially funded with trust funds, because the Pension Benefit Guaranty Corporation, which conducted the procurement, was a federal agency. Similarly, a procurement by a federal agency for a foreign government is subject to the statute, *Cosmos Eng'rs, Inc.,* Comp. Gen. Dec. B-220000.3, 86-1 CPD ¶ 186 (procurement by Agency for International Development for foreign government); *Yoosung T&S, Ltd.,* Comp. Gen. Dec. B-291407, 2002 CPD ¶ 204 (procurement conducted by the Army, but funded by the Republic of Korea); *Ahntech-Korea Co.,* Comp. Gen. Dec. B-400145.2, 2008 CPD ¶ 169 (although Republic of Korea made the award decision, the Army conducted the procurement — it issued the solicitation, evaluated the proposals, and made the award recommendation). But see *Environmental Tectonics Corp.,* 65 Comp. Gen. 504 (B-222483), 86-1 CPD ¶ 377, denying jurisdiction although the contract was financed by a federal agency, because the solicitation was issued and award made by the government of Egypt. See also *Peter Bauwens Bauunternehmung GmbH*

*& Co. KG*, Comp. Gen. Dec. B-277734, 97-2 CPD ¶ 98, dismissing a protest for lack of jurisdiction because the procurements were conducted by an agency of the government of Germany.

GAO will consider a protest when a nonappropriated fund instrumentality is acting only as a mere conduit for an agency, *Premiere Vending*, Comp. Gen. Dec. B-256560, 94-2 CPD ¶ 8 (protester alleged that agency was diverting vending machine requirements to employees' association in order to avoid applicable procurement statutes and regulations). In *Americable Int'l, Inc.*, Comp. Gen. Dec. B-251614, 93-1 CPD ¶ 336, GAO dismissed a protest, holding that in awarding franchise contracts for cable television services and telephone services, a nonappropriated fund instrumentality was not was acting as an agent for the Navy because there was no evidence of significant Navy participation in the procurement process.

Agencies may be exempted from the protest statute by provisions in their own statutes. See *Falcon Sys., Inc.*, 65 Comp. Gen. 584 (B-222549), 86-1 CPD ¶ 462, finding that United States Postal Service contracts were not subject to the protest statute based upon 39 U.S.C. § 410(a), which states that the Postal Service is exempted from any federal law dealing with public or federal contracts except those listed. Because the protest statute is not listed, it does not apply. The Court of Appeals for the Federal Circuit has reached the same conclusion that the United States Postal Service is not subject to GAO jurisdiction in *Emery Worldwide Airlines, Inc. v. United States*, 264 F.3d 1071 (Fed. Cir. 2001). Under Pub. L. No. 104-50, § 348, codified at 49 U.S.C. § 106, Congress directed the Federal Aviation Administration (FAA) to develop and implement a new Acquisition Management System and exempted the FAA from most provisions of federal acquisition law, one being the procurement protest system. Under the FAA management system, protesters should first seek informal resolution of any issues concerning protests with the contracting officer. If resolution at the contracting officer level is not desired or successful, offerors may file a protest with the FAA's Office of Dispute Resolution for Acquisition. Although initially Transportation Security Administration (TSA) procurements were placed under FAA's Acquisition Management System, Congress repealed this provision in order to place all Department of Homeland Security entities under the same system. GAO issued a final rule stating that it would hear protests of TSA procurements covered by TSA solicitations issued on or after June 23, 2008, 73 Fed. Reg. 32,427 June 9, 2008. The Presidio Trust is not subject to GAO jurisdiction because the Trust is statutorily exempt from all federal laws and regulations governing procurement by federal agencies, and CICA is not included in the list of statutes made applicable to the Trust, *Performance Excavators, Inc.*, Comp. Gen. Dec. B-291771, 2003 CPD ¶ 63. But see *MFM Lamey Group*, Comp. Gen. Dec. B-402377, 2010 CPD ¶ 81, where GAO held that the Overseas Private Investment Corporation (OPIC) was subject to GAO bid protest jurisdiction because the Foreign Assistance Act neither expressly exempts OPIC from FPASA, as amended by CICA, nor otherwise authorizes procurement procedures apart from CICA.

## b.  Procurement Contracts

GAO, in considering protests concerning the "procurement of property or services," will not take jurisdiction of protests over the procedures used in other types of transactions. Thus, jurisdiction will be denied over protests concerning grants or cooperative agreements as defined in 31 U.S.C. § 6303, *SBMA, Inc.,* Comp. Gen. Dec. B-255780, 93-2 CPD ¶ 292; cooperative research and development agreements under 15 U.S.C. § 3710a, *Spice Corp.,* Comp. Gen. Dec. B-258267, 94-2 CPD ¶ 257; and "other transactions" under 10 U.S.C. § 2371, *Energy Conversion Devices, Inc.,* Comp. Gen. Dec. B-260514, 95-2 CPD ¶ 121. See also *Exploration Partners,* Comp. Gen. Dec. B-298804, 2006 CPD ¶ 201 (NASA's issuance of Space Act agreements pursuant to its "other transactions authority" is not tantamount to the award of contracts for the procurement of goods and services); *Fred Schreiber,* Comp. Gen. Dec. B-272181, 96-2 CPD ¶ 71 (protests against nonselection of vocational rehabilitation counselors not a procurement of goods or services); and *Michael J. O'Kane,* Comp. Gen. Dec. B-257384, 94-2 CPD ¶ 120 (nonselection of attorneys for inclusion on a list from which attorneys will be selected for appointment to represent financially eligible defendants under the Criminal Justice Act not a procurement of goods or services).

GAO will review a protest that an agency is improperly using one of these instruments instead of a procurement contract, *Rocketplane Kistler,* Comp. Gen. Dec. B-310741, 2008 CPD ¶ 22 (protest alleged that agency improperly used Space Act agreement to avoid the requirements of procurement statutes and regulations). See also *Strong Envtl., Inc.,* Comp. Gen. Dec. B-311005, 2008 CPD ¶¶ 57 (no basis to conclude that the Library of Congress was required to use a procurement contract, or that it was improper for the library to use a cooperative agreement); *Sprint Commc'ns Co., L. P.,* Comp. Gen. Dec. B-256586, 94-1 CPD ¶ 300 (cooperative agreement was properly used - not to avoid the requirements of procurement statutes and regulations).

GAO lacks jurisdiction to consider a protest challenging the award of a "pure" concession contract; that is, a no-cost contract that merely authorizes a concessionaire to provide goods or services to the public, as opposed to the government, *Crystal Cruises, Inc.,* Comp. Gen. Dec. B-238347, 90-1 CPD ¶ 141. However, GAO has recognized that some concession contracts are hybrids that require the delivery of goods and/or services to the government. Where a transaction includes the delivery of goods or services of more than *de minimis* value to the government, it is a contract for the procurement of property or services within the meaning of CICA, *Great South Bay Marina, Inc.,* Comp. Gen. Dec. B-296335, 2005 CPD ¶ 135. See *Shields & Dean Concessions, Inc.,* Comp. Gen. Dec. B-292901.2, 2004 CPD ¶ 42, *recons. denied,* 2004 CPD ¶ 71 (concessionaire required to provide maintenance, repair and other services for government facility as well as facility improvement valued at over $800,000); *Starfleet Marine Transp., Inc.,* Comp. Gen. Dec. B-290181, 2002

CPD ¶ 113 (concessionaire for ferryboat services required to provide janitorial services for agency's docks and piers, equip ferries with public address systems for use by park rangers, and provide transportation for rangers). But see *White Sands Concessions, Inc.*, Comp. Gen. Dec. B-295932, 2005 CPD ¶ 62 (only services that concessionaire is required to furnish are those pertaining to the upkeep of the space in which it operates its business).

GAO will not exercise jurisdiction over subcontractor procurements unless specifically requested to do so by the agency, 4 C.F.R. § 21.5(h). This rule is derived from *U.S. West Commc'ns Servs., Inc. v. United States*, 940 F.2d 622 (Fed. Cir. 1991). In that case the court of appeals, construing language similar to that applicable to GAO, held that the GSBCA did not have jurisdiction over subcontract procurements that were conducted "for" a federal agency. In light of this decision, GAO stated in *Compugen, Ltd.,* Comp. Gen. Dec. B-261769, 95-2 CPD ¶ 103, that it will not exercise jurisdiction over subcontract procurements for the government without a written request from the agency that awarded the contract. Previously, GAO reviewed subcontractor procurements in cases where the contractor was acting "by or for the government," *St. Mary's Hosp. & Med. Ctr. of San Francisco, Cal.*, 70 Comp. Gen. 579 (B-243061), 91-1 CPD ¶¶597; *Ocean Enters., Ltd.,* 65 Comp. Gen. 585 (B-221851), 86-1 CPD ¶ 479. In *STR, LLC*, Comp. Gen. Dec. B-297421, 2006 CPD ¶ 11, GAO held that it would not consider a protest of an award of a subcontract as "by" the government where the contractor drafted the portion of the solicitation pertaining to evaluation of vendor responses, participated substantially in the evaluation of responses and selection of a product for award, and would be responsible for administration of the subcontract. In its analysis, GAO articulated the distinction between "for" and "by" the government, as follows:

> We continue to take jurisdiction where the subcontract is "by" the government. *RGB Display Corp.*, B-284699, May 17, 2000, 2000 CPD ¶ 80 at 3. We have considered a subcontract procurement to be "by" the government where the agency handled substantially all the substantive aspects of the procurement and, in effect, "took over" the procurement, leaving to the prime contractor only the procedural aspects of the procurement, i. e., issuing the subcontract solicitation and receiving proposals. *See St. Mary's Hosp. and Med. Ctr. of San Francisco, Calif., supra*, at 5-6; *University of Mich.; Industrial Training Sys. Corp.*, B-225756, B-225756.2, June 30, 1987, 87-1 CPD ¶ 643 at 5-6. In such cases, the prime contractor's role in the procurement was essentially ministerial, such that it was merely acting as a conduit for the government. On the other hand, we have found subcontractor procurements were not "by" the government where the prime contractor handled other meaningful aspects of the procurement, such as preparing the subcontract solicitation and evaluation criteria, evaluating the offers, negotiating with the offerors, and selecting an awardee. *See Kerr-McGee Chem. Corp — Recon.*, B-252979.2, Aug. 25, 1993, 93-2 CPD ¶ 120 at 4-6; *ToxCo, Inc.*, B-235562, Aug. 23, 1989, 89-2 CPD ¶ 170 at 4-5.

See also *Baron Servs., Inc.*, Comp. Gen. Dec. B-402109, 2009 CPD ¶ 264 (DOE's approval of the issuance of the RFP does not demonstrate that DOE took over the procurement); *Alatech Healthcare, LLC*, Comp. Gen. Dec. B-400925, 2009 CPD ¶ 57 (agency review, comment, and discussion of RFP with contractor did not show that procurement was "by" the government, where the contractor was responsible for significant aspects of the procurement); and *Addison Constr., Inc.*, Comp. Gen. Dec. B-293805, 2004 CPD ¶ 105 (contractor drafted the sections of the solicitation pertaining to the evaluation, evaluated the bids, and selected the awardee).

## *2. Nonstatutory Authority*

GAO's nonstatutory protests are conducted under its advance decision statute, 31 U.S.C. § 3529. This statute authorizes GAO to issue a decision on a question involving a payment the disbursing officer or head of an agency will make or a voucher presented to a certifying official for certification. Pursuant to 4 C.F.R. § 21. 13, GAO will hear procurement protests from a government agency not included in the definition of "federal agency" and protests involving sales of property from any government agency only if the agency agrees in writing to have GAO decide its protests. See, for example, *Delta Timber Co.*, Comp. Gen. Dec. B-290710, 2002 CPD ¶ 161 (protest involving timber sales); *OSRAM SYLVANIA Prods., Inc.*, Comp. Gen. Dec. B-287468, 2001 CPD ¶ 158 (protest involving Defense National Stockpile Center); *Total Spectrum Mfg., Inc.*, Comp. Gen. Dec. B-225400, 86-2 CPD ¶ 673 (procurements by the Architect of the Capitol, which is not a federal agency under the definition); and *Victory Salvage Co.*, Comp. Gen. Dec. B-253006, 93-2 CPD ¶ 92 (protest involving surplus property sales).

## B. Who May Protest

GAO is required to decide protests submitted by interested parties, 31 U.S.C. § 3553(a).31 U.S.C. § 3551(2) states that an interested party is "an actual or prospective bidder or offeror whose direct economic interest would be affected by the award of the contract or by failure to award the contract." This definition is the same as that under the repealed GSBCA protest authority statute, 40 U.S.C. § 759(h)(9). Because the General Services Board applied the same definition and used the same rationale as that of GAO, GSBCA cases are included in this section for illustrative purposes. The key phrases in the definition are "actual or prospective bidder or offeror" and "direct economic interest." The protester must meet both tests. The protest must relate to a particular solicitation or to the proposed award or award of a particular contract, *A. Moe & Co.*, 64 Comp. Gen. 755 (B-219762), 85-2 CPD ¶ 144 (protest against the denial of its application for a master agreement for repair and alteration of vessels does not pertain to a particular solicitation or to the proposed award or award of a particular contract and, thus, does not constitute a protest within the statute).

## *1. Actual or Prospective Bidder or Offeror*

Because *actual* bidders or offerors are determined by those who submit bids or proposals to the government, the major difficulties in this area have arisen in determining whether a party is a *prospective* bidder or offeror. The term has been taken to mean a potential competitor for the type of work being procured, *Tumpane Servs. Corp.,* Comp. Gen. Dec. B-220465, 86-1 CPD ¶ 95 (protester did not bid but would have if specifications were not defective). Parties are not potential competitors and, thus, are not interested parties, if they do not participate or do not have the capacity to participate in the market involved, *Polycon Corp.,* Comp. Gen. Dec. B-218304.2, 85-1 CPD ¶ 714 (firm's mere characterization of itself as a "prospective prime contractor" ineffective when it was a material supplier and had not bid for construction contract awards); *Julie Research Labs., Inc.,* Comp. Gen. Dec. B-219370, 85-2 CPD ¶ 185, *recons. denied,* 85-2 CPD ¶ 294 (offeror was required to do more than provide manufactured equipment, which was the only function the party contended it could perform); *Signal Corp.,* 69 Comp. Gen. 659 (B-240450), 90-2 CPD ¶ 116, *recons. denied,* 69 Comp. Gen. 725 (B-240450.2), 90-2 CPD ¶ 236 (party voluntarily released its proposed team and unequivocally asserted that it did not want to be further considered in the procurement). In *Federal Data Corp. v. United States,* 911 F.2d 699 (Fed. Cir. 1990), the court held that Federal Data was not an interested party because it knowingly removed itself from the bidding. The court also stated that the protester's desire to compete in a later solicitation if the board found the government's conduct unlawful was not sufficient to make Federal Data an interested party. See also *Robotic Sys. Tech.,* Comp. Gen. Dec. B-271760, 96-1 CPD ¶ 229, where GAO found that the protester was not an interested party where the protester during negotiations withdrew its proposed pricing with a promise to perform the contract at pricing to be provided in its BAFO but then did not submit a BAFO or otherwise confirm its earlier offer by the time specified for receipt of BAFOs.

Protesters have been considered interested parties if they would have submitted offers against a revised RFP. See *McRae, Indus., Inc.,* Comp. Gen. Dec. B-287609.2, 2001 CPD ¶ 127, where the protester alleged that the agency improperly waived the RFP's end-item test requirements which had deterred it from submitting a proposal. GAO reasoned that the protester would be a competitor if it sustained the protest and the agency revised the RFP to delete the requirement. Similarly, in *Poly-Pacific Techs., Inc.,* Comp. Gen. Dec. B-296029, 2005 CPD ¶ 105, the protester was found to be an interested party to protest a modification of the awarded contract that permitted the contractor to provide a product that Poly-Pacific was qualified to provide.

Prospective suppliers or subcontractors are not considered interested parties, *PPG Indus., Inc.,* Comp. Gen. Dec. B-272126, 96-1 CPD ¶ 285 (protester did not manufacture or sell equipment); *U.S. Polycon Corp.,* Comp. Gen. Dec. B-254655.3, 94-2 CPD ¶ 53 (protester was only a potential supplier to the ultimate awardee); *Allied Tube & Conduit,* Comp. Gen. Dec. B-252371, 93-1 CPD ¶ 345 (prospective supplier of pipe); *Control Techs., Inc.,* Comp. Gen. Dec. B-251335, 93-1 CPD ¶ 16 (mechanical and electrical subcontractor); *Industrial Combustion,* Comp. Gen. Dec. B-222043, 86-1 CPD ¶ 201 (manufacturer that may supply its product to bidders); *Polycon Corp.,* 64 Comp. Gen. 523 (B-218304), 85-1 CPD ¶ 567, *recons. denied,* 85-1 CPD ¶ 714 (protester that was solely a subcontractor/supplier); *ADB-ALNACO, Inc.,* 64 Comp. Gen. 577 (B-218541), 85-1 CPD ¶ 633 (manufacturer that supplied equipment to potential bidders or offerors).

Associations or organizations that do not perform contracts are not interested parties and cannot bring protests in their own name, *American Fed'n of Gov. Employees,* Comp. Gen. Dec. B-219590.3, 86-1 CPD ¶ 436 (government employees' union, protesting contracting-out cost comparison); *Northwest Forest Workers Assocs.,* Comp. Gen. Dec. B-218891.2, 85-1 CPD ¶ 685 (association representing organizations, some of which submitted bids); *Don Strickland's Consultant & Advisory Serv.,* Comp. Gen. Dec. B-217178, 85-1 CPD ¶ 141 (consultant who refused to identify prospective bidders it was representing). Compare *Windet Hotel Corp.,* Comp. Gen. Dec. B-220987, 86-1 CPD ¶ 138, accepting a protest filed by a representative on behalf of an identified interested party. Although an agent may represent an interested party in a protest where it files the protest on behalf of a specified party and has been authorized to act for that party, *E&R, Inc.,* Comp. Gen. Dec. B-255868, 94-1 CPD ¶ 218, the agent is not itself a prospective bidder or offeror and, thus, is not an interested party to protest on its own behalf, *Bulloch Int'l,* Comp. Gen. Dec. B-265982, 96-1 CPD ¶ 5; *Priscidon Enters., Inc.,* Comp. Gen. Dec. B-220278, 85-2 CPD ¶ 549. See *Total Procurement Servs., Inc.,* Comp. Gen. Dec. B-272343.2, 96-2 CPD ¶ 92, holding that a value-added network used to submit quotes by trading partners via FACNET was not an actual or prospective supplier because it did not submit quotes on its own behalf. Persons acting as private attorneys general are not interested parties, *Julie Research Labs., Inc.,* GSBCA 8070-P-R, 86-2 BCA ¶ 18,881.

Federal employees and/or their representatives qualify as "interested parties" for the purpose of protesting public-private competitions conducted pursuant to OMB Circular A-76, 4 C.F.R. § 21.0(a)(2). In 2004, GAO concluded that an in-house competitor in an A-76 competition did not meet the statutory definition of an "interested party," *Dan Duefrene,* Comp. Gen. Dec. B-293590.2, 2004 CPD ¶ 82. Following this decision, Congress enacted legislation that expanded the definition of an interested party. First, under the Ronald Reagan National Defense Authorization Act for Fiscal Year 2005, Pub. L. No. 108-375, the agency tender official became an interested party for GAO bid protest purposes for A-76 studies involving more than 65 full-time equivalent (FTE) employees initiated on or after January 26, 2005. See *James C. Trump,* Comp. Gen. Dec. B-2999370, 2007 CPD ¶ 40. Subsequently, under the National Defense Authorization Act for Fiscal Year 2008, Pub. L. No. 110-181, the definition of an interested party was again amended, eliminating the prior limitations with regard to the number of affected FTEs, and expanding the definition to include a designated employee agent. The Act provides:

(b)(1) In the case of an agency tender official who is an interested party under section 3551(2)(B) of this title, the official may file a protest in connection with the public-private competition for which the official is an interested party. At the request of a majority of the employees of the Federal agency who are engaged in the performance of the activity or function subject to such public-private competition, the official shall file a protest in connection with such public-private competition unless the official determines that there is no reasonable basis for the protest.

The Act also provided that, with regard to then-ongoing A-76 competitions, the expanded "interested party" definition was only applicable to a protest that "challenges final selection of the source of performance." See *Gary Johnson — Designated Employee Agent*, Comp. Gen. Dec. B-310910.3, 2009 CPD ¶ 22 (since none of the issues raised by the DEA's protest challenge the agency's source selection decision, the DEA was not an interested party).

## 2.  *Direct Economic Interest*

In order to have a direct economic interest, an actual or prospective offeror must be in line for award or be able to compete for award if its position in the protest is upheld. In reversing a holding of the General Services Board that the fourth lowest bidder in a sealed bid procurement had a sufficient economic interest to protest, the Federal Circuit held in *United States v. International Bus. Machs. Corp.*, 892 F.2d 1006 (Fed. Cir. 1989), that "Congress intended the phrase 'interested party' to be a meaningful limitation on the authority of the board to entertain" a protest. The court stated at 1011:

> The board was troubled by the "logic" that would allow the award of a questionable procurement to go unchallenged if the second-lowest bidder did not file a protest. It believed this result would be "contrary to the notions of full and open and fair and equal competition and would significantly undermine the integrity of the procurement and protest processes." *Id.* But, as the Supreme Court has said in an analogous context, the requirement that a party seeking review must allege facts showing that he is himself adversely affected does not insulate executive action from judicial review, nor does it prevent any public interests from being protected through the judicial process. It does serve as at least a rough attempt to put the decision as to whether review will be sought in the hands of those who have a direct stake in the outcome. *Sierra Club*, 405 U.S. at 740. Congress has decided that the coincidence of a disappointed bidder's "direct economic" interest with the public interest adequately accommodates both. By striking a different balance more solicitous of the latter, the board has upset this congressional scheme. Congress simply did not intend for the board to entertain the protests of innumerable disappointed bidders who have little or no chance of receiving the contract.

In negotiated procurement it is much more difficult to determine whether the protester has a direct economic interest in the award. GAO defined the problem in *Meridian Mgmt. Corp.*, Comp. Gen. Dec. B-271557, 96-2 CPD ¶ 64, as follows:

Determining whether a party is interested involves consideration of a variety of factors, including the nature of the issue raised, the benefit of relief sought by the protester, and the party's status in relation to the procurement. *Black Hills Refuse Serv.,* 67 Comp. Gen. 261 (1988), 88-1 CPD ¶ 151. A protester is not an interested party where it would not be in line for contract award were its protest to be sustained. *ECS Composites, Inc.,* B-235849.2, Jan. 3, 1990, 90-1 CPD ¶ 7.

It is easy to establish that a protester is an interested party if the relief being requested is to permit all the offerors to submit revised proposals. For example, in *Meridian*, the protester was held to be an interested party because it was arguing that the agency had improperly waived a mandatory contract requirement in selecting the winner. GAO reasoned that because the proper relief was notifying all offerors of the waiver and permitting them to submit revised proposals, all offerors were interested parties. Similarly, in *Loral Infrared & Imaging Sys., Inc.,* Comp. Gen. Dec. B-247127.3, 92-2 CPD ¶ 52, the protester was found to be an interested party because it claimed that the agency should have established a competitive range and conducted discussions instead of awarding without discussions, and GAO found that Loral's proposal would have been in the competitive range.

A protester will also be found to be an interested party if it claims that its proposal was improperly evaluated and that proper evaluation would have put it in line for award, *International Data Prods. Corp.,* Comp. Gen. Dec. B-274654, 97-1 CPD ¶ 34. See *Northwest EnviroService, Inc.,* 71 Comp. Gen. 453 (B-247380.2), 92-2 CPD ¶ 38 (contention that had its past performance been properly assessed, protester would have been the best value for the agency); *Rome Research Corp.,* Comp. Gen. Dec. B-245797.4, 92-2 CPD ¶ 194 (contention that proper evaluation of management experience and technical qualifications would have made protester the best value because it was the lowest-cost offeror); *A. G. Personnel Leasing, Inc.,* Comp. Gen. Dec. B-238289, 90-1 CPD ¶ 416 (contention that proper evaluation of its proposal would have placed protester in competitive range); and *SAMCA*, Comp. Gen. Dec. B-237981.3, 90-1 CPD ¶ 413 (contention that protester should have been placed in competitive range because deficiencies in its proposal were easily correctable).

If an offeror is challenging the evaluation of the winning offeror and not claiming that its proposal was improperly evaluated, it must challenge all higher-ranked offerors to be an interested party. See *Joint Mgmt. & Tech. Servs.,* Comp. Gen. Dec. B-294229.2, 2004 CPD ¶ 208, where GAO stated that the protester's proposal would have been ranked behind Firm A's, even if it had assumed that the protester's proposal should have received higher ratings than it did. Thus, since Firm A would be in line for award ahead of the protester, and the protester did not challenge the evaluation of Firm A's proposal, the protester was not an interested party. In *Abre Enters., Inc.,* Comp. Gen. Dec. B-251569.2, 93-1 CPD ¶ 239, the contracting officer's price analysis/source selection document showed that the protester was the lowest technically rated, second lowest-priced offeror. The protester did not challenge the evaluation of its own proposal nor the evaluation of the second rated proposal, and had the third highest combined total score for technical and price. GAO found that even if the protester's allegations against the awardee were sustained, the protester was not next in line for award based on the evaluation results and, therefore, not an interested party. See also *OMV Medical, Inc.*, Comp. Gen. Dec. B-281388; 99-1 CPD ¶ 53 (even if protester was correct that awardee should not have been awarded contract, all offerors were found technically acceptable with a low performance risk rating and the protester submitted the fourth lowest priced proposal); *Quaker Valley Meats, Inc./Supreme Sales, GmbH (J.V.)*, Comp. Gen. Dec. B-279217, 98-1 CPD ¶ 163 (protester's proposal was ranked third technically and the protester did not challenge the intervening offeror); *Property Analysts, Inc.*, Comp. Gen. Dec. B-277266, 97-2 CPD ¶ 77 (offeror that had submitted the highest priced of three technically equal proposals not an interested party because price was the determinative factor); *Government Tech. Servs., Inc.*, Comp. Gen. Dec. B-258082.2, 94-2 CPD ¶ 93 (protesters did not challenge the agency's evaluation of the proposals of the higher-ranked offerors vs. their own rankings); *Panhandle Venture V; Sterling Inv. Props., Inc.*, Comp. Gen. Dec. B-252982.3, 93-2 CPD ¶ 142 (protesters were fourth and sixth lowest offerors and neither challenged the eligibility of the intervening offerors for award); *ATD-American Co. — Recons.*, Comp. Gen. Dec. B-275926.2, 97-1 CPD ¶ 188 (protester not next in line for award); and *Ogden Support Servs., Inc. — Recons.*, Comp. Gen. Dec. B-270354.3, 97-1 CPD ¶ 212 (protester did not challenge the evaluation of a higher-ranked, lower-priced intervening proposal). Compare *J2A²JV, LLC*, Comp. Gen. Dec. B-401663.4, 2010 CPD ¶ 102, where the submitter of the tenth lowest price proposal in a low price, technically acceptable procurement was held to be an interested party to challenge the finding that a lower priced proposal was technically acceptable. GAO reached this conclusion because the agency had not determined the technical acceptability or the eligibility of the intervening lower priced proposals.

If an offeror is challenging the evaluation of the winning offeror and also claiming that its proposal was improperly evaluated, but loses on the latter challenge, it must challenge all higher-ranked offerors to be an interested party. See *EMS Ice, Inc.*, Comp. Gen. Dec. B-401688.3, 2009 CPD ¶ 211, where, after finding that the agency had properly determined that the protester's price was unreasonable, the protester was not an interested party to challenge the winning offeror's evaluation because there were intervening offerors in line for award. See also *DynCorp Int'l LLC*, Comp. Gen. Dec. B-294232, 2004 CPD ¶ 187, where GAO concluded that the agency reasonably decided that DynCorps proposal was ineligible for award as written, and since there was another technically acceptable proposal in line for award, even if it were to sustain DynCorps challenges, Offeror A would be in line for award, not DynCorp.

If an offeror not only challenges the award but also claims that evaluation of other proposals was inconsistent with stated evaluation factors and that its proposal represented the best value to the government, it will be found to be an interested party, *Wyle Labs., Inc.*, 69 Comp. Gen. 648 (B-239113), 90-2 CPD ¶ 107. See *Na-*

*tive Am. Indus. Distribs., Inc.,* Comp. Gen. Dec. B-310737.3, 2008 CPD ¶ 76 (offeror in a best value procurement whose price was low is an interested party even though another offeror had a higher technical score); *The Arora Group, Inc.,* Comp. Gen. Dec. B-288127, 2001 CPD ¶ 154 (recognizing an offeror whose proposal was ranked fifth as an interested party only because its protest challenged the agency's application of the evaluation criteria in general, and, if successful, could have placed the contractor in line for the award).

Parties that are ineligible for award do not have a direct economic interest in the award. Thus, they will normally not be interested parties unless they are contesting their ineligibility, *Philis Healthcare Informatics,* Comp. Gen. Dec. B-400733.8, 2009 CPD ¶ 246 (firm did not submit firm fixed price proposal as required by RFP); *Para Scientific Co.,* Comp. Gen. Dec. B-310976, 2008 CPD ¶ 54 (firm did not qualify as a small business concern under the appropriate NAICS code identified for the procurement); *ECI Def. Group,* Comp. Gen. Dec. B-400177, 2008 CPD ¶ 141 (protester had not acknowledged material amendment); *Boehringer Ingelheim Pharm., Inc.,* Comp. Gen. Dec. B-294944.3, 2005 CPD ¶ 32 (protester's drug had not been shown to be effective in the treatment of either of the two medical conditions identified in the solicitations); *Sterling Servs., Inc.,* Comp. Gen. Dec. B-291625, 2003 CPD ¶ 26 (protester had not acknowledged material amendment); *Yoosung T&S, Ltd.,* Comp. Gen. Dec. B-291407, 2002 CPD ¶ 204 (even if Army were to determine protester was a responsible prospective contractor, another offer, which submitted the only technically acceptable offer would still be in line for award); and *Qwest Commc'ns Int'l, Inc.,* Comp. Gen. Dec. B-287459, 2001 CPD ¶ 117 (protester was subject to restrictions imposed by Communications Act and therefore was unable to offer service). But see *Designer Assocs., Inc.,* Comp. Gen. Dec. B-293226, 2004 CPD ¶ 114, where GAO found the protester to be an interested party despite fact that the protester was not an 8(a) contractor, and the procurement was conducted under the 8(a) program, because the protester challenged the decision to place the procurement under the 8(a) program. See also *Allied Tech. Group, Inc.,* Comp. Gen. Dec. B-402135, 2010 CPD ¶ 152, where a protester that had submitted an "unacceptable" quotation was found to be an interested party to challenge the agency's determination that acceptability of the only vendor to submit an acceptable quotation.

Ineligibility for a procurement may result from the offeror's suspension or debarment, *Triton Elec. Enters, Inc.,* Comp. Gen. Dec., B-294221, 2004 CPD ¶ 139 (protester was proposed for debarment); *S. A. F. E. Export Corp.,* Comp. Gen. Dec. B-215022, 84-2 CPD ¶ 58 (protester was debarred). Ineligibility may also result from the restrictive nature of the procurement, *Sales Res. Consultants, Inc.,* Comp. Gen. Dec. B-284943, 2000 CPD ¶ 102 (protester not an FSS vendor); *Air Transport Ass'n,* Comp. Gen. Dec. B-278621, 98-1 CPD ¶ 56 (protester not a small business concern and RFP properly set aside for small business); *Precision Kinetics,* Comp. Gen. Dec. B-249975.2, 93-1 CPD ¶ 226 (protester not an approved source); *S. A. SABER,* Comp. Gen. Dec. B-249874, 92-2 CPD ¶ 403 (protester not a small disadvantaged business (SDB) in procurement properly set aside for SDBs); and *Cable*

*Antenna Sys.*, 65 Comp. Gen. 313 (B-220752), 86-1 CPD ¶ 168, *recons. denied*, 86-1 CPD ¶ 298 (incumbent not permitted to participate in a procurement intended to establish a second source for future competition).

Winners of multiple-award contracts are not interested parties because their economic interest is too speculative. In *Recon Optical, Inc.*, Comp. Gen. Dec. B-272239, 96-2 CPD ¶ 21, two awardees protested awards to each other under a solicitation for competitive proposals that proposed award of two contracts to develop an innovative product. The protests were dismissed on the ground that these parties lacked a direct stake in the outcome of the protests because neither protester could credibly allege that its contract would be reduced, increased, or otherwise affected by the other contract that had been awarded. GAO reasoned:

> While both protesters allege that they do have a direct economic interest in the protest because the contract awarded to the other protester essentially obligates funds which the agency would otherwise be able to apply to their own contract should the proposed costs of their respective proposal not be sufficient to cover the development and testing of the prototype camera, this type of speculative economic interest is not sufficiently direct to render the protesters interested parties. See Travenol Laboratories, Inc., B-215739; B-216961, Jan. 29, 1985, 85-1 CPD ¶ 114.

A potential competitor is an interested party in challenging the propriety of a sole source procurement, *Julie Research Labs., Inc.*, GSBCA 8070-P, 85-3 BCA ¶ 18,375. However, once the sole source procurement has been held to be proper, the potential competitor is no longer an interested party, *Julie Research Labs., Inc.*, GSBCA 8070-P, 85-3 BCA ¶ 18,375. See also *International Training, Inc.*, Comp. Gen. Dec. B-272699, 96-2 CPD ¶ 132, where GAO ruled that a protester was not an interested party to protest the failure of a contracting agency to follow sole source acquisition procedures because the solicitation contained restrictive requirements that made the protester ineligible for award, and the protester did not challenge these restrictive provisions.

## C. Time for Protest

Prior to the enactment of the statutory protest authority, GAO had adopted very restrictive time limitations on the filing of protests in order to ensure that the impact of protests on the procurement process was minimized. Although these time limitations remain in effect under the statutory protest authority, the statutes also contain additional protections when protests are timely filed — providing for limitations on contract award when a protest is filed before award and a stay of performance if the protest is filed quickly after award.

Neither a protester's unfamiliarity with GAO regulations, *Optical Energy Techs., Inc.*, Comp. Gen. Dec. B-401520, 2009 CPD ¶ 153, nor its decision to wait for a response to a congressional inquiry, provides a basis for suspending GAO timeliness regulations, *Professional Office Ctr.*, Comp. Gen. Dec. B-229704, 87-2 CPD ¶ 607. GAO Bid Protest Regulations are published in the Federal Register and the Code of Federal Regulations; protesters are charged with constructive notice of their contents.

## 1. Protests of Solicitation Improprieties

Protests of improprieties in solicitations are required to be filed before the closing date for receipt of proposals, 4 C.F.R. § 21.2(a)(1). The basis for this strict rule was explained in *Caddell Constr. Co.*, Comp. Gen. Dec. B-401281, 2009 CPD ¶ 130, as follows:

> Underlying our timeliness rules regarding solicitation improprieties is the principle that challenges which go to the heart of the underlying ground rules by which a competition is conducted, should be resolved as early as practicable during the solicitation process, but certainly in advance of an award decision if possible, not afterwards.

There are numerous protests that are dismissed because they concern solicitation improprieties. See, for example, *Ball Aerospace & Techs. Corp.*, Comp. Gen. Dec. B-402148, 2010 CPD ¶ 37 (allegation that evaluation scheme would not determine likely costs to the government); *CES Indus., Inc.*, Comp. Gen. Dec. B-401427, 2010 CPD ¶ 43 (allegation that agency improperly conducted the procurement on an unrestricted basis); *Sea Box, Inc.*, Comp. Gen. Dec. B- 401523, 2009 CPD ¶ 190 (conflict between the closing date listed on the GSA e-Buy system and the closing date listed on the RFQ); *General Dynamics — Ordnance & Tactical Sys.*, Comp. Gen. Dec. B-401658, 2009 CPD ¶ 217 (post-award challenge to evaluation scheme that could produce a misleading result); *Armorworks Enters., LLC*, Comp. Gen. Dec. B-400394, 2008 CPD ¶ 176 (allegation that RFP procedures and testing methods were inherently unreliable and deviated from industry practice); *Hart Sec. Ltd.*, Comp. Gen. Dec. B-400796.2, 2008 CPD ¶ 229 (post-closing challenge to agency's amendment requiring successful offeror to hold a facility security clearance); *Gentex Corp.*, Comp. Gen. Dec. B-400328, 2008 CPD ¶ 186 (challenge to inclusion of Federal Prison Industries in competition when it was apparent, prior to closing time for receipt of proposals, that it was a potential competitor); *Apptis, Inc.*, Comp. Gen. Dec. B-299457, 2008 CPD ¶ 49 (challenge that third-party contractor that was to assist in the evaluation of proposals had an OCI was known or should have been known before the closing date for receipt of proposals); *CAMSS Shelters*, Comp. Gen. Dec. B-309784, 2007 CPD ¶ 199 (allegation that brand name product itself fails to meet certain salient characteristics); *K9 Operations, Inc.*, Comp. Gen. Dec. B-299923, 2007 CPD ¶ 146 (challenge to evaluation provisions and that offeror's status as a service-disabled veteran would not be a factor in the evaluation process); *TransAtlantic Lines LLC*, Comp. Gen. Dec. B-296245, 2005 CPD ¶ 147 (challenge that RFP failed to include mandatory provision regarding limitations on subcontracting); *Pitney Bowes Inc.*, Comp.

Gen. Dec. B-294868, 2005 CPD ¶ 10 (challenge of patent ambiguity); *SouthWest Critical Care Assocs.,* Comp. Gen. Dec. B-279773, 98-2 CPD ¶ 22 (alleged defect in RFP); *Envirodyne Sys. Inc.,* Comp. Gen. Dec. B-279551.2, 98-1 CPD ¶ 174 (allegation of unduly restrictive specifications); *Thermolten Tech., Inc.,* Comp. Gen. Dec. B-278408.2, 98-1 CPD ¶ 35 (challenge of use of term "mature technology"); *Neal R. Gross & Co.,* Comp. Gen. Dec. B-275066, 97-1 CPD ¶ 30 (postaward protest that solicitation failed to provide for adequate evaluation of price); *Agriculture Tech. Partners,* Comp. Gen. Dec. B-272978, 96-2 CPD ¶ 226 (allegation that RFP failed to define "complexity," which was used to evaluate each offeror's corporate experience); and *Executive Court Reporters, Inc.,* Comp. Gen. Dec. B-272981, 96-2 CPD ¶ 227 (failure of RFP to include estimate quantities of the various types of transcripts).

Alleged solicitation improprieties that did not exist in the initial solicitation but which are subsequently incorporated into the solicitation by amendment, must be filed prior to the next closing time for receipt of proposals, 4 C.F.R. § 21.2(a) (1). GAO has recognized an exception, however, where a protester does not have a reasonable opportunity to file its protest before the due date for proposals. The cases where GAO has concluded that an offeror did not have a reasonable opportunity to protest solicitation terms, and thus applied the exception are those where the protester faced extremely limited time within which to challenge the solicitation provisions at issue. See, for example, *Dube Travel Agency & Tours, Inc.,* Comp. Gen. Dec. B-270438, 96-1 CPD ¶ 141 (amendment not received until 1 day before proposals due); *Skyline Indus., Inc.,* Comp. Gen. Dec. B-257340, 94-2 CPD ¶ 111 (time for receipt of proposals was "practically simultaneous with solicitation itself"); *Ling Dynamic Sys., Inc.,* Comp. Gen. Dec. B-252091, 93-1 CPD ¶ 407 (protester learned basis for challenging solicitation only 2 hours before bid opening); *G. Davidson Co.,* Comp. Gen. Dec. B-249331, 92-2 CPD ¶ 21 (2 hours and 45 minutes not a reasonable period of time within which to file a protest); *Bardes Servs., Inc.,* Comp. Gen. Dec. B-242581, 91-1 CPD ¶ 419 (protester was informed of basis of protest only one day before proposals due); *ImageMatrix, Inc.,* Comp. Gen. Dec. B-243170, 91-1 CPD ¶ 270 (protester received amendment only one day before proposals were due); *Culligan, Inc.,* 58 Comp. Gen. 307 (B-192581) (1979) (protester received amendment less than 3 hours before bid opening); and *Ampex Corp.,* Comp. Gen. Dec. B-190529, 78-1 CPD ¶ 212 ("the time for receipt of proposals was practically simultaneous with the solicitation, the entire process apparently taking only 10 minutes"). However, where there is a reasonable opportunity to file a protest, GAO will not waive the timeliness rule. See *WareOnEarth Commc'ns, Inc.,* Comp. Gen. Dec. B-298408, 2006 CPD ¶ 107 (protester received the amendments 4 days — or, as the protester describes them, 2 working days — before revised proposals were due and was able to prepare and timely submit the revised pricing information required by the agency); *Concepts to Operations, Inc.,* Comp. Gen. Dec. B-248606, 92-2 CPD ¶ 164 (3 calendar days, one business day, was sufficient time to file protest); *Mobile/Modular Express,* Comp. Gen.

Dec. B-246183, 91-2 CPD ¶ 459 (2 days reasonable period of time to file protest); *Pacific Instruments, Inc.*, Comp. Gen. Dec. B-228274, 87-2 CPD ¶ 380 ("only 2 working days" as argued by protester was reasonable opportunity to file protest); *R&B Equip. Co.*, Comp. Gen. Dec. B-219560.2, 85-2 CPD ¶ 272 (protester afforded "only 2 working days"); and *Reliance Steel Prods. Co.*, Comp. Gen. Dec. B-206754, 83-1 CPD ¶ 77 (2 days reasonable).

Protests of the ground rules of how a procurement will be conducted will be treated as challenges to the terms of a solicitation. See, for example, *Domain Name Alliance Registry*, Comp. Gen. Dec. B-310803.2, 2008 CPD ¶ 168 (post-closing argument that agency should have held discussions with protester untimely where agency unequivocally indicated prior to closing that agency did not contemplate holding discussions as part of corrective action). Similarly, in *Caddell Constr. Co.*, Comp. Gen. Dec. B-401281, 2009 CPD ¶ 130, the agency structured the procurement to allow for the prequalification of firms' eligibility as United States persons and publicly identified prequalified firms. This specifically provided offerors with an opportunity to challenge the eligibility of other potential offerors before the submission of proposals and would have allowed for the early resolution of any eligibility questions. GAO stated:

> Although, as a general rule, a protester is not required to protest that another firm should be excluded from the competition until after the firm has been selected for award, see, e. g., *REEP, Inc.*, B-290688, Sept. 20, 2002, 2002 CPD ¶ 158 at 1-2 (protest that awardee had impermissible organizational conflict of interest), we have applied a different rule where a protester is aware of the facts giving rise to its allegation that another firm should be ineligible to compete and where the protester has been expressly advised that the agency has determined that the firm in question is eligible. See *Abt Assocs., Inc.*, B-294130, Aug. 11, 2004, 2004 CPD ¶ 174 at 2; *International Sci. & Tech. Inst., Inc.*, B-259648, Jan. 12, 1995, 95-1 CPD ¶ 16 at 3-4. In such cases, we have found that the protester cannot wait until an award has been made to file its protest, but instead must protest before the closing time for receipt of proposals.

Generally where a solicitation for an IDIQ contract gives clear notice of an agency's intention to procure particular requirements under an IDIQ contract, any protest to those terms of the solicitation must be filed before the closing date for receipt of task order proposals. However, where the work statement is broad or vague and it is unclear what work will be placed under the task order a different rule has emerged. In *LBM, Inc.*, Comp. Gen. Dec. B-290682, 2002 CPD ¶ 157, the Army argued that LBM's protest of the transfer of the Fort Polk motor pool services to the LOGJAMSS contract should be dismissed as untimely. The Army believed that LBM should have been on notice from the LOGJAMSS solicitation that the Fort Polk motor pool services "could" be ordered under the LOGJAMSS contracts. GAO disagreed, stating:

We have recognized that the increasing use of IDIQ contracts with very broad and often vague statements of work may place an unreasonable burden upon potential offerors, who may be required to guess as to whether particular work, for which they are interested in competing, will be acquired under a particular IDIQ contract. *See Valenzuela Eng'g, Inc.*, B-277979, Dec. 9, 1997, 98-1 CPD ¶ 51 (Letter to the Acting Sec'y of the Army, Jan. 26, 1998, at 2). This burden may be particularly problematic for small businesses. *Id.* In our view, it is unreasonable to require a small business that believes that one specific acquisition should continue to be set aside for small businesses to identify the possibility, at the time proposals for IDIQ contracts to perform a broad and undefined scope of work are solicited, that the specific, and relatively small, acquisition it is interested in may ultimately be transferred to the IDIQ contracts.

The breadth and vagueness of the LOGJAMSS scope of work illustrate this, since it encompassed a "wide range of logistical functions and supporting tasks" and was undefinitized at the time the LOGJAMSS contracts were solicited. Accordingly, we conclude that LBM could not reasonably be aware, and required to protest, at the time the LOGJAMSS contracts were being competed (and apparently years before the Army considered using those contracts for the Fort Polk motor pool services), that the broad and nonspecific scope of work in the LOGJAMSS solicitation could be improperly used as a vehicle for the agency to perform the motor pool services at Fort Polk without first taking the steps legally required regarding a possible further acquisition of that work under a small business set-aside.

Similarly in *N&N Travel & Tours, Inc.*, Comp. Gen. Dec. B-285164.2, 2000 CPD ¶ 146, GAO found timely a challenge that travel management services must be set aside for small businesses, although not filed before the time set for receipt of proposals. Here, the agency advised and issued a draft solicitation that made clear that it would not use GSA's IDIQ contract for the Travis AFB travel service needs but rather would use DoD's contract and would set the procurement aside for small businesses. See also *Ocuto Blacktop & Paving Co.*, Comp. Gen. Dec. B-284165, 2000 CPD ¶ 32 (protest filed at time of task order for landfill capping is timely where solicitations for IDIQ contracts "do not provide clear notice that the [agency] will use these contracts to procure environmental remediation work at [particular] sites"). However, where the solicitation for the IDIQ contract is not broad and vague, but rather gives clear notice of the agency's intention to procure particular requirements under an IDIQ contract, any protest to those terms of the solicitation must be filed before the solicitation closing date, *Datamaxx Group, Inc.*, Comp. Gen. Dec. B-400582, 2008 CPD ¶ 231 (protest untimely where EAGLE solicitation provided clear notice that software development services would be acquired); and *MadahCom, Inc.*, Comp. Gen. Dec. B-297261.2, 2005 CPD ¶ 209 (protest that a solicitation improperly restricts competition to multiple-award task order contract holders, and that the task orders will exceed the scope of the underlying contracts timely when filed before the closing date for receipt of proposals).

## 2. Protests Not Apparent in Solicitation

Protests on any other ground are required to be filed at GAO within ten calendar days after the basis of the protest is known or should have been known, whichever is earlier, 4 C.F.R. § 21.2(a)(2). See, for example, *Rhonda Podojil — Agency Tender Official*, Comp. Gen. Dec. B-311310, 2008 CPD ¶ 94 (protest by agency tender official in competition conducted pursuant to OMB Circular A-76 dismissed as untimely where the ATO filed the protest more than ten days after it knew or should have known basis of protest); *Armorworks Enters., LLC*, Comp. Gen. Dec. B-400394, 2008 CPD ¶ 176 (challenge to solicitation amendment, issued after initial proposals had been submitted, and which did not provide offerors with an opportunity to submit revised proposals, should have been filed within 10 days of issuance of the amendment); *General Physics Fed. Sys. Inc.,* Comp. Gen. Dec. B-274795, 97-1 CPD ¶ 8 (protester's argument against the acceptance of an offer that included a particular subcontractor could and should have been made shortly after award); *Learjet, Inc.*, Comp. Gen. Dec. B-274385, 96-2 CPD ¶ 215 (protest over the interpretation of solicitation requirements untimely because it was not raised within 10 days after the protester was informed in writing during discussions of the agency's interpretation); and *Harris Corp.,* Comp. Gen. Dec. B-274566, 96-2 CPD | 205 (postaward complaint untimely because protester was challenging a defect in the procurement process that should have been raised well before discussions were concluded and an award was made).

There is an exception for protests challenging a procurement conducted on the basis of competitive proposals where a debriefing is requested and, when requested, is required. In this case, with respect to any protest basis that is known or should have been known either before or as a result of the debriefing, the initial protest cannot be filed before the debriefing date offered to the protester but must be filed not later than 10 calendar days after the date on which the debriefing is held, 4 C.F.R. § 21.2(a)(2). In other words, a post-debriefing protest will be considered timely if filed as late as ten days after the debriefing, even as to issues that should have been known before the debriefing, if that debriefing is "required." See *Dominion Aviation, Inc. — Recons.*, Comp. Gen. Dec. B-275419.4, 98-1 CPD ¶ 62 (challenge to protester's evaluation of its performance history as marginal untimely where not filed within 10 days of debriefing); *Black & Veatch Special Projects Corp.*, Comp. Gen. Dec. B-279492.2, 98-1 CPD ¶ 173 (protester had 10 days from date of debriefing to file protest concerning issues it first learned at debriefing); *WP Photographic Servs.*, Comp. Gen. Dec. B-278897.4, 98-1 CPD ¶ 151 (protester had 10 days to raise particular objections concerning the evaluation of its proposal after debriefing); *Global Eng'g & Constr. J. V.,* Comp. Gen. Dec. B-275999.4, 97-2 CPD ¶ 125 (protest untimely where issues were raised one month after they were addressed in written debriefing).

"Requested and required" debriefings also preclude protests submitted prior to the debriefing, *Real Estate Ctr.,* Comp. Gen. Dec. B-274081, 96-2 CPD ¶ 74. This rule is designed to encourage early and meaningful debriefings but to preclude strategic or defensive protests. See also *Minotaur Eng'g*, Comp. Gen. Dec. B-276843, 97-1 CPD ¶ 194.

The rule giving protesters ten days to file a protest after a "requested and required" debriefing is inapplicable where a protester's proposal is eliminated from a competition prior to award, and the protester chooses to delay receipt of a debriefing regarding elimination until after award. See 10 U.S.C. § 2305(b)(6)(A); 41 U.S.C. § 3705(a); FAR 15.505(a)(2); *United Int'l Investigative Servs., Inc.*, Comp. Gen. Dec. B-286327, 2000 CPD ¶ 173. In this situation, a protester may not passively await information providing a basis for protest; rather, a protester has an affirmative obligation to diligently pursue such information, *Automated Med. Prods. Corp.*, Comp. Gen. Dec. B-275835, 97-1 CPD ¶ 52. See *University of Massachusetts Donahue Inst.*, Comp. Gen. Dec. B-400870.3, 2009 CPD ¶ 173, where the protester delayed debriefing regarding the elimination of its proposal until after award. GAO held that challenging the agency's elimination of the proposal, filed more than three months after the protester received notice of the proposal's elimination, was untimely where the protester received all of the information on which the protest was based at the time the proposal was eliminated from the competition.

Protests originally filed with an agency must be filed at GAO within ten days of actual or constructive knowledge of initial adverse agency action, 4 C.F.R. § 21.2(a) (3); *International Garment Processors*, Comp. Gen. Dec. B-299743, 2007 CPD ¶ 130; *Lifecare Mgmt. Partners*, Comp. Gen. Dec. B-297078, 2006 CPD ¶ 8; *IBP, Inc.*, Comp. Gen. Dec. B-275259, 96-2 CPD ¶ 169; *Orbit Advanced Techs., Inc.*, Comp. Gen. Dec. B-275046, 96-2 CPD ¶ 228. In *Timothy J. Penny*, Comp. Gen. Dec. B-221710, Feb. 20, 1986, *Unpub.*, GAO held that these time limitations could not be avoided by having the protest filed through a member of Congress. A requested debriefing does not toll the requirement that a protest be filed within ten days of adverse action on an agency-level protest, *RTI Techs., LLC*, Comp. Gen. Dec. B-401075, 2009 CPD ¶ 86; *M2 Global Tech., Ltd.*, Comp. Gen. Dec. B-400946, 2009 CPD ¶ 13.

For the purposes of timeliness rules, the mechanical receipt of e-mail during a firm's regular business hours constitutes notice of an agency's award. In *Golight, Inc.*, Comp. Gen. Dec. B-401866, 2009 CPD ¶ 184, the protest was untimely because it was not filed within ten calendar days of the Friday that it was received during business hours. GAO rejected the protester's argument that its employee (to whom the e-mail was directed) had left for the day and did not open the e-mail until the following Monday. See also *American Office Servs., Inc.*, Comp. Gen. Dec. B-290511, 2002 CPD ¶ 122 (protester on notice of protest basis as of date of receipt of agency e-mail containing proposal deficiency information). Compare *Supreme Edgelight Devices, Inc.*, Comp. Gen. Dec. B-295574, 2005 CPD ¶ 58 (receipt of an agency-level protest decision on a non-business day did not constitute actual or constructive knowledge of initial adverse agency action). Where an e-mail notification of exclusion from the competitive range enters an offeror's computer system after close of business on a weekday or on a weekend or holiday and is not opened before the following business day, receipt of the notice is considered to have occurred on that business day, *International Res. Group*, Comp. Gen. Dec. B-286663, 2001 CPD ¶ 35. GAO stated that to construe receipt of an e-mail notification as occurring when the notification enters the offeror's computer system outside of normal business hours would lead to a reduction of the three-day period for requesting a debriefing granted by the FAR to a single day when the notification is transmitted after close of business on Friday or on Saturday of a weekend followed by a Monday holiday.

Constructive notice of award, starting the running of the ten day period, will be found where posting of the notice is made to fedbizopps, *CBMC, Inc.*, Comp. Gen. Dec. B-295586, 2005 CPD ¶ 2. But see *Worldwide Language Res., Inc.*, Comp. Gen. Dec. B-296984, 2005 CPD ¶ 206 (announcement of award on DoD's official website, *www. DefenseLink. mil*, did not place protesters on constructive notice of award and thus require protesters to file within ten days of the announcement because DefenseLink has not been designated by statute or regulation as the public medium for announcement of procurement actions).

GAO regulations permit consideration of late protests for "good cause" or if the protest raises "issues significant to the procurement system," 4 C.F.R. § 21.2(c). GAO, in order to maintain the value of the time limitations, has construed these exceptions strictly. The good cause exception is available only for a compelling reason beyond the protester's control, *Oracle Corp.*, Comp. Gen. Dec. B-260963, 95-1 CPD ¶ 231 (argument that dismissal of protest would be "particularly unfair" did not meet good cause exception); *John Cuneo, Inc.*, Comp. Gen. Dec. B-227983.2, 87-2 CPD ¶ 147 (protester's lack of awareness of the bid protest timeliness requirements not a good cause); *Arian Fashions, Inc.*, Comp. Gen. Dec. B-247314.3, 92-1 CPD ¶ 223 (fact that basis of protest arose during a holiday was not a good cause).

The "significant interest" exception is also applied strictly. See, for example, *Merck & Co.*, Comp. Gen. Dec. B-248655, 92-1 CPD ¶ 454, refusing to decide on a protest issue raised late and stating that "we strictly construe and seldom use the exception, limiting it to protests that raise issues of widespread interest to the procurement community." Other decisions finding no significant issue include *Goel Servs., Inc.*, Comp. Gen. Dec. B-310822.2, 2008 CPD ¶ 99 (argument that HUBZone price evaluation preference should have been included in solicitation); *Ervin & Assocs., Inc.*, Comp. Gen. Dec. B-279083, 98-1 CPD ¶ 126 (alleged over-breadth of the statement of work for an indefinite-quantity task order contract); *Source Diversified, Inc.*, Comp. Gen. Dec. B-259034, 95-1 CPD ¶ 119 (whether delegation of procurement authority should have been obtained for a particular procurement); *International Sci. & Tech. Inst., Inc.*, Comp. Gen. Dec. B-259648, 95-1 CPD ¶ 16 (organizational conflict of interest of awardee); *Pardee Constr. Co.*, Comp. Gen. Dec. B-256414, 94-1 CPD ¶ 372 (propriety of solicitation provisions that were incorporated by amendment); and *American Material Handling, Inc.*, Comp. Gen. Dec. B-255467.2, 94-1 CPD ¶ 158 (propriety of solicitation specifications).

GAO is most likely to find a significant issue when it has not ruled on an issue and believes that its decision will be of value to the procurement community. See, for example, *Tiger Truck, LLC*, Comp. Gen. Dec. B-400685, 2009 CPD ¶ 19 (the interplay between the obligation to conduct meaningful discussions and the rules governing TAA procurements); *Celadon Labs., Inc.*, Comp. Gen. Dec. B-298533, 2006 CPD ¶ 158 (the application of conflict of interest regulations to peer review evaluators in Small Business Innovation Research (SBIR) procurements); *Gene Quigley, Jr.*, 70 Comp. Gen. 273 (B-241565), 91-1 CPD ¶ 182 (newly promulgated regulations on individual sureties); *Discount Mach. & Equip., Inc.*, 70 Comp. Gen. 108 (B-240525), 90-2 CPD ¶ 420 (failure of an agency to refer an adverse agency nonresponsibility determination on a small business to Small Business Administration); *Golden N. Van Lines, Inc.*, 69 Comp. Gen. 610 (B-238874), 90-2 CPD ¶ 44 (failure to specify whether option prices would be evaluated); *Baszile Metal Serv.*, Comp. Gen. Dec. B-237925, 90-1 CPD ¶ 378 (DoD's regulatory requirements that SDB regular dealers provide a product manufactured by a small business concern when there is no SDB manufacturer in order to be eligible for an SDB evaluation preference in unrestricted procurements); *Cincinnati Milacron Mktg. Co.*, Comp. Gen. Dec. B-237619, 90-1 CPD ¶ 241 (interpretation of a congressional restriction on the use of appropriated funds); and *F. J. O'Hara & Sons, Inc.*, 69 Comp. Gen. 274 (B-237410), 90-1 CPD ¶ 197 (statutory restriction on the purchase of food). Earlier protest decisions were more liberal in using this exception to the timeliness rules. See *Department of the Navy; Fairchild Weston Sys., Inc.*, Comp. Gen. Dec. B-230013.2, 88-2 CPD ¶ 100 (unreasonable exclusion of a protester from the competitive range); *Sinclair Radio Labs, Inc.*, 67 Comp. Gen. 66 (B-227474.2), 87-2 CPD ¶ 470 (exclusion of a small business from competition); *Adrian Supply Co.*, 66 Comp. Gen. 367 (B-225440.2), 87-1 CPD ¶ 357 (actions by the contracting agency that are inconsistent with statute and regulation); and *Topley Realty Co.*, 65 Comp. Gen. 510 (B-221459), 86-1 CPD ¶ 398 (questionable application of definitive responsibility criteria).

## 3. Statutory Stay

Although the statutes do not limit the filing times for jurisdictional purposes, they do contain provisions that delay award or suspend contract performance pending the decision on a protest. These provisions were enacted to ensure that effective relief could be obtained by successful protesters. If a protest is filed before award, 31 U.S.C. § 3553(c) provides that while a protest is pending, "a contract may not be awarded in any procurement after the federal agency has received notice of the protest" from GAO. If a protest is filed after award but within specified time limitations, 31 U.S.C. § 3553(d) provides that the federal agency shall, on receipt of notice of the protest from GAO, "immediately direct the contractor to cease performance under the contract." Both of these stay provisions have exceptions based on urgency or compelling circumstances, 31 U.S.C. § 3553(c)(2) and (d)(3)(C). In addition, performance of a contract awarded prior to receipt of a protest may be continued during a protest based on a finding that it is "in the best interests of the United States," 31 U.S.C. § 3553(d)(3)(C). These findings must be made by "the head of the procuring activity," and the authority to make such findings may not be delegated, 31 U.S.C. § 3553(e).

The period for notice of the protest begins "on the date of contract award and ends on the later of (A) the date that is 10 [calendar] days after the date of the contract award; or (B) the date that is 5 [calendar] days after the debriefing date offered to an unsuccessful offeror for any debriefing that is requested and, when requested, is required." Thus, an agency must suspend contract performance if it receives notice of a protest by the tenth calendar day following contract award or the fifth calendar day following a timely requested debriefing, whichever is later, 31 U.S.C. § 3553.

Under 31 U.S.C. § 3553, an agency is required to suspend performance of a contract only if the agency receives notice *from the Comptroller General* within ten days of contract award. See *BDM Mgmt. Servs. Co.,* Comp. Gen. Dec. B-228287, 88-1 CPD ¶ 93, holding that there was no duty to suspend contract performance where a protest was filed on the eighth day after award (a Friday) and the agency was notified within one working day, on the eleventh day after award (a Monday). GAO is required to notify on the tenth calendar day after award but the agency received GAO notification of the protest on the eleventh calendar day. There is no recourse if GAO fails to notify the agency of the protest, *Florida Professional Review Org.,* Comp. Gen. Dec. B-253908.2, 94-1 CPD ¶ 17. Notice by the protester to the agency is insufficient to trigger suspension of contract performance, *Technology for Commc'ns Int'l v. Garrett,* 783 F. Supp. 1446 (D. D. C. 1992) (although protester notified Navy of protest, GAO did not notify the agency until the fourteenth day after contract award).

An agency can override a stay on a finding of urgent and compelling circumstances or, in the case of postaward protests, on a finding of urgent and compelling circumstances *or* if the override is in the government's best interests, 31 U.S.C. § 3553(c)(2) and (d)(3)(C). If an agency decides to award a contract or to proceed with performance in spite of the statutory stay, GAO has no authority to challenge this action. However, a protester can challenge the agency's decision to override the stay requirement by filing a suit in the Court of Federal Claims under the Administrative Procedure Act (APA), 5 U.S.C. § 706(2)(a). In *RAMCOR Servs. Group, Inc. v. United States,* 185 F.3d 1286 (Fed. Cir. 1999), the federal circuit held that the Court of Federal Claims had jurisdiction to rule on the validity of an agency's decision to override the automatic stay of an award when a timely protest was filed in GAO. This extends both to 31 U.S.C. § 3553(d)(3)(C) determinations premised upon asserted "best interests of the United States" as well as those based upon asserted "urgent and compelling circumstances that significantly affect interests of the United States," *PGBA, LLC v. United States,* 57 Fed. Cl. 655 (2003). Review of override decisions are guided by the standards as set forth in the Administrative Procedure Act. Under the APA a decision may be overturned only upon finding the agency's action to be arbitrary, capricious, an abuse of discretion, or otherwise not in accordance with law.

Although early Court of Federal Claims decisions suggested a more deferential standard of review should apply to judicial review of overrides, see, e. g., *Spherix, Inc. v. United States*, 62 Fed. Cl. 497 (2004) (deferential review of best interests override), the Court of Federal Claims has taken a far less deferential stance to agency override determinations since its decision in *Reilly's Wholesale Produce, Inc. v. United States*, 73 Fed. Cl. 705 (2006). In *Reilly*, the court identified the relevant factors an agency must consider and address when considering both "best interest" and "urgent and compelling circumstances" overrides at 711:

> (i) whether significant adverse consequences will necessarily occur if the stay is not overridden; (ii) conversely, whether reasonable alternatives to the override exist that would adequately address the circumstances presented; (iii) how the potential cost of proceeding with the override, including the costs associated with the potential that the GAO might sustain the protest, compare to the benefits associated with the approach being considered for addressing the agency's needs; and (iv) the impact of the override on competition and the integrity of the procurement system, as reflected in the Competition in Contracting Act. (Citations omitted)

In addition to these factors, the Court of Federal Claims has identified issues that the agency should not consider in exercising its override rights. For instance, the government's decision to override a stay may not be based simply on its view that the new contract is better than the old one or that the agency simply prefers to override the stay rather than await GAO's decision, *Advanced Sys. Dev., Inc. v. United States*, 72 Fed. Cl. 25 (2006) ("The allegation that the new contract is better than the old one in terms of cost or performance is not enough to justify a best interests determination."); *Superior Helicopter LLC v. United States*, 78 Fed. Cl. 181 (2007) (Forest Service's conclusion that exclusive-use contracts were more "advantageous" than the CWN contracts is an invalid justification for overriding automatic stay).

Justifications based on agency claims of cost savings have proven not likely to withstand judicial review, *Nortel Gov't Solutions, Inc. v. United States*, 84 Fed. Cl. 243 (2008) (rejecting government cost saving arguments on grounds that "similar amounts have been found insufficient to support a best interests override"). In *Automation Techs., Inc. v. United States*, 72 Fed. Cl. 723 (2006), the court held that the estimated $103,196.27 per month cost saving during an expected delay of almost three months in the context of an anticipated five-year $49,500,000 contract with options was insufficient to support an override. In *E-Management Consultants, Inc. v. United States*, 84 Fed. Cl. 1 (2008), the National Highway Traffic Safety Administration reasoned that the benefits of overriding the stay included avoiding termination costs of any replacement contract and maintaining uninterrupted performance beyond the calendar year. The court, however, stated "these are not the sorts of benefits envisioned in the cost-benefit calculation." If the agency will lose a significant amount of money without a stay, it may be able to justify the override, *Chapman Law Firm Co. v. United States*, 67 Fed. Cl. 188 (2005) (without the override the agency estimated it would lose $3 million per month and that government properties would be unmanaged and subject to vandalism).

When several offerors are available to perform the work or mechanisms like bridge contracts are available, the court is likely to sustain a challenge to the override, *Nortel Gov't Solutions, Inc. v. United States*, 84 Fed. Cl. 243 (2008) (agency override was arbitrary and capricious, in part, because the bridge contract provided a reasonable alternative); *Keeton Corrections, Inc. v. United States*, 59 Fed. Cl. 753 (2004) (agency override lacked a rational basis where the agency could have continued awarding short term sole source contracts to incumbent). But see *Alion Science & Tech. Corp. v. United States*, 69 Fed. Cl. 14 (2005) (upholding override noting the time-critical nature of the contract and the lack of multiple vendors).

In considering the effect of the override on the integrity of the procurement system, the court will not permit an agency to point to its likelihood of ultimately winning the contract. In *E-Management Consultants, Inc. v. United States*, 84 Fed. Cl. 1 (2008), the court held that the agency failed to consider the impact of its override on the procurement system and that the override memorandum failed to meet even the deferential standards of APA review, stating at 10:

> [T]he OM [override memorandum] failed to offer any reasoning that shows that it actually considered the integrity of the procurement system Congress created in CICA. . . . The text of the paragraphs in which the consideration is mentioned reads in full as follows:
>
> > I considered the impact on competition and on the integrity of the procurement process, should the agency decline to suspend performance.
> >
> > In my view, the competition process is best served by allowing the awardee to proceed. As noted above, I conclude from discussions with the relevant agency officials that the agency has a reasonable chance of prevailing. Moreover, the protester is not next in line for award. Taken together, these two points lead me to conclude that allowing the awardee to proceed is the fairest approach. As an extra safeguard, however, the awardee's performance will be limited to essential efforts during the pendency of the protest.

Id.

The claimed consideration of the impact on the procurement system do not recognize or vindicate the purpose of the automatic stay. NHTSA first states that it "has a reasonable chance of prevailing." . . . This observation does not relate to the integrity of the procurement system. It relates to the merits of the protest, not to the automatic stay in CICA. NHTSA also states that the protestor is not "next in line." . . . Again, this is not an appropriate evaluation of the impact of the override on the procurement system. The purpose of the procurement system as envisioned in CICA is a fair process in which disappointed bidders can seek review at GAO. GAO was given the automatic stay in CICA to promote these policies. *See* H. R. Rep. No 98-861 at 1435-36 (Conf. Rep. ). NHTSA then states that it has "limited [Centech's performance] to essential efforts during the pendency of the protest." . . . Again, this statement has nothing to do with the integrity of the procurement process. The CICA stay was meant to prevent the "fait accompli" of a contractor establishing a relationship in a new contract with an agency long before GAO issued its decision. *See* H. R. Rep. No. 99-138, at 4-5. Limiting the contractor to "essential efforts," . . . does not address Congress' concerns.

The agency must be able to demonstrate that its override determination was not arbitrary, capricious, or an abuse of discretion based upon the evidence in the record at the time the determination was made, *Advanced Sys. Dev., Inc. v. United States*, 72 Fed. Cl. 25 (2006) (rejecting notion that override "can be an evolving document"). See also *Cigna Gov't Servs., LLC v. United States*, 70 Fed. Cl. 100 (2006) (rationale for overriding the statutory stay in complex, costly procurement for Medicare claims processing was contained in a three and one-half page memorandum with little explanation and generalized conclusions); *PGBA, LLC v. United States*, 57 Fed. Cl. 65 (2003) (finding "nakedness of . . . assumption undercut other critical findings").

Some Court of Federal Claims judges have declined to apply the *Reilly* factors. In *PlanetSpace Inc. v. United States*, 86 Fed. Cl. 566 (2009), the court held that when considering injunctive relief in override cases, the court should only apply the APA four-factor test for injunctive relief and not the additional four *Reilly* factors. The court held that "Congress limited the court's review on an agency's decision in a CICA override action to the Administrative Procedure Act standards." In *PMTech, Inc. v. United States*, 95 Fed. Cl. 330 (2010), the court criticized the strict application of the four *Reilly* factors and found that the agency override was rational based on the urgency of remediation work of hazardous materials and the lack of an alternative course of action. Similarly in *Analysis Group, LLC v. United States*, 2009 U.S. Claims LEXIS 347 (Fed. Cl. 2009) the court stated that while these four additional factors may be helpful in analyzing the agency's override decision, they are not dispositive. The court went on to reason that even applying the *Reilly* factors, it was clear that the override was justified because the stay would jeopardize the Air Force's ability to meet its ongoing national security obligation such as its on going international treaties, health and welfare of military personnel, H1N1 virus planning, troop deployments, air flight planning for military operations in Afghanistan and similar locations, Air Force Counter-Radiological Warfare capabilities, and the implementation of toxins handling procedures and recommendations. Thus, national security was the significant factor in the court's decision. Overrides related to procurements involving national defense and security are more likely to withstand challenge, *Maden Tech Consulting Inc. v. United States*, 74 Fed.

Cl. 786 (2006) (procurement of electromagnetic spectrum engineering services to support war fighters in Iraq and Afghanistan); *Kropp Holdings, Inc. v. United States*, 63 Fed. CL. 537 (2005) ("where legitimate 'interests of national defense and national security' are raised and established to the court's satisfaction, the circumstances under which the court should find it 'necessary' to reach the merits of an override decision should be the exception, rather than the rule"); and *SDS Int'l, Inc. v. United States*, 55 Fed. Cl. 363 (2003) (absolutely essential to the success of the Weapons School and to the quality of our warriors that courseware development, production and presentation, as well as the contractor aircrew training not receive further interruption).

## D. Intervenors

4 C.F.R. § 21.0 defines an "intervenor" as:

an awardee if the award has been made or, if no award has been made, all bidders or offerors who appear to have a substantial prospect of receiving an award if the protest is denied.

Potential intervenors become aware of a protest by the fact that the contracting agency must immediately give notice of a protest to the awardee, if award has been made or, if award has not been made, to all bidders or offerors who appear to have a reasonable prospect of receiving an award, 4 C.F.R. § 21.3(a). Most often it is the awardee that files as an intervenor. See, for example, *B. L. Harbert-Brasfield & Gorrie, JV*, Comp. Gen. Dec. B-402229, 2010 CPD ¶ 89 (awardee filed as intervenor when protester challenged award on basis of organizational conflict of interest); *The Boeing Co.*, Comp. Gen. Dec. B-311344, 2008 CPD ¶ 114 (awardee filed as intervenor when protester challenged technical and cost evaluations of proposals); *Source One Mgmt., Inc.*, Comp. Gen. Dec. B-278044.4, 98-2 CPD ¶ 11 (awardee filed as intervenor when protester challenged technical evaluation of proposals); *EBA Eng'g, Inc.*, Comp. Gen. Dec. B-275818, 97-1 CPD ¶ 127 (awardee filed as intervenor when protester alleged that awardee used bait-and-switch tactics with proposed key personnel). However, offerors that are likely to win an award may also file as intervenors. See, for example, *Government Tech. Servs., Inc.*, Comp. Gen. Dec. B-258082.2, 94-2 CPD ¶ 93 (intervenor next offeror in line). Upon receiving notification of a protest, any intervenor may file a request for dismissal, it if believes that a protest or specific protest allegations should be dismissed before submission of an agency report, 4 C.F.R. § 21.3(b). If the protest is not dismissed, the agency must prepare the agency report and, subject to any protective order, simultaneously furnish a copy to the protester and any intervenors, 4 C.F.R. § 21.3(e). As with protesters, intervenors have ten days after receipt of the agency report to provide comments, 4 C.F.R. § 21.3(i). These comments must be given to the contracting agency and all other participating parties, 4 C.F.R. § 21.3(i).

Sometimes a party will find itself in the position of filing as an intervenor after having been a protester on the procurement. In *Executive Conference Ctr., Inc.,* Comp. Gen. Dec. B-275882.2, 97-1 CPD ¶ 138, the contracting officer, in response to a protest after award, terminated the award and awarded the contract to the protester, waiving its failure to acknowledge an amendment because the amendment was immaterial. The original awardee then protested and the original protester intervened to preserve its award. GAO sustained the protest holding that the amendment was material. Similarly, in *Alice Roofing & Sheet Metal Works, Inc.,* Comp. Gen. Dec. B-275477, 97-1 CPD ¶ 86, a protester persuaded a contracting officer to reverse the agency's award and was awarded the contract. When the original awardee protested, the original protester intervened and assisted the agency in persuading GAO to deny the protest.

## E. Procedures

Protests in GAO are governed by its protest procedures, 4 C.F.R. Part 21. The procedures can be found at *www.gao.gov.*

### 1. Filing a Protest

Protests are filed directly with GAO, not with the contracting agency. A copy of the protest, however, should be sent to the contracting agency at the time the protest is filed.

#### a. Manner of Protest

Protests must be filed in writing, 4 C.F.R. § 21.1(b). They may be hand delivered or sent by mail, commercial carrier, facsimile, or other electronic means. The filing party bears the risk that the delivery method chosen will not result in timely receipt at GAO. Protests are properly filed on a day if they are received by 5:30 p. m., eastern time, 4 C.F.R. § 21.0(g). The entire text of the protest must be received prior to this deadline in order for the protest to be timely, *Peacock, Myers & Adams*, Comp. Gen. Dec. B-279327, 98-1 CPD ¶ 94 (last page of protest received at 5:31 p.m.). Where a protest is transmitted to GAO (either by e-mail or fax) outside of business hours, GAO will consider the protest to have been filed at the time GAO next opens for business following receipt of the submissions, *FitNet Purchasing Alliance*, Comp. Gen. Dec. B-400553, 2008 CPD ¶ 177; *Guam Shipyard*, Comp. Gen. Dec. B-294287, 2004 CPD ¶ 181.

Protests should be addressed to:

General Counsel
General Accountability Office
441 G Street, N. W.
Washington, D. C. 20548
Attention: Procurement Law Control Group

4 C.F.R. § 21. 1(c) provides that the protest must:

(1) Include the name, street address, electronic mail address, and telephone and facsimile numbers of the protester,

(2) Be signed by the protester or its representative,

(3) Identify the contracting agency and the solicitation and/or contract number,

(4) Set forth a detailed statement of the legal and factual grounds of protest including copies of relevant documents,

(5) Set forth all information establishing that the protester is an interested party for the purpose of filing a protest,

(6) Set forth all information establishing the timeliness of the protest,

(7) Specifically request a ruling by the Comptroller General of the United States, and

(8) State the form of relief requested.

In addition, ¶ (d) provides that a protest may:

(1) Request a protective order,

(2) Request specific documents, explaining the relevancy of the documents to the protest grounds, and

(3) Request a hearing, explaining the reasons that a hearing is needed to resolve the protest.

Failure to specifically request a ruling by GAO or to state the form of relief requested has not been considered a fatal defect to the consideration of the protest on the merits, *Air Shunt Instruments*, Comp. Gen. Dec. B-293766, 2004 CPD ¶ 125; *Carolina Auto Processing*, Comp. Gen. Dec. B-226841, 87-2 CPD ¶ 8; *Container Prods. Corp.*, 64 Comp. Gen. 641 (B-218556), 85-1 CPD ¶ 727.

## b.  Copy to Contracting Agency

The protester must furnish a copy of the protest to the agency official designated in the solicitation — or if there is no such designation, to the contracting officer — within one day of filing at GAO, 4 C.F.R. § 21.1(e). A delay in providing a copy to the agency will not be considered prejudicial to the merits of the protest if the delay is not unreasonable and does not delay the preparation of the procuring agency's report to GAO, 4 C.F.R. § 21.1(i). For cases where notification to the agency was delayed but was not deemed prejudicial, see *Container Prods. Corp.*, 64 Comp.

Gen. 641 (B-218556), 85-1 CPD ¶ 727 (delay of one day), and *Land Mark Realty, Inc.,* Comp. Gen. Dec. B-224323, 86-2 CPD ¶ 620 (delay of two working days). But see *Alan Scott Indus.,* Comp. Gen. Dec. B-226012, 87-1 CPD ¶ 338, where a protest was dismissed because the copy to the procuring agency was received four working days after it was filed at GAO.

### c. Detailed Statement

The protest must include a detailed statement of its legal and factual grounds, 4 C.F.R. § 21.1(c). In *Mercer Prods. & Mfg. Co.,* Comp. Gen. Dec. B-251126, 92-2 CPD ¶ 385, GAO dismissed a request for reconsideration because the protester did not provide a detailed statement as to why it believed the awards to be improper. In *Image Contracting, Inc.,* Comp. Gen. Dec. B-245599, 91-2 CPD ¶ 588, GAO found that a detailed statement of the protest was insufficient because it merely stated that the technical specifications for the project were inadequate. In discussing the importance of the detailed statement, GAO stated:

> This requirement is intended to provide us and the agency with a sufficient understanding of the grounds for the protest and with an opportunity to consider and resolve the matter without disrupting the orderly process of government procurement.

In *Coffman Specialists, Inc.*, Comp. Gen. Dec. B-400706.2, 2008 CPD ¶ 211, GAO held that the protester failed to state sufficient legal and factual grounds for it to consider the protest, stating, "by [the protester's] own admission, in filing its protest 'prematurely,' it made 'certain assumptions . . . on the basis of belief,' acknowledging that it 'still does not have knowledge that the bases it makes [in its] protest are true and accurate,' and that it 'makes the allegations based on its good faith belief.'"

Protests will be denied if the legal or factual grounds are unconvincing on their face. See *FPM Remediations, Inc.*, Comp. Gen. Dec. B-401017.2, 2009 CPD ¶ 88 (protester's failure to receive a small business award resulted from its inaccurate representation that it was eligible for a HUBZone award, not from any violation of procurement law or regulation by the agency); *Med-South, Inc.*, Comp. Gen. Dec., B-401214, 2009 CPD ¶ 112 (no evidence to support contentions that the three offerors that responded to the solicitation cannot meet a solicitation requirement to be "established" in the state of Alabama and cannot comply with the "non-manufacturing rule" requirement); *View One, Inc.,* Comp. Gen. Dec. B-400346, 2008 CPD ¶ 142 (bare allegations that the agency "failed to perform a proper price/technical tradeoff" with neither evidence nor explanation to support it theory); *Herley Indus., Inc.,* Comp. Gen. Dec. B-242903, 91-1 CPD ¶ 449 (allegation that item did not meet salient characteristics of brand-name-or-equal specification without identifying the particular characteristics not met); *Blackhorse Servs. Co.,* Comp. Gen. Dec. B-244545, 91-2 CPD ¶ 30 (protest by a low bidder against a higher bidder without setting out and responding to the agency's basis for rejection); *Imaging Equip. Servs., Inc.,* Comp. Gen.

Dec. B-247201, 92-1 CPD ¶ 50 (unsupported assertion that agency's stated requirements were overly restrictive); *TAAS Israel Indus., Inc.,* Comp. Gen. Dec. B-251789, 94-1 CPD ¶ 197 (mere allegation that the agency's determination was wrong); *Federal Computer Int'l Corp.,* Comp. Gen. Dec. B-257618, 94-2 CPD ¶ 24 (protest that evaluation of proposals was improper without an explanation); *Automated Power Sys., Inc.,* Comp. Gen. Dec. B-257178, 95-1 CPD ¶ 76 (protest that merely listed allegedly ambiguous specifications without details or explanation); *Tidewater Marine, Inc.,* Comp. Gen. Dec. B-270602.5, 96-2 CPD ¶ 2 (protest that failed to articulate how or why the proposed work commencement date was unduly restrictive); *Siebe Envtl. Controls,* Comp. Gen. Dec. B-275999.2, 97-1 CPD ¶ 70 (protester's belief that it has been and would be a good contractor and that it submitted a proposal that met all necessary criteria so that it should not have been excluded from competitive range); and *Pacific Photocopy & Research Servs.,* Comp. Gen. Dec. B-278698, 98-1 CPD ¶ 69 (protest that estimates were not accurate without sufficient factual information).

## 2. Actions Following Receipt of Protest

Upon receipt of a protest, an agency has two courses of action. It can either take corrective action or fight the protest.

### a. Solving the Problem

Prior to GAO resolving a protest, an agency may, on its own initiative, take corrective action. In such cases GAO will dismiss the protest, *Canon USA, Inc.,* Comp. Gen. Dec. B-272414.7, 96-2 CPD ¶ 235.

#### (1) DISCRETION TO TAKE CORRECTIVE ACTION

Contracting officials in negotiated procurements have broad discretion to take corrective action, before or after a protest has been decided, when the agency determines that such action is necessary to ensure fair and impartial competition, *MayaTech Corp.,* Comp. Gen. Dec. B-400491.4, 2009 CPD ¶ 55; *Patriot Contract Servs., LLC,* Comp. Gen. Dec. B-278276.11, 98-2 CPD ¶ 77; *Rockville Mailing Serv., Inc.,* Comp. Gen. Dec. B-270161.2, 96-1 CPD ¶ 184; *Oshkosh Truck Corp. ; Idaho Norland Corp.,* Comp. Gen. Dec. B-237058.2, 90-1 CPD ¶ 274. The only constraint on this authority is that the corrective action must be appropriate to remedy the impropriety, *Computing Devices Int'l,* Comp. Gen. Dec. B-258554.3, 94-2 CPD ¶ 162. As long as the agency acts in good faith, GAO will find that the agency's corrective action is appropriate. In *ZAFER Constr. Co.,* Comp. Gen. Dec. B-401871.4, 2010 CPD ¶ 88, the protester argued that the Army's corrective action to permit new and complete proposals, including price revisions, was overbroad and contradicted the explicit representations from the agency counsel that the corrective action would be limited to the project management plan page limitation issue. The Army stated that due to the time lapse between proposal submission and the corrective action, the agency was concerned that the original price proposals submitted by the offerors would no longer accurately reflect the offerors' costs for the project and that the need to take corrective action also provided an opportunity to allow offerors to improve the quality of their technical submissions to account for any changed circumstances between the original proposal submission and the time of corrective action. GAO denied the protest holding that the agency has considerable discretion in these matters and it would not substitute its views for the Army's on how best to proceed, absent a showing that this discretion is being abused. In *Honeywell Tech. Solutions, Inc.,* Comp. Gen. Dec. B-400771.6, 2009 CPD ¶ 49, the protester argued that the agency's corrective action did not go far enough, insofar as offerors should be permitted to submit unlimited proposal revisions. GAO denied the protest finding that NASA's decision to update the past performance information from each offeror was a reasonable way to remedy the identified procurement impropriety while not affecting other portions of offerors' proposals and the evaluation thereof. See also *Pemco Aeroplex, Inc.,* Comp. Gen. Dec. B-310372.3, 2008 CPD ¶ 126 (since prior GAO decision was based on an informational deficiency in the agency's evaluation record, it was not unreasonable for the agency to correct that deficiency by performing and documenting the required analyses based on the information that was already available; protester's assertion that the agency was obligated to reopen discussions with all offerors was without merit); *ICON Consulting Group, Inc.,* Comp. Gen. Dec. B-310431.2, 2008 CPD ¶ 38 (reasonable to allow protester opportunity to compete for an award with remaining unsuccessful offerors, but not permitting protester to compete for one of the two 8(a) contracts already awarded); *CMKC & Maint., Inc.,* Comp. Gen. Dec. B-293803.2, 2004 CPD ¶ 243 (within the agency's discretion to reevaluate the quotations and make a new award determination based on a fully documented evaluation record); *Hyperbaric Techs., Inc.,* Comp. Gen. Dec. B-293047.2, 2004 CPD ¶ 87 (reasonable to solicit and evaluate revised proposals and make new best value determination); *PCA Aerospace, Inc.,* Comp. Gen. Dec. B-293042.3, 2004 CPD ¶ 65 (rescinding contract reasonable where dramatic price differentials may reasonably be interpreted to suggest that offerors had dissimilar understandings of the requirements); *Strand Hunt Constr., Inc.,* Comp. Gen. Dec. B-292415, 2003 CPD ¶ 167 (terminating contract reasonable); *Computer Assocs. Int'l, Inc.,* Comp. Gen. Dec. B-292077.2, 2003 CPD ¶ 157 (limited request for price information from each vendor reasonable way to remedy the suspected procurement impropriety while not affecting other portions of vendor's quotes and the evaluation thereof); *Johnson Controls World Servs., Inc.,* Comp. Gen. Dec. B-286714.3, 2001 CPD ¶ 145 (reasonable in organizational conflict of interest protest to require party to terminate its teaming relationship with conflicted organization and make the contents of a database available to mitigate prior awardee's potential competitive advantage and potential impaired objectivity); *Fisher-Cal Indus., Inc.,* Comp. Gen. Dec. B-285150.2, 2000 CPD ¶ 115 (terminating contract appropriate); *Landmark Constr. Corp.,* Comp. Gen. Dec. B-281957.3, 99-2 CPD ¶ 75 (reasonable to allow improperly awarded IDIQ contract to expire, and place no new delivery orders under the contract but allow delivery orders already issued to be performed pending recompetition and new award); *Patriot Contract Servs.*, Comp. Gen. Dec. B-278276.11, 98-2 CPD ¶ 77 (reasonable to rescind contracts, amend the solicitation, reopen negotiations, and request a second round of BAFOs, rather than a more limited corrective action approach as advocated by protester); *Southern Techs., Inc.,* Comp. Gen. Dec. B-278030, 97-2 CPD ¶ 167 (paying costs rather than recompeting procurement reasonable); *NavCom Defense Elecs., Inc.*, Comp. Gen. Dec. B-276163.3, 97-2 CPD ¶ 126 (reasonable to reopen discussions with all offerors in the competitive range and by request a second BAFO). It is not necessary for an agency to conclude that the protest is certain to be sustained before it may take corrective action. Even if the protest could be denied, the agency still has the prerogative to take corrective action, *Main Bldg. Maint., Inc.*, Comp. Gen. Dec. B-279191.3, 98-2 CPD ¶ 47.

Cases where GAO found the corrective action taken by the agency to have been unreasonable include *Ewing Constr. Co.,* Comp. Gen. Dec. B-401887.3, 2010 CPD ¶ 108 (agency downgraded rating from "significant weakness" to "deficiency" without reopening discussions to inform protester of downgrading); *American K-9 Detection Servs., Inc.,* Comp. Gen. Dec. B-400464.6, 2009 CPD ¶ 107 (disclosure of one offeror's price does not justify agency limiting of discussions to single issue which allowed one offeror to submit acceptable proposal but did not allow protester to improve its proposal); *Cooperativa Muratori Riuniti*, Comp. Gen. Dec. B-294980.5, 2005 CPD ¶ 144 (where agency amends request for proposals after closing and permits offerors to submit revised proposals, it should permit offerors to revise aspects of their proposals that were not the subject of the amendment absent evidence that the amendment could not reasonably have any effect on other aspects of proposals, or that allowing such revisions would have a detrimental impact on the competitive process); *Saltwater, Inc. — Recons.*, Comp. Gen. Dec. B-294121.3, 2005 CPD ¶ 33 (agency did not correct the issue that was raised in the original protest); *SYMVIONICS, Inc.*, Comp. Gen. Dec. B-293824.2, 2004 CPD ¶ 204 (agency provided material information concerning solicitation requirements to a single competitor in a post-award debriefing and the agency subsequently reopened the competition without providing the other competitors with the same information); *Gulf Copper Ship Repair, Inc.*, Comp. Gen. Dec. B-293706.5, 2004 CPD ¶ 108 (agency conducted discussions only with the awardee, rather than with all offerors whose proposals were in the competitive range); *Ridoc Enters., Inc./Myers Investigative & Sec. Servs., Inc.*, Comp. Gen. Dec. B-293045.2, 2004 CPD ¶ 153 (after restoring offerors to the competitive range in order to resolve an earlier protest, and having already conducted discussions with offeror that had continued to be in the competitive range, agency failed to conduct any discussions with the reinstated offerors); *Security Consultants Group, Inc.*, Comp. Gen. Dec. B-293344.2, 2004 CPD ¶ 53 (agency's decision to reopen competition, after making award to protester, in order to correct solicitation defect was unreasonable where record does not establish a reasonable possibility that any offeror was prejudiced by the defect; reopening of competition thus did not provide any benefit to the procurement system that would justify competitive harm to protester from resoliciting after exposure of protester's price); and *Rockwell Elec. Commerce Corp.*, Comp. Gen. Dec. B-286201.6, 2001 CPD ¶ 162 (agency did not correct original problems and only reopened discussions with one offeror in competitive range).

The Court of Federal Claims similarly recognizes contracting officals' broad discretion to take corrective action where the agency determines that such action is necessary to ensure fair and impartial competition, *DGS Contract Serv., Inc. v. United States*, 43 Fed. Cl. 227 (1999). See also *SP Sys., Inc. & DB Consulting Group, Inc. v. United States*, 86 Fed. Cl. 1 (2009) (agency decision to follow GAO recommendation to correct mistake in evaluation of proposals without reopening competition reasonable even though it resulted in selecting a different contractor); *Carahsoft Tech. Corp. v. United States*, 86 Fed. Cl. 325 (2009) (agency made reasonable decision to allow another round of price proposals but no revised technical proposals except permitting original protester to withdraw an unacceptable indemnification clause); *Consolidated Eng'g Servs., Inc. v. United States*, 64 Fed. Cl. 617 (2005) (agency decision to expand the scope of the corrective action to permit revisions to key personnel and subcontractors was reasonable, as was its decision to limit revisions to those areas). Compare *Sheridan Corp. v. United States*, 94 Fed. Cl. 663 (2010), where the court found that reopening the competition after award based on initial proposals when the protest issue was unfair evaluation of proposals, was totally unnecessary and unfairly allowed the losing competitors to submit new prices knowing the winning offeror's price.

## (2) TYPES OF CORRECTIVE ACTION

An agency may take any corrective action that GAO may recommend, such as amending the solicitation and requesting proposal revisions, *Computing Devices Int'l*, Comp. Gen. Dec. B-258554.3, 94-2 CPD ¶ 162; *Federal Sec. Sys., Inc.*, Comp. Gen. Dec. B-281745.2, 99-1 CPD ¶ 86; *International Res. Group*, Comp. Gen. Dec. B-286683, 2001 CPD ¶ 35; canceling the solicitation and resoliciting, *Noelke GmbH*, Comp. Gen. Dec. B-278324.2, 98-1 CPD ¶ 46; reopening negotiations, *Rockville Mailing Serv., Inc.,* Comp. Gen. Dec. B-270161.2, 96-1 CPD ¶ 184; terminating the contract and reevaluating proposals, *Strand Hunt Constr., Inc.,* Comp. Gen. Dec. B-292415, 2003 CPD ¶ 167; *Aquidneck Sys. Int'l, Inc.*, Comp. Gen. Dec. B-257170.2, 94-2 CPD ¶ 122; or payment of the protester's proposal preparation costs, *Southern Techs., Inc.,* Comp. Gen. Dec. B-278030, 97-2 CPD ¶ 167. In addition, subsequent to an ADR "outcome prediction," an agency may re-open a solicitation and allow offerors to make only limited revisions to their proposals, *Consol. Eng'g Servs., Inc. v. United States*, 64 Fed. Cl. 617 (2005).

## b.  Conducting the Protest

The Clinger-Cohen Act of 1996 shortened the time for GAO to decide a protest to 100 calendar days. To comply with this requirement, GAO protest procedures specify the precise times when the parties must take actions or deliver documents. These times are set to permit the parties adequate time to prepare documents while giving GAO time to decide the protest.

### (1) NOTIFICATION

GAO has one day to notify the contracting agency of GAO's receipt of the protest, 31 U.S.C. § 3553(b)(1); 4 C.F.R. § 21.3(a). As discussed above, the time for invoking a suspension of contract performance under 31 U.S. C § 3553(d) continues to run until the agency receives notice of the protest from GAO, and there is no recourse if GAO fails to comply with this one-day notification requirement.

### (2) REQUESTS FOR DISMISSAL

GAO may summarily dismiss a protest because the protest is untimely, the protester does not qualify as an interested party, or the protest fails to meet the requirement of specificity, 4 C.F.R. § 21.5. In addition, GAO rules specifically state that it will not consider the following issues:

1. A matter of contract administration

2. A matter that is in the purview of the SBA

3. Affirmative determinations of responsibility not involving definitive responsibility criteria

4. Violations of subsections (a), (b), (c), or (d) of Section 27 of the Procurement Integrity Act where the protester failed to report the information it believed constituted evidence of the offense to the federal agency responsible for the procurement within 14 days after the protester first discovered the possible violation; see *DME Corp.*, Comp. Gen. Dec. B-401924, 2010 CPD ¶ 44; *Honeywell Tech. Solutions, Inc.*, Comp. Gen. Dec. B-400771, 2009 CPD ¶ 49; *Frank A. Bloomer — Agency Tender Official*, Comp. Gen. Dec. B-401482, 2009 CPD ¶ 174

5. Protests not filed in GAO or the contracting agency within the time limits

6. Protests which lack a detailed statement of the legal and factual grounds or which fail to clearly state legally sufficient grounds

7. Procurements by other than federal agencies as defined in Section 3 of the Federal Property and Administrative Services Act of 1949; i.e.,

U.S. Postal Service, the Federal Deposit Insurance Corporation, and nonappropriated fund activities

8. Subcontract protests

9. Suspensions and debarments

10. Assertions that the protester's proposal should not have been included or kept in the competitive range

11. Decision of an agency tender official to file a protest or not file a protest in connection with a public-private competition

## (3) EARLY REQUEST FOR DOCUMENTS

A protest may include a request for the early release of documents relevant to the protest, 4 C.F.R. § 21.1(d)(2). In such cases the agency should send the documents to the protester as quickly as possible or arrange for an on-site review of documents. When such a request is made, the contracting agency must provide to all parties and GAO a list of the documents released and the documents that the agency intends to withhold from the protester, as well as the reasons for such withholding, 4 C.F.R. § 21.3(c). Objections to any proposed withholdings must be submitted to GAO within two days of the receipt of the list.

This procedure is intended to facilitate the resolution of disputes about the release of documents and to enable the protester to more easily meet the time limitations imposed after receipt of the agency report, 61 Fed. Reg. 39041 (July 26, 1996). However, the procedure is required only when the protester submits a specific request for release of documents at the time the protest is filed.

## (4) AGENCY REPORT

31 U.S.C. § 3553(f) requires that a protest file be made available to the parties to the protest. The contracting agency must file its report within 30 calendar days from the date it receives telephone notification from GAO of receipt of protest, 4 C.F.R. § 21.3(c). The agency must simultaneously send a copy of the report to the protester and any intervenors, 4 C.F.R. § 21.3(e). If a protective order has been issued, parties under the protective order will receive the entire file. Those not under the protective order will receive only a redacted version. If no protective order has been issued, only GAO will receive protected documents.

4 C.F.R. § 21.3(d) provides that the agency report should include:

the contracting officer's statement of the relevant facts, including a best estimate of the contract value, a memorandum of law, and a list and a copy of all relevant documents, or portions of documents, not previously produced, including, as appropriate: the protest; the bid or proposal submitted by the protester; the bid or proposal of the firm which is being considered for award, or whose bid or proposal is being protested; all evaluation documents; the solicitation, including the specifications; the abstract of bids or offers; and any other relevant documents. In appropriate cases, the contracting agency may request that the protester produce relevant documents, or portions of documents, that are not in the agency's possession.

The procuring agency may request an extension of time for submission of the agency report, 4 C.F.R. § 21.3(f). GAO will grant an extension of time on a case-by-case basis, *Blue Rock Structures, Inc.*, Comp. Gen. Dec. B-400811, 2009 CPD ¶ 26; *Military Agency Servs. Pty., Ltd.*, Comp. Gen. Dec. B-290414, 2002 CPD ¶ 130; *Land Mark Realty, Inc.*, Comp. Gen. Dec. B-224323, 86-2 CPD ¶ 620; *Adrian Supply Co.*, Comp. Gen. Dec. B-227022.6, 88-1 CPD ¶ 417.

## (5) REVERSE DISCOVERY

In appropriate cases, the contracting agency may request that the protester produce relevant documents, or portions of documents, that are not in the agency's possession," 4 C.F.R. § 21.3(d). This is known as the reverse discovery rule. This rule is narrowly construed. In *The Boeing Co.*, Comp. Gen. Dec. B-311344, 2008 CPD ¶ 114, Boeing objected to the Air Force request to produce broad categories of documents bearing upon, among other things, Boeing's interpretation of the solicitation and several of its protest allegations. The agency responded that its request was reasonable and limited, and sought relevant documents, which would be "necessary to allow GAO to perform a complete and accurate review of the issues in Boeing's protests." GAO denied the Air Force request, stating that its regulations do not provide for wide-open discovery requests by the agency.

## (6) ADDITIONAL DOCUMENTS

If a protester becomes aware of the existence of relevant documents after submission of the initial protest, it has two days from the time it first knew or should have known of the existence of additional documents to submit a written request for them to GAO and the agency, 4 C.F.R. § 21.3(g). This provision further provides that the agency must then respond within two days either with the documents, or a portion of the documents, and a list or with an explanation for why it is not required to produce the documents. GAO has stated that this procedure may not be used "to obtain information that will give rise to, or otherwise perfect a basis of protest," *Highland Eng'g, Inc.*, Comp. Gen. Dec. B-402634, 2010 CPD ¶ 137; *Quimba Software*, Comp. Gen. Dec. B-299000, 2007 CPD ¶ 14.

GAO will decide any dispute that arises concerning the release of withheld documents and whether this should be done under a protective order, 4 C.F.R. § 21.3(h).

When withheld documents are provided, the protester's comments on the agency report must be filed within the original comment filing period unless GAO determines that an extension is appropriate, 4 C.F.R. § 21.3(h).

### (7) COMMENTS ON AGENCY REPORT

Comments on the agency report must be filed with GAO within ten calendar days after receipt of the report, with a copy provided to the contracting agency and other participating parties, 4 C.F.R. § 21.3(i). Under this provision, if the protester fails to file comments or a written statement expressing continuing interest within the deadline, GAO will dismiss the protest, *Keymiaee Aero-Tech, Inc. — Recons.*, Comp. Gen. Dec. B-274803.3, 97-1 CPD ¶ 163; *Carmon Constr., Inc.*, Comp. Gen. Dec. B-271316.2, 96-2 CPD ¶ 3. In addition, if the protester fails to respond to the rebuttal of any protest issue, GAO will consider that the protester has abandoned that issue, *Dynamic Instruments, Inc.*, Comp. Gen. Dec. B-291071, 2002 CPD ¶ 183; *Strategic Resources, Inc.*, Comp. Gen. Dec. B-287398, 2001 CPD ¶ 131; *O. Ames Co.*, Comp. Gen. Dec. B-283943, 2000 CPD ¶ 20; *Analex Space Sys., Inc.*, Comp. Gen. Dec. B-259024, 95-1 CPD ¶ 106; *Carter Chevrolet Agency, Inc.*, Comp. Gen. Dec. B-254813, 94-1 CPD ¶ 5; *J.M. Yurick Assocs.*, Comp. Gen. Dec. B-243806.2, 91-2 CPD ¶ 245; *The Big Picture Co.*, Comp. Gen. Dec. B-220859.2, 86-1 CPD ¶ 218. Protests are rarely sustained where the protester does not file substantive comments on the report. See, for example *DUCOM, Inc.*, Comp. Gen. Dec. B-285485, 2000 CPD ¶ 144, where GAO noted that the Army provided a detailed response to each evaluation challenge raised in DUCOM's protest. DUCOM's comments on the agency report specifically addressed just two issues, which involved only six of 20 disadvantages noted by the SSEB. In the absence of any argument from DUCOM to the contrary, GAO held it had no basis to find the Army's evaluation unreasonable.

### (8) SUPPLEMENTAL ISSUES

A protester may raise new grounds for protest if the new grounds were first discovered upon receipt of the agency report and the protester raises these supplemental issues within ten days of its receipt of the agency report, *Anteon Corp.*, Comp. Gen. Dec. B-293523, 2004 CPD ¶ 51. The ten day period is strictly enforced. See *Planning & Dev. Collaborative Int'l*, Comp. Gen. Dec. B-299041, 2007 CPD ¶ 28, holding that the rule allowing a time extension for filing comments does not authorize an extension for raising supplemental protest issues.

### (9) FURTHER SUBMISSIONS

Although no further submissions are specifically provided for in the rules, GAO may permit or request further submissions by the parties, 4 C.F.R. § 21.3(j).

## 3.  Protective Orders

GAO is authorized by statute to issue protective orders, 31 U.S.C. § 3553(f)(2). 4 C.F.R. § 21.4(a) provides:

At the request of a party or on its own initiative, GAO may issue a protective order controlling the treatment of protected information. Such information may include proprietary, confidential, or source-selection-sensitive material, as well as other information the release of which could result in a competitive advantage to one or more firms. The protective order shall establish procedures for application for access to protected information, identification and safeguarding of that information, and submission of redacted copies of documents omitting protective information. Because a protective order serves to facilitate the pursuit of a protest by a protester through counsel, it is the responsibility of protester's counsel to request that a protective order be issued and to submit timely applications for admission under that order.

If there is no protective order, proprietary and procurement-sensitive documents must be furnished to GAO but not to nongovernmental parties, 4 C.F.R. § 21.4(b).

## a.  Admissible Parties

Three kinds of parties may be admitted under the protective order: (1) outside counsel, (2) in-house counsel, and (3) experts or consultants. The result is that if a protester is not represented by counsel, it will be denied access to proprietary and procurement-sensitive documents, *PPG-CMS-PSI JV*, Comp. Gen. Dec. B-298239, 2006 CPD ¶ 111; *JoaQuin Mfg. Corp.*, Comp. Gen. Dec. B-275185, 97-1 CPD ¶ 48. In such cases, a GAO attorney will review the withheld documents to determine if they support the protester's arguments, *Encompass Group LLC*, Comp. Gen. Dec. B-310940.3, 2009 CPD ¶ 60; *TEAM Support Servs., Inc.*, Comp. Gen. Dec. B-279379.2, 98-1 CPD ¶ 167. See also *Dominion Aviation, Inc., — Recons.*, Comp. Gen. Dec. B-275419.4, 98-1 CPD ¶ 62, denying a motion to reconsider issues found in the redacted GAO decision that was based on its review of proprietary materials that had not been released to the protester because it had no counsel. GAO stated that the protester had made a business decision not to retain counsel and obtain access to information under the protective order and could not later raise protest grounds based on information it essentially opted not to receive earlier.

In determining whether counsel should be admitted under a protective order, GAO will look to whether the attorney is involved in the competitive decision-making process, *Allied-Signal Aerospace Co.*, Comp. Gen. Dec. B-250822, 93-1 CPD ¶ 201. Where an attorney is involved in competitive decision making, the attorney will not be granted access to proprietary data of another company because there is an unacceptable risk of inadvertent disclosure of protected material, *U.S. Steel Corp. v. United States*, 730 F.2d 1465 (Fed. Cir. 1984).

Although it is often easier to establish that outside counsel is not involved in the decision-making process, GAO will determine the admission of counsel on a case-by-case basis. See *AirTrak Travel*, Comp. Gen. Dec. B-292101, 2003 CPD ¶ 117, where GAO admitted outside counsel based on evidence that the agency had competent in-house counsel to participate in competitive decision-making and the counsel was hired on a case-by-case basis. Compare *Allied-Signal Aerospace Co.*, Comp. Gen. Dec. B-250822, 93-1 CPD ¶ 201, where GAO excluded outside counsel because they were also officials involved in competitive decision-making for the firms they represented. See also *Colonial Storage Co.*, Comp. Gen. Dec. B-253501.5, 93-2 CPD ¶ 234, where GAO did not admit an interested party's counsel under a protective order because the counsel had represented the interested party at a presolicitation conference and had also participated in price discussions between the interested party and the agency. Although an individual outside counsel may be excluded from admission under the protective order, other attorneys from the same law firm may be admitted if adequate procedures are in place to guarantee access by only those attorneys admitted, *Mine Safety Appliances Co.*, Comp. Gen. Dec. B-242379.2, 91-2 CPD 506.

In-house counsel who are not involved in competitive decision making may be admitted under a protective order when the risk of inadvertent disclosure of proprietary or procurement-sensitive information is small, *Robbins-Gioia, Inc.*, Comp. Gen. Dec. B-274318, 96-2 CPD ¶ 222. In *Earle Palmer Brown Cos.*, Comp. Gen. Dec. B-243544, 91-2 CPD ¶ 134, GAO stated:

> In determining whether to grant access to protected material, we consider such factors as whether counsel primarily advises on litigation matters or also advises on pricing and production decisions, including the review of bids and proposals, the degree of physical separation and security with respect to those who participate in competitive decision-making and level of supervision to which in-house counsel is subject.

Here, GAO denied admittance under the protective order, stating that the direct relationship between the chief executive officer of the company and in-house counsel made the risk of inadvertent disclosure too high. Similarly in *McDonnell Douglas Corp.*, Comp. Gen. Dec. B-259694.2, 95-2 CPD ¶ 51, GAO denied admittance under the protective order because the in-house counsel were in the position of advising the firm's competitive strategists. See also *TRW, Inc.*, Comp. Gen. Dec. B-243450.2, 91-2 CPD ¶ 160, where in denying admittance under the protective order, GAO stated that there were only two attorneys in the office and, thus, the general legal counsel would likely be relied on to render legal advice on many subjects, including business-related decisions.

Similarly, with regard to experts or consultants, if the risk of inadvertent disclosure is too high, GAO will not admit such individuals under a protective order. In *Systems Research & Applications Corp.*, Comp. Gen. Dec. B-299818,

2008 CPD ¶ 28, GAO held that admission of a consultant to a GAO protective order was appropriate, over the objection that the consultant once held a position with the protester and that the consultant's daughter was currently employed by the protester. GAO stated that the record showed that the consultant had no continuing interest in the protester and the consultant's daughter held a relatively low-level position with the protester in a division that was unrelated to the work to be performed under the protested contract. In *Restoration & Closure Servs., LLC*, Comp. Gen. Dec. B-295663.12, 2005 CPD ¶ 92, GAO denied the consultants' applications for admission to the protective order. The applications agreed to restrict the consultants' activities only with regard to the particular site for the procurement being protested and thus permitted the consultants to engage or assist in the preparation of proposals for the same type of work at other sites where a party to the protest could be a competitor. *Bendix Field Eng'g Corp.*, Comp. Gen. Dec. B-246236, 92-1 CPD ¶ 227, is an interesting case where the agency requested that admission of experts to a protective order be made contingent upon a promise to avoid participation in future procurements for prepositioning for a period of five years. GAO found this to be reasonable given the large dollar value of the contract and the competition-sensitive nature of the information to be made available to the experts.

Even if there is little risk of inadvertent disclosure, if the information is highly sensitive, GAO may decline to admit experts or consultants, *EER Sys. Corp.*, Comp. Gen. Dec. B-256383, 94-1 CPD ¶ 354 (information contained proprietary engineering approaches and solutions that would be invaluable to any practicing engineer).

If the terms of the protective order are violated, both counsel and client are subject to a variety of sanctions, including dismissal of the protect. See *PWC Logistics Servs. Co. KSC(c)*, Comp. Gen. Dec. B-310559, 2008 CPD ¶ 25 (GAO dismissed protest after protester's attorney, who had been admitted under protective order, revealed protected information to protester); *Network Secs. Tech., Inc.*, Comp. Gen. Dec. B-290741.2, 2002 CPD ¶ 193 (GAO provides notice that, in a future case, it might impose the sanction of dismissal where protester's attorney discloses protected information to client).

### b. Procedure

An individual seeking admission under a protective order must submit an application to GAO with copies furnished to all other parties, 4 C.F.R. § 21.4(c). See Guide to GAO Protective Orders, GAO-09-770SP (June 2009) for sample forms. Although there is no time limit for filing an application, it should be done as soon as possible. Parties have two days to object to the applicant's admission, 4 C.F.R. § 21.4(c). GAO may, however, consider objections raised after that time.

## 4.  *Alternative Dispute Resolution*

GAO has also adopted alternative dispute resolution (ADR) procedures to more efficiently resolve protests. 4 C.F.R. § 21.0(h) provides:

> Alternative dispute resolution encompasses various means of resolving cases expeditiously, without a written decision, including techniques such as outcome prediction and negotiation assistance.

GAO may use alternative dispute resolution procedures at the request of one or more of the parties, or where GAO deems appropriate. This may take the form of negotiation assistance either before or after a protest is filed, or outcome prediction, where GAO will advise the parties of the likely outcome of the protest in order to allow the party likely to be unsuccessful to take appropriate action to resolve the protest without a written decision.

With negotiation assistance ADR, a GAO attorney acts as a facilitator. If settlement is reached, the protest is withdrawn or rendered academic. If no settlement is reached, GAO will issue a written decision.

With outcome prediction ADR, a GAO attorney concludes, based on precedent and/or facts, and with the concurrence of supervising attorneys, that one party is likely to prevail. It is initiated either by a party's request or by GAO attorney. The purpose is to share the view of GAO regarding the likely outcome, therein saving the parties' time and resources. These predictions have proven to be highly reliable — with the result that when a party is advised that it is likely to lose the protest, it should proceed in accordance with the prediction.

## 5.  *Hearings*

In 1991 GAO revised its bid protest regulations to permit a hearing on the protest at the request of one of the parties or on its own initiative, 4 C.F.R. § 21.7(a). The hearing replaced the former administrative conference proceedings. A hearing is not automatic but, rather, is held at the discretion of GAO, *Jack Faucett Assocs.*, Comp. Gen. Dec. B-254421, 94-2 CPD ¶ 72. Requests for hearings must set forth the reasons why a hearing is necessary, 4 C.F.R. § 21.7(a). See *Spectrum Sys., Inc.*, Comp. Gen. Dec. B-401130, 2009 CPD ¶ 110, denying a request for a hearing because the protester provided no reasonable basis for the necessity of a hearing and no legitimate reason for a hearing was apparent. GAO stated:

> As a general rule, we conduct hearings where there is a factual dispute between the parties which cannot be resolved without oral examination or without assessing witness credibility, or where an issue is so complex that developing the protest record through a hearing is more efficient and less burdensome than proceeding with written pleadings only. Absent evidence that a protest record is questionable

or incomplete, this Office will not hold a bid protest hearing merely to permit the protester to orally reiterate its protest allegations or otherwise search for additional grounds of protest since such action would undermine our ability to resolve protests expeditiously and without undue disruption of the procurement process.

A prehearing conference (usually by telephone) is generally conducted prior to the hearing to decide on the timing, the procedures to be followed, the issues to be considered, and the witnesses who will be called to testify, 4 C.F.R. § 21.7(b).

Generally, hearings are conducted as soon as practicable after receipt by the parties of the agency report and relevant documents, 4 C.F.R. § 21.7(c). Hearings are usually limited to one day and are conducted at GAO in Washington, D.C., or, at the discretion of GAO, at other locations, 4 C.F.R. § 21.7(c).

Witnesses are not sworn but are reminded that false testimony may subject them to criminal penalties. If a witness fails to appear or to answer a question, GAO may draw inferences unfavorable to the party for whom the witness would have testified, 4 C.F.R. § 21.7(f). In *HEROS, Inc.*, Comp. Gen. Dec. B-292043, 2003 CPD ¶ 111, GAO concluded that the sole source contractor did not have proprietary data blocking a competitive procurement, based partly on the fact the company refused to permit any cross-examination of its key witnesses. See also *Network Sec. Techs., Inc.*, Comp. Gen. Dec. B-290741.2, 2002 CPD ¶ 193 (GAO drew unfavorable inference regarding a violation of a protective order because of former counsel's failure to appear at GAO hearing); *Du & Assocs., Inc.*, Comp. Gen. Dec. B-280283.3, 98-2 CPD ¶ 156 (GAO inferred that a CO did not give a purported instruction to the protester because neither a witness nor a document alleged to prove the instruction were produced).

Posthearing comments are to be submitted within five days of the hearing unless GAO sets a different time, 4 C.F.R. § 21.7(g).

## 6. Time for Decision

Under the original statute in the CICA establishing GAO protest authority, GAO was given 90 working days to resolve a protest. The FASA restated this time as 125 calendar days. The Clinger-Cohen Act of 1996 shortened this time to 100 *calendar* days.

### a. Statutory Deadline

The 100 calendar days deadline for a decision begins the day the protest is submitted to GAO, 31 U.S.C. § 3554(a)(1). Although there is no specific exception authorizing an extension of time, where supplemental protests have been filed, GAO may "roll over" a protest — that is, dismiss the earlier protest and incorporate it into the last supplemental protest, 31 U.S.C. § 3554(a)(2). This, in effect, can extend the time taken to have the protest decided well beyond the 100-calendar-day period.

## b.  Express Option

In cases that can be decided on an expeditious basis, GAO may decide to use the "express option procedures." The FASA amended the express option process to require completion within 65 working days, Pub. L. No. 103-355, § 1403(a). The Clinger-Cohen Act of 1996 shortened this to 65 calendar days. A request for use of the express option may be submitted by any party in writing and must be received by GAO within five days after the protest or supplemental protest is filed, 4 C.F.R. § 21.10(c). When the express option is used, the following schedule applies, as set forth in 4 C.F.R. § 21.10(d):

> (1) The contracting agency shall file a complete report with GAO and the parties within 20 days after it receives notice from GAO that the express option will be used.

> (2) Comments on the agency report shall be filed with GAO and the other parties within 5 days after receipt of the report.

> (3) If a hearing is held, no separate comments on the agency report under paragraph (d)(2) of this section should be submitted unless specifically requested by GAO. Consolidated comments on the agency report and hearing shall be filed within 5 days after the hearing was held or as specified by GAO.

> (4) Where circumstances demonstrate that a case is no longer suitable for resolution using the express option, GAO shall establish a new schedule for submissions by the parties.

For cases using the express option procedures, see *B&S Transp., Inc.*, Comp. Gen. Dec. B-299144, 2007 CPD ¶ 16 (granted agency's request to use the express option where agency contended that fast-tracking would allow it to meet its deadlines in the Army's Base Realignment and Closure plan); *AshBritt Inc.*, Comp. Gen. Dec. B-297889, 2006 CPD ¶ 48 (express option used pursuant to agency request); *Integrated Support Sys. Inc.*, Comp. Gen. Dec. B-283137.2, 99-2 CPD ¶ 51; *Aalco Forwarding, Inc.*, Comp. Gen. Dec. B-277241.20, 98-2 CPD ¶ 1 (express option utilized in procurement with 99 protesters); and *Possehn Consulting*, Comp. Gen. Dec. B-278579, 98-1 CPD ¶ 10.

## c.  Summary Decision and Accelerated Schedule

At the request of a party or on its own initiative, GAO may set up an accelerated schedule for deciding a protest and may issue a summary decision on a protest, 4 C.F.R. § 21.10(e).

## d.  Decision Distribution

A hard copy of the decision is to be made available to each of the parties, as well as to the public, unless the decision is protected. If the decision is protected, only the parties under the protective order and the contracting agency will receive copies. Protected decisions are redacted and then made available to the public. Protest decisions are available electronically, per 4 C.F.R. § 21.12, at *http:// www. gpoaccess. gov/gaodecisions/index. html*. They are also available at *http:// gao. gov* (search for "legal decisions & opinions").

## 7. Reconsiderations

GAO will reconsider a bid protest decision at the request of a protester, an intervenor, or a federal agency involved in the protest, 4 C.F.R. § 21.14. Copies of the request must be sent to all parties that participated in the protest.

The request for reconsideration must be filed within ten calendar days of the date the basis for the request for reconsideration was or should have been known, 4 C.F.R. § 21.14(b). Normally, that is ten days after receipt of the decision, but if the protester learns of the decision in some other way, the ten-day rule will be enforced strictly. See *Speedy Food Serv., Inc.,* Comp. Gen. Dec. B-274406.2, 97-1 CPD ¶ 5, where the request for reconsideration was dismissed as untimely because it was not filed within ten days of the time the protester saw the decision on the Internet. In *Sodexho Mgmt., Inc. — Costs,* Comp. Gen. Dec. B-289605.3, 2003 CPD ¶ 136, GAO found an untimely request when the agency did not file within ten days of learning of the basis for its request for reconsideration when the protester submitted its initial cost claim with supporting documentation.

The request for reconsideration must do more than restate the arguments in the initial protest. 4 C.F.R. § 21.14(a) provides:

> GAO will not consider a request for reconsideration that does not contain a detailed statement of the factual and legal grounds upon which reversal or modification is deemed warranted, specifying any errors of law made or information not previously considered.

In *Tri-Star Indus.,* Comp. Gen. Dec. B-254767.3, 94-1 CPD ¶ 388, GAO stated that the request for reconsideration must be based on (1) the failure to consider evidence that should have been considered, (2) newly discovered evidence that the party could not reasonably have furnished for the initial consideration, or (3) errors of law. See *MadahCom, Inc. — Recons.,* Comp. Gen. Dec. B-297261.2, 2005 CPD ¶ 209 (wrong timeliness standard applied); *Department of the Navy,* Comp. Gen. Dec. B-237342.2, 90-2 CPD ¶ 39 (GAO misread agency record); and *Gracon Corp.,* Comp. Gen. Dec. B-236603.2, 90-1 CPD ¶ 496 (labor hours for electrical work considered in prior protest were in error). More often, the protester fails to provide a basis for reconsideration. See *Small Business Admin. — Recons.,* Comp. Gen. Dec. B-401057.2, 2009 CPD ¶ 148 (SBA's request for reconsideration primarily states its disagreement with GAO legal analysis regarding the statutory requirements for HUBZone set asides); *Metro Machine Corp. — Recons. &*

*Modification of Recommendation*, Comp. Gen. Dec. B-311245.5, 2008 CPD ¶ 167 (awardee/requester showed no error in, but simply disagreed with, GAO recommendation that the agency conduct meaningful discussions); *Shields & Dean Concessions, Inc. — Recons.*, Comp. Gen. Dec. B-292901.4, 2004 CPD ¶ 71 (decision contained no errors of fact or law, or present information not previously considered); *Social Security Administration; MCI WorldCom Commc'ns, Inc. — Recons.*, Comp. Gen. Dec. B-2086201.4, 2001 CPD ¶ 157 (GAO decision did not err in identifying the approximate potential value of Rockwell's price reduction under a fair and proper competition); and *RGII Techs., Inc. — Recons. & Protest*, B-278352.2, 98-1 CPD ¶ 130 (repetition of arguments made during consideration of the original protest and mere disagreement with GAO decision do not meet standard for reconsideration).

GAO rarely finds that the protester is offering newly discovered evidence that could not possibly have been furnished during the initial consideration, *Department of the Navy — Request for Modification of Remedy*, Comp. Gen. Dec. B-401102.3, 2009 CPD ¶ 162 (information not new where Navy failed to mention the DoD memoranda during the protest; it cannot now proffer this information and the associated arguments for the first time on reconsideration); *Allstate Van & Storage, Inc.*, Comp. Gen. Dec. B-270744.2, 96-2 CPD ¶ 72 (information proffered seven months after the protester had learned of the evidence not new).

There is no statutory deadline for issuing a decision on reconsideration. In addition, there is no requirement to withhold award or suspend performance during the pendency of the reconsideration, 4 C.F.R. § 21.14(c).

## F.  Standards of Review

31 U.S.C. § 3554(b)(1) provides that GAO will review an agency action to determine if it "complies with statute or regulation." Under this standard, a protester must establish that the contracting agency has prejudicially violated a statute or regulation or has taken a discretionary action without a rational basis. GAO has given agencies considerable latitude in applying this rational basis standard to discretionary actions. The federal circuit has made clear that administrative protest authorities are not permitted to substitute their judgment for that of the agency, *Unisys Corp. v. Department of the Air Force*, GSBCA 13129-P, 95-2 BCA ¶ 27,622, *rev'd*, 98 F 3d 1325 (Fed. Cir. 1996).

GAO traditionally acted in accordance with this guidance of the court, as shown by standard language in GAO decisions in protests challenging the rationality of discretionary decisions of contracting agencies. See, for example, *Red River Serv. Corp.*, Comp. Gen. Dec. B-253671.2, 94-1 CPD ¶ 385, stating:

> Where, as here, the RFP provides that technical considerations will be more important than cost, source selection officials have broad discretion in deter-

mining the manner in which they will make use of the technical and cost evaluation results in arriving at a source selection decision. *University of Dayton Research Inst.,* B-245431, Jan. 2, 1992, 92-1 CPD ¶ 6. Such cost/technical tradeoffs are governed only by the test of rationality and consistency with the RFP's stated evaluation criteria. *Miller Bldg. Corp.,* B-245488, Jan. 3, 1992, 92-1 CPD ¶ 21.

See also *JB Indus.,* Comp. Gen. Dec. B-251118.2, 93-1 CPD ¶ 297 (award to offeror with 13% higher price to obtain lower risk of unsuccessful performance); *University of Dayton Research Inst.,* Comp. Gen. Dec. B-245431, 92-1 CPD ¶ 6 (award to offeror with 27% higher cost and fee to obtain lower risk of technical failure). In none of these three cases was there any quantification of the technical and management evaluations. GAO stated a slightly different formulation of the standard in *Technology Vectors, Inc.,* Comp. Gen. Dec. B-252518.2, 94-1 CPD ¶ 345:

> Since the RFP here stated that award would be made to the offeror whose proposal was determined to be most advantageous to the government, considering price and other factors, the agency had the discretion to determine whether the technical advantages associated with [the winning offeror's] proposal was worth its higher price. Our Office will not object to that determination if the agency reasonably determined that the price premium involved is justified by the technical superiority of the proposal.

See *Ameriko Maint. Co.,* Comp. Gen. Dec., B-253274.2, 93-2 CPD ¶ 121 (award to higher-priced offeror to obtain more extensive experience); *D'Wiley's Servs., Inc.,* Comp. Gen. Dec., B-251912, 93-1 CPD ¶ 377, *DynCorp,* Comp. Gen. Dec. B-257037.2, 95-1 CPD ¶ 34, and *Scheduled Airlines Traffic Offices, Inc.,* Comp. Gen. Dec. B-257292.9, 95-2 CPD ¶ 113 (award to higher-priced offeror to obtain better staffing); *Centro Mgmt., Inc.,* Comp. Gen. Dec., B-249411.2, 92-2 CPD ¶ 387, and *Hornet Joint Venture,* Comp. Gen. Dec. B-258430.2, 95-1 CPD ¶ 55 (award to higher-priced offeror to obtain better staffing and lower risk of poor performance); *EG&G Team,* Comp. Gen. Dec. B-259917.2, 95-2 CPD ¶ 138 (award to higher-price offeror to obtain benefits of higher-rated proposal); *TRW, Inc.,* Comp. Gen. Dec. B-260623, 95-2 CPD ¶ 92 (award to higher-priced offeror to obtain lower risk); and *Tidewater Homes Realty, Inc.,* Comp. Gen. Dec. B-274689.5, 98-2 CPD ¶ 40 (award to lower-priced, lower-rated offer proper where agency determined that higher-rated offer was not so significantly superior as to be worth the associated cost premium). However, in *Strum, Ruger & Co.,* Comp. Gen. Dec. B-250193, 93-1 CPD ¶ 42, GAO overturned an award that required the agency to pay a large premium to an offeror that was rated only marginally superior to the protester. The source selection authority had selected the offeror with the highest technical score without making any tradeoff analysis. GAO stated that the source selection authority had "misapprehended applicable law" and sent the matter back to the agency to "document a reasoned source selection decision."

GAO continues to follow this broad standard of review. See *John Blood*, Comp. Gen. Dec. B-402133, 2010 CPD ¶ 30, stating:

> In reviewing a protest against the propriety of an evaluation, it is not our function to independently evaluate proposals and substitute our judgment for that of the contracting activity. *Barents Group, L. L. C.*, B-276082, B-276082.2, May 9, 1997, 97-1 CPD ¶ 164 at 6. Rather, we will review an evaluation to ensure that it was reasonable and consistent with the evaluation criteria in the solicitation and applicable procurement statutes and regulations; a protester's mere disagreement with the evaluation does not show it lacked a reasonable basis. *Id*. On the record here, we see no basis to question the evaluation of the protester's quotation or the source selection decision.

A protester's mere disagreement with the agency's judgment in its determination of the relative merit of competing proposals or quotes does not establish that the evaluation was unreasonable, *C. Lawrence Constr. Co.*, Comp. Gen. Dec. B-287066, 2001 CPD ¶ 70 (agency's judgment of past performance was reasonable and consistent with the stated evaluation criteria and applicable statutes and regulations). See also *La Dolce Vida Catering*, Comp. Gen. Dec. B-402421, 2010 CPD ¶ 96 (contracting officer concluded that the Regent proposal was most advantageous to the agency and selected it for award, noting various strengths in the proposal); *Domain Name Alliance Registry*, Comp. Gen. Dec. B-310803.2, 2008 CPD ¶ 168 (evaluation of an offeror's proposal or quote, including experience, is a matter within the agency's discretion). But see *Preferred Sys. Solutions, Inc.*, Comp. Gen. Dec. B-292322, 2003 CPD ¶ 166, where, GAO found the decision not reasonably based, stating:

> [T]he propriety of a cost/technical tradeoff turns not on the difference in technical score, per se, but on whether the contracting agency's judgment concerning the significance of that difference was reasonable in light of the solicitation's evaluation scheme. Where cost is secondary to technical considerations under a solicitation's evaluation scheme, as here, the selection of a lower-priced proposal over a proposal with a higher technical rating requires an adequate justification, i.e., one showing the agency reasonably concluded that notwithstanding the point or adjectival differential between the two proposals, they were essentially equal in technical merit, or that the differential in the evaluation ratings between the proposals was not worth the cost premium associated with selection of the higher technically rated proposal.

See also *The Boeing Co.*, Comp. Gen. Dec. B-311344, 2008 CPD ¶ 114 (record did not demonstrate the reasonableness of the agency's determination); *Shumaker Trucking & Excavating Contractors, Inc.*, Comp. Gen. Dec. B-290732, 2002 CPD ¶ 169 (decision to select a higher technically rated, higher priced proposal unreasonable where agency mechanically applied the solicitation's evaluation methodology; neither the source selection documentation nor the evaluation record establish a valid rationale for why the agency found the higher-priced, higher-technically-rated proposal to be most advantageous to the government).

## G. Prejudice

Competitive prejudice is an essential element of every viable protest, 51 Comp. Gen. 678 (B-174367) (1972); *Lithos Restoration Ltd.,* 71 Comp. Gen. Dec. 367 (B-247003.2), 92-1 CPD ¶ 379. The protester must establish that but for the agency's actions, it would have had a substantial chance of receiving the award, *Armorworks Enters., LLC,* Comp. Gen. Dec. B-400394.3, 2009 CPD ¶ 79. This is the same test as used in the courts, *Statistica, Inc. v. United States,* 102 F.3d 1577 (Fed. Cir. 1996); *Bannum, Inc. v. United States,* 404 F.3d 1346 (Fed. Cir. 2005); *Galen Med. Assocs., Inc. v. United States,* 369 F.3d 1324 (Fed. Cir. 2004); *Information Tech. & Applications Corp. v. United States,* 316 F.3d 1312 (Fed. Cir. 2003). In some instances GAO states the test as a "reasonable possibility that the protester would have otherwise been the successful offeror as a sufficient basis for sustaining a protest," *CDA Inv. Techs., Inc.,* Comp. Gen. Dec. B-272093.3, 97-1 CPD ¶ 103; *Truetech, Inc.,* Comp. Gen. Dec. B-402536.2, 2010 CPD ¶ 129. The court in *Statistica* stated that "reasonable likelihood" should be interpreted to be the same as "substantial chance."

General allegations of prejudice will not suffice. See *MCI Constructors, Inc.,* Comp. Gen. Dec. B-274347, 96-2 CPD ¶ 210, where GAO found a failure to show prejudice when the protester failed to present information showing how it could reduce its price by the nearly $7 million margin with the low offeror. See also *Labrador Airways Ltd.,* Comp. Gen. Dec. B-241608, 91-1 CPD ¶ 167, where the protester did not demonstrate to GAO that it was prejudiced because the agency relaxed specifications for commercial flight services for one offeror. The protester alleged in general terms that on past contracts this requirement resulted in a net cost to the protester, but failed to provide any information showing how it calculated this cost or how much of this cost was included in its offer.

Protesters have most readily demonstrated prejudice when they have been denied the opportunity to revise their proposals in the same manner as a competitor. For example, in *Global Assocs. Ltd.,* Comp. Gen. Dec. B-271693, 96-2 CPD ¶ 100, GAO found that the protester was prejudiced when the agency conducted discussions with only the awardee after the submission of best and final offers.

The failure to conduct meaningful discussions may be prejudicial. In *Cogent Sys., Inc.,* Comp. Gen. Dec. B-295990.4, 2005 CPD ¶ 179, GAO sustained a bid protest challenging the award of an Army contract for an automated fingerprint identification system because the agency's technical evaluators assigned the protester a significant weakness that was based upon the erroneous belief that the flatbed scanner offered in the protester's final proposal, which met technical requirements, was the same as the noncompliant flatbed scanner offered in the protester's initial proposal. The Army failed to raise this perceived significant weakness with the protester during discussions. See also *Ogden Support Servs., Inc.,* Comp. Gen. Dec.

B-270354, 96-1 CPD ¶ 175, sustaining a protest because the agency did not inform the protester of the evaluated weaknesses and deficiencies in its proposal. GAO concluded that the protester was prejudiced because it would have had an opportunity to improve its score to a level approaching the awardee's score and its proposal may well have remained low in cost. See also *Alliant Techsystems, Inc.,* Comp. Gen. Dec. B-260215.4, 95-2 CPD ¶ 79, stating that in these circumstances, it would "resolve any doubts concerning the prejudicial effect of the agency's action in favor of the protester." But see *McDonald-Bradley*, Comp. Gen. Dec. B-270126, 96-1 CPD ¶ 54, where an allegation that the protester was misled during discussions was denied because the protester did not demonstrate a reasonable possibility that it was prejudiced. The protester argued that the agency misled the firm during discussions into believing that its proposed wages had to be consistent with the Service Contract Act requirements, but GAO found no proof that the protester would have lowered its wages further in its BAFO or that an adjustment to the protester's price would have made its pricecompetitive. Similarly, in *Alliance Tech. Servs., Inc.,* Comp. Gen. Dec. B-311329, 2008 CPD ¶ 108, GAO found no prejudice by lack of meaningful discussions because even with a perfect score under the particular subfactor where the discussions were allegedly not meaningful, the total evaluated score would have remained lower technically than the other two awardees' proposals, and its price would remain higher than both awardees' prices. See also *D.N. Am., Inc.,* Comp. Gen. Dec. B-292557, 2003 CPD ¶ 188 (protester had not shown that it would have or could have identified contracts of a larger size or that its subcontractor's references would have included other than contracts for hardware support had these issues been raised during discussions).

Prejudice has also been demonstrated when the agency makes errors in initiating the procurement. In *Comint Sys. Corp.,* Comp. Gen. Dec. B-274853, 97-1 CPD ¶ 14, the agency's letter offering a requirement to the SBA for acceptance into the 8(a) program failed to give complete and accurate information regarding the proposed offering. GAO found prejudice because the failure to provide the information deprived the SBA of the opportunity to make a fully informed decision with respect to the acquisition and deprived the protester of a potential opportunity to participate in the procurement.

Prejudice has been found where an agency relaxes its requirements. See *George Hyman Constr. Co.,* Comp. Gen. Dec. B-265798, 95-2 CPD ¶ 173, where the agency relaxed a go/no go key personnel experience evaluation criterion. GAO noted that the key personnel experience requirements were very restrictive and that a prospective offeror had requested that the requirements be amended to be less restrictive, which the agency declined to do. Additionally, one offeror was rejected as technically unacceptable for failing to meet these requirements. Thus, GAO held that there was a reasonable possibility of prejudice by relaxing these requirements for the awardee. In *Lockheed Martin Corp.,* Comp. Gen. Dec. B-295402, 2005 CPD ¶ 24, prejudice was found where a senior procurement official, who was involved in discussions that culminated in the deletion of a performance requirement that favored the protester, acknowledged bias in favor of the ultimate awardee. However, where a proposal deviates from a specification by a negligible amount, prejudice is unlikely to be found. See *First Federal Corp. — Costs*, Comp. Gen. Dec. B-293373.2, 2004 CPD ¶ 94 (one-half mile deviation from the 25-mile requirement appears minor on its face and protester did not show how it would have altered its proposal to improve its competitive standing had it been given an opportunity to respond to the relaxed requirement); *Gulf Copper Ship Repair, Inc.*, Comp. Gen. Dec. B-292431, 2003 CPD ¶ 155 (deviation of 1 inch water depth specification); *L. A. Sys., Inc.*, Comp. Gen. Dec. B-276349, 97-1 CPD ¶ 206 (although agency relaxed the stated requirements, there was no reasonable possibility that the protester was prejudiced by the relaxation); and *Magnaflux Corp.*, Comp. Gen. Dec. B-211914, 84-1 CPD ¶ 4 (agency permitted to waive deviation from specification which was minor and did not result in prejudice).

When the procurement defect is a failure to evaluate proposals properly, the protester must show that proper evaluation would have given it a chance to win the competition. This test was met in *Labat-Anderson, Inc.,* 71 Comp. Gen. 252 (B-246071), 92-1 CPD ¶ 193, where the agency had so significantly deviated from its evaluation scheme that it was not clear how a reevaluation would have scored the competitors. Prejudice will not be found where the outcome of the evaluation is unchanged. In *Calnet, Inc.*, Comp. Gen. Dec. B-402558.2, 2010 CPD ¶ 130, GAO held that even if the protester were correct that the agency improperly failed to consider the protester's third past performance questionnaire, there was no prejudice. Including the scores of the third questionnaire in the calculation would have given the protester and awardee the same overall score but the awardee offered a lower price and therefore remained in line for award ahead of the protester. See also *Alsalam Aircraft Co.,* Comp. Gen. Dec. B-401298.4, 2010 CPD ¶ 23 (even if awardee failed to include the fringe benefit costs, a cost realism adjustment would not overcome the its $11.4 million advantage over the protester's overall price); *PM Servs. Co.*, Comp. Gen. Dec. B-310762, 2008 CPD ¶ 42 (even agreeing with protester regarding the agency's evaluation of its proposal, awardee's proposal remained technically superior and was offered at a 4.4% lower cost); *American Cybernetic Corp.*, Comp. Gen. Dec. B-310551.2, 2008 CPD ¶ 40 (even assuming that protester's technical proposal should have been assigned the highest possible rating, no reasonable possibly that the contracting officer would have concluded that protester's proposal was worth paying more than twice the price); *Med Optical*, Comp. Gen. Dec. B-296231.2, 2005 CPD ¶ 169 (even if protester received perfect scores in both areas where it challenged the agency's evaluation, its proposal would still be lower rated technically and substantially higher priced that the awardee's); *Restoration & Closure Servs., LLC*, Comp. Gen. Dec. B-295663.6, 2005 CPD ¶ 92 (protester's evaluated cost was $47 million higher than awardee's, and the protester made no claim that it would have been able to reduce its proposed costs); and *AVCARD*, Comp. Gen. Dec. B-293775.2, 2004 CPD ¶ 9 (given that protester's proposal was significantly higher priced than the awardee's, in order to prevail in its protest, protester would have had to demonstrate that agency should have rated proposal higher than awardee's proposal in at least one of the non-price evaluation areas to demonstrate prejudice).

When the evaluation errors are minor, prejudice is difficult to prove. See *SWR, Inc.*, Comp. Gen. Dec. B-294835, 2005 CPD ¶ 7 (although agency improperly failed to take into account the relative weights of the evaluation factors in scoring proposals, there was no basis for finding that correctly weighted scoring would have had any significant impact on the award decision); *Wadsworth Builders, Inc.*, Comp. Gen. Dec. B-291633, 2003 CPD ¶ 43 (even assuming the agency should have regarded the combat arms range project as relevant and considered it in evaluating the protester's past performance, there was no basis to conclude that this would have resulted in an increase in protester's past performance rating); *Innovative Mgmt., Inc.*, Comp. Gen. Dec. B-291375, 2003 CPD ¶ 11 (no prejudice by the agency's alleged error in not having protester's original transparencies available for use during its oral presentation); *SBC Fed. Sys.*, Comp. Gen. Dec. B-283693, 2000 CPD ¶ 5 (although agency may have improperly performed a price/technical tradeoff in violation of the solicitation's evaluation scheme, protester not prejudiced because proposal was technically unacceptable); *Northport Handling, Inc.*, Comp. Gen. Dec. B-274615, 97-1 CPD ¶ 3 (no prejudice by any errors that may have occurred during evaluation because even if agency assigned the highest rating to protester's performance as the incumbent, it would have no impact on past performance rating); *CDA Inv. Techs., Inc.*, Comp. Gen. Dec. B-272093, 97-1 CPD ¶ 102 (no prejudice by any errors that may have occurred in the evaluation of awardee's proposed use of a subcontractor because the subcontractor's task comprises only a relatively minor portion of the overall effort and will become obsolete early in the life of the contract); *Agriculture Tech. Partners*, Comp. Gen. Dec. B-272978, 96-2 CPD ¶ 226 (even if agency improperly evaluated staff evaluation factor, there were several superior proposals and protester had no reasonable chance for award); *Executive Court Reporters, Inc.*, Comp. Gen. Dec. B-272981, 96-2 CPD ¶ 227 (the slightly unequal weighting of the three factors in the evaluation did not have a material effect on protester's proposal score and resulting competitive position); *PADCO, Inc.*, Comp. Gen. Dec. B-270445, 96-1 CPD ¶ 142 (protester's own nominee had a similar deficiency and was found acceptable); and *Lithos Restoration Ltd.*, 71 Comp. Gen. Dec. 367 (B-247003.2), 92-1 CPD ¶ 379 (even if key personnel factor was evaluated under most important factor, as contemplated by RFP, protester's proposal would not have improved vs. the awardee's technically superior proposal).

Prejudice will not be found in circumstances where the protester does not demonstrate that it could have won the competition. See *SERAPH, Inc.*, Comp. Gen. Dec. B-297452, 2006 CPD ¶ 18 (no prejudice for alleged improper evaluation of key personnel because proposal was not selected for award due to the agency's evaluation conclusion that the proposal represented a moderate risk under the understanding of work evaluation factor, and not because of lack of experience); *Information Ventures, Inc.*, Comp. Gen. Dec. B-297225, 2005 CPD ¶ 216 (protester made no attempt to show that it could have met the agency's requirement, regardless of the time provided); *United Valve Co.*, Comp. Gen. Dec. B-295879, 2005 CPD ¶ 85 (agency had waived schedule specified in the solicitation for both competitors, and protester's own requested schedule was already longer than schedule granted to awardee, and protester's proposal offered a higher price); *United Enter. & Assocs.*, Comp. Gen. Dec. B-295742, 2005 CPD ¶ 67 (although SBA did not follow applicable certificate of competency procedures, the SBA agreed with the procuring agency that the 8(a) vendor was not responsible for this requirement, and thus SBA would not have exercised its right to appeal the agency's determination not to contract with that vendor, which was the only action under applicable regulations that SBA could take to contest the procuring agency's determination); *CourtSmart Digital Sys., Inc.*, Comp. Gen. Dec. B-292995.8, 2005 CPD ¶ 28 (protester did not show that it could or would have modified its quotation had it known of the agency's interpretation of the "fieldtested" requirement); *Kloppenburg Enters.*, Inc., Comp. Gen. Dec. B-294709, 2004 CPD ¶ 246 (although GAO recognizes that an agency is obligated to ensure that prospective contractors are registered in the CCR database before award, no prejudice where agency made award only after confirming that awardee would promptly register in the CCR database); *Cross Match Techs., Inc.*, Comp. Gen. Dec. B-293024.3, 2004 CPD ¶ 193 (solicitation provision that provides for incorporating into a BPA additional, unevaluated items, in quantities for which no estimates are provided in the solicitation, and at prices that are subsequently to be negotiated was improper, but record showed that the amount involved could have accounted for no more than small portion of awardee's overall price advantage); *Frasca Int'l, Inc.*, Comp. Gen. Dec. B-293299, 2004 CPD ¶ 38 (to the extent that protester was unable to compete, it was due to breakdown of teaming discussions caused by protester's untimely proposals submission, not to bundling); *Bath Iron Works Corp.*, Comp. Gen. Dec. B-290470, 2002 CPD ¶ 133 (agency's denial of protester's use of a decommissioned destroyer for testing while allowing the awardee to use such constituted unequal treatment but was not prejudicial because record showed protester would have obtained no material technical benefit or evaluation advantage had it been allowed to use of the destroyer); *Si-Nor, Inc.*, Comp. Gen. Dec. B-286910, 2001 CPD ¶ 1 (agency's failure to apply 10% SDB evaluation preference provided for in the solicitation where the awardee was an SDB making the preference inapplicable and there was no basis to conclude that protester inflated its bid price in reliance on application of the preference); *Charleston Marine Containers, Inc.*, Comp. Gen. Dec. B-283393, 99-2 CPD ¶ 84 (although agency failed to hold discussions, it was apparent from the record that the protester could not have improved its proposal enough through discussions to be in competition for award); *Motorola, Inc.*, Comp. Gen. Dec. B-277862, 97-2 CPD ¶ 155 (protester not prejudiced by an agency decision to ignore a requirement in the statement of work); *Brown & Root, Inc.*, Comp. Gen. Dec. B-270505.2, 96-2 CPD ¶ 143 (no evidence that had the protester been aware of the waiver of the security clearance requirement, it would have submitted a different proposal); and *Safety-Kleen Corp.*, Comp. Gen. Dec. B-274176, 96-2 CPD ¶ 200 (although the Army had improperly waived a provision requiring a certificate of environmental impairment liability insurance when it awarded the contract to a firm that did not meet the requirement, protester did not assert that it would have refrained from providing the insurance coverage had it known that the Army did not consider the coverage necessary).

Prejudice has also been found where an agency changes its requirements but does not issue an amendment to the solicitation. See *Symetrics Indus., Inc.*, Comp. Gen. Dec. B-274246.3, 97-2 CPD ¶ 59, sustaining the protest, finding that the agency was required to amend the solicitation upon receiving information that funds were unavailable for the purchase of a significant portion of an estimated quantity included in the RFP for an indefinite-quantity, indefinite-delivery contract. GAO stated that the change in quantity was material and there was a reasonable possibility that the protester was prejudiced by the failure to amend the solicitation. But see *M. K. Taylor Contractors, Inc.*, Comp. Gen. Dec. B-291730.2, 2003 CPD ¶ 97 (although agency improperly failed to issue amendment of the changed requirements, no prejudice found since, by protester's own calculations, increased quantities would not have led protester to reduce its price sufficiently to give it a substantial chance of receiving the award).

Prejudice cannot be proved if the protester is ineligible for award. See *Wyeth-Lederle Vaccines & Pediatrics*, Comp. Gen. Dec. B-274490, 96-2 CPD ¶ 229, holding that the protester suffered no prejudice as a result of the agency's inclusion of the single-award clause in the solicitation because even if the single-award clause were removed, the protester would still be ineligible for award because it did not possess the required license.

Prejudice will not be found where the agency accepts an expired offer if no changes are permitted to be made to the proposal, *Scot, Inc.*, Comp. Gen. Dec. B-295569, 2005 CPD ¶ 66 (acceptance of the expired offer did not prejudice the competitive system because no changes were made to awardee's proposal).

## H. Remedies

GAO can make recommendations to the agency but does not have the authority to direct the agency to take action or to refrain from doing so. Only in rare cases, however, do agencies fail to follow these recommendations. GAO is required to report annually to Congress all cases in which procuring agencies do not fully implement GAO's recommendations, 31 U.S.C. § 3554(e)(2). There are only a few instances where GAO's recommendations were not fully implemented by the respective agencies. See *Mission Critical Solutions*, Comp. Gen. Dec. B-401057, 2009 CPD ¶ 93; *Symplicity Corp.*, Comp. Gen. Dec. B-291902, 2003 CPD ¶ 89; *Consolidated Eng'g Servs., Inc.*, Comp. Gen. Dec. B-291345, 2002 CPD ¶ 220; *Rockwell Elec. Commerce Corp.*, Comp. Gen. Dec. B-286201.6, 2001 CPD ¶ 162, *modified*, 2002 CPD ¶ 47; *Aberdeen Tech. Servs., Inc.*, Comp. Gen. Dec. B-283727.2, 2000 CPD ¶ 46. See GAO Bid Protest Annual Reports to the Congress (Fiscal Years 2000-2008) available at *www.gao.gov/decisions/bidproan.htm*.

## 1.  *Nonmonetary Remedies*

GAO can recommend a variety of nonmonetary remedies. 31 U.S.C. § 3554(b)(1) states:

> If the Comptroller General determines that the solicitation, proposed award, or award does not comply with a statute or regulation, the Comptroller General shall recommend that the Federal agency —
>
> (A) refrain from exercising any of his options under the contract;
>
> (B) recompete the contract immediately;
>
> (C) issue a new solicitation;
>
> (D) terminate the contract;
>
> (E) award a contract consistent with the requirements of such statute and regulation;
>
> (F) implement any combination of recommendations under clauses (A), (B), (C), (D), and (E); or
>
> (G) implement such other recommendations as the Comptroller General determines to be necessary in order to promote compliance with procurement statutes and regulations.

If award has already been made, GAO, in making recommendations, is prohibited from considering any cost or disruption resulting from the termination, recompetition, or reaward of the contract, 31 U.S.C. § 3554(b)(2). In *Price Waterhouse*, Comp. Gen. Dec. B-220049, 86-1 CPD ¶ 333, an agency requested reconsideration of a decision that sustained a protest and recommended possible contract termination. GAO held that its decision would not be reconsidered based upon the estimated costs of termination where the agency proceeded with performance of the contract upon a finding that to do so would be in the best interests of the government. See also *Spherix, Inc.*, Comp. Gen. Dec. B-294572, 2005 CPD ¶ 3; *World-Wide Sec. Serv., Inc.*, 66 Comp. Gen. 195 (B-224277) (1987); and *Department of the Navy*, Comp. Gen. Dec. B-274944.4, 97-2 CPD ¶ 16.

GAO may recommend that the agency amend the solicitation, *FC Bus. Sys., Inc.*, Comp. Gen. Dec. B-278730, 98-2 CPD ¶ 9 (where RFP did not provide a common definition of a staff year, agency should amend solicitation to explain how it will take into consideration the differences in the number of hours per staff year proposed by the offerors or otherwise establish a uniform basis for preparing and evaluating offers); *Hoescht Marion Roussel, Inc.*, Comp. Gen. Dec. B-279073, 98-1 CPD ¶ 127 (where solicitation fails to realistically state agency's estimated requirements for various drug dosages, agency should amend RFP); *Comark Fed. Sys.*, Comp.

Gen. Dec. B-278343.2, 98-1 CPD ¶ 34 (where agency failed to advise vendors of the basis for the source selection, agency should amend RFQ to advise firms holding basic purchasing agreements of agency's needs, including whether agency is willing to conduct a cost/technical tradeoff).

GAO may also recommend that the agency make a new competitive range determination, *Trifax Corp.*, Comp. Gen. Dec. B-279561, 98-2 CPD ¶ 24, reinstate a wrongfully disqualified offeror to the competitive range, *KPMG Peat Marwick*, Comp. Gen. Dec. B-251902.3, 93-2 CPD ¶ 272, conduct new oral presentations, *e-LYNXX Corp.*, Comp. Gen. Dec. B-292761, 2003 CPD ¶ 219. See *Kathpal Techs., Inc.*, Comp. Gen. Dec. B-283137.3, 2000 CPD ¶ 6 (GAO recommended agency either afford all technically acceptable offerors an opportunity to make oral presentations or amend the solicitation to properly inform offerors that oral presentations would not be considered as part of offerors' proposals and obtain revised proposals).

A common remedy in negotiated procurement is to reopen discussions, request new revised proposals and reevaluate proposals, *Haworth, Inc.*, Comp. Gen. Dec. B-297077, 2005 CPD ¶ 215 (agency erroneously concluded that awardee's quotation met the stated requirements and erroneously downgraded protester's under the "environmental factors" evaluation factor); *Technical Support Servs., Inc.*, Comp. Gen. Dec. B-279665.2, 98-2 CPD ¶ 26 (agency had disregarded the solicitation's stated best value evaluation scheme); *Century Envtl. Hygiene, Inc.*, Comp. Gen. Dec. B-279378, 98-1 CPD ¶ 164 (evaluation of protester's proposal was inconsistent with the solicitation evaluation criteria); *Biosperics, Inc.*, Comp. Gen. Dec. B-278278, 98-1 CPD ¶ 161 (agency failed to inform firm that its cost/pricing was considered unrealistically low but instead twice encouraged the firm to reduce its proposed price); *Hughes STX Corp.*, Comp. Gen. Dec. B-278466, 98-1 CPD ¶ 52 (cost evaluation was unreasonable and discussions with the protester concerning its proposed direct labor rates were not meaningful); *CitiWest Props., Inc.*, Comp. Gen. Dec. B-274689.4, 98-1 CPD ¶ 3 (agency failed to conduct meaningful discussions); *Gardiner, Kamya & Assocs.*, Comp. Gen. Dec. B-258915.2, 95-1 CPD ¶ 193 (agency unreasonably downgraded protester's proposal); *National Med. Staffing, Inc.*, Comp. Gen. Dec. B-259402, 95-1 CPD ¶ 163 (agency did not conduct meaningful and equal discussions). In some cases GAO recommends that discussions be reopened but that they be of limited nature, *Boeing Sikorsky Aircraft Support*, Comp. Gen. Dec. B-277263.2, 97-2 CPD ¶ 91. Here, GAO recommended that the agency reopen negotiations regarding costs and fees with offerors in the competitive range and allow them to submit revised cost proposals.

In some instances GAO may recommend termination of the task order or contract. See *Tarheel Specialties, Inc.*, Comp. Gen. Dec. B-298197, 2006 CPD ¶ 140 (recommended that DHS/ICE terminate the task order to USIS, assess its requirements, and determine whether it is appropriate to obtain these services under the FSS program, and then either resolicit under the FSS program or by full and open competition).

In rare cases GAO recommends that award be made to the protester. See *Spectrum Sec. Servs., Inc.*, Comp. Gen. Dec. B-297320.2, 2005 CPD ¶ 227 (recommended that contract be terminated and that the agency consider award to protester or the other small business offeror); *Dismas Charities, Inc.*, Comp. Gen. Dec. B-292091, 2003 CPD ¶ 125 (in the event proposal is selected for award, the agency should terminate awardee's contract, and award a contract to the protester); *R. & W. Flammann GmbH*, Comp. Gen. Dec. B-278486, 98-1 CPD ¶ 40 (where agency improperly canceled procurement, GAO recommended that award be made to protester on the basis of its low offer); *For Your Information, Inc.*, Comp. Gen. Dec. B-278352, 97-2 CPD ¶ 164 (where agency had improperly awarded contract to technically unacceptable offeror, GAO recommended that the agency terminate the contract and make award to the protester, which was the only offeror that submitted a technically acceptable proposal); *Tri-State Gov't Servs., Inc.*, Comp. Gen. Dec. B-277315.2, 97-2 CPD ¶ 143 (where agency improperly accepted nonconforming offer, GAO recommended that contract be terminated and award be made to protester); *Aetna Gov't Health Plans, Inc.*, Comp. Gen. Dec. B-254397, 95-2 CPD ¶ 129 (where agency failed to recognize the significance of the organizational conflict of interest, GAO recommended that the agency terminate the existing contract and make award to protester); and *L&E Assocs.*, Comp. Gen. Dec. B-258808.4, 95-1 CPD ¶ 288 (where the record showed that the agency considered two technical proposals to be essentially equal, GAO recommended that award be made to the protester who offered a lower price and whose proposal had been improperly rejected for allegedly not providing firm labor rates).

## 2. Monetary Remedies

The monetary remedies that protesters have been able to recover are the costs of pursuing the protest, including attorneys' fees, and the costs of preparing the bid or proposal. Recovery of anticipated profits has been uniformly denied, *Baker Support Servs., Inc.*, Comp. Gen. Dec. B-256192.3, 95-1 CPD ¶ 75.

When GAO recommends payment of protest costs and/or bid or proposal preparation costs, it leaves it to the parties to agree on the amount. The protester is required to submit to the procuring agency a detailed and certified claim within 60 calendar days after receipt of GAO recommendation that the costs be paid, 4 C.F.R. § 21.8(f)(1). The protester seeking to recover the costs of pursuing its protest must submit sufficient evidence to support its monetary claim, *Consolidated Bell, Inc.*, 70 Comp. Gen. 358 (B-220425.4) (1991). In *Wind Gap Knitwear, Inc.*, Comp. Gen. Dec. B-251411.2, 95-2 CPD ¶ 94, GAO denied a claim for costs where the protester failed to file an adequately detailed claim with the agency within 60 days after the protester received a copy of the decision awarding protest costs. See also *Custom Prod. Mfg., Inc.*, Comp. Gen. Dec. B-235431.8, 95-2 CPD ¶ 40 (protester submitted its claim four-and-a-half years after it was entitled to such costs).

The procuring agency must decide the claim "as soon as practicable after the claim is filed" and notify GAO within 60 calendar days after GAO decision recommending the payment of costs, 4 C.F.R. § 21.8(f)(3). If the parties cannot reach agreement on the amount within a reasonable time, the protester may refer the matter to GAO for decision, 4 C.F.R. § 21.8(f)(2). A protester must diligently pursue a claim for protest costs, *Aalco Forwarding, Inc. — Costs*, Comp. Gen. Dec. B-277241.30, 99-2 CPD ¶ 36. Failure to timely pursue a claim may result in forfeiture of the right to recover protest costs, *Holloway & Co., PLLC — Costs*, Comp. Gen. Dec. B-311342.5, 2009 CPD ¶ 146 (request for recommendation for reimbursement of protest costs not diligently pursued where protester delayed filing at GAO until more than 8 months had passed without receiving a response from the contracting agency); *L-3 Commc'ns Corp., Ocean Sys. Div. — Costs*, Comp. Gen. Dec. B-281784.5, 2004 CPD ¶ 40 (although protester filed its claim with the agency in a timely fashion, the protester failed to continue pursuit of the claim for an extended period of time, nearly 3 years). GAO will not ordinarily recommend the amount of costs to be paid for pursuing the claim, *Princeton Gamma-Tech, Inc.*, 68 Comp. Gen. 401 (B-228052.5), 89-1 CPD ¶ 401, except where the parties cannot agree on the amount, 4 C.F.R. § 21.8(f)(2). See *ViON Corp.*, Comp. Gen. Dec. B-256363.3, 95-1 CPD ¶ 219, where GAO determined the amount of protest costs because the protester and the agency were unable to reach agreement. GAO, if determining the amount of costs to be paid, may also recommend that the agency pay the costs of pursuing this claim for costs before GAO, 4 C.F.R. § 21.8(f)(2).

## a.  Bid or Proposal Preparation Costs

31 U.S.C. § 3554(c)(1)(B) permits GAO to award the costs of preparing a bid or proposal to a successful protester. However, bid or proposal costs are not awarded merely if a protest is sustained; rather, recovery is appropriate only when a protester is unreasonably excluded from the competition and no other remedy is appropriate. This is often the case when performance of the contract is complete or when it is impractical to terminate the contract because performance has reached its latter stages, *Data Integrators, Inc.*, Comp. Gen. Dec. B-310928, 2008 CPD ¶ 27 (delivery had been completed — GAO recommended reimbursement of costs of quotation preparation and of filing and pursuing the protest, including reasonable attorneys' fees); *International Program Group, Inc.*, Comp. Gen. Dec. B-400278, 2008 CPD ¶ 172 (order for the requirement was completely performed — GAO recommended reimbursement of costs of filing and pursuing the protest); *Information Ventures, Inc.*, Comp. Gen. Dec. B-293518, 2004 CPD ¶ 76 (sole source contract was largely completed — protester had no proposal costs but GAO recommended reimbursement of costs of filing and pursuing the protest, including reasonable attorneys' fees); *Mechanical Contractors, S. A.*, Comp. Gen. Dec. B-277916.2, 98-1 CPD ¶ 68 (25% of the work had been completed and the agency had determined that urgent and compelling circumstances existed requiring several additional weeks to conduct discussions and reevaluate proposals — GAO recommended reimbursement

of proposal preparation costs); *Aerospace Design & Fabrication, Inc.*, B-278896.2, 98-1 CPD ¶ 139 ( unique circumstances created a situation where reevaluation and reconsideration of the selection decision could not return the parties to their respective positions prior to the agency error — GAO recommended reimbursement of proposal preparation costs); *Jack Faucett Assocs., Inc.*, Comp. Gen. Dec. B-279347, 98-1 CPD ¶ 155 (services had been substantially performed — GAO recommended reimbursement of quotation preparation costs); *International Data Sys.*, Comp. Gen. Dec. B-277385, 97-2 CPD ¶ 96 (contract had been fully performed — GAO recommended reimbursement of proposal preparation costs); *Adelaide Blomfield Mgmt. Co.*, Comp. Gen. Dec. B-253128.4, 95-1 CPD ¶ 7 (termination of the lease not feasible because the lease did not contain a termination for convenience clause — GAO recommended reimbursement of bid preparation and protest costs); and *Bush Painting, Inc.*, Comp. Gen. Dec. B-239904.3, 91-2 CPD ¶ 159 (performance was 90% complete — GAO recommended reimbursement of bid preparation costs).

GAO will not award proposal costs if the protester would not have been in line for the award, *Temps & Co.*, 65 Comp. Gen. 819 (B-221846.2), 86-2 CPD ¶ 236. But see *EHE Nat'l Health Servs.*, Inc., 65 Comp. Gen. 1 (B-219361.2), 85-2 CPD ¶ 362, where GAO found that a protester had a substantial chance of receiving the award when the protester was one of three firms in line for award.

If a solicitation is canceled for valid reasons not related to the protest, no bid or proposal preparation costs will be awarded. In *Orange Personnel Servs., Inc.*, Comp. Gen. Dec. B-256164.2, 95-1 CPD ¶ 26, cancellation precluded the award of bid preparation costs although the protester was in line for award. See also *Quan-Tech, Inc.*, Comp. Gen. Dec. B-278380.3, 98-1 CPD ¶ 165 (no proposal preparation costs awarded where agency reasonably canceled procurement in order to take corrective action); and *Fischer & Porter Co.*, Comp. Gen. Dec. B-227941.3, 88-1 CPD ¶ 327 (no bid preparation costs awarded where legislation passed subsequent to a GAO decision sustaining a protest had the effect of rendering the decision moot).

A protester is generally not entitled to the award of bid or proposal preparation costs if it will have an opportunity to compete for award of the contract under a resolicitation conducted as a result of its protest, *Lockheed Martin Corp. — Costs*, Comp. Gen. Dec. B-295402.2, 2005 CPD ¶ 192; *KIME Enters.*, Comp. Gen. Dec. B-241996.5, 91-2 CPD ¶ 523; 65 Comp. Gen. 268 (B-219667.2) (1986). However, GAO may recommend reimbursement where changed circumstances render no longer relevant a proposal that was previously submitted. In *COBRO Corp.*, Comp. Gen. Dec. B-287578.2, 2001 CPD ¶ 181, GAO recommended the award of bid and proposal costs where the protester had expended substantial cost and effort on a proposal which was likely to have virtually no value under a recompetition for a fundamentally different requirement. See also *Rockwell Elec. Commerce Corp. — Modification of Recommendation*, Comp. Gen. Dec. B-286201.8, 2002 CPD ¶ 47, recommending the reimbursement of proposal preparation costs since the agency stated it would not follow GAO's recommendation to cure the improprieties in the competition. GAO held that since the agency will not take appropriate corrective action, Rockwell will not have a meaningful opportunity to compete based on the proposal submitted. See *Aberdeen Tech. Servs. — Modification of Recommendation*, Comp. Gen. Dec. B-283727.3, 2001 CPD ¶ 146, recommending the reimbursement of protester's costs of preparing its proposal where the agency canceled the solicitation and acknowledged it would be unable to issue a new solicitation for "some 2 years" after GAO's original decision.

GAO has awarded bid preparation costs where a protester bid was improperly rejected even though the agency's subsequent review of the bid determined that it was not eligible for award, *Industrial Storage Equip. — Pac.*, Comp. Gen. Dec. B-228123.2, 88-1 CPD ¶ 328.

## b.  Protest Costs

GAO has the authority to grant protest costs, including reasonable attorneys' fees, 31 U.S.C. § 3554(c). Protest costs can be granted even when other corrective action is taken in a sustained protest, *Norse Inc.*, Comp. Gen. Dec. B-233534, 89-1 CPD ¶ 293 (protester was both reinstated into the contract competition and granted protest costs).

GAO has consistently rejected assertions that its cost reimbursement authority under CICA is properly applied to litigation costs incurred in connection with matters brought in another forum, since GAO does not view those costs as having been incurred in filing and pursuing a protest with GAO, *Sodexho Mgmt., Inc. — Costs*, Comp. Gen. Dec. B-289605.3, 2003 CPD ¶ 136 (GAO statutory authority to recommend reimbursement of costs does not extend to the costs associated with Sodexho's administrative appeal of the initial A-76 cost comparison). See also *Rice Servs., Ltd. — Costs*, Comp. Gen. Dec. B-284997.2, 2001 CPD ¶ 88; *Diverco, Inc., — Claim for Costs*, Comp. Gen. Dec. B-240639.5, 92-1 CPD ¶ 460.

### (1) GROUNDS FOR PROTEST COSTS

Generally, no protest costs will be granted if GAO has not made a decision on the merits, *Signal Corp.*, 69 Comp. Gen. 659 (B-240450), 90-2 CPD ¶ 116; *Moody Bros.*, Comp. Gen. Dec. B-237278.3, 89-2 CPD ¶ 590. For instance, if an agency cancels a solicitation for a valid reason unrelated to the protest, the protester will not be entitled to recover the costs of filing and pursuing its protest, *H. Watt & Scott Gen. Contractors, Inc.*, Comp. Gen. Dec. B-257776.3, 95-1 CPD ¶ 183 (cancellation based on inability to proceed with work due to weather conditions); *Digital Sys. Group, Inc.*, Comp. Gen. Dec. B-257835.2, 95-1 CPD ¶ 173 (agency did not receive any proposals that satisfied requirement); *Red River Serv. Corp.*, Comp. Gen. Dec. B-259462.2, 95-2 CPD ¶ 106 (bid acceptance period had expired). However, if the cancellation occurs after the date for the submission of the agency report, it may not be considered prompt corrective action with the result that protest costs may be allowed. See *KAES Enters., LLC — Protest & Costs*, Comp. Gen. Dec. B-402050.4, 2010 CPD ¶ 49, granting the protest costs incurred with regard to the single issue that was deemed meritorious in an outcome prediction conference – followed by cancellation of the procurement because the agency's requirements had changed.

As a general rule, GAO recommends reimbursement of costs incurred with respect to all issues pursued, not merely those upon which it prevails, *AAR Aircraft Servs. — Costs*, Comp. Gen. Dec. B-291670.6, 2003 CPD ¶ 100; *Main Bldg. Maint., Inc.*, Comp. Gen. Dec. B-60945.6, 97-2 CPD ¶ 163. However, in appropriate cases GAO will limit its recommendation for the award of protest costs where a part of their costs is allocable to a protest issue that is so clearly severable as to essentially constitute a separate protest, *Interface Floorings Sys., Inc. — Claim for Attorney Fees*, Comp. Gen. Dec. B-225439.5, 87-2 CPD ¶ 106. See *KAES Enters., LLC — Protest & Costs*, Comp. Gen. Dec. B-402050.4, 2010 CPD ¶ 49 (costs limited to specific ground on which protester was likely to prevail — agency's failure to consider price when excluding the firm's proposal from the competitive range); *Panacea Consulting, Inc. — Costs*, Comp. Gen. Dec. B-299307.3, 2007 CPD ¶ 133 (recovery of protest costs is limited to those issues upon which protester prevailed). In determining whether protest issues are so clearly severable as to essentially constitute separate protests, GAO considers, among other things, the extent to which the claims are interrelated or intertwined — i.e., the successful and unsuccessful claims share a common core set of facts, are based on related legal theories, or are otherwise not readily severable, *Sodexho Mgmt., Inc. — Costs*, Comp. Gen. Dec. B-289605.3, 2003 CPD ¶ 136. In *BAE Tech. Servs., Inc. — Costs*, Comp. Gen. Dec. B-296699.3, 2006 CPD ¶ 122, GAO held that the protester was entitled to recover costs attributed to almost all of the issues raised as they are "largely intertwined parts of [its] basic objection that the [agency] misevaluated proposals and treated offerors unequally." See also *Burns & Roe Servs. Corp. — Costs*, Comp. Gen. Dec. B-310828.2, 2008 CPD ¶ 81 (misevaluation of proposals, failure to hold meaningful discussions and treating offerors unequally involve the same core facts); *T Square Logistics Servs. Corp., Inc. — Costs*, Comp. Gen. Dec. B-297790.6, 2007 CPD ¶ 108 (reasonableness of the evaluation of proposals under the past performance factor and the failure to conduct meaningful discussions based on this evaluation were interconnected and based on common factual underpinnings); *Blue Rock Structures, Inc. — Costs*, Comp. Gen. Dec. B-293134.2, 2005 CPD ¶ 190 (all of protester's arguments pertained to the reasonableness of the agency's evaluation of proposals and source selection determination). But see *Al Qabandi United Co., Am. Gen. Trading & Contracting — Costs*, Comp. Gen. Dec. B-310600.3, 2008 CPD ¶ 112, where GAO recommended that the protester be reimbursed the reasonable costs of filing and pursuing its protest only as related to its challenge to the price evaluation. The protester's challenge to the affirmative determination of the awardee's responsibility and its assertion that the Army improperly relaxed performance requirements after award did not involve the same set of core facts as did its clearly meritorious challenge to the price evaluation. See also *Honeywell Tech. Solutions, Inc. — Costs*,

Comp. Gen. Dec. B-296860.3, 2005 CPD ¶ 226, where GAO did not recommend reimbursement of costs associated with the unresolved issues, which were severable from the organizational conflict of interest issue addressed during ADR.

## (2) CORRECTIVE ACTION

Where the contracting agency decides to take corrective action in response to a protest, GAO may recommend that the protester be reimbursed the reasonable costs of filing and pursuing the protest, including attorneys' fees and consultant and expert witness fees, 4 C.F.R. § 21.8(e). GAO will not, however, award bid and proposal costs, *Mapp Bldg. Servs. — Costs*, Comp. Gen. Dec. B-289160.2, 2002 CPD ¶ 60 ("[O]ur regulations do not provide for recovery of such costs where an agency has taken corrective action"). A protester will not be reimbursed its costs in every case in which an agency decides to take corrective action; rather, a protester should be reimbursed its costs where an agency *unduly delayed* its decision to take corrective action in the face of a *clearly meritorious* protest, *Griner's-A-One Pipeline Servs., Inc. — Entitlement to Costs*, Comp. Gen. Dec. B-255078.3, 94-2 CPD ¶ 41.

Undue delay in taking corrective action is generally found if the agency takes the action after the filing of the agency report, *CDIC, Inc. — Costs*, Comp. Gen. Dec. B-277526.2, 97-2 CPD ¶ 52. See *Core Tech Int'l Corp. — Costs*, Comp. Gen. Dec. B-400047.2, 2009 CPD ¶ 59 (corrective action occurring only after the agency report and ADR); *World Commc'ns Ctr., Inc. — Costs*, Comp. Gen. Dec. B-310398.4, 2008 CPD ¶ 19 (agency did not terminate the award and cancel the solicitation until after the agency had produced its report, the protester had filed its comments on the report, and GAO attorney assigned to the protest had requested additional information); *Salvation Army Comty. Corrs. Program*, Comp. Gen. Dec. B-298866.3, 2007 CPD ¶ 165 (corrective action after the protester filed its comments on the agency report and GAO informed the parties that a hearing would be conducted); *EBSCO Publishing, Inc. — Costs*, Comp. Gen. Dec. B-298918.4, 2007 CPD ¶ 90 (corrective action after the filing of the agency report); *Johnson Controls World Servs., Inc. — Costs*, Comp. Gen. Dec. B-295529.4, 2005 CPD ¶ 162 (agency did not investigate the protest allegations and withheld relevant protest documents until more than 70 days after the initial protest filing); *Miller Elevator Serv. Co. — Costs*, Comp. Gen. Dec. B-284870.3, 2000 CPD ¶ 126 (corrective action well after the agency had submitted its report and the protester had responded to it); *The Real Estate Ctr. — Costs*, Comp. Gen. Dec. B-274081.7, 98-1 CPD ¶ 105 (agency took three months and two weeks to acknowledge evaluation decision was insupportable and convene new evaluation panel); and *Pemco Aeroplex, Inc.*, Comp. Gen. Dec. B-275587.5, 97-2 CPD ¶ 102 (agency allowed four months to pass without revising the solicitation).

For cases finding that the protester was not entitled to award of costs of filing and pursuing its protest because the agency took prompt corrective action, see *Apptis, Inc. — Costs*, Comp. Gen. Dec. B-402146.3, 2010 CPD ¶ 123, and *Metalcraft*,

*Inc. — Costs*, Comp. Gen. Dec. B-402181.3, 2010 CPD ¶ 116 (agency's corrective action took place prior to the submission of its supplemental agency report); *AGFA HealthCare Corp. — Costs*, Comp. Gen. Dec. B-400733.6, 2009 CPD ¶ 90 (agency took corrective action on the date comments were due on the second supplemental report); *Intercontinental Constr. Contracting, Inc. — Costs*, Comp. Gen. Dec. B-400729.3, 2009 CPD ¶ 44 (agency promptly determined its evaluation was flawed and took corrective action within 18 days after the protester submitted its comments on the agency report); *Coronet Mach. Corp. — Costs*, Comp. Gen. Dec. B-400197.2, 2008 CPD ¶ 213 (Army initiated corrective action 10 days prior to the report due date); *Alaska Structures, Inc. — Costs*, Comp. Gen. Dec. B-298156.2, 2006 CPD ¶ 109 (decision to cancel the solicitation occurred prior to the date set for the filing of the agency's report); *Security Consultants Group, Inc. — Costs*, Comp. Gen. Dec. B-293344.6, 2004 CPD ¶ 228 (agency took prompt corrective action in cancelling the solicitation and notifying GAO of intent to reinstate protester's contract prior to the due date for the agency's report); *PTI Supply Co.*, Comp. Gen. Dec. B-276559.3, 97-2 CPD ¶ 11 (agency took responsive corrective action the same day); *Carlson Wagonlit Travel*, Comp. Gen. Dec. B-266337.3, 96-2 CPD ¶ 99 (38 working days before corrective agency action not unreasonable where four separate protests were filed against the agency); *Bionetics Corp.*, Comp. Gen. Dec. B-270323.3, 96-2 CPD ¶ 70 (agency took corrective action promptly after protester filed comments on agency report); *Veda Inc.*, Comp. Gen. Dec. B-265809.2, 96-2 CPD ¶ 27 (delay of almost five months not unreasonable); *Atlas Powder Int'l, Ltd.*, 73 Comp. Gen. 122 (B-254408.5), 94-1 CPD ¶ 278 (even though corrective action not taken for nearly two months, delay not unreasonable where corrective action taken within eight working days of telephone conference between the parties); *and Locus Sys., Inc.*, 71 Comp. Gen. 243 (B-241441.5), 92-1 CPD ¶ 177 (agency promptly investigated the protester's allegations and subsequently resolicited the requirement after determining that the protester was correct).

As a prerequisite to GAO recommending that costs be reimbursed where a protest has been settled by corrective action, not only must the protest have been meritorious, but it also must have been clearly meritorious, i.e., not a close question, *PADCO, Inc. — Costs*, Comp. Gen. Dec. B-289096.3, 2002 CPD ¶ 135; *J.F. Taylor, Inc. — Entitlement to Costs*, Comp. Gen. Dec. B-266039.3, 96-2 CPD ¶ 5; *Baxter Healthcare Corp. — Entitlement to Costs*, Comp. Gen. Dec. B-259811.3, 95-2 CPD ¶ 174; *GVC Cos. — Entitlement to Costs*, Comp. Gen. Dec. B-254670.4, 94-1 CPD ¶ 292. A protest is "clearly meritorious" when a reasonable agency inquiry into the protester's allegations would show facts disclosing the absence of a defensible legal position, *First Fed. Corp. Costs*, Comp. Gen. Dec. B-293373.2, 2004 CPD ¶ 94; *Department of the Army — Recons.*, Comp. Gen. Dec. B-270860.5, 96-2 CPD ¶ 23. The mere fact that an agency decides to take corrective action does not establish that a statute or regulation clearly has been violated, *Sun Chem. Corp. — Cost*, Comp. Gen. Dec. B-288466.4, 2001 CPD ¶ 199; *Spar Applied Sys. — Declaration of Entitlement*, Comp. Gen. Dec. B-276030.2, 97-2 CPD ¶ 70. Cases where GAO found the protest to be not clearly meritorious include *Contrack Int'l, Inc. — Costs*, Comp. Gen. Dec. B-401871.3, 2010 CPD ¶ 122 (although agency was unreasonable on two issues, it was reasonable on another protest issue with result that protest was not clearly meritorious); *AGFA HealthCare Corp. — Costs*, Comp. Gen. Dec. B-400733.6, 2009 CPD ¶ 90 (although agency's failure to evaluate alleged noncompliance with mandatory standards in RFP was a serious issue, GAO did not agree that the issue was so clearly meritorious as to reveal the absence of any defensible legal position); *Triple Canopy, Inc. — Costs*, Comp. Gen. Dec. B-310566.9, 2009 CPD ¶ 62 (while acknowledging that the issues presented were "close questions," protests not clearly meritorious); *New England Radiation Therapy Mgmt. Servs., Inc. — Costs*, Comp. Gen. Dec. B-297397.3, 2006 CPD ¶ 30 (whether or not solicitation was ambiguous and whether awardee's price was or was not in accordance with the RFP schedule was not apparent from the record); *J.F. Taylor, Inc.*, Comp. Gen. Dec. B-266039.3, 96-2 CPD ¶ 5 (interpretation of the solicitation's requirements and the awardee's compliance with the requirements not clearly meritorious); and *Baxter Healthcare Corp.*, Comp. Gen. Dec. B-259811.3, 95-2 CPD ¶ 174 (while contracting agency's technical evaluation was flawed it was not clearly meritorious). There are a number of cases where GAO has found a protest not clearly meritorious because corrective action has forestalled the assembly of the record on which the protest could be resolved. See *Yardney Tech. Prods., Inc.*, Comp. Gen. Dec. B-297648.3, 2006 CPD ¶ 65 (protest grounds not clearly meritorious where agency cancelled solicitation prior to final reports and GAO had not fully analyzed the parties' positions); *LENS, JV — Costs*, Comp,. Gen. Dec. B-295952.4, 2006 CPD ¶ 9 (protest not clearly meritorious where resolution of the protest required further record development such as a hearing to complete and clarify the record); *The Sandi-Sterling Consortium — Costs*, Comp. Gen. Dec. B-296246.2, 2005 CPD ¶ 173 (merits of protest would have required development of the protest record — including a complete agency report and the protester's comments on the report — and GAO would have had to conduct substantial further legal analysis); and *East Penn Mfg. Co. — Costs*, Comp. Gen. Dec. B-291503.4, 2003 CPD ¶ 83 (protest not clearly meritorious where decision would have required further steps to complete and clarify the record).

Clearly meritorious protests include *Facility Servs. Mgmt., Inc. — Costs*, Comp. Gen. Dec. B-402757.5, 2010 CPD ¶ 236 (agency selected offeror when its key personnel did not meet RFP requirements); *ManTech Sys. Eng'g Corp.*, Comp. Gen. Dec. B-401542.6, 2010 CPD ¶ 14 (notwithstanding clear misevaluation of cost proposal, agency elected to defend protest); *Commercial Design Group, Inc. — Costs*, Comp. Gen. Dec. B-400923.3, 2009 CPD ¶ 126 (had agency conducted a reasonable review of the allegations in initial protest, it would have discovered that awardee's proposed computer-aided design manager's resume did not provide a sufficient basis to conclude that he met RFP requirements); *Pond Sec. Group Italia JV — Costs*, Comp. Gen. Dec. B-400149.2, 2009 CPD ¶ 61 (alleged defect affected protester's ability to compete at the time the protest was pending); *Salvation Army Comty. Corrs. Program — Costs*, Comp. Gen. Dec. B-298866.3, 2007

CPD ¶ 165 (no reasonable explanation in the record for the agency's evaluation in a number of areas); *Shindong-A Express Tour Co., Ltd. — Costs*, Comp. Gen. Dec. B-292459.3, 2004 CPD ¶ 75 (initial protest provided ample information to permit the Army to conclude that the awardee's proposal was unacceptable under the solicitation's stated evaluation scheme); *Martin Elecs., Inc. — Costs*, Comp. Gen. Dec. B-291732.2, 2003 CPD ¶ 84 (agency's selection of one awardee was unreasonable and unsupported and agency's evaluation of another awardee's proposal was inconsistent with the solicitation's stated evaluation criteria); *Georgia Power Co.*, Comp. Gen. Dec. B-289211.5, 2002 CPD ¶ 81 (agency did not reasonably evaluate whether awardee's past performance was for services similar in size, magnitude, and complexity to the solicitation requirement); *PADCO, Inc. — Costs*, Comp. Gen. Dec. B-289096.3, 2002 CPD ¶ 135 (agency accepted, in its cost realism analysis, without any analysis, the awardee's unexplained final proposed rates, which were substantially less than those initially proposed, its historical rates, and its proposed ceiling rates); *Miller Elevator Serv. Co. — Costs*, Comp. Gen. Dec. B-284870.3, 2000 CPD ¶ 126 (evaluation deficiencies would reduce 6-point technical advantage and increase protester's price advantage, necessitating a new price/technical tradeoff); and *Browning-Ferris Indus. of Hawaii, Inc.*, Comp. Gen. Dec. B-278051.2, 98-1 CPD ¶ 122 (an inquiry into the protester's allegations would have revealed that estimates in the solicitation had no reasonable basis).

GAO's willingness to inform the parties through outcome prediction ADR that a protest is likely to be sustained is generally an indication that the protest is viewed as clearly meritorious, *National Opinion Research Ctr. — Costs*, Comp. Gen. Dec. B-289044.3, 2002 CPD ¶ 55. See *KAES Enters., LLC — Protest and Costs*, Comp. Gen. Dec. B-402050.4, 2010 CPD ¶ 49 (protest costs awarded with regard to issue identified during the ADR conference — exclusion of KAES's proposal from the competitive range without consideration of its price); *Panacea Consulting, Inc. — Costs*, Comp. Gen. Dec. B-299307.3, 2007 CPD ¶ 133 (ADR found that the record showed that the agency had weighted the evaluation criteria differently during the evaluations than the manner stated in the solicitation); and *TyeCom, Inc.*, Comp. Gen. Dec. B-287321.3, 2002 CPD ¶ 101 (during ADR conference GAO attorney handling the protest explained that protest was likely to be sustained because the agency had made an award to an offer which had submitted a substantially lower-rated technical proposal, on the basis of low proposed cost under a cost-reimbursement contract, without performing any meaningful cost realism analysis).

To be eligible for protest costs when the agency takes corrective action, the protester is required to file with GAO within 15 calendar days after being advised of the procuring agency's decision to take corrective action, 4 C.F.R. § 21.8(e). The protester must also file a copy with the procuring agency, which then has 15 calendar days to respond.

## c.  Amount Recoverable

GAO will award proposal preparation costs that are reasonable and sufficiently documented. See *Sodexho Mgmt., Inc — Costs*, Comp. Gen. Dec. B-289605.3, 2003 CPD ¶ 136, stating:

> A protester seeking to recover its proposal preparation costs must submit evidence sufficient to support its claim that those costs were incurred and are properly attributable to proposal preparation. *Stocker & Yale, Inc. — Claim for Costs*, B-242568.3, May 18, 1993, 93-1 CPD ¶ 387 at 4; *Patio Pools of Sierra Vista, Inc. — Claim for Costs*, B-228187.4, B-228188.3, Apr. 12, 1989, 89-1 CPD ¶ 374 at 3. The amount claimed may be recovered to the extent that it is adequately documented and is shown to be reasonable; a cost is reasonable if, in its nature and amount, it does not exceed that which would be incurred by a prudent person in the preparation of his or her proposal. *Patio Pools of Sierra Vista, Inc. — Claim for Costs, supra*; see also FAR § 31.201-3(a). Where a protester has aggregated allowable and unallowable costs in a single claim, such that our Office cannot tell from the record what portion is unallowable, we will recommend that the entire amount be disallowed even though some portion of the claim may be properly payable. *TRESP Assocs., Inc. — Costs*, B-258322.8, Nov. 3, 1998, 98-2 CPD ¶ 108 at 4. Although we recognize that the requirement for documentation may sometimes entail certain practical difficulties, we do not consider it unreasonable to require a protester to document in some detail the amount and purposes of its employees' claimed efforts and to establish that the claimed hourly rates reflect the employees' actual rates of compensation plus reasonable overhead and fringe benefits. *W. S. Spotswood & Sons, Inc. — Claim for Costs*, B-236713.3, July 19, 1990, 90-2 CPD ¶ 50 at 3. The mere submission of voluminous documentation in support of a claim is not enough to meet these standards.

GAO will award protest costs that are related to the protest. The costs incurred in protesting to the agency are not reimbursable, *Galen Med. Assocs., Inc. — Costs*, Comp. Gen. Dec. B-288661.6, 2002 CPD ¶ 114. Similarly, time spent attending a debriefing or in settlement discussions is not reimbursable, *Blue Rock Structures, Inc. — Costs,* Comp. Gen. Dec. B-293134.2, 2005 CPD 190, and a protester's time spent soliciting help from members of Congress is not recoverable, *Omni Analysis*, 69 Comp. Gen. 433 (B-233372.4), 90-1 CPD ¶ 436. However, costs of challenging an agency's corrective action have been found to be related costs, *T Square Logistics Servs. Corp., Inc. — Costs*, Comp. Gen. Dec. B-297790.6, 2007 CPD ¶ 108. Related costs have included the salaries of the protester's president and other employees for the time they worked on the protest, *Ultraviolet Purification Sys., Inc.,* Comp. Gen. Dec. B-226941.3, 89-1 CPD ¶ 376. See, however, *Berkshire Computer Prods.,* Comp. Gen. Dec. B-240327.3, 95-1 CPD ¶ 6, denying the award of protest costs because the protester did not establish that the costs claimed to have been paid to an unsalaried consultant and an attorney were related to the protest.

Generally, GAO will recommend that a protester with a clearly meritorious protest be paid all of its reasonable protest costs, not just those costs related to winning issues. However, in some cases, only the costs of severable issues will be paid. See *Burns & Roe Servs. Corp. — Costs*, Comp. Gen. Dec. B-310828.2, 2008 CPD ¶ 81, stating:

> As a general rule, we consider a successful protester entitled to be reimbursed costs incurred with respect to all issues pursued, not merely those upon which it prevails. *AAR Aircraft Servs. — Costs*, B-291670.6, May 12, 2003, 2003 CPD ¶ 100 at 9. In our view, limiting recovery of protest costs in all cases to only those issues on which the protester prevailed would be inconsistent with the broad, remedial, congressional purpose behind the cost reimbursement provisions of the Competition in Contracting Act of 1984, 31 U.S.C. § 3554 (c)(1) (a) (2006). *AAR Aircraft Servs. — Costs, supra*; *TRESP Assocs., Inc. — Costs*, B-258322.8, Nov. 3, 1998, 98-2 CPD ¶ 108 at 2. Nevertheless, failing to limit the recovery of protest costs in all instances of partial or limited success by a protester may also result in an unjust award determination. Accordingly, in appropriate cases, we have limited our recommendation for the award of protest costs where a part of those costs is allocable to an unsuccessful protest issue that is so clearly severable from the successful issues as to essentially constitute a separate protest. See, e. g., *BAE Tech. Servs., Inc. — Costs*, B-296699.3, Aug. 11, 2006, 2006 CPD ¶ 122 at 3; *Interface Floorings Sys., Inc. — Claim for Attorneys' Fees*, B-225439.5, July 29, 1987, 87-2 CPD ¶ 106 at 2-3. In determining whether protest issues are so clearly severable as to essentially constitute separate protests, we consider, among other things, the extent to which the issues are interrelated or intertwined — i.e., the successful and unsuccessful arguments share a common core set of facts, are based on related legal theories, or are otherwise not readily severable. See *Sodexho Mgmt., Inc. — Costs*, B-289605.3, Aug. 6, 2003, 2003 CPD ¶ 136 at 29.

Cases finding severable issues include *Facility Servs. Mgmt., Inc. — Costs*, Comp. Gen. Dec. B-402757.5, 2010 CPD ¶ 236 (meritorious challenge of evaluation of awardee's key personnel clearly severable from issues concerning evaluation of protester's proposal); *Core Tech Int'l Corp — Costs*, Comp. Gen. Dec. B-310600.3, 2009 CPD ¶ 58 (challenge to use of HUBZone price evaluation credit clearly severable from meritorious challenges of technical evaluation and adequate discussions); *Al Qabandi United Co.*, Comp. Gen. Dec. B-400047.2, 2008 CPD ¶ 112 (challenges of affirmative responsibility determination and relaxation of specification requirements severable from meritorious challenge of price evaluation); *Panacea Consulting, Inc. — Costs*, Comp. Gen. Dec. B-299307.3, 2007 CPD ¶ 133 (unrelated issues severable from meritorious challenge of inadequate documentation of source selection decision and improper weighting of evaluation factors). In the case where issues are severable and information submitted to support a claim is not detailed enough to establish how much of the claimed amount was incurred in pursuit of the successful protest issues, GAO has recognized a "page count" method — that is, an estimate based on the number of pages in the protester's submissions to GAO that were devoted to a particular issue — is a reasonable means of determining this amount, *ViON Corp. — Costs*, Comp. Gen. Dec. B-256363.3, 95-1 CPD ¶ 219. In *Intercon Assocs., Inc. — Costs*, Comp. Gen. Dec. B-296697.2, 2006 CPD ¶ 95, GAO held that, given the absence of more probative evidence from Intercon, it was reasonable for the agency to use a page count of Intercon's comments to segregate the costs attributable to a valid protest issue from the costs attributable to a mooted protest issue. See also *BAE Tech. Servs., Inc. — Costs*, Comp. Gen. Dec. B-296699.3, 2006 CPD ¶ 122, finding that the contemporaneous records documenting the time spent on the protest by BAE's attorneys and other legal staff were not sufficiently detailed to permit an allocation of hours to two severable issues where the protest was not sustained. GAO found it appropriate to reduce the claimed protest costs by 5.5% using a page count of the total number of pages in its submissions to GAO that were devoted to the two severable issues.

GAO will not allow the recovery of costs that may be related to the protest but are not properly documented, *W.S. Spotswood & Sons*, 69 Comp. Gen. 622 (B-236713.3), 90-2 CPD ¶ 50. The burden is on the protester to adequately document the costs incurred, and the protester cannot rely on standard rates to substantiate its claim. See *John Peeples*, 70 Comp. Gen. 661 (B-233167.2), 91-2 CPD ¶ 125. GAO will also disallow legal expenses or fees that are not adequately documented by the law firm, *Diverco, Inc.* (B-240639.5), 92-2 CPD ¶ 460. In *W. S. Spotswood & Sons*, 69 Comp. Gen. 622 (B-236713.3), 90-2 CPD ¶ 50, GAO disallowed costs due to data insufficiency. The protester submitted evidence showing the type and amount of work performed by the employees but did not demonstrate how the hourly rates were calculated or whether the rates claimed reflected actual compensation plus reasonable overhead and fringe benefits. In *Solutions Lucid Group, LLC — Costs*, Comp Gen. Dec. B-400967.2, 2009 CPD ¶ 198, GAO denied the protester's request for recommendation that it be reimbursed $52,800 in protest costs where the protester failed to furnish sufficient evidence to establish the number of hours worked and rates of compensation for the individuals who worked on the protest. See also *DTV Transition Group., Inc. — Costs*, Comp. Gen. Dec. B-401466.2, 2010 CPD ¶ 84 (claim not adequately documented where protester did not submit requested additional documentation — i.e., copies of the analysis performed by experts, documentation of attorneys' fees, and supporting records such as timesheets, calendars, expense reports, billing statements, and receipts); *Al Long Ford — Costs*, Comp. Gen. Dec. B-297807.2, 2007 CPD ¶ 189 (claim did not identify the dates on which the hours were worked or the nature of the tasks performed, nor did it include documentation supporting the claimed rates of compensation or establishing protester's obligation to compensate the consultant); *TRS Research — Costs, Comp Gen. Dec.* B-290644.2, 2003 CPD ¶ 112 (disallowed costs where the protester does not demonstrate adequate documentation demonstrating the reasonableness of outside counsel's hourly rates); *CAN Indus. Eng'g, Inc.*, Comp. Gen. Dec. B-271034.2, 97-2 CPD ¶ 149 (hours charged were unreasonable where sole supporting documentation consisted of a matrix showing only the employees' names, terse and very general descriptions of the type of work that each employee was doing over time periods of a week or two, and the total number of hours that the employees allegedly worked during those time periods); *Innovative Refrigeration Concepts*, Comp. Gen. Dec. B-258655.2, 97-2 CPD ¶ 19 (documentation failed to demonstrate how hourly rates were calculated or that the claimed rates reflected actual rates of compensation); *Custom Prod. Mfg., Inc.,* Comp. Gen. Dec. B-235431.7, 95-1 CPD ¶ 236 (protester's claim was denied because it consisted of lump-sum figures that prevented both the agency and GAO from reviewing the reasonableness of the amount claimed); and *McNeil Techs., Inc.,* Comp. Gen. Dec. B-254909.3, 95-1 CPD ¶ 207 (protester failed to identify which employees were involved in specific aspects of pursuing the protest, the purposes of the employees' claimed efforts, or what cost elements were reflected in the different hourly rates calculated for each individual).

## (1) ATTORNEYS' FEES

Attorneys' fees usually are the primary component of a claim for protest costs and may be part of proposal preparation costs. GAO generally accepts the number of attorney hours claimed, unless the agency identifies specific hours as excessive and articulates a reasonable analysis as to why payment for those hours should be disallowed, *Data Based Decisions, Inc. — Costs,* Comp. Gen. Dec. B-232663.3, 89-2 CPD ¶ 538. Simply concluding that the hours claimed are excessive or suggest duplication of effort is inadequate to justify denying a claim for protest costs, *Princeton Gamma-Tech, Inc. — Claim for Costs,* Comp. Gen. Dec. B-228052.5, 89-1 CPD ¶ 401; *Omni Analysis,* 69 Comp. Gen. 433 (B-233372.4), 90-1 CPD ¶ 436. In *BAE Tech. Servs., Inc. — Costs,* Comp. Gen. Dec. B-296699.3, 2006 CPD ¶ 122, GAO held that the agency's unsupported view that the hours claimed were excessive was insufficient to justify denying or reducing a claim when it had annotated each time charge by each BAE attorney for each day. GAO will examine the reasonableness of the attorney hours claimed to determine whether they exceed, in nature and amount, what a prudent person would incur in pursuit of his or her protest, *SKJ & Assocs., Inc.,* Comp. Gen. Dec. B-291533.3, 2003 CPD ¶ 130; *Price Waterhouse — Claim for Costs,* Comp. Gen. Dec. B-254492.3, 95-2 CPD ¶ 38. In *Pulau Elecs. Corp. — Costs,* Comp. Gen. Dec. B-280048.11, 2000 CPD ¶ 122, GAO held that Pulau's use of a five-person team was not unreasonable in the context of substantively and procedurally demanding protests. In *Galen Med. Assocs., Inc. — Costs,* Comp. Gen. Dec. B-288661.6, 2002 CPD ¶ 114, Galen's claim included a request that it be reimbursed for a total of 938.5 hours for various individuals at various hourly rates: 346.25 hours for an outside attorney, 220 hours for a consultant and 363 hours for Galen's president. GAO held that these claimed hours were far beyond what should have been necessary to reasonably pursue a protest that was relatively limited and straightforward in nature. GAO stated its file in this case was only open for approximately nine weeks, and yet these hours amount to 8.6 full-time (40-hour) work weeks for the attorney, nine full-time work weeks for Galen's president and 5.5 full-time work weeks for Galen's consultant. There was no hearing in the matter and the documents involved were not voluminous. The core government exhibit amounted to only 39 pages and the protester's submissions to GAO amounted to only 22 pages. The hours claimed equate to approximately 42 hours per page, and the cost amounts to approximately $7,154 per page. GAO stated that in its view, this amount was excessive and went well beyond what a prudent person would have expended in pursuit of the protest. See also *Armour of Am., Inc.,* Comp. Gen. Dec. B-237690.2, 92-1 CPD ¶ 257, where GAO determined that legal fees were excessive even though well documented. There, GAO disallowed all 36 hours of the attorneys' billed time for pursuit of issues that were clearly untimely, disallowed one fourth of Armour's attorneys' hours attributable to legal research and writing, and disallowed one third of the total time claimed by Armour's attorneys for travel to and from the informal bid protest conference held at GAO offices. In *Price Waterhouse*, Comp. Gen. Dec. B-254492.3, 95-2 CPD ¶ 38, GAO reviewed each hour billed to determine the reasonableness of the attorney hours claimed. GAO found that although 13.5 hours seemed to be high in preparing a protective order, it was not excessive. However, 4.5 hours to review the agency's notice to authorize contract performance pursuant to the statutory best interest clause was considered excessive by GAO. See also *CNA Indus. Eng'g, Inc.*, Comp Gen. Dec. B-271034.2, 97-2 CPD ¶ 149 (hours were excessive in that the protected documents were releasable only to individuals admitted to the protective order and the in-house employees, who were not admitted to the protective order, had no access to significant portions of the record); *Fritz Cos. — Costs*, Comp. Gen. Dec. B-246736.7, 94-2 CPD ¶ 58 (denied request for reimbursement where billing records showed that multiple attorneys performed duplicative work, and did not demonstrate a need for such efforts).

There is a statutory cap on attorneys' fees, except where the protester is a small business concern. The top rate reimbursable to large businesses for attorneys' fees is $150 per hour, 31 U.S.C. § 3554(c)(2)(B). However, the attorneys' fee cap may be increased where "the agency determines, based on the recommendation of GAO on a case-by-case basis, that an increase in the cost of living or a special factor, such as the limited availability of qualified attorneys for the proceedings involved, justifies a higher fee," 31 U.S.C. § 3554(c)(2)(B).

GAO routinely recommends an upward departure from the $150 cap to reflect the fact that the cost of living has increased, as measured by the Department of Labor's (DOL) Consumer Price Index (CPI). See *Sodexho Mgmt., Inc — Costs*, Comp. Gen. Dec. B-289605.3, 2003 CPD ¶ 136, discussing the § 3554 ceiling on attorneys' fees and the cost of living adjustment, and concluding that the statute contemplates an increase in the specified $150 per hour rate in order to offset any decrease in the value of the rate due to increases in the cost of living. Since *Sodexho*, GAO has found that the justification for an upward departure from the $150 cap is self-evident if the claimant asserts that the cost of living has increased, as measured by DOL's CPI. See, for example, *Transportation Sec. Admin. — Costs*, Comp. Gen. Dec. B-400340.8, 2010 CPD ¶ 119 (protester calculated fees at $210.77 to $211.12 per hour (depending on the month of billing) using DOL's CPI — All Urban Consumers); *Core Tech Int'l Corp. — Costs*, Comp. Gen. Dec. B-400047.3, 2009 CPD ¶ 121 (protester provided a detailed explanation of its calculation of the rates using DOL's CPI — All Urban Consumers); *EBSCO Publ'g, Inc. — Costs*, Comp. Gen. Dec. B-298918.4, 2007 CPD ¶ 90 (upward adjustment of attorney fees to reflect increase in cost of living as measured by the applicable CPI); *Department of the Army; ITT Fed. Servs. Int'l Corp. — Costs*, B-296783.4, 2006 CPD ¶ 72 (upward adjustment of attorneys' fees to a rate of $238 per hour using DOI's CPI for All Urban Consumers, U.S. City Average for Legal Services); and *Department of State — Costs*, Comp. Gen. Dec. B-295352.5, 2005 CPD ¶ 145 (Inter-Con's requested fees properly supported and reasonable).

Notwithstanding the lack of a fee cap for small business concern's attorneys' fees, GAO will only recommend rates charged by an attorney that are consistent with customary rates for similar work in the community, as well as the experience, reputation and ability of the practitioner, *Public Commc'ns Servs., Inc. — Costs*, Comp. Gen. Dec. B-400058.4, 2009 CPD ¶ 131 (finding reasonable an hourly rate of $705 per hour). GAO will also look to surveys of area law firms' hourly rates to determine the reasonableness of rates, *CourtSmart Digital Sys., Inc. — Costs*, Comp. Gen. Dec. B-292995.7, 2005 CPD ¶ 47 (hourly rate of $475 reasonable for an attorney experienced in government procurement law who was a partner in a Washington, D. C. firm; noting that according to an article published in the January 2003 edition of Legal Times, the hourly rates for partners from 19 Washington, D.C. area law firms surveyed ranged from $185 to $750). But see *TRS Research — Costs*, Comp. Gen. Dec. B-290644.2, 2003 CPD ¶ 112 (despite numerous requests by the agency, protester did not submit any documentation to show that the $425 hourly rate claimed by TRS counsel was representative of that charged for similar services in the Philadelphia area where he practices). GAO will also consider, where relevant and appropriate, the fee rates found allowable by it in other similarly complex proceedings, *Blue Rock Structures, Inc. — Costs*, Comp. Gen. Dec. B-293134.2, 2005 CPD ¶ 190 ("Given our approval of $475 as a reasonable hourly rate for a partner in a Washington firm in *CourtSmart*, we see no basis to object to the lower rate billed by Blue Rock's attorney, who is also a partner in a Washington firm.").

GAO will permit a protester to recover the work of support staff such as paralegals, but not library services, which GAO deems more appropriately to overhead, *Public Commc'ns Servs., Inc . — Costs*, Comp. Gen. Dec. B-400058.4, 2009 CPD ¶ 131; *Pulau Elecs. Corp. — Costs*, Comp. Gen. Dec. B-280048.11, 2000 CPD ¶ 122.

## (2) LABOR COSTS

A protester's internal labor costs for preparing a bid or proposal may be recovered where the rates reflect "actual rates of compensation plus reasonable overhead and fringe benefits," *Sodexho Mgmt., Inc — Costs*, Comp. Gen. Dec. B-289605.3, 2003 CPD ¶ 136. However, a protester may not recover profit, *Celadon Labs, Inc.*, Comp. Gen. Dec. B-298533.2, 2008 CPD ¶ 208; *Blue Rock Structures, Inc. — Costs*, Comp. Gen. Dec. B-293134.2, 2005 CPD ¶ 190; *SKJ & Assocs., Inc.*, Comp. Gen. Dec. B-291533.3, 2003 CPD ¶ 130. If a protester aggregates allowable and unallowable costs, the entire amount is disallowed even though some of the costs are reasonable, *TRESP Assocs., Inc. — Costs*, Comp. Gen. Dec. B-258322.8, 98-2 CPD ¶ 108. A protester may reasonably show the hours spent by employees through a general explanation of the tasks conducted and estimate of the time spent by those employees, *Data Based Decisions, Inc. — Costs*, Comp. Gen. Dec. B-232663.3, 89-2 CPD ¶ 538. There Data Based successfully supported the costs of its president salary for 133.75 hours and its out-of-pocket expenses by providing a document that listed by date a brief description of the work performed by the president and the amount of time spent. See, however, *International Program Group, Inc. — Costs*, Comp. Gen. Dec. B-400278.4, 2009 CPD ¶ 128, rejecting a claim for costs of a legal assistant at $80 per hour when the only evidence submitted was a lump-sum quarterly payment. GAO concluded this was not evidence of actual costs.

## (3) OUTSIDE CONSULTANTS & EXPERT WITNESSES

There is a statutory cap on fees for consultants and expert witnesses for large businesses. See 31 U.S.C. § 3554(c)(2)(A) limiting the rate to the "highest rate of compensation for expert witnesses paid by the Federal Government." FAR 33.104(h)(5)(i) provides that this will be the rate established under 5 U.S.C. § 3109 and 5 C.F.R. § 304.105. This is the rate of pay for a federal employee (GS-15, step 10), even where the consultant billed at a higher rate, *Department of the Army*, Comp. Gen. Dec. B-296783.4, 2006 CPD ¶ 72. In *Solutions Lucid Group, LLC — Costs*, Comp Gen. Dec. B-400967.2, 2009 CPD ¶ 198, GAO denied consultant costs because the evidence submitted did not show that the protester was obligated to reimburse the consultant even though it lost the protest or that the protester had actually paid the consultant.

## 3. Revision of Remedies

31 U.S.C. § 3554(e)(1) requires that GAO report promptly to the Senate's Committee on Governmental Affairs and Committee on Appropriations and the House's Committee on Government Reform and Oversight and the Committee on Appropriations any case in which a federal agency fails to implement fully a recommendation of the Comptroller General. The report is required to include "a comprehensive review of the pertinent procurement including the circumstances of the failure of the Federal agency to implement a recommendation of the Comptroller General," 31 U.S.C. § 3554(e)(1)(A). The report must also include a recommendation regarding whether "in order to correct an inequity or to preserve the integrity of the procurement process," Congress should consider (1) private relief legislation, (2) legislative recission or cancellation of funds, (3) further investigation by Congress, or (4) other action, 31 U.S.C. § 3554(e)(1)(B).

The details of implementing GAO recommendations for corrective action are within the sound discretion and judgment of the contracting agency, *Rel-Tek Sys. & Design, Inc. — Modification of Remedy*, Comp. Gen. Dec. B-280463.7, 99-2 CPD

¶ 1. Such discretion must be exercised reasonably and in a fashion that remedies the procurement impropriety that was the basis for GAO protest recommendation. In *The Futures Group Int'l*, Comp. Gen. Dec. B-281274.5, 2000 CPD ¶ 148, GAO had sustained the protest because the contemporaneous record did not evidence that USAID reasonably found the awardee's proposed rates realistic. In response to this decision the agency took corrective action by determining that the awardee's probable costs were the lowest and confirming award to that firm. GAO held this to be unreasonable because the agency was advised by the DCAA that the awardee's proposed uncapped indirect rates were understated by an amount that would have affected the outcome of the competition. See also *Rockwell Elec. Commerce Corp.*, Comp. Gen. Dec. B-286201.6, 2001 CPD ¶ 162, finding the agency did not act reasonably in its response to an earlier sustained decision by reopening discussions and requesting proposal revisions from only one offeror in the competitive range.

In some circumstances it may not be feasible or practicable for an agency to follow GAO's recommendation. In such cases the agency may request that GAO modify its recommendation for corrective action. See *Department of Commerce — Recons.*, Comp. Gen. Dec. B-277260.4, 98-2 CPD ¶ 35 (recommendation modified because agency established, through a site visit by GAO, that a significant portion of the contract work had been completed and that it would be impracticable to disturb award); *Department of Transp.; Computer Sci. Corp. — Recons. & Modification of Remedy*, Comp. Gen. Dec. B-278466.2, 98-1 CPD ¶ 140 (recommendation modified where original remedy would endanger agency's ability to address Year 2000 problem); *National Aeronautics & Space Admin. — Recons. & Modification,* Comp. Gen. Dec. B-274748.3, 97-1 CPD ¶ 159 (recommendation modified where it was not practicable to return the items because they had already been delivered and paid for); *ABA Indus., Inc. — Recons.*, Comp. Gen. Dec. B-250186.2, 93-1 CPD ¶ 415 (recommendation modified where only awardee could meet delivery schedule). Compare *Department of the Army — Request for Modification of Recommendation*, Comp. Gen. Dec. B-290682.2, 2003 CPD ¶ 23, where GAO would not modify its recommendation to open competition to all eligible small business concerns because CICA provides for full and open competition among eligible small business concerns for acquisitions required to be set aside for small businesses; *Department of Commerce — Request for Modification of Recommendation*, Comp. Gen. Dec. B-283137.7, 2000 CPD ¶ 27, where GAO would not modify its recommendation to permit offerors the opportunity to make oral presentations or amend the solicitation because the evaluation scheme may not be materially changed after receipt of proposals without providing offerors an opportunity to submit revised proposals based on the revised scheme; *Kumasi Ltd. /Kukawa Ltd. — Recons.*, 72 Comp. Gen. 331 (B-247975.12), 93-2 CPD ¶ 195, where GAO would not modify its recommendation to reopen negotiations on the basis of agency claim that continued performance of the contracts after best interest determination made implementation of recommendation impracticable; and *Gunn Van Lines — Recons.*, Comp. Gen. Dec. B-248131.2, 92-2 CPD ¶ 246, where GAO would not modify its recommendation of contract termination and award even though only one month remained on contract. Although an agency is not required to "formally" request modification before taking different corrective action, generally it will do so because of the requirement that GAO report noncompliance to Congress.

GAO may modify its recommendation if it finds the agency's request to be reasonable. See *Department of the Treasury, Bureau of Engraving and Printing — Request for Modification Remedy*, Comp. Gen. Dec. B-296490.6, 2007 CPD ¶ 101 (modification request on recommendation to reevaluate proposals and make new source selection decision granted where agency determined that its needs would be best met by splitting original requirements and competing under two new solicitations); *Department of State; Wackenhut Int'l, Inc. — Reconsideration and Modification of Recommendation*, Comp. Gen. Dec. B-295352.3, 2005 CPD ¶ 81 (modification request on recommendation to terminate reasonable in view of security concerns at the embassy as well as significant change in the agency's needs for guard service); *SMF Sys. Tech. Corp.*, Comp. Gen. Dec. B-292419.3, 2003 CPD ¶ 203 (disruption to agency's mission to provide medical services was considered in fashioning recommendation); and *J & J/BMAR Joint Venture, LLP — Costs*, Comp. Gen. Dec. B-290316.7, 2003 CPD ¶ 129 (wartime exigencies provide reasonable basis for delay in implementing corrective action).

The agency may decide to perform the work in-house, rather than take corrective action. In *Pemco Aeroplex, Inc.*, Comp. Gen. Dec. B-275587.9, 98-2 CPD ¶ 17, Pemco protested the evaluation of proposals and the award to Aero. In response to the protest, the Air Force determined that the evaluation of the offerors' past performance appeared to be inadequate. The Air Force decided to revise the solicitation, conduct discussions, solicit BAFOs, and reevaluate proposals. Because the Air Force decided to take corrective action, GAO dismissed Pemco's protest as academic. Subsequently, the Air Force decided not to complete the proposed corrective action but rather to perform the work in-house. In addition to arguing that the Air Force improperly failed to take the corrective action that it had promised and that the Air Force's actions were calculated to punish Pemco for protesting, the protesters argued that there was no reasonable basis for canceling the RFP. GAO denied the protest, stating:

> [S]o long as there is a reasonable basis for doing so, an agency may cancel a solicitation after the announcement of a different course of action in response to a GAO protest. *See Atlantic Scientific & Technology Corp.*, [Comp. Gen. Dec. B-276334.2, 97-2 CPD ¶ 116] at 1 - 2. In addition, if there is a reasonable basis for canceling a solicitation, notwithstanding some element of personal animus, we will not object to the cancellation. *Dr. Robert J. Telepak*, [Comp. Gen. Dec. B-247681, 92-2 CPD ¶ 4] at 4. Here, the protesters have offered no credible evidence showing that the cancellation was based upon animus toward either firm. In any event, since the Air Force has provided a reasonable basis for canceling the solicitation, neither the timing of the announcement of that basis nor the possibility of personal animus provides grounds for sustaining this protest.

See also *Southwest Anesthesia Servs.*, Comp. Gen. Dec. B-279176.2, 98-2 CPD ¶ 28, where GAO found proper an agency's decision to cancel a procurement and perform the services in-house, rather than take action, as promised.

In an unusual case, the Air Force defied a GAO recommendation. In *Pemco Aeroplex, Inc.*, Comp. Gen. Dec. B-280397, 98-2 CPD ¶ 79, GAO sustained a protest challenging the Air Force's decision to consolidate its depot workload requirements into a single solicitation. GAO recommended that the Air Force cancel the current solicitation and resolicit its requirements without bundling the workloads. The Air Force subsequently announced that it had gone ahead with the consolidated procurement, stating that awarding the depot work to one contractor will save up to $638 million during the nine-year life of the contract. In another interesting case, Symplicity contested the Office of Personnel Management's (OPM) award of a task order to TMP Worldwide, Inc. (Monster) for online employment information services. GAO sustained the protest, recommending that OPM reopen discussions and request revised quotations from vendors. *Symplicity Corp.*, Comp. Gen. Dec. B-291902, 2003 CPD ¶ 89. In July 2003 OPM formally declined to follow GAO's recommendation, on the basis that the recommendation was "incompatible with the best interest of Federal Government" and national security." See GAO Bid Protest Annual Report to the Congress for Fiscal Year 2003, B-158766 (2004). In August 2003, GAO reported the matter to Congress pursuant to 31 U.S.C. § 3554 and recommended that Congress consider an inquiry into OPM's failure to fully implement GAO's recommendation. Congressional hearings were held and the appropriations act for OPM was amended to cut funding for the procurement until OPM complied with GAO recommendations from the *Symplicity* decision. Funding was later restored in conference committee presumably after OPM agreed to cancel its contract with Monster and reopen the solicitation. Upon resolicitation of the procurement, OPM again awarded the contract to Monster. Another interesting case is *Mission Critical Solutions*, Comp. Gen. Dec. B-401057, 2009 CPD ¶ 93, *recons. denied*, 2009 CPD ¶ 148, where GAO held that HUBZone set-asides take precedence over the 8(a) program. Following GAO decision, on July 10, 2009 the Office of Management and Budget issued a memorandum directing executive branch agencies to disregard GAO's ruling pending legal review by the executive branch. On August 21, 2009, the Office of Legal Counsel (OLC) of the U.S. Department of Justice issued an opinion disagreeing with GAO's analysis, agreeing with the SBA's view that the HUBZone statute establishes "parity" with the 8(a) program. OLC stated further that its opinion was binding on the executive branch while GAO's decision was not, and directed agencies to disregard GAO decisions that are inconsistent with its opinion. Subsequently, the Court of Federal Claims agreed with GAO position, *Mission Critical Solutions v. United States*, 91 Fed. Cl. 386 (2010); *DGR Assocs., Inc. v. United States*, 94 Fed. Cl. 189 (2010), and GAO continued to grant protests when the HUBZone priority was not honored, *DGR Assocs., Inc.*, Comp. Gen. Dec. B-402494, 2010 CPD ¶ 115; *Rice Servs., Inc.*, Comp. Gen. Dec. B-402966.2, 2010 CPD ¶ 217. The matter was resolved by a statutory amendment providing for parity among the programs.

## IV. COURT OF FEDERAL CLAIMS

The Court of Federal Claims and its predecessors initially relied upon the Tucker Act, 28 U.S.C. § 1491(a)(1), to take jurisdiction over contract award controversies. This statute gives the court jurisdiction over claims "founded either upon the Constitution, or any Act of Congress, or any regulation of an executive department, or upon any express or implied contract with the United States." As early as 1956, the Court of Claims used the government's "implied contract to consider bids fairly" in holding that a disappointed bidder would be entitled to bid preparation costs if it could show that its bid had not been evaluated in good faith, *Heyer Prods. Co. v. United States*, 135 Ct. Cl. 63, 140 F. Supp. 409 (1956). The court again held that its jurisdiction extended to implied contracts to consider bids and proposals fairly and honestly in *Keco Indus., Inc. v. United States*, 203 Ct. Cl. 566, 492 F.2d 1200 (1974). However, lacking general equitable powers, the court could not grant injunctive relief but could only award damages.

Injunctive relief became available in 1982 when the following provision granting equitable powers to the Claims Court (renamed the Court of Federal Claims) was added to 28 U.S.C. § 1491(b)(3):

> To afford complete relief on any contract claim brought before the contract is awarded, the court shall have exclusive jurisdiction to grant declaratory judgments and such equitable and extraordinary relief as it deems proper, including but not limited to injunctive relief. In exercising this jurisdiction, the court shall give regard to the interests of national defense and national security.

The court held that this grant of jurisdiction also was limited to the implied contract to consider bids and proposals fairly and honestly. See *United States v. John C. Grimberg Co.*, 702 F.2d 1362 (Fed. Cir. 1983).

The Administrative Dispute Resolution Act of 1996 (ADRA), Pub. L. No. 104-320, repealed this provision but gave new "bid protest" jurisdiction to the court by enacting 28 U.S.C. § 1491(b), which states:

> (1) [T]he United States Court of Federal Claims . . . shall have jurisdiction to render judgment on any action by an interested party objecting to a solicitation by a Federal agency for bids or proposals for a proposed contract or to a proposed award or the award of a contract or any alleged violation of statute or regulation in connection with a procurement or a proposed procurement. . . . [T]he United States Court of Federal Claims . . . shall have jurisdiction to entertain such an action without regard to whether suit is instituted before or after award.

> (2) To afford relief in such an action, the courts may award any relief that the court considers proper, including declaratory and injunctive relief except that any monetary relief shall be limited to bid preparation and proposal costs.

Subsequently, some judges the Court of Federal Claims had decided that the court had protest jurisdiction under both 28 U.S.C. § 1491(a)(1) (damages) and 28 U.S.C. § 1491(b)(1) (injunction and/or damages). The Federal Circuit in *Resource Conservation Group, LLC v. Department of the Navy*, 597 F.3d 1238 (Fed. Cir. 2010), raised questions about this dual jurisdiction, holding that relief in the "procurement" context is exclusive under 28 U.S.C. § 1491(b)(1), while relief under 28 U.S.C. § 1491(a)(1) is still available when a claim arises from a federal solicitation which is not a procurement. In *Resource Conservation*, the protest arose from a solicitation to lease federal land and the protester contended the Court of Federal Claims had jurisdiction under 28 U.S.C. § 1491(a)(1) to consider a claimed breach of an implied contract of fair and honest consideration. The Court of Federal Claims dismissed the protest, holding it no longer had jurisdiction after the enactment of the ADRA to adjudicate the claim under § 1491(a)(1). The Court of Federal Claims also held it did not have jurisdiction under 28 U.S.C. § 1491(b)(1) over a bid protest involving a lease of government land, because relief under § 1491(b)(1) is limited to the procurement context, and the lease of land by the government is not a procurement. In addressing the question of implied-in-fact contract jurisdiction under § 1491(a)(1), the court noted that the legislative history clearly showed the ADRA was intended to unify bid protest law in one court under one standard, and § 1491(b)(1) jurisdiction was to be exclusive where § 1491(b)(1) provided a remedy. However, the Federal Circuit found it unlikely Congress intended § 1491(b)(1) to deny a pre-existing remedy without providing a new remedy. Here, because the protest involved a nonprocurement solicitation, the Court of Federal Claims had implied-in-fact contract jurisdiction under § 1491(a)(1). Two judges of the Court of Federal Claims have ruled that this dicta does not deprive the court of dual jurisdiction over procurement contract protests under § 1491(a)(1) and § 1491(b)(1), *FAS Support Servs., LLC v. United States*, 93 Fed. Cl. 687 (2010); *L-3 Commc'ns Integrated Sys., L. P. v. United States*, 94 Fed. Cl. 394 (2010). Two judges have followed *Resource Conservation* — *Metropolitan Van & Storage, Inc. v. United States*, 92 Fed. Cl. 232 (2010); *Linc Gov't Servs., LLC v. United States*, 96 Fed. Cl. 672 (2010). A fifth judge has held that a protester can assert breach of the implied contract to consider proposals fairly as part of its claim under § 1491(b)(1), *Bilfinger Berger AG Sede Secondaria Italiana v. United States*, 97 Fed. Cl. 96 (2010).

## A. Jurisdiction

Aside from the issue of whether the Court of Federal Claims has dual jurisdiction or only jurisdiction over "procurement" protests under 28 U.S.C. § 1491(b), there are other issued that must be addressed in deciding whether the court has jurisdiction.

### 1. Procurement Protests

28 U.S.C. § 1491(b)(1) gives the court jurisdiction to hear protests in connection with a procurement of a "federal agency."

## a.  Federal Agency

While the bid protest statute does not define the term "federal agency," it is defined in 40 U.S.C. § 472 as:

> any executive agency or any establishment in the legislative or judicial branch of the Government, including any wholly owned Government corporation.

The term "federal agency" is defined in other statutes, as well. Some definitions seem to be very broad. For example, 22 U.S.C. § 4802 states that "federal agency" "includes any department or agency of the United States Government." Some definitions do not include the legislative or judicial branches of the government within the definition. For example, 40 U.S.C. § 304e defines "federal agency" as "any executive department, independent establishment, commission, board, bureau, or office in the executive branch, or other agency of the United States." See also 5 U.S.C. § 804, which states that "federal agency" means any agency as is defined in § 551(1). This section defines "agency" as "each authority of the Government of the United States, whether or not it is within or subject to review by another agency, but does not include such entities as Congress, the courts, territories or possessions of the United States, the government of the District of Columbia, and courts martial and military commissions." Other statutory definitions include the legislative and judicial branches of the government. For example, 5 U.S.C. § 7901 defines "federal agency" as "an Executive agency as defined under Section 105 of title 5, United States Code, and shall include any agency of the legislative or judicial branch of Government." 40 U.S.C. § 612 is similar but excludes the Senate, the House of Representatives, and the Architect of the Capitol and any activities under his direction. 40 U.S.C. § 762, and 41 U.S.C. § 423 state that "federal agency" "has the meaning given such term by Section 3(b) of the Federal Property and Administrative Services Act of 1949" (40 U.S.C. § 472). The 28 U.S.C. § 451 definition of the term "agency" may also be used in bid protest cases. See *Emery Worldwide Airlines, Inc. v. United States*, 264 F.3d 1071 (Fed. Cir. 2001) (USPS is a "federal agency" within the meaning of the Tucker Act and the definition of "agency" in 28 U.S.C. § 451 governs that determination); *Hewlett-Packard Co. v. United States*, 41 Fed. Cl. 99 (1998) (Tucker Act as amended by the Administrative Disputes Resolution Act confers jurisdiction on court to hear protests challenging procurement decisions of the Postal Service).

## b.  In Connection with a Procurement

The phrase "in connection with a procurement" is very sweeping in scope. As long as a statute has a connection to a procurement proposal, an alleged violation suffices to supply protest jurisdiction, *RAMCOR Servs. Group, Inc. v. United States*, 185 F.3d 1286 (Fed. Cir. 1999). See also *LABAT-Anderson, Inc. v. United States*, 65 Fed. Cl. 570 (2005) (even though the protest did not involve review of a solicitation or award, it involved a government decision not to conduct a solicitation and thus was a challenge to an "alleged violation of statute or regulation in connection with a procurement"); and *Knowledge Connections, Inc. v. United States*, 79 Fed. Cl. 750 (2007) (court does not lose jurisdiction over a protest "because [an agency] allegedly only violated the APA, not a procurement statute"). In *Distributed Solutions, Inc. v. United States*, 539 F.3d 1340 (Fed. Cir. 2008), the Federal Circuit reversed the Court of Federal Claims decision, determining that the court possessed jurisdiction to entertain the complaint because 28 U.S.C. § 1491(b) expressly permits the filing of protests of pre-procurement decisions, such as an agency's determination of a need for property or services. The court adopted the definition of "procurement" from 41 U.S.C. § 403(2). This statute defines "procurement" as including "all stages of the process of acquiring property or services, beginning with the process for determining a need for property or services and ending with contract completion and closeout." The court concluded that "[t]o establish jurisdiction pursuant to this definition the contractors must demonstrate that the Government at least initiated a procurement, or initiated 'the process for determining a need' for acquisition and assistance solutions for JAMMS." Thus, it held that when the government issued an RFI to solicit information to determine the scope of services it required, there was jurisdiction to review such pre-procurement decisions. See also *Savantage Fin. Servs. v. United States*, 81 Fed. Cl. 300 (2008) (DHS's decision to migrate to the Oracle and SAP constituted a procurement because it reflected DHS's determination of a need to consolidate its financial management software systems, and its selection of the Oracle and SAP systems to meet that need); *K-LAK Corp. v. United States*, 93 Fed. Cl. 749 (2010) (claims challenging the decision to exit the 8(a) program and use the FSS concerned an alleged violation of statutes and regulations in connection with a procurement). But see *R&D Dynamics Corp. v. United States*, 80 Fed. Cl. 715 (2007) (declining to assume jurisdiction over a postaward protest related to the Army's Small Business Innovation Research Program because the claim did not arise "in connection with a procurement or proposed procurement" despite plaintiff's argument that GAO has routinely held that it has jurisdiction over protest actions related to the SBIR program). See also *Resource Conservation Group, LLC v. United States*, 597 F.3d 1238 (Fed. Cir. 2010), agreeing with the Court of Federal Claims (86 Fed. Cl. 475 (2009)) that the court lacked jurisdiction under § 1491(b)(1) to adjudicate protests involving leases of land where the government is the lessor, because a lease is not "in connection with a procurement or proposed procurement."

## 2. *Implied-in-Fact Jurisdiction*

28 U.S.C. § 1491(a)(1) confers jurisdiction over "any express or implied contract with the United States."

### a. *Contract of the United States*

The language of 28 U.S.C. § 1491(a)(1) permitting monetary relief is extremely broad, extending to "any contract of the United States." The following nonappropriated fund activities are explicitly included within the definition of the United States:

Army and Air Force Exchange Service

Navy Exchanges

Marine Corps Exchanges

Coast Guard Exchanges

Exchange Councils of the National Aeronautics and Space Administration

The only government agency excluded from coverage is the Tennessee Valley Authority, 28 U.S.C. § 1491(c). In *Slattery v. United States*, 635 F.3d 1298 (Fed. Cir. 2011), the court ruled in an en banc decision that this contract jurisdiction covered any entity that was acting on behalf of the government even though it had been given no appropriated funds. Earlier decisions had interpreted the statute as barring jurisdiction when an agency was receiving no appropriated funds and was not a listed agency. See *McDonald's Corp. v. United States*, 926 F.2d 1126 (Fed. Cir. 1991) (Navy resale and services support office covered even though it was not specifically listed in the statute because the legislative history showed that Congress intended to waive sovereign immunity for military organizations funded by resale activities); *Wolverine Supply, Inc. v. United States*, 17 Cl. Ct. 190 (1989) (Eielson AFB central base fund not covered because it was not included in the NAFI military exchanges set forth in the statute); *Eubanks v. United States*, 25 Cl. Ct. 131 (1992) (United States was not a party to the contract between housing authority and property owner, and its funding and regulating program did not establish any contractual obligation).

### b. Nonprocurement Contracts

Relief under 28 U.S.C. § 1491(a)(1) is available where an issue arises from a federal solicitation which is not a "procurement," i. e. where the federal solicitation concerns a sale, not an acquisition, or where a federal solicitation concerns the lease of federal real property, and not a federal "procurement" of property or services, *Resource Conservation Group, LLC v. Department of Navy*, 597 F.3d 1238 (Fed. Cir. 2010). As discussed above, the judges in the Court of Claims have reached different conclusions as to whether relief under this statute can be obtained on procurement contracts.

## B.  Standing — Who May Protest

"Standing is a threshold jurisdictional issue, which . . . may be decided without addressing the merits of a determination," *Castle v. United States*, 301 F.3d 1328 (Fed.

Cir. 2002). Before addressing the merits of a plaintiff's protest, a court must therefore determine whether a plaintiff has standing to invoke the court's jurisdiction.

## 1. Interested Parties — § 1491(b)(1)

The threshold issue in determining whether a party has standing under § 1491(b)(1) is whether a protester qualifies as an "interested party," *American Fed'n of Gov't Employees v. United States*, 258 F.3d 1294 (Fed. Cir. 2001). That section states that the Court of Federal Claims has jurisdiction "to render judgment on an action by an interested party objecting to a solicitation . . . ." The Federal Circuit has used the definition of "interested party" in the Competition in Contracting Act (CICA), 31 U.S.C. § 3551(2)(A), governing protests to GAO. See *Rex Serv. Corp. v. United States*, 448 F.3d 1305 (Fed. Cir. 2006). A two-part test is applied to determine whether a protester is an "interested party:" (1) the protester must show that it was an actual or prospective bidder; and (2) the protester must have a direct economic interest in the procurement, *Distributed Solutions, Inc. v. United States*, 539 F.3d 1340 (Fed. Cir. 2008).

### a. Actual or Prospective Bidder

Where the claim is that the government failed to engage in a competitive procurement, the plaintiff need not show that it would have received the award in a competition with other hypothetical bidders, but rather must show that it would have been a qualified bidder, *Myers Investigative & Sec. Servs., Inc. v. United States*, 275 F.3d 1366 (Fed. Cir. 2002). See *Savantage Fin. Servs. v. United States*, 81 Fed. Cl. 300 (2008) (plaintiff currently supplied a competitive financial management system to DHS and clearly could have competed for the contract if DHS had bid it out). In *RhinoCorps Ltd. Co. v. United States*, 87 Fed. Cl. 261 (Fed. Cl. 2009), the court found that the plaintiff had standing to continue its protest despite the fact that the company did not bid on the protested solicitation because the protest had been pending since well before the solicitation was issued and the protester claimed the solicitation was issued as a pretext to keep it from being awarded a follow-on contract. However, eventually RhinoCorps lost on the merits. See also *Magnum Opus Techs., Inc. v. United States*, 94 Fed. Cl. 512 (2010) (protester suing as a prospective bidder in a new competition that allegedly must be held because agency had no right to obtain services by exercising unpriced option); and *Totolo/King v. United States*, 87 Fed. Cl. 680 (2009) (prospective bidder if the solicitation were issued as a SDVOSB or small business set-aside). But see *Space Exploration Techs. Corp. v. United States*, 68 Fed. Cl. 1 (2005) (plaintiff is not an actual or prospective bidder and cannot qualify as an interested party with standing because it did not anticipate having full launch capability until the following fiscal year).

### b. Direct Economic Interest

A showing of direct economic interest requires the plaintiff to demonstrate that any alleged errors caused prejudice, *Myers Investigative & Sec. Servs., Inc. v. United*

*States*, 275 F.3d 1366 (Fed. Cir. 2002) (prejudice is a necessary element of standing). To prove a direct economic interest, the offeror is required to establish that, but for the alleged errors in the procurement, it had a substantial chance of receiving the contract, *Information Tech. & Applications v. United States*, 316 F.3d 1312 (Fed. Cir. 2003). Prejudice for standing is something less than prejudice on the merits because it is determined on the basis of the protester's allegations not the court's ruling on the validity of those allegations, *Linc Gov't Servs., LLC v. United States*, 95 Fed. Cl. 155 (2010) (calling this concept "allegational prejudice"). It can be demonstrated by cumulating the alleged errors, *USFalcon, Inc. v. United States*, 92 Fed. Cl. 436 (2010). Cases finding prejudice for standing purposes include *Coastal Int'l Sec., Inc. v. United States*, 93 Fed. Cl. 502 (2010) (plaintiff was in competitive range and record indicated that the competition between the two proposals was very close); *Hunt Bldg. Co. v. United States*, 61 Fed. Cl. 243 (2004) (protester was one of two offerors in the competitive range, with both deemed by the agency to be outstanding); *PGBA, LLC, v. United States*, 60 Fed. Cl. 196 (2004) (proposal was fully within the zone of consideration for a contractual award, and agency's handling of the data — access element showed unequal and unfair treatment). In *Systems Plus, Inc. v. United States*, 69 Fed. Cl. 757 (2006), the court held that the protester would have had a substantial chance of wining the contract. The protester was a qualified small business and its proposal was found to be technically acceptable. Also, as the incumbent supplier on many deliverables under the agreement, the protester demonstrated it was capable of performing the contract. But see *Homesource Real Estate Asset Servs., Inc. v. United States*, 94 Fed. Cl. 466 (2010), where the court held that even if plaintiff's protest grounds were sustained, there were eight vendors that did not receive any award and had higher technical ratings than plaintiff. Any of these eight vendors would have provided a better choice to the government. Therefore, even if plaintiff were to succeed in its protest on the merits, there was not a substantial chance it would be awarded the contract.

In a preaward context, a protester does not have to establish the prejudice necessary for standing by showing that it had a substantial chance of receiving the contract but only by showing a nontrivial injury which can be addressed by judicial relief, *Weeks Marine, Inc. v. United States*, 575 F.3d 1352 (Fed. Cir. 2009). In *Weeks Marine*, the court observed that in a preaward protest it is difficult for a prospective offeror to make the showing of prejudice because "there is no factual foundation for a 'but for' prejudice analysis." The court stated it would apply the standard used by the Court of Federal Claims that had previously been articulated in *Win-Star Commc'ns, Inc. v. United States*, 41 Fed. Cl. 748 (1998), in which standing is established by alleging "a non-trivial competitive injury which can be redressed by judicial relief." The Federal Circuit determined that this standard "strikes the appropriate balance" between § 1491(b)(1)'s "interested party" requirements and Article III standing requirements, and agreed that it is the appropriate standard to apply in a preaward challenge to an agency's solicitation. The court subsequently determined that Weeks had standing because it had alleged a facial defect in the solicitation that would materially affect how Weeks would be required to do business with the Corps for the duration of the IDIQ contract. See *Magnum Opus Techs., Inc. v. United States*, 94 Fed. Cl. 512 (2010) (if Magnum Opus succeeds in the protest, then it will be able to compete in any resolicitation for the services it alleges should have been subject to competition); *Knowledge Connections, Inc. v. United States*, 76 Fed. Cl. 6 (2007) (offeror had standing because it had effectively renewed its offer). But see *Camden Shipping Constr. Co. v. United States*, 89 Fed. Cl. 433 (2009) (protester's offer did not remain open for the required period).

## 2.  *Disappointed Bidders* — § 1491(a)(1)

The most common form of implied contract in contract award cases under § 1491(a)(1) arises when the government issues a solicitation, thereby making an offer to honestly and fairly consider responses, and the prospective contractor accepted this offer by submitting a bid or proposal, *Keco Indus., Inc. v. United States*, 192 Ct. Cl. 773, 428 F.2d 1233 (1970); *United States v. John C. Grimberg Co.*, 702 F.2d 1362 (Fed. Cir. 1983); *National Forge Co. v. United States*, 779 F.2d 665 (Fed. Cir. 1985). Such cases are usually characterized as "disappointed bidder" cases. In order to obtain jurisdiction on the basis of such implied contracts, the "disappointed bidder" must plead that it has accepted the government's offer contained in the solicitation. Thus, a party that did not submit a bid or proposal has no contract claim because it did not furnish the government the consideration requested for its promise, *Hero, Inc. v. United States*, 3 Cl. Ct. 413 (1983). In that case the plaintiff expended effort in preparing a bid but did not submit the bid, contending that the specifications were defective. The court refused to grant an injunction preventing award under the solicitation, reasoning that the mere expenditure of effort and money in preparing a bid without actually submitting it is not sufficient consideration for the government's implied promise. In *Harris Sys. Int'l, Inc. v. United States*, 5 Cl. Ct. 253 (1984), the court found no jurisdiction in an action by a small-business minority firm that had not submitted a proposal because the procuring agency had demanded that the SBA nominate another firm under the 8(a) set-aside. The court also held that the fact that the SBA had originally nominated the plaintiff to the Air Force did not establish an implied contract. In *Eagle Constr. Corp. v. United States*, 4 Cl. Ct. 470 (1984), the court found that the government's cancellation of a solicitation after technical proposals were received was not improper under the circumstances. Thus, the plaintiff who submitted a proposal under that solicitation but failed to submit one under the new solicitation for the same work had no disappointed bidder status under the new solicitation. See also *Control Data Sys., Inc. v. United States*, 32 Fed. Cl. 520 (1994) (incumbent contractor did not submit a proposal for follow-on contract, and the plaintiff's claim was therefore not a preaward protest within the jurisdiction of the court); *Howard v. United States*, 21 Cl. Ct. 475 (1990) (proposal submitted after closing date for receipt of proposals; thus, no valid offer that the government could accept); *Durable Metals Prods., Inc. v. United States*, 27 Fed. Cl. 472 (1993) (no jurisdiction because offeror withdrew from procurement); and *Data Transformation Corp. v. United States*, 13 Cl. Ct. 165 (1987) (informal presentation made to an agency of the plaintiff's technical ability to perform the work called for under the planned program was not the same as a response to a solicitation and did not create an implied-in-fact contract). While the court's rationale in nonbidder cases is clearly supportable where the plaintiff has not expended effort in reliance on the solicitation or decides to forgo the procurement, it is questionable where expenditures have been made in reliance on a solicitation that contains defective specifications or is otherwise improper.

The mere submission of a bid will not establish the necessary contractual relationship; the submission must be responsive to the invitation for bids. In *Yachts Am., Inc. v. United States*, 3 Cl. Ct. 447 (1983), *aff'd*, 779 F.2d 656 (Fed. Cir. 1985), the documents and letter submitted to the agency were found to be wholly nonresponsive and, thus, failed to give the plaintiff the status of a disappointed bidder. However, the court will review the bid and the solicitation to determine whether it is responsive and, if it so finds, will exercise its jurisdiction, *Olympia USA, Inc. v. United States*, 6 Cl. Ct. 550 (1984). See also *Blount, Inc. v. United States*, 22 Cl. Ct. 221 (1990) (court exercised jurisdiction to determine whether a clause in the IFB not addressed by the bid related to bidder responsiveness or responsibility). The disappointed bidder must also be able to show actual or threatened injury. In *Caddell Constr. Co. v. United States*, 9 Cl. Ct. 610 (1986), the court held that an offeror ranked sixth had no substantial chance for award and, thus, had no standing to sue. In addition, the firm submitting the offer must be eligible to receive the award, *ATL, Inc. v. United States*, 735 F.2d 1343 (Fed. Cir. 1984) (bids following a firm's suspension or debarment could not create implied contract because such firms are ineligible for award); *Gibraltar Indus., Inc. v. United States*, 2 Cl. Ct. 589 (1983), *vacated as moot*, 726 F.2d 747 (Fed. Cir. 1984) (bidder determined not to be a small business could not create implied contract by bidding on small business set-aside). However, a suspension or debarment issued after a bid or proposal has been submitted does not deprive the disappointed offeror of jurisdiction over such a previous bid or proposal, *Sterlingwear of Boston, Inc. v. United States*, 11 Cl. Ct. 517 (1987); *Electro-Methods, Inc. v. United States*, 728 F.2d 1471 (Fed. Cir. 1984). The court will take jurisdiction over claims alleging that the agency has improperly applied responsibility standards to an offeror, *Hayes Int'l Corp. v. United States*, 7 Cl. Ct. 681 (1985). See also *Skytech Aero, Inc. v. United States*, 26 Cl. Ct. 251 (1992), where an unsuccessful bidder alleged that the Army acted arbitrarily and capriciously by awarding a contract to a bidder that was not responsible and whose bid was nonresponsive. The court exercised jurisdiction and held that a preaward survey conducted by the Army allowed a reasonable conclusion that the bidder was responsible. The Court of Federal Claims has jurisdiction to review certificate of competency determinations by the SBA, *Cavalier Clothes, Inc. v. United States*, 810 F.2d 1108 (Fed. Cir. 1987); *Stapp Towing, Inc. v. United States*, 34 Fed. Cl. 300 (1995); *Related Indus., Inc. v. United States*, 2 Cl. Ct. 517 (1983).

In several rare cases the court has found preaward implied contracts to exist in situations other than disappointed bidder cases. See *Western Pioneer, Inc. v. United*

*States*, 8 Cl. Ct. 291 (1985), where the court held that a letter requesting that the plaintiff submit its proposed operating plan constituted "a sufficient request . . . such as to form an implied contract to fairly and honestly consider [the] responding proposal." See also *Standard Mfg. Co. v. United States*, 7 Cl. Ct. 54 (1984), where the plaintiff alleged that it responded to a *Commerce Business Daily* (CBD) notice in which the Air Force stated its intention to award a sole source contract and invited interested parties to identify interests in the procurement or to submit proposals for the work. The court held that such facts are sufficient to create an implied promise for the Air Force to give fair and impartial consideration to the response. Similarly, in *Magnavox Elec. Sys. Co. v. United States*, 26 Cl. Ct. 1373 (1992), the court held that a CBD notice of intent to conduct a sole source procurement and plaintiff's response that it could perform the work resulted in an implied contract to give plaintiff's response fair and impartial consideration. However, in *Motorola, Inc. v. United States*, 988 F.2d 113 (Fed. Cir. 1993), the court affirmed a decision of the Court of Federal Claims denying jurisdiction over a suit filed by a company that assisted the government in drafting the procurement specification but did not submit an offer because a bid sample was required. The Federal Circuit adopted the Court of Federal Claims decision, which disagreed with the rationale in *Standard Manufacturing*, stating that government requests for information and responses from prospective bidders are not the equivalents of offer and acceptance. The Federal Circuit quoted the Court of Federal Claims at 116:

> Such exchanges are not carried on with an expectation to presently affect legal relations. Rather, the parties are dealing — as they were here — exclusively with an eye to the future, each being free, in the meantime, to withdraw from the dialogue.
>
> The situation, therefore, is quite unlike that encountered where a bid has been submitted. In that circumstance there is a promise — the contractor's bid — which empowers the Government, upon acceptance, to bind the contractor to the terms of the solicitation. The essence of the contractor's engagement — the manifestation of an intention to be bound — warrants reading into the situation a reciprocal commitment from the Government, *i. e.,* a promise to fairly and honestly consider the contractor's bid. *Heyer Products Co. v. United States*, 135 Ct. Cl. 63, 69, 140 F. Supp. 409, 412 (1956).

See also *Garchik v. United States*, 37 Fed. Cl. 52 (1996), where the court denied jurisdiction over a proposal submitted in response to a CBD announcement that the agency proposed to enter into a sole source lease. In *American Hoist & Derrick, Inc. v. United States*, 3 Cl. Ct. 198 (1983), the plaintiff was a large business that was precluded from bidding on a solicitation because the procurement was set-aside for small businesses. However, the court took jurisdiction on the basis of an implied contract alleged to have been formed when the plaintiff released its proprietary data to the government in exchange for an agreement that it would be permitted to bid on the procurement. See also *Yachts Am., Inc. v. United States*, 3 Cl. Ct. 447 (1983), *aff'd*, 779 F.2d 656 (Fed. Cir. 1985). In *Airborne Data, Inc. v. United States*, 702 F.2d 1350 (Fed. Cir. 1983), the court held that an implied contract was formed when an unsolicited proposal was received in response to regulations inviting the submittal of such proposals. In *Pressman v. United States*, 33 Fed. Cl. 438 (1995), the court held that the agency's regulations prohibiting the release of confidential information did not give rise to an implied contract not to disclose confidential information contained in unsolicited proposals. The court distinguished *Airborne Data*, stating that in that case the text of the regulations contained an explicit promise of confidentiality, whereas in *Pressman* the regulations, although binding on the agency, could not be construed as suggesting that the agency was directing an offer to the general public to confidentially consider unsolicited proposals.

## C. Time for Protest

Unlike agency-level or GAO protests, there are no regulatory time limits for filing at the court, However, the Federal Circuit has established a waiver rule by stating that "a party who has the opportunity to object to the terms of a government solicitation containing a patent error and fails to do so prior to the close of the bidding process waives its ability to raise the same objection afterwards in a § 1491(b) action in the Court of Federal Claims," *Blue & Gold Fleet, L. P. v. United States*, 492 F.3d 1308 (Fed. Cir. 2007). *Blue & Gold* has been consistently interpreted as standing for the proposition that "[t]he proper time to challenge the provisions of a prospectus is before bids are required to be submitted," *Frazier v. United States*, 79 Fed. Cl. 148 (2007). Among the many reasons for this rule cited by the Federal Circuit is the need for "'expeditious resolution' of bid protests before this court." The waiver rule thus "avoids costly after the fact litigation," *Infrastructure Def. Techs., LLC v. United States*, 81 Fed. Cl. 375 (2008). Cases applying this rule include *Shamrock Foods Co. v. United States*, 92 Fed. Cl. 339 (2010) (terms of the solicitation); *Unisys Corp. v. United States*, 89 Fed. Cl. 126 (2009) (propriety of a price evaluation methodology that was explicitly described in the RFQ); *Blackwater Lodge & Training Center, Inc. v. United States*, 86 Fed. Cl. 488 (2009) (terms of solicitation); *Moore's Cafeteria Servs. v. United States*, 77 Fed. Cl. 180 (2007) (terms of solicitation amendment); *Scott v. United States*, 78 Fed. Cl. 151 (2007) (terms of solicitation); and *Erinys Iraq Ltd. v. United States*, 78 Fed. Cl. 518 (2007) (terms of solicitation). But see *Allied Materials & Equip. Co. v. United States*, 81 Fed. Cl. 448 (2008), finding no waiver to challenge a defect in an amendment because Allied had no knowledge of the amendment until after the date for submission of proposals. In *DGR Assocs., Inc. v. United States*, 94 Fed. Cl. 189 (2010), the court distinguished *Blue & Gold Fleet* and found a protest to a challenge to the solicitation impropriety timely even though it was not filed before the close of the bidding process. DGR had challenged the Air Force's solicitation before the closing date for receipt of proposals with an agency-level protest. When those actions proved unsuccessful DGR timely protested to GAO. At each step DGR followed applicable FAR and GAO protest procedures. The court held that the correct interpretation of *Blue & Gold Fleet* is that, if a party has challenged a solicitation impropriety before the close of the bidding process, the party is not precluded from later filing its protest at the Court of Federal Claims.

The court's only standard for determining if a post-award protest is untimely is whether the delay in bringing the protest was unreasonable and unexcused and prejudiced the government or other parties, *Software Testing Solutions, Inc. v. United States*, 58 Fed. Cl. 533 (2003). In one case, the court deemed timely a protest filed 14 months after the protester knew or should have known of the basis of the protest, *CW Gov't Travel, Inc. v. United States*, 61 Fed. Cl. 559 (2004).

## D. Intervenors

Intervenors are permitted under the Rules of the United States Court of Federal Claims (RCFC) 24, which states:

(a) Intervention of Right. On timely motion, the court must permit anyone to intervene who:

(1) is given an unconditional right to intervene by a federal statute; or

(2) claims an interest relating to the property or transaction that is the subject of the action, and is so situated that disposing of the action may as a practical matter impair or impede the movant's ability to protect its interest, unless the existing parties adequately represent that interest.

(b) Permissive Intervention.

(1) *In General*. On timely motion, the court may permit anyone to intervene who:

(A) is given a conditional right to intervene by a federal statute; or

(B) has a claim or defense that shares with the main action a question of law or fact.

(2) By a Government Officer or Agency.

[Not used.]

(3) *Delay or Prejudice*. In exercising its discretion, the court must consider whether the intervention will unduly delay or prejudice the adjudication of the original parties' rights.

The court has held that the requirements for intervention are to be construed in favor of intervention, *Cherokee Nation of Oklahoma v. United States*, 69 Fed. Cl. 148 (2005). Intervention is authorized where the applicant has an interest relating to the subject of the action and is so situated that disposition of the action may impair or impede its ability to protect that interest. Such intervention of right is mandated when the applicant's interests are not adequately represented by the existing parties to the litigation, *Che Consulting, Inc. v. United States*, 452 F.3d 1371 (2006). Here, the applicant to the motion to intervene asserted that its interests and the government's interests did not completely coincide. As a result, it argued that there was a likelihood that its interests may not be adequately protected by the government. The court agreed, stating that the issue before the court has a direct affect on the applicant, which may not be adequately articulated by the government, making intervention appropriate. See also *Northrop Grumman Information Tech., Inc. v. United States*, 74 Fed. Cl. 407 (2006), where the court granted the motion to intervene finding the intervenor's trade secrets and proprietary information constituted sufficient property interests to justify intervention. The record indicated a denial of the right to intervene might directly impair the intervenor's ability to protect its intellectual property. However, the court will not allow intervention to protect indirect or contingent interests, *American Maritime Transp. v. United States*, 870 F.2d 1559 (Fed. Cir. 1989); *Hage v. United States*, 35 Fed. Cl. 737 (1996).

A motion to intervene must be timely filed. Three factors are used to determine whether an intervention is timely: (1) the length of time during which the would-be intervenors actually knew or reasonably should have known of their rights; (2) whether the prejudice to the rights of existing parties by allowing intervention outweighs the prejudice to the would-be intervenors by denying intervention; and (3) the existence of unusual circumstances militating either for or against a determination that the application is timely, *Belton Indus., Inc. v. United States*, 6 F.3d 756 (Fed. Cir. 1993). See *Wackenhut Servs., Inc. v. United States*, 85 Fed. Cl. 273 (2008) (motion submitted two days after complaint, no party opposed motion and the court was unaware of any prejudice to the existing parties or any unusual circumstances); and *Information Scis. Corp. v. United States*, 73 Fed. Cl. 70 (2006) (submitted seven days after complaint, neither party opposed intervention, and court was unaware of any prejudice to existing parties or any unusual circumstances militating against intervention). However, in *TRW Envtl. Safety Sys., Inc. v. United States*, 16 Cl. Ct. 516 (1989), the Claims Court held that an unsuccessful bidder's motion to intervene in another unsuccessful bidder's suit for injunctive relief was untimely: the bidder waited 84 days from knowing of the suit before moving to intervene.

## E. Procedures

The Court of Federal Claims follows the rules set forth in the Rules of the United States Court of Federal Claims (RCFC) (as amended through January 11, 2010). These rules are based upon the Federal Rules of Civil Procedure. Appendix C to the RCFC, which is entitled "Procedures in Procurement Protest Cases Pursuant to 28 U.S.C. § 1491(b)" describes standard practices in Court of Federal Claims bid protest cases.

## 1.  Commencement of Action

### a.  Complaint and Service of Summons

A civil action in the Court of Federal Claims is commenced by filing a complaint with the clerk of court, RCFC 3. Service is made by the party, attorney of record, or any other person acting under the attorney of record's direction by executing a certificate of service, which contains the date and manner of service, the person or entity served, and the method of service employed, e.g., in person, by mail, or by electronic or other means, RCFC 5.3(a). The plaintiff must file an original and seven copies of the complaint with the court, RCFC 5.5. To serve a complaint on the United States, the clerk must deliver five copies of the complaint to the Attorney General or to an agent designated by authority of the Attorney General, RCFC 4(a). When serving a complaint, the clerk must enter the fact of service on the docket, and this entry will be prima facie proof of service, RCFC 4(b).

In order to expedite the proceeding, Appendix C to the RCFC requires that protester's "counsel must (except in exceptional circumstances to be described in moving papers) provide at least 24-hour advance notice of filing a protest" to the DOJ's Commercial Litigation Branch, the COFC Clerk, the procuring agency, and the apparently successful offeror(s) (if any)," Appendix C(2).

### b.  Filing Fee

A $350 filing fee must be paid to the clerk of the court when the action is commenced.

## 2.  Pleadings and Motion

### a.  Claim for Relief

Rule 8(a) states that the complaint must contain the following:

(1) a short and plain statement of the grounds for the court's jurisdiction, unless the court already has jurisdiction and the claim needs no new grounds to support;

(2) a short and plain statement of the claim showing that the pleader is entitled to relief; and

(3) a demand for the relief sought, which may include relief in the alternative or different types of relief.

In all averments of fraud or mistake, the circumstances constituting fraud or mistake must be stated with particularity, RCFC 9(b). See *Keco Indus., Inc. v.*

*United States*, 203 Ct. Cl. 566, 492 F.2d 1200 (1974), where the court held that a disappointed bidder's pleadings lacked particularity. In reaching this finding, the court stated that alleging general violations of the Armed Services Procurement Regulations fell far short of the specificity called for in the rule. See also *Baskett v. United States*, 2 Cl. Ct. 356 (1983) (although the Claims Court has adopted the notice pleading system found in the federal courts, this system does not do away with the requirement of particularity; unclear allegations of fraud and misrepresentation in pleadings of plaintiff are dismissed).

### b. Preliminary Hearings

Evidentiary hearings may be conducted by the Court of Federal Claims, RCFC 12(d). This rule provides that the following defenses must be heard and determined at a preliminary hearing unless the court orders deferral until trial:

(1) lack of subject-matter jurisdiction;

(2) lack of personal jurisdiction;

(3) improper venue [not used];

(4) insufficient process;

(5) insufficient service of process;

(6) failure to state a claim upon which relief can be granted; and

(7) failure to join a party under RCFC 19.

### 3. Administrative Record

When a protest is filed in court, the agency must file an "administrative record," RCFC 52.1. RCFC App. C, provision 22 provides a detailed list as guidance regarding the type of documents that may be appropriate for the United States to include as "core documents" in the administrative record pertaining to protests:

(a) the agency's procurement request, purchase request, or statement of requirements;

(b) the agency's source selection plan;

(c) the bid abstract or prospectus of bid;

(d) the Commerce Business Daily or other public announcement of the procurement;

(e) the solicitation, including any instructions to offerors, evaluation factors, solicitation amendments, and requests for best and final offers;

(f) documents and information provided to bidders during any pre-bid or pre-proposal conference;

(g) the agency's responses to any questions about or requests for clarification of the solicitation;

(h) the agency's estimates of the cost of performance;

(i) correspondence between the agency and the protester, awardee, or other interested parties relating to the procurement;

(j) records of any discussions, meetings, or telephone conferences between the agency and the protester, awardee, or other interested parties relating to the procurement;

(k) records of the results of any bid opening or oral motion auction in which the protester, awardee, or other interested parties participated;

(l) the protester's, awardee's, or other interested parties' offers, proposals, or other responses to the solicitation;

(m) the agency's competitive range determination, including supporting documentation;

(n) the agency's evaluations of the protester's, awardee's, or other interested parties' offers, proposals, or other responses to the solicitation, including supporting documentation;

(o) the agency's source selection decision including supporting documentation;

(p) preaward audits, if any, or surveys of the offerors;

(q) notification of contract award and the executed contract;

(r) documents relating to any pre- or post-award debriefing;

(s) documents relating to any stay, suspension, or termination of award or performance pending resolution of the bid protest;

(t) justifications, approvals, determinations, and findings, if any, prepared for the procurement by the agency pursuant to statute or regulation; and

(u) the record of any previous administrative or judicial proceedings relating to the procurement, including the record of any other protest of the procurement.

In many instances, the protester may believe that additional materials are necessary for the court to fully understand the basis for the protest. Motions to supplement the administrative record are governed by *Axiom Resource Mgmt., Inc. v. United States*, 564 F.3d 1374 (Fed. Cir. 2009). In *Axiom*, the court emphasized that "the parties' ability to supplement the administrative record is limited," and that the "focus of judicial review of agency action remains the administrative record," which should be supplemented only if the existing record is insufficient to permit meaningful review consistent with the Administrative Procedure Act. The court stated that determination of whether to order supplementation of the administrative record depends on whether supplementation is "necessary in order not 'to frustrate effective judicial review'" (quoting *Camp v. Pitts*, 411 U.S. 138, 142-43 (1973)). See also *Impresa Construzioni Geom. Domenico Garufi v. United States*, 238 F.3d 1324 (Fed. Cir. 2001). In a motion seeking testimony, the court in *Global Computer Enters., Inc. v. United States*, 88 Fed. Cl. 52 (2009), permitted supplementation of the administrative record because of the complexity of the case, the multitude of issues presented with respect to both jurisdiction and merits, the voluminous amount of information presented by the parties, and the necessity for supplementation in order to avoid frustrating judicial review. See also *Blue & Gold Fleet, LP v. United States*, 70 Fed. Cl. 487 (2006), *aff'd*, 492 F.3d 1308 (Fed. Cir. 2007) (supplementation is justified "when it is necessary for a full and complete understanding of the issues"); and *Mike Hooks, Inc. v. United States*, 39 Fed. Cl. 147 (1997) (considering evidence supplementing the record because it "help[s] explain the highly technical nature of the issues").

Supplementation of the administrative record is limited to cases in which "the omission of extra-record evidence precludes effective judicial review," *Murakami v. United States*, 46 Fed. Cl. 731 (2000), *aff'd*, 389 F.3d 1342 (Fed. Cir. 2005). The *Murakami* court stated that the purpose of limiting review to the record actually before the agency is to guard against courts using new evidence to "convert the 'arbitrary and capricious' standard into effectively 'de novo review.'" However, to perform an effective review pursuant to the APA, the court must have a record containing the information upon which the agency relied when it made its decision as well as any documentation revealing the agency's decision-making process. See *Citizens to Preserve Overton Park v. Volpe*, 401 U.S. 402, 420 (1971) ("[S]ince the bare record may not disclose the factors that were considered or the Secretary's construction of the evidence[,] it may be necessary for the [d]istrict [c]ourt to require some explanation in order to determine if the Secretary acted within the scope of his authority and if the Secretary's action was justifiable under the applicable standard.").

Cases permitting supplementation of the administrative record with declarations include *Totolo/King, a Joint Venture v. United States*, 87 Fed. Cl. 680 (2009) (affidavit attempted to explain why the government's failure to specify a bond estimate was unreasonable); and *Academy Facilities Mgmt. v. United States*, 87 Fed. Cl. 680 (2009) (affidavit of a source selection authority was an appropriate supplement to the record because it explicitly answered a question on a critical issue that was not clear in the administrative record). Cases rejecting supplementation include *Linc Gov't Servs., LLC v. United States*, 95 Fed. Cl. 155 (2010) (summary of past performance information not used by agency not included in record because it was unauthenticated and not sufficient to prove bad faith of agency officials); *DataMill, Inc. v. United States*, 91 Fed. Cl. 722 (2010) (rejecting supplementation of the record, stating that supplementation is justified (1) when required for meaningful judicial review, and (2) when necessary for a full and complete understanding of the issues); *Allied Tech. Group, Inc. v. United States*, 92 Fed. Cl. 226 (2010) (declarations offered by both parties were not included into the protest record because they were not before the contracting officer at the time the protested decision was made; they also constituted opinion testimony that would not assist the court in determining whether the agency's award decision was rational); and *L-3 Commc'ns Eotech, Inc. v United States*, 87 Fed. Cl. 565 (2009) (proffered documents were irrelevant to the court's APA review of the protester's elimination from competition and where other documents constituted "post-hoc contentions of fact and argument" that were not before the agency as it made its decision).

The court may permit supplementation of the record with information that the protester argues the agency either did consider or should have considered in making the protested decision. See *Montana Fish, Wildlife, & Parks Found., Inc. v. United States*, 91 Fed. Cl. 434 (2010) (Inspector General file when the agency decision was based, in part, on report); *Allied Tech. Group, Inc. v. United States*, 92 Fed. Cl. 226 (2010) (internet materials such as memoranda from the Office of Personnel Management and the Office of Management and Budget, Internet articles, and a screen short of an agency website); *PlanetSpace, Inc., v. United States*, 90 Fed. Cl. 1 (2009) (146 pages of documents received in response to a Freedom of Information Act request); and *Kerr Contractors, Inc. v. United States*, 89 Fed. Cl. 312 (2009) (agency's responses to questions regarding clarification of the solicitation).

Where bias is alleged, the administrative record frequently will not be complete or suffice to prove or disprove the allegation, *Pitney Bowes Gov't Solutions, Inc. v. United States*, 93 Fed. Cl. 327 (2010). Consequently, to address bias, the court will entertain extra-record evidence and permit discovery when there has been a "strong showing of bad faith or improper behavior" such that without discovery the administrative record cannot be trusted, *Alabama Aircraft Indus., Inc. v. United States*, 82 Fed. Cl. 757 (2008). The strong showing must have an evidentiary foundation and not rest merely on counsel's argument, suspicion, or conjecture, *Madison Servs., Inc. v. United States*, 92 Fed. Cl. 120 (2010). In *Pitney Bowes* the court determined that there were indicia of bias, including affidavits regarding pre-procurement discussions. The court ordered limited deposition testimony of the individual technical evaluation panel members in order to determine their views prior to finalization of the consensus reports. See also *Tech Sys., Inc. v. United States*, 97 Fed. Cl. 262 (2011) (witness statements showing actions of COTR sufficient to permit supplementation to demonstrate bias and bad faith); *L-3 Commc'ns Integrated Sys., L. P. v United States*, 91 Fed. Cl. 347 (2010) ("[A]llegations of bad faith and bias [must be] sufficiently well grounded to warrant supplementation of the [a]dministrative [r]ecord, [and] based upon hard facts."). A threshold showing of either a motivation for the governmental employee to have acted in bad faith or of conduct that is hard to explain absent bad faith is required, *Beta Analytics Int'l, Inc. v. United States*, 61 Fed. Cl. 223 (2004). Although the agency decision is entitled to a presumption of regularity, *Impresa Construzioni Geom. Domenico Garufi v. United States*, 238 F.3d 1324 (Fed. Cir. 2001), this presumption may be rebutted by an appropriate factual predicate, *OTI Am., Inc. v. United States*, 68 Fed. Cl. 108 (2005). Further, allowing for deposition testimony of the contracting officer or other governmental official in a bid protest, where appropriate, "may enable the court to satisfy its statutory duty to give due regard to the need for expeditious resolution of the action." *Asia Pac. Airlines v. United States*, 68 Fed. Cl. 8 (2005) (allowing supplementation where rationale of decision makers was not apparent from the administrative record); see also *Impressa Construzioni Geom. Domenico Garufi*, 238 F.3d 1324 (Fed. Cir. 2001) (allowing deposition of contracting officer to elucidate grounds for his decisions and determine whether a rational basis was lacking).

In some instances, a plaintiff will move to introduce portions of a prior GAO protest record into the court protest record. In *Bannum v. United States*, 89 Fed. Cl. 184 (2009), the court determined that documents related to contract performance should be supplements to the administrative record because without the documents, the court would not be able to assess whether the contracting agency provided a coherent and reasonable explanation of its exercise of discretion. In its reasoning the court cited RCFC Appendix C, provision 22(u), which explicitly anticipated the inclusion of the agency report submitted to GAO in the record in a subsequent protest filed at the Court of Federal Claims that involves the same procurement. See also *Holloway & Co., PLLC v. United States*, 87 Fed. Cl. 381 (2009), noting that the purpose of RCFC Appendix C, provision 22(u) is to ensure that the full record of all proceedings related to the procurement is before the court for review. The court allowed supplementation of the record with six documents generated before GAO because provision 22(u) indicates that core documents include the record of the previous protest. But see *Allied Tech. Group, Inc. v. United States*, 92 Fed. Cl. 226 (2010), stating that inclusion of documents in the record of a GAO protest is not automatic. The court denied the admission of declarations of a number of witnesses because they were opinion testimony proclaiming or denying the alleged superiority of the competing products, were not before the contracting officer at the time of the award decision, and were not necessary to organize or understand the administrative record.

The court may allow the introduction of information relevant to prejudice and the appropriate remedy, rather that the merits of the protest. See *AshBritt, Inc. v. United States*, 87 Fed. Cl. 344 (2009), stating at 366-67:

> In general, it is appropriate to add evidence pertaining to prejudice and the factors governing injunctive relief to the record in a bid protest — not as a supplement to the AR, but as part of this Court's record. Evidence directed at prejudice and remedy necessarily would not be before an agency decision maker effecting a

procurement decision such as a source selection award. Rather, evidence of the prejudicial effect vel non of a procurement decision or the ramifications of injunctive relief would necessarily post date and flow from such agency decision.

## 4. Depositions and Discovery

Parties may conduct discovery by oral examination (RCFC 30) or by written questions (RCFC 31). The scope of discovery is set forth in RCFC 26(b)(1):

> Parties may obtain discovery regarding any nonprivileged matter that is relevant to any party's claim or defense — including the existence, description, nature, custody, condition, and location of any documents or other tangible things and the identity and location of persons who know of any discoverable matter. For good cause, the court may order discovery of any matter relevant to the subject matter involved in the action. Relevant information need not be admissible at the trial if the discovery appears reasonably calculated to lead to the discovery of admissible evidence. All discovery is subject to the limitations imposed by RCFC 26(b)(2)(C).

Discovery sought in an effort to establish alleged bias of the agency in the procurement process is difficult to obtain. In *Information Tech. & Applications Corp. v. United States*, 316 F.3d 1312 (Fed. Cir. 2003), the appellant argued that the Court of Federal Claims improperly refused to allow discovery regarding alleged bias of the Air Force in the procurement process. In denying discovery, the federal circuit explained at 1323, n2:

> An agency decision is entitled to a presumption of regularity. [D]iscovery of the contracting officer's reasoning is not lightly to be ordered and should not be ordered unless record evidence raises serious questions as to the rationality of the contracting officer's [decision]. In this case, ITAC has pointed to no record evidence of bias. Instead it has merely reiterated its contentions that the Air Force erred in evaluating the proposals. This is not evidence of bias, and it is insufficient to overcome the presumption that the contracting officer acted in good faith.

See also *Alabama Aircraft Indus., Inc. — Birmingham v. United States*, 82 Fed. Cl. 757 (2008), denying discovery to probe the source selection decision when there was no evidence of impropriety.

Discovery must be conducted in a timely fashion early in the proceedings. If a party finds that unforeseen discovery is necessary during the argument of a case, it must request discovery at that time. In *Vanguard Sec., Inc. v. United States*, 20 Cl. Ct. 90 (1990), the plaintiff found, while arguing summary judgment motions, that the government was asserting new grounds to support the cancellation of a solicitation. The plaintiff did not indicate at the time that it needed discovery but made the request in its post-argument brief. The court denied this request, holding that it was untimely.

It is very difficult to obtain sanctions for failing to comply with discovery requests. In *ViON Corp. v. United States*, 906 F.2d 1564 (Fed. Cir. 1990), the court reversed the board's dismissal of a protest on the grounds that it was frivolous because the protester had not provided good faith answers to the government's interrogatories. The court quoted the board's reasoning, 90-1 BCA ¶ 22,287 at 111,941, as follows:

> Since this protest was filed, however, we have had the opportunity to observe the actions of protester first hand. We have reviewed in detail the answers ViON has provided to critical discovery requests. We have concluded that they were inadequate. We have likewise seen protester disregard important provisions in the Board's order authorizing discovery, with the result that the Board's control over the discovery process was diminished and the discovery accomplished was less efficient and less productive. In the absence of some redress from the Board, all of these actions on the part of ViON make it increasingly difficult for the agency to prepare a timely defense and, to that extent, provide ViON with an unfair advantage in pursuing the protest.

The court found that the interrogatories for which the board considered ViON nonresponsive did not relate to a matter that ViON had the burden to prove and held that a protest cannot be dismissed as frivolous unless the protest lacks an arguable basis in fact or law. The court held that noncompliance with a discovery order on issues that the protester did not have to prove and a finding by the board that the motive of the protester was not genuine did not make the protest frivolous. However, the court added in a footnote at 1566:

> This is not to say that the refusal to respond promptly and adequately to proper discovery request might not, in this or some other case, give rise to an inference that the protester's case lacks merits because the protester does not have the facts required for an arguable case.

## *5. Protective Orders*

When a party responding to a discovery request believes that it will have to provide confidential material, it can seek a protective order limiting the people that can review the material. RCFC 26(c) governs protective orders, providing that:

> A party or any person from whom discovery is sought may move for a protective order. The motion must include a certification that the movant has in good faith conferred or attempted to confer with other affected parties in an effort to resolve the dispute without court action. The court may, for good cause, issue an order to protect a party or person from annoyance, embarrassment, oppression, or undue burden or expense, including one or more of the following: . . . (G) requiring that a trade secret or other confidential research, development, or commercial information not be revealed or be revealed only in a specified way . . . .

See *Forest Prods. Northwest, Inc. v. United States*, 453 F.3d 1355 (Fed. Cir. 2006), affirming the denial of a protective order because the party had not met the "good cause" standard by submitting evidence that the material sought to be protected affected "its business operations, its public persona, or the privacy of its principals." In *Lakeland Partners, L.L.C. v. United States*, 88 Fed. Cl. 124 (2009), the court described the "good cause" standard as "strict," stating at 133:

> [T]he party . . . must make a particularized factual showing of the harm that would be sustained if the court did not grant a protective order. " Arthur R. Miller, *Confidentiality, Protective Orders, and Public Access to the Courts*, 105 Harv. L. Rev. 427, 433 (1991). "[T]he party seeking the protective order must show good cause by demonstrating a particular need for protection. " *Cipollone v. Liggett Group, Inc.*, 785 F.2d 1108, 1121 (3d Cir. 1986). Thus, broad allegations of harm, unsubstantiated by specific examples, are insufficient to justify issuance of a protective order.

In contrast, when competitors are involved in litigation, such as a protest including an intervener, courts frequently issue blanket protective orders as a means of allowing discovery to proceed efficiently, *Armour of Am. v. United States*, 73 Fed. Cl. 597 (2006) (emphasizing that such an order is not a determination that the protected material is proprietary). RCFC Form 8 is a standard form protective order to be used in protest cases. This form specifies that the only persons allowed access to protected information are "counsel for a party and independent consultants and experts assisting such counsel in connection with this litigation" as well as paralegal, clerical and administrative support personnel assisting counsel. Persons other than counsel must sign a RCFC Form 9 indicating that they have read and will abide by the order. Government attorneys and agency personnel are permitted access to protected material without any formalities.

A protective order can also deny discovery of confidential material when the court determines that the party does not need the information to pursue the litigation. Where a party seeking a protective order has shown that the information sought is confidential and that its disclosure might be harmful, the burden shifts to the party seeking discovery to establish that disclosure of trade secrets and confidential information is relevant and necessary to its case, *American Standard, Inc. v. Pfizer Inc.*, 828 F.2d 734 (Fed. Cir. 1987); *Heat & Control, Inc. v. Hester Indus., Inc.*, 785 F.2d 1017 (Fed. Cir. 1986). See *Pikes Peak Family Housing, LLC v. United States*, 40 Fed. Cl. 673 (1998), where the court held that the successful offeror was not entitled to a protective order forbidding disclosure of certain information by counsel for the disappointed offeror to its client. The court stated that the information, whether already in the administrative record or obtained through discovery, was pertinent to the disappointed offeror's own proposal. Thus, it was clear that discovery was not being used as a vehicle for the acquisition of proprietary information and trade secrets of other offerors.

The Court of Federal Claims can impose sanctions on attorneys who violate a protective order, *Pacific Gas & Elec. Co. v. United States*, 82 Fed. Cl. 474 (2008) (ordering attorney to pay costs incurred by government).

## F.  Standard of Review

The proper standard to be applied in protest cases is provided by 5 U.S.C. § 706(2)(A), which provides a reviewing court shall set aside the agency action if it is arbitrary, capricious, an abuse of discretion, or otherwise not in accordance with law, *Banknote Corp. of Am. v. United States*, 365 F.3d 1345 (Fed. Cir. 2004). In *Impresa Construzioni Geom. Domenico Garufy v. United States*, 238 F.3d 1324 (Fed. Cir. 2001), the court held that 28 U.S.C. § 1491(b), by its plain terms and according to its legislative history, "applies the Administrative Dispute Resolution Act standard of review previously applied by the district courts." Thus, the standards outlined in *Scanwell Labs., Inc. v. Shaffer*, 424 F.2d 859 (D.C. Cir. 1970), and the line of cases following that decision apply. Under the APA standard as applied in the *Scanwell* line of cases, and now in ADRA cases, an award may be set aside if either (1) the procurement official's decision lacked a rational basis, making it arbitrary or capricious, or (2) the procurement procedure involved a violation of statute or regulation.

The arbitrary and capricious standard is highly deferential, *Advanced Data Concepts, Inc. v. United States*, 216 F.3d 1054 (Fed. Cir. 2000). In *Keco Indus., Inc. v. United States*, 203 Ct. Cl. 566, 492 F.2d 1200 (1974), the court indicated that arbitrary or capricious action would not result from mere negligence by the government, but may be proved in a number of ways, stating at 574:

> One is that subjective bad faith on the part of the procuring officials, depriving a bidder of the fair and honest consideration of his proposal, normally warrants recovery of bid preparation costs. *Heyer Products Co. v. United States*, 135 Ct. Cl. 63, 140 F. Supp. 409 (1956). A second is that proof that there was "no reasonable basis" for the administrative decision will also suffice, at least in many situations. *Continental Business Enterprises v. United States*, 196 Ct. Cl. 627, 637-38, 452 F.2d 1016, 1021 (1971). The third is that the degree of proof of error necessary for recovery is ordinarily related to the amount of discretion entrusted to the procurement officials by applicable statutes and regulations. *Continental Business Enterprises v. United States*, *supra*, 196 Ct. Cl. at 637, 452 F.2d at 1021 (1971); *Keco Industries, Inc. v. United States*, *supra*, 192 Ct. Cl. at 784, 428 F.2d at 1240. The fourth is that proven violation of pertinent statutes or regulations can, but need not necessarily, be a ground for recovery.

In considering whether the government acted in bad faith, the court requires the protester to prove that the government acted with specific intent to injure it. See *Galen Med. Assocs., Inc. v. United States*, 369 F.3d 1324 (Fed. Cir. 2004), stating at 1330:

> [W]hen a bidder alleges bad faith, "in order to overcome the presumption of good faith [on behalf of the government], the proof must be almost irrefragable. " *Info.*

*Tech. Applications Corp. v. United States*, 316 F.3d 1312, 1323 n.2 (Fed. Cir. 2003). "Almost irrefragable proof" amounts to "clear and convincing evidence. " *Am-Pro Protective Agency, Inc. v. United States*, 281 F.3d 1234, 1239-40 (Fed. Cir. 2002). "In the cases where the court has considered allegations of bad faith, the necessary 'irrefragable proof' has been equated with evidence of some specific intent to injure the plaintiff. " *Torncello v. United States*, 231 Ct. Cl. 20, 681 F.2d 756, 770 (Ct. Cl. 1982).

See also *Aviation Enters., Inc. v. United States*, 8 Cl. Ct. 1 (1985) (refusing to find bad faith on the basis of "speculation and innuendo"); and *Shields Enters., Inc. v. United States*, 28 Fed. Cl. 615 (1993) (no evidence that the government specifically intended to injure the plaintiff or that the government operated with any prejudice toward the plaintiff). See, however, *Parcel 49C Ltd. P'ship v. United States*, 31 F.3d 1147 (Fed. Cir. 1994), affirming a decision that the General Services Administration abused its discretion when it canceled a solicitation for the lease of office space allegedly based on changes in the needs of the using agency. The court found that the using agency's needs did not change until five years into the future and concluded that the GSA had relied upon this interpretation merely as a pretext for ridding itself of the procurement. In a fact pattern similar to *Parcel 49C*, the court in *126 Northpoint Plaza L.P. v. United States*, 34 Fed. Cl. 105 (1995), found bad faith when GSA officials canceled a solicitation in an effort to accommodate the Immigration and Naturalization Service, which was trying to avoid contracting with a particular offeror

Absent bad faith, the protester must establish with clear and convincing evidence that the agency's determination lacked any rational basis or violated applicable statutes or regulations, *Vanguard Sec., Inc. v. United States*, 20 Cl. Ct. 90 (1990); *Northern Telecom, Inc. v. United States*, 8 Cl. Ct. 376 (1985). In finding that there was no rational basis for the action, the court in *Rockwell Int'l Corp. v. United States*, 4 Cl. Ct. 1 (1983), stated that: "To have a reasoned or rational basis, there must be a rational connection between the facts established and the choice made." See also *Prineville Sawmill Co. v. United States*, 859 F.2d 905 (Fed. Cir. 1988) (decision by Forest Service to reject all bids in timber sale had no reasonable basis). In *R. R. Donnelly & Sons, Co. v. United States*, 38 Fed. Cl. 518 (1997), the court rejected the argument that a postaward protester must prove a case by "clear and convincing" evidence and held that the burden was only "high." The court applied the standards traditionally applied in bid protests under *Keco Industries* but denied summary judgment because of unresolved factual issues between the parties.

If an award decision is challenged on the basis that it was made without a rational basis, the court will determine whether the contracting agency provided a coherent and reasonable explanation of its exercise of discretion, and the disappointed offeror bears "a heavy burden of showing that the award decision had no rational basis," *Centech Group, Inc. v. United States*, 554 F.3d 1029 (Fed. Cir. 2009). The court will sustain an agency action unless the action does not evince rational reasoning and consideration of relevant factors, *Weeks Marine, Inc. v. United States*, 575 F.3d 1352 (Fed. Cir. 2009). In *Weeks Marine*, a dredging contractor, filed a preaward bid protest challenging the Army Corps of Engineers' decision to solicit proposals for regional maintenance dredging and shore protection projects using multiple award, IDIQ task order contracts, rather than sealed bidding procedures. The Court of Federal Claims granted Weeks's motion for judgment on the administrative record, ruling that the Corps' solicitation violated 10 U.S.C. § 2304(a)(2), which provides that sealed bidding must be used when an agency plans to award a contract based solely on price and price-related factors, and finding that the Corps lacked a rational basis for departing from its traditional district-by-district procurement strategy, in which individual dredging efforts were sourced locally through sealed bidding. On appeal, the Federal Circuit reversed, holding that the solicitation for the regional multiple award contracts did call for evaluation of nonprice factors, and that the solicitation was rationally designed to address several of the Corps' goals. But see *Savantage Fin. Servs. v. United States*, 595 F.3d 1282 (Fed. Cir. 2010), finding no reasonable basis for the sole source decision because all the reasons cited by the agency in the justification as supporting its decision to use Oracle and SAP as the financial software system baseline were equally applicable to the Savantage system.

In negotiated procurement the court takes a more deferential view of whether an agency's actions were rational or reasonable than it does in sealed bidding, *Logicon, Inc. v. United States*, 22 Cl. Ct. 776 (1991). There, the court found that the government had a rational basis for reopening negotiations on a contract after having initially decided to award the contract to the plaintiff. In *Overstreet Elec. Co. v. United States*, 59 Fed. Cl. 99 (2003), the court characterized the standard of review as "near draconian." Further, in *Galen Med. Assocs., Inc. v. United States*, 369 F.3d 1324 (Fed. Cir. 2004), the court stated at 1330:

> Because the bid protest at issue here involved a "negotiated procurement," the protestor's burden of proving that the award was arbitrary, capricious, an abuse of discretion, or otherwise not in accordance with law is greater than in other types of bid protests. *LeBarge Prods., Inc. v. West*, 46 F.3d 1547, 1555 (Fed. Cir. 1995) (citing *Burroughs Corp. v. United States*, 617 F.2d 590, 597-98 (Ct. Cl. 1980)). "The higher burden exists because the contracting officer engages in what is 'inherently a judgmental process.'" *Omega World Travel v. United States*, 54 Fed. Cl. 570, 578 (2002) (citing *Burroughs*, 617 F.2d at 598). "[T]he greater the discretion granted to a contracting officer, the more difficult it will be to prove the decision was arbitrary and capricious." *Burroughs*, 617 F.2d at 597. "In formally advertised bidding the pertinent statutes and regulations are far more strict about the conduct of the procurement than in a negotiated one, consequently in negotiated procurement the contracting officer is entrusted with a relatively high degree of discretion." *Id.*

See *Blackwater Lodge & Training Ctr. v. United States*, 86 Fed. Cl. 488 (2009) (government reasonably determined awardee had instituted policies and procedures to resolve safety problems and there was no reason to disturb this judgment); *Medi-*

*cal Dev. Int'l, Inc. v. United States*, 89 Fed. Cl. 691 (2009) (government did not act arbitrary or capricious in conducting competitive range determination three months after the firm prices had expired because the contracting officer reasonably viewed the offers as definite enough to become binding upon the government's acceptance); *Dyonyx, L. P. v. United States*, 83 Fed. Cl. 460 (2008) (rational basis to exclude plaintiff from competitive range); *PHT Supply Corp. v. United States*, 71 Fed. Cl. 1 (2006) (risk rating based on past performance upheld because the solicitation did not limit the government's review to technically relevant contracts and assessment of the awardee's risk had a rational basis); *Avtel Servs., Inc. v. United States*, 70 Fed. Cl. 173 (2005) (contracting officer's decision not to disqualify the eventual awardee from competition not arbitrary and capricious); *Gulf Group, Inc. v. United States*, 61 Fed. Cl. 338 (2004) (risk rating based on past performance not arbitrary or capricious); *Mantech Telecomm. & Info. Sys. Corp. v. United States*, 49 Fed. Cl. 57 (2001) (proposed corrective action neither arbitrary, capricious nor otherwise contrary to law); *Cincom Sys., Inc. v. United States*, 37 Fed. Cl. 993 (1997) (government's award of software contract was supported by rational basis); *Delbert Wheeler Constr., Inc. v. United States*, 39 Fed. Cl. 239 (1997) (contracting officer's award to offeror who, in his opinion, provided best value, was reasonable); *W&D Ships Deck Works, Inc. v. United States*, 39 Fed. Cl. 638 (1997) (proposal was properly excluded from competitive range); *Compubahn, Inc. v. United States*, 33 Fed. Cl. 677 (1995) (offeror not entitled to relief because there was no evidence that the evaluators acted in bad faith or without a reasonable basis, notwithstanding the fact that four of the five evaluators were incapable of assessing the proposed technology); *IMS Servs., Inc. v. United States*, 33 Fed. Cl. 167 (1995) (Navy did not act arbitrarily, capriciously, or contrary to law when it reopened procurement competition and conducted new round of BAFOs). Compare *Turner Constr. Co. v. United States*, 94 Fed. Cl. 561 (2010) (agency acted arbitrarily in following GAO recommendation to cancel award and reopen competition because of an organizational conflict of interest of awardee); *Magnum Opus Techs., Inc. v. United* States, 94 Fed. Cl. 512 (2010) (agency arbitrarily exercised options that had no firm prices); *Systems Plus, Inc. v. United States*, 69 Fed. Cl. 757 (2006) (agency's price evaluation arbitrary because the contracting officer's methodology calculated a simple, nonweighted arithmetic formula to derive an average hourly rate for each bidder); *United Int'l Investigative Servs. v. United States*, 41 Fed. Cl. 312 (1998) (agency acted unreasonably in allowing an individual member of the technical evaluation board to rescore the offeror's technical proposal).

## G. Prejudice

In order for a protester to prevail in a bid protest, it must show not only that there was a significant error in the procurement process, but also that the error was prejudicial, *Data General Corp. v. United States*, 78 F.3d 1556 (Fed. Cir. 1996). There the court stated that the test was whether there was a "reasonable likelihood" that the protester would obtain award. In *Statistica, Inc. v. United States*, 102 F.3d

1577 (Fed. Cir. 1996), the court stated that to establish competitive prejudice, a protester must demonstrate that but for the alleged error, there was a "substantial chance" that it would receive an award. It concluded, however, that there was no difference between the "reasonable likelihood" test in *Data General* and the "substantial chance" test that had been used in older cases such as *CACI, Inc. — Fed. v. United States*, 719 F.2d 1567 (Fed. Cir. 1983), and *Morgan Bus. Assocs. v. United States*, 223 Ct. Cl. 325, 619 F.2d 892 (1980). The more recent Court of Appeals for the Federal Circuit cases all state a party has been prejudiced when it can show that but for the error, it would have had a substantial chance of securing the contract, *Labatt Food Serv., Inc. v. United States*, 577 F.3d 1375 (Fed. Cir. 2009); *Bannum, Inc. v. United States*, 404 F.3d 1346 (Fed. Cir. 2005); *Galen Med. Assocs., Inc. v. United States*, 369 F.3d 1324 (Fed. Cir. 2004). In *Afghan Am. Army Servs. Corp. v. United States*, 90 Fed. Cl. 341 (2009), the highest-priced offeror in a multiple-award competition for IDIQ trucking services contracts was prejudiced by the government's evaluation and selection errors because its proposal was within the competitive range, and it established there was a reasonable likelihood it would have received an award but for the errors. The protester was the most expensive offeror in a best-value procurement where price was weighed as approximately equal to past performance, past experience, and security approach and it received lower technical ratings than four other offerors also not awarded contracts. However, the result could have been different if the government had performed a proper price realism analysis, best-value tradeoff, and past experience evaluation. See also *Red River Holdings, LLC v. United States*, 87 Fed. Cl. 768 (2009) (improper evaluation of the awardee's proposal prejudicial).

De minimis errors by the agency are not sufficient grounds for overturning a contract award, *Andersen Consulting Co. v. United States*, 959 F.2d 929 (Fed. Cir. 1992) ("Any good lawyer can pick lint off any Government procurement, pundits say. We will not set aside an award, even if violations of law are found, unless those violations have some significance," quoting the GSBCA decision, 91-1 BCA ¶ 23,474). See also *Labatt Food Serv., Inc. v. United States*, 577 F.3d 1375 (Fed. Cir. 2009) (plaintiff did not show that government's improper acceptance of e-mails throughout the bid process interfered with its ability to receive the contract award); *Grumman Data Sys. Corp. v. Widnall*, 15 F.3d 1044 (Fed. Cir. 1994) (Air Force departure from standard accounting principles in conducting its best value analysis may have violated some technical accounting principles but was de minimis); and *Cubic Applications, Inc. v. United States*, 37 Fed. Cl. 345 (1997) (failure to follow statutory procedures in awarding the contract not prejudicial and thus nullification of the award was not warranted).

If there is a significant difference in price, the court is unlikely to make a finding of prejudice. In *Electronic Data Sys., LLC v. United States*, 93 Fed. Cl. 416 (2010), the court found the large price differential to preclude a finding of prejudice, stating at 436:

The difficulty for plaintiff in this regard is the sheer size of the differential between its price and that of BAE — in raw terms, slightly more than $50 million, representing nearly a 29 percent spread. This differential is the proverbial elephant in the parlor — and, strive as it might, plaintiff cannot squeeze that pachyderm out the door. That price variance weighed heavily on Treasury's best value determination because the two offerors had nearly identical merit ratings — ratings, to be sure, that plaintiff has challenged before this court, albeit unsuccessfully. While plaintiff correctly notes that prejudice may be found despite the existence of a price differential, it cannot be gainsaid that a significant difference in price, when accompanied by nearly identical technical ratings, can and often does preclude such a finding. And the cases so indicate. *See, e. g., Axiom Res. Mgmt., Inc. v. United States*, 78 Fed. Cl. 576, 590 (2007) (no prejudice where significant differences in price); *see also Data Gen.*, 78 F.3d at 1563 (indicating that price differential is a factor that may be considered in assessing prejudice).

See also *Allied Tech. Group, Inc. v. United States*, 92 Fed. Cl. 226 (2010) (assigning higher technical rating would not have affected award as evaluated price was at least 218% higher than awardee's); *Axiom Res. Mgmt., Inc. v. United States*, 78 Fed. Cl. 576 (2007) (despite apparent errors in the plaintiff's technical approach and past performance ratings, the awardee's lower price still trumped plaintiff's price); *Galen Med. Assocs., Inc. v. United States*, 369 F.3d 1324 (Fed. Cir. 2004) (proposal did not have requisite facilities required by the solicitation); *Candle Corp. v. United States*, 40 Fed. Cl. 658 (1998) (even if the government had complied with its legal obligations, the plaintiff's price still would have been considerably more expensive than the awardee's); *Analytical & Research Tech., Inc. v. United States*, 39 Fed. Cl. 34 (1997) (protester's price was 35% higher than the awardee's despite a violation of procurement laws); and *Data Gen. Corp. v. United States*, 78 F.3d 1556 (Fed. Cir. 1996) (despite pricing error, protester's prices remained substantially higher). See, however, *Alfa Laval Separation, Inc. v. United States*, 40 Fed. Cl. 215 (1998), *rev'd*, 175 F.3d 1365 (Fed. Cir. 1999), reversing a Court of Federal Claims decision that waiver of a mandatory specification was not prejudicial because there was a $5 million price difference between proposals. The appellate court concluded that the plaintiff had established prejudice because "[t]he only bid competing with Alfa Laval was unacceptable under the standards set out in the RFP," adding that because the plaintiff "submitted the only bid meeting all of the government's requirements, . . . it must have had a substantial chance to receive the contract award." As to the large differential in pricing, the court stated that "while price differential may be taken into account, it is not solely dispositive; we must consider all the surrounding circumstances in determining whether there was a substantial chance that a protester would have received an award but for a significant error in the procurement process."

In a best value procurement, an offeror has a relatively heavy burden to show prejudice, *Systems Plus, Inc. v. United States*, 69 Fed. Cl. 757 (2006). Here, the court found that although the government's methodology for evaluating proposed prices was irrational and arbitrary, the contracting officer determination that the awardee's proposal was sufficiently superior to the other offerors,' regardless of which measure of price was evaluated, was not arbitrary or capricious. The court in *Textron, Inc. v. United States*, 74 Fed. Cl. 11 (2006) would likely have ruled differently. The *Textron* court stated that if the court finds that the government has acted arbitrarily and capriciously, the analysis stops at that finding, reasoning that there should be no need to continue to rule on prejudice because a finding that the government has acted arbitrarily and capriciously invalidates the procurement.

## H. Remedies

The ultimate remedy sought by a protester is to receive award of the contract. However, such relief is granted in only the rarest of cases. More often, the agency will be directed to cure a defect in the procurement, and pending the action, the award of a contract will be delayed or the work under a contract will be suspended. In some cases the remedy may involve declarations of the rights of the parties or directions to recompete the contract. Monetary relief may also be granted. See 28 U.S.C. § 1491(b)(2) stating:

> [T]he courts may award any relief that the court considers proper, including declaratory and injunctive relief except that any monetary relief shall be limited to bid and proposal costs.

The court has discretion to award *both* injunctive relief and bid preparation costs, *CNA Corp. v. United States*, 83 Fed. Cl. 1 (2008), *aff'd*, 332 Fed. Appx. 638 (Fed. Cir. 2009). In *Alabama Aircraft Indus., Inc. — Birmingham v. United States*, 85 Fed. Cl. 558 (2009), *rev'd on other grounds*, 586 F.3d 1372 (Fed. Cir. 2009), in addition to the prior decision enjoining the Air Force from proceeding with a contract and requiring a resolicitation, the court awarded bid preparation and proposal costs in order to place Alabama Aircraft in the position it would have been but for the errors. Due to those errors, Alabama Aircraft was required to pay for and submit another proposal in a continuing effort to obtain an award of the contract. In *Geo-Seis Helicopters, Inc. v. United States*, 77 Fed. Cl. 633 (2007), when an injunction issued by the court was partial and only set aside part of the contract in question, the court found it appropriate to include bid preparation and proposal costs as part of the award. Other cases also have awarded complete, permanent injunctive relief along with bid preparation and proposal costs. See *United Payors & United Providers Health Servs., Inc. v. United States*, 55 Fed. Cl. 323 (2002) (ordered termination of the contract, allowed resolicitation of bids, and awarded bid preparation and proposal costs); *MVM, Inc. v. United States*, 47 Fed. Cl. 361 (2000) (awarded proposal and preparation costs in addition to the injunction previously ordered); *Seattle Sec. Servs. v. United States*, 45 Fed. Cl. 560 (2000) (awarded injunctive relief and bid preparation costs). But see *Ashbritt, Inc. v. United States*, 87 Fed. Cl. 344 (2009), where the court declined to award both injunctive and monetary relief because Ashbritt had achieved the goal of its protest — to secure, through injunctive relief, the chance to compete for further awards under the procurement on an even playing field.

## 1. Nonmonetary Remedies

The types of nonmonetary remedies that a protester may obtain in the Court of Federal Claims are either provisional (temporary restraining order (TRO) or preliminary injunction) or final relief (declaratory relief or permanent injunction).

The rules for granting a TRO or preliminary injunction are identical to those followed by the district courts. See RCFC 65. The four factors the court examines when determining whether a preliminary injunction should be granted are the same as in the district courts: (1) reasonable likelihood of success on the merits, (2) irreparable harm if the injunction is not granted, (3) substantial harm to the other parties if the stay is granted, and (4) consideration of the public interest, *Hydro Eng'g, Inc. v. United States*, 37 Fed. Cl. 448 (1997). The court seldom grants either a TRO or a preliminary injunction. As a general rule, courts interfere with the government procurement process "only in extremely limited circumstances," *Banknote Corp. of Am., Inc. v. United States*, 56 Fed. Cl. 377 (2003) (quoting *United States v. John C. Grimberg Co.*, 702 F.2d 1362, 1372 (Fed. Cir. 1983)), *aff'd*, 365 F.3d 1345 (Fed. Cir. 2004). In *Magellan Corp. v. United States*, 27 Fed. Cl. 446 (1993), the court denied a request for preliminary injunction, stating that the disruption to the ongoing procurement process would not be justified in view of the unlikelihood of success on the merits. In discussing its review of requests for preliminary injunctions, the court stated at 447:

> The court has the authority to enter an injunction blocking the award to any bidder other than Magellan. 28 U.S.C. § 1491(a)(3). The limited question is whether the status quo ante should be maintained while the plaintiff undertakes discovery and proofs on its request for permanent relief. Prior decisions of this court and of the United States Court of Appeals for the Federal Circuit, however, make it clear that such authority should not be routinely exercised. As the Federal Circuit wrote in *United States v. John C. Grimberg Co.*, 702 F.2d 1362 (Fed. Cir. 1983), equitable powers "should be exercised in a way which best limits judicial interference in contract procurement." *Id.* at 1372.

The decision on whether or not to grant an injunction is within the sound discretion of the trial court, *FMC Corp. v. United States*, 3 F.3d 424 (Fed. Cir. 1993); *Asociacion Colombiana de Exportadores de Flores v. United States*, 916 F.2d 1571 (Fed. Cir. 1990). Confirming the difficult nature of obtaining injunctive relief in a protest case, the Federal Circuit has stated that even if a trial court finds that the government's actions in soliciting and awarding a contract were arbitrary, capricious, or not in accordance with law, the trial court retains discretion on whether to issue an injunction, *PGBA, LLC v. United States*, 389 F.3d 1219 (Fed. Cir. 2004). In *PGBA*, the court reasoned that the statutory scheme for reviewing procurement decision "does not deprive a court of its equitable discretion in deciding whether injunctive relief is appropriate," and that 28 U.S.C. § 1491(b)(4) "does not automatically require a court to set aside an arbitrary, capricious, or otherwise unlawful contract award." Once injunctive relief is denied, "the movant faces a heavy burden of showing that the trial court abused its discretion, committed an error of law, or seriously misjudged the evidence," *FMC Corp. v. United States*, 3 F.3d 424 (Fed. Cir. 1993).

The court will examine whether a plaintiff can establish likely success on the merits before looking at the other factors for preliminary injunctive relief. In *Logicon, Inc. v. United* States, 22 Cl. Ct. 776 (1991), the court denied injunctive relief, finding that the agency's decision to reopen negotiations and conduct another round of BAFOs was not irrational or unreasonable; thus, the offeror did not establish by clear and convincing evidence a strong likelihood of success on the merits. In *Career Training Concepts, Inc. v. United States*, 83 Fed. Cl. 215 (2008), the court denied plaintiff's motion for injunctive relief, finding that an awardee's proposal was deemed timely because the contracting officer properly extended the deadline for receipt of proposals through a formal notice posted on the website used to conduct the solicitation, and the awardee submitted its offer within the extension period. The protester's attempt to characterize the extension as invalid based on the fact the contracting officer notified offerors of the extension via e-mail, rather than a formal solicitation amendment, was rejected. Similarly in *The Centech Group, Inc. v. United States*, 78 Fed. Cl. 496 (2007), *aff'd*, 554 F.3d 1029 (2009), the court held that Centech did not meet the first requisite for injunctive relief — demonstrated success on the merits. Here, Centech's proposal was unacceptable because it failed to comply with the Limitation on Subcontracting clause — a mandatory, material solicitation requirement. However, in *Isratex, Inc. v. United States*, 25 Cl. Ct. 223 (1992), the court issued a TRO upon finding a strong likelihood of success on the merits. The offeror was excluded from further participation in a negotiated procurement on the ground that its demonstration model did not satisfy one of the factors listed in the RFP, but the court found no indication in the RFP that automatic exclusion would follow from test failure. See also *Bona Fide Conglomerate, Inc. v. United States,* 96 Fed. Cl. 233 (2010), issuing a TRO finding that there was a likelihood of success on the merits because the agency's evaluation of proposals was questionable and there was a plausible allegation of conflict of interest and favoritism in the selection decision. The court also concluded that the agency could readily obtain the services being procured by awarding a bridge contract. Similarly, in *Bilfinger Berger AG Sede Secondaria Italiana v. United States*, 94 Fed. Cl. 389 (2010), the court issued a TRO based on the likelihood that the company would demonstrate that it had been declared ineligible on faulty grounds. A preliminary injunction was also issued in this case, 97 Fed. Cl. 96 (2010).

When assessing irreparable injury, "[t]he relevant inquiry in weighing this factor is whether the plaintiff has an adequate remedy in the absence of an injunction," *Magellan Corp. v. United States*, 27 Fed. Cl. 446, 447 (1993). In *Serco, Inc. v. United States*, 81 Fed. Cl. 463 (2008), the government was enjoined from proceeding with awards made under a governmentwide acquisition contract because it conducted an improper and flawed evaluation. The protesters demonstrated they would suffer irreparable injury if an injunction were not granted because the only other available relief—the potential for recovery of bid preparation costs—would not compensate them for the loss of valuable business over a contract term of potentially a decade.

The public interest must weigh in favor of injunctive relief, *Klinge Corp. v. United States*, 82 Fed. Cl. 127 (2008) (public interest weighs in favor of preventing the government from awarding a contract in contravention of the Trade Agreements Act and in preventing the government from failing to make proper inquiry into compliance when it had a duty to do so). The public interest is served by ensuring that the government conduct fair and legal procurement procedures, giving honest and fair consideration to all bids, *Aeroplate Corp. v. United States*, 67 Fed. Cl. 4 (2005). Preserving the integrity of the public procurement system is in the public interest, *MVM, Inc. v. United States*, 46 Fed. Cl. 137 (2000); *Day & Zimmerman Servs. v. United States*, 38 Fed. Cl. 591 (1997). The integrity of the procurement process includes the requirement that government officials follow applicable procurement law and regulation, *Rotech Healthcare, Inc. v. United States*, 71 Fed. Cl. 393 (2006) (procurement approach adopted by the VA violated the letter and the spirit of the nonmanufacturer rule and the Small Business Act as a whole). In *Serco, Inc. v. United States*, 81 Fed. Cl. 463 (2008), the court found the public interest would be served by granting the injunction, particularly in the context of a massive procurement that will impact the public potentially for a decade.

When an appeal is taken to the Court of Appeals for the Federal Circuit, an appellant may request a stay of contract award pending appeal under RCFC 62(c). However, the court follows a stringent test in determining whether to issue a stay pending appeal. This test mirrors the TRO test: "(1) a strong likelihood that the movant will prevail on the merits of the appeal; (2) irreparable injury to the movant unless the stay is granted; (3) no substantial harm to the other parties if the stay is granted; and (4) consideration of the public interest," *Aerolease Long Beach v. United States*, 31 Fed. Cl. 342 (1994).

The final relief by the Court of Federal Claims may take the form of a declaratory judgment or a permanent injunction. The test for a permanent injunction is almost identical to that for a temporary restraining order or preliminary injunction, but rather that the likelihood of success on the merits, a permanent injunction requires actual success on the merits, *Amoco Prod. Co. v. Village of Gambill, Alaska*, 480 U.S. 531 (1987). In *PGBA, LLC v. United States*, 389 F.3d 1219 (Fed. Cir. 2004), the court set out the test for a permanent injunction, stating at 1228-29, that a court must consider:

> (1) whether, as it must, the plaintiff has succeeded on the merits of the case; (2) whether the plaintiff will suffer irreparable harm if the court withholds injunctive relief; (3) whether the balance of hardships to the respective parties favors the grant of injunctive relief; and (4) whether it is in the public interest to grant injunctive relief.

The injunction may prohibit the agency from undertaking some activity or it may be mandatory, directing that certain actions be taken. See *Klinge Corp. v. United States*, 82 Fed. Cl. 127 (2008) (direction to terminate the contract); *Informatics Corp. v. United States*, 40 Fed. Cl. 508 (1998) (award of contract enjoined and reevaluation of plaintiff's proposal ordered); *ATA Def. Indus., Inc. v. United States*, 38 Fed. Cl. 489 (1997) (permanent injunction prohibiting continued performance of legally defective procurement); *Day & Zimmermann, Inc. v. United States*, 38 Fed. Cl. 591 (1997) (contract award enjoined unless and until discussions were held and resulting BAFOs were considered); and *126 Northpoint Plaza L. P. v. United States*, 34 Fed. Cl. 105 (1995) (original solicitation reinstated).

The court's grant of injunctive relief is limited in an otherwise meritorious protest when the procurement concerns national defense/national security issues, *Linc Gov't Servs., LLC v. United States*, 96 Fed. Cl. 672 (2010) (injunction denied based on testimony that it would impede effort in Iraq); *Geo-Seis Helicopters v. United States*, 77 Fed. Cl. 633 (2007) (national security considerations caused injunction to be limited in scope); *Filtration Dev. Co. v. United States*, 60 Fed. Cl. 371 (2004) (limited injunctive relief in light of national defense considerations); *Gentex Corp. v. United States*, 58 Fed. Cl. 634 (2003) (plaintiff found not to have met burden of demonstrating that injunctive relief is warranted, given urgency of procurement for the nation's military); and *Cincom Sys. v. United States*, 37 Fed. Cl. 226 (1997) (application for TRO and motion for preliminary injunction denied for national security reasons).

## 2. Monetary Remedies

The monetary remedies that protesters have been able to recover are generally limited to the costs of preparing the bid or proposal. In some instances the protester may receive attorneys' fees and expenses under the Equal Access to Justice Act (EAJA). Recovery of anticipated profits (or lost profits) has been uniformly denied. See *Keco Indus., Inc. v. United States*, 203 Ct. Cl. 566, 492 F.2d 1200 (1974) (improper to award lost profits in the absence of a contract and no certainty that protester would have received award); *Rockwell Int'l Corp. v. United States*, 8 Cl. Ct. 662 (1985) (prior precedent flatly precludes such an award); *La Strada Inn, Inc. v. United States*, 12 Cl. Ct. 110 (1987) (disappointed bidder may not recover anticipated profits on a contract improperly awarded to another); *Finley v. United States*, 31 Fed. Cl. 704 (1994) (lost profits are speculative in nature and have consistently been denied); and *Gentex Corp. v. United States*, 61 Fed. Cl. 49 (2004) (protester's attempt to recover a 15% "markup" on its bid and preparation costs was unsuccessful because profit is not an allowable cost).

### a. Bid or Proposal Preparation Costs

The Court of Federal Claims may award bid or proposal preparation costs in a protest action, 28 U.S.C. § 1491(a)(1); 28 U.S.C. §1491(b)(2). The Federal Circuit

COURT OF FEDERAL CLAIMS 1795

has held that "a losing competitor may recover the costs of preparing its unsuccessful proposal if it can establish that the Government's consideration of the proposals submitted was arbitrary or capricious," *E. W. Bliss Co. v. United States*, 77 F.3d 445 Fed. Cir. (1996) (quoting *Lincoln Servs., Ltd. v. United States*, 230 Ct. Cl. 416, 678 F.2d 157 (1982)). See also *Gentex Corp. v. United States*, 58 Fed. Cl. 634 (2003) ("[A] losing competitor may recover the costs of preparing its unsuccessful proposal if it can establish that the Government's consideration of the proposal submitted was arbitrary or capricious or in violation of applicable statute or regulation."). In finding the award of bid and proposal costs appropriate, the court in *MVM, Inc. v. United States*, 47 Fed. Cl. 361 (2000), observed at 366:

> An award of bid proposal and preparation costs . . . advance[s] the public interest and help[s] to ensure government compliance with procurement regulations. Offerors incur expenditures in preparing a bid proposal. When the government makes a prejudicial error, a disappointed bidder may expend additional funds on a bid protest action. If the disappointed bidder knows that it will be unable to recover any costs, it will have less incentive to bring a bid protest action. . . . By bringing a bid protest action, the disappointed bidder helps to ensure that the government complies with procurement regulations.

Bid or proposal cost may not be awarded if the protester has a reasonable chance of winning the competition when the corrective action is taken. Thus, if the court issues an injunction providing the protester with a fair opportunity to win the competition, the costs may be denied. See *AshBritt, Inc. v. United States*, 87 Fed. Cl. 344 (2009) *clarified*, 87 Fed. Cl. 654 (2009), stating at 379-80:

> Under the Tucker Act, this Court "may award any relief that the court considers proper," including declaratory and injunctive relief and bid and proposal preparation costs. 28 U.S.C. § 1491(b)(2). This provision of the Tucker Act, "through use of the permissive 'may,' provides the Court of Federal Claims with discretion in fashioning relief. " *PGBA, L. L. C. v. United States*, 389 F.3d 1219, 1226 (Fed. Cir. 2004). Because the Court grants AshBritt's request for injunctive relief, and AshBritt will have the opportunity to re-compete for additional awards, the Court declines to award bid and proposal preparation costs. While the Tucker Act does not preclude monetary damages if injunctive relief has been granted, the Court takes into account "the facts and circumstances of the particular case" in exercising its discretion whether to award both injunctive relief and bid and proposal preparation costs. See *CNA Corp. v. United States*, 83 Fed. Cl. 1, 11 (2008).

> Bid and proposal preparation costs are a form of reliance damages which are properly awarded when the costs have been wasted. See, e. g., *Centech Group, Inc. v. United States*, 79 Fed. Cl. 562, 564 (2007) (finding that the protestor may be entitled to bid and proposal preparation costs "if it can demonstrate that such costs were wasted. "). Here, AshBritt has achieved the goal of its protest — to secure, through injunctive relief, the chance to compete for further awards under this procurement on a level playing field. If AshBritt succeeds in winning additional awards, its bid and proposal preparation costs will not have been "wasted" in this procurement. Furthermore, AshBritt has already received both a primary

award and a reach back assignment under this procurement which were not displaced by the Court's injunction here, demonstrating that its bid and proposal preparation costs were not wasted. As such, the Court declines to award the additional relief of bid and proposal preparation costs.

However, such costs will be awarded if the protester has no chance to win the competition. See *Klinge Corp. v. United States*, 83 Fed. Cl. 773 (2008), *recons. denied*, 86 Fed. Cl. 713 (2009) (agency responded to injunction by recompeting using Federal Supply Schedule and protester had no Schedule contract); *L-3 Commc'ns Integrated Sys, L. P. v. United States*, 79 Fed. Cl. 453 (2007) (protester learned well after award that agency official had tilted award to competitor); *IDEA Int'l, Inc. v. United States*, 74 Fed. Cl. 129 (2006) (contract award based on defective procedures allowed to proceed because of urgency); *Morgan Bus. Assocs. v. United States*, 223 Ct. Cl. 325, 619 F.2d 892 (1980) (agency lost proposal). Costs have also been awarded when the court concludes that a losing protester has been required to expend excessive proposal costs because of a badly written RFP, *Centech Group, Inc. v. United States*, 79 Fed. Cl. 562 (2007), *aff'd*, 554 F.3d 1029 (Fed. Cir. 2009).

To be awarded bid or proposal preparation costs in a successful protest action, the protester must show those costs to be allocable and reasonable, *Coflexip & Servs., Inc. v. United States*, 961 F.2d 951 (Fed. Cir. 1992). Expenses compensable as bid preparation costs are those in the nature of researching specifications, reviewing bid forms, examining cost factors, and preparing draft and actual bids, *Finley v. United States*, 31 Fed. Cl. 704 (1994). Costs incurred in anticipation of or to qualify for a contract award are not recoverable bid preparation expenses, *Lion Raisins, Inc. v. United States*, 52 Fed. Cl. 115 (2002). In *Lion Raisins*, the costs of litigating a Small Business Administration size protest and obtaining a Certificate of Competency were not reimbursable bid and proposal preparation costs, because they were not incurred specifically for the bid. Here, the solicitation did not reference a set-aside for small business, eligibility to bid was not predicated on size, and the resolution of the size protest was irrelevant to contract award. However, although costs must support an initial or revised proposal, there is no requirement that a solicitation must be issued before such costs may be recovered, *Naplesyacht. com, Inc. v. United States*, 49 CCF ¶ 78,366 (2005). In *Naplesyacht*, the government had contested the costs as appearing to be related to procurements conducted under the GSA supply schedule and otherwise unrelated to the disputed solicitation. The court found, however, that the record sufficiently detailed that the protester began to prepare its proposal when it responded to requests for sources from the government. In addition, other correspondence established the government conducted pre-solicitation activities, including site visits to the protester's facilities. E-mail correspondence described the government's need for a specified foot length and other requirements that it later included in the boat manufacturing solicitation. The court found the costs allocable as related to research and preparation of the protester's initial and final proposals. If the parties cannot agree on the costs after the court has held the protester entitled to recover, the court can reopen the case and rule on the proper amount to be paid, *CNA Corp. v. United States*, 83 Fed. Cl. 1 (2008).

## b. Protest Costs

The costs of pursuing a protest in the Court of Federal Claims are not recoverable except under the Equal Access to Justice Act (EAJA), 28 U.S.C. § 2412, *Grumman Data Sys. Corp. v. United States*, 28 Fed. Cl. 803 (1993). See also *Coflexip & Servs., Inc. v. United States*, 20 Cl. Ct. 412 (1990) (court is without jurisdiction to award protest costs in the absence of a waiver of sovereign immunity); and *AT&T Techs., Inc. v. United States*, 18 Cl. Ct. 315 (1989) (damages for breach of the implied contract to fairly and honestly consider offers are limited exclusively to bid and proposal preparation costs).

Under the EAJA, an award of reasonable attorneys' fees may be made to a qualifying "party" who prevails in an action by or against the United States, provided that certain criteria are met, 28 U.S.C. § 2412(d)(1)(A). A qualifying "party" is a corporation or other organization with a net worth of less than $7 million and 500 or fewer employees, 28 U.S.C. § 2412(d)(2)(B). In *Lion Raisins, Inc. v. United States*, 57 Fed. Cl. 505 (2003), the court held that the net worth of two other business related to an entity that requested attorneys' fees and costs under the EAJA was irrelevant for purposes of determining whether the EAJA claimant was eligible to collect the fees. The government had asserted that Lion Raisins was an affiliate of two other business entities and that the net worth of these entities should be aggregated in determining Lion Raisin's net worth. The court explained that the plain language of EAJA counseled against aggregation, stating at 510:

> The jurisprudence makes clear that aggregation, if required at all, is necessary only when the underlying litigation pursued by the . . . claimant substantially benefitted another party, or if the claimant was not the real party in interest to the underlying litigation. This is not the situation in the case at bar. . . . Most important to the issue of aggregation, only plaintiff had a direct interest in the underlying lawsuit. While . . . [the other entities] may profit from plaintiff's ability to perform government contracts, even the more restrictive formulations of EAJA eligibility would not require aggregation for this type of attenuated benefit from the underlying litigation.

See also *Information Scis. Corp. v. United States*, 78 Fed. Cl. 673 (2007), where the government contended that the intervenor's net worth should include the assets and liabilities of its "working partners" and perhaps its principles. The court found that the intervenor did not have a formal legal or contractual relationship with any entity, and even if it had an implicit contractual relationship with its working partners, mere affiliation did not justify aggregating the net worth of affiliated companies under the EAJA. An applicant must present evidence showing its net worth was less than $7 million at the time the action is filed, *Ghanim Combined Group Co. v. United States*, 67 Fed. Cl. 494 (2005) (applicant's self-serving, nonprobative affidavit claiming a net worth below the threshold was inadequate to establish that its net worth did not exceed $7 million for purposes of EAJA).

Eligibility for such an award requires that: (1) the claimant be a "prevailing party;" (2) the government's position was not "substantially justified;" (3) no "special circumstances make an award unjust;" and (4) any fee application be submitted to the court within 30 days of final judgment in the action and be supported by an itemized statement, *Commissioner, INS v. Jean*, 496 U.S. 154 (1990); *Loomis v. United States*, 74 Fed. Cl. 350 (2006); *Lion Raisins, Inc. v. United States*, 57 Fed. Cl. 505 (2003).

The burden of establishing substantial justification rests upon the government, *White v. Nicholson*, 412 F.3d 1314 (Fed. Cir. 2005). In determining substantial justification, the court must "look at the entirety of the government's conduct [both prior to and during litigation] and make a judgment call whether the government's overall position had a reasonable basis in both law and fact," *Chiu v. United States*, 948 F.2d 711 (Fed. Cir. 1991). See also *Doty v. United States*, 71 F.3d 384 (Fed. Cir. 1995) ("[T]he term 'position of the United States' [in the EAJA] refers to the government's position throughout the dispute, including not only its litigating position but also the agency's administrative position."). See *Savantage Fin. Servs., Inc. v. United States*, 52 CCF ¶ 79,007 (Fed. Cl. 2008) (government's defense, which essentially argued its actions amounted to a software standardization decision that was not a procurement within the Court of Federal Claims' bid protest jurisdiction, was based on an unreasonable application of the Federal Acquisition Streamlining Act and a recent court decision); *Universal Fid. LP v. United States*, 70 Fed. Cl. 310 (2006) (restrictions were unreasonable and the government took corrective action late in the proceedings); and *Dubinsky v. United States*, 44 Fed. Cl. 360 (1999) (government assertion that procurement was conducted in accordance with simplified acquisition procedures was not reasonable because the protester successfully showed that the solicitation was conducted as a standard procurement, consequently making the government's discussions with the awardee improper). But see *Klinge Corp. v. United States*, 53 CCF ¶ 79,183 (2009), where an application for attorneys' fees and expenses under the EAJA was denied because the government's overall litigation position in the protest was substantially justified. In its EAJA application, the protester argued the government's decision to cancel the solicitation was based on its unreasonable conclusion that the protester did not comply with the Trade Agreements Act. Even though the government was mistaken in fact and law, the court found no government bad faith or animus toward the protester and no government desire to help the awardee.

The government's position will not be found to be reasonable or substantially justified when explicit, unambiguous regulations directly contradict that position, *Information Scis. Corp. v. United States*, 78 Fed. Cl. 673 (2007), 86 Fed. Cl. 269 (2009), 88 Fed. Cl. 626 (2009) (even though court resolved most of the protest challenges in the government's favor and did not rule the contracting officer's and SSA's decisions were unreasonable, violations of the FAR were ipso facto unreasonable in law); *Hillensbeck v. United States*, 74 Fed. Cl. 477 (2006) (government's position conflicted with unambiguous statutory definition and regulations); *Loomis v. United*

*States*, 74 Fed. Cl. 350 (2006) (military failed to comply with its own regulations); *Filtration Dev., Co. v. United States*, 63 Fed. Cl. 612 (2005) (government position contradicted unambiguous regulatory requirements relating to organizational conflicts of interest). In *Geo-Seis Helicopters, Inc. v. United States*, 79 Fed. Cl. 74 (2007), the government argued that its position in the underlying litigation was justified because there was significant GAO precedent supporting the contracting officer's position. The court determined that the plain language of the FAR precluded the government's position. The court held that the FAR and not GAO or the court, establish the parameters for the contracting officer's position.

The government's position may be found to be substantially justified even though the court previously overturned the government's actions. See *RAMCOR Servs. Group, Inc. v. United States*, 185 F.3d 1286 (Fed. Cir. 1999) ("Although INS had lost the underlying action, that outcome does not alone show that its position had no substantial justification.").

The court follows the Supreme Court's decision in *Buckhannon Board & Care Home, Inc. v. West Virginia Department of Health & Human Res.*, 532 U.S. 598 (2001) in deciding prevailing party status under EAJA, *Brickwood Contractors, Inc. v. United States*, 288 F.3d 1371 (Fed. Cir. 2002). In *Buckhannon*, the Supreme Court rejected the catalyst theory and set forth standards for a party to prevail under attorney fees statutes. Under the catalyst theory, a party "prevails" because the lawsuit brought about a voluntary change in the defendant's conduct. The Court found the catalyst theory insufficient because "[i]t allows an award where there is no judicially sanctioned change in the legal relationship of the parties." The Court then proceeded to construe the phrase "prevailing party" as requiring some judicial action that changes the legal relationship between the parties on the merits of the claim. In other words, to prevail, a party must have received a judicial imprimatur tantamount to a judgment in favor of that party on the merits of the original claim. That judicial action could take the form of a consent decree settling the claim in favor of the plaintiff, a judgment on the merits, or an award of damages. In *Rice Servs., LTD v. United States*, 405 F.3d 1017 (2005), an award of legal fees under the EAJA was reversed on appeal because the protester did not achieve prevailing party status as a result of the government's voluntary decision to withdraw a solicitation. The protester sought a reevaluation of the bids pursuant to the terms of the solicitation for dining services. The Court of Federal Claims granted the government's motion to dismiss the case, but included in its order a provision directing the government to follow through with its promise to reevaluate the solicitation. Subsequently, the protester was awarded its litigation costs as a prevailing party on the basis the dismissal order altered the parties' legal relationship. The Federal Circuit reversed finding that the dismissal order was not an enforceable judgment because the court did not reach the merits, and there was no evidence the order embodied an agreement between the parties and was incorporated into a consent decree. See also *Universal Fid. LP v. United States*, 70 Fed. Cl. 310 (2006) (contractor was a "prevailing party" because the court's order advised the parties the solicitation would be enjoined, the matter had been fully briefed, and the court and the parties agreed no hearing was necessary; the court's conclusions were legal in nature, exhibited an essence of finality and were made late in the proceedings, and an opinion granting injunctive relief would have been issued had the government declined curative action); and *Filtration Dev. Co., LLC v. United States*, 63 Fed. Cl. 612 (2005) (protester was a prevailing party because a permanent injunction granted in its favor altered the legal relationship between the parties). However, in *Knowledge Connections, Inc. v. United*, 76 Fed. Cl. 612 (2007), a court order remanding a bid protester's claim to the government procuring agency for further consideration was not sufficient to establish "prevailing party" status for purposes of recovering attorney's fees because the order did not grant any relief and the Court of Federal Claims retained jurisdiction over the appeal. Here, the remand order did not provide any resolution to the key question on the merits, which concerned whether the solicitation at issue was defective in a manner that prejudiced the protester. Accordingly the court held that a final judgment and a determination of whether the protester is a prevailing party will be achieved only after the court has had an opportunity to assess the government agency's determination on remand. The court ruled protester's EAJA application premature and denied it without prejudice. Similarly in *Advanced Sys. Tech., Inc. v. United States*, 74 Fed. Cl. 171 (2006), the protester filed an EAJA application, arguing it obtained "prevailing party" status when the court issued the preliminary injunction suspending the award pending the outcome of an SBA appeal. The court held that when a preliminary injunction only grants temporary relief preserving the status quo, "prevailing party" status is not conferred, because such a preliminary injunction is not a judicially sanctioned material alteration of the parties' legal relationship." Moreover, the remand to the SBA resulted from an agreement between the parties, not an adjudication of the court.

Attorneys' fees are compensable under the EAJA if adequately documented, specific to the protest, necessary, and reasonable, *Information Scis. Corp. v. United States*, 78 Fed. Cl. 673 (2007). Here, attorneys' expenses were compensable. The intervenor submitted law firm records itemizing miscellaneous expenses and confirmed the expenses were limited to the protest before the Court of Federal Claims, not the preceding GAO protest. The consultant worked for two days assisting the intervenor's counsel to review the administrative record, which the intervenor characterized as too large for an attorney to review unassisted. Given the consultant's expertise in reviewing administrative records in bid protests and assistance in preparing for the hearing within a small time-frame, the court held that his work was necessary and the associated fees were reasonable. Fees can include reasonable time preparing the application for EAJA fees, *Savantage Fin. Servs., Inc. v. United States*, 52 CCF ¶ 79,007 (Fed. Cl. 2008). Fees are compensable even if the protester does not win on all of the issues that are protested, *Information Scis. Corp. v. United States*, 86 Fed. Cl. 269 (2009), *recons. denied*, 88 Fed. Cl. 626 (2009).

Attorneys' fees are capped at $125 per hour unless the court makes special findings justifying a higher fee. See *Geo-Seis Helicopters, Inc. v. United States*, 79 Fed. Cl. 74 (2007) (entitled to cost of living adjusted allowing rate of $167.27). The fee application with supporting documentation must be submitted to the court within 30 days of final judgment.

## V. FEDERAL TORT CLAIMS ACT

Unsuccessful offerors and bidders may obtain relief in district court under the Federal Tort Claims Act (FTCA), 28 U.S.C. § 1346(b), but such actions have generally not been successful. In *Scanwell Labs., Inc. v. Thomas*, 521 F.2d 941 (D. C. Cir. 1975), *cert. denied*, 425 U.S. 910 (1976), an unsuccessful bidder bought an FTCA action in district court while its claim for recovery of bid preparation costs was pending in the Court of Claims, alleging in both actions that the government had violated its procurement regulations by awarding the contract to a nonresponsive bidder. The court first concluded that it need not decide the question of whether the plaintiff would be limited to proceeding under "one theory or the other," but stated that its "solution" would be "merely to prevent a double recovery." Turning then to the merits of the tort action, the court held that the plaintiff's claim was based upon alleged negligent misrepresentation and was therefore barred by the FTCA exceptions under 28 U.S.C. § 2680(h). The court in *Scanwell* also held that the government's action in evaluating the bids fell within the discretionary function exception to the Act, 28 U.S.C. § 2680(a), even though it had held in prior litigation that there was "no discretion to ignore the regulations regarding responsiveness of bids," 521 F.2d at 948.

In *Edelman v. Federal Hous. Admin.*, 382 F.2d 594 (2d Cir. 1967), the second circuit found that a claim by a disappointed bidder alleging that the government had failed to fairly consider its bid was barred by the misrepresentation exception. In *Covington v. United States*, 303 F. Supp. 1145 (N.D. Miss. 1969), a claim alleging that the Government had fraudulently misrepresented the amount of funds available for the solicited work, causing the bid to be rejected as nonresponsive for exceeding the funding limitation, was held to fall within this same exception. See also *Armstrong & Armstrong, Inc. v. United States*, 356 F. Supp. 514 (E.D. Wash. 1973), *aff'd*, 514 F.2d 402 (9th Cir. 1975), where the court held that a claim by an unsuccessful bidder that the Bureau of Reclamation had acted "negligently, arbitrarily, and capriciously" in denying it award of a contract was a claim based upon interference with contract rights and was thus barred under 28 U.S.C. § 2680(h), which expressly excepts claims based upon interference with contract rights from the waiver of sovereign immunity under 28 U.S.C. § 1336(b). It is evident from these decisions that even where disappointed bidders have succeeded in convincing a court that claims arising out of contract award decisions sound in tort, the breadth of the exceptions to the waiver of immunity set forth in 28 U.S.C. § 2680(a)-(m) has effectively precluded that class of plaintiffs from obtaining relief under the FTCA. See, however, *Myers & Myers, Inc. v. United States Postal Serv.*, 527 F.2d 1252 (2d Cir. 1975), where the second circuit held that refusal to renew a contract based upon a nonresponsibility determination might be a de facto debarment requiring a hearing and remanded the case to the district court for decision under the FTCA, with instructions that the discretionary function exception to the Act would not apply if it was found that the procurement official had "behave[d] unconstitutionally or outside the scope of . . . authority." In *Cecile Indus., Inc. v. United States*, 793 F.2d 97 (3d Cir. 1986), the court held that the government's failure to follow debarment regulations did not constitute actionable fraud.

# VI. INTERRELATIONSHIP OF FORUMS AND APPEALS

The current system gives protesters more than one available forum to hear protests; thus, protesters are able to select the forum best suited to their needs. This freedom of choice is recognized in GAO bid protest statute, 31 U.S.C. § 3556, which states that it "does not give the Comptroller General exclusive jurisdiction over protests" and that nothing "shall affect the right of any interested party" to bring suit in the Court of Federal Claims. However, care must be taken in selecting the forum because the filing of a protest may be held to be a binding election of that forum by the protester. There are a number of statutory provisions dealing with this issue.

## A. Government Accountability Office

GAO protest regulations provide that GAO will dismiss any protest where "the matter involved" is before a court of competent jurisdiction or where the matter has been decided on the merits by a court, unless the court requests a decision by GAO, 4 C.F.R. § 21.11(b). This rule applies to both initial protests and requests for reconsideration. 4 C.F.R. § 21.11(a) requires a protester to notify GAO immediately of any court proceedings that involve the subject matter of a protest and to file all relevant documents with GAO

When the subject matter is before a court of competent jurisdiction, GAO will dismiss the protest. In *Oahu Tree Experts*, Comp. Gen. Dec. B-282247, 99-1 CPD ¶ 69, the matter involved whether the contracting agency knew the "marginal" CPAR ratings to be motivated by bias, instead of an impartial assessment of the protester's performance. To answer this question, GAO stated that it must first determine whether bias did, in fact, taint the ratings — the same question posed in Oahu's federal complaint. GAO held that while Oahu correctly observed that its federal complaint does not mention the instant procurement and seeks different relief (i.e., the correction of the CPAR rather than the termination of the awardee's contract), these differences do not overcome the fact that Oahu has placed the same facts in issue before both the federal court.

A later-filed court action will also divest GAO of jurisdiction. In *Prince George's Contractors, Inc.*, 64 Comp. Gen. 786 (B-218640.2), 85-2 CPD ¶ 195, the protest was dismissed because the protester filed suit in the district court after filing a protest with GAO. In addition, GAO will not consider a request for costs and attorneys' fees for an action that was adjudicated in a court decision, *Pitney Bowes, Inc.*, 64 Comp. Gen. 623 (B-218241), 85-1 CPD ¶ 696. In that case the protest was first filed at GAO; but when the agency refused to suspend contract performance, the protester went to court and obtained an injunction. GAO ruled that its authority to award such remedies was ancillary to its jurisdiction to rule on the protest and that the district court injunction ousted it from jurisdiction in the case.

In determining whether the matter involved is before a court, GAO has ruled that it will not consider a protest where the court proceeding pertains to a matter that "might have been decided" by the court, even though it was not decided, *Santa Fe Corp.*, 64 Comp. Gen. 429 (B-218234.2), 85-1 CPD ¶ 361, *recons. denied*, 85-1 CPD ¶ 499; *Affiliated Textiles, Inc.*, Comp. Gen. Dec. B-242970.2, 91-2 CPD ¶ 127; *Techniarts Eng'g — Recons.*, Comp. Gen. Dec. B-238520.7, 92-1 CPD ¶ 504. Thus, GAO will not rule on a protest if any factual issue related to the protest is being litigated in a court. In *Meisel Rohrbau GmbH & Co.*, 67 Comp. Gen. 380 (B-228152.3), 88-1 CPD ¶ 371, GAO concluded that a pending court case requesting reinstatement of a prior solicitation was relevant to the current protest contesting the cancellation of the replacement solicitation. See also *North Shore Strapping Co.*, Comp. Gen. Dec. B-248003, 92-1 CPD ¶ 532, where GAO dismissed a protest alleging the use of restrictive specifications because it was within the scope of a pending court suit alleging unfair treatment of the protester by the procuring agency. But if the matter before the court is not relevant to the protest, GAO will not dismiss the protest. See *Rix Indus., Inc.*, Comp. Gen. Dec. B-241498, 91-1 CPD ¶ 165, finding that a pending litigation involving an offeror's alleged theft of trade secrets concerning the product to be manufactured under the contract was not relevant to the issue of whether that offeror could perform the pending contract. In *Sprint Commc'ns Co. LP*, Comp. Gen. Dec. B-288413.11, 2002 CPD ¶ 171, GAO dismissed a protest and request for reconsideration where the protester alleged that the agency had relied on misrepresented facts in determining that the awardee was responsible. GAO concluded that, although the award of the contract being protested was not being litigated, it could not reasonable rule of the protest because the misrepresentations of the awardee were the subject of a suit filed by the Securities Exchange Commission as well as grand jury indictments of officials of the company.

GAO dismisses protests when there is a case pending in court even if a party other than the protester files the court suit. See, for example, *Dawson Constr. Co.*, Comp. Gen. Dec. B-208547.2, 83-1 CPD ¶ 327, where GAO dismissed a protest of the cancellation of a procurement because a competitor had filed a suit in the Claims Court concerning the same procurement. This can result in a protest being dismissed because another party filed a subsequent suit in a court. *Test Sys. Assocs.*, Comp. Gen. Dec. B-256813.6, 96-2 CPD ¶ 161, is a good example of the peculiar nature of these cases. There an unsuccessful offeror filed a protest at GAO and shortly thereafter in district court challenging the award to TSAI. On its own initiative, the agency took corrective action and terminated TSAI's contract and notified TSAI of its intention to award to Dixon. TSAI filed its first protest with GAO (B-256813.3) on the basis of an ambiguous clause and for terminating its contract and rejecting its offer. In the meantime, Dixon choose not to withdraw its civil action in district court. TAO advised TSAI to intervene in Dixon's court action, but it did not. GEO then dismissed TSAI's protest, stating that the dispositive issue was before the district court. See also *Geronimo Serv. Co.,* Comp. Gen. Dec. B-242331.3, 91-1 CPD ¶ 321, where GAO refused to hear a protest of the award of a contract that was being litigated in district court in a suit filed by another protester. GAO noted that although the court had requested an advisory opinion from GAO, that opinion could not rule on Geronimo's protest because it had not intervened in the district court action An action filed in court will also deprive the government of the ability to obtain reconsideration by GAO if the protester files a suit in court after winning the protest, *Department of the Navy — Recons.,* Comp. Gen. Dec. B-253129.4, 96-1 CPD ¶ 175.

A court may specifically request that GAO provide an advisory opinion on the merits of a protest, *Academy Facilities Mgmt. — Advisory Opinion,* Comp. Gen. Dec. B-401094.3, 2009 CPD ¶ 139; *Career Training Concepts, Inc. — Advisory Opinion,* Comp. Gen. Dec. B-311429, 2009 CPD ¶ 97; *Patriot Contract Servs. — Advisory Opinion,* Comp. Gen. Dec. B-294777.3, 2005 CPD ¶ 10; *TEAC Am. Corp., Inc.,* Comp. Gen. Dec. B-259831, 95-1 CPD ¶ 273; *Test Sys. Assocs.,* Comp. Gen. Dec. B-256813.5, 94-2 CPD ¶ 153; *Florida Prof. Review Org., Inc.,* Comp. Gen. Dec. B-253908.2, 94-1 CPD ¶ 17. In such cases GAO will rule on the protest even if it would have been untimely if filed with GAO, *Adelaide Blomfield Mgmt. Co.,* 72 Comp. Gen. 335 (B-253128.2), 93-2 CPD ¶ 197. Once GAO gives a decision to the court, it will not reconsider that decision unless the court requests such action, *Ace Fed. Reporters, Inc.,* Comp. Gen. Dec. B-241309.3, 91-1 CPD ¶ 54.

## B. Appeals

There is no specified appeals procedure for GAO decisions because they are not in the nature of judicial decisions. If a protester is dissatisfied with a GAO decision, an action may be brought in the Court of Federal Claims, assuming that all requirements for jurisdiction are met, 31 U.S.C. § 3556. It is the agency's procurement award decision, not GAO's recommendation, that is subject to review by the court, *Advanced Constr. Servs., Inc. v. United States,* 51 Fed. Cl. 362 (2002) ("Construing § 1491(b)(1) in the expansive manner advocated by [the protester] would violate the well-established principle that it is the agency's decision, not the decision of GAO that is the subject of judicial review when a bid protester protests an award previously reviewed by GAO."); *Cubic Applications, Inc. v. United States,* 37 Fed. Cl. 339 (1997). Although the court is conducting its review of the agency's award decision under the APA, GAO recommendation is considered to be part of the agency record, 31 U.S.C. § 3556.

The Court of Federal Claims will not make a de novo review but, rather, will determine whether GAO's recommendation was rational, *Honeywell, Inc. v. United States*, 870 F.2d 644 (Fed. Cir. 1989). There, the contracting officer held that a competitor's bid was not responsive, but GAO ruled to the contrary and recommended that the Army award the contract to the competitor. When the Army stated that it would follow that recommendation, Honeywell, Inc., the second low bidder on the contract, filed suit in the Claims Court to enjoin the award. The Claims Court held that GAO did not have a rational basis for its recommendation and enjoined the award. The Court of Appeals for the Federal Circuit reversed because the court had retried the issue of whether the contracting officer's decision was correct rather than determining whether GAO decision was rational, stating at 647:

> The question before the Claims Court was whether the Army justifiably followed the GAO's recommendation that the bid identified Haz-Tad as the bidder and therefore was responsive to the solicitation. The Claims Court recognized that the controlling inquiry in deciding that question was whether the GAO's decision was a rational one. After paying lip service to that standard, however, the Claims Court impermissibly undertook what can fairly be characterized only as its own independent de novo determination of whether the bid documents identified Haz-Tad as the bidder.

*Carothers Constr., Inc. v. United States*, 18 Cl. Ct. 745 (1989), further articulated the scope of review at 751:

> Although Carothers Construction Inc. (Carothers) was not required to file a protest with the GAO, it elected to do so. This election precludes the Claims Court from conducting its own independent de novo determination. *Honeywell*, 870 F.2d at 647.

> Even if the court would come to a different conclusion, the procurement agency's decision to follow the Comptroller General's recommendation is proper, unless the Comptroller General's decision itself was irrational. *Honeywell*, 870 F.2d at 648. "If the court finds a reasonable basis for the agency's action, the court should stay its hand even though it might, as an original proposition, have reached a different conclusion as to the proper administration and application of the procurement regulations." *Id.* at 648 (citing *M. Steinthal & Co. v. Seamans*, 147 U.S. App. D.C. 221, 455 F.2d 1289, 1301 (D.C. Cir. 1971).

In *Centech Group, Inc. v. United States*, 79 Fed. Cl. 562 (2007), *aff'd*, 554 F.3d 1029 (2009), Centech argued that the Air Force irrationally ignored the responsibility determination of the SBA and followed GAO's independent finding of unacceptability. The court found GAO determination rational because Centech's proposal did not provide the information the RFP requested, making it unacceptable. The court found an agency decision to follow an irrational GAO decision itself irrational in *Turner Constr. Co. v. United States*, 94 Fed. Cl. 561 (2010), *motion to stay injunction denied*, 94 Fed. Cl. 586 (2010). There, the court concluded that GAO conducted an improper de novo review of the contracting officer's OCI determination without giving the agency the deference it was due. GAO had overturned the contracting officer's determination without highlighting any hard facts to base its OCI determination. The court held that the Army was arbitrary and capricious in implementing GAO's decision, stripping Turner of the contract.

There may be instances where the court will overturn agency actions that were validated by GAO, *Latecoere Int'l Inc. v. Department of the Navy*, 19 F.3d 1342 (11th Cir. 1994). There, the court disagreed with GAO's finding that the arbitrary rating of a proposal did not prejudice Latecoere. The court stated that GAO based its conclusion that "Latecoere was not prejudiced by the arbitrary elevation of [the other offeror's] ratings on two assumptions, one of which has no support in the record, and the other of which is flatly contradicted by the record." In *E.W. Bliss Co. v. United States*, 33 Fed. Cl. 123 (1995), *aff'd*, 77 F.3d 445 (Fed. Cir. 1996), the court, although acknowledging that GAO decisions should be given a high degree of deference, stated: "The Court of Claims is not bound by the views of the Comptroller General nor do they operate as a legal or judicial determination of the rights of the parties," quoting *Burroughs Corp. v. United States*, 223 Ct. Cl. 53, 63, 617 F.2d 590, 597 (1980) (citing *Font v. United States*, 219 Ct. Cl. 335, 593 F.2d 388 (1979)). In distinguishing *Honeywell*, the *Bliss* court stated that the Federal Circuit decision focused on the fact that the Claims Court did not give deference to either GAO or the contracting officer's decision but, rather, engaged in an independent de novo analysis. Thus, *Honeywell* should not be read as conferring on GAO a degree of deference beyond that set forth in *Burroughs*. The court stated at 135:

> The weight of precedent instructs that, although the review is not de novo and the GAO's decision is accorded deference, the court is to answer the question whether the agency's procurement decision or the GAO's decision on the protest was reasonable based on the record before the contracting officer or the GAO.

Although the court went to great lengths in analyzing the scope of its review, it in fact agreed with GAO's decision. Similarly, in *SP Sys., Inc. v. United States*, 86 Fed. Cl. 1 (2009), SP Systems originally won a NASA award, but, after GAO sustained a protest against the evaluations of cost realism, management approach, and past performance that led to that award, the agency followed GAO's specific recommendations for corrective action and (after re-evaluation) awarded the contract to a competitor. SP Systems then filed suit in the Court of Federal Claims, which found both GAO's decision and the agency's decision to follow it, reasonable, even though there were other ways the agency might have re-evaluated proposals.

If GAO's recommendation is plainly contrary to a statutory or regulatory requirement, that decision is irrational and an agency is not justified in following it. In *Firth Constr. Co. v. United States*, 36 Fed. Cl. 268 (1996), an offeror was the apparent low bidder but had failed to submit a completed Standard Form (SF) 1442. After bid opening, the offeror faxed a completed SF 1442 to the agency and was awarded the contract. Following a protest, the Office of Counsel of the agency advised the contracting division that the award was improper because the bid was nonresponsive due to the lack of an original signature on the SF 1442. Given this advice, the contracting officer canceled the award. The offeror protested to GAO, and GAO sustained the protest. The agency announced its intention to follow GAO's recommendation and award the contract to the offeror, and Firth Construction filed suit in the Court of Federal Claims. The court determined that the bid was nonresponsive because it lacked an original signature. Thus, the court held that GAO's decision was irrational and that the agency would be arbitrary and capricious to follow it. Similarly in *Grunley Walsh Int'l, LLC v. United States*, 78 Fed. Cl. 35 (2007), the Department of State disqualified plaintiff's prequalification based upon GAO's recommended interpretation of a statutory business-volume requirement. In holding that GAO's recommended interpretation is afforded no deference because it plainly lacked a reasonable basis and thus was arbitrary and capricious, the court stated at 43-44:

> Although the court does not specifically reach the question of whether the GAO afforded proper deference to the DOS's original interpretation under *Chevron, U.S.A., Inc. v. Natural Res. Def. Council, Inc.*, 467 U.S. 837 (1984), the court must address defendant's argument for affording deference to the DOS's new interpretation. Adoption of defendant's position would effectively strip this court of any real review in any case where the agency followed a recommendation of the GAO on an interpretation of a statute or regulation. The court declines to play that shell game. In entrusting this court with bid protest jurisdiction under APA standards, Congress necessarily meant for the court to undertake a meaningful review of agency action.

> Defendant cites *Honeywell, Inc. v. United States*, 870 F.2d 644 (Fed. Cir. 1989), in support of its argument. *Honeywell* stands for the rule that "a procurement agency's decision to follow the [GAO]'s recommendation . . . was proper unless the [GAO]'s decision itself was irrational." 870 F.2d at 648. In order to review an agency's action when it is based upon the recommendation of the GAO, it is necessary to examine the underlying decision of the GAO. *See Firth Const. Co. v. United States*, 36 Fed. Cl. 268, 271-72 (1996) (citing and applying *Honeywell* to overturn agency action that was based on a decision of the GAO). The GAO decision constitutes the very reason(s) for the agency action. Put another way, an agency action is not insulated from meaningful review simply because the GAO recommended it.

See also *Geo-Seis Helicopters, Inc. v. United States*, 77 Fed. Cl. 636 (2007), where the agency accepted amendments to the winning bid after the bid closing date in reliance on GAO precedent allowing agencies to issue amendments that extend the closing date after the closing date has passed. GAO denied a protest based on this precedent and Geo-Seis filed suit in the Court of Federal Claims. The court held that the agency violated the APA by relying on GAO precedent, stating that the refusal of the contracting officer to "adhere to the categorical reality of the 'late is late' rule renders arbitrary her decision to accept [the winning bidder's] first and second revised proposals."

## C. Appellate Review of Court of Federal Claims Protest Decisions

The Federal Circuit has jurisdiction over appeals from the Court of Federal Claims, 28 U.S.C. § 1295(a)(3). An appeal must be filed within 60 days from the date of entry of the judgment or order, Fed. R. App. P. 4(a)(1); R.C.F.C. 72. The Federal Circuit reviews legal decision of the Court of Federal Claims de novo, and applies the same standard of review as the Court of Federal Claims, *Dysart v. United States*, 369 F.3d 1303 (Fed. Cir. 2004).

## D. Precedential Authority

The Court of Federal Claims is bound by the decisions of the United States Supreme Court, the precedential decisions of the Federal Circuit, and the published decisions of the Federal Circuit's predecessor courts, the Court of Claims and the Court of Customs and Patent Appeals, *South Corp. v. United States*, 690 F.2d 1368 (Fed. Cir. 1982) (adopting as precedent the decisions of the predecessor Court of Claims and Court of Customs and Patent Appeals). Court of Federal Claims judges are not bound by the decisions of other Court of Federal Claims judges, *Casa De Cambio Comdiv S. A., de C. V. v. United States*, 291 F.3d 1356 (Fed. Cir. 2002).

# INDEX

## F

**H**

**I**